Who's Who
in
Scotland

6TH EDITION 1996

Carrick Media

Published by Carrick Media
2/7 Galt House, 31 Bank Street, Irvine KA12 0LL
01294 311322
01563 530830

Copyright 1995 Carrick Media

Printed in Great Britain by Bookcraft, Midsomer Norton, Avon

British Library Cataloguing-in-Publication Data
A catalogue record for this book is available from the British Library

ISBN 0 946724 35 0

THE EUROPEAN COMMISSION
REPRESENTATION IN SCOTLAND

FOR INFORMATION ON THE STRUCTURE AND POLICIES OF THE EUROPEAN UNION

* The Internal Market

* The Social Dimension

* The Common Agricultural Policy

* Grants

* R & D

* Enlargement

FULL READING LIBRARY AND DOCUMENTATION SERVICE

9 Alva Street
EDINBURGH EH2 4PH
Tel: 0131 225 2058
Fax: 0131 226 4105

KENNETH A. MUNRO
Head of
Representation
in Scotland

THE WHO'S WHO IN SCOTLAND DIRECTORY

AGRICULTURE, FISHERIES AND FOOD

ROWETT RESEARCH INSTITUTE
GREENBURN ROAD, BUCKSBURN, ABERDEEN AB2 9SB.
TEL.: 01224 712751. FAX: 01224 715349.

Contact: Professor W.P.T. James, Director, 01224 716601; Professor I. Bremner, Deputy Director, 01224 716602.

The remit of the Institute is to advance understanding of the biochemical and physiological aspects of mammalian nutrition and growth, and interaction with reproduction, and to investigate aspects of human nutrition. Its mission is to maintain the position of the Institute as the pre-eminent European nutrition centre for integrated research in biological sciences of relevance to health, food and agriculture.

SCOTTISH CROP RESEARCH INSTITUTE
INVERGOWRIE, DUNDEE DD2 5DA.
TEL.: 01382 562731. FAX: 01382 562426. e-mail: mail@scri.sari.ac.uk

Contact: Professor J.R. Hillman, Director; Dr. R.J. Killick, Secretary; Dr. W.H. Macfarlane Smith, Scientific Liaison Officer.

The Institute is financed principally by the Scottish Office Agriculture and Fisheries Department and external contracts (c. £13m. per annum). It undertakes research to advance knowledge in the biological sciences, to improve the quality of crops, and to control losses due to pests and diseases with due regard to the environment. It is the lead centre in the UK for research on potatoes and soft fruit, and has major inputs into barley, beans and brassicas, and other temperate, tropical and subtropical crops.

SCOTTISH FISHERMEN'S FEDERATION
16 BON ACCORD CRESCENT, ABERDEEN AB1 2DE.
TEL.: 01224 582583. FAX: 01224 574958.

Contact: Robert Allan, MBE, Chief Executive/Secretary; Miss Trudy C.U. Johnston, Assistant to the Chief Executive; Cecil T. Finn, MBE, President.

Aims to protect and promote the interests of Scottish fishermen engaged in commercial sea fishing, through contact and negotiation with the UK Government, the UK Parliament, the various institutions of the European Union, and the press and media, and generally to establish and maintain contact with all parties interested in the affairs of the Scottish fishing industry.

ARTISTIC

BBC SCOTTISH SYMPHONY ORCHESTRA
BBC BROADCASTING HOUSE, QUEEN MARGARET DRIVE, GLASGOW G12 8DG.
TEL.: 0141-338 2606. FAX: 0141-307 4312.

Contact: Hugh Macdonald, Head of Music, 0141-338 2489; Alan Davis, Manager, BBC SSO, 0141-338 2606.

Founded in December 1935, the BBC Scottish Orchestra as it was then called, was Scotland's first full-time professional orchestra. Since then it has developed an international reputation with concert tours throughout Europe and to Canada and Hong Kong, and regular appearances at the Edinburgh International Festival and BBC Proms in London. The orchestra is particularly noted for its performances of contemporary music and it has an ambitious commissioning policy, giving special prominence to Scottish composers. In recent years it has recorded extensively, winning *Gramophone* Awards in 1992 and 1993.

NATIONAL GALLERIES OF SCOTLAND
NATIONAL GALLERY OF SCOTLAND: THE MOUND, EDINBURGH EH2 2EL; SCOTTISH NATIONAL PORTRAIT GALLERY: 1 QUEEN STREET, EDINBURGH EH2 1JD; SCOTTISH NATIONAL GALLERY OF MODERN ART: BELFORD ROAD, EDINBURGH EH4 3DR. TEL.: 0131-556 8921. FAX: 0131-332 4939.
Contact: Timothy Clifford, Director.
The National Galleries of Scotland encompass the National Gallery of Scotland, the Scottish National Portrait Gallery and the Scottish National Gallery of Modern Art, and share a commom aim: to exhibit, acquire and conserve the finest and most significant works of art for the enjoyment and benefit of the public. The Galleries are run by the Director and Keepers and governed by the Board of Trustees, appointed by the Secretary of State for Scotland. Funds for running the Galleries and purchasing works of art are provided by the Government. The Galleries also benefit from the generous support of many private benefactors, lenders and sponsors.

ROYAL FINE ART COMMISSION FOR SCOTLAND
9 ATHOLL CRESCENT, EDINBURGH EH3 8HA. TEL.: 0131-229 1109. FAX: 0131-229 6031.
Contact: Charles Prosser, Secretary.
The Commission, established in 1927, advises government on the visual impact and quality of design of construction projects. It reports its views to Ministers and local authorities and may recommend that planning applications be called in by the Secretary of State for Scotland for his determination. It publicises its work in various ways including annual exhibitions, and publishes annual reports to HM The Queen through Parliament. Although the government finances it, the Commission remains totally independent and gives its opinions impartially.

SCOTTISH FILM COUNCIL
DOWANHILL, 74 VICTORIA CRESCENT ROAD, GLASGOW G12 9JN. TEL.: 0141-334 4445. FAX: 0141-334 8132. e-mail: sfc@cityscape.co.uk.
Contact: Maxine Baker, Director; Erika King, Deputy Director; Kevin Cowle, Corporate Relations.
The national body responsible for promoting all aspects of the moving image. With Scottish Office funding, SFC is particularly active in film exhibition (regional film theatres), training, media education, research, information services and international relations. SFC is also the home of *The Scottish Film Archive* which contains about four million feet of Scottish documentary.

SCOTTISH POETRY LIBRARY
TWEEDDALE COURT, 14 HIGH STREET, EDINBURGH EH1 1TE. TEL.: 0131-557 2876. e-mail: spl_queries@presence.co.uk
Contact: Tessa Ransford, Director; Penny Duce, Librarian.
With charitable status, a free reference and lending library for Scotland's poetry in its three languages throughout the centuries and up-to-date, Scottish Poetry Library also includes a wide range of international poetry. Lending is also by post, travelling van and branches offering books, audio and video tapes and magazines. Advice, specialist lists, indexes, and bibliographies are produced by the specially-devised computer programme, INSPIRE. Membership £10 (organisations £15) for reading room, newsletter and to support the work.

CHARITABLE

AGE CONCERN SCOTLAND
113 ROSE STREET, EDINBURGH EH2 3DT.
TEL.: 0131-220 3345; FAX: 0131-220 2779.

Contact: Maureen O'Neill, Director; Liz Mitchell, Information Manager.

Age Concern is committed to working throughout Scotland to ensure that all older people have their rights upheld, their needs addressed, their voices heard, and have choice and control over all aspects of their lives. We support a network of local groups providing practical services and friendship to older people. ACS is a campaigning organisation, seeking to influence policy and practice in all areas that affect older people.

ROYAL AIR FORCES ASSOCIATION (SCOTTISH AREA)
20 QUEEN STREET, EDINBURGH EH2 1JX.
TEL.: 0131-225 5221. FAX: RAF BENEVOLENT FUND 0131-220 0643.

Contact: Gerard M. Halloran, Director; David Hamer, Area Welfare Officer; Mrs Sandra Pottinger, Accountant.

Established by Royal Charter in 1943, RAFA promotes welfare and comradeship in remembrance of all who died in the Royal Air Force and Air Forces of the Commonwealth. Advice and assistance are provided on all aspects: pensions/appeal representation, nursing care, convalescence, sheltered housing, financial aid. RAFA Scottish Area has just under 5,000 members and 30 branches throughout Scotland. The Area is an integral part of the national organisation whose central headquarters are at 43 Grove Park Road, London W4 3RX.

SCOTTISH SOCIETY FOR AUTISTIC CHILDREN
HILTON HOUSE, ALLOA BUSINESS PARK, WHINS ROAD, ALLOA FK10 3SA.
TEL.: 01259 720044. FAX: 01259 720051.

Contact: Donald Liddell, Chief Executive; Helen Petrie, Appeals and Marketing Manager; Rae Gilmour, Administrator.

Autism is a lifelong condition which isolates the child or adult from the world as we know it. People with autism have great difficulty communicating, forming relationships and understanding emotions. Many are unable to speak and around 75 per cent have other learning difficulties. The SSAC provides specialist care, support and education to help people with autism, and their families, make the most of their lives. Fulfilling needs for family support services, telephone counselling, information and the development of respite care is heavily dependent upon the generosity of others.

CIVIL LIBERTIES

SCOTTISH COUNCIL FOR CIVIL LIBERTIES (SCCL)
146 HOLLAND STREET, GLASGOW G2 4NG.
TEL.: 0141-332 5960. FAX: 0141-332 5309.

Contact: Carole Ewart, Director; Brian Thomson, Research/Information Officer.

SCCL is an independent voluntary organisation which campaigns for the defence and promotion of civil liberties in Scotland. It is a membership organisation and constantly and actively seeks new people to join and organisations to affiliate. SCCL maintains a library of information which is freely available to the public.

CONSTITUTIONAL

SCOTTISH CONSTITUTIONAL CONVENTION
c/o ROSEBERY HOUSE, 9 HAYMARKET TERRACE, EDINBURGH EH12 5XZ.
TEL.: 0131-346 1222. FAX: 0131-346 0055.

Contact: Douglas Sinclair, Secretary; Esther Roberton, Co-ordinator; Canon Kenyon Wright, Chair of Executive Committee.

The membership of the SCC includes political parties, local government, trades unions, churches and a range of civic organisations who are working together to achieve three key objectives: to agree a scheme for a Parliament for Scotland; to mobilise Scottish opinion and ensure the approval of the Scottish people for that scheme; and to assert the right of the Scottish people to secure the implementation of that scheme.

CONSUMER INTERESTS

GAS CONSUMERS' COUNCIL – SCOTLAND
86 GEORGE STREET, EDINBURGH EH2 3BU.
TEL.: 0645 060708. FAX: 0131-220 3732.

Contact: Mr Euan Robson, Scottish Manager; Mrs Liz Futcher, Assistant Scottish Manager.

The Gas Consumers' Council is an independent autonomous body established under the Gas Act 1986. It represents the interests of consumers in Scotland. The Council has two main functions. First, it seeks to influence the policies of government departments or agencies, British Gas Scotland, and appropriate trade bodies to make them more sensitive to the needs of gas consumers. Secondly, it will deal with complaints from individual consumers unable to resolve their difficulties with British Gas Scotland or other gas supply and installation companies. The Gas Consumers' Council in Scotland retains solicitors, consulting engineers and architects to assist with more serious matters involving compensation.

SCOTTISH CONSUMER COUNCIL (SCC)
ROYAL EXCHANGE HOUSE, 100 QUEEN STREET, GLASGOW G1 3DN.
TEL.: 0141-226 5261. FAX: 0141-221 0731.

Contact: Deirdre Hutton, Chairman; Ann Foster, Director; Katie Carr, Press and Publications Officer.

The SCC was set up by the Government in 1975 to promote the interests of Scottish consumers, particularly those who experience disadvantage in society. We have no statutory powers and rely on careful research and persuasive lobbying. Although mainly funded through a grant-in-aid from the DTI, the SCC is independent of any political party and critically assesses the policies of successive governments using the consumer principles of access, choice, information, safety, redress and representation. The Council carries out research into the policies and practices of central and local government, business, industry and the professions and lobbies these bodies, when justified, to improve their services to the consumer.

DEVELOPMENT ORGANISATIONS

GLASGOW DEVELOPMENT AGENCY
ATRIUM COURT, 50 WATERLOO STREET, GLASGOW G2 6HQ.
TEL.: 0141-204 1111. FAX: 0141-248 1600.

Contact: Michael Lunn, Chairman; Stuart Gulliver, Chief Executive; Gordon P.

Kennedy, Director, Corporate Development.

Glasgow is the largest city in Scotland in terms of population, jobs, companies and investment. Its sphere of influence affects almost half of the Scottish population. Within the Scottish Enterprise network, Glasgow Development Agency's task of delivering economic development in Glasgow is unique, since it is the only Local Enterprise Company to serve an exclusively inner city area. Glasgow's urban context and scale presents a special set of challenges and problems, as well as genuine advantages and opportunities.

HIGHLAND OPPORTUNITY LIMITED
REGIONAL BUILDINGS, GLENURQUHART ROAD, INVERNESS IV3 5NX.
TEL.: 01463 702551. FAX: 01463 710848.
e-mail: gb1559_inverness.@vans.infonet.com OR eic@sprite.co.uk

Contact: Hugh F. Black, Company Manager, Ext. 2551; Isabel Crawford, Assistant Accountant, Ext. 2558; Caroline Gray-Stephens, European Executive, Ext. 2560.

Highland Opportunity Limited is the Enterprise Trust for the Highlands of Scotland providing financial assistance and business services, particularly to small and medium enterprises (SMEs). It provides low interest loans and related advisory support throughout Highland Region. It provides European business services from its Euro Info Centre throughout Northern Scotland. It presently operates four funds: the Opportunity Fund; the Fisheries Fund; the Caithness Fund; and the Prince's Scottish Youth Business Trust.

LANARKSHIRE DEVELOPMENT AGENCY
NEW LANARKSHIRE HOUSE, STRATHCLYDE BUSINESS CENTRE, BELLSHILL ML4 3AD.
TEL.: 01698 745454. FAX: 01698 842211.

Contact: Ian Livingstone, Chairman, Ext. 2001; Archie Bethel, Chief Executive, Ext. 2001.

Lanarkshire Development Agency is the driving force behind the regeneration of Lanarkshire. LDA aims to build a new Lanarkshire through partnership with the public and private sectors. Its goal is a strong and vibrant economy with successful companies and secure employment. LDA is a key player in flagship projects such as the Lanarkshire Enterprise Zone, The Eurocentral Channel Tunnel link and the reclamation of the Ravenscraig steel plant. The Agency has a range of powers in business development, property development and training.

EDUCATION

BELMONT HOUSE SCHOOL
SANDRINGHAM AVENUE, NEWTON MEARNS, GLASGOW G77 5DU.
TEL.: 0141-639 2922. FAX: 0141-639 9860.

Contact: John Mercer, Headmaster; C.A.S. Scott, Depute Head; G.D. Park, Assistant Head.

Our principal aim is to serve as well as we can the boys who are pupils with us. We believe that each boy is able to make a contribution to the school community. We aim to encourage this talent in every possible way and to open up new opportunities wherever they might exist. The life of the school is based upon a personalised approach and a caring attitude in the classroom where we seek to give the maximum amount of individual attention.

profession in Scotland. Has a Professional Association of Nursery Nurses section. Positively opposes strike action and never involves children in its disputes. Provides a highly personalised service to its members with a wide range of professional and non-professional services including free legal advice.

SCOTTISH CONSULTATIVE COUNCIL ON THE CURRICULUM
GARDYNE ROAD, BROUGHTY FERRY, DUNDEE DD5 1NY.
TEL.: 01382 455053. FAX: 01382 455046. e-mail: Reception @sccc.ac.uk

Contact: Cameron Harrison, Chief Executive, CHarrison@sccc.ac.uk; Tegwen Wallace, Senior Information Officer, TWallace@sccc.ac.uk; Anne Gerono, Public Relations and Promotions Officer, AGerono@sccc.ac.uk

The Scottish Consultative Council on the Curriculum is the principal advisory body to the Secretary of State on all curriculum matters relating to 3-18 year olds in Scottish schools. It has three main functions: to keep the curriculum under review and inform the government on those areas requiring attention; to consult with local authorities, teachers, parents and other representatives of the community; to provide guidance on curriculum development and practice. The Council publishes support materials for government programmes as well as guidance and discussion documents for teachers on aspects of the curriculum.

SCOTTISH EXAMINATION BOARD
IRONMILLS ROAD, DALKEITH, MIDLOTHIAN EH22 1LE.
TEL.: 0131-663 6601. FAX: 0131-654 2664.

Contact: Dr. H.A. Long, BSc, Chief Executive; Mr D. Miller, DUniv(Stirling), MA(Cantab), CIMgt, FIFD, FRSA, Chairman.

The Scottish Examination Board is a statutory body established by Act of Parliament to conduct examinations and award certificates relating to secondary education in Scotland. The Board advises the Secretary of State on matters relating to examinations for secondary school pupils; develops guidance material for issue to presenting centres and carries out research. The Board also has responsibility for the preparation, distribution and monitoring of tests for pupils in primary schools and at stages S1 and S2 in secondary schools.

SSERC LTD (TRADING AS SSERC)
24 BERNARD TERRACE, EDINBURGH EH8 9NX.
TEL.: 0131-668 4421. FAX: 0131-667 9344.

Contact: John Richardson, Executive Director; Allen Cochrane, Depute Director.

Technical resource support for science and technology education. Advisory, information, consultancy, testing and training services on anything connected with the purchase, use (including health and safety), maintenance and repair of equipment and materials for science and technology education.

ENERGY

ENERGY ACTION SCOTLAND (EAS)
21 WEST NILE STREET, GLASGOW G1 2PS.
TEL.: 0141-226 3064. FAX: 0141-221 2788.

Contact: Ann Marno, Director; Andrew Fairbairn, Development Officer; Allana Parker, PR/Information Officer.

The national organisation in Scotland promoting energy efficiency, energy conservation and affordable warmth for everyone. EAS has a rolling programme of assistance to local authorities and housing associations in developing energy efficiency strategies. It offers training in energy advice, energy auditing and related topics, consultancy and energy auditing services. It carries out educational and lobbying work, and information provision. Publications include: *Energy Review* (quarterly journal, free to members); *Developing an Energy Efficiency Strategy* (for local authorities); and *Fuel Poverty in Scotland.*

ENVIRONMENT AND CONSERVATION

EDINBURGH NEW TOWN CONSERVATION COMMITTEE
13A DUNDAS STREET, EDINBURGH EH3 6QG.
TEL.: 0131-557 5222. FAX: 0131-556 6355.
Contact: Richard Griffith, MA(Cantab), Dip Arch(Cantab), RIAS, Director; Caroline Sibbald, Grant Case Officer.
Established 1970 to halt decay of residential buildings in Georgian New Town. Funded by Scottish Office (Historic Scotland) and City of Edinburgh Council. Remit: to award grants for appropriate external repairs, promote building maintenance, and advise central and local government on major policy issues. Committee representation: City of Edinburgh Council; Historic Buildings Council for Scotland; Scottish Civic Trust; Cockburn Association; Architectural Heritage Society of Scotland; New Town Residents.

ROYAL COMMISSION ON THE ANCIENT AND HISTORICAL MONUMENTS OF SCOTLAND
JOHN SINCLAIR HOUSE, 16 BERNARD TERRACE, EDINBURGH EH8 9NX.
TEL.: 0131-662 1456. FAX: 0131-662 1477/1499.
Contact: Sir William Fraser, GCB, DLitt, FRSE; Mr R.J. Mercer, MA, FSA, FRSE.
The aims of the Royal Commission on the Ancient and Historical Monuments of Scotland are: to survey and record the man-made environment of Scotland; to compile and maintain in the National Monuments Record of Scotland a record of the archaeological and historical environment; and to promote an understanding of this information by all appropriate means.

THE SCOTTISH CIVIC TRUST
24 GEORGE SQUARE, GLASGOW G2 1EF.
TEL.: 0141-221 1466. FAX: 0141-248 6952.
Contact: John N.P. Ford, Director of Administration and Finance; John Gerrard MBE, DA(Edin), FRIAS, FRSA, Technical Director.
Founded in 1967 – has made its own influential contribution towards the improvement of Scotland's Built Environment and Heritage. We act both as catalysts and guardians to encourage: well informed public concern for the environment of both town and country; high quality in planning and in new architecture; the conservation and, where necessary, adaptation for re-use of older buildings of distinction or historic interest; knowledgeable and therefore effective comment in planning matters; the elimination of ugliness, whether resulting from social deprivation, bad design or neglect.

SOLWAY RIVER PURIFICATION BOARD
RIVERS HOUSE, IRONGRAY ROAD, DUMFRIES DG2 0JE.
TEL.: 01387 720502. FAX: 01387 721154.
The effective management of water resources in South West Scotland, taking into account the interests of all who are affected by our work. Actively improving and protecting the water quality of our rivers, lochs, seas around our coasts and groundwaters. From 1 April 1996 the Solway River Purification Board will become part of the Scottish Environment Protection Agency (SEPA).

FINANCIAL

ASSOCIATION OF BRITISH INSURERS
51 GRESHAM STREET, LONDON EC2V 7HQ.
TEL.: 0171-600 3333. FAX: 0171-696 8996.

Contact: Vic Rance, Manager, Media, 0171-216 7440; Suzanne Moore, Assistant Manager, Media, 0171-216 7411; Malcolm Tarling, Assistant Manager, Media, 0171-216 7410.

The Association of British Insurers represents around 430 insurance companies, which between them account for over 95 per cent of the business of UK insurance companies. The Association represents insurance companies to the Government and to regulatory and other agencies, and it provides a wide range of services to its members.

GENEALOGY

SCOTS ANCESTRY RESEARCH SOCIETY
29B ALBANY STREET, EDINBURGH EH1 3QN.
TEL.: 0131-556 4220. FAX: 0131-556 4220.

Contact: Alison Munro; Lorna Walker.

The Scots Ancestry Research Society was set up in 1945 by Mr Tom Johnston, then Secretary of State for Scotland, as a non-profit making organisation to assist persons of Scottish descent to trace facts about their ancestors in Scotland. The Society employs its own team of trained and experienced searchers, and is directed by a council representing Scottish historians and central and local archives and libraries. Over 60,000 enquiries from all over the world have so far been investigated.

HEALTH

NATIONAL BOARD FOR NURSING, MIDWIFERY AND HEALTH VISITING FOR SCOTLAND
22 QUEEN STREET, EDINBURGH EH2 1NT.
TEL.: 0131-226 7371. FAX: 0131-225 9970.

Contact: Mrs Isobel Mackinlay, Chairman, Ext. 214; Mrs Lyn Mitchell, Chief Executive, Ext. 211; Mr David Ferguson, Board Secretary, Ext. 202.

The National Board is the statutory body responsible in Scotland for ensuring professional standards of education and training for nurses, midwives and health visitors.

ROYAL COLLEGE OF PHYSICIANS AND SURGEONS
232-242 ST. VINCENT STREET, GLASGOW G2 5RJ.
TEL.: 0141-221 6072. FAX: 0141-221 1804.

Contact: Professor N. MacKay, President; Mr M.H. Lucas, Registrar; Mr J.J. Beaton, Librarian.

The College is responsible for postgraduate medical and dental training in the West of Scotland. Through its examinations in medicine, surgery and dentistry, and regular inspections of hospital posts which are accredited for training purposes, the College ensures that the highest standards are maintained. The College has a full programme of training courses, symposia and guest lectures on both general and specialist topics, which are attended by medical students, junior doctors, consultants, dentists and general practitioners. In addition the College occasionally offers lectures of wider interest (eg to schools) and there is an annual open day.

THE ROYAL COLLEGE OF SURGEONS OF EDINBURGH
NICOLSON STREET, EDINBURGH EH8 9DW.
TEL.: 0131-556 6206. FAX: 0131-557 6406. e-mail: royalcollsurglib@ed.ac.uk
Contact: Miss Margaret Bean MA, Clerk to the College, Ext. 227.

The Royal College of Surgeons of Edinburgh is a body incorporated by Royal Charter and is concerned with education and training for medical and surgical practice and with the maintenance of high standards of professional competence and conduct. The College shall comprise Honorary Fellows in surgery and Honorary Fellows in dental surgery, ordinary Fellows in surgery and ordinary Fellows in dental surgery.

SCOTTISH AMBULANCE SERVICE NHS TRUST
NATIONAL HEADQUARTERS, TIPPERLINN ROAD, EDINBURGH EH10 5UU.
TEL.: 0131-447 7711. FAX: 0131-447 4789.
Contact: Alan R. Devereux, CBE, DL, Chairman; Andrew W. Freemantle, MBE, Chief Executive; Andrew K. Marsden, FRCS, Consultant Medical Director.

The SAS purpose is to provide Scotland with a national ambulance service by delivering a comprehensive accident and emergency service, non-emergency patient transport services and other associated services to the ultimate benefit of patients. The SAS vision is by the year 2000 to be acknowledged as Scotland's finest public service and an international leader in the provision of ambulance services.

HOUSING AND HOMELESSNESS

SCOTTISH COUNCIL FOR SINGLE HOMELESS
9 FORREST ROAD, EDINBURGH EH1 2QH.
TEL.: 0131-226 4382. FAX: 0131-220 3107.
Contact: Claire Stevens, Director; Robert Aldridge, Information Officer; Wendy Mejka, Administration and Finance Officer.

Campaigns throughout Scotland to highlight the wide-ranging needs of single homeless people for access to secure accommodation according to individual requirements and the prevention of homelessness. SCSH also campaigns for improvements in the law and in the practices of service providers, publishes a bi-monthly newsletter, undertakes training and research, publishes reports and offers advice and information to individuals and agencies. SCSH works closely with others in the voluntary, statutory and independent sectors and has a particular interest in care in the community issues.

SCOTTISH FEDERATION OF HOUSING ASSOCIATIONS
38 YORK PLACE, EDINBURGH EH1 3HU.
TEL.: 0131-556 5777. FAX: 0131-557 6028.
Contact: David Orr, Director; Dave Alexander, Policy Manager; Rob Hughes, Member Services Manager.

As the voice of housing associations and co-operatives throughout Scotland, the SFHA promotes, encourages and assists the formation of housing associations and provides services to help them operate. It supports the provision of affordable quality housing for those in need. Negotiating new policy, practice and legislation, it seeks to influence Government and Scottish Homes. As well as conducting national campaigns, the SFHA provides training and advice for all those involved in, or interested in, the Scottish housing association movement.

LAND USE AND MANAGEMENT

SCOTTISH LANDOWNERS' FEDERATION
25 MARITIME STREET, EDINBURGH EH6 5PW.
TEL.: 0131-555 1031. FAX: 0131-555 1052.

Contact: Graeme H. Gordon, OBE, Convener; Brian Speed, OBE, FIMgt, Director.
Represents the whole spectrum of landowners in Scotland. There are approximately 4,000 members. The aims of the Federation are: to promote high standards of management and use of land; to ensure proper communication on matters relating to the ownership of land between its members, other organisations and the wider public; and to ensure that legislation and policies affecting landownership and use are prepared with proper consideration for the responsibilities and rights of landowners, in addition to the well-being of rural communities, the environment, and the wider public interests.

LEGAL

SCOTTISH CHILD LAW CENTRE
CRANSTON HOUSE, 108 ARGYLE STREET, GLASGOW G2 8BH.
TEL.: 0141-226 3434. FAX: 0141-226 3043.

Contact: Deirdrie Watson, Director; Valerie McIntyre, Training Officer; Alison Cleland, Information Officer.
The Scottish Child Law Centre provides advice, information, training and commentary on Scots Law for the benefit of under 18s in Scotland. We provide free telephone advice to adults on 0141-226 3737. We have a Freephone for under 18s on 0800-317 500.

LOCAL GOVERNMENT

CONVENTION OF SCOTTISH LOCAL AUTHORITIES
ROSEBERY HOUSE, HAYMARKET TERRACE, EDINBURGH EH12 5XZ.
TEL.: 0131-346 1222. FAX: 0131-346 0055.
e-mail: postmaster@cosla.demon.co.uk

Contact: Douglas Sinclair, Secretary General; Maureen Ferrier, Press Officer, maureen@cosla.demon.co.uk
COSLA is the local government organisation representing Scotland's local authorities. Its primary object is to promote the welfare and good government of the people of Scotland and to enhance and maintain the principles and values of local democracy. COSLA considers parliamentary legislation affecting councils; plays a significant role in the debate over local government finance and the amount of central government grant payable to councils; and acts as employers' association for member authorities.

POST OFFICES

POST OFFICE COUNTERS LTD
THE ATHENAEUM, 8 NELSON MANDELA PLACE, GLASGOW G2 1BT.
TEL.: 0141-353 7001. FAX: 0141-353 7020.

Contact: Mrs Wendy Goldstraw, Regional General Manager, Scotland and Northern

Ireland, 0141-353 7001.
Post Office Counters Ltd runs the country's largest retail chain – the nationwide network of Post Offices. We offer a wide range of retail services and products, are committed to providing excellent personal service to our customers and are proud of our unmatched presence in local communities.

PROFESSIONAL

BRITISH ASSOCIATION OF SOCIAL WORKERS
28 NORTH BRIDGE, EDINBURGH EH1 1QG.
TEL.: 0131-225 4549. FAX: 0131-220 0636.
Contact: David Colvin, CBE, Scottish Secretary.
The largest professional organisation of social workers in the United Kingdom, BASW aims to advance the practice and understanding of social work issues, to campaign for improvements in social conditions for vulnerable people and to represent members' interests. BASW also organises study conferences, publishes the *British Journal of Social Work, Rostrum* and *Professional Social Work* as well as many books on social work practice. BASW Scotland is also developing a consultancy service in social work.

THE ROYAL INCORPORATION OF ARCHITECTS IN SCOTLAND
15 RUTLAND SQUARE, EDINBURGH EH1 2BE.
TEL.: 0131-229 7545. FAX: 0131-228 2188.
Contact: Sebastian Tombs, Secretary and Treasurer; Kate Comfort, Director of Public Affairs.
The Royal Incorporation of Architects in Scotland (RIAS) aims to promote a wider awareness of architectural achievement in Scotland, current and historical. Activities furthering this objective include: architectural exhibitions – in the RIAS Gallery and elsewhere; the Rutland Press – which publishes the popular illustrated architectural guides to Scotland; and regular contributions to the mainstream press. The RIAS also assists clients in finding appropriate Chartered Architects, via the Client's Advisory Service, design competitions, Presidential nominations (for projects over £100,000), RIAS Consultancy and the biennial *Scottish Architects' Directory.*

THE ROYAL INSTITUTION OF CHARTERED SURVEYORS IN SCOTLAND
9 MANOR PLACE, EDINBURGH EH3 7DN.
TEL.: 0131-225 7078. FAX: 0131-226 3599.
Contact: Eileen Masterman, Director; Graeme Hartley, Deputy Director; Elizabeth Bruce, Assistant Director (Communications).
The principal objectives of the RICS in Scotland are to: promote the knowledge and skills of chartered surveyors and the services they offer; maintain high standards of qualification for membership of the Institution; maintain high standards of professional conduct; and ensure the continuing development of the knowledge and skill base of chartered surveyors.

RELIGIOUS

THE CHURCH OF SCOTLAND
121 GEORGE STREET, EDINBURGH EH2 4YN
TEL.: 0131-225 5722. FAX: 0131-220 3113.
Contact: Very Rev. Dr. James L. Weatherhead, Principal Clerk of the Genera

Assembly.

The Church of Scotland, part of the one Holy, Catholic and Apostolic Church, is the national church in Scotland, recognised by the State but independent in spiritual matters. Trinitarian in doctrine, Reformed in tradition and Presbyterian in polity, it exists to glorify God, to work for the advancement of Christ's kingdom throughout the world and to provide religious services for the people in Scotland, through parish ministry. It co-operates with other churches in various ecumenical bodies in Scotland and beyond.

RURAL

RURAL FORUM SCOTLAND
HIGHLAND HOUSE, 46 ST. CATHERINE'S ROAD, PERTH PH1 5RY.
TEL.: 01738 634565. FAX: 01738 638699.

Contact: Dermot Grimson, Director; Deirdre Hutton, Chairman; Barbara Kelly CBE, President.

Rural Forum is an alliance of non-governmental organisations that includes agricultural, environmental, business, trade union, consumer and community interests. A membership organisation, it brings together local authorities, community councils, government agencies and departments. It aims to address rural matters in an integrated way involving people living and working in the countryside. Three main areas of work: policy and innovation (includes undertaking and commissioning research, organising conferences, seminars, exchanges, etc); Rural Action Network (aims to support action at the local level by providing grants, advice and information); and Rural Housing Service (incorporates both a research and a community involvement element in respect of rural housing issues). Has a number of publications including a quarterly magazine, conference reports, case studies in rural development and reports on research and demonstration projects.

TRADE ORGANISATIONS

SCOTTISH & NORTHERN IRELAND PLUMBING EMPLOYERS' FEDERATION (SNIPEF)
2 WALKER STREET, EDINBURGH EH3 7LB.
TEL.: 0131-225 2255. FAX: 0131-226 7638.

Contact: Mr Robert D. Burgon, Director and Secretary; Miss Leslie Stark, Information Officer.

The Scottish & Northern Ireland Plumbing Employers' Federation is the national trade association for all types of firms involved in the plumbing and domestic heating industry in Scotland and Northern Ireland. SNIPEF has almost 1,000 member firms and requires each firm to satisfy a number of important criteria before being accepted into membership. It is widely regarded as one of the most effective and representative trade associations in the UK construction sector. SNIPEF operates a unique code of fair trading (including a guarantee of work scheme) in respect of customer complaints which consists of conciliation, and if necessary arbitration, to resolve customer complaints against member firms.

TRADE UNIONS

GMB SCOTLAND
FOUNTAIN HOUSE, 1/3 WOODSIDE CRESCENT, GLASGOW G3 7UJ.

TEL.: **0141-332 8641.** FAX: **0141-332 4491.**

Contact: Robert Thomson, Regional Secretary; David Falconer, Regional President; Alex McMillan, Finance Director, Scotland.

GMB – Britain's General Union has 800,000 members, 90,000 in Scotland alone. GMB has members in almost every industry and service, and is concerned not only with winning improvements in pay and conditions for its members, but also with providing services which are second to none. The GMB is a Union with a proud history, but rather than looking backward, it is known for its progressive and forward looking policies – policies which look at the industrial scene as it exists today.

UNISON, SCOTLAND
UNISON HOUSE, 14 WEST CAMPBELL STREET, GLASGOW G2 6RX.
TEL.: 0141-332 0006. FAX: 0141-331 1203.

Contact: Matt Smith, Scottish Secretary.

UNISON is the largest trade union in the country, representing a range of members across the public services – local government, the National Health Service, higher and further education, the electricity, gas and transport industries and a range of public and voluntary organisations. UNISON provides a range of membership services in addition to its professional negotiation and representation role. It has offices in Glasgow, Edinburgh, Perth, Aberdeen and Inverness. UNISON is committed to campaigning actively in support of public services in Scotland.

TRANSPORT

RAIL USERS' CONSULTATIVE COMMITTEE FOR SCOTLAND
CALEDONIAN MACBRAYNE USERS' CONSULTATIVE COMMITTEE
249 WEST GEORGE STREET, GLASGOW G2 4QE.
TEL.: 0141-221 7760. FAX: 0141-221 3393.

Contact: Helen Millar, Chairman; Bill Ure, Secretary; E.M. Norris, Assistant Secretary.

Exists to represent rail and ferry users' interests, to monitor quality of service provided by train operating companies and Caledonian MacBrayne; to undertake investigations into rail quality of service matters as directed by the Rail Regulator and Franchise Director; to act as "Court of Appeal" for passengers who are dissatisfied with how their complaints are handled by train operators. Holds four public meetings each year to question senior railway managers on quality of service matters. Reports annually to the Secretary of State for Scotland on rail matters.

YOUTH

THE GUIDE ASSOCIATION SCOTLAND
16 COATES CRESCENT, EDINBURGH EH3 7AH.
TEL.: 0131-226 4511. FAX: 0131-220 4828.

Contact: Miss P.M. Ashton, Executive Director; Mrs W.G. Robertson, Scottish Chief Commissioner; Mrs G.R. Patterson, Public Relations Adviser.

The Guide Association is the UK's largest voluntary movement for girls and women. Its purpose is to enable girls to mature into confident, capable and caring women, determined, as individuals to realise their potential in their career, home and personal life, and willing, as citizens, to contribute to their community and the wider world. We believe we can best develop these qualities in a mutually-supportive, female structure, within an environment of fun, friendship and adventure, underpinned by spiritual and moral values.

ZOOLOGICAL

ROYAL ZOOLOGICAL SOCIETY OF SCOTLAND
EDINBURGH ZOO, MURRAYFIELD, EDINBURGH EH12 6TS.
TEL.: 0131-334 9171. FAX: 0131-316 4050.

Contact: Professor Roger Wheater, Director; Dr. Miranda Stevenson, Curator (M.F.Stevenson@festival.ed.ac.uk); Amanda Alabaster Marketing Manager, 0131-334 7730.

Exists to promote, through the presentation of our living collections, the conservation of animal species and wild places by captive breeding, environmental education and scientific research. The Royal Zoological Society of Scotland is a charitable, non-profit making organisation devoted to the study and conservation of wildlife. Founded in 1909 to promote a greater knowledge of animal life among the Scottish people, today it is one of the nation's foremost conservation organisations, owning both Edinburgh Zoo and the Highland Wildlife Park.

SCOTRAIL

WHO'S WHO IN SCOTRAIL

Directors

John Ellis : *Director* (tel:0141 335 4500)
John Boyle : *Corporate Affairs* (tel:0141 335 4447)
Alex Lynch : *Finance* (tel:0141 335 4180)
Alan Somerville : *Commercial* (tel:0141 335 4665)
Peter Summerhayes : *Operations & Engineering* (tel:0141 335 4389)
Jim Logue : *Personnel* (tel:0141 335 4344)

Senior Management

Mike Ashton : *Marketing Manager, ScotRail services* (tel:0141 335 4606)
Peter Newbould : *Marketing Manager, SPTE services* (tel:0141 335 4635)
Theresa Houston : *Customer Services Manager* (tel:0141 335 4554)
Mike Price : *Contracts Manager* (tel:0141 335 3669)
Heather MacLeod : *Chief Accountant* (tel:0141 335 4634)
Alan Chaplin : *Fleet Engineer* (tel: 0141 335 4670)
Jeff Thomas : *Overnight Services Manager* (tel: 0141 335 4245)

Area Managers

Jacqueline Dey : Ayr
 Ayr Station
 Burns Statue Square
 Ayr KA7 3AU
 (tel : 0141 335 8500)

Stephen McCredie : Yoker
 Yoker Depot
 Matthew House
 55 Dyke Road
 Yoker G14 0LY
 (tel : 0141 335 7665)

Steve Montgomery : Edinburgh
 Waverley Station
 Edinburgh EH1 1BB
 (tel : 0131 550 2710)

Frank Callaghan : Glasgow Central
 Glasgow Central Station
 87 Union Street
 Glasgow G1 3TA
 (tel : 0141 335 4604)

Donald MacPherson : North
 Perth Station
 Leonard Street
 Perth PH2 8HF
 (tel : 01738 646400)

Alan Scott : Glasgow Queen Street
 Glasgow Queen Street Station
 North Hanover Street
 Glasgow G1 2AF
 (tel : 0141 335 3080)

Caledonian Chambers, 87 Union Street
Glasgow G1 3TA
Tel : 0141 332 9811
Fax: 0141 335 4592

Preface

This new, completely revised, edition of Who's Who in Scotland contains around 5,000 entries, many appearing for the first time.

All walks of Scottish life are represented: politics and public service, law, religion and education, business and finance, science and medicine, the arts and sport. Prominent Scots living outwith Scotland are not included.

Entries are arranged in alphabetical order, according to surname. A typical entry contains full name, present occupation, date and place of birth, followed by details of family, education and career, publications, recreations and address. The following abbreviations are commonly used: b. (born); m. (married); s. (son); d. (daughter).

Great care has been taken to ensure that information given is accurate and up to date, but during the period in which the book has been in preparation, it is inevitable that some circumstances will have changed. The publishers cannot accept liability for any errors.

A

Abbott, Mollie Pearson, CBE (1984), DPE, MEd; b. 4.2.28, Peebles. Educ. Edinburgh Ladies' College; Dunfermline College of Physical Education. Assistant Teacher of Physical Education in Edinburgh schools; Temporary Lecturer, Moray House College of Education, Edinburgh, 1952-56; Senior Lecturer, Ripon Training College, 1956-62; Principal Lecturer, Aberdeen College of Education, 1962-63; HM Inspector of Schools, 1964-70; Principal, Dunfermline College of Physical Education, 1970-83. Past Chairman: Association of Higher Academic Staff in Colleges of Education in Scotland, Scottish Central Committee on Physical Education, Scottish Joint Consultative Committee on Physical Education; former Member: General Teaching Council for Scotland, Court of Heriot Watt University, National Committee for the In-Service Training of Teachers, Scottish Arts Council, Scottish Council of Physical Education, Scottish Sports Council. Recreations: reading; skiing; swimming; walking; wind-surfing; handbell-ringing. Address: (h.) Janefield House, Kirkcudbright, DG6 4UR; T.-01557 30119.

Abercrombie, Ian R., Q.C., LLB (Hons); b. 7.7.55, Bulawayo. Educ. Milton High School; Edinburgh University. Recreations: travelling; walking. Address: (h.) 7 Lauder Road, Edinburgh, EH9 2EW; T.-0131-668 2489.

Aberdeen and Temair, June Marchioness of, CBE, DL, FRCM, FRSE. Musical Director and Conductor, Haddo House Choral and Operatic Society, since 1945. Educ. Southlands School, Harrow; Royal College of Music. Chairman: Scottish Children's League, 1969-84, NE Scotland Music School, since 1975, Advisory Council, Scottish Opera, 1979-90. Address: Haddo House, Aberdeen AB41 0ER; T.-01651 851216.

Abernethy, Hon. Lord, (John Alastair Cameron). Senator, College of Justice, since 1992; b. 1.2.38, Newcastle-upon-Tyne; m., Elspeth Mary Dunlop Miller; 3 s. Educ. St. Mary's School, Melrose; Glenalmond College, Perth; Pembroke College, Oxford. National Service, 2nd Lt., RASC, Aldershot and Malta, 1956-58. Called to the Bar, Inner Temple, 1963; admitted Member, Faculty of Advocates, 1966; Advocate-Depute, 1972-75; Standing Junior Counsel to Department of Energy, 1976-79, Scottish Development Department, 1978-79; QC (Scotland), 1979; Vice-Dean, Faculty of Advocates, 1983-92; President, Pensions Appeal Tribunals for Scotland, 1985-92 (Legal Chairman, 1979-85); Chairman, Faculty Services Ltd., 1983-89 (Director, 1979-89); Hon. Fellow, Pembroke College, Oxford, 1993; Vice-Chairman, Judges' Forum, International Bar Association, 1993-94, Chairman, since 1994; Member, Executive Committee, Society for the Welfare and Teaching of the Blind (Edinburgh and South East Scotland), 1979-92. Publications: Medical Negligence: an introduction, 1983; Reproductive Medicine and the Law (Contributor). Recreations: travel; sport; Africana. Address: (b.) Court of Session, Parliament House, Edinbrugh, EH1 1RQ; T.-0131-225 2595.

Adam, Edmund Ian, MBChB, DRCOG. Medical Adviser, Lothian Regional Council, 1985-95; Clinical Assistant, Department of Medicine, Western General Hospital, Edinburgh, since 1969; Medical Officer, Company of Merchants of City of Edinburgh, since 1973; b. 26.5.31, Edinburgh; m., Norma Barbara; 2 s. Educ. Daniel Stewart's College, Edinburgh; University of Edinburgh. House Officer (Surgery), General Hospital, Kirkcaldy, 1956-57; House Officer (Medicine), Bangour General Hospital, 1957; Medical Officer (Captain, RAMC), Intelligence Corps Depot, Sussex, 1957-59; House Officer (Obstetrics), Craigtoun Maternity Hospital, St. Andrews, 1959-60; Trainee Assistant, general practice, Dunkeld, 1960-61; Partner, general practice, Edinburgh, 1961-85; School Medical Officer, Daniel Stewart's and Melville College, Edinburgh, 1972-85. Moderator, Society of High Constables of Edinburgh, 1987-89; Honorary Physician: Scottish Schools Rugby Union, 1977-94, Scottish Badminton Union, 1977-90. Recreation: golf. Address: (h.) Norian, 60 Hillview Terrace, Edinburgh EH12 8RG; T.-031-334 3498.

Adam, Ian Clark, CA.Group Finance Director, Christian Salvesen plc, since 1994; b. 2.9.43, Dundee; m., Betty Anne; 1 s.; 1 d. Educ. Harris Academy, Dundee. Trained as CA, Henderson & Logie, Dundee, 1962-67; Price Waterhouse Peat & Co., Rio de Janeiro, 1967-70; Price Waterhouse, Bristol, 1970-76; Partner, Price Waterhouse, Edinburgh, 1976-86, Senior Partner, Scotland, 1986-94. Treasurer, Royal Burgess Golfing Society of Edinburgh; Treasurer, Royal Scottish Society for the Prevention of Cruelty to Children; Governor, Queen Margaret College, Stewarts Erskine Schools. Recreations: golf; reading; walking. Address: (b.) 50 East Fettes Avenue, Edinburgh, EH4 1EQ; T.-0131-559 3600.

Adam, Ian Simpson Thomson, QFSM, GIFireE. Firemaster, Central Region Fire Brigade, since 1984; b. 4.5.40, Dunfermline; m., Norma; 1 s. Educ. Beath Secondary, Cowdenbeath. Retained Firefighter, Fife, 1960; wholetime Firefighter, Fife, 1964; Leading Firefighter, Fife, 1968; Sub Officer, Fife, 1969; Station Officer, Fife, 1972; Assistant Divisional Officer, Fife, 1974; Divisional Officer, Fife, 1978; Third Officer, SDO, Fife, 1979; Depute Firemaster, Central, 1982. Recreations: gardening; photography. Address: (b.) Main Street, Maddiston, Falkirk, FK2 OLG.

Adams, David Anstey, MA. Principal, Northern College of Education, formerly Aberdeen College of Education, since 1983; b. 2.3.42, Wakefield, Yorkshire; m., Margaret Ishbel; 1 s.; 1 d. Educ. Harris Academy, Dundee; St. Andrews University. Teacher of English and History, High School of Dundee; Principal Teacher of English, Arbroath Academy; Assistant Director of Education: Angus County Council, Tayside Regional Council. Member, Committee of Scottish Higher Education Principals, General Teaching Council for Scotland, Open University Validation Board; Chairman, Independent Television Commission Viewer Consultative Council (Scotland). Recreations: fishing; shooting. Address: (b.) Northern College of Education, (Aberdeen Campus), Hilton Place, Aberdeen, AB9 1FA; T.-01224 283500.

Adams, Irene, JP. MP (Labour), Paisley North, since 1990; b. 1948. Address: House of Commons, London, SW1A 0AA.

Adams, James Gordon Leitch, MA, PhD. Director of Planning and Development, Scottish Tourist Board, since 1988 (formerly Director of Development); b. 17.10.40, Glasgow; m., Rowan Hopwood; 1 s.; 1 d. Educ. Dundee High School; St Andrews University; Queen's University, Canada; McGill University. Economist: Canadian Federal Government, 1966-70, Highlands and Islands Development Board, 1970-75; Lecturer, Glasgow University, 1975-82; Visiting Lecturer in Poland, 1978, and India, 1981. Recreations: mountaineering; golf. Address: (h.) 5 Corrennie Drive, Edinburgh; T.-0131-447 8073.

Adams, Robert William, OBE, FCMA, FCCA, JDipMA. Director, John Cairney & Co. Ltd., since 1983; Member, Committee of Management, Hanover Housing Association, since 1982; b. 27.9.22, Glasgow; m., Mary Ann Ritchie; 2 s.; 1 d. Educ. Shawlands Academy, Glasgow. H.C. Stewart & Co., CA, Glasgow; Lieutenant, Parachute Regiment; South of Scotland Electricity Board; James Colledge (Cocoa) Ltd., West Africa; Highland Home Industries Ltd.;

Managing Director, A.H. McIntosh & Co. Ltd., until 1982. Member, Glenrothes Development Corporation, 1976-84; former Member: Scottish Sports Council; Council, Institute of Cost and Management Accountants; Scottish Sports Council; former Convenor, Scottish Athletic Coaching Committee; former Scottish Chairman, Writers' Guild. Recreations: tennis; golf. Address: (h.) Achray, Shore Road, Aberdour, Fife; T.-01383 860269.

Adams, William Ralph McClymont, Esq., OStJ, FSA (Scot), FHSS. Vice President Heraldry Society of Scotland, since 1988 (Secretary, 1983-87) and Fellow of Society; b. 6.3.15, Banton, by Kilsyth; m., Joan Graham Barry; 1 s.; 2 d. Educ. Dollar Academy; Hillhead High School, Glasgow; Perth Academy; Heriot Watt College, Edinburgh; Edinburgh College of Art. Architectural training, Perth and Edinburgh; Civil Servant, 1939-80; specialised in conservation of carved stone, decorated plaster, painted ornament and heraldic blazons; Senior Conservation Officer for Scotland, from 1953; Officer, Most Venerable Order of St John of Jerusalem, since 1982; Honorary Guildsman, Ancient Royal Archers Guild of St Sebastian at Knokke, Belgium, 1984. Recreations: horticulture; photography; research and lecturing on heraldry, history, historic buildings and gardens. Address: (h.) Limegrove, High Street, Gifford, Haddington, East Lothian EH41 4QU; T.-01620 810617.

Adamson, James G., OBE. Vice President and Managing Director, AT&T (Scotland) Ltd.; b. 25.5.41, Rosyth; m., Ann May; 2 s.; 2 d. Educ. Heriot-Watt University. MoD (Navy), Rosyth; Honeywell Computer Systems; ITT; Marconi Space & Defence; NCR/AT&T. President, Fife Society for the Blind; Non-Executive Director: Scottish Higher Education Funding Council, Scottish Enterprise, East Board Bank of Scotland; Member, Scottish Economic Council; Member, Advisory Board, SCDI. Recreations: sailing; singing. Address: (b.) Kingsway West, Dundee; T.-01383 592368.

Adamson, Rev. Sidney, MA, BD. Minister, Church of Scotland; b. 3.8.11, Arbroath; m., Margaret T. Sharpe, JP; 1 s. Educ. Dumbarton Academy; Glasgow University and Trinity College; Royal Scottish Academy of Music and Drama. Ministries: St Ninian's, Sanquhar, 1937-47 (including war service), Trinity Church, Renfrew, 1947-54, High Kirk of Rothesay, 1954-59, St Michael's Inveresk, Musselburgh, 1959-85. Moderator of Presbytery: Dumfries, 1939, Dunoon, 1958, Dalkeith, 1964 and 1965; former Moderator, Synod of Lothian and Tweeddale; Army Chaplain, India, 1944-47; Territorial Army Chaplain, 1952-66; Chaplain, Royal British Legion (Scotland), Paisley, Renfrew, Rothesay, Musselburgh, and Honorary Vice President, Edinburgh & Lothian Area Council, 1973; Industrial Chaplain, Babcock & Wilcox Ltd., Renfrew, 1948-54; Chaplain, British Sailors' Society, 1955-85; Editor, Homeward Bound (Forces magazine, India), 1946-47. Publications: Two Centuries of Service (history of Sanquhar congregation), 1939; St Michael's Kirk at Inveresk (four editions between 1963 and 1984). Recreations: (at suitable periods) ballroom dancing; shooting; swimming; (always) reading; theatre; freelance journalism; ex-service welfare. Address: 48 Hailes Gardens, Colinton, Edinburgh, EH13 0JH; T.-0131-441 2471.

Addison, Alexander, MB, ChB, FRCGP, DObstRCOG. Senior Partner, Addison, Scott, Kane & Ferguson, since 1978; Chairman, Lanarkshire LMC, since 1989; Member, Scottish Committee, BMA, since 1984, and Fellow, BMA, since 1993; b. 23.8.30, Kerala; m., Joan Wood; 3 s. Educ. Keith Grammar School; Aberdeen Grammar School; Aberdeen University. House Surgeon and Physician, Woodend General Hospital, Aberdeen, 1954-55; Captain, RAMC; Junior Medical Specialist, Cowglen MH, 1955-58; SHO, Bellshill MH, 1958-59; GP in Douglas and Physician to Lady Home Hospital, since 1959; Member, West of Scotland Faculty of GP College, 1967-79 and of Scottish Council, 1976-78; Member, Lanarkshire LMC, since 1972, and of AMAC, since 1975; Chairman, Lanarkshire AMAC, 1982-86; Chairman, Scottish Association of General Practitioner Hospitals, 1985-87; Member, Scottish Committee of Medical Commission on Accident Prevention, since 1976; Member, National Medical Consultative Committee, 1977-83; Honorary Surgeon, St. Andrews Ambulance Association, 1959-89. Recreations: curling; golf; reading. Address: (h.) 7 Addison Drive, Douglas, Lanarkshire ML11 0PZ; T.-01555 851302.

Adler-Bell, Marianne. Dress Designer, since 1939; Member, Board of Directors, Citizens' Theatre, Glasgow, since 1973; b. 17.1.15, Berlin, Germany; m., John Bell (deceased); 1 s. Educ. Staatliche Augusta Schule, Berlin; Art School, Berlin. Former Vice-Chairman, Citizens' Theatre Society. Awarded Bundesverdienstkreuz (similar in Germany to OBE) for work in furthering Scottish-German relations. Recreations: opera; gardening. Address (h.) 348 Knightswood Road, Glasgow, G13 2BT; T.-0141-959 1696.

Affolter, Michael Theodore, BA (Hons), PhD, DipTP, MRTPI. Assistant Secretary, Scottish Office, since 1989; b. 11.5.40, Bangor, Northern Ireland; m., Margaret Elizabeth; 2 s. Educ. Bangor Grammar School; Queen's University of Belfast; Edinburgh College of Art. Planning Assistant, Ministry of Development, Northern Ireland, 1963-66; Scottish Development Department, 1967, Senior Planning Officer, 1973, then Principal. Recreations: hill-walking; skiing; badminton; cricket; golf. Address: (h.) 1 Mortonhall Road, Edinburgh EH9 2HS. T.-0131-667 4716.

Aggett, Kathleen McGregor, BSc. Head Teacher, Broxburn Academy, since 1991; b. 24.7.47, Dalbeattie; m., Graham Aggett; 1 d. Educ. Dalbeattie High School; Kirkcudbright Academy; Edinburgh University; Moray House College of Education. Castlebrae High School, Edinburgh: Teacher of Mathematics, 1970-76, Assistant Principal Teacher of Guidance to Assistant Head Teacher, 1976-88; Depute Head Teacher, Broxburn Academy, 1988-91. FRSA. Recreations: golf; gardening; reading; travel; backgammon. Address: (h.) Cardon Mews, 4A Mortonhall Road, Edinburgh, EH9 2HW; T.-0131-668 2468.

Agnew of Lochnaw, Sir Crispin Hamlyn. 11th Baronet (created 1629); Chief of the Agnews; Advocate, since 1982; Unicorn Pursuivant of Arms, 1981-86, Rothesay Herald of Arms, since 1986; b. 13.5.44, Edinburgh; m., Susan Rachel Strang Steel; 1 s.; 3 d. Educ. Uppingham School; Royal Military Academy, Sandhurst. Commissioned Royal Highland Fusiliers, 1964, as 2nd Lieutenant; Major, 1977; Retired, 1981. Member: Royal Navy Expedition to East Greenland, 1966; Joint Services Expedition to Elephant Island, Antarctica, 1970-71; Army Nuptse Himal Expedition, 1975; Army Everest Expedition, 1976; Leader: Army East Greenland Expedition, 1968; Joint Services Expedition to Chilean Patagonia, 1972-73; Army Api Himal Expedition, 1980. Publications: articles in various newspapers and journals. Recreations: mountaineering; offshore sailing. Address: 6 Palmerston Road, Edinburgh, EH9 1TN; T.-0131-667 4970.

Agnew, Ian, MA (Hons) (Cantab). Rector, Perth High School, 1975-92; b. 10.5.32, Newcastle-upon-Tyne; m., Gladys Agnes Heatherill; 1 d. Educ. King's College School, London; Pembroke College, Cambridge. Assistant Teacher of Modern Languages, Melville College, Edinburgh, 1958-63; Assistant Teacher of Modern Languages, then Principal Teacher of Russian, George Heriot's School, Edinburgh, 1964-70; Housemaster, Craigmount Secondary School, Edinburgh, 1970-73; Deputy, Liberton High School, Edinburgh, 1973-75. Non-Executive Director, Perth and Kinross Healthcare NHS Trust; Chairman, Tayside Regional Working Party on Religious Education, since 1977; Minute Secretary, Headteachers Association of

Scotland, 1979-81; Committee Member, SCCORE; President: Perthshire Musical Festival, 1978-88, Perth Chamber Music Society, 1982-89; Past President, Rotary Club of Perth St. John's; Past Chairman: Barnton and Cramond Conservative Association and West Edinburgh Conservative and Unionist Association; Elder, St. Andrew's Parish Church, Perth; Serving Officer (OStJ), Priory of Scotland of the Most Venenerable Order of St. John; Member, Society of High Constables, City of Perth; Governor: Balnacraig School, Perth, since 1981, Kilgraston School, Convent of the Sacred Heart, Bridge of Earn, since 1990. Recreations: music (opera); reading; tennis; gardening. Address: (h.) Northwood, Heughfield Road, Bridge of Earn, Perthshire, PH2 9BH; T.-01738 81 2273.

Ailsa, 8th Marquess of (Archibald Angus Charles Kennedy); b. 13.9.56; 2 d. Address: Cassillis House, Maybole, KA19 7JN.

Airlie, 13th Earl of (David George Coke Patrick Ogilvy), KT, GCVO, PC, JP. Lord Chamberlain of Her Majesty's Household; Ensign, Queen's Body-Guard for Scotland (Royal Company of Archers), since 1975; Chairman, General Accident Fire & Life Assurance Corporation plc, since 1987 (Deputy Chairman, 1975-87); Chancellor, University of Abertay, Dundee, since 1994; Director, Baring Stratton Investment Trust plc, since 1986; Lord Lieutenant, Angus; Chancellor of the Royal Victorian Order; Hon. President, Scottish Council, The Scout Association; b. 17.5.26, London; m., Virginia Fortune Ryan; 3 s.; 3 d. Educ. Eton College. Lieutenant, Scots Guards, 1944; serving 2nd Bn., Germany, 1945; Captain, ADC to High Commissioner and C-in-C Austria, 1947-48; Malaya, 1948-49; resigned commission, 1950; Chairman, Ashdown Investment Trust Ltd., 1968-82; Director, J. Henry Schroder Wagg & Co. Ltd., 1961-84 (Chairman, 1973-77); Chairman, Schroders plc, 1977-84; Scottish and Newcastle Breweries plc, until 1983; Director, Royal Bank of Scotland Group, 1983-93; Director, Royal Bank of Scotland plc, 1991-93. Address: (h.) Cortachy Castle, Kirriemuir, Angus; T.-Cortachy 231.

Aitchison, James Douglas, MA (Hons), MEd (Hons). Head Teacher, Boclair Academy, Bearsden, since 1991 (Head Teacher, Gleniffer High School, Paisley, 1984-91); b. 2.7.47, Glasgow. Educ. High School of Glasgow; Glasgow University; University of Marburg. Teacher, Lycee Faidherbe, Lille; Principal Teacher, Bearsden Academy; Assistant Head Teacher, Gryffe High School, Houston. Recreations: curling; walking; travel. Address: (h.) 44 Keystone Road, Milngavie, Glasgow G62 6QG; T.-041-956 6693.

Aitken, Professor Adam Jack, MA, DLitt. Editor, A Dictionary of the Older Scottish Tongue, 1956-86; Editorial Consultant and Pronunciation Editor, Concise Scots Dictionary, 1975-85; b. 19.6.21, Edinburgh; m., Norma Ward Manson; 3 s.; 1 d. Educ. Lasswade Secondary School; Edinburgh University. Assistant Lecturer in English Language, Edinburgh University, 1947-48; Research Fellow, Universities of Glasgow, Aberdeen and Edinburgh, 1948-54; Lecturer, Universities of Glasgow and Edinburgh, 1954-64 (Assistant Editor and Editor, Dictionary of the Older Scottish Tongue); Edinburgh University: Honorary Senior Lecturer, 1965-71, Senior Lecturer (part-time) in English Language, 1971-75, Reader (part-time) in English Language, 1975-79; Chairman, Language Committee, Association for Scottish Literary Studies, 1971-76; Chairman, Universities' Forum for Research on the Languages of Scotland, 1978-81; Vice-President, Scottish Text Society, since 1985; Hon. President, Forum for Research on the Languages of Scotland and Ulster, since 1991; Hon. Preses, Scots Language Society, since 1994; Biennial Sir Israel Gollancz Prize of British Academy, 1981; Honorary Professor, Edinburgh University, since 1984. Publications: Edinburgh Studies in English and Scots,

1971; The Computer and Literary Studies, 1973; Lowland Scots, 1973; Bards and Makars, 1977; Languages of Scotland, 1979. Address: (h.) 5 Bellevue Crescent, Edinburgh, EH3 6ND; T.-031-558 1534.

Aitken, Joan Nicol, MA (Hons), SSC. Solicitor, since 1978, formerly a Partner, Messrs Rollo Davidson and McFarlane, Cupar; Editor, Journal of the Law Society of Scotland; b. 26.2.53, Glasgow; m., Alistair Bruce Dodds; 1 d. Educ. James Gillespie's High School for Girls; Dundee University. Member: Scottish Consumer Council; former Member, Council, Law Society of Scotland; part-time Chairman, Industrial Tribunals (Scotland) and Child Support Appeal Tribunal; family law mediator and Vice-Convener, CALM; Member, General Dental Council; was first woman member, Society of Solicitors in the Supreme Courts of Scotland. Address: (h.) Shepherd's Lodge, Kiltarlity, Beauly IV4 7HR; T.-01463 741369.

Aitken, Professor Robert Cairns Brown, MB, ChB, DPM, MD, DSc (Hon), FRCPEdin, FRCPsych. Chairman, Royal Infirmary of Edinburgh NHS Trust, since 1994; Professor Emeritus of Rehabilitation Studies, Edinburgh University, 1974-94 (Dean, Faculty of Medicine, 1990-91, Vice-Principal, 1991-94); Honorary Consultant in Rehabilitation Medicine, Lothian Health Board, since 1994; b. 20.12.33, Dunoon; m., Audrey May Lunn; 1 s.; 1 d. Educ. Dunoon Grammar School; Cargilfield School, Edinburgh; Sedbergh School, Yorkshire; Glasgow University. Institute of Aviation Medicine, RAF, 1959-62; Orpington and Maudsley Hospitals, 1962-66; Senior Lecturer/Consultant Psychiatrist, Royal Infirmary and Royal Edinburgh Hospital, 1967-74. President, International College of Psychosomatic Medicine, 1985-87; Chairman, Napier Polytechnic of Edinburgh Governors, 1983-90; Member, Council for Professions Supplementary to Medicine, 1983-90; Member, General Medical Council, since 1991; Director, Lothian Health Board, 1991-93; Editor, Journal of Psychosomatic Research, 1979-85; occasional WHO consultant; Foundation Secretary, then President, Society for Research in Rehabilitation, 1981-83. Publications: papers on measurement of mood; flying phobia; management of disability. Recreations: people, places and pleasures of Edinburgh, Scotland and beyond. Address: (h.) 11 Succoth Place, Edinburgh, EH12 6BJ; T.-0131-337 1550.

Aitken, William Duff, MM (FG). Director, William Aitken Highland Exports Ltd., since 1973; Member, Board of Directors, Eden Court Theatre, 1984-88; Member, Inverness District Council, 1984-88; b. 12.3.27, Newton Mearns; m., Eva Alexandra Kjellsson; 2 d. Educ. Terra Nova, Birkdale; Merchant Taylors'; Liverpool Nautical College. Seafaring, 1943-53; tanning industry, 1953-72. Member, SSAT. Recreations: philately; swimming; RNXS; TNAUK. Address: (h) The Thistles, 24 MacLeod Road, Balloch, by Inverness, IV1 2JW; T.-01463 791234.

Aitken, William Russell, MA, PhD, FLA. Bibliographer; b. 7.2.13, Calderbank, Lanarkshire; m., Betsy Mary Murison; 1 d. Educ. Dunfermline High School; Edinburgh University. Assistant Librarian, Scottish Central Library, 1936-40; war service, RAF, 1941-46; County Librarian: Clackmannanshire, 1946-49, Perth and Kinross, 1949-58, Ayr, 1958-62; Lecturer, then Senior Lecturer, latterly Reader, Department of Librarianship, University of Strathclyde, 1962-78. President, Scottish Library Association, 1965; Friends Historical Society, 1989. Editor, Library Review, 1964-76. Books: A History of the Public Library Movement in Scotland, 1971; William Soutar's Poems in Scots and English (Editor), 1961, 1975; The Complete Poems of Hugh MacDiarmid (Editor, with Michael Grieve), 1978, 1985, 1993; Scottish Literature in English and Scots (a bibliographical guide), 1982; Poems of William Soutar: a new selection (Editor), 1988. Address:

(h.) 6 Tannahill Terrace, Dunblane, FK15 OAX; T.-Dunblane 823650.

Aitkenhead, John M., MA (Hons), MEd, JP. Principal and Founder, Kilquhanity House International School for Boys and Girls, since 1940; b. 21.5.10, Glasgow; m., Morag MacKinnon; 2 s.; 2 d. Educ. Ardrossan Academy; Glasgow University. Worked in Scottish education system until 1940; conscientious objector during World War II; established school inspired by work and writing of A.S. Neill; ardent Scottish nationalist. Recreations: singing; poetry; Scottish country dancing; Gaelic; gardening. Address: Kilquhanity, Castle Douglas DG7 3DB; T.-0155 650 597.

Alexander, Professor Alan, MA. Professor of Local and Public Management and Head, Department of Human Resource Management, Strathclyde University, since 1993 (Professor of Local Government, 1987-93); Director, Scottish Local Authorities Management Centre, 1987-93; b. 13.12.43, Glasgow; m., Morag MacInnes (Morag Alexander, qv); 1 s.; 1 d. Educ. Possil Secondary School, Glasgow; Albert Secondary School, Glasgow; Glasgow University. Lecturer/Assistant Professor, Political Science, Lakehead University, Ontario, 1966-71; Lecturer in Politics, Reading University, 1971-87. Member of Board, Housing Corporation, 1977-80; Member, Standing Research Committee on Local and Central Government Relations, Joseph Rowntree Memorial Trust, 1988-92; conducted inquiry into relations between Western Isles Islands Council and BCCI, 1991. Publications: Local Government in Britain since Reorganisation, 1982; The Politics of Local Government in the UK, 1982; L'amministrazione locale in Gran Bretagna, 1984; Borough Government and Politics: Reading, 1835-1985, 1985; Managing the Fragmented Authority, 1994. Recreations: theatre; cinema; hill-walking; avoiding gardening. Address: (b.) Department of Human Resource Management, The Graham Hills Building, 50 Richmond Street, Glasgow, G1 1XT; T.-0141-553 4167.

Alexander, Major-General David Crichton, CB. Commandant, Scottish Police College, 1979-87; b. 28.11.26, Aberdour; m., Diana Joyce (Jane) Fisher; 1 s.; 1 step-s.; 2 d. Educ. Edinburgh Academy; Staff College, Camberley; Royal College of Defence Studies. Royal Marines, 1944-77 (2nd Lieutenant to Major-General, including Equerry and Acting Treasurer to Duke of Edinburgh); Director-General, English Speaking Union, 1977-79. President, Corps of Commissionaires; Member, Civil Service Final Selection Board, 1978-88; Chairman, Edinburgh Academy, 1985-90; Freeman, City of London; Liveryman, Painter Stainers' Company; Member, Transport Users Consultative Committee for Scotland, 1989-93; President, SSAFA Fife, 1990-94. Recreations: fishing; golf; gardening. Address: (h.) Baldinnie, Park Place, Elie KY9 1DH; T.-01333 330882.

Alexander, David Richard Watson, CBE (1972), MA; b. 12.8.18, Montrose; m., Mrs M.A.E. James; 1 s., 1 d. by pr. m.; 3 step-s. Educ. Montrose Academy; Edinburgh University. Served World War II in Hong Kong, India, Ceylon and Malaya (2nd Royal Scots, 12th Frontier Force Regt. and Force 136 (S.O.E.)); final rank, Lieutenant Colonel; awarded MBE (Mil.) for gallant and distinguished service with S.O.E. behind Japanese lines in Malaya. Colonial Administrative Service: appointed Assistant District Officer, Nigeria, 1946; resigned, 1947; re-appointed, 1948, Administrative Officer, Somaliland - on secondment to Cyrenaica (Libya) for service with War Office, then Foreign Office Administration of African Territories, finally Government of Cyrenaica; appointments: PA to Chief Administrator, BMA Benghazi, Political Secretary, District Commissioner Derna, District Adviser, Benghazi, Chief Secretary, Ministry of Interior; transferred to Hong Kong, 1953; appointments: Commissioner

Essential Services Corps and Chief Staff Officer Civil Aid Services, Director of Social Welfare, Commissioner of Labour, Director of Urban Services and Chairman, Urban Council, Chairman, Housing Authority; Honourable Member, Legislative Council; retired, 1975. Elected Member, Lothian Regional Council, 1982-86 (Chairman, Planning and Development Committee). Address: (h.) 2 Crarae Avenue, Edinburgh, EH4 3JD.

Alexander, Rev. Douglas Niven, MA, BD. Minister, Erskine Parish Church, Bishopton, since 1970; Convener, Church of Scotland Board of Communication, 1987-91; b. 8.4.35, Eaglesham; m., Dr. Joyce O. Garven; 1 s.; 2 d. Educ. Hutchesons' Boys' Grammar School, Glasgow; Glasgow University (President, SRC, 1958); Union Theological Seminary, New York. Assistant Minister, St. Ninian's Church, Greenock, 1961-62; Warden, Iona Community House, Glasgow, 1963-70. Secretary, Scottish Union of Students, 1958; Assessor to Lord Rector, Glasgow University, 1969-71; Chaplain to Erskine Hospital, since 1970; Moderator, Paisley Presbytery, 1984; Mair Memorial Lecturer, Glasgow University, 1987; Chairman, British Churches Committee for Channel 4 TV, 1986-88; Member: Scottish Committee, IBA, 1988-90; Scottish Viewers Consultative Committee, ITC, 1991-92; National Religious Advisory Committee, IBA, 1988-90; National Religious Advisory Committee, ITC, 1991-92; Central Religious Advisory Committee, 1988-92. Recreation: researching ways of salmon poachers! Address: The Manse, Newton Road, Bishopton, Renfrewshire, PA7 5JP; T.-01505 862161.

Alexander, Rev. Eric J., MA, BD. Minister, St. George's-Tron Parish Church, Glasgow, since 1977; b. 9.5.32, Glasgow; m., Margaret D. Connell; 1 s.; 1 d. Educ. Allan Glen's School, Glasgow; Glasgow University. Publications: The Search for God, 1962; Plainly Teaching the Word, 1989. Address: (h.) 12 Dargarvel Avenue, Glasgow, G41.

Alexander, Professor James, BSc, PhD. Professor, Department of Immunology, Strathclyde University, since 1990; b. 14.11.49, Glasgow; m., Margaret Jean Wendon; 1 s. Educ. St. Mungo's Academy, Glasgow University. Scientific Staff, Division of Leprosy and Mycobacterial Research, National Institute for Medical Research, London, 1975-79; Research Fellow, Department of Biology, Imperial College of Science and Technology, London, 1979-85; Strathclyde University: Wellcome Trust Lecturer, Immunology, 1985, Senior Lecturer, 1989, Reader, 1990. Recreations: gardening; reading. Address: (b.) Todd Centre, Taylor Street, Strathclyde University, Glasgow G4 0NR; T.-0141-552 4400.

Alexander, John Huston, BLitt, MA, DPhil Oxon. Senior Lecturer in English, Aberdeen University, since 1984; Editor, Scottish Literary Journal; Field Editor, Abstracts of English Studies, since 1988; b. 5.4.41, Coleraine, Northern Ireland; m., Flora Ross; 2 s.; 2 d. Educ. Campbell College, Belfast; St. Edmund Hall, Oxford. Sessional Lecturer in English, University of Saskatchewan, Canada, 1966-67; Lecturer in English, Aberdeen University, 1968-84. Editor, The Scott Newsletter, since 1982. Publications: Two Studies in Romantic Reviewing, 1976; The Lay of the Last Minstrel: Three Essays, 1978; The Reception of Scott's Poetry By His Correspondents: 1796-1817, 1979; Marmion: Studies in Interpretation and Composition, 1981; Scott and his Influence (Editor, with David Hewitt), 1983; Reading Wordsworth, 1987; The Tavern Sages (Editor), 1992; Walter Scott, Kenilworth: A Romance (Editor), 1993; Scott in Carnival (Editor, with David Hewitt), 1993; Executive Editor, Edinburgh Edition of the Waverley Novels. Recreation: music. Address: (h.) 45A Queen's Road, Aberdeen, AB1 6YN; T.-01224 317424.

Alexander, Keith, BSc (Hons), BArch, RIBA, ARIAS, MBIM. Academic Director, Centre for Facilities

Management, Strathclyde University, since 1990; b. 20.9.49, Nottingham; m., Marie-Yvonne; 2 s.; 1 d. Educ. Wellingborough Grammar School; Welsh School of Architecture; University of Wales Institute of Science and Technology. Architect, new town development authorities, 1971-75; Principal, private practice, Northern Ireland and Scotland, 1975-78; Senior Lecturer, Ulster College, Northern Ireland Polytechnic, 1975-78; Consultant, Building Performance Design and Appraisal, 1978-90; Strathclyde University: Lecturer, Department of Architecture and Building Science, 1978-90, Director, Building Performance and Research Unit, 1984-90; Visiting Lecturer, School of Architecture, National University of Singapore, 1982-84; Architect, private practice, Singapore, 1982-84. President, European Facilities Management Network; Consultant Editor, Facilities and Facilities Management Journals. Recreations: rugby; golf. Address: (b.) Centre for Facilities Management, Strathclyde Graduate Business School, 199 Cathedral Street, Glasgow, G4 0QU. T.-0141-553 4165.

Alexander, Ken. Artistic Director, Byre Theatre, St. Andrews. Address: Abbey Street, St. Andrews, KY16 9LA.

Alexander, Sir Kenneth John Wilson, BSc (Econ), LLD, DUniv, FRSE, CBIM, Hon. Fellow, RIAS. Principal and Vice-Chancellor, Stirling University, 1981-86; b. 14.3.22, Edinburgh; m., Angela-May; 1 s.; 4 d. Educ. George Heriot's School, Edinburgh; School of Economics, Dundee. Taught at Universities of Leeds, Sheffield and Aberdeen; Professor of Economics, Strathclyde University, 1963-80; Chancellor, Aberdeen University, since 1986; Member, Advisory Committee on University of the Air, 1965; Chairman: Committee on Adult Education in Scotland, 1970-73, Social Science Research Council, 1975-76; President, Section F, British Association, 1974; Chairman, Highlands and Islands Development Board, 1976-80; Economic Consultant to the Secretary of State for Scotland, 1968-89; Member, Scottish Development Agency, 1975-85; Chairman, Council for Applied Science in Scotland, 1980-85; Governor, Technical Change Centre, 1981-87; Director, Scottish Television Ltd., since 1981; Member, Council for Tertiary Education in Scotland, 1981-82; Deputy Chairman, Scottish Council (Development and Industry), 1982-91; Honorary President: The Highland Fund, since 1983; Scottish National Dictionary Association Ltd., since 1983; President, Town and Country Planning (Scottish Section), since 1982; Director, Stakis plc, 1987-93; Chairman, Edinburgh Book Festival, 1987-91; Chairman, Scottish Industrial Trade Exhibitions, since 1990; Trustee, Aegean Archipelago, since 1994. Publications: The Economist in Business, 1967; Fairfields, a study of industrial change (with C.L. Jenkins), 1971; The Political Economy of Change (Editor), 1976. Recreation: Scottish antiquarianism. Address: (h.) 9 West Shore, Pittenweem, Fife, KY10 2NV; T.-01333 310593.

Alexander, Professor Michael Joseph, BA, MA (Oxon). Berry Professor of English Literature, St. Andrews University, since 1985; b. 21.5.41, Wigan; m., 1, Eileen Mary McCall (deceased); 2, Mary Cecilia Sheahan; 1 s.; 2 d. Educ. Downside School; Trinity College, Oxford; Perugia University; Princeton University. Editor, William Collins, London, 1963-65; Lecturer, University of California, 1966-67; Editor, Andre Deutsch, London, 1967-68; Lecturer: East Anglia University, 1968-69, Stirling University, 1969; Senior Lecturer, 1977; Reader, 1985. Publications: Earliest English Poems (Translator), 1966; Beowulf (Translator), 1973; Twelve Poems, 1978; The Poetic Achievement of Ezra Pound, 1979; History of Old English Literature, 1983; Macmillan Anthology of English Literature, 1989; Beowulf (Editor), 1995; Sons of Ezra (Editor), 1995. Address: (b.) School of English, St. Andrews University, St. Andrews KY16 9AL; T.-01334 462666.

Alexander, Morag, BA (Hons). Director, Equal Opportunities Commission, Scotland, since 1992; b. 10.10.43, Kilwinning; m., Professor Alan Alexander (qv); 1 s.; 1 d. Educ. Lourdes Secondary School, Glasgow; Glasgow University; Lakehead University, Ontario. Research Assistant, ASTMS, 1971-73; Editor and Researcher, RIPA, 1973-82; freelance journalist and consultant, 1982-90; Founding Editor, Women in Europe, 1985-89, and UK Correspondent, Women of Europe, 1987-92; Founding Director, Training 2000 (Scotland) Ltd., Scottish Alliance for Women's Training, 1990-92. Recreations: music; opera; visiting art galleries and museums; hill-walking. Address: (b.) E.O.C., Stock Exchange House, 7 Nelson Mandela Place, Glasgow, G2 1QW; T.-0141 248 5834.

Alexander, Samuel, BL. Honorary Sheriff, Dumbarton, since 1983; b. Glasgow; m., Isabella Kerr Ligertwood; 2 s. Educ. Govan High School; Glasgow University. Formerly Consultant and Senior Partner, Keyden Strang & Co., Solicitors, Glasgow. Recreations: golf; reading. Address: (h.) 1 Hillneuk Avenue, Bearsden, Glasgow, G61; T.-0141-942 4674.

Alexander, Walter Ronald, CBE. Chairman, Walter Alexander plc, 1979-90 (Managing Director, 1973-79); Company Director; b. 6.4.31; m., 1, Rosemary Anne Sleigh (m. diss.); 2 s.; 2 d.; 2, Mrs Lorna Elwes. Educ. Loretto School; Cambridge University (MA Hons). Chairman and Managing Director, Tayforth Ltd., 1961-71; Chairman, Scottish Automobile Company Ltd., 1971-73; Director: Scotcros plc, 1965-82 (Chairman, 1972-82); Investors Capital Trust plc, since 1967; Clydesdale Bank plc, since 1971; RIT and Northern plc, 1973-84; Dawson International plc, since 1979; Chairman, Scottish Appeals Committee, Police Dependants' Trust, 1974-81; President, Public Schools Golfing Society, 1973-79; Chairman: PGA, 1982-85; Royal and Ancient Golf Club of St. Andrews Trust, since 1987; Governor, Loretto School, 1961-89; Comr., Queen Victoria School, 1987-92; Scottish Free Enterprise Award, 1977. Recreation: golf. Address: Moonzie Mill, Balmullo, St. Andrews, KY16 0AH; T.-01334 870864.

Ali, Nasir, MB, BS, DPM, FRCPsych. Consultant Psychiatrist, since 1973; Honorary Senior Lecturer, Aberdeen University, since 1982; b. 21.8.39, Lucknow, India; m., D. Rosemary; 1 s.; 1 d. Address: (h.) Balmachree House, Dalcross, Inverness, IV1 2JQ; T.-Inverness 790602.

Ali, Yaqub, OBE. Chairman, Castle/AA Brothers Ltd.; Director, Strathclyde Vintners Ltd.; b. 12.12.31; m., Nancy; 1 s. Non-Executive Director, Landmark Cash & Carry Group; Member: Scottish Police Advisory Board, Scottish Industry Development Advisory Board, Queens College Council, Glasgow; Director, Ethnic Minority Enterprise Centre. Recreation: gardening. Address: (b.) 525 Crown Street, Glasgow, G5 9XR; T.-0141-429 6188.

Alison, Graham, BSc, MEd. General Secretary, Scottish Further and Higher Education Association, since 1982; b. 15.6.31, Clydebank; m., Norma McA. Perry; 2 d. Educ. Dumbarton Academy; Glasgow University. Education Officer, RAF; Educational Psychologist, Lecturer in Psychology and (until it closed) Vice-Principal, Hamilton College of Education. Recreations: theatre; golf; bowling. Address: (b.) 90 Mitchell Street, Glasgow, G1 3NQ; T.-0141-221 0118.

Allan, Bob, BSc (Hons), BSc (Hons), MA. Chief Executive, Clackmannanshire Council, since 1995; b. 20.6.52, Whitburn; m., Chrissie; 1 s.; 1 d. Educ. Bathgate Academy; Whitburn Academy; Aberdeen University; Queen's University, Kingston, Canada; Glasgow University. Formerly with COSLA; joined local government with City of Glasgow, 1980; Chief Executive, Clackmannan District Council, 1993-95. Recreations: family; reading (biography);

geology; sport; debunking the bumptious and pursuing the presumptuous. Address: 18 Cathkin Road, Glasgow; T.-0141-649 8639.

Allan, Charles Maitland, MA. Journalist, Economist and Farmer; b. 19.8.39, Stirling; m., Fiona Vine; 2 s.; 2 d. Educ. Dartington Hall; Aberdeen University. Lecturer in Economic History, Glasgow University, 1962-63; Lecturer in Economics, St. Andrews University, 1963-65; Lecturer and Senior Lecturer, Strathclyde University, 1965-74; Managing Editor, Leopard Magazine. Publications: Theory of Taxation; Death of a Papermill; Farmer's Diary I, II, III. Recreation: work. Address: (h.) Little Ardo, Methlick, Ellon, Aberdeenshire; T.-01651 806 218.

Allan, David Smith, BSc (Hons), DipEd. Headmaster, Preston Lodge High School, Prestonpans, since 1970; b. 17.1.35, Prestonpans; m., Alexandra; 2 s.; 1 d. Educ. Preston Lodge School, Prestonpans; Edinburgh University. Teacher, George Heriot's School, Edinburgh, 1958-63; Principal Teacher of Science, Preston Lodge High School, Prestonpans, 1963-70. Hon. President, Preston Lodge FP Club; Past President, Lothian Headteachers Association. Recreations: rugby committee work; golf. Address: (b.) Preston Lodge High School, Prestonpans, East Lothian; T.-Prestonpans 811170.

Allan, D. Stuart, LLB, NP. Solicitor and Notary Public; Director of Corporate Services, Fife Regional Council; b. 11.11.49, Dundee. Educ. Morgan Academy; Dundee University. Chairman, Society of Directors of Administration in Scotland, 1991-92. Address: (b.) Fife House, Glenrothes, KY7 5LT; T.-01592 414141.

Allan, Eric, MA (Hons). Head Teacher, St. Michael's Academy, Kilwinning, since 1994; b. 6.9.55, Inverness; m., Elaine; 2 d. Educ. Dingwall Academy; Glasgow University; Jordanhill College. Teacher: St. Andrew's Academy, Saltcoats, St. Brendan's High School, Linwood; Assistant Head Teacher, St. Brendan's, 1987-92; Depute Head Teacher, Trinity High School, Renfrew, 1992-94. Recreations: golf; supporting Kilmarnock FC; reading; music. Address: (h.) 3 Holmes Crescent, Kilmarnock; T.-01563 524199.

Allan, George Alexander, MA (Hons). Headmaster, Robert Gordon's College, Aberdeen, since 1978; b. 3.2.36, Edinburgh; m., Anne Violet Veevers; 2 s. Educ. Daniel Stewart's College, Edinburgh; Edinburgh University. Teacher of Classics, Glasgow Academy, 1958-60; Daniel Stewart's College: Teacher of Classics, 1960-63, Head of Classics, 1963-73 (appointed Housemaster, 1967); Schoolmaster Fellow Commoner, Corpus Christi College, Cambridge, 1972; Deputy Headmaster, Robert Gordon's College, 1973-77. Former Chairman and former Secretary, Headmasters' Conference (Scottish Division) (Member, National Committee, 1982 and 1983); Governor, Welbeck College, 1980-89; Council Member, Scottish Council of Independent Schools, since 1988. Recreations: gardening; golf; music. Address: 24 Woodend Road, Aberdeen, AB2 6YH; T.-01224 321733.

Allan, James Morrison, FRICS, ACIArb. Chartered Surveyor; b. 1.10.43, Edinburgh; m., Elizabeth Howie Sneddon Jack; 2 s. Educ. George Watson's College; Heriot Watt College. Joined Phillips Knox & Arthur as Apprentice Quantity Surveyor, 1960; qualified ARICS, 1965; FRICS, 1975; RICS: Chairman, National Junior Organisation, 1975-76; Chairman, Quantity Surveyors Committee in Scotland, 1988-89; Chairman, RICS in Scotland, 1991-92; Scottish nominee, RICS General Council; Member, RICS Management Board, 1992-95. Recreations: family; caravanning and motoring; golf. Address: (b.) 9 Park Crescent, Liberton, Edinburgh, EH16 6JD; T.-031-658 1113.

Allan, Professor James Robertson, DSc, PhD, BSc, CChem, FRSC. Professor, Department of Applied Chemical and Physical Sciences, Napier University, since 1994; b. 20.7.38, Coatbridge. Educ. Coatbridge High School; Strathclyde University. Lecturer in Chemistry, North Stafford Polytechnic, 1966-67; Lecturer, then Senior Lecturer in Inorganic Chemistry, Napier College/University, Edinburgh, 1967-94. Publications: two books; 152 papers. Recreation: bowls. Address: (h.) 12 Elliot Gardens, Edinburgh, EH14 1EH; T.-0131-442 5649.

Allan, Sheriff John Douglas, BL, DMS, FBIM. Sheriff of Lanark, since 1988; b. 2.10.41, Edinburgh; m., Helen E.J. Aiton; 1 s.; 1 d. Educ. George Watson's College, Edinburgh; Edinburgh University. Solicitor in private practice, Edinburgh, 1963-67; Procurator Fiscal Depute, Edinburgh, 1967-71; Solicitor, Crown Office, Edinburgh, 1971-76; Assistant Procurator Fiscal, then Senior Assistant Procurator Fiscal, Glasgow, 1976-79; Solicitor, Crown Office, Edinburgh, 1979-83; Procurator Fiscal for Edinburgh and Regional Procurator Fiscal for Lothians and Borders, 1983-88. Part-time Lecturer in Law, Napier College, Edinburgh, 1963-66; Holder, Scout "Medal of Merit". Recreations: Scouts; youth leadership; walking; Church. Address: (b.) Sheriff Court House, Lanark ML11 7NE; T.-01555 661531.

Allan, Robert, MBE. Chief Executive, Scottish Fishermen's Federation, since 1982; b. 14.11.33, Peterhead; m., Moira W. Morrison; 2 d. Educ. Aberdeen Grammar School. Audit Assistant, R.C. Kelman & Shirreffs, CA, Aberdeen, 1949-62; Assistant Secretary, latterly Secretary, Aberdeen Fishing Vessel Owners' Association Ltd. and Scottish Trawlers' Federation, 1962-71; Chief Executive, Aberdeen Fishing Vessel Owners' Association Ltd. and Aberdeen Fish Producers' Organisation Ltd., 1971-82. Recreation: keen follower of the fortunes of Aberdeen FC. Address: (h.) 40 Parkhill Circle, Dyce, Aberdeen, AB2 OFN; T.-01224 724366.

Allan, Scott Birnie, MA, DipEd. Vice-Principal, Queen Margaret College, since 1989; b. 16.3.37, Paisley; m., Margaret Coulthard; 2 s. Educ. Greenock Academy; King's School, Rochester; St. Andrews University; University of Surrey. Education Officer, Royal Army Education Corps, 1961-65; Lecturer, National Police Staff College, Bramshill, 1965-74; Senior Lecturer, latterly Head, Department of Communication and Information Studies, Queen Margaret College, 1974-89. Recreations: theatre; music; travel. Address: (b.) Queen Margaret College, Clerwood Terrace, Edinburgh, EH12 8TS; T.-0131-317 3203.

Allanbridge, Hon. Lord (William Ian Stewart), QC. Senator of the College of Justice in Scotland, since 1977; b. 8.11.25. Called to the Bar, 1951; Advocate-Depute, 1959-64; Home Advocate-Depute, 1970-72; Solicitor-General for Scotland, 1972-74; Temporary Sheriff Principal, Dumfries and Galloway, 1974.

Allcock, Ronald, FIWEM, CChem, FRSC. Director, Tay River Purification Board, since 1987; b. 9.1.40, Mancot; 1 s.; 1 d. Educ. Holywell Grammar School; Doncaster College of Technology. Research Chemist, Coalite Chemicals, 1962; District Inspector, Trent River Authority, 1966; Divisional Pollution Officer: Yorkshire Water, 1972, Clyde River Purification Board, 1978. Recreations: golf; reading; amateur football. Address: (b.) 1 South Street, Perth, PH2 8NJ; T.-Perth 627989.

Allen, Professor John Walter, MA, FSAS, FRSE. Professor of Solid State Physics, St. Andrews University, since 1980; b. 7.3.28, Birmingham. Educ. King Edward's High School, Birmingham; Sidney Sussex College, Cambridge. RAF, 1949-51; Staff Scientist, Ericsson Telephones Ltd., 1951-56; Services Electronics Research

Laboratory, 1956-68; Visiting Associate Professor, Stanford University, 1964-66; joined Department of Physics, St. Andrews University, 1968. Recreations: archaeology; country dancing. Address: (b.) Department of Physics and Astronomy, St. Andrews University, North Haugh, St. Andrews, Fife, KY16 9SS; T.-01334 463331.

Allison, Professor Arthur Compton, BSc, DipNumMath, PhD, FBCS. Vice Principal for Science and Engineering and Professor of Computing Science, Glasgow University, since 1986 (Director, Board of Studies in Information Technology); b. 24.3.41, Belfast; m., Dr. Joyce Allison; 3 d. Educ. Queen's University, Belfast; Glasgow University. Glasgow University, 1962-67; Smithsonian Institution, Boston, 1967-73; Glasgow University, 1973-83; Northeastern University, Boston, 1983-84; Glasgow University, since 1984. Elder, Church of Scotland. Recreations: running; squash; curling. Address: (b.) Department of Computing Science, Glasgow University, Glasgow, G12 8QQ; T.-0141-339 8855, Ext. 4453.

Allison, Charles William, MBChB, FFARCS. Consultant Anaesthetist, Stracathro Hospital, Brechin, since 1982; Consultant, Dundee teaching hospitals; Honorary Senior Lecturer, Dundee University; b. 1.7.52, Newport on Tay; m., Elspeth Stratton; 2 d. Educ. Madras College, St. Andrews; Dundee University. Training grades in anaesthesia, Dundee, 1976-81; Clinical Research Fellow, Hospital for Sick Children, Toronto, 1982. Publications: papers and book chapter. Recreations: golf; photography. Address: Summerbank House, Brechin, Angus DD9 6HL; T.-01356 623624.

Allison, Joseph Philip Sloan, MA (Cantab), CertEd. Headmaster, St. Mary's Music School, Edinburgh, since 1979; b. 6.2.44, Leeds; m., Caroline Margaret Paton; 3 s.; 1 d. Educ. Rugby; Churchill College, Cambridge; Moray House College of Education. Jardine Matheson & Co. Ltd., Hong Kong, 1967-70; Assistant Master, then Assistant Head, Belhaven Hill, Dunbar, 1970-77; Deputy Head, St. Mary's Music School, 1977-79. Recreations: sailing; birdwatching; hill-walking. Address: (h.) 4 Raeburn Street, Edinburgh, EH4 1HY; T.-0131-332 9768.

Allsop, Douglas Thomson, MBE. Executive Director, Scottish Council on Alcohol, since 1979; b. 5.11.32, Arbroath; m., Elizabeth Blair Marshall; 1 s. Educ. Arbroath High School. Clydesdale Bank Ltd., 1949-72 (latterly as Investment Manager); Regional Director, Slater, Walker Ltd., Merchant Bankers, 1973-77. Recreations: gardening; walking. Address: (b.) 137/145 Sauchiehall Street, Glasgow, G2 3EW; T.-0141-333 9677.

Allsop, Rev. Thomas Douglas, MA, BD. Minister, Beechgrove Church, Aberdeen, since 1977; b. 2.3.34, Kilmaurs; m., Marion Morrison Urie; 2 s.; 1 d. Educ. Kilmarnock Academy; Glasgow University and Trinity College. Assistant Minister, St. Marnock's, Kilmarnock; Minister: Kirriemuir South (after a union called Kirriemuir St. Andrew's), 1959-65; Minister, Knightswood St. Margaret's, Glasgow, 1965-77. Founder Chairman, Kirriemuir Round Table; Moderator, Dumbarton Presbytery, 1975, Aberdeen Presbytery, 1994-95; Burgess, City of Aberdeen. Recreations: photography; golf; musical appreciation. Address: 156 Hamilton Place, Aberdeen, AB2 4BB; T.-01224 642615.

Almaini, Professor A.E.A., BSc(Eng), MSc, PhD, CEng, FIEE. Associate Head, Department of Electrical, Electronic and Computer Engineering, Napier University, since 1991, Professor, since 1992; b. 1.7.45, Baghdad; m., Shirley May; 2 s.; 1 d. Educ. London University; Salford University; Loughborough University. Research Scientist, Scientific Research Foundation, 1970-78; Lecturer, then Senior Lecturer, Napier University, 1980-91. Recreation:

gardening. Address: (b.) EECE Department, Craiglockhart Campus, Edinburgh, EH14 1DJ; T.-0131-455 4364.

Alstead, Brigadier (Francis) Allan (Littlejohns), CBE, MPhil, FCIT, FBIM, FIPM, FInstAM, FRSA, FInstD. Chief Executive, Scottish Sports Council, since 1990; b. 19.6.35, Glasgow; m., Joy Veronica Edwards; 2 s. Educ. Glasgow Academy; Royal Military Academy, Sandhurst; Royal Naval Staff College; Joint Services Staff College; University of Wales, Aberystwyth. Commissioned into King's Own Scottish Borderers, 1955; commanded 1st Bn., KOSB, 1974-76; Military Assistant to Quarter-Master-General,, 1976-79; Instructor, Army Staff College, Camberley, 1979-81; Assistant Chief of Staff, BAOR, 1981-84 (Colonel); Commander, 51st Highland Brigade, 1984-87 (Brigadier); NATO Research Fellow, Edinburgh University, 1987-88; NATO Reinforcement Co-ordinator, 1988-90. Member, Royal Company of Archers (Queen's Bodyguard in Scotland); Regimental Trustee, KOSB; Deputy Hon. Colonel, Edinburgh and Heriot Watt Universities OTC; Governor, Moray House College; President, SSAFA, Edinburgh and Midlothian. Recreations: running; swimming; tennis; sailing. Address: (b.) South Gyle, Edinburgh, EH12 9DQ; T.-0131-317 7200.

Ambler, Professor Richard Penry, MA, PhD, FSAS. Professor of Protein Chemistry, Institute of Cell & Molecular Biology, Edinburgh University; b. 26.5.33, Bexley Heath; m.; 2 d. Educ. Haileybury and ISC; Pembroke College, Cambridge. Research Fellow, Pembroke College, Cambridge, 1959-62; scientific staff, MRC Laboratory of Molecular Biology, Cambridge, 1960-65; joined Department of Molecular Biology, Edinburgh University, 1965. Member, EMBO. Address: (b.) Institute of Cell & Molecular Biology, Darwin Building, University of Edinburgh EH9 3JR; T.-0131-650 5394.

Amin, Professor Sayed-Hassan, LLB, LLM, PhD. Advocate; International Lawyer; Author; President, Islamic Institute of International and Comparative Law; b. 25.11.48, Persia. Educ. University of Tehran; Glasgow University. Senior Lecturer, Reader, Professor, Glasgow Caledonian University (formerly Glasgow Polytechnic), 1981-95; Middle East Editor, Oil and Gas Law and Taxation Review, since 1985; Director and Representative for Scotland and N.I., World Development Movement, 1989-92; Member, Council for National Academic Awards, 1989-92; Member, Executive Committee, Royal Institute of International Affairs, Scottish Branch; Patron, Prisoners Abroad, Shaykh, Nagshbandi Sufi Order. Publications: 27 books on international, Middle Eastern and Islamic law. Recreations: walking; book collecting. Address: (b.) Advocates' Library, Parliament House, Parliament Square, Edinburgh EH1 1RF; T.-0131-557 2071.

Amyes, Professor Sebastian Giles Becket, BSc, MSc, PhD, DSc, MRCPath, FIBiol. Professor of Microbial Chemotherapy, Edinburgh University, and Joint Director, Scottish Antibiotic Reference Laboratory; b. 6.5.49, Stockton Heath; m., Dorothy Mary Gregory; 1 s.; 1 d. Educ. Cranleigh School; University College, London. Edinburgh University, since 1977; Reader, 1988; Professor, 1992. Royal Pharmaceutical Society annual conference award, 1984; C.L. Oakley lectureship, Pathological Society, 1987. Recreations: fishing; opera; golf; exploring parts of the world that the tour companies have not yet found. Address: (b.) Department of Medical Microbiology, Medical School, Teviot Place, Edinburgh, EH8 9AG; T.-0131-650 3163.

Andersen, Finn, MA. Director, Danish Cultural Institute in Britain, since 1985; b. 20.2.44, Denmark; m., Vivien Ann; 1 s.; 1 d. Educ. University of Arhus. Chairman, European Union Cultural Forum in Scotland. Recreations: the arts; travelling. Address: 3 Doune Terrace, Edinburgh, EH3 6DY; T.-0131-225 7189.

Anderson, Alastair, CA. Director of Finance, Napier University, since 1989; b. 10.8.49, Glasgow; m., Maureen Wilson; 1 s.; 1 d. Educ. Hutchesons' Boys Grammar School. CA apprentice and audit assistant, 1967-74; Assistant Accountant, 1975; Retail Trade Accountant, 1975-89. Recreations: sailing; squash. Address: (b.) 219 Colinton Road, Edinburgh, H14 1DJ; T.-0131-455 4656.

Anderson, Arthur Andrew, ARAgS. Head of Production, BBC Aberdeen, since 1993; Producer, Landward, since 1979; b. 21.11.44, Dumfries; m., Andrea Jane MacKenzie; 2 s.; 2 d. Educ. Barnard Castle School. Copy Boy, The Scotsman, 1961-64; Reporter, Scottish Farmer, 1964-65; Sub-Editor, Glasgow Herald, 1965-66; Agricultural Reporter, The Scotsman, 1967-69; Scottish Correspondent, Farmers Weekly, 1970-73; News/Farming Producer and Reporter, BBC Radio Carlisle, 1973-75; General Programme Producer, BBC Radio Scotland, 1975-77; joined BBC TV, Aberdeen, 1977. Winner RICS TV Award, John Deere Journalism Award, Norsk Hydro TV Award, One World Broadcasting Trust Prize, Netherthorpe Award. Recreation; lunching. Address: (h.) Denmill Cottage, Burnett Street, Auchenblae, AB30 1XQ; T.-01561 320248.

Anderson, Charles Mitchell, MA, DPA. Chief Executive, Ettrick and Lauderdale District Council, since 1985; b. 3.9.45, Kirkcaldy; m., Margaret; 2 s. Educ. Kirkcaldy High School; Edinburgh University; Strathclyde University (part-time). Divisional Assistant Secretary, Freight Transport Association; Administrative Officer, Irvine Development Corporation; Principal Administrative Officer, Highland Regional Council; Assistant Director of Administration and Legal Services, Central Regional Council; Assistant Secretary, Convention of Scottish Local Authorities. Address: (b.) PO Box 4, Council Chambers, Albert Place, Galashiels, TD1 3DL; T.-01896 754751.

Anderson, David Colville, VRD and Bar, QC, BA Oxon, LLB; b. 8.9.16, Cupar; m., Juliet Hill Watson; 2 s.; 1 d. Educ. Glenalmond College; Pembroke College, Oxford; Edinburgh University. RNVR, 1935-61; served World War II in destroyers; mentioned in Despatches, 1942; special operation, Norway, 1945; King Haakon VII Freedom Medal; Admiralty's Egerton Prize, 1943; Lieutenant Commander, 1947. Advocate, 1946; Lecturer in Scots Law, Edinburgh University, 1947-60; Standing Junior Counsel, Ministry of Works, 1954-55, and War Office, 1955-57; QC, 1957; Solicitor-General for Scotland, 1960-64; MP (Conservative) for Dumfries, 1963-64; Honorary Sheriff, 1965-72; Chairman, Industrial Appeal Tribunals, 1970-72; Chief Reporter for Public Inquiries and Under-Secretary, Scottish Office, 1972-74; Commissioner, Northern Lighthouses, 1960-64. Subject of play, The Case of David Anderson QC, by John Hale (Lyric, Hammersmith, 1981, etc.). Recreations: travel; hill-walking; golf. Address: (h.) 8 Arboretum Road, Edinburgh, EH3 5PD; T.-0131-552 3003.

Anderson, David Rae, MA (Hons), LLB, LLM, WS, NP. Solicitor, since 1961 (Senior Partner in private practice); part-time Legal Chairman, Industrial Tribunals, since 1971; Honorary Sheriff, since 1981; b. 27.1.36, Stonehaven; m., Jean Strachan. Educ. Mackie Academy, Stonehaven; Aberdeen University; Edinburgh University; Australian National University, Canberra. Barrister and Solicitor of Supreme Court of Victoria, Australia, 1962; Legal Officer, Attorney-General's Department, Canberra, 1962-65; part-time research student, Law Faculty, Australian National University, Canberra, and part-time Lecturer in Legal History, 1962-65; returned to Scotland, 1965, in private legal practice, Edinburgh, 1965-67, Alloa and Central Scotland, since 1967; Interim Town Clerk, Burgh of Alva, 1973; former part-time Reporter to Secretary of State for Scotland for public enquiries; former Dean, Society of Solicitors of Clackmannanshire; Member, Council, Law Society of Scotland; former Convener, International Relations Committee, 1992 Committee and Committee on

the Constitution; currently Convener, Specialist Accreditation Committee; former Member, UK Delegation, Council of the Bars and Law Societies of the European Community; Member, Stirling University Conference; Elder, Church of Scotland; Parliamentary candidate, 1970 and 1971; formerly served, RNVR; Past President, Alloa Rotary Club. Recreations: climbing and hill-walking; reading, especially historical biography and English literature; music, especially opera; interested in current affairs, architecture, stately homes and travel. Address: (h.) 3 Smithfield Loan, Alloa, FK10 1NJ; T.-01259 213096; (b.) 8 Shillinghill, Alloa, FK10 1JT; T.-01259 723201.

Anderson, Don S.H., IPFA, IRRV. Director of Finance and Central Services, Clydesdale District Council, since 1983; b. 9.1.43, Forfar; m., Irene R.; 3 d. Educ. Mackie Academy, Stonehaven. Trainee Accountant, Clackmannan County Council, 1961-66; Accountancy Assistant, Airdrie Town Council, 1966-69; Accountant, Kilmarnock Town Council, 1969-75; Finance Manager, Clydesdale District Council, 1975-83. Address: (b.) District Offices, South Vennel, Lanark, ML11 7JT; T.-01555 661331, Ext. 134.

Anderson, Dorothy Elizabeth, BSc (Hons), MB, ChB, MRCP(UK), DMRD, FRCR, FRCP(Glas). Consultant Radiologist, Glasgow Royal Infirmary, since 1981; Honorary Clinical Lecturer, then Senior Lecturer, Glasgow University, since 1982; b. 26.9.50, Glasgow; m., David Anderson; 1 s.; 1 d. Educ. Glasgow High School for Girls; Glasgow University. Pre-registration posts, Stobhill Hospital and Glasgow Royal Infirmary; post-registration year, Respiratory Unit, Knightswood Hospital; trained in radiology, Western Infirmary, Glasgow (Registrar, then Senior Registrar). Recreation: choral singing; walking; aerobics. Address: (h.) 18 Milverton Avenue, Bearsden, Glasgow G61 4BE; T.-0141-942 7510.

Anderson, Douglas Kinloch, OBE, MA. Chairman, Kinloch Anderson (Holdings) Ltd., Edinburgh, since 1975; Board Member, Scottish Tourist Board, 1986-92; Deputy Chairman, Edinburgh Marketing Ltd., 1990-92; Director: Lothian and Edinburgh Enterprise Ltd., Scottish Eastern Investment Trust PLC, Fidelity Special Values PLC, Carnegie Robertson Black Ltd.; b. 19.2.39, Edinburgh; m., Deirdre Anne; 2 s.; 1 d. Educ. George Watson's Boys College; St. Andrews University. Joined Kinloch Anderson Ltd., 1962 (fifth generation in family business); Assistant on Master's Court, Edinburgh Merchant Company, 1976-79; elected Honorary Member, St. Andrew's Society of Washington DC, 1985; Member, Edinburgh Festival Council, 1988-90; President, Edinburgh Royal Warrant Holders Association, 1987-88; Member, Scottish Committee, Institute of Directors; President, Edinburgh Chamber of Commerce, 1988-90; Master, Edinburgh Merchant Company, 1990-92; President, Royal Warrant Holders Association, 1994; elected Leith High Constable, 1993. Recreations: golf; fishing; watching rugby; travel (non-business). Address: (b.) Commercial Street/Dock Street, Leith, Edinburgh EH6 6EY; T.-0131-555 1355.

Anderson, Gavin Alan, DipArch, MPhil. Head, Community Care Division, Social Work Services Group, Scottish Office, since 1994; b. 5.7.39, Bridge of Allan; m., Margaret Clarke; 1 s.; 1 d. Educ. St. Modan's High School, Stirling; Edinburgh College of Art; Edinburgh University. Architect, Edinburgh University Architecture Research Unit, 1966-73; Architect, then Principal Architect, Scottish Development Department, 1973-85; Assistant Secretary, Scottish Home and Health Department, 1985-90; Deputy Chief Executive, NHS in Scotland, 1990-93. Recreations: reading; listening to music; art; walking. Address: (b.) 4 Jeffrey Street, Edinburgh, EH1 1DN; T.-0131-244 5452.

Anderson, Gordon Alexander, CA, FCMA. Chartered Accountant; b. 9.8.31, Glasgow; m., Eirene Cochran Howie Douglas; 2 s.; 1 d. Educ. High School of Glasgow

Apprentice CA, Moores Carson & Watson, Glasgow, 1949-54; qualified CA, 1955; National Service, Royal Navy, 1955-57 (Sub Lieutenant); Partner, Moores Carson & Watson, 1958 (firm name changed to McClelland Moores, 1958, Arthur Young McClelland Moores, 1968, Arthur Young, 1985, Ernst & Young, 1989); Chairman, Arthur Young, 1987-89; Deputy Senior Partner, Ernst & Young, 1989-90; Member, Council on Tribunals and of its Scottish Committee, since 1990; Chairman, Bitmac Ltd., since 1990; Director: TSB Group plc, since 1993, TSB Bank Scotland plc, since 1991 (Chairman, since 1994), High School of Glasgow Ltd., 1975-81 and since 1990, Chairman of Governors, since 1992; Director, Douglas Firebrick Co. Ltd., 1960-70; Member, Scottish Milk Marketing Board, 1979-85; Institute of Chartered Accountants of Scotland: Member, Council, 1980-84, Vice President, 1984-86, President, 1986-87. Recreations: golf; gardening; rugby football (as spectator). Address: (h.) Ardwell, 41 Manse Road, Bearsden, Glasgow, G61 3PN; T.-041-942 2803.

Anderson, Professor Gordon Charles, MA, FIPM, FITD, FBIM. Professor of Business Administration, Glasgow Caledonian University, since 1994; b. Aberfeldy; m., Marjory Ann Anderson; 2 s. Educ. Madras College, St. Andrews; St. Andrews University. After several years in personnel management, joined Strathclyde University as Lecturer in Management Studies; Director of MBA Programmes, 1984-92, Chairman, 1992-94; author of many articles and several books including Management Skills: Making the Most of People (Co-author) and Managing Performance Appraisal Systems. Recreations: swimming; golf; sailing; watching American football. Address: (h.) Upper Hatton, Dunkeld, Perthshire.

Anderson, Rev. Professor Hugh, MA, BD, PhD, DD, FRSE. Professor of New Testament Language, Literature and Theology, Edinburgh University, 1966-85; b. 18.5.20, Galston, Ayrshire; m., Jean Goldie Torbit; 1 s.; 1 s. (deceased); 1 d. Educ. Kilmarnock Academy; Glasgow University. Chaplaincy work, Egypt and Palestine, 1945-46; Lecturer in Old Testament, Glasgow University, 1946-51; Minister, Trinity Church, Pollokshields, Glasgow, 1951-57; Professor of Biblical Criticism, Duke University, North Carolina, 1957-66; special appointments including A.B. Bruce Lecturer in New Testament, Glasgow University, 1954-57; Katharine McBride Visiting Professor, Bryn Mawr College, Pennsylvania, 1972-73; Kenan Distinguished Visiting Professor, Meredith College, North Carolina, 1982-83; Pendergrass Visiting Professor, Florida Southern College, 1985-86, 1987-88. Awarded Schweitzer Medal from North Carolina History and Science Foundation. Publications: Psalms 1-45; Historians of Israel; The New Testament in Historical and Contemporary Perspective (Editor with W. Barclay); Jesus and Christian Origins; Jesus; The Gospel of Mark: Commentary; 3 and 4 Maccabees (Commentary). Recreations: golf; gardening; music. Address: (h.) 5 Comiston Springs Avenue, Edinburgh, EH10 6NT.

Anderson, Iain Buchanan, MA, DipEd, LGSM. Music Presenter/Sports Commentator, BBC, since 1985; b. 21.6.38, Stirling; m., Marion Elizabeth; 3 s.; 1 d. Educ. Bellahouston Academy, Glasgow; Glasgow University; Guildhall School. Lecturer in Speech and Drama, Jordanhill College, 1967; Arts Editor/Presenter, Radio Clyde, 1974. Rugby Correspondent, Scotland on Sunday. Address: (h.) Elmhurst, Station Road, Langbank, PA14 6YA; T.-047 554 733.

Anderson, James Alexander, BL, NP. Solicitor, since 1948; Member, Glasgow and North Argyll Legal Aid Committee, 1960-86; Honorary Sheriff at Oban, since 1980; b. 17.5.21, Glasgow; m., Jean Jeffrey Brown; 2 s.; 1 d. Educ. Elgin Academy; Edinburgh University. Army, 1942-46 (Staff Captain, RA); joined Anderson Banks & Co., Solicitors, Oban, 1950 (Senior Partner, until 1986); Local Representative, Legal Aid Committee, 1960-79; Dean of Faculty, Oban Procurators, 1975-78. Treasurer, Lorn & Mull Presbytery, 1963-82; Treasurer, Oban and District Christian Aid Committee; Elder, Church of Scotland. Recreations: writing; gardening; golf; pool. Address: (h.) Cottach, 1 Ferryfield Road, Connel, Argyll, PA37 1SR; T.-01631 710470.

Anderson, James Andrew, MA (Hons), DipEd, MRTPI. Director of Planning, Shetland Islands Council, since 1987; b. 19.11.45, Whalsay, Shetland. Educ. Anderson Educational Institute, Lerwick; Aberdeen University. Teachers For East Africa Scheme (Ministry of Overseas Development): recruited, 1967, Diploma in Education, Makerere University, Uganda, 1968, Education Officer, Kenya; Teacher, New Zealand, 1971; Hamilton City Council, New Zealand: Senior Town Planning Assistant, 1971, Assistant Town Planning Officer, Statutory Planning Department, 1974; Senior Planning Assistant, Shropshire County Council, 1976; Depute Director of Planning, Shetland Islands Council, 1978. Trustee, Shetland Amenity Trust. Recreations: hill walking; learning languages; foreign travel. Address: (h.) 12 Fogralea, Lerwick, Shetland Islands; T.-01595 3535.

Anderson, James Frazer Gillan, CBE, JP, DL. Member, Scottish Development Agency, 1986-89; Convener, Central Regional Council, 1974-86; b. 25.3.29, Maddiston, by Falkirk; m., May Harley; 1 s.; 1 d. Educ. Maddiston School; Graeme High School, Falkirk. Convener, Stirling County Council, 1971-75; Member: Health and Safety Commission, 1974-80; Montgomery Committee, 1982-84; Scottish Economic Council, 1983-87; Chairman, Maddiston Old Folks Association; awarded Honorary Degree, Doctor of University (Stirling). Recreations: gardening; walking; reading. Address: (b.) Viewforth, Stirling; T.-Stirling 442000.

Anderson, James Killoch, OBE, MB, ChB, FFCM, FCR, JP. Former Unit Medical Officer, Glasgow Royal Infirmary and Royal Maternity Hospital, Glasgow (retired, 1988); b. 3.2.23, Johnstone; m., Irene Webster Wilson; 1 s.; 2 d. Educ. High School of Glasgow; Glasgow University. Deputy Medical Superintendent, Glasgow Royal Infirmary and Associated Hospitals, 1954; appointed Medical Superintendent, 1957; District Medical Officer, Eastern District, Greater Glasgow Health Board, 1974; Unit Medical Officer, Unit East 1, Greater Glasgow Health Board, 1984. Corps Commandant and Council Member, St. Andrew's Ambulance Association, 1957-82; Member of Committee, Scottish Ambulance Service, 1957-74; Director, North Parish, Washing Green Society, Glasgow, since 1957; Member, Scottish Technical Education Council, since 1974; Member, Science Development Team, 16-18s Action Plan, Scottish Education Department. Recreations: gardening; golf. Address: (h.) 15 Kenilworth Avenue, Helensburgh, G84 7JR; T.-01436 3739.

Anderson, John. Regional Sheriff Clerk, Lothian and Borders. Address: Sheriff Court House, 27 Chambers Street, Edinburgh, EH1 1LB.

Anderson of Pittormie, Captain John Charles Lindsay, VRD (and clasp), OStJ, MA (Oxon), LLB, RNR. Solicitor; Consultant to Messrs J.L. Anderson; Honorary Sheriff, Tayside, Central and Fife, since 1986; Arable and Fruit Farmer; Quarrymaster, Fife Redstone and Brackmont Quarries; b. 8.9.08, Cupar; m., Elsie Margaret Begg; 1 s.; 2 d. Educ. St. Salvators, St. Andrews; Glenalmond College; Pembroke College, Oxford; Edinburgh University. Solicitor, since 1931; Member, St. Andrews Town Council, 1938-51 (Honorary Treasurer, 1945-51); Parliamentary candidate (Conservative), West Stirling, 1945; joined RNVR as Sub Lt., 1930; served World War II, Northern Patrol, Convoys, Gunnery Specialist; Captain, RNR, 1954; commanded HMS Unicorn, Tay Division RNVR/RNR,

1954-59; RNR ADC to The Queen, 1959-60; Founder Governor, Unicorn Preservation Society, since 1968; Member, Business Committee, Edinburgh University General Council, since 1982; Member, Council, Law Society of Scotland, 1983-86; former Dean of Faculty, Cupar; President, Royal Caledonian Curling Club, 1978-79; Chairman: Kirkcaldy Ice Rink, 1978-88, Scottish Ice Rinks Association, 1986-88, Fife Housing Co. Ltd., Cupar Corn Exchange Co. Ltd., Fife Redstone Quarry Co. Ltd., Brackmont Quarry Ltd.; Honorary President, St. Andrews Branch, Royal British Legion. Recreations: curling; shooting; golf; tennis. Address: (h.) Inverbeg, 22 Hepburn Gardens, St Andrews, KY16 9DE; T.-01334 72348.

Anderson, John Ferguson, LLB (Hons). Chief Executive, City of Glasgow Council, since 1995; b. 13.12.47, Kirkcaldy; m., Sandra; 1 s.; 1 d. Educ. Kirkcaldy High School; Queen's Park School, Glasgow; Edinburgh University. Various legal posts, Glasgow Corporation, 1969-75; Strathclyde Regional Council: Principal Solicitor, 1975-78, Assistant Director of Administration, 1978-80, Senior Executive Officer, 1980-86, Principal Executive Officer, 1986-90, Depute Chief Executive, 1990-95. Recreations: golf; football; transport; church activities. Address: (b.) City Chambers, Glasgow, G2 1DU; T.-0141-227 4739.

Anderson, Joseph Aitken, BA (Hons), CSD, MIMgt. Chief Executive, North of Scotland Milk Co-operative Society Ltd., since 1994 (Managing Director, North of Scotland Milk Marketing Board, 1982-94); Chairman, Company of Scottish Cheesemakers, since 1983; Director, Norlink Ltd., 1985-93; Chairman, ITC Viewers Consultative Council for Scotland, 1990-94; Director, Scottish Dairymen's Association, since 1994; b. 1.7.36, Prestonpans; m., Sheila Armstrong; 2 s. Educ. Preston Lodge; Open University. Managing Secretary: Carluke Co-operative Society, 1962-65, East Fife Co-operative Society, 1965-71; Depute Chief Executive, Central and East Fife Co-operative Society, 1971-79; Executive Officer and Secretary, Fife Regional Co-operative Society, 1979-82. Member, United Kingdom Dairy Association Council; Past Chairman, NE Branch, Society of Dairy Technology; Past President, Inverness and District Chamber of Commerce; Member, Highland Area Committee, Scottish Council (Development and Industry), since 1982. Recreations: golf; fly fishing; photography. Address: (b.) Balmakeith Industrial Estate, Forres Road, Nairn IV12 5QW; T-01667 453344.

Anderson, Kathleen Janette, OBE, FRSE, BSc, PhD, DSc, FScotVec, CBiol, FIBiol, CChem, FRSC. Depute Principal, Napier Polytechnic of Edinburgh, 1983-92; b. 22.5.27, Glasgow; m., Mark Elliot Muir Anderson; 1 s.; 1 d. Educ. Queens Park School, Glasgow; Glasgow University. Lecturer, West of Scotland Agricultural College, Glasgow, 1948-54; Johnson and Florence Stoney Research Fellow, University of Sydney, Australia, 1952-53; Commonwealth Travelling Research Fellow, Australia and New Zealand, 1953; Sir James Knott Research Fellow, Durham University, 1955-57; King's College, Durham University: Lecturer in Biochemistry, 1958-59, Lecturer in Microbiology, 1962-63, Lecturer (part-time) in Landscape Horticulture, 1963-65, Lecturer (part-time), Extra-Mural Department, 1959-65; Lecturer (part-time), Department of Extra-Mural Studies, Edinburgh University, 1965-68; Napier College, Edinburgh: Senior Lecturer, Department of Biological Sciences, 1968-69, Head of Department, Biological Sciences, 1969-83. Crown Trustee, National Library for Scotland, since 1981; Deacon, Church of Scotland, 1974-78, Elder, since 1978; CNAA Environmental Sciences Board, 1978-84; Chairman, Joint Committee for Biology, SCOTEC, 1979-85; Institute of Biology: Chairman, Scottish Branch, 1977-79, Member of Council, 1977-80, Fellowship Committee, 1980-83, Environment Division, 1982-86; Founder Chairman, Heads of Biology in Tertiary Education, 1975-77; Heads of Biology in Polytechnics, 1974-83; Nurse Education Committee, Royal Edinburgh Hospital, 1974-77; SCOTVEC: Council Member and Chairman, Education Policy Committee, 1984-92, Vice Chairman, 1989-92; Chairman, Edinburgh Branch, Glasgow Graduates' Association, 1985-86; Member, Scottish National Committee, English Speaking Union, 1987-92; Trustee, Royal Observatory (Edinburgh) Trust, since 1987; Member, Radioactive Waste Management Advisory Committee, 1988-92; Agriculture Industries Training Board, 1989-92; Scottish Committee, University Funding Council, 1989-92; Governor, St George's School, since 1989; Governor, George Watson's School, since 1990; founder Chairman, Women of Lothian Lunch, since 1987; Governor, Edinburgh's Telford College, since 1992. Publications: Discover Lothian Beaches; Holyrood Park Teacher's Handbook; Safety in Biological Laboratories. Recreations: grand-children; charity work; gardening; foreign travel. Address: (h.) 40 Barony Terrace, Edinburgh, EH12 8RD.

Anderson, Professor Malcolm, MA, DPhil (Oxon), FRSE. Professor of Politics, Edinburgh University, since 1979, and Dean, Faculty of Social Sciences; b. 13.5.34, Knutsford; m. Jacqueline Larrieu; 2 s.; 1 d. Educ. University College, Oxford. Lecturer in Government, Manchester University, 1960-63; Research Fellow, Institut National des Sciences Politiques, 1964-65 and 1986-87; Senior Lecturer, then Professor, Warwick University, 1965-79; Visiting Fellow, Institute of Higher Studies, Vienna, 1977-78; Associate Professor, Sorbonne-Pantheon, 1987-88. Chairman, European Community Studies Association. Publications: Government in France, 1970; Conservative Politics in France, 1974; Frontier Regions in Western Europe, 1983; Women, Equality and Europe (Co-editor), 1988; Policing the World, 1989; Policing Across National Boundaries (Co-Editor), 1994. Recreations: walking; reading; photography. Address: (h.) 72 Dundas Street, Edinburgh, EH3 6QZ; T. 031-556 9300.

Anderson, Moira, OBE. Singer; b. Kirkintilloch; m., D. Stuart Macdonald. Educ. Ayr Academy; Royal Scottish Academy of Music, Glasgow. Began with Kirkintilloch Junior Choir, aged six; made first radio broadcast for BBC in Scotland, aged eight; was Teacher of Music in Ayr before becoming professional singer; made first professional broadcast, White Heather Club, 1960; has toured overseas, had her own radio and TV series; has introduced Stars on Sunday, ITV; appeared in summer shows, cabaret, pantomime and numerous other stage shows; several Royal Variety performances.

Anderson, Peter David, MA, PhD, FSA Scot, FRHistS. Deputy Keeper, Scottish Record Office, since 1993; 10.3.47, Greenock; m., Jean Johnstone Smith; 1 s.; 1 d. Educ. Hutchesons' Grammar School, Glasgow; St. Andrews University; Edinburgh University. Teacher of History, 1972-73; Research Assistant, Scottish Record Office, 1975-80; Registrar, National Register of Archives (Scotland), 1980-83; Secretary, NRA(S), 1984-85; Conservation Officer, 1985-89; Head, Records Liaison Branch, 1989-93. Member: International Council on Archives Committee on Electronic Records, European Commission committee on new archive building; Secretary, Scottish Oral History Group, 1984-88, Deputy Convener, since 1988. Publications: Robert Stewart, Earl of Orkney, Lord of Shetland, 1533-93, 1982; Black Patie, 1993. Recreations: drawing and painting; drama. Address: (b.) Scottish Record Office, HM General Register House, Edinburgh, EH1 3YY; T.-0131-556 6585.

Anderson, Professor Robert David, MA, DPhil. Professor of Modern History, Edinburgh University, since 1994; 11.7.42, Cardiff. Educ. Taunton School, Somerset; Queen's and St. Antony's Colleges, Oxford. Assistant Lecturer, Glasgow University, 1967-69; Lecturer, then Senior

Lecturer and Reader, Edinburgh University, 1969-94. Publications: Education in France 1848-1870, 1975; France 1870-1914: Politics and Society, 1977; Education and Opportunity in Victorian Scotland, 1983 (winner, Scottish Arts Council Literary Award, 1984); The Student Community at Aberdeen, 1860-1939 (1988); Universities and Elites in Britain since 1800, 1992; Education and the Scottish People 1750-1918, 1995. Address: (b.) Department of History, Edinburgh University, Edinburgh; T.-0131-650 3786.

Anderson, Professor Thomas Alfred, CEng, FICE, FIWEM, FIHT, FIOSH, FIMgt. National Council Member and Director, Chartered Institution of Water and Environmental Management; Director, Strathclyde Greenbelt Company; Public Sector Management Consultant, Joint Board for Engineering Management; Visiting Professor, Department of Biology, Paisley University, since 1992; b. 9.11.34, Glasgow; m., Margaret; 3 d. Educ. Strathbungo Senior Secondary School; Royal Technical College, Glasgow; Paisley College of Technology. City Engineer's Department, Corporation of the City of Glasgow: Senior Civil Engineer, 1964-68, Assistant Chief Civil Engineer, 1968-75; Strathclyde Regional Council: Assistant Director of Sewerage, 1975-81, Depute Director of Sewerage, 1981-91, Director of Sewerage, 1991-94. Institution of Municipal Engineers National Medal and Prize Winner, 1980; Examiner/Reviewer, Institution of Civil Engineers, since 1977. Publications: technical papers. Recreations: gardening; golf; cricket. Address: (h.) Craigela, Ryefield Avenue, Drumpellier, Coatbridge, ML5 1LG; T.-01236 424146.

Anderson, William, CBE. Managing Editor, The Sunday Post (Editor, 1967-90); b. 10.2.34, Motherwell; m., Margaret Cross McClelland; 3 s. Educ. Dalziel High School; Glasgow University. Journalist since first producing school newspapers, with interruptions as cook steward, male nurse, medical student and Army officer. Recreations: fishing; sailing; cooking. Address: (b.) Courier Building, Meadowside, Dundee; T.-01382 23131.

Anderson, William. Leader of the Administration, Falkirk Council, since 1995; b. 22.5.43, Falkirk; m., Janet; 1 d. Educ. Camelon Junior Secondary; Falkirk Technical College. Recreations: music; fly fishing; golf. Address: (h.) 109 Garry Place, Grangemouth; T.-01324 486575.

Anderson, Professor Sir (William) Ferguson, Kt (1974), OBE, KStJ, MD, FRCP(Lond), (Glas), (Edin), (C), (I), FACP. Professor Emeritus, Geriatric Medicine, Glasgow University; Vice-President, Scottish Retirement Council; Honorary President, Crossroads (Scotland) Care Attendant Scheme; Honorary Vice-President, Age Concern (Scotland); Patron, Abbeyfield Society, Scotland; Vice-President, Marie Curie Cancer Care; b. 8.4.14, Glasgow; m., Margaret Gebbie; 1 s.; 2 d. Educ. Glasgow Academy; Glasgow University. Assistant Lecturer, Materia Medica, Glasgow University, 1939-41; Major, RAMC, 1941-46; Senior Lecturer, Materia Medica, Glasgow University, 1946-48; Senior Lecturer, Medicine, Welsh National School of Medicine, 1948-52; Honorary Consultant Physician, Cardiff Royal Infirmary, 1948-52; Consultant Physician in Geriatric Medicine and Advisor in diseases of old age and chronic sickness, Western Regional Board, 1952-65; Professor of Geriatric Medicine, Glasgow University, 1965-79. St. Mungo Prize, City of Glasgow; Ed Henderson Award, American Geriatrics Society; Brookdale Award, Gerontological Society of America. Recreation: golf. Address: (h.) Rodel, Moor Road, Strathblane, Glasgow, G63 9EX; T.-Blanefield 770862.

Andrews, Anthony Peter Hamilton, MA. Director, The British Council, Scotland, since 1990; b. 23.12.46. Royal Marines Officer, 1964-71; studied, St. Andrews University

and University College of North Wales, Bangor; British Council: Assistant Director, Kano, Nigeria, 1976-78, Assistant Representative, Yugoslavia, Belgrade, 1979-81, Assistant Representative, Oman, Muscat, 1981-85, Director, North East Brazil, Recife, 1985-89; Director, Glasgow, 1989-90; founded Scottish International Resource Project, 1990; leads Scottish EFL Consortium and set up British Council Edinburgh Centre for Training and Conferences, 1993. Recreations: river management; salmon fishing; sailing; natural history, especially trees and shrubs and entomology; literature; art; music. Address: (b.) The British Council, 3/4 Bruntsfield Crescent, Edinburgh EH10 4HD; T.-0131-447 4716.

Andrews, James, CIPFA, DPA. Director of Finance, City of Glasgow Council, since 1995; Treasurer, Glasgow Humane Society, since 1994; Secretary, Scottish Branch, CIPFA, since 1993; b. 28.11.38, Kilsyth; m., Mary; 1 s.; 2 d. Educ. Kilsyth Academy. Glasgow District Council, since 1976. Recreations: golf; walking; theatre. Address: (b.) City Chambers, Glasgow; T.-0141-227 4042.

Andrews, June, RMN, RGN, MA(Hons). Secretary to Scottish Board, Royal College of Nursing, since 1993; nurse, since 1980; b. Kilwinning. Educ. Ardrossan Academy; Glasgow University; Nottingham University. NHS nursing and management posts, Nottingham and London; adviser on ethics and Aids, RCN; Assistant Director Policy and Research, Royal College of Nursing. Member, Nuffield Council on Bioethics; Member, Alzheimer Scotland; regular contributor to nursing press. Address: (b.) RCN, 42 South Oswald Road, Edinburgh, EH9 2BB; T.-0131-662 1010.

Angus, Rev. James Alexander Keith, LVO, TD, MA. Minister, Braemar and Crathie Parish Churches, since 1979; Domestic Chaplain to The Queen; b. 16.4.29, Aberdeen; m., Alison Jane Daly; 1 s.; 1 d. Educ. High School of Dundee; St. Andrews University. Assistant Minister, Glasgow Cathedral, 1955-56; Minister: Hoddam Parish Church, 1956-67, Gourock Old Parish Church, 1967-79. TA: Captain, Royal Artillery, 1950-56, Chaplain, 1957-77; Convener, Committee of Chaplains to HM Forces, General Assembly, 1981-85; LVO, 1990. Recreations: hill-walking; fishing; golf. Address: (h.) The Manse of Crathie, Crathie, near Ballater, Aberdeenshire; T.-Crathie 208.

Angus, Rae, MA (Hons), MLitt, MIMgt, MITD. Principal, Aberdeen College, since 1993 (Depute Principal, Aberdeen College of Further Education, 1991-93); b. 1947, Ellon; m., Alison Hay; 2 d. Educ. Peterhead Academy; Aberdeen University. Further Education Lecturer, 1975; Research Fellow, Aberdeen University, 1978-80; Aberdeen College of Commerce, 1981-90, latterly as Depute Principal. Recreations: reading; walking; computing. Address: (h.) 4 Curlew Avenue, Newburgh, Aberdeen.

Angus, William Jestyn, FIPM, MIMC. Director, The Merchants House of Glasgow; Vice-President, Dumbarton Constituency Conservative Association; Vice-President, Glasgow and West of Scotland Outward Bound Association; b. 12.12.30, Northumberland; m., Eleanor Gillian Attwood; 1 s.; 1 d. Educ. Gordonstoun School; Harvard Business School. Eighteen years with George Angus & Co. Ltd., latterly part of Dunlop Holdings Ltd.; from 1953 in marketing, export sales, general management and group personnel management; joined Matthew Hall Group, 1971; Senior Consultant, MSL, 1973-82; Director Scotland, Knight Wendling Executive Search Ltd., 1982-92; Associate, Thomson Partners Ltd., 1993-94. Recreations: hill-walking; skiing; tennis; wine. Address: (h.) Braeriach, Helensburgh, G84 9AH; T.-01436 72393.

Angus, Col. William Turnbull Calderhead, CEng, MRAeS, FIMgt, FIQA. Honorary Sheriff, North Strathclyde, since 1986; b. 20.7.23, Glasgow; m., Nola

Leonie Campbell-Gillies; 2 s.; 2 d. Educ. Govan High School; Glasgow University; Royal Military College of Science. Commissioned Royal Regiment of Artillery, 1944; King's African Rifles and GSO2, DAAG (Major), HQ East Africa Command, 1945-47; Technical Staff Course, Royal Military College of Science, 1949-51; TSO2 (Major), Inspectorate of Armaments, 1951-54; BAOR and Cyprus, 1954-57; GSO2 (Major), G(Tech) HQ BAOR, 1957-60; TSO2 (Major), Ordnance Board, 1960-63; TSO2 (Major), Trials Establishment Guided Weapons, RA, 1963-65; postgraduate Guided Weapons Course, Royal Military College of Science, 1965-66; TSO1 (Lt. Col.), Royal Armament Research and Development Establishment, 1966-69; Assistant Director, Guided Weapons Trials (Col.), MOD Procurement Executive, 1970-73; Member (Col.), Ordnance Board, 1973-74; retired, 1974; self-employed holiday cottages proprietor, Scottish Manager, Blakes Holidays, 1976-93; Past President, Campbeltown Rotary Club. Recreations: wood-turning and manufacture of spinning wheels; creationism studies. Address: Kilchrist Castle, Campbeltown, Argyll, PA28 6PH; T.-01586 553210.

Annand, David Andrew, DA, ARBS. Sculptor; b. 30.1.48, Insch, Aberdeenshire; m., Jean; 1 s.; 1 d. Educ. Perth Academy; Duncan of Jordanstone College of Art, Dundee. Lecturer, Sculpture Department, Duncan of Jordanstone College of Art, Dundee, 1972-74; Art Department, St. Saviours High School, Dundee, 1975-88; full-time sculptor, since 1988; Latimer Award, 1976, Benno Schotz Award, 1978, Ireland Alloys Award, 1982; one man exhibition, Open Eye Gallery, Edinburgh, 1990; winner, High Street commission, Perth Partnership Sculpture Competition, 1990; winner, Irvine Development Corporation Almswall Road Sculpture Competition, 1990. Recreations: music; bird watching; children watching; cooking; eating; drinking wine. Address: Pigscrave Cottage, The Wynd, Kilmany, Cupar, Fife KY15 4PU. T.-0182 624 714.

Annand, Louise Gibson, MBE, MA (Hons), AMA. Artist; Member, Royal Fine Art Commission for Scotland, 1979-86; b. 27.5.15, Uddingston; m., 1, Alistair Matheson (deceased); 2, Roderick MacFarquhar (deceased). Educ. Hamilton Academy; Glasgow University. Teacher, primary and secondary schools, Glasgow, 1939-49; Assistant, Schools Museum Service, 1949-70; Museums Education Officer, 1970-80. Past Chairman: Scottish Educational Film Association (Glasgow Production Group); Glasgow Lady Artists Club Trust; National Vice-Chairman, Scottish Educational Media Association, 1979-84; President: Society of Scottish Women Artists, 1963-66 and 1980-85; Glasgow Society of Women Artists, 1977-79, 1988-91; Visiting Lecturer in Scottish Art, Regina University, 1982; Chairman, J.D. Fergusson Foundation, since 1982 (Trustee, since 1983); Member, Business Committee, General Council, University of Glasgow, 1981-85, 1988-91; Honorary Member, Saltire Society, since 1993; DUniv, Glasgow University, 1994; exhibited widely since 1945; produced numerous 16mm films, including the first on Charles Rennie Mackintosh, 1966. Recreations: mountaineering (Ladies Scottish Climbing Club). Address: (h.) 22 Kingsborough Gardens, Glasgow, G12 9NJ; T.-0141-339 8956.

Annandale and Hartfell, 11th Earl of (Patrick Andrew Wentworth Hope Johnstone of Annandale and of That Ilk). Farmer; Chief, Clan Johnstone; Baron of the Barony of the Lands of the Earldom of Annandale and Hartfell, and of the Lordship of Johnstone; Hereditary Steward, Stewartry of Annandale; Hereditary Keeper, Keys of Lochmaben Castle; Deputy Lieutenant, Dumfriesshire, since 1987; b. 19.4.41, Auldgirth, Dumfriesshire; m., Susan Josephine; 1 s.; 1 d. Educ. Stowe School; Royal Agricultural College, Cirencester. Member: Dumfriesshire County Council, 1970-75, Dumfries and Galloway Regional Council, 1975-85, Scottish Valuation Advisory Council, 1982, Solway River Purification Board, 1973-85; Underwriter, Lloyds, London, 1976. Address: (b.) House of Lords, London SW1.

Anstruther, Sir Ralph (Hugo), of that Ilk, 7th Bt. of Balcaskie and 12th of Anstruther, GCVO, MC, DL, BA. Equerry to the Queen Mother, since 1959, and Treasurer since 1961; b. 13.6.21. Educ. Eton; Magdalene College, Cambridge. Major (ret.), Coldstream Guards. Member, Queen's Bodyguard for Scotland (Royal Company of Archers); DL, Fife, 1960; DL, Caithness-shire, 1965. Address: Balcaskie, Pittenweem, Fife; Watten, Caithness.

Anton, Alexander Elder, CBE, MA, LLB, LLD (Hon), FBA; b. 1922; m., Doris May Lawrence; 1 s. Educ. Aberdeen University. Solicitor, 1949; Lecturer, Aberdeen, 1953-59; Professor of Jurisprudence, Glasgow University, 1959-73; Honorary Professor, 1984, Aberdeen University; Member, Scottish Law Commission, 1966-82; UK Delegate to Hague Conference on Private International Law, 1964-82; Chairman, Scottish Rights of Way Society, 1988-92. Publications: Private International Law, 1967; Civil Jurisdiction in Scotland, 1984. Recreation: hill-walking. Address: (h.) 5 Seafield Drive West, Aberdeen, AB1 7XA.

Arbuthnot, Peter Geoffrey. Managing Director, Christie's Scotland Limited, since 1989; b. 18.9.50, London; m., Belinda Terry-Engell; 1 s.; 1 d. Educ. Stowe School; Trinity College, Cambridge. Research in Indian Archaeology, 1974-76; Specialist, Ethnographic Art, Christie's Auctioneers, London, 1976-80; Commodity Trader, E.D. and F. Man, 1980-83; Christie's in the City, 1983-88. Recreations: squash; skiing; hockey; travel; public speaking. Address (b.) 164-166 Bath Street, Glasgow G2 4TG; T.-0141-332 8134.

Arbuthnott, 16th Viscount of (John Campbell Arbuthnott), CBE, DSC, FRSE, FRSA, BGCOStJ, MA. Lord Lieutenant, Grampian Region (Kincardineshire), since 1977; Director, Grampian Assured; Member, BP Scottish Advisory Board; b. 26.10.24; m.; 1 s.; 1 d. Educ. Fettes College; Gonville and Caius College, Cambridge. Member, Countryside Commission for Scotland, 1967-71; Chairman, Red Deer Commission, 1969-75; Member, Aberdeen University Court, 1978-84; President, Scottish Landowners Federation, 1974-79; President, Royal Scottish Geographical Society, 1984-87; Chairman, Scottish Widows' Fund and Life Assurance Society, 1984-87; Lord High Commissioner to the General Assembly of the Church of Scotland, 1986, 1987; President, Royal Zoological Society of Scotland, since 1976; President, Scottish Agricultural Organisation Society, 1980-83; President, Federation of Agricultural Cooperatives (UK), 1983-87; Deputy Chairman, Nature Conservancy Council, 1980-85, and Chairman, Scottish Committee, NCC; Chairman, Aberdeen and Northern Marts Ltd., 1986-91, Director, 1973-91; Director, Clydesdale Bank PLC, 1985-92 (Northern Area, 1975-85); Director, Britoil, 1988-90; Prior of Scotland, The Order of St. John, 1983-95; Member, Royal Commission on Historical Manuscripts, 1988-95. Address: (h.) Arbuthnott House, by Laurencekirk, Kincardineshire AB30 1PA.

Arbuthnott, Professor John Peebles, PhD, ScD, FIBiol, HonFTCD, FRSA, FRSE, FIIB. Principal and Vice Chancellor, Strathclyde University, since 1991; b. 8.4.39; m., Elinor Rutherford Smillie; 1 s.; 2 d. Educ. Glasgow University; Trinity College, Dublin. Assistant Lecturer, then Lecturer, Department of Bacteriology, Glasgow University, 1960-67; Fellow of the Royal Society, 1968-72; Senior Lecturer, Department of Microbiology, then Senior Lecturer, Department of Bacteriology, Glasgow University, 1972-75; Professor of Micriobiology, Trinity College, Dublin, 1976-88; Professor of Microbiology, Nottingham University, 1988-91. Member, Lister Institute, Board of Public Health Laboratory Service; Chairman, UK Forum for Microbiology; Chairman, Higher Education Councils' Joint

Information Systems Committee; Convener, Committee of Scottish Higher Education Principals; Member, Department of Trade and Industry Multimedia Advisory Group; Member, OST Committee on Dual Funding of Science and Technology. Recreations: attending soccer matches; golf. Address: (b.) Strathclyde University, Glasgow, G1 1XQ; T.-0141-552 4400.

Arbuthnott, The Hon. William David, MBE. Secretary, The Black Watch Association; b. 5.11.27, Colchester; m., Sonja Mary Thomson; 1 s.; 2 d. Educ. Fettes. Army Officer, The Black Watch, 1948-78. Recreations: gardening; reading; civil engineering. Address: (h.) The Old Manse, Trochry, by Dunkeld, PH8 ODY; T.-Trochry 723205; (b.) RHQ The Black Watch, Balhousie Castle, Hay Street, Perth, PH1 5HR; T.-Perth 623214.

Archer, Gilbert Baird, DL. Chairman,Tods of Orkney Ltd, since 1970; Chairman, John Dickson & Sons Ltd, since 1985; b. 24.8.42, Edinburgh; m., Irene Conn; 2 d. Educ. Melville College. Vice Convenor, George Watson's College, 1978-80; Governor, Fettes College, 1986-90; Director, Scottish Council of Independent Schools, 1988-91; Council Member, Governing Bodies Association of Independent Schools, 1988-91; Governor, Napier Polytechnic of Edinburgh; Governor, St. Columba's Hospice; Past President, Edinburgh Chamber of Commerce & Manufactures; Chairman, Scottish Chambers of Commerce; Chairman, Edinburgh Common Purpose, 1991-94; Past Moderator, High Constabulary of the Port of Leith; Liveryman, Worshipful Company of Gunmakers, London. Recreations: fishing; shooting. Address: (b.) 12 Broughton Place, Edinburgh EH1 3RX; T.-0131-556 4518.

Argent, Edward, DipRADA, FGSM. Director, School of Drama, Royal Scottish Academy of Music and Drama, since 1974; b. 21.8.31, London; m., Christine Tuck; 1 s.; 2 d. Educ. Mercers' School, London; RADA. Actor, Director, Stage Manager, 1954-70; Teacher, 1962-70; Principal Lecturer and Head, School of Theatre, Manchester Polytechnic, 1970-74. Director: Citizens' Theatre, Scottish Mask and Puppet Centre, Prime Productions, National Council for Drama Training, Conference of Drama Schools (Executive Committee). Recreations: theatre-going; reading; grandparenting. Address: (b.) 100 Renfrew Street, Glasgow, G2 3DB; T.-0141-332 4101.

Argyll, 12th Duke of, (Ian Campbell). Chief of Clan Campbell; Hereditary Master of the Royal Household, Scotland; Hereditary High Sheriff of the County of Argyll; Admiral of the Western Coast and Isles; Keeper of the Great Seal of Scotland and of the Castles of Dunstaffnage, Dunoon, and Carrick and Tarbert; b. 28.8.37; m. Iona Mary; 1 s.; 1 d. Address: Inverary Castle, Inverary, Argyll PA32 8XF.

Armour, Professor Sir James, CBE, PhD, Dr hc Utrecht, DVM&S (Edin), FRCVS, FRSE. Vice-Principal (Planning - External Relations), Glasgow University, since 1991; Dean, Faculty of Veterinary Medicine, 1986-91, and Professor of Veterinary Parasitology (Personal Chair), Glasgow University, since 1976; Chairman, Glasgow Dental Hospital and School NHS Trust, since 1995; b. 17.9.29, Basra, Iraq; m., Irene Morris (deceased); 2 s.; 2 d. Educ. Marr College, Troon; Glasgow University. Colonial veterinary service, Nigeria, 1953-60; Research Scientist, Wellcome Ltd., 1960-63; Glasgow University: Research Fellow, 1963-67, Lecturer/Senior Lecturer, 1967-73, Reader, 1973-76. Chairman, Government Committee on Animal Medicines, since 1987; Chairman, Editorial Board, In Practice (veterinary journal); Chairman, Governing Body, Institute of Animal Health. Publications: joint author of textbook on veterinary parasitology; editor, two books; 150 scientific articles. Recreation: golf. Address: (h.) Mokoia, 11 Crosbie Road, Troon, Ayrshire; T.-01292 314068.

Armour, Mary Nicol Neill, DA, RSA, RSW, RGI, LLD Glasgow (1980). Artist; b. 27.3.02, Blantyre; m., William Armour. Educ. Hamilton Academy; Glasgow School of Art. Elected ARSA, 1941; RSW, 1956; RSA, 1958; RGI, 1977; Honorary President: Glasgow School of Art, 1982; Royal Glasgow Institute of the Fine Arts, 1983; Vice President, Paisley Art Institute, 1983. Guthrie Award, RSA, 1937; Cargill Prize, RGI, 1972; Fellow, Paisley College of Technology, since 1989; Hon. Fellowship, Glasgow School of Art, 1993. Recreations: gardening; dress-making. Address: 2 Gateside Place, Kilbarchan, PA10 2LY; T.-01505 702873.

Armour, Robert Malcolm, MBA, LLB (Hons), DipLP, WS, NP. Director, Performance Development and Company Secretary, Scottish Nuclear Limited, since 1990; Director, IMS Trust, NIRA Limited, Electricity Producers Insurance Company Limited, IMS Scotland Limited, Scottish Nuclear International Ltd.; b. 25.9.59, Edinburgh; m., Anne Ogilvie White. Educ. Daniel Stewart's and Melville College, Edinburgh; Edinburgh University. Solicitor, Haldanes McLaren and Scott, WS, Edinburgh, 1983-86; Partner, Wright, Johnston and MacKenzie, Edinburgh, 1987-90. Recreations: golf; curling. Address: Scottish Nuclear, Peel Park, East Kilbride G74 5PR; T.-013552 62000.

Armstrong, Richard, CBE. Musical Director, Scottish Opera, since 1993; b. 7.1.43, Leicester. Educ. Wyggeston Grammar School, Leicester; Corpus Christi College, Cambridge. Musical Director, Welsh National Opera, 1973-86; Principal Guest Conductor, Frankfurt Opera, 1987-90. Address: (b.) Scottish Opera, 39 Elmbank Crescent, Glasgow, G2.

Arnold, James Edward, MBE, MA (Hon), BA, CertEd, FRIAS. Director, New Lanark Conservation Trust, since 1974; b. 16.3.45, Glasgow; m., Rose. Educ. Caludon Castle Comprehensive School; York University; London University. Recreations: New Lanark and life. Address: (b.) Mill Number Three, New Lanark, Lanark; T.-01555 661345.

Arnott, Rev. A. David K., MA, BD. Minister, Netherlee Parish Church, since 1977; Convener, Committee on Education for the Ministry, General Assembly, since 1995; b. 22.7.45, Dunfermline; m., Rosemary; 2 s.; 1 d. Educ. George Watson's College; St. Andrews University; Edinburgh University. Minister, Gorebridge Parish Church, 1971-77. Recreation: cooking. Address: 532 Clarkston Road, Glasgow, G44 3RT; T.-0141-637 2844.

Arnott, David Cleghorn, FILAM. Director of Leisure Services, Dunfermline District Council, since 1988; Member, Scottish Sports Council, since 1995; b. 6.2.42, Hamilton; m., Jean McFarlane Lennox; 2 s.; 1 d. Educ. Woodside Secondary, Hamilton. Joined local government with Lanarkshire County Council, 1957. Past Chairman, Scottish Branch, Institute of Leisure and Amenity Management; Hon. Life Member, Scottish Association of Local Sports Councils. Recreations: football; golf; beach-combing. Address: (h.) 9 Muirside Grove, Cairneyhill, Dunfermline; T.-01383 880751.

Arnott, James Mackay, TD, BL, WS, SSC. Solicitor; Partner, MacRoberts, Glasgow and Edinburgh, since 1963; b. 22.3.35, Blackford, Perthshire; m., Jean Barbara Allan; 3 s. Educ. Merchiston Castle School, Edinburgh University. National Service, RAF, 1957-60; TA, 1961-77. Council Member, Law Society of Scotland, 1983-85 (Convener, Law Reform Committee); Secretary, Scottish Building Contract Committee. Recreation: cricket. Address: (b.) 152 Bath Street, Glasgow, G2 4TB; T.-041-332 9988; 27 Melville Street, Edinburgh, EH3 7JF; T.-0131-226 2552.

Arnott, John Michael Stewart, BA. Director, Edinburgh Green Belt Trust, since 1992; Member, South East Regional Board, Scottish Natural Heritage, 1992-95; b. 12.6.33; m., Lynne Gladstone-Millar; 1 s.; 1 d. Educ. Peterhouse, Cambridge. Pilot, RAF, 1952-54; Announcer, Producer, Editor Talks and Features, Edinburgh Manager, BBC Scotland, 1960-90; Member, 1982-92, Vice-Chairman, 1986-92, Countryside Commission for Scotland; Chairman, Isle of May Bird Observatory, 1980-85; Chairman, Fair Isle Bird Observatory Trust, 1983-85; Member, Committee for Scotland, Nature Conservancy Council, 1986-91; Member, NCC Advisory Committee on Birds, 1990; Chairman, CCS Advisory Panel on Management of Mountain Areas, 1989-90; Member, National Parks of England and Wales Review Panel, 1990; President, Scottish Ornithologists' Club, 1984-87. Sony Award for Radio Feature, 1985. Recreations: ornithology; hill-walking. Address: (h.) East Redford House, 133 Redford Road, Edinburgh, EH13 0AS; T.-0131-441 3567.

Arnott, Professor Struther, BSc, PhD, ScD, FRSE, FRS. Principal and Vice-Chancellor, St. Andrews University, since 1986; b. 25.9.34, Larkhall; m., Greta Edwards; 2 s. Educ. Hamilton Academy; Glasgow University. King's College, London: Scientist, MRS Biophysics Research Unit, 1960-70, Demonstrator, Physics, 1960-67, Director of Postgraduate Studies in Biophysics, 1967-70; Purdue University, Indiana, USA: Professor of Molecular Biology, 1970, Head, Department of Biological Sciences, 1975-80, Vice-President for Research and Dean, Graduate School, 1980-86; Oxford University: Senior Visiting Research Fellow, Jesus College, 1980-81, Nuffield Research Fellow, Green College, 1985-86, Guggenheim Memorial Foundation Fellow, 1985. Recreations: birdwatching; botanizing. Address: (b.) College Gate, North Street, St. Andrews KY16 9AJ; T.-01334 462551.

Aronson, Sheriff Hazel Josephine, QC, LLB. Sheriff of Lothian and Borders at Edinburgh, since 1983; Temporary Judge, Court of Session and High Court, since 1992; Chairman, Mental Welfare Commission for Scotland; b. 12.1.46, Glasgow; m., John A. Cosgrove; 1 s.; 1 d. Educ. Glasgow High School for Girls; Glasgow University. Advocate at Scottish Bar, 1968-79; Sheriff of Glasgow and Strathkelvin at Glasgow, 1979-83. Recreations: swimming; langlauf; opera; foreign travel. Address: (h.) 14 Gordon Terrace, Edinburgh, EH16 5QR; T.-0131-667 8955.

Arthur, Adrian, BL. Editor, The Courier, Dundee, since 1993; b. 28.9.37, Kirkcaldy; m., Patricia Mill; 1 s.; 2 d. Educ. Harris Academy, Dundee; St. Andrews University. Joined staff of People's Journal; through the editorial ranks of The Courier (Deputy Editor, 1978-93). Recreations: golf; travel; Rotary. Address: (b.) 80 Kingsway East, Dundee, DD4 8SL; T.-01382 223131.

Arthur, Lt. General Sir Norman, KCB (1985); DL (Stewartry of Kirkcudbright); b. 6.3.31, London (but brought up in Ayrshire, of Scottish parents); m., Theresa Mary Hopkinson; 1 s.; 1 d.; 1 s. (deceased). Educ. Eton College; Royal Military Academy, Sandhurst. Commissioned Royal Scots Greys, 1951; commanded Royal Scots Dragoon Guards, 1972-74, 7th Armoured Brigade, 1976-77, 3rd Armoured Division, 1980-82; Director, Personal Services (Army), 1983-85; commanded Army in Scotland, and Governor of Edinburgh Castle, 1985-88; retired, 1988; Honorary Colonel, Royal Scots Dragoon Guards, 1984-92; Col. Comdt. Military Provost Staff Corps, 1983-88; Honorary Colonel, 205 (Scottish) General Hospital, Territorial Army, 1988-93; Colonel, The Scottish Yeomanry, since 1992; mentioned in Despatches, 1974. Officer, Royal Company of Archers; President, Scottish Conservation Projects Trust, since 1989; Vice President, Riding for the Disabled Association, Edinburgh and the Borders, 1988-94; Chairman, Cheshire Home, Dumfries, since 1994; Chairman, Army Benevolent Fund,

Scotland; Member, British Olympic equestrian team (three-day event), 1960. Recreations: riding; country sports; country life; reading. Address: (h.) Newbarns, Dalbeattie, Kirkcudbrightshire; T.-01556 630227.

Ashcroft, Professor Brian Kemp, BA (Hons), MA. Director, Fraser of Allander Institute, Strathclyde University, since 1989; Member, Secretary of State's Panel of Economic Consultants, since 1991; b. 5.3.47, Stockton-on-Tees; m., Janet; 1 s.; 2 d. Educ. Stockton Grammar School; Lancaster University. Rock musician, 1962-65; Construction Industry: labourer, clerk, office manager, 1965-70; Lecturer, Glasgow Polytechnic, 1974-76; Strathclyde University: Lecturer/Senior Lecturer, 1976-89, Research Director, Fraser of Allander Institute, 1989. Publications: over 30 academic papers/books. Recreations: photography; jogging; trying to hide his English origins. Address: (b.) 100 Cathedral Street, Glasgow, G4 0LN; T.-0141-552 4400.

Asher, Catherine Archibald, OBE, BA, RGN, SCM, RNT. Chairman, National Board for Nursing, Midwifery and Health Visiting for Scotland, 1993-95; b. 6.7.33, Edinburgh. Educ. Woodside School, Glasgow; Edinburgh University; Open University. Staff Nurse and Ward Sister, Glasgow Royal Infirmary, 1956-61; Nurse Teacher, Senior Tutor, Principal Nursing Officer (Teaching), Glasgow Royal Infirmary School of Nursing, 1963-74; Director of Nurse Education, Glasgow Eastern College of Nursing and Midwifery, 1974-91; Acting Principal, Glasgow College of Nursing and Midwifery, 1991-95. Recreations: gardening; golf; swimming. Address: (h.) 68 Fifth Avenue, Glasgow, G12 0AT; T.-0141-339 5072.

Ashmall, Harry Alfred, MA, MLitt, FIMgt. Rector, Morrison's Academy, since 1979; presenter of religious programmes on radio and television, since 1976; b. 22.2.39, Stirling; m., Edna Reid; 2 d. Educ. Kilsyth Academy; Glasgow University. Teacher and Careers Master, High School of Glasgow, 1961-66; Principal Teacher of History and Modern Studies, Lochend Secondary School; Principal Teacher of History, High School of Glasgow; Rector, Forfar Academy, 1971-79. Vice Chairman, UNICEF UK; Member, Governing Board and Management Committee, SCIS; Chairman, ISIS (Scotland); Member, Public Affairs Committee, ISJC. Publications: The High School of Glasgow: a history, 1976; Belief yet Betrayal, 1971; Preparing a Staff Manual, 1977; Pupils and their courses, 1981. Recreations: reading; skiing; golf. Address: (b.) Morrison's Academy, Crieff, PH7 3AN; T.-01764 653885.

Ashmore, Fionna Margaret, BA (Hons), FSA (Scot). Director, Society of Antiquaries of Scotland, since 1992; b. 21.5.50, London; m., P.J. Ashmore; 2 s.; 1 d. Educ. Oporto British School, Portugal; Convent of the Sacred Heart, Tunbridge Wells; University College, Cardiff; Glasgow University. Research on Portuguese Iron Age; archaeological indexer; Assistant Editor, Proceedings of the Society of Antiquaries of Scotland, 1978-90; Assistant Secretary, Cockburn Association, 1990-92. Recreations: reading; walking; visiting buildings and archaeological sites. Address: (b.) National Museums of Scotland, York Buildings, Queen Street, Edinburgh, EH2 1JD; T.-0131-225 7534, Ext. 327.

Ashton, Pauline Mary, BEd. Executive Director, Girl Guides Association (Scotland), since 1988; b. 1.1.59, Wincanton. Educ. Alcester Grammar School; St. Mary's College, Fenham. Teacher, Newcastle-upon-Tyne; Training Manager, Girl Guides Association. Recreations: good food and wine; travel; historic houses. Address: (b.) 16 Coates Crescent, Edinburgh, EH3 7AH; T.-0131-226 4511.

Ashworth, Bryan, MA, MD, FRCP(Lond), FRCP(Edin). Honorary Librarian, Royal College of Physicians of Edinburgh, 1982-91; Consultant Neurologist, Royal

Infirmary and Western General Hospital, Edinburgh, and Senior Lecturer in Medical Neurology, Edinburgh University, 1971-92; b. 5.5.29, Oundle, Northants. Educ. Laxton School; Oundle School; St. Andrews University. National Service, Captain RAMC, Northern Nigeria, 1953-55; junior hospital posts, Manchester and Bristol; Wellcome-Swedish Travelling Research Fellow, Karolinska Hospital, Stockholm, 1965-66; Lecturer in Clinical Neurology, Manchester University, and Honorary Consultant Physician, Manchester Royal Infirmary, 1967-71; Chairman and Director (non-executive), Robert Bailey and Son, PLC, Stockport, since 1978. Publications: Clinical Neuro-ophthalmology, 2nd edition, 1981; Management of Neurological Disorders, 2nd edition, 1985; The Bramwells of Edinburgh, 1986. Recreations: writing; walking. Address: (h.) 13/5 Eildon Terrace, Edinburgh, EH3 5NL; T.-0131-556 0547.

Ashworth, John Brian, OBE, FCA, CBIM. Vice Chairman, Seagram Distillers PLC (Managing Director, Chivas Brothers Ltd., 1974-93, and Seagram Distillers PLC, 1984-93); b. 2.9.36, Wakefield; m., Valerie; 2 s.; 1 d. Educ. Ackworth School; British College of Accountancy. Articled chartered accountancy, Leeds; Accountant, John Smiths Tadcaster Brewery Co. Ltd.; Commercial Director, Shaw Carpet Co. Ltd.; Founder/Managing Director, Crimpfil Ltd. Member, Council, CBI Scotland; Chairman, Renfrewshire Enterprise Ltd.; Governor, Paisley University; Member, Council, Scotch Whisky Association; Master, Keepers of the Quaich. Recreations: golf; travel. Address: (b.) 111 Renfrew Road, Paisley; T.-0141-842 2211.

Athanas, Christopher Nicholas, MA, LLB. Partner, Dundas & Wilson, Solicitors, Edinburgh, since 1969; b. 26.8.41, Aden; m., Sheena Anne Stewart; 1 s.; 2 d. Educ. Blairmore Preparatory School, Aberdeenshire; Fettes College, Edinburgh; Aberdeen University. Law Apprentice, then Legal Assistant, Paull & Williamsons, Advocates, Aberdeen, 1964-68; Legal Assistant, Dundas & Wilson, Solicitors, Edinburgh, 1968-69; Member, firm's Partnership Board, since 1992; Member, Society of Writers to the Signet; Notary Public; former Director, Edinburgh Junior Chamber of Commerce. Recreations: collecting; angling; golf; walking. Address: (b.) Dundas & Wilson, Saltire Court, 20 Castle Terrace, Edinburgh; T.-0131-228 8000.

Atherton, B.J. General Manager, Shetland Health Board. Address: (b.) Brevik House, South Road, Lerwick, ZE1 0RD.

Atholl, The Duke of ((George) Iain Murray), DL (Perthshire), MA. President, National Trust for Scotland, since 1994; Honorary President, Scottish Wildlife Trust, since 1974; b. 19.6.31, London. Educ. Eton; Christ Church, Oxford. Past President, Scottish Landowners Federation; Member, Committee on the Preparation of Legislation; Member, Red Deer Commission, 1969-83; Chairman, RNLI, 1979-89. Recreations: golf; bridge; shooting. Address: (h.) Blair Castle, Blair Atholl, Perthshire; T.-Blair Atholl 481212.

Atkinson, Professor David, BSc, PhD, MIBiol, CBiol, MIEEM, FRSA, MIPSS. Deputy Principal (R. & D.) and Dean, Edinburgh Centre, Scottish Agricultural College; Professor of Agriculture, Aberdeen University, and Head, Land Resources Department, Scottish Agricultural College, 1988-93; b. 12.9.44, Blyth; m., Elisabeth Ann Cocks; 1 s.; 2 d. Educ. Newlands County Secondary Modern School; Hull University; Newcastle-upon-Tyne University. East Malling Research Station, Maidstone, 1969-85; Macaulay Institute for Soil Research, 1985-87; Macaulay Land Use Research Institute, 1987-88. Individual Member, BCPC Council, since 1994; Member, IEEM Council, since 1995. Recreations: music; reading thrillers; quotations. Address: (b.) SAC, West Mains Road, Edinburgh, EH9 3JG.

Atkinson, Professor Michael David, MA, DPhil. Professor of Computational Science, St. Andrews University, since 1992; b. 4.5.46, Leeds; m., Helen Lawton Smith; 2 s.; 2 d. Educ. Leeds Grammar School; Queen's College, Oxford. Lecturer, University College, Cardiff, 1970-82; Professor, Carleton University, Ottawa, 1982-92. Recreations: bridge; walking; music. Address: 146 North Street, St. Andrews, KY16 9AF; T.-01334 478113.

Atkinson, Norman Keir, DipEd, FMA, AMA, FSA(Scot). Vice-Chair, Scottish Museums Council, since 1993; District Curator, Angus District Council, since 1977; b. 8.1.50, Arbroath; m., Noreen; 1 s; 1 d. Educ. Arbroath High; Dundee College of Education; Leicester University. Teacher, Angus County Council, 1972-75; Assistant Keeper, then Acting Keeper, Extension Services, Dundee Museum, 1975-77. Member, Heritage Committee, Society of Antiquaries of Scotland; Past President, Scottish Museums Federation. Recreations: football; archaeology; wildlife. Address: (b.) Meffan Institute, 20 West High Street, Forfar; T.-01307 464123/468813.

Atkinson, Valerie, MA (Hons).Editor Current Affairs, BBC Scotland, since 1995; Editor, Focal Point, BBC Scotland, 1988-94; b. 28.12.44, Glasgow; m., Ian Atkinson; 1 s.; 1 d. Educ. Hillhead High School, Glasgow; University of Glasgow. BBC Scotland, News and Current Affairs: Researcher, Radio, Reporter, TV, Director, TV, Producer, TV. Awards: BAFTA Scotland, 1993; ISDD National Television Award, 1993; Industrial Society, 1994. Address: (b.) BBC Current Affairs, Queen Margaret Drive, Glasgow, G12 8DG.

Austin, Professor Brian, BSc, PhD, DSc. Professor and Head, Department of Biological Sciences, Heriot-Watt University; b. 5.8.51, Barnet; m., Dawn Amy; 1 d. Educ. Mount Grace School, Potters Bar; University of Newcastle-upon-Tyne. Research Associate, 1977-78; Senior Scientific Officer, 1978-84; Lecturer, 1984-89; Reader, 1989-92. Recreations: reading; writing; walking. Address: (b.) Heriot-Watt University, Riccarton, Edinburgh, EH14 4AS; T.-0131-451 3452.

Austin, Juliet Leathes, BA (Hons). Headmistress, Kilgraston School, since 1993; b. 22.4.44, Reading; m., Anthony James Kirkpatrick Austin; 1 d. Educ. Downe House; Birmingham University. Downe House School, 1972-82, latterly as Head of English; Headmistress, Combe Bank School, 1982-93. Recreations: sailing; walking; painting. Address: (b.) Kilgraston School, Bridge of Earn, Perth, PH2 9BQ; T.-01738 812257.

Axford, Nicola Dawn, BA (Hons). General Manager, Royal Lyceum Theatre Company, since 1995; b. 17.10.60, London; m., Dr. Ian Brown. Educ. Bradford University. Director, Big Bird Music Theatre, 1982-86; Administrator, Major Road Theatre Company, 1986-87; Drama Finance Officer, Arts Council of Great Britain, 1987-91; Business Manager, PW Productions Ltd., 1991-92; Administrator, Manchester City of Drama 1994 Ltd., 1993-94. Address: (h.) 30 Haddington Place, Edinburgh, EH7 4AG; T.-0131-556 3987.

B

Bader, Douglas, MA, FRSA, FIL. Rector, Perth Grammar School, since 1985; b. 22.11.41, Stirling; m., May Heather; 3 s. Educ. Larbert High School. Teacher of Modern Languages, High School of Glasgow, 1965-69; Principal Assistant, then Principal Teacher, Alloa Academy, 1969-74; Assistant Rector, Forfar Academy, 1974-79; Depute Rector, Montrose Academy, 1979-85. Council Member, Headteachers' Association of Scotland. Recreations: singing; basketball; canoeing. Address: (b.) Perth Grammar School, Gowans Terrace, Perth, PH1 5AZ; T.-01738 620071.

Bagnall, John Michael, MA (Cantab), DipLib, MIInfSci. University Librarian, Dundee University, since 1987; b. 22.4.45, South Yorkshire; m., Carol. Educ. Mexborough Grammar School; Sidney Sussex College, Cambridge. Diploma in Librarianship, University College, London; Assistant Librarian and Sub-Librarian, Newcastle upon Tyne University. Recreations: music; bird-watching; languages. Address: University Library, Dundee, DD1 4HN; T.-01382 23181.

Baikie, Fiona M., BA (Hons), FRSA, MIM. Vice Principal, Edinburgh's Telford College, since 1994; b. 15.11.44, Leicester; m., Jim (dance band leader). Educ. John Neilson Institute, Paisley; Strathclyde University; Open University. Advertising and publishing assistant, 1965-69; Lecturer, then Senior Lecturer, Telford College, 1969-80; Head, Department of Commerce, Ayr College, 1980-82; Head, Department of Business Studies, 1982-88; Assistant Principal, Edinburgh's Telford College, 1988-94. Member, Board of Directors, Edinburgh Compact; Member, National Art Collections Fund. Recreations: languages and travel; collecting first editions; art. Address: (b.) Crewe Toll, Edinburgh, EH4 2NZ; T.-0131-332 2491.

Bailey, Michael, BA (Hons). Curator, Maclaurin Art Gallery, Ayr, since 1976; Visual Arts Development Officer, Kyle & Carrick District Leisure Service; b. 11.11.37, Stockport; m., Bernadette Donnelly; 4 s. Educ. Moseley Hall; Open University; Meteorological Office College. Meteorologist, 1956-61; marine biology research, UKAEA, 1961-64; meteorologist, 1964-76. Recreations: music and drama; visual arts; travel. Address: (b.) Rozelle House, Rozelle Park, Ayr, KA7 4NQ; T.-01292 445447.

Bailey, Raymond James, CEng, MIEE. Principal, Cardonald College, Glasgow, since 1986; b. 31.8.34, Glasgow; m., Maria Anne Mallon; 3 s. Educ. St. Mungo's Academy. Address: (b.) Cardonald College, Mosspark Drive, Glasgow, G52 3AY; T.-0141-883 6151.

Baillie, Ian David Hunter, CQSW. Director of Social Work, Church of Scotland Board of Social Responsibility, since 1990; Director, Social Care Association (Education), since 1987; Auxiliary Minister, United Reformed Church; b. 18.12.40, Dundee; m., Margaret MacCallum McFarlane; 3 d. Educ. Hutchesons Boys Grammar School. Eight years in life assurance; 25 years, to date, in social work; Member, Executive, International Christian Federation for Prevention of Alcoholism and Drug Addiction. Recreations: sport (watching); reading. Address: (b.) Charis House, 47 Milton Road East, Edinburgh, EH15 2SR; T.-0131-657 2000.

Baillie, Professor John, MA, CA. Visiting Professor of Accountancy, Heriot-Watt University, Edinburgh, since 1989; Johnstone-Smith Professor of Accountancy, Glasgow University, 1983-88; Partner, Scott-Moncrieff, since 1993; b. 7.10.44; m., Annette Alexander; 1 s.; 1 d. Educ. Whitehill School. Member, various technical and professional affairs committees, Institute of Chartered Accountants of Scotland.

Recreations: keeping fit; reading; music; golf. Address: (h.) The Glen, Glencairn Road, Kilmacolm, Renfrewshire; T.-Kilmacolm 3254.

Baillie, Marion, MA (Hons), FRSA. Chairman, Carers National Association (Strathclyde); Chairman, Advisory Committee, Carers National Association (Scotland). Educ. Glasgow University. Teacher of English, until 1963; Lecturer in English, until 1965; Headmistress, Morrison's Academy Girls' School, until 1972; Assistant Principal, Jordanhill College of Education, until 1987. Address: (h.) 12 Napier Road, Killearn, Glasgow; T.-Killearn 550 580.

Baillie, William James Laidlaw, PRSA, HRA, PPRSW, RGI, HRHA, HRWA, HFRBS, HBWS, HSSA, DAEdin. President, Royal Scottish Academy, since 1990; professional painter, since 1950; b. 19.4.23, Edinburgh; m. Helen Gillon; 1 s.; 2 d. Educ. Dunfermline High School; Edinburgh College of Art. Army Service (mainly Far East) 1942-47; Lecturer/Senior Lecturer in Drawing and Painting, Edinburgh College of Art, 1960-88; President, Royal Scottish Society of Painters in Water Colours, 1974-88; Royal Scottish Academy: Associate, 1968, Academician, 1979, Treasurer, 1986-90; 25 solo exhibitions in UK and abroad. Awards: 1980 EIS Award RSA, Cargill Award RGI, 1989 May Marshall Brown Award RSW, Sir William Gillies Award RSW. Recreations: music; travel. Address: 6A Esslemont Road, Edinburgh EH16 5PX; T.-0131-667 1538.

Bain, Aly. Fiddler; b. 1945, Lerwick. Co-founder, Boys of the Lough, 1972; Soloist; TV and radio anchorman.

Bain, Professor Andrew David, MA, PhD, FRSE. Visiting Professor, Glasgow University, since 1991; Board Member, Scottish Enterprise, since 1991; Economic Consultant, since 1991; b. 21.3.36, Glasgow; m., Eleanor Riches; 3 s. Educ. Glasgow University; Cambridge University. Various posts, Cambridge University, 1959-67; Professor of Economics: Stirling University, 1967-77, Strathclyde University, 1977-84; Group Economic Advisor, Midland Bank, 1984-90. Member: Committee to Review the Functioning of Financial Institutions, 1977-80, Monopolies and Mergers Commission, 1980-81; Member, TEC National Council, since 1994. Publications: The Control of the Money Supply, 1970; The Economics of the Financial System (2nd Edition), 1992. Address: (b.) Department of Political Economy, Glasgow University, Glasgow, G12 8RT; T.-041-339 8855.

Baird, Professor David Tennent, BA (Cantab), MB, ChB, DSc, FRCP Edin, FRCOG, FRS(Ed). Medical Research Council Professor of Reproductive Endocrinology, Edinburgh University, since 1985; Consultant Obstetrician and Gynaecologist, Simpson Memorial Maternity Pavilion, Edinburgh Royal Infirmary, since 1970; b. 13.3.35, Glasgow; m., Frances Hitchveld (m. dissolved); 2 s. Educ. Aberdeen Grammar School; Aberdeen University; Trinity College, Cambridge; Edinburgh University. After clinical training in endocrinology as well as obstetrics, spent three years (1965-68) as an MRC travelling Research Fellow at Worcester Foundation for Experimental Biology, Shrewsbury, Mass., USA, conducting research on reproductive endocrinology; Deputy Director, MRC Unit of Reproductive Biology, Edinburgh, 1972-77; Professor of Obstetrics and Gynaecology, Edinburgh University, 1977-85; served on a number of national and international committees. Publications: four books on reproduction. Recreations: ski mountaineering; music; sport. Address: (b.) Department of Obstetrics and Gynaecology, Edinburgh University, Centre for Reproductive Biology, 37 Chalmers Street, Edinburgh, EH3 9EW; T.-0131-229 2575.

Baird, John Alexander, MD, MRCPsych, DCH. Consultant Forensic Psychiatrist, Glasgow, since 1993; b. 28.8.47, Edinburgh; m., Ann Easson; 3 s. Educ. Daniel

Stewart's College, Edinburgh; Edinburgh University. Consultant Psychiatrist, State Hospital, Carstairs, 1981-85, Physician Superintendent, 1985-92. Standing Committee on Difficult Prisoners: Member, 1985-88, Chairman, 1988-91; Member, Parole Board for Scotland, 1992-94; Member, Advisory Committee on Prisoner Management, since 1993. Recreations: hill walking; wine; watching rugby. Address: (h.) 50 Munro Road, Jordanhill, Glasgow, G13 1SF.

Baird, Robert Grant, FRSE, MCIBS, MA. Executive Director, Scottish Financial Enterprise, since 1994; b. 13.1.43, Arbroath; m., Glynne Anne Ellis; 2 s. Educ. Arbroath High School; St. Andrews University; London School of Economics. Joined Bank of England, 1965; Royal Bank of Scotland, 1970; Chief Economist, Royal Bank of Scotland Group, 1985-91; Chief Executive, Scotland Europa (Brussels), 1991-94. Recreations: writing; opera; military history; European battlefields. Address: (b.) 91 George Street, Edinburgh, EH2 3ES; T.-0131-225 6990.

Baird, Susan, CBE, OStJ, JP, DUniv. Lord Provost of Glasgow, 1988-92; b. 26.5.40, Glasgow; m., George; 3 s.; 1 d. Educ. St. Mark's Secondary School, Glasgow. Worked in a city centre office; joined Labour Party, 1969; became Councillor for Parkhead, 1974; elected Bailie of the city, 1980; former Convener, Manpower Committee, latterly Vice-Convener, Parks and Recreation Committee. Address: (b.) City Chambers, George Square, Glasgow, G2 1DU; T.-0141-221 9600.

Baker, Frances J.T., MBE, MSc, BA, RGN, OHNC, Cert Ed. Senior Nursing Officer, British Gas Scotland, since 1982; Member, National Board for Nursing, Midwifery and Health Visiting for Scotland, 1988-93; President, FOHNEU; b. 29.4.34, Ayr; m., Alan; 1 s.; 1 d. Educ. Ayr Academy; London University (External); Manchester University. Casualty Staff Nurse, Ayr County Hospital; Sister, NCB, North Staffs; Lecturer, Senior Lecturer, Head of Health and Nursing Studies, Stoke on Trent Cauldon College, 1975-82. Publications: Role of Occupational Health Nurse in the Care of the Pregnant Woman at Work; Counselling Role of the Occupational Health Nurse. Recreations: opera and classical music; theatre; swimming; gardening; tapestry; reading. Address: (b.) Granton House, Marine Drive, Edinburgh, EH5 1YB.

Baker, Professor Michael John, TD, BA, BSc (Econ), DipM, CertITP (Harvard), DBA (Harvard), FCIM, F.SCOTVEC, FCAM, FRSA. Professor of Marketing, Strathclyde University, since 1971 (Deputy Principal, 1984-91); Chairman, Institute of Marketing, 1987; b. 5.11.35, Debden; m., Sheila; 1 s.; 2 d. Educ. Worksop College; Bede, Gosforth and Harvey Grammar Schools; Durham University; London University; Harvard University. Royal Artillery, 1956 (2nd Lt.); Richard Thomas & Baldwins (Sales) Ltd., 1958-64; Lecturer: Medway College of Technology, 1964-66, Hull College of Technology, 1966-68; FME Fellow, Harvard Business School, 1968-71; Member, Vice-Chairman and Chairman, SCOTBEC, 1973-85; Member, SSRC Management Committee, 1976-80; Dean, Strathclyde Business School, 1978-84; Chairman, Marketing Education Group, 1974-87; Member, SHERT, since 1983; Member, UGC Business and Management Sub-Committee, 1986-89; Member, Chief Scientist's Committee, since 1985; Governor, CAM; Director: Stoddard Sekers International PLC, STAMP Ltd.; Chairman, Westburn Publishers Ltd; Chairman, Scottish Management Projects Ltd.; Chairman, SGBS Ltd.; Governor, Lomond School. Publications: Marketing New Industrial Products; Market Development; Marketing Strategy and Management; Marketing, 5th edition, 1991; The Marketing Book (Editor); The Role of Design in International Competitiveness; Marketing and Competitive Success; Dictionary of Marketing & Advertising (2nd edition); Research for Marketing; Perspectives on Marketing Management (Editor); Marketing: Theory &

Practice (3rd edition) (Editor). Recreations: sailing; gardening; travel. Address: (b.) Strathclyde University, 173 Cathedral Street, Glasgow, G4 0RQ; T.-0141-552 4400.

Baker, Professor Michael John, BSc (Eng), ACGI, DIC, MICE, MIStructE, FSaRS. Professor of Safety Engineering, Aberdeen University, since 1991; b. 20.10.40, Oxford; m., Margaret Eleanor Lucas; 1 s.; 1 d. Educ. Leighton Park School, Reading; Imperial College of Science, Technology and Medicine, London. Civil Engineer, N.C.B., 1962-65; Research Assistant/Fellow, Imperial College, London, 1966-77; Lecturer in Structural Engineering, 1978-86; Reader in Structural Reliability, 1986-91. Vice-Chairman, Commission I, Comite Euro-International du Beton; Member of the Plenum, International Joint Committee on Structural Safety; Member, Research Strategy Board, Offshore Safety Division, Health and Safety Executive. Recreations: mountaineering; gardening. Address: (h.) 2 Thornton Place, Watson Street, Banchory, Kincardineshire, AB31 3UB; T.-01330 825495.

Baker, Ray, OBE. Chairman: Fife Enterprise, Fife Health Board, Fife College of Further and Higher Education, Association of Scottish Colleges, Fife Industry Council, Fife Euro Vocational Training Partnership, Fife Area Board Young Enterprise, Youth Clubs Fife; Vice Chairman, Fife Economic Forum; Director, GEC Scotland Ltd.; b. 15.10.26, Nuneaton. Educ. Lanchester and Dunchurch Colleges. Joined GEC, 1950. Recreations: music; reading; gardening; walking. Address: (b.) Fife Health Board, Springfield House, Cupar, KY15 5UP; T.-01334 656200.

Baker, Professor Thomas Neville, BMet, PhD, DMet, FIM, FInstP, CEng, CPhys. Professor, Department of Mechanical Engineering – Metallurgy and Engineering Materials Group, Strathclyde University; b. 11.1.34, Southport; m., Eileen May Allison. Educ. King George V School, Southport; Sheffield University. Research Metallurgist, Nelson Research Laboratories, English Electric Co., Stafford, 1958-60; Scientist, Project Leader, Tube Investments Research Laboratories, Hinxton Hall, Cambridge, 1961-64; Department of Metallurgy, Strathclyde University: SRC Research Fellow, 1965, Lecturer, 1966, Senior Lecturer, 1976, Reader, 1983, Professor, 1990, Professor of Metallurgy (1886 Chair), 1992, Vice Dean, School of Chemical and Materials Science, 1979-82, Head, Department of Metallurgy, 1986-87, Head, Division of Metallurgy and Engineering Materials, 1988-90; Committee Member, Institute of Metals, Metal Science Committee, 1980-94, Materials Technology Committee, since 1994; Chairman, Annual Conference on Metals and Materials, 1982-92. Publications: Yield, Flow and Fracture in Polycrystals (Editor), 1983; 90 research publications. Recreations: music; literature; creating a garden. Address: (b.) Department of Metallurgy and Engineering Materials, Strathclyde University, Colville Building, 48 N. Portland Street, Glasgow; T.-0141-552 4400.

Bale, Lesley Christine. Managing Director, Aberdeen Airport Ltd., since 1992; Director, Scottish Airports Ltd., since 1990; b. 14.4.59, Glasgow. Educ. Craigholme School, Glasgow; Strathclyde University. Deloitte Haskins & Sells (Glasgow), 1978-81; Coopers & Lybrand (Bermuda), 1981-83; Western International Financial Group (Bermuda): Vice-President, Treasurer and Director, 1983-87; Financial Controller, Prestwick Airport Ltd., 1988-90; Managing Director, Prestwick Airport Ltd., 1990-92. Alumnus of the Year, Strathclyde University, 1994. Recreations: bridge; golf. Address: Aberdeen Airport Ltd., Dyce, Aberdeen, AB2 0DU; T.-01224 725001.

Balekjian, Wahe Hagop, Dr (Law), Dr (pol sc), PhD. Honorary Senior Research Fellow, School of Law, Glasgow University, since 1990 (Reader in European Law, 1976-90, Head of Department, 1976-88); Visiting Titular Professor,

University of Salzburg, Austria, since 1981; Titular Professor, European Faculty, Land Use Planning, Strasbourg, since 1982; Honorary Senior Research Fellow, School of Law, Glasgow University, since 1990; b. 2.10.24, Cairo; m., Eva Birgitta. Educ. College of Arts and Sciences, Cairo; Vienna University; Manchester University. Diploma, Hague Academy of International Law. Lecturer, Vienna University, 1957-73; Simon Research Fellow, Manchester University, 1963-65; Head of Department, European Studies, National Institute of Higher Education, Limerick, 1973-76. Publications: Legal Aspects of Foreign Investment in the EEC, 1967 (awarded Prize of European Communities, 1967); The Status of Unrecognised States in International Law (published in German, 1971). Recreations: hill-walking; piano playing; languages. Address: (b.) School of Law, The University, Glasgow, G12 8QQ; T.-0141-339 8855, Ext. 5539.

Balfour of Burleigh, Lady (Janet Morgan), MA, DPhil, FRSAS. Writer; Company Director; b. 5.12.45, Montreal; m., Lord Balfour of Burleigh. Educ. Newbury County Girls' Grammar School; Oxford University; Sussex University; Harvard University. Member, Central Policy Review Staff, Cabinet Office, 1978-81; Member, Board, British Council, since 1989; Special Adviser to Director-General, BBC, 1983-86; Chairman, Cable & Wireless Resource Ltd., since 1993; Non-Executive Director: Cable & Wireless, W.H. Smith, Midlands Electricity, Scottish American Investment Co., Scottish Medical Research Fund; Member: Scottish Museums Council Development Resource, since 1988; Ancient Monuments Board for Scotland, since 1990; Book Trust Scotland, since 1992; Scottish Economic Council, since 1993; Chairman, Scotland's Book Campaign, since 1994; Editor, Diaries of a Cabinet Minister 1964-70 by Richard Crossman (3 volumes); Joint Editor, The Future of Broadcasting, 1982; author of Agatha Christie: a biography, 1984, and Edwina Mountbatten: a life of her own, 1991. Recreations: music of Handel; sea bathing; gardens.

Balfour of Burleigh, Lord. Chairman: United Artists Communications (Scotland) plc, Capella Nova, Canongate Press plc, until 1993; Deputy Governor, Bank of Scotland, 1977-91; b. 6.1.27, London. Educ. Westminster School, London. Graduate Apprentice, English Electric Company, 1951; various positions in manufacturing mangement; started English Electric's manufacturing operations in India as General Manager of new company in Madras, 1957-64; returned to Liverpool as General Manager; appointed General Manager, D. Napier & Son, before leaving the company in 1968; joined Bank of Scotland as a Director, 1968; also Director: Scottish Investment Trust plc; William Lawson Distillers Ltd.; Television Educational Network Ltd. Forestry Commissioner, 1971-74; Chairman, Scottish Arts Council, 1971-80; Chairman, Scottish Committee, ABSA, 1988-94; Chairman, Edinburgh Book Festival, 1982-87; Member, British Railways (Scottish) Board, 1982-92; Treasurer, Royal Society of Edinburgh, 1989-94; Treasurer, Royal Scottish Corporation; President, Friends of Vellore; President, Franco Scottish Society; Chancellor, Stirling University, since 1988. Recreations: woodwork; hill-climbing; music. Address: c/o Royal Society of Edinburgh, 22 George Street, Edinburgh.

Balfour, Alastair. Managing Director, The Insider Group, since 1993; b. 15.6.47, Edinburgh; m., Anne Johnstone; 2 s.; 3 d. Educ. Royal High School, Edinburgh. Trained as journalist with The Scotsman, 1966-68; became Industrial Reporter in Glasgow, 1974-78; joined Daily Record as Economics Correspondent, 1978-81; Business Editor, Sunday Standard, 1981-83; launched Scottish Business Insider, 1984; Editor, 1986-90; Editorial Director, until 1993. Director, Scottish Design; Chairman, Newsco Publications Ltd., Manchester; Founder Member, The Entrepreneurial Exchange; Member, Scottish Enterprise Business Birthrate Group. Recreations: family; sailing.

Address; (h.) 32 Glasgow Road, Blanefield, Stirlingshire G63 9BP; T.-01360 770750.

Balfour, 4th Earl of (Gerald Arthur James Balfour), JP; b. 23.12.25; m. Educ. Eton; HMS Conway. Member, East Lothian County Council, 1960-75. Address: (h.) The Tower, Whittingehame, Haddington.

Balfour, Ian Leslie Shaw, MA, LLB, BD, PhD, SSC, NP. Solicitor (Senior Partner, Balfour & Manson, since 1955; b. 16.6.32, Edinburgh; m., Joyce Margaret Ross Pryde; 3 s.; 1 d. Educ. Edinburgh Academy; Edinburgh University. Qualified as Solicitor, 1955; commissioned, RASC, 1955-57; Partner, Balfour & Manson, since 1959; Secretary, Oliver & Son Ltd., 1959-89; Fiscal to Law Society of Scotland, since 1981. Baptist Union of Scotland: President, 1976-77, Law Agent, since 1964, Secretary, Charlotte Baptist Chapel, Edinburgh, since 1980, Secretary, Scottish Bapist College, since 1983; Secretary, Elba Housing Society Ltd., 1969-92; Council, Society for Computers and Law, 1988-92; Director, Edinburgh Medical Missionary Society. Recreations: hill-walking; home computing; lay preaching. Address: (b.) 58 Frederick Street, Edinburgh; T.-0131-225 8291.

Balfour, Peter Edward Gerald, CBE. President, Scottish Council (Development and Industry), 1985-92 (Chairman, 1978-85); Director, Royal Bank of Scotland, 1972-90; Chairman, Charterhouse plc, 1985-91; b. 9.7.21, Woking; m., 1, Grizelda Ogilvy, 2, Diana Wainman; 3 s.; 2 d. Educ. Eton College. Served Scots Guards, 1940-54; joined William McEwan & Co., brewers, 1954; appointed Director, 1958; Director, Scottish Brewers, 1959; Scottish and Newcastle Breweries, 1961 (Chairman and Managing Director, 1970-83); Director and Vice Chairman, RBS Group, 1978. Recreations: farming; forestry. Address: (h.) Scadlaw House, Humbie, East Lothian; T.-01875 833252.

Balfour, William Harold St. Clair. Solicitor; b. 29.8.34, Edinburgh; m., 1, Patricia Waite (m. dissolved); 1 s.; 2 d.; 2, Alice Ingsay McFarlane; 2 step. d. Educ. Hillfield, Ontario; Edinburgh Academy; Edinburgh University. Partner, Balfour & Manson, Nightingale & Bell, since 1962; Clerk to Admission of Notaries Public, 1971-92; Prison Visiting Committee, 1965-70; Chairman, Basic Space Dance Theatre, 1980-86; Friends of Talbot Rice Art Centre, since 1982, Garvald Trustees, since 1980, Wellspring Management, since 1990; Secretary: Scottish Photography Gallery, Fruit Market Gallery, Edinburgh. Recreations: sailing; walking; wine. Address: (b.) 58 Frederick Street, Edinburgh, EH2 1LS; T.-0131 225 8291.

Ball, Derek William, MB, MRCPsych. Composer; Consultant Psychiatrist; b. 30.12.49, Letterkenny, Ireland; m., Marie Knox; 1 d. Educ. Kings Hospital, Dublin; Royal Irish Academy of Music; Trinity College, Dublin. Studied composition with Dr. Archie Potter; writes chamber and orchestral music; numerous performances in Dublin; pieces performed at festivals in Paris and Bordeaux. Founder Member, Association of Young Irish Composers; Secretary/Treasurer, Scottish Society of Composers. Address: (h.) Mazagon, 4 Glen Road, Lennoxtown, G65 7JX.

Ball, Geoffrey A., FCA. Chairman, CALA plc (Group Managing Director, since 1974); b. 4.8.43, Bristol; m., Mary Elizabeth; 3 s.; 1 d. Educ. Cotham Grammar School, Bristol. Former Managing Director, Greencoat Properties Ltd.; non-executive Director: Standard Life Assurance Company; Scottish Mortgage & Trust p.l.c. Recreations: golf; music. Address: 26 Hermitage Drive, Edinburgh, EH10 5BT; T.-0131-346 0194.

Ball, Graham Edmund, BDS, FDS, RCS (Eng), Cert MHS. Consultant in Dental Public Health, Fife and Borders Health Boards, since 1995; b. 14.12.53; m., Carolyn

Bowyer; 1 s.; 2 d. Educ. King Edward VI School, Southampton; Welsh National School of Medicine. Registrar, Oral and Maxillofacial Surgery, Portsmouth hospitals, 1979-81; Associate Specialist (part-time), Oral Surgery, Wessex Cardiothoracic Unit, 1982-84; general dental practice, 1984-88; Clinical Community Dental Officer, Orkney Health Board, 1988-91; Chief Administrative Dental Officer, Orkney Health Board, 1991-95. Recreations: sailing; walking. Address: (b.) Fife Health Board, Springfield House, Cupar, Fife; T.-01334 656200.

Ball, Professor John Macleod, BA (Cantab), DPhil. Professor of Applied Analysis, Department of Mathematics, Heriot-Watt University, Edinburgh, since 1996; Senior Fellow, Science and Engineering Research Council, 1980-85; b. 19.5.48, Farnham, Surrey. Educ. Mill Hill School; St. John's College, Cambridge. SERC postdoctoral research fellowship, 1972-74, at Department of Mathematics, Heriot-Watt University, and Lefschetz Center for Dynamical Systems, Brown University, Providence, Rhode Island, USA; Heriot-Watt University: Lecturer in Mathematics, 1974-78, Reader in Mathematics, 1978-82. Elected Fellow, Royal Society of Edinburgh, 1980; Whittaker Prize, Edinburgh Mathematical Society, 1981; Junior Whitehead Prize, London Mathematical Society, 1982; Keith Prize, Royal Society of Edinburgh, 1991; Naylor Prize, London Mathematical Society, 1995; elected Fellow, Royal Society, 1989; President, Edinburgh Mathematical Society, 1989-90; Visiting Professor, Institute for Advanced Study, Princeton, 1993-94; Council Member, Engineering and Physical Sciences Research Council, since 1994. Recreations: music; travel. Address: (h.) 11 Gloucester Place, Edinburgh, EH3 6EE.

Ballantyne, Professor Colin Kerr, MA, MSc, PhD. Professor in Physical Geography, St. Andrews University, since 1994; b. 7.6.51, Glasgow. Educ. Hutchesons' Grammar School; Glasgow University; McMaster University; Edinburgh University. Lecturer in Geography, St. Andrews University, 1980-89, Senior Lecturer in Geography and Geology, 1989-94. Gordon Warwick Award, 1987; Presidents' Medal, Royal Scottish Geographical Society, 1992. Publications: The Quaternary of the Isle of Skye, 1991; The Periglaciation of Great Britain, 1994. Recreations: music; travel; mountaineering; skiing; writing. Address: (h.) Birchwood, Blebo Craigs, Fife, KY15 5UF; T.-01334 850567.

Ballantyne, Fiona Catherine, MA, MCIM. Vice-Chair, BBC Broadcasting Council for Scotland, since 1991; Vice-Chair, Duncan of Jordanstone College of Art, 1988-94; Director, Network Scotland Ltd., since 1991; Director, Edinburgh Healthcare Trust, since 1994; b. 9.7.50, Bristol; m., A. Neil Ballantyne. Educ. Mary Erskine; Troon; Edinburgh University. Former Market Researcher and Market Research Manager; Research and Planning Manager, Thistle Hotels Ltd., 1975-77; Assistant Marketing Manager, Lloyds & Scottish Finance Group, 1977-79; Scottish Development Agency: Marketing Manager, Small Business Division, 1979-84, Head of Small Business Services, 1984-88, Director, Tayside and Fife, 1988-90; Managing Director, Ballantyne Mackay Associates, since 1990. Recreations: walking; swimming; tapestry; painting. Address: (b.) 2-8 Millar Crescent, Edinburgh, EH10 5HW; T.-0131-447 9700.

Ballantyne, Robert, MA (Hons). Assistant Editor, The Scotsman, since 1994; b. 12.4.53, Forfar; m., Aileen; 1 s. Educ. Beath Senior High School, Cowdenbeath; Edinburgh University. Journalist, Evening News, Edinburgh, 1974-79; joined The Times, 1979, Business Editor, 1993-94. Recreations: theatre; cycling; swimming. Address: (b.) 20 North Bridge, Edinburgh, EH1 1YT; T.-0131-243 3384.

Ballinger, Brian Richard, MA, BM, BCh, FRCPEd, FRCPsych, DPM. Consultant Psychiatrist, Dundee Psychiatric Service, since 1971; Honorary Senior Lecturer, Dundee University; Medical Director, Dundee Healthcare Unit and former Chairman, Dundee Division of Psychiatry; b. 1.6.37, Newport, Gwent; m., Dr. C. Barbara Ballinger; 2 s. Educ. Manchester Grammar School; University College, Oxford; St. Mary's Hospital Medical School, London. Postgraduate training in London, Oxford, Sheffield and Dundee; special interest in psychiatry of old age. Recreations: painting; music; travel. Address: (b.) Royal Dundee Liff Hospital, Dundee; T.-01382 580441.

Band, Thomas Mollison. Chairman, Made in Scotland, since 1994; Chairman, Andersons Enterprises Ltd., since 1994; Chairman, Edinburgh Europa Ltd., since 1994; Governor, Edinburgh Telford College, since 1990; Member, Board of Management, Perth Housing Association, since 1993; Director, Perth Theatre Ltd., since 1994; Adviser, Robert Gordon University Heritage Unit, since 1994; b. 28.3.34, Aberdeen; m., Jean McKenzie Brien; 1 s.; 2 d. Educ. Perth Academy. Principal, Tariff Division, Board of Trade, London, 1969-73; Director (Location of Industry), Department of Industry, Glasgow, 1973-76; Assistant Secretary (Industrial Policy), Scottish Economic Planning Department, 1976-78; Assistant Secretary (Housing), Scottish Development Department, 1978-82; Assistant Secretary (Finance), Scottish Office, 1982-84; Director, Historic Buildings and Monuments, Scottish Development Department, 1984-87; Chief Executive, Scottish Tourist Board, 1987-94. Recreations: gardening; skiing; shooting. Address: (h.) Heathfield, Pitcairngreen, Perthshire; T.-0173 883 403.

Banfill, Professor Phillip Frank Gower, BSc, PhD, CChem, MRSC. Professor of Construction Materials, Heriot-Watt University, since 1995; b. 20.3.52, Worthing; m., Patricia; 1 s.; 1 d. Educ. Lancing College; Southampton University; Liverpool University. Former Lecturer, Liverpool University. Publications: three books; 60 papers. Recreations: sailing; choral singing; bee-keeping. Address: (b.) Department of Building Engineering and Surveying, Heriot-Watt University, Riccarton, Edinburgh, EH14 4AS; T.-0131-449 5111.

Banks, Derek John, MA, MHSM. General Manager, Dumfries and Galloway Health Board, since 1993; b. 25.9.47, New York City; m., (Pauline) Moira; 2 s.; 1 d. Educ. St. Joseph's College, Dumfries; Glasgow University; Simon Fraser University, Canada. Civil Servant, 1973-86; Director of Planning and Information, Crewe Health Authority, 1986-88; Director of Corporate Planning and Estates, North Lincs Health, 1988-92. Recreations: hill-walking; cinema; chess. Address: (h.) Maxwell House, Corsock, Kirkcudbrightshire, DG7 3DH.

Banks, Iain. Novelist; b. 1954. Educ. schools in North Queensferry, Gourock, Greenock; Stirling University. Hitch-hiked through Europe, Scandinavia, Morocco, 1975, later worked for British Steel and IBM, and as a costings clerk in London. Books: The Wasp Factory, 1984; Walking on Glass, 1985; The Bridge, 1986; Consider Phlebas, 1987; Espedair Street, 1987; The Player of Games, 1988; Canal Dreams, 1989; Use of Weapons, 1990; The State of the Art, 1991; The Crow Road, 1992; Against a Dark Background, 1993; Complicity , 1993 (No. 1 bestseller in paperback); Feersum Endjinn, 1994; Whit, 1995.

Banks, Professor William McKerrell, BSc, MSc, PhD, CEng, FIMechE, FIM. Professor of Advanced Materials, Strathclyde University, since 1991; Academic Director, Centre for Advanced Structural Materials; Hon. Secretary, Scottish Branch, IMechE; b. 28.3.43, Irvine; m., Martha Ruthven Hair; 3 s. Educ. Irvine Royal Academy; Strathclyde University. Senior Research Engineer, G. & J. Weir Ltd., 1966-70; Lecturer, Senior Lecturer, Reader, Professor, Strathclyde University, since 1970. Recreations:

family; Bible teaching; gardening. Address: (h.) 19 Dunure Drive, Hamilton, ML3 9EY; T.-01698 823730.

Bannister, John Roy, Clerk to the Scottish Traffic Commissioner, since 1987; b. 3.11.46, London; m., Jan; 1 s., 1 d. Educ. Edmonton County Grammar School. Department of Transport: London, 1965-72, 1984-87, Newcastle upon Tyne, 1972-83; Manager, International Road Freight Office, Newcastle upon Tyne, 1983-84. Recreations: home brewing/wine; foreign travel; railways. Address: (h.) 13 Warrender Court, North Berwick, East Lothian; T.-01620 4683.

Barbenel, Professor Joseph Cyril, BDS, BSc, MSc, PhD, LDS RCS(Eng), CBiol, FIBiol, CPhys, FInstP, CEng, FBES, FRSE. Professor, Bioengineering Unit, Strathclyde University, since 1982 (Head, Tissue Mechanics Division, since 1970); b. 2.1.37, London; m., Lesley Mary Hyde Jowett; 2 s.; 1 d. Educ. Hackney Downs Grammar School, London; London Hospital Medical College; Queen's College, Dundee (St. Andrews University); Strathclyde University. Dental House Surgeon, London Hospital, 1960; National Service, RADC, 1960-61 (Lieutenant, 1960, Captain, 1961); general dental practice, London, 1963; student, 1963-67; Lecturer, Department of Dental Prosthetics, Dental School, Dundee, 1967-69; Senior Lecturer, Strathclyde University, 1970-82. Member, Steering Committee, Forum on Clinical Haemorheology; Member, Administrative Council, International Federation of Medical and Biological Engineering, and Chairman, European Working Group. Recreations: music; theatre. Address: (b.) University of Strathclyde, Bioengineering Unit, 106 Rottenrow, Glasgow, G4 ONW; T.-0141-552 4400.

Barbour, Very Rev. Robert Alexander Stewart, KCVO, MC, MA, BD, STM, DD, DipEd. Minister, Church of Scotland, since 1954; Dean, Chapel Royal in Scotland, 1981-91; Prelate, Priory of Scotland, Order of St. John, 1977-93; b. 11.5.21, Edinburgh; m., Margaret Pigot; 3 s.; 1 d. Educ. Rugby School; Balliol College, Oxford; St. Mary's College, St. Andrews. Army (Scottish Horse), 1940-45, Territorial Army, 1947-54; Editorial Assistant, Thomas Nelson & Sons, 1948-49; Secretary, Edinburgh Christian Council for Overseas Students, 1953-55; Lecturer and Senior Lecturer in New Testament Language, Literature and Theology, New College, Edinburgh University, 1955-71; Professor of New Testament Exegesis, Aberdeen University, 1971-86; Master, Christ's College, Aberdeen, 1977-82; Moderator, General Assembly of the Church of Scotland, 1979-80; Chaplain to the Queen in Scotland, 1976-91, Extra Chaplain, since 1991; Honorary Secretary, Novi Testamenti Societas, 1970-77. Recreations: music; forestry; walking. Address: (h.) Fincastle, Pitlochry, PH16 5RJ; T.-01796 473209.

Barclay, Kenneth Forsyth, BL, NP. Secretary, Scottish Law Commission; b. 1.2.38, Glasgow; m., Jean Broom Curwen; 1 s.; 1 d. Educ. Woodside Senior Secondary School, Glasgow; Glasgow University. Solicitor in private practice, 1960-71; Principal Solicitor, Cumbernauld Development Corporation, 1971-73; joined Office of Solicitor to Secretary of State for Scotland, 1973; Legal Secretary, Royal Commission on Legal Services in Scotland, 1976-80, then Divisional Solicitor, Scottish Office. Recreations: golf; walking; visiting Arran; reading. Address: (b.) 140 Causewayside, Edinburgh, EH19 1PR; T.-031-668 2131.

Barge, Ronald Mansfield, DSC, VRD, DL. Past Chairman, Otter Ferry Salmon Ltd.; Past Chairman, Bitmac Ltd.; b. 10.11.20, Rawal Pindi; m., Elizabeth Ann Lamberton; 3 s.; 3 d. Educ. Cargilfield; Glenalmond; Glasgow School of Art; Durham University; Royal College of Art, London. RNVR, 1937; Navy, 1939-46; Lt. Commander, Clyde Division, RNVR; former Director, Gem

Line Ltd., Glasgow; farming, Argyll, from 1971; a pioneer of salmon farming in Scotland; Vice President, Scottish Society for Prevention of Cruelty to Animals; Past Chairman, Glasgow and West of Scotland SPCA. Recreations: gardening; art. Address: (h.) Whistlers' Hill, Rhu, Dunbartonshire; T.-01436 820 285.

Barker, Alan. Music Director, The Scottish Ballet, since 1992; b. Australia. Educ. Melbourne University. Former Musical Director, New Zealand Ballet, and Artistic Director, New Zealand Opera; former Resident Conductor, Australian Ballet; joined American Ballet Theatre, 1978, as Associate Conductor, promoted to Principal Conductor, 1980; Music Director, Pittsburgh Ballet Theatre, 1988-90; has conducted National Ballet of Canada, Royal Danish Ballet, and Birmingham Royal Ballet. Address: (b.) Scottish Ballet, 261 West Princes Street, Glasgow, G4 9EE; T.-0141-331 2931.

Barker, Pamela Margaret Wentworth, BSc, MB, ChB, DPM, MRCPsych. Consultant Psychiatrist, Highland Health Board, since 1978; Clinical Senior Lecturer in Mental Health, Aberdeen University, since 1981; b. 5.11.29, London. Educ. Ipswich High School; Leeds University. House Physician and House Surgeon, General Infirmary, Leeds; Senior House Officer, Pinderfields General Hospital, Wakefield; Registrar, Stanley Royd Hospial, Wakefield; Assistant Psychiatrist, Yorkshire Regional Health Authority. Recreation: motor vehicle maintenance. Address: (h.) Burnside, Leachkin Road, Inverness, IV3 6NW; T.-01463 234101.

Barker, Ralph Fraser, MA (Hons), DipEd. Rector, Alloa Academy, since 1995; b. 10.7.51, Edinburgh; m., Suzanne; 2 s.; 1 d. Educ. Royal High School, Edinburgh; Edinburgh University. Teacher of Mathematics, then Assistant Principal Teacher, Royal High School, 1974-81; Principal Teacher, Knox Academy, 1981-84; Assistant Head Teacher, then Depute Head Teacher, Queensferry High School, 1984-94. Address: (b.) Claremont, Alloa, FK10 2EQ; T.-01259 214979.

Barlow, Professor (Arthur) John, PhD, DIC, BSc, ACGI, MIEE, CEng. Titular Professor, Electronics and Electrical Engineering Department, Glasgow University; b. 17.3.34, Nottinghamshire; m., Alma Marshall; 1 s.; 1 d. Educ. Nottingham High School; Imperial College. Turner and Newall Research Fellow, Imperial College, 1958-61; Glasgow University: Lecturer, 1961-66, Senior Lecturer, 1966-68, Reader, 1968-75. Address: (h.) 5 Auchencruive, Milngavie, Glasgow, G62 6EE.

Barnet, James Paul, MA, LLB. Partner, Macbeth Currie & Co., Solicitors, since 1965; Honorary Sheriff, Tayside Central and Fife, at Dunfermline; former Dean, Dunfermline District Society of Solicitors; b. 20.7.37, Darlington; m., Margaret Smart; 4 s. Educ. Dunfermline High School; Edinburgh University. Admitted as Solicitor, 1961. Council Member, Law Society of Scotland, 1985-88; Local Secretary, Scottish Garden City Housing Society Ltd.; Captain, Scottish Universities Golfing Society, 1980-81; President, Dunfermline Rotary Club, 1985-86. Recreations: golf; reading; quoting Dr. Johnson. Address: (h.) Bonnyton House, Dunfermline, Fife, KY12 9HT; T.-Dunfermline 731011.

Barnett, Robert Hall, FIMI. Managing Director, Barnetts Motor Group Ltd, since 1965; b. 22.1.36, Dundee; m., Alison; 1 s.; 1 d. Educ. Morgan Academy. Dundee and President, Tayside Chamber of Commerce, 1992-93; President, Scottish Motor Trade Association, 1982-84. Recreations: golf; sailing; motorcycling. Address: (b.) Riverside Drive, Dundee; T.-01382 668622.

Barnett, Robert James Charles, LLB (Hons). Director of Administration and Legal Services and Depute Chief

Executive, Western Isles Islands Council, since 1986; Returning Officer, Western Isles Islands Area, since 1986; b. 10.5.53, Birmingham; m., Christine Mary; 1 s.; 1 d. Educ. Homelands Technical High School, Torquay; Bristol Polytechnic; Guildford College of Law. Served articles with Torbay Borough Council, 1975-77; qualified as Solicitor, 1978; Assistant Solicitor, then Senior Assistant, then Principal Assistant Solicitor, Plymouth City Council, 1978-86. Recreations: music; reading; walking; family. Address: (b.) Western Isles Islands Council, Council Offices, Sandwick Road, Stornoway, Isle of Lewis, PA87 2BW; T.-01851 703773, Ext. 200.

Barr, Professor Allan David Stephen, BSc, PhD, CEng, FIMechE, FRSE. Jackson Professor of Engineering, Aberdeen University, since 1985; Dean, Faculty of Engineering and Mathematical and Physical Sciences; b. 11.9.30, Glasgow; m., Eileen Patricia Redmond. Educ. Daniel Stewart's College, Edinburgh; Edinburgh University. Student apprentice, Bristol Aeroplane Company; Lecturer, Department of Engineering, Edinburgh University; Fulbright Scholar, Visiting Associate Professor, Department of Theoretical and Applied Mechanics, Cornell University, USA; Senior Lecturer, then Reader, Department of Mechanical Engineering, Edinburgh University; Professor and Head, Department of Mechanical Engineering, Dundee University. Recreations: fly fishing; oil painting. Address: (b.) Department of Engineering, Kings College, University of Aberdeen, AB9 2UE.

Barr, David, DPE. Director of Physical Education, Dundee University, 1968-94 (retired); b. 7.3.34, Motherwell; m.; 1 s.; 1 d.; 1 step d. Educ. Dalziel High School, Motherwell; Scottish School of Physical Education, Jordanhill College of Education, Glasgow. Physical Fitness Officer, RAF, 1957-60; Games Master, Glyn Grammar School, Ewell, Surrey, 1960-63; Assistant Director of Physical Education, Aberdeen University, 1963-66; Director of Physical Recreation, Bradford University, 1966-68. Played water polo for Scotland, 1955-61, for Great Britain, 1958-61; national water polo coach, Great Britain, 1961-65; director of water polo, Scotland, 1972-75; team manager/coach, water polo, GB at World Student Games, Budapest, 1965, Turin, 1970, Moscow, 1973; President, Rotary Club of Claverhouse, 1993-94. Publications: A Guide to Water Polo, 1964; Play Better Water Polo, 1970; Water Polo, 1980. Recreations: golf; gardening. Address:(h.) 22 Tay Street, Newport-on-Tay, DD6 8HL; T.-01382 542120.

Barr, Rev. David, MA, BD. Hospital Chaplain, Glasgow Royal Infirmary and Canniesburn Hospital, 1962-84; b. 14.6.14, Airdrie. Educ. Airdrie Academy; Glasgow University and Trinity College. Student Assistant, New Monkland Parish Church, 1935-37; Minister, Kirkintilloch South Church, 1938-42; part-time Hospital Chaplain, Broomhill and Lanfine Hospitals; Minister, St. Mary's, Partick, 1942-62; part-time Hospital Chaplain, Glasgow Western Infirmary, 1960-62. Moderator, Glasgow Presbytery, 1969-70; Chairman, National Association of Whole-Time Hospital Chaplains for England, Scotland and Wales, 1978-82. Recreations: motoring; reading; topography; ecclesiology; medicine. Address: (h.) 17 Victoria Park Gardens South, Broomhill, Glasgow, G11 7BX; T.-0141-339 5364.

Barr, David George Dryburgh, MB, ChB, FRCPEd, DCH. Consultant Paediatrician, Lothian Health Board, since 1971; part-time Senior Lecturer, Department of Child Life and Health, Edinburgh University, since 1977; b. 14.2.36, Edinburgh; m., Anna Blair; 2 s.; 1 d. Educ. Daniel Stewart's College, Edinburgh; Edinburgh University. Senior Registrar, Royal Hospital for Sick Children, Edinburgh, 1965-69; Research Fellow, Children's hospital, Zurich, Switzerland, 1969-70; Consultant Paediatrician, Edinburgh Northern and West Fife Hospitals, 1971-77; Consultant Paediatrician, Royal Hospital for Sick Children

and Simpson Memorial Maternity Pavilion, since 1977; seconded to Ministry of Health and University of Riyadh, Saudi Arabia, 1980-83. Address: (b.) Royal Hospital for Sick Children, Sciennes Road, Edinburgh; T.-0131-667 1991.

Barr, Sheriff Kenneth Glen, MA, LLB. Sheriff, South Strathclyde, Dumfries and Galloway, at Dumfries, since 1976; b. 20.1.41.

Barr, William James, OBE, CEng, FICE, FIMgt. Chairman and Managing Director, Barr Limited (which includes W. & J. Barr and Sons (Scotland) Limited, Alpha Crane Limited, Alpha Services Limited, Alpha Access Limited, Econospace Limited, Barr Quarries Limited, Barmix Concrete, Barr Construction, Solway Engineers, Solway Precast, Solway Crane); b. 12.3.39, Ayr; m., Marlean Ramage; 2 s.; 1 d. Educ. Girvan High School; Glasgow University; Paisley University. Chairman, Freeport (Scotland) Ltd; Chairman, Thomas Telford Services Ltd; Chairman, Construction T.A. Services (Swindon) Ltd.; Member, Council and Executive, Institution of Civil Engineers; former Chairman, Glasgow and West of Scotland Association, Institution of Civil Engineers; Visiting Professor, Strathclyde University; former Chairman, Craigie College of Education; Chairman, Ayr College Board; Member of Court, Paisley University; Chairman, Ayr Locality Enterprise and Resources Trust; Member, Governing Council, ScotBIC; Vice-Chairman, Ayrshire Hospice; Founder Chairman, Laigh Milton Viaduct Conservation Project; former Vice-Chairman, Enterprise Ayrshire; Past President, Ayr Chamber of Commerce; Board Member, Ayrshire Chamber of Commerce and Industry; Past President, Association for Science and Education. Recreations: the works of Robert Burns and Thomas Telford; walking; reading. Address: (h.) Harkieston, Maybole, Ayrshire, KA19 7LP; T.-01655 83123; (b.) Heathfield, Ayr, KA8 9SL; T.-01292 281311.

Barratt, Michael, MA (Hons). Headmaster, Rannoch School, since 1982; b. 31.12.40, Edinburgh; m., Valerie Anne Dixon; 1 s.; 1 d. Educ. George Watson's College, Edinburgh; Merchiston Castle School; St. Andrews University; St. Edmund Hall, Oxford. Assistant Master, Epsom College, Surrey, 1964-73; Housemaster, Strathallan School, Perth, 1973-82. Recreations: golf; gardening; mountaineering; theatre. Address: Headmaster's House, Rannoch School, Rannoch, Perth, PH17 2QQ; T.-01882 632332.

Barrett, Professor Ann, MB, BS, FRCR, FRCP, MD. Professor of Radiation Oncology, Glasgow University, since 1986; Consultant, Royal Hospital for Sick Children, since 1986; b. 27.2.43, London; m., Adrian Bell; 1 s.; 2 d. Educ. Queen Elizabeth's Grammar School; St. Bartholomew's Hospital. Formerly Consultant in Radiotherapy and Oncology, Royal Marsden Hospital; Director, Beatson Oncology Centre, Glasgow, 1986-91; Member, MRC Molecular and Cell Medicine Board; Member, Council, Royal College of Radiologists. Publications: Cancer in Childhood (Co-editor); Practical Radiotherapy Planning (Co-author). Recreations: walking; music; novels. Address: (b.) Beatson Oncology Centre, Western Infirmary, Glasgow; T.-0141-339 8822.

Barrie, Alistair T., BSc (Hons), DipTP, MRTPI. Chief Planning Officer, City of Dundee District Council, since 1974; b. 19.2.38, Dundee; m., Elizabeth; 2 s.; 1 d. Educ. Harris Academy, Dundee; St. Andrews University; Heriot-Watt University. Past Chairman and former Hon. Secretary and Treasurer, Scottish Society of Directors of Planning. Recreation: athletics. Address: (b.) City of Dundee District Council, 21 City Square, Dundee, DD1 3BS; T.-01382 434400.

Barrie, Lesley, DPA, MHSM, DipHSM, MBIM. General Manager, Tayside Health Board, since 1993; General Manager, Forth Valley Health Board, 1991-93; b. 20.9.44, Glasgow. Educ. Glasgow High School for Girls; Glasgow University. NHS administrative trainee, 1963-66; hospital management, 1966-77; District General Manager: Inverclyde District, 1977-81, Glasgow South East, 1981-83; Director Administrative Services, Glasgow Royal Infirmary, Glasgow Royal Maternity Hospital, Glasgow Dental Hospital, 1983-87; Unit General Manager, Stirling Royal Infirmary, 1987-91. Member, Forth Valley Health Board, 1991-93 Member, Tayside Health Board, since 1993; Hon. Lecturer, Dundee University; Children's Panellist, 1975-79; Chairman, Social Security Appeal Tribunals, 1978-90; Table Tennis Internationalist for Scotland, 1963-70; formerly National and International Secretary, Scottish Table Tennis Association. Recreations: table tennis; badminton; reading. Address: (b.) P.O. Box 75, Vernonholme, Riverside Drive, Dundee, DD1 9NL.

Barron, Professor Laurence David, DPhil, BSc, MInstP, FRSE. Professor of Chemistry, Glasgow University, since 1984; b. 12.2.44, Southampton; m., Sharon Aviva Wolf; 1 s.; 1 d. Educ. King Edward VI Grammar School, Southampton; Northern Polytechnic, London; Lincoln College, Oxford. Post-doctoral research, Cambridge University, 1969-75; Ramsay Memorial Fellow, 1973-75; Glasgow University: Lecturer in Chemistry, 1975-80, Reader, 1980-84. Corday-Morgan Medal, Chemical Society, 1977; G.M.J. Schmidt Memorial Lecturer, Weizmann Institute of Science, 1984; F.L. Conover Memorial Lecturer, Vanderbilt University, 1987; Sir Harold Thompson Award, 1992. Publication: Molecular Light Scattering and Optical Activity, 1982. Recreations: water-colour painting; walking; music; radio-controlled model aircraft. Address: (b.) Chemistry Department, The University, Glasgow, G12 8QQ; T.-0141-339 8855.

Barrow, Professor Geoffrey Wallis Steuart, MA (Hons), BLitt, DLitt, FBA, FRSE, FSA, FSA Scot, FRHistS, Hon. DLitt (Glasgow and Newcastle upon Tyne). Sir William Fraser Professor of Scottish History and Palaeography, Edinburgh University, 1979-92; b. 28.11.24, Headingley, Leeds; m., Heather Elizabeth Agnes Lownie; 1 s.; 1 d. Educ. St. Edward's School, Oxford; Inverness Royal Academy; St. Andrews University; Pembroke College, Oxford. Royal Navy and RNVR (Sub-Lieutenant), 1943-46; Lecturer in History, University College, London, 1950-61; Professor of Medieval History, Newcastle-upon-Tyne University, 1961-74; Professor of Scottish History, St. Andrews University, 1974-79. Member, Royal Commission on Historical Manuscripts, 1984-90; Royal Historical Society: Council Member, 1963-74, Joint Literary Director, 1964-74, Vice President, 1982-86; Past Chairman of Council, Scottish History Society (President, 1973-77); President, Saltire Society, 1987-90; Vice-President, Commission Internationale de Diplomatique. Publications: Feudal Britain, 1956; Acts of Malcolm IV, 1960; Robert Bruce, 1965 and 1988; Acts of William I, 1971; The Kingdom of the Scots, 1973; The Scottish Tradition (Editor), 1974; The Anglo-Norman Era in Scottish History, 1980; Kingship and Unity: Scotland 1000-1306, 1981; Scotland and its neighbours, 1992. Recreations: hill-walking; visiting graveyards; travel. Address: (h.) 12A Lauder Road, Edinburgh, EH9 2EL; T.-0131-668 2173.

Barry, Rt. Rev. Mgr. John Charles McDonald, MA (Cantab), DCL. Parish Priest, Church of Our Lady, Star of the Sea, North Berwick, since 1989; b. 26.9.17, Edinburgh. Educ. Abbey School, Fort Augustus; Trinity College, Cambridge; University of Fribourg, Switzerland; Oscott College, Birmingham; Gregorian University, Rome. Ordained priest, 1944; appointed Curate, St. Patrick's, Kilsyth; sent to Rome to study canon law, 1946; appointed to St. Cuthbert's, Edinburgh, 1949; transferred to St.

Anthony's, Polmont, 1950; St. Andrew's College, Drygrange: Lecturer, 1953, Rector, 1960; St. Mark's, Edinburgh, 1977-89; Editor, Canon Law Abstracts, Canon Law Society of Great Britain, 1959-84; Consultor to the Pontifical Commission for the Revision of Canon Law, 1966-78. Recreations: golf; walking. Address: 9 Law Road, North Berwick, EH39 4PN; T.-01620 892195.

Bartholomew, John Christopher, MA, FRSE, FRSGS. President, Royal Scottish Geographical Society, 1987-93; b. 15.1.23, Edinburgh; m., Genevieve Achard-James; 5 s. Educ. Edinburgh Academy; Gordonstoun; Edinburgh University. Military Service, Royal Engineers (Survey), Middle East and East Africa, 1943-47; rejoined family firm on graduation, 1950, to share editorial responsibility for The Times Atlas of the World, mid-century edition and all subsequent editions, 1967-82, and other atlases; Editorial Director, John Bartholomew & Son Ltd., 1960-84. President, British Cartographic Society, 1970-71; Vice-President, International Cartographic Association, 1972-80; President, Edinburgh University Graduates' Association, 1980-82; Director, Scottish Rights of Way Society, since 1984.

Bartlett, Professor Christopher John, BA, PhD, FRHistS, FRSE. Professor of International History, Dundee University, since 1978 (Head of Modern History Department, 1983-88); Member, Scottish Examination Board; b. 12.10.31, Bournemouth; m., Shirley Maureen Briggs; 3 s. Educ. Queen Elizabeth's Grammar School, Wimborne; University College, Exeter; London School of Economics. Assistant Lecturer, Edinburgh University, 1957-59; Lecturer, University of the West Indies, Jamaica, 1959-62; Lecturer, Queen's College, Dundee, 1962-68; Reader, Dundee University, 1968-78. Publications: Great Britain and Sea Power 1815-53; Castlereagh; The Long Retreat; The Rise and Fall of the Pax Americana; A History of Postwar Britain 1945-74; The Global Conflict 1880-1990; British Foreign Policy in the Twentieth Century; The Special Relationship since 1945; Defence and Diplomacy 1815-1914; The Annual Register 1987-94 (UK and Scotland chapters). Address: (b.) Department of History, The University, Dundee.

Bartlett, Professor Robert John, MA, DPhil, FRHS. Professor of Mediaeval History, St. Andrews University, since 1992; b. 27.11.50, London; m., Honora Hickey; 1 s.; 1 d. Educ. Battersea Grammar School; Peterhouse, Cambridge; St. John's College, Oxford. Lecturer in History, Edinburgh University, 1980-86; Professor of Medieval History, University of Chicago, 1986-92. Publications: Gerald of Wales 1146-1223, 1982; Trial by Fire and Water: the medieval judicial ordeal, 1986; The Making of Europe, 1993. Recreations: walking; squash. Address: (b.) Department of Mediaeval History, St. Andrews University, St. Andrews, KY16 9AL; T.-01334 463308.

Barty, James Webster, OBE (1981), MA, LLB. Retired Solicitor; Honorary President, Scottish Law Agents Society, since 1984; b. 9.3.12, Dunblane; m., Elisabeth Beryl Roebuck; 1 s.; 2 d. Educ. Hurst Grange School, Stirling; Fettes College, Edinburgh; St. Andrews University; Edinburgh University. Qualified as Solicitor, 1935; Partner, Tho. & J.W. Barty, Dunblane, 1937-84; Scottish Law Agents Society: Secretary, 1940-82, President, 1982-84; Honorary Sheriff, since 1970. Clerk, Dunblane Cathedral Kirk Session, 1949-69; Council Member, Friends of Dunblane Cathedral, 1940-84 (Vice-Chairman, 1974-84). Recreations: life-long interest in sport (rugby, tennis, cricket, badminton) and in all arts, including theatre, opera, ballet, literature and painting. Address: (h.) Easterton, Argaty, Doune, Perthshire; T.-01786 841 372.

Bassett, Paul. Director, Mayfest. Address: (b.) Mayfest, 18 Albion Street, Glasgow, G1 1LH.

Basson, John Vincent, MB, ChB, BSc (Hons), MPhil, FRCPsych. Principal Medical Officer, Scottish Home and Health Department; b. 23.11.45, Manchester. Educ. De La Salle College, Salford; Edinburgh University. Fellowship in Community Psychiatry, 1976-78; Consultant Psychiatrist, Royal Edinburgh Hospital and HM Prison, Saughton, 1978-88. Member, Secretary of State's Committee on Difficult Prisoners, 1979-82; Past Chairman, Edinburgh Cyrenian Trust; Member, McClelland Committee on AIDS and Drug Abuse. Recreations: gardening; keep fit; golf; travel. Address: (b.) St. Andrew's House, Edinburgh; T.-0131-244 2805.

Bastable, Arthur Cyprian, OBE, BSc, CEng, FIEE, FIMgt. General Manager, Ferranti plc, Dundee, 1958-86; Director, Ferranti Astron Ltd., 1983-86; Director, Ferranti Industrial Electronics Ltd., 1984-86; Deputy Chairman, Dundee Port Authority, 1981-92 (Member, since 1967, Convener, Corporate Planning Committee, 1975-92); b. 9.5.23, Kobe, Japan; m., Joan Cardwell; 1 s.; 1 d. Educ. St. Georges School, Harpenden; Manchester University. Joined Ferranti, 1950; President, Dundee & Tayside Chamber of Commerce, 1970-71 (Convener, Overseas Trade and Development, 1973-91); Member, Tayside Development Authority, 1972-75; Vice-Chairman, Board of Governors, Dundee College of Technology, 1975-77; Member, Scottish Council, CBI, 1980; Member, Dundee Project Steering Committee, 1983-91; Director: Edinburgh Instruments Ltd., 1983-85; Taytec Ltd., 1985-88; Dundee and Tayside ITEC Ltd., 1985-88; Chairman, Tayside 1992 Committee, 1988-92. Recreations: sailing; skiing; ornithology. Address: (h.) Hunters Moon, 14 Lorne Street, Monifieth, Dundee, DD5 4DU.

Baster, Jeremy, BA, MPhil. Director of Economic Development, Orkney Islands Council, since 1985; b. 5.2.47, New York; m., Miriam Landor; 2 s.; 1 d. Educ. Leighton Park School, Reading; St. John's College, Oxford; University College, London. Early career in consultancy; Economist, Scottish Council (Development and Industry), 1975-80; Economist, Orkney Islands Council, 1980-85. Director, Soulisquoy Printmakers Ltd.; Director, Orkney Enterprise. Address: (b.) Council Offices, School Place, Kirkwall, KW15 1NY; T.-01856 3535.

Bates, Peter James, CertSocAdmin, DipSocWk. Director of Social Work, Tayside Regional Council, since 1987; b. 6.5.45, Birmingham; m., Ann Gordon; 1 s.; 3 d. Educ. Birmingham University. Left school at 15 and completed five year apprenticeship; became active in youth work and community action in Handsworth; attended Birmingham University from the age of 23; moved to Scotland, 1969, as a social worker in Greenock; senior social worker, Edinburgh, later Director of a Community Development Project in the Grassmarket; a Social Work Manager with Lothian Regional Council; Principal Child Care Officer, later Deputy Director of Social Work, Strathclyde Regional Council. Recreations: running; climbing; photography. Address: (b.) Social Work Department, Tayside House, 28 Crichton Street, Dundee, DD1 3RN; T.-Dundee 23281.

Bauckham, Professor Richard John, MA, PhD. Professor of New Testament Studies, St. Andrews University, since 1992; b. 22.9.46, London. Educ. Enfield Grammar School; Clare College, Cambridge. Fellow, St. John's College, Cambridge, 1972-75; Lecturer in Theology, Leeds University, 1976-77; Lecturer in the History of Christian Thought, Manchester University, 1977-87, Reader, 1987-92. Publications: Tudor Apocalypse; Jude, 2 Peter; Moltmann: Messianic Theology in the Making; The Bible in Politics; Jude and the Relatives of Jesus in the Early Church; The Theology of the Book of Revelation; The Climax of Prophecy; The Theology of Jurgen Moltmann. Recreations: walking; novels; poetry; gardening; sleeping. Address: (b.) St. Mary's College, St. Andrews, KY16 9JU; T.-01334 62830.

Baxby, Keith, BSc, MB, BS, FRCS. Consultant Urological Surgeon, Tayside Health Board, since 1977; Honorary Senior Lecturer, Dundee University, since 1977; Clinical Director, Special Surgical Services, Dundee Royal Infirmary, since 1991; b. 17.4.44, Sheffield. Educ. King Edward VII School, Sheffield; Durham University. House Officer, Royal Victoria Infirmary, Newcastle-upon-Tyne, 1968-69; Surgical Registrar, Newcastle University Hospitals, 1969-73; Northern Counties Kidney Fund Research Fellow, 1973-74; Senior Urological Registrar, Newcastle General Hospital, 1974-77; Visiting Professor of Urology, Louisiana State University, 1981; WHO Fellow in Clinical Urodynamics, 1984. Recreation: deer stalking. Address: (b.) Department of Urology, Royal Infirmary, Dundee; T.-01382 660111.

Baxter, Audrey Caroline, BA, DipACC. Managing Director, Baxters of Speyside Ltd.; b. 25.5.61; m., Colin McNiven. Educ. St. Leonard's School; Heriot-Watt University. International banking, Kleinwort Benson Ltd, London, 1983-87; Director, Corporate Planning, Baxters of Speyside, 1988-90. Director, Moray, Badenoch and Strathspey LEC, since 1991; Member, Council, CBI Scotland, since 1990; Director, Quality Scotland Foundation, since 1991. Recreations: fishing; tennis; water sports; reading; all music. Address: (b.) W.A. Baxter and Sons Ltd, Fochabers, Moray.

Baxter, Brian Newland, BSc, MSc, PhD, CEng, FRINA, FIES. Marine Consultant; Visiting Professor, Department of Ship and Marine Technology, Strathclyde University, since 1980; Nautical Assessor (Naval Architect), Home Office, since 1974; Moderator for Engineering Council Examinations, since 1977; b. London; m., Nadina McLeod; 2 d. Educ. King's College, Newcastle, Durham University. Scientific Officer, Royal Naval Scientific Service, 1948-50; Lecturer in Naval Architecture, King's College, Newcastle, 1950-57; Chief Representative, Bureau Veritas in the UK, 1957-62; Director, Yarrow & Co., Glasgow, 1962-79; Deputy Managing Director, Yarrow Shipbuilders, Glasgow, 1967-81; Director, British Shipbuilders Training and Education Co., 1981-84. President, Institution of Engineers and Shipbuilders in Scotland, 1979-81; Hon. Secretary, Seagull Trust, since 1984. Recreations: reading; writing; walking; golf. Address: (h.) Dunelm, Kilmacolm, Renfrewshire, PA13 4DQ; T.-0150 587 2092.

Baxter, Carole Mary, BSc. Co-Presenter, The Beechgrove Garden, BBC Scotland, since 1986 (Head Gardener, The Beechgrove Garden, since 1984); b. 30.6.57, Maidstone. Educ. Maidstone School for Girls; Sussex University. Undergardener, Kildrummy Castle Gardens Trust, Aberdeenshire, 1979-80; Gardener/Caretaker, Aberdeen University Air Squadron, 1980-83; Assistant Gardener, The Beechgrove Garden, Aberdeen, 1983-84. Publication: The Beechgrove Garden (Co-author). Recreations: skiing; walking; swimming; gardening. Address: (b.) BBC, Beechgrove Terrace, Aberdeen, AB9 2ZT; T.-01224 625233.

Baxter, Jim. Footballer; b. 1939, Fife. Glasgow Rangers, 1960-64, later Sunderland and Nottingham Forest. Capped 34 times for Scotland.

Baxter, Mary Ross, MBE, MA, LRAM. Immediate Past President, International PEN Scottish Centre; b. 23.9.27, Glasgow. Educ. Park School, Glasgow; Glasgow University. John Smith & Son, Booksellers, Glasgow, 1952-56; British European Airways, Glasgow Office, 1956-60; National Book League (now known as Book Trust), 1960-89; started the Scottish Office in 1961. Honorary Member, Scottish Library Association. Recreations: music; books; home-decorating; cooking; gardening. Address: (h.) 18 Crown Terrace, Glasgow, G12 9ES; T.-0141-357 0327.

Baxter, (William) Gordon, OBE, DL, LLD, DBA. President, W.A. Baxter & Sons Ltd., since 1994 (Chairman, 1970-94); b. 8.2.18, Fochabers, Moray; m., Ena E. Robertson; 2 s.; 1 d. Educ. Ashville College, Harrogate; Aberdeen University. ICI Explosives Ltd., 1940-45 (Research and Development Manager, various military projects); joined family business, 1946; Managing Director, 1947-71; Member, British Export Council Committee for Exports to USA, 1964-72; Member, North American Advisory Group, DTI, 1979-89; former Director, Grampian Regional Board, Bank of Scotland; Member of Council, Royal Warrant Holders Association, London; former Member, Scottish Conservative Party's Business Group. Recreations: fishing; tennis. Address: (h.) Speybank House, Fochabers, Moray; T.-01343 821234.

Bayliss, Anthony Paul, MB, ChB, FRCR, DMRD. Director of Radiology, Royal Aberdeen Hospitals NHS Trust; b. 7.2.44, Oldham; m., Margaret Anne; 3 s. Educ. Oldham Hulme Grammar School; St. Andrews University. Medical Intern., Mount Sinai Hospital, Minneapolis, 1969-70; House Officer, Ballochmyle Hospital, Ayrshire, 1970-71; Trainee Radiologist, Western Infirmary, Glasgow, 1971-75. Recreation: golf. Address: (h.) School House, Drumoak, Aberdeen; T.-01330 811650.

Baynham, John William, CBE, Doctor honoris causa (Edinburgh), BSc, PhD, DIC. Chairman, Lothian Health Board, since 1990; Chairman, Board of Governors, Moray House Institute of Education, Heriot Watt University, 1991-95; b. 20.1.29, Blantyre; m., Marie B. Friel; 1 d. Educ. Bathgate Academy; Aberdeen University; Imperial College, London. Scottish Agricultural Industries PLC, 1955-87, latterly as Agribusiness Director. Member, Lothian Health Board, 1987-90. Recreations: golf; grandchildren. Address: (h.) 2/18 Succoth Court, Succoth Park, Edinburgh, EH12 6BZ; T.-0131-337 2813.

Bealey, Professor Frank William, BSc (Econ), DSc (Econ). Professor of Politics, Aberdeen University, 1964-90; b. 31.8.22, Bilston, Staffordshire; m., Sheila Hurst; 1 s.; 2 d. Educ. King Edward VI Grammar School, Stourbridge; London School of Economics. Extra-Mural Lecturer, Manchester University, 1951-52; Lecturer, Keele University, 1952-64; Temporary Lecturer, Birmingham University, 1958-59. Treasurer and founder Member, Society for the Study of Labour History, 1960-63; Convener, Committee for Social Science, Aberdeen University, 1970-74 and 1986-89; Fellow, Royal Historical Society, 1971; Editorial Board, Political Studies, 1975-83; Visiting Fellow, Yale University, 1980; Organiser, Parliamentary All-Party Group, Social Science and Policy, 1984-89; Trustee, Jan Hus Educational Foundation, since 1981; Co-ordinator, EC Tempus Project, 1990-93. Publications: Labour and Politics 1900-1906 (Co-author); Constituency Politics (Co-author); The Social and Political Thought of the British Labour Party; The Post Office Engineering Union; The Politics of Independence (Co-author); Democracy in the Contemporary State. Recreations: reading poetry; darts; eating and drinking; watching football and cricket. Address: (h.) 2 Morag House, Oyne, AB52 6QT; T.-Old Rayne 457.

Beastall, Graham Hedley, BSc, PhD, MRCPath. Top Grade Biochemist (Endocrinology), Glasgow Royal Infirmary, since 1981; Honorary Senior Lecturer, Glasgow University, since 1983; b. 11.12.47, Liverpool; m., Judith; 2 s. Educ. Liverpool Institute High School for Boys; Liverpool University. Lecturer in Biochemistry, Liverpool University, 1971-72; Lecturer in Steroid Biochemistry, Glasgow University, 1972-76; Senior Biochemist (Endocrinology), then Principal Biochemist (Endocrinology), Glasgow Royal Infirmary, 1976-81.Chairman, Association of Clinical Biochemists, since 1994; Area Commissioner, Greater Glasgow Scout Council, 1980-88; Chairman, Scottish Programme and Training

Committee, since 1992. Recreations: Scouting; gardening; sport. Address: (b.) Department of Clinical Biochemistry, Royal Infirmary, Glasgow, G4 OSF; T.-0141-304 4632.

Beat, Janet Eveline, BMus, MA. Composer; Lecturer, Royal Scottish Academy of Music and Drama, since 1972; Artistic Director and Founder, Soundstrata (electro-acoustic ensemble); b. 17.12.37, Streetly. Educ. High School for Girls, Sutton Coldfield; Birmingham University. Freelance Orchestral Player, 1960s; Lecturer: Madeley College of Education, 1965-67, Worcester College of Education, 1967-71; founder Member and former Council Member, Scottish Society of Composers; a Director, Scottish Electro-Acoustic Music Association; writes musical criticism for The Scotsman; G.D. Cunningham Award, 1962; her works have been performed throughout Scotland as well as in Switzerland, Poland, North America, South America, Greece, Australia, and Japan. Recreations: travel; reading; photography. Address: (h.) 5 Letham Drive, Glasgow, G43 2SL; T.-041-637 1952.

Beath, Professor John Arnott, MA, MPhil. Professor of Economics, St. Andrews University, since 1991, and Head, School of Economics and Management, since 1992; Production Editor, Review of Economic Studies, since 1987; b. 15.6.44, Thurso; m., Dr. Monika Schroder. Educ. Hillhead High School; St. Andrews, London, Pennsylvania and Cambridge Universities. Research Officer, Department of Applied Economics, Cambridge University; Fellow, Downing College, Cambridge; Lecturer, then Senior Lecturer in Economics, Bristol University. Publication: The Economic Theory of Product Differentiation. Recreations: gardening; walking; music. Address: (h.) Simonden, Ceres, Cupar, KY15 5PP; T.-01334 858920.

Beattie, Alastair, MA, LLB. Chief Executive, Caithness District Council, since 1974; b. 11.10.37, Aberdeen; m., Rosaline; 2 s.; 1 d. Educ. Robert Gordon's College, Aberdeen; Aberdeen University. Legal/Principal Legal Assistant, Dumfries County Council, 1961-67; Caithness County Council: Depute County Clerk, 1967-74, Chief Executive, 1974. Recreations: swimming; gardening; bridge. Address: (b.) Council Offices, Market Square, Wick, Caithness; T.-01955 603761.

Beattie, Alistair Duncan, MD (Hons), FRCPGlas, FRCPLond. Consultant Physician, Southern General Hospital, Glasgow, since 1976; Honorary Clinical Lecturer, Glasgow University, since 1977; Chairman, West of Scotland Committee for Postgraduate Medical Education; b. 4.4.42, Laurencekirk; m., Gillian Margaret McCutcheon; 3 s.; 2 d. Educ. Paisley Grammar School; Glasgow University. Junior hospital appointments, Royal Infirmary and Western Infirmary, Glasgow, 1965-69; Department of Materia Medica, Glasgow University: Research Fellow, 1969-73, Lecturer, 1973-74; MRC Research Fellow, Royal Free Hospital, London, 1974-75. Honorary Treasurer, Medical and Dental Defence Union of Scotland. Recreations: golf; music. Address: (h.) 228 Queen Victoria Drive, Glasgow, G13 1TN; T.-0141-959 7182.

Beattie, Johnny. Comedian and entertainer; b. 1926, Glasgow. Established his career as principal comic in Robert Wilson's touring revue. Has appeared frequently in pantomime and in summer seasons at the Gaiety, Ayr.

Beaty, Robert T., FIEE, BSc (Hons). Director, IBM United Kingdom Ltd. Greenock Site, since 1993; b. 13.10.43, Kilmarnock; m., Anne; 2 s. Educ. Hamilton Academy; Glasgow University. Test engineer, Hoover Ltd., Cambuslang; joined IBM United Kingdom Ltd., as a quality engineer; has held various senior management positions at Greenock plant, as well as several international assignments in the United States and Europe, most recently Director of Operations for High Eng Systems, European HQ, Paris. Member, Board: Renfrewshire Enterprise

Company, Engineering Initiatives Programme in Scotland, Quality Scotland Foundation, Scottish Electronics Technology Group; Vice-Chairman, Scottish Electronics Forum, and Chairman, SEF Strategy Group. Recreations: hill-walking; jogging; cycling; golf; music; car restoration; foreign travel, especially France. Address: (b.) IBM United Kingdom Ltd., P.O. Box 30, Spango Valley, Greenock, PA16 0AH; T.-01475 895810.

Beaumont, Professor Phillip Barrington, BEcon (Hons), MEcon, PhD. Professor, Department of Social and Economic Research, Glasgow University, since 1990 (Senior Lecturer, 1984-86, Reader, 1986-90); b. 13.10.49, Melbourne, Australia; m., Patricia Mary Ann McKinlay; 1 s. Educ. Camberwell High School, Melbourne; Monash University, Melbourne; Glasgow University. Research Fellow, then Lecturer, Glasgow University, 1976-84; Visiting Professor: Massachusetts Institute of Technology, Boston, 1982, McMaster University, 1986, Case Western Reserve University, 1988, Cornell University, 1990. Publications: Bargaining in the Public Sector, 1978; Safety at Work and the Trade Unions, 1981; Job Satisfaction in Public Administration, 1983; The Decline of Trade Union Organization, 1987; Change in Industrial Relations, 1990; Public Sector Industrial Relations, 1991; Human Resource Management, 1993; The Future of Employment Management, 1995. Recreations: tennis; badminton; shooting; fishing. Address: (b.) The University, Glasgow, G12 8QQ; T.-0141-339 8855.

Beaumont, Professor Steven Peter, MA, PhD, CEng, MIEE, MIEEE. Titular Professor of Electronics and Electrical Engineering, Glasgow University, since 1989; b. 20.2.52, Norwich; m., Joanne Mary; 1 s.; 2 d. Educ. Norwich School; Corpus Christi College, Cambridge University. Research Fellow, Glasgow University, 1978-83; Barr and Stroud Lecturer in Electronics, Glasgow University, 1983-86, Senior Lecturer, 1986-89. Recreations: walking; small-holding. Address: (h.) 13 Kelvinside Terrace South, Glasgow, G20 6DW; T.-0141-330 5380.

Bechhofer, Professor Frank, MA. Professor of Social Research, Edinburgh University, since 1987 (Director, Research Centre for Social Sciences, since 1984); b. 10.10.35, Nurnberg, Germany; m., Jean Barbara Conochie; 1 s.; 1 d. Educ. Nottingham High School; Queens' College, Cambridge. Junior Research Officer, Department of Applied Economics, Cambridge University, 1962-65; Edinburgh University: Lecturer in Sociology, 1965-71, Reader in Sociology, 1971-87. Address: (b.) Research Centre for Social Sciences, Old Surgeons' Hall, High School Yards, Edinburgh, EH1 1LZ; T.-0131-650 6385.

Beck, Professor John Swanson, BSc, MD, FRCPGlas, FRCPEdin, FRCPath, FIBiol, FRSE. Emeritus Professor of Pathology, Dundee University, since 1993; Honorary Consultant Pathologist, Tayside Health Board, 1971-93; b. 22.8.28, Glasgow; m., Marion Tudhope Paterson; 1 s.; 1 d. Educ. Glasgow Academy; Glasgow University. House Officer, Western Infirmary and Royal Hospital for Sick Children, Glasgow, 1953-54; Trainee Pathologist, Western Infirmary and Glasgow University, 1954-63; Clinical Research Fellow, National Institute for Medical Research, London, 1960-61; Senior Lecturer in Pathology, Aberdeen University, 1963-71. Chairman, Clinical and Biomedical Research Committee, Chief Scientist Organisation, Scottish Home and Health Department, 1983-93 (Member, Chief Scientist Committee, 1983-93); Chairman, Breast Tumour Panel, Medical Research Council, 1979-89; Member, Tayside Health Board, 1983-91; Member, Medical Advisory Group, LEPRA, since 1988; Member, National Biological Standards Board, 1988-93; Chairman, Scientific Policy Advisory Committee, 1991-93; former Member, Cell Biology and Disorders Board, Medical Research Council; former Assistant Editor, Journal of Pathology. Recreation:

DIY. Address: (h.) 598 Perth Road, Dundee, DD2 1QA; T.-01382 562298.

Beckett, Rev. David Mackay, BA, BD. Minister, Greyfriars Tolbooth and Highland Kirk, Edinburgh, since 1983; Secretary, General Assembly Panel on Doctrine; b. 22.3.37, Glasgow; m., Rosalie Frances Neal; 2 s. Educ. Glenalmond; Trinity Hall, Cambridge; St. Andrews University. Assistant Minister, Dundee Parish Church (St. Mary's), 1963-66; Minister, Clark Memorial Church, Largs, 1966-83. Convener, Committee on Public Worship and Aids to Devotion, General Assembly, 1978-82; President, Church Service Society, 1986-88. Publication: The Lord's Supper, 1984. Address: (h.) 12 Tantallon Place, Edinburgh, EH9 1NZ; T.-0131-667 8671.

Bedborough, William F., MA (Hons), DipEdTech. Rector, Jordanhill School, since 1989 (Rector, Forfar Academy, 1979-89); b. 6.11.42, Glasgow; m., Sheena J. McLullich; 1 s.; 1 d. Educ. Hutchesons' Boys' Grammar School, Glasgow; Glasgow University. Assistant Teacher (History), Hutchesons' Boys Grammar School, 1965-68; Special Assistant Teacher (History), Hamilton Academy, 1968-69; Principal Teacher (History), Bellshill Academy, 1969-72; Assistant Rector, Arbroath Academy, 1972-75; Depute Rector, Galashiels Academy, 1975-79. Recreations: sailing; golf; hill-walking; travel; music. Address: (b.) Jordanhill School, Chamberlain Road, Glasgow; T.-0141-959 1897.

Beddie, Professor Lesley Anne, BSc, CEng, MBCS. Head, Department of Computer Studies, Napier University, since 1992; b. 3.11.53, London; m., Douglas Beddie; 2 d. Educ. Preston Manor Grammar School, Middlesex; Edinburgh University. Engineering programmer, Ferranti Ltd., 1975-77; senior programmer, Lothian Regional Council, 1977-79; Napier College/Polytechnic/University, since 1979. Publications: An Introduction to Computer Integrated Business (Co-author); An Introduction to Information and Knowledge Based Systems (Co-editor). Recreations: amateur drama; tap dancing; theatre. Address: (h.) 83 Balgreen Road, Edinburgh, EH12 5UA; T.-0131-346 2200.

Bedford, Geoff. Director, HMSO Scotland, since 1988. Address: (b.) South Gyle Crescent, Edinburgh, EH12 9EB; T.-0131-479 9000.

Bedi, Tarlochan Singh, JP, MB, BS, FRCPsych, DPM. Consultant Psychiatrist and Honorary Clinical Senior Lecturer, Southern General Hospital, Glasgow, since 1980; b. India; m., Dr. T.H. Ratani; 1 s. Educ. Poona University, India. Junior House Officer, Aga Khan Hospital, Nairobi; Senior House Officer, Glenside and Barrow Hospital, Bristol; Registrar, Coneyhill Hospital, Gloucester; Senior Registrar, Gartnavel and Southern General Hospital, Glasgow; Consultant Psychiatrist, Woodilee Hospital, Lenzie. Past President: Scottish Asian Action Committee, Glasgow; Indian Social and Cultural Association, Glasgow; Indian Graduates Society, Glasgow. Recreations: music; photography; culinary arts. Address: 156 Prestonfield, Milngavie, G62 7QA; T.-0141-445 2466.

Beevers, Professor Clifford, BSc, PhD. Professor of Mathematics, Heriot Watt University, since 1993; b. 4.9.44, Castleford; m., Elizabeth Ann; 2 d. Educ. Castleford Grammar School; Manchester University. Senior Lecturer, 1985; Director, CALM, 1985. Chairman, Edinburgh Branch, British Retinitis Pigmentosa Society. Recreations: walking; jogging; music; theatre. Address: (b.) Department of Mathematics, Heriot Watt University, Riccarton, Edinburgh, EH14 4AS; T.-0131-451 3233.

Begg, David, BA (Hons). Chair of Transport, Lothian Regional Council (Councillor, since 1986); Lecturer in Economics, Napier Polytechnic, since 1991; Secretary, Scottish Transport Studies Group; b. 12.6.56, Edinburgh. Educ. Portobello High School; Heriot-Watt University.

Economic Researcher, PIEDA, 1979; management employee, BR, 1979-81. Publications: articles on transport economics and local government finance. Recreations: golf; watching Hibernian F.C. Address: (b.) Parliament Square, Edinburgh; T.-0131-469 3347.

Begg, Professor Hugh MacKemmie, MA, PhD, DipTP, FRTPI, FRSA. Consultant Economist and Chartered Planner; Head, School of Town and Regional Planning, Dundee University; b. 25.10.41, Glasgow; m., Jane Elizabeth Harrison; 2 d. Educ. High School of Glasgow; St. Andrews University; University of British Columbia. Lecturer in Political Economy, St. Andrews University; Research Fellow, Tayside Study; Lecturer in Economics, Dundee University; Assistant Director of Planning, Tayside Regional Council; Visiting Professor, Technical University of Nova Scotia; Consultant, UN Regional Development Project, Egypt and Saudi Arabia; Consultant, Scottish Office Industry Department, Scottish Office Agriculture and Forestry Department; part-time Reporter, Scottish Office Inquiry Reporters Unit. Recreations: local history; reading; rugby. Address: (h.) 4 Esplanade, Broughty Ferry, Dundee; T.-01382 79642.

Begg, Ian McKerron, DA, FRIAS, FSA Scot. Architect (own practice), since 1983; Vice President, Architectural Heritage Society of Scotland; Member, Council, Saltire Society; b. 23.6.25, Kirkcaldy; 3 d. Educ. Kirkcaldy High School; Edinburgh College of Art. Partner, Robert Hurd & Partners, 1951-83; Interim Director, Edinburgh New Town Conservation Committee; Architectural Advisor, National Trust for Scotland; Interim Director, Edinburgh Old Town Committee for Conservation and Renewal. Recreations: travel, particularly to Paris; supporting Scotland's identity. Address: Ravens'Craig, Plockton, Ross-shire, IV52 8UB; T.-01599 544 265.

Begg, Norman Roderick Darroch, MA, LLB. Secretary, Aberdeen University; b. 23.12.41, London; m., Fiona Schofield; 3 d. Educ. Aberdeen Grammar School; Aberdeen University. Administrative Assistant, East Anglia University, 1964-66; Aberdeen University, since 1966: Administrative Assistant; Assistant Secretary; Registry Officer; Clerk to Senatus; Deputy Secretary. Member, Children's Panel, Grampian Region, 1984-87; Past Chairman, Aberdeen Studio Theatre Group; Director, Edinburgh Festival Fringe Society, 1980-83; Hon. Vice-President, Aberdeen Opera Company, since 1988. Recreation: amateur drama. Address: (b.)Aberdeen University, Regent Walk, Aberdeen AB9 1FX.

Begg, Robert William, CBE (1977), MA, CA, FRSA, DUniv (Glas). Member, Museums and Galleries Commission, 1988-91; b. 19.2.22; m., Sheena Margaret Boyd; 2 s. Educ. Greenock Academy; Glasgow University. Royal Navy, 1942-46 (Lt., RNVR) (Despatches). Consultant, Moores Rowland, since 1987 (Partner, Mann Judd Gordon, Glasgow, 1951-86). Honorary Treasurer, Royal Philosophical Society of Glasgow, 1952-62; Honorary Treasurer, Royal Glasgow Institute of Fine Arts, 1975-87, President, 1987-90; Member, Board of Governors, Glasgow School of Art, 1955-77 (Chairman, 1970-76); Trustee, National Galleries of Scotland, 1974-91 (Chairman, 1980-87); Council Member, National Trust for Scotland, 1984-90 (Executive, 1985-90); Member of Court, Glasgow University, 1986-90. Address: (h.) 3 Colquhoun Drive, Bearsden, Glasgow, G61 4NQ; T.-0141-942 2436.

Behan, Professor Peter Oliver, MD, ChB, FRCP(Lond), FRCP(I), FRCP(Glas), FACP. Consultant Neurologist, Greater Glasgow Health Board, since 1976; Professor of Neurology, Glasgow University; b. 8.7.35, Co. Kildare; m., Dr. Wilhelmina Behan; 2 s.; 1 d. Educ. Sir John Cass College, London; Leeds University Medical School. Demonstrator in Pathology, Cambridge University, 1965-66; Research Fellow in Psychiatry, Harvard University, 1966-67; Special Research Fellow, Oxford University, 1968-70; Lecturer in Neurology, then Senior Lecturer, then Reader, Glasgow University, from 1971. Patron, Motor Neurone Disease Association of Scotland; awarded Pattison Medal for contributions to neurology; International Dutch prize for study of fatigue states, 1995; Chief Editor, Journal of Neuroimmunology; papers and books on neurology; book on salmon and women (Co-author). Recreations: salmon fishing; Samuel Johnson. Address: (h.) 17 South Erskine Park, Bearsden, Glasgow; T.-0141-942 5713.

Belch, Sir Ross, CBE (1972), LLD Strathclyde (1978), BSc, FRSE, FRINA, CBIM, CEng. Company Director; b. 13.12.20, London; m., 1, Janette Finnie Murdoch (deceased); 4 d.; 2, Dorothy West. Educ. Morrison's Academy, Crieff; Glasgow University. Lithgows Ltd.: Director and General Manager, 1954, Managing Director, 1964; Managing Director, Scott Lithgow Group, 1969-80; Member, Board, British Shipbuilders, 1977-79; President, Shipbuilders and Repairers National Association, 1974-76; Chairman: Irvine Development Corporation, 1985-90, Murray Hotels (Crieff) Ltd., Kelvin Travel Ltd., Altnacraig Shipping plc, Altnamara Shipping plc, Ferguson Marine PLC; a Director, Jebsen Carriers Ltd., Ferguson Shipbuilders Ltd.; Chairman, Trustees, Scottish Maritime Museum. Address: (h.) Altnacraig House, Lyle Road, Greenock, PA16 7XT; T.-01475 721124.

Belfall, David J., BA (Hons). Under Secretary, Health Policy and Public Health Directorate, Scottish Office, since 1991; b. 26.4.47, Colchester; m., Lorna McLaughlan; 1 s.; 1 d. Educ. Colchester Royal Grammar School; St. John's College, Cambridge. Home Office, 1969-88 (Private Secretary to Permanent Under Secretary of State, 1973-74, Secretary to Lord Justice Scarman's Red Lion Square Inquiry, 1974-75); Scottish Office, since 1988. Recreations: squash; badminton. Address: (b.) St. Andrews House, Edinburgh, EH1 3DE.

Bell, Alexander Scott, FFA, FPMI. Group Managing Director, Standard Life Assurance Company, since 1988; b. 4.12.41, Falkirk; m., Veronica Jane Simpson; 2 s.; 1 d. Educ. Daniel Stewart's College, Edinburgh. Joined Standard Life, 1958; General Manager (Finance), 1985-88. Director: Bank of Scotland, Hammerson plc, Scottish Financial Enterprise. Recreations: golf; travel. Address: (b.) 3 George Street, Edinburgh, EH2 2XZ; T.-0131-245 6011.

Bell, Sheriff Andrew Montgomery, BL. Sheriff of Lothian and Borders, at Edinburgh, since 1990 (Sheriff of Glasgow and Strathkelvin, at Glasgow, 1984-90); b. 21.2.40, Edinburgh; m., Ann Margaret Robinson; 1 s.; 1 d. Educ. Royal High School, Edinburgh; Edinburgh University. Solicitor, 1961-74; called to Bar, 1975; Sheriff of South Strathclyde, Dumfries and Galloway, at Hamilton, 1979-84. Address: (h.) 5 York Road, Edinburgh, EH5 3EJ; T.-0131-552 3859.

Bell, Sheriff Archibald Angus, QC. Sheriff of Glasgow and Strathkelvin at Glasgow, since 1973; b. 13.4.23. Address: (b.) Sheriff Court House, 1 Carlton Place, Glasgow, G5 9DA.

Bell, Colin John, MA (Hons), HonLLD (Aberdeen). Broadcaster; Journalist; Author; Rector, Aberdeen University, 1991-93; b. 1.4.38, London; m., Caroline Rose Bell; 1 s.; 3 d. Educ. St. Paul's School; King's College, Cambridge. Journalist, The Scotsman, 1960-62 and 1975-78; Journalist/Contributor, London Life, Sunday Times, Sunday Telegraph, Daily Mirror, Sunday Mail, etc.; Lecturer, Morley College, 1965-68; College Supervisor, King's College, Cambridge, 1968-75; Parliamentary candidate (SNP), West Edinburgh, 1979; European Parliamentary candidate (SNP), North East Scotland, 1979; Vice-Chairman, SNP, 1978-84; Campaign Director, Euro Election, 1984; a Senior Fellow, the 21st Century Trust,

1990. Publications: City Fathers, 1969; Boswell's Johnson, 1971; Scotch Whisky, 1985; Radical Alternative (Contributor), 1978; The Times Reports (Series) (Editor). Recreations: jazz; Scottish history. Address: (h.) Cockburnhill, Balerno, Midlothian.

Bell, Professor Colin Roy, BA, MScEcon, FRSE. Professor of Sociology, Edinburgh University, since 1988; Vice Principal, since 1993; b. 1.3.42, Enfield; m., Dr. Janette Webb; 1 s.; 3 d. Educ. The Judd School, Tonbridge; Keele University; University of Wales. University teaching posts at Essex; Professor of Sociology, Universities of New South Wales and Aston; research posts, Universities of Leicester and Edinburgh. Publications: Middle Class Families; Community Studies; Doing Sociological Research; Property, Paternalism and Power; numerous other academic papers and books. Recreations: jazz and blues; Munros; Penguins; gardening. Address: (b.) Sociology Department, Edinburgh University, 18 Buccleuch Place, Edinburgh, EH8; T.-0131-667 1011.

Bell, Professor David Nevin Fraser, MA, MSc, PhD. Professor of Economics, Stirling University, since 1990; b. 16.12.51, Inverness; 1 s.; 1 d. Educ. Dornoch Academy; Aberdeen University; London School of Economics; Strathclyde University. Lecturer, St. Andrews University, 1974-75; Research Fellow, Fraser of Allander Institute, Strathclyde University, 1975-83, Macroeconomic Modelling Bureau, Warwick University, 1983-85; Lecturer, Glasgow University, 1985-90. Economic Consultant to Secretary of State for Scotland. Recreations: golf; hill walking; photography; more golf. Address: (b.) Department of Economics, Stirling University, Stirling, FK9 4LA; T.-01786 467486.

Bell, Donald Atkinson, BSc, PhD, FIMechE, CEng, MIEE, FBCS. Director, Marchland Consulting Ltd., since 1990 (Director, National Engineering Laboratory, 1983-90); b. 28.5.41, Belfast; m., Joyce Louisa Godber; 2 s. Educ. Royal Belfast Academical Institution; Queen's University, Belfast; Southampton University. National Physical Laboratory, Teddington, 1966-77; Electronics Applications Division, Department of Industry, 1978-82. Address: (b.) Marchland Consulting Ltd., 108 East Kilbride Road, Glasgow G76 8JF; T.-0141-644 2000.

Bell, George Armour, OBE, JP, BSc, MB, ChB. Chairman, Monklands and Bellshill Hospitals NHS Trust; Vice President, Tenovus-Scotland; b. 8.7.20, Bellshill; m., Elizabeth Davidson Porteous; 2 s. Educ. Bellshill Academy; Glasgow University. War Service, 609 Squadron — Normandy to Germany, SMO Prestwick, SMO Brize Norton, RAF. Retired General Practitioner, Bellshill; former Member, Lanarkshire Health Board; founder Chairman, Crime Prevention Panel, Bellshill and District; former Red Cross Detachment Medical Officer, Bellshill; founder Chairman, Community Council for Mossend; Honorary Medical Officer, Bellshill Bn., Boys Brigade; President, Bellshill Branch, Arthritis Care; Honorary Member, Rotary; Life Member, BMA; Life Member, RAF Association. Address: (h.) Chudleigh, 449 Main Street, Bellshill, Lanarkshire, ML4 1AX; T.-01698 749084.

Bell, G. Susan, ACIS, FSA (Scot). Founder Director, Scotland Direct (Holdings) Limited; Gourmet Scotland Limited; Bell Lawrie of Biggar (Developments) Ltd.; Wood Potters of Burolem Ltd.; Board Member: SCOTVEC, 1987-95, Southern General Hospital Trust, 1993-95; b. 31.8.46; m., Arthur J.A. Bell; 2 s.; 2 d. Educ. College of Commerce, Glasgow. Investment Analyst, Edinburgh, 1970-74; Conservative Parliamentary candidate: Motherwell, 1970, Caithness & Sutherland, February 1974; Chairman, Conservative Candidates Association, 1971-74; Member, Council, CBI Scotland, 1986-93; Board Member, Scottish Tourist Board, 1983-88; Member, Council, National Trust for Scotland, 1983-88; Council Member, Scottish

Landowners Federation; Chair, Women into Business. Recreations: garden; riding; reading. Address: (h.) Culter House, Coulter, Biggar; T.-01899 20064.

Bell, Rev. John L., MA, BD. Convener, Panel on Worship, Church of Scotland. Ordained, 1978. Joined Iona Community, 1988.

Bell, Robin, MA, MSc. Poet and Broadcaster; b. 4.1.45, Dundee; 2 d. Educ. Morrison's Academy, Crieff; St. Andrews University; Perugia University, Italy; Union College, New York; Columbia University, New York. Formerly: Director of Information, City University of New York, Regional Opportunity Program; Assistant Professor, John Jay College of Criminal Justice, City University of New York; Member, US Office of Education Task Force in Educational Technology; Audio-Visual Editor, Oxford University Press; Editor, Guidebook series to Ancient Monuments of Scotland; Secretary, Poetry Association of Scotland. Scottish Radio and Television Industries Award for Best Radio Feature, 1984; Sony Award, Best British Radio Documentary, 1985. Publications: The Invisible Mirror; Culdee, Culdee; Sawing Logs; Strathinver: A Portrait Album 1945-53; Collected Poems of James Graham, Marquis of Montrose (Editor); Radio Poems; The Best of Scottish Poetry; An Anthology of Living Scottish Poets (Editor); Bittersweet Within My Heart: collected poems of Mary Queen of Scots (Translator/Editor). Address: (h.) The Orchard, Muirton, Auchterarder, PH3 1ND.

Bell, Thomas Grant Law, LDS, RFPS(Glas). Regional Dental Officer, Scottish Home and Health Department, 1979-88; b. 17.2.26, Motherwell; m., Edith Barnett Porter; 1 s.; 1 d. Educ. Bellshill Academy; Anderson College of Medicine; Glasgow Dental Hospital and School. Captain, Royal Army Dental Corps, 1949-51; Assistant in general practice, 1951-54; Senior Dental Officer, Burgh of Motherwell and Wishaw, 1955-65; Principal in general practice, 1965-79; former Secretary and Treasurer and Past Chairman, Lanarkshire Section, BDA; Past Chairman, Local Dental Committee, Lanarkshire, and Lanarkshire Steering Committee, NHS Reorganisation; Lanarkshire Health Board: former Dental Secretary, Area Dental Committee, and former Member, GP Sub-Committee and Dental Service Committee; former Honorary Visiting Dental Surgeon, Edinburgh Dental Hospital. Recreations: fishing; shooting; photography; philately. Address: (h.) Cabrach, 10 Laburnum Crescent, Wishaw, ML2 7EH; T.-01698 384930.

Bellany, John, CBE, RA; b. June, 1942, Port Seton; m., 1, Helen Margaret Percy; 2, Juliet Gray Lister (deceased); 3, for second time, Helen Margaret Bellany; 2 s.; 1 d. Educ. Cockenzie Public School; Preston Lodge, Prestonpans; Edinburgh College of Art; Royal College of Art, London. Lecturer in Fine Art, Winchester School of Art, 1969-73; Head, Faculty of Painting, Croydon College of Art, 1973-78; Visiting Lcturer in Painting, R.C.A., 1975-85; Lecturer in Fine Art, Goldsmiths College, London University, 1978-84; elected Fellow Commoner, Trinity Hall, Cambridge, 1988; one-man exhibitions include: Arts Council touring show; Rosa Esman Gallery, New York; Christine Abrahams Gallery, Melbourne; Ikon Gallery, Birmingham; Walker Art Gallery, Liverpool; Roslyn Oxley Gallery, Sydney; National Portrait Gallery, London; Galerie Krikhar, Amsterdam; Fischer Fine Art, London; retrospective — Scottish National Gallery of Modern Art; Serpentine Gallery, London; Kimsthalle, Hamburg; Museum Ostral, Dortmund; Ruth Siegel Gallery, New York; Raab Gallery, Berlin; Fitzwilliam Museum, Cambridge; Kelvingrove Museum and Art Gallery (50th birthday tribute); Beaux Arts Gallery, Berkeley Square Gallery, London; elected Hon. RSA, 1987; joint 1st prize, Athena International Award, 1985. Recreation: motoring around Europe in search of beauty.

Bell-Scott, Euan Toddy Morison, LLB, NP, WS. Partner, Russel & Aitken, Falkirk, since 1981; Member, Forth Valley Health Board; b. 12.2.54, Edinburgh; m., Elizabeth Anne Hartley; 1 s.; 1 d. Educ. Edinburgh Academy; Aberdeen University. Recreations: family; road and cross-country running; tennis; golf; watching rugby internationals. Address: (h.) The Tower, 37 High Street, Dollar FK14 7AZ.

Beloff, Halla, BSc, PhD, MUniv, FBPS. Senior Lecturer, Department of Psychology, Edinburgh University, since 1963; b. 11.5.30; m., John Beloff; 1 s.; 1 d. Educ. South Hampstead High School; London University; Illinois University; Queen's University, Belfast. Former Editor, British Journal of Social and Clinical Psychology; former Member, Psychology Committee, Social Science Research Council; President, British Psychological Society, 1983-84. Occasional broadcaster, BBC Radio Scotland. Publications: Psychology Survey 5 (Co-Editor), 1984; Camera Culture, 1985, Getting into Life, 1986; Psychology Survey 6, 1987. Recreations: following the arts and not being shocked by the new; needlework. Address: (h.) 6 Blacket Place, Edinburgh, EH9 1RL; T.-0131-667 3200.

Belton, Neville Richard, BSc, PhD, CChem, MRSC. Senior Lecturer, Department of Child Life and Health, Edinburgh University, since 1975; Honorary Biochemist, Lothian Health Board; b. 5.10.37, Nottingham; m., Elisabeth Foster Inglis; 1 s.; 1 d. Educ. Nottingham High School; Birmingham University. Research Associate, Children's Memorial Hospital, Chicago, 1963-67; Lecturer in Pharmacology and Associate in Paediatrics, Northwestern University, Chicago, 1964-67; Lecturer, Department of Child Life and Health, Edinburgh University, 1967-75. Member: DHSS Working Party on the Composition of Infant Foods, 1974-80; Convenor, British Paediatric Nutrition, Metabolism and Pharmacology Group, 1978-81; Elder, Cramond Kirk; Assistant Secretary, Edinburgh Rotary Club, since 1995; President, Dean Lawn Tennis and Squash Club, since 1993. Publication: Textbook of Paediatric Nutrition (Joint Editor), 1991. Recreations: travel; sport (tennis, watching rugby); music. Address: (h.) 6 St. Bernards Crescent, Edinburgh, EH4 1NP; T.-0131-332 0392.

Beltrami, Joseph, BL, NP. Solicitor/Advocate (Beltrami & Co.); b. 15.5.32, Rutherglen; m., Brigid D.; 3 s. Educ. St. Aloysius College, Glasgow; Glasgow University. Intelligence Corps, 1954-56 (Sgt.); qualified as Solicitor, 1956; specialised in criminal law; has instructed in more than 500 murder cases; closely associated with two cases of Royal Pardon; in first batch of Solicitor/Advocates to have rights of audience in High Court and Court of Criminal Appeal. Chairman, soccer testimonials: Jim Johnstone and Bobby Lennox, 1976; Danny McGrain, 1980. Publications: The Defender, 1980; Glasgow - A Celebration (Contributor), 1984; Tales of the Suspected, 1988; A Deadly Innocence, 1989. Recreations: bowls; soccer; snooker; writing; boxing. Address: (h.) 5 St. Andrew's Avenue, Bothwell, Lanarkshire; T.-Bothwell 852374.

Benedetti, Giovanni. Chairman, Benedetti Holdings; Chairman, Pendigo Ltd.; Chairman, Wallace Cameron & Co. Ltd.; Chairman, JGT Marketing Services Ltd.; Chairman, GB Consulting and Management Services Ltd.; Director, Prince's Scottish Youth Business Trust; Director, ASSET; b. 6.3.43, Italy; m., Francesca; 2 d. Arrived in Britain aged 11; worked in uncle's cafe until age of 19; started his own business with two dry-cleaning shops; opened his first factory in Ardrossan, 1970; company bought by BET, 1989. Recreations: skiing; sailing.

Benington, (Charles) Kenneth, BSc, PhD, CEng, FIMechE. Industrial Adviser to Secretary of State for Scotland, since 1988; b. 1.4.31, Belfast; m., Margaret Malcolm; 1 s.; 1 d. Educ. Dalriada Grammar School, Ballymoney; Queen's University, Belfast; Heriot-Watt University. Graduate apprentice and design engineer, Associated Electrical Industries Ltd., 1953-60; Assistant Chief Engineer, Trials, British Ship Research Association, 1960-63; Lecturer, Heriot-Watt University, 1963-72; Senior Engineer, Marine Industries Centre, Newcastle University, 1972-74; Brown Brothers & Co. Ltd.: Systems Manager, 1974-75; Technical Manager, 1975-77; Technical Director, 1977-80; Assistant Managing Director and Technical Director, 1980-81; Managing Director, 1981-86; Technical Director, Vickers Marine Engineering Division, 1986-88;Member, Executive Committee, Scottish Employers' Association, 1984-86; Member, Board of Unilink, Heriot Watt University, 1987-90. Address: (b.) Scottish Office Industry Department, Meridian Court, 5 Cadogan Street, Glasgow, G2 6AT.

Bennet, Graham Alexander, QPM. Deputy Chief Constable, Fife, since 1991; b. 21.3.43, Insch; m., Alison; 2 s. Educ. Aberlour High School. Joined Fife Constabulary, 1963; Assistant Chief Constable, 1987. President, Phoenix Club for Disabled; President, Rosyth and District Scouts; Area Chairman, Fife Scouting. Recreations: gardening; keeping fish; football; exercising dog. Address: (h.) 8 Reid Avenue, Crossgates, Fife; T.-01383 510153.

Bennett, Bruce, MB, ChB (Hons), MD (Hons), FRCP, FRCPath, FRCPEd. Reader in Medicine, Aberdeen University; b. 5.7.38, Gorakphur, India; m., Dr. G. Adey Bennett. Educ. Brechin High School; Aberdeen University. Aberdeen University: Ashley Mackintosh Research Fellow, 1964; MRC Junior Research Fellow, 1965; Lecturer in Medicine, 1967; Eli Lilly Travelling Research Fellow, then Visiting Research Fellow, Case Western Reserve University, Cleveland, Ohio, 1970-72; Wellcome Senior Research Fellow, Aberdeen University, 1973; appointed Senior Lecturer, 1978. Address: (b.) Department of Medicine and Therapeutics, Polwarth Building, Foresterhill, Aberdeen; T.-01224 681818, Ext. 53025.

Bennett, David Andrew, MA, LLB, WS, NP. Partner, Bennett & Robertson, Solicitors, Edinburgh and Glasgow, since 1964; b. 27.3.38, Edinburgh; m., Marion Millar Park; 2 d. Educ. Melville College, Edinburgh; Fettes College, Edinburgh; Edinburgh University. Director, Jordan Group Ltd.; Member, Council, Law Society of Scotland, 1984-90. Session Clerk, Liberton Kirk, since 1975; Honorary Secretary, Scottish Hockey Association, 1973-82; Scottish Editor, Palmer's Company Law, since 1970, and Gore-Browne on Companies, since 1975. Recreations: most sports and arts. Address: (b.) 16 Walker Street, Edinburgh, EH3 7NN; T.-0131-225 4001.

Bennett, Helen Margaret, PhD, AMA, FSA Scot. Crafts Director, Scottish Arts Council, since 1993; Governor, Edinburgh College of Art, since 1992; b. 25.6.48, Newark; m., Philip Edwin Bennett; 1 d. Educ. Lilley and Stone High School for Girls, Newark; Exeter University; Edinburgh University. Assistant Curator, Borough of Weston-super-Mare, 1969-71; Curator of Agricultural and Social History, Bristol City Museums, 1971-72; Research Assistant, Costume and Textiles, National Museum of Antiquities of Scotland, 1974-81; freelance arts administrator, 1984-88; Head of Crafts Division, Scottish Development Agency, 1989-91; freelance cultural consultant, 1991-93. Recreations: walking; gardening; textile crafts. Address: (b.) 12 Manor Place, Edinburgh, EH3 7DD; T.-0131-226 6051.

Bennett, Ronald Alistair, CBE (1986), QC (Scot), MA, LLB. Vice-President for Scotland, Value Added Tax Tribunals, since 1977; b. 11.12.22; m., Margret Magnusson; 3 s.; 2 d.; 1 d. (dec.). Educ. Edinburgh Academy; Edinburgh University; Balliol College, Oxford. Lt., 79th (Scottish Horse) Medium Regiment, RA, 1943-45; Captain, attached RAOC, India and Japan, 1945-46; called to Scottish Bar, 1947; Standing Counsel to Ministry of Labour and National Service, 1957-59; Sheriff-Principal: Roxburgh, Berwick and Selkirk, 1971-74, South Strathclyde, Dumfries and Galloway, 1981-82, North Strathclyde, 1982-83, Highlands and Islands, 1990-91; Chairman, Medical Appeal Tribunals (Scotland), 1971-94; Chairman, Agricultural Wages Board for Scotland, since 1973; Chairman, Local Government Boundary Commission for Scotland, 1974-89; Chairman, Industrial Tribunals (Scotland), 1977-94; Chairman, Pension Appeal Tribunals (Scotland) since 1984. Address: (h.) Laxamyri, 46 Cammo Road, Barnton, Edinburgh, EH4 8AP.

Bennie, Robert William, BSc, IPFA. Director of Finance, Western Isles Islands Council, since 1992; b. 19.8.56, Edinburgh. Educ. Melville College, Edinburgh; Linlithgow Academy; Heriot-Watt University. Trainee Accountant/Accounting Assistant, Falkirk District Council; Chief Technical Assistant, Aberconwy B.C.; Principal Accountant, Vale of White Horse D.C.; District Finance Officer, Hinckley and Bosworth B.C.; Deputy Treasurer, South Northamptonshire D.C. Recreations: mountaineering; rugby; running; music; reading. Address: (b.) Stornoway, Isle of Lewis, PA87 2BW; T.-01851 703773, Ext. 230.

Benson, Professor Gordon Mitchell, AADip, SADG, FRIAS, ARIBA. Architect; b. 5.10.44, Glasgow; 1 s. 1 d. Educ. Glasgow High School; Glasgow University and Architectural Association. Partner in private practice, since 1978; recent prize work includes Cowgatehead Library, Edinburgh, 1995, New Museum of Scotland (international competition), 1991; Chair of Architecture, Strathclyde University, 1986-90; Visiting Professor, Edinburgh University, since 1991.

Berridge, David. Chief Executive, Scottish Equitable. Address: (b.) 28 St. Andrew Square, Edinburgh, EH2 1YF.

Berry, Professor David Richard, MA, MSc, PhD, DSc, CBiol, FIBiol, FIFST. Professor, Department of Bioscience and Biotechnology, Strathclyde University; b. 1.3.41, Huddersfield; m., Elisabeth Ann; 1 s.; 1 d. Educ. Holme Valley Grammar School; St. Peter's College, Oxford. Scientific Officer, Glaxo Ltd., Ulverston, 1962-64; graduate student, 1964-70; Lecturer, then Senior Lecturer, then Reader, Strathclyde University; Former Member, Scottish Examination Board Biology Panel; Chairman, Further and Higher Education Committee, Institute of Biology. Address: (b.) Department of Bioscience and Biotechnology, Strathclyde University, George Street, Glasgow; T.-0141-552 4400.

Berry, Graham, CA. Director of Finance and Administration, Scottish Arts Council, since 1989; b. 12.1.45, Edinburgh; 1 s.; 1 d. Educ. Royal High School, Edinburgh; CA Apprentice, Edinburgh, 1963-68; CA, Price Waterhouse, London, 1968-70; Divisional Chief Accountant, Trust House Forte, London, 1970-74; Company Secretary, 1974-86: Scottish Film Council, Scottish Council for Educational Technology, Glasgow Film Theatre, Filmhouse Ltd., Scetlander Ltd.; Finance Officer, Stirling University, 1986-89. Recreations: mountaineering; photography. Address: (b.) Scottish Arts Council, 12 Manor Place, Edinburgh, EH3 7DD; T.-0131-226 6051.

Berry, John, CBE (1968), DL (Fife) (1969), BA (Cantab), MA (Cantab), PhD (St. Andrews) Hon. LLD Dundee (1970), HonDSc St. Andrews (1991), FRSE (1936). Adviser and Consultant on environmental and wildlife conservation (retired); b. 5.8.07, Edinburgh; m., Hon. Bride Fremantle; 2 s.; 1 d. Educ. Ardvreck School, Crieff; Eton College; Trinity College, Cambridge. Salmon Research Officer, Fishery Board for Scotland, 1930-31; Biological Research Station, University College, Southampton; Research Officer, 1932-36; Director, 1936-39; Chief Press Censor for Scotland, 1940-44; Biologist and Information Officer, North of Scotland Hydro-Electric Board, 1944-49; Environment Conservation Adviser, 1944-89 (to South of Scotland Electricity Board, 1969-89, to Scottish Landowners Federation, 1984-87); Director of Nature Conservation in Scotland, 1949-67; consultancy work 1968-90. Honorary Life Member, Swiss League for Protection of Nature, 1946; founder Member (1948), International Union for Conservation of Natural Resources and first President, International Union Commission on Ecology; Member, Executive Board, International Waterfowl Research Bureau, 1963-72; Honorary Corresponding Member, Danish Natural History Society, since 1957; Vice-President and Honorary Life Fellow, Royal Zoological Society of Scotland, since 1959; Honorary Life Fellow: Wildfowl Trust, 1983; Glasgow Natural History Society, 1951; Member, Dundee University Court, 1970-78; Director, British Pavilion, Expo 71, Budapest; Member, Scottish Marine Biological Association, 1947-71 (Council, 1947-54 and 1957-66). Recreations: natural history (especially insects, water birds and fish); music. Address: (h.) The Garden House, Tayfield, Newport-on-Tay, Fife, DD6 8HA; T.-01382 543118.

Berry, William, MA, LLB, WS, NP. Senior Partner, Murray Beith & Murray, WS, Edinburgh; Chairman, Scottish Life Assurance Co.; Director: Scottish American Investment Co. Plc, Fleming Continental European Trust Plc, Alliance Trust plc, Dawnfresh Seafoods Ltd., Inchcape Family Investments Ltd., and other companies; b. 26.9.39, Newport-on-Tay; m., Elizabeth Margery Warner; 2 s. Educ. Ardvreck, Crieff; Eton College; St. Andrews University; Edinburgh University. Interests in farming, forestry, etc. Depute Chairman, Edinburgh Festival Society, 1985-89; Member Council/Board: New Town Concerts Society Ltd., Thistle Foundation. Performer in three records of Scottish country dance music. Recreations: music; shooting; forestry. Address: (b.) 39 Castle Street, Edinburgh, EH2 3BH; T.-0131-225 1200.

Bethel, Archibald A, BSc, MBA, CEng, MIMechE. Chief Executive, Lanarkshire Development Agency, since 1991; b. 9.2.53, Uddingston; m., Doreen; 1 s.; 1 d. Educ. Hamilton Academy; Strathclyde University. Vetco Gray Inc.; Managing Director, Engineering Division, Morrison Construction Group. Recreations: golf; computers; football. Address: (b.)New Lanarkshire House, Strathclyde Business Park, Bellshill, ML4 3AD; T.-01698 745454.

Bethell, John, BSc (Hons). Chief Executive, Scottish Seed Potato Development Council, since 1982; b. 30.4.39, Nuneaton; m., Gillian; 1 s.; 3 d. Educ. Hutchesons' Boys' Grammar School; Glasgow University. Geologist, Government of Sierra Leone; District Manager, Texaco Africa Ltd., Sierra Leone; Managing Director, Argus of Ayr Ltd.; Chairman, Argoventure Ltd.; Chairman, River Tyne Trust; Company Secretary, VT Growers Ltd., 1984-94; Company Secretary, SE Growers Ltd., 1989-94. Honorary Member, Kiev Rotary Club. Recreations: climbing; underwater fishing; fish-farming. Address: Gillisland, The Sands, Haddington, EH41 3EY; T.-0162 082 4133.

Bettison, Graeme Hayward, LLB(Hons). Chief Executive, Inverclyde Council, since 1995; b. 29.4.55, Edinburgh; m., Fiona. Educ. Royal High School, Edinburgh; Edinburgh University. West Lothian District Council, 1978-81; Dumfries and Galloway Regional Council, 1981-93; Senior Depute Director of Administration, Grampian Regional Council, 1993-95. President, Junior Chamber, Dumfries, 1984-85. Recreations: golf; reading; gardening. Address: (b.) Municipal Buildings, Greenock, PA15 1LY; T.-01475 882701.

Betts, Michael William, CBE, FCIT, FILog. Traffic Commissioner and Licensing Authority for Scotland, since 1992; b. 3.3.38, Bournemouth; m., Margaret Irene Lussi; 2 d. Educ. Hardye's School, Dorchester; Royal Military

Academy, Sandhurst. Commissioned Royal Army Service Corps, 1957 (Germany, Hong Kong, Oman); Royal Corps of Transport, 1965 (UK, Germany, Cyprus, Hong Kong); Staff College, Camberley, 1971; National Defence College, 1977; Commander (Brigadier), Royal Corps of Transport, British Army of the Rhine, 1986-87; Brigadier Logistics, British Army of the Rhine, 1987-90; Director of Movements (Army), Ministry of Defence, 1991-92; ADC to the Queen, 1990-92. Freeman, City of London, 1993; Freeman and Liveryman, Worshipful Company of Carmen, 1993. Recreations: sailing; skiing; bird-watching; bee-keeping. Address: (b.) Scottish Traffic Area Office, Floor J, Argyle House, 3 Lady Lawson Street, Edinburgh, EH3 9SE; T.-0131-529 8510.

Bevan, John Stuart, BSc (Hons), MBChB (Hons), MD, FRCP (Edin), FRSM. Consultant Physician and Endocrinologist, Aberdeen Royal Infirmary, since 1991; Honorary Senior Clinical Lecturer, Aberdeen University, since 1991; Member, Council, Endocrine Section, Royal Society of Medicine; b. 18.9.53, Portsmouth; m., Sheena Mary; 2 s.; 2 d. Educ. Portsmouth Northern Grammar School; Dunfermline High School; Edinburgh University. Registrar in Endocrinology, Radcliffe Infirmary, Oxford, 1981-83; Medical Research Council Training Fellow in Endocrinology, Oxford, 1984-86; Senior Registrar in Medicine and Endocrinology, University Hospital of Wales, Cardiff, 1987-90; Assistant Editor, Clinical Endocrinology, since 1994. Publications: papers on clinical neuroendocrinology, particularly the treatment of human pituitary tumours. Recreations: cricket; guitar; ornithology. Address: (b.) Department of Endocrinology, Aberdeen Royal Infirmary, Ward 47, Foresterhill, Aberdeen, AB9 2ZB; T.-01224 681818.

Beveridge, Crawford William, BSc, MSc. Chief Executive, Scottish Enterprise, since 1991; b. 3.11.45, Edinburgh; m., Marguerite Devoe; 1 s.; 1 d. Educ. Daniel Stewart's College; Edinburgh University; Bradford University Management Centre. Training Officer, Hewlett Packard, 1968; European Personnel Director, Digital, 1977; Vice President Human Resources, Analog Devices, 1982; Vice President Corporate Resources, Sun Microsystems, 1985. Recreations: cooking; music; paperweights. Address: (b.) Scottish Enterprise, 120 Bothwell Street, Glasgow, G2 7JP; T.-0141-248 2700.

Beveridge, George William, MB, ChB, FRCPE. Consultant Dermatologist, Edinburgh Royal Infirmary, since 1965; Honorary Senior Lecturer, Edinburgh University, since 1965; b. 23.2.32, Edinburgh; m., Janette Millar; 2 s.; 2 d. Educ. Dollar Academy; Edinburgh University. President, Scottish Dermatological Society, 1982-85; Elder, Church of Scotland. Recreations: golf; gardening. Address: (h.) 8 Barnton Park View, Edinburgh, EH4 6HJ.

Bewsher, Harold Frederick, LVO, OBE. Chairman, The Airborne Initiative (Scotland) Ltd., since 1995; Secretary, The Queen's Bodyguard for Scotland, 1982-94; b. 13.1.29, Glasgow; m., Susan Elizabeth Cruickshank; 2 s. Educ. Merchiston Castle School; Royal Technical College; Glasgow University; Royal Military Academy, Sandhurst. Regular Army, The Royal Scots, 1949-72; Director-General, Scotch Whisky Association, 1973-94. Chairman, New Club, Edinburgh, 1981-82; Chairman, Scottish Society for the Employment of Ex-Regular Soldiers, Sailors and Airmen, 1973-83. Recreations: outdoors — salmon fishing, field sports. Address: (b.) 33 Blacket Place, Edinburgh, EH9 1RJ; T.-0131-667 4600.

Bewsher, Peter Dixon, MB, ChB, MD, FRCPE. Reader in Therapeutics, Aberdeen University, since 1977; Honorary Consultant Physician, Grampian Health Board, since 1969; b. 6.4.34, Cockermouth; m., Marlyn Crichton; 2 s.; 1 d. Educ. Cockermouth Grammar School; St. Andrews University. Medical Registrar, Aberdeen Hospitals; Research Associate, Indiana University; Lecturer, then Senior Lecturer in Therapeutics, Aberdeen University. Recreations: music; golf; hill-walking. Address: (h.) 83 Abbotshall Drive, Cults, Aberdeen, AB1 9JJ; T.-Aberdeen 868078.

Biddulph, 5th Lord (Anthony Nicholas Colin). Interior Designer and Sporting Manager; b. 8.4.59; m., Hon. Sian Gibson-Watt; 1 s. Educ. Cheltenham; RAC, Cirencester. Recreations: shooting; design; fishing. Address: Address: (h.) Makerstoun, Kelso, TD5 7PA; T.-01573 460 234.

Biggart, Thomas Norman, CBE (1984), WS, MA, LLB. Partner, Biggart Baillie & Gifford, WS, Solicitors, Glasgow and Edinburgh, 1959-95; b. 24.1.30; m., Eileen Jean Anne Gemmell; 1 s.; 1 d. Educ. Morrison's Academy, Crieff; Glasgow University. Royal Navy, 1954-56 (Sub.-Lt., RNVR). Law Society of Scotland: Council Member, 1977-86; Vice-President, 1981-82; President, 1982-83; President, Business Archives Council, Scotland, 1977-86; Member, Executive, Scottish Council (Development and Industry), 1984-94; Member, Scottish Tertiary Education Advisory Council, 1984-87; Member, Scottish Records Advisory Council, 1985-91; Director: Clydesdale Bank, since 1985; Independent Insurance Group, since 1986 (Chairman, 1989-93); Chairman, Beechwood, Glasgow, since 1989; Trustee, Scottish Civic Trust, since 1989; Member, Council on Tribunals (Chairman, Scottish Committee), since 1990; Honorary Member, American Bar Association, 1982; OStJ, 1968. Recreations: golf; hill-walking. Address: (h.) Gailes, Kilmacolm, Renfrewshire, PA13 4LZ; T.-0150 587 2645.

Binnie, Frank Hugh. Chief Executive, Scottish Design, formerly Director, The Design Council Scotland, since 1990; Director, UK Clothing and Textile Initiative, since 1990; b. 1.3.50, Edinburgh; 3 s. Educ. Loughborough Grammar; De Montfort University. Design Management Trainee, Corahs Textiles, Leicester, 1970-73; Manufacturing Manager, Floreal Knitwear, Mauritius, 1973-76; Sales Manager, Kemptons Knitwear, Leicester, 1976-79; General Manager Design, Texport Unilever, 1979-82; Manufacturing Manager, Kilspindie Knitwear, 1982-85; Director and Company Secretary, Midlothian Enterprise, 1985-88; Managing Director, Perkins, Hodgkinson and Gillibrand (Coxmore plc), 1988-90. Visiting Professor in Engineering Design, Strathclyde University; Fellow, Chartered Society of Designers; Fellow, Royal Society of Arts, Design and Manufacturing; Chairman, Textile Institute Fashion, Product Design and Marketing Group. Recreations: yachting; running. Address: (b.) Ca' d'Oro Building, 45 Gordon Street, Glasgow, G1 3LZ; T.-0141-221 6121.

Binnie, John, MA (Hons). Artistic Director, Clyde Unity Theatre, since 1986; b. 30.7.65, Kilsyth. Educ. Kilsyth Academy; Glasgow University. Director/writer of 15 plays; Fringe First Awards for Beyond the Rainbow, 1989, and Accustomed to Her Face, 1993; A Little Older won 1992 Independent Theatre Award; Breadmakers won 1995 Paper Boat Award. Recreations: cinema-going; reading; eating; socialising. Address: (b.) The Old Athenaeum, 179 Buchanan Street, Glasgow, G1; T.-0141-353 1454.

Bird, Professor Colin C., MBChB, PhD, FRCPath, FRCPE, FRCSE, FRSE. Professor of Pathology and Head, Department of Pathology, Edinburgh University, since 1986; b. 5.3.38, Kirkintilloch; m., Ailsa M. Ross; 2 s.; 1 d. Educ. Lenzie Academy; Glasgow University. McGhie Cancer Research Scholar, Glasgow Royal Infirmary, 1962-64; Lecturer in Pathology: Glasgow University, 1964-67, Aberdeen University, 1967-72; MRC Goldsmiths Travelling Fellow, Chicago, 1970-71; Senior Lecturer in Pathology, Edinburgh University, 1972-75; Professor and Head, Department of Pathology, Leeds University, 1975-86.

Recreations: golf; skiing; hill walking; music. Address: (h.) 45 Ann Street, Edinburgh, EH4 1PL.

Bird, Jackie. Journalist; b. 31.7.62, Bellshill; m., Robert Bird; 1 d. Educ. Earnock High School. Music/Film/Television Editor, Jackie Magazine; Radio News Reporter and Presenter, Radio Clyde; Reporter, Evening Times; Reporter, Sun; Reporter/Presenter, TVS; Presenter, Reporting Scotland. Patron, Glasgow Cat and Dog Home. Recreations: swimming; aerobics; running; music; animal welfare. Address; (b.) BBC, Queen Margaret Drive, Glasgow; T.-0141-339 8844.

Birley, Tim(othy) Grahame, BSc(Eng), MSc, ACGI, FRTPI, FRICS, FRSA. Director, Centre for Human Ecology, Edinburgh University, since 1995; independent adviser on sustainable development and public policy; b. 13.3.47, Kent; m., Catherine Anne; 1 s.; 2 d. Educ. Sir Roger Manwood's Grammar School; Imperial College, London University; Edinburgh University. Local government, 1965-71; academic appointments, 1973-81; Director, Energy and Environment Research, 1982-85; Scottish Office: Inquiry Reporter, 1985-87, Principal Inquiry Reporter, 1987-88, Deputy Director of Building, 1988-90, Head, Rural Affairs Division, 1990-95. Non-Executive Director, RPT (Scotland), 1989-91; Central Scotland Woodlands, 1991-92. Recreation: family outings. Address: (h.) 6 Malta Terrace, Edinburgh, EH4 1HR; T.-0131-332 3499.

Birnie, George David, BSc, PhD. Senior Scientist, Beatson Institute for Cancer Research, since 1969; Honorary Lecturer in Biochemistry, Glasgow University, since 1982; b. 8.8.34, Gourock; m., Jean Gray McCaig; 2 s.; 1 d. Educ. Gourock High School; Greenock High School; Glasgow University. Assistant Lecturer in Biochemistry, Glasgow University, 1959-60; Postdoctoral Fellow, McArdle Memorial Laboratory, University of Wisconsin, 1960-62; Scientist, Imperial Cancer Research Fund Laboratories, London, 1962-69. Kitchener Scholarship, 1952-56; Fulbright Travel Scholarship, 1960-62; US Public Health Service Fellowship, 1960-62; Member, Editorial Advisory Panel, Biochemical Journal, 1981-92; Member, Editorial Board, Biochemical Journal, since 1992; editor of five books, author of more than 140 papers. Deacon, Giffnock Congregational Church, 1980-91. Recreation: gardening. Address: (b.) Beatson Institute for Cancer Research, Garscube Estate, Switchback Road, Bearsden, Glasgow, G61 1BD; T.-0141-942 9361.

Birss, Rev. Alan David, MA (Hons), BD (Hons). Minister, Paisley Abbey, since 1988; b. 5.6.53, Ellon; m., Carol Margaret Pearson. Educ. Glenrothes High School; St. Andrews University; Edinburgh University. Assistant Minister, Dundee Parish Church (St. Mary's), 1978-80; Minister, Inverkeithing Parish Church of St. Peter, 1982-88. Secretary, Scottish Church Society; Member, Council, Church Service Society; Chairman, Scottish Committee, Royal School of Church Music. Address: The Manse of Paisley Abbey, 15 Main Road, Castlehead, Paisley, PA2 6AJ; T.-0141-889 3587.

Bishop, Alan Henry, CB (1989), MA (Hons). HM Chief Inspector of Prisons for Scotland, 1989-94, retired; b. 12.9.29, Edinburgh; m., Marjorie Anne Conlan; 1 s.; 1 d. Educ. George Heriot's School, Edinburgh; Edinburgh University. Private Secretary to Parliamentary Under Secretaries of State for Scotland, 1958-59; Principal, Department of Agriculture and Fisheries for Scotland, 1959; First Secretary, Food and Agriculture, Copenhagen and The Hague, 1963-66; Assistant Secretary: Commission on the Constitution, 1969-73, Devolution Division, Scottish Office, 1973-76, Health Building and Liaison Divisions, SHHD, 1976-80; Assistant Under-Secretary of State, Scottish Office, London, 1980-84; Principal Establishment Officer, Scottish Office, 1984-89. President, Scottish Bridge Union, 1979-80. Recreations: contract bridge; theatre. Address: (h.) Beaumont Court, 19/8 Wester Coates Gardens, Edinburgh, EH12 5LT.

Bishop, Professor John Oliver, BSc, PhD, FRSE. Professor of Molecular Cell Biology, Edinburgh University, since 1989; Associate Director, Centre for Genome Research, since 1989; b. 14.5.35, Edinburgh; m., Gillian Clark Spowart; 1 s.; 1 d. Educ. George Heriot's; Edinburgh University. Scientist, City of Hope Medical Center, Duarte, CA, USA, 1959-60, University of Kentucky, Lexington, KY, USA, 1960-62; Edinburgh University: Lecturer in Genetics, 1962-74, Reader, 1974-89; Professor and Eminent Scholar, University of Maryland, 1990-92. FEBS Prize, 1974; Member, Academia Europaea, 1993. Recreation: cookery. Address: (b.) Centre for Genome Research, Edinburgh University, King's Buildings, Edinburgh, EH9 3JQ; T.-0131-650 5843.

Bisset, Raymond George, BSc. Provost, Gordon District Council, since 1992; Depute Convenor, Aberdeenshire Council, since 1995; Member, North of Scotland Water Authority, since 1995; b. 16.8.42, Ellon. Educ. Inverurie Academy; Aberdeen University. Past Chairman: Inverurie Round Table, Inverurie Angling Association, North of Scotland Anglers Federation; Chairman, Gordon Area Tourist Board. Recreations: angling; golf; hill-walking. Address: (h.) The Schoolhouse, Keithhall, Inverurie, AB51 0LX; T.-01467 621015.

Bisset-Johnson, Professor Alastair, LLB, LLM, Barrister. Professor of Private Law, Dundee University, since 1991; b. Northumberland; m., Dr. Winifred Bissett-Johnson (deceased). Educ. Royal Masonic School, Bushey. Assistant Lecturer, Sheffield University, 1963; Lecturer, Bristol University, 1963-67; Senior Lecturer, Monash University, Melbourne, 1968-71, Leicester University, 1971-76; Associate Professor, McGill University, Montreal, 1976-77; Professor, Dalhousie University, Halifax, Nova Scotia, 1977-90. Publications: Family Law in Australia (Co-author); Cases and Materials on Family Law (Co-author); Matrimonial Property Law in Canada (Co-author); The New Divorce Law (Co-author). Recreations: watercolour painting; music; food and wine. Address: (h.) 7 Shaftesbury Road, Dundee, DD2 1HF; T.-01382 645264.

Black, Professor Antony, MA (Cantab), PhD (Cantab). Professor in Political Science, Dundee University, since 1990; Author; b. 23.6.36, Leeds; m., Aileen Pow; 4 s.; 1 d. Educ. Shrewsbury School; King's College, Cambridge. Assistant Lecturer, Department of Political Science, Queen's College, Dundee, 1963-66; Lecturer, Department of Political Science, Dundee University, 1967-80; Visiting Associate Professor, School of Government and Public Administration, The American University, Washington, DC, 1975-76. Publications: Monarchy and Community: political ideas in the later conciliar movement (1430-50); Council and Commune: the Council of Basle and the 15th-century heritage; Guilds and civil society in European political thought from the 12th century to the present; State, Community and Human Desire; Community in Historical Perspective (Editor); Political Thought in Europe, 1250-1450. Address: (b.) Department of Political Science, Dundee University, Dundee; T.-Dundee 223181, Ext. 4592.

Black, Hugh Finlayson, BSc (Hons), MBA. Depute Director Development, Highland Regional Council, since 1984; Company Manager, Highland Opportunity Limited, since 1986; Regional Manager, Prince's Scottish Youth Business Trust, since 1988; Director: Business Information Source Ltd., Highland Birchwoods Ltd., North of Scotland European Partnership Ltd., Cesar Scotland Ltd.; b. 16.6.46, Johnstone; m., Lydia Mary McRae; 1 s.; 3 d. Educ. Paisley Grammar School; Aberdeen University; Strathclyde University; Glasgow University. Development Officer, West Cumberland Farmers, 1973-75; Regional Manager,

Pan Britannica Industries, 1976-79; Principal Officer, Grampian Regional Council, 1980-84. Recreations: family; education; farming; history; travel; walking. Address: (b.) Development Department, Highland Regional Council, Glenurquhart Road, Inverness, IV3 5NX; T.-01463 702000, Ext. 2551.

Black, Rev. James G., BD, DPS. Minister, Westwood Parish Church, East Kilbride, since 1986; b. 10.2.52, Motherwell; m., Isobel-Ann T. Hamilton; 1 d. Educ. Dalziel High School, Motherwell; Glasgow University. Minister: Hamilton North, 1978-82, Burnbank/Hamilton North, 1982-86. Editor, Church of Scotland Year Book; Secretary, Scottish Christian Conservative Forum. Recreations: reading; music. Address: 16 Inglewood Crescent, East Kilbride; T.-013552 23992.

Black, Laurie. Chairman, Taste of Scotland, since 1994; Chairman, Taste of Burns Country, since 1995; Joint Partner, Fouters Bistro, Ayr, since 1973; b. 10.7.48, West Germany; m., Fran; 1 s.; 1 d. Educ. Horley Secondary School; Bournemouth Technical College. Former policeman; left police, 1973, to open restaurant in Ayr. Committee Member, Ayrshire Tourism Industry Forum; Member, Scottish Tourist Board working party on natural cooking of Scotland; Director, Taste of Scotland, since 1993; Manager, Ayr Junior Ice Hockey Club. Recreations: cooking; travel; walking; music; computing; wine; golf. Address: (b.) 2A Academy Street, Ayr; T.-01292 261391.

Black, Professor Robert, QC, LLB (Hons), LLM, FRSA, FRSE. Professor of Scots Law, Edinburgh University, since 1981; General Editor, The Laws of Scotland: Stair Memorial Encyclopaedia, since 1988 (formerly Deputy and Joint General Editor); Temporary Sheriff, 1981-94; b. 12.6.47, Lockerbie. Educ. Lockerbie Academy; Dumfries Academy; Edinburgh University; McGill University, Montreal. Advocate, 1972; Lecturer in Scots Law, Edinburgh University, 1972-75; Senior Legal Officer, Scottish Law Commission, 1975-78; practised at Scottish bar, 1978-81; QC, 1987. Publications: An Introduction to Written Pleading, 1982; Civil Jurisdiction: The New Rules, 1983. Recreations: beer and books, not necessarily in that order. Address: (h.) 6/4 Glenogle Road, Edinburgh, EH3 5HW; T.-0131-557 3571.

Black, Robert Reid, MBE, ARSA, DA, ARIBA, FRIAS. Partner, Baxter Clark & Paul, Architects, Dundee, since 1965; b. 1.11.35, Arbroath; m., Moyra Christine Deuchar; 1 s.; 3 d. Educ. Arbroath High School; Dundee College of Art; Duncan of Jordanstone School of Architecture. Apprenticeship, Arbroath Town Council, 1951-55; Architectural Assistant, Arbroath Town Council, 1958; Northern Ireland Housing Trust, 1958-59; private practice, 1960; Baxter Clark & Paul, since 1961. Member, Housing Awards Panel, Saltire Society, since 1970 (currently Convener). Address: (b.) 20 South Tay Street, Dundee; T.-01382 27511.

Black, Robert William, MA (Hons, Econ), MSc (Town Planning), MSc (Public Policy). Controller of Audit, Accounts Commission for Scotland, since 1995; b. 6.11.46, Banff; m., Doreen Mary Riach; 3 s.; 1 d. Educ. Robert Gordon's College, Aberdeen; Aberdeen University; Heriot-Watt University; Strathclyde University. Nottinghamshire County Council, 1971-73; City of Glasgow Corporation, 1973-75; Strathclyde Regional Council, 1975-85; Chief Executive: Stirling District Council, 1985-90, Tayside Regional Council, 1990-95. Fellow, Royal Statistical Society. Recreations: hill-walking; cycling; golf; swimming; music and art. Address: (b.) 18 George Street, Edinburgh, EH2 2QU.

Black, W.J. Murray, BSc, PhD, ARICS, JP. Farms Director, Edinburgh School of Agriculture, since 1970; Honorary Senior Lecturer, Edinburgh University, since 1970; b. 26.7.35, Reading; m., Ann Warren; 3 d. Educ. Leighton Park School, Reading; Reading University; Durham University; College of Estate Management, Reading. Lecturer in Agriculture, Newcastle University, 1959-64; Principal Scientific Officer, Agricultural Institute, Dublin, 1964-70. Member: Farm Animal Welfare Council, London, since 1988, NCCS (SNH) S.E. Scotland Regional Board, since 1991, UK Register of Organic Food Suppliers R. & D. Committee, London, since 1989; Honorary Secretary/Treasurer, British Society of Animal Production, since 1980; Chairman, Governors, St. Margaret's School, Edinburgh. Publications: 45 scientific papers. Recreations: DIY houses and restoration of old cars; holidays in France. Address: The Pines, Bush, Penicuik, EH26 0PH; T.-0131-445 3136.

Blackadder, Elizabeth, OBE, RA, RSA. Artist; b. 24.9.31, Falkirk. Educ. Falkirk High School; Edinburgh University; Edinburgh College of Art. Lecturer, School of Drawing and Painting, Edinburgh College of Art, 1962-66; first Scottish woman painter elected full member, Royal Academy and Royal Scottish Academy.

Blackburn, John Daniel, MA. Past President, Association for Scottish Literary Studies; Vice-Convener, Advisory Council for the Arts in Scotland, since 1987; b. 2.7.31, Glasgow; m., Ailsa Cameron MacLachlan; 3 s. Educ. Eastwood Secondary School; Glasgow University. Teacher of English, 1957-68; Principal Teacher of English, Golspie High School, 1968-72; Lecturer in English, Moray House College of Education/Edinburgh University, 1972-82; freelance writing, lecturing and teaching, since 1982; long association with Scottish Examination Board (CSYS English). Publications include: A Writer's Journey: a study of the early poetry of Iain Crichton Smith, 1981; Gallery (poetry anthology), 1981; Hardy to Heaney (essays), 1986; The Poetry of Iain Crichton Smith, 1993. Recreations: music; countryside. Address: (h.) The Riggs, 9 South Back Road, Biggar, Lanarkshire; T.-01899 20550.

Blackburn, Richard A.M, BSC (Hons), MEd (Hons), MBA. Chief Executive, Banff and Buchan District Council, since 1990; b. 27.10.49, Rutherglen; m., Andrina; 2 d. Educ. Hamilton Academy; Glasgow University. Recreation: golf. Address (b.) St. Leonards, Sandyhill Road, Banff; T.-01261 813200.

Blackie, Professor John Walter Graham, BA (Cantab), LLB. Professor of Law, Strathclyde University, since 1991 (Senior Lecturer in Scots Law, Edinburgh University, 1988-91, Lecturer, 1975-88); Director, Blackie & Son Ltd., publishers, 1970-93; Advocate, since 1974; b. 2.10.46, Glasgow; m., Jane Ashman. Educ. Uppingham School; Peterhouse, Cambridge; Harvard; Merton College, Oxford; Edinburgh University. Open Exhibitioner, Peterhouse, Cambridge, 1965-68; St. Andrews Society of New York Scholar, Harvard, 1968-69; practised at Scottish bar, 1974-75. Recreations: music; sailing. Address: (h.) 17 Parsonage Square, Glasgow G1 1PX.

Blackshaw, Alan, OBE, VRD. Business Consultant and Author; Chairman, Career Development Associates Ltd., since 1995; Chairman, Caledonian Career Consultants Ltd., since 1994; Associate, Oakwood Environmental Ltd., since 1991; b. 7.4.33; m., 1, Jane Elizabeth Turner (m. dissolved); 1 d.; 2, Dr. Elspeth Paterson Martin; 1 s.; 2 d. Educ. Merchant Taylors' School, Crosby; Wadham College, Oxford (MA). Royal Marines (commissioned), 1954-56, and RM Reserve, 1956-76. Entered Home Civil Service, Ministry of Power, 1956; Principal Private Secretary to Minister of Power, 1967-69; Department of Energy: Under Secretary, 1974, Offshore Supplies Office, 1974-78 (Director-General, 1977-78), Coal Division, 1978-79; Consultant, N.C.B., 1979-86; Consultant Director, Strategy International, 1980-91; Member, Scottish Sports Council, 1990-95; Member, Scottish Natural Heritage, since 1992

(Chairman, Task Force on Access, 1992-94, Chairman, Audit Committee, since 1995); Patron, British Mountaineering Council, since 1979 (President, 1973-76); Chairman, Standing Advisory Committee on Mountain Training Policy, 1980-86 and since 1990; Chairman, Sports Council's National Mountain Centre, Plas y Brenin, since 1986; Chairman, Mountaineering Committee, UIAA, since 1990; Chairman, UK Mountain Training Board, 1991-94; Chairman, Scottish National Ski Council, 1991-94, President, since 1994; Freeman, City of London; FRGS; FInstPet. Publication: Mountaineering, 1965. Recreations: mountaineering; skiing. Address: (h.) 2 Clark Road, Edinburgh, EH5 3BD; T.-0131-467 3366.

Blair, Alastair William, MB, ChB, FRCPE, DCH. Consultant Paediatrician, Fife Area Health Board, latterly Kirkcaldy Acute Unit NHS Trust, since 1970; Honorary Senior Lecturer: Department of Biochemistry and Microbiology, St. Andrews University, since 1975; Department of Child Life and Health, Edinburgh University, since 1979; Secretary, Scottish Paediatric Society, 1987-94; b. 11.8.36, Preston; m., Irene Elizabeth McFee; 2 s. Educ. Harris Academy, Dundee; St. Andrews University. House Officer/Senior House Officer: Arbroath Infirmary; Maryfield Hospital, Dundee; Kings Cross Hospital, Dundee; Hospital for Sick Children, Great Ormond Street, London; Lecturer in Child Health, St. Andrews University; Registrar in Medical Paediatrics, Hospital for Sick Children, Great Ormond Street, London; Lecturer in Child Health, Aberdeen University; Wellcome-Swedish Research Fellow, Karolinska Children's Hospital, Stockholm; Senior Registrar in Paediatrics, Southmead Hospital, Bristol. Publication: Prenatal Paediatrics: a handbook for obstetricians and paediatricians (Co-author and Editor), 1971. Recreations: private aviation; camping; restoring old property; sailing; jazz. Address: (h.) Bellcraig Farm, by Leslie, Fife, KY6 3JE; T.-01592 741754.

Blair, (Ann) Kay, MA (Hons). Marketing Consultant, Business Perceptions, since 1982; Marketing Columnist, The Scotsman, since 1988; Board Member, Scottish Legal Aid Board, since 1994; Non-Executive Director, Edinburgh Sick Children's NHS Trust, since 1994; b. 12.4.53, Edinburgh; m., William; 1 s.; 2 d. Educ. James Gillespie's High School for Girls; St. Andrews University; School of Slavonic and Eastern European Studies, London University. Journalist/Researcher on Eastern Europe and Manager, Business Information Service, Financial Times, 1977-80; Marketing Information Manager, Scottish Development Agency, 1980-81. Recreations: skiing; cinema; travel. Address: (b.) 15b Moray Place, Edinburgh, EH3 6DT; T.-0131-220 6494.

Blair, Anna Dempster, DPE. Writer and Lecturer; b. 12.2.27, Glasgow; m., Matthew Blair; 1 s.; 1 d. Educ. Hutchesons' Girls Grammar School, Glasgow; Dunfermline College. Novels: A Tree in the West; The Rowan on the Ridge; Short Stories: Tales of Ayrshire; Scottish Tales; The Goose Girl of Eriska; Seed Corn; social history: Tea at Miss Cranston's; Croft and Creel; More Tea at Miss Cranston's. Recreations: film-making; travel; reading; friendship. Address: (h.) 20 Barrland Drive, Giffnock, Glasgow, G46 7QD; T.-0141-638 0676.

Blair, James Ballantyne, BL, InstAM (Dip). Honorary Sheriff, Grampian, Highland and Islands at Stonehaven, since 1989; b. 16.8.24, Dailly, Ayrshire; m., Margaret M.J. McCafferty (deceased); 2 s.; 2 d. Educ. Peebles High School; Edinburgh University. Post Office, Peebles, 1941-44; Royal Signals, 1944-48 (GHQ (I) Signals, New Delhi, 1945-47); Sheriff Clerk's Offices, Edinburgh, Inverness, Peebles, Dingwall, Glasgow, 1948-73; Sheriff Clerk of Aberdeenshire at Aberdeen, 1973-82. Recreations: opera/operetta; reading (current affairs and law reports). Address: 41 Woodcot Park, Stonehaven, AB3 2HG; T.-01569 762067.

Blair, James Eric, BL. Solicitor, since 1948; Honorary Sheriff, since 1980; b. 18.3.23, Airdrie. Educ. Glasgow Academy; Glasgow University. Past Captain, Airdrie Golf Club. Recreation: golf. Address: (h.) Dunedin, Forrest Street, Airdrie.

Blair, John Samuel Greene, OBE (Mil), TD, KStJ, BA, Hon. DLitt (St. Andrews), ChM, FRCSEdin, FICS, D(Obst)RCOG. Senior Lecturer, History of Medicine, St. Andrews University, since 1993; Honorary Lecturer, History of Medicine, Dundee University, since 1990 (Honorary Senior Lecturer in Surgery, 1967-90); President, British Society for the History of Medicine, 1993; President, Scottish Society for the History of Medicine, 1990-93; Member, Editorial Board, Vesalius, since 1994; Consultant Surgeon, Perth Royal Infirmary, 1965-90; b. 31.12.28, Wormit, Fife; m., Ailsa Jean Bowes; 2 s.; 1 d. Educ. Dundee High School; St. Andrews University (Harkness Scholar, 1946-50). National Service, RAMC, 1952-55; Tutor, Department of Anatomy, St. Salvator's College, St. Andrews, 1955; surgical and research training, Manchester, Dundee, Cambridge, London, 1957-65; Member, Court of Examiners, Royal College of Surgeons of Edinburgh, 1965; postgraduate Clinical Tutor, Perth, 1966-74; first North American Travelling Fellow, St. Andrews/Dundee Universities, 1971; Secretary, Tayside Area Medical Advisory Committee, 1974-83; Member, Education Advisory Committee, Association of Surgeons, 1984-88; Secretary, Perth and Kinross Division, British Medical Association, 1982-90; Member, Scottish Council and Chairman's Sub-Committee, BMA, 1985-89; Fellow of the BMA, 1990; Honorary Colonel (TA), RAMC; Member, Principal's Council, St Andrews University, since 1989; Elder, Church of Scotland; Hospitaller, Priory of Scotland, Order of St. John of Jerusalem; Mitchiner Lecturer, Army Medical Services, 1994. Publications:books on medical history and anatomy. Recreations: golf; history; travel; bridge. Address: (h.) 143 Glasgow Road, Perth; T.-Perth 623739.

Blair, Michael, FTS. Director of Tourism, Bute and Cowal Tourist Board, since 1993; b. 5.12.43, Glasgow; m., Margaret; 1 d. Educ. Rothesay Academy. Merchant Navy, 1961-66; Assistant Tourist Officer, Glasgow Corporation, 1966-75; Tourist Officer, Cunninghame District Council, 1975-91; Director, Dunoon and Cowal Tourist Board, 1991-93. Recreations: sailing; swimming. Address: (h.) 5 Eaglesham Terrace, Rothesay, PA20 9HL; T.-01700 503211.

Blair, Robin Leitch, MB, ChB, FRCSEdin, FRCS(C), FACS. Head, Department of Otolaryngology, Ninewells Hospital and Medical School, Dundee, since 1984; Clinical Director of Otolaryngology, Dundee Teaching Hospitals NHS Trust; b. 28.11.45, Gourock; m., Elizabeth Anne White; 2 d. Educ. Greenock Academy; Edinburgh University; University of Toronto. House Surgeon, Royal Infirmary, Edinburgh; Lecturer, Department of Anatomy, Glasgow University; Assistant Professor, Department of Otolaryngology, University of Toronto. Address: (b.) Department of Otolaryngology, Ninewells Hospital and Medical School, Dundee, DD1 9SY; T.-01382 60111, Ext. 2726.

Blair, Robin Orr, MA, LLB, WS. Partner, Dundas & Wilson, since 1967 (Managing Partner, 1976-83 and 1988-91); Chairman, Top Flight Leisure Group; Director, Tullis Russell & Co. Ltd. Educ. Rugby School; St. Andrews University; Edinburgh University. Purse Bearer to Her Majesty's High Commissioner to General Assembly of Church of Scotland. Address: (b.) Saltire Court, 20 Castle Terrace, Edinburgh, EH1 2EN; T.-0131-228 8000.

Blake, Professor Christopher, CBE, FRSE, MA, PhD. Bonar Professor of Applied Economics, Dundee University, 1974-88; Chairman, Glenrothes Development Corporation, since 1987; b. 28.4.26; m.; 2 s.; 2 d. Educ. Dollar Academy; St. Andrews University. Royal Navy, 1944-47; teaching posts, 1951-53; Assistant, Edinburgh University, 1953-55; Stewarts & Lloyds Ltd., 1955-60; Lecturer, then Senior Lecturer, St. Andrews University, 1960-67; Senior Lecturer, then Professor of Economics, Dundee University, 1967-74; Director, Alliance Trust plc, 1974-94; Director, William Low & Co. plc, 1980-90 (Chairman, 1985-90). Recreation: golf. Address: (h.) Westlea, 14 Wardlaw Gardens, St. Andrews, Fife, KY16 9DW.

Blakey, Rev. Ronald Stanton, MA, BD, MTh. Deputy Secretary, Department of Education, Church of Scotland, since 1981; Secretary, Assembly Council, from 1 Aug., 1988; b. 3.7.38, Glasgow; m., Kathleen Dunbar; 1 s. Educ. Hutchesons' Boys' Grammar School, Glasgow; Glasgow University. Minister: St. Mark's, Kirkconnel, 1963-67; Bellshill West, 1967-72; Jedburgh Old Parish with Edgerston and Ancrum, 1972-81. Member, Roxburgh District Council, 1974-80 (Chairman of Council, 1977-80); Religious Adviser, Border Television, 1973-81; Member, Borders Region Children's Panel, 1974-80; JP, 1974-80. Publication: The Man in the Manse, 1978. Recreation: collecting antiquarian books on Scotland. Address: (h.) 61 Orchard Brae Avenue, Edinburgh EH4.

Blanche, John Jamieson, OBE, CA. Chairman, West of Scotland Assured Homes PLC; Chairman, Scottish Veto Investment Company; Director, Chorus Trust Ltd.; b. 10.7.29, Paisley; m., Fiona; 1 s.; 1 d. Educ. Glasgow Academy; Strathallan School. Director, Allied-Lyons PLC, 1986-89; Chairman, Allied Distillers Ltd., 1987-89; William Teacher & Sons Ltd.: Managing Director, 1979-84, Chairman, 1984-89; Chairman and Managing Director, Stewart & Son of Dundee Ltd., 1969-79; Allied-Lyons Eastern Ltd.: Chief Executive, 1988-89, non-executive Director, 1989-91; Director, Clyde Port Authority, 1980-86; Member, East European Trade Council, 1988-91; Member, Food From Britain Council, 1989-92; President, Junior Chamber Scotland, 1967; Governor, Glasgow School of Art, 1991-93; Hon. Governor, Strathallan School, since 1993 (Governor, 1977-93). Recreations: golf; hill-walking; fishing; gardening; travel; music. Address: (b.) Daldrishaig, Aberfoyle, Stirling, FK8 3TQ; T.-01877 382223.

Bland, Roger, MA, LLB. Member, Legal Staff, Scottish Law Commission, since 1991; b. 22.3.37, Leicester; m., Diana Mary. Educ. George Watson's Boys College, Edinburgh; Edinburgh University. Depute Clerk of Court and Legal Assessor, Scottish Land Court, 1966-71; Deputy Secretary, National Industrial Relations Court, 1971-74; Member, Office of Solicitor to Secretary of State for Scotland, since 1974; Deputy Director, Scottish Courts Adinistration, 1982-91. Address: (b.) 140 Causewayside, Edinburgh, EH9 1PR; T.-0131-668 2131.

Blaxter, Professor John Harry Savage, MA (Oxon), DSc (Oxon), HonDUniv(Stirling), FIBiol, FRSE. Hon. Professor, Stirling University and St. Andrews University; Hon. Research Fellow, Scottish Association for Marine Science; b. 6.1.29, London; m., Valerie Ann McElligott; 1 s.; 1 d. Educ. Berkhamsted School; Brasenose College, Oxford. SO, then SSO, Marine Laboratory, Aberdeen, 1952-64; Lecturer, Zoology Department, Aberdeen University, 1964-69; PSO, 1969, SPSO, 1974, DCSO, 1985-91, Scottish Marine Biological Association, Oban. Recreations: sailing; gardening. Address: (h.) Dems Lodge, Barcaldine, Oban PA37 1SF.

Bleiman, David, MA, MBA, MIPD. Assistant General Secretary (Scotland), Association of University Teachers, since 1982; Member, STUC General Council, since 1990; Member, Industrial Tribunal, since 1992; b. 7.8.53, Cape Town; m., Maureen McGibbon; 1 s.; 1 d. Educ. Haberdashers' Aske's School; Christ's College and King's College, Cambridge. W.E.A. Tutor, 1978; General

Secretary, Scottish Further Education Association, 1979-82. Publication: Labour and Scottish Nationalism (Co-author), 1980. Recreations:listening to German language programmes; birdwatching. Address: (b.) 6 Castle Street, Edinburgh, EH2 3AT; T.-0131-226 6694.

Blyth, William, MA, LLB, BCom, SSC, NP. Chief Executive, City of Edinburgh District Council, since 1994; b. 3.8.37, Kirkcaldy; m., Anna Cecilia; 2 s.; 1 d. Educ. George Heriot's School, Edinburgh; Edinburgh University. Edinburgh Corporation: Head of Conveyancing and Contracts, 1971; Senior Depute Director of Administration, 1974; Director of Administration, 1980. Recreation: gardening. Address: City Chambers, High Street, Edinburgh; T.-0131-529 4252.

Boddy, Francis Andrew, MB, ChB, FRCPEdin, FFPHM, DPH. Director, Public Health Research Unit (formerly Social Paediatric and Obstetric Research Unit), Glasgow University, since 1978; b. 1.3.35, York; m., Adele Wirszubska; 2 d. Educ. Prince Henry's Grammar School, Otley; Edinburgh University. Research Associate, New York City Department of Health; Senior Lecturer, Department of Community Medicine, Glasgow University. Honorary Secretary, Society for Social Medicine, 1982-87; Chairman, 1996; Convener, Scottish Affairs Committee, Faculty of Public Health Medicine, 1991-94. Publications on socio-medical and public health topics. Recreations: fishing; photography. Address: (b.) 1 Lilybank Gardens, Glasgow, G12; T.-0141-339 3118.

Boe, Norman W., LLB (Hons). Deputy Solicitor to Secretary of State for Scotland, since 1987; b. 30.8.43, Glasgow; m., Margaret; 1 s.; 1 d. Educ. George Heriot's School, Edinburgh; Edinburgh University. Legal apprenticeship, Lindsays WS, 1965-67; Legal Assistant, Menzies & White, WS, 1967-70; Office of Solicitor, Scottish Office: Legal Assistant, 1970, Senior Legal Assistant, Divisional Solicitor. Recreations: golf; dog-walking; holidaying. Address: (b.) New St. Andrew's House, Edinburgh; T.-0131-244 4884.

Bogie, David Wilson, MA, LLB, FSAScot. Sheriff of Grampian, Highland and Islands at Aberdeen and Stonehaven, since 1985; b. 17.7.46, Dundee. Educ. George Watson's College; Grenoble University; Edinburgh University; Balliol College, Oxford. Admitted Member, Faculty of Advocates, 1972; Temporary Sheriff, 1981. Address: (b.) Sheriff's Chambers, Aberdeen; T.-01224 648316.

Bold, Alan. Writer; b. 20.4.43, Edinburgh; m., Alice Howell; 1 d. Educ. Broughton Secondary School; Edinburgh University. Full-time writer and visual artist since 1966; has published numerous books of poetry including: To Find the New; The State of the Nation; a selection in Penguin Modern Poets 15; In This Corner: Selected Poems 1963-83; collaborated on A Celtic Quintet, Haven and Homage to MacDiarmid; Editor, numerous anthologies, including: The Penguin Book of Socialist Verse; The Martial Muse; Cambridge Book of English Verse 1939-75; Making Love; The Bawdy Beautiful; Mounts of Venus; Drink To Me Only; The Poetry of Motion; books of criticism including: Thom Gunn & Ted Hughes; George Mackay Brown; The Ballad; Modern Scottish Literature; MacDiarmid: The Terrible Crystal; Muriel Spark; MacDiarmid: A Critical Biography (McVitie's Prize for Scottish Writer of the Year, 1989); Scotland: A Literary Guide; A Burns Companion; Editor: The Thistle Rises: a MacDiarmid Miscellany; The Letters of Hugh MacDiarmid; Rhymer Rab; author of novel, East Is West; has exhibited illuminated poems and oil paintings in a variety of venues; regular reviewer with Glasgow Herald and contributor to Sunday Times; Royal Philosophical Society of Glasgow annual arts award, 1990; Hon. President, Auchinleck Boswell Society, 1992. Recreations:

walking; playing alto saxophone; watching films; gardening. Address: (h.) Balbirnie Burns East Cottage, near Markinch, Glenrothes, Fife, KY7 6NE; T.-01592 757216.

Bolland, Alexander, QC (Scot),. BD, LLB; b. 21.11.50, Kilmarnock; m., Agnes Hunter Pate Moffat; 1 s.; 2 d. Educ. Kilmarnock Academy; St. Andrews University; Glasgow University. Admitted Faculty of Advocates, 1978; Captain, Army Legal Services, 1978-80; Standing Junior Counsel to Department of Employment in Scotland, 1988-92; QC (Scot), since 1992; Temporary Sheriff, since 1988; part-time Chairman, Industrial Tribunals, since 1992. Recreations: Hellenistics; walking; reading. Address: (h.) 60 North Street, St. Andrews, Fife; T.-01334 474599.

Bomont, Robert George, BSc (Econ), IPFA, JP. University Secretary, Stirling University, since 1973; b. 6.5.35, Preston; m., Marian; 1 s.; 2 d. Educ. Preston Grammar School; London University. Trainee and qualified accountant, Lancashire County Council, 1951-64; Assistant Finance Officer, Lancaster University, 1964-66; Accountant, then Accountant and Deputy Secretary, Stirling University, 1966-73. General Commissioner of Income Tax, since 1977; Chairman, Council of Management, Strathcarron Hospice. Recreations: golf; gardening; DIY. Address: (h.) Wester Ardoch, Feddal Road, Braco, by Dunblane, Perthshire.

Bonallack, Michael Francis, OBE. Secretary, Royal and Ancient Golf Club of St. Andrews, since 1983; b. 31.12.34. Address: (b.) St. Andrews, KY16 9JD.

Bond, Professor Sir Michael R., MD, PhD, FRCSEdin, FRCPsych, FRCPSGlas, DPM. Professor of Psychological Medicine, Glasgow University, since 1973 (Administrative Dean, Faculty of Medicine); b. 15.4.36, Balderton, Nottinghamshire; m., Jane; 1 s.; 1 d. Educ. Magnus Grammar School, Newark; Sheffield University. Vice-Principal, Glasgow University; Member, Scottish Higher Education Funding Council; Chairman, UK Medical Advisory Committee to Funding Councils; Member, SHHD Chief Scientist Committee; Fellow, Royal Society of Arts. Recreations: reading; music; painting. Address: (b.) Academic Centre, Gartnavel Royal Hospital, 1055 Great Western Road, Glasgow, G12 0XH.

Bone, (James) Drummond, MA. Dean, Faculty of Arts, Glasgow University, since 1992; b. 11.7.47, Ayr; m., Vivian. Educ. Ayr Academy; Glasgow University; Balliol College, Oxford. Lecturer in English and Comparative Literary Studies, Warwick University; Lecturer and Senior Lecturer, English Literature, Glasgow University. Academic Editor and Advisory Editor, The Byron Journal; Editor, Romanticism. Recreations: music; skiing. Address: (h.) The Old Manse, Bow of Fife, Cupar, Fife.

Bone, Professor Thomas R., CBE, MA, MEd, PhD, FCCEA. Professor and Deputy Principal, Strathclyde University, since 1993 (Principal, Jordanhill College, 1972-92); b. 2.1.35, Port Glasgow; m., Elizabeth Stewart; 1 s.; 1 d. Educ. Port Glasgow High School; Greenock High School; Glasgow University; Jordanhill College. Teacher of English, Paisley Grammar School, 1957-62; Lecturer in Education, Jordanhill College, 1962-63; Lecturer in Education, Glasgow University, 1963-67; Head of Education Department, Jordanhill College, 1967-71. Member, Dunning Committee, 1975-77; Chairman, Educational Advisory Council, IBA, 1985-88; Vice-Chairman: Scottish Examination Board, 1977-84; Scottish Tertiary Education Advisory Council, 1984-87; Chairman: Scottish Council for Educational Technology, 1981-87; Standing Conference on Studies in Education, 1982-84; Council for National Academic Awards Board for Organisation and Management, 1983-87; Chairman, Council for National Academic Awards Committee for Teacher Education, 1987-89; Chairman, General Teaching

Council for Scotland, 1990-91. Publication: School Inspection in Scotland, 1968. Recreation: golf. Address: (b.) Strathclyde University, Richmond Street, Glasgow, G1 1XQ; T.-0141-552 4400.

Bonnar, Anne Elizabeth, MA. Director, Bonnar Keenlyside; Arts Management Consultant; b. 9.10.55, St. Andrews; m., Fernley Thompson; 2 s.; 2 d. Educ. Dumbarton Academy; Glasgow University; City University, London; Jordanhill College of Education. Theatre Manager, Young Vic Theatre, London, 1980; Director, Circuit, 1982, 1983; Press and Publicity, Mayfest, 1984, 1985; Publicity Officer, Citizens' Theatre, Glasgow, 1981-85; Arts Public Relations Consultant, 1985-86; General Manager, Traverse Theatre, 1986-91. Address: (h.) The Grange, Burntisland, Fife KY3 0AA; T.-01592 874478.

Bonnar, David James. Director (National Lottery), Scottish Arts Council, since 1994; b. 20.10.50, Dunfermline; m., Sally Elizabeth Armour; 2 s. Educ. Dunfermline High School. Royal Bank of Scotland, 1968-73; Theatre Royal, Glasgow, 1975-80; Theatre Royal, Newcastle upon Tyne, 1980-84; General Manager, Perth Repertory Theatre, 1984-94. Recreations: singing; gardening; opera; architecture. Address: (b.) Scottish Arts Council, 12 Manor Place, Edinburgh; T.-0131-226 6051.

Bonnar, Desmond Michael, PhD, MBA, DipTP. Chief Executive, Lothian and Edinburgh Enterprise Ltd, since 1991; b. 26.7.47, Wishaw; m.. Maureen; 1 s.; 1 d. Educ. Reading University; Glasgow University; Glasgow School of Art. Scottish Development Agency: Regional Director, Edinburgh/Lothians, Head, Service Industry Group, Head, Special Projects Division, Project Executive, Glasgow Eastern Area Renewal Project. Recreations: skiing; windsurfing. Address: (b.) Apex House, 99 Haymarket Terrace, Edinburgh, EH12 5HD; T.-0131-313 4000.

Bonner, Geoff, BSc. Chief Executive, Stirling District Council, since 1990; b. 13.1.54, Luton. Educ. Luton Grammar School; Luton VI Form College; University of Aston in Birmingham; City of Birmingham Polytechnic. Planning Assistant, Luton Borough Council, 1975-79; Principal Planning Assistant, West Midlands County Council, 1979-85; Assistant Executive, West Midlands County Council, 1985-86; Assistant Chief Executive, Highland Regional Council, 1986-90. Member, SOLACE "Think Tank", since 1992; Member, SOLACE Scottish Branch Executive Committee, since 1993. Recreation: dabbling. Address: (b.) Municipal Buildings, Corn Exchange Road, Stirling; T.-01786 432000.

Bonomy, John, MA, LLB. Chief Executive and Director of Administration, Motherwell District Council, since 1983; b. 25.4.38, Motherwell; m., Isabella Margaret; 3 s. Educ. Dalziel High School, Motherwell; Glasgow University. Depute Town Clerk: Arbroath, 1966; Motherwell and Wishaw, 1966-74; Director of Administration, Motherwell, 1974-83. Recreations: golf; reading. Address: (b.) Civic Centre, Motherwell; T.-Motherwell 266166.

Booker-Milburn, Sheriff Donald, BA, LLB. Sheriff of Grampian Highland and Islands, since 1983. Address: Sheriff Court House, The Castle, Inverness, IV2 3EG.

Borland, Marjorie Kirsteen, DA, RIBA, ARIAS, SpDip, FRTPI. Commissioner, Royal Fine Art Commission for Scotland, since 1986; b. 13.1.25, Glasgow; m., John Charles Holmes, MC; 1 s.; 1 d. Educ. Westbourne School for Girls; Glasgow School of Architecture; School of Planning, London. Planner, London CC; Partner, Jack Holmes & Partners, Architects; Principal, The Jack Holmes Planning Group; Planning Consultant. Past Convener: RIAS Environment Committee, GIA Environment Committee. Address: (h.) Drumhead, Cardross, Dunbartonshire; T.- 0138 984 1217.

Borthwick, Professor Edward Kerr, MA (Aberdeen), MA, PhD (Cantab). Professor of Greek, Edinburgh University, 1980-89; b. 9.6.25, Aberdeen; m., Betty Jean Orton; 2 s.; 1 d. Educ. Aberdeen Grammar School; Aberdeen University; Christ's College, Cambridge. Croom Robertson Fellow, Aberdeen University, 1948-51; Lecturer in Classics, Leeds University, 1951-55; Edinburgh University: Lecturer in Greek, 1955-67, Senior Lecturer, 1967-70, Reader, 1970-80. Recreations: music; tennis; golf. Address: (h.) 9 Corrennie Drive, Edinburgh, EH10 6EQ; T.-0131-447 2369.

Borthwick of that Ilk, Lord (John Henry Stuart Borthwick), TD (1943), DL, JP, NN, OL, GCLJ. 23rd Lord Borthwick; Baron of Heriotmuir, Borthwick and Locherwart; Chairman: Heriotmuir Properties Ltd., since 1965; Heriotmuir Exporters Ltd., since 1972; b. 13.9.05, Borthwick; m., Margaret Frances Cormack (deceased); 2 s. Educ. Fettes College, Edinburgh; King's College, Newcastle-upon-Tyne. Diploma in Agriculture. Formerly RATA, re-employed 1939; served NW Europe, Allied Military Government Staff (Junior Staff College, SO 2), 1944; CCG (CO 1, Lt.-Col.), 1946; Department of Agriculture for Scotland, 1948-50; farming own farms, 1950-71; National Farmers Union of Scotland: Midlothian Branch Committee, 1963; Mid and West Lothian Area Committee, 1967-73 (President, 1970-72); Council Member, 1968-72; Member: Lothians Area Committee, NFU Mutual Insurance Society, 1969-85; Chairman, Monitoring Committee, Scottish Tartans, 1976; Scottish Southern Regional Committee, Wool Marketing Board, 1966-85; Chairman, Area Committee, South of Scotland Electricity Board Consultative Council, 1972-76; Member, Midlothian County Council, 1937-50; Member: Local Appeal Tribunal (Edinburgh and the Lothians), 1963-75; Midlothian Valuation Appeal Committee, 1966; Member: Standing Council of Scottish Chiefs; The Committee of the Baronage of Scotland; Member Corresponding, Istituto Italiano di Genealogie e Araldica, Rome and Madrid, 1964; Honorary Member: Council of Scottish Clans Association, USA, 1975; Royal Military Institute of Canada, 1976; Kt of Justice and Honour, GCLJ (Grand Croix, 1975); CL (Commander of the Rose of Lippe), 1971; NN, 1982. Recreations: shooting; travel; history. Address: Crookston, Heriot, Midlothian, EH38 5YS; T.-Heriot 232.

Borthwick, Kenneth White, CBE, DL, JP, CLM; b. 4.11.15, Edinburgh; m., Irene Margaret; 2 s.; 1 d. Educ. George Heriot's School, Edinburgh. War Service, RAF; Lord Provost and Lord Lieutenant, City of Edinburgh, 1977-80; Chairman, 1986 Commonwealth Games Organizing Committee; Dean of Consular Corps of Edinburgh and Leith, since 1991; Hon. Consul, Republic of Malawi, 1982-94. Recreations: golf; gardening; painting. Address: (h.) 17 York Road, Edinburgh, EH5 3EJ; T.-0131-552 2519.

Boswell, Lorne, BA. Scottish Secretary, Equity, since 1990; b. 9.1.59, Bridge of Allan; m., Noreen; 2 s.; 1 d. Freelance theatre worker and stage manager, 1981-89. Address: (b.) 114 Union Street, Glasgow, G1 3QQ; T.-0141 248 2472.1

Bouchier, Professor Ian Arthur Dennis, CBE, MB, ChB, MD, FRCP, FRCPEdin, FFPHM, Hon. FCP, FIBiol, FRSE, FRSA. Professor of Medicine, Edinburgh University, since 1986; b. 7.9.32, Cape Town, South Africa; m., Patricia Norma Henshilwood; 2 s. Educ. Rondebosch Boys High School; Cape Town University. Instructor in Medicine, School of Medicine, Boston University, 1964; London University: Senior Lecturer in Medicine, 1965; Reader in Medicine, 1970; Professor of Medicine, Dundee University, 1973-86. Member: Court, Dundee University; Chief Scientist, Scotland; Council, Royal Society, Edinburgh; Medical Research Council; President, World Organization of Gastroenterology; former Dean, Faculty of Medicine and Dentistry, Dundee University; President-elect, British Society of Gastroenterology. Publications: Clinical Skills (2nd edition), 1982; Gastroenterology (3rd edition), 1982; Gastroenterology: clinical science and practice (2nd edition), 1993. Recreations: music; history of whaling; cooking. Address: (b.) Department of Medicine, Royal Infirmary, Edinburgh, EH3 9YW; T.-031-536 2234.

Boulton, Professor Geoffrey Stewart, FRS, FRSE, BSc, PhD, DSc, FGS. Regius Professor of Geology and Mineralogy, Edinburgh University, since 1986; Provost and Dean, Faculty of Science and Engineering, since 1994; b. 28.11.40, Stoke-on-Trent; m., Denise Bryers; 2 d. Educ. Longton High School; Birmingham University. Geological Survey of GB, 1962-64; University of Keele, 1964-65; Birmingham University, 1965-67; Water Supply Department, Kenya, 1968; University of East Anglia, 1968-81; Extraordinary Professor, University of Amsterdam, 1981-86. President, Quaternay Research Association, 1991-94; President, British Glaciological Society, 1989-91; President, Geological Society of Edinburgh, 1991-94; Member, Nature Conservancy Council for Scotland Science Board, 1991-92; Member, Natural Environmental Research Council, since 1993 (Chairman, Earth Science and Technology Board); Chairman, UK Polar Science Board; Chairman, Royal Society Sectional Committee for Earth Science and Astronomy, 1993-95; Member, Royal Commission on Environmental Pollution; Kirk Bryan Award of the Geological Society of America, 1976. Recreations: violin; mountaineering. Address: (h.) 19 Lygon Road, Edinburgh, EH16 5QD; T.-0131-667 2531.

Bourne, Greg, BSc (Hons). Director and General Manager, BP Scotland, since 1995; b. 15.11.48, Devonport; m., Di; 1 d. Educ. University of Western Australia. Joined BP Exploration as a trainee drilling engineer, Abu Dhabi; worked extensively abroad; Operations Manager, Forties Field, 1985; Adviser on Energy and Transport, seconded to Prime Minister's Office, 1988; Chief Executive, BP Marine London, 1990; President and General Manager, Exploration and Gas, BP Developments, Australia, 1992; General Manager, BP Exploration, 1994. Recreations: skiing; sailing; hill-walking; golf; opera. Address: (b.) BP Exploration, Farburn Industrial Estate, Dyce, AB2 0PB; T.-01224 832507.

Bovey, Keith S., BL. Solicitor, since 1951; President, Scottish CND; b. 31.7.27, Renfrew; m., Helen Cameron; 1 s.; 1 d. Educ. Paisley Grammar School; Glasgow University. Army, 1944-48. Publication: Misuse of Drugs, A Handbook for Lawyers. Address: (b.) 126 Morningside Road, Edinburgh EH10 4DT; T.-0131-452 8822.

Bowen, Edward Farquharson, TD, QC, LLB. Advocate; b. 1.5.45, Edinburgh; m., Patricia Margaret Brown; 2 s.; 2 d. Educ. Melville College, Edinburgh; Edinburgh University. Admitted Solicitor, 1968; Advocate, 1970; Standing Junior Counsel, Scottish Education Department, 1976; Advocate Depute, 1979-83; Sheriff of Tayside, Central and Fife, at Dundee, 1983-90; Partner, Thorntons WS, 1990-91; resumed practice at Scottish Bar; QC, 1992; Governor, Dundee Institute of Technology, 1987-90. Served RAOC TA/TAVR, 1964-80. Recreation: golf. Address: (h.) The Old Manse, Lundie, Angus.

Bowie, Graham Maitland, CBE, MA, LLB. Chief Executive, Lothian Regional Council, since 1986 (Director of Planning, 1975-86); b. 11.11.31, Alloa; m., Jennifer; 1 s.; 2 d. Educ. Alloa Academy; St. Andrews University; Glasgow University. Glasgow Chamber of Commerce, 1957-59; Ford Motor Co., 1959-64; Edinburgh Corporation Education Department, 1964-69; Inner London Education Authority, 1969-75. Recreations: music; golf; walking. Address: (b.) Lothian Regional Council, Regional Headquarters, George IV Bridge, Edinburgh, EH1 1UQ; T.-0131-469 3001.

Bowler, David P., BA, MPhil, FSA (Scot). Director, Scottish Urban Archaeological Trust, since 1993; b. 9.12.55, Southampton. Educ. McGill University, Montreal; Lincoln College, Oxford. Address: (b.) 55 South Methven Street, Perth, PH1 5NX; T.-01738 622393.

Bowling, Dudley James Francis, DSc, BSc, PhD, CBiol, MIBiol. Reader in Plant Science, Aberdeen University, since 1981; b. 20.5.37, Kingston upon Hull; m., Sheila Mary Daun. Educ. Hull Grammar School; Nottingham University; Aberdeen University. Aberdeen University: Assistant in Botany, 1961; Lecturer in Botany, 1963; Senior Lecturer in Botany, 1974; Visiting Scientist, DSIR, Palmerston North, New Zealand, 1976-77. Publication: Uptake of Ions by Plant Roots, 1976. Recreations: gardening; model railways. Address: (b.) Department of Plant and Soil Science, St. Machar Drive, Old Aberdeen, AB9 2UD; T.-Aberdeen 272693.

Bowlt, Kenneth Stuart, BSc, ARICS. Chartered Surveyor; Member, Royal Institution of Chartered Surveyors Scottish Council, since 1990; b. 7.7.52, Nairn; m., Edith Bowman. Educ. Queen Victoria School, Dunblane; Edinburgh University. Voluntary Service Overseas, Zambia, 1975-80; set up Bowlts (chartered surveyors practice), 1991. Member, Royal Institution of Chartered Surveyors in Scotland Rural Practice Divisional Committee, since 1988; Secretary/Treasurer, West Ross Deer Management Group, since 1991. Recreations: fishing; stalking; five-a-side football; keep fit. Address: (h.) Muirfield, 27 Forteath Avenue, Elgin; T.-01343 549278.

Bowman, Allan John, MA, CQSW, DMS. Director of Social Work, Fife, since 1986; b. 3.1.50, Perth; m., Marilyn Norah Cosgrove; 1 s.; 3 d. Educ. Perth Academy; Edinburgh University; Robert Gordon's Institute of Technology; Anglian Regional Management Centre. Social Worker and Senior Social Worker, Dundee Corporation, then Tayside Region, 1972-78; Senior Social Worker, Depute Area Social Work Organiser and Area Social Work Organiser, Essex County Council, 1978-84; Depute Director and Director of Social Work, Fife Regional Council, 1985. Member, Tayside Education/ Industry Liaison Committee, 1977-78; Chair, Essex BASW, 1982-84. Recreations: horse racing; guitar; theatre; swimming; cricket; golf. Address: (b.) Social Work Department, Fife House, North Street, Glenrothes, KY7 5LT; T.-01592 414141, Ext. 3883.

Bowman, (Bernard) Neil, LLB, NP. Senior Partner, Bowman Gray Robertson & Wilkie, Solicitors, Dundee and Forfar, since 1984; first Lord President, Court of Deans of Guild of Scotland, 1989; Lord Dean of Guild of Guildry Incorporation of Dundee, 1987-90; President, Scottish Cricket Union, 1989; Secretary, Dundee Institute of Architects, since 1970; Director, High School of Dundee, 1980-90; Chairman, High School of Dundee Scholarship Fund, 1987-90; Clerk, Three United Trades of Dundee and to Mason Trade, Wright Trade and Slater Trade of Dundee, since 1970; Co-opted Member, Law Society of Scotland Committees — Public Relations and Conference, 1982-90, Complaints, 1987-90; Member, Working Party on "Corporate Conveyancing", 1989; Member, School Age Team Sports Enquiry, 1989; b. 11.11.43, Dundee; m., Pamela Margaret Munro Wright; 2 d. Educ. High School of Dundee; Edinburgh University; St. Andrews University. Apprenticeship, Sturrock Morrison & Gilruth, Solicitors, Dundee, 1967-69; admitted Solicitor, 1969; Notary Public, 1970; assumed Partner, Gray Robertson & Wilkie, 1971. Secretary: Dundee Building Trades (Employers) Association, 1970-89; Dundee Construction Industry Group Training Association, 1970-93; Tayside Construction Safety Association, 1975-89; Joint Secretary, Local Joint Council for Building Industry, 1970-89, and Local Joint Apprenticeship Committee for the Building Industry, 1970-89; President, Scottish Counties Cricket Board, 1981;

Committee Member and National Selector, Scottish Cricket Union, 1974-83; Selector, 1990. Recreations: cricketophile; breeding Highland cattle. Address: (b.) 27 Bank Street, Dundee; T.-01382 322267.

Bowman, Jack W., CBE. Chief Constable, Tayside Police. Address: P.O. Box 59, West Bell Street, Dundee, DD1 9JU.

Bowman, Pamela Margaret Munro, LLB, NP. Partner, Bowman Gray Robertson & Wilkie, Solicitors, Dundee and Forfar, since 1979; Secretary, Angus Society of Solicitors, 1984-94, Vice-Dean, since 1994; Non-Executive Member, Angus NHS Trust, since 1994; Member, Scottish Legal Aid Board, since 1994; Temporary Sheriff, since 1995; b. 1.8.44, Larbert; m., (Bernard) Neil Bowman; 2 d. Educ. Stirling High School; Queens College, Dundee, St. Andrews University. Apprenticeship, Shiell & Small, Solicitors, Dundee, 1965-67; admitted Solicitor and Notary Public, 1967; Assistant, Reid Johnston Bell & Henderson, Solicitors, Dundee, 1967-69; Assistant, Gray Robertson & Wilkie, Solicitors, Dundee, from 1975 until assumed Partner, 1979; Resident Partner at Forfar since 1981. Recreations: theatre; literature; clothes. Address:(b.) 37 East High Street, Forfar; T.-01307 464088.

Bowman, Professor William Cameron, BPharm, PhD, DSc, FIBiol, FRSE, FRSA, FRPharmS, HonFFARCS. Head, Department of Physiology and Pharmacology, Strathclyde University, 1966-87 and 1990-94; b. 26.4.30; m., Anne Wyllie Stafford; 1 s.; 1 d. Educ. London University. RAF (commissioned officer), 1955-57; Lecturer, then Reader in Pharmacology, London University, 1952-66. Dean, School of Pharmaceutical Sciences, Strathclyde University, 1974-77; Vice Principal, Strathclyde University, 1986-90; Visiting Professor: McGill University, Montreal; Cornell University, New York; Ohio Medical College. Member: Nomenclature Committee, BP Commission, 1964-67; Biology Committee, MOD, 1966-75; TCT and SEAR Sub-Committees, CSM, 1972-83; Biomedical Research Committee, SHHD, 1980-85; Chairman, Committee, British Pharmacological Society, 1981-84, Foreign Secretary since 1992; Chairman of Committee, Heads of UK Pharmacology Departments, 1990-94; Member, Executive Committee, European Federation of Pharmacologists, since 1991; Secretary General, International Union of Pharmacology, 1994-98. Publications: Textbook of Pharmacology, 1968, 1980; Pharmacology of Neuromuscular Function, 1980, 1990; Dictionary of Pharmacology, 1986; many research articles in scientific journals. Address: Department of Physiology and Pharmacology, Strathclyde University, Glasgow, G1 1XW; T.-0141-552 4400.

Bown, Professor Lalage Jean, OBE, MA (Oxon), DrUniv (Open University), DUniv (Paisley), Dr h.c. (Edinburgh), DUniv (Stirling), Hon. FITD, FRSA, FEIS, FRSE. Professor and Director, Department of Adult and Continuing Education, Glasgow University, 1981-92; Hon. Professor, Warwick University, since 1992; Distinguished Visitor, Curtin University, Perth, Australia, 1995; b. 1.4.27, Croydon. Educ. Wycombe Abbey School, Buckinghamshire; Cheltenham Ladies' College; Somerville College, Oxford. Resident Tutor: University College of the Gold Coast, 1949-55; Makerere University College, Uganda, 1955-59; successively Tutorial Advisor, Assistant Director, Deputy Director, Extra-Mural Department, Ibadan University, 1960-66 (Associate Professor, 1962-66); Director of Extra-Mural Studies and Professor Ad Personam, University of Zambia, 1966-70; Professor of Adult Education, Ahmadu Bello University, Nigeria, 1971-76; Commonwealth Visiting Professor, Edinburgh University, 1974; successively Professor of Adult Education and Dean of Education, Lagos University, 1977-80. Former Chairman, Scottish Community Education Council; Member: Board of Trustees, National Museums of Scotland; Council, INSITE Trust; former Board Member,

The British Council; former Member, Governing Body, Institute of Development Studies; Member, Commonwealth Standing Committee on Student Mobility and Higher Education Co-operation; Past President, British Comparative and International Education Society; Past President, Development Studies Association; Vice-President, National Union of Townswomen's Guilds; former Vice-President, WEA; Trustee, Womankind Worldwide; Vice-Chair, CODE Europe; Chair, Scottish Museums Council. Publications: 10 academic books. Recreation: travel. Address: (h.) 37 Partickhill Road, Glasgow G11 5BP; T.-0141-339 1714.

Bownes, Professor Mary, BSc, DPhil. Personal Chair of Developmental Biology, Edinburgh University, since 1994; b. 14.11.48, Drewsteignton; m., Michael J. Greaves; 1 d. Educ. Maldon Grammar School; Sussex University. Lecturer, Essex University; Lecturer, Senior Lecturer, Reader, Edinburgh University. Publications: 100 research articles and reviews. Address: (b.) Institute of Cell and Molecular Biology, Edinburgh University, Darwin Building, Mayfield Road, Edinburgh, EH9 3JR; T.-0131-650 5369.

Bowser of Argaty and the King's Lundies, David Stewart, JP, BA (Agric). Trustee, Scottish Forestry Trust, 1983-89 (Chairman, 1987); Member, Queen's Bodyguard for Scotland (Royal Company of Archers); Chairman, Scottish Council, British Deer Society, 1988-94; b. 11.3.26; m.; 1 s.; 4 d. Educ. Harrow; Trinity College, Cambridge. Captain, Scots Guards, 1944-47; Forestry Commissioner, 1974-82; President, Highland Cattle Society, 1970-72; Member, Perth County Council, 1954-61. Address: Auchlyne, Killin, Perthshire FK21 8RG.

Boxer, Professor David Howell, BSc, PhD. Professor of Biochemistry, Dundee University, since 1991, Head, Biochemistry Department, since 1988, Dean, Science and Engineering Faculty, since 1994; m., Dr. Maureen Boxer; 1 s.; 2 d. Educ. Aberdare Boys' Grammar School; Bristol University. Dundee University: Lecturer in Biochemistry, 1976, Senior Lecturer, 1985. Nuffield Research Fellow, 1983-84; Chairman, Biochemistry Biophysics Sub-Comittee, SERC, 1990-92. Recreations: travelling; skiing. Address: (b.) Department of Biochemistry, Medical Sciences Institute, Dundee University, Dundee, DD1 4HN; T.-01382 344834.

Boyd, Rev. A.C., MA, BD. Principal, Free Church College. Ordained, 1959. Address: (b.) The Mound, Edinburgh, EH1 2LS.

Boyd, Alan Robb, LLB, BA, SSC, NP. Legal Adviser, Irvine Development Corporation, since 1984; b. 30.7.53, Glasgow; m., Frances Helen Donaldson; 2 d. Educ. Irvine Royal Academy; Dundee University. Admitted Solicitor, 1976; Principal Legal Assistant, Shetland Islands Council, 1979-81; Principal Solicitor, Glenrothes Development Corporation, 1981-84. Council Member, Law Society of Scotland, since 1985 (Chairman, Public Service and Commerce Group, 1986-88, Convenor, Law Reform Committee, 1989-92, Convenor, Finance Committee, since 1992, Vice-President of the Society, 1994-95); President, European Company Lawyers' Association, 1992-94. Recreations: golf; music; gardening. Address: (b.) Perceton House, Irvine, Ayrshire, KA11 2AL; T.-01294 214100.

Boyd, Ian Mair, MSc, CA. Group Finance Director, The Weir Group PLC, since 1981; Director, Glasgow Income Trust plc, since 1990; Director, Inveresk PLC, since 1993; b. 4.9.44, Ayr; m., Theodora; 2 s.; 1 d. Educ. Ayr Academy; London Business School. The Weir Group PLC: Financial Controller International Division, 1975-78, Group Chief Accountant, 1978-81. Council Member, Institute of Chartered Accountants of Scotland, 1987-93; Chairman, Group of Scottish Finance Directors, 1990-91. Recreations:

golf; hill-walking; fishing. Address: (b.) The Weir Group PLC, Cathcart, Glasgow, G44 4EX; T.-0141-637 7111.

Boyd, James Edward, CA. Director and Financial Adviser, Denholm group of companies, since 1968; b. 14.9.28; m., Judy Ann Christey Scott; 2 s.; 2 d. Educ. Kelvinside Academy; The Leys School, Cambridge. President, Institute of Chartered Accountants of Scotland, 1982-83. Recreations: tennis; golf; gardening. Address: (h.) Dunard, Station Road, Rhu, G84 8LW; T.-01436 820441.

Boyd, John MacInnes, CBE, QPM. H.M. Chief Inspector of Constabulary for Scotland, since 1993; b. 14.10.33, Oban; m., Sheila MacSporran; 2 s. Educ. Oban High School. Paisley Burgh Police, 1956-67; Renfrew and Bute Constabulary, 1967-75; Strathclyde Police, 1975-84, Assistant Chief Constable, 1979-84; Chief Constable, Dumfries and Galloway, 1984-89; H.M. Inspector of Constabulary for Scotland, 1989-93. Recreations: golf; gardening; reading. Address: (b.) 2 Greenside Lane, Edinburgh, EH1 3AH; T.-0131-244 5614.

Boyd, John Morton, CBE, BSc, PhD, DSc, DLitt, FIBiol, CBiol, FRSE, FRSA, HonFRSGS, HonFRZSS. Consultant to Scottish Hydro-Electric plc, since 1985; Consultant to Forestry Commission, since 1985 (Honorary since 1992); Consultant to National Trust for Scotland, since 1985; b. 31.1.25, Darvel; m., Winifred Isobel Rome; 4 s. Educ. Darvel School; Kilmarnock Academy; Glasgow University. War service, 1943-47 (Flt. Lt., RAF). Nature Conservancy Council: Regional Officer, 1957-68, Assistant Director, 1969-70, Director (Scotland), 1971-85; Nuffield Travel Fellow, Mid-East and East Africa, 1964-65; Leader, British Jordan Expedition, 1966; Member, Royal Society Aldabra Expedition, 1967; Member, Council, Royal Zoological Society of Scotland, 1963-69, 1980-89, since 1990; Member, BBC Scotland Agricultural Advisory Committee, 1973-76; Member, Council, National Trust for Scotland, 1971-85; Member, Council, Royal Society of Edinburgh, 1978-81; Member, Seals Advisory Committee, NERC, 1973-79; Member, Consultative Panel on Conservation of Phoenix and Line Islands (Central Pacific), 1981-90; Co-Chairman, Area VI Anglo-Soviet Environmental Protection Agreement, 1977-85; Member, Council, Scottish Wildlife Trust, 1985-91; Vice-President, Scottish Conservation Projects Trust, since 1985; Member, Commission on Ecology, IUCN, 1976-92; Member, CCS Panel on Popular Mountain Areas, 1989; Member, Advisory Committee on Sites of Special Scientific Interest, SNH, since 1992; General Editor (Island Biology), Edinburgh University Press, 1985-92; Consultant Editor, Discover Scotland, 1989-90; Lecturer, Glasgow University (Honorary), Swan (Hellenic) Ltd., Serenissima Travel Ltd., Noble Caledonia Ltd.; Neill Prize, Royal Society of Edinburgh, 1985. Publications: St. Kilda Summer (Co-author), 1960; Mosaic of Islands, 1963; Highlands and Islands (Co-author), 1964; Travels in the Middle-East and East Africa, 1966; Island Survivors (Co-editor), 1974; The Natural Environment of the Hebrides (Co-editor), 1979 and 1983; Fraser Darling's Islands, 1986; The Hebrides — a natural history (Co-author), 1990; Fraser Darling in Africa, 1992. Recreations: hill-walking; travel; painting; photography. Address: (h.) 57 Hailes Gardens, Edinburgh, EH13 OJH; T.-0131-441 3220; Balephuil, Tiree, Argyll; T.-018792 521.

Boyd, Michael, MA (Hons). Artistic Director, Tron Theatre, Glasgow, since 1984; b. 6.7.55, Belfast; 1 s.; 1 d. Educ. Latymer Upper School, London; Daniel Stewart's College, Edinburgh; Edinburgh University. Director, Malaya Bronnaya Theatre, Moscow; Belgrade Theatre, Coventry; Crucible Theatre, Sheffield; freelance work, Royal Shakespeare Company, Royal National Theatre, Lyric Hammersmith, Haymarket Leicester, Royal Court, Traverse (Edinburgh), Cambridge Theatre Co., Harbourfront (Toronto), Stoney Brook (New York), Centaur (Montreal). Recreations:reading; music; travel.

Address: (b.) Tron Theatre, Trongate, Glasgow; T.-0141-552 3748.

Boyd, William Dalziel, MB, ChB, FRCPEdin, FRCPsych, DPM; b. 9.11.30, Cupar, Fife; m., Betty Ledingham Gordon; 3 s.; 1 d. Educ. Trinity College, Glenalmond; Edinburgh University. National Service, Royal Army Medical Corps; training posts at Rosslynlee Hospital, Midlothian; Edinburgh Royal Infirmary; Royal Edinburgh Hospital; Consultant Psychiatrist: Herdmanflat Hospital, Haddington; Royal Edinburgh Hospital; Physician Superintendent, Royal Edinburgh Hospital; Consultant Psychiatrist, Lothian Health Board (retired); former Vice-Chairman and Medical Commissioner, Mental Welfare Commission for Scotland; former Chairman, Age Concern Scotland. Recreation: improving old houses and old gardens. Address: (h.) 49/12 Belford Road, Edinburgh, EH4 3BR; T.-0131-226 5465.

Boyes, John, MA (Hons). HM Chief Inspector of Schools; b. 20.5.43, Greenock; m., Margaret Anne Peat; 1 s.; 1 d. Educ. Greenock High School; Glasgow University. Taught French and German, Alloa Academy and Denny High School, 1967-74. Recreation: mixing metaphors. Address: (b.) Scottish Office Education Department, New St. Andrew's House, Edinburgh; T.-0131-244 5136.

Boyle, Professor Alan Edward, MA, BCL, Barrister. Professor of International Law, Edinburgh University, since 1994; Barrister, Gray's Inn, since 1994; b. 28.3.53, Belfast; m., Caroline Patricia. Educ. Royal Belfast Academical Institution; Pembroke College, Oxford University. Lecturer, Senior Lecturer, Reader, Queen Mary and Westfield College, London University, 1978-94; Visiting Professor, College of William and Mary, VA, 1987; Visiting Professor, University of Texas, 1988, 1994. Publication: International Law and the Environment (Co-author), 1992. Recreations: gliding; walking; reading. Address: (b.) Faculty of Law, Edinburgh University, Old College, South Bridge, Edinburgh, EH8 9YL; T.-0131-650 2019.

Boyle, Rt. Rev. Mgr. Hugh Noonan, PhL, STL. Canon, Chapter of Metropolitan Cathedral Church of St. Andrew, Glasgow, since 1984; Chapter Secretary, since 1991; Prelate of Honour, since 1987; Archivist, Archdiocese of Glasgow, since 1973; b. 14.1.35, Glasgow. Educ. St. Aloysius' College, Glasgow; Glasgow University; Pontifical Scots College and Pontifical Gregorian University, Rome, 1956-63. National Service, RAF, 1954-56; ordained priest, Rome, 1962; Assistant Priest: St. Philomena's, Glasgow, 1963-66, St. Eunan's, Clydebank, 1966-76; Administrator, Metropolitan Cathedral Church of St. Andrew, Glasgow, 1983-92; Parish Priest, St. Leo's, Dumbreck, 1992-93; Archdiocese of Glasgow: Assistant Archivist, 1967-73; Chancellor, 1976-83. Editor, Catholic Directory for Scotland and Western Catholic Calendar, since issues of 1975; Member: Scottish Catholic Communications Commission, 1979-87; Scottish Catholic Heritage Commission, since 1981; Patron, Hutchesons' Hospital, since 1983. Recreations: music (listening); walking. Address: 1 Kelvinside Gardens, Glasgow, G20 6BG; T.-0141-946 0620.

Boyle, Iain Thomson, BSc (Hons), MB, ChB, FRCP, FRCP (London and Glasgow), FSA (Scot). Reader in Medicine, Glasgow University and Glasgow Royal Infirmary, since 1984; Medical Advisor, Strathclyde University, since 1991; Chairman, Board of Management, Scottish Medical Journal, since 1987; President, Bone and Tooth Society, since 1994; Vice President, Royal College of Physicians and Surgeons of Glasgow, since 1992, and Hon. Librarian, since 1994; b. 7.10.35, Glasgow; m., Elizabeth Johnston Carmichael; 1 s.; 2 d. Educ. Paisley Grammar School; Glasgow University. Lecturer in Medicine, Glasgow University and Glasgow Royal Infirmary, 1964-70; Hartenstein Research Fellow, Wisconsin University,

1970-72; Senior Lecturer in Medicine, Glasgow University and Glasgow Royal Infirmary, 1973-84. Editor, Scottish Medical Journal, 1978-83; Co-Editor, Bone, since 1983; Council Member, Royal College of Physicians and Surgeons, 1984-88; Secretary: Scottish Society for Experimental Medicine, 1984-88; Scottish Society of Physicians, 1984-88; President, Caledonian Philatelic Society, 1983-84; President, Association of Scottish Philatelic Societies, 1995-96; President, Harveian Society of Edinburgh, 1991; Fletcher Prize, Royal College of Physicians and Surgeons of Glasgow, 1973. Recreations: philately; Scottish social history; angling; gardening; golf. Address: (h.) 7 Lochbrae Drive, High Burnside, Rutherglen, Glasgow, G73 5QL.

Boyle, John Stirling, MA, DPA, FRSA. Director, Corporate Affairs (Scotland), ScotRail, since 1994; b. 17.9.39, Paisley; m., Helen Dickson; 2 s.; 1 d. Educ. Camphill School, Paisley; Glasgow University. School Teacher, 1960-61; Reporter, Sunday Post, 1961-62; Technical Writer, Harland Engineering Company, 1962-64; Health Education Officer, Stirling County, 1964-66; Public Relations Officer, Heriot-Watt University, 1966-73; Director, External Relations, Scottish Council (Development and Industry), 1973-83; Director of Public Affairs (Scotland), British Rail, 1983-92; Director, Corporate Affairs (Scotland), British Railways Board, 1992-94. Recreations: motor cycling; music; Munros. Address (b.) Caledonian Chambers, 87 Union Street, Glasgow, G1 3ET; T.-041-335 4447.

Boyle, Sandy, DGA. Deputy General Secretary (Scotland), BIFU, since 1992; Member, STUC General Council, since 1992; b. 23.12.45, Falkirk; m., Elizabeth Ross Cockrill; 1 s.; 1 d. Educ. Falkirk High School. Civil Servant, 1964-92. Vice-President, Society of Civil and Public Servants; Deputy President, National Union of Civil and Public Servants (President, NUCPS, 1989-92). Recreations: trade union badge collector; music; reading; bridge; watching Falkirk F.C. Address: (b.) 146 Argyle Street, Glasgow, G2 8BL; T.-0141-221 6475.

Bradley, Rev. Dr. Ian Campbell, MA, BD, DPhil. Writer and Broadcaster; Lecturer, Department of Divinity, Aberdeen University; b. 28.5.50, Berkhamsted; m., Lucy Patricia; 1 s.; 1 d. Educ. Tonbridge School, Kent; New College, Oxford; St. Andrews University. Research Fellow, New College, Oxford, 1971-75; Staff Journalist, The Times, 1976-82; ordained into Church of Scotland, 1990; Head, Religious Broadcasting, BBC Scotland, 1990-91. Publications: The Call to Seriousness, 1974; William Morris and his World, 1975; The Optimists, 1976; The Penguin Annotated Gilbert & Sullivan, 1980; The Strange Rebirth of Liberal Britain, 1982; Enlightened Entrepreneurs, 1986; The Penguin Book of Hymns, 1989; God is Green, 1990; O Love That Wilt Not Let Me Go, 1990; Marching to the Promised Land, 1992; The Celtic Way, 1993; The Power of Sacrifice, 1995. Recreations: music; walking; family; spas. Address: (h.) 7 Strathkinness High Road, St. Andrews KY16 9UA; T.-01334 475389.

Bradley, Professor Roy, BSc, MSc, PhD, FIMA, CMath. Head, Department of Mathematics, Glasgow Caledonian University, since 1992; b. 23.9.40, Wolverhampton; m., Ann; 1 s.; 1 d. Educ. Wolverhampton Grammar School; Durham University. Performance Engineer, 1963-65; Lecturer/Senior Lecturer/Principal Lecturer, Department of Mathematics and Statistics, Newcastle upon Tyne Polytechnic, 1965-86; Lecturer/Senior Lecturer, Department of Aerospace Engineering, Glasgow University, 1986-92. Recreation: mountaineering. Address: (b.) Department of Mathematics, Glasgow Caledonian University, Glasgow, G4 0BA; T.-0141-331 3610.

Brady, Paul A., BSc (Hons), PhD. Director Finance and Planning, Scottish Enterprise; b. 28.7.49, Glasgow; 2 s.; 1 d.

Educ. St. Mungo's Academy, Glasgow. Joined Scottish Office, 1974; posts in Industry, Police, and Energy areas, 1974-88; headed team advising on electricity privatisation, 1988-90; led on Higher Education reforms, 1991-92; Director of Policy, Scottish Higher Education Funding Council, 1991-92; Head, Finance Division (industry, transport and agriculture), Scottish Office, 1992-93. Recreations: walking; music; family. Address: (b.) Scottish Enterprise, 120 Bothwell Street, Glasgow, G2 7JP; T.-0141 248 2700.

Brady, Tom. Chief Executive, National Farmers Union of Scotland. Address: (b.) Rural Centre – West Mains, Ingliston, Newbridge, EH28 8LT.

Braidwood, Adam, BA (Hons), MBIM, FIPM. Director of Manpower, Highland Regional Council, since 1986; b. 28.3.44, Motherwell; m., Myra; 1 s.; 1 d. Educ. Dalziel High School; Strathclyde University; Glasgow University. Lanarkshire Education Authority; British Steel; Hoggett Bowers Consultants; Lothian Regional Council; Highland Regional Council. Recreations: angling; music. Address: (h.) 17 Trentham Court, Westhill, Inverness; T.-01463 791615.

Braithwaite, Robert Barclay, BSc, CEng, FICE, MASCE. General Manager, Aberdeen Harbour Board, since 1990 (Assistant, then Deputy General Manager and Harbour Engineer, 1986-89); b. 17.2.48, Glasgow; m., Christine Isobel Ross; 2 s. Educ. Hutchesons' Boys' Grammar School; Strathclyde University. Graduate/Assistant Engineer, Rendel Palmer & Tritton, Consulting Civil Engineers, London, 1969-74; Deputy Harbour Engineer, 1974-75, Harbour Engineer, 1976-86, Aberdeen Harbour Board. Chairman, Aberdeen Maritime Museum Appeal; Council Member, Aberdeen Chamber of Commerce; Council Member, British Ports Association. Recreations: hill-walking; badminton; reading. Address: (b.) Harbour Office, 16 Regent Quay, Aberdeen, AB9 1SS; T.-01224 592571.

Brand, David Allan, LLB (Hons), WS, NP. Solicitor; Partner, Thorntons WS, Dundee and Perth; b. 4.3.50, Dundee; 1 d. Educ. Grove Academy, Broughty Ferry; Dundee University. Former Member of Council, Law Society of Scotland; Dean, Faculty of Procurators and Solicitors in Dundee; Reporter to Scottish Legal Aid Board; former Member, Council, NHBC Scotland; Past Chairman: Solicitors Property Centres Group Scotland, Tayside Solicitors Property Centre, Social Security Tribunals. Recreations: all types of music; amateur operatics; theatre. Address: (b.) Whitehall Chambers, 11 Whitehall Street, Dundee, DD1 4AE; T.-01382 29111.

Brand, Hon. Lord (David William Robert Brand). Senator of the College of Justice in Scotland, 1972-89; b. 21.10.23.

Brand, Janet Mary Valentine, BA (Hons), DipTP, MRTPI. Senior Lecturer, Strathclyde University, since 1973 (Member of Senate, 1984-91 and since 1992; Member of Court, 1989-91; Convener, Programme of Opportunities for Women Committee, 1990-93); b. 19.4.44, Bath; 2 d. Educ. County High School for Girls, Brentwood; Exeter University. Local authority appointments in Departments of Planning, Essex County Council, London Borough of Barking and City of London, 1965-70; Senior Lecturer, Department of Planning, South Bank Polytechnic, 1970-73. Convener, Education Committee, Scottish Branch, RTPI, 1983-88). Recreations: the environment; gardening; family pursuits; travelling. Address: (b.) Centre for Planning, Strathclyde University, 50 Richmond Street, Glasgow; T.-0141-552 4400, Ext. 3905/6.

Brand, John Arthur. Reader in Government, formerly Politics, Strathclyde University; b. 4.8.34, Aberdeen; 1 d.

Educ. Aberdeen Grammar School; Aberdeen University; London School of Economics. Assistant in Politics, Glasgow University, 1959-61; Lecturer in Politics, Reading University, 1961-63; Lecturer in the Politics of Education, London University, 1963-64; joined Strathclyde University as Lecturer in Politics, 1964. Chairman: Campaign for a Scottish Assembly, 1979-83; Glasgow Community Relations Committee, 1968-71. Recreations: skiing; tennis; music. Address: (h.) 17 Kew Terrace, Glasgow, G12 OTE; T.-0141-339 1675.

Brannan, Micheline H., MA. Head, Civil Law Division, Scottish Office Home and Health Department, since 1995; b. 23.10.54, Glasgow; m., Michael N. Brannan; 2 s. Educ. Hutchesons' Grammar School; St. Hilda's College, Oxford. Scottish Office: joined as administrative trainee, 1976, promoted to Principal, 1982, Industry Department for Scotland, 1982-84, Scottish Education Department, 1985-88, Home and Health Department Criminal Justice Group, 1989-95. Recreations: Scottish country dancing; cycling; Jewish cultural activities. Address: (b.) Room 225, St. Andrews House, Edinburgh; T.-0131-244 2258.

Branscombe, Professor Peter John, MA (Oxon), PhD. Professor of Austrian Studies, St. Andrews University, since 1979; b. 7.12.29, Sittingbourne, Kent; m., Marina Riley; 2 s.; 1 d. Educ. Dulwich College; Worcester College, Oxford; Bedford College, London. Joined St. Andrews University, 1959, as Lecturer, then Senior Lecturer, in German. Governor, Royal Scottish Academy of Music and Drama, 1967-73; served on Awarding Panel for Schlegel-Tieck Prize, 1971-79 (Convener, 1974-77); Member: Music Committee, Scottish Arts Council, 1973-80; Scottish Arts Council, 1976-79; Chairman, SAC Working Party investigating the record industry in Scotland, 1976-77; Chairman, Conference of University Teachers of German in Scotland, 1983-85. Publications: Heine: Selected Verse, 1967 (2nd edition, 1986); Austrian Life and Literature 1780-1938:eight essays (Editor), 1978; Schubert Studies (Editor), 1982; Mozart: Die Zauberfloete, 1991. Recreations: natural history; walking; music; theatre. Address: (b.) 32 North Street, St. Andrews, KY16 9AQ; T.-01334 473367.

Brant, Douglas, IPFA, IRRV, MIMgt. Director of Finance, Strathkelvin District Council, since 1974; b. 27.6.42, Motherwell; m., Valerie Margaret; 1 s.; 1 d. Educ. Dalziel High School, Motherwell; Scottish College of Commerce. Trainee and Accountancy Assistant, Burgh of Motherwell and Wishaw, 1959-64; Burgh of Bishopbriggs: Assistant and Depute Town Chamberlain, 1964-68, Town Chamberlain, 1968-75. Past Chairman, Scottish Branch, CIPFA. Recreations: golf; curling. Address: (b.) PO Box 4, Tom Johnston House, Civic Way, Kirkintilloch, G66 4TJ.

Bray, Jeremy William, PhD. MP (Labour), Motherwell South, since 1983; Opposition Spokesman on Science and Technology, since 1983; b. 29.6.30, Hong Kong; m., Elizabeth Trowell; 4 d. Educ. Aberystwyth Grammar School; Kingswood School, Bath; Jesus College, Cambridge; Harvard University. Technical Officer, Wilton works, ICI, 1956-62; MP, Middlesbrough West, 1962-70; Member, Select Committee on Nationalised Industries, 1962-64; Chairman, Labour Science and Technology Group, 1964-66; Member, Economic Affairs Estimates Sub-Committee, 1964-66; Parliamentary Secretary, Ministry of Power, 1966-67; Joint Parliamentary Secretary, Ministry of Technology, 1967-69; Director, Mullard Ltd., 1970-73; Chairman, Fabian Society, 1971-72; Co-Director, Programme of Research into Econometric Methods, Imperial College, 1971-74; Consultant, Battelle Research Centre, Geneva, 1973; Senior Research Fellow, Strathclyde University, 1974, and Visiting Professor, 1974-79; Deputy Chairman, Christian Aid, 1972-83; MP, Motherwell and Wishaw, 1979-83; Member, Treasury and Civil Service Select Committee, 1979-83; Chairman, Sub-Committee,

Treasury and Civil Service Select Committee, 1981-82; Visiting Research Fellow, Imperial College, London, since 1989; Vice-Chairman, British-Chinese Parliamentary Group, since 1987; Vice-President, Parliamentary & Scientific Committee, since 1992; Vice Chairman, Parliamentary Group for Engineering Development, 1992-95; Chairman, All-Party Parliamentary Mental Health Group, since 1995. 1 Publications: Decision in Government, 1970; Production Purpose and Structure, 1982. Recreation: sailing. Address: (b.) House of Commons, London, SW1A 0AA.

Breaks, Michael Lenox, BA, DipLib. University Librarian, Heriot-Watt University, since 1985; b. 12.1.45, Plymouth; m., Barbara Lawson; 1 s.; 1 d. Educ. St. George's College, Weybridge; Leeds University. Assistant Librarian: University College, Swansea, York University; Social Sciences Librarian, University College, Cardiff, 1977-81; Deputy Librarian, University College, Dublin, 1981-85. Chairman, JANET National User Group, 1991-93; Non-Executive Director, UKERNA; Member, SCONUL Executive Board; Editor, New Review of Information Networking. Recreations: gardening; horse-riding; walking. Address: (h.) 15 Corrennie Gardens, Edinburgh, EH10 6DG; T.-0131-447 7193.

Breen, James William, DPE. Deputy Chief Executive, Scottish Sports Council, since 1989; b. 1.7.53, Lennoxtown; m., Fiona; 2 d. Educ. Victoria Drive Secondary School, Glasgow; Jordanhill College, Glasgow. Assistant Director of Leisure Services, Motherwell District Council, 1986-89. Address: (h.) 1 Castle Grove, Kilsyth, Glasgow, G65 9NB; T.-01236 825482.

Breeze, David John, BA, PhD, FSA, PPSA Scot, FRSE, MIFA. Chief Inspector of Ancient Monuments, Scotland, since 1989; Visiting Professor, Department of Archaeology, Durham University, since 1993; b. 25.7.44, Blackpool; m., Pamela Diane Silvester; 2 s. Educ. Blackpool Grammar School; Durham University. Inspector of Ancient Monuments, Scotland, 1969-88; Principal Inspector of Ancient Monuments, Scotland, 1988-89. Member, International Committee of the Congress of Roman Frontier Studies, since 1983; Member, Hadrian's Wall Advisory Committee, since 1977; Trustee, Senhouse Roman Museum, since 1985; Council Member, Society of Antiquaries of London, 1984-86; Chairman, 1989 Hadrian' Wall Pilgrimage; Chairman, British Archaeological Awards, since 1993; President, Society of Antiquaries of Scotland, 1987-90. Publications: The Building of Hadrian's Wall, The Army of Hadrian's Wall, Hadrian's Wall, and Roman Officers and Frontiers (all Co-author); Roman Scotland: a guide to the visible remains; Roman Scotland: some recent excavations (Editor); The Romans in Scotland (Co-author); The Northern Frontiers of Roman Britain; Roman Forts in Britain; Studies in Scottish Antiquity (Editor); Hadrian's Wall, a souvenir guide; A Queen's Progress, an introduction to the buildings associated with Mary Queen of Scots in Scotland; The Second Augustan Legion in North Britain; Service in the Roman Army (Co-editor); Invaders of Scotland (Co-author). Recreations: reading; walking; swimming; travel. Address: (b.) Historic Scotland, 20 Brandon Street, Edinburgh, EH3 5RA; T.-0131-244 3111.

Bremner, Ian, BSc, PhD, DSc. Deputy Director, Rowett Research Institute, Aberdeen, since 1988; b. 19.2.39, Aberdeen; m., Kathleen Stewart; 3 s. Educ. Robert Gordon's College, Aberdeen; Aberdeen University. Senior Research Biochemist, Fisons Pharmaceuticals Ltd., Cheshire, 1964-65; SSO, Nutritional Biochemistry Department, Rowett Research Institute, 1967, PSO, 1974; Grade 6, Biochemistry Division, 1985. Member, Parent Committee, and Hon. Treasurer, TEMA International: international symposia on trace elements in man and animals; Underwood Memorial Lecture, 1990; Member,

Management Committee, International Society for Trace Element Research in Humans. Address: (b.) Rowett Research Institute, Greenburn Road, Bucksburn, Aberdeen, AB2 9SB; T.-01224 716602.

Breslin, John Buchan, IPFA. Finance Director, Scottish Homes; b. 16.12.51, Kirkintilloch; 3 s.; 1 d. Educ. St. Ninian's High School, Kirkintilloch. Head of Finance, Glasgow District Council Housing Department, 1986-89; Head of Finance, Scottish Homes, 1989-91. Recreations: Munro bagging; jogging; badminton. Address: (h.) 15 Baberton Mains Row, Edinburgh, EH14 3EH; T.-0131-442 2583.

Brett, Timothy Edward William, BSc (Hons), FHSM, DipHSM, GradIPM. Chief Executive, Dundee Teaching Hospitals NHS Trust, since 1993; b. 28.3.49, Gravesend; m., Barbara Jane; 2 s; 1 d. Educ. Gravesend Grammar School for Boys; Bristol University. Unit Administrator, Plymouth General Hospital, 1981-85; Dundee General Hospitals Unit: Unit Administrator, 1985-87, Unit General Manager, 1987-93. Recreations: hill-walking; squash; swimming; theatre; church activities. Address: (h.) Woodend Cottage, Hazelton Walls, Cupar, KY15 4QL; T.-01382 632598.

Brew, David Allan, BA, MSc. Assistant Secretary, Scottish Office Industry Department, since 1990; b. 19.2.53, Kettering. Educ. Kettering Grammar School; Heriot-Watt University; Strathclyde University; European University Institute, Florence. Administration Trainee and HEO(D), Scottish Office, 1979-81; Administrator, DGV, Commission of the EC, 1981-84; Principal, Scottish Office Industry Department, Glasgow, 1984-88, Edinburgh, 1988-90; Assistant Secretary, since 1990; Head, Electricity Privatisation Division, 1990-91; Head, European Funds and Co-ordination Division, since 1991. Member, Court, Heriot-Watt University, 1985-91. Recreations: languages; music; film; gastronomy. Address (h.) Flat 4, 1 Dundas Street, Edinburgh, EH3 6QG; T.-0131-556 4692.

Brewster, Ernest Ralph, BSc, PhD, MBCS, FCIS, MIMgt, CChem. Director of Computer and Management Services, Borders Regional Council, since 1987; b. 29.12.47, Romford; 2 d. Educ. Royal Liberty Grammar School, Romford; Exeter University. Research Assistant, Exeter University, 1972-73; Research Fellow, Oxford University, 1973-75; Senior Scientific Officer, MAFF, 1975-80; Professional Technological Officer, later Principal, Central Computer and Telecommunications Agency, HM Treasury, 1980-85; Information Systems Manager, Norfolk County Council, 1985-87; Secretary, Borders Branch, Institute of Management, 1990-91, Chairman, 1992-95. Address: (b.) Regional Headquarters, Newtown St. Boswells, Melrose, TD6 0SA; T.-01835 823301.

Brian, Paul Vaughan, BSc. Rector, Lochaber High School, Fort William, since 1994; b. 14.6.42, Wokingham; m., Helen Margaret Balneaves; 1 s.; 1 d. Educ. Perth Academy; Edinburgh University; Heriot-Watt College. Depute Rector, Marr College, Troon, 1977; Headteacher, Gryffe High School, Bridge of Weir, 1979; Rector, Hutchesons' Grammar School, 1984; Rector, Biggar High School, 1985-94. Chairman, Lanarkshire Headteachers' Association, 1991-93; Scientific Officer, Scottish Hindu Kush expedition, 1968; Committee Member, Scottish Mountaineering Club. Recreations: mountaineering; golf; gardening. Address: (b.) Lochaber High School, Lochyside, Fort William.

Bridges, Professor Roy Charles, BA, PhD, FRGS, FRHistS. Professor of History, Aberdeen University, since 1988 (Chairman, African Studies Group, since 1983); b. 26.9.32, Aylesbury; m., Jill Margaret Bridges; 2 s.; 2 d. Educ. Harrow Weald County Grammar School; Keele University; London University. Lecturer in History,

Makerere University, Uganda, 1960-64; joined Aberdeen University as Lecturer, 1964; Senior Lecturer, 1971-88; Head, History Department, 1977-82, 1985-88, 1990-94; Secretary, African Studies Group, 1966-83. Member, History Panel, Scottish Examination Board, 1983- 89; Chairman, Joint Working Party on Higher and Post-Higher History, 1988-90; Council Member, Royal Historical Society, since 1995; Council Member, Hakluyt Society, since 1991; Treasurer, Scottish Institute of Missionary Studies. Publications: Nations and Empires (Co-author), 1969; J.A. Grant in Africa, 1982; Africa in Times Atlas of World Exploration. Recreations: cricket; geology; walking. Address: (b.) Department of History and Economic History, King's College, Aberdeen, AB9 2UB; T.-Aberdeen 272452.

Brindle, Anthony Warwick. Managing Director, The Scotsman Publications Limited, since 1994. Managing Director, Chester Chronicle and Associated Newspapers Limited, 1990-91; Managing Director, North Eastern Evening Gazette Limited, 1991-94. Director, Capital Enterprise Trust. Address: (b.) 20 North Bridge, Edinburgh, EH1 1YT; T.-0131-225 0268.

Britton, Professor Celia Margaret, MA (Cantab), PhD. Carnegie Professor of French, Aberdeen University, since 1991; b. 20.3.46, Stanmore, Middx. Educ. North London Collegiate School; New Hall, Cambridge. Temporary Lecturer in French, Kings College, London, 1972-74; Lecturer in French Studies, Reading University, 1974-91. Publications: Claude Simon: Writing The Visible, 1987; The Nouveau Roman: fiction, theory and politics, 1992; Claude Simon (Editor), 1993; articles on French literature and cinema. Address: (b.) Department of French, Aberdeen University, Old Aberdeen, AB9 2UB; T.-01224 272163.

Broadie, Professor Alexander, MA, PhD, DLitt, FRSE. Professor of Logic and Rhetoric, Glasgow University. Educ. Royal High School, Edinburgh; Edinburgh University; Balliol College, Oxford. Henry Duncan Prize Lecturer in Scottish Studies, Royal Society of Edinburgh, 1990-93; Gifford Lecturer, Aberdeen University, 1994. Publications: A Samaritan Philosophy, 1981; George Lokert: Late-Scholastic Logician, 1983; The Circle of John Mair, 1985; Introduction to Medieval Logic, 1987; Notion and Object, 1989; The Tradition of Scottish Philosophy, 1990; Paul of Venice: Logica Magna, 1990; Robert Kilwardby O.P.: on time and imagination, 1993; Introduction to Medieval Logic (2nd edition), 1993; The Shadow of Scotus, 1995. Address: (b.) Philosophy Department, The University, Glasgow, G12 8QQ; T.-0141-339 8855.

Brock, Professor David John Henry, BA (Oxon), PhD, FRCPath, FRSE, FRCPE. Professor of Human Genetics, Edinburgh University, since 1985; Director, Human Genetics Unit, Edinburgh University, since 1983; Chairman, Department of Medicine, Western General Hospital, since 1994; b. 5.6.36, London; m., Sheila Abercromby; 4 s. Educ. Diocesan College, Cape Town; Cape Town University; Oxford University. Postdoctoral Fellow: Massachussets Institute of Technology, 1962-63; Harvard University, 1963-66; Oxford University, 1966-67; Senior Scientific Officer, ARC Animal Breeding Research Organisation, 1967-68; joined Edinburgh University as Lecturer in Human Genetics, 1968; appointed Reader, 1978. Address: (b.) Human Genetics Unit, Western General Hospital, Edinburgh; T.-0131-332 7917.

Brock, Sheila Margaret, MA, PhD. Campaign Director, Museum of Scotland, since 1994; Chair, Visual Arts Committee, Scottish Arts Council, since 1993; b. Edinburgh; 4 s. Educ. George Watson's Ladies' College; Edinburgh University; St. Hugh's College, Oxford. Various teaching posts, Scotland, England, South Africa; Scholar, Radcliffe Institute, Cambridge; Education Department, Royal Scottish Museum, 1979-83; Head of Public Affairs, National Museums of Scotland, 1983-94. Recreations:

reading; music; gardening; travel. Address: (b.) Campaign Office, Royal Museum of Scotland, Chambers Street, Edinburgh, EH1 1JF; T.-0131-247 4389.

Brockington, John Leonard, MA, DPhil. Reader in Sanskrit, Edinburgh University, since 1989 (Senior Lecturer, 1982-89); b. 5.12.40, Oxford; m., Mary Fairweather; 1 s.; 1 d. Educ. Mill Hill School; Corpus Christi College, Oxford. Lecturer in Sanskrit, Edinburgh University, 1965-82. Publications: The Sacred Thread, 1981; Righteous Rama, 1984; Hinduism and Christianity, 1992. Address: (h.) 3 Eskvale Court, Penicuik, Midlothian EH26 8HT; T.-01968 678709.

Brocklebank, Ted. Head of Documentaries and Features, Grampian Television, since 1985 (Head of News and Current Affairs, 1977-85); b. 24.9.42, St. Andrews; 2 s. Educ. Madras College, St. Andrews. D.C. Thomson, Dundee, 1960-63; Freelance Journalist, 1963-65; Scottish TV, 1965-70; Reporter, Grampian TV, 1970-76. BAFTA Award for What Price Oil?; Radio Industries Club of Scotland Special Award (Documentary) for Tale of Two Cities; Norwegian Amanda award for eight-part series on world oil business, networked on Channel Four and throughout USA on PBS; BMA Award for Scotland the Grave. Recreations: rugby; music; reading; living in Scotland. Address: (b.) Grampian TV, Queen's Cross, Aberdeen, AB9 2XJ.

Brodie, Robert, CB, MA, LLB. Solicitor to Secretary of State for Scotland, since 1987 (Deputy Solicitor, 1984-87); b. 9.4.38, Dundee; m., Jean Margaret McDonald; 2 s.; 2 d. Educ. Morgan Academy, Dundee; St. Andrews University; Queen's College, Dundee. Scottish Office: Legal Assistant, 1965; Senior Legal Assistant, 1970; Deputy Director, Scottish Courts Administration, 1975; Assistant Solicitor, Scottish Office, 1982. Chairman, Scottish Tourette Syndrome Support Group, since 1993. Recreations: music; hill-walking. Address: (h.) 45 Stirling Road, Edinburgh; T.-0131-552 2028.

Brodie, William, BSc, CBiol, MIBiol. Rector, Wallace High School, Stirling, since 1984; b. 16.9.37, Hamilton; m. Helen Bland; 1 s.; 1 d. Educ. Hamilton Academy; Glasgow University; Paisley College of Technology. Teacher: Wishaw High School, 1965-67; Principal Teacher of Biology, Hutchesons' Grammar School, Glasgow, 1967-74; Assistant Rector, Graeme High School, Falkirk, 1974-79; Depute Rector, Kirkintilloch High School, 1979-81; Rector Balfron High School, 1981-84. Recreations: golf; tennis; gardening. Address: (b.) Wallace High School, Dumyat Road, Stirling, FK9 5BX; T.-01786 462166.

Brodie of Brodie, (Montagu) Ninian Alexander, DL, JP. b. 12.6.12, Forres; m., Helena Penelope Budgen (deceased); 1 s.; 1 d. Educ. Eton. Trained Webber-Douglas School of Dramatic Art, 1933-35; professional Actor and Director occasional broadcasts, 1935-40; served with Royal Artillery, including North Africa and Italy, 1940-45 returned to stage, with occasional films and broadcasts 1945-50; managed estate, market garden, etc., Brodie Castle, from 1950; transferred Brodie Castle and part of estate to National Trust for Scotland, 1979; voluntary work as guide etc., since 1980. Life Member, National Trust for Scotland. Recreations: shooting; hill-walking; collecting paintings. Address: (h.) Brodie Castle, Forres, Moray, IV36 0TE.

Broni, David Alexander Thomas. Head of Secretariat Scottish Enterprise, since 1991; b. 25.10.57, Glasgow; m. Ann Frances; 1 s.; 1 d. Educ. St. Mungo's Academy. Joined civil service, 1975; Manpower Services Commission, 12 years, Training Agency, 2 years, Scottish Office Industry Department, 2 years. Recreations: running; cycling; swimming; rugby; opera. Address: (b.) 120 Bothwell Street Glasgow, G2 7JP; T.-0141-228 2854.

Brooke, (Alexander) Keith, FRAgS. Director, Animal Diseases Research Association, now Moredun Foundation for Animal Health and Welfare, since 1981; Director, Scottish, English & Welsh Wool Growers Ld., since 1988; Director, Wigtownshire Quality Lamb Ltd.; Member of Council and Past Chairman, British Rouge de l'Ouest Sheep Society; Member, Panel of Agricultural Arbiters; b. 11.2.46, Minnigaff; m., Dilys K. Littlejohn; 1 s.; 3 d. Educ. George Watson's College, Edinburgh. President, Blackface Sheep Breeders Association, 1985-86, Hon. President, 1989-92; Director, Royal Highland and Agricultural Society of Scotland, 1986-93 and since 1994; Director, Wallets Marts PLC, 1989-91. Address: (h.) Carscreugh, Glenluce, Newton Stewart, DG8 0NU; T.-01581 300334.

Brooks, James, BTech (Hons), MPhil, PhD, FRSC, CChem, FGS, FInstPet, AssocBIT. Senior Partner, Brooks Associates Glasgow, since 1986; Visiting Lecturer, Glasgow University, since 1978; Chairman/Director, Petroleum Geology '86 Limited, since 1985; b. 11.10.38, Co. Durham; m., Jan Slack; 1 s.; 1 d. Educ. University of Bradford. Research Scientist, British Petroleum, 1969-75; Senior Research Fellow, Bradford University, 1975-77; Research Associate/Section Head/Senior Scientist, British National Oil Corporation/Britoil PLC, 1977-86. Geological Society: Vice President, 1984-87, Secretary, 1987-90; Founder and Chairman, The Petroleum Group; AAPG Distinguished Achievement Award for service to petroleum geology and human need, 1993; AAPG Distinguished Lecturer to North America, 1989-90; Chairman, Shawlands Academy School Board, since 1990; Church Secretary, Queen's Park Baptist Church, Glasgow; elected Member, Baptist Union of Scotland Council. Publications: 18 books; 80 research papers. Recreations:travel; reading; writing; sport (English soccer!); Christian work. Address: (h.) 10 Langside Drive, Newlands, Glasgow, G43 2EE; T.-0141-632 3068.

Brooks, Patrick William, BSc, MB, ChB, DPM, MRCPsych. Senior Medical Officer, Scottish Home and Health Department, since 1981; b. 17.5.38, Hereford. Educ. Hereford High School; Bishop Vesey's Grammar School, Sutton Coldfield; Edinburgh University. Royal Edinburgh and associated hospitals, including State Hospital, Carstairs, and Western General Hospital, Edinburgh: Senior House Officer, 1964-66; Registrar, 1966-69; Senior Registrar, 1969-74; Medical Officer, Scottish Home and Health Department, 1974-81. A founder Member, Edinburgh Festival Fringe Society, 1959 (Vice-Chairman, 1964-71); Chairman, Edinburgh Playhouse Society, 1975-81; Secretary, Lothian Playhouse Trust, 1981-83; Chairman, The Scottish Society; Joint Vice-Chairman, Royal Lyceum Theatre Club; Secretary, Friends of Scottish Ballet. Recreations: opera; ballet; music; theatre; cinema; modern Scottish art; travel. Address: (h.) 11 Thirlestane Road, Edinburgh, EH9 1AL.

Broun, Janice Anne, BA. Freelance journalist and author; b. 24.3.34, Tipton; m., Canon Claud Broun; 2 s.; 1 d. Educ. Dudley Girls High School; St. Anne's College, Oxford. Publications: Conscience and Captivity: Religion in Eastern Europe, 1988; Prague Winter, 1988; Albania: Religion in a Fortress State, 1989; Bulgaria: Religion Denied, 1989; Romania: Religion in a Hardline State, 1989. Recreations: swimming; cycling; table tennis; music; art history; travel. Address: Martin Lodge, Ardross Place, Alness, Ross-shire, IV17 0PX.

Brown, Alan Cameron, BSc (Hons), PhD, CBiol, MIBiol. Principal, Lauder College, Dunfermline, since 1987; b. 18.1.43, Rothesay; m., Noel Robertson Lyle. Educ. Rothesay Academy; Glasgow University. Assistant Teacher of Science, Ayr Academy, 1969-70; Principal Teacher of Biology, Loudon Academy, 1970-71; Principal Teacher of Biology, Ravenspark Academy, 1971-72; Depute Director of Education, Berwick County Council, 1972-75; Assistant

Director of Education, Borders Regional Council, 1975-80; Depute Principal, Galashiels College of FE, 1980-84; Depute Principal, Borders College of FE, 1984-87. Recreations: cycling; swimming. Address: (b.) Lauder College, Halbeath, Dunfermline, Fife; T.-Dunfermline 726201.

Brown, Professor Alan Geoffrey, BSc, MB, ChB, PhD, FRSE, FIBiol. Professor of Veterinary Physiology, Edinburgh University, since 1984; b. 20.4.40, Nottingham; m., Judith Allen; 1 s.; 1 d. Educ. Mundella School, Nottingham; Edinburgh University. Assistant Lecturer, then Lecturer in Veterinary Physiology, Edinburgh University, 1964-68; Beit Memorial Fellow for Medical Research, 1968-71; Research Fellow supported by MRC, 1971-74; Lecturer, then Reader in Veterinary Physiology, Edinburgh University, 1974-84; holder, MRC Research Fellowship for academic staff, 1980-85. Member, Editorial Boards, several scientific journals. Recreations: music; gardening; walking; reading. Address: (b.) Department of Preclinical Veterinary Sciences, Edinburgh University, Edinburgh, EH9 1QH; T.-0131-667 1011.

Brown, Alexander. Regional Sheriff Clerk, North Strathclyde. Address: (b.) Sheriff Court House, 106 Renfrew Road, Paisley, PA3 4DD.

Brown, Alistair M. Director of Information Technology, Scottish Office, since 1993; b. 1.3.57, Edinburgh; m., Sarah Thompson; 1 s.; 2 d. Educ. Linlithgow Academy. Scottish Office, since 1974; Personal Assistant to Chief Executive, S.D.A., 1987-89; Scottish Office Industry Department, 1989-93; Grade 5, 1993. Recreations: helping to bring up family; walking. Address: (b.) Saughton House, Broomhouse Drive, Edinburgh, EH11 3XD; T.-0131-244 8039.

Brown, Catherine, FSA Scot. Freelance Food Writer, since 1973; b. Glasgow; m., Iain Brown; 2 d. Educ. Hutchesons Grammar School; Queens College, Glasgow. Lecturer, catering subjects; professional cook in hotels and restaurants; senior researcher, Scottish Hotel School, for book, British Cookery, published 1976. Publications: Scottish Regional Recipes, 1981; Scottish Cookery, 1985; A Flavour of Edinburgh, 1986; Broths to Bannocks, 1990. Recreations: mountain climbing; cycling. Address: (h.) 4 Belhaven Terrace, Glasgow G12 0TF; T.-0141-357 4920.

Brown, Professor Charles Malcolm, BSc, PhD, DSc, FIBiol, FIBrew, FRSE. Professor of Microbiology, Heriot-Watt University, since 1979 (Head, Department of Biological Sciences, 1988-93; Dean of Science, 1993-95, Assistant Principal, since 1994); b. 21.9.41, Gilsland; m., Diane Mary Bryant; 3 d. Educ. Houghton-le-Spring Grammar School; Birmingham University. Lecturer in Microbiology, Newcastle-upon-Tyne University, 1966-73; Senior Lecturer, Dundee University, 1973-79. Deputy Chairman, C-MIST; Editor, Process Biochemistry. Recreations: music; walking. Address: (b.) Heriot-Watt University, Riccarton, Edinburgh, EH14 4AS; T.-0131-449 5111.

Brown, Craig. National Team Manager, Scottish Football Association. Formerly: Manager, Clyde Football Club, Lecturer, Craigie College of Education, Ayr. Address: (b.) 6 Park Gardens, Glasgow G3 7YF.

Brown, David Blair, MA, LLB. Rector, Dunfermline High School, since 1983; b. 6.5.38, Glasgow; m., Marjory Kathleen Muir; 2 s.; 1 d. Educ. Hutchesons' Boys Grammar School, Glasgow; Glasgow University; Jordanhill College of Education. Teacher, Hutcheson's Boys Grammar School; Principal Teacher of History, Renfrew High School, 1970-74; Assistant Rector, Stonelaw High School, 1974-78; Depute Rector and Acting Head, Dalbeattie High School, 1978-81; Assistant Rector, Musselburgh Grammar School,

1981-83. Member, Children's Panel, since 1976. Recreations: walking; cycling; swimming; gardening; theatre; music. Address: (b.) St Leonard's Place, Dunfermline KY11 3BG.

Brown, Professor Ewan, MA, LLB, CA, FRSA. Merchant Banker; Director: Noble Grossart Ltd., since 1971; Amicable Smaller Enterprises Trust Plc; John Wood Group Plc; Noble Grossart Investments Ltd.; Scottish Widows Bank plc; Stagecoach Holdings Plc; James Walker (Leith) Ltd.; Lovegrove and Associates Ltd.; b. 23.3.42, Perth; m., Christine; 1 s.; 1 d. Educ. Perth Academy; St. Andrews University. CA apprentice with Peat Marwick Mitchell, 1964-67. Honorary Professor in Finance, Heriot Watt University; Trustee, Carnegie Trust for the Universities of Scotland; Master, Merchant Company of Edinburgh; former Council Member, Institute of Chartered Accountants of Scotland; Council Member, Scottish Business School, 1974-80; Director: Scottish Transport Group, 1983-88, Scottish Development Finance, 1983-93, Pict Petroleum plc, 1973-95, Aberdeen Trust plc; Governor, Edinburgh College of Art, 1986-89; Session Clerk, Mayfield Church, 1983-88. Recreations: family; golf; skiing; Scottish watercolours; Mah Jongg. Address: (b.) 48 Queen Street, Edinburgh; T.-0131-226 7011.

Brown, Francis Henry, BA (Hons), MHSM, DipHSM. Chief Executive, Perth and Kinross Healthcare NHS Trust, since 1994; b. 17.4.47, Falkirk; m., Marion Muir Crawford; 2 s. Educ. Falkirk High School; Strathclyde University. Joined NHS as graduate trainee, 1975; various management/senior management posts, Border Health Board, Ayrshire and Arran Health Board, 1977-94. Recreations: music; swimming; cycling; golf. Address: (b.) Perth Royal Infirmary, Tay Mount Terrace, Perth; T.-01738 620540.

Brown, George Mackay, OBE, MA, Hon. MA (Open University), Hon. LLD (Dundee), Hon DLitt (Glasgow), FRSL. Poet and story-teller; b. 17.10.21, Stromness, Orkney. Educ. Stromness Academy; Newbattle Abbey College; Edinburgh University. Author of: (short stories) A Calendar of Love, A Time to Keep, Hawkfall, The Sun's Net, Andrina, The Masked Fisherman, Winter Tales; (poetry) Selected Poems, Winterfold, Voyages, The Wreck of the Archangel, Foresterhill, Orfco; (novels) Greenvoe, Magnus, Time in a Red Coat, The Golden Bird; Vinland, Beside the Ocean of Time; various plays for stage and television; three books for children; Editor, Selected Prose of Edwin Muir; two books on Orkney. Winner, 1988 James Tait Black prize for The Golden Bird. Address: (h.) 3 Mayburn Court, Stromness, Orkney, KW16 3DH.

Brown, Gordon Lamont. Scottish Rugby International and British Lion; author and after-dinner speaker; ITV rugby commentator; b. 1.11.47, Troon; m., Linda; 1 s.; 1 d. Educ. Marr College, Troon. Bank clerk, British Linen Bank, 1965-71; Building Society Manager: Leicester Building Society, 1971-76, Bristol & West Building Society, since 1976. Played for Scotland, 30 times; toured with British Isles Rugby Team ("Lions"), New Zealand 1971, South Africa 1974, New Zealand 1977; holds world record for number of tries scored by a forward on a tour (eight); Chairman, Stars Organisation for Spastics (Scotland); Vice Chairman, National Playing Fields Association (Scotland). Publications: Broon from Troon (autobiography); Rugby is a Funny Game (rugby anecdotes). Recreation: golf. Address: (h.) 65 Bentinck Drive, Troon, Ayrshire; T.-01292 314070.

Brown, Hamish Macmillan. Author, Lecturer, Photographer and Mountaineer; b. 13.8.34, Colombo, Sri Lanka. Educ. several schools abroad; Dollar Academy. National Service, RAF, Middle East/East Africa; Assistant, Martyrs' Memorial Church, Paisley; first-ever full-time appointment in outdoor education (Braehead School, Fife);

served many years on Scottish Mountain Leadership Board; has led expeditions world-wide for mountaineering, skiing, trekking, canoeing, etc. Publications: Hamish's Mountain Walk, 1979 (SAC award); Hamish's Groats End Walk, 1981 (Smith's Travel Prize shortlist); Time Gentlemen, Some Collected Poems, 1983; Eye to the Hills, 1982; Five Bird Stories, 1984; Poems of the Scottish Hills (Editor), 1982; Speak to the Hills (Co-Editor), 1985; Travels, 1986; The Great Walking Adventure, 1986; Hamish Brown's Scotland, 1988; Climbing the Corbetts, 1988; Great Walks Scotland (Co-author), 1989; Scotland Coast to Coast, 1990; Walking the Summits of Somerset and Avon, 1991; From the Pennines to the Highlands, 1992; The Bothy Brew & Other Stories, 1993; The Fife Coast, The Last Hundred, 1994. Recreations: books; music; Morocco. Address: 21 Carlin Craig, Kinghorn, Fife, KY3 9RX; T.-01592 890422.

Brown, Ian, CSSD, LUDipDA. Artistic Director, Traverse Theatre Company, since 1988; b. 8.3.51, Sawbridgeworth. Educ. The King's School, Ely; Central School of Speech and Drama, London. Drama Teacher; Community Arts Worker, Cockpit Theatre, London; English Language Teacher, Berlitz School, Paris; Director, Cockpit Youth Theatre, London; Associate Director, Theatre Royal, Stratford East; Artistic Director, TAG Theatre Company, Glasgow. Board, Sue McLennon Dance Company; Spirit of Mayfest Award for Great Expectations, 1988; Scotland on Sunday Paper Boat award for Bondagers, Mayfest, 1991. Address: (b.) Cambridge Street, Edinburgh, EH1 2ED; T.-0131-228 3223.

Brown, Ian. Chief Executive, Edinburgh Chamber of Commerce; b. 14.7.45, Hawick; m., Moira Blyth; 1 s.; 1 d. Educ. Hawick High School. Chief Executive, Chamber Developments Ltd., Who's Who in Business in Scotland Ltd., Edinburgh's Capital Ltd. Recreations: golf; curling; walking; music. Address: (b.) 3 Randolph Crescent, Edinburgh, EH3 7UD; T.-0131-225 5851.

Brown, Ian Forbes, FIB (Scot). Director:Wilson Distributors (Scotland) Ltd.; Credential Holdings Ltd.; Thorburn PLC; Norman Cordiner Ltd.; Chairman: Anglo Scottish Properties Plc; Allied London Scotland Ltd.; b. 5.3.29; m., Margaret Catherine; 1 s.; 1 d. Educ. Glasgow High School. Address: (h.) 8 Ardchoille Park, Strathmore Street, Perth PH2 7TL.

Brown, Ian James Morris, MA (Hons), MLitt, PhD, DipEd, FRSA. Playwright, since 1969; Reader in Drama, Queen Margaret College, Edinburgh, since 1994; b. 28.2.45, Barnet; m., 1, Judith Sidaway; 2, Nicola Axford; 1 s.; 1 d. Educ. Dollar Academy; Edinburgh University; Crewe and Alasager College. Schoolteacher, 1967-69, 1970-71; Lecturer in Drama, Dunfermline College, 1971-76; British Council: Assistant Representative, Scotland, 1976-77, Assistant Regional Director, Istanbul, 1977-78; various posts, Crewe and Alsager College, 1978-86, latterly Leader, BA (Hons) drama studies; Programme Director, Alsager Arts Centre, 1980-86; Drama Director, Arts Council of Great Britain, 1986-94. British Theatre Institute: Vice Chairman, 1983-85, Chairman, 1985-87; Member, International Advisory Committee, O'Neill Theatre Center, since 1994; plays include Mother Earth, The Bacchae, Carnegie, The Knife, The Fork, New Reekie, Mary, Runners, Mary Queen and the Loch Tower, Joker in the Pack, Beatrice, First Strike, The Scotch Play, Bacchai, Wasting Reality. Recreations: theatre; sport; travel; cooking. Address: (b.) Queen Margaret College, Clerwood Terrace, Edinburgh, EH12 8TS.

Brown, Ian Johnston Hilton, MA (Hons). Rector, Lanark Grammar School, since 1986 (Rector, Strathaven Academy, 1976-86); b. 5.10.37, Aberdeen. Educ. Royal High School, Edinburgh; Edinburgh University; Moray House College of Education. Teacher, Kirkcaldy High School, 1961-66; Principal Teacher, Bishopbriggs High School, 1966-71;

Assistant Head Teacher, Cathkin High School, 1971-74; Depute Rector, Hunter High School, 1974-76. Recreations: hill-walking; reading; swimming; theatre. Address: (b.) Lanark Grammar School, Lanark, ML11 9AQ; T.-Lanark 662471.

Brown, James Armour, RD, BL, FSA (Scot). Chancellor of the Priory of Scotland, Order of St. John of Jerusalem, since 1992; Partner, Kerr Barrie & Duncan (formerly Kerr, Barrie & Goss), Solicitors, Glasgow, 1957-91 (Consultant, 1991-93); b. 20.7.30, Rutherglen; m., Alexina Mary Robertson McArthur; 1 s. Educ. Rutherglen Academy; Glasgow University. National Service, Royal Navy, 1951-53; commissioned RNVR, 1952; served with Clyde Division, RNVR/RNR, 1953-72; Captain, 1972; Senior Reserve Supply Officer on staff of Admiral Commanding Reserves, 1973-76; Naval ADC to The Queen, 1975-76; Member, Suite of Lord High Commissioner to General Assembly of Church of Scotland, 1961-63; Session Clerk, Stonelaw Parish Church, Rutherglen, 1964-81; Member, Church of Scotland Committee on Chaplains to HM Forces, 1975-82 (Vice-Convener, 1979-82); Clerk, Incorporation of Bakers of Glasgow, 1964-89; Deacon, Society of Deacons and Free Preseses of Glasgow, 1978-80; Member, Glasgow Committee, Order of St. John of Jerusalem, since 1961 (Chairman, 1982-93, Honorary President, since 1995); Member, Chapter of the Priory of Scotland of the Order of St. John, since 1970; KStJ, 1975; Preceptor of Torphichen, Priory of Scotland, 1984-92; Hon. Chairman, Orders and Medals Research Society (Scottish Branch), 1987- 91. Recreations: music; historical research. Address: (h.) 6 Arran Way, Bothwell, Glasgow, G71 8TR; T.-0698 854226.

Brown, (James) Gordon. MA, PhD. MP (Labour), Dunfermline East, since 1983; Shadow Chancellor the Exchequer; b. 20.2.51. Educ. Kirkcaldy High School; Edinburgh University. Rector, Edinburgh University, 1972-75; Temporary Lecturer, Edinburgh University, 1976; Lecturer, Glasgow College of Technology, 1976-80; Journalist and Current Affairs Editor, Scottish Television, 1980-83. Contested (Labour) South Edinburgh, 1979; Chairman, Labour Party Scottish Council, 1983-84; Opposition Chief Secretary to the Treasury, 1987; Shadow Minister for Trade and Industry, 1989. Publications: the Red Paper on Scotland (Editor), 1975; The Politics of Nationalism and Devolution (Co-Editor), 1980; Scotland: The Real Divide, 1983; Maxton, 1986; Where There is Greed, 1989. Recreations: reading and writing; football; golf; tennis. Address: 21 Ferryhills Road, North Queensferry, Fife.

Brown, Jenny, MA (Hons). National Co-ordinator, Readiscovery Campaign; b. 13.5.58, Manchester; m., Alexander Richardson; 3 s. Educ. George Watson's College; Aberdeen University. Assistant Administrator, Edinburgh Festival Fringe Society, 1980-82; Director, Edinburgh Book Festival, 1983-91; Presenter, Scottish Television book programmes, 1989-94; Member, Press Complaints Commission; Commitee Member, Arvon at Moniack Mhor Writers' Centre. Address: (b.) Scottish Book Centre, 137 Dundee Street, Edinburgh, EH11 1BG.

Brown, Professor John Campbell, BSc, PhD, DSc, FRAS, FRSE. Astronomer Royal for Scotland, since 1995; Professor of Astrophysics, Glasgow University, since 1984; b. 4.2.47, Dumbarton; m., Dr. Margaret I. Brown; 1 s.; 1 d. Educ. Dumbarton Academy; Glasgow University. Glasgow University Astronomy Department: Research Assistant, 1968-70, Lecturer, 1970-78, Senior Lecturer, 1978-80, Reader, 1980-84; Nuffield Fellow, 1983-84; Kelvin Medallist, 1983-86; DAAD Fellow, Tubingen University, 1971-72; ESRO/GROC Fellow, Space Research Laboratory, Utrecht, 1973-74; Visitor: Australian National University, 1975, High Altitude Observatory, Colorado, 1977; NASA Associate Professor, Maryland University, 1980; NSF Fellow, University of California at San Diego,

1984; Brittingham Professor, University of Wisconsin, 1987. SERC Solar System Committee, 1980-83; Council, Royal Astronomical Society, 1984-87, 1990-93 (Vice-President, 1986-87); Member, International Astronomical Union, since 1976. Recreations: cycling; walking; painting; lapidary; conjuring; photography; woodwork. Address: (b.) Department of Physics and Astronomy, Glasgow University, Glasgow, G12 8QW; T.-0141-330 5182.

Brown, John Souter, MA (Hons), MIPR. Head of Public Relations, Strathclyde Regional Council, since 1993; b. 15.10.48, Glasgow; m., Angela McGinn; 1 s. Educ. Kirkcaldy High School; Edinburgh University. Statistics and Information Officer, Lanark County Council, 1970-72; Senior Officer (Research, Planning Publicity), Manchester City Social Services Department, 1972-75; Press Officer, Strathclyde Regional Council, 1975-80; Journalist and Presenter, Scottish Television, 1980-82; Editor, What's Your Problem?, 1982-84; Ways and Means, 1984-86; Senior Producer (Politics), Scottish Television, 1986-91; North of Scotland TV Franchise Team, 1991; Managing Director, Lomond Television, 1992-93; Chair, Volunteer Centre, Glasgow, since 1992; Director, Scottish Foundation, since 1990. Address: (b.) Public Relations Department, Strathclyde Regional Council, India Street, Glasgow, G2 4PF; T.-0141-227 3425.

Brown, Professor Kenneth Alexander, BSc, MSc, PhD, FRSE. Professor of Mathematics and Head of Department, Glasgow University; b. 19.4.51, Ayr; m., Irene M.; 2 s. Educ. Ayr Academy; Glasgow University; Warwick University. Recreations: reading; running. Address: (b.) Mathematics Department, Glasgow University, Glasgow, G12 8QW; T.-0141-330 5180.

Brown, Kenneth Clarke, CIPFA. Director of Finance, Nithsdale District Council, since 1984; Clerk and Treasurer, Solway River Purification Board, since 1989; b. 28.5.44, Dumfries; m., Olivia; 1 s.; 1 d. Educ. Dumfries Academy. Commenced career as Audit Examiner with District Audit in Chelmsford, 1966; moved to Carlisle; appointed Chief Internal Auditor, Skelmersdale and Holland UDC, 1971; moved to similar post, Chorley Borough Council, 1974; Depute Director of Finance, Nithsdale District Council, 1976-84. Honorary Treasurer, Ellisland Trust. Recreations: golf; football; keep-fit; DIY. Address: (h.) Kilmory, 51 Rotchell Park, Dumfries, DG2 7RL; T.-01387 254889.

Brown, Professor Kenneth J., BSc, PhD, FRSE. Professor in Mathematics, Heriot-Watt University, since 1993; b. 20.12.45, Torphins; m., Elizabeth Lobban; 1 s.; 2 d. Educ. Banchory Academy; Robert Gordon's College; Aberdeen University; Dundee University. Lecturer in Mathematics, Heriot Watt University, 1970-81, Senior Lecturer, 1981-91, Reader, 1991-93. Publications: 40 papers. Recreations: coaching athletics; reading. Address: (h.) 3 Highlea Grove, Balerno, Edinburgh, EH14 7HQ; T.-0131-449 5314.

Brown, Madeline, MB, ChB, MRCPsy, DPsy. Consultant Child Psychiatrist, Royal Aberdeen Children's Hospital, since 1982; b. 30.10.37, Aberdeen; m., Ian R. Brown; 2 s. Educ. Aberdeen Academy; Aberdeen University. Recreations: hill-walking; badminton; drama. Address: (h.) 37 Argyll Place, Aberdeen; T.-01224 633996.

Brown, Neil Dallas, DA. Painter; Lecturer, Department of Fine Art Studies (Painting Studios), Glasgow School of Art, since 1979; b. 10.8.38, Elgin; m., Georgina Ballantyne; 2 d. Educ. Bell Baxter High School, Cupar; Duncan of Jordanstone College of Art, Dundee; Royal Academy Schools, London. Visiting Lecturer, School of Design, Duncan of Jordanstone College of Art, since 1968; Visiting Lecturer in Painting, Glasgow School of Art, since 1976; since completing training, 38 one-man exhibitions, in Dundee, Manchester, Edinburgh, London (nine), Glasgow, York, Basle, Paris, Stirling, Belfast, Aberdeen and

Kirkcaldy; won 10 awards for painting; has been Guest Artist, Dollar Summer School for the Arts, Croydon College of Art, Strathclyde University, Ulster Polytechnic, Grays School of Art (Aberdeen), Maryland Institute College of Art (Baltimore), Newport College of Art (Wales). Recreations: fishing; running. Address: (h.) Aerie, 55 Abbeywall Road, Pittenweem, Fife, KY10 2NE; T.-311852.

Brown, Professor Peter Evans, PhD, FRSE. Professor of Geology, St. Andrews University, since 1990; b. 5.4.30, Kendal; m., Thelma Smith; 2 s. Educ. Kendal School; Manchester University. Mineralogist/Geologist, Geological Survey of Tanganyika; Lecturer/Senior Lecturer in Geology, Sheffield University; Professor of Geology, Aberdeen University. Recreations: mountaineering; exploration. Address: (b.) Department of Geography and Geology, Purdie Building, St. Andrews, KY16 9ST.

Brown, R. Iain F, MBE, MA, MEd, ABPsS, ChPsychol. Senior Lecturer, Department of Psychology, Glasgow University, since 1968; b. 16.1.35, Dundee; m., Catherine G. (qv); 2 d. Educ. Daniel Stewart's College, Edinburgh; St. Andrews University; Edinburgh University; Glasgow University. Education Department, Corporation of Glasgow; Department of Psychological Medicine, Glasgow University. National Training Adviser, Scottish Council on Alcohol, 1979-94; Member, Executive, Scottish Council on Alcohol, 1980-94; Chairman, Society for the Study of Gambling, London, 1987-92; Chairman, European Association for the Study of Gambling, since 1992; Chairman, Glasgow Council on Alcohol, since 1985; Chairman, Confederation of Scottish Counselling Agencies, 1989-93; Member, Lead Body on Advice, Guidance, Counselling and Psychotherapy (UK), since 1992. Recreations: travel; music. Address: (h.) 13 Kirklee Terrace, Glasgow, G12 0TH; T.-0141-339 7095.

Brown, Rob, MA (Hons). Media Editor, Scotland on Sunday, since 1993; b. 24.3.63, Glasgow; m., Margaret Graepel; 1 s. Educ. Armadale Academy; Glasgow University; University College, Cardiff; Queen's University, Ontario. News Reporter, Feature Writer, The Scotsman, 1986-88; Assistant Editor, Westminster Editor, Scotland on Sunday, 1988-90; Reporter, Scottish Television, 1990-92. Recreations: cinema; books; strolling round cities. Address: (b.) Regent Court, 70 West Regent Street, Glasgow; T.-0141-332 6163.

Brown, Professor Sally, BSc, MA, PhD. Professor of Education, Stirling University, since 1990; b. 15.12.35, London; m., Professor Charles Brown (deceased); 2 s. Educ. Bromley High School GPDST; University College, London; Smith College, Massachusetts; Stirling University. Lecturer in College of Education, London, and College of Technology, Nigeria; University Lecturer, Nigeria; School Science Teacher, Helensburgh; University Researcher, Stirling; Research Adviser to Scottish Education Department; Director, Scottish Council for Research in Education, 1986-90. Publications: 100 (articles, monographs, books) on educational research and education generally. Recreations: squash; reading; music. Address: (b.) Department of Education, Stirling University, Stirling, FK9 4LA.

Brown, Professor Stewart J., BA, MA, PhD, FRHistS. Professor of Ecclesiastical History, Edinburgh University, since 1988; b. 8.7.51, Illinois; m., Teri B. Hopkins-Brown; 1 s.; 1 d. Educ. University of Illinois; University of Chicago. Fulbright Scholar, Edinburgh University, 1976-78; Whiting Fellow in the Humanities, University of Chicago, 1979-80; Assistant to the Dean, College of Arts & Sciences, and Lecturer in History, Northwestern University, 1980-82; Associate Professor and Assistant Head, Department of History, University of Georgia, 1982-88; Visiting Lecturer, Department of Irish History, University College, Cork, 1986; Editor, Scottish Historical Review, since 1993.

Publication: Thomas Chalmers and the Godly Commonwealth in Scotland, 1982 (awarded Agnes Mure Mackenzie Prize from Saltire Society); Scotland in the Age of the Disruption (Co-author), 1993. Recreations: swimming; hill-walking. Address: (h.) 160 Craigleith Hill Avenue, Edinburgh, EH4 2NB; T.-0131-343 1712.

Brown, William, CBE (1971), Dr hc (Edin), DUniv (Strathclyde). Chairman, Scottish Arts Council; Chairman, Scottish Television, since 1991 (Managing Director, 1966-90); b. 24.6.29, Ayr; m., Nancy Jennifer Hunter; 1 s.; 3 d. Educ. Ayr Academy; Edinburgh University. STV: London Sales Manager, 1958-61, Sales Director, 1961-63, Deputy Managing Director, 1963-66. Lord Willis Award for services to TV, 1982; Royal Television Society Gold Medal for outstanding services to TV, 1984; Chairman, Council, ITCA, 1968-69, 1978-80; Director, ITN, 1972-77 and 1988-90; Director, ITP, 1968-89; Director, Channel 4, 1980-84; Director, Scottish Amicable Life Assurance Society, since 1981, Chairman, 1989-94. Recreation: golf. Address: (b.) STV, Cowcaddens, Glasgow, G2 3PR.

Brown, William, BL, WS, SSC, NP. Solicitor; Senior Partner, Tods Murray WS; b. 18.3.32, Dunfermline; m., Anne Sword; 2 d. Educ. Dunfermline High School; Edinburgh University. National Service commission, RAOC, 1952; Partner, Ranken & Reid, 1960-90. Recreations: golf; music; shooting. Address: (h.) Greenlawns, 45 Barnton Avenue, Edinburgh, EH4 6JJ; T.-0131-336 4227.

Browning, J. Robin, BA (Hons), FIB (Scot). General Manager, Bank of Scotland, since 1986 (Divisional General Manager, 1983-86); b. 29.7.39, Kirkcaldy; m., Christine Campbell; 1 s.; 1 d. Educ. Morgan Academy, Dundee; Strathclyde University; Harvard Business School. Bank of Scotland: Assistant Management Accountant, 1971-74, Assistant Manager (Corporate Planning), 1974-77; British Linen Bank Ltd.: Manager, 1977-79, Assistant Director, 1979-81, Director, 1981-82; Assistant General Manager, Bank of Scotland, 1982-83. Member of Council, Chartered Institute of Bankers in Scotland; Deputy Chairman, Association for Payment and Clearing Services. Recreations: curling; gardening; DIY enthusiast. Address: (b.) Bank of Scotland, Head Office, The Mound, Edinburgh, EH1 1YZ; T.-0131-243 5541.

Brownlie, Alistair Rutherford, OBE, MA, LLB, SSC. Solicitor Supreme Courts; Secretary, SSC Society, since 1970; b. 5.4.24, Edinburgh; m., Martha Barron Mounsey. Educ. George Watson's; Edinburgh University. Served as radio operator in 658 Air O.P. Squadron RAF, Europe and India; apprenticed to J. & R.A. Robertson, WS; qualified Solicitor, 1950; in private practice; Member, Committee on Blood Grouping (House of Lords); Solicitor for the poor, 1955-64, in High Court of Justiciary; Member, Council, Law Society of Scotland; Legal Aid Central Committee; Chairman, Legal Aid Committee, Scottish Legal Aid Board, 1986-90; founder Member, Past President, now Hon. Member, Forensic Science Society; Fellow, RSA; Elder, Church of Scotland and Congregational Union of Scotland. Publications: Drink, Drugs and Driving (Co-author); various papers on forensic science, criminal law and legal aid. Recreations: the pen, the spade, and the saw. Address: (h.) 8 Braid Mount, Edinburgh; T.-0131-447 4255.

Brownlie, William Steel, MC, TD, MA; b. 12.10.23, Cambusnethan; m., 1, Margaret Mitchell (deceased); 2, Netta Russell (deceased); 1 s.; 1 d. Educ. Greenock Academy; Glasgow University. Royal Armoured Corps, 1942-47; 2nd Fife and Forfar Yeomanry, 1944-47; Captain, NW Europe; Ayrshire (ECO) Yeomanry, 1950-68; Lt.-Col. Commanding, 1966-72; Teacher, John Neilson High School, Paisley, 1951-84 (Principal Teacher, Modern Languages); Contributor, Lingo Column, Times Educational Supplement; Editor, The Scottish

Schoolmaster; Editor, The Yeoman (Ayrshire Yeomanry). Publications: The Proud Trooper (History of the Ayrshire Yeomanry), 1964; Thirteen Letters from a Scottish Solider (Editor), 1988. Recreations: military history; philately; photography; philology. Address: (h.) Orchard Cottage, Law Brae, West Kilbride, KA23 9DD; T.-01294 822216.

Bruce, Andrew, MA (Hons), MEd. Headteacher, Craigmount High School, Edinburgh, since 1994; b. 26.3.46, Cowdenbeath; m., Jennifer Harkess; 1 s. Educ. Daniel Stewart's College, Edinburgh; Edinburgh University; Aberdeen University. Adviser in English, Dunbarton Division, Strathclyde Region; Assistant Head Teacher, Bankhead Academy, Aberdeen; Resources Development Officer, Grampian Region; Headteacher, Deans Community High School, Livingston; Head, Management Development Unit, Lothian Region. Recreations: squash; reading; motorcycling. Address: (b.) Craigs Road, Edinburgh, EH12 8NH; T.-0131-339 6823.

Bruce, David, MA.Writer and Consultant; Director, Scottish Film Council, 1986-94; b. 10.6.39, Dundee; m., Barbara; 1 s.; 1 d. Educ. Dundee High School; Aberdeen Grammar School; Edinburgh University. Freelance (film), 1963; Assistant Director, Films of Scotland, 1964-66; Director, Edinburgh International Film Festival, 1965-66; Promotions Manager, Mermaid Theatre, London, 1966-67; Executive Officer, British Universities Film Council, 1967-69; joined Scottish Film Council as Assistant Director, 1969; Depute Director, SFC and Scottish Council for Educational Technology, 1977-86. Chairman, Mental Health Film Council, 1982-84; Chairman, Scottish Society for History of Photography, 1983-86; Chairman, Association of European Film Institutes, 1990-94. Recreations: movies; music; photo-history. Address: (h.) Rosebank, 150 West Princes Street, Helensburgh, G84 8BH.

Bruce, Fraser Finlayson, RD, MA (Hons), LLB, FSA(Scot). Regional Chairman, Industrial Tribunals for Scotland, since 1993 (Permanent Chairman, 1982-93); Solicitor, since 1956; b. 10.10.31, Kirkcaldy; m., Joan Gwendolen Hunter; 2 step-s. Educ. St. Andrews University. National Service, Royal Navy, 1956-58, commissioned Sub-Lieutenant, RNVR; Legal Assistant: Lanark County Council, 1958-60, Inverness County Council, 1960-66; Depute County Clerk: Argyll County Council, 1966-70, Inverness County Council, 1970-72; County Clerk, Inverness County Council, 1972-75; Joint Director of Law and Administration, Highland Regional Council, 1975-82; Temporary Sheriff, 1984-92. Served RNVR, 1956-76, retiring as Lieutenant-Commander RNR. Recreations: hill walking; reading (in philosophy and naval/military history). Address: (h.) 1 Hazel Drive, Dundee DD2 1QQ; T.-01382 68501.

Bruce, George, OBE (1984), MA, DLitt. Writer/Lecturer; b. 10.3.09, Fraserburgh; m., Elizabeth Duncan; 1 s.; 1 d. Educ. Fraserburgh Academy; Aberdeen University. Teacher, English Department, Dundee High School, 1935-46; BBC Producer, Aberdeen, 1946-56; BBC Talks (Documentary) Producer, Edinburgh, with special responsibility for arts programmes, 1956-70; first Fellow in Creative Writing, Glasgow University, 1971-73; Visiting Professor, Union Theological Seminary, Richmond, Virginia, 1974; Visiting Professor of English, College of Wooster, Ohio, 1976-77; Scottish-Australian Writing Fellow, 1982; E. Hervey Evans Distinguished Fellow, St. Andrews Presbyterian College, North Carolina, 1985; Vice-Chairman, Council, Saltire Society; Council Member, Advisory Council of the Arts in Scotland; Extra-Mural Lecturer, Glasgow, St. Andrews and Edinburgh Universities; Executive Editor, The Scottish Review, 1975-76. Publications: verse: Sea Talk, 1944; Selected Poems, 1947; Landscapes and Figures, 1967; Collected Poems,

1970; The Red Sky, 1985; Perspectives: poems 1970-86, 1987; prose: Scottish Sculpture Today (Co-author), 1947; Anne Redpath, 1974; The City of Edinburgh, 1974; Festival in the North, 1975; Some Practical Good, 1975; A Scottish Postbag (Co-author), 1986; as Editor: The Scottish Literary Revival, 1962; Scottish Poetry Anthologies 1-6 (Co-Editor), 1966-72; The Land Out There, anthology (Editor), 1991. Recreation: visiting friends. Address: 25 Warriston Crescent, Edinburgh, EH3 5LB; T.-0131-556 3848.

Bruce, Malcolm Gray, MA, MSc. MP (Liberal Democrat, formerly Liberal), Gordon, since 1983; b. 17.11.44, Birkenhead; 1 s.; 1 d. Educ. Wrekin College; St. Andrews University; Strathclyde University. Trainee Journalist, Liverpool Daily Post & Echo, 1966-67; Section Buyer, Boots the Chemist, 1968-69; Fashion Retailing Executive, A. Goldberg & Sons, 1969-70; Research and Information Officer, NESDA, 1971-75; Marketing Director, Noroil Publishing, 1975-81; Director, Aberdeen Petroleum Publishing; Editor/Publisher, Aberdeen Petroleum Report, 1981-83; Co-Editor, Scottish Petroleum Annual, 1st and 2nd editions. Vice Chairman, Political, Scottish Liberal Party, 1975-84; Rector, Dundee University, 1986-89. Recreations: reading; music; theatre; hill-walking; cycling; travel. Address: (h.) House of Commons, London, SW1A 0AA.

Bruce, Professor Steve, BA, PhD. Professor of Sociology, Aberdeen University, since 1991; b. 1.4.54, Edinburgh; m., Elizabeth S. Duff; 1 s.; 2 d. Educ. Queen Victoria School, Dunblane; Stirling University. Variously Lecturer, Reader and Professor of Sociology, Queen's University of Be'fast, 1978-91. Publications: author of numerous books on religion, and on the Northern Ireland conflict. Recreation: farming. Address: (b.) Department of Sociology, Aberdeen University, Aberdeen, AB9 2TY; T.-01224 272761.

Bruce, Professor Victoria Geraldine, BA, MA, PhD, CPsychol, FBPsS. Professor of Psychology, Stirling University, since 1992; Member, Economic and Social Research Council, since 1992, and Chair, Research Programmes Board, since 1992; b. 4.1.53; m., Professor A.M. Burton. Educ. Newcastle-upon-Tyne Church High School for Girls; Newnham College, Cambridge. Lecturer, then Reader, then Professor of Psychology, Nottingham University, 1978-92. Member, Chief Executive's Research Advisory Group, Scottish Higher Education Funding Council, since 1993; Editor, British Journal of Psychology, since 1995; Chair, Psychology Panel for 1996 University Funding Councils' Research Assessment Exercise. Publications: numerous papers and several books on visual perception and cognition. Recreations: dogs; walking; games. Address: (h.) The Mill House, Fintry, Stirlingshire, G63 0YD; T.-0136 086 342.

Bruford, Alan James, BA, PhD. Archivist, School of Scottish Studies, Edinburgh University, since 1965; Editor, Tocher, since 1971; b. 10.5.37, Glasgow; m., Morag B. Wood; 1 d. Educ. Edinburgh Academy; Winchester College; St. John's College, Cambridge; Edinburgh University. Junior Research Fellow, 1965; Assistant Lecturer, 1965; Lecturer, 1968; Senior Lecturer, 1984; Reader, 1995; fieldwork throughout Scotland, especially Orkney and Shetland, collecting folktales and other traditions, songs, fiddle music and oral history; Treasurer, Scottish Association of Magazine Publishers, 1974-79; Convener, Scottish Oral History Group, 1987-93; Organising Secretary, 7th Congress, International Society for Folk-Narrative Research, 1979. Publications: Gaelic Folk-Tales and Mediaeval Romances, 1969; The Green Man of Knowledge and Other Scots Traditional Tales, 1982; Scottish Traditional Tales (Co-author), 1994. Recreations: music (traditional, baroque, composition); travel in Scotland; quizzes. Address: (h.) South Mains, West Linton, Peeblesshire, EH46 7AY.

Brumfitt, Professor John Henry, MA, DPhil (Oxon). Emeritus Professor, St. Andrews University, since 1986 (Professor of French, 1969-86); b. 5.4.21, Shipley; m., 1, Patricia Renee Grand; 2, Margaret Anne Ford; 1 s.; 2 d. Educ. Bradford Grammar School; Queen's College, Oxford. Laming Travelling Fellow, Queen's College, Oxford, 1947-48; Lecturer in French, University College, Oxford, 1948-51; St. Andrews University: Lecturer in French, 1951-59, Senior Lecturer, 1959-69; Member, Editorial Boards, French Studies and Forum for Modern Language Studies. Publications: The French Enlightenment; Voltaire Historian. Address: (h.) 22 Buchanan Gardens, St. Andrews, Fife; T.-01334 73079.

Brunt, Peter William, OBE, MD, FRCP(Lond), FRCP(Edin). Consultant Physician, Aberdeen Royal Infirmary, since 1970; Clinical Senior Lecturer in Medicine, Aberdeen University, since 1970; Physician to The Queen in Scotland, since 1984; b. 18.1.36, Prestatyn; m., Marina Evelyn Jane Lewis; 3 d. Educ. Manchester Grammar School; King George V School; Liverpool University. Recreations: mountaineering; music. Address:(h.) 17 Kingshill Road, Aberdeen, AB2 4JY; T.-Aberdeen 314204.

Bryant, Anthony B., FRICS. Regional Director, Highlands, National Trust for Scotland, since 1986; b. 25.1.38; m., Jane E.A.; 1 s.; 1 d. Educ. Bryanston School. Trained as land agent, Chatsworth Estate, 1956-60, returning there 1964-69 after working for the Duchy of Cornwall; joined National Trust for Scotland as Depute Factor, 1969; Factor, 1976; Head Factor, 1984. Recreations: music; painting. Address: (b.) Abertarff House, Church Street, Inverness 1V1 1EU; T.-Inverness 232034.

Bryant, Professor David Murray, BSc, PhD, ARCS, DIC. Professor, Department of Biological and Molecular Sciences, Stirling University, since 1989; b. 24.9.45, Norwich; m., Victoria Margaret Turton; 1 s.; 1 d. Educ. Greshams School, Holt; Imperial College, London. Lecturer/Senior Lecturer/Reader, Stirling University, since 1970. Member. Committees, National Environment Research Council; Chairman, Research and Surveys Committee, and Council Member, British Trust for Ornithology. Recreations: skiing; birds; theatre. Address: (h.) Kenilworth Road, Bridge of Allan, FK9 4EH.

Bryce, Professor Charles F.A., BSc, PhD, DipEdTech, CBiol, FIBiol, CChem, FRSC. Professor, Dean, Faculty of Science, and Head, Department of Biological Sciences, Napier University, since 1983; b. 5.9.47, Lennoxtown; m., Maureen; 2 s. Educ. Lenzie Academy; Shawlands Academy; Glasgow University; Max Planck Institute, Berlin. Executive Editor, Computer Applications in the Biosciences; Member, EFB Task Group on Public Perceptions of Biotechnology; Adviser to the Committee on Science and Technology in Developing Countries (India); Chairman, UK Deans of Science Committee; Convener, UCAS Biology Panel. 1Recreations:competitive bridge; collecting wine. Address: (b.) Napier University, 10 Colinton Road, Edinburgh, EH10 5DT; T.-0131-455 2525.

Bryce, Colin Maxwell, DA (Edin), FCSD, FRSA. Head, Department of Design, Napier University, since 1992; b. 14.9.45, Edinburgh; m., Caroline Joy; 2 s. Educ. Royal High School, Edinburgh; Edinburgh College of Art; Moray House College of Education. Art and Design Teacher, Portobello High School, 1968-75; Head of Art and Design, Wester Hailes Education Centre, 1975-85; Education Advisory Officer/Senior Education Officer/Director, The Design Centre Scotland, 1985-90; Managing Director, Quorum Graphic Design, 1990-91; Principal, Hunter Maxwell Associates, 1991-92. Member, Society of High Constables of Edinburgh. Recreations: looking, listening, and talking. Address: (b.) Napier University, 10 Colinton Road, Edinburgh, EH10 5DT; T.-0131-455 2560.

Bryce, Professor Tom G.K., BSc, MEd, PhD, CPsychol. Professor, Department of Educational Studies, Faculty of Education, Strathclyde University, Jordanhill Campus, since 1993; b. 27.1.46, Glasgow; m., Karen Douglas Stewart; 1 s.; 1 d. Educ. King's Park Secondary School, Glasgow; Glasgow University. Teacher of Physics, Jordanhill College School, 1968-71; P.T. of Physics, King's Park Secondary School, 1971-73; part-time Lecturer in Psychology, Glasgow University, 1972-75; Open University Tutor, 1979-84; Lecturer, 1973, Head of Psychology, 1983, Head, Division of Education and Psychology, 1987-94, Jordanhill College of Education. Chairman, Editorial Board, Scottish Educational Review. Publications include: How to Assess Open-ended Practical Investigations in Biology, Chemistry and Physics, 1991. Recreations: moutaineering; badminton. Address: (b.) Jordanhill Campus, Southbrae Drive, Glasgow, G13 1PP; T.-0141-950 3366.

Brydon, Norman, BSc, FBIM, MCIM. Chief Executive, formerly General Secretary, Scottish Squash, since 1991; b. 18.2.36, Spennymoor. Educ. Spennymoor Grammar School; University College, London. Director of Finance and Administration, Scottish Sports Council, 1985-88; Director of Finance, industrial services group, 1988-91. Organist and Choirmaster, Corstorphine Old Kirk. Recreations: most sports; music (semi-professional); bridge (Senior Life Master and international trialist). Address: (b.) Caledonia House, South Gyle, Edinburgh, EH12 9DQ; T.-0131-317 7343.

Bryson, Norval MacKenzie, MSc, DPhil, FFA. Deputy Group Managing Director, Scottish Provident; b. 22.1.49, Dundee; m., Pamela Judith Sallie; 1 s.; 2 d. Educ. High School of Dundee; St. Andrews University; Magdalen College, Oxford. Joined Scottish Provident, 1974. Former Member of Council, Faculty of Actuaries. Recreation: walking the dog. Address: (h.) Achmore, 1 Hillview Terrace, Corstorphine, Edinburgh, EH12 8RA; T.-0131-334 2614.

Buccleuch, 9th Duke of, and Queensberry, 11th Duke of (Walter Francis John Montagu Douglas Scott), KT (1978), VRD, JP. Hon. Captain, RNR; Captain, Queen's Bodyguard for Scotland (Royal Company of Archers); Lord Lieutenant of Roxburgh, since 1974, and of Ettrick and Lauderdale, since 1975; b. 23.9.23, London; m., Jane McNeill, daughter of John McNeill, QC, Appin, Argyll; 3 s.; 1 d. Educ. Eton; Christ Church, Oxford. Served World War II, RNVR; MP (Conservative), Edinburgh North, 1960-73; PPS to the Scottish Office, 1961-64; Chairman, Conservative Party Forestry Committee, 1967-73; Chairman, Royal Association for Disability and Rehabilitation, since 1978, and President, since 1993; President: Royal Highland and Agricultural Society of Scotland, 1969, St. Andrew's Ambulance Association, Royal Scottish Agricultural Benevolent Institution, Scottish National Institution for War Blinded, Royal Blind Asylum and School, Galloway Cattle Society, East of England Agricultural Society, 1976, Commonwealth Forestry Association; President (Scotland), Malcolm Sargent Cancer Fund for Children; President, Royal Scottish Forestry Society, since 1994; Chairman, Living Landscape Trust, since 1985; Chairman, Buccleuch Heritage Trust, since 1986; Vice-President: Royal Scottish Society for Prevention of Cruelty to Children, Disablement Income Group Scotland, Disabled Drivers Motor Club, Spinal Injuries Association; Honorary President: Animal Diseases Research Association, Scottish Agricultural Organisation Society; DL: Selkirk, 1955, Midlothian, 1960, Roxburgh, 1962, Dumfries, 1974; Chancellor, Most Ancient & Most Noble Order of the Thistle, since 1992; Chairman, Association of Lord Lieutenants, since 1990. Recreations: travel; country sports; painting; photography; classical music. Address: Bowhill, Selkirk; T.-Selkirk 20732; and Drumlanrig Castle, Thornhill; T.-Thornhill 30248.

Buchan, Alexander Stewart, MB, ChB, FRCA. Consultant in charge of Obstetric Anaesthesia, Simpson Memorial Maternity Pavilion, Edinburgh, since 1988; b. 7.9.42, Aberdeen; m., Henrietta Young Dalrymple; 1 s. Educ. Loretto School; Edinburgh University. Anaesthetic training in Edinburgh, apart from work in Holland, 1972; appointed Consultant in NHS, 1975; Royal Infirmary, Edinburgh, Royal Hospital for Sick Children, and Princess Margaret Rose Orthopaedic Hospital. Publication: Handbook of Obstetric Anaesthesia, 1991. Recreations: sailing; fishing; golf. Address: (h.) 21 Chalmers Crescent, Edinburgh, EH9 1TS; T.-0131-667 1127.

Buchan of Auchmacoy, Captain David William Sinclair, JP, KStJ. Chief of the Name of Buchan; b. 18.9.29; m., The Hon. Susan Blanche Fionodbhar Scott-Ellis; 4 s.; 1 d. Educ. Eton; Royal Military Academy, Sandhurst. Commissioned Gordon Highlanders, 1949; served Berlin, BAOR and Malaya; ADC to GOC-in-C, Singapore, 1951-53; retired 1955. Member, London Stock Exchange; Senior Partner, Messrs Gow and Parsons, 1963-72. Changed name from Trevor through Court of Lord Lyon King of Arms, 1949, succeeding 18th Earl of Caithness as Chief of Buchan Clan. Member: Queen's Body Guard for Scotland (Royal Company of Archers); The Pilgrims; Friends of Malta GC; Alexandra Rose Day Council; Council, St. John's Ambulance, London; Council, Royal School of Needlework, 1987; Conservative Industrial Fund Committee, 1988; Governor, London Clinic, 1988; Vice-President, Bucks CCC, since 1984; Member, Council for London, Order of St. John; Master, Worshipful Company of Borderers, 1992; President, Ellon Cricket Club. Recreations: cricket; tennis; squash. Address: Auchmacoy House, Ellon, Aberdeenshire.

Buchanan, Duncan. Director, Highland River Purification Board. Address: (b.) Graesser House, Foddarty Way, Dingwall, IV15 9XB.

Buchanan, James Glen Stewart, MB, ChB, FRCGP, DCH, DRCOG. Chairman, Scottish Council on Alcohol, 1987-95; b. 11.6.24, Annan; m., Elizabeth Urquhart Macgregor; 2 s. Educ. Dumfries Academy; Edinburgh University. General Practitioner, Vale of Leven, 1958-87; Past President, Glasgow Psychosomatic Society. Recreations: hill-walking; fishing; reading. Address: (h.) Landalla Cottage, Glenisla, Blairgowrie, PH11 8PH; T.-01575 582318.

Buchanan, James S., BSc, PhD, MIBiol, MIFM. Executive Director, Association of Scottish Shellfish Growers; Member of Council, Scottish Association for Marine Science; Assistant Editor, Journal of Fish Biology; Specialist Lecturer, Napier University; b. 1.4.38, Khartoum; m., Ann Neilson Ferrier; 3 d. Educ. Fettes College; U.C.N.W., Bangor; Stirling University. NERC Research Fellow, Institute of Aquaculture, Stirling University; Head of Environmental Toxicology, Huntingdon Research Centre; Lecturer in Microbiology, Napier Polytechnic, Edinburgh; Business Manager, Inveresk Research International; Technical Director, Scottish Salmon Growers Association, 1988-92. Fellow, Royal Geographic Society; Past President, Glencorse Pipe Pand; Past President, Rotary Club of Lochhead and Roslin. Recreations: sailing; music. Address: (h.) The Old Parsonage, Roslin, EH25 9LF; T.-0131-440 2116.

Buchanan, Professor John (Iain) Thomson, BSc, MSc, PhD. Professor of Computer Science, Strathclyde University, since 1988; b. 25.7.46, Glasgow; m., Margaret Moffat. Educ. Allan Glen's School, Glasgow; Glasgow University; Strathclyde University. Lecturer, Manchester University, 1971-75; Lecturer, Strathclyde University, 1976-88. Recreations: yachting; mountains; music; food and wine. Address: (b.) Department of Computer Science, Strathclyde University, Glasgow, G1 1XH; T.-0141-552 4400.

Buchanan, Joyce Mary, BA, Dip SW. Deputy Director (Elderly Services), Board of Social Responsibility, Church of Scotland, since 1987; b. 9.4.49, Ayr. Educ. Larkhall Academy; Strathclyde University; Edinburgh University. Social Worker, 1971-74; Training Officer, Board of Social Responsibility, 1974-87; External Asessor to Certificate on Social Service, 1981-86. Secretary of State Appointee, Saughton Prison Visiting Committee; External Verifier for SVQ; Member, Residential Forum, Standards Project Group. Recreations: handcrafts; reading; involvement with local churches in setting up care groups for elderly people. Address: (b.) Church of Scotland, Charis House, 47 Milton Road East, Edinburgh, EH15 2SR; T.-0131-657 2000.

Buchanan, Paul, MA, MSc, MTS. Tourism Manager, City of Dundee Tourist Board, since 1987; b. 29.2.60, Barnet; m., Elizabeth; 2 s. Educ. Lochaber High School; Edinburgh University; Strathclyde University. Assistant Area Tourist Officer, Kincardine and Deeside Tourist Board. Vice-Chairman, Great British Cities Marketing Group. Recreation: photography. Address: (b.) 4 City Square, Dundee, DD1 3BA; T.-01382 434277.

Buchanan, William Menzies, DA. Head of Fine Art, 1977-90, Acting Director, 1990-91, Deputy Director, 1991-92, Glasgow School of Art; b. 7.10.32, Caroni Estate, Trinidad, West Indies. Educ. Glasgow School of Art. Art Teacher, Glasgow, 1956-61; Exhibitions Officer, then Art Director, Scottish Arts Council, 1961-77. Chairman, Stills Gallery, Edinburgh, 1987-92; Member, Fine Art Board, Council for National Academic Awards, 1978-81. Publications: Scottish Art Review, 1965, 1967, 1973; Seven Scottish Painters catalogue, IBM New York, 1965; The Glasgow Boys catalogue, 1968; Joan Eardley, 1976; Mr Henry and Mr Hornel Visit Japan catalogue, 1978; Japonisme in Art (Contributor), 1980; A Companion to Scottish Culture (Contributor), 1981; The Stormy Blast catalogue, Stirling University, 1981; The Golden Age of British Photography (Contributor), 1984; The Photographic Collector (Contributor), 1985; Willie Rodger: A Retrospective (Contributor to catalogue), 1986; Scottish Photography Bulletin (Contributor), 1988; History of Photography (Conrtributor), 1989; Mackintosh's Masterwork (Editor), 1989; British Photography in the 19th Century (Contributor), 1989; The Art of the Photographer J. Craig Annan, 1992; Photography 1900 (Contributor), 1993; J. Craig Annan: selected texts and bibliography, 1994. Recreations: gardening; cooking. Address: (h.) Allan Water School House, by Skelfhill, Hawick, TD9 0PH; T.-01450 850311.

Buchanan-Jardine, Sir Andrew Rupert John, MC. Landowner; Deputy Lieutenant; b. 2.2.23, London; 1 s.; 1 d. Educ. Harrow; Royal Agricultural College. Joined Royal Horse Guards, 1941; served NW Europe; retired as Major, 1949. Joint Master, Dumfriesshire Foxhounds, 1950; JP. Recreation: country pursuits. Address: (h.) Dixons, Lockerbie, Dumfriesshire; T.-Lockerbie 2508.

Buchanan-Smith, Robin D., BA, ThM. Member, Board of Directors, Scottish Television, since 1982; Chancellor's Assessor, St. Andrews University, 1981-85; Chairman, Scotland's Heritage Hotels, 1988-91; b. 1.2.36, Currie, Midlothian; m., Sheena Mary Edwards; 2 s. Educ. Edinburgh Academy; Glenalmond; Cambridge University; Edinburgh University; Princeton Theological Seminary. Minister, Christ's Church, Dunollie, Oban, 1962-66; Chaplain, St. Andrews University, 1966-73. Chaplain: 8th Argylls, 1962-66, Highland Volunteer, 1967-69; British Council of Churches Preacher to USA, 1968; Commodore, Royal Highland Yacht Club, 1977-81. Recreations: sailing; Scotland. Address: Isle of Eriska, Ledaig, Argyll, PA37 1SD; T.-01631 720371.

Buckland, Professor Roger, MA, MPhil. Professor of Accountancy, Aberdeen University, since 1993, and Head, Department of Accountancy, since 1993; b. 22.4.51, Sheffield; m., Dr. Lorna McKee; 2 d. Educ. Aston Woodhouse High School; Selwyn College, Cambridge. Research Fellow, York University; Lecturer, University of Aston. Publications: The Unlisted Securities Market; Finance for Growing Enterprises. Recreation: hot air balloon pilot; family. Address: (b.) Dunbar Street, Aberdeen, AB9 2TY; T.-01224 272206.

Buckland, Professor Stephen T., BSc, MSc, PhD, CStat. Professor of Statistics, St. Andrews University, since 1993; Head, Wildlife Population Assessment Research Group, since 1993; b. 28.7.55, Dorchester; m., Patricia A. Peters; 1 d. Educ. Foster's School, Sherborne; Southampton University; Edinburgh University; Aberdeen University. Lecturer in Statistics, Aberdeen University, 1977-85; Senior Scientist, Tuna/Dolphin Program, Inter-American Tropical Tuna Commission, San Diego, 1985-87; Senior Consultant Statistician, Scottish Agricultural Statistics Service, 1988-93, Head, Environmental Modelling Unit, 1991-93. Publications: The Birds of North-East Scotland (Co-editor), 1990; Distance Sampling: estimating abundance of biological populations (Co-author), 1993. Recreations: natural history; walking; reading. Address: (b.) School of Mathematical and Computational Sciences, St. Andrews University, North Haugh, St. Andrews, KY16 9SS; T.-01334 463787.

Buckley, Ernest Graham, MD, FRCPE, FRCGP. Director, Scottish Council for Postgraduate Medical and Dental Education, since 1993; b. 16.10.45, Oldham; m., Dr. Felicity Buckley; 2 s.; 1 d. Educ. Manchester Grammar School; Edinburgh University. General Practitioner, Livingston, 1974-93; Editor, British Journal of General Practice, 1982-90. Recreations: gardening; history; upholstery. Address: (b.) 12 Queen Street, Edinburgh, EH2 1JE; T.-0131-225 4365.

Bunch, Antonia Janette, MA, FLA, FIInfSc, FSA Scot. Director, Scottish Science Library, since 1987; b. 13.2.37, Croydon. Educ. Notting Hill and Ealing High School; Strathclyde University. Assistant Librarian, Scottish Office, 1962-65; Librarian, Scottish Health Service Centre, 1965-81; Lecturer, Strathclyde University, 1981-86. Founding Chairman, Association of Scottish Health Sciences Librarians; Member, Standing Committee on Science and Technology Libraries, IFLA, 1987-91; Member, Advisory Committee, British Library Science Reference and Information Service, since 1987. Publications: Libraries in Hospitals (Co-author), 1969; Hospital and Medical Libraries in Scotland: an Historical and Sociological Study, 1975; Health Care Administration: an Information Sourcebook, 1979. Recreations: breeding and showing Welsh mountain ponies; gardening; music; travelling in Italy. Address: (b.) National Library of Scotland, 33 Salisbury Place, Edinburgh, EH9 1SL; T.-0131-226 4531.

Buncle, Tom, BA, MA. International Marketing Director, Scottish Tourist Board, since 1994; b. 25.6.53, Arbroath; m., Janet; 2 s. Educ. Trinity College, Glenalmond; Exeter University; Sheffield University. Various posts, British Tourist Authority, 1978-91; Deputy Overseas Marketing Director, Scottish Tourist Board, 1991-94. Recreations: wind-surfing; scuba diving; cycling; walking. Address: (b.) Scottish Tourist Board, 23 Ravelston Terrace, Edinburgh, EH4 3EU; T.-0131-332 2433.

Bundy, Professor Alan Richard, BSc, PhD, FRSA, FAAAI. Professor, Department of Artificial Intelligence, Edinburgh University, since 1990; b. 18.5.47, Isleworth; m., D. Josephine A. Maule; 1 d. Educ. Heston Secondary Modern School; Springgrove Grammar School; Leicester University. Tutorial Assistant, Department of Mathematics, Leicester University, 1970-71; Edinburgh University:

Research Fellow, Metamathematics Unit, 1971-74; Lecturer, Department of Artificial Intelligence, 1974-84; Reader, 1984-87; Professorial Fellow, 1987-90. Editorial Board: Artificial Intelligence Journal, Journal of Automated Reasoning, AJ & Society Journal. Publications: Artificial Intelligence: An Introductory Course, 1978; The Computer Modelling of Mathematical Reasoning, 1983; The Catalogue of Artificial Intelligence Tools, 1984. Recreations: wine and beer making; walking; bridge. Address: (b.) Department of Artificial Intelligence, Edinburgh University, 80 South Bridge, Edinburgh, EH1 1HN; T.-0131-650 2716.

Bunn, Professor Philip Robertson, BSc, MSc, PhD, MInstMC, MIEE, CEng. Director of International Relations, Paisley University (Head, Department of Electrical Engineering, Dean, Faculty of Engineering, 1990-93); b. 19.2.43, Hertford; m., Katrina McKenzie; 1 s.; 1 d. Educ. St. Albans School; Leicester University; Bradford University. Elliott Automation Ltd (later GEC Elliott Process Automation Ltd), 1964-72; International Combustion Ltd, 1972-73; Principal Lecturer, Computer Engineering, Teesside Polytechnic, 1973-88. Recreation: golf. Address: Department of Electrical and Electronic Engineering, Paisley University, High Street, Paisley, PA1 2BE; T.-0141-848 3400.

Bunney, Herrick, LVO, BMus, FRCO, FRSAMD, ARCM. Honorary Fellow, Edinburgh University; Organist and Master of the Music, St. Giles' Cathedral, Edinburgh, since 1946; b. 1915, London; m., Mary Howarth Cutting; 1 s.; 1 d. Educ. University College School; Royal College of Music. Organist to Edinburgh University, until 1981; former Conductor: Edinburgh Royal Choral Union, Edinburgh University Singers, The Elizabethan Singers (London), St. Cecilia Singers. Recreations: hill-walking; bird-watching. Address: (h.) 3 Upper Coltbridge Terrace, Edinburgh, EH12 6AD; T.-0131-337 6494.

Burchell, Professor Brian, BSc (Hons), PhD, MRCPath. Professor of Medical Biochemistry and Clinical Director, University Department of Biochemical Medicine, Dundee; Honorary Professor, St. Andrews University; b. 1.10.46, Bosworth; m., Ann; 1 s.; 1 d. Educ. King Edward VII Grammar School, Coalville; St. Andrews University. Lecturer in Biochemistry: Loughborough University of Technology, 1974-75; Dundee University, 1976-78; Wellcome Trust Special Research Leave Fellow, 1978-80; Wellcome Trust Senior Lecturer in Biochemistry, Dundee University, 1980-88. Editor and Deputy Chairman, Editorial Board, Biochemical Journal. Publications: over 150 scientific papers and reviews. Recreation: golf. Address: (b.) University Department of Biochemical Medicine, Ninewells Hospital and Medical School, Dundee, DD1 9SY; T.-01382 60111, Ext. 2164.

Burdon, Professor Roy Hunter, BSc, PhD, CBiol, FIBiol, FRSA, FRSE. Professor of Molecular Biology, Strathclyde University; m., Margery Grace Kellock; b. 27.4.38, Glasgow; 2 s. Educ. Glasgow Academy; St. Andrews University. Assistant Lecturer, Glasgow University, 1959; Research Fellow, New York University, 1963; Glasgow University: Lecturer in Biochemistry, 1964, Senior Lecturer, 1967, Reader, 1974, Professor of Biochemistry (Titular), 1977; Guest Professor of Microbiology, Polytechnical University of Denmark, 1977-78; Governor, West of Scotland College of Agriculture; Biochemical Society (UK): Honorary Meeting Secretary, 1981-85, Honorary General Secretary, 1985-89, Chairman, 1989-92; Chairman, British Co-ordinating Committee for Biotechnology, 1991-93; Chairman, Scientific Advisory Committee, European Federation of Biotechnology, 1991; Auditor, International Union of Biochemistry and Molecular Biology, 1991-94. Recreations: music; painting; golf. Address: (h.) 144 Mugdock Road, Milngavie, Glasgow, G62 8NP; T.-0141-956 1689.

Burgess, Charles Douglas, FRICS, IRRV, ACIArb. Partner, David Watson, Property Agents, Surveyors and Valuers, Glasgow, since 1973; Honorary Secretary, Royal Institution of Chartered Surveyors in Scotland, since 1993; b. 20.12.33, Glasgow; m., Margaret (Rita) Helen Blackwood; 2 d. Educ. High School of Glasgow; Royal Technical College, Glasgow. National Service, 1956-58; Assistant Surveyor, Hendry & Steel, 1958-65; Partner, 1965-73. Chairman, Royal Institution of Chartered Surveyors in Scotland, 1990-91; President, Property Owners and Factors Association, Glasgow, Ltd., 1977-79; President, Property Owners and Factors Association, Scotland Ltd., 1987-88; Past Deacon, Society of Deacons and Free Preseses of Glasgow; Past Preses, Weavers Society of Anderston; Past President, Sandyford Burns Club, Glasgow; Past President, Glasgow and District Burns Association. Recreations: sailing; music; the works of Robert Burns. Address: (b.) 926 Govan Road, Glasgow, G51 3AE; T.-0141-445 3741.

Burgess, Professor Robert Arthur, LLB, PhD. Professor of Business Law, Strathclyde University, since 1989; b. 24.2.46, Northwich; m., Frances I.L. Burns; 1 s.; 1 d. Educ. Sir John Deane's Grammar School, Northwich; University College, London; Edinburgh University. National Provincial Bank, 1967-69; Lecturer in Law, Southampton University, 1969-72; Lecturer in Taxation and Investment Law, Edinburgh University, 1972-78; Reader in Law, University of East Anglia, 1978-89. Chairman, Glasgow Royal Infirmary University NHS Trust, since 1994. Publications: Perpetuities in Scots Law; Corporate Finance Law; Law of Borrowing. Recreations: food and drink; travel. Address: (b.) Law School, Strathclyde University, 173 Cathedral Street, Glasgow, G4 0RQ; T.-0141-552 4400.

Burgon, Robert Douglas, BA, MLitt, APMI. Director and Secretary, Scottish & Northern Ireland Plumbing Employers' Federation, since 1988; Secretary and Pensions Manager, Plumbing Pensions (UK) Ltd., since 1988; b. 3.8.55, Haddington; m., Sheila Georgina Bryson. Educ. North Berwick High School; Heriot Watt University. SNIPEF: Assistant Industrial Relations Officer, 1978, Assistant to the Director, 1979, Secretary, 1983. Recreation: music (church organist). Address: (b.) 2 Walker Street, Edinburgh, EH3 7LB; T.-0131-225 2255.

Burley, Elayne Mary, BA (Hons). Director, Napier Enterprise Centre, Napier University, since 1991; b. 17.10.44, Cheshire; 2 s.; 1 d. Educ. Astley Grammar School for Girls; Leeds University. Leeds Polytechnic, 1966-68; Lecturer, Gordon Institute of Technology, Victoria, Australia, 1970-72; Lecturer, Open University in Scotland, 1972-84; Head of Training, Scottish Council for Voluntary Organisations, 1984-91. Convenor, Confederation of Scottish Counselling Agencies; Member, Council, Rotary Club of Edinburgh. Recreations: golf; bridge; performing arts; walking on the beach; collecting blue and white china. Address: (b.) 10 Colinton Road, Edinburgh; T.-0131-455 2311.

Burley, Lindsay Elizabeth, MB, ChB, FRCPE, MRCGP, MHSM. Director of Planning and Development, Lothian Health Board; b. 2.10.50, Blackpool; m., Robin Burley. Educ. Queen Mary School, Lytham; Edinburgh University. Address: (b.) Lothian Health, Deaconess House, 148 Pleasance, Edinburgh, EH8 9RS; T.-0131-536 9000.

Burn, Richard Armstrong, FCIH. Director of Housing Management, Scottish Homes, since 1992; b. 6.7.52, Dundee; m., Fiona. Educ. Kirkton High School, Dundee; Dundee College of Commerce. Director of Housing, Western Isles Council, 1984-89; District Manager, Fife District, Scottish Homes, 1989-92. Director, Community Business Fife. Recreation: badminton (SBU coach).

Address: (b.) Scottish Homes, Carlyle House, Carlyle Road, Kirkcaldy, KY1 1DB; T.-01592 641055.

Burnet, George Wardlaw, LVO, BA, LLB, WS, KStJ, JP. Lord Lieutenant, Midlothian, since 1992; Chairman, Caledonian Research Foundation, since 1988; b. 26.12.27, Edinburgh; m., Jane Elena Moncrieff; 2 s.; 1 d. Educ. Edinburgh Academy; Lincoln College, Oxford; Edinburgh University. Senior Partner, Murray Beith & Murray, WS, 1983-91; Chairman, Life Association of Scotland Ltd., 1985-93. Brigadier, Queen's Bodyguard for Scotland (Royal Company of Archers); former Midlothian County Councillor; Convenor, Church of Scotland Finance Committee, 1980-83; Hon. Fellow, Royal Incorporation of Architects in Scotland. Address: (h.) Rose Court, Inveresk, Midlothian, EH21 7TD.

Burnett, Charles John, KStJ, DA, AMA, FSAScot, FHSS, MLitt. Ross Herald of Arms; Curator of Fine Art, Scottish United Services Museum, Edinburgh Castle, since 1985; Vice-President, Heraldry Society of Scotland, since 1986; Vice-Patron, Genealogical Society of Queensland, since 1986; b. 6.11.40, Sandhaven, by Fraserburgh; m., Aileen E. McIntyre; 2 s.; 1 d. Educ. Fraserburgh Academy; Gray's School of Art, Aberdeen; Aberdeen College of Education. Advertising Department, House of Fraser, Aberdeen, 1963-64; Exhibitions Division, Central Office of Information, 1964-68 (on team which planned British pavilion for World Fair, Montreal, 1967); Assistant Curator, Letchworth Museum and Art Gallery, 1968-71; Head, Design Department, National Museum of Antiquities of Scotland, 1971-85. Heraldic Adviser, Girl Guide Association in Scotland, since 1978; Librarian, Priory of the Order of St. John in Scotland, since 1987; Vice President, Society of Antiquaries of Scotland, since 1992; Honorary Citizen of Oklahoma, 1989. Recreations: reading; visiting places of historic interest. Address: (h.) 7 Spottiswoode Road, Edinburgh, EH9 1BH; T.-0131 447 3111.

Burnett, James Murray, FRICS, DipTP. Partner, Donaldsons, Chartered Surveyors, since 1987; Board Member, Cumbernauld Development Corporation, since 1990; Director, Broadwood Developments plc, since 1992; b. 7.2.44, Edinburgh; m., Elizabeth Anne; 1 s.; 2 d. Educ. Boroughmuir School; Heriot-Watt University; Edinburgh College of Art. Joined Donaldsons in 1970, giving development consultancy advice for large shopping centres. Vice-Chairman, Royal Institution of Chartered Surveyors in Scotland, 1992-93. Recreations: golf; gardening. Address: (h.) 438 Lanark Road, Colinton, Edinburgh; T.-0131-441 2200.

Burnett, Robert Gemmill, LLB, SSC, NP. Solicitor, since 1972; b. 18.1.49, Kilmarnock; m., Patricia Margaret Masson; 1 s.; 2 d. Educ. George Heriot's School, Edinburgh; Edinburgh University. Apprentice, then Assistant, then Partner, Drummond Miller WS; Partner, Burnett Christie. Solicitor to General Teaching Council. Recreations: golf; gardening. Address: (b.) 53 George IV Bridge, Edinburgh; T.-031-225 3456.

Burnett, Rodney Alister, MB, ChB, MRCP, FRIPHH, FRCPath. Consultant Pathologist responsible for diagnostic services, University Department of Pathology, Western Infirmary, Glasgow, since 1985; b. 6.6.47, Congleton; m., Maureen Elizabeth Dunn; 2 d. Educ. Sandbach School; St. Andrews University. Lecturer in Pathology, Glasgow University, 1974-79; Consultant in administrative charge, Department of Pathology, Stobhill Hospital, Glasgow, 1979-85. Member of Council, Royal Institute for Public Health and Hygiene, and Chairman, Board of Education and Examination for Anatomical Pathology Technology. Address: (h.) 134 Brownside Road, Cambuslang, Glasgow, G72; T.-0141-641 3036.

Burnett, Rupert Gavin, BCom, CA, FCMA; b. 6.11.39, India; m., Elspeth Maclean; 2 s.; 1 d. Educ. George Watson's College; Edinburgh University; Harvard Business School. Procter & Gamble Ltd., 1963-65; Management Consultant, McLintock, Moores and Murray, 1965-68; Chartered Accountant, Arthur Young (latterly Ernst & Young), 1968-91, Partner, 1970; Honorary Professor, Stirling University, since 1991; Member, Council, Institute of Chartered Accountants of Scotland, since 1990; Chairman, Glasgow & North Strathclyde Area Committee, 1992-95; CCAB Audit Practices Committee, 1986-91; Vice-Chairman, Church of Scotland Investors Trust, since 1995; General Trustee, Church of Scotland, since 1995; various non-executive directorships. Recreations: watching amateur rugby; wild brown trout fishing; croft; family. Address: (h.) 7 Ralston Road, Bearsden, Glasgow.

Burnett-Stuart of Crichie, George Slessor. Farmer and Landowner, since 1969; b. 3.1.48, Cobham; m., Patricia De Lavenne; 2 d. Educ. Winchester College; Bordeaux University. Elected Member, Council and Executive, National Trust for Scotland; Member, Council, and Past Chairman, Stewart Society; Chairman, Grampian Farming Forestry Wildlife Group; Regional Board Member, Scottish Natural Heritage; Treasurer, Friends of Grampian Stones. Recreations: kite-flying; travelling; tree-planting. Address: Crichie House, Stuartfield, Peterhead, AB4 8DY; T.-01771 24202.

Burns, Dr. Harry J.G. Director of Public Health, Greater Glasgow Health Board. Address: (b.) 112 Ingram Street, Glasgow, G1 1ET.

Burns, Jessica Martha, BA (Hons), LLB, SSC. Chairman, Independent Tribunal Service with responsibility for Child Support Appeal Tribunals, since 1992; b. 4.10.52, Dumfries; m., Bill Findlay; 2 d. Educ. Carlisle and County High School for Girls; Stirling University; Edinburgh University. Lecturer in Law, Glasgow University, 1983-85; Senior Lecturer, Faculty of Law, Aberdeen University, 1986-92. Member, Parole Board for Scotland, 1990-92; Member, Police Advisory Board for Scotland, 1988-92; Governor, Scottish Police College, 1988-92; Visiting Professor, School of Law, Maryland University, 1988. Recreations: relaxing with family; theatre; music; good company. Address: (b.) ITS, Wellington House, 134 Wellington Street, Glasgow, G2 2XL; T.-0141-353 1441.

Burstall, Professor Rodney M., MA, MSc, PhD. Professor of Computer Science, Edinburgh University, since 1979; b. 11.11.34, Liverpool; m., Seija-Leena (deceased); 3 d. Educ. George V Grammar School, Southport; King's College, Cambridge; Birmingham University. Operational Research Consultant, Brussels, 1959; Operational Research and Programming, Reed Paper Group, Kent, 1960; Research Fellow, Birmingham University, 1962; Research Fellow, Lecturer, Reader, Professor, Department of Artificial Intelligence, Edinburgh University, 1964-79. Emissary to UK for Venerable Chogyam Trungpa Rinpoche, Buddhist Meditation Master, 1982; Member, Academia Europaea, 1989; Fellow, Royal Society of Edinburgh, since 1995. Address: (b.) Department of Computer Science, Edinburgh University, King's Buildings, Mayfield Road, Edinburgh, EH9 3JZ; T.-0131-650 5155.

Burt, Gillian Robertson, MA (Hons). Headmistress, Craigholme School, Glasgow, since 1991; b. 7.2.44, Edinburgh; m., Andrew Wallace Burt; 1 s.; 1 d. Educ. Mary Erskine School; Edinburgh University; Moray House College of Education. Teacher of Geography, Tabeetha Church of Scotland School, Jaffa, Israel, 1966-67; Teacher of Geography, Boroughmuir Secondary School, 1967-70; Head of Geography, St. Hilary's School, Edinburgh, 1970-71, 1976-86, Head of Careers, 1986-91 (merged with St.

Margaret's School, 1983). Recreations: music; theatre; walking; cooking; foreign travel. Address: (h.) 277 Nithsdale Road, Glasgow, G41 5LX; T.-0141-427 2034.

Burton, Anthony Winston, OBE, BA (Hons). Managing Director, The Planning Exchange, since 1975; b. 14.10.40, Leicester; 2 s.; 1 d. Educ. Wyggeston; Keele University. Council Member, Consumers' Association; Member, UK Ecolabelling Board. Recreations: cooking; sailing. Address: (h.) 9 Marchmont Terrace, Glasgow, G12; T.-0141-334 7697.

Burton, Derek Arthur, BSc, MA, ABPsS. Honorary Senior Lecturer in Clinical Psychology, St. Andrews University, since 1977; b. 27.8.32, Staffordshire. Educ. North Staffordshire College; Leicester University; Hull University. Research Assistant, Institute of Neurology, London; Senior Psychologist, Leicester; Principal Psychologist, Leicester Area Psychology Service; Consultant Psychologist, Fife Adult Psychology Service. Collingwood Philosophy Prizewinner; Honorary Fellow, Edinburgh University. Recreations: hill walking; music; theatre. Address: (b.) Department of Psychology, St. Andrews University, St. Andrews; T.-St. Andrews 76161.

Burton, Lord (Michael Evan Victor Baillie). Landowner and Farmer; Executive Member, Scottish Landowners Federation, 1963-92; b. 27.6.24, Burton-on-Trent; m., 1, Elizabeth Ursula Foster Wise (m. diss.); 2, Coralie Denise Cliffe; 2 s.; 4 d. Educ. Eton; Army. Scots Guards, 1942 (Lt., 1944); Lovat Scouts, 1948; Member, Inverness County Council, 1948-75; JP, 1961-75; Deputy Lieutenant, Inverness, 1963-65; has served on numerous committees. Recreations: shooting, fishing and hunting (not much time); looking after the estate. Address: Dochfour, Inverness; T.-01463 861252.

Busby, John Philip, NDD, DA (Edin), RSW, ARSA, PPSSA; b. 2.2.38, Bradford; m., Joan; 1 s.; 2 d. Educ. Ilkley Grammar School; Leeds College of Art; Edinburgh College of Art. Lecturer in Drawing and Painting, Edinburgh College of Art, 1956-58; Founder Member, Society of Wildlife Artists; Board Member, Artists for Nature Foundation; illustrated 30 books on natural history; author and illustrator: Birds in Mallorca, Drawing Birds, John Busby Nature Drawings, The Living Birds of Eric Ennion. Recreations: music; bird-watching; travel. Address: (h.) Easter Haining, Ormiston Hall, East Lothian, EH35 5NJ; T.-01875 340512.

Bush, Professor Peter Williams, BA, PhD, FRGS, FRSA. Vice-Principal, Glasgow Caledonian University, since 1989; b. 8.11.45, Liverpool; m., Judy; 1 s.; 1 d. Educ. St. Mary's College, Crosby, Liverpool; University College, London; Leeds University. Lecturer, Senior Lecturer, Principal Lecturer in Geography, Staffordshire University, 1970-81; Head, Department of Humanities, Glasgow College of Technology, 1981-84; Assistant Director, Glasgow Polytechnic, 1985-89. Chair, Scottish Advisory Committee on Credit and Access, since 1993; Academic Auditor, Higher Education Quality Council, since 1993; Member, Board of Governors, St. Andrew's College of Education, 1987-95; Member, Northern Ireland Higher Education Council, since 1993. Recreations: sports; music; travel. Address: (b.) Glasgow Caledonian University, Cowcaddens Road, Glasgow, G4 0BA; T.-0141-331 3133.

Bushe, Frederick, OBE, RSA (1987), DA, DAE. Sculptor, since 1956; Director, Scottish Sculpture Workshop, since 1979; b. 1.3.31, Coatbridge; m., Fiona M.S. Marr; 1 d.; 3 s., 1 d. by pr. m. Educ. Our Lady's High School, Motherwell; Glasgow School of Art. Lecturer in Sculpture: Liverpool College of Education, 1962-69, Aberdeen College of Education, 1969-79; full-time Artist since 1979; established Scottish Sculpture Workshop and Scottish Sculpture Open Exhibition; exhibited in numerous one man and group exhibitions, since 1962. Recreations: music; cooking. Address: (h.) Rose Cottage, Lumsden, Huntly, Aberdeenshire.

Busuttil, Professor Anthony, MD, FRCPath, FRCP(Glas), FRCPE, DMJ(Path). Regius Professor of Forensic Medicine, Edinburgh University, since 1987; Honorary Consultant Pathologist, Lothian Health Board, since 1976; Police Surgeon, Lothian and Borders Police, since 1980; b. 30.12.45, Rabat, Malta; m., Angela; 3 s. Educ. St. Aloysius' College, Malta; Royal University of Malta. Junior posts, Western Infirmary, Glasgow; Lecturer in Pathology, Glasgow University. Address: (h.) 78 Hillpark Avenue, Edinburgh, EH4 7AL; T.-0131-336 3241.

Bute, 7th Marquess of (John Colum Crichton-Stuart); b. 26.4.58; m.; 1 s.; 2 d.

Butler, Anthony Robert, BSc, PhD, DSc, AKC. Reader in Chemistry, St. Andrews University, since 1965; b. 28.11.36, Croydon, Surrey; m., Janet Anderson. Educ. Selhurst Grammar School; King's College, London; Cornell University. Lecturer, Fleming Centenary Celebration, Darvel, 1981. Recreations: hill-walking; road-running; music; writing Chinese characters. Address: (h.) Red Gable, Denhead, St. Andrews; T.-01334 850521.

Butler, Vincent Frederick, RSA, RGI. Sculptor. Address: (h.) 17 Deanpark Crescent, Edinburgh, EH4 1PH; T.-0131-332 5884.

Butlin, Ron, MA, DipAECD. Poet and Novelist; b. 17.11.49, Edinburgh. Educ. Dumfries Academy; Edinburgh University. Writer in Residence, Lothian Region Education Authority, 1979, Edinburgh University, 1981, 1984-85; Scottish/Canadian Writing Exchange Fellow, University of New Brunswick, 1983-84; Writer in Residence for Midlothian, 1989-90. Publications: poetry: Stretto, 1976; Creatures Tamed by Cruelty, 1979; The Exquisite Instrument, 1982 (Scottish Arts Council Book Award); Ragtime in Unfamiliar Bars, 1985 (SAC Book Award, Poetry Book Society recommendation); prose: The Tilting Room (short stories), 1983 (SAC Book Award); The Sound of My Voice (novel), 1987; Blending In (play), 1989; Histories of Desire (poetry), 1995. Recreations: music; travel. Address: (h.) 7 West Newington Place, Edinburgh, EH9 1QT; T.-0131-667 0394.

Butter, Sir David Henry, KCVO, MC. Lord Lieutenant, Perth and Kinross, 1975-95; Landowner and Company Director; b. 18.3.20, London; m., Myra Alice Wernher; 1 s.; 4 d. Educ. Eton College; Oxford University. Served in World War II, 2nd Lt., Scots Guards, 1940; served in Western Desert, North Africa, Sicily and Italy (ADC to GOC 8th Army, 1944); Temporary Major, 1946; retired, 1948; Ensign, Queen's Bodyguard for Scotland (Royal Company of Archers); President, Highland TAVR, 1979-84; Member, Perth County Council, 1955-74; Deputy Lieutenant, Perthshire, 1956; Vice Lieutenant, Perthshire, 1960-71; Lord Lieutenant of County of Perth, 1971-75, of Kinross, 1974-75; Governor, Gordonstoun School, 1954-86; Honorary President, Perthshire Battalion, Boys Brigade. Recreations: golf; skiing; travel; shooting. Address: Cluniemore, Pitlochry, Perthshire; T.-01796 2006.

Butter, Professor Peter Herbert. Regius Professor of English Language and Literature, Glasgow University, 1965-86; b. 7.4.21, Coldstream; m., Bridget Younger; 1 s.; 2 d. Educ. Charterhouse; Balliol College, Oxford. Royal Artillery, 1941-46; Lecturer in English, Edinburgh University, 1948-58; Professor of English, Queen's University, Belfast, 1958-65. Secretary/Treasurer, International Association of University Professors of English, 1965-71. Publications: Shelley's Idols of the Cave, 1954; Francis Thompson, 1961; Edwin Muir, 1962; Edwin Muir: Man and Poet, 1966; Shelley's Alastor, Prometheus Unbound and Other Poems (Editor), 1971; Selected Letters of Edwin Muir (Editor), 1974; William Blake: Selected Poems (Editor), 1982; The Truth of Imagination: Uncollected Prose of Edwin Muir (Editor), 1988; Complete Poems of Edwin Muir (Editor), 1991. Recreations: gardening; hill-walking. Address: (h.) Ashfield, Prieston Road, Bridge of Weir, Renfrewshire, PA11 3AW; T.-Bridge of Weir 613139.

Butterfield, Alan W., MA, DipEd, JP. Rector, Hamilton Grammar School, since 1971; b. 1.5.33, Dundee; m., Rosemary; 1 s.; 1 d. Educ. Dundee High School; St. Andrews University. Teacher of English and History, Harris Academy, Dundee; Special Assistant of English and History, Dunfermline High School; Principal Teacher of English: Broxburn Academy, Trinity Academy, Edinburgh; Depute Rector, Falkirk High School. President, Headteachers' Association of Scotland, 1984-85. Recreation: Rotary. Address: (h.) 23 Langside Road, Bothwell, Lanarkshire; T.-853505.

Butterworth, Neil, MA, HonFLCM. Chairman, Scottish Society of Composers, since 1991; Music Critic, Times Educational Supplement, since 1983; Broadcaster; b. 4.9.34, Streatham, London; m., Anna Mary Barnes; 3 d. Educ. Rutlish School, Surrey; Nottingham University; London University; Guildhall School of Music, London. Lecturer, Kingston College of Technology, 1960-68; Head, Music Department, Napier College, Edinburgh, 1986-87. Conductor: Sutton Symphony Orchestra, 1960-64, Glasgow Orchestral Society, 1975-83 and since 1989; Chairman, Incorporated Society of Musicians, Edinburgh Centre, since 1981; Chairman, Inveresk Preservation Society, since 1988; Churchill Fellowship, 1975. Publications: Haydn, 1976; Dvorak, 1980; Dictionary of American Composers, 1983; Aaron Copland, 1984; Samuel Barber, 1988; Vaughan Williams, 1989; Neglected Music, 1991; over 300 compositions. Recreations: autographs; collecting books and records; giant jigsaw puzzles. Address: (h.) The White House, Inveresk, Musselburgh, Midlothian; T.-0131-665 3497.

Buxton, Paul Kenneth, MA (Cantab), MB, BChir, FRCP(C), FRCPEdin. Consultant Physician in Dermatology, Fife Health Board and Royal Infirmary, Edinburgh, since 1981; Member, Clinical Teaching Staff, Edinburgh University, since 1981; b. 28.2.36, Harrar, Ethiopia; m., Heather; 1 s.; 1 d. Educ. Trinity College, Cambridge; St. Thomas's Hospital, London. Dermatologist, Royal Jubilee Hospital, Victoria, BC, Canada, 1971-81. President, Fife Branch, BMA, 1986-87; Fellow, Royal Society of Medicine; Member, Ethical Committee, Fife Health Board; Member, Editorial Board, Ethics and Medicine. Publication: ABC of Dermatology. Recreations: seafaring; books; art; country pursuits. Address: (h.) Old Inzievar House, Dunfermline, KY12 8HA; T.-01383 880297.

Byrne, John. Dramatist and stage designer; b. 1940, Paisley. Plays include: The Slab Boys, Cuttin' A Rug, Still Life (trilogy); Normal Service; Cara Coco; television series: Tutti Frutti; Your Cheatin' Heart.

C

Caddie, James Murdoch, MBIM. Adviser to voluntary organisations; Chief Executive, Clyde Development Corp Trust, since 1992; b. 2.11.27, Glasgow; m., Grace Betty (deceased); 2 d. Educ. Whitehill Senior Secondary School, Glasgow. Administrator: South of Scotland Electricity Board, 1948-71, NHS, 1971-77; formerly Chief Executive Officer, Epilepsy Association of Scotland. Member: local Health Council, 1978-83; Glasgow Council for Welfare of the Disabled; Chairman, Joint Epilepsy Associations Committee, 1980-88. Recreations: gardening; travel. Address: (h.) 35 Baldric Road, Glasgow, G13 3QJ; T.- 0141-959 7250.

Cadell, Colin Simson, CBE, DL, MA, AMIEE; b. 7.8.05, Colinton; m., Rosemary Elizabeth Pooley; 2 s.; 1 d. Educ. Merchiston; Edinburgh University; Ecole Superieure d'Electricite. Commissioned RAF, 1926; Director of Signals, RAF, 1944; AOC, 66 Group, 1946; Managing Director, International Aeradio, 1947; Vice-Lieutenant for West Lothian, 1972-86; Chairman, Edinburgh Airport Consultative Committee, 1972-83. Member, Royal Company of Archers (Queen's Bodyguard for Scotland); Legion of Merit (US). Address: (h.) 2 Upper Coltbridge Terrace, Edinburgh, EH12.

Cadell, Patrick Moubray, BA, FSA (Scot). Keeper of the Records of Scotland, since 1991; b. 17.3.41, Linlithgow; m., Sarah King; 2 s.; 1 d. Educ. Merchiston Castle School, Edinburgh; Cambridge University; Toulouse University. Information Officer, British Museum; Assistant Keeper, Department of MSS, British Museum; Keeper of Manuscripts, National Library of Scotland, 1983-90. Bailie, Abbey Court of Holyrood; Past President, West Lothian History and Amenity Society. Recreations: walking; the French language. Address: (b.) Scottish Record Office, HM General Register House, Edinburgh EH1 3YY; T.-0131-535 1312.

Cadell of Grange, William Archibald, DL, MA (Cantab), FRIAS. Architect; Commissioner, Royal Fine Art Commission for Scotland; b. 9.3.33, Aldershot; m., Mary-Jean Carmichael; 3 s. Educ. Merchiston Castle; Trinity College, Cambridge; Regent Street Polytechnic. Robert Matthew, Johnson Marshall and Partners; William A. Cadell Architects, 1968-95; DL, West Lothian, 1982; Member, Executive and Curatorial Committees, National Trust for Scotland; former Chairman, RIAS Conservation Working Group; former Chairman, West Lothian History and Amenity Society. Recreations: gardening; local history; theatre. Address: Grange, Linlithgow, West Lothian; T.- 01506 842946.

Caie, Professor Graham Douglas, MA, PhD. Professor of English Language, Glasgow University, since 1990; b. 3.2.45, Aberdeen; m., Ann Pringle Abbott; 1 s.; 1 d. Educ. Aberdeen Grammar School; Aberdeen University; McMaster University, Canada. Teaching Assistant, McMaster University, 1968-72; Amanuensis and Lektor, Copenhagen University, 1972-90. Chairman, Medieval Centre, Copenhagen University, 1985-90; Visiting Professor: McMaster University, 1985-86, Guelph University, 1989; Associate Fellow, Clare Hall, Cambridge, 1977-78; Secretary, Scottish Professors of English; Member, Board, McMaster Old English Texts series; Committee, Scottish Texts Society; Erasmus Academic Advisory Group (EC Commission); Board, European Society for the Study of English. Publications: The Theme of Doomsday in Old English Poetry; Beowulf; Bibliography of Junius XI MS; numerous articles. Address: (h.) 12B Upper Glenburn Road, Bearsden, Glasgow, G61 4BW; T.- 0141-943 1192.

Cairns, Rev. John Ballantyne, LTh, LLB. Parish Minister, Riverside Church, Dumbarton, since 1985; b. 15.3.42, London; m., Dr. Elizabeth Emma Bradley; 3 s. Educ. Sutton Valence School, Kent; Bristol University; Edinburgh University. Messrs Richards, Butler & Co., Solicitors, City of London, 1964-68; Administrative Assistant, East Lothian County Council, 1968-69; Assistant Minister, St. Giles, Elgin, 1973-75; Minister, Langholm, Ewes and Westerkirk Parish Churches, 1975-85, also linked with Canonbie, 1981-85; Clerk, Presbytery of Annandale and Eskdale, 1980-82; Convener, Maintenance of the Ministry Committee and Joint Convener, Board of Ministry and Mission, Church of Scotland, 1984-88; Chairman, Judicial Commission of General Assembly, since 1993; Convener, General Assembly Committee on Chaplains to Her Majesty's Forces, since 1993; Moderator, Presbytery of Dumbarton, 1993-94; Chaplain to Moderator of General Assembly, 1995; Divisional Chaplain, Strathclyde Police. Publications: Keeping Fit for Ministry, 1988; Democracy and Unwritten Constitutions, 1989. Recreations: golf; curling. Address: (b.) High Street, Dumbarton, G82 1NB; (h.) 5 Kirkton Road, Dumbarton, G82 4AS.

Cairns, Robert, MA, DipEd. Member, City of Edinburgh District Council, since 1974 (Convener, Planning and Development Committee, since 1986); b. 16.7.47, Dundee; m., Pauline Reidy; 2 s. Educ. Morgan Academy; Edinburgh University; Moray House College of Education. Assistant Editor, Scottish National Dictionary, 1969-74; Parliamentary candidate (Labour), North Edinburgh, 1973, February 1974; Teacher, James Gillespie's High School, since 1975; Board Member: Edinvar Housing Association, Old Town Renewal Trust, Old Town Community Development Project. Recreations: gardening; theatre. Address: (h.) 70 Ratcliffe Terrace, Edinburgh; T.-0131-667 1741.

Cairns, Professor Robert Alan, BSc, PhD, FInstP. Professor, School of Mathematical and Computational Sciences, St. Andrews University, since 1991 (Reader, 1985-91); b. 12.3.45, Glasgow; m., Ann E. Mackay. Educ. Allan Glen's School, Glasgow; Glasgow University. Lecturer in Applied Mathematics, St. Andrews University, 1970-83; Senior Lecturer, 1983-85; Consultant, UKAEA Culham Laboratory, since 1984. Committee Member, Plasma Physics Group, Institute of Physics, 1981-84; Member, SERC Laser Committee, 1990-93; Member, SERC Atomic and Molecular Physics Sub-Committee, 1990-93; Member, Editorial Board, Plasma Physics, 1983-85; Editor, Journal of Plasma Physics, since 1995. Publications: Plasma Physics, 1985; Radiofrequency heating of plasmas, 1991. Recreations: music (listening to and playing recorder and baroque flute); golf; hill-walking. Address: (b.) Department of Mathematical and Computational Sciences, St. Andrews University, North Haugh, St. Andrews, Fife, KY16 9SS; T.-01334 63743.

Cairns, Walter. Literature Director, Scottish Arts Council. Address: (b.) 12 Manor Place, Edinburgh, EH3 7DD.

Calder, Professor Andrew Alexander, MD, FRCS(Edin), FRCP (Glas and Edin), FRCOG. Professor of Obstetrics and Gynaecology, Edinburgh University, since 1987; Consultant Gynaecologist, Edinburgh Royal Infirmary and Consultant Obstetrician, Simpson Memorial Maternity Pavilion, Edinburgh, since 1987; b. 17.1.45, Aberdeen; m., Valerie Anne Dugard; 1 s.; 2 d. Educ. Glasgow Academy; Glasgow University. Clinical training posts in obstetrics and gynaecology, 1969-72: Queen Mother's Hospital, Western Infirmary, Royal Maternity Hospital and Royal Infirmary, (all Glasgow); Research Fellow, Nuffield Department of Obstetrics and Gynaecology, Oxford University, 1972-75; Lecturer in Obstetrics and Gynaecology, Glasgow University, 1975-78, Senior Lecturer, 1978-86. Secretary, Munro Kerr Society for the Study of Reproductive Biology, 1980-86, Chairman, since 1989; Blair Bell Memorial

Lecturer, RCOG, 1977; WHO Travelling Fellow, 1985; British Exchange Professor, UCLA, 1992. Recreations: music; golf; curling. Address: (h.) 21 Braid Avenue, Edinburgh, EH10 4SR; T.-0131-447 0490.

Calder, Angus Lindsay, MA, DPhil. Writer; Reader and Staff Tutor in Arts, Open University in Scotland, 1979-93; b. 5.2.42, Sutton, Surrey; m., 1, Jennifer Daiches; 1 s.; 2 d.; 2, Catherine Kyle; 1 s. Educ. Wallington County Grammar School; Kings College, Cambridge. Lecturer in Literature, Nairobi University, 1968-71; Visiting Lecturer, Chancellor College, Malawi University, 1978; Visiting Professor of English, University of Zimbabwe, 1990; Member, Board of Directors, Royal Lyceum Theatre Company; Editorial Committee, Cencrastus; Member, Panel of Judges, Saltire Society Scottish Book of the Year Award, since 1983; Eric Gregory Award for Poetry, 1967. Publications: The People's War: Britain 1939-1945, 1969 (John Llewellyn Rhys Memorial Prize); Revolutionary Empire, 1981 (Scottish Arts Council Book Award); The Myth of the Blitz, 1991; Revolving Culture: notes from the Scottish Republic, 1994 (SAC Book Award). Recreations: curling; cricket. Address: (h.) 15 Leven Terrace, Edinburgh, EH3 9LW; T.-0131-229 8196.

Calder, Finlay, OBE. Grain Exporter; b. 20.8.57, Haddington; m., Elizabeth; 1 s.; 1 d. Educ. Daniel Stewart's and Melville College. Played rugby for Scotland, 1986-90; captained Scotland, 1989; captained British Isles, 1989. Recreation: work! Address: (b.) 3 John's Place, Leith, EH6 7EL; T.-0131-554 6263.

Calder, George D., BA (Hons), LLB, MIPM. Assistant Secretary, Scottish Office, since 1987; b. 20.12.47, Edinburgh; m., Kathleen Bonar; 2 d. Educ. George Watson's College; Pembroke College, Cambridge; Edinburgh University. Department of Employment, 1971-73; European Commission, 1973-76; HM Treasury, 1976-79; Manpower Services Commission Scotland, 1979-83; MSC Director for Northern England, 1983-85; MSC Director for Scotland, 1985-87. Recreations: hill-walking; football; reading; writing; book collecting. Address: (b.) 16 Waterloo Place, Edinburgh; T.-0131-244 3848.

Calder, Jenni, BA, MPhil. Freelance Writer; Head of Publications, National Museums of Scotland, Edinburgh, since 1987; b. 3.12.41, Chicago, Illinois; 1 s.; 2 d. Educ. Perse School for Girls, Cambridge; Cambridge University; London University. Freelance writer, 1966-78; taught and lectured in Scotland, England, Kenya and USA; Lecturer in English, Nairobi University, 1968-69; Education Officer, Royal Scottish Museum, 1978-87. Publications: Chronicles of Conscience: a study of George Orwell and Arthur Koestler, 1968; Scott (with Angus Calder), 1969; There Must be a Lone Ranger: the Myth and Reality of the American West, 1974; Women and Marriage in Victorian Fiction, 1976; Brave New World and Nineteen Eighty Four, 1976; Heroes: from Byron to Guevara, 1977; The Victorian Home, 1977; The Victorian Home from Old Photographs, 1979; RLS, A Life Study, 1980; The Robert Louis Stevenson Companion (Editor), 1980; Robert Louis Stevenson and Victorian Scotland (Editor), 1981; The Strange Case of Dr Jekyll and Mr Hyde (Editor), 1979; Kidnapped (Editor), 1981; Catriona (Editor), 1981; The Enterprising Scot (Editor), 1986; Island Landfalls (Editor), 1987; Bonny Fighters: The Story of the Scottish Soldier, 1987; Open Guide to Animal Farm and Nineteen Eighty Four, 1987; The Wealth of a Nation (Editor), 1989; St. Ives, a new ending, 1990; Scotland in Trust, 1990; Treasure Island (Editor); Margaret Oliphant, 1995; Mediterranean (poems, as Jenni Daiches). Recreations: music; films; walking the dog. Address: (h.) 31 Station Road, South Queensferry, West Lothian; T.-0131-331 1287.

Calder, Robert Russell, MA. Critic, Philosophical Writer, Historian of Ideas, Poet, Freelance Journalist, Book Reviewer; b. 22.4.50, Burnbank. Educ. Hamilton Academy; Glasgow University; Edinburgh University. Co-Editor, Chapman, 1974-76 and since 1988; Editor, Lines Review, 1976-77; Theatre Critic and Feature Writer, Scot, 1983-86; books: A School of Thinking, 1995; Narcissism, Nihilism, Simplicity (Editor), 1992; poetry: Il Re Giovane, 1976, Ettrick & Annan, 1981; Serapion, 1993. Recreations: music - opera singing; jazz piano. Address: (h.) 23 Glenlee Street, Burnbank, Hamilton, ML3 9JB; T.-01698 824244.

Calderwood, Sir Robert, Kt. Deputy Chairman, Scottish Opera, since 1991; Chairman, Greater Glasgow Health Board, since 1993; Chief Executive, Strathclyde Regional Council, 1980-92; b. 1.3.32; m., Meryl Anne; 3 s.; 1 d. Educ. William Hulme's School, Manchester; Manchester University (LLB Hons). Town Clerk: Salford, 1966-69, Bolton, 1969-73, Manchester, 1973-79. Director, Glasgow Garden Festival 1988 Ltd., 1985-88; Chairman, Strathclyde Buses Ltd., 1989-93; Member: Parole Board for England and Wales, 1971-73; Society of Local Authority Chief Executives, since 1974 (President, 1989-90); Scottish Consultative Committee, Commission for Racial Equality, 1981-88; Director, European Summer Special Olympic Games 1990 (Strathclyde) Ltd., 1989-90; Member, Council, Industrial Society, since 1983; Director, GEC (Scotland) Ltd., since 1991; Director, Scottish Opera, since 1991; Member, Court of Governors, Glasgow Caledonian University, since 1994. Hon. Fellow, IWEM, 1992. Recreations: theatre; watching rugby; interested in United Nations activities. Address:(h.) 6 Mosspark Avenue, Milngavie, Glasgow, G62 8NL.

Calderwood, Robert. Chief Executive, Southern General Hospital NHS Trust. Address: (b.) 1345 Govan Road, Glasgow, G51 4TF.

Caldwell, David Cleland, SHNC, MA, BPhil. Secretary, The Robert Gordon University, since 1984; b. 25.2.44, Glasgow; m., Ann Scott Macrae; 1 s.; 1 d. Educ. George Watson's College, Edinburgh; St. Andrews University; Glasgow University. Warwick University: Lecturer in Politics, 1969-76, Administrative Assistant, 1976-77, Assistant Registrar, 1977-80; Registry Officer, Aberdeen University, 1980-84. Member: Warwick District Council, 1979-80, Grampian Regional Council, 1983-84; Parliamentary candidate (Labour), North East Fife, 1988; Member, Aberdeen Grammar School Council, 1983-88 (Chairman, 1985-88); Member, St. Andrews University Court, 1986-94 (Convener, Audit Commitee, 1990-94); Member, Board of Management, Moray College, since 1995; Director, Viscom (Aberdeen) Ltd., since 1992 (Chairman, 1994-95). Address: (b.) The Robert Gordon University, Schoolhill, Aberdeen, AB9 1FR; T.-01224 262010.

Caldwell, David Hepburn, MA, PhD, FSAScot. Curator in Charge of the Scottish Medieval Collections, Royal Museum of Scotland; b. 15.12.51, Kilwinning, Ayrshire; m., Margaret Anne McGovern; 1 s.; 2 d. Educ. Ardrossan Academy; Edinburgh University. Joined staff, National Museum of Antiquities, 1973. Publications: The Scottish Armoury, 1979; Scottish Weapons and Fortifications, 1981. Recreation: travelling. Address: (h.) 3 James Park, Burntisland, Fife, KY3 9EW; T.-872175.

Caldwell, Sheila Marion, BA (Hons). General Secretary, Glasgow Association of Women Graduates; Member, Committee, Royal Scottish Geographical Society; b. England; m., Major Robert Caldwell, TD. Educ. Tunbridge Wells Grammar School; University College, London. Founder/Principal, Yejide Girls' Grammar School, Ibadan, Nigeria; first Principal, Girls' Secondary (Government) School, Lilongwe, Malawi; Depute Head, Mills Grammar School, Framlingham, Suffolk; Head, St. Columba's School, Kilmacolm, 1976-87; Treasurer, Secondary Heads' Association, Scotland, 1984-87. Recreations: travel; art history and architecture; music, opera and ballet; cooking. Address: (h.) 27 Oxford Road, Renfrew, PA4 0SJ; T.-0141-886 2296.

Calman, Professor Kenneth Charles, MD, PhD, FRCP, FRCS, FRSE. Chief Medical Officer, Department of Health, since 1991; Chief Medical Officer, Scottish Home and Health Department, 1989-91; b. 25.12.41, Glasgow; m., Ann; 1 s.; 2 d. Educ. Allan Glen's School, Glasgow; Glasgow University. Lecturer in Surgery, Western Infirmary, Glasgow, 1968-72; MRC Clinical Research Fellow, London, 1972-73; Professor of Oncology, Glasgow University, 1974-84; Dean of Postgraduate Medicine, 1984-89. Recreations: golf; jogging; gardening. Address: (h.) 585 Anniesland Road, Glasgow; T.-0141-954 9423.

Calvocoressi, Richard. Keeper, Scottish National Gallery of Modern Art, since 1987; b. 5.5.51; m.; 1 s.; 2 d. Educ. Eton; Magdalen College, Oxford.

Cameron, Alan Iain, BSc. Rector, Ellon Academy, since 1981; b. 21.9.41, Southend, Argyll; m., Elizabeth Margaret Logan; 2 s. (1 dec.); 1 d. Educ. Campbeltown Grammar School; Glasgow University; Jordanhill College. Teacher of Physics/Chemistry, Campbeltown Grammar School, 1964-67; Head of Science, Invergordon Academy, 1967-74; Head of Chemistry, Mackie Academy, 1974-77; Depute Head Teacher, Selkirk High School, 1977-81. President, Ellon Rotary Club, 1988-89; Council, Headmasters' Association of Scotland, 1992-96; Founder and President, Ellon Burns Club, Ellon Gaelic Choir. Recreations: singing (Gaelic choir); bagpipes; church choir; golf. Address: (h.) Ceol Nan Craobis, 5 Fechil Brae, Ellon, AB41 8NS; T.-01358 720 130.

Cameron, Alasdair, FSA Scot. Farmer and Crofter; Commissioner and Vice Chairman, Crofters Commission; b. 12.6.44, Dingwall; m., Jeannette Benzie; 2 d. Educ. Dingwall Academy. Member, Scottish Agricultural Arbiters Association; Member, Northern Counties Valuators Association; Chairman, Highland Farming and Forestry Advisory Group; Hon. President, Black Isle Farmers Society; Member, Scottish Vernacular Buildings Working Group; Member, Historic Farm Buildings UK; Past Chairman, Dingwall Round Table. Recreations: photography; industrial archaeology; local history; the countryside. Address: Wellhouse Farm, Black Isle, Muir of Ord, Ross-shire, IV6 7SF; T.-01463 870416.

Cameron, Alexander, BA, CertASS, CQSW. Director of Social Work, Borders Regional Council, since 1987; b. 29.4.50, Glasgow; m., Linda Dobbie; 2 s. Educ. Duncanrig Senior Secondary; East Kilbride; Strathclyde University; Aberdeen University. Social Worker, Clackmannan County Council, 1973-75; Central Regional Council; Research/Planning Officer, 1975-79, Principal Officer (Fieldwork), 1979-81, Assistant Director of Social Work, 1981-87. Secretary, Association of Directors of Social Work. Recreations: rugby; Scottish country dancing. Address: (h.) Glencairn, Gattonside, Melrose, Roxburghshire; T.-01896 82 2831.

Cameron, Allan John, DL, MBE, VL, JP. Convener, Ross and Cromarty District Council; Farmer and Landowner, since 1947; b. 25.3.17, Edinburgh; m., Elizabeth Vaughan-Lee; 2 s.; 2 d. Educ. Harrow; Royal Military College. Regular officer, Queen's Own Cameron Highlanders, 1936-47 (ret. Major); Member, Ross and Cromarty County Council, 1955-75 (Chairman, Education Committee, 1962-75); Member, Ross and Cromarty District Council, since 1975 (Convener, since 1991); former Commissioner: Red Deer Commission, Countryside Commission for Scotland; former Member, BBC Council for Scotland; President, Royal Caledonian Curling Club, 1963; President, International Curling Federation, 1965-69. Recreations: curling; golf; shooting; fishing; gardening. Address: (h.)

Allangrange, Munlochy, Ross and Cromarty, IV8 8NZ; T.-014638 11249.

Cameron, Rt. Rev. Andrew Bruce. Bishop of Aberdeen and Orkney, Scottish Episcopal Church, since 1992; b. 2.5.41, Glasgow; m., Elaine Cameron; 2 s. Educ. Eastwood Secondary School; Edinburgh Theological College. Curate, Helensburgh and Edinburgh, 1964-70; Chaplain, St. Mary's Cathedral, Edinburgh, 1970-75; Diocesan and Provincial Youth Chaplain, 1969-75; Rector, St. Mary's Church, Dalmahoy, and Anglican Chaplain, Heriot Watt University, 1975-82; Churches Development Officer, Livingston Ecumenical Parish, 1982-88; Rector, St. John's Episcopal Church, Perth, 1988-92; Convener, Mission Board, Scottish Episcopal Church, 1988-92. Recreations: music; theatre; various sports; gardening. Address: Bishop's House, Ashley House, Ashley Gardens, Aberdeen, AB1 6RQ; T.-01224 208142.

Cameron, Colin. Head of Television, BBC Scotland, since 1991; b. 30.3.50; m., Christine Main; 2 s. Educ. Glasgow Academy; Duke of York School, Nairobi; Polytechnic of Central London. Journalist, Current Affairs, BBC Scotland, 1973-76; Film Director, That's Life, 1976-77; Producer/Director, Everyman and Heart of the Matter, 1977-85; Editor, Brass Tacks, BBC North, 1985-88; Head of Documentary Features, BBC Television, 1988-91. Board Member, Scottish Film Production Fund; RTS International Current Affairs Award, 1984; UN Association Media Peace Prize, 1984. Recreations: dinghy sailing; cycling; cinema; Scottish art. Address: (b.) BBC Scotland, Queen Margaret Drive, Glasgow, G12 8DG; T.-0141-338 2424.

Cameron, David Roderick Simpson, RIBA, ARIAS, MRTPI, FSA (Scot). Architect/Planner; Chairman, The Saltire Society, since 1990; Convener, Historic Burghs Association of Scotland (Steering Committee), since 1993; Convener, Charles Cameron Conservation Campaign (St. Petersburg), since 1944; Chairman, Sir Patrick Geddes Memorial Trust, since 1991; Depute Director of Planning, City of Edinburgh District Council, since 1983; European Union, ECOS Project Manager (of Edinburgh and Berlin team) for revival of Kazimierz quarter of Krakow, Poland, since 1993; b. 2.6.41, Inverness; m., Filitsa Boulton; 1 s.; 2 d. Educ. Angusfield and George Watson's College; Edinburgh College of Art; Newcastle University. Architect, Rowand Anderson, Kininmonth and Paul, 1968-71; Conservation Officer, Edinburgh Corporation and Edinburgh District Council, 1971-83. Secretary, Saltire Arts and Crafts in Architecture Award Panel, 1987-94; Secretary, Saltire Housing Award Panel, 1974-83; Hon. Secretary, Edinburgh Architectural Association, 1972-75; and Editor, EAA Review, 1980-84; Member, Executive Committee, Scottish Society of Directors of Planning, since 1988; Member, Clan Cameron Council, since 1988, and Honorary Treasurer, since 1995; Member of Council, National Trust for Scotland, since 1994. Recreations: art; fishing; Scottish and Greek history. Address: The Saltire Society, 9 Fountain Close, 22 High Street, Edinburgh, EH1 1TF; T.-0131-556 1836.

Cameron, Younger of Lochiel, Donald Angus, MA, FCA, DL. Director, J. Henry Schroder Wagg & Co. Limited, since 1984; b. 2.8.46, London; m., Lady Cecil Kerr; 1 s. 3 d. Educ. Harrow; Christ Church, Oxford. 2nd Lieutenant, Queen's Own Cameron Highlanders (TA), 1966-68; Chartered Accountant, 1971. DL, Lochaber, Inverness, Badenoch and Strathspey. Address: (h.) Achnacarry, Spean Bridge, Inverness-shire.

Cameron of Lochiel, Colonel Sir Donald (Hamish), KT (1973), CVO, TD, JP. 26th Chief of the Clan Cameron; Lord Lieutenant, County of Inverness, 1971-86; Chartered Accountant; b. 12.9.10; m., Margaret Gathorne-Hardy; 2 s.; 2 d. Educ. Harrow; Balliol College, Oxford. Lt.-Col. commanding: Lovat Scouts, 1944-45; 4/5th Bn. (TA),

Queen's Own Cameron Highlanders, 1955-57; Colonel, 1957 (TARO); Vice-Chairman, Royal Bank of Scotland, 1969-80; Chairman, Culter Guard Bridge Holdings Ltd., 1970-76; Chairman, Scottish Widows Life Assurance Society, 1964-67; President, Scottish Landowners Federation, 1979-84; President, Royal Highland and Agricultural Society of Scotland, 1971, 1979, 1987; Member, Scottish Railways Board (Chairman, 1959-64). Address: (h.) Achnacarry, Spean Bridge, Inverness-shire.

Cameron, Rt. Rev. Douglas M. Bishop of Argyll and Isles, since 1993; b. 23.3.35, Natal; m., Anne Patricia Purnell; 2 d. Educ. Eastwood Grammar School; Edinburgh Theological College; University of the South, Sewanee, Tennessee. Curator, Christ Church, Falkirk, 1962-65; Priest, Papua New Guinea, 1965-74, Archdeacon, 1972-74; Rector: St. Fillan's and St. Hilda's, Edinburgh, 1974-88, St. Mary's, Dalkeith, and St. Edward's, Lasswade, 1988-92; Canon and Synod Clerk, Diocese of Edinburgh, 1990-92; Dean of Edinburgh, 1991-92. Recreations: hill-walking; music; cooking. Address: (b.) The Pines, Ardconnel Road, Oban, PA34 5DR; T.-01631 66912.

Cameron, Professor Dugald, DA, FCSD, FRSA. Director, Glasgow School of Art, since 1991; Hon. Professor, Glasgow University, since 1993; Director, Squadron Prints, since 1977; Industrial Design Consultant, since 1965; b. 4.10.39, Glasgow; m., Nancy Inglis. Educ. Glasgow High School; Glasgow School of Art. Industrial Designer, Hard Aluminium Surfaces Ltd., 1962-65; Visiting Lecturer, Glasgow School of Art, 1963-70; Head of Product Design, Glasgow School of Art, 1970-82; Head of Design, 1982-91. Member: Engineering Advisory Committee, Scottish Committee, Council of Industrial Design, since 1966, Industrial Design (Engineering) Panel and 3D Design Board, CNAA, since 1978, Scottish Committee of Higher Education, Design Council; commission RAFVR (T), 1974. Publications: Glasgow's Own (a history of 602 City of Glasgow Squadron, Royal Auxiliary Air Force), 1987; Glasgow's Airport, 1990. Recreations: railways; flying (lapsed private pilot). Address: (h.) Achnacraig, Skelmorlie, Ayrshire.

Cameron, Duncan Inglis, OBE, JP, BL, DUniv, CA, FRSGS. Director of Administration and Secretary, Heriot-Watt University, 1965-90; b. 26.8.27, Glasgow; m., Elizabeth Pearl Heron; 2 s.; 1 d. Educ. Glasgow High School; Glasgow University. RAF, 1945-48; CA apprentice, Alfred Tongue & Co., 1948-51; Qualified Assistant, Cooper Brothers & Co., 1951-52; Assistant Accountant, Edinburgh University, 1952-65; Commonwealth Universities Administrative Fellow, 1972. President, Edinburgh Junior Chamber of Commerce, 1962-63; Governor, Keil School, Dumbarton, 1967-85; Chairman of Council, Royal Scottish Geographical Society, 1983-88 (Trustee, since 1973); Governor, Scottish College of Textiles, since 1991; Chairman, Bioscot Ltd., 1983-84; Chairman, Edinburgh Conference Centre Ltd., 1987-90; Director, Heriot-Watt Computer Application Services Ltd., 1987-90; Chairman, SCOT Innovation and Development Ltd., since 1991; Member, Universities Central Council on Admissions, 1967-90; Member, Directing Group, Programme on Institutional Management in Higher Education, OECD, Paris, 1986-90; Member, Executive Committee, Federated Superannuation System for Universities, since 1988; Member, Executive Committee, Scottish Norwegian Business Forum, since 1991; Member, Board of Management, Petroleum Science and Technology Institute, 1989-93; Chairman, Edinburgh Society of Glasgow University Graduates, 1984-85; Session Clerk, St. Ninian's Church, Corstorphine, since 1969; Honorary Fellow, Royal Scottish Geographical Society, 1989; Honorary Doctor, Heriot-Watt University, 1991; Officer of the Royal Norwegian Order of St. Olav, 1979. Recreations: travel; photography. Address: (h.) 11 The Hermitage, 11 Kinellan Road, Edinburgh, EH12 6ES; T.-0131 346 4454.

Cameron, Brigadier Ewen Duncan, OBE. Director of Administration and Personnel, National Trust for Scotland, since 1986; b. 10.2.35, Bournemouth; m., Joanna Margaret Hay; 2 d. Educ. Wellington College; Royal Military Academy, Sandhurst. Commissioned The Black Watch, 1955; DS, The Staff College, 1972-75; Commanding Officer, 1st Bn., The Black Watch, 1975-78; Commander, Royal Brunei Armed Forces, 1980-82; Indian College of Defence Studies, Delhi, 1983; Divisional Brigadier, Scottish Division, 1984-86. Member, Queen's Bodyguard for Scotland (Royal Company of Archers). Recreations: music; bird-watching; squash; skiing; gardening. Address: (h.) The Old Manse, Arngask, Glenfarg, Perthshire, PH2 9QG; T.-01577 830394.

Cameron, Professor George Gordon, BSc, PhD, DSc, FRSE. Professor of Physical Chemistry, Aberdeen University, since 1984; b. 1.12.32, Stirling; m., Aileen Elizabeth Sinclair; 1 s.; 2 d. Educ. Stirling High School; Glasgow University. Lecturer in Chemistry, St. Andrews University, 1961; Lecturer in Physical Chemistry, then Senior Lecturer, then Reader, Aberdeen University, 1966-84. Recreations: outdoor activities (walking, skiing); music. Address: (b.) Department of Chemistry, Aberdeen University, Aberdeen, AB9 2UE; T.-01224 272903.

Cameron, Professor Iain Thomas, BSc (Hons), MA (Cantab), MD (Edin), MRCOG, MRACOG. Regius Professor, Obstetrics and Gynaecology, Queen Mother's Hospital, Glasgow; b. 21.2.56, Flixton; m., Heidi D. Wade; 1 s.; 2 d by pr. m. Educ. Hutton Grammar School; Edinburgh University. Research Fellow, Department of Obstetrics and Gynaecology, Edinburgh University, 1982-84; Lecturer and Registrar, 1984-86; Clinical Research Fellow, Monash University, 1986-88; Senior Registrar, Royal Women's Hospital, Melbourne, 1988-89; Lecturer, Cambridge University, 1989-92. Recreation: solo piping. Address: (b.) Department of Obstetrics and Gynaecology, Queen Mother's Hospital, Glasgow, G3 8SJ; T.-0141-201 0567.

Cameron, Sheriff Ian Alexander, MA, LLB. Sheriff of Grampian, Highland and Islands, at Wick, Dornoch and Stornoway, since 1993; b. 5.11.38, Elgin; m., Dr. Margaret Anne Cameron; 1 s. Educ. Elgin Academy; Edinburgh University; Aberdeen University. Partner, Stewart and McIsaac, Solicitors, Elgin, 1962-86; Sheriff at Edinburgh, 1987-93. Recreations: travel; railway history. Address: Achnacarry, Elgin, IV30 1NU; T.-0343 542731; 19/4 Damside, Dean Village, Edinburgh, EH4 3BB; T.-031-220 1548.

Cameron, Professor Rev. James Kerr, MA, BD, PhD, FRHistS. Professor of Ecclesiastical History, St. Andrews University, 1970-89; b. 5.3.24, Methven; m., Emma Leslie Birse; 1 s. Educ. Oban High School; St. Andrews University; Hartford Theological Seminary, Hartford, Connecticut. Ordained as Assistant Minister, Church of the Holy Rude, Stirling, 1952; appointed Lecturer in Church History, Aberdeen University, 1955; Lecturer, then Senior Lecturer in Ecclesiastical History, St. Andrews University; Dean, Faculty of Divinity, 1978-83. President: Ecclesiastical History Society, 1976-77, British Sub-Commission, Commission Internationale d'Histoire Ecclesiastique Comparee, 1979-92; Vice-President, International Association for Neo-Latin Studies, 1979-81. Publications: Letters of John Johnston and Robert Howie, 1963; First Book of Discipline, 1972; contributions to: Acta Conventus Neo-Latini Amstelodamensis, 1973; Advocates of Reform, 1953; The Scottish Tradition, 1974; Renaissance and Renewal in Christian History, 1977; Reform and Reformation: England and the Continent, 1979; Origins and Nature of the Scottish Enlightenment, 1982; A Companion to Scottish Culture. Recreation: gardening. Address: (h.) Priorscroft, 71 Hepburn Gardens, St. Andrews, KY16 9LS; T.-01334 473996.

Cameron, J. Gordon, MA, LLB, DipLP, WS, NP. Partner, Stuart & Stuart WS, since 1987; b. 15.11.57, Edinburgh; m., Deborah Jane; 1 s. Educ. George Watson's College; Aberdeen University. Joined Stuart & Stuart WS as assistant, 1985. Hon. Secretary and Treasurer, Royal Celtic Society. Recreations: hill-walking; cycling; keep-fit. Address: (b.) 23 Rutland Street, Edinburgh, EH1 2RN; T.-0131-228 6449.

Cameron, John Bell, CBE, FRAgricS, AIAgricE. Chairman, British Railways (Scottish) Board, 1988-93; Member, British Railways Board, 1988-94; Farmer, since 1961; b. 14.6.39, Edinburgh; m., Margaret Clapperton. Educ. Dollar Academy. Vice President, National Farmers' Union, 1976-79, President, 1979-84; Member, Agricultural Praesidium of EEC, 1979-84; Chairman, EEC Advisory Committee for Sheepmeat, 1982-90; Chairman, World Meats Group, (IFAP), since 1983; Chairman, Board of Governors, Dollar Academy, since 1985; Chairman, United Auctions Ltd., since 1985; Member, Board of Governors, Macaulay Land Use Research Institute, since 1987. Long Service Award, Royal Observer Corps. Recreations: flying; shooting; travelling. Address: (h.) Balbuthie Farm, by Leven, Fife; T.-01333 730210.

Cameron, Hon. Lord (John Cameron), KT (1978), Kt (1954). Senator of the College of Justice in Scotland and Lord of Session, 1955-85; b. 1900. Sheriff of Inverness, Elgin and Nairn, 1945; Sheriff of Inverness, Moray, Nairn and Ross and Cromarty, 1946-48; Dean, Faculty of Advocates, 1948-55.

Cameron, (John Roderick) Hector, LLB, NP. Solicitor; Director, Telecom Service Centres Ltd.; Director, McColl McGregor Ltd.; b. 11.6.47, Glasgow; m., Rosemary Brownlee; 1 s.; 1 d. Educ. High School of Glasgow; Friends School, Wigton; St. Andrews University. Admitted Solicitor, 1971; Partner, Bishop, Milne Boyd & Co., 1973; Chairman, Glasgow Junior Chamber of Commerce, 1981; Managing Partner, Bishop & Co., 1985; Partner, Dorman Jeffrey & Co., 1990; Director, Merchants House of Glasgow, 1986; Director, Glasgow Chamber of Commerce, 1987. Chairman, Strathclyde Appeal Committee, Help the Aged, 1987. Recreations: reading; gardening; sailing; golf. Address: (h.) 5 Cleveden Crescent, Glasgow, G12 0PD.

Cameron, Rev. Dr. John Urquhart, BA, BSc, PhD, BD, ThD. Minister, Parish of Broughty Ferry, since 1974; b. 10.6.43, Dundee; m., Jill Sjoberg; 1 s.; 1 d. Educ. Falkirk High School; St. Andrews University; Edinburgh University; University of Southern California. Marketing Executive, Beechams, London, 1969-73; Assistant Minister, Wellington Church, Glasgow, 1973-74; Chaplain, Royal Naval Reserve, 1976-81; Marketing Consultant, Pergamon Press, Oxford, 1977-81; Religious Education Department, Dundee High School, 1980-87; Sports Journalist and Travel Writer, Hill Publications, Surrey, since 1981; Physics Department, Dundee College of Further Education, since 1987; Moderator, Presbytery of Dundee, since 1993; Chaplain, Royal Caledonian Curling Club. National and international honours in both summer and winter sports, 1960-85; sports scholarship, University of Southern California, 1962-64. Recreations: golf; skiing; curling. Address: St. Stephen's Manse, 33 Camperdown Street, Broughty Ferry; T.-01382 77403.

Cameron of Lochbroom, Lord (Kenneth John Cameron), Life Baron (1984), PC (1984), MA (Oxon), LLB, QC, FRSE, Hon. FRIAS. Senator of the College of Justice, since 1989; Chairman, Royal Fine Art Commission for Scotland; b. 11.6.31, Edinburgh; m., Jean Pamela Murray; 2 d. Educ. Edinburgh Academy; Corpus Christi College, Oxford; Edinburgh University. Advocate, 1958; Queen's Counsel, 1972; President, Pensions Appeal Tribunal for Scotland, 1976; Chairman, Committee of Investigation Under Agricultural Marketing Act 1958,

1980; Advocate Depute, 1981; Lord Advocate, 1984; Hon. Bencher, Lincoln's Inn; Hon. Fellow, Corpus Christi College, Oxford. Recreations: fishing; sailing. Address: (h.) 10 Belford Terrace, Edinburgh.

Cameron, Sheriff Lewis, MA, LLB. Solicitor, since 1962; Sheriff of South Strathclyde Dumfries and Galloway at Hamilton, since 1994, at Dumfries, 1988-94; b. 12.8.35, Glasgow; m., Sheila Colette Gallacher; 2 s.; 2 d. Educ. St. Aloysius College; Blairs College; St. Sulpice, Paris; Glasgow University. RAF, 1954-56; admitted Solicitor, 1962. Member, Legal Aid Central Committee, 1970-80; Legal Aid Secretary, Airdrie, 1978-87; Chairman, Social Security Appeal Tribunals, 1983-88; Dean, Airdrie Society of Solicitors, 1984-85; Tutor, Strathclyde University, 1981-88; Treasurer, Monklands Victim Support Scheme, 1983-88; Chairman, Dumfries and Galloway Family Conciliation Service, 1988-92; Chairman, Dumfries and Galloway, Scottish Association for the Study of Delinquency, 1988-92; Member, Scotland Committee, National Children's Homes; Trustee, Oscar Marzaroli Trust; Chairman, PHEW. Address: (b.) Sheriff Court House, Beckford Street, Hamilton.

Cameron, Roy, QPM, BA, MPhil. Chief Constable, Dumfries and Galloway Constabulary. Address: (b.) Cornwall Mount, Dumfries, DG1 1PZ.

Cameron, Thomas Anthony (Tony). Under Secretary (Agriculture), Scottish Office, since 1992; b. 3.2.47; m., Elizabeth Christine Sutherland; 2 s. Educ. Stranraer High School. Department of Agriculture and Fisheries for Scotland, 1966; Private Secretary to Deputy Under Secretary of State, Scottish Office, 1972, to Permanent Under Secretary of State, 1973-74; HEO(D), DAFS, 1974-77; Principal, DAFS, 1977-82; Assistant Secretary, DAFS, 1982-87; Scottish Office Finance Division, 1987-92. Recreations: reading; mountaineering; cycling. Address: Scottish Office Agriculture and Fisheries Department, Pentland House, 47 Robb's Loan, Edinburgh.

Campbell, Alan Grant, LLB. Chief Executive, Grampian Regional Council, since 1991; b. 4.12.46, Aberdeen; m., Susan Black; 1 s.; 2 d. Educ. Aberdeen Grammar School; Aberdeen University. Aberdeen County Council: Law apprentice/Solicitor, 1968-72, Senior Legal Assistant, 1972-75; Grampian Regional Council: Assistant Director of Law and Administration, 1975-79, Depute Director, 1979-84, Director of Law and Administration, 1984-91; Seminar Leader, Diploma in Legal Practice, Aberdeen University. Recreation: cycling. Address: Woodhill House, Westburn Road, Aberdeen, AB9 2LU; T.-01224 682222, Ext. 4400.

Campbell, Alasdair, MA. Writer; b. 27.5.41, Ness, Lewis; m., Alison Munro; 3 s.; 3 d. Educ. Nicolson Institute, Stornoway; Aberdeen University. Gaelic play broadcast by BBC Scotland (radio), 1981, followed by various plays, short stories, and novels; Writer in Residence, Sabhal Mor Ostaig, Skye, 1988-90. Address: (h.) Druim Fraoich, Garrie View, Conon Bridge, Ross-shire; T.-01349 861460.

Campbell of Airds, Alastair Lorne. Chief Executive, Clan Campbell, since 1984; Archivist, Inveraray Castle, since 1984; H.M. Unicorn Pursuivant of Arms, Court of the Lord Lyon, since 1987; b. 11.7.37, London; m., Mary-Ann Campbell-Preston; 3 s.; 1 d. Educ. Eton; R.M.A., Sandhurst. Regular Army, 1955-63 (commissioned Argyll and Sutherland Highlanders); Reid Pye and Campbell, 1963-71 (Managing Director, 1970-71); Waverley Vintners Ltd., 1972-83 (Marketing Director, 1972, Managing Director, 1977). Member, Queen's Bodyguard for Scotland (Royal Company of Archers); FSA Scot; Patron, Armorial and Heraldry Society of Australasia; Chairman, Advisory Committee on Tartan to the Lord Lyon. Publications: Two Hundred Years — The Highland Society of London; The Life and Troubled Times of Sir Donald Campbell of

Ardnamurchan. Recreations: painting; fishing; walking. Address: (h.) Inverawe Barn, Taynuilt, Argyll, PA35 1HU; T.-0186 62 207.

Campbell, Professor Alexander George Macpherson, MB, ChB, FRCPEdin, DCH. Emeritus Professor of Child Health, Aberdeen University; b. 3.2.31, Glasgow; m., Sheila Mary Macdonald; 1 s.; 2 d. Educ. Dollar Academy; Glasgow University. Paediatric Registrar, Royal Hospital for Sick Children, Edinburgh, 1959-61; Senior House Officer, Hospital for Sick Children, London, 1961-62; Assistant Chief Resident, Children's Hospital of Philadelphia, 1962-63; Fellow in Paediatric Cardiology, Hospital for Sick Children, Toronto, 1963-64; Fellow in Fetal and Neonatal Physiology, Nuffield Institute for Medical Research, Oxford, 1964-66; Lecturer in Child Health, St. Andrews University, 1966-67; Assistant, then Associate Professor of Paediatrics, Yale University School of Medicine, 1967-73; Professor of Child Health, Aberdeen University, 1973-92. Chairman, Joint Committee for Vaccination and Immunisation, Department of Health. Recreation: golf. Address: (h.) 34 Woodburn Crescent, Aberdeen; T.-01224 319152.

Campbell, Alistair Bromley, OBE. Farmer; Agricultural Consultant and Valuer; Chairman of Council, Scottish Conservation Projects Trust, since 1984; Director Training, Craft Ltd. and Pathcraft Ltd.; b. 23.6.27, Charing, Kent; m., Rosemary Pullar; 1 s.; 2 d. Educ. Tonbridge School. Training in agriculture, 1944-47; self-employed Farmer, 1948-81; Agricultural Consultant, Arbiter, Valuer, 1968-81; Agricultural Adviser and Valuer, South of Scotland Electricity Board, 1972-81; Vice-Chairman, Countryside Commission for Scotland, 1972-81 (Member from 1969); Member, Secretary of State's Panel of Agricultural Arbiters, 1968-81; Member, Scottish Land Court, 1981-92; Chairman, Executive Committee of Council of Management, Strathcarron Hospice, Denny; former Council Member, British Trust for Conservation Volunteers (Chairman, Scottish Regional Committee, 1975-84); Church Warden, St. Mary's Episcopal Church, Dunblane, since 1960; Honorary Vice-President and a Director, Doune and Dunblane Agricultural Society; former Convener, Legal Committee, NFU of Scotland; General Commissioner of Income Tax, since 1971; Chairman, Scottish Executive Committee, Association of Agriculture, 1980-86. Recreations: work; shooting; enjoying countryside; farming. Address:(h.) Grainston Farm, Kilbryde, Dunblane, Perthshire, FK15 9NF; T.-01786 823304.

Campbell, Allan. Chief Executive, Comunn na Gaidhlig. Address: (b.) 5 Mitchell Lane, Inverness, IV2 3HQ.

Campbell, Catherine, JP, BSc, BA (Hons), MSc. Educational Psychologist; Member, Scottish Milk Marketing Board, 1981-92; Chairman, Cumbernauld "I" Tech, 1984-88; b. 10.1.40, Glasgow; m., John Campbell; 2 s.; 1 d. Educ. Notre Dame High School; Glasgow University; Open University; Strathclyde University. Teacher of Mathematics, 1962-68; Member, Cumbernauld and Kilsyth District Council, 1969-78; Member, Cumbernauld Development Corporation, 1975-84. Jubilee Medal, 1977; CACDP (stage 3 sign language). Recreations: promotion of equal opportunities for deaf people; cooking; homecrafts. Address: (h.) 10 Westray Road, Cumbernauld, G67 1NN; T.-0123 67 24834.

Campbell, Colin Malcolm, QC; b. 1.10.53. Address: (b.) Advocates' Library, Parliament House, Edinburgh, EH1 1RF.

Campbell, Sir Colin Moffat, Bt, MC. Chairman, James Finlay plc, 1975-90; b. 4.8.25; m., Mary Anne Chichester Bain; 2 s.; 1 d. (deceased). Educ. Stowe. Scots Guards, 1943-47 (Captain); joined James Finlay & Co. Ltd., 1947. President, Federation of Kenya Employers, 1962-70;

Chairman, Tea Board of Kenya, 1961-71; Chairman, East African Tea Trade Association, 1960-61, 1962-63, 1966-67; Member, Scottish Council, CBI, 1979-85; Member, Council, CBI, 1981-92; Deputy Chairman, Commonwealth Development Corporation, 1983-89, Board, 1981-89. Recreations: gardening; racing; cards. Address: (h.) Kilbryde Castle, Dunblane, Perthshire.

Campbell, David (Daibhidh), MA; b. 1934; m. Chairman, Project Trust, since 1994; Chairman, Penkill Trust, 1992-93; soldier, diplomat, memorialist, petty bureaucrat, 1956-94. Address: (h.) Old Costerton, Midlothian; T.-Humbie 833 682.

Campbell, Donald. Writer; b. 25.2.40, Wick; m., Jean Fairgrieve; 1 s. Educ. Boroughmuir High School, Edinburgh. Playwright, essayist, lyricist and poet; stage plays include: The Jesuit, 1976; The Widows of Clyth, 1979; Blackfriars Wynd, 1980; Till All The Seas Run Dry, 1981; Howard's Revenge, 1985; Victorian Values, 1986; The Fisher Boy and the Honest Lass, 1990; The Ould Fella, 1993; also active as writer and director in a number of community projects; script co-ordinator, The Dundee Mysteries, Dundee Rep; poetry includes: Rhymes 'n Reasons, 1972; Blether, 1979; Selected Poems: 1970-1990, 1990; other work includes: A Brighter Sunshine (theatre history), 1983, four television plays, 50 radio programmes; Fellow in Creative Writing, Dundee Universit'r, 1987-89; William Soutar Fellow, Perth, 1991-93; awards include: three Fringe Firsts; Silver Medal, 1983 New York Radio Festival for A Clydebuilt Man; Radio Industries Club Award for The Miller's Reel, 1987. Address: (h.) 85 Spottiswoode Street, Edinburgh, EH9 1BZ; T.-0131-447 2305.

Campbell, Doris Margaret, MD, FRCOG. Senior Lecturer in Obstetrics and Gynaecology and Reproductive Physiology, Aberdeen University, since 1984; b. 24.1.42, Aberdeen; m., Alasdair James Campbell; 1 s.; 1 d. Educ. Aberdeen High School for Girls; Aberdeen University. Resident house officer posts, Aberdeen, 1967-69; Research Fellow, Aberdeen University, 1969-73; Registrar in Obstetrics and Gynaecology, Aberdeen Hospitals, 1973-74; Lecturer in Obstetrics and Gynaecology and Physiology, Aberdeen University, 1974-84. Former Member, Scottish Women's Hockey Council. Recreations: bridge; badminton; guiding. Address: (h.) 77 Blenheim Place, Aberdeen; T.-Aberdeen 639984.

Campbell, Elizabeth (Libby), RGN, RM, MSc. Executive Director, Nursing and Quality, West Lothian NHS Trust, since 1993 (Director of Nursing, 1989-93); National Chairman, National Association of Theatre Nurses; b. 9.8.50, Dundee. Educ. Mary Erskine School for Girls, Edinburgh; Edinburgh University. Assistant, then Deputy, Director of Nursing Services, Bangour General Hospital, West Lothian, 1985-89. Member, UK Central Council for Nurses, Midwives and Health Visitors. Recreations: singing; travelling; Munro bagging; music. Address: (h.) 8 Fettes Row, Edinburgh, EH3 6SE; T.-0131-556 5116.

Campbell, Fraser David, MA, MSc, FCIBS. General Manager, Bank of Scotland (International Division), since 1994; b. 7.8.44, Glasgow; 1 s.; 1 d. Educ. Dollar Academy; Edinburgh University; London Business School. Product Manager, Beecham Group, 1968; Consultant, Hoskyns Group, 1970; British Linen Bank Ltd., 1973; Director, Coopers & Lybrand, 1984; Bank of Scotland: Assistant General Manager, 1988, General Manager (Centrebank), 1992. Governor, Scottish Film Council. Recreations: swimming; hill-walking; sailing; shooting. Address: (b.) Orchard Brae House, Edinburgh, EH4 2UG; T.-0131-343 7000.

Campbell, Wing Commander George, MBE, EsqStJ, DL, MBIM; b. 24.11.22, Renton; m., Marion T.H. Halliday; 1 s.;

1 d. Educ. Vale of Leven Academy. Joined RAF, 1941; served in UK, India, Burma, Malaya, Singapore; demobilised, 1946, and continued in Royal Air Force Voluntary Reserve (Training Branch), serving with Air Training Corps; formed 2319 (Vale of Leven) Squadron, 1956; appointed to Wing Staff, Glasgow, and Western Wing, 1973; promoted to Wing Commander, 1978; retired, 1983; attended Bisley as competitor, coach, and team captain for 48 years; Vice Chairman, 602 City of Glasgow Squadron, Royal Auxiliary Air Force Squadron Museum; Vice Chairman, Duke of Edinburgh Award (County Co-ordinating Committee); Elder, Church of Scotland; County Representative, Royal Air Forces Benevolent Fund; Past President, Dumbarton Rotary Club; Past Chairman, RNLI, Dumbarton Branch. Address: (h.) Valeview, Comley Bank, Oxhill, Dumbarton; T.-Dumbarton 63700.

Campbell of Croy, Baron (Gordon Thomas Calthrop Campbell), PC (1970), MC (and Bar). Consultant, oil industry, 1975-94; Director, Alliance and Leicester Building Society and Chairman of its Scottish Board, 1975-94; Chairman, Stoic Insurance Services, 1979-93; b. 8.6.21; m.; 2 s.; 1 d. Educ. Wellington. Commissioned, Regular Army, 1939; RA, 1942 (Major); wounded and disabled, 1945; entered HM Foreign Service, 1946 and served in the Foreign Office, at the UN, in the Cabinet Office (Private Secretary to the Secretary of the Cabinet) and in the Embassy in Vienna; MP (Conservative), Moray and Nairn, 1959-74; Government Whip, 1961-62; Lord Commissioner of the Treasury and Scottish Whip, 1962-63; Parliamentary Under-Secretary of State, Scottish Office, 1963-64; Secretary of State for Scotland, 1970-74; Chairman, Scottish Committee, International Year of Disabled, 1981; Partner, Holme Rose Estate and Farms; Trustee, Thomson Foundation, since 1980; Chairman, Advisory Committee on Pollution of the Sea, 1987-89; Chairman, Scottish Council of Independent Schools, 1976-80; Vice Lord Lieutenant of Nairnshire, since 1988; President, Anglo-Austrian Society, since 1991. Address: (h.) Holme Rose, Cawdor, Nairnshire.

Campbell, Hugh Hall, QC, BA (Hons), MA (Oxon), LLB (Hons), FCIArb. Queen's Counsel, since 1983; b. 18.2.44, Glasgow; m., Eleanor Jane Hare; 3 s. Educ. Glasgow Academy; Trinity College, Glenalmond; Exeter College, Oxford; Edinburgh University. Called to Scottish Bar, 1969; Standing Junior Counsel to Admiralty, 1976. Recreations: music; hill-walking; golf. Address: (h.) 12 Ainslie Place, Edinburgh, EH3 6AS; T.-0131-225 2067.

Campbell, Sir Ian, CBE, OStJ, VRD, JP. Deputy Chairman, Heath (Scotland) Ltd., since 1987; Chairman, Select Assured Properties PLC, since 1989; Director, Travel System Ltd., 1987-90; Director, Hermiston Securities, since 1990; b. 3.2.23, Edinburgh; m., Marion Kirkhope Shiel; 1 d. Educ. Daniel Stewart's College, Edinburgh. Royal Navy, 1942-46; Royal Naval Reserve, 1946-64 (retired with rank of Commander); John Line & Sons, 1948-61 (Area Manager, West of England); Managing Director, MacGregor Wallcoverings Ltd., 1965-77; Finance Director, Scottish Conservative Party, 1977-89. Councillor, City of Edinburgh, 1984-88; Member, Transport Users Consultative Committee for Scotland, 1981-87; Freeman, City of Glasgow, 1991. Recreations: golf; vintage cars; water colour painting. Address: (h.) Merleton, 10 Boswall Road, Edinburgh, EH5 2PR; T.-031-552 4825.

Campbell, Sir Ilay Mark, MA (Oxon). Chairman, Christie's Scotland, since 1978; Director, High Craigton Farming Co.; b. 29.5.27, Edinburgh; m., Margaret Minette Rohais Anderson; 2 d. Educ. Eton; Christ Church, Oxford. Christie's: Scottish Agent, 1968, Joint Scottish Agent, 1973-92; Honorary Vice-President, Scotland's Garden Scheme; Trustee, Crarae Gardens Charitable Trust, since 1978; Trustee, Tree Register of the British Isles, since 1988; Chairman, Church Buildings Renewal Trust (Glasgow), since 1993; Past President, Association for the Protection of

Rural Scotland; former Convener, Church of Scotland Committee on Artistic Matters; Member, Historic Buildings Council for Scotland; Member, Gardens Committee, National Trust for Scotland; former Scottish Representative, National Arts Collection Fund. Recreations: heraldry; genealogy; collecting heraldic bookplates. Address: (h.) Crarae Lodge, Inveraray, Argyll, PA32 8YA; T.-01546 86274/370.

Campbell, James Hugh, BL. Senior Partner, Bird Semple Fyfe Ireland, WS, 1987-91, Consultant until 1993; b. 13.11.26, Old Kilpatrick; m., Iris Burnside Hercus; 2 s.; 1 d. Educ. Bearsden Academy; Glasgow University. Senior Partner, Bird Son & Semple, 1965-73, and Bird Semple Crawford Herron, 1973-87. Member, Council, Law Society of Scotland, 1986-95 (President, 1991-92); Past President, Glasgow Juridical Society. Recreations: music; reading; golf. Address: (h.) 24 Woodvale Avenue, Giffnock, Glasgow, G46 6RQ; T.-041-638 2630.

Campbell, John Alexander, BCom, CA. Chief Executive, Glasgow North Limited, since 1995; b. 19.10.56, Falkirk; m., Wendy Judith; 1 s. Educ. Falkirk High School; Edinburgh University. Trainee to Manager, Arthur Young, Chartered Accountants, 1978-85; Partner, Campbell, Rennie & Co., CA, Aberdeen, 1986-88; Manager, Stoy Hayward, CA, Glasgow, 1990-92; Business Development Executive, Govan Initiative Limited, 1992-95. Recreations: golf; rugby; football. Address: (b.) St. Rollox House, 130 Springburn Road, Glasgow, G21 1YN; T.-0141-552 5413.

Campbell, Joseph. Managing Director, West Sound Radio PLC, since 1983; b. 16.8.39, Glasgow; m., Sheila Margaret Craig; 1 s.; 2 d. Educ. Kirkcudbright Academy. Managing Director, United Scottish Farmers, 1969-77; Managing Director, Kintyre Farmers, 1977-83. Chairman, Scottish Agricultural Managers' Association, 1975-77; Scottish Council Member, Animedica International, 1977-79; Council Member, Scottish Agricultural Organisation Society, 1979-83; Chairman, Ayrshire Nursing Homes Federation, 1985-90 and since 1991; Director, Ayr Chamber of Commerce, 1985; Director, Ayrshire Local Enterprise Company, 1990-92; Managing Director, South West Sound, since 1990; Vice Chairman, Opera West, since 1986; Director, Scottish/Irish Radio Sales, since 1990; Managing Director, Beechgrove Homes Ltd., since 1992; Chairman, ASA Security, since 1994. Royal Humane Society Award, 1963. Recreations: music; painting; reading; golf. Address: (h.) 30 Racecourse Road, Ayr, KA7 2UX; T.-01292 266033.

Campbell, Malcolm, MA (Hons), PhD. Reader in Greek, St. Andrews University, since 1984 (Chairman, 1987-91); b. 10.11.43, Shrewsbury; m., Dorothy Helen Fear; 2 s. Educ. Boroughmuir School, Edinburgh; Edinburgh University; Balliol College, Oxford. Lecturer, St. Andrews University, since 1968. Publications: A Commentary on Quintus Smyrnaeus, Posthomerica XII, 1981; Echoes and Imitations of Early Epic in Apollonius Rhodius, 1981; Index verborum in Apollonium Rhodium, 1983; Studies in the Third Book of Apollonius Rhodius' Argonautica, 1983; A Lexicon to Triphiodorus, 1985; Index verborum in Moschum et Bionem, 1987; Index in Arati Phaenomena, 1988; Moschus Europa (Editor), 1991; A Commentary on Apollonius Rhodius, Argonautica III, 1994. Recreations: music; philately. Address: (b.) Department of Greek, The University, St. Andrews, Fife.

Campbell, Melfort Andrew. Director, Water Weights Ltd., since 1985; Director, Hiremerit Ltd., since 1990; Member, CBI Scottish Council, since 1989; b. 6.6.56, Exeter; m., Lucy Jane Nickson (Hon. Mrs); 3 d. Educ. Ampleforth College. Joined Water Weights Ltd., 1979; Managing Director, since 1985; founded IMES Ltd., 1994. Member, Queen's Bodyguard for Scotland (Royal Company of Archers). Recreations: rugby; cricket; fishing; shooting.

WHO'S WHO IN SCOTLAND 83

Address: (h.) Mains of Altries, Maryculter, Aberdeen, AB1 0BN; T.-01224 734381.

Campbell, Niall Gordon, BA. Under Secretary, Social Work Services Group, Scottish Office Home and Health Department, since 1989; b. 9.11.41, Peebles; m., Alison M. Rigg; 3 s. Educ. Edinburgh Academy; Merton College, Oxford. Entered Scottish Office 1964; Assistant Secretary, 1978; various posts in Scottish Education Department and Scottish Development Department. Address (h.) 15 Warriston Crescent, Edinburgh.

Campbell, Robert Craig, BSc, MCIM. Chief Economist, Scottish Council (Development and Industry), since 1988; b. 29.4.47, Glasgow; m., Elizabeth Helen C.; 2 d. Educ. Glasgow Academy; St. Andrews University. Scottish Council: Research Executive, 1970-77, Research Director, 1977-84, Director, Overseas Projects Unit, 1984-86, Policy Research Director, 1986-88. Recreation: angling. Address: (b.) Scottish Council (Development and Industry), 23 Chester Street, Edinburgh; T.-0131-225 7911.

Campbell, Rev. Roderick D.M., TD, BD, FSA Scot. Minister, Mearns Parish Church, since 1979; Vice Chairman, Greater Glasgow Health Board, since 1994; b. 1.8.43, Glasgow; m., Susan Norman; 2 d. Educ. Daniel Stewart's College, Edinburgh; Arbroath High School; Jordanhill College of Education; New College, Edinburgh University. Teacher, Technical Subjects, Glasgow, Tanzania and London, 1967-70; Associate Minister, St. Andrew's, Nairobi, 1975-78; Chieftain, Caledonian Society of Kenya, 1978; founder Member, Undugu Society of Kenya, 1975; Chairman, Institute of Advanced Motorists (Kenya), 1977-78. Convener, Lodging House Mission, Glasgow Presbytery, 1981-86; Convener, National Church Extension Committee, Church of Scotland, 1987-89; Chaplain, 1/52 Lowland Volunteers, TA; Vice-Convener, Maintenance of the Ministry Committee, General Assembly; Member, Greater Glasgow Health Board; Chairman, The 1988 Forum, 1988-91; Chairman, Glasgow Churches Council for Overseas Students, 1987-94; Vice Chairman, Eastwood Conservative Association, 1988-94. Recreations: swimming; horse-riding; hill-walking. Address: The Manse of Mearns, Newton Mearns, Glasgow, G77 5BU; T.-0141-616 2410.

Campbell, Steven. Painter; b. 1953, Glasgow. Studied, Glasgow School of Art; Fulbright Scholarship; one-man exhibition, New York, 1983, followed by exhibitions in Chicago, Munich, Berlin, Edinburgh, London and other cities.

Campbell, (Walter) Menzies, CBE (1987), QC, MA, LLB. MP (Liberal Democrat), North East Fife, since 1987; Advocate, since 1968; Queen's Counsel, since 1982; Member, Select Committee on Defence, since 1992; Member, Parliamentary Assembly of CSCE, since 1992; Member, North Atlantic Assembly, since 1989; Party Spokesman on Defence and Sport, since 1988, Foreign Affairs, since 1994; b. 22.5.41, Glasgow; m., Elspeth Mary Urquhart. Educ. Hillhead High School, Glasgow; Glasgow University; Stanford University, California. President, Glasgow University Union, 1964-65; took part in Olympic Games, Tokyo, 1964; AAA 220-yards champion, 1964, 1967; Captain, UK athletics team, 1965-66; 1966 Commonwealth Games, Jamaica; UK 100-metres record holder, 1967-74. Advocate Depute, 1977-80; Standing Junior Counsel to the Army in Scotland, 1980-82. Parliamentary candidate (Liberal): Greenock and Port Glasgow, February, 1974, and October, 1974, East Fife, 1979, North East Fife, 1983; Chairman, Scottish Liberal Party, 1975-77; Member: UK Sports Council, 1965-68; Scottish Sports Council, 1971-81; Chairman, Royal Lyceum Theatre, Edinburgh, 1984-87; Member, Broadcasting Council for Scotland, 1984-87. Recreations: all sports;

music; theatre. Address: (b.) House of Commons, London, SW1A 0AA; T.-0171-219 4446.

Campbell, William Kilpatrick, MA (Hons). Director, Mainstream Publishing, since 1978; Director, Edinburgh Book Festival, since 1992; b. 1.3.51, Glasgow; m., Marie-France Callie; 2 d. Educ. Kilmarnock Academy; Edinburgh University. Postgraduate research, Universities of Edinburgh and California; world travel, 1975; Publications Manager, Edinburgh University Student Publications, 1976-78. Publications: Alternative Edinburgh (Co-Editor), 1972; Another Edinburgh, 1976. Recreations: soccer; tennis; swimming; wine; books; people. Address: (b.) 7 Albany Street, Edinburgh, EH1 3UG; T.-0131-557 2959.

Campbell-Brown, Robert Colin, BSc. Executive Director, Crossroads (Scotland) Care Attendant Scheme, since 1990; b. 13.7.32, Dolphinton; m., (Dr.) Beatrice Mary Catto; 1 s.; 2 d. Educ. Trinity College, Glenalmond; St. Andrews University. British Petroleum Company, 1957-90: Chief Petroleum Engineer; Executive Manager, Qatar General Petroleum Company; Senior Adviser, Health, Safety and Environmental Protection, BP Exploration UK. Member, Council and Executive Committee, Scottish Conservation Projects Trust. Recreations: conservation; bee-keeping; sailing. Address: (h.) 15 Trinity, Lynedoch Place, Glasgow, G3 6AA; T.-0141-332 1487.

Campbell-Gibson, Lt.Comdr. R.N. (Ret.) Hugh Desmond. Member, Council, Association for Protection of Rural Scotland; Member, Executive Committee, and County Organiser, Argyll, Scotland's Gardens Scheme; b. 18.8.24; m., Deirdre Wilson; 2 s.; 1 d. Educ. Royal Naval College, Dartmouth. Naval cadet, 1937-41; served Royal Navy, 1941-60; war service convoy duties, Atlantic and Mediterranean; farmed Glenlussa, by Campbeltown, 1960-68; farmed and ran hotel, Dunmor, Seil, Argyll, 1969-83; now manages family woodlands at Melfort. Recreations: gardening; skiing. Address: (h.) Tighnamara, Melfort, Kilmelford, Argyll; T.-Kilmelford 224.

Campbell-Preston, Robert Modan Thorne, OBE, MC, TD. Deputy Lieutenant of Argyll and Bute (Vice Lieutenant, 1966-90); b. 7.1.09; m., The Hon. Angela Murray (deceased); 1 d. Educ. Eton; Christ Church, Oxford. Lt., Scottish Horse, 1930; Lt.-Col., 1945; Hon. Col., Fife & Forfar Yeomanry/Scottish Horse, 1962-67; retired Member, Royal Company of Archers (Queen's Bodyguard for Scotland); Joint Managing Director, Alginate Industries Ltd., 1949-74; DL, 1951; JP, 1950; Silver Star, USA, 1945; President, Argyll and Bute Trust. Recreations: shooting; fishing; gardening. Address: Ardchattan Priory, by Oban, Argyll; T.-Bonawe 274.

Campsie, Alistair Keith, SDA. Author, Journalist and Piper; b. 27.1.29, Inverness; m., Robbie Anderson; 2 s.; 1 d. Educ. West Sussex High School; Lanark Grammar School; West of Scotland College of Agriculture. Inspector of Agriculture, Sudan Government Service, 1949; Cocoa Survey Officer, Nigeria, 1951; experimental staff, National Institute of Agricultural Engineering (Scotland), 1953; Country Editor, Weekly Scotsman, 1954; Sub-Editor, Verse Writer, Scottish Daily Mail, 1955; Founder Editor, East African Farmer and Planter, 1956; Chief Sub-Editor, Weekly Scotsman, 1957; designed and appointed first Editor, Geneva Weekly Tribune, 1958; Chief Feature Writer, Scottish Daily Mail, 1959; Columnist, Science Correspondent and Senior Writer, Scottish Daily Express, 1962-73; founded The Piper's Press, 1988; two Scottish Arts Council writer's bursaries; two SAC publisher's awards. Publications: Poems and a Pibroch (with Hugh MacDiarmid), 1972; By Law Protected, 1976; The MacCrimmon Legend or The Madness of Angus Mackay, 1980; We Bought a Country Pub (under pen-name Alan Mackinnon), 1984; Perfect Poison, 1985; Pibroch: the Tangled Web (radio series), 1985; Dundas or How They

Murdered Robert Burns (play), 1987; The Clarinda Conspiracy, 1989; The True Story of The Ball of Kirriemuir, 1989; Cary Grant Stopped Me Smoking, 1991; Hunt Down A Prince, 1994; Traitors of the '45 (in press). Recreations: bagpipes (playing and composing); good whisky; self-important people. Address: Piper's Restaurant and Private Hotel, Union Place, Montrose; T.-01674 72298.

Canavan, Dennis, BSc (Hons), DipEd. MP (Labour), Falkirk West, since 1983; b. 8.8.42, Cowdenbeath. Educ. St. Bride's and St. Columba's Schools, Cowdenbeath; Edinburgh University. Principal Teacher of Mathematics, St. Modan's High School, Stirling, 1970-74; Assistant Head, Holyrood High School, Edinburgh, 1974; Leader, Labour Group, Stirling District Council, 1974; MP, West Stirlingshire, 1974-83; Chairman, Scottish Parliamentary Labour Group, 1980-81; Chair, PLP Northern Ireland Committee, since 1989; Member, Foreign Affairs Select Committee, since 1982; Founder and Convener, All Party Parliamentary Scottish Sports Group, since 1987; Parliamentary Spokesman for Scottish Committee on Mobility for Disabled, since 1976, and Scottish Spina Bifida Association, since 1976; Honorary President, Milton Amateurs Football Club. Recreations: marathon running; hill-climbing; fishing; swimming; football (former Scottish Universities football internationalist). Address: (b.) Constituency Office, 37 Church Walk, Denny FK6 6DF; T.-01324 825922.

Canavan, Sheriff Vincent Joseph, LLB. Sheriff of South Strathclyde, Dumfries and Galloway at Hamilton, since 1987; b. 13.12.44. Address: (b.) Sheriff Court House, Beckford Street, Hamilton, ML3 6AA.

Candlish, Kenneth Henry, BL, JP, DL. Retired Solicitor; Deputy Lieutenant, Berwickshire; b. 22.8.24, Edinburgh; m., Isobel Robertson-Brown; 2 d. Educ. George Watson's; Edinburgh University. Depute County Clerk, West Lothian, 1951-64; County Clerk, Berwickshire, 1964-75. Recreations: photography; wine-making; music. Address: (h.) The Elms, Duns, Berwickshire; T.-Duns 883298.

Cannon, Steven, MA (Hons). Deputy Secretary, Dundee University, since 1994; College Secretary, Duncan of Jordanstone College of Art, 1993-94; b. 19.12.57, Keighley; m., Joyce. Educ. St. Bedes Grammar School, Bradford; Dundee University. Administrative Assistant, then Admissions Officer, Warwick University, 1983-86; Financial and Administration Manager, Warwick University Science Park, 1986-88; Financial Manager, Ninewells Hospital and Medical School, Dundee, 1988-93. Recreations: family interests; golf; cricket; music. Address: (b.) Dundee University, Nethergate, Dundee, DD1 4HT; T.-01382 344008.

Cant, Harry Wallace, MA, LLB, WS, NP. Solicitor since 1954; Clerk and Treasurer, Iona Cathedral Trust, 1965-85; b. 5.7.18, Edinburgh; m., Mary Fleming Hamilton; 3 s.; 1 d. Educ. George Watson's College, Edinburgh; Edinburgh University. War Service, 1939-46 (Capt., Royal Artillery, 51st Highland Division, Western Desert, Sicily, France and Germany); wounded France, 1944; Partner: Menzies & Thomson, WS, 1954, J. & F. Anderson, WS, 1966; Consultant, J. & F. Anderson, WS, 1984-87; Secretary, Edinburgh Musical Festival Association, 1958-67; Secretary, Scottish Society of Women Artists, 1960-68; Treasurer, Scottish Action on Dementia, 1987-89. Recreations: golf; reading. Address: (h.) 77 Craiglockhart Road, Edinburgh, EH14 1EL; T.-0131-441 3512.

Cantley, Maurice, BSc, PhD. Director, Highlands and Islands Enterprise, since 1991; b. 6.6.37, Cambuslang; m., Rosalind Diana Jones; 2 d. Educ. Bedford Modern and Bristol Grammar; Bristol University. Unilever Ltd., 1961-67; McCann Erickson Advertising, London, 1967-76; Director of Recreation and Tourism, Tayside Regional Council, 1976-82; Head of Tourism, HIDB, 1982-85; Marketing Director, Highlands and Islands Development Board, 1985-91. Chairman, Association of Directors of Recreation, Leisure and Tourism, 1980-82; Hon. Education Officer, Society of Cosmetic Chemists of GB, 1963-66. Recreations: driving north of Ullapool; natural history; hill-walking. Address: (h.) Oldshorebeg, Kinlochbervie, Sutherland, IV27 4RS; T.-01971 521257.

Capewell, Simon, MB, BS, MD, MSc, MRCP (UK). Senior Medical Officer, Scottish Office Home and Health Department, since 1990; b. Honiton. Educ. Monmouth School; Newcastle upon Tyne Medical School. Surgical and medical posts in Newcastle, Oxford, Teesside, Cardiff and Edinburgh. Recreations: walking; skiing. Address: (b.) St. Andrews House, Edinburgh; T.-0131-244 2275.

Caplan, Hon. Lord (Philip Isaac Caplan), MA, LLB, QC. Senator of the College of Justice, since 1989; b. 24.2.29, Glasgow; m., Joyce Stone (2nd m.); 2 s.; 2 d. Educ. Eastwood School; Glasgow University. Solicitor, 1952-56; called to Bar, 1957; Standing Junior Counsel to Accountant of Court, 1964-70; Chairman, Plant Varieties and Seeds Tribunal, Scotland, 1977-79; Sheriff of Lothian and Borders, at Edinburgh, 1979-83; Sheriff Principal of North Strathclyde, 1983-88; Member, Sheriff Courts Rules Council, 1984-88; Commissioner, Northern Lighthouse Board, 1983-88; Chairman, Scottish Association for the Study of Delinquency, 1985-89, Hon. Vice President, 1990; Member, Advisory Council on Messengers at Arms and Sheriff Officers, 1987-88; Chairman, Scottish Association of Family Conciliation Services, 1989-94, Honorary President, since 1994; Chairman, James Powell UK Trust. FRPS (1988), AFIAP (1985). Recreations: photography; bridge; music; reading. Address: (b.) Court of Session, Parliament House, Edinburgh.

Capperauld, Ian, MB, ChB, DObst, RCOG, FRCSEdin, FRCSGlas, FRCSEng. Executive Director, Research and Development, Ethicon Ltd., since 1969; Consultant Surgeon, since 1962; Medical Director, Huntly Nursing Home, since 1981; Member, Lothian Health Board, since 1981; b. 23.10.33, New Cumnock; m., Wilma Hyslop Young; 2 s. Educ. Cumnock Academy; Glasgow University; Edinburgh University. Served as Major, RAMC, 1959-69 (Consultant Surgeon). Recreations: fishing; shooting. Address: (b.) Ethicon Ltd., PO Box 408, Bankhead Avenue, Edinburgh; T.-0131-453 5555.

Carbery, Emeritus Professor Thomas Francis, OBE, MSc, PhD, DPA. Former Professor, Strathclyde Business School, Strathclyde University; Chairman, South of Scotland Consumers Committee/Office of Electricity Regulation, since 1990; Member, Data Protection Tribunal, since 1985; b. 18.1.25, Glasgow; m., Ellen Donnelly; 1 s.; 2 d. Educ. St. Aloysius' College, Glasgow; Glasgow University; Scottish College of Commerce. Cadet navigator/meteorologist, RAF, 1943-47; civil servant, 1947-61; Lecturer, then Senior Lecturer, Scottish College of Commerce, 1961-64; Strathclyde University: Senior Lecturer in Government-Business Relations, 1964-75, Head, Department of Office Organisation, 1975-79, Professor of Office Organisation, 1979-85, Professor of Business Information, 1985-88; part-time Professor of Marketing, 1988-90. Member: Independent Broadcasting Authority, 1970-79, Broadcasting Complaints Commission, 1981-86, Royal Commission on Gambling, 1975-77, Transport Users Consultative Committee (Chairman, Scottish TUCC), 1975-81, Press Council, 1987-90, Scottish Consumer Council (latterly Vice-Chairman), 1976-84; Chairman, Scottish Transport Research Group, 1983-87; Member, Scottish Legal Aid Board, 1986-92; Member, Church of Scotland Committee on Higher Education, 1986-87; Chairman, Strathclyde University Inter-denominational Chaplaincy Committee, 1981-87; Joint Editor, Bulletin of Society for Co-operative Studies; Chairman, Scottish

Catholic Communications Commission; Member, Scottish Catholic Education Commission, 1980-93. Recreations: conversation; watching television; spectating at association football; very bad golf. Address: (h.) 24 Fairfax Avenue, Glasgow, G44 5AL; T.-0141-637 0514.

Cargill, Kenneth George, MA, LLB. Head of News, Current Affairs and TV Sport, BBC Scotland, since 1988; b. 17.2.47, Arbroath; m., Una Gallacher. Educ. Arbroath High School; Edinburgh University. BBC TV Scotland: Researcher, Current Affairs, 1972; Reporter, Current Account, 1973; Film Director, Public Account, 1978; Producer, Current Account, 1979, Agenda, 1981, People and Power (London), 1983; Editor of the day, Reporting Scotland, 1983; Editor, Scotland 2000, 1986-87; Deputy Editor, News and Current Affairs, Television, 1984-88; Head of TV News, Current Affairs and Sport, 1988-94. Publication: Scotland 2000 (Editor), 1987. Address: (b.) Broadcasting House, Queen Margaret Drive, Glasgow, G12 8DG; T.-0141-338 2250.

Carlaw, David Jackson. Vice-Chairman, Scottish Conservative Party, since 1995; Chairman, Scotland, Northern Ireland, Cumbria Ford Dealers, since 1994; Managing Director, Wylies Group, since 1987; b. 12.4.59, Glasgow; m., Wynne Stewart; 2 s. Educ. Glasgow Academy. Wylies Group, since 1977. Vice-Chairman, Scottish Conservative Party, 1992-94; Chairman, Eastwood Conservatives, 1988-92; Chairman, Scottish Young Conservatives, 1984-86. Recreations: reading; theatre; film; opera; design. Address: (b.) Wylies Ltd., 370 Pollokshaws Road, Glasgow, G41 1QR; T.-0141-423 6644.

Carmichael of Kelvingrove, Baron (Neil George Carmichael). Life Peer; b. 1921. MP (Labour), Woodside, 1962-74, Kelvingrove, 1974-83.

Carmichael, Peter, CBE, DSc; b. 26.3.33, Dunblane; m., June; 2 s.; 4 d. by pr. m. Educ. McLaren High School, Callander; Glasgow University. Design engineer, Ferranti Ltd., Edinburgh, 1958-65; Hewlett-Packard, South Queensferry: Project Leader, 1965-67, Production Engineering Manager, 1968-73, Engineering Manager, 1973-75, Manufacturing Manager, 1975-76, Division General Manager, 1976-82, Joint Managing Director, 1980-82; Scottish Development Agency: Director, Small Business and Electronics, 1982-88, Group Director East, 1988-89. Chairman, Esmee Fairbairn Economic Institute. Recreations: fishing; antique clock restoration. Address: (h.) 86 Craiglea Drive, Edinburgh; T.-0131-447 6334; Marchbank Cottage, Ballantrae, Ayrshire; T.-0146 5831355.

Carmichael of Carmichael (Richard John). 26th Baron of Carmichael, since 1980; 30th Chief of Name and Arms of Carmichael, since 1981; Chartered Accountant; Farmer; b. 1.12.48, Stamford; m., Patricia Margaret Branson; 1 s.; 2 d. Educ. Hyton Hill Preparatory School; Kimbolton School; Coventry College of Technology. Audit Senior, Coopers and Lybrand, Tanzania, 1972; Audit Manager, Granger Craig Tunnicliffe, Tauranga, New Zealand, 1974; ACA, 1971; FCA, 1976; Factor/Owner, Carmichael Estate, 1980; Director: Carmichael Heritage Leisure Ltd., Clydesdale Development Co. Ltd., Scottish Orienteering 6-Day Event Co. Ltd.; claims family titles: Earldom of Hyndford, Viscountcies of Inglisberry and Nemphlar, and Lordship Carmichael of Carmichael. Member, Supreme Council of Scottish Chiefs; Secretary Carmichael Anstruther District Charitable Association; New Zealand Orienteering Champion, 1977; International Controller, International Orienteering Federation, 1994. Recreations: orienteering; skiing; Clan Carmichael Association. Address: Carmichael House, Carmichael, by Biggar, Lanarkshire, ML12 6PG; T.-01899 308336.

Carmichael, William George, BL. Regional Procurator Fiscal, Hamilton, since 1987; b. 26.2.33, Glasgow; m., Elizabeth Anne Gemmel; 1 s.; 2 d. Educ. Eastwood School; Glasgow University. Legal Assistant: Hamilton Town Council, 1958-59, Argyll County Council, 1959-60, Ayr Town Council, 1961-62, Glasgow Corporation, 1963-65; Procurator Fiscal's Service, since 1965. Recreations: golf; walking; music. Address: (b.) Cameronian House, 3/5 Almada Street, Hamilton, ML3 0HG; T.-01698 284000.

Carnall, Geoffrey Douglas, MA, BLitt. Honorary Fellow, Department of English Literature, Edinburgh University, since 1994; b. 1.2.27, Croydon, Surrey; m., Elisabeth Seale Murray; 1 s.; 2 d. Educ. Perse School, Cambridge; Magdalen College, Oxford. Lecturer in English, Queen's University, Belfast, 1952-60; Lecturer, then Senior Lecturer in English Literature, Edinburgh University, 1960-69, Reader, 1969-94. Chairman, Edinburgh Council for Nuclear Disarmament, 1963-70; Elder, South-East Scotland Monthly Meeting, Society of Friends (Quakers), 1970-87; Chairman, Edinburgh Christian Campaign for Nuclear Disarmament, 1982-85; Vice-Chair, Scottish Christian CND, 1987. Publications: Robert Southey and His Age, 1960; Robert Southey, 1964; The Mid-Eighteenth Century (Volume 8, Oxford History of English Literature) (Co-author), 1979; The Impeachment of Warren Hastings (Co-editor), 1989. Recreation: subverting the war system. Address: (b.) Department of English Literature, David Hume Tower, George Square, Edinburgh, EH8 9JX; T.-0131-667 1011.

Carnegie, Leslie Thompson, CBE (1980), BL, JP, Solicitor. Chief Executive, Dumfries and Galloway Regional Council, 1974-85; Honorary Sheriff, since 1960; b. 16.8.20, Aberdeen; m., Isobel Jane McCombie, JP. Educ. Aberdeen Grammar School; Aberdeen University. Legal Department, Aberdeen Corporation, 1939-48; Depute County Clerk, East Lothian, 1948-54; County Clerk, Dumfries County Council, 1954-75. Past President, Society of County Clerks in Scotland; Clerk, Dumfries Lieutenancy, 1954-85. Recreations: gardening; music appreciation; sporting activities. Address: (h.) Marchhill Park, Dumfries.

Carnegy-Arbuthnott, David, TD, DL, LLD, CA. Landowner; b. 17.7.25, London; m., Helen Adamson Lyell; 2 s.; 2 d. Educ. Stowe. Emergency commission, The Black Watch, 1944-47; Chartered Accountant, 1953; in practice, Dundee, 1956-86; TA, 1955-69; Brevet Colonel, 1969; Hon. Colonel, 1st Bn., 51st Highland Volunteers (TA), 1980-89; Deputy Lieutenant, County of City of Dundee, 1973-89, Angus, since 1989; Member, Queen's Bodyguard for Scotland (Royal Company of Archers), since 1959; Governor, Dundee College of Education, 1985-87; Governor, Northern College of Education, 1987-91; President, Dundee Chamber of Commerce, 1971-72; Member of Court, Dundee University, 1977-85; Convener, Standing Committee, Scottish Episcopal Church, 1987-92. Recreations: shooting; country pursuits. Address: (h.) Balnamoon, Brechin, Angus, DD9 7RH; T.-01356 660208.

Carnegy of Lour, Baroness (Elizabeth Patricia), DL. Life Peer, since 1982; Member, House of Lords Select Committee on European Communities; Member, Council and Finance Committee, Open University, since 1984; Member, Court, St. Andrews University, since 1991; b. 28.4.25. Educ. Downham School. Cavendish Laboratory, Cambridge, 1943-46; Girl Guides Association: Training Adviser for Scotland, 1958-62 and for Commonwealth HQ, 1963-65; co-opted Angus County Council Education Committee, 1967-75; Councillor, Tayside Regional Council, 1974-82; Chairman, Education Committee, 1976-82; Chairman, Working Party on Professional Training in Community Education Scotland, 1975-77; Commissioner, Manpower Services Commission, 1979-82, and Chairman, Committee for Scotland, 1980-83; Member, Scottish Economic Council, 1980-92; President for Scotland, Girl

Guides Association, 1979-89; Member, Scottish Council for Tertiary Education, 1979-84; Chairman, Scottish Council for Community Education, 1980-88; Honorary Sheriff, 1969-84; Deputy Lieutenant, District of Angus, 1988; Fellow, Royal Society of Arts, 1987; Honorary LLD, Dundee University, 1991. Address: (h.) Lour, Forfar, Angus, DD8 2LR; T.-01307 82 237.

Carr, Isabel Anne, BA. General Secretary (Scotland), YWCA, since 1992; b. 23.6.54, Gifford. Educ. Berwickshire High School; Edinburgh University; Jordanhill College of Education. Rhodesia Ministry of Education, 1976; Lothian Regional Council Community Education, 1978-80; Church of Scotland Board of World Mission and Unity, Pakistan, 1981-85; Area Secretary, South Scotland, Christian Aid, 1985-92. Address: (b.) 7 Randolph Crescent, Edinburgh, EH3 7TH; T.-0131-225 7592.

Carr, John Roger, CBE, JP, FRICS. Chairman, Countryside Commission for Scotland, 1985-92 (Member, since 1979); Member, Macaulay Land Use Research Institute, since 1987; Director, UK 2000 Scotland, 1990-93; Vice President, FWAG Scotland, since 1993; b. 18.1.27, Ackworth, Yorkshire; m., Cathrine Elise Dickson-Smith; 2 s. Educ. Ackworth & Ayton (Quaker) School. Royal Marines, 1944-47; Gordon Highlanders TA, 1950-55; Factor, Walker Scottish Estates Co., Ballater; Factor, subsequently Director and General Manager, Moray Estates Development Co., Forres; former Convenor, Scottish Recreational Land Association; former Council Member, Scottish Landowners' Association; former District Councillor, Moray. Recreations: most country pursuits. Address: (b.) Bradbush, Darnaway, Moray, IV36 0SH; T.-01309 641249.

Carr, Walter. Comedian and actor; b. 1925, Larkhall. Professional debut, 1940; many comic roles and as dame in pantomime; theatre work includes Edinburgh Festival production of The Three Estates; seasons at Royal Lyceum, Perth, and Pitlochry.

Carrol, Charles Gordon, MA, DipEd. Director, Commonwealth Institute, Scotland, since 1971; b. 21.3.35, Edinburgh; m., Frances Anne Sinclair; 3 s. Educ. Melville College, Edinburgh; Edinburgh University; Moray House College of Education. Education Officer: Government of Nigeria, 1959-65, Commonwealth Institute, Scotland, 1965-71. Lay Member, Press Council, 1978-83. Recreations: walking; angling; reading; cooking. Address: (h.) 11 Dukehaugh, Peebles; T.-01721 721296.

Carroll, Professor Robert Peter, MA, PhD. Professor, Department of Biblical Studies, Glasgow University, since 1991 (Dean, Faculty of Divinity, 1991-94); b. 18.1.41, Dublin; m., Mary Anne Alice Stevens; 2 s.; 1 d. Educ. High School, Dublin; Trinity College, Dublin University; Edinburgh University. After postgraduate degree, worked as swimming pool attendant, barman, brickie's mate, secondary school teacher; Glasgow University: Assistant Lecturer in Semitic Languages, 1968, Lecturer in Old Testament Language and Literature, 1969, Senior Lecturer in Biblical Studies, 1981; Reader, 1986. Publications: When Prophecy Failed, 1979; From Chaos to Covenant, 1981; Jeremiah: A Commentary, 1986; Jeremiah (JSOT Guide), 1989; Wolf in Sheepfold, 1991. Recreations: cinema; daydreaming; writing imaginary books in my head. Address: (h.) 5 Marchmont Terrace, Glasgow, G12 9LT; T.-0141-339 0440.

Carse, George, MA, BL; b. 30.10.19, Edinburgh; m., Ann Elisabeth C. Rankine; 1 d. Educ. Edinburgh Academy; Edinburgh University. Assistant, St. Cuthbert's Parish Church, Edinburgh, 1943-44; Chaplain, Royal Navy, 1944-47; Minister: Lethendy and Kinloch Parish Church, 1947-49, Liberton Northfield Parish Church, 1949-59; admitted Faculty of Advocates, 1965. President, Edinburgh Natural History Society, 1967-70; President, Lothians Branch, Scottish Wildlife Trust, since 1978; Chairman, Liberton Association, 1967-73. Recreations: walking; ornithology; natural history. Address: (h.) 121 Liberton Brae, Edinburgh, EH16 6LD; T.-0131-664 2070.

Carter, Christopher John, BA (Hons), PhD, MRTPI, FIMgt, FRSA. Director, Duncan of Jordanstone College and Deputy Principal, Dundee University, since 1994; b. 5.2.41, Capel, Surrey; m., Ann Fisher Prince; 1 s.; 1 d. Educ. Ottershaw School, Chertsey, Surrey; Birmingham University; Glasgow University. Town Planning Assistant, Cumbernauld Development Corporation, 1963-64 and 1967-68; Visiting Lecturer in Geography, Brock University, St. Catharines, Ontario, 1968-69; Lecturer/Senior Lecturer in Planning, Glasgow School of Art, 1969-76; Principal Lecturer in Planning, Coventry (Lanchester) Polytechnic, 1976-78; Senior Lecturer/Head, Department of Town and Regional Planning, Duncan of Jordanstone College of Art, 1978-81; Vice Principal, Duncan of Jordanstone College of Art, 1981-93, Acting Principal, 1993-94. Winner, RTPI Prize, 1970. Member: Board of Governors, Dundee Institute of Technology, 1989-91; Scottish Committee, Universities Funding Council, 1989-92; Scottish Higher Education Funding Council, 1992-93; Member, Board of Governors, Northern College, since 1994. Publications: Innovations in Planning Thought and Practice at Cumbernauld New Town 1956-62; The Designation of Cumbernauld New Town (case study) (Co-author). Recreations: skiing; running; photography; music. Address: (h.) 39 Haston Crescent, Kinnoull, Perth; T.-01738 636802.

Carter, Professor David Craig, MB, ChB, MD, FRCSEdin, FRCSGlas, FRCPEdin. Regius Professor of Surgery, Edinburgh University, since 1988; Honorary Clinical Consultant, Edinburgh Royal Infirmary, since 1988; Surgeon to the Queen in Scotland, since 1993; President-elect, Surgical Research Society; Member, Broadcasting Council for Scotland, since 1989; Chairman, Scottish Council for Postgraduate Medical and Dental Education; Member, Medical Advisory Committee, Higher Education Funding Council, since 1994; Co-editor, British Journal of Surgery; Non-executive Director, Lothian Health Board, since 1994; b. 1.9.40, Penrith; m., Ilske; 2 s. Educ. St. Andrews University. Lecturer in Clinical Surgery, Edinburgh University, 1969-74; 12-month secondment as Lecturer in Surgery, Makerere University, Kampala, Uganda, 1972; Senior Lecturer in Surgery, Edinburgh University, 1974-79; St. Mungo Professor of Surgery, Glasgow University, 1979-88; Honorary Consultant, Glasgow Royal Infirmary, 1979-88; 12-month secondment as Associate Professor of Surgery, University of California, 1976. Council Member, Royal College of Surgeons of Edinburgh, 1980-89. Moynihan Prize, 1973; James IV Association of Surgeons Travelling Fellow, 1975. Recreations: golf; music. Address: (b.) University Department of Surgery, Royal Infirmary, Edinburgh, EH3 9YW; T.-0131-536 3812.

Carter, Tom, OBE, ACIS, ACMA, CIPFA. Chairman, Partnership Housing Ltd.; Chairman, Grampian Epilepsy Centre; b. 27.12.23, Carlisle; 2 s. Educ. Birkenhead Park High School. 7th Bn., Royal Tank Rgt., 1942-44; various clerical posts, mainly with former LMS Railway, 1939-47: Birkenhead: Clerk, Parks and Cemeteries Department 1947-48, Accountancy Assistant, 1948-55; Technical Assistant, rising to Assistant Secretary, former IMTA 1955-61; Deputy County Treasurer, Holland (Lincolnshire) 1961-68; County Treasurer, Moray and Nairn, 1968-75; Director of Finance, Grampian Regional Council, 1975-87; Acting Director of Finance, Western Isles Island Council 1991-92. Governor, Robert Gordon's University (formerly RGIT), 1989-94; Past Chairman, Directors of Finance (Scotland) Section, CPFA; Member, Local Government Finance Working Party; former Commissioner, Public

Works Loan Board. Recreations: walking; bridge; gardening; wine-making; reading. Address: (h.) 24 Gordon Road, Mannofield, Aberdeen, AB1 7RL.

Carty, Matthew John, MB, ChB, FRCSEdin, FRCPSGlas, FRCOG. Consultant Obstetrician and Gynaecologist, Southern General Hospital, Glasgow, since 1977; b. 8.3.42, Hamilton; m., Caroline Martin; 2 s.; 2 d. Educ. St. Aloysius College, Glasgow; Glasgow University. Lecturer in Midwifery, Nairobi University, Kenya, 1970-71; Lecturer in Midwifery, Glasgow University, 1972-77. Recreations: squash; golf; tennis; jogging. Address: (h.) 31 Monreith Road, Newlands, Glasgow; T.-0141-632 1033.

Cash, John David, BSc, MB, ChB, PhD, FRCPath, FRCPGlas, FRCPE, FRCSEdin. National Medical and Scientific Director, Scottish National Blood Transfusion Service, since 1979; Honorary Professor, Department of Medicine, Edinburgh University, since 1987; b. 3.4.36, Reading; m., Angela Mary Thomson; 1 s.; 1 d. Educ. Ashville College, Harrogate; Edinburgh University. Edinburgh and South East Scotland Blood Transfusion Service: Deputy Director, 1969, Regional Director, 1974. President, Royal College of Physicians of Edinburgh, 1994; Adviser in Blood Transfusion, WHO. Recreations: fishing; gardening. Address: (b.) Scottish National Blood Transfusion Service, Headquarters, Ellen's Glen Road, Liberton, Edinburgh EH17 7QT; T.-0131-664 2317.

Cassels, James Rendall Thomson, BSc, MSc, PhD, CChem, FRSC. Head Teacher, Bellahouston Academy, Glasgow, since 1986; b. 23.4.45, Irvine; m., Angela; 3 d. Educ. Irvine Royal Academy; Strathclyde University; Glasgow University. Assistant Head Teacher, Camphill High School, Paisley, 1977-84; Depute Head Teacher, Mearns Castle High School, Glasgow, 1984-86. Formerly: Member, Chemistry Panel, Scottish Examination Board; Chairman, Joint Working Party on Standard Grade Chemistry; Member, advisory committee, Scottish Council for Research in Education; awarded medal, Education Division, Royal Society of Chemistry, 1980. Recreation: bird-watching. Address: (b.) 30 Gower Terrace, Glasgow, G42 5QE; T.-0141-427 2251.

Cassidy, Anthony (Tony) F., BSc (Hons). Chief Executive, Renfrewshire Enterprise, since 1991; Non-Executive Director, EFM Dragon Investment Trust, EFM Japan Investment Trust, Castle Cairn Investment Trust; b. 17.11.44, Kilbarchan; m., Laura Jane; 2 s. Educ. Glasgow University. Lecturer, Mechanical Engineering, Glasgow University, 1969-72; British Council official: India, 1972-76, Japan, 1976-81, France, 1983-84; Director, Japan/Asia, Locate in Scotland, 1984-91. Recreations: opera; orchestral music; rowing; sailing; skiing. Address: (b.) 25 Causeyside Street, Paisley, PA1 1UL; T.-0141-848 0101.

Cater, Isabel McGregor, MCSP. Chairman, North-East Fife District Council, since 1992; b. 20.5.39, Swansea; m., Dr. John I. Cater; 3 d. Educ. Morrisons Academy, Crieff; School of Physiotherapy, Royal Infirmary, Edinburgh. Chartered Physiotherapist, 1961-83. JP, since 1989; Director, Scottish Rights of Way Society, 1981-85. Recreations: walking; swimming; gardening; reading. Address: (h.) Woodlands, Gauldry, Newport-on-Tay, DD6 8RW; T.-01382 330 284.

Catto, Professor Graeme R.D., MB, ChB (Hons), MD (Hons), DSc, FRCP, FRCPE, FRCPGlas. Vice-Principal, since 1995, Dean, Faculty of Clinical Medicine, since 1992, and Professor in Medicine and Therapeutics, Aberdeen University, since 1988; Honorary Consultant Physician/Nephrologist, since 1977; Vice Chairman, Aberdeen Royal Hospitals NHS Trust, since 1992; b. 24.4.45, Aberdeen; m., Joan Sievewright; 1 s.; 1 d. Educ. Robert Gordon's College; Aberdeen University. Research Fellow/Lecturer/Senior Lecturer/Reader in Medicine,

Aberdeen University, 1970-88; Harkness Fellow of Commonwealth Fund of New York, 1975-77 (Fellow in Medicine, Harvard Medical School and Peter Bent Brigham Hospital, Boston). Recreations: curling; fresh air; France. Address: (b.) Department of Medicine, Aberdeen University, Foresterhill, Aberdeen, AB9 2ZB; T.-01224 681818.

Cawdor, 7th Earl of (Colin Robert Vaughan Campbell); b. 30.6.62. Address: Cawdor Castle, Nairn.

Cawthra, David Wilkinson, BSc, FEng, FICE, FIHT, CBIM. Chief Executive, The Miller Group Limited, since 1992; b. 5.3.43, Halifax; m., Maureen Mabel Williamson; 1 s.; 1 d. Educ. Heath Grammar School, Halifax; Birmingham University. Mitchell Construction Company Ltd., 1964-73; Tarmac Construction Ltd., 1973-79; Balfour Beatty Ltd., 1979-91. Member, NEDO Construction Industry Sector Group, 1990-92. Recreations: hill-walking; American history. Address: (b.) Miller House, 18 South Groathill Avenue, Edinburgh, EH4 2LW; T.-0131-332 2585.

Chalmers, David Watson Penn. Director and Deputy Chief Executive, Dunfermline Building Society, since 1995; b. 28.4.46, Dundee; m., Jacky; 1 d. Educ. Harris Academy, Dundee. Joined Dunfermline Building Society, 1974. Director, South Fife Enterprise Trust Ltd.; Member, Committee of Management, Kingdom Housing Association Ltd.; Member, Mortgage Practitioners Panel, Council of Mortgage Lenders; Member, Business Support Group, Whitfield Partnership, Dundee; Trustee, Scottish Housing Association's Charitable Trust. Recreations: golf; chess; hill-walking; running. Address: (b.) Caledonia House, Carnegie Avenue, Dunfermline, KY11 5PJ; T.-01383 627727.

Chalmers, Professor Ian Donald, BSc, PhD, CEng, MInstP, FIEE, SMIEEE. Professor, Department of Electronic and Electrical Engineering, Strathclyde University, since 1988; b. 4.6.40, London; 1 s.; 1 d. Educ. Montrose Academy; Dundee Technical College; Strathclyde University. CEGB Research Fellow, 1968-73; Lecturer, Department of Electrical Engineering, Strathclyde University, 1973-83, Senior Lecturer, 1983-86, Reader, 1986-88, Professor, 1988. SHEFC Teaching Quality Assessor, since 1993. Publications: 70 research papers. Recreations: golf; walking. Address: (h.) Flat 23, 46 Speirs Wharf, Glasgow, G4 9TB; T.-0141-353 0874.

Chalmers, Rev. John Pearson, BD. Depute Secretary, Department of Ministry, Church of Scotland, since 1995; Vice Chairman, Board of Governors, Donaldson's College, since 1991; b. 5.6.52, Bothwell; m., Elizabeth; 2 s.; 1 d. Educ. Marr College; Strathclyde University; Glasgow University. Minister, Renton Trinity, 1979-86; Clerk, Dumbarton Presbytery, 1982-86; Minister, Palmerston Place, Edinburgh, 1986-95; Convener, Board of Ministry, since 1994. Recreations: golf; bee-keeping. Address: (b.) 121 George Street, Edinburgh, EH2 4YN; T.-0131-225 5722.

Chalmers, Rev. Murray, MA. Convener, Nomination Committee, General Assembly, Church of Scotland. Ordained, 1965; hospital chaplain.

Chalmers, Patricia, MA (Hons). Councillor, Glasgow District Council, since 1982 (Personnel Convener, since 1992); Member, Historic Buildings Council for Scotland, since 1989; b. Glasgow; m., Walter Scott Chalmers; 1 s.; 2 d. Educ. Rothesay Academy; Glasgow University. Member, Board, Scottish Opera, since 1991; Member, Board, Theatre Royal, since 1985; Member, Board, Tron Theatre, since 1992; a Director, Glasgow Cultural Enterprises Ltd., since 1991, Glasgow Building Preservation Trust, since 1991, Redundant Churches Trust, since 1991. Recreations: work;

the arts. Address: (b.) City Chambers, Glasgow, G2 1DU; T.-0141-227 4007.

Chambers, Ernest George Wilkie, MBA, BSc (Hons). Chief Executive, West of Scotland Water Authority; b. 10.5.47, Dundee; m., Jeanette; 1 s.; 1 d. Educ. Harris Academy, Dundee. Assistant Engineer, East of Scotland Water Board and Lower Clyde Water Board, 1969-75; Strathclyde Regional Council Water Department: Area Engineer (Renfrew), 1975-79, Divisional Operations Engineer, Lower Clyde Division, 1979-84, Assistant Divisional Manager, 1984-86, Assistant Director (Operations & Maintenance), 1986-88; Director, 1988-94; SRC Water Services Department: Director, 1994-95. National Senior Vice President, Institution of Water Officers, 1995-96; President, Scottish Area, Association of Water Officers, 1991-92. Recreations: sailing; DIY; gardening. Address: (b.) 419 Balmore Road, Glasgow, G22 6NU; T.-0141-355 5101.

Chaplin, Peter D. Chief Executive, Sea Fish Industry Authority. Address: (b.) 18 Logie Mill, Logie Green Road, Edinburgh, EH7 4HG.

Chapman, Francis Ian, CBE, FRSA, CBIM. Chairman, Scottish Radio Holdings PLC, since 1972; Director, United Distillers PLC, 1988-93; Chairman and Managing Director, Chapmans Publishers Ltd., 1989-91; Chairman, Guinness Publishing, since 1991; b. 26.10.25, St. Fergus, Aberdeenshire; m., Marjory Stewart Swinton; 1 s.; 1 d. Educ. Shawlands Academy, Glasgow; Ommer School of Music. War Service: RAF air crew cadet, 1943-44; National Service coal mines, 1945-47. William Collins: trainee, 1947, Sales Representative, New York Branch, 1951, General Sales Manager, London, 1955, appointed to main operating Board as Group Sales Director, 1960; appointed to Board, William Collins (Holdings) Ltd. as Joint Managing Director, 1967; Deputy Chairman, William Collins (Holdings) Ltd., 1976; Chairman, William Collins Publishers Ltd., 1979; Chairman and Chief Executive, William Collins PLC, 1981-89; Chairman, Hatchards Ltd., 1976-89; Board Member, Pan Books Ltd., 1962-84; Chairman, Harvill Press Ltd., 1976-89; Board Member, Book Tokens Ltd., since 1981; Member, Governing Council, SCOTBIC, since 1983; Board Member, IRN Ltd., 1983-85; President, Publishers Association, 1979-81; Trustee, Book Trade Benevolent Society, since 1982; Board Member, Scottish Opera Theatre Royal Ltd., 1974-79; Director, Stanley Botes Ltd., 1985-89; Non-Executive Director, Guinness PLC, 1986-91; Joint Chairman and Chief Executive, Harper and Row, New York, 1987-89; Deputy Chairman, Orion Publishing Group, 1993-94. Scottish Free Enterprise Award, 1985; Hon. DLitt, Strathclyde, 1990. Recreations: golf; swimming; music; grandchildren. Address: (b.) Radio Clyde, Clydebank Business Park, Clydebank.

Chapman, Professor John N., MA, PhD, FInstP, FRSE. Titular Professor, Physics and Astronomy, Glasgow University, since 1988; b. 21.11.47, Sheffield; m., Judith M.; 1 s.; 1 d. Educ. King Edward VII School, Sheffield; St. John's College and Fitzwilliam College, Cambridge. Research Fellow, Fitzwilliam College, Cambridge; Lecturer, Glasgow University. Publication: Quantitative Electron Microscopy (Co-Editor). Recreations: photography; walking; squash. Address: (b.) Department of Physics and Astronomy, Glasgow University, Glasgow, G12 8QQ; T.-0141-330 4462.

Chapman, Robert Sutherland, MB, ChB (Hons), FRCP(Glas), FRCP(Edin), FRCP(Lond). Consultant Dermatologist, Greater Glasgow Health Board and Forth Valley Health Board, since 1971; Clinical Lecturer, Glasgow University, since 1973; b. 4.6.38, Cults, Aberdeenshire; m., Dr. Rosalind S. Slater; 2 s.; 1 d. Educ. Turriff Academy; Aberdeen University. House Officer,

Aberdeen Royal Infirmary; Research Fellow, Department of Materia Medica and Therapeutics, Aberdeen University; Registrar and Senior Registrar in Dermatology, Aberdeen Hospitals; Senior Registrar in Dermatology, Middlesex Hospital and St. John's Hospital for Diseases of the Skin, London. Recreations: gardening; hill-walking. Address: (h.) 4 Seafield Avenue, Bearsden, Glasgow, G61 3LB; T.-0141-942 8993.

Charlton, Professor Graham, BDS, MDS, FDSRCS. Professor of Conservative Dentistry and Head of Department, Edinburgh University, 1978-91; b. 15.10.28, Newbiggin-By-Sea, Northumberland; m., Stella Dobson; 2 s.; 1 d. Educ. Bedlington Grammar School; St. John's, York; Durham University. CertEd. Teacher in Northumberland, 1948-52 (including period of National Service); Dental School, 1952-58; general dental practice, 1958-64; Lecturer, then Senior Lecturer/Honorary Consultant, Bristol University, 1964-78 (Clinical Dean, Dental School, Bristol, 1975-78). Dean of Dental Studies, Edinburgh University, 1978-83. Address: (h.) 7A Thorn Road, Bearsden, Glasgow, G61 4PP; T.-0141-942 9188.

Chatfield, William Robertson, MD, ChB, FRCS Glas, FRCS Edin, FRCOG, DFM. Consultant Obstetrician, Queen Mother's Hospital, Glasgow; Consultant Gynaecologist, Western Infirmary, Glasgow; Honorary Senior Lecturer, Glasgow University; b. 19.9.39, Glasgow; m., Mary McIndeor McArthur; 2 s.; 1 d. Educ. Glasgow Academy; Glasgow University. Hall Tutorial Fellow, Glasgow University; Lecturer, Nairobi University, Kenya; Senior Lecturer, Otago University, New Zealand. Recreation: golf. Address: (h.) 11 The Loaning, Whitecraigs, Glasgow, G46 6SE; T.-0141-639 1840.

Chatterji, Professor Monojit, BA, MA, PhD. Bonar Professor of Applied Economics, Dundee University, since 1989 (Head, Department of Economics and Management, since 1993); b. 15.1.51, Bombay; m., Anjum Rahmatulla; 1 s.; 2 d. Educ. Cathedral School, Bombay; St. Columba's, Delhi; Elphinstone College, Bombay; Christ's College, Cambridge. Recreations: tennis; cinema; history; theology. Address: (b.) Department of Economics, Dundee University, Dundee; T.-01382 23181.

Cheetham, Professor Juliet, MA. Professor and Director, Social Work Research Centre, Stirling University, since 1986; b. 12.10.39, Jerusalem; m., Christopher Paul Cheetham; 1 s.; 2 d. Educ. St. Andrews University; Oxford University. Probation Officer, Inner London, 1959-65; Lecturer in Applied Social Studies and Fellow of Green College, Oxford University, 1965-86. Member: Committee of Enquiry into Working of the Abortion Act; Northern Ireland Human Rights Commission; Commission of Racial Equality; Social Security Advisory Committee; Council for National Academic Awards; Economic and Social Research Council. Recreation: canal boats. Address: (b.) Social Work Research Centre, Stirling University, Stirling, FK9 4LA; T.-0786 67724.

Chester, Richard Waugh, ARAM, GRSM, ARCM, FRSA. Director, National Youth Orchestra of Scotland, since 1987; b. 19.4.43, Hutton Rudby; m., Sarah Chapman-Mortimer; 1 s.; 2 d. Educ. The Friends' School, Great Ayton; Huddersfield University; Royal Academy of Music. Flautist: BBC Northern Ireland, 1965, Royal Scottish National Orchestra, 1967; Conductor; Teacher; Examiner. Director, Glasgow Festival Strings; Governor, St. Mary's Music School, Edinburgh. Recreations: tennis; swimming; good food. Address: (h.) Milton of Cardross, Port of Menteith, Stirling, FK8 3JY; T.-01877 384634.

Cheyne, Rev. Professor Alexander Campbell, MA (Hons), BLitt, BD, HonDLitt (Memorial University, Newfoundland). Professor of Ecclesiastical History, Edinburgh University, 1964-86; Principal, New College,

Edinburgh, 1984-86; Moderator, Edinburgh Presbytery, Church of Scotland, 1987-88; b. 1.6.24, Errol, Perthshire. Educ. Kirkcaldy High School; Edinburgh University; Oriel College, Oxford; Basel University, Switzerland. National Service, Black Watch and RAEC (Instructor, Army School of Education), 1946-48; Glasgow University: Assistant Lecturer, 1950-51, Lecturer in History, 1951-53; New College and Basel University, 1953-57; Lecturer in Ecclesiastical History, Edinburgh University, 1958-64. Carnegie Scholar, 1948-50; Aitken Fellow, 1956-57; Visiting Professor, Wooster College, Ohio, 1973; Chalmers Lecturer (Trinity College, Glasgow, and Christ's College, Aberdeen), 1976-80; Visiting Fellow, Wolfson College, Cambridge, 1979; Burns Lecturer, Knox College, Dunedin, New Zealand, 1980; Lee Lecturer, 1993; President, Scottish Church History Society, 1986-89. Publications: The Transforming of the Kirk: Victorian Scotland's Religious Revolution, 1983; The Practical and the Pious: Essays on Thomas Chalmers 1780-1847 (Editor), 1985; The Ten Years' Conflict and the Disruption, 1993; contributions to: Reformation and Revolution: Essays presented to Hugh Watt, 1967, The Westminster Confession in the Church Today, 1982; In Divers Manners, 1990; Christ, Church and Society: essays, 1993; introduction to Movements of Religious Thought in Britain during the Nineteenth Century, 1971. Recreations: classical music; walking; foreign travel. Address: (h.) 12 Crossland Crescent, Peebles, EH45 8LF; T.-01721 722288.

Chezeaud, Jacques-Marcel, BA (Hons). Rector, St. Joseph's College, Dumfries, since 1994; b. 16.8.52, Bourges, France; m., Joan I. Campbell; 1 s.; 1 d. Educ. Lycee Alain Fournier, France; Orleans University; Stirling University. Foreign language assistant, Wallace Hall and Sanquhar Academies, 1974-75; manager, wine trade, 1979-80; Teacher, English/French, Biggar High School and St. Mary's Academy, Bathgate, 1980-82; Principal Teacher, Modern Languages, Our Lady's High School, Broxburn, 1982-85; Depute Rector, St. Columba's High School, Perth, 1985-91; Depute Head, St. David's High School, Dalkeith, 1991-94. Member, Executive Committee, Scottish Association for Language Teaching. Recreations: long-distance running; reading; good food and wines. Address: (b.) St. Joseph's College, Craigs Road, Dumfries, DG1 4UU; T.-01387 252893.

Chick, Jonathan Dale, MA (Cantab), MB, ChB, MPhil, FRCPE, FRCPsych. Consultant Psychiatrist, Royal Edinburgh Hospital, since 1979; part-time Senior Lecturer, Edinburgh University, since 1979; b. 23.4.45, Wallasey; m., Josephine Anna; 2 s. Educ. Queen Elizabeth Grammar School, Darlington; Corpus Christi College, Cambridge; Edinburgh University. Posts in Edinburgh teaching hospitals, 1971-76; scientific staff, MRC Unit for Epidemiological Studies in Psychiatry, 1976-79. Adviser, WHO, Department of Transport; awarded Royal College of Psychiatrists Research Medal and Prize. Publication: Drinking Problems (Co-author). Recreations: wheels, reels, spiels and stichomythia. Address: (h.) 8 Abbotsford Park, Edinburgh.

Chisholm, Duncan Douglas, MB, ChB, MRCPsych, DPM, DPsychother. Consultant Child and Adolescent Psychiatrist, Department of Child and Family Psychiatry, Royal Aberdeen Children's Hospital, since 1975; Clinical Senior Lecturer, Department of Mental Health, Aberdeen University, since 1975; b. 8.10.41, Grantown-on-Spey; m., Rosemary Galloway Doyle; 2 d. Educ. Grantown Grammar School; Aberdeen University. Pre-registration House Officer, Aberdeen, 1965-66; post-registration Senior House Officer/Registrar, Royal Cornhill Hospital and Ross Clinic, Aberdeen, 1966-70; Senior Registrar in Child and Adolescent Psychiatry, 1970-75 (including one-year sabbatical, Clarke Institute of Psychiatry, Toronto, 1973-74). Vice-President, Family Mediation Grampian; Academic Secretary, Scottish Child and Adolescent

Section, Royal College of Psychiatrists. Recreations: reading; chess; crosswords; literature, history and culture of Scotland and Scottish Highlands; bowls. Address: (h.) Figurettes, 51 Fountainhall Road, Aberdeen, AB2 4EU; T.-01224 620786.

Chisholm, Duncan Fraser. Managing Director, Duncan Chisholm & Sons Ltd., Inverness, since 1979; Vice-Chairman, Inverness, Loch Ness and Nairn Tourist Board, since 1988; b. 14.4.41, Inverness; m., Mary Rebecca MacRae; 1 s.; 1 d. Educ. Inverness High School. Member, Inverness District Council, 1984-92; Member, Board of Governors, Eden Court Theatre, Inverness, 1984-88; President, Inverness and Highland Chamber of Commerce, 1983-84 (Vice-President, 1982-83); President, Clan Chisholm Society, 1978-89; Past President, Inverness Wine Appreciation Society; Assistant Area Scout Commissioner, 1975-78. Recreations: swimming; badminton. Address: (b.) 47-53 Castle Street, Inverness; T.-01463 234599.

Chisholm, Duncan John, FRICS. Regional Assessor, Fife Regional Council, since 1990; Electoral Registration Officer, Fife Regional Council, since 1990; Community Charges Registration Officer, Fife Regional Council, since 1990; b. 21.1.53, Musselburgh; m., Ann Thomson; 1 s.; 1 d. Educ. Trinity Academy, Edinburgh. Apprentice Surveyor, Midlothian County Assessor, 1970-74; Valuer, Midlothian County Assessor, 1974-75; Valuer, Senior Valuer, Divisional Assessor, Lothian Regional Assessor, 1975-89. Recreations: golf; music; eating; real ale. Address (b.) Fife House (03), North Street, Glenrothes, Fife; T.-Glenrothes 414141.

Chisholm, Malcolm. MP (Labour), Edinburgh Leith, since 1992; b. 7.3.49; m.; 2 s.; 1 d. Former teacher. Address: (b.) House of Commons, London, SW1A 0AA.

Chiswick, Derek, MB, ChB, MPhil, FRCPsych. Honorary Senior Lecturer in Forensic Psychiatry, Edinburgh University; Consultant Forensic Psychiatrist, Lothian Health Board; b. 7.1.45, Hampton, Middlesex; m., Ann Williams; 3 d. Educ. Preston Manor County School, Wembley; Liverpool University. Parole Board for Scotland: Member, 1983-88, Vice-Chairman, 1984-88; Member, Home Office Advisory Board on Restricted Patients. Recreation: relaxing with family. Address: (h.) 6 St. Catherine's Place, Edinburgh, EH9 1NU; T.-0131-667 2444.

Christian, Professor Reginald Frank, MA (Hons) (Oxon). Professor of Russian and Head of Department, St. Andrews University, 1966-92, now Honorary Professor; b. 9.8.24, Liverpool; m., Rosalind Iris Napier; 1 s.; 1 d. Educ. Liverpool Institute High School; Queen's College, Oxford. RAF, 1943-46 (aircrew), flying on 231 Sqdn. and 6 Atlantic Ferry Unit (Pilot Officer, 1944); Foreign Office (British Embassy, Moscow), 1949-50; Lecturer and Head of Russian Department, Liverpool University, 1950-55; Senior Lecturer, then Professor of Russian and Head of Department, Birmingham University, 1955-66; Visiting Professor: McGill University, Montreal, 1961-62, Institute of Foreign Languages, Moscow, 1964-65; Dean, Faculty of Arts, St. Andrews University, 1975-78; Member, University Court, 1971-73, 1981-85. President, British Universities Association of Slavists, 1967-70; Member, International Committee of Slavists, 1970-75; Honorary Vice-President, Association of Teachers of Russian; Member, UGC Arts Sub-Committee on Russian Studies. Publications: Russian Syntax (with F.M. Borras), 1959 and 1971; Korolenko's Siberia, 1954; Tolstoy's War and Peace: A Study, 1962; Russian Prose Composition (with F.M. Borras), 1964 and 1974; Tolstoy: A Critical Introduction, 1969; Tolstoy's Letters, edited, translated and annotated, 1978; Tolstoy's Diaries, edited, translated and annotated, 1985 and 1994. Recreations: violin; fell-walking; formerly association football. Address: (h.) Culgrianach, 48 Lade Braes, St.

Andrews, Fife; T.-01334 474407; Scioncroft, Knockard Road, Pitlochry; T.-01796 472993.

Christie, Alexander Duncan, PhD, BSc, CEng, MIEE, AFRAeS. Head, Department of Diagnostic Ultrasound, Ninewells Medical School, Dundee, since 1971; b. 14.6.30, Detroit; m., Beatrice R. Phemister; 2 d. Educ. Robert Gordon's College, Aberdeen; Aberdeen University. Pilot, RAF, 1953-63; Lecturer, Bristol College of Technology, 1963-67; Lecturer, Aberdeen University, 1967-70; Principal Physicist, Tayside Health Board, and Honorary Senior Lecturer, Dundee University, since 1971; Consultant Clinical Scientist, Dundee Teaching Hospitals (NHS Trust), since 1990; Professor, WHO Collaborating Centre, University of Zagreb, since 1986; Visiting Professor, University of Hong Kong, 1988-89. Publication: Ultrasound and Infertility, 1981. Address: (b.) Department of Obstetrics and Gynaecology, Dundee University, Dundee; T.-0382 60111.

Christie, Andrew John McPhedran, BAcc, CA, ATII. Partner, Arthur Andersen (Chartered Accountants), since 1983; b. 17.7.50, Glasgow; m., Barbara Isabel Tait; 2 s. Educ. Hillhead High School, Glasgow; Glasgow University. Joined Arthur Andersen, 1971; appointed Honorary Professor, Heriot-Watt University, 1990. Past Convener, Taxation Committee, ICAS; Member of Council, ICAS; Governor, Edinburgh College of Art. Recreations: golf; skiing. Address: (b.) 18 Charlotte Square, Edinburgh, EH2 4DF; T.-031-225 4554.

Christie, Campbell. General Secretary, Scottish Trades Union Congress, since 1986; b. 23.8.37, Carsluith, Kirkcudbrightshire; m., Elizabeth Brown Cameron; 2 s. Educ. Albert Senior Secondary School, Glasgow; Woolwich Polytechnic, London. Civil Servant, Department of Health and Social Security, 1954-72; National Officer, then Deputy General Secretary, Society of Civil and Public Servants, 1972-86. Member, EEC Economic and Social Committee; Member, Scottish Economic Council, Glasgow Development Agency; Director, Wildcat Theatre Company, Theatre Royal Opera Company. Address: (h.) 31 Dumyat Drive, Falkirk; T.-01324 624555; (b.) 16 Woodlands Terrace, Glasgow, G5; T.-0141-332 4649.

Christie, Ian, BSc, CEng, MIEE. Director and Business Strategy Development Manager, ABB Power T&D Ltd., since 1995; Director, ABB Transformers PLC (Ireland), since 1988; Vice President, Scottish Council Development and Industry, since 1993; b. 1.1.37, Rutherglen; m., Irene M.L.; 1 s.; 1 d. Educ. Rutherglen Academy; Glasgow University. Chairman, Tayside Committee, SCDI; Fellow, University of Abertay, Dundee. Recreations: reading; walking; entomology. Address: (b.) ABB Power T&D Ltd., East Kingsway, Dundee, DD4 7RP; T.-01382 454500.

Christie, Rev. James, SJ, MA, MSc, CQSW, MInstGA. Director, The Garnethill Centre, Glasgow, since 1980; b. 3.7.40, Bellshill, Lanarkshire. Educ. Our Lady's High School, Motherwell; St. Aloysius College, Glasgow; Campion Hall, Oxford; Columbia University; Southampton University; London School of Economics. Ordained Priest, Society of Jesus, 1970; parish work and training in Paris, 1970-71; on staff of Fons Vitae Institute, Johannesburg, 1971-72; School Counsellor, Wimbledon College, 1973-75; Depute Director, The Dympna Centre, London, 1977-80; Training Group Analyst, IGA, since 1995. Chairman, Scottish Section, The Group-Analytic Society (London), since 1992. Recreation: hill-walking. Address: 23 Oakfield Avenue (2/2), Glasgow, G12 8JF; T.-0141-337 6960.

Christie, Robert Alexander, LLB. Chief Executive and Director of Administration, Berwickshire District Council, since 1977; b. 24.1.45, Preston. Educ. Balshaw's Grammar School, Leyland, Lancashire; St. Andrews University. Dumfries County Council: Principal Legal Assistant, 1969-71, Depute County Clerk, 1971-73; Depute County Clerk, Argyll County Council, 1973-75; Depute Director of Administration, Argyll and Bute District Council, 1975-76; Chief Executive, Lochaber District Council, 1976-77. Recreations: cooking; reading; listening to music. Address: (b.) District Council Offices, 8 Newtown Street, Duns, Berwickshire, TD11 3DT; T.-01361 882600.

Christie, Robert Johnstone Stevenson, BSc (Hons), FRSA. Scottish Secretary, Professional Association of Teachers, since 1989; b. 7.8.46, Edinburgh; m., Anne Elisabeth Fraser Macleod; 3 d. Educ. Grangemouth High School; Paisley College of Technology; Jordanhill College of Education; Glasgow University. Chemist, British Petroleum Chemicals Ltd., 1964-68; Principal Teacher of Physics, Tain Royal Academy, 1976-88. Recreations: family; music; history; sailing; Rotary. Address: (b.) 4/6 Oak Lane, Edinburgh, EH12 6XH; T.-0131-317 8282.

Christie, Terry, BSc (Hons). Headteacher, Musselburgh Grammar School, since 1987; Manager, Stenhousemuir Football Club, since 1992; b. 16.12.42, Edinburgh; m., Susan; 2 s.; 1 d. Educ. Holy Cross Academy, Edinburgh. Headteacher, Ainslie Park, 1982-87. Former professsional footballer; Manager, Meadowbank Thistle, 1980-92; President, Lothian Schools FA. Recreations: reading; golf. Address: (h.) 76 Meadowfield Terrace, Edinburgh, EH8 7NU; T.-0131-661 1486.

Christie, Sheriff William James, LLB. Sheriff of Tayside, Central and Fife, at Kirkcaldy, since 1979; b. 1.11.32.

Clapham, David Charles, LLB, SSC. Solicitor (Principal, private practice, since 1984); President, Glasgow Bar Association, 1992-93; Secretary, Strathclyde Region Local Valuation Panel, since 1988; part-time Chairman, Social Security Appeal Tribunals, since 1992; Secretary, Scottish Law Agents Society, since 1994; b. 16.10.58, Giffnock; m., Debra Harriet Samuels; 1 s.; 2 d. Educ. Hutchesons' Boys' Grammar School, Glasgow; Strathclyde University. Legal apprenticeship, 1979-81; admitted Solicitor, 1981; admitted Notary Public, 1982; founded own legal practice, 1984; Tutor, Strathclyde University, 1984-92; part-time Lecturer, Glasgow University, 1991-94. Secretary, Glasgow Bar Association, 1987-91, Vice President, 1991-92. Recreations: reading and collecting books. Address: (b.) 79 West Regent Street, Glasgow, G2 2AW; T.-0141-332 5537.

Clark, Alastair Trevor, CBE (1976), LVO (1974), MA (Oxon), FSA Scot. Barrister; Member, Race Relations Assessors Panel, Scottish Sheriff Courts, since 1983; a Governor, Edinburgh Filmhouse, 1980-84 and since 1987; Member, National Museums of Scotland Charitable Trust, since 1987; Member, Museums Association Council, 1983-86 and since 1990; Member, Edinburgh International Festival Council, 1980-86 and since 1990; Member, Almond Valley Heritage Trust, since 1990 (Vice Chairman, since 1993); Trustee, Stirling Smith Art Gallery and Museum, since 1993; b. 10.6.23, Glasgow; m., Hilary Agnes Mackenzie Anderson. Educ. Giffnock Academy; Glasgow Academy; Edinburgh Academy; Magdalen College, Oxford; Inns of Court (Middle Temple); Ashridge Management College. War service, Queen's Own Cameron Highlanders and Royal West African Frontier Force, Nigeria, India and Burma, 1942-46; Administrative Branch, HM Colonial Service (later HMOCS): Nigeria, 1949-59 (Secretary to Cabinet, Northern Region; Senior District Officer), Hong Kong, 1960-72 (Director of Social Welfare; Deputy and Acting Director of Urban Services; Acting Chairman Urban Council; Clerk of Councils; Principal Assistant Colonial Secretary, etc.), Western Pacific, 1972-77 (Chief Secretary Western Pacific High Commission; Deputy and Acting Governor, Solomon Islands); retired, 1977; Vice-President, Hong Kong Scout Association, 1965-72; Joint Founder, HK Outward Bound School; Honorary Secretary, St. John's Cathedral Council, 1963-72; Country

Leader Fellowship to USA, 1972; Selector, Voluntary Service Overseas, 1978-80; Leverhulme Trust Grant, 1979-81; Chairman, Scottish Museums Council, 1981-84 and 1987-90; Vice-Chairman, Committee of Area Museum Councils, 1983-84; Member, Secretary of State's Museums Advisory Board, 1983-85; Trustee, National Museums of Scotland, 1985-87; a Director, Royal Lyceum Theatre Company, 1982-84; Member, Lothian Health Board, 1981-89; Member, City of Edinburgh District Council, 1980-88; Member, Court of Directors, Edinburgh Academy, 1979-84. Publication: A Right Honourable Gentleman — Abubakar from the Black Rock, 1991. Recreations: music; books; theatre; netsuke; cartophily. Address: (h.) 11 Ramsay Garden, Edinburgh, EH1 2NA; T.-0131-225 8070.

Clark, Alex. Member, Board of Directors: Mayfest (Founder and Hon. President), Scottish Ballet, Glasgow Jazz Festival, Glasgow Film Theatre, Arran Theatre and Arts Trust; Trustee, James Milne Memorial Trust; Trustee, Hugh MacDiarmid Memorial Trust; b. 2.1.22, Larkhall; m., Jessie Beveridge McCulloch; 1 s.; 1 d. Educ. Larkhall Academy. Grain miller, 1936-39; coal miner, 1939-53; political organiser, 1953-69; Scottish and Northern Ireland Secretary, British Actors Equity Association, 1969-84; created the post of STUC Arts Officer, 1985-87; founder Member, Boards, Scottish Youth Theatre, Scottish Theatre Company, Royal Lyceum Theatre Company; also served on Boards of Pitlochry Festival Theatre and Cumbernauld Theatre Company; Member, Scottish Arts Council's Review Committee on Scottish Theatre Company, 1987; Member, Working Party on a National Theatre for Scotland, 1987; Lord Provost's Award for services to the city of Glasgow, 1987; Member, STUC Entertainment and Arts Committee, 1975-94; Winner, ABSA-Goodman & Reed Elsevier Award for Services to the Arts, 1994. Recreations: reading; music; theatre; walking; gardening. Address: (h.) Ponfeigh, 8 Strathwhillan, Brodick, Isle of Arran.

Clark, Alistair Campbell, MA, LLB, WS. Partner, Blackadder, Reid, Johnston (formerly Reid, Johnston, Bell & Henderson), Solicitors, Dundee, since 1961; President, Law Society of Scotland, 1989-90 (Council Member, since 1982); Honorary Sheriff, Tayside Central & Fife, since 1986;Chairman, Dovetail Enterprises, since 1993; Trustee, Dundee Disabled Children's Association, since 1993; b. 4.3.33, Dundee; m., Evelyn M. Clark; 3 s. Educ. Grove Academy, Broughty Ferry; St. Andrews University. Dean, Faculty of Procurators and Solicitors in Dundee, 1979-81, Hon. Life Member, since 1991; founder Chairman, Broughty Ferry Round Table; Founder President, Claverhouse Rotary Club, Dundee. Recreations: family; travel; erratic golf. Address: (b.) 34 Reform Street, Dundee; T.-01382 29222.

Clark, David Findlay, OBE, DL, MA, PhD, CPsychol, FBPsS, ARPS. Deputy Lieutenant, Banffshire, since 1992; Consulting Clinical Psychologist; former Director, Area Clinical Psychology Services, Grampian Health Board and Clinical Senior Lecturer, Department of Mental Health, Aberdeen University; b. 30.5.30, Aberdeen; m., Janet Ann Stephen; 2 d. Educ. Banff Academy; Aberdeen University. Flying Officer, RAF, 1951-53; Psychologist, Leicester Industrial Rehabilitation Unit, 1953-56; Senior, then Principal Clinical Psychologist, Leicester Area Clinical Psychology Service, and part-time Lecturer, Leicester University and Technical College, 1956-66; WHO short-term Consultant, Sri Lanka, 1977; various lecturing commitments in Canada and USA, since 1968. Honorary Sheriff, Grampian and Highlands; former Governor, Aberdeen College of Education; Member, Grampian Children's Panel, 1970-85; Safeguarder (in terms of Social Work Scotland Act), since 1985; Past Chairman, Clinical Division, British Psychological Society. Publications: Help, Hospitals and the Handicapped, 1984; book chapters and technical articles. Recreations: photography; sailing; chess; guitar playing; painting and drawing; golf; hill-walking.

Address: (h.) Glendeveron, 8 Deveron Terrace, Banff, AB45 1BB; T.-01261 812624.

Clark, Professor Frank, CBE, MHSM, DipHSM. General Manager, Lanarkshire Health Board, since 1985; Visiting Professor, Glasgow Caledonian University, since 1993; b. 17.10.46, Aberdeen; m., Linda Margaret; 2 d. Educ. Aberdeen Academy. Greater Glasgow Health Board: Assistant District Administrator, 1977-81, District General Administrator, 1981-83; Lanarkshire Health Board: Director of Administrative Services, 1983-84, Secretary, 1984-85. Chairman, Scottish Health Board General Managers Group, since 1993; Member: National Nursing Strategy Group, Scottish Overseas Health Support Policy Board, West of Scotland Dental Educational Trust Distance Learning Unit Appeal Committee, Joint Working Group on Purchasing; Chairman, West of Scotland Health Service Research Network; Board Member, New Lanarkshire Ltd. Recreations: reading; music; gardening; driving; swimming; DIY; poetry. Address: (b.) Lanarkshire Health Board, 14 Beckford Street, Hamilton, ML3 0TA; T.-01698 281313.

Clark, Graham M. BSc, PhD, CChem, FRSC, FIMgt, FRSA. Principal, Falkirk College of Technology, since 1992; b. 2.8.41, Dumfries; m., Linda A.; 3 d. Educ. George Watson's College, Edinburgh; Edinburgh University. Research Fellow, Hull University, 1966-67; Lecturer, Huddersfield Polytechnic, 1967-79; Head of Applied Science, North East Surrey College of Technology, 1980-85; Deputy Director, Nene College, Northampton, 1986-89; Principal, Angus College of Further Education, 1990-92. Editor, Thermal Analysis Reviews and Abstracts, 1986-93. Recreations: golf; hill walking; UK philately. Address: (b.) Falkirk College of Technology, Grangemouth Road, Falkirk, FK2 9AD; T.-01324 24981.

Clark, Guy Wyndham Nial Hamilton, JP, DL. Deputy Lieutenant, Renfrewshire, since 1987; Director, Greig, Middleton & Co. Ltd., since 1986; b. 28.3.44; m., Brighid Lovell; 2 s.; 1 d. Educ. Eton. Commd. Coldstream Guards, 1962-67; Investment Manager, Murray Johnstone Ltd., Glasgow, 1973-77; Partner, R.C. Greig & Co. (Stockbrokers), Glasgow, 1977-86; Member, Executive Committee, Erskine Hospital; Chairman, JP Advisory Committee, since 1991. Recreations: hunting; shooting; fishing; racing. Addrss: (h.) Braeton, Inverkip, PA16 0DU; T.-01475 520 619.

Clark, Rev. James, MA, DipTheol. Minister, Glasgow R.P. Church of Scotland, since 1991; Clerk of Synod, since 1993; b. Glasgow. Educ. Edinburgh University. Publications: Life and Works of Samuel Rutherford; booklets on James Begg, DD, and the National Covenants; The Christian Faith, by Theodore Beza (translator). Address: 4 Burnbrae Avenue, Glasgow, G61 3ES.

Clark, J. Hamish, OBE. Chairman, North of Scotland Milk Marketing Board. Address: Milton of Connage, Ardersier, IV1 2SX.

Clark, John Kenneth, BA (Hons), MA. Glasspainter; b. 1.12.57, Dumbarton. Educ. Dumbarton Academy; Glasgow School of Art. Commissions include: Cafe Gandolfi, Glasgow (Saltire Award); Paisley Abbey (Saltire Award); Heaton Memorial Window, Ledbury; Lockerbie Memorial Window; Queens Park Synagogue, Glasgow; Beirut Hostages Windows, Broxted; St Petrus Worms — Herrnsheim; St. Konrad, Amberg-Ammersicht. Address: (h.) 11A Maxwell Drive, Glasgow, G41 5DR; T.-0141-429 0987.

Clark, Kenneth James, CBE, MA, LLB, JP. Chief Executive, Borders Regional Council, since 1974; b. 30.4.33, Perth; m., Marion; 3 s. Educ. Dundee High School; St. Andrews University. National Service, Queen's Own Cameron Highlanders, 1955-57; Legal and Administrative

Assistant, Roxburgh County Council, 1962-63; Banff County Council: Legal and Administrative Assistant, 1963-64, Assistant County Clerk, 1964-65, Depute County Clerk, 1965-66; Depute County Clerk, Berwick County Council, 1966-71; County Clerk, Ross and Cromarty County Council, 1971-74. Member, Working Group for Scotland on Handling of Complaints against the Police, 1974; Member, Committee of Inquiry into Local Government in Scotland (The Stodart Committee), 1981. Address: (b.) Regional Headquarters, Newtown St. Boswells, Melrose, TD6 OSA; T.-01835 823301.

Clark, M. Lynda, QC. Admitted Advocate, 1977; called to English Bar, 1988; contested Fife North East (Labour), 1992. Address: (b.) Advocates' Library, Parliament Square, Edinburgh, EH1 1RF.

Clark, Pamela Ann Dean, LLB (Hons). Executive Director, Highland Community Care Forum, since 1994; b. 18.10.60, Inverness. Educ. Lossiemouth High School; Edinburgh University; Aberdeen College of Education. Welfare Benefits Adviser, Central Regional Council; Legal Services Adviser, Citizens Advice Scotland; Director, Tenant Participation Advisory Service. Member, Scottish Council of Voluntary Organisations Policy Committee; Member, Scottish Homes Advisory Committee on Housing Information and Advice. Recreations: Irish wolfhound; swimming; cinema. Address: (h.)8 Burnfarm Cottages, Killen, Munlochy, Ross-shire.

Clark, Robert John Whitten. Head, Fisheries Regimes Fishstock Management, Marketing and Trade Division, Department of Agriculture and Fisheries for Scotland, 1985-87; b. 29.9.32, Edinburgh; m., Christine Margaret Reid; 1 s.; 1 d. Educ. George Heriot's School, Edinburgh. Scottish Education Department: various appointments, 1949-69, including Private Secretary to Secretary of Department, 1960-61, Head, Teacher Training Branch, 1967-69, Head, Schools Branch, 1969-73, Head, Children's Hearings Branch, Social Work Services Group, 1973-75, Head, Children's Division, Social Work Services Group, 1975-76, Head, List D (Approved) Schools Division, Social Work Services Group, 1976-79; Head, Home Defence and Emergency Services Co-ordination Division, Scottish Home and Health Department, 1979-85. Former Captain and Past President, Edinburgh and District Civil Service Golfing Society; Captain, Scottish Education Department Golf Club, 1984-85; former Vice-Captain, Scottish Civil Service Golfing Society. Recreations: travel; golf; reading; gardening. Address: (h.) 39 Gordon Road, Edinburgh, EH12 6LZ; T.-0131-539 1017.

Clark, Robert Phillip, SSC, NP. Solicitor (retired); b. 20.4.20, Dundee; m., Helen Joan Forman; 3 s. Educ. Logie Secondary School, Dundee; University College, Dundee. Commenced legal training, 1937; War service, 1940-45: Royal Armoured Corps; Royal Military College, Sandhurst; commissioned 2nd Fife & Forfar Yeomanry; Regimental Signals Officer; wounded 1944; resumed legal training, 1947-50; qualified Solicitor, 1950; Court procurator, 1952-56; Honorary Sheriff of Tayside Central and Fife at Dundee, since 1977; former Dean, Faculty of Procurators and Solicitors in Dundee; former Vice-President, Scottish Law Agents Society; Clerk, Hammerman Incorporation of Dundee. Recreations: tennis and golf; hill-walking; photography. Address: (h.) Kilry Lodge, Alyth, Perthshire.

Clark, Terence Gilbert, CEng, MIEE, MMS, MHSM. Director of Administration, Tayside Health Board, since 1986; b. 19.3.39, Bristol; m., Jennifer Mary; 1 s.; 1 d. Educ. Katharine Lady Berkeley's Grammar School; Bristol College of Science and Technology. Design engineer, 1955-64; work study officer, East Anglian Regional Health Board, 1964-70; Chief Work Study Officer, then General Administrator, Tayside Health Board, 1970-86. Recreations: classic cars and motorcycles. Address: (b.)

Vernonholme, Riverside Drive, Dundee; T.-Dundee 645151.

Clarke, (Christopher) Michael, BA (Hons). Keeper, National Gallery of Scotland, since 1987; b. 29.8.52, York; m., Deborah Clare Cowling; 2 s.; 1 d. Educ. Felsted School, Essex; Manchester University. Art Assistant, York City Art Gallery, 1973-76; Research Assistant, British Museum, 1976-78; Assistant Keeper in charge of prints, Whitworth Art Gallery, Manchester, 1978-84; Assistant Keeper, National Gallery of Scotland, 1984-87. Visiting Fellow, Yale Center for British Art, 1985. Publications include: The Tempting Prospect; A Social History of English Watercolours; The Arrogant Connoisseur (Co-Editor); Richard Payne Knight; Lighting Up the Landscape – French Impressionism and its Origins; Corot and the Art of Landscape; Eyewitness Art – Watercolours. Recreations: listening to music; tennis; golf. Address: (b.) National Gallery of Scotland, The Mound, Edinburgh, EH2 2EL; T.-0131-556 8921.

Clarke, Eric Lionel. MP (Labour), Midlothian, since 1992; b. 9.4.33, Edinburgh; m., June; 2 s.; 1 d. Educ. Holy Cross Academy; W.M. Ramsey Technical College; Esk Valley Technical College. Coal miner, 1949-77; General Secretary, NUM Scottish Area, 1977-89; County Councillor, Midlothian, 1962-74; Regional Councillor, Lothian, 1974-78. Recreations: fly fishing; gardening; carpentry. Address: (h.) 32 Mortonhall Park Crescent, Edinburgh; T.-0131-654 1585.

Clarke, Matthew G., QC. Admitted, Faculty of Advocates, 1978.

Clarke, Owen James. Controller, Inland Revenue, Scotland, since 1990; b. 15.3.37, Edinburgh; m., Betty; 2 s.; 1 d. Educ. Portobello High. Entered Civil Service, 1955; served in London, Merseyside, North of England; in Scotland: Greenock, Falkirk, Wick, Edinburgh; three years in Revenue fraud squad; six years, special anti-avoidance office. Recreations: judo; golf; jogging; hill-climbing. Address: (b.) 80 Lauriston Place, Edinburgh, EH3 9SL; T.-0131-229 9344.

Clarke, Peter, CBE, BSc, PhD, LLD (Hon), CChem, FRSC, DEd(Hon), FInstPet. President, Association for Educational and Training Technology, 1993-95; Chairman, Industrial Training Centre, Aberdeen, 1989-95; b. 18.3.22, Mansfield; m., Ethel; 2 s. Educ. Queen Elizabeth's Grammar School, Mansfield; University College, Nottingham. Principal, Robert Gordon's Institute of Technology, Aberdeen, 1970-85. Chairman, Scottish Vocational Education Council, 1985-91; Chairman, Aberdeen Enterprise Trust, 1984-92; President, Association of Principals of Colleges, 1980-81; Member, Science and Engineering Research Council, 1978-82; Trustee, Gordon Cook Foundation, since 1988. Recreations: walking; gardening. Address: (h.) Dunaber, 12 Woodburn Place, Aberdeen, AB1 8JR; T.-01224 311132.

Clarke, Professor Roger John, ALCM, BA, BTech, MSc, PhD, CEng, MIEE, MIEEE. NCR Professor of Electronic Engineering, Heriot Watt University, since 1989; b. 1.10.40, Ewell, Surrey; m., Yvonne Clarke; 1 s. Educ. Gravesend Grammar School; Loughborough University. Development Engineer, STC Ltd., Woolwich, 1962-64; Research Associate, then Lecturer in Electrical Engineering, Loughborough University, 1964-86; Reader in Electrical Engineering, Heriot Watt University, 1986-89. Recreations: gardening; playing the cello; Shakespeare. Address: (b.) Department of Computing and Electrical Engineering, Heriot Watt University, Riccarton, Edinburgh, EH14 4AS; T.-0131-451 3323.

Clarke, Thomas, CBE, JP. MP (Labour), Monklands West, since 1983; Member Shadow Cabinet; Shadow Secretary of

State for Scotland, 1992-93; b. 10.1.41, Coatbridge. Educ. Columba High School, Coatbridge. Former Assistant Director, Scottish Council for Educational Technology; Provost of Monklands, 1975-82; Past President, Convention of Scottish Local Authorities; MP, Coatbridge and Airdrie, 1982-83; author, Disabled Persons (Services Consultation and Representation) Act, 1986. Recreations: films; walking; reading. Address: (h.) 37 Blairhill Street, Coatbridge, ML5 1PG; T.-01236 422550.

Clarkson, Graeme Andrew Telford, LLB. Senior Partner, Baird & Company, Solicitors, Kirkcaldy, since 1990; b. 6.9.53, Fraserburgh; m., Moira; 3 s. Educ. High School of Dundee; Aberdeen University. Law Apprentice, Allan MacDougall & Co., Edinburgh; Assistant, Ranken & Reid, Edinburgh; Assistant, then Partner, Baird & Company. Past Chairman, Kirkcaldy Round Table; Council Member, Law Society of Scotland. Address: (b.) 2 Park Place, Kirkcaldy, Fife; T.-01592 268608.

Clayson, Christopher William, CBE (1974), OBE (1966), MB, ChB, DPH, MD, FRCPEdin, FRCPLond, Hon.FACP, Hon.FRACP, Hon.FRCP(Glas), Hon.FRCGP, Hon. FRCP Edin. Physician (retired); b. 11.9.03, Ilford. Educ. George Heriot's School, Edinburgh; Edinburgh University. Assistant Physician: Southfield Sanatorium, Edinburgh, 1931-44, City Hospital, Edinburgh, 1939-44; Lecturer, Edinburgh University, 1939-44; Medical Superintendent, Lochmaben Sanatorium, 1944-48; Consultant Physician, Dumfries and Galloway Hospitals, 1948-68; President, RCPEdin, 1966-70; Chairman, Departmental Committee on Scottish Licensing Law, 1971-73; Chairman, Scottish Council on Postgraduate Medical Education, 1970-74; William Cullen Prizeman, RCPEdin, 1978. Address: (h.) Cockiesknowe, Lochmaben, Lockerbie, DG11 1RL; T.-01387 810231.

Cleall, Charles, MA(Wales), BMus(Lond), ADCM, FRCO(CHM), GTCL, LRAM, HonTSC. Author and Writer; b. 1.6.27, Heston, Middlesex; m., Mary Turner; 2 d. Educ. Hampton School, Middlesex; Trinity College of Music; London University; Jordanhill College of Education, Glasgow; University College of North Wales. Organist and Choirmaster, St. Luke's, Chelsea, 1945-46; Command Music Adviser to Royal Navy, Plymouth Command (Instr. Lieut., RN) 1946-48; Professor of Solo Singing and Voice Production, and of ear-training and of choral repertoire, Trinity College of Music, London, 1949-52; Choral Scholar, Westminster Abbey, 1949-52; Organist and Choirmaster, Wesley's Chapel, City Road, London, 1950-52; Conductor, Morley College Orchestra, 1950-52; Conductor, Glasgow Choral Union, 1952-54; BBC Music Assistant, Midland Region, 1954-55; Music Master, Glyn County School, Ewell, 1955-66; Conductor, Aldeburgh Festival Choir, 1957-60; Organist and Choirmaster, St. Paul's, Portman Square, W1, 1957-61; Organist and Choirmaster, Holy Trinity, Guildford, 1961-65; Lecturer in Music, The Froebel Institute, Roehampton, 1967-68; Adviser in Music, London Borough of Harrow, 1968-72; Northern Divisional music specialist, HM Inspectorate of Schools in Scotland, 1972-87; Editor, Journal, Ernest George White Society, 1983-88; has given many lectures on singing and choir training; has written scores of articles and book reviews. Limpus Fellowship Prizeman, Royal College of Organists; International Composition Prizeman, Cathedral of St. John the Divine, New York. Publications: Voice Production in Choral Technique, 1955/1970; The Selection and Training of Mixed Choirs in Churches, 1960; Sixty Songs from Sankey, 1960; John Merbecke's Music for the Congregation at Holy Communion, 1963; Music and Holiness, 1964; Plainsong for Pleasure, 1969; Authentic Chanting, 1969; A Guide to Vanity Fair, 1982; Walking round the Church of St. James the Great, Stonehaven, 1993. Recreations: writing; reading; natural history; walking. Address: (h.) 10 Carronhall, Stonehaven, Aberdeen, AB3 2HF.

Cleland, John, BSc (Hons). Depute Principal, Kilmarnock College, since 1984; b. 3.11.35, Darvel; m., Janet G. Ross; 1 s.; 1 d. Educ. Darvel Junior Secondary School; Kilmarnock Academy; Glasgow University. Assistant Teacher of Mathematics, then Assistant Teacher of Science, Kilmarnock Academy; Assistant Teacher of Chemistry, then Senior Assistant Teacher, then Head of Department, Kilmarnock Technical College; Head, Department of Mathematics and Science, Kilmarnock College. FE Representative, SCEEB Chemistry Syllabus Panel, 1974-77; Joint Setter, SCE "H" Grade Chemistry, 1984; Member, Ayr Friends of the Hospice Committee. Recreations: bridge; golf. Address: (b.) Holehouse Road, Kilmarnock, KA3 7AT; T.-01563 23501.

Clements, Professor John Barklie, BSc, PhD, FRSA, FRSE. Professor of Virology, Glasgow University, since 1995; b. 14.3.46, Belfast. Educ. Belfast Royal Academy; Queen's University, Belfast. Research Fellow, California Institute of Technology, 1971-73; joined Institute of Virology, Glasgow University, 1973; Cancer Research Campaign Travelling Fellow, Department of Biochemistry and Molecular Biology, Harvard University, 1983; Council Member, Society for General Microbiology, 1984-88; Member, MRC Physiological Systems and Disorders Board, 1990-94; Chairman, Grants Committee B, PMIB, 1992-94; Member, Clinical and Biomedical Research Committee, Scottish Home and Health Department, 1990-93. Recreations: walking; golf; music. Address: (b.) Institute of Virology, Glasgow University, Glasgow; T.-0141-330 4027.

Clemson, Gareth, BMus (Auckland), BMus (Edinburgh). Teacher of violin and viola, since 1975; Composer; b. 1.10.33, Thames, New Zealand; m., Thora Clyne; 2 s.; 1 d. Educ. St. Peter's School, New Zealand; King's College, New Zealand; Auckland University; Edinburgh University. Music teaching, New Zealand, Edinburgh and West Lothian, 1960-75; String Teacher, West Lothian, 1975-85, Fife Region, since 1985; lessons in composition from Thomas Wilson, 1963-65; chamber works including Nexus I and II, Waters of Separation, The Singing Cat, Invocation; broadcasts, New Zealand and Scotland; recent compositions, Trumpet in the Dust and Blackbird. Recreations: drawing and painting; photography; philately; cats. Address: (h.) Tillywhally Cottage, Milnathort, Kinross-shire, KY13 7RN; T.-Kinross 864297.

Clerk of Penicuik, Sir John Dutton, 10th Bt, CBE (1966), VRD, FRSE, JP. Lord Lieutenant of Midlothian, 1972-92; b. 30.1.17; m.; 2 s.; 2 d. Educ. Stowe. Ensign,, Queen's Bodyguard for Scotland (Royal Company of Archers). Address: (h.) Penicuik House, Penicuik, Midlothian, EH26 9LA.

Clifford, Nigel Richard, MA (Cantab), DipInstM, DipCAM, MBA, FIMgmt. Chief Executive, Glasgow Royal Infirmary University NHS Trust, since 1994; b. 22.6.59, Emsworth; m., Jeanette; 2 s.; 1 d. Educ. Portsmouth Grammar School; Downing College, Cambridge; Strathclyde University. British Telecom, 1981-92, latterly as Head of Business Strategy, BT Mobile Communications. Founding Trustee, Herald Foundation for Women's Health. Recreations: family life; walking; running. Address: (b.) 84 Castle Street, Glasgow, G4 0SF; T.-0141-304 4924.

Clifford, Timothy Peter Plint, BA, AMA, FRSA, FSAScot. Director, National Galleries of Scotland, since 1984; b. 26.1.47; m., Jane Olivia Paterson; 1 d. Educ. Sherborne; Perugia University; Courtauld Institute, London University. Manchester City Art Galleries: Assistant Keeper, Department of Paintings, 1968-72, Acting Keeper, 1972; Assistant Keeper: Department of Ceramics, Victoria and Albert Museum, London, 1972-76, Department of Prints and Drawings, British Museum, London, 1976-78; Director, Manchester City Art Galleries, 1978-84.

Chairman, International Committee for Museums of Fine Art, 1980-83; Member, Museums and Galleries Commission, 1983-88; Member, Executive Committee, Scottish Museums Council; Vice President, Turner Society, 1984; Hon. Vice-President, Frigate Unicorn Preservation Society, since 1987; Member, Academic Committee, Accademia Italiana, since 1987; British Institute of Management's Special Award, 1991. Cavaliere all'Ordine del Merito della Repubblica Italiana, 1988; Member, Advisory Council, Friends of Courtauld Institute, since 1990; Vice-President, NADFAS, since 1990. FRSA; FSA (Scot). Recreations: shooting; bird-watching; collecting butterflies and moths. Address: (b.) National Galleries of Scotland, The Mound, Edinburgh, EH2 2EL.

Clouting, David Wallis, BDS, MSc, LDSRCS (Eng), DDPH. Chief Administrative Dental Officer, Borders Health Board, since 1990, Borders Community Health Services NHS Trust, since 1995; b. 29.3.53, London; m., Dr. Margaret M.C. Bacon; 3 s.; 1 d. Educ. Leyton County High School for Boys; University College Hospital Dental School, London; Institute of Dental Surgery, London; Joint Department of Dental Public Health, London Hospital Medical College and University College, London. Senior Dental Officer for Special Needs, East and North Hertfordshire Health Authorities, 1983-90. Recreations: amateur radio; DIY; swimming; hill walking; sailing. Address: (b.) Borders Community Health Services NHS Trust, Huntlyburn House, Melrose, TD6 9BP; T.-01896 754333.

Clow, Robert George Menzies. Chairman (since 1979) and Managing Director (1969-94), John Smith & Son (Glasgow) Ltd.; b. 27.1.34, Sian, Shensi, North China; m., Katrina M. Watson. Educ. Eltham College, London. Interned by Japanese as a child; National Service, RAF; trained as a bookseller, Bumpus London; worked in Geneva; joined John Smith & Son (Glasgow), 1960. Founded, with others, The New Glasgow Society, 1965 (Chairman 1967, 1968); worked for 12 years in rehabilitating St. Vincent Crescent, Glasgow, as founder member, St. Vincent Crescent Area Association; Secretary, First Glasgow Housing Association, since 1978; restored Aiket Castle (winner of an Europa Nostra Merit Award, 1989), 1976-79; National Trust for Scotland: elected to Council 1978 and 1991; Executive Member, Committee, Strathclyde Building Preservation Trust, 1986; appointed to Architectural Heritage Fund Executive, 1989. Recreations: farming; bee keeping; opera; restoring old houses; swimming; skiing; reading on holiday. Address: Aiket Castle, Dunlop, Ayrshire; T.-(b.) 0141-221 7472.

Clyde, Hon. Lord (James John Clyde), DUniv (Heriot Watt), BA (Oxon), LLB. Senator of the College of Justice, since 1985; b. 29.1.32, Edinburgh; m., Ann Clunie Hoblyn; 2 s. Educ. Edinburgh Academy; Corpus Christi College, Oxford; Edinburgh University. Called to Scottish Bar, 1959; QC, 1971; Advocate Depute, 1973-74; Chancellor to Bishop of Argyll and the Isles, 1972-85; a Judge of the Courts of Appeal of Jersey and Guernsey, 1979-85; Chairman, Medical Appeal Tribunal, 1974-85; Chairman, Committee of Investigation for Scotland on Agricultural Marketing, 1984-85; Chairman, Scottish Valuation Advisory Council, since 1987 (Member, since 1972); Member, UK Delegation to CCBE, 1978-84 (Leader, 1981-84); Chairman of the Inquiry into the removal of children from Orkney, 1991-92. Vice-President, Royal Blind Asylum and School, since 1987; President, Scottish Young Lawyers' Association, since 1988; Vice Chairman, Court, Edinburgh University, since 1993; Director, Edinburgh Academy, 1979-88; Chairman, St. George's School for Girls, since 1989; Governor, Napier Polytechnic of Edinburgh, since 1989; Assessor to Chancellor of Edinburgh University, 1989-94; Trustee and Manager, St. Mary's Music School, 1976-93; Trustee, National Library of Scotland, 1978-94. Recreations: music; gardening.

Address: (h.) 9 Heriot Row, Edinburgh, EH3 6HU; T.-0131-556 7114.

Clydesmuir, Baron (Ronald John Bilsland Colville), KT (1972), CB (1965), MBE (1944), TD. Lord Lieutenant, Lanarkshire, 1963-92; Captain General, Queen's Bodyguard for Scotland (Royal Company of Archers); b. 21.5.17; m.; 2 s.; 2 d. Educ. Charterhouse; Trinity College, Cambridge. Served in The Cameronians (Scottish Rifles), 1939-45; commanded 6/7th Bn., The Cameronians, TA, 1953-56; Director, Colvilles Ltd., 1958-70; Governor, British Linen Bank, 1966-71; Governor, Bank of Scotland, 1972-81; Director, Scottish Provident Institution, 1954-88; Director, Barclays Bank, 1972-82; Chairman, North Sea Assets Ltd., 1972-88; Scottish Council (Development and Industry): Chairman, Executive Committee, 1966-78, President, 1978-87; President, Scottish Council of Physical Recreation, 1964-72; Hon. LLD, Strathclyde, 1968; Hon. DSc, Heriot-Watt, 1971. Address: (h.) Langlees House, Biggar, Lanarkshire ML12 6NP.

Coates, Leon, MA (Cantab), LRAM, ARCO. Lecturer in Music, Edinburgh University, since 1965; b. 15.6.37, Wolverhampton; m., Heather Patricia Johnston. Educ. Derby School; St. John's College, Cambridge. Composer, pianist, organist, St. Andrew's and St. George's Church, Edinburgh, since 1981; Conductor: Edinburgh Chamber Orchestra, 1965-75, Edinburgh Symphony Orchestra, 1973-85; Conductor, Edinburgh Studio Orchestra, since 1986; Harpsichordist, Scottish Baroque Ensemble, 1970-77; broadcasts as pianist and harpsichordist; compositions broadcast on Radio 3, Radio 4 Scotland and Radio Eireann. Recreation: hill-walking. Address: (h.) 35 Comely Bank Place, Edinburgh EH4 1ER; T.-0131-332 4553.

Coats, Sir William David, Kt, DL, HonLLD (Strathclyde), 1977. Chairman, Coats Patons PLC, 1981-86; Deputy Chairman, Clydesdale Bank PLC, 1985-93; b. 25.7.24, Glasgow; m., The Hon. Elizabeth L.G. MacAndrew; 2 s.; 1 d. Educ. Eton College. Joined J. & P. Coats Ltd., 1948, as management trainee; held various appointments and became a Director, 1957; appointed Director, Coats Patons PLC, on its formation, 1960; Deputy Chairman, 1979. Recreations: golf; shooting. Address: (h.) The Cottage, Symington, Ayrshire, KA1 5QG.

Cobbe, Professor Stuart Malcolm, MA, MD, FRCP. Professor of Medical Cardiology, Glasgow University, since 1985; b. 2.5.48, Watford; m., Patricia Frances; 3 d. Educ. Royal Grammar School, Guildford; Cambridge University. Training in medicine, Cambridge and St. Thomas Hospital, London; qualified, 1972; specialist training in cardiology, National Heart Hospital, London, and John Radcliffe Hospital, Oxford; research work, University of Heidelberg, 1981; Consultant Cardiologist and Senior Lecturer, Oxford, 1982-85. Recreation: walking. Address: (b.) Department of Medical Cardiology, Queen Elizabeth Building, Royal Infirmary, Glasgow, G31 2ER; T.-0141-552 3535, Ext. 4722.

Cochran, Hugh Douglas, BA (Oxon), LLB. Advocate in Aberdeen, since 1958; b. 26.4.32, Aberdeen; m., Sarah Beverly Sissons; 4 s.; 2 d. Educ. Loretto; Trinity College, Oxford; Edinburgh University. Partner: Cochran & Macpherson, 1958-80, Adam, Cochran, 1980-93. Secretary, Aberdeen Association for the Prevention of Cruelty to Animals, since 1972; Registrar, Diocese of Aberdeen and Orkney, since 1984. Recreations: cycling; collecting stamps. Address: 6 Bon Accord Square, Aberdeen, AB9 1XU; T.-Aberdeen 588913.

Cochrane of Cults, 4th Baron (Ralph Henry Vere Cochrane), DL; b. 20.9.26; m.; 2 s. Address: Cults, Cupar, KY15 5RD.

Cockburn, Professor Forrester, MD, FRCPGlas, FRCPEdin, DCH. Samson Gemmell Professor of Child Health, Glasgow University, since 1977; b. 13.10.34, Edinburgh; m., Alison Fisher Grieve; 2 s. Educ. Leith Academy; Edinburgh University. Early medical training, Edinburgh Royal Infirmary, Royal Hospital for Sick Children, Edinburgh, and Simpson Memorial Maternity Pavilion, Edinburgh; Research Fellow in Paediatric Metabolic Disease, Boston University; Visiting Professor, San Juan University, Puerto Rico; Nuffield Fellow, Institute for Medical Research, Oxford University; Wellcome Senior Research Fellow, then Senior Lecturer, Department of Child Life and Health, Edinburgh University. Publications: a number of textbooks on paediatric medicine, neonatal medicine, nutrition and metabolic diseases. Recreation: sailing. Address: (b.) University Department of Child Health, Royal Hospital for Sick Children, Yorkhill, Glasgow, G3 8SJ; T.-0141-201 0236.

Cockburn, James Masson Thomson, BSc (Hons), CEng, FICE, FIWEM, FIWO, FIMgt. Director of Water Services, Grampian Regional Council, since 1988; b. 22.1.47, Aberdeen; m., Avril; 2 s. Educ. Robert Gordon's College; Dundee University. Assistant Engineer, East of Scotland Water Board, 1969-75; Assistant Divisional Manager (Dundee), Department of Water Services, Tayside Regional Council, 1975-76; Assistant Director, Department of Water and Sewerage, Dumfries and Galloway Regional Council, 1976-79; Depute Director, Department of Water Services, Grampian Regional Council, 1979-88. Past President, Scottish Section, Institution of Water Engineers and Scientists; Member of Council, Institution of Water and Environmental Management, 1987-91; President, Scottish Area Institution of Water Officers, 1994-95; Secretary, Scottish Association of Directors of Water and Sewerage, since 1989. Recreations: hill-walking; sailing; skiing; curling; Rotary. Address: (b.) Grampian Regional Council, Woodhill House, Westburn Road, Aberdeen, AB9 2LU; T.-01224 664900.

Cocker, Douglas, DA, ARSA. Sculptor, since 1968; Lecturer in Sculpture, Grays School of Art, Aberdeen, 1982-90; b. 23.3.45, Alyth, Perthshire; m., Elizabeth Filshie; 2 s.; 1 d. Educ. Blairgowrie High School; Duncan of Jordanstone College of Art, Dundee. SED Travelling Scholar, Italy and Greece, 1966; RSA Andrew Carnegie Travelling Scholar, 1967; RSA Benno Schotz Award, 1967; Greenshields Foundation (Montreal) Fellowship, 1968-69 (studies in New York and Greece); RSA Latimer Award, 1970; Arts Council of GB Award, 1977; East Midlands Arts Award, 1979; Scottish Arts Council Major Bursary, 1989; Essex Fine Art Fellowship, 1991-92; Visiting Artist: Newcastle Polytechnic, Duncan of Jordanstone College of Art, Edinburgh College of Art and Tyler University, Philadelphia. Fourteen one-man exhibitions, 1969-92; numerous group and mixed exhibitions, 1970-85; various commissions. Recreations: reading; travel; sport. Address: (h.) Mount Pleasant, Pleasance Road, Coupar Angus, Perthshire; T.-01828 627509.

Coffey, Daniel, JP. Provost, Kilmarnock and Loudoun District, since 1992 (SNP councillor, since 1988); Councillor, SNP Group Leader, and Leader of the Opposition, Strathclyde Region, since 1994; Convenor, Convention of Scottish Local Authorities SNP Group, since 1992; Member, European Union Committee of the Regions; Member, SNP National Executive Committee and National Council; Member, SNP National Assembly; Treasurer: Association of Nationalist Councillors, Kilmarnock FC Supporters Travel Club, Association of Kilmarnock FC Supporters; Hon. President, Burns Federation; b. 19.7.54, Kilmarnock. Educ. St. Joseph's, Kilmarnock. Recreations: football supporter; marathon runner. Address: (h.) 7 Craufurdland Road, Kilmarnock, KA3 2HT; T.-01563 531916.

Cogdell, Professor Richard John, BSc, PhD, FRSE. Hooker Professor of Botany, Glasgow University, since 1993; b. 4.2.49, Guildford; m., Barbara; 1 s.; 1 d. Educ. Royal Grammar School, Guildford; Bristol University. Post-doctoral research, USA, 1973-75; Botany Department, Glasgow University, 1975-94, now Institute of Biomedical and Life Sciences. Recreations: cricket; aerobics; Scottish dancing; theatre. Address: (b.) Division of Biochemistry and Molecular Biology, Glasgow University, Glasgow, G12 8QQ; T.-0141-330 4232.

Coggins, Professor John Richard, MA, PhD, FRSE. Professor of Biochemistry, Glasgow University, since 1986; Director, Postgraduate Studies, Institute of Biomedical and Life Sciences, Glasgow University, since 1995; b. 15.1.44, Bristol; m., Dr. Lesley F. Watson; 1 s.; 1 d. Educ. Bristol Grammar School; Queen's College, Oxford; Ottawa University. Post-doctoral Fellow: Biology Department, Brookhaven National Laboratory, New York, 1970-72, Biochemistry Department, Cambridge University, 1972-74; Lecturer, Biochemistry Department, Glasgow University, 1974-78, Senior Lecturer, 1978-86. Chairman, Molecular Enzymology Group, Biochemical Society, 1982-85; Chairman, Biophysics and Biochemistry Committee, SERC, 1985-88; Managing Director, Biomac Ltd., 1988-94; Member, DTI-Research Councils Biotechnology Joint Advisory Board, 1989-94; Member of Council, AFRC, 1991-94; Biochemistry Adviser to UFC, 1989-92; Member of Council, Hannah Research Institute, since 1994; Governing Member, Caledonian Research Foundation, since 1994; Chairman, HEFC Research Assessment Panel for Biochemistry, 1995-96. Recreations: sailing; travelling. Address: (b.) Division of Biochemistry and Molecular Biology, IBLS, Glasgow University, Glasgow, G12 8QQ; T.-0141-330 5267.

Cohen, Professor Anthony Paul, BA, MSc (SocSc), PhD, FRSE. Professor and Head, Department of Social Anthropology, Edinburgh University, since 1989; University Convener of Postgraduate Studies; b. 3.8.46, London; m., Dr. Bronwen J. Cohen; 3 s. Educ. Whittingehame Collge, Brighton; Southampton University. Assistant Professor, Queen's University, Kingston, Ontario, 1970-71; Lecturer/Senior Lecturer in Social Anthropology, Manchester University, 1971-89. Publications: The Management of Myths; The Symbolic Construction of Community; Whalsay: Symbol, Segment and Boundary in a Shetland Island Community; Self Consciousness: an alternative anthropology of identity; Belonging (Editor); Symbolising Boundaries (Editor); Humanising the City? (Co-Editor). Recreations: thinking; music; novels; political spectating. Address: (b.) Adam Ferguson Building, Edinburgh University, George Square, Edinburgh, EH8 9LL; T.-0131-650 3934, Ext. 6373.

Cohen, Cyril, OBE, JP, FRCPEdin, FRCPGlas. Honorary Fellow, Dundee University; Past President, Forfarshire Medical Association; retired Consultant Physician, Geriatric Medicine, and Hon. Senior Lecturer, Geriatric Medicine, Dundee University; Chairman, Angus Community Care Forum; b. 2.11.25, Manchester; m., Dr. Sarah E. Nixon; 2 s. Educ. Manchester Central High School; Victoria University, Manchester. Embarked on career in geriatric medicine, 1952. Former Chairman, Advisory Group on Health Education for Elderly People, Health Education Board for Scotland; former Member/Chairman, Angus District and Tayside Area Medical Committees; Secretary/Chairman, Tayside Area Hospital Medical Services Committee; Member, Scottish and UK Central Committee, Hospital Medical Services, and Chairman, Geriatric Medicine Sub-committee; Past Chairman, Scottish Branch, British Geriatric Society (former Council Member); Member, Panel on Nutrition of the Elderly, COMA; Honorary Vice-President, Dundee and District Branch, British Diabetic Association; Life Member, Manchester Medical Society; Past Member, Chief Scientist's

Committee for Research on Equipment for the Disabled and Health Services Research Committee; Vice-Chairman, Angus Access Panel; Honorary Vice-President, Dundee and District Branch, British Diabetic Society; Chairman, Radio North Angus (Hospital Radio); former Member, Brechin and Forfar School Councils, Forfar Academy School Board and Central Committee on Primary Education; Secretary, Aberlemno Community Council; Vice-Chairman, Angus Association of Voluntary Organisations and Member, Brechin Day Care Centre Committee; former Director, Scottish Hospital Advisory Service; Past President, Montrose Burns Club and Brechin Arts Guild; Member, Executive, Age Concern Scotland; Member, League of Friends, Forfar Hospitals; Past Chairman, Angus Care of the Elderly Group. Publications: many on geriatric medicine and care of the elderly. Recreations: photography; short walks; being at home. Address: (h.) Mansefield, Aberlemno, Forfar, DD8 3PD; T.-0130-783 259.

Cohen, George Cormack, MA, LLB. Advocate; b. 16.12.09, Glasgow; m., Elizabeth Wallace; 1 s.; 1 d. Educ. Kelvinside Academy, Glasgow; Glasgow University. Admitted to Faculty of Advocates, 1935; Sheriff of Caithness at Wick, 1944-51; Sheriff of Ayrshire at Kilmarnock, 1951-55; Sheriff of Lothians and Peebles at Edinburgh, 1955-66. Recreations: gardening; travel. Address: (h.) 37B Lauder Road, Edinburgh, EH9 1UE; T.-0131-668 1689.

Cohen, Patricia Townsend Wade, BSc, PhD. Head of Molecular Biology and Special Appointments Scientist, Medical Research Council Protein Phosphorylation Unit, Department of Biochemistry, Dundee University; b. 3.5.44, Worsley, Lancashire; m., Professor Philip Cohen (qv); 1 s.; 1 d. Educ. Bolton School; University College, London. Postdoctoral Research Fellow, Department of Medical Genetics, Washington University, Seattle, USA, 1969-71; Department of Biochemistry, Dundee University: Science Research Council Fellowship, 1971-72, Research/Teaching Fellow (part-time), 1972-83, Lecturer (part-time), 1983-90, Senior Lecturer, 1990-91. Publications: 100 papers and reviews in scientific journals. Recreations: reading; skiing; golf. Address: (h.) Inverbay II, Invergowrie, Dundee, DD2 5DQ; T.-01382 562328.

Cohen, Professor Philip, BSc, PhD, FRS, FRSE. Royal Society Research Professor, Dundee University, since 1984; Honorary Director, Medical Research Council Protein Phosphorylation Unit, since 1990; b. 22.7.45, London; m., Patricia Townsend Wade (qv); 1 s.; 1 d. Educ. Hendon County Grammar School; University College, London. Science Research Council/NATO postdoctoral Fellow, Department of Biochemistry, University of Washington, 1969-71; Dundee University: Lecturer in Biochemistry, 1971-78, Reader in Biochemistry, 1978-81, Professor of Enzymology, 1981-84. Publications: 300 papers and reviews, one book. Recreations: chess; golf; natural history. Address: (h.) Inverbay II, Invergowrie, Dundee; T.-01382 562328.

Coid, Donald Routledge, MSc, BMedSci, BM, BS, FRACMA, FAFPHM, MRCP, MFPHM. Chief Administrative Medical Officer and Director of Public Health, Tayside Health Board, since 1994; b. 13.6.53, Wallingford; m., Susan Kathleen Ramus Crocker; 3 d. Educ. Bromley Grammar School for Boys; Harrow County School for Boys; Nottingham University; London University. Field Medical Officer, Royal Flying Doctor Service of Australia, 1979-80; Medical Officer, Community Health Services, Western Australia, 1981-82; Regional Director of Public Health, Eastern Goldfields, Western Australia, 1982-85; Medical Superintendent, Kalgoorie Regional Hospital, 1984-85; Fife Health Board: Consultant in Public Health, 1985-92; Assistant General Manager, 1992-93. Recreations: golf; singing; cricket; piano.

Address: (h.) 90 Hepburn Gardens, St. Andrews, KY16 9LN; T.-01334 472710.

Coke, Professor Simon, MA (Oxon). Professor of International Business, Edinburgh University, since 1972; b. 27.6.32, Bicester, Oxfordshire; m., Diana Margaret Evison; 1 s.; 2 d. Educ. Ridley College, Ontario; Pembroke College, Oxford. Marketing Executive, Beecham Overseas, 1958-64; General Manager, Japan, etc., Johnson & Johnson, 1964-68; Head, Department of Business Studies, Edinburgh University, 1984; Dean, Scottish Business School, 1981-83; Director, Edinburgh University Management School; Director: Nippon Asset Trust, Ivory and Sime Optimum Income Trust PLC, Jiig-Cal Ltd., Lastolite Ltd. Address: (b.) Edinburgh University Management School, 7 Bristo Square, Edinburgh EH8 9AL.

Cole-Hamilton, Arthur Richard, CBE, BA, CA, FIB(Scot). Chairman, Stakis plc; Chairman, General Committee, Royal and Ancient Golf Club of St. Andrews; b. 8.5.35, Kilwinning; m., Prudence Ann; 1 s.; 2 d. Educ. Ardrossan Academy; Loretto School; Cambridge University. Partner, Brechin Cole-Hamilton & Co., CA, 1962-67; various appointments, Clydesdale Bank, 1967-82; appointed Chief Executive, 1982, Director, 1984; retired 1992. Former Council Member, Institute of Chartered Accountants of Scotland (Chairman, Finance and General Purposes Committee, 1981-85); Chairman, Committee of Scottish Clearing Bankers, 1991-92; President, Institute of Bankers in Scotland, 1988-90; former Chairman, Scottish Council (Development and Industry); Director, Glasgow Chamber of Commerce, 1985-91; Trustee, National Galleries of Scotland, since 1986. Recreation: golf. Address: (h.) 26 Lady Margaret Drive, Troon, KA10 7AL; T.-01292 311338.

Cole-Hamilton, Professor David John, BSc, PhD, FRSC, FRSE. Irvine Professor of Chemistry, St. Andrews University, since 1985; b. 22.5.48, Bovey Tracey; m., Elizabeth Ann Brown; 2 s.; 2 d. Educ. Haileybury and ISC Hertford; Edinburgh University. Research Assistant Temporary Lecturer, Imperial College, 1974-78; Lecturer Senior Lecturer, Liverpool University, 1978-85. Sir Edward Frankland Fellow, Royal Society of Chemistry, 1984-85; Corday Morgan Medallist, 1983; President, Chemistry section, British Association for the Advancement of Science, 1995. Address: (b.) Department of Chemistry, The Purdie Building, St. Andrews, Fife, KY16 9ST; T.-01334 76161.

Collie, George Francis, CBE (Civil), MBE (Military), JP, BL. Honorary Sheriff, Grampian Region, at Aberdeen since 1974; retired Advocate in Aberdeen and Notary Public; b. 1.4.09, Aberdeen; m., Margery Constance Fullarton Wishart; 2 s. Educ. Aberdeen Grammar School; Aberdeen University. Partner, then Senior Partner, James & George Collie, Solicitors and Advocates in Aberdeen. Deputy Chairman, then Chairman, Board of Management for Aberdeen Special Hospitals, 1952-68. Honorary Colonel, 51st Highland Division, RASC (TA) and later Honorary Colonel, 153 Highland Regiment, RCT (V) 1964-72. Address: (h.) Morkeu, Cults, Aberdeen, AB1 9PT; T.-01224 867636.

Collier, H. Bruce, DCA, MITSA. Director of Consumer and Trading Standards, Strathclyde Regional Council, since 1991; b. 24.5.46, Dumbarton; m., Margaret; 3 d. Educ. Clydebank High School. Assistant Director, Department of Consumer and Trading Standards, Strathclyde Regional Council, 1985. Chairman, Association of Petroleum and Explosives Acts Administration, 1973; Chairman, Institute of Trading Standards Scotland, 1986; Vice President, European Inter-Regional Institute of Consumer Affairs, since 1991; Secretary, Cunninghame CAB; Member, Scottish Consumer Council; Council Member, Institute of Trading Standards Administration. Recreations: reading;

walking. Address: (b.) Strathclyde House, 20 India Street, Glasgow, G2 4PF; T.-0141-227 3105.

Colligan, Professor Ian Cunningham, BSc, MBCS, MIMgt, CEng. Head, Department of Mathematical and Computer Sciences, University of Abertay, Dundee, since 1985; b. 20.11.39, Dundee; 1 s.; 1 d. Educ. Harris Academy, Dundee; St. Andrews University; Durham University. Mathematician/Programmer, C.A. Parsons & Co. Ltd., Newcastle, 1961-62; Computer Specialist, International Research & Development Ltd., Newcastle, 1962-63; Programmer/Chief Programmer/Deputy Manager, NCR Scottish Computing Centre, 1963-67; Head, Management Sciences Department, NCR (Manufacturing) Ltd., Dundee, 1968-70; Manager Director, Infobanx Ltd., Consultants, 1971-80; Lecturer/Senior Lecturer, Dundee Institute of Technology, 1980-85. Recreations: hill-walking; travel. Address: (b.) Department of Mathematical and Computer Sciences, University of Abertay, Dundee, Bell Street, Dundee, DD1 1HG; T.-01382 308600.

Collin, William Robert, BSc. Headteacher, Dunbar Grammar School, since 1983; b. 3.7.43, Edinburgh; m., Valerie; 2 s.; 1 d. Educ. Eyemouth High School; Berwickshire High School; Edinburgh University; Moray House College of Education. Teacher, then Principal Teacher: Eyemouth High School, Arbroath High School; Assistant Head Teacher, Dunbar Grammar School; Depute Head Teacher, Selkirk High School. Elder, Church of Scotland. Recreations: history of east coast fishing industry; gardening; walking. Address: (h.) Rosebery Place, Dunbar, EH42 1AQ; T.-01368 863162.

Collins, Dennis Ferguson, MA, LLB, WS. Senior Partner, Carlton Gilruth, Solicitors, Dundee (retired); Honorary Sheriff; b. 26.3.30, Dundee; m., Elspeth Margaret Nicoll; 1 s.; 1 d. Educ. High School of Dundee; St. Andrews University. Part-time Lecturer in Scots Law, St. Andrews University, then Dundee University, 1960-79; Agent Consulaire for France in Dundee, since 1976; Hon. Secretary, Dundee Society for Prevention of Cruelty to Children, 1962-90; Treasurer, Dundee Congregational Church, since 1966; Past President, Dundee and District Philatelic Society; Past President, Association of Scottish Philatelic Societies; Dean, Faculty of Procurators and Solicitors in Dundee, 1987-89. Recreations: Chinese postal history; gardening; Sherlock Holmes pursuits; travelling in France. Address: (h.) Stirling House, Craigiebarn Road, Dundee, DD4 7PL; T.-01382 458070.

Collins, Kenneth Darlingston, BSc (Hons), MSc. Member (Labour), European Parliament, since 1979; b. 12.8.39, Hamilton; m., Georgina Frances Pollard; 1 s.; 1 d. Educ. St. John's Grammar School; Hamilton Academy; Glasgow University; Strathclyde University. Steelworks apprentice, 1956-59; University, 1960-65; Planning Officer, 1965-66; WEA Tutor, 1966-67; Lecturer: Glasgow College of Building, 1967-69, Paisley College of Technology, 1969-79; Member: East Kilbride Town and District Council, 1973-79, Lanark County Council, 1973-75, East Kilbride Development Corporation, 1976-79; Chairman, NE Glasgow Children's Panel, 1974-76; European Parliament: Deputy Leader, Labour Group, 1979-84, Chairman, Environment Committee, 1979-84 and since 1989 (Vice-Chairman, 1984-87), Socialist Spokesman on Environment, Public Health and Consumer Protection, 1984-89; Fellow, Royal Scottish Geographical Society; Hon. Fellow, Chartered Institute of Water and Environment Management; Hon. Senior Research Fellow, Department of Geography, Lancaster University; Member, Advisory Committee, European Public Policy Institute, Warwick University; Director, Institute for European Environmental Policy, London; Fellow, Industry and Parliament Trust. Recreations: music; boxer dogs; cycling. Address: (b.) 11 Stuarton Park, East Kilbride, G74 4LA; T.-013552 37282.

Collins, Kenneth E., MPhil, PhD, MRCGP. Vice President, Glasgow Jewish Representative Council; b. 23.12.47, Glasgow; m., Irene Taylor; 1 s.; 3 d. Educ. High School of Glasgow; Glasgow University. General medical practitioner in Glasgow, since 1976; Medical Officer, Newark Lodge, Glasgow, since 1978; Research Associate, Wellcome Unit for the History of Medicine, Glasgow University. Past Chairman, Glasgow Board of Jewish Education. Publications: Aspects of Scottish Jewry, 1987; Go and Learn: International Story of the Jews and Medicine in Scotland, 1988; Second City Jewry, 1990. Address: (h.) 3 Glenburn Road, Giffnock, Glasgow, G46 6RE.

Colquhoun of Luss, Captain Sir Ivar (Iain), 8th Bt, JP, DL. Honorary Sheriff; Chief of the Clan; b. 4.1.16.

Coltart, George John Letham, TD, MA, MSc, CEng, MICE. Priory Secretary, Order of St. John of Jerusalem, since 1991; b. 2.2.29, Edinburgh; m., Inger Christina Larsson; 1 s.; 1 d. Educ. George Watson's College, Edinburgh; Royal Military Aademy, Sandhurst; King's College, Cambridge; Cornell University, USA. Commissioned, Royal Engineers, 1949; Captain, Adjutant, 23 Engineer Regiment, 1957-58; Staff College, Camberley, 1962; DAA & QMG 5 Bde, 1963-65; OC 51 Field Squadron, 1965-66; trasferred to Reserve, 1966; Senior Lecturer in Civil Engineering, Heriot-Watt University, 1966-91 (Deputy Head of Department, 1987-90). Convener, Edinburgh and Heriot-Watt Universities Joint Military Education Committee, 1988-91; Commanding Officer, Edinburgh and Heriot-Watt UOTC, 1971-74; TA Colonel, Lowlands, 1975-80; Chairman, Lowland TAVRA, 1987-90. Recreations: reserve forces; forestry; DIY. Address: Napier House, 8 Colinton Road, Edinburgh EH10 5DS; T.-0131-447 6314; Polskeoch, Thornhill, DG3 4NN.

Coltrane, Robbie, DA. Actor/Director; b. 31.3.50, Glasgow. Educ. Trinity College, Glenalmond; Glasgow School of Art. Film credits: Subway Riders, 1979, Balham Gateway to the South, 1980, Britannia Hospital, 1981, Scrubbers, 1982, Krull, 1982, Ghost Dance, 1983, Chinese Boxes, 1984, The Supergrass, 1984, Defense of the Realm, 1985, Revolution, 1985, Caravaggio, 1985, Absolute Beginners, 1985, Mona Lisa, 1985, Eat the Rich, 1987, The Fruit Machine, 1987, Slipstream, 1988, Bert Rigby, You're a Fool, 1988, Danny Champion of the World, 1988, Let It Ride, 1988, Henry V, 1988, Nuns on the Run, 1989, Perfectly Normal, 1989, Pope Must Die, 1990, Oh What A Night, 1991, Adventures of Huck Finn, 1992, Goldeneye, 1995; theatre credits: The Bug, 1976, Mr Joyce is Leaving, 1978, The Slab Boys, 1978, The Transfiguration of Benno Blimpie, 1978, The Loveliest Night of the Year, 1979-80, Dick Whittington, 1979, Snobs and Yobs, 1980, Yr Obedient Servant (one-man show), 1987, Mistero Buffo (one-man show), 1990; television credits include: roles in several The Comic Strip Presents productions, lead role in Tutti Frutti (BBC Scotland), Alive and Kicking, 1991, Coltrane in a Cadillac, 1992, Cracker, 1993. Recreations: vintage cars; sailing; painting; reading; movies. Address: c/o CDA, 47 Courtfield Road, London, SW7; T.-0171-370 0708.

Comley, David John, BSc, PhD, FIH. Director of Housing, Glasgow City Council, since 1988; b. 25.4.50, Carshalton. Educ. Ashlyns School, Berkhamsted; Birmingham University. Housing Management Trainee, then District Housing Manager, Dudley Metropolitan Borough, 1976-80; District Housing Manager, then Assistant Director, then Depute Director, Glasgow City Council,since 1980. Adviser to COSLA, since 1988; Member, Hamish Allan Trust; Council Member, Institute of Housing; Member, Joseph Rowntree Foundation Committee on Housing Standards; Board Member, Department of Environment Good Practice Unit in Housing Management. Recreations: jazz; classical music; saxophone; hill-walking; literature; cinema; theatre.

Address: (b.) Wheatley House, 25 Cochrane Street, Glasgow, G1 1HZ.

Conboy, William Morgan, MA (Oxon), FRSA. Principal, Newbattle Abbey College, since 1993; b. 8.5.31, Edinburgh; m., Irene; 1 s.; 1 d. Educ. Royal High School; Ruskin College and Jesus College, Oxford. Assistant Research Officer, Institute of Economics and Statistics, Oxford University, 1966-69; Staff Tutor, Economics and Industrial Relations, Oxford University, 1969-79; Vice Principal, Ruskin College, Oxford, 1979-94; Acting Principal, Newbattle Abbey College, 1990-93. External Adviser, Singapore Institute of Labour Studies, since 1990; National President, WEA, since 1991. Recreations: choral singing; golf. Address: (h.) Principal's Flat, Newbattle Abbey College, Dalkeith, EH22 3LL.

Conn, Derrick. Chief Manager, Girobank Scotland. Address: (b.) 93 George Street, Edinburgh, EH2 3JL.

Conn, Stewart. Poet and playwright; b. 1936, Glasgow, brought up Kilmarnock. Educ. Glasgow University. Author of numerous stage plays, including The Burning, Herman, The Aquarium; television work includes The Kite, Bloodhunt; recent poetry includes In the Kibble Palace, The Luncheon of the Boating Party and In the Blood; his production of Carver (by John Purser) won Gold Medal Award, International Radio Festival, 1991; left BBC, 1992.

Connarty, Michael, BA, DCE. MP (Labour), Falkirk East, since 1992; Chair, Economy, Industry and Energy Committee, Scottish PLP Group; Secretary, PLP Science and Technology Committee; b. 3.9.47, Coatbridge; m., Margaret Mary; 1 s.; 1 d. Educ. Stirling University; Jordanhill College of Education; Glasgow University. Member, Scottish Executive, Labour Party, 1981-92; Chair, Labour Party Scottish Local Government Committee, 1988-90; Member, Convention of Scottish Local Authorities, 1980-90 (Depute Labour Leader, 1988-90); Member, Stirling District Council, 1977-90 (Council Leader, 1980-90); Vice-Chair, Socialist Educational Association, 1983-85; Council Member, Educational Institute of Scotland, 1984-85; Founding Secretary, Labour Coordinating Committee (Scotland); Vice-Chairman, Scottish MAP, since 1988. Recreations: family; hill-walking; reading; music; Falkirk FC; Bo'ness United FC. Address: (b.) 47 Bo'ness Road, Grangemouth FK3 8AP; T.-01324 474832.

Connell, Anthony Anderson, LLB (Hons). Chief Executive, The Moray Council, since 1995; b. 27.7.53, Aberdeen; m., Sandra; 2 s.; 2 d. Educ. Robert Gordons College, Aberdeen; Aberdeen University. Grampian Regional Council: Principal Solicitor (Litigation), Assistant Director (Law and Administration), Depute Director (Law and Administration), Depute Chief Executive and Director of Administration. Group Leader (Public Administration), Aberdeen University. Recreations: reading; music; collecting; photography; politics as an observer. Address: (b.) Council Headquarters, High Street, Elgin, IV30 1BX; T.-01343 543451.

Connell, Douglas Andrew, LLB, NP, WS, FRSA. Member, Scottish Arts Council, since 1994; Chairman, Lottery Committee, Scottish Arts Council, since 1994; Chairman, Edinburgh Book Festival, 1991-95; b. 18.5.54, Callander; m., Marjorie Elizabeth; 2 s. Educ. McLaren High School; Edinburgh University. Qualified as a solicitor, 1976; admitted as a Writer to the Signet, 1976; Partner, Dundas and Wilson, 1979; President, Scottish Young Lawyers Association, 1975-76; Tutor in Scots Law, Edinburgh University, 1974-76; Member, Revenue Committee, Law Society of Scotland, 1979-92; Member, Partnership Board, Dundas and Wilson, since 1991; Trustee, Pushkin Prizes in Scotland; Member, Development Resource, Scottish Museums Council; Patron, National Galleries of Scotland; Fellow, Royal Society of Arts.

Recreations: books; travel; good food. Address: (b.) Saltire Court, 20 Castle Terrace, Edinburgh, EH1 2EN; T.-0131-228 8000.

Connell, Professor John Muir Cochrane, MD, FRCP. Senior Clinical Scientist, MRC Blood Pressure Unit, since 1987; Hon. Consultant Physician, Western Infirmary, Glasgow, since 1987; Hon. Professor, Glasgow University, since 1993; b. 10.10.54, Irvine; m., Lesley Elizabeth Armstrong; 3 s.; 1 d. Educ. Hutchesons' Grammar School; Glasgow University. Clinical Scientist, MRC Blood Pressure Unit, 1983; Visiting Research Fellow, Howard Florey Institute, Melbourne, 1986-87. Treasurer, Scottish Society for Experimental Medicine. Recreation: golf. Address: (b.) Western Infirmary, Glasgow.

Connelly, David, MA (Oxon), FSAScot. Secretary, Buildings of Scotland Trust, since 1990; Chairman, Cockburn Conservation Trust, Edinburgh, since 1990; b. 23.2.30, Halifax; m., Audrey Grace Salter; 1 s.; 1 d. Educ. Heath Grammar School, Halifax; Queen's College, Oxford. Colonial Administrative Service, Tanganyika, 1954-62; Assistant Secretary, St. Andrews University, 1962-63; Principal, Commonwealth Relations Office, 1963-64; First Secretary, British High Commission, New Delhi, 1964-66; Principal, Scottish Office, 1966-73; Assistant Secretary, 1973-87; Director, Historic Buildings and Monuments, Scotland, 1987-90. Recreations: opera; literature; history; architecture; walking the hills; country life. Address: c/o Royal Bank of Scotland plc, 36 St. Andrew Square, Edinburgh, EH2 2YB.

Connon, Iain Urquhart, MRTPI. Director of Environment Division, Dunfermline District Council, since 1991; b. 14.8.39, Perth; m., Eileen Margaret; 2 d. Educ. Perth Academy; Dundee College of Art. Rowand, Anderson, Kinninmouth & Paul, Architects, Edinburgh, 1962-67; Robert Matthew, Johnson Marshall & Partners, Architects, Edinburgh, 1967-70; Planning Department, Burgh of Dunfermline, 1970-75; Dunfermline District Council, since 1975. Recreations: landscape gardening; childcare. Address:(b.) 3 New Row, Dunfermline, KY12 7NN; T.-01383 736321.

Connon, Joyce Blair. Scottish Secretary, Workers Educational Association, since 1992; b. 11.6.47, Edinburgh; m., Neil Connon; 1 s.; 1 d. W.E.A. Tutor Organiser, Lothian, 1988; District Secretary, South-East Scotland, 1989. Recreations: reading; theatre; walking. Address: (b.) W.E.A., Riddle's Court, 322 Lawnmarket, Edinburgh, EH1 2PG; T.-0131-226 3456.

Connor, Professor James Michael, MD, BSc (Hons), MB, ChB (Hons), FRCP. Professor of Medical Genetics and Director, West of Scotland Regional Genetics Service, since 1987 (Wellcome Trust Senior Lecturer and Honorary Consultant in Medical Genetics, Glasgow University, 1984-87); b. 18.6.51, Grappenhall, England; m., Dr. Rachel A.C. Educ. Lymm Grammar School, Cheshire; Liverpool University. House Officer, Liverpool Royal Infirmary; Resident in Internal Medicine, Johns Hopkins Hospital, USA; University Research Fellow, Liverpool University; Instructor in Internal Medicine, Johns Hopkins Hospital, USA; Consultant in Medical Genetics, Duncan Guthrie Institute of Medical Genetics, Yorkhill, Glasgow. Publications: Essential Medical Genetics (Co-author), 1984 (4th edition, 1993); various articles on aspects of medical genetics. Recreation: windsurfing. Address: (h.) East Collarie Farm, by Fenwick, Ayrshire; T.-Fenwick 600790.

Conroy, Stephen, Painter; b. 1964, Helensburgh. Educ. Glasgow School of Art. Group exhibitions, Royal Glasgow Institute of Fine Arts, Scottish National Gallery of Modern Art, Cincinnati and tour; one-man exhibitions, London.

Considine, John, MA, MEd. Rector, Inverness Royal Academy, since 1993; b. 26.11.50, Glasgow; m., Hellen L. Campbell; 1 s.; 2 d. Educ. St. Aloysius College; Glasgow University. Teacher: St. Margaret Mary's, Glasgow, 1973, Inverness High, 1974, Millburn Academy, Inverness, 1976; Principal Teacher, then Assistant Rector, Charleston Academy, Inverness, 1978-88; Depute Rector, Woodmill High, Dunfermline, 1988-93. Member, Inverness College Board of Management, and Chair, College Personnel Sub-Committee. Recreations: hill-walking; running; squash. Address: (b.) Inverness Royal Academy, Culduthel Road, Inverness; T.-01463 222884.

Constable, Alan W., BSc (Hons), CertEd. Rector, Morgan Academy, Dundee, since 1987; b. 30.8.46, Blairgowrie; m., Irene M.; 2 s. Educ. Blairgowrie High School; Heriot Watt University, Edinburgh; Moray House College, Edinburgh. Design engineer, 1970-71; Teacher/Principal Teacher/Assistant Headteacher, 1972-83; HMI Technology, Scottish Education Department, 1983-84; Depute Rector, Montrose Academy, 1984-86. Recreations: golf; hockey. Address: (b.) Morgan Academy, Forfar Road, Dundee, DD4 7AY; T.-01382 453805.

Constable, Provost John Grant. Provost, Falkirk District Council, since 1992; b. 21.7.46, Falkirk. Educ. Bo'ness Academy; Falkirk Technical College. Member, Falkirk District Council, since 1974; S.N.P. Group Leader, 1980-92. Address: (b.) Municipal Buildings, Falkirk; T.-Falkirk 24911.

Conti, Rt. Rev. Mario Joseph, STL, PhL, DD. Bishop of Aberdeen, since 1977; Member, Pontifical Council for the Promotion of Christian Unity, Rome, since 1984; Member, International Commission for English in the Liturgy, 1978-87; b. 20.3.34, Elgin. Educ. St. Marie's Convent; Springfield School, Elgin; Blairs College, Aberdeen; Scots College, Pontifical Gregorian University, Rome. Ordained priest, Rome, 1958; Curate, St. Mary's Cathedral, Aberdeen, 1959-62; Parish Priest, St. Joachim's, Wick and St. Anne's, Thurso, 1962. Commendatore, Order of Merit, Italian Republic; President-Treasurer, SCIAF, 1977-85; President, National Liturgy Commission, 1978-86; Chairman, Scottish Catholic Heritage Commission; President, Commission for Christian Doctrine and Unity, since 1986; first Convener, Central Council, ACTS, 1990; Member, Pontifical Commission for the Cultural Heritage of the Church, since 1994; Knight Commander of the Holy Sepulchre, 1989; Conventual Chaplain Ad Honorem, Knights of Malta, 1991, Principal Chaplain to British Association of the Order, since 1995. Recreations: music; art. Address: Bishop's House, 156 King's Gate, Aberdeen; T.-01224 319154.

Convery, Sheriff Daniel. Sheriff of Glasgow and Strathkelvin. Address: (b.) Sheriff Court House, 1 Carlton Place, Glasgow, G5 9DA.

Conway, Rt. Rev. Mgr. Michael Joseph, BA, MSc (Econ). Catholic Chaplain, Glasgow University, since 1977; Prelate of Honour, since 1988; b. 5.3.40, Newry. Educ. St. Colman's College, Newry; St. Kieran's College, Kilkenny; University College, Dublin; London School of Economics. St. James's, Coatbridge, 1963-65; St. David's, Plains, Airdrie, 1965-66; St. Theresa's, Newarthill, 1966-69; St. Monica's, Coatbridge, 1975-77. Recreations: golf; hill-walking; reading; listening to music. Address: (b.) Scotus College, 2 Chesters Road, Bearsden, Glasgow, G61 4AG; T.-0141-942 8384.

Cook, Alexander Bethune, BSc (Hons). Chief Planning Officer, Dunfermline District Council, since 1991; b. 3.10.46, Kirkcaldy; m., Jennifer; 2 s. Educ. Kirkcaldy High School; Heriot Watt University. Planning Assistant, Cumbernauld Development Corporation; Senior Planning Assistant, Dumfries and Galloway Regional Council; joined Dunfermline D.C. as Principal Planning Officer. Recreations: guitar music; hill-walking; golf. Address: (b.) 3 New Row, Dunfermline, KY12 7NN; T.-01383 736321.

Cook, Fraser Murray, OBE, BSc, MIMechE, CEng, FInstPet. Chairman, Highlands and Islands Development Consultative Council, 1986-88; Vice Chairman, Forth Ports Authority, 1985-88; Member, Court, Stirling University, 1986-94; b. 29.12.17, Conon Bridge, Ross-shire; m., Eve Smith Reid (deceased). Educ. Inverness Royal Academy; Morgan Academy, Dundee; St. Andrews University. Engineering graduate apprentice, Pumpherston Oil Co. Ltd., 1939-41; REME, South East Asia Command, 1941-46; Assistant to Manager, Pumpherston Oil Co. Ltd., 1946-48; Production Engineer, latterly Oil Construction Engineer, Southern Africa, 1948-53; Engineer, BP Oil Grangemouth Refinery Ltd., 1953-56; Manager, Pumpherston Oil Co. Ltd., 1956-62; Works Manager: BP Oil Grangemouth Refinery Ltd., 1962-66, BP Oil Llandarcy Refinery Ltd., 1966-69; General Manager, then Managing Director and General Manager, BP Oil Grangemouth Refinery Ltd., 1969-77. Chairman, Cumbernauld Development Corporation, 1983-86; Chairman, East Strathearn Community Council, since 1989. Recreations: some golf; photography. Address: Littleton Cottage, Cultoquhey, by Crieff, Perthshire, PH7 3NF; T.-Crieff 653537.

Cook, Rev. James Stanley Stephen Ronald Tweedie, BD, DipPSS. Minister, Hamilton West Parish Church, since 1974; b. 18.8.35, Tullibody; m., Jean Douglas McLachlan; 2 s.; 1 d. Educ. Whitehill Secondary School, Glasgow; St. Andrews University. Apprentice quantity surveyor, Glasgow, 1953-54; regular soldier, REME, 1954-57; Assistant Preventive Officer, Waterguard Department, HM Customs and Excise, 1957-61; Officer, HM Customs and Excise, 1961-69; studied for the ministry, 1969-74. Chairman, Cruse (Lanarkshire), 1983-93, since 1994; Chairman, Cruse — Scotland, since 1992; Member, Council, Cruse UK, 1988-94; Member, National Training Group, Cruse, 1987-94; Chairman, Hamilton Crime Prevention Panel, 1986-87; Member, Action Research for Crippled Child Committee, 1977-94; Substitute Provincial Grand Master, Lanarkshire (Middle Ward), 1983-88; Honorary Provincial Grand Chaplain, since 1989; founder Member, Wishaw Victim Support Scheme, 1985; President, Hamilton Rotary Club, 1994-95; Member, Hamilton Crime Prevention Panel, since 1976, Chairman, 1986-87. Recreations: music; photography; DIY; computer work. Address: West Manse, 43 Bothwell Road, Hamilton, ML3 0BB; T.-Hamilton 458770.

Cook, Michael Blyth, BSc, AHWU. Rector, Queen Anne High School, Dunfermline, since 1988; b. 8.6.39, Dunfermline; m., Sheena Rodger; 4 d. Educ. Beath High School, Cowdenbeath; Edinburgh University; Heriot Watt University. Teacher, Special Assistant, Beath High School, 1963-68; Principal Teacher of Maths, St. Columba's, Dunfermline, 1968-71, and Buckhaven High School, 1971-74; Assistant Rector, then Depute Rector, Woodmill High School, 1974-87. Recreations: golf; bridge; hill-walking. Address: (b.) Queen Anne High School, Broomhead, Dunfermline; T.-Dunfermline 728188.

Cook, Robin. MP (Labour), Livingston, since 1983 (Edinburgh Central, 1974-83); Shadow Foreign Secretary; b. 28.2.46. Formerly: Opposition Spokesman on Trade and Industry; Opposition Spokesman on Health and Social Security. Address: (b.) House of Commons, London, SW1A 0AA.

Cooke, Professor David John, BSc, MSc, PhD, CPsych, FBPsS. Professor of Forensic Psychology, Glasgow Caledonian University, since 1992; Head of Forensic Clinical Psychology, Greater Glasgow Health Board, since 1984; Honorary Lecturer, since 1984, and Honorary Senior Research Fellow, Glasgow University, since 1989; b.

13.7.52, Glasgow; m., Janet Ruth Salter; 2 d. Educ. Larbert High School; St. Andrews University; Newcastle-upon-Tyne University; Glasgow University. Clinical Psychologist, Gartnavel Royal Hospital, 1976-83; Cropwood Fellow, Institute of Criminology, Cambridge University, 1986. Recreations: sailing; opera; cooking. Address: (b.) Douglas Inch Centre, 2 Woodside Terrace, Glasgow, G3 7UY; T.-0141-332 3844.

Cooke, Joseph Henry, BSc (Hons), MA, DipEd. Head Teacher, Kyle Academy, Ayr, since 1985; b. 30.12.32, Kingston, St. Vincent, West Indies; m., Mary A. Marshall; 3 s. Educ. Methodist College, Belfast; Queen's University, Belfast. Teacher, Down High School, Downpatrick, 1956-67; Head, Geography Department: Strathearn School, Belfast, 1967-74, Ravenspark Academy, Irvine, 1975-79; Assistant Head Teacher, then Depute Head Teacher, Garnock Academy, Kilbirnie, 1979-85. Session Clerk, Alloway Parish Church. Recreations: travel; bowls; photography; gardening; DIY. Address: (h.) 3 Corsehill Park, Ayr, KA7 2UG; T.-01292 284745.

Cooke, Nicholas Huxley, MA (Oxon), FRSA. Director, The Scottish Conservation Projects Trust, since 1984; b. 6.5.44, Godalming, Surrey; m., Anne Landon; 2 s.; 3 d. Educ. Charterhouse School; Worcester College, Oxford. Retail management, London, 1967; chartered accountancy training, London, 1968-71; British International Paper, London, 1972-78; Director (Scotland), British Trust for Conservation Volunteers, 1978-84. Member: Policy Committee, Scottish Council for Voluntary Organisations; Executive Group, UK 2000 Scotland; Chairman, Scottish Advisory Panel, Shell Better Britain Campaign; Member, Scottish Committee, European Year of the Environment, 1987-88. Recreations: fishing; walking; photography; outdoor conservation work. Address: (b.) Balallan House, 24 Allan Park, Stirling, FK8 2QG; T.-01786 79697.

Cooke, Professor Timothy, MD, FRCS, MB, ChB. St. Mungo Professor of Surgery, Glasgow University, since 1989; Honorary Consultant Surgeon, Royal Infirmary, Glasgow; b. 16.9.47, Liverpool; m., Lynn; 1 s.; 1 d. Educ. Birkenhead Institute; Liverpool University. Surgical training, Liverpool University, 1973-79; Lecturer in Surgery, Southampton University, 1980-83; Senior Lecturer and Honorary Consultant Surgeon, Charing Cross & Westminster Medical School, 1983-86; Senior Lecturer and Honorary Consultant Surgeon, Liverpool University and Royal Liverpool and Broadgreen Hospitals, 1986-89. Hunterian Professor, Royal College of Surgeons of England. Publications: numerous scientific articles about cancer research. Recreations: playing wide range of indoor and outdoor sports; lifetime supporter, Liverpool FC. Address: (b.) University Department of Surgery, Royal Infirmary, Glasgow, G31 2ER; T.-0141-552 3535, Ext. 5429.

Coombs, Professor Graham H., BSc, PhD, FRSE. Professor of Zoology, Glasgow University, since 1990; b. 22.9.47, Coventry; m., Isabel; 1 d. Educ. King Henry VIII School, Coventry; University College, London. Research Fellow, University of Kent, 1972-74; Lecturer, Department of Zoology, Glasgow University, 1974-86, Senior Lecturer, 1986-88, Reader, 1988-90, Head, Department of Zoology, 1991-94. Recreation: golf. Address: (b.) Parasitology, Joseph Black Building, Glasgow University, Glasgow, G12 8QQ; T.-0141-339 8855, Ext. 4777.

Cooper, Patricia, BA, DMS, CertEd. Lecturer in Consumer Studies, The Robert Gordon University, Aberdeen, since 1983; Council Member, Scottish Consumer Council, 1987-93; Member, Food Policy Committee, National Consumer Council, 1988-93; Member, MAFF Working Party on Food Additives; Member, Regional Advisory Board, Scottish Agricultural College (Aberdeen), 1991-94; b. 24.11.42, South Elmsall; m., John M. Cooper; 2

s. Teacher/Lecturer in Home Economics, since 1963. Member, British Telecom Consumer Liaison Panel, 1986; Secretary, Aberdeen Consumer Group, 1985. Recreations: entertaining; reading diverting novels. Address: (b.) The Robert Gordon University, Kepplestone Premises, Queens Road, Aberdeen, AB9 2PG.

Cooper, Sheena M.M., MA. Rector, Aboyne Academy and Deeside Community Centre; b. 7.3.39, Bellshill. Educ. Dalziel High School, Motherwell; Glasgow University. Teacher of History, Dalziel High School, Motherwell, 1962-68; Lecturer in History, Elizabeth Gaskell College of Education, Manchester, 1968-70; Woman Adviser, then Assistant Rector, Montrose Academy, 1970-76; Rector, John Neilson High School, Paisley, 1976-83. Member: Council for Tertiary Education in Scotland, 1979-83, Scottish Examination Board, 1984-92, Scottish Vocational Education Council, 1985-88, Religious Advisory Council, BBC, 1980-91, Broadcasting Council for Scotland, since 1991; President, Education Section, British Association for Advancement of Science, 1978-79. Recreations: walking; skiing. Address: (b.) Aboyne Academy and Deeside Community Centre, Aboyne; T.-01339 86222, Ext. 24.

Copeland, Professor Laurence Sidney, BA (Hons), MA (Econ), PhD. Ivory Professor of Finance, Stirling University, since 1991; b. 8.9.46, Manchester; m., Rebecca; 2 s. Educ. Manchester Grammar School; Brasenose College, Oxford. Lecturer, Manchester University, 1976-91. Visiting Professor, New York University, 1982, 1983; Visiting Research Fellow, Lancaster University, 1990. Publication: Exchange Rates and International Finance, 1989, 1994. Recreation: running. Address: Department of Accounting and Finance, Stirling University, Stirling, FK9 4LA; T.-01786 467283.

Coppock, Professor John Terence, CBE, MA, PhD, FBA, FRSE. Secretary and Treasurer, Carnegie Trust for the Universities of Scotland, since 1986; Emeritus Professor of Geography, Edinburgh University; b. 2.6.21, Cardiff; m., Sheila Mary Burnett (deceased); 1 s.; 1 d. Educ. Penarth County School; Queens' College, Cambridge. Civil Servant, 1938-47 (Lord Chancellor's Department, Ministry of Works, Customs and Excise); War Service, Army, 1939-46 (Commissioned, 1941); Departmental Demonstrator, Department of Geography, Cambridge University, 1949-50; University College, London: Assistant Lecturer, 1950-52, Lecturer, 1952-64, Reader, 1964-65; Ogilvie Professor of Geography, Edinburgh University, 1965-86. Institute of British Geographers: Vice-President, 1971-73, President, 1973-74; Vice-President, Royal Scottish Geographical Society, since 1975; Vice-President, British Academy, 1985-87. Recreations: walking; natural history; listening to music. Address: (b.) Carnegie Trust for the Universities of Scotland, Cameron House, Abbey Park Place, Dunfermline, KY12 7PZ; T.-01383 622148.

Corbet, Professor Philip Steven, BSc, PhD, DSc, ScD, FIBiol, FESC, FRSE, FRSA. Biologist and Author; Professor of Zoology, Dundee University, 1980-90 (Head, Department of Biological Sciences, 1983-86); Professor Emeritus, since 1990; b. 21.5.29, Kuala Lumpur, Malaysia; m., Mary Elizabeth Canvin; 1 d. by pr. m. Educ. Dauntsey's School, Wiltshire; Reading University; Gonville and Caius College, Cambridge. Zoologist, East African Fisheries Research Organisation, Jinja, Uganda, 1954-57; Entomologist: East African Virus Research Organisation, Entebbe, Uganda, 1957-62; Entomology Research Institute, Canada Department of Agriculture, Ottawa, 1962-67; Director, Research Institute, Canada Department of Agriculture, Belleville, Ontario, 1967-71; Professor and Chairman, Department of Biology, Waterloo University, Ontario, 1971-74; Professor and Director, Joint Centre for Environmental Sciences, Canterbury University and Lincoln College, New Zealand, 1974-78; Professor, Department of Zoology, Canterbury University, New

Zealand, 1978-80. Entomological Society of Canada: President, 1971, Gold Medal, 1974, Fellow, 1976; Commonwealth Visiting Professor, Cambridge University, 1979-80; Member, New Zealand Government Independent Fact-Finding Group on Nuclear Energy, 1975-77; Member, New Zealand Environmental Council, 1976-79; Member, Committee for Scotland, Nature Conservancy Council, 1986-90; Societas Internationalis Odonatologica, Member of Honour, 1985; British Dragonfly Society: President, 1983-92, Honorary Member, since 1991. Publications: Dragonflies (Co-author), 1960; A Biology of Dragonflies, 1962; The Odonata of Canada and Alaska, Vol. 3 (Co-author), 1975; research papers on medical entomology and pest management. Recreations: natural history; music. Address: (h.) 29 Mentone Terrace, Edinburgh EH9 2DF; T.-031-662 4696.

Cormack, John James Callender, MD, FRCPE, FRCGP. General Medical Practitioner; Apothecary to HM Household at the Palace of Holyroodhouse, since 1991; Chairman, Corstorphine Trust, since 1995; b. 21.2.34, Edinburgh; m., Joy Mackenzie Gourlay; 1 s.; 2 d. Educ. Edinburgh Academy; Edinburgh University. House Officer, Grenfell Mission, Canada, 1960-61; Medical Officer, CCAP Hospital, Nyasaland, 1961-62; Principal in general practice, Corstorphine, since 1964; part-time Lecturer, Department of General Practice, Edinburgh University, 1966-76; Member, Panel of Examiners, Royal College of General Practitioners, 1971-82. Joint Session Clerk, Corstorphine Old Parish Church; Hon. Librarian and Trustee, Royal Medical Society. Publications: Practice – Clinical Management in General Practice (Co-editor); Teaching General Practice (Co-editor). Recreations: cycling; walking; painting; Scottish history. Address: (b.) Ladywell Medical Centre, Ladywell Road, Edinburgh, EH12 7TB; T.-0131-334 3602.

Corner, David John, BA (Oxon), FRHS. Secretary, St. Andrews University, since 1991; Honorary Lecturer, Department of Mediaeval History, St. Andrews University, since 1991; b. 24.10.47, Birmingham; m., Carol Ann; 2 s. Educ. King Edward VI Grammar School, Aston, Birmingham; Worcester College, Oxford. Prize Fellow, Magdalen College, Oxford, 1972-75; Lecturer, Department of Mediaeval History, St. Andrews University, 1975-91. Governor, Newbattle Abbey College, since 1991; President, St. Andrews Association of University Teachers, 1985-88. Recreations: cinema; sport. Address: St. Andrews University, College Gate, North Street, St. Andrews, KY16 9AJ; T.-01334 462549.

Corner, Douglas Robertson, FIB (Scot). General Manager, Banking, Clydesdale Bank PLC, since 1992; Director, Quality Scotland Foundation; b. 13.5.44, Glasgow; m., Alice Cairns; 1 s.; 1 d. Educ. Duncanrig Secondary School, East Kilbride. Royal Bank of Scotland, 1962-68; Rolls-Royce Ltd., 1968-69; Clydesdale Bank, since 1969. Director: Quarriers Homes; Clyde General Finance Ltd.; Scottish Agricultural Securities Corporation; Vice-President, Chartered Institute of Bankers in Scotland; Director, Hairmyres and Stonehouse Hospitals NHS Trust. Recreations: golf; bowls; walking. Address: (b.) 30 St. Vincent Place, Glasgow, G1 2HZ; T.-0141-248 7070.

Cornish, Melvyn David, BSc, PGCE. Deputy Secretary, Edinburgh University, since 1991; b. 29.6.48, Leighton Buzzard; m., Eileen Joyce Easterbrook; 1 s.; 1 d. Educ. Cedars Grammar School, Leighton Buzzard; Leicester University. Chemistry Teacher, Jamaica and Cumbria, 1970-73; Administrator, Leicester Polytechnic, 1973-78; Senior Administrative Officer, Assistant Secretary, Director of Planning, Edinburgh University, 1978-91. Recreations: walking; photography; travel; family. Address: (b.) Old College, South Bridge, Edinburgh; T.-0131-650 2136.

Cornwell, Professor John Francis, PhD, BSc, DIC, ARCS, FRSE. Professor of Theoretical Physics, St. Andrews University, since 1979 (Chairman, Physics Department, 1984-85); b. 28.1.37, London; m., Elizabeth Margaret Burfitt; 2 d. Educ. Ealing Grammar School; Imperial College, London. Lecturer in Applied Mathematics, Leeds University, 1961-67; St. Andrews University: Lecturer in Theoretical Physics, 1967-73, Reader, 1973-79. Publications: Group Theory in Physics, three volumes, 1984, 1989; Group Theory and Electronic Energy Bands in Solids, 1969. Recreations: sailing; hill-walking; tennis; badminton; golf. Address: (b.) Department of Physics and Astronomy, St. Andrews University, North Haugh, St. Andrews, Fife, KY16 9SS; T.-01334 476161.

Cornwell, Professor Keith, BSc, PhD, DEng, FIMechE. Professor, Department of Mechanical Engineering, Heriot-Watt University; Dean of Engineering, since 1993; b. 4.4.42, Abingdon; m., Sheila Joan Mott; 1 s.; 1 d. Educ. City University, London. Research Fellow, then Lecturer, Middlesex Polytechnic; Lecturer, Heriot-Watt University. Member, UK Committee on Heat Transfer; UK Representative on Eurotherm Committee. Publications: The Flow of Heat; numerous journal papers. Recreations: travelling; gardening. Address: (h.) Strathview, Templar Place, Gullane, EH39 2AH.

Corrie, John Alexander. Farmer; Member (Conservative), European Parliament for Worcestershire and Warwickshire, since 1994; Vice-Chair, 1979 Backbench Committee of European Conservatives; Chairman, Scottish Transport Users Consultative Committee, since 1989; Vice Chairman, Central Transport Consultative Committee, since 1992; Director, Ayrshire Agricultural Society, since 1990; Council Member for Scotland, Royal Agricultural Society of England, since 1992; Member, Health and Safety Committee, since 1993; Member, Railways Industry Advisory Committee, since 1993; b. 1935; m.; 1 s.; 2 d. Educ. Kirkcudbright Academy; George Watson's College, Edinburgh; Lincoln Agricultural College, New Zealand. Commissioned from the ranks, New Zealand Army, 1957; National Chairman, Scottish Young Conservatives, 1964; Council Member, National Farmers Union of Scotland, 1965; Chairman, Kirkcudbright Conservative Association, 1966; Lecturer, British Wool Marketing Board, 1967-74, and Agricultural Training Board, 1969-74; MP (Conservative), Bute and North Ayrshire, 1974-83, North Cunninghame, 1983-87; appointed Scottish Conservative spokesman on education, 1974; Member, European Parliament, 1975 and 1977-79; Vice President, EEC/Turkey Committee; appointed Opposition Whip, 1975 (resigned, 1976); elected to Council, Belted Galloway Cattle Society, 1978; PPS to Secretary of State for Scotland, 1979-81; elected to Council, National Cattle Breeders Association, 1979; introduced private member's Bill on abortion law reform, 1979; Chairman, Scottish Conservative Backbench Committee, 1981; elected Leader, Conservative Group on Scottish Affairs, 1982; Member, Council of Europe, 1983-87; Member, Western European Union (Defence Committee), 1983-87; Industry Fellowship with Conoco Oil, 1987; Vice Chairman, FAO Committee in Rome for Council of Europe; awarded Wilberforce Plaque for humane work, 1981; farms family farm in Kirkcudbright. Address: (h.) Park of Tongland, Kirkcudbright, DG6 4NE.

Corsar, Charles Herbert Kenneth, LVO, OBE, TD, JP, DL, MA. Farmer, since 1953; Secretary for Scotland, Duke of Edinburgh's Award, 1966-87; b. 13.5.26, Edinburgh; m., The Honourable Dame Mary Corsar, DBE (qv) ; 2 s.; 2 d. Educ. Merchiston Castle; King's College, Cambridge. Commissioned, The Royal Scots TA, 1948; commanded 8/9 Bn.,The Royal Scots TA, 1964-67; Edinburgh and Heriot-Watt Universities OTC, 1967-72; TA Colonel, 1972-75; Hon. ADC to The Queen, 1977-81; Honorary Colonel, 1/52 Lowland Volunteers, 1975-87; Chairman, Lowland TA and VR Association, 1984-87; Zone Commissioner, Home

Defence, East of Scotland; County Councillor, Midlothian, 1958-67; Vice-Lieutenant, Midlothian; Vice President, The Boys Brigade, 1970-91 and President, Edinburgh Bn., Boys Brigade, 1969-87 (Hon. President, Edinburgh Bn., since 1987); Chairman, Scottish Standing Conference of Voluntary Youth Organisations, 1973-78; Governor: Merchiston Castle School, Clifton Hall School; Chairman, Wellington List D School, 1978-84; Chairman, Earl Haig Fund Scotland, 1984-90; Secretary, Royal Jubilee and Princes' Trusts (Lothian and Borders); Member, Scottish Sports Council, 1972-75; Elder, Church of Scotland, since 1956. Recreations: gardening; bee-keeping; shooting. Address: (h.) Burg, Torloisk, Ulva Ferry, Isle of Mull PA74 6NH; T.-Ulva Ferry 289; 11 Ainslie Place, Edinburgh, EH3 6AS; T.-0131-225 6318.

Corsar, The Hon. Dame Mary Drummond, DBE (1993), MA; b. 8.7.27, Edinburgh; m., Colonel Charles H.K. Corsar (qv); 2 s.; 2 d. Educ. Westbourne, Glasgow; St. Denis, Edinburgh; Edinburgh University. Chairman, Women's Royal Voluntary Service, 1988-93; Chairman, Scotland, WRVS, 1981-88; Midlothian Girl Guides: Secretary, 1951-66, County Commissioner, 1966-72; Deputy Chief Commissioner, Girl Guides Scotland, 1972-77; Member: Parole Board for Scotland, 1982-89; Executive Committee, Trefoil Centre, since 1975; Visiting Committee, Glenochil Detention Centre, 1976; Management Committee, Church of Scotland Youth Centre, Carberry, 1976-82; Governor, Fettes College; Member of Convocation, Heriot Watt University; Chairman, TSB Foundation for Scotland. Recreation: hill-walking. Address: (h.) Burg, Torloisk, Ulva Ferry, Isle of Mull, PA74 6NH; T.-0168 8500289.

Coull, James West. Honorary Sheriff, Dundee, since 1971; b. 30.5.14, Dundee; m., Jean Fairley; 1 s.; 1 d. Educ. Morgan Academy, Dundee; St. Andrews University. Solicitor (retired) and Notary Public; Burgh Prosecutor, Carnoustie, 1963-75; Dean, Faculty of Procurators and Solicitors in Dundee, 1971-73. Recreations: gardening; watercolour painting. Address: (h.) 2A Guthrie Street, Carnoustie, Angus.

Coulsfield, Hon. Lord (John Taylor Cameron), QC, BA, LLB. Senator of the College of Justice, since 1987; b. 24.4.34, Dundee; m., Bridget Deirdre Sloan. Educ. Fettes College; Corpus Christi College, Oxford; Edinburgh University. Admitted to Faculty of Advocates, 1960; Queen's Counsel, 1973; Lecturer in Public Law, Edinburgh University, 1960-64; Advocate Depute, 1977-80; Keeper of the Advocates Library, 1977-87; Chairman, Medical Appeal Tribunals, 1985-87; Judge of the Appeal Courts of Jersey and Guernsey, 1986-87.

Coulter, Stewart, BA (Hons), DipEd, FMA. Depute Director, Glasgow Museums, since 1989; b. 13.6.42, Antrim; m., Frances Day; 1 s.; 1 d. Educ. Ballymena Academy; Queens University, Belfast. Teacher/Housemaster, Coleraine Academical Institution, 1965-69; Head of Geography, Markham College, Lima, Peru, 1969-72; Assistant Museum Education Officer, Glasgow Museums, 1972-80, Museum Education Officer, 1980-89. Vice-Chairman, Glasgow Art Galleries and Museums Association. Publication: Museum Education in Scotland — a Directory (Co-author), 1981. Recreations: theatre; bridge; swimming. Address: (b.) Art Gallery and Museum, Glasgow, G3 8AG; T.-0141-305 2601.

Coulthard, William George, LLB. Solicitor, since 1971; Honorary Sheriff, since 1988; b. 13.3.48, Whitehaven; m., Fiona Jane McQueen; 1 s.; 2 d. Educ. Glasgow Academy; Glasgow University. Partner in legal firm, since 1974; Dean, Faculty of Procurators, Stewartry of Kirkcudbright, 1986-88; Chairman, Castle Douglas High School Board, 1990-94; President, Castle Douglas Rotary Club, 1995. Recreations: golf; swimming; hill-running. Address: (h.) Netherby, Castle Douglas, DG7 1BA; T.-01556 502965.

Couper, Jean, BSc. Independent Management Consultant, since 1995; Member, Scottish Legal Aid Board, since 1994; Member, Health Education Board for Scotland, since 1994; Vice Chairman, The Wise Group, since 1988; Vice Chairman, Heatwise Glasgow Ltd., since 1988; b. 31.8.53, Kilmarnock; m., John Anderson Couper; 1 s.; 1 d. Educ. Kilmarnock Academy; Glasgow University. Production engineer, foundry manager, quality assurance manager, 1974-79; materials manager, 1979-82; Management Consultant: Arthur Young, 1982-87, Price Waterhouse, 1987-95. Senator, Junior Chamber International. Recreations: gardening; skiing. Address: Lismore, 13 Otterburn Drive, Giffnock, Glasgow, G46 6PZ; T.-0141-638 4880.

Courtney, Professor James McNiven, BSc, PhD, Dr sc nat, ARCST, EurChem, CChem, FRSC, FIM. Professor, Bioengineering Unit, Strathclyde University, since 1989 (Reader, 1986-89, Senior Lecturer, 1981-86); Tenured Professor, International Faculty for Artificial Organs, since 1992; Secretary/Treasurer, International Society for Artificial Organs, since 1994; b. 25.3.40, Glasgow; m., Ellen Miller Courtney; 2 s.; 1 d. Educ. Whitehill Senior Secondary School; Royal College of Science and Technology; Strathclyde University. Rubber technologist: MacLellan Rubber Ltd., Glasgow, 1962-65, Uniroyal Ltd., Dumfries, 1965-66; Lecturer, Bioengineering Unit, Strathclyde University, 1969-81. Recreation: football supporter (Glasgow Rangers). Address: (b.) Strathclyde University, Bioengineering Unit, 106 Rottenrow, Glasgow; T.-0141-552 4400.

Cousin, (David) Alastair (Henry), BVMS, MRCVS, DBR, JP. Partner, veterinary practice, Kintyre, since 1972; Honorary Sheriff, Campbeltown Sheriff Court, since 1990; b. 19.4.44, Kincardine on Forth; m., Anne Macleod; 1 s.; 1 d. Educ. Balfron High School; Glasgow University; Liverpool University. Veterinary practice, Campbeltown: Veterinary Assistant, 1966, Junior Partner, 1972, Senior Partner, 1982. Commodore, Campbeltown Sailing Club, 1995. Recreations: sailing; shooting; gardening; music. Address: (h.) Southpark, Kilkerran Road, Campbeltown; T.-01586 553108.

Coutts, Findlay Macrury, MA, LLB. Director of Central Services, Dunfermline District Council, since 1991 (Director of Administration, 1975-91); b. 16.3.43, Aberdeen; m., Christine; 1 s.; 1 d. Educ. Aberdeen Grammar School; Aberdeen University. Law apprentice/Legal Assistant, Hamilton Town Council, 1966-69; Town Clerk, Cupar, 1969-75. Recreations: good food; golf; town twinning. Address: (b.) City Chambers, Dunfermline; T.-Dunfermline 722711.

Coutts, Rev. Fred, MA, BD. Hospital Chaplain, Aberdeen Royal Hospitals NHS Trust; b. 13.1.47, Forfar; m., Mary Lawson Fraser Gill; 2 s.; 1 d. Educ. Brechin High School; Dollar Academy; St. Andrews University; Edinburgh University. Assistant Minister, Linwood Parish Church, 1972-74; Minister: Buckie North, 1974-84, Mastrick, Aberdeen, 1984-89. Chairman: Buckie Community Council, 1981-83, Moray Firth Community Radio Association, 1982-83. Recreations: music; photography; computing. Address: 9A Millburn Street, Aberdeen, AB1 2SS; T.-Aberdeen 583805.

Coutts, Herbert, SBStJ, AMA, FMA, FSAScot. City Curator, Edinburgh City Museums and Art Galleries, since 1973; b. 9.3.44, Dundee; m., Angela E.M. Smith; 1 s.; 3 d. Educ. Morgan Academy, Dundee. Assistant Keeper of Antiquities and Bygones, Dundee City Museums, 1965-68; Keeper, 1968-71; Superintendent, Edinburgh City Museums, 1971-73; Vice-President, Museum Assistants Group, 1969-70; Member: Government Committee on future of Scotland's National Museums and Galleries, 1979-80; Council, Museums Association, 1977-78, 1987-88;

Council, Society of Antiquaries of Scotland, 1981-82; Board, Scottish Museums Council, 1985-88; Museums Adviser, COSLA, 1985-90; Member, Paxton House Trust, since 1988; Member, East Lothian Community Development Trust, since 1989; External Examiner, St. Andrews University, since 1994. Contested Angus South (Lab), 1970. Publications: Ancient Monuments of Tayside; Tayside Before History; Edinburgh: An Illustrated History; Huntly House; Lady Stair's House; Gold of the Pharaohs (Editor); Dinosaurs Alive! (Editor); Sweat of the Sun — Gold of Peru (Editor); Golden Warriors of the Ukrainian Steppes (Editor). Recreations: family; gardening; opera; writing; reading; walking. Address: (h.) Kirkhill House, Queen's Road, Dunbar, EH42 1LN; T.-01368 63113.

Coutts, John R.T., BSc, PhD. Reader in Obstetrics and Gynaecology/Reproductive Medicine, Glasgow University, since 1987; b. 10.7.41, Dundee; m., Marjory R.B.; 1 s.; 2 d. Educ. Morgan Academy, Dundee; St. Andrews University. Dundee University: Research Fellow in Obstetrics and Gynaecology, 1966-69, Honorary Lecturer in Obstetrics and Gynaecology, 1969-70; Lecturer, then Senior Lecturer, Glasgow University, 1970-87. Publications: The Functional Morphology of the Human Ovary (Editor); many journal articles. Recreation: bowling. Address: (b.) Department of Obstetrics and Gynaecology, Glasgow Royal Infirmary, 10 Alexandra Parade, Glasgow; T.-0141-552 3535.

Coutts, Norman Alexander, BSc, MB, ChB, FRCP(Glas), FRCP(Edin), FRCP(Lond). Consultant Paediatrician, Argyll and Clyde Health Board, since 1969; Honorary Senior Clinical Lecturer, Paediatrics, Glasgow University, since 1980; b. 20.1.33, Glasgow; m., Margaret Sargeant; 2 s.; 1 d. Educ. Woodside School, Glasgow; Glasgow University. House Officer posts, Glasgow, 1958-59; Captain, RAMC, 1959-61; Registrar posts, Lincoln, Leeds, York and Glasgow, 1961-69. Member of Council, British Paediatric Association, 1985-88. Recreations: walking; philately. Address: (h.) 1 Elm Gardens, Bearsden, Glasgow, G61 3BH; T.-0141-942 7194.

Coutts, T(homas) Gordon, MA, LLB, QC, FCIArb. Queen's Counsel, since 1973; b. 5.7.33, Aberdeen; m., Winifred K. Scott; 1 s.; 1 d. Educ. Aberdeen Grammar School; Aberdeen University. Advocate, 1959; Chairman, Industrial Tribunals, 1972; Chairman, Medical Appeal Tribunals, 1984; Chairman, VAT Tribunals, 1990; Temporary Judge, Court of Session, 1991; Member, Panel of Arbitration, CIArb, 1995. Recreations: travel; stamp collecting. Address: (h.) 6 Heriot Row, Edinburgh.

Cowan, Brigadier Colin Hunter, CBE, MA, FRSA, CEng, MICE. Chief Executive, Cumbernauld Development Corporation, 1970-85; b. 16.10.20, Edinburgh; m., 1, Elizabeth Williamson (deceased); 2 s.; 1 d.; 2, Mrs Janet Burnett. Educ. Wellington College; Trinity College, Cambridge. Commissioned, Royal Engineers, 1940; service in India and Burma, Royal Bombay Sappers and Miners, 1942-46; staff and regimental appointments, UK and Malta, 1951-60; commanded Field Engineer Regiment, Germany, 1960-63; Defence Adviser, UK Mission to UNO, New York, 1964-66; Chief Staff Officer to Engineer-in-Chief (Army), Ministry of Defence, 1966-68; Brigadier, Engineer Plans (Army), Ministry of Defence, 1968-70. Recreations: hill-walking; photography; music. Address: (h.) 12B Greenhill Gardens, Edinburgh, EH10 4BW; T.-0131-447 9768.

Cowan, David Lockhart, MB, ChB, FRCSEdin. Consultant Otolaryngologist, City Hospital, Royal Hospital for Sick Children and Western General Hospital, Edinburgh, since 1974; Honorary Senior Lecturer, Edinburgh University; b. 30.6.41, Edinburgh; m., Eileen M. Masterton; 3 s.; 1 d. Educ. George Watson's College, Edinburgh; Trinity College, Glenalmond; Edinburgh University. Scottish Representative, Council, British

Association of Otolaryngologists. Publications: Logan Turner's Diseases of the Ear, Nose and Throat (Co-author); Paediatric Otolaryngology (Co-author). Recreations: golf; all sport. Address: (h.) 28 Braid Hills Road, Edinburgh, EH10 6HY; T.-0131-447 3424.

Cowan, John, MBE, BA, BSc (Hons), MSc, PhD, DEng, FIStructE, FEIS. Director, Open University in Scotland, since 1987 (Professor of Engineering Education, Heriot Watt University, 1982-87); b. 19.3.32, Glasgow; m., Audrey Walker Cowan; 3 s.; 1 d. Educ. High School of Glasgow; Edinburgh University; Heriot-Watt University. Design engineer, Blyth & Blyth, Edinburgh, 1952-64; joined Heriot-Watt College as Lecturer, 1964; awards, Institution of Structural Engineers and Czech Ministry of Higher Education, for work in engineering education research. Recreations: reading; music; photography. Address: (b.) 10 Drumsheugh Gardens, Edinburgh, EH3 7QJ; T.-0131-226 3851.

Cowan, Lt. Col. John Mervyn, TD, MCIBS. Chairman, Earl Haig Fund (Scotland), since 1993; Chairman, Royal Artillery Association Scottish Region, since 1991; b. 13.2.30, Oban; m., Marion Neilson Kidd; 1 s.; 2 d. Educ. Oban High School. National Bank of Scotland, National Commercial Bank of Scotland, Royal Bank of Scotland, 1946-90 (retired); TA commission, 1963; commanded 207 (City of Glasgow) Battery RA(V), 1980-82; J.L.S.O., HQ Scotland, 1982-90; Member, RA Council for Scotland. Recreations: travel; charitable works; sport. Address: (h.) 43 Hunter Grove, Bathgate, EH48 1NN; T.-01506 655784.

Cowan, Margaret Morton (Lady Cowan), MA, JP. Member, Executive Committee, National Trust for Scotland, since 1991; Member, Scottish Committee, British Council, since 1991; b. 4.11.33, Newmilns; m., Sir Robert Cowan ; 2 d. Educ. St. George's School for Girls, Edinburgh; Edinburgh University. British Petroleum Company, 1955-59; Teacher, West Midlands Education Authority, 1965-76; Consultant and Lecturer in Use of Language, Hong Kong, 1976-81; Convener, The Highland Festival; Member, Justice of the Peace Committee, Inverness, since 1985. Address: (h.) The Old Manse, Farr, Inverness-shire, IV1 2XA; T.-0180 83 209.

Cowe, Alan Wilson, MA, LLB. Secretary and Clerk, Church of Scotland General Trustees, since 1964; b. 9.8.38, Kelso; m., Agnes Cunningham Dick. Educ. Dunfermline High School; Edinburgh University. Law apprentice, Simpson Kinmont & Maxwell, WS, Edinburgh; Assistant to Secretary, Church of Scotland General Trustees, 1963-64. Recreations: long-distance running; hill-walking. Address: (b.) 121 George Street, Edinburgh, EH2 4YR; T.-0131-225 5722.

Cowie, Professor John McKenzie Grant, BSc, PhD, DSc, CChem, FRSC, FRSE. Professor of Chemistry of Materials, Heriot-Watt University, since 1988 (Professor of Chemistry, Stirling University, 1973-88); b. 31.5.33, Edinburgh; m., Agnes Neilson Campbell; 1 s.; 1 d. Educ. Royal High School, Edinburgh; Edinburgh University. Assistant Lecturer, Edinburgh University, 1956-58; Research Officer, National Research Council of Canada, Ottawa, 1958-67; Lecturer, Essex University, 1967-69; Senior Lecturer, Stirling University, 1969-73. Staff Assessor, Bangladesh Agricultural College; Chairman, Scottish Spinal Cord Injury Association, 1991-94; Hon. President, Scottish Council on Disability (Stirling District); Vice Chairman, Scottish Council on Disability, 1989-90; Hon. President, Stirling Association of Voluntary Services.. Recreations: reading; painting; listening to music. Address: (h.) Traquair, 50 Back Road, Dollar, Clackmannanshire; T.-Dollar 742031.

Cowie, Hon. Lord (William Lorn Kerr Cowie), MA (Cantab), LLB (Glas). Senator of the College of Justice in

Scotland, since 1977; b. 1.6.26, Glasgow; m., Camilla Henrietta Grizel Hoyle; 2 s.; 2 d. Educ. Fettes College, Edinburgh; Clare College, Cambridge; Glasgow University. RNVR, 1944-47 (Sub. Lt.); Member, Faculty of Advocates, 1952; QC, 1967. Scottish rugby internationalist, 1953. Recreation: fishing. Address: (h.) 20 Blacket Place, Edinburgh; T.-0131-667 8238.

Cowley of Innerwick, Col. Victor Charles Vereker, TD, JP, DL. Land Owner and Farmer; b. 4.4.18, Glasgow; m., Moyra McClure; 1 s.; 2 d. Educ. St. Mary's, Melrose; Merchiston Castle School. Young master printer, 1937; commissioned, RATA, 1939; served France, North Africa, Sicily, Italy, Burma, Indo China; Col. Depute CRA 51st Highland Division; Chairman, Brownlie Scandrett and Graham Ltd. (retired 1960); Vice Convener, East Lothian County Council, 1973; Regional Councillor, Lothian, 1975; Commissioner of Income Tax, East Lothian, 1965-87. Recreations: shooting; golf. Address: Crowhill, Innerwick, Dunbar, EH42 1QT; T.-01368 840279.

Cox, Gilbert Kirkwood, DL, JP. General Manager Scotland, Associated Perforators & Weavers Ltd., since 1971; Director/Trustee, Airdrie Savings Bank, since 1987 (Vice President, 1992); b. 24.8.35, Chapelhall, Airdrie; m., Marjory Moir Ross Taylor; 2 s.; 1 d. Educ. Airdrie Academy. National Coal Board, 1953-63; David A. McPhail & Sons Ltd., 1963-68; D.A. Monteith Holdings, 1968-71. Deputy Lieutenant, Lanarkshire; founder Member and Past President, Monklands Rotary Club; Member, Scottish Kidney Research Fund. Recreations: golf; gardening; walking. Address: (h.) Bedford House, Commonhead Street, Airdrie, ML6 6NS; T.-01236 763331.

Cox, Sheriff Principal Graham Loudon, QC, MA, LLB, Sheriff Principal of South Strathclyde Dumfries and Galloway, since 1993; b. 22.12.33, Newcastle-upon-Tyne; m., Jean Nelson; 3 c. by pr. m. Educ. Hamilton Academy; Grove Academy; Edinburgh University. Army 1956-61 (latterly Major, Directorate of Army Legal Services); called to the Bar, 1962; Advocate-Depute, 1966-68; Sheriff of Tayside Central and Fife, at Dundee, 1968-93; QC, 1993; Secretary, Sheriffs' Association, 1987-91, President, 1991-93. Recreations: skiing; golf; restoration of decaying property. Address: (h.) Crail House, Crail, Fife; T.-01333 450270.

Cracknell, Professor Arthur Philip, MA, MSc, DPhil, CPhys, FInstP, FRSE, FRSA. Carnegie Professor of Physics, Dundee University, since 1993; b. 18.5.40, Ilford; m., Margaret Florence Grant; 1 s.; 2 d. Educ. Chigwell School; Pembroke College, Cambridge; Queen's College, Oxford. Lecturer in Physics: University of Singapore, 1964-67, University of Essex, 1967-70; Senior Lecturer in Physics, then Reader, Dundee University, 1970-78; Professor of Theoretical Physics, 1978-93; Editor, International Journal of Remote Sensing. Publications: 25 books; 250 scientific papers. Address: (b.) Dundee University, Dundee, DD1 4HN; T.-01382 223181.

Cracknell, (William) Martin. Chief Executive, Glenrothes Development Corporation, 1976-93; b. 24.6.29, Leicester; m., Gillian Goatcher; 2 s.; 2 d. Educ. St. Edwards School, Oxford; Royal Military Academy, Sandhurst. Army, Royal Green Jackets, 1947-69; British Printing Industries Federation, 1969-76. Board Member, Glenrothes Enterprise Trust, 1983-89; Member, Executive, Scottish Council (Development and Industry), 1984-89; Chairman, Glenrothes University Industry Dining Club, 1976-93; Chairman, Committee for Scotland, German Chamber of Industry and Commerce in the UK, 1987-92. Address: (h.)West End Cottage, Freuchie, Fife, KY7 7EZ; T.-01337 857849.

Craft, Professor John Anthony, BSc, PhD. Professor of Biochemistry, Glasgow Caledonian University, since 1990;

b. 16.12.46, London; m., Anne McCord; 1 s.; 3. Educ. Horley County Secondary School; University College, London. Research Fellow, University College London; Lecturer, Glasgow College of Technology; Reader, Glasgow Polytechnic. Recreations: mountaineering; skiing; orchids; gardening. Address: (b.) Biological Sciences, Glasgow Caledonian University, Cowcaddens Road, Glasgow, G4 0BA; T.-0141-331 3220.

Craig, Emeritus Professor Gordon Younger, BSc, PhD, CGeol, FRSE. Emeritus Professor of Geology, Edinburgh University, since 1984; President, International Commission on the History of the Geological Sciences, 1984-89; b. 17.1.25, Milngavie; m., Mary Thornton; 2 s.; 2 step s.; 1 step d. Educ. Hillhead High School; Bearsden Academy; Glasgow University; Edinburgh University. Joined Edinburgh University as Lecturer, 1947; James Hutton Professor of Geology, 1967-84; Visiting Professor, University of Colorado, 1958-59, UCLA, 1959, 1965; Leverhulme Fellow, ANU, Canberra, 1978; Distinguished Foreign Scholar, Mid-America State Universities, 1980; Green Professor, University of British Columbia, 1977, Texas Christian University, 1994; President, Edinburgh Geological Society, 1967-69; Clough Medal, Edinburgh Geological Society, 1987; History of Geology Division Award, Geological Society of America, 1990. Publications: Geology of Scotland (Editor), 1991 (3rd ed.); James Hutton: The Lost Drawings (Co-author), 1977; A Geological Miscellany (Co-author), 1982. Recreations: golf; gardening. Address: (h.) 14 Kevock Road, Lasswade, Edinburgh, EH18 1HT; T.-0131-663 8275.

Craig, Rev. Maxwell Davidson, MA, BD, ThM. General Secretary, Action of Churches Together in Scotland, since 1990 (Minister, St. Columba's Parish Church, Bridge of Don, Aberdeen, 1989-91); Chaplain to the Queen in Scotland, since 1986; Convener, Church and Nation Committee, Church of Scotland, 1984-88; b. 25.12.31; m., Janet Margaret Macgregor; 1 s.; 3 d. Educ. Bradford Grammar School; Harrow School; Oriel College, Oxford; Edinburgh University. National Service, 1st Bn., Argyll and Sutherland Highlanders (2nd Lt.), 1954-56. Assistant Principal, Ministry of Labour, 1957-61; Private Secretary to Parliamentary Secretary, 1959-61; left London and civil service to train for ministry of Church of Scotland, 1961; ThM, Princeton, 1965; Minister, Grahamston Parish Church, Falkirk, 1966-73; Minister, Wellington Church, Glasgow, 1973-89; Chairman: Falkirk Children's Panel, 1970-72, Hillhead Housing Association Ltd., 1975-89; Member, Strathclyde Children's Panel, 1973-86. Recreations: hill-walking; choral singing. Address: (h.) 9 Kilbryde Crescent, Dunblane, Perthshire FK15 9BA; T.-01786 823147.

Craig, Robert, BA, MA, ALA. Director, Scottish Library Association, since 1984; b. 2.7.43, Hamilton; m., Ann Beaton; 1 s.; 1 d. Educ. Dalziel High School; Strathclyde University. Depute County Librarian, Lanark County Council, 1974-75; Principal Education Librarian, Glasgow Division, Strathclyde Regional Council, 1975-79; Lecturer, Strathclyde University, 1979-84. Publications: Scottish Libraries (Editor); Lights in the Darkness (Co-Editor); Scotland 1939 (Co-author). Recreations: reading; gardening; football. Address: (b.) Motherwell Business Centre, Coursington Road, Motherwell, ML1 1PW; T.-01698 252526.

Craig, Robert Harvey, RD, CA. Chartered Accountant in professional practice, since 1955; Honorary Sheriff, North Strathclyde at Campbeltown, since 1986; b. 18.12.29, Campbeltown; m., Marion Caldwell; 1 s.; 1 d. Educ. Campbeltown Grammar School; Glasgow University. Admitted to Institute of Chartered Accountants of Scotland, 1953; Fleet Air Arm, 1953-55; later commanded a Naval Reserve minesweeper; Director of various companies.

Recreations: sailing; skiing. Address: (h.) Ferndean, Campbeltown, Argyll, PA28 6EN; T.-01586 552495.

Craik, Professor Alexander Duncan Davidson, BSc, PhD, FRSE. Professor of Applied Mathematics; St. Andrews University, since 1988 (Reader, 1974-87); b. 25.8.38, Brechin; m., Elizabeth Mary Farmer; 1 s.; 1 d. Educ. Brechin High School; St. Andrews University; Cambridge University. St. Andrews University: Lecturer in Applied Mathematics, 1963-70, Senior Lecturer, 1970-74. Publication: Wave Interactions and Fluid Flows, 1985. Address: (h.) 92 Hepburn Gardens, St. Andrews, KY16 9LN.

Craik, Professor Robert John McArthur, BSc, MSc, PhD, FIOA, MCIBSE, CEng. Professor, Department of Building Engineering and Surveying, Heriot Watt University, since 1992; b. Haddington; m., Susan Margaret Scott; 1 s.; 3 d. Educ. Dunbar Grammar School; Heriot Watt University. Heriot-Watt: Lecturer, 1983, Reader, 1990. Recreations: swimming; cycling. Address: (b.) Department of Building Engineering and Sruveying, Heriot Watt University, Riccarton, Edinburgh; T.-0131-449 5111.

Craik, Sheriff Roger George, QC (Scot). Sheriff of Lothian and Borders, at Edinburgh, since 1984; b. 22.11.40.

Cramb, Rev. Erik McLeish, LTh. Organiser for Tayside, Scottish Churches Industrial Mission, since 1989; b. 26.12.39, Glasgow; m., Elizabeth McLean; 2 s.; 3 d. Educ. Woodside Secondary School, Glasgow; Glasgow University and Trinity College. Minister: St. Thomas' Gallowgate, Glasgow, 1973-81, St. Paul's United Church, Kingston, Jamaica, 1981-84, Yoker, Glasgow, 1984-89. Socialist; Member, Iona Community; Member, Disablement Income Group; Chair, Dundee Money Advice Project. Recreation: supports Partick Thistle. Address: (h.) 65 Clepington Road, Dundee, DD4 7BQ; T.-01382 458764.

Cramond, Ronald Duncan, CBE (1987), MA, FIMgt, FSA (Scot). Chairman, Strathclyde Greenbelt Company, since 1992; Trustee: National Museums of Scotland, since 1985, Scottish Civic Trust, since 1988, Cromarty Arts Trust, 1988-91, Bo'ness Heritage Trust, since 1989; Vice President, Architectural Heritage Society of Scotland, 1989-94; b. 22.3.27, Leith; m., Constance MacGregor (deceased); 1 s.; 1 d. Educ. George Heriot's School; Edinburgh University. Commissioned Royal Scots, 1950; entered War Office, 1951; Private Secretary to Parliamentary Under Secretary of State, Scottish Office, 1956; Principal, Department of Health for Scotland, 1957; Mactaggart Fellow, Glasgow University, 1962; Haldane Medallist in Public Administration, 1964; Assistant Secretary, Scottish Development Department, 1966; Under Secretary, 1973; Under Secretary, Department of Agriculture and Fisheries for Scotland, 1977. Deputy Chairman, Highlands and Islands Development Board, 1983-88; Member, Scottish Tourist Board, 1985-88; Chairman, Scottish Museums Council, 1990-93; Commissioner, Countryside Commission for Scotland, 1988-92. Recreations: golf; hill-walking; testing a plastic hip. Address: (b.) c/o National Museums of Scotland, Chambers Street, Edinburgh, EH1 1JF.

Crampin, Professor Stuart, BSc, PhD, ScD, FRSE, FRAS. Professor of Seismic Anisotropy, Department of Geology and Geophysics, Edinburgh University, since 1992; Director, Edinburgh Anisotropy Project, British Geological Survey, since 1988; b. 22.10.35, Tiptree, Essex; m., Roma Eluned Williams; 2 d. Educ. Maldon Grammar School; King's College, London; Pembroke College, Cambridge. Research Fellow, Uppsala University, 1963-65; Gassiot Fellow in Seismology, NERC, 1966-69; Principal Scientific Officer, Institute of Geological Sciences, 1969-76; Senior Principal Scientific Officer (Individual Merit), 1976-87, Deputy Chief Scientific Officer (Individual Merit), British Geological Survey, 1987-92; Honorary

Professor, Geophysics Department, Edinburgh University, 1988-92. Conrad Schlumberger Award, EAEG, 1986; Virgil Kauffman Gold Medal, SEG, 1988. Publications: 160 research papers. Recreations: hill-walking; travelling. Address: (b.) Department of Geology and Geophysics, Edinburgh University, Grant Institute, West Mains Road, Edinburgh, EH9 3JW; T.-0131-650 4908.

Crampsey, Robert A. McN., MA (Hons), ARCM. Freelance Broadcaster and Writer; b. 8.7.30, Glasgow; m., Dr. Veronica R. Carson; 4 d. Educ. Holyrood School, Glasgow; Glasgow University; London University (External). RAF, 1952-55 (demobilised in rank of Flt. Lt.); Head of History Department, St. Aloysius College, Glasgow, 1967-71; Assistant Head Teacher, Holyrood Secondary School, 1971-74; Rector, St. Ambrose High School, Coatbridge, 1974-86. Winner, Brain of Britain, BBC, 1965; Churchill Fellow, 1970; semi-finalist, Mastermind, 1972-73; BBC Sports Commentator. Publications: History of Queen's Park FC; Puerto Rico; The Manager; The Scottish Footballer; The Edinburgh Pirate (Arts Council Award); The Run Out; Mr Stein (a biography); The Young Civilian; The Glasgow Golf Club 1787-1987; The Empire Exhibition; The Somerset Cricket Quiz Book; The Surrey Cricket Quiz Book; Ranfurly Castle Golf Club — a centenary history; The Official Centenary History of the Scottish Football League; Scottish Railway Connections. Recreations: travel; things Hispanic; listening to and playing music; cricket. Address: (h.) 15 Myrtle Park, Glasgow, G42; T.-0141-423 2735.

Cranston, Colin. Firemaster, Lothian and Borders. Address: (b.) Brigade Headquarters, Lauriston Place, Edinburgh, EH3 9DE.

Cranston, Professor William Ballantyne, PhD, CEng, FICE, FIStructE, FACI, MIESIS, MIABSE, MIOD. Research Professor, Department of Civil Engineering, Paisley University; b. 7.12.33, Edinburgh; m., Agnes Muir Anderson; 4 s.; 1 d. Educ. Dollar Academy; Glasgow University. Assistant to Professor of Civil Engineering, Glasgow University, 1957-61; Cement and Concrete Association: Research Engineer, 1961-77, Head, Design Department, 1977-83, Director (Technical Applications), 1984-87; Professor and Head, Department of Civil Engineering, Paisley University, 1988-92. Recreations: sailing; fly-fishing. Address: (h.) Flat 8, 8 Riverview Place, Glasgow, G5 8EB; T.-0141-429 8169.

Crawford, James, MA, LLB, NP. Honorary Sheriff, Greenock, since 1987; retired Solicitor; b. 10.10.23, Greenock; m., Ruth Gibson; 1 s.; 1 d. Educ. Greenock Academy; Glasgow University. Army, 1942-46, commissioned Reconnaissance Corps, 1944, and served in West Africa and Burma; private practice, Gourock, 1949-88; 277th Field Regiment, RA, TA, 1949-53, retiring as Captain; General Commissioner for Income Tax, Renfrewshire, 1989; Hon. Secretary, Inverkip Society, 1962-83 (now Trustee); Chairman, Greenock Provident Bank, 1965-66. Recreations: gardening; fishing; travel. Address: (h.) 4 Edinburgh Drive, Gourock, PA19 1AG; T.-01475 631413.

Crawford, Robert, MA, DPhil. Lecturer in Modern Scottish Literature, School of English, St. Andrews University, since 1989; Associate Director, St. Andrews Scottish Studies Institute, since 1993; Co-Editor, Verse Magazine, 1984-95; Poetry Editor, Polygon, since 1991; Poet and Critic; b. 23.2.59, Bellshill; m., Alice Wales; 1 s. Educ. Hutchesons' Grammar School, Glasgow; Glasgow University; Balliol College, Oxford. Snell Exhibitioner & Carnegie Scholar, Balliol College, Oxford, 1981-84; Elizabeth Wordsworth Junior Research Fellow, St. Hugh's College, Oxford, 1984-87; British Academy Postdoctoral Fellow, Department of English Literature, Glasgow University, 1987-89. Publications: The Savage and the City in the Work of T.S. Eliot, 1987; A Scottish Assembly, 1990; Sharawaggi (Co-author), 1990; About Edwin Morgan (Co-Editor), 1990; Other Tongues: young Scottish poets in English, Scots and Gaelic (Editor), 1990; The Arts of Alasdair Gray (Co-Editor), 1991; Devolving English Literature, 1992; Talkies, 1992; Reading Douglas Dunn (Co-Editor), 1992; Identifying Poets, 1993; Liz Lochhead's Voices (Co-Editor), 1993; Twentieth Century Literature of Scotland: a selected bibliography, 1995; Talking Verse (Co-Editor), 1995. Recreation: being private. Address: (b.) School of English, St. Andrews University, St. Andrews, KY16 9AL; T.-01334 76161, Ext. 2666.

Crawford, 29th Earl of, and Balcarres, 12th Earl of (Robert Alexander Lindsay), PC, DL. Premier Earl of Scotland; Head of House of Lindsay; b. 5.3.27; m., Ruth Beatrice Meyer; 2 s.; 2 d. Educ. Eton; Trinity College, Cambridge. Grenadier Guards, 1945-49; MP (Conservative), Hertford, 1955-74, Welwyn and Hatfield, February to September, 1974; Opposition Front Bench Spokesman on Health and Social Security, 1967-70; Minister of State for Defence, 1970-72; Minister of State for Foreign and Commonwealth Affairs, 1972-74; Chairman, Lombard North Central Bank, 1976-80; Director, National Westminster Bank, 1975-88; Director, Scottish American Investment Co., 1978-88; Vice-Chairman, Sun Alliance & London Insurance Group, 1975-91; President, Rural District Councils Association, 1959-65; Chairman, National Association of Mental Health, 1963-70; Chairman, Historic Buildings Council for Scotland, 1976-83; Chairman, Royal Commission on Ancient and Historical Monuments of Scotland, 1985-95; First Crown Estate Commissioner, 1980-85; Deputy Lieutenant, Fife; Chairman, National Library of Scotland, since 1990; Chairman, Joint Committee, RSA and NGS, since 1993. Address: (h.) Balcarres, Colinsburgh, Fife, KY9 1HL.

Crawford, Robert Caldwell. Composer; b. 18.4.25, Edinburgh; m., Alison Braedine Orr; 1 s.; 1 d. Educ. Melville College, Edinburgh; Keswick Grammar School; Guildhall School of Music, London. Freelance Composer and Critic until 1970; BBC Music Producer, 1970-85; Chairman, Music Advisory Committee for Sir James Caird's Travelling Scholarships Trust, 1978-93. Recreations: carpentry; hill-walking; gardening; beekeeping. Address: (h.) 12 Inverleith Terrace, Edinburgh, EH3 5NS; T.-0131-556 3600.

Crawford, Robert Hardie Bruce, JP. Leader, Perthshire and Kinross Council, since 1995; b. 16.2.55, Perth; m., Jacqueline; 3 s. Educ. Kinross High School; Perth High School. Civil servant, Scottish Office, since 1974; elected District Councillor, Perth and Kinross, 1988, SNP Group Leader, since 1992. Recreations: watching Dunfermline Athletic; family. Address: (h.) 12 Douglas Crescent, Kinross; T.-01577 863531.

Crawford, Professor Robert MacGregor Martyn, BSc, DocSciNat (Liege), FRSE, FInstBiol. Professor of Plant Ecology, St. Andrews University, since 1977; b. 30.5.34, Glasgow; m., Barbara Elizabeth Hall; 1 s. Educ. Glasgow Academy; Glasgow University; Liege University; Moscow University. Lecturer, then Reader in Botany, St. Andrews University; Past President, Edinburgh Botanical Society; Editor, Flora. Recreations: European languages; music; photography. Address: (b.) The University, St. Andrews, KY16 9AJ; T.-01334 463370.

Crawford, Robert MacKay, BA, PhD, FRSA. Managing Director, Scottish Enterprise Operations; b. 14.6.51, Largs; m., Linda; 1 s.; 1 d. Educ. St. Michael's Adademy, Kilwinning; Strathclyde University; Harvard University; Glasgow University. Assembler, IBM, 1969-71; Research Officer, SNP, 1977-79; Citibank, London, 1982-83; Research Fellow, Fraser of Allander Institute, 1983-86; joined Locate in Scotland, 1986, apppointed Director, 1991.

Recreations: running; hill walking; reading (literature, history of ideas). Address: (b.) 120 Bothwell Street, Glasgow, G2 7JP; T.-0141-248 2700.

Crawford, Rudy, BSc (Hons), MBChB, FRCS (Glas). Consultant in Accident and Emergency Care, Royal Infirmary, Glasgow, since 1990; Honorary Clinical Senior Lecturer, Glasgow University, since 1991; b. 5.5.49, Glasgow; m., Jane Crawford; 1 s.; 1 d. Educ. Glasgow University. Temporary Lecturer in Anatomy, Glasgow University; general surgery training; specialist training in accident and emergency medicine and surgery, Glasgow and Aberdeen; formerly member of offshore specialist team providing medical support for North Sea oil emergencies including Piper Alpha Disaster; founder Member and Local Project Director, Scottish Trauma Audit Group and Scottish Child Accident Research and Audit Group; Member, Council, St. Andrew's Ambulance Association; Member, Scottish Management Efficiency Group Working Party on Accident and Emergency Services. Recreations: running; photography; travel; Rotary International. Address: (b.) Accident and Emergency Department, Royal Infirmary, Glasgow, G4 0SF; Ext. 0141-552 3535, Ext. 5116.

Crawford, Thomas, MA. Hon. Reader in English, Aberdeen University, since 1985; Convener, Publications Board, Association for Scottish Literary Studies, since 1988; b. 6.7.20, Dundee; m., Jean Rennie McBride; 1 s.; 1 d. Educ. Dunfermline High School; Edinburgh University; University of Auckland. University of Auckland: Lecturer in English, 1953-60, Senior Lecturer, 1960-62, Associate Professor, 1963-65; Lecturer in English, Edinburgh University, 1965; Commonwealth Research Fellow, Hamilton, Ontario, 1966; Senior Lecturer in English, then Reader, Aberdeen University, 1967-85; Warnock Fellow, Yale University, various times, since 1978. Past President, Association for Scottish Literary Studies; former Editor, Scottish Literary Journal; Council Member, Scottish Text Society. Publications: Burns: a study of the poems and songs, 1960; Scott, 1965; Scott, selected poems (Editor), 1972; Love, Labour, and Liberty, 1976; Society and the Lyric, 1980; Boswell, Burns and the French Revolution, 1990. Recreations: walking and rambling; music. Address: (h.) 61 Argyll Place, Aberdeen, AB2 4HU; T.-01224 635862.

Crean, Gerard Patrick, PhD, FRCPE, FRCPG, FRCPI. Consultant Physician, Ross Hall Hospital, Glasgow; Consultant Physician and Physician-in-charge, Gastro-Intestinal Centre, Southern General Hospital, Glasgow, 1967-92; b. 1.5.27, Courtown Harbour, County Wexford; m., Janice Dodds Mathieson; 1 s.; 2 d. Educ. Rockwell College, Cashel, County Tipperary; University College, Dublin. House appointments, Mater Misericordiae Hospital, Dublin, Western General Hospital, Edinburgh and Edinburgh Royal Infirmary; Registrar, then Senior Registrar, Western General Hospital, Edinburgh; Member, scientific staff, Medical Research Council Clinical Endocrinology Unit, Edinburgh; Honorary Lecturer, Department of Therapeutics, Edinburgh University; Visiting Professor in Physiology, Pennsylvania University. Clarke Prize, Edinburgh Pathological Club; contributed to several textbooks. Past President, British Society of Gastroenterology; President, Scottish Fiddle Orchestra. Recreations: fiddle playing; traditional music; history of Antarctic exploration; golf. Address: (h.) St. Ronan's, Duchal Road, Kilmacolm, PA13 4AY; T.-Kilmacolm 2504.

Cresser, Professor Malcolm Stewart, PhD, DIC, BSc, ARCS, FRSC, CChem. Professor of Plant & Soil Science, Aberdeen University, since 1989; b. 17.4.46, London; m., Louise Elizabeth Blackburn; 1 s.; 2 d. Educ. St. Ignatius College, Tottenham; Imperial College, London. Lecturer, Senior Lecturer, Reader, Department of Soil Science, Aberdeen University, 1970-89; awarded 11th SAC Silver Medal, 1984. Publications: Solvent Extraction in Flame

Spectroscopic Analysis; Flame Spectrometry in Environmental Chemical Analysis; Environmental Chemical Analysis (Co-author); Acidification of Freshwaters (Co-author); Soil Chemistry and its Applications (Co-author). Recreations: painting; drawing; gardening. Address: (b.) Department of Plant and Soil Science, Meston Building, Old Aberdeen, AB9 2UE; T.- 01224 272259.

Cresswell, Lyell Richard, BMus (Hons), MusM, PhD. Composer; b. 13.10.44, Wellington, New Zealand; m.; Catherine Mawson. Educ. Victoria University of Wellington; Toronto University; Aberdeen University. Music Organiser, Chapter Arts Centre, Cardiff; Forman Fellow, Edinburgh University, 1980-82; Canadian Commonwealth scholarship, 1969-70; Dutch Government bursary, 1974-75; Ian Whyte Award, 1978; APRA Silver Scroll, 1979; Cramb Fellow, Glasgow University, 1982-85. Address: (h.) 4 Leslie Place, Edinburgh, EH4 1NQ; T.- 0131-332 9181.

Crichton, Maurice, CA. Director, Woolwich Building Society and Chairman, Scottish and Northern Ireland Local Board, since 1977; Chairman, Irvine Development Corporation, since 1991; b. 4.6.28, Glasgow; m., Diana Russell Lang; 3 s.; 1 d. Educ. Kelvinside Academy; Cargilfield School; Sedbergh School. Partner, Touche Ross & Co., Chartered Accountants, 1955-86. Deacon Convener, Trades House of Glasgow, 1988-89; Member, Board, Bield Housing Association; Elder, Paisley Abbey. Recreations: golf; music; trout fishing; shooting. Address: (b.)Irvine Development Corporation, Perceton House, Irvine KA11 2AL.

Critchley, Frank. Honorary Sheriff, Grampian, Highland and Islands, since 1984; b. 7.10.14, Inverness; m., Joyce; 1 s.; 1 d. Educ. Inverness Royal Academy; George Watson's College, Edinburgh; Edinburgh University. Solicitor, 1938- 84, retiring as Senior Partner of MacNeill & Critchley, Inverness; Royal Corps of Signals, 1939-46 (Major); President, Inverness Rotary Club, 1954-55; Member, Craig Dunain Hospitals Board of Management, 1952-58 (Chairman of Finance); Registrar, Diocese of Moray Ross and Caithness, 1971-86; Member, Council, Law Society of Scotland, 1971-77; Dean, Faculty of Solicitors of Inverness-shire, 1979-82; Chairman, Regional Advisory Committee, North of Scotland Conservancy, Forestry Commission, 1989-93; Chairman, Inverness Civic Trust, 1991-94. Recreations:reading; walking; gardening; theatre. Address: (h.) Malwa, 9 Mayfield Road, Inverness; T.-Inverness 233516.

Critchlow, Howard Arthur, BDS, FDSRCS(Eng), FDSRCPS(Glas). Consultant Oral Surgeon (Honorary Senior Lecturer), Glasgow Dental Hospital, Stobhill General Hospital and Royal Hospital for Sick Children, Glasgow, since 1976; b. 22.4.43, Littleborough; m., Avril; 1 s.; 1 d. Educ. Nottingham High School for Boys; Sheffield University. General dental practice, Sheffield; oral surgery training post, Sheffield, Southampton, Odstock and Newcastle. Chairman, Greater Glasgow Health Board Dental Ethical Committee. Recreations: gardening; hill-walking; running. Address: (b.) Glasgow Dental Hospital and School, 378 Sauchiehall Street, Glasgow, G2 3JZ; T.- 0141-211 9600.

Croall, Alastair. Chief Executive, Scottish Borders Council, since 1995. Address: (b.) c/o Regional HQ, Newtown St. Boswells, Melrose, TD6 0SA.

Croan, Sheriff Thomas Malcolm, MA, LLB. Sheriff of North Strathclyde at Kilmarnock, since 1983; b. 7.8.32, Edinburgh; m., Joan Kilpatrick Law; 1 s.; 3 d. Educ. St. Joseph's College, Dumfries; Edinburgh University. Admitted to Faculty of Advocates, 1956; Standing Junior Counsel, Scottish Development Department, 1964-65 and

(for highways work), 1967-69; Advocate Depute, 1965-66; Sheriff of Grampian, Highland and Islands at Banff and Peterhead, 1969-83. Recreation: sailing. Address: (h.) Overdale, 113 Bentinck Drive, Troon.

Crofton, Sir John Wenman, KB, MA, MD, Dr h.c., FRCP, FRCPE. Vice-Chairman, Scottish Committee, Chest, Heart and Stroke Association, 1976-90; Chairman, Tobacco and Health Committee, International Union Against Tuberculosis and Lung Disease, 1984-88; b. 27.3.12, Dublin; m., Eileen Chris Mercer, MBE; 2 s.; 3 d. Educ. Tonbridge; Sidney Sussex College, Cambridge. Professor of Respiratory Diseases, Edinburgh University, 1952-77; Dean, Faculty of Medicine, 1963-66; Vice-Principal, 1969- 70; President, Royal College of Physicians of Edinburgh, 1973-76; Chairman, Scottish Health Education Co-ordinating Committee, SHHD, 1981-86; Edinburgh Medal for Science and Society, 1995. Recreations: history; music; mountains. Address: (h.) 13 Spylaw Bank Road, Edinburgh, EH13 0JW; T.-0131-441 3730.

Crofts, Roger Stanley, BA, MLitt, CertEd. Chief Executive, Scottish Natural Heritage, since 1991; Visiting Professor in Geography, Royal Holloway, London University; b. 17.1.44, Leicester. Educ. Hinckley Grammar School; Liverpool University; Leicester University. Research Assistant in Geography: Aberdeen University, 1966-72, University College, London, 1972-74; entered Scottish Office, 1974; Senior Research Officer, 1974-78; Principal Research Officer, 1978-84; Assistant Secretary, Highlands and Tourism Division, Industry Department, 1984-88; Assistant Secretary, Rural Affairs Division, Scottish Development Department, 1988-91. Member, Council: Royal Scottish Geographical Society, National Trust for Scotland, Scottish Wildlife Trust. Recreations: gardening; choral singing; hill-walking; wildflower photography. Address: (h.) 19 Manor Place, Edinburgh, EH3 7DX; T.-0131-225 1177.

Cromartie, 5th Earl of (John Ruaridh Grant Mackenzie). Chief of the Clan Mackenzie; b. 12.6.48; m.; 2 s. Address: Castle Leod, Strathpeffer, IV14 9AA.

Cromarty, Professor John Alfred, BSc, MSc, MRPharmS. Professor of Clinical Pharmacy, The Robert Gordon University, Aberdeen, since 1993; National Specialist in Clinical Pharmacy (Scotland), since 1993; Honorary Consultant Clinical Pharmacist, Dundee Teaching Hospitals NHS Trust; Honorary Clinical Pharmacist, Grampian Health Board, Grampian Healthcare NHS Trust, Aberdeen Royal Hospitals NHS Trust; b. 26.8.51, Kirkwall; m., Evelyn McKenzie; 2 d. Educ. Kirkwall Grammar School; Heriot Watt University; Strathclyde University; Aberdeen College of Education; Aberdeen University. Principal Pharmacist, North West Thames RHA, 1980-81; Principal Pharmacist/Senior Lecturer, North West Thames RHA/London University, 1981-89; Director, Post Qualification Education for Pharmacists in Scotland/Senior Lecturer, Strathclyde University, 1989-93. Recreations: wine; natural history; rugby (spectating); the ba' (player); poetry. Address: (b.) Clinical Pharmacy Practice Unit, School of Pharmacy, The Robert Gordon University, Schoolhill, Aberdeen, AB9 1FR; T.-01224 262540.

Crompton, Professor David William Thomasson, MA, PhD, ScD, FIBiol, FRSE. John Graham Kerr Professor of Zoology, Glasgow University, since 1985, Vice-Dean of Science, since 1993; b. 5.12.37, Bolton; m., Effie Mary Marshall; 1 s.; 2 d. Educ. Bolton School; Sidney Sussex College, Cambridge. National Service, commission, King's Own Royal Regiment, 1957; Assistant in Research, Cambridge University, 1963-68; Fellow, Sidney Sussex College, 1964-85; Vice-Master, 1981-83; Lecturer in Parasitology, Cambridge University, 1968-85; Joint Editor, Parasitology, 1972-82; Adjunct Professor, Division of Nutritional Sciences, Cornell University, New York, since

1981; Aquatic Life Sciences Committee, Natural Environment Research Council, 1981-84; Director, Company of Biologists Ltd., since 1985; Member, WHO Expert Committee on Parasitic Diseases, since 1985; Scientific Medal, Zoological Society of London, 1977; Head, WHO Collaborating Centre for soil-transmitted helminthiases, Glasgow University. Recreations: mountain walking; fishing; books; bull terriers. Address: (b.) Institute of Biomedical and Life Sciences, Glasgow University, Glasgow, G12 8QQ; T.-0141-330 5395; (h.) 7 Kirklee Terrace, Glasgow, G12 0TQ; T.-0141-357 2631.

Crompton, Graham Kenneth, MB, ChB, FRCPE, FCCP. Consultant Physician, Lothian Health Board, since 1969; Senior Lecturer (part-time) in Medicine and Respiratory Medicine, Edinburgh University, since 1969;Member, National Asthma Campaign Therapy Task Force, since 1991; President, British Thoracic Society 1994-95; President, Scottish Thoracic Society, 1994-96; b. 14.2.35, Salford; 2 s. Educ. Salford Grammar School; Edinburgh University. Appointed Consultant Physician, 1969; Director of Studies, Faculty of Medicine, 1977-88; Member, Medical Advisory Committee, Asthma Society, 1981-88. Publications: Diagnosis and Management of Respiratory Diseases; chapters in 12 medical text books; numerous papers. Recreation: watching sport. Address: (h.) 14 Midmar Drive, Edinburgh, EH10 6BU; T.-0131-447 1022.

Crosby, William Scott, CBE (1982), BL. Lawyer; b. 31.7.18, Hawick; m., Margaret Elizabeth Bell; 3 s. Educ. Hawick High School; Edinburgh University. Army Service, 1939-46; Croix de Guerre, 1945; acted as Brigade Major 152 Brigade, 1945; Former Senior Partner, Storie, Cruden & Simpson, Advocates, Aberdeen; Chairman, Grampian Health Board, 1973-82; President, Society of Advocates in Aberdeen, 1984-85. Recreations: golf; swimming; walking; gardening. Address: (h.) 16 Golf Place, Aboyne, AB34 5GA; T.-013398 85357.

Crosfield, Rev. Canon George Philip Chorley, OBE, MA (Cantab). Provost, St. Mary's Cathedral, Edinburgh, 1970-90; Hon. Canon, St. Mary's Cathedral, since 1991; b. 9.9.24, London; m., Susan Mary Jullion; 1 s.; 2 d. Educ. George Watson's College, Edinburgh; Selwyn College, Cambridge. Royal Artillery, 1942-46 (Captain); Priest, 1952; Assistant Curate: St. David's, Pilton, Edinburgh, 1951-53, St. Andrew's, St. Andrews, 1953-55; Rector, St. Cuthbert's, Hawick, 1955-60; Chaplain, Gordonstoun School, 1960-68; Canon and Vice-Provost, St. Mary's Cathedral, Edinburgh, 1968-70. Recreations: gardening; walking; carpentry. Address: (h.) 21 Biggar Road, Silverburn, near Penicuik EH26 9LQ; Tel.-01968 676607.

Crowden, Kenneth Harry, FIPD, MIMgt. Principal Consultant, Ardgowan Associates, since 1993; Director, Scottish Export Agency; General Manager Scotland, Astra Training Services Limited, since 1990; b. 22.6.47, Edinburgh; m., Isobel Mary. Educ. Boroughmuir School, Edinburgh. Ministry of Labour, Employment Benefits Service; Manpower Services Commission, Job Centre Manager, Regional Marketing and Sales Manager; exchange with French Civil Service; Marketing and Product Development Manager/Regional Operations Manager/ Director for Scotland, Skills Training Agency, Department of Employment. Past President, Rutherglen Junior Chamber; Senator, Junior Chamber International; Past Chairman, Scottish Senate, JCI. Recreations: sailing; skiing. Address: (h.) 686 Clarkston Road, Netherlee, Glasgow G44 3YS; T.-0141-633 2011.

Cruickshank, Alistair Booth, MA. Director and Secretary, Royal Scottish Geographical Society, since 1986; b. 3.8.31, Dumfries; m., Sheena Carlin Brown; 2 s.; 1 d. Educ. High School of Stirling; Glasgow University; Georgia University. RAF, 1956-58; Glasgow University, 1958-61; Nottingham University, 1961-65; Glasgow University, 1965-86.

ordained Auxiliary Minister, Church of Scotland, 1991; Deputy Lieutenant, County of Clackmannan, since 1991. Recreations: fly fishing; peoples and places. Address: (b.) 40 George Street, Glasgow; T.-0141-552 3330.

Cruickshank, Harvey. Honorary Sheriff at Perth, since 1966; b. 25.5.15, Perth; m., Muriel Helen Marshall; 1 s.; 1 d. Educ. Perth Academy. Apprenticeship, 1932-37, qualifying as Solicitor, 1937; Assistant, Condie, Mackenzie & Co., WS, Perth, 1937-39; enlisted, RAOC, 1940; commissioned, RAOC, 1941; Staff Captain, War Office, 1942; Major, 1944; demobbed 1945; Condie, Mackenzie & Co., WS: Partner, 1945, Senior Partner, 1962, retired, 1984; Moderator, Society of High Constables of Perth, 1963-65; President, Perth Rotary Club, 1972-73; Vice-Convener, Church of Scotland Committee on Maintenance of the Ministry, 1980-83. Recreations: golf; photography. Address: (h.) 13 Viewlands Road, Perth, PH1 1BL; T.-01738 621882.

Crummy, Helen Murray, MBE, DLitt, DL, JP; b. 10.5.20, Edinburgh; m., Larry Crummy; 3 s. Educ. James Clark's School. Founder Member and Organising Secretary, 23 years, Craigmillar Festival Society; served on Morris Committee (Housing and Social Work); former Member: Scottish Council for Community Education, Scottish Arts Council Development Committee, various Gulbenkian committees, DHSS Appeals Tribunal, Lothian Regional Council Education Advisory Committee. Recreations: writing; historical research; reading; gardening. Address: (h.) 4 Whitehill Street, Newcraighall, Musselburgh, EH21 8RA; T.-0131-669 7344.

Cruttenden, Timothy Peter, BEd, DipPhysEd, FILAM. Director of Leisure Services, East Kilbride District Council, since 1980; b. 6.9.45, Portsmouth; m., Hazel; 2 s. Educ. Warblington School, Havant; Bristol University; St. Paul's, Cheltenham. Taught in Hampshire and Gloucestershire, 1967-72; sports centre management, 1973-77; recreation administration, since 1977. Past Chairman, Association of Directors of Recreation, Leisure and Tourism. Recreations: squash; hockey; golf; sailing. Address: (b.) Civic Centre, East Kilbride, G74 1AB; T.-0135 52 71277.

Cubie, Andrew, LLB (Hons), NP, WS. Senior Partner, Fyfe Ireland WS, since 1994; Chairman, Bird Semple Fyfe Ireland WS, 1991-94; b. 24.8.46, Northallerton; m., Dr. Heather Ann Cubie; 1 s.; 2 d. Educ. Dollar Academy; Edinburgh University. Partner, Fyfe Ireland & Co., WS, 1971; Senior Partner, Corporate Department, Bird Semple Fyfe Ireland, WS, 1987; non-executive Director of a number of private companies; formerly:Examiner, Law Society of Scotland and External Examiner, Edinburgh University; Chairman, Scottish Council, CBI; Chairman of Governors, George Watson's College; Vice Chairman, RNLI Scotland; Member, Committee of Management, and Deputy Chairman, Fund-Raising Committee, RNLI. Recreation: sailing. Address: (b.) Orchard Brae House, 30 Queensferry Road, Edinburgh, EH4 2HG; T.-0131-343 2500.

Cullen, The Hon. Lord (William Douglas Cullen), LLD, DUniv, FRSE, HonFEng. Senator of the College of Justice, since 1986; b. 18.11.35, Edinburgh; m., Rosamond Mary Downer; 2 s.; 2 d. Educ. Dundee High School; St. Andrews University (MA); Edinburgh University (LLB). Called to the Scottish Bar, 1960; QC, 1973; Advocate-Depute, 1977-81; Chairman of the Inquiry into the Piper Alpha Disaster, 1988-90. Member, Royal Commission on the Ancient and Historical Monuments of Scotland, since 1987; Chairman, Cockburn Association, 1984-86; Chairman, Board of Governors, St. Margaret's School, Edinburgh, since 1994. Recreations: gardening; natural history. Address: (b.) Court of Session, Parliament House, Edinburgh; T.-0131-225 2595.

Culliven, John. Convener, Perthshire and Kinross Council, since 1995; b. 6.2.37, Glasgow; m., Sheila Elizabeth Grant MacKenzie; 4 s. Regional Councillor, since 1989. Recreations: bagpipes; horse-riding. Address: (h.) Craigmhor, Calvine, Pitlochry; T.-01796 483 250.

Cumming, Lt. Col. Alaistair Michael, OBE. Regimental Secretary to The Highlanders (Seaforth, Gordons and Camerons), since 1995; Commandant, Queen's Own Highlanders Battalion Army Cadet Force; b. 22.12.41, Singapore; m., Hilary Katharine Gray; 2 s. Educ. Bradfield College, Berkshire. Cadet, RMA Sandhurst, 1960-61; commissioned into The Gordon Highlanders, 1962; Major/Company Commander, Northern Ireland, 1976-77; Major/Staff Officer, Edinburgh, 1978-79; Battalion Second in Command, Hong Kong, 1980-81; Major/Staff Officer, Londonderry, 1982-84; Lt. Col.: Commander Ground Liaison Team, Germany, 1985-88; Naval and Military Attache, British Embassy, Poland, 1989-92; Commander Support Weapons Wing, Netheravon, 1992-95. Recreations: cricket; golf; tennis; shooting; skiing. Address: (b.) RHQ, The Highlanders, Cameron Barracks, Inverness, IV2 3XD.

Cumming, Alexander James, MA (Hons), CIMA, IPFA. Chief Executive, Aberdeen Royal Hospitals NHS Trust, since 1994; b. 7.3.47, Aberdeen; m., Margaret Callan; 1 s., 2 d. Educ. Fordyce Academy; Robert Gordon's College; Aberdeen University. VSO, 1968-70; Accountant, Company Secretary, Chief Accountant, 1970-75; joined Grampian Health Board, 1975. Treasurer, Langstane Housing Association. Address: (b.) Foresterhill House, Ashgrove Road West, Aberdeen; T.-01224 681818.

Cumming, Eric Alexander, MIMgt, AInstAM, FSA (Scot). Principal, Scottish Court Service HQ, since 1995; b. 9.5.54, Glasgow; m., Isabel Rodger. Educ. Albert Senior Secondary School; Glasgow College of Commerce. Entered Scottish Court Service (Sheriff Clerk's Branch), 1972; posts in Glasgow, Nairn, Ayr, Dumbarton; Depute Clerk of Session and Justiciary, 1983; Sheriff Clerk, Ayr, 1990-92; Deputy Principal Clerk of Justiciary, 1992-95. Recreations: Clyde steamers; reading; naval history. Address: (b.) Hayweith House, 23 Lauriston Street, Edinburgh; T.-0131 221 6822.

Cumming, Robert Currie, BL, FCIBS, ACIB, FRCSEdin (Hon.). Chairman, English Speaking Union — Scotland, 1984-90; b. 21.5.21, Strathaven; m., Mary Jean McDonald Crombie. Educ. Hutchesons' Grammar School, Glasgow; Glasgow University. Former Executive Director, Royal Bank of Scotland Group PLC and Royal Bank of Scotland PLC. Trustee, Royal Scottish Geographical Society. Recreations: fishing; golf; walking. Address: (h.) 3 Succoth Park, Edinburgh, EH12 6BX; T.-0131-337 1910.

Cummings, John Andrew, BA, MA. Headmaster, Keil School, since 1993; b. 15.5.49, Eastbourne; m., Claire; 1 s.; 1 d. Educ. Eastbourne Grammar School; University of Kent; London University. Assistant Master: Glasgow Academy, 1975-80, Tonbridge School, Kent, 1980-89; Head of English and Drama/Head of Sixth Form, Wycliffe College, 1989-93. Recreations: reading; theatre; hill-walking; tennis. Address: (b.) Keil School, Helenslee Road, Dumbarton, G82 4AL; T.-01389 62003.

Cummins, John George, MA, PhD. Reader in Spanish, Aberdeen University, since 1980 (Head, Department of Spanish, 1979-90); b. 26.9.37, Hull; m., Elaine S. Rockett; 2 s.; 1 d. Educ. Malet Lambert School, Hull; Manchester University. Assistant in Spanish, St. Andrews University, 1961-63; Lecturer in Spanish, Birmingham University, 1963-64; Aberdeen University: Lecturer in Spanish, 1964-72, Senior Lecturer in Spanish, 1972-80. Recreations: shooting; fishing. Address: (b.) Department of Spanish, King's College, Aberdeen University, Old Aberdeen; T.-Aberdeen 272540.

Cunliffe, Michael James Paton, BSc, MSc. Director of Corporate Services, East of Scotland Water Authority, since 1995; b. 9.3.47, Sunderland; m., Jocelyn Mary Willoughby; 1 s.; 1 d. Educ. Kendal Grammar School; Edinburgh University. Administration Trainee, Scottish Development Department, 1971-73; Higher Executive Officer, Scottish Economic Planning Department, 1973-75; Principal, Scottish Development and Education Departments, 1975-82; Assistant Secretary, Scottish Development, Industry, and Education Departments, 1982-95. Elder, St. Andrew's and St. George's Church, Edinburgh. Recreations: sailing; country walks; listening to music. Address: (b.) 27 Perth Street, Edinburgh, EH3 5RB; T.-0131-244 2924.

Cunningham, David Kenneth, BEd, MEd (Hons), FRSA. Head Teacher, Hillhead High School, Glasgow, since 1993; b. 19.4.48, Saltcoats; m., Marion S. Shedden; 2 d. Educ. Ardrossan Academy; Glasgow University; Jordanhill College of Education. Principal Teacher of English, North Kelvinside Secondary, 1976-80; Assistant Head Teacher, Garthamlock Secondary, 1980-82; Adviser in English, Dunbarton Division, 1982-90, Education Officer (Acting), 1989-90; Inspector, Quality Assurance Unit, Strathclyde Regional Council, 1990-93. Member, National Council, Headteachers Association of Scotland. Recreations: various sports; reading; photography; travel; family. Address: (h.) 7 Waterfoot Road, Newton Mearns, Glasgow; T.-0141-639 3367.

Cunningham, Edward, CBE, MA (Cantab), MBA (Harvard), FRSE. Director (Non-Executive), TSB Bank Scotland Plc, since 1986, Watson & Philip Plc, since 1989; Chairman: Scottish Exhibition Centre Ltd.,1992-95; The PHQ Agency, since 1990; Agrilay Ltd., since 1994; BUE Marine Ltd., since 1994; b. 15.9.31, Pakistan; m., Sylvia; 2 s. Educ. Trinity Hall, Cambridge; Harvard Business School. World Bank, Washington DC, 1968-77; Scottish Development Agency, 1977-90; Business Options Ltd., since 1990. Address: (b.) TSBBank Scotland, Henry Duncan House, 120 George Street, Edinburgh, EH2 4LH.

Cunningham, Ian Campbell, MA, BPhil. Keeper of Manuscripts, Maps and Music, National Library of Scotland, since 1991; b. 17.9.38, Falkirk; m., Morvern; 2 d. Educ. Campbeltown Grammar School; Glasgow University; Oxford University. Assistant Keeper, National Library of Scotland, 1963-90. Former Secetary and President, Edinburgh Bibliographical Society. Publications: editions of Herodas and of Auchinleck ms facsimile; Greek Manuscripts in Scotland; David Livingstone: a catalogue of documents. Address: (b.) National Library of Scotland, George IV Bridge, Edinburgh, EH1 1EW; T.-0131-226 4531.

Cunningham, Professor Ian M.M., CBE, FRSE, FIBiol, FRAgS, Hon. Assoc. RCVS, Bsc, PhD. Member, Executive Committee, National Trust for Scotland, and Chairman, Countryside and Nature Conservation Committee; Chairman, Board, Macaulay Land Use Research Institute; General Council Assessor, Court, Edinburgh University; Director, Edinburgh Technopole Co. Ltd; b. 30.9.25, Kirknewton; m., Agnes Whitelaw Frew. Educ. Lanark Grammar School; Edinburgh University. Assistant Economist, West of Scotland Agricultural College, 1946-47; Lecturer in Agriculture, Durham School of Agriculture, 1947-50; Lecturer, then Senior Lecturer, Edinburgh University, 1950-68; Director, Hill Farming Research Organisation, 1968-80; Professor of Agriculture, Glasgow University, and Principal, West of Scotland Agricultural College, 1980-87. Member: Farm Animal Welfare Council, Hill Farming Advisory Committee, Scotland; George Hedley Memorial Award for services to the sheep industry; Massey Ferguson Award for services to British agriculture; Sir William Young Award for services to livestock production in Scotland; Hon. Assoc., RCVS. Address: (h.) Bruaich, Hazlieburn, West Linton, Peeblesshire.

Cunningham, Very Rev. Monsignor John, JCD. Parish Priest, St. Patrick's Greenock, since 1992; Chairman, Roman Catholic Scottish National Tribunal, 1986-92; Papal Chaplain, since 1994; b. 22.2.38, Paisley. Educ. St. Mary's College, Blairs, Aberdeen; St. Peter's College, Cardross; Scots College and Gregorian University, Rome. Assistant Priest, Our Lady of Lourdes, Bishopton, 1964-69; Professor of Canon Law, St. Peter's College, Cardross and Newlands (Glasgow), 1967-81; Advocate of the Roman Catholic Scottish National Tribunal, 1970-82; Assistant Priest, St. Columba's, Renfrew, 1974-86; Vice-President, RC Scottish National Tribunal, 1982-86. Address: 5 Orangefield Place, Greenock, PA15 1YX; T.-01475 720223.

Cunningham, Roseanna, MP. MP (SNP), Perth and Kinross, since 1995; b. 27.7.51, Glasgow. Educ. University of Western Australia. SNP Research Department, 1976-79; law degree, Edinburgh University; Trainee Solicitor, Dumbarton District Council, 1983-86; Glasgow District Council, 1986-89; private practice as a Solicitor, 1989-90; called to the Scottish Bar, 1990. Recreations: martial art; reading; cinema; cats. Address: (b.) House of Commons, Westminster, London, SW1A 0AA.

Cunningham-Jardine, Ronald Charles. Lord Lieutenant, Dumfries, since 1991; Farmer; b. 19.9.31, Edinburgh; m., Constance Mary Teresa Inglis; 1 s.; 1 d. Educ. Ludgrove; Eton; Royal Military Academy, Sandhurst. Royal Scots Greys (retired as Captain), 1950-58. Recreations: all country sports. Address: (h.) Fourmerkland, Lockerbie, Dumfriesshire, DG11 1EH; T.-01387 810226.

Curnow, John, BMedSci (Hon), BM, BS. Consultant, Communicable Disease and Environmental Medicine, Grampian Health Board, since 1990; Senior Clinical Lecturer in Public Health Medicine, Aberdeen University, since 1990; Medical Officer, No. 2 Maritime Headquarters Unit, since 1991; b. 25.8.42, Bodmin, Cornwall; m., Mary Elizabeth; 1 s.; 2 d. Educ. Churston Ferras Grammar School; Nottingham University. Commissioned Officer, RAF (Pilot), 1962-80; Nottingham University, 1980-85; NHS, 1985-86; Registrar, Senior Registrar, Trent Training Scheme for Community Medicine, 1986-89; Consultant, Public Health Medicine, Central Nottingham Health Authority, 1989-90. Member, Executive Council, Royal Environmental Health Institute of Scotland, since 1994; Fellow, Society of Public Health; Expedition Trainer, Duke of Edinburgh Award Scheme. Recreations: mountain walking; field sports. Address: (h.) Chapel Croft, Arbuthnott, Laurencekirk, AB30 1NA.

Curran, Professor Sir Samuel Crowe, Kt, DL, MA, BSc, PhD, DSc, FInstP, FInstE, FRSE, FRS, CEng, DEng, FEng. Visiting Professor of Energy Studies, Glasgow University; Scientific Adviser to various organisations; Fellow of Strathclyde University; b. 23.5.12, Ballymena, Northern Ireland; m.; 3 s.; 1 d. Educ. Wishaw High School; Glasgow University; Cambridge University; California University. Research, Glasgow University, Cambridge University; war research, MAP and Ministry of Supply in radar and atom bomb (Manhattan project); staff, Physics Department, Glasgow University; Chief Scientist, UKAEA at AWRE (also on management board, UKAEA, Harwell); Principal, Royal College of Science and Technology, Glasgow; Principal and Vice-Chancellor, Strathclyde University. Publications: books on nuclear radiation, energy, and issues in science and higher education. Recreations: golf; horology. Address: (h.) 93 Kelvin Court, Glasgow, G12 OAH; T.-0141-334 8329.

Currie, Alexander Monteith, OBE, BA, BLitt, Dr hc (Edin), HonLLD (Sheffield). Secretary, Edinburgh University, 1978-89; b. 2.5.26, Stevenston; m., Pamela Mary Breeze; 2 s. Educ. Stevenston Higher Grade School; Portmadoc Grammar School; Bangor University; St. Catherine's College, Oxford. Administrative Officer, Manchester University, 1952-61; Academic Secretary, Liverpool University, 1962-65; Registrar and Secretary, Sheffield University, 1965-78. Officer (First Class), Royal Order of the Polar Star (Sweden). Address: (h.) 13 Moray Place, Edinburgh, EH3 6DT; T.-0131-225 7775.

Currie, Heriot Whitson, QC; b. 23.6.52. Admitted, Faculty of Advocates, 1979; called to the Bar, Gray's Inn, 1991.

Currie, John (Ian) C., CChem, MRSC, FIWEM. Director and River Inspector, Tweed River Purification Board, since 1964; b. 19.10.33, Glasgow; m., Margaret A.; 3 s.; 1 d. Educ. Shawlands Academy, Glasgow; Paisley Technical College. Assistant Inspector and Chemist, Tweed River Purification Board, 1955-61; Assistant Inspector, Clyde River Purification Board, 1961-64; Pollution Prevention Officer, Usk River Authority, 1964. Recreation: golf. Address: (b.) Burnbrae, Mossilee Road, Galashiels; T.-01896 752425.

Currie, Ken. Painter; b. 1960, North Shields. Educ. Paisley College; Glasgow School of Art. Worked on two films about Glasgow and Clyde shipbuilding, 1983-85; specialises in political realism, including a series of murals for the People's Palace Museum, Glasgow, on the socialist history of the city.

Curtis, Professor Adam Sebastian Genevieve, MA, PhD. Professor of Cell Biology, Glasgow University, since 1967; b. 3.1.34, London; m., Ann Park; 2 d. Educ. Aldenham School; Kings College, Cambridge. University College, London: Honorary Research Assistant, 1957-62, Lecturer in Zoology, 1962-67. Director, Company of Biologists Ltd., since 1961; Governor, Westbourne School, 1985-90; Council Member, Royal Society of Edinburgh, 1983-86; President, Society of Experimental Biology, 1991-93; Editor, Scottish Diver magazine, 1978-91, and since 1994; President, Scottish Sub-Aqua Club, 1972-76. Recreations: sports diving; gardening. Address: (h.) 2 Kirklee Circus, Glasgow, G12 OTW; T.-0141-339 2152.

Curtis, Professor David James, BSc, PhD, FZS, CBiol, FIBiol. Professor of Biology, Paisley University, since 1990; Tutor in Biology and Psychology, Open University, since 1973; Ecologist; b. 5.4.45, Liverpool; m., Margaret Angela Lacey; 2 d. Educ. St. Mary's College, Crosby; Liverpool University. Lecturer in Biology, Paisley College of Technology, 1970-81; Senior Lecturer in Biology, Paisley College of Technology, 1981-90; edited five books, written many scientific papers and reports; organised international conferences about environmental conservation; Hon. Secretary, Scottish Environmental Education Council and Director, Scottish Environmental Information Network for Education, 1983-91; Co-Director, Scottish Chough Study Group, since 1988; Founding Co-Director, European Forum on Birds and Pastoralism, since 1988; Board Member, Clyde River Purification Board, 1984-92; Member, Species Survival Commission (Steppe and Grassland Birds), IUCN - World Conservation Union, since 1992. Recreations: motor-caravanning; walking; bird-watching; jogging. Address: (b.) Department of Biological Sciences, Paisley University, High Street, Paisley, PA1 2BE; T.-0141-848 3119.

Cuschieri, Professor Alfred, MD, ChM, FRCSEd, FRCSEng, FIBiol. Professor and Head, Department of Surgery, Dundee University, since 1976; b. 30.9.38, Malta; m., Dr. M.P. Holley; 3 d. Educ. St. Aloysius College; Royal University of Malta; Liverpool University. Lecturer/Senior Lecturer/Reader in Surgery, then Professor of Surgery, Liverpool University. Recreations: fishing; music. Address: (h.) 6 Balnacarron Avenue, St. Andrews, KY16 9LT; T.-01382 60111.

Cusine, Professor Douglas James, LLB. Professor, Department of Conveyancing and Professional Practice of Law, Aberdeen University, since 1990; Member, Council, Law Society of Scotland, since 1988; Member, Lord President's Advisory Council on Messengers-at-Arms and Sheriff Officers, since 1989; b. 2.9.46, Glasgow; m., Marilyn Calvert Ramsay; 1 s.; 1 d. Educ. Hutchesons' Boys' Grammar School; Glasgow University. Solicitor, 1971; Lecturer in Private Law: Glasgow University, 1974-76, Aberdeen University, 1977-82; Senior Lecturer, 1982-90. Publications: Marine Pollution: Law and Practice (Co-Editor), 1980; Cases and Materials in Commercial Law (Co-Editor), 1987; A Scots Conveyancing Miscellany (Editor), 1987; New Reproductive Techniques: a legal perspective, 1988; Law and Practice of Diligence (Co-author), 1989; Reproductive Medicine and the Law (Co-Editor), 1990; Standard Securities, 1990; various articles on medico-legal issues and conveyancing. Recreations: swimming; walking; bird-watching. Address: (b.) Aberdeen University, Taylor Building, Regent Walk, Old Aberdeen AB9 2UB.

Cuthbert, James R., MA, MSc, DPhil. Chief Statistician, Scottish Office, since 1988; b. 20.7.46, Irvine. Educ. Glasgow University; Sussex University. Lecturer in Statistics, Glasgow University, 1970-74; civil servant (Scottish Office and HM Treasury), since 1974. Address: (b.) Scottish Office, New St. Andrew's House, Edinburgh, EH1 3SX.

Cuthbert, Thomas Paterson, MA (Hons), MEd. Regional Manager (Scotland), ATB — Landbase, since 1993; b. 20.12.57, Dunfermline; m., Margaret; 2 d. Educ. Queen Anne High School, Dunfermline; Edinburgh University. British Universities Soccer Internationalist, 1980. Teacher, Alloa Academy, 1981-87; Research and Development Officer, Scottish Vocational Education Council, 1987-88; Project Development Officer, Fife Education Department, 1989-91; Business Development and Training Manager, Scottish Association of Master Bakers, 1991-93. Recreations: sport, including football, tennis and golf; current affairs; cinema; collecting classic Westerns; reading history. Address: (b.) The Rural Centre, West Mains, Ingliston, Newbridge, Midlothian, EH28 8NZ; T.-0131-335 3830.

Cuthbertson, Iain, MA (Hons), FRSAMD. Actor; b. 4.1.30. Educ. Glasgow Academy; Aberdeen Grammar School; Aberdeen University. General Manager/Director of Productions, Citizens' Theatre, Glasgow, 1962-65; Associate Director, Royal Court Theatre, London, 1965; Director, Perth Theatre, 1967-68; sometime Administrator, Playhouse Theatre, Nottingham; stage performances include title roles in Armstrong's Last Goodnight (Citizens'), The Wallace (Edinburgh Festival), Serjeant Musgrave's Dance (Royal Court), Sutherland's Law (TV series); 1,500 broadcasts; TV work includes Budgie, Charles Endell Esq.; premiere of A Drunk Man Looks at the Thistle, set to music and dance; Hon. LLD, Aberdeen University; former Board Member, Scottish Theatre Company; former Hon. President, SCDA; Visiting Stage Director and Tutor, Royal Scottish Academy of Music and Drama. Recreations: countryside; sailing. Address: (b.) Janet Welch, Personal Management, 32 Hill Street, Richmond, Surrey, TW9 1TW.

Cuthbertson, Ian Jardine, LLB, NP, MIPA, MSPI, FInstD. Solicitor, Notary Public and Licensed Insolvency Practitioner; Partner, Dorman, Jeffrey & Co., Solicitors, Glasgow and Edinburgh, since 1979; b. 8.5.51, Glasgow; m., Sally Jane; 1 s.; 2 d. Educ. Jordanhill College School, Glasgow; Glasgow University. Apprenticeship, Messrs Boyds; admitted as Solicitor, 1974; Partner, Messrs Boyds, 1978; jointly founded firm of Dorman Jeffrey & Co., 1979. Honorary Legal Adviser, Glasgow Group, Riding for the Disabled Association. Recreations: watching football and rugby. Address: (b.) Madeleine Smith House, 6/7 Blythswood Square, Glasgow; T.-041-221 9880; 20 Ainslie Place, Edinburgh; T.-0131-225 9999.

Cutler, Timothy Robert (Robin), CBE, BSc, DSc. Director General, Forestry Commission, since 1990; b. 24.7.34, India; m., Ishbel W.M.; 1 s.; 1 d. Educ. Banff Academy; Aberdeen University. Colonial Forest Service, Kenya, 1958-64; New Zealand Government Forestry, 1964-90, latterly Chief Executive, New Zealand Ministry of Forestry. Recreations: Rotary; tennis; golf; travel. Address: (b.) 231 Corstorphine Road, Edinburgh, EH12 7AT; T.-0131-334 0303.

Czerkawska, Catherine Lucy, MA (Hons); MA (postgraduate). Novelist and Dramatist; b. 3.12.50, Leeds; m., Alan Lees; 1 s. Educ. Queen Margaret's Academy, Ayr; St. Michael's Academy, Kilwinning; Edinburgh University; Leeds University. Wrote and published two books of poetry (White Boats and a Book of Men); taught EFL in Finland and Poland for three years; returned to Scotland to work as Community Writer in Fife; thereafter, full-time freelance writer working on radio and television drama, original plays and adaptations, short stories, features, etc.; author, Shadow of the Stone and The Golden Apple; Pye Radio Award for Best Play of 1980, O Flower of Scotland; Scottish Radio Industries Club Award, 1983, for Bonnie Blue Hen. Recreations: travel; films; local history; swimming; genealogy. Address: c/o Peters Fraser and Dunlop, 5th Floor, The Chambers, Chelsea Harbour, Lots Road, London, SW10 0XF; T.-0171-376 7676.

D

Dagg, John Hunter, MD (Hons), FRCPGlas, FRCPEdin. Consultant Physician, Western Infirmary, Glasgow, since 1972; Honorary Lecturer in Medicine, Glasgow University, since 1962; b. 23.3.33, Rutherglen. Educ. High School of Glasgow; Glasgow University. Junior hospital posts, Glasgow and Paisley, 1958-65; Senior US Public Health Service Fellow, University of Washington Medical School, 1965-67; Senior Wellcome Fellow in Clinical Science, University Department of Medicine, Western Infirmary, Glasgow, 1968-72. Member, Board of Examiners, Royal Colleges of Physicians, UK. Recreations: classical music, especially as pianist; hill-walking; gardening. Address: (h.) Ardvulan, Gartmore, By Stirling, FK8 3RJ.

Daiches, Professor David, CBE, MA (Edin), DPhil (Oxon), Hon. DLitt (Edinburgh, Glasgow, Sussex, Brown, Guelph), Docteur de l'Universite (Sorbonne), DUniv (Stirling), Dottore in Lettere (Bologna). Writer; b. 2.9.12, Sunderland; m., Isobel J. Mackay (deceased); 1 s.; 2 d. Educ. George Watson's College, Edinburgh; Edinburgh University; Balliol College, Oxford. Professor of English, Cornell University, 1946-51; University Lecturer in English and Fellow of Jesus College, Cambridge, 1951-61; Professor of English, Sussex University, 1961-77; Director, Institute for Advanced Studies in the Humanities, Edinburgh University, 1980-86. President, Saltire Society, 1981-87, now Hon. President; Past President, Association for Scottish Literary Studies. Publications: numerous works of criticism and biography, including A Critical History of English Literature; Robert Burns; Sir Walter Scott and His World; The Paradox of Scottish Culture; God and the Poets (Gifford Lectures, 1983). Recreations: music; talking. Address: (h.) 22 Belgrave Crescent, Edinburgh, EH4 3AL.

Daiches, Lionel Henry, MA, LLB. Queen's Counsel, since 1956; Fellow, International Academy of Trial Lawyers, since 1976; b. 8.3.11, Sunderland; 2 s. Educ. George Watson's College, Edinburgh; Edinburgh University. Solicitor, Scotland, 1936-39; Army service, 1940-46, including Judge Advocate-General's Branch, Central Mediterranean Forces, North Africa and Italy (including Anzio Beachhead); Advocate, Scots Bar, 1946; QC Scotland, 1956; broadcaster on television and radio. Publication: Russians at Law, 1960. Recreations: walking and talking. Address: (h.) 10 Heriot Row, Edinburgh, EH3 6HU; T.-0131-556 4144.

Dake, Laurence Patrick, OBE, BSc (Hons). Consultant, Reservoir Engineering (Hydrocarbon), since 1982; Honorary Professor, Petroleum Engineering, Heriot Watt University, since 1982; b. 11.3.41, Warrington; m., Grace Anderson. Educ. Douglas High School, Isle of Man; Glasgow University. Reservoir Engineer, Shell International, 1964-74; Head of Reservoir Engineering Training, The Hague, Holland, 1974-78; Chief Reservoir Engineer, BNOC, Glasgow, 1978-82. Adviser to governments, the Bank of Scotland, and oil companies; worked on more than 100 projects worldwide; awarded OBE for services to reservoir engineering. Publications: Fundamentals of Reservoir Engineering, 1978; The Practice of Reservoir Engineering, 1994. Recreations: golf; cooking. Address: The Chapel, 10 Dublin Meuse, Edinburgh, EH3 6NW; T.-0131-558 3147.

Dalby, Martin, BMus, ARCM. Composer; freelance music producer; b. 25.4.42, Aberdeen; m., Hilary. Educ. Aberdeen Grammar School; Royal College of Music. Music Producer, BBC Radio 3, 1965-71; Cramb Research Fellow in Composition, Glasgow University, 1971-72; Head of Music, BBC Scotland, 1972-90; Executive Music Producer, BBC Scotland, 1990-93. Recreations: flying; railways; bird-watching; hill-walking. Address: (h.) 23 Muirpark Way, Drymen, near Glasgow, G63 ODX; T.-01360 660427.

Dale, Brian Graeme, LLB, WS, NP. Partner, Brooke & Brown, WS, Dunbar, since 1974; Convener, Standing Committee, General Synod, Scottish Episcopal Church, since 1992; b. 20.11.46, London; m., Judith Gail de Beaufort Franklin; 4 s.; 2 d. Educ. Bristol Grammar School; Aberdeen University. Legal apprentice, Shepherd & Wedderburn, WS, Edinburgh, 1968-70; Assistant, then Partner, Stuart & Stuart WS, Edinburgh, 1970-85; Treasurer, 1971-95, Secretary, 1974-90, Registrar, 1974, Diocese of Edinburgh, Scottish Episcopal Church; Honorary Secretary, Abbeyfield Society (Dunbar) Ltd. Recreations: music; armchair sport; singing; family life. Address: (h.) 5 The Doon, Spott, Dunbar, East Lothian; T.-Dunbar 862059.

Dale, Professor John Egerton, BSc, PhD, FRSE, FIBiol. Emeritus Professor of Plant Physiology, Edinburgh University, since 1993; b. 13.2.32, London; m., Jacqueline Joyce Benstock; 1 s.; 2 d. Educ. City of London School; Kings College, London. Plant Physiologist, Empire Cotton Growing Corporation, Uganda, 1956-61; Edinburgh University: Lecturer in Botany, then Reader, 1961-85, Professor of Plant Physiology, 1985-93, Head, Division of Biological Sciences, 1990-93. Secretary, Society for Experimental Biology, 1974-79; Secretary General, Federation of European Societies of Plant Physiology, 1978-84. Publications: 100 papers on growth of leaves and related topics. Recreations: travel; gardening. Address: (h.) The Old Bothy, Drem, North Berwick, EH39 5AP; T.-01620 850394.

Dalhousie, Earl of (Simon Ramsay), KT, GCVO, GBE, MC, LLD. Lord Lieutenant, County of Angus, 1967-89; Lord Chamberlain to Queen Elizabeth, the Queen Mother, 1965-92; Chancellor, Dundee University, 1977-92; b. 17.10.14, London; m., Margaret Elizabeth Mary Stirling; 3 s.; 2 d. Educ. Eton; Christ Church, Oxford. Major, 4/5 Black Watch TA; served overseas, 1939-45 (prisoner); MP, Forfar, 1945-50; Conservative Whip, 1946-48; Governor-General, Federation of Rhodesia and Nyasaland, 1957-63. Address: (h.) Brechin Castle, Brechin, Angus; T.-0135-62 2176.

Dalkeith, Earl of (Richard Walter John Montagu Douglas Scott). Member: Scottish Natural Heritage, since 1992, Independent Television Commission, since 1991, Millennium Fund Commission, since 1994; b. 14.2.54; m., Lady Elizabeth Kerr; 2 s.; 2 d. Son and heir of 9th Duke of Buccleuch (qv). Address: (h.) Dabton, Thornhill, Dumfriesshire.

Dalrymple, Major The Hon. Colin James, DL, JP, BA. Farmer and Landowner, since 1956; b. 19.2.20, Ford, Midlothian; m., Fiona Jane Edwards (qv); 1 s.; 3 d. Educ. Eton College; Trinity College, Cambridge. Served with Scots Guards, 1939-56; Member, Midlothian County Council, 1967-75; President, Scottish Landowners Federation. Recreations: shooting; fishing. Address: Oxenfoord Mains, Dalkeith.

Dalrymple, Fiona Jane, OBE. Chairman, Home Grown Cereals Authority Advisory Committee, Food From Britain, since 1992; Board Member, Scottish Agricultural College; b. 15.1.34, London; m., Hon. Colin Dalrymple (qv); 1 s.; 2 d. Educ. Downham. Former Convener, Pigs Committee and Animal Health and Welfare Group, National Farmers Union of Scotland; former Hon. President, NFU of Scotland; former Chairman, Large White Breed Council. Organiser, Midlothian, Scotland's Gardens Scheme. Recreations: gardening; needlework; bridge. Address: (h.) Oxenfoord Mains, Dalkeith, Midlothian; T.-01875 320208.

Dalrymple, Sir Hew (Fleetwood) Hamilton-, 10th Bt (created 1697), KCVO, 1985 (CVO, 1974). Lord Lieutenant, East Lothian, since 1987; Vice-Chairman, Scottish & Newcastle Breweries, 1983-86 (Director, 1967-86); Chairman, Scottish American Investment Co., 1985-91 (Director, since 1967); b. 9.4.26; m., Lady Anne-Louise Mary Keppel; 4 s. Educ. Ampleforth; Staff College, Camberley, 1957. Commissioned Grenadier Guards, 1944; DAAG HQ 3rd Division, 1958-60; Regimental Adjt., Grenadier Guards, 1960-62; retired, 1962; Captain, Queen's Bodyguard for Scotland (Royal Company of Archers). DL, East Lothian, 1964; JP, 1987. Address: Leuchie, North Berwick, East Lothian; T.-North Berwick 2903.

Dalrymple, John Francis, BA, PhD, MInstP, CPhys, FSS. Director, Scottish Quality Management Centre, Stirling University, since 1990 (Head, Department of Management Science, 1990-92, Senior Lecturer, 1989-90, Lecturer, 1979-89); Governor, BMT Quality Assurance Ltd., since 1990; Chairman, Scottish Association of Children's Panels, 1983-88; b. 18.9.49, Rosyth; 1 s.; 3 d. Educ. St. Andrew's High School, Kirkcaldy; Stirling University; Strathclyde University. Research Fellow, then Lecturer, Department of Applied Physics, Strathclyde University, 1974-79. Member, Strathclyde Region Children's Panel, since 1977. Recreations: skiing; walking; reading; swimming. Address: (b.) Management Science, School of Management, Stirling University, Stirling, FK9 4LA; T.-01786 467360.

Dalrymple-Hamilton, Christian Margaret, MBE, DL; b. 20.9.19, Devon. President, Wigtownshire Girl Guides. Address: (h.) Cladyhouse, Cairnryan, Stranraer, Wigtownshire.

Dalrymple-Hamilton of Bargany, Captain North Edward Frederick, CVO, MBE, DSC, JP, DL (Ayrshire). Lieutenant, Queen's Bodyguard for Scotland (Royal Company of Archers); b. 17.2.22; m., 1, Hon. Mary Colville (deceased); 2 s.; 2, Antoinette Beech. Educ. Eton. Director of Naval Signals, 1965, Director, Weapons Equipment Surface, 1967, retired, 1970. Address: (h.) Lovestone House, Bargany, Girvan, Ayrshire, KA26 9RF; T.-01465 871227.

Dalyell, Tam. MP (Labour), Linlithgow (formerly West Lothian), since 1962; Weekly Columnist, New Scientist, since 1967; b. 9.8.32, Edinburgh; m., Kathleen Wheatley; 1 s.; 1 d. Educ. Edinburgh Academy; Harecroft; Eton; King's College, Cambridge; Moray House, Edinburgh. National Service, Scots Greys; Teacher, Bo'ness Academy, 1957-61; Deputy Director of Studies, Ship-School Dunera, 1961-62; Member, Public Accounts Committee, 1962-66; PPS to R.H.S. Crossman, 1964-70; Vice-Chairman, Parliamentary Labour Party, 1974-76; Member, European Parliament, 1975-78; Member, National Executive Committee, Labour Party, 1986-87;Member, Advisory Council on Biological Sciences, Edinburgh University; a Vice-President, Research Defence Society; Hon. Doctor of Science, Edinburgh University, 1994. Publications: Case for Ship Schools, 1959; Ship-School Dunera, 1961; Devolution: the end of Britain?, 1978; A Science Policy for Britain, 1983; One Man's Falklands, 1983; Misrule, 1987; Dick Crossman: a portrait, 1989. Address: (h.) The Binns, Linlithgow, EH49 7NA; T.-0506-83 4255.

Dalzel-Job, Lt. Cdr. Patrick. Deputy Lieutenant, Lochalsh, since 1979; b. 1.6.13, London; m., Bjorg Bangsund (deceased); 1 s. Educ. Berkhamsted; in Switzerland. Owner/Master, topsail schooner Mary Fortune, mainly Norwegian and Arctic waters, until start of Second World War; as a junior Sub Lt., organised landing of Allied Expeditionary Force, North Norway, 1940, and evacuation of civilians from Narvik before German bombing; thanked by King of Norway; awarded Knight's Cross (1st Class) of St. Olav with swords; Special Service Operations, Norway, France, Germany; Canadian Navy, post-war; retired to West Highlands, 1960. Publications: The Settlers, 1957; From Arctic Snow to Dust of Normandy, 1991. Recreations: skiing; sailing; woodland garden. Address: (h.) Nead-An-Eoin, by Plockton, Ross-shire; T.-01599 544 244.

Daniels, Peter William, MA (Hons). Chief Executive, Clydesdale District Council, since 1983; b. 8.6.49, Wishaw; m., Anne; 3 s.; 1 d. Educ. Brandon High School, Motherwell; Dalziel High School, Motherwell; Glasgow University; Jordanhill College of Education. Lecturer (A) in Public Administration, Bell College of Technology, Hamilton, 1972-75; Personal Assistant to Chief Executive, Renfrew District Council, 1975-81; Assistant Chief Executive, Leicester City Council, 1981-83. Former elected Member, East Kilbride District Council; former Vice-Chairman, Manpower Committee, COSLA. Recreations: family; running; anything to do with Motherwell Football Club; classical music; playing piano and clarinet. Address: (b.) Clydesdale District Council, District Offices, South Vennel, Lanark, ML11 7JT; T.-Lanark 661331.

Darby, John Kenneth, BSc, PhD, CEng, MBCS, CPhys, FInstP. Assistant Principal, Napier University, since 1985; b. 7.2.40, Aldridge; m., Marion Christina; 2 s.; 1 d. Educ. King Edward VI School, Lichfield; Sheffield University. Research Officer, Oxford University, 1964; ICI Research Fellow, Edinburgh University, 1965; Computer Instructor, Rolls-Royce Ltd., 1968; Consultant, SPL Ltd., 1971; Principal Lecturer, Teesside Polytechnic, 1973, Head, Department of Computer Science, 1978. Member, SHEFC, since 1992. Recreations: game fishing; collecting. Address: (b.) 219 Colinton Road, Edinburgh, EH14 1DJ; T.-0131-444 2266.

Dareau, Margaret Grace, MA. Senior Editor, Dictionary of the Older Scottish Tongue, since 1984; b. 11.3.44, Dumfries; m., Michel Dareau; 1 s.; 2 d. Educ. Annan Academy; Edinburgh University. Research Assistant on Middle English Dialects Atlas, 1967; Kennedy Scholarship to study linguistics, MIT, 1967; began work at Dictionary of Older Scottish Tongue, 1968; Editor, Concise Scots Dictionary, 1976-77, 1980-84. Recreation: horse riding. Address: (h.) The Old Manse, Howgate, Penicuik, EH26 8QB; T.-01968 673028.

Darling, Alistair Maclean, LLB. MP (Labour), Edinburgh Central, since 1987; Member, Faculty of Advocates, since 1984; b. 28.11.53, London; m., Margaret Vaughan; 1 s.; 1 d. Educ. Loretto School; Aberdeen University. Solicitor, 1978-83; Advocate, since 1984; Member, Lothian Regional Council, 1982-87; Member, Lothian and Borders Police Board, 1982-87; Governor, Napier College, 1985-87; Front-Bench Spokesman, Treasury Affairs, since 1992. Address: (b.) 78 Buccleuch Street, Edinburgh; T.-0131-662 0123.

Darwent, Rt. Rev. Frederick Charles, LTh (Hon), JP. Bishop of Aberdeen and Orkney, 1978-92; b. 20.4.27, Liverpool; m., 1, Edna Lilian Waugh (deceased); 2 d.; 2, Roma Evelyn Fraser. Educ. Warbreck School, Liverpool; Ormskirk Grammar School; Wells Theological College, Somerset. Followed a banking career, 1943-61; War Service, Far East, 1945-48; ordained Deacon, 1963, Priest, 1964, Diocese of Liverpool; Curate, Pemberton, Wigan, 1963-65; Rector: Strichen, 1965-71, New Pitsligo, 1965-78, Fraserburgh, 1971-78; Canon, St. Andrew's Cathedral, Aberdeen, 1971; Dean of Aberdeen and Orkney, 1973-78. Recreations: amateur stage (acting and production); calligraphy; music. Address: (h.) 107 Osborne Place, Aberdeen, AB2 4DD; T.-01224 646497.

Das, Sachinandan, MB, BS, FRCR, DMRT. Consultant in administrative charge, Ninewells Hospital, Dundee, and Head, University Department, Dundee University, since 1987, Clinical Director, since 1991; Chairman, Area Oncology Committee, since 1987; Council Member, Scottish Radiological Society, since 1987; Regional

Postgraduate Education Advisor in Radiotherapy and Oncology, since 1987; b. 1.8.44, Cuttack, India; m., Dr. Subhalaxmi; 1 s.; 1 d. Educ. Ravenshaw Collegiate School; SCB Medical College, Cuttack, India; Utkal University. Senior House Officer in Radiotherapy, Plymouth General Hospital, 1969-70; Registrar in Radiotherapy and Oncology, then Senior Registrar, Mersey Regional Centre for Radiotherapy, Liverpool, 1970-77; Member: Standing Scottish Committee, National Medical Consultative Committee, Scottish Paediatric Oncology Group, Joint Radiological Safety Committee, Radiation Hazards Sub-Committee, Unit Medical and Dental Advisory Committee. Recreations: hill-walking; table tennis; reading. Address: (h.) Grapevine, 42 Menzieshill Road, Dundee, DD2 1PU; T.-Dundee 642915.

Datta, Dipankar, MB, BS, FRCPGlas. Consultant Physician (with special interest in gastroenterology), since 1975; Honorary Senior Clinical Lecturer and Clinical Sub-Dean, Glasgow University; Chairman, Scottish India Forum; Founder Director, Scottish Overseas Aid; b. 30.1.33, Chittagong, India; m., Dr. J.B. Datta (qv); 1 s.; 1 d. Educ. Calcutta University. Former Member, Central Executive Committee, Scottish Council, United Nations Association; former Vice Chairman, UN Association, Glasgow; former Chairman, Overseas Doctors' Association, Scottish Division; former Member, Lanarkshire Health Board; Member, Executive Committee, Scottish Council, Royal Commonwealth Society for the Blind; former Member, Senate, Glasgow University; Member, General Medical Council; Chairman, British Medical Association, Lanarkshire; Member, Scottish Council, BMA; Chairman, South Asia Voluntary Enterprise. Recreations: reading - history, economics and international politics. Address: (h.) 9 Kirkvale Crescent, Newton Mearns, Glasgow, G77 5HB; T.-0141-639 1515.

Davenport, Professor John, BSc, MSc, PhD, DSc, FIBiol, FZS. Director, University Marine Biological Station, Millport, since 1991; Professor of Marine Biology, London University; b. 12.2.46; m., Julia Ladner; 2 d. Educ. Bablake School, Coventry; London University; Southampton University; University of Wales. Demonstrator in Marine Biology, University of Wales at Bangor, 1970-72; Researcher, NERC Unit of Marine Invertebrate Biology, 1972-83 (promoted Principal Scientific Officer, 1980); Lecturer, then Senior Lecturer, School of Animal Biology, University of Wales at Bangor, 1983-88; Reader in Marine Biology, School of Ocean Sciences, Marine Sciences Laboratories, Menai Bridge, 1988-91. Publications: Animal Osmoregulation (Co-Author), 1981; Environmental Stress and Behavioural Adaptation, 1985; Animal Life at Low Temperature, 1992. Recreations: skiing; sailboarding; swimming; birding; badminton. Address: (b.) University Marine Biological Station, Isle of Cumbrae, KA28 0EG.

Davidson, Alan Ingram, ChM, FRCSEdin, DObstRCOG. Consultant Surgeon, Aberdeen Royal Infirmary, since 1974; Honorary Senior Lecturer in Surgery, Aberdeen University, since 1974; b. 25.3.35, Aberdeen; m., Margaret Elizabeth Mackay; 1 s.; 1 d. Educ. Robert Gordon's College, Aberdeen; Aberdeen University. House Officer, Aberdeen Royal Infirmary, 1959-60; National Service, Royal Army Medical Corps, 1960-62; Lecturer, Department of Pathology, Aberdeen, 1963-64; Registrar and Senior Registrar, Aberdeen Royal Infirmary, 1964-74. Recreations: gardening; watching TV; music. Address: (h.) 20 Hillview Road, Cults, Aberdeen; T.-Aberdeen 867347.

Davidson, Hon. Lord (Charles Kemp Davidson), MA, LLB, FRSE. Chairman, Scottish Law Commission, since 1988; Senator of the College of Justice, since 1983; Deputy Chairman, Boundaries Commission for Scotland, since 1985; b. 13.4.29, Edinburgh; m., Mary Mactaggart; 1 s.; 2 d. Educ. Fettes College, Edinburgh; Oxford University; Edinburgh University. Advocate, 1956; QC (Scot), 1969; Keeper, The Advocates Library, 1972-77; Vice Dean, Faculty of Advocates, 1977-79; Dean, 1979-83; Procurator to the General Assembly of the Church of Scotland, 1972-83; Chairman, National Health Service Tribunal for Scotland, 1970-83. Address: (h.) 22 Dublin Street, Edinburgh, EH1 3PP; T.-0131-556 2168.

Davidson, Professor Colin William, BSc, DipER, PhD, CEng, FIEE, FRSA. Consulting Engineer; b. 18.9.34, Edinburgh; m., Ranee M.N. Cleland; 2 d. Educ. George Heriot's School; Edinburgh University. Lecturer, Edinburgh University, 1956-61; Electronics Engineer, Nuclear Enterprises (GB) Ltd., 1961-64; Lecturer, Heriot-Watt College/University, 1964-67; Associate Professor, Chulalongkorn University, Bangkok, 1967-68; Heriot-Watt University: Senior Lecturer, 1968-85, Professor of Electrical Engineering, 1985-88, Dean of Engineering, 1976-79 and 1984-87, Head of Department, 1979-87. Member, Lothian Regional Council, 1990-94; Vice-President, Institution of Electrical Engineers, 1990-93; Liveryman, Worshipful Company of Engineers, City of London. Recreation: sailing (Royal Highland Yacht Club). Address: (h.) 20 East Barnton Avenue, Edinburgh, EH4 6AQ; T.-0131-336 5806.

Davidson, Professor Donald Allen, BSc, PhD. Professor of Environmental Science, Stirling University, since 1991; b. 27.4.45, Lumphanan; m., Caroline E. Brown; 1 s.; 2 d. Educ. Robert Gordon's College, Aberdeen; Aberdeen University; Sheffield University. Lecturer, St. David's University College, Wales, 1971-76; Lecturer, Senior Lecturer, Reader, Strathclyde University, 1976-86; Reader, Stirling University, 1986-91. Member of Council, Royal Scottish Geographical Society. Publications include: The Evaluation of Land Resources, 1992; many papers. Recreations: exploring the countryside; real ale. Address: (b.) Department of Environmental Science, Stirling University, FK9 4LA; T.-01786 467840.

Davidson, Duncan Lewis Watt, BSc (Hons), MB, ChB, FRCPEdin. Consultant Neurologist, Tayside Health Board, since 1976; Honorary Senior Lecturer in Medicine, Dundee University, since 1976; b. 16.5.40, Kingston, Jamaica; m., Dr. Anne V.M. Maiden; 4 s.; 1 d. Educ. Knox College, Jamaica; Edinburgh University. House Officer, Senior House Officer, Registrar and Senior Registrar posts in medicine and neurology, Edinburgh, 1966-75; Peel Travelling Fellowship, Montreal, 1973-74; MRC clinical scientific staff, MRC Brain Metabolism Unit, Edinburgh, 1975-76. Recreations: gardening; golf. Address: (h.) Brooksby, Queens Terrace, St. Andrews, Fife; T.-01334 76108.

Davidson, Eric Dalgleish, DA (Edin), RIBA, FRIAS. Director, Scottish Health Service, Common Services Agency, Building Division, 1985-89; b. 7.9.28, Musselburgh; m., June Mary Ryman; 2 s.; 2 d. Educ. Musselburgh Grammar School; Heriot-Watt University; Edinburgh College of Art. Assistant Regional Architect, South Eastern Regional Hospital Board, 1961-74; Lecturer in Advanced Practice and Management, Department of Architecture, Edinburgh University, 1966-74; Assistant Director and Chief Architect, Scottish Health Service, Common Services Agency, Building Division, 1974-85. Council Member, RIAS, 1984-88; Member, Scottish Building Contracts Committee, 1987-91; Member, Scottish Building Standards Committee (Research Sub-Committee), 1986-91; Committee Member, Disability Scotland; Vice Chairman, Corstorphine Trust. Address: (h.) 27 Belgrave Road, Edinburgh, EH12 6NG; T.-0131-334 5231.

Davidson, Ian Graham, MA (Hons). MP (Labour), Glasgow Govan, since 1992; b. 8.9.50, Jedburgh; m., Morag Mackinnon; 1 s.; 1 d. Educ. Jedburgh Grammar School; Galashiels Academy; Edinburgh University; Jordanhill College of Education. Chairman, Strathclyde

Education Committee, 1990-92; Chairman, COSLA Education Committee, 1990-92. Address: (b.) Constituency Office, 1829 Paisley Road West, Glasgow, G52 3SS; T.-0141-883 8336.

Davidson, Rev. Ian Murray Pollock, MBE, MA, BD. Minister, Allan Park South Church and Church of the Holy Rude, Stirling, 1985-94; Chairman, General Trustees, Church of Scotland, since 1993; b. 14.3.28, Kirriemuir; m., Isla; 2 s. Educ. Montrose Academy; St. Andrews University. National Service, 1949-51; Minister: Crieff North and West Church (St. Andrew's), 1955-61, Grange Church, Kilmarnock, 1961-67, Cambuslang Old Church, 1967-85; Convener, Maintenance of the Ministry Committee and Board, Church and Ministry Department, 1981-84; General Trustee, since 1975. Publications: At the Sign of the Fish (history of Cambuslang Old Parish Church), 1975; A Guide to the Church of the Holy Rude. Recreations: travel; photography; reading; writing. Address: (h.) 13/8 Craigend Park, Edinburgh, EH16 5XX; T.-0131-664 0074.

Davidson, John F., MB, ChB, FRCPEdin, FRCPath. Consultant Haematologist, Glasgow Royal Infirmary, since 1969; b. 11.1.34, Lumphanan; m., Laura G. Middleton; 1 s.; 1 d. Educ. Robert Gordon's College, Aberdeen; Aberdeen University. Surgeon Lt., RN; Registrar in Medicine, Aberdeen Royal Infirmary; Research Registrar in Medicine, then Senior Registrar in Haematology, Glasgow Royal Infirmary; Honorary Clinical Senior Lecturer, Glasgow University; Honorary Consultant Haematologist, Strathclyde University. Secretary, British Society for Haematalogy, 1983-86; President, British Society for Haematology, 1990-91; Chairman, BCSH Haemostasis and Thrombosis Task Force, 1986-81; Chairman, Steering Committee NEQAS in blood coagulation, 1986-91; Member, Council, Royal College of Pathologists, two terms; Secretary, Joint Committee on Haematology, Royal College of Pathologists and Royal College of Physicians; Editor, Progress in Fibrinolysis, Volumes I to VII; Chairman, International Committee on Fibrinolysis, 1976-84; Co-Editor in Chief, Fibrinolysis. Recreation: gardening. Address: (b.) Department of Haematology, Glasgow Royal Infirmary, Glasgow; T.-0141-304 4669.

Davidson, John Knight, OBE, MD, FRCPEdin, FRCPGlas, FRCR, FACR (Hon), FRACR (Hon). Consultant Radiologist; b. 17.8.25, Edinburgh; m., Edith E. McKelvie; 2 s.; 1 d. Educ. George Watson's Boys College, Edinburgh; Edinburgh University. Member, Council, Medical and Dental Defence Union; Member, Scottish Council, Scottish Conservative and Unionist Association; Member, BBC Medical Advisory Group; Non-Executive Director, Yorkhill NHS Trust, 1993-95; Consultant Radiologist in administrative charge, Western Infirmary and Gartnavel General, Glasgow, 1967-90; Royal College of Radiologists: Member, Council, 1984-87, Chairman, Examining Board, 1976-79, Scottish Committee, 1985-89; Member, Council, Royal Glasgow Institute of Fine Arts, 1978-88; Adviser in Hyperbaric Research, MRC and Aberdeen, 1970-92; Deputy President, Glasgow and Renfrewshire, British Red Cross Society, 1988-93. International Skeletal Society Silver Medal, 1992; Beaven Williams Professor, Australasia, 1977; Aggarwal Memorial Oration, India, 1988; Editor, Aseptic Necrosis of Bone and numerous publications. Recreations: golf; painting; bridge; meeting people; skiing. Address: (h.) 31 Newlands Road, Glasgow, G43 2JG; T.-0141-632 3113.

Davidson, Julie Wilson. Writer and Broadcaster; Television Critic/Columnist, The Herald, since 1981; Freelance Contributor, BBC, Granada TV, The Times, The Observer, etc., since 1981; b. Motherwell; m., Harry Reid (qv); 1 d. Educ. Aberdeen High School for Girls. Trainee Journalist, D.C. Thomson Ltd., Dundee, 1961-64; Feature Writer and Sub-Editor, Aberdeen Press & Journal, 1964-67;

The Scotsman: Feature Writer, 1967-77, Columnist, 1977-81. Columnist/Critic of the Year, Scottish Press Awards, 1985; Critic of the Year, Scottish Press Awards, 1988-89-92-94-95; Canada Travel Award, 1992. Recreations: reading; walking; travelling; lunching. Address: (h.) 15 Albion Buildings, Ingram Street, Glasgow; T.-041-552 8403.

Davidson, Neil Forbes, QC, BA, MSc, LLB, LLM; b. 13.9.50. Admitted, Faculty of Advocates, 1979; called to the Bar, Inner Temple, 1990; Commissioner, Scottish Council for International Arbitration, since 1990.

Davidson, Sheriff Richard Alexander, LLB, NP. Sheriff of Tayside Central and Fife at Dundee, since 1994; b. 3.11.47, Lennoxtown; m., Shirley Margaret Thomson; 1 s.; 1 d. Educ. Oban High School; Glasgow University. Apprentice Solicitor, 1969-72; Assistant Solicitor, 1972-76; Partner, Tindal Oatts, 1976-94. Member, Glasgow and North Argyll Legal Aid Committee, 1984-89. Recreations: popular music; golf; football; swimming; tennis; rearing children. Address: (b.) Sheriff Courthouse, West Bell Street, Dundee; T.-01382 226513.

Davidson, Professor Robert, MA, BD, DD, FRSE. Moderator, General Assembly of the Church of Scotland, 1990-91; Professor of Old Testament Language and Literature, Glasgow University, 1972-91; Principal, Trinity College, Glasgow, 1981-91; b. 30.3.27, Markinch, Fife; m., Elizabeth May Robertson; 5 s.; 4 d. Educ. Bell-Baxter School, Cupar; St. Andrews University. Lecturer in Biblical Studies, Aberdeen University, 1953-60; Lecturer in Hebrew and Old Testament Studies, St. Andrews University, 1960-66; Lecturer/Senior Lecturer in Old Testament, Edinburgh University, 1966-72. Publications: The Bible Speaks, 1959; The Old Testament, 1964; Geneses 1 - 11, 1973; Genesis 12 - 50, 1979; The Bible in Religious Education, 1979; The Courage to Doubt, 1983; Jeremiah Volume 1, 1983; Jeremiah Volume 2, Lamentations, 1985; Ecclesiastes, Song of Songs, 1986; Wisdom and Worship, 1990; A Beginner's Guide to the Old Testament, 1992. Recreations: music; gardening. Address: (h.) 30 Dumgoyne Drive, Bearsden, Glasgow, G61 3AP; T.-0141-942 1810.

Davidson, William Keith, CBE, JP; b. 20.11.26, Glasgow; m., Dr. Mary W.A. Davidson; 1 s.; 1 d. Educ. Coatbridge Secondary School; Glasgow University. Medical Officer, 1st Bn., RSF, 1950; Maj. 2 i/c 14 Field Ambulance, 1950-51; Medical Officer, i/c Holland and Belgium, 1952; General Medical Practitioner, 1953-90; Chairman, Glasgow Local Medical Committee, 1971-75; Chairman, Scottish General Medical Services Committee, 1972-75; Member, Scottish Council on Crime, 1972-75; Fellow, BMA, 1975; Deputy Chairman, General Medical Services Committee (UK), 1975-79; Member, Scottish Medical Practices Committee, 1968-80; Chairman, Scottish Council, BMA, 1978-81; Chairman, Scottish Health Services Planning Council, 1984-89; Member, Scottish Health Services Policy Board, 1985-89; Vice President, BMA, since 1983; Hon. President, Glasgow Eastern Medical Society, 1984-85; Member, General Medical Council, 1984-94; Fellow, Royal College of General Practitioners, since 1980; Member, Greater Glasgow Health Board, 1989-91; Chairman, Strathclyde Aids Forum, 1990-93; Chairman, Greater Glasgow Health Board Aids Forum, 1990-93; Chairman, Greater Glasgow Health Board Drugs & Alcohol Forum, 1990-93; Vice Chairman, Chryston High School Board, since 1990; Elder, Church of Scotland, since 1956. Recreation: gardening. Address: (h.) Dunvegan, Hornshill Farm Road, Stepps, Glasgow, G33 6DE; T.-0141-779 2103.

Davidson, William Powell, MREHIS, MInstWM, MILAM. Director of Environmental Health & Leisure Services, Stewartry District Council, since 1982; Chairman, Scottish Food and Drugs Co-ordinating Committee, since 1991; b. 28.8.48, Paisley; m., Elizabeth Ann Davidson; 1 s.

Educ. Camphill Senior Secondary School, Paisley; Langside College, Glasgow; Bell College, Hamilton. Trainee, then Assistant Sanitary Inspector, Renfrew County Council, 1966-71; Sanitary Inspector, Paisley Burgh Council, 1971-72; Assistant District Sanitary Inspector, Perth and Kinross Joint County Council, 1972-75; Area Environmental Health Officer, Argyll and Bute District Council, 1975-76; Regional Manager, Ciba Geigy Public Hygiene Project, Saudi Arabia, 1976-77; Senior Environmental Health Officer, Perth and Kinross District Council, 1977-79; Depute Director of Environmental Health, Stewartry District Council, 1979-82. Recreations: golf; gardening; travel; jogging; football. Address: (b.) Environmental Health & Leisure Services Department, Cannonwalls, High Street, Kirkcudbright.

Davie, Elspeth, DA. Writer; b. Kilmarnock; m., George Elder Davie; 1 d. Educ. George Watson's College; Edinburgh University; Edinburgh Art College. Taught Art for several years in the Borders, Aberdeen and Northern Ireland; author of four novels: Providings, Creating A Scene, Climbers on a Stair, Coming to Light; five collections of short stories: The Spark, The High Tide Talker, The Night of the Funny Hats, A Traveller's Room, Death of a Doctor; two Arts Council Awards; received Katherine Mansfield Prize, 1978. Recreations: reading; walking; films. Address: (h.) 155/17 Orchard Brae Gardens, Edinburgh, EH4; T.-0131-332 8297.

Davie, Ivor Turnbull, MB, ChB, FRCA, HonFCPS(Bd). Consultant Anaesthetist, Western General Hospital, Edinburgh, since 1971; Honorary Senior Lecturer, Edinburgh University, since 1979; Lecturer, Central Midwives Board (Scotland), since 1974; b. 23.2.35, Edinburgh; m., Jane Elizabeth Fleischmann; 1 s.; 1 d. Educ. Royal High School, Edinburgh; Edinburgh University. Member, Board of Examiners, Faculty of Anaesthetists, Royal College of Surgeons of England and Royal College of Anaesthetists, 1978-91; President, Edinburgh and East of Scotland Society of Anaesthetists, 1990-91; Tutor, Faculty of Anaesthetists, 1979-87; Regional Educational Adviser, College of Anaesthetists, since 1988; Member, Editorial Board, British Journal of Obstetrics and Gynaecology, 1980-84; Visiting Medical Officer, Westmead Centre, Sydney, NSW, 1983. Address: (b.) Department of Anaesthesia, Western General Hospital, Edinburgh, EH4 2XU; T.-0131-537 1652.

Davies, Professor Alun Millward, BSc, MB, ChB, PhD. Professor in Medical Science, St. Andrews University, since 1993; b. 2.8.55, Tredegar. Educ. Pontllanfraith Grammar School; Liverpool University; London University. Lecturer, Middlesex Hospital Medical School, London, 1982-83; Lecturer, then Senior Lecturer, then Reader in Neurobiology, St. George's Hosital Medical School, London, 1983-93. Recreations: playing piano and harpsichord; sketching; building musical instruments. Address: (b.) Bute Medical Building, St. Andrews University, St. Andrews, KY16 9TS; T.-01334 63219.

Davies, David Somerville, FTCL, ARCM. Conductor, Artistic Director, Paragon Ensemble Scotland, since 1985; b. 13.6.54, Dunfermline. Educ. Dunfermline High School; Royal Scottish Academy of Music; Edinburgh University; Marseille Conservatoire. Assistant Principal Flute, Scottish National Orchestra; Principal Flute, Scottish Opera; Freelance Conductor at home and overseas; recordings: two volumes of Contemporary Scottish Music, 1991, 1993; Lecturer and Head of Woodwind, Royal Scottish Academy of Music and Drama; Tovey Memorial Prize; Clutterbuck Scholarship; Sir James Caird Scholarship; Scottish Arts Council Music Award; Scottish International Education Trust Award; Performing Rights Society/Scottish Society of Composers Award for services to contemporary Scottish music. Recreations: reading; photography; computing.

Address: (b.) c/o Paragon Ensemble Scotland, 2 Port Dundas Place, Glasgow G2 3LB; T.-0141-332 9903.

Davies, Professor Graeme John, BE, MA, PhD, ScD, FEng. Principal and Vice-Chancellor, Glasgow University, since 1995; b. 7.4.37, New Zealand; m., Florence; 1 s.; 1 d. Educ. Mt. Albert Grammar School, Auckland; University of Auckland; Cambridge University. Junior Lecturer, University of Auckland, 1960-62; Lecturer, Cambridge University, 1962-77; Professor of Metallurgy, Sheffield University, 1978-86; Vice-Chancellor, Liverpool University, 1986-91; Chief Executive, Universities Funding Council, 1991-93; Chief Executive, Higher Education Funding Council for England, 1992-95. Hon. LLD, Liverpool, 1991; Hon. FRSNZ, 1993; Hon. DMet, Sheffield, 1995; Hon. DSc, Nottingham, 1995; Hon. FTCL, 1995; FIMechE; FIM; FRSA; CBIM; DL, Merseyside, 1989-93. Recreations: bird-watching; golf. Address: (b.) Glasgow University, Glasgow, G12 8QQ; T.-0141-330 4250.

Davies, Hywel William, MA. Chief Executive, Royal Highland and Agricultural Society of Scotland, since 1991; Director, Scottish Agricultural and Rural Development Centre, since 1991; Director, Scottish Farming and Countryside Educational Trust, since 1991; b. 28.6.45, Wales; m. Patricia Thornhill; 1 s.; 1 d. Educ. Harrow; Magdalene College, Cambridge. Army Officer, commissioned Royal Horse Guards (The Blues), 1965-87; commanded The Blues and Royals, 1984-87; defence and allied industries, 1988-91. Member, Committee, Order of St. John Association (Central Region); Panel Judge, British Driving Society. Recreations: country sports and horses (represented Great Britain at 4-in-hand carriage driving). Address: (h.) Peatland, Gatehead, Ayrshire, KA2 9AN; (b.) Ingliston, Edinburgh, EH28 8NF; T.-0131-333 2444.

Davies, Ivor, MA, DipEd, PhD, MILAM. Director of Planning, Scottish Sports Council, since 1975, and Director, Lottery Sports Fund, since 1994; b. Scotland. Educ. Edinburgh University. Founded and developed Department of Geography, Lakehead University, Thunder Bay, Ontario, and became first Chairman of Department. Recreations: sport; music. Address: (b.) Caledonia House, South Gyle, Edinburgh, EH12 9DQ; T.-0131-317 7200.

Davies, Professor Peter Anthony, BSc, DipEd, PhD, FRSE. Professor of Fluid Dynamics, Dundee University, since 1994; b. 7.11.44, N. Yorks; m., Ann Smith; 1 s. Educ. Grammar School, Yarm-on-Tees; Newcastle upon Tyne University. Royal Society Postdoctoral Fellow, International Meteorological Institute, Stockholm, 1971-73; Senior Research Associate, Department of Physics, Newcastle upon Tyne University, 1973-80; Lecturer, Senior Lecturer, Reader, Professor, Department of Civil Engineering, Dundee University, since 1981. Vice-President, European Geophysical Society, 1981-83. Publications: two books; 100 scientific publications. Recreations: sport; reading. Address: (b.) Department of Civil Engineering, The University, Dundee, DD1 4HN; T.-01382 344346.

Davies (a.k.a. Glasse-Davies), Professor R. Wayne, MA, PhD, ScD. Robertson Professor of Biotechnology, Glasgow University, since 1989; b. 10.6.44, Cardiff; m., Victoria Glasse; 3 s.; 1 d. Educ. Queen Elizabeth's Hospital, Bristol; St. John's College, Cambridge. Research Fellow, University of Wisconsin, 1968-71; H3 Professor, Universitat Zu Koln, FRG, 1971-77; Lecturer, University of Essex, 1977-81; Senior Lecturer, UMIST, 1981-83; Vice-President, Scientific and Research Director, Allelix Biopharmaceuticals, Toronto, 1983-89. Recreations: poetry and literature; cello; skiing. Address: (b.) Robertson Laboratory of Biotechnology, Institute of Biomedical and Life Sciences, Glasgow University, 54 Dumbarton Road, Glasgow, G11 6NU.

Davies, Terry, BSc (Hons), MSc, MInstP, FIPC. Principal, James Watt College of Further and Higher Education, since 1990; b. 14.12.40, Llanelli. Educ. Llanelli Boys' Grammar School; University College of Swansea; Nottingham University. Lecturer (Physics), Middlesex Polytechnic, then Preston Polytechnic, 1964-73; Depute Head, Department of Engineering, Science and Construction, Lewes Technical College, 1973-79; Head, Department of Science, Mathematics and Computing, Telford College of Further Education, Edinburgh, 1979-85; Depute Principal, Telford College of FE, 1985-90. Recreations: rugby; cricket; squash; tennis. Address: (b.) James Watt College, Finnart Street, Greenock, PA16 8HF; T.-01475 24433.

Davis, Alan Angus, BSc (Hons). Manager, BBC Scottish Symphony Orchestra, since 1992; b. 7.2.58, Glasgow. Educ. Queen Anne High School, Dunfermline; Aberdeen University. Publicity and Publications Assistant, The Poetry Society, 1981-82; Marketing Officer, Incorporated Society of Musicians, 1982-84; freelance administrator, 1984-92. Council Member, Society for the Promotion of New Music; Director, Edinburgh Contemporary Arts Trust; Director, Chamber Group of Scotland. Recreations: cooking; gardening; American literature. Address: (b.) Broadcasting House, Queen Margaret Drive, Glasgow, G12; T.-0141-330 2606.

Davis, Christine A.M., MA, DipEd. Chairman, Scottish Legal Aid Board, since 1991; Member, Scottish Agricultural Wages Board, since 1990; Chairman, The Quaker Tapestry at Kendal Ltd.; b. 5.3.44, Salisbury; m., Robin John Davis; 2 d. Educ. Perth Academy; Ayr Academy; St. Andrews University; Aberdeen University; Aberdeen College of Education. Teacher of History and Modern Studies, Cumbernauld High School and High School of Stirling, 1967-69; joined Dunblane Town Council and Perth and Kinross Joint County Council, 1972; undertook research in Canada on Ontario Hydro and small claims in Ontario courts, 1977-78; Chairman, Electricity Consultative Council for North of Scotland, 1980-90; Member: North of Scotland Hydro Electric Board, 1980-90, Scottish Economic Council, 1987-95, Scottish Committee of the Council on Tribunals, 1989-95; Clerk, Britain Yearly Meeting, Society of Friends (Quakers), 1991-95; President, Council of Churches for Britain and Ireland, 1990-92. Recreations: embroidery; bird-watching; walking. Address: (h.) 24 Newton Crescent, Dunblane, Perthshire, FK15 ODZ; T.-Dunblane 823226.

Davis, Margaret Thomson. Novelist; b. Bathgate; 2 s. Educ. Albert Secondary School. Worked as children's nurse; Red Cross nurse; short story writer; novelist; author of autobiography, The Making of a Novelist; novels include The Breadmakers, A Baby Might Be Crying, A Sort of Peace, The Prisoner, The Prince and the Tobacco Lords, Roots of Bondage, Scorpion in the Fire, The Dark Side of Pleasure, A Very Civilised Man, Light and Dark, Rag Woman Rich Woman, Daughters and Mothers, Wounds of War, A Woman of Property, A Sense of Belonging, Hold Me Forever, Kiss Me No More. Committee Member: International PEN (Scottish Branch); Society of Authors; Lecturer in Creative Writing; Honorary President, Strathkelvin Writers Club; Committee Member, Swanwick Writers' School. Recreations: reading; travelling; being with friends. Address: c/o Heather Jeeves Literary Agency, 9 Dryden Place, Edinburgh, EH9 1RP.

Davis, Robert Clive, CEng, MIMarE. Marine Engineer Superintendent, Scottish Fisheries Protection Agency, since 1991; b. 29.8.38, Brighton; m., Elizabeth Mary Warren; 2 s. Educ. Marist Brothers, Durban, South Africa; Glasgow College of Nautical Studies. Apprenticeship, James Brown, Durban, South Africa; joined Merchant Navy, 1959; served with Safmarine, Bank Line, Jardine Matheson; Boiler Inspector, 1970-72; joined Scottish Office, 1972; promoted Chief Engineer, 1979. Recreations: golf; gardening; DIY.

Address: (h.) 19 Duddingston Park South, Edinburgh, EH15 3NY; T.-0131-669 5320.

Davis, Robert Gunn. Member, Mental Welfare Commission for Scotland, since 1984; Social Work Adviser (Mental Health), Strathclyde Region, since 1977; b. 11.5.38, Edinburgh; m., Mildred Bennett; 1 s.; 1 d. Educ. Daniel Stewart's College, Edinburgh. Certificate of Qualification in Probation Work, Jordanhill College, 1968. Probation Officer, City of Glasgow, before 1969; Senior Social Worker, then Social Work Training Officer, Lanark County Council, 1970-75; Recruitment and Training Officer, Strathclyde Region Social Work Department, 1975-77. Founder Member, British Association of Social Workers. Recreations: vintage/classic motorcycle and vehicle rallies. Address: (h.) 5 Braid Green, Livingston, West Lothian, EH54 8PN; T.-Livingston 39148.

Davison, Edward Cowper. Secretary, Local Government Staff Commission; b. 31.10.40, Darlington; m., Anna Fay Henderson; 2 d. Educ. Dame Allan's School, Newcastle-upon-Tyne; Glasgow University; London University Institute of Education. Assistant Master, Tottenham County School, 1964-68; administrative staff, Glasgow University, 1969-75; Principal, Scottish Office, 1975-84; Assistant Secretary, 1984-94. Address: (b.) 48 Manor Place, Edinburgh, EH3 7EH.

Davison, Timothy Paul, BA (Hons), MHSM, DipHSM, MBA. Chief Executive, Greater Glasgow Community and Mental Health Services NHS Trust, since 1994; b. 4.6.61, Newcastle upon Tyne; m., Hilary Williamson; 1 s. Educ. Kenton School, Newcastle upon Tyne; Stirling University; Glasgow University. Appointments in Stirling Royal Infirmary, Royal Edinburgh Hospital, Glasgow Royal Infirmary, 1984-90; Sector General Manager, Gartnavel Royal Hospital, 1990-91; Unit General Manager, Mental Health Unit, Glasgow, 1991-92, Community and Mental Health Unit, Glasgow, 1992-94. Member, Executive Committee, Glasgow Association of Mental Health; Member, Council, Glasgow and West of Scotland Institute of Public Administration. Recreations: tennis; military and political history. Address: (b.) Gartnavel Royal Hospital, 1055 Great Western Road, Glasgow, G12 0XH; T.-0141-211 3782.

Dawson, Professor John Alan, BSc, MPhil, PhD, MIPDM. Professor of Marketing, Edinburgh University, since 1990; b. 19.8.44, Hyde; m., Jocelyn Barker; 1 s.; 1 d. Educ. Lady Manners School, Bakewell; University College, London; Nottingham University. Lecturer, Nottingham University; Lecturer, Senior Lecturer, Reader, St. David's University College, Wales; Fraser of Allander Professor of Distributive Studies, Stirling University; Visiting Lecturer, University of Western Australia; Visiting Research Fellow, Australian National University; Visiting Professor: Florida State University, Chuo University. Former Member, Distributive Trades Committee, NEDC; former Honorary Secretary, Institute of British Geographers; Board Member, Cumbernauld Development Corporation; Chairman, National Museums of Scotland Trading Co. Publications: Evaluating the Human Environment, 1973; Man and His World, 1975; Computing for Geographers, 1976; Small-Scale Retailing in the UK, 1979; Marketing Environment, 1979; Retail Geography, 1980; Commercial Distribution in Europe, 1982; Teach Yourself Geography, 1983; Shopping Centre Development, 1983; Computer Methods for Geographers, 1985; Retailing in Scoland 2005, 1988; Evolution of European Retailing, 1988; Retailing Environments in Developing Countries, 1990; Competition and Markets, 1992. Recreations: sport; writing. Address:(b.) Edinburgh University, 50 George Square, Edinburgh; T.-0131-650 3827.

Dawson, Thomas Cordner, QC (Scot). Solicitor-General for Scotland, since 1992; b. 14.11.48. Advocate, 1973; QC, 1986.

Deane, Robert Fletcher, MB, ChB, MSc, FRCSEdin, FRCSGlas. Consultant Urological Surgeon, since 1971; b. 25.3.38, Glasgow; m., Sylvia Alison Yuill; 3 s. Educ. Hillhead High School, Glasgow; Glasgow University. Consultant Urologist, Western Infirmary, Glasgow, since 1971; Senior Consultant Surgeon to Family Planning Association, Glasgow; Member, Specialist Advisory Committee (Urology); Founder, Board of Intercollegiate Specialty Board in Urology. Publication: Urology Illustrated. Recreations: golf; music. Address: (h.) 27 Bellshaugh Lane, Glasgow, G12 0PE; T.-0141-334 8102.

Deans, Joyce Blair, MBE, BArch, PPRIAS, RIBA, ACIArb, FRSA. Architect; President, Royal Incorporation of Architects in Scotland, 1991-93 (first woman President); b. 29.1.27, Glasgow; m., John Albert Gibson Deans; 2 s.; 2 d. Educ. Laurel Bank School for Girls; Strathclyde University. Re-entered profession as Assistant, private practice, 1968; appointed Associate, 1972; established own practice, 1981; elected Member, Council, Glasgow Institute of Architects, 1975-90 (first female President, 1986-88); elected Member, Council, Royal Incorporation of Architects, 1979-95; first female Vice President, Royal Incorporation of Architects in Scotland, 1986-88; Member, Building Standards Advisory Committee, since 1987; Chairman, BSAC (Research), since 1988; Member, Scottish Construction Industry Group, since 1991; Director, Cairn Housing Association, since 1988; Director, Glasgow West Conservation Trust, since 1987; Governor, Laurel Bank School for Girls, since 1981; Governor, Glasgow School of Art, since 1989; Member, Court, Strathclyde University, since 1992 (Deputy Chairman of Court (Estates)), since 1993; elected Vice President, Royal Institute of British Architects, 1993-95; Member, RIBA Council, since 1993. Recreations: gardening; golf; walking; reading; theatre. Address: 11 South Erskine Park, Bearsden, Glasgow, G61 4NA; T.-0141-942 6795.

DeFelice, Hilda, BA (Hons). Headteacher, St. Luke's High School, Barrhead, since 1993; b. 16.2.49, Glasgow; m. Gordon Herriot; 1 s.; 1 d. Educ. Holyrood Secondary School, Glasgow; Strathclyde University. Teacher, 1973-76; Assistant Principal Teacher, 1976-79; Principal Teacher, 1979-86; Assistant Head Teacher, St. Ninian's High School, Giffnock, 1986-90; Depute Head Teacher, St. Bride's High School, East Kilbride, 1990-93. Recreations: reading; guitar; music. Address: (b.) St. Luke's High School, Springfield Road, Barrhead, G78 2SG; T.-0141-881 9321.

Della Sala, Professor Sergio F., MD, PhD. Chair of Psychology, Aberdeen; b. 23.9.55, Milan. Senior Neurologist, Milan teaching hospital; Head, Neuropsychology Unit, Veruno, Italy. Address: (b.) King's College, Aberdeen University, Aberdeen.

Demarco, Professor Richard, OBE, RSW, SSA, Hon. FRIAS, DA, Hon. DFA, ACA. Artist and Writer; Director, Richard Demarco Gallery, since 1966; External Assessor, Stourbridge College of Art, since 1988; b. 9.7.30, Edinburgh; m., Anne Muckle. Educ. Holy Cross Academy, Edinburgh; Edinburgh College of Art. National Service, KOSB, 1954-56; Art Master, Duns Scotus Academy, Edinburgh, 1957-67; Vice-Chairman, Board, Traverse Theatre Club, 1963-67; Director, Sean Connery's Scottish International Education Trust, 1972-73; Member, Board of Governors, Carlisle School of Art, 1970-74; Member, Edinburgh Festival Society, since 1971; Contributing Editor, Studio International, 1982-84. Gold Order of Merit, Polish People's Republic; awarded insignia of Chevalier de L'Ordre Des Arts Et Des Lettres; Order of Cavaliere Della Republica d'Italia; Scottish Arts Council Award for services to Scotland's visual arts, 1975; Arts Medal, Royal Philosophical Society of Glasgow, 1995; awarded Honorary Doctorate, Atlanta College of Art, 1993; Honorary Member, Scottish Arts Club; Artistic Director, European Youth Parliament, since 1993; Professor, Kingston University, since 1993; Director, Demarco European Art Foundation, since 1993; Trustee, Kingston-Demarco European Cultural Foundation, since 1993. Publications: The Road to Meikle Seggie; The Artist as Explorer. Recreation: walking "The Road to Meikle Seggie". Address: (h.) 23(a) Lennox Street, Edinburgh; T.-0131-343 2124.

Dempster, Alastair Cox, FCIBS. Chief Executive, TSB Bank Scotland plc, since 1992; Deputy Chairman, TSB Bank Channel Islands Ltd., since 1992; Chairman, Committee of Scottish Clearing Bankers, since 1993; b. 22.6.40, Glasgow; m., Kathryn; 2 s. Educ. Paisley Grammar School. Royal Bank of Scotland, 1955-62; various managerial appointments, Scotland, Hong Kong, New York, 1962-81; AGM, International Division, Royal Bank of Scotland, 1981-86; Director of Commercial Banking and International/Executive Director, TSB Scotland plc, 1986-91; Chief Executive, TSB Bank Channel Islands Ltd., 1991-92. President, Chartered Institute of Bankers in Scotland; Member, Scottish Council Development and Industry Board and Executive Committee; Member, CBI Scottish Council; Convener, Heriot Watt Audit Committee; Member, Heriot Watt University Court; Director, Scottish Homes; Director, Office of the Banking Ombudsman; Direct Aberforth Split Level Trust plc; Member, Board of Governors, Edinburgh College of Art. Recreations: golf; tennis; bridge. Address: (b.) TSB Bank Scotland plc, Henry Duncan House, 120 George Street, Edinburgh, EH2 4TS; T.-0131-225 4555.

Denholm, James Allan, CBE, CA. Director, William Grant & Sons Ltd., since 1975; Chairman, East Kilbride Development Corporation, 1983-94 (Member, since 1979); Director, Scottish Mutual Assurance Society, since 1987 (Deputy Chairman, since 1992); Director, Scottish Cremation Society Limited, since 1980; Director, Abbey National plc, since 1992; President, Institute of Chartered Accountants of Scotland, 1992-93; b. 27.9.36, Glasgow; m., Elizabeth Avril McLachlan, CA; 1 s.; 1 d. Educ. Hutchesons Boys Grammar School, Glasgow; Institute of Chartered Accountants of Scotland. Apprenticed, McFarlane Hutton & Patrick, CA, Glasgow (Sir William McLintock prizeman); Chief Accountant, A. & W. Smith & Co. Ltd., Glasgow, 1960-66; Secretary, William Grant & Sons Ltd., since 1968; Council Member, Institute of Chartered Accountants of Scotland, 1978-83, 1989-93; Director and Treasurer, Glasgow YMCA, 1966-79; Chairman, Glasgow Junior Chamber of Commerce, 1972-73; Member, CBI Scottish Legal Panel, since 1987; Elder, New Kilpatrick Parish Church, since 1971; Visitor of the Incorporation of Maltmen in Glasgow, 1980-81; President, The Deacons' Association of Glasgow, 1994-95; Presis, The Weavers' Society of Anderston, 1994-95; President, Wine and Spirit Club of Scotland, 1983-84; Trustee, Scottish Cot Death Trust; Fellow, Society of Antiquaries of Scotland, since 1987; Fellow, Royal Society for the Encouragement of Arts, Manufactures and Commerce, 1993. Recreations: shooting; golf. Address: (h.) Greencroft, 19 Colquhoun Drive, Bearsden, Glasgow; T.-0141-942 1773.

Denholm, John Clark, MA (Hons), MIPA. Managing Director, Leith Advertising Agency Ltd., since 1984; Chairman, One to One Direct Communications Ltd., since 1990; b. 10.9.50, Chesterfield; m., Julia; 1 s.; 1 d. Educ. Buckhaven High School; St. Andrews University. Product Manager, The Boots Company, Nottingham, 1972-76; Brand Manager, Scottish & Newcastle Breweries, 1976-80; Account Director, Hall Advertising, Edinburgh, 1980-84. Recreation: golf. Address: (b.) 1 Canon Street, Edinburgh; T.-0131-557 5840.

Dennis, Richard Benson, PhD, BSc. Managing Director, Edinburgh Instruments Ltd.; Director, Edinburgh Sensors Ltd.; Senior Lecturer, Heriot-Watt University; Founder, Mintek GmbH, West Germany; b. 15.7.45, Weymouth; m.,

Beate Stamm; 2 d. Educ. Weymouth Grammar School; Reading University. SRC Postdoctoral Fellow, Reading; Guest Fellow, Freiburg University, 1968-70; Lecturer/Senior Lecturer, Heriot-Watt University, 1970-91; Alexander von Humboldt Fellow, Munich University, 1976-78; Treasurer, UK Laser and Electro-Optic Trade Association; Council Member, Scottish Consultative Committee on the Curriculum, since 1991; Chairman, Balerno High School Board; Joint Winner, Department of Industry EPIC Award (Education in Partnership with Industry and Commerce), 1982. Recreations: bridge; sport. Address: (b.) Edinburgh Instruments Ltd., Riccarton, Currie, Edinburgh; T.-0131-449 5844.

Dennis, Roy, MBE. Wildlife Consultant/Ornithologist, since 1991; Main Board Member, Scottish Natural Heritage, since 1992; Hill Farmer, since 1985; b. 4.5.40; m., Marina MacDonell; 2 s.; 1 d. Educ. Price's School. Migration Research Assistant, UK Bird Observatories, 1958-59; Warden, Lochgarten Osprey Reserve, 1960-63; Warden, Fair Isle Bird Observatory, 1963-70; Highland Officer, RSPB, 1971-87, Regional Officer (North Scotland), 1987-91; Author/Lecturer/Broadcaster. Publications: Ospreys and Speyside Wildlife; Birds of Badenoch and Strathspey; Puffins; Ospreys; Peregrine Falcons; Divers; The Loch. Recreations: travel; photography; cross-country skiing; bird-watching. Address: Inchdryne, Nethybridge, Inverness-shire, PH25 3EF; T.-01479 831 384.

Dennison, Brigadier Malcolm Gray. Lord Lieutenant of Orkney, since 1990; b. 19.3.24, Nyasaland. Educ. Lincoln School; Edinburgh University. RAF, 1942-52: Bomber Command, 1944-45, Senior Intelligence Officer, 219 and 205 Groups, Egypt, 1946-47, MECAS, 1947-48, HQ Middle East Air Force Intelligence, 1948-51; Bahrain Petroleum Co., 1953-55; Intelligence, Sultan Armed Forces, Oman, 1955-75, Adviser to Sultan, 1975-83. Order of Oman (Military); DSM (Oman). Address: (h.) Roeberry House, St. Margaret's Hope, Orkney, KW17 2TW; T.-01856 83 228.

Denny, Margaret Bertha Alice, OBE, DL, BA (Hons), PhD. Member, Council and Executive Committee, National Trust for Scotland, since 1974 (Vice President, 1981-91); b. 30.9.07, Chatham; m., Edward Leslie Denny. Educ. Dover County School; Bedford College for Women, London University. Entered Civil Service as Principal, Ministry of Shipping, 1940; Assistant Secretary, 1946; Under Secretary, 1957; Governor, Bedford College; Member, Scottish Advisory Council for Civil Aviation, 1958-67; Member, Western Regional Hospital Board, 1960-74; Member, Scottish Committee, Council of Industrial Design, 1961-71; Member, General Advisory Council, BBC, 1962-66; Member, General Nursing Council, Scotland, 1963-78; Member, Board of Management, State Hospital, Carstairs, 1966-76; Vice-Chairman, Argyll and Clyde Health Board, 1974-77; County Commissioner, Girl Guides, Dunbartonshire, 1958-68; DL, Dunbartonshire, since 1973; Officer, Order of Orange Nassau, 1947. Recreations: gardening; needlework; music. Address: (h.) Dalnair House, Croftamie, Glasgow, G63 0EZ; T.-01360 660106.

Denyer, Professor Peter Brian, BSc, PhD. Managing Director, VLSI Vision Ltd. and Professor of Integrated Electronics, Edinburgh University, since 1986; b. 27.4.53, Littlehampton; m., Fiona Margaret Lindsay; 2 d. Educ. Worthing Technical High School; Loughborough University. Wolfson Microelectronics Institute, 1976-80; Lecturer, then Reader, Edinburgh University, 1981-86. Chairman, SERC/DTI Microelectronics Design Sub-Committee, 1989-91; Director, VLSI Vision Ltd., since 1990. Publications: Introduction to MOSLSI Design, 1983; VLSI Signal Processing: A Bit-Serial Approach, 1985. Recreations: family; walking; renovation. Address: (h.) 91 Colinton Road, Edinburgh, EH10 5DF; T.-0131-337 3432.

Deregowski, Professor Jan Bronislaw, BSc, BA, PhD, DSc, FBPsS, FRSE. Professor of Psychology, Aberdeen University, since 1986 (Reader, 1981-86); b. 1.3.33, Pinsk, Poland; m., Eva Loft Nielsen; 2 s.; 1 d. Educ. London University. Lecturer, then Senior Lecturer, Aberdeen University, 1969-81. Publications: Illusions, Patterns and Pictures: a cross-cultural perspective; Distortion in Art; Perception and Artistic Style (Co-author). Address: (b.) Department of Psychology, King's College, Old Aberdeen, AB9 2UB; T.-Aberdeen 272247.

Dervaird, Hon. Lord (John Murray), MA (Oxon), LLB (Edin), FCIArb. Dickson Minto Professor of Company Law, Edinburgh University, since 1990, Dean, Faculty of Law, since 1994; Chairman, Scottish Council for Arbitration, since 1989; Council Member, London Court of International Arbitration, since 1990; Trustee, David Hume Institute, since 1992; Member, ICC Committee on Business Law, Paris, since 1992; Chairman, Scottish Ensemble, since 1988; Member, City Disputes Panel, since 1994; Member, Panel of Arbitrators, International Centre for Settlement of Investment Disputes; Hon. President, Advocates' Business Law Group, since 1988; b. 8.7.35, Stranraer; m., Bridget Jane Godfrey; 3 s. Educ. Stranraer schools; Edinburgh Academy; Corpus Christi College, Oxford; Edinburgh University. Advocate, 1962; QC, 1974; Law Commissioner (part-time), 1979-88; Senator of the College of Justice, 1988-89. Publications: Stair Encyclopaedia of Scots Law (Contributor); articles on legal and ornithological subjects. Recreations: farming; gardening; bird-watching; music; curling. Address: (b.) Faculty of Law, Old College, South Bridge, Edinburgh.

Devereux, Alan Robert, CBE, DL, CEng, MIEE, CBIM. Chairman, Scottish Ambulance Service NHS Trust, since 1995; Founder, Quality Scotland Foundation; International Director, Gleneagles PLC, since 1990; Director, Scottish Mutual Assurance Society, since 1976; b. 18.4.33, Frinton-on-Sea; m., 1, Gloria Alma Hair (deceased); 1 s.; 2, Elizabeth Tormey Docherty. Educ. Colchester School; Clacton County High School; Mid Essex Technical College. Marconi's Wireless Telegraph Company: apprentice, 1950-55, Standards Engineer, 1955-56; Technical Production Manager, Halex Division, British Xylonite Company, 1956-58; Technical Sales Manager, SPA Division, Sanitas Trust, 1958-65; General Manager, Dobar Engineering, 1965-67; various managerial posts, Norcros Ltd., 1967-69; Group Managing Director, Scotcros Ltd., 1969-78; Deputy Chairman, Scotcros Ltd., 1978-80. CBI: Chairman, Scotland, 1977-79 (Deputy Chairman, 1975-77), Council Member, 1972-84, Member, President's Advisory Committee, 1979; UK Regional Chairman, 1979; Chairman, Small Industries Council for Rural Areas of Scotland, 1975-77; Member, Scottish Development Agency, 1977-83; Chairman, Scottish Tourist Board, 1980-90; Chairman, Glasgow City Mission; Director, Children's Hospice Association for Scotland; Scottish Free Enterprise Award, 1978; Deputy Lieutenant, Renfrewshire, since 1985. Recreations: work; amateur radio; reading. Address: (h.) South Fell, 24 Kirkhouse Road, Blanefield, Glasgow, G63 9BX; T.-0360 770464.

Devine, John, FRICS, IRRV. Member, Lands Tribunal for Scotland, since 1991; b. 23.10.29, Glasgow; m., Agnes Susan McLaughlin; 2 s.; 1 d. Educ. St. Mary's College, Blairs, Aberdeen; Glasgow College of Technology; College of Estate Management. Apprentice and qualified assistant, Thomas Binnie & Hendry, Chartered Valuation Surveyors, 1947-57; Senior Valuer, Fife County Council's Assessor's Department, 1957-62; Partner, then Senior Partner, Graham & Sibbald, Chartered Surveyors, 1962-91. Member, Board of Management, Fife College of Further and Higher Education, since 1992. Recreation: golf. Address: (h.) 80 Milton Road, Kirkcaldy, KY1 1TP; T.-01592 264806.

Devine, Rt. Rev. Joseph. Bishop of Motherwell, since 1983; b. 7.8.37. Ordained priest in Glasgow, 1960. Address: (b.) 17 Viewpark Road, Motherwell, ML1 3ER.

Devine, Professor Thomas Martin, BA, PhD, DLitt, FRHistS, FRSE, FBA. Professor of Scottish History, Strathclyde University, since 1988 (Dean, Faculty of Arts and Social Studies, 1993-94); Deputy Principal of the University; b. 30.10.46, Motherwell; m., Catherine Mary Lynas; 2 s.; 3 d. Educ. Our Lady's RC High School, Motherwell; Strathclyde University. Lecturer, then Senior Lecturer and Reader, Department of History, Strathclyde University, 1969-88; Visiting Professor, University of Guelph, Canada, 1983 and 1988 (Adjunct Professor in History, since 1988); Governor, St. Andrews College of Education; Joint Founding Editor, Scottish Economic and Social History, 1980-84; British Academy/Leverhulme Trust Senior Research Fellow, 1992-93. Publications: The Tobacco Lords, 1975; Lairds and Improvement in Enlightenment Scotland, 1979; Ireland and Scotland 1600-1850 (Co-Editor), 1983; Farm Servants and Labour in Lowland Scotland 1770-1914, 1984; A Scottish Firm in Virginia 1767-77, 1984; People and Society in Scotland 1760-1830 (Co-Editor), 1988; The Great Highland Famine, 1988; Improvement and Enlightenment (Editor), 1989; Conflict and Stability in Scottish Sociey (Editor), 1990; Irish Immigrants and Scottish Society in the Eighteenth and Nineteenth Centuries (Editor), 1991; Scottish Emigration and Scottish Society, 1992; Scottish Elites, 1993; The Transformation of Rural Scotland (Co-Editor), 1994; Clanship to Crofters' War, 1994; Industry, Business and Society in Scotland since 1700, 1994; Glasgow: I, Beginnings to 1830, 1995. Recreations: walking and exploring the Hebrides; watching skilful football; travelling in Italy. Address: (b.) Department of History, McCance Building, 16 Richmond Street, Glasgow, G1 1XQ; T.-0141-552 4400, Ext. 4531.

de Vink, Peter Henry John, BComm. Managing Director, Edinburgh Financial and General Holdings Ltd., since 1978; b. 9.10.40, Amsterdam; m., Julie Christine (Krista) Quarles van Ufford; 1 s.; 1 d. Educ. Edinburgh University. National Service, Dutch Army, 1961-63; Edinburgh University, 1963-66; Ivory and Sime Investment Managers, 1966-78, latterly as Director. Address: (b.) 7 Howe Street, Edinburgh, EH3 6TE; T.-0131-225 6661; (h.) Huntly Cot, Temple, Midlothian.

Dewar, Donald Campbell, MA, LLB. MP (Labour), Glasgow Garscadden, since 1978 (Labour Chief Whip); b. 21.8.37, Glasgow; 1 s.; 1 d. Educ. Glasgow Academy; Glasgow University. Practised as Solicitor in Glasgow; MP, Aberdeen South, 1966-70; PPS to Tony Crosland, 1967; Chairman, Select Committee on Scottish Affairs, 1980-81; Member, Scottish front bench team, 1981-83; elected to Shadow Cabinet, 1984; Opposition Spokesman on Scottish Affairs, 1983-92, Social Security, 1992-95. Address: (h.) 23 Cleveden Road, Glasgow, G12; T.-0141-334 2374.

Dewar, Douglas, MA (Hons), CA. Finance Director, Scottish Airports Ltd., since 1992; b. 18.6.47, Glasgow; m., Nancy; 1 s.; 1 d. Educ. High School of Glasgow; Glasgow University. Arthur Young McClelland Moores; Scotish Co-ordinated Investments Ltd.; Scottish Express Ltd. (Finance Director); Stansted Airport Ltd. (Finance Director). Address: (b.) Scottish Airports Ltd., St. Andrews Drive, Glasgow Airport, Glasgow, PA3 2SW; T.-0141-848 4298.

Dewar, Lawrence, MIGD. Chief Executive, Scottish Grocers' Federation, since 1980; b. 12.1.36, Blackford; m., Nancy Kelly; 2 s.; 2 d. Educ. Dunfermline High School. Grocer of the Year, 1967; President, Scottish Grocers' Federation, 1975; Member, Board, SCOTBEC, 1981-85; Member, Sector Sector Board 5, SCOTVEC, since 1986; Secretary, Institute of Grocery Distribution (Scottish Branch), 1984. Recreations: golf; reading; TV. Address:

(b.) 3 Loaning Road, Edinburgh, EH7 6JE; T.-0131-652 2482.

Dewar Dury, Andrew. Managing Director, Allied Distillers. Address: (b.) 2 Glasgow Road, Dumbarton.

Dick, David, OBE, DIC, CEng, FIEE. H.M. Lay Inspector of Fire Services for Scotland, since 1994; Principal, Stevenson College of Further Education, Edinburgh, 1969-87; Chairman, Fire Services Examination Board (Scotland), 1968-86; Member, Construction Industry Training Board, 1976-85; Member, Electrical Engineering Services Committee, CITB, 1976-88; b. 20.3.29, Edinburgh; m., Muriel Elsie Margaret Buchanan; 5 d. Educ. Boroughmuir School, Edinburgh; Heriot-Watt College, Edinburgh; Imperial College, London. Electrical Engineer, North of Scotland Hydro-Electric Board, 1951-54; Lecturer, Dundee College of Technology, 1954-60; Head, Department of Electrical Engineering, Coatbridge Technical College, 1960-64; Depute Principal, Napier College of Science and Technology, Edinburgh, 1964-69. Manpower Services Commission: Chairman, Lothian District Manpower Committee, 1981-82, Member, Lothian and Borders Area Manpower Board, 1982-85; Member and Chairman, various committees: Scottish Technical Education Council, Scottish Business Education Council, 1969-87; Member, General Convocation, Heriot-Watt University, Edinburgh, 1970-73; Past Chairman, Scottish Committee, Institution of Electronic and Radio Engineers; former Honorary President, Edinburgh and District Spastics Association. Publication: Capital Walks in Edinburgh – The New Town, 1994. Recreations: music (flute); gardening; writing historical biographies. Address: (h.) West Lodge, Clerkington, near Haddington, East Lothian.

Dick, Maria M., MA. Head Teacher, Auchenharvie Academy, since 1989; b. 3.3.49, Irvine; m., James Dick, BSc. Educ. Irvine Royal Academy; Glasgow University. Teacher of English, then Assistant Principal Teacher, Irvine Royal Academy, 1972-77; Principal Teacher of English: James Hamilton Academy, 1977-80, Ravenspark Academy, 1980-83; Divisional Curriculum Development Officer, 1983-84; Assistant Head Teacher, then Temporary Depute Head Teacher, Auchenharvie Academy, 1984-89. Recreations: large dogs — Belgian Shepherds. Address: (b.) Auchenharvie Academy, Saltcoats Road, Stevenston, Ayrshire, KA20 3JW.

Dickie, Thomas, JP. Chairman, Housing Committee, Cunninghame District Council, since 1992 (Member of Council, since 1975); b. 5.12.30, Beith; m., Janette Coulter Brown. Educ. Beith Academy; Speirs' Secondary School; Glasgow and West of Scotland Commercial College. From office boy to Personnel Manager, Redpath Engineering Ltd., 1946-80; Member, Board, Irvine Development Corporation, 1981-84; Chairman, Garnock Valley Development Executive, 1984-88; Secretary, Cunninghame North Constituency Labour Party, 1990-92. Recreations: caravanning; walking; music. Address: (h.) 45 Loadingbank Court, Kilbirnie, Ayrshire, KA25 6JX; T.-01505 682205.

Dickinson, Professor Harry Thomas, BA, DipEd, MA, PhD, DLitt, FRHistS. Professor of British History, Edinburgh University, since 1980; Professor of British History, Nanjing University, since 1987; b. 9.3.39, Gateshead; m., Jennifer Elizabeth Galtry; 1 s.; 1 d. Educ. Gateshead Grammar School; Durham University; Newcastle University. Teacher of History, Washington Grammar School, 1961-64; Earl Grey Fellow, Newcastle University, 1964-66; History Department, Edinburgh University: Assistant Lecturer, 1966-68, Lecturer, 1968-73, Reader, 1973-80; Associate Dean (Postgraduate), 1992-96; Visiting Professor, Nanjing University, China, 1980-83-87-94; Fulbright Scholar, 1973; Huntington Library Fellowship, 1973; Folger Shakespeare Library Fellowship, 1973; Winston Churchill Fellow, 1980; Leverhulme Award,

1986-87; Ahmanson Fellowship, UCLA, 1987; Anstey Lecturer, University of Kent, 1989; Chairman, Publications Committee, Historical Association, 1991-94; Vice-President, Royal Historical Society, 1991-95; Member, Humanities Committee, CNAA, 1991-93; National Auditor, Higher Education Quality Council, 1993-95; Member, Marshall Aid Commonwealth Commission, since 1987. Publications: Bolingbroke; Walpole and the Whig Supremacy; Liberty and Property; British Radicals and the French Revolution; The Correspondence of Sir James Clavering; Politics and Literature in the 18th Century; The Political Works of Thomas Spence; Caricatures and the Constitution 1760-1832; Britain and the French Revolution; The Politics of the People in Eighteenth-century Britain; Editor, History; many essays and reviews. Recreations: reading; films. Address: (h.) 44 Viewforth Terrace, Edinburgh, EH10 4LJ; T.-0131-229 1379.

Dickson, Captain Alexander Forrest, OBE, RD, FRIN. Commissioner of Northern Lighthouses, since 1979; b. 23.6.20, Edinburgh; m., Norma Houston; 3 s.; 2 d. Educ. George Watson's; Leith Nautical College. Apprentice, P. Henderson and Co., 1936-39; Royal Navy service in destroyers, 1939-45; Lecturer, Leith Nautical College, 1945-49; Shell International Marine Co. Ltd., 1949-79 (Director Operations, 1968-79). Honorary Sheriff, Perth. Recreations: fishing; gardening; golf. Address: (h.) Birchburn, Kenmore, Perthshire; T.-018873 283.

Dickson, Campbell S., MA, DipEd. Rector, Nairn Academy, since 1987; b. 25.11.44, Edinburgh; 2 s. Educ. Boroughmuir High School, Edinburgh; Edinburgh University. Teacher of Modern Languages, Dunfermline High School, 1968-71; Principal Teacher of Modern Languages, Golspie High School, 1971-79; Assistant Rector, Banff Academy, 1979-82; Depute Rector, Lochaber High School, 1982-87. Member, Scottish Central Committee on Modern Languages, 1977-80. Recreations: sport (curling, golf); walking; bridge; reading. Address: (b.) Nairn Academy, Duncan Drive, Nairn, IV12 4RD; T.-01667 53700.

Dickson, Ian Archibald. Secretary to Northern Lighthouse Board, since 1987; b. 3.5.42, Edinburgh; m., Moira Evelyn McLean; 1 s. Educ. George Heriot's, Edinburgh. Northern Lighthouse Board: Executive Officer, 1960-73, Personnel Officer, 1973-77, Deputy Secretary, 1977-86. Elder, Church of Scotland. Address: (b.) 84 George Street, Edinburgh; T.-0131-226 7051.

Dickson, Leonard Elliot, CBE, MC, TD, DL, BA (Cantab), LLB. Retired Solicitor; b. 17.3.15, Edinburgh; m., Mary Elisabeth Cuthbertson; 1 s.; 1 d. Educ. Uppingham; Magdalene College, Cambridge; Glasgow University. 1st Bn., Glasgow Highlanders HLI, 1939-46; former Senior Partner, Dickson, Haddow & Co., Solicitors, Glasgow (retired, 1985); Clerk, Clyde Lighthouses Trust, 1953-65; Secretary, Glasgow Society of Sons of Clergy, 1953-83; serving Officer, TA, 1939-55 (Lt. Col. commanding 1st Bn., Glasgow Highlanders, 1952-55); Chairman, Lowland TAVR, 1968-70; Member, Glasgow Executive Council, NHS, 1956-74 (Vice Chairman, 1970-74). Recreations: travel; gardening. Address: (h.) Bridge End, Gartmore, Stirling, FK8 3RR; T.-01877 382 220.

Dickson, Sheriff Robert Hamish, LLB, WS. Sheriff of South Strathclyde, Dumfries & Galloway at Airdrie, since 1988; b. 19.10.45, Glasgow; m., Janet Laird Campbell; 1 s. Educ. Glasgow Academy; Drumtochty Castle; Glenalmond; Glasgow University. Solicitor, Edinburgh, 1969-71, and Glasgow, 1971-86; Partner, Brown Mair Gemmill & Hislop, Solicitors, Glasgow, 1973-86; apppointed floating Sheriff of South Strathclyde, Dumfries & Galloway at Hamilton, 1986. Recreations: golf; music; reading. Address: (b.) Airdrie Sheriff Court, Airdrie; T.-Airdrie 751121.

Dickson, William Thomas. Convener, Development and Planning, Central Regional Council, since 1991; Director, Stirling Enterprise Park; Director, Venture Forth Ltd.; b. 5.6.53, Dumfries; m., Elizabeth; 1 s.; 1 d. HM Forces (KOSB), 1970-76; elected, Central Regional Councillor, 1990. Member, Executive, Age Concern (Scotland). Recreation: sport (spectator). Address: (b.) Central Regional Council, Viewforth, Stirling, FK8 2ET; T.-01786 443379.

Dillon, J. Shaun H., DRSAM (Comp), FSA Scot. Professional Musician; Composer, Oboist and Teacher of Woodwind; b. 30.12.44, Sutton Coldfield. Educ. Berwickshire High School; Fettes College; Royal Scottish Academy of Music; Guildhall School of Music. Studied composition with Frank Spedding and Edmund Rubbra; awarded prize for composition for Leicestershire Schools Orchestra, 1965; commissions from various bodies, including Scottish Amateur Music Association; Instructor of Woodwind: Edinburgh Corporation, 1967-72, Aberdeen Corporation (latterly Grampian Region), 1972-81; Freelance Musician, since 1981; sometime Director of Music, St. Mary's Cathedral, Aberdeen; two suites of Airs and Graces for strings published; Secretary, Association of Instrumental and Vocal Specialists, 1975-78. Recreations: reading, especially history, literature; crosswords; playing flute (badly) in ceilidh bands. Address: (b.) 34 Richmond Street, Aberdeen, AB2 4TR; T.-Aberdeen 630954.

Dilworth, Rt. Rev. Gerard Mark, OSB, MA, PhD, FRHistS, FSA Scot. Abbot, Fort Augustus Abbey, since 1991; b. 18.4.24. Educ. St. Andrew's School, Edinburgh; Fort Augustus Abbey School, Invernessshire; Oxford University; Edinburgh University. Fort Augustus Abbey School: Senior Modern Languages Master, 1956-59, Headmaster, 1959-72; Parish Priest, Fort Augustus, 1974-79; Editor, The Innes Review, 1979-84; Keeper, Scottish Catholic Archives, Edinburgh, 1979-91. Publications: The Scots in Franconia; George Douglas: priest and martyr; Scottish Monasteries in the Late Middle Ages, 1995. Address: (b.) The Abbey, Fort Augustus, Inverness, PH32 4DB; T.-01320 366232.

Dinsdale, Professor Jack, MA, MSc, CEng, MIMechE, MIEE, FIQA. NCR Professor of Mechatronics, Dundee University, since 1989; b. 25.12.37, London; 4 s.; 1 d. Educ. Mill Hill School, London; Trinity College, Cambridge; Cranfield Insitute of Technology. Project Manager, Elliott Automation (now GEC), 1960; Principal Research Engineer, Cranfield Unit for Precision Engineering (CUPE), 1968; Professor of Machine Systems, Cranfield Institute of Technology, 1984. Recreations: music-making; photography. Address: (b.) Dundee University, Dundee, DD1 4HN; T.-01382 223181.

Dixon, Brian Ringrose, ACIB. Scotland Director, Barclays Bank PLC, since 1983; Member, Court, Strathclyde University; b. 4.1.38, Market Weighton; m., Annette Robertson; 2 s. Educ. Pocklington School, York. Member, Executive Council, Scottish Council Development and Industry. Recreations: rugby; gardening; golf; walking. Address: (b.) 90 St. Vincent Street, Glasgow, G2 5UQ; T.-0141-221 9585.

Dixon, Professor Geoffrey Richard, BSc, PhD, FIHort, FIBiol, CBiol. Professor of Horticulture, University of Strathclyde, since 1987; Head, Vice-Dean, Department of Horticulture, Director, Scottish Horticultural Advisory Service, SAC — Auchincruive; b. 13.6.42, London; m., Kathleen Hilda Edwards; 1 s.; 1 d. Educ. Pewley County School, Guildford; Wye College, University of London. Plant Pathologist, National Institute of Agricultural Botany, Cambridge, 1968-78; Head, Horticulture Division and Chairman, Crop Production and Protection Group, and Senior University Lecturer, Aberdeen School of Agriculture, 1978-87; Chairman, International Clubroot Working Group; Visiting Professor, Mansourah University,

Egypt; Visiting Professor, Von Humboldt University, Berlin; Senior Research Scholar, University of Wisconsin; Visiting Lecturer, University of Horticulture, Budapest; Vice-Chairman, Education and Training Committee, Scottish Branch, Institute of Horticulture; Member, Examinations Board, Royal Horticultural Society; created Freeman Citizen of Glasgow and Member, Incorporation of Gardeners of Glasgow; Member of the Master Court. Wain Fellowship, BBSRC; Nuffield Foundation Fellowship, European Community Erasmus Programme Co-ordinator. Publications: Vegetable Crop Diseases; Plant Pathogens and their control in Horticulture; 100 scientific papers. Recreations: gardening; photography; travel; hill-walking. Address: (h.) Helenton Mote, Symington, by Ayr, KA1 5PP; T.-01563 830251.

Dixon-Carter, Clare. Vice-Chairman, British Red Cross Society; Chairman, Scottish Central Council Branch, British Red Cross Society; b. 18.9.38, London. Educ. Moira House School, Eastbourne. Technical staff, EMI; hotel management, 1959-65; Assistant Regional Organiser for Scotland, World Worldlife Fund, 1969-77; joined Inverness-shire Branch, British Red Cross Society, 1965; Branch Director, 1979-86; awarded British Red Cross Society Voluntary Medical Service Medal, 1983; BRCS Badge of Honour for distinguished service and life membership of society, 1986; Vice-Chairman, Scottish Central Council Branch, 1986-90. Recreations: photography; travel; music. Address: (h.) Easter Balnabaan, Drumnadrochit, Inverness-shire, IV3 6UX; T.-0456 450310.

Dobie, Margaret G.C., OBE, MA, DipSocStud. Hon. Vice President, Scottish Association for the Study of Delinquency; Chair, Dumfries & Galloway Valuation Panel, since 1987; Chairman, Dumfries & Galloway Family Mediation Service Executive Committee; b. Galloway; m., James T.J. Dobie; 3 s. Educ. Benedictine Convent, Dumfries; Dumfries Academy; Edinburgh University. Medical Social Worker; Chair, Dumfries and Galloway Regional Children's Panel, 1971-77; Social Worker, Child Guidance Service, Dumfries; National Secretary, Scottish Association for the Study of Delinquency, 1982-87; Member, Broadcasting Council for Scotland, 1987-91; Chair, Dumfries and Galloway Children's Panel Advisory Committee, 1982-89; Chair, Children's Panel Advisory Group, 1985-88. Recreations:travel; tennis; reading. Address: (h.) Ardlui, Merse Road, Rockcliffe, Dalbeattie, DG5 4QH; T.-01556 630272.

Dobie, Rev. Rachel Jean Wayland, LTh. Minister, since 1990; Vice-Convener, General Assembly Board of Parish Education, since 1993; b. 17.8.42, Forres; m., Kirkpatrick H. Dobie; 1 s.; 1 d. Educ. Dumfries Academy; Jordanhill College; Edinburgh University. Primary schoolteacher, 1963-80; Auxiliary Minister, Dalbeattie with Urr, 1990-93; Church of Scotland Sunday School Adviser, 1976-86; Reader, 1982-90; Chair, Marriage Guidance, Dumfries, 1984-86; Member, General Assembly Youth Education Committee, 1985-93. Publication: Time Together, 1981. Recreations: music; fine arts. Address: (h.) Glenfiddich, Corbelly Hill, Dumfries; T.-01887 254806.

Dobson, Ronald Matthew, MA, PhD. Honorary Lecturer in Zoology, Glasgow University (Lecturer in Agricultural Zoology, 1959-74, Senior Lecturer, 1974-90); b. 18.12.25, Blackburn, Lancashire; m., Ruth Hilda Nash; 2 s.; 3 d. Educ. Queen Elizabeth's Grammar School, Blackburn; Cambridge University; London University. Insect Infestation Inspector, Ministry of Food, then Department of Agriculture for Scotland, 1945-49; Research Assistant, Wye College, London University, 1950-53; Scientific Officer, then Senior Scientific Officer, Rothamsted Experimental Station, 1953-59. Fellow, Royal Entomological Society of London; Honorary Editor, Glasgow Naturalist, 1983-95. Publications: Insects and Other Invertebrates in Colour

(adaptation); numerous scientific and natural history articles. Recreations: music; house renovation; boating. Address: (h.) 7 Netherburn Avenue, Glasgow, G44 3UF; T.-0141-637 3659.

Docherty, Michael. Chief Executive, Hamilton District Council; b. 12.1.52, Glasgow; m., Linda; 2 s.; 1 d. Educ. St. Mungo's Academy, Glasgow. Trainee Accountant, Electricity Board, 1971-74; Accountancy Assistant, Coatbridge Town Council, 1974-75; Accountant, Monklands District Council, 1975-77, Stirling District Council, 1977-79; Senior Accountant, Monklands District Council, 1979-82; Principal Accountant, Renfrew District Council, 1982-84; Depute Director of Finance, Motherwell District Council, 1984-91; Director of Finance, Hamilton District Council, 1991-92. Recreations: running; reading; hill-walking. Address: (b.) Town House, 102 Cadzow Street, Hamilton, ML3 6HH; T.-01698 282323.

Dodd, Raymond Henry, MA, BMus, ARAM. Cellist and Composer; b. 31.3.29; m., Doreen Joyce; 1 s.; 1 d. Educ. Bryanston School; Royal Academy of Music; Worcester College, Oxford. Music Master, Sedbergh School, 1951-55; Aberdeen University: Lecturer in Music, 1956, Senior Lecturer in Music, 1971-91; Visiting Professor of Music, Wilson College, USA, 1972-73. Various orchestral and chamber music compositions; awarded Szymanowski Medal, Polish Ministry of Art and Culture, 1982. Address: (h.) 14 Giffordgate, Haddington, East Lothian, EH41 4AS; T.-0162 082 4618.

Doig, Andrew, MB, ChB, FRCPEdin, FRCP. Consultant Physician, Edinburgh Royal Infirmary, 1963-89; Senior Lecturer in Medicine, Edinburgh University, 1963-89; b. 18.12.24, Edinburgh; m., Anne Bisset Duthie; 1 s.; 1 d. Educ. Boroughmuir School, Edinburgh; Edinburgh University; Illinois University. Junior medical posts, Edinburgh Royal Infirmary, Victoria Hospital (Burnley), Edinburgh University; postdoctoral Research Fellow, United States Public Health Service; President, Scottish Society of Physicians, 1985-86; President, Harveian Society of Edinburgh, 1989-90. Recreations: hill-walking; photography; 18th-century history. Address: (h.) 13 Nile Grove, Edinburgh, EH10 4RE; T.-0131-447 4160.

Doig, Very Rev. Andrew Beveridge, MA, BD, DD. Moderator, General Assembly of the Church of Scotland, 1981-82; b. 18.9.14, Carluke; m., 1, Nan Carruthers (deceased); 1 d.; 2, Barbara Young; 1 s.; 1 d. Educ. Hyndland Secondary School, Glasgow; Glasgow University; Trinity College, Glasgow; Union Theological Seminary, New York. Missionary, Church of Scotland, to Nyasaland, 1939; Senior Chaplain to the Forces, East Africa Command, 1940-45; Secretary, Blantyre Mission Council, 1946-53; Member: Government Advisory Committee on African Education, 1948-53, Nyasaland Legislative Council, 1946-53; seconded from missionary service to be Nominated Member for African Interests, Central Africa Federal Assembly, 1953-58; General Secretary, Blantyre Synod, Church of Central Africa, Presbyterian, 1958-62; Minister, St. John's and King's Park, Dalkeith, 1962-72; Clerk, Dalkeith Presbytery, 1965-72; Member, Overseas Council, Church of Scotland, and Convener, Christian Aid, 1967-70; General Secretary, National Bible Society of Scotland, 1972-82; Member, Executive Committee for Europe in worldwide United Bible Societies, 1974-82. Recreation: golf. Address: (h.) The Eildons, Moulin Square, Pitlochry, PH16 5EW; T.-01796 472892.

Doig, Ian, IPFA, FCCA. Scottish Secretary, CIPFA, since 1986; Secretary, Local Authority (Scotland) Accounts Advisory Committee, since 1986; b. 25.11.45, Glasgow; m., Barbara; 1 d. Educ. Alva and Alloa Academies; Strathclyde University. Address: (b.) CIPFA Scottish Office, 8 North West Circus Place, Edinburgh, EH3 6ST; T.-0131-220 4316.

Doig, John Scott. Regional Sheriff Clerk, Tayside Central and Fife; b. 24.11.38, Dundee; m., Margaret; 1 s.; 1 d. Educ. Harris Academy, Dundee. Sheriff Clerk Service since 1956 in Glasgow, Perth, Campbeltown, Linlithgow, Dumbarton, Inverness; Secretary, Sheriff Court Rules Council, 1973-79. Recreations: bowls; curling; snooker. Address: (b.) Sheriff Courthouse, 6 West Bell Street, Dundee; T.-01382 229961.

Doig, P. Michael R., MA (Hons). Head Teacher, Cumbernauld High School, since 1992; b. 2.5.48, Glasgow; m., Catherine; 2 s. Educ. High School of Glasgow; Glasgow University. Teacher/Assistant Principal Teacher/Principal Teacher of Modern Languages, 1972-81; Assistant Head Teacher, Hermitage Academy, Helensburgh, 1981-85; Depute Head Teacher, Kirkintilloch High School, 1985-92. Member, National Council, Headteachers' Association of Scotland. Recreations: music; golf. Address: (b.) Cumbernauld High School, Ring Road, S. Carbrain, Glasgow, G67 2UF; T.-01236 725511.

Donachie, Professor William David, BSc, PhD, MAcadEurop. Professor of Bacterial Genetics, Edinburgh University, since 1993; b. 27.4.35, Edinburgh; m.,Millicent Masters, BS, MS, PhD; 1 s. Educ. Dunfermline High School; Edinburgh University. Assistant Lecturer in Genetics, Edinburgh University, 1958-62; Research Associate in Biochemical Sciences, Princeton University, 1962-63; Lecturer in Genetics, Edinburgh University, 1963-65; Scientific Staff, MRC Molecular Genetics Unit, London and Edinburgh, 1965-74; Senior Lecturer/Reader in Molecular Biology, Edinburgh University, 1974-93. Publications: 70 research papers. Recreations: drawing; natural history; T'ai Chi. Address: (b.) Institute of Cell and Molecular Biology, Edinburgh University, Darwin Building, King's Buildings, Mayfield Road, Edinburgh, EH9 3JR; T.-0131-650 5354.

Donald, Colin Dunlop, BA (Cantab), LLB, DUniv, FRSA, DL. Partner and latterly Consultant, McGrigor Donald, Solicitors, Glasgow, 1966-94; b. 24.7.34, Strathaven; m., Theresa Ann Gilliland; 2 s.; 1 d. Educ. Cargilfield; Rugby; Gonville and Caius College, Cambridge; Glasgow University. National Service, 1953-55, 2nd Lt., The Cameronians (Scottish Rifles). President and Chairman, Council, The Thistle Foundation, Edinburgh and Renfrew; Member, Court, Glasgow University, since 1980, as an Assessor of the General Council; Member, Executive, National Trust for Scotland; Director, Universities Superannuation Scheme Ltd.; Trustee, TSB Foundation for Scotland; Member, Council, Scottish Conservation Projects Trust; a Deputy Lieutenant of Stirling and Falkirk. Recreations: golf and other outdoor sports. Address: (h.) 23 Park Terace, Stirling, FK8 2JS; T.-01786 473565.

Donald, George Malcolm, RSA, RSW, DA, ATC, MEd. Lecturer, Edinburgh College of Art; Director, ECA Summer School; b. 12.9.43, Ootacamund, South India; 1 s.; 1 d. Educ. Robert Gordon's College; Aberdeen Academy; Edinburgh College of Art; Hornsey College of Art; Edinburgh University. Joined Edinburgh College of Art as Lecturer, 1969; Visiting Lecturer, five Faculties of Art in India, 1979; Visiting Professor of Art, 1981, and Visiting Professor, Drawing and Anatomy, 1985, University of Central Florida; Visiting Professor, Strasbourg, 1986, Belgrade, 1987, Sechuan Fine Art Institute, China, 1989; Chinese Academy of Fine Art, 1994; Latimer Award, RSA, 1970; Guthrie Award, RSA, 1973; Scottish Arts Council Bursary, 1973; RSA Gillies Bequest Travel Award to India, 1978; SAC Travel and Study Award, Indiana, 1981; RSA Gillies Prize, 1982; RSW Mary Marshall Brown Award, 1983; RGI Cargill Award, 1987; former Council Member, Printmakers Workshop (Edinburgh); one man shows, Florida, 1985, Helsinki, 1985, Edinburgh Festival, 1985, Belgrade, 1987, Florida, 1987, Edinburgh, 1988, 1990, London, 1992-94, Edinburgh 1993-94-95. Address: (h.)

Bankhead, by Duns, Berwickshire, TD11 3QJ; T.-01361 883014.

Donald, Patricia Mary, BSc, MB, ChB, DRCOG, FRCGP. General Practitioner, since 1981; Honorary Secretary, Scottish Council, Royal College of General Practitioners, since 1994, and Co-ordinator, Scottish Council Clinical Guidelines, since 1995; b. 17.3.53, Edinburgh; m., Dr. Crawford Thurston. Educ. St. George's School for Girls; Edinburgh University. Founder Member, SHARP; Member, Joint Working Group on Primary Care, Scottish Office; Member, Council, St. George's School for Girls. Recreations: skiing; hill-walking; riding. Address: (h.) 26 York Road, Edinburgh, EH5 3EH; T.-0131-551 3035.

Donald, Peter. Secretary, Scottish Football League. Address: (b.) 188 West Regent Street, Glasgow, G2 4RY.

Donaldson, Alistair. General Manager, Scotland, Meat and Livestock Commission. Address: (b.) 3 Atholl Place, Perth, PH1 5ND.

Donaldson, Rev. David, MA, BD (Hons), DipEd. Minister, Duddingston Kirk, Edinburgh, since 1990; b. 6.7.43, Glasgow; m., Jean Lacey; 1 s.; 3 d. Educ. Glasgow Academy; Glasgow University. Missionary, Church of Scotland, Taiwan, 1969-75; Minister: St. David's Bathgate, 1975-83, Whitfield, Dundee, 1983-90. Convener, Diaconate Committee, Church of Scotland, 1990-95. Recreations: tennis; badminton. Address: (h.) Duddingston Manse, 5 Old Church Lane, Edinburgh, EH15 3PX; T.-0131-661 4240.

Donaldson, David Abercrombie, RSA, RP, RGI, LLD, DLitt, HonDLitt (Glasgow), HonDA. Painter; Painter and Limner to The Queen in Scotland, since 1977; b. 29.6.16, Chryston; m., 1, Kathleen Boyd Maxwell; 1 s.; 2, Maria (Marysia) Mora-Szorc; 2 d. Educ. Coatbridge Secondary School; Glasgow School of Art. Head of Painting School, Glasgow School of Art, 1967-81; Hon. LLD, Strathclyde, 1971; HonDA, Glasgow School of Art, 1993. Recreations: music; cooking. Address: (h.) 5 Cleveden Drive, Glasgow, G12 0SB; T.-0141-334 1029.

Donaldson, Professor Gordon Bryce, MA, PhD, FInstP, FRSE. Professor of Applied Physics and Head of Department, Strathclyde University, since 1993; b. 10.8.41, Edinburgh; m., Christina Martin; 1 s.; 1 d. Educ. Glasgow Academy; Christ's College, Cambridge. Cavendish Laboratory, Cambridge, 1962-65; Lecturer in Physics, Lancaster University, 1966-75; Strathclyde University: Lecturer, 1976, Senior Lecturer, 1978; Visiting Scientist and Fulbright Scholar, University of California, 1975; Visiting Professor, University of Virginia, 1981; Chairman, Institute of Physics Low Temperature Group, 1990-93; DTI/SERC Coordinator for National Superconductivity Programme, 1990-93. Address: (b.) Department of Physics and Applied Physics, Strathclyde University, Glasgow, G4 ONG.

Donaldson, Professor Iain Malcolm Lane, BSc, MB, ChB, MA, FRCPE, MRCP. Professor of Neurophysiology, Edinburgh University, since 1987; b. 22.10.37; m.; 1 s. Educ. Edinburgh University. House Physician and Surgeon, Research Fellow, Honorary Lecturer, Honorary Senior Registrar, Departments of Medicine and Surgical Neurology, Edinburgh University, 1962-69; Anglo-French Research Scholarship, University of Paris, 1969-70; Research Officer, University Laboratory of Physiology, Oxford, 1970-79; Fellow and Tutor in Medicine, St. Edmund Hall, Oxford, 1973-79; Professor of Zoology, Hull University, 1979-87; Emeritus Fellow, St. Edmund Hall, Oxford, since 1979. Recreation: studying the past. Address: (b.) Centre for Neuroscience, Edinburgh University, Appleton Tower, Crichton Street, Edinburgh, EH8 9LE.

Donaldson, James Andrew, BDS, BA, DFM. Principal in general dental practice; b. 28.2.57, Glasgow; m., Patricia H. Winter; 1 s.; 3 d. Educ. Coatbridge High School; Dundee University; Open University; Glasgow University. Dental Adviser, British Antarctic Survey, since 1986; Member: National Council, General Dental Practitioners Association, since 1989, Scottish General Dental Services Committee, 1991-93, Aberdeen District Council, 1984-86, Grampian Regional Council, 1986-88; Director, "Open Wide" Dental Courses. Recreations: skiing; squash; scuba diving. Address: (h.) Ellon Castle, Ellon, AB41 9QN; T.-01358 21865.

Donaldson, James T., BA (Hons), MEd. HM Chief Inspector of Schools, since 1988 (HM Inspector of Schools, 1982-88); Director of Quality Assessment, Scottish Higher Education Funding Council, since 1992; Director of Teaching and Learning, Scottish Higher Education Funding Council, since 1993; b. 4.3.45, Ecclefechan; m., Maureen; 1 s.; 2 d. Educ. Wallace Hall Academy; Strathclyde University; Edinburgh University. Lecturer, Edinburgh College of Commerce, 1968-73; Lecturer/Senior Lecturer, Queen Margaret College, Edinburgh, 1973-79; Head, Department of Business Studies, Telford College of Further Education, Edinburgh, 1979-82. Recreations: golf; running. Address: (b.) Scottish Higher Education Funding Council, 97 Haymarket Terrace, Edinburgh, EH12 5HD.

Donaldson, James W.G., CBE. Chairman, Ayrshire and Arran Health Board. Address: (b.) P.O. Box 13, Hunters Avenue, Ayr.

Donaldson, Marion. Fashion Designer; b. 1944, Glasgow. Trained as primary school-teacher; with husband, founded fashion company, mid-1960s.

Donaldson, William, MA, PhD. Writer, Researcher, Traditional Musician; b. 19.7.44, Fraserburgh. Educ. Fraserburgh Academy; Aberdeen University. Publications: Popular Literature in Victorian Scotland, 1986; The Jacobite Song, 1988; The Language of the People, 1989. Recreation: piobaireachd player. Address: (b.) 13 Mile End Avenue, Aberdeen.

Donnachie, Ian, MA, MLitt, PhD, FRHistS, FSA (Scot). Senior Lecturer in History, Open University in Scotland, since 1985, and Staff Tutor, since 1970; b. 18.6.44, Lanark. Educ. Lanark Grammar School; Glasgow University; Strathclyde University. Research Assistant, Galloway Project, Strathclyde University, 1967-68; Lecturer in Social Studies: Napier Polytechnic, 1968-70, Deakin University, Victoria, 1982; Visiting Fellow: Deakin University, Victoria and Sydney University, NSW, 1985; Vice-Chairman, Scottish Brewing Archive; Consultant: National Library of Scotland, Scottish Tourist Board, Scottish Office Education Department, Scottish Consultative Committee on the Curriculum; Member: Universities Association for Continuing Education (Scotland), International Council for Distance Education; Conference Secretary, Economic and Social History Society of Scotland. Publications include: A History of the Brewing Industry in Scotland; Industrial Archaeology in the British Isles (jointly); Scottish History 1560-1980 (jointly); That Land of Exiles: Scots in Australia (jointly); Forward! Labour Politics in Scotland 1888-1988 (Co-Editor); A Companion to Scottish History from the Reformation to the Present (jointly); The Manufacture of Scottish History (Co-editor); Historic New Lanark: the Dale and Owen Industrial Community since 1785 (Co-author). Recreations: walking; curling; eating; drinking. Address: (b.) 10 Drumsheugh Gardens, Edinburgh, EH3 7QJ; T.-0131-226 3851.

Donnelly, Dougie. Radio and Television Broadcaster, since 1976; b. 7.6.53, Glasgow; m., Linda; 3 d. Educ. Hamilton Academy; Strathclyde University. Studied law at University; Presenter, BBC Sports: Grandstand, Sportscene, World Championship snooker and bowls, golf; Radio Clyde mid-morning show, 1979-91. Scottish Radio Personality of Year, 1979, 1982 and 1985; Scottish TV Personality of Year, 1982; Member: Stars Organisation for Spastics, Lords Taverners. Recreations: golf; reading; socialising; work. Address: (b.) c/o David John Associates, 90 Barrington Drive, Glasgow, G4 9ET; T.-0141-357 0532.

Donnison, Professor David. Honorary Research Fellow, Glasgow University; Visiting Professor, Warwick University; b. 19.1.26. Lecturer: Manchester University, 1950-53, Toronto University, 1953-55; London School of Economics and Political Science: Reader, 1956-61, Professor, 1961-69; Director, Centre for Environmental Studies, London, 1969-75; Chairman, Supplementary Benefits Commission, 1975-80; Professor of Town and Regional Planning, Glasgow University, 1980-90. Address: (b.) Glasgow University, Glasgow, G12 8RT.

Donohoe, Brian H. MP (Labour), Cunninghame South, since 1992; b. 10.9.48, Kilmarnock; m., Christine; 2 s. Educ. Irvine Royal Academy; Kilmarnock Technical College. Secretary, Irvine and District Trades Council, 1973-81; Chair, North Ayrshire and Arran LHC, 1977-79; Chair, Cunninghame Industrial Development Committee, 1975-79; former full-time trade union official (NALGO). Recreation: gardening. Address: (h.) 5 Greenfield Drive, Irvine, Ayrshire; T.-01294 274419.

Donovan, Professor Robert John, BSc, PhD, CChem, FRSC, FRSE. Professor of Chemistry, Edinburgh University, since 1979; b. 13.7.41, Nantwich; m., Marion Colclough; 1 d. Educ. Sandbach School; University College of Wales, Aberystwyth; Cambridge University. Research Fellow, Gonville and Caius College, 1966-70; Edinburgh University: Lecturer in Physical Chemistry, 1970-74, Reader in Chemistry, 1974-79. Member, Physical Chemistry Panel, Science & Engineering Research Council, 1977-80; Member, Management Committee, SERC Synchrotron Radiation Source, Daresbury, 1977-80; Member, SERC Synchroton Radiation Facility Committee, 1979-84; Chairman, SERC Laser Facility Committee, 1989-92; Member, SERC Science Board, 1989-92; Chairman, Facilities Commission, SERC, 1993-94; awarded Corday-Morgan Medal and Prize, Royal Society of Chemistry, 1975; Member, Faraday Council, Royal Society of Chemistry, 1981-83, 1991-93. Recreations: hill-walking; skiing; sail-boarding; cross-country riding. Address: (b.) Department of Chemistry, Edinburgh University, West Mains Road, Edinburgh, EH9 3JJ; T.-0131-650 4722.

Dorman, Arthur Brian, LLB, FIMgt. Solicitor; Founding and Senior Partner, Dorman, Jeffrey & Co., Glasgow and Edinburgh; b. 21.6.45, Glasgow; 1 s.; 1 d. Educ. Hillhead High School; Glasgow University. Recreation: occasional golf. Address: (b.) Madeleine Smith House, 6/7 Blythswood Square, Glasgow, G2 4AD; T.-0141-221 9880.

Dorward, Adam Paterson, FCFI. Member, Borders Health Board (Convener, Finance Committee), 1978-89; b. 11.6.22, Galashiels; m., Jean MacPherson Ovens; 2 s. Educ. Sedbergh School; St. John's College, Cambridge; Dundee School of Economics; Tailor & Cutter Academy; Stevenson College. RAF, 1942-46 (Flt. Lt. Pilot, Flying Instructor); J. & J. Dorward Ltd., Gala Forest: joined, 1946, appointed Designer/Production Manager, 1948, appointed Director, 1952, Managing Director, 1972, Chairman, 1978; negotiated amalgamation with Dawson International, remaining Managing Director for 18 months; administration, Youth Opportunities Programme and Youth Training Scheme, Borders Regional Council, 1982-84; Business Consultant, 1984; Production Co-ordinator, clothing manufacturer, 1985-87. Former Governor, Scottish College of Textiles; Town and County Councillor, 1955-60; Member, Board, Galashiels Further Education College, 1955-60; Deacon, Galashiels Manufacturers' Corporation,

1960; a Governor, St. Mary's Preparatory School, Melrose, 1960; Council Member, Clothing Manufacturers' Federation of GB, 1973-81; Chairman, Scottish Clothing Manufacturers' Association, 1975-79; Past Chairman, Border Counties TSB; former Trustee, TSB of South of Scotland; Member, Eildon Housing Association, since 1978; Trustee, R.S. Hayward Trust. Recreations: sports; gardening. Address: (h.) Letham, Tweedmount Road, Melrose, TD6 9ST; T.-0896 82 2723.

Dorward, David Campbell, MA, GRSM, LRAM. Composer, since 1944; Music Producer, BBC, 1962-91; b. 7.8.33, Dundee; m., Janet Offord; 1 s.; 2 d. Educ. Morgan Academy, Dundee; St. Andrews University; Royal Academy of Music. Teaching, 1960-61; Freelance, 1961-62. Arts Adviser, Lamp of Lothian Collegiate Trust, since 1967; Member, Scottish Arts Council, 1972-78; Consultant Director, Performing Right Society, 1985-90; Patron's Fund Award, 1958; Royal Philharmonic Prizewinner, 1958; compositions include four string quartets, symphony, four concertos, Tonight Mrs Morrison (one-act opera), A Christmas Carol (musical), and incidental music for TV, radio, film and stage. Recreations: photography; computers; walking in the country. Address: (h.) 10 Dean Park Crescent, Edinburgh, EH4 1PH; T.-0131-332 3002.

Dorward, David Philip, MA (Hons), LLB. Honorary Sheriff, Tayside, Central and Fife at Cupar, since 1995; b. 10.4.31, Dundee; m., Joy Stewart; 2 s. Educ. Dundee High School; St. Andrews University. Joined St. Andrews University as Administrative Assistant, 1959; successively Assistant Secretary, Deputy Secretary, Secretary; retired. Publications: Scottish Surnames; Scotland's Place-Names. Recreations: music; golf; gardening; walking; European travel. Address: (h.) 7 Drumcarron Crescent, Strathkinness, KY16 9XT; T.-0133 4850630.

Douglas, Alan. Journalist and Broadcaster; b. 16.10.51, Dundee; m., Viv Lumsden (qv); 2 d. Educ. Forfar Academy. Local newspapers, 1970-74; BBC Local Radio Reporter and Producer, 1974-78; Reporter/Presenter, BBC TV Scotland, 1978-89; freelance broadcaster and journalist, BBC TV and Radio, Scottish TV, and corporate; Partner, The Broadcasting Business (media consultancy). Recreations: home improvement and renovation. Address: 9 Lethington Road,k Glasgow, G46 6TA.

Douglas, David Pringle, DipTP, MRTPI. Chief Executive, Scottish Borders Enterprise, since 1990; b. 13.5.39, Edinburgh; m., Diane; 1 s.; 1 d. Local government, 1957-86; Material International, USA, 1986-87; Roger Tym & Partners, Glasgow, 1987-90. Recreations: golf; walking. Address: (b.) Bridge Street, Galashiels, TD1 1SW; T.-01896 758991.

Douglas, Gavin Stuart, RD, QC, MA, LLB; b. 12.6.32. Educ. South Morningside School; George Heriot's School; Edinburgh University. Solicitor, 1955; admitted to Faculty of Advocates, 1958; Member, Lord Advocate's Department in London, 1961-64; returned to practice at Scots Bar, 1964; Counsel to Scottish Law Commission, since 1965; Hon. Sheriff, 1965-71; a Chairman of Industrial Tribunals, 1966-78; Senior Counsel to Secretary of State for Scotland under Private Legislation Procedure (Scotland) Act 1936, since 1975; Member, Lothian Health Board, 1981-85; Editor, Session Cases, seven volumes, 1976-82. Recreations: golf; skiing. Address: (b.) Parliament House, Parliament Square, Edinburgh, EH1 1RF.

Douglas, James Hall, MA, LLB. Honorary Sheriff, since 1983; b. 16.9.21, Glasgow; m., Louisa Hemsworth. Educ. Whitehill Senior Secondary School, Glasgow; Glasgow University. RAF, 1940-46; Procurator Fiscal service, 1951-82, at Ayr, Glasgow, Stranraer and Dunfermline; Procurator Fiscal, Dunfermline, 1967-82. Recreations: reading;

gardening; music; philately. Address: (h.) 1 Canmore Grove, Dunfermline, KY12 OJT; T.-Dunfermline 725486.

Douglas, John Aitken, DPE, DMS, MBIM, FILAM. Director of Recreation Services, Inverclyde District Council, since 1974; b. 8.4.41, Duns; m., Anne; 1 s.; 1 d. Educ. Berwickshire High School, Duns; Scottish School of Physical Education, Jordanhill College of Education; Glasgow College of Technology. Teacher of Physical Education, Dollar Academy, 1963-65; Assistant Lecturer in Physical Education, Glasgow University, 1965-66; Lecturer in Physical Education, Strathclyde University, 1966-67; Manager, Bellahouston Sports Centre, Glasgow, 1967-71; Recreation Officer, Bishopbriggs Burgh Council, 1971-74. Churchill Fellow, 1970; Past Chairman: British and Irish Basketball Federation, 1972-73, Association of Recreation Managers, 1973-74 and 1979-80; Member, National Executive, Institute of Leisure and Amenity Management, and Past Chairman, Scottish Region; former Member, Executive, Association of Directors of Recreation, Leisure and Tourism; former Officer Adviser, COSLA. Recreations: hockey; squash; caravanning; skiing. Address: (b.) Municipal Buildings, Greenock; T.-01475 24400.

Douglas, Professor Neil James, MD, FRCP. Professor of Respiratory and Sleep Medicine, Edinburgh University; Director, Scottish National Sleep Laboratory; Dean, Royal College of Physicians of Edinburgh; Consultant Physician, since 1983; b. 28.5.49, Edinburgh; m., Dr. Sue Galloway; 1 s.; 1 d. Educ. Dundee High School; Trinity College, Glenalmond; St. Andrews University; Edinburgh University. Lecturer in Medicine, Edinburgh University, 1974-83; MRC Travelling Fellow, University of Colorado, 1980-81. Recreations: fishing; gardening; eating. Address: (b.) Respiratory Medicine Unit, Department of Medicine, Royal Infirmary, Lauriston Place, Edinburgh, EH3 9YW; T.-0131 536 3252.

Douglas, Patricia, MBE. Director, Charles Rennie Mackintosh Society; m., Thomas H. Douglas; 2 s. Recreations: tennis; bridge. Address: (b.) Queen's Cross, 870 Garscube Road, Glasgow, G20 7EL; T.-0141-946 6600.

Douglas, Sadie Naomi, MBE. Administrative Director, Scottish Civic Trust, 1983-93; b. Huddersfield; m., Alexander Douglas (deceased); 1 s. Educ. Longley Hall, Huddersfield; Huddersfield Technical College. Worked with Oxfam, 1966-70; Organising Secretary, Facelift Glasgow, 1970-73; Trust Secretary, Scottish Civic Trust, 1973-83. Member, Countrywide Holiday Association (Past President, Glasgow CHA Club); Member, Scottish Countryside Activities Council; Vice-Chairman, West Kilbride Amenity Society. Recreation: hill-walking. Address: (h.) Hillhouse, Ardneil Avenue, West Kilbride, Ayrshire, KA23; T.-01294 822465.

Douglas-Hamilton, Lord James Alexander, MA, LLB. MP (Conservative), Edinburgh West, since 1974; Minister of State for Health and Home Affairs, Scottish Office (Parliamentary Under Secretary of State for Education and Housing, 1992-95, Home Affairs and Environment, 1989-92); Honorary Secretary, Conservative Parliamentary Constitutional Committee and Conservative Parliamentary Aviation Committee; b. 31.7.42, Strathaven; m., Susan Buchan; 4 s. Educ. Eton; Balliol College, Oxford; Edinburgh University. Advocate at Scots Bar, 1968; Member, Edinburgh Town Council, 1972; Scottish Conservative Whip, 1977; a Lord Comr, HM Treasury, and Government Whip for Scottish Conservative Members, 1979-81; PPS to Malcolm Rifkind MP, at Foreign Office, later Scottish Office; Captain, Cameronian Coy., 2nd Bn., Lowland Volunteers (RARO), 1972; Honorary President, Scottish Amateur Boxing Association, since 1975; President, Royal Commonwealth Society in Scotland, 1979-87; President, Scottish Council, United Nations

Association, 1981-87. Oxford Boxing Blue, 1961; President, Oxford Union Society, 1964. Publications: Motive For A Mission: The Story Behind Hess's Flight to Britain, 1971; The Air Battle for Malta: The Diaries of a Fighter Pilot, 1981; Roof of the World, 1983; The Truth about Rudolf Hess, 1993. Recreations: golf; forestry; debating; history; boxing. Address: House of Commons, London, SW1A 0AA; T.-0171-219 4399.

Douglas-Home, Hon. (Lavinia) Caroline, FSA Scot. Estate Factor, Douglas and Angus Estates, since 1959; Trustee, National Museum of Antiquities of Scotland, 1982-85; Deputy Lieutenant, Berwickshire, since 1983; b. 11.10.37 (daughter of Baron Home of the Hirsel, KT, PC). Educ. privately. Woman of the Bedchamber (Temporary) to Queen Elizabeth the Queen Mother, 1963-65; Lady-In-Waiting (Temporary) to HRH Duchess of Kent, 1966-67. Recreations: fishing; reading; antiquities. Address: (h.) Heaton Mill House, Cornhill-on-Tweed, Northumberland; T.-01890 882303.

Douglas Home, Mark. Deputy Editor, Scotland on Sunday, since 1995. Address: (b.) 20 North Bridge, Edinburgh, EH1 1YT.

Dover, Sir Kenneth James, BA, MA, DLitt, Hon.LLD (St. Andrews, Birmingham), Hon.LittD (St. Andrews, Bristol, London, Liverpool, Durham), Hon.DHL (Oglethorpe), FRSE, FBA. Chancellor, St. Andrews University, since 1981; b. 11.3.20, Croydon; m., Audrey Ruth Latimer; 1 s.; 1 d. Educ. St. Paul's School, London; Balliol College, Oxford; Merton College, Oxford. Fellow and Tutor, Balliol College, Oxford, 1948-55; Professor of Greek, St. Andrews, 1955-76; President, Corpus Christi College, Oxford, 1976-86. Served in Royal Artillery, 1940-45; President, Hellenic Society, 1971-74; President, Classical Association, 1975; President, British Academy, 1978-81; Foreign Honorary Member, American Academy of Arts and Sciences, since 1979; Foreign Member, Royal Netherlands Academy, since 1979; Honorary Fellow, Balliol, Corpus Christi and Merton Colleges, Oxford. Recreations:lonely country; historical linguistics. Address: (h.) 49 Hepburn Gardens, St. Andrews, Fife, KY16 9LS; T.-01334 473589.

Dow, Professor Alexander Carmichael, MA, PhD. Professor and Head, Department of Economics, Glasgow Caledonian University, since 1989; b. 28.8.46; m., Sheila Christine; 2 d. Educ. Perth Academy; St. Andrews University; Simon Fraser University; University of Manitoba. Research Officer, Commonwealth Secretariat; Lecturer and Assistant Professor, University of Toronto; Lecturer, Stirling University. Recreations: curling; travel. Address: (b.) Department of Economics, Glasgow Caledonian University, Cowcaddens Road, Glasgow, G4 0BA; T.-041-331 3310.

Dow, Rear-Admiral Douglas Morrison, CB. Director, National Trust for Scotland, since 1992; b. 1.7.35; m., Felicity Margaret Mona Napier; 2 s.; Educ. George Heriot's School; BRNC Dartmouth. Joined RN, 1952; served Staff of C-in-C Plymouth, 1959-61; HMS Plymouth, 1961-63; RN Supply Sch., 1963-65; Staff of Comdr FEF, 1965-67; HMS Endurance, 1968-70; BRNC Dartmouth, 1970-72; Cdr 1972; Assistant Director, Officer Appointments (S), 1972-74; Sec to Comdr British Navy Staff, Washington, 1974-76; HMS Tiger, 1977-78; NDC Latimer, 1978-79; Captain 1979; CSO(A) to Flag Officer Portsmouth, 1979; Sec to Controller of Navy, 1981; Captain, HMS Cochrane, 1983; Commodore, HMS Centurion, 1985; RCDS, 1988; Rear Admiral, 1989; Director General, Naval Personal Services, 1989-92; FBIM. Recreations: rugby union; fly fishing; shooting; golf; gardening. Address: (b.) National Trust for Scotland, 5 Charlotte Square, Edinburgh, EH2 4DU; T.-0131-226 5922.

Dow, Sheila Christine, MA (Hons), PhD. Reader in Economics, Stirling University, since 1988; b. 16.4.49, Dumfries; m., Professor Alexander Dow; 2 d. Educ. Hawick High School; St. Andrews University; University of Manitoba; McMaster University; Glasgow University. Overseas Office, Bank of England, 1970-72; Economist, then Senior Economist, Department of Finance, Government of Manitoba, 1973-77; Lecturer, Department of Economics, Stirling University, 1979-88. Publications: Macroeconomic Thought, 1985; Financial Markets and Regional Economic Development, 1990; Money Matters (Co-author), 1982; Money and the Economic Process, 1993. Recreations: travel; various sports. Address: (b.) Department of Economics, Stirling University, Stirling, FK9 4LA; T.-01786 473171, Ext. 7474.

Downes, Robert, DipTP, BPhil. Director, Industry and Skills, Scottish Enterprise, since 1994; b. 10.8.51, Belfast; m., Pauline; 2 s. Educ. Portora Royal School, Enniskillen; Dundee University. Local government, 1976-82; Dundee Project, 1982-84; SDA, 1984-87; Director, North East, SDA, 1987-90; Director, Conran Roche Planning, London, 1990-92; independent consultant, 1992-93; Chief Executive, Dumfries and Galloway Enterprise, 1993-94; Director, Scottish and International Operations, Scottish Enterprise, 1994. Advisor, Ulster Community Conference and Flax Trust, Belfast, since 1994; Director, CTF Training Ltd., since 1990; Director, Investors in People, Scotland, since 1994; part-time Lecturer, Strathclyde University, since 1994. Recreations: running; cycling; live music; travelling; films; pub crack; Jim Thompson novels; journalists' biographies; Kelvin walkway. Address: (h.) 18 Cleveden Gardens, Kelvinside, Glasgow, G12 0PT; T.-0141-357 1651.

Downie, Professor Robert S., MA, BPhil, FRSE. Professor of Moral Philosophy, Glasgow University, since 1969 (Stevenson Lecturer in Medical Ethics, 1984-88); b. 19.4.33, Glasgow; m., Eileen Dorothea Flynn; 3 d. Educ. High School of Glasgow; Glasgow University; Queen's College, Oxford. Tutor, Worcester College, Oxford, 1958-59; Glasgow University: Lecturer in Moral Philosophy, 1959-68, Senior Lecturer, 1968-69; Visiting Professor: Syracuse University, New York, 1963-64, Dalhousie University, Nova Scotia, 1976. Publications: Government Action and Morality, 1964; Respect for Persons, 1969; Roles and Values, 1971; Education and Personal Relationships, 1974; Caring and Curing, 1980; Healthy Respect, 1987; Health Promotion: models and values, 1990; The Making of a Doctor, 1992; Francis Hutcheson, 1994; The Healing Arts: an Oxford illustrated anthology, 1994. Recreation: music. Address: (b.) Department of Philosophy, Glasgow University, G12 8QQ; T.-0141-339 8855.

Downs, Ian, DipArch, DipTP, RIBA, MRTPI, FRIAS. Chief Architect/Planner and Technical Director, Irvine Development Corporation; b. 21.2.37, Withernsea, East Yorkshire; 1 s.; 1 d. Educ. Withensea High School; Hull School of Architecture; Manchester University. Architect, Cumbernauld Development Corporation, 1960-63; Architect/Planner: United States (private practice, working on New Towns), 1964-65, Wilson & Womersely, 1965-66; Group Architect, Livingston Development Corporation, 1966-69; Assistant Chief Architect: Redditch Development Corporation, 1969-76, West Midlands Metropolitan County Council, 1976-79. Recreation: sailing. Address: (b.) Irvine Development Corporation, Perceton House, Irvine; T.-Irvine 214100.

Dowson, Henry Richard, BSc, PhD, FRSE. Reader in Mathematics, Glasgow University, since 1975; Editor-in-Chief, Glasgow Mathematical Journal, since 1975; b. 2.3.39, Newcastle-upon-Tyne. Educ. Royal Grammar School, Newcastle-upon-Tyne; King's College, Newcastle-upon-Tyne; St. John's College, Cambridge. Assistant Lecturer, Department of Pure Mathematics, University

College of Swansea, 1963-65; Lecturer, Department of Mathematics, Newcastle-upon-Tyne University, 1965-66; Assistant Professor, Illinois University, 1966-68; Department of Mathematics, Glasgow University: Lecturer, 1968-73, Senior Lecturer, 1973-75. Publication: Spectral Theory of Linear Operators, 1978. Recreation: bridge; numismatics. Address: (b.) Department of Mathematics, University Gardens, Glasgow, G12 8QW; T.-041-339 8855, Ext. 6537.

Doyle, Professor Christopher John, BA, MSc. Head of Economics, Marketing and Management Department, Scottish Agricultural College, Auchincruive, since 1989; Adjunct Professor of Agricultural Economics, Glasgow University, since 1989; Vice Dean (Education), 1991-94, and Professor of Agricultural Economics, since 1994, Scottish Agricultural College, Auchincruive; b. 21.8.48, Sale, Cheshire; m., Alice; 1. d. Educ. St Ambrose College, Cheshire; Keele University; Newcastle upon Tyne University. Departmental Demonstrator in Agricultural Economics, Oxford University, 1972-76; Research Officer, Centre for Agricultural Strategy, Reading University, 1976-79; Principal Scientific Officer, Institute for Grassland and Animal Production, 1979-86; Senior Economist, Ruakura Research Centre, MAF, New Zealand, 1987; Principal Scientific Officer, Institute for Grassland and Animal Production, 1988-89. Publications: 80 scientific papers and publications. Recreations: languages; foreign travel; modern history; theatre. Address: (b.) Scottish Agricultural College, Auchincruive, Ayr, KA6 5HW; T.-01292 520331.

Doyle, Rev. Ian Bruce, MA, BD, PhD. Pastoral Assistant, Palmerston Place Church, Edinburgh, since 1989; General Secretary, Department of National Mission, 1984-89; b. 11.9.21, Methil, Fife; m., Anne Watt Wallace; 2 s. Educ. Buckhaven High School; St. Andrews University; New College, Edinburgh. Served with Church of Scotland Huts, Germany, 1945-46; Assistant to Rev. D.P. Thomson, Evangelist, 1946; Minister: St. Mary's, Motherwell, 1946-60, Eastwood, Glasgow, 1960-77; Convener: Home Mission Committee, 1970-74, Home Board, 1974-77; Secretary, Department of Home Mission, 1977-84; Joint Secretary, Department of Ministry and Mission, 1984-89; General Secretary, Board of National Mission, 1989-91; Secretary, Prison Chaplaincies Board, 1977-89. Publications: This Jesus; Reformation and Revolution (Contributor); The Word for All Seasons (Contributor); Local Church Evangelism (Contributor); D.P.: a memoir of Dr. D.P. Thomson. Recreation: reading. Address: (h.) 21 Lygon Road, Edinburgh; T.-0131-667 2697.

Draper, Professor Paul Richard, BA, MA, PhD. Professor of Finance, Strathclyde University, since 1986 (Head, Department of Accounting and Finance, since 1990); Vice Dean, Strathclyde Business School, since 1993; b. 28.12.46, Hayes; m., Janet Margaret; 1 s.; 1 d. Educ. Exeter, Reading and Stirling Universities. Lecturer: St. Andrews and Edinburgh Universities. Publication: Scottish Financial Sector (Co-author), 1988; Investment Trust Industry in the UK, 1989. Recreations: renovating country cottages; home computing. Address: (h.) 19 Upper Gray Street, Newington, Edinburgh; T.-0131-667 4087.

Drewry, James Michael, FITSA, DCA. Director of Trading Standards, Lothian Regional Council, since 1989; b. Hexham. Trained, Northumberland County Council; Inspector of Weights and Measures, Cheshire County Council; Senior Assistant Chief Trading Standards Officer, Humberside County Council, 1976-79; County Consumer Protection Officer, Durham County Council, 1980-89. Past Chairman, Institute of Trading Standards Administration; Chairman, Prosafe (Product Safety Enforcement Forum of Europe); President, European Consumer Product Safety Association; Member, Sheriff Court Rules Council. Recreations: squash; golf; travel. Address: (b.) Chesser House, 500 Gorgie Road, Edinburgh EH11 3YJ; T.-0131-469 5454.

Drummond, Elizabeth, BSc (Econ) (Hons). Director of Information, Scottish Office, since 1992; b. 12.1.47, Stevenston, Ayrshire. Educ. Rhyl Grammar School; LSE. Economist, Lazard Brothers & Co. Ltd., 1967-69; Writer, Central Office of Information, 1969-73; Government Spokesman for Price Commission, 1973-77; Department of Trade, 1977-80; Prime Minister's Office, 1980-82; Chief Press Officer, Northern Ireland Office, 1982-83; Chief Press Officer (later Deputy Director), Home Office, 1983-86; Chief Information Officer, Department of Education and Science, 1986-88; Director of Public Affairs, Institute of Chartered Accountants in England and Wales, 1988-89; Head of Public Relations, Westminster City Council, 1989-92. Recreations: reading; walking; music; gardening; cooking. Address: (b.) New St. Andrew's House, Edinburgh, EH1 3TG; T.-0131-244 4969.

Drummond, Humphrey, MC. Writer and Farmer; Proprietor and Managing Director, The Historical Press; b. 18.9.22, Old Buckenham, Norfolk; m., Cherry Drummond, 16th Baroness Strange; 3 s.; 3 d. Educ. Eton; Trinity College, Cambridge. Captain, 1st Mountain Regiment; former General Secretary, Council for Preservation of Rural Wales; Welsh Representative, National Trust; Chairman, Society of Authors (Scotland), 1976-82. Publications: Our Man in Scotland; The Queen's Man; The King's Enemy; Falconry For You; Falconry; Balkan Assault; Nazi Gold. Recreations: mechanical musical instruments; pre-Raphaelitism. Address: Megginch Castle, Errol, Perthshire; T.-01821 642 222.

Drummond, Rev. Norman Walker, MA, BD. National Governor and Chairman, Broadcasting Council for Scotland, since 1994; Headmaster, Loretto School, 1984-95; b. 1.4.52, Greenock; m., Lady Elizabeth Kennedy; 3 s.; 2 d. Educ. Crawfordton House, Dumfriesshire; Merchiston Castle School; Fitzwilliam College, Cambridge; New College, Edinburgh. Chaplain to the Forces, 1976-82; Depot, The Parachute Regiment and Airborne Forces, 1977-78; 1st Bn., The Black Watch (Royal Highland Regiment), 1978-82; Chaplain, Fettes College, 1982-84; Chaplain to Her Majesty the Queen in Scotland; Member, Queen's Bodyguard for Scotland (Royal Company of Archers); former Member of Court, Heriot-Watt University; President, Victoria League in Scotland, since 1995; Member, Scottish Committee for Imperial Cancer Research; Trustee, Foundation for Skin Research; Member, Scottish Committee, Duke of Edinburgh's Award Scheme; Chairman, Musselburgh and District Council of Social Services; President, Edinburgh Bn., Boys' Brigade. Publications: The First Twenty Five Years (the official history of the Black Watch Kirk Session); Mother's Hands. Recreations: rugby football; cricket; golf; curling; traditional jazz; Isle of Skye. Address: BBC Scotland, Broadcasting House, Queen Margaret Drive, Glasgow, G12 8DG; T.-0141 338 2835.

Drummond, Thomas Anthony Kevin, LLB, QC. Advocate Depute, Crown Office, 1985-90; Member, Criminal Injuries Compensation Board, since 1990; Joint Chairman, Institute of Chartered Accountants of Scotland Discipline Tribunal; Member, Firearms Consultative Committee, since 1989; b. 3.11.43, Howwood, Renfrewshire; m., Margaret Broadley; 1 d. Educ. Blairs College, Aberdeen; St. Mirin's Academy, Paisley; Edinburgh University. Civil Service, 1962-66; Solicitor, 1970-74; Bar, since 1974; QC, 1987. Cartoonist (Tak), Scots Law Times, since 1981. Recreations: shooting; hill-walking; hobbies. Address: (h.) Pomathorn House, Howgate, Midlothian; T.-Penicuik 674046.

Drummond-Young, James Edward, QC, BA, LLB; b. 17.2.50. Advocate, 1976.

Dry, Philip John Seaton, LLB. Partner, Biggart Baillie & Gifford WS, Solicitors, since 1971; b. 21.4.45, Lincolnshire; m., Joyce Christine Hall; 1 s.; 1 d. Educ George Watson's College; Greenock Academy; Glasgow University. Apprenticeship with Biggart Lumsden & Co., 1966-68; Assistant Solicitor, 1968-70; Director, Westscot Homes PLC and Westscot Homes II PLC; Director, Fyfe Chambers (Glasgow) Ltd.; Council Member, Law Society of Scotland, since 1991; Convener, Practice Management Committee, since 1992; Vice Convenor, Guarantee Fund, since 1993; Member, Post Office Users' Council for Scotland, since 1995; Director, Glasgow Renfrewshire Society. Recreations: sailing; the garden; opera; swimming; travel. Address: (b.) Dalmore House, 310 St. Vincent Street, Glasgow, G2 5QR; T.-0141-228 8000.

Dryden, Professor Myles Muir, BSc (Econ), MBA, PhD. Professor of Management Studies, Glasgow University, since 1972; b. 21.9.31, Dundee; m., Margaret Mary Cargill; 1 s.; 1 d. Educ. Kirkcaldy High School; London School of Economics; Cornell University. National Service, 1st Bn., Black Watch, BAOR, 1950-52; Assistant Professor of Finance, Sloan School of Industrial Management, Massachusetts Institute of Technology, 1960; Lecturer, then Reader in Economics, Edinburgh University, 1963-72; appointed to first Chair of Management Studies, Glasgow University, 1972 (Head of Department, until 1980); Member, Scottish Business School Council, 1975-79; has published in a number of professional journals; research on capital budgeting, share price behaviour and portfolio management. Recreations: pottering about in the garden or with microcomputers. Address: (b.) Department of Management Studies, 55 Southpark Avenue, Glasgow, G12 8LF; T.-0141-330 4664.

Drysdale, Thomas Henry, LLB, WS. Solicitor; Deputy Keeper of Her Majesty's Signet, since 1991; Partner, Shepherd & Wedderburn, WS, Edinburgh, since 1967 (Managing Partner, 1988-94); b. 23.11.42, Buchlyvie; m., Caroline Shaw; 1 s.; 2 d. Educ. Cargilfield; Glenalmond; Edinburgh University. Chairman, Edinburgh Solicitors Property Centre, 1981-88. Recreations: skiing; walking; reading. Address: (b.) Saltire Court, 20 Castle Terrace, Edinburgh, EH1 2ET; T.-0131-228 9900.

Dudgeon, Alexander (Sandy) Stewart, MA, CA. Managing Director, Martin Currie Unit Trusts Ltd., since 1994; b. 16.10.57, Edinburgh; m., Jennifer J.K. Waddell; 2 s.; 1 d. Educ. Trinity College; Glenalmond; Aberdeen University. Adam & Company PLC: Company Secretary, 1983-86, Director, 1983-94; Member, Horseracing Advisory Council, 1985-90. Recreations: racing; farming; squash; golf; bridge. Address: (h.) 3 Cluny Drive, Edinburgh, EH10 6DW; T.-0131-229 5252.

Dudley Edwards, Owen, BA, FRHistS. Reader in History, Edinburgh University; b. 27.3.38, Dublin; m., Barbara Balbirnie Lee; 1 s.; 2 d. Educ. Belvedere College, Dublin; University College, Dublin; Johns Hopkins University, Baltimore. Visiting Lecturer in History, University of Oragon, 1963-65; Assistant Lecturer in History, Aberdeen University, 1966-68; Lecturer in History, Edinburgh University, 1968-79; Visiting Lecturer, California State University of San Francisco, 1972-73; Visiting Associate Professor, University of South Carolina, 1973; Sir David Owen Evans Lecturer, University College of Wales, Aberystwyth, 1987; Journalist and Broadcaster, notably for Irish Times, since 1959, and BBC, since 1969; contributor to various journals, especially The Scotsman. Life Member: American Historical Association, Organisation of American Historians, Royal Medical Society (Edinburgh University), Royal Lyceum Theatre Club; External Examiner: Queen's University, Belfast, Bradford University, Manchester University, Sorbonne, University College Cardiff. Publications: Celtic Nationalism (with Gwynfor Evans, Ioan Rhys and Hugh MacDiarmid), 1968; The Sins of Our Fathers - Roots of Conflict in Northern Ireland, 1970; The Mind of an Activist - James Connolly, 1971; P.G. Wodehouse - a Critical and Historical Essay, 1977; Burke and Hare, 1980; The Quest for Sherlock Holmes: a Biographical Study of Arthur Conan Doyle, 1982; Eamon de Valera, 1987; Macaulay (Historians on Historians), 1988; The Edinburgh Festival, 1990; City of 1000 Worlds — Edinburgh in Festival, 1991; as Editor/Contributor: 1916 - The Easter Rising (with Fergus Pyle), 1968; Conor Cruise O'Brien Introduces Ireland, 1969; James Connolly: Selected Political Writings (with Bernard C. Ransom), 1973; Scotland, Europe and the American Revolution (with George Shepperson), 1976; Christmas Observed (with Graham Richardson), 1981; Edinburgh (with Graham Richardson), 1983; A Claim of Right for Scotland, 1989; The Fireworks of Oscar Wilde, 1989; A. Conan Doyle: The Exploits of Brigadier Gerard, 1991; The Oxford Sherlock Holmes (General Editor), 1993. Address: (b.) Department of History, Edinburgh University, George Square, Edinburgh.

Duff, John Hume, MA (Cantab), MA (Edin), DipEd (Oxon). Rector, Kelvinside Academy, since 1980; b. 24.4.40, Edinburgh. Educ. St. Mary's School, Melrose; Edinburgh Academy; Corpus Christi College, Cambridge; Edinburgh University; Brasenose College, Oxford. Housemaster and Head of History Department, Kelly College, Tavistock, Devon, 1967-80. Major, TA. Recreations: squash rackets; skiing; hill-walking; foreign travel. Address: (b.) Kelvinside Academy, 33 Kirklee Road, Glasgow, G12 OSW; T.-0141-357 3376.

Duffty, Paul, MB, ChB, FRCP, LMCC. Consultant Paediatrician, since 1982; Senior Lecturer in Child Health, Aberdeen University, since 1982; b. 1.9.46, Leeds; m., Lesley Marjory Macdonald; 2 d. Educ. Leeds Central High School; Aberdeen University. Lecturer in Child Health, Aberdeen University, 1972-75; Trainee in General Practice, Aberdeen, 1975-76; Lecturer in Child Health, Aberdeen University, 1976-78; Fellow in Neonatology, Toronto University, 1978-80; Staff Paediatrician, Hospital for Sick Children, Toronto, and Assistant Professor, Toronto University, 1980-82. Recreations: hill-walking; cross-country skiing; philately. Address: (h.) 13 Louisville Avenue, Aberdeen; T.-01224 317072.

Duffus, George McKay, FREHIS. City Environmental Development Officer, City of Aberdeen District Council, since 1991; b. 10.7.45, Aberdeen; m., Patricia; 2 s. Educ. Aberdeen Grammar School. Corporation of City of Aberdeen, 1964-79; City of Aberdeen District Council, since 1979. Recreations: walking; reading; listening to music. Address: (b.) Environmental Development Division, St. Nicholas House, Broad Street, Aberdeen; T.-01224 522210.

Duffus, John Henderson, BSc, PhD, DSc, CBiol, MIBiol, CChem, FRSC. Director, Edinburgh Centre for Toxicology (EdinTox); Senior Lecturer in Environmental Toxicology, Heriot-Watt University, since 1980. Educ. Arbroath High School; Edinburgh University; Heriot-Watt University. Research Fellow: Warwick University, 1965-67, Edinburgh University, 1967-70; Lecturer, Heriot-Watt University, 1970-80; WHO Consultant, Toxicology and Chemical Safety, since 1981; Member, UK Department of the Environment Advisory Committee on Hazardous Substances, since 1991; Titular Member, IUPAC Commission on Toxicology, since 1991; Member, RSC Committee on Environment, Health and Safety. Publications: Environmental Toxicology, 1980; Carbohydrate Metabolism in Plants (Co-author), 1984; Environmental Toxicology and Ecotoxicology, 1986; Magnesium in Mitosis and the Cell Cycle (Co-author), 1987; Yeast: A Practical Approach (Co-Editor), 1988; The Toxicology of Chemicals, Series 1, Carcinogenicity, Vol III , Vol IV (Co-Editor), 1991-93; Toxic Substances in Crop

Plants (Co-Editor/Author), 1991; Cancer and Workplace Chemicals, 1995. Address: (b.) Heriot-Watt University, Riccarton, Edinburgh, EH14 4AS; T.-0131-451 3456.

Duffy, Mgr. Francis, Former Vicar General to RC Bishop of Galloway; Resident Chaplain, Nazareth House, Kilmarnock, since 1992; b. 15.10.14, Edinburgh. Educ. Holy Cross Academy, Edinburgh; Blairs College, Aberdeen; Pontifical Scots College, Rome; Gregorian University, Rome. Ordained Priest (Rome), 1938; Curate, Ayr, 1939-41; Professor, Blairs College, Aberdeen, 1941-55; parish work in various towns, since 1955; Monsignor, since 1972. RC Religious Adviser, Scottish Television, 1958-78; Member, Dumfries Education Committee, 1963-72; Composer of congregational Church music and hymns. Address: Nazareth House, 23 Hill Street, Kilmarnock, KA3 1HG.

Duffy, Graham Woodburn. Partner, Graphic Partners Design Consultants, since 1971; Director, Edinburgh Chamber of Commerce, since 1992; Director, Scottish Design, since 1994; Fellow, Royal Society of Arts; b. 19.6.42, Edinburgh; m., Rosemary Jean; 1 s.; 1 d. Educ. Royal High School, Edinburgh; Heriot Watt College/Edinburgh College of Art. Andrew Grant Scholarship, Edinburgh College of Art, 1961-63; Graphic Designer, Pillans and Wilson, 1963-67; Graphic Designer/Typographer, Forth Studios, 1967-68; self-employed Design Consultant, 1969-71. Recreations: masters rowing; skiing; English literature; music; theatre; film. Address: (b.) 179 Canongate, Edinburgh; T.-0131-557 3558.

Duffy, John Alastair, BSc, PhD, DSc, CChem, FRSC. Reader in Chemistry, Aberdeen University, since 1991; Quality Assessor for Scottish Higher Education Funding Council, 1993-94; b. 24.9.32, Birmingham; m., Muriel F.L. Ramsay; 1 s.; 1 d. Educ. Solihull School, Warwickshire; Sheffield University. Research Chemist, Albright & Wilson, Oldbury, 1958-59; Lecturer in Inorganic Chemistry, Wolverhampton Polytechnic, 1959-61; Senior Lecturer in Inorganic Chemistry, NE Wales Institute, 1961-65; Lecturer in Chemistry, Aberdeen University, 1966-77; Assessor in Inorganic Chemistry for Ordinary and Higher National Certificates and Diplomas in Scotland, 1971-82; Consultant to Schott Glaswerke, Mainz, West Germany, 1984-86; Past Chairman, NE Scotland Section, Royal Society of Chemistry; Consultant to British Steel Corporation, 1987-91. Publications: General Inorganic Chemistry, 1966; Bonding Energy Levels and Bands in Inorganic Solids, 1990. Recreations: 20th-century opera; music. Address: (h.) 35 Beechgrove Terrace, Aberdeen, AB2 4DR; T.-01224 641752.

Duffy, John Charles, BSc, MSc, CStat. Director, Statistics and Information, Alcohol Research Group, since 1990; Hon. Secretary, Association of University Teachers (Scotland), since 1992; b. 6.3.49, Glasgow; m., Rosemary Clare Arthur; 2 s.; 1 d. Educ. St. Andrew's High School, Kirkcaldy; Edinburgh University; Reading University. Lecturer, Department of Statistics, Edinburgh University, and Non-Clinical Scientist, Medical Research Council, 1970-89; Senior Lecturer, Department of Statistics, Edinburgh University, since 1990. President, Association of University Teachers (Scotland), 1988-90. Recreations: reading; music; computers; puzzles; conversation. Address: (b.) Alcohol Research Group, Department of Psychiatry, Edinburgh University, Kennedy Tower, Morningside Park, Edinburgh, EH10 5HF; T.-0131-537 6505.

Duffy, Sheila Sinclair, MA. Women's Editor, Radio Clyde, since 1973; Freelance Journalist, since 1967; b. 6.8.46, Silloth, Cumberland; m., Paul Young; 2 d. Educ. St. Joseph's, Nicosia; Boroughmuir School, Edinburgh; Edinburgh University. Auxiliary nurse, Edinburgh Royal Infirmary, 1965-66; croupier, Edinburgh night club, 1966-67; graduate trainee, Scottish Television, 1967-68; Reporter, Scottish Television, 1968-73; Presenter, Dateline Early/Edinburgh Film Festival programmes/Moneywise; Member, Visiting Committee, Glenochil Young Offenders Institution, since 1995. Glenfiddich Food Writer Award, 1986. Recreations: children; husband; genealogy; cooking; reading; cake decorating; walking; sampler embroidery. Address: c/o Young Casting Agency, 7 Beaumont Gate, Glasgow; T.-0141-339 5180.

Duggan, Professor Arthur William, BSc, MB, BS, MD, PhD, FRSE. Professor of Veterinary Pharmacology, Edinburgh University, since 1987; b. 14.6.36, Brisbane; m., Gwyndolyn Helen Randall; 2 s.; 1 d. Educ. Brisbane Grammar School; Queensland University. Medical practice, 1961-67; medical research, Institute of Advanced Studies, Australian National University, Canberra, 1968-87. Publications: over 100 scientific papers. Address: (h.) 5c Strathalmond Road, Edinburgh, EH4 8AB.

Duggan, Connell, MA, JP. Headteacher, St. Augustine's R.C. High School, Edinburgh, since 1992; b. 19.8.37, Edinburgh; m., Theresa Mary Clair; 2 s.; 1 d. Educ. St. Mary's Academy, Bathgate; Edinburgh University; Moray House College of Education. Teacher, St. Mary's, West Calder, 1959-62; Special Assistant, St. Mary's, Bathgate, 1962-70; Senior Housemaster, St. Aidan's, Wishaw, 1970-73; Assistant Headteacher, St. Kentigern's, Blackburn, 1973-79; Deputy Headteacher, St. Augustine's, Edinburgh, 1979-92. President, Scottish Schools Football Association, 1984-86, 1992-94; Council Member, SFA, 1992-94, Life Member, since 1994; Member, East Calder District Council, 1963-76; Board, Livingston Development Corporation, 1967-75. Recreations: literature; cinema; theatre; music; soccer; bowls; bridge. Address: (h.) 2 Burngrange Gardens, West Calder, EH55 8ES; T.-01506 873822.

Dukes, Professor Paul, BA (Cantab), MA, PhD. Professor of History, Aberdeen University, since 1988; b. 5.4.34, Wallington; m., Rosemary Mackay; 1 s.; 1 d. Educ. Wallington County Grammar School; Cambridge University. Advisory Editor, History Today. Publications: several books on aspects of Russian, American, European and world history. Recreations: hill-walking; travel. Address: (b.) History Department, Aberdeen University, Aberdeen; T.-01224 272465.

Dun, Thomas Dixon Connochie. Farmer; Hon. Secretary, Royal Highland Agricultural Society, since 1995; Hon. President, North Country Cheviot Sheep Society, since 1970; b. 16.8.30, Selkirk; m., Jacqueline Joan Bruce; 3 s.; 1 d. Educ. Dollar Academy; Edinburgh Agriculture College. Farming, since 1953. Chairman, Royal Highland Agricultural Society, 1992-93, Director, 1972-94; President, North Country Cheviot Sheep Society, 1967-68; Council Member, National Sheep Association, since 1960; winner, George Hedley Memorial Award, 1991. Recreations: horse-racing; rugby. Address: Nether Brotherstone, Heriot, Midlothian, EH38 5YS; T.-01875 835225.

Dunbar, Sir Archibald Ranulph, MA, DipAgric (Cantab), DTA (Trin). Retired; b. 8.8.27, London; m., Amelia M.S. Davidson; 1 s.; 2 d. Educ. Wellington College; Pembroke College, Cambridge. Military Service, Cameron Highlanders (attached Gordon Highlanders), 1945-48; Imperial College of Tropical Agriculture, Trinidad, 1952-53; Agricultural Officer, Colonial Service, Uganda (later Overseas Civil Service, Uganda) 1953-70; Landowner, Duffus Estate, Elgin, since 1970. Honorary Sheriff, Sheriff Court District of Moray, since 1989; Knight of Honour and Devotion, Sovereign Military Order of Malta, 1989. Recreations: swimming; railways; model railways; military models. Address: (h.) The Old Manse, Duffus, Elgin, Moray; T.-01343 830270.

130 WHO'S WHO IN SCOTLAND

Dunbar, Ian Duncan, LLB. President, Law Society of Scotland, 1993-94; Partner, Miller Hendry, Solicitors, since 1990; b. 31.10.48, Dundee; m., Susan Young. Educ. Lawside Academy, Dundee; Queens College, Dundee/St. Andrews University. Law apprentice, Soutar Reid & Mill, Dundee, 1969-71; Assistant Solicitor, Sneddon Campbell & Munro, Perth, 1971-72, Partner, 1972-85; merged to form Miller Sneddon, 1985; Partner, 1985-90; merged to form Miller Hendry, 1990. Recreations: golf; rugby; cooking; wine. Address: (h.) Craigrownie, Forgandenny Road, Bridge of Earn, Perth, PH2 9HA; T.-01738 812255.

Dunbar, John Greenwell, MA, FSA, FSA Scot, HonFRIAS. Secretary, Royal Commission on the Ancient and Historical Monuments of Scotland, 1978-90; b. 1.3.30, London; m., Elizabeth Mill Blyth. Educ. University College School, London; Balliol College, Oxford. joined staff, Royal Commission on the Ancient and Historical Monuments of Scotland, 1953; Member, Ancient Monuments Board for Scotland, 1978-90. Publications: The Historic Architecture of Scotland, 1966; Accounts of the Masters of Works, Volume 2 (1616-1649), (Joint Editor), 1982. Address: (h.) Paties Mill, Carlops, by Penicuik, Midlothian, EH26 9NF; T.-01968 660250.

Dunbar, Lennox Robert, DA, ARSA. Head of Printmaking, Grays School of Art, since 1987; Painter and Printmaker; b. 17.5.52, Aberdeen; m., Jan Storie; 2 s.; 1 d. Educ. Aberdeen Grammar School; Grays School of Art. Part-time Lecturer, 1975-82; Etching Technician, Peacock Printmakers, 1978-82; Education Officer, Peacock Printmakers, 1982-86; appointed Lecturer in Painting and Printmaking, Grays School of Art, 1986; Visiting Lecturer, Duncan of Jordanstone College of Art, Dundee, and Newcastle University; Visiting Artist/Tutor, Louisiana State University; participated in many group and one-man exhibitions; numerous awards including Latimer Award, 1978, Guthrie Award, 1984, Shell Expro Premier Award, 1991 and 1993; work in many private and public collections.

Dunbar, Morrison Alexander Rankin, FCIOB, FFB, FBIM, FRSAMD, FRSA. Chairman, Royal Scottish National Orchestra, since 1993; Chairman, Royal Scottish Academy of Music and Drama Trust, since 1992; Chairman, Scottish Philharmonic Trust; Director, Dunberon Flats Ltd., since 1962; b. 27.4.29, Glasgow; m., Sally Joan Sutherland; 2 s.; 1 d. Educ. Belmont House; Gresham House. Managing Director, Morrison Dunbar Ltd. Builders, 1957-81. President: Scottish Building Contractors Association, 1968, Scottish Building Employers Federation, 1975, Building Employers Confederation, 1980, Builders Benevolent Institution, 1987; Lord Dean of Guild, Merchants House of Glasgow, 1991-93; Chairman, Epilepsy Association of Scotland, 1990-93; Chairman, Royal Scottish Academy of Music and Drama, 1987-91; Trustee and Director, St. Mary's Music School, Edinburgh; Trustee, University of Strathclyde Foundation; Member, Lloyds of London; Member, Trades House of Glasgow. Recreations: music; art galleries; golf. Address: (h.) 18 Devonshire Terrace Lane, Glasgow, G12 9XT; T.-0141-357 1289.

Dunbar-Nasmith, Rear Admiral David Arthur, CB, DSC, DL. Chairman, Moray and Nairn Newspaper Company, 1982-91; Director, Cairngorm Chairlift Company, 1973-91; b. 21.2.21, Glen of Rothes, Rothes; m., Elizabeth Bowlby; 2 s.; 2 d. Educ. Lockers Park; Royal Naval College, Dartmouth. To sea, 1939; War service, Atlantic and Mediterranean; Commanding Officer, HM Ships Haydon, 1943-44, Peacock, 1945-46, Moon, 1946, Rowena, 1946-48, Enard Bay, 1951, Alert, 1954-56, Berwick and 5th Frigate Squadron, 1961-63, Commodore Amphibious Forces, 1966-67; Naval Secretary, 1967-70; Flag Officer Scotland and Northern Ireland, 1970-72; Member, Highlands and Islands Development Board, 1972-

83 (Chairman, 1981-82, Deputy Chairman, 1972-81); Member: Countryside Commission for Scotland, 1972-76, British Waterways Board, 1980-87, North of Scotland Hydro Electric Board, 1982-85; Gentleman Usher of the Green Rod to the Order of the Thistle; Vice Lieutenant, County of Moray; Member, Queen's Bodyguard for Scotland (Royal Company of Archers). Recreations: sailing; shooting; skiing. Address: (h.) Glen of Rothes, Rothes, Moray; T.-01340 831216.

Dunbar-Nasmith, Professor Emeritus James Duncan, CBE, BA, DA, RIBA, PPRIAS, FRSA, FRSE. Professor and Head, Department of Architecture, Heriot-Watt University and Edinburgh College of Art, 1978-88; Partner, The Law and Dunbar-Nasmith Partnership, Architects, Edinburgh, Forres, and Wiesbaden, since 1957; b. 15.3.27, Dartmouth. Educ. Lockers Park; Winchester College; Trinity College, Cambridge; Edinburgh College of Art. Lt., Scots Guards, 1945-48; ARIBA, 1954; President: Edinburgh Architectural Association, 1967-69, Royal Incorporation of Architects in Scotland, 1971-73; Member, RIBA Council, 1967-73 (Vice-President and Chairman, Board of Architectural Education, 1972-73); Council, ARCUK, 1976-84, Board of Education, 1976-88 (Vice Chairman, 1977); Member: Royal Commission on Ancient and Historical Monuments of Scotland, since 1972, Ancient Monuments Board for Scotland, 1969-82 (interim Chairman, 1972-73), Historic Buildings Council for Scotland, 1966-93; Trustee: Scottish Civic Trust, Architectural Heritage Fund, Theatres Trust, Holyrood Brewery Foundation; Member: Edinburgh New Town Conservation Committee, Council of Europa Nostra; Deputy Chairman, Edinburgh Festival Society, 1981-85. Recreations: music; theatre; skiing; sailing. Address: (b.) 16 Dublin Street, Edinburgh, EH1 3RE; T.-0131-556 8631.

Duncan, Sheriff Agnes Lawrie Addie, LLB. Sheriff of Glasgow and Strathkelvin, since 1982; b. 17.6.47. Admitted Solicitor, 1969; called to the Scottish Bar, 1976.

Duncan, Alan James, BSc (Hons), MS, PhD, CPhys, FInstP, FRSE. Reader in Physics, Stirling University, since 1989; b. 4.11.38, North Berwick; m., Helen Irene Thompson; 1 s.; 1 d. Educ. North Berwick High School; St. Andrews University; Stanford University. Research Officer: Tube Investments Ltd., 1961-63, International Research and Development Company Ltd., 1963-65; Research Assistant, Stanford University, 1965-70; Lecturer in Physics, Stirling University, 1970-89. Chairman, Scottish Branch, Institute of Physics, 1983-85; Member, Atomic Molecular and Optical Physics Committee, Institute of Physics, 1990-93; Lead Assessor, Physics in Scotland, 1993-94. Recreations: reading; swimming. Address: (h.) 13 Newton Crescent, Dunblane, FK15 0DZ; T.-01786 822806.

Duncan, Professor Archibald Alexander McBeth, MA, FBA, FRSE, FRHistS. Professor of Scottish History, Glasgow University, 1962-93; b. 17.10.26, Pitlochry; m., Ann Hayes Sawyer; 2 s.; 1 d. Educ. George Heriot's School, Edinburgh; Edinburgh University; Balliol College, Oxford. Lecturer: Balliol College, 1950-51, Queen's University, Belfast, 1951-53, Edinburgh University, 1953-61; Leverhulme Fellow, 1961-62; Clerk of Senate, Glasgow University, 1978-83. Publications: Scotland, The Making of the Kingdom; revised 3rd edition of W.C. Dickinson's Scotland from Earliest Times to 1603; Regesta Regum Scottorum, v., The Acts of Robert I 1306-29, 1988. Recreation: swimming. Address: (h.) 17 Campbell Drive, Bearsden, Glasgow, G61 4NF; T.-0141-942 5023.

Duncan, David Graham Bruce, DipArch, DipTP, RIBA, MRTPI, RIAS, FRSA. Director of Planning, City of Edinburgh District Council, since 1988; b. 23.8.36, Derby; m., Helen Teresa; 2 s. Educ. George Heriot's School, Edinburgh; Edinburgh College of Art. Architect/Planner, R.E. & B.L.C. Moira, Architects and Planning Consultants,

Edinburgh, 1960-63; Architect/Planner, Government of State of Singapore, 1963-67; Assistant Planner, then Depute County Planning Officer, East Lothian County Council, 1967-75; Director of Planning, East Lothian District Council, 1975-88. Address: 1 Cockburn Street, Edinburgh; T.-0131-225 2424.

Duncan, Geoffrey Cheyne Calderhead, BL, NP. Lord Dean of Guild, Merchants House of Glasgow, 1993-95; b. 6.10.29, Whitecraigs, Glasgow; m., Lorna Dowling; 1 s.; 1 d. Educ. Belmont House School; Glasgow Academy; Glasgow University. Partner, Aitken, Hamilton & Duncan, 1951-70; Partner, Kerr, Barrie & Duncan, 1970-91; Chairman, Glasgow Junior Chamber of Commerce, 1963-64; Director, The Girls' School Company Ltd., 1964-90 (Chairman, 1977-90); Chairman, St. Columba's School, 1972-83; Director, The West of Scotland School Company Ltd., since 1972 (Chairman, since 1989); Member, Board of Management, Glasgow South Western Hospitals, 1964-69; Member, Clyde River Purification Board, 1969-75; Director, Glasgow Chamber of Commerce, 1972-92; Chairman, Glasgow Post Office Advisory Committee, 1974-84; Member, Post Office Users' National Council, 1974-87; Chairman, Post Office Users' Council for Scotland, 1984-87; Chairman, Advisory Committee on Telecommunications for Scotland, 1984-87; Secretary, Clyde Cruising Club, 1964-69; Council Member, Clyde Yacht Clubs' Association, 1967-73; Member, Scottish Council, Royal Yachting Association, 1967-73; Director, The Merchants' House of Glasgow, since 1982; Member, Glasgow Committee, Royal National Lifeboat Institution, since 1980; Council Member, Royal Faculty of Procurators in Glasgow, 1981-84; Trustee, George Craig Trust Fund, since 1980 (Chairman, since 1989); Trustee, Ferguson Bequest Fund, since 1987; Member, Executive Committee, Abbeyfield Quarrier's Society, since 1981 (Chairman, since 1988); Member, Council of Management, Quarrier's Homes, 1985-93; Director, The Scottish Cremation Society Ltd. (Chairman, since 1993); Member, Iona Cathedral Management Board, 1990-93; Director, Iona Abbey Ltd., since 1993; Deputy Chairman, Strathclyde Region Valuation Panel, since 1993; General Commissioner for Income Tax, since 1994. Recreations: golf; curling; gardening; photography. Address: (h.) Mid Clevans, Bridge of Weir, Renfrewshire; T.-Bridge of Weir 612566.

Duncan, Professor James Lindsay, BVMS, PhD, MRCVS. Professor in Veterinary Parasitology, Glasgow University, since 1987, Vice-Dean, Faculty of Veterinary Medicine, since 1994; b. 26.2.41, Law, Carluke; m., Helen M.; 1 s.; 1 d. Educ. Wishaw High School; Glasgow University. Veterinary Practice, UK, and clinical teaching posts, Kenya, 1964-70; Glasgow University: Research Fellow, Department of Veterinary Parasitology, 1970-76, Lecturer, 1976-79, Senior Lecturer, 1979-82, Reader, 1982-87; Consultant, joint FAO/IAEA Animal Health Division, International Atomic Energy Agency, Vienna, and several multinational pharmaceutical companies; Co-author of several textbooks. Recreations: tennis; squash; golf; music. Address: (h.) Eastfield of Wiston, Biggar, Lanarkshire; T.-Lamington 270.

Duncan, James Wann, MBE, JP, MIMFT. Rector's Assessor, Dundee University; former Vice-Chairman, Tayside Health Board (Convener, General Purposes Committee); Convener, Personnel and Accommodation Sub-Committee, Management Committee, Common Services Agency; retired Senior Chief Maxillofacial Technician, Dundee Royal Infirmary; b. 14.7.25, Dundee; m., Hilda Mackenzie Gray; 3 d. Educ. Stobswell Secondary School; Dundee College of Technology. Former Convener, Property Equipment Supplies Committee, General Board of Management, Dundee General Hospitals; former Vice-Convener, General Purposes Committee, General Board of Management, Dundee Northern Hospitals; former Member, Dundee Town Council (Senior Magistrate); former

Convener: Dundee Art Galleries and Museums Committee, Further Education Committee, Dundee Police Committee; former Member, Board of Governors, Scottish Police College; Member, Dundee District Council, 1974-77 (Convener, Planning and Development Committee); Chairman, Dundee City Labour Party, 1960-62; former Member, Scottish Council, SDP; former Scottish Representative, National Committee for Dental Technicians, USDAW; former Member: STUC Health and Social Services Committee, Dundee University Court. Recreations: golf; gardening; DIY. Address: (h.) 13 Clive Road, Downfield, Dundee, DD3 8LP; T.-01382 825488.

Duncan, Leslie James, CA. Managing Partner, Scottish Region, Grant Thornton, since 1989; b. 17.11.44, Cupar; m., Liz; 2 s. Educ. George Heriot's, Edinburgh; Robert Gordon's, Aberdeen; Aberdeen University. Grant Thornton: Partner, Glasgow Office, 1975, Managing Partner, Glasgow Office, 1988. Recreation: Treasurer, Riley RM Club. Address: (b.) 112 West George Street, Glasgow, G2 1QF; T.-0141-332 7484.

Duncan, Malcolm, MA, LLB, JP. Chief Executive, East Lothian District Council, since 1987; b. 14.7.45, Cupar; m., Stephanie; 1 s.; 1 d. Educ. Royal High School, Edinburgh; Edinburgh University. Legal apprentice, Midlothian County Clerk, 1969-72; East Lothian District Council: Legal Assistant, 1972-75, Director of Administration, 1974-87. Address: (b.) Council Buildings, Haddington, East Lothian, EH41 3HA; T.-01620 824161.

Duncan, Professor William. MBChB, FRCPE, FRCSE, FRCPC, FRCR, FACR (Hon), FRACR (Hon). Professor of Radiation Oncology, Edinburgh University, since 1971; Head, Department of Clinical Oncology, Edinburgh University, since 1990; b. 29.4.30, Aberdeeen; m., Joyce Mary Gellatly; 3 s. Educ. Robert Gordon's College, Aberdeen; Aberdeen University. Consultant, Christie Hospital and Holt Radium Institute, Manchester; Lecturer, Manchester University; Director, South East Scotland Regional Radiotherapy Services; Honorary Consultant, Lothian Health Board; Chief, Department of Radiation Oncology, Ontario Cancer Institute, Princess Margaret Hospital, Toronto. Publication: Clinical Radiobiology (Co-author). Recreations: painting; gardening; music. Address: 30A Inverleith Place, Edinburgh, EH3 5QB; T.-0131-552 2898.

Duncan Millar, Ian Alastair, CBE, MC, MA, MICE, CEng, FIFM, DL. Chairman, Consultative Committee on Freshwater Fisheries, 1981-86; Vice President, Scottish Landowners Federation, 1986-90; Member, Queen's Bodyguard for Scotland (Royal Company of Archers); b. 22.11.14, Alloa; m., Louise Reid McCosh; 2 s.; 2 d. Educ. Greshams School, Holt; Trinity College, Cambridge. Civil Engineer, Sir Alexander Gibb & Partners, 1937-51 (except War years); War Service, Corps of Royal Engineers, Western Desert, Europe (with Highland Division); wounded; twice mentioned in Despatches; retired as Major; Resident Engineer i/c Pitlochry Dam and Power Station, 1946-51; Member: Perth and Kinross County Council, 1946-74 (Convener, 1970-74), Tayside Regional Council, 1974-78 (Convener, 1974-78), North of Scotland Hydro Electric Board, 1956-70 (Depute Chairman, 1970-72); Director: Macdonald Fraser & Co., Perth, 1961-84, United Auctions (Scotland) Ltd., 1963-74 (Chairman, 1967-74); fought Parliamentary elections as Liberal, Banff, 1945, Kinross and West Perth, 1949 and 1963. Director, Hill Farming Research Organisation, 1966-78; Chairman, Scottish Branch, Institute of Fisheries Management, 1980-83; Vice President, Royal Highland and Agricultural Society of Scotland, 1972. Publication: A Countryman's Cog, 1990. Recreations: fishing; shooting; knowing about salmon. Address: (h.) Reynock, Remony, Aberfeldy, Perthshire; T.-Kenmore 400.

Dundas, Ronald Edgar, MA (Hons). Chief Financial Editor, The Herald, since 1993; b. 11.7.42, Glasgow; m., Elizabeth; 1 s.; 1 d. Educ. Hutchesons' Grammar School, Glasgow; St. Salvators College, St. Andrews University. Glasgow Herald: Sub-Editor, 1964, Leader Writer, 1965, Chief Leader Writer, 1967, Business Editor, 1973. Conservative candidate: Greenock, 1966, Glasgow Kelvingrove, 1970; Chairman, East Renfrewshire Conservative Association, 1971-73. Recreations: travel; food and wine; watching cricket. Address: (b.) The Herald, 195 Albion Street, Glasgow; T.-0141-552 6255.

Dundas-Bekker, Althea Enid Philippa, DL. Deputy Lieutenant, Midlothian, since 1991; Vice Chairman, Midlothian Tourist Association, since 1988; b. 4.11.39, Gorebridge; m., Aedrian Ruprecht Bekker (deceased); 2 d. Educ. Business College, Auckland. Secretarial work abroad, in London, and with the National Trust for Scotland; inherited Arniston House, 1970, and restoring ever since. Trustee, Scottish Mining Museum; Trustee, Scottish Businessmen's Achievement Award Trust; Member, Curatorial Committee, National Trust for Scotland; Member, Royal Commission on Historical Manuscripts; Trustee, Arniston Village Improvement Trust; Chairman, Gorebridge Local History Society. Recreation: walking dogs. Address: (h.) Arniston House, Gorebridge, Midlothian, EH23 4RY; T.-0187530 238.

Dundee, 12th Earl of (Alexander Henry Scrymgeour). Hereditary Royal Standard-Bearer for Scotland; b. 5.6.49; m.; 1 s.; 3 d. Address: Farm Office, Birkhill, Cupar, Fife.

Dundonald, 15th Earl of (Iain Alexander Douglas Blair); b. 17.2.61; m., Marie Beatrice Louise Russo; 1 s.; 1 d. Educ. Wellington College; Royal Agricultural College, Cirencester. Company Director; Hon. Chilean Consul to Scotland. Recreations: marine and rural environment; rural housing; Scottish affairs. Address:Lochnell Castle, Ledaig, Argyll.

Dunion, Kevin Harry, MA (Hons), MSc. Director, Friends of the Earth Scotland, since 1991; b. 20.12.55, Bridge of Allan; 2 s. Educ. St. Andrew's High School, Kirkcaldy; St. Andrews University; Edinburgh University. HM Inspector of Taxes, 1978-80; Administrator, Edinburgh University Students Association, 1980-84; Scottish Campaigns Manager, Oxfam, 1984-91. Editor, Radical Scotland, 1982-85; Chair, Scottish Education and Action for Development, 1990-92, Board Member since 1989; Board Member, Lothian and Edinburgh Environmental Partnership; Trustee, Kathmandu Environmental Education Project; Member, Advisory Committee, UK Foundation for the Peoples of the South Pacific; Treasurer, Friends of the Earth International; Chair, Scottish Environmental Forum. Address: (b.) Bonnington Mill, 72 Newhaven Road, Edinburgh, EH6 5QG; T.-0131-554 9977.

Dunlop, Alastair Barr, OBE, FRICS. Deputy Chairman, Lothians Ethics of Medical Research Committee; Chairman, Edinburgh Branch, World Wildlife Fund; General Commissioner for Income Tax, since 1991; b. 27.12.33, Calcutta; m., Catriona C.L.H. MacLaurin; 1 s.; 1 d. Educ. Radley. National Service, 1952-54 (active service, Malaya: 2nd Lt., 1st Bn., RWK); commerce, City of London, 1954-58; agricultural student, 1959-61; Land Agent, Inverness, 1962-71 (Partner, Bingham Hughes & Macpherson); Joint Founding Director, Martin Paterson Associates Ltd., 1971. Member, Lothian Health Board, 1983-91 (Vice-Chairman, 1989-91); Chairman, Edinburgh and Borders Branch, RICS, 1977; Trustee, Paintings in Hospitals Scotland; Life Member, Institute of Directors; President, Edinburgh South Conservative Association; Chairman, South Edinburgh Conservative Association, 1980-84 and 1992-95; Chairman, Central and South, Scottish Conservative and Unionist Association, 1985-88; elected Member, Council, National Trust for Scotland, since 1992; Trustee, Paintings in Hospitals Scotland. Recreations: golf; skiing; fine arts. Address: 46 Dick Place, Edinburgh, EH9 2JB; T.-0131-667 5343.

Dunlop, Arnie, BA, DipArch, DipM, ARIAS, MCIM. Architect; a Director, Edinburgh Chamber of Commerce, since 1995; President, Edinburgh Junior Chamber of Commerce, since 1995; b. 14.12.58, Newcastle upon Tyne; m., Louise. Educ. Royal Grammar School, Newcastle upon Tyne; Liverpool Polytechnic; Heriot-Watt University. Recreations: golf; football. Address: (b.) Campbell & Arnott Ltd., 4 Albany Lane, Edinburgh; T.-0131-557 1725.

Dunlop, Eileen. Children's Writer; b. 13.10.38, Alloa; m., Antony Kamm (qv). Educ. Alloa Academy; Moray House College. Publications: Robinsheugh, 1975; A Flute in Mayferry Street, 1976; Fox Farm, 1978; The Maze Stone, 1982 (SAC Book Award); Clementina, 1985 (SAC Book Award); The House on the Hill, 1987 (commended, Carnegie Medal); The Valley of Deer, 1989; Finn's Island, 1991; Tales of St. Columba, 1992; Green Willow's Secret, 1993; (with Antony Kamm) Scottish Verse to 1800, 1985; A Book of Old Edinburgh, 1983; Finn's Roman Fort, 1994; Tales of St. Patrick, 1995. Recreations: reading; gardening; theatre. Address: (h.) 46 Tarmangie Drive, Dollar, FK14 7BP; T.-01259 742007.

Dunlop, Professor John, BSc, MSc, PhD, CEng, MIEE, MIEEE. Professor of Electronic Systems Engineering, Strathclyde University, since 1989; b. 18.4.44, Cardiff; m., Irene Margaret; 1 d. Educ. Canton High School for Boys, Cardiff; University College of Swansea. Lecturer, Senior Lecturer, Reader, Professor, Strathclyde University. Publications: Telecommunications Engineering (Co-author); numerous technical papers. Recreations: sailing; cycling; railway modelling. Address: (b.) Strathclyde University, 204 George Street, Glasgow, G1 1XW; T.-0141-552 4400.

Dunn, Bill, BA. Chief Executive, Ayr Locality Enterprise Resource Trust (ALERT), since 1988 (Managing Director, Garnock Valley Development Executive, 1984-88); b. 26.2.48, Ayr; m., Sheila; 2 s.; 2 d. Educ. Ayr Academy; Strathclyde University. Transport Manager, National Freight Corporation/British (later Scottish) Road Services, 1970-73; Administrator, Ayrshire Joint Police Committee, 1973; Internal Audit Department, British Steel Corporation, Glasgow, 1973-81; Garnock Valley Task Force: Project Co-ordinator, 1981-83, Business Development Consultant, 1983-84. Recreations: family; golf; football; music; DIY; model railways. Address: (b.) 16 Smith Street, Ayr, KA7 1TD; T.-01292 264181.

Dunn, Professor Douglas Eaglesham, BA, FRSL, Hon.LLD (Dundee, 1987), Hon.DLitt (Hull, 1995). Professor, Department of English, St. Andrews University, since 1991, and Director, St. Andrews Scottish Studies Institute, since 1993; b. 23.10.42, Inchinnan. Educ. Renfrew High School; Camphill Senior Secondary School, Paisley; Hull University. Books of poems: Terry Street, 1969, The Happier Life, 1972, Love or Nothing, 1974, Barbarians, 1979, St. Kilda's Parliament, 1981, Elegies, 1985, Selected Poems, 1986, Northlight, 1988, Dante's Drum-Kit, 1993; Secret Villages (short stories), 1985; Boyfriends and Girlfriends (short stories), 1995; Andromache (translation), 1990; Poll Tax: The Fiscal Fake, 1990; books edited: Choice of Lord Byron's Verse, 1974, The Poetry of Scotland, 1979, A Rumoured City: New Poets from Hull, 1982; Two Decades of Irish Writing: a Critical Survey, 1975; The Essential Browning, 1990; Scotland: an anthology, 1991; Faber Book of Twentieth Century Scottish Poetry, 1992; Oxford Book of Scottish Short Stories, 1995; author of plays, and TV films using commentaries in verse. Gregory Award, 1968; Somerset Maugham Award, 1972; Geoffrey Faber Memorial Prize, 1975; Hawthornden Prize, 1982; Whitbread Award for Poetry and Whitbread Book of the Year Award, 1985; Cholmondeley Award, 1989. Honorary Visiting Professor, Dundee University, 1987; Fellow in Creative Writing, St. Andrews University, 1989-91; Honorary Fellow, Humberside College, 1987. Address (b.) School of English, St. Andrews University, St. Andrews, KY16 9AL.

Dunnachie, James Francis, JP. MP (Labour), Glasgow Pollok, since 1987; b. 17.11.30. Address: (b.) House of Commons, London, SW1A 0AA.

Dunne, John Joseph, MA (Hons), MPhil, PhL, AFBPsS, CPsychol. Consultant Clinical Psychologist and Head, Community Clinical Psychology Service, Forth Valley Health Board, since 1985; Honorary Lecturer in Psychology, Stirling University, since 1986 (Director, Macmillan Nursing Research Project, since 1987); Honorary Senior Lecturer, since 1994; b. 31.8.42, Kirkcaldy; m., Marie Anne Cecile. Educ. Blairs College, Aberdeen; Gregorian University, Rome; St. Andrews University; Edinburgh University. Clinical Psychologist, Royal Edinburgh Hospital, 1977-81; Senior Clinical Psychologist (Primary Care), Dedridge and Craigshill Health Centres, Livingston, 1981-85; Honorary Fellow, Edinburgh University, since 1984; Member, Scottish Office Home & Health Department's National Panel for the Care of the Dying and Bereaved in Scotland, 1992-96; Member, steering group for establishment of BACUP (Scotland), since 1995; Member, working group to develop guidelines in palliative and cancer care, 1993; Consultant in Clinical Psychology, Cancer Relief Macmillan Fund, since 1993; Member, Advisory Group to "Partnership in Cancer Care". Address: (b.) Community Clinical Psychology Service, Department of Psychology, Stirling University, Stirling; T.-01786 67680.

Dunnet, Professor George Mackenzie, CBE, BSc, PhD, DSc, FRSE, FIBiol, FRSA. Regius Professor of Natural History, Aberdeen University, 1974-92 (Dean, Faculty of Science, 1984-87); Chairman, Salmon Advisory Committee, since 1986; Chairman, Fish Farming Advisory Committee, since 1990; Member of Council, Scottish Natural Heritage, and Chairman, its Research Board, 1992-95; Chairman, Shetland Oil Terminal Environmental Advisory Group, since 1977; b. 19.4.28, Dunnet, Caithness; m., Margaret Henderson Thomson; 1 s.; 2 d. Educ. Peterhead Academy; Aberdeen University. Research Fellow, Oxford University, 1952; Research Officer, CSIRO, Australia, 1953-58; Lecturer/Senior Lecturer in Zoology, Aberdeen University, 1958-71; Professor of Zoology, Aberdeen University, 1971-74; Director, Culterty Field Station, Aberdeen University, 1958-88; Senior Research Fellow, DSIR, New Zealand, 1968-69. Member, Committees: The Nature Conservancy, Nature Conservancy Council, Natural Environment Research Council, British Council; Chairman, Advisory Committees for Protection of Birds (Scotland, and England and Wales), 1979-81; Council Member, Scottish Marine Biological Association; President, British Ecological Society, 1979-81; Member, Red Deer Commission, 1975-80; Chairman, Advisory Committee on Science, NCC, 1990-91; Chairman, Science Research and Development Board, NCCS, 1991-92. Recreations: walking; croquet. Address: (h.) Whinhill, Inverebrie, Ellon, Aberdeen, AB41 8PT; T.-01358 761 215.

Dunnett, Sir Alastair (MacTavish), HonLLD (Strathclyde). Director, Thomson Scottish Petroleum Ltd., 1979-87; b. 26.12.08, Kilmacolm; m., Dorothy Halliday (see Dorothy Dunnett); 2 s. Educ. Overnewton School; Hillhead High School, Glasgow. Entered Commercial Bank of Scotland Ltd., 1925; Co-Founder, The Claymore Press, 1933-34; Glasgow Weekly Herald, 1935-36; The Bulletin, 1936-37; Daily Record, 1937-40; Chief Press Officer, Secretary of State for Scotland, 1940-46; Editor: Daily Record, 1946-55; The Scotsman, 1956-72; Managing Director, Scotsman Publications Ltd., 1962-70 (Chairman,

1970-74); Chairman, Thomson Scottish Petroleum Ltd., Edinburgh, 1971-79; Member, Executive Board, Thomson Organisation Ltd., 1973-78; Director, Scottish Television, 1975-79; a Governor, Pitlochry Festival Theatre, 1958-84; Member: Press Council, 1959-62, Scottish Tourist Board, 1962-70, Council, National Trust for Scotland, 1962-70, Scottish International Education Trust, Scottish Theatre Ballet Committee, Scottish Opera Committee. Publications: Treasure at Sonnach, 1935; Heard Tell, 1946; Quest by Canoe, 1950 (new edition published as The Canoe Boys, 1995); Highlands and Islands of Scotland, 1951; The Donaldson Line, 1952; The Land of Scotch, 1953; The Duke's Day, No Thanks to the Duke, 1978; Among Friends (autobiography), 1984; The Scottish Highlands (Co-author), 1988; End of Term, 1989; author of plays: The Original John Mackay, 1956; Fit to Print, 1962 (Duke of York's, London). Recreations: sailing; riding; walking. Address: (h.) 87 Colinton Road, Edinburgh, EH10 5DF; T.-0131-337 2107.

Dunnett, Dorothy, OBE. Writer, since 1960; Portrait Painter, since 1950; b. 25.8.23, Dunfermline; m., Sir Alastair M. Dunnett (qv); 2 s. Civil Service: Assistant Press Officer, Scottish Government Departments, Edinburgh, 1940-46, Executive Officer, Board of Trade, Glasgow, 1946-55; Trustee for the Secretary of State for Scotland, Scottish National War Memorial, since 1962; Director, Scottish Television p.l.c., 1979-92; Fellow, Royal Society of Arts, since 1986; Trustee, National Library of Scotland, since 1986; Director, Edinburgh Book Festival, since 1990. Publications (novels): Game of Kings, 1961; Queens' Play, 1964; The Disorderly Knights, 1966; Dolly and the Singing Bird, 1968; Pawn in Frankincense, 1969; Dolly and the Cookie Bird, 1970; The Ringed Castle, 1971; Dolly and the Doctor Bird, 1971; Dolly and the Starry Bird, 1973; Checkmate, 1975; Dolly and the Nanny Bird, 1976; King Hereafter, 1982; Dolly and the Bird of Paradise, 1983; Niccolo Rising, 1986; The Spring of the Ram, 1987; The Scottish Highlands (Co-author), 1988; Race of Scorpions, 1989; Moroccan Traffic, 1991; Scales of Gold, 1991; The Unicorn Hunt, 1993; To Lie with Lions, 1995; Contributor to Scottish Short Stories, anthology, 1973. Recreations: travel; medieval history; opera; orchestral music; ballet. Address (h.) 87 Colinton Road, Edinburgh, EH10 5DF; T.-0131-337 2107.

Dunning, Norman Moore, BA (Oxon), CQSW. Director, Enable, since 1991; b. 15.4.50, Crewe; m., Diana Mary; 2 s. Educ. Sandbach School; Jesus College, Oxford; Manchester University. Probation Officer, City of Manchester and Salford, 1973-75; Social Worker, NSPCC, 1975-77; Leader, RSSPCC Overnewton Centre, Glasgow, 1978-87; Divisional Manager (East and North Scotland), RSSPCC, 1987-91. Recreations: running; cycling; swimming. Address: (h.) 7 The Ness, Dollar, Clackmannanshire; T.-01259 43354.

Dunrossil Viscount (John William Morrison), CMG, JP, MA, KStJ. Lord Lieutenant, Western Isles, since 1993; Consultant, Bank of Bermuda, since 1989; Chairman, Bison Books Ltd., since 1989; Director, International Registries Inc., since 1993; b. 22.5.26, London; m., Diana; 3 s.; 3 d. Educ. Fettes College; Oriel College, Oxford. RAF (Pilot), 1945-48 and 1951; HM Diplomatic Service, 1951-88; served in Australia, East Pakistan, South Africa; International Maritime Consultative Organization, 1968-70; Counsellor and Head of Chancery, Ottawa, 1970-74; Counsellor, Brussels, 1975-78; High Commissioner: Fiji and Tuvalu, 1978-82, Barbados, 1982-83; Governor, Bermuda, 1983-88. Recreation: music. Address: (h.) Dunrossil House, Clachan Sands, Lochmaddy, Isle of North Uist, HS6 5AY; T.-01876 500 213.

Dunsire, Thomas, MA, LLB, WS. Partner, then Consultant, J. & J. Milligan, WS, Edinburgh (now Morton, Fraser & Milligan, WS), 1951-90; b. 16.11.26, Rangoon,

134 WHO'S WHO IN SCOTLAND

Burma; m., Jean Mary. Educ. Morrison's Academy, Crieff; Edinburgh University. Royal Navy; Solicitor and WS, 1950. Chairman, Governors, Morrison's Academy, since 1984. Recreations: formerly rugby, football, golf and cricket. Address: (h.) 40 Liberton Brae, Edinburgh.

Dunsmuir, David. Director, Disability Scotland. Address: (b.) Princes House, 5 Shandwick Place, Edinburgh, EH2 4RG.

Durham, Jane Mary Stow, MBE. Commissioner, Royal Commission for Ancient and Historical Monuments of Scotland, 1983-95; Member, Council, Society of Antiquaries for Scotland, since 1995; Vice President, Architectural Heritage Society of Scotland, since 1985; President, Tain and Easter Ross Civic Trust, since 1990; Trustee, Scottish Historic Buildings Trust; b. 26.5.24, Invergordon; m., P.E. Durham, RN (retd.); 3 s. FSA Scot; former Chairman, Scottish Vernacular Buildings Group. Recreations: trying to save church buildings within medieval parish boundaries; identifying settlement patterns from the past; driving a gig. Address: (h.) Scotsburn, Kildary, Ross-shire, IV18 0PE; T.-0186 284 2241.

Durrani, Professor Tariq Salim, BSc (Hons), MSc, PhD, FIEE, CEng, FIEEE. Professor, Department of Electronic and Electrical Engineering, Strathclyde University, since 1986; b. 27.10.43, Amraoti, India; m., Clare Elizabeth; 1 s.; 2 d. Educ. Marie Colaco High School, Karachi; Engineering University, Dacca; Southampton University. Research Fellow, Southampton University, 1970-76; joined academic staff, Strathclyde University, 1976; Director, SERC/DTI Scottish Regional Transputer Centre, since 1987; Director, DTI Centre for Parallel Signal Processing, since 1988; Director/Chairman, Scottish Electronics Technology Group; President, IEEE Signal Processing Society; Chairman, Management Committee, IT Associate Companies Scheme (ITACS). Publications: six books; over 200 technical research papers. Recreation: playing occasional golf badly. Address: (b.) Department of Electronic and Electrical Engineering, Strathclyde University, Glasgow; T.-0141-552 4400, Ext. 2883.

Durward, William Farquharson, MB, ChB, FRCP(Edin), FRCP(Glas). Consultant Neurologist, Greater Glasgow and Lanarkshire Health Boards, since 1977; Honorary Clinical Senior Lecturer in Neurology, Glasgow University, since 1978; Director, Cloburn Quarry Co. Ltd.; b. 16.9.44, Kilmarnock; m., Ann Roy Paterson; 1 s.; 1 d. Educ. Kilmarnock Academy; Glasgow University; Boston University. Employed by NHS, since 1968; specialist training grades, 1969-77. Recreations: walking; reading; railway conservation. Address: (h.) Overdale, 20 South Erskine Park, Bearsden, Glasgow, G61 4NA; T.-0141-942 3143.

Duthie, Sir Robert (Robin) Grieve, CBE (1978), CA, LLD, CBIM, FRSA, FRIAS, DTech (Napier). Chairman, Neill Clerk Group plc, since 1993; Director: Carclo Engineering Group PLC, since 1986, Royal Bank of Scotland plc, since 1978, British Assets Trust plc, since 1977, Devol Engineering Ltd., since 1993; Chairman, Tay Residential Investments plc, since 1988; Member, Board of Governors, Beatson Institute for Cancer Research, since 1989; Vice Chairman, BP Advisory Board Scotland, since 1990; b. 2.10.28, Greenock; m., Violetta Noel Maclean; 2 s.; 1 d. Educ. Greenock Academy. Apprentice Chartered Accountant, Thomson Jackson Gourlay and Taylor, CA, 1946-51; joined Blacks of Greenock, 1952; appointed Managing Director, 1962; Chairman, Black & Edgington, 1972-83. Chairman, Inverkip Society, 1966; Director, Greenock Chamber of Commerce, 1966; Member, Clyde Port Authority, 1971-83 (Chairman, 1977-80); Chairman, Scottish Development Agency, 1979-88; Chairman, Britoil PLC, 1988-90; Director, Greenock Provident Bank, 1969-75 (Chairman, 1975); Member, Scottish Telecommunications Board, 1972-77; Council Member, Institute of Chartered Accountants of Scotland, 1973-78; Member: East Kilbride Development Corporation, 1976-78, Strathclyde Region Local Valuation Appeal Panel, 1976-83; CBI Tax Liaison Officer for Scotland, 1976-79; Chairman, Made Up Textile Association of Great Britain, 1972; Member: British Institute of Management Scottish Committee, 1976, Glasgow and West of Scotland Committee, Scottish Council (Development and Industry), 1975-79; Chairman, Greenock Club, 1972; Captain, Greenock Cricket Club, 1960-61; Commissioner, Queen Victoria School, Dunblane, 1972-89; Commissioner, Scottish Congregational Ministers Pension Fund, since 1973; Member, Scottish Economic Council, since 1980; Member of Council, Royal Caledonian Curling Club, 1984-88; Treasurer, Nelson Street EU Congregational Church, Greenock, since 1970. Awarded Honorary Degree of Doctor of Laws, Strathclyde University, 1984. Recreations: curling; golf. Address: (h.) Fairhaven, 181 Finnart Street, Greenock, PA16 8JA; T.-Greenock 22642.

Dutton, Ian Murray, BSc, MSc, DipEd. Director of Education, Borders Regional Council, since 1990; b. 26.4.41, West Bridgeford; m., Margaret; 2 d. Educ. Jarrow Grammar School; Durham University; Bristol University. Chemistry Teacher, 1963-74; Northumberland County Council: Assistant Director of Education, 1975-87, Deputy Director of Education, 1988-90. Recreations: fishing; golf; gardening. Address: (b.) Regional Headquarters, Newtown St. Boswells, Melrose, TD6 0SA; T.-01835 23301.

Duxbury, Professor Geoffrey, BSc, PhD, CPhys, FInstP. Professor, Chemical Physics, Strathclyde University; b. 6.11.42, Blackburn; m., Mary R.; 1 s.; 1 d. Educ. Cheadle Hulme School; Sheffield University. Junior Research Fellow, National Physical Laboratory, 1967-69; Research Assistant, Research Associate, Lecturer in Chemical Physics, Bristol University, 1970-80; Senior Lecturer/Reader, Strathclyde University, 1981-86. Marlow Medal, Faraday Division, Royal Society of Chemistry, 1975. Address: (b.) Department of Physics and Applied Physics, Strathclyde University, Glasgow, G4 0NG; T.-0141-552 4400.

Dyer, James A.T., MB, ChB (Hons), FRCPsych. Medical Commissioner, Mental Welfare Commission for Scotland, since 1991, and Director, since 1993; b. 31.12.46, Arbroath; m., Suzanne Whitaker; 2 s.; 1 d.; 1 step-s.; 2 step d. Educ. Bo'ness Academy; Robert Gordon's College, Aberdeen; Aberdeen University. Trainee General Practitioner, Skene, Aberdeenshire, 1971-72; junior clinical appointments, then Senior Registrar in Psychiatry, Royal Edinburgh Hospital, 1972-77; Scientific Officer, MRC Unit for Epidemiological Studies in Psychiatry, Edinburgh, 1977-80; Consultant Psychiatrist, Royal Edinburgh Hospital, 1981-91; Chairman, Royal College of Psychiatrists, Section for Social, Community and Rehabilitation Psychiatry; Member, Medical Action for Global Security. Recreations: walking; reading; photography. Address: (b.) 37 Lauder Road, Edinburgh, EH9 1UE; T.-0131-667 2479.

E

Eagles, John Mortimer, MBChB, MPhil, FRCPsych. Consultant Psychiatrist, Royal Cornhill Hospital, Aberdeen, since 1985; Honorary Senior Lecturer in Mental Health, Aberdeen University, since 1985; b. 21.10.52, Newport-on-Tay; m., Janette Isobel Rorke; 2 d. Educ. Bell-Baxter High School, Cupar; Aberdeen University; Edinburgh University. Resident House Officer posts, Aberdeen, 1977-78; Senior House Officer/Registrar in Psychiatry, Royal Edinburgh Hospital, 1978-82; Lecturer, Department of Mental Health, Aberdeen University, 1982-85; Psychiatric Tutor for trainee psychiatrists, Aberdeen, 1987-92. Chairman, North-East Regional Postgraduate Medical Education Committee, since 1990. Recreations: cricket; golf; travel; reading. Address: (h.) 41 Binghill Park, Milltimber, Aberdeen, AB1 0EE; T.-01224 732434.

Eastmond, Clifford John, BSc, MD, FRCP, FRCPE. Consultant Rheumatologist, Aberdeen Royal Hospitals NHS Trust, since 1979; Clinical Senior Lecturer, Aberdeen University, since 1979; b. 19.1.45, Ashton-under-Lyne; m., Margaret Wadsworth; 2 s.; 1 d. Educ. Audenshaw Grammar School; Edinburgh University. House Officer posts, Edinburgh, one year; moved to Liverpool for further training, subsequently to Rheumatism Unit, Leeds. Elder, Church of Scotland. Recreations: skiing; hill-walking; music. Address: (h.) Whinmoor, 34 Leslie Crescent, Westhill, Skene, Aberdeenshire; T.-01224 741009.

Easton, Rev. David John Courtney, MA, BD. Minister, Burnside Parish Church, Glasgow, since 1977; Moderator, Glasgow Presbytery, 1989-90; 7.10.40, Bogota, Colombia; m., Edith Stevenson; 2 s.; 1 d. Educ. Arbroath High School; Aberdeen University. Minister, Hamilton-Bardrainney Parish Church, Port Glasgow, 1967-77. Past Chairman, Scottish Tear Fund Advisory Committee; Member, Rutherford House Council. Recreation: music. Address: 59 Blairbeth Road, Burnside, Rutherglen, Glasgow, G73 4JD; T.-0141-634 1233.

Easton, Sir Robert William Simpson, CBE (1980), DUniv, CEng, FIMechE, FIMarE, FRINA. Chairman, Yarrow Shipbuilders Ltd., 1979-94; Chairman, GEC Scotland, since 1990; Chairman, GEC Naval Systems, 1991-94; Director, Glasgow Development Agency, 1990-94; Chairman, Clyde Port Authority, 1983-93; Director, Supermarine Consortium Ltd., 1986-94; Director, Brumac Engineering, since 1994; Chancellor, University of Paisley, since 1993; b. 30.10.22, Glasgow; m., Jean Fraser; 1 s.; 1 d. Educ. Govan High School, Glasgow; Royal Technical College, Glasgow. Apprentice, Marine Engineer, 1939-51; Manager, Yarrow & Co. Ltd., 1951-65; Yarrow Shipbuilders Ltd.: Director, 1965-70, Deputy Managing Director, 1970-77, Managing Director, 1977-91; Main Board Director, Yarrow & Co. Ltd., 1971-77. Vice-President, Clyde Shipbuilders Association, 1972-79; Member, Worshipful Company of Shipwrights, 1982; Freeman, City of London, 1982; Council Member, RINA, 1983; Trustee, Seagull Trust, 1984; Director, Merchant House of Glasgow, 1994; Member, Incorporation of Hammermen, 1989; Past President, Institute of Welding. Recreations: sailing; golf; walking; family. Address: (h.) Springfield, Stuckenduff Road, Shandon, Dunbartonshire, G84 8NW; T.-01436 820 677.

Easton, Robin Gardner, OBE, MA, DipEd. Rector, High School of Glasgow, since 1983; b. 6.10.43, Glasgow; m., Eleanor Mary McIlroy; 1 s.; 1 d. Educ. Kelvinside Academy; Sedbergh School; Christ's College, Cambridge; Wadham College, Oxford. Teacher of French and German, Melville College, Edinburgh, 1966-72; Housemaster and Deputy Head, French Department, Daniel Stewart's and Melville College, 1972-78; Head, Modern Languages, George Watson's College, 1979-83. Elder, Church of Scotland. Recreations: watching rugby; tennis; hill-walking; visiting ancient monuments. Address: (h.) 21 Stirling Drive, Bearsden, Glasgow, G61 4NU; T.-0141-943 0368.

Eastwood, Martin Anthony, MB, MSc, FRCPE. Honorary Librarian, Royal College of Physicians of Edinburgh; retired Gastroenterologist; b. 7.8.35, Hull; m., Jenny; 3 s.; 1 d. Educ. Minster Grammar School, Southwell; Edinburgh University. Publications: papers on physiology of the colon and nutrition; Human Nutrition and Dietetics (Co-Editor), 1986. Address: (h.) Hill House, North Queensferry, KY11 1JJ.

Eccles, Alexander Charles William Anderson, RD—, BA, LLB, WS. Temporary Sheriff, since 1984; part-time Chairman, Social Security Appeals Tribunals, since 1985, and Rent Assessment Committee, since 1975; part-time Chairman, Industrial Tribunals, since 1991; b. 8.1.33, Newcastle upon Tyne; m., Judith Margaret Hardy; 2 s.; 2 d. Educ. Loretto; Gonville and Caius College, Cambridge; Edinburgh University. National Service, 1951-53 (commissioned HLI); TA, Royal Scots, 1953-59; qualified Solicitor and WS, 1960; Assistant with various firms and local authorities, 1960-68; Partner, J.L. Anderson & Co., Solicitors, Cupar, Kinross, Glenrothes and Cowdenbeath, 1968-84. Lt. Cdr., RNR, 1966-85; Rugby Blue, Edinburgh University (played for Scottish Universities and Durham County). Recreations: rugby; squash; reading military history. Address: (h.) Ringwood House, 33A High Street, Auchtermuchty, Fife.

Eckford, James Millar, OBE, FCIS, FHSM, FBIM, FRSA. Board General Manager, Ayrshire and Arran Health Board, since 1985; b. 8.7.36, Edinburgh; m., Joan Miller. Educ. George Heriot's School, Edinburgh. General Administrator, Aberdeen General Hospitals; Senior Administrator, Dundee General Hospitals; Hospital Secretary, Western General Hospital, Edinburgh; Assistant Secretary, South-Eastern Regional Hospital Board; Deputy Secretary and Treasurer, Acting Secretary and Treasurer, Edinburgh Northern Hospitals Group; District Administrator, East Fife District, Fife Health Board, 1974-79; Secretary, Forth Valley Health Board, 1979-85. Board of Management, Ayr College; Chairman, Dalmellington and District Conservation Trust. Recreations: bowling; fishing; curling; Ayr United FC. Address: (h.) 22 Abbot's Way, Doonfoot, Ayr; T.-01292 42323.

Edge, David Owen, BA, MA, PhD, FRSE, FRAS, FRSA. Reader Emeritus, since 1992, Reader in Science Studies, 1979-92, Edinburgh University; b. 4.9.32, High Wycombe; m., Barbara Corsie; 2 s.; 1 d. Educ. Aberdeen Grammar School; Leys School, Cambridge; Gonville and Caius College, Cambridge. Assistant Physics Master, Perse School, Cambridge; Producer, Science Unit, Talks Department, BBC Radio, London, 1959-66; Senior Fellow, Society for the Humanities, and Senior Research Associate, Science, Technology and Society Program, Cornell University, 1973; Member, Edinburgh University Court, 1983-86; Scottish HQ Adviser for Students, Scout Association, 1966-85; President (Past Chairman), Scout & Guide Graduate Association; Circuit Steward, Methodist Church, Edinburgh and Forth Circuit, 1983-86; Editor, Social Studies of Science, since 1971; Member, various CNAA panels and committees, since 1972; Chair, Board of Science, Policy Support Group, 1989-93; Member, DQA Auditing Team, HEQC, 1991-93; Member, ABRC Working Party on Peer Review, 1990-91; President, Society for Social Studies of Science (4S), 1985-87; John Desmond Bernal Prize, 1993; Fellow, American Association for the Advancement of Science. Publications: Astronomy Transformed (Co-author), 1976; Science in Context (Co-Editor), 1982. Recreations: hill-walking; music; watching sport - especially soccer and baseball. Address: (h.) 25 Gilmour Road, Edinburgh, EH16 5NS; T.-0131-668 4008.

Edward, Judge David Alexander Ogilvy, CMG, QC, MA, LLD, FRSE. Judge of the Court of Justice of the European Communities, since 1992 (Judge of the Court of First Instance, 1989-92); Advocate, since 1962; Trustee, National Library of Scotland, since 1966; b. 14.11.34, Perth; m., Elizabeth Young McSherry; 2 s.; 2 d. Educ. Sedbergh School; University College, Oxford; Edinburgh University. National Service, RNVR, 1956-57 (Sub-Lt.); Clerk, Faculty of Advocates, 1967-70, Treasurer, 1970-77; President, Consultative Committee, Bars and Law Societies of the European Community, 1978-80; Salvesen Professor of European Institutions, Edinburgh University, 1985-89 (Hon. Professor, since 1990, Hon.LLD, 1993); Hon. Bencher, Gray's Inn, 1992; Member, Law Advisory Committee, British Council, 1974-88; Chairman, Continental Assets Trust plc, 1986-89; Director, Adam & Company plc, 1984-89; Director, Harris Tweed Association Ltd., 1985-89; Member, Panel of Arbitrators, International Centre for Settlement of Investment Disputes, 1981-89; Specialist Adviser to House of Lords Select Committee on the European Communities, 1985-88; Trustee, Hopetoun House Preservation Trust (Chairman, 1988-92); Hon. President, Scottish Council for International Arbitration, 1988-89. Address: (h.) 32 Heriot Row, Edinburgh EH3 6ES; (b.) EC Court of Justice, L-2925 Luxembourg; T.-010-352-43032203.

Edwards, Frederick Edward, LVO, RD, DUniv, MUniv. Director of Social Work, Strathclyde Regional Council, 1976-93; b. 9.4.31, Liverpool; 2 s.; 1 d. Educ. St. Edward's College, Liverpool; Glasgow University. Midshipman to Second Officer, Alfred Holt & Co., 1948-57; awarded Perm. Commn. RNR, 1953; Lt.-Cmdr., 1963; Reserve Decoration, 1972; Clasp, 1982; Management Trainee, Morgan Crucible Group, 1957-60; Probation Service, Liverpool, 1960-69; Director of Social Work, Joint County Council of Moray and Nairn, 1969-75; Director of Social Work, Grampian Region, 1975-76; Visiting Professor of Social Administration and Social Work, Glasgow University, 1988-93; awarded Hon. Doctorate, Paisley University, 1993; Trustee, New Lanark Conservation Trust, since 1993; President, Volunteer Development Scotland, since 1993. Recreations: hill-walking; natural history; Scottish country dancing. Address: (h.) Gardenfield, Ninemileburn, by Penicuik, EH26 9LT; T.-01968 674566.

Edwards, George Lowden, CEng, MIMechE, MIEE, FIM, FInstPet. Head of Corporate Affairs, Clydesdale Bank PLC; Trustee, Scottish Civic Trust; Deputy Chairman, Scottish National Committee, English-Speaking Union; b. 6.2.39, Kirriemuir; m., Sylvia Izatt; 1 d. Educ. Webster's Seminary, Kirriemuir; Dundee Institute of Technology. Production Engineer, Burroughs Machines Ltd., Cumbernauld, 1961-64; Development Division, Scottish Council (Development and Industry), Edinburgh, 1964-67; General Manager, GR Designs Ltd., Perth, 1967-68; London Director, Scottish Council (Development and Industry), 1968-78; Manager, Public Affairs Scotland, Conoco (UK) Ltd., Aberdeen, 1978-83; Manager, Public Affairs, Conoco (UK) Ltd., London, 1983-85. Recreations: music; travel; food and wine. Address: (h.) 1 Back Dean, Ravelston Terrace, Edinburgh, EH4 3UA.

Edwards, Neil, DMS, DCA, MITSA. Director of Trading Standards and Consumer Protection, Fife, since 1988; b. 6.10.45, Wrexham, N. Wales. Educ. Yale High School, Wrexham; Liverpool Polytechnic. Inspector of Weights and Measures, Denbighshire CC, 1967-74; Area Officer, Department of Trading Standards, Clwyd CC, 1974-78; retail management, Italy, 1978-81; Trading Standards Officer, Durham CC, 1981-83; Principal Trading Standards Officer, West Midlands CC, 1983-86; Depute Director of Trading Standards, Dumfries and Galloway RC, 1986-88. Recreation: sport. Address: (b.) Fife House (03), North Street, Glenrothes, Fife KY7 5LT; T.-01592 416353.

Edwards, Robin Anthony, CBE, WS. Partner, Dundas & Wilson CS, since 1965; Member, Lands Tribunal for Scotland, since 1991; b. 7.4.39. Address: (b.) Saltire Court, 20 Castle Terrace, Edinburgh, EH1 2EN.

Eilbeck, Professor John Christopher, BA, PhD, FIMA, FRSE. Professor, Department of Mathematics, Heriot-Watt University, since 1986 (Head of Department, 1984-89); b. 8.4.45, Whitehaven; m., Lesley; 3 s. Educ. Whitehaven Grammar School; Queen's College, Oxford; Lancaster University. Royal Society European Fellow, ICTP, Trieste, 1969-70; Research Assistant, Department of Mathematics, UMIST, Manchester, 1970-73; Heriot-Watt University: Lecturer, Department of Mathematics, 1973-80, Senior Lecturer, 1980-85, Reader, 1985-86; Long-term Visiting Fellow, Center for Nonlinear Studies, Los Alamos National Laboratory, New Mexico, 1983-84. Publications: Rock Climbing in the Lake District (Co-author), 1975; Solitons and Nonlinear Wave Equations (Co-author), 1982. Recreation: mountaineering. Address: (b.) Department of Mathematics, Heriot-Watt University, Riccarton, Edinburgh, EH14 4AS; T.-0131-451 3220.

Elder, Dorothy-Grace. Columnist, Scotland on Sunday, since 1992; Television Scriptwriter and Producer; m., George Welsh; 1 s.; 2 d. D.C. Thomson newspapers; Glasgow Herald as reporter, news feature writer, leader writer; TV and radio news, BBC Scotland; feature writer and columnist, Scottish Daily News Co-operative; feature writer and columnist, Scottish Daily Express; freelance feature writer and columnist, Sunday Mail; productions for Scotland and the network, BBC and Scottish TV. Trustee, Yorkhill Children's Fund, Royal Hospital for Sick Children; Member, ACHE UK Committee (opposing child pornography); Winner, Oliver Award. Address: Scotland on Sunday, 20 North Bridge, Edinburgh, EH1 1YT.

Elders, Rev. (Iain) Alasdair, MA, BD. Minister, Broughton St. Mary's Parish Church, Edinburgh, since 1992; b. 17.4.39, Sunderland; m., Hazel Stewart Steven; 1 s.; 1 d. Educ. Daniel Stewart's College, Edinburgh; Edinburgh University. Assistant Minister: Edinburgh: St. Andrew's, 1961-63, Edinburgh: High (St. Giles Cathedral), 1963-65; Minister, Cumbernauld: Abronhill (church extension charge), 1965-73; Minister, Edinburgh: Broughton McDonald, 1973-92; Secretary, Cumbernauld Council of Churches, 1967-72; Chairman, Council of East End Churches of Edinburgh, 1978-82; Chairman, New Town Community Council, 1986-89 and since 1992; Scout Commissioner, 1966-90; Secretary, East End Churches Together, since 1989; Vice-Chairman, Edinburgh and East of Scotland Society for the Deaf; Moderator, Edinburgh Presbytery, 1994. Address: Broughton St. Mary's Manse, 103 East Claremont Street, Edinburgh, EH7 4JA; T.-0131-556 7313.

Elgin, 11th Earl of, and Kincardine, 15th Earl of, (Andrew Douglas Alexander Thomas Bruce), KT (1981), DL, JP; 37th Chief of the Name of Bruce; Lord Lieutenant, Fife Region, since 1987; Ensign, Queen's Bodyguard for Scotland (Royal Company of Archers); President, Royal Scottish Automobile Club; b. 17.2.24; m., Victoria Usher; 3 s.; 2 d. Educ. Eton; Balliol College, Oxford. President, Scottish Amicable Life Assurance Society, 1975-94; Chairman, National Savings Committee for Scotland, 1972-78; Member, Scottish Postal Board, since 1980; Lord High Commissioner, General Assembly, Church of Scotland, 1980-81; Grand Master Mason of Scotland, 1961-65; President, Royal Caledonian Curling Club, 1968-69; Hon. LLD, Dundee, 1977, Glasgow, 1983. Address: (h.) Broomhall, Dunfermline, KY11 3DU.

Eliott of Redheugh, Margaret Frances Boswell. Chief of Clan Elliot; Chairman, Elliot Clan Society and Sir Arthur Eliott Memorial Trust; b. 13.11.48; m., 1, Anthony Vaughan-Arbuckle (deceased); 1 s.; 1 d.; 2, Christopher

Powell Wilkins. Educ. Hatherop Castle School. Address: Redheugh, Newcastleton, Roxburghshire.

Ellington, Professor Henry Irvine, BSc, PhD, CEng, FIEE, CPhys, FInstP, FCollP. Director, Educational Development Unit, The Robert Gordon University, since 1988; Professor, since 1990; b. 17.6.41, Aberdeen; m., Lindsay Moir Sheldon; 1 s.; 1 d. Educ. Robert Gordon's College, Aberdeen; Aberdeen University. Scientific Officer, AERE, Harwell, 1963-65; Robert Gordon's Institute of Technology: Lecturer, School of Physics, 1966-73, Senior Lecturer in charge, Educational Technology Unit, 1973-88; consultancy work in educational technology for numerous organisations. Publications: eight books; over 150 papers. Recreations: reading; music; golf. Address: (h.) 164 Craigton Road, Aberdeen; T.-01224 316274.

Ellington, Marc Floyd, DL. Baron of Towie Barclay (Feudal Barony); Laird of Gardenstown and Crovie; Deputy Lieutenant, Aberdeenshire, since 1984; b. 16.12.45; m., Karen Leigh; 2 d. Member, National Committee, Architectural Heritage Society of Scotland; Member, British Heritage Commission (representing Scottish Tourist Board); Vice-President, Buchan Heritage Society; Trustee, Scottish Historic Building Trust; Chairman, Grampian Regional Council Tourism Task Force; Chairman, Heritage Press (Scotland); Director: Grampian Enterprise Ltd., Aberdeen University Research Ltd., Gardenstown Estates Ltd., Soundcraft Audio; Partner, Heritage Sound Recordings; awarded Saltire Award, 1973, Civic Trust Award, 1975, European Architectural Heritage Award, 1975; Producer, documentary films and television programmes; Member, Historic Buildings Council for Scotland, since 1980; SBStJ; FSA. Recreations: sailing; historic architecture; art collecting; music. Address: Towie Barclay Castle, Auchterless, Turriff, Aberdeenshire, AB5 8EP; T.-018884 347.

Elliot, Sir Gerald Henry. Chairman, Scottish Opera, 1987-92; Chairman, Biotal Limited, 1987-90; Chairman, Martin Currie Unit Trusts, 1988-90; b. 24.12.23, Edinburgh; m., Margaret Ruth Whale; 2 s.; 1 d. Educ. Marlborough College; New College, Oxford. Chairman, Christian Salvesen PLC, 1981-88; Chairman, Scottish Provident Institution, 1983-89; Chairman, Scottish Arts Council, 1980-86; Vice Chairman, Scottish Business in the Community, 1987-89; Chairman, Prince's Scottish Youth Business Trust, 1987-94; Trustee, National Museums of Scotland, 1987-91; Member of Court, Edinburgh University, 1984-93; Chairman, Scottish Unit Managers Ltd., 1984-88; Chairman of Trustees, David Hume Institute, 1985-95; Chairman, Institute of Directors, Scottish Division, 1989-92; Trustee and Director, Edinburgh Festival Theatre, since 1995; Member, Court of Regents, Royal College of Surgeons, since 1990; President, UN50 Scotland, since 1993; Fellow, Royal Society of Edinburgh, since 1977; Honorary Consul for Finland in Edinburgh and Leith, 1957-89; Hon. d.h.c., Edinburgh University, 1989; Hon. LLD, Aberdeen University, 1991. Address: (b.) 8 Howe Street, Edinburgh, EH3 6TD; T.-0131-220 3739.

Elliot, John. Farmer; Vice Chairman, British Wool Marketing Board and Member for Southern Scotland; b. 29.5.47, Duns, Berwickshire; m., Joan Kathleen Wight; 1 s.; 1 d. Educ. St. Mary School, Melrose; Edinburgh Academy. Nuffield Scholar, US and Canada, 1982. Recreations: spectator sports; reading; writing; agriculture. Address: Roxburgh Mains, Kelso, TD5 8NJ.

Elliot, Robert John, LLB, WS. Solicitor; b. 18.1.47, Edinburgh; m., Christine; 1 s.; 1 d. Educ. Loretto School; Edinburgh University. Partner, Lindsays WS, since 1973; Council Member, Law Society of Scotland; Board Member, Queensberry House Hospital, Edinburgh. Recreations: golf; Scottish country dancing; detective novels; argument.

Address: (b.) 11 Atholl Crescent, Edinburgh, EH3 8HE; T.-0131-229 1212.

Elliot, Thomas, MBE, JP. Farmer; a Director, Animal Diseases Research Association; Member, Hill Farming Advisory Committee for Scotland; b. 6.4.26, Galashiels; m., Patrena Jennifer Mundell; 1 s.; 2 d. Educ. St. Mary's School; Loretto. President, Border Area, NFU of Scotland, 1974-76; Chairman, Selkirk Branch, 1968; President, South Country Cheviot Society, 1971-73; Member, Southern Regional Committee, British Wool Board. Played rugby, Gala RFC, 1945-58; 14 caps for Scotland, 1955-58; Barbarians, 1956; British Lions, South African tour, 1955. "Border Man of the Year", Tweeddale Press, 1979; Elder and Session Clerk, Caddonfoot Church. Recreations: watching rugby; reading books; farming. Address: Newhall, Clovenfords, Galashiels; T.-Clovenfords 260.

Elliott, Professor Alex, BA, PhD, DSc, CPhys, FInstP, FIPSM. Director, West of Scotland Health Boards' Department of Clinical Physics and Bioengineering, since 1990; Professor of Clinical Physics, Glasgow University, since 1991; b. 1.2.49, Edinburgh; m., Barbara; 2 d. Educ. Trinity Academy, Edinburgh; Stirling University; Glasgow University. Temporary Lecturer, Nuclear Medicine Unit, Strathclyde University, 1974-75; Lecturer in Nuclear Medicine, Middlesex Hospital Medical School, 1975-77; Principal Physicist, Department of Nuclear Medicine, St. Bartholomew's Hospital, London, 1977-81; Chief Physicist, Western Infirmary/Gartnavel General Hospital, Glasgow, 1981-90. Publications: 200 papers and presentations. Recreations: cycling; orienteering; squash. Address: (b.) 22 Western Court, 100 University Place, Glasgow, G12 8SQ; T.-0141-211 2948.

Elliott, Professor Robert F., BA (Oxon), MA. Professor of Economics, Aberdeen University, since 1990; b. 15.6.47, Thurlow, Suffolk; m., Susan Elliott Gutteridge; 1 s. Educ. Haverhill Secondary Modern School, Suffolk; Ruskin College and Balliol College, Oxford; Leeds University. Joined Aberdeen University, 1973, as Research Fellow, then Lecturer; acted as Consultant to numerous public and private sector organisations, including Megaw Committee of Inquiry into Civil Service Pay, the EEC Commission, HM Treasury OECD, Highlands and Islands Development Board, on issues of pay and employment. Publications: books on Pay in the Public Sector, 1981; Incomes Policies, Inflation and Relative Pay, 1981; Incomes Policy, 1981; Unemployment and Labour Market Efficiency, 1989; Labour Market Analysis, 1990. Recreations: music; reading; golf. Address: (h.) 11 Richmondhill Place, Aberdeen, AB2 4EN; T.-01224 314901.

Elliott, Hon. Lord (Walter Archibald Elliott), QC, MC, BL. President, Lands Tribunal for Scotland, 1971-92; Chairman, Scottish Land Court, 1978-92; Brigadier, Queen's Bodyguard for Scotland (Royal Company of Archers); b. 6.9.22, London; m., Susan Isobel MacKenzie Ross; 2 s. Educ. Eton College; Edinburgh University. 2nd Bn., Scots Guards, 1943-45 (Staff Captain, 1947); Advocate and at the Inner Temple, Barrister-at-Law, 1950; QC (Scotland), 1963; conducted Edinburgh ring road inquiry, 1967. Publications: Us and Them: a study of group consciousness, 1986; Esprit de Corps, 1995. Recreations: gardening; shooting. Address: (h.) Morton House, 19 Winton Loan, Edinburgh, EH10 7AW; T.-031-445 2548.

Ellis, Charles William, OBE, BA (Hons), LLD. Chairman, Grampian Health Board, 1982-89; Member, Whitley Council for Professions Allied to Medicine, 1987-89; b. 15.11.21, Horsham, Sussex; m., Maureen Patricia Radley; 1 s.; 3 d. Educ. Oxted County School; University College London. Indian Army and Royal Artillery, 1941-64; completed degree in modern history, 1964-66 (begun in 1940-41); Junior Lecturer to Head, School of Social Studies, Robert Gordon's Institute of Technology,

Aberdeen, 1966-85. Councillor, City of Aberdeen, 1971-75 (Convener, Education Committee, 1974-75); Councillor, Grampian Regional Council, 1974-78 (Leader, Labour Group). Recreations: International affairs; family; genealogy. Address: (h.) 78 Kirk Brae, Cults, Aberdeen, AB1 9QQ; T.-Aberdeen 861581.

Ellis, Frank, MA, BA (Hons), MEd. Rector, Denny High School, since 1987; b. 30.1.44, Shotts; m., Moreen Russell McLean; 1 s. Educ. Our Lady's High School, Motherwell; Glasgow University; London University; Stirling University. Teacher of Classics, Cumbernauld High School, 1966-71; Principal Teacher of Classics: Cumbernauld High School, 1971-73, Lornshill Academy, Alloa, 1973-78; Assistant Rector, Falkirk High School, 1978-84; Depute Rector, McLaren High School, Callander, 1984-87. Member, CCC, 1980-83. Recreations: squash; hill-walking; reading; music (listening); skiing. Address: (h.) 43 Westerlea Drive, Bridge of Allan, Stirling, FK9 4DQ; T.-Bridge of Allan 833177.

Ellis, Jean B.M., OBE, BSc, MB, ChB, JP. Member, Mental Welfare Commission for Scotland, 1984-88; Member, Scottish Hospital Endowment Research Trust, 1978-90; b. 13.9.20, Poona, India; m., Richard T. Ellis (qv); 2 s.; 2 d. Educ. Malvern Girls College; Aberdeen University. Past Chairman: Aberdeen Marriage Guidance Council, Royal Cornhill and Associated Hospitals Board of Management, Grampian and Islands Family Trust; former Member: NE Regional Hospital Board, Nurses and Midwives Whitley Council (Management Side), Grampian Health Board. Address: (h.) 18 Rubislaw Den North, Aberdeen, AB2 4AN; T.-01224 316680.

Ellis, John Russell, BA (Oxon). Director, ScotRail, since 1995; b. 21.5.38, Chipping Campden; m., Jean Eileen; 2 d. Educ. Rendcomb College, Cirencester; Pembroke College, Oxford. Joined BR as management trainee, 1962; Deputy General Manager, Southern Region, 1985-87; General Manager, ScotRail, 1987-90, Southern Region, 1990-91; Director, Total Quality Management and Deputy Managing Director, InterCity, 1992-93; Director Production, Railtrack, 1993-95. Recreations: hockey; cricket; gardening; walking. Address: (b.) Caledonian Chambers, 87 Union Street, Glasgow, G1 3TA; T.-0141-335 4500.

Ellis, Richard Tunstall, OBE, DL, MA, LLB, LLD (Hon); b. 6.9.18, Liverpool; m., Jean Bruce Maitland Porter (see Jean B.M. Ellis); 2 s.; 2 d. Educ. Merchant Taylors School, Crosby; Silcoates School, Wakefield; Aberdeen University. Captain, Royal Signals, 1939-45 (POW, Germany); Partner, Paull & Williamsons, Advocates, Aberdeen, 1949-83, Senior Partner, 1970-83; Chairman, Trustee Savings Bank Scotland, 1983-86; Chairman, TSB Scotland p.l.c., 1986-89; Director, TSB Group p.l.c., 1986-89; Chairman, Board of Governors, Dunfermline College of Physical Education, 1964-67; Governor, Aberdeen College of Education, 1969-75; Member: Scottish Board, Norwich Union Insurance Society, 1973-80, Aberdeen Board, Bank of Scotland, 1972-82, Aberdeen University Court, 1984-93, Council, National Trust for Scotland, 1984-89; Chairman, Scottish Division, Institute of Directors, 1988-89. Recreations: golf; hill-walking; skiing. Address: (h.) 18 Rubislaw Den North, Aberdeen, AB2 4AN; T.-01224 316680.

Elphinstone, 18th Lord (James Alexander Elphinstone); b. 22.4.53; m.; 3 s.; 1 d. Address: Drumkilbo, Meigle, Blairgowrie, PH12 8QS.

Elvidge, John William, BA (Oxon). Under Secretary, Scottish Office Industry Department; b. 9.2.51, Edmonton, Middlesex. Educ. Sir George Monoux School, Walthamstow; St. Catherine's College, Oxford. Recreations: appreciating other people's creativity; observing other people's politics. Address: (b.) Victoria Quay, Edinburgh, EH6; T.-0131-244 4609.

Embrey, John Derek, FCA, MCT.Director, Nimrod House Ltd., since 1994; Finance Director, Dawson International PLC, 1983-94; b. 14.7.45, Shrewsbury; m., Carol Anne. Educ. Bishop Vesey's School. Member, Investment Committee, Carnegie Trust for the Universities in Scotland; Non-Executive Director, Company Growth Team, Scottish Enterprise. Recreations: equestrian activities; theatre. Address: (b.) Nimrod House, Muckhart, Dollar, Clackmannanshire, FK14 7JN.

Emmanuel, Professor Clive Robert, BSc (Econ), MA, PhD, ACIS. Professor of Accounting and Director of CIFA; b. 23.5.47; m.; 1 s.; 2 d. Educ. UWIST; Lancaster University; UCW, Aberystwyth. Steel Company of Wales, Port Talbot, 1964-68; Lecturer, Lancaster University, 1974-78; Senior Lecturer, then Reader, UCW, Aberystwyth, 1978-87; Associate Professor, University of Kansas, 1980-82; Visiting Professor, Denkin University, Australia, 1994. Address: (b.) Department of Accounting and Finance, Glasgow University, Glasgow.

Emmanuel, Francis Xavier Soosaipillai, MB, BS, MSc, PhD, MRCPath. Consultant Medical Mircobiologist, Lothian Health Board, since 1986; Honorary Senior Lecturer in Medical Microbiology, Edinburgh University, since 1988; Regional Adviser, Royal College of Pathologists, since 1993; b. 24.8.48, Jaffna, Sri Lanka; m., Jacintha; 2 d. Educ. Ceylon University; Birmingham University. Lecturer, Ceylon University, 1973-77; Research Fellow, Birmingham University, 1977-80; Registrar in Microbiology, Western General Hospital, Edinburgh, 1980-83; Senior Registrar in Microbiology, Oxfordshire Health Authority, 1983-86. Recreations: cooking; reading. Address: (h.) 14 Polwarth Terrace, Merchiston, Edinburgh, EH11 1ND; T.-0131-228 4476.

Emond, Professor William John, BSc, FIMA, FSS, CMath, C Stat. Vice Principal, University of Abertay, Dundee (formerly Dundee Institute of Technology), since 1985; b. 23.8.42, Bellshill; m., Helen Catherine Elliott; 1 s.; 2 d. Educ. Allan Glen's School; Strathclyde University. Lecturer, then Senior Lecturer, polytechnics in England; former Head, Department of Mathematics and Computer Studies, Dundee Institute of Technology; Member, General Teaching Council; Past Chairman: Alyth Musical Society, Perthshire Youth Brass Association. Recreations: golf; sailing; choral singing. Address: (h.) Kinbrae, Alyth, Perth, PH11 8ES; T.-01828 632446.

Emslie, Hon. Derek Robert Alexander, QC, BA, LLB; b. 21.6.49. Advocate, 1974; Advocate-Depute, 1985-88; part-time Chairman: Pension Appeal Tribunal (Scotland), since 1988; Medical Appeal Tribunal (Scotland), since 1990.

Emslie, Rt. Hon. Lord (George Carlyle), MBE, PC, LLD, FRSE. Lord Justice General of Scotland, 1972-89; Lord President of the Court of Session, 1972-89; b. 6.12.19, Glasgow; m., Lilias Ann Mailer Hannington; 3 s. Educ. High School of Glasgow; Glasgow University. Commissioned A. & S.H., 1940; served War of 1939-45 (Despatches), North Africa, Italy, Greece, Austria, 1942-46; p.s.c. Haifa, 1944; Brigade Major (Infantry), 1944-46; Advocate, 1948; Advocate-Depute (Sheriff Courts), 1955; QC (Scotland), 1957; Sheriff of Perth and Angus, 1963-66; Dean, Faculty of Advcoates, 1965-70; Senator of the College of Justice, 1970-72; Chairman, Scottish Agricultural Wages Board, 1969-73; Member, Council on Tribunals (Scottish Committee), 1962-70; Hon. Bencher, Inner Temple, 1974, and Inn of Court of N. Ireland, 1981; PC, 1972; Baron (Life Peer), created 1980. Recreation: golf. Address: (h.) 47 Heriot Row, Edinburgh, EH3 6EX; T.-0131-225 3657.

Emslie, Hon. (George) Nigel (Hannington), QC; b. 17.4.47. Admitted to Faculty of Advocates, 1972; part-time Chairman, Medical Appeal Tribunals, since 1988.

Emslie-Smith, Donald, OStJ, MD (Hons), ChB, FRCP, FRCPEdin, FSA Scot. Honorary Fellow, Dundee University (Reader in Medicine, 1971-87, Head, Department of Medicine, 1986-87); Honorary Consultant Physician (Cardiologist), Tayside Health Board, 1961-87; b. 12.4.22, Aberdeen; m., Ann Elizabeth Milne; 1 s.; 1 d. Educ. Trinity College, Glenalmond; Aberdeen University. House Physician, Aberdeen Royal Infirmary; RAFVR (Medical Branch), UK and Middle East; Registrar in Cardiology, Dundee Royal Infirmary; Edward Wilson Memorial Research Fellow, Baker Institute, Melbourne; Tutor and Senior Registrar in Medicine, Royal Postgraduate Medical School and Hammersmith Hospital, London; Senior Lecturer in Medicine, St. Andrews University. Council Member, Association of Physicians of Great Britain and Ireland, 1977-80; Chairman, British Cardiac Society, 1987; President, Harveian Society of Edinburgh, 1986-87; Harveian Orator, 1987. Publications: Textbook of Physiology (Co-author and Editor) (8th to 11th editions); Accidental Hypothermia, 1977. Recreations: fly-fishing; dinghy-sailing; music; painting. Address: (b.) University Department of Medicine, Ninewells Hospital and Medical School, Dundee, DD1 9SY; T.-01382 660111.

Engeset, Jetmund, FRCSE, FRCSG. Consultant Surgeon, Grampian Health Board, since 1987; Surgeon to the Queen in Scotland, since 1985; b. 22.7.38.

English, Peter Roderick, BSc (Hons), NDA (Hons), PhD. Reader in Animal Husbandry, Aberdeen University; b. 9.3.37, Glen Urquhart, Inverness-shire; m., Anne Dunlop Mackay; 2 s.; 1 d. Educ. Balnain Public School; Arnisdale School; Glen Urquhart Senior Secondary School; Inverness Royal Academy; Aberdeen University. Farm Manager, Aberdeen University: Assistant Lecturer, Research Fellow, Lecturer Senior Lecturer, Reader. Won David Black Award, 1984, for major contribution to British pig industry. Publications: Glen Urquhart; The Sow — improving her efficiency; The Growing and Finishing Pig; Stockmanship. Recreations: athletics; shinty (Founder and first Editor, Shinty Yearbook); writing; travel; hard labour. Address: (h.) Arnisdale, 13 Fintray Road, Aberdeen, AB1 8HL; T.-Aberdeen 319306.

Entwistle, Professor Noel James, BSc, PGCE, PhD, FilDr (h.c.), FBPsS. Bell Professor of Education, Edinburgh University, since 1978; Director, Godfrey Thomson Unit for Educational Research and Centre for Research on Learning and Instruction, since 1978; b. 26.12.36, Bolton; m., Dorothy Bocking; 1 d. Educ. King's School, Ely; Sheffield University; Aberdeen University. Teacher, Rossall School, Fleetwood, 1961-64; Research Fellow, Aberdeen University, 1964-68; Department of Educational Research, Lancaster University: Lecturer, 1968, Senior Lecturer, 1971, Professor, 1972. Editor, British Journal of Educational Psychology, 1975-79; Editor, Higher Education, since 1993. Recreations: reading; walking; golf. Address: (b.) 10 Buccleuch Place, Edinburgh, EH8 9JT; T.-0131-667 1011.

Entwistle, Raymond Marvin, FCIB. Managing Director, Adam & Company Group Plc, since 1993; b. 12.6.44, Croydon; m., Barbara Joan Hennessy; 2 s.; 1 d. Educ. John Ruskin Grammar School. Several managerial appointments with Lloyds Bank. Governor, Edinburgh College of Art; Chairman, Fruit Market Gallery, Edinburgh; Non-executive Director, John Davidson (Holdings) Ltd. Recreations: golf; shooting; fishing; antiques. Address: (b.) 22 Charlotte Square, Edinburgh, EH2 4DF; T.-0131-225 8484.

Erdal, David Edward, MA, MBA. Chairman, Tullis Russell & Co. Ltd., since 1985; Director, Job Ownership Ltd.; Chairman, Baxi Partnership Ltd.; Trustee, FI Group Shareholders' Trust; b. 29.3.48, Umtali, Zimbabwe; 1 s.; 1 d. Educ. Glenalmond; Brasenose College, Oxford; Harvard Business School. English Language Teacher, London,

1972-74; Foreign Language Institute, People's Republic of China, 1974-76; joined Tullis Russell, 1977. Trustee, Baxi Partnership; Fellow, Royal Society of Arts. Recreations: sailing; skiing; reading. Address: (b.) Tullis Russell & Co. Ltd., Markinch, Glenrothes, KY7 6PB; T.-01592 753311.

Erickson, Professor John, MA, FRSE, FBA, FRSA. Director, Centre for Defence Studies, Edinburgh University, since 1967; b. 17.4.29, South Shields; m., Ljubica; 1 s.; 1 d. Educ. South Shields High School; St. John's College, Cambridge. Research Fellow, St. Antony's College, Oxford; Lecturer, Department of History, St. Andrews University; Lecturer/Reader, Department of Government, Manchester University; Reader/Professor, Defence Studies, Edinburgh University. President, Association of Civil Defence and Emergency Planning Officers, until 1984; Visiting Professor, Yale University, 1987; Hon. Fellow, Aerospace Academy of Ukraine, 1995. Publications: The Soviet High Command, 1962; The Road to Stalingrad, 1975; The Road to Berlin, 1984; Soviet Ground Forces, An Operational Assessment, 1986; Barbarossa, The Axis and the Allies (Editor and Contributor), 1994. The Russian General Staff 1700-1994, forthcoming. Recreation: model-making. Address: (b.) 31 Buccleuch Place, Edinburgh; T.-0131-650 4263.

Ermarth, Professor Elizabeth Deeds, BA, MA, PhD. Saintsbury Professor of English Literature, Edinburgh University, since 1994; b. 30.11.39, Denver, Colorado; m., Professor Thomas Vargish; 1 s. Educ. Carleton College, Minn.; University of California at Berkeley; University of Chicago. Northwestern University, Illinois, 1969-71; Dartmouth College, New Hampshire, 1972-74; Reed College, Oregon, 1974-78; University of Maryland, Baltimore, 1979-94 (Presidential Research Professor, 1991-95); Fullbright Senior Fellow and Overseas Fellow, Churchill College, Cambridge, 1992-93. Publications: Sequel to History: Postmodernism and the Crisis of Representational Time; George Elliot; Realism and Consensus in the English Novel. Recreations: singing; hiking; travel. Address: (b.) English Department, Edinburgh University, David Hume Tower, George Square, Edinburgh, EH8 9JX; T.-0131-447 0617.

Erroll, 24th Earl of (Merlin Sereld Victor Gilbert Hay). Hereditary Lord High Constable of Scotland; Chief of the Hays; b. 20.4.48; m.; 2 s.; 1 d. Lives in Hampshire.

Erskine, Donald Seymour, DL, FRICS. Factor and Director of Estates, National Trust for Scotland, 1961-89; b. 28.5.25, London; m., Catharine Annandale McLelland; 1 s. 4 d. Educ. Wellington College. RA (Airborne), 1943-47 (Captain); Pupil, Drumlanrig Estate, 1947-49; Factor, Country Gentlemen's Association, Edinburgh, 1950-55; Factor to Mr A.L.P.F. Wallace, 1955-61. Member, Queen's Bodyguard for Scotland (Royal Company of Archers); Deputy Lieutenant, Perth and Kinross; Elder and General Trustee, Church of Scotland. Recreations: golf; shooting; singing. Address: (h.) Cleish House, Cleish, Kinross-shire, KY13 7LR; T.-01577 850232.

Essery, David James. Under Secretary, Scottish Office Home and Health Department, since 1991; b. 10.5.38, Greenock; m., Nora Loughlin Sim; 2 s.; 1 d. Educ. Royal High School, Edinburgh. Entered Department of Health for Scotland, 1956; Private Secretary to Minister of State, Scottish Office, 1968-69; Principal, Scottish Development Department, 1969-76; Assistant Secretary, Scottish Economic Planning Department, 1976-81; Scottish Development Department, 1981-85; Under Secretary, Department of Agriculture and Fisheries for Scotland, 1985-91. Recreations: reading; music; cricket. Address: (b.) St. Andrew's House, Edinburgh EH1 3DE; T.-0131-244 2127.

Evans Charles, CEng, MIMechE, MIRTE. Chief Executive and Managing Director, Lothian Region Transport plc, since 1986 (Director of Public Transport, Lothian Regional Council, 1978-86); Chairman, Bus and Coach Council — Scotland, 1987-88; b. 30.8.37, Chadderton, Lancashire; m., Cherie; 3 s.; 1 d. Educ. North Chadderton Secondary Modern School; Oldham Technical College. Apprentice Engineer/Engineer, Oldham Corporation Passenger Transport, 1952-63; Assistant Engineer, Manchester Corporation, 1963-65; Edinburgh Corporation: Assistant Chief Engineer, 1965-71, Chief Engineer, 1971-75; Depute Director, Lothian Regional Council, 1975-78. President, Bus and Coach Council, 1986-87; Director, Edinburgh Chamber of Commerce, 1990-93. Recreations: golf; caravanning. Address: (b.) 1-4 Shrub Place, Leith Walk, Edinburgh, EH7 4PA; T.-0131-554 4494.

Evans, David Pugh, ARCA, RSA, RSW; paints in Edinburgh; b. 20.11.42, Gwent. Educ. Newbridge Grammar School; Newport College of Art; Royal College of Art. Lecturer, Edinburgh College of Art, 1965-68; Fine Art Fellow, York University, 1968-69; Lecturer, Edinburgh College of Art, since 1969; travelled and painted throughout USA, 1975; solo exhibitions: Marjorie Parr Gallery, London; Mercury Gallery, London; York University; Fruitmarket Gallery, Edinburgh; Open Eye Gallery, Edinburgh. Address: (h.) 17 Inverleith Gardens, Edinburgh, EH3 5PS; T.-0131-552 2329.

Evans, Sheriff George James, MA, LLB. Sheriff of Glasgow and Strathkelvin, at Glasgow, since 1983; b. 16.7.44.

Evans, James, MBE, RD, JP, DL, BSc, CEng, FRINA, MIMechE. Managing Director, Thomas Evans (Berwick) Ltd.; Chairman, Berwickshire District Council, since 1980; Chairman, Fishing Boat Builders Association, 1979- 90; b. 9.5.33, South Shields; m., Patricia Alexena Kerr; 1 s.; 2 d. Educ. Merchiston Castle School; Kings College, Durham. Apprenticeship, 1950-56; Royal Navy, 1956-58; YARD, 1958-63; UKAEA, 1963-68; RNR, 1956-80 (retired as Captain (E) RNR); Member, Eyemouth Burgh Council, 1972-75; Berwickshire County Council; Vice-Chairman and Finance Chairman, Berwickshire District Council, 1974-80; awarded Silver Medal, Nuclear Engineering Society, 1962; Hon ADC, The Queen, 1979-80; Deputy Lieutenant, Berwickshire, since 1978; Chairman, Berwick Freemen's Guild, since 1975; Lord President, Court of Deans of Guild Scotland, 1994-95. Address: (h.) Makore, Northburn View, Eyemouth, Berwickshire; T.-Eyemouth 50231.

Evans, Martyn Robert Rowlinson, BA (Hons), MA (Econ). Chief Executive Officer, Citizens Advice Scotland, since 1992; Visiting Professor (Social Welfare Law), Strathclyde University Law School, since 1993; b. 11.7.52, Hamilton; m., Angela May Morton; 2 s. Educ. Warwick School; City of Birmingham Polytechnic; Manchester University. Department of Health and Social Security, 1974-75; Stockport Council for Voluntary Services, 1975-76; Tameside MBC, 1976-78; Centre for Housing Research, Glasgow University, 1979-80; Housing Aid Worker, Shelter, 1980-83; Depute Director, Shelter Scotland, 1983-87; Director, 1987-92; Chair, Glasgow Council for Single Homeless, 1984-87; Convener, Board of Trustees, Glasgow Stopover, 1986-87; Non-Executive Director, Scottish Council for Voluntary Organisations; Trustee, Hamish Allen Trust; Member, STU Action 2000 Committee, since 1992. Recreations: golf; music. Address: (h.) 30 Teviotdale Place, Edinburgh; T.-0131-332 1463.

Eveling, Stanley, BA, BPhil. Fellow, Edinburgh University; Playwright; b. 4.8.25, Newcastle upon Tyne; m., Kate Howell; 2 s.; 2 d. Educ. King's College, Durham University; Lincoln College, Oxford. Recreations: golf;

tennis; going abroad. Address: (b.) Fettes College, Edinburgh, EH4 1QX.

Everett, Peter, BSc (Hons), SPMB. Director, Scottish Hydro-Electric, since 1989; Director, Forth Ports Authority, since 1989; Director, Edinburgh Java Trust plc, since 1995; Director, Ramco Energy Ltd., since 1993; b. 24.9.31, London; m., Annette Patricia Hyde; 3 s.; 1 d. Educ. George Watson's College; Edinburgh University. Royal Engineers, 1953-55 (2nd Lt.); joined Shell International Petroleum Company, 1955; Managing Director, Brunei Shell Petroleum Co. Ltd., 1979-84; Managing Director, Shell UK Exploration and Production, 1985-89; retired, 1989. Honorary Professor, Heriot Watt University, 1989. Recreation: golf. Address: (h.) Cluain, Castleton Road, Auchterarder, Perthshire PH3 1JW.

Ewart, Carole, MA (Hons). Director, Scottish Council for Civil Liberties, since 1988; b. 3.11.61, Glasgow. Educ. Glasgow University; Jordanhill College of Education. Address: (b.) 146 Holland Street, Glasgow, G2 4NG; T.-0141-332 5960.

Ewing, David John, MA, MD, FRCP(Ed). Senior Medical Officer, Scottish Office Home and Health Department; b. 27.8.40, London; m., E. Anne Bellamy; 2 d. Educ. Dulwich College; Jesus College, Cambridge; Guy's Hospital, London. Lecturer in Medicine, Edinburgh University, 1970-80; Wellcome Trust Senior Lecturer in Medicine, Edinburgh University, and Hon. Consultant Physician, Lothian Health Board, 1980-91. Castelli-Pedroli Prize, 1987, European Association for the Study of Diabetes. Recreations: walking; reading; cathedral and church architecture. Address: (b.) Scottish Office Home and Health Department, St. Andrew's House, Edinburgh, EH1 3DE.

Ewing of Kirkford, Lord (Harry Ewing), Joint Chair, Scottish Constitutional Convention; b. 20.1.31; m., Margaret; 1 s.; 1 d. MP (Labour), Stirling and Falkirk Burghs, 1971-74, Stirling, Falkirk and Grangemouth, 1974-83, Falkirk East, 1983-92; Under Secretary of State for Scotland, 1974-79; Opposition Spokesman on Scottish Affairs, 1979-83, UK Trade and Industry, 1983-84, Scottish Affairs, 1984-87; Chairman, Ewing Inquiry into availability of housing for wheelchair disabled, since 1993; Chairman, Scottish Disability Foundation, since 1994; Member, Council of Europe, 1987-92; Opposition Spokesman on Transport and Scottish Affairs, House of Lords, since 1992. Address: (h.) Gowanbank, 45 Glenlyon Road, Leven, KY8 4AA.

Ewing, Margaret Anne, MA, BA (Hons). MP (Moray), since 1987; Parliamentary Leader, SNP, since 1987; b. 1.9.45, Lanark; m., Fergus Stewart Ewing. Educ. Biggar High School; Glasgow University; Strathclyde University; Jordanhill College. Schoolteacher, 1968-74 (Principal Teacher of Remedial Education, St. Modan's, Stirling, 1972-74); SNP MP (East Dunbartonshire), 1974-79; Freelance Journalist, 1979-81; Co-ordinator, West of Scotland CSS Scheme, 1981-87. Recreations: grdening; reading; arts in general. Address: (h.) Burns Cottage, Tulloch's Lane, Tulloch's Brae, Lossiemouth, Moray, IV31 6QY; T.-0134381 3218/2222.

Ewing, Winifred Margaret, MA, LLB, NP. Member (SNP), European Parliament, since 1975; President, Scottish National Party; President, European Free Alliance, since 1991; b. 10.7.29, Glasgow; m., Stewart Martin Ewing; 2 s.; 1 d. Educ. Queen's Park School; Glasgow University. Solicitor, since 1952; former Secretary and President, Glasgow Bar Association; President, Soroptimist Club (Glasgow), 1966; MP (SNP), Hamilton, 1967-70, Moray and Nairn, 1974-79; Doctor, Open University. Recreations: walking; reading; painting; swimming. Address: (h.) Goodwill, Miltonduff, Elgin, IV30 3TL.

F

Fair, James Stuart, MA, LLB, WS, LLD. Solicitor; Senior Partner, now Consultant, Thorntons, WS, Dundee; Honorary Sheriff and Temporary Sheriff; Clerk, Commissioners of Inland Revenue (Dundee District); Director of private investment trust companies; b. 30.9.30, Perth; m., Anne Lesley Cameron; 2 s.; 1 d. Educ. Perth Academy; St. Andrews University; Edinburgh University. Past Chairman, University Court, Dundee; Chairman, Dundee Port Authority; Past President, Dundee and Tayside Chamber of Commerce & Industry; Past Chairman, Review Committee, Perth Prison; Member, Scottish Solicitors' Discipline Tribunal, 1978-88; Past President, Dundee Choral Union; Trustee, Sir James Caird's Travelling Scholarship Trust; Member, Committee on Medical Ethics, Ninewells Hospital and Medical School, Dundee; Chairman, Dundee Teaching Hospitals NHS Trust; Hon. Doctor of Laws, Dundee University. Address: (h.) Beechgrove House, 474 Perth Road, Dundee, DD2 1LL.

Fairbairn, Douglas McKay, CBE, LLB, CA, ATII. Managing Partner, Ernst & Young, Glasgow, since 1990; Chairman, Institute of Directors, West of Scotland, since 1991; Member, Council, CBI Scotland, since 1993; b. 28.1.48, Greenock; m., Allison; 1 s.; 1 d. Educ. Strathallan School; Edinburgh University. Law degree; qualified as CA, 1973; admitted to Institute of Taxation, 1975; Tax Partner, Grahams Rintoul & Co. (now Ernst & Young), 1975; Head of Tax, Ernst & Young, 1982. Recreations: golf; tennis; hill-walking; music. Address: (b.) 50 George Square, Glasgow; T.-041-553 4272.

Fairbairn, The Hon. Mrs Elizabeth, BA. Secretary/Administrator, Edinburgh International Festival Endowment Fund; Secretary/Administrator, The Gulliver Award for the Performing Arts in Scotland; Chairman: Castle Rock Housing Association, Lothian Housing Association, and Live Music Now! Scotland; Trustee, Glasite Meeting House Trust; Council Member, The Cockburn Association; President, Clan Mackay Society; b. 21.6.38; 3 d. Address: 38 Moray Place, Edinburgh, EH3 6BT; T.-0131-225 2724.

Fairgrieve, Brian David, OBE, DL, MB, ChB, FRCSEd. General Surgeon, Falkirk Royal Infirmary, 1960-87; Deputy Lieutenant, Falkirk and Stirling Districts; b. 21.2.27, Glasgow. Educ. Glasgow Academy; Glasgow University. RMO, 2/6th Gurkha Rifles, 1952-54; initial medical training, Western Infirmary, Glasgow, Stobhill General Hospital, Kilearn Hospital; Area Scout Commissioner, 21 years; President, Forth Valley Area Scout Council; Past President, Rotary Club of Falkirk; Lecturer and Examiner, Scotish Police College; Member, Council, St. Andrew's Ambulance Association; former Director, Incorporated Glasgow Stirlingshire & Sons of the Rock Society; Hon. Vice President, Grangemouth Rugby Club; awarded Silver Wolf, 1983, and OBE, 1986, for services to International Scouting. Recreations: photography; travel. Address: (h.) 19 Lyall Crescent, Polmont, Falkirk, FK2 0PL; T.-01324 715449.

Fairgrieve, James Hanratty, DA, ARSA, RSW. Painter; Senior Lecturer in Drawing and Painting, Edinburgh College of Art, since 1968; b. 17.6.44, Prestonpans; m., Margaret D. Ross; 2 s.; 1 d. Educ. Preston Lodge Senior Secondary School; Edinburgh College of Art. Postgraduate study, 1966-67; Travelling Scholarship, Italy, 1968; President, SSA, 1978-82; exhibited in Britain and Europe, since 1966. Recreation: angling. Address: (h.) Burnbrae, Gordon, Berwickshire; T.-Gordon 357.

Fairgrieve, Sir (Thomas) Russell, CBE, TD, JP. Chairman, Quality Guaranteed PLC; Chairman, Bain Hogg Scotland; b. 3.5.24, Galashiels; m., Millie Mitchell; 1 s.; 3 d. Educ. St. Mary's School, Melrose; Sedbergh School, Yorkshire. Commissioned, 8th Gurkha Rifles (Indian Army), 1943; Company Commander, 1/8th Gurkha Rifles, 1944-46 (Burma, Malaya and Java); TA, 4th KOSB, 1947-63 (Major). Director, Laidlaw & Fairgrieve Ltd., 1953-68 (Managing Director, 1958-68); Director, Dawson International PLC, 1961-73 (Group Yarn Sales Director, 1965-68); Chairman, Scottish Young Conservatives, 1950-51; President, Scottish Conservative Association, 1965-66; MP, Aberdeenshire West, 1974-83; Chairman, Scottish Conservative Group for Europe, 1974-78; Scottish Conservative Whip, 1975; Chairman, Scottish Conservative Party, 1975-80; Under-Secretary of State for Scotland, 1979-81; Member, Consultative Assembly, Council of Europe and WEU, 1982-83. Address: (h.) Pankalan, Bolside, Galashiels; T.-01896 752278.

Fairhead, Nigel Derek, FCA. Director of Finance, National Trust for Scotland, since 1991; b. 17.10.52, Malaya; m., Morag McGregor; 1 s.; 1 d. Educ. Brighton College; Hendon College. Trained with Spain Brothers & Co., Kent; qualified as a chartered accountant, 1976; Price Waterhouse, Paris, 1978-79; Marcus Hazelwood, Cheltenham, 1979-81; joined National Trust for Scotland, 1981. Address: (b.) 5 Charlotte Square, Edinburgh, EH2 4DU; T.-0131-226 5922.

Fairlie of Myres, David Ogilvy, MBE. Landowner; Chairman, East Fife Branch, Arthritis and Rheumatism Council; b. 1.10.23, Edinburgh; m., Jane Bingham-Newland. Educ. Ampleforth College, York; Oriel College, Oxford. Officer, Royal Signals, Europe, Ceylon, Singapore, Java, Malaya, Korea, SHAPE Paris; retired, 1959; former Cupar District Commissioner and Fife Area Commissioner for Scouts; awarded Silver Acorn and Silver Wolf; DL, Fife; JP; Member, Queen's Bodyguard for Scotland; Knight Commander of the Equestrian Order of the Holy Sepulchre of Jerusalem, Lieutenant of Scotland. Publication: Fairlie of that Ilk. Recreations: genealogy; photography; walking; shooting; gardening; bee-keeping. Address: Myres Castle, Auchtermuchty, Cupar, Fife, KY14 7EW.

Fairlie, Peter James Morrison. Managing Director, Glenturret Distillery Ltd., since 1989; b. 18.12.57, Bridge of Allan; m., Anne (Louise) Moon; 1 s.; 1 d. Educ. Strathallan School. Glenturret Distillery Ltd., since 1977. Vice Chairman, Association of Scottish Visitor Attractions, 1988-94; Member, Scottish Sports Council, 1990-93; Member, Scottish Tourist Board Seasonality Working Group, since 1994; Member, Board of Governors, Strathallan School, since 1994. Recreations: squash (Internationalist, 1980-87); golf; skiing; angling. Address: (b.) Glenturret Distillery, Crieff, PH7 4HA; T.-01764 656565.

Fairweather, Andrew Burton, OBE, TD, BA, MIMgt. General Secretary, Abbeyfield Society for Scotland, since 1991; b. 26.2.31, Edinburgh; m., Elizabeth Brown; 3 s. Educ. Royal High School, Edinburgh; Edinburgh University; Open University. Clerical Officer, HM Customs and Excise, 1949; Executive Officer: Accountant of Court for Scotland, 1949, Department of Health for Scotland, 1951 (Secretary, Scottish Medical Practices Committee, 1954-58); Higher Executive Officer, Department of Health for Scotland and Scottish Development Department, 1958; Senior Executive Officer, Scottish Development Department, 1965 (Secretary, Rent Assessment Panel for Scotland, 1965-67); Principal: Chief Administrative Officer, Civil Service College, Edinburgh, 1970, Scottish Economic Planning Department, 1972, Scottish Development Department, 1974 (Secretary, Local Government Staff and Property Commissions, 1974-77), Scottish Office Central Services, 1981; Senior Principal,

Scottish Office Central Services, 1982. Rifle Brigade, RAEC; Royal Scots (TA) and Royal Corps of Transport (TA); Commanding Officer, 495 Liaison Unit (BAOR), Royal Corps of Transport (TA), 1977-81; Colonel, Regular Army Reserve of Officers, 1982. Address: (h.) 127 Silverknowes Gardens, Edinburgh.

Fairweather, Clive Bruce, OBE. HM Chief Inspector of Prisons for Scotland, since 1994; b. 21.5.44, Edinburgh; m., Ann; 1 s.; 1 d. Commanding Officer, Scottish Division Depot, 1984-87; Commanding Officer, 1st Bn., King's Own Scottish Borderers, 1987-89; Divisional Colonel, The Scottish Division, 1991-94. Address: (b.) Scottish Office, St. Andrews House, Edinburgh; T.-0131-244 8481.

Fairweather, Rev. Ian C.M., MA (Hons), BD. Associate Minister, Glasgow Cathedral, 1985-90; b. 7.3.20, Glasgow; m., Joan Margaret Dickinson. Educ. Hutchesons' Boys' Grammar School, Glasgow; Glasgow University. Professor of Philosophy, Scottish Church College, Calcutta, and Murray College, Sialkot, 1945-47; Minister, Perceton & Dreghorn Parish Church, 1948-63; Lecturer in Religious Studies and Religious Education, Jordanhill College of Education, 1964-82. Church of Scotland Representative, General Teaching Council for Scotland, 1983-91; Hon. Fellow, New College, Edinburgh, 1984-85. Publications: The Quest for Christian Ethics: an inquiry into ethics and Christian ethics (Co-author); Religious Education (Co-author). Recreation: gardening. Address: (h.) Seaforth, 10 Hillside Road, Cardross, G82 5LX; T.-01389 841551.

Falconer, Alexander. Member (Labour), Mid Scotland and Fife, European Parliament, since 1984; b. 1.4.40, Dundee; 1 s.; 1 d. Educ. St. John's Junior Secondary School, Dundee. Former foundry worker; Royal Navy stoker, 1959-68; Rosyth Dockyard, 1969-84; Shop Steward, TGWU, 1970-84; Chair, Fife Federation of Trades Councils. Address: (b.) 25 Church Street, Inverkeithing, Fife, KY11 1LH; T.-01383 419330.

Falconer, Ian McLeod, BSc, CEng, MICE. Director of Estates and Buildings, Dundee University, since 1979; b. 21.7.31, Aberdeen; m., Brenda; 2 s.; 1 d. Educ. Aberdeen Academy; Aberdeen University. Worked in hydro-electric, building and civil engineering contracting throughout Scotland until 1979; commissioned in Royal Engineers during National Service, 1956; appointed Specialist Adviser, House of Commons Committee on Scottish Affairs, 1982, for inquiry into dampness in housing. Recreations: swimming; golf; reading. Address: (b.) The University, Dundee; T.-0382 223181.

Falconer, Professor Kenneth John, MA, PhD (Cantab). Professor in Pure Mathematics, St. Andrews University, since 1993; b. 25.1.52, Middlesex; m., Isobel Jessie Nye; 1 s.; 1 d. Educ. Kingston Grammar School; Corpus Christi College, Cambridge. Research Fellow, Corpus Christi College, Cambridge, 1977-80; Lecturer, then Reader, Bristol University, 1980-93; Visiting Professor, Oregon State University, 1985-86. Publications: The Geometry of Fractal Sets; Fractal Geometry — Mathematical Foundations and Applications; Unsolved Problems in Geometry (Co-author); 60 papers. Recreations: hill-walking and long distance walking (National Committee Member, Long Distance Walkers Association, 1987-92, and Editor of its magazine Strider). Address: (h.) Lumbo Farmhouse, St. Andrews, Fife; T.-01334 478507.

Falconer, Lake. Solicitor (retired); b. 21.10.27, Oban; m., Winifred Margaret Payne; 2 s. Educ. Oban High School; Glasgow University. RAF, 1946-48; qualified Solicitor, 1951; Partner, then Senior Partner, D.M. MacKinnon & Co., WS, Oban, 1953-89; Council Member, Law Society of Scotland, 1980-90; Vice President, 1985-86; Dean, Oban Faculty of Solicitors, 1983-86; Honorary Sheriff of North Strathclyde at Oban, since 1988; Chairman, Oban Social

Security Appeal Tribunal; Commodore, Royal Highland Yacht Club, 1974-77; Chairman and Depute Launching Authority, Oban Lifeboat, since 1972; Chairman, North Argyll District Scout Council, since 1982; Session Clerk, Kilmore and Oban Church of Scotland, 1974-93. Recreation: sailing. Address: (h.) Birkhill, Glenmore, Oban, PA34 4PG; T.-01631 562940.

Falkland, 15th Viscount of (Lucius Edward William Plantagenet Cary). Premier Viscount of Scotland; b. 8.5.35; m.; 1 s.; 1 s., 2 d. by pr. m.

Fallon, Edward Brian. Deputy Leader, Lothian Regional Council, since 1990 (Chair, General Purposes Committee, since 1986); Convener, COSLA Protective Services Committee, since 1990; b. 10.11.47, Edinburgh; m., Jennifer Mary; 1 s.; 1 d. Educ. St. Anthony's School, Edinburgh; Napier College; Edinburgh School of Building. Elected, Lothian Regional Council, 1982. Vice President, ECOSA; Hon. President, ITSA; Member, PNB; Member, NJC Fire Service. Recreations: golf; football; reading; swimming. Address: (b.) Regional Chambers, Parliament Square, Edinburgh, EH1 1TT; T.-0131-469 3325.

Fane, Venetia Sophia Diana, MBE. Administrative Secretary, Malcolm Sargent Cancer Fund for Children, Committee for Scotland, since 1971. Address: Drumwhill, Mossdale, by Castle Douglas, DG7 2NL; T.-01644 450 269.

Fannin, A. Lorraine, BA (Hons), DipEd. Director, Scottish Publishers Association, since 1987; b. Belfast; m., Nigel Fannin; 2 s.; 1 d. Educ. Victoria College, Belfast; Queen's University, Belfast; Reading University. Teacher of Modern Languages, Henley-on-Thames and Edinburgh; opened children's bookshop, 1979. Recreations: theatre; gardening; antique-hunting; reading. Address: (b.) 137 Dundee Street, Edinburgh, EH11 1BG; T.-0131-228 6866.

Fargus, Col. Brian Alfred, OBE, DL; b. 3.1.18, Ollerton; m., Shiona Margaret Lay MacKichan; 1 s.; 1 d. Educ. Cargilfield; Rugby; Royal Military College, Sandhurst; Staff College, Camberley. Commissioned The Royal Scots, 1938; served Hong Kong, 1938-41, and North West Europe - Adjutant, 8th Bn., The Royal Scots, 1944-45; C.O. Depot The Royal Scots, 1957-59; Senior Intelligence Officer, Middle East Command, 1966-67; Colonel General Staff, HQ Scotland, 1968-70; Military Attache, British Embassy, Pretoria, 1971-72; Assistant Regimental Secretary, then Regimental Secretary, The Royal Scots, 1973-83. Recreations: golf; gardening; fishing. Address: St. Arvans, Nisbet Road, Gullane, East Lothian, EH31 2BQ; T.-01620 842440.

Farley-Sutton, Captain Colin David, RN, CEng, FIMechE, DL. ~~Independent Consulting Engineer;~~ Deputy Lieutenant, Caithness, since 1986; ~~Director, Highland Community Care Forum, since 1993; Member, Caithness and Sutherland Local Health Council, 1993-95;~~ b. 20.12.31, Rugby; m., Sheila Wilson Baldwin; 2 s.; 2 d. Educ. Rugby College of Technology and Arts; RN Engineering College, Plymouth; RN College, Greenwich. Royal Navy, 1950-82 ~~(Captain Superintendent, HMS Vulcan, Dounreay, 1980-82); Bookseller, Thurso, 1983-87; Lecturer, Thurso Technical College, 1984-87;~~ President, Caithness Branch, Red Cross, ~~1984-1997.~~ Address: (h.) Shepherd's Cottage, Lynegar, Watten, Caithness, KW1 5YJ; T.-01955 621697.

Farmer, Tom, CBE. Chairman and Chief Executive, Kwik-Fit Holdings PLC, since 1984; b. 10.7.40, Edinburgh; m., Anne Drury Scott; 1 s.; 1 d. Educ. Holy Cross Academy. Address: (b.) 17 Corstorphine Road, Edinburgh; T.-0131-337 9200.

Farquhar, Agnes B.F., MA, LLB. Consultant, R.D. Hunter & Co.; Member, Council, Law Society of Scotland, 1985-91; Member, Scottish Solicitors Discipline Tribunal; b.

Kilmarnock; m., James W. McGirr (deceased); 1 s. Educ. Kilmarnock Academy; Glasgow University. Elder, Church of Scotland. Address: (h.) Moorfield, Cumnock, Ayrshire; T.-01290 421185.

Farquhar, Charles Don Petrie, JP, DL. Member, Dundee District Council, since 1974; b. 4.8.37, Dundee; 2 d. Educ. Stobswell Secondary School; Dundee Trades College; NCLC. Time-served engineer; elected Dundee Corporation, 1965; former Magistrate and Chairman of various Committees; served Royal Engineers (TRG NCO); Supervisory Staff, Plant Engineering Division, NCR; elected Dundee District Council, 1974; Lord Provost and Lord Lieutenant, City of Dundee District, 1975-77; Chairman, Leisure and Recreation Committee, Dundee District Council; Past Chairman, Tayside and Fife Committee for Employment of Disabled People. Recreations: fresh-water angling; numismatics; DIY; pool; golf. Address: (h.) 2 Killin Avenue, Dundee, DD3 6EB.

Farquhar, William John, MA, DSA, FHSM. Secretary, Clinical Resource and Audit Group, NHS in Scotland, since 1989; b. 29.5.35, Maud, Aberdeenshire; m., Isabel Henderson Rusk; 4 s. Educ. Peterhead Academy; Aberdeen University; Manchester University. National Administrative Trainee, Scottish Health Service; Hospital Secretary, Whitehaven Hospital, Cumberland; Deputy Secretary and Treasurer, West Cumberland Hospital Management Committee; Regional Staff Officer, South-Eastern Regional Hospital Board; Deputy Secretary, Eastern Regional Hospital Board; Lothian Health Board: District Administrator, South Lothian District, then Administrator, Operational Services. Secretary, Scottish Health Service Planning Council, 1985-89; Director, Planning Unit, Scottish Home and Health Department, 1987-90; Secretary, Scottish Health Service Advisory Council, 1989-93; Council of Europe Medical Fellowship, 1988; Elder, Colinton Parish Church; Vice-Convener, Church of Scotland Board for National Mission, 1991-94; Convener, Health Care Advisory Group, Board of World Mission, since 1991; Member, Executive Committee, Crossroads, Edinburgh. Recreations: gardening; walking. Address: (h.) Craigengar, 7 Harelaw Road, Colinton, Edinburgh, EH13 0DR; T.-0131-441 2169.

Farquharson, Angus Durie Miller, DL, MA, FRICS. Vice Lord Lieutenant, Aberdeenshire, since 1988 (DL, 1984); b. 27.3.35, Haydon Bridge; m., Alison Mary Farquharson of Finzean; 2 s.; 1 d. Educ. Trinity College, Glenalmond; Downing College, Cambridge. Chartered Surveyor, Estate Factor, Farmer and Forester; Council Member, Scottish Landowners Federation, 1980-88; Member: Deeside Advisory Committee, Forestry Commission, 1980-94; Red Deer Commission, 1986-92; Nature Conservancy Committee for Scotland, 1986-91; NE Committee, SNH, 1991-94; Hon. President, Kincardine/Deeside Scouts; Director, Lathallan School; Member, Church of Scotland Judicial Committee. Recreations: shooting; fishing; gardening; nature conservation. Address: (h.) Finzean House, Finzean, Banchory, Aberdeenshire, AB31 3NZ; T.-01330850 229.

Farquharson, Captain Colin Andrew, JP, DL, FRICS. Lord Lieutenant of Aberdeenshire, since 1987; Chartered Surveyor and Land Agent, since 1953; Member, Grampian Health Board, 1981-87; Director, MacRobert Farms (Douneside), 1971-87; b. 9.8.23; m., 1, Jean Sybil Mary Hamilton (deceased); 2 d.; 1 d. deceased; 2, Clodagh, JP, DL, widow of Major Ian Houldsworth of Dallas, Morayshire; 3 step s.; 2 step d. Educ. Rugby. Grenadier Guards, 1942-48; ADC to Field Marshal Sir Harald Alexander (Earl Alexander of Tunis), 1945; Member, Board of Management, Royal Cornhill Hospitals, 1962-74; Chairman, Gordon Local Health Council, 1975-81; DL, Aberdeenshire, 1966; Vice Lord Lieutenant, Aberdeenshire, 1983-87; Member, Queen's Bodyguard for Scotland (Royal

Company of Archers), since 1964. Recreations: shooting; fishing; farming. Address: Whitehouse, Alford, Aberdeenshire, AB33 8DP.

Farquharson, Sir James Robbie, KBE, BSc, CEng, FICE. Upland farmer, since 1965; b. 1.11.03, Kirriemuir; m., Agnes Binny Graham; 2 s. Educ. Websters High School, Kirriemuir; Royal Technical College, Glasgow; Glasgow University. Trainee Civil Engineer, LMS Railway, 1923-25; Civil Engineer, Kenya and Uganda Railway, 1925-37; Tanganyika Railway: Assistant to General Manager, 1937-41, Chief Engineer, 1941-45, General Manager, 1945-48; Deputy General Manager and Chief Engineer, East African Railways andHarbours, 1948-52; General Manager, Sudan Railways, 1952-57; General Manager, East African Railways and Harbours, 1957-61; Assistant Crown Agent and Engineer-in-Chief, Crown Agents, 1961-65. Fellow, Scottish Council Development and Industry; Former Member, Executive Committee, Scottish Council Development and Industry; undertook missions to Nigeria, Malawi, Jordan and Philippines for Overseas Development Administration; advised African Development Board on transport matters. Publication: Tanganyika Transport, 1945. Recreation: farming in retirement. Address: (h.) Kinclune, Kirriemuir, Angus, DD8 5HX; T.-01575 574710.

Farrell, Sheriff James Aloysius, MA, LLB. Sheriff of Lothian and Borders, since 1986; b. 14.5.43, Glasgow; m., Jacqueline Allen; 2 d. Educ. St. Aloysius College; Glasgow University; Dundee University. Admitted to Faculty of Advocates, 1974; Advocate-Depute, 1979-83; Sheriff of Glasgow and Strathkelvin, 1984-85; Sheriff of South Strathclyde, Dumfries and Galloway, 1985-86. Recreations: sailing; cycling; hill-walking. Address: (b.) Sheriff's Chambers, Edinburgh; T.-0131-226 7181.

Farrell, William John. Secretary, Board of Stewardship and Finance, Church of Scotland, since 1993; b. 10.5.35, Glasgow; m., Mary Elizabeth Kelly. Educ. Whitehill School; Glasgow Technical College. Church of Scotland Elder and Reader. Recreations: walking; swimming; reading; joking. Address: (b.) 121 George Street, Edinburgh; T.-0131-225 5722.

Farrington, Dennis Joseph, BSc, DPhil, LLM, CChem, MRSC, FIMgt, FRSA. Deputy Secretary and Registrar, Stirling University, since 1986; b. 13.8.47, Ellesmere Port; m., Julia Baverstock; 1 s.; 1 d. Educ. Ellesmere Port County Grammar School; University of Kent; University of Ulster. Civil Service, 1972-81: Customs and Excise, 1972-73, Northern Ireland Office, 1973-78, HM Stationery Office, 1978-81; Personnel Officer, Hull University, 1981, Administrative Secretary, 1986. Secretary, Conference of University Administrators, 1982-88; Chairman, Cancer Research Campaign, Stirling, 1987-91. Publications: Universities and the Law (Co-author), 1990; The Law of Higher Education, 1994. Recreations: DIY; home computing. Address: (b.) Stirling University, Stirling, FK9 4LA; T.-01786 467020.

Farry, James. Chief Executive, The Scottish Football Association Ltd., since 1990 (Secretary, The Scottish Football League, 1979-89); b. 1.7.54, Glasgow; m., Elaine Margaret; 1 s.; 1 d. Educ. Queens Park Secondary School; Hunter High School; Claremont High School. Recreations: occasional fishing; regular spectating football matches. Address: (b.) 6 Park Gardens, Glasgow, G3 7YF; T.-0141-332 6372.

Fass, Rev. Michael J., MA. Director, Partners in Economic Development Ltd., since 1992; Director, West Lothian Enterprise Ltd., 1983-92; b. 22.6.44, Sonning, Berks; m., Iola Mary Ashton; 1 s.; 2 d. Educ. Eton College; Trinity College, Cambridge; IMD, Lausanne. Served C Squadron (Berkshire Yeomanry) Berkshire and Westminster Dragoons (TA), 1963-68; worked in industry at Hays

Wharf, Miles Druce-GKN, and DTI's Small Firms Service; Director, Prince's Scottish Youth Business Trust; Non-Stipendiary Minister, Scottish Episcopal Church; Correspondent, Scotland on Sunday. Publication: The Vital Economy, Integrating Training and Enterprise (Co-Author). Address: 20 Fountainhall Road, Edinburgh, EH9 2NN.

Faulkner, Professor Douglas, WhSch, PhD, DSc, RCNC, FEng, FRINA, FIStructE, FRSA, FSNAME. President, Institution of Engineers and Shipbuilders in Scotland, since 1995; Professor and Head, Department of Naval Architecture and Ocean Engineering, Glasgow University, until October 1995; b. 29.12.29, Gibraltar; m., Isobel Parker Campbell; 3 d. Educ. Sutton High School, Plymouth; HM Dockyard Technical College, Devonport; Royal Naval College, Greenwich. Aircraft carrier design, 1955-57; production engineering, 1957-59; structural research, NCRE Dunfermline, 1959-63; Assistant Professor of Naval Construction, RNC, Greenwich, 1963-66; Structural Adviser to Ship Department, Bath, 1966-68; Naval Construction Officer attached to British Embassy, Washington DC, 1968-70; Member, Ship Research Committee, National Academy of Sciences, 1968-71; Research Associate and Defence Fellow, MIT, 1970-71; Structural Adviser, Ship Department, Bath, and Merrison Box Girder Bridge Committee, 1971-73; UK Representative, Standing Committee, International Ship Structures Congress, 1973-85; Member, Marine Technology Board, Defence Scientific Advisory Council; Head, Department of Naval Architecture and Ocean Engineering, Glasgow University, since 1973; awarded: David W. Taylor Medal; William Froude Medal; Peter the Great Medal. Recreations: hill-walking; music; chess; GO. Address: (h.) 4 Murdoch Drive, Milngavie, Glasgow, G62 6QZ; T.-0141-956 5071.

Featherstone, Simon Mark, FCA, BA. Director of Finance, NHS in Scotland, since 1995; b. 15.3.53, Northallerton; m., Sarah; 2 s. Educ. Northallerton Grammar School; Newcastle upon Tyne University. Arthur Young McLelland Moores & Co., London, 1974-78; Alexander & Alexander, Bermuda, 1978-80; McAlpine Aviation, Luton, 1980-82; Bristol and West Building Society, 1982-88; North of England Building Society, 1989-94. Recreations: fell-walking; golf; family. Address: (b.) St. Andrew's House, Edinburgh, EH1 3DE; T.-0131-244 3464.

Fee, Kenneth, MA, FRCS. Editor, Scots Independent, since 1985; b. 14.7.31, Glasgow; m., Margery Anne Dougan; 3 s.; 1 d. Educ. Gourock High School; Hamilton Academy; Glasgow University. President, Glasgow University SRC and Scottish Union of Students; Editor, Gum, Ygorra and GU Guardian; sometime in military intelligence; Sub-Editor, Glasgow Herald; Strathclyde Publishing Group; itinerant teaching; Member, Scottish Executive, NASUWT, since 1983; various SNP branch, constituency and national offices, since 1973. Publication: How to Grow Fat and Free. Recreations: chess; gastronomy; campaigning. Address: (h.) 157 Urrdale Road, Dumbreck, G41 5DG; T.-0141-427 0117.

Fenton, Professor Emeritus Alexander, CBE, MA, BA, DLitt, HonDLitt (Aberdeen), FRSE, FSA, FRSGS, FSA Scot. Director, National Museum of Antiquities of Scotland, 1978-85; Research Director, National Museums of Scotland, 1985-89; Director, European Ethnological Research Centre, since 1989; Chair of Scottish Studies and Director, School of Scottish Studies, Edinburgh University, 1990-94; b. 26.6.29, Shotts; m., Evelyn Elizabeth Hunter; 2 d. Educ. Turriff Academy; Aberdeen University; Cambridge University. Senior Assistant Editor, Scottish National Dictionary, 1955-59; part-time Lecturer, English as a Foreign Language, Edinburgh University, 1958-60; National Museum of Antiquities of Scotland: Assistant Keeper, 1959-75, Deputy Keeper, 1975-78; part-time Lecturer, Department of Scottish History, Edinburgh

University, 1974-80; Honorary Fellow, School of Scottish Studies, since 1969; Foreign Member: Royal Gustav Adolf Academy, Sweden, since 1978, Royal Danish Academy of Sciences and Letters, since 1979; Honorary Member: Volkskundliche Kommission fur Westfalen, since 1980, Hungarian Ethnographical Society, since 1983; Jury Member, Europa Prize for Folk Art, since 1975; President, Permanent International Committee, International Secretariat for Research on the History of Agricultural Implements; Secretary, Permanently Standing Organising Board, European Ethnological Atlas; President, Scottish Vernacular Buildings Working Group; President, Scottish Country Life Museums Trust; Secretary and Trustee, Friends of the Dictionary of the Older Scottish Tongue; Secretary and Trustee, Scotland Inheritance Fund; Co-Editor: Tools and Tillage, since 1968, The Review of Scottish Culture, since 1984. Publications: The Various Names of Shetland, 1973, 1977; Scottish Country Life, 1976 (Scottish Arts Council Book Award); The Diary of a Parish Clerk (translation from Danish), 1976; The Island Blackhouse, A Guide to the Blackhouse at 42 Arnol, Lewis, 1978 (re-issued, 1989); A Farming Township, A Guide to Auchindrain, the Museum of Argyll Farming Life, 1978; The Northern Isles, Orkney and Shetland, 1978 (Dag Stromback Award); The Rural Architecture of Scotland (Co-author), 1981; The Shape of the Past 1, 1985; If All The World Were a Blackbird (translation from Hungarian), 1985; The Shape of the Past II, 1986; 'Wirds an' Wark 'e Seasons Roon on an Aberdeenshire Farm, 1987; Country Life in Scotland, Our Rural Past, 1987; Scottish Country Life, 1989; The Turra Coo, 1989. Recreation: languages. Address: (b.) European Ethnological Research Centre, National Museums of Scotland, Queen Street, Edinburgh, EH2 1JD; T.-0131-225 7534.

Fenton, Professor George Wallace, MB, FRCPEdin, FRCPLond, FRCPsych, MRCP, DPM. Professor of Psychiatry, Dundee University, since 1983; Honorary Consultant Psychiatrist, Tayside Health Board, since 1983; Chairman, Scottish Division, Royal College of Psychiatrists, 1988-93; b. 30.7.31, Londonderry; m.; 1 s. Educ. Ballymena Academy; Queen's University, Belfast. Lecturer, Academic Department of Psychiatry, Middlesex Hospital, 1964-66; Maudsley Hospital, London: Consultant Psychiatrist, 1967-75, Consultant in Charge, Epilepsy Unit, 1969-75, Consultant Neurophysiologist, 1968-75; Senior Lecturer, Institute of Psychiatry, London University, 1967-75; Professor of Mental Health, Queen's University, Belfast, 1976-83. Publications: Event Related Potentials in Personality and Psychopathology (Co-author), 1982; numerous papers on clinical neurophysiology and neuropsychiatry. Recreations: sailing; history; literature. Address: (b.) University Department of Psychiatry, Ninewells Hospital and Medical School, Dundee, DD1 9SY; T.-01382 660111, Ext. 3111.

Fenwick, Hubert Walter Wandesford. Architectural Historian and Lecturer; Chairman, Royal Martyr Church Union; b. 17.7.16, Glasgow. Educ. Huntley School, New Zealand; Royal Grammar School, Newcastle-upon-Tyne. Architectural student; qualified, 1950; office of Ian G. Lindsay, then Lorimer & Matthew, Edinburgh; gave up architectural career, 1958; RIBA Examiner for Scotland in History of Architecture, until post abolished; Assistant Secretary and PRO, Scottish Georgian Society, 1960-65; Council Member, Cockburn Association, 1966; Scottish Editor, Church Illustrated, 1959-64; Editor and Manager, Edinburgh Tatler and Glasgow Illustrated, 1966-67; regular contributor to Scots Magazine, 25 years, and other journals. Publications: Architect Royal; Auld Alliance; Scotland's Historic Buildings; Scotland's Castles; Chateaux of France; Scotland's Abbeys and Cathedrals; View of the Lowlands; Scottish Baronial Houses. Recreations: foreign travel; architectural history; sketching and photography (for own books and articles); gardening. Address: 15 Randolph Crescent, Edinburgh, 3; T.-0131-225 7982.

Ferguson, Professor Allister Ian, BSc, MA, PhD, FInstP, CPhys. Professor of Photonics, Strathclyde University, since 1989; b. 10.12.51, Aberdeen; m., Kathleen Ann Challenger. Educ. Aberdeen Academy; St. Andrews University. Lindemann Fellow, Stanford University, 1977-79; SERC Research Fellow, St. Andrews, 1979-81; SERC Advanced Fellow, Oxford, 1981-83; Junior Research Fellow, Merton College, Oxford, 1981-83; Lecturer, then Senior Lecturer, Southampton University, 1983-89. Fellow, Royal Society of Edinburgh, since 1993. Address: (b.) Department of Physics and Applied Physics, Strathclyde University, Glasgow, G4 0NG; T.-0141-552 4400.

Ferguson, James Murray, BSc (Econ), MPhil, DipEd, FCIS, FIPM, FBIM, FRSA, FSA Scot. Principal and Chief Executive, Aberdeen College, 1990-93; b. 21.4.28, Almondbank, Perthshire; m., Moira McDougall, BA; 2 d. Educ. Perth Academy; London University; Edinburgh University; Dundee University; Moray House College of Education. Military Service, 1946-79: full-time, Army Emergency Reserve, Territorials, T&AVR, Regular Army Reserve of Officers (final rank of Major); variety of business appointments, mainly in insurance, investment and finance, 1952-64; lectureships in range of management subjects, various higher educational establishments, 1965-76; Principal, Elmwood College, Fife, 1976-82; Principal, Aberdeen College of Commerce, 1982-90. Governor: Further Education Staff College, Coombe Lodge, Bristol, 1982-87, Aberdeen College of Education, 1983-87. Recreations: sporting: badminton, tennis, hill-walking; non-sporting: reading, writing, public speaking, local history studies. Address: (h.) Crosslands, Meethill Road, Alyth, PH11 8DE; T.-Alyth 2701.

Ferguson, Joan P.S., MA, ALA, FRCPEdin. Librarian, Royal College of Physicians of Edinburgh, 1966-94; Hon. Secretary, Scottish Genealogy Society, since 1960; b. 15.9.29, Edinburgh. Educ. George Watson's Ladies College; Edinburgh University. Scottish Central Library, 1952-66. Member, Scottish Records Advisory Council, 1987-83; Compiler: Scottish Newspapers, Scottish Family Histories; Contributor, Companion and New Companion to Scottish Culture. Recreations: genealogy; gardening; reading. Address: (h.) 21 Howard Place, Edinburgh, EH3 5JY; T.-0131-556 3844.

Ferguson, Professor Michael Anthony John, BSc (Hons), PhD. Professor of Molecular Parasitology, Department of Biochemistry, Dundee University, since 1994; b. 6.2.57, Bishop Auckland; m., Dr. Maria Lucia Sampaio Guther; 1 s. Educ. St. Peters School, York; UMIST; London University. Research Associate, Rockefeller University, New York, 1982-85; Research Assistant, Oxford University, 1985-88; Lecturer, then Reader, Dundee University, 1988-94. FRSE; Colworth Medal, 1991; Howard Hughes International Research Scholar. Address: (b.) Department of Biochemistry, Dundee University, Dundee, DD1 4HN; T.-01382 229595.

Ferguson, Moira, BA (Hons). National Executive Officer, Scottish Pre-school Play Association, since 1988; b. 28.5.35, Glasgow; m., Douglas Ferguson; 3 d. Educ. Glasgow High School for Girls; Open University. J. & P. Coats; Glasgow Education Department; Greater Glasgow Health Board. Chairman, SPPA, 1982-84; Chairman, Scope in Scotland, 1984-85; President, Scottish Childminding Association; Secretary, Association of Chief Officers of Scottish Voluntary Organisations. Recreations: reading; theatre. Address: (b.) 29 Elmwood Avenue, Glasgow, G11 7ED; T.-0141 339 0390.

Ferguson, Patricia Ann Hatrick, BSc, JP. Member, Fife College Board of Management, since 1992; Director, Hatrick-Bruce Group, since 1977; b. Dundee; m., Euan Ferguson. Educ. St. Margaret's, Aberdeen; St. Andrews University; Royal Military College of Science. Chairman,

Fife Health Board, 1987-93. Recreation: dressage. Address: Lydiard House, Milton of Balgonie, Fife.

Ferguson, Robert Greig, MREHIS, MIWM. Director of Environmental Health, Caithness District Council, since 1974; b. 30.7.42, Saltcoats; m., Ruth; 1 s.; 2 d. Educ. Ardrossan Academy; School of Building, Cambuslang; David Dale College, Glasgow; Coatbridge Technical College; Dundee University. Student sanitary inspector, Ayr County Council, 1961-65; assistant sanitary inspector: Ayr County Council, 1965-66, Clackmannan County Council, 1966-67; District Sanitary Inspector, Angus County Council, 1967-70; Caithness County Council: Depute County Sanitary Inspector, 1970-71; County Sanitary Inspector, 1971-74. Recreations: golf; snooker; cartophily; bowls. Address: (b.) County Offices, 77 High Street, Wick; T.-Wick 603761, Ext. 236.

Ferguson, Rev. Ronald, MA, BD, ThM. Minister, St. Magnus Cathedral, Orkney, since 1990 (Leader, Iona Community, 1981-88); b. 27.10.39, Dunfermline; m., Cristine Jane Walker; 2 s.; 1 d. Educ. Beath High School, Cowdenbeath; St. Andrews University; Edinburgh University; Duke University. Journalist, Fife and Edinburgh, 1956-63; University, 1963-71; ordained Minister, Church of Scotland, 1972; Minister, Easterhouse, Glasgow, 1971-79; exchange year with United Church of Canada, 1979-80; Deputy Warden, Iona Abbey, 1980-81. Publications: Geoff: A Life of Geoffrey M. Shaw, 1979; Grace and Dysentery, 1986; Chasing the Wild Goose, 1988; The Whole Earth Shall Cry Glory (Co-Editor), 1985; George MacLeod, 1990; Daily Readings by George MacLeod (Editor), 1991; Black Diamonds and the Blue Brazil, 1993; Every Blessed Thing (play), 1993. Recreation: supporting Cowdenbeath Football Club. Address: (h.) Cathedral Manse, Berstane Road, Kirkwall, Orkney, KW15 1NA; T.-0856 3312.

Ferguson, R. Scott, BA. Editor, News, Sport and Current Affairs, Scottish Television, since 1993; b. 10.11.58, Glasgow; m., Teri Lally; 1 d. Educ. Cumbernauld High School; Strathclyde University. Journalist, D.C. Thomson, 1980-82; Researcher, BBC Network Current Affairs, London, 1982-84; Assistant Producer, BBC Scotland News and Current Affairs, 1984-86; Scottish Television: Producer/Director, 1986-90, Senior Producer, 1990-93. Gold Medallist, New York Television Festival. Recreations: television; cinema; football; cooking. Address: (b.) Scottish Television, Cowcaddens, Glasgow, G2 3PR; T.-0141-332 9999.

Ferguson, William James. Farmer, since 1954; Vice Chairman, Aberdeen Milk Company; Vice Chairman, Scottish Agricultural College; Director, Rowett Research Institute, Aberdeen; Director, Hannah Research Institute, since 1995; Deputy Lieutenant, Grampian Region; b. 3.4.33, Aberdeen; m., Carroll Isobella Milne; 1 s.; 3 d. Educ. Turriff Academy; North of Scotland College of Agriculture. National Service, 1st Bn., Gordon Highlanders, 1952-54, serving in Malaya during the emergency. Member, Scottish Country Life Museums Trust Ltd. Recreations: golf; field sports. Address: Rothiebrisbane, Fyvie, Turriff, Aberdeenshire, AB53 8LE; T.-01651 891 213.

Fergusson of Kilkerran, Sir Charles, 9th Bt; b. 10.5.31; m., Hon. Amanda Mary Noel-Paton; 2 s.

Fergusson, Professor David Alexander Syme. MA, BD, DPhil. Professor of Systematic Theology, Aberdeen University, since 1990; b. 3.8.56, Glasgow; m., Margot McIndoe; 2 s. Educ. Kelvinside Academy; Glasgow University; Edinburgh University; Oxford University. Assistant Minister, St. Nicholas Church, Lanark, 1983-84; Associate Minister, St. Mungo's Church, Cumbernauld, 1984-86; Lecturer, Edinburgh University, 1986-90. Chaplain to Moderator of the General Assembly, 1989-90.

Publications: Bultmann, 1992; Christ, Church and Society, 1993. Recreations: football; golf; jogging. Address: 44 Ashley Road, Aberdeen, AB1 6RJ; T.-01224 583817.

Fernie, Professor Eric Campbell, CBE, BA, FSA, FSA Scot, FRSE. Watson Gordon Professor of Fine Art, Edinburgh University, since 1984; Chairman, Ancient Monuments Board for Scotland, since 1989; b. 9.6.39, Edinburgh; m., Margaret Lorraine; 1 s.; 2 d. Educ. Marist Brothers College, Johannesburg; Witwatersrand University; London University. Lecturer, Witwatersrand University, 1964-67; East Anglia University: Lecturer, 1967-74, Senior Lecturer, 1974-84, Dean, School of Fine Art and Music, 1977-81. Publications: An Architectural History of Norwich Cathedral; The Architecture of the Anglo-Saxons; The Communar and Pitancer Rolls of Norwich Cathedral Priory (Co-author). Address: (b.) 19 George Square, Edinburgh, EH8 9LD; T.-0131-667 1011.

Ferrell, William Russell MBChB, PhD, MRCP (Glas). Reader in Physiology, since 1991, Head of Department, 1993-94, Glasgow University; b. 5.3.49, St. Louis, USA; m., Anne Mary Scobie; 3 s. Educ. St. Aloysius College, Glasgow; Glasgow University. House Officer, NHS, 1973-74; Lecturer in Physiology, 1977; Senior Lecturer in Physiology, 1989. Recreations: computing; tennis; classical music. Address: (b.) Division of Neuroscience and Biomedical Systems, Institute of Biomedical and Life Sciences, Glasgow University, G12 8QQ; T.-0141 330 4100.

Ferrier, Professor Robert Patton, MA (Cantab), BSc, PhD, FInstP, FRSE. Professor of Natural Philosophy, Glasgow University, since 1973; Head, Department of Physics and Astronomy, since 1989; b. 4.1.34, Dundee; m., Valerie Jane Duncan; 2 s.; 1 d. Educ. Morgan Academy, Dundee; Queen's College, Dundee, St. Andrews University. Scientific Officer, AERE Harwell, 1959-61; Research Associate, Massachusetts Institute of Technology, 1961-62; Senior Research Assistant, Cavendish Laboratory, Cambridge, 1962-65; Fellow, Fitzwilliam College, Cambridge, 1964-73; Assistant Director of Research, Cavendish Laboratory, Cambridge, 1965-71; Lecturer in Physics, Cambridge University, 1971-73; Guest Scientist, IBM Research Division, California, 1972-73. Member, Physics Committee, SERC, 1979-82 (Chairman, Semiconductor and Surface Physics Sub-Committee, 1979-82). Recreations: tennis; reading crime novels; garden and house maintenance. Address: Department of Physics and Astronomy, The University, Glasgow, G12 8QQ; T.-0141-330 5388.

Fewson, Professor Charles Arthur, BSc, PhD, FRSE, FIBiol. Professor and Director, Institute of Biomedical and Life Sciences, Glasgow University, since 1982; b. 8.9.37, Selby, Yorkshire; m., Margaret C.R. Moir; 2 d. Educ. Hymers College, Hull; Nottingham University; Bristol University. Research Fellow, Cornell University, New York, 1961-63; Department of Biochemistry, Glasgow University: Assistant Lecturer, 1963-64, Lecturer, 1964-68, Senior Lecturer, 1968-79, Reader, 1979-82; Titular Professor, 1982-94. Address: (h.) 39 Falkland Street, Glasgow, G12 9QZ; T.-0141-339 1304.

Field, Christopher David Steadman, MA, DPhil, ARCM. Senior Lecturer in Music, Edinburgh University, 1987-95, and Dean, Faculty of Music, 1993-95; b. 27.4.38, Frimley; m., Elizabeth Ann. Educ. Winchester College Choir School; Radley College; New College, Oxford. Lecturer in Music, St. Andrews University, 1974-76, Senior Lecturer, 1976-87; Associate Director, Scottish Early Music Consort, since 1979; Member, Governing Board, RSAMD, 1973-82. Recreation: gardening. Address: (h.) 2 Maynard Road, St. Andrews, KY16 8RX.

Fife, 3rd Duke of (James George Alexander Bannerman Carnegie); b. 23.9.29; m., Hon. Caroline Cecily Dewar (m. diss.); 1 s.; 1 d. Educ. Gordonstoun. National Service, Scots Guards, Malaya, 1948-50; Royal Agricultural College; Clothworkers' Company and Freeman, City of London; President, ABA, 1959-73, Vice-Patron, 1973; Vice Patron, ABA, 1973-94; Ships President, HMS Fife, 1964-87; a Vice-Patron, Braemar Royal Highland Society; a Vice-President, British Olympic Association. Address: Elsick House, Stonehaven, Kincardineshire, AB3 2NT.

Findlay, A.F. (Sandy). Chairman and Chief Executive, Hewden Stuart Plc; b. 19.5.36, Mintlaw; m., Marty; 2 d. Educ. Peterhead Academy; Robert Gordon's Technical College. Engineer/draughtsman; design/development engineer; engineer/area manager, Atlas Copco, 1963-69; joined Hewden Stuart Plc, 1969, and worked through the ranks to main board; main board, since 1982. Recreations: golf; gardening; grand-children. Address: (h.) Pitfour, 1 Leewood Park, Dunblane, FK15 0NX.

Findlay, Alastair Donald Fraser, MA. Fisheries Secretary, Scottish Office Agriculture and Fisheries Department, since 1993; b. 3.2.44, Perth; m., Morag Cumming Peden; 1 s.; 3 d. Educ. Pitlochry High School; Kelso High School; Edinburgh University. Assistant Principal, DAFS, 1966-70; Private Secretary to Joint Parliamentary Under Secretary, Scottish Office, 1970-71; Principal, 1971-74; on loan to Diplomatic Service as First Secretary (Agriculture and Food), The Hague, 1975-78; Assistant Secretary, Higher Education, SED, 1979-82; Fisheries Division, 1982-85, Livestock Products Division, 1985-88, DAFS; Under Secretary, Scottish Office Industry Department, 1988-93. Recreations: golf; walking; watching rugby and football. Address: (b.) Pentland House, 47 Robb's Loan, Edinburgh, EH14 1TW; T.-0131-244 6034.

Findlay, Donald Russell, QC, LLB (Hons), MPhil. Advocate, since 1975; Vice-Chairman, Glasgow Rangers FC; b. 17.3.51, Cowdenbeath; m., Jennifer E. Borrowman. Educ. Harris Academy, Dundee; Dundee University; Glasgow University. Sometime Lecturer in Commercial Law, Heriot-Watt University. Recreations: Glasgow Rangers FC; Egyptology; archaeology; wine; ethics. Address: (b.) Advocates Library, Parliament House, Parliament Square, Edinburgh, EH1 1RF; T.-0131-226 2881.

Findlay, Hugh, OBE. Regional Sheriff Clerk, South Strathclyde, Dumfries and Galloway. Address: (b.) Sheriff Court House, Graham Street, Airdrie, ML6 6EE.

Findlay, Richard Martin, LLB, NP. Entertainment Lawyer and Partner, Tods Murray WS, Edinburgh, since 1990 (Partner, Ranken & Reid SSC, Edinburgh, 1979-90); b. 18.12.51, Aberdeen. Educ. Gordon Schools, Huntly; Aberdeen University. Trained, Wilsone & Duffus, Advocates, Aberdeen; Legal Assistant, Commercial Department, Maclay Murray & Spens, Glasgow and Edinburgh, 1975-78. Company Secretary: Edinburgh Capital Group Limited, Edinburgh Arts and Entertainment Limited, Filmhouse Limited, Scottish Arts Lobby, French Film Festival Ltd., Edinburgh International Jazz Festival, Italian Film Festival, Arts Research and Development Scotland, Grampian and Highland Distribution Ltd. Recreations: music; theatre; opera; cinema. Address: (b.) 66 Queen Street, Edinburgh, EH2 4NE; T.-0131-226 4771.

Fink, Professor George, MB, BS, MD, MA, DPhil, FRSE. Director, MRC Brain Metabolism Unit, since 1980; Honorary Professor, Edinburgh University, since 1984; b. 13.11.36, Vienna; m., Ann Elizabeth; 1 s.; 1 d. Educ. Melbourne High School; Melbourne University; Hertford College, Oxford. House Officer appointments, Royal Melbourne and Alfred Hospitals, 1961-62; Demonstrator and Lecturer, Department of Anatomy, Monash University,

1963-64; Nuffield Dominions Demonstrator, Oxford, 1965-67; Senior Lecturer, Monash University, 1968-71; University Lecturer, Oxford, 1971-80; Official Fellow and Tutor in Physiology and Medicine, Brasenose College, Oxford, 1974-80. Member of Council, European Neuroscience Association, 1980-82, since 1994; President, European Neuroendocrine Association, since 1991. Publications: Neuropeptides: Basic and Clinical Aspects (Co-Editor), 1982; Neuroendocrine Molecular Biology (Co-Editor), 1986; 300 papers. Recreations: skiing and squash. Address: (b.) MRC Brain Metabolism Unit, Department of Pharmacology, Edinburgh University, 1 George Square, Edinburgh, EH8 9JZ; T.-0131-650 3548.

Finlay, Ian, CBE, MA, HRSA, FRSA. Professor of Antiquities, Royal Scottish Academy; Writer and Art Historian; b. 2.12.06, Auckland, New Zealand; m., Mary Scott Pringle; 2 s.; 1 d. Educ. Edinburgh Academy; Edinburgh University. Joined Royal Scottish Museum, 1932; Deputy Regional Information Officer Scotland (Ministry of Information), 1942-45; Secretary, Royal Fine Art Commission for Scotland, 1953-61; Royal Scottish Museum: Keeper, Department of Art and Ethnography, 1955-61, Director, 1961-71. Former Member: International Council of Museums, Counseil de Direction Gazette des Beaux Arts; former Vice-Chairman, Scottish Arts Council; Freeman, City of London; Member, Livery Worshipful Company of Goldsmiths; Guest, State Department, US, 1960. Publications: Scotland, 1945; Scottish Art, 1945; Art in Scotland, 1948; Scottish Crafts, 1948; A History of Scottish Gold and Silver Work, 1956; Scotland (enlarged edition), 1957; The Lothians, 1960; The Highlands, 1963; The Lowlands, 1967; Celtic Art: An Introduction, 1973; Priceless Heritage: The Future of Museums, 1977; Columba, 1979 (Scottish Arts Council Award); A History of Scottish Gold and Silver Work (new edition, 1991). Address: (h.) Currie Riggs, Balerno, Midlothian, EH14 5AG; T.-0131-449 4249.

Finlay, Ian Gardner, BSc, MB, ChB, FRCS. Consultant Colorectal Surgeon, Royal Infirmary, Glasgow, since 1987; b. 24.5.52, Leven; m., Patricia Mary Whiston; 1 s.; 1 d. Educ. St. Andrews University; Manchester University. House Surgeon; Casualty Officer; Demonstrator in Anatomy; Registrar in Surgery; Senior Registrar in Surgery: Royal Infirmary, Glasgow; St. Mark's Hospital, London; University of Minnesota. Hon. Treasurer, Royal College of Physicians and Surgeons of Glasgow. Publications: more than 100 relating to disorders of the large bowel. Recreations: sailing; skiing; ornithology; antique furniture. Address: (b.) Department of Coloproctology, Ward 61, Royal Infirmary, Glasgow; T.-0141-211 4000, Ext. 4084.

Finlay, Ian Hamilton. Artist and Writer; b. 1925, Bahamas. Played leading role in foundation of concrete poetry movement; moved, 1966, to farmhouse near Dunsyre, transforming the grounds into a modern version of a classical garden, including sculptures and other works.

Finlay, Robert Derek, BA, MA. Chairman, Dawson International PLC, since 1995; b. 16.5.32, London; m., Una Ann Grant; 2 s.; 1 d. Educ. Kingston Grammar School; Emmanuel College, Cambridge. Ltd., Gordon Highlanders, 1950-52; Mobil Oil Co. UK, 1953-61; Associate, Principal, Director, McKinsey & Co., 1961-79; Managing Director, H.J. Heinz Co. Ltd., 1979-81; Senior Vice-President, World HQ, H.J. Heinz Co., 1981-93; Non-Executive Director, Dawson International PLC, 1990-95. Recreations: tennis; rowing; music; theatre. Address: (h.) Grantully Castle, by Aberfeldy, PH15 2EG.

Finlayson, Michael. Chief Executive, SCDC (Scottish Co-operatives Development Company) Ltd., since 1993; Company Secretary, CVCS Ltd., since 1993; Council Member, UKCC, since 1993; Non-Executive Director, Out

of This World Ltd.; b. 12.8.52, Taunton; 1 s.; 1 d. Educ. John Hush's Grammar School, Taunton. Address: (b.) SCDC Ltd., Templeton Business Centre, Glasgow, G40 1DA; T.-0141-554 3797.

Finn, Anthony, MA (Hons). Rector, St. Andrew's High School, Kirkcaldy, since 1988; Member, General Teaching Council and Convener of its Education Committee; Assessor Teacher Education, Scottish Higher Education Funding Council, 1994-95; Teachers' Representative, National Committee for the Staff Development of Teachers; Member, EIS National Council; Governor, Moray House College of Education; Vice Chair, Fife Secondary Head Teachers Association; b. 4.6.51, Irvine; m., Margaret Caldwell. Educ. St. Joseph's Academy, Kilmarnock; Glasgow University. Teacher, Principal Teacher, Assistant Head Teacher, Depute Head Teacher, Acting Head Teacher, St. Andrew's Academy, Saltcoats, 1975-88. Recreations: sport; travel; literature; current affairs. Address: (h.) 1 Blair Place, Kirkcaldy, KY2 5SQ; T.-01592 640109.

Finn, Kathleen, DCE. Schoolteacher; Past President, Educational Institute of Scotland (now Parliamentary Convener); Member, TUC and STUC Women's Committees and Member, STUC General Council; Chair, STUC Education and Training Committee; b. 22.2.43, Glasgow. Educ. Possil Secondary School; Jordanhill College. Union activist since start of teaching career. Member, Board of Directors, Wildcat. Recreations: swimming; reading; political theatre; cat lover. Address: (h.) 18 Marywood Square, Glasgow, G41 2BJ; T.-0141-423 1796.

Finnie, James Ross, CA. Member, Inverclyde District Council, since 1977; Ross Finnie & Co., Chartered Accountants; Chairman, Systems Reliability Scotland Ltd., Finance Director, Buko Holdings Ltd., b. 11.2.47, Greenock; m., Phyllis Sinclair; 1 s.; 1 d. Educ. Greenock Academy. Member, Executive Committee, Scottish Council (Development and Industry), 1976-87; Chairman, Scottish Liberal Party, 1982-86. Address: (h.) 91 Octavia Terrace, Greenock, PA16 7PY; T.-01475 631495.

Firth, Professor William James, BSc, PhD, CPhys, FRSE. Professor of Physics, Strathclyde University (Head, Department of Physics and Applied Physics, 1990-93); b. 23.2.45, Holm, Orkney; m., Mary MacDonald Anderson; 2 s. Educ. Perth Academy; Edinburgh University; Heriot-Watt University. Lecturer to Reader, Physics, Heriot-Watt University, 1967-85. Recreation: sports (Edinburgh University Hockey Blue, 1967-68). Address: (b.) John Anderson Building, 107 Rottenrow, Glasgow, G4 0NG.

Fisher, Archie. Folk singer, guitarist, composer, broadcaster; b. 1939, Glasgow. First solo album, 1966; presenter, Travelling Folk, BBC Radio; Artistic Director, Edinburgh International Folk Festival, 1988-92.

Fisher, Gregor. Actor (television, theatre, film). Credits include (BBC TV): Rab C. Nesbitt series (leading role), Naked Video series, Scotch and Wry, Para Handy. Best Actor award, Toronto Festival, for One, Two, Three. Address: (b.) c/o William Morris UK Ltd., 31-32 Soho Square, London, W1V 5DG.

Fisher, Howard Andrew Powell, BSc, PhD, MRSC, CChem. Director of Economic Development and Planning, Grampian Regional Council, since 1989; b. 15.7.40, London; m., Fiona Elizabeth Munro; 1 s.; 1 d. Educ. Cranleigh; Glasgow University. Civil Service, 1967-88. Recreations: painting; interest in design. Address: (b.) Woodhill House, Westburn Road, Aberdeen, AB9 2LU.

Fisher, Kenneth Holmes, BA, ACIS, AInstM, DipABCC. Depute Principal, North Glasgow College, since 1987; b. 19.3.41, Glasgow. Educ. Hillhead High School, Glasgow.

Administrative appointments, Colvilles Ltd., 1957-67; Lecturer and Senior Lecturer, Anniesland College, Glasgow, 1967-75; Head, Department of Business Studies, Cumbernauld College, 1975-80; Head, Department of Commerce, Anniesland College, Glasgow, 1980-86. Address: (b.) 110 Flemington Street, Glasgow, G21 4BX; T.-0141-558 9001.

Fitzgerald, Professor Alexander Grant, BSc, PhD, DSc, CPhys, FInstP. Professor of Analytical Electron Microscopy, Dundee University, since 1992; b. 12.10.39, Dundee; m., June; 1 s.; 2 d. Educ. Perth Academy; Harris Academy; St. Andrews University; Cambridge University. Research Fellow, Lawrence Berkeley Laboratory, University of California; Lecturer, Senior Lecturer, Reader, Professor, Dundee University. Publications: 105 conference and journal papers; book: Quantitative Microbeam Analysis (Co-editor). Recreations: swimming; golf. Address: (b.) Department of Applied Physics and Electronic and Mechanical Engineering, Dundee University, Dundee, DD1 4HN; T.-01382 344553.

Fitzgerald, Brian John, BSc, CEng, FICE. Chairman and Managing Director, Laing Scotland, since 1989; Director, John Laing Construction Ltd., since 1989; Chairman, Environment Committee, CBI (Scotland); b. 17.9.46, Glasgow; 2 s. Educ. Salesian College, Farnborough; Glasgow University. Whatlings plc: Engineer, Manager, Director, Managing Director, 1969-88; Director: Alfred McAlpine Construction Ltd., 1985-88, Norcity Homes plc, since 1988, Norcity II plc, since 1989, Norhomes plc, since 1989, Manchester Village Homes plc, since 1989. Address: (b.) John Laing Construction Ltd., 175 Elderslie Street, Glasgow; T.-041-332 7055.

Fitzgerald, Maren L., LLB, MICFM. Depute Campaign Director, Children 1st, since 1994; b. 20.4.47, Glasgow; 2 s. Educ. Glasgow High School for Girls; Glasgow University. Appeal Director, Strathcarron Hospice, 1989-92; Director of Fundraising, Scottish Medical Research Fund, 1992-94; Administrator, Scottish Hospital Endowments Research Trust, 1993-94; Member, Business Committee, General Council, Glasgow University, 1982-92, and Convenor, Social Affairs Committee of the Business Committee, 1988-92; Trustee, University of Glasgow Trust, since 1989. Recreation: golf. Address: (b.) 41 Polwarth Terrace, Edinburgh, EH11 1NU; T.-0131 346 4552.

Fitzsimons, Sheriff J.T. Sheriff of North Strathclyde. Address: (b.) Dumbarton Sheriff Court, Sheriff Court House, Church Street, Dumbarton, G82 1QR.

Fleming, Archibald Macdonald, MA, BCom, PhD, FRSA. Director of Continuing Education, Strathclyde University, since 1987 (Director, Management Development Programmes, Strathclyde Business School, 1984-87); Lecturer, Department of Information Science, Strathclyde University, since 1968; Consultant on Management Training and Development, since 1970; b. 19.6.36, Glasgow; m., Joan Moore; 1 s.; 1 d. Educ. Langholm Academy; Dumfries Academy; Edinburgh University. W. & T. Avery, 1961-63; IBM (UK) Ltd., 1963-64; Sumlock Comptometer Ltd., 1964-68; Consultancies: Scottish Co-operative Wholesale Society, 1969, Hotel and Catering Industry Training Board, 1971, Scottish Engineering Employers Association, 1973. Member, Strathclyde Children's Panel; Member, Committee on Food Processing Opportunities in Scotland, Scottish Council (Development and Industry); Vice-Chairman, Universities Council for Adult and Continuing Education (Scotland), since 1990; Member, Church of Scotland Education Committee; Member, American Association of Adult and Continuing Education. Publication: Collins Business Dictionary (with B. McKenna). Recreation: reading, observing and talking on Scotland and the Scots. Address: (b.) 16 Richmond Street, Glasgow, G1 1XQ.

Fleming, Professor George, BSc, PhD, FEng, FRSE, FICE, MIWEM. Professor of Civil Engineering, Strathclyde University, since 1985; b. 16.8.44, Glasgow; m., Irene Fleming; 2 s.; 1 d. Educ. Knightswood Secondary School, Glasgow; Strathclyde University; Stanford University, California. Research Assistant, Strathclyde University, 1966-69, Stanford University, 1967; Senior Research Hydrologist, Hydrocomp International, California, 1969-70; Research Associate, Stanford University, 1969-70; Director and Vice President, Hydrocomp International, Palo Alto and Glasgow, 1970-79; Lecturer, then Senior Lecturer, then Reader in Civil Engineering, Strathclyde University, 1971-85; Visiting Professor, University of Padova, Italy, since 1980; Vice Dean, Engineering Faculty, Strathclyde University, 1984-87; Member, Overseas Projects Board, DTI, 1991. Publications: Computer Simulation in Hydrology, 1975; The Sediment Problem, 1977; Deterministic Models in Hydrology, 1979. Recreations: farming; fishing; food; film-making. Address: (b.) John Anderson Building, 107 Rottenrow, Glasgow, G4 0NG; T.-0141-552 4400, Ext. 3168.

Fleming, Sheriff Grahame R, QC. Sheriff of Lothian and Borders, since 1993; b. 13.2.49. Address: (b.) Linlithgow Sheriff Court, Sheriff Court House, Court Square, Linlithgow, EH49 7EQ.

Fleming, Maurice. Editor, The Scots Magazine, 1974-91; b. Blairgowrie; m., Nanette Dalgleish; 2 s.; 1 d. Educ. Blairgowrie High School. Trained in hotel management before entering journalism; worked on various magazines; has had five full-length plays performed professionally, as well as one-act plays by amateurs; founder Member: Traditional Music and Song Association of Scotland, Scottish Poetry Library; Past Chairman, Blairgowrie, Rattray and District Civic Trust; Past Chairman, Blair in Bloom. Publications: The Scots Magazine — A Celebration of 250 Years (Co-Editor); The Ghost O' Mause and Other Tales and Traditions of East Perthshire. Recreations: theatre; reading; bird-watching; enjoying the countryside; folksong and folklore. Address: (h.) Craigard, Perth Road, Blairgowrie; T.-Blairgowrie 873633.

Fleming, Tom, OBE. Actor and Director; b. 29.6.27, Edinburgh. Professional theatre debut, 1945, in company led by Edith Evans; Co-Founder, Edinburgh Gateway Company, 1953; joined Royal Shakespeare Company at Stratford upon Avon, 1962, and played several classical roles, including Prospero, Brutus, Cymbeline, Buckingham and Kent; toured with RSC in USSR, USA and Europe, 1964; appointed Director, new Royal Lyceum Theatre Company, 1965; there played title role in Galileo; Director, Scottish Theatre Company, 1982-87; awarded Roman Szlydowski Prize for his production of The Thrie Estaites, Warsaw, 1986; TV work includes portrayals of Robert Burns, William Wallace, Jesus of Nazareth, Henry IV, Weir of Hermiston, and Sir John Reith; Television commentator on royal and state occasions, including silver jubilee celebrations, two royal weddings, 10 state funerals, Queen's birthday parade and annual Cenotaph service (30 years), D-Day remembrance service and VE Day 50th anniversary celebrations; commentator, Edinburgh Military Tattoo, since 1966; Hon. doctorate, Heriot-Watt University; FRSAMD.

Fletcher, Colonel Archibald Ian, OBE. Justice of the Peace for Argyll and Bute, since 1971; Lord Lieutenant, since 1993; Hon. Sheriff (Rothesay), since 1994; b. 9.4.24, London; m., Helen Clare de Salis; 1 s.; 2 d. Educ. Ampleforth College. Recruit, Guards Depot, 1942; Troop Leader, 3rd Tank Bn., Scots Guards, NW Europe, 1944-45; served Palestine, N. Africa, Malaya, Kenya; commanded 1st Bn., Scots Guards, 1963-66, Malaya and Borneo, and Regiment, 1967-70; retired to farm in Argyll; County Councillor, 1972-74; Member, NFU of Scotland Council, 1972-85, Honorary President, 1985-86, President, Cowal

Area, 1987-89; Council Member, Timber Growers UK, 1986-91; Director (Deputy Chairman), Argyll and the Islands Enterprise, since 1991; Chairman, Colintraive and Glendaruel Community Council, since 1977; Chieftain, Cowal Highland Gathering, 1994. Recreation: country pursuits. Address: (h.) Dunans, Glendaruel, Colintraive, Argyll; T.-Glendaruel 235.

Fletcher, Sheriff Michael John, LLB. Sheriff of South Strathclyde Dumfries & Galloway at Dumfries, since 1994; b. 5.12.45, Dundee; m., Kathryn Mary; 2 s. Educ. High School of Dundee; St. Andrews University. Solicitor, 1968-94. Recreations: golf; gardening. Address: (h.) Kilgour, Barhill, Dalbeattie, DG5 4HX; T.-01556 610635.

Fletcher, Professor Roger, MA, PhD, FIMA, FRSE. Professor of Optimization, Department of Mathematics and Computer Science, Dundee University, since 1984; b. 29.1.39, Huddersfield; m., Mary Marjorie Taylor; 2 d. Educ. Huddersfield College; Cambridge University; Leeds University. Lecturer, Leeds University, 1963-69; Principal Research Fellow, then Principal Scientific Officer, AERE Harwell, 1969-73; Senior Research Fellow, then Senior Lecturer, then Reader, Dundee University, 1973-84. Publications: Practical Methods of Optimization, 2nd edition, 1987. numerous others. Recreations: hill-walking; music; bridge. Address: (h.) 43 Errol Road, Invergowrie, Dundee, DD2 5BX; T.-01382 562452.

Flett, Ian Stark, CBE (1984), MA, MEd, ABPS. Chairman, Scottish Centre for Tuition of the Disabled, 1980-89; Chairman, National Association for Gifted Children Scotland, 1985-93; b. 26.1.20, Aberdeen; m., Moyra. Educ. Aberdeen Grammar School; Aberdeen University; Aberdeen College of Education. RAF, Signals and Intelligence Branch, 1940-46; Teacher, Aberdeen, 1947-49; Adviser, Durham, 1949-54; Assistant Education Officer, Lancashire, 1954-59; Deputy, 1959-63; Deputy Education Officer, City of Hull, 1963-66; Member, Dalegacy Institute of Education, Hull University, 1963-66; Director of Education, Fife, 1966-85; General Secretary, Association of Directors of Education in Scotland, 1975-85; President, 1979-80; Adviser to Association of County Councils, 1970-74; Principal Adviser, Convention of Scottish Local Authorities, 1975-84; Member, Consultative Committee on the Curriculum, 1977-87; Member, General Teaching Council, 1976-84; Governor, Craiglockhart College of Education, 1977-83; Chairman, Scottish Association of Educational Management and Administration, 1981-84. Publication: The Years of Growth 1945-75, 1989. Recreations: music; gardening. Address: (h.) 5 Townsend Place, Kirkcaldy, Fife, KY1 1HB; T.-01592 260279.

Flett, James. JP. Honorary Sheriff, Lothians and Borders; Past Chairman, City of Edinburgh Valuation Appeal Committee; b. 26.1.17, Findochty; m., Jean Walker Ross; 1 s. Educ. Findochty Public School; Heriot-Watt University; Royal Military College, Sandhurst. Commissioned Seaforth Highlanders; Chief Official, Royal Burgh of Linlithgow (retired). Governor, West Lothian Educational Trust; former Member, JP Advisory Committee; former Member, Scottish Home Department Interviewing Committee at Edinburgh Prisons; former Member, West Lothian Licensing Board. Recreations: gardening; travel; walking. Address: (h.) Craigenroan, Linlithgow, West Lothian; T.-Linlithgow 842344.

Flint, Professor David, TD, MA, BL, CA, FRSA. Professor of Accountancy, Glasgow University, 1964-85 (Vice-Principal, 1981-85); b. 24.2.19, Glasgow; m., Dorothy Mary Maclachlan Jardine; 2 s.; 1 d. Educ. High School of Glasgow; Glasgow University. Royal Signals, 1939-46 (Major; mentioned in Despatches); Partner, Mann Judd Gordon & Company, Chartered Accountants, Glasgow, 1951-71; Lecturer (part-time), Glasgow

University, 1950-60; Dean, Faculty of Law, 1971-73; Council Member, Scottish Business School, 1971-77; Institute of Chartered Accountants of Scotland: President, 1975-76, Vice-President, 1973-75, Convener, Research Advisory Committee, 1974-75 and 1977-84, Convener, Working Party on Future Policy, 1976-79, Convener, Public Sector Committee, 1987-89, Convener, Taxation Review and Research Sub-Committee, 1960-64; Trustee, Scottish Chartered Accountants Trust for Education, 1981-87; Member, Management Training and Development Committee, Central Training Council, 1966-70; Member, Management and Industrial Relations Committee, Social Science Research Council, 1970-72 and 1978-80; Member, Social Sciences Panel, Scottish Universities Council on Entrance, 1968-72; Chairman, Association of University Teachers of Accounting, 1969; Member, Company Law Committee, Law Society of Scotland, 1976-85; Scottish Economic Society: Treasurer, 1954-62, Vice-President, 1977-88, Hon. Vice-President, since 1988; Member, Commission for Local Authority Accounts in Scotland, 1978-80; President, European Accounting Association, 1983-84. Publication: Philosophy and Principles of Auditing, 1988. Recreation: golf. Address: (h.) 16 Grampian Avenue, Auchterarder, Perthshire, PH3 1NY; T.-01764 663978.

Flockhart, (David) Ross, OBE, BA, BD. Director, Scottish Council for Voluntary Organisations, 1972-91; b. 20.3.27, Newcastle, NSW, Australia; m., Pamela Ellison Macartney; 3 s.; 1 d.; 1 d. (deceased). Educ. Knox Grammar School, Sydney; Sydney University; Edinburgh University. Royal Australian Engineers, 1945-46; Chaplain to Overseas Students, Edinburgh, 1955-58; Parish Minister (Church of Scotland), Northfield, Aberdeen, 1958-63; Warden, Carberry Tower, Musselburgh, 1963-66; Lecturer and Senior Lecturer, School of Community Studies, Moray House College of Education, 1966-72; Member, Scottish Arts Council, 1976-82; Member, Court, Stirling University, since 1989; Trustee and Vice-Chairman, Community Projects Foundation. Recreations: bee-keeping; sailing. Address: (h.) Longwood, Humbie, East Lothian, EH36 5PN; T.-01875 833208.

Florey, Professor Charles du Ve, MD, MPH, FFCM, FRCPE. Professor of Epidemiology and Public Health, Dundee University, since 1983. Instructor, Assistant Professor, Yale University, 1963-69; Member, Scientific Staff, MRC, 1969-71; Senior Lecturer, then Reader, then Professor, St. Thomas's Hospital Medical School, 1971-83; Member, Committee on Data Protection, 1976-78. Publications: Introduction to Community Medicine; Methods for Cohort Studies of Chronic Airflow Limitation. Address: (b.) Department of Epidemiology and Public Health, Ninewells Hospital and Medical School, Dundee, DD1 9SY; T.-01382 632124.

Fluendy, Malcolm A.D., MA, DPhil, DSc, CChem, FRSC, MInstP, CPhys, FRSE. Reader in Chemistry, Edinburgh University; b. 28.3.35, London; m., Annette Pidgeon; 2 s. Educ. Westminster City School; Balliol College, Oxford. National Service, 1953-55 (Lt., Royal Signals); Royal Naval Scientific Service, 1955-56; Balliol College, Oxford, 1956-62; Research Fellow: University of California, Berkeley, 1962-63, Harvard University, 1963-64; joined Edinburgh University as Lecturer, 1964. Chairman, Molecular Beam Group, Chemical Society, 1974-79; Physical Secretary, RSE, 1990-93. Publication: Molecular Beams. Recreations: sailing; cruising (yachtmaster). Address: (b.) Department of Chemistry, West Mains Road, Edinburgh, EH9 3JJ; T.-0131-667 1081.

Flynn, Professor Peter, MA (Oxon). Director, Institute of Latin American Studies, Glasgow University, since 1972; Chairman, Centre for Amazonian Studies, since 1991; b. 30.12.35; 1 s.; 2 d. Educ. Balliol College and St. Antony's College, Oxford. Senior Scholar, St. Antony's College,

150 WHO'S WHO IN SCOTLAND

1964-67; Visiting Scholar, Institute of Latin American Studies, Columbia University, 1965; Lecturer in Latin American Studies, Glasgow University, 1967-68; Lecturer in Latin American Politics, Liverpool University, 1968-72. Publications: Brazil: A Political Analysis, 1979; various papers. Recreations: fly fishing; motor caravanning; running; weight training; music. Address: (h.) King's Gate, 37 Victoria Crescent Road, Glasgow, G12 9DD; T.-0141-334 9537.

Foley, Hugh Smith. Principal Clerk of Session and Justiciary, since 1989; b. 9.4.39, Falkirk; m., Isobel King Halliday. Educ. Dalkeith High School. Entered Scottish Court Service (Court of Session Branch), 1962; Assistant Clerk of Session, 1962-71; Depute Clerk of Session, 1972-80; seconded to Sheriff Court, Edinburgh, 1980-81; Principal Sheriff Clerk Depute, Glasgow, 1981-82; Sheriff Clerk, Linlithgow, 1982; Deputy Principal Clerk of Session, 1982-86; Senior Deputy Principal Clerk, 1986-89. Member, Lord President's Committee on Procedure in Personal Injuries Litigation in Court of Session, 1978-79. Recreations: walking; painting. Address: (b.) Parliament House, Edinburgh, EH1 1RQ; T.-031-225 2595.

Foot, Professor Hugh Corrie, BA, PhD, FBPsS. Professor of Psychology, Strathclyde University, since 1992; b. 7.6.41, Northwood, Middx; m., Daryl M.; 1 s.; 1 d. Educ. Durham University; Queen's College, Dundee. Research Fellow, Dundee University, 1965-68; University of Wales Institute of Science and Technology: Lecturer, 1968-77, Senior Lecturer, 1977-88; Reader, University of Wales College of Cardiff, 1989-91. Recreations: tennis; hill walking. Address: Department of Psychology, Strathclyde University, Turnbull Building, 155 George Street, Glasgow, G1 1RD; T.-0141-552 4400, Ext. 2580.

Forbes, Professor Charles Douglas, DSc, MD, MB, ChB, FRCP, FRCPGlas, FRCPEdin, FRSA, FRSE. Professor of Medicine, Dundee University, and Honorary Consultant Physician, Tayside Health Board, since 1987; b. 9.10.38, Glasgow; m., Janette MacDonald Robertson; 2 s. Educ. High School of Glasgow; Glasgow University. Assistant Lecturer in Materia Medica, Glasgow University; Lecturer in Medicine, Makerere, Uganda; Registrar in Medicine, Glasgow Royal Infirmary; Reader in Medicine, Glasgow University; Fellow, American Heart Association; Fullbright Fellow; Director, Regional Haemophilia Centre, Glasgow. Recreation: gardening. Address: (h.) East Chattan, 108 Hepburn Gardens, St. Andrews, KY16 9LT; T.-01334 472428.

Forbes, David Fraser, LLB (Hons). General Secretary, Scottish Health Visitors' Association, since 1988; b. 11.4.56, Glasgow; m., Isabel Hamilton; 3 d. Educ. Greenock Academy; Edinburgh University. Porter, Royal Edinburgh Hospital, and Senior Shop Steward, NUPE, 1978-87; Diploma in Accountancy, Stirling University, 1987-88. Recreations: football; cricket; golf. Address: (b.) 94 Constitution Street, Leith, Edinburgh, EH6 6AW; T.-0131-553 4061.

Forbes, Very Rev. Graham J.T., MA, BD. Provost, St. Mary's Cathedral, Edinburgh, since 1990 (Provost, St. Ninian's Cathedral, Perth, 1982-90); b. 10.6.51, Edinburgh; m., Jane Miller; 3 s. Educ. George Heriot's School, Edinburgh; Aberdeen University; Edinburgh University. Curate, Old St. Paul's, Edinburgh, 1976-82; Chairman, Canongate Youth Project, 1977-83; Chairman, Lothian Association of Youth Clubs, 1981-88; Member, Scottish Community Education Council, 1982-88; Chairman, Scottish Intermediate Treatment Resource Centre, 1982-89; Member, Edinburgh Area Board, Manpower Services Commission, 1980-83; Chairman, Youth Affairs Group, Scottish Community Education Council, 1982- 88; Non-Executive Director, Radio Tay, 1987-90; Member, Parole Board for Scotland, 1991-95; HM Lay Inspector of

Constabulary, since 1995. Address: 8 Lansdowne Crescent, Edinburgh, EH12 5EQ.

Forbes, Sheriff John Stuart, MA, LLB. Sheriff of Tayside, Central and Fife, at Dunfermline, since 1980; b. 31.1.36.

Forbes, 22nd Lord (Nigel Ivan Forbes), KBE (1960), JP, DL. Premier Lord of Scotland; Chairman, Rolawn Ltd., since 1975; b. 19.2.18; m., Hon. Rosemary Katharin Hamilton-Russell; 2 s.; 1 d. Educ. Harrow; Sandhurst. Retired Major, Grenadier Guards; Representative Peer of Scotland, 1955-63; Minister of State, Scottish Office, 1958-59; Member, Scottish Committee, Nature Conservancy 1961-67; Member, Aberdeen and District Milk Marketing Board, 1962-72; Chairman, River Don District Board, 1962-73; President, Royal Highland and Agricultural Society of Scotland, 1958-59; President, Scottish Scout Association, 1970-88; Member, Sports Council for Scotland, 1966-71; Chairman, Scottish Branch, National Playing Fields Association, 1965-80; Deputy Chairman, Tennant Caledonian Breweries Ltd., 1964-74. Address: (h. Balforbes, Alford, Aberdeenshire,AB33 8DR; T.-01975 62516.

Ford, Gordon J.W., BA, DipEd. Headmaster, Broughton High School, since 1993;' b. 1.5.52, Inverkeithing; m. Audrey; 1 s.; 2 d. Educ. Kirkcaldy High School; Knox Academy; Stirling University. Teacher of History, Modern Studies, 1974-87; Assistant Headteacher, Greenhall High School, 1987-89; Depute Headteacher, Ainslie Park High School, 1989-91; Depute Headteacher, Armadale Academy, 1991-93. Recreations: coaching rugby (Livingston RFC); tennis; music; tai chi. Address: (b.) Broughton High School, Carrington Road, Edinburgh, EH4 1EG; T.-0131-332 7805.

Ford, Professor Ian, BSc, PhD. Professor of Statistics and Head of Department, Glasgow University, since 1991; b. 4.2.51, Glasgow; m., Carole Louise Ford; 1 s. Educ. Hamilton Academy; Glasgow University. Visiting Lecturer, University of Wisconsin, Madison, 1976-77; Lecturer, then Senior Lecturer, Reader and Titular Professor, Glasgow University, since 1977. Publications: 50 papers. Recreations: gardening; travel. Address: (b.) Robertson Centre for Biostatistics, Boyd Orr Building, Glasgow University, Glasgow; T.-0141-330 4744.

Ford, James Allan, CB, MC. Author; Trustee, National Library of Scotland, 1981-91; b. 10.6.20, Auchtermuchty; m., Isobel Dunnett; 1 s.; 1 d. Educ. Royal High School, Edinburgh; Edinburgh University. Employment Clerk Ministry of Labour, 1938-39; Executive Officer, Inland Revenue, 1939-40; Captain, The Royal Scots, 1940-44 (POW, Far East, 1941-45); Executive Officer, Inland Revenue, 1946-47; Department of Agriculture for Scotland 1947-66 (Assistant Secretary, 1958); Registrar General for Scotland, 1966-69; Under Secretary, Scottish Office, 1969-79. Publications (novels): The Brave White Flag, 1961 Season of Escape, 1963; A Statue for a Public Place, 1965 A Judge of Men, 1968; The Mouth of Truth, 1972 Recreations: trout fishing; gardening. Address: (h.) Hillpark Court, Edinburgh, EH4 7BE; T.-0131 336 5398.

Ford, James Angus, MB, ChB, FRCPEdin, FRCPGlas, FRCP (Lond), DCH. Consultant Paediatrician, since 1975 Chairman, Scottish Joint Consultants Committee Chairman, National Medical Advisory Committee; Past Chairman, Scottish Council, British Medical Association; b. 5.11.43, Arbroath; m., Dr. Veronica T. Reid. Educ. Kelvinside Academy; Glasgow University. House appointments: Glasgow Royal, Southern General, Stobhill Belvidere; Registrar/Senior Registrar, Stobhill; Consultant appointments: Rutherglen Maternity Hospital, Royal Hospital for Sick Children, Glasgow; Territorial Army: six years, 6/7th Bn., Cameronians (Scottish Rifles), Captain, BMA: Chairman, Hospital Junior Staff Committee

(Scotland), Deputy Chairman, HJSC (UK), Member of Council (Scottish and UK), Member, Joint Consultants Committee (Scottish and UK). Recreation: gardening. Address: (h.) 20 Ralston Road, Bearsden, Glasgow; T.-0141-942 4273.

Ford, John Noel Patrick, OStJ, FInstD. Director of Administration and Finance, Scottish Civic Trust, since 1993; Regional Chairman, Glasgow, Princes Scottish Youth Business Trust, since 1993; Chairman, Glasgow Committee, Order of St. John, since 1993; Trustee, New Lanark Conservation Trust, since 1994; b. 18.12.35, Surbiton; m., Roslyn Madeleine Penfold; 2 s.; 2 d. Educ. Tiffin School, Kingston on Thames. Retired, 1992, as Chairman, Scotland and Northern Ireland, and Marketing Director, OCS Group Ltd. Deacon, Incorporation of Masons of Glasgow, 1985-86; Deacon Convener, Trades House of Glasgow, 1991-92; Governor, Hutchesons' Educational Trust, since 1986; General Commissioner of Inland Revenue, Glasgow North. Recreations: golf and sport in general; gardening. Address: (b.) 24 George Square, Glasgow, G2 1EF; T.-0141-221 1466.

Forrest, Professor Sir (Andrew) Patrick (McEwen), Kt (1986), BSc, MD, ChM, FRCS, FRCSEdin, FRCSGlas, DSc (Hon), LLD (Hon), FACS (Hon), FRACS (Hon), FRCSCan (Hon), FRCR (Hon), FIBiol, FRSE. Professor Emeritus, Edinburgh University; Associate Dean of Clinical Studies, International Medical College, Malaysia; b. 25.3.23, Mount Vernon, Lanarkshire; m., Margaret Anne Steward; 1 s.; 2 d. Educ. Dundee High School; St. Andrews University. House Surgeon, Dundee Royal Infirmary; Surgeon Lieutenant, RNVR; Mayo Foundation Fellow; Lecturer and Senior Lecturer, Glasgow University; Professor of Surgery, Welsh National School of Medicine; Regius Professor of Clinical Surgery, Edinburgh University; Visiting Scientist, National Cancer Institute, USA; Chief Scientist (part-time), Scottish Home and Health Department, 1981-87; Chairman, Working Group, Breast Cancer Screening, 1985-86; President, Surgical Research Society, 1974-76; President, Association of Surgeons of Great Britain and Ireland, 1988-89; Lister Medal, Royal College of Surgeons of England, 1987; Member, Kirk Session, St. Giles Cathedral. Publications: Prognostic Factors in Breast Cancer (Co-author), 1968; Principles and Practice of Surgery (Co-author), 1985; Breast Cancer: the decision to screen, 1990. Recreations: sailing; golf. Address: (h.) 19 St. Thomas Road, Edinburgh, EH9 2LR; T.-0131-667 3203.

Forrest, Peter, ATI. Managing Director, Dawson International PLC, since 1995, Main Board Director, since 1994; Managing Director, Todd & Duncan Ltd., Kinross, since 1991; b. 2.5.38, Dewsbury; m., Evelyn Margaret; 3 s. Educ. Batley Grammar School; Huddersfield College of Textiles. Yorkshire textile industry, 1959-70; founded and become Managing Director, Dundee Fabrics Ltd., 1971-76; Dundee Fabrics taken over, 1976, continuing as MD until 1980, also joining board of Courtaulds Northern Weaving Division; Operations Director, Legler Industria Tessile, Italy, 1980-91. Recreations: sailing; walking; classical music. Address: (h.) Whinfield House, Kinross, KY13 7AU; T.-01577 862989.

Forrest, Robert Jack, FRAgS. Director, Royal Highland & Agricultural Society of Scotland, since 1979, Hon. Treasurer, 1985-88, Chairman, 1989-90, Hon. Secretary since 1991; b. 4.1.39, Duns; m., Jennifer McCreath; 2 s.; 1 d. Educ. Loretto School; East of Scotland College of Agriculture. Director, Robert Forrest Ltd. (Farmers), since 1960, Chairman since 1986; President, British Simmental Cattle Society, 1983-84; judged pedigree cattle and sheep at home and abroad; President, Scottish Agricultural Arbiters Association, 1993-94; Vice Chairman, Scottish Agricultural Benevolent Institution, 1991; Council Member, Royal Agricultural Society of the Commonwealth; Director,

Scottish Borders Enterprise, since 1994; Elder, Bonkyl Church. Address: (h.) Preston, Duns, Berwickshire, TD11 3TQ; T.-01361 882826.

Forrester, Professor Alexander Robert, BSc, PhD, DSc, FRSC, FRSE. Professor of Chemistry, Aberdeen University, since 1985 (Head of Department, 1987-90, Dean, Faculty of Engineering and Mathematical and Physical Sciences, 1990-91); Vice-Principal (Sciences), since 1991; b. 14.11.35, Kelty, Fife; m., Myrna Ross; 1 s.; 3 d. Educ. Alloa Academy; Stirling High School; Heriot-Watt University; Aberdeen University (PhD). Chairman, North of Scotland Section, Royal Society of Chemistry, 1987-90; Council Member: Royal Society of Chemistry, 1987-90, Perkin Division, Royal Society of Chemistry, since 1991; Member, Committee, Scottish National Library, since 1988; Member, Grants Committee, 1988-91, and BP Fellowship Committee, 1988-91, Royal Society Edinburgh; Director, Aberdeen University Research and Industrial Services, since 1990, Offshore Medical Services, since 1992. Recreations: golf; cricket; football (free transfers from Third Lanark and Partick Thistle). Address: (b.) Chemistry Department, Aberdeen University, Aberdeen; T.-Aberdeen 272944.

Forrester, Rev. Professor Duncan Baillie, MA (Hons), BD, DPhil. Principal, New College, Edinburgh, since 1986, and Professor of Christian Ethics and Practical Theology, since 1978; Member, WCC Faith and Order Commission, since 1983; President, Society for Study of Theology, 1991-93; President, Society for Study of Christian Ethics, 1991-94; Church of Scotland Minister; b. 10.11.33, Edinburgh; m., Rev. Margaret McDonald; 1 s.; 1 d. Educ. Madras College, St. Andrews; St. Andrews University; Chicago University; Edinburgh University. Part-time Assistant in Politics, Edinburgh University, 1957-58; Assistant Minister, Hillside Church, Edinburgh, and Leader of St. James Mission, 1960-61; as Church of Scotland Missionary, Lecturer and then Professor of Politics, Madras Christian College, Tambaram, South India, 1962-70; ordained Presbyter, Church of South India, 1962; part-time Lecturer in Politics, Edinburgh University, 1966-67; Chaplain and Lecturer in Politics, Sussex University. Publications: Caste & Christianity, 1980; Encounter with God (Co-author), 1983; Studies in the History of Worship in Scotland (Co-Editor), 1984; Christianity and the Future of Welfare, 1985; Theology and Politics, 1988; Just Sharing (Co-author), 1988; Beliefs, Values and Policies, 1989; Worship Now Book II (Co-editor), 1989; Theology and Practice (Editor), 1990. Recreations: hill-walking; reading; listening to music. Address: (h.) 25 Kingsburgh Road, Edinburgh, EH12 6DZ; T.-0131-337 5646.

Forrester, Frederick Lindsay, MA (Hons), DipEd, FEIS. Depute General Secretary, Educational Institute of Scotland, since 1992; b. 10.2.35, Glasgow; 1 s.; 1 d. Educ. Victoria Drive Senior Secondary School, Glasgow; Glasgow University; Jordanhill College of Education. Teacher of English, Glasgow secondary schools, 1962-64; Teacher of English and General Studies, Coatbridge Technical College, 1964-67; Assistant Secretary, Educational Institute of Scotland, 1967-75, Organising Secretary, 1975-92. Recreations: walking; cycling; swimming; foreign travel. Address: (h.) 2/6 East Farm of Gilmerton, Edinburgh, EH17 8TQ; T.-0131 672 1638.

Forrester, Ian Stewart, QC, MA, LLB, MCL. Honorary Visiting Professor in European Law, Glasgow University, since 1991; Member, European Advisory Board, Tulane University Law School, since 1992; b. 13.1.45, Glasgow; m., Sandra Anne Therese Keegan; 2 s. Educ. Kelvinside Academy, Glasgow; Glasgow University; Tulane University of Louisiana. Admitted to Faculty of Advocates, 1972; admitted to Bar of State of NY, 1977; Maclay, Murray & Spens, 1968-69; Davis Polk & Wardwell, 1969-72; Cleary Gottlieb Steen & Hamilton, 1972-81; established independent chambers, Brussels, 1981; Co-Founder, Forrester & Norall, 1981 (Forrester Norrall & Sutton, 1989), practising before European Commission and Courts. Chairman: British Conservative Association, Belgium, 1982-86; European Trade Law Association, since 1989 ; Member, European Committee of British Invisibles; Elder, St. Andrew's Church of Scotland, Brussels. Recreations: politics; wine; cooking; restoring old houses. Address: Advocates' Library, Parliament House, Edinburgh, EH1 1RF.

Forrester, Professor John V., MD (Hons), FRCS(Ed), FRCOphth, FRCS(G). Cockburn Professor of Ophthalmology, since 1984; Editor, British Journal of Ophthalmology, since 1992; b. 11.9.46, Glasgow; m., Anne Gray; 2 s.; 2 d. Educ. St. Aloysius College, Glasgow; Glasgow University. Various hospital appointments, Glasgow, 1971-78; MRC Travelling Fellow, Columbia University, New York, 1976-77; Consultant Ophthalmologist, Southern General Hospital, 1979-83. Recreation: family. Address: (b.) Department of Ophthalmology, Aberdeen University, Aberdeen AB9 2ZD; T.-01224 681818.

Forrester, Rev. Margaret Rae, MA, BD. Minister, St. Michael's, Edinburgh, since 1980; Convener, Board of World Mission and Unity, Church of Scotland, since 1992; b. 23.11.37, Edinburgh; m., Duncan B. Forrester; 1 s.; 1 d. Educ. George Watson's Ladies' College; Edinburgh University and New College. Assistant Pastor, Madras; Minister, Telscombe Cliffs URC, Sussex; Assistant Minister, St. George's West, Edinburgh; Chaplain, Napier College, Edinburgh. Recreation: gardening. Address: 25 Kingsburgh Road, Edinburgh, EH12 6DZ; T.-0131-337 5646.

Forsyth of That Ilk, Alistair Charles William, JP, KHS, FSCA, FSA Scot, FInstPet, CStJ. Baron of Ethie; Chief of the Name and Clan of Forsyth; b. 7.12.29; m., Ann Hughes; 4 s. Educ. St. Paul's School; Queen Mary College, London. Company Director; CStJ, 1982; KHS, 1992; Freeman of the City of London; Liveryman of the Scriveners Company. Recreations: Scottish antiquities; hill-walking. Address: (h.) Ethie Castle, by Arbroath, Angus, DD11 5SP.

Forsyth, Bill. Film Director and Script Writer; b. 1947, Glasgow. Films include: Gregory's Girl, 1981, Local Hero, 1983, Comfort and Joy, 1984, Housekeeping, 1988, Breaking In, 1990, Being Human, 1993. BAFTA Awards: Best Screenplay, 1982, Best Director, 1983.

Forsyth, Rt. Hon. Michael Bruce, PC, MA. MP (Conservative), Stirling, since 1983; Secretary of State for Scotland, since 1995; b. 16.10.54, Montrose; m., Susan Jane; 1 s.; 2 d. Educ. Arbroath High School; St. Andrews University. National Chairman, Federation of Conservative Students, 1976; Member, Westminster City Council, 1978-83; Member, Select Committee on Scottish Affairs; Parliamentary Private Secretary to the Foreign Secretary, 1986-87; Past Chairman, Scottish Conservative Party; former Parliamentary Under Secretary of State and Minister of State, Scottish Office; former Minister of State, Department of Employment. Recreations: mountaineering; astronomy. Address: House of Commons, London, SW1.

Forte, Professor Angelo D.M., LLB, MA. Professor of Commercial Law, Aberdeen University, since 1993; b. 9.5.49, Lower Largo; m., Janina Rak; 1 d. Educ. St. Joseph's College, Dumfries; Edinburgh University. Lecturer in Private Law, Glasgow University, 1977-80, Dundee University, 1980-84; Lecturer, then Senior Lecturer in Scots Law, Edinburgh University, 1985-92. Publications: Cases and Material in Commercial Law (Co-editor); Gloag and Henderson's Introduction to Scots Law (10th edition) (Co-editor); various publications on commercial law.

Recreations: fishing; Scottish railways; reading. Address (h.) The Rowans, 3 Markethill, Ellon, Aberdeenshire.

Forteviot, 4th Baron (John James Evelyn Dewar) Director, John Dewar & Sons Ltd., since 1965; Member Queen's Bodyguard for Scotland (Royal Company o Archers); b. 5.4.38. Educ. Eton. Black Watch (RHR), 1956- 58. Address: (h.) Aberdalgie House, Perth.

Forty, Professor Arthur John, CBE, BSc, PhD, DSc LLD, DUniv, FRSE. Principal and Vice-Chancellor Stirling University, 1986-94; b. 4.11.28, Shrivenham; m. Alicia Blanche Hart Gough; 1 s. Educ. Headlands School Swindon; Bristol University. RAF, 1953-56; Senior Scientist, Tube Investments Ltd., 1956-58; Lecturer, Bristo University, 1958-64; founding Professor of Physics Warwick University, 1964-86; Pro-Vice-Chancellor Warwick Univ., 1970-86; Member, Physics and Materials Science Committees, SERC, 1970-74; Member, UGC 1982-86 (Vice-Chairman, 1985-86); Member, Computer Board, Universities and Research Councils, 1982-85 (Chairman, 1988-91); Chairman, Committee of Scottish University Principals, 1990-92; Member, British Library Board, 1987-94; Chairman, Information Systems Committee, UFC, 1991-92; Hon. Fellow and Chairman EPCC, Edinburgh University, since 1994; author of "Forty Report" on future facilities for advanced research computing. Recreations: dinghy sailing; gardening Address: (h.) Port Mor, St. Fillans, Perthshire, PH6 2NF.

Forwell, Harold Christie. Member, Fife Health Board 1981-89; Member, Industrial Tribunals (Scotland), 1978-94; b. 16.8.25, Kirkcaldy; m., Isobel Russell Stuart; 1 s.; 1 d. Educ. George Watson's College, Edinburgh; Queen's University, Belfast. Past Chairman, National Joint Committee for Scottish Baking Industry; former Member Retail Wages Council (BFCS Scotland); Past President. Scottish Association of Master Bakers, Kirkcaldy Rotary Club. Queen's Jubilee Medal, 1977. Recreations: sailing; travel. Address: (h.) 4 West Fergus Place, Kirkcaldy, Fife; T.-01592 260474.

Foster, Ann, MA. Director, Scottish Consumer Council, since 1991; b. 28.9.49, St. Andrews. Educ. Hutchesons' Girls' Grammar School, Glasgow; St. Andrews University; Reading University. Lecturer, ILEA, 1972-78; Consultant National Consumer Council, 1978-91; Member, UK Ecolabelling Board; Member, Nutrition Task Force; Member, Committee on Medical Aspects of Food Policy; Member, Scottish Diet Action Group; Member, Advisory Group on Sustainable Development. Recreations: skiing; theatre; opera. Address: (b.) Royal Exchange House, 100 Queen Street, Glasgow, G1 3DN; T.-0141-226 5261.

Foster, James Richard Charles, pce, jsdc, RN (Retd). General Manager, WS Society, since 1993; b. 7.11.48, Arbroath; m., Kathryn Taylor; 1 s.; 2 d. Educ. George Heriot's School; Hampton School; Britannia Royal Naval College. Former naval officer, submariner and sometime commander of a Polaris submarine. Recreations: hill-walking (Munros); sailing. Address: (b.) The Signet Library, Parliament Square, Edinburgh, EH1 1RF; T.-0131-225 4923.

Foster, John, CBE, FRICS, FRTPI, RIBA, ARIAS, FRSA. President, Ramblers Association (Scotland); b. 13.8.20, Glasgow; m., Daphne Househam. Educ. Whitehill School, Glasgow; Royal Technical College, Glasgow. Surveyor with private firm in Glasgow, 1937; Air Ministry during War; Assistant Planning Officer: Kirkcudbright County Council, 1945-47, Holland Joint Planning Committee, Lincolnshire, 1947-48; Deputy County Planning Officer, Holland County Council, 1948-52; Deputy Planning Officer, Peak Park Planning Board, 1952-54; Director, Peak District National Park Board, 1954-68; Director, Countryside Commission for Scotland, 1968-85. Honorary

Vice-President, Countrywide Holidays Association; Honorary Fellow, Royal Scottish Geographical Society; Member, Executive Committee, Scottish Council for National Parks; Hon. Member, European Federation of Nature and National Parks; Vice-Chairman, Heritage Unit Advisory Board, Robert Gordon University, Aberdeen; Life Member, National Trust for Scotland; George Waterston Memorial Award, 1991. Recreations: walking; swimming; photography; philately; reading; travel. Address: (h.) Birchover, Ferntower Road, Crieff, PH7 3DH; T.-01764 652336.

Foster, Professor John Odell, MA, PhD. Professor of Applied Social Studies, Paisley University, since 1981; b. 21.10.40, Hertford; m., Renee Prendergast. Educ. Guildford Grammar School; St. Catherine's College, Cambridge. Postdoctoral Research Fellow, St. Catherine's College, Cambridge, 1965-68; Lecturer in Politics, Strathclyde University, 1966-81. Secretary, Scottish Committee, Communist Party of Britain, since 1988. Publications: Class Struggle and the Industrial Revolution, 1974; Politics of the UCS Work-In, 1986; Track Record: the Caterpillar Occupation, 1988. Recreation: hill-walking. Address: (h.) 845 Govan Road, Glasgow, G51.

Foster, Professor Roy, MA, DPhil, DSc, FRSC, FRSE. Emeritus Professor; Professor of Physical-Organic Chemistry, Dundee University, 1969-86; b. 29.7.28, Leicester; m., Delwen Eluned Rodd; 1 s.; 2 d. Educ. Wyggeston School, Leicester; Wadham College, Oxford. Research Fellow, Department of Pharmacology, Dundee University, 1953-56; Queen's College, Dundee (St. Andrews University): Senior Edward A. Deeds Fellow, 1956-59, Lecturer in Organic Chemistry, 1959-63, Senior Lecturer, 1963-66, Reader, 1966-67 (thence Dundee University, 1967-69). British Association for the Advancement of Science: Member of Council, Member, General Committee, Chairman, Tayside and Fife Branch, 1977-84; Dundee University: sometime Member of Court, Dean, Faculty of Science, Head, Department of Chemistry. Recreation: gardening. Address: 19 Adelaide Place, Dundee, DD3 6LE; T.-01382 25082.

Fothergill-Gilmore, Linda Adams, BS, PhD, FSA Scot. Reader in Biochemistry, Edinburgh University, since 1989; b. 16.4.43, Boston, Massachusetts; m., John Frederick Bruce Hole; 1 s.; 1 d. Educ. Provincetown High School; Michigan State University; Aberdeen University. Research Fellow in Biochemistry, then Research Officer in Biochemistry, Aberdeen University, 1969-83; Lecturer in Biochemistry, Aberdeen University, 1983-86; Senior Lecturer in Biochemistry, Edinburgh University, 1986-89. Recipient, Wellcome Trust University Award, 1986-91. Recreations: sailing; choral singing; travel; house renovations. Address: (b.) Department of Biochemistry, Edinburgh University, George Square, Edinburgh, EH8 9XD; T.-0131-650 3728.

Foulds, Emeritus Professor Wallace Stewart, CBE, MD, ChM, FRCS, FRCSGlas, DO, Hon. FRCOphth, Hon. DSc (Strathclyde), Hon. FRACO, Hon. FCMSA. Emeritus Professor of Ophthalmology, Glasgow University; Visiting Professor, National University of Singapore and Singapore National Eye Centre; b. 26.4.24, London; m., Margaret Holmes Walls; 1 s.; 2 d. Educ. George Watson's Boys College, Edinburgh; Paisley Grammar School; Glasgow University. RAF Medical Branch, 1946-49; training posts, Moorfields Eye Hospital, London, 1952-54; Research Fellow, Institute of Ophthalmology, London University, and Senior Registrar, University College Hospital, London, 1954-58; Consultant Ophthalmologist, Addenbrookes Hospital, Cambridge, 1958-64; Tennent Professor, Glasgow University, 1964-89; Honorary Lecturer, Cambridge University and Research Fellow, London University, 1958-64; Past President: Ophthalmological Society of UK, Faculty of Ophthalmologists; Past Chairman, Association

for Eye Research; Past President, Royal College of Ophthalmologists. Recreations: sailing; diving; DIY; natural history. Address: (b.) Ross Hall Hospital, 221 Crookston Road, Glasgow, G63 3NQ; T.-0141-810 3151.

Foulis, Alan Keith, BSc, MD, MRCPath, FRCP(Ed). Consultant Pathologist, Royal Infirmary, Glasgow, since 1983; b. 25.5.50, Glasgow; m., Anne Don Martin; 1 s.; 1 d. Educ. Glasgow Academy; Glasgow University. Trained in pathology, Western Infirmary, Glasgow, following brief flirtation with surgery at Aberdeen Royal Infirmary; C.L. Oakley Lecturer, Pathological Society, Oxford, 1987; Bellahouston Medal, Glasgow University, 1987; R.D. Lawrence Lecturer, British Diabetic Association, Manchester, 1989. Publications: research papers on diseases of the pancreas. Recreations: choral and Leider singing; walking; cycling; arctophilia; natural history. Address: (h.) 32 Tannoch Drive, Milngavie, Glasgow; T.-0141-956 3092.

Foulkes, George, JP, BSc. MP (Labour and Co-operative), Carrick, Cumnock and Doon Valley, since 1979; Opposition Spokesman on Foreign Affairs, 1984-92, Defence, 1992-93, Overseas Development, since 1994; b. 21.1.42, Oswestry; m., Elizabeth Anna; 2 s.; 1 d. Educ. Keith Grammar School; Haberdashers' Aske's School; Edinburgh University. President, Scottish Union of Students, 1964-66; Director: European League for Economic Co-operation, 1967-68, Enterprise Youth, 1968-73, Age Concern Scotland, 1973-79; Chairman: Lothian Region Education Committee, 1974-79, Education Committee, COSLA, 1975-79; Rector's Assessor, Edinburgh University, 1968-71; Chairman, John Wheatley Centre; Director, The Co-operative Press; Treasurer, Parliamentarians for Global Action. Recreations: boating; watching football (Heart of Midlothian and Ayr United). Address: (h.) 8 Southpark Road, Ayr, KA7 2TL; T.-Ayr 265776.

Fourman, Professor Michael Paul, BSc, MSc, DPhil. Professor of Computer Systems, Edinburgh University, since 1988; Director, Abstract Hardware Ltd., since 1986; b. 12.9.50, Oxford; m., Jennifer Robin Head; 2 s.; 1 d. Educ. Allerton Grange, Leeds; Bristol University; Oxford University. Junior Research Fellow, Wolfson College, Oxford, 1974-78; J.F. Ritt Assistant Professor of Mathematics, Columbia University NY, 1976-82; Department of Electrical & Electronic Engineering, Brunel University: Research Fellow, 1983-86, Hirst Reader in Integrated Circuit Design, 1986, Professor of Formal Systems, 1986-88. Recreations: cooking; sailing. Address: (b.) Computer Science Department, JCMB, King's Buildings, Edinburgh, EH9 3JZ; T.-0131-650 5197.

Fowkes, Professor Francis Gerald Reid, MB, ChB, PhD, FRCPE, FFPHM. Professor of Epidemiology, Edinburgh University, since 1994; Director, Wolfson Unit for Prevention of Peripheral Vascular Diseases, since 1989; Hon. Consultant Public Health Medicine, since 1985; b. 9.5.46, Falkirk; 1.s.; 1 d. Educ. George Watson's College, Edinburgh; Edinburgh University. Senior Lecturer, University of Wales, 1980-85; Reader/Professor, Edinburgh University, since 1985. Address: (b.) Department of Public Health Sciences, Edinburgh University, Teviot Place, Edinburgh, EH8 9AG; T.-0131-650 3220.

Fowler, Agnes Isobel, BSc. Director of Finance and Administration, Royal Scottish Academy of Music and Drama; b. 13.2.42, Glasgow; m., William M. Fowler; 2 s.; 1 d. Educ. Jordanhill College School; Glasgow University. Governor, Associated Board, Royal Schools of Music. Recreations: hill-walking; swimming; gardening; Church. Address: (h.) Hillside, 7 Main Street, Drymen, Glasgow; T.-01360 660009.

Fowlie, Hector Chalmers, OBE, MB, ChB, FRCPEdin, FRCPsych, DPM. Retired Consultant Psychiatrist;

Chairman, Dundee Healthcare NHS Trust; Member of Court, Abertay University, Dundee; b. 21.6.29, Dundee; m., Christina N.M. Walker; 2 s.; 1 d. Educ. Harris Academy, Dundee; St. Andrews University. House Officer, Maryfield Hospital, Dundee, and Perth Royal Infirmary; Registrar, Dundee Royal Mental Hospital; Lecturer, Department of Psychiatry, Medical School, Dundee University; Consultant Psychiatrist and Deputy Physician Superintendent, Gartnavel Royal Hospital, Glasgow; Physician Superintendent, Royal Dundee Liff and Strathmartine Hospitals; Consultant Psychiatrist, Tayside Health Board. Vice-Chairman, Mental Welfare Commission for Scotland, 1984-89; sometime Vice-Chairman, Parole Board for Scotland; Member, Tayside Health Board; Council of Europe Scholar; Consultant, WHO; Past Chairman, Dundee Association for Mental Health. Recreations: reading; walking. Address: (h.) 21 Clepington Road, Dundee; T.-01382 456926.

Fox, Christopher Howard Christian, MRAC, ARICS. Regional Director, South West Region, Scottish Natural Heritage, since 1992; b. 13.1.41, Whitehaven; m., Caroline Jane Porter; 1 s.; 1 d. Educ. Fettes College, Edinburgh; Royal Agricultural College, Cirencester. Assistant Land Agent: W.H. Cooke & Arkwright, Chartered Surveyors, Hereford, 1963-69, Nature Conservancy Council, Edinburgh, 1969-73; Area Land Agent, North Scotland, Nature Conservancy Council, 1973-83; Senior Land Agent (Scotland), Nature Conservancy Council, 1983-91; Regional Director, South West Scotland, Nature Conservancy Council for Scotland, 1991-92. Director, Scottish Agricultural College, Auchincruive, 1991-94; Member, Advisory Committee, Scottish Agricultural College. Recreations: country sports; contemporary Scottish painters; music. Address: (h.) 6 Afton Terrace, Edinburgh, EH5 3NG; T.-0131-552 5894.

Fox, Professor Keith Alexander Arthur, BSc (Hons), MB, ChB, FRCP. Duke of Edinburgh Professor of Cardiology, Edinburgh University, since 1989; b. 27.8.49, Salisbury, Rhodesia; m., Aileen E.M.; 1 s.; 1 d. Educ. Falcon College; Edinburgh University. Assistant Professor of Medicine, Washington University School of Medicine, 1980-85; Senior Lecturer in Cardiology and Consultant Cardiologist, University Hospital of Wales College of Medicine, 1985-89. Address: (b.) Cardiovascular Research Unit, Edinburgh University, Hugh Robson Building, George Square, Edinburgh, EH8 9XF; T.-0131-650 3696.

Fraile, Professor Medardo, PhD. Writer; Emeritus Professor in Spanish, Strathclyde University, since 1985; b. 21.3.25, Madrid; m., Janet H. Gallagher; 1 d. Educ. Madrid University. Teacher of Spanish language and literature, Ramiro de Maeztu Secondary School, Madrid, 1956-64; Assistant in Spanish, Southampton University, 1964-67; Strathclyde University: Assistant Lecturer in Spanish, 1967-68, Lecturer, 1968-79, Reader, 1979-83, Personal Professor, 1983-85. Travelling Scholarship for authors, 1954; Premio Sesamo for short story writing, 1956; literary grant, Juan March Foundation, 1960; Book of the Year award, 1965; La Estafeta Literaria Prize for short stories, 1970; Hucha de Oro Prize for short stories, 1971; research grant, Carnegie Trust, 1975; Ibanez Fantoni Prize for journalism, 1988. Publications: several collections of short stories (Complete Short Stories, Madrid, 1991), five books for children, a novel and books of essays and literary criticism. Recreations: swimming; walking. Address: (h.) 24 Etive Crescent, Bishopbriggs, Glasgow, G64 1ES; T.-0141-772 4421.

Frame, John Neil Munro, LLB. Director, Stocktrade; Member, Scottish Sports Council; Trustee, The Sportsman's Charity; b. 8.10.46, Edinburgh; m., Susan Macmillan; 2 s.; 2 d. Educ. Edinburgh University. Recreations: jogging slowly downhill; golfing erratically; reading profusely.

Address: 30 Murrayfield Road, Edinburgh, EH12 6ER; T.-0131-346 0077.

Frame, Roger Campbell Crosbie, CA. Secretary, Royal Scottish Society of Painters in Water Colours, since 1986; Secretary, Glasgow Eastern Merchants and Tradesmen's Society, since 1983; Treasurer, Glasgow Group of Artists, 1983-88; b. 7.6.49, Glasgow; m., Angela M. Evaristi; 2 s.; 1 d. Educ. Glasgow Academy. Qualified CA, 1973; formed Frame & Co., CA, 1976. Deacon, Incorporation of Coopers of Glasgow, 1985-86. Recreations: clay pigeon shooting; art. Address: (b.) 29 Waterloo Street, Glasgow, G2 6BZ; T.-0141-226 3838.

France, Anthony James, MA, MB, BChir, MRCP. Consultant Physician, Tayside Health Board, since 1989; Honorary Senior Lecturer, Dundee University, since 1989; b. 5.4.54, London; m., Rosemary; 1 s.; 2 d. Educ. Perse School, Cambridge; Magdalene College, Cambridge; St. Thomas' Hospital, London. Qualified 1978; specialises in management of HIV infection and other communicable diseases. Recreations: photography; gardening; decorating an old house. Address: (b.) King's Cross Hospital, Clepington Road, Dundee, DD3 8EA; T.-01382 660111.

France, Professor Peter, MA, PhD, FBA. Professor of French, Edinburgh University, 1980-90, Endowment Fellow, since 1990; b. 19.10.35, Londonderry; m., Sian Reynolds; 3 d. Educ. Bradford Grammar School; Magdalen College, Oxford. Fellow, Magdalen College, Oxford, 1960-63; Lecturer, then Reader in French, Sussex University, 1963-80; French Editor, Modern Language Review, 1979-85; President, British Comparative Literature Association, since 1992; President, International Society for the History of Rhetoric, 1993-95. Publications: Racine's Rhetoric, 1965; Rhetoric and Truth in France, 1972; Poets of Modern Russia, 1982; Diderot, 1982; Rousseau: Confessions, 1987; Politeness and its Discontents, 1992; New Oxford Companion to Literature in French, 1995.. Address: (b.) 60 George Square, Edinburgh, EH8 9JU; T.-0131-650 8417.

Francis, Professor Arthur, BSc, ACGI, FRSA. Professor of Corporate Strategy, Glasgow University, since 1992; b. 16.12.44, Leamington Spa; m., Janice Mary; 1 s.; 2 d. Educ. Warwick School; Imperial College, London. Research Officer, Imperial College, 1967-73; Nuffield College, Oxford, 1973-76; Lecturer/Senior Lecturer, Imperial College, 1976-92, Head, Business Policy Group, 1986-92. Member, Council, British Academy of Management; Fellow, Royal Society of Arts. Publications: six books; numerous journal articles. Recreations: music; literature. Address: (b.) 59 Southpark Avenue, Glasgow, G12 8LF; T.-0141-330 4130.

Francis, John Michael, BSc, ARCS, PhD, DIC, FRSGS, FRSE, FRZSS. Assistant Secretary, Scottish Office, since 1981; b. 1.5.39, London; m., Eileen; 2 d. Educ. Gowerton Grammar School, near Swansea; Imperial College of Science and Technology, London University. CEGB Berkeley Nuclear Laboratories, 1963-70; Director, Society, Religion and Technology Project, Church of Scotland, 1970-74; Senior Research Fellow, Heriot-Watt University, 1974-76; Principal, Scottish Development Department, 1976-81; Director, Scotland, Nature Conservancy Council, 1984-91, then Chief Exective, Nature Conservancy Council for Scotland. Consultant, World Council of Churches, 1971-83; Chairman, SRT Project, Church of Scotland, 1979-94; Member, Oil Development Council for Scotland, 1973-76; Member, Advisory Committee for Scotland, Nature Conservancy Council, 1973-76; Council Member, National Trust for Scotland, 1984-92; Chairman, Edinburgh Forum, 1986-92; Professional Member, World Future Society, Washington DC, since 1992; Member, John Muir Trust, since 1994. Publications: Scotland in Turmoil, 1972; Changing Directions, 1973; Facing Up to Nuclear Power, 1976; The Future as an Academic Discipline, 1975; The

Future of Scotland, 1977; North Sea Oil and the Environment (Jointly), 1992; contributions to scientific journals. Recreations: theatre; hill-walking; ecumenical travels. Address: (h.) 49 Gilmour Road, Newington, Edinburgh, EH16 5NU; T.-0131-667 3996.

Fraser, Alan Alexander, BSc (Hons), MBChB, MRCPsych. Consultant Psychiatrist, Southern General Hospital, Glasgow, since 1987; Honorary Senior Lecturer in Psychiatry, Glasgow University, since 1988; b. 17.10.55, Kilbirnie. Educ. Spier's School, Beith; Glasgow University. Address: (h.) 50 Westbourne Gardens, Glasgow, G12 9XF; T.-0141-357 2283.

Fraser, Alan William, BSc, PhD. Rector, Arbroath High School, since 1995; b. 12.3.47, Forres; m., Edith; 1 s.; 3 d. Educ. Forres Academy; Aberdeen University. Teacher, Buckhaven High, Kirkcaldy High; Assistant Rector, Montrose Academy, 1985-88; Depute Rector, Webster's High School, Kirriemuir, 1988-95; served on a number of national science committees and projects. Recreations: hill-walking; sports; music; church work. Address: (h.) 8 Redfield Road, Montrose; T.-01674 675128.

Fraser, Alan William, MA (Hons). Head, Enterprise Networks and Tourism Division, Scottish Office Education and Industry Department, since 1993; b. 17.12.51, Lennoxtown; m., Joan; 2 s.; 1 d. Educ. Daniel Stewart's College; Banff Academy; Aberdeen University. Entered Scottish Office, 1973; Assistant Secretary to Inquiry into UK Prison Services, 1978-79; Private Secretary to Minister of State, 1979-81; secondment to Aberdeen District Council, 1981-82; Head, New Towns Branch, IDS, 1982-85; Manager, Scottish Office Efficiency Unit, 1985-88; Head, Industrial Policy and Technology Division, SOID, 1988-91; Principal Private Secretary to Secretary of State for Scotland, 1991-93. Recreations: hill-walking; skiing; wind-surfing. Address: (b.) Scottish Office Education and Industry Department, Victoria Quay, Edinburgh, EH6 6QQ; T.-0131-244 7588.

Fraser, Brian Mitchell, BA (Hons), PhD, DGA, FIPM. Senior Assistant Principal, Glasgow Caledonian University; b. 31.7.43, Paisley; m., Hannah Orr Weir Burt; 3 s. Educ. Camphill High School, Paisley; London University; Strathclyde University. Civil Servant, 1962-70; Senior Administrator, Paisley College of Technology, 1970-78; Director of Personnel, Glasgow University, 1978-91; Boys' Brigade historian and leader. Publications: Sure and Stedfast - A History of the Boys' Brigade (Co-author), 1983; A Legacy of Scots (Co-author), 1988; Kirk and Community, 1990. Recreations: youth work; historical research. Address: (h.) Dunedin, Holehouse Road, Eaglesham; T.-Eaglesham 302416.

Fraser, Callum George, BSc, PhD, FAACB. Top Grade Biochemist, Ninewells Hospital and Medical School, since 1983; Honorary Senior Lecturer, Dundee University, since 1983; Honorary Senior Lecturer, St. Andrews University, since 1988; b. 3.1.45, Dundee; m., Stella Sim; 2 d. Educ. Dunfermline High School; Perth Academy; Aberdeen University. Postdoctoral Fellow, National Research Council of Canada, 1969-70; Lecturer in Chemical Pathology, Aberdeen University, and Honorary Biochemist, Grampian Health Board, 1970-75; Chief Clinical Biochemist, Flinders Medical Centre, South Australia, 1975-83; Honorary Senior Lecturer, then Honorary Associate Professor, Flinders University of South Australia, 1975-83. Former Chairman, Education Division, International Federation of Clinical Chemistry; former Member, Commission on Teaching of Clinical Chemistry, International Union of Pure and Applied Chemistry; Member, Editorial Board, Advances in Clinical Chemistry. Recreations: sailing; gardening; reading; travel. Address: (b.) Department of Biochemical Medicine, Ninewells Hospital, Dundee, DD1 9SY; T.-01382 60111.

Fraser, Sir Charles Annand, KCVO, WS, DL. Partner, W. & J. Burness, 1956-92 (retired); Chairman, Adam and Company PLC; Director: British Assets Trust PLC, Scottish Television PLC, Scottish Business in the Community; Vice Chairman, United Biscuits (Holdings) PLC; b. 16.10.28, Humbie, East Lothian; m., Ann Scott-Kerr; 4 s. Educ. Hamilton Academy; Edinburgh University. Purse Bearer to Lord High Commissioner to General Assembly of Church of Scotland, 1969-88; served on Court, Heriot-Watt University, 1972-78; Council Member, Law Society of Scotland, 1966-72; Chairman, Lothian & Edinburgh Enterprise, 1991-94; Trustee, Scottish Civic Trust. Recreations: gardening; skiing; squash; piping. Address: (h.) Shepherd House, Inveresk, Midlothian; T.-0131-665 2570.

Fraser, David James, MA, MHSM, MIPD. Chief Executive, North Ayrshire and Arran NHS Trust, since 1993; b. 1.7.52, Fraserburgh; m., Anne; 1 s. Educ. Peterhead Academy; Aberdeen University. Peat Marwick Mitchell & Co., City of London, 1974-75; Scottish Health Service Management Training Scheme, 1975-77; Lothian Health Board, 1977-93. Recreations: gardens; photography; opera. Address: (b.) Crosshouse Hospital, Kilmarnock, KA2 0BE; T.-01563 572230.

Fraser, Douglas Jamieson. Poet; b. 12.1.10, Edinburgh; m., Eva Nisbet Greenshields; 2 s.; 1 d. Educ. George Heriot's School. Spent 44 years with Standard Life Assurance Company, Edinburgh; awarded Queen's Silver Jubilee Medal. Publications: Landscape of Delight; Rhymes o' Auld Reekie; Where the Dark Branches Part; Treasure for Eyes to Hold. Recreation: painting. Address: (h.) 2 Keith Terrace, Edinburgh, EH4 3NJ; T.-0131-332 5176.

Fraser, Elwena D.A. Honorary Sheriff, Tayside, Central and Fife, since 1982; Member, Rateable Valuation Appeal Committee, 1975-85; Governor, Dundee Institute of Technology, 1969-89; Fellow of Dundee Institute, since 1990; b. 5.9.31, Lowestoft; m., Dr. Ian Tuke Fraser; 2 s.; 1 d. Educ. Craigholm School, Glasgow; Calder Girls' School, Seascale. Journalist, Scottish Daily Express, 1950-54; Member, Perth Town Council, 1969-72; Member, Education Committee, Perth County Council, 1969-72; Member, Dundee University Adult Education Committee, 1969-72; Member, Executive Committee, Perth Tourist Association, 1969-72; Member, Executive Committee, Perth Festival of the Arts, 1971-81; Board Member, Perth College of Further Education, 1972-78 (Chairman, 1975-78); Honorary Manager, Trustee Savings Bank (Perthshire), 1973-75; Member, Gas Consumers Council for Scotland, 1973-93; Member, BBC Broadcasting Council for Scotland, 1977-80. Recreation: gardening. Address: (h.) 15 Spoutwells Avenue, Scone, Perthshire, PH2 6RP; T.-01738 551310.

Fraser, Eugenie. Writer, since 1980; b. 10.12.05, Archangel, Russia; m., Ronald Fraser; 2 s. Educ. Archangel; Bruce's Business College, Dundee. Housewife since marriage in 1935; spent 26 years travelling to and from India; four years to and from Thailand. Scottish Arts Council Award-winner. Recreations: swimming; sewing; embroidery; travel. Address: (h.) 5 Braid Crescent, Edinburgh, EH10 6AX; T.-0131-447 3855.

Fraser, Hugh Donald George, MBE, QPM, DipSM, OStJ, FBIM, MIPM, MIIRSM. Former Senior Assistant Secretary, Heriot-Watt University; Member, Lothian Regional Council, since 1982; Honorary Secretary, Scottish Chamber of Safety, since 1979; b. Edinburgh; m., Margaret Jane Stothard; 1 s.; 2 d. War Service, RAF Aircrew, 1939-45 (Pilot); Edinburgh City Police, 1941-71; Chief Superintendent, Research and Planning Branch, Home Office, London, 1966-68; Deputy Commandant, Scottish Police College, 1968-71. Honorary Secretary, Edinburgh and District Spastic Association, 14 years; Member:

Edinburgh Accident Prevention Council, Lothian Retirement Committee. Recreations: Burns' enthusiast; work with senior citizens; jogging; the theatre. Address: (h.) 181 Braid Road, Edinburgh, EH10 6JA; T.-0131-447 1270.

Fraser, Ian Scott, BSc (Econ), LLB, DEc, DPA, FBIM. Barrister-at-Law; Advocate; b. 21.7.18, Dundee; m., Kathleen Mary Fraser; 1 s.; 1 d. Educ. Fort William High School; London University. Civil Service: Admiralty, 1936-46, Ministry of Pensions and National Insurance, 1946-55 and 1961-63, Treasury, 1955-57 (seconded to NATO (Shape) Paris 1956-57); United Nations official, 1957-61 and 1963-76, serving in Ethiopia and other African countries, New York, Middle East, and South America; travel and further education, 1976-81; practising Advocate, 1981-86; Chairman, Board of Directors, Scottish Rights of Way Society Ltd., 1983-86; Life Member, National Trust for Scotland and Royal Scottish Geographical Society. Recreations: travel; photography; motor caravanning; walking. Address: (h.) 1 Mayfield Gardens, Edinburgh, EH9 2AX; T.-0131-667 3681.

Fraser, James Edward, CB, MA (Aberdeen), BA (Cantab), FSA (Scot). Secretary of Commissions for Scotland, 1992-94; b. 16.12.31, Aberdeen; m., Patricia Louise Stewart; 2 s. Educ. Aberdeen Grammar School; Aberdeen University; Christ's College, Cambridge. Royal Artillery, 1953-55 (Staff Captain, "Q", Tel-El-Kebir, 1954-55); Assistant Principal, Scottish Home Department, 1957-60; Private Secretary to Permanent Under-Secretary of State, Scottish Office, 1960-62; Private Secretary to Parliamentary Under-Secretary of State, Scottish Office, 1962; Principal, 1962-69: SHHD, 1962-64, Cabinet Office, 1964-66, HM Treasury, 1966-68, SHHD, 1968-69; Assistant Secretary: SHHD, 1970-76, Scottish Office Finance Division, 1976; Under Secretary, Local Government Finance Group, Scottish Office, 1976-81, Scottish Home and Health Department, 1981-91. President, Scottish Hellenic Society, Edinburgh and Eastern Scotland, 1987-93. Recreations: reading; music; walking; Greece, ancient and modern; DIY. Address: (h.) 59 Murrayfield Gardens, Edinburgh, EH12 6DH; T.-0131-337 2274.

Fraser, James Mackenzie, MA (Hons), MEd, MIMgt. Secretary, Paisley University (formerly Paisley College), since 1989; b. 29.7.48, Poolewe; m., Sheila; 1 s.; 2 d. Educ. Plockton High School; Edinburgh University; Stirling University. Lecturer in Liberal Studies, Inverness College of Further Education, 1971-77; Assistant Registrar, Stirling University, 1977-87; Secretary, Queen Margaret College, Edinburgh, 1987-89. Director, Centre for Environmental Management Ltd., since 1992; General Trustee, Free Church of Scotland; Chairman, Thomas Chalmers Housing Association. Recreations: music; theatre; films; reading; genealogy; Paisley Burns Club. Address: (h.) Tanera, 30 West Banlton Place, Livingston, EH54 9ED.

Fraser, Sheriff James Owen Arthur, MA, LLB. Sheriff of Grampian, Highland and Islands, since 1984; b. 9.5.37. Solicitor, 1967-84. Address: (b.) Sheriff Court House, Ferry Road, Dingwall, IV15 9QX.

Fraser, Jeremy William, LLB (Hons), DipLP, NP. Solicitor; Legal Adviser and Company Secretary, TSB Bank Scotland PLC, since 1990; b. 2.5.62, Inverness; m., Claudia Bolling; 1 d. Educ. Alloa Academy; Edinburgh University. Lindsay Duncan & Black WS; Lloyds Bowmaker Ltd. Recreations: hockey; squash; golf; hill-walking. Address: (b.) 120 George Street, Edinburgh; T.-0131-225 4555.

Fraser, John, MA (Hons), FRSA. Rector, Mackie Academy, Stonehaven, since 1975; b. 8.8.36, Inverness; m., Judith Helen Procter; 2 d. Educ. Inverness Royal Academy; Aberdeen University; Aberdeen College of Education. Teacher, Harris Academy, 1960-66; Principal Teacher of History, Buckie High School, 1966-72; Assistant Head Teacher and Depute Rector, Peterhead Academy, 1972-75; Governor, Aberdeen College of Education, since 1984; Member: GTC, 1979-83 and 1990-91, Grampian Region Education Committee, 1975-78; Regional Convener, SSTA, 1976-86. Conductor: Buckie Choral Union, 1968-72, Peterhead Choral Society, 1972-75; Organist in various churches; President, Stonehaven Rotary Club, 1988-89. Recreations: music; DIY. Address: (b.) Slug Road, Stonehaven; T.-01569 762071.

Fraser, John A.W., MA, FEIS, JP, DL. Deputy Lieutenant for Shetland, since 1985; b. 9.11.28, Lerwick; m., Jane Ann Jamieson; 2 s. Educ. Anderson Educational Institute; Edinburgh University; Moray House College of Education. Education Officer, RAF, 1950-52; Teacher, Baltasound Junior Secondary School, 1952-54; Head Teacher: Haroldswick Primary School, 1954-59, Aith Junior High School, 1959-66, Scalloway Junior High School, 1966-88. Former Member, National Council, EIS; Chairman, Scalloway Development Association; Member, Shetland Valuation Appeals Committee; Director, Scalloway Waterfront Trust; General Commissioner of Income Tax; Chairman, Shetland Probus Club. Recreations: genealogy; travel; gardening. Address: (h.) Broadwinds, Castle Street, Scalloway, Shetland; T.-Scalloway 644.

Fraser, Rev. John Gillies. Chairman, Lord's Day Observance Society, Scottish Council, 1985-89; Chairman, Church of Scotland Total Abstainers Society, since 1980; Vice-Chairman, National Church Association, since 1986; Minister, Macgregor Memorial Church, Glasgow, 1960-70, Elderpark Macgregor Memorial Church, 1970-86; 5.7.14, Glasgow; m., Jessie MacKenzie Mayer; 1 s.; 3 d. Educ. Shawlands Academy; Glasgow University and Trinity College. Public Assistance Department (later Social Service Department), Glasgow Corporation, 1931-48; Ministry of National Insurance, 1948; divinity student, 1948-50; Minister/Missionary, Church of Scotland, Northern Rhodesia, 1950-60; Minister, Macgregor Memorial Church, 1960-70. Scottish Assistant Secretary, Crusaders' Union, 1935-47; Secretary, South West Glasgow Sunday School Union, 1942-47. Recreation: gardening. Address: (h.) 17 Beaufort Gardens, Bishopbriggs, Glasgow, G64 2DJ; T.-0141-772 2987.

Fraser, Lindsey M., BA (Hons), PGCE. Executive Director, Book Trust Scotland, since 1991; Head of Young Book Trust; b. 15.8.61, Edinburgh. Educ. George Watson's College; York University; Froebel Institute, London. Manager, Heffers Children's Bookshop, Cambridge, 1986-91. Recreations: reading; music. Address: (b.) Book Trust Scotland, Scottish Book Centre, 137 Dundee Street, Edinburgh, EH11 1BG; T.-0131-229 3663.

Fraser, Lady Marion Anne, MA, LRAM, ARCM, LLD. Chair, Board, Christian Aid, since 1990; Chairman, Scottish International Piano Competition, since 1995; Chair, Scottish Association of Mental Health, since 1995; b. 17.10.32, Glasgow; m., Sir William Kerr Fraser; 3 s.; 1 d. Educ. Hutchesons' Girls' Grammar School; University of Glasgow; RSAMD. Lord High Commissioner to General Assembly of the Church of Scotland, 1994; Her Majesty's High Commissioner to the General Assembly of the Church of Scotland, 1995. Formerly Director: RGI, Scottish Opera, Laurel Bank School; Founder Chairman, Friends of the RSA; Director, St. Mary's Music School; Trustee, Scottish Churches Architectural Heritage Trust. Recreations: family and friends; people and places. Address: (h.) Broadwood, Edinburgh Road, Gifford, East Lothian EH41 4JE; T.-01620 810 319.

Fraser of Carmyllie, Lord (Peter Fraser), PC, QC. Minister of State, Department of Trade and Industry; former Minister of State, Scottish Office; b. 29.5.45. MP (Conservative), Angus South, 1979-83, Angus East, 1983-

87; Solicitor-General for Scotland, 1982-89; Lord Advocate, 1989-92.

Fraser, Robert Dunbar, MA (Hons), MIMgt. Rector, Kirkcaldy High School, since 1989; b. 30.11.45, Dingwall; m., Annice; 2 s.; 2 d. Educ. Dingwall Academy; Aberdeen University. Depute Rector, Culloden Academy, 1979-84; Rector, Keith Grammar School, 1984-89. Board Member, Fife College. Recreations: sports; DIY; being with family. Address: (h.) Elphinstone Lodge, 77 Hepburn Gardens, St. Andrews, Fife.

Fraser, Robert W., OBE, BSc (Hons), CEng, FICE, FCIWEM. Director, Water and Drainage Services, Borders Regional Council, since 1981; b. 13.5.39, Kirkcaldy; m., Elizabeth; 1 s.; 1 d. Educ. Kirkcaldy High School; Edinburgh University. Address: (b.) West Grove, Waverley Road, Melrose, TD6 9SJ; T.-0896 822056.

Fraser, Simon Cumming. Director, Scottish Landowners' Federation, since 1989; b. 18.9.35, Sevenoaks; m., Elspeth Dickson; 1 s.; 1 d. Educ. RN College, Dartmouth. Royal Navy, 1949-88, as a Commander, Staff Planning Officer to Flag Officer Scotland, 1984-88. Recreations: hill-walking; gardening. Address: (b.) 25 Maritime Street, Edinburgh; T.-0131-555 1031.

Fraser, Sheriff Simon William Hetherington, LLB, NP. Sheriff of North Strathclyde at Dumbarton, since 1989; b. 2.4.51, Carlisle; m., Sheena Janet; 1 d. Educ. Glasgow Academy; Glasgow University. Solicitor, 1973; Partner, Flowers & Co., Solicitors, Glasgow, 1976-89; Temporary Sheriff, 1987-89. Glasgow Bar Association: Secretary, 1977-79, President, 1981-82. Recreation: cricket. Address: (b.) Sheriff Court, Church Street, Dumbarton; T.-01389 63266.

Fraser, Provost William Alexander Elrick, OStJ, JP. Provost, Inverness District Council, since 1992; Councillor, since 1962; b. 19.8.27, Inverness; m., Margaret Elizabeth; 2 s.; 2 d. Educ. Inverness Royal Academy. Past President: Inverness Round Table, Inverness Rotary, Inverness Master Butchers, Inverness Amateur Swimming Club, Highland District Swimming Association; Chairman: Inverness Harbour Trust, Governors of Eden Court Theatre; Director: Highland Hospice Ltd., Highland Prospect Ltd., Highland Opportunity Ltd., Inverness and Loch Ness Horizons Ltd.; Patron, Inverness Sea Cadets; Hon. President, Inverness Opera Company, Inverness Festival Association, Inverness Tattoo Committee; Past President, Scottish Accident Prevention Council. Address: (h.) Balwearie, Drummond Road, Inverness, IV2 4NA; T.-01463 233345.

Fraser, Professor William Douglas, BSc, MSc, PhD, FRICS. Professor and Head, Department of Land Economics, Paisley University, since 1986; b. 3.1.40, Edinburgh. Educ. Edinburgh Academy; London University; Strathclyde University. Partner, Bingham, Hughes and Macpherson, Chartered Surveyors, Inverness, 1970-72; Lecturer, Department of Land Economics, Paisley College, 1972-83; Lecturer, Centre for Property Valuation and Management, City University, London, 1983-86. Publication: Principles of Property Investment and Pricing, 1984. Recreations: climbing; gardening. Address: (b.) Department of Land Economics, Paisley University, High Street, Paisley, PA1 2BE; T.-0141-848 3450.

Fraser, William Hamish, MA, DPhil. Reader in History, Strathclyde University (Dean, Faculty of Arts and Social Studies, 1987-93); b. 30.6.41, Keith; m., Helen Tuach; 1 d. Educ. Keith Grammar School; Aberdeen University; Sussex University. Lecturer in History, Strathclyde University, 1966-77. Publications: Trade Unions and Society 1850-1880, 1973; Workers and Employers, 1981; The Coming of the Mass Market, 1982; Conflict and Class: Scottish Workers 1700-1838, 1988; People and Society in Scotland 1830-1914, 1990. Recreations: hill-walking; skiing; cleaning canals. Address: (h.) 112 High Station Road, Falkirk, FK1 5LN; T.-01324 622868.

Fraser, Sir William Kerr, GCB (1984), LLD, FRSE. Principal and Vice Chancellor, Glasgow University, 1988-95; Permanent Under Secretary of State, Scottish Office, 1978-88; b. 18.3.29; m., Marion Anne Forbes; 3 s.; 1 d. Educ. Eastwood Secondary School; Glasgow University. RAF, 1952-55; various posts in Scottish Office, 1955-78, including Principal Private Secretary to Secretary of State for Scotland, 1966-67. Director, Scottish Mutual Assurance Society; Governor, Caledonian Research Foundation. Address: (h.) Broadwood, Edinburgh Road, Gifford, East Lothian, EH41 4JE; T.-01620 810 319.

Freeman, Christopher Paul, BSc, MB, ChB, MPhil, FRCPsych. Consultant Psychiatrist, Royal Edinburgh Hospital, Edinburgh, since 1980; Senior Lecturer, Department of Psychiatry, Edinburgh University, since 1980; Psychiatric Tutor, Royal Edinburgh Hospital, since 1983; b. 21.4.47, York; m., Katherine; 2 s. Educ. Nunthorpe School, York; Edinburgh University. Royal College of Psychiatrists Gaskell Gold Medal. Publication: Research Methods in Psychiatry (Co-author), 1989. Recreations: tennis; squash; growing bonsaii trees. Address: (h.) The Old Farmhouse, Wester Pencaitland, East Lothian, EH34 5DE; T.-01875 340 612.

Freemantle, Andrew, MBE, FIMgt. Chief Executive, Scottish Ambulance Service, since 1991; b. 26.9.44, Bournemouth; m., Patricia Mary; 4 d. Educ. Framlingham College; Royal Military College of Science. Commissioned, Royal Hampshire Regiment (Germany, Malaya, Borneo), 1965-69; Australian SAS Regiment (Australia, South Vietnam), 1969-72; Royal Hampshire Regiment, (Hong Kong, UK, Northern Ireland), 1972-76; Staff College, Camberley, 1978; Directing Staff, Staff College, 1983-84; Commanding Officer, Royal Hampshire Regiment (mention in Dispatches, 1987), 1985-87; Commander, 19 Infantry Brigade (Brigadier), 1987-89; Member, Royal College of Defence Studies, 1990. Recreations: running; cooking; field sports. Address: (b.) National Headquarters, Scottish Ambulance Service NHS Trust, Tipperlinn Road, Edinburgh, EH10 5UU; T.-0131-447 7711.

Freer, Professor John Henry, BSc, MSc, PhD. Titular Professor in Microbiology, Glasgow University, since 1986; Deputy Director, Institute of Biomedical and Life Sciences; b. 17.11.36, Kasauli, India; m., Jocelyn Avril Williams; 4 d. Educ. Durham University; Nottingham University; Birmingham University. Lecturer in Microbiology, New South Wales University, Australia, 1962-65; New York University Medical Centre: Associate Research Scientist, then Assistant Professor, Microbiology, 1965-68; Senior Lecturer, Microbiology Department, Glasgow University, 1968-82; Reader in Microbiology, 1982-86; Editor-in-Chief, Journal of General Microbiology, 1990-95. Publications: Bacterial Protein Toxins (Joint Editor), 1988, 1990, 1992; Sourcebook of Bacterial Protein Toxius, 1991; 100 scientific articles. Recreations: sailing; painting. Address: (b.) Joseph Black Building, Microbiology, Glasgow University, Glasgow, G12 8QQ; T.-0141-330 4002.

Friend, James, MA, MB, ChB, FRCPEdin. Consultant in Thoracic Medicine, Grampian Health Board, since 1973; Clinical Senior Lecturer in Medicine, Aberdeen University, since 1973; b. 2.6.38, Edinburgh; m., Elizabeth; 1 s.; 2 d. Educ. Edinburgh Academy; Gonville and Caius College, Cambridge; Edinburgh University. Hospital posts in Edinburgh and Oxford; Dorothy Temple Cross Fellowship, Seattle, 1971-72; British Thoracic Society: Council Member, 1983-91, Treasurer, 1984-91; Chairman, Grampian Action on Smoking and Health, since 1989.

158 WHO'S WHO IN SCOTLAND

Recreation: the Scottish hills. Address: (b.) Aberdeen Royal Infirmary, Aberdeen, AB9 2ZD.

Frier, Brian Murray, BSc (Hons), MD, FRCP (Edin), FRCP (Glas). Consultant Physician, Royal Infirmary, Edinburgh, since 1987; part-time Reader in Medicine, Edinburgh University, since 1995; b. 28.7.47, Edinburgh; m., Dr. Isobel M. Wilson; 1 d. Educ. George Heriot's School, Edinburgh; Edinburgh University. Medical Registrar, Ninewells Hospital, Dundee, 1974-76; Research Fellow in Diabetes and Metabolism, Cornell University Medical Centre, The New York Hospital, 1976-77; Senior Medical Registrar, Royal Infirmary, Edinburgh, 1978-82; Consultant Physician, Western Infirmary and Gartnavel General Hospital, Glasgow, 1982-87. R.D. Lawrence Lecturer, British Diabetic Association, 1986; Governor, George Heriot's Trust, Edinburgh, 1988-94. Recreations: appreciation of the arts; ancient and modern history. Address: (h.) 100 Morningside Drive, Edinburgh, EH10 5NT; T.-0131-447 1653.

Frizzell, Edward W. MA (Hons). Chief Executive, Scottish Prison Service, since 1991; Board Member, Quality Scotland Foundation, since 1991; b. 4.5.46, Paisley; m., Moira Calderwood; 2 s.; 1 d. Educ. Paisley Grammar School; Glasgow University. Scottish Milk Marketing Board, 1968-73; Scottish Council (Development and Industry), 1973-76; DAFS, Scottish Office, 1976-78; First Secretary, Fisheries, Office of the UK Permanent Representative to European Communities, Brussels (Foreign and Commonwealth Office), 1978-82; Assistant Secretary (Grade 5), Scottish Education Department, Higher Education Division, 1982-86; Scottish Office Finance Division, 1986-89; Director, Locate in Scotland, Scottish Office Industry Department (Grade 4), 1989-91. Address: (b.) Calton House, 5 Redheughs Rigg, Edinburgh, EH12 9HW; T.-0131-244 8522.

Frost, Patricia. General Manager, Fife Health Board. Address: Springfield House, Cupar, Fife.

Frutin, Bernard Derek, MBE, MInstPkg. Inventor; Chairman and Managing Director: Rocep Lusol Holdings Ltd., since 1973, Rocep Pressure Packs Ltd., since 1987; b. 7.2.44, Glasgow; 3 d. Educ. Kelvinside Academy, Glasgow. Winner of nine international innovator awards since 1989, including John Logie Baird and British Institute of Packaging Environmental Awards; Innovator of the Year, 1989 (Institute of Packaging); Finalist, 1992 Prince of Wales Award. Recreations: sailing; skiing; fine food; listening to music. Address: (b.) Rocep Lusol Holdings Ltd., Rocep Business Park, Kings Inch Road, Deanpark, Renfrew, PA4 8XY; T.-0141-885 2222.

Fry, Professor Stephen C., BSc, PhD, FRSE. Professor of Plant Biochemistry, Edinburgh University, since 1995; b. 26.11.53, Sheffield; m., Verena Ryffel; 3 d. Educ. Thornbridge School, Sheffield; Leicester University. Postdoctoral Research Fellow, Cambridge University, 1978-79; Royal Society Rosenheim Research Fellow, Cambridge University, 1979-82; Senior Research Associate, University of Colorado, 1982-83; Lecturer in Botany, then Reader in Plant Biochemistry, Edinburgh University, 1983-95. President's Medal, Society for Experimental Biology, 1988. Publication: The Growing Plant Cell Wall: Chemical and Metabolic Analysis, 1988. Recreations: hill-walking; paper chromatography. Address: (b.) Division of Biological Sciences, Edinburgh University, King's Buildings, Mayfield Road, Edinburgh, EH9 3JH; T.-0131-650 5320.

Fullarton, John Hamilton, ARIAS, DipTP. Consultant Architect and Town Planner; Director of Technical Services, Scottish Special Housing Association, 1979-89; b. 21.2.31, Dalry, Ayrshire; m., Elvera Peebles; 1 s. Educ. Dalry High School; Glasgow School of Art; Royal Technical College, Glasgow; Edinburgh College of Art. Architect with local authorities before joining Scottish Office, 1964; Superintending Architect, Scottish Development Department, 1970-78; Head of New Towns, Construction Industry Division, Scottish Economic Planning Department, 1978-79. Research Fellowship, Urban Planning, Edinburgh College of Art, 1966-67. Publication:Waverley Park Conservation Study, 1977. Address: (h.) 7 Queens Crescent, Edinburgh, EH9 2AZ; T.-0131-667 5809.

Fullerton, Hance. Chief Executive, Grampian Enterprise Ltd. Address: (b.) 27 Albyn Place, Aberdeen, AB1 1YL.

Fulton, Rev. John Oswald, BSc, BD. General Secretary, United Free Church of Scotland, since 1994; b. 9.7.53, Glasgow; m., Margaret P.; 1 d. Educ. Clydebank High School; Glasgow University. Ordained as minister, 1977; Minister, Croftfoot U.F. Church, Glasgow, 1977-94. Recreations: reading; gardening; photography. Address: (b.) 11 Newton Place, Glasgow, G3 7PR; T.-0141-332 3435.

Fulton, Rikki, OBE, DLitt. Actor; b. 15.4.24, Glasgow; m., Kate Matheson. Educ. Whitehill Secondary School. Invalided out of RNVR as Sub-Lt., 1945; began professional career broadcasting with BBC in Glasgow; Presenter, BBC Showband, London, 1951-55; appeared in numerous pantomimes and revues with Howard & Wyndham from 1955, including Five Past Eight shows; television work including Scotch & Wry (creator, Rev. I.M. Jolly) and starring roles in The Miser and A Winter's Tale; films including The Dollar Bottom, Gorky Park, Local Hero, Comfort and Joy and The Girl in the Picture. Scottish TV Personality of the Year, 1963 and 1979; Best Light Entertainment Performance of the Year, 1969 and 1983; President's Award, Television and Radio Industries Club, 1988; Lifetime Achievement Award, BAFTA Scotland, 1993. Recreations: bridge; chess; reading; music (listening and piano); writing; painting.

Fulton, William Francis Monteith, BSc, MD (Hons), MB, ChB, FRCP, FRCPGlas, FRCPEdin. Reader, Department of Materia Medica, Glasgow University, 1977-84; Consultant Physician, Stobhill General Hospital, Glasgow, 1958-84; b. 12.12.19, Aberdeen; m., Dr. Frances I. Melrose; 1 s.; 1 d. Educ. Bryanston School, Dorset; Glasgow University. Resident Physician and Surgeon, Western Infirmary, Glasgow, 1945-46; National Service, Merchant Navy, 1946-48 (Ship's Surgeon); joined National Health Service, 1950; Research Assistant, Cardiology, Edinburgh University, 1952-53; Senior Lecturer, Department of Materia Medica, Glasgow University, 1958-77; Senior Fellow, Cardiology, Johns Hopkins Hospital, Baltimore, 1963-64; Foundation Professor of Medicine, Nairobi University, 1967-72. Publications: The Coronary Arteries, 1965; Modern Trends in Pharmacology and Therapeutics, 1967. Address: (h.) Woodhill, Braemar, AB3 5XX; T.-0133 97 41239.

Fulton, Sheriff William J. Sheriff of Grampian, Highland and Islands at Inverness. Address: (b.) The Castle, Inverness, IV2 3EG.

Furnell, James R.G., MA (Hons), DCP, PhD, LLB, FBPsS, DipLP. Consultant Clinical Psychologist (Child Health), Forth Valley Health Board, since 1980; Advocate (called to Scottish Bar, 1993); Honorary Fellow, Edinburgh University, since 1987; b. 20.2.46, London; m., Lesley Anne Ross; 1 s.; 1 d. Educ. Leighton Park Society of Friends School, Reading; Aberdeen University; Glasgow University; Stirling University; Dundee University. Clinical Psychologist, Royal Hospital for Sick Children, Glasgow, 1970-72; Senior Clinical Psychologist, Forth Valley Health Board, 1972-80. Member, National Consultative Committee of Scientists in Professions Allied to Medicine, 1984-87 (Secretary, Clinical Psychology Sub-Committee); Member,

Forth Valley Health Board, 1984-87; Chairman, Division of Clinical Psychology, British Psychological Society, 1988-89. Recreations: flying; cross-country skiing. Address: (h.) Glensherup House, Glendevon, by Dollar, Perthshire, FK14 7JY; T.-01259 781234.

Furness, Professor Raymond Stephen, BA, MA, PhD. Professor of German, St. Andrews University, since 1984; b. 25.10.33, Builth Wells; m., Janice Fairey; 1 s.; 2 d. Educ. Welwyn Garden City Grammar School; University College, Swansea. Modern Languages Department, University of Manchester Institute of Science and Technology; Department of German, Manchester University. Publications: Expressionism; Literary History of Germany 1890-1945; Wagner and Literature; A Companion to Twentieth Century German Literature; An Introduction to German Literature 1871-1989; The Dedalus Book of German Decadence. Recreation: sleeping. Address: (h.) The Dirdale, Boarhills, St. Andrews, KY16 8PP; T.-0133 488 469.

Furness, Col. Simon John, DL. Landowner; Vice Lord Lieutenant, Berwickshire, since 1990; b. 18.3.36, Ayton. Educ. Charterhouse; RMA, Sandhurst. Commissioned Durham Light Infantry, 1956, 2nd Lt.; served Far East, UK, Germany; active service, Borneo, Northern Ireland; retired, 1978; Deputy Colonel (Durham) The Light Infantry, 1989-93. Member, Executive, National Trust for Scotland (Chairman, Gardens Committee). Recreations: field sports; gardening. Address: The Garden House, Netherbyres, Eyemouth, Berwickshire, TD14 5SE; T.-018907 50337.

Furness, William Arthur, BA, MSc. National Manager for Scotland, BT; b. 6.9.45, London. Educ. St. Benedict's Abbey School, Ealing; Exeter University; London University. Various posts within BT. Board Member: Edinburgh Chamber of Commerce, Edinburgh Science Festival, Quality Foundation Scotland; Executive Committee Member: Scottish Council Development and Industry, Scottish Business in the Community. Recreations: travel; dogs; reading; art. Address: (b.) Caledonian House, Room E18, 19A Canning Street, Edinburgh, EH3 8TA; T.-0131-345 6000.

Fyfe, Alistair J., BSc (Hons). Depute Chief Executive, SCET (Scottish Council for Educational Technology), since 1992; b. 21.6.46, Glasgow; m., Aileen M. Dandie; 1 s.; 1 d. Educ. Allan Glen's School; Glasgow University; Jordanhill College of Education. Teacher, then Principal Teacher of Mathematics, 1969-76; Lecturer, Computer Education, Jordanhill College of Education, 1976-81; Consultant, Scottish Microelectronics Development Programme, 1981-87; Assistant Director, Scottish Council for Educational Technology, 1987-92. Recreations: badminton; golf. Address: (b.) 74 Victoria Crescent Road, Glasgow, G12 9JN; T.-0141-337 5000.

Fyfe, Andrew, MA (Hons). Director of Operations, Scottish Homes, since 1992; b. 26.6.54, Glasgow; m., Louise Drummond; 2 d. Educ. Hutchesons', Glasgow; Glasgow University. Research Assistant, Strathclyde University, 1975-78; Senior Development Officer, Govanhill Housing Association, 1978-81; Director, Shettleston Housing Association, Glasgow, 1982-89; Director of Strategic Development, Scottish Homes, 1989-92. Member, Executive Council, Scottish Business in the Community; Chairman, Scotish Federation of Housing Associations, 1987-89. Address: (b.) Thistle House, 91 Haymarket Terrace, Edinburgh, EH12 5HE; T.-0131-479 5353.

Fyfe, Maria, BA (Hons). MP, Glasgow Maryhill, since 1987; Opposition Spokesperson on Women, 1988-91; Scottish Affairs Spokesperson, since 1992; b. 25.11.38, Glasgow; 2 s. Educ. Notre Dame High School, Glasgow; Strathclyde University. Glasgow District Councillor, 1980-87; Senior Lecturer, Central College of Commerce, 1977-87; Member, Scottish Executive Committee, Labour Party, 1981-87. Address: (b.) House of Commons, London, SW1A 0AA; T.-071-219 4430; 0141-945 1495.

Fyfe, William Stevenson, CBE (1992), FIIM. Chairman, Greater Glasgow Health Board, 1993; b. 10.6.35, Glasgow; m., Margaret H.H. Auld; 1 s.; 1 d. Educ. Dollar Academy; Scottish College of Commerce. Town Councillor, Prestwick, 1967-73; Ayr County Councillor, 1970-73; apppointed to Ayrshire and Arran Health Board, 1973 (Financial Convener, 1973-81); Chairman, Ayrshire and Arran Health Board, 1981-93; Chairman, Scottish Health Services Advisory Council, 1989-93; Member, General Whitley Council, 1989-93. Address:(h.) Ford House, Pennyglen, Culzean, KA19 8JW.

G

Galbraith, Rev. David Douglas, MA, BD, BMus, MPhil. Administrative Secretary, Panel on Worship, Panel on Doctrine, Advisory Committee on Artistic Matters, Church of Scotland, since 1995; b. 22.6.40, Kirkintilloch; 2 d. Educ. Ardrossan Academy; Dundee High School; St. Andrews University; Glasgow University. Associate Minister, Craigmillar, Edinburgh, 1970-77; Minister, Strathkinness Parish Church, 1977-80; Lecturer in Practical Theology, St. Andrews University, 1980-81; Professor of Ministry and Mission, Trinity Theological College, Brisbane, 1981-86; Chaplain to St. Andrews University, 1987-93. Music Director, Craigmillar Festival Society, 1972-77; Chair, Lothian and Borders Branch, Royal School of Church Music, since 1995; Journal Editor, One Voice (church music), Trinity Occasional Papers (theology). Publications: Square Dance in Heaven, 1966; Worship in the Wide Red Land (Editor), 1975. Address; (h.) 9 Bonnington Terrace, Edinburgh, EH6 4BP; T.-0131-555 0701.

Galbraith, Professor Roderick Allister McDonald, BSc, PhD (Cantab), CEng, MRAeS. Head of Aerospace Engineering, Glasgow University, since 1989; b. 4.8.47, Lowmoor, England; m., Lynn Margaret Fraser. Educ. Greenock High School; James Watt Memorial College; Paisley College of Technology; Cambridge University. Apprentice Draughtsman/Engineer, Scott's Shipbuilding & Engineering Co. Ltd., 1964-72; Department of Aerospace Engineering, Glasgow University: joined 1975; Reader, 1989, Professor, 1992. Publications: over 100 reports and publications on aerodynamics. Recreations: sailing; walking. Address: (b.) Department of Aerospace Engineering, Glasgow University, Glasgow, G12 8QQ; T.-0141-330 5295.

Galbraith, Samuel Laird, BSc, MBChB, MD, FRCSGlas. MP (Labour), Strathkelvin and Bearsden, since 1987; Neurosurgeon; b. 18.10.45. Address: (b.) House of Commons, London, SW1A 0AA.

Galbraith, William C., QC, BA, LLB; b. 25.2.35. Parliamentary Counsel, Scottish Law Commission, since 1975.

Gale, William Stuart, QC, LLB (Hons). Advocate, 1980. Address: Advocates' Library, Parliament House, Edinburgh EH1 1RF.

Gallacher, Tom. Writer; b. 16.2.34, Alexandria. Stage plays: Our Kindness to 5 Persons, 1969; Mr Joyce is Leaving Paris, 1971; Revival, 1972; Three to Play, 1972; Schellenbrack, 1973; Bright Scene Fading, 1973; The Only Street, 1973; Personal Effects, 1974; A Laughing Matter, 1975; Hallowe'en, 1975; The Sea Change, 1976; A Presbyterian Wooing (adapted from Pitcairne's The Assembly), 1976; The Evidence of Tiny Tim, 1977; Wha's Like Us - Fortunately!, 1978; Stage Door Canteen, 1978; Deacon Brodie (adapted from Stevenson and Henley), 1978; Jenny, 1979; Natural Causes, 1980; The Parole of Don Juan, 1981; The Treasure Ship (adapted from Brandane), 1982. Publications: (fiction): Hunting Shadows, 1981; Apprentice, 1983; Journeyman, 1984; Survivor, 1985; The Jewel Maker, 1986; The Wind on the Heath, 1987; The Stalking Horse, 1989; Gainful Perjury, 1990. Address: (b.) 25 Linn Walk, Garelochhead, Dunbartonshire G84 0DS.

Gallagher, Jim, BSc, MSc. Director (Human Resources), Scottish Prison Service, since 1991; b. 23.9.54, Clydebank; m., Una Green; 1 s.; 2 d. Educ. St. Aloysius College, Glasgow; Glasgow University; Edinburgh University. Administration Trainee, Scottish Office, 1976; Private Secretary to Minister for Home Affairs and Environment,

1980-82; Principal, Criminal Justice Division, 1982-86; Secretary, Scottish Office Management Group, 1986-88; Head, Urban Policy Division, 1988-89; Private Secretary to successive Secretaries of State for Scotland, 1989-91. Address: (b.) Calton House, Redheughs Rigg, Edinburgh; T.-0131-244 8572.

Gallagher, Sister Maire T., CBE, MA (Hons), MEd FScotVec, DCE. Retired Headteacher; Sister of Notre Dame Religious Congregation, since 1959; Chairman, Scottish Consultative Council on the Curriculum, 1987-91; b. 27.5.33, Glasgow. Educ. Notre Dame High School, Glasgow; Glasgow University; Notre Dame College of Education. Principal Teacher of History, Notre Dame High School, Glasgow; Lecturer in Secondary Education, Notre Dame College of Education; Headteacher, Notre Dame High School, Dumbarton, 1974-87. Member, Consultative Committee on the Curriculum, since 1976; Member, Executive, Secondary Heads Association (Scottish Branch), 1976-83; Coordinator, Christian Life Movement Groups, West of Scotland. Recreations: reading; dress-making; bird-watching. Address: (h.) Sisters of Notre Dame, 67 Moorpark Avenue, Penilee, Glasgow, G52 4ET; T.-0141 810 4214.

Gallie, Philip Roy, TEng, MIPlantE. MP (Conservative), Ayr, since 1992; Vice-Chairman, Scottish Conservative and Unionist Party, since 1995; b. 3.6.39, Portsmouth; m., Marion Wands. Educ. Dunfermline High School; Kirkcaldy Technical College. Apprenticeship, H.M. Dockyard, Rosyth, 1955-60; Merchant Navy, 1960-64; electricity industry, 1964-92. Recreations: sports; politics. Address: (b.) 1 Wellington Square, Ayr; T.-01292 263991.

Galloway, George. MP (Glasgow Hillhead), since 1987; Vice-Chair, Parliamentary Foreign Affairs Committee; b. 16.8.54, Dundee; 1 d. Educ. Harris Academy, Dundee. Production Worker, Michelin Tyres, 1974; Dundee Labour Party Organiser, 1977; General Secretary, War on Want, 1983. Chairman, Scottish Labour Party, 1981-82; Member, Scottish Labour Party Executive Committee, 1974-84; Founder and first General Secretary, Trade Union Friends of Palestine, 1979. Recreations: football; music; films. Address: (b.) House of Commons, Westminster, London; T.-0171-219 4084.

Galloway, Janice. Writer/Music Critic; b. 2.12.56, Kilwinning. Educ. Ardrossan Academy; Glasgow University. Variety of paid and unpaid work, including 10 years' teaching English in Ayrshire; music criticism for Glasgow Herald, The Observer, Scotland on Sunday; fiction writing, including one collection of short stories and two novels. Publications: The Trick Is To Keep Breathing, 1990; The Trick, 1991; Blood, 1991; Foreign Parts, 1994; New Writing Scotland (Co-Editor), 1990-92.

Galloway, Peter George, BA, DipComm. Rector, Trinity Academy, Edinburgh, since 1983; b. 21.3.44, St. Andrews; m., Elizabeth; 1 d. Educ. Buckhaven High School; Heriot Watt University; Moray House College of Education. Teacher, Broughton Secondary, Edinburgh, 1967-69; Principal Teacher, Liberton High School, 1969-76; Assistant Rector, Royal High School, Edinburgh, 1976-80; Depute Head, James Gillespie's High School, Edinburgh, 1980-83. Recreations: rugby football, as a spectator; golf; tennis; cinema; travel; cooking. Address: (b.) Trinity Academy, Craighall Avenue, Edinburgh, EH6 4RT; T.-0131-552 8101.

Galloway, 13th Earl of (Randolph Keith Reginald Stewart); b. 14.10.28; m. Address: Senwick House, Brighouse Bay, Borgue, Kirkcudbrightshire, DG6 4TP.

Galt, Sheriff Eric. Sheriff of Glasgow and Strathkelvin. Address: (b.) Sheriff Court House, 1 Carlton Place, Glasgow, G5 9DA.

Galt, Rose Ann, MA (Hons), FEIS. Depute Registrar (Education), General Teaching Council for Scotland; b. 19.3.37, Glasgow; m., William Galt; 1 d. Educ. Possil Secondary School, Glasgow; Glasgow University; Jordanhill College. Started teaching, Albert Secondary, Glasgow, 1960; appointed Principal Teacher (Guidance), 1970; after career break, resumed teaching, Our Lady's High School, Cumbernauld, 1971, and became Principal Teacher of English, Greenfaulds High School, 1975; EIS: Chairman, Glasgow Local Association, 1970-71, President, Dumbarton Local Association, 1976-77, National Vice-President, 1978-79, National President, 1979-80, Convener, Parliamentary Committee, 1987-89, Member, National Executive, 1987-89; Convener, Education Committee, General Teaching Council, 1982-86, Vice-Chairperson, 1985-87, Chairperson, 1987-89; Member, Scottish Examination Board, 1982-90; Member, European Executive Committee, World Confederation of Organisations of the Teaching Profession (WCOTP), 1988-89; Member, Equal Opportunities Commission Education Advisory Group, since 1994. Recreations: reading; cooking; fiendishly difficult crosswords. Address: (h.) 38 Meadow View, Cumbernauld, Glasgow; T.-01236 722028.

Gammell, James Gilbert Sydney, MBE, CA; b. 4.3.20, Camberley; m., Susan Patricia Bowring; 5 s.; 1 d. Educ. Winchester College. Major, Grenadier Guards, Second World War; Partner, Ivory & Sime, 1949, Chairman, 1974-85; former Director, Bank of Scotland, Standard Life. Recreation: farming. Address: (h.) Foxhall, Kirkliston, West Lothian, EH29 9ER; T.-0131-333 3275.

Gani, Professor David, BSc, DPhil, CChem, FRSC, FRSE. Professor of Organic Chemistry, St. Andrews University, since 1990; b. 29.9.57, Beckenham; m., Julie Margaret; 4 d. Educ. Rawlins Grammar School, Quorn; Sussex University; Croydon Technical College. Royal Society University Fellow, Southampton University, 1983-88; Lecturer in Bioorganic Chemistry, then Senior Lecturer, Southampton University, 1988-90, Research Co-ordinator and Financial Controller, Institute of Biomolecular Sciences, 1987-90. ICI Research Award, 1990; Corday Morgan Medal and Prize, 1991; Hickinbottom Prize Fellowship, 1992-93. Publications: 90 papers; one book. Recreations: chess; guitar; music; swimming. Address: (b.) School of Chemistry, Purdie Building, St. Andrews University, St. Andrews; T.-01334 63860.

Garbutt, David Charles Gemmell, QPM. Deputy Chief Constable, Grampian Police, since 1992; Secretary, Association of Chief Police Officers in Scotland Communications Committee, since 1991, and Member, Personnel and Training Committee, since 1992; b. 16.8.45, Harthill; m., Moira Murdoch; 1 s.; 1 d. Educ. College of Commerce, Hull; Napier, Edinburgh. Joined Edinburgh City Police, 1964; transferred to Kingston upon Hull, 1967; returned to Edinburgh, 1970; promoted Chief Superintendent, 1987, as Divisional Commander, West Lothian; promoted Assistant Chief Constable, Lothian and Borders Police, 1991. Recreations: hill-walking; cycling; curling. Address: (b.) Police HQ, Queen Street, Aberdeen, AB9 1BA; T.-01224 639111.

Garden, Neville Abbot. Broadcaster; Writer and Lecturer on musical and media matters; b. 13.2.36, Edinburgh; m., Jane Fowler; 1 s., 1 d.; 3 d. by pr. m. Educ. George Watson's College, Edinburgh. Reporter, Sub-Editor, Feature Writer, Evening Dispatch, 1953-63; Daily Columnist and Music Critic, Edinburgh Evening News, 1963-64; Senior Feature Writer, Scottish Daily Express, 1964-78; Presenter, Good Morning Scotland, BBC Radio Scotland, 1978-90, Queen Street Garden, 1990-93; Music Critic and Columnist, Sunday Standard, 1981-83; Music Writer, Scotland on Sunday, since 1988; Conductor: Edinburgh Grand Opera, seven years; Edinburgh Ballet Theatre, nine years. Publication: Bloomsbury Good Music Guide.

Gardiner, Iain Derek, FRICS. Chartered Surveyor, since 1957; Senior Partner, Souter & Jaffrey, Chartered Surveyors, since 1986; Chairman, Royal Institution of Chartered Surveyors in Scotland; b. 22.12.33, Glasgow; m., Kathleen Elizabeth Johnson; 2 s.; 1 d. Educ. Hutcheson's Grammar School, Glasgow; Royal Technical College, Glasgow. Trainee and Assistant Quantity Surveyor, John H. Allan & Sons, Glasgow, 1950-57; National Service, Royal Engineers, 1957-59; Souter & Jaffrey, Inverness: Quantity Surveyor, 1959-63, Partner, 1963-86. Chairman, Inverness Area, RICS in Scotland, 1969-70; Chairman, Quantity Surveyors Committee, RICS in Scotland, 1989-90; Chairman, Friends of Eden Court Theatre, 1981-82; Chairman, Inverness Area Scout Council. Recreations: swimming; travel; cookery. Address: (b.) 33 Academy Street, Inverness, IV1 1JN; T.-01463 239494.

Gardner, Angela Joy, BSc (Hons). Independent Public Affairs Consultant, AJ Enterprises, since 1994; b. 16.9.62, Wolverhampton; m., Andrew Ronald Gardner. Educ. Codsall High School; UMIST. BP Chemicals Ltd., South Wales and Grangemouth, 1984-90; BP Schools Link Officer, 1985-90; Senior Public Affairs Officer, BP, 1990-94. Member, General Teaching Council for Scotland, since 1990. Address: (h.) 72 Craigcrook Road, Edinburgh, EH4 3PN; T.-0131-336 5164.

Gardner, Dianne Alicia, BA (Hons). Headmistress, Wellington School, Ayr, since 1988; b. 15.9.47, Wolverhampton; m., John W. Gardner. Educ. Ounsdale School; Liverpool University. Museum Assistant, 1969-71; Teacher of History, 1971-72; Head of History, then Senior Mistress, Wellington School, 1972-88. Recreations: painting; gardening. Address: (b.) Carleton Turrets, Ayr, KA7 2XH; T.-01292 269321.

Gardner, James, BSc. Rector, Dunblane High School, since 1989; b. 3.2.41, Glasgow; m., Margaret Catherine; 1 s.; 1 d. Educ. Allan Glen's School, Glasgow; Glasgow University; Strathclyde University. Teacher of Mathematics, Allan Glen's School, 1968-76; Principal Teacher of Mathematics, Cranhill Secondary, Glasgow, 1976-80; Assistant Head Teacher, Dunoon Grammar School, 1980-84; Depute Rector, Wallace High School, Stirling, 1984-89. Member, British Antarctic Survey, 1963-66. Recreations: climbing; skiing; orienteering; chess. Address: (b.) Dunblane High School, Highfields, Dunblane; T.-01786 823823.

Garland, Professor David William, LLB, MA, PhD. Professor of Penology, Faculty of Law, Edinburgh University, since 1992; b. 7.8.55, Dundee; m., Anne Jowett; 2 d. Educ. Harris Academy, Dundee; Edinburgh University; Sheffield University. Edinburgh University: Lecturer, Faculty of Law, 1979-90, Reader, 1990-92; Davis Fellow, History Department, Princeton University, 1984-85; Visiting Professor: Boalt Law School, University of California, Berkeley, 1988, Department of Sociology, New York University, 1992, School of Law, New York University, 1992-93. Sellin-Glueck Prize, American Society of Criminology, 1993. Publications: Punishment and Welfare, 1985 (winner of Denis Carroll Prize, International Society of Criminology); Punishment and Modern Society (awarded Distinguished Scholar Award, American Sociological Association and Outstanding Scholarship Award, American Society for the Study of Social Problems). Recreations: cinema; squash; sociology. Address: Old College, South Bridge, Edinburgh, EH8 9YL; T.-0131-650 2032.

Garland, Harry Mitchell, MBE, CQSW, FBIM. Chairman, Secretary of State's Advisory Committee on Scotland's Travelling People, since 1987; b. 7.7.28,

Aberdeen; m., Phyllis Sandison; 1 s.; 1 d. Educ. Rockwell Academy, Dundee; Robert Gordon's College, Aberdeen; Moray House College, Edinburgh; Edinburgh University. Probation Officer/Senior Probation Officer/Principal Probation Officer, 1958-69; Depute Director of Social Work, Aberdeen and Kincardine Counties, 1969-73; Director of Social Work: Paisley Burgh, 1973-74, Western Isles, 1974-78, Central Region, 1978-86. Chairman, National Association of Probation Officers in Scotland, 1968-69; President, Association of Directors of Social Work, 1983; Member, Forth Valley Health Board, 1986-90. Recreations: voluntary work; church; golf; walking. Address: (h.) 7 Cromarty View, Nairn, IV12 4HX; T.-01667 453684.

Garner, John Angus McVicar, MB, ChB, DRCOG, DCH, MRCGP. Principal in general practice, since 1980; Chairman, Scottish General Medical Services Committee, since 1992; Member, Scottish Council, British Medical Association, since 1989; Chairman, Lothian Local Medical Committee, 1991-92; b. 4.9.50, London; m., Catherine Lizbeth; 1 s.; 1 d. Educ. Eltham College; Edinburgh University. Secretary, Lothian Local Medical Committee, 1986-89; Member, General Medical Services Committee, since 1989; Member, National Medical Advisory Committee, since 1989. Recreations: amphibians and photographing fungi. Address: (h.) 25 Murrayfield Avenue, Edinburgh, EH12 6AU; T.-0131-337 6120.

Garraway, Professor William Michael, MD, MSc, FRCPE, FRCGP, FFCM, FACE, DObstRCOG, DCH. Professor of Public Health, Edinburgh University, since 1983; b. 26.1.42, Dumfries; m., Alison Mary Haggart; 1 s.; 1 d. Educ. Carlisle Grammar School; Edinburgh University; London University; Mayo Graduate School of Medicine. Lecturer, Department of Community Medicine, Edinburgh University, 1972-77 (Senior Lecturer, 1978-81); Consultant Epidemiologist, Mayo Clinic, Rochester, USA, 1981-83. Recreations: hill-walking; cross-country skiing. Address: (b.) Medical School, Teviot Place, Edinburgh, EH8 9AG.

Garrett, Graeme Frederick, LLB, SSC. Solicitor; Partner, Robin Thompson & Partners, Edinburgh, since 1991; b. 23.1.53, Milan; m., Kathleen McGowan; 2 d. Educ. Royal High School, Edinburgh; Edinburgh University. Partner, Allan McDougall & Co., SSC, 1979-91. Council Member, Law Society of Scotland, since 1993. Recreations: rugby; fishing; reading; whisky. Address: (b.) 16 Castle Street, Edinburgh; T.-0131-225 4297.

Garrett, James Allan, MB, ChB, FRCSEdin, FRCSGlas. Consultant Surgeon, Stobhill Hospital, Glasgow, since 1967; b. 8.3.28, Glasgow; m., Margaret Keddie; 1 s.; 1 d. Educ. Hutchesons' Grammar School, Glasgow; Glasgow University. Captain, RAMC, 1952-54; House Officer, Registrar and Senior Registrar, Glasgow Royal Infirmary, 1954-67. Address: (h.) 12 Richmond Drive, Cambuslang, Glasgow, G72 8BH; T.-0141-641 3333.

Garrick, Sir Ronald, FEng, FRSE. Managing Director and Chief Executive, Weir Group, since 1982; b. 21.8.40; m.; 2 s.; 1 d. Non-Executive Director, Scottish Power, Shell UK; Member, Scottish Economic Council; Deputy Chairman, Scottish Enterprise Board. Address: (b.) Weir Group PLC, 149 Newlands Road, Glasgow, G44 4EU.

Garrod, Professor Neil, BSc (Hons), PhD, ACIS. Professor of Financial Analysis and Head, Department of Accounting and Finance, Glasgow University, since 1993; b. 7.6.54; m., Sonja Gortnar; 1 s.; 1 d. Educ. Guthlaxton Upper School, Wigston; Manchester Institute of Science and Technology. Lecturer in Business Finance, University College of Wales, Aberystwyth, 1979-87; Associate Professor, Graduate Management Institute, Union College, New York, 1987-89; Senior Lecturer in Accounting and Finance, University of Wales, Bangor, 1989-90, Royal Insurance Professor of Finance and Accounting, 1990-93 Recreation: running. Address: (b.) Department of Accounting and Finance, Glasgow University, Glasgow G12 8LE; T.-0141-339 8855, Ext. 5426.

Gartside, Peter, BEd (Hons). UNICEF Educational Representative; Freelance education and training consultant; Research Officer, Scottish Council for Research in Education, 1987-88; b. 31.10.32, Oldham; m., Kathleen; 1 s. Educ. East Oldham High School; Chester Diocesan Training College; Charlotte Mason College of Education National Service, Royal Scots Greys, 1951-53; Teacher Hollinwood County Secondary School, Oldham, 1955-57; Housemaster, The Blue Coat School, Oldham, 1957-68; Head of House, Hattersley County Comprehensive School 1968-70; Warden, Workington Teachers' Centre, Cumbria 1970-76; Education Department, Independent Broadcasting Authority, 1977-78; Warden, West Cumbria Teachers Centre, 1978-79; Adviser, Scottish Council for Educational Technology, 1980-86; Secretary, Scottish Committee on Open Learning, 1983-86; Secretary, National Committee of Teachers' Audio/Visual Aids Groups; former Member, BBC Radio Carlisle Education Education Advisory Panel Recreations: walking; travel; music. Address (h.) 73 Argyle Way, Dunblane, FK15 9DY.

Garvie, Alexander Femister, MA, FRSE. Reader Department of Classics, Glasgow University, since 1987 (Head of Department, since 1991); b. 29.1.34, Edinburgh; m., Jane Wallace Johnstone; 1 s.; 1 d. Educ. George Watson's College, Edinburgh; Edinburgh University; Cambridge University. Assistant, then Lecturer, Department of Greek, Glasgow University, 1960-72; Visiting Gillespie Professor, College of Wooster, Ohio, 1967-68; Visiting Assistant Professor, Ohio State University, 1968; Visiting Professor, University of Guelph, 1986. Publications: Aeschylus' Supplices: Play and Trilogy, 1969; Aeschylus Choephori: Introduction and Commentary, 1986; Homer Odyssey Books VI-VIII, 1994. Recreations: music; hill-walking. Address: (h.) 93 Stirling Drive, Bishopbriggs, Glasgow; T.-0141-772 4140.

Garvie, Ian Graham Donaldson, MA (Hons), BLitt, DipEd. Rector, Auchmuty High School, Glenrothes, 1976-90; b. 7.6.29, Perth; m., Margaret M.C. McIntosh. Educ. Perth Academy; Edinburgh University; Moray House College; Exeter College, Oxford. Vice-Chairman, Scottish Talking Newspaper Group. Recreation: hill-walking. Address: (h.) 23 Lakeside Road, Kirkcaldy, KY2 5QJ; T.- 01592 266886.

Gaskin, Professor Maxwell, DFC (and bar), MA. Jaffrey Professor of Political Economy, Aberdeen University, 1965-85; b. 18.11.21, Liverpool; m., Brenda Stewart; 1 s.; 3 d. Educ. Quarry Bank School, Liverpool; Liverpool University. War Service, RAF, 1941-46; Lecturer and Senior Lecturer in Economics, Glasgow University, 1951-65; Head, Department of Political Economy, Aberdeen University, 1965-81; Economic Consultant to Secretary of State for Scotland, 1965-87; Member, Scottish Agricultural Wages Board, 1972-90; Chairman, Foresterhill and Associated Hospitals Board, 1972-74; Chairman, Flax and Hemp and Retail Bespoke Tailoring Wages Councils, 1978-93; Member, Civil Engineering EDC, 1978-84; Chairman, Section F, British Association, 1978-79; President, Scottish Economic Society, 1981-84; Fellow, Royal Economic Society. Publications: The Scottish Banks: A Modern Survey, 1965; North East Scotland: A Survey of its Development Potential (Co-author), 1969; Economic Impact of North Sea Oil on Scotland (Co-author), 1978; Employment in Insurance, Banking and Finance in Scotland, 1980; The Political Economy of Tolerable Survival (Editor), 1981. Recreations: music; gardening. Address: (h.) Westfield, Ancrum, Roxburghshire, TD8 6XA; T.-018353 830237.

Gautam, Prasanna Chandra, MBBS (Hon), MRCP (UK), FRCPEdin; MFCH. Consultant Physician, Grampian Health Board, since 1989; Clinical Senior Lecturer in Medicine, Medical School, Aberdeen, since 1989; b. 3.4.45, Nepal; m., Leela Mani; 1 s.; 1 d. Educ. Padmodaya High School, Kathmandu; Bangalore Medical College, India. HMG of Nepal: Medical Officer, 1970-76, Senior Medical Officer, 1977-78; Senior House Officer in General Medicine, UK, 1977-81; Registrar in Cardiology, Liverpool, 1981-84; Registrar in Geriatric Medicine, Liverpool, 1984-86; Senior Registrar in General Medicine and Geriatrics, 1986-89. Chairman, Nepalese Doctors Association (UK); Executive Member, Scottish Branch, BGS. Publications: several books in Nepali; publications on hypothermia and cardiac problems in the elderly. Recreations: chess; travelling; gardening; walking. Address: (b.) Department of Medicine for the Elderly, Woodend Hospital, Aberdeen; T.-01224 663131, Ext. 56319.

Gavin, Anthony John, BSc, DipEd. Head Teacher, St. Margaret's Academy, Livingston, since 1993; b. 11.10.41, Perth; m., Charlotte Duffy; 2 d. Educ. Perth Academy; St. Andrews University. Teacher, St. Andrew's High School, Kirkcaldy, 1964-71; Principal Teacher/Assistant Headteacher, St. David's High School, Dalkeith, 1971-77; Depute Headteacher, St. Augustine's High School, Edinburgh, 1977-79; Headteacher, St. Saviour's High School, Dundee, 1979-93; TVEI Adviser Scotland, 1986-90. Member, Scottish Community Education Council, since 1993; Chair, Catholic Headteachers' Association of Scotland, since 1994. Recreations: music; golf. Address: (h.) 5 Colinton Court, Glenrothes, KY6 3PE; T.-01592 743462.

Gavin, Derek, FRICS, IRRV. Chartered Surveyor, since 1971; Executive Director, Stirling Enterprise Park and Stirling Enterprise, since 1984; Board Director, Stirling Business Links Ltd.; b. 12.12.46, Perth; m., Terry; 1 s. Educ. Perth Academy; College of Estate Management. Trainee Surveyor, Bell Ingram, Perth, 1964-69; Management Surveyor, Scottish Industrial Estates Corporation, Glasgow, 1969-72; Valuation Surveyor, Bell Ingram, Perth, 1972-77; Estates Property Manager, Central Regional Council, 1977-84. Recreations: veteran hockey player; golf. Address: (b.) John Player Building, Players Road, Stirling; T.-01786 463416.

Gavin, Kevin George, MA (Hons), DipEd. Chief Adviser, Strathclyde Regional Council Education Department, since 1990 (HM Inspector of Schools, 1985-90); b. 4.7.48, Aberdeen; m., Jessie M.C. Connell; 1 d. Educ. Aberdeen Academy; Aberdeen University; Aberdeen College of Education. Assistant Head Teacher, Silverwood Primary School, Kilmarnock, 1974-77; Head Teacher, Monkton Primary School, 1977-80; Adviser in Primary Education: Grampian, 1980-83, Strathclyde, 1983-85. Recreations: walking; gardening; food and drink; art; motor-cycling. Address: (h.) Monymusk, Benslie Village, by Kilwinning, KA13 7QY; T.-01294 554440.

Gawthrop, Professor Peter John, MA, DPhil, MIEE, MInstMC, CEng, EurIng. Wylie Professor of Mechanical Engineering, Glasgow University, since 1987; b. 10.3.52, Seascale; 2 d. Educ. Whitehaven Grammar School; Queen's College, Oxford. W.W. Spooner Research Fellow, New College, Oxford; Lecturer, then Reader, Sussex University. Recreation: hill-walking. Address: (b.) Department of Mechanical Engineering, James Watt Building, Glasgow University, Glasgow, G12 8QQ; T.-0141-339 8855.

Gayre of Gayre and Nigg, Lt. Col. Robert, MA, DPhil, DFSc, DSc; Grand Commander, Order of St. Lazarus; b. 6.8.07; m., Mary Nina Terry (deceased); 1 s. Educ. Edinburgh University; Exeter College, Oxford. Commissioned Officer, Supplementary Reserve Royal Artillery, 1931; War Service, 1939; transferred to Regular Army Reserve, 1941; Staff Officer for Education, HQ Airborne Forces, 1941; Major HQ, Oxford District, 1941; Lt. Col., Educational Adviser, Allied Military Government for Italy, 1943; Professor of Anthropology, University of Saugor, India, 1954. Member, Royal Society of Naples. Recreation: reading. Address: Minard Castle, Argyll.

Geddes, Keith, BEd. Leader, Labour Group, Lothian Regional Council, since 1990; Board Member: Lothian and Edinburgh Enterprise Ltd., Edinburgh Old Town Renewal Trust; Senior Vice President, COSLA; Board Member, Edinburgh International Conference Centre; b. 8.8.52, Selkirk; m., Linda McCracken. Educ. Galashiels Academy; Edinburgh University; Moray House College. Regional Councillor, since 1982; Chair, LRC Education Committee, 1987-90; Chair, LRC Policy and Resources Committee, since 1990. Recreations: hill-walking; golf; film. Address: (h.) 9 Willowbrae Avenue, Edinburgh; T.-0131-661 7935.

Gemmell, Curtis Glen, BSc, PhD, MIBiol, FRCPath. Reader in Bacteriology, Glasgow University, since 1990 (Senior Lecturer, 1976-90); Honorary Bacteriologist, Greater Glasgow Health Board, since 1976; b. 26.8.41, Beith, Ayrshire; m., Anne Margaret; 2 d. Educ. Spier's School, Beith; Glasgow University. Glasgow University: Assistant Lecturer, 1966-68, Lecturer, 1968-69; Paisley College of Technology: Lecturer, 1969-71, Senior Lecturer, 1971-76; Visiting Assistant Professor, University of Minnesota, Minneapolis, 1979-80. Recreations: gardening; golf. Address: (h.) Sunninghill, 19 Lawmarnock Crescent, Bridge of Weir, PA11 3AS; T.-Bridge of Weir 613350.

Gemmell, Gavin John Norman, CA. Senior Partner, Baillie, Gifford & Co., since 1989 (Partner, since 1967); Chairman, Toyo Trust Baillie Gifford Ltd., since 1989; Director, Scottish Widows Fund & Life Assurance Society, since 1984, Guardian Baillie Gifford Ltd., since 1990, TSB Bank Scotland PLC, since 1991; b. 7.9.41, Edinburgh; m., Kathleen Fiona Drysdale; 1 s.; 2 d. Educ. George Watson's College. Qualified CA, 1964; joined Baillie, Gifford & Co., 1964; Chairman, AITC Tax Committee, 1980-89; Member, Court, Heriot Watt University, since 1993. Recreations: golf; squash; foreign travel. Address: (b.) 1 Rutland Court, Edinburgh, EH3 8EY; T.-0131-222 4000.

Gemmill, Robert, MA, FIMC. Member, Business Committee, General Council, Glasgow University, since 1987 and Assessor of the General Council on the Court, since 1990; b. 20.2.30; m., 1, Anne MacMurchy Gow (deceased); 2, Elisabeth Mary MacLennan; 2 s.; 1 d. Educ. High School of Glasgow; Glasgow University. Manufacturing management, Procter & Gamble Ltd., 1953-56; Management Consultant, PA Management Consultants Ltd., 1956-85. Played rugby football for Glasgow High School FP, Northumberland, Cheshire, Barbarians and Scotland, 1950-51. Recreations: golf; travel; music. Address: (h.) 31 Newark Drive, Glasgow, G41 4QA; T.-0141-423 1860.

Gennard, Professor John, BA (Econ), MA (Econ), FIPM. Professor of Industrial Relations, Strathclyde University, since 1981; b. 26.4.44, Manchester; m., Florence Anne Russell; 1 s.; 1 d. Educ. Hulme Grammar School for Boys; Sheffield University; Manchester University. Research Officer, Industrial Relations Department, then Lecturer in Industrial Relations, London School of Economics, 1968-81. Publications: The Reluctant Militants (Co-author), 1972; Financing Strikers, 1978; Industrial Relations and Job Security, 1979; The Closed Shop in British Industry, 1984; A History of the National Graphical Association, 1990. Recreations: football; swimming; politics; trade unions; food and drink. Address: (h.) 4 South Avenue, Carluke, Lanarkshire; T.-01555 51361.

George, John Charles Grossmith, FSAScot, FHS. Kintyre Pursuivant of Arms, since 1986; b. 15.12.30, London; m.,

Margaret Mary Maria Mercedes Weld. Educ. Ampleforth. Lt., Hertfordshire Yeomanry, 1951-54; films and television advertising, 1952-62; College of Arms, 1962-72; Earl Marshal's Liaison Officer with the Churchill family, 1965; Green Staff Officer, Prince of Wales's Investiture, 1969; Garioch Pursuivant, 1976. Chairman, Philbeach Light Opera Society, 1961-63; Vice President, BBC "Mastermind" Club, 1979-81; Knight of Obedience, Sov. Mil. Ord. of Malta; Commander, Ord. Pro Merito Melitensi; Knight Constantinian Order of St. George. Publications: The Puffin Book of Flags, 1975; The French Heralds (paper), 1985; numerous historical articles. Recreations: English light opera and musical comedies; hagiographies; sports. Address: (h.) 115 Henderson Row, Edinburgh, EH3 5BB; T.-0131-557 1605.

George, Judith Wordsworth, MA (Oxon), PhD. Deputy Scottish Director, The Open University, since 1984; b. 26.8.40, Bradford; 2 d. Educ. Heath Grammar School, Halifax; Somerville College, Oxford. Tutor in Philosophy, St. Andrews University; Lecturer in History of Fine Art, Manchester University; Tutor in Classics, Open University; Senior Counsellor, Open University in Scotland. Recreations: gardening; classical music; hill-walking. Address: (b.) 10 Drumsheugh Gardens, Edinburgh, EH3 7QJ; T.-0131-260 7130.

George, Professor William David, MB, BS, FRCS, MS. Professor of Surgery, Glasgow University, since 1981; b. 22.3.43, Reading; 1 s.; 3 d. Educ. Henley Grammar School; London University. Lecturer in Surgery, Manchester University, 1973-77; Senior Lecturer in Surgery, Liverpool University, 1977-81. Member, National Committees, British Association of Surgical Oncology and Surgical Research Society. Recreations: veteran rowing; golf. Address: (b.) University Department of Surgery, Western Infirmary, Glasgow, G11 6NT; T.-0141-339 8822.

Gerber, Cyril, OBE. Founding Director, Compass Gallery, since 1969; Director, Cyril Gerber Fine Art, since 1982; b. 4.11.17, Glasgow; m., Pat Gerber (qv); 1 s.; 2 d. Educ. Albert Road Academy, Glasgow. Commissioned Officer, Royal Artillery, World War II (served in India and Ceylon). Life Member, Friends of Glasgow School of Art; Lord Provost of Glasgow's Medal, 1990 for services to the arts; National Arts Collection Fund award, 1991. Recreations: tennis; travel; music; theatre; walking; family. Address: (b.) 148 West Regent Street, Glasgow, G2 2RQ; T.-0141 221 3095.

Gerber, Pat, MA (Hons). Writer, since 1982; Lecturer (part-time), Glasgow University, since 1985; b. 17.3.34, Glasgow; m., Cyril Gerber (qv); 3 s.; 2 d. Educ. St. Leonard's School; Glasgow University. Committee Member: Scottish Book Marketing Group, Society of Authors in Scotland, Saltire Society (Glasgow Branch), International Pen (Scottish Centre). Publications: The Search for the Stone of Destiny; Maiden Voyage; several plays. Recreations: reading; travel; swimming; tennis; hill-walking; sailing; cars; sewing; music. Address: (h.) 6 Golf Road, Clarkston, Glasgow, G76 7LZ; T.-0141-638 2269.

Gerrard, John Henry Atkinson, MBE, FRIAS, DA (Edin), MA (Cantab), FRSA. Technical Director, Scottish Civic Trust, since 1984; b. 15.9.34, Leicester; m., Dr. Margaret Mackay. Educ. Abbotsholme; Corpus Christi College, Cambridge; Edinburgh College of Art. Assistant Architect: Sheffield Corporation, 1961-63, Planning Department, Oxford City Council, 1965-68; Assistant Director, Scottish Civic Trust, 1968-84. Recreation: travelling hopefully. Address: (b.) Scottish Civic Trust, 24 George Square, Glasgow; T.-0141-221 1466.

Gerson, Jack Barton. Dramatist and Novelist; b. 31.7.28, Glasgow; 1 d. Educ. Hillhead High School, Glasgow. RAF, two years; worked in advertising and cinema distribution,

1949-59; writing full-time since 1959; won BBC Television Play Competition, 1959, for Three Ring Circus; has written more than 100 hours of television drama; created two series The Regiment and The Omega Factor; 14 radio plays; novels include Whitehall Sanction, Assassination Run, Treachery Game, The Back of the Tiger, Deaths Head Berlin, The Evil Thereof, The Fetch. Recreations: cinema; reading; swimming; Caribbean Islands; sleeping in front of television set. Address: (b.) c/o Harvey Unna & Stephen Durbridge, 24 Pottery Lane, Holland Park, London, W11 4LZ.

Gerstenberg, Frank Eric, MA (Cantab), PGCE, FRSA. Principal, George Watson's College, Edinburgh, since 1985; b. 23.2.41, Balfron; m., Valerie MacLellan; 1 s.; 2 d. Educ. Trinity College, Glenalmond; Clare College, Cambridge; London University. Assistant Master, Kelly College, Tavistock, 1963-67; Housemaster and Head of History, Millfield School, 1967-74; Headmaster, Oswestry School, 1974-85. Governor, Beaconhurst School, Bridge of Allan. Recreations: skiing; sailing; travelling; music. Address: (h.) 27 Merchiston Gardens, Edinburgh, EH10 5DD; T.-0131-337 6880.

Gerver, Professor Elisabeth, BA (Hons), MA, PhD. Professor of Continuing Education and Director, Centre for Continuing Education, Dundee University, since 1990; b. 15.4.41, Winnipeg; m., Dr. David Gerver (deceased); 1 s.; 1 d. Educ. Wolfville High School, Nova Scotia; Dalhousie University, Canada; Toronto University; King's College, London. Lecturer in Communications, Newcastle upon Tyne Polytechnic, 1968-69; part-time staff, Open University, 1971-84; Lecturer in Communication, Queen Margaret College, Edinburgh, 1974-83; Director, Scottish Community Education Microelectronics Project, Glasgow, 1981-82; Director, Scottish Institute of Adult and Continuing Education, 1983-90. Council Member, Scottish Community Education Council, 1979-83; Member, BBC Continuing Education Advisory Council, 1983-86; Vice-President, European Bureau of Adult Education, 1986-90; Executive Member, Universities Association for Continuing Education, since 1992; Governor, Queen Margaret College, 1985-88; Chair, Editorial Board, Computers in Adult Education and Training, 1986-92; Board Member, Tayside Education Business Partnership, since 1992; Member, IBA Educational Advisory Council, 1988-90. Publications: Computers and Adult Learning, 1984; Humanising Technology, 1985; Strategic Women: how do they manage in Scotland? (Co-author), 1991. Recreations: travel; the performing arts; hill-walking; sailing. Address: (h.) 13 Chester Street, Edinburgh, EH3 7RF; T.-0131-225 1776.

Gibbons, John Ernest, PhD, DipArch, DipTP, ARIBA, ARIAS, FSA(Scot), FRSA. Director of Building and Chief Architect, Scottish Office, since 1984; b. 20.4.40, Halesowen; m., Patricia Mitchell; 1 s.; 2 d. Educ. Oldbury Grammar School; Birmingham School of Architecture, Aston University; Edinburgh University. Lecturer, Birmingham School of Architecture and Aston University, 1962-65; Research Fellow, Architecture Research Unit, then Lecturer in Architecture, Edinburgh University, 1966-72; Principal, Architect's Division, Scottish Development Department, 1972-78; Visiting Research Scientist, CSIRO, Melbourne, 1975; Assistant Director, Building Directorate, SDD, 1978; Deputy Director, Scottish Office Building Directorate, 1982-84. Member of Council, EAA and RIAS, 1977-80; Member, Council, ARCUK, since 1984; Assessor, Design Council, 1984-88. Address: (h.) Crichton House, Pathhead, Midlothian, EH37 5UX; T.-01875 320085.

Gibbs, Lavinia. Trustee, National Galleries of Scotland, since 1986; Member, Brodick Country Park Committee, since 1980; b. 7.6.39, London; m., Stephen Gibbs; 2 s.; 1 d. Educ. Heathfield, Ascot; Ipswich Civic College. Librarian, Courtauld Institute of Art, London, 1960-66; Child Care Officer/Social Worker, Royal Borough of Kensington and

Chelsea, 1968-73; Representative for Norfolk, National Art Collections Fund, 1968-73; Member, Council, National Trust for Scotland, 1975-80, and Curatorial Committee, 1982-92; President, Isle of Arran Branch, Save the Children Fund. Recreation: gardening. Address: (h.) Dougarie Lodge, Isle of Arran, KA27 8EB; T.-0177 084 0229.

Gibbs, Ronald Percy, OBE. President, Phab Scotland, since 1992 (Chairman, 1984-92); a Director, Handicabs (Lothian), since 1985; Convener, History Section, The Cramond Association, since 1983; b. 1.6.21, London; m., Margaret Eleanor Dean; 1 d. Educ. Owen's School, Islington. Ministry (later Department) of Transport, 1938-81; set up the Ports Office for Scotland in Edinburgh, 1973, and remained head of that Office until retiral in 1981. Recreations: transport and communications; music; Scottish and industrial history; photography. Address: (h.) 13 Inveralmond Drive, Edinburgh, EH4 6JX; T.-0131-312 6034.

Gibbs, Stephen Cokayne, Director, Vaux Group PLC, since 1970; b. 18.7.29, Hertingfordbury, England; m., Lavinia Bacon; 2 s.; 1 d. Educ. Eton College. Served with KRRC (60th Rifles), 1947-49; TA, service with QVR (TA), 1951-63: Lt., 1951, Captain, 1956, Major, 1958; Port Line Ltd., 1949-62: Assistant Manager, 1957, London Manager, 1959; Charles Barker PLC, 1962-87: Director, 1962, Deputy Chairman, 1982-87. Member, Executive, National Trust for Scotland, since 1987, and Council, since 1991; Member, TUCC for Scotland, since 1992; Member, Red Deer Commission, since 1993; Chairman, Association of Deer Management Groups, since 1994. Recreations: shooting; fishing. Address: The Estate Office, Dougarie, Isle of Arran, KA27 8EB; T.-01770 840259.

Gibson, Edgar Matheson, MBE, TD, DL, DA. Chairman, St. Magnus Cathedral Fair, since 1982; Honorary Sheriff, Grampian, Highlands and Islands, since 1992; Member, Orkney Health Board, since 1991; Deputy Lieutenant, Orkney, since 1976; Chairman, Orkney Branch, SSAFA, since 1990; Vice Chairman, Italian Chapel Preservation Committee, since 1994; Hon. President, Society of Friends of St. Magnus Cathedral, since 1994; b. 1.11.34, Kirkwall; m., Jean McCarrick; 2 s.; 2 d. Educ. Kirkwall Grammar School; Gray's College of Art, Aberdeen. National Service, 1958-60; TA and TAVR service to 1985 with Lovat Scouts, reaching Lt. Col.; Battalion Second in Command, 2/51 Highland Volunteers, 1973-76; Joint Services Liaison Officer for Orkney, 1980-85; Cadet Commandant, Orkney Lovat Scouts ACF, 1979-86, Honorary Colonel, since 1986; Chairman, Northern Area, Highland TA&VR Association, 1987-93. Recreations: painting; sculpture; whisky tasting. Address: (h.) Transcona, New Scapa Road, Kirkwall, Orkney; T.-0856 2849.

Gibson, Rev. Henry Montgomerie, MA, BD, PhD. Minister, The High Kirk, Dundee, since 1979; b. 11.6.36, Wishaw; m., Dr. Anne Margaret Thomson; 1 s. Educ. Wishaw Academy; Hamilton Academy; Glasgow University. Assistant Minister, Glasgow Cathedral, 1960; Minister: Carmunnock Parish Church, Glasgow, 1961-71, Aberfeldy, 1971-79; Convener, Church of Scotland Working Party on Alcohol and Drugs, 1975-81. Recreations: reading; table tennis (occasionally). Address: High Kirk Manse, 6 Adelaide Place, Dundee, DD3 6LF; T.-Dundee 322955.

Gibson, John Alan, MB, ChB, MD, FRCGP, DObstRCOG, CBiol, FIBiol, FLS, FZS, FRGS, FRMS, FGS, FSA (Scot). Senior Honorary Secretary, British Medical Association, since 1979; Chairman, Scottish Natural History Library, since 1974; Editor, the Scottish Naturalist, since 1972; b. 15.5.26, Kilbarchan; m., Dr. Mary M. Baxter; 1 d. Educ. Lindisfarne School; Paisley Grammar School; Glasgow University. Family doctor, village of Kilbarchan; Hon. Secretary, Renfrewshire Division, BMA,

1957-95; last Secretary, Renfrewshire Local Medical Committee; first Secretary, Argyll and Clyde Area Medical Committee; Member, Central Council, Central Ethical Committee, Scottish Council and Scottish GMS Committee, BMA; Hon. President, Renfrewshire BMA; Fellow, Royal Society of Medicine; Life Fellow, Royal College of General Practitioners; Scottish Representative and Vice-President, Society for the Bibliography of Natural History; Scientific Meetings Secretary, Vice-President and Hon. Member, Society for the History of Natural History; Chairman, Friends of Glasgow University Library; Chairman, Scottish Natural History Trust; Chairman, Clyde Area Branch, Scottish Wildlife Trust; President, Renfrewshire Natural History Society; Secretary and Honorary Life Member, Scottish Society for the Protection of Birds; Life Fellow, RSPB; Chairman, Clyde Bird Club; Secretary, Royal Physical Society of Edinburgh; Gold Medal, Scottish Society for the Protection of Birds, 1967; Life Fellow, Royal Zoological Society of Scotland; Queen's Silver Jubilee Medal, 1977; Fellowship, BMA, 1982. Publications: Mammals of West of Scotland; Birds of Clyde Area; Atlas of Clyde Vertebrates; Regional Bibliography of West of Scotland Vertebrates; Bibliography of Scottish Vertebrate Zoology; 300 scientific papers on Scottish natural history, 1943-95. Recreations: natural history; golf (Royal Troon). Address: (h.) Foremount House, Kilbarchan, PA10 2EZ; T.-01505 702410.

Gibson, Rev. Professor John Clark Love, MA, BD, DPhil. Professor of Hebrew and Old Testament Studies, Edinburgh University, 1987-94; b. 28.5.30, Coatbridge; m., Agnes Gilmour Russell, MA ; 4 s.; 1 d. Educ. Coatbridge High School; Glasgow University; Magdalen College, Oxford. Licensed as Probationer, Church of Scotland, 1956; Assistant Minister, Bellshill West, 1956; Minister, Newmachar, 1959-62; Edinburgh University: Lecturer in Hebrew and Semitic Languages, 1962-73, Reader, 1973-87; Associate Minister, St. Philip's, Joppa, since 1994; President, Society for Old Testament Studies, 1994. Publications: Textbook of Hebrew Inscriptions, 1971; Textbook of Aramaic Inscriptions, 1975; Canaanite Myths and Legends, 1978; Textbook of Phoenician Inscriptions, 1982; Daily Study Bible (Old Testament) (General Editor and author of volumes on Genesis and Job), 1981-86; Reader's Digest Family Guide to the Bible (Features Editor), 1984; The Bible in Scottish Life and Literature (Contributor), 1988; Hebrew Syntax, 1994. Recreations: the Bible in Scots; Burns; golf. Address: 10 South Morton Street, Edinburgh; T.-0131-669 3635.

Gibson, William Erle, BA, LLB. Sheriff, since 1989; b. 30.8.34, Glasgow; m., Anne; 1 s.; 2 d. Educ. Dollar Academy; Trinity Hall, Cambridge; Glasgow University. Solicitor in Glasgow, 1961-89; Clerk to General Commissioners of Taxes, City of Glasgow, 1968-89; Clerk to General Council, Glasgow University, 1976-86. Member, European Ethical Review Committee, since 1976. Recreations: golf; fishing; piping; hill-walking; the family. Address: (h.) 7A Briarwell Road, Milngavie, Glasgow; T.-0141-956 2770.

Gibson, William John Alexander, MB, ChB, DMRD (Lond), FRCR. Consultant Diagnostic Radiologist with administrative responsibility, Stracathro Hospital, Brechin; Hon. Senior Lecturer, Dundee University; President, Scottish Radiological Society, 1991-93; b. 20.5.36, Ayr; m., Daphne Gardiner; 2 s. Educ. Douglas-Ewart High School, Newton Stewart; Glasgow University. Various posts, Victoria Infirmary and Glasgow Royal Infirmary; Senior Registrar, Dundee Royal Infirmary; appointed Consultant, Stracathro Hospital, 1968; Secretary, Scottish Radiological Society, 1977-80. Recreations: bowling; motor sport; TV sport; philately. Address: (h.) 12 Cedar Road, Broughty Ferry, Dundee, DD5 3BB; T.-01382 79446.

Gibson-Smith, Chris, BSc, MSc, PhD. Chief Executive, BP Exploration Europe, since 1992; b. 8.9.45, Newcastle; m., Marjorie; 2 d. Educ. Taunton School; Durham University; Newcastle University; Stanford University. Oil exploration and production geologist with BP in a variety of world-wide posts, 1970-84; Sloan Fellow, Stanford University, 1984; President, BP Alaska Exploration Inc., 1985-87; Assistant General Manager, BP Corporate Planning Department, 1987-89; General Manager, Developments, BPX Europe, 1989-91; Deputy Chief Executive, BP Exploration Europe, 1991-92. Council Member, CBI Scotland. Recreations: sport; music; modern art; history; literature. Address: (b.) Farburn Industrial Estate, Dyce, Aberdeen, AB2 0PB.

Gilbert, Colin, BA (Hons). Head of Comedy, BBC Scotland, since 1986; b. 3.4.52, Glasgow; m., Joanna; 1 s.; 1 d. Educ. St. Paul's School; York University. Script Editor, Not The 9 O'Clock News, 1980-82; Producer: A Kick Up the Eighties, 1983, Naked Radio, 1984, Naked Video and City Lights, 1986-89, Rab C. Nesbitt, 1990-95, I, Lovett, 1990, Tales of Para Handy, 1993-94, The Baldyman, 1994, Bad Boys, 1994; holder, RTS Reith Award; BAFTA Scotland Award for outstanding contribution to film or TV production. Address: (b.) BBC Scotland, Queen Margaret Drive, Glasgow, G12 8DG.

Gilchrist, Allan C., BSc, DipEd, FRSA. Director of Education, Highland Region, since 1994; b. 12.9.38, Paisley; m., Margaret Porteous; 2 s. Educ. John Neilson Institution; Glasgow University. Teacher, 1962-69; Head Teacher, 1969-74; Education Officer, 1974-85; Depute Director of Education, 1985-94. Recreations: walking; golf; travel; reading. Address: (b.) Highland Regional Council, Glenurquhart Road, Inverness, IV3 5NX; T.-01463 702801.

Gilchrist, Archibald, MA. Director, Caledonian MacBrayne Ltd., since 1990; Director, RMJM Ltd., since 1988; Board Member, Scottish Legal Aid Board, since 1986; b. 17.11.29, Glasgow; m., Elizabeth Jean; 2 s.; 1 d. Educ. Loretto School; Pembroke College, Cambridge. Barclay Curle & Co. Ltd., 1954-64; Brown Bros. & Co. Ltd., 1964-72; Govan Shipbuilders Ltd., 1972-79; Vosper Pte Ltd., Singapore, 1980-86. Recreations: shooting; fishing; golf. Address: (h.) 35 Barnton Avenue, Edinburgh, EH4 6JJ; T.-0131-336 4288.

Gilchrist, Bernard, MBE, MA (Hons) (Oxon); b. 20.5.19, Manchester; m., Jean W. Gregory; 2 s.; 1 d. Educ. Manchester Grammar School; Queen's College, Oxford. Tanganyika: Forest Officer, HM Colonial/Overseas Civil Service, 1942-62 (Conservator of Forests, 1960), Conservator of Forests, Tanganyika/Tanzania Government Service, 1962-65; Chief Executive, Scottish Wildlife Trust, 1965-85. Recreations: countryside; natural history; hill-walking; photography. Address: (h.) 9 Murrayfield Gardens, Edinburgh, EH12 6DG; T.-0131-337 3869.

Gilchrist, Thomas, BSc, PhD, CChem, FRSC. Managing Director, Ross Fraser Ltd. and Giltech Ltd., since 1984; b. 18.6.36, Ayr; m., Fiona Christina Brown; 2 d. Educ. Ayr Academy; Glasgow University. Assistant Lecturer in Chemistry, Glasgow University, 1961-62; Research Chemist: Canadian Industries Ltd., Quebec, 1962-64, ICI Ltd., Stevenston, Ayrshire, 1964-69; Strathclyde University: Lecturer in Bioengineering, 1969, Head, Division of Artificial Organs, Bioengineering Unit, 1972, Senior Lecturer in Bioengineering, 1975-84. Recreations: golf; curling. Address: (h.) The Lodge, 67 Midton Road, Ayr, KA7 2TW; T.-Ayr 266088.

Giles, Cecilia Elspeth, CBE, MA. Member, Rail Users Consultative Committee for Scotland, since 1989; Member, Church of Scotland Board of Stewardship and Finance, 1986-93, Vice Convener 1990-93; Member, Assembly Council, since 1993; b. Dumfries. Educ. Queen Margaret's School, Yorkshire; Edinburgh University. Administrative staff, Khartoum University, 1956-57; joined Administrative staff, Edinburgh University, 1957; Assistant Secretary, Edinburgh University, 1972-87; Committee of Vice-Chancellors and Principals' Administrative Training Officer (seconded part-time), 1983-85. President, Edinburgh University Graduates' Association, 1889-91; Member, Business Committee, General Council, Edinburgh University, 1988-93, Convener, Constitutional Sub-Committee, 1991-93. Publication: Scotland for the Tourist (Co-author). Recreations: entertaining friends, family and godchildren; theatre. Address: (b.) Graduates' Association, 5 Buccleuch Place, Edinburgh, EH8 9LW.

Gill, Hon. Lord (Brian Gill), MA, LLB, PhD. Senator of the College of Justice in Scotland, since 1994; b. 25.2.42; m.; 5 s.; 1 d. Educ. St. Aloysius College; Glasgow University; Edinburgh University. Advocate, 1967; Advocate-Depute, 1977-79; Standing Junior Counsel: Foreign and Commonwealth Office (Scotland), 1974-77, Home Office (Scotland), 1979-81, Scottish Education Department, 1979-81; QC, 1981; called to the Bar, Lincoln's Inn, 1991; Keeper, Advocates' Library, 1987-94. Address: (b.) Court of Session, Parliament House, Parliament Square, Edinburgh, EH1 1RQ.

Gill, Professor Roger William Thomas, BA (Hons), BPhil, MA, PhD, AFBPsS, FIPD, FIMgt, CPsychol. Professor of Business Administration (Human Resource Management), Strathclyde University Graduate Business School, since 1992; Director, Management Development and Consultancy Services; b. 3.10.45, Cumbria; 1 s.; 1 d. Educ. Merchant Taylors' School, Crosby; St. Peter's College, Oxford; Liverpool University; Bradford University. English Electric, 1967-68; Inbucon/AIC Management Consultants, 1969-71; Personnel Manager, De La Rue, 1971-72; Manpower Manager, Associated Weavers, 1972-74; Lecturer, Bradford University Management Centre, 1974-78; Assistant Professor, State University of New York at Binghamton, 1979-82; Managing Director, Roger Gill & Associates, Singapore, 1982-90; Regional Manager (Asia), PA Consulting Group, Singapore, 1990-91. Publications: numerous articles and research reports. Recreations: music; theatre; food and wine; reading; doing nothing. Address: (b.) 199 Cathedral Street, Glasgow, G4 0QU; T.-0141-553 6141.

Gillespie, Archibald, CA, ACMA, IPFA. Director of Finance, Strathclyde Regional Council, since 1986; b. 4.9.35, Greenock; m., Alice Finlayson; 2 s.; 2 d. Educ. Greenock High School. Chief Internal Auditor, Greenock Corporation, 1964-67; County Treasurer, Bute County Council, 1967-75; Senior Depute Director of Finance, Strathclyde Regional Council, 1975-86. Commissioner, Public Works Loan Board; Member, Scottish Valuation Advisory Council. Recreations: golf; badminton. Address: (h.) 64 South Street, Greenock; T.-01475 81904.

Gillespie, Professor William John, TD, BSc, MB, ChB, ChM, FRCSEd, FRACS. Professor of Orthopaedic Surgery, Edinburgh University, since 1993; b. 16.6.40, Stirling; m., Lesley Diane Wood; 2 s. Educ. George Watson's College; Edinburgh University. Professor of Orthopaedic Surgery, Christchurch School of Medicine, University of Otago, 1981-89; Professor of Orthopaedic Surgery, University of Newcastle, New South Wales, 1989-93. Address: (b.) Princess Margaret Rose Orthopaedic Hospital, Fairmilehead, Edinburgh, EH10 7ED; T.-0131-536 4667.

Gillies (nee McCall-Smith), Anne Bethea, MA, LLB. Advocate; Honorary Sheriff of South Strathclyde, Dumfries and Galloway, at Lanark, since 1960; Member, Valuation Appeal Panel, Strathclyde, 1974-88; b. 12.4.22, Lochgilphead, Argyll; m., Sheriff Principal M.G. Gillies, T.D., Q.C. (qv). Educ. Sherborne School for Girls, Dorset; Edinburgh University. Served in WAAF, until 1946; called to Scottish Bar, 1951; married, 1954. Recreations: gardening; cats. Address: (h.) 1 The Warren, Gullane, East Lothian, EH31 2BE; T.-Gullane 842857.

Gillies, Anne Lorne, MA, PhD, PGCE, LRAM, Drhc. Singer and Writer, since 1962; education and community development, since 1985; Television Producer, since 1993; b. 21.10.44, Stirling; 1 s.; 2 d. Educ. Oban High School; Edinburgh University; London University; Jordanhill College of Education; Glasgow University. Singer: TV, radio, concert, recital, theatre, recording; writer: scripts, children's books, novels, articles, autobiography (Song of Myself); education/community development: teacher, resource development; National Education Officer, Comunn na Gaidhlig, 1988-90; Arts Development Officer, Govan Initiative Ltd., 1991-93; currently employed as Producer, Scottish Television; patron of many charitable and/or cultural organisations. Recreation: watching the weans. Address: (h.) 54 Terregles Avenue, Glasgow, G41 4LX; T.-0141-423 6002.

Gillies, Norman Neil Nicolson, BA, MIMgt, FRSA. Director, Sabhal Mor Ostaig, since 1988; Vice Chairman, Skye & Lochalsh Local Enterprise Company, since 1990; b. 1.3.47, Flodigarry, Isle of Skye; m., Jean Brown Nixon; 1 s.; 2 d. Educ. Portree High School; Strathclyde University; Open University. College Secretary, Sabhal Mor Ostaig, 1983-88; Director: Development Partners Ltd., Canan Ltd, UHI Ltd.; Member: Barail (Centre for Highlands and Islands Policy Studies); Leirsinn Research Centre; University of the Highlands and Islands Academic Council; Gaelic Television Committee; Gaelic Television Training Trust. Recreations: reading; television; family. Address: (h.) Innis Ard, Ardvasar, Isle of Skye, IV45 8RU; T.-01471 844 281.

Gillies, Rev. Dr. Robert Arthur, BD, PhD. Rector, St. Andrew's Episcopal Church, St. Andrews, since 1991; b. 21.10.51, Cleethorpes; m., Elizabeth; 3 s. Educ. Barton-upon-Humber Grammar School; Edinburgh University; St. Andrews University. Medical Laboratory Technician, 1968-72; Curate, Christ Church, Falkirk, 1977-80; Curate, Christ Church Morningside, and Chaplain, Napier College, 1980-84; Chaplain, Dundee University, 1984-90. Hon. Lecturer, Department of Philosophy, Dundee University, 1985-95. Publication: A Way for Healing, 1995. Recreations: family; garden; Scotland's mountains. Address: St. Andrew's Rectory, Queen's Terrace, St. Andrews, Fife, KY16 9QF; T.-01334 73344.

Gillies, Professor William, MA (Edin), MA (Oxon). Professor of Celtic, Edinburgh University, since 1979; b. 15.9.42, Stirling; m., Valerie; 1 s.; 2 d. Educ. Oban High School; Edinburgh University; Corpus Christi College, Oxford; Dublin University. Dublin Institute for Advanced Studies, 1969-70; Lecturer, Edinburgh University, 1970-79; Fellow, Royal Society of Edinburgh, 1990. Director, SNDA Ltd. Recreations: walking; gardening; music. Address: (h.) 67 Braid Avenue, Edinburgh, EH10 6ED.

Gillis, Charles Raphael, MD, FRCP(Glas), FFCM. Director, West of Scotland Cancer Surveillance Unit, since 1973; Director, WHO Collaborating Centre; Honorary Clinical Senior Lecturer, Glasgow University, since 1973; b. 23.10.37, Glasgow; m., Judith Ann Naftalin; 1 s.; 1 d. Educ. High School of Glasgow; Glasgow University. Lecturer in Epidemiology and Preventive Medicine, then Senior Lecturer and Honorary Consultant Epidemiologist, Glasgow University, 1965-73. Past Chairman, Cancer Education Co-ordinating Group of the UK and Republic of Ireland; Past Chairman, West of Scotland Oncological Organisation. Address: (b.) West of Scotland Cancer Surveillance Unit, Ruchill Hospital, Bilsland Drive, Ruchill, Glasgow, G20 9NB; T.-0141-946 7120.

Gillon, Hamish William, FFA, FPMI. Group Actuary, Scottish Provident Institution, since 1988; b. 22.1.40, Edinburgh; m., Sandra; 1 s.; 1 d. Educ. Royal High School, Edinburgh. Various appointments, Scottish Provident Institution, since 1965. Vice President, Faculty of Actuaries; Hon. Treasurer (Scotland), The Scout Association. Address: (b.) 6 St. Andrew Square, Edinburgh, EH2 2YA; T.-0131-556 9181.

Gilmour, Colonel Sir Allan Macdonald, KCVO, OBE, MC (and Bar), DSC (USA). Lord Lieutenant of Sutherland, 1972-91; Chairman, Highland River Purification Board, since 1994; Member, Highland Regional Council, since 1976; President, Highland Territorial & Auxiliary Reserve Association, 1989-91; b. 23.11.16, Edinburgh; m., Jean Wood; 3 s.; 1 d. Educ. Cargilfield, Edinburgh; Winchester College; Trinity College, Oxford. Commissioned Seaforth Highlanders, 1939; served War in Middle East, Sicily and NW Europe; Regimental and Staff appointments, 1945-69, including Instructor, Staff College, Quetta, and Chief of Staff, Ghana Armed Forces; Member, Sutherland County Council, 1970; Member, Highland Health Board, 1974 (Chairman, 1982-84); DL, Sutherland, 1969; Member, Highlands and Islands Development Consultative Council, 1980-88; Chairman, Sutherland District Council, 1974-78; Chairman, East Sutherland Council of Social Service, 1972-76; Board Member, Scottish National Orchestra Society, 1976-86. Recreation: fishing. Address: (h.) Invernauld, Rosehall, Lairg, Sutherland; T.-0154 984 204.

Gilmour, Andrew Parr, BSc (Hons). Rector, Rothesay Academy, since 1983; b. 26.4.46, Glasgow; m., Elizabeth Morrison MacPherson; 1 s.; 2 d. Educ. Allan Glen's School, Glasgow; Glasgow University. Teacher of Chemistry, Allan Glen's School, 1969; Dunoon Grammar School: Principal Teacher of Chemistry, 1972, Assistant Rector, 1975; Depute Head Teacher, Mearns Castle High School, 1981. Recreations: golf; badminton; rugby (spectating nowadays); swimming; cycling; windsurfing; gardening. Address: (h.) Millford, 34 Mount Stuart Road, Rothesay, Isle of Bute; T.-Rothesay 503336.

Gilmour, Douglas Graham, BSc (Hons), MB, ChB, MD, FRCS. Consultant Vascular Surgeon, Glasgow Royal Infirmary, since 1983; b. 15.4.47, Glasgow; m., Evelyn Jean; 2 s.; 2 d. Educ. Kelvinside Academy, Glasgow; Glasgow University. House Surgeon/Physician, then Senior House Officer/Registrar in Surgery, Western Infirmary, Glasgow, 1971-77; Glasgow Royal Infirmary: Senior Registrar in Surgery, 1977-80, Senior Lecturer (Honorary Consultant) in Surgery, 1980-83. Recreations: family; golf; skiing. Address: (b.) Vascular Surgery Department, Royal Infirmary, Glasgow; T.-0141-552 3535, Ext. 5503.

Gilmour, John, DL, MFH. Farmer; b. 15.7.44, Edinburgh; m., Valerie Jardine Russell; 2 s.; 2 d. Educ. Eton; Aberdeen College. Captain, FFY/SH (TA); Member, Queen's Bodyguard for Scotland (Royal Company of Archers); Chairman, Point-to-Point Racing Advisory Committee; Trustee, ADRA (Moredun Foundation). Recreations: fishing; reading. Address: Balcormo Mains, Leven, Fife; T.-0133 336 229.

Gilmour, John Andrew George, MA, LLB, NP. Solicitor; Marketing Consultant; Honorary Sheriff at Dumbarton, since 1991; b. 17.11.37, Balloch; m., Roma Aileen; 3 d. Educ. Morrison's Academy, Crieff; Edinburgh University. Partner, McArthur Brown Robertson; Partner, McArthur Stanton; President, Strathclyde Junior Chamber of Commerce, 1973; Director, Dumbarton Enterprise Trust, since 1985; Dean, Faculty of Dunbartonshire Solicitors, 1988-90; Law Society accredited Liquor Licensing Specialist, 1993. Recreations: sport; music; gastronomy. Address: (h.) Cramond Cottage, 19 East Lennox Drive, Helensburgh; T.-01436 75057.

Gilmour, Sir John Edward, 3rd Bt, DSO, TD, JP, BA. Lord Lieutenant of Fife, 1980-87; b. 24.10.12, Edinburgh; m., Ursula Mabyn Wills; 2 s. Educ. Eton College; Trinity Hall, Cambridge; Dundee School of Economics. Served with Fife and Forfar Yeomanry, 1939-45; served on Fife County Council, 1951-61; MP (Conservative), East Fife, 1961-79; Chairman, Conservative Party in Scotland, 1965-67; Lord High Commissioner, General Assembly, Church of Scotland, 1982, 1983. Recreation: gardening. Address: (h.) Montrave, Leven, Fife, KY8 5NY; T.-Leven 426159.

Gilmour, William McIntosh, OStJ, BL. Honorary Sheriff, Dumbarton; Lawyer; b. 9.3.23, Newcastle-upon-Tyne; m., Elinor Adams. Educ. Hillhead High School; Cally House, Gatehouse of Fleet; Glasgow University. Early experience with legal firms in Glasgow; became Partner, latterly Senior Partner, in firm in Dunbartonshire; now retired; former Dean, Faculty of Solicitors in Dunbartonshire; former Member and Past President, Clydebank Rotary Club; Past Deacon, Society of Deacons and Free Presces; former Chairman for Dunbartonshire, Order of St. John; Member, Incorporation of Gardeners (Glasgow Trades House). Recreations: dog-walking (formerly, motor sport). Address: (h.) 65 Killermont Road, Bearsden, Glasgow; T.-0141-942 0498.

Gimingham, Professor Charles Henry, OBE, BA, PhD, ScD, FRSE, FIBiol. Regius Professor of Botany, Aberdeen University, 1981-88; b. 28.4.23, Leamington; m., Elizabeth Caroline Baird; 3 d. Educ. Gresham's School, Holt, Norfolk; Emmanuel College, Cambridge. Research Assistant, Imperial College, London, 1944-45; Department of Botany, Aberdeen University: Assistant, 1946-48, Lecturer, 1948-61, Senior Lecturer, 1961-64, Reader, 1964-69, Professor, since 1969, Head of Department, 1981-88; Member: Scottish Committee of Nature Conservancy, 1966-69, Scottish Advisory Committee, Nature Conservancy Council, 1970-80, Countryside Commission for Scotland, 1980-92; President, Botanical Society of Edinburgh, 1982-84; Vice-Chairman, NE Regional Board, Nature Conservancy Council for Scotland, 1991-92; Member, NE Regional Board, SNH, since 1992; Member, Board of Management, Hill Farming Research Organisation, 1981-87; Member, Governing Body, Aberdeen College of Education, 1981-87; Member, Council of Management, Macaulay Institute for Soil Research, 1983-87; Member, Board of Management, Macaulay Land Use Research Institute, 1987- 90; British Ecological Society: Joint Secretary, 1956-61, Vice-President, 1962-64, Joint Editor, Journal of Ecology, 1975-78, President, 1986-87. Publications: Ecology of Heathlands, 1972; Introduction to Heathland Ecology, 1975; Lowland Heathland Management Handbook, 1992. Recreations: hill-walking; photography; history and culture of Japan. Address: (h.) 4 Gowanbrae Road, Bieldside, Aberdeen.

Gimson, George Stanley, QC (Scot). Chairman, Pensions Appeals Tribunals, Scotland, since 1975; b. 1915. Educ. High School of Glasgow; Glasgow University. Advocate, 1949; Sheriff Principal of Aberdeen, Kincardine and Banff, 1972-74; Sheriff Principal of Grampian, Highland and Islands, 1975-82; Member, Edinburgh Central Hospitals Board, 1960-70 (Chairman, 1964-70); Director, SNO Society Ltd., 1962-80; Trustee, National Library of Scotland, 1963-76; Chairman, RSSPCC, Edinburgh, 1972-76; Hon. LLD, Aberdeen, 1981. Address: (h.) 11 Royal Circus, Edinburgh, EH3 6TL.

Girdwood, Professor Ronald Haxton, CBE, MB, ChB (Hons), MD, PhD, FRCPEd, FRCP, FRCPI, FRCPath, Hon. FACP, Hon. FRACP, FRSE. President, Royal College of Physicians of Edinburgh, 1982-85; Chairman, Scottish National Blood Transfusion Association, 1980-95; b. 19.3.17, Arbroath; m., Mary Elizabeth Williams; 1 s.; 1 d. Educ. Daniel Stewart's College, Edinburgh; Edinburgh University; Michigan University. Army service, RAMC,

UK and India, 1942-46, successively as Lt., Captain, Major and Lt.-Col. (when posted to Burma); Lecturer, then Senior Lecturer, Reader in Medicine, Edinburgh University, 1946-62; Research Fellow, Michigan University, 1948-49; Consultant Physician, Edinburgh Royal Infirmary, 1950-82; Professor of Therapeutics and Clinical Pharmacology, Edinburgh University, 1962-83 (Dean, Faculty of Medicine, 1975-79); Chairman, Scottish Group, Nutrition Society, 1961-62; President, British Society for Haematology, 1963-64; Chairman, Executive Committee, Edinburgh and SE Scotland Blood Transfusion Association, 1970-95; Member, UK Committee on Safety of Medicines, 1972-83; Chairman, Medico-Pharmaceutical Forum, 1985-87; President, University of Edinburgh Graduates' Association, 1991-92; Member, Board of Governors, St. Columba's Hospice, since 1985; Suniti Panja Gold Medal, Calcutta School of Tropical Medicine, 1980; given the Freedom of Sirajgunj, Bangladesh, 1984; Oliver Memorial Award for services to blood transfusion, 1991. Publications: Travels with a Stethoscope, 1991; editor of four medical books and more than 300 medical papers. Recreations: writing; photography. Address: (h.) 2 Hermitage Drive, Edinburgh, EH10 6DD; T.-0131-447 5137.

Glasby, Michael Arthur, BM, BCh, MA, MSc (Oxon), MA (Cantab), CBiol, MIBiol, FRCS (Edin), FRCS (Eng). Reader in Anatomy, Edinburgh University, since 1992; b. 29.10.48, Nottingham; m., Celia M.E. Robinson. Educ. High Pavement Grammar School, Nottingham; Christ Church, Oxford; Oxford Medical School. Senior Scholar and Assistant Tutor in Physiology, Christ Church, Oxford, 1971-76; Surgeon, Harefield Hospital Transplant Trust, 1981-83; Fellow and Lecturer in Anatomy, New Hall, Cambridge, 1983-87; Lecturer in Anatomy, Royal College of Surgeons of England, 1984-87; joined Edinburgh University as Lecturer, 1987. Editor, anatomy textbook for surgeons and physiology textbook for surgeons; numerous articles. Recreations: golf; Latin and Greek literature; music; beekeeping; wine. Address: (b.) Department of Anatomy, Edinburgh University, Edinburgh, EH8 9AG; T.-0131-650 3112.

Glasgow, 10th Earl of (Patrick Robin Archibald Boyle). Television Director/Producer; b. 30.7.39; m., Isabel Mary James; 1 s.; 1 d. Educ. Eton; Paris University. Sub.-Lt., RNR, 1959-60; Producer/Director, Yorkshire TV, 1968-70; freelance Film Producer, since 1971; formed and manage Kelburn Country Centre, 1977. Address (b.) Kelburn Castle, Fairlie, Ayrshire, KA29 0BE; T.-01475 568685.

Glasier, Anna, MB, ChB, BSc, MRCOG, MD. Director, Lothian Health Board Family Planning and Well Woman Services, since 1990; Senior Lecturer, Department of Obstetrics and Gynaecology, Edinburgh University, since 1990; Consultant Gynaecologist, Lothian Health Board, since 1989; b. 16.4.50, Salisbury. Educ. Lord Digby's School, Sherborne. Clinical Research Scientist, Medical Research Council Centre for Reproductive Biology, Edinburgh, 1989-90. Recreations: ski mountaineering; sailing. Address: (b.) 18 Dean Terrace, Edinburgh, EH4 1NL; T.-0131-332 7941.

Glass, Alexander, OBE, MA, DipEd. Rector, Dingwall Academy, since 1977; b. 1.6.32, Dunbar; m., Edith Margaret Duncan Baxter; 3 d. Educ. Dunbar Grammar School; Edinburgh University; Heidelberg University; University of Aix-en-Provence. Teacher of Modern Languages, Montrose Academy, 1958-60; Special Assistant Teacher of Modern Languages, Oban High School, 1960-62; Principal Teacher of Modern Languages, Nairn Academy, 1962-65; Principal Teacher of French and Assistant Rector, Perth Academy, 1965-72; Rector, Milne's High School, Fochabers, 1972-77. Chairman, COSPEN; former President, Highland Secondary Headteachers' Association; former Chairman, Highland Region Working Party for Modern Languages; Regional Chairman, Highland

Region Children's Panel; former Chairman, Children's Panel Chairmen's Group; Reader, Church of Scotland; Licentiate, Auxiliary Ministry, Church of Scotland; Chairman, Inverness District, Scottish Community Drama Association; Chairman and Secretary, Scottish Secondary Schools' Travel Trust; Churchill Fellow, 1991. Recreations: amateur drama; foreign travel; Rotary. Address: (h.) Craigton, Tulloch Avenue, Dingwall, IV15 9LH; T.-01349 863258.

Glen, Alastair Campbell Agnew, MD, BSc, FRCP(Glas). Consultant Clinical Biochemist, Victoria Infirmary, Glasgow, since 1970; Honorary Senior Lecturer, Glasgow University, since 1991; Clinical Director, Victoria Infirmary Laboratories, since 1994; b. 3.8.36, Glasgow; m., Lesley Gordon; 2 s.; 1 d. Educ. Glasgow Academy; Glasgow University. Research Associate, Massachusetts Institute of Technology, 1966. Recreations: almost anything from skiing and angling to Scottish politics. Address: (h.) 276A Nithsdale Road, Glasgow, G41 5LP; T.-0141-427 2131.

Glen, Alexander Iain Munro, MB, ChB, FRCPsych, FRCP(Glas), DPM. Hon. Consultant Psychiatrist, Highland Health Board; Hon. Senior Lecturer, Aberdeen University, since 1986; Research Director, Highland Psychiatric Research Group, since 1981; Member (SNP), Highland Regional Council, since 1990; Member, SNP National Council; SNP Shadow Health Spokesperson; b. 25.5.30, Glasgow; m., Dr. Evelyne Glen; 2 s.; 2 d. Educ. Albert Road Academy, Glasgow; Glasgow University. National Service as Surgeon Lt., RNVR, 3rd Frigate Squadron, Far East, 1955-57; Research Fellow, Psychiatry, Glasgow University, 1964-68; Medical Research Council Clinical Psychiatry Unit, 1968-72; MRC Brain Metabolism Unit, Research Fellow, Pharmacology, Edinburgh University, 1972-81. Recreations: politics; poetry; Scotland. Address: (h.) Dalnavert Community Co-operative, Dalnavert, by Kincraig, PH21 1NG; T.-0154 04 347.

Glen, Duncan Munro. Writer and Lecturer; Sole Owner, Akros Publications, since 1960; b. 11.1.33, Cambuslang; m., Margaret Eadie; 1 s.; 1 d. Educ. West Coats, Cambuslang; Edinburgh College of Art. Book Designer, HM Stationery Office, London; Lecturer in Typography; Editor, Robert Gibson & Co. Ltd.; Lecturer, then Senior Lecturer, then Head of Graphic Design, Lancashire Polytechnic; Professor and Head, Department of Visual Communication, Nottingham Trent University (Emeritus Professor); Editor, Akros, poetry magazine, 1-51. Author and editor of many books including Hugh MacDiarmid and The Scottish Renaissance, Selected Essays of Hugh MacDiarmid, In Appearances: Poems, The Autobiography of a Poet, Makars' Walk, The Poetry of the Scots, Selected Poems 1965-1990, A Journey Into Scotland, Hugh MacDiarmid: Out of Langholm and Into the World; A Nation in a Parish. Recreation: walking. Address: (h.) 18 Warrender Park Terrace, Edinburgh, EH9 1EF; T.-0131-229 3680.

Glen, Eric Stanger, MB, ChB, FRCSGlas, FRCSEdin. Consultant Urological Surgeon, Walton Urological Teaching and Research Centre, Southern General Hospital, Glasgow; Honorary Clinical Senior Lecturer, Glasgow University; Member, Surgical Examination Panel, Royal College of Physicians and Surgeons of Glasgow; b. 20.10.34, Glasgow; m., Dr. Patricia. Educ. Glasgow University. Pre-Consultant posts, Western and Victoria Infirmaries, Glasgow; Ship Surgeon, Royal Fleet Auxiliary. Chairman, Greater Glasgow Health Board Incontinence Resource Group; Past Chairman, Area Medical Committee; Founder and former Secretary, International Continence Society; Founder, Urological Computing Society. Publications: chapters in books; papers on urodynamics, urology and computing. Recreations: travel; writing;

computer applications. Address: (h.) 9 St. John's Road, Pollokshields, Glasgow, G41 5RJ; T.-0141-423 0759.

Glen, Norman MacLeod, CBE, TD, MA, JP. Member, Dumbarton District Council, since 1974; b. 22.12.11, Glasgow; m., Dr. Janet M.S. Glen (deceased); 2 s.; 2 d. Educ. Glasgow Academy; Glasgow University. Retail trade as Buyer, Director and Managing Director, John Glen & Co. Ltd., Glasgow, 1932-74; War Service, six years; TA (mostly 474 HAA Regt RA), 1938-56 (Lt. Colonel, 1954-56); Parliamentary candidate (Liberal), 1945, (Conservative), 1951, 1955, 1959, 1964, 1966 and By-Election, Woodside, 1962; elected, Helensburgh Town Council, 1966 (last Provost of Helensburgh, 1970-75); Elder, West Kirk of Helensburgh. Recreation: walking. Address: (h.) Flat 11, Queen's Court, Helensburgh, G84 7AH; T.-01436 3497.

Glen, Robbie, BA, FIMgt. Governor, H.M. Institution, Cornton Vale, since 1994; b. 31.5.46, Hamilton; m., Elspeth Reyburn; 2 d. Educ. Hamilton Academy; Strathclyde University. Assistant Governor, Polmont Borstal, 1969; Assistant Governor, Longriggend Remand Institution, 1972; Deputy Governor, Edinburgh Prison, 1976; seconded to Prison HQ Admin Branch, 1979; Governor, Castle Huntly Borstal, 1981; Governor, Dungavel Prison, 1984; seconded to Prisons Inspectorate, 1986; returned to Dunvagel, 1987, transferred to Prisons HQ Operations Branch; Deputy Governor/Acting Governor, Barlinnie Prison, 1991. Trustee, Hamilton and District International Sports Trust; Barker, Variety Club of Great Britain. Recreations: golf; reading. Address: (b.) Cornton Vale, Cornton Road, Stirling, FK9 5NY; T.-01786 832591.

Glen, William Hamish. Artistic Director, Dundee Rep, since 1992; b. 20.12.57, Edinburgh; m., Denise Maria Winford. Educ. Edinburgh Academy. ASM, Traverse Theatre, 1979-81; Trainee Director, Tron Theatre, 1986-87, Associate Director, 1988-89; Artistic Director, Winged Horse, 1990-92; worked as freelance director in Lithuania and Finland. Address: (b.) Tay Square, Dundee; T.-01382 227684.

Glenarthur, 4th Baron (Simon Mark Arthur), Bt, DL, MCIT, FRAeS. Chairman, St. Mary's Hospital, Paddington, NHS Trust, since 1991; Consultant, British Aerospace PLC, since 1989, Hanson PLC, since 1989, Chevron UK Ltd., since 1994; Deputy Chairman, Hanson Pacific Ltd., since 1994; Chairman, British Helicopter Advisory Board, since 1992; President, National Council for Civil Protection, since 1991; DL, Aberdeenshire, since 1987; b. 7.10.44; m.; 1 s.; 1 d. Educ. Eton. Retired Major, 10th Royal Hussars (PWO); Helicopter Captain, British Airways, 1976-82; a Lord in Waiting, 1982-83; Parliamentary Under Secretary of State: Department of Health and Social Security, 1983-85, Home Office, 1985-86; Minister of State, Scottish Office, 1986-87; Minister of State, Foreign and Commonwealth Office, 1987-89; Member (Brigadier), Queen's Bodyguard for Scotland (Royal Company of Archers); Scottish Patron, The Butler Trust, since 1994. Address: (b.) House of Lords, London, SW1A 0PW.

Gloag, Ann. Group Managing Director, Stagecoach Holdings. Address: (b.) Charlotte House, 20 Charlotte Street, Perth, PH1 5LL.

Gloag, Matthew Irving. Director, Matthew Gloag & Son Ltd., since 1971; b. 1.12.47, Perth; m., Dilly Moon; 2 d. Chairman, Scottish Licensed Trade Association, 1984-85 and 1995-96. Address: (b.) 33 Kinnoull Street, Perth, PH1 5EU; T.-01738 621101.

Glover, Professor David Moore, BA, PhD, FRSE. Professor of Molecular Genetics, Dundee University, since 1989; Director, Cancer Research Campaign Cell Cycle Group, since 1989; b. 28.3.48, Chapeltown; m., Barbara A.

Spruce. Educ. Broadway Grammar School, Barnsley; Fitzwilliam College, Cambridge. Postdoctoral Fellow, Stanford University, California, 1972-75; Imperial College, London, 1975-89, latterly as Head, Biochemistry Department. Publications: 100 scientific papers; two books; Editor, eight books. Address: (b.) CRC Laboratories, Medical Sciences Institute, Dundee, DD1 4HN; T.-01382 344793.

Glover, John, BSc (Econ). Rules Secretary, Royal and Ancient Golf Club of St. Andrews, since 1981; b. 3.3.33, Belfast; m., Maureen Elizabeth; 3 d. Educ. Campbell College, Belfast; Queens University, Belfast. Address: (h.) Braetrees, 96A Hepburn Gardens, St. Andrews, KY16 9LN; T.-01334 475595.

Glover, John McTaggart (Ian). Director and Deputy Chief Executive, Dunfermline Building Society, since 1981; b. 6.4.35, Hawick; m., Jessie Nicholson Stewart; 1 d. Educ. Hawick High School. Standard Life Assurance Co., 1956-61; Scottish Life Assurance, 1961-72; Edinburgh Building Society, 1972-80; Edinburgh and Paisley Building Society, 1980-81. Recreations: rugby; curling; hill-walking; Rotary. Address: (h.) 17 Hillpark Crescent, Edinburgh, EH4 7BG; T.-0131-336 5637.

Glover, Rev. Robert Lindsay, BMus, BD, ARCO. Minister, St. George's West, Edinburgh, since 1985; b. 21.7.45, Watford; m., Elizabeth Mary Brown; 2 s.; 2 d. Educ. Langholm Academy; Dumfries Academy; Glasgow University. Minister, Newton Parish, near Dalkeith, 1971-76; Minister, St. Vigeans Parish, Arbroath, 1976-85. Recreations: music (organ, piano, accordion); caravanning; following Heart of Midlothian FC; reading. Address: 58 Shandwick Place, Edinburgh, EH2 4RT.

Glover, Sue, MA. Writer; b. 1.3.43, Edinburgh; m., John Glover; 2 s. Educ. St. George's School, Edinburgh; Montpellier University; Edinburgh University. Original drama and other scriptwriting for radio, television and theatre; theatre productions include The Seal Wife, Edinburgh Festival, 1980, An Island in Largo, Byre Theatre, 1981, The Bubble Boy, Glasgow Tron, 1981, The Straw Chair, Traverse Theatre, 1988; Bondagers, Traverse Theatre, 1991 (winner, 1990 LWT Plays on Stage Award); Sacred Hearts, 1994; television work includes The Spaver Connection and Mme Montand and Mrs Miller, Dear Life; televised version of The Bubble Boy won a silver medal, New York Film and Television Festival, and a merit, Chicago International Film Festival, 1983. Recreations: house and garden. Address: Castlefield Cottage, Castlebank Road, Cupar, Fife; T.-Cupar 653664.

Goddard, Kenneth George, BA, IPFA. Director of Finance, Skye and Lochalsh District Council, since 1981; b. 14.1.47, Pembroke Dock; m., Jennifer; 2 s. Educ. Pembroke Grammar School; St. Davids University, Lampeter. Inland Revenue, 1970-72; Pembroke Borough Council, 1972-74; South Pembrokeshire District Council, 1974-78; joined Skye and Lochalsh District Council, 1978. Address: (b.) Park Road, Portree, Isle of Skye, IV51 9EP; T.-01478 2341.

Godden, Anthony John, BSc (Hons), FRSH, AIHE. Principal, West Lothian College, since 1987; b. 26.3.46, Swansea; m., Kelly; 1 s.; 1 d. Educ. Dynevor Grammar School; North East London Polytechnic; Open University. Lecturer, Bridgnorth College of Further Education, 1970-73; Social Tutor, Airedale and Wharfedale College of Further Education, 1973-75; Warden, Mildmay Hall, and Head, Section of General Studies and Information Sciences, Essex Institute of Higher Education, 1975-78; Assistant Inspector, Kent County Council Education Department, 1978-82; Principal, Gainsborough College of Further Education, 1982-86.Knight of the Holy Sepulchre of Jerusalem; Chairman, Almond Housing Association, Livingston. Recreations: armchair sport; theatre; guitar;

travel. Address: (b.) West Lothian College, Marjoribanks Street, Bathgate, EH48 1QJ; T.-01506 634300.

Godden, Tony Richard Hillier, CB, BSc (Econ). Member, The Council on Tribunals and its Scottish Committee, 1988-94; Member, Advisory Board on Ancient Monuments, since 1990; Secretary, Friends of the Royal Scottish Academy, since 1988; Secretary, Scottish Development Department, 1980-87; b. 13.11.27, Barnstaple; m., Marjorie Florence Snell; 1 s.; 2 d. Educ. Barnstaple Grammar School; London School of Economics. Commissioned, RAF Education Branch, 1950; entered Civil Service, 1951; first appointed to Colonial Office; Private Secretary to Parliamentary Under Secretary of State, 1954-55; seconded to Cabinet Office, 1957-59; joined Scottish Home Department, 1961; Assistant Secretary, Scottish Development Department, 1964; Under Secretary, 1969; Secretary, Scottish Economic Planning Development, 1973-80. Address:9 Ross Road, Edinburgh, EH16 5QN.

Godfray, Martin Francis, BSc, CChem, FRSC, MChemA. Public Analyst, Official Agricultural Analyst and Scientific Adviser, Lothian, Borders and Highland Regional Councils and Orkney and Shetland Islands Councils, since 1980; b. 10.5.45, Barry, Glamorgan; m., Heather Jean; 1 s.; 2 d. Educ. Barry Boys Grammar Technical School; Birmingham University. Deputy Public Analyst and Deputy Agricultural Analyst, London Boroughs of Southwark, Greenwich, Islington and Tower Hamlets, 1973-80. Address: (b.) Regional Laboratory, 4 Marine Esplanade, Edinburgh, EH6 7LU; T.-0131-553 1171.

Godfrey, Professor Alan Dearn, BA (Hons), FCCA. Professor of Accounting and Head, Department of Finance and Accounting, Glasgow Caledonian University; b. 12.5.46, Falkirk; 1 s.; 1 d. Educ. Falkirk High School; Strathclyde University. Financial Consultant, Engineering Services Ltd., 1972-76; Lecturer, then Senior Lecturer, Glasgow College, 1976-88; Depute Head of Department, then Acting Head of Department, Glasgow Polytechnic, 1988-93. Recreations: music; golf. Address: (b.) Department of Finance and Accounting, Glasgow Caledonian University, Glasgow, G4 0BA; T.-0141-331 3361.

Godman, Norman. MP (Labour), Greenock and Port Glasgow, since 1983; b. 1938. Address: (b.) House of Commons, London, SW1A 0AA.

Gold, Lex. Director, CBI in Scotland; former Managing Director, Scottish Enterprise; b. 14.12.40, Rigside; m., Eleanor; 1 s.; 1 d. Educ. Lanark Grammar School. Sub-Editor, Daily Record; professional footballer; joined Civil Service, Glasgow, 1960; Inland Revenue, two years; Civil Service Department, four years; Home Office, 21 years; Training Agency, three years. Address: (b.) 5 Claremont Terrace, Glasgow, G3 7XT.

Goldberg, Professor Sir Abraham, KB, MD, DSc, FRCP, FRCPEdin, FRCPGlas, FRSE. Regius Professor of the Practice of Medicine, Glasgow University, 1978-89; Founder President, Faculty of Pharmaceutical Medicine of Royal Colleges of Physicians of UK, 1989; b. 7.12.23, Edinburgh; m., Clarice Cussin; 2 s.; 1 d. Educ. Sciennes School, Edinburgh; George Heriot's School, Edinburgh; Edinburgh University. House Physician, Royal Hospital for Sick Children, Edinburgh, 1946-47; RAMC, 1947-49 (granted rank of honorary Major on discharge); Nuffield Research Fellow, UCH Medical School, London, 1952-54; Eli Lilly Travelling Fellow in Medicine (MRC), Department of Medicine, Utah University, 1954-56; Glasgow University: Lecturer in Medicine, 1956-59, Titular Professor of Medicine, 1967-70, Regius Professor of Materia Medica, 1970-78. Chairman, Grants Committee 1, Clinical Research Board, MRC, 1973-77; Member, Chief Scientist's Committee, SHHD, 1977-83; Chairman,

Biomedical Research Committee, SHHD, 1977-83; Editor, Scottish Medical Journal, 1962-63; Chairman, Committee on Safety of Medicines, 1980-86; Fitzpatrick Lecturer, Royal College of Physicians, London, 1988; Goodall Memorial Lecturer, Royal College of Physicians and Surgeons of Glasgow, 1989; City of Glasgow Lord Provost's Award, 1988. Publications: Disorders of Porphyrin Metabolism (Co-author), 1987; Recent Advances in Haematology (Joint Editor), 1971; Clinics in Haematology "The Porphyrias" (Co-author), 1980. Recreations: medical history; literature; writing; walking; swimming. Address: (h.) 16 Birnam Crescent, Bearsden, Glasgow, G61 2AU.

Golden, Gerry. Managing Director, Lilley plc. Address: (b.) 331 Charles Street, Glasgow, G21 2QX.

Goldie, Annabel Macnicoll, DL, LLB, NP. Deputy Lord Lieutenant, Renfrewshire, since 1993; Deputy Chairman, Scottish Conservative Party, since 1995; Director, Prince's Scottish Youth Business Trust, since 1994; b. 27.2.50, Glasgow. Educ. Greenock Academy; Strathclyde University. Solicitor in private practice, since 1978. Elder, Church of Scotland; Member, West of Scotland Advisory Board, Salvation Army; Member, Strathclyde University Court. Recreations: weeding; walking; dogs; swimming. Address: (h.) Levernholm, Gledstane Road, Bishopton, PA7 5AU; T.-0141-248 3020.

Goldie, David. Farmer; Director, Royal Highland and Agricultural Society, since 1976 (Chairman of Directors, 1987-88); b. 30.7.37, Dumfries; m., Ann Irving; 3 s. Educ. Wallace Hall Academy, Closeburn, Thornhill. Chairman, Annandale Young Farmers Club, 1958-59; Elder and Treasurer, Ruthwell Church, since 1968; founder Chairman, local Community Council, 1978-81; Chairman, Dumfries Agricultural Society, 1977-79; Member, Scottish Training Committee, Agricultural Training Board, 1982-86; Member, Scottish Agricultural Development Council, 1983-86. Address: (h.) Longbridgemuir, Clarencefield, Dumfries; T.-0138 787 210.

Good, John Russell. Secretary, Royal Highland and Agricultural Society of Scotland, since 1981; b. 9.8.41, Kirkcudbright; m., Muriel Law Bathgate; 2 s.; 1 d. Educ. Kirkcudbright Academy. Trainee and junior bank officer, 1958-64; Group Secretary in North Lanarkshire, NFU of Scotland, 1964--66; Procedures Analyst, Caterpillar Tractor Co., Uddingston, 1966-67; joined RHASS, 1967. Recreations: gardening; swimming; skiing; music. Address: (h.) 4 Chesterhall Steading, Longniddry, East Lothian, EH32 0PQ; T.-0187 585 2888.

Goodall, Alexander, MA (Hons). Principal, Wester Hailes Education Centre, since 1982; b. 25.8.38, Dolphinton, Peebles-shire; 1 s.; 1 d. Educ. Portobello High School; Edinburgh University; Moray House College of Education. Teacher of History, Niddrie Marischal Secondary School, 1961-64; Education Officer, Teso College, Uganda, 1964-69; Preston Lodge High School: Principal Teacher of History, 1969-74, Assistant Head Teacher, 1974-78; Depute Principal, Wester Hailes Education Centre, 1978-82. Editor, Scottish History Teaching Review. Publication: Economics and Development (Co-author). Recreations: trout angling; rubber bridge. Address: (b.) 5 Murrayburn Drive, Edinburgh; T.-0131-442 2201.

Gooday, Professor Graham W., BSc, PhD, FRSE. Professor of Microbiology, Aberdeen University, since 1984; b. 19.2.42, Colchester; m., Margaret A. Mealing; 1 s.; 2 d. Educ. Hove Grammar School for Boys; Bristol University. VSO, Sierra Leone, 1964; Research Fellowships: Leeds University, 1967, Glasgow and Oxford Universities, 1969; Lecturer, Senior Lecturer, Reader, Aberdeen University, 1972-84; Member, Aquatic Life Sciences Committee, NERC, 1984-87; Council Member,

British Mycological Society, 1974-77, President, 1993; Council Member, Society for General Microbiology, 1976-80; awarded first Fleming Lectureship, Society for General Microbiology, 1976. Recreation: open countryside. Address: (b.) Department of Molecular and Cell Biology, Marischal College, University, Aberdeen, AB9 1AS; T.-01224 273147.

Goodman, Professor Anthony Eric, MA (Oxon), BLitt (Oxon), FRHistS. Professor of Medieval and Renaissance History, Edinburgh University, since 1993; b. 21.7.36, London; m., Jacqueline; 1 d. Educ. Selhurst Grammar School, Croydon; Magdalen College, Oxford. Joined staff, Edinburgh University, 1961. Secretary, Edinburgh Branch, Historical Association, since 1975. Publications: The Loyal Conspiracy, 1971; A History of England from Edward II to James I, 1977; The Wars of the Roses, 1981; A Traveller's Guide to Medieval Britain (Co-author), 1986; The New Monarchy, 1471-1534, 1988; John of Gaunt, 1992. Address: (h.) 23 Kirkhill Gardens, Edinburgh, EH16 5DF; T.-0131-667 5988.

Goodman, Professor Timothy Nicholas Trewin, BA, MSc, DPhil. Professor of Applied Analysis, Dundee University, since 1994; b. 29.4.47, London; m., Choo-Tin; 3 d. Educ. Judd School; St. John's College, Cambridge; Warwick University; Sussex University. Teacher, VSO, 1973; Teacher, Singapore, 1974-75; Lecturer, Universiti Sains Malaysia, 1975-79; Lecturer, Dundee University, 1979-90; Professor Texas A&M University, 1990-91; Reader, Dundee University, 1992-94. Recreations: walking; Scottish country dancing; music. Address: (b.) Department of Mathematics and Computer Science, Dundee University, Dundee; T.-01382 344488.

Goodsman, James Melville, CBE. Managing Director, Michael Fraser & Co. Ltd; Director, Consensus Ltd.; Director, Conservative Party in Scotland, 1990-92; b. 6.2.47, St. Andrews; m., Victoria Smitherman. Educ. Elgin Academy. Conservative Party Agent, 1968-80; Deputy Central Office Agent, North West Area, 1980-84; Assistant Director (Community Affairs), CCO, 1984-89; Head, Community and Legal Department, CCO, 1989-90. Recreations: golf; Church music; Scotland's heritage. Address: (b.) Treeton House, Ardersier, Inverness; T.-01667 462111.

Goodwin, Sir Matthew Dean, CA. Former Chairman, Hewden Stuart PLC; b. 12.6.29, Dalserf; m., Margaret Eileen Colvil; 2 d. Educ. Glasgow Academy.

Goodwin, Michael David, OBE. Managing Director, Electrical Contractors' Association of Scotland, since 1991; Director, Scottish Electrical Contractors' Insurance, since 1991; Executive Trustee, Scottish Electrical Charitable Training Trust, since 1991; b. 18.1.40, Colombo; m., Anne Dundas, nee Finlay; 2 s.; 2 d. Educ. Stowe School; Britannia Royal Naval College, Dartmouth. Graduated as full career commission officer, Royal Navy, 1960; Sub Lt., 1961; Lt., 1962; graduated RN Junior Staff Course, 1964; exchange service with Royal Australian Navy, 1968-70; Lt. Commander, 1970; graduated RAF Senior Staff Course, 1973; Commander, 1978; NATO appointments, 1980-86; retired, 1988; Assistant Director, Administration, Information and Settlement Division, International Stock Exchange, 1988-91. Recreations: tennis; theatre; music; reading; clay shooting; swimming. Address: (b.) Bush House, Bush Estate, Midlothian, EH26 0SB; T.-0131-445 5577.

Goodwin, Michael John, BSc, DipEd. Rector, Carrick Academy, since 1990; b. 17.9.45, Aberdeen; m., Winifred Ann; 1 s.; 1 d. Educ. High School of Glasgow; Glasgow University; University of East Africa. Teacher of Physics, Uganda, 1968-70; Teacher of Mathematics, Dumbarton and Glasgow, 1970-74; Principal Teacher of Mathematics,

Cleveden Secretary, Glasgow, 1974-84; Depute Headteacher, Doon Academy, 1984-90. Recreations: hill-walking; rugby; traditional music; classical music. Address: (h.) 23 Ashgrove Street, Ayr; T.-01292 284026.

Goold, Lord (James Duncan), Life Peer (1987), Kt (1983), CA, DUniv., FRSA, FCIOB, FFB. Lord Lieutenant of Renfrewshire, since 1994; Chairman, Mactaggart & Mickel Ltd., since 1993 (Director since 1965); Director: American Trust PLC, since 1984, Gibson & Goold Ltd., since 1978, Edinburgh Oil & Gas PLC, since 1987, b. 28.5.34, Glasgow; m., Sheena Paton (deceased); 2 s.; 1 d. Educ. Glasgow Academy. President: Scottish Building Contractors' Association, 1971, Scottish National Federation of Building Trades Employers, 1977-78; Honorary Treasurer, Scottish Building Employers' Federation, 1979-81; Chairman, Conservative Board of Finance Scotland, 1980-83; Honorary Treasurer, Scottish Conservative and Unionist Association, 1980-83; Honorary President, Eastwood Conservative Association, 1978-95; Chairman, East Renfrewshire Conservative Association, 1974-77; Chairman, CBI Scotland, 1981-83; Chairman, Scottish Conservative Party, 1983-89; Chairman, Royal Scottish Orchestra, 1991-93; Member, Scottish Hospital Endowments Research Trust; Chairman of Court, Strathclyde University, since 1993; President, Glasgow Bn., Boys Brigade, 1987-93; Elder, Mearns Parish Church; Trustee, Ferguson Bequest; Vice President, Tenovus-Scotland. Recreations: golf; walking. Address: (b.) 126 West Regent Street, Glasgow, G2 2BH; T.-0141-332 0001.

Gordon, Alexander Grant. Chairman, William Grant & Sons Distillers Ltd. Address: (b.) Phoenix Crescent, Strathclyde Business Park, Motherwell, ML4 3AN.

Gordon, Boyd. Fisheries Consultant; Fisheries Secretary, Department of Agriculture and Fisheries for Scotland, 1982-86; b. 18.9.26, Musselburgh; m., Elizabeth Mabel Smith; 2 d. Educ. Musselburgh Grammar School. Military Service, Royal Scots; joined Civil Service, initially with Ministry of Labour, then Inland Revenue; joined Department of Agriculture and Fisheries for Scotland, 1953; Principal dealing with Salmon and Freshwater Fisheries Administration and Fisheries Research and Development, 1962-73; Assistant Secretary, Agriculture Economic Policy, EEC Co-ordination and Agriculture Marketing, 1973-82. Recreations: golf; gardening; local Church matters; violin playing. Address: (h.) 87 Duddingston Road, Edinburgh; T.-0131-669 4380.

Gordon, Professor George, MA (Hons), PhD. Director of Academic Practice, Strathclyde University, since 1987; Governor, Jordanhill College of Education, 1982-93 (Chairman, 1987-93); b. 14.11.39, Edinburgh; m., Jane Taylor Collins; 2 d. Educ. George Heriot's School; Edinburgh University. Edinburgh University: Vans Dunlop Scholar, 1962-64, Demonstrator, 1964-65; Strathclyde University: Assistant Lecturer, 1965-66, Lecturer, 1966-80, Dean, Faculty of Arts and Social Studies, 1984-87; served on SUCE and SCE Geography Panels, SCOVACT, and General Teaching Council for Scotland; Convener, Publications Committee, Royal Scottish Geographical Society; Vice President, British Association for the Advancement of Science; former Member, General Assembly of Open University; Member, Senate, Strathclyde University. Publications: Regional Cities of the UK 1890-1980 (Editor), 1986; Perspectives of the Scottish City (Editor), 1985; Scottish Urban History, 1983; The Making of Scottish Geography (Co-author), 1984; Settlement Geography, 1983; Urban Geography, 1981. Recreations: theatre-going; watching sport. Address: (b.) Centre for Academic Practice, Strathclyde University, 50 George Street, Glasgow; T.-0141-552 4400, Ext. 2637.

Gordon, George, MB, ChB, FRCSE, FRCOG. Consultant Obstetrician and Gynaecologist, Dumfries and Galloway, since 1969; b. 4.9.36, Markinch, Fife; m., Rosemary Gould Hutchison; 1 s.; 1 d. Educ. Bell Baxter School; Edinburgh University. Senior Registrar, Western General Hospital, Edinburgh, 1966-69; Chairman, Scottish Confidential Enquiry into Maternal Mortality; Member, Central Midwives Board for Scotland, 1978-84; Examiner, FRCS Edinburgh, MRCOG and DRCOG London; Clinical Director, Local Acute and Maternity Hospitals Trust; Honorary Secretary, Dumfries and Stewartry Division, BMA, 1975-87; Fellow of BMA. Recreations: music; Scottish literature; golf; gardening. Address: (b.) Dumfries and Galloway Royal Infirmary, Bankend Road, Dumfries, DG1 4AP.

Gordon, George Park Douglas, BSc (Hons). HM Chief Inspector of Schools, Western Division; b. 23.10.37, Peterhead; m., Karein L.M.; 1 s.; 1 d. Educ. Peterhead Academy; Aberdeen University; Aberdeen College of Education. Teacher of Science, Peterhead Academy, 1961-64; Principal Teacher of Science, Dornoch Academy, 1964-67; Assistant Adviser in Science, Glasgow, 1967-69; HM Inspector of Schools, 1969-75, Higher Grade, 1975-86; HM Chief Inspector of Schools: Education (Basic and Special), 1986-88, Education 5-14 and Special Educational Needs, 1988-89, Western Division and Special Educational Needs, 1989-92, Western Division and Staff Development and Training, 1992-95. Recreations: golf; squash; gardening; reading; walking; spending winter Saturdays watching football and supporting Aberdeen FC. Address: (h.) Suilven, 8 Ewing Walk, Fairways, Milngavie, G62 6EG; T.-0141-956 5131.

Gordon, Sheriff Gerald Henry, QC, MA, LLB, PhD, LLD. Sheriff of Glasgow and Strathkelvin, since 1978; Temporary Judge, Court of Session and High Court of Justiciary, since 1992; b. 17.6.29, Glasgow; m., Marjorie Joseph; 1 s.; 2 d. Educ. Queen's Park Senior Secondary School; Glasgow University. Advocate, 1953; Procurator Fiscal Depute, Edinburgh, 1960-65; Edinburgh University: Head, Department of Criminal Law and Criminology, 1965-72, Personal Professor of Criminal Law, 1969-72, Dean, Faculty of Law, 1970-73, Professor of Scots Law, 1972-76; Sheriff of South Strathclyde, Dumfries and Galloway, at Hamilton, 1976-77; Member: Interdepartmental Committee on Scottish Criminal Procedure, 1970-77, Committee on Criminal Appeals and Miscarriages of Justice, since 1995. Publications: Criminal Law of Scotland, 1967, 1978; Renton & Brown's Criminal Procedure (Editor), 1972, 1983. Recreations: Jewish studies; coffee conversation; swimming. Address: (h.) Sheriff Court, Glasgow; T.-0141-429 8888.

Gordon, Rev. Canon Hugh. Chaplain, St. Joseph's House, Edinburgh; b. 18.11.10, Inverness. Educ. Stonyhurst College, Lancashire; Heriot-Watt College, Edinburgh; Oscott College, Birmingham. Ordained, 1937; Curate, Inverness, 1937; Army Chaplain, 1940 (Egypt and El Alamain, 51st Highland Division); Osnabruck, 1946, developing civilian parish church and first Catholic school in Germany after the fall of Hitler; Priest: Stirling, Selkirk, St. Andrews, Edinburgh St. Margaret's and St. John the Evangelist, Linlithgow St. Michael's; founded Linlithgow Scripture Centre for Christian Unity; former Executive Member, Scottish Catholic Lay Apostolate Council; Member: Commission for Christian Doctrine and Unity; Order of Christian Unity; Fellowship of St. Andrew. Recreations: anything to help restoration of Christian unity; stopped tennis, golf, fishing. Address: 47 Gilmore Place, Edinburgh, EH3 9NG; T.-0131-229 1929.

Gordon, James Stuart, CBE, DLitt., MA (Hons). Managing Director, Radio Clyde, since 1973; Chief Executive, Scottish Radio Holdings, since 1991; Member, BP Scottish Advisory Board, since 1991; Director, Clydeport Holdings Ltd., since 1992; Member, Glasgow University Court, since 1984; b. 17.5.36, Glasgow; m.,

Anne Stevenson; 2 s.; 1 d. Educ. St. Aloysius College, Glasgow; Glasgow University (President of the Union, 1958-59). Political Editor, STV, 1965-73. Winner, Observer Mace Debating Tournament, 1957; Sony Special Award for Services to Radio, 1984. Chairman, Scottish Exhibition Centre, 1983-89; Member, Scottish Development Agency, 1981-90. Recreations: his children; genealogy; golf. Address: (b.) Radio Clyde, Clydebank Business Park, Clydebank; T.-0141-306 2202.

Gordon, Canon Kenneth Davidson, MA. Rector, St. Devenick's Episcopal Church, Bieldside, Aberdeen, since 1971; Examining Chaplain to Bishop of Aberdeen and Orkney, 1978-86; Warden of Lay Readers, Diocese of Aberdeen and Orkney, since 1978; b. 27.12.35, Edinburgh; m., Edith Jessica Newing; 2 s. Educ. George Heriot's School, Edinburgh; Edinburgh University; Tyndale Hall, Bristol. Curate, St. Helens Parish Church, Lancashire, 1960-66 (with charge of St. Andrew's Mission Church, 1962-66); Vicar, St. George the Martyr's Parish Church, Bolton, 1966-71; Canon, St. Andrew's Cathedral, Aberdeen, since 1981. Member, Mission Board, General Synod, Scottish Episcopal Church. Address: The Rectory, Bieldside, Aberdeen, AB1 9AP; T.-01224 861552.

Gordon, Richard. Director, Scotch Malt Whisky Society. Address: (b.) 87 Giles Street, The Vaults, Leith, Edinburgh, EH6 6BZ.

Gordon, Robert Smith Benzie, MA. Director of Administrative Services (Under Secretary), Scottish Office, since 1991; b. 7.11.50, Aberdeen; m., Joyce Cordiner; 2 s.; 2 d. Educ. Gordon Schools, Huntly; Aberdeen University. Joined Scottish Office, 1973; Principal, Scottish Development Department, 1979-85; Principal Private Secretary to Secretary of State for Scotland, 1985-87; Assistant Secretary, Department of Agriculture and Fisheries, 1988-90; Assistant Secretary, Management, Organisation and Industrial Relations Division, Scottish Office, 1990-91. Address: (b.) St. Andrew's House, Edinburgh; T.-0131-556 8400.

Gordon, Professor William Morrison, MA, LLB, PhD, FRSE. Douglas Professor of Civil Law, Glasgow University, since 1969; Solicitor (non-practising), since 1956; b. 3.3.33, Inverurie; m., Isabella Evelyn Melitta Robertson; 2 s.; 2 d. Educ. Inverurie Academy; Robert Gordon's College, Aberdeen; Aberdeen University. National Service, Royal Navy, 1955-57; Assistant in Jurisprudence, Aberdeen University, 1957-60; Glasgow University: Lecturer in Civil Law, 1960-65, Senior Lecturer in Law, 1965-69 (and Sub-Dean of Faculty); Dean of Faculty, 1974-76. Elder and Session Clerk, Jordanhill Parish Church; Literary Director, The Stair Society. Publications: Studies in Transfer of Property by Tradition, 1970; Scottish Land Law, 1989; Stair Society Miscellany III, 1992; European Legal History (2nd Ed.), (with others), 1994. Recreation: golf. Address: (b.) School of Law, Stair Building, University, Glasgow, G12 8QQ; T.-0141-339 8855, Ext. 5387.

Gordon-Duff-Pennington, Patrick Thomas, OBE, DL. Chairman, Red Deer Commission, since 1993; b. 12.1.30, London; m., Phyllida Rosemary; 4 d. Educ. Eton; Trinity College, Oxford. Farmed in Dumfriesshire, 1959-82; Hon. President, Scottish NFU, 1981-83; Convenor, Scottish Landowners Federation, 1988-91; Managing Director, family estate in Inverness-shire, since 1990; Chairman, Scottish Committee, Association of Electricity Producers, since 1991; DL, Cumbria; Vice-President: Field Studies Council, Scottish Conservation Projects; Member, Executive, Rural Forum. Address: (b.) 82 Fairfield Road, Inverness, IV3 5LH; T.-01463 231751.

Gorman, Professor Daniel Geelan, BSc, PhD, CEng, FIMechE. Head, School of Mechanical and Offshore

Engineering, Robert Gordon University, since 1989; Editor-in-Chief, Machine Vibration, since 1991; b. 9.8.48, Bellshill; m., Dr. June Neilson; 1 s.; 1 d. Educ. Holy Cross High School, Hamilton; Strathclyde University. Honeywell Ltd., 1968-69; E. Scragg & Sons Ltd., 1969-74; PhD student, 1974-77; Trinity College, Dublin, 1977-80; University of Limerick, 1980-81; Queen Mary and Westfield College, London, 1981-89. Recreations: golf; motor cars. Address: (h.) The Linns, Catterline, Stonehaven, Kincardineshire; T.-01569 750273.

Gorrie, Donald Cameron Easterbrook, OBE, MA, JP. Leader, Liberal Democrat Group: City of Edinburgh District Council, since 1980; Lothian Regional Council, since 1974; b. 2.4.33, India; m., Astrid Salvesen; 2 s. Educ. Hurst Grange, Stirling; Oundle School; Corpus Christi College, Oxford. Schoolmaster: Gordonstoun School, 1957-60, Marlborough College, 1960-69; Scottish Liberal Party: Director of Research, 1969-71, Director of Administration, 1971-75; Edinburgh Town Councillor, 1971-75. Director, 'Edinburgh Translations'; Member, Board: Edinburgh Festival, Scottish Chamber Orchestra, Royal Lyceum Theatre Company, Queens Hall, Lothian Association of Youth Clubs, Edinburgh Youth Cafe; former Scottish native record holder, 880 yards. Address: (h.) 54 Garscube Terrace, Edinburgh, EH12 6BN; T.-0131-337 2077.

Gossip, Michael A.J., OBE, JP, BL, FBIM. Chief Executive, Argyll and Bute District Council, since 1974; Honorary Sheriff, Dunoon, since 1989; b. 27.4.33, Edinburgh; m., Margaret; 1 s.; 2 d. Educ. George Watson's Boys' College, Edinburgh; Edinburgh University. Legal Assistant, Midlothian County Council, 1955-57; Dumfries County Council: Senior Legal Assistant, 1957-60, Depute County Clerk, 1960-71; Argyll County Council: Depute County Clerk, 1971-72, County Clerk, 1972-75. Recreations: bowls; gardening. Address: (b.) Kilmory Castle, Lochgilphead, Argyll; T.-01546 602127.

Gotts, Iain McEwan, DipLE, DipTP, FRICS, MRTPI. Chief Executive, PIEDA plc, Planning, Economic and Development Consultants, since 1976; b. 26.2.47, Glasgow; m., Pamela; 1 s.; 2 d. Educ. Jordanhill College School, Glasgow; Paisley College of Technology; Heriot-Watt University/Edinburgh College of Art. Trainee Surveyor, British Rail Property Department, Glasgow, 1965-68; further education, 1968-72; Surveyor/Land Economist, Wright & Partners, Edinburgh, 1972-76. Recreations: music; golf; rugby. Address: (b.) 10 Chester Street, Edinburgh, EH3 7RA; T.-0131-225 5737.

Gould, Robert. Leader, Strathclyde Regional Council, since 1992; Leader, Glasgow Unitary Council, since 1995; b. 8.2.35; m., Helen; 2 s.; 2 d. Elected to Glasgow Corporation, 1970; JP and magistrate, 1971; elected to Strathclyde Regional Council, 1974; Chair, National Joint Council Manual Workers, 1980-92; Chair, National Joint Council Fire Brigades, 1980-88; elected Depute Leader, SRC, 1986; Chairman, National Joint Council (Employer), APT&C and Manual Workers, 1986; Director: SECC, Glasgow Cultural Enterprises Ltd., Royal Concert Hall Board. Recreations: golf; hill-walking; sports; theatre. Address: (b.) Strathclyde House, 20 India Street, Glasgow; T.-0141-227 3000.

Gow, Sir (James) Michael, GCB, DL (Edinburgh), FSAScot. President, Royal British Legion Scotland, since 1986; President, Earl Haig Fund (Scotland), since 1986; b. 3.6.24; m., Jane Emily Scott; 1 s.; 4 d. Educ. Winchester College. Enlisted, Scots Guards, 1942; commissioned, 1943; served NW Europe 1944-45, Malayan Emergency, 1949; Equerry to the late HRH Duke of Gloucester, 1952-53; Brigade Major, 1955-57; Regimental Adjutant, Scots Guards, 1957-60; Instructor, Army Staff College, 1962-64; Command, 2nd Bn Scots Guards, Kenya and England, 1964-66; GSO1, HQ London District, 1966-67; Command,

4th Guards Brigade, 1968-69; Imperial Defence College, 1970; Brigadier General Staff (Int.) HQ, BAOR and Assistant Chief of Staff, G2 HQ, Northag, 1971-73; GOC 4th Div., BAOR, 1973-75; Director of Army Training, 1975-78; General Officer Commanding, Scotland, Governor of Edinburgh Castle, 1979-80; Commander-in-Chief, BAOR and Commander, Northern Army Group, 1980-83 (awarded die Plakette des deutschen Heeres); ADC Gen. to the Queen, 1981-84; Commandant, Royal College of Defence Studies, 1984-86. Colonel Commandant: Intelligence Corps, 1973-86, Scottish Division, 1979-80; Brigadier, Queen's Body Guard for Scotland, (Royal Company of Archers); UK Member, Eurogroup US Tour, 1983; UK Kermit Roosevelt Lecturer, USA, 1984; Vice President: Queen Victoria School, Dunblane, 1979-80, Royal Caledonian Schools, Bushey, since 1980; County Commissioner, British Scouts, W. Europe, 1980-83 (Silver Acorn); Elder, Church of Scotland, since 1988; President, National Association of Sheltered Employment, since 1993; Freeman: City of London, 1980, State of Kansas, USA, 1984; Freeman and Liveryman, Painters' and Stainers' Company, 1980. Publications: Trooping the Colour: A History of the Sovereign's Birthday Parade by the Household Troops, 1989; Jottings in a General's Notebook, 1989; General Reflections, 1991. Recreations: sailing; music; travel; reading. Address: (h.) 18 Ann Street, Edinburgh EH4 1PJ; T.-0131-332 4752.

Gow, Sheriff Neil, QC (Scot). Sheriff of South Strathclyde, at Ayr, since 1976; b. 24.4.32.

Grace, Professor John, BSc, PhD. Professor of Environmental Biology, Edinburgh University, since 1992; b. 19.9.45, Northampton; m., Elizabeth Ashworth; 2 s.; 1 d. Educ. Bletchley Grammar School; Sheffield University. Lecturer, then Reader in Ecology, Edinburgh Univrsity, 1970-92. Co-Editor, Functional Ecology, since 1986; Technical Editor, International Society for Biometeorology, since 1983; Member, Terrestrial Life Sciences Committee, Natural Environment Research Council, 1986-89; Council Member, British Ecological Society, since 1983. Publications: Plant Response to Wind, 1977; Plants and their Atmospheric Environment (Co-Editor), 1981; Plant-atmosphere Relationships, 1983. Recreations: hill-walking; cycling; fishing; bridge. Address: (h.) 25 Craiglea Drive, Edinburgh, EH10 5PB; T.-0131-447 3030.

Gracie, Alistair. Head of News and Current Affairs, Grampian Television, since 1986; b. 25.2.48, Aberdeen; m., Wendy; 1 s.; 2 d. Educ. Aberdeen Grammar School. Joined Aberdeen Journals as Trainee Journalist, 1966; worked on Press and Journal as Reporter and Evening Express as Sub-Editor; moved into television as Researcher/Reporter, 1972; Grampian Television: News Editor, 1974, Programme Editor, 1978. Recreations: mountaineering; squash; running; photography; reading; painting. Address: (b.) Grampian TV, Queen's Cross, Aberdeen, AB9 2XJ.

Graeme, Malcolm Laurie, OStJ, VRD, MA, MB, BChir, MFPHM, DPH, MRCS, LRCP; b. 16.9.19, Guernsey; m., Dr. Patricia Doreen Shurly, MB, BS, MRCP; 1 d. Educ. Stowe; Jesus College, Cambridge; St. George's Hospital Medical School (Devitt-Pendlebury Scholarship). Surgeon, Lt.-Surgeon, Lt. Cdr., RNVR/RNR, 1944-64; Public Health Service, London County Council, London Borough of Barnet and London Borough of Enfield, 1957-70; Medical Branch, Civil Service, Departments of Education and Science and Health and Social Security, 1970-79; Ordained Elder, Church of Scotland, 1970; Member, Kirk Session, Ceres Parish Church, since 1987; Life Governor, Royal Scottish Corporation of London; District Councillor (Conservative), NE Fife, 1980-84; Member, Fife Health Board, 1983-87; Hon. Vice-President, NE Fife Conservative Association, 1987; Chairman, Fife and Kinross Committee, King George's Fund for Sailors and Member, Scottish Council, 1987-90; Life Member, St. John

Association of Scotland and Chairman, Fife Order Committee. Recreation: gardening. Address: (h.) Little Baltilly, Ceres, by Cupar, Fife, KY15 5QG; T.-01334 828 238.

Graham, Rev. A. David M., BA, BD. Minister, Rosemount Parish Church, Aberdeen, since 1990; b. 17.7.40, Tralee; m., Mary A. Taylor; 2 s.; 1 d. Educ. Wesley College, Dublin; Methodist College, Belfast; Queen's University, Belfast; Glasgow University. Assistant, South Leith Parish; Secretary for Christian Education, Scottish National Council of YMCAs; Minister, Anderston Parish, Glasgow; Warden, Iona Abbey; Minister, Rutherford Parish, Aberdeen. Recreations: jogging; climbing. Address: 22 Osborne Place, Aberdeen, AB2 4DA; T.-01224 648041.

Graham, Professor David I., MB, ChB, PhD, FRCPath, FRCPS, FRSE. Professor of Neuropathology, Glasgow University, since 1983; b. 20.7.39, Glasgow; m., Joyce; 1 s.; 1 d. Educ. Penarth County Grammar School; Welsh National School of Medicine, Cardiff. Registrar, Western Infirmary, Glasgow, 1965-68; Lecturer, Department of Neuropathology, Glasgow, 1968-72; Fogarty Fellow, Laboratory of Neuropathology, Philadelphia, 1972-74; Senior Lecturer, Glasgow, 1974-83. Publications: several books; 300 papers. Recreations: hill-walking; music. Address: (b.) Department of Neuropathology, Institute of Neurological Sciences, Southern General Hospital, Govan Road, Glasgow, G51 4TF; T.-0141-201 2113.

Graham, Lord Donald, BSc, MBA. Director of Information Technology, Adam & Company, since 1991; Director, Fruit Market Gallery, since 1992; Director, KDCL Ltd., Property Developers, since 1992; b. 28.10.56, Salisbury, Southern Rhodesia; m., Bridie; 3 d. Educ. St. Andrews College, South Africa; St. Andrews University; INSEAD. Recreations: piping; music. Address: (b.) Adam & Company plc, 22 Charlotte Square, Edinburgh, EH2 4DF; T.-0131-225 8484.

Graham, Elspeth Forbes, MA, PhD. Lecturer in Geography, St. Andrews University, since 1980; Member, Local Government Boundary Commission for Scotland, since 1994; b. 7.2.50, Edinburgh; 1 s.; 1 d. Educ. George Watson's Ladies College, Edinburgh; St. Andrews University; Durham University. Visiting Lecturer, University of Minnesota, 1979-80. Publications: Postmodernism and the Social Sciences (Co-editor), 1992; research papers on population policies and issues. Recreations: horse-riding; Celtic music. Address: (b.) Department of Geography, St. Andrews University, St. Andrews, KY16 9ST; T.-01334 463908.

Graham, Ian, BSc(Econ) (Hons), DipEdTech (CNAA). Principal, John Wheatley College, Glasgow, since 1992; b. 26.6.51, Devizes. Educ. Queen Victoria School, Dunblane; London Universty (External). Lecturer/Senior Lecturer, Reid Kerr College, Paisley, 1975-86; Head of Department, Clydebank College, 1986-88; Further Education Officer, Strathclyde Regional Council, 1988-89; HM Inspector of Schools, 1989-90; Assistant Director of Education (FE), Strathclyde Region, 1990-92. Fellow, Royal Society of Arts; Fellow, Institute of Personnel and Development; Member, Board, Scottish Community Education Council; Member, Strathclyde European Partnership Management Board. Recreations: reading; cinema; foreign travel; admiring Burmese cats. Address: (b.) 1346 Shettleston Road, Glasgow, G32 9AT; T.-0141-778 2426.

Graham, John James, OBE, MA, FEIS. Joint Editor, The New Shetlander, since 1956; b. 12.7.21, Lerwick; m., Beryl Smith; 3 s.; 2 d. Educ. Lerwick Central Secondary School; Edinburgh University. RAF Training Command, 1941-44; Bomber Command, 1944-46; Principal Teacher of English, Anderson Educational Institute, Lerwick, 1950-66; Headmaster: Lerwick Central Secondary School, 1966-70,

Anderson High School, Lerwick, 1970-82; Member: Consultative Committee on the Curriculum, 1976-80, Broadcasting Council for Scotland, 1981-84; President, Shetland Folk Society. Publications: A Grammar and Usage of the Shetland Dialect (Co-author); Northern Lights (Joint Editor); The Shetland Dictionary; Shadowed Valley (novel); Strife in the Valley (novel). Recreations: local history; golf. Address: (h.) 10 Reform Lane, Lerwick, Shetland; T.-Lerwick 3425.

Graham, John Michael Denning, LLB (Hons), NP. Solicitor and Notary Public, since 1970; Senior Partner, Paterson Roberson & Graham, since 1971; Deputy Chairman, Kilmacolm Developments Limited; Director: Select Assured Properties PLC, John Smith & Son (Glasgow) Ltd.; Non Executive Director, West Glasgow Hospitals University NHS Trust; Chairman, Rent Assessment Committee, Glasgow, since 1983; Chairman, Child Support Appeal Tribunal, since 1993; Senior Tutor in Law, Glasgow University; Governor, Glasgow Caledonian University; b. 7.9.44, Kirkintilloch; m., Christina Jeanne Sinclair; 2 s. Educ. Royal Belfast Academical Institution; Queen's University, Belfast. Recreations: tennis; golf; hang-gliding. Address: (b.) 12 Royal Crescent, Glasgow, G3 7SL; T.-0141-353 0550.

Graham, John Strathie, BA. Under Secretary, Local Government Group, Scottish Office Environment Department, since 1991; b. 27.5.50, Edinburgh; m., Anne Graham; 2 s.; 1 d. Educ. Edinburgh Academy; Corpus Christi College, Oxford. Joined Scottish Office, 1972; Principal, Scottish Economic Planning Department, 1976; Assistant Secretary, Industry Department for Scotland, 1982; Private Secretary to Secretary of State, 1983; Assistant Secretary: Planning Division, Scottish Development Department, 1985, Finance Division 1, 1990. Recreations: exploring Scotland; listening to music. Address: (b.) New St. Andrews House, Edinburgh, EH1 3TG.

Graham, Keith H.R., LLB, WS. Principal Clerk, Scottish Land Court, since 1972; b. 29.5.47, Edinburgh; m., Patricia; 2 d. Educ. George Watson's College; Edinburgh University. Apprenticeship, Davidson & Syme, WS, 1968-70; private practice, 1970-72; Legal Assessor, Scottish Land Court, 1972-82. Publication: The Scottish Land Court: Practice and Procedure. Address: (b.) 1 Grosvenor Crescent, Edinburgh, EH12 5ER; T.-0141-225 3595.

Graham, Kenneth. Chairman, Scottish Post Office Board. Address: (b.) West Port House, 102 West Port, Edinburgh, EH3 9HS.

Graham, Martin. Secretary of the Library (Keeper), National Library of Scotland. Address: (b.) George IV Bridge, Edinburgh, EH1 1EW.

Graham, Professor Neil Bonnette, BSc, PhD, CChem, FRSC, FIM, FRSE. Professor in Chemical Technology, Strathclyde University, since 1973; b. 23.5.33, Liverpool; 1 s.; 3 d. Educ. Alsop High School, Liverpool; Liverpool University. Research Chemist, Research Scientist, Canadian Industries Ltd., MacMasterville PQ, Canada, 1956-67; Assistant Group Head, then Group Head, Polymer Chemistry, ICI, Runcorn, Cheshire. Member: Advisory Committee on Dental and Surgical Materials, 1980-86, and sometime member of various committees, Society of Chemical Industry, Royal Society of Chemistry and Plastics and Rubber Institute; Chairman, Glasgow Membrane Group, since 1986; Member, International Editorial Boards, Biomedical Polymers and Journal of Controlled Release; Governor and Trustee, Keil School; Trustee, James Clerk Maxwell Trust. Recreations: music; walking. Address: (b.) Strathclyde University, Department of Pure and Applied Chemistry, Thomas Graham Building, 295 Cathedral Street, Glasgow, G1 1XL; T.-0141-552 4400, Ext. 2133.

Graham, Nigel John O. Member, Highland Regional Council, since 1983; b. 28.7.27, Worcestershire; m., Margaret; 2 s.; 2 d. Educ. Marlborough College. Highland Light Infantry, 1945-53; TA, Queen's Own Cameron Highlanders, 1953-61; farmer, 1953-83; Member, Nairn County Council, 1966-72; Member, N.E. Board, Scottish Natural Heritage. Recreation: bird-watching; photography. Address: (h.) Househill, Nairn; T.-Nairn 453241.

Graham, Sir Norman William, Kt (1971), CB (1961), MA, DLitt (Heriot-Watt), DUniv (Stirling), FRSE; b. 11.10.13, Dundee; m., Catherine Mary Strathie; 2 s.; 1 d. Educ. High School of Glasgow; Glasgow University. Assistant Principal, Department of Health for Scotland, 1936; Principal, Ministry of Aircraft Production, 1941; Principal Private Secretary to Minister, 1944; Assistant Secretary, Department of Health for Scotland, 1945; Under Secretary, 1956; Secretary, Scottish Education Department, 1964-73. Recreations: golf; gardening. Address: (h.) 6 Chesterhall Steading, Longniddry, East Lothian; T.-01875 852130.

Graham, Ronald Cairns, MB, ChB, DipSocMed, FRCP, FFCM. General Manager, Tayside Health Board, 1985-93; Honorary Senior Lecturer, Dundee University, since 1969; b. 8.10.31, Airdrie; m., Christine Fraser Osborne; 2 s.; 1 d. Educ. Airdrie Academy; Glasgow University. Deputy Medical Superintendent, Edinburgh Royal Infirmary; Assistant Senior Administrative Medical Officer, South-Eastern Regional Hospital Board; Eastern Regional Hospital Board: Deputy Senior Administrative Medical Officer, Senior Administrative Medical Officer; Chief Administrative Medical Officer, Tayside Health Board, 1973-85. Recreation: fishing. Address: (h.) 34 Dalgleish Road, Dundee; T.-Dundee 455426.

Graham, Thomas. MP (Labour), Renfrew West and Inverclyde, since 1987; b. 1944. Address: (b.) House of Commons, London, SW1A 0AA.

Graham, Rev. William Peter, MA, BD. Clerk, Edinburgh Presbytery, since 1993; b. 24.11.43, Edinburgh; m., Isabel Arnot Brown; 2 s. Educ. George Watson's College, Edinburgh; Edinburgh University. Assistant Minister, Dundee (St. Mary's) Parish Church, 1966-68; Minister, Chirnside Parish Church, 1968-93, Bonkyl & Preston, 1973-93, Edrom-Allanton, 1978-93; Clerk, Duns Presbytery, 1982-93; Convener, General Assembly's Nomination Committee, 1990-93. Recreations: golf; theatre; reading. Address: (b.) 10 Palmerston Place, Edinburgh, EH12 5AA; T.-0131-225 9137.

Graham-Bryce, Ian James, DPhil. Principal and Vice-Chancellor, Dundee University, since 1994; Head, Environmental Affairs Division, Shell Internationale Petroleum Maatschappij BV, 1986-94; b. 20.3.37; m., Anne Elisabeth Metcalf; 1 s.; 3 d. Educ. William Hulme's Grammar School, Manchester; University College, Oxford; BA, MA, BSc, FRSC, CChem. Lecturer, UCNW, Bangor, 1961-64; Senior Scientific Officer, Rothamsted Experimental Station, 1964-70; Senior Research Officer, ICI Plant Protection Division, Berks, 1970-72; Special Lecturer in Pesticide Chemistry, Department of Zoology and Applied Entomology, Imperial College of Science and Technology, 1970-72; Rothamsted Experimental Station: Head, Department of Insecticides and Fungicides, 1972-79, Deputy Director, 1975-79; Director, East Malling Research Station, 1979-86; Cons. Director, Commonwealth Bureau of Horticulture and Plantation Crops, 1979-86; Society of Chemical Industry, London: President, 1982-84, Member, Council, 1969-72, 1974-89, Hon. Secretary, Home Affairs, 1977-80; Member, NERC, since 1989. Publications: Physical Principles of Pesticide Behaviour, 1980; papers on soil science, plant nutrition, and crop protection. Recreations: music (especially opera); fly fishing;

windsurfing. Address: (b.) Dundee University, Dundee, DD1 4HN.

Grainger, John McGregor Leighton, MBE, FTS. Director of Tourism, Perthshire Tourist Board, since 1982; b. 3.9.43, Aberdeen; m., Kathleen; 1 s. (deceased); 2 d. Assistant Tourist Officer, Aberdeen Town Council, 1959-67; Tourism Manager, Dunbar Town Council, 1967-69; Tourism Manager, Perth Tourist Association, 1969-74; Senior Tourist Officer, Tayside Regional Council, 1974-82. Secretary, Scottish Tourism Awards Scheme; Secretary, Society of High Constables of the City of Perth. Recreations: fishing; hill-walking. Address: (b.) Lower City Mills, West Mill Street, Perth, PH1 5QP; T.-01738 627958.

Grains, Florence Barbara, OBE, JP. Chairman, Shetland Health Board, since 1985; Member, Shetland Islands Council, since 1986; Director, Shetland Careers Service; Chairman, Shetland Council of Social Service; b. 2.11.32, Shetland; m., Alistair M. Grains; 4 s. Educ. Whiteness School, Shetland; Lerwick FE Centre. Retired Sub-postmaster, Whiteness, Shetland. Chairman, Alting Debating Society; Trustee, Shetland Amenity Trust; Chairman, Shetland Branch, Post Office Users Council for Scotland; Member, Shetland Area Licensing Board; Trustee, Walls and District Agricultural Society; Supervisor, Whiteness and Weisdale Playgroup; Cub Scout Leader; Chairman, Shetland Family History Society; Chairman, Foula Electricity Trust. Address: (h.) Hoove, Whiteness, Shetland; T.-01595 84 243.

Grant, Donald Blane, CBE, TD, LLD, CA. Chairman, Scottish Legal Aid Board, 1986-91; Partner, Thomson, McLintock & Co., 1950-86; Chairman, Tayside Health Board, 1984-91; b. 8.10.21, Dundee; m., Lavinia Margaret Ruth Ritchie; 3 d. Educ. Dundee High School. Royal Artillery, 1939-46 (retired as Major). Chairman: Mathew Trust, Caird Travelling Scholarships Trust. Recreations: golf; fishing; shooting; gardening. Address: (h.) 24 Albany Road, Broughty Ferry, Dundee, DD5 1NT.

Grant, Donald Patrick James, FBIM, FRSA. Honorary Sheriff, Rothesay; b. 12.5.19, Fulwood, Yorkshire; m., Joan Winfield Grant; 1 s.; 1 d. Educ. Kings School, Macclesfield; Kings College, Durham University. Royal Navy, 1940-46, serving as Lieutenant RNVR in submarines, and as air engineering officer Flag Officer Air's staff, East Indies station; Vickers Ltd., Engineering Group, 1946-74, in various appointments as General Manager and Managing Director; Consultant, 1974-76. Address: (h.) Heathmount, 22 Crichton Road, Rothesay, PA20 9JR; T.-01700 503409.

Grant, Gary J., MA. Chief Executive, Campbeltown & Kintyre Enterprise Trust Ltd., since 1994; Kintyre Project Officer, Argyll & The Islands Enterprise, since 1994; b. 19.4.69, Inverness; partner, Sarah; 1 s. Educ. Millburn Academy, Inverness; Aberdeen University. Research Assistant, MacKay Consultants, Inverness, 1990-92; Project Executive, Argyll and The Islands Enterprise, 1992-94. Recreations: sports, principally rugby. Address: (b.) Hazelburn Business Park, Millknowe, Campbeltown, Argyll, PA28 6HA; T.-01586 552338.

Grant, (Helen) Rae. Administrator, Scottish Liberal Democrats, since 1989; b. 17.12.40, Edinburgh; m., James Sturrock Grant; 2 d. Educ. Boroughmuir High School; Torphichen Commercial College. Party Secretary, 1974-89. Recreations: reading; swimming; walking. Address: (b.) 4 Clifton Terrace, Edinburgh, EH12 5DR; T.-0131-337 2314.

Grant, Ian David, CBE, FRAgS. Chairman, Scottish Tourist Board, since 1990; b. 28.7.43, Dundee; m., Eileen May Louisa Yule; 3 d. Educ. Strathallan School; East of Scotland College of Agriculture. Chairman, EEC Cereals Working Party, 1982-88 and International Federation of Agricultural Producers, Grains Committee, 1984-90;

President, NFU of Scotland, 1984-90; Director: Scottish Hydro Electric, East of Scotland Farmers Ltd., NFU Mutual Insurance Society Ltd., Clydesdale Bank PLC; Member: Scottish Council, CBI, since 1984, Board, British Tourist Authority, since 1990. Recreations: shooting; swimming; music. Address: (h.) Leal House, Alyth PH11 8JQ. Tel.: 01828 632695.

Grant, Ian Faulconer Heathcoat, JP, DL. Managing Director, Glenmoriston Estates Limited; Chairman, Pacific Assets Trust PLC; Director: Royal Bank of Scotland PLC, Royal Bank of Scotland Group plc, Worldwide Value Fund Inc. (USA), Banco Santander S.A., Holland Pacific Fund N.V.; b. 3.6.39, Singapore; m., Sally; 1 s.; 3 d. Educ. Cargilfield; Sedbergh; Liverpool College of Commerce. ICI Ltd., 1957-62; various positions, Jardine Matheson & Co. Ltd., Hong Kong, 1962-73, culminating in directorship on Main Board. Address: (b.) Glenmoriston Estates Ltd., Glenmoriston, near Inverness; T.-01320 351202.

Grant, Rev. James Gordon, MA, BD. Minister, Dean Church, Edinburgh, since 1987 (Portland Church, Troon, 1965-87); b. 5.7.32, Glasgow; m., Susan Ann Hewitt; 2 s.; 1 d. Educ. High School of Stirling; St. Andrews University. Ordained, 1957; Probationer Assistant, St. Mungo's Parish Church, Alloa, 1957-59; Minister, Dyce Parish Church, Aberdeen, 1959-65; Convener, Inter-Church Relations Committee, 1983-84. Recreations: golf; climbing; ornithology. Address: (h.) 1 Ravelston Terrace, Edinburgh, EH4 3EF; T.-0131-332 5736.

Grant, Major James MacAlpine Gregor, TD, NDA, MRAC. Landowner and Farmer, since 1961; b. 18.2.38, Nakuru, Kenya; m., Sara Marjory; 3 d. Educ. Eton; Royal Agricultural College, Cirencester. National Service, Queen's Own Cameron Highlanders, 1957-58; TA with 4/5th Queen's Own Cameron Highlanders; Volunteers with 51st Highland Volunteers. Address: Roskill House, Munlochy, Ross-shire, IV8 8PA; T.-Munlochy 207.

Grant, James Shaw, CBE, LLD, FRSE, FRAgS, MA. Author; b. 22.5.10, Stornoway; m., Catherine Mary Stewart. Educ. Nicolson Institute, Stornoway; Glasgow University. Editor, Stornoway Gazette, 1932-63; Governor, Pitlochry Festival Theatre, 1954-84 (Chairman, 1971-83); Member, Crofters Commission, 1955-78 (Chairman, 1963-78); Director, Grampian TV, 1969-80; Member: Highlands and Islands Development Board, 1970-82, Scottish Advisory Committee, British Council, 1972-94; Chairman, Harris Tweed Association Ltd., 1972-84; Member, Council, National Trust for Scotland, 1979-84; Governor, Eden Court Theatre, since 1980 (Vice Chairman, since 1987); author of plays: Tarravore, The Magic Rowan, Legend is Born, Comrade the King. Publications: Highland Villages, 1977; Their Children Will See, 1979; The Hub of My Universe, 1982; Surprise Island, 1983; The Gaelic Vikings, 1984; Stornoway and the Lews, 1985; Discovering Lewis and Harris, 1987; Enchanted Island, 1989; A Shilling for Your Scowl, 1992. Address: (h.) Ardgrianach, Inshes, Inverness; T.-Inverness 231476.

Grant, Professor John Paxton, LLB, LLM. Professor, School of Law, Glasgow University, since 1988 (Dean, Faculty of Law and Financial Studies, 1985-89 and since 1992); b. 22.2.44, Edinburgh; m., Elaine E. Sutherland. Educ. George Heriot's School, Edinburgh; Edinburgh University; Pennsylvania University. Lecturer, Faculty of Law: Aberdeen University, 1967-71, Dundee University, 1971-74; Senior Lecturer, Department of Public International Law, Glasgow University, 1974-88; Visiting Professor: Saint Louis University School of Law, 1981, Northwestern School of Law, Lewis and Clark College, 1984 and 1986. Editor, The Juridical Review, since 1988. Publications: Independence and Devolution (Editor), 1976; The Impact of Marine Pollution: Law and Practice (Joint Editor), 1980; The Encyclopaedic Dictionary of

International Law (Joint General Editor), 1985; Legal Education 2000 (Joint Editor), 1988; English–Estonian Law Glossary (Joint Editor), 1993; English for Lawyers (Joint Editor), 1995. Recreations: walking; travelling. Address: (h.) 87 Warrender Park Road, Edinburgh, EH9 1EW; T.-0131-229 7705.

Grant, Lesley Dunbar, MBE, MA. Member, Scottish Sports Council; b. 10.1.33, Banchory. Educ. Banchory Academy; Aberdeen University; Aberdeen College of Education. Former teacher/head teacher; Past Chairman, Northern Area, Scottish Conservative and Unionist Association; former Councillor, Dean of Guild and Hon. Treasurer, Banchory Town Council; former Handicap Adviser and Selector, Scottish Ladies Golf Association; Elder, Banchory-Ternan East Church. Recreations: current affairs; travel; caring. Address: (h.) Ordeans, Arbeadie Terrace, Banchory, AB31 3TN; T.-01330 822782.

Grant, Very Rev. Malcolm Etheridge, BSc (Hons), BD (Hons). Provost and Rector, Cathedral Church of S. Andrew, Inverness, Rector, S. Paul's, Strathnairn and Priest-in-charge, S. Mary's-in-the-Fields, Culloden, since 1991; b. 6.8.44, Maidstone; m., Katrina Russell Nuttall; 1 s.; 1 d. Educ. Dunfermline High School; Edinburgh University; Edinburgh Theological College. Assistant Curate: S. Mary's Cathedral, Glasgow, 1969-72, Grantham Parish Church, in charge of Church of the Epiphany, Earlesfield, 1972; Team Vicar, Earlesfield, Grantham Team Ministry, 1972-78; Priest-in-charge, S. Ninian's, Invergordon, 1978-81; Provost and Rector, Cathedral Church of S. Mary the Virgin, Glasgow, 1981-91; Examining Chaplain to Bishop of Moray, Ross and Caithness, 1979-81; Member, Highland Region Education Committee, 1979-81. Address: 15 Ardross Street, Inverness, IV3 5NS; T.-01463 233535.

Grant, Sir (Matthew) Alistair. Chairman, Argyll Group PLC, since 1988; b. 6.3.37, Haddington; m., Judith Mary Grant; 2 s. ; 1 d. Educ. Woodhouse Grove School, Yorkshire. Unilever, 1958-63; J. Lyons, 1963-65; Connell May & Steavenson, 1965-68; Marketing Director, Fine Fare Ltd., 1968-72; Managing Director, Oriel Foods Ltd., 1973-77; Managing Director of companies which formed Argyll Group, 1977-86; Deputy Chairman and Chief Executive, Argyll Group, 1986. Chairman, Biotechnology and Biological Sciences Research Council; Ordinary Director, Bank of Scotland; Non-Executive Director, Scottish & Newcastle PLC; Visiting Professor, Strathclyde University; Trustee, National Museums of Scotland; Regent, Royal College of Surgeons, Edinburgh. Recreations: hunting; fishing; reading; music.

Grant, Professor Nigel Duncan Cameron, MA, MEd, PhD, FRSE. Professor of Education, Glasgow University, 1978-95; b. 8.6.32, Glasgow; m., Valerie Keeling Evans; 1 s.; 1 d. Educ. Inverness Royal Academy; Glasgow University. Teacher of English, Glasgow secondary schools, 1957-60; Lecturer in Education, Jordanhill College of Education, 1960-65; Lecturer in Educational Studies, then Reader, Edinburgh University, 1965-78. Past Chairman and President, British Comparative and International Education Society; former Executive Member, Comparative Education Society in Europe; Past Chairman: Scottish Educational Research Association, Scottish Universities Council for Studies in Education; Educational Consultant, Comann Sgoiltean Da-Chananach Ghlaschu; Member, Executive Committee, Advisory Council for the Arts in Scotland; Member, Editorial Board, Comparative Education; Trustee, Urras Foghlam na Gaidhlig; Member, Scottish Constitutional Steering Committee; Hon. President, Glasgow Educational Colloquium. Publications: Soviet Education, 1964; Society, Schools and Progress in Eastern Europe, 1969; Education and Nation-Building in the Third World (Editor and Co-author), 1971; A Mythology of British Education (Co-author), 1974; Scottish Universities:

The Case for Devolution (Co-author), 1976; Patterns of Education in the British Isles (Co-author), 1977; The Crisis of Scottish Education, 1982. Recreations: theatre; music; poetry; natural history; languages; art; travel; calligraphy.

Grant, Peter James. Chairman, Sun Life Corporation PLC, since 1983; Chairman, Sun Life Assurance Society PLC, since 1983 (Director, since 1973); b. 5.12.29, London; m., Paula Eugster; 2 s.; 3 d. Educ. Winchester; Magdalen College, Oxford. Lieutenant, Queen's Own Cameron Highlanders. Vice-Chairman, 1983-85, Deputy Chairman, 1985-88, Lazard Bros & Co.; Director, Scottish Hydro, 1990-95; Director, London Merchant Securities PLC, BNP UK Holdings Ltd.; Member, Civil Aviation Authority; Chairman, Highlands & Islands Airports Ltd.; Member, Council, Institute of Directors; Member, Cromarty Firth Port Authority, since 1994. Recreations: fishing; shooting; golf. Address: (h.) Mountgerald, near Dingwall, Ross-shire, IV15 9TT; T.-01349 62244.

Grant, Professor Peter Mitchell, BSc, PhD, CEng, FIEE. Professor of Electronic Signal Processing, Edinburgh University, since 1987; Director, EUMOS, Edinburgh, since 1985; b. 20.6.44, St. Andrews; m., Marjory Renz; 2 d. Educ. Strathallan School; Heriot-Watt University; Edinburgh University. Honorary Editor, Proceedings IEE (Part F). Publication: Adaptive Filters (Co-Editor), 1985; Signal Processing and Coding (Co-author), 1988. Address: (b.) Department of Electrical Engineering, Edinburgh University, Edinburgh, EH9 3JL; T.-0131-650 5569.

Grant, Richard Anthony, BSocSc, MSc. Head of Division, Land Use and Crofting, Scottish Office Agriculture and Fisheries Department, since 1991; b. 12.6.48, Leicester; m., Jacqueline Claire; 1 s.; 1 d. Educ. Loughborough College School; Birmingham University; Strathclyde University. Research Officer/Senior Research Officer, Scottish Education Department and Scottish Development Department, 1969-75; Principal Research Officer, Housing Research Unit, Scottish Development Department, 1975-77; Principal, Sports Policy Branch, Scottish Education Department, 1977-79; Principal Research Officer, Housing and Urban Renewal Research Unit, Scottish Development Department, 1979-85; Principal, Land Use and Conservation Branch, Department of Agriculture and Fisheries, 1986-89; Principal, NHS Management Executive, 1989-91. Recreations: cycling; hill-walking; cross-country skiing. Address: (b.) Room 102, Pentland House, Robbs Loan, Edinburgh; T.-0131-224 6190.

Grant of Dalvey, Sir Patrick Alexander Benedict, 14th Bt, FSA Scot, LLB. Chieftain of Clan Donnachy; Company Director; b. 5.2.53.

Grant of Rothiemurchus, John Peter, DL. Landowner; Chairman, Scot Trout Limited; Director, Cairngorm Recreation Trust; Member, Council, National Trust for Scotland; Vice President, Scottish Landowners Federation; b. 22.10.46, Rothiemurchus; m., Philippa (qv); 1 s.; 2 d. Educ. Gordonstoun. Past Chairman: Scottish Recreational Land Association; British Deer Producers Society; Highland Region Forestry, Farming and Wildlife Advisory Group; former Member, Forestry Commission Regional Advisory Committee; Patron, Highland Hospice. Recreations: skiing; shooting. Address: (b.) Doune of Rothiemurchus, by Aviemore; T.-01479 810647.

Grantham, Michael. Secretary, Crofters Commission. Address: (b.) 4-6 Castle Wynd, Inverness, IV2 3EQ.

Gravestock, Martin John. Crown Estate Receiver for Scotland, since 1985; b. 31.8.52, Carshalton, Surrey; m., Olwyn Claire; 3 s. Educ. Sutton County Grammar School. Crown Estate Office, since 1969: Legal, Foreshore and Seabed, General, and London Branches; Head, Personnel

Branch, 1984; Head, Foreshore and Seabed Branch, 1984-85. Recreations: cars; gardening. Address: (b.) 10 Charlotte Square, Edinburgh; T.-0131-226 7241.

Gray, Adam, OBE, NDA, NDD, ARAgS. Farmer; President, Scottish Agricultural Arbiters Association, since 1989; Chairman, UK Milk Publicity Council, since 1989; Director, Scottish Pride Ltd., since 1994; b. 6.8.29, Borgue, Kirkcudbright; m., Elaine West Russell; 3 s. Educ. George Watson's Boys College; West of Scotland Agricultural College. Nuffield Scholar, 1955; Past President, Stewartry NFU; Member, NFU Council; Director, Royal Highland & Agricultural Society (Honorary Vice-President, 1994-95); Director, Scottish Milk Marketing Board, 1981-94; former Council Member, British Simmental Cattle Society; Past Chairman, SW Scotland Grassland Society; former Chairman, Kirkcudbright District Council; Honorary President, Stewartry Agricultural Society; Secretary, Kirkcudbright Burns Club; Past President, Kirkcudbright Rotary Club. Recreations: rugby; local history. Address: (h.) Ingleston, Borgue, Kirkcudbright; T.-015577 208.

Gray, Alasdair. Artist and Writer; b. 28.12.34, Glasgow; m., Morag McAlpine; 1 s. Educ. Whitehill Senior Secondary School; Glasgow Art School. Part-time Art Teacher, 1958-62; Scene Painter, 1963-64; has since lived by drawing, painting, writing; Glasgow People's Palace has a collection of his portraits and cityscapes; extant murals: Palacerigg nature reserve, Cumbernauld; Abbots House local history museum, Dunfermline. Publications: novels: Lanark; 1982 Janine; The Fall of Kelvin Walker; Something Leather; McGrotty and Ludmilla; A History Maker; Poor Things; short story collections: Unlikely Stories, Mostly; Lean Tales (this last also containing work by Jim Kelman and Agnes Owens); Ten Tales Tall and True; Five Glasgow Artists (an exhibition catalogue); Saltire Self-Portrait No. 4; Why Scots Should Rule Scotland. Scottish National Library has a collection of his unpublished plays and other material. Recreations: reading; talking to friends; drinking; walking.

Gray, Alexander, MA, LLB, DUniv, FSA Scot. Honorary Sheriff, Dumbarton; b. 6.5.12, Glasgow; m., Margaret; 2 s. Educ. Hillhead High School; Glasgow University; Edinburgh University. Town Clerk, Cove and Kilcreggan, 1948-67; Queen's Coronation Medal, 1953; Dean, Faculty of Procurators, Dumbarton, 1972; Clerk of Peace, Dunbartonshire,1974. Recreations: archaeology; Gaelic; arthritis charity. Address: (h.) (h.) Borraichill, 116 Frederick Crescent, Port Ellen, Isle of Islay, PA42 7BQ.

Gray, 22nd Lord (Angus Diarmid Ian Campbell-Gray); b. 3.7.31; m.; 1 s.; 3 d. by pr. m. Address: Airds Bay House, Taynuilt, Argyll, PA35 1JR.

Gray, Charles Ireland, CBE, FRSA, JP. Leader, Strathclyde Regional Council, 1986-92 (Depute Leader, 1978-86); Member, Scottish Enterprise Board, since 1990; b. 25.1.29, Gartcosh; m., Catherine; 3 s.; 2 d. Educ. Coatbridge High School. Local government, since 1958; former Director, Scottish Exhibition and Conference Centre; former Vice-Chairman, East Kilbride Development Corporation; former Member: Scottish Development Agency, Clyde Port Authority; former Vice-Chairman, Planning Exchange; UK Vice-President, European Committee of Regions. Recreations: music; reading; local government. Address: (b.) Strathclyde House, 20 India Street, Glasgow, G2 4PF.

Gray, David, DipArch (Aberdeen), RIBA, FRIAS, DipTP (Strath). Director of Architectural and Related Services, Strathclyde Regional Council, since 1991; b. 2.10.37, Aberdeen; m., Margaret Ross Allen Gordon; 1 s.; 2 d. Educ. Robert Gordon's College; Scott Sutherland School of Architecture; Strathclyde University. Apprentice architect/architect, Aberdeen, 1956-62; architect, Lanark County Council, 1962-66; architect/planner, East Kilbride

Development Corporation, 1966-67; Group Leader/Assistant County Architect, then Depute County Architect, Renfrew County Council, 1967-75; Strathclyde Regional Council: Area Architect (Renfrew Division), 1975-76, Depute Director (Renfrew/Dumbarton/Argyll), 1976-78, Depute Director (Glasgow Division), 1978-87, Senior Depute Director, 1987-91. President, Association of Chief Architects of Scottish Local Authorities; Council Member, Royal Institute of Architects in Scotland; Scottish Member, Public Sector Group, Royal Incorporation of British Architects. Recreations: sport; theatre; gardening. Address: (b.) Strathclyde Regional Council, Strathclyde House 2, 20 India Street, Glasgow, G2 4PF; T.-0141-227 2100.

Gray, Ethel Marian, CBE, JP, MA, LLD, DUniv, FEIS. Director, LEAD - Scotland, and Chairman, Advisory Committee; Convener, Adult Access to Education, Scottish Institute of Adult and Continuing Education, 1988-89 (President of Institute, 1984-87); Vice-Chairman, Board of Governors, The Queen's College, Glasgow, 1980-88; Chairman, Education Project for Older People, Age Concern Scotland, 1982-85; b. 19.4.23, Glasgow; m., George Deans Gray (qv). Educ. Hutchesons' Girls Grammar School; Paisley Grammar School; Glasgow University. Teacher of English, 1946-52; Lecturer in English and Drama, Jordanhill College, 1952-63; Founding Principal, Craigie College of Education, Ayr, 1963-75; Director, Scottish Adult Literacy Agency, 1976-79; Chairman, National Book League Scotland, 1977-81; Member of Court, Chairman of Staffing Committee and Joint Faculty Staff Review Board, Heriot-Watt University, 1979-84; Adviser in Adult Education, IBA, 1983-88; Member, Scottish Tertiary Education Advisory Council, 1984-87; Member, Scottish Advisory Committee, British Council, 1968-89; Member, STV Education Advisory Committee, 1981-92; Member, Scottish Community Education Council, 1979-85 (Chairman, Communications and Technology Group and Chairman, Management Committee, Micro-Electronics Project); Member, Crawford Commission on Radio and Television Coverage, 1973-75; Member, Committee of Enquiry on the Police, 1977-79; Member, Consultative Committee on the Curriculum, 1965-71. Recreations: reading; travelling; theatre. Address: (h.) 7 Greenbank Crescent, Edinburgh, EH10 5TE; T.-0131-447 5403.

Gray, George Bovill Rennie, OBE, DL, CDA, FBIM. Farmer; Chairman, G.B.R. Gray Ltd., since 1952; Chairman, Board of Management, Hanover (Scotland) Housing Association Ltd., 1992-95; Trustee, Scottish Society for Crop Research; Director, Moredun Animal Health Ltd.; b. 5.3.20, Edinburgh; m., Anne Constance Dale; 4 s.; 2 d. Educ. Clayesmore School, Dorset; Edinburgh and East of Scotland College of Agriculture. Past Chairman, East Lothian Area, National Farmers Union of Scotland; former Convenor, Cereals Committee, NFU of Scotland; former Member, Seed Production Committee, National Institute of Agricultural Botany, Cambridge; a Director, West Cumberland Farmers Ltd., 1955-85; Director, Scottish Society for Research in Plant Breeding, 1957-81; Director, Animal Diseases Research Association, 1958-93; Member, Pig Industry Development Authority, 1958-68; Chairman, Oxford Farming Conference, 1972; Member, Agricultural and Veterinary Sub-Committee, UGC, 1972-82; Member, Lothian Regional Council, 1974-82; Member, Scottish Advisory Board, British Institute of Management, 1978-90; Member, Scientific Research Panel, Home Grown Cereals Authority, 1973-80;Director, Cruden Foundation. Recreations: gardening; arboriculture. Address: Smeaton-Hepburn, East Linton, EH40 3DT; T.-01620 860275.

Gray, George Deans, CBE, MA; b. 23.5.08, Edinburgh; m., Ethel Marian Rennie (see Ethel Marian Gray). Educ. Royal High School, Edinburgh; Edinburgh University.

Teacher of Classics: Musselburgh Grammar School, 1931-37, George Watson's College, Edinburgh, 1937-45; Principal Teacher, Royal High School, Edinburgh, 1946-59; Secretary, Scottish Council for the Training of Teachers, 1959-66; Registrar (first), General Teaching Council for Scotland, 1966-72; Honorary General Secretary, Scottish Secondary Teachers Association, 1945-59; Chairman: Classical Association (Edinburgh and SE Centre), 1968-73, Scottish Dyslexia Association, 1980-82. Recreations: choral singing; classical music; piano; gardening. Address: (h.) 7 Greenbank Crescent, Edinburgh, EH10 5TE; T.-0131-447 5403.

Gray of Contin, Lord (Hamish Gray), PC, DL. Business and Parliamentary Consultant, since 1986; b. 28.6.27, Inverness; m., Judith W. Brydon; 2 s.; 1 d. Educ. Inverness Royal Academy. Queen's Own Cameron Highlanders, 1945-48; Director, family and other private companies, 1949-70; MP, Ross and Cromarty, 1970-83; Government Whip, 1971-74; Opposition Spokesman on Energy, 1975-79; Minister of State for Energy, 1979-83; Minister of State for Scotland, 1983-86; Spokesman for Government in Lords for Scotland, Employment and Energy, 1983-86. Vice President, Neighbourhood Energy Action; President, Energy Action Scotland; Vice President, Scottish Association of Youth Clubs. Recreations: golf; cricket; hill-walking; rugby. Address: (h.) Achneim House, Flichity, Inverness-shire, IV1 2XE.

Gray, Iain George Fowler. Scottish Office Industry Department, since 1990; b. 3.5.39, Glasgow. Educ. Albert Road Academy, Glasgow; Roseburn, Edinburgh; Royal High School, Edinburgh. Joined War Office as Executive Officer, 1960; PS/DUS (B), 1964-65; joined Scottish Office as Assistant Principal, 1965, Principal, 1969; SED to 1971; Private Secretary to Minister of State, 1971-72; SDD, 1973; SEPD, 1973-77; DAFS (Assistant Secretary), 1978-84; Finance Officer, DAFS/SED, 1985-89; Scottish Office Home and Health Department, 1989-90. Recreation: golf. Address:(b.) St. Andrews House, Edinburgh; T.-0131-244 4680.

Gray, James Allan, MB, ChB, FRCPEdin. Consultant in Communicable Diseases, City Hospital, Edinburgh, 1969-95; Honorary Senior Lecturer, Department of Medicine, Edinburgh University, 1992-95; Principal Medical Officer, Scottish Widows' Fund, Edinburgh, since 1990; President, British Society for the Study of Infection, 1989-91; b. 24.3.35, Bristol; m., Jennifer Margaret Newton Hunter; 1 s.; 2 d. Educ. St. Paul's School, London; Edinburgh University. House Surgeon and Physician posts, Edinburgh and Middlesbrough; Short Service Commission, RAF Medical Branch, 1960-63; Senior House Officer, Research Fellow and Registrar posts, Edinburgh, 1965-67; Registrar, Bristol Royal Infirmary, 1967-68; Senior Registrar, Royal Free Hospital (Department of Infectious Diseases), London, 1968-69; Assistant Director of Studies (Medicine), Edinburgh Post-Graduate Board, 1976-84; Fellow, Royal Medical Society (Senior President, 1958-59); Founder Editor, Res Medica, 1957-58; Assistant Editor, Journal of Infection, 1979-86. Publications: Antibacterial Drugs Today (Co-author), 1983; Infectious Diseases (Co-author), 1984, 1992. Recreations: hill-walking; pottery collecting; photography. Address: (h.) St. Andrews Cottage, 15 Lauder Road, Edinburgh, EH9 2EN; T.-0131-667 4124.

Gray, Professor James Robertson, OBE, BSc, DipActMaths, FFA, FIMA, CMath, FSS. Professor and Head, Department of Actuarial Mathematics and Statistics, Heriot-Watt University, 1971-89 (now Emeritus); Member, Council, Royal Scottish Geographical Society and Convener, Lecture Committee; b. 21.2.26, Dundee; m., Catherine McAulay Towner. Educ. High School of Dundee; Edinburgh University. Actuarial Trainee, Scottish Life Assurance Company, 1947-49; St. Andrews University: Lecturer in Mathematics, 1949-50, Lecturer in Statistics,

1950-62, Senior Lecturer in Statistics (also Head of Department), 1962-71; Heriot-Watt University: established first Department of Actuarial Science in UK; Dean, Faculty of Science, 1978-81; Council Member, Faculty of Actuaries, 1969-87 (Vice President, 1983-87); Vice-Chairman, Scottish Examination Board, 1984-90 (Convener of Examinations Committee, 1982-90); former Vice-Chairman, Scottish Universities Council on Entrance; Past Chairman: Scottish Branch, Institute of Mathematics and Its Applications, Edinburgh Branch, Royal Statistical Society. Recreations: golf; hill-walking; bridge; music; Probus. Address: (h.) Green Gables, 9 Cammo Gardens, Edinburgh, EH4 8EJ; T.-0131-339 3330.

Gray, John William Reid, MA, LLB, Advocate; b. 24.12.26, Aberdeen. Educ. Aberdeen Grammar School; Aberdeen University. Resident Magistrate, Uganda, 1954-62; Temporary Procurator-Fiscal Depute, Glasgow, 1962-63; Lecturer in Private Law, Queen's College, Dundee, then Dundee University, 1964-84; Warden, Airlie Hall, 1966-75; Member of Senate, 1971-75. Fellow, Saltzberg Seminar, 1964. Publications: articles in legal journals; The Administration of Justice Act, 1982. Address: (h.) Rhynuie, 41 Golf Road, Ballater, Aberdeenshire AB35 5RS. T.-013397 55656.

Gray, Michael Maxwell, OBE, DL. Chairman and Chief Executive, McQueen Ltd., since 1982; b. 5.5.47, Galashiels; m., Trish; 2 s. Educ. Galashiels Academy. Joined McQueen as management trainee, 1964; management buy-out, 1976. Board Member, Scottish Enterprise; Member, IR Committee, Scottish Print Employers Federation. Recreations: rugby; cricket; golf; reading. Address: (b.) McQueen Ltd., Nether Road, Galashiels, TD1 3HE; T.-01896 754866.

Gray, Muriel, BA (Hons). Broadcaster; Joint Managing Director, Ideal World Productions; b. Glasgow. Educ. Glasgow School of Art. Worked as an illustrator; then as a designer with National Museum of Antiquities; was member of rock band, The Family Von Trapp; had own show with Radio Forth; was frequent presenter on Radio 1; co-presented The Tube, Channel 4; had own arts programme, The Works, Tyne Tees; own music programme, Studio 1, Border TV; presented Casebook Scotland, BBC Scotland; Frocks on the Box, Thames TV; Acropolis Now, ITV; presented The Media Show, Channel 4; Co-Producer and Presenter, Walkie Talkie, Channel 4; first woman Rector, Edinburgh University; Producer/Presenter/Director, The Munro Show, Scottish TV; Producer/Presenter, Art is Dead...Long Live TV!, Channel Four; The Golden Cagoule, BBC. Publications: The First Fifty; The Trickster (novel). Recreation: being in the Scottish Highlands — gets grumpy and miserable if can't be up a mountain every few weeks.

Gray, Professor Peter Michael David, MA, DPhil, FBCS. Professor, Department of Computing Science, Aberdeen University, since 1989; b. 11.2.40, Abingdon; m., Doreen F. Ross; 1 s.; 1 d. Educ. Abingdon School; Queens' College, Cambridge; Jesus College, Oxford. Systems Analyst, Plessey Co., Poole, 1966-68; Research Fellow, Computer Research Group, Aberdeen University, 1968-72; Lecturer in Computing Science, Aberdeen University, 1972-84; Visiting Associate Professor, University of Western Ontario, 1985; Senior Lecturer, 1985-89. Reader, Church of Scotland. Publication: Logic, Algebra and Databases. Recreation: croquet. Address: (b.) Department of Computing Science, King's College, Aberdeen, AB9 2UB; T.-01224 272292.

Gray, Robert, CBE, OStJ, JP, LLD, DL, MICW. Chairman, Mayfest; b. 3.3.28, Glasgow; m., Mary McCartney; 1 d. Educ. St. Mungo's Academy; Glasgow College of Building. Joiner; Clerk of Works; Lecturer and Senior Lecturer in Building Subjects; elected Member,

Glasgow District Council, 1974; Chairman, Licensing Committee, 1975-77; Vice Chairman, JP Committee, 1976-77; City Treasurer, 1980-84; Lord Provost and Lord Lieutenant of Glasgow, 1984-88; Chairman, Greater Glasgow Tourist Board, 1984-88. Address: (b.) 18 Albion Street, Glasgow, G1 1LH.

Gray, Professor Robert Hugh, BSc (Econ), MA (Econ), FCA, FRSA. Mathew Professor of Accounting and Information Systems, Dundee University, since 1990; b. 1.4.52, Manchester; 2 s. Educ. De La Salle College, Salford; Hull University; Manchester University. Qualified as accountant with KPMG Peat Marwick, 1976; Lecturer, Lancashire Polytechnic, UCNW Bangor, University of East Anglia; Member, Research Board, Scottish National Heritage; Editor, Social and Environmental Accounting; Director, Centre for Social and Environmental Accounting Research; Member, Council, Institute of Environmental Managers. Publications: various books including Accounting for the Environment; The Greening of Accountancy. Recreations: golf; sailing; rock music. Address: (b.) Department of Accountancy and Business Finance, Dundee University, Dundee, DD1 4HN; T.-01382 307789.

Gray, Sir William (Stevenson), Kt (1974), JP, DL, HonLLD (Strathclyde), HonLLD (Glasgow). Solicitor and Notary Public, since 1958; Chairman, Norcity Homes PLC, since 1988; b. 3.5.28, Glasgow; m., Mary Rodger; 1 s.; 1 d. Educ. Hillhead High School, Glasgow; Glasgow University. Chairman: Scottish Special Housing Association, 1966-72, Clyde Tourist Association, 1972-75, Scotland West Industrial Promotion Group, 1972-75, WPHT Scotland Ltd. (formerly World of Property Housing Trust Scottish Housing Association Ltd.), since 1974, Irvine New Town Development Corporation, 1974-76, Scottish Development Agency, 1975-79, The Oil Club, since 1975, Research Trust for Institute of Neurological Sciences, 1978-94, Glasgow Independent Hospital Ltd., 1982-89, Webtec Industrial Technology Ltd., 1984-91, Barrell Selection Ltd., since 1987, Gap Housing Association Ltd., since 1988, Gap Housing Association (Ownership) Ltd., since 1988, Clan Homes plc, since 1988, Manchester Village Homes plc, since 1989, Norhomes plc, since 1989, Norcity II Plc, since 1989, Paragon Group, since 1990, Home Partners Plus Plc, since 1991, Paragon Protected Growth, since 1993, Norcity III and IV plc, since 1993. Member: Lower Clyde Water Board, 1971-72, National Trust for Scotland, 1971-72, Scottish Opera Board, 1971-72, Executive, Scottish Council (Development and Industry), 1971-75, Convention of Royal Burghs, 1971-75, Clyde Port Authority, 1972-75, Scottish National Orchestra Society, 1972-75, Advisory Council for Energy Conservation, 1974-84, Scottish Economic Council, 1975-83, Central Advisory Committee on JPs, since 1975, Glasgow Advisory Committee on JPs, since 1975, Third Eye Centre, 1984-91 (Chairman, 1975-84), Hodgson Martin Ltd. Advisory Board, 1988-94, Dermalase Ltd., 1989-91. Vice President: Charles Rennie Mackintosh Society, since 1974, Glasgow Citizens' Theatre, since 1975 (Member, Board of Directors, 1970-75), Strathclyde Theatre Group, 1975-86, Scottish Association for Care and Resettlement of Offenders, 1982-86 (Chairman, 1975-82); Governor, Glasgow School of Art, 1961-75; Patron: Scottish Youth Theatre, 1978-86, Scottish Pakistani Society, since 1984; Member: Court, Glasgow University, 1972-75, Council, Strathclyde University Business School, 1978-88, Glasgow Corporation, 1958-75 (Chairman, Property Management Committee, 1964-67); Treasurer, City of Glasgow, 1971-72; Lord Provost and Lord Lieutenant of the City of Glasgow, 1972-75. Recreations: sailing; theatre. Address: (b.) 13 Royal Terrace, Glasgow G3 7NY; T.-0141-332 8877.

Green, Malcolm Robert, MA, DPhil. Chairman, Environment Committee, Strathclyde Regional Council, since 1990 (Chairman, Education Committee, 1982-90); Chairman, Education Committee, Convention of Scottish Local Authorities, 1978-90; Lecturer in Roman History, Glasgow University, since 1967; b. 4.1.43, Leicester; m., Mary Margaret Pratley; 1 s.; 2 d. Educ. Wyggeston Grammar School, Leicester; Magdalen College, Oxford. Address: (b.) Strathclyde House, 20 India Street, Glasgow, G2 4PF; T.-0141-227 3885.

Greenberg, Rabbi Philip T., BA, MPhil. Rabbi, Giffnock and Newlands Hebrew Congregation, Glasgow, since 1981; b. 28.6.37, Liverpool; m., Hannah Barber-Kestenberg; 1 s.; 1 d. Educ. Quarry Bank Grammar, Liverpool; Jews College, London University. Minister, Chingford Hebrew Congregation, 1959-68; Rabbi, Nottingham Hebrew Congregation, 1968-72; Head, Mishna Stream, Hasmonean Boys Grammar School, London, 1972-81. Member, Executive, Glasgow Council of Christians and Jews. Recreations: music; reading; photography. Address: (h.) 20 Ayr Road, Giffnock, Glasgow, G46 6RY; T.-0141-638 0309.

Greene, John Gerald, MA, PhD, FBPsS. Head of Psychological Services, Western District, Greater Glasgow Health Board; Clinical Lecturer, Glasgow University; b. 10.3.38, Glasgow; m., Dr. Elisabeth Rose Hamil; 2 s.; 2 d. Educ. St. Aloysius College, Glasgow; Glasgow University. Clinical Tutor, Glasgow University Master of Applied Science degree in Clinical Psychology; Registrar, Board of Examiners for Master's Degree in Clinical Psychology; Chairman, National (Scotland) Scientific Consultative Committee on Clinical Psychological Services, 1985-87; Secretary and Treasurer, Scottish Branch Committee, Division of Clinical Psychology, 1977-81. Publications: The Social and Psychological Origins of the Climacteric Syndrome, 1984; Clinical Psychology in the Scottish Health Service (Co-author), 1984. Recreations: music; tennis. Address: (b.) Psychology Department, Gartnavel Royal Hospital, Glasgow, G12 0XH.

Greene, John Henderson, MA, LLB. former Partner, MacRoberts, Solicitors, Glasgow, Edinburgh and London; b. 2.6.32, Kilmarnock; m., Catriona McGillivray Scott; 1 s. Educ. Merchiston Castle School, Edinburgh; Edinburgh University. Assistant, Joseph Kirkland & Son, Solicitors, Saltcoats, 1958-60; Assistant, MacRoberts, Solicitors, 1960 (appointed Partner, 1961); Law Society of Scotland: former Vice-Convener, Company Law Committee, former Member, Bankruptcy and Liquidation Committee; former Council Member, Royal Faculty of Procurators, Glasgow; founder Chairman, Troon Round Table, 1964; Captain, Royal Troon Golf Club, 1989-90; Elder, Portland Church, Troon; President, Glasgow Ayrshire Society, 1985-86 and 1993-94; Vice-Chairman, Ayrshire and Arran Health Board. Publication: Law and Practice of Receivership in Scotland (Co-author). Recreations: golf; gardening. Address: (h.) Silvertrees, 7 Lady Margaret Drive, Troon, KA10 7AL; T.-Troon 312482.

Greenman, Professor Jonathan Vaughan, BA, MA, PhD. Professor of Mathematics and Its Applications, Stirling University, since 1990; b. 3.3.39, Cardiff; m., Barbara Phyllis; 2 s. Educ. Kingston Grammar School; Cambridge University. Harkness Scholar, University of California, Berkeley; Department of Physics, MIT; Stanford Research Institute, California; Department of Mathematics, Essex University; Tutor, Open University; Senior Analyst, Corporate Planning, British Petroleum plc; Industry Analyst, Centre for Global Energy Studies. Recreations: cinema; walking; travel. Address: (b.) Department of Mathematics, Stirling University, Stirling, FK9 4LA; T.-01786 467460.

Greenock, William, MA. Principal, Clydebank College, since 1984; b. 3.2.37, Glasgow; 2 d. Educ. Allan Glen's School; Glasgow University. Teacher, secondary schools, 1959-65; David Dale College, 1965-68; Langside College,

1968-70; Reid Kerr College, 1970-75; Anniesland College, 1975-82; Ayr College, 1982-84. Session Clerk, Langside Parish Church, Glasgow. Recreation: golf. Address: (b.) Clydebank College, Kilbowie Road, Clydebank, G81 2AA; T.-0141-952 7771.

Greensted, Professor Christopher Stanford, BSc, MSc. Director, Strathclyde Graduate Business School, since 1986; b. 10.9.41, Leeds; m., Candace Helen; 1 s.; 1 d.; 1 s. by pr. m. Educ. Cranbrook School, Kent; Sir John Cass College, London; Strathclyde University. Chemist in pharmaceuticals, 1960-65; operational research/consultancy in food industry, 1966-68; appointed Lecturer in OR, Strathclyde, 1969, then in Accounting and Finance, 1974; was part-time Director of yacht chandlery company, eight years. RNR officer, eight years. Publications: three books; several articles on business statistics and management development. Recreations: sailing; golf; theatre and concerts. Address: (h.) 18 Carrick Drive, Glasgow, G32 0RW; T.-0141-778 9120.

Greer, Professor Ian Andrew, MB, ChB, MD (Glas), MRCP(UK), FRCP(Glas), MFFP, MRCOG. Muirhead Professor and Head, Department of Obstetrics and Gynaecology, Glasgow University, since 1991; Honorary Consultant Obstetrician and Gynaecologist, Glasgow Royal Infirmary and Glasgow Royal Maternity Hospital, since 1991; b. 16.4.58, Glasgow; m., Anne Smith; 2 s. Educ. Allan Glen's School, Glasgow; Glasgow University. Registrar in General Medicine, Glasgow Royal Infirmary; Registrar in Obstetrics and Gynaecology, Glasgow Royal Maternity Hospital and Glasgow Royal Infirmary; Lecturer in Obstetrics and Gynaecology, Edinburgh University; Clinical Research Scientist/Consultant Obstetrician and Gynaecologist, MRC Reproductive Biology Unit, Edinburgh. MRCOG Gold Medal; Blair-Bell Lectureship, Royal Collge of Obstetricians and Gynaecologists 1989; Travelling Fellowship, RCOG, 1989; Watson Prize Lecture, Royal College of Physicians and Surgeons of Glasgow, 1990. Address: (b.) Department of Obstetrics and Gynaecology, Glasgow University, Glasgow Royal Infirmary, Glasgow, G31 2ER; T.-0141-552 8316.

Gregory, Paul, BA, DipTP, MRTPI. Director of Planning and Development, Borders Regional Council, since 1986. Educ. King Edward VII Grammar School, King's Lynn; Manchester University. Norfolk County Council; Scottish Development Department; Borders Regional Council. Address: (b.) Regional HQ, Newtown St. Boswells, Melrose, TD6 0SA; T.-01835 823301.

Gregson, William Derek Hadfield, CBE, DL, DFH, CEng, FIEE, CBIM, FRSA. Commissioner of Northern Lighthouses; Director: Anderson Strathclyde, Brammer plc, East of Scotland Industrial Investments PLC; Consultant, ICI; b. 27.1.20; m., Rosalind Helen Reeves; 3 s.; 1 d. Educ. UK and Switzerland. Director, Ferranti Holdings, 1983-85; Deputy Chairman, British Airports Authority, 1975-85; Director, British Telecom (Scotland), 1977-85; Past President, EEA; Past President, BEAMA. Recreations: woodwork; books; automation in the home. Address: (h.) Murrayfield House, 66 Murrayfield Avenue, Edinburgh EH12 6AU. T.-0131-337 3858.

Greig, G. Andrew, MA. Author; b. 23.9.51, Bannockburn. Educ. Waid Academy, Anstruther; Edinburgh University. Full-time writer, since 1979; Writer-in-Residence, Glasgow University, 1979-81; Scottish-Canadian Exchange Fellow, 1981-82; Writer-in-Residence, Edinburgh University, 1993-94; climbed on Himalayan expeditions. Publications: six volumes of poetry including Men on Ice, Surviving Passages, The Order of the Day, Western Swing; two mountaineering books; a novel, Electric Brae. Recreations: climbing; fishing; music. Address: Stirling's Dairy, 2 Brewery Close, South Queensferry; T.-0131-331 2535.

Grier, Arnold Macfarlane, MB, ChB, FRCSEdin. Consultant Ear, Nose and Throat Surgeon, Highland Health Board, since 1962; National Vice-President, Scottish Association for the Deaf; b. 5.9.21, Musselburgh; m., Elisabeth J. Kluten; 2 s.; 1 d. Educ. Musselburgh Grammar School; Edinburgh University. Recreations: gardening; aviculture; painting. Address: (h.) Elmbank, 68 Culduthel Road, Inverness; T.-Inverness 234682.

Grier, Scott, OBE, MA, CA, MCIT. Managing Director, Loganair Limited, since 1983; b. 7.3.41, Kilmacolm; m., Frieda Gardiner; 2 s. Educ. Greenock High School; Glasgow University. Apprenticed, Grahams Rintoul & Co., 1962-66; Accountant, Ardrossan Harbour Company, 1967-75; Loganair: Financial/Commercial Manager and Secretary, 1976, Financial Director, 1977; Director, Glasgow Chamber of Commerce, since 1990; Member, Scottish Tourist Board, since 1992; Governor, Scottish Sports Aid Foundation, since 1993. Recreations: golf; philately. Address: (h.) Lagavulin, 15 Corsehill Drive, West Kilbride, KA23 9HU; T.-01294 823138.

Grieve, Professor Andrew Robert, DDS, BDS, FDS RCSEd. Professor of Conservative Dentistry, Dundee University, since 1980 (Dean of Dentistry, since 1993); Consultant in Restorative Dentistry, Tayside Health Board, since 1980; b. 23.5.39, Stirling; m., Frances M. Ritchie; 2 d. Educ. Perth Academy; St. Andrews University. Junior hospital appointments and general dental practice, 1961-65; Lecturer in Operative Dental Surgery and Dental Therapeutics, St. Andrews University, 1963-65; Lecturer in Conservative Dentistry, Birmingham University, 1965; appointed Senior Lecturer and Consultant in Restorative Dentistry, Birmingham Area Health Authority (Teaching), 1975. Member, Dental Council, Royal College of Surgeons of Edinburgh, 1983-88 and since 1989; President, British Society for Restorative Dentistry, 1986-87; President, Royal Odonto-Chirurgical Society of Scotland, 1994-95 (Council Member, 1985-88); Chairman, Tayside Area Dental Advisory Committee, 1987-90; Member, General Dental Council, since 1989. Recreation: hill-walking. Address: (b.) Department of Conservative Dentistry, Dental School, The University, Dundee, DD1 4HN; T.-01382 26041.

Grieve, John. Actor; b. 14.6.24, Glasgow. Trained, Royal Scottish Academy of Music and Drama (James Bridie Gold Medallist), followed by five full seasons, Citizens' Theatre, Glasgow; also appeared in Guthrie's production of The Anatomist, Citizens', 1968; numerous other performances on the Scottish stage, including leading roles in The Bevellers, The Flouers o' Edinburgh, The Good Soldier Schweik, Twelfth Night; television work includes The Vital Spark, Oh Brother, Doctor at Sea, New Year shows; numerous appearances in pantomime; appeared with Scottish Theatre Company in Waiting for Godot and The Thrie Estaites. Address: (b.) c/o David White Associates, 2 Ormond Road, London, Surrey, TW10 6TH.

Grieve, Professor Sir Robert, Kt (1969). Honorary Professor, Heriot-Watt University; Professor Emeritus, Glasgow University; b. 11.12.10. Chief Planner, Scottish Office, 1960-64; Professor of Town and Regional Planning, Glasgow University, 1964-74; Chairman, Highlands and Islands Development Board, 1965-70; former President, Saltire Society; Hon. Vice-President, Scottish Youth Hostels Association.

Grieve, Professor Robert, MA, PhD, CPsych, FBPsS. Professor of Psychology, Edinburgh University, since 1987; b. 2.8.44, Bathgate; m., Anne; 1 s.; 2 d. Educ. Edinburgh University. Lecturer in Psychology, St. Andrews University; Senior Lecturer in Psychology, then Associate Professor of Psychology, University of Western Australia. Address: (b.) Department of Psychology, Edinburgh University, 7 George Square, Edinburgh, EH8 9JZ; T.-0131-650 3441.

Grieve, Hon. Lord (William Robertson Grieve), VRD (1958), QC (Scot), MA, LLB. Senator of the College of Justice in Scotland, 1972-88; Chairman, Board of Governors, St. Columba's Hospice, since 1983; b. 21.10.17, Glasgow; m., Lorna St. John Benn (deceased); 1 s.; 1 d. Educ. Glasgow Academy; Sedbergh School; Glasgow University. Served with Royal Navy as an RNVR officer, 1939-45; Advocate, Scots Bar, 1947; QC, 1957; Sheriff Principal, Renfrew and Argyll, 1964-72; Judge of Appeal, Jersey and Guernsey, 1971-72; Procurator, Church of Scotland, 1968-72; Chairman, Governors, Fettes Trust, 1978-86. President, Glasgow University Union, 1938. Recreations: golf; painting. Address: (h.) 20 Belgrave Crescent, Edinburgh, EH4 3AJ; T.-0131-332 7500.

Griffiths, Nigel, JP. MP (Labour), Edinburgh South, since 1987; Opposition Spokesman on Consumer Affairs, since 1989; b. 20.5.55; m., Sally McLaughlin. Educ. Hawick High School; Edinburgh University; Moray House College of Education. Secretary, Lothian Devolution Campaign, 1978; Rights Adviser, Mental Handicap Pressure Group, 1979-87; City of Edinburgh District Councillor, 1980-87 (Chairperson, Housing Committee); Member, Edinburgh Festival Council, 1984-87; Member, Edinburgh Health Council, 1982-87; Executive Member, Edinburgh Council of Social Service, 1984-87; Member, Wester Hailes School Council, 1981; Executive Member, Scottish Constitutional Convention (Chair, Finance Committee). Recreations: travel; live entertainment; badminton; hill-walking; rock-climbing; architecture; reading; politics. Address: (h.) 30 McLaren Road, Edinburgh, EH9 2BN; T.-0131-667 1947.

Griffiths, Professor Peter Denham, CBE, BSc, MD, LRCP, MRCS, FRCPath, FIMgt, FRSA. Emeritus Professor of Biochemical Medicine, Dundee University (Vice-Principal, 1979-85, Dean of Medicine and Dentistry, 1985-89); Consultant, Tayside Health Board, 1986-89; Director and Trustee, Scottish Hospitals Endowment Research Trust, since 1994; b. 16.6.27, Southampton; m., Joy Burgess; 3 s.; 1 d. Educ. King Edward VI School, Southampton; Guy's Hospital, London University. House appointments, Guy's Hospital, 1956-57; Junior Lecturer in Physiology, Guy's Hospital, 1957-58; Registrar and Senior Registrar, Guy's and Lewisham Hospitals, 1958-64; Consultant Pathologist, Harlow Hospitals Group, 1964-66; Senior Lecturer in Clinical Chemistry/Honorary Consultant, St. Andrews University, then Dundee University, 1966-68. Member, General Medical Council, 1986-93; President, 1987-89, and sometime Chairman of Council, Association of Clinical Biochemists; former Director, Dundee Repertory Theatre. Recreations: music; domestic activities. Address: (h.) 52 Albany Road, West Ferry, Dundee, DD5 1NW; T.-01382 776772.

Grimmond, Iain William, BAcc (Hons), CA. Treasurer, Erskine Hospital for Disabled Ex-Servicemen, since 1981; b. 8.8.55, Girvan; m., Marjory Anne Gordon Chisholm; 1 s.; 2 d. Educ. Hutchesons' Boys Grammar School; Glasgow University. Trainee CA, Ernst & Whinney, Glasgow, 1976-79; Assistant Treasurer, Erskine Hospital, 1979-81. Elder, Giffnock South Parish Church; Honorary Auditor, Paisley Art Institute. Recreations: golf; football; reading. Address: (h.) 9 Wemyss Avenue, Crookfur, Newton Mearns, Glasgow, G77 6AR; T.-0141-639 4894.

Grimson, Dermot, MRTPI. Director, Rural Forum, since 1987; Secretary, Trans European Rural Network; Board Member, Enterprise Music Scotland; Secretary, Forum on the Environment; b. 22.5.52, Glasgow. Educ. Kelvinside Academy; Glasgow School of Art. Planner, Renfrew District Council; Planner, Banff and Buchan District Council. Former Member of Banff and Buchan Health Council; Past Chairman, Buchan Countryside Group; former Secretary, Banff and Buchan Constituency Labour Party; Chairman, Perth Civic Trust. Address: (h.) 10 St. John's Place, Perth; T.-01738 630014.

Grinyer, Professor John Raymond, MSc, FCA. Professor of Accountancy and Business Finance, Dundee University, since 1976 (Head, Department of Accountancy and Business Finance, 1976-90, Dean, Faculty of Law, 1984-85 and 1993); b. 3.3.35, London; m., Shirley Florence Marshall; 1 s.; 2 d. Educ. Central Park Secondary Modern School, London; London School of Economics. London Electricity Board, 1950-53; National Service, RAMC, 1953-55; Halifax Building Society, 1955-56; Martin Redhead & Co., Accountants, 1956-60; Hope Agar & Co., Chartered Accountants, 1960-62; Kemp Chatteris & Co., Chartered Accountants, 1962-63; Lecturer, Harlow Technical College, 1963-66; City of London Polytechnic, 1966-71; Cranfield School of Management, 1971-76; Chairman, British Accounting Association, 1980-81 and 1990, and Scottish Representative, 1984-93. Recreations: golf; dinghy sailing; Member, Royal Tay Yacht Club. Address: (b.) The University, Dundee, DD1 4HN; T.-Dundee 307192.

Grinyer, Professor Peter Hugh, MA (Oxon), PhD. Emeritus and Honorary Professor, St. Andrews University; b. 3.3.35, London; m., Sylvia Joyce Boraston; 2 s. Educ. Balliol College, Oxford; London School of Economics. Senior Managerial Trainee, Unilever Ltd., 1957-59; Personal Assistant to Managing Director, E.R. Holloway Ltd., 1959-61; Lecturer and Senior Lecturer, Hendon College of Technology, 1961-64; Lecturer, The City University, London, 1965-69; The City University Business School: Senior Lecturer and Co-ordinator of Research, 1969-72, Reader, 1972-74, Professor of Business Strategy, 1974-79; Esmee Fairbairn Professor of Economics (Finance and Investment), St. Andrews University, 1979-93; Chairman, Department of Economics, 1979-85; Vice-Principal, 1985-87 (Acting Principal, 1986); Chairman, Department of Management, 1987-89; Chairman, St. Andrews Management Institute, since 1989; Chairman, St. Andrews Strategic Management Ltd., since 1989. Member, Sub-Committee on Management and Business Studies, University Grants Committee, 1979-85; Consultant to NEDO on Sharpbenders Project, 1984-86; Non-Executive Director: Glenrothes Enterprise Trust, 1983-86, John Brown plc, 1984-86, Don Bros. Buist plc (now Don and Low (Holdings) Ltd.) 1985-91, Ellis and Goldstein plc, 1987-88; Chairman (non-executive), McIlroy Coates, since 1991; Member, Scottish Legal Aid Board, since 1992. Recreations: mountain walking; golf; listening to music. Address: (b.) St. Andrews Management Institute, 3 St. Mary's Place, St. Andrews, KY16 9UY; T.-01334 62871.

Groat, John Malcolm Freswick, MBE, JP, DL. Company Director: J.M.F. Groat & Sons Ltd., Orkney Seaport Supplies Ltd.; Member, Orkney Health Board, 1979-91; Postmaster, Longhope, Orkney, since 1964; Secretary, Longhope Lifeboat, 1962-95; b. 9.9.23, Longhope, Orkney; m., Edna Mary Yule. War service: joined RAFVR as Air Crew Cadet, 1943; operational service with No. 576 and No. 150 Lancaster Squadrons No. 5 Group, Bomber Command, RAF, until 1945, then in India and as Officer i/c transport, Air Command South East Asia, Changi, Singapore, until 1947; Clerk, Hoy and Walls District Council, 1953-74; Clerk, School Management Committee, Walls and Flotta, 1953-74; Registrar of Births etc., Hoy and Walls, 1953-74; Provincial Grand Master, Orkney and Zetland, 1979-84; Trustee, Longhope Lifeboat Disaster Fund, since 1969; Agent, Shipwrecked Mariners Society; Secretary, Longhope British Legion, 1948-53; Secretary, Longhope Sailing Club, 1950-60; former Member, Orkney Pilotage Committee; Director, Orkney Islands Shipping Co., 1974-87; Member, Coastguard Lifesaving Company, Longhope, 1947-61; Founder Member, Orkney Flying Club, 1949; Secretary/Treasurer, Walls and Hoy Agricultural Society, 1950-60; R.W. Master, Lodge St. Colm No. 1022, 1964-69. Address: (h.) Moasound, Longhope, Orkney, T.-241.

Groom, Brian William Alfred, BA. Editor, Scotland on Sunday, since 1994; b. 26.4.55, Manchester; m., Carla May; 1 s.; 1 d. Educ. Manchester Grammar School; Balliol College, Oxford. Reporter, Goole Times, 1976-78; Financial Times, 1978-88: Sub-Editor, International Edition, 1978-81, Labour Reporter, 1981-85, UK News Editor, 1985-88; Deputy Editor, Scotland on Sunday, 1988-94. Recreations: walking; cricket; cinema; reading. Address: (b.) 20 North Bridge, Edinburgh, EH1 1YT; T.-0131-225 2468.

Grossart, Angus McFarlane McLeod, CBE, LLD, MA, CA. Advocate; Merchant Banker; Chairman of the Trustees, National Galleries of Scotland, since 1988; Director: Hewden Stuart plc, since 1988, Alexander and Alexander, New York, since 1984, American Trust PLC, since 1973, Edinburgh Fund Managers PLC, since 1983 (Deputy Chairman), Noble Grossart Limited, since 1969, The Royal Bank of Scotland plc, since 1982, The Scottish Investment Trust PLC, since 1973 (Chairman), Scottish Television plc, since 1989; b. 6.4.37, Glasgow; m., Gay Kerr Dodd; 1 d. Educ. Glasgow Academy; Glasgow University. CA apprentice, Thomson McLintock, 1958-62; Advocate, Scottish Bar, 1963-69; Managing Director, Noble Grossart Ltd., since 1969. Former Scottish Editor, British Tax Encyclopaedia and British Tax Review. Recreations: golf; decorative arts. Address: (b.) 48 Queen Street, Edinburgh, EH2 3NR; T.-0131-226 7011.

Grosset, Alan George, MA, LLB, WS, NP. Partner, Alex. Morison & Co., WS; b. 18.1.42, Edinburgh; 1 s.; 1 d. Educ. Royal High School, Edinburgh; Edinburgh University. Law Society of Scotland "Troubleshooter" from inception of scheme, until 1987; President, Scottish Lawn Tennis Association, 1983-84; Council Member, Lawn Tennis Association, 1980-89; first Chairman, Scottish Sports Association, 1984-90; Member, Scottish Sports Council, 1984-94, Vice-Chairman, since 1994; Captain, Duddingston Golf Club, 1992-94; Founder Member, Scottish Branch, Society for Computers and Law; Secretary, British Sports Forum, since 1991. Recreations: golf; tennis; squash. Address: (b.) 68 Queen Street, Edinburgh; T.-0131-226 6541.

Grosz, David Peter, BA (Hons). Chairman, Ramblers' Association Scottish Council, since 1985; Founding Member and Committee Member, Scottish Council for National Parks, 1991-95; b. 2.4.39, London. Educ. Wyggeston Boys' Grammar School, Leicester; Nottingham University; School of Education, Leicester University. School Teacher, Leicester, 1962-78, West Lothian, 1978-84. Member, RA National Executive Committee, since 1983; Member, Board of Directors, Scottish Rights of Way Society, 1984-92; Chairman, Friends of New Lanark, 1985-89; Member, Council, National Trust for Scotland, 1989-94. Recreations: walking; reading; campaigning with passion for public access and countryside conservation. Address: (h.) 57 Harburn Avenue, Deans, Livingston, EH54 8NH; T.-01506 410493.

Groves, C. Arthur, JP. Chairman, Borders Region Valuation Panel, since 1991; Chairman, Justices Committee, Ettrick and Lauderdale, since 1984; Chairman, General Inland Revenue Commissioners, since 1983; b. 28.11.24, London. Educ. Raine's Foundation, London. Selkirk Town Council, 1961-75 (Hon. Treasurer); former Selkirk County Councillor (Chairman, Finance Committee). Recreation: equestrian activities. Address: (h.) 24 Hillview Crescent, Selkirk, TD7 4AZ; T.-01750 21126.

Grundy, David Stanley, MA, MPhil. Commissioner Policy and Resources, Forestry Commission, since 1990; b. 10.4.43, Leigh; m., Elizabeth Jenny Schadla Hall; 1 s. Educ. De La Salle College, Manchester; Jesus College, Cambridge; Jesus College, Oxford. Assistant Principal, MOP, 1967-70; Assistant Private Secretary to Minister,

Ministry of Technology, 1970-71; Principal, DTI, 1971-78; DOE, 1978-79; Chief Economic Adviser, Government of Vanuatu, 1979-81; Chief Economist, Forestry Commission, 1982-90. Recreations: angling; bird-watching; gardening; tennis. Address: (b.) 231 Corstorphine Road, Edinburgh, EH12 7AT; T.-0131-334 0303.

Guest, Charles Drysdale Graham, FRICS. Chartered Surveyor; Partner, Ryden Property Consultants and Chartered Surveyors, since 1981; b. 26.7.47, Edinburgh; m., Gail Meikle; 1 s.; 2 d. Educ. George Watson's College, Edinburgh; Merchiston Castle School, Edinburgh; Liverpool Polytechnic. Richard Ellis, Chartered Surveyors, Johannesburg, 1970-72; Weatherall Green & Smith, London, 1972-77; joined Ryden, 1977. Recreations: shooting; fishing; skiing; tennis. Address: (b.) 46 Castle Street, Edinburgh, EH2 3BM; T.-0131-225 6612.

Guild, Ivor Reginald, CBE, FRSE, MA, LLB, WS; b. 2.4.24, Dundee. Educ. Cargilfield; Rugby; New College, Oxford; Edinburgh University. Director, Fulcrum Investment Trust; Trustee, Edinburgh University; former Partner, Shepherd & Wedderburn, WS; former Procurator Fiscal to the Lyon Court. Recreations: golf; genealogy. Address: (b.) 16 Charlotte Square, Edinburgh, EH2 4YS; T.-0131-225 8585.

Guild, Stuart Alexander, TD, BL, WS, NP. Writer to the Signet, since 1950; Senior Partner, Guild and Guild WS, 1958-89; b. 25.1.24, Edinburgh; m., Fiona Catherine MacCulloch; 1 s.; 2 d. Educ. Edinburgh Academy; George Watson's College, Edinburgh; Queen's University, Belfast; Edinburgh University. Royal Artillery, 1942-47; Territorial Army (RA), 1947-65; County Cadet Commandant, Lothian Bn., ACF, 1967-69 (Hon. Lt-Col.); Honorary Treasurer, 1976-91, and Shooting Convener, Army Cadet Force Association (Scotland), 1969-94; Council Member, Army Cadet Force Association, 1976-91; Member, Royal Artillery Council of Scotland, 1982-84 and 1985-93; President, Lothian & Peebles Home Guard Rifle Association, 1980-91; Vice-President, Lothian Smallbore Shooting Association, 1985-92; Governor, Melville College Trust, 1976-91 (now Hon. Governor); Chairman, Sandilands Memorial Trust, 1980-94; Assistant, The Company of Merchants of the City of Edinburgh, 1972-75; Vice-Convener, Mary Erskine School for Girls, 1973-75. Recreations: golf; target shooting; photography. Address: (h.) 7 Lockharton Gardens, Edinburgh, EH14 1AU.

Gulliver, Stuart, BSc (Econ). Chief Executive, Glasgow Development Agency, since 1991; b. 10.1.42, Sheffield; m., Barbara McKewan; 3 s.; 1 d. Educ. Firth Park Grammar School; London School of Economics. Research Fellow in Economics, Leeds University; Senior Lecturer, Leeds Polytechnic; commercial development, Warrington New Town Development Corporation; Regional Director, Scottish Development Agency. Visiting Professor in Economic and Social Research, Glasgow University. Recreations: cricket; tennis; watching football; music, especially modern jazz; theatre. Address: (b.) Atrium Court, 50 Waterloo Street, Glasgow, G2 6HQ; T.-0141-204 1111.

Gunn, Alexander MacLean, MA, BD. Minister, Aberfeldy with Amulree and Strathbraan with Dull and Weem, since 1986; b. 26.2.43, Inverness; m., Ruth T.S.; 1 s.; 1 d. Educ. Edinburgh Academy; Beauly; Dingwall Academy; Edinburgh University and New College. Parish Minister: Wick St. Andrews and Thrumster, 1967-73; Member, Caithness Education Committee, 1968-73; Parish Minister, Glasgow St. David's Knightswood, 1973-86; Convener, Church of Scotland Rural Working Group, 1988-90; Convenor, General Assembly's Presbytery Development Committee, 1990-92; Convenor, General Assembly's Mission and Evangelism Resource Committee, since 1992. Chairman, Breadalbane Academy School Board, 1989-92.

Address: The Manse, Taybridge Terrace, Aberfeldy, PH15 2BS; T.-01887 820656.

Gunn, James Forsyth Grimmond, BSc, CEng, FICE, FIStructE, ACIArb, MConsE. Chairman, Blyth & Blyth Group, since 1986; Director, Blyth & Blyth Associates, since 1976; b. 5.8.36, Edinburgh; m., Brenda; 1 s.; 1 d. Educ. George Watson's Boys' College; Edinburgh University. Construction Engineer, Bovis, London and Manchester, 1960-61; joined Blyth & Blyth, 1962; Manager, Belfast Office, 1964-70; Associate, Edinburgh Office, 1970; Partner/Director, Edinburgh, 1976. Former Member, Scottish Council, CBI; Member, Committee, Institution of Structural Engineers, Scottish Branch. Recreations: golf; fishing; hill-walking; music. Address: (h.) 8A Glencairn Crescent, Edinburgh, EH12 5BS; T.-0131-226 6975.

Gurdon, Col. Robert Temple, FBIM. Regimental Secretary, The Black Watch, since 1992; b. 23.6.32, Colchester; m., Elizabeth Ann Terry; 1 s.; 1 d. (dec.). Educ. Rugby School. Commissioned The Black Watch, 1952; Staff College, 1963; National Defence College, 1973; commanded 1/51 Highland Volunteers, 1975-77; Chief of Staff Scotland, 1979-83; retired as Colonel, 1983; Schools Liaison Officer for Army in Scotland, 1983-92. Recreations: shooting; golf. Address: (h.) 4 Middleby Street, Edinburgh, EH9 1TD; T.-0131-667 3875.

Guy, Professor John Alexander, MA, PhD, FRHistS. Professor of Modern History, St. Andrews University, since 1991, and Head, School of History and International Relations, 1992-94; Provost, St. Leonard's College, since 1994; b. 16.1.49, Australia; m., Rachel Hooper; 1 s.; 1 d. Educ. King Edward VII School, Lytham; Clare College, Cambridge. Research Fellow, Selwyn College, Cambridge, 1970-73; Assistant Keeper of Public Records, Public Record Office, London, 1973-78; Visiting Lecturer in British History, University of California, Berkeley, 1977; History Department, Bristol University, 1978-90; British Academy Marc Fitch Research Reader, 1987-89; John Hinkley (Visiting) Professor, Johns Hopkins University, Baltimore, 1990; Richard L. Turner Professor of Humanities, and Professor of History, University of Rochester, 1990-91. Publications: The Cardinal's Court; The Public Career of Sir Thomas More; Law and Social Change in British History (Co-editor); The Court of Star Chamber and its Records to the Reign of Elizabeth I; Christopher St. German on Chancery and Statute; Reassessing the Henrician Age (Co-author); The Complete Works of Thomas More, Vol. X (Co-Editor); Tudor England; The Tudors and Stuarts (Co-author). Address: Office of the Principal, St. Andrews University, College Gate, St. Andrews, KY16 9AJ.

Gwilt, George David, MA, FFA, FBCS. Director: European Assets Trust NV, since 1979, Scottish Mortgage & Trust plc, since 1983, Hodgson Martin Ltd., since 1989, Edinburgh Festival Society Ltd., 1989-95; b. 11.11.27, Edinburgh; m., Ann Sylvester; 3 s. Educ. Sedbergh; St. John's College, Cambridge. Standard Life, 1949-88, latterly as Managing Director; President, Faculty of Actuaries, 1981-83; Trustee, South of Scotland TSB, 1966-83; Member, Younger Committee on Privacy, 1970-72; Member, Monopolies and Mergers Commission, 1983-87; Convener, Scottish Poetry Library, since 1988. Recreations: flute playing; squash. Address: (h.) 39 Oxgangs Road, Edinburgh, EH10 7BE; T.-0131-445 1266.

H

Haddington, 13th Earl of (John George Baillie-Hamilton); b. 21.12.41; m.; 1 s.; 2 d. Address: Mellerstain, Gordon, Berwickshire, TD3 6LG.

Haddow, Margaret Maureen, BA, MSc, MIMgt. Head, Department of Business Information Management, Napier University, since 1992; b. 25.5.46, Glasgow. Educ. Dalziel High School, Motherwell; Strathclyde University. Lecturer/Senior Lecturer, West Lothian College of Further Education, 1968-79; joined Napier University, 1979, as a Senior Lecturer. Elder, St. Andrew's and St. George's Church, Edinburgh. Publication: Administrative Management Case Studies, 1992. Recreations: music; singing — alto in Scottish Chorus and church choir. Address: (b.) Department of Business Information Management, Napier University, Sighthill Court, Edinburgh, EH11 4BN; T.-0131-455 3458.

Hadley, Geoffrey, BSc (Hons), PhD. Honorary Senior Lecturer, Aberdeen University, since 1985; Consultant Microbiologist, since 1985; b. 7.2.32, Stoke-on-Trent; 3 d. by pr. m. Educ. Longton High School; Birmingham University. Research Fellow, Nottingham University, 1956-58; Lecturer, Glasgow University, 1958-60; Lecturer, then Senior Lecturer, Aberdeen University, 1960-85; seconded to University of Malaya, 1967-68; Member, Aberdeen County Council, 1973-75; Grampian Regional Council, 1974-94; Convener, Grampian Regional Council, 1986-90; Vice-President, British Mycological Society, 1987; Chairman, Aberdeen Civic Society; Chairman, Grampian Heart Campaign; Member, Management Committee, Hanover (Scotland) Housing Association. Recreations: walking; music; home brewing and wine-making; cricket; classical music; home brewing and wine-making; cricket; cycling; DIY. Address: (h.) 74 Don Street, Old Aberdeen, Aberdeen, AB2 1UU; T.-01224 494472.

Hagart-Alexander of Ballochmyle, Sir Claud, Bt, DL, JP, BA, CEng, MInstMC. Vice Lord-Lieutenant, Ayrshire and Arran, since 1983; b. 6.1.27, Peking; m., Hilda Etain Acheson; 2 s.; 2 d. Educ. Sherborne; Corpus Christi College, Cambridge. Address: (h.) Kingencleugh House, Mauchline, Ayrshire, KA5 5JL; T.-01290 550217.

Haggart, Rt. Rev. Alastair Iain Macdonald, MA, LLD. Retired Bishop; b. 10.10.15, Glasgow; m., 1, Margaret Agnes Trundle; 2 d.; 2, Mary Scholes. Educ. Edinburgh Theological College; Durham University. Curate, St. Mary's Cathedral, Glasgow; Curate. St. Mary's, Hendon, London; Precentor, St. Ninian's Cathedral, Perth; Rector, St. Oswald's, King's Park, Glasgow; Synod Clerk, Diocese of Glasgow; Provost, St. Paul's Cathedral, Dundee; Principal, Theological College, Edinburgh; Bishop of Edinburgh; Primus, Scottish Episcopal Church. Recreations: walking; reading; music; asking people questions. Address: (h.) 19 Eglinton Crescent, Edinburgh, EH12 5BY; T.-0131-337 8948.

Haggart, David Ballantine, JP, MA. Writer and Broadcaster; Head of Careers Service, Aberdeen University, 1963-92; b. 15.3.34, Dundee; m., Gwendolen Hall; 3 s. Educ. Aberdeen Grammar School; Aberdeen University. National Service, Band of Royal Corps of Signals, 1956-58; Teacher, Perth and Kinross County Council, 1958-59; Youth Employment Officer, City of Aberdeen, 1959-63; Member, Justices' Committee, Aberdeen, since 1976; Member, Justice of the Peace Advisory Committee, since 1991; Chairman, Ferryhill Community Council, 1976-82; Chairman, Castlehill Housing Association, 1991-94; Chairman, Aberdeen and NE Scotland Music Festival, 1982-84; Writer and Producer, educational television programmes, including The Interview (Royal Television

Society award); Editor, Current Vacancies, 1986-93; Columnist, Prospects Today, Evening Express; regular radio broadcasts, mainly on religious programmes; Presenter, Sunday Best, Northsound Radio, since 1981, Producer, since 1988. Recreations: music; motoring; local history. Address: (h.) 24 Polmuir Road, Aberdeen, AB1 2SY; T.-01224 584176.

Haggart, Mary Elizabeth, OBE; b. 8.4.24, Leicester; m., Rt. Rev. A.I.M. Haggart (qv). Educ. Wyggeston Grammar School for Girls, Leicester; Leicester Royal Infirmary and Children's Hospital. Leicester Royal Infirmary: Staff Nurse, 1947-48, Night Sister, 1948-50, Ward Sister, 1950-56, Night Superintendent, 1956-58, Assistant Matron, 1958-61; Assistant Matron, Brook General Hospital, London, 1962-64; Matron, Dundee Royal Infirmary and Matron Designate, Ninewells Hospital, Dundee, 1964-68; Chief Nursing Officer, Board of Managements, Dundee General Hospitals and Ninewells Hospital, 1968-73; Chief Area Nursing Officer, Tayside Health Board, 1974-82; President, Scottish Association of Nurse Administrators, 1972-77; Member, Scottish Board, Royal College of Nursing, 1965-70; Member, General Nursing Council for Scotland, 1965-70 and 1978-82; Chairman, Scottish Board of Nursing Midwifery and Health Visiting, 1980-83; Member, Standing Nursing and Midwifery Committee, 1971-74 (Vice Chairman, 1973-74); Member, Action on Smoking and Health Scotland, 1978-82 (Chairman, Working Party, Smoking and Nurses); Governor, Dundee College of Technology, 1978-82; Honorary Lecturer, Department of Community Medicine, Dundee University and Medical School, 1980-82; Member, Management Committee, Carstairs State Hospital, 1982-92; Member, United Kingdom Central Council for Nursing Midwifery and Health Visiting, 1980-82; Member, Scottish Hospital Endowments Research Trust, since 1986. Recreations: walking; music; travel. Address: (h.) 19 Eglinton Crescent, Edinburgh, EH12 5RY; T.-0131-337 8948.

Haggarty, William McLaughlan, TD, BL. Solicitor, since 1950; Senior Partner, Mathie-Morton Black & Buchanan, Ayr; Honorary Sheriff, South Strathclyde, Dumfries and Galloway; b. 22.2.26, Glasgow; m., Olive Dorothy Mary Speirs; 1 s.; 1 d. Educ. High School of Glasgow; Glasgow University. War Service, Merchant Navy, 1943-47; Chairman, National Insurance Tribunal, North and South Ayrshire, 1963-88; Lt. Col. Commanding 264 (Scottish) Regiment, Royal Corps of Transport (TA), 1966; Dean, Ayr Faculty of Solicitors, 1982; Governor, Craigie College of Education, Ayr, 1983-91. Recreations: golf; travel; gardening. Address: (b.) 4 Alloway Place, Ayr; T.-01292 263549.

Hague, Clifford Bertram, MA, DipTP, MRTPI. Head, School of Planning and Housing, Heriot-Watt University/Edinburgh College of Art, since 1990; b. 22.8.44, Manchester; m., Irene; 1 s.; 3 d. Educ. North Manchester Grammar School; Magdalene College, Cambridge; Manchester University. Planning Assistant, Glasgow Corporation Planning Department, 1968-69; Lecturer, Department of Town and Country Planning, Heriot-Watt University/Edinburgh College of Art, 1969-73, Senior Lecturer, 1973-90; Council Member, Royal Town Planning Institute, 1979-87 and since 1991 (Past Chairman, Scottish Branch). Publication: The Development of Planning Thought: A Critical Perspective, 1984. Recreation: cricket. Address: (b.) School of Planning and Housing, Edinburgh College of Art, Edinburgh, EH3 9DF; T.-0131-221 6160.

Haig, Andrew James Newton, BSc, PhD, CBiol, FIBiol, FCIWEM. Depute Director (Chief Scientist), Clyde River Purification Board, since 1992; b. 2.4.47, London; m., Barbara Mary Jackson; 1 s.; 1 d. Educ. King's School, Bruton; London University; Leeds University. Research Assistant, Leeds University Marine Laboratory, 1968-71;

Clyde River Purification Board: Marine Biologist, 1971-74, Assistant Marine Survey Officer, 1974-75, Marine Survey Officer, 1975-89, Assistant Director, 1989-92. Member, Scottish Council, Institute of Biology, 1978-81; Consultant/Adviser, World Health Organisation, Copenhagen 1978, Lisbon 1978, Athens 1979; NATO Invited Specialist, Lisbon 1977; Member, Fish Farming Advisory Committee, since 1994. Recreations: natural history; gardening; angling. Address: (b.) Rivers House, Murray Road, East Kilbride, Glasgow, G75 0LA; T.-013552 38181.

Haig of Bemersyde, The Earl (George Alexander Eugene Douglas), OBE, DL, MA, ARSA, KStJ. Painter; b. 15.3.18, London; 1 s.; 2 d. Educ. Cargilfield; Stowe School; Christ Church, Oxford. 2nd Lt., Royal Scots Greys, 1938; retired on account of disability, 1951 (rank of Captain); attended Camberwell School of Arts and Crafts; paintings in many public and private collections; served Second World War; taken prisoner, 1942; Member, Royal Fine Art Commission for Scotland, 1958-61; Chairman, SE South East Scotland Disablement Advisory Committee, 1960-73; Trustee, Scottish National War Memorial, since 1961 (present Chairman); Trustee, National Galleries of Scotland, 1962-72; Member, Scottish Arts Council, 1968-74; Past Chairman, Royal British Legion Scotland; President, Earl Haig Fund Scotland/Royal British Legion Scotland, 1980-86; President, Scottish Branch, Officers Association; President, Scottish Craft Centre, 1952-73; Vice President, Scottish National Institution for War Blinded and of Royal Blind Asylum, since 1960. Recreations: fishing; shooting. Address: (h.) Bemersyde, Melrose, TD6 9DP; T.-018352 2762.

Haines, Gerald, MA. Rector, Keith Grammar School, since 1989; b. 28.7.38, Glamorgan; m., Avril Esther Shearer; 1 s.; 1 d. Educ. Eastwood Senior Secondary, Glasgow; Glasgow University. Teacher of English, Cumbernauld High School, 1964-69; Principal Teacher of English, then Assistant Head Teacher, Lossiemouth High School, 1969-78; Depute Rector, Keith Grammar School, 1978-89. Recreations: bridge; cricket; gardening; golf. Address: (b.) School Road, Keith, AB55 3ES; T.-01542 882461.

Hajducki, Andrew Michael, QC, MA. Advocate, since 1979; QC (Scot), since 1994; Temporary Sheriff, since 1987; b. 12.11.52, London; 2 s.; 1 d. Educ. Dulwich College; Cambridge University (Downing). Called to English Bar (Gray's Inn), 1976; Reporter, Session Cases, 1980; Tutor, Edinburgh University, 1979-81; Safeguarder, Lothian Children's Panel, since 1987. Fellow, Royal Society of Antiquaries of Scotland. Publications: two books on the railways of East Lothian; Scottish Civic Government Licensing Law (Co-author). Recreations: travel by train, tram, and Land Rover; reading fiction, topography, and history. Address: (b.) Advocates Library, Parliament House, Edinburgh.

Halcrow, James George, MA, BMus (Hons), DipEd. Director of Education, Shetland Islands Council, since 1992; b. 28.2.45, Lerwick; m., Anne; 2 d. Educ. Anderson Educational Institute, Lerwick; Edinburgh University. Teacher of Music, Royal High School, Edinburgh, 1970-71; Principal Teacher of Music, Anderson High School, Lerwick, and part-time County Music Organiser, 1971-74; Adviser in Music, Shetland Islands Council, 1974-89; Home/School Adviser, Shetland Islands Council, 1989-92. Chairman, Association of Music Advisers in Scotland, 1988-90; Convenor, Music Panel, Scottish Examination Board, 1991. Recreations: performing music; DIY. Address: (b.) Education Office, Schlumberger Base, Gremista Industrial Estate, Lerwick, ZE1 0PX; T.-01595 698800, Ext. 3222.

Halcrow, William. Director, Forth River Purification Board. Address: (b.) Avenue North, Heriot-Watt Research Park, Riccarton, Edinburgh, EH14 4AP.

Haldane of Gleneagles, James Martin, MA, CA, FRSA. 26th Laird of Gleneagles; Partner, Chiene & Tait, CA, since 1989; Director, Scottish Life Assurance Co., since 1990; Chairman, Queen's Hall (Edinburgh) Ltd., since 1987; Director, Investors Capital Trust PLC, since 1995; Director, Wellington Members Agency Ltd., since 1955; b. 18.9.41, Edinburgh; m., Petronella Victoria Scarlett; 1 s.; 2 d. Educ. Winchester College; Magdalen College, Oxford. Partner, Arthur Young, 1970-89. Member of Council, National Trust for Scotland, since 1992; Treasurer, Queen's Bodyguard for Scotland (Royal Company of Archers), since 1992; Chairman, Craighead Investments PLC, 1982-90; Trustee, D'Oyly Carte Opera Trust, 1985-92; Member of Council, Edinburgh Festival Society, 1985-89; Member, Northern and Scottish Board, Legal and General Assurance Co., 1984-87; Chairman, Scottish Chamber Orchestra, 1978-85. Recreations: music; golf. Address: (h.) Gleneagles, Auchterarder, PH3 1PJ; T.-01764 682 388.

Haldane, Professor John Joseph, BA, PGCE, BA, PhD. Professor of Philosophy, St. Andrews University, since 1994; Director, Centre for Philosophy and Public Affairs, St. Andrews University, since 1988; b. 19.2.54, London; m., Hilda Marie Budas; 2 s.; 2 d. Educ. St. Aloysius College, Glasgow; Wimbledon School of Art; London University. Art Master, St. Joseph's Grammar School, Abbey Wood, 1976-79; Visiting Lecturer, School of Architecture, University of Westminster, since 1983; Lecturer in Moral Philosophy, St. Andrews University, 1983-90, Reader, 1990-94. Member, Editorial Board, The Philosophical Quarterly, since 1984; Member, Editorial Boards: Journal of Medical Ethics, Journal of Philosophy of Education, American Journal of Jurisprudence; Fellow, Royal Society of Edinburgh. Recreations: reading; photography; gardening; art. Address: (b.) Department of Moral Philosophy, St. Andrews University, St. Andrews, KY16 9AL; T.-01334 462488.

Halford-MacLeod, Col. (ACF), Retired Lt. Col. Aubrey Philip Lydiat, MA (Hons), late Black Watch (RHR); retired Army officer; Director, Living History in Scotland and Living History Ltd., since 1993; b. 28.4.42, Bagdad; m., Alison Fiona Brown; 2 s.; 1 d. Educ. Winchester College; RMA Sandhurst; Magdalen College, Oxford. Commissioned into Black Watch, 1962; Lt., 1964; Capt., 1968; Maj., 1975; Lt. Col., 1985; appointed Commanding Officer, Glasgow and Strathclyde Universities OTC, 1985; Chief of Staff, The Scottish Division, 1988; UK Liaison Officer (as Colonel), US European Command Stuttgart, 1991; SO1 G1 Action and Support Team (Demob Cell), Army HQ Scotland, 1992; Commandant, The Black Watch ACF Battalion, 1993. Recreations: walking the dogs; shooting; fishing; opera; model soldiers; curling; country dancing. Address: (h.) The Old Manse, 28 Skene Street, Strathmiglo, KY14 7QL; T.-01337 860715.

Halford-MacLeod, Aubrey Seymour, CMG, CVO, MA (Oxon); b. 15.12.14, Birmingham; m., Giovanna M. Durst; 3 s.; 1 d. Educ. King Edward's School, Birmingham, and abroad; Magdalen College, Oxford. HM Diplomatic Service, Third Secretary, Foreign Office, 1937; Bagdad, 1939; Office of Minister of State, Algiers, 1943; reopened Embassy, Rome, 1944; Secretary, Advisory Council Italy, and Political Adviser to Allied Control Commission, 1943-46; PPS to Permanent Under Secretary, Foreign Office, 1946-49; Deputy Secretary-General, Council of Europe, 1949-52; Tokyo, 1953-55; Libya, 1955-57; Kuwait, 1957-59; Munich, 1959-65; Ambassador to Iceland, 1966-70. Director, Scottish Opera, 1972-77; President, Scottish Society for Northern Studies, 1972-75; Vice-President, Clan MacLeod Society of Scotland, 1973-77; Adviser, Scottish Council (Development and Industry), 1970-77. Recreations: fishing; ornithology. Address: (h.) Mulag House, North Harris, Western Isles, PA85 3AB; T.-Harris 2054.

Hall, Professor Denis R., BSc, MPhil, PhD, FInstP, FIEE, CEng, FRSE. Professor of Optoelectronics, Heriot-Watt

University, since 1986; b. 1.8.42; m.; 1 s.; 1 d. Educ. Manchester University; London University; Case Western Reserve University. NRC Postdoctoral Fellow, NASA Goddard Space Flight Center, 1971-72; Senior Research Scientist, AVCO Everett Research Laboratory, Boston, 1972-74; Principal Scientific Officer, Royal Signal and Radar Establishment, 1974-79; Senior Lecturer/Reader, Department of Applied Physics, Hull University, 1979-86. Address: (b.) Heriot-Watt University, Riccarton, Edinburgh, EH14 4AS.

Hall, Jacqueline, MA (Hons), DMS, DipM. Executive Director, Gordon Enterprise Trust, since 1990; b. 17.1.65, Aberdeen. Educ. Bankhead Academy, Aberdeen; Aberdeen University; Robert Gordon's Institute of Technology. Executive Officer, Civil Service, 1986-87; Assistant Director, Moray Enterprise Trust, 1987-90. Scottish Young Career Woman of the Year, 1991; Board Member, Grampian, Young Enterprise Scotland; Assessment Panel Member, Investors in People Scotland; Advisor, Young Enterprise Scotland; Advisor, Princes Scottish Youth Business Trust. Recreations:scuba diving; running; swimming; aerobics; reading; salmon fishing. Address: (b.) The Business Development Centre, Thainstone Agricultural Centre, Inverurie, AB51 9WU; T.-01467 621166.

Hall, Major General Jonathan Michael Francis Cooper, OBE (1987). GOC Scotland and Governor of Edinburgh Castle, since 1995; b. 10.8.44, Wilmslow; m., Sarah Linda Hudson; 2 d. Educ. Taunton School; RMA Sandhurst. Cmmnd 3rd Carabiniers, 1965; Staff College, Camberley, 1977; Comd Offr, Royal Scots Dragoon Guards, 1984-86; Higher Cmd and Staff Course, 1988; Comd 12th Armoured Bde, 1989-90; Member, Royal College of Defence Studies, 1991; Dep Mil Sec (A), Ministry of Defence, 1992-94; Director, RAC, 1994-95. Member, Cavalry and Guards' General Club, since 1981; Col Comdt The Scottish Division, since 1995; Col Comdt The Royal Army Veterinary Corps, since 1995; Chairman, Her Majesty's Commissioners, Queen Victoria School, Dunblane, since 1995; Hon. Vice-President, Royal British Legion Scotland; Vice-President, Earl Haig Fund Scotland; Member, Council, Scottish National Institution for the War Blinded; Hon. President, Princess Louise's Scottish Hospital (Erskine Hospital); Member, Executive Council, Scottish Veterans' Residences; Patron, Scottish Society for the Employment of Ex-Regular Sailors, Soldiers and Airmen; Hon. President, Scottish Veterans' Garden City Association; Member, Council, Scottish Union Jack Association; Trustee, Scottish National War Memorial; Committee Member, Army Benevolent Fund. Recreations: country pursuits; tennis; skiing; travel. Address: (b.) Army HQ Scotland, Craigiehall, South Queensferry, West Lothian, EH30 9TN; T.-0131-310 2061.

Hall, Martin R., BSc (Hons), MREHIS, MIEH. Director of Environmental Services, Shetland Islands Council, since 1992; b. 30.3.56, Irvine; m., Joyce; 1 s.; 2 d. Educ. St. Michael's Academy, Kilwinning; Strathclyde University. Student EHO, Saltcoats Town Council, 1974; EHO, Cunninghame DC, 1975-86; Depute Director, Environmental Health and Trading Standards, Shetland Islands Council, 1986-90; Director, EH&TS, 1990-92. Recreations: Scouting; golf. Address: (b.) Greenhead, Gremista, Lerwick, ZE1 0PY; T.-01595 696789.

Hall, Professor Peter Anthony, BSc, PhD, MD, MRCPath. Professor of Cellular Pathology, Dundee University, since 1993; b. 2.2.58, Italy. Educ. Tunbridge Wells Technical School; London University. Lecturer in Pathology, London University; Research Fellow, Imperial Cancer Research Fund; Senior Lecturer, Royal Postgraduate Medical School; Professor of Histopathology, London University. Recreation: walking.

Hall, Samuel James, BL, NP, WS. Solicitor, since 1951; Partner, Robson, McLean WS, since 1957; former Legal Assessor, Professional Conduct Committee, United Kingdom Central Council for Nursing, Midwifery and Health Visiting; Solicitor to the Ministry of Defence (Navy Department) in Scotland; b. 29.5.30, Edinburgh; m., Olive Douglas Kerr; 2 s.; 1 d. Educ. Daniel Stewart's College, Edinburgh; Edinburgh University. Officer, Royal Army Service Corps, until 1953. Recreations: golf; reading history of Second World War. Address: (h.) Carron Vale, 2 Wardie Road, Edinburgh; T.-0131-552 1836.

Hall, William, CBE, DFC, FRICS. Member, Lands Tribunal for Scotland, 1971-91; Member, Lands Tribunal for England and Wales, 1979-91; Honorary Sheriff, Paisley, since 1974; b. 25.7.19, Paisley; m., Margaret Semple Gibson; 1 s.; 3 d. Educ. Paisley Grammar School. Pilot, RAF, 1939-45 (Despatches); Senior Partner, R. & W. Hall, Chartered Surveyors, Paisley, 1949-79; Chairman, Royal Institution of Chartered Surveyors in Scotland, 1971; Member, Valuation Advisory Council, 1970-80; Executive Member, Erskine Hospital, since 1976. Recreation: golf. Address: (h.) Windyridge, Brediland Road, Paisley, PA2 9HF; T.-Brediland 3614.

Hall, William Andrew McDonald, MA (Hons). Head Teacher, Dalry Secondary School, Kirkcudbrightshire, since 1973; b. 12.2.37, Airdrie; m., Catherine R.; 1 s.; 2 d. Educ. Airdrie Academy; Glasgow University. Teacher of History, Hamilton Academy, 1962-66; Principal Teacher of History, Mackie Academy, Stonehaven, 1966-73. Recreations: reading; golf; Airdrieonians Football Club; cinema. Address: (b.) Dalry Secondary School, St. John's Town of Dalry, Kirkcudbrightshire, DG7 3UU; T.-0164 43 259.

Hall, (William) Douglas, OBE (1985), BA, FMA. Keeper, Scottish National Gallery of Modern Art, 1961-86; b. 9.10.26, London; m., 1, Helen Elizabeth Ellis (m. diss.); 1 s.; 1 d.; 2, Matilda Mary Mitchell. Educ. University School, Hampstead; University College and Courtauld Institute of Art, London University, 1948-52. Intelligence Corps, 1945-48 (Middle East); Manchester City Art Galleries: Keeper, Rutherston Collection, 1953-58, Keeper, City Art Gallery, 1958-59, Deputy Director, 1959-61. Recreations: music; travel; gardening; wall-building. Address: (h.) 4 Northumberland Place, Edinburgh, EH3 6LQ; T.-031-557 3393; Laidlaws, Spottiswood, Gordon, Berwickshire, TD3 6NQ; T.-01578 740277.

Halliburton, Ian Scott. Director, James Finlay Investment Management Ltd., since 1978; b. 30.1.43, Huddersfield; m., Anne Whitaker; 1 s.; 1 d. Educ. Royal High School, Edinburgh; Royal Scottish Academy of Music and Drama. General banking training, Royal Bank of Scotland, 1961-63; RSAMD, 1963-66; professional actor, 1967-70; sales consultant, 1970-71; insurance broker, 1971-78. Director, New Beginnings (Strathclyde) Ltd; Director, Enterprise Music Scotland. Recreations: hill-walking; listening to music; supporting the arts. Address: (h.) 259 Garrioch Road, Glasgow, G20 8QZ; T.-0141-946 5426.

Halliday, James, MA, MLitt, JP. Chairman, Scots Independent Newspapers; b. 27.2.27, Wemyss Bay; m., Olive Campbell; 2 s. Educ. Greenock High School; Glasgow University. Teacher: Ardeer FE Centre, 1953, Kildonan Secondary School, Coatbridge, 1954-56, Uddingston Grammar School, 1956-58, Dunfermline High School, 1958-67; Lecturer in History, Dundee College of Education, 1967-79; Principal Lecturer in History, 1979-87. Chairman, Scottish National Party, 1956-60; Parliamentary candidate: Stirling and Falkirk Burghs, 1955 and 1959, West Fife, 1970. Publications: World in Transformation — America; Scotland The Separate; A Concise History of Scotland; 1820: The Radical War; Story of Scotland (Co-author). Recreations: reading; folk music; football spectating. Address: (h.) 15 Castleroy Crescent, Broughty Ferry, Dundee, DD5 2LU; T.-01382 477179.

Halliday, Rt. Rev. Robert Taylor, MA, BD. Bishop of Brechin, since 1990; b. 7.5.32, Glasgow; m., Dr. Gena M. Chadwin; 1 d. Educ. High School of Glasgow; Glasgow University; Trinity College, Glasgow; Episcopal Theological College, Edinburgh. Deacon, 1957; Priest, 1958; Assistant Curate, St. Andrew's, St. Andrews, 1957-60, St. Margaret's, Newlands, Glasgow, 1960-63; Rector, Holy Cross, Davidson's Mains, Edinburgh, 1963-83; External Lecturer in New Testament, Episcopal Theological College, Edinburgh, 1963-74; Canon, St. Mary's Cathedral, Edinburgh, 1973-83; Rector, St. Andrew's, St. Andrews, 1983-90; Tutor in Biblical Studies, St. Andrews University, 1984-90. Recreations: walking; reading; gardening. Address: 35 Carlogie Road, Carnoustie, DD7 6ER.

Halling, Professor Peter James, BA, PhD. Professor of Biocatalyst Science, Strathclyde University, since 1990; b. 30.3.51, London. Educ. Calday Grammar School; Churchill College, Cambridge; Bristol University. Postdoctoral Fellow, University College, London, 1975-78; Research Scientist, Unilever Research, Bedford, 1978-83. Recreation: orienteering. Address: (h.) 34 Montague Street, Glasgow, G4 9HX; T.-0141-552 4400.

Halls, Michael, FREHIS, FRSH, MIWM. Director of Environmental Services, Ettrick and Lauderdale District Council, since 1975; President, International Federation of Environmental Health, from 1996; b. 6.12.39, Galashiels; m., Sheila; 1 s.; 1 d. Educ. Galashiels Academy; Heriot-Watt. Trainee Burgh Surveyor, Galashiels Town Council, 1959-63; Additional Public Health Inspector, Thame Urban District Council, 1963-64; Galashiels Town Council: Assistant Burgh Surveyor and Sanitary Inspector, 1964-68, Depute Burgh Surveyor, 1968-71, Burgh Surveyor, 1971-75. Last Honorary Secretary, Scottish Institute of Environmental Health, 1978-83; first Senior Vice-President, Royal Environmental Health Institute of Scotland. Recreation: golf; philately; wine-making/drinking; music; eating; photography. Address: (b.) PO Box 4, Paton Street, Galashiels, TD1 3AS; T.-01896 754751.

Hamblen, Professor David Lawrence, MB, BS, PhD, FRCS, FRCSEdin, FRCSGlas. Professor of Orthopaedic Surgery, Glasgow University, since 1972; Honorary Consultant in Orthopaedic Surgery, Greater Glasgow Health Board, since 1972; Visiting Professor to National Centre for Training and Education in Prosthetics and Orthotics, Strathclyde University, since 1981; Hon. Consultant Orthopaedic Surgeon to Army in Scotland; Non-Executive Director, West Glasgow Hospitals University NHS Trust, since 1994; b. 31.8.34, London; m., Gillian; 1 s.; 2 d. Educ. Roan School, Greenwich; London University. The London Hospital, 1963-66; Teaching Fellow in Orthopaedics, Harvard Medical School/Massachusetts General Hospital, 1966-67; Lecturer in Orthopaedics, Nuffield Orthopaedic Centre, Oxford, 1967-68; Senior Lecturer in Orthopaedics/Honorary Consultant, Edinburgh University/South East Regional Hospital Board, 1968-72; Member, Chief Scientist Committee and Chairman, Committee for Research on Equipment for Disabled, 1983-90; Member, Editorial Board, Journal of Bone and Joint Surgery, 1978-82 and 1985-89; Secretary and Treasurer, JBJS Council of Management, since 1992; Member, Physiological Systems Board, Medical Research Council, 1983-88; President, British Orthopaedic Association, 1990-91 (Chairman, Education Sub-Committee, 1986-89). Recreation: golf. Address: (b.) University Department of Orthopaedic Surgery, Western Infirmary, Glasgow, G11 6NT; T.-0141-211 2678/2264.

Hamer-Hodges, David William, MS, FRCS, FRCSE. Consultant Surgeon, Western General Hospital, Edinburgh, since 1979; Honorary Senior Lecturer, Edinburgh University, since 1979; b. 17.10.43, Portsmouth; m., Gillian Landale Kelman; 3 s.; 1 d. Educ. Portsmouth Grammar School; University College London. Senior Registrar,

Aberdeen Teaching Hospitals; Research Fellow, Harvard Medical School; Resident Surgical Officer, St. Mark's Hospital, London. Address: (b.) 38 India Street, Edinburgh; T.-0131-226 5720.

Hamill, Hamish. Secretary, Scottish Office Home and Health Department. Address: (b.) St. Andrew's House, Edinburgh, EH1 3DG.

Hamill, Sir Patrick, Kt (1984), QPM, OStJ, BA. Chief Constable of Strathclyde, 1977-85; b. 29.4.30, Clydebank; m., Nellie Gillespie; 4 s.; 1 d. Educ. St. Patrick's High School, Dumbarton. Joined Dunbartonshire Constabulary, 1950, and rose through the ranks until promoted Chief Superintendent, 1970; transferred to City of Glasgow Police, 1972; appointed Assistant Chief Constable, 1974; joined Strathclyde Police, 1975, and attended the Royal College of Defence Studies, 1976; President, Association of Chief Police Officers (Scotland), 1982-83, Honorary Secretary and Treasurer, 1983-85; Member, Board of Governors: St. Aloysius College, Glasgow, 1983-90, St. Andrew's College of Education, Bearsden, 1987-88; Chairman, Management and Development Board, St. Margaret's Hospice, Clydebank, since 1986. Recreations: walking; reading history; golf.

Hamilton, Alex. Writer of fiction; b. 14.4.49, Glasgow. Publications: Three Glasgow Writers, 1976; Gallus, Did You Say?, 1982; Abdul the Tobacco Curer, forthcoming; The Formulae, forthcoming; many articles, songs, stories, reviews, broadcasts. Recreations: language; literature; music; theatre. Address: (h.) 12 Woodlands Drive, Glasgow, G4 9EH; T.-0141-339 2258.

Hamilton, Alexander Macdonald, CBE, JP, MA, LLB. Vice Chairman, Royal Bank of Scotland Group plc; Vice Chairman, Royal Bank of Scotland plc; b. 11.5.25, Motherwell; m., Catherine; 2 s.; 1 d. Educ. Hamilton Academy; Glasgow University. Former Senior Partner, subsequently Consultant, McGrigor Donald, Solicitors, Glasgow; former Member, Council, Law Society of Scotland, now Convener, Insolvency and Diligence Committees; President of the Society, 1977-78; former Member, Court House Committee, Royal Faculty of Procurators of Glasgow; Past President, Glasgow Juridical Society; former Chairman, Scottish Committee, The Scout Association; Secretary, Cambuslang Old Parish Church; former Vice-Chairman and Legal Adviser, Cambuslang Community Council. Recreations: sailing; golf. Address: (h.) 30 Wellshot Drive, Cambuslang; T.-0141-641 1445.

Hamilton, 15th Duke of, and Brandon, 12th Duke of (Angus Alan Douglas Douglas-Hamilton), MA. Premier Peer of Scotland; Hereditary Keeper of Palace of Holyroodhouse; b. 13.9.38; m., Sarah Scott; 2 s.; 2 d. Educ. Eton; Balliol College, Oxford. Flt.-Lt., RAF (retired, 1967); flying instructor, 1965; Instrument Rating Examiner, 1966; Test Pilot, Scottish Aviation, 1971-72; Member, Queen's Bodyguard for Scotland (Royal Company of Archers), since 1975; KStJ, 1975, Prior for Scotland, 1975-82; Honorary Member, Royal Scottish Pipers, 1977; Council Member, Cancer Research Campaign, 1978; Honorary Air Commodore, Maritime Headquarters Unit 2, R.Aux.AF, 1982. Publication: Maria R, 1991. Address: (h.) Lennoxlove, Haddington, East Lothian.

Hamilton, Arthur Campbell, QC, BA, LLB. Queen's Counsel, since 1982; Judge of the Courts of Appeal of Jersey and of Guernsey, since 1988; President, Pensions Appeal Tribunals for Scotland, since 1992; b. 10.6.42, Glasgow; m., Christine Ann; 1 d. Educ. High School of Glasgow; Glasgow University; Worcester College, Oxford; Edinburgh University. Advocate, 1968; Standing Junior Counsel to Scottish Development Department, 1975-78, Inland Revenue (Scotland), 1978-82; Advocate Depute, 1982-85. Recreations: hill-walking; fishing; music; history.

Address: (h.) 8 Heriot Row, Edinburgh, EH3 6HU; T.-0131-556 4663.

Hamilton, Christine M., MA. Depute Director and Director Planning and Development, Scottish Arts Council, since 1991; b. 9.8.54, Hamilton. Educ. Kirkcaldy High School; Harris Academy, Dundee; Glasgow University; City University, London (Diploma, Arts Administration). House Manager, Citizens' Theatre, Glasgow; Administrator: 7:84 Theatre Company, Tag Theatre Company; Arts Officer, Scottish Trades Union Congress. Recreations: arts: hill-walking; swimming. Address: (b.) 12 Manor Place, Edinburgh, EH3 7DD; T.-0131-226 6051.

Hamilton, Gordon MacMillan, MB, ChB, DFM, MPhil. Medical Director, Glasgow University Health Service, since 1989; Hon. Senior Lecturer, Department of General Practice, Glasgow University, since 1989; Branch Medical Officer, Glasgow and Renfrewshire Branch, British Red Cross, since 1992; b. 6.2.54, Motherwell. Educ. Glasgow University. Various hospital appointments, 1977-89. Past Chairman, Friends of the S.N.O. Recreations: tennis: squash; keep-fit; art; antiques; music. Address: (h.) Gorrisholm, 2 Holm Road, Crossford, ML8 5RG; T.-01555 860 877.

Hamilton, Ian Robertson, QC (Scot), BL; b. 13.9.25, Paisley; m., Jeannette Patricia Mari Stewart; 1 s.; 1 s., 2 d. by pr. m. Educ. John Neilson School, Paisley; Allan Glen's School, Glasgow; Glasgow University; Edinburgh University. RAFVR, 1944-48; called to Scottish Bar, 1954, and to Albertan Bar, 1982; Founder, Castle Wynd Printers, Edinburgh, 1955; Advocate Depute, 1962; Director of Civil Litigation, Republic of Zambia, 1964-66; Hon. Sheriff of Lanarkshire, 1967; retired from practice to work for National Trust for Scotland and later to farm in Argyll, 1969; returned to practice, 1974; Sheriff of Glasgow and Strathkelvin, May-December, 1984; returned to practice. Chief Pilot, Scottish Parachute Club, 1979-90; Student President, Heriot-Watt University, 1990-93; Rector, Aberdeen University, 1994-96. Publications: No Stone Unturned, 1952; The Tinkers of the World, 1957 (Foyle award-winning book); A Touch of Treason, 1990; The Taking of the Stone of Destiny, 1991; A Touch More Treason. Recreation: motor-biking. Address: (b.) Advocates' Library, Parliament House, Edinburgh, EH1 1RF.

Hamilton, Loudon Pearson, CB (1987), MA (Hons). Chairman, Scottish Food Quality Certification Company since 1995; Chairman, Scottish Agricultural and Rural Development Centre, since 1992; b. 12.1.32, Glasgow; m., Anna Mackinnon Young (deceased); 2 s. Educ. Hutchesons Grammar School, Glasgow; Glasgow University. National Service, RA, 1953-55 (2nd Lt.); Inspector of Taxes, Inland Revenue, 1956-60; Assistant Principal, Department of Agriculture and Fisheries for Scotland, 1960; Private Secretary to Parliamentary Under Secetary of State for Scotland, 1963-64; First Secretary, Agriculture, British Embassy, Copenhagen and The Hague, 1966-70; Assistant Secretary, Department of Agriculture and Fisheries for Scotland, 1973-79; Principal Establishment Officer, Scottish Office, 1979-84; Secretary, Scottish Office Agriculture and Fisheries Department, 1984-92. Chairman, Corstorphine Trust, 1990-95. Address: (h.) 5 Belgrave Road, Edinburgh, EH12 6NG; T.-0131-334 5398.

Hamilton, Thomas Banks, BAcc, CA. Chief Executive and Director, Ashbourne PLC, since 1988; Managing Director, Elders PLC, since 1988; b. 22.11.55, Glasgow; 3 s.; 1 d. Educ. Glasgow Academy; Glasgow University. Director, Independent Healthcare Association; Chairman, Bon Secours Health Systems Ltd. Recreations: hill-climbing; golf; painting; drawing. Address: (b.) Ashbourne House, 58 West Regent Street, Glasgow, G2 2QZ; T.-0141-331 2222.

Hamilton, William, MB, ChB, MD, FRCPGlas, FRCPEdin, DPH, DCH. Paediatric Endocrinologist, in private practice; Paediatrician and Paediatric Endocrinologist, Department of Child Health, Royal Hospital for Sick Children, Glasgow, 1961-89; University Senior Lecturer, 1962-89; b. 22.12.22, Holytown, Lanarkshire; m., Elizabeth Janet Beveridge; 2 s. Educ. Holytown Public School; Dalziel High School, Motherwell; Glasgow University. House Physician/House Surgeon posts, Glasgow, 1952-54; general practice, 1954-56; Registrar medical post, Inverness, 1957-61; Senior Registrar in Paediatrics, 1961-62. Advisor on Postgraduate and Undergraduate Education and Training, Fatah Medical School, Tripoli, Libya. Publications: Clinical Paediatric Endocrinology, 1972; Surgical Treatment of Endocrine Disease; chapters in Diseases of the Fetus and Newborn, 1994. Recreations: gardening; vintage car enthusiast. Address: (h.) 81 Woodend Drive, Glasgow, G13 1QF; T.-0141-954 9961.

Hamilton-Grierson, Philip John, OBE, MA. Chairman, State Hospital, Carstairs; Chairman, Northern College; Chairman, Highland Hospice Ltd.; Director: Cromarty Firth Port Authority, Investors in People Scotland Ltd., Jade in Scotland Ltd., A1 Welders Ltd.; b. 10.10.32, Inveresk; m., Pleasaunce Jill Cardew; 1 s.; 2 d. Educ. Rugby School; Corpus Christi College, Oxford. Contracts Manager, Bristol Aircraft Ltd.; Economic Adviser, Joseph Lucas Industries Ltd.; Secretary to Liberal Parliamentary Party; Director, Gallaher Ltd. Fellow, Royal Society of Arts. Recreations: hill-walking; tennis; music. Address: Pitlundie, North Kessock, Ross-shire, IV1 1XG; T.-Kessock 392.

Hammerton, Professor Desmond, OBE, BSc, CBiol, FIBiol, FIWEM, FIMgt, FRSE. Visiting Professor, Department of Biology, Paisley University; b. 17.11.29, Wakefield, Yorkshire; m., Jean Taylor; 2 s.; 2 d. Educ. Harrow Weald County School; Birkbeck College, London University. Assistant Biologist, Metropolitan Water Board, 1953-55; Research Biologist, Bristol Waterworks, 1955-58; Principal Assistant, Lothians River Purification Board, 1958-62; Director, Hydrobiological Research Unit, Khartoum University, 1962-71; Deputy Director, Clyde River Purification Board, 1971-74, Director, 1975-94; Consultant, World Health Organisation, 1977-90; Member, Aquatic Life Sciences Grants Committee, Natural Environment Research Council, 1975-79; Member, Marine Pollution Monitoring Management Group and its Steering Committee, 1974- 91; Member, Steering Committee for the Development of Environmental Quality Objectives and Standards, Department of Environment, 1981-94; Member, Scottish Council, Institute of Biology, 1973-76; elected to Committee of Environment Division, Institute of Biology, 1977 (Chairman, Environment Division, 1980-82); Member, Terrestrial and Freshwater Sciences Committee, Natural Environment Research Council, 1985-89; Member, Court, University of Paisley. Recreations: chess; tennis; hill-walking. Address: (h.) 7 Fairfield Place, Bothwell, Glasgow, G7 8RP; T.-01698 852261.

Hampson, Stephen F., MA, BPhil. Under Secretary, Scottish Office, since 1993; b. 27.10.45, Grimsby; m., Gunilla Brunk; 1 s.; 1 d. Educ. The Leys School, Cambridge; University College, Oxford. Lecturer, Department of Political Economy, Aberdeen University, 1969-71; Economist, National Economic Development Office, 1971-75; Economic Adviser, Scottish Office, 1975-78 and 1982-84; First Secretary, British High Commission, New Delhi, 1978-81; Assistant Secretary, Scottish Office, 1984-93. Recreations: hill-walking; theatre. Address: (h.) Glenelg, Park Road, Kilmacolm, Renfrewshire; T.-Kilmacolm 872615.

Hampton, Robert. Principal Dancer, Scottish Ballet, since 1986; b. London. Trained, Legat Russian Ballet School; joined Scottish Ballet, 1979, making his principal debut as

James in La Sylphide, 1983; has danced all the danseur noble roles in the company's repertoire: La Sylphide, Giselle, Swan Lake, The Nutcracker, Coppelia, and Cinderella; Patron, Russian Ballet Society, since 1992. Address: (b.) Scottish Ballet, 261 West Princes Street, Glasgow, G4 9EE.

Hanley, Clifford. Writer and Performer; Emeritus Professor, York University, Toronto; b. 28.10.22, Glasgow; m., Anna Clark (deceased); 1 s.; 2 d. Educ. Eastbank Academy, Glasgow. Journalist, since 1940; Novelist, since 1957; Songwriter; Broadcaster; Member, Scottish Arts Council, 1965-72; Member, Inland Waterways Advisory Council, 1970-73; Professor of Literature, York University, Toronto, 1979-80. Publications: Dancing in the Streets; Love from Everybody; The Taste of Too Much; Nothing but the Best; The System; The Redhaired Bitch; It's Different Abroad; The Italian Gadget; The Chosen Instrument; The Scots; Another Street, Another Dance; History of Scotland. Recreations: music; talk. Address: (h.) 35 Hamilton Drive, Glasgow, G12 8DW.

Hann, James, CBE, FCIM, FInstPet, FInstD. Chairman, Scottish Nuclear Ltd., since 1990; Chairman, Northern Lighthouse Board, since 1993; Member, Nationalised Industries Chairman's Group, since 1990; b. 18.1.33. Address: (b.) 3 Redwood Crescent, Peel Park, East Kilbride, G74 5PR.

Hannay of Kirkdale and That Ilk, Ramsay William Rainsford. Landowner, Farmer, Caravan Park Operator, since 1964; Barrister-at-Law, Inner Temple; b. 15.6.11, India; m., Margaret Wiseman; 1 s.; 1 d. Educ. Winchester College; Trinity College, Cambridge (Hons. degree in Law). Called to the Bar and practised in the Bankruptcy Court; called up for service in the Forces, 1939; commissioned, HLI; served throughout the War in Europe, with a short spell in USA and Canada; demobilised with rank of Major; Legal Assistant, then Assistant Solicitor, Board of Trade, 1946-64; Honorary Sheriff, Stewartry of Kirkcudbright; Member, Queen's Bodyguard for Scotland (Royal Company of Archers); President, Dumfries and Galloway Boy Scouts Association; Chief of the Clan Hannay; President, Drystane Walling Association of Great Britain. Recreations: sailing; shooting; fishing. Address: (h.) Cardoness, Gatehouse-of-Fleet, Kirkcudbrightshire; T.-Mossyard 207.

Hanson, William Stewart, BA, PhD, FSA, FSA Scot. President, Council for Scottish Archaeology, since 1989; Senior Lecturer in Archaeology, Glasgow University, since 1990; b. 22.1.50, Doncaster; m., Lesley Macinnes. Educ. Gravesend Grammar School; Manchester University. Lecturer in Archaeology, Glasgow University, 1975; Chairman, Scottish Field School of Archaeology, 1982-89; Chairman, Scottish Archaeological Link, since 1990; Member, Executive Committee, Council for British Archaeology, since 1989; Director, large-scale archaeological excavations at several sites in Scotland and northern England, including complete excavation of the Roman Fort at Elginhaugh, Dalkeith; recipient, Glenfiddich Living Scotland Award, 1987. Publications include: Agricola and the conquest of the north; Rome's north-west frontier: the Antonine Wall (Co-author); Scottish archaeology: new perceptions (Co-editor); papers and articles. Recreations: tennis; film. Address: (h.) 4 Victoria Road, Stirling, FK8 2RH; T.-01786 465506.

Hanvey, Rev. James, BA, MTh, DPhil (Oxon). Jesuit Priest, since 1983; Headmaster, St. Aloysius College, Glasgow, since 1990; b. 6.1.51, Belfast. Publications: papers published in theology and spirituality. Recreations: walking; cooking; music. Address: (b.) 45 Hill Street, Glasgow, G3 6RJ; T.-0141-332 3190.

Happs, John Henderson, MA (Hons). Head Teacher, Mainholm Academy, Ayr, since 1994; b. 1.9.47, Irvine; m., Jean; 4 s.; 1 d. Educ. Irvine Royal Academy; Glasgow University; Jordanhill College. Teacher of English/Principal Teacher of English, Ravenspark Academy, 1970-80; Assistant Head Teacher/Depute Head Teacher/Acting Head Teacher, Kilwinning Academy, 1980-88. Recreations: caravanning; music; reading; computing; playing with grand-daughter. Address: (b.) Mainholm Academy, Mainholm Road, Ayr, KA8 0QQ; T.-01292 267300.

Hardie, Andrew Rutherford, QC (Scot). Dean, Faculty of Advocates, since 1994; b. 8.1.46, Alloa; m., Catherine Storrar Elgin; 2 s.; 1 d. Educ. St. Modan's High School, Stirling; Edinburgh University. Enrolled Solicitor, 1971; Member, Faculty of Advocates, 1973; Advocate Depute, 1979-83. Address: (b.) Advocates' Library, Parliament House, Edinburgh, EH1 1RF.

Hardie, Professor David Grahame, MA, PhD. Professor of Cellular Signalling, Dundee University, since 1994; b. 25.4.50, Liverpool; m., Linda Margaret; 4 s. Educ. Merchant Taylor's School, Crosby; Cambridge University; Heriot-Watt University. Lecturer/Senior Lecturer/Reader, Dundee University, 1977-94. Recreation: hill-walking. Address: (b.) Biochemistry Department, Dundee University, Dundee, DD1 4HN; T.-01382 344253.

Hardie, Donald Graeme, TD, JP, FIM. Director, Hardie Polymers Ltd., since 1976; Director, Ronaash Ltd., since 1988; Director, Hardie Polymers (England) Ltd., since 1989; b. 23.1.36, Glasgow; m., Rosalind Allan Ker; 2 s. Educ. Blairmore and Merchiston Castle. Commissioned 41st Field Regiment RA, 1955; Battery Commander 277 (Argyll & Sutherland Highlanders) Regiment RA (TA), 1966; Commanding Officer GSVOTC, 1973; TA Col. Lowlands, 1976; TA Col. DES, 1980; TA Col. Scotland, 1985; ACF Brigadier Scotland, 1987. UTR Management Trainee, 1956-59; F.W. Allan & Ker, Shipbrokers, 1960-61; J. & G. Hardie & Co. Ltd., 1961-81; Director, Gilbert Plastics Ltd., 1973-76. Lord Lieutenant, Strathclyde Region (Districts of Dumbarton, Clydebank, Bearsden & Milngavie, Strathkelvin, Cumbernauld & Kilsyth), since 1990; Hon. Col. 105, Air Defence Regiment RA (V); Hon. Col. Glasgow & Lanarkshire ACF; Vice Chairman, Scottish Gunner Council; Member, Executive Committee, Erskine Hospital; Vice President, ACFA Scotland. Recreations: skiing; sailing; shooting; fishing. Address: (h.) Dun Ruadh, Gartocharn, Dunbartonshire, G83 8SB.

Hardie, Sir Douglas Fleming, CBE, LLD, FRSA, CBIM. Chairman, Edward Parker & Co. Ltd., since 1960; Chairman, Grampian Television PLC, 1989-93; b. 26.5.23, Dundee; m., Dorothy Alice Warner; 2 s.; 1 d. Educ. Trinity College, Glenalmond. Trooper, 58 Training Regt., RAC, 1941; commissioned RMA Sandhurst, 1942, 1 Fife & Forfar Yeomanry Flamethrowing Tank Regt., NW Europe, 1942-46 (Despatches), Major. Director: Dayco Rubber (UK) Ltd., 1956-86, Clydesdale Bank plc, 1981-92, The Alliance Trust plc, 1982-93, The Second Alliance Trust plc, 1982-93, Alliance Trust (Finance) Ltd., 1982-93, SECDEE Leasing, 1982-93, Alliance Trust (Nominees) Ltd., 1982-93; Chairman, A.G. Scott Textiles, 1985-87; Deputy Chairman, Scottish Development Agency, 1978-91; Member: CBI Grand Council, London, 1976-85, Scottish Economic Council, 1977-91; Councillor, Winston Churchill Memorial Trust, since 1985; Director, Prince's Scottish Youth Business Trust, 1987; Past President, Dundee Rotary Club; Vice-President, Fife & Forfar Yeomanry Regimental Association; Deacon Convener, Nine Incorporated Trades of Dundee, 1951-54; Elder, Dundee Parish Church (St. Mary's). Recreations: golf; fishing. Address: (h.) 6 Norwood Terrace, West Park, Dundee, DD2 1PB.

Hardie, John Donald Morrison, OBE, DL, FRSA, MA, MSc. Director, Scottish Division, Institute of Directors, since 1980; Director, Bute Fabrics Ltd., since 1970; b. 27.9.28; m., Sally Patricia Connally (see Sally Hardie); 2 s.; 1 d. Educ. Beckenham Grammar School; St. Andrews University; Indiana University. Major, Queen's Own Cameron Highlanders; founder Director, Wood, Hardie Ltd.; organised Scotland in Europe campaign for 1975 Referendum. Session Clerk, Humbie; Deputy Chairman, Patrons' Council, Museum of Scotland. Recreations: golf; shooting. Address: (h.) Chesterhill House, Humbie, East Lothian, EH36 5PL; T.-Humbie 833 648.

Hardie, Sally Patricia Connally, BA. Member, Executive, National Trust for Scotland, since 1985; Member of Court, St. Andrews University, since 1987; Lothians Chairman, National Art Collections Fund, since 1987; Trustee, Robert T. Jones Jr. Memorial Scholarship Fund; b. 6.2.26, Atlanta; m., John Donald M. Hardie (qv); 2 s.; 1 d. Educ. The Spence School, New York; Vassar College. Recreations: conservation and study of our heritage; gardening; politics. Address: (h.) Chesterhill House, Humbie, East Lothian, EH36 5PL; T.-Humbie 648.

Hardie, William Dunbar, MBE, MA, BA, MUniv. Writer and Entertainer; b. 4.1.31, Aberdeen; m., Margaret Elizabeth Simpson; 1 s.; 1 d. Educ. Robert Gordon's College, Aberdeen; Aberdeen University; Sidney Sussex College, Cambridge. Administrative Assistant, then Assistant Secretary, NE Regional Hospital Board; District Administrator, North District, Grampian Health Board; Secretary, Grampian Health Board, 1976-83. Co-writer and performer, Scotland The What? (comedy revue); writer, Dod'N'Bunty column, Aberdeen Evening Express. Recreations: reading; TV-watching; film and theatre-going; sport; avid and totally biased follower of Aberdeen's football team, Scotland's rugby team, and England's cricket team. Address: (h.) 50 Gray Street, Aberdeen, AB1 6JE; T.-01224 310591.

Hare, Professor Paul Gregory, BA, BPhil, DPhil. Professor of Economics and Director, Centre for Economic Reform and Transformation, Heriot-Watt University, since 1985; b. 19.3.46, Hull; m., Susan Jennifer Robertson; 1 s.; 2 d. Educ. Malet Lambert High School, Hull; St. John's College, Cambridge; Nuffield College, Oxford. Technical Officer, ICI, 1967-68; Lecturer, Birmingham University, 1971-72; Lecturer, Senior Lecturer, Reader, Stirling University, 1972-85. Member, Lothian Region Children's Panel, 1981-89. Recreations: hill-walking; reading; listening to choral music. Address: (h.) 34 Saughtonhall Drive, Edinburgh, EH12 5TN; T.-0131-337 7329.

Hare Duke, Rt. Rev. Michael Geoffrey, BA, MA, DD. Bishop of St. Andrews, Dunkeld and Dunblane, 1969-94 (retired); Chairman, Age Concern Scotland, since 1994; b. 28.11.25, Calcutta; m., Grace Lydia Frances Dodd; 1 s.; 3 d. Educ. Bradfield College; Trinity College, Oxford; Westcott House, Cambridge. Sub-Lt., RNVR, 1944-46; Deacon, 1952; Priest, 1953; Curate, 1952-56; Vicar, Bury, 1956-62; Pastoral Director, Clinical Theology Association, 1962-64; Vicar, St. Paul's Daybrook and Officiating Chaplain, E. Midlands District HQ, 1964-69. Chairman, Scottish Association for Mental Health; Member, Anglican Communion Peace and Justice Network, Convener, 1992-94. Publications: The Caring Church (Co-author); First Aid in Counselling (Co-author); Understanding the Adolescent; The Break of Glory; Freud; Good News; Stories Signs and Sacraments of the Emerging Church; Praying for Peace, reflections on the Gulf crisis; Hearing the Stranger. Recreations: walking; writing; broadcasting. Address: (h.) 2 Balhousie Avenue, Perth, PH1 5HN; T.-01738 622642.

Hargreave, Timothy Bruce, MB, MS, FRCSEdin, FRCS. Consultant Urological Surgeon, Western General Hospital, Edinburgh, since 1978; b. 23.3.44, Lytham; m., Molly; 2 d. Educ. Harrow; University College Hospital, London University. Senior Registrar: Western Infirmary, Glasgow,

University College Hospital, London; Medical Officer, Paray Mission Hospital, Lesotho. Publications: Diagnosis and Management of Renal and Urinary Disease; Male Infertility (Editor); Practical Urological Endoscopy; The Management of Male Infertility. Recreation: skiing. Address: (h.) 20 Cumin Place, Edinburgh.

Harkess, Ronald Dobson, OBE, BSc, MS, PhD, NDA, CBiol, MIBiol, FRAgS, FRSA. Agricultural Scientist and Consultant; Member, Scottish Panel, Royal Agricultural Societies, since 1994; b. 11.7.33, Edinburgh; m., Jean Cuthbert Drennan; 2 d. Educ. Royal High School, Edinburgh; Edinburgh University; Cornell University. Senior Fison Research Fellow, Nottingham University, 1969-62; Assistant Grassland Adviser, West of Scotland Agricultural College, Ayr, 1962-72; Senior Agronomist, 1972-86; Technical Secretary, Council, Scottish Agricultural Colleges, 1986-90, Company Secretary, 1987-90; Company Secretary, Scottish Agricultural College, 1990-91; Assistant Principal, Scottish Agricultural College, 1991-93. Recreations: amateur radio; philately; gardening. Address: (h.) Friarton Bank, Rhynd Road, Perth, PH2 8PT; T.-01738 643435.

Harkness, Rt. Rev. James, CB, OBE, MA, FRSA, OStJ. Moderator, General Assembly of the Church of Scotland, 1995-96; Extra Chaplain to The Queen; b. 20.10.35, Thornhill; m., Elizabeth Anne; 1 s.; 1 d. Educ. Dumfries Academy; Edinburgh University. Assistant Minister, North Morningside Parish Church, 1959-61; Chaplain, KOSB, 1961-65; Chaplain, Queen's Own Highlanders, 1965-69; Singapore, 1969-70; Deputy Warden, RAChD, 1970-74; Senior Chaplain, Northern Ireland, 1974-75; 4th Division, 1975-78; Staff Chaplain, HQ BAOR, 1979-80; Assistant Chaplain, Scotland, 1980-81; Senior Chaplain, 1st British Corps, 1981-82; BAOR, 1982-84; Deputy Chaplain General, 1985-86; Chaplain General to the Forces, 1987-95. QHC, 1982-95; Hon. Chaplain to BLESMA, Royal British Legion Scotland; Patron, St. Mary's Music School, Edinburgh, Napier University. Recreations: walking; reading; watching sport. Address: (h.) 13 Saxe-Coburg Place, Edinburgh, EH3 5BR; T.-0131-343 1297.

Harlen, Professor Wynne, OBE, MA (Oxon), MA (Bristol), PhD. Director, Scottish Council for Research in Education, since 1990; Visiting Professor, Liverpool University, since 1990; b. 12.1.37, Swindon; 1 s.; 1 d. Educ. Pate's Grammar School for Girls, Cheltenham; St. Hilda's College, Oxford; Bristol University. Teacher/Lecturer, 1958-66; Research Associate, Bristol University School of Education, 1966-73; Research Fellow, Project Director, Reading University, 1973-77; Research Fellow, Centre for Science Education, King's College, London, 1977-84; Sidney Jones Professor of Science Education, Liverpool University, 1985-90. Chair, Children in Scotland Early Years Forum, 1991-95; Member, Secretary of State's Working Party on the Development of the National Curriculum in Science, 1987-88; President, British Educational Research Association, 1993-94. Publications: 22 books; 110 papers. Recreations: concerts; opera; hill-walking. Address: (h.) 26 Torphin Road, Colinton, Edinburgh, EH13 0HW; T.-0131-441 6130.

Harper, Professor Alexander Murray, MB, ChB, MD (Hons). Professor of Surgical Physiology, Glasgow University, since 1981; Honorary Consultant Clinical Physiologist, Greater Glasgow Health Board, since 1970; b. 31.5.33, Glasgow; m., Charlotte Maria Fossleitner; 2 s.; 1 d. Educ. Hutchesons' Grammar School; Glasgow University. House Physician and Surgeon, Southern General Hospital and Glasgow Royal Infirmary, 1957-58; McIntyre Research Scholar in Clinical Surgery, Glasgow Royal Infirmary, 1958-60; Scientific Assistant, Medical Research Council, 1960-63; Wellcome Senior Research Fellow in Clinical Science and Honorary Lecturer in Surgery, Glasgow University, 1963-68; Glasgow University: Senior Lecturer in Surgery and Surgical Physiology, 1968-69, Reader, 1969-81. Editor in Chief, Journal of Cerebral Blood Flow and Metabolism, 1981-89; Editor, Cerebrovascular and Brain Metabolism Reviews, since 1989; David Patey Prize, Surgical Research Society, 1966; H.G. Wolff Award, American Association for Study of Headache, 1968; Gold Medal, British Migraine Association, 1976; Honorary Fellow, American Heart Association (Stroke Council), 1980. Recreations: fishing; contract bridge; gardening. Address: (b.) Wellcome Surgical Institute, Glasgow University, Garscube Estate, Bearsden Road, Glasgow, G61 1QH; T.-0141-330 5826.

Harper, Rev. Anne J. McInroy, BD, STM, MTh. Chaplain, Glasgow Royal Infirmary University NHS Trust, since 1990; b. 31.10.49, Glasgow. Educ. Camphill Senior Secondary School, Paisley; Glasgow University; Union Theological Seminary, New York. Graduate Fellow, Union Theological Seminary, and Assistant Minister, 2nd Presbyterian Church, New York City, 1974-75; research, Church history and liturgics, Glasgow University, 1975-78; Assistant Minister, Abronhill Church, Cumbernauld, 1978-79; Christian Education Field Officer, Church of Scotland Department of Education, 1979-84; Minister, Linthouse St. Kenneth's Parish Church, 1984-90. Holder (first woman), The Scots Fellowship awarded by Union Theological Seminary, New York, 1974. Address: The Chaplain's Office, Glasgow Royal Infirmary, Glasgow, G4 0SF; T.-0141-552 3535.

Harper, Professor Anthony John, BA, MA, PhD, CertEd. Professor of German Studies, Strathclyde University, since 1979; b. 26.5.38, Bristol; m., Sandra; 1 s.; 2 d. Educ. Clifton College, Bristol; Bristol University; Exeter University. Lecturer, Department of German, Edinburgh University, 1962-79. Publications: German Today (Co-author), 1967; David Schirmer - A Poet of the German Baroque, 1977; Time and Change, Essays on German and European Literature, 1982; Schriften zur Lyrik Leipzigs 1620-1670, 1985; The Song-Books of Gottfried Finckelthaus, 1988 ; Studien zum deutschen, Weltlichen Lied (Co-author), 1992; The European Emblem (Co-author), 1992; edition of Chr. Brehme; Lustige Gediehte, 1994. Address: (b.) Department of Modern Languages, Strathclyde University, 26 Richmond Street, Glasgow, G1 1XQ; T.-0141-552 4400.

Harper, Rev. David Little, BSc, BD (Hons). Minister, St. Meddan's Church, Troon, since 1979; Moderator, Presbytery of Ayr, 1991-92; b. 31.10.47, Moffat; m., Janis Mary Clark; 2 s. Educ. Morton Academy, Thornhill; Dumfries Academy; Edinburgh University. Assistant Minister, Cumbernauld St. Mungo's, 1971-72; first Minister, New Erskine Parish Church, 1972-79. Member, Scottish Advisory Committee, Independent Broadcasting Authority, 1974-79; Scottish Member, Religious Advisory Panel, IBA, 1978-79. Recreations: golf; hill-walking; swimming. Address: St. Meddan's Manse, 27 Bentinck Drive, Troon, Ayrshire; T.-01292 311784.

Harper, Douglas Ross, BSc, MD, FRCSEdin, FRCSEng, FRCSGlas. Consultant Surgeon, since 1976, Medical Director, since 1994, Falkirk and District Royal Infirmary NHS Trust; Examiner, Royal College of Surgeons of Edinburgh, since 1979; Examiner, Royal College of Surgeons of Glasgow, since 1987; Honorary Senior Lecturer, Department of Clinical Surgery, Edinburgh University, since 1976; b. 16.2.40, Aberdeen; m., Dorothy Constance Wisely; 1 s.; 3 d. Educ. Aberdeen Grammar School; Aberdeen University. House Officer, Registrar and Fellow in Vascular Surgery, Aberdeen Royal Infirmary, 1967-73; Senior Registrar, Edinburgh Royal Infirmary, 1973-76. Elder, Bridge of Allan Chalmers Church of Scotland. Recreations: hill-walking; geology; woodwork. Address: (h.) Glenallan, 16 Upper Glen Road, Bridge of Allan, Stirlingshire, FK9 4PX; T.-01786 832242.

Harper, Edward James, MA, BMus, ARCM, LRAM. Composer, since 1957; Reader in Music, Edinburgh University, since 1990; Director, New Music Group of Scotland, since 1973; b. 17.3.41, Taunton; m., Dorothy Caroline Shanks. Educ. King Edward VI School, Guildford; Royal College of Music, London; Christ Church, Oxford. Main works as a Composer: Piano Concerto, 1971, Bartok Games, 1972, Ricercari in Memoriam Luigi Dallapiccola, 1975, Fanny Robin (chamber opera), Chester Mass, 1979, Clarinet Concerto, 1981, Hedda Gabler (opera, commissioned for Scottish Opera), 1985; Fantasia V (for chamber orchestra), 1985; The Mellstock Quire (chamber opera), 1987; Homage to Thomas Hardy (baritone and orchestra), 1990. Address: (h.) 7 Morningside Park, Edinburgh, EH10 5HD; T.-0131-447 5366.

Harper, John Ross, CBE, MA, LLB. Senior Partner, Ross Harper & Murphy and Harper Macleod, Solicitors, since 1962; b. 20.3.35, Glasgow; m., Ursula; 2 s.; 1 d. Educ. Hutchesons' Boys' Grammar School; Glasgow University. Parliamentary Commissioner; Professor of Law, Strathclyde University; Past President, Law Society of Scotland; Chairman, Section on General Practice, International Bar Association; former President, Scottish Conservative & Unionist Association; former Chairman, Society of Scottish Conservative Lawyers; former Parliamentary candidate (Conservative), Hamilton and West Renfrewshire; Vice-President, International Bar Association; Joint Chairman, Mining (Scotland) Ltd. Publications: Glasgow Rape Case; My Client My Lord; A Practitioner's Guide to the Criminal Courts; Fingertip Criminal Law; Rates Revaluation; Devolution. Recreations: angling; bridge; shooting. Address: (b.) The Ca'd'oro, 45 Gordon Street, Glasgow, G1 3PE; T.-0141-221 8888.

Harris, Rev. John William Forsyth, MA. Minister, Bearsden South Church, since 1987; b. 10.3.42, Hampshire; m., Ellen Lesley Kirkpatrick Lamont; 1 s.; 2 d. Educ. Merchant Taylors' School, London; St. Andrews University; New College, Edinburgh. Ordained Assistant, St. Mary's Church, Haddington, 1967-70; Minister: St. Andrew's Parish Church, Irvine, 1970-77, St. Mary's Parish Church, Motherwell, 1977-87. Convener, Scottish Churches' Christian Aid Committee, 1986-90; Convener, Scottish Christian Aid Committee, since 1990; Member, Board, Christian Aid, since 1990; Member, Executive, Church and Nation Committee, 1985-91, Convener of its Media Interests Sub-Committee, 1985-87, and its Economic and Industrial Interests Sub-Committee, 1987-91; Member, Executive, Scottish Churches' Council, 1986-90; Convener, Scottish Television's Religious Advisory Committee, since 1990; Member, Executive, Board of World Mission, since 1992, and Convener of its Sub-Committee on the Caribbean, Central and South America, since 1993; Moderator, Dumbarton Presbytery, 1994-95. Fencing Blue, St. Andrews and Edinburgh; Scottish Fencing Team, 1963-66. Recreations: holiday home in Kintyre; Cruban walking. Address: 61 Drymen Road, Bearsden, Glasgow, G61 2SU; T.-0141-942 0507.

Harris, Marshall James, DPA. Director, Scottish Educational Trust for United Nations and International Affairs, since 1986; b. 14.3.28, Edinburgh; m., Matilda Currie Main; 2 s.; 1 d. Educ. Armadale Secondary; Glasgow University. Accountancy, pre-1958; Scottish National Officer, UN Association, 1958-86; Secretary, Scottish Standing Committee for Voluntary International Aid. Former Liberal and Alliance candidate. Recreations: reading; member of Rotary, Liberal International and Royal Institute of International Affairs. Address: (h.) Hopetoun, Charlotte Street, Brightons, Falkirk; T.-01324 715203.

Harrison, Albert, MA, BA, ALA, MIInfSc. Librarian, Strathclyde University, since 1982; b. 19.7.34, Lancaster; m., Margaret. Educ. Storey's Institute, Lancaster; University of Cape Town. Librarian: University of

Zimbabwe, 1976-78; St. Patrick's College, Maynooth, 1980-82. Recreations: tennis; sailing. Address: (b.) University Library, Strathclyde University, Glasgow, G4 0NS; T.-0141-552 3701.

Harrison, Professor Bryan Desmond, CBE, BSc, PhD, FRS, FRSE, Hon. DAgric. Professor of Plant Virology, Dundee University, since 1991; b. 16.6.31, Purley, Surrey; m., Elizabeth Ann Latham-Warde; 2 s.; 1 d. Educ. Whitgift School, Croydon; Reading University. Agricultural Research Council Postgraduate Research Student, 1952-54; Scientific Officer, Scottish Horticultural Research Institute, 1954-57; Senior and Principal Scientific Officer, Rothamsted Experimental Station, 1957-66; Scottish Horticultural Research Institute/Scottish Crop Research Institute: Principal Scientific Officer, 1966, Senior Principal Scientific Officer (Individual Merit), 1969, Deputy Chief Scientific Officer (Individual Merit), 1981; Head, Virology Department, 1966-91; Honorary Professor, Department of Biochemistry and Microbiology, St. Andrews University, 1987; Honorary Visiting Professor, Dundee University, 1988-91; Past President, Association of Applied Biologists. Recreation: gardening. Address: (b.) Department of Biological Sciences, Dundee University, Dundee, DD1 4HN; T.-01382 562731.

Harrison, Cameron, BSc (Hons), MEd. Chief Executive, Scottish Consultative Council on the Curriculum, since 1991; Rector, The Gordon Schools, Huntly, 1982-91; b. 27.8.45, Mauchline, Ayrshire; m., Pearl; 1 s.; 1 d. Educ. Cumnock Academy; Strathclyde University; Glasgow University; Stirling University. Teacher, Greenock Academy, 1968-71; Principal Teacher of Physics, Graeme High School, Falkirk, 1971-79; Depute Rector, Kirkcudbright Academy, 1979-82; Member, SEB; CCC Sub-Committees (Member, JWP on Higher Physics, 1976-79); Member, several research advisory committees; Chairman, Scottish Central Committee for Physical Recreation; General Secretary, CIDREE. Recreations: lay preacher; used to play rugby (still pretends to!); music. Address: (b.) Gardyne Road, Broughty Ferry, Dundee, DD5 1NY.

Harrison, Professor Robert Graham, BSc (Hons), PhD, FRSE. Professor of Physics, Heriot-Watt University, since 1987; b. 26.2.44 Oxford; m., Rowena Indrania; 1 s.; 1 d. Educ. Wanstead High School; London University. Postgraduate and postdoctoral research, Royal Holloway College, London, and Culham Laboratories, UKAEA, 1966-72; Lecturer, Bath University; joined Physics Department, Heriot-Watt University. Publications: 200 scientific publications, including editorship of four books. Address: (b.) Physics Department, Heriot-Watt University, Riccarton, Currie, Edinburgh, EH14 4AS; T.-0131-449 5111.

Harrison, Sydney, OBE. Proprietor, Paisley and Renfrewshire Gazette Group, 1963-87; Chairman, James Paton Ltd., Printers, 1970-87; Editor, Scot, 1981-87; b. 13.4.13, Glasgow; m., Joan Morris. Educ. Whitehill School, Glasgow. Journalist, various newspapers, 1927-37; Sub-Editor, Glasgow Herald, 1938-39; Army, 1939-46 (Lt.-Col., 1944); Editor, Scottish Field, 1946-63; Director, Scottish Counties Newspapers, 1950-63; Councillor, 4th District, Renfrewshire, 1956-67; Member, Council of Industrial Design, Board of Trade, 1955-65; Honorary Member, Scottish PEN; President, Paisley Burns Club, 1984-85; Past President, Rotary Club of Paisley. Recreations: curling; motoring; caravanning; travel. Address: (h.) Aviemore, Brookfield, Renfrewshire, PA5 8UG; T.-Johnstone 20634.

Hart, Maidie (Jenny Marianne), MA (Hons); b. 15.12.16, Brookfield, Renfrewshire; m., William Douglas Hart; 2 d. Educ. St. Columba's School for Girls, Kilmacolm; St. Andrews University. Church of Scotland: Vice Convener, Home Board, 1967-70, National Vice-President, Woman's Guild, 1967-70, National President, Woman's Guild, 1972-75, Elder, since 1974; Executive Member, Women's National Commission, 1974-76; Member, Coordinating Committee, UK International Woman's Year, 1974-76 (Chairwoman, Scottish Steering Committee); first Chairwoman, Scottish Convention of Women, 1977; Vice President, British Council of Churches, 1978-81; Church of Scotland Delegate to World Council of Churches, 5th Assembly, 1975, WCC European Conference, 1978, WCC Human Rights and Mission Women's Conference, 1980, WCC Sheffield International Conference, 1981. Recreations: travel; walking; family; reading; garden; cooking. Address: (h.) Westerlea, Chapelhill, Dirleton, East Lothian, EH39 5HG; T.-0620 850 278.

Hart, Morag Mary, JP, DL, RGN, RSCN. Deputy Lieutenant, Dunbartonshire, since 1989; Director, Scotsell Ltd., since 1982; b. 19.4.39, Glasgow; m., Tom Hart; 1 s.; 1 d. Educ. Westbourne School for Girls, Glasgow. Sick Children's Hospital, Glasgow, 1956-59; Western General Hospital, Edinburgh, 1960-62. County Commissioner, Dunbartonshire Girl Guides, 1982-90; Chairman, Dunbartonshire Area Scouts, since 1994. Recreations: reading; gardening; sailing; walking. Address: (h.) 18 Campbell Drive, Bearsden, Glasgow, G61 4NE; T.-0141-942 1216.

Hart, Professor Robert Albert, BA (Hons), MA. Professor of Economics, Stirling University, since 1986, and Head, School of Management, 1991-94; b. 7.1.46, Hartlepool; m., Shirley; 3 d. Educ. Hartlepool Grammar School; Liverpool University. Economics Lecturer, Aberdeen University, 1969-73, Leeds University, 1974-75; Senior Lecturer, Strathclyde University, 1976-80; Senior Research Fellow, Science Centre, Berlin, 1980-86. Recreations: walking; reading; drinking beer. Address: (b.) Department of Economics, Stirling University, Stirling, FK9 4LA; T.-01786 467471.

Hart, Professor Susan Jane Ritchie, BA (Hons), PhD, DipMRS. Professor of Marketing, Heriot-Watt University, Edinburgh, since 1993; b. 18.7.60, Edinburgh. Educ. Bearsden Academy; Strathclyde University. Universite de Technologie de Compiegne, 1982-83; Procter and Gamble PLC, 1983-84; Research Assistant/Lecturer/Senior Lecturer, Department of Marketing, Strathclyde University, 1984-93. Publications: Marketing and Competitive Success (Co-author); papers. Recreations: hill-walking; skiing. Address: (b.) Department of Business Organisation, Heriot-Watt University, Riccarton, Edinburgh, EH14 4AT; T.-0131-449 5111, Ext. 4772.

Harte, Professor Ben, BA, MA, PhD(Cantab), FRSE. Professor of Metamorphism, Edinburgh University, since 1991; b. 30.5.41, Blackpool; m., Angela Elizabeth; 1 s.; 2 d. Educ. Salford Grammar School; Trinity College, Cambridge University. Lecturer/Reader, Edinburgh University, 1965-91; Guest Research Investigator, Carnegie Institution of Washington, 1974-75; Visiting Associate Professor, Yale University, 1982; Visiting Research Fellow, University of Cape Town, 1990. Address: (b.) Department of Geology and Geophysics, King's Buildings, Edinburgh, EH9 3JW; T.-0131-650 8528.

Hartley, Clive, BA, DipTP, MRTPI. Director of Tourism, Dumfries and Galloway Tourist Board, since 1995, on secondment from Dumfries and Galloway Regional Council (Depute Director); b. 20.4.47; m, Joyce Walker. Educ. Nelson Secondary Technical School; Hull University; Central London Polytechnic. Assistant Research Officer, Countryside Commission for England and Wales; Research Officer, Department of the Environment; Principal Planning Officer, Dumfries and Galloway Regional Council. Past President, Galloway Mountaineering Club; Past President, Dumfries and Galloway Architectural and Engineering Society. Recreations: hill-walking; gardening; natural

194 WHO'S WHO IN SCOTLAND

history; photography. Address: (b.) Campbell House, Bankend Road, Dumfries, DG1 4TH; T.-01387 250434.

Hartley, Graeme Edward, BA. Deputy Director, Royal Institution of Chartered Surveyors in Scotland, since 1990; b. 9.4.61, Edinburgh; m., Lee Adams Rankine; 1 s. Educ. Perth High School; Napier University. Dundee Chamber of Commerce, 1983-85; Electrical Contractors' Association of Scotland, 1985-90. Member, Scottish Building Contract Committee, since 1986; Member, Scottish Joint Consultative Committee for Building, since 1986. Recreations: golf; running: X-C skiing. Address: (b.) 9 Manor Place, Edinburgh, EH3 7DN; T.-0131-225 7078.

Hartnett, Frank Ernest Lawrence, OBE, BSc (Econ), CertEd, DipEdTech. General Manager, Grampian Health Board, since 1991; b. 3.9.40, Alton; m., Catherine Mary Adams; 1 s.; 1 d. Educ. Lord Wandsworth College; London University; Southampton University; Sussex University. Head, Economics Department, Cheshunt Grammar School; commissioned RAF, 1965; lead role in achieving organisational change in RAF training, 1972-75; involved in fast jet operations, RAF Germany, 1975-78; introduction of Tornado into RAF, 1978-81; OFFR and aircrew selection, 1982; OC Trg WG, RAF Hereford, 1982-85; OC Admin WG, RAF Cosford, 1985-87; General Manager, Maternity and Child Health, 1987-89, General Manager, Mental Health, 1989-91, Grampian Health Board. Recreations: hill-walking; shooting; badminton. Address: (b.) Summerfield House, 2 Eday Road, Aberdeen, AB9 1RE; T.-01224 404000.

Hartnoll, Mary C., CBE, Hon. LLD, BA (Hons). Director of Social Work, Strathclyde Regional Council, since 1993 (Director of Social Work, Grampian Regional Council, 1978-93); b. 31.5.39, Bristol. Educ. Colston's Girls School, Bristol; Bedford College, London University; Liverpool University. Child Care Officer, Dorset County Council, 1961-63; various posts, Reading County Borough, 1963-74; Berkshire County Council: Assistant Director, 1974-75, Divisional Director, 1975-77. Recreations: natural history; walking. Address: (b.) Strathclyde House, 20 India Street, Glasgow, G2 4PF.

Hartshorn, Christina, BA, MSc, DipCG. Enterprise Officer for Women in Scotland, since 1986; b. 18.12.46, Birmingham; 1 d. Educ. Bartley Green Girls' Grammar School, Birmingham; Essex University; Stirling University. Careers Officer, Senior Careers Officer, Fife Regional Council; Lecturer, Napier College, Edinburgh; Tutor, Extra Mural Department, Edinburgh University; Freelance Careers Advisor and Counsellor. Equal Opportunities Fellowship, German Marshall Fund of the United States, 1987. Recreations: friends; hill-walking; clarinet. Address: (b.) Scottish Enterprise Foundation, Stirling University, Stirling; T.-01786 467353.

Harvey, Professor Alan L., BSc, PhD, MBA. Director, Strathclyde Institute for Drug Research, since 1988; Professor in Physiology and Pharmacology, Strathclyde University, since 1986; b. 23.6.50, Glasgow. Educ. Hutchesons', Glasgow; Strathclyde University. Lecturer in Physiology and Pharmacology, Strathclyde University, 1974-83; Senior Lecturer, 1983-86. British Pharmacological Society Sandoz Prize, 1983; British Pharmaceutical Conference Science Award, 1983. Publications: Toxicon (Editor); Snake Toxins, 1991. Address: (b.) Department of Physiology and Pharmacology, Strathclyde University, Glasgow, G1 1XW; T.-0141-553 4155.

Harvey, Jake, DA, RSA. Sculptor and Lecturer; Lecturer, Edinburgh College of Art; b. 3.6.48, Kelso; m., Anne Penelope; 1 s.; 2 d. Educ. Kelso High School; Edinburgh College of Art. Latimer Award, RSA, 1975; Benno Schotz Sculpture Prize, RSA, 1976; ARSA, 1977; Hugh MacDiarmid Memorial Sculpture, 1982-85; William Gillies

Bursary, 1989; RSA, 1989; has shown in many solo and group exhibitions; major retrospective exhibition, Talbot Rice Gallery, 1993; commissions include: Hugh MacDiarmid Memorial Sculpture, 1982, Charles Rennie Mackintosh Sculpture, Glasgow, 1985, Newcraighall Mining Sculpture, 1987, Poacher's Tree, 1991. Recreations: fishing; walking. Address: (h.) Maxton Cross, Maxton, St. Boswells, Roxburghshire; T.-01835 22650.

Harvey, Susan, MA, MIL. President, International Orienteering Federation, since 1994; Board Member, SE Regional Board, Scottish Natural Heritage, since 1992; b. 3.7.43, Harpenden; m., Robin Harvey, MBE; 1 s. Educ. Claremont, Esher; Edinburgh University. General Secretary, World Orienteeering Championships, 1974-76; Director, Harvey Map Services Ltd., since 1977; President, Scottish Orienteering Association, 1979-80; Secretary General, International Orienteering Federation, 1983-86; Commissioner, Countryside Commission for Scotland, 1988-92. British Ladies Open Champion Orienteering, 1971. Recreations: orienteering; guitar; gardening; carpentry. Address: (h.) Mile End, Doune, FK16 6BJ; T.-01786 841202.

Harvey, Rev. William John, BA (Hons), BD (Hons). Minister, Church of Scotland, since 1964; Leader, The Iona Community, 1988-95; b. 17.5.37, Glasgow; m., Isabel Mary Douglas; 2 s.; 2 d. Educ. Fettes College, Edinburgh; Oxford University; Glasgow University. National Service, Argyll & Sutherland Highlanders, 1956-58; Ordained Assistant, Govan Old Parish Church, 1964-66; Member, Gorbals Group Ministry, 1963-71; Minister, Laurieston-Renwick Parish Church, Glasgow, 1968-71; Warden, Iona Abbey, 1971-76; Minister, Raploch Parish Church, Stirling, 1976-81; Minister, Govan Old Parish Church, 1981-88. Member, Church of Scotland Committee on Church and Nation, 1978-86; Kerr Lecturer, Glasgow University, 1987. Recreations: reading; history; bread and wine-making; sea-bird watching. Address: (h.) Flat 2/1, 99 McCulloch Street, Glasgow, G41 1NT; T.-0141-429 3774.

Harvey-Jamieson, Lt.-Col. Harvey Morro, OBE, TD, DL, WS; b. 9.12.08, Edinburgh; m., Frances Ridout; 3 s. Educ. Edinburgh Academy; RMC, Sandhurst; Edinburgh University (BL). 2nd Lt., 1st Bn., King's Own Scottish Borderers, 1928; Captain, 1938; Major, RA TA, 1939; Lt. Col., 1943; CO 3rd Edinburgh Home Guard Bn. Royal Scots, 1954-57; Member, Royal Company of Archers (Queen's Bodyguard for Scotland), since 1934; Secretary and Legal Adviser, The Company of Merchants of City of Edinburgh, 1946-71; Member, Committee on Conveyancing Legislation, 1964-66; Chairman, Scottish Committee HMC Association of Governing Bodies of Boys and Girls Public Schools, 1956-70; Member, Council, Cockburn Association, 1957-78; Deputy Lieutenant, Edinburgh, since 1968. Recreation: travel. Address: (h.) 20 Dean Terrace, Edinburgh; T.-0131-332 4589.

Haslett, Professor Christopher, BSc (Hons), MBChB (Hons), FRCP Edin, FRCP Lond. Professor of Respiratory Medicine, Edinburgh University, since 1990; Honorary Consultant Physician, Lothian Health Board, since 1990; Visiting Professor, Department of Medicine, Royal Postgraduate Medical School, since 1990; b. 2.4.53, Chester; m., Jean Margaret; 1 s.; 1 d. Educ. Wirral Grammar School; Edinburgh University Medical School. House Physician, Department of Medicine, Royal Infirmary, Edinburgh, 1977-87; Rotating Medical Registrar, Ealing Hospital and Hammersmith Hospital, London, 1980-82; MRC Travelling Fellow, National Jewish Hospital, Denver, Colorado, 1982-85; MRC Senior Clinical Fellow and Senior Lecturer, Department of Medicine, Royal Postgraduate Medical School, Hammersmith Hospital, London, 1986-90. Vice-Chairman, National Asthma Campaign Research Committee; Member, MRC Molecular and Cellular Medicine Board; Member and Vice Chairman,

MRC Systems "A" Grants Committee; Secretary, Lung Injury Section, European Respiratory Society. Recreation: rugby union. Address: (b.) Respiratory Medicine Unit, Department of Medicine, Royal Infirmary, Edinburgh, EH3 9YW; T.-0131-229 2477.

Hastings, Gavin. Rugby player; b. 1962, Edinburgh. Educ. George Watson's College, Edinburgh; Cambridge University. Made debut for Scotland, 1986; played in World Cups, 1987-91-95; member, Scottish team which won Grand Slam, 1990; played three times for British Lions.

Hastings, Gerard Bernard, BSc, PhD. Director, Centre for Social Marketing, Department of Marketing, Strathclyde University, since 1987; Member, Forth Valley Health Board; b. 5.10.54, Ilkley; 3 s. Educ. St. Michael's College, Leeds; Newcastle upon Tyne Polytechnic; Strathclyde University. Recreations: hill-walking; travel; books. Address: (b.) Department of Marketing, Strathclyde University, 173 Cathedral Street, Glasgow, G4 0RQ; T.-0141-552 4400.

Hatwell, Anthony, DFA(Lond). Sculptor; Head, School of Sculpture, Edinburgh College of Art, 1969-90; b. 21.6.31, London; m., Elizabeth; 2 d. Educ. Dartford Grammar School; Slade School of Fine Art; Borough Polytechnic; Bromley College of Art. Some exhibitions: Scottish Arts Council Edinburgh Festival Exhibition, 1978; British Sculpture in the 20th Century, Whitechapel Gallery, 1981; Built in Scotland exhibition in Edinburgh, Glasgow, and London, 1983; Slade Postgraduate Scholarship, 1956; Boise Travelling Scholarship, 1957; Assistant to Henry Moore, 1958; Member, London Group, 1959-69 (Vice-President, 1961-63); works in collections of Scottish National Gallery of Modern Art, Arts Council of GB, Scottish Arts Council and private collections. Address: (h.) 4 North Street, Belhaven, Dunbar, East Lothian.

Havergal, Giles, OBE, MA, DLitt, FRSE, FRSAMD. Director, Citizens' Theatre, Glasgow, since 1969; b. 9.6.38.

Hawkins, Anthony Donald, BSc, PhD, FSA Scot, FRSE. Director of Fisheries Research for Scotland, since 1987 (Deputy Director, 1983-87); Honorary Professor, Aberdeen University; b. 25.3.42, Dorset; m., Susan Mary; 1 s. Educ. Poole Grammar School; Bristol University. Entered Scottish Office as Scientific Officer, Marine Laboratory, Aberdeen, 1965; Senior Scientific Officer, 1969, Principal Scientific Officer, 1972, Senior Principal Scientific Officer, 1978, Deputy Chief Scientific Officer, 1983; conducts research into behaviour and physiology of fish; awarded A.B. Wood Medal, Institute of Acoustics, 1978; Honorary Lecturer in Marine Biology, St. Andrews University. Publications: books on fish physiology and aquarium systems. Recreations: reading; angling; soccer; breeding whippets. Address: (b.) Marine Laboratory, PO Box 101, Victoria Road, Torry, Aberdeen; T.-01224 876544.

Haworth, John Roger, BA (Hons),MRTPI, MCIT. Director of Economic Development, Ross and Cromarty District Council; b. 4.2.46, Worsley, Manchester; m., Margaret; 2 s.; 2 d. Educ. Bolton School; Manchester University. Planning Assistant, Stirling County Council, 1968-71; Ross and Cromarty County Council: Assistant Planning Officer, 1971-73, Assistant Planning Officer (Western Isles), 1973-74; Director of Planning and Development, Western Isles Islands Council, 1974-87. Recreations: reading; music; films; history; travel. Address: (b.) Council Offices, Dingwall, Ross & Cromarty, IV15 9QN; T.-01349 868626.

Hay, Ann Catherine, OBE. Secretary, Scottish Conservative and Unionist Association, since 1981; Deputy Director, Scottish Conservative Party, since 1990; b. Forres. Educ. Forres Academy. Agent, Edinburgh Pentlands Conservative Association, 1963-65; National Organiser, Scottish Young Conservatives, 1965-68; Secretary, Federation of Conservative Students, 1969-72; Agent, High Peak (Derbyshire) Conservative Association, 1973-76; Deputy Director, Scottish Conservative Party, 1976-81. Recreations: reading; music; sewing; DIY. Address: (b.) Suite 1/1, 14 Links Place, Leith, Edinburgh, EH6 7EZ; T.-0131-555 2900.

Hay, Francis (Frank) Walker Christie, OBE, DL, MA (Hons). Deputy Lieutenant, Banffshire, since 1988; Honorary Sheriff, Banff, since 1992; Member, Committee of Management, Cairn Housing Association Ltd.; Member, National Council, Royal British Legion Scotland; b. 20.3.23, Aberdeen; m., Margaret Anne Castel; 2 s.; 1 d. Educ. Robert Gordon's College, Aberdeen; Aberdeen University. Commissioned into Reconnaissance Corps, 1943; gazetted Captain, 1947; Teacher of History, 1950-58; Special Assistant, Turriff Academy, 1958-63; Principal Teacher of History, Breadalbane Academy, Banff Academy, 1963-74; Assistant Rector, Banff Academy, 1974-88; Member, Banffshire Education Committee, 1961-75. Recreations: furniture making; Banff Choral Society. Address: (h.) 11 Fife Street, Banff, AB45 1JB; T.-01261 812285.

Hay, Ian, FCIBS, MIBC, MACE, MIAH. Chief Executive, Scottish Association of Master Bakers, since 1989; b. 31.8.39, Aberdeen; m., Amelia Robertson; 3 s.; 1 d. Educ. Ellon Academy. Thirty years with Clydesdale Bank PLC, including senior positions as General Manager London and Regional Director with responsibilities for East of Scotland; appointed Chief Executive, Craft Baking Training Organisation, 1993; Chairman, National Council of Industry Training Organisations (Scotland), since 1995. Recreations: golf; reading; hypnotherapy. Address: (b.) 4 Torphichen Street, Edinburgh, EH3 8JQ; T.-0131-229 1401.

Hay, J. Iain, FRICS, IRRV. Chairman, Royal Institution of Chartered Surveyors in Scotland, 1993-94; Consultant to Knight Frank & Rutley, 1991-93; J. Iain Hay, Chartered Surveyors, since 1992; b. 17.7.44, Ayr; m., Elizabeth; 2 d. Educ. Kelvinside Academy. Thomas Binnie & Hendry, Chartered Surveyors, 1962-66; Dunbarton County Assessors Office, 1966-69; Bovis Homes, 1969-70; Senior Surveyor, Millar Macrae and Stewart, 1970-72, Partner, 1972-86; Partner, Knight Frank & Rutley, 1986-91; Director, Montrose Estates (1982) Ltd., 1986-93; Director, KDCL Ltd., since 1992. Past President, Property Agents International. Recreations: golf; gardening. Address: (h.) Castle House, Drymen, Glasgow; T.-01360 660550.

Hay, James Taylor Cantlay, MBE, BSc (Hons), DTech, FInstPet, AAPG. Oil and Gas Consultant; Chairman, Scottish Sub-sea Technology Group, since 1991; Chairman, Grampian Enterprise Training Services, since 1992; Chairman, Operational Command Training Organisation, since 1991; Director, The Scottish Ballet, since 1993; b. 13.6.35, Huntly; m., Mary Gordon Davidson; 1 s.; 2 d. Educ. Banchory Academy; Aberdeen University. Geologist, Iraq Petroleum Co. Ltd., Iraq, 1958-66; Head of Geology, Abu Dhabi Petroleum Co. Ltd., Abu Dhabi, 1967-71; Lecturer in Geology, Aberdeen University, 1971-74; Senior Production Geologist, Burmah Oil, London, 1974-76; various management roles, BNOC, Aberdeen and Glasgow, 1977-80; General Manager, BNOC/Britoil, Aberdeen, 1980-87; General Manager, BP Exploration, Aberdeen, 1988-91. Recreations: golf; shooting. Address: (h.) 67 Fountainhall Road, Aberdeen; T.-01224 645955.

Hay, John McWhirter. Sheriff Clerk, Kirkcaldy, since 1993; b. 27.4.43, Glasgow; m., Mary Wilkie Munro; 3 d. Educ. Clydebank High School. Clerical Officer: Glasgow Sheriff Court, 1960-63, Dumbarton Sheriff Court, 1963-65; Second Class Depute, Glasgow Sheriff Court, 1965-71; First Class Depute, Ayr Sheriff Court, 1971-80; Sheriff

Clerk, Dunfermline, 1980-88; Project Sponsor, Scottish Courts Administration, 1988-93. Captain, Troon St. Meddans Golf Club, 1975; Captain, Dunfermline Golf Club, 1989-91. Recreations: versatile sportsman, first love golf (single figure handicap, since 1972). Address: (b.) Sheriff Clerk's Office, Whytescauseway, Kirkcaldy; T.-01592 260171.

Hay, Michael James, BSc (Hons), DipEd. Head Teacher, Tynecastle High School, since 1987; b. 8.3.47, Newport Pagnell; m., Rosalind Margaret Gibling; 1 s.; 1 d. Educ. Perth Academy; Edinburgh University. Teacher of Mathematics, Royal High School, 1968-71; Principal Teacher of Mathematics: John Watson's School, 1971-73, Leith Academy, 1973-79; Assistant Head Teacher, Penicuik High School, 1979-83; Depute Head Teacher, Tynecastle High School, 1983-87. Chair, Lothian Branch, Headteachers Association of Scotland; Secretary, Lothian Headteachers' Association. Recreations: music (organist and choirmaster); hill-walking; recreational computing. Address: (b.) Tynecastle High School, McLeod Street, Edinburgh, EH11 2NJ; T.-0131-337 3488.

Hay, Sheriff Principal Robert Colquhoun, CBE, MA, LLB, WS. Sheriff Principal of North Strathclyde, since 1989; b. 22.9.33, Glasgow; m., Olive Black; 2 s.; 2 d. Educ. Edinburgh University. Legal practice, 1956-63, 1968-76; Depute Procurator Fiscal, 1963-68; Chairman, Industrial Tribunals (Scotland), 1976-81, President, 1981-89; Commissioner of Northern Lights, since 1989, Chairman, 1992-93; Member, Sheriff Court Rules Council, since 1990, Chairman, since 1993; Commissioner for Clan Hay, since 1995. Address: (b.) Sheriff Principal's Chambers, Sheriff Court House, Renfrew Road, Paisley, PA3 4DD; T.-0141-887 5291.

Hay, Robert King Miller, BSc, MSc, PhD, MIBiol. Director, Scottish Agricultural Science Agency, since 1990; b. 19.8.46, Edinburgh; m., Dorothea Harden Vinycomb; 2 s.; 1 d. Educ. Forres Academy, Moray; Aberdeen University; University of East Anglia. AFRC Research Fellow, Edinburgh University, 1971-74; Lecturer in Crop Production: University of Malawi, 1974-76, Edinburgh University, 1976-77; Lecturer in Environmental Sciences, Lancaster University, 1977-82; Leverhulme European Fellow, Agricultural University of Norway, 1981; Head of Plant Sciences, Scottish Agricultural College, Ayr, 1982-90; British Council Research Fellow, University of Western Australia, 1989. Publications: Environmental Physiology of Plants; Chemistry for Agriculture and Ecology; Introduction to the Physiology of Crop Yield; Volatile Oil Crops (Editor); Science Policies in Europe: unity and diversity (Editor); 50 scientific papers. Recreations: walking; building walls; music; Scotland. Address: (h.) 16 Polton Road, Lasswade, EH18 1AA.

Hay, Professor Robert Walker, BSc, PhD, CChem, FRSC, FRSE. Professor of Chemistry, St. Andrews University, since 1988; Pro Dean of Science (Graduate Studies), since 1993; b. 17.9.34, Stirling; m., Alison Laird; 1 s.; 3 d. Educ. Stirling High School; Glasgow University. Assistant Lecturer, Glasgow University, 1959; subsequently worked at Esso Research; Lecturer, Senior Lecturer and Reader, Victoria University, Wellington, New Zealand, 1961; Reader, Stirling University, 1971; Professor, Stirling University, 1984. Publications: Bioinorganic Chemistry, 1984; numerous scientific papers. Recreations: walking; travel; caravanning; reading. Address: (b.) Chemistry Department, St. Andrews, KY16 9AJ; T.-01334 76161.

Hay, William Flett, CBE (1986). Hon. President, Scottish Fishermen's Federation; b. 7.10.29, Findochty; m., Sheila Reid; 1 s.; 1 d. Educ. Portsoy School. Took up sea going career in the fishing industry at the age of 14; took command of own vessel, 1954; retired from active sea going career, 1984; Chairman, Scottish White Fish Producers' Association, 1976-82.

Hayes, Sir John Osler Chattock, KCB, OBE; b. 9.5.13; m., Hon. Rosalind Mary Finlay; 2 s.; 1 d. Educ. Royal Naval College, Dartmouth. War service, 1939-45, Atlantic/HMS Repulse/Singapore/Russian Convoys/Malta; Real Admiral, Naval Secretary to First Lord of Admiralty, 1962-64; Vice Admiral/Rear Admiral, Flag Officer 2nd in command Western Fleet, 1964-66; Vice Admiral, Flag Officer Scotland and Northern Ireland, 1966-68; President, King George's Fund for Sailors, Scotland, 1968-79; Vice Patron, Royal National Mission for Deep Sea Fishermen, 1968-94; Deputy Chairman, Gordonstoun School, 1977-86; Lord Lieutenant of Ross and Cromarty, Skye and Lochalsh, 1977-88. Publication: Face the Music: a sailor's story, 1991. Recreations: music; writing; walking. Address: (h.) Wemyss House, Nigg, Tain, Ross and Cromarty, IV19 1QW; T.-Nigg 212.

Hayes, Michael George, BA, MCD, MRTPI. Director of Planning and Building Control, City of Glasgow, since 1995 (Director of Planning, 1993-95); b. 20.2.47, Liverpool; m., Elizabeth; 1 s.; 2 d. Educ. Bootle Grammar School; Leeds University; Liverpool University. Assistant Planner, Bootle CB, 1971; Principal Planning Officer, Sefton MD, 1974; Assistant Divisional Planning Officer, Liverpool, 1979; City Planning Officer, Liverpool, 1985. Member, Historic Areas and Buildings Advisory Committee, English Heritage; Member, Executive Committee, Scottish Society of Directors of Planning. Recreations: Reader in Anglican church; cycling; hill-walking; music; theatre. Address: (b.) 231 George Street, Glasgow, G1 1RX; T.-0141-227 5903.

Haythornthwaite, Professor Josephine Angela, BA, PhD, FLA, FInstInfSc. Chief Librarian, Glasgow Caledonian University, since 1989; Visiting Profesor in Information Management, Leicester De Montfort University, since 1993; b. 24.6.38, Leamington Spa. Educ. St. Margaret's School, Ludlow, Strathclyde University. Began career as librarian, 1962; Depute Librarian, Glasgow College of Technology, 1971-78; Lecturer, Strathclyde University, 1978-82; Lecturer, Loughborough University, 1983-89. Publications: Distance Education in Library and Information Studies (Co-author); Business Information Maze; Scotland in the Nineteenth Century. Recreations: theatre; music; cooking; entertaining; travel. Address: (b.) Glasgow Caledonian University, Cowcaddens Road, Glasgow, G12 0PQ; T.-0141-331 3860.

Heading, Robert Campbell, BSc, MD, FRCP. Consultant Physician, Edinburgh Royal Infirmary, since 1975; Reader in Medicine, Edinburgh University, since 1992; b. 3.7.41, Stepps, Lanarkshire; m., Patricia Mary Goldie; 2 s.; 1 d. Educ. Birkenhead School; King Edward's School, Birmingham; Edinburgh University. Address: (h.) 20 Frogston Road West, Edinburgh, EH10 7AR; T.-0131-445 1552.

Heald, Professor David Albert, BA, ACMA. Professor of Accountancy, Aberdeen University, since 1990; Specialist Adviser, Scottish Affairs Committee, House of Commons, since 1993; Specialist Adviser, Treasury and Civil Service Committee, House of Commons, since 1989; b. 25.9.47, York; m., Yvonne Duncan. Educ. Nunthorpe Grammar School, York; Leicester University; Jordanhill College. Accountant, Raleigh Industries, 1969-70, British Steel Corporation, 1971-72; Lecturer in Economics, Glasgow College of Technology, 1972-78; Lecturer in Economics, later in Management Studies, Glasgow University, 1978-90. Labour Parliamentary candidate, Roxburgh, Selkirk and Peebles, 1979. Publications: several books and numerous articles, including: Making Devolution Work; Financing Devolution within the UK; a study of the lessons from failure; Public Expenditure: its defence and reform;

Financing a Scottish Parliament: options for debate. Recreations: theatre; cinema; everything French; squash; boating on the Moray Firth; hoping for the next Grand Slam. Address: (b.) Department of Accountancy, Aberdeen University, Edward Wright Building, Aberdeen, AB9 2TY; T.-01224 272213.

Healy, Brendan. Chief Executive, St. Andrew's Ambulance Association. Address: (b.) 48 Milton Street, Glasgow, G4 0HR.

Healy, Raymond Michael, BSc. Headmaster, Lourdes Secondary School, Glasgow, since 1987 (Rector, Our Lady's High School, Cumbernauld, 1976-86); b. 8.7.40, Glasgow; m., Margaret Bradburn; 2 s. Educ. St. Aloysius College, Glasgow; Glasgow University; Jordanhill College of Education. Research Department: Babcock & Wilcox Ltd., Renfrew, 1961-62; Sandeman Bros., Glasow, 1962-63; Teacher: St. Margaret Mary's Secondary School, Glasgow, 1964-65, St. Aloysius College, Glasgow, 1965-69; Principal Teacher of Chemistry, St. Aloysius College, Glasgow, 1969-72; Assistant Headteacher, St. Andrew's High School, Clydebank, 1972-74; Depute Headteacher, St. Patrick's High School, Dumbarton, 1974-76. Member, Scottish Central Committee on Science, 1978-81. Recreation: golf. Address: (b.) Lourdes Secondary School, 47 Kirriemuir Avenue, Glasgow, G52 3DF.

Heaney, Henry Joseph, MA, FLA, FRSE. University Librarian and Keeper of the Hunterian Books and MSS, Glasgow University, since 1978; b. 2.1.35, Newry, Northern Ireland; m., Mary Elizabeth Moloney. Educ. Abbey Grammar School, Newry; Queen's University, Belfast. Assistant Librarian, Queen's University, Belfast, 1959-62; Librarian, Magee University College, Londonderry, 1962-69; Deputy Librarian, New University of Ulster, 1967-69; Assistant Secretary, Standing Conference of National and University Libraries, 1969-72; Librarian: Queen's University, Belfast, 1972-74, University College, Dublin, 1975-78. Member, Advisory Committee on Public Library Service, Northern Ireland, 1965; Chairman, NI Branch, Library Association, 1966, 1973; Trustee, National Library of Scotland, 1980-91; Chairman, British Library Ad Hoc Working Party on Union Catalogues, 1982; Member: British Library Board, 1989-95, British Library Reference Division Advisory Committee, 1982-89, British Library Lending Division Advisory Committee, 1983-86, British Eighteenth Century Short Title Catalogue Committee, since 1983, Standing Committee, University Libraries Section, IFLA, 1986-91; Trustee, National Manuscripts Conservation Trust, 1989-95; Chairman, Consortium of University Research Libraries, since 1995; Editor, World List of Abbreviations of Organisations; President, Scottish Library Association, 1990. Address: (b.) Glasgow University Library, Hillhead Street, Glasgow, G12 8QE; T.-0141-330 5633.

Hearne, John Michael, BMus, MMus. Publisher (Longship Music); Freelance Composer and Professional Singer; b. 19.9.37, Reading; m., Margaret Gillespie Jarvie. Educ. Torquay Grammar School; St. Luke's College, Exeter; University College of Wales, Aberystwyth. Teaching, Rugeley, Staffordshire, 1959-60; Warehouseman/Driver, Torquay, 1961-64; Teaching: Tonlistarskoli Borgarfjardar, Iceland, 1968-69, UCW Aberystwyth, 1969-70; Lecturer, Aberdeen College of Education, 1970-87; Composer, vocal, instrumental and incidental music; Member, John Currie Singers; McEwen Commission, Glasgow University, 1979; Past Chairman, Scottish Society of Composers; Chairman, Scottish Music Advisory Committee, BBC, 1986-90; Chorus Manager, Aberdeen International Youth Festival, since 1978; won Radio Forth Trophy, 1985, for most outstanding work on Edinburgh Festival Fringe; BBC commission for BBCSSO, 1990 (trumpet concerto); joint winner, Gregynog Composers' Award for Wales, 1992; Chairman, Gordon

Forum for the Arts, 1991-94; Conductor, Stonehaven and District Choral Society; District Councillor, Incorporated Society of Musicians; Member, Executive Committee, Composers' Guild GB. Recreations: motoring and travel (1954 Daimler Roadster). Address: (h.) Smidskot, Fawells, Keith-Hall, Inverurie, AB51 OLN; T.-01651 882 274.

Heatly, Sir Peter, CBE, DL, BSc, CEng, FICE. Chairman, Peter Heatly & Co. Ltd., since 1958; Chairman, Scottish Sports Council, 1975-87; Chairman, Commonwealth Games Federation, 1982-90; b. 9.6.24, Edinburgh; m., Mae Calder Cochrane. Educ. Leith Academy; Edinburgh University. Structural Designer, Redpath Brown & Co. Ltd., 1946; Lecturer in Civil Engineering, Edinburgh University, 1948. Chairman, International Diving Committee, 1984-88; Master, Edinburgh Merchant Company, 1988-90; awarded Honorary Doctorate, Edinburgh University, 1992, Queen Margaret College, 1994. Recreations: swimming; gardening; travel. Address: (h.) Lanrig, Balerno, Edinburgh, EH14 7AJ; T.-0131-449 3998.

Hector, Gordon Matthews, CMG, CBE (OBE, 1955), MA (Oxon). Honorary Vice President, The St. Andrew Society; Secretary to Assembly Council, General Assembly of Church of Scotland, 1980-85; b. 9.6.18, Aberdeen; m., Dr. Mary Forrest Gray; 1 s.; 2 d. Educ. St. Mary's School, Melrose; Edinburgh Academy; Lincoln College, Oxford. HM Colonial Administrative Service and Overseas Civil Service, 1946-66: District Commissioner, Kenya, Secretary, Kenya Road Authority, Secretary to Government of Seychelles, 1952-55, Acting Governor, 1953, Deputy Resident Commissioner and Government Secretary, Basutoland (now Lesotho), 1956-64, Deputy British Government Representative, Lesotho, 1965-66; Aberdeen University: Clerk to University Court, 1967, Deputy Secretary, 1976-80. OBE, 1955. Fellow, Commonwealth Fund, 1939; Burgess of Guild, Aberdeen; Chairman, West End Community Council, Edinburgh, 1986-89; Court of Directors, Edinburgh Academy, 1967-75; Chairman, Great North of Scotland Railway Association, 1990-92; Chairman, Scottish Council, Victoria League, 1983-88; Member, sometime Chairman, Board of Managers, Oakbank List D School, 1969-90. Recreations: town and country walking; railways ancient and modern; grandchildren. Address: (h.) 4 Montgomery Court, 110 Hepburn Gardens, St. Andrews, KY16 9LT; T.-01334 73784.

Hedderwick, Alexander Mark. Managing Director, Adam & Company Investment Management, since 1989; Director, Adam & Company Group PLC, since 1992; b. 13.12.48. Hedderwick Borthwick, Stockbrokers, 1969-73; Langton Underwriting Agents, Lloyds, 1973-84. Recreations: family; gardening; bee-keeping. Address: (b.) 22 Charlotte Square, Edinburgh, EH2 4DF; T.-0131-225 8484.

Hedderwick, Mairi Crawford, DA (Edin). Illustrator, Writer and Public Speaker; b. 2.5.39, Gourock; 1 s.; 1 d. Educ. St. Columba's School, Kilmacolm; Edinburgh College of Art; Jordanhill College of Education. Art Teacher, mid-Argyll primary schools, 1962; Hebridean "dropping out", crofting, child rearing, 1964-73; part-time art teaching 1979-86; community co-operative worker, Highlands and Islands, 1986-88. Publications: for children: Katie Morag series, Peedie Peebles series, Carpenter MacPheigh; for adults: An Eye on the Hebrides, Highland Journey. Recreations: a day outside ending round a table with friends, food and wine. Address: Isle of Coll, Argyll, PA78 6TB.

Heggie, Professor Douglas Cameron, MA, PhD, FRAS, FRSE. Professor of Mathematical Astronomy, Edinburgh University, since 1994; b. 7.2.47, Edinburgh; m., Linda Jane Tennent; 2 d. Educ. George Heriot's School, Edinburgh; Trinity College, Cambridge. Research Fellow, Trinity College, Cambridge, 1972-76; Lecturer in

Mathematics, Edinburgh University, 1975-85, Reader, 1985-94; Council Member, Royal Astronomical Society, 1982-85; President, Commission 37, International Astronomical Union, 1985-88. Publications: Megalithic Science; scientific papers on dynamical astronomy. Recreations: family life; walking; music. Address: (b.) Edinburgh University, Department of Mathematics and Statistics, King's Buildings, Edinburgh, EH9 3JZ; T.-0131-650 5035.

Heller, Martin Fuller Vernon, FRSAMD. Actor, since 1947; b. 20.2.27, Manchester; m., Joyce Allan; 2 s.; 4 d. Educ. Rondebosch Boys High School, Cape Town; Central School of Speech Training and Dramatic Art, London. Compass Players, 1948-52; repertory seasons and/or individual productions at following Scottish theatres: St. Andrews Byre, Edinburgh Gateway, Glasgow Citizens' (eight seasons), Edinburgh Royal Lyceum, Edinburgh Traverse, Dundee Repertory, Perth Repertory, Pitlochry Festival; Founder/Artistic Director, Prime Productions; extensive television and radio work; Member, Scottish Arts Council, 1975-82 (latterly Chairman, Drama Committee); Board Member, Pitlochry Festival Theatre; Governor, Royal Scottish Academy of Music and Drama, 1982-94. Recreations: politics; history; listening to music. Address: (h.) 54 Hermiston, Currie, Midlothian, EH14 4AQ; T.-0131-449 4055.

Helms, Professor Peter Joseph, MB, BS, PhD, FRCP. Professor of Child Health, Aberdeen University, since 1991; Consultant Paediatrician, since 1982; b. 26.6.47, Melbourne; m., Kathleen Mary; 1 s.; 3 d. Educ. Wimbledon College; Royal Free Hospital School of Medicine; London University. SHO, Hospital for Sick Children, Great Ormond Street, 1976; Lecturer in Paediatrics, Charing Cross Hospital Medical School, 1977-78; Research Fellow, Institute of Child Health, London, 1978-81, National Heart and Lung Institute, London, 1981-82; Senior Lecturer, Institute of Child Health, 1982-91; Honorary Consultant Paediatrician, Hospital for Sick Children, Great Ormond Street, 1982-91. Recreations: music; hill-walking; European history. Address: (b.) Department of Child Health, Foresterhill, Aberdeen, AB9 4ZD; T.-01224 681818.

Hemingway, Dennis, BSc, FSS, AFIMA. Secretary, Scottish Nursery Nurses' Board, since 1974; Consultant, Education Training and Administrative Services, since 1988; b. 28.6.35, Wakefield; m., Rosalie; 1 s.; 3 d. Educ. Normanton Grammar School; Leeds University. Technical Engineer, Bristol Aeroplane Company, 1955-60; Assistant Lecturer, Lecturer and Senior Lecturer, Bristol Technical College, 1960-65; Deputy Secretary, then Secretary, Union of Lancashire and Cheshire Institutes, 1965-74; Chief Officer, Scottish Technical Education Council, 1974-85; Depute Director, Scottish Vocational Education Council, 1985-87. Treasurer, Ayrshire Branch, Leukaemia Research Fund; Past President, Dundonald Historical Society. Recreations: bridge; sailing; swimming. Address: (h.) 6 Kilnford Crescent, Dundonald, Kilmarnock, KA2 9DW; T.-01563 850057.

Hemingway, Professor R. Gordon, MSc, PhD. Professor of Veterinary Animal Husbandry, Glasgow University Veterinary School, 1969-90; b. 6.4.25, Sheffield; m., Dorothy E. Adam; 2 d. Educ. King Edward VII School, Sheffield; Leeds University. Ministry of Agriculture and Fisheries, 1946-48; Royal Agricultural College, Cirencester, 1948-53; joined Glasgow University, 1953. Past Chairman: Agriculture Group, Society of Chemical Industry, Scottish Group, Nutrition Society. Recreations: golf; gardening; grandchildren. Address: (h.) Eaglesfield, Milndavie Road, Strathblane, Glasgow, G63 9EL; T.-01360 770044.

Henderson, Andrew Kerr, MB, ChB, FRCP. Consultant Physician and Clinical Director, Lorn and the Islands District General Hospital, Oban; Honorary Clinical Senior Lecturer, Glasgow University; b. 1.3.46, Hawick; m., Doreen Innes Wilkinson; 1 s.; 2 d. Educ. Glasgow Academy; Glasgow University. Medical Registrar, Western Infirmary, Glasgow; Medical Registrar/Senior Registrar, Glasgow Royal Infirmary. Chairman, Counties Branch, Scottish Schoolboys' Club. Recreations: gardening; hill-walking. Address: (h.) Birkmoss, North Connel, Argyll; T.-Connel 379.

Henderson, Douglas Mackay, CBE, BSc, FLS, FRSE, VMH. Queen's Botanist in Scotland, since 1987; b. 30.8.27, Blairgowrie; m., Julia Margaret Brown; 1 s.; 2 d. Educ. Blairgowrie High School; Edinburgh University. Scientific Officer, Department of Agriculture, Scotland, 1948-50; Research Botanist, Royal Botanic Garden, Edinburgh, 1950-70; Curator, Royal Society of Edinburgh, 1978-87; Secretary, International Association of Botanical Gardens, 1969-81; Regius Keeper, Royal Botanic Garden, Edinburgh, 1970-87; Honorary Professor, Edinburgh University, since 1982; Administrator, Inverewe Garden, National Trust for Scotland, 1987-92; Council Member, National Trust for Scotland, since 1993. Recreations: natural history; painting; sailing; cooking. Address: (h.) Larachan, 54 Lonemore, Gairloch, Ross-shire, IV21 2DB; T.-01445 2391.

Henderson, Elizabeth Kidd, MA (Hons), MEd (Hons). Member, Church of Scotland Education Committee; Governor, Glasgow Academy; Headmistress, Westbourne School, 1970-88; b. 25.5.28, Dunfermline. Educ. Dunfermline High School; Edinburgh University; St. Andrews University. Mathematics Teacher, Morrison's Academy, Crieff; Second Master, Mathematics, Dundee High School; Principal Teacher of Mathematics, Aberdeen High School; former Secretary, Mathematics Panel, Scottish Examination Board; President, Scottish Area, Secondary Heads Association; President, Glasgow Mathematical Association. Chairman, Community Council. Publication: Modern Mathematics for Schools (Co-author). Recreations: walking; golf. Address: (h.) 16 George Reith Avenue, Glasgow, G12 0AN; T.-0141-334 8545.

Henderson, Hamish Scott, MA, Hon.LLD, Hon.DUniv, Dr.h.c. Lecturer/Research Fellow, School of Scottish Studies, Edinburgh University, since 1952 (Honorary Fellow, since 1988); b. 11.11.19, Blairgowrie; m., Felicity Schmidt; 2 d. Educ. Blairgowrie High School; Dulwich College; Downing College, Cambridge University. Wartime: Intelligence Officer, 51st Highland Division and other Infantry Divisions, Egypt, Libya, Tunisia, Sicily, Italy; mentioned in Dispatches, 1945; District Secretary, WEA, 1947-49; Assistant to Alan Lomax in folklore collection and editing, 1950-51; first translator of gramsci into English. Publications:Elegies for the Dead in Cyrenaica, 1948 (Somerset Maugham Award, 1949); Ballads of World War II (published by Lili Marlene Club of Glasgow), 1947. Recreations: writing; singing; song-writing. Address: (h.) 20 Melville Terrace, Edinburgh; T.-0131-667 5143.

Henderson, James. Registrar of Companies for Scotland, since 1992; b. 22.11.48, Kilmarnock; m., Patricia Mazs; 2 d. Educ. Kilmarnock Academy. Joined the Queen's and Lord Treasurer's Remembrancer, 1967; Department of Trade and Industry, 1981; became Companies House DTI's first agency, 1988. Recreations: bowls (playing; spectating); reading; gardening. Address: (b.) 37 Castle Terrace, Edinburgh, EH1 2EB; T.-0131-535 5855.

Henderson, James Gunn. Editor, Northern Times, since 1975; b. 10.7.31, Wick; m., 1, Catherine Maclean (deceased); 2 d.; 2, Christine Mackay; 4 s. Educ. Wick High School. Reporter, John O'Groat Journal, 1948-53; Scottish Daily Express: Reporter, 1953-60, Deputy Chief, Edinburgh, 1960-65, Deputy News Editor, Glasgow, 1965-69, News Features Editor, Glasgow, 1969-75.Trustee,

Moray Firth Radio Charity, Highland Community Foundation. Recreation: reading newspapers. Address: (b.) Sutherland Press House, Golspie; (h.) Littleferry, Golspie, KW10 6TD; T.-01408 633993/633548.

Henderson, John Harley, JP. Member, City of Dundee District Council, since 1974 (Convener of Housing, 1984-92); Teacher of Mathematics, St. John's High School, Dundee, since 1976; b. 17.8.41, Dundee; m., Peggy Henderson; 1 s.; 1 d. Educ. Lawside Academy, Dundee; Dundee College of Technology. Former Divisional Council Secretary, AUEW-TASS; Dundee District Council: former Secretary and Leader, Administration Group, former Convener of Cleansing, former Convener of Planning and Development; Secretary, Dundee Labour Party, since 1993. Address (h.) 24 Burrelton Gardens, Dundee; T.-01382 811982.

Henderson, Major Richard Yates, TD, JP, BA (Oxon), LLB. Lord Lieutenant, Ayrshire and Arran, since 1991; b. 7.7.31, Nitshill; m., Frances Elizabeth Chrystal; 3 s. (inc. 1 s. dec.); 1 d. Educ. Rugby; Hertford College, Oxford; Glasgow University. Royal Scots Greys, 1950-52; TA Ayrshire (ECO) Yeomanry, 1953-69 (Major); Deputy Lieutenant, Ayrshire and Arran, 1970-90; Partner, Mitchells Roberton, Solicitors, 1958-90, Consultant, 1991-92; Member, Queen's Bodyguard for Scotland (Royal Company of Archers). Chairman, SSAFA/FHS, Ayrshire. Recreations: shooting; tennis; golf. Address: (h.) Blairston, by Ayr; T.-01292 441601.

Henderson, Robert Ewart, QC, BL; b. 29.3.37. Admitted to Faculty of Advocates, 1963; Chairman, Medical Appeal Tribunal (Scotland), since 1985, War Pensions Appeal Tribunal, since 1986. Address: (b.) Advocates' Library, Parliament House, Edinburgh, EH1 1RF.

Henderson, Stewart Alexander, RIBA, FRIAS. Executive Director of Property Services, Edinburgh District Council; b. 18.1.47, Glasgow; m., Gilian Wallace; 1 s.; 1 d. Educ. Falkirk High School; Glasgow School of Art. Private practice, Glasgow; Principal Architect, Stewartry District; Depute Director of Architectural Services, Stornoway; Chief Architect, Clydesdale District; Chief Architect, Scottish & Newcastle. Council Member, RIAS, EAA. Recreations: shooting; stalking; fishing. Address: (b.) 329 High Street, Edinburgh; T.-0131-529 4916.

Henderson, Thomas Wilson. Director, John Turnbull & Sons Ltd., Hawick, since 1983; Member, Ettrick and Lauderdale District Council, since 1974; Provost of Selkirk, since 1978; b. 28.9.41, Selkirk; m., Catherine Helen Herbert; 2 s. Educ. Selkirk Public School; Selkirk High School; Scottish College of Textiles; Paisley College of Technology. Served apprenticeship as dyer with George Roberts & Co. Ltd., Selkirk, 1957-61; Dyer, Grays Carpets, Ayr, 1961-70; Assistant Manager, John Turnbull & Sons Ltd., Hawick, 1978-83; involved in management buy-out, 1983; Member, Selkirk Town Council, 1973-75; Corporate Member, Society of Dyers and Colourists; holder of various offices, Transport and General Workers Union, since 1970; Organiser, Scottish National Party, Ayr Constituency, 1967-70. Recreations: hill-walking; horse-riding; reading; folk music; jazz; football; cricket. Address: (h.) Triglav, 29 Shawpark Crescent, Selkirk; T.-01750 20821.

Hendrie, Eric. Chairman/Director, Grampian Careers Co. Ltd.; Director, GEL Step-Ahead; b. 11.9.25, Glasgow; m., Isabel; 1 s.; 1 d. Educ. Lambhill School, Glasgow; Royal Technical College, Glasgow. Councillor: Aberdeen Corporation, 1970-75, Grampian Regional Council, 1975-94 (Convener of Education, 1990-94). Address: (h.) 37 New Park Road, Aberdeen, AB2 6UT; T.-0224 691723.

Hendry, Professor Alan, BSc (Hons), PhD, CEng, FIM, MInstP, FRSA. Professor of Metallurgy and Engineering Materials, Strathclyde University, since 1988 (Reader in Ceramics, 1985-88); b. 29.1.47, Ochiltree; m., Jean Carey Kerr; 1 s.; 1 d. Educ. Cumnock Academy; Strathclyde University. Postdoctoral Research Associate, Newcastle University, 1971-75; Research Officer, Midlands Region, CEGB, 1975-76; Lecturer in Metallurgy and Assistant Director, Wolfson Research Group for High Strength Materials, Newcastle University, 1976-85; President, Scottish Association for Metals, 1990-92; Member, Materials Commission, SERC, 1989-92, Materials Programme, EPSRC, since 1994; Member, International Academy of Ceramics; Allan B. Dove Medal, Wire Assoc. Int., 1993. Address: (h.) Ardleven, 23 Campbell Drive, Bearsden, Glasgow, G61 4NF; T.-0141-942 3169.

Hendry, Professor Emeritus Arnold William, BSc, PhD, DSc, FICE, FIStructE, FRSE. Professor of Civil Engineering, Edinburgh University, 1964-88; b. 10.9.21, Buckie; m., Elizabeth Lois Alice Inglis; 1 s.; 1 d. Educ. Buckie High School; Aberdeen University. Assistant Civil Engineer, Sir William Arrol & Co. Ltd., Glasgow, 1941-43; Lecturer in Civil Engineering, Aberdeen University, 1943-49; Reader in Civil Engineering, King's College, London, 1949-51; Professor of Civil Engineering and Dean, Faculty of Engineering, Khartoum University, 1951-57; Professor of Building Science, Liverpool University, 1957-63. Recreations: walking; DIY; travel. Address: (h.) 146/6 Whitehouse Loan, Edinburgh, EH9 2AN; T.-0131-447 0368.

Hendry, Joy McLaggan, MA (Hons), DipEd. Editor, Chapman Magazine, since 1972; Writer; Writer-in-Residence, Stirling District Council, 1991-93; b. 3.2.53, Perth; m., Ian Montgomery. Educ. Perth Academy; Edinburgh University. Former teacher; Co-Editor, Chapman, 1972-76, Sole Editor, since 1976; Deputy Convener, Scottish Poetry Library Association, 1983-88; Convener, Committee for the Advancement of Scottish Literature in Schools; Member AdCas; Scottish National Theatre Steering Committee; Campaign for a Scottish Assembly; Member, Drama Committee, Scottish Arts Council; writes poetry; gives lectures and talks and performances of poetry and song; radio critic, The Scotsman; theatre reviewer. Publications:Scots: The Way Forward; Poems and Pictures by Wendy Wood (Editor); The Land for the People (Co-Editor); Critical Essays on Sorley MacLean (Co-Editor); Critical Essays on Norman MacCaig (Co-Editor); Gang Doun wi a Sang (play); radio play: The Wa' at the Warld's End, Radio 3. Recreations: going to theatre; cinema; reading. Address: 4 Broughton Place, Edinburgh, EH1 3RX.

Hendry, Professor Leo Brough, MSc, MEd, PhD, FBPS. Professor of Education, Aberdeen University, since 1989; b. 12.11.35, Glasgow; m., Philomena Walsh; 2 d. Educ. Hermitage Academy, Helensburgh; Jordanhill College of Education, Glasgow; Bradford University; Leicester University; Aberdeen University. School Teacher in Scottish and English schools, including two posts as Head of Department, 1957-64; Lecturer in Education and Physical Education, College of St. Mark and St. John's, Chelsea, London University Institute, 1964-66; Head of Human Movement Studies, Trinity and All Saints' Colleges, Leeds University Institute, 1966-71; Lecturer in Education, then Senior Lecturer, Aberdeen University, 1971-88; Head, Education Department, 1988-94; Member, Scottish Council for Research in Education, 1983-86. Publications: School, Sport, Leisure: three dimensions of adolescence, 1978; Adolescents and Leisure, 1981; Growing Up and Going Out, 1983; Personality and Performance in Physical Education and Sport (Co-author), 1974; Physical Education in England (Co-author), 1976; Towards Community Education (Co-author), 1980; The Nature of Adolescence (Co-author), 1990; Young People's Leisure and Lifestyles (Co-author), 1993; book chapters; research articles. Recreations: golf; writing; broadcasting;

presenting papers at international conferences. Address: (b.) Department of Education, Aberdeen University, Aberdeen, AB9 2UB; T.-01224 272729 and 272731.

Hendry, Stephen, Professional snooker player; b. 13.1.69; m., Mandy. Youngest-ever Scottish Amateur Champion (aged 15); has won 54 major titles worldwide; youngest player to attain No. 1 ranking; youngest player to win World Championship, 1990; World Champion five times; UK Champion, three times; Masters Champion, five times. Address: (b.) Cuemasters Ltd., Kerse Road, Stirling, FK7 7SG; T.-01786 462634.

Henley, Rt. Rev. Michael Harry George, CB. Bishop of St. Andrews, Dunkeld and Dunblane, since 1995; b. 16.1.38; m.; 2 d.

Henriksen, Henry Neil, BSc, MEd. Rector, The James Young High School, since 1982; b. 2.9.33, Edinburgh; m., Edith Robb; 2 s. Educ. Royal High School, Edinburgh; Edinburgh University; Strathclyde University. Taught at Portobello, Falkirk High, Forrester; Depute Head, Penicuik High School. Recreations: television; climbing Allermuir. Address: (h.) 16 Redford Loan, Edinburgh, EH13 0AX; T.-0131-441 2282.

Henry, Sheriff A.C., MA, LLB. Sheriff of Glasgow and Strathkelvin, at Glasgow. Admitted, Faculty of Advocates, 1969. Address: (b.) Sheriff Court House, 1 Carlton Place, Glasgow, G5 9DA.

Henry, Gordon Edward, DA, MCSD. Chief Executive, Grampian Highlands & Aberdeen Tourism Marketing Company, since 1993; b. 23.9.37, Elgin; m., Elizabeth Browne; 2 s. Educ. Elgin Academy; Grays School of Art; Aberdeen College of Education. Art Teacher, Lecturer and Freelance Designer, 1960-63; Aberdeen University Press: Staff Designer, 1963-69, Design Manager, 1969-71, Company Director, 1971-75; Director of Tourism, City of Aberdeen, 1976-93; President, British Association of Tourism Officers. Recreations: painting; golf; swimming; reading. Address: (b.) St. Nicholas House, Aberdeen, AB9 1DE; T.-01224 522450.

Henry, Captain Michael Charles, DL, RN (Rtd.) Deputy Lieutenant, Dunbartonshire, since 1989; Director, Merchants House of Glasgow, since 1990; b. 4.6.28, London; m., Nancie Elma Nicol; 2 s.; 3 d. Educ. Royal Naval College, Dartmouth. Naval career, Cadet to Captain, 1942-78; submarine specialist; commanded HM Submarines Seraph, Trump and Resolution, Britain's first Polaris submarine; fired first British missile, Cape Canaveral, and conducted first deterrent patrol, 1968; commanded 10th (Polaris) Submarine Squadron, Faslane, and Queen's Harbour Master, Clyde, 1972-74; commanded HMS Hampshire, 1975-76; Director of Naval Operations and Trade, 1976-78; Marine Manager, British National Oil Corporation, Aberdeen, 1978-80; Naval Regional Officer Scotland and Northern Ireland, Glasgow, 1980-90. Recreation: sailing. Address: (h.) Aldavhu, Garelochhead, Dunbartonshire, G84 0EL; T.-01436 810533.

Henshelwood, James, JP, FISMM, MCIM, MInstM, AMNI. Director, Glasgow Building Preservation Trust, since 1982; President, Glasgow Bute Benevolent Society; Member, St. John Association of Scotland; Member, Central Advisory Committee on Justices of the Peace; b. 18.2.22, Glasgow; m., Mavis Irene Watson (deceased); 3 s.; 2 d. Educ. Allan Glen's School; Whitehill Senior Secondary School; Royal Technical College, Glasgow. Joined Merchant Navy as cadet, 1938, and "swallowed the anchor" in 1953 as Master Mariner; Special Services, RNR; Independent Councillor, Johnstone, 1966-69 (Burgh Treasurer); President, Chartered Institute of Marketing, Strathclyde Branch; Immediate Past Chairman, Nautical Institute, West of Scotland; Governor, RNLI; Vice-

Chairman, Scottish Pre-Retirement Council; former Director, Glasgow Chamber of Commerce. Recreations: golf; sailing; walking. Address: (h.) 72 Globe Court, Calderwood, East Kilbride, Glasgow, G74 3QZ; T.-013552 38851.

Hepburn, Professor Ronald William, MA, PhD. Professor of Moral Philosophy, Edinburgh University, since 1975; b. 16.3.27, Aberdeen; m., Agnes Forbes Anderson; 2 s.; 1 d. Educ. Aberdeen Grammar School; Aberdeen University. Assistant, then Lecturer, Department of Moral Philosophy, Aberdeen University, 1952-60; Visiting Associate Professor, New York University, 1959-60; Professor of Philosophy and Head of Department, Nottingham University, 1960-64; Professor of Philosophy, Edinburgh University, 1964-75; Stanton Lecturer, Cambridge University, 1965-68; Heslington Lecture, York University, 1970; Margaret Harris Lectures on Religion, Dundee University, 1974. Publications: Christianity and Paradox, 1958; Wonder and Other Essays, 1984. Recreation: hill-walking; photography. Address: (b.) Department of Philosophy, David Hume Tower, George Square, Edinburgh, EH8 9JX; T.-0131-667 1011.

Herald, Sheriff John Pearson, LLB, NP, SSC. Sheriff of North Strathclyde at Greenock and Rothesay, since 1992; b. 12.7.46, Glasgow; m., Catriona; 1 d. Educ. Hillhead High School, Glasgow; Glasgow University. Partner, Carlton Gilruth, Solicitors, Dundee, 1970-91; Depute Town Clerk, Newport-on-Tay, 1970-75; Member, Angus Legal Aid Committee, 1970-79, Secretary, 1979-87; Member, Legal Aid Central Committee, 1981-87; Temporary Sheriff, 1984-91; part-time Chairman, Industrial Tribunals, 1984-91. Chairman, Dundee Citizens Advice Bureau, 1972-79 and 1982-91; President, Rotary Club of North Fife, 1989. Recreations: football; golf; reading. Address: (b.) Sheriff Court House, Nelson Street, Greenock; T.-01475 787073.

Herbert, Jean, BSc, MBA. Chief Executive, West Glasgow Hospitals University NHS Trust. Address: (b.) Administration Building, Western Infirmary, Dumbarton Road, Glasgow, G11 6NT.

Herbert, Professor Rodney Andrew, BSc, PHD, CBiol, MIBiol. Professor of Microbiology, Dundee University, since 1992; b. 27.6.44, York; m., Helen Joyce Macpherson Millard; 2 s. Educ. Archbishop Holgate's Grammar School, York; Bradford University; Aberdeen University. Research Fellow, Edinburgh University, 1970-71; Lecturer/Reader in Microbiology, Dundee University, 1971-92. General Secretary, Society for General Microbiology; Senior Visiting Scientist: British Antarctic Survey, 1976-77, Ross Sea, Antarctica, 1982-83. Recreations: music; walking; gardening. Address: (b.) Department of Biological Sciences, Dundee University, Dundee, DD1 4HN; T.-Dundee 23181, Ext. 4262.

Herbison, Rt. Hon. Margaret McCrorie, PC (1964), MA, LLD (Hon.); b. 11.3.07, Shotts. Educ. Bellshill Academy; Glasgow University. Teacher, 1930-45; MP for Lanarkshire North, 1945-70; Joint Under-Secretary of State, Scottish Office, 1950-51; Minister of Pensions and National Insurance, 1964-66; Minister of Social Security, 1966-67; Chairman, Select Committee on Overseas Aid, 1968-70; Lord High Commissioner to General Assembly of Church of Scotland, 1970; Hon. LLD, Glasgow University, 1970; Scotswoman of the Year, 1970; Member, Royal Commission on Standards of Conduct in Public Life, 1975-76; Lay Observer, 1975-76; Chairman, Labour Party, 1956-57. Recreations: reading; gardening. Address: (h.) 8 Mornay Way, Shotts, ML7 4EG; T.-Shotts 21944.

Herd, James Peter, MBE, WS, NP. Partner, Beveridge, Herd & Sandilands, WS, Kirkcaldy, since 1951; Honorary Sheriff, Kirkcaldy, since 1987; b. 18.5.20, Kirkcaldy; m., Marjory Phimister Mitchell; 3 s.; 2 d. Educ. Edinburgh

Academy; St. Andrews University; Edinburgh University. Army Service as Major, Black Watch, UK and South East Asia, 1939-46; Local Director, Royal Insurance Group, since 1951; Trustee, Kirkcaldy and District Trustee Savings Bank, 1952-83; Director, Kirkcaldy Ice Rink Limited, 1982-88; Director, Kirkcaldy Abbeyfield Society, 1970-92. Recreations: curling; gardening. Address: (b.) 1 East Fergus Place, Kirkcaldy, Fife, KY1 1XT; T.-01592 261616.

Herdman, John Macmillan, MA (Hons), PhD (Cantab), DipTh. Writer, since 1963; b. 20.7.41, Edinburgh. Educ. Merchiston Castle School, Edinburgh; Magdalene College, Cambridge. Creative Writing Fellow, Edinburgh University, 1977-79; Scottish Arts Council bursaries, 1976 and 1982; Scottish Arts Council Book Awards, 1978 and 1993; Hawthornden Writer's Fellowship, 1989 and 1995; William Soutar Fellowship, 1990-91. Publications: Descent, 1968; A Truth Lover, 1973; Memoirs of My Aunt Minnie/ Clapperton, 1974; Pagan's Pilgrimage, 1978; Stories Short and Tall, 1979; Voice Without Restraint: Bob Dylan's Lyrics and Their Background, 1982; Three Novellas, 1987; The Double in Nineteenth Century Fiction, 1990; Imelda and Other Stories, 1993. Recreations: reading; walking; listening to music. Address: (h.) 18 Clyde Place, Perth, PH2 0EZ; T.-01738 633504.

Heron, Garth McAllen Drennan, BA, FIPM. Personnel Director, United Distillers, since 1993; b. 21.5.49, Belfast; m., Louise Dick; 1 s.; 1 d. Educ. Friend's School, Lisburn; Queen's University, Belfast; Strathclyde University. Personnel Officer, United Dominions Trust Ltd., 1971-73; Personnel Manager, Alcan Aluminium Ltd., 1973-76; Personnel Manager, Bourns Ltd., Fife, 1976-78; Personnel Director, Honeywell Ltd., Bracknell, 1978-87; General Manager, Personnel Division, Clydesdale Bank, 1987-93. Elder, Cramond Kirk. Recreations: family; church; sports; cinema. Address: (b.) 2 Pentland Road, Edinburgh, EH13 0JA.

Herron, Very. Rev. Andrew, ATCL, MA, BD, LLB, DD, LLD. Moderator, General Assembly of Church of Scotland, 1971; b. 29.9.09, Glasgow; m., Joanna Fraser Neill; 4 d. Educ. Strathbungo H.G. School; Albert Road Academy; Glasgow University and Trinity College. Minister: Linwood, 1936-40, Houston and Killellan, 1940-59; Clerk, Glasgow Presbytery, 1959-81. Baird Lecturer, 1985; William Barclay Lecturer, 1989. Publications: Record Apart, 1972; Guide to the General Assembly, 1976; Guide to Congregational Affairs, 1979; Guide to the Presbytery, 1982; Kirk by Divine Right, 1985; The Law and Practice of the Kirk, 1985; Guide to the Ministry, 1987; Guide to Ministerial Income, 1987; Minority Report, 1990. Address: (h.) 36 Darnley Road, Glasgow, G41 4NE; T.-0141-423 6422.

Hetherington, Professor (Hector) Alastair, Dhc (Lille), MA. Emeritus Professor in Media Studies, Stirling University, since 1987; b. 31.10.19, Llanishen, Glamorgan; m., 1, Miranda; 2 s.; 2 d.; 2, Sheila; 1 step s.; 2 step d. Educ. Corpus Christi College, Oxford. Army, 1940-46; Glasgow Herald, 1946-50; The Guardian, 1950-75 (Foreign Editor, 1953-56, Editor, 1956-75); BBC Scotland, 1976-79; Director, Scotquest (film company), since 1982; Chairman, The Scott Trust (owners, The Guardian and Manchester Evening News), 1984-89; various films for Channel Four. Publications: Guardian Years, 1981; News, Newspapers and Television, 1985; Perthshire in Trust, 1988; News in the Regions, 1989; Highlands and Islands, a generation of progress, 1990; Cameras in the Commons, 1990; Inside BBC Scotland 1975-1980, 1992; A Walker's Guide to Arran, 1995. Recreation: hill-walking. Address: (h.) High Corrie, Isle of Arran, KA27 8GB; T.-01770 810 562.

Hewitt, Professor David S., MA, PhD. Professor in Scottish Literature, Aberdeen University, since 1994 (Reader, 1991-94); b. 22.4.42, Hawick; m., Angela Catherine Williams; 1 s.; 1 d. Educ. Melrose Grammar School; George Watson's College, Edinburgh; Edinburgh University; Aberdeen University. Aberdeen University: Assistant Lecturer in English, 1964, Lecturer, 1968, Senior Lecturer, 1982; Treasurer, Association for Scottish Literary Studies, since 1973; Editor-in-Chief, Edinburgh Edition of the Waverley Novels, 1984; President, Edinburgh Sir Walter Scott Club, 1988-89; Elder, Cathedral Church of St. Machar, Old Aberdeen; Managing Editor, New Writing Scotland, 1983-86. Publications: Scott on Himself (Editor), 1982; Literature of the North, 1983; Scott and His Influence, 1984; Longer Scottish Poems, Vol. 2 1650-1830, 1987; Scottish Carnival, 1993; The Antiquary, 1995. Address: (b.) Department of English, Aberdeen University, Aberdeen, AB9 2UB; T.-01224 273777.

Hewitt, Margaret Irene Montague, OBE (Mil.), TD. Council Member, National Trust for Scotland, 1987-95; Life Vice President and Associate of Honour, National Association of Flower Arrangement Societies of Great Britain; m., Dr. Fred Hewitt. Auxiliary Territorial Service (ATS), 1939-47; retired as Chief Commander (Lt. Col.); raised 319 West Lancashire Bn., Women's Royal Army Corps (Territorial), 1948-53; Chairman, National Association of Flower Arrangement Societies of Great Britain, 1971-73; Chairman, Perth and Kinross Members' Group, National Trust for Scotland, 1982-86 (now President). Recreations: flower arranging and decor; gardening; travel; photography; theatre; wildlife and conservation; Airedale dogs. Address: (h.) Croft Cappanach, Pitlochry, Perthshire, PH16 5JT; T.-01796 482 366.

Heywood, Barry Keith, MA, LLB. Regional Procurator Fiscal, Dundee, since 1991; b. 24.7.46, Oldham; m., Mary A.; 1 s.; 1 d. Educ. Kirkcaldy High School; Edinburgh University. Procurator Fiscal Depute, Ayr, 1971-77, Glasgow, 1977-78; Procurator Fiscal, Wick, 1978-83; Assistant Procurator Fiscal, Glasgow, 1983-86; Procurator Fiscal, Inverness, 1986-91. Recreations: walking; Roman and Byzantine history; "railway buff". Address: (b.) 15 West Bell Street, Dundee, DD1 1HB; T.-01382 27535.

Hickman, Richard Michael, BA (Hons), MA, DipTP, MRTPI. Deputy Chief Inquiry Reporter, since 1989; b. 30.4.42, Beckenham; m., Sandie Randall; 2 s; 1 d. Educ. Kingswood School, Bath; London School of Economics; University of British Columbia. Work in town and country planning for London County Council, Greater London Council, Lower Mainland Regional Planning Board (British Columbia), Scottish Development Department; Scottish Office Inquiry Reporters Unit, since 1979. Hon. Visiting Fellow, Department of Planning and Housing, Edinburgh College of Art. Recreations: walking; cycling; sailing; skiing. Address: (b.) 2 Greenside Lane, Edinburgh, EH1 3AG; T.-031-244 5641.

Hider, Calvin Fraser, MB, ChB, FFARCS. Consultant Anaesthetist, Edinburgh Royal Infirmary, since 1964; Honorary Senior Lecturer, Faculty of Medicine, Edinburgh University; b. 29.5.30, Glasgow; m., 1, Jean M.D. Dott (deceased); 3 d.; 2, Frances Ann Smithers. Educ. George Watson's Boys College, Edinburgh; Edinburgh University. Medical training, Dumfries and Galloway Royal Infirmary and Edinburgh Royal Infirmary; RNVR, Surgeon (Lt.-Cdr.), 1955-64. Recreations: sailing; sheep-breeding (Jacob). Address: (h.) Marchwell Cottage, Penicuik, Midlothian, EH26 OPX; T.-01968 672680.

Higgins, Sheriff Colin Kirk, LLB. Sheriff of North Strathclyde at Paisley, since 1990; b. 9.11.45, Slough; m., Anne Marie McMahon; 1 s.; 2 d. Educ. St. Patrick's High School, Coatbridge; Glasgow University. Law Apprentice, Coatbridge, 1967-69; Legal Assistant, Coatbridge, 1969-70; Legal Assistant, James Bell & Sons, 1970-73; Partner, Bell, Russell & Co., 1973-90. Dean, Airdrie Society of Solicitors,

1989-90. Recreations: reading; travel; walking; theatre. Address (b.) Court House, St. James' Street, Paisley; T.-041-887 5291.

Higgs, Professor Peter Ware, BSc, MSc, PhD, FRS, FRSE. Professor of Theoretical Physics, Edinburgh University, since 1980; b. 29.5.29, Newcastle-upon-Tyne; m., Jo Ann Williamson; 2 s. Educ. Cotham Grammar School, Bristol; King's College, London. Postdoctoral Fellow, Edinburgh University, 1954-56, and London University, 1956-58; Lecturer in Mathematics, University College, London, 1958-60; Lecturer in Mathematical Physics, then Reader, Edinburgh University, 1960-80. Hughes Medal, Royal Society, 1981; Rutherford Medal, Institute of Physics, 1984; James Scott Prize, Royal Society of Edinburgh, 1993. Recreations: music; walking; swimming. Address: (h.) 2 Darnaway Street, Edinburgh, EH3 6BG; T.-0131-225 7060.

Highgate, Sir James Brown, CBE (1981), MA, LLB, JP. Consultant, Miller, Beckett and Jackson, Solicitors; former Senior Partner, Brownlie Watson & Beckett, Solicitors; b. 18.6.20, Glasgow. Educ. High School of Glasgow; Glasgow University. Served, Royal Artillery and Royal Indian Artillery, 1941-46 (demobilised as Major); appointed General Commissioner of Income Tax, 1969 (appointed Chairman, Glasgow North Division, 1981); Member, Strathclyde Advisory Board, Salvation Army, since 1970, Vice Chairman, since 1990; Joint Honorary Secretary, Scottish Conservative and Unionist Association, 1973-86 (President, 1987-89); Honorary President, Motherwell North Conservative Constituency; Elder, Park Church of Scotland, Uddingston. Recreations: golf; travel. Address: (h.) Broomlands, 121 Kylepark Drive, Uddingston, Glasgow; T.-Uddingston 813377.

Hill, Richard Inglis, BSc (Hons), FICE, FIHT. Director of Roads and Transportation, Borders Regional Council, since 1974; b. 8.5.33, Callander; m., Margaret; 2 s. Educ. McLaren High School, Callander; Royal College of Science and Technology, Glasgow. Perth and Kinross Joint County Council: student assistant, 1951-53, graduate assistant, 1954-56, Assistant Engineer, 1958-59, Senior Engineer, 1959-61, Senior Supervisory Engineer, 1961-65, Assistant County Surveyor, 1965-72; County Surveyor and Engineer, Selkirk County Council, 1972-75. Past Secretary and Chairman, Scottish Branch, County Surveyors' Society; former Secretary and Chairman, Institution of Highways and Transportation, Central and Southern Scotland Branch; Secretary, Scottish Branch, County Surveyors' Society; Adviser, Roads and Transportation Committee, COSLA; Past Chairman, Edinburgh and East of Scotland Division, Association of Municipal Engineers. Recreations: walking; music. Address: (b.) Regional HQ, Newtown St. Boswells, Melrose, TD6 OSA; T.-St. Boswells 23301.

Hill, Professor William George, BSc, MS, PhD, DSc, FRSE, FRS. Professor of Animal Genetics, Edinburgh University, since 1983; Head, Department of Genetics, 1989-90, Institute of Cell, Animal and Population Biology, 1990-93, Division of Biological Sciences, since 1993; b. 7.8.40, Hemel Hempstead; m., C. Rosemary Austin; 1 s.; 2 d. Educ. St. Albans School; London University; University of California; Iowa State University; Edinburgh University. Edinburgh University: Assistant Lecturer, 1965-67, Lecturer, 1967-74, Reader, 1974-83; Visiting Research Associate, Iowa State University, 1967-68-69-72; Visiting Professor: University of Minnesota, 1966, Iowa State University, 1978, North Carolina State University, 1979, since 1985; Consultant Geneticist: Cotswold Pig Development Co., since 1965, Holstein Friesian Society, since 1978; Member, AFRC Animals Research Grant Board, 1986-92; Member, Director's Advisory Group, AFRC Animal Breeding Research Organisation, 1982-86, AFRC Institute of Animal Physiology and Genetics Research, 1986-93, Roslin Institute, since 1994; Member,

Council, Royal Society, 1993-94. Recreations: farming; bridge. Address: (h.) 4 Gordon Terrace, Edinburgh, EH16 5QH; T.-0131-667 3680.

Hillhouse, Sir (Robert) Russell, KCB, FRSE. Permanent Under-Secretary of State, Scottish Office, since 1988; b. 23.4.38, Glasgow; m., Alison Fraser; 2 d. Educ. Hutchesons' Grammar School, Glasgow; Glasgow University. Entered Home Civil Service as Assistant Principal, Scottish Education Department, 1962; Principal, 1966; HM Treasury, 1971; Assistant Secretary, Scottish Office, 1974; Scottish Home and Health Department, 1977; Principal Finance Officer, Scottish Office, 1980; Under-Secretary, Scottish Education Department, 1985; Secretary, 1987. Recreation: making music. Address: (b.) St. Andrew's House, Regent Road, Edinburgh, EH1 3DG; T.-0131-556 8400.

Hillier, Professor Stephen Gilbert, BSc, MSc, PhD, DSc, MRCPath. Professor, Department of Obstetrics and Gynaecology, Edinburgh University, since 1985, and Director, Reproductive Medicine Laboratory, since 1985; Member, Human Fertilisation and Embryology Authority, since 1991; b. 16.1.49, Hillingdon; m., Ameneh; 2 d. Educ. Hayes County Grammar School; Leeds University; Welsh National School of Medicine. Postdoctoral Research Fellow, National Institutes of Health, USA, 1976-78; Research Scientist, University of Leiden, 1978-82; Senior Lecturer, Reproductive Biochemistry, RPMS, London University, 1982-85. Member, Interim Licensing Authority for Human Fertilisation and Embryology, 1987-91; 1991 Society for Endocrinology Medal. Publications: Ovarian Endocrinology, 1991; Scientific Essentials of Reproductive Medicine, 1996. Recreations: fly-fishing; walking. Address: (b.) Edinburgh University Centre for Reproductive Biology, 37 Chalmers Street, Edinburgh, EH3 9EW; T.-0131-229 2575.

Hillman, John Richard, BSc, PhD, HonDSc, CBiol, FIBiol, FLS, FBIM, FRSE. Director, Scottish Crop Research Institute, since 1986; Visiting Professor, Dundee University, Edinburgh University, Glasgow University and Strathclyde University; Deputy Chairman, Mylnefield Research Services Ltd.; Chairman Agriculture, Natural Resources and Environment Sector Panel, UK Technology Foresight Programme; b. 21.7.44, Farnborough, Kent; m., Sandra Kathleen Palmer; 2 s. Educ. Chislehurst and Sidcup Grammar School; University of Wales. Assistant Lecturer, 1968, and Lecturer, 1969, Physiology and Environmental Studies, Nottingham University; Lecturer, 1971, Senior Lecturer, 1977, Reader, 1980, Professor of Botany, 1982, Glasgow University. Recreations: landscaping; building renovations; horology; reading. Address: (b.) Scottish Crop Research Institute, Invergowrie, Dundee, DD2 5DA; T.-01382 562731.

Hills, Professor Sir Graham (John), PhD, DSc, LLD, FRSE, Hon DSc (Lodz, Southampton, Lisbon), Hon. LLD (Glasgow, Waterloo and Strathclyde), DUniv (Paisley). National Governor for Scotland, BBC, 1989-94; President, Society of Chemical Industry, 1991-93; Principal and Vice-Chancellor, Strathclyde University, 1980-91; b. 9.4.26, Leigh-on-Sea; m., 1, Brenda Stubbington; 2, Mary Jane McNaughton; 1 s.; 3 d. Educ. Westcliff High School for Boys; Birkbeck College and Imperial College, London University. Lecturer in Physical Chemistry, Imperial College, 1949-62; Professor of Physical Chemistry, Southampton University, 1962-80; Visiting Professor, University of Western Ontario, 1968; Visiting Professor and National Science Foundation Fellow, Case-Western Reserve University, Ohio, 1968-69; Visiting Professor, Buenos Aires University, 1976; Member, Advisory Council on Science and Technology, 1987-93; (Non-Executive) Member, Scottish Post Office Board, since 1986; Non-Executive Director, Scottish Enterprise, 1988-94; Fellow, Birkbeck College; Fellow, Royal Scottish Academy of

Music and Drama; Fellow, University of East London; Director, Glasgow Chamber of Commerce, since 1981; President, Friends of Glasgow Cathedral, since 1987; Chairman, Quarriers Homes, since 1992; Commander Insignia, Order of Merit of Polish People's Republic; Commander Insignia, Royal Norwegian Order of Merit. Publications: Reference Electrodes, 1961; Polarography, 1964. Recreations: music; hill-walking; European politics. Address: (b.) Sunnyside of Threepwood, Laigh Threepwood, Beith, Ayrshire, KA15 2JW.

Hind, Archie. Novelist and Playwright; b. 1928. Author of The Dear Green Place, 1966.

Hine, Professor Harry Morrison, MA, DPhil (Oxon). Scotstarvit Professor of Humanity, St. Andrews University, since 1985; b. 19.6.48, Portsmouth; m., Rosalind Mary Ford; 1 s.; 1 d. Educ. King Edward's School, Birmingham; Corpus Christi College, Oxford. P.S. Allen Junior Research Fellow, Corpus Christi College, 1972-75; Lecturer in Humanity, Edinburgh University, 1975-85. Editor (Joint), The Classical Review, 1987-93. Publication: An Edition with Commentary of Seneca, Natural Questions, Book Two, 1981. Recreations: walking; reading. Address: (h.) 33 Drumcarrow Road, St. Andrews, Fife, KY16 8SE; T.-01334 474459.

Hingston, David Robert, LLB, NP. Procurator Fiscal, Dingwall; 29.7.48, Assam, India; m., Sylvia Isobel Reid; 2 s.; 1 d. Educ. Morrison's Academy, Crieff; Edinburgh University. Private practice, Edinburgh; joined Procurator Fiscal service, 1975 (Kirkcaldy, Dunfermline, Edinburgh); seconded to Scottish Law Commission; then Edinburgh Office; Procurator Fiscal, Wick; Tutor in Criminal Law, Demonstrator Criminal Procedure. Publication: Stair Memorial Encyclopaedia (Contributor); Criminal Procedure (Co-author). Recreations: fitting 36 hours into 24; fishing. Address: (b.) Procurator Fiscal's Office, Sheriff Court House, Ferry Road, Dingwall; T.-Dingwall 862122.

Hird, David Forbes, CA. General Manager, Forth Valley Health Board, since 1993; b. 11.5.43, Aberdeen; m., Irene; 1 s.; 2 d. Educ. Robert Gordon's College, Aberdeen; Aberdeen University. Range of finance posts in NHS, since 1966; District Finance Officer, East Fife District, 1974, North Lothian District, 1979; Director of Finance, Forth Valley Health Board, 1984. Recreation: curling. Address: (b.) 33 Spittal Street, Stirling; T.-01786 457248.

Hirst, Sir Michael William, LLB, CA, FRSA. Chairman, Scottish Conservative and Unionist Party, since 1993; b. 2.1.46, Glasgow; m., Naomi Ferguson Wilson; 1 s.; 2 d. Educ. Glasgow Academy; Glasgow University. Partner, Peat Marwick Mitchell & Co., Chartered Accountants, until 1983; Director of and Consultant to various companies; Partner, Hirst & Associates; contested: Central Dunbartonshire, February and October, 1974, East Dunbartonshire, 1979; MP (Conservative), Strathkelvin and Bearsden, 1983-87; Member, Select Committee on Scottish Affairs, 1983-87; Parliamentary Private Secretary, Department of Energy, 1985-87; Vice-Chairman, Scottish Conservative Party, 1987-89; President, Scottish Conservative and Unionist Association; Chairman, Scottish Conservative Candidates Association, 1978-81; Hon. Secretary, British Diabetic Association; Chairman, The Park School Educational Trust; Member, Court, Glasgow Caledonian University; Director, Children's Hospice Association Scotland; Member, Executive Committee, Princess Louise Scottish Hospital, Erskine; Elder, Kelvinside Hillhead Parish Church. Recreations: golf; hill-walking; skiing. Address: (h.) Enderley, Baldernock Road, Milngavie, Glasgow, G62 8DU; T.-0141-956 1213.

Hitchman, Professor Michael L., BSc, DPhil, CChem, FRSC, FRSA, FRSE. Young Professor of Chemistry, Strathclyde University, since 1984 (Chairman, Department of Pure and Applied Chemistry, 1986-89; Vice-Dean, Faculty of Science, 1989-92); b. 17.8.41, Woburn, Bedfordshire; m., Pauline J. Thompson; 1 s.; 2 d. Educ. Stratton Grammar School, Biggleswade; Queen Mary College and King's College, London University; University College, Oxford. Assistant Lecturer in Chemistry, Leicester Regional College of Technology, 1963-65; Junior Research Fellow, Wolfson College, Oxford, 1968-70; ICI Postdoctoral Research Fellow, Physical Chemistry Laboratory, Oxford University, 1968-70; Chief Scientist, Orbisphere Corporation, Geneva, 1970-73; Staff Scientist, Laboratories RCA Ltd., Zurich, 1973-79; Lecturer, then Senior Lecturer, Salford University, 1979-84. Royal Society of Chemistry: Chairman, Electroanalytical Group, 1985-88; Treasurer, Electrochemistry Group, 1984-90; Member, Chemistry and Semiconductor Committees, Science and Engineering Research Council; Member, since 1985, Chairman, 1989-92, International Advisory Board, EUROCVD; Medal and Prize, British .... Council, 1993. Publications: Ring-disk Electrodes (Co-author), 1971; Measurement of Dissolved Oxygen, 1978; Chemical Vapor Deposition (Co-editor), 1993. Recreations: humour; cooking; eating; rambling; losing weight. Address: (b.) Department of Pure and Applied Chemistry, Strathclyde University, 295 Cathedral Street, Glasgow, G1 1XL; T.-0141-552 4400.

Hobbs, Grete. Hotelier, Inverlochy Castle, since 1969; b. Copenhagen; m., Joseph B. Hobbs (deceased); 1 s.; 1 d. Educ. Ballerup. Numerous hotel awards; Free Enterprise Award; Hotelier of the Year, 1989. Recreations: golf; bridge. Address: (b.) Inverlochy Castle, Fort William, PH33 6SN; T.-01397 702177.

Hobsbaum, Professsor Philip Dennis, MA, PhD, DLitt, LRAM, LGSM. Poet and Critic; Titular Professor in English Literature, Glasgow University, since 1985 (Reader in English Literature, 1979-85); b. 29.6.32, London; m., Rosemary Phillips. Educ. Belle Vue Grammar School, Bradford; Downing College, Cambridge; Sheffield University. Lecturer in English, Queen's University, Belfast, 1962-66; Lecturer, then Senior Lecturer in English Literature, Glasgow University, 1966-79; Chairman of writers' groups in London, 1955-59, Belfast, 1962-66, Glasgow, 1966-75. Publications: A Group Anthology (Co-Editor), 1963; The Place's Fault, 1964; In Retreat, 1966; Coming Out Fighting, 1969; Ten Elizabethan Poets (Editor), 1969; A Theory of Communication, 1970; A Reader's Guide to Charles Dickens, 1972; Women and Animals, 1972; Tradition and Experiment in English Poetry, 1979; A Reader's Guide to D.H. Lawrence, 1981; Essentials of Literary Criticism, 1983; A Reader's Guide to Robert Lowell, 1988; Wordsworth: Selected Poetry and Prose (Editor), 1989; Channels of Communication (Co-editor), 1992; Metre, Rhythm and Verse Form, 1995. Recreations: walking the dog; playing the piano. Address: (b.) Department of English Literature, Glasgow University, Glasgow; T.-0141-339 8855.

Hodges, Desmond W.H., OBE, FRIAS. Director, Architectural Heritage Society of Scotland; b. 25.9.28, Dublin; m., Margaret Elisabeth Anderson; 2 d. Educ. St. Columba's College, Rathfarnham, Co. Dublin. Founder Member, Ulster Architectural Heritage Society; Director, Edinburgh New Town Conservation Committee, 1972-94; Representative, Royal Incorporation of Architects in Scotland on Council, National Trust for Scotland. Address: (h.) 14 Shandon Street, Edinburgh, EH11 1QH; T.-0131 337 4929.

Hogg, Ian Alisdair Lawrence, MA, CA. Chief Executive, Scottish Rugby Union, since 1991; b. 13.6.40, Edinburgh; m., Louise; 1 s.; 1 d. Educ. George Watson's College; Edinburgh University. Chartered Accountant, 1961-78; Treasurer, Scottish Rugby Union, 1978-83, Secretary, since 1983. Recreations: rugby; cricket. Address: (b.) Scottish

Rugby Union, Murrayfield, Edinburgh, EH12 5PJ; T.-0131-346 5000.

Hogg, Norman, MP, Cumbernauld and Kilsyth, since 1979; Non-executive Director, Kelvin Central Buses Ltd., since 1991; b. 12.3.38, Aberdeen; m., Elizabeth M. Christie. Educ. Ruthrieston Secondary School, Aberdeen. Local Government Officer, Aberdeen Town Council, 1953-67; District Officer, NALGO, 1967-79; MP, East Dunbartonshire, 1979-83; Member: Transport Users Consultative Committee for Scotland, 1977-79, Select Committee on Scottish Affairs, 1979-82; Scottish Labour Whip, 1982-83; Chairman, Scottish Parliamentary Labour Group, 1981-82; Deputy Chief Opposition Whip, 1983-87; Scottish Affairs Spokesman, 1987-88; Member, Chairman's Panel, since 1988; Member, Public Accounts Committee, 1991-92. Recreation: music. Address: House of Commons, Westminster, London SW1A 0AA; T.-0171-219 5095.

Hogwood, Professor Brian Walter, BA, PhD. Professor of Politics, Department of Government, Strathclyde University, since 1991; b. 29.6.50, Glasgow; m., Patricia Brearey. Educ. Hamilton Academy; Glenrothes High School; Keele University. Economics Sub-Editor, Cambridge University Press, 1974-75; appointed Lecturer in Politics, Strathclyde University, 1975; Senior Lecturer, 1985; Reader, 1988. Recreations: cooking; computing; cross-country running. Address: (b.) Department of Government, Strathclyde University, McCance Building, 16 Richmond Street, Glasgow; T.-0141-552 4400, Ext. 2919.

Hollands, Clive, OBE. Secretary, St. Andrew Animal Fund, 1970-94; b. 1929, London; m.; 1 s.; 1 d. Educ. St. Clement Dane's School, London; St. Mary's College, Liverpool. Scottish Society for the Prevention of Vivisection: Assistant Secretary, 1966-70, Director, 1970-88; Secretary, Committee for the Reform of Animal Experimentation; Member, Farm Animal Welfare Council; Advisory Director, World Society for Protection of Animals; Vice-President, Royal Society for Prevention of Cruelty to Animals, 1980-82; Chairman, Animal Welfare Year, 1976-77. Address: (h.) Burnbank Cottage, Soonhope, Peebles, EH45 8BH; T.-01721 729550.

Holloway, Most Rev. Richard Frederick, BD, STM, DUniv (Strathclyde), DD (Aberdeen). Bishop of Edinburgh, since 1986; Primus of the Scottish Episcopal Church, since 1992; b. 26.11.33; m., Jean Elizabeth Kennedy; 1 s.; 2 d. Educ. Kelham Theological College; Edinburgh Theological College; Union Theological Seminary, New York. Curate, St. Ninian's, Glasgow, 1959-63; Priest-in-charge, St. Margaret and St. Mungo's, Glasgow, 1963-68; Rector, Old St. Paul's, Edinburgh, 1968-80; Rector, Church of the Advent, Boston, Mass, 1980-84; Vicar, St. Mary Magdalen's, Oxford, 1984-86. Recreations: running; long-distance walking; reading; going to the cinema; listening to music. Address: (h.) 3 Eglinton Crescent, Edinburgh, EH12 5DH.

Holmes, George Dennis, CB (1979), FRSE, FICfor. Forestry Consultant, since 1987; b. 9.11.26, Conwy; m., Sheila Rosemary; 3 d. Educ. John Bright's School, Llandudno; University of Wales, Bangor. Forestry Commission, 1948-86 (Director General, 1976-86). Chairman, Scottish Council for Spastics, since 1986. Recreations: fishing; sailing; golf. Address: (h.) 7 Cammo Road, Barnton, Edinburgh, EH4 8EF; T.-0131-339 7474.

Holy, Professor Ladislav, PhD. Professor of Social Anthropology, St. Andrews University, since 1987; b. 4.4.33, Prague. Educ. Charles University, Prague. Research Officer, Czechoslovak Academy of Sciences; Director, Livingstone Museum, Zambia; Lecturer and Reader in Social Anthropology, Queen's University, Belfast; Reader in Social Anthropology, St. Andrews University. Recreations: gardening; hill-walking. Address: (b.) Department of Social Anthropology, St. Andrews University, St. Andrews, KY16 9AL.

Home Robertson, John David. MP (Labour), East Lothian, since 1983 (Berwick & East Lothian, 1978-83); b. 5.12.48, Edinburgh; m., Catherine Brewster; 2 s. Educ. Ampleforth College; West of Scotland Agricultural College. Farmer; Member: Berwickshire District Council, 1974-78, Borders Health Board, 1975-78; Chairman, Eastern Borders Citizens' Advice Bureau, 1976-78; Member, Select Committee on Scottish Affairs, 1979-83; Chairman, Scottish Group of Labour MPs, 1983; Scottish Labour Whip, 1983-84; Opposition Front Bench Spokesman on Agriculture, 1984-87, on Scotland, 1987-88, on Agriculture, 1988-90; Member, Select Committee on Defence, since 1990; Member, British-Irish Parliamentary Body, since 1993. Address: (b.) House of Commons, Westminster, London, SW1A OAA; T.-0171-219 4135; 01368 63679.

Homfray, John L., MBE, TD, FCA. Chairman, Iona Cathedral Trust Management Board, 1982-92; Director, Iona Abbey Ltd., since 1993; b. 5.8.16, Darjeeling, India; m., Elizabeth M. Shand; 2 s.; 1 d. Educ. Sherborne. Captain, RA 80 Field Regiment, 1940-45 (mentioned in Despatches); Director, Clyde Shipping Co. Ltd., Glasgow, 1948-81; Deputy Lieutenant, Dunbartonshire, 1975-90. Lt. Col., City of Glasgow Artillery, RATA, 1953-57; Chairman, Glasgow Aged Seamen Relief Fund; Director, Sailors Orphan Society of Scotland. Recreations: shooting; travelling. Address: (h.) Ardballachan, Bracklinn Road, Callander, Perthshire; T.-01877 30256.

Hood, Evelyn. Novelist and Playwright; b. 9.3.36, Paisley; m., James R. Hood; 2 s. Educ. John Neilson Institution, Paisley; Glasgow College of Commerce. Author of 19 novels and six one-act plays; former journalist; Lecturer and Tutor. Recreations: reading; amateur drama. Address: (h.) 17 Kilbarchan Road, Johnstone, PA5 8RD; T.-01505 321409.

Hood, James. MP (Labour), Clydesdale, since 1987; b. 16.5.48. Address: House of Commons, London, SW1A 0AA.

Hood, Professor Neil, FRSE, MA, MLitt. Professor of Business Policy, Department of Marketing, Strathclyde University, since 1979; Director, Strathclyde International Business Unit, since 1992; b. 10.8.43, Wishaw; m., Anna Watson Clark; 1 s.; 1 d. Educ. Wishaw High School; Glasgow University. Research Fellow, Scottish College of Textiles, 1966-68; Lecturer/Senior Lecturer, Paisley College of Technology, 1968-78; Economic Adviser, Scottish Economic Planning Department, 1979; Director, Locate in Scotland, 1987-89; Director, Employment and Special Initiatives, SDA, 1989-90; Visiting Professor of International Business, University of Texas, Dallas, 1981; Visiting Professor, Institute of International Business, Stockholm School of Economics, since 1982; Director, Euroscot Meat Exports Ltd., 1981-85; Economic Consultant to Secretary of State for Scotland, 1980-87; Director, Scottish Development Finance Ltd., 1984-90 and since 1993; Investment Adviser, Castleforth Fund Managers, 1984-87; Director, LIFE Ltd., 1984-86; Board Member, Irvine Development Corporation, 1985-87; Director, Prestwick Holdings PLC, 1986-87; Director: Lamberton (Holdings) Ltd., 1989-92, GA (Holdings) Ltd., 1990-92, Shanks and McEwan PLC, 1990-94, I & S UK Smaller Companies Trust plc, since 1993, I & S Trustlink Ltd., since 1994, Kwik-Fit plc, since 1991, Grampian Holdings plc, since 1993; Corporate Adviser, Scottish Power, since 1989; Chairman, John Dickie Group Ltd., since 1995; President, European International Business Association, 1985-86. Publications: Industrial Marketing — A Study of Textiles (Co-author), 1970; Chrysler UK: A Corporation in Transition (Co-author), 1977; The Economics of

Multinational Enterprise (Co-author), 1979; European Development Strategies of US Multinationals Located in Scotland (Co-author), 1980; Multinationals in Retreat: The Scottish Experience (Co-author), 1982; Multinational Investment Strategies in the British Isles (Co-author), 1983; Industry, Policy and the Scottish Economy (Co-Editor), 1984; Transnational Corporations in the Textile Industry (Co-author), 1984; Foreign Multinationals and the British Economy (Co-author), 1987; Strategies in Global Competition (Co-Editor), 1987; Scottish Financial Sector (Co-author), 1988. Recreations: swimming; reading; gardening. Address: (h.) Teviot, 12 Carlisle Road, Hamilton, ML3 7DB; T.-01698 424870.

Hook, Professor Andrew Dunnet, MA, PhD. Bradley Professor of English Literature, Glasgow University, since 1979; b. 21.12.32, Wick; m., Judith Ann (deceased); 2 s.; 1 d. Educ. Wick High School; Daniel Stewart's College, Edinburgh; Edinburgh University; Manchester University; Princeton University. Edinburgh University: Assistant Lecturer in English Literature, 1961-63, Lecturer in American Literature, 1963-70; Senior Lecturer in English, Aberdeen University, 1970-79; Chairman, Committee for Humanities and Member, Committee for Academic Affairs, CNAA, 1987-92; Chairman, Scottish Universities Council on Entrance English Panel, 1986-92; Chairman, Universities and Collegesd Admissions Service English Panel, since 1995; Member, Scottish Examination Board, 1984-92; President, Eighteenth-Century Scottish Studies Society, 1990-92. Publications: Scotland and America 1750-1835, 1975; American Literature in Context 1865-1900, 1983; Scott's Waverley (Editor), 1971; Charlotte Bronte's Shirley (Editor, with Judith Hook), 1974; Dos Passos: A Collection of Critical Essays (Editor), 1974; The History of Scottish Literature II, 1660-1800 (Editor), 1987; Scott Fitzgerald, 1992. Recreations: theatre; opera; catching up on reading. Address: (b.) Department of English Literature, Glasgow University, Glasgow, G12 8QQ; T.-0141-339 8855, Ext. 4226.

Hooper, Ian Ross, BA. Depute Director (Resources), National Museums of Scotland, since 1989; Director, Museum of Scotland Project, since 1990; b. 26.5.49, Edinburgh; m., Julie Ellen Vaughan; 1 s.; 1 d. Educ. Hornchurch Grammar School; University of East Anglia. Administrator, Department of the Environment, 1973-89; seconded to English Heritage, 1984-85, responsible for historic buildings policy. Recreations: historic buildings; hill-walking; golf. Address: (b.) Royal Museum of Scotland, Edinburgh, EH1 1JF; T.-0131-225 7534.

Hope, Colin John Filshill, OStJ, BA, FCII, FCIS, FCIT, FBIM, MCIM, DipM. Member, Council, Insurance Ombudsman Bureau, 1981-94; Director, Merchants House of Glasgow, 1981-87, 1988-94, 1995; Member, Air Transport Committee, Association of British Chambers of Commerce, 1986-90; Governor, Keil School, 1986-91; Governor, Glasgow Educational and Marshall Trust, since 1986; Member, General Convocation, Strathclyde University, 1980-90; Member, South of Scotland Electricity Consultative Committee, 1990-91; b. 24.6.24, Dullatur; m., Jean Calder Douglas; 1 s.; 2 d. Educ. Glasgow High School; Glasgow Academy; Open University. RAF, 1942-47; joined Stenhouse & Partners, 1947; appointed Director, 1949; served in many capacities, including Managing Director, Stenhouse International; joined Norman Frizzell Scotland Ltd. as Managing Director, 1974; additionally Director, Norman Frizzell UK Ltd., 1976-81; Director, G.T. Senior, 1981-83 (Consultant, 1983-85); a Director, Glasgow Chamber of Commerce, 1979-88. Member: Scottish Consumer Council, 1979-85, Electricity Consultative Council for Scotland, 1979-87, Glasgow Airport Consultative Committee, since 1984; former Chairman, Transport Users Consultative Committee; Director, Glasgow Native Benevolent Association, 1988-91 and since 1992; Member, Dumbartonshire Committee, Order of St.

John, 1987-93. Address: (h.) Omaha, 4 Munro Drive East, Helensburgh, G84 9BS; T.-01436 673091.

Hope of Craighead, Rt. Hon. Lord (James Arthur David Hope), PC. A Senator of the College of Justice, Lord Justice General of Scotland, and Lord President of the Court of Session, since 1989; b. 27.6.38, Edinburgh; m., Katharine Mary Kerr; 2 (twin) s.; 1 d. Educ. Edinburgh Academy; Rugby School; St. John's College, Cambridge (BA); Edinburgh University (LLB); Hon. LLD, Aberdeen (1991), Strathclyde (1993), Edinburgh (1995). National Service, Seaforth Highlanders, 1957-59; admitted Faculty of Advocates, 1965; Standing Junior Counsel to Inland Revenue, 1974-78; QC, 1978; Advocate Depute, 1978-82; Chairman, Medical Appeal Tribunal, 1985-86; Legal Chairman, Pensions Appeal Tribunal, 1985-86; Dean, Faculty of Advocates, 1986-89; President, The Stair Society, 1993; Hon. Professor of Law, Aberdeen, 1994; Baron (Life Peer), 1995. Publications: Gloag and Henderson's Introduction to Scots Law (Joint Editor, 7th edition, Assistant Editor, 8th and 9th editions); Armour on Valuation for Rating (Joint Editor, 4th and 5th editions); (Contributor) Stair Memorial Encyclopaedia of Scots Law. Address: (h.) 34 India Street, Edinburgh, EH3 6HB; T.-0131-225 8245.

Hope, William, MA. Rector, Elgin High School, since 1978; b. 26.9.43, Scotland; m., Patricia Miller. Educ. Dalbeattie High School; Kirkcudbright Academy; Edinburgh University; Jordanhill College of Education. Alloa Academy: Assistant Teacher, Principal Teacher of Guidance; Assistant Rector, Lochaber High School. Chairman, Moray Branch, UNICEF; Vice Chairman, Elgin and District Branch, Cancer Relief; President, Forres St. Lawrence Cricket Club; Vice President, North of Scotland Cricket Association. Recreations: umpiring hockey and cricket; fishing; public speaking. Address: (b.) Elgin High School, High School Drive, Elgin, Moray; T.-01343 545181.

Hopwood, Sylvia Elaine, MB, ChB, DPM. Psychiatrist, Tayside Region, and Honorary Lecturer, Dundee University, since 1962; b. 25.2.38, Salford; 2 d. Educ. Leeds University. Medical and neurological training, Leeds, 1960-62; psychiatric training, Dundee, 1962. Chairman, Gowrie Housing Association; Member, National Schizophrenia Fellowship and Manic Depressive Fellowship. Publications: many articles on alcoholism, depression and schizophrenia. Recreations: lace-making; embroidery; gardening. Address: (h.) 6 Strips of Craigie Road, Dundee, DD4 7PZ; T.-01382 462265.

Horden, Professor John Robert Backhouse, MA, MLitt, DHL, FSA, FSA(Scot), FRSL. Professor Emeritus of Bibliographical Studies, Stirling University; b. Warwickshire; m., Aileen Mary Douglas (deceased); 1 s. Educ. Oxford University; Cambridge University; Heidelberg University; Sorbonne; Lincoln's Inn. Former Director, Centre for Bibliographical Studies, Stirling University; former Director, Institute of Bibliography and Textual Criticism, Leeds University; former Tutor and Lecturer in English Literature, Christ Church, Oxford; Visiting Professorial appointments, Universities of Pennsylvania State, Saskatchewan, Erlangen-Nurnberg, Texas at Austin, Munster; Editor, Dictionary of Scottish Biography, since 1982; Cecil Oldman Memorial Lecturer, 1971; Marc Fitch Prize for Bibliography, 1979. Publications: Francis Quarles: A Bibliography of his Work to 1800, 1953; Francis Quarles' Hosanna and Threnodes (Editor), 1960; Annual Bibliography of English Language and Literature (Editor), 1967-75; English and Continental Emblem Books (22 vols.) (Editor), 1968-74; Art of the Drama, 1969; Dictionary of Concealed Authorship, Vol. 1 (Editor), 1980; initiator and first editor, Index of English Literary Manuscripts, seven volumes, 1980-90; Everyday Life in Seventeenth-Century England, 1974; Techniques of

Bibliography, 1977; John Freeth: Political Ballad Writer and Inn Keeper, 1985; Bibliographia (Editor), 1992. Recreations: golf (represented England, Warwickshire, Oxford, Cambridge); music; painting. Address: (b.) Department of English Studies, Stirling University, Stirling, KF9 4LA.

Horn, David Bowes, BSc, PhD, CChem, FRSC, FRCPath, CBiol, FIBiol, FRSE. Head, Department of Clinical Chemistry, Western General Hospital, Edinburgh, 1966-87; Honorary Senior Lecturer in Clinical Chemistry, Edinburgh University, 1966-87; b. 18.8.28, Edinburgh; m., Shirley Kay Riddell; 2 d. Educ. Daniel Stewart's College, Edinburgh; Heriot-Watt University, Edinburgh; Edinburgh University. Senior Grade Biochemist: Vale of Leven Hospital, Alexandria, 1956, Queen Elizabeth Hospital, Birmingham, 1959; Biochemist, Royal Victoria Infirmary, Newcastle-upon-Tyne, and Honorary Lecturer, Department of Clinical Biochemistry, Newcastle-upon-Tyne University, 1959. Past Chairman, Scottish Region, Association of Clinical Biochemists (former Member, ACB National Council); Past Chairman, Scientific Services Advisory Group Clinical Chemistry Sub-Committee; Royal Society of Chemistry Representative, Mastership in Clinical Biochemistry Examination Board, 1973-88. Recreations: computation; gardening; walking. Address: (h.) 2 Barnton Park, Edinburgh, EH4 6JF; T.-0131-336 3444.

Horne, Allan Maxwell, BL. Solicitor (retired); Honorary Sheriff, Elgin, since 1981; b. 24.2.17, Brora; m., Margaret Ross; 1 d. Educ. Elgin Academy; Edinburgh University. Royal Artillery, 1940-46: commissioned 128th Field Regiment, 51st (H) Division, served as Air Observation Pilot, 1945-46, demobilised with rank of Captain; Legal Assistant, Inverness, 1946-49; Partner, Grigor & Young, Solicitors, Elgin, 1949-83, retiring as Senior Partner; Burgh Prosecutor, Elgin, 1950-75. Recreation: golf. Address: (h.) Melford, 11 Fleurs Place, Elgin; T.-Elgin 542833.

Horner, Professor Robert Malcolm Wigglesworth, CEng, BSc, PhD, MICE, MBIM. Professor of Engineering Management, since 1986, and Head, Department of Civil Engineering, 1985-91, Dundee University; Non-executive Direcor, Atlantic Power and Gas Ltd., since 1991; b. 27.7.42, Bury; m., Beverley Anne Wesley; 1 s.; 1 d. Educ. The Bolton School; University College, London. Civil Engineer, Taylor Woodrow Construction Ltd., 1966-77; Lecturer, Department of Civil Engineering, Dundee University, 1977-83, Senior Lecturer, 1983-86. Founder Chairman, Dundee Branch, Opening Windows on Engineering; Winner, CIOB Ian Murray Leslie Award, 1980 and 1984; Director, Dundee Rep., since 1991; Member, Council, National Conference of University Professors, 1989-93; Director, Scottish International Resource Project, since 1994; Chairman, Friends of St. Paul's Cathedral, since 1993. Recreations: squash; gardening. Address: (h.) Westfield Cottage, 11 Westfield Place, Dundee, DD1 4JU; T.-01382 225933.

Hornibrook, John Nevill, OBE, VRD, FEng, FIChemE. A Director, Renfrewshire Healthcare NHS Trust; Chairman,Awarding Body for Vocational Qualifications for the Chemical and Pharmaceutical Industries; Vice-Chairman, Garnock Valley Development Executive; Member, Court, University of Paisley; Chairman, Waste Management Centre, University of Paisley; Director, Scotvec; Member, Scottish and National CBI Education and Training Committees; Consultant, RPS Cairns Ltd., Edinburgh; b. 25.10.28, Gerrards Cross, Buckinghamshire; m., Dr. (Norma) Gillian Newbury; 2 d. Educ. Wellington College; Birmingham University. National Service, Royal Navy, 1949-51; various industrial appointments at home and overseas; Roche Products, Dalry, 1972-93, Divisional Director, 1981-93. Former Chairman, Enterprise Ayrshire. Recreations: sailing; gardening. Address: (h.) Cruachan, West Glen Road, Kilmacolm, PA13 4PN; T.-01505 873265.

Horobin, John Charles, BSc, PhD. Head of Conference and Group Services, St. Andrews University, since 1989; Chairman, St. Andrews and Fife Conference Bureau Ltd; b. 13.2.45, Long Eaton; 1 s.; 1 d. Educ. Long Eaton Grammar School; King's College, London University; Durham University. Tutor-Organiser, WEA, Plymouth and West Devon, 1971-74; Assistant Director of Adult Education, St. Andrews University, 1974-89. Address: (b.) Residence and Business Services, St. Andrews University, 79 North Street, St. Andrews, KY16 9AJ; T.-01334 462520.

Horsburgh, Sheriff John Millar Stewart, QC. Sheriff of Lothian and Borders, at Edinburgh, since 1990; b. 15.5.38. Admitted to Scots Bar, 1965. Address: (b.) Sheriff Court House, 27 Chambers Street, Edinburgh, EH1 1LB.

Horsfall, Sheriff A.C., MA, LLB. Member, Lands Tribunal for Scotland. Admitted Faculty of Advocates, 1953.

Horsman, Graham Joseph Vivian, OBE (1977), JP, MA. Chairman, Forth Valley Health Board, 1977-85; Member, Scottish Health Service Planning Council, 1977-85; Extra-Parliamentary Commissioner Under Private Legislation Procedure (Scotland) Act, 1976-86; b. 10.11.19, London; m., Ruth Guest; 2 s.; 2 d. Educ. Whitgift School; Trinity College, Oxford. Councillor, County Borough of Reading, 1946-47; Member, Stirling and Clackmannan Hospitals Board of Management, 1966-69; Chairman, Stirling, Falkirk and Alloa Hospitals Board of Management, 1970-74; Member, Forth Valley Health Board, 1973-77; Member, Committee to Review Assessment in the Third and Fourth Years of Secondary Education in Scotland (Dunning Committee), 1975-77. Chairman, Dollar Civic Trust, 1970-78; Vice-Chairman, Scottish Association of Citizens' Advice Bureaux, 1976-78 (Council Member, 1973-78). Recreations: music; reading; walking. Address: (h.) 9 Tarmangie Drive, Dollar, Clackmannanshire; T.-Dollar 2575.

Horspool, William McKie, BSc, PhD, DSc, CChem, FRSC, FRSE. Reader in Organic Chemistry, Dundee University, since 1972; b. 12.8.36, Kilmarnock; m., Una Macfarlane Hamill; 1 s.; 1 d. Educ. Kilmarnock Academy; Strathclyde University; Glasgow University. Postdoctoral Associate, Columbia University, New York, 1964-65; Lecturer in Organic Chemistry, Queen's College, St. Andrews, 1965-72; Visiting Professor, Wisconsin University, 1974; Visiting Professor, Complutense University, Madrid, 1985. Publications: Aspects of Organic Photochemistry, 1976; Synthetic Organic Photochemistry (Editor), 1984; Organic Photochemistry: a comprehensive treatment, 1992; numerous papers in scientific journals. Recreations: gardening; DIY construction; choral singing (Treasurer, Dundee Choral Union); local church affairs (Session Clerk, Fowlis and Liff). Address: (h.) Waulkmill, Liff, Dundee, DD2 5LR.

Housden, Stuart David, BSc (Zoology). Director Scotland, RSPB, since 1993; b. 24.6.53, Croydon; m., Catherine Juliet Wilkin; 3 d. Educ. Selhurst Grammar School; Royal Holloway College, London University. Freshwater biologist, Thames Water, 1976; RSPB: Species Investigation Officer, 1977-79, Parliamentary Officer, 1979-82, Manager — Government Unit, 1982-85, Head, Conservation Planning Department, 1985-90, Head, Conservation Planning, 1990-93. Churchill Fellow, 1992. Publications: Important Bird Areas in the UK (Co-Editor); numerous articles. Recreations: ornithology; travel; rugby football; politics; work. Address: (b.) 17 Regent Terrace, Edinburgh, EH7 5BN; T.-0131-557 3136.

House, Professor Charles Randall, PhD, DSc, FRSE. Professor of Cell Physiology, Edinburgh University, since 1985; b. 16.7.38, Glasgow; 1 s.; 1 d. Educ. Queens Park School, Glasgow; Glasgow University; Birmingham University; Edinburgh University. Assistant Lecturer in

Biophysics, Edinburgh University; Senior Research Associate in Biophysics, University of East Anglia; Research Associate in Neurophysiology, Columbia University, NY; Lecturer, then Reader in Physiology, Edinburgh University; Visiting Professor in Physiology, St. George's University School of Medicine, Grenada, WEst Indies; Editor, Journal of Physiology; Editor, Experimental Physiology. Address: (b.) Department of Preclinical Veterinary Sciences, Edinburgh University, Edinburgh, EH9 1QH; T.-0131-650 6105.

Houslay, Professor Miles Douglas, BSc, PhD, FRSE, FRSA, FIBiol, CBiol. Gardiner Professor of Biochemistry, Glasgow University, since 1984; b. 25.6.50, Wolverhampton; m., Rhian Mair; 2 s.; 1 d. Educ. Grammar School, Brewood, Stafford; University College, Cardiff; King's College, Cambridge; Cambridge University. ICI Research Fellow and Fellow, Queens' College, Cambridge, 1974-76; Lecturer, then Reader in Biochemistry, UMIST, 1976-82; Selby Fellow, Australian Academy of Science, 1984; Colworth Medal, Biochemical Society of Great Britain, 1984; Honorary Research Fellow, California Metabolic Research Foundation, since 1981; Editor in Chief, Cellular Signalling; Deputy Chairman, Biochemical Journal, 1984-89; Editorial Board, Biochimica Biophysica Acta; Committee Member, Biochemical Society, 1982-85; Member, Research Committee, British Diabetic Association, 1986-91; Chairman, Grant Committee A, Cell and Disorders Board, Medical Research Council, 1989-92; Member, Scientific and Medical Grant Committee, Scottish Home and Health Department, 1991-94; Member, Advisory Board for External Appointments, London University, 1990-92. Publication: Dynamics of Biological Membranes; over 300 scientific papers. Address: (b.) Department of Biochemistry, Glasgow University, Glasgow, G12 8QQ; T.-0141-339 8855, Ext. 4624.

Housley, Edward, MB, ChB, FRCPEdin, FRCP. Consultant Physician, Edinburgh Royal Infirmary, since 1970; Honorary Senior Lecturer, Department of Medicine, Edinburgh University, since 1970; b. 10.1.34, Chester, USA; m., Alma Mary; 1 d. Educ. Mundella Grammar School, Nottingham; Birmingham University. Postgraduate training, Department of Medicine, Birmingham University and McGill University, Montreal; Chairman, MRCP (UK) Part I Examining Board. Recreation: crossword puzzles. Address: (h.) 16 Sunbury Place, Edinburgh, EH4 3BY.

Houston, Major General David, CBE. Lord Lieutenant of Sutherland, since 1991; b. 24.2.29.

Houston, Rev. Graham Richard, BSc (Hons), BD (Hons), MTh. Chaplain, Heriot-Watt University, since 1990; b. 3.5.50, Glasgow; m., Irene Elizabeth Robertson; 1 s.; 2 d. Educ. Hutchesons' Boys' Grammar School, Glasgow; Strathclyde University; Aberdeen University. Assistant, project, Govan, 1972-73; Assistant Minister, Palmerston Place Church, Edinburgh, 1976-77; Minister, Kildonan and Loth Church, Sutherland, 1978-82; Minister, Letham St. Mark's Church, Perth, 1982-90. Recreations: squash; golf; cricket. Address: (h.) 3 Ramsay Place, Penicuik, Midlothian, EH26 9JS; T.-01968 672752.

Houstoun, Andrew Beatty, OBE, MC, DL, JP. Vice President, Scottish Landowners Federation, since 1984; b. 15.10.22, Cranleigh; m., Mary Elizabeth Spencer-Nairn; 4 s. Educ. Harrow. Regular Army, 1941-56; retired as Major, 1st The Royal Dragoons; farming, Angus and Perthshire, since 1956; commanded Fife and Forfar Yeomanry/Scottish Horse (TA), 1962-65; Angus County Councillor, 1966-75 (Vice Chairman, Education Committee); Convener, Scottish Landowners Federation, 1979-82; Chancellor's Assessor, Dundee University Court, 1981-92; Vice Lord Lieutenant, Angus, since 1986. Address: Lintrathen Lodge, Kirriemuir, Angus, DD8 5JJ; T.-0157 56 228.

Howard, Ian, MA (Hons), ARSA. Head of Painting, Duncan of Jordanstone College of Art, Dundee, since 1986; b. 5.11.52, Aberdeen; m., Ruth D'Arcy; 2 d. Educ. Aberdeen Grammar School; Edinburgh College of Art; Edinburgh University. Travelling scholarship to Italy, 1976; part-time Lecturer in Painting, Gray's School of Art, Aberdeen, 1977 (appointed full-time, 1980); Scottish Arts Council Award, 1979, Bursary, 1985-86; numerous one-man and group exhibitions. Recreations: reading; music; cooking. Address: (h.) 66 Camphill Road, Broughty Ferry, Dundee; T.-Dundee 79395.

Howe, Professor James Alexander Macgregor, MA, PhD, FAAAI. Head, Department of Artificial Intelligence, Edinburgh University, since 1978 (Professor of Artificial Intelligence, since 1985); b. 7.7.37, Glasgow; m., Nan Harvie Bell; 1 s.; 2 d. Educ. Kelvinside Academy, Glasgow; St. Andrews University; Cambridge University. Senior Assistant in Research, Laboratory of Experimental Psychology, Cambridge University, 1964-66; Research Fellow, Lecturer, Senior Lecturer, Reader, Department of Artificial Intelligence, Edinburgh University, 1967-85; Founder Director, Conversational Software Ltd., 1969-73; Founder and Chairman, Artificial Intelligence Applications Institute, Edinburgh University, since 1984; Governor, Scottish Council for Educational Technology, 1981-84; Chairman, Society for the Study of Artificial Intelligence and the Simulation of Behaviour, 1982-85; Chairman, Alvey Directorate's IKBS Advisory Group, 1983-88; Chairman, SERC/DTI Systems Engineering – Committee A, 1988-91; Member, Ordnance Survey Science and Technology Advisory Committee, 1987-92; Member, Court, Edinburgh University, since 1994. Recreations: skiing; curling; gardening; golf. Address: (h.) 26 Essex Road, Edinburgh, EH4 6LJ; T.-0131-339 5390.

Howett, Kevin, BSc (Hons). National Officer, Mountaineering Council of Scotland, since 1989; b. 27.12.57, Alnwick. Educ. King Edward VI School, Morpeth; Exeter University; University College of North Wales. Outdoor Activities Instructor, Newcastle upon Tyne LEA. Publications: Rock Climbing in Scotland; articles. Recreations: rock climbing; winter snow and ice climbing; bird-watching. Address: Buddleia Cottage, Gwydyr Road, Crieff, PH7 4BS.

Howie, Andrew Law, CBE, FRAgrS. Chairman, Robert Howie & Sons, since 1982; Chairman, Scottish Milk Marketing Board, 1982-94, Scottish Milk Ltd., 1994-95; b. 14.4.24, Dunlop; m., Joan Duncan; 2 s.; 2 d. Educ. Glasgow Academy. Joined Robert Howie & Sons, 1941; War Service, RN; became Director, 1965; President, Scottish Compound Feed Manufacturers, 1968-70 and 1983-85; President, Compound Animal Feed Manufacturers National Association, 1971-72; Director, Scottish Corn Trade, 1976-78; Vice-President/Feed, UK Agricultural Supply Trade Association, 1980-81; Chairman, Scottish Council, UKASTA, 1985-87; Director, Scottish Milk Marketing Board, 1980-94; Member, CBI Scottish Council, since 1989. Recreations: golf; gardening. Address: (h.) Newmill House, Dunlop, Kilmarnock, KA3 4BQ; T.-01560 484936.

Howie, Sir James William, Kt (1969), LLD, MD, FRCP, FRCPath, FIMLS, Hon. ARCVS; b. 31.12.07, Oldmeldrum, Aberdeenshire; m., Isabella Winifred Mitchell; 2 s.; 1 d. Educ. Robert Gordon's College, Aberdeen; Aberdeen University. Specialised in bacteriology as applied to infectious diseases and agriculture; RAMC, 1939-45, Nigeria and War Office; Professor of Bacteriology, Glasgow University, 1951-63; Medical Director, Public Health Laboratory Service, 1963-73; Honorary Physician to the Queen, 1965-68; Past President: BMA, Royal College of Pathologists, Association of Clinical Pathologists, Institute of Sterile Services Management. Recreations: golf; music. Address: (h.) 34 Redford Avenue, Edinburgh, EH13 0BU; T.-0131-441 3910.

Howie, John Cameron, IPFA, IRRV. Chief Executive, Stewartry District Council, since 1988; b. 22.9.41, Perth; m., Kathleen N.; 1 d. Educ. Perth Academy. Chief Accountant, Perth and Kinross Joint County Council, 1967; Depute County Treasurer, Ross and Cromarty County Council, 1970; County Treasurer, Kirkcudbright County Council, 1972; Director of Finance and Housing, Stewartry District Council, 1975-88. Recreations: golf; swimming; all sports; reading. Address: (h.) Kinclaven, Hardgate, Castle Douglas, DG7 3LD.

Howie, Professor John Garvie Robertson, MD, PhD, FRCPE, FRCGP. Professor of General Practice, Edinburgh University, since 1980; b. 23.1.37, Glasgow; m., Elizabeth Margaret Donald; 2 s.; 1 d. Educ. High School of Glasgow; Glasgow University. Registrar, Laboratory Medicine, Western Infirmary, Glasgow, 1962-66; General Practitioner, Glasgow, 1966-70; Lecturer/Senior Lecturer in General Practice, Aberdeen University, 1970-80; Member: Biomedical Research Committee, SHHD, 1977-81, Health Services Research Committee, SHHD, 1982-86, Chief Scientist Committeee, SHHD, since 1987, Committee on the Review of Medicines, since 1986; Chairman, Heads of Departments of General Practice Group. Publication: Research in General Practice. Recreations: golf; gardening; music. Address: (h.) 4 Ravelrig Park, Balerno, Midlothian, EH14 7DL; T.-0131-449 6305.

Howie, Professor John Mackintosh, CBE, MA, DPhil, DSc, FRSE. Regius Professor of Mathematics, St. Andrews University, since 1970; b. 23.5.36, Chryston, Lanarkshire; m., Dorothy Joyce Miller; 2 d. Educ. Robert Gordon's College, Aberdeen; Aberdeen University. Assistant in Mathematics, Aberdeen University, 1958-59; Assistant, then Lecturer in Mathematics, Glasgow University, 1961-67; Senior Lecturer in Mathematics, Stirling University, 1967-70; visiting appointments:Tulane University, 1964-65, State University of New York at Buffalo, 1969-70, University of Western Australia, 1968, Monash University, 1979, Northern Illinois University, 1988; Dean of Science, St. Andrews University, 1976-79. President, Edinburgh Mathematical Society, 1972-73; Vice-President, London Mathematical Society, 1984-86 and since 1990; Convener, SCEEB Mathematics Panel, 1970-73; Chairman, Scottish Central Committee on Mathematics, 1975-81; Member, Committee to Review Examinations (Dunning Committee), 1975-77; Chairman, Governors, Dundee College of Education, 1983-87; Keith Prize, Royal Society of Edinburgh, 1979-81; Chairman, Committee to review Fifth and Sixth Years (Howie Committee), 1990-92. Publications: An Introduction to Semigroup Theory, 1976; Automata and Languages, 1991; Fundamentals of Semigroup Theory, 1995; papers in mathematical journals. Recreations: music; gardening. Address: (b.) Mathematical Institute, St. Andrews University, North Haugh, St. Andrews, KY16 9SS; T.-01334 63746.

Howie, Professor Peter William, MD, FRCOG, FRSE, FRCP (Glas). Professor of Obstetrics and Gynaecology, Dundee University, since 1981 (Dean, Medicine and Dentistry, 1990-93); b. 21.11.39, Aberdeen; m., Anne Jardine Quigg; 1 s.; 1 d. Educ. High School of Glasgow; Glasgow University. Astor Foundation Research Fellow, Royal College of Pathologists, 1970-71; Lecturer, then Senior Lecturer, Department of Obstetrics and Gynaecology, Glasgow University, 1971-78; Clinical Consultant, Medical Research Council Reproductive Biology Unit, Edinburgh, 1978-81. Recreations: golf; music. Address: (h.) 8 Travebank Gardens, Monifieth, Dundee, DD5 4ET; T.-01382 534802.

Howie, William Forbes, DL, JP, BSc, CEng, MIEE, BA. Justice of the Peace, since 1974; Deputy Lieutenant, Stirling and Falkirk District, since 1981; General Commissioner of Income Tax, since 1983; b. 13.8.20, Falkirk; m., Janet M. Campbell; 2 s.; 1 d. Educ. Falkirk High School; Glasgow University; Open University. RAF, during Second World War (demobbed as Flight Lieutenant); Managing Director, Thomas Laurie & Co. Ltd., 1956-81; appointed Chairman, Children's Panel Advisory Committee, Falkirk, 1970; Chairman, Supplementary Benefit Appeal Tribunal, Stirling and Falkirk, 1973-88; Past Chairman, Forth Valley Scouts; former Session Clerk St. Andrews Church, Falkirk; set up Stirling and District Amateur Football Association, 1951 (its first Secretary); set up Falkirk Section, Scottish Wildlife Trust, 1984. Recreations: golf; bowls; colour photography; gardening; wildlife. Address: 12 Gartcows Crescent, Falkirk, FK1 5QH; T.-Falkirk 24128.

Howison, John Andrew, BSc, MSc, CEng, MICE, ACIArb. Deputy Chief Engineer, Roads Directorate, Scottish Office Industry Department, since 1992; b. 12.8.46, Ruislip; m., Teresa Maria; 2 s.; 2 d. Educ. Surbiton Grammar School; Edinburgh University; Heriot Watt University. Edinburgh Corporation, 1968-70; Livingston Development Corporation, 1970-73; Department of Environment/Department of Transport/Scottish Office, since 1973. Address: (b.) New St. Andrews House, St. James Centre, Edinburgh; T.-0131-244 5177.

Howitt, Lewis Finnigan, MB, ChB, DPH, FFCM, FRCP. Consultant Public Health Medicine, Lothian Health Board, retired; b. 27.5.28, Aberdeen; m., Sheila Helen Elizabeth Burns; 1 s.; 1 d. Educ. Aberdeen Central School; Aberdeen University. Medical Officer, RAF; Medical Officer, Counties of Roxburgh and Selkirk Public Health Department; Medical Officer, then Senior Medical Officer, City of Edinburgh Public Health Department; Deputy Medical Officer of Health, Counties of Midlothian and Peebles Public Health Department; Senior Medical Officer, Scottish Home and Health Department. Recreations: gardening; golf. Address: (h.) 27 Cluny Drive, Edinburgh, EH10 6DT; T.-0131-447 5849.

Howson, Peter. Painter; b. 1958, London. Studied, Glasgow School of Art, 1975-77. Official artist, Gulf War.

Ho-Yen, Darrel Orlando, BMSc (Hons), MBChB, MD, MRCPath. Consultant Microbiologist, Raigmore Hospital, Inverness, since 1987; Director, Scottish Toxoplasma Reference Laboratory, since 1987; Honorary Clinical Senior Lecturer, Aberdeen University, since 1987; b. 1.5.48; m., Jennifer Nicholls; 2 s. Educ. Dundee University. Ninewells Hospital and Medical School, Dundee, 1974-83; Regional Virus Laboratory, Ruchill Hospital, Glasgow, 1983-87. Publications: Better Recovery from Viral Illnesses; Diseases of Infection (Co-author); Unwind; Human Toxoplasmosis (Co-author); Climbing Out. Address: (b.) Microbiology Department, Raigmore Hospital, Inverness, IV2 3UJ; T.-01463 704206.

Hubbuck, Professor John Reginald, MA (Cantab), MA, DPhil (Oxon), FRSE, FRSA, CMath, FIMA. Professor of Mathematics, Aberdeen University, since 1978; b. 3.5.41, Girvan; m., Anne Neilson; 1 s.; 1 d. Educ. Manchester Grammar School; Queens' College, Cambridge; Pembroke College, Oxford. Fellow: Gonville and Caius College, Cambridge, 1970-72, Magdalen College, Oxford, 1972-78; President, Edinburgh Mathematical Society, 1985-86. Recreation: hill-walking. Address: (h.) 8 Fonthill Terrace, Aberdeen, AB1 2UR; T.-01224 588738.

Huckle, Derek Arthur, CA, FIMgt, FCCA. Principal, Fife College of Further and Higher Education, since 1984; b. 25.1.30, Newtown St. Boswells; m., Janette; 2 d. Educ. Galashiels Academy. National Service, 1954-56; paper making, 1956-70; further education, since 1970. Member, Committees, Institute of Chartered Accountants of Scotland, Institute of Management, SCOTVEC. Address: (b.) Fife College of Further and Higher Education, St. Brycedale Avenue, Kirkcaldy, KY1 1EX; T.-01592 268591.

Hudson, Christopher Sydney, DSO (and Bar), FInstM, CIPD; b. 1.8.16, Tunbridge Wells; m., Ruth Julia Risse; 1 d. Educ. privately, in Switzerland. Army Service, Royal Fusiliers and SOE, 1940-45 (Lt.-Col.); Control Commission for Germany (British and US Sectors), 1946-53; Personnel Manager in overseas companies, Shell International Petroleum Co., Israel, Trinidad, Zaire, Algeria; seconded to International Labour Organisation, Geneva, 1966; Executive in charge of Personnel, Training and Industrial Relations, Bank of Scotland, 1968-80. Croix de Guerre with Palme. Recreations: golf; swimming. Address: (h.) Invereil House, North Berwick, East Lothian, EH39 5DH; T.-01620 3646.

Hudson, Rev. Eric Vallance, LTh. Minister, Westerton Fairlie Memorial Church, since 1990; b. 22.2.42, Glasgow; m., Lorna Mary Miller; 1 s.; 1 d. Educ. Paisley Grammar School; Wollongong High School, NSW; Christ's College, Aberdeen and Aberdeen University. Sub-Editor, D.C. Thomson & Co. Ltd., Dundee, 1961-66; Senior Assistant Minister, New Kilpatrick Parish Church, Bearsden, 1971-73; Minister, Kintore Parish Church, 1973-78; Religious Programmes Officer, Scottish Television, 1978-89. Address: 3 Canniesburn Road, Bearsden, Glasgow, G61 1PW.

Huggins, Martin, MA, FRSA. Co-Founder and Principal, Edinburgh School of English, since 1969; b. 11.4.39, Edinburgh; m., 1, Astrid Chalmers Watson (m. diss.); 2 d.; 2, Margot Learmond. Educ. George Watson's College; Edinburgh University. Chairman, Scottish Craftsmanship Association, 1977-84; Governor, Edinburgh College of Art, 1980-92; Director, Edinburgh Chamber of Commerce, 1982-86; Chairman, ARELS, 1984-86; Member, British Council Recognition Advisory Committee, 1984-86; Chairman, Board of Governors, Edinburgh College of Art, 1990-92; President, Scottish Arts Club, 1990-92; Assistant, Masters Court, Edinburgh Merchant Company, 1992-95; Trustee, Hospitalfield Trust, since 1994. Recreations: music; travel; lunching at the Arts Club. Address: (h.) 16 McLaren Road, Edinburgh, EH9 2BN; T.-0131-667 1751.

Hughes, Professor James, BSc, CEng, MIEE, FBIM. Professor of Management, Strathclyde University, since 1989; b. 15.6.30, Ayr; m., Margaret Brown Hughes; 1 s.; 1 d. Educ. Ayr Academy; Strathclyde University. Project Manager, GEC Ltd.; general management, latterly Corporate Director Scotland, Honeywell Ltd.; Director and General Manager, Security Division, Microwave & Electronic Systems Ltd.; Director and General Manager, Tannoy Ltd.; Personnel Director, Ellerman Scotland; Human Relations Director, Thorn EMI plc. Recreations: music; squash; hill-walking; painting. Address: (h.) 41 Craigleith View, Edinburgh, EH4 3JY; T.-0131-337 5169.

Hughes, Professor John, BSc, CEng, FIMechE, FISPO. Professor and Director, National Centre for Prosthetics and Orthotics, Strathclyde University, since 1972; b. 20.4.34, Renfrew; m., Margaret Scoular Crichton; 2 d. Educ. Camphill School; Strathclyde University. Worked in shipbuilding and engineering, 1950-63; Strathclyde University: Lecturer in Mechanical Engineering Design, 1963-67, Senior Lecturer, Bioengineering Unit, 1967-72; Past President, International Society for Prosthetics and Orthotics. Recreations: golf; gardening. Address: (b.) Strathclyde University, Curran Building, 131 St. James' Road, Glasgow, G4 OLS; T.-0141-552 4049.

Hughes, Paul Michael. Chief Executive, Royal Scottish National Orchestra, since 1993; b. 16.6.56, Malvern. Educ. King's School, Worcester; Trinity College of Music, London. Staff accompanist and vocal coach, TCM, 1980-82; Librarian, ECYO, 1983-85; freelance tour manager, 1982-85; General Manager, Academy of Ancient Music, 1985-89; executive in touring department, Harrison/Parrott Ltd., 1985-89; artist manager and Artistic Director of Events, IMG Artists, 1989-93. Recreations: cinema; theatre; walking. Address: (b.) RSNO Centre, 73 Claremont Street, Glasgow, G3 7HA; T.-0141-226 3868.

Hughes, Robert. MP (Labour), Aberdeen North, since 1970; b. 3.1.32; m.; 2 s.; 3 d. Educ. Powis Secondary School, Aberdeen; Robert Gordon's College, Aberdeen; Benoni High School, Transvaal; Pietermaritzburg Technical College, Natal. Engineering apprenticeship, South African Rubber Company, Natal, 1949-54; draughtsman, C.F. Wilson & Co., Aberdeen, 1954-70; Member, Aberdeen City Council, 1962-71; Chairman, Aberdeen City Labour Party, 1961-69; Member, Select Committee on Scottish Affairs, 1971; Opposition Junior Spokesman on Scottish Affairs, 1972-74; Parliamentary Under Secretary of State, Scottish Office, 1974-75; Chairman, Select Committee on Scottish Affairs, 1981; Opposition Junior Spokesman on Transport, 1981-83; Opposition Principal Spokesman on Agriculture, 1984-85, on Transport, 1985-87; Member, General Medical Council, 1976-79; Chairman, Anti Apartheid Movement, 1976-94; Chairman, Action for Southern Africa (ACTSA), since 1994; Vice-Convenor, Scottish Group, Labour MPs, 1989; Convenor, Scottish Group of Labour MPs, 1990-91; Member, Select Committee on Scottish Affairs, since 1992. Address: (b.) House of Commons, London SW1A 0AA.

Hughes, Rt. Hon. Lord (William Hughes), PC (1970), CBE (1956), DL, LLD. Company Director; b. 22.1.11, Dundee; m., Christian Clancher Gordon (deceased); 2 d. Educ. Balfour Street School; Dundee Technical College. ARP Controller, Dundee, 1939-43; Armed Forces, 1943-46 (commissioned 1944, demobilised as Captain, 1946, served India, Labuan and Burma); Member, Dundee Town Council, 1933-36 and 1937-61; City Treasurer, 1946-47; Lord Provost, 1954-60; Chairman, Eastern Regional Hospital Board, 1948-60; Member, Court, St. Andrews University, 1954-63; Member, Council, Queen's College, Dundee, 1954-63; Member, Committee on Civil Juries, 1958-59; Member, Committee to Inquire into Registration of Title to Land, 1960-62; Member, North of Scotland Hydro Electric Board, 1957-64; Member, Scottish Transport Council, 1960-64; Chairman, Glenrothes Development Corporation, 1960-64; Chairman, East Kilbride Development Corporation, 1975-82; Chairman, Royal Commission on Legal Services in Scotland, 1976-80; Joint Parliamentary Under Secretary of State for Scotland, 1964-69; Minister of State for Scotland, 1969-70 and 1974-75; President, Scottish Federation of Housing Associations, 1975-93; Member, Council of Europe and Western European Union, 1976-87; Hon. Member, Council of Europe, since 1987. Recreation: gardening. Address: (h.) The Stables, Ross, Comrie, Perthshire; T.-01764 670557.

Hughes, William Young, CBE. Chairman and Chief Executive, Grampian Holdings plc, since 1985 (Chief Executive, 1976-85); Chairman, Aberforth Smaller Companies Trust PLC, since 1990; Treasurer, Scottish Conservative Party, since 1993 (Deputy Chairman, 1989-92); Director, Central Scotland Healthcare NHS Trust, since 1994; b. 12.4.40, Milnrow, Lancaster; m., Anne Macdonald Richardson; 2 s.; 1 d. Educ. Firth Park Grammar School, Sheffield; Glasgow University; Strathclyde University; Heriot-Watt University. Partner, R. Gordon Drummond, 1966-70; Managing Director, MSJ Securities Ltd., 1970-76. Chairman, CBI Scotland, 1987-89; Member, Governing Council, Scottish Business in the Community. Recreations: Member, Glenbervie and Gleneagles Golf Clubs. Address: (b.) Stag House, Castlebank Street, Glasgow, G11 6DY; T.-0141-357 2000.

Hughes Hallett, Professor Andrew Jonathan, BA (Hons), MSc (Econ), DPhil, FRSA. Professor of Economics, Strathclyde University, since 1989; Research Fellow, Centre for Economic Policy Research, since 1985; Consultant to World Bank, UN, EEC, etc., since 1986; b. 1.11.47, London; m., Claudia; 2 s.; 1 d. Educ. Radley

College; Warwick University; LSE; Oxford University. Lecturer in Economics, Bristol University, 1973-77; Associate Professor, Erasmus University, Rotterdam, 1977-85; David Dale Professor, Newcastle University, 1985-89. Publications: four books; 145 papers. Address: (b.) 100 Cathedral Street, Glasgow, G4 0LN; T.-0141-552 4400.

Hughes Hallett, David. Director, Scottish Wildlife Trust. Address: (b.) Cramond House, Cramond Glebe Road, Edinburgh, EH4 6NS.

Hughson, A.V. Mark, MD, MB, ChB, MRCPsych, DPM. Consultant Psychiatrist, Leverndale Hospital, Glasgow, since 1990; Honorary Clinical Senior Lecturer, Glasgow University, since 1991; b. 12.3.47, Edinburgh; m., Joan Scally; 2 s. Educ. George Watson's College, Edinburgh; Glasgow University. Recreations: playing the organ (not too badly); skiing (badly). Address: (h.) 1 Cleveden Gardens, Glasgow, G12 0PU; T.-0141-334 2473.

Hull, John Hewett, FRSE, BSc (Hons), MSc, CGeol, FGS. Assistant Director, British Geological Survey, 1982-94; Senior Officer in Scotland and Head, Geological Survey of Scotland, N. Ireland and Northern England, 1982-94; Head, Petroleum Geology, Geophysics and Offshore Surveys, 1985-94; b. 18.6.34, Manchester; m., Peggy Dunning. Educ. Manchester Central Grammar School; Birmingham University. H.M. Geological Survey of Great Britain, 1958-94; Hon. Research Fellow, Edinburgh University; Vice-President, Edinburgh Geological Society, since 1993. Publications: numerous books, professional papers and maps. Recreations: sport and music. Address: (h.) 14 Laverockdale Park, Colinton, Edinburgh, EH13 0QE; T.-0131-441 7563.

Hume, Sir Alan (Blyth), Kt, CB, MA; b. 5.1.13, Broxburn; m., Marion Morton Garrett; 1 s.; 1 d. Educ. George Heriot's School, Edinburgh; Edinburgh University. Scottish Office: entered, 1936, Under Secretary, Scottish Home Department, 1957-59, Assistant Under Secretary of State, 1959-62, Under Secretary, Ministry of Public Building and Works, 1963-64, Secretary, Scottish Development Department, 1965-73. Chairman, Ancient Monuments Board for Scotland, 1973-81; Chairman, Edinburgh New Town Conservation Committee, 1975-90. Recreations: golf; fishing. Address:(h.) 12 Oswald Road, Edinburgh, EH9 2HJ; T.-0131-667 2440.

Hume, James Douglas Howden, CBE, BSc, CEng, FIMechE, Hon. LLD (Strathclyde). Chairman and Managing Director, Drimard Limited, since 1988; Chairman, Magnum Power Solutions Ltd.; b. 4.5.28, Melbourne, Australia; m., June Katharine Spriggs; 1 s.; 2 d. Educ. Loretto; Strathclyde University; Glasgow University. Royal Artillery, 1944-46 (2nd Lt.); engineering training: James Howden & Company Limited, 1948-54, Production Engineering Limited, 1954-55; James Howden & Company Limited: Production Manager, 1955-56, appointed Director, 1957, Joint Managing Director, 1960, Managing Director, 1963; Howden Group PLC: Managing Director, 1968, Deputy Chairman and Managing Director, 1973, appointed Chairman, 1987 (resigned, November 1987). Member, Court, Strathclyde 1989-92. Address: (b.) Drimard Limited, 22 East Lennox Drive, Helensburgh, Dunbartonshire, G84 9JD; T.-01436 75132.

Hume, John Robert, BSc, ARCST, FSA, FSA Scot. Chief Inspector of Historic Buildings, Historic Scotland; Member, Inland Waterways Amenity Advisory Council, since 1974; Member, Industrial Archaeology Sub-Committee, English Heritage, since 1985; Chairman, Seagull Trust, 1978-93; Trustee, Scottish Maritime Museum, since 1983; Honorary Vice-President, Association for Industrial Archaeology; b. 26.2.39, Glasgow; m., Catherine Hope Macnab; 4 s. Educ. Hutchesons' Boys' Grammar School; Glasgow University; Royal College of Science and Technology. Assistant Lecturer, Lecturer, Senior Lecturer in Economic History, Strathclyde University, 1964-91. Member, Ancient Monuments Board for Scotland, 1981-84; Director, Scottish Industrial Archaeology Survey, 1978-84. Publications: The Industrial Archaeology of Glasgow; The Industrial Archaeology of Scotland; as Co-author: Workshop of the British Empire: Engineering and Shipbuilding in the West of Scotland; Beardmore: the History of a Scottish Industrial Giant; The Making of Scotch Whisky; A Bed of Nails: a History of P. MacCallum & Sons Ltd.; Shipbuilders to the World: a History of Harland and Wolff; Steam Entertainment; Historic Industrial Scenes: Scotland; Industrial History in Pictures: Scotland; Glasgow's Railway Stations. Recreations: photography; reading. Address: (h.) 28 Partickhill Road, Glasgow, G11 5BP.

Hume, Krystyna D., BSc. Head Teacher, St. Serf's School, Edinburgh, since 1992; b. 2.10.43, Edinburgh; m., Bill Hume; 2 s. Educ. James Gillespie's High School for Girls; Edinburgh University. Teacher of Mathematics: Portobello Secondary School, 1966-74 (Housemistress, 1970-74), St. Serf's School, 1981-92. Recreations: reading; going to the theatre and concerts; listening to music. Address: (b.) St. Serf's School, 5 Wester Coates Gardens, Edinburgh, EH12 5LT; T.-0131-337 1015.

Hume, Robert, BSc, MBChB, PhD, FRCP(Edin). Reader in Developmental Medicine, Dundee University; Consultant Paediatrician, Dundee Teaching Hospitals NHS Trust, since 1993; b. 5.4.47, Edinburgh; m., Shaena Finlayson Blair; 2 d. Educ. Dalkeith High School; Edinburgh University. MRC Fellow, Department of Biochemistry, Edinburgh University, 1975-78; Lecturer, Department of Child Life and Health, Edinburgh University, 1978-80; Senior Lecturer, Department of Child Life and Health, Edinburgh University, 1980-92. Member Royal College of Obstetricians and Gynaecologists (Birthright) Research Advisory Committee; Medical and Dental Defence Union of Scotland Specialist Advisor. Address: (b.) Centre for Research into Human Development, Departments of Child Health, Obstetrics and Gynaecology, Ninewells Hospital and Medical School, Dundee, DD1 9SY; T.-01382 60111.

Humphrey, James Malcolm Marcus, CBE, DL, OStJ, MA, FRICS. Grand Master Mason of Scotland, 1983-88; Member, Grampian Regional Council, 1974-94; Deputy Lieutenant, Aberdeenshire, since 1989; Alternate Member, European Committee of the Regions; Non-Executive Director, Grampian Healthcare NHS Trust; b. 1.5.38, Montreal, Canada; m., Sabrina Margaret Pooley; 2 s.; 2 d. Educ. Eton College; Oxford University. Conservative Parliamentary candidate, North Aberdeen, 1966, Kincardine and Deeside, 1991; Council Member, National Farmers' Union of Scotland, 1968-73; Member, Aberdeen County Council, 1970-75 (Chairman of Finance, 1973-75); Chairman of Finance, Grampian Regional Council, 1974-78 (Leader, Conservative Group, 1974-78); former Chairman, Clinterty Agricultural College Council; Member, Queen's Bodyguard for Scotland (Royal Company of Archers); Chairman, North of Scotland Board, Eagle Star Group, 1973-91. Recreations: shooting; fishing; photography. Address: (h.) Dinnet, Aboyne, Aberdeenshire.

Hunt, David, BSc, DipURP, CEng, MICE, MCIT. Managing Director, Clydeport PLC, since 1994; b. 29.11.47, Glasgow; m., Christine; 2 s. Educ. Allan Glen's School; Paisley College of Technology; Strathclyde University. Civil engineering, 1970-81; sales and general management, 1981-86; joined Clyde Port Authority, 1986; Clydeport Holdings Ltd., 1992. Address: (b.) Clydeport PLC, 16 Robertson Street, Glasgow, G2 8DS; T.-0141-221 8733.

Hunter, A. Colin J., BA. Head Teacher, Tiree High School, since 1985; b. 26.9.47, Falkirk; m., June Sinclair Stark; 2 s.; 1 d. Educ. Falkirk High School; Stirling

University. Entered teaching, 1972; Teacher, Falkirk High School and Forres Academy; Principal Teacher of Biology, Whitfield High School, Dundee; Depute Head Teacher, Auchtercairn Secondary School, Gairloch. Recreations: gardening; golf; walking. Address: (h.) Cornaigmore Schoolhouse, Isle of Tiree, Argyll, PA77 6XA; T.-01879 220556.

Hunter, Allison Carnegie. Director of Organisation, Scottish National Party, since 1990; b. 8.1.42, Glasgow; m., Ian James Hunter; 1 s.; 2 d. Educ. Pollokshields Senior Secondary School; Jordanhill College of Education. Schoolteacher, 1961-65 and 1971-90. Recreations: cooking; reading; music. Address: (h.) 4 Tantallon Road, Shawlands, Glasgow, G41 3BX; T.-0141-649 1093.

Hunter, Archibald Sinclair, CA. Senior Partner, Scotland, KPMG Peat Marwick (and UK Board Member); b. 20.8.43, Glasgow; m., Pat; 2 s.; 1 d. Educ. Queen's Park School, Glasgow. Trained with Mackie & Clark, CA, Glasgow; qualified as CA, 1966; joined Thomson McLintock, 1966; Partner, 1974. Vice President, Institute of Chartered Accountants of Scotland; Member, Executive, Scottish Council Development and Industry. Recreations: golf; swimming; walking. Address: (b.) 24 Blythswood Square, Glasgow, G2 4QS; T.-0141-226 5511.

Hunter, Colin M., MB, ChB, DRCOG, FRCGP. Hon. Treasurer, Scottish Council, Royal College of General Practitioners, since 1994; Hon. Secretary, N.E. Scotland Faculty, RCGP, since 1989; Hon. Member, Association of Managers in General Practice (Scotland), since 1992; b. 28.4.58, Stirling. Educ. High School of Stirling; Aberdeen University. Principal in general practice, Skene Medical Group, 1986; Teaching Fellow, Aberdeen University, 1988; first member, RCGP in Scotland, to attain Fellowship of Royal College of Assessment, 1993. Recreations: hill-walking; singing. Address: The Langdales, 1 Craigston Gardens, Westhill, Aberdeen, AB32 6NL; T.-01224 742594.

Hunter, Professor Geoffrey, BSc, PhD, CChem, FRSC. Professor of Chemistry, Dundee University, since 1993, and Head, Department of Chemistry, since 1990; b. 28.6.43, Co. Durham; m., Jacqueline; 1 d. Educ. Stanley Grammar School; Sheffield University; Newcastle-upon-Tyne University. Research Fellow, Simon Fraser University, Vancouver, 1967; Scientific Officer, Atomic Energy Research Establishment, Harwell, 1968; Lecturer, Dundee University, 1969, Senior Lecturer, 1988; Gast Professor, University of Vienna, 1994. Publications: author/co-author of more than 80 publications. Recreation: sailing. Address: (b.) Chemistry Department, Dundee University, Dundee, DD1 4HN.

Hunter, George Alexander, OBE (1980), CStJ. Secretary, Commonwealth Games Council for Scotland, since 1978; Founder Governor, Scottish Sports Aid Foundation, since 1980; Member, Edinburgh District Council, since 1992; b. 24.2.26, Edinburgh; m., Eileen Elizabeth. Educ. George Watson's College, Edinburgh. Served with Cameronians, seconded to 17th Dogara Regiment, Indian Army, 1944-47 (Captain); Lawson Donaldson Seeds Ltd., 1942-82 (Director, 15 years); Secretary, Scottish Amateur Rowing Association, 1948-78 (President, 1978-84); Adviser, Sports Aid Foundation since 1979; Treasurer, Commonwealth Games Council for Scotland, 1962-78; Member, Scottish Sports Council, 1976-84 (Chairman, Games and Sports Committee, 1976-84); Chairman, Scottish Standing Conference for Sport, 1977-84. Address: (h.) 139 Old Dalkeith Road, Edinburgh; T.-031-664 1070.

Hunter, James, MA (Hons), PhD. Writer, Historian, Journalist and Broadcaster; Member, Board, Highlands and Islands Enterprise; Member, North West Regional Board, Scottish Natural Heritage; b. 22.5.48, Duror, Argyll; m.,

Evelyn; 1 s.; 1 d. Educ. Oban High School; Aberdeen University; Edinburgh University. Former Director, Scottish Crofters Union. Publications: The Making of the Crofting Community, 1976; Skye: The Island, 1986; The Claim of Crofting, 1991; Scottish Highlanders: A People and their Place, 1992; A Dance Called America: The Scottish Highlands, the United States and Canada, 1994. Address: (b.) 22 Borve, Portree, Isle of Skye, IV51 9PE; T.-01470 532421.

Hunter, Hon. Lord (John Oswald Mair Hunter), VRD. Senator of the College of Justice in Scotland, 1961-86; b. 21.2.13. Chairman, Scottish Law Commission, 1971-81.

Hunter, John Andrew Adam, BSc, MB, ChB, FRCPE. Consultant Physician in Rehabilitation Medicine, Edinburgh Healthcare NHS Trust, since 1976; part-time Senior Lecturer in Rehabilitation Studies, Edinburgh University, since 1977 (Head, Rehabilitation Studies Unit, 1988-90); b. 20.10.43, Perth; m., Hazel Watson; 1 s.; 1 d. Educ. Bell Baxter High School, Cupar; St. Andrews University. House Officer in Medicine and Orthopaedic Surgery, 1968-69; Lecturer in Biochemistry, Rheumatism Research Centre, Manchester University, 1969-72; Senior House Officer in Medicine, University Hospitals of South Manchester, 1972-74; Lecturer in Rheumatology, Manchester Royal Infirmary and Manchester University, 1974-76; Chairman, Disability and Continuing Healthcare Committee, Chief Scientist's Office, Scottish Home and Health Department; Member, Disability Living Allowance Advisory Board, Department of Social Security; Temporary Advisor to WHO on Rehabilitation. Recreations: singing; deep sea fishing. Address: (h.) 37 Gilmour Road, Edinburgh, EH16 5NS; T.-0131-667 5333.

Hunter, Professor John Angus Alexander, BA, MD, FRCPEdin. Grant Professor of Dermatology, Edinburgh University, since 1981; b. 16.6.39, Edinburgh; m., Ruth Mary Farrow; 1 s.; 2 d. Educ. Loretto School; Pembroke College, Cambridge; Edinburgh University. Research Fellow, Institute of Dermatology, London, 1967; Registrar, Department of Dermatology, Edinburgh Royal Infirmary, 1968-70; Exchange Research Fellow, Department of Dermatology, Minnesota University, 1968; Lecturer, Department of Dermatology, Edinburgh University, 1970-74; Consultant Dermatologist, Lothian Health Board, 1974-80; Member: Executive Committee of Investigative Group, British Association of Dermatologists, 1974-76; Executive Committee, British Association of Dermatologists, 1977-79; SEC, Scottish Dermatological Society, 1980-82; Specialist Advisory Committee, (Dermatology), Joint Committee on Higher Medical Training, 1980-87 (Chairman, 1986-90); Medical Appeal Tribunal, since 1982; Scottish Committee for Hospital Medical Services, 1983-85; President, Section of Dermatology, Royal Society of Medicine, 1993-94; President, Scottish Dermatological Society, 1994-97. Publications: Common Diseases of the Skin (Co-Editor); Clinical Dermatology (Co-Editor). Recreations: music; gardening; tropical fish; golf. Address: (h.) Leewood, Rosslyn Castle, Roslin, Midlothian, EH25 9PZ; T.-0131-440 2181.

Hunter, Sir Laurence Colvin, Kt, MA, DPhil, FRSE. Professor of Applied Economics, Glasgow University, since 1970; b. 8.8.34, Glasgow; m., Evelyn Margaret Green; 3 s.; 1 d. Educ. Hillhead High School, Glasgow; Glasgow University; University College, Oxford. Assistant Lecturer, Manchester University, 1958-59; 2nd Lt., RAEC, 1959-61; Walgreen Postdoctoral Fellow, University of Chicago, 1961-62; joined Glasgow University as Lecturer, 1962; Vice-Principal, 1982-86; Director of External Relations, 1987-90. Council Member, ACAS, 1974-86; Chairman, Police Negotiating Board, since 1986; Council Member, Economic and Social Research Council, 1989-92; Editor, Scottish Journal of Political Economy, since 1966; President, Scottish Economic Society, since 1993.

Recreations: golf; painting; curling. Address: (h.) 23 Boclair Road, Bearsden, Glasgow, G61 2AF; T.-0141-942 0793.

Hunter, Mollie. Writer; Past Chairman, Society of Authors in Scotland; b. 30.6.22, Longniddry; m., Thomas McIlwraith; 2 s. Educ. Preston Lodge School. Freelance Journalist, until 1960; Writer of various types of fiction (fantasy, historical novels, "realism") for children of varying age groups; 30 titles published, including Talent Is Not Enough, on the craft of writing for children; travelled extensively (Australia, New Zealand, Canada, USA); Lecturer on writing for children; Writer-in-Residence, Dalhousie University, Halifax, Canada, on two occasions; awarded Arbuthnot Lectureship, 1975, and Carnegie Medal, 1975. Recreations: reading; gardening; music. Address: Rose Cottage, 7 Mary Ann Court, Inverness IV3 5BZ; T.-01463 713914.

Hunter, Russell. Actor; b. 18.2.25, Glasgow. Former shipyard worker; began acting as an amateur; made professional debut with Glasgow Unity Theatre, 1947; appeared in repertory with Edinburgh Gateway, Edinburgh Traverse and Glasgow Citizens'; acted with the RSC, Bristol Old Vic and at the Old Vic, London; played title role in The Servant o' Twa Maisters, 1965, opening production of Edinburgh Civic Theatre Company; played The Pope in Galileo, also at Royal Lyceum; played The Gravedigger in Hamlet, Assembly Hall, Edinburgh Festival; took title role in Cocky, one-man play, 1969; played Jock, solo play, 1972.

Hunter, William, MA. Columnist, The Herald; b. 16.8.31, Paisley; m., Mo (deceased); 1 s.; 1 d. Educ. Paisley Grammar School; Glasgow University. Publications: The Saints; Bell the Cage!; Dear Happy Ghosts. Recreation: weeding. Address: (h.) 233 Fenwick Road, Glasgow; T.-0141-638 1323.

Hunter, William Hill, CBE, CA, JP, DL. Partner, McLay, McAlister & McGibbon, CA, 1946-91, Consultant, since 1991; Director, J. & G. Grant, Glenfarclas Distillery, 1966-92; b. 5.11.16, Cumnock; m., Kathleen Cole; 2 s. Educ. Cumnock Academy. Enlisted as private, RASC, 1940; commissioned Royal Artillery, 1941; Staff Captain, Middle East, 1944-46; Director: Abbey National Building Society (Scottish Advisory Board), 1966-86, City of Glasgow Friendly Society, 1966-88 (President, 1980-88); Member, CBI Scottish Council, 1978-84; Member, Institute of Directors West of Scotland Committee, 1980-91; President, Renfrew West and Inverclyde Conservative and Unionist Association, since 1972; President, Scottish Young Unionist Association, 1958-60; President, Scottish Unionist Association, 1964-65; contested (Unionist), South Ayrshire, 1959 and 1964; Hon. Treasurer, Quarrier's Homes, 1972-94; Hon. Financial Advisor, Erskine Hospital, since 1980; Session Clerk, Kilmacolm Old Kirk, 1972-77; Chairman, Salvation Army Advisory Board in Strathclyde, 1982-93; Chairman, Salvation Army Housing Association Scotland Ltd., 1986-91; admitted to Distinguished Order of Auxiliary Service of Salvation Army, 1981; Deacon Convener, Trades House of Glasgow, 1986-87; Honorary Vice President, Royal Scottish Agricultural Benevolent Institution, since 1994; Honorary President, Friends of Glasgow Botanic Gardens, since 1994. Recreations: gardening; golf; swimming; music. Address: (h.) Armitage, Kilmacolm, PA13 4PH; T.-0150587 2444.

Hunter Blair, Francis, JP. Hill Farmer; Vice-President and Past Chairman, Galloway Cattle Society of Great Britain and Ireland; b. 29.10.30, Lincoln; m., Joyce Adeline Mary Graham; 4 s.; 1 d. Educ. Royal Naval College, Dartmouth; West of Scotland Agricultural College. President, Stewartry Branch, National Farmers' Union of Scotland, 1968-69; Council Member, NFU of Scotland, 1969-70; Vice President, Royal Highland and Agricultural Society of

Scotland, 1987; several periods of office as Secretary and President, local agricultural shows; Past Chairman, Carsphairn Community Council; Elder and Session Clerk, Carsphairn Kirk. Recreations: country pursuits; reading. Address: Marbrack, Carsphairn, Castle Douglas, Stewartry of Kirkcudbright; T.-Carsphairn 207.

Hunter Blair, James, DL. Landowner and Forester; b. 18.3.26, Ayr. Educ. Eton; Oxford. Scots Guards, 1944-48; University, 1948-50; merchant bank, London, 1951-53; managed family estate, since 1953. Past President, Royal Scottish Forestry Society; former Vice-President, Royal Highland Society; Past Chairman, Historic Houses Association for Scotland; Trustee, National Galleries of Scotland. Recreations: shooting; fishing; going to the opera. Address: Blairquhan, Maybole, Ayrshire; T.-Straiton 239.

Huntly, 13th Marquess of (Granville Charles Gomer Gordon). Premier Marquess of Scotland; Chief, House of Gordon; b. 4.2.44; m.; 1 d.; 1 s., 2 d. by pr. m. Address: Aboyne Castle, Aberdeenshire, AB34 5JP.

Hurford, Professor James Raymond, BA, PhD. Professor of General Linguistics, Edinburgh University, since 1979; b. 16.7.41, Reading; m., Sue Ann Davis; 2 d. Educ. Exeter School; St. John's College, Cambridge; University College, London. Assistant Professor, Department of English, University of California, Davis, 1968-71; Lecturer, then Senior Lecturer, Department of Linguistics, Lancaster University, 1972-79. Publications: Language and Number: the emergence of a cognitive system; Semantics: a coursebook (Co-author); The Linguistic Theory of Numerals; Grammar: a student's guide. Address: (b.) Edinburgh University, Edinburgh, EH8 9YL.

Hurman, David Charles, MBChB, DTM&H, DMRT, FRCR, HonMD (Manitoba). Consultant in Radiotherapy and Oncology, Aberdeen Royal Hospitals NHS Trust (Head of Department, since 1991); Visiting Consultant, Shetland Health Board, since 1988; Clinical Senior Lecturer, Aberdeen University, since 1988; b. 9.2.52, London; m., Dr. Dorothy Elizabeth McMurray; 1 s.; 1 d. Educ. Ashford County Grammar School; Liverpool University. Pre-registration and junior medical posts, Southport General Infirmary and Christiana Hartley Maternity Hospital, 1975-77; Medical Officer, Trans-Borneo Expedition, 1978; Mersey Regional Centre for Radiotherapy and Oncology, Clatterbridge Hospital, Bebington, 1979-86; Clinical Research Fellow, Cross Cancer Institute and University of Alberta, 1986-87; Senior Medical Officer, International Scientific Support Trust Expedition to Java and Kalimantan, 1994. Recreations: foreign travel; football; cricket; hills and mountains; rock music. Address: (h.) 85 Cairnfield Place, Aberdeen, AB2 4LX; T.-01224 638411.

Hurst, Professor Andrew, CGeol, FGS. Shell Professor of Production Geoscience, Aberdeen University, since 1992; Director, PSTI Production Geoscience Unit, since 1992; b. 5.9.53, Stoke-on-Trent; m., Liv Christiansen; 1 s.; 1 d. Educ. Cheadle Grammar School; Aberdeen University; Reading University. Geologist, Norway, 1981-82; Senior Geologist, Norway, 1982-90; Senior Geologist, Unocal UK, 1990-91; Advising Geologist, Unocal UK, 1991-92. Executive Editor, Sedimentary Geology; William Smith Fund Award, Geological Society of London, 1993; Chief Editor, Petroleum Geoscience; editor of two books. Recreations: squash; music; natural history. Address: (b.) Department of Geology and Petroleum Geology, King's College, Aberdeen, AB9 2UE; T.-01224 273713.

Hutcheon, Rev. Douglas John. Superintendent, Baptist Union of Scotland, since 1993; b. 27.7.38, Buckie; m., Helen Smith; 2 s.; 2 d. Educ. Buckie High School; Milnes High School, Fochabers; Bible Training Institute. Bank of Scotland, 1953-57; Minister of the Baptist Church, since 1962. Recreations: reading; hill-walking; watching (occasionally playing) football; music. Address: (b.) 14 Aytoun Road, Glasgow, G41 5RT; T.-0141-423 6169.

Hutcheson, John Mitchell. Executive Officer, Royal Scottish Pipe Band Association, since 1990; b. 25.5.31, Glasgow. Educ. Allan Glen's School, Glasgow. Director, Hugh Baird & Sons Ltd., 1976-85; Chairman, Institute of Brewing (Scotland), 1986-88. Recreations: golf; cricket; reading; philately. Address: (h.) 29 Victoria Park Drive North, Glasgow, G14 9NL; T.-0141-959 3501.

Hutcheson, Rev. Norman McKenzie, MA, BD. Minister, Dalbeattie and Urr Parish Churches; b. 11.10.48, Leven; m., Elizabeth; 2 d. Educ. Hillhead High School, Glasgow. Minister, St. Andrews, Kirkcaldy, 1973-88. Vice-Convener, Committee on Education, Church of Scotland. Recreations: photography; travel; reading. Address: (h.) 36 Mill Street, Dalbeattiew, DG5 4HE; T.-01556 610029.

Hutchinson, Peter, PhD, FIFM. Assistant Secretary, North Atlantic Salmon Conservation Organization, since 1986; b. 26.5.56, Glasgow; m., Jane MacKellaig; 1 s.; 1 d. Educ. Queen Elizabeth's Grammar School, Blackburn; Edinburgh University. Project Co-ordinator, Surface Water Acidification; Research Biologist: Institute of Terrestrial Ecology, Edinburgh University; Member, Consular Corps in Edinburgh and Leith, since 1991. Recreations: golf; squash; rugby union; angling. Address: (h.) 57 Craiglea Drive, Morningside, Edinburgh.

Hutchison, David, MA, MLitt. Senior Lecturer in Communication Studies, Glasgow Caledonian University, since 1975; b. 24.9.44, West Kilbride; m., Pauleen Frew; 2 d. Educ. Ardrossan Academy; Glasgow University. Tutor/Organiser, WEA (West of Scotland), 1966-69; Teacher, Reid Kerr College, Paisley, 1969-71; Lecturer in Communication Studies, Glasgow College of Technology, 1971-75; Member, West Kilbride District Council, 1970-75 (Chairman, 1972-75); Governor, Scottish Film Council, 1987-95; Member, General Advisory Council, BBC, since 1988; author of play, Deadline, Pitlochry Festival Theatre, 1980. Publications: The Modern Scottish Theatre, 1977; Headlines: the Media in Scotland (Editor), 1978; various articles/chapters. Recreations: walking; swimming; the arts. Address: (b.) Department of Language and Media, Caledonian University, Cowcaddens Road, Glasgow, G4 0BA; T.-0141-331 3255.

Hutchison, Ian Somerville, OBE, JP. Chairman, Eastwood District Licensing Board; Member, Eastwood District Council (Chairman of Planning); Vice Chairman, Scottish National Housing & Town Planning Council; Member, Scottish Valuation Advisory Council, 1982-86; Member, Historic Buildings Council for Scotland, since 1983; Member, Glasgow West Conservation Trust; Managing Director, Timbertection Ltd., since 1973; b. 10.4.28, Glasgow; m., Aileen Wallace; 2 s.; 2 d. Educ. Hutchesons' Boys' Grammar School. Elected to First (Eastwood) District Council, 1967, Renfrew County Council, 1970, Eastwood District Council, 1974; Provost, Eastwood, 1974-80; Delegate, COSLA, since 1975 (Vice President, COSLA, 1979-82); Vice Chairman, Planning Exchange; Member, Renfrewshire Valuation Appeals Committee; Governor, The Queen's College, Glasgow, since 1973 (Chairman of Governors, 1980-88); Member, Management Committee, Renfrewshire Enterprise. Recreations: gardening; fishing. Address: (h.) 39 Hazelwood Avenue, Newton Mearns, Glasgow, G77 5QT; T.-0141-639 2186.

Hutchison, Sir Peter Craft, CBE, Bt, BA. Chairman, Hutchison & Craft Ltd., Insurance Brokers, and associated/subsidiary companies; Chairman, Forestry Commission, since 1994; b. 5.6.35, London; m., Virginia Colville; 1 s. Educ. Eton; Magdalene College, Cambridge. National Service, Royal Scots Greys (2nd Lt.); Northern Assurance Co. (London); Director of various companies;

Past Chairman, Ailsa Shipbuilding Co. Ltd.; Director, Stakis plc, 1979-91; Board Member, Scottish Tourist Board, 1981-87; Vice Chairman, British Waterways Board, since 1988; Chairman, Board of Trustees, Royal Botanic Garden, Edinburgh, 1985-94; Chairman, Loch Lomond and Trossachs Working Party, 1991-93; Deacon, Incorporation of Hammermen of Glasgow, 1984-85. Recreations: plant hunting; gardening; calligraphy. Address: (h.) Milton House, Milton, by Dumbarton, G82 2TU; T.-Dumbarton 61609.

Hutton, Alasdair Henry, OBE, TD. Managing Consultant, Coutts Career Consultants, Aberdeen, since 1995; writer and broadcaster; European political consultant; Chairman, Calchou Electronics; Chairman, Disease Prevention Organisation; Member, Roxburgh District Advisory Committee, Scottish Borders Enterprise; former Director, Scottish Agricultural College; former Chairman, Crime Concern Scotland; b. 19.5.40, London; m., Deirdre Mary Cassels (see Deirdre Mary Hutton); 2 s. Educ. Dollar Academy; Brisbane State High School. Trainee technician, Radio 4BH Brisbane, 1956; Clemenger Advertising, Melbourne, 1957-59; Journalist, The Age, Melbourne, 1959-61, Aberdeen Journals, 1962-64; Broadcaster, BBC, 1964-79; Member, European Parliament, 1979-89. Member, Queen's Bodyguard for Scotland (Royal Company of Archers); Former Member, 15th (Scottish Volunteer) Bn., The Parachute Regiment; Vice-President, Kelso Branch, Royal British Legion; Trustee, Community Service Volunteers; Vice-Chairman, John Buchan Society; Fellow, Industry and Parliament Trust; Honorary President, Scottish Association of CB Clubs; Patron, Kelso Laddies' Association; Member, Ancient Order of Mosstroopers; Honorary Chairman, Hawick Conservative Club; Member, CVHQ; Narrator, Edinburgh Military Tattoo, since 1992; Member, International Relations Committee, Law Society of Scotland, since1991; Member, Church and Nation Committee, Church of Scotland, since 1992; Member, Board, UK 2000 Scotland, since 1991. Address: (b.) Rosebank, Shedden Park Road, Kelso, TD5 7PX; T.-01573 224369.

Hutton, Deirdre Mary. Chairman, Scottish Consumer Council, since 1991; Member, National Consumer Council, since 1991; Chairman, Rural Forum, since 1992; Member, Board, Enterprise Music Scotland, since 1992 (formerly Founder Chairman); Member, Parole Board for Scotland, since 1993; Deputy Chairman, Personal Investment Authority Ombudsman Bureau, since 1995; Member, Personal Investment Authority Consumer Panel, since 1994; b. 15.3.49, Haddington; m., Alasdair Hutton (qv); 2 s. Educ. Sherborne School for Girls; secretarial college. Research Assistant, Glasgow Chamber of Commerce, 1976-81; seconded to Scotland is British Campaign and Scotland Says No Campaign during devolution referendum, 1979; Secretary, Kelso Music Society. Recreations: music; reading. Address: (h.) Rosebank, Shedden Park Road, Kelso, TD5 7PX; T.-01573 224368.

Hutton, James Thomas, ARCM. Composer; Visiting Teacher of Music, since 1960; b. 12.5.23, Glasgow; m., Anne Jamieson Bowes; 1 s. Educ. Provanside Secondary School; Glasgow University; Royal Scottish Academy of Music. Worked for Renfrewshire Education Authority, 1960-64, Lanarkshire Education Authority, since 1964; entirely self-taught Composer of orchestral music; works include two symphonies, two concert-overtures, piano concerto, chamber music, and works for brass band, solo piano and organ; has also composed and arranged music for jazz orchestras and groups. Recreation: playing jazz piano. Address: (h.) 88 Warwick, East Kilbride; T.-East Kilbride 25895.

I

Ibbett, Professor Roland Norman, BSc, MSc, PhD, FRSE, CEng, FBCS, FRSA. Professor of Computer Science, Edinburgh University, since 1985, Vice-Principal, since 1994; b. 21.6.41, Burton upon Trent; m., Janet; 3 s.; 3 d. Educ. Burton upon Trent Grammar School. Lecturer in Computer Science, Manchester University, 1967-75, Senior Lecturer, 1975-82, Reader, 1982-85. Chairman, Conference of Professors and Heads of Computing, 1993-95. Publications: two books; 40 papers. Recreations: gardening; DIY; listening to music. Address: (b.) Department of Computer Science, Edinburgh University, King's Buildings, Edinburgh, EH9 3JZ; T.-0131-650 5119.

Idiens, Dale, BA, DipEd. Depute Director (Collections) and Keeper, Department of History and Applied Art, National Museums of Scotland; b. 13.5.42, Prestatyn. Educ. Wycombe High School, High Wycombe; Leicester University. Royal Scottish Museum, Department of Art and Archaeology: Assistant Keeper in Charge of Ethnography, 1964, Deputy Keeper, 1979, Keeper, 1983. Address: (b.) Royal Museum of Scotland, Chambers Street, Edinburgh; T.-0131-225 7534.

Ingham, Keith Philip Dudley, BA (Hons), MA. Senior Lecturer, Department of Economics, Strathclyde University, since 1989; International Student Officer, Strathclyde Business School, since 1985; Member, Scottish Arts Council, 1990-93; b. 23.4.45, Grimsby. Educ. Wintringham Boys' Grammar School, Grimsby; University of East Anglia. Teaching Assistant, Carleton University, Ottawa; Lecturer, Department of Economics, Strathclyde University; Senior Lecturer, Department of Economics, Lund University, Sweden. Publications include: Understanding the Scottish Economy. Recreations: skiing; trying to keep fit; learning to like opera. Address: (b.) Department of Economics, Strathclyde University, Glasgow, G4 0LN; T.-0141-552 4400.

Ingle, Professor Stephen James, BA, MA (Econ), DipEd, PhD. Professor of Politics, Stirling University; b. 6.11.40, Ripon; m., Margaret Anne; 2 s.; 1 d. Educ. The Roan School, London; Sheffield University; Wellington University, NZ. Lecturer in Politics, Hull University, 1967-80; Senior Lecturer, 1980-91; Head of Department, 1985-90. Secretary, Political Studies Association, 1988-89. Publications: Socialist Thought in Imaginative Literature, 1979; Parliament and Health Policy, 1981; British Party System, 1987, 1989; George Orwell: a political life, 1993. Recreations: reading; music; hill-walking. Address: (b.) Department of Politics, Stirling University, Stirling, FK9 4LA; T.-01786 467593.

Inglis, George Finlay, CA. Director of Finance and Administration, Scottish Tourist Board, since 1988; b. 2.1.46, Edinburgh; m., Catherine; 1 s.; 1 d. Educ. Royal High School, Edinburgh. Recreations: sport; literature; good wine; good food. Address: (h.) 67 Hillpark Avenue, Edinburgh, EH4 7AL; T.-0131-336 2338.

Inglis, Hamish. Chairman, Scottish Equitable. Address: (b.) 28 St. Andrew Square, Edinburgh, EH2 1YF.

Inglis, Professor James Alistair Macfarlane, CBE (1984), MA, LLB. Professor of Conveyancing, Glasgow University, 1979-93; Professor of Professional Legal Practice, Glasgow University, 1984-93; Consultant, McClure, Naismith, Anderson & Gardiner, Solicitors, Glasgow (Partner, 1956-93); Dean, Royal Faculty of Procurators in Glasgow, 1989-92; b. 24.12.28, Kilmarnock; m., Mary Elizabeth Howie; 2 s.; 3 d. Educ. Kilmarnock Academy; Fettes College; St. Andrews University; Glasgow University. Qualified as Solicitor, 1952; Member: Board of Management, Victoria and Leverndale Hospitals, 1964-74, Greater Glasgow Health Board, 1975-83; President, Rent Assessment Panel for Scotland, 1976-87; Chairman, Glasgow Hospitals Auxiliary Association, since 1985; Convener, Ad Hoc Committee, Church of Scotland, into Legal Services of Church, 1978-79; Session Clerk, Caldwell Parish Church, since 1963; General Trustee, Church of Scotland, since 1993. Address: (h.) Crioch, Uplawmoor, Glasgow; T.-Uplawmoor 850315.

Inglis, John, RSW, FSA(Scot), DA. Painter and Lecturer; b. 27.7.53, Glasgow; m., Heather; 2 s.; 2 d. Educ. Hillhead High School; Gray's School of Art. Travelling scholarships to Italy, 1976; Member, Dundee Group, 1979-84; one-man exhibitions: Aberdeen, 1976 and 1977; Glasgow, 1980, Skipton, 1981, Aberdeen Hospitals, 1989, Alloa Museum, 1989; Smith Art Gallery, Stirling, 1993; Scottish Arts Council Award, 1981; RSA Keith Prize, 1975; SAC Bursary, 1982; RSA Meyer Oppenheim Prize, 1982; RSW EIS Award, 1987; SAC Grant, 1988; May Marshall Brown Award, 1994. Address: (h.) 21 Hillview Road, Larbert, Stirlingshire; T.-01324 558891.

Ingram, Adam. MP (Labour), East Kilbride, since 1987; b. 1.2.47, Glasgow; m., Maureen McMahon. Educ. Cranhill Senior Secondary School. Programmer/analyst, 1965-1970; systems analyst, 1970-77; full-time union official, 1977-87; Councillor, East Kilbride District Council, 1980-87 (Leader of the Council, 1984-87); PPS to Neil Kinnock, Leader of the Opposition, 1988-92; Labour Opposition Spokesperson on Social Security, since 1993; JP. Recreations: fishing; cooking; reading. Address: (b.) House of Commons, London, SW1A 0AA; T.-0171-219 4093.

Ingram, Adam Hamilton, BA (Hons). Executive Vice-Convener Organisation, Scottish National Party, since 1994; b. 1.5.51, Kilmarnock; m., Gerry; 3 s.; 1 d. Educ. Kilmarnock Academy; Paisley College. Senior Economic Assistant, MSC, Edinburgh, 1985-86; Researcher/part-time Lecturer, Paisley College, 1987-88; Head of Research, Development Options Ltd., 1989; Consultant, EES Consultants Ltd., 1990-95; self-employed economic consultant, since 1995. Recreations: politics; golf; supporting Kilmarnock F.C. Address: (h.) 3 Woodside Avenue, Kilmarnock, KA1 1TU; T.-01563 541690.

Ingram, Professor David Stanley, BSc, PhD, MA, ScD, FLS, FIBiol, FRSE. Regius Keeper (Director), Royal Botanic Garden, Edinburgh, since 1990; Hon. Professor, Edinburgh University, since 1991; Visiting Professor, Glasgow University, since 1991; Honorary Professor of Horticulture, Royal Horticultural Society, since 1995; b. 10.10.41, Birmingham; m., Alison W.; 2 s. Educ. Yardley Grammar School, Birmingham; Hull University; Cambridge University. Research Fellow, Glasgow University, 1966-68, Cambridge University, 1968-69; Senior Scientific Officer, Unit of Developmental Botany, Cambridge, 1969-74; Lecturer, then Reader in Plant Pathology, Botany Department, Cambridge University, 1974-90; Fellow (also Tutor, Dean and Director of Studies in Biology), Downing College, Cambridge, 1974-90; author of several books and many papers in learned journals; Editor, Annals of Botany. Recreations: literature; film; theatre; music; travel. Address: (b.) Royal Botanic Garden, Edinburgh, EH3 5LR; T.-0131-552 7171.

Ingram, Greig Webster, MA. Rector, High School of Stirling, since 1994; b. 20.11.47, Burnhervie; m., Patricia Annette Miller. Educ. Mackie Academy, Stonehaven; Aberdeen University; Aberdeen College of Education. Teacher of Modern Studies and History, 1970-74; Principal Teacher of Modern Studies, St. Margaret Mary's Secondary, Glasgow, 1974-84; Assistant Head Teacher, Eastbank Academy, Glasgow, 1984-89, Depute Head Teacher, 1989-94. Recreations: reading; music; travel; running; soccer.

Address: (b.) Ogilvie Road, Stirling, FK8 2PA; T.-01786 472451.

Ingram, Hugh Albert Pugh, BA (Cantab), PhD (Dunelm). Senior Lecturer (formerly Lecturer) in Botany (Ecology), Dundee University, since 1966; Trustee, National Museums of Scotland, 1987-94; Editor, Journal of Applied Ecology, since 1991; b. 29.4.37, Rugby; m., Dr. Ruth Hunter; 1 s.; 1 d. Educ. Lawrence Sheriff School, Rugby; Rugby School; Emmanuel College, Cambridge; Hatfield College, Durham. Demonstrator in Botany, University College of North Wales, Bangor, 1963-64; Staff Tutor in Natural Science, Department of Extra-Mural Studies, Bristol University, 1964-65; Member, UK Committee, International Peat Society; Member, Executive Committee, Scottish Field Studies Association, since 1989; Member, Museums and Galleries Commission Working Party on the non-national museums of Scotland, 1984-86; Vice-Chairman (Conservation and Science), Scottish Wildlife Trust, 1982-87. Recreations: music (clarinet, piano); literature; rural history; hill-walking. Address: Johnstonfield, Dunbog, Cupar, Fife, KY14 6JG.

Ingram, Professor Malcolm David, BSc, PhD, DSc, CChem, FRSC. Professor of Chemistry, Aberdeen University, since 1993; b. 18.1.39, Wallasey; m., Lorna Hardman; 1 s.; 1 d. Educ. Oldershaw Grammar School; Liverpool University. Aberdeen University: Lecturer in Physical Chemistry, 1965-78, Senior Lecturer in Chemistry, 1978-90, Reader, 1990-93. Chairman, Aberdeen and North of Scotland Section, Royal Society of Chemistry, 1990-93. Publications: 125 in scientific journals. Recreations: gardening; foreign travel. Address: (b.) Department of Chemistry, Aberdeen University, Aberdeen, AB9 2UE; T.-01224 272905.

Innes, James, BSc, CEng, MICE, FIHT. Director of Roads and Chief Road Engineer, Scottish Office Industry Department, since 1995; Visiting Professor of Civil Engineering, Strathclyde University, since 1992; b. 7.8.44, Helmsdale; m., June Pearson; 1 s.; 1 d. Educ. Woodside Secondary School, Glasgow; Strathclyde University. Lanark County Council, 1966-67; Inverness County Council, 1967-73; Scottish Development Department, 1973-84; Department of Transport (Superintending Engineer), 1984-85; Assistant Chief Road Engineer, Scottish Office Industry Department, 1985-88; Deputy Chief Road Engineer, Scottish Office Industry Department, 1988-95. Recreation: golf. Address: (b.) Room 3/102, New St. Andrews House, Edinburgh, EH1 3SZ; T.-0131-244 5178.

Innes, Professor John, BCom, PhD, CA, FCMA. Professor of Accountancy, Dundee University, since 1991; b. 11.7.50, Edinburgh; m., Ina. Educ. George Watson's College; Edinburgh University. Student accountant and staff auditor, KPMG, 1972-75; International Operational Auditor, Uniroyal Inc., 1975-78; Lecturer and Senior Lecturer in Accounting, Edinburgh University, 1978-91. Canon Foundation Visiting Research Fellow, 1992-93; SHEFC Lead Assessor in Accounting, 1995-96. Recreations: golf; squash; tennis. Address: (b.) Department of Accountancy & Business Finance, Dundee University, Dundee, DD1 4HN; T.-01382 344197.

Innes, Norman Lindsay, OBE, BSc, PhD, DSc, FIBiol, FIHort, FRSE. Agricultural Research Consultant; Deputy Director, Scottish Crop Research Institute, 1986-94 (Head, Plant Breeding Division, 1984-89); b. 3.5.34, Kirriemuir; m., Marjory Niven Farquhar; 1 s.; 1 d. Educ. Websters High School, Kirriemuir; Aberdeen University; Cambridge University. Senior Cotton Breeder: Sudan, 1958-66, Uganda, 1966-71; Head, Cotton Research Unit, Uganda, 1972; National Vegetable Research Station, Wellesbourne: Head, Plant Breeding Section, 1973-84, Deputy Director, 1977-84; Honorary Lecturer, then Honorary Professor,

Birmingham University, 1973-84; Governing Board Member, International Crops Research Institute for Semi-Arid Tropics, India, 1982-88; Honorary Professor, Dundee University, since 1988; Governing Board Member, International Potato Centre, Peru, since 1988, Chairman, 1991-95; Vice-President, Association of Applied Biologists, 1990-92, President, 1993-94; Chairman, British Association of Plant Breeders, 1982-84; Member, Oxfam Council of Trustees, 1982-85. Recreations: golf; photography; travel. Address: (b.) Scottish Crop Research Institute, Invergowrie, Dundee, DD2 5DA; T.-01382 562731.

Innes of Edingight, Sir Malcolm Rognvald, KCVO, MA, LLB, WS, FSA Scot, KStJ. Lord Lyon King of Arms, since 1981; Secretary to Order of the Thistle, since 1981; b. 25.5.38, Edinburgh; m., Joan Hay; 3 s. Educ. Edinburgh Academy; Edinburgh University. Carrick Pursuivant, 1958; Marchmont Herald, 1971; Lyon Clerk and Keeper of the Record, 1966; Member, Queen's Bodyguard for Scotland (Royal Company of Archers); President, Scottish Heraldry Society. Recreation: shooting. Address: (b.) Court of the Lord Lyon, HM New Register House, Edinburgh; T.-0131-556 7255.

Ireland, James Cecil Hardin. Trustee, Scottish Rugby Union, 1951-91 (President, 1950-51); b. 10.12.03, Glasgow; m., Margaret Stewart McLean. Educ. High School of Glasgow. Singer Manufacturing Co. Ltd.; William Younger & Co. Ltd.; War service, RNVR and Royal Marines, 1940-46; Dundee Manager, William Younger & Co. Ltd.; London Manager, Scottish & Newcastle Breweries (retired, 1968); rugby international, 1925-26-27; Scottish Rugby Union Committee, 1936; international Referee, 1938-39; Chairman, four Home Unions Tours Committee, 1946-51; Honorary Vice President, South Africa Rugby Board, 1964; President, Glasgow High School Club, 1964-65; Elder, St. Columba's Church of Scotland, London, 1960-68. Recreations: spectating at all sports; renewing friendships. Address: (h.) 10 Abbots View, Polmont, FK2 OQL; T.-Polmont 713400.

Ireland, Dr. Kenneth, OBE, DUniv, BL, FRSA, FTS. Consultant, Hanover Fine Arts (Edinburgh); b. 17.6.20, Edinburgh; m., Moira Lamb; 2 s. Educ. Edinburgh Academy; Edinburgh University. Law Apprentice, Steedman Ramage & Co., WS, Edinburgh, 1938-41; War service: Royal Artillery, L. Bdr., 1941-42, Intelligence Corps, WO II, 1942-46; Lt. (TA), 1948-52; General Manager: Park Theatre, Glasgow, 1946-49, Pitlochry Festival Theatre, 1951-52; Pitlochry Festival Society Ltd.: General Manager and Secretary, 1953-57, Festival Director and Secretary, 1957-83 (retired, 1984); Board Member, Scottish Tourist Board, 1966-69; Chairman, Tourist Association of Scotland, 1967-69; Deputy Chairman, Scottish Tourist Consultative Council, 1977-83; ESU Scotland Thyne Scholarship, 1970; Bill Heron Trophy, 1981 (first recipient for services to tourism). Recreations: foreign travel; drama; music; art; literature. Address: (h.) 10 Ravelston Rise, Edinburgh, EH4 3LH; T.-0131-346 2292.

Ireland, Kenny. Artistic Director, Royal Lyceum Theatre Company. Address: (b.) Grindlay Street, Edinburgh, EH3 9AX.

Ireland, Sheriff Ronald David, QC, HonLLD. Sheriff Principal, Grampian, Highland and Islands, 1988-93; b. 13.3.25, Edinburgh. Educ. George Watson's College, Edinburgh; Balliol College, Oxford (Scholar); Edinburgh University. Advocate, 1952; Clerk, Faculty of Advocates, 1957-58; Professor of Scots Law, Aberdeen University, 1958-71; QC, 1964; Dean, Faculty of Law, Aberdeen University, 1964-67; Chairman, Board of Management, Aberdeen General Hospitals, 1964-71; Sheriff, Lothian and Borders at Edinburgh, 1972-88; Director, Scottish Courts Administration, 1975-78. Address: (h.) 6A Greenhill Gardens, Edinburgh, EH10 4BW.

Irgens, Professor Christopher S., BEng (Hons), DipBS, MSc, MBCS, CEng. University of Paisley: Professor, Department of Mechanical and Manufacturing Engineering, since 1995; Dean, Faculty of Information, Social and Management Sciences, 1991-95; Professor, Department of Computing Science, 1991-95; Chairman, University Computer Integrated Manufacturing Group; Elected Member, IFIP WG5.7; Non-Executive Chairman, Ai Airliner Ltd.; b. 10.5.45, Bergen; m., Sophie Christine Tough; 2 d. Educ. Bergen Katedralskole; Liverpool University. CAD-CAM Systems Designer, Ferranti Ltd., Edinburgh, 1971-75; Systems Consultant, CSL, Edinburgh, 1975-76; Product Manager, EMMA AS, Bergen, 1976-77; Lecturer, then Senior Lecturer, Paisley College, 1979-91. Recreations: skiing; curling. Address: (b.) Department of Computing Science, Paisley University, High Street, Paisley, PA1 2BE; T.-0141-848 3304.

Irons, Lord Provost Norman MacFarlane, CBE, Hon.DLitt, CEng, MIMechE, MCIBSE, Hon. FRCSE, JP. Lord Provost and Lord Lieutenant of the City of Edinburgh, since 1992; Partner, Building Services Consulting Engineers, since 1993; b. 4.1.41, Glasgow; m., Anne Buckley; 1 s.; 1 d. Held various posts as Consulting Engineer; founded own practice, 1983. SNP Member, City of Edinburgh District Council, since 1976. Recreation: rugby football. Address: (h.) 141 Saughtonhall Drive, Edinburgh, EH12 5TS; T.-0131-337 6154.

Ironside, Leonard. Chairman, Grampian Initiative; Member, Grampian Regional Council, since 1982; Member, Board of Directors, Grampian Enterprise Ltd., since 1994; Chairman, Grampian Regional Labour Group; Patron, Grampian Special Olympics for Handicapped; Commonwealth Professional Wrestling Champion, since 1981; Director, Aberdeen Exhibition and Conference Centre; Director, International Downhole Drilling and Technology Centre;Director, Scottish Sub-Sea Technology Group; Director, Grampian Health Board Heart Disease Campaign; b. 16.2.50, Aberdeen. Educ. Hilton Academy, Aberdeen. Inspector, contributions agency, DHSS, since 1990. Won Commonwealth Professional Wrestling Championship at Middleweight, 1979; lost Championship, 1981; regained title, 1981; gained European Lightweight title, 1985, relinquished title, 1989. Recreations: yoga teacher; also plays tennis, squash, badminton; cycling. Address: (h.) 42 Hillside Terrace, Portlethen, Kincardineshire; T.-Aberdeen 780929.

Irvine, Andrew Robertson, MBE (1979), BSc, FRICS. Rugby Player; b. 16.9.51, Edinburgh; m., Audrey; 1 s.; 3 d. Educ. George Heriot's School, Edinburgh; Edinburgh University. Captained George Heriot's School, Scottish Schools, Heriots FP, Edinburgh, Scotland; holds record for most tries scored by a full back (10); made international debut against All Blacks, 1972; 51 Scottish caps.

Irvine, J. Alastair, BA. President, Scottish Provision Trade Association, 1993-94; Director, A. McLelland & Son Ltd., since 1992; Director, Caledonian Cheese Company, since 1995; Panel Member, SCOTVEC, 1991-94; b. 6.11.65, Kilmarnock. Educ. Strathallan School; Paisley University. Recreations: skiing; motorcycling; football; hill-walking; photography. Address: (b.) A. McLelland & Son Ltd., New Cheese Market, Townhead, Glasgow, G4; T.-0141-552 2962.

Irvine, Professor John Maxwell, BSc, MSc, PhD, FInstP, ChPhys, FRAS, FRSA, FRSE. Principal and Vice-Chancellor, Aberdeen University, since 1991; b. 28.2.39, Edinburgh; m., Grace Ritchie; 1 s. Educ. George Heriot's School; Edinburgh University; University of Michigan; Manchester University. English-Speaking Union Fellow, University of Michigan, 1961-62; Lecturer in Theoretical Physics, Manchester University, 1964 (Senior Lecturer, 1973, Reader, 1976, Professor, 1983); Dean of Science,

Manchester University, 1989. Research Associate, Cornell University, 1966-68; Head, Nuclear Theory Group, SERC Daresbury Laboratory, 1974-76. Member, Council, Institute of Physics, 1981-92 (Vice President, 1982-87); Member, Council, European Physical Society, 1989-92; Member, Executive Committee, SCDI, since 1992; Member, Scottish Economic Council, since 1993. Address: (b.) Principal's Office, Aberdeen University, Regent Walk, Aberdeen, AB9 1FX; T.-01224 272134.

Irvine, Joseph Andrew, BSc. Head Teacher, Brae High School, since 1988; b. 18.6.44, Lerwick; m., Ishbel; 2 s. Educ. Anderson Educational Institute, Lerwick; Aberdeen University. Teacher of Maths/Science, Lerwick Central School, 1967-68; Teacher of Maths, Assistant Principal Teacher, Principal Teacher, Anderson High School, 1968-84; Field Officer, Shetland Islands Council, 1984-88. Chairman, Northern Sports Development Trust. Recreations: sailing; photography. Address: (b.) Brae High School, Brae, Shetland, ZE2 0QG; T.-01806 522 370.

Irvine-Fortescue, James William, MA (Hons), CA, JP, DL, KLJ, FSA Scot. Commissioner of Income Tax, County of Kincardine, 1957-92; Chairman, Grampian Region Valuation Appeal Committee, 1975-90; b. 7.6.17, Wilmslow; m., Margaret Guise Yates; 3 s.; 1 d. Educ. Aberdeen Grammar School; Edinburgh Academy; Aberdeen University. War Service: Royal Army Pay Corps, 1940-46, service in India and Ceylon, 1942-46 (Major and Staff Paymaster); JP and Magistrate, Kincardineshire, 1957; Member, Kincardine County Council, 1952-73; Chairman, Lower Deeside District Council, 1964-73. President, Deeside Field Club, 1981-86; a Vice President, Royal Society for Asian Affairs, 1983-88; Past President, Auchinleck Boswell Society; Past Chairman, Aberdeen Music Festival. Recreations: family history research; foreign travel. Address: (h.) Kingcausie, Maryculter, Kincardineshire, AB1 0AR; T.-01224 732224.

Irving, Gordon, MA (Hons). Writer, Journalist and Broadcaster; b. 4.12.18, Annan; m., Elizabeth Dickie (deceased); 1 s. Educ. Dumfries Academy; Edinburgh University. Staff Journalist, Daily Record, Edinburgh and Glasgow; Reuters' News Agency, London; TV Guide, Scotland; The Viewer, Scotland; Freelance Writer/Journalist, since 1964; Travel Correspondent, UK and overseas media; Scotland Correspondent, Variety, New York. Publications: Great Scot! (biography of Sir Harry Lauder); The Good Auld Days; The Solway Smugglers; The Wit of the Scots; The Wit of Robert Burns; The Devil on Wheels; Brush Up Your Scotland; Annie Laurie; Take No Notice and Take No More Notice! (World's Funniest Signs); The First 200 Years (Story of Dumfries and Galloway Royal Infirmary). Recreations: making video films of personal travels; collecting trivia; researching Scottish music-hall history; fighting bumbling bureaucrats. Address: (h.) 36 Whittingehame Court, Glasgow, G12 OBG; T.-0141-357 2265.

Irving, John Bruce, BSc, MSc, PhD, FInstM, FSA Scot. Director of Information Technology, Dumfries and Galloway Regional Council, since 1986; b. 19.6.42, Lenzie; m., Margaret Anne McWilliam, MB, ChB, MFCH; 2 s.; 1 d. Educ. Lenzie Academy; Glasgow University. Owner, Bonshaw Tower, the seat of the Irving clan since 1022; research, National Engineering Laboratory, East Kilbride, 1969-78; Project Co-ordinator, then Information Systems Manager, Chloride Technical Ltd., Manchester, 1978-85. Past President: Ayrshire Philatelic Society, Dumfries Philatelic Society; Chairman, Dumfries and Galloway Family History Society; Past Chairman, Dumfries and Galloway International Family Association; Chairman, Data General User Group. Recreations: outdoor pursuits; family history; philately. Address: (h.) Bonshaw Tower, Kirtlebridge, Lockerbie, DG11 3LY; T.-01461 500256.

Irving, Margaret Anne, MBChB, MFCH. Lead Clinician, Child and Family Health Specialty, Dumfries and Galloway Community HS Trust; b. 28.4.43, Glasgow; m., Dr. John Bruce Irving; 2 s.; 1 d. Educ. Bathgate Academy; Glasgow University. Registrar in Bacteriology, Western Infirmary, Glasgow; Principal in general practice, Ayrshire; CMO in Child Health, Salford Health Authority; Senior Clinical Medical Officer in Child Health, Dumfries & Galloway Health Board; Medical Adviser to Regional Adoptions and Fostering Panel; Chairman, Scottish Medical Group, British Agencies for Adoption and Fostering, 1990-93. Recreations: gardening; opera. Address: (h.) Bonshaw Tower, Kirtlebridge, Lockerbie, Dumfriesshire, DG11 3LY; T.-01461 500256.

Irving, Ronald Eckford Mill, MA, DPhil (Oxon). Reader in Politics, Edinburgh University, since 1981; b. 14.7.39, Glasgow; m., Christine Mary Gaudin; 4 d. Educ. Merchiston Castle School; St. Edmund Hall, Oxford. Schoolmaster, 1961-65; Lecturer in Politics: Bristol University, 1968-69, Edinburgh University, 1969-81. Publications: Christian Democracy in France, 1973; The First Indochina War: French and American Policy in Vietnam 1945-54, 1975; The Christian Democratic Parties of Western Europe, 1979. Recreations: golf; piping. Address: (h.) 43 Ormidale Terrace, Edinburgh, EH12 6ED; T.-0131-337 3663.

Irwin, Professor David George, MA, PhD, FSA, FRSA. Professor of History of Art and Head of Department, Aberdeen University, since 1970; b. 24.6.33, London; m., Francina Sorabji; 1 s.; 1 d. Educ. Holgate Grammar School, Barnsley; Queen's College, Oxford (Exhibitioner); Courtauld Institute of Art, London University. Lecturer in History of Fine Art, Glasgow University, 1959-70; Past President, British Society for 18th Century Studies; former Council Member, Walpole Society; former Member, Art Panel, Scottish Arts Council; Member, Editorial Board, British Journal of 18th Century Studies; Committee Member, Aberdeen Art Gallery; Committee Member, Architectural Heritage Society of Scotland; elected Member, International Association of Art Critics; won Laurence Binyon Prize, Oxford, 1956. Publications: English Neoclassical Art; Paul Klee; Visual Arts, Taste and Criticism; Designs and Ornaments of Empire Style; Winckelmann, Writings on Art; John Flaxman, Sculptor, Illustrator, Designer; Scottish Painters, At Home and Abroad, 1700 to 1900 (with Francina Irwin). Recreations: travel; swimming. Address: (b.) Department of History of Art, King's College, Old Aberdeen, Aberdeen, AB9 2UB; T.-01224 272458.

Ivory, Brian Gammell, MA (Cantab), CA, FRSA. Group Chief Executive, The Highland Distilleries Company plc, since 1994; b. 10.4.49, Edinburgh; m., Oona Mairi MacPhie Bell-Macdonald (see Oona Mairi MacPhie Ivory); 1 s.; 1 d. Educ. Eton College; Magdalene College, Cambridge. CA apprentice, Thomson McLintock, 1971-75; joined Highland Distilleries, 1976, became Director, 1978, Managing Director, 1988; Director, Matthew Gloag and Son Ltd., 1987, Chairman, since 1994; Director, Orpar SA, since 1990; Director, Remy Cointreau SA, since 1991; Member, Scottish Arts Council, 1983-92 (Vice-Chairman, 1988-92); Member, Arts Council of GB, 1988-92. Recreations: the arts; farming; hill-walking. Address: (h.) Brewlands, Glenisla, by Blairgowrie, Perthshire, PH11 8PL; 12 Ann Street, Edinburgh, EH4 1PJ; (b.) 106 West Nile Street, Glasgow, G1 2QY; T.-0141-332 7511.

Ivory, Oona Mairi MacPhie, MA (Cantab), ARCM. Professional Musician; Vice Chairman, The Scottish Ballet; Governor, Royal Scottish Academy of Music and Drama; Director, Theatre Royal, Glasgow; Trustee, The Piping Trust; Director, The Piping Centre; b. 21.7.54, Ayr; m., Brian Gammell Ivory (qv); 1 s.; 1 d. Educ. King's College, Cambridge; Royal Scottish Academy of Music and Drama; Royal Academy of Music. Recreations: visual arts; sailing. Address: (h.) Brewlands, Glenisla, by Blairgowrie, Perthshire, PH11 8PL; 12 Ann Street, Edinburgh, EH4 1PJ.

Izat, Alexander John Rennie, MA. Chairman, United Auctions (Scotland) Ltd., since 1992; Director, Shires Investment PLC, since 1988; Partner, John Izat & Partners (Farmers), since 1975; Director, Glasgow Investment Managers, since 1990; Director, Moredun Animal Health Ltd., since 1992; b. 14.7.32, London; m., Frederica Ann McNiel; 1 s.; 2 d. Educ. Glenalmond; Oriel College, Oxford. Partner, Williams de Broe & Co., Stockbrokers, 1955-75; farming at Balliliesk and Naemoor, 1975-87; farming at High Cocklaw, since 1987; former Member, Council, Scottish NFU; Past President, Fife and Kinross NFU and Kinross Agricultural Association; Director, Royal Highland Agricultural Society, since 1985 (Hon. Treasurer, since 1992); Member, Council, Glenalmond College, since 1975 (Chairman, Committee of Council, since 1989); President, Northern Area, Suffolk Sheep Society, 1989-91; Trustee, Animal Diseases Research Association, since 1988. Address: (b.) High Cocklaw, Berwick-upon-Tweed, TD15 1UZ; T.-01289 86591.

Izatt, Mark Andrew, BSc (Hons). Special Adviser to Scottish Office Ministers, since 1994; b. 23.3.69, Dunfermline. Educ. Woodmill High School, Dunfermline; Aberdeen University. Technical Officer, Timber Growers UK, 1991-92; Rersearch Assistant to George Kynoch, MP, and Raymond Robertson, MP, 1992-93; Research Assistant to Raymond Robertson, MP, 1993-94. Recreations: hill-walking; travel. Address: (b.) St. Andrew's House, Edinburgh, EH1 3DG; T.-0131-244 2439.

Izod, (Kenneth) John, BA (Hons), PhD. Senior Lecturer, Department of Film and Media Studies, Stirling University, since 1978; b. 4.3.40, Shepperton; m., Irene Chew Geok Keng (divorced 1994); 1 s.; 1 d. Educ. Prince Edward School, Harare City, Zimbabwe; Leeds University. Clerk articled to Chartered Accountant, 1958-63; Projectionist, mobile cinema unit, 1963; Lecturer in English, New University of Ulster, 1969-78; former Governor, Scottish Film Council; Chairman, Stirling Film Theatre, 1982-89 and 1991-92. Publication: Reading the Screen, 1984; Hollywood and the Box Office 1895-1986, 1988; The Films of Nicolas Roeg, 1991. Address: (b.) Film and Media Studies, University, Stirling, FK9 4LA; T.-01786 473171.

J

Jack, Professor Robert Barr, CBE, MA, LLB. Senior Partner, McGrigor Donald, Solicitors, Glasgow, Edinburgh and London, 1990-93 (Partner, 1957-93); Professor of Mercantile Law, Glasgow University, 1978-93; b. 18.3.28; m., Anna Thorburn Thomson; 2 s. Educ. Kilsyth Academy; High School of Glasgow; Glasgow University. Admitted a Solicitor in Scotland, 1951; Member, Scottish Law Commission, 1974-77; Scottish Observer, Department of Trade's Insolvency Law Review Committee, 1977-82; Member, Council for the Securities Industry, 1983-85; Lay Member, Council of the Stock Exchange, 1984-86; Independent Member, Board, Securities and Futures Authority (formerly Securities Association), 1986-94; Board Member, Securities and Investment Board, since 1994; Chairman, Review Committee on Banking Services Law, 1987-89; Member, Panel on Takeovers and Mergers, since 1992; Member, Financial Law Panel, since 1993; Chairman: Brownlee plc, Timber Merchants, Glasgow, 1984-86 (Director, 1974-86); Joseph Dunn (Bottlers) Ltd., Soft Drink Manufacturers, Glasgow, since 1983; Director: Bank of Scotland, since 1985, Scottish Metropolitan Property plc, since 1980 (Deputy Chairman, since 1991), Scottish Mutual Assurance plc, since 1987 (Chairman, since 1992), Clyde Football Club Ltd., since 1980, Gartmore Scotland Investment Trust PLC, since 1991, Glasgow Development Agency, since 1992; President, Scottish National Council of YMCAs, since 1983 (Chairman, 1966-73); Governor, Hutchesons' Educational Trust, Glasgow, 1978-87 (Chairman, 1980-87); Chairman, The Turnberry Trust, since 1983; Member, Scottish Higher Education Funding Council, since 1992; Governor, Beatson Institute for Cancer Research, since 1989. Publications: lectures and articles on various aspects of company law, the statutory regulation and self-regulation of the City, and banking and insolvency law. Recreations: golf; music; hopeful supporter of one of Glasgow's less fashionable football teams; a dedicated lover of Isle of Arran. Address: (h.) 50 Lanton Road, Lanton Park, Newlands, Glasgow, G43 2SR; T.-0141-637 7302.

Jack, Professor Ronald Dyce Sadler, MA, PhD. Professor of Scottish and Medieval Literature, Edinburgh University, since 1987; b. 3.4.41, Ayr. Educ. Ayr Academy; Glasgow University; Edinburgh University. Department of English Literature: Assistant Lecturer, 1965, Lecturer, 1968, Reader, 1978, Associate Dean, Faculty of Arts, 1971-73; Visiting Professor, Virginia University, 1973-74; Director, Universities Central Council on Admissions, 1988-94 (Member, 1973-76); Pierpont Morgan Scholar, British Academy, 1976; Advising Editor, Scotia, since 1980; Member, Scottish Universities Council on Entrance, since 1981; Governor, Newbattle Abbey College, 1984-89; Beinecke Fellow, Yale, 1992; Visiting Professor, Strathclyde University, 1993. Publications: Robert MacLellan's Jamie the Saxt (Co-Editor), 1970; Scottish Prose 1550-1700, 1972; The Italian Influence on Scottish Literature, 1972; A Choice of Scottish Verse 1560-1660, 1978; The Art of Robert Burns (Co-author), 1982; Sir Thomas Urquhart, The Jewel (Co-author), 1984; Alexander Montgomerie, 1985; Scottish Literature's Debt to Italy, 1986; The History of Scottish Literature, Volume 1, 1988; Patterns of Divine Comedy, 1989; The Road to the Never Land, 1991; Of Lion and of Unicorn, 1993. Address: (b.) Department of English Literature, Edinburgh University, David Hume Tower, George Square, Edinburgh, EH8 9JX.

Jackson, Anthony Arthur, MA, MSc, FICDDip. Senior Lecturer, School of Town and Regional Planning, Duncan of Jordanstone College, Dundee University, since 1991; Vice President (Scotland), Institute of Civil Defence and Disaster Studies, since 1991; Founding Partner, St. Andrews Economic Services, 1986; b. 18.6.46, London; m., Alicia; 3 d. Educ. Westminster City School; Gonville and Caius College, Cambridge; Reading University. Agricultural Economist, Malawi Government, 1968-71; St. Andrews University: Stanley Smith Senior Fellow, 1971-73, Lecturer in Economics, 1973-91; FAO/FFHC Food and Nutrition Consultant, Malawi Government, 1973-76; Warning Officer, 1975-81, and Sector Scientific Adviser, UKWMO, 1981-91; Editor, Journal of Institute of Civil Defence, 1982-89; Group Leader, Conservative Group, Fife Regional Council, 1982-86; Director, WS Training, since 1992; Director, Byre Theatre, 1980-89; Diploma, Institute of Civil Defence and Gerald Drewitt Medal, 1980. Recreations: theatre; cricket; philately. Address: (h.) Creinch, Peat Inn, by Cupar, Fife, KY15 5LH; T.-01334-840275.

Jackson, Eileen. Author; b. 18.4.26, Bristol; m., John Tunnard Jackson; 3 d. Short story/article writer, 1935-74; novels, since 1974; first novel, published USA, 1976, UK, 1978; 21 novels in over 65 editions and 10 languages; pseudonyms: Helen May, Linda Comer, Elizabeth Warne; also publishes as Eileen Jackson; President, Strathclyde Writers, since 1985; Lecturer. Recreations: reading; book collecting; swimming; golf; travel. Address: (h.) Girvan Lodge, Blairquhan, Maybole, Ayrshire, KA19 7QP; T.-01655 770639.

Jackson, Gavin W. General Manager, Orkney Health Board. Address: (b.) Garden House, New Scapa Road, Kirkwall, KW15 1BQ.

Jackson, Jack, BSc (Hons), PhD, MIBiol, CIBiol. HM Staff Inspector of Schools with responsibility for science subjects; b. 31.5.44, Ayr; m., Sheilah Margaret Fulton; 1 s.; 3 d. Educ. Ayr Academy; Glasgow University; Jordanhill College of Education. Demonstrator, Zoology Department, Glasgow University, 1966-69; Lecturer in Zoology, West of Scotland Agricultural College, 1969-72; Assistant Teacher of Biology, Cathkin High School, 1972-73; Principal Teacher of Biology, Ayr Academy, 1973-83. Senior Examiner and Setter, Scottish Examination Board, 1978-83; Director, Board, Scottish Youth Theatre, 1979-82; Member, Scottish Council, Institute of Biology, 1980-83; Member, School Board, Balerno High School, since 1989. Recreations: family life; gardening; hill-walking; conservation. Address: (b.) HM Inspector of Schools' Office, Saughton House, Broomhouse Drive, Edinburgh EH11 3XD; T.-0131-244 8324.

Jackson, Jim, BA. Executive Director, Alzheimer's Scotland – Action on Dementia, since 1994; b. 10.2.47, Bradford; m., Jennifer; 1 s.; 1 d. Educ. Stand Grammar School; West Ham College of Technology; Open University. Playleader, 1969-72; Community Development Worker, 1972-77; Principal Assistant, Community Services and Development, Wirral, 1977-81; Consultant, Home Office Voluntary Services Unit, 1981-84; Assistant Director, Scottish Council for Voluntary Organisations, 1984-93; Director, Alzheimer's Scotland, 1993-94. Recreations: hill-walking; modern jazz. Address: (b.) 8 Hill Street, Edinburgh, EH2 3JZ; T.-0131-225 1453.

Jackson, Professor Michael Herbert, BA, PhD, CBiol, MIBiol, FRSH, MREHIS, MIEH. Professor and Head, Division of Environmental Health, Strathclyde University; b. 17.7.40, Hornchurch; m., Diana Evans; 2 d. Educ. Nantwich and Acton Grammar School; Open University; Strathclyde University. Lecturer in Environmental Health, Strathclyde University, 1977-86; previously public health inspector and environmental health officer. President, Strathendrick Speakers Club. Recreations: gardening; reading; holidaying. Address: (b.) Department of Civil Engineering, Strathclyde University, John Anderson Building, Glasgow, G4 0NG; T.-0141-552 4400, Ext. 3437.

Jackson, Professor Michael Peart, BA, MA, GradIPM. Deputy Principal, Stirling University, since 1991; b. 1.7.47, Oldham; m., Sylvia; 1 s.; 1 d. Educ. Hulme Grammar School, Oldham; Hull University. Lecturer and Senior Lecturer in Sociology, Professor of Human Resource Management, Stirling University. JP; author of 12 books on industrial relations and employment policy. Address: (b.) Deputy Principal's Office, Stirling University, Stirling; T.-01786 467013.

Jackson, Richard Dodds, MA, DipEd. Assistant Secretary (Vocational Education), Scottish Office Education Department, since 1990; b. 13.9.37, Galashiels; m., Brenda Routledge Jackson; 1 s.; 1 d. Educ. St. Mary's School, Melrose; Royal High School, Edinburgh; St. Andrews University; Moray House College of Education. Teacher of English, Broughton Secondary School, Edinburgh, and Daniel Stewart's College, Edinburgh, 1961-70; HM Inspector of Schools and FE Colleges, 1970-75; Scottish Education Department: Temporary Principal, Arts Branch, 1975-78, Assistant Secretary, Social Work Services Group, 1978-82; Deputy Director (Personnel and Supplies), Scottish Prison Service, 1982-86; Assistant Secretary (Primary Health Care), Scottish Home and Health Department, 1986-90. Recreations: theatre and opera work. Address: (b.) 43 Jeffrey Street, Edinburgh; T.-0131-244 5382.

Jackson, Robert Penman, MIBM. Director of Public Works, City of Dundee District Council, since 1984; b. 2.4.47, Dunfermline; m., Helen Paxton; 1 s.; 1 d. Educ. Beath Senior High School, Cowdenbeath; Napier College of Science and Technology, Edinburgh. RSAS Diploma. Burgh Surveyor and Sanitary Inspector, Lochgelly Town Council, 1971-75; Assistant Director of Technical Services, Dunfermline District Council, 1975-84. Honorary Secretary, Lochgelly Old Folks' Reunion Committee. Recreation: golf. Address: (b.) 353 Clepington Road, Dundee; T.-Dundee 434729.

Jackson, William Gordon, QC, LLB. Queen's Counsel; b. 5.8.48, Saltcoats; m., Anne; 1 s.; 2 d. Educ. Ardrossan Academy; St. Andrews University. Advocate Depute, 1987-90. Address: (b.) Advocates Library, Parliament House, Edinburgh; T.-0131-226 2881.

Jacobs, Raymond Alexander. Golf Correspondent, The Herald, since 1963; b. 13.1.31, Accrington. Educ. Loretto School. Recreation: catching up. Address: (b.) 195 Albion Street, Glasgow, G1 1QP; T.-0141-552 6255.

Jamal, Goran A., MB, ChB (Hons), MD, PhD, MRCP, FRCP. Consultant, Department of Neurology, Southern General Hospital, Glasgow, since 1988; Senior Clinical Lecturer, Glasgow University, since 1989; Senior Lecturer in Neuroscience, Strathclyde Region, since 1989; b. 19.7.53, Iraqi Kurdistan; m., Dr. Vian M.S. Anber; 1 s.; 1 d. Educ. Central Secondary School, Baghdad; Glasgow University. Research Fellow, Glasgow University Department of Neurology, 1981-86; Senior Registrar, Department of Neuroscience, St. Bartholomew's Hospital and London University, 1986-88. Chairman, Kurdish Relief Association. Publications: several chapters in books and more than 100 papers. Recreation: member, Pond Leisure Club, Glasgow. Address: (b.) Department of Neurology, I.N.S., Southern General Hospital, Glasgow, G51 4TF; T.-0141-201 2462.

James, David Sheard, MB, ChB, DipEd, DCH, DPM, FRCPsych, FRCP (Glas). Consultant Child Psychiatrist, Royal Hospital for Sick Children, Glasgow, since 1971; Honorary Clinical Senior Lecturer, Child and Adolescent Psychiatry, Glasgow University, since 1991; b. 19.2.39, Harrogate; m., Hilary; 1 s.; 2 d. Educ. Warwick School; Sheffield University. Paediatrics, Sheffield Children's Hospital; Registrar in Psychiatry, Mapperley Hospital,

Nottingham; Research Registrar, United Sheffield Hospitals; Senior Registrar, Child Psychiatry, Birmingham Children's Hospital and Charles Burns Clinic. Publication: Families Without Hope (Co-author), 1975. Recreations: motor vehicles; model railway. Address: (h.) Waterside, Lochlibo Road, Uplawmoor, Glasgow, G78 4AA; T.-01505 850269.

James, Professor Keith, BSc, PhD, DSc, FIBiol, FRCPath, FRSE. Professor in Immunology, Edinburgh University, since 1991; b. 15.3.38, Cumbria; m., Valerie Spencer Jubb; 3 s. Educ. Whitehaven Grammar School; Birmingham University. Research Fellow, Birmingham University, 1962-64; Research Assistant, University of California, 1964-65; Senior Lecturer, Edinburgh University, 1965-77, Reader, 1977-91; Past Chairman, Treasurer and Education Secretary, British Society for Immunology (now a Trustee); Secretary General, International Union of Immunological Societies; serves on the editorial board of a number of journals. Publications: Introducing Immunology (Co-author); numerous scientific papers. Recreations: hill-walking; photography. Address: (h.) 23 Crosswood Crescent, Balerno, Edinburgh, EH14 7LX; T.-0131-449 5583.

James, Mary Charlotte, BA (Hons). Headmistress, St. Leonards School, St. Andrews, since 1988; b. 2.4.44, Bilston, Staffs; m., Lawrence Edwin James; 2 s. Educ. St. Leonards School; York University; St. Anne's College, Oxford. Head of History, Casterton School, Kirkby Lonsdale, 1979-84; Headmistress, Queen Ethelburga's School, Harrogate, 1984-88. Member, Scottish Council, ISCO; Member, SCIS working party on marketing and PR. Recreations: reading; cooking; walking; sleeping. Address: St. Leonards House, St. Andrews, Fife; T.-01334 472126.

James, Stuart, BA, FLA, MIInfSc, FRSA. Librarian, Paisley University, since 1989; b. 17.3.44, Borehamwood; m., Gillian Margaret Buckman; 1 s.; 1 d. Educ. Bushey Grammar School; Birmingham University. Leeds City Libraries, 1965-69; Northampton Development Corporation, 1970-71; Irvine Development Corporation (Librarian/ Information Specialist), 1971-78; Depute Librarian, Paisley College, 1978-89. Editor, Library Review; Editor, Reference Reviews; Convenor, Scottish Academic Libraries Co-operative Training Group, 1987-92; Member, Council of Polytechnic Librarians Executive Committee, 1991-93; Honorary Secretary, Library Association Cataloguing and Indexing Group, since 1992; Member, British Library National Bibliographic Service Advisory Board. Recreations: history of aviation; reading; book collecting. Address: (b.) Library, Paisley University, High Street, Paisley, PA1 2BE; T.-0141-848 3750.

James, Thomas William, Head of Strategic Affairs, Scottish Power; b. 23.8.40, Motherwell; m., Anne Fiona MacDonald; 2 d. Educ. Dalziel High School. Journalist, Glasgow Herald; The Scotsman: Journalist, Parliamentary Correspondent, Political Correspondent, Chief Political Correspondent; Scottish Political Editor, Sunday Standard; SSEB: Press Officer, Public Relations Officer, Director of Public Affairs. Recreations: walking; bird watching; music; theatre; clay pigeon shooting. Address: (b.) Corporate Office, Atlantic Quay, Glasgow, G2 8SP; T.-0141-248 8200.

James, Professor (William) Philip (Trehearne), CBE, MA, MD, DSc, FRCP, FRCPEdin, FRSE, MFPHM. Director, Rowett Research Institute, Aberdeen, since 1982; Research Professor, Aberdeen University, since 1983; b. 27.6.38, Liverpool; m., Jean Hamilton Moorhouse; 1 s.; 1 d. Educ. Bala School, North Wales; Ackworth School, Yorkshire; University College, London. Senior House Physician, Whittington Hospital, London, 1963-65; Clinical Research Scientist, Medical Research Council Tropical Metabolism Research Unit, Kingston, Jamaica, 1965-68;

Harvard Research Fellow, Massachusetts General Hospital, 1968-69; Wellcome Trust Research Fellow, MRC Gastroenterology Unit, London, 1969-70; Senior Lecturer, Department of Human Nutrition, London School of Hygiene and Tropical Medicine, and Honorary Consultant, UCH, 1970-74; Assistant Director, MRC Dunn Nutrition Unit, and Honorary Consultant Physician, Addenbrooke's Hospital, Cambridge, 1974-82. Sir David Cuthbertson Lecturer; Van den Berghs & Jurgens Reporting Award; Amos Memorial Lecturer; Sir Thomas Middleton Memorial Lecturer; Sir Stanley Davidson Memorial Lecturer; Minshull Lecture; Member, COMA and its Sub-Committees; Chairman, Panel on Novel Foods; Member: Nutrition Task Force; Advisory Committee on Novel Foods and Processes; Sectional Committee 1, Royal Society of Edinburgh; Chief Executive's Research Advisory Group, Scottish Higher Education Funding Council; President, National Food Alliance; Chairman: Coronary Prevention Group; WHO Committee on Nutrition Policy, 1989; FAO Commission on National Energy Needs, 1987-88; Department of Health Task Force on Obesity, 1994; Royal College of Physicians of Edinburgh Working Party on Management of Obesity in the NHS, since 1994; Association of Professors of Human Nutrition, since 1994; International Task Force on Obesity Management, since 1995; Planning Group, European Young Nutrition Leadership Courses, since 1994; European Panel for European Heart Foundations' Analysis of Cardiovascular Risk, since 1994; Member: EC Scientific Committee for Food, since 1992, World Cancer Research Fund International Panel on Diet and Cancer, since 1994; Adviser, European Directors of Agricultural Research on Diet and Health, since 1995; author, WHO report on Nutrition and European Health; author, FAO book on human energy requirements; editor, textbook on human nutrition and dietetics, 1992. Address: (b.) Rowett Research Institute, Greenburn Road, Bucksburn, Aberdeen, AB2 9SB; T.-01224 712751.

Jameson, John, FIMgt, AIFireE. Firemaster, Strathclyde Fire Brigade, since 1991; b. 12.4.46, Chapelhall; m., Helen Mulvey; 1 s.; 1 d. Educ. St. Aloysius and St. Patrick's High School, Coatbridge. Lanarkshire Fire Brigade, 1965-70; Glasgow Fire Service, 1970-75; Strathclyde Fire Brigade: joined 1975, Assistant Firemaster, 1987-88, Deputy Firemaster, 1988-91. Fire Brigade Long Service and Good Conduct Medal, 1985; Strathclyde Regional Council Medal for Bravery, 1987; Churchill Fellowship, 1983. Recreations: historic buildings; golf. Address: (b.) Fire Headquarters, Bothwell Road, Hamilton, ML3 0EA.

Jameson, John Valentine McCulloch, OBE, JP, DL, BSc, FRICS. Chairman Designate, West of Scotland Water Authority, 1995; Member, Dumfries and Galloway Regional Council, 1974-94 (Convener, 1983-90); Partner, G.M. Thomson & Co., Chartered Surveyors, since 1970; b. 5.10.33, Twynholm, Stewartry of Kirkcudbright; m., Mary Irene Butters; 1 s.; 2 d. Educ. Rugby School; College of Estate Management (External). Commissioned 4/7 Royal Dragoon Guards, 1952-54; Shell Petroleum Co., London, 1954-57; Richard Costain (Canada) Ltd., Toronto, 1958-64. Member and Bailie, Gatehouse-of-Fleet Town Council, 1970-75; Chairman, Finance Committee, Dumfries and Galloway Regional Council, 1974-83; Chairman, Dumfries and Galloway Tourist Association, 1978-82; Chairman, Royal Institution of Chartered Surveyors in Scotland, 1981-82; Council Member, National Trust for Scotland, 1980-84; Chairman, Dumfries & Galloway Enterprise Co. Ltd., 1993-94; Treasurer, Anwoth and Girthon Kirk Session. Recreations: golf; shooting; squash; hill-walking. Address: (h.) Laghead, Gatehouse-of-Fleet; T.-01557 814389.

Jamie, David Mitchell, FRICS, MRTPI, FCIT. Director of Planning, Lothian Regional Council, since 1986; b. 11.8.41, Edinburgh; m., Eileen; 1 s.; 1 d. Educ. North Berwick High School; Heriot-Watt University; Edinburgh College of Art.

Chartered Surveyor in private practice, Edinburgh and Glasgow, 1959-67; Town Planner in local government, since 1967. Chairman, Planning and Development Division, RICS in Scotland, 1986-88 and 1994-95. Recreations: sailing; theatre. Address: (b.) 12 St. Giles Street, Edinburgh, EH1 1PT; T.-0131-469 3888.

Jamie, Kathleen, MA. Writer; b. 13.5.62, Johnstone. Educ. Currie High School; Edinburgh University. Publications: The Way We Live; The Autonomous Region; The Queen of Sheba; The Golden Peak.

Jamieson, David. Honorary Sheriff, South Strathclyde, Dumfries and Galloway, since 1976; b. 10.8.17, Glasgow; m., Pauline Bainbridge; 1 d. Educ. Albert Road Academy, Glasgow; Glasgow University. Six years in HM Forces during Second World War; former practising Solicitor in Hamilton. Publications: Uddingston, The Village (parts one to five), 1974-84; Uddingston in Picture Postcards, 1984. Recreation: local history. Address: (b.) 22 Clydesdale Street, Hamilton; T.-Hamilton 281767.

Jamieson, Rev. Gordon David, MA, BD. Minister, Barnhill St. Margaret's Parish Church, Dundee, since 1986; Interim Convener, Church of Scotland Board of Ministry, since 1995; b. 1.3.49, Glasgow; m., Annette; 1 s.; 1 d. Educ. Hamilton Academy; Edinburgh University. Assistant Minister, Tron Moredun, Edinburgh, 1973-74; Minister, Schaw Kirk, Drongan, 1974-79; Minister, Elie Parish Church, linked with Kilconquhar and Colinsburgh Parish Church, 1979-86; Vice-Convener, Committee on the Maintenance of the Ministry, 1993-95. Address: The Manse, Invermark Terrace, Broughty Ferry, Dundee, DD5 2QU; T.-01382 779278.

Janes, Derek Charles, MA, AMA. Assistant Head of Museums and Galleries, Edinburgh City Museums, since 1985; President, Scottish Museums Federation, since 1993; b. 24.3.48, Bristol; m., Diane; 1 s.; 1 d. Educ. Bristol Grammar School; George Watson's College; Edinburgh University. Lancaster City Museum, 1969-71; Assistant Curator, Bury County Borough Museum and Art Gallery, 1972-74; Keeper of Social History, Bury Metropolitan Borough Museum, 1974-76; Senior Keeper, Social History, Coventry City Council Herbert Art Gallery, 1976-84. Publication: Lancaster. Recreations: garden; house; music; towns; reading. Address: (b.) City Art Centre, 2 Market Street, Edinburgh EH1 1DE. T.-0131-529 3951.

Jardine, Sir (Andrew) Rupert (John) Buchanan-, 4th Bt, MC, DL. Landowner; b. 2.2.23; m., Jane Fiona Edmonstone (m. diss.); 1 s.; 1 d. Educ. Harrow; Royal Agricultural College. Retired Major, Royal Horse Guards; Joint Master, Dumfriesshire Foxhounds, 1950; Deputy Lieutenant, Dumfriesshire, 1978. Address: (h.) Dixons, Lockerbie, Dumfriesshire.

Jardine, Ian William, BSc, PhD. Regional Director (North East Scotland), Scottish Natural Heritage, since 1992; b. 22.5.59, Edinburgh; m., Anne Daniel; 2 s. Educ. Royal High School, Edinburgh; Durham University; Leeds University. Joined Scottish Office, 1984; worked in various departments, including Scottish Development and Industry Departments; Private Secretary to Ian Lang MP; involved in setting-up of urban partnership initiatives and management of Castlemilk Partnership. Recreations: acting; gardening; natural history. Address: (b.) 17 Rubislaw Terrace, Aberdeen, AB1 1XE; T.-01224 642863.

Jardine, Sheriff James Christopher Macnaughton, BL. Sheriff, of Glasgow and Strathkelvin at Glasgow, 1979-95 (from 1969 of North Strathclyde at Dumbarton, and of Stirling, Dunbarton and Clackmannan at Dumbarton); b. 18.1.30, Glasgow; m., Vena Kight; 1 d. Educ. Glasgow Academy; Gresham House; Glasgow University. Lt., RASC, 1950-52; admitted as Solicitor in Scotland, 1953; in practice as principal (Nelson & Mackay), from 1955; Partner, McClure Naismith Brodie & Co., Glasgow, 1956-69; Secretary, Glasgow University Graduates Association, 1956-66; Member, Business Committee, Glasgow University General Council, 1964-67; a Vice-President, Sheriffs Association, 1976-79; Member, Joint Probation Consultative Committee for Strathclyde Region (subsequently Social Work in the Criminal Justice System), 1981-94. Recreations: enjoyment of theatre, opera and music; swimming.

Jardine, Leslie Thomas, LLB. Director of Economic Development, Dumfries and Galloway Regional Council, since 1986; b. 4.6.49, Dumfries; m., Angela; 1 s. Educ. Dumfries Academy; Glasgow University. Law apprentice, then Legal Assistant, Dumfries County Council, 1972-75; Policy Planning Assistant, then Regional Public Relations Officer, Dumfries and Galloway Regional Council, 1975-86. Solicitor. Recreation: riding (Chairman, Dumfries and Galloway Branch, British Horse Society). Address: (b.) 118 English Street, Dumfries; T.-01387 61234.

Jarman, Richard Neville, MA (Oxon). General Director, Scottish Opera, since 1991; b. 24.4.49, Sawbridgeworth. Educ. King's School, Canterbury; Trinity College, Oxford. Publicity Officer/Assistant to Administrative Director, English National Opera, 1971-76; Touring Officer: Dance, Arts Council of GB, 1976-77; Artistic Assistant/Administrator, Edinburgh International Festival, 1978-84; General Administrator, English National Ballet, 1984-90. Fellow, Royal Society of Arts. Recreations: theatre; music; travel; gardening. Address: (b.) Scottish Opera, 39 Elmbank Crescent, Glasgow, G2 4PT; T.-0141-248 4567.

Jarvie, Norman Dobson, MB, ChB, FRCGP, DObstRCOG. General Practitioner, Crieff; Chairman, National Medical Advisory Committee, since 1990; b. 31.3.36, Glasgow; m., Dr. Anne Jarvie; 2 s.; 1 d. Educ. Rutherglen Academy; Glasgow University. Medical Officer to Crieff Cottage Hospital, Ardvreck School and Morrison's Academy, since 1964; Chairman, Local Medical Committee, Perth and Kinross Division, 1978-80; President, Perth and Kinross Division, BMA, 1980; Chairman, Scottish Association of General Practitioner Community Hospitals, 1981-85; General Practitioner Tutor, Dundee University; Chairman, Scottish Council, Royal College of General Practitioners, 1987-90; Provost, East Scotland Faculty, RCGP, 1987-90. Recreations: skiing; sailing; golf. Address: (b.) Health Centre, Crieff, PH7 3SA; T.-01764 652456.

Jarvis, Geoffrey, FRIBA, FRIAS. Architect in private practice; Consultant in historic buildings; b. 9.1.28, London; m., Rosalind Bailey; 2 s.; 2 d. Educ. Kelvinside Academy; Glasgow Academy; Glasgow School of Architecture. Worked for two years in Philadelphia and New York (Marcel Breuer); returned to Glasgow, setting up in private practice; Consultant to National Trust for Scotland, 1972-87; principal works include Culzean Country Park Centre; Clan Donald Centre, Skye; Chatelherault, Hamilton; Edinburgh Castle Visitor Reception Feasibility Study; Past Chairman, Glasgow Tree Lovers' Society; Founder, former Honorary Secretary and Chairman, New Glasgow Society; Co-Founder and Vice-Chairman, Clyde Fair International, 1972-73; Co-founder, Clydebuilt, 1991; Director, Clyde Maritime Trust; RIBA national award, Regenerating Scotland Award, three Europa Nostra Diplomas of Merit; two Civic Trust Awards; Chairman, Glasgow Buildings Guardian Committee; Founder Director, Clyde Festival Gardens 1999 Ltd. Recreations: travel and sight-seeing; local and Scottish history; Glasgow; family. Address: (b.) 7 Fitzroy Place, Glasgow, G3 7RH; T.-041-226 4981.

Jarvis, Professor Paul Gordon, PhD, Fil dr, FRSE, FRS Uppsala, FIBiol, FIChFor. Professor of Forestry and Natural Resources, Edinburgh University, since 1975; b. 23.5.35, Tunbridge Wells; m., Margaret Susan Gostelow; 1 s.; 2 d. Educ. Sir Anthony Brown's School, Brentwood; Oriel College, Oxford. PhD study, Sheffield University, 1957-60; Postdoctoral Fellow, NATO, Institute of Plant Physiology, Uppsala University, 1960-62; Fil dr, Uppsala University, 1963; Senior Lecturer in Plant Physiology, Royal College of Agriculture, Uppsala; Aberdeen University: Lecturer in Botany, 1966-72, Senior Lecturer, 1972-75. Council Member, Society for Experimental Biology, 1977-80, President, 1993-95; Commissioner, Countryside Commission for Scotland, 1976-78; Council Member, National Trust for Scotland, since 1987; Trustee, John Muir Trust, since 1989; Member, Governing Body, Scottish Crops Research Institute, 1977-86; Co-Founder and Sectional Editor, Plant, Cell and Environment; present interests: environmental change, biodiversity, forest ecology; serves on various editorial and review boards. Recreations: hill-walking; gardening; growing trees. Address: (h.) Belmont, 47 Eskbank Road, Dalkeith, Midlothian, EH22 3BH; T.-0131-663 8676.

Jauncey of Tullichettle, Lord (Charles Eliot Jauncey), PC. Lord of Appeal in Ordinary, since 1988; Senator of the College of Justice in Scotland, 1979-88; b. 8.5.25; m., Sarah Camilla Cathcart; 2 s.; 2 d. Educ. Radley; Christ Church, Oxford; Glasgow University. Advocate, 1949; Kintyre Pursuivant of Arms, 1955; QC, 1963; Sheriff Principal of Fife and Kinross, 1971. Member, Historic Buildings Council for Scotland, 1971-92. Recreations: fishing; shooting; bicycling; genealogy. Address: (h.) Tullichettle, Comrie, Perthshire, PH6 2HU; T.-01764 670349.

Jeary, Peter, IPFA. Director of Finance, Borders Regional Council, since 1983; b. 16.8.44, Durham; m., Margaret; 1 s.; 1 d. Ministry of Pensions and National Insurance, 1960-63; District Audit Service, Lincoln, 1963-67; Reading Corporation, 1967-68; Northampton Corporation, 1968-71; Inverness County Council, 1971-75; Highland Regional Council, 1975-83. Address: (b.) Regional HQ, Newtown St. Boswells, Melrose, TD6 0SA; T.-01835 823301.

Jeeves, Professor Malcolm Alexander, CBE, MA, PhD (Cantab), Hon. DSc (Edin), FBPsS, FRSE. Vice-President, Royal Society of Edinburgh, 1990-93; Professor of Psychology, St. Andrews University, since 1969; b. 16.11.26, Stamford, England; m., Ruth Elisabeth Hartridge; 2 d. Educ. Stamford School; St. John's College, Cambridge University. Lt., 1st Bn., Sherwood Foresters, BAOR, 1945-48; Exhibitioner, St. John's College, Cambridge, 1948-52; research and teaching, Cambridge and Harvard Universities, 1952-56; Lecturer, Leeds University, 1956-59; Professor and Head, Department of Psychology, Adelaide University, 1959-69 (Dean, Faculty of Arts, 1963-64); Member: Council, SERC, 1985-89, Neuroscience and Mental Health Board, MRC, 1985-89, Council, Royal Society of Edinburgh, 1985-88 (Vice President, 1990-93); Director, Medical Research Council Cognitive Neuroscience Research Group, 1983-88; Vice-Principal, St. Andrews University, 1981-85; Chairman, Executive Committee, International Neuropsychological Symposium, since 1986; Editor, Neuropsychologia; Cairns Memorial Lecturer, Australia, 1986; New College Lecturer, University of NSW, 1987. Honorary Sheriff, Fife, since 1986. Publications: Analysis of Structural Learning (Co-author); Psychology Survey No. 3 (Editor); Experimental Psychology: An introduction for biologists; The Effects of Structural Relations upon Transfer (Co-author); Thinking in Structures (Co-author); Behavioural Science and Christianity (Editor); Free to be Different (Co-author); Psychology and Christianity: The View Both Ways; The Scientific Enterprise and Christian Faith; Psychology: Through the eyes of faith (Co-author); Mind Fields. Recreations: walking; music; fishing. Address: (b.) Department of Psychology, St. Andrews University, St. Andrews, KY16 9JU; T.-01334 76161.

Jeffares, Professor Alexander Norman, AM, MA, PhD, DPhil, Ddel'U, DLitt, FAHA, FRSE, FRSL, FRSA. Professor of English Studies, Stirling University, 1974-86; Honorary Professor, since 1987; Managing Director, Academic Advisory Services Ltd.; Director, Colin Smythe Ltd.; b. 11.8.20, Dublin; m., Jeanne Agnes Calembert; 1 d. Educ. The High School, Dublin; Trinity College, Dublin; Oriel College, Oxford. Lecturer in Classics, Trinity College, Dublin, 1943-45; Lector in English, Groningen University, 1946-48; Lecturer in English Literature, Edinburgh University, 1949-51; Professor of English Language and Literature, Adelaide, 1951-56; Professor of English Literature, Leeds, 1957-74. Secretary, Australian Humanities Research Council, 1954-57; Honorary Fellow, Australian Academy of Humanities; Founding Chairman, Association for Commonwealth Literary and Language Studies, 1966-68 (Honorary Life Fellow); Founding Chairman, International Association for Study of Anglo-Irish Literature, 1968-70 (Honorary Life President, since 1973); Member, Scottish Arts Council (Chairman, Literature Committee, 1977-83, Vice Chairman, 1980-84); Member, Arts Council of GB, 1980-84; Chairman, National Book League Scotland, 1985-87, Book Trust Scotland, 1987-89; Board Member, Book Trust, 1987-89; President, International PEN, Scottish Centre, 1986-89; Vice-President, Royal Society of Edinburgh, 1988-89; Vice-Chairman, Muckhart Community Council, 1979-86; Chairman of Judges, McVitie Prize, 1988-91. Publications: Yeats: Man and Poet; Seven Centuries of Poetry; The Scientific Background (Co-author); A Commentary on the Poems of Yeats; A Commentary on the Plays of Yeats (Co-author); History of Anglo-Irish Literature; Restoration Drama; New Commentary on Poems of Yeats; Brought up in Dublin (poems); Brought up to Leave (poems); An Irish Childhood (Co-Editor); A Jewish Childhood (Co-Editor); Yeats: a new biography; Yeats's Poems; Yeats's Vision; Yeats: the love poems; Always Your Friend (Co-Editor); Swift, the selected poems; Joycechoyce (Co-editor); Ireland's Women (Co-editor); Collins Dictionary of Quotations (Co-editor); Images of Imagination (essays). Recreations: drawing; painting; restoring old houses. Address: (h.) Craighead Cottage, Fife Ness, Crail, Fife; T.-01333 50898.

Jeffcoat, Marilyn Annette, BCom, FCCA. Senior Partner, D.M. Vaughan & Co., Accountants, since 1979; Member of Court, Napier University, since 1990; Commissioner, Mental Welfare Commission, since 1992; b. 7.4.47, Birmingham; 5 s.; 1 d. Educ. Erdington Grammar School, Birmingham; Edinburgh University. Worked in investment management, tax accountancy and audit with Baillie Gifford, Ivory & Sime, and Coopers & Lybrand until 1976, qualifying as a certified accountant in 1976; public practice since 1979. Director: Scottish Council for Single Parents, St. Mary's Cathedral Workshop Ltd.; Treasurer: Society of Scottish Artists, St. Mary's Episcopal Cathedral, Edinburgh; Trustee, Scottish Hospital Trust. Recreations: theology; mathematics; dance. Address: (b.) 10 Gloucester Place, Edinburgh; T.-0131-225 8282.

Jefferson, Gordon Cort, BSc, MSc, PhD, FRPharmS. Secretary, Scottish Department, Royal Pharmaceutical Society of Gt. Britain, since 1988 (Head, Department of Pharmacy, Heriot-Watt University, 1983-88); Member, National Pharmaceutical Advisory Committee; Member, Scottish PQE Board for Health Service Pharmacists; b. 12.9.35, Edenfield, Lancs; m., Jean Margaret Perkin; 2 s. Educ. Bacup and Rawtenstall Grammar School; Lancaster Royal Grammar School; Manchester University. Benger Research Fellow, then Teaching Assistant, Department of Pharmacology, Manchester University, 1960-62; Lecturer/Senior Lecturer in Pharmacology, Department of Pharmacy, Heriot-Watt College/University, 1962-83. Recreations: golf; railway history; amateur interest in architecture. Address: (h.) 5 Cherry Tree Crescent, Balerno, Edinburgh, EH14 5AY; T.-0131-449 3549.

Jeffery, Professor Jonathan, MA, BSc, DPhil, DSc, CChem, FRSC, CBiol, FIBiol, FRSA, FRSE. Professor of Biochemistry, Aberdeen University, since 1983; b. 29.7.35, Liverpool; m., Christa Torriano-Williams; 2 d. Educ. Liverpool Institute High School; Jesus College, Oxford University. Research Biochemist, ICI, 1962-66; Aberdeen University: Lecturer in Chemical Pathology, 1966-72, Lecturer in Biochemistry, 1972-74, Senior Lecturer in Biochemistry, 1974-83. Recreations: country walks; some interest in theatre, visual arts and music. Address: (b.) Department of Molecular and Cell Biology, Aberdeen University, Marischal College, Aberdeen, AB9 1AS; T.-01224 272000.

Jeffrey, John J., BSc (Hons), BA (Ed), DipEd, CEng, MRINA. Depute Principal, Inverness College, since 1970; b. 29.7.35, Greenock; m., Norma May McGregor; 1 s.; 2 d. Educ. Greenock High School; Strathclyde University; Open University; Aberdeen University; Paisley College of Technology. Began career as apprentice/design draughtsman, Scott Lithgow (Shipbuilders), 1950-61; Nuclear power design Engineer, English Electric, Leicester, 1961-63; Lecturer in Naval Architecture/Engineering, then Senior Lecturer, Kirkcaldy College of Technology, 1963-67; Second Depute Principal, Aberdeen Technical College, 1967-70. Recreations: golf; tennis; computing. Address: (b.) Inverness College, 3 Longman Road, Longman South, Inverness; T.-01463 236681.

Jeffrey, Dr. Robin Campbell, FEng, FIMechE, FIChemE. Chief Executive, Scottish Nuclear Ltd., since 1992; b. 19.2.39, Kirkintilloch; m., Barbara; 2 s.; 1 d. Educ. Lenzie Academy; Kelvinside Academy; Royal College of Science and Technology, Glasgow; Glasgow University; Cambridge University. Babcock and Wilcox, Renfew, 1956-60 and 1964-79; joined SEEB (later ScottishPower), 1979; Technical Services Manager, 1979-80, Torness Project Manager, 1980-88, Chief Engineer, 1988-89, Managing Director, Engineering Resources Business, 1989-92. Visiting Professor, University of Strathclyde. Recreations: squash; tennis; real tennis; skiing. Address: (h.) 71D Partickhill Road, Glasgow; T.-0141-357 3079.

Jeffreys-Jones, Rhodri, BA (Wales), PhD (Cantab), FRHistS. Reader in History, Edinburgh University, since 1990; b. 28.7.42, Carmarthen; m., Mary Fenton; 2 d. by pr. m. Educ. Ysgol Ardudwy; University of Wales; Cambridge University; Michigan University; Harvard University Tutor: Harvard, 1965-66, Fitzwilliam College, Cambridge, 1966-67; Assistant Lecturer, then Lecturer, then Senior Lecturer, Edinburgh University, 1967-90; Fellow, Charles Warren Center for the Study of American History, Harvard, 1971-72; Canadian Commonwealth Visiting Fellow and Visiting Professor, University of Toronto, 1993. Publications: Violence and Reform in American History; American Espionage: From Secret Service to CIA; Eagle Against Empire: American Opposition to European Imperialism 1914-82 (Editor); The Growth of Federal Power in American History (Joint Editor); The CIA and American Democracy; North American Spies (Joint Editor); Changing Differences: Women and the Shaping of American Foreign Policy, 1917-1994. Recreations: snooker; vegetable gardening. Address: (b.) Department of History, Edinburgh University, William Robertson Building, George Square, Edinburgh, EH8 9JY; T.-0131-650 3773/3780.

Jenkins, Blair, MA (Hons). Director of Broadcasting, Scottish Television, since 1994; b. 8.1.57, Elgin; m., Jennifer Smillie; 3 d. Educ. Elgin Academy; Edinburgh University. Joined Evening Express, Aberdeen, from school, 1974; Young Journalist of the Year, Scottish Press Awards, 1977; university, 1976-80; joined BBC in London, becoming chief sub-editor, Television News, 1982; Producer, Nine O'Clock News, 1983; returned to Scotland, 1984, to produce Reporting Scotland, BBC; joined Scottish TV, 1986, to re-launch Scotland Today; Editor, News and

Current Affairs, 1990-93; Head of Regional Broadcasting, 1993-94. Recreations: his daughters; good books; Aberdeen Football Club. Address: (b.) Scottish Television plc, Cowcaddens, Glasgow, G2 3PR; T.-0141-332 9999.

Jenkins, David, BMus, PhD. Academic Registrar, Moray House College of Education, since 1984; b. 30.5.44, Dundee; m., Dr. Janet Jenkins; 2 s.; 1 d. Educ. Perth Academy; Edinburgh University. Assistant Teacher, Tynecastle Secondary School, Edinburgh, 1968-70; Lecturer, then Vice-Principal, Callendar Park College of Education, Falkirk, 1970-82; Lecturer and Clerk to Board of Studies, Moray House College of Education, 1982-84. Recreations: music; gardening. Address: (h.) 18 Blacket Place, Edinburgh, EH9 1RL; T.-0131-667 2885.

Jenkins, Robin, MA. Novelist; b. 11.9.12. Author of: Happy for the Child, The Thistle and the Grail, The Cone-Gatherers, Guests of War, The Missionaries, The Changeling, Some Kind of Grace, Dust on the Paw, The Tiger of Gold, A Love of Innocence, The Sardana Dancers, A Very Scotch Affair, The Holy Tree, The Expatriates, A Toast to the Lord, A Far Cry from Bowmore, A Figure of Fun, A Would-be Saint, Fergus Lamont, The Awakening of George Darroch, Just Duffy, Poverty Castle, Willie Hogg. Address: (h.) Fairhaven, Toward, Dunoon, PA23 7UE.

Jennett, Professor Bryan, MD, FRCS. Professor of Neurosurgery, Glasgow University, 1968-91 (Dean, Faculty of Medicine, 1981-86); Member, Court, Glasgow University, 1987-91; b. 1.3.26, Twickenham, Middlesex; m., Professor Sheila Jennett; 3 s.; 1 d. Educ. King's College, Wimbledon; King George V School, Southport; Liverpool University. Lecturer in Neurosurgery, Manchester University; Rockefeller Travelling Fellow, University of California; Hunterian Professor, Royal College of Surgeons of England. Member, Medical Research Council, 1979-83; Member, Chief Scientist Committee, Scotland; Rock Carling Fellow. Publications: Epilepsy After Non-Missile Head Injuries; Introduction to Neurosurgery; High Technology Medicine - Benefits and Burdens. Recreations: writing; cruising under sail. Address: (h.) 83 Hughenden Lane, Glasgow, G12 9XN.

Jennings, James, JP. Convener, Strathclyde Regional Council, since 1986; Honorary Sheriff, Kilmarnock, since 1991; Chairman, Police Negotiating Board, since 1990; b. 18.2.25; m., 1, Margaret Cook Barclay (deceased); 3 s.; 2 d.; 2, Margaret Mary Hughes, JP; 2 d. Educ. St. Palladius School, Dalry; St. Michael's College, Irvine. Steel industry, 1946-79. Member: Ayr County Council, 1958, Strathclyde Regional Council, 1974 (Vice-Convener, 1982-86); Chairman: Ayr CC Police and Law Committee, 1964-70, Ayrshire Joint Police Committee, 1970-75, North Ayrshire Crime Prevention Panel, 1970-82, Police and Fire Committee, Strathclyde Regional Council, 1978-82; contested Perth and East Perthshire, 1966; Vice-President, St. Andrew's Ambulance Association; Patron, Association of Youth Clubs in Strathclyde; Honorary President: Scottish Retirement Council, Princess Louise Scottish Hospital (Erskine Hospital); Honorary Vice-President: SNO Chorus, Royal British Legion Scotland (Dalry and District Branch); JP, Cunninghame, 1969 (Chairman, Cunninghame Justices Committee, since 1974); Vice-Chairman, Official Side, Police Negotiating Board, 1984-86, Chairman, 1986-88; Chairman, Garnock Valley Development Executive, since 1988. Recreation: local community involvement. Address: (h.) 4 Place View, Kilbirnie, KA25 6BG; T.-Kilbirnie 3339.

Jennings, Kevin, MB, FRCP. Consultant Cardiologist, Aberdeen Royal Infirmary, since 1983; b. 9.3.47, Charleville, Eire; m., Heather; 2 s.; 1 d. Educ. Downside; St. Bartholomew's Hospital, London. Registrar: King's College Hospital, London, London Chest Hospital; Senior Registrar, Freeman Hospital, Newcastle-upon-Tyne. Recreations: theatre; ballet; golf; windsurfing. Address: 58

Rubislaw Den South, Aberdeen, AB2 6AX; T.-Aberdeen 311466.

Jessop, Sheriff Alexander Smethurst, MA, LLB. Sheriff at Aberdeen, since 1990; b. 17.5.43, Montrose; m., Joyce Isobel Duncan; 2 s.; 1 d. Educ. Montrose Academy; Fettes College; Aberdeen University. Partner, Campbell, Middleton, Burness and Dickson, Montrose; Procurator Fiscal Depute, Perth, 1976-78; Assistant Solicitor, Crown Office, 1978-80; Senior Assistant Procurator Fiscal, Glasgow, 1980-84; Regional Procurator Fiscal, Aberdeen, 1984-87, Glasgow, 1987-90. Chairman, Aberdeen Victim Support. Recreation: golf. Address: (b.) Sheriff Court House, Aberdeen, AB9 1AP; T.-01224 648316.

Jessop, Thomas Findlay. Collector of Customs and Excise, Glasgow, 1989-94; b. 19.8.34, Edinburgh; m., Elizabeth; 1 s.; 1 d. Educ. George Heriot's School, Edinburgh; Edinburgh University. Royal Navy (National Service), 1954-56; Officer of Customs and Excise, 1956-72; Surveyor of Customs and Excise, 1972-78; Assistant Collector of Customs and Excise, 1978-86; Senior Principal, Alcoholic Drinks Policy, 1986-89. Recreations: sailing; gardening; badminton (when time permits). Address: (h.) Spinningdale, 3 Barrcraig Road, Bridge of Weir, PA11 3HG.

Johnsen, Konrad W.M., BCom, CA (SA). Chief Executive, Howden Group PLC, since 1987; b. 20.11.42, South Africa; m., Dorothy; 2 d. Educ. Selborne College, South Africa; Rhodes University, Grahamstown; University of Witwatersrand. Trained as Accountant, Thomson McLintock, Johannesburg and London; joined Howden in South Africa, 1973; transferred to UK, 1984. Recreations: golf; tennis; skiing. Address: (b.) Old Govan Road, Renfrew, PA4 0XJ; T.-0141-885 2245.

Johnson, Professor Brian Frederick Gilbert, FRSC, FRS, BSc, MA, PhD. Crum Brown Professor of Inorganic Chemistry, Edinburgh University, since 1991; b. 11.9.38, Northampton; m., Christine; 2 d. Educ. Northampton Grammar School; Nottingham University. Lecturer: Manchester University, 1965-67, University College, London, 1967-70; Lecturer, then Reader, Cambridge University, 1970-90; Fitwilliam College: Fellow, 1970-90, President and Acting Master, 1988-90, Hon. Fellow, since 1991. Recreations: hiking; painting. Address: (b.) Department of Chemistry, Edinburgh University, West Mains Road, Edinburgh, EH9 3JJ; T.-0131-650 4706.

Johnson, David (Charles), MA, BA, PhD. Composer; Musical Historian; Cellist; McGibbon Ensemble, since 1979; 27.10.42, Edinburgh; 1 s. Educ. Aberdeen University; St. John's College, Cambridge. Research Fellow in Scottish Music, Napier University, 1995; Tutor, Edinburgh University Music Faculty, 1988-94; awarded Scottish Arts Council composer's bursary, 1992-93; compositions include four operas, an orchestral suite, chamber music, songs, a piano concerto, church music. Publications: Music and Society in Lowland Scotland, 1972; Scottish Fiddle Music in the 18th Century, 1984; contributions to the New Grove Dictionary of Music, 1981; The Scots Cello Book, 1990; Stepping Northward, 1991; 12 Preludes and Fugues, 1995. Address: (h.) 1 Hill Square, Edinburgh, EH8 9DR; T.-0131-667 7054.

Johnson, Ian M., BA, FLA, MIInfSc, MIMgt. Head, School of Information and Media Studies, Robert Gordon University, Aberdeen, since 1989; b. 17.3.45, Sheffield; m., Jean Trevena. Educ. King Edward VII School, Sheffield; Liverpool College of Commerce; Leeds Polytechnic. Sheffield City Libraries, 1962-74; Department of Education and Science (Office of Arts and Libraries), 1970-72 (on secondment); Rotherham M.B. Council, 1974-78; College of Librarianship Wales, 1978-89. Chairman, Professional Board, International Federation of Library Associations and

Institutions, 1993-95; Chairman, Library Association Personnel Training and Education Group, 1994-95. Recreations: theatre; cinema; travel. Address: (b.) 352 King Street, Aberdeen, AB9 2TQ; T.-Aberdeen 262951.

Johnson, James Henry, DipArch, ARIAS. Executive Director, Edinburgh Old Town Renewal Trust, since 1991; b. 21.5.33, Southend-on-Sea; m., Krystyna Maria Anna Dobraczynska; 1 s.; 2 d. Educ. King Edward VI School, Southampton; Northern Polytechnic, London. Architect, Cumbernauld Development Corporation, 1961-63; Lecturer/Senior Lecturer/Reader, Strathclyde University, 1963-83; Director, Assist housing rehabilitation unit, 1973-83; Member, Assist architects' co-operative, 1983-86; Director, Edinburgh Old Town Committee for Conservation and Renewal, 1986-91. Recreation: self-build restoration of Galloway stables. Address: (b.) EOTRT, 8 Advocates Close, 357 High Street, Edinburgh, EH1 1PS; T.-0131-225 8818.

Johnson, Sir Ronald (Ernest Charles), Kt (1970), CB (1962), MA (Cantab). Retired Civil Servant; b. 3.5.13, Portsmouth; m., Elizabeth Gladys Nuttall; 2 s.; 1 s. deceased. Educ. Portsmouth Grammar School; St. John's College, Cambridge. RNVR, Intelligence Eastern Fleet, 1944-45; entered Scottish Office, 1935; Secretary, Scottish Home and Health Department, 1963-72; Secretary of Commissions for Scotland, 1972-78. Chairman, Civil Service Savings Committee for Scotland, 1963-78; Member, Scottish Records Advisory Council, 1975-81; Member, Committee on Administration of Sheriffdoms, 1981-82; Chairman, Fire Service Research and Training Trust, 1976-89; President, Edinburgh Bach Society, 1973-86; President, Edinburgh Society of Organists, 1980-82; JP, Edinburgh, since 1971. Recreation: church organ. Address: (h.) 14 Eglinton Crescent, Edinburgh, EH12 5DD; T.-0131-337 7733.

Johnston, Hon. Lord (Alan Charles Macpherson), BA (Hons) (Cantab), LLB. Senator of the College of Justice, since 1994; Queen's Counsel (1980); b. 13.1.42, Stirling; m., Anthea Jean Blackburn; 3 s. Educ. Edinburgh Academy; Loretto School; Jesus College, Cambridge; Edinburgh University. Advocate, 1967; Standing Junior Counsel, Scottish Home and Health Department, 1972; Advocate Depute, 1978-82; Chairman: Industrial Tribunal, 1982-85, Medical Appeal Tribunal, 1985-89; Treasurer, Faculty of Advocates, 1977-89, Dean, Faculty of Advocates, 1989-93. Publication: Introduction to Law of Scotland 7th Edition (Joint Editor). Address: (h.) 3 Circus Gardens, Edinburgh; T.-0131-225 1862.

Johnston, Alastair J.C., OBE, BSc. Chairman, Duncan Honeyman Ltd., Stirling, and Lyndalware Ltd., Auchterarder; b. 16.9.28, Dundee; m., Morag Campbell; 2 s. Educ. Harris Academy, Dundee; St. Andrews University. Apprenticeship, Caledon Shipyard, Dundee; Industrial Engineering Manager, North British Rubber Co., Edinburgh; Plant Manager, Armstrong Cork Co., Gateshead; Director and General Manager, William Briggs Ltd., Dundee; Managing Director: Permanite Ltd., Waltham Abbey, Trident Equipment Ltd., Ware, Gates Rubber Co. Ltd., Dumfries. Address: (h.) Roseburn, 15 West Moulin Road, Pitlochry, Perthshire PH16 5EA; T.-01796 473900.

Johnston, Sheriff Alexander Graham, LLB, BA. Sheriff of Glasgow and Strathkelvin, at Glasgow, since 1985 (Grampian, Highland and Islands, 1982-85); b. 16.7.44.

Johnston, Alistair, BSc (Hons). Rector, Kelso High School, since 1975; b. 2.5.39, Stirling; m., Elizabeth; 2 s.; 1 d. Educ. High School of Stirling; Glasgow University. Teacher, George Heriot's School, 1962-65; Principal Teacher of Physics, Galashiels Academy, 1965-71; Depute Rector, Banff Academy, 1971-75. Conference Convener, Headteachers' Association of Scotland. Recreations:

gardening; walking; sailing; skiing; golf. Address: (b.) Kelso High School, Bowmont Street, Kelso, TD5 7EG; T.-01573 224444.

Johnston, Frederick Patrick Mair, CBE, FRSA, MA. Executive Chairman, Johnston Press plc (formerly F. Johnston & Co. Ltd.), since 1973; Chairman, Dunn & Wilson Ltd., since 1976; b. 15.9.35, Edinburgh; m., Elizabeth Ann Jones; 2 s. Educ. Morrison's Academy, Crieff; Lancing College, Sussex; New College, Oxford. Editorial Department, Liverpool Daily Post and Echo, 1959; Assistant Secretary, The Times Publishing Co. Ltd., 1960; Company Secretary, F. Johnston & Co. Ltd., 1969; Chairman, Central Scotland Manpower Committee, 1976-83; Member, Press Council, 1974-88; President, Scottish Newspaper Proprietors' Association, 1976-78; Treasurer, Society of Master Printers of Scotland, 1981-86; President, The Newspaper Society, 1989-90; Director, Scottish Mortgage & Trust plc, since 1991. Recreations: reading; travelling. Address: (b.) 53 Manor Place, Edinburgh, EH3 7EG; T.-0131-225 3361.

Johnston, Geoffrey Edward Forshaw, LLB, CA, FCIT. Managing Director, Cambria Investments Ltd. (Arbuckle, Smith Group), since 1972; Director, Petrasco Services Ltd., since 1974; President, Glasgow Chamber of Commerce, 1994-95 (Director since 1981); b. 20.6.40, Burton, Wirral; m., Elizabeth Anne Lockhart; 2 d. Educ. Loretto School; St. Andrews University. Wilson, Stirling & Co., 1959-65; joined Arbuckle, Smith Holdings Ltd., 1965; Director, 1968; Managing Director, 1972; management buy-out; Director, British International Freight Association; Member, Scottish Valuation Advisory Council; Governor, Lomond School. Recreations: sailing; skiing; hill-walking; golf; DIY. Address: (b.) Ferry Road, Yorkhill, Glasgow, G3 8QU; T.-0141-337 8000.

Johnston, George Hermiston, Dip., Youth and Community Work. Director, Scottish Standing Conference of Voluntary Youth Organisations, since 1992; b. 22.11.36. Director, Clermiston Centre and Youth Secretary, Edinburgh YMCA, 1964-70; General Secretary, Belfast YMCA, 1970-74; Training Officer, Northern Ireland Association of Youth Clubs, 1974-76, Director, 1976-92. Former Vice-Chairman, Voluntary Youth Network for Northern Ireland (Youthnet); Past President, European Confederation of Youth Clubs. Recreations: photography; music; walking; art. Address: (b.) SSCVYO, Central Hall, West Tollcross, Edinburgh, EH3 9BP; T.-0131-229 0339.

Johnston, Grenville Shaw, OBE, TD, KCSG, DL, CA. Chartered Accountant, since 1968; Territorial Army Officer, 1964-89 (Lt. Col.); b. 28.1.45, Nairn; m., Marylyn Jean Picken; 2 d. Educ. Blairmore School; Fettes College. Qualified in Edinburgh with Scott Moncrieff Thomson & Sheills; Thomson McLintock & Co., Glasgow, 1968-70; joined family firm, W.D. Johnston & Carmichael, Elgin, 1970; Senior Partner, 1975. Commanding Officer, 2nd 51st Highland Volunteers, 1983-86; Deputy Lieutenant of Moray, since 1980; Knight Commander, Order of St. Gregory, 1982, for work for Pluscarden Abbey; OBE for services to Territorial Army; Chairman, Grampian Committee, Royal Jubilee Trusts, 1982-91; Member, Cairngorm Recreation Trust Ltd.; Governor, Gordonstoun School; Chairman, Moray Venture Capital Fund Ltd.; Director, Moray & Nairn Newspaper Co. Ltd.; Council Member, Institute of Chartered Accountants of Scotland (Highland Area); Trustee and Council Member, Queens Own Highlanders; Council Member, The Highlanders; Member, Grampian Committee, Princes Scottish Youth Business Trust. Recreations: shooting; fishing; hockey; running; golf; skiing; singing (tenor). Address: (h.) Spynie Kirk House, Spynie, By Elgin, Moray, IV30 3XJ.

Johnston, Professor Ian Alistair, BSc, PhD, FRSE. Professor of Comparative Physiology (Personal Chair),

Director, Gatty Marine Laboratory, St. Andrews University, since 1985; b. 13.4.49, Barking, Essex; m., Dr. Rhona S. Johnston. Educ. Addey and Stanhope Grammar School, London; Hull University. NERC Postdoctoral Research Fellow, Bristol University, 1973-75; Lecturer in Physiology, St. Andrews University, 1976-84; Reader, 1984-85; Visiting Senior Lecturer, Department of Veterinary Physiology, Nairobi University, 1981; Visiting Scientist, British Antarctic Survey base, Signy Island, South Orkneys, 1983-84; awarded Scientific Medal, Zoological Society of London. Recreations: photography; walking; reading. Address: (b.) School of Biological and Medical Sciences, St. Andrews University, St. Andrews, KY16 8LB; T.-01334 463440.

Johnston, James George, BSc (Hons), AdvDipEd, FRSA, MIM. Headteacher, Leverhulme Memorial School, Leverburgh, Harris, since 1984; b. 1.5.54, Glasgow; m., Marilyn; 1 s. Educ. Cumbernauld High School; Glasgow University. Recreations: golf; painting; reading; music; voluntary work. Address: Rosevilla, Main Street, Tarbert, Isle of Harris; T.-01859 502060.

Johnston, James Kenneth Buchanan, TD, BL. Former Senior Partner, Brown Mair Mackintosh & Co., Solicitors, Glasgow; Past Chairman, Royal Yachting Association Scotland; b. 4.9.15, Stirling; 1 d. Educ. Stirling High School; Glasgow University. Organist and Choirmaster, 1930-39; Service in Territorial Army, 1936-39; War Service in Middle East and Far East, 1939-44 (rank of Lt.-Col.); graduated a Solicitor, 1945. Commodore, Royal Scottish Motor Yacht Club, 1968-71, Hon. Commodore, since 1987; Legal Adviser, Royal Yachting Association Scotland; awarded RYA Award, 1983, for services to yachting. Address: (h.) 47 Poplar Avenue, Newton Mearns, Glasgow; T.-0141-639 7238.

Johnston, John Robert, BSc, PhD, FIBiol. Reader, Department of Bioscience and Biotechnology, Strathclyde University, since 1983; b. 6.10.34, Leven, Fife; m., Janet Bonthrone Reekie; 3 s. Educ. Buckhaven High School; St. Andrews University. Teaching Associate, University of California, Berkeley; Research Scientist, Brewing Research Foundation, Nutfield, Surrey; Royal Society Latin America Exchange Fellow, 1970-71, Mexico City; Lecturer, then Senior Lecturer, Strathclyde University, 1964-83; Visiting Research Professor, University of California, Berkeley, 1987-95; Vice-President, Royal Philosophical Society of Glasgow, 1987-90. Recreations: outdoor activities; theatre and music; community affairs. Address: (h.) 83 Castlehill Road, Bearsden, Glasgow, G61 4DX; T.-0141-942 1461.

Johnston, Professor Marie, BSc, PhD, DipClinPsych, FBPsS, CPsychol. Professor in Psychology, St. Andrews University, since 1992; b. 6.7.44, Aberdeen; m., Derek Johnston. Educ. High School for Girls, Aberdeen; Aberdeen University; Hull University. Research Officer, Oxford University, 1971-77; Lecturer/Senior Lecturer/Reader, Royal Free Hospital School of Medicine, 1977-90; Reader/Professor of Psychology, St. Andrews University, since 1990; Honorary Clinical Psychologist, Tayside and Fife Health Boards, since 1991; first Chair, Section of Health Psychology, British Psychological Society; President, European Health Psychology Society. Recreation: gardening. Address: (b.) School of Psychology, St. Andrews University, St. Andrews, KY16 9JU; T.-01334 62060.

Johnston, Peter William, MA, LLB, FRSA. Chief Executive and Secretary, Institute of Chartered Accountants of Scotland, since 1989; b. 8.2.43, Peebles; m., Patricia Sandra; 1 s.; 1 d. Educ. Larbert High School; Glasgow University. Partner, MacArthur & Co., Solicitors, Inverness, 1971-76; Procurator Fiscal Service, 1976-89. Recreations: music; languages; sailing. Address: (b.) 27 Queen Street, Edinburgh, EH2 1LA; T.-0131-225 5673.

Johnston, Robin Alexander, BSc, MB, BCh, BAO, MD, FRCS (Edin). Consultant Neurosurgeon, since 1985; Honorary Clinical Senior Lecturer, Glasgow University, since 1990; b. 30.3.49, Belfast; m., Ann. Educ. Belfast Royal Academy; Queens University, Belfast. Various surgical posts, UK, 1974-77; neurosurgical training, Belfast, Dallas, Glasgow, 1977-85. Address: (b.) Institute of Neurological Sciences, Southern General Hospital, Glasgow; T.-0141-445 2466.

Johnston, Sir Russell, MA (Hons). MP (Liberal Democrat), Inverness, Nairn and Lochaber (formerly Inverness), since 1964; b. 28.7.32, Edinburgh; m., Joan Graham Menzies; 3 s. Educ. Carbost Public School; Portree High School; Edinburgh University; Moray House College of Education. National Service: commissioned into Intelligence Corps and 2nd i/c British Intelligence Unit, Berlin, 1958-59; History Teacher, Liberton Secondary School, Edinburgh, 1961-63; Research Assistant, Scottish Liberal Party, 1963-64; Joint Parliamentary Adviser, Educational Institute of Scotland, 1964-70; Member, Royal Commission on Local Government in Scotland, 1966-69; Parliamentary Spokesman for Scottish National Federation for the Welfare of the Blind, since 1967; Parliamentary Representative, Royal National Institute for the Blind, since 1977; Member, Select Committee on Scottish Affairs, 1969; Parliamentary Adviser, Scottish Police Federation, 1971-75; Scottish Liberal Party: elected to Executive, 1961, and Organisation Committee, 1962, Vice Chairman, 1965, Chairman, 1970-74, Leader, 1974-88, President, since 1988; Liberal Party Spokesman on Education, 1964-66, on Foreign Affairs, 1970-75 and 1979-85, on Scotland, 1970-73, 1975-83, 1985-88, on Devolution, 1975, on Defence, 1983-88; Member, House of Commons Committee on Privileges, 1988-92; Liberal Democrat Parliamentary Spokesman, Foreign and Commonwealth Affairs, 1988-89, European Affairs, 1988-94, East/West Relations, 1989-94, Central and Eastern Europe, since 1994; Leader, Council of Europe Liberal Democrat and Reform Group, since 1994; President, Council of Europe Sub Committee on Youth and Sport, since 1992; Vice President, Liberal International, since 1994; Member, European Parliament, 1973-75 and 1976-79; Vice President, European Liberal Group and Group Spokesman on Regional Policy, 1973-75; Vice President of the Parliament's Political Committee, 1976-79; Member, Western European Union Assembly and Representative to Council of Europe, 1984-85, and since 1987; Leader, Scottish Liberal Democrats, 1988-94; Deputy Leader, Parliamentary Party, 1988-92; Vice President, ELDR, 1990-92. Recreations: reading; photography; shinty (Vice Chief, Camanachd Association, 1987-90). Address: House of Commons, London, SW1A 0AA; T.-0171-219 5180.

Johnston, Thomas Lothian, MA, PhD, DL, FRSA, FRSE, CIMgt, DrHC, DEd, LLD, DUniv, FEIS. President, Royal Society of Edinburgh, since 1993; Chairman, Scottish Committee, Royal Society of Arts, 1991-95; Director, Hodgson Martin Ltd., Scottish Life Assurance Company; Chairman, Academic Residences in Scotland plc; b. 9.3.27, Whitburn; m., Joan Fahmy; 2 s.; 3 d. Educ. Hawick High School; Edinburgh University; Stockholm University. Lecturer in Political Economy, Edinburgh University, 1953-65; Professor of Economics, Heriot-Watt University, 1966-76; Vice-Chancellor, Heriot-Watt University, 1981-88; Chairman, Manpower Services Committee for Scotland, 1977-80; Scottish Chairman, Industry Year, 1986, and Industry Matters, 1987-89; Trustee, National Galleries of Scotland, since 1989; industrial relations arbitrator and mediator; academic appointments in other countries: Illinois University, 1957, 1962-63; Queen's University, Canada, 1965, Western Australian Institute of Technology, 1979, Visiting Professor, International Institute for Labour Studies, Geneva, 1973. Publications: Collective Bargaining in Sweden, 1962; Economic Expansion and Structural Change, 1963; The Structure and Growth of the Scottish

Economy (Co-author), 1971; Introduction to Industrial Relations, 1981. Recreations: gardening; walking. Address: (h.) 14 Mansionhouse Road, Edinburgh, EH9 1TZ; T.-031-667 1439.

Johnston, Very Rev. William Bryce, MA, BD, DD, DLitt. Minister, Colinton Parish Church, 1964-91; Chaplain to The Queen in Scotland, 1981-91, Extra Chaplain, since 1991; b. 16.9.21, Edinburgh; m., Ruth Margaret Cowley; 1 s.; 2 d. Educ. George Watson's College, Edinburgh; Edinburgh University. Chaplain to the Forces, 1945-49; Minister: St. Andrew's Church, Bo'ness, 1949-55, St. George's Church, Greenock, 1955-64; Chaplain, HM Prison, Greenock, 1959-64; Convener, General Assembly Committees: Adult Christian Education, 1970-72, Church and Nation, 1972-76, Inter-Church Relations, 1979-81; Moderator of the General Assembly, 1980; Cunningham Lecturer, New College, 1968-71; Visiting Lecturer in Social Ethics, Heriot-Watt University, 1966- 88; Member, Broadcasting Council for Scotland, 1983-87. Publications: translations of Karl Barth and John Calvin; Ethics and Defence (Contributor). Recreations: organ music; bowls. Address: (h.) 15 Elliot Road, Edinburgh, EH14 1DU; T.-0131-441 3387.

Johnston, William John, BSc (Hons), DipEd(Tech). Rector, Aberdeen Grammar School, since 1987; b. 17.8.47, Kilmarnock; m., Katie Mary Maclean; 3 d. Educ. Spier's School, Beith; Glasgow University. Marketing Assistant, ICI Silicones, 1969-70; Teacher: Cranhill Secondary, 1971-73, Perth High School, 1973-75; Assistant Principal Teacher, Glenrothes High School, 1975-78; Principal Teacher, Millburn Academy, 1978-81; Assistant Rector, Kingussie High School, 1981-84; Depute Rector, Culloden Academy, 1984-87. Address: (b.) Aberdeen Grammar School, Skene Street, Aberdeen; T.-01224 642299.

Johnstone, Professor Alexander Henry, BSc, PhD, DipREd, CChem, FRSC. Professor in Science Education, Glasgow University, since 1990 (Head, Science Education Research Group, since 1972); Director, Centre for Science Education, Glasgow University, since 1989; Director, Teaching and Learning Service, Glasgow University, since 1994; b. 17.10.30, Edinburgh; m., Martha Y. Cuthbertson; 2 s. Educ. Leith Academy; Edinburgh University; Glasgow University; Moray House College of Education. Commissioned, Royal Corps of Signals; Assistant Teacher of Chemistry, George Watson's College, Edinburgh; Head, Chemistry Department, High School of Stirling; Lecturer, then Senior Lecturer in Chemistry, then Reader in Chemical Education, Glasgow University. Vice-President, Royal Society of Chemistry (President, Education Division); Consultant to Consultative Committee on the Curriculum. Recreations: hill-walking; photography; archaeology; lay preaching. Address: (b.) Department of Chemistry, The University, Glasgow, G12 8QQ; T.-0141-339 8855, Ext. 5172.

Johnstone, Professor Eve Cordelia, MD, FRCP, FRCPsych, DPM. Professor of Psychiatry, Edinburgh University; Honorary Consultant Psychiatrist; Honorary Member, Scientific Staff, Medical Research Council; b. 1.9.44, Glasgow. Educ. The Park School, Glasgow; Glasgow University. Junior hospital appointments, 1968-72; Lecturer in Psychological Medicine, Glasgow University, 1972; Member, Scientific Staff, Medical Research Council, 1974-89. Publications: 160 papers. Recreations: cultivating plants; playing bridge; foreign travel. Address: (b.) Kennedy Tower, Royal Edinburgh Hospital, Edinburgh; T.-0131-447 2011.

Johnstone, Sir Raymond, CBE, BA, CA. Chairman, Forestry Commission, 1989-94; Director, RJ KILN & Co. Ltd., since 1995; Director, Lomond Underwriting plc (Chairman, since 1993); Chairman, Murray Johnstone Ltd., 1984-91; (Managing Director, 1968-88); b. 27.10.29, London; m., Susan Sara; 5 step s.; 2 step d. Educ. Eton;

Trinity College, Cambridge. Investment Analyst, Robert Fleming & Co. Ltd., London, 1955-60; Partner (CA), Brown, Fleming & Murray (later Whinney Murray & Co.), 1960-68; Director: Dominion Insurance Co. Ltd., 1973-95 (Chairman, 1978-95); Scottish Financial Enterprise, 1986-91 (Chairman, 1989-91); Summit Group PLC (Chairman, since 1989); Glasgow Cultural Enterprises Ltd., since 1988; Murray Income PLC, since 1989; Murray International PLC, since 1989; Murray Smaller Markets PLC, since 1989; Murray Ventures PLC, since 1984; Murray Enterprise PLC, since 1989; Chairman, Murray Split Capital Trust PLC, since 1991; Director, Scottish Amicable Life Assurance Society, since 1971 (Chairman, 1983-85); Member, Scottish Economic Council; Hon. President, Scottish Opera. Recreations: fishing; shooting; opera; farming. Address: (h.) Wards, Gartocharn, Dunbartonshire.

Johnstone, Professor William, MA (Hons), BD. Professor of Hebrew and Semitic Languages, Aberdeen University, since 1980; Minister, Church of Scotland, since 1963; b. 6.5.36, Glasgow; m., Elizabeth M. Ward; 1 s.; 1 d. Educ. Hamilton Academy; Glasgow University; Marburg University. Lecturer in Hebrew and Semitic Languages, Aberdeen University, 1962-72, Senior Lecturer, 1972-80, Dean, Faculty of Divinity, 1983-87; President, Society for Old Testament Study, 1990. Recreation: alternative work. Address: (h.) 37 Rubislaw Den South, Aberdeen, AB2 6BD; T.-Aberdeen 316022.

Jolliffe, Professor Ian, BSc, DPhil. Professor of Statistics, Aberdeen University, since 1992; b. 22.12.45, Isle of Wight; m., Jean Peddar; 1 s.; 1 d. Educ. Sandown Grammar School; Sussex University. Lecturer, then Senior Lecturer, Kent University; visiting positions, Dalhousie University, University of Guelph. Recreations: running; dinghy sailing; folk music. Address: (b.) Department of Mathematical Sciences, Aberdeen University, Edward Wright Building, Dunbar Street, Aberdeen, AB9 2TY; T.-01224 272611.

Jolly, Douglas, BSc (Hons). Rector, Viewforth High School, 1981-95; Council Member, Headteachers' Association of Scotland; b. 30.6.38, Dundee; m., Elizabeth Smith; 2 d. Educ. Grove Academy, Broughty Ferry; St. Andrews University. Principal Teacher of Physics, Lawside Academy, 1964-72; Assistant Rector, Craigie High School, 1972-75; Depute Rector, Arbroath High School, 1975-81; Member, Central Committee for Science Teaching in Scotland, 1972-75. Elder, Markinch Parish Church. Recreations: golf; gardening; travel. Address: (h.) 16 Orchard Drive, Glenrothes, Fife; T.-Glenrothes 757039.

Jones, Professor Charles, MA, BLitt, FRSE. Forbes Professor of English Language, Edinburgh University, since 1990; b. 24.12.39, Glasgow; m., Isla Shennan. Educ. St. Aloysius College, Glasgow; Glasgow University. Lecturer in Linguistics, Hull University, 1964-67; Lecturer, Department of English Language, Edinburgh University, 1967-78; Professor of English Language, Durham University, 1978-90. Convenor, Scots Language Resource Centre Association; Council Member, Saltire Society, since 1995 (Convenor, Education Committee); Member, Edinburgh University Court, since 1993. Publications: An Introduction to Middle English; Phonological Structure and the History of English; Grammatical Gender in English; A History of English Phonology; A Treatise on the Provincial Dialect of Scotland (Editor); Historical Linguistics (Editor). Recreation: breeding Soay sheep. Address: (h.) Laggan Cottage, Faladam, Midlothian, EH37 5SU; T.-01875 33 652.

Jones, David Adams, MA, MSc, DipStat, FSS. Director, Information and Statistics Division, Scottish Health Service, since 1986; b. 23.4.33, Fochriw; m., Fiona Janet Hill; 2 s.; 2 d. Educ. The Lewis School, Pengam, Glamorgan; Jesus College, Oxford. Lt., Royal Navy; Industrial Statistician, British Nylon Spinners; Lecturer in Statistics, UWIST;

Statistician and Chief Statistician, Welsh Office; Director of Statistics, Scottish Health Service. Recreations: squash; gentle hill-walking. Address: (b.) Trinity Park House, Edinburgh; T.-0131-551 8562.

Jones, Professor Huw, BA, MA. Professor of Geography, Dundee University; b. Llanidloes; 2 s. Educ. Newtown Boys Grammar School, Powys; University College of Wales, Aberystwyth. Editor, International Journal of Population Geography. Address: (b.) Department of Geography, Dundee University, Dundee, DD1 4HN; T.-01382-344 427.

Jones, Keith Greig, LLB. Director of Legal Services and Depute Chief Executive, Kincardine and Deeside District Council, since 1985; b. 10.9.48, Edinburgh; m., Margaret. Educ. Aberdeen Grammar School; Aberdeen University. Various appointments in private legal practice, 1969-75; joined Law and Administration Department, Kincardine and Deeside District Council, 1975. Trustee, Grampian Transport Museum Trust. Address: (b.) Viewmount, Stonehaven, AB3 2DQ; T.-01569 762001.

Jones, Mark Ellis Powell, MA, FSA, FSA Scot, FRSA. Director, National Museums of Scotland, since 1992; b. 5.2.51, Bogota; m., Dr. A.C. Toulmin; 2 s.; 2 d. Educ. Eton College; Oxford University; London University. Assistant Keeper of Coins and Medals, British Museum, 1974-90; Keeper of Coins and Medals, 1990-92. President, Federation Internationale de la Medaille; Secretary, British Art Medal Society. Address: (h.) 39 Regent Street, Portobello, Edinburgh, EH15 2AY; T.-0131-657 3335.

Jones, Professor Peter (Howard), MA, FRSE, FRSA, FSA Scot. Professor of Philosophy, University of Edinburgh, since 1984; Director, Institute for Advanced Studies in the Humanities, since 1986; b. 18.12.35, London; m., Elizabeth Jean Roberton; 2 d. Educ. Highgate School; Queens' College, Cambridge. Regional Officer, The British Council, London, 1960-61; Research Scholar, University of Cambridge, 1961-63; Assistant Lecturer in Philosophy, Nottingham University, 1963-64; University of Edinburgh: Lecturer in Philosophy, 1964-77, Reader, 1977-84; Visiting Professor of Philosophy: University of Rochester, New York, 1969-70, Dartmouth College, New Hampshire, 1973, 1983, Carleton College, Minnesota, 1974, Oklahoma University, 1978, Baylor University, 1978, University of Malta, 1993; Distinguished Foreign Scholar, Mid-America State Universities, 1978; Visiting Fellow, Humanities Research Centre, Australian National University, 1984; Calgary Institute for the Humanities, 1992; Lothian Lecturer, 1993; Gifford Lecturer, University of Aberdeen, 1994-95; Trustee, National Museums of Scotland, since 1987; Trustee, University of Edinburgh Development Trust; Governor, Morrison's Academy, Crieff, since 1984; Founder Member, The Hume Society, 1974. Publications: Philosophy and the Novel, 1975; Hume's Sentiments, 1982; A Hotbed of Genius, 1986; Philosophy and Science in the Scottish Enlightenment, 1988; The Science of Man in the Scottish Enlightenment, 1989; Adam Smith Reviewed, 1992. Recreations: opera; chamber music; the arts; architecture. Address: (b.) Institute for Advanced Studies in the Humanities, Hope Park Square, Edinburgh, 8; T.-0131-650 4671.

Jones, Trevor, IPFA, FCCA, ACIS, MIMgt. General Manager, Lothian Health Board, since 1995; b. 23.12.50, Penshaw, Co. Durham; m., Hazel Oliver. Entered NHS, 1978; Northern Regional Health Authority; South Manchester Health Authority; Waltham Forest Health Authority; Chief Executive, Forest Healthcare NHS Trust, 1991-95. Recreations: golf; squash; Durham CCC; Sunderland AFC. Address: (b.) Lothian Health Board, 148 Pleasance, Edinburgh, EH8 9RS; T.-0131-536 9001.

Jones, Rev. William Gerald, MA, BD, ThM. Minister, Kirkmichael with Straiton St. Cuthbert's, since 1985; b. 2.11.56, Irvine; m., Janet Blackstock. Educ. Dalry High School; Garnock Academy, Kilbirnie; Glasgow University; St. Andrews University; Princeton Theological Seminary, Princeton, New Jersey. Assistant Minister, Glasgow Cathedral, 1983-85. Freeman Citizen of Glasgow, 1984; Member, Incorporation of Gardeners of Glasgow, 1984; Convener, Administration Committee, Presbytery of Ayr, 1988-91; Member, General Assembly Panel on Worship, 1987-91; Member, Council, Church Service Society, since 1986; Member, Committee to Nominate the Moderator of the General Assembly, 1988-92; Member, Societas Liturgica, since 1989; AssChLJ (Assistant Chaplain, Order of St. Lazarus of Jerusalem), 1995. Publication: Prayers for the Chapel Royal in Scotland, 1989. Recreations: music; redundant churches; reading; writing; travel. Address: The Manse, Kirkmichael, Maybole, Ayrshire, KA19 7PJ; T.-01655 750286.

Jordan, Professor Grant, MA, PhD. Professor of Politics, Aberdeen University, since 1990; b. 12.10.48, Forfar; m., Susan Allardice; 1 s.; 2 d. Educ. Forfar Academy; Aberdeen University. Entered market research, 1971; moved to Keele University, 1973, Aberdeen University, 1974. Recreations: books; skiing; Montrose FC. Address: (b.) Department of Politics and International Relations, Aberdeen University, Aberdeen, AB9 2TY; T.-01224 272722.

Jordan, Brigadier Howard Alfred John, MBE, FCIT. Chief Executive, Scottish Engineering, since 1980; Vice Chairman, Lowland TAVRA, since 1994; b. 26.3.36, Edinburgh; m., Patricia Ann Tomlin; 1 s.; 1 d. Army, 1954-80; Lt. Col., Royal Corps of Transport; commanded 154 (Lowland) Transport Regiment RCT(V). Chairman, Carmunnock Community Council, since 1980; Chairman, Strathclyde Group, National Council for Conservation of Plants and Gardens, since 1983; Honorary President, Carmunnock British Legion, since 1980; Member, Lowland TA Council, since 1981; Commandant, ACF Scotland, Chairman, ACFA Scotland, since 1994. Address: (b.) 105 West George Street, Glasgow, G2 1QL; T.-0141-221 3181.

Joughin, Sir Michael, CBE, JP, CBIM, FRAgS; Member, Bank of Scotland East of Scotland Board, 1990-95; b. 26.4.26, Devonport; m., 1, Lesley Roy Petrie; 2, Anne S.H. Hutchison; 1 s.; 1 d. Educ. Kelly College, Tavistock, Devon. Royal Marines, 1944-52 (Lt.); seconded, Fleet Air Arm, 1946-49 (ditched off Malta, 1949, invalided, 1952). Chairman, North of Scotland Hydro-Electric Board, 1983-90; Member, South of Scotland Electricity Board, 1983-88; Chairman, Scottish Hydro Electric plc, 1990-93; Chairman, North of Scotland Milk Marketing Board, 1974-83; Past Chairman, Grassland and Forage Committee, JCC; Chairman, Scottish Agricultural Development Council, 1971-80; Chairman, Governors, North of Scotland College of Agriculture, 1969-72; President, National Farmers Union of Scotland, 1964-66; Deputy Lieutenant, County of Moray, 1974-80; Governor: Rowett Research Institute, Aberdeen, 1968-74, Scottish Plant Breeding Station, 1969-74, Animal Diseases Research Association, Edinburgh, 1969-74; Chairman, Governors, Blairmore Preparatory School, near Huntly, 1966-72; Member: Scottish Constitutional Committee (Douglas-Home Committee), 1969-70, Intervention Board for Agricultural Produce, 1972-76, National Economic Development Council for Agriculture, 1967-70; Past Chairman, NEDC Working Party on Livestock; Member: Agricultural Marketing Development Executive Committee, 1965-68, British Farm Produce Council, 1965-66; former Member: Selection Committee, Nuffield Farming Scholarships, Awards Committee, Massey-Ferguson National Award for Services to UK Agriculture; Chairman: North of Scotland Grassland Society, 1970-71, Elgin Market Green Auction Co., 1969-70; Founder Presenter, Country Focus (farming programme), Grampian Television, 1961-64 and 1967-69;

Captain, 11th Bn., Seaforth Highlanders (TA), 1952-53. Recreation: sailing. Address: (h.) Elderslie, Findhorn, Moray; T.-01309 690277.

Jowitt, Professor Paul William, PhD, DIC, BSc(Eng), ACGI, CEng, FICE. Professor of Civil Engineering Systems, Heriot-Watt University, since 1987 (Head, Civil Engineering Department, 1989-91; Head, Civil and Offshore Engineering, since 1991); Editor, Civil Engineering Systems, since 1985; b. 3.8.50, Doncaster; m., Jane Catriona Urquhart; 1 s.; 1 d. Educ. Maltby Grammar School; Imperial College. Lecturer in Civil Engineering, Imperial College 1974-86 (Warden, Falmouth Hall, 1980-86); Director, Tynemarch Systems Engineering Ltd., 1984-91 (Chairman, 1984-86). Recreations: painting; Morgan 3-wheelers; restoring old houses. Address: (h.) 22 Fountainhall Road, The Grange, Edinburgh, EH9 2LW; T.-0131-667 5696.

Jung, Roland Tadeusz, BA, MA, MB, BChir, MD, MRCS, LRCP, MRCP, FRCPEdin, FRCPLond. Consultant Physician (Specialist in Endocrinology and Diabetes), since 1982; Honorary Reader, Dundee University, and Clinical Director of General Medicine, Dundee Teaching Hospitals Trust; b. 8.2.48, Glasgow; m., Felicity King; 1 d. Educ. St. Anselm's College, Wirral; Pembroke College, Cambridge; St. Thomas Hospital and Medical School, London. MRC Clinical Scientific Officer, Dunn Nutrition Unit, Cambridge, and Honorary Senior Registrar, Addenbrooke's Hospital, Cambridge, 1977-79; Senior Registrar in Endocrinology and Diabetes, Royal Postgraduate Medical School, Hammersmith Hospital, London, 1980-82. Publication: Endocrine Problems in Oncology (Co-Editor), 1984; Colour Atlas of Obesity, 1990. Recreation: gardening. Address: (b.) Department of Medicine, Ninewells Hospital and Medical School, Dundee; T.-Dundee 60111.

K

Kamm, Antony, MA. Author; b. 2.3.31, London; m., Eileen Dunlop (qv). Educ. Charterhouse; Worcester College, Oxford. Editorial Director, Brockhampton Press, 1960-72; Senior Education Officer, Commonwealth Secretariat, 1972-74; Managing Editor (Children's Books), Oxford University Press, 1977-79; Consultant to UNESCO and other international organisations, 1963-76; part-time Lecturer in Publishing Studies, Stirling University, since 1988; Chairman, Children's Book Group, The Publishers Association, 1963-67, and of Children's Book Circle, 1963-64; played cricket for Middlesex, 1952. Publications include: Choosing Books for Younger Children, 1976; Scotland, 1989; A Dictionary of British and Irish Authors, 1990; Collins Biographical Dictionary of English Literature, 1993; The Jacobites, 1995 (with Eileen Dunlop):Edinburgh, 1982; The Story of Glasgow, 1983; Kings and Queens of Scotland, 1984; and other information books for children on Scottish themes; several anthologies. Recreations: work; watching sport on TV. Address: (h.) 46 Tarmangie Drive, Dollar, FK14 7BP; T.-01259 742007.

Kane, Jack, OBE, JP, DL, Dr hc (Edin). Honorary Vice-President, Age Concern Scotland, since 1986; Honorary President: Workers Educational Association (SE Scotland), Craigmillar Festival Society, Jack Kane Centre; b. 1.4.11, Addiewell, Midlothian; m., Anne Murphy; 1 s.; 2 d. Educ. Bathgate Academy. Librarian, 1937-55; War Service, Royal Artillery, 1940-46; District Secretary, Workers Educational Association (SE Scotland), 1955-76; Chairman, South of Scotland Electricity Consultative Council, 1977-80; Chairman, Board of Trustees, National Galleries of Scotland, 1975-80; Councillor, Edinburgh, 1938-75 (Bailie, 1947-51, Lord Provost, 1972-75). Recreations: reading; walking.

Kane, Liam James, ACMA. Chief Executive, Caledonian Publishing Ltd., since 1991; b. 11.1.50, Glasgow; m., Gillian Willie; 2 s.; 3 d. Educ. Holyrood Senior Secondary School; Central College, Glasgow. Commercial apprentice, G. & J. Weir, 1967-70; Accountant to Deputy Managing Director, Scottish Daily Record and Sunday Mail Ltd., 1970-84; M.D., Grant Forrest Advertising Ltd., 1985; Deputy General Manager, News Group Newspapers, 1985; General Manager, News (Scotland) Ltd., 1986; General Manager, Today newspaper, 1987-89; General Manager, Sky Television PLC, 1989-91. Governor, Glasgow Caledonian University Court. Address: (b.) 195 Albion Street, Glasgow, G1 1QP; T.-0141-552 6255.

Kane, Patrick Mark, MA (Hons). Lead Singer, Hue and Cry (pop group); former Rector, Glasgow University; Writer and Broadcaster; b. 10.3.64, Glasgow; m., Joan McAlpine; 1 d. Educ. St. Ambrose RC Secondary, Coatbridge; Glasgow University. Worked in London as a freelance writer; returned to Scotland to start professional music career with brother Gregory; achieved Top 10 and Top 20 singles and albums successes, 1987-89; Columnist, The Scotsman; TV arts presenter. Recreations: being with family; listening to music; reading abstruse social theory.

Kay, Michael, BSc, PhD. Head, Animal and Feed Technology Department, Estate Manager, and Vice-Dean, Scottish Agricultural College's Centre in Aberdeen, since 1979; b. 10.3.38, York; m., Moira G. Kay; 1 s.; 1 d. Educ. St. Peter's School, York; Leeds University; Aberdeen University. Joined Rowett Research Institute, 1963. Recreations: sport; gardening; DIY. Address: (b.) School of Agriculture, 581 King Street, Aberdeen, AB9 1UD; T.-01224 480291.

Kay, William, MA. Freelance Broadcaster/Writer/Producer; b. 24.9.51, Galston, Ayrshire; m., Maria Joao de Almeida da Cruz Dinis; 1 s.; 2 d. Educ. Galston High School; Kilmarnock Academy; Edinburgh University. Producer, Odyssey series, Radio Scotland; produced about 40 documentaries on diverse aspects of working-class oral history; Writer/Presenter, TV documentaries, including Miners, BBC Scotland; Presenter, Kay's Originals, Scottish TV. Commandeur d'Honneur, Commanderie du Bontemps de Medoc et des Graves; won Australasian Academy of Broadcast Arts and Sciences Pater award, 1987, 1988; Medallist, International Radio Festival of New York, 1990-92; Sloan Prize for writing in Scots, 1992; Wine Guild of UK 1994 Houghton Award, for Fresche Fragrant Clairettis. Publications: Odyssey: Voices from Scotland's Recent Past (Editor); Odyssey: The Second Collection (Editor); Knee Deep in Claret: A Celebration of Wine and Scotland (Co-author); Made in Scotland (poetry); Jute (play for radio); Scots — The Mither Tongue; They Fairly Mak Ye Work (for Dundee Repertory Theatre); Lucky's Strike (play for radio); The Dundee Book. Recreations: the weans; languages; films; Dundee United. Address: (h.) 72 Tay Street, Newport on Tay, Fife, DD6 8AP.

Kayne, Steven Barry, PhD, MBA, BSc, MRPharmS, MCPP, DAgVetPharm, MPS (NZ), ACNZP, MIPharmM, MBIM. Consultant Homoeopathic and Veterinary Pharmacist; medical journalist; b. 8.6.44, Cheltenham Spa; m., Sorelle; 2 s. Educ. Westcliff High School; Aston University; Strathclyde University; Glasgow University. Lecturer; Visiting Lecturer in Pharmacy Practice, University of Otago; Pharmacy Tutor to UK Faculty of Homoeopathy; Member: UK Faculty of Homoeopathy Council and Education Committee; Faculty of Homoeopathy (Scotland) Council and Education Committee; Council, British Homoeopathic Association; Natural Medicine Advisory and Research Committee; Adjudication Panel, British Pharmaceutical Conference; Government Advisory Board on Homoeopathic Registration; Homoeopathic Medical Research Council; Chairman, Joint Services Committee, Epilepsy Association of Scotland. Recreations: walking in Spey Valley; watching rugby; photography. Address: (h.) 79 Milverton Road, Whitecraigs, Giffnock, Glasgow; T.-0141-638 3216.

Keane, Sheriff Francis Joseph, PhL, LLB. Sheriff of Lothians and Borders, since 1993; b. 5.1.36, Broxburn; m., Lucia Corio Morrison; 2 s.; 1 d. Educ. Blairs College, Aberdeen; Gregorian University, Rome; Edinburgh University. Partner, McCluskey, Keane & Co., 1959; Procurator Fiscal Depute, Perth, 1961, Edinburgh, 1963; Senior PF Depute, Edinburgh, 1971; Senior Legal Assistant, Crown Office, Edinburgh, 1972; Procurator Fiscal, Airdrie, 1976; Regional Procurator Fiscal, South Strathclyde, Dumfries and Galloway, 1980; Sheriff of Glasgow and Strathkelvin, 1984-93. President, Procurators Fiscal Society, 1982-84. Recreations: music; tennis; walking; painting. Address: (b.) 27 Chambers Street, Edinburgh EH1 1LB; T.-0131-225 2525.

Keane, Professor Simon Michael, MA, LLB, PhD, CA. Professor of Accountancy, Glasgow University, since 1983; b. 8.4.35, Glasgow; m., Mary; 1 d. Educ. St. Aloysius College; Glasgow University. Investigating Accountant, Admiralty, 1965-67; Lecturer, Glasgow College of Commerce, 1967-69; Glasgow University: Lecturer, 1969-81, Reader, 1981-83. Publications: Efficient Market Hypothesis, 1980; Stock Market Efficiency, 1983. Recreations: golf; painting. Address: (b.) 67 Southpark Avenue, Glasgow, G12; T.-0141-339 8855.

Kearney, Sheriff Brian, MA, LLB. Sheriff of Glasgow and Strathkelvin, since 1977; b. 25.8.35.

Kee, Professor A. Alistair, MA, BD, STM, PhD, DLitt. Professor of Religious Studies and Head, Department of Theology and Religious Studies, Edinburgh University (Head, Department of Religious Studies, Glasgow

University, 1976-88); b. 17.4.37, Alexandria; m., Anne Paterson; 1 s.; 1 d. Educ. Clydebank High School; Glasgow University; Union Theological Seminary, New York. Lecturer: University College of Rhodesia, 1964-67, Hull University, 1967-76; Senior Lecturer, then Reader, Glasgow University, since 1976; Visiting Professor: Augusta College, Georgia, 1982-83, Dartmouth College, New Hampshire, 1990,1995; Director, SCM Press Ltd.; delivered Jaspers Lectures, Ripon Hall, Oxford, 1975; Ferguson Lectures, Manchester University, 1986. Publications: The Way of Transcendence; A Reader in Political Theology; Constantine Versus Christ; Being and Truth; Domination or Liberation; The Roots of Christian Freedom; Marx and the Failure of Liberation Theology; From Bad Faith to Good News. Address: (b.) Department of Theology and Religious Studies, Edinburgh University, New College, Mound Place, Edinburgh, EH1 2LX; T.-0131-650 8953.

Keeble, Neil Howard, BA, DPhil, DLitt, FRHistS. Reader in English, Stirling University, since 1988; b. 7.8.44, London; m., Jenny Bowers; 2 s.; 1 d. Educ. Bancroft's School, Woodford Green; St. David's College, Lampeter; Pembroke College, Oxford. Foreign Lektor, Department of English, University of Aarhus, Denmark, 1969-72; Lecturer in English, Aarhus, 1972-74; Lecturer in English, Stirling University, 1974-88. Publications: Richard Baxter: Puritan Man of Letters; The Literary Culture of Nonconformity in later seventeenth-century England; The Autobiography of Richard Baxter (Editor); The Pilgrim's Progress (Editor); John Bunyan: Conventicle and Parnassus (Editor); A Handbook of English and Celtic Studies in the United Kingdom and the Republic of Ireland (Editor); The Cultural Identity of Seventeenth-Century Woman (Editor); Lucy Hutchinson, Memoirs of the Life of Colonel Hutchinson (Editor); Calendar of the Correspondence of Richard Baxter (Co-Compiler). Recreations: books and book-collecting; films (especially Westerns); the Midi; gardening. Address: Duncraggan House, Airthrey Road, Stirling, FK9 5JS; T.-01786 473758.

Keegan, James Douglas, LLB, DFM, SSC, FCIArb, NP. Solicitor Advocate; Senior Partner, Keegan Walker & Co., Solicitors, since 1987; Chairman, Caledonian Nursing Care Group, since 1990; Member, Council, Law Society of Scotland, since 1992; Member, Scottish Council, Chartered Institute of Arbiters, since 1994; b. 25.9.51, Uddingston; m., Karen Keegan; 3 d. Educ. Our Lady's High School, Motherwell; Strathclyde University; Glasgow University. Partner, Drummond and Co., WS, Edinburgh, 1978-87. Recreations: swimming; reading; football; rugby. Address: (b.) Pentland House, Almondvale, Livingston, West Lothian, EH54 6NG; T.-01506 430042.

Keen, Richard Sanderson, LLB (Hons). Queen's Counsel; b. 29.3.54, Rustington; m., Jane Carolyn Anderson; 1 s.; 1 d. Educ. King's School, Rochester; Dollar Academy; Edinburgh University. Admitted to Faculty of Advocates, 1980; Standing Junior Counsel in Scotland to DTI, 1986-93; QC, 1993. Recreations: golf; skiing; shooting; opera. Address: (b.) Parliament House, Parliament Square, Edinburgh; T.-0131-226 5071.

Keir, Professor Hamish Macdonald, BSc, PhD, DSc, CBiol, FIBiol, CChem, FRSC, FRSE. Professor of Biochemistry, Aberdeen University, since 1968 (Vice-Principal, 1982-84); Vice-Chairman, Governors, Macaulay Land Use Research Institute, since 1987; Chairman, Board of Governors, Rowett Research Institute, 1989-93; b. 5.9.31, Moffat; m., 1, Eleanor Campbell; 1 s.; 2 d.; 2, Linda Gerrie; 2 d. Educ. Ayr Academy; Glasgow University; Yale University. Hon. Secretary, The Biochemical Society, 1970-77, Chairman, 1986-89; Member, Cell Board, Medical Research Council, 1970-74; Scottish Home and Health Department, BRC, 1974-78; Ethical and Research Committees, Grampian Health Board; Science and Engineering Research Council (Biology), 1980-84; University Grants Committee (Biology), 1984-90; Royal Society — British National Committee for Biochemistry, 1986-90; Board of Governors, North of Scotland College of Agriculture, 1976-91; Tenovus — Scotland, Grampian Region, 1980-86; Board of Governors, Longridge Towers School, since 1988; Committees of the International Union of Biochemistry, 1974-82; Chairman, Natural Environment Research Council, Institute of Marine Biochemistry, 1969-84; Chairman, Universities of Scotland Purchasing Consortium, since 1988; President, European Union of Societies for Experimental Biology, since 1989; European Science Foundation, since 1989; President, Council, Federation of European Biochemical Societies, 1980-83. Recreations: piano; golf; travel. Address: (b.) Department of Molecular and Cell Biology, Aberdeen University, Marischal College, Aberdeen, AB9 1AS; T.-01224 273121.

Kelbie, Sheriff David, LLB (Hons); Sheriff of Grampian, Highland and Islands, at Aberdeen and Stonehaven, since 1986 (North Strathclyde, at Dumbarton, 1979-86); b. 28.2.45, Inverurie; m., Helen Mary Smith; 1 s.; 1 d. Educ. Inverurie Academy; Aberdeen University. Passed Advocate, 1968; Associate Lecturer, Heriot-Watt University, 1971-76; Secretary, Scottish Congregational College, 1974-82; Member, UK/Ireland Committee of Christian Aid, 1986-90. Recreations: sailing; reading. Address: (h.) 38 Earlspark Drive, Bieldside, Aberdeen.

Kellas, Professor James Grant, MA, PhD, FRHistS. Professor in Politics, Glasgow University, since 1984; b. 16.5.36, Aberdeen; m., Norma Rennie Craig; 2 s.; 1 d. Educ. Aberdeen Grammar School; Aberdeen University; London University. Tutorial Fellow in History, Bedford College, London University, 1961-62; Assistant in History, Aberdeen University, 1962-64; Glasgow University: Lecturer in Politics, 1964-73; Senior Lecturer, 1973-77, Reader, 1977-84. Member, Study of Parliament Group. Publications: Modern Scotland, 1968, 1980; The Scottish Political System, 1973, 1975, 1984, 1989; The Politics of Nationalism and Ethnicity, 1991. Recreations: mountaineering; music. Address: (b.) Department of Politics, Glasgow University, Glasgow, G12 8RT; T.-0141-339 8855.

Kelly, Alexander Joseph, MA, MEd. Rector, Auchmuty High School, Glenrothes, since 1990; b. 18.6.46, Dunoon; m., Ann Smith; 3 s.; 1 d. Educ. Dunoon Grammar School; Glasgow University. Teacher, Assistant Principal Teacher, Principal Teacher, St. Mary's, Glasgow, 1969-75; Principal Teacher, St. Mungo's Academy, 1975-79; Assistant Head Teacher, St. Columba's, Dunfermline, 1979-84; Deputy Head Teacher, St. Andrew's High, Kirkcaldy, 1984-90. Recreations: Rotary; golf; photography; walking. Address: (h.) Blythswood, 101 Main Street, Aberdour, Fife; T.-01383 860369.

Kelly, Barbara Mary, CBE, DipEd. President, Rural Forum Scotland; Member, Scottish Economic Council; Chairman, Rural Affairs Advisory Committee, BBC Scotland; Member, Scottish Enterprise Board; Director, Clydesdale Bank plc; Member, Scottish Tourist Board; Member, Scottish Advisory Board, BP plc; Chair, Training 2000; Journalist and Broadcaster; Partner in dairy farming enterprise; b. 27.2.40, Dalbeattie; m., Kenneth A. Kelly (qv); 1 s.; 2 d. Educ. Dalbeattie High School; Kirkcudbright Academy; Moray House College. Past Chairman, Scottish Consumer Council; former Member, National Consumer Council; former Vice-Chairman, SWRI; Duke of Edinburgh's Award: former Chairman, Scottish Advisory Committee and former Member, UK Advisory Panel; former Member, Priorities Board, MAFF; former EOC Commissioner for Scotland; Past Chairman, Dumfries and Galloway Area Manpower Board, Manpower Services Commission; Trustee, Scottish Children's Bursary Fund. Recreations: painting; music. Address: (h.) Barncleugh, Irongray, Dumfries, DG2 9SE; T.-01387 73210.

Kelly, Kenneth Archibald. Dairy Farmer; b. Glasgow; m., Barbara Mary Prentice (see Barbara Mary Kelly); 1 s.; 2 d. Educ. Glasgow Academy; Sedbergh; West of Scotland College of Agriculture. Elected to Stewartry County Council, 1969, Dumfries and Galloway Regional Council, 1974 (Chairman, Planning); Past Chairman, North British Hereford Breeders Association; Past President, Dumfries Rugby Club; Session Clerk, Irongray Kirk. Recreations: shooting; fishing; curling; music. Address: (h.) Barncleugh, Irongray, Dumfries, DG2 9SE; T.-01387 730210.

Kelly, Michael, CBE (1983), OStJ, JP, BSc(Econ), PhD, LLD, DL, FRSA. Public Relations Consultant, since 1984; Chairman, Royal Scottish Society for the Prevention of Cruelty to Children, since 1987; Member, National Arts Collection Fund, since 1990; b. 1.11.40, Glasgow; m., Zita Harkins; 1 s.; 2 d. Educ. St. Joseph's College, Dumfries. Assistant Lecturer in Economics, Aberdeen University, 1965-67; Lecturer in Economics, Strathclyde University, 1967-80; Lord Provost of Glasgow, 1980-84; Rector, Glasgow University, 1984-87; Director, Drumkinnon Development Company; British Tourist Authority Medal for services to tourism, 1984; Robert Burns Award from University of Old Dominion, Virginia, for services to Scottish culture, 1984; Scot of the Year, 1983; Radio Scotland News Quiz Champion, 1986, 1987; Radio Scotland Christmas Quiz Champion, 1987; Honorary Mayor of Tombstone, Arizona; Kentucky Colonel, 1983. Recreations: philately; golf. Address: (b.) 95 Bothwell Street, Glasgow, G2 7HY; T.-0141-204 2580.

Kelly, Michael W., MBA, MIPM, MBIM. Chief Executive, Falkirk and District Royal Infirmary NHS Trust, since 1992; b. 9.5.46, Northampton; m., Patricia Ann. Educ. Cavendish County, Eastbourne; Glasgow Caledonian. Nurse; Nursing Officer; Head of Nursing; Director of Nursing; General Manager. Recreations: horse-riding; Highland cattle; gardening. Address: (b.) Majors Loan, Falkirk, FK1 5QE; T.-01324 624000.

Kelman, James. Novelist; b. 1946, Glasgow. Works include: The Busconductor Hines; A Chancer; Greyhound for Breakfast; A Disaffection; How Late It Was How Late (Booker Prize, 1994).

Kelnar, Christopher J.H., MA, MD, FRCP, DCH. Consultant Paediatric Endocrinologist, Royal Hospital for Sick Children, Edinburgh, since 1983; Senior Lecturer, Department of Child Life and Health, Edinburgh University, since 1983; b. 22.12.47, London; m., Alison; 1 s.; 2 d. Educ. Highgate School, London; Trinity College, Cambridge; St. Bartholomew's Hospital, London. Research Fellow, Paediatric Endocrinology, Middlesex Hospital, London, 1979-81; Senior Registrar, Hospital for Sick Children, Great Ormond Street, London, and Tutor, Institute of Child Health, London, 1981-83. Publications: The Sick Newborn Baby, 1981 (3rd edition, 1995); Childhood and Adolescent Diabetes, 1995; chapters and papers on paediatric endocrinology. Recreations: music; gardening. Address: (b.) Royal Hospital for Sick Children, Sciennes Road, Edinburgh, EH9 1LF; T.-0131-536 0000.

Kelso, David Elliot, BSc, MEd. HM Chief Inspector, Scottish Office Education Department; b. 25.3.45, Glasgow; m., Dorothy Louise Christie; 1 s.; 2 d. Educ. St. Joseph's College, Dumfries; Edinburgh University; Glasgow University; Dundee University. Personnel Officer, Singer (UK) Ltd., Clydebank, 1968-69; Personnel Manager, Rank Organisation, Kirkcaldy, 1969-71; Lecturer in Management, Glasgow College, 1971-73; Senior Lecturer, Dundee College of Commerce, 1973-76; Head, Department of Commerce and Business Studies, Falkirk College, 1976-83; Assistant Principal, 1983-85; HMI, 1985. Recreations: running; esperanto; hill-walking. Address: (h.) Lomond, St. Mary's Drive, Dunblane, Perthshire; T.-01786 822605.

Kemball, Professor Emeritus Charles, CBE, MA, ScD, HonDSc, CChem, FRSC, MRIA, FRSE, FRS. Emeritus Professor of Chemistry, Edinburgh University, since 1983; b. 27.3.23, Edinburgh; m., Kathleen Purvis Lynd; 1 s.; 2 d. Educ. Edinburgh Academy; Trinity College, Cambridge. Fellow, Trinity College, 1946-54 (Junior Bursar, 1949-51, Assistant Lecturer, 1951-54); Demonstrator in Physical Chemistry, Cambridge University, 1951-54; Professor of Physical Chemistry, Queen's University, Belfast, 1954-66 (Dean, Faculty of Science, 1957-60, Vice-President, 1962-65); Professor of Chemistry, Edinburgh University, 1966-83 (Dean, Faculty of Science, 1975-78). President, Royal Institute of Chemistry, 1974-76; President, Royal Society of Edinburgh, 1988-91; Meldola Medal, RIC, 1951; Corday-Morgan Medal, 1958; Tilden Lecturer, 1960; Surface and Colloid Chemistry Award, Chemical Society, 1972; Ipatieff Prize, American Chemical Society, 1962; Gunning-Victoria Jubilee Prize, Royal Society of Edinburgh, 1976-80. Recreations: hill-walking; card games; wine-making. Address: (h.) 24 Main Street, Tyninghame, Dunbar, East Lothian, EH42 1XL; T.-01620 860710.

Kemp, Professor Alexander George, MA (Hons). Professor of Economics, Aberdeen University, since 1983; b. Blackhall, Drumoak, Aberdeenshire. Educ. Robert Gordon's College, Aberdeen; Aberdeen University. Economist, Shell International Petroleum, London, 1962-64; Lecturer in Economics, Strathclyde University, 1964-65; Lecturer, then Senior Lecturer, then Reader, Aberdeen University, 1966-83. Specialist Adviser to House of Commons Select Committee on Energy, 1980-92; Economic Consultant to Secretary of State for Scotland; Consultant to: UN Centre for Transnational Corporations, Commonwealth Secretariat, World Bank; Member, Energy Advisory Panel, UK government. Publications: 135 books and papers on petroleum economics. Address: (b.) Department of Economics, King's College, Aberdeen, AB9 2TY; T.-01224 272168.

Kemp, Arnold, MA. Editor, The Herald, 1981-94; b. 15.2.39; 2 d. Educ. Edinburgh Academy; Edinburgh University. Sub-Editor: The Scotsman, 1959-62, The Guardian, 1962-65; The Scotsman: Production Editor, 1965-70, London Editor, 1970-72, Deputy Editor, 1972-81. Recreations: music; reading; theatre.

Kemp, Donald Douglas, LLB, DipLP, NP. Solicitor, since 1983; b. 5.3.60, Dumbarton; m., Carole Anne Kemp; 1 s. Educ. Montrose Academy; Aberdeen University. Partner, T. Duncan & Co., Solicitors, Montrose, since 1986; Dean, Society of Procurators and Solicitors of Angus, since 1993. Recreations: golf; football; music. Address: (b.) 192 High Street, Montrose, Angus; T.-01674 672533.

Kempton, Rodney Alistair, MA, BPhil, CStat. Director, Biomathematics and Statistics Scotland (formerly Scottish Agricultural Statistics Service), since 1986; b. 2.7.46, London; m., Annelise; 2 s.; 1 d. Educ. Chislehurst and Sidcup Grammar School; Wadham College, Oxford. Rothamsted Experimental Station, Harpenden, 1970-76; Head, Statistics Department, Plant Breeding Institute, Cambridge, 1976-86. President, British Region, International Biometric Society, 1994-96. Recreations: hill-walking; cycling. Address: (b.) BioSS, The King's Buildings, Edinburgh University, EH9 3JZ; T.-0131-650 4902.

Kendell, Robert Evan, CBE, MD, FRCP, FRCPsych. Chief Medical Officer, Scottish Office Home and Health Department; b. 28.3.35, Rotherham; m., Ann Whitfield; 2 s.; 2 d. Educ. Mill Hill School; Cambridge University; King's College Hospital Medical School. Visiting Professor, University of Vermont College of Medicine, 1969-70; Reader in Psychiatry, Institute of Psychiatry, London University, 1970-74; Professor of Psychiatry, Edinburgh University, 1974-91, and Dean, Faculty of Medicine, 1986-90. Gaskell Medal, Royal College of Psychiatrists, 1967;

Paul Hoch Medal, American Psychopathological Association, 1988; Marcé Society Medal, 1994; Fellow, Royal Society of Edinburgh, 1993. Publications: The Classification of Depressive Illnesses, 1968; The Role of Diagnosis in Psychiatry, 1975; Companion to Psychiatric Studies (Editor), 1983, 1988, 1993. Recreations: walking up hills; overeating. Address: (h.) 3 West Castle Road, Edinburgh, EH10 5AT.

Kendle, Professor Keith Emery, BPharm (Hons), PHD, MRPharmS. Professor of Clinical Pharmacy, Robert Gordon University, since 1992; b. 24.8.41, Hetton-Le-Hole. Educ. Houghton Le Spring Grammar School; School of Pharmacy, London University. Endocrinologist,. then Deputy Head of Endocrinology, BDH Research Ltd.; Senior Lecturer, Robert Gordon's Institute of Technology. Recreations: hill-walking; music. Address: (b.) School of Pharmacy, Robert Gordon University, Schoolhill, Aberdeen;' T.-01224 262537.

Kennedy, Alison Louise, BA (Hons). Writer; b. 22.10.65, Dundee. Educ. High School of Dundee; Warwick University. Community Arts Worker, 1988-89; Writer in Residence, Project Ability, 1989-94; Writer in Residence, Hamilton/East Kilbride Social Work Department, 1990-92; fiction critic for Scotsman, etc.; two S.A.C. book awards; Saltire Best First Book Award; John Llewellyn Rees/Mail on Sunday Prize; listed, Sunday Times Best of Young British Novelists; Festival Fringe First; Social Work Today Award. Publications: Night Geometry; Garscadden Trains; Looking for the Possible Dance; Now That You're Back; So I Am Glad; The Audition (play). Recreations: cinema; clarinet; fencing.

Kennedy, (Alistair James) Spencer, MA, LLB, SSC, NP. Partner, Balfour & Manson Nightingale & Bell, since 1991; Past President, Society of Solicitors in the Supreme Courts of Scotland; b. 3.5.45, Dumfries; m., Joan Margaret Whitelaw. Educ. Royal High School of Edinburgh; Edinburgh University. Estate Duty Office, 1965-68; Connell & Connell, 1968-70; Nightingale & Bell, SSC, 1970-90. Recreations: hill-walking; horticulture. Address: (b.) 58 Frederick Street, Edinburgh, EH1 1LS; T.-0131-225 8291.

Kennedy, Professor Angus Johnston, MA, PhD, Officier dans l'Ordre des Palmes Academiques. Professor of French Language and Literature, Glasgow University; b. 9.8.40, Port Charlotte; m., Marjory McCulloch Shearer; 2 d. Educ. Bearsden Academy; Glasgow University. Glasgow University: Assistant Lecturer in French, 1965, then Lecturer, Senior Lecturer, Reader; former Secretary, British Branch, International Arthurian Society. Publications: books on Christine de Pizan. Address: (b.) French Department, Glasgow University, Glasgow; T.-0141-339 8855.

Kennedy, Professor Arthur Colville, CBE, MD, FRCP(Lond), FRCPE, FRCP(Glas), FRCPI, FRSE, FACP(Hon.), FRACP (Hon.). Consultant Physician, Royal Infirmary, Glasgow, 1959-88; Muirhead Professor of Medicine, Glasgow University, 1978-88; President, Royal College of Physicians and Surgeons of Glasgow, 1986-88; b. 22.10.22, Edinburgh; m., Agnes White Taylor; 1 s. (deceased); 2 d. Educ. Whitehill School, Glasgow; Glasgow University. Medical Officer, RAFVR, 1946-48; junior NHS posts, 1948-57; Lecturer in Medicine, Glasgow University, 1957; Senior Lecturer, 1961; Reader, 1966; Titular Professor, 1969; responsible for establishment of Kidney Unit, Glasgow Royal Infirmary, 1959; Chairman, MRC Working Party in Glomerulonephritis, 1976-88; Member, Executive Committee, National Kidney Research Fund, 1976-83; Expert Adviser to WHO on Renal Disease; Adviser to EEC on Nephrology in Developing Countries; Chairman, Professional and Linguistic Assessments Board (PLAB), GMC, 1987-89; President, Royal Medico-Chirurgical Society of Glasgow, 1971-72; President, European Dialysis and Transplant Association, 1972-75; President, Scottish Society of Physicians, 1983-84; President, Harveian Society

of Edinburgh, 1985; Member, Greater Glasgow Health Board, 1985-89; Member, General Medical Council, 1989-92; President, British Medical Association, 1991-92. Recreations: gardening; walking; reading; photography. Address: (h.) 16 Boclair Crescent, Bearsden, Glasgow, G61 2AG; T.-0141-942 5326.

Kennedy, Charles Peter, MA (Hons). MP (SLD, formerly SDP), Ross, Cromarty and Skye, since 1983; President, Liberal Democrats, 1989-94; Liberal Democrat Spokesman on Europe, since 1992; b. 25.11.59, Inverness. Educ. Lochaber High School, Fort William; Glasgow University; Indiana University. President, Glasgow University Union, 1980-81; Winner, British Observer Mace for Student Debating, 1982; Journalist, BBC Highland, Inverness, 1982; Fulbright Scholar, Indiana University (Bloomington Campus), 1982-83. Chairman, SDP Council for Scotland, 1986-88; SDP Spokesman on Health and Social Services, and Scotland, 1983-87; Alliance Election Spokesman, Social Security, Jan.-June, 1987; Member, Select Committee on Social Services, 1985-87; SLD Interim Joint Spokesman, Social Security, 1988; SLD Spokesman, Trade and Industry, 1988-89; Liberal Democrat Spokesman, Health, 1989-92; Member, Select Committee on House of Commons Televising, 1988. Recreations: reading; writing. Address: (b.) House of Commons, London, SW1A 0AA; T.-0171-219 5090.

Kennedy, Frederick John, OBE, LLB. Regional Reporter, Strathclyde Regional Council; b. 22.6.40, Grantham; m., Eleanor Mae Watson; 1 s.; 1 d. Educ. High School of Glasgow; Glasgow University. Private, industrial and local government legal practice; former Reporter to the Children's Panel, City of Glasgow; former Director of Administration, Fife Regional Council. Recreations: golf; reading; gardening. Address: (b.) Merchant Exchange, 10-20 Bell Street, Glasgow, G1 1LG; T.-0141-225 7970.

Kennedy, Professor Gavin, BA, MSc, PhD, FCIM. Professorial Fellow, Esmee Fairbairn Research Centre, Heriot-Watt University; Managing Director, Negotiate Ltd., Edinburgh; b. 20.2.40, Collingham, Yorkshire; m., Patricia Anne; 1 s.; 2 d. Educ. London Nautical School; Strathclyde University. Lecturer: Danbury Management Centre, NE London Polytechnic, 1969-71, Brunel University, 1971-73. Lecturer, National Defence College, Latimer, 1972-74; Senior Lecturer in Economics, Strathclyde University, 1973-85. Publications: Military in the Third World, 1974; Economics of Defence, 1975; Bligh, 1978 (Yorkshire Post Book of the Year, 1979); Death of Captain Cook, 1978; Burden Sharing in NATO, 1979; Mathematics for Innumerate Economists, 1982; Defence Economics, 1983; Invitation to Statistics, 1983; Everything is Negotiable, 1984; Negotiate Anywhere, 1985; Macro Economics, 1985; Superdeal, 1985; The Economist Pocket Negotiator, 1987; Captain Bligh: the man and his mutinies, 1988; Do We Have A Deal?, 1991; Simulations for Training Negotiators, 1993; The Perfect Negotiation, 1993; Negotiation, 1994; Local Pay Bargaining, 1995.. Recreation: reading. Address: (h.) 22 Braid Avenue, Edinburgh; T.-0131-447 3000.

Kennedy, Professor Peter Graham Edward, MB, BS, MPhil, PhD, MD, DSc, MRCPath, FRCPLond, FRCPGlas, FRSE. Burton Professor of Neurology and Head of Department, Glasgow University, since 1987; Consultant Neurologist, Institute of Neurological Sciences, Southern General Hospital, Glasgow, since 1986; b. 28.3.51, London; m., Catherine Ann; 1 s.; 1 d. Educ. University College School, London; University College, London; University College Medical School. Medical Registrar, University College Hospital, 1977-78; Hon. Research Assistant, MRC Neuroimmunology Project, University College, London, 1978-80; Research Fellow, Institute of Virology, Glasgow University, 1981; Registrar and Senior Registrar, National Hospital for Nervous Diseases, London, 1981-84; Assistant Professor of Neurology, Johns Hopkins University School of

Medicine, 1985; "New Blood" Senior Lecturer in Neurology and Virology, Glasgow University, 1986-87. BUPA Medical Foundation "Doctor of the Year" Research Award, 1990; Linacre Medal and Lectureship, Royal College of Physicians of London, 1991; T.S. Srinivasan Endowment Lecturer and Gold Medal, 1993; Member, Medical Research Advisory Committee, Multiple Sclerosis Society; Chairman, Research Committee, Scottish Motor Neurone Disease Association. Publications: Infections of the Nervous System (Co-author); numerous papers on neurology, neurovirology and neurobiology. Recreations: reading and writing; music; astronomy; tennis; walking in the country. Address: (b.) Institute of Neurological Sciences, Southern General Hospital, Glasgow, G51; T.-0141-445 2466.

Kennedy, Peter Norman Bingham, TD, CA, DL. Investment Director, since 1979; Landowner; b. 11.10.42, Kings Lynn; m., Priscilla Ann; 4 d. Educ. Rugby. Qualified as CA, 1967; worked for R.C. Greig & Co., Alex. Lawrie Factors Ltd. and Duncan Lawrie Ltd.; Managing Director, Gartmore Scotland Limited, since 1988. Served with Ayrshire Yeomanry/Queen's Own Yeomanry (TA), 12 years; Chairman, River Doon Fishery Board, since 1980; Deputy Lieutenant, Ayrshire and Arran. Address: (b.) Charles Oakley House, 125 West Regent Street, Glasgow, G2 2SG.

Kent, Roger Williamson, CBE, CQSW, DipAppSocStud. Convener, Scottish Council for Voluntary Organisations, since 1990; b. 27.12.31, Portsmouth; m., Angela Mary; 1 d. Educ. Royal Naval College, Dartmouth. Royal Navy, 1945-61; approved schools, 1962-64; social worker, 1964-73; Director of Social Services, Doncaster, 1973-79; Director of Social Work, Lothian Region, 1979-89; Director, Waverley Care Trust, 1989-95. Commissioner for Scotland, CRE, 1989-93. Recreations: watching cricket; walking dog. Address: (h.) 5 Fidra Road, North Berwick, EH39 4LY; T.-01620 894658.

Kermack, Sheriff Stuart Ogilvy, BA (Oxon), LLB. Sheriff of Tayside, Central and Fife, at Forfar and Arbroath, 1971-93; b. 9.7.34, Edinburgh; m., Barbara Mackenzie; 3 s.; 1 d. Educ. Glasgow Academy; Jesus College, Oxford; Glasgow University. Called to Scottish Bar, 1958. Address: (h.) 7 Littlecauseway, Forfar, Angus; T.-Forfar 64691.

Kernohan, Robert Deans, OBE, MA. Journalist, Writer and occasional Broadcaster; b. 9.1.31, Mount Vernon, Lanarkshire; m., Margaret Buchanan Bannerman; 4 s. Educ. Whitehill School, Glasgow; Glasgow University; Balliol College, Oxford. RAF, 1955-57; Editorial Staff, Glasgow Herald, 1957-67 (Assistant Editor, 1965-66, London Editor, 1966-67); Director-General, Scottish Conservative Central Office, 1967-71; Freelance Journalist and Broadcaster, 1972; Editor, Life and Work, The Record of the Church of Scotland, 1972-90. Chairman, Federation of Conservative Students, 1954-55; Conservative Parliamentary candidate, 1955, 1959, 1964; Member, Newspaper Panel, Monopolies and Mergers Commission, since 1987; Member, Ancient Monuments Board for Scotland, since 1990; Member, Broadcasting Standards Council, since 1994; Chairman, Scottish Christian Conservative Forum, 1991; HM Inspector of Constabulary for Scotland (Lay Inspector), 1992-95; Elder, Cramond Kirk, Edinburgh. Publications: Scotland's Life and Work, 1979; William Barclay, The Plain Uncommon Man, 1980; Thoughts through the Year, 1985; Our Church, 1985; The Protestant Future, 1991; The Road to Zion, 1995. Recreations: rugby-watching; travel; pontification. Address: (h.) 5/1 Rocheid Park, Edinburgh, EH4 1RP; T.-0131-332 7851.

Kerr, Allan MacDonald, LLB. Solicitor; Director of Law and Administration, Nairn District Council, since 1984, and Chief Executive, since 1989; b. 10.6.53, Glasgow; m., Mairi; 2 s. Educ. Bishopbriggs High School; Glasgow University. Law apprentice, later qualified Assistant, McGettigan & Co.,

Solicitors, Glasgow, 1976-78; Principal Legal Assistant, later Solicitor, Western Isles Islands Council, 1978-82; Clerk of Court, Motherwell District, 1982-84. Recreations: family; motoring; reading. Address: (b.) The Court House, High Street, Nairn; T.-01667 455523.

Kerr, Sheriff B.A., QC, BA, LLB. Sheriff of Glasgow and Strathkelvin at Glasgow. Admitted to Faculty of Advocates, 1973. Address: (b.) Sheriff Court House, 1 Carlton Place, Glasgow, G5 9DA.

Kerr, David Alexander, MC, TD, JP, DL; b. 30.9.16, Inverkip; m., Elizabeth Phoebe Coxwell Cresswell; 1 s.; 1 d. Educ. Canford School. Joined Westburn Sugar Refineries Ltd., Greenock, 1936; joined 5/6 Bn., Argyll & Sutherland Highlanders, 1936; mobilised, 1939, serving in France, Belgium, North Africa, Italy, Palestine and Syria; MC, 1945; mentioned in Despatches; Territorial Decoration, 1948; returned to Westburn, 1946; Technical Director, 1949; Refinery Director, 1955; Joint Managing Director, 1960; Managing Director, 1967; Chairman, 1972; Director, The Sankey Sugar Company Ltd., 1965; Managing Director, Maubre Sugars Ltd., 1972; Director, Tate & Lyle Refineries Ltd., 1976-79; retired, 1979. County Commissioner, County of Renfrew Scout Association, 1964-70, County Chairman, 1971-73; Area President, 1976-93; Chief Commissioner for Scotland, 1977-81; Honorary Chief Commissioner, since 1981; a County Vice-President, Renfrewshire Guide Association. Recreations: garden; philately; photography. Address: (h.) Whitefarland, 88 Octavia Terrace, Greenock, PA16 7PY; T.-01475 631980.

Kerr, Finlay, MB, ChB, DObsRCOG, FRCPEdin, FRCPGlas. Consultant Physician, Raigmore Hospital, Inverness, since 1976; Honorary Senior Lecturer, Aberdeen University, since 1976; Board Director, Highland Hospice, 1985-90 (Chairman, Board of Directors, 1985-87); b. 8.8.41, Edinburgh; m., Margaret Ann Carnegie Allan; 1 s.; 2 d. Educ. Keil School; Glasgow University. House Physician and Surgeon, Western Infirmary, Glasgow; House Physician, Ruchill Hospital, Glasgow; House Surgeon, Queen Mother's Hospital, Glasgow; Senior House Officer, Western Infirmary, Glasgow; Fellow, University of Southern California; Lecturer in Medicine, then Senior Registrar in Medicine, Edinburgh Royal Infirmary. Recreations: sailing; skiing; walking. Address: (h.) The Birks, 2 Drummond Place, Inverness.

Kerr, Francis Robert Newsam, OBE, MC; b. 12.9.16, Ancrum; m., Anne Frederica Kitson; 2 s.; 1 d. Educ. Ampleforth College. Officer, Royal Scots (Lt-Col.), retired, 1960. Address: (h.) The Coach House, New Howden, Jedburgh, TD8 6QP; T.-01835 864193.

Kerr, Rev. Philip John, PhB, STL. Parish Priest, Sacred Heart, Cowie; R.C. Chaplain, Stirling University; Lecturer in Systematic Theology, Scotus College, Bearsden; b. 23.4.56, Edinburgh. Educ. Holy Cross Academy; St. Augustine's High School, Edinburgh; Scots College and Gregorian University, Rome. Assistant Priest, St. Francis Xavier's, Falkirk, 1980-82; Lecturer in Systematic Theology, St. Andrew's College, Drygrange, 1982-86; Vice-Rector and Lecturer in Systematic Theology, Gillis College, Edinburgh, 1986-93. Secretary: Joint Commission for Doctrine (CofS/RC); Joint Study Group (Scottish Episcopal Church/RC). Recreations: squash; walking. Address: Sacred Heart Presbytery, Bannockburn Road, Cowie, FK7 7BG; T.-01786 813466.

Kerr, Robert James, MA (Hons), PhD. Rector, Peebles High School, since b. 14.6.47, Jedburgh; m., Isobel Grace Atkinson; 2 s.; 1 d. Educ. Kelso High School; Edinburgh University. Assistant Teacher, Lochaber High School, 1973-75; Assistant Principal Teacher of Geography, Forrester High School, 1976-77; Principal Teacher of Geography, Douglas Ewart High School, 1977-82; Assistant

Rector, Elgin High School, 1982-85; Depute Rector, Forres Academy, 1985-86. Chairman, "Higher Still" Specialist Group in PSE, since 1994. Recreations: fishing; rugby supporter; hill-walking/mountainering; ornithology; skiing; travel. Address: (h.) Enniskerry, Eshiels, Peebles, EH45 8NA; T.-01721 722131.

Kerr, Professor William John Stanton, BDS, FDS, RCSEdin, MDS, FFD, RCSIrel, DOrthRCS, FDS RCPS Glas, DDS. Professor of Orthodontics, Glasgow Dental Hospital and School, since 1993; Honorary Consultant in Orthodontics, since 1978; b. 12.7.41, Belfast; m., Marie-Francoise; 1 d. Educ. Campbell College, Belfast; Queen's University, Belfast. Address: (b.) Glasgow Dental Hospital and School, 378 Sauchiehall Street, Glasgow, G2 3JZ; T.-0141-332 7020.

Kerrigan, Herbert Aird, QC, MA, LLB (Hons); b. 2.8.45, Glasgow; 1 s. Educ. Whitehill School, Glasgow; Aberdeen University; Keele University; Hague Academy. Admitted to Faculty of Advocates, 1970; Lecturer in Criminal Law and Criminology, Edinburgh University, 1969-73; Lecturer in Scots Law, Edinburgh University, 1973-74; Visiting Professor, University of Southern California, since 1979; Member, Longford Commission, 1972; Church of Scotland: Elder, 1967 (now at Greyfriars Tolbooth and Highland Kirk), Reader, 1969, elected Member, Assembly Council, 1981-85; President, Edinburgh Royal Infirmary Samaritan Society, since 1992; called to the English Bar (Middle Temple), 1990; joined Chambers of Edmund Lawson, QC, 1991; appointed QC in Scotland, 1992. Publications: An Introduction to Criminal Procedure in Scotland, 1970; Ministers for the 1980s (Contributor), 1979; The Law of Contempt (Contributing Editor), 1982; The Law of Sport (2nd edition) (Contributor), 1995. Recreation: travel. Address: (h.) 20 Edinburgh Road, Dalkeith, Midlothian, EH22 1JY; T.-0131-660 3007.

Kesting, Rev. Sheilagh M., BA, BD. Secretary, Committee on Ecumenical Affairs, Church of Scotland. Ordained, 1980. Address: (b.) 121 George Street, Edinburgh, EH2 4YN.

Kidd, Professor Cecil, BSc, PhD, FIBiol, FRSA. Regius Professor of Physiology, Aberdeen University, since 1984; b. 28.4.33, Shotley Bridge, Co. Durham; m., Margaret Winifred; 3 s. Educ. Queen Elizabeth Grammar School, Darlington; King's College, Newcastle-upon-Tyne; Durham University. Demonstrator in Physiology, King's College, Newcastle-upon-Tyne; Lecturer/Senior Lecturer/Reader in Physiology, Senior Research Associate in Cardiovascular Studies, Leeds University; Head, Department of Biomedical Sciences. Recreations: squash; gardening. Address: (b.) Department of Biomedical Sciences, Marischal College, Aberdeen University, Aberdeen; T.-01224 273006.

Kidd, David Hamilton, LLB, LLM, WS, NP. Partner, Biggart Baillie & Gifford, since 1978; Solicitor Advocate, since 1994; b. 21.9.49, Edinburgh; m., Geraldine Stephen; 2 s.; 1 d. Educ. Edinburgh Academy; Edinburgh University. Research Assistant, Law Faculty, Queen's University, Belfast, 1976-77. Recreations: cycling; skiing; sailing. Address: (b.) 11 Glenfinlas Street, Edinburgh, EH3 6YY; T.-0131-226 5541.

Kidd, Frank Forrest, CA, ATII. Partner, Coopers & Lybrand, Chartered Accountants, since 1979; b. 4.5.38, Dundee; m., Beryl Ann Gillespie; 2 s.; 2 d. Educ. George Heriot's School; Ballards. CA Apprentice, 1955-60; Partner, Wylie & Hutton, 1962-79; Honorary Professor, Department of Accountancy and Business Law, Stirling University; President, Institute of Chartered Accountants of Scotland, 1988-89. Recreations: golf; walking. Address: (b.) Erskine House, P.O. Box 90, 68/73 Queen Street, Edinburgh, EH2 4NH; T.-0131-226 4488.

Kidd, Professor Ian Gray, MA (St. Andrews), MA (Oxon), FBA. Emeritus Professor of Greek, St. Andrews University; b. 6.3.22, Goretty, Chandernagore, India; m., Sheila Elizabeth Dow; 3 s. Educ. Dundee High School; St. Andrews University; Queen's College, Oxford. St. Andrews University: Lecturer in Greek, 1949, Senior Lecturer, 1965; Visiting Professor, University of Texas at Austin, 1965-66; Member, Institute for Advanced Study, Princeton, 1971-72; St. Andrews University: Personal Professor of Ancient Philosophy, 1973-76, Professor of Greek, 1976-87, Provost of St. Leonard's College, 1978-83, Chancellor's Assessor, University Court, since 1989; Member, Institute for Advanced Study, Princeton, 1979-80; Hon. Fellow, St. Leonard's College, since 1987; Hon. Fellow, Institute for Research in Classical Philosophy and Science, Princeton, USA, since 1989. Publication: Posidonius, Vol. I, The Fragments, 1972, 1989, Vol. II, The Commentary, 1989. Recreations: music; reading. Address: (h.) Ladebury, Lade Braes Lane, St. Andrews, Fife, KY16 9EP; T.-01334 474367.

Kidd, Jean Buyers, BA, DipMusEd, LRAM, ARCM. Music Director, Junior and Youth Choruses, Scottish National Orchestra, since 1978; b. Macduff, Banffshire; widow. Educ. Buckie High School; Royal Scottish Academy of Music; Open University. Taught in various Glasgow schools and for many years, Principal Teacher of Music, Bellahouston Academy; former Conductor, Bellahouston Music Society; gave instruction in music and drama to women in Duke Street Prison; former Secretary, Scottish Certificate of Education Examination Board. Recreations: reading; playing chamber music; gardening; craft work. Address: (h.) Carolside, Gowanlea Road, Comrie, Perthshire, PH6 2HD; T.-Comrie 70856.

Kidd, Mary Helen (May), JP, MA. National Chairman, Scottish Women's Rural Institutes, since 1993; Member, Scottish Consumer Council, since 1991; Member, Advisory Board, Scottish Agricultural College, Edinburgh, since 1991; m., Neil M.L. Kidd; 2 s. Educ. Brechin High School; Edinburgh University. Partner in family farming business. Recreations: playing piano and organ; creative writing. Address: (h.) Holemill of Kirkbuddo, Forfar, Angus, DD8 2NQ; T.-01307 820 318.

Kiddie, Charles, BSc (Hons). Rector, Perth High School, since 1993; b. 3.4.49, Dundee; m., Esther Linda Power; 2 s. Educ. Harris Academy, Dundee; Aberdeen University; University of Kansas; Dundee College of Education. Teacher, Forfar Academy; Principal Teacher, Breadalbane Academy, Aberfeldy; Assistant Head Teacher, Whitfield High School, Dundee; Adviser in Social Subjects, Tayside Regional Council; Rector, Auchterarder High School. Recreation: family. (b.) Perth High School, Oakbank Road, Perth; T.-01738 628271.

Killeen, Jan Mary, BSc, DipASS, Assistant Director, Public Policy, Alzheimer's Scotland – Action on Dementia; Secretary, Scottish Dementia Appeal, since 1990; b. 5.7.46, Farnborough, Kent; m., Damian Killeen; 2 s. Educ. London University; University College, Swansea; Leeds University. Library Assistant, BBC, 1965-66; Housing Welfare Officer, Lambeth Borough Council, 1969-70; Community Development Officer, Coventry Corporation, 1970-73; Community Development Officer, Doncaster Metropolitan Borough Council, 1975-78; Doncaster Metropolitan Institute for Higher Education: Lecturer, 1973-79, Tutor, 1979-81; Co-ordinator, Scottish Action on Dementia, 1985-88; Training Officer, Age Concern Scotland, 1981-89; Director, Scottish Action on Dementia, 1987-94. Publications: several in the field of social policy and dementia and service development in day care. Recreation: walking on the beach after dinner. Address: (h.) Eastbourne House, 21 Bedford Terrace, Joppa, Edinburgh, EH15 2EJ; T.-0131-669 2888.

Killick, Roger John, BSc, MBA, MA, PhD, CBiol, MIBiol. Secretary, Scottish Crop Research Institute, since 1988; b. 27.5.45, London; m., E. Marion Smith; 1 s.; 1 d. Educ. Purley County Grammar School for Boys; London University; Birmingham University; Dundee University; Leicester University. Research Geneticist, Scottish Plant Breeding Station, 1969-82; Assistant to Director, Scottish Crop Research Institute, 1982-88. Recreations: hill-walking; watching ballet. Address: (h.) Hilltops, 19 Sidlaw Terrace, Birkhill, Dundee, DD2 5PY; T.-01382 580396.

Kilshaw, David Andrew George. Solicitor, since 1979; Chairman, Borders Health Board, since 1993; b. 18.3.53, Glencoe; 3 s. Educ. Keil School, Dumbarton. Traineeship, Brunton Miller, Solicitors, Glasgow, 1975-80; Solicitor, Borders Regional Council, 1980-83; Partner, Cullen Kilshaw Solicitors, Galashiels and Melrose, since 1983. Safeguarder, Borders Region Children's Panel, since 1987. Recreations: coach, Peebles Rugby Football Club; golf; fishing; walking; listening to music. Address: (b.) 27 Market Street, Galashiels; T.-01896 758311.

Kimbell, Professor David Rodney Bertram, MA, DPhil, LRAM, FRSA. Professor of Music, Edinburgh University, since 1987 (Professor of Music, St. Andrews University, 1979-87); b. 26.6.39, Gillingham, Kent; m., Ingrid Else Emilie Lubbe; 1 s.; 2 d. Educ. Dartford Grammar School; Kent College, Canterbury; Worcester College, Oxford. Lecturer in Music, Edinburgh University, 1965-78. Publication: Verdi in the Age of Italian Romanticism, 1981; Italian Opera, 1991. Address: (h.) 3 Bellevue Crescent, Edinburgh, EH3 6ND; T.-0131-556 5480.

Kincraig, Hon. Lord (Robert Smith Johnston), QC (Scot), BA (Hons), LLB. Senator of the College of Justice in Scotland, 1972-88; Chairman, Parole Review Body for Scotland; b. 10.10.18, Glasgow; m., Margaret Joan Graham (deceased); 1 s.; 1 d. Educ. Strathallan; St. John's College, Cambridge; Glasgow University. Member, Faculty of Advocates, 1942; Advocate-Depute, 1953-55; QC (Scot), 1955; Home Advocate Depute, 1959-62; Sheriff of Roxburgh, Berwick and Selkirk, 1964-70; Dean, Faculty of Advocates, 1970-72. Recreation: gardening. Address: (h.) Westwood Cottage, Southfield Farm, Longniddry, EH32 0PL; T.-Longniddry 853583.

Kinder, Anthony Kenneth, BSc, MA, MBA. Chair, Lothian Enterprise Board; Secretary, Labour Group, West Lothian Council; b. 19.6.49, Middlesborough; m., Kathleen Greenwood. Lecturer, Falkirk College, 1980-95. Recreation: golf. Address: (h.) 53 West Main Street, Broxburn, West Lothian; T.-01506 853162.

King, Professor Bernard, MSc, PhD, FIWSc, CBiol, FIBiol. Principal and Vice-Chancellor, University of Abertay, Dundee, since 1992; b. 4.5.46, Dublin; m., Maura Antoinette Collinge; 2 d. Educ. Synge St. Christian Brothers School, Dublin; College of Technology, Dublin; University of Aston in Birmingham. Research Fellow, University of Aston, 1972-76; Dundee Institute of Technology, 1976-91: Lecturer, Senior Lecturer, Head, Department of Molecular and Life Sciences, Dean, Faculty of Science; Assistant Principal, Robert Gordon Institute of Technology/Robert Gordon University, 1991-92. Director: Higher Education Quality Council, Dundee Enterprise Trust; Governor, Unicorn Preservation Society; Chairman, Committee of Principals of Scottish Centrally-Funded Colleges. Recreations: reading; music; sailing. Address: (h.) 11 Dalhousie Place, Arbroath, DD11 2BT; T.-01382 308012.

King, Elspeth Russell, MA, FMA.Director, Smith Art Gallery and Museum, Stirling, since 1994; Director, Dunfermline Heritage Trust, 1991-94; b. 29.3.49, Lochore, Fife. Educ. Beath High School; St. Andrews University; Leicester University. Curator, People's Palace, Glasgow, 1974-91, with responsibility for building up the social

history collections for the city of Glasgow. Address: (b.) Abbot House, Maygate, Dunfermline, KY12 7NG; T.-01383 733 266.

King, Erika Elizabeth, BA, ACIS. Deputy Director, Scottish Film Council, since 1990; Company Secretary, Scottish Film Production Fund, since 1990; Company Secretary, Scottish Screen Locations, since 1990; b. 4.11.52, Edinburgh. Educ. Trinity Academy, Edinburgh; Lancaster University; City University, London. Arts Council of Great Britain, 1975-79; Administrator, Third Eye Centre, Glasgow, 1979-90. Scottish Representative, Ski Club of G.B., since 1984; Opera Correspondent, Jewish Echo, 1986-91; Board Member, A.B.S.A. Recreations: skiing; hill-walking; violin playing. Address: (h.) 100 Novar Drive, Glasgow, G12 9JN; T.-0141-334 4445.

King, Robert Lees Lumsden. Secretary, Post Office Users' Council for Scotland, since 1988; Secretary, Scottish Advisory Committee on Telecommunications, since 1988; b. 23.3.49, Peebles; m., Yvonne Mary Black. Educ. Leith Academy. Department of Agriculture and Fisheries for Scotland, 1966-70; Department of Environment, 1970-72; Forestry Commission, 1972-79; Nature Conservancy Council, 1979-88. Recreations: country life; shooting; reading; travel. Address: (b.) 2 Greenside Lane, Edinburgh, EH1 3AH; T.-0131-244 5576.

Kinnaird, Alison, MA, FGE. Glass Engraver and Artist; Clarsach Player; b. 30.4.49, Edinburgh; m., Robin Morton; 1 s.; 1 d. Educ. George Watson's Ladies College; Edinburgh University. Freelance glass artist, since 1971; exhibitions in Edinburgh, 1978, 1981, 1985, in London, 1988, 1995; work in many public and private collections; professional musician, since 1970; has produced three LPs as well as film and TV music; served on Council, Scottish Craft Centre, 1974-76; Council, SSWA, 1975-76; Member, BBC Scottish Music Advisory Committee, 1981-84; Member, BBC Broadcasting Council for Scotland, 1984-88; Member, SAC Crafts Commitee, 1993-95; awarded SDA/CCC Craft Fellowship, 1980; Glass-Sellers of London Award, 1987. Recreations: children; cooking; garden. Address: (h.) Shillinghill, Temple, Midlothian, EH23 4SH; T.-Temple 328.

Kinnis, William Kay Brewster, PhD, FRSA. Solicitor and Notary Public; Consultant Lawyer with Cannon, Orpin & Murdochs, Solicitors, Glasgow, since 1995; Director, East Neuk Properties Ltd., Kilrymont Properties Ltd., Culdee Properties Ltd., Madras Properties Ltd., Swilcan Properties Ltd., Rock & Spindle Properties Ltd., Christian Action Glasgow Housing Trust Ltd.; b. 5.1.33, St. Andrews; m., Agnes Inglis Erskine, MA; 2 d. Educ. Hamilton Academy; Glasgow University; London University (External). Partner: MacArthur Stewart & Orr, Solicitors, Oban and Lochgilphead, 1959-62; Town Clerk and Burgh Chamberlain, Lochgilphead, 1960-62; Partner, Murdoch Jackson, Solicitors, Glasgow, 1963-92; Senior Partner, Miller Jackson, Solicitors, Lenzie, 1982-92; Senior Partner, Cannon, Orpin & Murdochs, 1992-95; Council Member, Member, Royal Faculty of Procurators, 1980-83; Governor, Baillie's Institution, 1983-94. Choral Scholar, Glasgow University, 1954-58; Choirmaster, Lochgilphead Parish Church, 1959-62; Reader, Church of Scotland, since 1960; Member, Church of Scotland Board of Practice and Procedure and Law Committee, since 1990. Recreations: choral singing; swimming; reading; travel. Address: (b.) 78 Queen Street, Glasgow, G1 3DW; T.-0141-204 1155.

Kinnoull, 15th Earl of (Arthur William George Patrick Hay); b. 26.3.35; m.; 1 s.; 3 d. Lives in London.

Kinross, Lord (Christopher Patrick Balfour), LLB, WS. Solicitor, since 1975; b. 1.10.49, Edinburgh; m., Susan Jane Pitman; 2 s. Educ. Eton College; Edinburgh University. Member, Royal Company of Archers, Queen's Bodyguard for Scotland; James IV Association of Surgeons. Recreation: off-road motorsport. Address: (b.) Saltire Court, 20 Castle Terrace, Edinburgh; T.-0131 228 9900.

Kintore, 13th Earl of (Michael Canning William John **Keith**); b. 22.2.39; m.; 1 s.; 1 d. Address: The Stables, Keith Hall, Inverurie, AB51 0LD.

Kirby, Professor Gordon William, MA, PhD, ScD, CChem, FRSC, FRSE. Regius Professor of Chemistry, Glasgow University, since 1972; b. 20.6.34, Wallasey; 2 s. Educ. Liverpool Institute High School; Liverpool Technical College; Gonville and Caius College, Cambridge. Imperial College, London: 1851 Exhibition Senior Studentship, 1958-60, Assistant Lecturer, 1960-61, Lecturer, 1961-67; Professor of Organic Chemistry, Loughborough University of Technology, 1967-72. Corday-Morgan Medal and Prize, Royal Society of Chemistry, 1969; Tilden Lectureship, Royal Society of Chemistry, 1974-75. Recreation: hill-walking. Address: (b.) Department of Chemistry, Glasgow University, Glasgow, G12 8QQ; T.-0141-339 8855, Ext. 4416/4417.

Kirk, David, MA, BM, BCh, DM, FRCS (Eng), FRCS-RCPS (Glas). Consultant Urological Surgeon, Greater Glasgow Health Board, since 1982; Honorary Professor, Glasgow University, since 1995; Honorary Clinical Lecturer, Glasgow University, 1984-95; b. 26.5.43, Bradford; m., Gillian Mary Wroot; 1 s.; 2 d. Educ. King Edwards School, Birmingham; Balliol College, Oxford; Oxford University Clinical Medical School. Resident House Physician and House Surgeon, Radcliffe Infirmary, Oxford; University Demonstrator, Oxford; clinical surgical posts, Oxford and Bristol; Arris and Gale Lecturer, Royal College of Surgeons (England), 1980-81; surgical Registrar appointment, Sheffield; academic surgical research, Sheffield University; Senior Registrar in General Surgery, then in Urology, Bristol. Secretary/Treasurer, 1983-85, Chairman, 1985-88, Scottish Urological Oncology Group; Council Member, Urology Section, Royal Society of Medicine, 1984-87; Council Member, British Association of Urological Surgeons, 1988-91; Chairman, Prostate Forum, 1991-94; Chairman, Intercollegiate Board in Urology. Recreations: skiing; hill-walking; classical music. Address: (h.) Woodend, Prospect Road, Dullatur, Glasgow, G68 0AN; T.-01236 720778.

Kirk, Professor Gordon, MA, MEd, FRSA. Principal, Moray House College of Education, since 1981; Vice-Chairman, Committee of Scottish Higher Principals, 1993-94; Vice-Chairman, General Teaching Council, since 1992; b. 8.5.38, Dunfermline; m., Jane D. Murdoch; 1 s.; 1 d. Educ. Camphill Secondary School, Paisley; Glasgow University. Lecturer in Education, Aberdeen University, 1965-74; Head, Education Department, Jordanhill College of Education, 1974-81; Member, Munn Committee on the Curriculum of the Secondary School, 1974-77; Chairman, Educational Broadcasting Council, Scotland, 1985-91; Chairman, Scottish Council for Research in Education, 1984-92; Member: General Teaching Council for Scotland, since 1984, Consultative Committee on the Curriculum, 1984-91, Council for National Academic Awards, 1979-93. Publications: Scottish Education Looks Ahead (Assistant Editor), 1969; Curriculum and Assessment in the Scottish Secondary School, 1982; Moray House and Professional Education (Editor), 1985; The Core Curriculum, 1986; Teacher Education and Professional Development, 1988; Handbook of Educational Ideas and Practices (Associate Editor), 1990; Scottish Education and the European Community (Editor), 1992; 5-14: Scotland's National Curriculum (Editor), 1994; Moray House and Change in Higher Education (Editor), 1995; Professional Issues in Education series (Co-Editor). Recreations: walking; golf; bridge. Address: (h.) Craigroyston, Broadgait, Gullane, East Lothian; T.-01620 843299.

Kirk, James, MA, PhD, DLitt, FRHistS, FRSE. Reader in Scottish History, Glasgow University, since 1991; b. 18.10.44, Falkirk. Educ. Stirling High School; Edinburgh University. Lecturer in Scottish History, Glasgow University, 1972-89; Senior Lecturer, 1989-91; David Berry Prize, Royal Historical Society, 1973; Wolfson Award, 1977; British Academy Major Research Awards, 1989-93; ESRC Research Award, 1993-95. President, Scottish Church History Society, 1989-92; Hon. Secretary, Scottish Record Society, since 1973; Hon. Secretary, Scottish Society for Reformation History, since 1980; Member, Council, Scottish History Society, 1989-93; Section Editor, Royal Historical Society, Annual Bibliography of British and Irish History. Publications: The University of Glasgow 1451-1577, 1977; Records of the Synod of Lothian and Tweeddale, 1977; The Second Book of Discipline, 1980; Stirling Presbytery Records, 1981; Visitation of the Diocese of Dunblane, 1984; Patterns of Reform, 1989; Humanism and Reform (Editor), 1991; The Books of Assumption of the Thirds of Benefices, 1995; Scotland's History (Editor), 1995; The Medieval Church in Scotland (Editor), 1995; Contributor to Dictionary of Scottish Church History and Theology, 1993, Encyclopedia of the Reformation, 1995. Recreations: living in Wester Ross; viticulture. Address: (h.) Woodlea, Dunmore, Stirlingshire, FK2 8LY; T.-01324 831240.

Kirk, James Foster, BSc. Rector, Tain Royal Academy, since 1979; b. 31.8.41, Bellshill; m., Margo McFarlane; 1 s.; 1 d. Educ. Hamilton Academy; Glasgow University. Entered teaching, 1963; promoted to Principal Teacher of Science, then Principal Teacher of Guidance, then Assistant Rector; moved from Lanarkshire to Highlands, 1975. Recreations: gardening; golf; hill-walking. Address: (h.) The Barn House, Delny, Invergordon, Ross-shire; T.-Kildary 842564.

Kirkbride, George, CEng, FICE, FIHTE, FIBM, Eur.Ing, ACIArb. Part-time Reporter, Scottish Office; Consultant Managing Director, GK Skill Time Ltd.; Conciliator, Institution of Civil Engineers; retired Director of Roads, Grampian Regional Council; b. 26.5.33, Willington; 1 s.; 2 d. Educ. Aireborough Grammar School; Bradford Technical College. Pupil, Aireborough Urban District Council, 1949-54; Senior Engineer, Bradford Corporation, 1956-59; Senior Engineer, then Chief Assistant, Crewe Borough, 1959-66; Principal Engineer, then Project Coordinator, Wolverhampton Borough, 1966-72; Depute City Engineer, Dundee City, 1972-75; Regional Roads Engineer, Fife Regional Council, 1975-83. Past President, FUMPO; County Surveyors' Society: Member, 1992 Group, Secretary, European Liaison Group; Fellow, Dundee College of Technology. Recreations: cycling; swimming. Address: (h.) 18 Redwood Crescent, Cove, Aberdeen, AB1 4NZ.

Kirkham, Norman, DA, RGI. Hon. Secretary, Royal Glasgow Institute, since 1991; b. 20.11.36, Glasgow. Educ. North Kelvinside Senior Secondary School; Glasgow School of Art. Interior Designer, 1960-76; full-time painter, since 1976; part-time Lecturer, Glasgow School of Art, since 1977; Past President, Glasgow Art Club; elected RGI, 1987. Recreations: cooking; reading; theatre-going. Address: (h.) 6 Hampden Terrace, Glasgow, G42 9XG; T.-0141-632 2708.

Kirkhill, Baron (John Farquharson Smith). Life Peer; b. 7.5.30. Lord Provost, Aberdeen, 1971-75; Minister of State, Scottish Office, 1975-78; former Chairman, North of Scotland Hydro-Electric Board; Delegate to Parliamentary Assembly of Council of Europe, since 1987 (Chairman, Committee on Legal Affairs and Human Rights, since 1991); Hon.LLD.

Kirkness, Professor Colin Maitland, BMedBiol, MBChB, FRCS(Edin), FRCOphth, FRCS (Glas). Tennent Professor of Ophthalmology, Glasgow University, since 1991; Vice President, European Board of Ophthalmology; Secretary, EUPO; b. 4.5.49, Kirkwall. Educ. Fraserburgh Academy; Aberdeen University. Resident Surgical Officer and Senior

Resident, Moorfields Eye Hospital, London, 1980; Lecturer, 1983, Senior Lecturer and Director, 1989, Pocklington Eye Transplant Unit, Institute of Ophthalmology, London; Honorary Consultant, Moorfields Eye Hospital, 1987. Publications: books on ophthalmology; papers. Address: (b.) Tennent Institute, 38 Church Street, Glasgow, G11 6NT; T.-0141-211 2000, Ext. 2640.

Kirkwood, Archy, BSc. MP (Liberal Democrat), Roxburgh and Berwickshire, since 1983; Liberal Democrat Chief Whip, since 1992; b. 22.4.46, Glasgow; m., Rosemary Chester; 1 s.; 1 d. Educ. Cranhill School; Heriot-Watt University. Solicitor, Notary Public; Aide to Sir David Steel, 1971-75, 1977-78; Liberal Spokesman on Health and Social Services, and on Social Security, 1985-87; Alliance Spokesman on Overseas Development, 1987; Liberal Spokesman on Scotland, 1987-88; Social and Liberal Democrat Convener on Welfare, Health and Education, 1988-89; Liberal Democrat Deputy Chief Whip, and Spokesman on Welfare and Social Security, 1989-92; Spokesman on Community Care, since 1994. Trustee, Joseph Rowntree Reform Trust, since 1985. Recreations: music; photography. Address: (b.) House of Commons, London, SW1A 0AA.

Kirkwood, Hon. Lord (Ian Candlish Kirkwood). Senator of the College of Justice, since 1987; b. 8.6.32. Advocate, 1957; QC, 1970. Address: (b.) Court of Session, Parliament House, Edinburgh, EH1 1RQ.

Kirkwood, Professor (James) Michael, MA, DipSovStud, MA. Professor in Slavonic Languages and Literatures, Glasgow University, since 1993; b. 6.3.41, Glasgow; m., Melanie Claire McMath; 1 s.; 1 d. Educ. Hillhead High School, Glasgow; Glasgow University. Assistant Lecturer, Lecturer, Senior Lecturer in Russian, Lancaster University, 1966-82; Senior Lecturer in Russian, School of Slavonic and East European Studies, London University, 1982-92; Reaer in Russian Studies, SSEES, 1992-93. Recreations: skiing; windsurfing; hill-walking; bird-watching; squash; golf. Address: (b.) Department of Slavonic Languages and Literatures, Hetherington Building, Glasgow University, Glasgow, G12 8QQ; T.-0141-330 4731.

Kirkwood, Ralph C., BSc, PhD, FRSE. Reader in Biology, Strathclyde University, since 1981, and Research Coordinator, Graduate School of Environmental Studies, since 1993; b. 6.7.33, Glasgow; m., Mair Enid; 3 s. Educ. Jordanhill College School, Glasgow; Glasgow University; University of Wales, Aberystwyth. Lecturer, Botany Department, West of Scotland Agricultural College, 1959-64; Strathclyde University: Lecturer, Biology Department, 1964-72, Senior Lecturer, 1972-81; Member, Regional Advisory Committee, Scottish Agricultural College; Member, Scientific Advisory Committee, S.N.H. Publications: Target sites for herbicide action (Editor); Clean Technology and the Environment (Co-Editor). Recreations: sailing; photography; natural history; walking. Address: (b.) Department of Bioscience and Biotechnology, Todd Centre, Strathclyde University, Glasgow, G1 1XW; T.-0141-552 4400.

Kitchen, John Philip, MA, BMus, PhD (Cantab), FRCO, LRAM. Senior Lecturer in Music, Edinburgh University, since 1987 (Lecturer in Music, St. Andrews University, 1976-87); Harpsichord Consultant, Royal Scottish Academy of Music and Drama; Concert Organist, Harpsichordist, Pianist; b. 27.10.50, Airdrie. Educ. Coatbridge High School; Glasgow University; Cambridge University. Harpsichordist/Organist, Scottish Early Music Consort, Stanesby Recorder Trio, St. Andrews Baroque Trio; BBC and commercial recordings; music reviewer. Recreations: more music; entertaining. Address: (b.) Faculty of Music, Alison House, 12 Nicolson Square, Edinburgh, EH8 9DF; T.-0131-650 2432.

Klein, Bernat, CBE, FCSD, Hon. FRIAS. Chairman and Managing Director, Bernat Klein Ltd., 1981-92; b. 6.11.22, Senta, Yugoslavia; m., Margaret Soper; 1 s.; 2 d. Educ. Senta, Yugoslavia; Bezalel School of Arts and Crafts, Jerusalem; Leeds University. Designer: Tootal, Broadhurst, Lee, 1948-49, Munrospun, Edinburgh, 1949-51; Chairman and Managing Director, Colourcraft, 1952-62; Managing Director, Bernat Klein Ltd., 1962-66; Chairman and Managing Director, Bernat Klein Design Ltd., 1966-81. Member, Design Council, 1962-68; Member, Royal Fine Art Commission for Scotland, 1981-87. Publications: Eye for Colour, 1965; Design Matters, 1975. Recreations: tennis; reading. Address: High Sunderland, Galashiels; T.-01750 20730.

Kleinpoppen, Professor Hans, DiplPhysicist, Chart Phys, Dr re nat & habil, FInstPhys, FRAS, FRSA, FRSE, Fellow, American Physical Society. Professor of Experimental Physics, Stirling University, since 1968; b. 30.9.28, Duisburg, Germany. Educ. Giessen University; Heidelberg University; Tuebingen University. Visiting Fellow, Colorado University, 1967; Visiting Associate Professor, Columbia University, New York, 1968; Stirling University: Head, Physics Department, 1970-72, Director, Institute of Atomic Physics, 1975-81, Head, Unit of Atomic and Molecular Physics, School of Natural Sciences, since 1989. Visiting Professor, Bielefeld University, since 1979; Visiting Fellow, Fritz Haber Institut, Max Planck Gessellschaft, since 1991. Co-Director, three International Summer Schools; Chairman, several national and international Conferences on Atc nic Physics. Publications: editor of 11 books; research papers; articles in many journals; monograph series on physics of atoms and molecules (Co-editor). Address: (b.) Unit of Atomic and Molecular Physics, Stirling University, Stirling.

Knight, Alanna, FSA Scot. Novelist; b. Co. Durham; m., Alistair Knight; 2 s. Educ. Jesmond High School. Writing career began, 1965; novels: Legend of the Loch, 1969 (RNA First Novel Award), The October Witch, 1971, This Outward Angel, 1971, Castle Clodha, 1972, Lament for Lost Lovers, 1972, The White Rose, 1974, A Stranger Came By, 1974, The Wicked Wynsleys, 1977; historical novels: The Passionate Kindness, 1974, A Drink for the Bridge, 1976, The Black Duchess, 1980, Castle of Foxes, 1981, Colla's Children, 1982, The Clan, 1985; Estella, 1986; detective novels: Enter Second Murderer, 1988, Blood Line, 1989, Deadly Beloved, 1989, Killing Cousins, 1990, A Quiet Death, 1991, To Kill A Queen, 1992; The Evil that Men Do, 1993, The Missing Duchess, 1994, Inspector Faro and the Edinburgh Mysteries, 1994, The Bull Slayers, 1995; crime novels: the Sweet Cheat Gone, 1992, This Outward Angel, 1994; plays: The Private Life of R.L.S., 1973, Girl on an Empty Swing, 1977; non-fiction: The Robert Louis Stevenson Treasury, 1985; RLS in the South Seas, 1986, Bright Ring of Words (Co-author), 1994; radio short stories, plays and documentaries. Recreations: walking; reading; painting. Address: (h.) 24 March Hall Crescent, Edinburgh, EH16 5HL; T.-0131-667 5230.

Knight, Raymond Stewart, AAIB. General Manager Projects, Clydesdale Bank, since 1994; b. 12.6.44, Australia; m., Phyllis; 2 s.; 1 d. National Australia Bank, 1981-91; General Manager Retail East, 1991, General Manager Regional Banking, 1992, Clydesdale Bank. Address: (b.) 30 St. Vincent Place, Glasgow; T.-0141-223 2841.

Knill-Jones, Jennifer Gillian, MB, BS, LRCP, MRCS, MRCPsych. Consultant Psychiatrist, since 1986; b. 15.8.36, Stockton-on-Tees; 3 d. Educ. Sutton High School; St. Bartholomew's Hospital Medical School. House Officer posts, Luton and Dunstable Hospital, Elizabeth Garrett Anderson Hospital, London, St. Bartholomew's Hospital, London; Clinical Assistant, Gartnavel Royal Hospital, Glasgow; Senior Registrar in Psychiatry, Greater Glasgow Health Board. Recreations: walking; Scottish country dancing. Address: (b.) Parkhead Hospital, Salamanca Street, Glasgow, G32; T.-0141-554 7951.

Knops, Professor Robin John, BSc, PhD, FRSE. Professor of Mathematics, Heriot-Watt University, Edinburgh, since 1971 (Vice Principal, since 1988); b. 30.12.32, London; m., Margaret; 4 s.; 2 d. Educ. Nottingham University. Nottingham University: Assistant Lecturer in Mathematics, 1956-59, Lecturer in Mathematics, 1959-62; Newcastle-upon-Tyne University: Lecturer in Applied Mathematics, 1962-68, Reader in Continuum Mechanics, 1968-71; Head, Department of Mathematics, Heriot-Watt University, 1971-83; Visiting Professor: Cornell University, 1967 and 1968; University of California, Berkeley, 1968; Pisa University, 1974; Ecole Polytechnique Federale Lausanne, Switzerland, 1980; Royal Society of Edinburgh: Council Member, 1982-92, Executive Committee Member, 1982-92, Meetings Secretary, 1982-87, Chief Executive Editor, Proceedings A, 1982-87, Curator, 1987-92; President, Edinburgh Mathematical Society, 1974-75; President, International Society for the Interaction of Mechanics and Mathematics, since 1991. Publications: Uniqueness Theories in Linear Elasticity (Co-author), 1971; Theory of Elastic Stability (Co-author), 1973. Recreations: walking; reading. Address: (b.) Lord Balerno Building, Heriot-Watt University, Edinburgh, EH14 4AS; T.-0131-449 5111.

Knowler, Professor John T., PhD, CBiol, FIBiol. Head, Department of Biological Sciences, Glasgow Caledonian University, since 1990; b. 19.10.42, Whitstable; m., Susan Penelope; 2 d. Educ. Canterbury Technical School; Glasgow University. Insecticide and pharmaceutical industries, 1962-69; research, 1969-72; post-doctoral research, 1972-73; Lecturer in Biochemistry, Senior Lecturer, Glasgow University, 1973-90. Publications: 75 papers, 11 chapters in academic books, two authored books. Recreations: bird-watching and other aspects of natural history; gardening. Address: (b.) Department of Biological Sciences, Glasgow Caledonian University, Cowcaddens Road, Glasgow, G4 0BA; T.-0141-331 3210.

Knox, Col. Sir Bryce Muir, KCVO, MC (and Bar), CStJ, TD, BA (Cantab); b. 4.4.16, Edinburgh; m., Patricia Mary Dunsmuir; 1 s.; 1 d. Educ. Stowe; Trinity College, Cambridge. County of Ayr: Deputy Lieutenant, 1953, Vice Lieutenant, 1970-74, Ayrshire and Arran Lord Lieutenant, 1974-91; Chairman, W. & J. Knox Ltd., Kilbirnie, 1970-78; Vice-Chairman, Lindustries Ltd., 1979 (Director, 1953-79); served with Ayrshire (ECO) Yeomanry, 1939-45, North Africa and Italy (CO, 1953-56, Hon. Col., 1960-71); Honorary Colonel, Ayrshire Yeomanry Squadron, Queen's Own Yeomanry, 1971-77; President, Royal Highland Agricultural Society of Scotland, 1990-91. Publications: brief historical notes of the Ayrshire Yeomanry; History of the Eglinton Hunt. Recreation: country sports. Address: (h.) Martnaham Lodge, by Ayr, KA6 6ES; T.-Dalrymple 204.

Knox, John, BA, BD. General Secretary, Scottish National Council of YMCAs, since 1992; b. 28.1.35, Larne, Co. Antrim; m., Patricia Ringland; 1 s.; 1 d. Educ. Larne Grammar School; Queen's University, Belfast; Edgehill College; London University. Methodist Minister, Dublin, Donegal and Belfast, 1959-69; General Secretary, Methodist Youth Department, Ireland, 1969-78; Associate Secretary, Irish Council of Churches, 1978-82; Chief Officer, Scottish Standing Conference of Voluntary Youth Organisations, 1982-92. Recreations: gardening; mountain walking; music. Address: (b.) 11 Rutland Street, Edinburgh, EH1 2AE; T.-0131-228 1464.

Knox, Professor John Henderson, BSc, PhD, DSc, FRSC, CChem, FRSE, FRS. Director, Wolfson Liquid Chromatography Unit, Edinburgh University, since 1972 (Emeritus Professor of Physical Chemistry and Honorary Fellow since 1984); b. 21.10.27, Edinburgh; m., Josephine Anne Wissler; 4 s. Educ. George Watson's Boys College,

Edinburgh; Edinburgh University; Cambridge University. Edinburgh University: Lecturer, 1953-66, Reader, 1966-74, Professor, 1974-84. Recreations: skiing; hill-walking; sailing. Address: (h.) 67 Morningside Park, Edinburgh; T.-0131-447 5057.

Knox, Robert, MA, LLB, WS. Senior Maritime Partner, Henderson Boyd Jackson, Edinburgh, since 1993; Solicitor, since 1959; Solicitor to Ministry of Defence (Army) in Scotland, since 1980; Honorary Consul for Belgium in Edinburgh, since 1982; b. 23.5.35, Paisley; m., Jill Mackness; 2 s.; 1 d. Educ. Paisley Grammar School; Glasgow University; Manchester University; Edinburgh University. Member, Lord Maxwell's Committee on Civil Jurisdiction and Enforcement. Recreations: gardening; photography; foreign travel; music; painting; railways past and present; model railways. Address: (b.) 19 Ainslie Place, Edinburgh; T.-0131-226 6881.

Knox, William. Author and Journalist; b. 20.2.28, Glasgow; m., Myra Ann McKill; 1 s.; 2 d. Educ. Eastwood School. Deputy News Editor, Evening News, Glasgow, 1957; Scottish Editor, Kemsley Newspapers, Glasgow, 1957-60; News Editor, Scottish Television, 1960-62; Freelance Author and Broadcaster, since 1962; author of more than 60 books, including novels of crime, sea and adventure; awarded Police Review Award for best novel of British police procedures, 1987 (The Crossfire Killings); Presenter Crime Desk, STV, 1977-88; William Knox Collection established Boston University, USA; Past President and Honorary Member, Association of Scottish Motoring Writers; former Member, Scottish Committee, Society of Authors; Past President, Glasgow Rotary Club; Honorary Editor, Scottish Lifeboat, RNLI; Fellow, Paul Harris Foundation, Rotary International, 1989. Recreations: motoring; photography; dogs. Address: (h.) 55 Newtonlea Avenue, Newton Mearns, Glasgow, G77 5QF.

Knox, William James. Member, Council, ACAS, since 1992; Chairman, UK Federation of Small Businesses, 1989-92; Chairman, Inverclyde Megawatt Festival, since 1994; b. 4.8.44, Glasgow; m., Ann May; 1 d. Educ. Greenock High School; Reid Kerr College, Paisley. Partner, A.F. McPherson & Co., Builders and Merchants, since 1962; Board Member, Scottish National Federation of Building Trade Employers, 1970-79; Member, Social Security Tribunal, 1978-84; Director, Morton Football and Athletic Club, 1986-89; Chairman, Morton Development Club, 1986-89; Member, Board of Directors, Greenock Arts Guild, since 1993; Member, Executive, Scottish Constitutional Convention, 1989-90. Recreations: football; bowling; photography; canals. Address: (h.) 3 Moorfield Road, Gourock, PA19 1DD; T.-01475 633327.

Kristiansen, Professor Bjorn, BSc, MSc, PhD. Robertson Professor of Bioprocess Technology, Strathclyde University, since 1990; Director, Strathclyde Fermentation Centre, since 1988; b. 1.2.47, Baerum, Norway; m., Joan Linden Kristiansen; 2 s.; 2 d. Educ. UMIST; Imperial College. Address: (b.) Department of Bioscience and Biotechnology, Strathclyde University, 204 George Street, Glasgow, G1 1XQ.

Kuenssberg, Nicholas Christopher D., BA (Hons) (Oxon), FCIS, CIMgt. Director, 1991, Managing Director, since 1994, Dawson International plc; Non-executive Director, Scottish Power Plc, since 1984; Director, Standard Life Assurance Company, since 1988. b. 28.10.42, Edinburgh; m., Sally Robertson; 1 s.; 2 d. Educ. Edinburgh Academy; Wadham College, Oxford. Director, J. & P. Coats Ltd., 1978-91; Director, Coats Patons Plc, 1985-91; Director, Coats Viyella PLC, 1986-91; Visiting Professor, Strathclyde Business School, 1988-91. Recreations: languages; opera; travel; sport. Address: (b.) Dawson Intrnational Plc, 9 Charlotte Street, Edinburgh, EH2 4DR.

Kyle, James, CBE, DSc, MCh, FRCS. Chairman, Raigmore Hospital NHS Trust, Inverness; b. 26.3.25, Ballymena, Northern Ireland; m., Dorothy Elizabeth Galbraith; 2 d. Educ. Ballymena Academy; Queen's University, Belfast. Scholarship to Mayo Clinic, USA, 1950; Tutor in Surgery, Royal Victoria Hospital, Belfast, 1952; Lecturer in Surgery, Liverpool University, 1957; Senior Lecturer in Surgery, Aberdeen University, 1959-60, and Surgeon, Aberdeen Royal Infirmary, 1959-89. Member, Grampian Health Board, 1973-77, Chairman, 1989-93; Chairman, Scottish Committee for Hospital Medical Services, 1976-79; elected Member, General Medical Council, since 1979; Chairman, Scottish Joint Consultants Committee, 1984-89; Chairman, Representative Body, British Medical Association, 1984-87; President, Aberdeen Medico-Chirurgical Society, 1989-90. Publications: Peptic Ulcer; Pye's Surgical Handicraft; Crohn's Disease; Scientific Foundations of Surgery. Recreations: Fellow, Royal Philatelic Society, London; licensed radio amateur, GM4 CHX. Address: (h.) 7 Fasaich, Gairloch, IV21 2BD; T.-01445 712398.

Kyle, Peter McLeod, MBChB, FRCS(Edin), FRCS(Glas), FCOphth. Consultant Ophthalmologist, Greater Glasgow Health Board, since 1982; Honorary Clinical Senior Lecturer, Glasgow University, since 1985; Member, Medical Appeal Tribunals, Scotland, since 1986; b. 19.8.51, Rutherglen; m., Valerorie Anne Steele; 1 s.; 2 d. Educ. High School of Glasgow; Glasgow University. Lecturer in Ophthalmology, Glasgow University, 1980-84. Ophthalmic Adviser, Queens College, Glasgow, since 1985; Vice-Chairman, Examination Council, British Orthopic Society, since 1990. Recreations: walking; skiing. Address: (h.) 36 Sutherland Avenue, Glasgow; T.-0141-427 4400.

Kyle, Robert, MBE, DL, NP. Honorary Sheriff, Strathclyde, at Airdrie; Deputy Lieutenant, County of Dunbarton; b. 28.3.19, Strathaven; m., Pauline Watson; 3 s.; 1 d. Educ. Strathaven Academy; Hamilton Academy; Glasgow University. War service, six years; Legal Assistant, Kilmarnock Town Council, 1946-48; Depute Town Clerk, Airdrie Town Council, 1948-52; Town Clerk, Kirkintilloch Town Council, 1952-68; Town Clerk and Manager, Cumbernauld Town Council, 1968-74; Chief Executive, Cumbernauld and Kilsyth District Council, 1974-81. Past President: Dumbartonshire Golf Union, Kirkintilloch & District Agricultural Society, Strathaven Golf Club, Rotary Club of Kirkintilloch. Recreations: golf; angling. Address: (h.) 23 Middlemuir Road, Lenzie, Glasgow, G66 4NA; T.-0141-776 1861.

Kynoch, George Alexander Bryson, BSc. MP (Conservative), Kincardine and Deeside, since 1992; Parliamentary Under Secretary of State for Scotland – Minister for Industry and Local Government; b. 7.10.46, Keith; m., Dr. Rosslyn Marget McDevitt; 1 s.; 1 d. Educ. Cargilfield School, Edinburgh; Glenalmond College, Perth; Bristol University. Plant Engineer, ICI Ltd., Nobel Division, 1968-71; G. and G. Kynoch PLC, 1971-92, latterly as Group Executive Director; Non-Executive Director: Kynoch Group PLC, Aaadvark Clear Mine Ltd., since 1992; Member, Aberdeen and District Milk Marketing Board, 1988-92; Director, Moray Badenoch and Strathspey Local Enterprise Co. Ltd., 1991-92; Chairman, Scottish Woollen Publicity Council, 1983-90; President, Scottish Woollen Industry, 1990-91; Vice Chairman, Northern Area, Scottish Conservative and Unionist Association, 1991-92. Recreations: golf; skiing; travel. Address: (b.) House of Commons, London, SW1A 0AA; T.-0171-219 5808.

L

Lacey, Robert Anderson Geddes, BMus, CQSW. Executive Director, Scottish Central Council Branch, British Red Cross Society, since 1992; b. 313.53, Greenock; m., Marion; 1 s.; 1 d. Educ. Lenzie Academy; Glasgow University; Stirling University. Music Assistant, Glasgow Arts Centres, 1976-78; Scottish Project Organiser, One-to-One Scotland, 1978-80; Development Officer, Care of the Young Disabled Scheme, Scottish Central Council Branch, British Red Cross, 1980-85; Manager, Care of the Young Disabled Scheme, 1985-92. Recreations: sailing; music. Address: (b.) Alexandra House, 204 Bath Street, Glasgow, G2 4HL; T.-0141-332 9591.

Laidlaw, Bruce, ACIS. Administrative Secretary, Royal Scottish Academy, since 1995; b. 11.7.45, Edinburgh; m., Sandra; 1 s.; 1 d. Educ. Royal High School; Napier College, Edinburgh. Assistant Secretary, Cranston London Hotels Co. Ltd., 1963-65; public service, Edinburgh City, 1966-74; Elections Officer, Lothian Regional Council, 1975-79; public service, Lothian Regional Council, 1980-95. Recreations: fishing; skiing. Address: (b.) Royal Scottish Academy, The Mound, Edinburgh, EH2 2EL; T.-0131-225 6671.

Laidlaw, Professor James Cameron, MA, PhD. Emeritus Professor of French, Aberdeen University (Professor of French, 1975-92); Honorary Fellow, Arts Faculty, Edinburgh University; b. 3.3.37, Ecclefechan; m., Elizabeth Fernie Bosomworth; 1 s.; 2 d. Educ. George Watson's College, Edinburgh; Edinburgh University; Trinity Hall, Cambridge. Research Fellow, Trinity Hall, Cambridge, 1961-63; Lecturer in Medieval French, Queen's University, Belfast, 1963-65; University Assistant Lecturer (from 1969 University Lecturer) in French, and Fellow, Trinity Hall, Cambridge, 1965-74; Visiting Fellow, Gonville and Caius College, Cambridge, 1986-87; Visiting Professor, Victoria University of Wellington, New Zealand, 1990-91; Vice-Principal, Aberdeen University, 1984-86. Member Arts Sub-Committee, University Grants Committee, 1980-89; Adviser in Modern Languages, Universities Funding Council, 1989-91; Honorary Secretary, Modern Humanities Research Association, 1961-67. Publications: The Future of the Modern Humanities (Editor), 1969; The Poetical Works of Alain Chartier, 1974; Alain Chartier: poemes, 1988. Recreations: walking; cycling. Address: (h.) Orchard Walls, Traquair, Innerleithen, EH44 6PU; T.-01896 831227.

Laing, The Hon. Mark Hector, MA. Managing Director, Simmers Biscuits, since 1990; Chairman, Capital Enterprise Trust; Member, Executive Council, Scottish Business in the Community; b. 22.2.51, London; m., Susanna Crawford; 1 s.; 2 d. Educ. Eton College; Cambridge University. United Biscuits p.l.c., since 1972: Factory Director, Glasgow, 1985; Production Director, McVities, 1988. Recreations: walking; gardening; fishing; shooting. Address: (b.) Simmers, Romano House, 43 Station Road, Corstorphine, Edinburgh, EH12 7AQ; T.-0131-334 0852.

Laing, Marshall George, MA, LLB. Solicitor; Honorary Sheriff; b. 31.1.23, Aberdeen; m. Educ. Robert Gordon's College, Aberdeen; Aberdeen University. Legal Assistant: Guild & Guild, WS, Edinburgh, 1949-50, Davidson & Garden, Aberdeen, 1950-55, Wilkinson & Grist, Hong Kong, 1955-59, J.L. Anderson & Co., Cupar, 1960-62; Partner: Craig and Geddes, Dumfries 1962-76, Symons & MacDonald, Dumfries, 1976-88. Recreation: golf. Address: (h.) 3 Richmond Avenue, Dumfries; T.-Dumfries 53871.

Laird, David Logan, FRICS, JP, DL. Solicitor; Partner, Thorntons WS, since 1985; Chartered Surveyor and Consultant, Smiths Gore; Chairman, Cairngorms Partnership, since 1994; Member, Scottish National Heritage (Regional Chairman, North East Region), since 1992; b. 13.4.37, St. Andrews; m., Ann Ruth Thorley; 2 s.; 1 d. Educ. Bell Baxter School, Cupar; Edinburgh University; Edinburgh College of Agriculture. Partner, Clark Oliver Dewar & Webster, SSC, 1971-85. Deputy Lieutenant, Angus, since 1989; Member, Nature Conservancy Council for Scotland, 1990-92. Recreations: stalking; gardening; shooting; fishing. Address: (h.) West Memus, Forfar, Angus, DD8 3TY; T.-01307 860251.

Lally, Patrick James, JP, DL, HRGI, FRSA. Leader, City of Glasgow District Council, 1986-92 and since 1994; Chairman, Greater Glasgow Tourist Board, since 1994; Chairman, Glasgow Cultural Enterprises, since 1988; b. Glasgow; m., Margaret Beckett McGuire; 2 s. Elected, Corporation of Glasgow, 1966-75 (Deputy Leader of Corporation, 1972-75); elected City of Glasgow Council, 1974-77, since 1980; City Treasurer, 1984-86; Director, Greater Glasgow Tourist Board and Convention Bureau; Director, Scottish Exhibition and Conference Centre; Hon. Member, Royal Glasgow Institute of Fine Arts; Director, Mayfest International Arts Festival; Director, Citizens Theatre; Chairman, Glasgow International Jazz Festival; Hon. Director, Chinese Peoples Association for Friendship with Foreign Countries; Director, Castlemilk Economic Development Agency; Director, 7:84 Theatre Company. Recreations: enjoying the arts; reading; watching TV and football. Address: (b.) City Chambers, George Square, Glasgow; T.-0141-227 4100.

Lamb, Rev. A. Douglas, MA, FSA (Scot). Parish Minister, Dalry: St. Margaret's, since 1973; Convener, Mission and Evangelism Resource Committee, Board of National Mission, Church of Scotland, since 1995; b. 9.11.36, Glasgow; m., Jean A. Beattie; 3 s.; 1 d. Educ. Hermitage School, Helensburgh; Glasgow University; Princeton Seminary. Assistant Minister: First Presbyterian, Philadelphia, Airdrie West; Parish Minister, Unst (Shetland). Recreations: hill-walking; history; continental travel. Address: St. Margaret's Manse, Dalry, KA24 4DA; T.-01294 832234.

Lamb, Professor Joseph Fairweather, MB, ChB, BSc, PhD, FRCPEdin, FRSE, FRSA. Honorary Professor; Chandos Professor of Physiology, St. Andrews University, 1969-93; Chairman, Save British Science Society, since 1986; b. 18.7.28, Brechin; m., 1, Olivia Jane Horne; 3 s.; 1 d.; 2, Bridget Cecilia Cook; 2 s. Educ. Brechin High School; Edinburgh University. National Service, 1947-49; House Surgeon, Dumfries Royal Infirmary, 1955-56; House Physician, Eastern General Hospital, Edinburgh, 1956; Research Scholar, then Lecturer, Edinburgh University, 1957-61; Lecturer, then Senior Lecturer, Glasgow University, 1961-69; Editor, Journal of Physiology, 1968-74; Senior Secretary, Physiological Society, 1982-85. Publication: Essentials of Physiology, 1980. Recreations: boat-building; sailing; amateur radio. Address: (h.) Kenbrae, 23 Millbank, Cupar, KY15 5DP.

Lamb, Colonel Tom Bell Maxwell, OBE, CStJ, MA, FSA (Scot), DL. Retired Colonel, HM Forces; Deputy Lord Lieutenant, Argyll & Bute, since 1987; b. 23.11.18, Lanark; m., Sheina Barclay Dempster; 2 s.; 1 d. Educ. Lanark Secondary School; Heriot-Watt College. Commercial Bank of Scotland, 1935-38; Chartered Bank of India, 1938-39; Regular Officer, Queen's Own Cameron Highlanders, 1940-70; staff, Stirling University, 1970-75; Controller, The Burn, Edzell, 1975-84. Croix de Guerre, 1945; Meritorious Service Decoration (Singapore), 1964; mentioned in Despatches, 1945; Commander of St. John, 1982. Recreation: golf (Member, R. & A.). Address: (h.) Seafield, Kilchattan Bay, Isle of Bute; T.-Kilchattan Bay 682.

Lambie, David, BSc (Hons), DipEd, FEIS. Chairman, Development Committee, Cunninghame Housing

Association, since 1992; Chairman, Saltcoats Labour Party, since 1992; MP (Labour), Cunninghame South, 1970-92; b. 13.7.25, Saltcoats; m., Netta Merrie; 1 s.; 4 d. Educ. Ardrossan Academy; Glasgow University; Geneva University. Teacher, Glasgow Corporation, 1950-70. Secretary, All Party Committee for Energy Studies, 1980-92; chaired Select Committee on Scottish Affairs, 1981-87; UK Member, Council of Europe and Western European Union, 1987-92; Chairman, PLP Aviation Committee, 1988-92. Recreation: watching junior football. Address: (h.) 11 Ivanhoe Drive, Saltcoats, Ayrshire, KA21 6LS; T.-01294 464843.

Lammie, Neil Robertson, FCCA. Director of Finance, Ayrshire and Arran Health Board, since 1991; b. 4.11.41, Ayr; m., Winnie; 2 s.; 1 d. Educ. Marr College, Troon. Treasurer, Fife Health Board, 1979-85; Treasurer, Ayrshire and Arran Health Board, 1985-91. Chairman, Health Board Directors of Finance Purchaser Finance Support Group. Recreations: sport in general, rugby union and golf in particular. Address: (b.) Seafield House, Doonfoot Road, Ayr, KA7 4DW; T.-01292 611040.

Lamont, Alan McGregor, MA, DipEd. General Secretary, Scottish Secondary Teachers' Association, since 1994 (Deputy General Secretary, 1985-94); b. 23.2.40, Glasgow; m., Alison Rae; 2 s. Educ. Glasgow Academy; Aberdeen University. Royal Artillery, 1961-64; Teacher of Mathematics, 1965-75; Principal Teacher, Alness Academy, 1975-81; Assistant General Secretary, SSTA, 1981-85. Captain, Niddry Castle Golf Cub, 1992-94. Recreations: golf; walking. Address: (h.) 52 Tippetknowes Park, Winchburgh.

Lamont, Colin C., MA, PhD. Headteacher, Ross High School, Tranent, since 1989; b. 6.10.44, Glasgow; m.; 2 s. Educ. Robert Gordon's College, Aberdeen; Aberdeen University; Edinburgh University. Teacher, Merchiston Castle School, Edinburgh; Principal Teacher, Robert Gordon's College, Aberdeen; Adviser in English, Renfrew Division, Strathclyde; Headteacher, Gracemount High School, Edinburgh. Address: (b.) Ross High School, Well Wynd, Tranent, East Lothian, EH33 2EQ; T.-01875 610433.

Lamont, Rev. Stewart Jackson, BSc, BD. Minister, Church of Scotland, since 1972; Freelance Journalist and Broadcaster (Religious Affairs Correspondent, Glasgow Herald), since 1980; Parish Minister, Kinning Park, Glasgow, since 1991; b. 8.1.47, Broughty Ferry; m., Larisa V. Gaydakova. Educ. Grove Academy, Broughty Ferry; St. Andrews University. General Council Assessor, St. Andrews University Court, 1970-82; Producer, BBC Religious Department, 1972-80; Freelance Radio and Television Presenter and Producer, 1980-91; part-time Minister, Abernyte, 1980-82. Publications: The Third Angle, 1978; Is Anybody There?, 1980; Religion and the Supernatural (Co-author), 1985; 'Religion Inc.' (Scientology), 1986; Scotland 2000 (BBC TV, 1987; Church and State, 1989; In Good Faith, 1989; The Swordbearer: John Knox, 1991; Glasgow Herald Book of Glasgow (Contributor); St. Andrews Rock, 1993. Winner, Scottish Schools Debating Competition, 1965; President of the Union, St. Andrews, 1969. Recreations: cooking; music; foreign travel. Address: Apartment 9, 10 Mavisbank Gardens, Glasgow, G51 1HF; T.-0141-427 2191.

Lamont, William David Dawson, CA, IRRV. Director of Finance, Argyll & Bute District Council, since 1990; b. 14.11.49, Irvine; m., Eleanor; 1 s.; 1 d. Educ. Irvine Royal Academy; Institute of Chartered Accountants of Scotland (Glasgow University). Trained and worked as chartered accountant with Alexander Sloan & Company, Glasgow, 1966-73; Depute Burgh Chamberlain, Royal Burgh of Irvine, 1973-75; Depute Director of Finance, Argyll & Bute District Council, 1975-90. Treasurer, Ardrishaig Parish

Church. Recreations: family; travel; music; Rotary; messing about in boats. Address: (b.) Department of Finance, Kilmory, Lochgilphead, PA31 8RT; T.-01546 604220.

Lamont-Brown, Raymond, MA, AMIET, MJS, FSA (Scot). Author and Broadcaster; Lecturer, Centre for External Services, St. Andrews University, since 1978, Centre for Continuing Education, Dundee University, since 1988; Founder, Japan Research Projects, since 1965; b. 20.9.39, Horsforth, Leeds; m., Dr. Elizabeth Moira McGregor. Educ. Wheelwright Grammar School, Dewsbury; Bradford Technical College; SOAS; Nihon Daigaku, Japan. Honorary Secretary/Treasurer, Society of Authors in Scotland, 1982-89; Past President, St. Andrews Rotary Club; Vice-Chairman, St. Andrews Community Council, 1988-91; Chairman, Arthritis Care Liaison Committee (Central, Fife and Tayside), since 1991; Member, Council, Arthritis Care, since 1991. Publications: 42 published books, including Discovering Fife; Phantoms of the Sea; The Life and Times of Berwick-upon-Tweed; The Life and Times of St. Andrews; Royal Murder Mysteries; Scottish Epitaphs; Scottish Superstitions; Scottish Traditions and Festivals; Famous Scots; Scottish Witchcraft. Address: (h.) Crawford House, 132 North Street, St. Andrews, Fife, KY16 9AF; T.-01334 474897.

Lamprell-Jarrett, Peter Neville, KCSG, KCHS, PPIAAS, FIAS, FFB, FSA(Scot), FRSA. Partner, Archard & Partners, Architects and Surveyors, since 1954; b. 23.6.19, Margate; m., Kathleen Furner; 1 s.; 1 d. Educ. Vernon House Preparatory School; Cliftonville College. Architectural Assistant, LCC (later GLC) Housing Department, 1947-49; Deputy Controller of Works, Land Settlement Association, 1950-54; President, Incorporated Association of Architects and Surveyors, 1967-68; Kt. Commander, Equestrian Order Holy Sepulchre of Jerusalem, 1974; Kt. Commander, Pontifical Order of St. Gregory the Great, 1975; responsible for design of many Catholic schools and churches; Freeman, City of London; Life Vice President, London Caledonian Catholic Association; Past Chairman, Archdiocese of Westminster Catholic Parents and Electors Association; Liveryman, Worshipful Company of Wheelwrights, since 1978. Recreations: painting; walking; fishing; classical music. Address: (h.) Carrick House, Carrick Castle, by Lochgoil, Argyll, PA24 8AF; T.-Lochgoilhead 703394.

Landale, Sir David William Neil, KCVO, DL. Chairman, T.C. Farries & Company Limited; Secretary and Keeper of the Records, Duchy of Cornwall, 1987-93; b. 27.5.34, London; m., (Norah) Melanie; 3 s. Educ. Eton College; Balliol College, Oxford (MA). Black Watch, Royal Highland Regiment, 1952-54; Jardine Matheson & Co. Ltd., 1958-75, served in Hong Kong, Thailand, Taiwan and Japan (Director, 1967-75); Director, Matheson & Co. Ltd., 1975; Member, Royal Company of Archers, Queen's Bodyguard for Scotland, since 1966. Recreations: all countryside pursuits; theatre; reading (history). Address: (h.) Dalswinton, Dumfries; T.-01387 740 208/279.

Dalswinton Ho. DG2 OXZ

Lander, Ronald, BSc. Chairman and Managing Director: Scotlander plc, since 1985, Scetlander Ltd., since 1986; Director, Centre for Entrepreneurial Development, Glasgow University, 1985-88; b. 5.8.42, Glasgow; m., Elizabeth Stirling; 2 s. Educ. Allan Glen's School; Glasgow University. Chairman and Managing Director, Lander Grayburn & Co. Limited, 1970-83; Deputy Managing Director, Lander Alarm Company (Scotland) Limited, 1975-79; Managing Director, Lander Alarms Limited and Lander Alarms (Scotland) Limited, 1979-85; Chairman, Lander & Jess Limited, 1983-87. Member, CBI Scottish Council, 1977-83, 1984-90, since 1992; founding Chairman, CBI Scotland's Smaller Firms' Working Group, 1977-80; founder Member, CBI Industrial Policy Committee, London, 1978-86; Chairman, CBI Scotland Smaller Firms' Committee, since 1993; Chairman, Scottish

Fire Prevention Council, 1979-80; Member, Glasgow University Appointments Committee, since 1979; CBI Representative, Home Office/CBI/TUC Joint Committee on Prison Industries, 1980-87; Industrial Member, Understanding British Industry, Scotland, 1981-89; Member, Council, Scottish Business School, 1982-87; Director, British Security Industry Association Council, 1984-85; Governor, Scottish Sports Aid Foundation, 1985-88; Vice-Chairman, CBI Scotland Education and Training Committee, 1986-87; Member: Kincraig Committee (review of parole system and related matters), 1987-89, Manpower Services Committee for Scotland (later the Training Agency), 1987-88; founder Chairman, Local Employer Network (LENS) Scottish Co-ordinating Committee, 1987; Chairman, CBI Scotland Education and Training Committee, 1987-89; Director, SCOTVEC, 1987-93; Member, CBI Business/Education Task Force (the Cadbury Report), 1988; Member, Scottish Consultative Council on the Curriculum, 1988-91; Vice-Convener, Scottish Education/Industry Committee, 1988-91; founder Member, Glasgow Action, 1985; Member, Secretary of State for Scotland's Crime Prevention Committee, 1984-87; Companion IEE, 1986; Board Member, Glasgow Development Agency, since 1991; Visiting Professor, Glasgow University, since 1991; National Judge, National Training Awards, 1989-92. Address: (b.) Lander Software, Glasgow Software Centre, 1 Atlantic Quay, Broomielaw, Glasgow, G2 8JE; T.-0141 226 5611.

Lane, Professor David Philip, BSc, PhD, FRSE. Professor of Molecular Oncology, Department of Biochemistry, Dundee University, since 1990; Director, Cancer Research Campaign Cell Transformation Group, since 1990; Gibb Fellow, Cancer Research Campaign, since 1990; b. 1.7.52, London; m., Professor Ellen Birgitte Lane (qv); 1 s.; 1 d. Educ. John Fisher School, Purley; University College, London. Lecturer in Zoology, then Lecturer in Biochemistry, Imperial College, London; Principal Scientist, Imperial Cancer Research Fund, South Mimms. Publications: (book) Antibodies, a laboratory manual; 170 articles. Recreations: walking; tennis; motor bikes. Address: (b.) CRC Laboratories, Dundee University, Dundee, DD1 4HN; T.-01382 344982.

Lane, Professor Ellen Birgitte, BSc, PhD. Cox Professor of Anatomy and Cell Biology, Dundee University, since 1991; Director, Cancer Research Campaign Cell Structure Research Group, since 1990; b. 24.12.50, Welwyn Garden City; m., David Philip Lane (qv); 1 s.; 1 d. Educ. Withington Girls' School, Manchester; University College, London. Research Assistant, Imperial College of Science and Technology, 1975-77, University College, 1977-78, Cold Spring Harbour Laboratories, New York, 1978-80; Imperial Cancer Research Fund, 1980-90; ICRF Clare Hall Laboratories, 1985-90. Publications: scientific papers in cell biology and cancer research. Recreation: enjoying the children growing up. Address: (b.) CRC Laboratories, Department of Anatomy and Physiology, Medical Sciences Institute, Dundee University, Dundee, DD1 4HN; T.-01382 344921.

Lang, Lt.-Gen. Sir Derek, KCB (1967), DSO (1944), MC (1941), DL; b. 7.10.13, Guildford; 1 s.; 1 d. Educ. Wellington College; RMC, Sandhurst. Director of Army Training, 1964-66; GOC-in-C, Scottish Command, and Governor of Edinburgh Castle, 1966-69. President, Army Cadet Force Association (Scotland), 1974-86. Recreations: golf; fishing; shooting; music. Address: (h.) Templeland, Kirknewton, Midlothian, EH27 8DJ; T.01506 883211.

Lang, Ian Bruce, PC, OStJ, BA. MP (Conservative) Galloway and Upper Nithsdale, since 1983 (Galloway, 1979-83); Secretary of State for Scotland, since 1990 (Minister of State, Scottish Office, 1987-90, Parliamentary Under Secretary of State, Scottish Office, 1986-87, and at Department of Employment, 1986); b. 27.6.40, Glasgow;

m., Sandra Caroline Montgomerie; 2 d. Educ. Lathallan School; Rugby School; Sidney Sussex College, Cambridge. Member, Select Committee on Scottish Affairs, 1979-81; Honorary President, Scottish Young Conservatives, 1982-84; Trustee, Glasgow Savings Bank and West of Scotland TSB, 1969-82; Lord Commissioner of HM Treasury, 1983-86; Scottish Whip, 1981-83; Vice-Chairman, Scottish Conservative Party, 1983-87; Member, Queen's Bodyguard for Scotland (Royal Company of Archers), since 1974; Insurance Broker and Company Director, 1962-81. Address (b.) House of Commons, Westminster, London, SW1A OAA.

Langford, Professor David Anthony, FCIOB, MSc, MPhil, MBIM, FRSA. Barr Professor of Construction, Strathclyde University, since 1991; b. 6.5.50, Notingham; m., Victoria; 1 d. Educ. Barstable School, Basildon; Bristol Polytechnic; Aston University; Cranfield School of Management. MSc Course Director, Department of Building Technology, Brunel University, 1975; Director of Postgraduate Studies, Bath University, 1987. Address: (b.) Department of Civil Engineering, Strathclyde University, Glasgow, G4 0NG; T.-0141-552 4400.

Langley, Crawford James, LLB (Hons), DPA, ACIS. Director of Law and Administration, Tayside Regional Council, since 1991; Director of Legal Services, Aberdeen City Council, since 1995; b. 21.11.51, Glasgow; m., Janette. Educ. Bellahouston Academy, Glasgow; Glasgow University. Legal apprentice, Corporation of Glasgow, 1973-75; various legal posts, Strathclyde Regional Council, 1975-89, Principal Solicitor, 1984-89; Depute Director of Law and Administration, Tayside Regional Council, 1989-91. Part-time Tutor in Public Administration, Dundee University; Assistant Area Commissioner, Scout Association. Recreations: travel; gardening. Address: (h.) Canouan, Eassie, Angus, DD8 1SG; T.-Glamis 518.

Lansdowne, 8th Marquess of (George John Charles Mercer Nairne Petty-Fitzmaurice); b. 27.11.12; 2 s.; 1 d. Minister of State for Colonial Affairs, 1962-64, for Commonwealth Relations, 1963-64. Address: Meikleour House, Perthshire, PH2 6EA.

Larkin, Professor Maurice John Milner, MA, PhD. Professor of Modern European History, Edinburgh University, since 1976; b. 12.8.32, Harrow on the Hill; m., Enid Thelma Lowe; 1 s.; 1 d. Educ. St. Philip's Grammar School, Birmingham; Trinity College, Cambridge. Assistant Lecturer, then Lecturer, Glasgow University, 1958-65; Lecturer, then Senior Lecturer, then Reader, Kent University, 1965-76. Publications: Gathering Pace: Continental Europe 1870-1945, 1969; Church and State after the Dreyfus Affair, 1974; Man and Society in Nineteenth-Century Realism, 1977; France since the Popular Front, 1988; Religion, politics and preferment in France since 1890, 1995. Recreations: bird-watching; music; films. Address: (b.) History Department, Edinburgh University, Edinburgh, EH8 9JY; T.-0131-650 3754.

Larner, Professor John Patrick, MA, FRHistA. Titular Professor of History, Glasgow University, since 1979; b. 24.3.30, London; m., Christina Ross (deceased); 2 s. Educ. Finchley Grammar School; New College, Oxford. Rome Medieval Scholar, British School of Rome, 1954-57; Lecturer, Glasgow University, 1957-79. Publications: Lords of Romagna, 1965; Culture and Society in Italy, 1971; Florentine Society 1382-1494, 1972; Italy in the Age of Dante, 1980. Recreations: hill-walking; photography. Address: (b.) Department of Medieval History, The University, Glasgow, G12 8QQ; T.-0141-339 8855.

Last, Professor Frederick Thomas, DSc, ARCS, FRSE, SHM. Applied Biologist; Honorary Professor, Forestry and Natural Resources, Edinburgh University, since 1972; b. 5.2.28, Wembley; m., Pauline Mary Cope; 2 s. Educ.

Haberdashers' Aske's Hampstead School; Imperial College of Science and Technology, London. Rothamsted Experimental Station, Herts, 1950-61; Chief Plant Pathologist to Government of Sudan, 1956-58; Head, Mycology and Bacteriology, Glasshouse Crops Research Institute, Sussex, 1961-69; Visiting Professor, Pennsylvania State University, 1969-70; Member of Directorate, Institute of Terrestrial Ecology, Midlothian, 1970-86; Commissioner, Red Deer Commission, 1981-86; Visiting Professor, Agriculture and Environmental Science, Newcastle upon Tyne University, 1986-94; Chairman, Advisory Committee on Sites of Special Scientific Interest, since 1992; Chairman, Tree Advice Trust, since 1993; Programme Convener, Royal Society of Edinburgh, since 1993; Advisor, Chongqing Institute of Environmental Science, since 1993. Publications: Tree Physiology and Yield Improvement (Joint Editor), 1976; Land and its Uses, Actual and Potential: An Environmental Appraisal (Joint Editor), 1986; Acidic Deposition, Its Nature and Impacts (Joint Editor). Recreations: gardening; philately; travelling. Address: (h.) Furuly, Seton Mains, Longniddry, East Lothian, EH32 0PG; T.-01875 852102.

Lathe, Professor Richard Frank, BSc, Dr es Sci. Professorial Fellow, Edinburgh University, since 1989; Director, AFRC Centre for Genome Research, since 1989; b. 23.4.52, London; m., Margaret. Educ. Edinburgh University; Universite Libre de Bruxelles. Assistant Scientific Director, Transgene SA, Strasbourg; Principal Scientific Officer, ABRO, Edinburgh; Professor of Genetics/Genetic Engineering, University of Strasbourg; Director/Scientific Director, Ecole Superieure de Biotechnologie de Strasbourg. Publications: more than 100 scientific papers. Recreations: guitar; squash. Address: (b.) King's Buildings, West Mains Road, Edinburgh, EH9 3JQ; T.-0131-650 5890.

Lauderdale, Earl of (Patrick Francis Maitland), BA (Hons) (Oxon). Company Director; b. 17.3.11, Walsall; m., Stanka Lozanitch; 2 s.; 2 d. Educ. Lancing College; Brasenose College, Oxford. Journalist, Fleet Street, 1934-39; War Correspondent, Poland, 1939; Balkans/Danubian Correspondent, The Times, 1939-41; War Correspondent, the Pacific, News Chronicle, 1941-43; Foreign Office, 1943-45; Editor, The Fleet Street Letter Service, 1945-51; MP (Conservative), Lanark, 1951-59; Peer, since 1968; Chairman, Lords Energy Committee, 1974-79; Founder/Deputy Chairman, Parliamentary Group for Energy Studies, since 1983; Guardian, Shrine of Our Lady of Walsingham, since 1955 (now Emeritus); Chairman, Parliamentary 'Church in Danger' Group, 1988-95; Hereditary Bearer of the National Flag of Scotland. Recreations: reading; travel; pilgrimages to St. Mary's, Haddington. Address: (h.) 12 St. Vincent Street, Edinburgh; T.-031-556 5692.

Laurenson, Arthur Bruce, OBE, FRSA. Consultant; Chairman, Shetland Catch Ltd., since 1992; Director, Shetland Enterprise Company, since 1991; b. 22.7.31, Lerwick; m., Janet S. Mullay; 2 d. Educ. Anderson High School. Assistant Clerk and Collector, Lerwick Harbour Trust, 1947-64; appointed Clerk and Treasurer, 1968; General Manager and Clerk, 1972; Consultant, since 1991. Honorary Sheriff; Member, Lerwick Lifeboat Committee. Recreations: crofting; breeding Shetland ponies; gardening. Address: (h.) Vatnagarth, 2 Lovers Loan, Lerwick, Shetland, ZE1 0BA; T.-01595 2799.

Laurenson, James Tait, FCA. Non-Executive Director: Alvis PLC, since 1972, I & S UK Smaller Companies Trust plc, since 1983, Hiscox Holdings Ltd., since 1992, NSM plc, since 1994, Fidelity Special Values plc, since 1994; Chairman, Assets Investments SA, since 1983, Roksafe Sysems Ltd., since 1995; b. 15.3.41, Farnborough; m., Hilary Josephine; 1 s.; 3 d. Educ. Eton College; Magdalene

College, Cambridge. Ivory & Sime PLC: joined 1968; Partner, 1970; Director, 1975; left 1983; Managing Director, Tayburn Design Group Limited, 1983-84 (Chairman, 1984-88); Managing Director, Adam & Company Group plc, 1984-93; Chairman, Erskine Stewart's Melville Governing Council. Recreations: spending time with the family; gardening. Address: (h.) Hill House, Kirknewton, Midlothian, EH27 8DR; T.-01506 881990.

Laurie, Ian Cameron, FCIH. Chief Executive, Bearsden and Milngavie District Council, since 1985; b. 18.1.40, Bishopbriggs; m., Jean; 1 s. Educ. Bishopbriggs High School; GlasgowCollege of Building. Accountancy Assistant, then Housing Manager, Burgh of Kirkintilloch, 1963-74; Director of Housing, Strathkelvin District Council, 1974-85. Clerk to Lord Lieutenant of Dunbartonshire. Recreations: bowling; curling; music; reading; calligraphy. Address: (b.) 100 Milngavie Road, Bearsden, Glasgow, G61 2TQ; T.-0141-942 2262.

Laver, Professor John David Michael Henry, MA (Hons), DipPh, PhD, FBA, FRSE, FIOA. Chairman, Humanities Research Board of the British Academy; Professor of Phonetics, Centre for Speech Technology Research, Edinburgh University, since 1985; Director, Centre for Speech Technology Research, Edinburgh University, 1984-89, Vice Principal, since 1994; b. 20.1.38, Nowshera, Pakistan; m., Sandy Hutcheson; 3 s.; 1 d. Educ. Churcher's College, Petersfield; Edinburgh University. Assistant Lecturer, then Lecturer in Phonetics, Ibadan University, 1963-66 (Exchange Lecturer, Edinburgh University, 1964-65); Lecturer, then Senior Lecturer in Phonetics, Edinburgh University, 1966-80; Reader in Phonetics, 1980-84; Visiting Assistant Professor, Department of Linguistics, University of California, 1971; Visiting Research Fellow, Macquarie University, Sydney, 1982; Information Technology Fellowship, Edinburgh, 1983-84; President, International Phonetic Association, 1991-95. Publications: Communication in Face to Face Interaction (Joint Editor), 1972; Phonetics in Linguistics (Joint Editor), 1973; Voice Quality, 1979; The Phonetic Description of Voice Quality, 1980; The Cognitive Representation of Speech (Joint Editor), 1981; The Prospect of Future Speech Technology (Co-author), 1987; Proceedings of the European Conference on Speech Technology (Co-Editor), 1987; Aspects of Speech Technology (Co-Editor), 1988; The Gift of Speech, 1991; Principles of Phonetics, 1994; Menschen imd ihre Stimmen, 1994. Address: (b.) Humanities Research Board of the British Academy, Edinburgh University, Playfair Library, Old College, Edinburgh; T.-0131-650 2088.

Laverock, Edward, MA, LLB. Retired Solicitor; b. 21.10.19, Dunlop; m., Helen Moffat Harriet Mackison; 1 s.; 1 d. Educ. Hutchesons' Grammar School, Glasgow; Glasgow University. Partner, J. & W. Buchan, Peebles, 1945-86 (Senior Partner, 1954-86); Town Clerk, Peebles, 1948-75. Honorary Sheriff, since 1983. Address: (h.) Craigmount, Bonnington Road, Peebles; T.-01721 720314.

Law, Graham Couper, MA (Cantab), RSA, RIBA, FRIAS. Former Partner, The Law & Dunbar-Nasmith Partnership, Architects; b. 28.9.23, Glasgow; m., Isobel Evelyn Alexander Drysdale; 1 s.; 3 d. Educ. Merchiston Castle School; Kings College, Cambridge. Royal Engineers, 1941-46; ARIBA, 1951; Council Member: Edinburgh Architectural Association, 1964-69, Royal Incorporation of Architects in Scotland, 1965-67; Member: Architects Registration Council, 1967-75, ARCUK Professional Purposes Committee, 1967-73; Chairman, Workshop and Artists Studio Provision (Scotland) Ltd., 1977-81; Member, RIAS Investigation Committee, 1979-85; Associate, Royal Scottish Academy, 1980, Academician, 1995. Recreations: drawing; fishing. Address: (b.) 16 Dublin Street, Edinburgh, EH1 3RE; T.-0131-556 8631.

Law, James, QC, MA, LLB. Queen's Counsel, since 1971; b. 7.6.26, Irvine; m., Kathleen Margaret Gibson (see Kathleen Margaret Law); 2 s.; 1 d. Educ. Kilmarnock Academy; Girvan High School; Glasgow University. Admitted to Faculty of Advocates, 1951; Advocate Depute, 1957-64; Member, Criminal Injuries Compensation Board, since 1970. Address: 7 Gloucester Place, Edinburgh, EH3 6EE; T.-0131-225 2974.

Lawrence, Professor Andrew, BSc, PhD, FRAS. Regius Professor of Astronomy, Edinburgh University, since 1994; b. 23.4.54, Margate; partner, Debbie Ann Carel; 1 s.; 1 d. Educ. Chatham House Grammar School, Ramsgate; Edinburgh University; Leicester University. Exchange Scientist, Massachusetts Institute of Technology, 1980-81; Senior Research Fellow, Royal Greenwich Observatory, 1981-84; Research Assistant, then SERC Advanced Fellow, School of Mathematical Sciences, Queen Mary College, London, 1984-89; Lecturer, Physics Department, Queen Mary and Westfield College, London, 1989-94. Publications: over 60 in learned journals. Recreations: painting electrons and teasing publishers; acting. Address: (b.) Institute for Astronomy, Edinburgh University, Royal Observatory, Blackford Hill, Edinburgh.

Lawrence, John Henry, FCA. Honorary Sheriff, Kilmarnock; b. 4.5.05, Cardiff; m., Kathleen Clare Craig; 3 s. Educ. Cardiff High School. Senior Clerk, Deloitte & Co., CA, London, 1929-37; Assistant Secretary, Richardsons Westgarth & Co., Wallsend, 1938-42; Director and Secretary, Glenfield & Kennedy Ltd., Kilmarnock, 1942-70; former Council Member, Glasgow Management Association; Past Chairman, Glasgow Branch, Institute of Office Management; former Director, Kilmarnock Chamber of Industries; former Member, Taxation Committee, CBI; former Committee Member, Athlone Foundation; former Secretary and President, Kilmarnock Rotary Club; former Director, Ayrshire Branch, British Red Cross Society; former Chairman, Ayrshire Branch, English Speaking Union. Recreations: music; golf; bridge. Address: (h.) 10 Wilson Avenue, Troon, KA10 7AF; T.-01292 312776.

Lawrie, Frank James. Director (Heritage Policy), Historic Scotland, since 1991; b. 30.10.45, Edinburgh; m., Ann Macamon Kerr; 2 s.; 1 d. Educ. Royal High School, Edinburgh. Executive Officer, Department of Agriculture and Fisheries for Scotland, 1964-70; Higher Executive Officer, Scottish Office Finance Division, 1970-78; Senior Executive Officer, 1978-81; Principal, Department of Agriculture and Fisheries for Scotland, 1981-88; Deputy Director, Historic Buildings and Monuments, Scotland, 1988-91. Recreations: railway archaeology; cricket; golf. Address: (b.) Longmore House, Salisbury Place, Edinburgh, EH9 1SH; T.-0131 668 8727.

Lawrie, Nigel Gilbert, BSc, PhD. Head Teacher, Port Glasgow High School, since 1985; b. 2.6.47, Edinburgh; m., Janet Clark Warnock; 1 d. Educ. Bearsden Academy; Strathclyde University. Chemistry Teacher, Hermitage Academy, Helensburgh, 1972-75; Principal Teacher of Chemistry, Dunoon Grammar School, 1975-81; Assistant Head Teacher, Garnock Academy, 1981-84; Depute Head Teacher, Castlehead High School, Paisley, 1984-85. President, Scottish Association for Teachers of Social and Vocational Skills, 1984-88; Member, National Council, Headteachers' Association of Scotland, since 1991; Member, Scottish Examination Board, since 1994. Recreations: reading; gardening; football. Address: (b.) Port Glasgow High School, Marloch Avenue, Port Glasgow; T.-01475 705921.

Lawson, Alexander Adamson Hutt, MD, FRCPEdin. Consultant Physician, Fife Health Board, 1969-95; Honorary Senior Lecturer, Edinburgh University, 1979-95; Medical Adviser, War Pensions Appeal Tribunal, Scotland, since 1979; b. 30.7.37, Dunfermlihe; m., Barbara Helen Donnet; 3 s.; 1 d. Educ. Dunfermline High School; Edinburgh University. Consultant Member, Clinical Teaching Staff, Faculty of Medicine, Edinburgh University, 1971-95; Postgraduate Tutor in Medicine, West Fife, 1973-81; Medical Assessor, General Medical Council, since 1982; Member, Fife Health Board, 1981-91 (Vice-Chairman, 1989-91); President, Scottish Society of Physicians, 1989-90; President, West Fife Medical Society, 1982-83; Life Trustee, Carnegie Dunfermline Trust and Carnegie United Kingdom Hero Fund, since 1980; Life Trustee, Carnegie United Kingdom Trust, since 1983; Member, Committee of Safety, Efficacy and Adverse Reactions of Drugs (Committee, Safety of Medicines, DHSS, London), 1982-84; Member, Specialist Advisory Committee (UK) HCMT - General (Internal) Medicine, 1984-88; UK Representative to European Union of Medical Specialties, Monospecialty Committee for General Medicine, since 1986. Publications: Common Acute Poisonings; Acute Poisoning in Principles and Practice of Medicine; Toxicology and Drug Monitoring in Chemical Diagnosis of Disease; scientific papers. Address: (h.) 2 Park Avenue, Dunfermline, Fife, KY12 7HX; T.-Dunfermline 726435.

Lawson, Rev. Alexander Hamilton, THM, ThD, FPhS. Retired Minister (Kilbowie Parish Church, Clydebank, 1955-88); b. 16.9.21, Toronto, Canada; m., Martha Stevenson Macdonald; 1 s.; 1 d. Educ. Coatbridge Senior Secondary School; Glasgow University and Trinity College; American Bible College, Chicago; Metropolitan College of Law, St. Albans. RAF, 1941-46; Minister, Prestonpans Grange, 1950-55; Moderator, Dumbarton Presbytery, 1970-71; Member, Education Committee, General Assembly, eight years; served 15 years on Dunbartonshire Education Committee (Chairman, General Sub-Committee, 1967-70); Joint Chairman, Religious Education/EIS Group, 1963-74; Governor, Hamilton College of Education, 1967-72; Member, British Atlantic Committee and Representative Speaker, International Conferences, Wolfheze, 1983, and Amsterdam, 1986; Leader, fact-finding mission to South AFrica, 1986. Publication: The Moral Challenge of Defence Controversy in Our Nuclear Era. Recreations: watercolour and oil paintings; Probus; President, Riverside Church Men's Bowling Club; President and Secretary, Trinity College 1950 Club; reading; gardening. Address: 1 Glebe Park, Mansewood, Dumbarton, G82 3HE; T.-Dumbarton 742030.

Lawson, Fettes Grafton. Retired Solicitor (Lawson, Coull & Duncan, Dundee); Honorary Sheriff, Tayside, Central and Fife at Dundee; b. 27.6.18, Dundee; m., Lily Norrie Latto; 1 s.; 2 d. Educ. Alloa Academy. Apprenticeship, 1937 (War Service, 1939-45); qualified, 1946; retired, 1987. Dean, Faculty of Procurators and Solicitors in Dundee, 1973-75. Recreations: reading; walking. Address: (h.) 2 Taypark, 30 Dundee Road, West Ferry, Dundee, DD5 1LX.

Lawson, John Philip, BSc, FEIS. Chairman, Scottish Youth Hostels Association, since 1980; Headteacher, St. Joseph's School, Linlithgow, 1974-94; b. 19.8.37, Bathgate; m., Diana Mary Neal. Educ. St. Mary's Academy, Bathgate; Edinburgh University; Moray House College of Education. Teacher, West Lothian, 1962-94; Member, West Lothian Children's Panel, 1972-81; Member, SYHA National Executive, since 1966; Vice-Chairman, SYHA, 1975-80; Member, International Youth Hostel Federation delegation to China, 1984; awarded Richard Schirrmann Medal by German Youth Hostels Association, 1988; a Director, Scottish Rights of Way Society Ltd., since 1979; a Director, Gatliff Hebridean Hostels Trust, since 1988; President, West Lothian Headteachers Association, 1986-88; President, Federation of Youth Hostels Associations in the European Community, since 1990; First Vice-President, International Youth Hostel Federation, since 1994.

Recreations: hill-walking;music; reading. Address: (h.) 25 Bolam Drive, Burntisland, Fife, KY3 9HP; T.-0592 872132.

Lawson, Rev. Kenneth Charles, MA. Tutor-Organiser, Department of Parish Education, Church of Scotland, since 1984; Director, Human Relations and Ecumenical Spirituality Programmes, Scottish Churches Open College, since 1991; b. 24.12.34, Agadir, Morocco; m., Mary Elizabeth Anderson; 3 s. Educ. Royal High School, Edinburgh; Preston Lodge School; Stranraer High School; Edinburgh University. Assistant Minister, Brechin Cathedral; Sub-Warden, St. Ninian's Training Centre, Crieff; Minister: Paisley South, Cumbernauld St. Mungo. Recreations: walking; reading; painting. Address: (b.) St. Colm's Education Centre and College, 20 Inverleith Terrace, Edinburgh, EH3 5NS; T.-0131-332 0343.

Lawson, Lilian Keddie, BSc (Hons), MBA. Service Director, Scotland, Royal National Institute for Deaf People, since 1993; b. 23.2.49, Pittenweem; m., John McDonald Young, OBE; 2 d. Educ. Donaldson's School, Edinburgh; Mary Hare Grammar School, Newbury; Edinburgh University; Strathclyde University. Administrative Assistant, progressing to Head of Administration, British Deaf Association, 1981-92; Manager, Sign Language Interpreting Services, Strathclyde Regional Council, 1992-93. Publication: Words in Hand (Co-author), 1984. Recreations: gardening; her children. Address: (b.) 9 Clairmont Gardens, Glasgow, G3 7LW; T.-0141-332 0343.

Laybourn, Professor Peter John Robert, MA (Cantab), PhD, FIEE, FRSE. Titular Professor in Electronics and Electrical Engineering, Glasgow University, since 1985, and Head, Department of Electronics and Electrical Engineering; b. 30.7.42, London; m., Ann Elizabeth Chandler; 2 d. Educ. William Hulme's Grammar School; Bristol Grammar School; Clare College, Cambridge. Research Assistant, Leeds University, 1963-66; Research Fellow, Southampton University, 1966-71; Lecturer, then Senior Lecturer, then Reader, Glasgow University, 1971-85; Honorary Editor, IEE Proceedings: Optoelectronics. Recreations: sailing; boat-building; plant collecting. Address: (h.) Ashgrove, Waterfoot Row, Thorntonhall, Glasgow; T.-0141-644 3992.

Lazarowicz, Mark, MA, LLB, DipLP. Member, Edinburgh District Council, since 1980 (Leader of the Council, 1986-93, Chairperson, Labour Group, 1993-94); b. 8.8.53. Educ. St. Andrews University; Edinburgh University. Vice-Chairperson, Labour Party in Scotland, 1988-89, Chairperson, 1989-90; Chairperson, Edinburgh International Conference Centre Ltd., 1992-93; Chairperson, Edinburgh Tourist Board, 1993-94. Address: (h.) 17 Bellevue Place, Edinburgh; T.-0131-556 4438.

Leach, Professor Donald, BSc, CMath, FIMA, CPhys, MInstP, CEng, MBCS, FRSA. Principal, Queen Margaret College, Edinburgh, since 1985; b. 24.6.31, Croydon; m., June Valentine Reid; 2 s.; 1 d. Educ. John Ruskin Grammar School, Croydon; London University (External). Pilot Officer, Navigator, RAF, 1951-53; Physicist, British Jute Trade Research Association, Dundee, 1955-65; Technical Director, A.R. Bolton & Co. Ltd., Edinburgh, 1965-66; Napier College: Lecturer and Senior Lecturer in Mathematics, 1966-68, Head, Department of Mathematics and Computing, 1968-74, Assistant Principal/Dean, Faculty of Science, 1974-85. Member, South-Eastern Regional Hospital Board, 1969-74, and Lothian Health Board, 1977-81; Member: Scottish Health Service Common Services Agency's Advisory Panel on Information Processing, 1979-86, Scottish Health Service Planning Council's Information and Computer Systems Advisory Group, 1981-86, Information Steering Committee (Chairman), 1981-86; Institute of Mathematics: Council Member, 1978-81, Chairman, Scottish Branch, 1980-83, Member, Joint IMA-

Royal Society of London Mathematical Education Committee, 1981-84; Council for National Academic Awards: Member, Combined Studies Science Board, 1975-79, Science Technology and Society Board, 1979-82 (Chairman, 1981-82), Interfaculty Studies Board, 1981-85, Committee for Science and Technology, 1981-84, Committee for Scotland, 1987-92; Chairman, Science Technology and Society Association, 1982-85; Chairman, Mathematics and Computing Course Committees, SCOTEC/SCOTBEC, 1981-85; Hon. Secretary, Committee of Principals and Directors of Scottish Central Institutions (COPADOCI), 1985-88, Chairman, 1988-92; Member, Council for Professions Supplmentary to Medicine, since 1985; Member, Executive, Scottish Council (Development and Industry), since 1987; Member, Board of Directors, Edinburgh Chamber of Commerce, since 1991; Member, Council, World Association for Cooperative Education, since 1991; Member, Board of Directors, Higher Education Quality Council, since 1992; Member, Board of Directors, Capital Enterprise Trust, since 1993; President, Leith Chamber of Commerce, since 1994; Honorary Fellow, Society of Chiropodists and Podiatrists, 1991; Liberal candidate, West Edinburgh, 1959, East Fife, 1961; Labour candidate, West Perthshire, 1970. Recreations: badminton; walking; skiing; cooking. Address: (b.) Queen Margaret College, Edinburgh, EH12 8TS; T.-0131-317 3200.

Leake, Professor Bernard Elgey, BSc (Hons), PhD, DSc. Professor of Geology and Keeper of the Geological Collections in the Hunterian Museum, Glasgow University, since 1974; b. 29.7.32, Grimsby; m., Gillian Dorothy Dobinson; 5 s. Educ. Wirral Grammar School; Liverpool University. Leverhulme Postdoctorate Research Fellow, Liverpool University, 1955-57; Lecturer in Geology, then Reader, Bristol University, 1957-74. Lyell Medal, Geological Society, 1977; President, Geological Society, 1986-88, Treasurer, 1981-85 and since 1989. FRSE. Address: (b.) Department of Geology, Glasgow University, Glasgow; T.-0141-339 8855, Ext. 5435.

Lederer, Peter J. Managing Director, Gleneagles Hotels plc, since 1987; General Manager, The Gleneagles Hotel, since 1983; Director, Guinness Enterprises, since 1987; b. 30.11.50; m., Marilyn Ruth MacPhail. Four Seasons Hotels, Canada, 1972-79; Vice President, Wood Wilkings Ltd., Toronto, 1979-81; General Manager, Plaza Group of Hotels, Toronto, 1981-83. Governor, Ardvreck School, Crieff; Director, Scottish Enterprise Tayside Ltd.; Chairman, Tourism Training Scotland; Chairman, Hospitality Industry Trust Scotland; Chairman, Tourism Forum; Freeman, City of London; Member, Advisory Scottish Council for Education and Training Targets; FHCIMA; Master Innholder. Recreations: Matthew and Mark. Address: (b.) The Gleneagles Hotel, Auchterarder, Perthshire, PH3 1NF; T.-01764 62231.

Ledger, Philip Stevens, CBE, FRSE, HonLLD (Strathclyde), MA, MusB, FRCM, HonRAM, FRNCM, HonGSM, FRCO. Principal, Royal Scottish Academy of Music and Drama, since 1982; b. 12.12.37, Bexhill-on-Sea; 1 s.; 1 d. Educ. Bexhill Grammar School; King's College, Cambridge. Master of the Music, Chelmsford Cathedral, 1962-65; East Anglia University: Director of Music, 1965-73, Dean, School of Fine Arts and Music, 1968-71; Conductor, Cambridge University Musical Society, 1973-82; Director of Music and Organist, King's College, Cambridge, 1974-82; President, Royal College of Organists, 1992-94; President, Incorporated Society of Musicians, 1994-95; Editor, Anthems for Choirs 2 and 3; Composer/Editor, Six Carols with Descants. Publication: The Oxford Book of English Madrigals (Editor). Recreations: swimming; theatre. Address: (b.) Royal Scottish Academy of Music and Drama, 100 Renfrew Street, Glasgow, G2 3DB; T.-0141-332 4101.

Ledingham, Major James Norman, TD, DL, MA, LLB. Retired Farmer and Solicitor; Deputy Lieutenant, Sutherland, 1964-94; b. 12.11.11, Perth; m., Helen Matheson Murray; 1 d. Educ. Allan Glen's School, Glasgow; Strathallan School; Glasgow University. Trained and qualified as Solicitor, 1934-39; joined TA, 1938; 2nd Bn., Glasgow Highlanders HLI, 1939; Co. Commander, 1941-42; attached Commando Mountain Warfare School, Wales, 1943; posted as Signal Officer to Lovat Scouts, 1944; Italian Campaign, 1944-45; wounded; mentioned in Despatches; Chairman, Sutherland TA Association, since 1964; Sutherland NFU Representative, 1970-76; Vice President, Scottish Mountaineering Club, 1979-81; Sutherland Member, N. Committee, T.A. & A.F., 1970-82. Recreations: mountaineering; golf. Address: (h.) Kintradwell, Brora, Sutherland, KW9 6LU; T.-0140 8621251.

Lee, Professor Clive Howard, MA, MLitt (Cantab). Professor of Historical Economics, Aberdeen University, since 1991; Editor, Scottish Economic and Social History, 1989-93, Convener of Council, since 1994; b. 21.4.42, Leeds; m., Christine Ann. Educ. West Leeds High School; Fitzwilliam College, Cambridge. Assistant Lecturer to Professor, Aberdeen University, since 1966. Publications include: The British Economy since 1700: a macroeconomic perspective, 1986; British Regional Employment Statistics 1841-1971, 1979. Recreations: watching and playing football; gardening; going to pub. Address: (b.) Department of Economics, Aberdeen University, Regent Walk, Aberdeen; T.: 01224 272198.

Lee, Professor Michael Radcliffe, MA, DM, DPhil (Oxon), FRCP, FRCPE, FRSE. Professor of Clinical Pharmacology, Edinburgh University, since 1984; b. 21.11.34, Manchester; m., Judith Ann Horrocks; 1 s.; 1 d. Educ. Manchester Grammar School; Brasenose College, Oxford. Beit Memorial Fellow for Medical Research; Lecturer in Medicine, Oxford University; Lecturer in Medicine, St. Thomas's Hospital Medical School; Medical Director, then Managing Director, Weddel Pharmaceuticals Ltd.; Senior Lecturer in Clinical Pharmacology, Leeds University. Publications: books on medicine and hypertension. Recreations: gardening; walking; old trains; old books. Address: (h.) 112 Polwarth Terrace, Edinburgh, EH11 1NN; T.-0131-337 7386.

Lees, James George Grahame, MA, LLB, NP. Partner, McLean & Stewart, Solicitors, Dunblane, since 1974; Vice Chairman, Judicial Commission, Church of Scotland; b. 22.6.46, Perth; m., Hazel Margaret Raffan; 1 s.; 2 d. Educ. Dundee High School; St. Andrews University; Edinburgh University. Solicitor, J. & F. Anderson, WS, Edinburgh, 1969-72; Solicitor, McLean & Stewart, Solicitors, Dunblane, since 1972. Elder, Dunblane Cathedral Church of Scotland. Recreations: walking; photography; fishing. Address: (h.) Northbank, St. Margaret's Drive, Dunblane, FK15 ODP; T.-Dunblane 822928.

Lees, Robert Ferguson, LLB. Regional Procurator Fiscal, Lothian and Borders, since 1991; b. 15.9.38, Bellshill; m., Elizabeth. Educ. Bellshill Academy; Strathclyde University. Entered Procurator Fiscal Service, 1972; Legal Assistant, Paisley, 1972-75; Legal Assistant/Senior Legal Assistant/Senior Depute Procurator Fiscal, Glasgow, 1975-81; Assistant Procurator Fiscal, Dundee, 1982-88; Regional Procurator Fiscal, North Strathclyde, 1989-91. Recreations: music; travel; foreign languages. Address: (b.) Procurator Fiscal's Office, Sheriff Court House, 29 Chambers Street, Edinburgh, EH1 1LD.

Lefevre, Frank Hartley, MA, LLB, NP. Solicitor and Advocate in Aberdeen, since 1959; Senior Partner, Frank Lefevre Practice, since 1988; Chairman, Quantum Claims Compensation Specialists Ltd., since 1988; b. 4.12.34, Aberdeen; m., Hazel Gray; 1 s.; 2 d. Educ. Robert Gordon's College, Aberdeen; Aberdeen University. Commenced legal practice, 1959; set up, 1988, Britain's first no-win no-fee professional compensation company. Treasurer, Aberdeen Society of Advocates, 1994, President 1995; Past President, Grampian Squash Racquets Association (now Honorary President); Member, Council, Royal Aberdeen Golf Club, 1993-95. Recreations: squash; golf; music. Address: (h.) Braco Lodge, 11 Rubislaw Den North, Aberdeen; T.-01224 317170.

Leggat, James, BA, DipEd. Rector, Annan Academy, since 1994; b. 8.5.53, Glasgow; m., Susan Renshaw. Educ. Glasgow Academy; Stirling University. Teacher of English, Renfrewshire and Glasgow; Principal Teacher of English, Eastbank Academy, Glasgow; Assistant Rector, Carluke High School; Depute Rector, Hunter High School, East Kilbride. Address: (b.) Annan Academy, St. John's Road, Annan, DG12 6AP.

Leggate, Peter James Arthur, JP, FRICS. Chartered Surveyor, since 1967; Chairman, Lowland Insurance Brokers Ltd.; Director: Isla Mines Ltd., James Gammell & Son Ltd., Ptarmigan International Capital Trust Plc, Cheviot Investments Ltd.; b. 17.10.43; m., Jennifer Susan Gammell; 1 s.; 1 d. Educ. Wrekin College. Qualified as Chartered Surveyor, 1967; Kenneth Ryden & Partners, 1967-70; P.G. Matineau, Jedburgh, 1970-72; Founder, P.J. Leggate & Co., Edinburgh, 1973-79 (Sole Principal, since 1979). Recreations: horses; sailing; skiing. Address: (h.) Greenlandean House, Greenlaw, Berwickshire, TD10 6XP.

Leiper, Joseph, MA, DipEd, ACII. Rector, Oldmachar Academy, since 1983; b. 13.8.41, Aberdeen; m., Moira Taylor; 2 d. Educ. Aberdeen Grammar School; Aberdeen University. Inspector, Commercial Union Assurance, until 1967; Aberdeen University, 1967-72; Aberdeen College of Education, 1971-72; Teacher of English, since 1972. Recreation: sailing. Address: (b.) Oldmachar Academy, Jesmond Drive, Bridge of Don, Aberdeen, AB2 8ZJ; T.-01224 820887.

Leishman, Brian Archibald Scott. Business Manager, Edinburgh Military Tattoo, since 1978; b. 16.9.36; 1 s.; 1 d. Educ. Fettes College, Edinburgh. Retired Regular Army Officer; commissioned The Cameronians (Scottish Rifles); re-badged King's Own Scottish Borderers; service in the Arabian Gulf, East Africa and Europe; Italian Staff College, 1971-73; Assistant Defence Attache, British Embassy, Rome, 1974-76; Ticketing Consultant, XIII Commonwealth Games in Edinburgh, 1986; Board Member, Edinburgh Military Tattoo Ltd. and Edinburgh Military Tattoo (Charities) Ltd.; Chairman, Edinburgh International Jazz and Blues Festival; Board Member, Edinburgh Tourist Board; Founder Member and Board Member, Edinburgh Capital Group (Edinburgh Entertains); Board Member, Box Office Management International, New York. Recreations: sailing; music; photography. Address: (b.) Tattoo Office, 22 Market Street, Edinburgh, EH1 1QB; T.-0131-225 4783.

Leishman, Marista Muriel, MA, FRSA. Director, The Insite Consultancy for Management and Training; b. 10.4.32, Beaconsfield; m., Murray Leishman; 1 s.; 3 d. Educ. St. George's School, Ascot; St. Andrews University. First Head of Education, National Trust for Scotland, 1979-86; two National Training Awards for Insite. Recreations: music; painting; writing; hill-walking; gardening. Address: 9/1 St. Leonard's Crag, Edinburgh, EH8 9SP; T.-0131-667 1246.

Leishman, Mark Murray. Head of Corporate Affairs, BBC Scotland, since 1995; b. 4.3.62, Perth. Educ. Firrhill High School, Edinburgh; Napier College, Edinburgh. Press and PR, National Trust for Scotland, 1979-81; Reporter, United News Service, 1982-84; Reporter, Fife Free Press, Kirkcaldy, 1986-87; Chief Reporter, Radio Forth/Tay, 1987-88; Reporter, Radio Clyde, 1988-90; Reporter,

Political Correspondent, Sunday Times, 1990-93; Presenter, Good Morning Scotland, BBC Scotland, 1993-95. Recreations: fishing; running; golf; gym work; reading; cinema; music. Address: (h.) 106 Novar Drive, Glasgow, G12 9SU; T.-0141-338 2000.

Leitch, Donald H., DMS, MHCIMA, MCFA. Depute Principal, Glasgow College of Food Technology, since 1991; b. 2.4.48, Glasgow; m., Mary B.; 2 s. Educ. Hyndland Senior Secondary School; Langside College, Glasgow; Glasgow College of Technology. Catering management, Health Service, 1967-70; Depute Catering Officer, Glasgow University, 1970-74; Lecturer/Senior Lecturer, Glasgow College of Food Technology, 1974-85; Head of Department, Cambuslang College, Glasgow, 1985-91. Immediate Past Chairman, Scottish Division, Cookery and Food Association. Recreations: hill-walking; gardening. Address: (b.) 230 Cathedral Street, Glasgow, G1 2TG; T.-0141-552 3751.

Lello, Glenn Edward, BDS, FDSRCS, LRCP, MRCS, MB, BCh, FRCS, PhD, MKGChir. Consultant Maxillofacial Surgeon; Senior Lecturer; b. 31.1.47, Pretoria; m., Judith Farquharson; 1 s.; 2 d. Consultant, Rochester University, 1977-79, Zurich University, 1979-82; Senior Specialist, Witwatersrand University, 1982-85; Professor/Head of Department, Medical University, South Africa, 1985-88; Consultant, Manchester University, 1988-90; Consultant, Maxillofacial Surgery, Edinburgh, since 1990. Publications: 38 scientific articles; seven chapters. Recreations: squash; skiing; watersports. Address: (b.) Department of Maxillofacial Surgery, City Hospital, Greenbank Drive, Edinburgh, EH10 5SB.

Leng, James William. Group Chief Executive, Low & Bonar PLC, since 1992; b. 19.11.45; m., Carole Ann. Joined Low & Bonar Group, 1984, as Managing Director of Flotex; moved to Scotland, 1986, and established group's Plastics Division; took over responsibility for all European operations, 1988; Main Board Director, since 1989. Recreations: golf; squash; music. Address: (b.) Bonar House, Faraday Street, Dundee, DD1 9JA; T.-01382 818171.

Lenman, Professor Bruce Philip, MA (Aberdeen), MLitt, LittD (Cantab), FRHistSoc. Professor of Modern History, St. Andrews University, since 1992 (formerly Reader in Modern History); b. 9.4.38, Aberdeen. Educ. Aberdeen Grammar School; Aberdeen University; St. John's College, Cambridge. Assistant Professor, Victoria University, Canada, 1963; Lecturer in Imperial and Commonwealth History, Queen's College, Dundee (St. Andrews University), 1963-67; Lecturer, Dundee University, 1967-72; United College, St. Andrews: Lecturer, Department of Modern History, 1972-78, Senior Lecturer, 1978-83; British Academy Fellow, Newberry Library, Chicago, 1982; John Carter Brown Library Fellow, Brown University, Providence, RI, 1984; Harrison Professor, College of William & Mary, VA, 1988-89. Publications: Esk to Tweed, 1975; An Economic History of Modern Scotland 1660-1976, 1977 (Scottish Arts Council Award); The Jacobite Risings in Britain 1689-1746, 1980 (Scottish Arts Council Award); Scotland 1746-1832, 1981; The Jacobite Clans of the Great Glen 1650-1784, 1984; The Jacobite Cause, 1986; The Jacobite Threat (Co-author), 1990; The Eclipse of Parliament, 1992. Recreations: golf; squash; badminton; Scottish country dancing; hill-walking. Address: (b.) Department of Modern History, St. Andrews University, St. Andrews, KY16 9AL; T.-01334 476161.

Leonard, Wilfred. Member, Island Policy Committee, Scottish Accident Prevention Council; b. 9.5.12, Humberton, Brafferton, Yorkshire; m., Margaret Ross (deceased); 1 s.; 2 d. Educ. Brafferton Church of England School. Staffordshire County Police, 1935-67 (retired in rank of Inspector); Member, Inverness County Council,

1973-74; Past Chairman: Harris District Council, South Harris Agricultural Society, Harris Council of Social Service; former Member: Highlands and Islands Consultative Council; Highlands and Islands Manpower Board, MSC; Member, Western Isles Islands Council, 1974-86 (Chairman, Planning and Development, 1980-86). Recreation: gardening. Address: (h.) Cnoc-Na-Ba, Finsbay, Isle of Harris; T.-Manish 232.

Leslie, Allan Eunson, FRSH, MREHIS, MIWEM. Director of Environmental Health, Orkney Islands Council, since 1975; b. 15.11.41, Garmouth, Morayshire; m., Vivia Mary Stewart. Educ. Mackie Academy, Stonehaven; Harris Academy, Dundee; Strathclyde University. Assistant Sanitary Inspector, Kincardine County Council, 1964-70; Area Sanitary Inspector, Sutherland County Council, 1970-72. Recreations: gardening; walking; sea fishing; bowls; bridge; reading. Address: (b.) Orkney Islands Council, Environmental Health Department, Council Offices, School Place, Kirkwall, Orkney Isles; T.-01856 873535.

Leslie, Professor Frank Matthews, JP, BSc, PhD, DSc, FIMA, FInstP, FRSE, FRS. Professor of Mathematics, Strathclyde University, since 1982; Chairman, British Liquid Crystal Society, 1987-91; b. 8.3.35, Dundee; m., Ellen Leitch Reoch; 1 s.; 1 d. Educ. Harris Academy; Queen's College, Dundee; Manchester University. Assistant Lecturer, Manchester University, 1959-61; Research Associate, MIT, USA, 1961-62; Lecturer, Newcastle University, 1962-68; Visiting Assistant Professor, Johns Hopkins University, USA, 1966-67; Strathclyde University: Senior Lecturer, 1968-71, Reader, 1971-79, Personal Professor, 1979-82; Consultant, DRA Malvern; Annual Award, British Society of Rheology, 1982. Recreations: golf; hill-walking. Address: (b.) Department of Mathematics, Strathclyde University, Livingstone Tower, 26 Richmond Street, Glasgow, G1 1XH; T.-0141-552 4400.

Leslie, John, MRPharmS. Chairman, Orkney Health Board, since 1991; b. 1.1.35, Kirkwall; m., Evelyn MacGillivray; 1 s. Educ. Kirkwall Grammar School; Robert Gordon's Institute of Technology, Aberdeen. Member, NHS Executive Council for Orkney, 1968-74; Chairman, Kirkwall Chamber of Commerce, 1973-74; Member, Orkney Health Board, 1979-85 and since 1987. Past President, Kirkwall Rotary Club. Recreations: participating in amateur music and drama groups; simple electronics/computing. Address: (h.) Failte, Bignold Park Road, Kirkwall, Orkney; T.-01856 874002.

Lessels, Norman, CBE, CA. Senior Partner, Chiene & Tait, CA; Chairman, Standard Life Assurance Company; Chairman, Cairn Energy PLC; Chairman, Havelock Europa PLC; Director, Bank of Scotland; Director, Scottish Eastern Investment Trust PLC; Director, Robert Wiseman Diaries PLC; b. 2.9.38, Edinburgh; m., Christine Stevenson; 1 s. Educ. Edinburgh Academy. Partner, Ernst & Whinney, until 1980; President, Institute of Chartered Accountants of Scotland, 1987-88. Recreations: golf; music; bridge. Address: (b.) 3 Albyn Place, Edinburgh; T.-0131-225 7515.

Lessnoff, Michael Harry, MA, BPhil. Reader in Politics, Glasgow University, since 1986; b. 23.1.40, Glasgow. Educ. High School of Glasgow; Glasgow University; Balliol College, Oxford. Assistant Principal, Department of Education and Science, 1965-66; Lecturer, then Senior Lecturer, Department of Politics, Glasgow University, 1966-86; Visiting Associate Professor, College of William and Mary, Williamsburg, USA, 1977-78. Won Snell Exhibition, 1963. Publications: The Structure of Social Science, 1974; Social Contract, 1986; Social Contract Theory, 1990; The Spirit of Capitalism and the Protestant Ethic, 1994. Recreations: literature; art; science; travel. Address: (h.) 58 White Street, Glasgow, G11 5EB; T.-0141-334 1799.

Levein, Charles Peter Alexander, MA, PhD. Chief Research Officer, Scottish Office, since 1988; b. 16.5.40, Devonport; 1 s.; 2 d. Educ. Dunfermline High School; Edinburgh University. Demonstrator, Geography Department, Edinburgh University; Research Officer, Central Planning Research Unit, Scottish Development Department; Senior Research Officer, WC Scotland Planning Team; Principal Research Officer, Scottish Office Urban Deprivation Unit; Senior Principal Research Officer, Scottish Office. Recreations: golf; bowls; tennis. Address: (h.) 45 The Wynd, Dalgety Bay, Fife; T.-01383 822952.

Leven and Melville, Earl of (Alexander Robert Melville). Lord Lieutenant, Nairn; Company Director; President, British Ski Federation, 1981-85; Honorary President, Scottish National Ski Council; Chairman, Governors, Gordonstoun School, 1971-89; b. 13.5.24, London; m., Susan Steuart-Menzies; 2 s.; 1 d. Educ. Eton. Coldstream Guards, 1942-52 (retired as Captain); ADC to Governor General of New Zealand, 1951-52; Convener, Nairn County Council, 1970-74. Address: (h.) Glenferness House, Nairn, IV12 5UP; T.-01309 651202.

Lever, Professor William Fred, MA, DPhil. Professor in Urban Studies, Associate Dean, Faculty of Social Sciences, Glasgow University, since 1982; b. 17.4.43, Accrington; m., Marian Frances Hardman; 1 s.; 2 d. Educ. Accrington Grammar School; St. Peter's College, Oxford. Tutor in Geography, Oxford University, 1965-67; Lecturer, Reader, in Urban Studies, Glasgow University, 1967-82. Publications: Industrial Relocation and Employment Change; The City in Transition; Industrial Change in the UK; Social and Economic Change in Metropolitan Areas. Recreations: travel; theatre; skiing. Address: (h.) 34 Kirkhouse Road, Blanefield, Glasgow; T.-01360 770536.

Levinthal, Terrence Scott, BES, DipUD. Secretary, The Cockburn Association (Edinburgh Civic Trust), since 1992; b. 9.12.61, Winnipeg. Educ. University of Waterloo; Heriot-Watt/Edinburgh College of Art. Investigator, Royal Fine Art Commission for Scotland, 1988-92. Chairman, Lothian Environmental Action Forum. Recreations: hill-walking, skiing, cycling and other outdoor pursuits; the arts; woodworking. Address: (b.) Trunk's Close, 55 High Street, Edinburgh, EH1 1SR; T.-0131-557 8686.

Levison, Professor David Annan, MD, FRCPath. Professor of Pathology, Ninewells Hospital and Medical School, Dundee, since 1995; b. 4.1.44, Perth; m., Rosemary Ann; 4 s.; 2 d. Educ. George Watson's Boys College; Kirkcaldy High School; St. Andrews University. Lecturer in Pathology, Dundee University, 1969-77; Senior Lecturer (Hon. Consultant) in Histopathology, St. Bartholomew's Hospital, London, 1978-88; Professor of Clinical Histopathology, UMDS, Guy's Hospital, London, 1988-94. Treasurer, Pathological Society of Great Britain and Ireland; Pathology Editor, Surgery; author of 100 scientific papers. Recreations: sailing; hill-walking; family. Address: (h.) Huntly, 8 Glamis Drive, Dundee, DD2 1QL; T.-01382 668150.

Levison, Rev. Mary Irene, BA, BD, DD. Minister of the Church of Scotland (retired); (Extra) Chaplain to the Queen in Scotland, since 1991; b. 8.1.23, Oxford; m., Rev. Frederick Levison. Educ. St. Leonard's School, St. Andrews; Oxford University; Edinburgh University. Administrative Assistant, Scottish Home Department, 1943-46; Deaconess, Church of Scotland, Musselburgh, 1954-58; Tutor, St. Colm's College, 1958-61; Assistant Chaplain, Edinburgh University, 1961-64; Assistant Minister, St. Andrew's and St. George's Church and Chaplain to the retail trade, Edinburgh, 1978-83; Moderator, Edinburgh Presbytery, 1988. Publication: Wrestling with the Church, 1992. Recreations: gardening; music; travel. Address: (h.) 2 Gillsland Road, Edinburgh, EH10 5BW; T.-0131-228 3118.

Levy, Professor Roger P., BA (Hons), MPhil, PhD. Head, School of Public Administration and Law, Robert Gordon University, since 1991; b. 14.12.50, London. Educ. Southgate Technical College; Leicester University; Glasgow University; McGill University. Tutor in Government, Glasgow University, 1974-75; Lecturer in Public Administration, Bell College, 1975-79; worked in Canada, 1979-83; Education Development Officer, Scottish Civil Liberty Trust, Glasgow, 1983; Lecturer/Senior Lecturer in Public Administration, Glasgow Polytechnic, 1983-91. Publications (books): A Guide to Civil Liberties in Scotland (Co-author), 1980; Young People and the Law (Co-author), 1985; Scottish Nationalism at the Crossroads, 1990; numerous book chapters and articles. Address: (b.) Robert Gordon University, School of Public Administration and Law, 352 King Street, Aberdeen, AB9 2TQ; T.-01224 262900.

Liddell, Colin. Corporate Communications Director, Scottish Power plc, since 1993; b. 28.8.47, Falkirk; m., Sheena Wood Mackay. Educ. Denny High School. Journalist, Johnston Newspaper Group, 1964-69; Editor, Linlithgow Journal & Gazette, 1968-69; Journalist, Scotsman Publications, 1969-77; Senior Press Officer, Scottish Development Agency, 1977-82; PR Director, then Chief Executive, Charles Barker Scotland, 1982-86; Public Affairs Director, United Distillers, 1986-93. Non-Executive Director: Quality Scotland Foundation, Barclays Bank (Scottish Regional Board). Recreations: golf; gardening. Address: (h.) Friarbank, Manse Road, Linlithgow, West Lothian; T.-01506 843734.

Liddell, David, BSc (Hons), DipSW. Director, Scottish Drugs Forum since 1986; b. 1957, Kingston. Educ. Riddlesdown School; Sheffield University; Edinburgh University. Project Worker, Bristol Cyrenians and Dublin Simon Community; Researcher, Queen Charlotte's Hospital, London; Biochemist, Children's Hospital, Dublin; Youth Worker, Dublin Committee for Travelling People; Field Worker, Standing Conference on Drug Abuse. Publications: Drug Problems in Edinburgh District, 1987 (Co-author); Drugfax (Co-author), 1991. Recreations: travel; cycling; working on allotment. Address: (b.) 5 Oswald Street, Glasgow, G1 4QR; T.-0141-221 1175.

Liddell, Helen Lawrie, BA. MP (Labour), Monklands East, since 1994; Chief Executive, Business Venture Programme, 1993-94; Director of Corporate and Public Affairs, Scottish Daily Record and Sunday Mail Ltd., 1991-92 (Director of Personnel and Public Affairs, 1988-91); b. 6.12.50, Coatbridge; m., Dr. Alistair H. Liddell; 1 s.; 1 d. Educ. St. Patrick's High School, Coatbridge; Strathclyde University. Head, Economic Department, STUC, 1971-76; Scottish Secretary, Labour Party, 1977-88; Labour candidate, East Fife, 1974; Economics Correspondent, BBC, 1976-77. Publication: Elite, 1990. Address: (h.) Glenisla, Main Road, Langbank, Renfrewshire; T.-Langbank 344.

Liddell, John Chalmers, MA, LLB. Depute Chief Executive, Grampian Regional Council, since 1979; b. 25.3.46, Dumfries; m., Laura; 2 s.; 1 d. Educ. High School of Glasgow; St. Andrews University. Depute County Clerk, Berwickshire; Assistant Director of Administration, Borders Region; Depute Director of Law and Administration, Grampian Region. Vice-President, Scottish National Ski Council. Recreations: skiing; golf. Address: (b.) Woodhill House, Westburn Road, Aberdeen, AB9 2LU; T.-01224 682222, Ext. 4403.

Liddle, Robert Christie, CA, ATII. Partner, Robb Ferguson CA, since 1966; Secretary, Royal Glasgow Institute of the Fine Arts, since 1986; Secretary, Scottish Artists Benevolent Association, since 1993; b. 2.8.33, Hamilton; m., Elizabeth Jean Smith; 2 s.; 1 d. Educ. Hamilton Academy. Partner, Russ Ferguson & Maclennan,

CA, 1958. Recreations: travel; bowling. Address: (b.) 5 Oswald Street, Glasgow, G1 4QR; T.-0141-248 7411.

Lidgate, Professor David, BEng, PhD, CEng, FIEE, FInstE. Professor and Head, Department of Electrical, Electronic and Computer Engineering, Napier University, since 1994; b. 11.7.46, Gosforth; m., Janet; 1 d. Educ. Royal Grammar School, Newcastle upon Tyne; Liverpool University. Research Engineer, A. Reyrolle & Co. Ltd., 1965-75; Lecturer, UMIST, 1975-88; Head, School of Engineering, Greenwich University, 1988-94. Member, Electricity Consumers Committee for Southern Scotland. Recreations: genealogy; model railways. Address: (b.) 219 Colinton Road, Edinburgh, EH14 1DJ; T.-0131-455 4361.

Light, John V. Rector, The Edinburgh Academy. Address: (b.) 42 Henderson Row, Edinburgh, EH3 5BL.

Lilley, Professor David Malcolm James, FRSE. Professor of Molecular Biology, Dundee University, since 1989; b. 28.5.48, Colchester; m., Patricia Mary; 2 d. Educ. Gilberd School, Colchester; Durham University. Joined Biochemistry Department, Dundee University, 1981; awarded Colworth Medal by Biochemical Society, 1982. Publications: over 150 scientific papers. Recreation: foreign languages. Address: (b.) Department of Biochemistry, Dundee University, Dundee, DD1 4HN; T.-01382 344243.

Lilwall, Nicholas Brier, BSc, MA, PhD. Head, Rural Resource Management Department, The Scottish Agricultural College, Aberdeen, since 1985; b. 15.8.37, Liverpool; m., Anne; 2 s.; 1 d. Educ. Truro School, Cornwall; Leeds University; Minnesota University. Assistant Lecturer, Leeds University, 1964-66; Research Assistant, Minnesota University, 1967-71; Economist, Edinburgh School of Agriculture, since 1971. Recreation: tennis. Address: (b.) The Scottish Agricultural College, West Mains Road, Edinburgh, EH9 3JG; T.-0131-667 1041.

Lincoln, Professor Dennis W., DSc, FRSE. Director, Medical Research Council Reproductive Biology Unit, Edinburgh, since 1982; b. 21.7.39, Gt. Ellingham; m., Rosemary A. Barrell; 1 s.; 1 d. Educ. Nottingham University; Cambridge University. Research Fellow, Corpus Christi College, Cambridge, 1966-67; Lecturer, Reader, Professor, Faculty of Medicine, Bristol University. Honorary Professor, Faculty of Medicine, Edinburgh University, since 1985. Recreation: ornithology. Address: (b.) Centre for Reproductive Biology, 37 Chalmers Street, Edinburgh, EH3 9EW; T.-0131-229 2575.

Lindsay of Dalry and Balmaclellan, Alistair, MA, LLB, NP, FSA Scot. Editor, Clan Lindsay Society Publications, since 1947; Consultant, Stewarts, Nicol, D. & J. Hill (Partner, 1948-82); b. 5.2.23, Glasgow; m., Agnes Calder Hamilton Neilson; 1 s.; 1 d. Educ. Pollokshields Secondary School; Larkhall Academy; Glasgow University. Governor, Baillies Institution Free Public Library, six years; Secretary, Old Glasgow Club, 12 years; Secretary, (Glasgow) Ballad Club, 24 years; Life Member, Glasgow Art Gallery and Museums Association; Director: Barloch Proprietors Ltd., Popular Properties Ltd., PIN Computers Ltd. Publications: The Laird of Barloch 1632-1984, 1985; The Clachan Fair 1872, 1995; Dictionary of National Biography (Contributor). Recreations: genealogy; local history. Address: (h.) Brucewell, Midtown, St. Johns Town of Dalry, Castle Douglas; T.-0164 43 306.

Lindsay, David Cameron, OBE, BSc, DUniv, FEng, FICE. Assessor, General Council, and Member of Court, Glasgow University, since 1984; b. 12.12.20, Glasgow; m., Catherine; 2 s.; 1 d. Educ. Allan Glen's School; Glasgow University. Captain, Royal Engineers, India and Burma, 1944-47; Whatlings Ltd., 1947-85, latterly as Chairman; Chairman, Institution of Civil Engineers (Glasgow and West of Scotland), 1968; Elder, Church of Scotland;

Chairman, Federation of Civil Engineering Contractors (Scottish Secton), 1973-76. Recreations: bowling; golf; oil painting. Address: (h.) 49 Stewarton Drive, Cambuslang, Glasgow, G72 8DQ; T.-0141-641 1323.

Lindsay, Frederic, MA (Hons). Writer; Chair, Society of Authors in Scotland; b. 12.8.33, Glasgow; m., Shirley; 1 s.; 3 d. Educ. North Kelvinside Senior Secondary School; Glasgow University; Jordanhill College; Edinburgh University. Worked as library assistant, teacher, lecturer; since becoming full-time writer in 1979, has published four novels: Brond, 1984, Jill Rips, 1987, A Charm Against Drowning, 1988, After the Stranger Came, 1992; has written plays for Scottish Youth Theatre; radio plays for children; adapted Brond as serial for Channel 4. Member, Scottish Arts Council Literature Committee. Recreations: cinema; theatre; television; reading; walking in the Pentlands. Address: (h.) 2a Hopelands Road, Silverburn, Penicuik, EH26 9LH; T.-01968 678498.

Lindsay, James, CBE, BL, CA. Honorary President, Scottish Golf Union, since 1960; Honorary Sheriff, Falkirk; b. 31.10.12, Larbert; m., Margaret Craig Wyllie; 4 s.; 1 d. Educ. Falkirk High School; Glasgow University. Macfarlane Lang & Co. Ltd.: Accountant and Secretary, 1937-57, Director, 1955-73; Director, United Biscuits Ltd., 1957-73; Chairman, The Cake and Biscuit Alliance, 1970-73; President, Scottish Golf Union, 1958-60. Recreations: golf; gardening. Address: (h.) 8 Neilson Street, Falkirk, FK1 5AQ; T.-Falkirk 622248.

Lindsay, James Kerr, MA. Manager, Scottish Fisheries Museum Trust Ltd., since 1989; Director, Campbeltown Shipyard Ltd., since 1990; Director, Landcatch Ltd., since 1991; b. 13.7.34, Dundee; m., Dorothy Pattullo; 1 s.; 1 d. Educ. Morgan Academy, Dundee; St. Andrews University. Production Controller/Finishing Manager, Alex. Pirie & Sons, 1958-66; Head of Fisheries Division, Highlands and Islands Development Board, 1966-89. Governor, Unicorn Preservation Society, Dundee; Council Member, Scottish Museums Council, Edinburgh. Recreations: ornithology; chess. Address: (h.) 5 St. Ayles Crescent, Anstruther, Fife; T.-01333 310028.

Lindsay, 16th Earl of (James Randolph Lindesay-Bethune). Parliamentary Under Secretary of State, Scottish Office, since 1995; b. 19.11.55; m., Diana Mary Chamberlayne-Macdonald. Educ. Eton; Edinburgh University; University of California, Davis. President, International Tree Foundation, since 1995; Trustee, Gardens for the Disabled Trust, since 1984; Member, Advisory Panel, Railway Heritage Trust, since 1990; Director, Tay Forth Marketing Group Ltd., since 1990; Member, Advisory Council, World Resource Foundation, since 1994; Lord in Waiting (Government Whip), 1995; Green Ribbon political award, 1995; practises as a landscape architect and environmental consultant. Address: (h.) Lahill, Upper Largo, Fife, KY8 6JE.

Lindsay, John. Chief Executive, East Lothian Council. Address: (b.) Council Buildings, Haddington, East Lothian, EH41 3HA.

Lindsay, Professor John Gordon, BSc, PhD. Professor of Biochemistry, Glasgow University, since 1992; b. 9.8.45, Birkenhead; m., Joan Cameron Barr; 2 s. Educ. Bellshill Academy; Glasgow University. Lecturer in Biochemistry, then Senior Lecturer, then Reader, Glasgow University, 1973-92. Fulbright Scholar, 1979-80; Editorial Adviser, Biochemical Journal; 110 publications in learned journals. Recreations: playing and coaching cricket; golf; classical music. Address: (b.) Division of Biochemistry and Molecular Biology, Institute of Biomedical and Life Sciences, Glasgow University, Glasgow, G12 8QQ; T.-0141-330 5902.

Lindsay, John Maurice, CBE, TD, DLitt, HonFRIAS. Consultant, Scottish Civic Trust (Director, 1967-83); Secretary-General, Europa Nostra, 1983- 91; b. 21.7.18; m., Aileen Joyce Gordon; 1 s.; 3 d. Educ. Glasgow Academy; Scottish National Academy of Music. Drama Critic, Scottish Daily Mail, 1946-47; Music Critic, The Bulletin, 1946-60; Border Television: Programme Controller, 1961-62, Production Controller, 1962-64, Features Executive and Chief Interviewer, 1964-67. Atlantic-Rockefeller Award, 1946; Editor: Scots Review, 1949-50, The Scottish Review, 1975-85; Member, Historic Buildings Council for Scotland, 1976-87; Council Member, Association of Scottish Literary Studies, since 1983, President, 1988-90; Trustee, New Lanark Conservation Trust, 1985-94; Trustee, National Heritage Memorial Fund, 1980-84; HonDLitt, Glasgow, 1982. Publications: poetry: The Advancing Day, 1940; Perhaps To-morrow, 1941; Predicament, 1942; No Crown for Laughter: Poems, 1943; The Enemies of Love: Poems 1941-45, 1946; Selected Poems, 1947; Hurlygush: Poems in Scots, 1948; At the Wood's Edge, 1950; Ode for St. Andrew's Night and Other Poems, 1951; The Exiled Heart: Poems 1941-56, 1957; Snow Warning and Other Poems, 1962; One Later Day and Other Poems, 1964; This Business of Living, 1969; Comings and Goings: Poems, 1971; Selected Poems 1942-72, 1973; The Run from Life, 1975; Walking Without an Overcoat, Poems 1972-76, 1977; Collected Poems, 1979; A Net to Catch the Winds and Other Poems, 1981; The French Mosquitoes' Woman and other diversions and poems; Requiem for a Sexual Athlete; Collected Poems 1940-90; On the Face Of It: Collected Poems, Vol. 2; News of the World: Last Poems; prose: Pocket Guide to Scottish Culture; The Scottish Renaissance; The Lowlands of Scotland: Glasgow and the North; Robert Burns: The Man, His Work, The Legend; Dunoon: The Gem of the Clyde Coast; The Lowlands of Scotland: Edinburgh and the South; Clyde Waters: Variations and Diversions on a Theme of Pleasure; The Burns Encyclopedia; Killochan Castle; By Yon Bonnie Banks: A Gallimaufry; Environment: A Basic Human Right; Portrait of Glasgow; Robin Philipson; History of Scottish Literature; Lowland Scottish Villages; Francis George Scott and the Scottish Renaissance; The Buildings of Edinburgh (Co-author); Thank You For Having Me: A Personal Memoir; Unknown Scotland (Co-author); Castles of Scotland: A Constable Guide; Count All Men Mortal: The Story of the Scottish Provident Institution; Victorian and Edwardian Glasgow; An Illustrated Guide to Glasgow; The Comic Poems of William Tennant (Co-editor); Edinburgh Past and Present (Co-author); The Youth and Manhood of Cyril Thornton (Editor); The Scottish Dog (Co-author); A Pleasure of Gardens (Co-author); The Scottish Quotation Book (Co-author); The Music Quotation Book (Co-author); The Theatre and Opera Lover's Quotation Book (Co-author); The Burns Quotation Book (Co-author); The Chambers Guide to Good Scottish Gardens (Co-author). Recreations: music; walking. Address: (h.) 7 Milton Hill, Milton, Dumbarton, G82 2TS; T.-Dumbarton 762655.

Lingard, Joan Amelia. Author; b. Edinburgh; 3 d. Educ. Bloomfield Collegiate School, Belfast; Moray House College of Education, Edinburgh. Member, Scottish Arts Council, 1980-85; Chair, Society of Authors in Scotland, 1980-84; Director, Edinburgh Book Festival, since 1994; first novel published, 1963; has also written plays for TV, including 18-part series, Maggie, adapted from quartet of teenage books; novels: Liam's Daughter, 1963; The Prevailing Wind, 1964; The Tide Comes In, 1966; The Headmaster, 1967; A Sort of Freedom, 1968; The Lord on our Side, 1970; The Second Flowering of Emily Mountjoy, 1979; Greenyards, 1981; Sisters By Rite, 1984; Reasonable Doubts, 1986; The Women's House, 1989; After Colette, 1993; Dreams of Love and Modest Glory, 1995; 30 children's books. Recreations: reading; walking; travelling. Address: (b.) David Higham Associates, 5-8 Lower John Street, Golden Square, London, W1R 4HA.

Lingard, Robin Anthony, MA, FTS. Project Director, University of the Highlands and Islands Project, since 1993; Director of Training and Social Development, Highlands and Islands Enterprise, 1991-93; Member, Scottish Tourist Board, 1988-92; b. 19.7.41, Enfield; m., Margaret; 2 d. Educ. Felsted School; Emmanuel College, Cambridge. Joined Ministry of Aviation, 1963; Private Secretary to Joint Parliamentary Secretary, Ministry of Technology, 1966-68; appointments, Department of Industry, DTI, etc., to 1984; Head, Enterprise Unit, Cabinet Office, 1984-85; Head, Small Firms and Tourism Division, Department of Employment, 1985-87; full-time Board Member, Highlands and Islands Development Board, 1988-91. Chairman, Prince's Trust Committee for Highlands, Western Isles and Orkney; Member, Management Board, Prince's Trust and Royal Jubilee Trusts. Recreations: watching birds; walking; reading; aviation history. Address: (h.) Kinnairdie House, Dingwall, IV15 9LL; T.-01349 61044.

Linklater, John Richard Gordon. Journalist, The Herald, Glasgow; b. 29.1.52, Dumfries; 1 s.; 1 d. Educ. Royal High School, Edinburgh; Stirling University; Glasgow University. Recreations: music; theatre; chess; Hibernian FC. Address: (b.) 195 Albion Street, Glasgow, G1 1QP.

Linklater, Karl Alexander, BVM&S, PhD, CBiol, FIBiol, ARAgS, FRCVS. Director, Scottish Agricultural Colleges Veterinary Investigation Service, since 1986; Member, Veterinary Products Committee, since 1990; Director, Animal Diseases Research Association, since 1991; b. 1.9.39, Stromness, Orkney; m., Margaret Carr Gibb; 1 s.; 1 d. Educ. Robert Gordon's College, Aberdeen; Edinburgh University. General veterinary practice, Tarland, Aberdeenshire, 1962-66; North of Scotland College of Agriculture, Aberdeen, 1966-67; Royal (Dick) School of Veterinary Studies, Edinburgh University, 1967-73; East of Scotland College of Agriculture, St. Boswells, 1973-86. President, Sheep Veterinary Society, 1983-85; Vice-President, British Veterinary Association, since 1994; President, Association of Veterinary Teachers and Research Workers (Scotland), 1988-90; President, Scottish Branch, British Veterinary Association, 1992-94; President, Scottish Metropolitan Division, BVA, 1979-80; Alan Baldry Award, 1982. Recreations: sport; gardening; sheep breeding. Address: (h.) Bridge Park, Old Bridge Road, Selkirk; T.-01750 20571.

Linklater, Magnus Duncan. Writer and Broadcaster; Editor, The Scotsman, 1988-94; Chairman, Edinburgh Book Festival; b. 21.2.42, Harray, Orkney; m., Veronica Lyle; 2 s.; 1 d. Educ. Eton College; Cambridge University. Reporter, Daily Express, Manchester, 1965-66; London Evening Standard: Diary Reporter, 1966-67, Editor, Londoner's Diary, 1967-69; Sunday Times: Editor, Spectrum, 1969-72, Editor, Colour Magazine, 1972-75, News Editor/Features Editor, 1975-83; Managing Editor, The Observer, 1983-86; Editor, London Daily News, 1986-87. Publications: Hoax: the Howard Hughes-Clifford Irving Affair (Co-author); Jeremy Thorpe: A Secret Life (Co-author); The Falklands War (with Sunday Times Insight team); Massacre — the story of Glencoe; The Fourth Reich — Klaus Barbie and the Neo-Fascist Connection (Co-author); Not With Honour — the inside story of the Westland Affair (Co-author); For King and Conscience — John Graham of Claverhouse, Viscount Dundee (Co-author); Anatomy of Scotland (Co-editor); Highland Wilderness. Honorary Doctor of Arts, Napier University. Recreations: book-collecting; fishing. Address: (h.) 5 Drummond Place, Edinburgh, EH3 6PH; T.-0131-557 5705.

Linklater, Marjorie; b. 19.3.09, Edinburgh; m., Eric Linklater (deceased); 2 s.; 2 d. Educ. St. George's School, Edinburgh; Downe House, Newbury, Berkshire; Royal Academy of Dramatic Art, London. Stage career ended, 1930, after appearing in three plays in West End; returned to Scotland and married Eric Linklater, 1933; SSAFA

Representative, 1942-45; Member, Ross and Cromarty County Council, 1953-69; served on Inverness Hospital Board; Member, Scottish Arts Council, 1957-63; former Member, Advisory Council, HIDB; Council Member, European Architectural Heritage Year, 1972-75; joined Scottish National Party, 1979, having progressed from Conservative via Liberal; as Chairman of Orkney Heritage Society, 1977-81, led "No Uranium" campaign to prevent uranium mining in Orkney; Secretary, Stormy Bank Group opposed to dumping nuclear waste in seabed off Orkney; founder Chairman, Pier Arts Centre Management Committee; helped to initiate Orkney Folk Festival; Hon. Vice President, St. Magnus Festival; President, Orkney Heritage Society, since 1994. Recreation: the arts. Address: (h.) 20 Main Street, Kirkwall, Orkney, KW15 1BU; T.-01856 3619.

Linkston, Alexander Millar, IPFA. Chief Executive Officer/Director of Finance, West Lothian District Council, since 1990; b. 13.12.49, Bathgate; m., Margaret Cuddihy; 2 d. Educ. Lindsay High School, Bathgate; Glasgow College of Commerce. Joined West Lothian County Council as trainee accountant, 1965. Secretary, West Lothian Municipal Bank; Treasurer, Forth Valley Tourist Board. Recreations: horse riding; swimming; Rotary. Address: (b.) District Headquarters, South Bridge Street, Bathgate, EH48 1TS; T.-01506 637000.

Linlithgow, 4th Marquess of (Adrian John Charles Hope); b. 1.7.46; m.; 1 s.; 1 d.; 2 s. by pr. m. Address: Hopetoun House, South Queensferry, West Lothian, EH30 9SL.

Lisgo, John, BSc (Econ) (Hons), DipEd (Hons). Principal, Jewel and Esk Valley College, Edinburgh, since 1986 (Lauder Technical College, Dunfermline, 1983-86); b. 8.7.40, Seaham, Durham; m., Norma Ranson Peel; 1 s. Educ. Ryhope School, Sunderland; London School of Economics and Political Science; Durham University. Assistant Teacher of History and Mathematics, Boldon Secondary School, 1962-63; Assistant Lecturer in Economics, then Liaison Officer for Adult Education, Monkwearmouth College of Further Education, 1963-72; Stevenson College of Further Education: Senior Lecturer in Social Studies, 1972-75, Head, Department of Language and Social Studies, 1975-80, Assistant Principal, 1980-83. Chairman, Association of Principals (Scotland); Board Member, JEVCEL; Board Member, Craigmillar Opportunities Trust; Board Member, Midlothian Enterprise. Recreation: swimming. Address: (b.) 24 Milton Road East, Edinburgh, EH15 2PP; T.-0131-669 8461.

Lishman, Professor Joyce, MA (Oxon), PhD, DipSW. Head, School of Applied Social Studies, Robert Gordon University, since 1993; m., Dr. J.R. Lishman; 1 s.; 1 d. Educ. Normanton Girls High School; St. Hilda's College, Oxford University; Edinburgh University; Aberdeen University. Social Worker/Senior Social Worker, Departments of Child and Family Psychiatry, Edinburgh; Research Assistant/Research Fellow, Aberdeen University; Editor, Research Highlights Series; Malcolm Sargent Social Worker, Royal Aberdeen Children's Hospital; Lecturer/Senior Lecturer, RGIT. Publications: Handbook of Theory for Practice; Teachers in Social Work (Editor); Communication in Social Work. Recreations: family and friends; music; theatre; reading; cycling; swimming. Address: (b.) The Robert Gordon University, Schoolhill, Aberdeen, AB9 1FR.

Lister-Kaye, Sir John, 8th Bt. of Grange. Naturalist, Author, Lecturer; Member, International Committee, World Wilderness Foundation, since 1984; Chairman, Scottish Committee, RSPB, 1985-92; Member, Committee for Scotland, NCC, 1989-90; NW Regional Chairman, NCCS, 1991; NW Regional Chairman, Scottish Natural Heritage, since 1992; b. 8.5.46; m., 1, Lady Sorrel Deirdre Bentinck;

1 s.; 2 d.; 2, Lucinda Anne Law. Educ. Allhallows School. Founded Field Studies Centre, Highlands, 1970; founder Director, Aigas Trust, 1979. Publications: The White Island, 1972; Seal Cull, 1979; The Seeing Eye, 1980; One for Sorrow, 1994. Address: (h.) House of Aigas, Beauly, Inverness-shire, IV4 7AD.

Lithgow, Sir William (James), 2nd Bt. of Ormsary, DL, LLD, CEng, FRINA, CBIM. Industrialist; Farmer; Chairman, Lithgows Limited, since 1959 (Director, since 1956); b. 10.5.34; m., 1, Valerie Helen Scott (deceased); 2, Mary Claire Hill; 2 s.; 1 d. Educ. Winchester College. Chairman, Hunterston Development Company Limited, 1987 (Director, since 1971); Director: Campbeltown Shipyard Ltd., Landcatch Limited, Lithgows Limited, Lithgows Pty Limited; Chairman, Scott Lithgow Drydocks Ltd., 1967-78; Vice-Chairman, Scott Lithgow Ltd., 1968-78; Chairman, Western Ferries (Argyll) Ltd., 1972-85; Director, Bank of Scotland, 1962-86. Member: British Committee, Det Norske Veritas, 1966-92, Greenock District Hospital Board, 1961-66, General Board (Royal Society Nominee), Nat. Physical Lab., 1963-66; Honorary President, Students Association, and Member, Court, Strathclyde University, 1964-69; Member: Executive Committee, Scottish Council Development and Industry, 1969-85, Scottish Regional Council, CBI, 1969-76, Clyde Port Authority, 1969-71, West Central Scotland Plan Steering Committee, 1970-74, Board, National Ports Council, 1971-78, Scottish Milk Marketing Board, 1979-83; Chairman, Iona Cathedral Trustees Management Board, 1979-83; Council Member, Winston Churchill Memorial Trust, 1979-83; Member, Queen's Body Guard for Scotland (Royal Company of Archers), 1964; Fellow, Scottish Council Development and Industry. Recreations: rural life; invention; photography. Address: (b.) PO Box 7, Lochgilphead, Argyll PA31 8JH; T.-01880 770244.

Little, Professor John Anthony, BSc, MSc, PhD, CEng, MICE, FGS. Professor and Head, Department of Civil Engineering, Paisley University, since 1992; Associate Dean, Faculty of Engineering, since 1993; b. 24.11.48, Catterick; m., Gail; 1 s.; 2 d. Educ. Chatham House Grammar School, Ramsgate; University of Wales; Durham University; City University. Research engineer, construction industry, 1972-76; Senior Lecturer, Hatfield Polytechnic, 1976-86; Lecturer/Senior Lecturer, Heriot-Watt University, 1986-92. Chairman, Scottish Geotechnical Group, since 1992. Address: (b.) Department of Civil Engineering, Paisley University, High Street, Paisley, PA1 2BE; T.-0141-848 3250.

Little, Keith, MB, ChB, MD, FRCP, FRCSEdin, FFAEM. Consultant in Accident and Emergency Medicine, Edinburgh Royal Infirmary; b. 26.4.43, Yeadon, Yorkshire; m., Margaret R.; 2 s.; 2 d. Educ. Dalbeattie High School; Dumfries Academy; Edinburgh Medical School. First posts in Edinburgh; moved to Derby as a Registrar in Accident and Emergency Medicine; Consultant, Chester Royal Infirmary, 1974-78. President, British Association for Accident and Emergency Medicine; President-Elect, Faculty of Accident and Emergency Medicine. Publication: Accident and Emergency Resuscitation (Co-author). Recreations: golf; tennis. Address: (b.) Accident and Emergency Department, Royal Infirmary, Edinburgh; T.-0131-536 4007.

Littlejohn, Professor David, BSc, PhD, CChem, FRSC. UNICAM Professor of Analytical Chemistry, Strathclyde University, since 1988; b. 1.5.53, Glasgow; m., Lesley Shaw MacDonald. Educ. Duncanrig Secondary School, East Kilbride; Strathclyde University. Technical Officer, ICI Petrochemicals Division, Wilton, Middlesborough, 1978-80; Lecturer/Senior Lecturer in Chemistry, Strathclyde University, 1981-88. Awarded 15th SAC Silver Medal by Royal Society of Chemistry, 1987; joint Editor in Chief, Talanta, International Journal of Pure and Applied

Analytical Chemistry, 1989-91. Publications: 120 research papers, 10 reviews. Address: (b.) Department of Pure and Applied Chemistry, Strathclyde University, 295 Cathedral Street, Glasgow, G1 1XL; T.-0141-552 4400.

Littlejohn, William Hunter, DA, RSA, RSW, RGI. Head of Fine Art, Gray's School of Art, Aberdeen, 1980-85; b. 16.4.29, Arbroath. Educ. Arbroath High School; Dundee College of Art. Art Teacher: Angus Schools, 1953-56, Arbroath High School, 1956-66; Lecturer, then Head of Painting, Gray's School of Art, 1970-80. Address: (h.) 16 Colvill Place, Arbroath, Angus; T.-Arbroath 874402.

Livingstone of Bachuil, Alastair, MA, LLB, FSA Scot. Baron of Bachuil; b. 1.9.14, Blantyre, Nyasaland; m., Valerie Collins; 2 s.; 3 d. Educ. Loretto School; Edinburgh University; Cambridge University. Sudan Political Service, 1938-40; 1940-43: commissioned into West Yorkshire Regiment in Khartoum, later Brigade Intelligence Officer, 9th Indian Infantry Brigade, active service in Eritrea and Western Desert; seconded to Palestine Government as Assistant District Commissioner, 1943-47; Executive, Iraq Petroleum Company Ltd., 1948-73. Chairman, Lismore Community Council, 1977-80; Member, Convention of the Baronage of Scotland; Hereditary Keeper of the Pastoral Staff of Saint Moluag; Past Chairman, 1745 Association; Co-editor, Muster Roll of Prince Charles Edward Stuart's Army, 1746. Recreations: genealogy; Scottish history; country pursuits. Address: (h.) Bachuil, Isle of Lismore, Argyll; T.-01631 760 256.

Livingstone, Andrew Hugh, BSc (Hons), DipEd. Rector, St. Columba's School, Kilmacolm, since 1987; b. 7.12.44, Campbeltown; m., Christine Margaret Henderson (deceased); 1 s.; 1 d. Educ. Campbeltown Grammar School; Aberdeen University; Glasgow University. Assistant Teacher, High School of Glasgow, 1968-70; Principal Teacher of Mathematics, Paisley Grammar School, 1970-78; Assistant Rector, Williamwood High School, 1978-83; Depute Rector, Paisley Grammar School, 1983-87. Treasurer, Scottish Mathematical Council, 1978-83. Recreations: golf; bridge; walking. Address: (h.) 38 Lanfine Road, Paisley, PA1 3NL; T.-0141-840 2125.

Livingstone, Ian Lang, OBE, BL, NP. Chairman, Lanarkshire Health Board, since 1993; Chairman, Lanarkshire Development Agency, since 1991; Chairman, Board, Motherwell College, since 1992; Consultant Solicitor, since 1989; b. 23.2.38, Hamilton; m., Diane; 2 s. Educ. Hamilton Academy; Glasgow University. Qualified as Solicitor, 1960; Partner, Senior Partner, Ballantyne & Copland, Solicitors, Motherwell, 1962-86; Chairman and Director, family property investment and development company, since 1987. Former Chairman, Motherwell Football Club; Member, Dalziel High School Board; Hon. President, Motherwell Conservative Association; Governor, David Livingstone Memorial Trust; Elder, St. Mary's Parish Church, Motherwell. Recreations: walking; football; music. Address: (h.) 223 Manse Road, Motherwell, ML1 2PY; T.-01698 253750.

Livingstone, Rognvald Maitland, BA, PhD, NDA, NDAgrE, JP. Company Director; b. 27.1.35, Aberdeen; m., Rona Scholes; 2 s.; 2 d. Educ. Aberdeen Grammar School; North of Scotland College of Agriculture; Essex Institute of Agriculture; Aberdeen University; Open University. Military service, Royal Armoured Corps; agricultural research service, 1958-85; Managing Director, Rowett Research Services, 1985-90; Governor, North of Scotland College of Agriculture, 1987-90; Deputy Convener, Grampian Regional Council, 1990-94. Recreations: skiing; swimming; hill-walking; gardening; reading. Address: (h.) Kirkstane House, Skene, Aberdeenshire, AB32 6XX; T.-01224 743586.

Lloyd-Jones, Glyn Robin, MA, BA. Author and Novelist; Vice President, Scottish PEN International, since 1993; b.

5.10.34, London; m., Sallie Hollocombe; 1 s.; 2 d. Educ. Blundell's School, Tiverton; Selwyn College, Cambridge University; Jordanhill College of Education. Teaching in Scottish secondary schools; Director, Curriculum Development Centre, Clydebank; English-Speaking Union Thyne Travel Scholarship to America, 1974; President, Scottish Association of Writers, 1981-86; Adviser, Education Department, Dunbartonshire, 1972-89; radio drama, Ice in Wonderland, 1992 (winner, Radio Times new drama script award). Publications: children's: Where the Forest and the Garden Meet, 1980; novels: Lord of the Dance (Winner, BBC/Arrow First Novel Competition, 1983); The Dreamhouse, 1985; Fallen Angels, 1992; education books: Assessment: From Principles to Action, 1985; How to Produce Better Worksheets, 1985; non-fiction: Argonauts of the Western Isles, 1989. Recreations: mountaineering; sea-kayaking; photography; chess. Address: (h.) 26 East Clyde Street, Helensburgh, G84 7PG; T.-01436 672010.

Lo, Professor Kwok Lun, MSc, PhD, CEng, FIEE. Professor of Power Systems, Strathclyde University, since 1989; Visiting and Consultant Professor to several overseas universities, since 1987; power systems consultant, since 1970; b. 23.6.43; m., Dr. K.K.N. Lo; 2 s. Educ. St. Joseph's College, Hong Kong; UMIST. Began career with South Wales Switchgear Ltd., Central Electricity Generating Board, South Wales Electricity Board; joined Department of Electrical Engineering, Paisley College of Technology, 1971; joined Strathclyde University, 1977, as Lecturer, then Senior Lecturer, then Reader; author/co-author of more than 200 technical publications. Recreations: swimming; walking. Address: (b.) Department of EEE, Royal College, 204 George Street, Strathclyde University, Glasgow; T.-0141-552 4400, Ext. 2169.

Lobban, Alexander James, MIFireE. Firemaster, Grampian Region, since 1993; b. 16.2.47, Aberdeen; m., Caroline; 2 d. Educ. Inverurie Academy. Joined Fire Service, 1966; Course Director — Command Studies, Fire Service College, Moreton-in-Marsh, 1984; joined Grampian as Deputy Firemaster, 1989. Recreations: sailing; skiing. Address: (b.) 19 North Anderson Drive, Aberdeen, AB9 2TP; T.-01224 696666.

Lochhead, Liz. Poet and Playwright; b. 1947, Motherwell. Educ. Glasgow School of Art. Combined teaching art and writing for eight years; became full-time writer after selection as first holder, Scottish/Canadian Writers' Exchange Fellowship, 1978; former Writer in Residence, Tattenhall Centre, Chester. Publications include: Memo for Spring, Islands, Grimm Sisters, Dreaming of Frankenstein, True Confessions; plays include: Blood and Ice, Dracula, Same Difference, Sweet Nothings, Now and Then, True Confessions, Mary Queen of Scots Got Her Head Chopped Off, The Big Picture.

Lockett, Patrick Gordon, CA. Partner, Ernst & Young, since 1979; Director, Cumbernauld Development Corporation, since 1989; b. 3.5.46, Glasgow; m., Erica; 1 s.; 1 d. Educ. Wellington College, Berkshire; Harvard Business School. Partner, Whinney Murray & Co., 1979. Recreations: field sports; tennis; travel. Address: (h.) Swindridgemuir, Dalry, Ayrshire; T.-01294 832079.

Lockhart, Sheriff Brian Alexander, BL. Sheriff, Glasgow and Strathkelvin, since 1981; b. 1.10.42, Ayr; m., Christine Ross Clark; 2 s.; 2 d. Educ. Glasgow Academy; Glasgow University. Partner, Robertson Chalmers and Auld, Solicitors, 1967-79; Sheriff, North Strathclyde, at Paisley, 1979-81. Recreations: fishing; golf; squash; family. Address: (h.) 18 Hamilton Avenue, Glasgow, G41; T.-0141-427 1921.

Lockhart of the Lee, Angus Hew; b. 17.8.46, Dunsyre; m., Susan Elizabeth Normand; 1 s.; 1 d. Educ. Rannoch School,

Perthshire; North of Scotland College of Agriculture. Recreations: shooting; skiing. Address: (h.) Newholm, Dunsyre, Lanark, ML11 8NQ; T.-01968 682254.

Lockhead, Moir, IEng, MCIT, MIRTE. Chairman and Managing Director, GRT Holdings PLC, since 1989; Executive Chairman, GRT Bus Group PLC; b. 25.4.45, Sedgefield; m., Audrey; 3 s.; 1 d. Educ. West Cornforth Secondary School; Darlington Technical College; Middlesborough Polytechnic. Former Head of Engineering, Strathclyde Passenger Transport Executive; joined Grampian Regional Transport as General Manager, 1985. Address: (b.) 395 King Street, Aberdeen, AB9 1SP; T.-01224 637047.

Lockley, Stephen Randolph, BSc, CEng, MICE, FICT, MIMunE, MIHT, DipTE. Director General, Strathclyde Passenger Transport Executive, since 1986; b. 19.6.43, Manchester; m., Angela; 2 d. Educ. Morecambe Grammar School; Manchester University. Highway and Planning Engineer, Lancashire County Council, 1964-72; Transportation and Planning Engineer, Lanarkshire County Council, 1972-75; Strathclyde Regional Council: Principal Engineer (Transportation), 1975-77, Depute Director of Policy Planning, 1977-80, Principal Executive Officer, 1980-86. Address: (b.) Consort House, 12 West George Street, Glasgow, G2 1HN; T.-0141-332 6811.

Logan, Alec, MB, ChB, MRCGP. Vice-Chairman, Scottish Council, Royal College of General Practitioners, since 1993; Editor, Hoolet (Scottish magazine, RCGP), since 1994; b. 18.11.59, Bellshill; m., Janice Crofts; 2 s. Educ. Hutchesons' Grammar School; Glasgow University. Medical Officer, Royal Navy, 1980-88; GP, Wishaw, since 1988. Recreations: sailing; reading; music. Address: (h.) 47 Orchard Street, Motherwell, ML1 3JE; T.-01698 258201.

Logan, Andrew, SDA, NDA, FIHort. Farmer; Governor, Scottish Crop Research Institute, since 1986; Director, Scottish Nuclear Stock Association, since 1983; Member, Horticultural Development Council, since 1986; Chairman, Dorward Gray Ltd.; b. 24.3.40, Cupar; m., M.L. Fleming; 3 s.; 1 d. Educ. Strathallan School; Edinburgh School of Agriculture. Director: Fifegro, 1973-79, Elba, 1979-84, Central Farmers, 1974-83; Chairman, Soft Fruit and Field Vegetable Committee, Scottish NFU, 1979-83; Member, Scottish Agricultural Development Council, 1983-86; Governor: National Vegetable Research Station, 1977-87; Strathallan School, since 1986; Director, East of Scotland Growers, 1987-89; Member, Home Grown Cereals Authority Research and Development Committee, 1987-89; Director, Scotfresh, 1984-89; Governor, Institute of Horticultural Research, 1987-89; Member, Scottish Agricultural Research and Development Advisory Council, 1987-90; Director, Futursky, since 1988; Director, Top Hat Holdings, since 1989; Council Member, Scottish Agricultural Organisation Society, since 1991. Recreations:skiing; golf. Address: (h.) Tarvit Home Farm, Cupar, Fife; T.-Cupar 652808.

Logan, Brian. Director, Scottish Charities Office. Address: (b.) 25 Chambers Street, Edinburgh, EH1 1LA.

Logan, Jimmy. Actor/Manager; Comedian; b. 4.4.28, Glasgow. One of five children who appeared on stage as The Logan Family; toured as an accordionist, juvenile lead and comedian's feed; for many years starred in Five Past Eight (summer revue) and numerous pantomimes; wrote and produced Lauder (one-man show); nine appearances at Royal performances.

Logan, Rev. Robert James Victor, MA, BD. Minister, Crown Church, Inverness, since 1970; Clerk, Synod of the Southern Highlands, 1976-92; Clerk, Inverness Presbytery, since 1980; b. Kilmarnock. Educ. Dundee High School; St. Andrews University; Edinburgh University. Assistant

Minister, Auld Kirk of Ayr, 1962-64; Minister, Newton Parish Church, Dalkeith, 1964-70; Member, Church Boundaries' Commission, 1974-75; Clerk, Synod of Moray, 1972-75; Convener, Nomination Committee, General Assembly, 1979-82; Chairman, successful group applying for franchise to operate Moray Firth Radio, 1979-81. Publication: The Lion, The Pit and the Snowy Day. Recreations: classical music; opera; bridge; reading history. Address: (h.) 39 Southside Road, Inverness, IV2 4XA; T.-01463 231140.

Logan, Rt. Rev. Vincent, DipRE. Roman Catholic Bishop of Dunkeld, since 1981; b. 30.6.41, Bathgate. Educ. Blairs College, Aberdeen; St. Andrew's College, Drygrange. Ordained Priest, 1964; Assistant Priest, St. Margaret's, Edinburgh, 1964-66; Corpus Christi College, London, 1966-67; Chaplain, St. Joseph's Hospital, Rosewell, Midlothian, 1966-67; Adviser in Religious Education, Archdiocese of St. Andrews and Edinburgh, 1967; Parish Priest, St. Mary's, Ratho, 1977-81; Vicar Episcopal for Education, Edinburgh, 1978. Address: Bishop's House, 29 Roseangle, Dundee, DD1 4LS; T.-01382 24327.

Logan, (William) Bruce, BA (Cantab), LLB, NP, WS. Partner, W. & J. Burness, WS, Solicitors, since 1969; b. 7.9.41, Forfar; m., Jennifer Mary; 3 d. Educ. Fettes College, Edinburgh; Cambridge University; Edinburgh University. Hon. Consul of Venezuela at Edinburgh; Director, Art in Partnership Scotland Ltd.; Secretary, Edinburgh Galleries Association. Recreations: music; contemporary art; cycling; walking. Address: (b.) 16 Hope Street, Edinburgh; T.-0131-226 2561.

Logie, John Robert Cunningham, MB, ChB, PhD, FRCS(Eng), FRCS(Edin), FRCS(Glas). Consultant General Surgeon, Inverness Hospitals, since 1981; b. 9.9.46, Aberdeen; m., Sheila C. Will. Educ. Robert Gordon's College, Aberdeen; Trinity College, Glenalmond; Aberdeen University. House Officer, then Senior House Officer, then Lecturer, Department of Surgery, then Senior Registrar, Aberdeen Royal Infirmary. Recreations: rugby refereeing; garden; railways; ornamental waterfowl. Address: (h.) The Darroch, Little Cantray, Culloden Moor, Inverness, IV1 2AG.

Logue, James, CEng, FIMechE, MIMgt. Personnel Director, ScotRail Train Operating Unit, since 1994; Board Member, Institution of Mechanical Engineers, since 1990; Board Member, Strathkelvin Enterprise Trust, since 1987; b. 13.5.39, Glasgow; m., Pamela; 1 s.; 2 d. Educ. St. Mungo's, Glasgow; Stow College, Glasgow. ScotRail: base Engineer, 1978-89, Quality Programmes Manager, 1989-92, Retail Manager, 1992-94; Chairman, IMechE Railway Division, Scottish Branch. Recreations: golf; DIY; car maintenance; socialising. Address: (h.) 1 Linnhe Avenue, Bishopbriggs, Glasgow, G64 1HG; T.-0141-772 6268.

Long, Hamish Arthur, BSc, PhD. Chief Executive, Scottish Examination Board, since 1990 (Assistant Director, 1985-89); b. 21.9.41, Edinburgh; m., Elizabeth Anne Stephen; 1 s.; 1 d. Educ. Daniel Stewart's College; Edinburgh University; Moray House College of Education. X-ray crystallographic research, Edinburgh University, 1963-66; Technical Officer, ICI, 1966-67; Science Teacher/Special Assistant, North Berwick High School, 1968-72; Principal Teacher of Science, Dunbar Grammar School, 1972-73; Examination Officer, then Senior Examination Officer, then Statistics and Development Officer, Scottish Examination Board, 1973-85. Recreations: music; gardening; painting; golf. Address: (b.) Ironmills Road, Dalkeith, Midlothian, EH22 1LE; T.-0131-663 6601.

Lonie, James William Laing, MA. Assistant Secretary, Scottish Office Environment Department, since 1992; b. 24.6.41, Falkirk; m., Nuala Clare Ward. Educ. Falkirk High School; Edinburgh University; Gonville and Caius College,

Cambridge. HM Treasury, 1967-76; joined Scottish Office, 1976. Recreations: music; walking; languages. Address: (b.) 27 Perth Street, Edinburgh; T.-0131-244 2920.

Lord, Geoffrey, OBE, MA, AIB, FRSA. Founder Director, The ADAPT Trust, since 1992; Secretary and Treasurer, Carnegie UK Trust, 1977-93; Chairman, The Unemployed Voluntary Action Fund, since 1990; President, Centre for Environmental Interpretation; b. 24.2.28, Rochdale; m., Jean; 1 s.; 1 d. Educ. Rochdale Grammar School; Bradford University. Midland Bank Ltd., 1946-58; Greater Manchester Probation and After-Care Service, 1958-76 (Deputy Chief Probation Officer, 1974-76); Vice-President, Selcare Trust; Chairman, Pollock Memorial Missionary Trust; Honorary Fellow, Manchester Metropolitan University, 1987; Trustee, HomeStart UK. Publications: The Arts and Disabilities, 1981; Interpretation of the Environment, 1984. Recreations: the arts; philately; walking; enjoying life. Address: (h.) 9 Craigleith View, Edinburgh.

Lord, John, BA, FRSA. Director Strategy, Scottish Enterprise, since 1993; b. 15.4.52, Bristol; m., Wendy; 2 s.; 1 d. Educ. Australia; Woking County Grammar School; Kingston College of Further Education; Warwick University. Freelance journalist and writer; Administrative Trainee, Department of Employment; Area Manager, Training Agency, 1989-90; Chief Executive, Enterprise Ayrshire, 1990-93. Director, Borderline Theatre. Publication: The Floating Harbour – A Landsape History of Bristol City Docks. Recreations: architectural history; football; the arts. Address: (b.) Scottish Enterprise, 120 Bothwell Street, Glasgow; T.-0141-248 2700.

Lord, Jonathan Christopher, MA. Secretary, Royal Scottish Automobile Club, since 1991; b. 29.4.53, Alverstoke; m., Angela Phillips; 1 s. Educ. Dollar Academy; St. Andrews University. Ministry of Defence (Naval), 1975-76; Royal Scottish Automobile Club, since 1976; Member, RAC British Motor Sports Council, since 1991; RAC Rallies Committee, since 1981; FIA Observer for International Rallies; RACMSA Steward; Clerk of the Course, RSAC International Scottish Rally, since 1982; Standing Joint Committee of RAC, AA and RSAC: Joint Secretary, 1986, Member, since 1991; Secretary, Scottish Motor Sport Federation, since 1985. Recreations: music (especially choral singing); cricket; motor sport. Address: (h.) 11 Melrose Gardens, Glasgow, G20 6RB; T.-0141-946 5045.

Lorimer, A. Ross, MD, FRCP, FRCPGlas, FRCPEdin. Honorary Professor, Glasgow University; Consultant Physician and Cardiologist, Glasgow Royal Infirmary, since 1970; b. 5.5.37, Bellshill; m., Fiona Marshall; 3 s. Educ. Uddingston Grammar School; High School of Glasgow; Glasgow University. Recreations: reading; walking. Address: (b.) Department of Cardiology, Royal Infirmary, Glasgow.

Lorimer, Robert Lewis Campbell, MA, FSAScot. Publisher to the Trustees, W.L. Lorimer Memorial Trust Fund, since 1979; Hon. Fellow, School of Scottish Studies, Edinburgh University, since 1979; Vice-President, Scottish National Dictionary Association, since 1993; b. 7.9.18, Glasgow; m., Priscilla Johnston Packard; 1 s.; 4 d. Educ. Shrewsbury School; Balliol College, Oxford; 123 OCTU, RA. Enlisted in Royal Artillery, 1939, commissioned 1940, served at 1st Battle of Alamein, 1942; ADC to GOC III Corps, 1943; promoted Captain, 1943; Political IO (Hungary) at GHQ MEF, 1943-44, and at AFHQ, Caserta, 1944-45; mentioned in despatches, 1946; also served in the Scottish Horse RAC TA, 1953-58; employed in Edinburgh by: Nelsons as General Editor, 1947-55; Oliver & Boyd as General Editor, 1955-69, and as Director, 1968-69; Irish University Press as Scottish Editor, 1970-72; Southside as Chairman, Managing Director, and General Editor, 1969-

75; Member, Council, Scottish National Dictionary Association, 1967-93; founded Scottish Publishers' Association, 1973, Chairman, 1973-75; edited and published his father W.L. Lorimer's New Testament in Scots, 1983. Recreations: studying musical form in preliterate Highland bagpipe music; military music; military history; Balkan politics and current affairs; hill-walking (when younger); sightseeing; reading; talking. Address: (h.) Balcorrachy, Strathtummel, Pitlochry, PH16 5RX.

Lothian, Sheriff Andrew, MA, LLB. Sheriff of Lothian and Borders at Edinburgh. Advocate, 1968. Address: (b.) Sheriff Court House, 27 Chambers Street, Edinburgh, EH1 1LB.

Lothian, Professor Niall, BA, CA, FRSA. Professor of Accounting, Heriot-Watt University, since 1987; b. 27.2.48, Edinburgh; m., Carol Miller; 1 s.; 1 d. Educ. Daniel Stewart's College, Edinburgh; Heriot-Watt University. Lecturer, then Senior Lecturer, Department of Accountancy and Finance, Heriot-Watt University, 1973-87; Visiting Professor: IMEDE, Lausanne, 1979-80, INSEAD, Fontainebleau, 1984; Consultant, United Nations Industrial Development Organisation, Vienna, since 1980; President, Institute of Chartered Accountants of Scotland, 1995-96. Publications: Accounting for Inflation: Issues and Managerial Practices, 1978; Audit Quality and Value for Money, 1983; How Companies Manage R. & D., 1984; Corporate Performance Indicators, 1987. Address: (b.) Department of Accountancy and Finance, Heriot-Watt University, PO Box 807, Riccarton, Edinburgh, EH14 4AT; T.-0131-449 5111.

Lothian, 12th Marquess of (Peter Francis Walter Kerr), KCVO, DL; b. 8.9.22, Melbourne, near Derby; m., Antonella Newland; 2 s.; 4 d. Educ. Ampleforth College, York; Christ Church, Oxford. Parliamentary Under Secretary, Ministry of Health, 1964; Parliamentary Under Secretary, Foreign and Commonwealth Office, 1970-72; Lord in Waiting, 1972-73; Lord Warden of the Stannaries, 1977-83. Knight of Malta; Ensign, Queen's Bodyguard for Scotland; Chairman of Council, Scottish Branch, British Red Cross, 1973-83. Recreations: music; shooting. Address: Ferniehirst Castle, Jedburgh, Roxburghshire; T.-01835 864021/0835 862872.

Loudon, Alasdair John, LLB, NP, WS. Senior Partner, Loudons WS, Edinburgh, since 1992; Vice President, Edinburgh Bar Association, since 1995; b. 7.4.56, Edinburgh; m., Mary V.; 2 s.; 1 d. Educ. Edinburgh Academy; Dundee University. Apprentice, Tods, Murray and Jamieson, WS, 1978-80; Qualified Assistant, Warner & Co., 1980-82, Partner, 1982-92; founded Loudons WS, 1992. Recreations: golf; football (Heart of Midlothian supporter). Address: (b.) 29 St. Patrick Square, Edinburgh; T.-0131-662 4193.

Loudon, John Alexander, LLB, NP, SSC. Solicitor, Messrs J. & A. Hastie, SSC, Edinburgh (Senior Partner); Member, Council, Law Society of Scotland (Convenor, Guarantee Fund); specialist in Liquor Licensing Law; b. 5.12.49, Edinburgh; m., Alison Jane Bruce Laird; 2 s. Educ. Edinburgh Academy; Dundee University. Apprenticeship, Tindal, Oatts and Roger, Solicitors, Glasgow. Secretary, Scottish Division, British Hospitality Association; Legal Adviser (Scotland), British Association of Shooting and Conservation; Secretary and Legal Adviser, Edinburgh and Lothians Decorators' Association; High Constable, City of Edinburgh Ward XV. Recreations: children; shooting; stalking; skiing; occasional use of a mountain bike and even more occasional golf. Address: (b.) 43 York Place, Edinburgh, EH1 3HT; T.-0131-556 7951.

Loudon, John Bruce, MB, ChB, FRCPsych, DPM. Head, Mental Health Service, Edinburgh Healthcare NHS Trust; Consultant Psychiatrist, Royal Edinburgh Hospital, since

1978 (Clinical Director, General Psychiatry, 1991-94); Honorary Senior Lecturer, Department of Psychiatry, Edinburgh University; b. 12.8.43, Edinburgh; m., Susan Mary Lay; 3 s. Educ. Edinburgh Academy; Edinburgh University. Address: (b.) Andrew Duncan Clinic, Morningside, Edinburgh, EH10 5HF; T.-0131-537 6452.

Loughran, Thomas Joseph, MA, BA (Hons). Head Teacher, Holy Cross RC High School, Hamilton, since 1986; b. 26.8.38, Airdrie; m., Maireen Keddilty; 2 s.; 1 d. Educ. Our Lady's High School, Motherwell; Glasgow University; Strathclyde University. Depute Head Teacher, St. Margaret's RC High School, Airdrie, 1976-78; Head Teacher, St. Andrew's RC High School, East Kilbride, 1978-86. Recreations: football; wine-making. Address: (b.) Holy Cross RC High School, Muir Street, Hamilton, ML3 6EY; T.-Hamilton 283888.

Lovat, Sheriff Leonard Scott, BL. Sheriff of South Strathclyde, Dumfries and Galloway, at Hamilton, 1978-93; b. 28.7.26, Gourock; m., Elinor Frances McAlister (deceased); 1 s.; 1 d. Educ. St. Aloysius' College, Glasgow; Glasgow University. Solicitor, 1948; in partnership, 1955-59; also Assistant to Professor of Roman Law, Glasgow University, 1954-63; Procurator Fiscal Depute, Glasgow, 1960; Cropwood Fellow, Institute of Criminology, Cambridge University, 1971; Senior Assistant Procurator Fiscal, Glasgow and Strathkelvin, 1976. Member, Board of Governors, St. Aloysius' College, Glasgow, 1986-93; Board of Governors, The Garnethill Centre, Glasgow, 1989-93; Member, West of Scotland Committee, Council of Christians and Jews, 1990-93. Publication: Climbers' Guide to Glencoe and Ardgour (two volumes), 1959 and 1965. Recreations: music; hill-walking; bird-watching. Address: (h.) 38 Kelvin Court, Glasgow, G12 OAE; T.-0141-357 0031.

Lovat, 18th Baron (Simon Fraser); b. 13.2.77. Educ. Harrow.

Love, Frances Mary. Director, Marriage Counselling Scotland, since 1987; Tutor and Lecturer, Scottish Human Relations and Counselling Course, since 1986; Organisational Consultant, SIHR, since 1986; b. 2.7.38, Edinburgh; m., James Love; 1 d. Educ. Broughton Secondary School. Edinburgh Public Library Service; voluntary playleader, Edinburgh Toddlers Playcentres; Pre-School Playgroup Association: playgroup supervisor, fieldworker, Scottish Adviser; General Secretary, Pre-School Playgroups Association; Executive Officer/Company Secretary, Scottish Council for Opportunities in Play Experience (SCOPE). Member, Management Board, Scottish Council of Voluntary Organisations; Member, Executive Committees, Scottish Child & Family Alliance and Scottish Council for Single Parents. Recreations: gardening; reading; theatre; dress-making. Address: (b.) 105 Hanover Street, Edinburgh, EH2 1DJ; T.-0131-225 5006.

Love, James Derek. Director of Cricket, Scottish Cricket Union, since 1992; b. 22.4.55, Leeds; m., Janice Hazel; 2 s. Educ. Brudenell, Leeds. Yorkshire County Cricket Club, 1975-89; England (three one-day internationals), 1981. Recreations: golf; shooting; rugby league. Address: (b.) Caledonia House, South Gyle, Edinburgh, EH12 9DQ; T.-0131-317 7247.

Love, Robert Malcolm, MA (Hons), FRSAMD. Controller of Drama, Scottish Television, since 1979; b. 9.1.37, Paisley. Educ. Paisley Grammar School; Glasgow University; Washington University, St. Louis. Actor and Director, various repertory companies, including Nottingham Playhouse, 1962-65; Producer, Thames TV, 1966-75, including Public Eye, Van Der Valk; freelance Producer, 1976-79, including Thames TV, LWT, Seacastle Film Productions, Scottish TV. Awards including:

Commonwealth Festival, New York TV and Film Festival, Chicago Film Festival, BAFTA Scotland, nominated for International Emmy, New York, 1982; productions for Scottish include Taggart, Take the High Road, Doctor Finlay. Recreations: reading; music; theatre; travel. Address: (b.) Scottish Television, Cowcaddens, Glasgow.

Lovelace, 5th Earl of (Peter Axel William Locke King); b. 26.11.51; m. Address: Torridon House, Torridon, IV22 2HA.

Low, Alistair James, BSc, FFA. Director, William M. Mercer Ltd., Actuaries and Employee Benefit Consultants, since 1986; Non-Executive Director, Scottish Widows Fund, since 1984; b. 2.8.42, Dundee; m., Shona Wallace; 2 s.; 1 d. Educ. Dundee High School; St. Andrews University. Recreations: golf; skiing; bridge. Address: (h.) Thornfield, Erskine Loan, Gullane, East Lothian.

Low, Bet, ARSA, RSW, RGI. Freelance Artist; b. 27.12.24, Gourock. Educ. Greenock Academy; Glasgow School of Art; Hospitalfield College of Art. Joined Unity Theatre Company, set designing etc., 1946; exhibited in international exhibition, Warsaw, 1954; co-founder and exhibitor, first open-air exhibition on railings at Botanic Gardens, Glasgow; worked part-time as art therapist, early 60s; Co-Founder and Co-Director, New Charing Cross Gallery, Glasgow, 1963-68; major retrospective exhibition, Third Eye Centre, 1985; exhibited widely in Britain and Europe and recently in Hong Kong. Recreations: reading; Scottish Opera; Glasgow Art Club; beach-combing; just pottering. Address: 53 Kelvinside Gardens, Glasgow, G20 6BQ; T.-0141-946 1377.

Low, Ian Campbell, BSc, CA, LLD. b. 15.12.12, Newport, Fife; m., Nora Bolton; 2 d. Educ. Fettes College; St. Andrews University. Deputy Chairman, then Chairman, Low & Bonar PLC, Dundee, 1937-77; Chairman, Dundee and London Investment Trust PLC, 1950-87; Chairman, J.T. Inglis & Sons Ltd., 1945-95. Recreations: shooting; fishing; gardening. Address: (h.) Holly Hill, 69 Dundee Road, Broughty Ferry, Dundee, DD5 1NA; T.-01382 779148.

Low, Sir James (Richard) Morrison-, 3rd Bt, DL, DFH, CEng, MIEE. Director, Osborne & Hunter Ltd., Glasgow, 1956-89; b. 3.8.25; m., Ann Rawson Gordon; 1 s.; 3 d. Educ. Ardvreck; Harrow; Merchiston; Faraday House, London. Royal Corps of Signals, 1943-47 (Captain). President, Electrical Contractors Association of Scotland, 1982-84; Director, National Inspection Council of Electrical Installation Contractors, 1982-88 (Chairman, Scottish Committee, 1982-88); Chairman, Electrical Industry Liaison Committee, 1986-88; Chairman, Fife Area Scout Council, 1966-84; Chairman, Cupar Branch, East Fife Conservative Association, 1965-78; Trustee, TSB, 1960-80; President, Elecrical Contractors Association of Scotland, 1982-84; DL, Fife, 1978. Address: (h.) Kilmaron, Cupar, Fife.

Low, William, CBE, LLD, JP, CIMgt. Chairman, Scottish Enterprise Tayside, 1991-94; Chairman, Dundee Heritage Trust, since 1986; Director, Dundee Enterprise Trust, since 1987; b. 12.9.21, Dundee; m., Elizabeth Ann Stewart Sime; 2 s. Educ. Merchiston Castle School, Edinburgh. Chairman, Don & Low (Holdings) Ltd., 1975-89; Chairman, UBI Scotland, 1984-89; Chairman, European Association for Textile Polyolefins, 1982-85; Chairman, British Polyolefin Association, 1971-73 and 1978-79; President, Dundee & Tayside Chamber of Commerce & Industry, 1973-74. Past President, Scottish Lawn Tennis Association; Provost, Burgh of Kirriemuir, 1973-75; appointed Fellow, Scottish Council (Development & Industry), 1989. Recreations: shooting; fishing; golf; gardening. Address: (h.) Herdhill Court, Kirriemuir, Angus, DD8 5LG; T.-01575 572215.

Lowden, Professor Gordon Stuart, MA, LLB, CA. Director, Dundee and London Investment Trust PLC, since 1981; b. 22.5.27, Bangkok; m., Kathleen; 2 s.; 1 d. Educ. Dundee High School; Strathallan School; St. John's College, Cambridge; St. Andrews University. Trained with Moody Stuart & Robertson, CA, Dundee; became Partner, 1959; part-time Lecturer/Senior Lecturer, Dundee University, 1955-83; Honorary Professor, Department of Accountancy and Business Finance, Dundee University, since 1987; Member, Board of Governors, Strathallan School; Member, University Court, Dundee University; former Chairman, Dundee Port Authority; Past President, Institute of Chartered Accountants of Scotland. Recreations: golf; watching rugby; bridge. Address: (h.) 169 Hamilton Street, Barnhill, Dundee, DD5 2RE; T.-01382 778360.

Lowe, Professor Gordon Douglas Ogilvie, MB, ChB, MD, FRCPEdin, FRCPGlas, FRCPLond. Professor of Medicine, Glasgow University, since 1993; Consultant Physician, Glasgow Royal Infirmary, since 1985; Director, West of Scotland Haemophilia Centre, since 1987; b. 2.1.49, London; m., Ann Harvie; 1 s.; 1 d. Educ. Dundee High School; St. Andrews University. House Officer, Royal Infirmary and Maryfield Hospital, Dundee, 1972-73; Senior House Officer, City Hospital, Nottingham, 1973-74; Registrar, Royal Infirmary, Glasgow, 1974-77; Lecturer, Glasgow University, 1978-85, Senior Lecturer, 1985-92, Reader, 1992-93. Past President, British Society for Haemostasis and Thrombosis. Publications: editor of books and author of publications on thrombosis and bleeding disorders. Recreations: travel; railways; gardening. Address: (b.) Department of Medicine, Royal Infirmary, Glasgow, G31 2ER; T.-0141-552 3535.

Lowe, John Duncan, CB, MA, LLB. Crown Agent, since 1991; b. 18.5.48, Alloa; m., Jacqueline M.; 2 s. Educ. Hamilton Academy; Glasgow University. Procurator Fiscal Depute, Kilmarnock, 1974-77; Legal Assistant, Crown Office, 1977-79; Senior Procurator Fiscal Depute, Glasgow, 1979-80; Assistant Procurator Fiscal, Glasgow, 1980-83; Assistant Solicitor, Crown Office, 1983-84; Deputy Crown Agent, 1984-88; Regional Procurator Fiscal, Lothian and Borders, 1988-91. Address: (b.) Crown Office, 25 Chambers Street, Edinburgh EH1 1LA; T.-0131-226 2626.

Lowe, Martin John Brodie, BSc, PhD. Secretary to Edinburgh University, since 1990; b. 10.4.40, Dorking; m., Janet MacNaughtan; 3 s.; 1 d. Educ. Dunfermline High School; St. Andrews University. British Council Officer, with service in Tanzania and South India, 1965-69; Strathclyde University: Administrative Assistant, 1969-71, Assistant Registrar, 1971-73, Secretary to Senate, 1973-81; Secretary and Registrar, St. Andrews University, 1981-89. National Council, Voluntary Service Overseas, 1976-83; Honorary Secretary, then Chairman, Glasgow and West of Scotland VSO Committee, 1973-81. Recreations: piping; hill-walking; family interests. Address: (b.) Old College, South Bridge, Edinburgh, EH8 9YL; T.-0131-650 2143.

Lowis, Professor C. Ann, MedDipN, RGN, OHNC. Professor and Director of Nursing, Robert Gordon University, Aberdeen, since 1992; b. 27.3.41, Liverpool; m., Richard Walker Lowis; 2 d. Educ. Bellerive Convent; Liverpool; Dundee; Abedeen. Former staff nurse, sister, nursing officer, senior nursing officer, senior nursing advisor. Secretary of State appointment to UK Central Council for Nursing, Midwifery and Health Visiting. Recreations: cooking; wine; walking. Address: (h.) Whitemyres Stud, Lang Stracht, Aberdeen; T.-01224 317154.

Lucas, Michael Hudson, BSc (Hons). Registrar, Royal College of Physicians and Surgeons of Glasgow, since 1990; b. 26.8.47, Dundee; m., Erika Esther Rogerson; 1 s.; 1 d. Educ. Grove Academy, Dundee; St. Andrews University. Statistical research, 1969-70; Lecturer in Statistics, St. Andrews University, 1971-72; Higher Scientific Officer, Civil Aviation Authority, 1973; Edinburgh University: Administrative Assistant, 1974, Senior Administrative Officer, 1978, Assistant Secretary, 1985. Fulbright Fellowship, 1986. Recreations: Times crossword; keeping up with his children. Address: (h.) 707 Clarkston Road, Glasgow, G44 3UD; T.-0141-637 4809.

Ludlam, Christopher A., BSc (Hons), MB, ChB, PhD, FRCP, FRCPath. Consultant Haematologist, Edinburgh Royal Infirmary, since 1980; Director, Edinburgh Haemophilia Reference Centre, since 1980; part-time Senior Lecturer in Medicine, Edinburgh University, since 1980; b. 6.6.46, Edinburgh. Educ. Edinburgh University. MRC Research Fellow, 1972-75; Senior Registrar in Haematalogy, University Hospital of Wales, Cardiff, 1975-78; Lecturer in Haematology, University of Wales, 1979. Address: (b.) Department of Haematology, Royal Infirmary, Edinburgh; T.-0131-536 2122.

Lumsden, Iain C., MA, FFA. Group Finance Director and Appointed Actuary, Standard Life Assurance Company, since 1990; b. 6.6.46, Perth; m., Rosemary; 1 s.; 1 d. Educ. Exeter College, Oxford University. Standard Life, since 1967. Address: (b.) 3 George Street, Edinburgh, EH2 2XZ; T.-0131-225 2552.

Lumsden, James Alexander, MBE, TD, MA, LLB, DL. Director, Bank of Scotland, 1958-85; Director, Scottish Provident Institution, 1968-85; b. 24.1.15, Arden, Dunbartonshire; m., Sheila Cross; 3 s. Educ. Cargilfield School, Edinburgh; Rugby School; Corpus Christi College, Cambridge; Glasgow University. Territorial Army, 1937-46; Partner, Maclay Murray & Spens, Solicitors, Glasgow and Edinburgh, 1947-82; Director of certain Investment Trust companies managed by Murray Johnstone Ltd., 1967-85; Director, Burmah Oil, 1957-76; Member, Queen's Body Guard for Scotland (Royal Company of Archers), 1963; Commissioner of Income Tax, County of Dumbarton, 1964-90; Member, Committee on Company Law, 1960-62; Fellow, Law Society of Scotland and Royal Faculty of Procurators, Glasgow. Recreations: shooting; fishing; other country pursuits. Address: (h.) Bannachra, by Helensburgh, Dunbartonshire, G84 9EF; T.-01389 850653.

Lumsden, Professor Keith Grant, MA, PhD, FRSE. Professor and Director, Esmee Fairbairn Research Centre, Heriot-Watt University, Edinburgh, since 1975; b. 7.1.35, Bathgate; m., Jean Baillie MacDonald; 1 s. Educ. Bathgate Academy; Edinburgh University; Stanford University, California. Instructor, Department of Economics, then Assistant Professor, Graduate School of Business, Stanford University, 1960-67; Research Associate, Stanford Research Institute, 1965-71; Director, Stanford University Conference: NDTE, 1966, RREE, 1968; Associate Professor, Graduate School of Business, Stanford University, 1968-75; Visiting Professor of Economics, Heriot-Watt University, 1969-70; Director: Economics Education Project, 1969-74, Behavioral Research Laboratories, 1970-72, Capital Preservation Fund Inc., 1971-75, Nielsen Engineering Research Inc., 1972-75; Member, American Economic Association Committee on Economic Education, 1978-81; Academic Director, Service and Transport Executive Programme (STEP), since 1979; Professor of Economics, Advanced Management College, Stanford University, since 1971; Affiliate Professor of Economics, INSEAD, France; Member, Economics Education 14-16 Project, Manchester University; Member, Advisory Council, David Hume Institute, since 1984; Member, Board of Directors, Hewlett Packard Ltd., 1982-92. Publications: The Free Enterprise System, 1963; The Gross National Product, 1964; International Trade, 1965; Microeconomics: A Programmed Book, 1966; Macroeconomics: A Programmed Book, 1966; New Developments in the Teaching of Economics (Editor), 1967; Excess Demand and Excess Supply in World Tramp

Shipping Markets, 1968; Recent Research in Economics Education (Editor), 1970; Basic Economics: Theory and Cases, 1973; Efficiency in Universities: The La Paz Papers (Editor), 1974; Economics Education in the United Kingdom, 1980; Economics: a distance learning study programme, 1991. Recreations: tennis; deep sea sports fishing. Address: (h.) 40 Lauder Road, Edinburgh, EH9 1UE.

Lumsden, Vivien Dale Victoria, DSD, CDS. Presenter, Scottish Television, since 1989; b. 22.11.52, Edinburgh; m., Alan Douglas (qv); 1 s.; 1 d. Educ. James Gillespie's High School for Girls, Edinburgh; RSAMD. Full-time mother, 1975-82; AA Traffic News Reporter, 1982-84; BBC Scotland: Breakfast Newsreader, 1984-85, Reporting Scotland Presenter, 1985-89, Garden Party, 1988; joined Scottish TV as Presenter, Scotland Today, 1989; also presented chat show, Telethon, BAFTA Awards, Business Game, Home Show. Trustee, Parents Oncology Support Yorkhill. Recreations: learning Italian; food (reading, cooking, eating); interior design; drinking more champagne than her husband. Address: (b.) Scottish Television, Cowcaddens, Glasgow; T.-0141-332 9999.

Lumsden, William Hepburn Russell, DSc, MD, DTM, DTH, FIBiol, FRCPEdin, FRSE. Scientific and Medical Writer; b. 27.3.14, Forfar; m., Pamela Kathleen Bartram; 2 s.; 1 d. (deceased). Educ. Queen Elizabeth's Grammar School, Darlington; Glasgow University; Liverpool University. MRC Fellow in Tropical Medicine, 1938-41; active service, Malaria Field Laboratories, RAMC, 1941-46; Yellow Fever (subsequently East African Virus) Research Institute, Entebbe, 1947-57; Director, East African Trypanosomiasis Research Organisation, Tororo, 1957-63; Lecturer, Department of Bacteriology, Edinburgh University Medical School, 1963-64; Senior Lecturer, Department of Animal Health, Royal (Dick) School of Veterinary Studies, Edinburgh University, 1964-68; Visiting Professor, Toronto University, 1968; Professor of Medical Protozoology, London School of Hygiene and Tropical Medicine, London University, 1968-79; Senior Editor, Advances in Parasitology, 1978-82; Council Member, Royal Society of Tropical Medicine and Hygiene, 1969-73, 1974-77; Council Member, Royal Zoological Society of Scotland, 1967-68; Member, Expert Advisory Panel on Parasitic Diseases (Trypanosomiasis), WHO, 1962-84; Member, Trypanosomiasis Panel, Ministry of Overseas Development, 1973-79; Member, International Malaria Review Teams, Bangladesh, 1978, Nepal, 1979, Sri Lanka, 1980; Editing Secretary, Berwickshire Naturalists' Club, 1988-91. Publications: Techniques with Trypanosomes, 1973; Biology of the Kinetoplastida (Editor), 1976 and 1979. Recreations: trout fishing; hill-walking. Address: (h.) 16A Merchiston Crescent, Edinburgh, EH10 5AX; T.-0131-229 2702.

Lunan, Charles Burnett, MD, FRCOG, FRCS. Consultant Obstetrician, Royal Maternity Hospital, Glasgow, since 1977; Consultant Gynaecologist, Royal Infirmary, Glasgow, since 1977; b. London; m., Helen Russell Ferrie; 2 s.; 1 d. Educ. High School of Glasgow; Glasgow University. Lecturer, Obstetrics and Gynaecology, Aberdeen University, 1973-75; Senior Lecturer, University of Nairobi, 1975-77; WHO Consultant, Family Planning Programme, Bangladesh, 1984-85. Treasurer, 1982-90, Vice-President, 1990-91, President, Royal Medico-Chirurgical Society of Glasgow, 1991-92; Secretary, Glasgow Obstetrical and Gynaecological Society, 1978-82. Recreations: gardening; photography; hill-walking. Address: (h.) 1 Moncrieff Avenue, Lenzie, Glasgow, G66 4NL; T.-0141-776 3227.

Lunan, Duncan Alasdair, MA (Hons), FBIS, DipEd. Author; b. 24.10.45; m., Linda Joyce Donnelly (m. diss.). Educ. Marr College, Troon; Glasgow University. Management Trainee, Christian Salvesen (Managers) Ltd.,

1969-70; self-employed (Author), 1970-78 and since 1980; Manager, Astronomy Project, Glasgow Parks Department, 1978-79; SF Critic, Glasgow Herald, 1971-82 and 1985-91; Photo-Archivist, Glasgow 1990 Press Centre, 1990-91; regular astronomy column in various papers and magazines; Council Member, Association in Scotland to Research into Astronautics (ASTRA), since 1963 (President, 1966-72, 1978-85, and since 1990; Secretary, 1985- 89). Publications: Man and the Stars, 1974; New Worlds for Old, 1979; Man and the Planets, 1983; Starfield (Editor), 1989. Recreation: folk music. Address: c/o Campbell, 16 Oakfield Avenue, Hillhead, Glasgow, G12 8JE; T.-0141-339 2558.

Lundie, Mary Elizabeth, JP, RGN. Matron, The Princess Louise Scottish Hospital, Erskine, since 1977; b. 11.10.36, Barrhead; m., Peter Lundie; 3 s.; 3 d. Educ. St. Margaret's Convent, Paisley. Trained, Western Infirmary, Glasgow, 1954-58; Staff Nurse, Knightswood Hospital, 1962-65; Southern General Hospital, Glasgow, 1965-66; Sister, Gartloch Hospital, Glasgow, 1966-67; Sister and Nursing Officer, Ruchill Hospital, Glasgow, 1967-75; Nursing Officer, The Princess Louise Scottish Hospital, Erskine, 1975-77. Recreations: reading; walking dogs. Address: (h.) Matron's House, Erskine Hospital, Bishopton, Renfrewshire.

Lunn, George Michael, BSc, DipHWU. Chairman, Glasgow Development Agency; former Chairman and Chief Executive, The Whyte & Mackay Group PLC; former Chairman, Invergordon Distillers Group plc; b. 22.7.42, Stirling; m., Jennifer Burgoyne; 3 s.; 1 d. Educ. Kelvinside Academy; Glasgow University; Heriot-Watt University. North of Scotland Distilling Co. Ltd., 1965-68; Distillers Co. (Carbon Dioxide) Ltd., 1968-70; PA Management Consultants, 1970-72; British Carpets Ltd., 1972-78; joined Whyte & Mackay Distillers Ltd., 1978. Recreations: golf; tennis; sailing.

Lunny, Sheriff William Francis, MA, LLB. Sheriff of South Strathclyde, Dumfries and Galloway, since 1984; b. 10.12.38. Advocate, 1977. Address: (b.) Sheriff Court House, Beckford Street, Hamilton, ML3 6AA.

Luscombe, Rt. Rev. Lawrence Edward, OStJ, MA, MPhil, PhD, LLD, DLitt, CA, FRSA, FSA Scot. Primus of the Scottish Episcopal Church, 1985-90, and Bishop of Brechin, 1975-90; b. 10.11.24; m., Dr. Doris Morgan (deceased); 1 d. Educ. Kelham College; King's College, London; Dundee University. Indian Army, 1942-47; Major; Chartered Accountant, 1952; Partner, Galbraith Dunlop & Co. (later Watson and Galbraith), CA, 1953-63; Curate, St. Margaret's, Glasgow, 1963-66; Rector, St. Barnabas', Paisley, 1966-71; Provost, St. Paul's Cathedral, Dundee, 1971-75. Honorary Canon, Trinity Cathedral, Davenport, Iowa, since 1983; Member, Education Committee, Renfrew County Council, 1967-71; Chairman, Governing Body: Glenalmond College, Edinburgh Theological College, 1985-90; Governor: Lathallan School, Dundee College of Education; Chairman, Inter-Anglican Finance Committee, 1989-93; Member, Tayside Health Board, 1989-93; Honorary Research Fellow, Dundee University, since 1993; Member, Court, Corporation of Sons of the Clergy. Address: (h.) Woodville, Kirkton of Tealing, by Dundee, DD4 0RD; T.-Tealing 331.

Lyall, Fiona Jane, DL, MB, ChB, DPH. Family Doctor, Laurencekirk, since 1959; Director, Grampian Television PLC, since 1980; Non-Executive Director, Aberdeen Royal Hospitals NHS Trust, since 1992; Non-Executive Director, Templehill Community Council, since 1990; Deputy Lieutenant, Kincardineshire, since 1985; b. 13.4.31, Inverness; m., Dr. Alan Richards Lyall; 1 s.; 1 d. Educ. Inverness Royal Academy; Aberdeen University. Former Member, Laurencekirk Burgh Council; former Kincardine County and Grampian Regional Councillor; Member,

Grampian Health Board, 1974, and Kincardine & Deeside Health Council, 1974; Member, Children's Panel Advisory Committee, 1974; Member, Grampian Valuation Appeals Committee; Member, Prince's and Royal Jubilee Trust for Grampian; Treasurer, Action Research for Crippled Child. Recreations: skiing; riding; gardening. Address: Melrose Bank, Laurencekirk, AB30 1AL; T.-01561 377220.

Lyall, Ian Alastair, DSC, VRD, DL, FICS; b. 16.3.17, Bangor, Co. Down; m., Eileen Patricia Bennet; 1 d. Educ. Hillhead High School, Glasgow; College of Nautical Studies, Glasgow. Chairman and Managing Director, Roxburgh Henderson & Co. Ltd., 1967-80; Director: British & Burmese Steam Navigation Co. Ltd., 1971-80, Henderson Line Ltd., 1971-80; President, Glasgow Chamber of Commerce, 1978-79; retired Lt. Commander, RNR, 1963. Recreations: sailing; fishing; shooting. Address: (h.) 21 Chapelacre, Helensburgh, G84 7SH; T.-01436 673976.

Lyall, Michael Hodge, MB, ChB, ChM, FRCSEdin. Consultant Surgeon, Tayside Health Board, since 1975; Honorary Senior Lecturer, Dundee University, since 1975; b. 5.12.41, Methilhill, Fife; m., Catherine B. Jarvie; 3 s. Educ. Buckhaven High School; St. Andrews University. President, Tayside Division, Ileostomy Association of Great Britain; Past President, North Fife Rotary Club. Recreation: computing. Address: (h.) 26 Linden Avenue, Newport on Tay, Fife, DD6 8DU.

Lyddon, William Derek Collier, CB, DLitt, BA, RIBA, DipTP, FRTPI. Chairman, The Planning Exchange; Chairman, Management Committee, Edinburgh School of Environmental Design; Chief Planner, Scottish Development Department, 1967-85; Honorary Professor, Heriot-Watt University; Governor, Edinburgh College of Art; b. 17.11.25, Loughton, Essex; m., Marian Louise Kaye Charlesworth; 2 d. Educ. Wrekin College; University College, London. Depute Chief Architect Planner, Cumbernauld Development Corporation; Chief Architect Planner, Skelmersdale Development Corporation. President, International Society of City and Regional Planners, 1981-84. Address: (h.) 38 Dick Place, Edinburgh; T.-0131-667 2266.

Lyell, 3rd Baron (Charles Lyell), Bt. Parliamentary Under-Secretary of State, Northern Ireland Office, 1984-89; b. 27.3.39. Educ. Eton; Christ Church, Oxford. Scots Guards, 1957-59; CA; Opposition Whip, 1974-79; Government Whip, 1979-84; Member, Queen's Bodyguard for Scotland (Royal Company of Archers); DL, Angus, 1988. Address: (h.) Kinnordy House, Kirriemuir, Angus.

Lyle, Lt.-Col. (Archibald) Michael, OBE, DL, JP, MA, BA. Landowner and Farmer; b. 1.5.19; m., Hon. Elizabeth Sinclair; 4 d. (1 dec.). Educ. Eton College; Trinity College, Oxford. Hon. Attache, Rome, 1938-39; served 1939-46 with The Black Watch RHR (wounded Normandy, 1944, discharged with wounds, 1946); Lt.-Col., The Scottish Horse RAC (TA), 1953-56; Chairman, T&AFA, 1959-64; Member, Royal Company of Archers, since 1946; Member, Perth and Kinross County Council, 1946-74, Tayside Regional Council, 1974-79; Chairman, Perth College of Further Education, since 1978; JP, Perth, 1950; DL, Perthshire, 1961; Vice Lord Lieutenant, Perth and Kinross, since 1984. Recreations: fishing; shooting; music. Address: Riemore Lodge, Dunkeld, Perthshire; T.-0135 04 205.

Lyle, David Angus, MA, LLB, NP, SSC, FCIS, FInstM, FInstD, FIAM, FRSA. Consultant, Solicitor, and Chartered Company Secretary, in private practice, since 1993; b. 7.9.40; m., Dorothy Ann Clark; 1 s.; 3 d. Educ. George Watson's College, Edinburgh; Edinburgh University. Account Executive, Advertising Agencies, London; Indentured, Edinburgh Corporation; Solicitor, Lloyds and Scottish Finance Ltd., Edinburgh; Depute County Clerk,

East Lothian County Council; Director of Administration and Law, Dumfries and Galloway Regional Council; Agency Secretary, Scottish Development Agency; Director/Company Secretary, Scottish Enterprise. Recreations: shooting; golf; bridge. Address: (b.) The Caledonian Suite, St Andrew House, 141 West Nile Street, Glasgow G1 2RN; T.-0141-333 1119.

Lynch, Alexander McKay, ACMA, MCIT. Deputy Director/Financial Director, ScotRail, since 1994; b. 6.10.49, Greenock; m., Christina Keenan; 2 d. Educ. St. Columba's High School, Greenock; Central College of Commerce and Distribution, Glasgow. BR management posts, since 1976. Hon. President, Railway Staff Association, Scotland. Recreations: youth football; TV; music. Address: (b.) Caledonian Chambers, 87 Union Street, Glasgow, G1 3TA; T.-0141-335 4180.

Lyon, Robert Alexander, MA, CA, CMA. Dean, Faculty of Law and Accountancy, Dundee University, since 1994; Member, Council, Institute of Chartered Accountants of Scotland, since 1994; Non-Executive Director, Dundee Teaching Hospitals NHS Trust, since 1993; b. 18.2.48, Dundee. Educ. Morgan Academy, Dundee; Dundee University. CA student, Dundee, 1969-73; Senior Accountant, Peat, Marwick, Mitchell & Co., USA, Germany, Scotland, 1972-76; Lecturer, then Senior Lecturer, Dundee University, since 1976. Address: (b.) Faculty of Law and Accountancy, Dundee University, Dundee, DD1 4HN; T.-01382 344195.

Mc/Mac

McAleese, Professor Ray, MA, PhD, MIInfSc, FRSA. Centre for Combined Studies, Heriot Watt University; b. 22.3.44, Coleraine; m., Dr. Sybil McAleese; 2 s. Educ. Coleraine Academical Institution; Trinity College, Dublin. Aberdeen University: Research Fellow, 1973, Lecturer, 1975, Senior Lecturer, 1982. Elder, Church of Scotland; School Board Chairman; Council Member, SRHE, AETT, ALT. Publications:books on educational technology. Recreations: golf; running; water colour painting; photography; arguing. Address: (h.) 242 Colinton Road, Edinburgh, EH14 1DL; T.-0131-443 9209.

McAllion, John, MA (Hons). MP (Lab), Dundee East, since 1987; b. 13.2.48, Glasgow; m., Susan Jean; 2 s. Educ. St. Augustine's Secondary, Glasgow; St. Andrews University. Teacher, History and Modern Studies, St. Saviour's Secondary, Dundee, 1973-78, Social Studies, Balgowan List D School, Dundee, 1978-82; Research Assistant to Bob McTaggart, MP, 1982-86; Regional Councillor, 1984-87; Convener, Tayside Regional Council, 1986-87. Member, Scottish Executive, Labour Party, 1986-88; Senior Vice Chairperson, Dundee Labour Party, 1986, 1987. Recreations: football; reading; music. Address: (h.) 3 Haldane Street, Dundee, DD3 0HP; T.-01382 200329.

McAlpine, Thomas, BSc, CEng, MIEE. Business Consultant; b. 23.9.29, Motherwell; m., Isobel Lindsay; 2 s.; 1 d. Educ. Dalziel High School, Motherwell; Strathclyde University. National Service, REME, 1952-54 (2nd Lt.); Chief Engineer, Belmos Co. Ltd., Bellshill, 1954-58; Chief Development Engineer, Mine Safety Appliances, Glasgow, 1958-62; Managing Director: Rowen Engineering Co. Ltd., Glasgow, 1962-71, Chieftain Industries PLC, Livingston, 1971-85. Former Executive Vice Chairman Administration, Scottish National Party (former Vice President, SNP); Parliamentary candidate, Clydesdale (Lanark), 1974, 1979, 1983, Dumfries, 1987; District Councillor, Clydesdale, since 1988. Recreations: when young, played rugby, swimming and tennis. Address: (h.) 9 Knocklea Place, Biggar, Lanarkshire, ML12 6DZ; T.-01899 20423.

McAndrew, Nicolas, CA. Chairman, Murray Johnstone Ltd., since 1992; b. 9.12.34, London; 2 s.; 1 d. Educ. Winchester College. National Service (The Black Watch) commission, 1953-55; articled clerk, Peat Marwick Mitchell, 1955-61; qualified CA, 1961; S.G. Warburg & Co. Ltd., Merchant Bankers, 1962-78; became Chairman, Warburg Investment Management Ltd., and Director, Mercury Securities Ltd.; Managing Director, N.M. Rothschild & Sons Ltd., Merchant Bankers, 1979-88. Master, Worshipful Company of Grocers, 1978-79. Recreations: fishing; shooting; golf. Address: (h.) Kilcoy Castle, Killearnan, Muir of Ord, Ross-shire IV6 7RX; T.- 01463 871 393.

McArdle, Colin S., MD, FRCS, FRCSEdin, FRCSGlas. Consultant Surgeon, University Department of Surgery, Glasgow Royal Infirmary, since 1981; Honorary Professor, Glasgow University, since 1991; b. 10.10.39, Glasgow; m., June M.C. Merchant; 2 s.; 1 d. Educ. Jordanhill College School; Glasgow University. Senior Registrar in General Surgery, Western Infirmary, Glasgow, 1972-75; Consultant Surgeon: Victoria Infirmary, Glasgow, 1975-78, Glasgow Royal Infirmary, 1978-80. Address: (h.) 4 Collylinn Road, Bearsden, Glasgow.

MacArthur, Rev. Allan Ian, BD, JP. Minister, Lochcarron Parish, since 1973; District Councillor, since 1984; b. 22.5.28, Marvig, Isle of Lewis; m., Effie Macleod; 1 s.; 6 d. Educ. Nicolson Institute, Stornoway; Glasgow University and Trinity College. Meteorologist, Air Ministry and Falkland Islands Dependencies Survey, Antarctica; teaching; Minister of Religion and Presbytery Clerk. Member, Crofters Commission, 1984-90. Address: Church of Scotland Manse, Lochcarron, Ross-shire, IV54 8YD; T.- 05202 278.

McArthur, Douglas B., BSc (Hons). Managing Director, Radio Advertising Bureau, since 1992; Director, Balgray Communications Group Ltd. and subsidiaries, 1984-92; b. 17.3.51, Dundee; m., Elizabeth M.A.; 3 d. Educ. Kirkton High School, Dundee; Glasgow University. Marketing management roles, Proctor and Gamble, Scottish & Newcastle, Campbell's Soups Ltd., Radio Clyde; marketing and advertising consultancy roles with Hall Advertising and Baillie Marshall Advertising. Director, Drumchapel Opportunities Ltd.; Member, Scottish Arts Council (Chairman, Drama Committee). Recreations: swimming; music; visual arts; drama. Address: (h.) 33 Victoria Crescent Road, Glasgow, G12 9DD.

Macarthur, Edith. Actress; b. Ardrossan, Ayrshire. Educ. Ardrossan Academy. Began career, 1948, with Wilson Barrett Company, then Perth Repertory, Gateway Theatre Company, Citizens' Theatre, Glasgow, Bristol Old Vic, Royal Shakespeare Company, Ochtertyre Theatre, Royal Lyceum Theatre Company, West End; television work includes The Borderers, Sunset Song, Weir of Hermiston, Sutherland's Law; Take the High Road; nominated for Scottish BAFTA award in The Long Roads, 1993; recent stage appearances: solo-performance play, Marie of Scotland, Jamie the Saxt and The Thrie Estates for the Scottish Theatre Company at Edinburgh Festivals and Warsaw International Festival, 1986, Judith Bliss in Hay Fever, Royal Lyceum Theatre, 1987, Charley's Aunt, Death of a Salesman, Royal Lyceum, 1988, Daphne Laureola, Pygmalion, Pride and Prejudice, Pitlochry Festival Theatre, 1988; The Cherry Orchard, Royal Lyceum, 1989; The Cherry Orchard, The Circle, Arsenic and Old Lace, Pitlochry, 1990; Driving Miss Daisy, Perth, 1991; Cinderella, Glasgow and Edinburgh, 1990, 1991; Good, Glasgow and Edinburgh, 1992; Long Day's Journey into Night, Dundee, 1994; The Prime of Miss Jean Brodie, London, 1994-95. Recreations: music; books. Address: c/o Larry Dalzell Associates Ltd., Suite 12, 17 Broad Court, London, WC2B 5QN.

McArthur, George, OBE. Convener, Consultative Committee on Church Properties, Church of Scotland, since 1994; Chairman, Scottish Churches Housing Agency, since 1993; Convener, Edinburgh Peace and Justice Resource Centre, since 1992; b. 22.7.30, Edinburgh; m., Margaret Moffat Wilson; 1 s.; 1 d. Educ. Leith Academy. Missionary (youth worker), Church of Scotland, South Africa, 1956-71; Official Correspondent for Church of Scotland's List D schools, 1972-77; involved in formation of Kirk Care Housing Association Ltd., 1973, becoming its first Director, 1978, retired, 1992. Chairman, Council, Scottish Federation of Housing Associations, 1984-86; a Vice-President, Churches National Housing Coalition, 1995. Recreations: golf; supporting Hibernian F.C.; walking; reading. Address: (h.) 3 Craigcrook Road, Edinburgh, EH4 3NQ; T.-0131-477 0312.

McArthur, John Duncan, BSc (Hons), MB, ChB (Hons), DM, FRCPGlas, MRCP, FRCPEdin. Consultant Physician and Cardiologist, Western Infirmary and Gartnavel General Hospital, Glasgow, since 1978; Honorary Clinical Senior Lecturer, Glasgow University, since 1978; b. 7.1.38, Hamilton; m., Elizabeth A. Bowie; 2 s.; 1 d. Educ. Hamilton Academy; Glasgow University. Junior doctor, Royal Infirmary, Glasgow, and in Ayrshire, 1963-67; St. Colm's College, Edinburgh, 1967-68; Missionary, Church of Scotland, working as Cardiologist at Christian Medical College Hospital, Vellore, India, 1968-73; Senior Registrar, Glasgow Teaching Hospitals, 1974-78. Elder, Killermont Parish Church; Council Member, Interserve, Scotland.

Recreations: DIY; gardening. Address: (h.) 8 Durness Avenue, Bearsden, Glasgow, G61 2AQ; T.-041-942 7330.

Macartney, W.J. Allan, MA, BLitt, PhD. Member of the European Parliament for North East Scotland, since 1994; Staff Tutor, Social Sciences, The Open University in Scotland, 1975-94; Honorary Fellow, Edinburgh University, since 1981; Member, National Executive Committee, Scottish National Party, since 1984, Vice President, 1990-92, Senior Vice-Convener and Foreign Affairs Spokesperson, since 1992; b. 1941, Accra, Ghana; m., J.D. Anne Forsyth; 2 s.; 1 d. Educ. Elgin Academy; Tuebingen University; Marburg University; Edinburgh University; Glasgow University. Teacher, Eastern Nigeria, 1963-64; Lecturer, University of Botswana, Lesotho and Swaziland, 1966-74; Executive Member, Unit for the Study of Government in Scotland, Scottish Self-Government College, Saint Andrew Society; Church of Scotland Elder, since 1979; Member, Church and Nation Committee, since 1989; Chairman, National Flag Trust, since 1991; Parliamentary candidate (SNP), 1970, 1979, 1983, 1987 (International Relations Spokesperson, 1982-91, Agriculture, Forestry, Fisheries and Rural Affairs, 1991-92); Euro candidate, 1989; President, UN Association (Edinburgh), since 1991. Publications: Readings in Boleswa Government, 1971; The Referendum Experience, 1981; Islands of Europe, 1984; Self-Determination in the Commonwealth, 1987; Towards 1992, 1989; Asking the People, 1992. Recreations: music; languages; walking; vexillology. Address: (b.) 70 Rosemount Place, Aberdeen, AB2 4XJ; T.-01224 623150.

MacAskill, Norman Alexander, OBE, JP. Vice-Chairman, Crofters Commission, 1966-86; b. 1.11.24, Lochinver; m., Joan Logan Brown; 2 s. Educ. Lochinver Public School; Golspie High School. Customs and Excise Officer; Social Welfare Officer, North West Sutherland; former Secretary, North and West Sutherland Council of Social Service; former Chairman, Sutherland Tourist Organisation. Recreations: fishing; music; history; archaeology. Address: (h.) 8 Cruamer, Lochinver, Lairg, Sutherland; T.-0571 844291.

McAulay, Alexander Davidson, BA. Headteacher, Leith Academy, since 1995; b. 30.4.53, Aberdeen; m., Linda Margaret; 1 s.; 1 d. Educ. Stirling University. Began teaching career, Firrhill High; Principal Teacher of Business Studies, Tynecastle High; Depute Regional Co-ordinator, TVEI; Regional Co-ordinator; Depute Headteacher, Forrester High. Recreations: football; music. Address: (b.) 20 Academy Park, Edinburgh; T.-0131-554 0606.

Macaulay, Rev. Donald, OBE, JP. Former Minister, Park, Isle of Lewis; former Convener, Western Isles Council; b. 25.2.26, Great Bernera; m., Catherine Macleod; 3 s.; 3 d. Educ. Great Bernera School; Aberdeen University. Several years a fisherman; Member: Ross and Cromarty County Council, 1969-75, Lewis District Council, 1969-75; Member, COSLA Policy Committee, 1975-82; Director, Western Isles Enterprise. Recreations: fishing; travel; local history; silviculture. Address: Garymilis, Great Bernera, Isle of Lewis; T.-01851 612341.

MacAulay, Professor Donald, MA, BA, DipGenLing. Professor of Celtic, Glasgow University, since 1991; b. 21.5.30, Isle of Lewis; m., Ella Murray Sangster; 1 s.; 1 d. Educ. Nicolson Institute, Stornoway; Aberdeen University; Cambridge University. Lecturer in English Language, Edinburgh University, 1957-60; Lecturer in Irish and Scottish Gaelic, Trinity College, Dublin, 1960-63; Lecturer in Applied Linguistics, Edinburgh University, 1963-67; Senior Lecturer in Celtic, then Reader in Celtic, Aberdeen University, 1967-91. Chairman, Gaelic Books Council; Chairman of Governors, Catherine McCaig's Trust. Publications: Seobhrach as a' Chlaich; Nua-bhardachd

Ghaidhlig; The Celtic Languages. Recreations: poetry; surviving. Address: (b.) Department of Celtic, Glasgow University, Glasgow, G12 8QQ; T.-0141-330 4222.

Macaulay of Bragar, Rt. Hon. Lord (Donald Macaulay), QC. Advocate, 1963; QC (Scot), 1975; Life Peer, since 1989. Address: (b.) Advocates' Library, Parliament House, Edinburgh, EH1 1RF.

McAvoy, Peter, BA (Hons). Headteacher, Islay High School, since 1994; b. 14.10.57, Paisley; m., Anne Todd; 1 s.; 1 d. Educ. St. Mirin's Academy, Paisley; Paisley College; Jordanhill College. Teacher of Modern Studies/Economics, Strathclyde Region, 1979-84; Principal Teacher, Staff Tutor, Assistant Headteacher, Adviser in Social Subjects, Tayside Region, 1984-94. Past Chairman, Modern Studies Association. Recreations: football; fantasy fitness training. Address: (h.) Port Charlotte Schoolhouse, Port Charlotte, Island of Islay, Argyllshire; T.-01496 850 353.

McAvoy, Thomas McLaughlin. MP (Labour and Co-operative), Glasgow Rutherglen, since 1987; b. 14.12.43, Rutherglen; m., Eleanor Kerr; 4 s. Member, Strathclyde Regional Council, 1982-87; an Opposition Chief Whip, 1990-93. Address: (b.) House of Commons, London, SW1A 0AA.

McBain, Ian G. Director, Scottish Council for Spastics. Address: (b.) 22 Corstorphine Road, Edinburgh, EH12 6HP.

McBryde, Professor William Wilson, LLB, PhD, LLD, FRSE. Professor of Scots Law, Dundee University, since 1987, Deputy and Vice Principal, 1991-94; Solicitor, since 1969; b. 6.7.45, Perth; m., Joyce Margaret Gossip; 1 s; 2 d. Educ. Perth Academy; Edinburgh University. Apprentice and Assistant, Morton, Smart, Macdonald & Milligan, WS, Edinburgh, 1967-70; Court Procurator, Biggart, Lumsden & Co., Glasgow, 1970-72; Lecturer in Private Law, Glasgow University, 1972-76; Member, Scottish Law Commission Working Party on Contract Law, since 1975; Senior Lecturer in Private Law, Aberdeen University, 1976-87; Specialist Parliamentary Adviser to House of Lords Select Committee on the European Communities, 1980-83; Member, Scottish Consumer Council, 1984-87; Member, Scottish Advisory Committee on Arbitration, since 1986; Director, Scottish Universities' Law Institute, since 1989; Honorary Sheriff, Tayside, Central and Fife, at Dundee, since 1991; Member, DTI Working Party on Rights in Security over Moveables, since 1994. Recreations: walking; photography. Address: (b.) Faculty of Law, Dundee University, Dundee, DD1 4HN; T.-01382 23181.

McBurnie, Gavin John, MB, ChB, MBA, DRCOG, MHSM. Director, Primary Care, Fife Health Board, since 1994; b. 9.9.59, Edinburgh; m., Doreen Elizabeth; 3 s. Educ. Royal High School, Edinburgh; Glasgow University; Edinburgh University. Junior doctor, 1982-86; general medical practitioner, 1986-91; Assistant Director, Strategic Planning and Contracts, 1993-94. Recreations: rugby union; r. and b. Address: (h.) 25 Ferryfield, Cupar, Fife; T.-01334 656572.

McCabe, Primrose Smith, CA. Partner, Primrose McCabe & Co., CA, Linlithgow, since 1987; President, Institute of Chartered Accountants of Scotland, 1994-95; Member, Commission for Local Authority Accounts, 1988-92; Non-executive Director, Dunfermline Building Society, since 1990; Honorary Treasurer, Hospitality Industry Trust Scotland, since 1994; b. 21.9.40, Gorebridge; m., Ernest Henry Elfred McCabe. Educ. Ayr Academy. Trained CA, Stewart Gilmour & Co., Ayr, 1958-63; joined Romanes & Munro as Qualified Assistant, 1963; progressed through manager ranks to Partner, Deloitte Haskins & Sells, 1981; Hon. Treasurer, YWCA, seven years until 1987; set up own practice, 1987; first Convener, General Practitioners

Committee, ICAS. Recreations: walking dogs; dress-making. Address: (b.) Regent House, Regent Centre, Linlithgow, EH49 7HU; T.-01506 842466.

McCabe, Thomas. Leader, South Lanarkshire Council, since 1995; Leader, Hamilton District Council, since 1992; b. 28.4.54, Hamilton. Educ. St. Martin's Secondary; Bell College of Technology. Senior shop steward, Hoover Ltd., 1974-93; welfare rights officer, since 1993. Recreations: walking; reading; gardening; cinema. Address: (b.) South Lanarkshire Council, Council Offices, Almada Street, Hamilton, ML3 0AA; T.-01698 454192.

MacCaig, Norman, OBE, MA, DLitt (Edinburgh), DUniv (Stirling), Lld (Dundee), FRSE, FRSC, ARSA. Poet; b. 14.11.10, Edinburgh; m., Isabel; 1 s.; 1 d. Educ. Royal High School, Edinburgh; Edinburgh University. Former schoolteacher; former Writer in Residence, Edinburgh University; former Reader in Poetry, Stirling University; publications of poetry: Far Cry, 1943, The Inward Eye, 1946, Riding Lights, 1955, The Sinai Sort, 1957, A Common Grace, 1960, A Round of Applause, 1962, Measures, 1965, Surroundings, 1966, Rings on a Tree, 1968, A Man in my Position, 1969, The White Bird, 1973, The World's Room, 1974, Tree of Strings, 1977, The Equal Skies, 1980, A World of Difference, 1983; Selected Poems, 1971; Penguin Modern Poets 21, 1972; Old Maps and New selected poems), 1978; Collected Poems, 1985; Voice-over, 1988; Collected Poems (paperback), 1988; New Collected Poems, 1990; Queen's Gold Medal for Poetry, 1986; eight Scottish Arts Council awards, two Society of Authors awards; Heinemann Award, Cholmondely Award. Recreations: literature; music; fishing. Address: 7 Leamington Terrace, Edinburgh, EH10 4JW; T.-0131-229 809.

McCall, Professor James, BSc, MEd, PhD, CPsychol, AFBPsS, FRSA. Professor and Dean, Faculty of Education, Strathclyde University, since 1993; b. 14.7.41, Kilmarnock; m., Mary Elizabeth Stuart Maclean; 3 s. Educ. Kilmarnock Academy; Glasgow University; Aberdeen University; Jordanhill College of Education. Teacher of Science, Hillhead High School, Glasgow; Principal Teacher of Physics, Queen's Park Secondary School, Glasgow; Lecturer in Educational Psychology, Aberdeen College of Education; Head, Psychology Department, Jordanhill College of Education;Vice Principal, Jordanhill College of Education, 1983-92, Acting Principal, 1992-93; Member, Board of Governors, Glasgow School of Art, since 1986; Member, CNAA Committee on Teacher Education, 1989-92; Member, General Teaching Council for Scotland, since 1992. Publications: Techniques for the Assessment of Practical Skills in Foundation Science, 1983; Techniques for Assessing Process Skills in Practical Science, 1988; Teacher Education in Europe, 1990; How to assess open-ended practical investigations in Biology, Chemistry and Physics, 1991. Recreations: bridge; golf. Address: (b.) Jordanhill Campus, Strathclyde University, Southbrae Drive, Glasgow, G13 1PP; T.-0141-950 3200.

McCall, Kathleen Mary, DL, LRAM. Deputy Lieutenant for Borders Region, District of Tweeddale, since 1988; Patron, Tweeddale Branch, British Red Cross Society, since 1993; b. 20.2.33, Karachi; m., J.A.G. McCall, CMG. Educ. Calder Girls' School, Seascale; Royal Scottish Academy of Music and Drama. Held various teaching posts; voluntary offices with Red Cross in Nigeria. Recreations: music; walking; the arts. Address: (h.) Burnside, West Linton, EH46 7EW; T.-01968 660488.

McCall-Smith, Professor Alexander, LLB, PhD. Professor, Faculty of Law, Edinburgh University; Author; b. 24.8.48, Zimbabwe; m., Dr. Elizabeth Parry; 2 d. Educ. Christian Brothers' College, Bulawayo; Edinburgh University. Lecturer, Queen's University, Belfast, 1973-74; Head, Department of Law, University of Botswana, 1981;

Professor of Law, Southern Methodist University, Dallas, Texas, 1988. Publications: (non-fiction): Law and Medical Ethics (Co-author); Butterworth's Medico-Legal Encyclopaedia (Co-author); Scots Criminal Law (Co-author); The Criminal Law of Botswana; fiction: Children of Wax; Heavenly Date; numerous books for children. Recreation: wind instruments. Address: (h.) 16A Napier Road, Edinburgh, EH10 5AY; T.-0131-229 6083.

MacCallum, Alasdair Norman, BSc (Hons). Chief Executive, Don & Low Holdings, since 1986; Non-Executive Chairman, Lassalle Engineering Ltd.; Director, Hamish Morison Ltd., Vico Properties PLC; b. 27.1.36, Connel, Argyll; m., Helga Diana; 1 s.; 1 d. Educ. Keil School; Glasgow University. National Service Commission, Royal Artillery; Unilever, six years; Culter Guard Bridge Paper Co. Ltd., seven years; Devro Ltd. (Production Director, Managing Director), 14 years; Baxters of Fochabers (Managing Director), one year. Chairman, Montrose Harbour Trust; Chairman, CBI Scotland, 1991-93; Governor, Scottish Crop Research Institute; Fellow, Dundee Institute of Technology. Recreations: angling; shooting; gardening; theatre; music; reading. Address: (h.) Inverossie, Rossie Braes, Montrose, DD10 9TJ; T.-0674 673013.

McCallum, Sir Donald Murdo, CBE, DL, BSc, DSc, LLD, DUniv, FEng, FIEE, FRAeS, CBIM, FRSE, FScotVec, FRSGS. Chairman, Scottish Council Development and Industry, 1985-91, President, 1991-93; Chairman, Laser Ecosse Ltd., since 1990; b. 6.8.22, Edinburgh; m., 1, Barbara Black (deceased); 1 d.; 2, Margaret Illingworth (nee Broadbent). Educ. George Watson's Boys' College; Edinburgh University. Admiralty Signal Establishment, 1942-46; Standard Telecommunication Laboratories, 1946; joined Ferranti, 1947; General Manager, Ferranti Scottish Group, 1968-85; Director, Ferranti plc, 1970-87; Chairman, Scottish Tertiary Education Advisory Council, 1984-87; Chairman, Scottish Committee, Universities Funding Council, 1989-91; Trustee, National Library of Scotland; Member, Court, Napier University; Governor, Edinburgh College of Art, 1987-93; Member, Scottish Economic Council, 1983-91. Recreations: fishing; photography. Address: (h.) 46 Heriot Row, Edinburgh, EH3 6EX; T.-0131-225 9331.

MacCallum, Professor James Richard, BSc, PhD, DSc, CChem, FRSC, FRSE. Professor of Polymer Chemistry, St. Andrews University (Vice-Principal, since 1992); b. 3.5.36, Kilmartin; m., Eleanor Margaret Thomson; 2 s.; 1 d. Educ. Dumfries Academy; Glasgow University. Technical Officer, ICI Fibres Division, 1961-62; ICI Research Fellow, Aberdeen University, 1962-63; Lecturer, St. Andrews University, 1964; Master, United College, 1988-92. Elder, St. Leonards Church, St. Andrews. Recreation: golf. Address: (h.) 9 Cairnsden Gardens, St. Andrews, Fife; T.-01334 473152.

MacCallum, Neil Robb. Poet, Critic and Editor; Convener, Edinburgh Branch, Scots Language Society, since 1995 (Preses of the Society, 1993-95); Committee Member, Poetry Association of Scotland, since 1995; Committee Member, Scottish Poetry Library, 1989-95; Vice-Convener, Scots Language Society Resource Centre, 1993-95; b. 15.5.54, Edinburgh. Educ. Firrhill High School; Napier College, Edinburgh. Lothian Health Board, 1973-87; Edinburgh City Councillor, 1977-80; Assistant National Secretary, SNP, 1980-81, National Secretary, 1981-86; Arts Columnist, Scots Independent; Poetry Critic, Scottish Book Collector; Editor, Scots Glasnost. Publications: Report of the SNP Commission of Inquiry (Editor), 1984; Portrait of a Calvinist, 1991; Mak It New (Co-Editor), 1995. Recreations: reading; theatre; fitness and weight-training; running. Address: (h.) 18 Redford Avenue, Edinburgh, EH13 0BU; T.-0131-441 3724.

Maccallum, Professor Norman Ronald Low, BSc, PhD, CEng, FIMechE. Professor, Department of Mechanical Engineering, Glasgow University, since 1992; b. 18.2.31, Walston, Lanarkshire; m., Mary Bentley Alexander; 1 s.; 2 d. Educ. Allan Glen's School, Glasgow; Glasgow University. Assistant in Mechanical Engineering, Glasgow University, 1952-55; National Service, Royal Navy, 1955-57 (final rank: Sub-Lt.); Lecturer in Mechanical Engineering, Glasgow University, 1957-61; Performance Engineer, Rolls-Royce Ltd. (Scottish Group), 1961-62; Lecturer in Mechanical Engineering/Senior Lecturer/Reader, Glasgow University, 1962-92. Joint Session Clerk, Trinity St. Paul's Church, Cambuslang. Recreation: singing. Address: (h.) 43 Stewarton Drive, Cambuslang, Glasgow, G72 8DQ.

McCann, Fergus John, MBA, CA. Chairman and Managing Director, Celtic plc; b. Stirling; moved to Canada 1963 to work for Touche Ross & Co.; financial executive posts: Cott Beverages (Canada) Ltd., Distillers Corporation Seagrams Limited, Pretty Polly Canada Ltd.; founded International Golf Inc., Montreal, 1973; joined Board, Celtic Football Club, 1994. Address: (b.) 95 Kerrydale Street, Glasgow, G40 3RE.

McCann, James Aloysius, MA, LLB. Solicitor and Notary Public; a founding Director, Legal Defence Union in Scotland, 1987, Chairman, since 1990; b. 14.8.39, Glasgow; m., Jane Marlow; 3 s.; 1 d. Educ. St. Mungo's Academy, Glasgow; Glasgow University. Former Member, Legal Aid Central Committee; Dean, Faculty of Dunbartonshire Solicitors, 1986-88; Convenor for Law Society PQLE Advocacy Training Courses, 1983-91; Senior Tutor (Professional Legal Practice), Glasgow University, 1981-91; Member, Law Society of Scotland Legal Aid Committee; Reporter, Scottish Legal Aid Board (Co-opted Member, Criminal Applications Committee, 1987-93); appointed Honorary Sheriff at Dumbarton, 1990; commission as Temporary Sheriff, 1991. Recreations: sailing/windsurfing; chess; music. Address: (b.) 499 Kilbowie Road, Clydebank, G81 2AX.

McCann, Peter Toland McAree, CBE (1977), OStJ, DL, JP, BL. Solicitor and Notary Public, since 1947; b. 2.8.24, Glasgow; m., Maura Eleanor Ferris; 1 s. Educ. St. Mungo's Academy, Glasgow; Glasgow University. Councillor, Corporation of Glasgow, 1961-75; River Bailie, 1962; Magistrate, 1963-66; Police Judge, 1967-74; JP, since 1967; Lord Lieutenant, 1975-77; Lord Provost, City of Glasgow District, 1975-77; Depute Lieutenant, since 1977; Chairman, St. Thomas More Society for Lawyers, 1960; Chairman, McCann Committee for Provision of Secondary Education for Physically Disabled Children, 1968; awarded two Golden Swords from HRH Prince Fawaz of Saudi Arabia, 1977-78; awarded Silver and Golden Swords from City of Jeddah, 1975-78; awarded Medal of King Faisal of Saudi Arabia, 1976. Recreations: music; history; model railways; collecting model cars and model soldiers. Address: (h.) Craig En Ross, 31 Queen Mary Avenue, Crosshill, Glasgow, G42 8DS.

McCarrison, Robert, BSc, CBiol, FIBiol, FRSA. Rector, Marr College, Troon, since 1978; b. 3.11.37, Oxford; m., Janet M. Gibson; 1 s.; 1 d. Educ. Ayr Academy; Glasgow University; Institute of Biology. Assistant Science Teacher, Principal Teacher (Biology), Assistant Rector, Cumnock Academy, 1959-76; Depute Rector, James Hamilton Academy, Kilmarnock, 1976-78. Past President: Ayrshire Science Teachers Association, Ayrshire Biology Panel, Rotary Club of Troon; Treasurer, Kingcase Parish Church, Prestwick; President, Headteachers' Association of Scotland, 1994-95. Recreations: golf (Prestwick St. Nicholas). Address: (b.) Marr College, Dundonald Road, Troon; T.-01292 311082.

McCarthy, James, BSc, FRZSS (Hon). Lecturer/Conservation Consultant; Deputy Director (Scotland), Nature Conservancy Council, 1975-91; b. 6.5.36, Dundee; m.; 2 s.; 1 d. Educ. Harris Academy, Dundee; Aberdeen University; University of East Africa, Kampala. Military Service, 1954-56 (Royal Marines commissioned Black Watch, seconded King's African Rifles); Leverhulme Scholar, Makerere College, Kampala, 1959-61; Assistant Conservator of Forests, Tanzania, and Lecturer in Forest Ecology, Forest Training School, 1961-63; Deputy Regional Officer (North England), Nature Conservancy, 1963-69. Churchill Fellow, USA, 1976; Nuffield/Leverhulme Fellow, 1988. Recreation: cross-country skiing. Address: (h.) 6a Ettrick Road, Edinburgh; T.-0131-229 1916.

McClellan, John Forrest, MA, Hon. FDIT. Director, Scottish International Education Trust, since 1986; Member, Management Committee, Hanover (Scotland) Housing Association, since 1986; b. 15.8.32, Glasgow; m., Eva Maria Pressel; 3 s.; 1 d. Educ. Aberdeen Grammar School; Aberdeen University. 2nd Lt., Gordon Highlanders and Nigeria Regiment, Royal West African Frontier Force, 1954-56; entered Civil Service, 1956; Assistant Principal, Scottish Education Department, 1956-59; Private Secretary to Permanent Under Secretary of State, Scottish Office, 1959-60; Principal, Scottish Education Department, 1960-68; Civil Service Fellow, Glasgow University, 1968-69; Scottish Education Department: Assistant Secretary, Schools Division, 1969-71; Assistant Secretary, Higher Education Division, 1971-77; Assistant Under Secretary of State, Scottish Office, 1977-80; Under Secretary, Industry Department for Scotland, 1980-85 (retired). Publication: Then A Soldier (novel), 1991. Recreations: gardening; walking. Address: (h.) Grangeneuk, West Linton, Peeblesshire; T.-West Linton 60502.

McClelland, Professor John Ferguson, CBE, CIMgt, FRSA, FRSE. Vice-President, Worldwide Manufacturing, Digital Corporation, since 1995; Visiting Professor and Fellow, Paisley University, since 1993; Main Board Member, Digital UK Ltd., since 1995; b. 27.3.45, Glasgow; m., Alice; 1 d. Educ. North Kelvinside School; Glasgow College. South of Scotland Electricity Board, 1963-68; IBM Corporation, 1968-95: Controller, Greenock Manufacturing, 1977, European Director of Operations, 1980, European Manufacturing Controller, 1983, Director of Manufacturing, Greenock, 1987, Director of UK Manufacturing, 1992, Vice-President, Worldwide Manufacturing, 1994. Chairman, Judging Panel, Quality Scotland Excellence Award; Member, Scottish Higher Education Funding Council; Chairman, CBI UK Technology and Innovation Committee. Recreations: golf; football; gardening. Address: (b.) Digital Ltd., Crompton Way, Irvine, KA11 4DY; T.-01294 203162.

McClements, Rev. Duncan Elliott, MA (Hons), BD (Hons), MTh. Parish Minister, Falkirk Grahamston United since 1976; Clerk, Falkirk Presbytery, since 1989; Convener, Committee on Ecumenical Affairs, Church of Scotland, since 1994; b. 28.8.40, Glasgow; m., Dorothy Jean Easton; 1 s.; 1 d. Educ. Daniel Stewart's College; Edinburgh University. Assistant Minister, Carrick Knowe Parish, Edinburgh, 1965-66; Parish Minister, Hurlford Reid Memorial, 1966-76. Sometime Chairman, Kirk Care Housing Association; Secretary, Editorial Board, Contact (pastoral studies journal). Recreations: gardening; reading; watching sport; Rotary. Address: 30 Russel Street, Falkirk, FK2 7HS; T.-01324 624461.

McClure, Judith, MA (Oxon), DPhil, FSAScot. Head, St. George's School, Edinburgh, since 1994; b. 22.12.45, Stockton; m., Dr. Roger Collins. Educ. Newlands Grammar School, Middlesbrough; Somerville College, Oxford. Sir Maurice Powicke Research Fellow, Lady Margaret Hall, Oxford, 1976-77; Lecturer in Medieval Latin and Medieval History, Liverpool University, 1977-79; Lecturer in

History, Oxford University (Jesus, Somerville and Worcester Colleges), 1979-81; Teacher and Head of Department in History and Politics, School of St. Helen & St. Katherine, Abingdon, 1981-84; Deputy Head, Kingswood School, Bath, 1984-87; Head, Royal School, Bath, 1987-93. Member, Court, University of Bath, 1989-92; Member, General Convocation, Heriot Watt University, since 1994; Member, Board of Governors, Clifton Hall School, since 1995; Member, Governing Body, Scottish Council of Independent Schools, since 1995. Publication: Bede: The Ecclesiastical History (Co-author), 1994. Recreations: reading; using a computer; travelling. Address: (b.) St. George's School for Girls, Garscube Terrace, Edinburgh, EH12 6BG; T.-031-332 4575.

McCluskey, Baron (John Herbert McCluskey), LLD (Dundee). Senator of the College of Justice in Scotland, since 1984; Life Peer, since 1976; b. 12.6.29, Glasgow; m., Ruth Friedland; 2 s.; 1 d. Educ. St. Bede's Grammar School, Manchester; Holy Cross Academy, Edinburgh; Edinburgh University; MA, LLB. Admitted Faculty of Advocates, 1955; Standing Junior Counsel to Ministry of Power (Scotland), 1963; Advocate-Depute, 1964-71; QC (Scot), 1967; Chairman, Medical Appeal Tribunals for Scotland, 1972-74; Sheriff Principal of Dumfries and Galloway, 1973-74; Solicitor General for Scotland, 1974-79. Chairman, Scottish Association for Mental Health, 1985-94; Independent Chairman: Scottish Football League Compensation Tribunal, SFA Appeals Tribunal; Reith Lecturer, BBC, 1986; Editor, Butterworth's Scottish Criminal Law and Practice series. Publications: Law, Justice and Democracy, 1987; Criminal Appeals, 1992. Recreations: tennis; pianoforte. Address: (b.) Court of Session, Parliament House, Edinburgh, EH1 1RF; T.-0131-225 2595.

McCoist, Ally. Footballer; b. 1962, Bellshill. Debut for St. Johnstone aged 16; signed for Sunderland, 1981; joined Rangers, 1983; became club's leading post-war league goal-scorer. First capped for Scotland, 1986.

McColgan, Elizabeth. Athlete; b. 24.5.64, Dundee; m., Peter Conor McColgan. Educ. University of Alabama. Commonwealth Games Gold medallist (10,000 metres), 1986; Silver medallist, World Cross-Country Championships, 1987; Olympic Games Silver medallist (10,000 metres), 1988; Silver medallist, World Indoor Championships, 1989; Gold medallist (10,000 metres) and Bronze medallist (3,000 metres), Commonwealth Games, 1990.

McColl, James Hamilton, NDH, SDH, SHM. Horticulturalist; b. 19.9.35, Kilmarnock; m., Billie; 1 s.; 1 d. Educ. Kilmarnock Academy; West of Scotland Agricultural College. Staff Member, WSAC, Auchincruive, Ayr, 1956-59; Assistant Head Gardener, Reading University Botanic Garden, 1959-61; Horticultural Adviser/Lecturer, Shropshire Education Authority, 1961-67; Horticultural Adviser: MAFF, Leicestershire, Northants and Rutland, 1967-73, North of Scotland College of Agriculture, 1973-78; PRO, Morrison Bowmore Distillers Ltd.; Co-Presenter, The Beechgrove Garden, BBC TV Scotland, 1978-89, since 1994; former Trustee, Royal Botanic Gardens, Edinburgh. Recreations: golf; music; rugby. Address: (h.) Ayrshire House, Oldmeldrum, Aberdeenshire; T.-01651 873955.

McCombie, John, FRICS, IRRV. General Manager, Glenrothes Development Corporation. Address: (b.) Balgonie Road, Markinch, Glenrothes, KY7 6AH.

McConnell, Charles Stephen, BA (Hons), MPhil. Executive Director, Scottish Community Education Council, since 1993; Board Member, International Association for Community Development, since 1990; b. 20.6.51, Harrogate. Educ. Huyton Hill School, Ambleside; Granby Park School, Harrogate; City of Birmingham Polytechnic; Paisley College of Technology. Community Educator; Lecturer in Community Studies, Clydebank Technical College; Action Researcher, Community Education, Scottish Local Government Unit; Lecturer in Community Education, Dundee College of Education; Senior Policy Development Officer, National Consumer Council; Development Director, Action Resource Centre; Public and European Affairs Director, Community Development Foundation. Publications: Community Worker as Politiciser of the Deprived; Deprivation, Participation and Community Action; Community Education and Community Development; Post 16 — Developments in Continuing Education in Scotland; Classroom Commercials — business sponsorship of education; Consumer Action and Community Development; Community Development — the European dimension; A Citizen's Europe; Promoting Community Development in Europe; Community Development and Urban Regeneration; Community Education in Scotland – A Reader. Recreations: fell-walking; reading political biography. Address: (b.) Rosebery House, 9 Haymarket Terrace, Edinburgh, EH12 5EZ; T.-0131-313 2488.

McConnell, Jack Wilson, BSc, DipEd. General Secretary, Scottish Labour Party, since 1992; b. 30.6.60, Irvine; m., Bridget; 1 s.; 1 d. Educ. Arran High School; Stirling University. Mathematics Teacher, Lornshill Academy, 1983-92; Member, Stirling District Council, 1984-92, Council Leader, 1990-92, Treasurer, 1988-92, Chair, Leisure and Recreation Committee, 1986-88, Equal Opportunities Committee, 1986-90; President, 1980-82, Hon. President, 1991-93, Stirling University Students Association; Chair, Board of Directors, Stirling Windows Ltd., 1988-92; Member, Labour Party Scottish Executive Committee, 1989-92; Parliamentary candidate, Perth and Kinross, 1987. Publication: Proposals for Scottish Democracy, 1989. Address: (h.) 10a Argyll Avenue, Stirling, FK8 1UL; T.-01786 479470.

McConnell, Walter Scott, OBE, FRPharmS, PhC. Community Pharmacist, since 1962; Vice Chairman, Ayrshire and Arran Community Health Care Trust; Chairman, Advisory Committee on Prisoner Management, Scottish Prison Service; Member, Local Review Committee, HM Prison, Dungavel; b. 7.4.36, Kilmarnock; m.; 1 s.; 3 d. Educ. Kilmarnock Academy; Royal Technical College, Glasgow. Former Chairman, Pharmaceutical General Council (Scotland). Recreations: curling; golf. Address: (h.) 27 Mauchline Road, Hurlford, Kilmarnock, KA1 5AB; T.-01563 525393.

McCool, Thomas Joseph, CBE, BSc (Hons), HonDEd, FRSA. Chief Executive, Scottish Vocational Education Council, since 1986; b. 1.3.39, Bellshill; m., Anne McGurk; 2 d. Educ. Our Lady's High School, Motherwell; Glasgow University; Jordanhill College of Education. Various teaching appointments, 1961-71; Assistant Director of Education, then Depute Director, Renfrewshire, 1971-76; Divisional Education Officer, Renfrew Division, Strathclyde, 1976-86. Member, Munn Committee, 1975-78; Member, Scottish Certificate of Education Examination Board, 1978-86; Chairman, Scottish Central Committee on Guidance, 1981-86; Member, SCDI Policy Review Committee, 1990-92; Member, Educational Broadcasting Council for Scotland, 1988-92; Member, Universities' Funding Council — Scottish Committee, 1989-92; Member, CBI (Scotland) Training Committee, 1990-92; Member, CNAA Committee for Scotland, 1986-92; Member, National Forum for Management Education and Development, since 1989; Member, Open University Validation Board, since 1993; Member, CBI Standing Education and Training Committee, since 1995; Trustee, Kibble Education and Care Centre, since 1993; Governor, Scottish Council for Educational Technology, since 1994. Recreations: golf; walking. Address: (b.) Hanover House, Douglas Street, Glasgow, G2 7NQ; T.-0141-242 2052.

MacCormack, Professor Geoffrey Dennis, BA, LLB, MA, DPhil. Professor of Jurisprudence, Aberdeen University, since 1971; b. 15.4.37, Canterbury; 1 d. Educ. Parramatta High School, Sydney; Sydney University; Oxford University. Recreation: walking. Address: (b.) Department of Jurisprudence, Aberdeen University, Aberdeen; T.-01224 27 2418.

McCormack, Ian Andrew. Editor, West Highland Free Press, since 1976; b. 5.2.48, Kilmarnock; 2 d. Educ. Kilmarnock Academy. Trainee Journalist, Evening Times, Glasgow, 1965, Kilmarnock Standard, 1966-67; Reporter, Glasgow Herald, 1968-69; joined West Highland Free Press, 1975. Address: (b.) Broadford, Isle of Skye; T.-01471 822464.

McCormack, Jean Elizabeth Wallace, JP. Provost, Perth and Kinross District Council, since 1992; b. 13.6.38, Duundee; m., Peter McCormack; 1 s.; 1 d. Educ. Harris Academy, Dundee; Dundee College of Education. Address: (b.) Council Chambers, 2 High Street, Perth, PH1 5PH; T.-01738 39911.

MacCormick, Donald, MA. Broadcasting Journalist; b. 16.4.39, Glasgow; m., Elizabeth Elton; 3 s.; 2 d. Educ. King's Park Secondary School, Glasgow; Glasgow University. Reporter/Presenter: Grampian TV, 1968-70, BBC Scotland, 1970-75, BBC1 Tonight, 1975-79, BBC2 Newsnight, 1981-89; Deputising Chairman, BBC1 Question Time, 1985; Presenter, LWT/ITV Special Inquiry, 1990-92; Presenter, political programmes, Scottish TV, since 1992; Presenter, BBC World (international news channel), since 1995. Address: (b.) Scottish Television plc, Cowcaddens, Glasgow, G2 3PR; T.-0141-332 9999.

MacCormick, Professor (Donald) Neil, MA, LLD, Hon. LLD (Uppsala), HonLLD (Saarland), FRSE, FBA. Regius Professor of Public Law, Edinburgh University, since 1972; Vice President, International Association for Legal and Social Philosophy, 1991-95; Vice President, Royal Society of Edinburgh, 1991-94; b. 27.5.41, Glasgow; m., 1, Karen (Caroline) Rona Barr (m. diss.); 3 d.; 2, Flora Margaret Britain. Educ. High School of Glasgow; Glasgow University; Balliol College, Oxford. Lecturer in Jurisprudence, Queen's College, Dundee, 1965-67; Fellow, Balliol College, Oxford, 1967-72; Oxford University: CUF Lecturer, 1968-72, Pro-Proctor, 1970-71; Dean, Faculty of Law, Edinburgh University, 1973-76 and 1985-88; Senate Assessor, University Court, 1982-85; Provost, Faculty Group of Law and Social Sciences, 1993-96; Member, Broadcasting Council for Scotland, 1985-89. President, Oxford Union, 1965; Executive Member, Scottish National Party, 1978-81, Council Member, 1978-84 and since 1989; Foreign Member, Finnish Academy of Science. Publications: as author or editor, books on philosophy of law, political philosophy, etc. Address: (h.) 19 Pentland Terrace, Edinburgh, EH10 6AA; T.-0131-447 7945.

McCormick, John, MA, MEd. Controller, BBC Scotland, since 1992; b. 24.6.44; m., Jean Frances Gibbons; 1 s.; 1 d. Educ. St. Michael's Academy, Irvine; Glasgow University. Former schoolteacher; joined BBC as Education Officer, 1970; Senior Education Officer, Scotland, 1975-82; Secretary and Head of Information, BBC Scotland, 1982-87; The Secretary of the BBC, 1987-92. Member, Glasgow Children's Panel, 1972-77; Visiting Committee, Glenochil Young Offenders' Institution, 1979-85; Vice-Chairman, Youth-At-Risk (Scotland); Director, Edinburgh Film Festival; Hon. President, Edinburgh International Television Festival; Hon. Joint Chairman, BAFTA Scotland. Recreations: theatre; cinema; biography; newspapers. Address: (b.) Broadcasting House, Queen Margaret Drive, Glasgow, G12 0TT; T.-0141-339 8844.

McCormick, John William Penfold, BSc, PhD. Chairman, Scottish Association for Public Transport, since 1988; Information Technology Manager, Weir Group Management Systems, since 1979; b. 9.6.46, Renfrew; m. Linda M.L.; 1 d. Educ. Paisley Grammar School; Glasgow University. Research Fellow, Glasgow University, 1971-74; computer management, since 1975. Recreations: hillwalking; transport; music. Address: (b.) 5 St. Vincent Place, Glasgow, G1 2HT; T.-0141-639 3697.

McCormick, Patrick. Chairperson, General Council Scottish TUC, 1995-96; Scottish Divisional Officer, USDAW, since 1985; Member, Industrial Tribunals, since 1986; b. 21.5.33, Greenock; m., May; 1 d. Educ. St. Columba's High School, Greenock. Recreations: photography; walking; music; DIY. Address: (b.) USDAW, 342 Albert Drive, Glasgow, G41 5PG; T.-0141-427 6561.

McCosh, Professor Andrew Macdonald, BSc, DBA, HonMBA, CA. Professor of the Organisation of Industry & Commerce, Edinburgh University, since 1986; b. 16.9.40, Glasgow; m., Anne; 3 d. Educ. Edinburgh Academy; Edinburgh University; Harvard University. Associate Professor of Accounting, University of Michigan, 1964-71; Research Assistant, Visiting Professor of Business Administration, Harvard Business School, 1964-75; Professor of Management Accounting, Manchester Business School, 1971-85. Recreations: mountaineering; fishing; golf. Address: (b.) Department of Business Studies, William Robertson Building, 50 George Square, Edinburgh, EH8 9JY; T.-0131-650 3801.

McCosh, James, LLB, DL. Solicitor, since 1976; b. 28.8.48, Irvine; m., Sheila Joan Loudon; 2 s. Educ. Wellington College; Dundee University. Deputy Lieutenant, since 1982; Secretary/Treasurer, Dalry Farmers Society. Address: (h.) Pitcon, Dalry, Ayrshire; T.-01294 835776.

McCourt, Arthur David, BSc (Hons). Chief Executive, Highland Council, since 1995; b. 11.7.47, Newburgh, Fife; m., Jan; 1 d. Educ. Bell-Baxter High School, Cupar; Edinburgh College of Art; Heriot-Watt University. Various posts with Northumberland County Council, Central Regional Council, Stirling District Council; Assistant Chief Executive, Tayside Regional Council, 1990-93. Recreation: mountaineering. Address: (b.) Regional Buildings, Glenurquhart Road, Inverness, IV3 5NX; T.-01463 702831.

McCrae, William Morrice, MB, ChB, FRCPE, FRCP(G). Consultant Physician, Royal Hospital for Sick Children, Edinburgh, 1965-91; Senior Lecturer, Department of Child Life and Health, Edinburgh University, 1965-91; b. 11.3.32, Hurlford; m., Jennifer Jane Graham. Educ. Kilmarnock Academy; Glasgow University. House Physician/House Surgeon, Royal Infirmary, Glasgow; Captain, RAMC; Hall Fellow in Medicine, Glasgow University; Lecturer, Department of Child Health, Glasgow University. Recreations: gardening; history. Address: (h.) Seabank House, Aberdour, Fife.

McCreadie, Robert Anderson, LLB, PhD, Advocate; b. 17.8.48, St. Andrews. Educ. Madras College, St. Andrews; Edinburgh University; Christ's College, Cambridge. Lecturer, Dundee University, 1974-78, Edinburgh University, 1978-93; called to Scottish Bar, 1992; Standing Junior Counsel, Department of Transport, 1994; Member: Scottish Consumer Council, 1977-82, Social Security Appeal Tribunals, 1987-92; Labour Parliamentary Candidate, Edinburgh South, 1983; joined Scottish Liberal Party, 1985; Parliamentary Candidate: Livingston, 1987, Glasgow Central, 1989, Edinburgh South, 1992; Vice Chairman, Scottish Liberal Democrats, 1988-92; Executive Committee, Scottish Constitutional Convention, 1989-82, Executive Committee, Child Poverty Action Group, 1974-76; Chairman, Scottish Legal Action Group, 1980-82; Fellow, British-American Project, 1985. Publication: You and Your Rights: An A to Z Guide to the Law in Scotland,

1984 (Joint Editor). Recreations: music; Scottish history; walking. Address: (h.) 40 Marchmont Crescent, Edinburgh EH9 1HG; T.-0131-667 1383.

McCreadie, Robin G., DSc, MD, FRCPsych. Director of Clinical Research, Crichton Royal Hospital, Dumfries, since 1982; Medical Commissioner, Mental Welfare Commission, Edinburgh, since 1994; b. 21.2.42, Troon; 2 d. Educ. Ayr Academy; Glasgow University. Lecturer in Psychological Medicine, Glasgow University; Consultant Psychiatrist, Gartnavel Royal Hospital, Glasgow. Recreations: hill-walking; all things Italian. Address: (b.) Crichton Royal Hospital, Dumfries; T.-01387 255301.

McCreath, Thomas Crawford, JP, DL. Farmer; b. 28.6.29, Whithorn; 3 s.; 1 d. Educ. Fettes College. Nuffield Farming Scholar, to New Zealand and Australia, 1956; farming, since 1948; Past Chairman, SWS Grassland Society and Milk Records Association; General Commissioner of Income Tax. Recreations: music; walking; sailing; trout fishing. Address: (h.) Garlieston Home Farm, Garlieston, Newton Stewart, DG8 8HF; T.-01988 600 267.

McCrone, Iain Alistair, CBE (1987), SDA. Farmer and Company Director; b. 29.3.34, Glasgow; m., Yvonne Findlay; 4 d. Educ. Glasgow Academy; Trinity College, Glenalmond; West of Scotland Agricultural College. Farming on own account, since 1956; Managing Director, McCrone Farmers Ltd., since 1958; began fish farming, 1968; Director, Highland Trout Co. (now Marine Harvest McConnell); Director, Otter Ferry Salmon Ltd., since 1974; Member, Fife Regional Council, 1978-82; Parliamentary candidate (Conservative), Central Fife, 1979; Council Member, National Farmers Union of Scotland, 1977-82; Board Member, Glenrothes Development Corporation, since 1980; Member, Fife Health Board, 1983-91; Nuffield Farming Scholar, 1966; President, Scottish Conservative and Unionist Association, 1985-87. Recreations: golf; rugby (spectator). Address: (h.) Cardsknolls, Markinch, Fife, KY7 6LP; T.-01337 830267.

McCrone, Professor Robert Gavin Loudon, CB, MA, MSc, PhD, LLD, FRSE. Visiting Professor, Department of Business Studies, since 1994, and Hon. Fellow of the Europa Institute, since 1992, Edinburgh University; Deputy Chairman, Royal Infirmary of Edinburgh NHS Trust, since 1994; Board Member, Scottish Opera, since 1992; b. 2.2.33, Ayr; m., Alexandra Bruce Waddell; 2 s.; 1 d. Educ. St. Catharine's College, Cambridge; University of Wales; Glasgow University. Fisons Ltd., 1959-60; Lecturer in Economics, Glasgow University, 1960-65; Fellow, Brasenose College, Oxford, .1965-70; Consultant, UNESCO, 1964; Member, NEDC Working Party on Agricultural Policy, 1967-68; Adviser, House of Commons Select Committee on Scottish Affairs, 1969-70; Senior Economic Adviser, Scottish Office, 1970-72; Under Secretary, 1972-80; Secretary, Industry Department for Scotland, 1980-87; Secretary, Scottish Office Environment Department, 1987-92; Chief Economic Adviser, Scottish Office, 1972-92. Council Member: Economic and Social Research Council, 1986-89, Royal Economic Society, 1977-82, Scottish Economic Society, 1982-91; Member, Advisory Committee, Inquiry into Implementation of Constitutional Reform, since 1995. Publications: The Economics of Subsidising Agriculture, 1962; Scotland's Economic Progress 1951-60, 1963; Regional Policy in Britain, 1969; Scotland's Future, 1969; Housing Policy in Britain and Europe (Co-author), 1995. Recreation: walking. Address: (b.) Department of Business Studies, Edinburgh University, 50 George Square, Edinburgh, EH8 9JY; T.-0131 650 4603.

McCrorie, Ian, BSc. Chorusmaster, Scottish Festival Singers, since 1991; Assistant Rector, Greenock Academy, since 1975; b. 6.5.41, Greenock; m., Olive Simpson Bolton; 2 s. Educ. Greenock Academy; Glasgow University.

Founded Toad Choir, Greenock, which appeared in numerous BBC Songs of Praise programmes (and won 1975 National Choral Competition, Royal Albert Hall, London); this choir became the nucleus of the Scottish Philharmonic Singers (1976-91); Organist and Choirmaster, Mid Kirk of Greenock, 1964-93; conducted at Festivals in France and Poland, and took SPS to Israel and the London Proms; Member, Greenock Presbytery, and Panel on Worship, General Assembly; Past President and Convener of Cruising, Clyde River Steamer Club; author of numerous books and articles on Clyde and West Highland steamers. Recreations: as above! Address: (h.) 72 Newton Street, Greenock; T.-01475 26689.

McCue, William, OBE (1982), LRAM, ARAM. Bass Singer; b. 17.8.34, Allanton, Shotts; m., Patricia Carrick; 1 d. Educ. Calderhead High School; Royal Scottish Academy of Music; Royal Academy of Music. Began professional singing career in 1960; his work has included opera, oratorio, recital, concert, cabaret, pantomime and stage musical, radio and TV; has travelled throughout the world, making numerous visits to USA, Canada, USSR, Iceland, Europe and Israel; has made various recordings of Scots songs and Negro spirituals; Director, Scottish Singers Company; Honorary Life Member, Saltire Society; former Member, Scottish Arts Council. Recreations: watching all sport; listening to all kinds of music; gardening; escaping to the Scottish countryside. Address: (h.) Sweethope House, Bothwell, Glasgow, G71 8BT; T.-01698 853241.

McCulloch, Professor Alistair John Andrew, BA (Hons), PhD. Professor of Public Administration, Robert Gordon University, since 1994; b. 4.8.50, Edinburgh; m., Gillian Elizabeth Reeves; 1 s.; 2 d. Educ. Queen Elizabeth Grammar School, Darlington; Huddersfield Polytechnic; Exeter University. Lecturer, Huddersfield Technical College; Researcher and Lecturer, Huddersfield Polytechnic; Lecturer, Robert Gordon Institute of Technology; Reader in Public Administration, Robert Gordon University. Editorial Board Member, Greener Management International; author of articles and reports on environmental politics, policy and management. Recreations: reading; music; travelling. Address: (b.) School of Public Administration and Law, Robert Gordon University, 352 King Street, Aberdeen; T.-01224 262909.

McCulloch, Ian, DA, ARSA. Painter and Printmaker; b. 4.3.35, Glasgow; m., Margery Palmer; 2 s. Educ. Eastbank Academy; Glasgow School of Art. Elected Member, Society of Scottish Artists, 1964; elected Associate, Royal Scottish Academy, 1989; paintings in many private and public collections; numerous one-man and group exhibitions; 1st prize, Stirling Smith Biennial, 1985; winner, Glasgow International Concert Hall Mural Competition, 1989-90; Fine Art Fellow, Strathclyde University, since 1994.. Recreation: university teaching. Address: (h.) 51 Victoria Road, Lenzie, Glasgow, G66 5AP; T.-0141-776 1053.

McCulloch, Professor James, BSc, PhD. Professor of Neuroscience, Glasgow University, since 1988; b. 7.4.51, Irvine; m., Mailis Christina; 2 s. Educ. Spiers School, Beith; Glasgow University. Lecturer, 1978-86, Reader, 1986-88, Glasgow University; Secretary, International Society for Cerebral Blood Flow and Metabolism, since 1989. Publications: four books; 180 scientific papers. Recreations: squash; skiing. Address: (b.) Glasgow University, Bearsden Road, Glasgow, G61 1QH; T.-0141-330 5828.

McCulloch, Margery Palmer, BA, MLitt, PhD, LRAM. University teacher and writer; m., Ian McCulloch; 2 s. Educ. Hamilton Academy; London University; Glasgow University. Convener, Glasgow Branch, Saltire Society. Publications: The Novels of Neil M. Gunn: a critical study, 1987; The Man Who Came Back: short stories and essays by Neil M. Gunn, 1991; Edwin Muir: poet, critic and novelist, 1993. Recreation: music. Address: (h.) 51 Victoria Road, Lenzie, Glasgow, G66 5AP; T.-0141-776 1053.

McCulloch, Tony, BSc, MEd, MA, FRSA. Rector, Charleston Academy, Inverness, since 1991; President, Highland Secondary Headteachers Association, since 1994; Convener, Friends of Balnain House, since 1993; b. 12.12.50, Glasgow; m., Anne C.; 1 s.; 1 d. Educ. St. Pius Secondary, Glasgow; University of Ulster; Edinburgh University; Open University. Taught in Glasgow, Cumbernauld, Edinburgh, and Armadale. Recreations: traditional music; mandolin. Address: (b.) Charleston Academy, Kinmylies, Inverness; T.-01463 234324.

McCunn, Archibald Eddington, OBE, BSc (Hons), CEng, MIMechE, FBIM. Hon. Vice-President, Scottish Salmon Growers Association; Board Member: State Hospital, Scottish Natural Heritage (South West); Trustee, Argyll and Bute Countryside Trust; b. 27.5.27, Motherwell; m., Olive Isobel Johnston; 1 s.; 1 d. Educ. Dalziel High School; Strathclyde University. Engineering management, Colvilles Ltd./ BSC, 1952-63; Senior Consultant, Inbucon/AIC, 1963-67; Divisional Chairman, Stenhouse Industries, 1967-71; Divisional Chairman/Consultant, Grampian Holdings plc, 1971-89; Board Member, Highlands and Islands Development Board, 1985-89; Director: A.E. McCunn Consultants Ltd., 1985-95, McConnell Salmon Ltd., 1990-94. Recreations:painting; music; walking; gardening. Address: (h.) 2 McIntosh Way, Motherwell, ML1 3BB; T.-01698 253500.

McDaid, Professor Seamus, CA, MBA. Professor of Accounting and Dean, Faculty of Business, Glasgow Caledonian University; b. 23.7.52, Glasgow; m., Alice; 2 d. Educ. St. Mungo's Academy; Glasgow University; Strathclyde University. Qualified as CA, 1974; trained with Wylie & Bisset, CA; worked for Coopers & Lybrand; joined Glasgow College as Lecturer, 1976; Senior Lecturer, 1980. Recreations: football; badminton. Address: (h.) 4 Hexham Gardens, Maxwell Park, Glasgow, G41 4AQ; T.-0141-423 1066.

McDevitt, Professor Denis Gordon, DSc, MD, FRCP, FRCPI, FRCPEd, FFPM. Professor of Clinical Pharmacology, Dundee University Medical School, since 1984, Dean, Faculty of Medicine and Dentistry; Honorary Consultant Physician, Tayside Health Board, since 1984; President, Association of Physicians of Great Britain and Ireland, 1987-88; Civil Consultant in Clinical Pharmacology, RAF, since 1987; Member, Medicines Commission, since 1986; b. 17.11.37, Belfast; m., Anne McKee; 2 s.; 1 d. Educ. Campbell College, Belfast; Queen's University, Belfast. Assistant Professor of Medicine and Consultant Physician, Christian Medical College, Ludhiana, North India, 1968-71; Senior Lecturer in Clinical Pharmacology and Consultant Physician, Queen's University Medical School, 1971-76; Merck International Fellow in Clinical Pharmacology, Vanderbilt University, Nashville, Tennessee, 1974-75; Reader in Clinical Pharmacology, Queen's University Medical School, 1976-78; Professor of Clinical Pharmacology, Queen's University of Belfast and Consultant Physician, Belfast Teaching Hospitals, 1978-83. Chairman, Clinical Section, British Pharmacological Society, 1985-88 (Secretary, 1978-82). Recreations: golf; classical music. Address: (h.) 1 Godfrey Street, Barnhill, Dundee, DD5 2QZ.

MacDiarmid, Gordon, MA (Hons). Depute Leader, City of Glasgow Council, since 1995; Depute Leader, Glasgow District Council, since 1994; City Treasurer, since 1992; b. 10.6.51, Glasgow. Educ. Allan Glen's School, Glasgow; Glasgow University; Jordanhill College. Teacher: appointed to Renfrew High School, 1973, Principal Teacher of Modern Studies, since 1981; elected to Glasgow District Council, 1985; Convener of Personnel, 1987; Vice-Convener of Finance, 1990; Convener of Finance, 1992;

Member, Boards, Royal Scottish National Orchestra, Centre for Contemporary Arts, Glasgow Cultural Enterprises Ltd. Recreations: music; theatre; pets; watching Rangers; reading; food and wine. Address: (h.) 122 Wedderlea Drive, Cardonald, Glasgow, G52 2SY; T.-0141-882 2474.

McDonald, Rev. Alexander, BA, CMIWS. General Secretary, Department of Ministry, Church of Scotland, since 1988; b. 5.11.37, Bishopbriggs; m., Essdale Helen McLeod; 2 s.; 1 d. Educ. Bishopbriggs Higher Grade School; Whitehill Senior Secondary School, Glasgow; Glasgow University and Trinity College. Management in timber trade, 1952-54; RAF, 1954-56; management in timber trade, 1956-58, motor trade, 1958-62; student, 1962-68; Minister, St. David's Bathgate, 1968-74, St. Mark's, Old Hall, Paisley, 1974-88. Trustee, Scottish Television Staff Trust; wide range of involvement with Boys' Brigade in Scotland, Scottish Spastics, mentally handicapped children, ACCORD, Christian Aid and many others; regular broadcaster. Recreations: reading; walking; fishing. Address: Church of Scotland, 121 George Street, Edinburgh, EH2 4YN; T.-0131-225 5722.

McDonald, Alexander John. Breed Secretary, Galloway Cattle Society, since 1990; b. 12.6.39, Fochabers. Educ. Milnes High School. RAF, 1958-90. Editor and Publsher, The Galloway Journal. Recreations: country pursuits; photography. Address: (b.) 15 New Market Street, Castle Douglas, DG7 1HY; T.-01556 502753.

MacDonald, Sheriff Alistair Archibald, MA, LLB, DL, KHS. Sheriff of Grampian, Highland and Islands, at Kirkwall and Lerwick, 1968-91; b. 8.5.27, Edinburgh; m., Jill Russell; 1 s.; 1 d. Educ. Broughton School; Edinburgh University. Army Service, Intelligence Corps, 1945-48; called to Scottish Bar, 1954; Sheriff Substitute of Caithness, Sutherland, Orkney and Shetland, at Lerwick, 1961-68; Deputy Lieutenant of Shetland, since 1986; Knight of the Equestrian Order of the Holy Sepulchre of Jerusalem, 1987. Address: (h.) Westhall, Shetland Isles; T.-Lerwick 2711.

Macdonald, Alister Gordon, BSc, PhD, DSc. Reader in Physiology, Aberdeen University, since 1984; b. 25.1.40, London; m., Jennifer; 1 s.; 2 d. Educ. Boys' High School, Trowbridge, Wiltshire; Bristol University. University of East Anglia, 1963-69; joined Aberdeen University as Lecturer in Physiology, 1969. Publications: Physiological Aspects of Deep Sea Biology, 1975; Effects of High Pressure on Biological Systems, 1993. Recreations: hill-walking; badminton; music; Scottish country dancing. Address: (b.) Department of Biomedical Sciences, Marischal College, Aberdeen, AB9 1AS; T.-Aberdeen 273021.

MacDonald, Allan, MA. Head of Gaelic Television, Grampian TV, 1992-94; Managing Director, MNE Television, since 1989; Managing Director, Corrodale Ltd., since 1988; Member, Board of Management, Lews Castle F.E. College, since 1992; b. 11.6.53, Eriskay; m., Marion Margaret; 1 d. Educ. St. Vincent's College, Langbank; Blairs College, Aberdeen; Glasgow University. Senior Producer, BBC Highland, Inverness; Senior Producer/Manager, BBC Radio Nan Eilean, Stornoway; Manager, BBC Highland, Inverness; Television Producer, BBC Scotland, Glasgow. Address: (h.) 62 Moorfoot Way, Bearsden, Glasgow, G61 4RL.

Macdonald, Angus David, MA (Hons) (Cantab), DipEd. Headmaster, Lomond School, Helensburgh, since 1986; b. 9.10.50, Edinburgh; m., Isabelle Marjory Ross; 2 d. Educ. Portsmouth Grammar School; Cambridge University; Edinburgh University. Assistant Teacher, Alloa Academy, 1972-73; Assistant Teacher, Edinburgh academy, 1973-82 (Exchange Teacher, King's School, Parramatta, NSW, 1978-79); George Watson's College, Edinburgh: Principal Teacher of Geography, 1982, Deputy Principal, 1982-86.

Recreations: outdoor recreation; sport; piping; gardening. Address: 8 Millig Street, Helensburgh, Dunbartonshire; T.-0436 679204.

Macdonald, Angus Stewart, CBE, DL, FRAgS; b. 7.4.35, Edinburgh; m., Janet Ann Somerville; 3 s. Educ. Conon Bridge School; Gordonstoun School. Chairman, Scottish Agricultural Development Council, 1980-85; Past Chairman, former Vice President and former Treasurer, Royal Highland and Agricultural Society; Director, British Wool Marketing Board and associated companies; Chairman, Dingwall Auction Mart Ltd.; Director, Grampian Television PLC; Chairman, Gordonstoun School; former Director, Hill Farming Research Organisation; Trustee, ÄTSMoredun Animal Health Trust Fund and MacRobert Trust; Member,Highlands and Islands Enterprise; Crown Commissioner for Crown Estates in Scotland; Trustee, British Wool Marketing Board Pension Fund; former Chairman, SCOTVEC Sector Board; Member, Queen's Bodyguard for Scotland (Royal Company of Archers); Recreation: field sports. Address: Torgorm, Conon Bridge, Dingwall, Ross-shire; T.-01349 861365.

MacDonald, Calum Alasdair, PhD. MP (Labour), Western Isles, since 1987; b. 7.5.56, Stornoway. Address: (b.) House of Commons, London, SW1; T.-071-219 4609.

MacDonald, Professor Caroline Mary, BSc, PhD, CBiol, FIBiol. Professor and Head, Department of Biological Sciences, Paisley University, since 1992; b. 4.9.51, Edinburgh; m., Alastair MacDonald; 2 d. Educ. Glasgow High School for Girls; Glasgow University. Lecturer/Senior Lecturer, Strathclyde University, 1983-92; Chairman, European Society for Animal Cell Technology, since 1994 (Secretary and Treasurer, 1991-94); Chief Editor, Genetic Engineer and Biotechnologist; Member, Executive Committee, Heads of University Biological Sciences. Recreations: family; gardening; travel. Address: (b.) Department of Biological Sciences, Paisley University, High Street, Paisley, PA1 2BE; T.-0141-848 3101.

MacDonald, Colin Cameron, BA. Under Secretary, Principal Establishment Officer, Scottish Office; b. 13.7.43, Glasgow; m., Kathryn Campbell; 1 s.; 1 d. Educ. Allan Glen's School; Strathclyde University. Scottish Development Department: Research Officer, Research Services, 1967-70, Senior Research Officer, Research Services, 1970-71, Principal Research Officer, Central Planning Research Unit, 1971-75; Senior Principal Research Officer, Scottish Office Central Research Unit, 1975-81; Chief Research Officer, 1981-88; Assistant Secretary, Housing, 1988-91. Non-Executive Director, TSB Bank Scotland PLC, since 1994. Recreations: tennis; fishing; music. Address: (b.) 16 Waterloo Place, Edinburgh, EH1 3DN; T.-0131-244 3938.

MacDonald, Professor Donald Gordon, RD*, BDS, PhD, FRCPath, FDSRCPS(G). Professor in Oral Pathology, Glasgow University, since 1991; Consultant Oral Pathologist, Glasgow Dental Hospital, since 1974; b. 5.7.42, Glasgow; m., Emma Lindsay Cordiner; 2 s. Educ. Kelvinside Academy, Glasgow; Glasgow University. Assistant, then Lecturer, Glasgow University, 1964-69; Visiting Associate Professor in Oral Pathology, University of Illinois, 1969-70; Lecturer, Senior Lecturer, Reader in Oral Medicine and Pathology, Glasgow University, 1970-91; Editor, Glasgow Dental Journal, 1969-75; Honorary Consultant Forensic Odontologist, Strathclyde Police, since 1976; Vice President, Association of Head and Neck Oncologists of Great Britain, 1987-90; President, British Society for Oral Pathology, 1988-91. Recreations: Royal Naval Reserve; golf; curling. Address: (h.) 2 Dougalston Gardens South, Milngavie, Glasgow; T.-0141-956 2075.

MacDonald, Donald John, BSc. Rector, Nicolson Institute, Stornoway, since 1989 (Rector, Thurso High School, 1980-89); b. 25.5.39, Glasgow; 1 s.; 2 d. Educ. Hill's Trust School, Glasgow; Lionel School, Lewis; Govan High School, Glasgow; Glasgow University; Jordanhill College of Education. Teacher of Science, Govan High School; Principal Teacher of Physics: Kirkwall Grammar School, Govan High School; Assistant Head, Linwood High School; Depute Rector, Dingwall Academy; Assistant Divisional Education Officer, Highland Region. Address: (b.) Springfield Road, Stornoway, PA87 2PZ.

MacDonald, Donald John, BA, MREHIS, MCIEH. Chief Food and Dairy Officer, Scottish Office Agriculture and Fisheries Department, since 1990; b. 14.3.48, Dingwall. Educ. Dingwall Academy; Inverness College; Aberdeen University; Open University. Environmental Health Officer: Kincardine and Deeside District Council, 1970-76, Inverness District Council, 1976-84; Food and Dairy Officer, SOAFD, 1984-90. Recreations: geology; walking; literature. Address: (b.) Room 358 (C), Pentland House, 47 Robb's Loan, Edinburgh; T.-0131-244 6427.

MacDonald, Donald Murray, MCIBS. Retired Bank Manager; Honorary Sheriff, since 1984; b. 10.6.32, Inverness; m., Irene Foubister Kemp; 2 d. Educ. Inverness Royal Academy. Entered service of Union Bank of Scotland Ltd., 1947; worked in a number of offices throughout Scotland; appointed Accountant, Stornoway Branch, Bank of Scotland, 1971; Assistant Manager, Kirkwall, 1973; Manager, Lochmaddy and Benbecula, 1977; Manager, Portree, 1982 (retired 1986). Treasurer, Church of Scotland, Portree. Recreations: gardening; piping; stalking. Address: (h.) Hillview, Hill Place, Staffin Road, Portree, Isle of Skye, IV51 9HP.

McDonald, Sir Duncan, Kt (1983), CBE (1976), DEng, DSc, BSc, FEng, FH-WC, Hon.FIEE, CBIM, SMIEEE, FRSE, FRSA. Director: Barclays Bank, Scotland; Northern Rock Building Society, Scotland; b. 20.9.21, Inverkeithing; m., Jane Anne Guckian; 3 s.; 1 d. Educ. Inverkeithing Public School; Dunfermline High School; Edinburgh University. Early experience, British Thomson Houston, Rugby (Head, R & D., BTH transformer interests); appointed Chief Transformer Designer, Bruce Peebles, Edinburgh, 1954; became Chief Engineer of company, 1959; Managing Director, 1962; following merger, joined Board, C.A. Parsons, 1969, and Board, Retrofle Parsons Group, 1973; became Chief Executive of Group; first Group Managing Director, Northern Engineering Industries plc, 1977; appointed Chairman and Chief Executive, 1980; Honorary Fellow, Heriot-Watt College, 1962; DSc Heriot-Watt University, 1982; Honorary Fellow, Institution of Electrical Engineers, 1984; awarded first Hon. Doctorate of Engineering by Newcastle upon Tyne University, 1984; Fellow, Scottish Council (Development and Industry). Recreations: golf; fishing; gardening. Address: (h.) Duncliffe, Kinellan Road, Edinburgh, EH12 6ES; T.-0131-337 4814.

Macdonald, Rev. Fergus, MA, BD. General Secretary, National Bible Society of Scotland, since 1981; b. 2.3.36, Evanton; m., Dolina H. Mackay; 1 s.; 4 d. Educ. Edinburgh University. Assistant Minister, Hope Street Free Church, Glasgow, 1960-62; Minister, St. Andrew's Evangelical Presbyterian Church, Lima, Peru, 1962-67; Minister, Cumbernauld Free Church of Scotland, 1968-81. Address: (b.) 7 Hampton Terrace, Edinburgh, EH12 5XU; T.-0131-337 9701.

Macdonald, Rev. Finlay Angus John, MA, BD, PhD. Minister, Jordanhill Parish Church, Glasgow, since 1977; b. 1.7.45, Watford; m., Elizabeth Mary Stuart; 2 s. Educ. Dundee High School; St. Andrews University. Assistant Minister, Bo'ness Old Kirk, 1970-71; Minister, Menstrie Parish Church, 1971-77; Junior Clerk and Treasurer, Stirling and Dunblane Presbytery, 1973-77; Convener, General Assembly Board of Practice and Procedure, 1988-

92; Convener, General Assembly Business Committee, 1989-92; Depute Clerk, General Assembly, since 1993; Member, Strathclyde University Court. Recreations: music; hill-walking; reading; gardening. Address: (h.) 96 Southbrae Drive, Glasgow, G13 1TZ; T.-0141-959 1310.

Macdonald, Fiona Margaret Taylor, LLB, NP. Solicitor, since 1981; Member, Council, Law Society of Scotland, since 1992; Member, Western Isles Health Board, since 1993; b. 14.4.56, Glasgow; m., Norman Lewis Macdonald. Educ. Hillpark Secondary School; Dundee University. Solicitor, Inverclyde District Council, 1981-83; Solicitor, Bird Semple & Crawford Heron, Stornoway, 1983-89; Solicitor, Western Isles Islands Council, since 1989. Local Secretary, Cancer Research Campaign (Scotland). Recreation: founder member, Goathill Ceilidh Band. Address: (h.) Valasay, Goathill Crescent, Stornoway, PA87 2TA; T.-01851 70 6364.

Macdonald, Gibson Torbett. Provost, Kyle and Carrick District Council, 1984-88 and since 1992; b. 21.1.33; m., Muirkirk; m., Mary Hastings Logan Lambie; 1 s.; 1 d. Educ. Kilmarnock Academy. National President, Junior Chamber Scotland; Executive Vice President, Junior Chamber International; Chairman, Ayr Branch, Ayr Conservative Association; Chairman, Ayr Conservative Constituency; Town Councillor, Royal Burgh of Ayr; District Councillor, Kyle and Carrick District (held Convenership of Planning, Employment and Policy and Resources Committees); Chairman, Culzean Country Park Joint Committee; Member, COSLA Planning and Town Twinning Committees. Treasurer, Ayrshire Decorative and Fine Arts Society; Past President, Ayr Town Twinning Association; Secretary, Franco Scottish Society (Ayrshire); President, Ayr Chamber of Commerce, 1990-92; Dean of Guildry, 1991-92; Vice-President, Ayrshire Chamber of Commerce and Industry, since 1993. Recreations: bowling; bridge; computing; philately. Address: (h.) 14 Belmont Avenue, Ayr, KA7 2JN.

Macdonald, 8th Baron, (Godfrey James Macdonald of Macdonald). Chief of the Name and Arms of Macdonald; b. 28.11.47; m., Claire Catlow; 1 s.; 3 d. Address: (h.) Kinloch Lodge, Isle of Skye.

Macdonald, Gus. Managing Director, Scottish Television; Television Journalist; b. 20.8.40, Larkhall; m., Teen; 2 d. Educ. Allan Glen's School, Glasgow. Marine engineer, Stephens, Linthouse, 1955-62; Circulation and Publicity Manager, Tribune, 1963-65; Investigative Journalist, The Scotsman, 1965-67; Editor, Financial Scotsman, 1966-67; Investigative Bureau, World in Action, Granada, 1967-69; Editor/Executive Producer, World in Action, 1969-75; successively Head of Current Affairs, Head of Regional Programmes, Head of Features, Granada; Writer/Presenter, Camera: Early Photography, 1979-80, MacDiarmid: Hammer and Thistle; Presenter, variously, World in Action, What the Papers Say, Devil's Advocate, Union World; Election and Party Conference coverage; C4 Viewers Ombudsman, Right to Reply, 1982-88; BAFTA Award, current affairs; National Viewers and Listeners' Association Award, 1985; founder Chairman, Edinburgh International Television Festival, 1976; Visiting Professor, Film and Media Studies, Stirling University, since 1985; Chairman, Edinburgh International Film Festival, since 1993; Governor, National Film and Television School; Vice President, Royal Television Society; Board, GMTV; Chairman, ITV Broadcast Board, 1993-94; Fellow, Royal Society of Arts. Publications: Grierson: Television and Documentary, 1977; Camera: Victorian Eyewitness, 1979. Recreations: words; music; pictures; exploring Scotland. Address: (b.) Scottish Television, Cowcaddens, Glasgow, G2 3PR.

Macdonald, Hugh. Head of Music, BBC Scotland. Address: (b.) Queen Margaret Drive, Glasgow, G12 8DG.

McDonald, Ian Alexander, MB, ChB, FFCM. Director of Public Health, Borders Health Board. Address: (b.) Huntlyburn House, Melrose, TD6 9BP.

Macdonald, Ian Hamish, OBE, FCIBS, CIMight. Chairman, Clan Donald Lands Trust; Director, AIB Group Northern Ireland PLC; b. 30.12.26, Inverness; m., Patricia Lace; 1 d. Educ. Inverness Royal Academy; Inverness Technical High School. RAFVR, 1944; Queen's Own Cameron Highlanders, 1945 (Hon. Captain, 1948); Mercantile Bank, 1948-59; The Hongkong and Shanghai Banking Corporation: Manager, 1959-72, General Manager, India, 1972-73, General Manager International, 1973-80, Executive Director, 1980-83; Chairman, Hongkong Bank of Canada, 1981-83; Chief General Manager, TSB Scotland, 1983-86, and TSB Scotland PLC, 1986-87; Director, TSB Group PLC, 1986-87; Director, Scottish Power PLC, 1987-92; Chairman, Clairmont PLC, 1987-91, First Edinburgh Homes PLC, 1988-92, EFM Dragon Trust, 1987-92, Scottish Council Foundation, 1983-92; Director, Macdonald Orr, 1987-93, TSB Northern Ireland PLC, 1987-92, Morgan Grenfell Scotland Ltd., 1987-91; Member, Court, Edinburgh University, 1989-92. Recreations: fishing; golf; bridge. Address: (h.) Minewood Cottage, 11 Abercromby Drive, Bridge of Allan, FK9 4EA.

Macdonald, Professor Ian Robert, MA, PhD. Professor in Spanish, Aberdeen University, since 1991 (Vice-Principal and Dean, Faculty of Arts and Divinity); b. 4.5.39, The Hague; m., Frances Mary; 3 s. Educ. Whitgift School; St. Andrews University. United Steel Cos. Ltd., 1961-64; research student, 1964-65; Lecturer, then Senior Lecturer, Aberdeen University, 1965-90. Recreations: walking; digging; carpentry. Address: (h.) 47 North Deeside Road, Peterculter, Aberdeen; T.-01224 732284.

McDonald, Rev. James Ian Hamilton, MA, BD, MTh, PhD, FEIS. Reader in Christian Ethics and New Testament Studies, Edinburgh University, since 1992; b. 7.2.33, Stonehouse; m., Jenny Paterson Fleming. Educ. Rutherglen Academy; Glasgow University; Edinburgh University. Parish Minister, Johnstone West; Baird Research Fellow in Christian Education; Lecturer in Religious Education, Moray House, Edinburgh; Lecturer in Christian Ethics and Practical Theology, then Senior Lecturer in Christian Ethics and New Testament, Edinburgh University; Associate Dean, Faculty of Divinity, 1991-94; Head, Department of Christian Ethics, since 1995; Convener, Church of Scotland Education Committee, 1985-89. Recreations: walking; reading; painting. Address: (b.) New College, Mound Place, Edinburgh, EH1 2LX; T.-0131-650 8923.

McDonald, Professor James Rufus, BSc, MSc, PhD, CEng, MIEE, MIEEE. Rolls-Royce Chair in Power Engineering, Strathclyde University, since 1994; b. 28.4.57, Glasgow; m., Eileen M.T. Greene; 2 d. Educ. St. Gerards, Glasgow; Strathclyde University. Assistant Engineer, Scottish Electrical Training Scheme, 1978-79; Project Engineer, South of Scotland Electricity Board, 1979-84; Lecturer, then Senior Lecturer, then Professor, Strathclyde University, since 1984; Manager, Centre for Electrical Power Engineering, since 1990. Director, Pollok School Company. Publications: three books; over 150 technical papers. Recreations: music; theatre; reading; football; golf; skiing; tennis. Address: (h.) 48 Colonsay Drive, Newton Mearns, Glasgow, G77 6TY; T.-0141-639 6783.

McDonald, James Stevenson, BL, NP. President, Scottish Law Agents Society, 1992-94; Solicitor; b. 5.10.32, Castle Douglas; m., Margaret Mary Campbell; 1 s.; 1 d. Educ. Edinburgh Academy; Edinburgh University. Solicitor, private practice. Past President, Kilmarnock Rotary Club; Clerk to Board of Management, Dundonald Parish Church. Recreations: walking; gardening. Address: (h.) 6 Laurieston Court, Dundonald, Kilmarnock; T.-01563 851185.

McDonald, Professor Janet B.I., MA, FRSE, FRSAMD, FRSA. Professor of Drama, Glasgow University, since 1979; b. 28.7.41, Netherlee, Renfrewshire; m., Ian James McDonald; 1 d. Educ. Hutchesons' Girls' Grammar School; Glasgow University. Member, Governing Body, Royal Scottish Academy of Music and Drama, 1979-94; Member, Board, Citizens' Theatre, 1979-82 and since 1989 (Chair, since 1991); Council Member, Royal Society of Edinburgh, since 1994; Chairman, Drama and Theatre Board, Council for National Academic Awards, 1981-85; Chairman, Standing Committee of University Departments of Drama, 1982-85; Chairman, Drama Committee, Scottish Arts Council, 1985-88; Chair, Creative and Performing Arts Committee, CNAA, 1989-91. Address: (b.) 53 Hillhead Street, Glasgow, G12 8QF; T.-0141-339 8855.

Macdonald, Father John Angus, STB, MA, MLitt. Parish Priest, Fort William, and R.E. Adviser, Diocese of Argyll and the Isles, since 1991; Member, Scottish Catholic Education Commission, since 1993; Commissioner for South Argyll, Argyll Islands and Southern Isles, Crofters Commission, since 1992; b. 6.12.45, Askernish, South Uist. Educ. Daliburgh J.S. School; St. Mary's College, Blairs; Royal Scots College, Spain (Comillas University); Aberdeen University. Ordained, 1970; Curate, 1970-72; Staff, St. Mary's College, Blairs, 1972-83, Depute Rector, 1978-83; Administrator, St. Mary's, Arisaig, 1983-85; Parish Priest: St. Mary's, Bornish, 1985-87, St. Peter's, Daliburgh, 1987-91. School Board Member, Fort William R.C. School, since 1991; Editor, Crann, Aberdeen University Celtic Society magazine, 1974-78; Spanish language translator for Concilium, 1981-90; Member, Western Isles Islands Council Education Committee, 1985-91; Member, Gaelic Advisory Committee, BBC, 1986-90; Member, Western Isles Health Board, 1989-92. Recreations: music; reading; local and church history; hillwalking; languages; DIY. Address: (h.) St. Mary's, Belford Road, Fort William, PH33 6BT; T.-01397 702174.

MacDonald, Major-General John Donald, CB, CBE. Joint Secretary, Royal British Legion Scotland, and The Earl Haig Fund (Scotland); b. 5.4.38; m., Mary Warrack; 1 s.; 2 d. Educ. George Watson's College, Edinburgh; RMA, Sandhurst; RMCS, Shrivenham; DSSC, India; National Defence College, Latimer. Commissioned King's Own Scottish Borderers, 1958, RASC, 1963, Royal Corps of Transport, 1976-78; Commander, Armd. Division Transport Regiment, BAOR, 1978-80 (Lt.-Col.); Exchange Instructor, Australian Army Cmd. and Staff College, 1980-82; Head of Personnel and Logistics, Armd. Division, BAOR, 1983-86 (Col.); Head of Personnel and Officer for Human Resources, MoD, London, 1987-88; Distribution and Transport Director, 1 Br Corps, BAOR, 1988-91 (Brigadier); Director General, Transport and Movement (Distribution), Army, 1991-93 (Major-General). FCIT; FILDM. Recreations: travel; music; art; rugby (internationalist); athletics (internationalist); golf; skiing. Address: (b.) New Haig House, Logie Green Road, Edinburgh, EH7 4HR.

MacDonald, Margo. Freelance journalist and broadcaster; b. Hamilton; m., Jim Sillars; 1 step s.; 2 d.; 1 step-d. Educ. Hamilton Academy; Dunfermline College. Teacher, 1963-65; barmaid and mother, 1965-73; Member of Parliament, 1973-74; Broadcaster/Writer, 1974-78; Director, Shelter, Scotland, 1978-81; Radio Forth: Broadcaster, 1981-83, Editor, Topical Programmes, 1983-85; political and current affairs broadcasting as reporter/presenter, 1985-91; former Chief Executive, Network Scotland. Address: (h.) 97 Grange Loan, Edinburgh, EH9 2ED.

Macdonald, Rev. Professor Murdo Ewen, MA, BD, DD (St. Andrews), DD (McGill University). Emeritus Professor, Trinity College, Glasgow University; b. 28.8.14, Isle of Harris; 2 s. Educ. Sir Edward Scott School, Harris; Kingussie Secondary School; St. Andrews University.

Minister, Portree, Isle of Skye, 1939-40; Chaplain to 4th Camerons, 1940-42; Chaplain to 2nd Paras, 1942; wounded and taken prisoner, North Africa, and spent rest of War in Germany (acted as Chaplain to American Air Force); awarded Bronze Star; Pollock Lecturer in Preaching, Canada; Syme Lecturer in Theology and Preaching, Lutheran Colleges, USA; Ferrie Lecturer in Preaching and Theology, Australia. Publications: Vitality of Faith; Need to Believe; Call to Obey; Crisis of Belief; Call to Communicate; Lost Provinces of Religion. Address: (h.) 68 Lauderdale Gardens, Glasgow, G12 9QW; T.-041-334 2087.

Macdonald, Rev. Neil, MA. Free Church Minister, Fearn, Ross-shire; Moderator, General Assembly, Free Church of Scotland, 1996; b. 1932, Skye; m.; 1 s.; 2 d. Educ. Portree High School; Edinburgh University; Moray House College; Free Church College. Ordained and inducted, 1959; first charge, Lochalsh; Minister, Fearn, 25 years.

Macdonald, Norman Malcolm. Writer and Dramatist; b. 24.7.27, Thunder Bay, Canada; m., Mairi F. Educ. Nicolson Institute; Newbattle Abbey College. New Zealand Air Force, 1949-57; journalism and administration at various periods; Administrator, Fir Chlis (Gaelic theatre company), 1978-80; Secretary, Sabhal Mor Ostaig Gaelic College, 1982-83. Publications: Calum Tod (novel); An Sgaineadh (novel); Fad (poetry); Bathach Chaluim, Anna Chaimbeul, The Catechist, The Brahan Seer, Sublime Savage, Aimhreit Aignis, The Teuchtar's Tale, Or an Amadain, Ordugh na Saorsa (plays); Call Na h'Iolaire, Clann-Nighean a Sgadain (historical); The Shutter Falls (television). Recreation: walking. Address: 14 Tong, Isle of Lewis.

Macdonald, Peter Cameron, DL, SDA. Vice-President, Scottish Landowners' Federation, since 1990 (Convener, 1985-88); Farmer, since 1961; Director, J. Dickson & Son, Gunmakers, since 1968; b. 14.12.37, Edinburgh; m., Barbara Helen Drimmie Ballantyne; 2 step-s. Educ. Loretto; East of Scotland College of Agriculture. Council Member: Scottish Landowners Federation, since 1976, Blackface Sheepbreeders Association, 1970-74; Member, Forth River Purification Board, 1979-87; Director, Royal Highland and Agricultural Society of Scotland, 1985; Deputy Lieutenant, West Lothian, since 1987. Recreations: fishing; shooting; golf. Address: Colzium Farm, Kirknewton, Midlothian, EH27 8DH; T.-01506 880607.

Macdonald, Rhoda Mairi, MA. Head of Gaelic, Scottish Television, since 1991; b. 18.10.58, Stornoway. Educ. Nicolson Institute, Stornoway; Glasgow University; Jordanhill College. Freelance Television Presenter, 1979-88; Scottish Television: Researcher, 1988, Programme Executive, Gaelic, 1989. Director, Scottish Television Enterprises; Executive Member, Celtic Film and Television Association. Recreations: reading; cinema; cooking. Address: (b.) Scottish Television, Cowcaddens, Glasgow, G2 3PR; T.-0141-332 9999.

McDonald, Hon. Lord (Robert Howat McDonald), MC (1944), MA, LLB. Senator of the College of Justice in Scotland, 1973-89; b. 15.5.16, Paisley; m., Barbara Mackenzie. Educ. John Neilson Institution, Paisley; Glasgow University. Admitted Solicitor, 1938; KOSB, 1939-46 (mentioned in Despatches); admitted, Faculty of Advocates, 1946; QC (Scot), 1957; Sheriff of Ayr and Bute, 1966-71; Member, Criminal Injuries Compensation Board, 1964-71; Chairman, Mental Welfare Commission for Scotland, 1964-83; Chairman, General Nursing Council for Scotland, 1970-73. Address: (h.) 5 Doune Terrace, Edinburgh, EH3 6EA.

Macdonald, Roderick, BSc(Agri), MSc. Member, Scottish Land Court, since 1986; b. 6.2.27, Benbecula; m., Elizabeth MacLeod; 3 d. Educ. Portree High School; Aberdeen University; Michigan State University, USA. Bayer

Agriculture, 1952-54; Lands Division, Department of Agriculture and Fisheries for Scotland, 1954-67 and 1972-86, latterly as Assistant Chief; Head, Land Development Division, Highlands and Islands Development Board, 1967-72; appointed Gaelic Speaking Member, Scottish Land Court, 1986; Trustee and Surveyor, Glebes Committee, Church of Scotland, since 1994; Secretary, Highland Fund, since 1993. Recreations: golf; fiddle playing; fishing. Address: 19 Cherrytree Loan, Balerno, Edinburgh; T.-0131-449 3600.

Macdonald, Vice-Admiral Sir Roderick (Douglas), KBE (1978). Painter; b. 25.2.21, Java; m., 1, Joan Willis (m. diss.); 2 s.; 1 s. deceased; 2, Mrs Pamela Bartosik. Educ. Fettes (Captain, Scottish Schoolboys' rugby, 1937-38). Entered Royal Navy, 1939; served at sea throughout War, 1939-45; Comd. six HM ships, one minesweeper and two frigate squadrons; Cyprus (Despatches, 1957); Commander, Naval Forces Borneo, 1965 (CBE); Captain of the Fleet, 1970; COS to C-in-C, Naval Home Command, 1973-76; ADC to The Queen, 1975; COS to Comdr., Allied Naval Forces Southern Europe, 1976-79. Chieftain, Skye Highland Games; President, Skye Piping Society; Fellow, Nautical Institute (Vice-President, 1976-85); Trustee and Executive, Clan Donald Lands Trust; President, Inverness Sea Cadets Unit; own exhibitions, Naples, Edinburgh (2), London (5). Publication: The Figurehead, 1993. Recreations: sailing; Highland bagpipe, gardening. Address: (h.) Ollach, Braes, Skye, IV51 9LJ.

Macdonald, Roderick Francis, QC; b. 1.2.51. Advocate, 1975. Address: (b.) Advocates' Library, Parliament House, Edinburgh, EH1 1RF.

MacDonald, Professor Ronald, BA, MA, PhD. Professor of International Finance, Strathclyde University, since 1993; b. 23.4.55, Glasgow. Educ. Falkirk High School; Heriot Watt University; Manchester University. Midland Bank Fellow in Monetary Economics, Loughborough University, 1982-84; Lecturer in Economics, Aberdeen University, 1984-88; Senior Lecturer, 1988-89; Robert Fleming Professor of Finance and Investment, Dundee University, 1989-93; Visiting Professor, Queen's University, Canada, 1988, University of New South Wales, Australia, 1989; Visiting Scholar, International Monetary Fund, Washington DC, since 1991. Publications: Floating Exchange Rates; International Money: theory evidence and institutions (Co-author); five co-edited books; 90 journal articles. Recreations: music; photography; hill-walking. Address: (b.) Department of Economics, Strathclyde University, Glasgow, G4 0LN; T.-0141-552 4400.

McDonald, Sheena Elizabeth, MA. Broadcaster/Journalist. Educ. George Watson's Ladies' College; Edinburgh University; Bristol University. Presenter, currently, of The Vision Thing, Channel 4.

MacDonald, Professor Simon Gavin George, MA, PhD, FInstP, FRSE. Professor of Physics, Dundee University, 1973-88 (Head, Department of Physics, 1979-85); Chairman, Statistics Committee, Universities Central Council on Admissions, 1989-93; b. 5.9.23, Beauly, Inverness-shire; m., Eva Leonie Austerlitz; 1 s.; 1 d. Educ. George Heriot's, Edinburgh; Edinburgh University. Junior Scientific Officer, Royal Aircraft Establishment, Farnborough, 1943-46; Lecturer in Physics, St. Andrews University, 1948-57; Senior Lecturer in Physics: University College of the West Indies, 1957-62, St. Andrews University, 1962-67; Dundee University: Senior Lecturer in Physics, 1967-73, Dean of Science, 1970-73, Vice-Principal, 1974-79; Member, Scottish Universities Council on Entrance, 1969-82 (Vice-Convener, 1973-77, Convener, 1977-82); Chairman, Technical Committee, UCCA, 1979-83; Deputy Chairman, UCCA, 1983-89; Chairman, Board of Directors, Dundee Repertory Theatre, 1975-89. Publications: Problems and Solutions in General Physics; Physics for Biology and Premedical Students; Physics for

the Life and Health Sciences. Recreations: bridge; golf; fiction writing. Address: (b.) 10 Westerton Avenue, Dundee, DD5 3NJ; T.-01382 78692.

McDonald, William, JP, CA. Bursar, The Carnegie Trust for the Universities of Scotland, since 1990; b. 9.11.29, Perth; m., Anne Kidd Laird McDonald; 1 s.; 1 d. Educ. Perth Academy. RAF, 1952-54; Secretary, South Mills and Grampian Investment, Dundee, 1957-62; The Company of Merchants of the City of Edinburgh: Chamberlain, 1962-90, Secretary, 1971-90; Clerk and Treasurer, Incorporation of Guildry in Edinburgh, 1975-90; Joint Secretary, Scottish Council of Independent Schools, 1978-90. Scout Association: Deputy Chief Commissioner of Scotland, 1977-79, Honorary Treasurer, Scotland, 1989-93, Chairman, UK Finance Sub-Committee, since 1993; Member, High Constables of Edinburgh, since 1982; Chairman, Scottish Environmental and Outdoor Education Centres, 1987-92; Member, Lothian Region Valuation Appeal Committee, since 1989. Recreations:Scout Association; bridge. Address (h.) 1/3 Wyvern Park, The Grange, Edinburgh, EH9 2JY; T.-0131-662 4145.

McDonald, Very Rev. William James Gilmour, MA, BD, Hon. DD (Edinburgh). Minister, Mayfield Parish Church, Edinburgh, 1959-92; Moderator, General Assembly of Church of Scotland, 1989-90; b. 3.6.24, Edinburgh; m., Patricia Watson; 1 s.; 2 d. Educ. Daniel Stewart's College; Edinburgh University; Gottingen University. Royal Artillery and Indian Artillery, 1943-46; Parish Minister, Limekilns, 1953-59. Convener, Committee on Education for the Ministry, 1974-78; Convener, Assembly Council, 1984-87; Chaplain, Edinburgh Merchant Company; Warrack Lecturer, 1993-95; Turnbull Trust Preacher, Melbourne, 1993-94. Recreations: music; cinema. Address: (h.) 7 Blacket Place, Edinburgh, EH9 1RN; T.-0131-667 2100.

MacDonell of Glengarry, Air Cdre. Aeneas Ranald Donald, CB, DFC. 22nd Chief of Glengarry; Member, Standing Council of Scottish Chiefs; Trustee, Clan Donald Lands Trust; Trustee, Finlaggan Trust; b. 15.11.13, Baku, Russia; m., 1, Diana Dorothy Keane; 2 s.; 1 d.; 2, Lois Eirene Frances Streatfeild; 1 s.; 1 d. Educ. Hurtspierpoint College; Royal Air Force College, Cranwell. RAF Officer, 1931-64; seconded to Fleet Air Arm, 1935-37; Flying Instructor, 1938-39; Air Ministry; Officer Commanding Spitfire Squadron during Battle of Britain; POW, Germany, 1941-45; Chief Flying Instructor, RAF College, Cranwell; Air Attache, Moscow, 1956-58; Director of Management and Work Study, Ministry of Defence, 1960-64; retired from RAF; Construction Industry Training Board, 1967-72; Head, Commercial Department, Industrial Society, 1972-76; Partner, John Courtis & Partners, Management Selection Consultants; finally retired and moved to Scotland, 1981. Honorary President, Ross and Cromarty Branch, Soliders', Sailors' and Airmen's Families Association. Recreation: bird watching. Address: (h.) Elonbank, 23 Castle Street, Fortrose, Ross-shire, IV10 8TH; T.-01381 620121.

McDonnell, Michael Anthony, BD, DipCE, MIRSO. Regional Road Safety Manager, ROSPA Scotland, since 1990; Secretary, Scottish Accident Prevention Council, since 1990; b. 13.5.55, Bellshill; m., Rosemary Boyle; 1 s. Educ. St. Patrick's High School, Coatbridge; Hamilton College of Education; Chesters College, Glasgow. Strathclyde Regional Council, 1976-81, 1982-83, 1988-90, latterly as Assistant Road Safety Training Officer. Recreations: football; golf; cinema. Address: (b.) Slateford House, 53 Lanark Road, Edinburgh, EH14 1TL; T.-0131-455 7457.

McDougall, Professor Bonnie S., BA, MA, PhD. Professor of Chinese, Edinburgh University, since 1990; b. 12.3.41, Sydney; m., A. Hansson; 1 s. Educ. University of Sydney.

Lecturer in Chinese, University of Sydney; Nuffield Fellow, London University; Visiting Lecturer, Harvard University; editor, translator and teacher, Peking; Professor of Modern Chinese, University of Oslo. Council Member, British Association of Chinese Studies. Recreations: reading; travelling. Address: (b.) Department of East Asian Studies, Edinburgh University, 8 Buccleuch Place, Edinburgh, EH8 9LW; T.-0131-650 4227.

MacDougall, John William, JP, FIIM. Leader of Administration, Fife Regional Council, since 1987 (Chairman, Policy and Resources Committee); b. 8.12.47, Dunfermline; m., Catherine; 1 s.; 1 d. Educ. Templehall Secondary Modern; Rosyth Dockyard College; Fife College; Glenrothes College. Vice-President/Treasurer, Association of European Regions; Member, COSLA International Affairs Committee; Board Member: Glenrothes Development Corporation, Fife Enterprise Company. Recreations: DIY; sport. Address: (b.) Fife House, North Street, Glenrothes, Fife; T.-01592 754411, Ext. 6209.

McDougall, Peter. Screenwriter; b. 1947, Greenock. Television and film work includes: Just Another Saturday, 1974 (Prix Italia); Elephant's Graveyard, 1976; Just A Boy's Game, 1979; Shoot for the Sun, 1985; Down Where The Buffalo Go, 1988; Down Among The Big Boys, 1993.

MacDougall, Robert Hugh, MB, ChB, DMRT, FRCS, FRCR. Clinical Director, Department of Clinical Oncology, Western General Hospitals, Edinburgh, and Honorary Senior Lecturer in Clinical Oncology, Edinburgh University, since 1986; Honorary Senior Lecturer, St. Andrews University; b. 9.8.49, Dundee; m., Moira Jean Gray; 1 s.; 2 d. Educ. High School of Dundee; St. Andrews University; Edinburgh University. Demonstrator in Anatomy, St. Andrews University; Registrar in Surgery, Aberdeen Royal Infirmary; Lecturer in Clinical Oncology, Edinburgh University; Consultant Radiotherapist and Oncologist, Tayside Health Board. Recreations: curling; fishing; reading. Address: (b.) Department of Clinical Oncology, Western General Hospital, Edinburgh.

McDowall, Linda, MA. Chief Executive, East Kilbride Business Centre, since 1993; Member, Lanarkshire Health Board, since 1995; b. 29.1.55, Glasgow; m., Colin McDowall. Educ. Glenwood Secondary School; Glasgow University. Entered civil service, 1977; joined Motherwell Enterprise Development Co., 1989. Panel Member, Investors in People (Scotland) Ltd. Recreations: swimming; keep-fit; sailiong; skiing. Address: (b.) Platthorn Road, East Kilbride, Glasgow, G74 1NW; T.-013552 38456.

McDowall, Stuart, CBE, MA (Hons). Economic Consultant; Deputy Chairman, Boundary Commission for Scotland, since 1983; Deputy Chairman, Central Arbitration Committee, since 1976; b. 19.4.26. Address: (b.) New St. Andrew's House, Edinburgh, EH1 3TG.

MacDowell, Professor Douglas Maurice, MA, DLitt, FRSE, FBA. Professor of Greek, Glasgow University, since 1971; b. 8.3.31, London. Educ. Highgate School; Balliol College, Oxford. Schoolmaster, 1954-58; Manchester University: Assistant Lecturer, 1958-61, Lecturer, 1961-68, Senior Lecturer, 1968-70, Reader, 1970-71; Visiting Fellow, Merton College, Oxford, 1969; President, Glasgow Centre, Classical Association of Scotland, 1973-75, 1977-79, 1982-84, 1988-90; Chairman, 1973-76, and Vice President, since 1976, Scottish Hellenic Society; Chairman, Council, Classical Association of Scotland, 1976-82. Publications: Andokides: On the Mysteries, 1962; Athenian Homicide Law, 1963; Aristophanes: Wasps, 1971; The Law in Classical Athens, 1978; Spartan Law, 1986; Demosthenes: Against Meidias, 1990; Aristophanes and Athens, 1995. Address: (b.) Glasgow University, Glasgow, G12 8QQ.

McEachran, Colin Neil, QC, MA, LLB, JD. QC, since 1981; b. 14.1.40, Glasgow; m., Kathrine Charlotte; 2 d. Educ. Glenalmond College; Merton College, Oxford; Glasgow University; University of Chicago. Advocate, since 1968; Advocate Depute, 1974-77; QC, 1981; Member, Scottish Legal Aid Board, since 1990; part-time Chairman, Medical Appeal Tribunals, Disability and Pension. Vice Chairman, Commonwealth Games Council for Scotland. Recreations: target shooting; hill-walking. Address: 1 Saxe Coburg Place, Edinburgh; T.-0131-332 6820.

McElroy, Professor(Arthur) Rennie, MA, MBA, DipLib, FLA. Chief Librarian, Napier University, since 1985; b. 21.10.45, Falkirk; 1 d. Educ. George Heriot's School; Edinburgh, Strathclyde and Glasgow Universities. Napier College: Assistant Librarian, 1968-70, Tutor Librarian, 1970-79, Depute Librarian, 1980-84. President, Scottish Library Association, 1989; Member of Council, Library Association, 1989-92; Member, Scottish Library and Information Council; author/editor of several books, reports, articles. Recreations: sport; travel; walking; reading. Address: (b.) Napier University, Sighthill, Edinburgh, EH11 4BN; T.-0131-455 3301.

McEwan, Helen Purdie, MD, FRCOG, FRCSGlas. Consultant Obstetrician and Gynaecologist, Royal Infirmary and Royal Maternity Hospital, Glasgow, since 1972; President, Royal Medico Chirurgical Society, Glasgow, 1984-85; b. Glasgow. Educ. Jordanhill College School; Glasgow University. Chairman, Scottish Executive, Royal College of Obstetricians and Gynaecologists; Member, Advisory Board, Women's Health Concern. Recreations: visiting Western Highlands and Islands; music. Address:(h.) 47 Westland Drive, Glasgow, G14 9PE.

McEwan, Iain, MA (Hons). Rector, Pitlochry High School, since 1986; b. 26.10.39, Perth; m., Nancy Graham; 2 d. Educ. Blairgowrie High School; Aberdeen University. Teacher of History, Lenzie Academy, 1963-67; Principal Teacher of History, Arbroath Academy, 1967-74, Morgan Academy, 1974-81; Depute Rector, Pitlochry High School, 1981-86. Convener, SEB History Panel, 1980-82; Vice President, Scottish Schoolboys' Hockey Association, 1985-87; Vice-Chairman (Administration), Scottish Youth Hockey Board, 1987-89; Hon. Vice-President, Scottish Hockey Union and SYHB. Recreations: photography; hockey; historic aircraft; amateur drama. Address: (h.) 7 Fenton Terrace, Pitlochry, Perthshire; T.-01796 2188; (b.) East Moulin Road, Pitlochry, Perthshire; T.-01796 2900.

McEwan, Sheriff Robin Gilmour, QC, LLB, PhD. Sheriff of Ayr, since 1988 (of Lanark, 1982-88); Temporary Judge, Court of Session and High Court of Justiciary, since 1991; b. 12.12.43, Glasgow; m., Sheena McIntyre; 2 d. Educ. Paisley Grammar School; Glasgow University. Faulds Fellow in Law, Glasgow University, 1965-68; admitted to Faculty of Advocates, 1967; Standing Junior Counsel, Department of Energy, 1974-76; Advocate Depute, 1976-79; Chairman, Industrial Tribunals, 1981; Member, Scottish Legal Aid Board, since 1989. Publications: Pleading in Court, 1980; A Casebook on Damages (Co-author), 1983; Contributor to Stair Memorial Encyclopaedia of the Laws of Scotland, 1986. Recreations: formerly: football, boxing; now: golf, skating. Address: (b.) Sheriff Court, Ayr, KA7 1DR; T.-Ayr 268474.

McEwan, Roy James, BSc (Econ), DAARL. Managing Director, Scottish Chamber Orchestra, since 1993; b. 12.5.51, Dumfries. Educ. Dumfries High School; Carlisle Grammar School; London School of Economics; Polytechnic of Central London. House Manager, St. George's Theatre, London, 1977-78; Manager, Whitechapel Art Gallery, 1978-79; Administrator, then Director, MacRobert Arts Centre, Stirling, 1979-91; Director of Arts Development, North West Arts Board, Manchester, 1991-

93. Chairman, Federation of Scottish Theatres, 1988-91; Member, Drama Committee, Scottish Arts Council, 1991. Address: (b.) 4 Royal Terrace, Edinburgh, EH7 5AB.

McEwen, Professor James, MB, ChB, FRCP (Glasgow), FFPHM, FFOM, DIH. Henry Mechan Professor of Public Health, Glasgow University, since 1989; Consultant in Public Health Medicine, Greater Glasgow Health Board; b. 6.2.40, Stirling; m., Elizabeth May Archibald; 1 s.; 1 d. Educ. Dollar Academy; St. Andrews University. Lecturer in Industrial Medicine, Dundee University; Senior Lecturer in Community Medicine, Nottingham University; Chief Medical Officer, The Health Education Council; Professor of Community Medicine, King's College, University of London. Recreations: church; gardening. Address: (b.) 2 Lilybank Gardens, Glasgow G12 8RZ. T.-0141-330 5013.

McEwen, John, MB, ChB, PhD, FRCPE, FFPM. Medical Director, Drug Development (Scotland) Ltd., since 1983; Honorary Senior Lecturer, Dundee University, since 1983; Honorary Consultant, Tayside Health Board, since 1984; b. 11.4.43, Uddingston; m., Veronica Rosemary Iverson; 1 s.; 1 d. Educ. Ecclesfield Grammar School; St. Andrews University. Resident Physician/Surgeon, Dundee Hospitals, 1966-67; Lecturer in Therapeutics, Dundee University, 1969-75; Visiting Fellow in Clinical Pharmacology, Vanderbilt University, Tennessee, 1972-74; Head of Clinical Pharmacology, Hoechst, UK, 1975-82. Recreations: keyboard instruments; hill-walking; choral singing. Address: (h.) 1 Osborne Place, Dundee, DD2 1BE; T.-Dundee 641060.

MacEwen, Martin, LLB, DLitt, ACIoH, MIMgt, NP. Vice Principal, Edinburgh College of Art, since 1995; Director, Scottish Ethnic Minorities Research Unit, since 1985; b. 21.12.43, Edinburgh; m., Jessica; 2 d. Educ. George Heriot's School; Aberdeen University; Edinburgh University; Heriot Watt University. District Officer/Assistant Secretary for Protectorate Affairs, Solomon Islands, 1967-70; Legal Assistant and Assistant Solicitor, Dunfermline Burgh, 1970-72; Assistant Conciliation Officer, Race Relations Board, 1972-74; Lecturer in Planning and Housing Law, Edinburgh College of Art/Heriot Watt University, 1974-86; Senior Lecturer, 1986-90; Assistant Principal, 1991-95. Recreations: squash; chess; tennis; walking. Address: (h.) 9 Ross Gardens, Edinburgh; T.-0131-667 3725.

MacEwen, Robert Rule (Robin), BL. Solicitor; Honorary Sheriff, Inverness, since 1984; b. 31.1.07, Inverness; m., 1, Elsie Ellis; 2, Marion Pringle or Jack; 1 s. Educ. Inverness Royal Academy; St. Peter's School, York; Edinburgh University. Partner, Stewart, Rule & Co., 1930-67, Rule MacEwen & Co., 1967-77; Consultant, MacLeod & MacCallum, 1977-81; War Service: RAOC, France and Germany, 1944-45 (mentioned in Despatches); Member, Inverness Town Council, 1950-56 (Magistrate and Chairman, Planning Committee); Member, Northern Regional Hospital Board, 1953-56; Dean, Faculty of Solicitors of the Highlands, 1976-79; Chairman, Federation of Scottish Film Societies, 1955; Chairman, Inverness Civic Trust, 1967-72; Chairman, Highlands and Islands Film Guild, 1974-77; Chairman, The Balnbin Trust, 1974-87, Hon. President, since 1987; Member, National Trust Advisory Committee on Culloden; Chairman, Inverness Liberal Association, 1980-81. Address: (h.) Brangan Cottage, 7 Crown Circus, Inverness, IV2 3NH; T.-01463 225385.

McFadden, Jean Alexandra, CBE, JP, DL, MA, LLB. Leader, Glasgow District Council, 1980-86, 1992-94; Lecturer in Law, Strathclyde University; Vice Lord Lieutenant, City of Glasgow, since 1980; b. 26.11.41, Glasgow; m., John (deceased). Educ. Hyndland Secondary School; Glasgow University; Strathclyde University. Principal Teacher of Classics, Strathclyde schools, 1967-86;

entered local government as Member, Cowcaddens Ward, Glasgow Corporation, 1971; Glasgow District Council: Member, Scotstoun Ward, 1984, Chairman, Manpower Committee, 1974-77, Leader, Labour Group, 1977-86, Leader of the Council, 1980-86, Treasurer, 1986-92; President, COSLA, 1990-92; Convener, Scottish Local Government Information Unit, since 1984; Member, Board, Scottish Development Agency, 1989-91, GDA, since 1992; Chairman, Mayfest, since 1983. Recreations: cycling; theatre; walking; golf; West Highland terriers. Address: (h.) 16 Lansdowne Crescent, Glasgow G20 6NG; T.-0141-334 3522.

MacFadyen, Hon. Lord (Donald James Dobbie), LLB, FCIArb. Senator of the College of Justice; b. 8.9.45, Glasgow; m., Christine Balfour Gourlay Hunter; 1 s.; 1 d. Educ. Hutchesons' Grammar School, Glasgow; Glasgow University. Advocate, 1969; Standing Junior Counsel, Department of Agriculture and Fisheries for Scotland, 1977-79, Scottish Home and Health Department, 1982-83; Advocate-Depute, 1979-82; QC, 1983; part-time Chairman, Medical Appeal Tribunals, 1989-95; Vice-Dean, Faculty of Advocates, 1992-95; Temporary Judge, Court of Session, 1994-95. Address: (h.) 66 Northumberland Street, Edinburgh, EH3 6JE; T.-0131-556 6043.

McFadyen, Thomas, MB, ChB. Senior Medical Officer, Erskine Hospital, since 1978; b. 30.11.39, Glasgow. Educ. Allan Glen's School; Glasgow University. Appointments, Glasgow Royal Infirmary, Law Hospital, Carluke and Royal Alexandra Infirmary, Paisley. Recreation: golf. Address: (h.) Tigh-Na-Coille, Erskine Hospital, Bishopton, PA7 5PU; T.-0141-812 7555.

McFall, John, BSc (Hons), BA, MBA. MP (Labour), Dumbarton, since 1987; Deputy Shadow Secretary of State for Scotland; b. 4.10.44, Glasgow; m., Joan Ward; 1 d. Educ. Schoolteacher, Assistant Head Teacher, 1974-87; Opposition Whip, 1989-91; Visiting Professor, Strathclyde Business School; Treasurer, British/Hong Kong Group; Vice-Chairman, British/Italian Group; Joint Secretary, British/Peru Group; Secretary, Retail Industry Group, Roads Study Group; Treasurer, Scotch Whisky Group. Recreations: jogging; reading; golf. Address: (b.) House of Commons, Westminster, London.

MacFarlane, Professor Alistair George James, CBE, PhD, DSc, MA, ScD, FIEE, FEng, FRS, FRSE. Principal and Vice Chancellor, Heriot-Watt University, since 1989; Chairman, Scottish Council for Research in Education, since 1993; Chairman, Scottish Library and Information Council, since 1994; b. 1931, Edinburgh; m., Nora; 1 s. Educ. Hamilton Academy; Glasgow University. Metropolitan-Vickers Electrical Company Ltd.: Electronic Engineer, Radar and Servo Division, Group Leader, Moving Target Indication and Receiver Laboratories; Lecturer, Electrical Engineering, Queen Mary College, London University, 1959 (Reader, 1965); UMIST: Reader in Control Engineering, 1966, Professor, 1969; Cambridge University: Chair, Engineering, 1974, Head, Information Engineering Division, Fellow, Selwyn College, 1974 (Vice-Master, 1980-88); Consultant Editor, International Journal of Control. Past Member: SERC Computer Board, Joint Policy Committee for National Facilities for Advanced Research Computing, Advisory Committee on Safety of Nuclear Installations. American Society of Mechanical Engineers Centennial Medal, 1980; Sir Harold Hartley Medal, Institute of Measurement and Control,1982; IEE Achievement Medal, 1992; IEE Faraday Medal, 1993. Address: (b.) Heriot-Watt University, Riccarton, Edinburgh, EH14 4AS.

Macfarlane, Rev. Alwyn James Cecil, BA, MA; b. 14.6.22, Edinburgh; m., Joan Cowell Harris; 1 s.; 1 d. Educ. Cargilfield School, Edinburgh; Rugby School; New College, Oxford; New College, Edinburgh. Captain, 6th

Black Watch, North Africa, Italy and Greece, 1940-45; entered Ministry, Church of Scotland, 1951; Minister: Fodderty and Strathpeffer, 1952-59, St. Cuthbert's Church, Edinburgh (Associate), 1959-63, Portobello Old, Edinburgh, 1963-68, Newlands (South), Glasgow, 1968-85; Associate Minister, The Scots' Church, Melbourne, 1985-88. Chaplain to The Queen in Scotland; Member, The Queen's Household in Scotland. Recreations: photography; travel. Address: 4/9 Belhaven Place, Edinburgh.

Macfarlane, Professor Colin John, BSc, CEng, FRINA, MIMarE. Lloyd's Register Professor of Subsea Engineering, Strathclyde University, since 1986; Governor, Centre for Advanced Maritime Studies, since 1988; b. 4.3.50, Inverkip; m., Sheila Gardner; 1 s.; 1 d. Educ. Uddingston Grammar School; Strathclyde University. P&O Steam Navigation Company and Three Quays Marine Services, 1973-80; BP Engineering (specialist naval architect), 1981-86. Recreations: family; reading; gardening. Address: (b.) Strathclyde University, Department of Ship and Marine Technology, 100 Montrose Street, Glasgow; T.-0141-552 4400.

Macfarlane, James C., OBE. Chairman, Tayside Health Board. Address: (b.) P.O. Box 75, Vernonholme, Riverside Drive, Dundee, DD1 9NL.

Macfarlane, Neil Gerard, FRICS, IRRV, FIMgt. Director of Estates, Strathclyde Regional Council; b. Glasgow; m., Agnes Beatrix; 2 d. Educ. St. Mungo's Academy, Glasgow; Royal College of Science and Technology. Assessor's and Estates Departments, Corporation of City of Glasgow; appointed Head of Estates, Strathclyde Regional Council, 1974, Director, 1987. Executive Member, Scottish Branch, Local Authority Valuers Association; Executive Member, General Practice Division, Royal Institution of Chartered Surveyors in Scotland. Recreations: bowling; walking; light music. Address: (b.) 20 India Street, Glasgow, G2 4PF; T.-0141-204 2900.

Macfarlane of Bearsden, Lord, (Norman (Somerville) Macfarlane), DL, FRSE, HRSA, HRGI, Hon.FRIAS, Hon.FScotvec, Hon.FRCPSGlas, Hon. LLD (Strathclyde, 1986; Glasgow, 1988; Glasgow Caledonian, 1993; Aberdeen, 1995), DUniv (Stirling, 1992); Dr. h.c. (Edinburgh, 1992). Chairman, Macfarlane Group (Clansman) PLC, since 1973 (Managing Director, 1973-90); Chairman, United Distillers UK, since 1987; Lord High Commissioner, General Assembly of Scotland, 1992-93; b. 5.3.26; m., Marguerite Mary Campbell; 1 s.; 4 d. Educ. High School of Glasgow. Commissioned, Royal Artillery, 1945, served Palestine, 1945-47; founded N.S. Macfarlane & Co. Ltd., 1949 (became Macfarlane Group (Clansman) PLC, 1973); Underwriting Member of Lloyd's, since 1978; Chairman: The Fine Art Society PLC, since 1976, American Trust PLC, since 1984 (Director, since 1980), Guinness PLC, 1987-89 (Joint Deputy Chairman, 1989-92); Director: Clydesdale Bank PLC, since 1980, General Accident Fire and Life Assurance Corporation plc, since 1984, Edinburgh Fund Managers plc, since 1980, Glasgow Chamber of Commerce, 1976-79; Member: Council, CBI Scotland, 1975-81, Board, Scottish Development Agency, 1979-87; Chairman, Glasgow Development Agency, 1985-92; Vice-Chairman, Scottish Ballet, 1983-87 (Director, since 1975); Director, Scottish National Orchestra, 1977-82; President, Royal Glasgow Institute of the Fine Arts, 1976-87; Member, Royal Fine Art Commission for Scotland, 1980-82; Scottish Patron, National Art Collection Fund, since 1978; Governor, Glasgow School of Art, 1976-87; Trustee: National Heritage Memorial Fund, since 1984, National Galleries of Scotland, since 1986; Director, Third Eye Centre, 1978-81; Chairman, Governors, High School of Glasgow, 1979-87; Member, Court, Glasgow University, 1979-87; President: Stationers' Association of GB and Ireland, 1965, Company of Stationers of Glasgow, 1968-70, Glasgow High School Club, 1970-72; Hon. Fellow,

Glasgow School of Art, since 1993; knighted, 1982; created a Life Peer, 1991. Recreations: golf; cricket; theatre; art. Address: (b.) Macfarlane Group (Clansman) PLC, Sutcliffe Road, Glasgow, G13 1AH; (h.) 50 Manse Road, Bearsden, Glasgow, G61 3PN.

Macfarlane, Professor Peter Wilson, BSc, PhD, FBCS, FESC, FRSE. Professor in Medical Cardiology, Glasgow University, since 1991; b. 8.11.42, Glasgow; m., Irene Grace Muir; 2 s. Educ. Hyndland Senior Secondary School, Glasgow; Glasgow University. Glasgow University: Assistant Lecturer in Medical Cardiology, 1967, Lecturer, 1970, Senior Lecturer, 1974, Reader, 1980; President, 5th International Congress on Electrocardiology, Glasgow, 1978; Chairman, 15th and 18th Annual Conferences, International Society of Computerised Electrocardiography, 1990, 1993; Author/Editor, 12 books. Recreations: watching football; running half-marathons; playing violin. Address: (h.) 12 Barrcraig Road, Bridge of Weir, PA11 3HG; T.-Bridge of Weir 614443.

Macfarlane, Professor Thomas Wallace, DDS, DSc, FRCPath, FDSRCPSGlas. Professor in Oral Microbiology, Glasgow University, since 1991; Honorary Consultant in Oral Microbiology; Dean Designate of Dental Education, 1994-95; Head, Department of Oral Sciences, 1992-95; b. 12.12.42, Glasgow; m., Nancy McEwan; 1 s. Educ. Hyndland Senior Secondary School; Glasgow University. Assistant Lecturer, Dental Histology and Pathology, 1966-69; trained in Medical Microbiology and Histopathology, Glasgow Royal Infirmary; Lecturer in Oral Medicine and Pathology, 1969-77; organised and ran the diagnostic service in Oral Microbiology, Glasgow Dental Hospital and School; Senior Lecturer in Oral Medicine and Pathology and Consultant in Oral Microbiology, 1977; Reader in Oral Medicine and Pathology, 1984-91. Recreations: music; reading; painting; walking. Address: (b.) Oral Microbiology Unit, Dental Hospital and School, 378 Sauchiehall Street, Glasgow, G2 3JZ; T.-0141-211 9600.

McFarlane, William Stewart, CA; b. 26.3.33, Glasgow; m., Sandra; 1 d. Educ. High School of Glasgow. Trained as Chartered Accountant, Wilson Stirling (now Touche, Ross & Co.), Glasgow; Parlane McFarlane CA, 1957-58; National Service (Second Lieutenant, Royal Corps of Signals), 1959-60; Partner, McFarlane, Son & Co., CA, 1961-62 (merged with Dickson, McFarlane & Robinson, CA, 1963-84, merged with Wylie & Bisset, CA, since 1985). Member, Council, Institute of Chartered Accountants of Scotland, 1971-76, Institute's representative, directorate of Glasgow Chamber of Commerce, 1970-88; President, Glasgow Chamber of Commerce, 1990-92; Past Finance Convener, Scottish Golf Union; Past Treasurer, Scottish Squash Rackets Association; Captain, Association of Golf Club Secretaries, 1980; Director, The Park School (Glasgow) Limited; Past Deacon, Incorporation of Masons of Glasgow; President, Rotary Club of Charing Cross. Recreations: golf; curling; swimming; squash. Address: (b.) 135 Wellington Street, Glasgow, G2 2XE; T.-0141-248 3904.

McGeough, Professor Joseph Anthony, FRSE, BSc, PhD, DSc, CEng, FIMechE, FIEE. Regius Professor of Engineering, Edinburgh University, since 1983; Honorary Professor, Nanjing Aeronautical and Astronautical University, China, since 1991; Visiting Professor, University Federico II of Naples, 1994; b. 29.5.40, Kilwinning; m., Brenda Nicholson; 2 s.; 1 d. Educ. St. Michael's College; Glasgow University; Aberdeen University. Research Demonstrator, Leicester University, 1966; Senior Research Fellow, Queensland University, Australia, 1967; Research Metallurgist, International Research and Development Co. Ltd., Newcastle-upon-Tyne, 1968-69; Senior Research Fellow, Strathclyde University, 1969-72; Lecturer in Engineering, Aberdeen University, 1972-77 (Senior Lecturer, 1977-80, Reader,

1980-83). Chairman, Dyce Academy College Council, 1980-83; Honorary Vice-President, Aberdeen University Athletic Association, since 1981; Chairman, Edinburgh and S.E. Scotland Panel, IMechE, 1988-92; Chairman, Scottish Branch, IMechE, 1993-95; Hon. President, Lichfield Science and Engineering Society, 1987-88; Member, Engineering Research Board, AFRC, 1992-94; Editor, Journal of Processing of Advanced Materials, since 1991. Publications: Principles of Electrochemical Machining, 1974; Advanced Methods of Machining, 1988. Recreations: gardening; golf; athletics. Address: (h.) 39 Dreghorn Loan, Colinton, Edinburgh, EH13 ODF; T.-0131-441 1302.

McGettrick, Professor Bartholomew John, OBE, FRSAMD, KHS, FRSA, BSc (Hons), MEd (Hons). Honorary Professor, Glasgow University; Principal, St. Andrew's College of Education, since 1985; Member, Scottish Consultative Council on the Curriculum, since 1988 (Deputy Chairman, since 1991); Member, General Teaching Council for Scotland, since 1986; Member, various CNAA committees; Chairman, Committee on Assessment 5-14; b. 16.8.45, Glasgow; m., Elizabeth Maria McLaughlin; 2 s.; 2 d. Educ. St. Aloysius' College, Glasgow; Glasgow University. Teacher and Head, Department of Geography, St. Aloysius' College, Glasgow, 1968-72; Educational Psychologist, Scottish Centre for Social Subjects, 1972-75; Assistant Principal, then Vice-Principal, Notre Dame College of Education (latterly St. Andrew's College of Education), 1975-85. Chairman, Catholic Education Commission for Scotland, 1981-87; Chair, "Higher Still" Task Group – Staff Development; Member, Council for Educational Technology, 1982-86; Member, SCOTVAC, 1984-88; Chairman, Committee of Principals of Colleges of Education, 1990-92; Vice-Chairman, Association Catholique Internationale des Institutions de Sciences de L'Education, 1990-92; Chairman, Board of Governors, St. Aloysius' College, Glasgow; Governor: Kilgraston School, Craighalbert Centre; Chairman, Governors, Craighead Institute; Member, International Committee for the Education of Teachers; Vice Chair: Educational Broadcasting Council for Scotland, Advisory Group on Sustainable Development. Recreations: sports (squash, rugby). Address: (h.) 174 Carmunnock Road, Glasgow, G44 5AJ; T.-0141-637 8112.

McGhee, Rev. Robert, DD. Minister, Falkirk St. Andrew's West, since 1990 (Falkirk St. Andrew's, 1972-90); b. 29.7.29, Port Glasgow; m., Mary Stevenson Cunningham; 1 s.; 2 d. Educ. Port Glasgow High School; Greenock High School; Glasgow University and Trinity College. Trained as cashier/bookkeeper, 1945-54; RAF, 1947-49; ordained and inducted to Pulteneytown St. Andrew's, Wick, 1959; Minister, Wick St. Andrew's and Thrumster, 1961-66; Minister, Newbattle, Dalkeith, 1966-72; Convener, Board of Social Responsibility, Church of Scotland, 1985-89 (Convener, Community Care, Social Responsibility, 1977-85); Convener, Personnel Committee, Church of Scotland, since 1992; Chairman, Lord's Day Observance Society, Scotland, 1970-74; President, Scottish Evangelistic Council, 1982-85; Moderator: Presbytery of Caithness, 1964-65, Presbytery of Falkirk, 1983-84, Synod of Forth, 1985-86. Address: St. Andrew's West Manse, 1 Maggie Woods Loan, Falkirk, FK1 5SJ; T.-Falkirk 23308.

McGhie, James Marshall, QC, LLB (Hons). Queen's Counsel, since 1983; Member, Criminal Injuries Compensation Board, since 1992; b. 15.10.44, Perth; m., Ann M. Cockburn; 1 s.; 1 d. Educ. Perth Academy; Edinburgh University. Advocate-Depute, 1983-86; part-time Chairman, Medical Appeal Tribunals, 1987-92. Address: (b.) Advocates Library, Parliament House, High Street, Edinburgh; T.-0131-226 5071.

McGibbon, Alistair, MA, MEd. Rector, Woodlands High School, Falkirk, since 1983; b. 3.10.37, Glasgow; m., Jean Ronald; 2 s.; 1 d. Educ. North Kelvinside School; Glasgow University; Stirling University. Teaching appointments in Glasgow, Guildford, Perth (Western Australia), Papua New Guinea, Central Region. Recreations: golf; Church activities. Address: (b.) Woodlands High School, Rennie Street, Falkirk, FK1 5AL; T.-01324 29615.

McGill, Rt. Rev. Stephen, PSS, STL. Bishop of Paisley, 1968-88; b. 4.1.12, Glasgow. Educ. St. Aloysius College, Glasgow; Blairs College, Aberdeen; Institut Catholique, Paris. Staff, Le Grand Seminaire, Bordeaux, 1939, Le Grand Seminaire, Aix-en-Province, 1940; Spiritual Director, then Rector, Blairs College, Aberdeen, 1940-60; Bishop of Argyll and the Isles, 1960-68. Recreations: caligraphy; golf. Address: 13 Newark Street, Greenock, PA16 7UH.

McGillivray, Rev. (Alexander) Gordon, MA, BD, STM; b. 22.9.23, Edinburgh; m., Winifred Jean Porter; 2 s.; 2 d. Educ. George Watson's Boys' College, Edinburgh; Edinburgh University; Union Theological Seminary, New York. Royal Artillery, 1942-45; Assistant Minister, St. Cuthbert's Parish Church, Edinburgh; Minister: Waterbeck Church, 1951-58, Nairn High Church, 1958-73; Clerk, Presbytery of Edinburgh, 1973-93; Clerk, General Assembly of Church of Scotland, 1971-94, retired. Recreations: golf; theatre. Address: 7 Greenfield Crescent, Balerno, Midlothian, EH14 7HD; T.-0131-449 4747.

McGillivray, Elizabeth Norma, LLB (Hons), NP. Solicitor, since 1982; part-time University Lecturer, since 1984; b. 16.1.48, Perth; m., Robert Gordon McGillivray. Educ. Grove Academy, Broughty Ferry; Dundee University. Partner, Bowmans Solicitors, Dundee, since 1985; part-time Tutor, Dundee University, 1984-92, part-time Lecturer, since 1989. Member, Council, Law Society of Scotland; Member, Board of Management, Angus College; Founder Chairman, Tayside Cancer Support Group. Recreations: music; walking; reading; enjoying life. Address: (h.) Lochtyknowe, Carnoustie, Angus; T.-01241 854887.

McGilvray, Professor James William, MA, MLitt. Professor of Economics, Strathclyde University, since 1975; Director, Fraser of Allander Institute, 1980-86; b. 21.2.38, Glasgow; m., Alison Ann; 1 s.; 1 d. Educ. St. Columba's College, Dublin; Edinburgh University. Recreations: golf; gardening. Address: (b.) 100 Cathedral Street, Glasgow, G4 0LN; T.-0141-552 4400.

McGinlay, Alan Douglas, BSc. Head Teacher, Hillpark Secondary School, since 1991; b. 14.4.50, Glasgow; m., Lynn; 1 s.; 1 d. Educ. Queen's Park Secondary School; Glasgow University. Assistant Head Teacher, then Depute Head and Acting Head, James Hamilton Academy, 1984-91; Head Teacher, Govan High School, 1991-94. Address: (b.) 36 Cairngorm Road, Glasgow, G43 2XA; T.-0141-637 1071.

McGirr, Professor Edward McCombie, CBE, BSc, MD, DSc (Hon.), FRCP, FRCPEdin, FRCPGlas, FFCM, FACP (Hon.), FRSE. Chairman, Scottish Council for Postgraduate Medical Education, 1979-85; Emeritus Professor, Glasgow University, since 1981 (Dean of Faculties, 1992-94); b. 15.6.16, Hamilton; m., Diane Curzon Woods; 1 s.; 3 d. Educ. Hamilton Academy; Glasgow University. RAMC, 1941-47, including posts as graded physician and specialist in medicine ; appointments in University Department of Medicine, Glasgow Royal Infirmary, 1947-78, latterly Muirhead Chair of Medicine, Glasgow University, and Physician in charge of wards, Glasgow Royal Infirmary; Dean, Faculty of Medicine, Glasgow University, 1974-81; Administrative Dean and Professor of Administrative Medicine, Glasgow University, 1978-81. President, Royal College of Physicians and Surgeons of Glasgow, 1970-72; Chairman, Scottish Health Service Planning Council, 1978-84; Honorary Physician to the Army in Scotland, 1975-81;

sometime Member: Greater Glasgow Health Board, National Radiological Protection Board, General Nursing Council for Scotland, National Board for Nursing, Midwifery and Health Visiting; Past President, Royal Medico-Chirurgical Society of Glasgow; Chairman, Scottish Council for Opportunities for Play Experience (SCOPE), 1985-87; Chairman, Clyde Estuary Amenity Council, 1986-90. Recreations: reading; curling. Address: (h.) Anchorage House, Bothwell, by Glasgow, G71 8NF; T.-01698 852194.

McGlynn, Archie Smith, BA (Hons), MPhil, DipComm. HM Chief Inspector of Schools, since 1987; b. Tarbert, Argyll; m., Leah Sutherland Ross; 1 s.; 1 d. Educ. Tarbert Secondary School; Campbeltown Grammar School; Strathclyde University; Glasgow University. Industry and commerce, 1962-64 and 1966-67; Teacher in schools and further/higher education colleges, 1964-69; Depute Principal, Glenrothes College, 1969-75; HM Inspector of Schools, 1976-87. Recreations: hedgehog preservation; following Fife Flyers. Address: (b.) Room 4/35, New St. Andrew's House, Edinburgh; T.-0131-244 4569.

McGlynn, Rt. Rev. Lord Abbot (James Aloysius) Donald, OCSO, STL, SLJ. Monk, Order of Cistercians of Strict Observance, since 1952; Abbot of Nunraw, since 1969; b. 13.8.34, Glasgow. Educ. Holyrood School, Glasgow; St. Bernardine's School, Buckinghamshire; Gregorian University, Rome. President, Scottish Council of Major Religious Superiors, 1974-77; President, British Isles Regional Council of Cistercian Abbeys, 1980-84; Chairman, Union of Monastic Superiors, 1985-89; Official Roman Catholic Visitor to the General Assembly, Church of Scotland, 1976 and 1985; Commandeur Ecclesiastique, Military & Hospitaller Order of St. Lazarus of Jerusalem, 1985; Patron, Friends of the Beatitudes, Madras; Patron, Haddington Pilgrimage of St. Mary & the Three Kings. Recreations: iconography; farm work; computer printing. Address: Sancta Maria Abbey, Nunraw, Garvald, Haddington, EH41 4LW; T.-0162 083 223.

McGowan, Daniel, MILAM. Director of Community Services, Cumbernauld and Kilsyth District Council, since 1989 (Director of Leisure and Recreation, 1978-89); b. 23.9.41, Coatbridge; m.; 4 s.; 1 d. Educ. St. Patrick's High School, Coatbridge; Coatbridge Technical College. Chairman, Scottish Swimming Coaches Association, 1980-90. Recreations: swimming; golf. Address: (b.) Council Offices, Bron Way, Cumbernauld, G67 1DZ; T.-012367 22131.

McGowan, Professor David Alexander, MDS, PhD, FDSRCS, FFDRCSI, FDSRCPSG. Professor of Oral Surgery, Glasgow University, since 1977, Dean of Dental Education, 1990-95; Consultant Oral Surgeon, Greater Glasgow Health Board, since 1977; b. 18.6.39, Portadown, Co. Armagh; m., Margaret Vera Macaulay; 2 d. Educ. Portadown College; Queen's University, Belfast. Oral surgery training, Belfast and Aberdeen, 1961-67; Lecturer in Dental Surgery, Queen's University, Belfast, 1968; Lecturer, then Senior Lecturer and Deputy Head, Oral and Maxillofacial Surgery, London Hospital Medical College, 1968-77. Postgraduate Adviser in Dentistry, Glasgow University, 1977-90; Chairman, Dental Committee, Scottish Council for Postgraduate Medical Education, 1980-90; Dean, Dental Faculty, and Member of College Council, Royal College of Physicians and Surgeons of Glasgow, 1989-92; Member and Vice-Chairman of Executive, General Dental Council; Member, Conference of Deans of Dental Schools; Chairman, National Dental Advisory Committee; Member, EC Advisory Committee on training of dental practitioners; former Council Member, British Association of Oral and Maxillofacial Surgeons. Recreations: sailing; music. Address: (b.) Department of Oral Surgery, Glasgow Dental Hospital and School, 378 Sauchiehall Street, Glasgow, G2 3JZ; T.-0141-211 9700.

McGowan, Ian David, MA, PhD. Director, Centre for Publishing Studies, Stirling University, since 1988, and Senior Lecturer in English Studies, since 1992; Member, Scottish Arts Council, and Chairman, Literature Committee, since 1993; b. Glasgow. Educ. Pembroke College, Oxford. Joined Stirling University as Lecturer in English Studies, 1973. Member and Chairman, Grants to Publishers Panel, since 1985, Chairman, Grants to Magazines Panel, since 1992, Scottish Arts Council; Member, Executive Committee, Book Trust Scotland, 1986-93. Publications: The Restoration and the Eighteenth Century; Charles Dickens: Little Dorrit; articles and chapters. Address: (b.) Centre for Publishing Studies, Stirling University, Stirling, FK9 4LA; T.-01786 473171.

McGowan, Ian Duncan, BA. Librarian, National Library of Scotland, since 1990 (Secretary of the Library, 1988-90); b. 19.9.45, Liverpool; m., Elizabeth Ann Weir; 2 d. Educ. Liverpool Institute; Exeter College, Oxford. Assistant Keeper, National Library of Scotland, 1971-78; Keeper (Catalogues and Automation), 1978-88. Address: (b.) National Library of Scotland, George IV Bridge, Edinburgh, EH1 1EW; T.-0131-226 4531.

McGowan, John, LLB. Sheriff in Glasgow, since 1993; Temporary Sheriff, 1986-93; b. 15.1.44, Kilmarnock; m., Elise Smith; 2 s. Educ. St. Joseph's Academy, Kilmarnock; Glasgow University. Admitted Solicitor, 1967; Council Member, Law Society of Scotland, 1982-85. Recreations: golf; tennis; curling; cricket; listening to music. Address: (h.) 19 Auchentrae Crescent, Ayr.

McGown, Archibald M. Director, Scottish Pre-Retirement Council, since 1987; b. 15.11.33, Paisley; m., Janet Robertson; 1 s.; 2 d. Educ. Rutherglen Academy. Managing Director, Elvestead Canned Meat Co. Ltd., 1976-86. Chairman, Royal Scottish Automobile Club, 1992-94. Recreations: curling; bowling. Address: (b.) Alexandra House, 204 Bath Street, Glasgow, G2 4HL; T.-0141-332 9427.

McGrath, John. Playwright; Theatre, Film and TV Director; Artistic Director, 7:84 Theatre Company (Scotland), 1973-88; Producer/Director, Freeway Films, since 1982; b. 1.6.35, Birkenhead; m., Elizabeth MacLennan; 2 s.; 1 d. Educ. Alun Grammar School, Mold, Clwyd; St. John's College, Oxford. Playwright (more than 40 plays produced professionally in UK and abroad); Writer of film screenplays for feature films and TV plays; Director in theatre and TV; Poet and Songwriter; plays for theatre including Events While Guarding the Bofors Gun, The Cheviot, The Stag and the Black, Black Oil, Blood Red Roses, Border Warfare, John Brown's Body, Watching for Dolphins, The Wicked Old Man. Visiting Judith E. Wilson Fellow, Cambridge, 1979 and 1989; recent film and television productions: Border Warfare, John Brown's Body, The Dressmaker, Mairi Mhor, Carrington, Half the Picture. Publications: A Good Night Out (lectures); The Bone Won't Break. Address: (b.) Freeway Films, 67 George Street, Edinburgh, EH2 2JG; T.-0131-225 3200.

McGrath, Professor John Christie (Ian), BSc, PhD. Regius Professor of Physiology, Glasgow University, since 1991; Co-Director, Clinical Research Initiative in Heart Failure, since 1994; b. 8.3.49, Johnstone; m., Wilma Nicol; 1 s.; 1 d. Educ. John Neilson Institution, Paisley; Glasgow University. Glasgow University: Research Fellow in Pharmacology and Anaesthesia, 1973-75, Lecturer, 1975-83, Senior Lecturer, 1983-88, Reader, 1988-89, Titular Professor, 1987-91. Sandoz Prizewinner, British Pharmacological Society, 1980; Pfizer Award for Biology, 1983. Recreations: running; politics; travel. Address: (b.) Institute of Physiology, Glasgow University, Glasgow; T.-041-330 4483.

McGrath, Tom. Playwright and Poet; b. 1940, Rutherglen. Educ. Glasgow University. Founder Editor, International Times, 1966-67; Musical Director, Great Northern Welly Boot Show; Director, Third Eye Centre, Glasgow, 1974-77; plays include: Laurel and Hardy, 1976, The Hardman, 1977.

McGregor, Rev. Alistair Gerald Crichton, QC, BD, BA, LLB, WS. Minister, North Leith Parish Church, Edinburgh, since 1987; Temporary Sheriff, 1984-87; b. 15.10.37, Sevenoaks, Kent; m., Margaret Dick Lees or McGregor; 2 s.; 1 d. Educ. Charterhouse; Pembroke College, Oxford; Edinburgh University. Solicitor; Advocate; QC; former Standing Junior Counsel to Queen's and Lord Treasurer's Remembrancer, to Scottish Home and Health Department and to Scottish Development Department; Past Chairman, Discipline Committee, Potato Marketing Board; former Clerk, Rules Council, Court of Session; former Tutor in Scots Law, Edinburgh University; former Chairman, Family Care; Director, Apex (Scotland) Ltd; Executive Committee, Kirk Care Housing Association Ltd. Publication: Obscenity (Co-author). Recreations: squash; tennis; swimming; travel; cinema. Address: (h.) 22 Primrose Bank Road, Edinburgh, EH5; T.-0131-551 2802.

MacGregor, Professor Bryan Duncan, BSc, MSc, PhD, DipSurv, MRTPI, ARICS. MacRobert Professor of Land Economy, Aberdeen University, since 1990; b. 16.10.53, Inverness. Educ. Inverness Royal Academy; Edinburgh University; Heriot Watt University; Cambridge University. Lecturer, Department of Land Management, Reading University, 1981-84; Lecturer, Department of Town and Regional Planning, Glasgow University, 1984-87; Deputy, then Property Research Manager, Prudential Portfolio Managers, 1987-90. Recreations: hill-walking; football; literature; music; thinking. Address: (b.) Department of Land Economy, St. Mary's College, Aberdeen University, Aberdeen, AB9 2UF; T.-01224 272356.

McGregor, Very Rev. Canon Charles Cameron, BA. Parish Priest, Banchory, since 1982; b. 6.9.26, Buckie. Educ. Our Lady's High School, Motherwell; Blairs College, Aberdeen; Allen Hall, St. Edmund's College, Ware. Army Service, 1945-48; ordained Priest, St. Bridget's, Baillieston, 1954; Parish Priest, Inverurie, 1956-62, Kincorth, 1962-72; Cathedral Administrator, Aberdeen, 1972-82; Dean, St. Mary's, since 1979; Dean, St. Columba's, since 1982; appointed to Cathedral Chapter, 1994; Broadcaster, BBC, 1958-84; Religious Adviser, Grampian TV, 1965-85; Army Chaplain, TAVR, 1965-72, 1st Bn., Lowland Volunteers; Chairman, Scottish Catholic International Aid Fund, 1988-92. Recreations: reading; theatre; historical buildings; Doric prose and verse. Address: (h.) Corsee Cottage, High Street, Banchory, AB31 3RP; T.-01330 822835.

Macgregor, Rt. Rev. George, MA, BD (Hons). Bishop of Moray, Ross and Caithness, since 1994; b. 17.11.33, Glasgow; m., Elizabeth Jean; 1 s.; 3 d. Educ. Hutchesons' Boys Grammar School, Glasgow; St. Andrews University. Deaconed and priested, 1977; St. Michael's, Elie, 1978-81; St. Luke's, Glenrothes, 1981-86; St. James', Dollar, 1986-90; St. Luke's, Wester Hailes, 1991-93. Recreations: hill-walking; rugby. Address: (b.) 11 Kenneth Street, Inverness, IV3 5NR; T.-01463 226255.

MacGregor of MacGregor, Brigadier Sir Gregor, 6th Bt. 23rd Chief of Clan Gregor; b. 22.12.25; m., Fanny Butler; 2 s. Educ. Eton. Commissioned, Scots Guards, 1944; commanding 1st Bn., Scots Guards, 1966-69; Col. Recruiting, HQ Scotland, 1971; Lt.-Col. commanding Scots Guards, 1971-74; Defence and Military Attache, British Embassy, Athens, 1975-78; Comdr., Lowlands, 1978-80; Grand Master Mason of Scotland, 1988-93; Member, Queen's Bodyguard for Scotland (Royal Company of Archers). Address: (h.) Bannatyne, Newtyle, Blairgowrie, Perthshire.

McGregor, Iain. Honorary Secretary, SABRE (Scotland Against Being Ruled By Europe); b. 19.3.37, Stirling. Educ. Selkirk High School; Kelso High School. Army Service, REME; International Trade Exhibitions Publicist, London; Editor, BIPS International Photo-Feature Agency; Journalist, Fleet Street and provinces; Writer and Lecturer in Journalism, Asia, Europe, North America; Founding Director, Institute for Christian Media (Canada); Member, Social Credit Secretariat; Editor, The Patriot for Scotland; Scotland Representative, European Anti-Maastricht Alliance; Council Member, Heritage Society of Scotland. Recreations: local history; travel; music; theatre; film; books. Address: (h.) 170 Portobello High Street, Edinburgh, EH15 1EX.

MacGregor, Ian George Stewart, OBE, MA, MEd, FIMgt; b. 29.12.24, Newcastle-upon-Tyne. Educ. Altrincham Grammar School; Bell-Baxter School, Cupar; St. Andrews University; Edinburgh University; New York University. Assistant Principal, Ministry of Finance, Government of Northern Ireland, 1947-50; Teacher, Buckhaven High School, 1952-53 and 1954-55 (Teaching Fellowship in Psychology, New York University, 1953-54); Principal Administrative Assistant, Edinburgh Corporation Education Department, 1955-59; Assistant Director of Education, Aberdeenshire, 1959-64; Senior Depute Director of Education, West Lothian, 1964-70; Rector, Bathgate Academy, 1970-88. General Council Assessor, Edinburgh University Court; Chairman of Governors, Compass School, Haddington. Recreations: Scouting; photography; Rotary; travel. Address: (h.) 20 Stewart Avenue, Bo'ness, EH51 9NL; T.-01506 822462.

Macgregor, Janet Elizabeth, OBE, BSc, MB, ChB, MD, FRCPath, FRCOG. Director, Harris Birthright Research Centre, Aberdeen University, since 1988; b. 12.1.20, Glasgow; m., Professor A.G. Macgregor (deceased); 3 s.; 1 d. Educ. Bearsden Academy; Glasgow University. Captain, RAMC, 1943-45; Medical Officer, Maternity and Child Welfare, Glasgow, Sheffield and Edinburgh, 1946-59; Research Fellow, Department of Obstetrics and Gynaecology, Aberdeen University, 1960-66; Medical Assistant, Grampian Health Board, 1966-73; appointed Senior Lecturer, Aberdeen University, 1973. Member, Cytology Sub-Committee, Royal College of Pathologists, 1980-82; Chairman and President, British Society for Clinical Cytology, 1977-83; Member, Medical Advisory Committee, Women's National Cancer Control Campaign, since 1977; Member, IARC (WHO) Study Group on Cervical Cancer, 1978-84; Fellow, International Academy of Cytology, since 1963. Address: (h.) Ardruighe, Clachan, Isle of Seil, Argyll; T.-0185-23-427.

Macgregor, Jimmie, MBE, DA. Radio and Television Presenter; Author; Lecturer. Educ. Springburn Academy; Glasgow School of Art. Forefront of British folk revival for more than 20 years; countless radio and TV appearances, tours in Britain and abroad; more than 20 albums recorded; own daily radio programme, Macgregor's Gathering, for more than 10 years; regular TV series on long-distance walks; various books on folk song and the outdoors; has written theme music for TV and radio, illustrated books; gives regular lectures and slide shows; Life Member, RSPB; President, Friends of River Kelvin; Vice-President, Scottish Conservation Projects and Scottish Youth Hostels Association; twice Scot of the Year; Hon. Fellow, Royal Zoological Society of Scotland. Recreations: collecting paintings, pottery, glass, furniture; the outdoors; wildlife; hill-walking; theatre; art; music; antiques; old cars; anything and everything Scottish. Address: (b.) BBC, Queen Margaret Drive, Glasgow.

McGregor, John Cummack, BSc (Hons), MB, ChB, FRCS, FRCSEdin. Consultant Plastic and Reconstructive Surgeon, Lothian Region, based at Regional Plastic Surgery

Unit, Bangour General Hospital, since 1980; b. 21.4.44, Paisley; m., Moira Imray; 1 s.; 1 d. Educ. Paisley Grammar School; Glasgow University. Initial medical and surgical training, Paisley Royal Alexandra Infirmary, Western Infirmary, Glasgow, Stobhill Hospital, Glasgow, Nottingham City Hospital, Canniesburn Plastic Surgery Unit, Glasgow and Bangour General Hospital. Recreations: tennis; badminton; golf; cacti collecting; budgerigar breeding/showing. Address: (b.) Department of Plastic Surgery, Bangour General Hospital, West Lothian; Murrayfield Hospital, 122 Corstorphine Road, Edinburgh, EH12 6UD.

Macgregor, William. Chief Agricultural Officer, Scottish Office Agriculture and Fisheries Department. Address: (b.) Pentland House, 47 Robb's Loan, Edinburgh, EH14 1TY.

McGregor, William, MA, MEd. Rector, James Hamilton Academy, Kilmarnock, since 1989; b. 14.2.44, Kilmarnock; m., Elspeth Barbara Greene; 1 s.; 1 d. Educ. Kilmarnock Academy; Glasgow University. Teacher, Assistant Rector, Depute Rector, Mainholm Academy, Ayr, 1968-89. Publications: bus histories. Recreations: photography (transport); writing. Address: (h.) 25 Blackburn Drive, Ayr, KA7 2XN; T.-01292 282043.

McGrigor, Captain Sir Charles Edward, 5th Bt. A Vice-President, RNLI; Member, Queen's Bodyguard for Scotland (Royal Company of Archers); a Deputy Lieutenant, Argyll and Bute; b. 5.10.22; m., Mary Bettine (eldest daughter of the late Sir Archibald Edmonstone, 6th Bt. of Duntreath); 2 s.; 2 d. Educ. Eton. Joined Army, 1941; Rifle Brigade, North Africa, Italy, Austria (mentioned in Despatches); ADC to Duke of Gloucester, 1945-47.

McGuire, Edward, ARCM, ARAM. Composer; b. 15.2.48, Glasgow. Educ. Junior Department, RSAMD; Royal Academy of Music, London; State Academy of Music, Stockholm. Won National Young Composers Competition, 1969; Rant selected as test piece for 1978 Carl Flesch International Violin Competition; Proms debut, 1982, when Source performed by BBC SSO; String Quartet chosen for 40th Anniversary Concert, SPNM, Barbican, 1983; featured composer, Park Lane Group series, Purcell Room, 1993; frequent commissions and broadcasts including Euphoria (EIF/Fires of London), Songs of New Beginnings (Paragon Ensemble), Quintet II (Lontano), Peter Pan (Scottish Ballet), A Glasgow Symphony (NYOS), The Loving of Etain (Paragon Opera), Trombone Concerto (Aix-en-Provence Festival), Mistral (Glasgow Wind Band); plays flute with and writes for Whistlebinkies folk group. Address: c/o Scottish Music Information Centre, 1 Bowmont Gardens, Glasgow, G12 9LR; T.-0J41-334 6393.

McGurk, John. Editor, Evening News, since 1995. Address: (b.) 20 North Bridge, Edinburgh, EH1 1YT.

McHardy, Stuart Andrew, MA (Hons), FSA (Scot). Director, Scots Language Resource Centre, Perth, since 1993; b. 19.4.47, Dundee; m., Sandra Davidson; 1 s. Educ. Morgan Academy, Dundee; Edinburgh University. Formerly worked in advertising and marketing and as professional musician, writer, broadcaster and journalist. Publications: Strange Secrets of Ancient Scotland; Tales of Whisky and Smuggling. Recreations: music; hill-walking. Address: (b.) S.L.R.C., A.K. Bell Library, 2-8 York Place, Perth, PH2 8EP.

McIldowie, James Robert, MA, LLB, NP. Solicitor, since 1962; Honorary Sheriff, since 1986; b. 24.9.37, Crieff; m., Isabella Junor (June) Anderson; 2 d. Educ. Morrison's Academy, Crieff; Edinburgh University. Apprentice and Assistant in Edinburgh; joined McLean & Stewart, Dunblane and Callander, 1962; became a Partner, 1963; now Senior Partner. Accredited Expert in Agricultural Law; former Secretary and Treasurer, Highland Pony Society.

Recreations: golf; music; theatre; all sports. Address: (b.) 51-53 High Street, Dunblane, Perthshire; T.-01786 823217.

McIlvanney, William. Novelist and Poet; b. 1936, Kilmarnock. Educ. Kilmarnock Academy; Glasgow University. Teacher (Assistant Rector (Curriculum), Greenwood Academy, Irvine, until 1975); Creative Writing Fellow, Strathclyde University, 1972-73; author of Remedy is None, 1966 (joint winner, Geoffrey Faber Memorial Award, 1967), A Gift from Nessus, 1968 (Scottish Arts Council Publication Award, 1969), Docherty, 1975 (Whitbread Award for Fiction, 1975), Laidlaw, 1977, The Papers of Tony Veitch, 1983, The Big Man, 1985, Strange Loyalties, 1990; three books of poetry: The Longships in Harbour, 1970, Weddings and After, 1983, In Through the Head, 1985; Surviving the Shipwreck (essays and collected journalism), 1991.

McIlwain, Alexander Edward, CBE, MA, LLB, SSC, WS. Senior Partner, Leonards, Solicitors, Hamilton; Honorary Sheriff, South Strathclyde, Dumfries and Galloway, at Hamilton, since 1981; b. 4.7.33, Aberdeen; m., Moira Margaret Kinnaird; 3 d. Educ. Aberdeen Grammar School; Aberdeen University. Commissioned, Royal Corps of Signals, 1957-59; Burgh Prosecutor then District Prosecutor, Hamilton, 1966-76; Dean, Society of Solicitors of Hamilton, 1981-83; Chairman, Legal Aid Central Committee, 1985-87; President, Law Society of Scotland, 1983-84; Member: Central Advisory Committee for Scotland on Justices of the Peace; Lanarkshire Health Board; The Scout Council (UK); Honorary Member, American Bar Association; Honorary Vice President, Scottish Lawyers for Nuclear Disarmament; Chairman, Lanarkshire Scout Area, 1981-91; Chairman, Hamilton Sheriff Court Project, 1990-94; Temporary Sheriff, since 1984; Vice President, Temporary Sheriffs Association, since 1993. Publications: Time Costing and Time Recording (in collaboration); Supporting Victims in the Criminal Justice System. Recreations: work; gardening; golf. Address: (h.) 7 Bothwell Road, Uddingston, Glasgow; T.-01698 813368.

MacInnes, Donald, BA, MBA. Chief Executive, Dunbartonshire Enterprise, since 1991; b. 8.8.47, Isle of Harris; m., Catherine; 3 s.; 1 d. Educ. Inverness Royal Academy; Strathclyde University. Former building society manager and development surveyor. Recreation: sailing. Address: (h.) 83 Woodend Drive, Jordanhill, Glasgow; T.-0141-950 1374.

MacInnes, Hamish, OBE, BEM. Writer and Designer; b. 7.7.30, Gatehouse of Fleet. Educ. Gatehouse of Fleet. Mountaineer with numerous expeditions to Himalayas, Amazon and other parts of the world; Deputy Leader, 1975 Everest SW Face Expedition; film Producer/Advisor/safety expert, with Zinnemann, Connery, Eastwood, Putnam, etc.; Advisor, BBC TV live outside broadcasts on climbing; author of 20 books on travel and adventure, including two autobiographies and fiction; designed the first all-metal ice axe, Terodactyl ice climbing tools, the MacInnes stretchers; Founder, Search and Rescue Dog Association; Honorary Member, Scottish Mountaineering Club; former President, Alpine Climbing Group; world authority on mountain rescue; Doctor of Laws (Hons), Glasgow University; Hon. DSc, Heriot Watt University; Hon. DSc, Aberdeen University; President, Guide Dogs Adventure Group; former Leader, Glencoe Mountain Rescue Team. Recreations: as above. Address: (h.) Glencoe, Argyll; T.-0855 811258.

McInnes, Sheriff John Colin, QC, BA (Hons) (Oxon), LLB, HonLLD (St. Andrews). Advocate; Sheriff, Tayside, Central and Fife, since 1974; b. 21.11.38, Cupar, Fife; m., Elisabeth Mabel Neilson; 1 s.; 1 d. Educ. New Park School, St. Andrews; Cargilfield School, Edinburgh; Merchiston Castle School, Edinburgh; Brasenose College, Oxford;

Edinburgh University. 2nd Lt., 8th Royal Tank Regiment, 1956-58; Lt., Fife and Forfar Yeomanry, Scottish Horse, TA, 1958-64; Advocate, 1963; Director, R. Mackness & Co. Ltd., 1963-70; Chairman, Fios Group Ltd., 1970-72; Parliamentary candidate (Conservative), Aberdeen North, 1964; Tutor, Law Faculty, Edinburgh University, 1965-72; in practice, Scottish Bar, 1963-72; Sheriff of Lothian and Peebles, 1972-74. Member, St. Andrews University Court, 1983-91; Chairman, Fife Family Conciliation Service, 1988-90; Member and Vice-President, Security Service Tribunal, since 1989; Member and Vice-President, Intelligence Services Tribunal, since 1994. Publication: Divorce Law and Practice in Scotland, 1990. Recreations: fishing; shooting; hill-walking; skiing; photography. Address: (h.) Sheriff Court, Tay Street, Perth, PH2 8NL.

McInnes, Professor William McKenzie, MSc, PhD, CA, FRSA. Professor of Accounting, Stirling University, since 1994; b. 24.5.42, Hawick; m., Christine Mary; 1 s.; 1 d. Educ. George Watsons College, Edinburgh; Durham University; Glasgow University. Management Accountant, IBM (UK) Ltd., 1966-68; Lecturer, Kirkcaldy Technical College, 1968-70; Audit Senior, Coopers and Lybrand, Bermuda, 1970-72; Senior Lecturer, Newcastle upon Tyne Polytechnic, 1974-76; Lecturer, then Senior Lecturer, Strathclyde University, 1976-91; Director of Research, Institute of Chartered Accountants of Scotland, 1992-93; Elder, Cadder Parish Church. Recreations: golf; tennis; music. Address: (b.) Department of Accountancy and Finance, Stirling University, Stirling, FK9 4LA; T.-01786 467280.

McIntosh, Rev. Colin George, MA, BD (Hons). Minister, Dunblane Cathedral, since 1988 (St. John's-Renfield Church, Glasgow, 1976-88); b. 5.4.51, Glasgow; m., Linda Mary Henderson; 2 d. Educ. Govan High School; Glasgow University. Assistant Minister, Corstorphine, Edinburgh, 1975-76. Chairman, Leighton Library Trustees; Trustee, Dunblane Cathedral Museum; Director, Church of Scotland Selection Schools, since 1992. Recreations: gardening; music; reading. Address: (h.) Cathedral Manse, The Cross, Dunblane, FK15 0AQ.

McIntosh, David Bainbridge, MA, MHSM, FIPD. General Manager, Scottish National Blood Transfusion Service, since 1990 (Director, Scottish Health Service Management Development Group, 1987-90); b. 28.10.46, Oxford; m., Judith Mary Mitchell; 4 d. Educ. Edinburgh Academy; Christ Church, Oxford; London School of Economics. Industrial Relations Adviser, Coats Patons (UK) Ltd., 1972-73; Personnel Manager: J. & P. Coats (UK) Ltd., 1974-79, J. & P. Coats Ltd., 1979-81; Mill Manager: Comphanhia De Linha Coats & Clark LDA Portugal, 1981-84, Hilos Cadena SA Colombia, 1984-87. Member, Executive Board, European Plasma Fractionation Association; Committee Member, Edinburgh & South East Scotland Outward Bound Association; Member, Court of Directors, The Edinburgh Academy; former Chief Instructor, Loch Earn Sailing School. Recreations: golf; sailing; skiing; squash; fishing. Address: (b.) Ellen's Glen Road, Edinburgh, EH17 7QT; T.-0131-664 2317.

Macintosh, Farquhar, CBE, MA, DipEd, DLitt, Dr. hc (Edinburgh), FEIS, FScotvec. Chairman, Sabhal Mor Ostaig, since 1991; Chairman, Highlands and Islands Education Trust, since 1988; Chairman, Education Committee, European Movement (Scotland), since 1993; Chairman, Scottish Examination Board, 1977-90; b. 27.10.23, Isle of Skye; m., Margaret M. Inglis; 2 s.; 2 d. Educ. Portree High School; Edinburgh University; Glasgow University; Jordanhill College of Education. Taught, Greenfield Junior Secondary School, Hamilton, Glasgow Academy and Inverness Royal Academy; Headmaster: Portree High School, Oban High School; Rector, Royal High School, Edinburgh, 1972-89; Member, Highlands and Islands Development Consultative Council and Convener,

Education Sub-Committee, 1965-82; Chairman, Jordanhill Board of Governors, 1970-72; Chairman, BBC Secondary Programme Committee, 1972-80; Chairman, School Broadcasting Council for Scotland, 1981-85; Vice-Chairman, School Broadcasting Council for UK, 1984-86; Member, Court, Edinburgh University, 1976-91; Governor, St. Margaret's School, since 1989, Royal Blind School, Edinburgh, since 1990; Gaelic Correspondent, Weekly Scotsman, 1953-57. Recreations: hill-walking; travel; Gaelic. Address: 12 Rothesay Place, Edinburgh, EH3 7SQ; T.-0131-225 4404.

McIntosh, Professor Francis George, BSc, MSc, CEng, MIEE, FRSA. Professor of Electronic and Electrical Engineering, Robert Gordon University, since 1984 (Assistant Principal and Dean of Science and Technology, since 1988); b. 19.3.42; 1 d. Previously Head, School of Electronic and Electrical Engineering, RGIT. Register of advisors, IEE accreditation; former Member, IEE Accreditation Committee; Member, NBS Research and Development Committee. Address: (b.) Robert Gordon University, Schoolhill, Aberdeen, AB9 1FR; T.-01224 262020.

McIntosh, Iain Redford. Sculptor; b. 4.1.45, Peterhead; m., Freida; 2 d. Educ. Peterhead Academy; Gray's School of Art. Recreation: sculpture. Address: (h.) 2 Middlefield Brae, Cupar, Fife.

McIntosh, Professor Jean Barbara, PhD, BSc, SRN, CMB. Professor of Community Nursing Research, Glasgow Caledonian University, since 1993; Non-Executive Director, Greater Glasgow Community and Mental Health Services NHS Trust, since 1994; b. 16.8.44, Fulmer; m., Dr. James R.B. McIntosh; 2 s. Educ. Watford Girls' Grammar School; LSE; University College Hospital, London. Former student nurse and staff nurse; Research Fellow, Aberdeen University, 1972-76; Senior Nurse Research, Greater Glasgow Health Board, 1981-88; Reader, then Professor, Glasgow Caledonian University, since 1989. Publications: one book; numerous papers. Recreations: hill-walking; gardening; classical music. Address: (b.) Department of Nursing and Community Health, Glasgow Caledonian University, 70 Cowcaddens Road, Glasgow, G4 0BA; T.-0141-331 3461.

Macintosh, Joan, CBE (1978), MA (Oxon), LLD (Hon., Dundee and Strathclyde), DUniv. (Stirling). Member, Commission, Scottish Constitutional Convention, 1993; Member, Council, Victim Support Scotland, since 1992; Hon. President, Scottish Legal Action Group; b. 23.11.19. Chairman, Scottish Consumer Council, 1975-80; Vice-Chairman, National Consumer Council, 1976-84; Lay Observer for Scotland, 1982-89; Chairman, Scottish Child Law Centre, 1989-92. Address: (h.) Wynd End, Auchterarder, Perthshire, PH3 1AD.

Macintosh, Keith William, LLB. Company Secretary, Clydesdale Bank PLC, since 1987; b. 21.6.49, Cardross; m., Diana Clark; 2 s. Educ. High School of Glasgow; Glasgow University. Partner, Macintosh Humble & Co., Solicitors, Dumbarton, 1977-87. Scottish Amateur Golf Champion, 1979; Secretary, Society of Scottish Golf Internationalists; Council Member, Royal Faculty of Procurators in Glasgow; Member, Committee of Managers, Western Club, Glasgow. Recreation: golf. Address: (b.) 30 St. Vincent Place, Glasgow, G1 2HL; T.-0141-223 2041.

McIntosh, Neil William David, CBE, ACIS, FIPM, FRSA. Chief Executive, Strathclyde Regional Council, since 1992; b. 30.1.40, Glasgow; m., Marie Elizabeth Lindsay. Educ. King's Park Senior Secondary School, Glasgow. O. and M. Trainee, Honeywell Controls Ltd., Lanarkshire, 1959-62; O. and M. Assistant, Berkshire, Oxford and Reading Joint Management Services Unit, 1962-64; O. and M. Officer, Stewarts and Lloyds Ltd., Lanarkshire, 1964-66; Senior O.

and M. Officer, Lanark County Council, 1966-69; Establishment/O. and M. Officer, Inverness County Council, 1969-75; Personnel Officer, Highland Regional Council, 1975-81; Director of Manpower Services, Highland Regional Council, 1981-85; Clerk, Dumfries Lieutenancy, 1985; Chief Executive, Dumfries and Galloway Regional Council, 1985-92; Director: Training 2000 (Scotland) Ltd., Sportability Scotland, Quality Scotland Foundation. Hon. Doctorate, Syracuse University. Recreations: bowling; hill-walking; antique bottle collecting; local history; youth work; dry-stane dyking. Address: (b.) Strathclyde House, 20 India Street, Glasgow, G2 4PF.

McIntosh, Peter William, BA, FIMgt. Assistant Principal, Robert Gordon University, since 1988, and Dean, Faculty of Management, since 1988; b. 9.4.51, Dunfermline; m., Christine; 1 s.; 1 d. Educ. Dunfermline High School; Strathclyde University. Lecturer in Economics, Strathclyde University, 1974-75; Lecturer in Business Studies, Bell College, Hamilton, 1975-78; Lecturer, Senior Lecturer, Head of Department and Dean, Faculty of Professional Studies, Napier Polytechnic, 1978-88. Recreations: sport; music; travel. Address: (b.) Faculty of Management, Robert Gordon University, Hilton Place, Aberdeen; T.-01224 283804.

Macintosh, Robert Macfarlan, MA, LLB. Solicitor; Chairman, Rent Assessment Committee, Glasgow, since 1966; Honorary Sheriff Substitute, Dumbarton, since 1975; b. 16.6.17, Dumbarton; m., Ann McLean Kelso; 1 s. Educ. Dumbarton Academy; George Watson's College, Edinburgh; Glasgow University. Qualified as Solicitor, 1949; Local Secretary, Dumbarton Legal Aid Committee, 1950-84; Chairman: Dunbartonshire Rent Tribunal, 1960, Glasgow Rent Tribunal, 1974; Clerk to Commissioners of Income Tax, East and West Dunbartonshire, since 1973; President, Dumbarton Burns Club; President, Cardross Golf Club. Recreation: golf. Address: (h.) Ardmoy, Peel Street, Cardross, Dunbartonshire.

McIntyre, Alasdair Duncan, CBE, BSc, DSc, FRSE, FIBiol, FRSA. Chairman, Marine Forum for Environmental Issues, since 1990; President, Estuarine and Coastal Sciences Association, since 1992; President, Sir Alister Hardy Foundation for Ocean Science, since 1992; Chairman, Buckland Foundation, since 1994; Member, Research Board, Scottish Natural Heritage, since 1992; Emeritus Professor of Fisheries and Oceanography, Aberdeen University, since 1986; b. 17.11.26, Helensburgh; m., Catherine Helen; 1 d. Educ. Hermitage School, Helensburgh; Glasgow University. Senior Principal Scientific Officer in charge of environmental team, Marine Laboratory, Aberdeen, 1973-79; Deputy Director, Department of Agriculture and Fisheries for Scotland, Marine Laboratory, Aberdeen, 1979-83; Director of Fisheries Research for Scotland, 1983-86; Co-ordinator, UK Fisheries Research and Development, 1986; Editor, Fisheries Research. Recreations: reading; food and wine; walking. Address: (h.) 63 Hamilton Place, Aberdeen, AB2 4BW; T.-01224 645633.

McIntyre, Archibald Dewar, CBE, MB, ChB, DPH, FFCM, FRCPE, DIH, DTM&H. Principal Medical Officer, Scottish Home and Health Department, 1977-93; b. 18.2.28, Dunipace; m., Euphemia Hope Houston; 2 s.; 2 d. Educ. Falkirk High School; Edinburgh University. Senior Medical Officer, Overseas Civil Service, Sierra Leone; Depute Medical Officer of Health, Stirling County Council; Depute Secretary, Scottish Council for Postgraduate Medical Education; Senior Medical Officer, Scottish Home and Health Department. Recreations: gardening; photography. Address: (h.) Birchlea, 43 Falkirk Road, Linlithgow, EH49 7PH; T.-01506 842063.

Macintyre, Iain Melfort Campbell, MB, ChB, MD, FRCSE. Consultant Surgeon, Edinburgh, since 1979; Chairman, Edinburgh Postgraduate Board for Medicine, since 1995; b. 23.6.44, Glasgow; m., Tessa Lorna Mary Millar; 3 d. Educ. Daniel Stewart's College, Edinburgh; Edinburgh University. Lecturer in Surgery, Edinburgh University, 1974-78; Visiting Professor, University of Natal, 1978-79; Council of Europe Travelling Fellow, 1986; Member, Council, Royal College of Surgeons of Edinburgh, since 1991; Member, National Medical Advisory Committee, 1992-95. Recreations: historical postcards; photography; flying light aircraft; skiing. Address: (b.) Department of Surgery, Western General Hospital, Edinburgh; T.-0131-332 2525.

McIntyre, Very Rev. Professor John, CVO, MA, BD, DLitt, DD, DHL, Dr hc, FRSE. Professor of Divinity, Edinburgh University, 1956-86; Honorary Chaplain to The Queen in Scotland, 1974-86 (Extraordinary Chaplain, since 1986); Dean of the Order of the Thistle, 1974-89; b. 20.5.16, Glasgow; m., Jessie Brown Buick; 2 s.; 1 d. Educ. Bathgate Academy; Edinburgh University. Ordained, 1941; Locum Tenens, Parish of Glenorchy and Inishail, 1941-43; Minister, Fenwick, Ayrshire, 1943-45; Hunter Baillie Professor of Theology, St. Andrew's College, Sydney University, 1946-56; Principal, St. Andrew's College, 1950-56, Hon. Fellow, since 1991; Principal Warden, Pollock Halls of Residence, Edinburgh University, 1960-71; Acting Principal and Vice-Chancellor, Edinburgh University, 1973-74, 1979; Principal, New College, and Dean, Faculty of Divinity, 1968-74; Moderator, General Assembly of the Church of Scotland, 1982; Convener, Board of Education, Church of Scotland, 1983-87; former Council Member and Vice President, Royal Society of Edinburgh. Publications: St. Anselm and his Critics, 1954; The Christian Doctrine of History, 1957; On the Love of God, 1962; The Shape of Christology, 1966; Faith, Theology and Imagination, 1987. Recreation: travel. Address: (h.) 22/4 Minto Street, Edinburgh, EH9 1RQ; T.-0131-667 1203.

Macintyre, Lorn, BA (Hons), PhD. Freelance Writer; b. 7.9.42, Taynuilt, Argyll; m., Mary. Educ. Stirling University; Glasgow University. Novelist and Short Story Writer; publications include Cruel in the Shadow and The Blind Bend in Chronicles of Invernevis Series. Recreation: work. Address: (h.) Priormuir, by St. Andrews, Fife; T.-01334 476428.

McIntyre, Robert Douglas, MB, ChB, DPH, DUniv, JP, FSC. Honorary Consultant, Stirling Royal Infirmary, since 1974; Chancellor's Assessor, Stirling University, 1978-88; b. 15.12.13, Dalziel; m., Letitia S. MacLeod; 1 s. Educ. Hamilton Academy; Daniel Stewart's College; Edinburgh University; Glasgow University. Consultant Chest Physician, Stirling and Clackmannan Counties, 1951-79; MP, Motherwell and Wishaw, 1945; Chairman, SNP, 1948-56; President, SNP, 1958-80; Honorary Treasurer, Royal Burgh of Stirling, 1958-64; Provost of Stirling, 1967-75; Freeman, Royal Burgh of Stirling. Recreations: sailing; conversation. Address: (h.) 8 Gladstone Place, Stirling; T.-Stirling 73456.

Macintyre, Professor Sally, BA, MSc, PhD. Director, Medical Research Council Medical Sociology Unit, since 1983; Honorary Professor, Glasgow University, since 1991; b. 27.2.49, Edinburgh; m., Dr. Guy Muhlemann. Educ. Durham, London and Aberdeen Universities. Research Fellow, Aberdeen University, 1971-75; Researcher, MRC Medical Sociology Unit, Aberdeen, 1975-83. Fellow, Royal Society of Medicine; Hon. Member, Faculty of Public Health Medicine. Recreations: skiing; hill-walking; climbing. Address: (b.) MRC Medical Sociology Unit, 6 Lilybank Gardens, Glasgow, G12 8QQ; T.-0141-357 3949.

MacIver, Alistair. Acting President, Scottish Crofters Union, since 1994; Chairman, Caithness and Sutherland

Constituency Labour Party, since 1985; Branch Secretary, General, Municipal and Boilermakers' Union, since 1971; b. 13.5.30, Brora. Educ. Lairg Senior School. Member: Rogart Community Council, since 1982, Sutherland Council on Alcohol, since 1990. Recreations: reading; indoor bowling. Address: (h.) Elcama, Inchcape, Rogart, IV28 3UD; T.-01408 641373.

MacIver, Donald John Morrison, MA (Hons). Researcher and Adviser in Bilingual Education, Western Isles Islands Council, since 1989 (Principal Teacher of Gaelic, Nicolson Institute, 1973-89); b. 12.11.42, Stornoway; m., Alice Macleod; 1 s. Educ. Nicolson Institute; Aberdeen University. Teacher of Gaelic, 1968-73. President, An Comunn Gaidhealach, 1985-90; former Director, National Gaelic Arts Project; former Member, Gaelic Books Council; Director, Acair Publishing Co.; former Editor, Sruth (newspaper of An Comunn Gaidhealach). Publications: Gaelic Oral Composition; Gaelic Language Practice; Gaelic O-Grade Interpretation; Sgriobh Seo; Feuch Seo; Feuch Freagairt; Faic Is Freagair; Camhanaich; Eadar Peann Is Paipear; Coinneach Odhar; Grian is Uisge; Co Rinn E?; A'Chlach. Recreations: writing (prose and poetry); computing; reading poetry; gardening; Coronation Street. Address: (h.) 32 Goathill Road, Stornoway, Isle of Lewis, PA87 2NL; T.-01851 702582.

MacIver, Duncan Malcolm, CBE. Deputy Director, Scottish Prison Service, 1978-86 (retired); b. 7.5.22, Meerut, India; m., Jessie D.T. Neilson; 2 s.; 1 d. Educ. McLaren High School, Callander. Served in Black Watch and Royal Scots, 1939-47, in Ceylon, India and Burma (14th Army), rank of Sgt.; joined Scottish Prison Service as a prison officer, 1948; promoted to Governor grade, 1960; Assistant Governor, Polmont and Barlinnie; Deputy Governor, Polmont and Perth; Governor: Castle Huntly Borstal, 1969-70, Aberdeen Prison, 1970-73; Assistant Inspector of Prisons, 1973-75; Governor (HQ), 1975-76; Governor, Edinburgh Prison, 1976-78; Controller of Operations (Deputy Director), Scottish Prison Service. Recreations: golf; gardening; bowls. Address: (h.) 3 Caiystane Drive, Edinburgh; T.-0131-445 1734.

MacIver, Iain Boyd, CA, IPFA, IRRV. Director of Finance, Tayside Regional Council, since 1982; b. 18.7.42, Glasgow; m., Joyce Goldie; 2 s. Educ. Hillhead High School, Glasgow University. Qualified as CA, 1964; private practice, 1964-66; Senior Accountant, Renfrew County Council, 1966-69; Depute Town Chamberlain, Royal Burgh of Rutherglen, 1969-72; Town Chamberlain, Burgh of Alloa, 1972-75; Chief Assistant Director of Finance, Central Regional Council, 1975-79; Depute Director of Finance, Tayside Regional Council, 1979-82. Chairman, Scottish Branch, Chartered Institute of Public Finance and Accountancy; Director, Dundee Repertory Theatre. Recreations: walking; cycling; gardening; theatre. Address: (b.) Tayside House, Crichton Street, Dundee; T.-01382 303555.

MacIver, Ian, BSc, DipEd, MSc, PhD. Principal, Coatbridge College, since 1989; b. 25.11.38, Stornoway; m., Anne Maureen Ramsay; 3 s.; 2 d. Educ. Nicolson Institute, Stornoway; Portree High School; Glasgow University. Secondary school teacher, 1962-64; studied and taught, University of Alberta, University of Chicago, and York University, Toronto, 1964-73; returned to Scotland and held posts, Langside College, 1973-74, Jordanhill College, 1975-76, James Watt College, 1977-82, Anniesland College, 1982-89. Elder, Free Church of Scotland. Recreations: distance running; reading; loafing. Address: (b.) Coatbridge College, Kildonan Street, Coatbridge, ML5 3LS; T.-01236 422316.

MacIver, Matthew M., MA, MEd, FRSA. Rector, Royal High School, Edinburgh, since 1989; b. 5.7.46, Isle of Lewis; m., Katrina; 1 s.; 1 d. Educ. Nicolson Institute,

Stornoway; Edinburgh University; Moray House College. History Teacher, 1969-72; Principal Teacher of History, Craigmount High School, 1972-80; Assistant Rector, Royal High School, 1980-83; Depute Head Teacher, Balerno High School, 1983-86; Rector, Fortrose Academy, 1986-89. Chairman, Joint Working Party on Classical Studies, since 1988; Member, Gaelic Television Committee, since 1991; Member, Business Council, Edinburgh University; Member, Board of Governors, Moray House Institute of Education; Member, Higher Still Specialist Group on Classical Studies. Recreation: Gaelic culture. Address: (h.) 21 Durham Road, Edinburgh, EH15 1NY; T.-0131-669 5029.

MacIver, Roy, MA, LLB. Secretary General, Convention of Scottish Local Authorities, 1986-95; b. 15.10.42, Stornoway; m., Anne; 3 s. Educ. Nicolson Institute, Stornoway; Edinburgh University; Glasgow University. Legal Assistant, Paisley Corporation; Solicitor/Administrator, Dunfermline Town Council, 1970-72; Assistant County Clerk (Lewis), Ross and Cromarty County Council, 1972-75; Chief Executive, Western Isles Islands Council (Comhairle nan Eilean), 1974-86. Recreation: jazz. Address: (b.) Rosebery House, 9 Haymarket Terrace, Edinburgh; T.-0131-346 1222.

Mackay, Angus Victor Peck, MA, BSc (Pharm), PhD (Cantab), MB, ChB, FRCPsych, FRCP (Ed). Physician Superintendent and Clinical Director, Argyll and Bute Hospital, and MacKintosh Lecturer in Psychological Medicine, Glasgow University, since 1980; Hon. Senior Lecturer, Department of Psychology, St. Andrews University; Medical Director, Argyll & Bute NHS Trust; Chairman, National Working Group on Mental Illness, since 1993; Psychiatric Representative, Committee on Safety of Medicines, DHSS, since 1983; b. 4.3.43, Edinburgh; m., Elspeth M.W. Norris; 2 s.; 2 d. Educ. George Heriot's School, Edinburgh; Edinburgh University; Churchill and Trinity Colleges, Cambridge. MRC Research Fellow, Cambridge; Member, senior clinical staff, MRC Neurochemical Pharmacology Unit, Cambridge, with appointment as Lecturer in Pharmacology, Trinity College (latterly, Deputy Director of Unit). Deputy Chairman, Health Services Research Committee of the Chief Scientist for Scotland; Member, Research Committee, Mental Health Foundation; Chairman, Argyll and Clyde Area Psychiatric Sub-Committee; Member, Scottish Executive, Royal College of Psychiatrists; Chairman, Research and Clinical Section, Royal College of Psychiatrists (Scotland). Recreations: rowing; sailing; rhododendrons. Address: (h.) Tigh an Rudha, Ardrishaig, Argyll; T.-01546 603272.

McKay, Sheriff Archibald Charles, MA, LLB. Sheriff of Glasgow and Strathkelvin, since 1979; b. 18.10.29; m., Ernestine Maria Tobia; 1 s.; 3 d. Educ. Knocknacarry, Co. Antrim; St. Aloysius' College, Glasgow; Glasgow University. National Service Commission, 1955-56; Solicitor, Glasgow, 1957; established own firm of solicitors, 1961; President, Glasgow Bar Association, 1967-68; appointed to the bench, 1978. Recreations: flying light aircraft; motor cycling; amateur radio; tennis. Address: (h.) 96 Springkell Avenue, Pollokshields, Glasgow, G41 4EL; T.-0141-427 1525.

Mackay, Charles, CB, BSc, MSc, FIBiol. Chief Agricultural Officer, Department of Agriculture and Fisheries for Scotland, 1975-87; b. 12.1.27, Kinloch, Sutherland; m., Marie A.K. Mitchell; 1 s.; 1 d. Educ. Strathmore School; Lairg Higher Grade Public School; Aberdeen University; Kentucky University. DAFS: Temporary Inspector, 1947-48, Assistant Inspector, 1948-54, Inspector, 1954-64, Senior Inspector, 1964-70, Technical Development Officer, 1970-73, Deputy Chief Agricultural Officer, 1973-75. Recreations: fishing; golf. Address: (h.) 4/3 Craufurland, Edinburgh, EH4 6DL; T.-0131-339 8770.

McKay, Sheriff Colin Graham, MA, LLB. Sheriff of North Strathclyde, since 1990; b. 20.1.42. Solicitor, 1966; private practice, 1966-90.

MacKay, Colin Hinshelwood, MA (Hons), FSA Scot. Partner, Colin MacKay Associates; Broadcaster and Writer; b. 27.8.44, Glasgow; m., Olive E.B. Brownlie; 2 s. Educ. Kelvinside Academy, Glasgow; Glasgow University; Jordanhill College of Education. Reporter/Presenter: Border Television Ltd., 1967-70, Grampian Television Ltd., 1970-73; Political Editor, Scottish Television PLC, 1973-92 (Presenter, Ways and Means, 1973-86); recent programmes include: People and Power (BBC Radio Scotland); Talk-In Sunday (Radio Clyde); Westminster File (Border TV); Eikon (Scottish TV); ITV Commentator: Papal Visit to Scotland, 1982, CBI Conference, Glasgow, 1983. Winner, Observer Mace, 1967 (British Universities Debating Championship); Member, two-man British Universities Canadian Debating Tour, 1967; Commonwealth Relations Trust Bursary to Canada, 1981; Member, Scottish Arts Council, 1988-94. Publications: Kelvinside Academy: 1878-1978, 1978; The Scottish Dimension in Central and Eastern Canada, 1981. Recreations: music (especially opera); reading; writing.

McKay, David Sutherland. Director and General Manager, JVC Manufacturing UK Ltd., since 1988; Director, SETG Ltd., since 1984; Chairman, Lanarkshire Quality Forum; b. 28.8.38, Wick; m., Catherine Margaret; 2 d. Educ. Wick High School; Robert Gordon's College. Apprenticeship in control engineering; Design Engineer, British Oxygen Co.; joined Honeywell Control Systems as Design Engineer; appointed Technical Director, 1983. Member, Bell College Management Board; Member, Scottish Electronic Forum. Recreation: worrying about cost of sailing. Address: (h.) Green Garth, Nethan Glen, Crossford, ML8 5QU; T.-Crossford 309.

Mackay, Professor David William, CBiol, FIBiol, FIWEM, FBIM, MIFM. Chief Officer, North East River Purification Board, since 1990; Visiting Professor, Institute of Aquaculture, Stirling University, since 1992; Board Member, Scottish Marine Biological Association, since 1991; b. 6.4.36, Stirling; m., Maureen. Educ. High School of Stirling; Strathclyde University; Paisley College. Experimental Officer, Freshwater Fisheries Laboratory, Pitlochry; Freshwater Biologist, then Marine Survey Officer, Clyde River Purification Board; Principal Environmental Protection Officer, Government of Hong Kong; Depute Director, Clyde River Purification Board; Head of Environmental Services, Ove Arup and Partners, Hong Kong; General Manager and Clerk, North East River Purification Board, Aberdeen. Vice President and Secretary, Scottish Anglers National Association, 1970-89. Recreations: farming; scuba diving; fishing. Address: (b.) NERPB, Greyhope House, Greyhope Road, Torry, Aberdeen, AB1 3RD; T.-01224 248338.

Mackay, Professor Donald Iain, MA, FRSE. Chairman, Scottish Enterprise, since 1993; Chairman, PIEDA plc, since 1976; Honorary Professor, Heriot-Watt University, since 1982; b. 27.2.37, Kobe, Japan; m., Diana Marjory Raffan; 1 s.; 2 d. Educ. Dollar Academy; Aberdeen University. Professor of Political Economy, Aberdeen University, 1971-76; Professor of Economics, Heriot-Watt University, 1976-82; Director, Grampian Holdings; Vice President, Scottish Association of Public Transport; Member, Scottish Economic Council; Economic Consultant to Secretary of State for Scotland; Governor, National Institute of Economic and Social Research. Recreations: tennis; bridge. Address: (h.) Newfield, 14 Gamekeepers Road, Edinburgh; T.-0131-336 1936.

Mackay, Donald John, MA, FRSA, FIMgt. Chairman, Highland Communities NHS Trust, since 1994; Chief Executive, Harris Tweed Association, 1982-93; b. 8.6.30, North Uist; m., Rhona MacLeod; 3 d. Educ. Portree High School; Aberdeen University; London University. District Commissioner and Private Secretary/Aide de Camp to Governor, Sierra Leone, 1954-58; Scottish Agricultural Organisation Society, 1958-61; AEA, Dounreay, 1961-63; British Aluminium, 1964-65; Director, An Comunn Gaidhealach, 1965-70; Primary Division, British Aluminium, 1970-82. Member, Red Deer Commission, 1966-74; Member, Highland Disablement Committee, since 1970-91, Chairman, 1991-94; Member, Highland Area Group, Scottish Council, 1971-93; Member, North of Scotland Electricity Council, 1981-84; Secretary, CBI Highland Area Group, 1978-87, Chairman, 1988-91; Member, HIDB Consultative Council, 1978-81, 1988-91; Member, Nature Conservancy Council Scottish Advisory Committee, 1979-86; MSC Chairman, Highlands & Islands, 1981-88; Member, Executive Committee, Scottish Council, 1982-93; Chairman, CNAG, 1984-86; Chairman, Albyn Housing Society, 1979-83; Chairman, CNAG, 1984-86; Chairman, Albyn Housing Society, 1979-83; Director, Fearann Eilean Iarmain, 1972-91; Member, Industrial Tribunal Panel, since 1986; Deputy Chairman, Sabhal Mor Ostaig, 1981-85; Member, Highland River Purification Board, 1981-83; Member, Highland Health Board, 1991-93. Recreations: sailing; shooting; fishing; Gaelic. Address: (h.) Kildonan, Teandalloch, Beauly, by Inverness.

Mackay, Donald Sage, QC, LLB, LLM; b. 30.1.46. Called to Scottish Bar, 1976; Member, Criminal Injuries Compensation Board, since 1989. Address: (b.) Advocates' Library, Parliament House, Edinburgh, EH1 1RF.

Mackay, Rev. Canon Douglas Brysson. Rector, Church of the Holy Rood, Carnoustie, since 1972; Synod Clerk, Diocese of Brechin, since 1981; Canon, St. Paul's Cathedral, Dundee, since 1981; b. 20.3.27, Glasgow; m., Catherine Elizabeth; 2 d. Educ. Possil Senior Secondary School; Edinburgh Theological College. Precentor, St. Andrew's Cathedral, Inverness, 1958; Rector, Gordon Chapel, Fochabers, 1961 (also Priest-in-Charge, St. Margaret's Church, Aberlour, 1964); Canon, St. Andrew's Cathedral, Inverness, 1965; Synod Clerk, Diocese of Moray, Ross, Caithness, 1965; Honorary Canon, St. Andrew's Cathedral, Inverness, 1972; Convenor of Youth, Moray Diocese, 1965; Brechin Diocese: Convenor, Social Service Board, 1974, Convenor, Joint Board, 1974, Convenor, Administration Board, 1982; Chairman, Truth and Unity Movement, 1980-87. President, British Red Cross, Carnoustie, 1974-82; President, British Legion, Carnoustie, 1981; Vice-Chairman, Carnoustie Community Care, 1981; Chairman, Carnoustie Community Council, 1979-81; President, Carnoustie Rotary Club, 1976. Recreations: golf; snooker; reading; music. Address: Holyrood Rectory, Carnoustie, DD7 6AB; T.-Carnoustie 52202.

Mackay, Douglas Ian, QC, LLB; b. 10.8.48. Advocate, 1980. Address: (b.) Advocates' Library, Parliament House, Edinburgh, EH1 1RF.

Mackay, Eileen Alison, MA. Principal Finance Officer, Scottish Office; b. 7.7.43, Helmsdale, Sutherland; m., A. Muir Russell (qv). Educ. Dingwall Academy; Edinburgh University. Research Officer, Department of Employment, 1965-72; Principal: Scottish Office, 1972-78, HM Treasury, 1978-80; Adviser, Central Policy Review Staff, Cabinet Office, 1980-83; Assistant Secretary, Scottish Development Agency and New Towns Division, Industry Department for Scotland, 1983-87; Rural Environment and Nature Conservation Division, Scottish Development Department, 1987-88; Under Secretary, Housing and Local Government, SDD, 1988-91. Address: (b.) New St. Andrews House, Edinburgh.

MacKay, Gregor D.R., MA (Hons). Special Adviser to Secretary of State for Scotland, since 1994; b. 23.7.69,

Torphins. Educ. Daniel Stewart's and Melville College, Edinburgh; St. Andrews University. Special Adviser to Scottish Office Ministers, 1992-94. Recreations: golf; tennis. Address: (b.) Scottish Office, St. Andrew's House, Edinburgh, EH1 3DG; T.-0131-244 2757.

Mackay of Talmine, Rev. Hugh, GCLJ, MA, FSAScot, CF(ACF). Minister, Duns Parish Church, since 1967; Clerk, Synod of the Borders, 1982-92; b. 5.1.30, Edinburgh. Educ. Daniel Stewart's College, Edinburgh; Edinburgh University and New College. Student Assistant, Canongate Kirk, Edinburgh, 1955-57; Senior Assistant, St. Machar's Cathedral, Old Aberdeen, 1957-58; Minister, St. Bride's Parish Church, Glasgow, 1958-67. Chaplain to Moderator of General Assembly, 1972-73; Founder Chairman, Duns Community Council, 1977-78; Principal Chaplain, ACF Scotland, since 1987; Chancellor of Grand Bailiwick of Scotland, Order of St. Lazarus of Jerusalem, 1988-91; Depute Grand Master of Grand Lodge of Scotland, 1988-91; Third Grand Principal, SG Royal Arch Chapter; Grand Prior, Great Priory of the Temple & Malta. Recreations: singing; drawing; Heraldry; too many other things. Address: Manse of Duns, Berwickshire, TD11 3DP; T.-Duns 883755.

Mackay, Ian Munro, BCom, CA. Principal, Mackay & Co., Chartered Accountants, Golspie and Dornoch, since 1979; Honorary Sheriff, Dornoch Sheriff Court, since 1985; b. 14.9.47, Brora; m.; Maureen; 2 s.; 1 d. Educ. Golspie High School; Edinburgh University. Trained as CA in Edinburgh, qualifying in 1973; has worked in the profession since, spending three years in United Arab Emirates, returning to UK in 1979 to set up own practice. Auditor, Treasurer, Secretary of several local charities and sporting organisations; Secretary, Dornoch Curling Club; President, Sutherland Curling Province, 1991-93; Treasurer, Brora Ice Rink Club. Recreations: curling; local history; garden; following most sports. Address: (h.) 4 Sutherland Road, Dornoch, Sutherland; T.-01862 810333.

Mackay, James Alexander, MA, DLitt. Author and Journalist; Numismatic and Philatelic Correspondent, Financial Times, since 1972; Editor, the Burns Chronicle, 1978-91, and The Burnsian, 1986-89; b. 21.11.36, Inverness; m., Renate Finlay-Freundlich. Educ. Hillhead High School, Glasgow; Glasgow University. Lt., RA Guided Weapons Range, Hebrides, 1959-61; Assistant Keeper, Department of Printed Books, British Museum, in charge of philatelic collections, 1961-71; returned to Scotland as a full-time Writer, 1972; Editor-in-Chief, IPC Stamp Encyclopedia, 1968-72; Columnist on antiques, Financial Times, 1967-72, philately and numismatics, 1972-85; Trustee, James Currie Memorial Trust, since 1987, Burns-Gaelic Trust, since 1992; Publisher of books on philately and postal history; author of 150 books on aspects of the applied and decorative arts, numismatics, philately, postal history; Scottish books include Robert Bruce, King of Scots, 1974; Rural Crafts in Scotland, 1976; Scottish Postmarks, 1978; The Burns Federation 1885-1985, 1985; The Complete Works of Robert Burns, 1986; The Complete Letters of Robert Burns, 1987; Burnsiana, 1988; Burns-Lore of Dumfries and Galloway, 1988; Burns at Ellisland, 1989; Scottish Post Offices, 1989; Burns A-Z, 1990; Kilmarnock, 1992; Burns, a biography, 1992; Vagabond of Verse, 1995; William Wallace Brave Heart, 1995. Recreations: travel; languages; music (piano-playing); photographing post offices. Address: (h.) 75/5 Lancefield Quay, Glasgow, G3 8HA; T.-0141-221 2797.

Mackay of Clashfern, Lord (James Peter Hymers), Baron (1979), PC (1979), FRSE, Hon. FRICE. Lord High Chancellor of Great Britain, since 1987; Chancellor, Heriot Watt University, since 1991; b. 2.7.27, Edinburgh; m., Elizabeth Gunn Hymers; 1 s.; 2 d. Educ. George Heriot's School, Edinburgh; Edinburgh University. Lecturer in Mathematics, St. Andrews University, 1948-50; Major Scholar, Trinity College, Cambridge, in Mathematics, 1947,

taken up, 1950; Senior Scholar, 1951; BA (Cantab), 1952; LLB Edinburgh (with distinction), 1955; admitted, Faculty of Advocates, 1955; QC (Scot), 1965; Standing Junior Counsel to: Queen's and Lord Treasurer's Remembrancer, Scottish Home and Health Department, Commissioners of Inland Revenue in Scotland; Sheriff Principal, Renfrew and Argyll, 1972-74; Vice-Dean, Faculty of Advocates, 1973-76; Dean, 1976-79; Lord Advocate of Scotland, 1979-84; a Senator of the College of Justice in Scotland, 1984-85; a Lord of Appeal in Ordinary, 1985-87. Part-time Member, Scottish Law Commission, 1976-79; Hon. Master of the Bench, Inner Temple, 1979; Fellow, International Academy of Trial Lawyers, 1979; Fellow, Institute of Taxation, 1981; Director, Stenhouse Holdings Ltd., 1976-77; Member, Insurance Brokers' Registration Council, 1977-79; a Commissioner of Northern Lighthouses, 1975-84; Hon. LLD: Edinburgh, 1983, Dundee, 1983, Strathclyde, 1985, Aberdeen, 1987, Birmingham, 1990; Hon. DCL, Newcastle, 1990; Hon. Doctor of Laws, College of William and Mary, 1989; Hon. Fellow, Trinity College, Cambridge, 1989; Hon.LLD, Cambridge, 1989; Hon. Fellow, Royal College of Surgeons, Edinburgh, 1989; Fellow, American College of Trial Lawyers, 1990. Recreation: walking. Address: Lord Chancellor's Residence, House of Lords, London, SW1A 0PW.

MacKay, John, OBE, MB, ChB, FRCGP. Retired General Medical Practitioner; Member, General Medical Council; Member, Scottish National Board for Nursing, Midwifery and Health Visiting; b. 24.7.26, Glasgow; m., Matilda MacLennan Bain; 2 s.; 2 d. Educ. Govan High School; Glasgow University. Junior House Doctor, Victoria Infirmary and Southern General Hospital, Glasgow, 1949; Ship's Surgeon, 1950; Assistant in General Practice, Govan, 1951-52 (Principal, since 1953); Member, Board of Management, Glasgow South West Hospitals, prior to 1973; Tutor, University Department of General Practice, Glasgow; part-time Medical Referee, Scottish Home and Health Department; Honorary Life Manager, Govan Weavers Society; Member, Scottish General Medical Services Committee. Recreations: angling; golf; gardening. Address: (h.) Moorholm, Barr's Brae, Kilmacolm, Renfrewshire, PA13 4DE; T.-Kilmacolm 3234.

Mackay, John, TD, MA, FInstD. Director and General Manager, Royal Mail Scotland and N. Ireland, since 1986; Board Member, Royal Mail, Scottish Post Office Board, since 1985; Board Member, Scottish Business in the Community; Governing Member, Quality Scotland; Committee Member: Scottish Higher Education Funding Council, Quality Assessment Committee, Lowland Employers Liaison Committee (Army), Army Benevolent Fund Scotland; Chairman, Edinburgh Common Purpose; b. 14.9.36, St. Andrews; m., Barbara Wallace; 1 s.; 2 d. Educ. Madras College; Dunfermline High School; Kirkcaldy High School; Edinburgh University. Army (Lt., East Anglian Regiment), 1959-63; TA, 1964-86, Royal Engineers (Postal and Courier), Colonel; Post Office: Controller Personnel and Finance, Eastern Region, 1977-79, Director Philately, Post Office HQ, 1979-84, Operations Director, Royal Mail HQ, 1991-92. Recreations: golf; watching rugby; cricket; reading; walking dog; convivial company. Address: (b.) 102 West Port, Edinburgh, EH3 9HS; T.-0131-228 7400.

Mackay, John Angus, MA. Director, Gaelic Television Fund, since 1991; Board Member, Highlands and Islands Enterprise; Director, Comunn Na Gaidhlig, since 1985; b. 24.6.48, Shader, Stornoway; m., Maria F.; 4 s. Educ. Nicolson Institute; Aberdeen University; Jordanhill College. Aberdeen Circulation Rep., D.C. Thomson, 1970-71; Jordanhill College, 1971-72; Teacher, 1972-77; Field Officer, then Development Officer, then Senior Administrative Officer, HIDB, 1977-85. Chairman, Gaelic Youth Radio Trust; Chairman, Gaelic Television Training Trust; Director, Acair; Chairman, Sabhal Mor Ostaig, 1987-91. Recreations: reading; skiing; swimming; running.

Address: (h.) Druimard, Arnol, Isle of Lewis; T.-01851 71479.

McKay, John Henderson, CBE (1987), DL, JP, BA (Hons), PhD, Dr h.c. (Edinburgh). Chairman, Scottish Working Peoples' History Trust, since 1992; Convener, Business Committee, General Council, Edinburgh University, since 1992; Vice President, Royal Caledonian Horticultural Society, since 1993; Hon. Vice-President, St. Andrew Society, since 1989; Hon. President, Scottish Craftsmanship Association, since 1987; Patron, Scotland Yard Adventure Centre, since 1988; b. 12.5.29, Kirknewton; m., Catherine Watson Taylor; 1 s.; 1 d. Educ. West Calder High School; Open University. Labourer and Clerk, Pumpherston Oil Co. Ltd., 1948-50; National Service, Royal Artillery, 1950-52; Customs and Excise, 1952-85; Lord Provost of Edinburgh, 1984-88. Recreations: gardening; reading; listening to music. Address: (h.) 2 Buckstone Way, Edinburgh, EH10 6PN; T.-0131-445 2865.

MacKay of Ardbrecknish, Lord (John Jackson MacKay), BSc, DipEd, JP. Life Peer, since 1991; Minister of State, Social Security, since 1994; Under Secretary of State, Department of Transport, January-July, 1994; Lord in Waiting (Government Whip in the House of Lords), 1993-94; b. 15.11.38, Lochgilphead; m., Sheena Wagner; 2 s.; 1 d. Educ. Dunoon Grammar School; Campbeltown Grammar School; Glasgow University; Jordanhill College of Education. Member, Oban Town Council, 1969-74; Member, Argyll Water Board, 1969-74; Principal Teacher of Mathematics, Oban High School, 1969-79; MP for Argyll, 1979-83, for Argyll & Bute, 1983-87; Parliamentary Private Secretary to Secretary of State for Scotland, 1982; Parliamentary Under Secretary of State, Scottish Office, 1982-87; Chief Executive, Scottish Conservative Party, 1987-90; Chairman, Sea Fish Industry Authority, 1990-93; Member, Select Committee on the European Communities; Justice of the Peace for the City of Glasgow. Recreations: fishing; sailing. Address: (h.) Innishail, 51 Springkell Drive, Pollokshields, Glasgow, G41 4EZ.

Mackay, Rev. Professor John L., MA, MLitt, BD. Principal Clerk of Assembly, Free Church of Scotland. Address: (b.) 15 North Bank Street, The Mound, Edinburgh, EH1 2LS.

McKay, Rev. Johnston Reid, MA (Glasgow), BA (Cantab). Senior Producer, Religious Programmes, BBC, since 1987; b. 2.5.42, Glasgow. Educ. High School of Glasgow; Glasgow University; Cambridge University. Assistant Minister, St. Giles' Cathedral, 1967-71; Church Correspondent, Glasgow Herald, 1968-70; Minister, Bellahouston Steven Parish Church, 1971-78; frequent Broadcaster; Governor, Paisley College; Minister, Paisley Abbey, 1978-87; Editor, The Bush (newspaper of Glasgow Presbytery), 1975-78; Chairman, Scottish Religious Advisory Committee, BBC, 1981-86; Stanley Mair Lecturer on Preaching, Glasgow University, 1995. Publications: From Sleep and From Damnation (with James Miller), 1970; Essays in Honour of William Barclay (Joint Editor), 1976; Through Wood and Nails, 1982. Recreations: good music and bad golf. Address: (b.) 41 Stakehill, Largs, KA30 9NH; T.-01475 672960.

MacKay, Professor Norman, MD, FRCP(Glas), FRCP(Edin), FRCS (Edin), FRCGP, FCPSP, FACP (Hon). Dean of Postgraduate Medicine and Professor of Postgraduate Medical Education, Glasgow University, since 1989; Consultant Physician, Victoria Infirmary, Glasgow, since 1974; President, Royal College of Physicians and Surgeons of Glasgow, since 1994; b. 15.9.36, Glasgow; m., Grace Violet McCaffer; 2 s.; 2 d. Educ. Govan High School; Glasgow University. Honorary Secretary: Royal College of Physicians and Surgeons of Glasgow, 1973-83, Standing Joint Committee, Scottish Royal Colleges, 1978-82, Conference of Royal Colleges and Faculties in Scotland,

1982-91; Speciality Adviser in Medicine, West of Scotland Committee of Postgraduate Medical Education, 1982-89; President, Royal Medico-Chirurgical Society of Glasgow, 1982-83; Member, Area Medical Committee, Greater Glasgow Health Board, 1987-89; President, Southern Medical Society, 1989-90. Recreations: gardening; walking; golf; association football. Address: (h.) 4 Erskine Avenue, Dumbreck, Glasgow, G41 5AL; T.-0141-427 1900.

Mackay, Peter, CB, MA. Secretary and Chief Executive, Scottish Office Industry Department, since 1990; b. 6.7.40, Arbroath; m., Sarah Holdich; 1 s.; 2 d. Educ. Glasgow High School; St. Andrews University. Teacher, New South Wales, Australia, 1962-63; Assistant Principal, Scottish Development Department, 1963; Private Secretary to Secretaries of State for Scotland, 1973-75; Director for Scotland, Manpower Services Commission, 1983-85; on secondment from Scottish Office to Department of Employment, London, 1985; Under Secretary, Scottish Education Department (Further and Higher Education, Arts and Sport), 1987-89. Nuffield Travelling Fellowship, 1978-79. Recreations: Scotland; high altitudes and latitudes; dinghy sailing; sea canoeing; tennis. Address: (h.) 6 Henderland Road, Edinburgh, EH12 6BB; T.-0131-337 2830.

Mackay, Robert Ostler. Solicitor, since 1930; Notary Public, since 1955; b. 25.12.07, Greenock; m., 1, Dorothy Lilian Johnson (deceased); 2, Irene Isobel Ray Anderson; 1 s.; 2 d. Educ. Greenock Academy; Alyth Public School; Blairgowrie High School; Edinburgh University. Partner: J.C. Richards & Morrice, Solicitors, Fraserburgh, 1939-45, Ferguson & Petrie, Solicitors, Duns, 1945-85; Honorary Sheriff, Lothian and Borders, at Duns, since 1981; Council Member, Law Society of Scotland, 1958-79 (Vice-President, 1967-68); Founding Member, Agricultural Law Association; Life Member, Cairngorm Club. Address: (h.) Nethercraigs, Tighnabruaich, Argyll; T.-01700 811 368.

Mackay, William Kenneth, BSc, CEng, FICE, FIHT. Consultant, JMP Consultants Ltd. (formerly Jamieson Mackay & Partners), since 1965; Commissioner, Royal Fine Arts Commission for Scotland, 1981-92; Board Member, Clyde Port Authority, 1985-93; b. 6.6.30, Moyobamba, Peru. Educ. Hillhead High School, Glasgow; Glasgow University. Engineer, NCB, West Fife Area, 1954-57; Senior Engineer, Fife County Council, 1957-59; Group Engineer, Cumbernauld New Town Development Corporation, 1959-65; Consultant, since 1965; Past Chairman, Scottish Branch, Institution of Highways and Transportation; former Member, Planning and Transport Research Advisory Council to UK Government. Recreations: swimming; walking. Address: (b.) Stewart House, 123 Elderslie Street, Glasgow, G3 7AR; T.-0141 221 4030.

McKean, Professor Charles Alexander, BA, FRSA, FSA Scot, HonFRIBA, Hon FRIAS. Professor of Architecture, Duncan of Jordanstone College, Dundee University; Secretary, Royal Incorporation of Architects in Scotland, 1979-94; b. 16.7.46, Glasgow; m., Margaret Yeo; 2 s. Educ. Fettes College; Bristol University. RIBA: Secretary, London Region, 1968-76, Secretary, Eastern Region, 1972-79, Secretary, Community Architecture, 1976-79; Architectural Correspondent, The Times, 1977-83; Trustee, Thirlestane Castle; author of architectural guides to Edinburgh, Dundee, Stirling, London, Cambridge, Moray, Central Glasgow, Banff and Buchan; General Editor, RIAS/Landmark Trust Guides to Scotland. Publications: The Scottish Thirties; Edinburgh: Portrait of a City. Recreations: books; glasses; gardens; stately homes. Address: (b.) Duncan of Jordanstone College, Perth Road, Dundee, DDH 4HT; T.-01382 223261.

McKechnie, George. Editor, The Herald, since 1994; Editor, Glasgow Evening Times, 1981-94; b. 28.7.46,

Edinburgh; m., Janequin Claire Seymour Morris; 2 s. Educ. Portobello High School, Edinburgh. Reporter: Paisley & Renfrewshire Gazette, 1964-66, Edinburgh Evening News, 1966, Scottish Daily Mail, 1966-68, Daily Record, 1968-74; Deputy News Editor/News Editor, Sunday Mail, 1974-76; Assistant Editor, Evening Times, 1976-80. Recreation: reading. Address: (b.) 195 Albion Street, Glasgow, G1 1QP; T.-0141-552 6255.

McKee, Graham Hamilton, BSc, BPhil. Chief Executive, Scottish Enterprise Tayside, since 1994; b. 11.9.51; m., Pilar; 1 s.; 2 d. Educ. Hutchesons' Grammar School, Glasgow; Glasgow University; Newcastle-upon-Tyne University. Assistant Planner, Burnley Borough Council, 1975-77; Scottish Development Agency, 1977-91, latterly as Regional Manager; Director Economic Development, Scottish Enterprise Tayside, 1991-93. Recreation: family. Address: (b.) Scottish Enterprise Tayside, Enterprise House, 45 North Lindsay Street, Dundee, DD1 1HT; T.-01382 223100.

McKee, Professor (James Clark St. Clair) Sean, BSc, MA, PhD, DSc, FIMA, CMath. Professor of Mathematics, Strathclyde University, since 1988; b. 1.7.45, Belfast. Educ. George Watson's College, Edinburgh; St. Andrews University; Dundee University; Oxford University. NCR Research Fellow, 1970-72; Lecturer in Numerical Analysis, Southampton University, 1972-75; Fellow, Hertford College, Oxford, 1975-86; Professor of Industrial Mathematics, Strathclyde University, and Consultant Mathematician, Unilever Research, 1986-88. Member, Council, ECMI; Committee Member, Scottish Branch, Institute of Mathematics and Its Applications; Member, IMA Programmes Committee. Publications: 100 papers; Industrial Numerical Analysis (Co-Editor), 1986; Vector and Parallel Computing (Co-Editor), 1989; Artificial Intelligence in Mathematics (Co-Editor), 1994. Recreations: climbing Munros; golf; theatre; running conferences. Address: (b.) Department of Mathematics, Strathclyde University, Glasgow, G1 1XH; T.-0141-552 4400.

McKee, John Joseph, KCSG, JP, MA (Hons), FEIS. Vice Chairman, Scottish Catholic International Aid Fund; b. 11.11.05, Johnstone; m., Margaret M.A. McGuire; 2 s.; 1 d. Educ. St. Mungo's Academy, Glasgow; Glasgow University. Forty-five years' teaching service in Glasgow, latterly as Headteacher, Holyrood Secondary School, 1959-71; Education Officer to Roman Catholic Hierarchy of Scotland, 1971-82; Secretary, Catholic Education Commission Scotland, 1972-82; Member of Justice and Peace Commission for Scotland, 1966-76. Recreation: gardening. Address: (h.) 30 Lanton Road, Glasgow, G43 2SR; T.-0141-633 0070.

McKellar, Kenneth, BSc. Singer, Composer, Writer; b. 23.6.27, Paisley. Gave first concert in local hall, aged 13; continued singing while at school, university and during his first two years working in forestry; has made numerous records of classical and popular music; numerous tours, especially in Australia and New Zealand; has appeared a number of times at the London Palladium.

McKelvey, William. MP (Labour), Kilmarnock and Loudoun, since 1979; b. 1934. Chairman, Select Committee on Scottish Affairs, since 1992. Address: (b.) House of Commons, London, SW1A 0AA.

McKelvie, Campbell John, BSc (Hons), ARCST, FICE, FIMgt, MIMBM. Director of Building and Works, Strathclyde Region; b. 1.2.32, Tarbert, Argyll; m., Rhona Paton Smith; 2 s. Educ. Marr College, Troon; Glasgow University; Royal College of Science and Technology; Oxford University Business School. Private sector, 1955-75; Senior Depute Head of Direct Works, Strathclyde Region, 1975-79. Recreations: golf; curling; bridge.

Address: (b.) Philip Murray Road, Bellshill, Lanarkshire; T.-Bellshill 749121.

McKenna, Rosemary, CBE, DCE, JP. President, Convention of Scottish Local Authorities; Policy and Resources Convener, Cumbernauld and Kilsyth District Council; Member, Board, Cumbernauld Development Corporation; Member, Board, Scottish Enterprise; Member, Committee, Regions of European Union; Member, Executive, Scottish Council Development and Industry; Member, Secretary of State's Advisory Panel on Sustainable Development; b. 8.5.41, Kilmacolm; m., James Stephen McKenna; 3 s.; 1 d. Educ. St. Augustine's Secondary School, Glasgow; St. Andrew's College, Bearsden. Taught in various primary schools, 1974-93; Leader of Council, Cumbernauld and Kilsyth, 1984-88, Provost 1988-92, Leader of Council, 1992-94; Policy Board Member: Local Government Management Board, Local Government International Bureau; Member, Executive, Scottish Constitutional Convention. Recreations: reading; cooking. Address: (h.) 9 Westray Road, Cumbernauld, G67 1NN.

MacKenzie, Angus Alexander, CA. Chartered Accountant, since 1955; b. 1.3.31, Nairn; m., Catherine; 1 d. Educ. Inverness Royal Academy; Edinburgh University. National Service, RAF, 1955-57; in private practice as CA Assistant in Edinburgh, 1957-59, Inverness, 1959-61; commenced in practice on own account, 1961; Chairman, Highland Group, Riding for the Disabled Association; Director, PLM Helicopters Ltd. Recreations: shooting; stalking; hill-walking; gardening. Address: (h.) Tigh an Allt, Tomatin, Inverness-shire; T.-Tomatin 511270.

MacKenzie, Archibald MacIntosh, DL. Vice Lord Lieutenant, Dunbartonshire, since 1990; b. 3.6.33, Inveraray; m., Margaret Young Ritchie; 1 s.; 1 d. Educ. Hermitage School, Helensburgh. Chairman, Dumbarton Branch, Royal National Lifeboat Institution; Vice Convenor, Scottish Lifeboat Council; Chairman, Scottish Lifeboat Executive Committee; Member, Committee of Management, Royal National Lifeboat Institution; Director, Dunbartonshire Branch, British Red Cross; Member, Loch Lomond Rescue Committee; Elder, Church of Scotland. Recreations: sailing; golf; reading; classical music. Address: (h.) Millerston, 10 Boghead Road, Dumbarton; T.-Dumbarton 763654.

Mackenzie, Major Colin Dalzell, MBE, MC, DL. Lord Lieutenant, Inverness-shire, since 1986; b. 23.3.19, Fawley; m., Lady Anne Fitz Roy; 1 s.; 3 d. Educ. Eton; RMC, Sandhurst. Page of Honour to King George V, 1932-36; joined Seaforth Highlanders, 1939; ADC to Viceroy of India, 1945-46; Deputy Military Secretary to Viceroy of India, 1946-47; retired, 1949; TA, 1950-56; Inverness County Council, 1949-52; Director, various companies. Recreation: fishing. Address: (h.) Farr House, Inverness, IV1 2XB; T.-Farr 521202.

Mackenzie, Sheriff Colin Scott, DL, BL, NP. Sheriff of Grampian Highland and Islands, at Lerwick and Kirkwall, since 1992; b. 7.7.38, Stornoway; m., Christeen E.D. MacLauchlan. Educ. Nicolson Institute; Fettes College; Edinburgh University. Procurator Fiscal, Stornoway, 1969-92; Burgh Prosecutor, Stornoway, 1971-75; JP Fiscal, 1971-75; Deputy Lieutenant and Clerk to Lieutenancy of the Western Isles, 1975-92; Vice Lord Lieutenant of Islands Area, Western Isles, 1984-92; Founder President, Stornoway Flying Club, 1970; Founding Dean, Western Isles Faculty of Solicitors; elected Council Member, Law Society of Scotland, 1985-92; Convener, Criminal Law Committee, 1991-92; Elder, Church of Scotland, since 1985; Member, Board of Social Responsibility, Church of Scotland; Convener, Assembly Study Group on Young People and the Media, 1991-93; author of article on Lieutenancy, Stair Memorial Encyclopaedia of Law of Scotland, 1987; President, Stornoway Rotary Club, 1977;

President, Lewis Pipe Band. Recreation: fishing. Address: (h.) Park House, Matheson Road, Stornoway, Lewis; Middlebank, Bells Road, Lerwick, Shetland.

MacKenzie, Graham Alexander, MA (Hons). Rector, Alness Academy, since 1993; b. 4.1.50, Helensburgh; m., Mary; 2 s.; 1 d. Educ. St. Patrick's High School, Dumbarton; Edinburgh University. Teacher/Assistant Principal Teacher, St. Patrick's High School, 1974-78; Principal Teacher of English, St. Ninian's High, Kirkintilloch, 1978-89; Assistant Rector, then Depute Rector, Campbeltown Grammar, 1989-93. Recreations: most sports. Address: 19 Drumdyre Road, Dingwall, IV15 9RW; T.-01349 862628.

MacKenzie, Hugh D., MA (Hons), FEIS, JP, FRSA. Headteacher, Craigroyston Community High School, 1972-93; Director, Craigroyston Curriculum Project, since 1980; b. 29.5.33, Edinburgh; m., Helen Joyce; 1 s.; 1 d. Educ. Royal High School; Edinburgh University; Moray House College of Education, Edinburgh. Education Officer, RAF, 1956-58; Assistant Teacher, Niddrie Marischal Junior Secondary School and Falkirk High School, 1958-62; Principal Teacher: Broxburn Academy, 1962-64, Liberton High School, 1964-70; Deputy Headteacher, Craigmount High School, 1970-72; Scottish Representative, Northern Regional Examination Board, 1973-88; Vice-Chairman, Lothian Regional Consultative Committee, 1984-87; a Director, Royal Lyceum Theatre, Edinburgh, since 1985, Scottish Community Education Council, 1985-88; President, Royal High School Rugby Club; President and Founder Member, Edinburgh Golden Oldies Rugby Club. Publication: Craigroyston Days, 1995. Recreations: rugby; squash; golf; ornithology; philately; jazz. Address: (h.) 3 Beechwood Mains, Edinburgh.

MacKenzie, Ian Kenneth, OBE, JP. Member, Council and Executive Committee, National Trust for Scotland; Chairman, Red Deer Commission, 1984-92; Chairman, Highlands and Islands Development Consultative Council, 1988-91; Landowner; b. 1.3.31, Nairn; m., Margaret Vera Matheson; 2 s.; 2 d. Educ. Inverness Royal Academy. Member, Scottish Agricultural Consultative Panel; Member, Secretary of State's Panel of Arbiters; Director, Royal Highland and Agricultural Society of Scotland, 1980-84. Recreation: field sports. Address: Leanach House, Culloden Moor, Inverness, IV1 2EJ.

Mackenzie, Rev. Ian Murdo. Church of Scotland Minister; Writer, Broadcaster, Organist; b. b. 3.8.31, Fraserburgh; m., Elizabeth Alice Whitley; 1 s.; 1 d. Educ. Strichen School; Fettes College; Edinburgh University. Assistant Organist, St. Giles Cathedral, 1952-58; Editor, The Student, Sooth and Breakthrough; Founder Member, Telephone Samaritans Scotland, 1960; Columnist, Edinburgh Evening Dispatch; Conductor, Calton Singers; Music Organiser, Iona Abbey; Assistant Minister, St. Giles, 1960-62; Founder, Edinburgh University CND, 1962; Scottish Secretary, Student Christian Movement, 1962-63; Assistant General Secretary, Student Christian Movement, 1963-64; Secretary, University Teachers Group, 1963-65; Religious Adviser and Executive Producer, Religious Programmes, ABC TV, 1964-68; LWT, 1968-69; conceived and produced From Inner Space, Looking for an Answer, Don't Just Sit There, Question '68, Roundhouse; Religious Columnist, The Times, 1966-68; Minister, Peterhead Old Parish Church, 1969-73; Presenter, For Christ's Sake and What The Religious Papers Say, Grampian TV; Chairman, Scottish Religious Panel, IBA, 1970-72; Head of Religious Programmes, BBC Scotland, 1973-89; conceived Eighth Day, Voyager, Angles, Gates to Space, The Quest; Writer/Presenter, He Turned Up, Channel Four, 1990; Baird Lectures on Church Music, 1990; Presenter/Improviser on hymns and other programmes, Radio Scotland. Publications: Tunes of Glory; Vision and Belief; various papers, articles and essays. Recreations: attending concerts,

cathedrals, and newsagents; driving with majestic care and attention; writing novels; wondering about God; preaching about wondering. Address: (h.) 1 Glenan Gardens, Helensburgh, Dunbartonshire, G84 8XT; T.-01436 673429.

MacKenzie, Robert. Chief Executive, Fife Enterprise. Address: (b.) Huntsman House, 33 Cadham Centre, Glenrothes, KY7 6RU.

McKenzie Smith, Ian, OBE, RSA, PRSW, LLD, FSA (Scot), FMA; City Arts and Recreation Officer, City of Aberdeen, since 1989 (Director, Aberdeen Art Gallery and Museums, 1968-89); b. 3.8.35; m., Mary Rodger Fotheringham; 2 s.; 1 d. Educ. Robert Gordon's College, Aberdeen; Gray's School of Art, Aberdeen; Hospitalfield College of Art, Arbroath. Teacher of Art, 1960-63; Education Officer, Council of Industrial Design, Scottish Committee, 1963-68. Work in permanent collections: Scottish National Gallery of Modern Art, Scottish Arts Council, Arts Council of Northern Ireland, Contemporary Art Society, Aberdeen Art Gallery and Museums, Glasgow Art Gallery and Museums, Abbot Hall Art Gallery, Kendal, Hunterian Museum, Glasgow, Nuffield Foundation, Carnegie Trust, Strathclyde Education Authority, Lothian Education Authority, Royal Scottish Academy, Department of the Environment, City Art Centre, Edinburgh, Perth Art Gallery; Member, Scottish Arts Council, 1970-77; Member, Scottish Museums Council; President, RSW, 1988; Deputy President, RSA, 1990-91, Treasurer, 1990, Secretary, since 1991; Governor: Edinburgh College of Art, 1976-88, The Robert Gordon University, 1989; FSS; FRSA. Address: (h.) 70 Hamilton Place, Aberdeen, AB2 4BA; T.-01224 644531.

Mackenzie-Stuart, Lord (Alexander John Mackenzie-Stuart); b. 18.11.24; m., Anne Burtholme Millar; 4 d. Educ. Fettes College; Sidney Sussex College, Cambridge; Edinburgh University (LLB). Admitted Faculty of Advocates (Scottish Bar), 1951; Honorary Keeper, Advocates' Library, 1969; Sheriff-Principal of Aberdeen, Kincardine and Banff, 1971; Senator of the College of Justice, 1972; Judge of the Court of Justice of the European Communities, 1973; elected President of the Court, 1984; retired from Court of Justice, 1988; since retirement, Woodrow Wilson Center for International Scholars, Washington; lectures on Community Law and other matters in UK and Europe; Honorary Doctorates: Stirling, Exeter, Edinburgh, Glasgow, Aberdeen, Cambridge, Birmingham; Prix Bech for services to Europe, 1989; Honorary Bencher, Middle Temple, King's Inn, Dublin; created Life Baron, 1988, as Lord Mackenzie-Stuart of Dean; FRSE; President, British Academy of Experts, 1989-92. Address: (h.) 7 Randolph Cliff, Edinburgh, EH3 7TZ; T.-0131-225 1089.

McKerrell, Douglas Gordon, LLB. Partner, Kidstons & Co., Solicitors, Glasgow, since 1992; Partner, Maclay Murray and Spens, 1976-92; b. 18.8.44, Edinburgh; m., Elizabeth Anne (Lizanne) Brown; 3 s.; 1 d. Educ. Royal High School, Edinburgh; High School of Glasgow; Glasgow University. After training and qualifying, spent several years in private practice in London and Glasgow; Tutor/Senior Tutor, Finance and Investment, Diploma in Legal Practice, Glasgow University, 1980-89; Chairman, Rent Assessment Panel for Scotland, 1980-89; Scottish Representative, UK Committee, UNICEF, 1985-88; Chairman, Scottish Music Information Centre, 1990-93; Chairman, Scottish SPCA, 1988-93; Trustee, Scottish International Piano Competition; Secretary, Children's Music Foundation in Scotland; Trustee, Scottish Musicians' Benevolent Fund; Governor, Laurel Bank School; Board Member, Edinburgh International Film Festival. Publication: The Rent Acts: A Practitioner's Guide, 1985. Recreations: music; theatre; cinema; collecting records. Address: (b.) 1 Royal Bank Place, Buchanan Street, Glasgow; T.-0141-221 6551.

Mackey, Professor James Patrick, PhD, LPh, BD, STL, DD, BA. Thomas Chalmers Professor of Theology, Edinburgh University, since 1979; b. 9.2.34; m., Hanorah Noelle Quinlan; 1 s.; 1 d. Educ. Mount St. Joseph College, Roscrea; National University of Ireland; Pontifical University, Maynooth; Queen's University, Belfast; Oxford University; London University; Strasbourg University. Lecturer in Philosophy, Queen's University, Belfast, 1960-66; Lecturer in Theology, St. John's College, Waterford, 1966-69; Associate Professor and Professor of Systematic and Philosophical Theology, San Francisco University, 1969-79; Visiting Professor: University of California, Berkeley, 1974, Dartmouth College, New Hampshire, 1989; Member, Centre for Hermeneutical Studies, Berkeley, 1974-79; Dean, Faculty of Divinity, Edinburgh University, 1984-88, Associate Dean and Director of Graduate School, since 1995; Editor, Studies in World Christianity (international journal), since 1995. Publications: The Modern Theology of Tradition, 1962; Life and Grace, 1966; Tradition and Change in the Church, 1968; Contemporary Philosophy of Religion, 1968; Morals, Law and Authority (Editor), 1969; The Church: Its Credibility Today, 1970; The Problems of Religious Faith, 1972; Jesus: The Man and the Myth, 1979; The Christian Experience of God as Trinity, 1983; Religious Imagination (Editor), 1986; Modern Theology: A Sense of Direction, 1987; New Testament Theology in Dialogue, (Co-Author), 1987; Introduction to Celtic Christianity, 1989; The Cultures of Europe: the Irish contribution, 1993; Power and Christian Ethics, 1994. Recreations: yachting; rediscovery of original Celtic culture of these islands. Address: (h.) 10 Randolph Crescent, Edinburgh EH3 7TT; T.-0131-225 9408.

McKichan, Duncan James, OBE, BL. Solicitor; Partner, Maclay Murray & Spens, 1952-91; Honorary Consul for Canada, 1986-92; Dean, Royal Faculty of Procurators in Glasgow, 1983-86; b. 28.7.24, Wallington, Surrey; m, Leila Campbell Fraser; 2 d. Educ. George Watson's College, Edinburgh; Solihull School; Downing College, Cambridge; Glasgow University. Royal Navy, 1943-46; qualified as Solicitor, 1950. Recreations: gardening; walking; sailing; skiing. Address: (h.) Invermay, Queen Street, Helensburgh; T.-01436 674778.

Mackie, Michael James, BMedBiol, MBChB, MD, FRCP, FRCPath. Consultant Haematologist, since 1981; Area Director, Haematology Services, 1991-93; b. 17.11.48, Aberdeen; 1 s.; 1 d. Educ. Robert Gordon's College, Aberdeen; Aberdeen University. Junior appointments in Aberdeen and Canada; Consultant and Senior Lecturer, Liverpool University, 1981-86; Consultant Haematologist, Western General Hospital, Edinburgh, since 1986. Recreation: tennis. Address: (b.) Department of Haematology, Western General Hospital, Crewe Road, Edinburgh; T.-0131-537 1902.

MacKie, Professor Rona McLeod, MD, DSc, FRCP, FRCPGlas, FRCPLond, FRCPath, FRSE, FInstBiol. Professor of Dermatology, Glasgow University, since 1978; Honorary Consultant Dermatologist, Greater Glasgow Health Board, since 1978; b. 22.5.40, Dundee; 1 s.; 1 d. Educ. Laurelbank School, Glasgow; Glasgow University. Registrar, Department of Dermatology, Western Infirmary, Glasgow, 1970-71; Lecturer in Dermatology, Glasgow University, 1971-72; Consultant Dermatologist, Greater Glasgow Health Board, 1972-78. Recreation: skiing. Address: Department of Dermatology, Glasgow University, Glasgow, G11 6NU; T.-0141-339 8855, Ext. 4006.

McKiernan, Professor Peter, BA, MA, PhD, MIM, FRSA. Professor of Strategic Management, St. Andrews University, since 1992; b. 28.12.53, Accrington; m., Morna; 1 s.; 1 d. Educ. Preston Catholic College; Lancaster University; Surrey University. Former M.D. of mechanical engineering company; Lecturer in Management, St. Andrews University; Senior Lecturer in Strategic Management, Warwick University. Publications: Sharpbenders; Strategies of Growth; Inside Fortress Europe; Historical Evolution of Strategic Management. Recreations: cricket; poetry. Address: (b.) Department of Management St. Andrews University, KY16 9AL; T.-01334 62795.

McKillop, Professor James Hugh, BSc, MB, ChB, PhD, FRCP, FRCR. Muirhead Professor of Medicine, Glasgow University, since 1989; Honorary Consultant Physician, Glasgow Royal Infirmary, since 1982; b. 20.6.48, Glasgow; m., Caroline A. Oakley; 2 d. Educ. St. Aloysius' College Glasgow; Glasgow University. Hall Fellow in Medicine, then Lecturer in Medicine, Glasgow University, 1974-82; Postdoctoral Fellow, Stanford University Medical Center, California, 1979 and 1980; Senior Lecturer in Medicine, Glasgow University, 1982-89. Watson Prize Lectureship Royal College of Physicians and Surgeons of Glasgow, 1979; Harkness Fellowship, Commonwealth Fund of New York, 1979-80; Robert Reid Newall Award, Stanford University, 1980; Honorary Treasurer, Scottish Society of Experimental Medicine, 1982-87; Honorary Secretary, British Nuclear Cardiology Group, 1982-87; Symposium Editor, Scottish Medical Journal, 1984-93; Council Member, British Nuclear Medicine Society, 1985-94 (Hon. Secretary, 1988-90, President, 1990-92); Editor, Nuclear Medicine Communications, since 1990; Congress President Elect, European Association of Nuclear Medicine. Recreations: music (especially opera); history. Address: (b.) University Department of Medicine, Royal Infirmary, Glasgow, G31 2ER; T.-0141-552 4014.

McKinlay, Professor David Gemmell, BSc, PhD, ARCST, CEng, FICE, FASCE, FGS, FRSE. Emeritus Professor, Strathclyde University; Geotechnical Consultant; b. 23.8.24, Glasgow; m., Muriel Lees Donaldson; 1 s.; 1 d Educ. Allan Glen's School, Glasgow; Royal Technical College, Glasgow; Glasgow University. War Service commissioned RNVR; County Engineer's staff, Dumfries County; civil engineering consultancy; teaching and research, Royal College of Science and Technology, then Strathclyde University. Member, Subsidence Compensation Review Committee, 1984; Council Member, Institution of Civil Engineers, 1979-82, 1983-86; Chairman, Ground Engineering Group Board, 1981-86; Governor, Rotary International District 123, 1987-88. Recreations: estate development; freshwater fishing; travel. Address: (h. Spylawbank, 39 Burn Road, Darvel, KA17 ODB; T.-01560 322552.

McKinlay, Peter, MA (Hons). Chief Executive, Scottish Homes, since 1991; Chairman, Campbeltown and Kintyre Enterprise Trust, since 1992; Chairman, Bute Partnership since 1993; Director, Common Purpose since 1993; Director, St. Mary's Cathedral Workshop, since 1994; b 29.12.39, Campbeltown; m., Anne Thomson; 2 s.; 1 d Educ. Campbeltown Grammar School; Glasgow University Assistant Postal Controller, GPO HQ, Edinburgh; Assistant Principal, PS to Secretary, Scottish Development Department; Principal, Housing, SDD; Principal Private Secretary to Rt. Hon. Bruce Millan, Minister of State Principal, Local Government Finance; Assistant Secretary Finance; Assistant Secretary, Industry Department fo. Scotland; Director, Scottish Prison Service, 1988-91. Non Executive Director, D.S. Crawford; Badminton Blue Glasgow University; Member, National Executive, First Division Association, 1977-80. Recreations: reading; gardening; family; friends. Address: (b.) Thistle House, 91 Haymarket Terrace, Edinburgh, EH12 5HE; T.-0131-313 0044.

McKinney, Alan. National Director, Scottish Decorators Federation; Director of Organisation and Headquarters Scottish National Party, 1977-90; b. 16.10.41, Glasgow; m. Elma; 1 s.; 1 d. Educ. Brechin High School. Time-served refrigeration engineer before entering politics full-time as National Organiser, SNP, 1977; former Election Agent

Dundee East; former elected Member, NEC. Played football for Brechin City. Recreation: golf. Address: (b.) 1 Grindlay Street Court, Edinburgh, EH3 9AR; T.-0131-221 1527.

McKinnon, Andrew, MA (Hons). Artistic Director, Perth Theatre, since 1993; b. 1949, Glasgow. Educ. Allan Glen's School, Glasgow; Glasgow University; Balliol College, Oxford. Associate Director, Perth Theatre; Drama Officer, Arts Council of Great Britain; Associate Director, Nottingham Playhouse; Director, York Theatre Royal; Artistic Director, Northern Stage; Director, The Actors Centre. Recreations: music; architecture; pulp fiction; social history. Address: (b.) Perth Theatre, Perth, PH1 5UW; T.-01738 38123.

McKinnon, David Douglas, BSc, FFA, CMath, FIMA. Director, General Manager and Actuary, Scottish Mutual Assurance Society, 1982-90, Director, 1981-91, Director, Scottish Mutual Assurance plc, since 1992; b. 18.7.26, Larbert; m., Edith June Kyles; 1 s.; 2 d. Educ. High School of Stirling; Glasgow University. Faculty of Actuaries: Fellow, since 1951, President, 1979-81; Member of Council, International Actuarial Association, 1972-89 and Secretary for the UK, 1975-89; Member, Investment Advisory Committee, Glasgow University Court, since 1982; Chairman, Associated Scottish Life Offices, 1988-90; Member, Board of Association of British Insurers, 1988-90; Session Clerk, Larbert West Church, 1968-87; Vice-Chairman, Church of Scotland Trust, 1984-89, Chairman, since 1991; Member, Church of Scotland Assembly Council, since 1987; Director, Church of Scotland Insurance Company Ltd., since 1992; Director, Scotsure Insurance Company Ltd., since 1992; Member, Trinity College (Glasgow) Financial Board, since 1977; President, Falkirk and District Battalion, The Boys' Brigade, 1972-77. Recreations: golf; gardening. Address: (h.) 4 Carronvale Road, Larbert, Stirlingshire; T.-01324 562373.

MacKinnon, Major John Farquhar, MC, DL, JP; b. 27.1.18, Melbourne; m., Sheila Pearce (deceased); 1 s.; 1 d. (deceased); 2, Mrs Anne Swann. Educ. Geelong, Australia; Corpus Christi College, Cambridge (MA). Army, Queen's Own Cameron Highlanders, 1939-46 (Major); twice wounded; Middle East, 1940-41; ADC, Governor General, Union of South Africa, 1942; Staff, UK, 1943-46 (left service due to wounds); Staff TA, 1949-54; ICI Ltd., 1949-73, Regional Manager; Secretary, British Field Sports Society, Berwickshire, 1974-80; Elder, Kirk of Lammermuir; JP, Deputy Lieutenant, Berwickshire, since 1987. Recreations: shooting; fishing. Address: (h.) Craigie Lodge, Longformacus, by Duns, Berwickshire; T.-Longformacus 890251.

McKinnon, Niall I., MA (Hons), DipEd. Head Teacher, Vale of Leven Academy, since 1994; b. 6.4.39, Daliburgh, South Uist; m., Eileen; 2 s.; 2 d. Educ. Portree High School; Glasgow University. Teacher, Hillhead High School, 1962-69; Principal Teacher of Classics, Hermitage Academy, 1969-76; Assistant Head Teacher, then Depute Head Teacher, Vale of Leven Academy, 1976-85; Head Teacher, Braidfield High School, Clydebank, 1985-94. Publication: Discovering the Greeks (Co-author), 1977. Recreations: church; hill-walking; golf; bridge. Address: (b.) Vale of Leven Academy, Alexandria, Dunbartonshire, G83 0TS.

Mackintosh of Mackintosh, Lachlan Ronald Duncan, OBE, JP, FSA Scot. 30th Chief of Clan Mackintosh, since 1957; Lord Lieutenant of Inverness, Lochaber, Badenoch and Strathspey, since 1985; Member, Highland Regional Council, since 1974; b. 27.6.28, Camberley; m., Mabel Cecilia Helen ("Celia") Bruce; 1 s.; 2 d.; 1 d. deceased. Educ. R.N. College, Dartmouth. Seaman Officer, Specialist in Communications, Royal Navy, retiring as Lt.-Cdr., 1963; President, Clan Chattan Association, since 1958; Chairman, Highland Exhibitions Ltd., 1964-85; Vice President, Scottish Conservative and Unionist Association, 1969-71;

Member, Inverness County Council, 1970-75; Chairman, Inverness Prison Visiting Committee, 1973-86. Address: Moy Hall, Tomatin, Inverness, IV13 7YQ; T.-01808 511211.

Mackintosh, Peter, MIEOD, FInstP, FRSA. Director of Development, Highland Regional Council, since 1980; Company Manager, Highland Prospect Ltd.; b. 7.6.39, Nairn; m., Una; 2 s. Educ. Roses Academic Institute, Nairn. Architectural Assistant: Inverness County Council, 1958-60, Fife County Council, 1960-62; Ross and Cromarty County Council: Senior Architectural Assistant, 1962-72, Assistant Development Officer, 1972-75; Highland Regional Council: Divisional Development Officer, 1975-78, Assistant Director of Development, 1978-80. Chairman, Clan Chattan Association; Trustee, Fresson Trust; Company Member, Highland Hospice. Recreations: walking; gardening; travel; world affairs; family activities. Address: (b.) Regional Buildings, Glenurquhart Road, Inverness, IV3 5NX; T.-01463 702000.

McLachlan, Alastair Stevenson, MA (Hons). Rector, Lornshill Academy, Alloa, since 1988; b. 7.8.40, Glasgow; m., Anne Rutherford; 1 s.; 1 d. Educ. High School of Glasgow; Glasgow University. Recreations: family; golf; after-dinner speaking; singing. Address: (b.) Lornshill Academy, Tullibody Road, Alloa, FK10 2ES; T.-01259 214331.

Maclachlan, Alistair Andrew Duncan, BA (Hons). Rector, Forres Academy, since 1982; b. 14.3.46, Perth; m., Alison M.S. Love; 2 s. Educ. Perth Academy; Strathclyde University. Teacher in various schools, 1969-71; Principal Teacher of Economics and Business Studies, 1971-74; Assistant Rector, Keith Grammar School, 1974-78; Depute Rector, Elgin High School, 1978-82; Member, SCCC. Secretary and Treasurer, Keith Agricultural Show, 1972-82; Chairman, Elgin Squash Club, since 1982. Recreations: keeping fit; squash; reading; music. Address: (h.) 82 Duncan Drive, Elgin, Moray, IV30 2NH; T.-Elgin 542193.

McLaren, Alistair C., TD, MB, ChB, DPH. Hon. President, Scottish Official Board of Highland Dancing, since 1974; b. 23.11.07, Edinburgh; m., Margaret Field Martell (deceased); 1 s. Educ. George Watson's Boys' College; Edinburgh University. General practice, Edinburgh, 1932-73; Major, RAMC (T), 1939-45. Former Chairman, Clan MacLaren Society. Recreations: Highland dancing and adjudicating; walking. Address: (h.) 15 Merchiston Park, Edinburgh, EH10 4PW; T.-0131-229 3561.

McLaren, Archie, FRICS. Chief Valuer (Scotland), Valuation Office Agency, since 1992; b. 28.1.40, Kilsyth; m., Dolina Archina MacIsaac; 1 s.; 1 d. Educ. Kilsyth Academy; College of Estate Management, London. Partner, W.R. Patterson & Houston, 1964-67; Estates Surveyor, Glenrothes Development Corporation, 1968-70; Principal Valuer, Valuation Office Inland Revenue, 1971-74, First Class Valuer, 1975-77; District Valuer, Dumbarton & Argyll, 1977-91. Recreations: photography; gardening. Address: (b.) Meldrum House, 15 Drumsheugh Gardens, Edinburgh, EH3 7UN; T.-0131-225 8511, Ext. 501.

McLaren, Bill. Rugby Union Commentator, BBC; b. 16.10.23. Played wing forward for Hawick; had trial for Scotland but forced to withdraw because of illness; became reporter on local newspaper; first live radio broadcast, Glasgow v. Edinburgh, 1953; former teacher of physical education.

MacLaren, Duncan MacGregor, MA (Hons), MTh. Director, Scottish Catholic International Aid Fund (SCIAF), since 1986; b. 22.3.50, Dumbarton. Educ. Clydebank High School; Glasgow University; New College, Edinburgh University. Assistant Principal, English Section, Institut auf dem Rosenberg, Switzerland, 1973-74; Researcher, Historical Dictionary of Scottish Gaelic, Glasgow University, 1974-75; Researcher, House of Commons, 1975-77; Press Officer, SNP, Edinburgh, 1977-83; Education/Promotion Officer, SCIAF, Glasgow, 1983-86. Member, Third Order of St. Dominic; Vice-President, CIDSE. Publications: Amannan; Dialogue for Development (Editor); Focus on Peace and Justice; The Radical Tradition; New Writing Scotland. Recreation: hill-walking in the Highlands. Address: (b.) 5 Oswald Street, Glasgow, G1 4QR; T.-0141-221 4447.

MacLaren, Iain Ferguson, MB, ChB, FRCSEdin, FRCS, FRCP Edin. Consultant Surgeon, Royal Infirmary, Edinburgh, 1974-92; b. 28.9.27, Edinburgh; m., Dr. Fiona Barbara Heptonstall; 1 s.; 1 d. Educ. Edinburgh Academy; Fettes College; Edinburgh University. Captain, RAMC, Egypt, 1950-52; Surgical Registrar, Royal Hospital for Sick Children, Edinburgh, 1956-58; Senior Surgical Registrar, Royal Infirmary, 1959-63 and 1964-67; Fellow in Surgical Research, Hahnemann Medical College and Hospital, Philadelphia, 1963-64; Consultant Surgeon, Deaconess Hospital, Edinburgh, 1967-85; Vice-President, Royal College of Surgeons of Edinburgh, 1983-86 (Council Member, 1977-83 and 1987-94); Fellow, Royal Medical Society (Honorary Treasurer, 1979-85); Chairman, Royal Medical Society Trust, since 1985; Honorary Pipe-Major, Royal Scottish Pipers' Society, 1959-62; Honorary Secretary: Harveian Society of Edinburgh, 1968-87, Aesculapian Club, since 1978; Hon. Secretary, Royal College of Surgeons of Edinburgh, 1972-77; Secretary, Edinburgh University General Council, since 1993; Chairman, Clan MacLaren Society, 1968-91; Chieftain, Clan Lathran, 1991. Recreations: music; the study of military history; all aspects of Scottish culture. Address: (h.) 3 Minto Street, Edinburgh, EH9 1RG; T.-0131-667 3487.

McLatchie, Cameron, OBE, LLB. Chairman and Chief Executive, British Polythene Industries, formerly Scott & Robertson PLC, since 1988; Non-executive Director, Motherwell Bridge Holdings; Board Member, Scottish Enterprise; b. 18.2.47, Paisley; m., Helen Leslie Mackie; 2 s.; 1 d. Educ. Boroughmuir School, Edinburgh; Largs High School; Ardrossan Academy; Glasgow University. Whinney Murray & Co., Glasgow, 1968-70; Thomas Boag & Co. Ltd., Greenock, 1970-75; Chairman and Managing Director, Anaplast Ltd., Irvine, 1975-83; this company purchased by Scott & Robertson. Recreations: bridge; golf. Address: (b.) 96 Port Glasgow Road, Greenock; T.-01475 45432.

McLaughlin, Andrew James, BSc (Hons), MSc, FRPharmS. Chief Administrative Pharmaceutical Officer, Ayrshire and Arran Health Board, since 1978; b. 8.1.44, Greenock; m., Sheila; 2 d. Educ. St. Columba's High School, Greenock; Glasgow University; Heriot Watt University. Community pharmacy, Boots The Chemist; hospital pharmacy, Hairmyres Hospital, East Kilbride; Principal Pharmacist, Western Infirmary, Glasgow; Fellow, Royal Pharmaceutical Society. Recreations: golf; hill-walking; photography. Address: (h.) 40 Bathurst Drive, Alloway, Ayr, KA7 4QY; T.-01292 442404.

McLaughlin, Mary, MA. Head Teacher, Notre Dame High School, Glasgow, since 1990; b. 18.8.48, Glenboig; m., William J. McLaughlin; 1 d. Educ. St. Patrick's High School, Coatbridge; Glasgow University; Notre Dame College of Education. Principal Teacher of Modern Languages, St. Margaret's High, Airdrie; Assistant Head Teacher, Taylor High School, New Stevenston. Recreations: reading; music; cycling; walking. Address: (b.) 160 Observatory Road, Glasgow, G12 9LN; T.-0141-339 3015.

McLay, Charles. Regional Sheriff Clerk, Glasgow and Strathkelvin. Address: (b.) Sheriff Court House, 1 Carlton Place, Glasgow, G5 9DA.

Maclay, Baron (Joseph Paton Maclay), 3rd Baron; Bt. Deputy Lieutenant, Renfrewshire, since 1986; Director, Altnamara Shipping Plc, since 1994; b. 11.4.42; m., Elizabeth Anne Buchanan; 2 s.; 1 d. Educ. Winchester; Sorbonne. Managing Director: Denholm Maclay Co. Ltd., 1970-83, Denholm Maclay (Offshore) Ltd., Triport Ferries (Management) Ltd., 1975-83; Deputy Managing Director, Denholm Ship Management Ltd., 1982-83; Director: Milton Shipping Co. Ltd., 1970-83, Marine Shipping Mutual Insurance Company, 1982-83; President, Hanover Shipping Inc., 1982-83; Director: British Steamship Short Trades Association, 1978-83, North of England Protection and Indemnity Association, 1976-83; Chairman, Scottish Branch, British Sailors Society, 1979-81; Vice-Chairman, Glasgow Shipowners & Shipbrokers Benevolent Association, 1982-83; Director, Denholm Ship Management (Holdings) Ltd., 1991-93. Address: (h.) Duchal, Kilmacolm, Renfrewshire.

McLay, Louisa Mary, MA. Headmistress, Fernhill School, Rutherglen, since 1992; b. 14.8.45, Glasgow; m., Dr. Arthur McLay. Educ. Notre Dame High School; Glasgow University. Primary Teacher, 1966-73; Fernhill School: Teacher of English, French, History, 1973-76, Principal Teacher of English, 1976-94, Deputy Headmistress, 1978-92. Recreations: music; gardening. Address: (b.) Fernhill School, Fernbrae Avenue, Burnside, Rutherglen, Glasgow; T.-0141-634 2674.

MacLean, Rev. Andrew Thomas, BA, BD. Parish Minister, St. Andrew's, Port Glasgow, since 1993; b. 1.2.50, Abadan, Iran; m., Alison Douglas Blair; 1 s.; 1 d. Educ. Bearsden Academy; Clydebank Technical College; Stirling University; Edinburgh University. Co-operative Insurance Society, 1967-70; Partner, Janus Enterprises, 1970-72; Probationer, Loanhead, 1979-80; Minister, Aberdeen Stockethill, 1980-85; Chaplain, Strathclyde University, 1985-93. Convener, Church of Scotland Board of Social Responsibility, 1989-93. Recreations: sound recording; running; photography; parachuting. Address: St. Andrew's Manse, Barr's Brae, Port Glasgow, PA14 5QA; T.-01475 741486.

McLean, Angus, BL, SSC. Solicitor; Honorary Sheriff, Argyll (Dunoon); b. 26.10.12, Kilmartin, Argyll; m., Celia Jane Oliver; 1 s.; 1 d. Educ. Dunoon Grammar School; Glasgow University. Solicitor (Corrigall Ritchie & McLean, Dunoon), 1935; Royal Artillery, 1940-46; seconded Indian Army, 1942, Major (DAAG), 1945. Member, Council, Law Society of Scotland, 1950-74 (Vice President, 1964); Past President, Dunoon Business Club and Dunoon Rotary Club. Publications: History of Dunoon; Place Names of Cowal. Recreations: travel; gardening. Address: (h.) 21 Ravelston Dykes, Edinburgh, EH4 3JE; T.-0131-332 4774.

MacLean, Charles Hector, BL, AE, DL. Former Senior Partner, Montgomerie & Co., Solicitors, Glasgow; Chairman, Association for Relief of Incurables in Glasgow and West of Scotland, 1964-94; Deputy Lieutenant, County of Renfrew, since 1987; b. 9.12.13, Glasgow; m., Rachael Malcolm Hutchesson; 2 s.; 2 d. Educ. Canford School; Glasgow University. Pilot Officer, 602 Squadron Auxiliary Air Force, 1936; mobilised, 1939; severely wounded, 1940, as Flt. Commander in Battle of Britain; released in rank of Wing Commander, 1945; re-commissioned as Wing Commander, RAuxAF to raise and command 3602 Fighter Control Unit. Vice President, Officers Association, Scottish Branch; Member, Committee, Earl Haig Fund Scotland, 1965-94. Address: (h.) 71 Lochwinnoch Road, Kilmacolm, Renfrewshire.

McLean, Colin, BSc, MRTPI, FSA (Scot). Director, Scottish Mining Museum, since 1988; Council Member, Association of Independent Museums, since 1991; b. 7.1.55, Falkirk; m., Kirsty Forbes; 2 d. Educ. George Heriot's School, Edinburgh; Kirkcudbright Academy;

Edinburgh University; Edinburgh College of Art/Heriot Watt University. Assistant Planner, East Lothian District Council, 1978-84; Depute Director, Scottish Mining Museum, 1984-88. Recreations: reading; hill-walking; badminton; sailing. Address: (b.) Scottish Mining Museum, Lady Victoria Colliery, Newtongrange, Midlothian, EH22 4QN; T.-0131-663 7519.

Maclean, Sir Donald, FBCO. Deputy Chairman, Scottish Conservative Party, 1985-89, Vice Chairman, 1989-91; President, Scottish Conservative and Unionist Association, 1983-85; Ophthalmic Optician, since 1952; Dean of Guildry, Ayr Guildry, since 1993; Chairman, Ayrshire Medical Support Ltd.; b. Annan; widower; 1 s.; 1 d. Educ. Morrison's Academy, Crieff; Heriot-Watt, Edinburgh. Ophthalmic Optician in Edinburgh, Newcastle, Perth and now Ayr; Chairman, Ayrshire Local Optical Committee, 1986-88; former Member, Transport Users Local Consultative Committee; Chairman, Ayr Constituency Conservative Association, 1971-75; Chairman, West of Scotland Area Council, Scottish Conservative Association, 1977-78-79; Member, National Union Executive Committee, 1979-89 (Member, GP Committee, 1983-85); Elder, Church of Scotland; Past President, West Highland Steamer Club; Liveryman of the Worshipful Copany of Spectacle Makers; Freeman, City of London. Recreations: photography; reading. Address: (b.) 59 Newmarket Street, Ayr, KA7 1LL.

McLean, Donald, OBE, FRICS. Development Director, Cumbernauld Development Corporation, since 1984; b. 20.2.45, Hamilton; m., Nancy; 2 s. Educ. Hamilton Academy. Lanark CC, 1962-68; West Lothian CC, 1968-69; Ronald Lyon Group, 1969-70; Dundee Corporation, 1970-73; Forth Ports Authority, 1973-74; Livingston Development Corporation, 1974-80; Northampton Development Corporation, 1980-84. Member, Dunbartonshire Valuation Appeal Committee. Recreations: golf; gardening; walking; reading; rugby. Address: (b.) Cumbernauld House, Cumbernauld; T.-01236 721155.

Maclean of Dunconnel, Sir Fitzroy Hew, 1st Bt, KT, CBE (Mil). 15th Hereditary Keeper and Captain of Dunconnel; b. 11.3.11; m., Hon. Mrs Alan Phipps; 2 s. Educ. Eton; Cambridge. Entered Foreign Office, 1933; served Second World War, Queen's Own Cameron Highlanders and Special Air Service Regiment (Brigadier commanding British Military Mission to Yugoslav partisans, 1943-45); MP (Conservative), Lancaster, 1941-59, Bute and North Ayrshire, 1959-74; Parliamentary Under Secretary of State for War and Financial Secretary, War Office, 1954-57; Member, UK Delegation to North Atlantic Assembly, 1962-74; Member, Council of Europe and WEU, 1972-74; Hon. LLD, Glasgow, 1969, Dundee, 1984; Croix de Guerre, France; Order of Kutuzov, USSR; Partisan Star, 1st Class, Yugoslavia; Order of the Yugoslav Star with Ribbon; Order of Merit, Yugoslavia; President, British Yugoslav Society; Past President, Great Britain-USSR Association; author of works of military history and other books. Address: (h.) Strachur House, Strachur, PA27 8BX.

MacLean, Sheriff Hector Ronald. Sheriff of Lothian and Borders, at Linlithgow, since 1988; b. 6.12.31. Advocate, 1959. Address: (b.) Sheriff Court House, Court Square, Linlithgow, EH49 7EQ.

MacLean, Ian Hamish, MBChB, FFPHM. Chief Administrative Medical Officer and Director of Public Health, Dumfries and Galloway Health Board, since 1989; Honorary Clinical Senior Lecturer, Glasgow University, since 1989; b. 9.10.47, Bishop's Stortford, Herts; m., Anne; 1 s.; 1 d. Educ. Felsted School; Dundee University. Consultant in Public Health Medicine, Borders Health Board, 1980-89. Recreations: music; sailing; flying; house restoration; photography. Address: (b.) Dumfries and Galloway Health Board, Nithbank, Dumfries, DG1 2SD; T.-01387 246246.

MacLean, Ian Teasdale, MA, LLB. Solicitor; Senior Partner, Mackie & Dewar, since 1982 (Partner, since 1968); Honorary Treasurer, Aberdeen YMCA, since 1970; b. 3.6.40, Stornoway; m., Lavinia May Symonds; 1 s.; 1 d. Educ. Nicolson Institute, Stornoway; Aberdeen University. Qualified as Solicitor, 1964, after three years' indenture with Morice & Wilson, Advocates in Aberdeen; salaried Solicitor, J.D. Mackie & Dewar, Advocates in Aberdeen, 1965-68. Address: (b.) 18 Bon-Accord Square, Aberdeen; T.-01224 596341.

McLean, Jack, DA, MSIAD. Journalist and Broadcaster; b. Irvine, Ayrshire. Educ. Allan Glen's School, Glasgow; Edinburgh College of Art. Apprentice Welder, 1962-65; various jobs until 1968; Studio Artist, uncertificated Art Teacher, 1968-70; Edinburgh Art College; Jordanhill College of Education; Teacher of Art in Glasgow schools, until 1988; began writing with Times Educational Supplement with regular column; Columnist, The Scotsman, 1967-81; Columnist, Glasgow Herald, since 1981; Scottish Vice-Chairman and National Executive Member, National Union of Students, 1970-74; Member, Scottish Council, Educational Institute of Scotland, 1981-82; Member, Strathclyde Regional Council Education Committee, 1986-88. Commendation, Scottish Press Awards, 1985, 1986; Runner-up, Columnist of the Year, British Press Awards, 1985; Scottish Feature Writer of the Year, 1989; commended Columnist of the Year, 1989. Publications: The Bedside Urban Voltaire; More Bedside Urban Voltaire; The Sporting Urban Voltaire; City of Glasgow. Recreations: drinking in public houses (see A. Hind); flashy dressing; talking. Address: Glasgow Herald, 195 Albion Street, Glasgow, G1 1QP; T.-0141-423 0380, 0141-552 6255.

McLean, John David Ruari, CBE, DSC, Croix de Guerre. Typographer and Author; b. 10.6.17, Minnigaff; m., Antonia Maxwell Carlisle; 2 s.; 1 d. Educ. Dragon School, Oxford; Eastbourne College. Royal Navy, 1940-45; Tutor in Typography, Royal College of Art, 1948-51; Typographic Adviser, Hulton Press, 1953-60; The Observer, 1960-62; Art Editor, The Connoisseur, 1962-73; Founder-Partner, Rainbird, McLean Ltd., 1951-58; Founder Editor, Motif, 1958-67; Honorary Typographic Adviser to HM Stationery Office, 1966-80; Senior Partner, Ruari McLean Associates Ltd., 1960-81; Trustee, National Library of Scotland, 1981. Publications include: Modern Book Design, 1958; Victorian Book Design and Colour Printing, 1963; Magazine Design, 1969; Jan Tschichold, Typographer, 1975; The Thames & Hudson Manual of Typography, 1980; Benjamin Fawcett, Engraver and Colour Printer, 1988; Edward Bawden, war artist, and his letters home 1940-45 (Editor), 1989; Nicolas Bentley drew the pictures, 1990; Typographers on Type (Editor), 1995. Recreations: sailing; acquiring books. Address: (h.) Pier Cottage, Carsaig, Mull, PA70 6HD; T.-01681 704 216.

Maclean, John Robert, DL; b. 24.5.51, Lossiemouth; m., Veronica Mary Lacy Hulbert-Powell; 1 s.; 2 d. Educ. Milton Abbey School. Commissioned into Queen's Own Highlanders, 1971; left Army, 1978, and returned home to farm via Royal Agricultural College, Cirencester; Deputy Lieutenant, County of Moray, since 1987; Member, Royal Company of Archers (Queen's Bodyguard for Scotland), since 1988; Chairman, Elgin Branch, Earl Haig Fund; Member, Committee, Highland Branch, Scottish Landowners Federation. Recreations: shooting; field sports. Address: (h.) Westfield House, near Elgin, Moray.

MacLean, Hon. Lord (Ranald Norman Munro MacLean), BA, LLB, LLM. Senator of the College of Justice, since 1990; Queen's Counsel, since 1977; b. 18.12.38, Aberdeen; m., Pamela Ross; 2 s.; 1 d. Educ.

Inverness Royal Academy; Fettes College, Edinburgh; Cambridge University; Edinburgh University; Yale University. Advocate, 1964; Advocate Depute, 1972-75; Advocate Depute (Home), 1979-82. Recreations: hill-walking; bird watching. Address: (h.) 38 Royal Terrace, Edinburgh, EH7 5AH.

Maclean, Sir Robert (Alexander), KBE (1973), Kt (1955), LLD. Honorary Life President, A.F. Stoddard & Co. Ltd.; Deputy Lieutenant, Renfrewshire; b. 11.4.08, Cambuslang; m., Vivienne Neville Bourke; 2 s.; 2 d. Educ. High School of Glasgow. Partner, later a Senior Partner, James Templeton & Co., Glasgow, 1937-45; Chairman, A.F. Stoddard & Co. Ltd., 1946-83. Chairman, Glasgow Junior Chamber of Commerce, 1940; President, Glasgow Chamber of Commerce, 1956-58; Chairman, Scottish Council of Chambers of Commerce, 1960-62; President, Association of British Chambers of Commerce, 1966-68; Regional Controller (Scotland), Board of Trade, 1944-46; Regional Controller, Factory and Storage Control, 1941-44; Chairman, Scottish Industries Exhibitions, 1949, 1954, 1959; Chairman, Scottish Exports Committee, 1966-70; Chairman, Scottish Industrial Estates Corporation, 1955-72; President, British Industrial Exhibition, Moscow, 1966; Member, BNEC, 1966-70; Member, Scottish Aerodromes Board, 1950-61; Member, Export Council for Europe, 1960-64; Vice-Chairman, Scottish Board for Industry, 1952-60; a Vice-President, Scottish Council (Development and Industry), 1955-82. Recreations: golf; fishing. Address: (h.) South Branchal Farm, Bridge of Weir, Renfrewshire, PA11 3SJ; T.-Kilmacolm 2162.

MacLean, Sorley, MA (Hons). Poet; b. 1911, Osgaig, Raasay; m., Renee Cameron; 3 d. Educ. Portree High School; Edinburgh University. Teacher of English, Portree and Tobermory; Head, English Department, Boroughmuir School, Edinburgh; Headmaster, Plockton High School; Writer in Residence, Edinburgh University, 1973-75; Filidh (Resident Poet), Sabhal Mor Ostaig, 1975-76; author of: 17 Poems for 6d (with Robert Garioch), 1940; Dain do Eimhir, 1943; Four Points of a Saltire (Co-author), 1970; Poems to Eimhir (translated from the Gaelic by Iain Crichton Smith), 1971; Reothairt is Contraigh, Spring Tide and Neap Tide, Selected Poems 1932-72, 1977.

McLean, Una. Actress; b. 1930, Strathaven. Trained, Royal Scottish Academy of Music and Drama; professional debut, Byre, St. Andrews, 1955 ; pantomime debut, Mother Goose, 1958; joined Citizens' Theatre, Glasgow, 1959; appeared in Five Past Eight revue, 1960s; many television appearances.

Maclean, Professor William James, DA, RSA, FSA Scot. Professor of Fine Art, Duncan of Jordanstone College, University of Dundee; b. 12.10.41, Inverness; m., Marian Forbes Leven; 2 s.; 1 d. Educ. Inverness Royal Academy; HMS Conway; Grays School of Art, Aberdeen. Postgraduate and Travel Scholarship, Scottish Education Trust Award, Visual Arts Bursary, Scottish Arts Council; Benno Schotz Prize; one-man exhibitions in Rome, Glasgow, Edinburgh and London; group exhibitions in Britain, Europe and North America; represented in private and public collections including Arts Council, British Museum, Scottish National Gallery of Modern Art, Fitzwilliam Museum, Cambridge, and several Scottish galleries. Address: (h.) Bellevue, 18 Dougall Street, Tayport, Fife.

MacLeary, Alistair Ronald, MSc, DipTP, FRICS, FRTPI, FBIM, FRSA. Honorary Fellow, Commonwealth Association of Surveying and Land Economy; Member, Lands Tribunal for Scotland; MacRobert Professor of Land Economy, Aberdeen University, 1976-89 (Dean, Faculty of Law, 1982-85); President, Planning and Development Division, Royal Institution of Chartered Surveyors, 1984-85; b. 12.1.40, Glasgow; m., Claire Leonard; 1 s.; 1 d. Educ.

Inverness Royal Academy; College of Estate Management; Heriot-Watt University; Strathclyde University. Assistant Surveyor, Gerald Eve & Co., Chartered Surveyors, 1962-65; Assistant to Director, Murrayfield Real Estate Co. Ltd., 1965-67; Assistant Surveyor and Town Planner/Partner, Wright & Partners, 1967-76; seconded to Department of the Environment, London, 1971-73; Member, Committee of Inquiry into the Acquisition and Occupancy of Agricultural Land, 1977-79; Member, Home Grown Timber Advisory Committee, Forestry Commission, 1981-87; Chairman, Board of Education, Commonwealth Association of Surveying and Land Economy, 1981-90; Editor, Land Development Studies, 1986-90; Member, Natural Environment Research Council, 1988-91. Recreations: shooting; skiing; hill-walking. Address: (h.) St. Helen's, St. Andrew's Road, Ceres, Fife, KY15 5NQ; T.-01334 828862.

MacLeay, Very Rev. John Henry James, MA. Dean of Argyll, since 1987; Rector, St. Andrew's, Fort William, since 1978; Canon, St. John's Cathedral, Oban, since 1980; b. 7.12.31, Inverness; m., Jane Speirs Cuthbert; 1 s.; 1 d. Educ. St. Edmund Hall, Oxford. Ordained Deacon, 1957; Priest, 1958; Curate: St. John's, East Dulwich, 1957-60, St. Michael's, Inverness, 1960-62; Rector, St. Michael's, Inverness, 1962-70; Priest-in-Charge, St. Columba's, Grantown-on-Spey and St. John's, Rothiemurchus, 1970-78. Recreations: fishing; reading; visiting churches and cathedrals. Address: St. Andrew's Rectory, Parade Road, Fort William, PH33 6BA; T.-01397 2979.

MacLehose of Beoch, Baron (Crawford Murray MacLehose), KT (1983), GBE (1976), KCMG (1971), KCVO (1975), DL, Hon. LLD (York, 1983, Strathclyde, 1984). Chairman, School of Oriental and African Studies, 1983-91; Chairman, Scottish Trust for the Physically Disabled and Margaret Blackwood Housing Association, 1983-91; Life Peer; 16.10.17; m.; 2 d. Educ. Rugby; Balliol College, Oxford. Served Second World War (Lt., RNVR); joined Foreign Service, 1947; Governor and C-in-C, Hong Kong, 1971-82. Address: (h.) Beoch, Maybole, Ayrshire.

McLeish, Henry Baird. MP (Labour), Central Fife, since 1987; b. 15.6.48; 1 s.; 1 d. Educ. Buckhaven High School, Methil; Heriot-Watt University. Former Research Officer and Planning Officer in local government; former Member, Kirkcaldy District Council and Fife Regional Council (Leader, 1982-87); Scottish Front Bench Spokesman for Education and Employment, 1988-89, for Employment and Training, 1989-92; Shadow Scottish Minister of State, 1992-94; Shadow Minister of Transport, since 1994. Recreations: reading; history; life and work of Robert Burns; malt whisky; Highlands and Islands. Address: (h.) 27 Braid Drive, Glenrothes, KY7 4ES; T.-01592 755330.

McLellan, Rev. Andrew Rankin Cowie, MA, BD, STM. Minister, St. Andrew's and St. George's, Edinburgh, since 1986; b. 16.6.44, Glasgow; m., Irene L. Meek; 2 s. Educ. Kilmarnock Academy; Madras College, St. Andrews; St. Andrews University; Glasgow University; Union Theological Seminary, New York. Assistant Minister, St. George's West, Edinburgh, 1969-71; Minister, Cartsburn Augustine, Greenock, 1971-80; Minister, Viewfield, Stirling, 1980-86; Member, Inverclyde District Council, 1977-80; Tutor, Glasgow University, 1978-82; Chaplain, HM Prison, Stirling, 1982-85; Convener, Church and Nation Committee, General Assembly, since 1992. Recreations: golf; family; theatre; travel; books. Address: 25 Comely Bank, Edinburgh, EH4 1AJ; T.-031-332 5324.

McLellan, Douglas Richard, MD, MRCPath, DFM. Consultant Pathologist, Victoria Infirmary, Glasgow, since 1989; Honorary Senior Lecturer, Glasgow University, since 1989; b. 13.6.55, Glasgow; m., Caitriona; 3 s. Educ. High School of Glasgow; Glasgow University. Registrar in Pathology, Southern General Hospital, Glasgow, 1978-81; Honorary Senior Registrar in Neuropathology (MRC Head

Injury Project), Institute of Neurological Sciences, Glasgow, 1981-84; Senior Registrar in Pathology, Western Infirmary, Glasgow, 1984-89. Recreations: bibliomania; Celtology. Address: (h.) 8 Calderwood Road, Newlands, Glasgow, G43 2RP.

McLellan, James Alexander, LLB. Director of Administration, Argyll and Bute District Council, since 1978; b. 23.12.50, Lochgilphead; m., Alexis; 2 s.; 1 d. Educ. Keil School; Glasgow University. Recreations: fishing; gardening. Address: (h.) Kilmory, Lochgilphead, Argyll, PA31 8RT; T.-01546 602127.

McLelland, John, BVMS, MVSc, PhD, MRCVS. Reader, Department of Preclinical Veterinary Sciences, Edinburgh University, since 1981; b. 11.6.37, Kilmarnock; m., Morar; 1 s.; 2 d. Educ. Kilmarnock Academy; Glasgow Academy; Glasgow University; Liverpool University. Pig Industry Development Authority Scholar, Veterinary Hospital, Glasgow University, 1962-63; Egg Marketing Board Scholar, Department of Veterinary Anatomy, Liverpool University, 1964; Assistant Lecturer, then Lecturer, Department of Veterinary Anatomy, Liverpool University, 1964-72; Lecturer, then Senior Lecturer, Department of Veterinary Anatomy, Edinburgh University, 1972-81; Chairman, Sub-Committee on Systema Digestorium, International Committee on Avian Anatomical Nomenclature. Publications: Outlines of Avian Anatomy (Co-author), 1975; Form and Function in Birds (Co-editor), 1979, 1981, 1985, 1989; An Introduction to the Functional Anatomy of the Limbs of the Domestic Animals (Co-author), 1984; Birds: Their Structure and Function (Co-author), 1984; A Colour Atlas of Avian Anatomy, 1990. Recreations: cooking; travel. Address: (h.) 117/10 W. Savile Terrace, Edinburgh; T.-0131-662 4588.

MacLennan, David Neall, BSc, FIOA, FInstP, CEng. Deputy Director, Marine Laboratory, since 1986; b. 26.9.40, Aberdeen; m., Sheila Cormack; 1 s.; 1 d. Educ. Rober Gordon's College; Aberdeen University. Scientific Officer, AERE Harwell, 1962-67; Marine Laboratory, 1967-73; Head Office, Department of Agriculture and Fisheries for Scotland, 1973-75; returned to Marine Laboratory, 1976. Vice President, ICES, since 1993. Recreation: bridge. Address: (h.) 2 Stronsay Avenue, Aberdeen; T.-0224 876544.

Maclennan, Professor Duncan, MA, MPhil. Mactaggart Professor of Land Economics and Finance, Glasgow University; Director, Centre for Housing Research and Urban Studies, since 1983; Economic Adviser to OECD, Paris, since 1981; Board Member, Scottish Homes, since 1988; b. 12.3.49, Glasgow; 1 s.; 1 d. Educ. Allan Glen's Secondary School; Glasgow University. Lecturer in Applied Economics, Glasgow University, 1974-76; Lecturer in Political Economy, Aberdeen University, 1976-78; Lecturer in Applied Economics, Glasgow University, 1979-82; Chairman, National Steering Group for Care and Repair. Past President, Allan Glen's Rugby Club. Recreations: watching rugby; gardening; housework. Address: (b.) Centre for Housing Research, 25 Bute Gardens, Glasgow; T.-0141-330 4615.

MacLennan, Finlay, QPM, FBIM. Deputy Chief Constable, Northern Constabulary, since 1985; Member, National Broadcasting Council for Scotland, 1987-91; b. 10.4.36, Harris; m., Barbara Patricia; 1 s.; 1 d. Educ. Portree High School; Garnett College, London. National Service, Cameron Highlanders, 1956-58; Metropolitan Police, 1958-85. Member, Board of Management, YMCA, Lambeth, 1979-82. Recreations: squash; shooting; hill-walking; sailing; fishing. Address: (b.) Police Headquarters, Perth Road, Inverness, IV2 3SY; T.-01463 239191.

Maclennan, Robert Adam Ross. MP (Lib. Dem.), Caithness and Sutherland; Lib. Dem. President and Spokesman on Constitutional Affairs, National Heritage and Broadcasting; Barrister-at-Law; b. 26.6.36, Glasgow; m., Helen Cutter Noyes; 2 s.; 1 d. Educ. Glasgow Academy; Balliol College, Oxford; Trinity College, Cambridge; Columbia University, New York. Parliamentary Private Secretary to Secretary of State for Commonwealth Affairs, 1967; Opposition Spokesman on Scottish Affairs and Defence, 1970; Parliamentary Under-Secretary of State, Department of Prices and Consumer Protection, 1974-79; Opposition Spokesman on Foreign Affairs, 1979; Founder Member, SDP, 1981, and author of party's constitution; Parliamentary Spokesman on Agriculture, 1981, Home Affairs, 1983, Economic Affairs, 1987; elected Leader, SDP, 1987. Recreations: music; theatre; visual arts. Address: (b.) House of Commons, London, SW1A 0AA; T.-0171-219 6553.

MacLennan, Professor William Jardine, MD, FRCP, FRCPEdin, FRCPGlas. Professor of Geriatric Medicine, Edinburgh University, since 1986; Honorary Consultant Physician in Geriatric Medicine, Lothian Health Board, since 1986; b. 11.2.41, Glasgow; m., Fiona Hannah Campbell; 2 s. Educ. Hutchesons' Boys' Grammar School; Glasgow University. House Physician, Stobhill Hospital, Glasgow, 1964; Hansen Research Scholar, then Assistant Lecturer, then Lecturer, Department of Materia Medica, Glasgow University, 1965-69; Senior Registrar in Geriatric Medicine, Stobhill General Hospital and Glasgow Western Infirmary, 1969-71; Senior Lecturer in Geriatric Medicine, Southampton University, 1971-80; Senior Lecturer, then Reader in Geriatric Medicine, Dundee University, 1980-86; Convener of Trustees, Dementia Services Development Centre; Member, Council of Professions Supplementary to Medicine. Publications: books on clinical care of the elderly, drugs in the elderly and bone disease in the elderly, metabolic and endocrine disorders in the elderly, infections in elderly patients. Recreations: hill-walking; ship-modelling; playing classical guitar badly. Address: (h.) 26 Caiystane Avenue, Fairmilehead, Edinburgh; T.-0131-445 1755.

MacLeod, Ally. Football manager; b. 1931, Glasgow. Played for Third Lanark, St. Mirren, Blackburn, Hibernian, Ayr United; Manager, Ayr United, Aberdeen, Motherwell, Airdrie, Queen of the South; led Scotland to World Cup, Argentina, 1978.

MacLeod, Andrew Kenneth, BA. Chief Executive, Scottish Fisheries Protection Agency, since 1991; b. 28.3.50, Elgin; m., Sheila Janet; 2 d. Educ. Fettes College, Edinburgh; St. John's College, Oxford. Nuffield College, Oxford, 1971-74; National Economic Development Office, 1974-78; Economic Adviser, Manpower Services Commission, Office for Scotland, 1978-83; Economic Adviser/Principal, Scottish Office, 1983-90; Head, Fisheries Division III, 1990-91. Address: (b.) Pentland House, 47 Robb's Loan, Edinburgh, EH14 1TY; T.-0131-244 6059.

MacLeod, Archibald, OBE, NDA, NDD. Member, Red Deer Commission, since 1989; Member, Scottish Advisory Committee, RSPB, since 1993; b. 23.3.28, Kames, Argyll; m., Sheena Fleming Ferguson; 2 s.; 1 s deceased. Educ. Greenock High School; West of Scotland Agricultural College. Research Assistant, West of Scotland Agricultural College, 1949-53; Officer-in-Charge, Lephinmore Research Farm, Hill Farming Research Organisation, 1953-56; Senior Adviser (North Argyll), West of Scotland Agricultural College, 1956-66; Head of Advisory Services, Argyll Area, 1966-86. Chairman, Crofters Commission, 1986-89; Past President; Oban Rotary Club, Oban Speakers Club; founder Chairman, West Cowal YFC; Honorary Vice-President, Lorn Agricultural Society. Recreations: shooting; curling; gardening; reading. Address: (h.) Craigielea, Kames, By Tighnabruaich, Argyll, PA21 2AE.

MacLeod, Calum Alexander, CBE, MA, LLB, LLD. Chairman, Grampian Television PLC, since 1993;

Chairman, Grampian Health Board, since 1993; Chairman, Britannia Building Society, since 1994; Chairman, Abtrust Scotland Investment Company PLC, since 1986; Chairman, Albyn of Stonehaven Ltd., since 1973; Deputy Chairman, Scottish Eastern Investment Trust PLC, since 1988; Director, Bradstock Group PLC, since 1994; Aberdeen Board Member, Bank of Scotland, since 1980; b. 25.7.35, Stornoway; m., Elizabeth M. Davidson; 2 s.; 1 d. Educ. Nicolson Institute; Glenurquhart High School; Aberdeen University. Partner, Paull & Williamsons, Advocates, Aberdeen, 1964-80; Member, White Fish Authority, 1973-80; Member, North of Scotland Hydro-Electric Board, 1976-84; Member, Highlands and Islands Development Board, 1984-91; Chancellor's Assessor, Aberdeen University, 1979-90; Chairman of Governors, Robert Gordon's College, 1981-94; Chairman, Scottish Council of Independent Schools, since 1991. Recreations: golf; motoring; hill-walking; reading; music. Address: (h.) 6 Westfield Terrace, Aberdeen, AB2 4RU; T.-01224 641614.

Macleod, Rev. Professor Donald, MA. Professor of Systematic Theology, Free Church College, since 1978; Editor, The Monthly Record, 1977-90; Vagrant Preacher, since 1978; b. 24.11.40, Ness, Isle of Lewis; m., Mary Maclean; 3 s. Educ. Nicolson Institute, Stornoway; Glasgow University; Free Church College. Ordained Guy Fawkes Day, 1964; Minister: Kilmallie Free Church, 1964-70, Partick Highland Free Church, Glasgow, 1970-78. Recreations: dreaming about cricket, fishing and gardening; Gaelic music.

Macleod, Donald Angus David, MB, ChB, FRCS Edin, FISM. Consultant General Surgeon, since 1976; b. 4.3.41, Selkirk; m., Lucile Janette Kirkpatrick; 1 s.; 2 d. Educ. Gordonstoun; Edinburgh University. Chairman, Lothian Health Board Basic Surgical Training Committee, 1986-91; Director of Studies (Surgery), Edinburgh Postgraduate Board for Medicine, 1976-86; Chairman, Scottish Committee, Medical Commission for Accident Prevention, 1980-85; Chairman, West Lothian Medical Staff Committee, 1986-89; Member, West Lothian Unit Management Team, 1987-89; Hon. Medical Adviser, Scottish Rugby Union since 1969; Member, International Rugby Football Board Medical Advisory Committee, since 1978; Vice-Chairman, Medical Advisory Committee, 13th Commonwealth Games, Scotland, 1984-86; Chairman, Sports Medicine and Sports Science Consultative Group, Scottish Sports Council, 1990-93; Associate Post Graduate Dean, Lister Post Graduate Institute, since 1993; Councillor, Royal College of Surgeons of Edinburgh, since 1992; awarded Robert Atkins Award for services to sports medicine, 1992. Recreation: orienteering. Address: (h.) The Haining, Woodlands Park, Livingston, West Lothian, EH54 8AT.

MacLeod, Donald Ian Kerr, RD—, MA, LLB, WS. Partner, Shepherd & Wedderburn, WS, since 1964; b. 19.4.37, Edinburgh; m., Mary St. Clair Bridge; 1 s.; 2 d. Educ. Aberdeen Grammar School; Aberdeen University; Edinburgh University. Apprentice, MacPherson & Mackay, WS, 1957-60; Assistant, Shepherd & Wedderburn, 1960-64; Solicitor in Scotland to HM Customs and Excise and Department of Employment, since 1970, and Health and Safety Executive, since 1974. Lt.-Cdr. RNR (Retd.); Member, Court of Session Rules Council; Church Elder. Recreations: hockey; golf; walking. Address: (b.) Saltire Court, Castle Terrace, Edinburgh, EH1 2ET; T.-0131-228 9900.

MacLeod, Fraser. Director, Scottish Crofters Union. Address: (b.) Old Mill, Broadford, Isle of Skye, IV49 9AQ.

McLeod, Helen R. General Secretary, The Girls' Brigade Scotland, since 1981; b. 2.9.44, Glasgow. Educ. Hyndland Secondary School; Jordanhill College of Education. Local government officer, 1961-78; community education worker, 1980-81. Secretary, Strathclyde Conference of Voluntary Youth Organisations, 1988-91. Recreations: music; photography; reading. Address: (b.) Boys' Brigade House, 168 Bath Street, Glasgow, G2 4TQ; T.-0141-332 1765.

MacLeod, Professor Iain Alasdair, BSc, PhD, CEng, FICE, FIStructE. Professor of Structural Engineering, Strathclyde University, since 1981; b. 4.5.39, Glasgow; m., Barbara Jean Booth; 1 s.; 1 d. Educ. Lenzie Academy; Glasgow University. Design Engineer, Crouch and Hogg, Glasgow, 1960-62; Assistant Lecturer in Civil Engineering, Glasgow University, 1962-66; Design Engineer, H.A. Simons Ltd., Vancouver, 1966-67; Structural Engineer, Portland Cement Association, Illinois, 1968-69; Lecturer in Civil Engineering, Glasgow University, 1969-73; Professor and Head, Department of Civil Engineering, Paisley College of Technology, 1973-81; Chairman, Scottish Branch, Institution of Structural Engineers, 1985-86; Vice-President, Institution of Structural Engineers, 1989-90; Member, Standing Committee on Structural Safety, since 1989. Recreations: climbing; sailing. Address: (b.) Department of Civil Engineering, Strathclyde University, 107 Rottenrow, Glasgow; T.-0141-552 4400.

Macleod, Ian Buchanan, BSc, MB, ChB, FRCSEdin. Honorary Secretary, Royal College of Surgeons of Edinburgh, since 1993; Consultant Surgeon, Royal Infirmary, Edinburgh, 1969-93; Honorary Senior Lecturer, Department of Clinical Surgery, Edinburgh University, 1969-93; Surgeon to the Queen in Scotland, 1987-93; b. 20.5.33, Wigan; m., Kathleen Gillean Large; 1 s.; 1 d. Educ. Wigan Grammar School; Edinburgh University. House Surgeon and House Physician, Royal Infirmary, Edinburgh, 1957-59; National Service, RAMC, Malaya, Singapore, Nepal, 1959-61; appointments, Department of Clinical Surgery, Edinburgh University and Royal Infirmary, Edinburgh, since 1961. Editor, Journal, Royal College of Surgeons of Edinburgh, 1982-87. Publications: Principles and Practice of Surgery (Co-author), 1985, 1989, 1995; Farquharson's Text Book of Operative Surgery (Contributor), 1986; Companion to Medical Studies (Contributor), 1981, 1985. Recreations: golf; photography. Address: (h.) Derwent House, 32 Cramond Road North, Edinburgh, EH4 6JE; T.-0131-336 1541.

Macleod, Iseabail Campbell, MA. Editorial Director, Scottish National Dictionary Association Ltd., since 1986; b. 27.5.36, Glasgow. Educ. Clydebank High School; Lenzie Academy; Glasgow University. Teacher, 1958-64; Editorial Assistant, Europa Publications, 1965-66; Editor of bilingual dictionaries, Collins, Glasgow, 1966-74; Dictionaries Editor, Editorial Director, W. & R. Chambers, Edinburgh, 1974-77. Publications: Pocket Guide to Scottish Words, 1986; Pocket Scots Dictionary (Co-editor), 1988; Scots Thesaurus (Co-editor), 1990; Concise English-Scots Dictionary (Co-editor), 1993. Recreations: hill-walking; cooking; languages; music. Address: (h.) 11 Scotland Street, Edinburgh, EH3 6PU; T.-0131-556 5683.

MacLeod, Professor James Summers, LLM, CA, FTII. Partner, Ernst & Young, Edinburgh, since 1973; Professor, Department of Accountancy, Edinburgh University, since 1986; b. 3.8.41, Dumfries; m., Sheila Stromier; 2 s.; 1 d. Educ. Dumfries Academy; Glasgow University. Lecturer, Edinburgh University, 1965-68; Lecturer, Heriot Watt University, 1968-71; joined Arthur Young (now Ernst & Young), 1971. Publications: Taxation on Insurance Business (Co-author), 3rd edition, 1992; 200 papers. Recreations: bridge; music; reading. Address: (h.) 2 Bonaly Road, Edinburgh; T.-0131-441 4144.

MacLeod of MacLeod, John. 29th Chief of Clan MacLeod; b. 10.8.35; m.; 1 s.; 1 d. Educ. Eton. Address: Dunvegan Castle, Isle of Skye.

McLeod, John, FRAM, FTCL, LRAM, ARCM. Composer, Conductor and Lecturer; Director, Post Graduate course in Composing for Film and Television, London College of Music, since 1991; Visiting Professor, Royal Academy of Music, since 1993; b. 8.3.34, Aberdeen; m., Margaret Murray; 1 s.; 1 d. Educ. Aberdeen Grammar School; Royal Academy of Music, London. Director of Music, Merchiston Castle School, 1974-85; Visiting Lecturer, RSAMD, 1985-89; Ida Carroll Research Fellow, Royal Northern College of Music, 1988-89; Guest Conductor: Scottish National Orchestra, Scottish Chamber Orchestra, BBC Scottish Symphony Orchestra; Associate Composer, Scottish Chamber Orchestra, 1980-82; Guinness Prize for British Composers, 1979; Radio Forth Award for Composition, 1981; UK Music Education Award, 1982. Recreations: travelling; books; art; films; theatre; walking; conversation; gardening; cooking; wine; malt whisky. Address: (h.) Aldourie House, 9 Redford Crescent, Colinton, Edinburgh, EH13 OBS.

Macleod, John Alasdair Johnston, DL, FRCGP, DCH, DObsRCOG. General Practitioner, North Uist, since 1973; Secretary, Western Isles Local Medical Committee (GP), 1977-91; Deputy Lieutenant, Western Isles, since 1979; b. 20.1.35, Stornoway; m., Lorna Jean Ferguson; 2 s.; 1 d. Educ. Nicolson Institute; Keil School; Glasgow University. National Service, Royal Navy, 1957-59; hospital posts, Glasgow and London, 1963-73; Non-Executive Director, Olscot Ltd., 1969-93; trainer in general practice, 1975-95; Visiting Professor, Department of Family Medicine, University of North Carolina, 1985; Member, World Organisation of National Colleges Academique of Family Practice, since 1989 (Member, WONCA World Group "Recruitment for Rural Practice", since 1992); Member, General Practitioner Writers Association, since 1986. Member, Committee of North Uist Highland Gathering; Fellow, Royal Society of Medicine; Admiralty Surgeon and Agent, 1974-91; author of papers and articles, singly and jointly, on aspects of isolated practice. Recreations: boating; horticulture; photography; time-sharing. Address: (h.) Tigh-Na-Hearradh, Lochmaddy, Isle of North Uist, HS6 5AE; T.-018763 224.

Macleod, John Francis Matheson, MA, LLB, NP. Solicitor in Inverness, 1959-94; Dean, Faculty of Solicitors of the Highlands, 1988-91; Chairman, Crofters Commission, 1978-86; Member, Council, Law Society of Scotland, 1988-92; b. 24.1.32, Inverness; m., Alexandra Catherine; 1 s. Educ. Inverness Royal Academy; George Watson's College; Edinburgh University. Solicitor, Fife County Council, 1957-59; in private practice, 1959-94; Parliamentary candidate (Liberal): Moray and Nairn, 1964, Western Isles, 1966; Chairman, Highland Region, Scottish Liberal Party, until 1978; former Vice-Chairman, Broadcasting Council for Scotland. Address: (h.) Bona Lodge, Aldourie, Inverness; T.-01463 751327.

Macleod, John Murray, MA. Freelance Journalist and Broadcaster; b. 15.4.66, Kilmallie, Inverness-shire. Educ. Jordanhill College School, Glasgow; James Gillespie's High School, Edinburgh; Edinburgh University. Columnist, The Herald and The Scotsman, 1989-92; Columnist/Writer-at-large, The Herald, since 1992; also writer of interviews/profiles. Scottish Journalist of the Year, 1991; Young Scottish Journalist of the Year, 1991-92. Recreations: cycling; corresponding; photography; poaching; applied Free Presbyterianism. Address: (h.) 1 Maraig, Harris, Western Isles, PA85 3AG; T.-01859 50 2127.

MacLeod, Emeritus Professor Malcolm, MD (Hons), FRCPEdin. Professor Emeritus in Renal Medicine, Aberdeen University; b. 9.12.16, Glasgow; m., Elizabeth Shaw Ritchie; 1 s. Educ. Nicolson Institute, Stornoway; Aberdeen University. Military Service, Africa, India, SE Asia, 1940-46 (Medical Specialist, RAMC); Lecturer,

Senior Lecturer, Reader in Medicine, 1947-80; Personal Professor in Renal Medicine, Aberdeen University, 1981; Honorary Consultant Physician, Aberdeen Royal Infirmary, 1955-82 and Honorary Consultant in charge, Medical Renal Unit, 1966-82; President, Scottish Society of Physicians, 1980. Recreation: natural history. Address: (h.) 76 Hamilton Place, Aberdeen, AB2 4BA; T.-0224 635537.

McLeod, Professor Malcolm Donald, MA, BLitt (Oxon), FRSE. Director, Hunterian Museum and Art Gallery, Glasgow University, since 1990; b. 19.5.41, Edinburgh; m., I.V. Barry; 2 s.; 1 d. Educ. Birkenhead School; Hertford and Exeter Colleges, Oxford. Research Assistant, Institute of Social Anthropology, Oxford, 1964-65; Lecturer, Sociology Department, University of Ghana, 1967-69; Assistant Curator, Museum of Archaeology and Ethnology, Cambridge, 1969-74; College Lecturer and Director of Studies, Magdalene and Girton Colleges, Cambridge, 1969-74; Fellow, Magdalene College, 1972-74; Keeper of Ethnography, British Museum, 1974-90; Honorary Lecturer, Department of Anthropology, UCL, 1976-81; Honorary Lecturer, Department of Archaeology, University of Glasgow, since 1992. Publications: The Asante, 1981; Treasures of African Art, 1981; Ethnic Sculpture (Co-author), 1985; Jacob Epstein Collector (Co-author), 1989. Address: (h.) Mossfennan, Bowden, Melrose, TD6 0ST; 13 Kirklee Terrace, Glasgow G12 8QQ.

Macleod, Murdoch, MBE, JP. General Manager, Secretary and Treasurer, Stornoway Pier and Harbour Commission, since 1975; Honorary Sheriff; b. 11.8.32, Shawbost, Isle of Lewis; m., Crisybil; 1 s.; 1 d. Educ. Nicolson Institute, Stornoway. Ross and Cromarty Council: Highways Department, 1955-57, Education Department, 1957-65; Stornoway Town Council: Town Clerk's Department, 1965-68, Town Clerk, 1968-75. Former Deputy Chairman, Transport Users Consultative Committee for Scotland; Past Chairman, District Courts Association; Chairman, Western Isles Justices Committee; Member, Council, British Ports Asssociation; Chairman, Scottish Port Members, British Ports Association; Director, Western Isles Development Fund Ltd.; Honorary President, Lewis Pipe Band; Member, British Airways Consumer Council for Highlands and Islands; Chairman, League of Friends, Stornoway Hospitals and Homes. Recreation: reading. Address: (h.) 46 Barony Square, Stornoway, Isle of Lewis; T.-01851 703024.

Macleod, Sheriff Principal Norman Donald, QC, MA, LLB. Sheriff Principal of Glasgow and Strathkelvin, since 1986; Commissioner of Northern Lighthouses, since 1986; b. 6.3.32, Perth; m., Ursula Jane Bromley; 2 s.; 2 d. Educ. Mill Hill School; George Watson's Boys College; Edinburgh University; Hertford College, Oxford. Called to the Bar, 1956; District Officer and Crown Counsel, Colonial Service, East Africa, 1957-63; at the Bar, 1963-67; Sheriff at Glasgow, 1967-86. Recreation: rustic pursuits. Address: (b.) 1 Carlton Place, Glasgow, G5 9DA; T.-0141-429 8888.

McLeod, Norman Duff, FCCA. Group Finance Director, Low & Bonar PLC, since 1990; b. 2.8.51, Dundee; m., Alison; 1 s.; 1 d. Educ. Grove Academy, Dundee. Henderson & Loggie, CAs, Dundee, 1968-77; Bonar Long Ltd., 1977-84, latterly as Finance Director and Company Secretary; Low & Bonar PLC, since 1984. Recreation: golf. Address: (b.) Bonar House, Faraday Street, Dundee, DD1 9JA; T.-01382 818171.

MacLeod, Peter, MCIBS. Retired Banker; yachting journalist; Honorary Sheriff, Oban, since 1988; b. 9.6.33, Ruaig, Isle of Tiree; m., Jean MacDonald Buchanan; 2 s. Educ. Oban High School. Served as Captain, Royal Signals, AER; joined Royal Bank of Scotland, 1949; Bank Manager: Tobermory, Kinlochleven, Wick, Oban. Past Commodore, Royal Highland Yacht Club. Publication: History of Royal Highland Yacht Club, 1881-1986. Recreations: sailing;

island wandering; impromptu ceilidhs; beachcombing. Address: (h.) The Wheelhouse, Ganavan, Oban, Argyll; T.-01631 563577.

MacLeod, Rev. Roderick, MA (Hons), BD, PhD (Edin), PhD (Open). Minister, Cumlodden, Lochfyneside and Lochgair, Argyll, since 1985; b. 24.6.41, Lochmaddy. Educ. Paible Secondary School; Portree High School; Edinburgh University. Minister, Berneray, North Uist, 1966-85; Member: Western Isles Islands Council, 1974-82, Western Isles Health Board, 1975-79; Clerk, Uist Presbytery, 1981-85; Mackinnon Memorial Lecturer, Cape Breton College, 1979; Visiting Scholar, Harvard Divinity School, 1981; Editor, Gaelic Supplement, Life and Work, since 1980; Founder, Cruisgean (Gaelic newspaper); author of several Gaelic books; writes and broadcasts on Highland affairs in Gaelic and English. Recreations: walking; shinty. Address: Furnace, Inveraray, Argyll, PA32 8XU; T.-014995 288.

MacLeod, Roderick John, LLB (Hons). Advocate; Member, Broadcasting Council for Scotland, since 1992; b. 7.12.52, Skye; m., Lorna Jane Robertson. Educ. Portree High School; Edinburgh University. Research Assistant, BBC Scotland, 1976-78; Solicitor, 1979-93. Director, Highland Fund Ltd.; former Chairman, Club Gniomhachas nan Gaidheal; Founder Director, Comunn na Gaidhlig. Recreations: Gaelic literature; reading; cycling; football. Address: (h.) 19 South Oswald Road, Edinburgh, EH9 2HQ; T.-0131-667 2829.

McLernan, Sheriff Kieran Anthony, KHS, MA, LLB. Sheriff of Grampian Highlands and Islands at Banff and Peterhead, since 1991; b. 29.4.41, Wemyss Bay; m., Joan Doherty; 1 s.; 3 d. Educ. St. Aloysius College, Glasgow; Glasgow University. Solicitor, 1965-91; Temporary Sheriff, 1986-91; Tutor, Glasgow University, 1987-91. Recreations: golf; hockey; skiing. Address: (h.) Peockstone Farm, Lochwinnoch, Renfrewshire; T.-01505 842128.

McLetchie, David William, LLB (Hons), WS. Solicitor, since 1976; President, Scottish Conservative and Unionist Association; b. 6.8.52, Edinburgh; m., Barbara Gemmell Baillie (deceased); 1 s. Educ. George Heriot's School; Edinburgh University. Apprentice Solicitor, 1974-76; Solicitor, Tods Murray WS, 1976-80; Partner, Tods Murray WS, since 1980. Recreations: golf; football (Heart of Midlothian); rock and pop music. Address: (h.) 13 Keith Crescent, Edinburgh, EH4 3NH; T.-0131-332 4691.

McLevy, Harry. Member, STUC General Council; Regional Officer, Amalgamated Engineering Union, since 1985; b. 28.8.36, Dundee; m., Doris Laburn; 3 s.; 1 d. Educ. Logie Junior Secondary. Address: (b.) 145 West Regent Street, Glasgow; T.-0141-248 7131.

McMahon, Hugh Robertson, MA (Hons). Member (Labour), European Parliament, Strathclyde West, since 1984; b. 17.6.38, Saltcoats; m., Helen Paterson Grant; 1 s.; 1 d. Educ. Stevenston High School; Ardrossan Academy; Glasgow University. Schoolteacher in Ayrshire (Largs High, Stevenston High, Irvine Royal Academy, Mainholm Academy); Assistant Head, Ravenspark Academy, 1971-84. Vice-Chair, EP Social Affairs, Employment and Working Environment Committee, 1992-94; Member, Budgetary Control and Environment Committees; Chair, EP Delegation with Norway, 1989-92; currently Member, Delegation with Hungary. Recreation: golf. Address: (b.) Euro Office, 9 Low Road, Paisley PA2 6AQ.

McMahon, Peter, BSc (Hons). Scottish Political Editor, The Scotsman, since 1995; b. 31.7.59, Dublin; m., Seonal MacKinnon; 2 s.; 1 d. Educ. St. Augustine's High School, Edinburgh; St. Andrews University. Reporter, Cambrian News Agency, Cardiff; Reporter, Northampton Chronicle and Echo; Political Correspondent, Central Press Features, Westminster; Political Correspondent, Daily Star;

Westminster Editor, Scotland on Sunday; Political Editor, Sunday Mirror. Recreations: music; sport. Address: (b.) 20 North Bridge, Edinburgh, EH1 1YT; T.-0131-225 2468.

McManus, Professor John, DSc, PhD, ARCS, DIC, FRSE, CGeol, MIEnvSci. Professor of Geology, St. Andrews University, since 1993 (Reader, 1988-93); Honorary Director, Tay Estuary Research Centre, 1979-92; b. 5.6.38, Harwich; m., J. Barbara Beveridge; 2 s.; 1 d. Educ. Harwich County High School; Imperial College, London University. Assistant, then Lecturer, St. Andrews University, 1964-67; Lecturer, Senior Lecturer, Reader, Dundee University, 1967-88; UNESCO Representative, International Commission on Continental Erosion, 1980-84 and 1986; Member, Scottish Natural Heritage S.E. Region Board and Scientific Advisory Committee; Member, Secretary of State's Committee on Waste Discharges into the Marine Environment; President, Estuarine and Brackish Water Sciences Association, 1995-98; Member, Eden Estuary Nature Reserve Management Committee; former Treasurer, British Sedimentological Research Group; Consultant on Coastal Erosion and Protection to four Regional Councils; Executive Editor, Transactions of the Royal Society of Edinburgh, Earth Sciences, 1988-95; Associate Editor, Continental Shelf Research. President: Cupar Choral Association, 1968-78, Cupar Amateur Opera, 1979-91. Recreations: music; bird-watching; swimming; stamp collecting. Address: (b.) School of Geography and Geology, Purdie Building, St. Andrews University, St. Andrews, Fife, KY16 9ST.

McManus, Rev. Matthew Francis. Parish Priest, Kilwinning; Convenor, Association of Scottish Local Health Councils, 1983-92; b. 22.9.40, Rutherglen. Educ. Sacred Heart High School, Girvan; St. Andrew's College, Drygrange. Ordained, 1965, Assistant Priest, St. Margaret's, Ayr; Parish Priest, New Cumnock, Kirkconnel and Sanquhar, 1976-81, Kirkcudbright, 1981-88; Chairman, Dumfries and Galloway Local Health Council, 1985-87; Chairman, Castle Douglas District CAB, 1984-87; Chairman, Stewartry Council of Voluntary Service, 1985-88; Chairman, Stewartry School Council, 1985-87; Member, Scottish Consumer Council, 1983-90; Member, Complaints Committee, Law Society of Scotland, since 1985; Secretary, Association of Vocations Directors of Scotland, since 1987. Address: St. Winin's, St. Winning's Lane, Kilwinning, KA13 6EP; T.-Kilwinning 552276.

McMaster, Brian John, CBE. Director, Edinburgh International Festival, since 1991; b. 9.5.43. General Administrator, subsequently Managing Director, W.N.O., 1976-91. Address: (b.) 21 Market Street, Edinburgh, EH1 1BW.

McMaster, Gordon James, MP, MIHort, CertEd. MP (Labour), Paisley South, since 1990; Scottish Labour Whip, since 1992; Assistant Deputy Chief Whip, since 1994; Secretary, All-Party Disablement Group, since 1992; Vice Chair, All Party Gardening Club, since 1994; b. 13.2.60, Johnstone. Educ. Johnstone High School; Langside College; West of Scotland Agricultural College, Jordanhill College. Began career as apprentice gardener, 1976; Lecturer, then Senior Lecturer in Horticulture, Langside College, 1980-89; Co-ordinator, Growing Concern (Strathclyde), 1989-90. Former Member, Renfrew District Council (Leader, 1988-90). Recreations: gardening; reading; writing. Address: (b.) The Gatehouse, 22 Neilston Road, Paisley, PA2 6LN.

MacMillan, Emeritus Professor Andrew, OBE, RSA, MA, FRIAS, RIBA. Emeritus Professor, University of Glasgow, since 1994; Professor of Architecture and Head, Mackintosh School of Architecture, Glasgow University, 1973-94; b. 11.12.28, Glasgow; m., Angela Lillian McDowell; 1 s.; 3 d. Educ. North Kelvinside Secondary School; Glasgow School of Architecture. Glasgow Corporation, 1945-52; East Kilbride Development

Corporation, 1952-54; joined Gillespie Kidd & Coia, 1954 (Partner, 1966); has served as a Member of: CNAA Architecture Board, ARCUK Board of Architectural Education, Scottish Arts Council WASPS Board, GIA Education Committee; Vice President for Education, RIBA; Vice President, Prince and Princess of Wales Hospice, 1981; RIBA Bronze Medal, 1965; RIBA Award for Architecture, four times; RSA Gold Medal, 1975; Concrete Society Award, 1978; Carpenter Award, 1982, 1983; various Saltire Society and Civic Trust awards; Member, Forum, Scottish Churches Architectural Heritage Trust; Patron, Arts Education Trust, since 1988. Recreations: travel; sailing; water colour. Address: (b.) Mackintosh School of Architecture, Glasgow University and Glasgow School of Art, 177 Renfrew Street, Glasgow, G3 6RQ.

Macmillan, Angus. Director of Tourism, Western Isles Tourist Board; b. 3.12.55, Ness, Isle of Lewis; m., Isabel; 2 d. Educ. Govan High School, Glasgow. Address: (b.) 26 Cromwell Street, Stornoway, PA87 2DD; T.-01851 703088.

MacMillan, George Gordon, MA (Cantab). Chief of Clan MacMillan; Deputy Lieutenant, Renfrewshire; b. 20.6.30, London; m., (Cecilia) Jane Spurgin; 2 s. Educ. Aysgarth School; Eton; Trinity College, Cambridge. Schoolmaster, Wellington College, 1953-63; Lecturer, Trinity College, Toronto, 1963-64; Lecturer, Bede College, Durham, 1965-74. Owner, small historic house with gardens and woods open to the public. Address: (h.) Finlaystone, Langbank, Renfrewshire, PA14 6TJ; T.-01475 540285.

MacMillan, Very Rev. Gilleasbuig Iain, MA, BD. Minister, St. Giles', The High Kirk of Edinburgh, since 1973.

MacMillan, Hector. Playwright; b. 1929, Glasgow. Plays include: The Rising, 1970; The Sash, 1973.

MacMillan, Hugh, CBE, QPM, MIAM. Chief Constable, Northern Constabulary. Address: (b.) Perth Road, Inverness, IV2 3SY.

Macmillan, Professor Hugh Colin, MA, MBA, CEng, MBCS. Professor of Business Policy, Edinburgh University, since 1992; b. 24.8.42, Edinburgh; m., Sheina Thorburn Templeton; 2 d. Educ. Radley College; Clare College, Cambridge; Harvard Business School. Engineer, Systems Engineer, Data Processing Manager, 1964-71; student, Harvard Business School, 1971-73; various management jobs, 1973-80; Principal, Nolan, Norton & Co., London, 1980-87; Partner, KPMG Management Consulting, London, 1987-92. Recreations: music; sailing. Address: (b.) William Robertson Building, 50 George Square, Edinburgh, EH8 9JY; T.-0131-650 4598.

Macmillan, Iain Alexander, CBE, LLD, BL. Sheriff of South Strathclyde, Dumfries and Galloway, at Hamilton, 1981-92; b. 14.11.23, Oban; m., Edith Janet McAulay; 2 s.; 1 d. Educ. Oban High School; Glasgow University; Scottish Commercial College. RAF (France, Germany, India), 1944-47; Solicitor (Sturrock & Co., Kilmarnock), 1952-81; Council Member, Law Society of Scotland, 1964-79 (President, 1976-77); Chairman, Lanarkshire Branch, Scottish Association for the Study of Delinquency, 1986-92; President, Temporary Sheriffs Association, since 1993. Recreations: golf; music. Address: (h.) 2 Castle Drive, Kilmarnock, Ayrshire; T.-01563 525864.

MacMillan, James Loy, BMus, PhD. Composer and Conductor; Affiliate Composer, Scottish Chamber Orchestra, since 1990; Visiting Composer, Philharmonia, since 1992; Composer in Residence, RSAMD, since 1990; b. 16.7.59, Kilwinning; m., Lynne; 1 s.; 2 d. Educ. Cumnock Academy; Edinburgh University; Durham University. Principal compositions: The Confession of Isobel Gowdie, London Proms, 1990; Busqueda, Edinburgh

International Festival, with Diana Rigg, 1990; featured composer, Musica Nova, 1990, Huddersfield Contemporary Music Festival, 1991; Veni, Veni, Emmanuel, percussion concerto for Evelyn Glennie, London P:roms, 1992; featured composer, Edinburgh International Festival, 1993; recording of Tryst and The Confession of Isobel Gowdie by BBC SSO won Gramophone Award, contemporary music category, 1993; Seven Last Words, BBC TV, 1994; nominated for Mercury Music Prize, 1995.

McMillan, John Boyd, BSc. Rector, Invergordon Academy, since 1986; b. 16.12.41, Irvine; m., Kathleen Miller (deceased); 2 s. Educ. Irvine Royal Academy; Glasgow University; Jordanhill College of Education. Mathematics Teacher: Irvine Royal Academy, 1964-67, Gloucester School, Hohne, 1967-72, Invergordon Academy, 1972-74; Principal Teacher of Mathematics, Thurso High School, 1974-82; Assistant Rector, Alness Academy, 1982-86; In-Service Training Co-ordinator, HRC, Inverness, 1986; Chairman, Highland Education Industry Liaison Committee, 1990-91; President, Highland Secondary Heads Association, 1988-90; President, Invergordon Highland Gathering. Football Blue. Recreations: gardening; public speaking; genealogy. Address: (b.) Invergordon Academy, Academy Road, Invergordon, IV18 0LD; T.-0349 852362.

Macmillan, Professor (John) Duncan, MA, PhD, FRSA, HRSA. Professor of the History of Scottish Art, Edinburgh University; Curator, Talbot Rice Gallery and University Collections, Edinburgh University, since 1979; Hon. Keeper of Portraits, Royal College of Surgeons, Edinburgh; b. 7.3.39, Beaconsfield; m., Vivien Rosemary Hinkley; 2 d. Educ. Gordonstoun School; St. Andrews University; London University; Edinburgh University. Lecturer, then Senior Lecturer, then Reader, Department of Fine Art, Edinburgh University. Chairman, Edinburgh Galleries Association. Recreation: walking. Address: (h.) 20 Nelson Street, Edinburgh; T.-0131-556 7100.

MacMillan, John MacFarlane Bute, MBE, MC. Chairman, Taste of Scotland Scheme Ltd.; Chairman, The Murrayfield PLC; b. 12.8.17, Rothesay; m., Rosaline Daphne May Spencer; 1 s.; 1 d. Educ. Allan Glen's School, Glasgow. Regular Army Officer, Royal Artillery, 1939-57; General Manager, then Managing Director, D.S. Crawford Ltd., 1958-62; Director, United Biscuits (Holdings) Ltd., 1962-82; Chairman, D.S. Crawford Ltd., 1979-82; Chairman, UB Restaurants Ltd., 1979-82. Recreations: bird-watching; walking; swimming; tennis. Address: (h.) 24 Cammo Gardens, Edinburgh, EH4 8EQ; T.-0131-339 6501.

McMillan, Joyce Margaret, MA (Hons), DipEd. Journalist and Theatre Critic; Scotland on Sunday: Social/Political Columnist, since 1989, Theatre Critic, since 1993; b. 29.8.52, Paisley. Educ. Paisley Grammar School; St. Andrews University; Edinburgh University. Theatre Reviewer, BBC Radio Scotland and The Scotsman, 1979-81; Theatre Critic, Sunday Standard, 1981-83; Radio Critic, The Herald, 1983-95; Scottish Theatre Critic, The Guardian, 1984-93. Chair, NUJ Freelance Branch, Edinburgh; Vice-Chair, NUJ Freelance Industrial Council, London; Chair, Scottish Constitutional Commission, 1994; Executive Member, Helsinki Citizens' Assembly, Prague. Publications: The Traverse Story, 1963-88, 1988; Charter for the Arts in Scotland, 1992. Recreations: food; drink; films; music; talking politics. Address: 8 East London Street, Edinburgh, EH7 4BH; T.-0131-557 1726.

McMillan, Michael Dale, BSc, LLB, NP. Managing Partner, Burnett & Reid, Solicitors, Aberdeen; Partner, Macdonalds Sergeants, Solicitors, East Kilbride and Glasgow, 1971-92; b. 15.2.44, Edinburgh; m., Isobel Ross Mackie; 2 s.; 1 d. Educ. Edinburgh Academy; Edinburgh University. Secretary: East Kilbride Chamber of Commerce, 1971-86, East Kilbride Chamber of Trade, 1971-92; Member, East Kilbride Development Corporation,

1979-84; Secretary, Pilgrim Legal Users' Group, 1985-92; Captain, East Kilbride Golf Club, 1979; Chairman, Strathaven Academy School Board, 1991-92; President, East Kilbride Burns Club, 1989-91. Recreations: golf; sailing; skiing. Address: (h.) 9 Tillybrake Road, Banchory, Kincardineshire; T.-01330 824527.

Macmillan, Michael Muirdoch, MA, LLB. Solicitor, since 1967; b. 14.3.41, Conon Bridge; m., Maureen Mary Hoey; 2 s.; 2 d. Educ. Dingwall Academy; St. Andrews University; Edinburgh University. Member, Council, Law Society of Scotland; Labour candidate, Ross, Cromarty and Skye, 1987; Labour Euro-candidate, Highlands and Islands, 1994. Recreation: relishing a challenge. Address: 87/89 High Street, Alness, IV17 0SH; T.-01349 883338.

McMillan, William Alister, BL. Solicitor, since 1955; b. 19.1.34, Ayr; m., Elizabeth Anne; 3 d. Educ. Strathallan; Glasgow University. Clerk of the Peace, County of Ayr, 1974-75; Honorary Sheriff, Ayr; Governor, Strathallan School. Recreations:sailing; golf; philately. Address: (h.) Afton Lodge, Mossblown, by Ayr; T.-01292 520 710.

Macmillan, Very Rev. William Boyd Robertson, MA, BD, HonLLD (Dundee), Hon. DD (Aberdeen). Minister, Dundee Parish Church (St. Mary's), 1978-93; Chaplain in Ordinary to The Queen in Scotland, since 1988; President, Scottish Church Society, since 1993; Prelate, Order of St. John of Jerusalem (Scotland), since 1993; b. 3.7.27, Keith; m., Mary Adams Bisset Murray. Educ. Royal High School, Edinburgh; Aberdeen University. Royal Navy, 1946-48; Aberdeen University, 1948-54 (President, SRC, 1953-54); Minister: St. Andrew's Church, Bo'ness, 1955-60, Fyvie Parish Church, 1960-67, Bearsden South Church, 1967-78. Convener, Board of Practice and Procedure, 1984-88, and of Business Committee, 1985-88, General Assembly, Church of Scotland; Moderator, General Assembly, 1991-92; Chaplain, City of Dundee District Council, 1978-93; Freeman of Dundee, 1991; Chairman of Directors, High School of Dundee, since 1993; Chairman, The Murray Home for Scottish Veterans, since 1994; Trustee, Scottish National War Memorial, since 1994. Recreations: golf; reading. Address: (h.) 17 Braehead Drive, Edinburgh, EH4 6QJ.

Macnab of Macnab, Hon. Mrs, DL. Honorary Vice President, Scotland's Gardens Scheme, since 1991 (Chairman, 1983-91); Member, Executive Committee, National Trust for Scotland, since 1991; Deputy Lieutenant, Fife, since 1992; b. 6.6.36, Edinburgh; m., J.C. Macnab of Macnab (qv); 2 s.; 2 d. Address: (h.) Leuchars Castle Farmhouse, Leuchars, St. Andrews, KY16 0EY; T.-01334 838777.

Macnab of Macnab, James Charles — The Macnab. Senior Consultant, Hill Samuel Investment Services Ltd., 1982-92, now retired; 23rd Chief, Clan Macnab; b. 14.4.26, London; m., Hon. Diana Mary Anstruther-Gray (see Hon. Mrs. Macnab of Macnab); 2 s.; 2 d. Educ. Radley College; Ashbury College, Ottawa. Served, RAF and Scots Guards, 1944-45; Lt., Seaforth Highlanders, 1945-48; Assistant Superintendant and Deputy Superintendant, Federation of Malaya Police Force, 1948-57; Captain, Seaforth Highlanders (TA), 1960-64; managed family estate and farms, 1957-82; County Councillor, Perth and Kinross Joint County Council, 1964-75; District Councillor, Perth, 1961-64; JP, 1968-86; Member, Central Regional Council, 1978-82; Member, Queen's Bodyguard for Scotland (Royal Company of Archers). Address: (h.) Leuchars Castle Farmhouse, Leuchars, St. Andrews, KY16 0EY; T.-01334 838777.

McNair, James Burt Oliver, BSc (Hons), DipEd. Secretary, Headteachers' Association of Scotland; b. 20.7.33, Bargeddie, Lanarkshire; m., Muriel Eadie; 1 s.; 2 d. Educ. Woodside Secondary School, Glasgow; Glasgow University. Taught, Gambia High School; Principal Teacher of Physics and Assistant Head, North Kelvinside Secondary School; Depute Head, John Street Secondary School; Head, Waverley Secondary School, 1976-92. Chairman, SED Joint Working Party on Social and Vocational Skills; Member, Scottish Examination Board; Chairman, Drumchapel Citizens' Advice Bureau, 1981-84; Chairman, Scripture Union — Scotland. Publication: Basic Knowledge Physics. Address: (b.) Strathclyde University, Jordanhill Campus, Southbrae Drive, Glasgow, G13 1PP.

Macnair, Terence Crawford, LLB, NP. Solicitor, since 1967; Honorary Sheriff, North Strathclyde, since 1988; b. 16.12.42, Kingston, Jamaica; m., Ishbel Ross Hunter; 1 s. Educ. High School of Glasgow; Glasgow University. Town Clerk, Lochgilphead, 1970-75; Partner, MacArthur Stewart & Orr, 1970-81; Senior Partner, MacArthur Stewart, since 1981; Assistant Clerk, Tarbert Harbour Authority, since 1970; Clerk, Awe District Salmon Fishery Board, since 1979; President, Oban Rotary Club, 1988-89; Past Chairman, Oban Tennis and Squash Club; Secretary/Treasurer, Oban and District Licensed Trade Association, since 1977; Chairman, North Argyll Development Agency, since 1994. Recreations: tennis; squash; golf; curling; bridge; music. Address: (b.) Boswell House, Oban; T.-01631 562215.

McNally, Rt. Rev. Anthony Joseph. Rector, Gillis College, Edinburgh, since 1987; Vicar General, Archdiocese of St. Andrews and Edinburgh, since 1985; b. 27.5.32, Edinburgh. Educ. Blairs College, Aberdeen; Seminaire St. Sulpice, Paris. Ordained Priest, 1955; Assistant Priest, Methil, Fife, 1955-63; Missioner, Calabar and Bauchi Province, Nigeria, 1963-67; Assistant Priest, Bonnybridge, 1967-72; Parish Priest, Burntisland, 1972-80, St. Peter's, Morningside, 1980-85; Parish Priest, Musselburgh, and Vicar General, Archdiocese, 1985; Parish Priest, St. Columba's, Edinburgh, since 1993. Recreations: reading; walking. Address: (b.) St. Columba's, 9 Upper Gray Street, Edinburgh EH9 1SN.

McNaught, Peter Cairn, MA, MLitt, FRSA. Principal, Craigie College of Education, Ayr, 1976-87; b. 29.5.25, Glasgow; m., Else Kristine Sandvad; 1 s.; 1 d. Educ. Hutchesons' Boys' Grammar School, Glasgow; Glasgow University. Teacher, Queen's Park and Hutchesons' Boys' Grammar Schools, Glasgow, 1952-58; Lecturer in English, Moray House College of Education, Edinburgh, 1958-60; Principal Lecturer in English, Aberdeen College of Education, 1960-61; Moray House College of Education: Principal Lecturer in Educational Methods and Senior Assistant Principal, 1961-70, Vice-Principal, 1970-75. Vice-Chairman, Scottish Council for the Validation of Courses for Teachers; Member, General Teaching Council for Scotland; Vice-Chairman, West Sound; Chairman, STV Education Committee; Member, STV Staff Trust; United Kingdom Award, Council for Educational Technology, 1982; Visiting Professor in English Studies, Strathclyde University, 1988; Director, Wider Access Programme, 1988-1992. Address: (h.) 36 Arran Gardens, Troon, KA10 6TE; T.-01292 312200.

McNaughton, John Ewen, OBE, JP, FRAgS. Chairman, Scotch Quality Beef & Lamb Association, since 1981; Member, British Wool Marketing Board, since 1975; Member, Panel of Agricultural Arbiters, since 1973; Member, Red Deer Commission, 1975-92; b. 28.5.33, Edinburgh; m., Jananne Ogilvie Honeyman; 2 s.; 2 d. Educ. Cargilfield; Loretto. Born and bred a hill sheep farmer; after a short spell in America, began farming at Inverlochlarig with father; served on Council, NFU of Scotland; Elder, Church of Scotland. Recreations: yachting; stalking. Address: Inverlochlarig, Balquhidder, Lochearnhead, Perthshire, FK19 8PH; T.-0187 74 232.

Macnaughton, Professor Sir Malcolm Campbell, MD, LLD, FRCPGlas, FRCOG, FRSE, FSLCOG (Hon.),

FACOG (Hon.), FRCA (Hon.), FRACOG (Hon.). Vice President, Royal College of Midwives; Professor of Obstetrics and Gynaecology, Glasgow University, 1970-90; b. 4.4.25, Glasgow; m., Margaret-Ann Galt; 2 s.; 3 d. Educ. Glasgow Academy; Glasgow University. RAMC, 1949-51; Lecturer in Obstetrics and Gynaecology, Aberdeen University, 1957-61; Senior Lecturer, St. Andrews University, 1961-66; Consultant, Eastern Regional, 1966-70. Member, Chief Scientist Committee, SHHD; Member, Biomedical Research Committee and Health Service Research Committee, SHHD; Member, MRC Grant Committee and Cell Systems Board, MRC; Member, Scientific Committee, Hospital Recognition Committee, RCOG; President, RCOG, 1984-87; President, British Fertility Society, 1993-95; Chairman, Scottish Perinatal Mortality Advisory Group; Chairman, SCOTMEG Working Party on Accident and Emergency Services in Scotland. Recreations: walking; fishing; curling. Address: (h.) 15 Boclair Road, Bearsden, Glasgow, G61 2AF; T.-0141-942 1909.

McNay, W. Gordon, OBE, DL, JP, BL; b. 11.12.25, Wishaw; m., Margaret C. MacKay. Educ. Wishaw High School; Glasgow University. Depute Town Clerk, Burgh of Airdrie, 1952-53; Senior Depute Town Clerk, Burgh of Motherwell and Wishaw, 1953-63; Town Clerk, Burgh of East Kilbride, 1963-75; Chief Executive, East Kilbride District Council, 1975-88. Deputy Lieutenant, County of Lanark; Honorary Freeman, East Kilbride District. Recreations: golf; photography; philately. Address: (h.) Solbakken, 17 Kibblestane Place, Strathaven, ML10 6EL; T.-01357 520889.

McNee, Sir David Blackstock, Kt, QPM, FBIM, FRSA, KStJ. President, National Bible Society of Scotland; Non-Executive Director and Adviser to a number of public limited companies; b. 23.3.25; m., Isabella Clayton Hopkins; 1 d. Educ. Woodside Senior Secondary School, Glasgow. Joined City of Glasgow Police, 1946; Deputy Chief Constable, Dunbartonshire Constabulary, 1968; Chief Constable: City of Glasgow Police, 1971-75, Strathclyde Police, 1975-77; Commissioner, Metropolitan Police, 1977-82. Honorary Vice-President, Boys' Brigade, since 1980; Vice-President, London Federation of Boys Clubs, since 1982; Patron, Scottish Motor Neurone Association, since 1982; Freeman, City of London, 1977; President, Glasgow City Committee, Cancer Relief, 1987-92. Recreations: fishing; golf; music.

McNee, Ian. Member, Parole Board for Scotland, since 1989 (Chairman, since 1995); b. 22.4.32, Edinburgh; m., Betty; 1 s.; 1 d. Educ. Boroughmuir School. Former Managing Director, now Chairman, MacDonald Lindsay Pindar PLC. Member, Lothian Region Children's Panel, 1972-88, Chairman, 1985-88; Past President, Edinburgh Master Printers; Past Captain, Kingsknowe Golf Club. Recreation: golf. Address: (h.) 16 Camptoun, Drem, East Lothian, EH39 5BA; T.-01620 880 631.

MacNee, William, MB, ChB, MD (Hons), FRCP(Glas), FRCP(Edin). Reader in Medicine, Edinburgh University; Visiting Professor, Department of Biological Sciences, Napier University; Honorary Consultant Physician, Lothian Health Board, since 1987; Clinical Director, Respiratory Medicine Unit; b. 18.12.50, Glasgow; m., Edna Marina Kingsley; 1 s.; 1 d. Educ. Coatbridge High School; Glasgow University. House Physician/House Surgeon, Glasgow and Paisley, 1975-76; SHO/Registrar in Medicine, Western Infirmary/Gartnavel Hospitals, Glasgow, 1976-79; Registrar in Respiratory Medicine, City Hospital, Edinburgh, 1979-80; MRC Research Fellow/Honorary Registrar, Department of Respiratory Medicine, Royal Infirmary, Edinburgh, 1980-82; Lecturer, Department of Respiratory Medicine, City Hospital, Edinburgh, 1982-83; Senior Registrar, Respiratory Medicine/Medicine, Lothian Health Board, 1983-87; MRC Research Fellow, University of British Columbia, Vancouver, 1985-86; Senior Lecturer in Respiratory Medicine, 1987-93. Member, Council, Scottish Thoracic Society, 1990-93. Recreations: music; theatre; squash. Address: (b.) Department of Medicine, Royal Infirmary, Lauriston Place, Edinburgh, EH3 9XW; T.-0131-229 2477.

Macneil of Barra, Ian Roderick, BA, LLB, FSA Scot. Wigmore Professor of Law, Northwestern University, Chicago, since 1980; b. 20.6.29, New York City; m., Nancy C. Wilson; 2 s.; 1 d. Educ. Scarborough School; Vermont University; Harvard University. Lt., AUS, 1951-53; Commissioned Officer, USAR, 1950-67; practised law, 1956-59; Member, Cornell Law School Faculty, 1959-72, 1974-80; Visiting Professor, University College, Dar es Salaam, 1965-67, Duke Law School, 1971-72; Professor of Law and Member, Centre for Advanced Studies, Virginia University, 1972-74; Visiting Fellow, Centre for Socio-Legal Studies, Wolfson College, Oxford, 1979, and Edinburgh University Faculty of Law, 1979, 1987; Visiting Professor, Harvard University, 1988-89; Guggenheim Fellow, 1978-79. Member, Standing Council of Scottish Chiefs; author of numerous books and articles. Recreations: walking; reading; historical studies. Address: (h.) Kisimul Castle, Isle of Barra, PA80; T.-Castlebay 300; 5/8 Fountainhall Road, Edinburgh, EH9 2NL; T.-0131-667 6068.

McNeil, Neil, MB, ChB, DPH, DPA, FFCM, FFPHM, MREHIS. Retired Unit Consultant in Public Health Medicine/Director of Community Medicine/Unit Medical Officer/District Medical Officer, Lanarkshire Health Board, 1976-92; Honorary Senior Clinical Lecturer/Honorary Clinical Lecturer, Department of Public Health, Glasgow University, 1976-92; b. 4.6.31, Glasgow; m., Florence Ward Butterworth; 2 s.; 1 d. Educ. Govan High School; Glasgow University. SHO, Senior Resident, House Physician and House Surgeon, Western Infirmary, Glasgow, 1956-58; Hall Fellow, Glasgow University, 1958-60; Registrar, Western Infirmary, Glasgow, 1960-61; Divisional Medical Officer of Health, City of Glasgow, 1962-65; Principal Lecturer in Health Education and Medical Officer, Jordanhill College, Glasgow, 1965-68; Medical Officer of Health, North-East Hampshire, and Honorary Consultant, Aldershot, 1968-69; Medical Officer, Scottish Home and Health Department, 1969-73; Honorary Lecturer, Departments of Materia Medica and Community Medicine, Glasgow University, 1973-74; Consultant Epidemiologist, Communicable Diseases (Scotland) Unit, Ruchill Hospital, 1973-74; Senior Medical Officer, Scottish Home and Health Department, 1974-76. Dr. MacKinlay Prize in Public Health and Preventive Medicine, Glasgow University, 1962. Publications on community medicine, environmental medicine, public health, immunisation and infectious disease control. Recreations: tennis; photography; natural history; Gaelic language and culture; Scottish history and archaeology. Address: (h.) Claddach, 25 Waterfoot Road, Newton Mearns, Glasgow, G77 5RU.

MacNeill, Hector Fletcher, MA. Honorary Sheriff of North Strathclyde at Campbeltown, since 1981; b. 28.9.18, South Knapdale, Argyll; m., Iona Mary Pursell; 1 s.; 2 d. Educ. Keil School; Edinburgh University. RNVR, 1939-46; in action with HMS Hotspur at Battles of Narvik, Matapan and Crete; commanded HM Frigate Keats, 1945-46; Assistant Master, Campbeltown Grammar School, 1947-53, Oban High School, 1953-56; Head Master, Campbeltown primary schools, 1956-83. Member, crew, Campbeltown Lifeboat, 1950-53; President, Campbeltown Horticultural Society, 1963-84; Commodore, Campbeltown Sailing Club, 1968-69; Chairman, Campbeltown Sea Cadets, 1978-83; Member, Presbytery of South Argyll, 1986-92. Recreations: gardening; sailing; woodworking; climbing in Scotland. Address: (h.) Davaar House, Campbeltown, Argyll, PA28 6RE; T.-01586 552349.

McNeill, Ian Cameron, DSc, PhD, BSc. Reader in Chemistry, Glasgow University, since 1977; b. 29.4.32, Glasgow; m., Jessie Robertson Howard; 2 s.; 1 d. Educ. Allan Glen's School, Glasgow; Glasgow University. Assistant in Chemistry, Glasgow University, 1956; ICI Research Fellow, Londonderry Laboratory for Radiochemistry, Durham University, 1958; Lecturer in Chemistry, then Senior Lecturer, Glasgow University, 1961-77. Member, Editorial Board, Polymer Degradation and Stability; Committee Member, Polymer Degradation Discussion Group; Elder, Church of Scotland. Recreations: hill-walking; photography; classical music. Address: (b.) Department of Chemistry, Glasgow University, Glasgow, G12 8QQ; T.-0141-339 8855, Ext. 4441/6580.

McNeill, James Louis, DA, FRSA. Head Teacher, St. Ninian's High School, Kirkintilloch, since 1989; b. 25.8.36, Kirkintilloch; m., Kathleen Shinwell; 1 s.; 1 d. Educ. St. Ninian's High School, Kirkintilloch; Salesian College, Macclesfield; Glasgow School of Art; Jordanhill College of Education. Teacher of Art/Learning Support, 1965-72; Principal Teacher of Guidance, 1972-76; Assistant Head Teacher, Cardinal Newman High School, 1976-78; Adviser in Guidance, Glasgow Division, 1978-85; Head Teacher, St. Gerard's Secondary, Glasgow, 1985-89. Recreations: reading; walking; watching professional soccer. Address: (h.) 12 Southwood Drive, King's Park, Glasgow, G44 5SH; T.-0141-637 6467.

McNeill, James Walker, QC. Advocate, since 1978; b. 16.2.52, Dunoon; m., Katherine Lawrence McDowall; 2 s.; 1 d. Educ. Dunoon Grammar School; Sidney Sussex College, Cambridge; Edinburgh University. QC, 1991; Standing Junior Counsel, Department of Transport in Scotland, 1984-88, Inland Revenue, 1988-91. Member of Council, Scottish Universities Law Institute. Recreations: music; hill-walking; golf; sailing; travel. Address: (b.) Advocates' Library, Parliament House, Edinburgh, EH1 1RF; T.-0131-226 5071.

McNeill, John, BA (Hons), MSc, MPhil, FInstD, FIMgt. Chief Executive, SACRO, since 1991; b. 7.7.45, Belfast; m., Margaret Alison McCartney; 1 s.; 2 d. Educ. Annandale Grammar School; Queen's University, Belfast; Open University; Edinburgh University. Governor, N.I. Prison Service, 1973-80, Scottish Prison Service, 1980-85; Depute Director, SACRO, 1985-91. Hon. Treasurer, International Federation of Settlements; Cropwood Fellow, Institute of Criminology, Cambridge University, 1985; Associate, Centre for Criminology and the Social and Philosophical Study of Law, Edinburgh University. Recreations: fly fishing; golf. Address: (b.) 31 Palmerston Place, Edinburgh, EH12 5AP; T.-0131-226 4222.

McNeill, Sheriff Peter Grant Brass, PhD, MA (Hons), LLB, QC. Sheriff of Lothian and Borders at Edinburgh, since 1982; b. 3.3.29, Glasgow; m., Matilda Farquhar Rose; 1 s.; 3 d. Educ. Hillhead High School, Glasgow; Morrison's Academy, Crieff; Glasgow University. Law apprentice, Biggart Lumsden & Co., Glasgow, 1952-55; Carnegie Fellowship, 1955; Faulds Fellowship, 1956-59; Scottish Bar, 1956; Honorary Sheriff Substitute of Lanarkshire, and of Stirling, Clackmannan and Dumbarton, 1962; Standing Junior Counsel to Scottish Development Department (Highways), 1964; Advocate Depute, 1964; Sheriff of Lanarkshire, subsequently of Glasgow and Strathkelvin, at Glasgow, 1965-82; President, Sheriffs' Association, 1982-85; Chairman, Council, Stair Society, 1990; Chairman, Scottish Legal History Group, 1990. Publications: Balfour's Practicks (Editor), 1962-63; An Historical Atlas of Scotland c. 400 - c. 1600 (Co-Editor), 1975; Adoption of Children in Scotland, 1982, 2nd ed., 1986. Recreations: legal history; gardening; book-binding. Address: (b.) Sheriffs' Chambers, Sheriff Court House, Lawnmarket, Edinburgh, EH1 2NS; T.-0131-226 7181.

MacNeill, Seumas, MA, MInstP. Principal, The College of Piping, since 1945; Editor, The Piping Times, since 1950; Hon. President, Saltire Society, since 1993; b. 12.9.17, Glasgow; m., Janet Boyd; 1 s. Educ. Hyndland School; Glasgow University. Physicist, Royal Technical College, Glasgow, 1940-41; Lecturer, Natural Philosophy Department, Glasgow University, 1941-82. Honorary Secretary, Glasgow District, SYHA, 1943-45; awarded Loving Cup by City of Glasgow, 1993. Publications: Tutor for the Bagpipe, Parts 1, 2 and 3 (Co-author); Piobaireachd, the Classical Music for the Bagpipe; Piobaireachd and its Interpretation (Co-author). Recreations: hill-walking; bridge; physics. Address: (h.) 22 Mosshead Road, Bearsden, Glasgow; T.-0141-334 3587.

McNicol, George Paul, CBE, MD, FRSE, FRCP, FRCPG, FRCPE, FRCPath, HonFACP, FRSA, Hon.DSc (Wabash Coll.), Hon. LLD (Aberdeen). Principal and Vice-Chancellor, Aberdeen University, 1981-91; b. 24.9.29, Glasgow; m., Susan Moira Ritchie; 1 s.; 2 d. Educ. Hillhead High School, Glasgow; Glasgow University. House Surgeon, Western Infirmary, Glasgow, 1952; House Physician, Stobhill General Hospital, Glasgow, 1953; Regimental MO, RAMC, 1953-55; Assistant, Department of Materia Medica and Therapeutics, and Registrar, University Medical Unit, Stobhill General Hospital, 1955-57; University Department of Medicine, Glasgow Royal Infirmary: Registrar, 1957-59, Honorary Senior Registrar, 1961-65; Lecturer in Medicine, 1963-65; Honorary Consultant Physician, 1966-71; Senior Lecturer in Medicine, 1966-70; Reader in Medicine, 1970-71; Professor of Medicine and Honorary Consultant Physician, Leeds General Infirmary, 1971-81; Chairman, Board, Faculty of Medicine, Leeds University, 1978-81; Harkness Fellow, Commonwealth Fund, Department of Internal Medicine, Washington University, 1959-61; Honorary Clinical Lecturer and Honorary Consultant Physician, Makerere UC Medical School Extension, Kenyatta National Hospital, Nairobi, 1965-66. Former Member, Advisory Council on Misuse of Drugs; Chairman, Part I Examining Board, Royal College of Physicians (UK); Member of Council, Committee of Vice-Chancellors and Principals of the Universities of the UK, 1989-91; Chairman, Medical Advisory Committee, CVCP, 1985-91; Member, Committee on Academic Standards and International Advisory Committee (European Sub-Group), CVCP; Member, Advisory Committee for Medical Training, European Community, 1987-94, Co-Chairman, 1990-94; Member of Council, Association of Commonwealth Universities, 1988-91; Non-executive Director and Vice-Chairman, Raigmore Hospital NHS Trust, 1993-95. Recreations: skiing; sailing. Address: (h.) Chanonry Green, Kincurdie Drive, Rosemarkie, Ross-shire, IV10 8SJ; T.-01381 621211.

McNicoll, Professor Iain Hugh, BA, PhD. Professor of Applied Economics, Strathclyde University, since 1987; Senior Research Advisor, Fraser of Allander Institute, since 1991; b. 24.6.51, Glasgow; m. Educ. St. Mungo's Academy, Glasgow; Stirling University. Leverhulme Research Fellow, Industrial Science, Stirling University, 1974-76; Lecturer, Business Studies, Edinburgh University, 1976-79; Fellow/Senior Fellow, Director of Research, Acting Director/Director, Fraser of Allander Institute, 1979-89. Publications: two books; ten monographs; 45 academic journal and book articles. Recreations: hi-fi; golf; astronomy. Address: (b.) Department of Economics, Strathclyde University, 100 Cathedral Street, Glasgow; T.-0141-552 4400.

MacNish, Alastair J.H., FCCA, MIPD. Chief Executive, South Lanarkshire Council, since 1995; b. 4.2.47, Greenock; m., Jean Ferguson Bell; 1 s.; 2 d. Educ. Gourock High School. Chief Auditor, Renfrew High School, 1973-75; Principal Accountant, then Assistant Director of Education, then Depute Director of Social Work,

Strathclyde Regional Council, 1975-95. Recreations: golf; curling; bridge. Address: (b.) South Lanarkshire Council, Regional Offices, Almada Street, Hamilton, ML3 0AA; T.-01698 454208.

Macniven, Duncan, TD, MA, MLitt. Deputy Director, Historic Scotland, since 1990; b. 1.12.50, Edinburgh; m., Valerie Clark (see Valerie Macniven); 2 d. Educ. Melville College, Edinburgh; Aberdeen University. Graduate trainee, Scottish Office, 1973-78, Principal, 1978-86, Assistant Secretary, 1986-90. Recreations: walking; Scottish dancing; swimming; cycling; exploring; Scottish history. Address: (b.) Longmore House, Salisbury Place, Edinburgh EH9 1SH; T.-0131-668 8735.

Macniven, Valerie Margaret, MA (Hons). Assistant Secretary, Scottish Office Education Department, since 1992; b. 14.1.51, Perth; m., Duncan Macniven (qv); 2 d. Educ. Aberdeen High School for Girls; Edinburgh University. Scottish Office, 1973-82 and since 1987. Elder, Church of Scotland. Recreations: Scottish country dancing; tennis; travel. Address: (b.) New St. Andrews House, Edinburgh, EH1 3TG; T.-0131-244 5111.

McNulty, Howard, BPharm, PhD, FRPharmS. Chief Administrative Pharmaceutical Officer, Greater Glasgow Health Board, since 1990; b. 8.11.46, Colne; m., Laura Jean; 1 s.; 2 d. Educ. Nelson Secondary Technical School, Lancs; Bradford University. Began career as pharmacist, Timothy White's/Boots, 1969; joined Greater Glasgow Health Board as District Pharmaceutical Officer, Western District, 1983. Recreations: watching cricket and rugby. Address: (h.) 14 Coronation Way, Bearsden, Glasgow, G61 1DA; T.-0141-942 8427.

McOwan, Rennie, FSA Scot. Writer and Broadcaster; b. Stirling; m., Agnes Mooney; 3 s.; 1 d. Educ. Alva Academy. Reporter, Stirling Journal; Sub-Editor, Kemsley Newspapers, Daily Record; Public Relations, Roman Catholic Church; Sub-Editor, Features Writer, Scotsman Publications; Assistant Publicity Secretary, National Trust for Scotland; now: Correspondent in Scotland for NC News Agency, Washington, and RNS Agency, New York; Scottish Arts Council Lecturer under Writers in Schools scheme; Tutor to writing groups; Contributor to newspapers and magazines in Britain and overseas; radio and TV scripts and research. Publications: Light on Dumyat; The White Stag Adventure; The Day the Mountain Moved; Walks in the Trossachs and the Rob Roy Country; The Green Hills; Kilchurn Castle: A History; contributed to: Walking in Scotland; Poetry of the Scottish Hills; Speak to the Hills; Wild Walks; The Story of Scotland; Discover Scotland; Great Walks, Scotland; Classic Coastal Walks of Britain; On Foot Through History. Recreations: mountaineering; Scottish history and literature. Address: 7 Williamfield Avenue, Stirling, FK7 9AH; T.-01786 461316.

McPartlin, Sheriff Noel, MA, LLB. Sheriff of Grampian, Highland and Islands, at Elgin, since 1985; b. 25.12.39.

McPhail, Angus William, MA (Oxon). Headmaster, Strathallan School, since 1993; b. 25.5.56, Ipswich; m., Elizabeth Hirsch; 2 s.; 1 d. Educ. Abingdon School; University College, Oxford. Overseas Department, Bank of England, 1978-82; Assistant Master, Glenalmond College, 1982-85; Head of Economics and Housemaster, Sedbergh School, 1985-93. Recreations: cricket; golf; walking; music; theatre. Address: (h.) Headmaster's House, Strathallan School, Forgandenny, Perth, PH2 9EG; T.-01738 812546.

Macphail, Sheriff Iain Duncan, QC, MA (Hons), LLB. Sheriff of Lothian and Borders at Edinburgh, since 1995; b. 24.1.38; m., Rosslyn Graham Lillias Hewitt; 1 s.; 1 d. Educ. George Watson's College; Edinburgh University; Glasgow University. Admitted Faculty of Advocates, 1963; practice, Scottish Bar, 1963-73; Faulds Fellow in Law, Glasgow University, 1963-65; Lecturer in Evidence and Procedure, Strathclyde University, 1968-69, Edinburgh University, 1969-72; Standing Junior Counsel to Scottish Home and Health Department and Department of Health and Social Security, 1971-73; Extra Advocate-Depute, 1973; Sheriff of Glasgow and Strathkelvin (formerly Lanarkshire), 1973-81; Sheriff of Tayside, Central and Fife at Dunfermline and Alloa, 1981-82; Sheriff of Lothian and Borders at Linlithgow, 1982-88, at Edinburgh, 1988-89. Member, Scottish Law Commission, 1990-94; Chairman, Scottish Association for the Study of Delinquency, 1978-81; Hon. LLD, Edinburgh, 1992. Publications: Evidence, 1987; Sheriff Court Practice, 1988. Address: (b.) Sheriff Court House, 27 Chambers Street, Edinburgh EH1 1LB; T.-0131-225 2525.

McPhee, George, MBE, BMus, FRCO, DipMusEd, RSAM, Hon. FRSCM. Visiting Professor of Organ, St. Andrews University; Chairman, Paisley International Organ Festival; Organist and Master of the Choristers, Paisley Abbey, since 1963; b. 10.11.37, Glasgow; m., Margaret Ann Scotland; 1 s.; 2 d. Educ. Woodside Senior Secondary School, Glasgow; Royal Scottish Academy of Music and Drama; Edinburgh University. Studied organ with Herrick Bunney and Fernando Germany; Assistant Organist, St. Giles' Cathedral, 1959-63; joined staff, RSAMD, 1963; Conductor, Scottish Chamber Choir, 1971-75; Conductor, Kilmarnock and District Choral Union, 1975-84; since 1971, has completed 12 recital tours of the United States and Canada; has been both Soloist and Conductor with Scottish National Orchestra; numerous recordings and broadcasts; has taken part in numerous music festivals as Soloist; Adjudicator; Examiner, Associated Board, Royal Schools of Music; Special Commissioner, Royal School of Church Music; Silver Medal, Worshipful Company of Musicians. Recreations: golf; walking. Address: (h.) 17 Main Road, Castlehead, Paisley, PA2 6AJ; T.-0141-889 3528.

Macpherson, Sheriff Alexander Calderwood, MA, LLB. Sheriff of South Strathclyde, Dumfries and Galloway, at Hamilton, since 1978; b. 14.6.39.

McPherson, Professor Andrew Francis, BA, DPSA, FBA, FEIS, FSCRE. Co-Director, Centre for Educational Sociology, and Professor of Sociology, Edinburgh University; b. 6.7.42, Louth; 1 s.; 1 d. Educ. Ripon Grammar School; Queen's College, Oxford. Lecturer, Glasgow University, 1965-68; Edinburgh University: Research Fellow, 1968-72, Lecturer, 1972-79, Senior Lecturer, 1979-83, Reader, 1983-89, Professor, since 1989. Publications: The Scottish Sixth, 1976; Tell Them from Me, 1980; Reconstructions of Secondary Education, 1983; Governing Education, 1988. Address: (b.) CES, 7 Buccleuch Place, Edinburgh, EH8 9LW.

Macpherson, Archie. Sports broadcaster and journalist; b. 1935, Glasgow. Former headmaster; football commentator, BBC Scotland, until 1990; reported Olympic Games, 1984 and 1988, for BBC network; author of Action Replays, 1991.

McPherson, Duncan James, CBE, MA, SDA. Farmer; Convener, Highland Regional Council; b. 29.10.30, Santos, Brazil; m., Vivian Margaret; 1 s.; 1 d. Educ. Robert Gordon's College, Aberdeen; Aberdeen University. Member, Cromarty Town Council, 1964-75, Ross and Cromarty County Council, 1972-75; Fellow, Scottish Council (Development and Industry), since 1990; Member, Board, Scottish Natural Heritage; President, Rosemarkie Golf Club; Chairman, Cromarty Firth Port Authority. Recreations: golf; curling; formerly rugby (Scottish trialist, 1951-56). Address: Cromarty Mains, Cromarty, Ross-shire; T.-01381 600 232.

Macpherson, Ian George, BSc, DipEd. Rector, Eastwood High School, 1977-95; b. 29.4.37, Perth; m., Gillian Brian;

2 s. Educ. Perth Academy; St. Andrews University; Edinburgh University; Moray House College of Education. Assistant Teacher of Physics, George Heriot's School, Edinburgh, 1959-62; Principal Teacher of Science, Dornoch Academy, Sutherland, 1962-64; Principal Teacher of Physics, Liberton High School, Edinburgh, 1964-69; Adviser in Science, Renfrewshire, 1969-73; Headmaster, Barrhead High School, 1973-77. Recreations: yachting; Ocean Youth Club; Rotary. Address: (h.) 20A Park Road, Paisley, PA2 6JW; T.-0141-884 2807.

McPherson, James Alexander Strachan, CBE, MA, BL, LLB, FSA Scot, JP. Lord Lieutenant, Grampian Region (Banffshire), since 1987; Senior Partner, Alexander George & Co., Solicitors, Macduff; Chairman, JP Advisory Committee, Banff and Buchan, since 1987; Honorary Sheriff, Grampian, Highland and Islands at Banff, since 1972; b. 20.11.27, Wormit, Fife; m., Helen Marjorie Perks, MA; 1 s.; 1 d. Educ. Banff Academy; Aberdeen University. Member, Macduff Town Council and Banff County Council, 1958-75; Provost of Macduff, 1972-75; Convener, Banff County Council, 1970-75; Member, Grampian Health Board, 1974-82; Member, Post Office Users National Council for Scotland, 1976-80; Member, Police Advisory Board for Scotland, 1974-86; Member, Grampian Regional Council, 1974-90; Chairman, Public Protection Committee, 1974-86; Governor, Scottish Police College, 1974-86; Chairman, Banff and Buchan JP Advisory Committee, since 1987; Member, Scottish Solicitors Discipline Tribunal, since 1990; Member, Aberdeen University Court, since 1993. Recreations: reading; sailing; swimming. Address: (h.) Dun Alastair, 126 Gellymill Street, Macduff; T.-Macduff 832377.

Macpherson of Drumochter, Lord (James) Gordon Macpherson), 2nd Baron, JP, FRES, FRSA, FZS. Chairman and Managing Director, Macpherson, Train & Co. Ltd., since 1964; Chairman, A.J. Macpherson & Co. Ltd., since 1973; b. 22.1.24; m., 1, Dorothy Ruth Coulter (deceased; 2 d.; 1 s. deceased; 2, Catherine MacCarthy; 1 s.; 2 d. Educ. Loretto; Wells House, Malvern. RAF, 1939-45. Freeman, City of London. Address: (h.) Kyllachy, Tomatin, Inverness-shire.

Macpherson, John Hannah Forbes, CBE, OStJ, CA. Lord Dean of Guild, Glasgow; Chairman, Glasgow Development Agency, since 1990; Chairman, Scottish Mutual Assurance Society, since 1971; b. 23.5.26, Glasgow; m., Margaret Graham Roxburgh; 1 s. Educ. Glasgow Academy; Merchiston Castle School, Edinburgh. Royal Naval Volunteer Reserve, 1943; Apprentice CA, Wilson Stirling & Co., 1947 (qualified, 1949); Partner, Wilson Stirling & Co. (subsequently Touche Ross & Co.), 1956-86; Chairman: Glasgow Junior Chamber of Commerce, 1965; Scottish Industrial Estates Corporation, 1972, Irvine Development Corporation, 1976; President, Glasgow Chamber of Commerce, 1980; Director, Scottish Metropolitan Property plc, 1986; Chairman, TSB Scotland plc, 1984; Director, TSB Group plc, 1985; Deputy Chairman, Hill Samuel Bank Ltd., 1991; Director, PCT Group plc, 1992; Governor, Merchiston Castle School, 1988; Member, Charity Appeals Committee for Prince and Princess of Wales Hospice; Director, Glasgow Native Benevolent Society; Member of Court, Glasgow University, 1987. Recreations: travel; gardening; reading. Address: (h.) 16 Collylinn Road, Bearsden, Glasgow; T.-0141-942 0042.

MacPherson, Margaret Hope, MA. Children's Author; b. 29.6.08, Colinton; m., Duncan MacPherson; 7 s. Educ. St. Denis School, Edinburgh; Edinburgh University. Married, farmed, brought up family; local government, 1945-49; Member, Commission of Inquiry into Crofting, 1951-54 (wrote minority report); Secretary, Skye Labour Party, 1961-84. Publications (children's books): Shiny Boys, 1963; The Rough Road, 1965; Ponies for Hire, 1967; The New Tenants, 1968; Battle of the Braes, 1970; The Boy on

the Roof, 1972. Recreations: gardening; watching shinty; football; swimming. Address: (h.) Ardrannach, Torvaig, Portree, Skye; T.-01478 2758.

Macpherson, Peter, FRCP, FRCR, DTCD, FLS. President, British Society of Neuroradiologists, 1990-92; President, Botanical Society of the British Isles, 1991-93; Emeritus Consultant Neuroradiologist, Institute of Neurological Sciences; b. 16.10.25, Inveraray; m., Agnes Cochrane Davidson; 4 d. Educ. Inveraray Grammar School; Keil School, Dumbarton; Anderson College, Glasgow. House Surgeon, Royal Infirmary, Stirling; Junior Hospital Medical Officer, Robroyston Hospital, Glasgow; Chest Physician, Argyll; Registrar/Senior Registrar, Western Infirmary, Glasgow. Commodore, Oban Sailing Club, 1958-60; President, Glasgow Natural History Society, 1979-81 and 1983-86; Honorary Secretary, Botanical Society of the British Isles, Committee for Scotland, since 1977; Plant Recorder for Lanarkshire, since 1978; Elder, Church of Scotland, since 1957. Recreations: natural history; sailing. Address: (h.) Ben Alder, 15 Lubnaig Road, Glasgow; T.-0141-632 0723.

Macpherson of Cluny (and Blairgowrie), The Honourable Sir William, KB (1983), TD, MA. 27th Hereditary Chief of the Clan Macpherson (Cluny-Macpherson); b. 1.4.26; m., Sheila McDonald Brodie; 2 s.; 1 d. Educ. Summer Fields, Oxford; Wellington College; Trinity College, Oxford. Scots Guards, 1944-47 (Captain); 21st Special Air Service Regiment (TA), 1951-65 (Lt.-Col. Commanding, 1962-65); Honorary Colonel, 21st SAS, 1983-91. Called to the Bar, Inner Temple, 1952; Queen's Counsel, 1971-83; Recorder of the Crown Court, 1972-83; Member, Senate and Bar Council, 1979-83; Bencher, Inner Temple, 1978; Judge of the High Court of Justice (of England and Wales), Queen's Bench Division, 1983; Honorary Member, Northern Circuit, since 1987. Member, Queen's Bodyguard for Scotland (Royal Company of Archers), since 1976, Brigadier, 1989; Vice President, Royal Scottish Corporation; President, Highland Society of London, 1991-94. Recreations: golf; fishing; rugby football. Address: (h.) Newton Castle, Blairgowrie, Perthshire; (b.) Royal Courts of Justice, Strand, London, WC2.

Macphie, Charles Stewart. Chairman and Managing Director, Macphie of Glenbervie Ltd., since 1965; Vice Chairman, Rowett Research Institute; Farmer; b. 22.9.29, Baltimore, Maryland; m., Elizabeth Margaret Jill Pearson; 1 s.; 1 d. Educ. Dalhousie Castle School; Rugby. Member, Scottish Export Forum. Address: (h.) Glenbervie, Kincardineshire; T.-01569 740226.

McQuaid, John, MA (Hons), MEd, PhD. Composer and Psychologist; b. 14.3.09, Lochgelly; m., Mary Darkin; 1 s.; 1 d. Educ. St. Mungo's Academy, Glasgow; Glasgow University; Edinburgh University. Taught, 1935-40; War Service, 1941-46 (Intelligence Corps), Africa and SE Asia; taught, 1946-51; Psychologist, 1952-77; studied music under Erik Chisholm; numerous broadcasts and public performances of compositions (piano, chamber music, orchestra, etc.); Visiting Lecturer, Galway University, 1971. Address: (h.) St. Anne's, 8 Ardrossan Road, Saltcoats, KA21 5BW; T.-01294 463737.

Macquaker, Donald Francis, MA (Oxon), LLB. Chairman, Scottish Health Service Common Services Agency, 1987-91; Chairman, Greater Glasgow Health Board, 1983-87; Partner, T.C. Young & Son, Writers, Glasgow, 1957-93, Consultant, since 1993; Director, Lithgows Limited, since 1987; b. 21.9.32, Stair; m., Susan Elizabeth Finlayson; 1 s.; 1 d. Educ. Winchester College; Trinity College, Oxford; Glasgow University. Former Member, Board of Management, Glasgow Royal Maternity Hospital and Associated Women's Hospitals (latterly Vice-Chairman); Chairman, Finance and General Purposes Committee, Greater Glasgow Health Board, 1974-83;

Director, Prince and Princess of Wales Hospice, Glasgow, 1991-94. Recreations: shooting; fishing; gardening. Address: (h.) Blackbyres, by Ayr; T.-0292 441088.

MacQueen, Professor Jack (John), MA (Glasgow), MA (Cantab), Hon DLitt. Professor Emeritus, Edinburgh University, since 1988, and Hon. Fellow, Faculty of Arts, since 1993; b. 13.2.29, Springboig; m., Winifred W. MacWalter; 3 s. Educ. Hutchesons' Boys Grammar School; Glasgow University; Christ's College, Cambridge. RAF, 1954-56 (Pilot Officer, Flying Officer); Assistant Professor of English, Washington University, St. Louis, Missouri, 1956-59; Edinburgh University: Lecturer in Medieval English and Scottish Literature, 1959-63, Masson Professor of Medieval and Renaissance Literature, 1963-72; Director, School of Scottish Studies, 1969-88; Professor of Scottish Literature and Oral Tradition, 1972-88; Endowment Fellow, 1988-92. Publications: St. Nynia, 1961, 1990; Robert Henryson, 1967; Ballattis of Luve, 1970; Allegory, 1970; Progress and Poetry, 1982; Numerology, 1985; Rise of the Historical Novel, 1989; Scotichronicon III and IV (with W. MacQueen), 1989; Scotichronicon I and II (with W. MacQueen), 1993; Scotichronicon V and VI (with W. MacQueen and D.E.R. Watt), 1995; Oxford Book of Scottish Verse (with T. Scott), 1966; A Choice of Scottish Verse 1470-1570 (with W. MacQueen), 1972; Humanism in Renaissance Scotland (Co-author), 1990. Recreations: walking; occasional archaeology; music. Address: (h.) Slewdonan, Damnaglaur, Drummore, Stranraer, DG9 9QN.

McQueen, James Donaldson Wright, MA, PhD. Chief Executive, Scottish Dairy Association; UK Representative, European Dairy Association; Deputy Member, EC Milk Advisory Committee; Council Member, Royal Scottish Geographical Society; Member, Advisory Committee for Scotland and N. Ireland, Understanding British Industry; b. 14.2.37, Dumfries; m., Jean Evelyn Brown; 2 s.; 1 d. Educ. King's Park School, Glasgow; Glasgow University. Assistant Lecturer, Department of Geography, Glasgow University, 1960-61; Junior Manager, Milk Marketing Board (England and Wales), 1961-62; Scottish Milk Marketing Board, 1963-89 (Deputy Managing Director, 1985-89); Member, CBI Scottish Council, 1987-89; Member, CBI National Council, 1991-94. Recreations: golf; gardening; photography. Address: (h.) Ormlie, 53 Kingston Road, Bishopton, Renfrewshire, PA7 5BA; T.-Bishopton 862380.

MacRae, Kenneth. Chief Executive, Student Awards Agency for Scotland. Address: (b.) Gyleview House, 3 Redheughs Rigg, Edinburgh, EH12 9HH.

Macrae, Col. Sir Robert Andrew Alexander Scarth, KCVO, MBE (1953). Lord Lieutenant of Orkney, 1972-90; Farmer; b. 14.4.15; m., Violet Maud Maclellan; 2 s. Educ. Lancing; RMC, Sandhurst. Commissioned Seaforth Highlanders, 1935; active service, BEF 1940 (PoW, 1940-45), NW Europe, 1945 (Despatches, 1945), Korea, 1952-53, East Africa, 1953-54; retired from Army, 1968; farming in Orkney, since 1967; Councillor, Orkney CC, 1970-74; Orkney Islands Council, 1974-78; Vice-Chairman, Orkney Hospital Board, 1971-74; Orkney Health Board, 1974-79; Honorary Sheriff, Grampian Highlands and Islands, 1974; JP, 1975; Freedom of Orkney, 1990. Recreations: sailing; gardening (watching the cabbages being blown out to sea). Address: (h.) Grindelay, Orphir, Orkney, KW17 2RD.

McSwan, Malcolm, OBE, CA. Managing Director, Racal-MESL Ltd., since 1983; Director, Wolfson Microelectronics Ltd., since 1984; Proprietor, Knapp Tree Farm; b. 31.8.39, Glasgow; m., Juliet Cowper-Jackson; 2 s. Educ. Royal High School, Edinburgh. Recreations: renovation; trees. Address: (b.) Lochend Industrial Estate, Newbridge, Midlothian; T.-0131-333 2000.

MacSween, Donald John. Chief Executive, An Comunn Gaidhealach. Address: (b.) 91 Cromwell Street, Stornoway, PA87 2QG.

MacSween, Iain MacLean, BA (Econ), MPhil. Chief Executive, Scottish Fishermen's Organisation, since 1982; b. 20.9.49, Glasgow; m., Jean Gemmill Martin; 3 s.; 1 d. Educ. Knightswood Secondary School; Strathclyde University; Glasgow University. Fisheries Economics Research Unit, 1973-75; Department of Agriculture and Fisheries for Scotland, 1975-77; Scottish Fishermen's Organisation, since 1977; President, European Federation of Fishermen's Organisations. Address: (b.) 601 Queensferry Road, Edinburgh, EH2 6EA; T.-0131-339 7972.

MacSween, Professor Roderick Norman McIver, BSc, MD, FRCPGlas, FRCPEdin, FRCPath, FRSE, FIBiol. Professor of Pathology, Glasgow University, since 1984; Honorary Consultant Pathologist, Western Infirmary, Glasgow, since 1970; b. 2.2.35, Kinloch, Lewis; m., Marjory Pentland Brown; 1 s.; 1 d. Educ. Inverness Royal Academy; Glasgow University. Successively Lecturer, Senior Lecturer, Reader and Titular Professor in Pathology, Glasgow University, 1965-84; Physician/Research and Education Associate, Colorado University Medical Center, Denver, 1968-69; Honorary Fellow, South African Society of Pathologists, 1982; Otago Savings Bank Visiting Professor, Otago University, 1983; Hans Popper Lecturer in Liver Pathology, Columbia University College of Physicians and Surgeons, New York, 1988; Henry Moon Lecturer, University of California, San Francisco, 1993; President, Royal Medico-Chirurgical Society of Glasgow, 1978-79; President, International Academy of Pathology, British Division, 1988-90; Editor, Histopathology (Journal). Publications: Muir's Textbook of Pathology, 13th edition (Co-Editor); Pathology of the Liver, 3nd edition (Co-Editor); Recent Advances in Histopathology, Nos. 11-15; Recent Advances in Hepatology, No. 1. Former Captain, Dunaverty and Machrihanish Golf Clubs. Recreations: golf; gardening; opera; hill-walking; more golf! Address: (b.) University Department of Pathology, Western Infirmary, Glasgow, G11 6NT; T.-0141-211 2233.

MacTaggart, Kenneth Dugald, BA, PhD. Head of Economics, Highlands and Islands Enterprise, since 1988; b. 15.4.53, Glasgow; m., Caroline McNicholas; 2 d. Educ. Allan Glen's School, Glasgow; Glasgow University; Paisley College; Aston University. Economic research, Aston University, 1976-80; Editor, Export Times, London, 1980-84; Editor, Property International, London and Bahrain, 1984-87; Director, Inc Publications, London, 1987-88. Recreations: hill-walking; piano; photography. Address: (h.) The Sutors, 28 Broadstone Park, Inverness, IV2 3LA; T.-01463 233717.

MacVicar, Angus, MA, DUniv. Author; b. 28.10.08, Argyll; m., Jean Smith McKerral (deceased); 1 s. Educ. Campbeltown Grammar School; Glasgow University. Reporter, Campbeltown Courier, 1931-33; Freelance Author; Army Service, 1940-45 (Captain, RSF); Freelance Author, Journalist, Radio and TV Scriptwriter; published 78 books, including adult novels, children's novels, adult and children's non-fiction, plays; Honorary Sheriff-Substitute, Argyll, 1965; Doctorate, Stirling University, 1985. Recreations: golf; gardening; amateur drama. Address: (h.) Achnamara, Southend, Campbeltown, Argyll, PA28 6RW; T.-01586 830228.

McVicar, George Christie, DipMusEd, RSAM; Hon.FTSC. Chairman, Scottish Amateur Music Association, 1982-95; Founder and Director, Lennox Singers, since 1990; b. 17.3.19, Dumbarton. Educ. Dumbarton Academy; Royal Scottish Academy of Music and Drama. Teacher of Music, Dunbartonshire Schools, 1946-54; Lecturer in Music, Moray House College of Education, 1954-56; Adviser in Music to Stirlingshire and subsequently Central Region, 1956-79. Adjudicator Member, British Federation of Music Festivals; Examiner, Trinity College of Music, 1979-91; Convenor, Saltire Scots Song Competitions, 1986-93. Publications: The Saltire Scottish Song Book (formerly Oxford Scottish Song Book); Saltire Two-Part Scottish Song Book; The New Scottish Song Book. Address: (h.) 22 Queen Street, Stirling, FK8 1HN; T.-01786 72074.

MacVicar, Rev. Kenneth, MBE, TD, MA. Extra Chaplain to the Queen in Scotland, since 1991; b. 25.8.21. Minister, Kenmore and Lawers, 1950-90.

McVie, John, BL, WS, NP. Consultant, McVies WS; Honorary Sheriff-Substitute, Lothian and Borders; b. 7.12.19, Edinburgh; m., Lindsaye Woodburn Mair; 1 s.; 1 d. Educ. Royal High School; Edinburgh University. Captain, 7/9th Bn., The Royal Scots, 1940-46 (Signal Officer, North West Europe); mentioned in Despatches; Town Clerk, Royal Burgh of Haddington, 1951-75. Recreations: fishing; golf; motoring. Address: (h.) Ivybank, Haddington, East Lothian; T.-0162-082 3727.

MacWalter, Ronald Siller, BMSc (Hons), MB, ChB (Hons), MRCP(UK); FRCP(Edin); FRCP (Glas). Consultant Physician in Medicine for the Elderly, Royal Victoria Hospital, Dundee, since 1986; Honorary Senior Lecturer in Medicine, Dundee University, Ninewells Hospital, Dundee, since 1986; b. 14.12.53, Broughty Ferry; m., Sheila Margaret Nicoll; 2 s. Educ. Harris Academy, Dundee; Dundee University. Registrar in Medicine and Haematology, Department of Clinical Pharmacology, Ninewells Hospital, Dundee; Senior Registrar in General Medicine and Geriatric Medicine, Nuffield Department of Medicine, John Radcliffe Hospital, Oxford. Publication: Aids to Clinical Examination. Recreations: gardening; DIY; watercolour painting; music; skiing; swimming. Address: (h.) Ellangowan, 8 Hillcrest Road, Dundee, DD2 1JJ; T.-01382 566125.

McWhirter, Malcolm, MRCP, MFPHM. Director of Public Health and Chief Administrative Medical Officer, Forth Valley Health Board. Address: (b.) 33 Spittal Street, Stirling, FK8 1DX.

McWilliam, James, OBE, MA (Hons), DipEd. Rector, Lochaber High School, 1970-88; Chairman, Highland Health Board, 1983-91; b. 4.10.27, Portsoy, Banffshire; m., Helen C. Brodie; 3 d. Educ. Fordyce Academy, Banffshire; Glasgow University. Teacher of English, Calderhead School, Shotts, 1951; National Service (Royal Army Education Corps), 1951-53; Teacher, Coatbridge High School, 1953; Special Assistant, Beath High School, Cowdenbeath, 1958; Principal Teacher of English, Campbeltown Grammar School, 1961-70. Member, Highland Health Board, since 1978 (Chairman, Practitioners' Committee, 1981); Honorary Sheriff, Grampian, Highlands and Islands, since 1978; Past President: Lochaber Rotary Club, Lochaber EIS, Highland Secondary Headteachers Association. Recreations: music; TV; golf (occasionally). Address: (h.) 19 Seafield Street, Portsoy, Banff; T.-01261 43148.

McWilliam, Rev. Thomas Mathieson, MA, BD. Minister, Lylesland Parish Church, Paisley, since 1980; b. 12.11.39, Glasgow; m., Patricia Jane Godfrey; 1 s.; 1 d. Educ. Eastwood Secondary School; Glasgow University; New College, Edinburgh. Assistant Minister, Auld Kirk of Ayr, 1964-66; Minister: Dundee St. David's North, 1966-72, East Kilbride Greenhills, 1972-80; Convener, Youth Education Committee, General Assembly, 1980-84; Moderator, Paisley Presbytery, 1985-86; Convener, Board of Practice and Procedure, General Assembly, since 1992. Recreations: walking; reading; gardening; bowling. Address: (h.) 36 Potterhill Avenue, Paisley, PA2 8BA; T.-0141-884 2882.

M

Maan, Bashir Ahmed, JP, DL; b. 22.10.26, Maan, Pakistan; 1 s.; 3 d. Educ. D.B. High School, Quila Didar Singh; Punjab University. Involved in the struggle for creation of Pakistan as a student, 1943-47; organised rehabilitation of refugees from India in Maan and surrounding areas, 1947-48; emigrated to UK and settled in Glasgow, 1953; Founder Secretary, Glasgow Pakistan Social and Cultural Society, 1955-65 (President, 1966-69); Member, Executive Committee, Glasgow City Labour Party, 1969-70; Vice-Chairman, Glasgow Community Relations Council, 1970-75; Member, Glasgow Corporation, 1970-75 (Magistrate, City of Glasgow, 1971-74; Vice-Chairman, then Chairman, Police Committee, 1971-75); Member, National Road Safety Committee, 1971-74 and Scottish Accident Prevention Committee, 1971-75; Member, BBC Immigrant Programmes Advisory Committee, 1972-80; Convenor, Pakistan Bill Action Committee, 1973; contested East Fife Parliamentary seat, February 1974; President, Standing Conference of Pakistani Organisations in UK and Eire, 1974-77; Police Judge, City of Glasgow, 1974-75; Member, City of Glasgow District Council, 1975-84; Deputy Chairman, Commission for Racial Equality, 1977-80; Member, Scottish Gas Consumers Council, 1978-81; Bailie, City of Glasgow, 1980-84; Member, Greater Glasgow Health Board, 1981-92; Deputy Lieutenant, Glasgow, since 1982; Hon. Research Fellow, Glasgow University, 1988-91; Founder Chairman, Scottish Pakistani Association, 1984-91, and since 1994; Judge, City of Glasgow District Courts; Chairman, Strathclyde Community Relations Council, 1986-93 and since 1994; Member, BBC General Advisory Council, since 1992; a Governor, Jordanhill College of Further Education, 1987-91; Chairman, Mosque Committee, Islamic Centre, Glasgow, 1986-91. Publication: The New Scots. Recreations: golf; reading. Address: (h.) 8 Riverview Gardens, Glasgow, G51 8EL; T.-0141-429 7689.

Mabon, Rt. Hon. Dr. Dickson, PC (1977), KStL, MB, ChB, DHMSA, MFHom, FRSA, FInstPet, FInstD. Chairman, Ashtree & Son Ltd.; Deputy Chairman, Cairn Energy plc; Chairman, Royal London Homoeopathic Hospital NHS Trust; Member, Energy Saving Trust; b. 1.11.25, Glasgow; m., Elizabeth Zinn; 1 s. Educ. North Kelvinside School; Glasgow University. MP, Greenock and Port Glasgow, 1955-83; Joint Parliamentary Under Secretary of State for Scotland, 1964-67; Minister of State for Scotland, 1967-70; Minister of State for Energy, 1976-79; Treasurer, Parliamentary Group for Energy Studies. Address: (h.) 2 Sandringham, Largs, KA30 8BT; T.-01475 672293.

Machin, Professor George Ian Thom, MA, DPhil, FRHistS. Professor of British History, Dundee University, since 1989, Head, Department of Modern History, since 1992; b. 3.7.37, Liverpool; m., Dr. Jane Margaret Pallot; 2 s. Educ. Silcoates School, near Wakefield; Jesus College, Oxford. Research Student and Tutor, Oxford University, 1958-61; Assistant Lecturer, then Lecturer in History, Singapore University, 1961-64; Lecturer in Modern History, St. Andrews University, 1964-67; Lecturer, then Senior Lecturer, then Reader, Dundee University, 1967-89; Course Tutor, Open University in Scotland, 1971-82. Member, History Panel, Scottish Universities Council on Entrance, 1990-94; Observer, Scottish Examination Board, 1991-94; sometime External Examiner, Universities of Cambridge, St. Andrews, Aberdeen, Hull, Sussex, Stirling; Treasurer, Abertay Historical Society, 1966-73; Treasurer, Dundee Branch, Historical Association, 1981-92, President, 1992-95; Elder, Church of Scotland, since 1981. Publications: The Catholic Question in English Politics 1820 to 1830, 1964; Politics and the Churches in Great Britain 1832 to 1868, 1977; Politics and the Churches in Great Britain 1869 to 1921, 1987; The Liberal Governments 1905-15, 1991; Disraeli, 1995. Recreations: the arts; hill-walking; photographing historic sign-posts. Address: (h.) 50 West Road, Newport-on-Tay, Fife, DD6 8HP; T.-01382 543371.

Maciocia, Mario G.A. Chairman, OHP Ltd., since 1991; b. 17.5.49, Kirkcaldy; m., Hilary Anne; 2 s.; 1 d. Educ. St. Andrews High School; George Watson's College; Heriot Watt University. Chairman and Chief Executive, Alma Holdings, 1988-90; Chief Executive, Alma Confectionery Ltd., 1985-88; Director, Continental Sweets NV, 1985-90. Recreations: fishing; shooting; skiing; cricket; golf; rugby. Address: (h.) Pittormie, Dairsie, Fife; T.-01334 870374.

Mack, Douglas Stuart, MA, PhD, FRSE. Reader, Stirling University, since 1994; General Editor, Association for Scottish Literary Studies, 1980-90; General Editor, Stirling/South Carolina Edition of James Hogg, since 1990; President, The James Hogg Society, since 1982; b. 30.1.43, Bellshill; m., Wilma Stewart Grant; 2 s. Educ. Uddingston Grammar School; Glasgow University; Stirling University. Research Assistant, National Library of Scotland, 1965-66; Assistant Librarian: St. Andrews University, 1966-70, Stirling University, 1970-86; Lecturer, Stirling University, 1986-94. Editor of various books by James Hogg and Sir Walter Scott. Recreations: watching Hamilton Accies; sailing on paddle steamers. Address: (h.) 2 Law Hill Road, Dollar, FK14 7BG; T.-Dollar 742452.

Mack, Jimmy. Broadcaster and Journalist; Presenter, The Jimmy Mack Show, Radio Clyde 2, since 1990; b. 26.6.34, Greenock; m., Barbara; 1 s.; 1 d. Educ. Lenzie Academy; Bathgate Academy. Insurance Inspector, Guardian Royal Exchange Assurance Co., 1956-70; Producer and Presenter, various programmes, BBC Radio Medway, Kent, 1970-79; Presenter, Radio 1 Club, BBC Radio 1, 1967-70; Presenter, The Early Show, Night Ride, Junior Choice, BBC Radio 2, 1971-76; Producer, You and Yours, Woman's Hour, In Britain Now, BBC Radio 4, 1977-78; Presenter, The Jimmy Mack Show and Jimmy Mack's Old Gold, BBC Radio Scotland, 1979-89; Presenter, Top Club and Best Years of Their Lives, Grampian TV, 1980-84; Presenter, Scotland Today, Scottish TV, 1984-85; Presenter, I Believe You Believe, BBC TV, 1986. Television and Radio Industries Club of Scotland Award for best live radio programme, 1986. Publication: Jimmy Mack Show Book, 1984. Recreation: photography. Address: (b.) Radio Clyde, Clydebank Business Park, Glasgow, G81 2RX; T.- 0141-306 2200.

Mackie, Alistair Graham, MCIBS, AIQA. Chief Executive, Clydesdale Development Company, since 1993; b. 7.4.39, Glasgow; m., Barbara; 1 s.; 2 d. Educ. Kilmarnock Academy. Senior Manager, Royal Bank of Scotland. Recreations: golf; cycling; bowling. Address: (b.) Clydesdale Business Centre, Lanark; T.-01555 665064.

Mackie, Professor Andrew George, MA, PhD, FRSE, FIMA. Professor of Applied Mathematics, Edinburgh University, 1968-88; b. 7.3.27, Tain; m., Elizabeth Maud Hebblethwaite; 1 s.; 1 d. Educ. Tain Royal Academy; Edinburgh University; Cambridge University; St. Andrews University. Lecturer, Dundee University, 1948-50; Bateman Research Fellow and Instructor, California Institute of Technology, 1953-55; Lecturer: Strathclyde University, 1955-56, St. Andrews University, 1956-62; Professor of Applied Mathematics, Victoria University of Wellington, New Zealand, 1962-65; Research Professor, Maryland University, 1966-68; Visiting Professor, California Institute of Technology, 1984 and University of New South Wales, Australia, 1985; Vice-Principal, Edinburgh University, 1975-80; Chairman, Scottish Mathematical Council, 1980-84; President, Edinburgh Mathematical Society, 1982-83. Publication: Boundary Value Problems, 1965. Recreation:

golf. Address: (h.) 47 Cluny Drive, Edinburgh, EH10 6DU; T.-0131-447 2164.

Mackie of Benshie, Baron (George Yull Mackie), CBE, DSO, DFC, LLD. Farmer; Liberal Democrat Spokesman, House of Lords, on Devolution, Agriculture, Scotland, Industry; Member, Council of Europe and Western European Union, since 1986; b. 10.7.19, Aberdeen; m., 1, Lindsay Lyall Sharp; 1 s. (deceased); 3 d.; 2, Mrs Jacqueline Lane. Educ. Aberdeen Grammar School; Aberdeen University. Bomber Command and Air Staff, 1944. Contested South Angus, 1959; Vice-Chairman (Organisation), Scottish Liberal Party, 1959-64; MP (Liberal), Caithness and Sutherland, 1964-66; Chairman, Scottish Liberal Party, 1965-70; contested Caithness and Sutherland, 1970; contested NE Scotland, European Parliamentary Election, 1979; Member, EEC Scrutiny Committee (D), House of Lords; Executive, Inter-Parliamentary Union; Chairman, Industrial Appeal Committee, Pitlochry Festival Theatre, 1979; Chairman, Angus Committee, Salvation Army, 1976-84; Rector, Dundee University, 1980-83; Director, Scottish Ballet, 1986-88. Address: (h.) Cortachy House, by Kirriemuir, Angus; T.-0575 4229.

Mackie, Joyce Grant, BA (Hons), DipCE, DL. Vice-President, National Trust for Scotland, since 1988; Partner, farming business, since 1963; b. 7.5.40, Forfar; m., Bruce Stephen Mackie; 2 s.; 2 d. Educ. St. Margaret's School for Girls, Aberdeen; Moray House College of Education. Teacher, Dalmilling School, Ayr, 1961-63. National Trust for Scotland: Member, Council, 1974-79, 1985-90, Member, Executive Committee, 1976-86; Member, Aberdeen Committee, Scottish Children's League (RSSPCC); Trustee, David Gordon Memorial Trust, since 1977; Director, Lathallan Preparatory School, Montrose, since 1979, Chairman, since 1990; Member, Council, Glenalmond College, since 1991; Member, Church of Scotland Nomination Committee, 1985-88; Member, Executive Committee, Aberdeen University Quincentenary Campaign, since 1993. Recreations: gardening; art; tennis; Scotland. Address: (h.) Balquhindachy, Methlick, Ellon, Aberdeenshire AB41 0BY; T.-016514 373.

Mackie, Maitland, CBE, BSc, MA. Farmer; Owner, Mackie's; Chairman, MADCO, Farmdata; Chairman, Farm Assured Scotch Livestock; Member, Priorities Board for Agricultural Research; b. 21.9.37, Aberdeen; m., Dr. Halldis Mackie; 1 s.; 2 d. Educ. Aberdeen Grammar School; Aberdeen University. Former Chairman, Food and Animal Committees, Agricultural and Food Research Council; former Vice-President, National Farmers Union of Scotland; Chairman, Scottish Pig Industry Initiative; Chairman, Grampian Enterprise Ltd; Director, Rowett Research Institute and Rowett Research Services. Recreations: skiing; sailing; Norway. Address: Westertown, Rothienorman, Aberdeenshire; T.-01467 671466.

Mackie, Marie Watson-Watt, MA (Hons), EdB (Dip). National Chairman, Scottish Women's Rural Institutes, 1987-93; Non-Executive Director, Borders Community Health NHS Trust; b. Kilmarnock; m., Alex. O. Mackie, MA (Hons), FSA Scot. Educ. Kilmarnock Academy; Glasgow University. County Federation Chairman, SWRI, Roxburghshire, 1975-81; National Vice-Chairman, SWRI, 1981-87; Member, Women's National Commission, 1987-89; former Executive Member, Scottish Institute of Adult Education; Producer, Lecturer and Adjudicator, amateur drama; Chairman, Roxburghshire Drama Association; Britain in Bloom Judge, 1975-84; SWRI Delegate to ACWW Hague conference, 1992; Member, Borders Enterprise Focus on Community Sustainability Group, 1993; Council Member, Scottish Association of Young Farmers Clubs, 1987-94; Council Member, Rural Forum (Scotland), 1987-90; House Management Committee, Sue Ryder Home (Borders). Recreations: interior design; 19th-century pottery; Samoyed dogs; enjoying the countryside of Scotland; art and architecture. Address: (h.) Linton Downs, Kelso, Roxburghshire.

Macklon, Alan Edward Stephen, BSc, PhD. Project Leader, Plants Division, Macaulay Land Use Research Institute; b. 2.10.36, Dover; m., Bridget Jessamine Carr; 4 s. Educ. Cambridgeshire High School for Boys; Nottingham University; Aberdeen University. Joined Macaulay Institute for Soil Research, 1962; spent a year as Research Associate, Washington State University, 1966-67. Recreation: gardening. Address: (b.) Macaulay Land Use Research Institute, Craigiebuckler, Aberdeen, AB9 2QJ; T.-Aberdeen 318611.

Maddox, Professor Christopher Edward Ralph, BSc, PhD, CBiol, MIBiol, DipManEd. Principal, Scottish College of Textiles, Galashiels, since 1988 (Vice Principal, Queen Margaret College, Edinburgh, 1983-88); Professor, Heriot-Watt University, since 1991; b. 21.11.40; m., Janet; 2 s. Educ. Priory School, Shrewsbury; Birmingham University. MRC Research Fellow, Warwick University, 1965-66; Senior Lecturer, Luton College of Technology, 1966-67; Senior Lecturer, then Principal Lecturer, then Assistant Dean of Studies, Manchester Polytechnic, 1967-77; Head, Department of Molecular and Life Sciences, Dundee College of Technology, 1977-83. Member, SCOTEC Committees for Biology and Medical Laboratory Sciences, 1978-83; Member, Council, Scottish Branch, Institute of Biology, 1979-82; Member, CNAA Combined Studies Board, 1983-87; Member, CNAA Health Studies Committee, 1987-89; Member, Health Visiting Joint Committee, UK Central Council for Nursing, Midwifery and Health Visiting, 1983-88; Director, Scottish Borders Enterprise Company, since 1990; Director, SCOT Innovation & Development, since 1992; Director, Higher Education Statistics Agency, since 1993; Member, Scottish Examination Board, since 1992. Recreations: reading; watching sports. Address: (b.) Scottish College of Textiles, Galashiels, TD1 3HF; T.-01896 753351.

Madsen, Johan, BA, MBA, DipM, MBIM, MCIM. Managing Director, Garnock Valley Development Executive Ltd., since 1988; Director, Ayrshire Marketing Ltd., since 1991; b. 15.4.40, Aarhus, Denmark; m., Dr. Sheila Madsen; 2 d. Educ. Open University; Strathclyde University; Chartered Institute of Marketing. Manager, subsidiary of Danish company, 1969-72; Sales Manager for Scotland, Stimorol (UK) Ltd., 1972-86. Recreations: music; photography. Address: (b.) 44 Main Street, Kilbirnie, Ayrshire; T.-01505 685455.

Magee, William F., LLB. Secretary, Accounts Commission for Scotland, since 1995; b. 25.1.50, Glasgow; m., Helen McCann; 2 s. Educ. St. Aloysius College, Glasgow; Glasgow University. Legal work with various Scottish local authorities; Depute Director of Administration, Edinburgh District, 1984-88; Director of Administration and Legal Services, Central Region, 1988-95. Past Chairman, Society of Directors of Administration in Scotland. Recreations: music; golf. Address: (b.) 18 George Street, Edinburgh; T.-0131-477 1234.

Maguire, Sheriff John, PhD, LLB, QC. Sheriff Principal, Tayside, Central and Fife, since 1990; b. 30.11.34, Kirkintilloch; m., Eva O'Hara; 2 s.; 2 d. Educ. St. Ninian's High School, Kirkintilloch; St. Mary's College, Blairs; Pontifical Gregorian University, Rome; Edinburgh University. Standing Junior Counsel, Ministry of Public Buildings and Works, 1962-68; Sheriff at Airdrie, 1968-73; Sheriff at Glasgow, 1973-90; Secretary, Sheriffs Association, 1982-87, President, 1988-90. Co-Founder and Chairman, PHEW, 1985-90. Recreations: reading; thinking about doing the garden. Address: (b.) Sheriff Principal's Chambers, Perth Sheriff Court, Tay Street, Perth; T.-01738 620546.

Magnusson, Magnus, KBE (Hon.), MA (Oxon), FRSE, FRSA, FSA Scot. Writer and Broadcaster; Chairman, Scottish Natural Heritage, since 1992; b. 12.10.29, Reykjavik, Iceland; m., Mamie; 1 s.; 3 d. Educ. Edinburgh Academy; Jesus College, Oxford. Reporter, Scottish Daily Express; Features Writer, The Scotsman; Co-Presenter, Tonight, BBC TV, 1964-65; Presenter: Chronicle, Cause for Concern, Checkpoint, All Things Considered, Mainly Magnus, BC - The Archaeology of the Bible Lands, Living Legends, Vikings!, Mastermind; Rector, Edinburgh University, 1975-78.

Mahmood, Tahir Ahmed, MB, BSc, DObstRCP, MD, MRCOG, FRCP(Ireland); MFFP. Consultant Obstetrician and Gynaecologist, Forth Park Hospital, Kirkcaldy, since 1990; Clinical Senior Lecturer, Obstetrics and Gynaecology, Aberdeen University, since 1990; Hon. Secretary, Division of Obstetrics and Gynaecology and Paediatrics, Fife, 1991-94; b. 7.10.53, Pakistan; m., Aasia Bashir; 2 s. Educ. King Edward Medical College, Lahore, Punjab University. Member, Scottish Hospital Staffing Review Committee, sub-speciality of obstetrics and gynaecology, 1986-88; Member, Minimal Invasive Surgery Subgroup and Clinical Resource Management — Procurement Group for Acute Unit, Fife, 1991-92; Ethicon RCOG Travelling Fellowship, 1991; Member, Senate, Aberdeen University, since 1992; Hon. Secretary, Northern Obstetrical and Gynaecological Society, since 1993; Member, Area Medical Committee, Fife, since 1993, and Vice Chairman, since 1994; RCOG: District Tutor, since 1993, Member, Scottish Executive Council, since 1994. Recreations: squash; jogging; reading; history; walking. Address: (b.) Forth Park Hospital, 30 Bennochy Road, Kirkcaldy, Fife; T.-01592 261155.

Main, Professor Brian G.M., BSc, MBA, MA, PhD. Professor of Economics, Edinburgh University, since 1991 b. 24.8.47, St. Andrews; m., June Lambert; 2 s.; 1 d. Educ. Buckhaven High School; St. Andrews University; University of California, Berkeley. Lecturer, then Reader in Economics, Edinburgh University, 1976-87; Professor of Economics and Chairman, Department of Economics, St. Andrews University, 1987-91. Recreation: fishing. Address: (b.) Department of Economics, Edinburgh University, George Square, Edinburgh, EH8 9JY; T.-0131-650 8361.

Main, Carol B.L.D., BA. Director, National Association of Youth Orchestras, since 1979; Scottish Director, Live Music Now, since 1984; Classical Music Editor, The List, since 1985; b. 21.12.58, Kirkcaldy; m., Colin Heggie; 1 d. Educ. Kirkcaldy High School; Edinburgh University. Freelance music critic, mainly with Scotsman. Board Director, Edinburgh Festival Fringe Society; Committee Member, Scottish Arts Council. Address: (b.) Ainslie House, 11 St. Colme Street, Edinburgh, EH3 6AG; T.-0131-225 4606.

Main, John Duguid, MHort (RHS), DHE, FIHort. Curator, Royal Botanic Garden, Edinburgh, since 1988; b. 1.9.40, Carlisle; m., Jean Marisa Melville; 2 s. Educ. Irthing Valley School, Brampton; Askham Bryan College, York; Royal Botanic Garden, Edinburgh. Garden Supervisor, Royal Botanic Garden, Edinburgh, 1965-75; Superintendent, Harlow Car Gardens, Harrogate, 1975-80; Curator, Royal Horticultural Society Garden, Wisley, 1980-88. Council member, Borde Hill Garden Ltd.; President, Royal Caledonian Horticultural Society; Vice-President, Lakeland Horticultural Society; Council Member, National Council for the Conservation of Plants and Gardens. Recreations: gardening; art; aviculture; photography. Address: (h.) East Gate House, 7B Inverleith Row, Edinburgh, EH3 5LP; T.-0131-551 5686.

Main, Kirkland, ARSA, RSW, DA, FEIS. Head, School of Drawing and Painting, Edinburgh College of Art, and Deputy Principal, since 1991; b. 1.7.42, Edinburgh; m.,

Geraldine Francis; 1 d. Educ. Daniel Stewart's College; Edinburgh College of Art. Assistant to Vice Principal, Edinburgh College of Art, 1980-83 (Governor, 1979-85); Member, Central Institutions Staffs Salaries Committee, 1977-81; Member, Scottish Joint Negotiating Committee, Further Education, 1982-87; Chairman, Association of Lecturers in Scottish Central Institutions, 1982-86. Address: (h.) 15 Cramond Village, Edinburgh, EH4 6NU.

Main, Sir Peter (Tester), ERD, MD, LLD (Hon.), FRCPE, CIMgt; b. 21.3.25, Aberdeen; m., 1, Margaret Tweddle (deceased); 2 s.; 1 d.; 2, May Heatherington McMillan. Educ. Robert Gordon's College; Aberdeen University. House Surgeon, Aberdeen Royal Infirmary, 1948-49; Captain, RAMC, 1949-51; Medical Officer with Field Ambulance (Suez), 1956; Lt. Col., RAMC (AER), retired 1964; general practice, 1953-57; The Boots Co. PLC: joined Research Department, 1957; Director of Research, 1968; Managing Director, Industrial Division, 1979; Director, 1973-85, Vice Chairman, 1980-81, Chairman, The Boots Co. PLC, 1982-85; Director, Scottish Development Agency, 1986-91; Director, W.A. Baxter & Sons Ltd., 1985-91. Member, National Economic Development Council, 1984-85; Chairman, Committee of Inquiry into Teachers' Pay and Conditions, Scotland, 1986; Governor, Henley Management College, 1983-86. Recreations: fishing; Scottish music. Address: Ninewells House, Chirnside, Duns, Berwickshire, TD11 3XF; T.-01890 818191.

Mair, Alexander, MBE (1967). Chairman, RGIT Ltd., since 1988; Governor, Robert Gordon's College, Aberdeen, since 1988; b. 5.11.22, Echt; m., Margaret Isobel. Educ. Skene Central School; School of Accountancy, Glasgow. Company Secretary, Grampian TV, 1961-70; appointed Director, 1967; Director and Chief Executive, 1970-87. President, Aberdeen Chamber of Commerce, 1989-91; Chairman, Aberdeen International Football Festival, 1988-91; Chairman, Oil Industry Community Fund, since 1993. Recreations: golf; skiing; gardening. Address: (h.) Ravenswood, 66 Rubislaw Den South, Aberdeen, AB2 6AX; T.-01224 317619.

Mair, Alistair S.F., MBE, DL, BSc, FIMgt. Chairman, since 1991, Managing Director, since 1977, Caithness Glass Ltd.; Chairman, CBI Scotland, 1989-91, and Member, CBI Council; Deputy President, British Glass Manufacturers Confederation; b. 20.7.35, Drumblade; m., 1, Anne Garrow (deceased); 2, Mary Bolton; 4 s.; 1 d. Educ. Robert Gordon's College, Aberdeen; Aberdeen University. Rolls Royce, Glasgow, 1957-71: graduate apprentice, PA to General Manager, Production Control Manager, Product Centre Manager; RAF, 1960-62 (short-service commission, Technical Branch); Managing Director, Caithness Glass Ltd., 1971-75; Marketing Director, Worcester Royal Porcelain Co., 1975-76. Non-Executive Director: Grampian Television, since 1986, Crieff Hydro Ltd., since 1994; Governor, Morrison's Academy, Crieff; Commissioner, Queen Victoria School, Dunblane; Member, Aberdeen University Court; Chairman, Crieff Auxiliary Association (Richmond House). Recreations: gardening; walking; current affairs. Address: (h.) Dungora, Heathcote Road, Crieff, Perthshire, PH7 4AG; T.-01764 652191.

Mair, Henry. Poet; b. 4.3.45, Kilmarnock; m., Etta; 1 s.; 1 d. Educ. St. Joseph's High School, Kilmarnock. Originator, 1972, and Secretary, Scottish National Open Poetry Competition; guest, USSR Writers' Union, 1980. Publications: I Rebel, 1970; Alone I Rebel, 1974; Flowers in the Forest, 1978; The Prizewinners, 1987. Address: (h.) 42 Tollerton Drive, Irvine, Ayrshire; T.-Irvine 76381.

Mair, William Wallace, MA, MBA. Secretary, Faculty of Actuaries in Scotland, since 1974; Secretary, Associated Scottish Life Offices; b. 19.6.49, Bellshill; m., Sandra Cunningham; 1 s.; 1 d. Educ. Uddingston Grammar School; Glasgow University; Edinburgh University. Assistant

Secretary, Royal Institution of Chartered Surveyors, 1969-72; Secretary, Scottish National Federation of Building Trades Employers, 1972-73. Recreations: badminton; cricket; hill-walking; lay preaching. Address: (b.) 40 Thistle Street, Edinburgh EH2 1EN; T.-0131-220 4555.

Maitland-Carew, The Hon. Gerald Edward Ian, DL; b. 28.12.41, Dublin; m., Rosalind Averil Speke; 2 s.; 1 d. Educ. Harrow School. Army Officer, 15/19 The Kings Royal Hussars, 1960-72; looked after family estates, since 1972; Member, Royal Company of Archers; Chairman, Lauderdale Hunt; Chairman, Lauderdale and Galawater Branch, Royal British Legion Scotland; Deputy Lieutenant, Ettrick and Lauderdale and Roxburgh, 1989; elected Member, Jockey Club, 1989; Chairman, Musselburgh Racecourse, 1993; Member, Border Area, TA Committee. Recreations: racing; hunting; shooting. Address: (h.) Thirlestane Castle, Lauder, Berwickshire; T.-01578 722 254.

Makin, Keith, BSc, MSc, DipSocAdmin, CQSW, MInstM. Director of Social Services, Dumfries and Galloway Council, since 1995; b. 22.4.53, Luton; m., Margaret Louise; 1 s.; 2 d. Educ. Kingsbury Grammar School, Dunstable; Cardiff University; Manchester University; Birmingham University. Social Worker, Cheshire County Council, 1975080; Senior Social Worker, Oxfordshire, 1980-83; Team Manager/Operations Manager, Warwickshire, 1983-89; Divisional Director, Northumberland, 1990-93; Depute Director, then Director of Social Work, Dumfries and Galloway Regional Council, 1994-95. Executive Committee Member, Association of Directors of Social Work. Recreations: fishing; driving; music; cookery; sailing. Address: (b.) Irongray Technology Park, Irongray Road, Dumfries, DG2 0HS.

Malcolmson, Peter, OBE, JP, CQSW. Administration Manager, Shetland Oil Industries Group; Councillor, Shetland Islands Council (Vice Chairman, Education Committee); former Director of Social Work, Shetland Islands Council; b. 27.7.39, Lerwick; m., Grace Eleanor Robson; 2 s.; 2 d. Educ. Anderson High School, Lerwick; Moray House College, Edinburgh. Social Worker, 1963-90. Recreations: voluntary social work; guizing and sailing Viking Longship. Address: (h.) Skersund, Upper Sound, Lerwick, Shetland Isles, ZE1 0RQ.

Mallinson, Edward John Harold, MPharm, FRPharmS, FIMgt, FRSH. Chief Administrative Pharmaceutical Officer, Lanarkshire Health Board, since 1984; b. 15.3.50, Bingley; m., Diana Gray; 2 d. Educ. Bradford Grammar School; Bradford University. Staff Pharmacist (Ward Pharmacy Services), Bradford Royal Infirmary, 1973-78; District Pharmaceutical Officer, Perth and Kinross District, 1978-83. Chairman, Scottish Chief Administrative Officers, 1990-92; Royal Pharmaceutical Society of Great Britain: Hon. Secretary, Bradford & District Branch, 1978, Hon. Secretary, Dundee & Eastern Scottish Branch, 1979-83, Hon. Secretary and Treasurer, Lanarkshire Branch, since 1984; Member of Council, Royal Society of Health; Vice Chairman and Secretary, Pharmaceutical Group, Royal Society of Health, 1986-89; Chairman, Strathclyde Police/Lanarkshire Health Board Drug Liaison Committee, 1985-91; Member, General Synod, Scottish Episcopal Church, 1986-95; Honorary Treasurer, Comunn Gaidhlig na h-Eaglais Easbaigich; Secretary, Lanarkshire Branch, British Institute of Management, 1989-91, Chairman, 1991-94. Recreations: genealogy; Gaelic language and culture; walking and cooking. Address: (h.) Malden, North Dean Park Avenue, Bothwell, Glasgow, G71 8HH; T.-01698 852973.

Mangan, Professor J.A., BA, DLC, ACSE, PhD, FRHistS, FRAI, FAAPE. Professor of Education, Strathclyde University, since 1993; Visiting Professor, Faculty of Arts, University of California, since 1985; b. 25.3.39, Liverpool; m., Doris; 1 s.; 1 d. Has lectured in Europe, North America, Asia and Australasia; Founder and Academic Executive Editor, International Journal of the History of Sport; Series Editor, International Studies in the History of Sport. Publications: Athleticism in Victorian and Edwardian Public School; The Games Ethic and Imperialism; Manliness and Morality (Co-editor); From Fair Sex to Feminism (Co-editor); Industrial and Post-Industrial Eras (Co-editor); Pleasure, Profit and Proseyltism (Editor); Sport in Africa (Co-editor); The Cultural Bond (Editor); Benefits Bestowed? (Editor); Making Imperial Mentalities (Editor); The Imperial Curriculum (Editor). Recreations: gardening; hill-walking; local history. Address: (b.) Strathclyde University, Glasgow, G1 1XQ.

Mann, Charles John Howell, OBE, OStJ, TD, DL, MB, BS, DPH, FSA(Scot). Medical Practitioner, since 1949; b. 21.2.26, London; m., Dr. Evelyn M.F. Mann; 1 s. (dec.); 2 d. Educ. Epsom College; St. Mary's Hospital Medical School, London. Chairman, St. Andrew's Ambulance Association, Aberdeen; Medical Adviser, Scotoil Services Ltd.; Hon. Medical Adviser, RNLI, Aberdeen. Recreations: gardening; walking; fishing; shooting. Address: (h.) Altmore, Myrtle Den Road, Milltimber, Aberdeen; T.-01224 867682.

Mann, David George, BSc, PhD. Deputy Regius Keeper (Deputy Director), Royal Botanic Garden, Edinburgh, since 1990; b. 25.2.53, Romford, Essex; m., Lynn Barbara; 1 s.; 1 d. Educ. Brentwood School; Bristol University. Edinburgh University: Demonstrator, 1978-81, Lecturer, 1981-90, Director of Studies, 1989-90. Member, Council, International Society for Diatom Research; Editor, Diatom Research; G.W. Prescott Award, 1991. Publications: editor/author of 60 papers and books. Recreations: classical piano; watercolour painting. Address: (b.) Royal Botanic Garden, Inverleith Row, Edinburgh, EH3 5LR; T.-0131-552 7171.

Mann, Gordon Laurence, DipTP, MRTPI, MInstPet. Director of Physical Planning, Dumfries and Galloway Regional Council, since 1987 (Director of Planning, Shetland Islands Council, 1980-87); b. 28.4.48, Dundee. Address: (b.) English Street, Dumfries, DG1 2DD; T.-01387 261234.

Manning, Professor Aubrey William George, BSc, DPhil, FInstBiol, Dr (h c) (Toulouse), FRSE. Professor of Natural History, Division of Biological Sciences, Edinburgh University, since 1973; b. 24.4.30, London; m.; 3 s., inc. 2 by pr. m. Educ. Strode's School, Egham; University College, London; Merton College, Oxford. Research, 1951-54; National Service, Royal Artillery, 1954-56; Lecturer, then Reader in Zoology, Edinburgh University, 1956-73; Secretary-General, International Ethological Committee, 1971-79; President, Association for the Study of Animal Behaviour, 1981-84; President, Biology Section, British Association for the Advancement of Science, 1993; Member, Scottish Advisory Committee, Nature Conservancy Council, 1982-89; Member, Advisory Committee on Science, NCC, 1985-89; Chairman of Council, Scottish Wildlife Trust, since 1990. Publication: An Introduction to Animal Behaviour, 1992; research papers in biological journals. Recreations: woodland conservation; walking; architecture. Address: (h.) The Old Hall, Ormiston, East Lothian; T.-Pencaitland 340536.

Manojlovic-Muir, Ljubica, BSc, PhD, CChem, FRSC. Reader in Chemistry, Glasgow University, since 1989; b. 31.10.31, Topola, Yugoslavia; m., Dr Kenneth W. Muir; 1 s.; 1 d. Educ. Arandjelovac Gimnazia, Yugoslavia; University of Belgrade. Scientific Officer, Boris Kidrich Institute of Nuclear Sciences, Vincha, Belgrade, 1955-67; 1967-72: Research Fellow, Brookhaven National Laboratory, Upton, New York, Northwestern University, Evanston, Illinois, University of Sussex; Lecturer,

Chemistry, Glasgow University, since 1972. Member: Royal Society of Chemistry, British Crystallographic Association; New York Academy of Sciences. Publications: 205 papers published in chemistry journals. Recreations: reading; music; gardening; travel. Address: Department of Chemistry, Glasgow University, Glasgow G12 8QQ; T.-0141-339 8855, Ext. 4506.

Mansfield and Mansfield, 8th Earl of (William David Mungo James Murray), JP, DL; b. 7.7.30; m., Pamela Joan Foster; 2 s.; 1 d. Educ. Eton; Christ Church, Oxford. National Service, Malayan Campaign; called to Bar, Inner Temple, 1958; Barrister, 1958-71; Member, British Delegation to European Parliament, 1973-75; Minister of State, Scottish Office, 1979-83; Minister of State, Northern Ireland Office, 1983-84; Director: General Accident Fire and Life Assurance Corporation Ltd., 1972-79, and since 1985; The American Trust Ltd., since 1985; Pinneys of Scotland Ltd., 1985-89; Ross Breeders Ltd., 1989-90; Hon. President, St. Andrews Society of Glasgow, 1972-92; President, Royal Scottish Country Dance Society, since 1977; Hon. Member, RICS; First Crown Estate Commissioner, since 1985. Address: (h.) Scone Palace, Perthshire, PH2 6BE.

Manson, Alexander Reid, CBE, SDA, ARAgS. Farmer; Member, Meat and Livestock Commission, since 1986; General Commissioner of Income Tax, since 1991; Director, National Animal Data Centre, since 1992; b. 2.9.31, Oldmeldrum; m., Ethel Mary Philip; 1 s.; 2 d. Educ. Robert Gordon's College; North of Scotland College of Agriculture. Member, Oldmeldrum Town Council, 1960-65; founder Chairman, Aberdeen Beef and Calf Ltd., 1962; Past President, Scottish Agricultural Organisation Society Ltd.; Chairman, Buchan Meat Producers Ltd., 1982-92; Past President, Federation of Agricultural Cooperatives; Member, Williams Committee of Enquiry, 1989. Recreations: golf; bird-watching. Address: (h.) Kilblean, Oldmeldrum, Inverurie, AB51 ODN; T.-Oldmeldrum 872226.

Manson, Richard U., MCIH. General Manager, State Hospital, Carstairs, since 1990; b. 2.5.51, Glasgow; m., Barbara; 2 s.; 1 d. Educ. Shawlands Academy; Glasgow College of Commerce; Glasgow College of Building. District Housing Manager, then Management Auditor, Glasgow District Council, 1979-87; Operations Director, Quality Street Ltd., 1987-89; Managing Director, Homesense Ltd., 1989-90. Recreations: golf; music; the arts. Address: (b.) State Hospital, Carstairs, Lanark ML11 8RP; T.-01555 840293.

Manwaring, Gaye Melodie Anne, MBE, BSc, PhD, FRSA. Development Director, Tertiary Education, Northern College of Education, since 1987; Director, Medical Open Learning Service, since 1987; b. 15.10.45, Margate; m., Andrew Henry Wilson. Educ. Exeter University; Edinburgh University. Research Fellow, Glasgow University, 1969-75; Senior Lecturer in Educational Technology, Dundee College of Education, 1975-87. Former Governor, SCET; Member, various Committees of SCET, CET, CNAA; work with MSC, Open Tech, National Extension College, Open College, British Council, SOED. Recreations: theatre; gardening; reading; friends; cats. Address: (b.) Northern College of Education (Dundee Campus), Gardyne Road, Dundee, DD5 1NY; T.-01382 464000.

Mar and Kellie, Earl of (James Thorne Erskine). Boat Builder; Estate Worker; Scottish Liberal Democrat Peer; b. 10.3.49, Edinburgh; m., Mary Irene; 1 step s.; 4 step d. Educ. Eton; Moray House College of Education. Youth and Community Worker, Craigmillar, 1971-73; Social Worker, Sheffield, 1973-76, Grampian Region, 1976-78; Social Worker, Prison Social Worker, Community Service Supervisor, Highland Region, 1979-87; Builder, Kincardine, 1990-92; Project Worker, SACRO, Falkirk,

1992-93. Recreations: canoeing; hill-walking; boat building; Alloa Tower. Address: House of Lords, London, SW1A 0PW.

Maran, Professor Arnold George Dominic, MB, ChB, MD, FRCS, FACS, FRCP, FRCS (Eng), FDS (Hon). Professor of Otolaryngology, Edinburgh University, since 1988; Vice President, Royal College of Surgeons; Consultant Surgeon, Royal Infirmary and City Hospital, Edinburgh, since 1974; b. 16.6.36, Edinburgh; m., Anna; 1 s.; 1 d. Educ. Daniel Stewart's College; Edinburgh University; University of Iowa. Trained in Otolaryngology in Edinburgh and America; former Consultant Otolaryngologist, Tayside Health Board, and Professor of Otolaryngology, West Virginia University. Fifteen Visiting Professorships to foreign universities. Publications: six books and 150 scientific papers. Recreations: golf; music; travel. Address: (h.) 15 Cluny Drive, Edinburgh, EH10 6DW; T.-0131-447 8519.

Marjoribanks, Gerald Brian, BA, LRAM, ALAM. Officer for Scotland, Independent Television Commission, previously Independent Broadcasting Authority, since 1983; b. 22.7.42, Falkirk; m., Kathleen; 2 s.; 2 d. Educ. Falkirk High School; Edinburgh College of Speech and Drama; Open University. Sports Presenter, Sportsreel, Sportscene, Sportsound, BBC Scotland, 1966-83; Lecturer in Drama, Notre Dame College of Education, 1967-79; Co-ordinator of Learning Resources, Dunfermline College of Physical Education, 1979-80; Head of Public Relations, Cumbernauld Development Corporation, 1980-83. Recreations: drama adjudication; badminton; photography. Address: (h.) Underwood, 33 Maggie Wood's Loan, Falkirk, FK1 5HR.

Marjoribanks, Sir James Alexander Milne, KCMG (1965), MA. HM Diplomatic Service, 1934-71; b. 29.5.11, Edinburgh; m., Sonya Patricia Stanley de Brandon (deceased); 1 d. Educ. Edinburgh Academy; Edinburgh University; Strasbourg University. Served in Peking, Hankow, Marseilles, Jacksonville, New York, Bucharest, Canberra, Luxembourg, Bonn, Brussels, London; Assistant Under-Secretary of State, Foreign Office, 1962-65; Ambassador to European Communities, 1965-71. Director, Distillers PLC, 1971-76; Member, Edinburgh University Court, 1976-80; Governing Member, Caledonian Research Foundation; Chairman, Scotland in Europe, 1979-91; Member, Committee for European Community Cultural Co-operation. Recreation: hill-walking. Address: (h.) 13 Regent Terrace, Edinburgh, EH7 5BN; T.-031-556 3872; Lintonrig, Kirk Yetholm, Kelso; T.-01573 420 384.

Marker, Cdr. John (Iain) Hamilton, VRD (and bar), BA, MLitt, FIL, FRMetS, RNR (Rtd.). Depute Principal, Napier College of Commerce and Technology, 1974-87; b. 23.9.24, Greenock; m., Elizabeth Urie Macfarlane. Educ. Ulverston Grammar School; Kings College, Durham University. Assistant Master, Middlesex County Secondary School, 1952-54; Assistant Lecturer in Economics, Kingston College of Advanced Technology, 1954-57; Assistant Lecturer/Lecturer in Economics, Isleworth Polytechnic, 1957-62; Head of Department, West London College, 1962-68; Head of Department, then Depute Principal, Edinburgh College of Commerce, 1968-74. Recreations: golf; reading; gardening. Address: (h.) 2 Cherry Tree Gardens, Balerno, Midlothian, EH14 5SR; T.-0131-449 3936.

Markland, John A., MA, PhD, ACIS. Chief Executive, Fife Regional Council, since 1986; b. 17.5.48, Bolton; m., Muriel Harris; 4 d. Educ. Bolton School; Dundee University. Demographer, Somerset County Council, 1974-76; Senior Professional Assistant, Tayside Regional Council; Personal Assistant to Chief Executive, then Assistant Chief Executive, Fife Regional Council, 1979-86; Chairman, Scottish Branch, Society of Local Authority Chief Executives, 1993-95; Director, UK 2000 (Scotland);

Director, Fife Enterprise; Clerk to Lord Lieutenant of Fife. Recreations: climbing Scotland's Munros; cycling. Address: (b.) Fife House, North Street, Glenrothes, Fife; T.-01592 414141.

Marks, Frederick Charles, OBE, MA, LLB, FIMgt. Commissioner for Local Administration in Scotland (Local Government Ombudsman); Vice Chairman, Queen Margaret Hospital, Dunfermline, NHS Trust; b. 3.12.34, Bellshill; m., Agnes M. Bruce; 3 s.; 1 d. Educ. Wishaw High School; Glasgow University. Depute Town Clerk, Dunfermline, 1963-68; Town Clerk, Hamilton, 1968-75; Chief Executive, Motherwell, 1974-83; General Manager, Scottish Special Housing Association, 1983-89; Deputy Chairman, Local Government Boundary Commission for Scotland, 1989-94. Address: (b.) 23 Walker Street, Edinburgh EH3 7HX; T.-0131-225 5300.

Marnoch, Hon. Lord (Michael Stewart Rae Bruce), QC (Scot), MA, LLB. Senator of the College of Justice, since 1990; b. 26.7.38; m., Alison M. Stewart; 2 d. Educ.; Loretto; Aberdeen University. Advocate, 1963; QC, 1975; Standing Counsel to Department of Agriculture and Fisheries for Scotland, 1973; to Highlands and Islands Development Board, 1973; Advocate-Depute, 1983-86; Member, Criminal Injuries Compensation Board, 1986-89. Chairman for Scotland, Salmon and Trout Association, 1989-94. Recreations: golf; fishing. Address: (b.) Parliament House, Edinburgh; T.-0131-225 2595.

Marnoch, Derek George, BSc, ACMA. Chief Executive, Aberdeen Chamber of Commerce, since 1983; b. 30.10.35, Aberdeen; m., Kathleen Howard; 3 s. Educ. Aberdeen Grammar School; Aberdeen University. Recreation: golf. Address: (h.) The Gables, Kirk Road, Stonehaven, AB3 2DX; T.-01569 762709.

Marquis, Alistair Forbes, BA, MEd, DipCE, FCollP. Chairman, Scottish Committee of The Boys' Brigade, since 1991; elected Representative, UK Brigade Executive for East Lowland District, since 1989; Scottish Member, UK Management Committee, since 1991; b. 13.1.50, Glasgow; m., Margaret Jarvie Greenlees; 1 d. Educ Queen's Park Secondary School; Jordanhill College, Glasgow; Open University; Edinburgh University. Teacher/Assistant Head Teacher/Head Teacher; Inspector of Schools, 1989. Member, Scottish Committee on Special Educational Needs, 1985-88; Chairman, Lanthorn Community Complex Management Committee, 1979-82; SFA Football Referee, 1972; Church of Scotland Elder. Recreations: gardening; reading; walking. Address: (h.) 39 Bankton Drive, Murieston, Livingston, EH54 9EJ; T.-01506 414406.

Marr, Derek Shepherd, QFSM, FIFireE. Firemaster, Tayside Fire Brigade, since 1990; Secretary, Scottish Chief & Assistant Chief Fire Officers Association, since 1991; b. 6.7.48, Arbroath; m., Edna; 1 s.; 1 d. Educ. Arbroath High School. Joined fire service, 1967. Chairman, Tayside Fire Liaison Panel; COSLA Adviser to Protective Services Committee; Council Member, Chief & Assistant Chief Fire Officers Association. Recreations: reading; golf. Address: (b.) Fire Brigade Headquarters, Blackness Road, Dundee.

Marr, Norman G., CStJ, DipArch, ARIBA, FRIAS. Consultant Architect/Planner; Director of Planning and Development, Kincardine and Deeside District Council, 1975-92; b. 19.5.37, Aberdeen. Educ. Aberdeen Grammar School; Scott Sutherland School of Architecture, Aberdeen. Architectural Assistant, Aberdeen County Council, 1961-66; Senior Research Assistant, Corporation of the City of Aberdeen, Town Planning Department, 1967-69 (Principal Development Assistant, 1970-75). Organist and Choirmaster, Denburn Parish Church, Aberdeen, since 1956; Secretary, Scottish Federation of Organists, 1970-92 (President, 1993-94); Member, Aberdeen Order of St. John Committee; Member, Church of Scotland Property Commission; Vice-Chairman, Friends of St. Machar's Cathedral, Aberdeen, and Friends of the Kirk of St. Nicholas, Aberdeen. Recreations: organ playing/building; swimming; long-distance running; hill-walking; books; entertaining. Address: (h.) 63 Devonshire Road, Aberdeen, AB1 6XP; T.-01224 322937.

Marrian, Ian Frederic Young, MA, CA. Deputy Secretary, Institute of Chartered Accountants of Scotland, since 1991 (Director of Education, since 1981); b. 15.11.43, Kilwinning; m., Moira Selina McSwan; 1 s.; 2 d. Educ. Royal Belfast Academical Institution; Queens University, Belfast; Edinburgh University. Qualified as CA, 1969; Deloitte Haskins & Sells: audit practice, Rome, 1969-72, London, 1972-73, Audit Partner, Edinburgh, 1973-78, Technical Partner, London, 1978-81. Recreations: gardening in the grand scale; wines. Address: (h.) Bowerhouse, Dunbar, EH42 1RE; T.-0131-479 4815.

Marrian, Valerie Jean, MB, ChB, FRCP(Lond), FRCP(Edin), DCH. Consultant Paediatrician, since 1967; Honorary Senior Lecturer in Child Health, since 1967; b. 16.8.32, London; m., Douglas Fraser Hooper. Educ. Mary Erskine School, Edinburgh; Edinburgh University. Member, Children's Panel Advisory Committee, 1971-74; Member, Scottish Sports Council, 1974-80, Vice-Chairman, 1980-88; Member, The Sports Council, 1983-88. Recreations: skiing; classical music; opera; dog obedience/agility; cats. Address: (h.) 25 Hamilton Place, Perth, PH1 1BD; T.-01738 621018.

Marshall, David. MP (Labour), Glasgow Shettleston, since 1979; b. 1941. Address: (b.) House of Commons, London, SW1A 0AA.

Marshall, Enid Ann, MA, LLB, PhD, Assoc. RICS, ACIArb, FRSA. Solicitor; Reader, Scots Law Research Unit, Stirling University, since 1994; Editor, Scottish Law Gazette, since 1983; Chairman, Social Security Appeal Tribunal, Stirling and Falkirk, since 1984; b. 10.7.32, Boyndie, Banffshire. Educ. Banff Academy; Bell-Baxter School, Cupar; St. Andrews University. Apprentice Solicitor, 1956-59; Lecturer in Law, Dundee College of Technology, 1959-72; Lecturer, then Senior Lecturer, then Reader in Business Law, Stirling University, 1972-94. Departmental Editor, Arbitration Section, Journal of Business Law, since 1976. Publications: General Principles of Scots Law; Scottish Cases on Contract; Scottish Cases on Agency; Scottish Cases on Partnerships and Companies; Scots Mercantile Law; Gill on Arbitration; Charlesworth and Cain Company Law (Scottish Editor); Notes on the Law of Property in Scotland (Editor, 3rd edition); M.C. Oliver's Company Law (10th, 11th, 12th editions). Recreations: veganism; animal welfare. Address: (h.) 24 Easter Cornton Road, Stirling, FK9 5ES; T.-Stirling 478865/467285.

Marshall, Professor Ian Howard, MA, BD, PhD (Aberdeen), BA (Cantab). Professor of New Testament Exegesis, Aberdeen University, since 1979; b. 12.1.34, Carlisle; m., Joyce Elizabeth; 1 s.; 3 d. Educ. Aberdeen Grammar School; Aberdeen University; Cambridge University; Göttingen University. Assistant Tutor, Didsbury College, Bristol; Methodist Minister, Darlington; Lecturer, then Senior Lecturer and Reader in New Testament Exegesis, Aberdeen University. Publications: Kept by the Power of God; Luke: Historian and Theologian; The Origins of New Testament Christology; New Testament Interpretation (Editor); The Gospel of Luke; I Believe in the Historical Jesus; The Epistles of John; Acts; Last Supper and Lord's Supper; Biblical Inspiration; 1 and 2 Thessalonians; Jesus the Saviour; 1 Peter; Philippians; The Acts of the Apostles. Address: (b.) Department of Divinity with Religious Studies, King's College, Aberdeen, AB9 2UB; T.-01224 272388.

Marshall, Professor Ian Henry, BSc, PhD, CEng, FIMechE, FIEE, FIM, FRSA. Head, Department of

Mechanical and Manufacturing Engineering, Paisley University, since 1991, and Dean, Faculty of Engineering, since 1993; Editor-in-Chief, International Journal of Composite Structures, since 1983; b. 10.11.48, Irvine; m., Nan; 2 s.; 1 d. Educ. St. Bridget's School, Kilbirnie. Apprenticeship as fitter/turner, ICI Ltd., Ardeer; Lecturer/Senior Lecturer/Professor, Paisley College of Technology. Publications: 21 books on composite structures, numerous technical papers. Recreation: antique guns. Address: (b.) Paisley University, High Street, Paisley, PA1 2BE; T.-0141-848 3562.

Marshall, Janet Ann, ALA. Chairman, Scottish Society for the Prevention of Cruelty to Animals, since 1993; b. 3.7.47, Inchinnan; m., Allan W. Marshall; 2 s. Educ. John Neilson Institution, Paisley; Strathclyde University. Glasgow Public Libraries, 1965-67; Children's Librarian, 1969-73; School Librarian, 1973-75; Senior Education Resources Librarian, 1975-79; Farmer, 1979-92. Chairman, Dunlop Primary School Board, since 1989; Member, Strathclyde Region Children's Panel, since 1988. Recreation: gardening. Address: (h.) Silverhill Farm, Dunlop, Kilmarnock, KA3 4BN; T.-01560 484807.

Marshall, Professor Mary Tara, MA, DSA, DASS. Director, Dementia Services Development Centre, Stirling University; b. 13.6.45, Darjeeling, India. Educ. Mary Erskine School for Girls; Edinburgh University; London School of Economics; Liverpool University. Child Care Officer, London Borough of Lambeth, 1967-69; Social Worker, Personal Service Society, Liverpool, 1970-74; Research Organiser, Age Concern, Liverpool, 1974-75; Lecturer in Social Studies, Liverpool University, 1975-83; Director, Age Concern Scotland, 1983-89. Publication: Social Work with Old People, 1983; Working with Dementia, 1990. Recreations: photography; bird-watching. Address: (b.) Dementia Services Development Centre, Stirling University, Stirling, FK9 4LA; T.-01786 467740.

Marshall, Maud Evelyn, MA (Hons), MSc, MRTPI. Member, Building Standards Advisory Committee, since 1992; Member, Lottery Committee, Scottish Arts Council, since 1994; b. 24.1.50, Glasgow. Educ. Park School, Glasgow; Edinburgh University; Swiss Federal Institute of Technology; Strathclyde University. Director of Consultancy and Chief Policy Advisor, Scottish Homes, since 1992. Recreations: skiing; music; travel. Address: (b.) Thistle House, 91 Haymarket Terrace, Edinburgh, EH12 5HE; T.-0131-479 5255.

Marshall, Susan Muriel, ALAM. Reporter to the Children's Panel, Western Isles Islands Area, since 1990; b. 8.6.49, St. Andrews; m., John Lawrence Marshall; 2 d. Educ. St. Denis School, Edinburgh; Edinburgh College of Speech & Drama. O. & M. analyst, 1970-74; Member, Western Isles Children's Panel, 1976-90, Chairman, 1983-90. Recreations: walking; cooking; France. Address: (b.) 10 Harbour View, Stornoway, Isle of Lewis; T.-01851 706317.

Martin, Daniel, MA, BSc, PhD, FRSE, CMath, FIMA. Honorary Lecturer in Mathematics, Glasgow University, since 1980; b. 16.4.15, Carluke. Educ. High School of Glasgow; Glasgow University. Lecturer in Mathematics, Royal Technical College, Glasgow, 1938-47; Scientific Officer, Air Navigation Section, Royal Aircraft Establishment, Farnborough, 1941-45; Lecturer/Senior Lecturer in Mathematics, Glasgow University, 1947-80; Snell Visitor to Balliol College, Oxford, 1975-76. President, Glasgow Mathematical Association, 1958-59; President, Edinburgh Mathematical Society, 1960-61; former Assessor, Church of Scotland's selection schools for candidates for the Ministry. Publications: Solving Problems in Complex Numbers, 1968; An Introduction to Vector Analysis (Reviser), 1970; Manifold Theory: an introduction for mathematical physicists, 1991. Recreations: theology; local history; Gaelic. Address: (b.) Department of

Mathematics, Glasgow University, Glasgow, G12 8QW; T.-0141-339 8855, Ext. 6537.

Martin, David McLeod, DA, RSW, RGI. Painter; b. 30.12.22, Glasgow; m., Isobel Agnes Fowlie Smith; 4 s. Educ. Govan High School; Glasgow School of Art; Jordanhill College of Education. RAF, 1942-46. Principal Teacher, Hamilton Grammar School, 1973-83; retired early to paint full-time; exhibits regularly in Scotland; exhibited RA, 1984; numerous group shows; one man shows, Glasgow, Edinburgh, Perth, Greenock, Newcastle, Stenton, London; former Vice President, RSW. Address: (h.) The Old Schoolhouse, 53 Gilmour Street, Eaglesham, Glasgow, G76 0LG.

Martin, David Weir, BA (Econ). Member (Labour), European Parliament, for Lothians, since 1984; Vice-President, European Parliament, since 1989; b. 26.8.54, Edinburgh; m., Margaret Mary Cook; 1 s.; 1 d. Educ. Liberton High School; Heriot-Watt University. Worked as stockbroker's assistant and animal rights campaigner; became Lothian Regional Councillor, 1982; Vice-President, National Playbus Association; Member, Committee, Advocates for Animals; Director, St. Andrew Animal Fund; Member, West Lothian Develement Council; Rapporteur, Intergovernmental Conferences; Vice President, International Institute for Democracy. Publications: Bringing Common Sense to the Common Market — A Left Agenda for Europe; European Union and the Democratic Deficit; Europe — An Ever Closer Union; Towards a Wider, Deeper, Federal Europe. Recreations: soccer; reading. Address: (b.) 4 Lothian Street, Dalkeith EH22 1DS.

Martin, Ged, BA, MA, PhD, FRHistS. Director, Centre of Canadian Studies, and Reader in History, Edinburgh University, since 1983; Past President, British Association for Canadian Studies; b. 22.5.45, Hornchurch; m., Ann Barry. Educ. Royal Liberty School, Romford; Magdalene College, Cambridge. Research Fellow, Magdalene College, Cambridge, 1970-72, Australian National University, 1972-77; Lecturer, then Statutory Lecturer, University College, Cork, 1977-83. Canadian High Commissioner's Award for Service to British-Canadian Relations, 1989. Publications: ten books, including Canada's Heritage in Scotland (Co-author), 1989. Recreations: reading and writing history; music; talking to cats. Address: (b.) 21 George Square, Edinburgh, EH8 9LD; T.-0131-667 1011, Ext. 6801.

Martin, Rev. James, MA, BD, DD. Minister, High Carntyne, Glasgow, 1954-87; b. 21.1.21, Motherwell; m., Marion Gordon Greig; 2 d. Educ. Dalziel High School, Motherwell; Glasgow University. Minister, Newmilns West Church, 1946-54; Convener, Publications Committee, General Assembly, 1978-83 and Board of Communications, 1983-87. Publications: Did Jesus Rise from the Dead?; The Reliability of the Gospels; Letters of Caiaphas to Annas; Suffering Man, Loving God; The Road to the Aisle; People in the Jesus Story; A Plain Man in the Holy Land; Listening to the Bible; William Barclay: A Personal Memoir; My Friend Bobby; It's You, Minister; It's My Belief; Travels in the Holy Land; God-Collared; William Barclay in a Nutshell; You Can't Be Serious. Recreations: football; tennis; conversation. Address: 9 Magnolia Street, Wishaw; T.-Cambusnethan 385825.

Martin, John. Managing Director, Northsound Radio. Address: (b.) 45 King's Gate, Aberdeen, AB2 6BL.

Martin, John Sharp Buchanan, BSc. Under Secretary, School Education and Sport, Scottish Office, since 1992; b. 7.7.46, West Kilbride; m., Catriona Meldrum; 1 s.; 1 d. Educ. Bell-Baxter High School, Cupar; St. Andrews University. Assistant Principal, 1968-73; Private Secretary to Parliamentary Under Secretary of State, 1971-73; Principal, 1973-79; Rayner Scrutinies, 1979-80; Assistant

Secretary, Highlands and Tourism Division, 1980-84; Housing Division 1, 1984-89; Transport and Local Roads Division, 1989-92. Recreations: tennis; cricket; philately. Address: (b.) New St. Andrews House, Edinburgh; T.-0131-244 4413.

Martin, Michael John. MP (Labour), Glasgow Springburn, since 1979; Chairman, Scottish Grand Committee, since 1987; b. 3.7.45, Glasgow; m., Mary McLay; 1 s.; 1 d. Educ. St. Patrick's Boys' School, Glasgow. Member, Glasgow Corporation, 1973-74, and Glasgow District Council, 1974-79. Member, Speaker's Panel of Chairmen, since 1987; Fellow, Parliament and Industry Trust; Secretary, British-Italian Parliamentary Group; Member, College of Piping. Recreations: hill-walking; studying history of Forth and Clyde Canal; listening to pipe band music. Address: (h.) 144 Broomfield Road, Glasgow, G21 3UE; T.-0141-558 2975.

Martin, Robert (Roy) Logan, QC, LLB. Advocate, since 1976; Barrister, since 1990; b. 31.7.50, Glasgow; m., Fiona Frances Neil; 1 s.; 2 d. Educ. Paisley Grammar School; Glasgow University. Solicitor, 1973-76; Member, Sheriff Courts Rules Council, 1981-84; Standing Junior Counsel, Department of Employment (Scotland), 1983-84; Advocate-Depute, 1984-87; admitted to Bar of New South Wales, 1987; Queen's Counsel, 1988; called to the Bar, Lincoln's Inn, 1990; Chairman (part-time), Industrial Tribunals, since 1990; Chairman, Scottish Planning, Local Government and Environmental Bar Group, since 1991. Honorary Secretary, The Wagering Club, 1982-91. Recreations: shooting; skiing; modern architecture; vintage motor cars. Address: (h.) Hardengreen House, Dalkeith, EH22 3LF; T.-0131-660 5997.

Martin, Professor Roderick, MA, DPhil, DLitt. Director, Glasgow University Business School and Professor of Organizational Behaviour, since 1992; b. 18.10.40, Lancaster; 1 s.; 2 d. Educ. Royal Grammar School, Lancaster; Balliol College, Oxford; University of Pennsylvania; Nuffield College, Oxford. Lecturer, York Univrsity, 1964-66; Lecturer in Sociology, Oxford University, 1966-69; Fellow and Tutor in Politics and Sociology, Trinity College, Oxford, 1969-84; Professor of Industrial Sociology, Imperial College, London, 1984-88; Fellow, Templeton College, Oxford, 1988-91. Member, ESRC Research Grants Board, 1987-91. Publications: eight books, including Bargaining Power, 1992. Recreations: reading; listening to music. Address: (b.) 55-59 Soth Park Avenue, Glasgow, G12 8LF; T.-0141-330 5410.

Martin, Professor Ursula Hilda Mary, MA, PhD, CEng, FRSA. Professor, School of Mathematical and Computational Sciences, University of St Andrews, since 1992; b. 3.8.53, London. Educ. Cambridge University. Lecturer, London University, 1978-81; Visiting Professor, University of Illinois, 1981-83; Lecturer, Manchester University, 1983-87; Reader, then Professor, London University, 1987-92. Address: (b.) School of Mathematical and Computational Sciences, University of St Andrews, North Haugh, St. Andrews, KY16 9SS; T.-01334 63252.

Martin-Bates, Robert Stuart, BL. Honorary Sheriff, Perth, since 1989; b. 8.5.21, Perth; m., Ursula Louise Sarena; 2 s. Educ. Glenalmond College; Edinburgh University. Served in Royal Navy, 1941-46; private practice as solicitor in Perth and Pitlochry, 1948-90; Burgh Prosecutor, Crieff, 1960-74; Depute Burgh Prosecutor, Perth, 1963-74. Member and Past Moderator, Perth Society of High Constables, since 1957; Past President, Society of Solicitors of the City and County of Perth; Member, Committee, Perth Model Lodging House Association, 1950-85 (Chairman, 1968-85); Member, Committee, Perthshire & Kinrosshire Society for the Blind, 1979-89, including three years as Chairman, now Hon. Vice-President. Recreations:

golf; gardening; reading. Address: (h.) Immeriach, Glencarse, Perth, PH2 7NF; T.-01738 860284.

Marwick, George Robert, SDA, DL, JP. Chairman, Swannay Farms Ltd., since 1972; Chairman, Campbeltown Creamery (Holdings) Ltd., 1974-90; Deputy Lieutenant, County of Orkney, since 1976; Member, Countryside Commission for Scotland, 1978-86; b. 27.2.32, Edinburgh; m., 1, Hanne Jensen; 3 d.; 2, Norma Gerrard. Educ. Port Regis; Bryanston; Edinburgh School of Agriculture. Councillor, local government, 1968-78; Vice-Convener, Orkney County Council, 1970-74, Convener, Orkney Islands Council, 1974-78; Chairman, North of Scotland Water Board, 1970-73; Member, Scottish Agricultural Consultative Panel, since 1972 (formerly Winter Keep Panel, 1964-72); Director, North Eastern Farmers Ltd., since 1968; Director, Orkney Islands Shipping Co., 1972-87; Council Member, National Trust for Scotland, 1979-84. Recreations: shooting; tennis; motor sport. Address: (h.) Swannay House, by Evie, Orkney; T.-0185-672 365.

Mason, Christopher Michael, MA, PhD. Chairman, Clyde Maritime Trust Ltd., since 1991; Member, City of Glasgow Council, since 1995; Leader, Strathclyde Liberal Democrat Group, 1986-96; Member, Strathclyde Regional Council, 1982-96; Lecturer in Politics, Glasgow University, 1966-93; b. 8.3.41, Hexham; m., Stephanie Maycock; 2 d. Educ. Marlborough College; Magdalene College, Cambridge. Alliance candidate, Glasgow, European Elections, 1984; Liberal Democrat candidate, Glasgow Hillhead, General Election, 1992; Chairman, Scottish Liberal Party, 1987-88; Member, Scottish Constitutional Convention, since 1989. Publication: Effective Management of Resources: The International Politics of the North Sea, 1979. Recreation: sailing. Address: (h.) 18 Randolph Road, Glasgow, G11 7LG; T.-0141-339 2840.

Mason, Professor Sir David Kean, KB, CBE, BDS, MD, Hon. DChD, FRCS, FDS, FRCPath, Hon. FFD, Hon. FDS, Hon. LLD. President, General Dental Council, 1989-94; Professor of Oral Medicine, Glasgow University, 1967-92 (Dean of Dental Education, 1980-90); Honorary Consultant Dental Surgeon, since 1965; b. 5.11.28, Paisley; m., Judith Armstrong; 2 s.; 1 d. Educ. Paisley Grammar School; Glasgow Academy; St. Andrews University; Glasgow University. RAF Dental Branch, 1952-54; Registrar in Oral Surgery, Dundee, 1954-56; Senior Lecturer in Dental Surgery and Pathology, Glasgow University, 1964-67; Chairman, National Dental Consultative Committee, 1976-80; Member: Medicines Commission, 1976-80, Dental Committee, MRC, 1973-83, Physiological Systems Board, MRC, 1976-80, GDC, 1976-93, Dental Strategy Review Group, 1980-81, Dental Review Working Party, UGC, 1986-87, WHO Expert Committee on Oral Health, since 1991; Convener, Dental Council, RCPSGlas, 1977-80; John Tomes Prize, RCS England, 1979; Colyer Prize RCS England, 1993; Honorary Member, British Dental Association, 1993; Honorary Member, American Dental Association, 1994. Publications: Salivary Glands in Health and Disease (Co-author); Introduction to Oral Medicine (Co-author); Self Assessment: Manuals I and II (Co-Editor); Oral Manifestations of Systemic Disease. Recreations: golf; tennis; gardening; enjoying the pleasure of the countryside. Address: (h.) Greystones, Houston Road, Kilmacolm, Renfrewshire; T.-Kilmacolm 2001.

Mason, Derek Stevens, CBE (1986), JP, FRICS, FFB. Partner, John Baxter, Dunn and Gray, Chartered Quantity Surveyors, since 1970; Governor (Vice-chairman, since 1987), Hutchesons' Educational Trust, since 1972; b. 21.5.34, Glasgow; m., Jeanette M. Mason, OBE, JP; 2 s.; 1 d. Educ. Allan Glen's School, Glasgow; Royal Technical College (part-time). RICS: Chairman, West of Scotland Junior Sub-Branch, 1965-66, Chairman, Scottish Junior Branch, 1966-67; Councillor, Glasgow Corporation, 1970 and 1972-75, Glasgow District Council, 1974-84 (Deputy

Leader, Conservative Group, 1977-80; Bailie, 1977-80); Chairman, Glasgow Sports Promotion Council, 1977-80 (Hon. Vice-President, since 1980); Preceptor, Hutchesons' Hospital, 1978-80; JP, since 1977; Member, Master Court, Incorporation of Masons of Glasgow, since 1983, Collector, 1989-90, Deacon, 1991-92; Member, Merchants House of Glasgow; Chairman, Scottish Special Housing Association, 1981-89; Member, SCOTVEC Council, since 1993. Recreations: reading; current affairs; watching Clyde FC. Address: (h.) Carinya, 77 Newlands Road, Glasgow, G43 2JP; T.-0141-649 2665.

Mason, Douglas C., BSc. Member, Glenrothes Development Corporation, since 1985; Parliamentary Research Assistant, since 1979; Freelance Journalist, since 1977; b. 30.9.41, Dunfermline. Educ. Bradford Grammar School; St. Andrews University. Conservative Party Organising Secretary, 1969-77; Member, Fife County Council, 1967-70; Member, Kirkcaldy District Council, 1974-88; Member, Scottish Housing Advisory Committee, 1978-80; contested Central Fife, General Election, 1983; Vice-Convener, General Council Business Committee, St. Andrews University. Domestic Policy Adviser, Adam Smith Institute, since 1984. Publications: Allocation and Transfer of Council Houses (Co-author), 1980; The Qualgo Complex, 1984; Revising the Rating System, 1985; Room for Improvement, 1985; University Challenge, 1986; Time to Call Time, 1986; Ex Libris, 1986; Expounding the Arts, 1987; Licensed to Live, 1988; Pining for Profit, 1988; A Home for Enterprise, 1989; Privatizing the Posts, 1989; Wiser Councils and Shedding a Tier, 1989; Wood for the Trees, 1991; City in the Mist (Co-author), 1995. Recreations: books; music. Address: (h.) 84 Barnton Place, Glenrothes, Fife; T.-01592 758766.

Mason, Gavin John Finlay, MA, LLB. Solicitor; Secretary and Legal Adviser, Strathclyde Passenger Transport Executive, since 1984; b. 15.5.31, Bargeddie, Lanarkshire; m., Patricia Hunter Anderson; 1 s.; 1 d. Educ. Hamilton Academy; Glasgow University. Solicitor in private practice, until 1979, then local government service. Address: (h.) 3 Newark Drive, Glasgow, G41 4QJ; T.-0141-423 7496.

Mason, Jeanette Miller, OBE, JP. Deputy Chairman, Irvine Development Corporation, since 1991 (Member, 1983-91); Member, Rail Users Consultative Committee for Scotland, since 1987; b. 12.10.35, Glasgow; m., Derek S. Mason, CBE, JP (qv) 2 s.; 1 d. Educ. Strathbungo. Member, Scottish Committee, IBA, 1972-77; Children's Panel (Glasgow), 1971-77; Member, Scottish Gas Consumers' Council, 1982-86; Councillor, Strathclyde Regional Council, 1978-86; Chairman, Strathclyde Lunch Committee, Action Research for the Crippled Child, 1985-87, Chairman, Special Events Committee, since 1990; Member, DSS Appeals Tribunal, 1987-94; Panel Member for Scotland, Gas Consumers Council, 1986-94; Chairman, Irvine Housing Association, since 1994; Chairman, Whitley Council (Employers Side) for New Towns, since 1993. Recreations: current affairs; politics; reading; gardening. Address: (h.) Carinya, 77 Newlands Road, Glasgow, G43 2JP; T.-0141-649 2665.

Mason, Professor Emeritus John Kenyon French, CBE, MD, LLD, FRCPath, DMJ. Regius Professor of Forensic Medicine, Edinburgh University, 1973-85; b. 19.12.19, Lahore; m., Elizabeth Latham (deceased); 2 s. Educ. Downside School; Cambridge University. St. Bartholomew's Hospital. Regular Officer, Medical Branch, RAF, following War Service; Consultant in charge, RAF Department of Aviation and Forensic Pathology, 1957-73. President, British Association in Forensic Medicine, 1981-83; Swiney Prize in Jurisprudence, 1978. Publication: Forensic Medicine for Lawyers, 2nd Edition; Law and Medical Ethics, 4th Edition (Co-author); Medico-legal Aspects of Reproduction and Parenthood; Human Life and

Medical Practice. Address: (h.) 66 Craiglea Drive, Edinburgh, EH10 5PF; T.-0131-447 2301.

Mason, Professor John Stanley, BSc, PhD, CEng, FIMechE, FIMarE, MIMinE. Principal and Vice-Chancellor, Glasgow Caledonian University, since 1988; b. 30.1.34, Wigan; m., Florence; 2 s. Educ. Wigan Grammar School; Nottingham University. NCB, 1950-54 and 1958-59; Mathematics Master, 1959-62; Lt., Royal Navy; Middle East and Royal Naval Engineering College, Manadon, 1963-66; Principal Lecturer, Mechanical Engineering, Liverpool Polytechnic, 1966-68; Head of Division, Fluid Mechanics and Thermodynamics, Liverpool Polytechnic, 1969-73; Senior Research Fellow, Nottingham University, 1968-69; Head, School of Mechanical Engineering/Dean, Faculty of Engineering/Dean, Faculty of Technology, Thames Polytechnic, 1973-87; Depute Director, Glasgow College, 1987-88; Council Member, SERC, since 1990; Member, Link Steering Group, since 1989; Board Member, Glasgow Development Agency, since 1992; industrial consultancy; published 125 papers, 1971-91; awarded Silver Plate, International Powder and Bulk Solids Conference, 1985. Recreations: travel; sport. Address: (b.) Glasgow Caledonian University, Cowcaddens Road, Glasgow, G4 0BA; T.-041-331 3113.

Mason, Keith Stirling, LLB (Hons), NP. Chief Administrative Officer, Dunfermline District Council, since 1991; Clerk of the Peace, Dunfermline, since 1991; b. 4.6.55, Montrose. Educ. Kirkcaldy High School; Edinburgh University. Legal apprenticeship, Dundas & Wilson, CS, Edinburgh; Legal Assistant, Dunfermline District Council, 1979-82, Senior Legal Assistant, 1982-85; Principal Solicitor, 1985-91. Clerk to Standing Conference of Local Authorities in the Forth Estuary. Recreations: squash; public transport systems; Church elder; Crusaders leader. Address: (b.) City Chambers, Kirkgate, Dunfermline; T.-01383 722711.

Mason, Rev. Canon Kenneth Staveley, BD, BSc, ARCS. Canon, St. Mary's Cathedral, Edinburgh; Pantonian Professor of Theology, since 1989; b. 1.11.31, Winnipeg, Canada; m., Barbara Thomson; 1 s.; 1 d. Educ. Imperial College of Science and Technology, London; Wells Theological College. Vicar, Allerthorpe with Thornton and Melbourne, Diocese of York, 1963-69; Sub-Warden and Librarian, St. Augustine's College, Canterbury, 1969-76; Director and Principal, Canterbury School of Ministry, 1976-89; Examining Chaplain to Archbishop of Canterbury, 1977-91. Recreation: bird watching. Address: (b.) 9c Rosebery Crescent, Edinburgh EH12 5JP; T.-0131-337 0500.

Massie, Allan Johnstone, BA, FRSL. Author and Journalist; b. 16.10.38, Singapore; m., Alison Langlands; 2 s.; 1 d. Educ. Drumtochty Castle; Trinity College, Glenalmond; Trinity College, Cambridge. Schoolmaster, Drumtochty Castle, 1960-71; taught EFL, 1972-75; Creative Writing Fellow, Edinburgh University, 1982-84, Glasgow and Strathclyde Universities, 1985-86; Editor, New Edinburgh Review, 1982-84; Fiction Reviewer, The Scotsman, since 1975; Television Critic, Sunday Standard, 1981-83 (Fraser of Allander Award, Critic of the Year, 1982); Sports Columnist, Glasgow Herald, 1985-88; Columnist: Daily Telegraph, Daily Mail. Publications: (novels): Change and Decay in all around I see; The Last Peacock; The Death of Men (Scottish Arts Council Book Award); One Night in Winter; Augustus; A Question of Loyalties; The Sins of the Father; Tiberius; The Hanging Tree; Caesar; These Enchanted Woods; The Ragged Lion; King David; (non-fiction): Muriel Spark; Ill Met by Gaslight; The Caesars; Portrait of Scottish Rugby; Colette; 101 Great Scots; Byron's Travels; Glasgow; Edinburgh; (as Editor): Edinburgh and the Borders in Verse; (radio play): Quintet in October; (plays): The Minstrel and the Shirra; First-Class Passengers. Recreations: reading; watching rugby, cricket, racing; walking the dogs. Address: (h.) Thirladean House, Selkirk, TD7 5LU; T.-Selkirk 20393.

Masson, Alastair H.B., BA, MB, ChB, FRCSEdin, FFARCS. President, British Society of the History of Medicine; Consultant Anaesthetist, Edinburgh Royal Infirmary (retired); b. 30.1.25, Bathgate; m., Marjorie Nan Paisley-Whyte; 3 s.; 1 d. Educ. Bathgate Academy; Edinburgh University. Visiting Professor of Anesthesiology, South Western Medical School, Dallas, Texas, 1962-63. President, Scottish Society of Anaesthetists, 1978-79; Honorary Archivist, Royal College of Surgeons, Edinburgh; President, Scottish Society of the History of Medicine, 1984-87. Recreations: golf; hill-walking; music; travel. Address: (h.) 28 Beechmount Park, Edinburgh.

Masterman, Eileen Mary, MA (Hons). Director, Royal Institution of Chartered Surveyors in Scotland, since 1992; Member, Building Standards Advisory Committee, since 1994; Director, Edinburgh Chamber of Commerce, since 1994; b. Spennymoor, Co. Durham; m., Norman A. Fiddes; 2 d. Educ. St. Anthony's School for Girls, Sunderland; Dundee University. Research Assistant, Dundee University, 1976-80; Investigator and Complaints Examiner, Commissioner for Local Administration in Scotland, 1980-90; Advocates' Clerk/Business Manager, Faculty of Advocates, 1990-92. Recreation: aerobics. Address: (b.) 9 Manor Place, Edinburgh, EH3 7DN; T.-0131-225 7078.

Masters, Christopher, BSc (Hons), PhD, AKC. Chief Executive, Christian Salvesen PLC, since 1989; b. 2.5.47, Northallerton; m., Gillian Mary Hodson; 2 d. Educ. Richmond School; King's College, London; Leeds University. Shell Research BV/Shell Chemicals UK Ltd., 1971-77; joined Christian Salvesen as Business Development Manager, 1979; transferred to Christian Salvesen Inc., USA, 1982, as Director of Planning; Managing Director, Christian Salvesen Seafoods, 1983; Managing Director, Industrial Services Division, 1985; appointed a Director, Christian Salvesen PLC, 1987. Member, Scottish Economic Council, since 1991; Chairman, Scottish Board of Young Enterprise, since 1994; Chairman, Quality Assessment Committee of Higher Education Funding Council, since 1991; Non-Executive Director: British Assets Trust, since 1989, Scottish Widows, since 1991, Scottish Chamber Orchestra Trust, since 1993; Scottish Opera, since 1994. Recreations: wines; music. Address: (b.) 50 East Fettes Avenue, Edinburgh, EH4 1EQ; T.-0131-552 7101.

Masterton, Gavin George, FIB (Scot). General Manager, Bank of Scotland, since 1986, Deputy Treasurer, since 1992; b. 19.11.41, Dunfermline; m., Sheila; 3 d. Educ. Dunfermline High School; Harvard University (AMP). Began banking career with British Linen Bank, 1957; branch banking for several years, then to various Head Office functions; appointed Assistant General Manager; initiated bank's move into management buy-out market. Address: (b.) Bank of Scotland, The Mound, Edinburgh.

Mather, John, CBE, FSCA, FCIS, FCIT. Executive Chairman, Clydeport Ltd.; b. 17.12.36, Glasgow. Chairman, Ardrossan Harbour Co. Ltd.; Member, Council, British Ports Association; Member, Council, Company and Commercial Accountants; Immediate Past President, International Association of Ports and Harbors of the World; Visiting Professor, Strathclyde University Department of Engineering. Address: (b.) 16 Robertson Street, Glasgow, G2 8DS; T.-0141-221 8733.

Matheson, Alexander, OBE, FRPharmS, MRSH, DL, JP. Chairman, Western Isles Health Board (Member, since 1973; Vice-Chairman, 1991-93); b. 16.11.41, Stornoway; m., Irene Mary Davidson, BSc, MSc; 2 s.; 2 d. Educ. Nicolson Institute, Stornoway; Robert Gordon's Institute of Technology, Aberdeen. Chairman, Stornoway Pier and Harbour Commission, since 1991 (Member, since 1968); Member, Stornoway Trust Estate, since 1967 (Chairman, 1971-81); Chairman, Stornoway Historical Society; Chairman, Western Isles Development Fund, since 1972; Member, Stornoway Town Council, 1967-75; Provost of Stornoway, 1971-75; Member, Ross and Cromarty County Council, 1967-75; Member, Western Isles Islands Council, 1974-94 (Chairman, Development Services, 1974-80, Vice-Convener, 1980-82, Convener, 1982-90); President, Islands Commission of the Conference of Peripheral Maritime Regions of Europe, 1987-91 and 1993-94; Honorary Sheriff, since 1972; Vice Lieutenant, Western Isles Islands Area; Director, Western Isles Enterprise; Director, Callanish Ltd.; Chairman and Superintendent Pharmacist, Roderick Smith Ltd., Stornoway. Address: (h.) 33 Newton Street, Stornoway, Isle of Lewis; T.-01851 702082.

Matheson, Allen Short, FRIBA, PPRIAS, MRTPI. Retired Partner, Matheson Gleave Partnership; Member, Royal Fine Art Commission for Scotland; b. 28.2.26, Egypt; m., Catherine Anne; 2 s. Educ. George Watson's College; Edinburgh College of Art. Past President, Royal Incorporation of Architects in Scotland; Past Chairman, Scottish Construction Industry Group; former Vice-Chairman, Board of Governors, Glasgow School of Art; former Director, Glasgow Chamber of Commerce; Past Chairman, Joint Standing Committee of Architects, Surveyors and Building Contractors. Address: (h.) 11 Spence Street, Glasgow, G20 0AW; T.-0141-946 5670.

Matheson, Andrew James, BSc, PhD. Assistant Secretary, Food Safety and Animal Health Division, Scottish Office, Agriculture and Fisheries Department, since 1994; b. 13.10.37, Inverness; m., Muriel Oliver Davidson; 3 d. Educ. Inverness Royal Academy; Edinburgh University. Research Fellow, Department of Electrical Engineering, Glasgow University, 1962-65; Lecturer, then Senior Lecturer, Department of Chemistry, Essex University, 1965-75; Principal, Scottish Office, 1975-89; Director of Manpower, NHS in Scotland Management Executive, 1990-94. Recreations: Church organist; choral singing; Munros compleated. Address: (b.) Pentland House, 47 Robb's Loan, Edinburgh EH14 1TW; T.-0131-244 6159.

Matheson, Very Rev. James Gunn, MA, BD. Moderator, General Assembly of the Church of Scotland, 1975-76; Minister, Portree, 1973-79; b. 1.3.12.

Matheson, Lindsay S.G., MA, MLitt. Headmaster, Milne's High School, Fochabers, since 1985; b. 2.10.44, Edinburgh; m., Katherine R.; 2 d. Educ. Otago Boys' High School, Dunedin; George Watson's, Edinburgh; St. Andrews University; Oxford University. History Teacher, Banff Academy, 1970-72; Principal Teacher of History, Lochaber High School, 1972-80; Assistant Rector, Inverurie Academy, 1980-85. Recreations: cycling; golf; bridge. Address: (h.0 15 Woodside Place, Fochabers; T.-01343 820864.

Matheson, Susan Margaret Graham, BSc (Soc Sci). Director, Family Mediation Scotland, since 1988; b. 6.6.49, Tarbert, Harris; 1 d. Educ. St. George's School for Girls, Edinburgh; Edinburgh University. Antique dealer, 1971-73; Research Officer, then Senior Research Officer, Scottish Office Central Research Unit, 1973-88. Vice-Convener, Scottish Council for Single Parents, since 1993; Committee Member, Stepfamily Scotland, since 1993. Publications: several Government research reports and other publications. Recreation: skiing. Address: (b.) 127 Rose Street South Lane, Edinburgh, EH2 4BB; T.-0131-220 1610.

Mathewson, David Carr, BSc, CA. Merchant Banker; Director, Noble Grossart Limited, since 1989; b. 26.7.47, Broughty Ferry; m., Jan McIntyre; 1 s.; 1 d. Educ. Daniel Stewart's College, Edinburgh; St. Andrews University.

Deloitte Haskins & Sells, Edinburgh, 1968-72; Williams Glyn & Co., London, 1972-75; Nedbank Group, South Africa, 1976-86; Noble Grossart Limited, since 1986; Director, Quicks Group plc, since 1991, Rodime plc, since 1992. Recreations: family interests; golf; skiing; athletics. Address: (b.) 48 Queen Street, Edinburgh, EH2 3NR; T.-0131-226 7011.

Mathewson, George Ross, CBE, BSc, PHD, MBA, LLD, FRSE, CEng, MIEE, CBIM, FCIBS. Group Chief Executive, Royal Bank of Scotland Group plc, Royal Bank of Scotland plc, since 1992; Director, Strategic Planning and Development, Royal Bank of Scotland Group plc, Royal Bank of Scotland plc, since 1987; Director: Scottish Investment Trust Ltd., since 1981, EFTPOS UK Ltd., since 1988, Royal Bank Group Services Ltd., since 1987, Citizens Financial Group, since 1989, Royal Scottish Assurance plc, since 1989, Royal Santander Financial Services SA, since 1989, Direct Line Insurance plc, since 1990; b. 14.5.40, Dunfermline; m., Sheila Alexandra Graham Bennett; 2 s. Educ. Perth Academy; St. Andrews University; Canisius College, Buffalo, New York. Assistant Lecturer, St. Andrews University, 1964-67; Systems Engineer (various positions), Bell Aerospace, Buffalo, New York, 1967-72; ICFC: Executive in Edinburgh Area Office, 1972-81, Area Manager, 1974-79, Director and Assistant General Manager, 1979-81; Chief Executive, Scottish Development Agency, 1981-87. Recreations: tennis; skiing; geriatric rugby; golf; business. Address: (h.) 29 Saxe Coburg Place, Edinburgh, EH3 5BP.

Mathie, Hugh Alexander, MA, MEd. Rector, McLaren High School, Callander, since 1985; b. 30.7.35, Dundee; m., Margaret Black; 2 s.; 1 d. Educ. Morgan Academy, Dundee; St. Andrews University. Teacher of Classics, Kilsyth Academy and Kirkton High School, Dundee; Principal Teacher of Classics, Kilsyth Academy and Cumbernauld High School; Assistant Rector, Depute Rector, Greenfaulds High School; Rector, Kilsyth Academy. Recreations: hillwalking; golf. Address: (h.) Welwyn, Firpark Terrace, Cambusbarron, Stirling; T.-Stirling 472900.

Mathieson, John George, CBE, TD, DL, BL, WS. Solicitor; Chairman, Thorntons, WS, Tayside; b. 15.6.32, Argyll; m., Shirley Bidder; 1 s.; 1 d. Educ. George Watson's College, Edinburgh; Glasgow University. Territorial Army, 1951-86: Commanding Officer The Highland Regiment RA, TA Colonel for Highlands, Honorary Colonel 105 Regiment RA(TA), Chairman, Highlands TA Association; ADC TA, the Queen, 1975-80. Commenced practice as Solicitor, Glasgow, 1955; Clark Oliver, Arbroath, 1957; Scottish Director, Woolwich Building Society, 1975; Chairman, Independent Tribunal, 1992; Chairman, Arbroath Branch, Royal British Legion and Earl Haig Fund; Deputy Lieutenant, Angus, 1977; Chairman, Royal Artillery Council for Scotland; Honorary President, Angus Bn., Boys' Brigade; Elder, Colliston Parish Church. Recreations: shooting; golf; gardening. Address: (h.) Willanyards, Colliston, Arbroath, Angus; T.-01241 890286.

Matthews, Baird, BL. Solicitor in private practice, since 1950; Honorary Sheriff, Kirkcudbright and Stranraer; b. 19.1.25, Newton Stewart; m., Mary Thomson Hope; 2 s.; 1 d. Educ. Douglas Ewart High School; Edinburgh University. Commissioned, Royal Scots Fusiliers, 1944; demobilised as Captain, 1st Bn., 1947; Partner, A. B. & A. Matthews, Solicitors, Newton Stewart, since 1950; Clerk to General Commissioners of Income Tax, Stranraer and Newton Stewart Districts, from 1952; Burgh Prosecutor, Newton Stewart, from 1968; Depute Procurator Fiscal for Wigtownshire, 1970; Chairman, Board of Local Directors, General Accident Fire and Life Assurance Corporation, 1988; Dean of Faculty of Stewartry of Kirkcudbright Solicitors, 1979; Dean of Faculty of Solicitors of the District of Wigtown, 1983; Chairman, Appeals Tribunal,

1984. Recreations: golf; curling. Address: (b.) Bank of Scotland Buildings, Newton Stewart, Wigtownshire; T.-01671 404100.

Matthews, Herbert Eric, MA (Oxon), BPhil (Oxon). Head, Department of Philosophy, Aberdeen University, since 1989; Reader in Philosophy, since 1993; b. 24.10.36, Liverpool; m., Hellen Kilpatrick Matthews; 2 s. Educ. Liverpool Institute High School for Boys; St. John's College, Oxford. Lecturer, Department of Logic, Aberdeen University, 1963. Publications: numerous articles in learned journals; translations of works of German philosophy; The Philosophy of Thomas Reid (Editor); Philosophy and Health Care (Editor). Recreations: cinema; reading; walking; cycling. Address: (b.) Department of Philosophy, Aberdeen University, Aberdeen, AB9 2UB; T.-01224 272367.

Matthews, Professor John Burr Lumley, MA, DPhil, FRSE. Director and Secretary, Scottish Association for Marine Science; Honorary Professor, Stirling University, since 1984; b. 23.4.35, Isleworth; m., Jane Rosemary; 1 s.; 2 d. Educ. Warwick School; Oxford University. Research Scientist (Zooplankton), Oceanographic Laboratory, Edinburgh, 1961-67; Senior Lecturer, Department of Marine Biology, then Professor of Marine Biology, University of Bergen, 1967-84; Visiting Professor, University of British Columbia, 1977-78; Director, NERC Dunstaffnage Marine Laboratory, 1988-94. Recreations: cross country skiing; gardening; wine-making. Address: (h.) Grianaig, Rockfield Road, Oban, PA34 5DH; T.-01631 62734.

Mattock, Professor John Nicholas, MA, PhD. Professor of Arabic and Islamic Studies, Glasgow University, since 1987; b. 6.1.38, Horsham. Educ. Christ's Hospital; Pembroke College, Cambridge. Research Fellow, Pembroke College, Cambridge, 1963-65; Lecturer in Arabic and Islamic Studies, then Senior Lecturer, Glasgow University, 1965-87. Member, Editorial Board, Journal of Arabic Literature, since 1970; British Representative, European Union of Arabists and Islamists, since 1986; President, European Union of Arabists and Islamists, 1990-94. Address: (b.) Department of Arabic and Islamic Studies, Glasgow University, Glasgow, G12 8QQ; T.-0141-330 5586.

Mauchline, John, PhD, DSc, CBiol, FIBiol, FRSE. Research Biologist, Scottish Association for Marine Science, since 1962; UK Editor, Marine Biology, 1977-95; b. 1.7.33, Motherwell; m., Isobel Hopkins Warden; 1 s.; 2 d. Educ. High School of Glasgow; Glasgow University. Research Biologist, UKAEA, 1958-62. Visiting Professor, University of Tokyo, 1976; Visiting Scholar, Memorial University of Newfoundland, 1987. Recreations: fly fishing; painting. Address: (b.) Dunstaffnage, Marine Research Laboratory, P.O. Box 3, Oban, PA34 4AD; T.-Oban 62244.

Maund, Robert Graham, BSc, DipTP, FRTPI. Director of Physical Planning, Strathclyde Regional Council, since 1984; b. 10.11.38, Cheshire; m., Judith L.; 3 s.; 1 d. Educ. Manchester University. City of Manchester: trainee graduate engineer, various planning posts, Assistant City Planning Officer; Greater Manchester Council: Assistant County Planning Officer, Deputy County Planning Officer. Recreations: walking; photography; listening to music; reading; theatre. Address: (b.) Strathclyde House, 20 India Street, Glasgow, G2 4PF; T.-0141-227 3626.

Maurel, Paul Dominic. Theatre Director, Eden Court Theatre, Inverness, since 1994; b. 27.5.62, London. Educ. Guildhall School of Music and Drama. Executive Administrator, Belfast Civic Arts Theatre, 1992-94. Member, Board of Directors, SALVO. Recreations: travel; food and drink; Star Trek movies. Address: (b.) Eden Court Theatre, Bishops Road, Inverness, IV3 5SA; T.-01463 239841.

Maver, Professor Thomas Watt, BSc (Hons), PhD, FInstE, FRSA, HonFRIAS. Professor of Computer Aided Design, Department of Architecture and Building Science, and Director of the Graduate School, Strathclyde University, since 1982 (Head of Department, 1983-85, 1988-91); b. 10.3.38, Glasgow; m., Avril Elizabeth Cuthbertson; 2 d. Educ. Eastwood Secondary School; Glasgow University. Special Research Fellow, Engineering Faculty, Glasgow University, 1961-67; Strathclyde University: Research Fellow, School of Architecture, 1967-70, Director, Architecture and Building Aids Computer Unit, Strathclyde, since 1970; Visiting Professor: Technical University Eindhoven, Universiti Sains Malaysia, University of Rome (La Sapienza); Past Chairman, Design Research Society; Royal Society Esso Gold Medal, 1989; Founder, CAAD Futures and FCAADE. Recreations: family; farming. Address: (h.) 8 Kew Terrace, Glasgow, G12; T.-0141-339 7185.

Mavor, Professor John, BSc, PhD, DSc (Eng), FRSE, FEng, FIEEE, CPhys, FInstP, CEng, FIEE. Principal and Vice-Chancellor, Napier University, since 1994; b. 18.7.42, Kilwinning; m., Susan Christina; 2 d. Educ. Bromley Technical High School; City University; London University. AEI Research Laboratories, London, 1964-65; Texas Instruments Ltd., Bedford, 1968-70; Emihus Microcomponents Ltd., Glenrothes, 1970-71; Edinburgh University: joined 1971, first holder, Lothian Chair of Microelectronics, 1980-86, Head, Department of Electrical Engineering, 1984-89, Chairman, School of Engineering, 1987-89, Dean, Faculty of Science & Engineering, 1989-94, Chair of Electrical Enginering, 1986-94. Recreations: gardening; hill-walking. Address: (b.) Napier University, Craiglockhart Campus, 219 Colinton Road, Edinburgh EH14 1DJ; T.-0131-455 4600.

Maxton, John Alston. BA (Oxon), DipEd (Oxon). MP (Labour), Glasgow Cathcart, since 1979; b. 5.5.36, Oxford; m., Christine Elspeth; 3 s. Educ. Lord Williams Grammar School, Thame; University College, Oxford. Lecturer in Social Studies, Hamilton College of Education, before entering Parliament; Chairman, Association of Lecturers in Colleges of Education in Scotland, 1974-78; Member, Scottish Select Committee, 1980-83, Public Accounts Committee, 1983-84; Opposition Treasury and Scottish Whip, 1984-85; Opoosition Scottish Front Bench Spokesperson on Health, Local Government and Transport, 1985-87, on Industry and Local Government Finance, 1987-92; Member, National Heritage Select Committee. Recreations: listenng to jazz (Director, Glasgow International Jazz Festival); running. Address: (h.) 37 Larch Grove, Hamilton, ML3 8NF; T.-01698 43847.

Maxwell, Donald, MA. Professional Singer; b. 12.12.48, Perth; m., Alison Jayne Norman. Educ. Perth Academy; Edinburgh University. Former Teacher of Geography; since 1976, professional Singer with British opera companies and orchestras; Principal Baritone, Scottish Opera, 1978-82; Principal Baritone, Welsh National Opera, 1982-85; guest appearances, Royal Opera House, London, as well as France, Belgium, Germany, Canada, Argentina, USA, Italy, Japan; Edinburgh Festival, notably as Falstaff; The Music Box, with Linda Ormiston. Recreation: railways. Address: (b.) c/o 6 Murray Crescent, Perth.

Maxwell, Gordon Stirling, MA, FSA, FSA Scot. Archaeologist and Author; b. 21.3.38, Edinburgh; m., Kathleen Mary King; 2 d. Educ. Daniel Stewart's College, Edinburgh; St. Andrews University. Investigator (Archaeological), Royal Commission on the Ancient and Historical Monuments of Scotland, 1964-86; Head of Field Survey, RCAHMS, 1986-91, Head of Archaeology, 1991-95; President, Society of Antiquaries of Scotland, since 1993. Publications: Rome's North-West Frontier: The Antonine Wall (Co-author), 1983; The Impact of Aerial Reconnaissance on Archaeology (Editor), 1983; The Romans in Scotland, 1989; A Battle Lost: Romans and Caledonians at Mons Graupius, 1990. Recreations: archaeology; gardening; aviation; Scottish literature. Address: (h.) Micklegarth, 72A High Street, Aberdour, Fife, KY3 0SW; T.-01383 860796.

Maxwell, Ingval, DA, RIBA, FRIAS, FSA Scot. Director, Technical Conservation Research and Education, Historic Scotland, since 1993; b. 28.5.44, Penpont; m., Susan Isabel Maclean; 1 s.; 1 d. Educ. Dumfries Academy; Duncan of Jordanstone College of Art, Dundee. Joined Ministry of Public Buildings and Works as Architect, 1969; Area Architect, then Principal Architect, Ancient Monuments Branch, 1972-85; Assistant Director of Works, Historic Scotland, 1985-93; RIBA Research Award, 1970-71; RIAS Thomas Ross Award, 1988; Chairman, Scottish Vernacular Buildings Working Group, 1990-94; Member, Great Britain Technical Forum; Member, RIAS Conservation Working Group; Member, SDA Conservation Bureau Advisory Panel, 1989-91. Recreations: photography; astronomy; aircraft; farm buildings. Address: (h.) 135 Mayfield Road, Edinburgh, EH9 3AN.

Maxwell, (Thomas) Fordyce, MBE. Diary Editor, Columnist, Agricultural Editor, The Scotsman, since 1989; b. 21.8.45, Northumberland; m., Liz (Elizabeth Duncan); 1 s.; 1 d. Educ. Berwick Grammar School; Harper Adams Agricultural College. Farming News, 1967-69; The Scotsman: Assistant Agricultural Editor, 1969-75, Agricultural Editor, 1975-77; farming/freelance, 1977-89; rejoined The Scotsman, 1989. Seaton Award, 1992; author of three books. Recreations: family; gardening; reading. Address: (b.) 20 North Bridge, Edinburgh; T.-0131-243 3323.

Maxwell, Professor Thomas Jefferson, BSc, PhD. Director, Macaulay Land Use Research Institute, since 1987 (Head, Animal Production Department, Hill Farming Research Organisation, 1981-87); Honorary Research Professor, Aberdeen University; b. 7.10.40, Aspatria, Cumbria; m., Christine Patrick Speedie; 1 s.; 1 d. Educ. Silcoates School, Wakefield; Edinburgh University. Specialist Animal Production Adviser, East of Scotland College of Agriculture, 1967-70; Research Scientist, Animal Production Department, Hill Farming Research Organisation, 1970-81. Recreations: reading; hill-walking; gardening. Address: (b.) Macaulay Land Use Research Institute, Craigiebuckler, Aberdeen.

Maxwell-Irving, Alastair Michael Tivey, BSc, CEng, MIEE, MIMgt, FSAScot. Antiquarian and Archaeologist; b. 1.10.35, Witham, Essex; m., Esther Mary Hamilton, MA, LLB. Educ. Lancing College; London University; Stirling University. General Electric Company, 1957; English Electric Company, 1960; Assistant Factor, Annandale Estates, 1966; Weir Pumps Ltd., 1970-91; founder Member and Secretary, 1975-78, Central Scotland Branch, British Institute of Management; Treasurer, Logie Community Council. Publications: Genealogy of the Irvings of Dumfries, 1965; The Irvings of Bonshaw, 1968; The Irvings of Dumfries, 1968; Lochwood Castle, 1968; Early Firearms and their Influence on the Military and Domestic Architecture of the Borders, 1974; Cramalt Tower: Historical Survey and Excavations, 1977-79, 1982; Borthwick Castle: Excavations 1979, 1982; Andrew Dunlop (Clockmakers' Company 1701-32), 1984; Hoddom Castle: A Reappraisal of its Architecture and Place in History, 1989; Lochwood Castle, 1990; The Castles of Buittle, 1991; Lockerbie Tower, 1992. Recreations: architecture and history of the Border towers of Scotland; archaeology; family history and genealogy; Florence and the art and architecture of Tuscany; horology; heraldry; photography; gardening. Address: (h.) Telford House, Blairlogie, Stirling, FK9 5PX.

Maxwell-Scott, Dame Jean (Mary Monica), DCVO (1984). Lady in Waiting to Princess Alice, Duchess of

Gloucester, since 1959; b. 8.6.23. VAD Red Cross Nurse, 1941-46; great-great-great grand-daughter of Sir Walter Scott. Address: (h.) Abbotsford, Melrose, Roxburghshire, TD6 9BQ.

Maxwell-Scott, Patricia Mary, OBE. Honorary Sheriff of Selkirk, since 1971; b. 11.3.21, Curragh, Dublin; m., Harold Hugh Christian Boulton. Educ. Convent des Oiseaux, Westgate on Sea, Kent. ATP, 1942-45. Great-great-great grand-daughter of Sir Walter Scott. Recreations: travelling; reading. Address: (h.) Abbotsford, Melrose, TD6 9BQ; T.-01896 2043.

May, David Jeans, MA (Hons). Rector, Craigie High School, Dundee, since 1990; b. 28.12.45, Aberdeen; m., Anne Elizabeth Raeside Eastop; 1 s.; 1 d. Educ. Robert Gordon's College, Aberdeen; Aberdeen University; Jordanhill College of Education. Teacher, St. Columba's, Gourock, 1973-74; Assistant Principal Teacher of Social Subjects, Castlehead High, Paisley, 1974-78; Principal Teacher of Modern Studies/Economics, Grange Secondary, Glasgow, 1978-84; Assistant Head Teacher, Dunoon Grammar School, 1984-87; Deputy Rector, Montrose Academy, 1987-90. Convener, SEB Modern Studies Panel; Member, Secretary of State for Scotland's Working Group on Environmental Education. Recreations: hill-walking; squash; gardening. Address: (h.) Evanston, Lamondfauld Lane, Hillside, Montrose, DD10 9HY; T.-0167 4830673.

May, Douglas James, LLB. Queen's Counsel, since 1989; b. 7.5.46, Edinburgh. Educ. George Heriot's; Edinburgh University. Advocate, 1971; Temporary Sheriff, since 1990; Social Security Commissioner, Child Support Commissioner, since 1993; Parliamentary candidate (Conservative), Edinburgh East, 1974, Glasgow Cathcart, 1983. Recreations: golf (Captain, Scotland Universities Golfing Society, 1990-91); photography (LRPS, 1995); travel. Address: 23 Melville Street, Edinburgh; T.-0131-225 2201.

May, Malcolm Stuart, BA, BD, STM, CQSW. Chief Officer, Dundee Voluntary Action, since 1979; b. 9.9.40, Isle of Shapinsay, Orkney; m., Alison Wood; 1 s.; 1 d. Educ. Kilmarnock Academy; The Gordon Schools, Huntly; Hamilton Academy; Queen's University, Belfast; Glasgow University; Union Theological Seminary, New York. Assistant Minister, The Old Kirk, West Pilton, Edinburgh, 1966-68; staff, Iona Community, Glasgow, 1968-72; social work training, 1972-73; Training Officer, Scottish Council for Voluntary Organisations, 1973-78. Member, Board of Management, Dundee College; Non-Executive Director, Tayside Health Board. Recreations: reading; choral singing; hill-walking. Address: (b.) Kandahar House, 72 Meadowside, Dundee, DD1 1EN.

Mayfield, Hon. Lord (Ian MacDonald), MC (1945), QC (Scot). Former Senator of the College of Justice in Scotland; b. 26.5.21. Sheriff Principal of Dumfries and Galloway, 1973; President, Industrial Tribunals for Scotland, 1973-81; Scottish Chairman, Employment Appeal Tribunal, 1986-92.

Mearns, Anne, MA (Hons), DipTP, MRTPI, MIMgt. Chief Executive, Aberdeen District Council, since 1994; b. 20.8.47, Glasgow. Educ. Hyndland Secondary School; Glasgow University; Strathclyde University. Planning Assistant, Coatbridge Burgh, 1969; Planner, Lanark County Council, 1969-73; Senior Planner (Research), Glasgow Corporation, 1973-75; Supervisory Planner (Policy Analysis), 1975-78, Assistant Chief, 1978-79, Chief Planner (Policy and Intelligence), 1979-87, Chief Corporate Planner, Town Clerk's Office, Glasgow District Council, 1987-89; Depute Town Clerk (Corporate Policy Development), Glasgow District Council, 1989-94. Member, Editorial Board, British Urban and Regional Information Systems Association; Member, Council,

Glasgow and West of Scotland Institute of Public Administration; Member, Advisory Board, Graduate School of Environmental Studies, Strathclyde University. Recreations: cities; canine rambles; cultural and cerebral pursuits; clarsach. Address: (b.) The Town House, Aberdeen AB9 1FY; T.-01224 522500.

Meek, Brian Alexander, OBE, JP. Columnist, The Herald; Member, Conservative Group, Edinburgh District Council, since 1992; b. 8.2.39, Edinburgh; m., Frances C. Horsburgh; 1 s.; 1 d. Educ. Royal High School, Edinburgh; Edinburgh Secretarial College. Joined Scotsman Publications as trainee, then Sub-Editor, Features Writer; transferred to Express Newspapers as Feature Writer, Leader Writer and Rugby Correspondent; elected, Edinburgh Corporation, 1969; Leader, Conservative Group, 1970-72; elected as Bailie, 1972; Convener, Lothian Regional Council, 1982-86; Vice-President, Scottish Conservative and Unionist Association, 1989-92. Address: (b.) Lothian Regional Council, Parliament Square, Edinburgh; T.-0131-229 9292.

Meek, David, MA, MEd. Rector, Portree High School, since 1994; b. 20.7.54, Bonnybridge; m., Sheena Flora Meek; 2 s. Educ. Falkirk High School; Glasgow University. Teacher, Renfrew High School; Assistant Principal Teacher, Vale of Leven Academy; Principal Teacher of English, then Assistant Head Teacher, Boclair Academy; Inspector, Quality Assurance Unit, Strathclyde. Recreations: music; reading; theology; education. Address: (h.) An Acarsaid, Viewfield Road, Portree, Isle of Skye, IV51 9ES; T.-01478 612252.

Meek, Professor Donald Eachann MacDonald, MA (Cantab), MA, PhD (Glas), FRHistS. Professor of Celtic, Aberdeen University, since 1993; b. 16.5.49, Glasgow, brought up in Tiree; m., Rachel Jane Rogers; 2 d. Educ. Oban High School; Glasgow University; Emmanuel College, Cambridge. Lecturer, Senior Lecturer and Reader in Celtic, Edinburgh University, 1979-92. Assistant Editor, Historical Dictionary of Scottish Gaelic, Glasgow University, 1973-79; Honorary Secretary, Gaelic Society of Glasgow, 1974-79; Member, Gaelic Advisory Committee to Broadcasting Council for Scotland, 1976-78; Member, Gaelic Panel, National Bible Society of Scotland, since 1978; President, Edinburgh and Lothians Baptist Association, 1992-93; Clerk and Treasurer, Board of Celtic Studies (Scotland), since 1994; Editor, 1992 edition, Gaelic Bible; a General Editor, Dictionary of Scottish Church History and Theology, 1993; Baptist lay preacher. Publications: books include Mairi Mhor nan Oran, 1977; The Campbell Collection of Gaelic Proverbs and Proverbial Sayings, 1978; Island Harvest: A History of Tiree Baptist Church, 1988; Sunshine and Shadow: the story of the Baptists of Mull, 1991; A Mind for Mission: essays (Editor), 1992. Recreations: family activities; getting to know the Highlands. Address: (h.) 50 Dunecht Road, Westhill, Skene, AB32 6RH; T.-01224 742668.

Meldrum, Angus Alexander, BSc, DIA. Managing Director, Tennent Caledonian Breweries Ltd., since 1992; Director, Bass Ireland Ltd., since 1981; Director, Maclay's Brewery & Co. Ltd., since 1992; b. 7.11.45, Stornoway; m., Anne-Marie; 1 s. Educ. Kingussie School; Edinburgh University; Bath University Management School. Joined Bass plc, London, 1971; Tennent Caledonian Breweries Ltd., 1978; Brands Marketing Director, Bass Brewers Ltd., Burton-on-Trent, 1990-92. President, Brewers Association of Scotland, 1992-94. Recreations: fishing; shooting; sport. Address: (b.) 110 Bath Street, Glasgow, G2 2ET; T.-0141-552 6552.

Meldrum, James, MA. Registrar General for Scotland, since 1994; b. 9.8.52, Kirkintilloch. Educ. Lenzie Academy; Glasgow University. Administration Trainee/HEO (Admin), Scottish Office, 1973-79; Principal grade posts, Scottish

Economic Planning Department, Scottish Development Department, Scottish Office Personnel Division, 1979-86; Deputy Director, Scottish Courts Administration, 1986-91; Head, Investment Assistance Division, Scottish Office Industry Department, 1991-94. Address: (b.) New Register House, Edinburgh EH1 3YT; T.-0131-334 0380.

Mellon, Sir James, KCMG, MA. Chairman, Scottish Homes, since 1989; Chairman, Regent Pacific Corporate Finance; Vice-President, English-Speaking Union Scotland, since 1991; Director, Scottish American Investment Company PLC, since 1989; Chairman, Thamesmead Town, since 1993; b. 25.1.29, Glasgow; m., 1, Frances Murray (dec.); 2, Philippa Shuttleworth; 1 s.; 3 d. Educ. Glasgow University. Department of Agriculture for Scotland, 1953-60; Agricultural Attache, Copenhagen and The Hague, 1960-63; Foreign Office, 1963-64; Head of Chancery, Dakar, 1964-66; UK Delegation to European Communities, 1967-72; Counsellor, 1970; Foreign and Commonwealth Office: Head, Science and Technology Department, 1973-75, Commercial Counsellor, East Berlin, 1975-76, Head, Trade Relations and Export Department, 1976-78; High Commissioner in Ghana and Ambassador to Togo, 1978-83; Ambassador to Denmark, 1983-86; Director-General for Trade and Investment, USA, and Consul General, New York, 1986-88. Publications: A Danish Gospel, 1986; Og gamle Danmark, 1992. Recreations: music; theatre. Address: (b.) Thistle House, 91 Haymarket Terrace, Edinburgh, EH12 5HE; T.-0131-313 0044.

Mellows, Susan Mary, BSc, PhD, DIC. Academic Registrar, Strathclyde University, since 1993; b. 20.1.44, Brackley, Northants. Educ. Brackley High School; Edinburgh University; Imperial College, London. Kodak Ltd., 1966-67; Science and Engineering Research Council, London, 1970-85; YARD Ltd., Glasgow, 1985-90 (Manager, System Dynamics and Underwater Engineering Group); joined Strathclyde University, 1990, as Deputy Registrar. Recreations: hill-walking; other outdoor activities; books; music. Address: (b.) John Anderson Campus, Strathclyde University, Glasgow, G1 1XG; T.-0141-552 4400, Ext. 2002.

Melville, Ian Dunlop, MB, ChB, FRCPGlas, FRCPLond. Consultant Neurologist, Institute of Neurological Sciences, Glasgow, 1965-88; Honorary Clinical Lecturer, Glasgow University, 1968-88; b. 9.11.27, Glasgow; m., Eliza Duffus; 1 s.; 3 d. Educ. Shawlands Academy; Glasgow University. RAF Medical Branch; Medical Registrar, Glasgow Royal Infirmary; Academic Registrar, National Hospital for Nervous Diseases, London; Clinical Research Fellow, Medical Research Council, London; Senior Medical Registrar, Glasgow. Member, Council of Management, Quarrier's Village, Bridge of Weir; Editor, Bulletin of Royal College of Physicians and Surgeons, Glasgow. Recreations: golf; photography; watercolour painting. Address: (h.) 9 Mirrlees Drive, Glasgow, G12 OSH; T.-0141-339 7085.

Mennie, Alastair Douglas, LLB, PhD, FSA Scot. Academic and practising lawyer; b. 2.10.57, Aberdeen. Educ. Aberdeen University; Edinburgh University. Advocate, since 1982; Part-time Lecturer in European and International Law, 1987-92; Professor of Law, ESADE Business School, Barcelona, 1992-94; Visiting Professor, University of Toulouse, 1994-95. Publications: Domicile Flowcharts, 1991; numerous articles in British and foreign law journals. Recreations: visiting prehistoric sites; modern art exhibitions. Address: (h.) 25 Panmure Place, Edinburgh, EH3 9HP; T.-0131-229 5604.

Mennie, William Patrick, BL, NP. Partner, Grigor & Young, Solicitors, Elgin and Buckie, since 1964 (Senior Partner, since 1984); b. 11.10.37, Elgin; m., Patricia Leslie Bogie; 2 s.; 1 d. Educ. Elgin Academy; Edinburgh University. Solicitor, 1960; part-time Town Clerk,

Dufftown, 1973-75; part-time Depute Procurator Fiscal, Elgin, 1966-74; Honorary Sheriff at Elgin, since 1993; specialist in agricultural law, accredited by Law Society of Scotland; Secretary, Malt Distillers Association of Scotland; Member, Property Marketing Committee, Law Society of Scotland, 1985-93. Recreation: game shooting. Address: (h.) Innesmill, Urquhart, Elgin; T.-01343 842643.

Menzies, Duncan A.Y., QC, MA (Oxon), LLB. Queen's Counsel, since 1991; b. 28.8.53, Edinburgh; m., Hilary Weston; 2 s. Educ. Edinburgh Academy; Cargilfield; Glenalmond; Wadham College, Oxford; Edinburgh University. Advocate, 1978; Standing Junior Counsel to The Admiralty, 1984-91. Parliamentary Candidate, Midlothian, 1983, Edinburgh Leith, 1987; founder, Scottish Wine Society, 1976. Recreations: shooting; golf; wines. Address: (h.) Leaston House, Humbie, East Lothian; T.-01875 833219.

Menzies, George Macbeth, BA, LLB. Partner, W. & J. Burness, Solicitors, since 1974; b. 18.4.43, Edinburgh; m., Patricia Mary; 1 s.; 2 d. Educ. Edinburgh Academy; Corpus Christi College, Oxford; Edinburgh University. Past Chairman, North British Steel Group (Holdings) PLC; Non-Executive Director, Cairn Petroleum Oil & Gas Ltd., 1986-88; Chairman, Fruitmarket Gallery, 1984-88; President, Edinburgh Academical Football Club, 1990-92; Chairman, Endeavour Training (Scotland) Ltd., since 1983; Director, Scottish Council (Development and Industry), since 1990. Recreations: walking; contemporary arts; rugby. Address: (b.) 16 Hope Street, Edinburgh; T.-0131-226 2561.

Menzies, Gordon, MA (Hons), DipEd. Independent Producer (retired Head of Educational Broadcasting, BBC Scotland); b. 30.7.27, Logierait, Perthshire; m., Charlotte; 2 s.; 1 d. Educ. Breadalbane Academy, Aberfeldy; Edinburgh University. Producer/Director, Who Are the Scots?, 1971, The Chiel Amang Us, 1974, Ballad Folk, 1975, History Is My Witness, 1976, Play Golf with Peter Alliss, 1977, Scotch and Wry, 1978-79, Two Views of Burns, 1979, Barbara Dickson in Concert, 1981-84-86, The World of Golf, 1982, The Celts, 1987, Play Better Golf with Peter Alliss, 1989, Scotch and Wry Hogmanay, 1980-91; Editor, The Afternoon Show, 1981-85; Play Snooker with Dennis Taylor, 1990; Play Bridge with Zia, 1991. Publications: Who Are the Scots?, 1971; The Scottish Nation, 1972; History Is My Witness, 1976; Play Golf, 1977; The World of Golf, 1982; Scotch and Wry, 1986; Double Scotch and Wry, 1988; Play Better Golf, 1989. Recreations: golf; snooker; curling; theatre. Address: (h.) 8 Ingleside, Lenzie, Glasgow, G66 4HN.

Menzies, John Maxwell. Chairman, John Menzies PLC, since 1952; b. 13.10.26; m., Patricia Eleanor Dawson; 4 d. Educ. Eton. Lt., Grenadier Guards; Member, Berwickshire County Council, 1954-57; Director: Scottish American Mortgage Co., 1959-63, Standard Life Assurance Co., 1960-63, Vidal Sassoon Inc., 1969-80, Gordon & Gotch plc, 1970-85, Atlantic Assets Trust, 1973-88, Ivory and Sime Enterprise Capital PLC (formerly Independent Investment Co. plc), since 1973 (Chairman, since 1983), Fairhaven International, 1980-88, Rocky Mountains Oil & Gas, 1980-85, Ivory & Sime plc, 1980-83, Personal Assets PLC, 1981-92, Bank of Scotland, 1984-94, Guardian Royal Exchange, since 1985, Malcolm Innes & Partners Ltd., since 1989. Trustee, Newsvendors' Benevolent Institution, since 1974 (President, 1968-74); Member, Royal Company of Archers, Queen's Bodyguard for Scotland; Member, Board of Trustees, National Library of Scotland, since 1991. Recreations: farming; shooting; reading; travel. Address: (b.) 108 Princes Street, Edinburgh, EH2 3AA; T.-0131-225 8555.

Menzies, Neil Graham Finlay, BSc, FRSA. Corporate Adviser; Scottish Adviser to Chemical Industries Association; b. 14.10.41, Meiklour; 2 d. Educ. Lower

School of John Lyon, Harrow; St. Andrews University. Voluntary Service Overseas, Nigeria, 1964-66; ICI, 1966-93, lately Scottish Affairs Adviser; Member, Prince's Trusts Advisory Fund-raising Committee for Scotland; Director, Royal Lyceum Theatre Company; Member, Investors in People Recognition Panel for Scotland; Lay Member, Scottish Office, Education Department, HM Inspectorate; Non-Executive Director, Scottish Ambulance Service. Address: (h.) 13 Northumberland Street, Edinburgh, EH3 6LL; T.-0131-557 4321.

Mercer, John, MA, DipEd. Headmaster, Belmont House School, since 1972; b. 11.8.40, Glasgow; m., Eileen Margaret; 2 s.; 1 d. Educ. Eastwood Senior Secondary School; Glasgow University; Jordanhill College of Education. Teacher of English/History, Mossvale Secondary School, Paisley, 1962-66; Head Teacher of English, Belmont House School, 1966-72. Elder and former Session Clerk, Mearns Parish Kirk; President, Eastwood Rotary Club, 1986-87. Recreations: golf; skiing; walking; reading; palaeontology. Address: (b.) Belmont House School, Newton Mearns, Glasgow, G77 5DU; T.-0141-639 2922.

Mercer, Roger James, MA, FSA, FSA Scot, MIFA. Secretary, Royal Commission for the Ancient and Historical Monuments (Scotland); b. 12.9.44, London; m., Susan; 1 s.; 1 d. Educ. Harrow County Grammar School; Edinburgh University. Inspector of Ancient Monuments, AM Division, Department of the Environment, London, 1969-74; Lecturer and Reader, Department of Archaeology, Edinburgh University, 1974-89. Treasurer, Society of Antiquaries of Scotland, 1977-87; Vice President, Society of Antiquaries of Scotland, 1988-91; Vice President, Prehistoric Society, 1987-91; Vice-President, Council for British Archaeology, 1991-94. Recreations: music; reading; learning. Address: (b.) RCAHMS, John Sinclair House, 16 Bernard Terrace, Edinburgh, EH8 9NX.

Merchant, Bruce Alastair, OBE, LLB. Solicitor; Partner, South, Forrest, Mackintosh & Merchant, Inverness, since 1971; Dean, Faculty of Solicitors of the Highlands; Member, Accounts Commission for Scotland; b. 17.5.45, Edinburgh; m., Joan Isobel Sinclair Hamilton; 1 s.; 2 d. Educ. Inverness Royal Academy; Aberdeen University. Council Member, Law Society of Scotland, 1982-88 (Convener, Guarantee Fund Committee, 1984-87, Convener, Finance Committee, 1987-88); Member: Highland Health Board, 1981-91, Board of Management for Inverness Hospitals, 1971-74, Inverness Local Health Council, 1975-81. Address: (h.) 3 Crown Circus, Inverness; T.-01463 239980.

Merrills, Austin, OBE. Chairman, Ireland Alloys (Holdings) Ltd., since 1971; Director, Johnston Press PLC, since 1985; b. 15.4.28, Sheffield; m., Daphne Olivia Coates; 1 s.; 2 d. Educ. King Edward VII School, Sheffield; Sheffield University. Governor, Glasgow School of Art. Address: (b.) PO Box 18, Hamilton, ML3 0EL; T.-01698 822461.

Merrylees, Andrew, BArch, DipTP, RSA, RIBA, FRIAS, FCSD, FRSA. Architect; Principal, Andrew Merrylees Associates, since 1985; b. 13.10.33, Newmains; m., Maie Crawford; 2 s.; 1 d. Educ. Wishaw High School; Strathclyde University. Sir Basil Spence, Glover and Ferguson: joined, 1957, Associate, 1968, Partner, 1972; awards: RIBA Bronze Medal, Saltire Award, Civic Trust Award, Art in Architecture Award, Royal Scottish Academy Gold Medal, Concrete Society Award, SCONUL Award. Recreations: painting; cooking; tennis; walking. Address: (b.) Quadrant, 17 Bernard Street, Edinburgh, EH6 6PW; T.-0131-555 0688.

Meston, Professor Michael Charles, MA, LLB, JD. Professor of Scots Law, Aberdeen University, since 1971; b. 13.12.32, Aberdeen; m., Dorothea Munro; 2 s. Educ. Robert Gordon's College, Aberdeen; Aberdeen University; Chicago University. Lecturer in Private Law, Glasgow University, 1959-64; Aberdeen University: Senior Lecturer in Comparative Law, 1964-68, Professor of Jurisprudence, 1968-71; Dean, Faculty of Law, 1970-73 and 1988-91; Honorary Sheriff, Grampian Highland and Islands, since 1972; Temporary Sheriff, since 1993; Vice Principal, Aberdeen University, 1979-82; Trustee, National Museum of Antiquities of Scotland, 1982-85; Governor, Robert Gordon's College, Aberdeen; Member, Grampian Health Board, 1985-91; Non-Executive Director, Aberdeen Royal Hospitals NHS Trust, since 1992. Publications: The Succession (Scotland) Act 1964; The Matrimonial Homes (Family Protection) (Scotland) Act 1981; The Scottish Legal Tradition, 1991. Recreations: golf; photography. Address: (h.) 4 Hamilton Place, Aberdeen, AB2 4BH; T.-Aberdeen 641554.

Michels, David Micheal Charles, FHCIMA. Chief Executive, Stakis plc, since 1991; b. 8.12.46, London; m., Michele; 1 s.; 1 d. Educ. Hendon College. Sales and Marketing Manager: Grand Metropolitan Hotels, Ladbroke Leisure; Managing Director: Ladbroke Leisure, Ladbroke Hotels; Executive Vice President, Hilton International; Non Executive Director: Aberforth, Split Level Trust PLC. DLitt, Caledonian. Address: (b.) 3 Atlantic Quay, York Street, Glasgow, G2 8JH; T.-0141-204 4321.

Michie, Professor David Alan Redpath, RSA, RGI, RWA, DA, FRSA. Professor, Heriot Watt University, 1988-90; Head, School of Drawing and Painting, Edinburgh College of Art, 1982-90; b. 30.11.28, St. Raphael, France; m., Eileen Anderson Michie; 2 d. Educ. Hawick High School; Edinburgh College of Art. Travelling Scholarship, Italy, 1954-55; Lecturer, Grays School of Art, Aberdeen, 1957-61; Lecturer, Edinburgh College of Art, 1961 (Vice Principal, 1974-77). President, Society of Scottish Artists, 1961-63; Member, General Teaching Council for Scotland, 1975-80; Member, Court, Heriot-Watt University, 1979-82; Council Member, British School at Rome, 1980-85; Guthrie Award, RSA, 1964; David Cargill Prize, RGI, 1977; Lothian Region Award, 1977; Sir William Gillies Award, 1980; RGI Prize, 1990; Cornelissen Prize, RWA, 1992; one-man exhibitions, Mercury Gallery, London, seven times, 1966-92, Lothian Region Chambers, 1977, The Scottish Gallery, 1980, 1994, Loomshop Gallery, Lower Largo, 1981, 1987, Mercury Gallery, Edinburgh, 1986; Baarn and Amsterdam, 1991; Visiting Professor, Faculty of Art Studio Department, UCLA, Santa Barbara, 1992. Address: (h.) 17 Gilmour Road, Edinburgh, EH16 5NS.

Michie, (Janet) Ray. MP (Lib. Dem.), Argyll and Bute, since 1987; b. 4.2.34; m.; 3 d. Educ. Aberdeen High School for Girls; Lansdowne House School, Edinburgh; Edinburgh School of Speech Therapy. Former Area Speech Therapist, Argyll and Clyde Health Board. Address: (b.) House of Commons, SW1A 0AA.

Micklem, Professor Henry Spedding, MA, DPhil (Oxon). Professor of Immunobiology, Edinburgh University, 1980-92, Honorary Fellow, since 1992; b. 11.10.33, Oxford; m., Lisel Ruth Thomas; 3 s. 1 d. Educ. Rugby School; Oriel College, Oxford. Scientific Staff, Medical Research Council; Research Fellow, Institut Pasteur, Paris; Academic Staff, Department of Zoology, Edinburgh University; Visiting Professor, Department of Genetics, Stanford University; Visiting Fellow, Department of Pathology, New York University Medical School; Member, Scientific Advisory Committee, Melville Trust, 1986-92. Address: (b.) Division of Biological Sciences, Edinburgh University, West Mains Road, Edinburgh, EH9 3JT; T.-0131-650 5496.

Middleton, Francis, MA, LLB; b. 21.11.13, Rutherglen; m., Edith Muir; 2 s.; 1 d. Educ. Rutherglen Academy; Glasgow University. Solicitor, 1937; Indian Army, 1939

(11 Sikh Regiment); injured, 1942; Judge Advocate General's Branch, 1942-45; 1st Class Interpreter, Urdu, Examiner for India in Punjabi; Advocate, 1946; Sheriff, 1948-78. Serves on boards of various charitable bodies. Recreations: reading; walking; water divining. Address:(h.) 20 Queens Court, Helensburgh, G84 7AH; T.-01436 678965.

Middleton, Robert, JP, Hon. DLitt, HonLLD. Convener, Grampian Regional Council, since 1990; President, North Sea Commission of the Conference of Peripheral Maritime Regions, since 1992; b. 28.7.32, Aberdeen; m., Audrey Ewen; 2 s. Educ. Aberdeen Grammar School. Started apprenticeship with Post Office Telephones, 1948; Aberdeen Town Council: elected, 1961, appointed Magistrate, 1963, Chairman of Magistrates, 1965-66, Chairman, Education Committee, 1966-69; Chairman, Labour Party in Scotland, 1986-87; contested Banffshire as Labour candidate, 1966; contested Aberdeen South, 1974 (twice) and 1983; elected, Grampian Regional Council, 1975. Publications: North Sea Brose; Grampian Homeland. Recreations: golf; reading; writing not very good poetry; travel; bridge; bowls. Address: (h.) 9 Stronsay Avenue, Aberdeen, AB2 6HX; T.-01224 313366.

Middleton, Ruth Charlotte, LLB. Secretary/Director, Ark Housing Association Ltd., since 1978; b. 9.9.42, Edinburgh; m., Norman A. Middleton; 1 s.; 1 d. Educ. Berwickshire High School; Edinburgh University. Legal practice, 1965-78. Address: The Priory, Canaan Lane, Edinburgh, EH10 4SG; T.- 0131-447 9027.

Midgley, Professor John Morton, BSc, MSc, PhD, CChem, FRSC, FRPharmS. Professor of Pharmaceutical and Medicinal Chemistry, Strathclyde University, since 1984 (Chairman and Head of Department, 1985-90); b. 14.7.37, York; m., Jean Mary Tillyer; 2 s. Educ. Nunthorpe Grammar School, York; Manchester University; London University. Demonstrator, Manchester University, 1959-61; Assistant Lecturer, School of Pharmacy, London University, 1962-65; Research Associate, Massachusetts Institute of Technology, 1965-66; Lecturer, then Senior Lecturer, School of Pharmacy, London University, 1966-83; Member: Committee on the Review of Medicines, 1984-92, British Pharmacopoie Committee, since 1985, Committee on the Safety of Medicines, since 1990, Council of Royal Pharmaceutical Society of GB, 1991-92, Science and Engineering Research Council Pharmacy Panel, since 1985. Recreations: fly fishing; fisheries management; training labradors; gardening; music. Address: (b.) Strathclyde University, Department of Pharmaceutical Sciences, Royal College, 204 George Street, Glasgow, G1 1XW; T.-0141-552 4400, Ext. 2125.

Milburn, Professor George Henry William, PhD, CChem, FRSC, FBIM, Dr (h.c.), FRSA. Head, Department of Applied Chemical and Physical Sciences, Napier University, since 1973; b. 25.11.34, Wallasey; m., Jean Muriel; 1 s.; 1 d. Educ. Wallasey Grammar School; Leeds University. Short service commission, Royal Corps of Signals, 1959-63; Staff Demonstrator, Leeds University, 1963-66; Research Fellow, Sydney University, 1967-68; Senior Scientific Officer, Agricultural Research Council, 1968-69; Lecturer, Plymouth Polytechnic, 1969-70; Senior Lecturer, Sheffield Polytechnic, 1970-73.Convener, Committee of Scottish University Heads of Chemistry Departments; Honorary Doctorate, Technical University, Budapest, 1988. Publications: more than 50 scientific publications including a textbook on crystal structure analysis. Recreations: golf; bridge; photography. Address: (h.) 9 Orchard Court, Longniddry, East Lothian; T.-0875 853228.

Mill, Douglas Russell, LLB, BA, MBA, NP. Partner, MacFarlane Young & Co., Solicitors, Paisley, since 1987; Depute Director, Centre for Professional Legal Studies, Strathclyde University, since 1993; Member of Council, Law Society of Scotland, since 1993; b. 3.1.57, Paisley; m., Christine; 2 s.; 1 d. Educ. Paisley Grammar School; Glasgow University. Publication: Successful Practice Management, 1992. Recreations: golf; rugby. Address: (h.) Foxburn, South Avenue, Paisley, PA2 7SP; T.-0141-884 6164.

Millan, Rt. Hon. Bruce, PC, CA. European Commissioner, 1989-95; b. 5.10.27, Dundee; m., Gwendoline May Fairey; 1 s.; 1 d. Educ. Harris Academy, Dundee. MP, Glasgow Craigton, 1959-83, Glasgow Govan, 1983-88; Parliamentary Secretary for the RAF, 1964-66; Parliamentary Secretary, Scottish Office, 1966-70; Minister of State, Scottish Office, 1974-76; Secretary of State for Scotland, 1976-79; Opposition Spokesman on Scottish Affairs, 1979-83. Address: (h.) 10 Beech Avenue, Glasgow, G41; T.-0141-427 6483.

Millan, William Robert, LLB, NP. Chief Executive, since 1993, and Director of Administrative and Legal Services, since 1986, Roxburgh District Council; Clerk to the JP Advisory Committee, since 1993; Clerk of the Peace (Roxburgh Commission Area), since 1986; Clerk to the Licensing Board and District Court, since 1986; b. 17.8.52, Glasgow; m., Margaret Hamilton McCulloch; 1 s.; 1 d. Educ. Hillhead High School; Glasgow University. Bannatyne, Kirkwood, France & Co., Writers, Glasgow, 1973-75; Senior Legal Assistant, Cumnock and Doon Valley District Council, 1975-79; Depute Director of Administrative and Legal Services, Roxburgh District Council, 1979-86. Recreations: reading; DIY; gardening; skiing; badminton; golf; photography. Address: (b.) District Council Offices, High Street, Hawick, TD9 9EF; T.-01450 75991.

Millar, Bob, MA, CA. Director of Strategy, Scottish Homes, since 1990; b. 30.3.50, Edinburgh; m., Sandra; 1 s.; 1 d. Educ. George Heriot's School; Edinburgh University. Chartered Accountant, Touche Ross; Financial Accountant, Bredero UK Ltd., Castle Rock Housing Association; Head of Registration, Housing Corporation. Recreations: sports; socialising. Address: (h.) 5 Craiglea Place, Edinburgh; T.-0131-447 7401.

Millar, Helen Jean, MA, FRSA. Member, Air Transport Users Council, since 1991; Member, Advisory Committee on Novel Foods and Processes, since 1991; Convenor, Glasgow Local Health Council; Lecturer in charge, Children's Panel Training, Glasgow University, since 1980; b. 10.10.31, Glasgow; 3 s.; 2 d. Educ. Craigholme School, Glasgow; Glasgow University. Chairman, Consumers in European Community Group, 1988-91; Chairman, Consumer's Committee for Scotland, 1980-89; Member and Vice-Chairman, Scottish Consumer Council, 1979-87; Chairman, Strathclyde Children's Panel, 1979-81; Vice-Chairman, New Glasgow Society, 1980-87; Founder Member, Board, Tron Theatre Club, Glasgow. Recreations: theatre; arts in general; Glasgow; arguing. Address: (h.) 33 Aytoun Road, Glasgow, G41; T.-0141-423 4152.

Millar, Henry Rankin, MB, ChB, BMedBiol (Hons), FRCPsych. Consultant Psychiatrist, Royal Cornhill Hospital, Aberdeen, since 1991; b. 23.4.47, Aberdeen; m., Frances Morgan; 3 d. Educ. Aberdeen Grammar School; Aberdeen University. House Officer, Aberdeen Royal Infirmary, 1972-73; Junior Fellow in Community Medicine and Honorary Senior House Officer in Medicine, Aberdeen University and Aberdeen Royal Infirmary, 1973-74; Senior House Officer/Registrar in Psychiatry, Royal Edinburgh Hospital, 1975-77; Senior Registrar and Lecturer, Dundee Psychiatric Services and Dundee University, 1977-80; Consultant Psychiatrist, Southern General Hospital, Glasgow, 1980-91. Recreation: walking. Address: (h.) Failte, Quarryhill, Mid Auguston, Peterculter, Aberdeen, AB1 OPP.

Millar, Professor Keith, BA, PhD, CPsychol, FBPsS. Titular Professor of Behavioural Science, Medical Faculty, Glasgow University, since 1984; b. 27.6.50, Dundee; m., Dr. Margaret Elspeth Reid; 1 step s. Educ. Dundee High School; Stirling University; Dundee University. Research Scientist, MRC Applied Psychology Unit, Cambridge, 1976-79; Lecturer, Department of Psychiatry, University Hospital and Medical School, Nottingham, 1979-84; Senior Lecturer, Behavioural Sciences Group, Medical Faculty, Glasgow University, 1984-88. Publications: papers and edited book on topics relating psychology to medicine. Recreations: reading; travelling; procrastination. Address: (h.) 33 West Chapelton Crescent, Bearsden, Glasgow, G61 2DE; T.-0141-942 4978.

Millar, Mary Armour, MB, ChB, FRCPGlas, FRCR. Consultant Radiologist, Victoria Infirmary, Glasgow, since 1972; b. 10.8.39, Glasgow. Educ. Queen's Park Senior Secondary School; Glasgow University. Resident House Officer: Stobhill Hospital, Glasgow Royal Infirmary; Victoria Infirmary: Registrar in Medicine, Registrar in Radiology, Senior Registrar. Medical Advisor, Overseas Missionary Fellowship in Scotland; Member, Congregational Board, Sandyford Henderson Memorial Church. Recreations: reading; gardening; hill-walking. Address: (h.) 1 Rosslea Drive, Giffnock, Glasgow, G46 6JW; T.-0141-638 3036.

Millar, Peter Carmichael, OBE, MA, LLB, WS. Deputy Keeper of Her Majesty's Signet, 1983-91; Chairman, Church of Scotland General Trustees, 1973-85; Chairman, Mental Welfare Commission for Scotland, 1983-91; Chairman, Medical Appeal Tribunals, since 1991; Chairman, Pension Appeal Tribunals, since 1992; b. 19.2.27, Glasgow; m., Kirsteen Lindsay Carnegie; 2 s.; 2 d. Educ. Aberdeen Grammar School; Glasgow University; St. Andrews University; Edinburgh University. Royal Navy, 1944-47; Partner, W. & T.P. Manuel, WS, 1954-62; Partner, Aitken Kinnear & Co., WS, 1963-87; Partner, Aitken, Nairn WS, 1987-92; Clerk, Society of Writers to HM Signet, 1964-83. Recreations: golf; hill-walking; music. Address: (h.) 25 Cramond Road North, Edinburgh, EH4 6LY.

Millar, William McIntosh, OBE, BL, FRSAMD. Solicitor (retired); Partner and latterly Consultant, McClure Naismith Anderson & Gardiner, Solicitors, Glasgow, 1955-92; Editor, Journal of the Law Society of Scotland, 1983-89; b. 10.9.25, Edinburgh; 3 s.; 2 d. Educ. Glasgow Academy; Fettes College; Glasgow University. Royal Signals, 1943-47 (Captain, 1947); Secretary, Fife Kinross & Clackmannan Charitable Society, 1955-88 (President, 1961-62, and Patron, 1985); Chairman, Strathclyde Housing Society Ltd. and 11 associated housing societies, 1966-75; Member, Scottish Housing Advisory Committee, 1970-75; Founder Member, Scottish Federation of Housing Associations, 1976-78; Trustee, Scottish Housing Associations Charitable Trust, 1980-91 (Chairman, from 1985); Director, Citizens Theatre Ltd. and Chairman, Close Theatre Club, 1969-72; Governor, Royal Scottish Academy of Music and Drama, 1969-90; Chairman, Scottish Early Music Association, 1984-91. Recreations: music; writing; avoiding golf and politics. Address: (h.) 5 Reef, Uig, Isle of Lewis, HE5 9HU; T.-01851 672245.

Miller, Professor Alan, BSc, PhD, CPhys, FInstP. Professor of Semiconductor Physics, St. Andrews University, since 1993; Professor of Physics and Electrical Engineering, University of Central Florida, since 1989; b. 5.6.49, Dunfermline; m., Susan Linklater; 3 d. Educ. Gibraltar Grammar School; Edinburgh University; Bath University. Research Fellow, Heriot-Watt University, 1974-79; Visiting Assistant Professor, North Texas University, 1979-81; Senior Principal Scientific Officer, Royal Signals and Radar Establishment, Malvern, 1981-89. Publications: Optical and Quantum Electronics (Editor); Modern Optics

series of monographs (Editor). Address: (b.) Department of Physics and Astronomy, North Haugh, St. Andrews, KY16 9SS; T.-01334 463122.

Miller, Alan Cameron, MA, LLB, FCIT. Advocate; Past Chairman (Scotland), Institute of Transport; b. 10.1.13, Killin, Perthshire; m., Audrey Main; 1 s.; 1 d. Educ. Fettes College; Edinburgh University. Member, Faculty of Advocates, since 1938; Royal Navy, 1940-45; Sheriff, Fort William, 1946-52; Legal Adviser (Scotland) to: British Transport Commission, 1952-62, British Railways Board, 1962-72. Voluntary Tutor, Fettes College, 1974-93. Recreations: golf; music. Address: (h.) 12A Quality Street, North Berwick; T.-01620 5035.

Miller, Alan Douglas, LLB (Hons), DipLP. Principal Reporter, Scottish Children's Reporter Administration, since 1995; b. 30.11.59, Edinburgh; m., Alison; 1 s.; 2 d. Educ. Stewart's/Melville College, Edinburgh; Edinburgh University. Assistant/Area Reporter, Strathclyde, 1985-90; Regional Reporter, Dumfries and Galloway, 1990-95; Secretary, Association of Children's Reporters, 1990-93. Associate Member, Iona Community; Elder, Church of Scotland.

Miller, Alastair Robert John Dunlop, BSc, MAg, NDA, FRAgS. Farmer; Chairman, Top Hat Holdings Ltd.; b. 5.3.37, Tranent; m., Margaret Eileen Lees-Brown; 3 d. Educ. Edinburgh Academy; Rugby; Edinburgh University; Purdue University, USA. Scottish Horticulture Medal. Recreations: golf; travel. Address: (h.) Ferrygate, North Berwick, East Lothian.

Miller, Professor Andrew, MA, BSc, PhD, FRSE, FIBiol. Principal and Vice-Chancellor, University of Stirling, since 1994; b. 15.2.36, Kelty, Fife; m., Rosemary S.H. Fyvie; 1 s.; 1 d. Educ. Beath High School; Edinburgh University. Assistant Lecturer in Chemistry, Edinburgh University, 1960-62; Postdoctoral Fellow, CSIRO, Melbourne, and Tutor in Chemistry, Ormond College, Melbourne University, 1962-65; Staff Scientist, MRC Laboratory of Molecular Biology, Cambridge, 1965-66; Lecturer in Molecular Biophysics, Oxford University and (from 1967) Fellow, Wolfson College, 1966-83 (Honorary Fellow, since 1994); on secondment as first Director, European Molecular Biology Laboratory, Grenoble Antenne, France, 1975-80. Committee Member: British Biophysical Society, 1972-74, SERC Synchrotron Radiation Facility Committee, 1979-82, Biological Sciences Committee, 1982-85, Neutron Beam Research Committee, 1982-85; Council Member, Institut Laue-Langevin, 1981-85; Member: MRC Joint Dental Committee, 1984-86, UGC Biological Sciences Committee, 1985-89; (part-time) Director of Research, European Synchrotron Radiation Facility, Grenoble, 1986-91; Member, Advisory Board, AFRC Food Research Institute, since 1985; Member, UFC Advisory Groups on Biological Sciences and Pre-clinical Medicine, since 1989; Member, Scientific Council, Grenoble University, since 1989; Vice-Dean of Medicine, Edinburgh University, 1991-93; Professor of Biochemistry, Edinburgh University, 1984-94; Vice-Principal, Edinburgh University, 1993-94. Address: (b.) University of Stirling, Stirling FK9 4LA.

Miller, Andrew, MA, FLA. Director of Libraries, Glasgow City Council, since 1981; b. 25.12.36, Hamilton; m., Jean Main Freeland; 2 d. Educ. St. John's Grammar School; Hamilton Academy; Glasgow and West of Scotland Commercial College. Assistant, Hamilton Public Libraries and Glasgow District Libraries; Depute Burgh Librarian, Motherwell and Wishaw, 1963-74; Depute Director of Libraries, Glasgow District Council, 1974-81. Chairman of Council and Past President, Scottish Library Association; Past President, Strathclyde Librarians' Club; Vice President, Motherwell Speakers' Forum. Recreations: reading; travelling; public speaking; planning. Address: (b.)

Mitchell Library, North Street, Glasgow, G3 7DN; T.-0141-305 2801.

Miller, Brian, BSc (Hons). Rector, Dalziel High School, Motherwell, since 1990; b. 4.1.51, Glasgow; m., Margaret; 1 s.; 1 d. Educ. High School of Glasgow; Strathclyde University. Teacher of Mathematics, 1974-77; Assistant Principal Teacher, 1977-80; Principal Teacher, 1980-84; Assistant Head Teacher, Cranhill Secondary School, Glasgow, 1984-86; Depute Head Teacher, Stonelaw High School, Glasgow, 1986-90. Recreation: bowls. Address: (b.) Cranford Street, Motherwell, ML1 3AG.

Miller, Rev. Charles W., MA. Chaplain, Royal Dundee Liff Hospital, since 1980; b. 4.2.26, Kinross; m., Isabella Russell Stewart, MA; 3 s. Educ. St. Mary's School, Dunblane; McLaren High School, Callander; Aberdeen University; St. Andrews University. Assistant Minister, Auld Kirk of Ayr, 1953-54; Minister: Torthorwald, Dumfries, 1953-59, Munro Church, Rutherglen, 1959-65, Cruden, Aberdeenshire, 1965-72, Anstruther Parish Church, 1972-80, Fowlis Easter and Liff Parish Church, 1980-94; former Convener: Overseas Committee, Dumfries Presbytery; Church and Nation and Social Responsibility Committees, Aberdeen Presbytery; Social Responsibility Committee, St. Andrews Presbytery; Member, Scottish Churches Consultative Committee on Road Safety; Member, Governing Council, Institute of Advanced Motorists, since 1964 (President, Scottish Groups Association); Chairman, Tayside League of Hospital Friends. Recreations: caravanning; swimming; landscape painting. Address: Palm Springs, Parkside, Auchterhouse, Dundee, DD3 0RF; T.-01382 320407.

Miller, Sheriff Colin Brown, LLB, SSC. Sheriff of South Strathclyde, Dumfries and Galloway, since 1991; b. 4.10.46, Paisley; m., Joan Elizabeth Blyth; 3 s. Educ. Paisley Grammar School; Glasgow University. Partner, McFadyen & Semple, Solicitors, Paisley, 1971-91 (Senior Partner, 1987-91); Council Member, Law Society of Scotland, 1983-91 (Convener, Conveyancing Committee, 1986-89; Convener, Judicial Procedure Committee, 1989-91; Chairman, Working Party on Rights of Audience in Supreme Courts, 1990-91); Member, Joint Law Society Committee with Keeper of Registers, 1982-91; Chairman, Blythswood Housing Association Ltd., 1981-91; Honorary Legal Adviser, Waverley Steam Navigation Co., 1976-91; Dean, Faculty of Procurators in Paisley, 1991. Recreations: sailing (PS Waverley); Clyde steamers; railways; photography. Address: (b.) Ayr Sheriff Court, Wellington Square, Ayr; T.-01292 268474.

Miller, Sir Donald John, DUniv, BSc, FEng, FIMechE, FIEE, FRSE. Chairman, Scottish Power (formerly SSEB), 1982-92; b. 9.2.27, London; m., Fay G. Herriot; 1 s.; 2 d. Educ. Banchory Academy; Aberdeen University. Metropolitan-Vickers, 1947-53; British Electricity Authority, 1953-55; Preece Cardew & Rider (Consulting Engineers), 1955-66; Chief Engineer, North of Scotland Hydro-Electric Board, 1966-74; Director of Engineering, SEEB, 1974; appointed Deputy Chairman, 1979. Chairman, Power Division, IEE, 1977. Recreations: gardening; walking; sailing. Address: (h.) Puldohran, Gryffe Road, Kilmacolm, Renfrewshire; T.-Kilmacolm 3652.

Miller, Edward, CBE, MA, MEd, MLitt. Director of Education, Strathclyde Regional Council, 1974-88; b. 30.3.30, Glasgow; m., Margaret T. McLean; 2 s. Educ. Eastbank Academy; Glasgow University. Junior Depute Director of Education, West Lothian, 1959-63; Senior Assistant Director of Education, Stirlingshire, 1963-66; Depute and Senior Depute Director of Education, Glasgow, 1966-74. Recreations: swimming; boating; reading; golf; gardening.

Miller, George Richardson. National Chairman, Royal British Legion Scotland, since 1992; Director, L.S. Starrett

Co. Ltd., Jedburgh, since 1993; b. 31.3.32, Jedburgh; m., Margaret; 1 s.; 1 d. Educ. Jedburgh Grammar School; Galashiels Technical College. Recreations: curling; fishing; rugby football. Address: (h.) 3 Howden Drive, Jedburgh; T.-01835 862202.

Miller, Hugh Craig, BSc, MB, ChB, FRCPEdin. Consultant Cardiologist, Edinburgh Royal Infirmary, since 1975; b. 7.4.42, Edinburgh; m., Isobel Margaret; 1 s.; 1 d. Educ. George Watson's College; Edinburgh University. Registrar, Edinburgh Royal Infirmary, 1969-72; Senior Registrar, Brompton Hospital, London, 1972-75; Research Fellow, Duke University, North Carolina, 1973-74; Fulbright Scholar. Recreations: skiing; sailing. Address: (h.) 12 Dick Place, Edinburgh; T.-0131-667 4235.

Miller, Professor Hugh Graham, BSc, PhD, DSc, FICFor, FIBiol, FRSE, FRSA. Professor and Head, Department of Forestry, Aberdeen University, since 1984; b. 22.11.39, Ndola, Zambia; 1 s.; 1 d. Educ. Kaptagat School, Kenya; Strathallan School; Sutton High School; Aberdeen University. Joined Department of Peat and Forest Soils, Macaulay Institute for Soil Research, 1986. Awarded Institute of Foresters Silvicultural Prize, 1974; selected for International Union of Forest Research Organization's Scientific Achievement Award, 1981; President, Institute of Chartered Foresters, 1994-96. Recreation: curling. Address: (b.) Department of Forestry, Aberdeen University, St. Machar Drive, Aberdeen, AB9 2UD; T.-01224 272666.

Miller, Ian George Tweedie, BSc, AFIMA, MBCS, CEng, FRSA. Principal, North Glasgow College, since 1990; Chairman, Skill (Scotland), since 1992; b. 5.8.42, Hamilton; m., Una; 1 s.; 1 d. Educ. George Heriot's, Edinburgh; Heriot Watt University. Research Assistant, Hatfield Polytechnic; Lecturer, Computer Science, Strathclyde University; Director, Computer Centre, Paisley College; Depute Principal, Stevenson College. Recreations: golf; bowling. Address: (b.) 110 Flemington Street, Glasgow, G21 4BX; T.-0141-558 9001.

Miller, Rev. Ian Hunter, BA, BD. Minister, Bonhill, since 1975; b. 30.5.44, Johnstone; m., Joan Elizabeth Parr; 2 s. Educ. Johnstone High School; Glasgow University; Open University. Travel agent, latterly Branch Manager, A.T. Mays, 1962-69; Assistant Minister, Renfrew Old Kirk, 1974-75. Moderator, Dumbarton Presbytery, 1985-87 (Convener, Planning Committee, since 1985). Recreations: golf; badminton; music; drama. Address: Bonhill Manse, 1 Glebe Gardens, Bonhill, Alexandria, G83 9HR; T.-Alexandria 53039.

Miller, Ian James, MA, LLB. Secretary and Academic Registrar, Napier University, Edinburgh, since 1987; b. 21.10.38, Fraserburgh; m., Sheila Mary Hourston; 1 s.; 2 d. Educ. Fraserburgh Academy; Aberdeen University; Edinburgh University. Private legal practice, 1963-68; Senior Legal Assistant, Inverness County Council, 1968-70; Depute County Clerk, then County Clerk, Ross and Cromarty County Council, 1970-75; Chief Executive, Inverness District Council, 1975-77; Director of Law and Administration, Grampian Regional Council, 1977-84; Director, Kildonnan Investments Ltd., Aberdeen, 1984-87. Recreations: golf; curling. Address: (b.) 219 Colinton Road, Edinburgh, EH14 1DJ; T.-0131-455 4603.

Miller, Dr. Jack Elius, OBE, JP, OStJ, FRCGP. Consultant Occupational Medical Officer, since 1965; Director, The Medical Insurance Agency Ltd., since 1978; Director and Chairman, Echo Publications Ltd., since 1988; Trustee, The Cameron Fund (London), since 1981; b. 7.3.18, Glasgow; m., Ida Warrens; 1 s. Educ. Hillhead High School; Glasgow University. General Medical Practitioner in Glasgow (retired); Captain, Royal Army Medical Corps, 1944-46; Chairman (founder Member), Glasgow Marriage Guidance Council, 1956-61 (Hon. Vice-President, since 1961); Hon.

Vice-President, Scottish Marriage Guidance Council, since 1967; Chairman, Scottish General Services Committee, 1969-72; Chairman, Association of Jewish Ex-Servicemen and Women of Scotland, 1952-61 and 1964-68; President, Glasgow Jewish Representative Council, 1969-72; Member, Council, BMA, 1964-81 (National Treasurer, 1972-81; Gold Medallist, 1982); Freeman, City of London; Member, Board of Deputies of British Jews, 1979-88; Vice-President, Prince and Princess of Wales Hospice, since 1981; Co-Chairman, Scottish Jewish Archives Committee, since 1986; Chairman, Scottish Health Authorities Review of Priorities for the Eighties, 1985-87. Publication: Glasgow Doctors' Handbook (three editions). Recreations: travel; reading; communal affairs. Address: (h.) 38 Fruin Court, Fruin Avenue, Newton Mearns, Glasgow, G77 6HJ; T.-0141-639 7869.

Miller, James, CBE (1986), MA, FCIOB, FCIArb, CBIM. Chairman, since 1970, Managing Director, 1970-91, The Miller Group Ltd. (formerly James Miller & Partners); Director, British Linen Bank Ltd., since 1983; Member, Advisory Board, British Petroleum; Chairman, Court, Heriot-Watt University, since 1990; Director, Bank of Scotland, since 1993; b. 1.9.34, Edinburgh; m., 1, Kathleen Dewar (deceased); 2, Iris Lloyd-Webb; 1 s.; 3 d. Educ. Edinburgh Academy; Harrow School; Balliol College, Oxford. National Service, Royal Engineers. James Miller & Partners Ltd.: joined, 1958, appointed Director, 1960; Scottish Representative, Advisory Committee to the Meteorological Services, 1980-92; Chairman, Federation of Civil Engineering Contractors, 1985-86, President, 1990-93; Deacon Convener, Incorporated Trades of Edinburgh, 1974-77; President, Edinburgh Chamber of Commerce, 1981-83; Assistant, 1982-85, Treasurer, 1990-92, Master, 1992-94, Merchant Company of Edinburgh. Recreation: shooting. Address: (b.) The Miller Group Ltd., Miller House, 18 South Groathill Avenue, Edinburgh, EH4 2LW; T.-0131-332 2585.

Miller, James David Frederick, DUniv (Stirling), MA (Cantab), CBIM, FIPM. Chairman, Wolverhampton and Dudley Breweries; Chairman, SCOTVEC; Chairman, Scottish Examination Board; Director, Institute of Management; Director, Forth Valley Enterprise; Director, Scottish Life Assurance Co. Ltd; Director, Edinburgh Military Tattoo; b. 5.1.35, Wolverhampton; m., Saffrey Blackett Oxley; 2 s.; 1 s. (deceased); 1 d. Educ. Edinburgh Academy; Emmanuel College, Cambridge; London School of Economics. National Service, Argyll and Sutherland Highlanders, Cameron Highlanders, commissioned in South Staffords, 1953-55. Chairman, Court, Stirling University, since 1992; Commissioner, Queen Victoria School, Dunblane, 1987. Recreations: gardening; tennis; golf. Address: (h.) Blairuskin Lodge, Kinlochard, Aberfoyle, by Stirling, FK8 3TP; T.-01377 387 346.

Miller, Rev. John Stewart Abercromby Smith, MA, BD, STM. Minister, Morningside United Church, Edinburgh, since 1980; b. 3.5.28, Gibraltar; m., Lorna Vivien Fraser; 1 s.; 1 d. Educ. Lanark Grammar School; Edinburgh University; Union Theological Seminary, New York. Assistant Minister, St. Giles' Cathedral, Edinburgh, 1953-54; Minister: St. Andrew's, Hawick, 1954-59, Sandyhills, Glasgow, 1959-67, Mortlach and Cabrach, Banffshire, 1967-75, North Morningside, Edinburgh, and Morningside Congregational Church, 1975-80; Visiting Instructor, Columbia Theological Seminary, Georgia, 1986; Honorary Associate Minister, Peachtree Presbyterian Church, Atlanta, 1986; Chaplain, Sea Cadet Corps. Recreations: reading; listening to music; exploring Britain. Address: (h.) 1 Midmar Avenue, Edinburgh; T.-0131-447 8724.

Miller, Keith. Chief Executive, The Miller Group. Address: (b.) Miller House, 18 South Groathill Avenue, Edinburgh, EH4 2LP.

Miller, Professor Kenneth, LLB, LLM, PhD. Professor of Law, Strathclyde University, since 1992; b. 11.12.51, Paisley; m., Margaret Macleod. Educ. Paisley Grammar School; Strathclyde University; Queen's University, Canada. Lecturer in Law, then Senior Lecturer, Strathclyde University, 1975-91; Deputy General Editor, Stair Memorial Encyclopaedia of the Laws of Scotland, since 1990; Member, Employment Law Committee, Law Society of Scotland. Publications: Employment Law in Scotland (Co-author); Property Law (Co-author). Recreations: reading; golf; theatre. Address: (b.) Law School, Strathclyde University, 173 Cathedral Street, Glasgow; T.-0141-552 4400.

Miller, Sir Ronald Andrew Baird, CBE (1985), CA, DSc. former Chairman, Dawson International PLC; Chairman, British Knitting and Clothing Export Council; b. 13.5.37, Edinburgh. Non-Executive Director: Christian Salvesen PLC, Scottish Amicable Life Assurance Society, Securities Trust of Scotland; Member, Court, Napier University. Address: (b.) 7 Doune Terrace, Edinburgh EH3 6DY.

Miller, Professor Timothy John Eastham, PhD, BSc, MIEE, CEng, SMIEEE, FRSE. Lucas Professor in Power Electronics, Glasgow University, since 1986; b. 25.9.47, Wigan; m., Janet Ann; 3 d. Educ. Atlantic College; Glasgow University; Leeds University. Research Fellow, Department of Electrical and Electronic Engineering, Leeds University, 1973-77; joined Corporate Research and Development Center, General Electric, NY, 1979, Manager, Power Electronics Control Program, 1983-86; appointed GEC Titular Professor in Power Electronics, Glasgow University, 1986. Publications: five textbooks and reference book; 100 papers. Ten patents. Recreation: racing cyclist. Address: (b.) Department of Electronics and EE, Glasgow University, Glasgow, G12 8LT; T.-0141-330 4922.

Miller, William, BSc, DipTP. Member, European Parliament, Glasgow, since 1994; b. 22.7.54, Gartocharn; 1 s.; 1 d. Educ. Paisley Technical College; Kingston Polytechnic. Strathclyde Regional Councillor, 1986-94. Recreations: ties; records; Kilmarnock F.C. Address: 9 Chisholm Street, Glasgow, G1 5HA; T.-0141-552 2234.

Miller, William Brown, OBE, BSc (Hons), ARCST (Hons). Company Director; b. 14.4.32, Kilmarnock; m., Brenda; 1 s.; 1 d. Educ. Hutchesons Grammar School, Glasgow; Glasgow University; Strathclyde University (RCST). Apprentice, Rolls-Royce, Glasgow and Derby; Quality Engineer, Trans Canada Airlines, Winnipeg, Toronto, Montreal; Development Engineer, Rolls-Royce, Derby and Scotland; Site Manager, Rolls-Royce, Hamilton; founder, Prestwick Circuits Ltd., Ayr, 1969; Managing Director, until 1991; Chairman, until 1992; founding Director, West Sound Radio; founding Director, PIK Holdings Ltd., Prestwick, 1991; Council Member, Scottish Council Development and Industry; Council Member, CBI, Scotland and nationally; Chairman, UBI Scotland; Director, Magnum Power PLC, since 1993; Director, Sheldahl Inc. Minnesota, USA, since 1991; Board Member, Irvine Development Corporation, since 1993. Recreations: church; skiing. Address: (h.) Whiteleys, Alloway, Ayr; T.-01292 443968.

Miller, Professor William L., MA, PhD, FBA. Edward Caird Professor of Politics, Glasgow University, since 1985; b. 12.8.43, Glasgow; m., Fiona Thomson; 2 s.; 1 d. Educ. Aberdeen Grammar School; Royal High School, Edinburgh; Edinburgh University; Newcastle University. Formerly Lecturer, Senior Lecturer and Professor, Strathclyde University; Visiting Professor, Virginia Tech., Blacksburg, Virginia, 1983-84; also taught at Universities of Essex and Cologne; frequent Contributor to Press and TV; Member, Editorial Boards: Electoral Studies, Political Studies. Publications: Electoral Dynamics, 1977; The End of British Politics?, 1981; The Survey Method in the Social and Political Sciences, 1983; Elections and Voters, 1987; The Quality of Local Democracy, 1988; How Voters Change, 1990; Media and Voters, 1991; Alternatives to Freedom, 1995. Address: (b.) Department of Politics, Glasgow University, G12 8RT; T.-0141-339 8855.

Milligan, Eric. Convener, Lothian Regional Council, since 1990; Convenor, City of Edinburgh Council, since 1995; b. 27.1.51, Edinburgh; m., Janis. Educ. Tynecastle High School; Napier College of Commerce and Technology. Edinburgh District Councillor, 1974-78; Lothian Regional Councillor, since 1978; Chairman, Finance Committee, 1980-82, 1986-90; President, COSLA, 1988-90.

Milligan, Hon. Lord (James George Milligan). Senator of the College of Justice, since 1988; b. 10.5.34. Advocate, 1959; QC, 1972; Advocate Depute, 1971-78; Chairman, Medical Appeal Tribunal (Scotland), 1979-88; Chairman, RSSPCC, 1978-92. Address: (b.) Court of Session, Parliament House, Edinburgh, EH1 1RQ.

Mill Irving, Robert Martin. Marine Superintendent, Scottish Fisheries Protection Agency; b. 18.6.37, Suez; m., Alison Machray Loudon; 1 s.; 2 d. Educ. Merchiston Castle; Thames Nautical Training College. Joined Shell Tanker Company as Apprentice, 1955; Department of Agriculture and Fisheries for Scotland: Second Officer, 1966, First Officer, 1971, Commanding Officer, 1977, Assistant Marine Superintendent, 1981. Recreation: riding. Address: (h.) Station House, Gifford, East Lothian; T.-0162081 404.

Mills, Professor Colin Frederick, OBE, MSc, PhD, CChem, FRSC, FRSE. Professorial Research Fellow and Director, Postgraduate Studies, Rowett Research Institute, since 1986 (Head, Biochemistry Division, 1966-86); Co-ordinator, Nutrition Monitoring Unit for Relief Programmes; b. 8.7.26, Swinton, Lancashire; m., D. Beryl; 1 d. Educ. Altrincham Grammar School; Reading University; London University. ARC Unit for Micronutrient Research, Long Ashton Research Station, Bristol University, 1946-47; Assistant Lecturer in Biochemistry, Wye College, London University, 1947-51; joined Rowett Research Institute, 1951. Member, WHO/FAO Experts Committee on Trace Elements in Human Nutrition; Chairman, International Committee for Symposia on Trace Elements in Man and Animals; Royal Society for Chemistry John Jeye Gold Medallist (Environmental Studies); Visiting Professor, Nutritional Biochemistry, University of Newcastle-upon-Tyne. Recreations: music; sailing. Address: (b.) Rowett Research Institute, Bucksburn, Aberdeen, AB2 9SB; T.-01224 712751.

Mills, Harold Hernshaw, CB, BSc, PhD. Secretary, Scottish Office Environment Department, since 1992; b. 2.3.38, Greenock; m., Marion Elizabeth Beattie. Educ. Greenock High School; Glasgow University. Cancer Research Scientist, Roswell Park Memorial Institute, Buffalo, New York, 1962-64; Lecturer, Chemistry Department, Glasgow University, 1964-69; Principal, Scottish Home and Health Department, 1970-76; Assistant Secretary: Scottish Office, 1976-81, Privy Council Office, 1981-83, Scottish Development Department, 1983-84; Under Secretary, Scottish Development Department, 1984-88; Principal Finance Officer, Scottish Office, 1988-92. Address (b.) Scottish Office, New St. Andrew's House, Edinburgh, EH1 3TB; T.-0131-244 4714.

Mills, Kenneth Leslie George, MA, BSc, MB, BChir, FRCS, FRCSEdin, FRCSCanada. Consultant Orthopaedic Surgeon, since 1968; b. 16.8.29, Birmingham; 2 d. Educ. High School of Glasgow; Cambridge University; Westminster Hospital, London. Medical Officer, RAF; Senior Lecturer in Orthopaedic Surgery, Dundee University. Publications: Guide to Orthopaedics (Trauma), 1979; Colour Atlas of Accidents and Emergencies, 1984. Address: (h.) 29 Craigiebuckler Avenue, Aberdeen, AB1 7SL; T.-01224 314077.

Milne, Brian, MB, ChB, FRCOG. Consultant Gynaecologist and Obstetrician, Raigmore Hospital NHS Trust, Inverness, since 1978; Clinical Senior Lecturer, Aberdeen University, since 1978; b. 9.1.42, Elgin; m., Mary I.B.; 2 s. Educ. Keith Grammar School; Aberdeen University. House Officer and Senior House Officer appointments, Aberdeen Royal Infirmary; Registrar appointments, Raigmore Hospital, Inverness and Southern General Hospital, Glasgow; Senior Registrar, Obstetrics and Gynaecology, Leicester Royal Infirmary, 1974-78. Recreations: golf; curling. Address: (h.) Muirfield House, 28 Muirfield Road, Inverness; T.-01463 222134.

Milne, George, BSc (Hons), MEd. Headteacher, Peterhead Academy since 1991; b. 4.6.49, Aberdeen; m., Elizabeth Kerr; 2 s.; 1 d. Educ. Aberdeen Grammar School; Aberdeen University. Maths Teacher, 1972-81; Principal Teacher of Maths, Peterhead Academy, 1981-84; Assistant Head Teacher, then Depute Head, Mintlaw Academy, 1984-91. Recreations: Rotary activities; golf; reading. Address: (b.) Peterhead Academy, Prince Street, Peterhead, AB42 6QQ; T.-01779 72231.

Milne, John Alexander, BA, BSc (Hons), PhD. Deputy Director and Head, Animals and Grazing Ecology Division, Macaulay Land Use Research Institute; b. 22.11.43, Edinburgh; m., Janet Erskine; 1 s. Educ. Waid Academy; Edinburgh University; London University; Open University. Deputy Editor, Grass and Forage Science; Address: (b.) Craigiebuckler, Aberdeen, AB9 2QJ.

Milne, Professor John Sim, BSc (Hons), CEng, FIMechE. Professor of Mechatronics, University of Abertay, Dundee, since 1993; b. 22.6.36, Arbroath; m., Isabella Paton; 2 s. Educ. Arbroath High School; Strathclyde University. Lecturer, then Senior Lecturer in Mechanical Engineering, Dundee Institute of Technology, 1958-93. Member, IEE professional group PGI6; Member, Higher Still Specialist Group on Design, Engineering and Technology; co-author of two textbooks and invited contributor to two engineering reference books. Recreations: cycling; hill-walking. Address: (h.) 45 Monymusk Road, Arbroath, DD11 2BZ; T.-01241 873988.

Milne, Robert Hughes, MBE, JP. Managing Director, Aberdeen Fish Curers and Merchants Association Ltd., since 1987 (Chief Executive/Secretary, 1983-87); b. 4.6.39, Pittenweem; m., Helen Wilma Masson; 1 s. Educ. Waid Academy, Anstruther. Assistant Chief Fisheries Advisor, then Regional Officer, Herring Industry Board, 1962-73; Development Officer/Secretary, then Secretary General, Scottish Federation of Fishermen's Co-operatives Ltd., Fishing Co-operative Trading (Scotland) Ltd. and Fishing Co-operatives (Manufacturing) Ltd., 1973-83. Served, European Community Social Problems Fisheries Committee, European Community Advisory Committee on Fisheries and Association of European Agricultural and Fisheries Co-operatives, 1973-83; Member, Isle of Man Government's Commission of Inquiry, 1982-83; Secretary, Scottish Fish Merchants Federation Ltd., since 1984; Member, Sea Fish Industry Authority Research and Development Committee and Sea Fish Training Council, since 1983. Burgess of Guild, City of Aberdeen; Council Member, Aberdeen Chamber of Commerce; Vice Chairman, Grampian Region Fisheries Committee. Recreations: gardening; church activities. Address: (h.) South Esplanade West, Aberdeen, AB9 2FJ; T.-01224 897744.

Milne Home, John Gavin, JP, TD, FRICS. Lord Lieutenant, Dumfries and Galloway, 1988-91; Chartered Surveyor and Land Agent; b. 20.10.16, Dumfriesshire; m., Rosemary Elwes; 2 s.; 1 d. Educ. Wellington College; Trinity College, Cambridge. Served 4th Bn., King's Own Scottish Borderers, 1938-45; Factor, Buccleuch Estates Ltd., on Eskdale, Liddesdale and Branxholm Estates, 1945-

74; Member, Dumfries County Council, 1949-74; Chairman, Dumfries and Galloway Region, British Field Sports Society, 1976-88. Recreations: country sports; nature study. Address: Kirkside of Middlebie, Lockerbie, Dumfriesshire, DG11 3JW; T.-01576 300204.

Milner, Professor A.D., MA, DipPsych, PhD, FRSE. Professor of Neuropsychology, St. Andrews University, since 1990 (Dean, Faculty of Science, 1992-94, Head, School of Psychology, since 1994); b. 16.7.43, Leeds. Educ. Bradford Grammar School; Lincoln College, Oxford. Research Worker, Institute of Psychiatry, London, 1966-70; Lecturer, then Senior Lecturer, St. Andrews University, 1970-85, Reader, 1985-90. Publications: The Neuropsychology of Consciousness (Editor); The Visual Brain in Action, 1995. Address (b.) Psychological Laboratory, St. Andrews University, St. Andrews, KY16 9JU; T.-01334 462065.

Milton, Ian Murray, MCIM. Chairman, Milton Hotels Ltd.; Director, Nevis Range Development Company PLC; Board Member, Scottish Tourist Board; Director, Lochaber Ltd.; b. 25.7.45, Glasgow; m., Ann; 1 s.; 3 d. Educ. Lochaber High School; Scottish Hotel School, Glasgow. Began Milton Hotels with brother, 1965. Recreations: golf; skiing; computing. Address: (b.) Milton Hotels Ltd., North Road, Fort William, PH33 6TG; T.-01397 703139.

Minto, 6th Earl of (Gilbert Edward George Lariston Elliot-Murray-Kynynmound), OBE (1986), JP. Brigadier, Queen's Bodyguard for Scotland (Royal Company of Archers); President, Scottish Council on Alcohol, since 1988; Vice Lord-Lieutenant, Borders Region, Roxburgh, Ettrick and Lauderdale, since 1992; Convener, Borders Regional Council, since 1990; b. 19.6.28; m., 1, Lady Caroline Child-Villiers (m. diss.); 1 s.; 1 d.; 2, Mary Elizabeth Ballantine (deceased); 3, Mrs Caroline Larlham. Educ. Eton; Sandhurst. Former Captain, Scots Guards. Address: (h.) Minto, Hawick.

Miquel, Raymond Clive, CBE (1981), CIM. Chairman, Lees of Scotland Ltd., since 1993; b. 28.5.31. Managing Director, Arthur Bell & Sons Ltd., 1973-85; Chairman, Scottish Sports Council, 1987-91.

Misra, Prem Chandra, BSc, MBBS, DPM (RCP&S, Edin and Glas), FAGS. Consultant Psychiatrist, Parkhead Hospital; Deputy Clinical Services Manager, Eastern Psychiatric Services, Glasgow, since 1992; Deputy Physician Superintendent, Gartloch and Parkhead Hospitals, Glasgow, 1984-92; Clinical Senior Lecturer, Glasgow University, since 1976; b. 24.7.41, Lucknow, India; m., Sandhya; 1 s.; 2 d. Educ. KK Degree College and King George's Medical College, Lucknow, India; Lucknow University. Rotating Intern, King George's Medical College Hospital, Lucknow, 1967; Demonstrator, Department of Human Physiology, Lucknow University, 1967; Resident Senior House Officer, General Medicine and Geriatrics, Wigan and Leigh Group of Hospitals, 1968-69; Resident House Surgeon, General Surgery, Wigan Royal Infirmary, 1968-69; Resident House Physician, General Medicine, Whelley Hospital, Wigan, 1969-70; Resident Senior House Officer in Psychiatry, then Resident Registrar in Psychiatry, Bolton District General Hospital, 1970-73; Senior Psychiatric Registrar (Midland Area Consultant Training Scheme), Hollymoor Hospital, Birmingham, 1973-76; Consultant Psychiatrist, Solihull Area Health Authority, 1976; appointed Consultant Psychiatrist, Glasgow Royal Infirmary and Duke Street Hospital, 1976; Consultant in Charge, Acorn Street Day Hospital, 1979. President, Indian Association of Strathclyde, since 1981; Member, Executive Committee: Strathclyde Community Relations Council, 1981-85, Scottish Council for Racial Equality, 1982; Member, Social and Welfare Committee, CRC, for Ethnic Groups and Vietnam Refugees, 1982; Member, Board of Directors, Scottish Refugee Council, since 1995; awarded Ludwika Bierkoskigo Medal by Polish Medical Association for "outstanding contributions in the prevention and treatment of disabilities"; Secretary, Division of Psychiatry, Eastern District of Glasgow, 1980-94; Member: Executive Committee, British Society of Research on Sex Education, International Scientific Committee on Sexuality and Handicap, International Advisory Board of Israel Society of Clinical and Experimental Hypnosis; Executive Committee Member, European Society of Hypnosis; Member, International Committee of Sexologists; Justice of the Peace; President, British Society of Medical and Dental Hypnosis (Scotland), 1987-89. Publications: Modern Trends in Hypnosis; research papers. Address: (b.) Parkhead Hospital, 81 Salamanca Street, Glasgow, G31 5BA; T.-0141-554 7951.

Mitcalfe, Kirsteen, BA. Deputy Lieutenant of Moray, since 1991; Member, Gordonstoun School Board of Governors, 1982-94; b. 23.7.36, Edinburgh; m., Hugh Mitcalfe; 4 d. Educ. Oxenfoord Castle School; Open University. Recreations: skiing; tennis; reading. Address: (h.) Milton Brodie, Forres, Moray, IV36 0UA; T.-01343 850281.

Mitchell, Anne Clouston, MA (Hons). Principal, St. Margaret's School, Edinburgh, since 1994; b. 24.2.46, Aberdeen. Educ. Lossiemouth High School; Elgin Academy; Aberdeen University. Assistant Teacher of English, Kirkcaldy and Lossiemouth; Teacher of English as a Foreign Language, Germany; Teacher of English/Assistant Housemistress, St. Leonards School; Principal Teacher of English, North Berwick High School and Balerno High School; Assistant Headteacher, then Depute Head, Dunbar Grammar School; seconded as Lothian Region Arts Co-ordinator. Co-author, Heinemann Core English Series. Recreations: theatre; reading; gardening. Address: (h.) 22 Cedar Drive, Port Seton, EH32 0SN; T.-01875 815187.

Mitchell, Colin Malcolm, BSc, CBiol, MIBiol, MIMgt. Headteacher, Dumfries High School, since 1990; b. 11.6.50, Paisley; m., Pamela Margaret; 2 s. Educ. Forrester Secondary School, Edinburgh; Heriot Watt University. Teacher of Science/Biology, then Principal Teacher of Biology, Craigroyston High School, Edinburgh; Assistant Headteacher, then Depute Headteacher, Maxwelltown High School, Dumfries. Deputy team leader, Moffat Mountain Rescue Team; Chairman, Dumfries Group, Scottish Wildlife Trust; Chairman, Dunscore Community Council. Recreations: mountaineering; bird-watching. Address: (b.) Dumfries High School, Marchmont, Dumfries, DG1 1PX.

Mitchell, David William, CBE. Joint Managing Director, M & N Norman (Timber) Ltd., since 1992; Chairman, Cumbernauld New Town, since 1987; b. 4.1.33, Glasgow; m., Lynda Guy; 1 d. Educ. Merchiston Castle School. Director, Mallinson-Denny (Scotland) Ltd., 1980-87; Director, Hunter Timber (Scotland) Ltd., 1987-92; Member, Western Regional Hospital Board, 1965-73; Member, Glasgow Rating Valuation Appeal Committee, 1970-74; Council Member, CBI Scotland, 1979-85; Executive Member, Scottish Council (Development and Industry), since 1979; President, Scottish Timber Trade Association, 1980-82; Executive Member, Institute of Directors in Scotland, 1983-91; President, Scottish Conservative and Unionist Association, 1980-82; Treasurer, Scottish Conservative Party, 1990-93; Member, Board of Management, Craighalbert Centre. Recreations: golf; shooting; fishing. Address: (h.) Dunmullin House, Blanefield, Stirlingshire, G63 9AJ; T.-01505 329124.

Mitchell, Rev. Duncan Ross, BA (Hons), BD (Hons). Minister, St. Andrews Church, West Kilbride, since 1980; b. 5.5.42, Boddam, Aberdeenshire; m., Sandra Brown; 2 s.; 1 d. Educ. Hyndland Senior Secondary School, Glasgow; Strathclyde University; Glasgow University. Worked in insurance industry, four years; Minister, Craigmailen UF

Church, Bo'ness, 1972-80; Convener, Assembly Youth Committee, UF Church, 1974-79; Member: Scottish Joint Committee on Religious Education, 1974-79, Multilateral Conversation in Scotland, 1976-79, Board of Social Responsibility, Church of Scotland, 1983-86;Ardrossan Presbytery: Convener, World Mission and Unity, 1984-88, Convener, Stewardship and Finance, 1988-91; Convener, General Assembly Board of World Mission and Unity, Local Involvements Committee, and Executive Member of the Board, 1987-92; Church of Scotland Delegate to Council of Churches for Britain and Ireland Assembly; Moderator, Ardrossan Presbytery, 1992-93; Member, Scottish Christian Aid Committee. Recreations: cycling; supporting Partick Thistle. Address: St. Andrew's Manse, 7 Overton Drive, West Kilbride; T.-01294 823142.

Mitchell, Professor Falconer, BCom, CA. Professor of Management Accounting, Edinburgh University; b. 24.11.50, Stirling; m., Maureen Wilson; 2 s. Educ. High School of Stirling; Edinburgh University. Audit apprenticeship, KPMG Edinburgh; Lecturer in Accounting, Heriot Watt University; Lecturer, Senior Lecturer, Edinburgh University. Canon Foundation in Europe Visiting Fellow, 1990-91. Recreations: bowling; gardening; reading; travel. Address: (b.) Department of Accounting, Edinburgh University, George Square, Edinburgh, EH8 9JY; T.-0131-650 8340.

Mitchell, George Watson, MA. Director of Programmes, Grampian TV, since 1989; Board Member, Scottish Film Production Fund, since 1993; Director, Central Scotland Radio, since 1993; b. 24.3.49, Edinburgh. Educ. Royal High School, Edinburgh; Edinburgh University. Thomson Regional Newspapers, 1971-73; BBC, 1974-80; ATV, Birmingham, 1980-81; Central Television, 1982-88 (Editor, Current Affairs, East Midlands TV Centre); Programme Controller, Grampian TV, 1988-89. Recreations: watching TV; hill-walking; tennis. Address: (b.) Grampian TV, Queen's Cross, Aberdeen; T.-01224 646464.

Mitchell, Iain Grant, QC, LLB (Hons), FSA Scot, FRSA. Queen's Counsel, since 1992; Temporary Sheriff, since 1992; Honorary Secretary, Scottish Conservative and Unionist Association, since 1993; b. 16.11.51, Edinburgh. Educ. Perth Academy; Edinburgh University. Called to Scottish Bar, 1976; Past President, Diagnostic Society of Edinburgh; former Vice-President, Edinburgh University Conservative Association; Conservative candidate, Falkirk West, General Election, 1983, Kirkcaldy, General Election, 1987, Cumbernauld and Kilsyth, General Election, 1992; Chairman, Trust for an International Opera Theatre of Scotland; Vice-Chairman, Scottish Baroque Ensemble Ltd.; Member, Scottish Committee, Royal Institute of International Affairs; Member, Executive Committee of European Movement (Scottish Council); Member, Executive Committee, Scottish Lawyers' European Group; Member, Conservative Group for Europe. Recreations: music and the arts; photography; cinema; walking; history; travel; writing; finding enough hours in the day. Address: (b.) Advocates Library, Parliament House, High Street, Edinburgh; T.-0131-226 5071.

Mitchell, Ian, BSc. Managing Director, Tay Salmon Fisheries Co. Ltd., since 1982; Chairman, Tay District Salmon Fisheries Board, since 1987 (Member, since 1976); Chairman, Tay River Purification Board, since 1992 (Member, since 1975); b. 26.2.49, Aberdeen; m., Frances Barbara Hutchison; 3 s.; 1 d. Educ. Forres Academy; Edinburgh University. Joined Tay Salmon Fisheries, 1971; Member, Esk District Salmon Fisheries Board, 1975-94; Member, Salmon Net Fishing Association Council, 1982-87 (Chair, 1987-94); Member, Association of Scottish District Salmon Fishery Boards, 1982-94 (Chairman, 1995); Member, Government Salmon Advisory Committee, 1986-95. Recreations: salmon fishing; walking. Address: (b.) St. Leonards Bank, Perth, PH2 8EB; T.-01738 636407.

Mitchell, Sheriff J.K., LLB. Sheriff of Glasgow and Strathkelvin at Glasgow. Advocate, 1979. Address: (b.) Sheriff Court House, 1 Carlton Place, Glasgow, G5 9DA.

Mitchell, John, BSc. Head Teacher, Kilsyth Academy, since 1985; b. 4.1.45, Kirkintilloch; m., Irene; 1 s.; 1 d. Educ. Lenzie Academy; Glasgow University. Taught in Glasgow; Principal Teacher of Physics, Balfron High School and Bishopbriggs High School; Assistant Head Teacher, Kilsyth Academy; Deputy Head Teacher, Knightswood Secondary School. Address: (h.) Kilsyth Academy, Balmalloch, Kilsyth, G65 9NF; T.-01236 822244.

Mitchell, (John) Angus (Macbeth), CB, CVO, MC, LLD(Hon), DUniv (Stirling). b. 25.8.24, Ootacamund, India; m., Ann Williamson; 2 s.; 2 d. Educ. Marlborough College; Brasenose College, Oxford. Royal Armoured Corps (Captain), 1943-46; Scottish Office, 1949-84; Principal Private Secretary to Secretary of State for Scotland, 1958-59; Under Secretary, Social Work Services Group, 1969-74; Secretary, Scottish Education Department, 1976-84. Order of Orange-Nassau, 1946; Chairman, Scottish Marriage Guidance Council, 1965-69; Vice-Convener, Scottish Council of Voluntary Organisations, 1986-91; Member, Commission for Local Authority Accounts in Scotland, 1985-89; Chairman of Court, Stirling University, 1984-92; Chairman, Scottish Action on Dementia, 1986-94; Member, Historic Buildings Council for Scotland, 1988-94; Co-ordinator, Recording Scottish Graveyards Project, since 1992. Publications: Scottish Office Ministers 1885-1985; Procedures for the Reorganisation of Schools in England, 1986. Recreations: old Penguins; gravestones; maps. Address: (h.) 20 Regent Terrace, Edinburgh, EH7 5BS; T.-0131-556 7671.

Mitchell, John Gall, QC, MA, LLB. Social Security (formerly National Insurance) Commissioner, since 1979, and Child Support Commissioner, since 1992; b. 5.5.31, Edinburgh; m., 1, Anne Bertram Jardine (deceased); 3 s.; 1 d.; 2, Margaret Galbraith. Educ. Royal High School, Edinburgh; Edinburgh University. Advocate, 1957; Standing Junior Counsel, Customs and Excise, Scotland, 1964-70; a Chairman, Industrial Tribunals, Scotland, 1966-80; Honorary Sheriff of Lanarkshire, 1970-74; Chairman, Supreme Court Legal Aid Committee, 1974-79; a Chairman, Pensions Appeal Tribunals, Scotland, 1974-80. Address: (b.) 23 Melville Street, Edinburgh; T.-0131-225 2201.

Mitchell, John Logan, QC, LLB (Hons). Queen's Counsel, since 1987; Advocate Depute, 1981-85; b. 23.6.47, Dumfries; m., Christine Brownlee Thomson; 1 s.; 1 d. Educ. Royal High School, Edinburgh; Edinburgh University. Called to Bar, 1974; Standing Junior Counsel to Forestry Commission; Standing Junior Counsel, Department of Agriculture and Fisheries. Past President, Royal High School F.P. Club. Recreations: running; golf. Address: (h.) 17 Braid Farm Road, Edinburgh; T.-031-447 8099.

Mitchell, Jonathan James, BA, LLB, QC. Deputy Social Security Commissioner, since 1995; Queen's Counsel, since 1992; Temporary Sheriff, since 1988; b. 4.8.51, Edinburgh; m., Melinda McGarry; 1 s.; 1 d. Advocate, 1979; QC, 1992. Publication: Eviction and Rent Arrears, 1995. Address: (h.) 30 Warriston Crescent, Edinburgh T.-0131-557 0854.

Mitchell, Lyn, BSc (SocSci), MMedSci, RGN, SCM, RSCN, RNT. Chief Executive, National Board for Nursing, Midwifery and Health Visiting for Scotland, since 1986; b. 26.4.40, Elgin; m., David Mitchell; 1 step s.; 1 step d. Educ. Elgin Academy; Edinburgh University; Nottingham University. Ward Sister: Sheffield Children's Hospital, Aberdeen Royal Infirmary; Nurse Teacher, Foresterhill College, Aberdeen; Senior Health Education Officer, Grampian Health Board; Lecturer, Department of Nursing

Studies, Edinburgh University; Nursing Adviser, Scottish Health Education Group. Address: (b.) 22 Queen Street, Edinburgh, EH2 1NT; T.-0131-226 7371.

Mitchell, Ross, MA, DSA, FHSM, MIPM. Secretary, Mental Welfare Commission for Scotland; b. Glasgow; m., Marion; 1 s. Educ. Hillhead High School, Glasgow; Glasgow University; Manchester University. Eastern Regional Hospital Board: National Administrative Trainee, 1956-58, Administrative Assistant, 1958-60, Work Study Officer, 1960-61; Hospital Secretary, Bridge of Earn Hospital, 1961-65; Deputy Secretary and Treasurer, East Fife Board of Management, 1965-69; Secretary and Treasurer, West Lothian Board of Management, 1969-73; Secretary, Fife Health Board, 1973-81; Secretary, Lothian Health Board, 1981-87; Associate Director, Scottish Hospital Advisory Service, 1987-94. Recreations: squash; golf; tennis. Address: (h.) 43 Braehead Road, Edinburgh, EH4 6BD; T.-0131-339 1279.

Mitchell, Professor Ross Galbraith, MD, FRCPEdin, DCH. Professor of Child Health, Dundee University, 1973-85, now Emeritus; Member, General Medical Council, 1983-85; b. 18.11.20; m., June Phylis Butcher; 1 s.; 3 d. Educ. Kelvinside Academy, Glasgow; Edinburgh University. Surgeon Lt., Royal Naval Volunteer Reserve, 1944-47; junior medical posts, Edinburgh, Liverpool and London, 1947-52; Rockefeller Research Fellow in Physiology, Mayo Clinic, USA, 1952-53; Lecturer in Child Health, St. Andrews University, 1952-55; Consultant Paediatrician, Dundee Teaching Hospitals, 1955-63; Professor of Child Health, Aberdeen University, 1963-72. Chairman, Editorial Board, Mac Keith Press, 1980-95; Chairman, Scottish Advisory Council on Child Care, 1966-68; Dean, Faculty of Medicine and Dentistry, Dundee University, 1978-81; Chairman, Aberdeen Association of Social Service, 1971-72; President, Scottish Paediatric Society, 1982-84; President, Harveian Society of Edinburgh, 1982-83; Vice-Chairman, Scottish Child and Family Alliance, 1985-92. Recreations: fishing; gardening; languages. Address: (h.) Craigard, Abertay Gardens, Barnhill, Dundee, DD5 2SQ; T.-01382 776983.

Mitchell, Ruthven, BSc (Hons), MB, ChB, MD, FRCPath, FRCPGlas, FRCPEdin. Regional Director, Glasgow and West of Scotland Blood Transfusion Service, since 1978; b. 28.3.36, Cambuslang; m., Eleanor Forbes Burnside; 1 s.; 1 d. Educ. Hamilton Academy; Glasgow University. Glasgow Royal Infirmary: Medical and Surgical House Officer, 1961-62; Senior House Officer in Pathology, 1962-63; Registrar in Pathology, 1963-65; University Lecturer in Pathology, 1965-68; Consultant Pathologist, Ministry of Health, Tanzania, 1965-67; Deputy Medical Director, Glasgow and West of Scotland Blood Transfusion Service, 1967-78. Recreations: gardening; fishing. Address: (h.) 2 Byron Court, Sweethope Farm Steading, Bothwell, Lanarkshire; T.-01698 853255.

Mitchison, Professor John Murdoch, ScD, FRS, FRSE. Professor Emeritus and Honorary Fellow, Edinburgh University (Professor of Zoology, 1963-88); b. 11.6.22; m., Rosalind Mary Wrong; 1 s.; 3 d. Educ. Winchester College; Trinity College, Cambridge. Army Operational Research, 1941-46; Research Scholar, then Fellow, Trinity College, Cambridge, 1946-54; Lecturer, then Reader in Zoology, Edinburgh University, 1953-62; Member, Edinburgh University Court, 1971-74, 1985-88; Dean, Faculty of Science, 1984-85; Member, Academia Europaea; Member, Scottish Marine Biological Association, 1961-67; Executive Committee Member, International Society for Cell Biology, 1964-72; Member: Biological Committee, SRC, 1972-75, Royal Commission on Environmental Pollution, 1974-79, Science Board, SRC, 1976-79, Working Group on Biological Manpower, DES, 1968-71, Advisory Committee on Safety of Nuclear Installations, Health and Safety Executive, 1981-84; President, British Society for Cell

Biology, 1974-77. Publication: The Biology of the Cell Cycle. Address: (h.) Great Yew, Ormiston, East Lothian, EH35 5NJ; T.-Pencaitland 340530.

Mitchison, Naomi, CBE. Writer; b. 1.11.97, Edinburgh; m., Dick Mitchison; 3 s.; 2 d. Educ. Dragon School, Oxford; St. Anne's College, Oxford. Member: Argyll County Council, 1945-65, Highland Panel, 1945-65, Highland and Island Advisory Council, 1965-75; contested Scottish Universities Parliamentary constituency for Labour; author of about 80 books, including: The Corn King and the Spring Queen; Blood of the Martyrs; The Bull Calves; The Big House; Lobsters on the Agenda; Five Men and a Swan; Cleopatra's People; volumes of autobiography; The Cleansing of the Knife; Images of Africa; Memoirs of a Space Woman; Travel Light; Early in Orcadia; A Girl Must Live. Address: (h.) Carradale House, Carradale, Campbeltown, Argyll.

Mitchison, Professor Rosalind Mary, Hon DLitt, FRSE, FRHistS, MA. Professor of Social History, Edinburgh University, 1981-86; b. 11.4.19, Manchester; m., J.M. Mitchison (qv); 1 s.; 3 d. Educ. Channing School, Highgate; Lady Margaret Hall, Oxford. Assistant Lecturer, Manchester University, 1943-46; Tutor, Lady Margaret Hall, Oxford, 1946-47; Assistant: Edinburgh University, 1954-57, Glasgow University, 1962-63; Lecturer, Glasgow University, 1966-67; Lecturer, then Reader, Edinburgh University, 1967-81. President, Scottish History Society, 1981-84. Publications:A History of Scotland, 1970; British Population Change since 1860, 1977; Life in Scotland, 1978; Lordship to Patronage: Scotland 1603-1745, 1983; Sexuality and Social Control: Scotland 1660-1780 (Co-author), 1989; Coping with destitution: poverty and relief in Western Europe, 1991. Recreation: walking. Address: (h.) Great Yew, Ormiston, East Lothian, EH35 5NJ; T.-Pencaitland 340530.

Mithen, Dallas Alfred, CB, BSc, FICFor. President, Institute of Chartered Foresters, 1984-86; Chairman, Forestry Training Council, 1984-92; b. 5.11.23; m., 1, Peggy Clarke (deceased); 2, Avril Teresa Dodd; 1 s.; 1 d. Educ. Maidstone Grammar School; University College of North Wales, Bangor. Fleet Air Arm, 1942-46; joined Forestry Commission as District Officer, 1950; Deputy Surveyor, New Forest, and Conservator, SE (England), 1968-71; Senior Officer, Scotland, 1971-75; Head, Forest Management Division, Edinburgh, 1975-76; Commissioner for Harvesting and Marketing, Forestry Commission, 1977-83. Trustee, Central Scotland Countryside Trust, since 1985; President, Forestry Section, BAAS, 1985. Recreations: swimming; walking; gardening. Address: (h.) Kings Knot, Bonnington Road, Peebles, EH45 9HF; T.-01721 720738.

Mochrie, Ronald George. Deputy Chief Executive/Director Support Services, Scottish SPCA, since 1988; b. 10.8.36, Bonnybridge; m., Helen Joan Farquhar; 1 s.; 1 d. Educ. Denny High School; Falkirk Technical College. Company Secretary/Accountant, Gilbert Plastics Ltd., 1974-77; Secretary and Treasurer, Glasgow and West of Scotland SPCA, 1977-87. Leader Trainer, Scottish Adult Leader Training Team. Recreations: gardening; walking; photography; Scouting. Address: (b.) 19 Melville Street, Edinburgh, EH3 7PL; T.-0131-225 6418.

Moffat, Alistair Murray, MA (Hons), MPhil. Chief Executive, Scottish Television Enterprises, since 1993 (Director of Programmes, 1990-93); b. 16.6.50, Kelso; m., Lindsay Thomas; 1 s.; 2 d. Educ. Kelso High School; St. Andrews University; Edinburgh University; London University. Ran Edinburgh Festival Fringe, 1976-81; Arts Correspondent/Producer/Controller of Features, Scottish Television. Publications: The Edinburgh Fringe, 1978; Kelsae — A History of Kelso from Earliest Times, 1985; Remembering Charles Rennie Mackintosh, 1989.

Recreations: sleeping; supporting Kelso RFC. Address: (b.) Scottish Television, Cowcaddens, Glasgow, G2 3PR.

Moffat, Leslie Ernest Fraser, BSc, MB, ChB, FRCS. Consultant Urological Surgeon, since 1986; Clinical Senior Lecturer, Aberdeen University; b. 23.11.49, Lanark; m., Elaine Elizabeth Theakston; 3 d. Educ. Lanark Grammar School; Edinburgh University. Professorial house officer posts, Edinburgh; SHO, Department of Surgery, Royal Infirmary, Edinburgh; Rotating Surgical Registrar, Edinburgh, 1977-79; Urological Senior Registrar, Glasgow teaching hospital, 1982-86; Chairman, Grampian Division, BMA. Recreation: country life. Address: (h.) Tillery House, Udny, Ellon, Aberdeenshire; T.-01651 842898.

Mogendorff, Professor Dolf A., FRSA, FHCIMA, MIMgt. Head of Department and Professor, Department of Hospitality, Tourism and Leisure Management, Glasgow Caledonian University, since 1993; b. 9.6.46, Holland; 4 s. Educ. Strathclyde University; Aberdeen University. Hotel and catering management in Holland and UK, 1965-75; Lecturer in Hospitality Management, Robert Gordon University, Aberdeen, 1975-88; Principal Lecturer, University of Central England, Birmingham, 1988-93. National Chairman, Council for Hospitality Management Education. Recreations: music; walking; literature. Address: (b.) Glasgow Caledonian University, 1 Park Drive, Glasgow, G3 6LP; T.-0141-337 4313.

Moir, Alan C., MA (Hons), DipEd. Rector, Ayr Academy, since 1989; b. 18.4.47, Elgin; m., Margaret; 2 s. Educ. Elgin Academy; Aberdeen Grammar School; Aberdeen University. Teacher of History, Assistant Principal Teacher, Belmont Academy, Ayr; Principal Teacher of History, Auchinleck Academy; Assistant Rector, then Depute Rector, Carrick Academy, Maybole. Session Clerk, Prestwick South Church; Secretary, Ayrshire Branch, Head Teachers Association of Scotland. Recreations: music; reading; gardening. Address: (h.) 89 Ayr Road, Prestwick, KA9 1RR; T.-01292 476883.

Moir, Alexander Thomas Boyd, MB, ChB, BSc, PhD, FRCPEdin, FRCPGlas, FRCPath, FFPHM, MFOM, FIBiol, FIFST. Director and Deputy Chief Scientist, Chief Scientist Office, Scottish Office Home and Health Department; b. 1.8.39, Bolton; m., Isabel May Sheehan; 1 s.; 2 d. Educ. George Heriot's School, Edinburgh; Edinburgh University. Intern appointment, New York City Hospitals; MRC Scientific/Clinical Scientific Staff, Honorary Registrar/Senior Registrar, Honorary Fellow, Edinburgh University; Senior/Principal Medical Officer, Scottish Home and Health Department. Recreations: playing games; listening to music; reading. Address: (b.) Scottish Office Home and Health Department, St. Andrews House, Edinburgh, EH1 3DE; T.-0131-556 8400.

Moir, Dorothy Carnegie, MB, ChB, MD, FFPHM, DipMgt. Chief Administrative Medical Officer/Director of Public Health, Lanarkshire Health Board, since 1994; Community Medicine Specialist, since 1979; Honorary Senior Clinical Lecturer in Public Health, Aberdeen University; Honorary Senior Clinical Lecturer, Department of Public Health, Glasgow University; b. 27.3.42, Aberdeen; m., Alexander D. Moir; 3 s. Educ. Albyn School for Girls, Aberdeen; Aberdeen University. Research Fellow in Therapeutics and Pharmacology, 1966-69; Lecturer in Community Medicine, 1970-79; Chief Administrative Medical Officer/Director of Public Health, Forth Valley Health Board, 1988-94. Address: (b.) 14 Beckford Street, Hamilton ML3 0TA.

Moir, Rev. Ian Andrew, MA, BD. Church of Scotland Adviser for Urban Priority Areas, since 1991; Minister, Old Kirk of Edinburgh, 1983-91; b. 9.4.35, Aberdeen; m., Elizabeth; 3 s. Educ. Aberdeen Grammar School; Aberdeen University. Sub-Warden, St. Ninian's Training Centre,

Crieff, 1959-61; Superintendent, Pholela High School, Natal, 1962-73; Assistant Secretary, Church of Scotland Overseas Council, 1974-83. Recreations: walking; golf. Address: (h.) 47 Millersneuk Drive, Lenzie, G66 5JE.

Molana, Professor Hassan, BA, MA, PhD. Professor of Economics, Dundee University, since 1993; b. 16.5.53, Tehran. Educ. Southampton University; Essex University. Research Assistant, Essex University; Research Officer, Southampton University; Lecturer, then Senior Lecturer, Glasgow University; Senior Lecturer, Dundee University. Recreation: classical music. Address: (b.) Department of Economics, Dundee University, DD1 4HN; T.-01382 344375.

Mole, George Alexander (Sandy). Vice President, National Farmers Union of Scotland, since 1990; Director, Coastal Grains Ltd., since 1988; Director, Scottish Agricultural and Rural Centre Ltd., since 1992; b. 7.6.43, Duns; m., Jean Mitchell; 1 s.; 2 d. Educ. St. Mary's, Melrose; Merchiston Castle. NFU of Scotland: President, Mid and East Berwick; Convener, Cereals Committee; Member, EEC Commission Cereals Advisory Committee; Chairman, AFRC Cereal Consultative; Member, Home Grown Cereals Authority R. & D. Committee; Member, Institute of Brewing Cereal Publicity. Recreations: golf; shooting. Address: Greenburn, Reston, Eyemouth, TD14 5LP.

Mollison, Professor Denis, ScD. Professor of Applied Probability, Heriot-Watt University, since 1986; Trustee, John Muir Trust, since 1986 (Co-Founder,1983); b. 28.6.45, Carshalton; m., Jennifer Hutton; 1 s.; 3 d. Educ. Westminster School; Trinity College, Cambridge. Research Fellow, King's College, Cambridge, 1969; Lecturer in Statistics, Heriot-Watt University, 1973. Elected Member of Council, National Trust for Scotland, 1979-84; Chairman, Mountain Bothies Association, 1978-94. Address: (h.) The Laigh House, Inveresk, Musselburgh, EH21 7TD; T.-0131-665 2055.

Molloy, Daniel Frances. Convener, Midlothian District Council, since 1992; Chairman, Midlothian Tourism Association, since 1988; b. 16.10.52, County Donegal; m., Mara; 1 s.; 1 d. Educ. St. Connells School, Co. Donegal. Member, Lothian Health Board, 1979-87; Vice-Convener, Midlothian District Council, 1988-92. Recreations: reading; walking in the countryside. Address: (h.) 57 Woodburn Bank, Dalkeith, EH22 2HP; T.-0131-663 2120.

Monaghan, Thomas John, IPFA. Town Clerk and Chief Executive, City of Glasgow District, since 1991; b. 24.11.46, Airdrie; m., Anna-Frances; 3 s. Educ. St. Patrick's High School, Coatbridge. Qualified as an accountant, 1970; held various appointments in Finance Department before becoming Senior Depute Town Clerk, 1988. Recreations: golf; opera. Address: (b.) City Chambers, Glasgow, G2 1DU; T.-0141-227 4501.

Moncreiff, 5th Baron (Harry Robert Wellwood Moncreiff), Bt; b. 4.2.15; m., Enid Marion Watson Locke (deceased); 1 s. Educ. Fettes College, Edinburgh. Lt.-Col. (Hon.), RASC (retired). Address: (h.) Tulliebole Castle, Fossoway, Kinross-shire.

Moncur, Charles C., MA (Hons), MIPR. Chairman, Commission on Scottish Education, since 1994; b. 22.3.41, Aberdeen; m., Sheila; 2 d. Educ. Culter School; Aberdeen University. Economic Analyst, ICI, Harrogate, 1969-72; Economic Adviser, Scottish Office Industry Department, 1972-85; Senior Planning Officer, BP Exploration, Aberdeen, 1985-88; Manager Community Affairs, BP Exploration, Glasgow, 1988-92; Manager Public Affairs Scotland, British Petroleum Co. plc, 1992-95. Member, Executive Council, Scottish Business in the Community; Member, Executive Council, Scottish Council Development and Industry; Board of Management, Marine Biological Research Station, Millport; Advisory Committee, UBI Scotland. Recreations: golf; football. Address: (h.) 60 Cammo Gardens, Barnton, Edinburgh EH4 8HF; T.-0131-339 5219.

Mone, Rt. Rev. John Aloysius. Bishop of Paisley, formerly Titular Bishop of Abercorn and Auxiliary Bishop of Glasgow; b. 22.6.29, Glasgow. Educ. Holyrood Secondary School; Seminaire St. Sulpice and Institut Catholique, Paris. Ordained Priest, 1952; Assistant: St. Ninian's, Knightswood, Glasgow, 1952-75, Our Lady and St. George, Glasgow, 1975-79; Parish Priest, St. Joseph's, Tollcross, Glasgow, 1979-84. National Chairman, Catholic Marriage Advisory Council, 1981; Chairman, Scottish Catholic International Aid Fund, 1975-77; President, National Justice and Peace Commission, 1987; President/Treasurer, Scottish Catholic International Aid Fund, since 1985.

Monelle, Raymond, MA, BMus, PhD, ARCM. Writer on music; Reader in Music, Edinburgh University; b. 19.8.37, Bristol; 2 d. Educ. Bristol Grammar School; Pembroke College, Oxford; Royal College of Music. Publication: Linguistics and Semiotics in Music, 1992. Address: (h.) 80 Marchmont Road, Edinburgh, EH9 1HR.

Monro, Sir Hector, AE, DL, JP, FRAgS, MP (Conservative), Dumfries, since 1964; Under Secretary of State, Scottish Office, since 1992; Farmer; b. 4.10.22, Edinburgh; m., 1, Lady (Anne) Monro (deceased); 2 s.; 2, Lady (Doris) Monro. Educ. Canford School; Cambridge University; Dundee School of Economics. RAF, 1941-46; Royal Auxiliary Air Force, 1946-53, Honorary Air Commodore, since 1981, Inspector General since 1990; Member, Dumfries County Council, 1952-67 (Chairman, Planning Committee and Joint Police Committee); Scottish Conservative Whip, 1967-70; Lord Commissioner, HM Treasury, 1970-71; Minister of Health and Education, Scottish Office, 1971-74; Opposition Spokesman on Scottish Affairs, 1974-75, Sport, 1974-79; Minister of Sport and Rural Affairs, 1979-81; Member, Nature Conservancy Council, 1982-91; Member, Area Executive, NFU, since 1964; Member, Council, National Trust for Scotland, 1983-92; Vice-President, Scottish Rugby Union, 1975, President, 1976-77; Member, Queen's Bodyguard for Scotland (Royal Company of Archers); President: NSRA, 1987-92, ACU, 1983-90. Recreations: rugby; golf; flying; vintage cars; country sports. Address: (h.) Williamwood, Kirtlebridge, Lockerbie, Dumfriesshire; T.-01461 500213.

Montagu-Smith, Group Captain Arthur, DL, RAF (Retd); b. 17.7.15; m., Elizabeth Hood Alexander; 1 s.; 1 d. Educ. Whitgift School; RAF Staff College. Commissioned RAF, 1935; Adjutant 99 Squadron, 1938-39; served Second World War, European Theatre, North Africa and Mediterranean; Flt. Cdr., 264 Squadron, 1940, and 221 Squadron, 1941; OC 248 Squadron, 1942-43; Battle of Britain Gold Rosette, 1940; mentioned in Despatches, 1942; Deputy Director, RAF Training, USA (Washington), 1944; OC 104 Wing, France, 1945; Hon. ADC, Governor, N.I., 1948-49; Air Adviser, New Delhi, 1949-50; RAF Representative, Chiefs of Staff Committee, UN, New York, 1951-53; HM Air Attache, Budapest, 1958-60; retired at own request, 1961; Regional Executive, Small Industries Council and Scottish Development Agency, 1962-80; Member, Elgin District Council, 1967-75; Member, Moray TAFA, 1961-68; Director, Elgin and Lossiemouth Harbour Company, 1966-90; Deputy Lieutenant, Morayshire, 1970-91; Hon. County Representative, Moray and Nairn, RAF Benevolent Fund, since 1964; Chairman, Elgin and Lossiemouth Scottish SPCA, 1971-82; Past President, Victoria League, Moray and Nairn; Past Chairman, Moray Association of Youth Clubs. Recreations: outdoor interests; travel; animal welfare. Address: (h.) Woodpark, by Elgin, Moray; T.-0134 384 2220.

Montgomery, Sir (Basil Henry) David, 9th Bt, JP, DL. Lord Lieutenant, Perth and Kinross, since 1995; Chairman, Forestry Commission, 1979-89; b. 20.3.31.

Montgomery, David Andrew, MA, CertEd. Chief Executive, East Ayrshire Council, since 1995; b. 22.10.46, Irvine; 2 s.; 1 d. Educ. Irvine Royal Academy; Glasgow University; Jordanhill College of Education. Teacher, Principal Teacher, Assistant Head Teacher, 1969-81; Strathclyde Regional Council: Principal Officer (Teacher Staffing), 1982-84; Education Officer, 1984-86; Assistant Director of Education, then Depute Director of Education, then Senior Depute, 1990-93. Recreations: photography; aviation. Address: (b.) London Road Centre, London Road, Kilmarnock, KA3 7DG; T.-01563 574057.

Montgomery, Rev. Robert Aitken. MA, Chaplain to Quarrier's Homes and Parish Minister, Quarrier's Village, 1978-92; b. 25.7.27, Ruthwell, Dumfries; m., Elizabeth Hay; 2 s. Educ. Hutchesons' Grammar School; Glasgow University and Trinity College. Parish Minister: Portsoy, 1955, Fordyce, 1972; Moderator: Presbytery of Fordyce, 1965, of Strathbogie and Fordyce, 1972, of Greenock, 1983; former Chairman, various Committees, County of Banff and Grampian Region, including Chairman, Children's Panel Advisory Committees; Hon. President, Abbeyfield Strathgryffe Society. Recreations: fishing; hill-walking. Address: (h.) 11 Myreton Avenue, Kilmacolm, PA13 4LJ.

Montrose, 8th Duke of (James Graham), OStJ. Brigadier, Queen's Bodyguard for Scotland (Royal Company of Archers), since 1986 (Member, since 1965); b. 6.4.35; m., Catherine Elizabeth MacDonell; 2 s.; 1 d. Educ. Loretto. Council Member, National Farmers' Union of Scotland, 1982-84, 1987-90. Address: (h.) Buchanan, Drymen, Glasgow.

Moodie, William McD., CBE. Chief Constable, Fife. Address: (b.) Police HQ, Wemyss Road, Dysart, Kirkcaldy, KY1 2YA.

Moon, Brenda Elizabeth, MA, MPhil, FLA, FRSE. Librarian, Edinburgh University, since 1980; b. 11.4.31, Stoke on Trent. Educ. Oxford University. Assistant Librarian, Sheffield University, 1955-62; Sub-Librarian, then Deputy Librarian, Hull University, 1962-79. Recreations: walking; gardening; canal cruising. Address: (b.) Edinburgh University Library, George Square, Edinburgh; T.-0131-650 3378.

Moonie, Lewis George, MB, ChB, DPM, MRCPsych, MSc, MFCM. MP (Labour), Kirkcaldy, since 1987; b. 25.2.47, Dundee; m., Sheila Burt; 2 s. Educ. Nicolson Institute, Stornoway; Grove Academy, Dundee; St. Andrews University. A variety of junior and senior medical posts, 1970-87, latterly Consultant in Public Health Medicine, Fife Health Board. Member, Fife Regional Council, 1982-86; Member, Social Services Select Committee, 1987-88; Treasury Select Committee, 1989-90; Opposition Front-Bench Spokesman on Technology, 1990-92, Science and Technology, 1992-94, Industry, since 1994. Address: (b.) 25 High Street, Kirkcaldy, Fife; T.-01592 201873.

Moore, Andrew F., BL. Commerce and Education Consultant; b. 5.12.39, Leven; m., Anne MacGregor; 2 s.; 1 d. Educ. Buckhaven High School; Edinburgh University. Examiner, Estate Duty Office, Edinburgh, 1958-63; Assistant, then Depute Secretary, Scottish Council for Commercial Education, 1963-73; Depute Chief Officer, Scottish Business Education Council, 1973-80; Chief Officer, SCOTBEC, 1980-85; seconded to Stirling University, 1987-89; Director, Scottish Chambers of Commerce, 1989-95; Director, Chinese Enterprise Management Development Programmes, 1989-94. Governor, Scottish Council for Educational Technology,

1976-84; Director, Filmhouse, Edinburgh, 1980-85; British Association for Commercial and Industrial Education; Honorary Treasurer, 1979-81, Honorary Secretary, 1966-80; President, International Society for Business Education, 1993; President, Pedagogical Committee, International Society for Business Education and Member, ISBE/SIEC Executive, since 1980; Member, Scottish Council for Research in Education, 1984-87; Hon. Secretary, Scottish Students' Song Book Committee Ltd., 1980-93; Session Clerk, Scoonie Kirk, Leven, 1982-92; President, Leven YMCA 1972-95; Member: Council, Association of British Chambers of Commerce; Executive Committee, Scottish Business in the Community; Executive Committee, Scottish Council (Development & Industry); Forces Resettlement Committee for Scotland; Member, RNIB Alwyn House Advisory Committee; Director: Fife Enterprise, 1994; Director, North of Scotland European Partnership, 1994. Recreations: golf; youth work; Rotary International; foreign travel. Address: (h.) Annandale, Linksfield Street, Leven, Fife; T.-01333 425164.

Moore, George, LLB (Hons). Solicitor and Solicitor Advocate; Joint Senior Partner, Hamilton Burns Moore, since 1973; b. 7.11.47, Kilmarnock; m., Ann Beattie; 2 s.; 1 d. Educ. High School of Glasgow; Glasgow University. Member, Glasgow and North Argyll Legal Aid Committee, 1979; Reporter to Scottish Legal Aid Board, 1986; part-time Chairman, Industrial Tribunals in Scotland, 1986; Member, Sheriff Court Rules Council, 1987. Recreations: tennis; golf; windsurfing. Address: (b.) 13 Bath Street, Glasgow, G2 1HY; T.-0141-353 2121.

Moore, Kenneth William, BSc, PhD. Agricultural Research, Education and Advisory Services Division, Scottish Office Agriculture and Fisheries Department, since 1990; b. 31.5.41, Glasgow; m., Sheila Blackwood; 2 d. Educ. Allan Glen's School, Glasgow; Glasgow University. Joined Civil Service, 1967; variously responsible for Land Tenure Reform, Health Services, Scottish Development Agency; Finance Officer, Scottish Education Department, 1980-83, and Department of Agriculture and Fisheries for Scotland, 1983-84; Head, Local Government Division, 1984-87; Head, Housing (Private Sector) Division, 1987-90. Recreations:hill-walking; mathematics and computing; cycling; language and languages; bird-watching; music. Address: (h.) 22 Morningside Park, Edinburgh; T.-0131-447 2051.

Moore, Rev. William Haisley, MA. Secretary for Scotland, Boys Brigade, since 1990; b. 9.7.35, Donaghadee; m., Geraldine Ann Moorhead; 1 s.; 2 d. Educ. Bangor Grammar School; Magee University College, Londonderry; Dublin University; Presbyterian College, Belfast. Chaplain to the Forces, attached Royal Highland Fusiliers, 1966-70; Minister, Church of Scotland, 1970-90. Convener, Church of Scotland Youth Education Committee. Recreations: golf; gardening. Address: (b.) Boys Brigade, Scottish HQ, Carronvale House, Larbert, FK5 3LH; T.-0324 562008.

Moorhouse, John Edwin. Director, Scottish Business in the Community, since 1990; b. 7.10.41, Stone, Staffs; m., Susan; 2 s.; 2 d. Educ. Bridlington School. With Royal Dutch/Shell Group of companies, 1963-94; Director: CTF Training, The Scottish Ballet, Young Enterprise Scotland, and various other charitable organisations. Recreations: music; swimming; theatre. Address: (b.) 43 Station Road, Corstorphine, Edinburgh, EH12 7AF; T.-0131-334 9876.

Moos, Khursheed Francis, OBE, MB, BS, BDS, FRCSEdin, FDS RCS (Eng, Edin), FDS RCPS (Glas). Consultant Oral and Maxillofacial Surgeon; Honorary Professor, Glasgow University; President, Cranio-facial Society of Great Britain, 1994-95; President, British Association of Oral and Maxillofacial Surgeons, 1991-92; Dean, Faculty of Dental Surgery, Royal College of Physicians and Surgeons of Glasgow, since 1992; b.

1.11.34, London; m., Katharine Addison; 2 s.; 1 d. Educ. Dulwich College; Guy's Hospital, London; Westminster Hospital. National Service, RADC, Lt., 1959, Capt., 1960; Registrar in Oral Surgery, Mount Vernon Hospital, Middlesex, 1966-67; Senior Registrar, Oral Surgery, University of Wales, Cardiff, 1967-69; Consultant Oral Surgeon, S. Warwicks and Coventry Hospitals, 1969-74; Consultant Oral and Maxillofacial Surgeon, Canniesburn Hospital, Glasgow, since 1974; Civilian Consultant to Royal Navy, since 1976; Down Surgical Prize, 1988. Publications include contributions to books and various papers. Recreations: music; natural history; philately; Eastern philosophy; gardening. Address: (h.) 43 Colquhoun Street, Helensburgh, Dunbartonshire, G84 9JW; T.-01436 73232.

Moray, Earl of (Douglas John Moray Stuart), BA, FRICS. Chairman, Moray Estates Development Co., since 1974; b. 13.2.28, Johannesburg; m., Malvina Dorothea Murray; 1 s.; 1 d. Educ. Hilton College, Natal; Trinity College, Cambridge. Address: (h.) Darnaway Castle, Forres, Moray.

Moreland, John Scotland, OBE, BSc, CEng, FIMechE. Board Member, Cumbernauld Development Corporation, since 1976; Director, Scottish Nuclear Ltd., since 1990; b. 6.5.31, Bellshill; m., May; 2 s.; 1 d. Educ. Dalziel High School, Motherwell; Glasgow University. Early career in engineering design and production management; Motherwell Bridge Group, 1967-82: Production Director, General Manager of Motherwell Brige Offshore, latterly Group Marketing Director; BP Exploration/Britoil, 1982-90: Construction Manager then Project Manager for Clyde offshore oil field development, latterly Venture Manager for all BP non-operated oil fields in UK continental shelf. Recreations: theatre; opera; music; climbing mountains. Address: (h.) 24 Falkland Street, Glasgow, G12 9PR; T.-0141-334 5676.

Morgan, Alasdair, MA, BA. National Secretary, Scottish National Party, since 1992; Project Manager, Lothian Regional Council, since 1986; b. 21.4.45, Aberfeldy; m., Anne Gilfillan; 2 d. Educ. Breadalbane Academy, Aberfeldy; Glasgow University. SNP: National Treasurer, 1983-90, Senior Vice-Convener, 1990-91. Recreation: hill-walking. Address: (h.) 2 Park Place, Dunfermline, Fife; T.-01383 736559.

Morgan, Edwin (George), OBE, MA, Hon. DLitt (Loughborough, Glasgow, Edinburgh), Hon.DUniv (Stirling, Waikato); Hon. MUniv (Open). Freelance Writer (Poet, Critic, Translator), since 1980; Emeritus Professor of English, Glasgow University, since 1980; Visiting Professor of English, Strathclyde University, 1987-90; Honorary Professor, University College of Wales, Aberystwyth, since 1990; b. 27.4.20, Glasgow. Educ. Rutherglen Academy; High School of Glasgow; Glasgow University. War Service, Royal Army Medical Corps, 1940-46; Glasgow University: Assistant Lecturer in English, 1947, Lecturer, 1950, Senior Lecturer, 1965, Reader, 1971, Titular Professor, 1975; received Cholmondeley Award for Poets, 1968; Hungarian PEN Memorial Medal, 1972; Scottish Arts Council Book Awards, 1968, 1973, 1977, 1978, 1983, 1985, 1988, 1991, 1992; Saltire Society and Royal Bank Scottish Literary Award, 1983; Soros Translation Award (New York), 1985. Publications: (poetry): The Vision of Cathkin Braes, 1952, Beowulf, 1952, The Cape of Good Hope, 1955, Poems from Eugenio Montale, 1959, Sovpoems, 1961, Collins Albatross Book of Longer Poems (Editor), 1963, Starryveldt, 1965, Emergent Poems, 1967, Gnomes, 1968, The Second Life, 1968, Proverbfolder, 1969, Twelve Songs, 1970, The Horseman's Word, 1970, Scottish Poetry 1-6 (Co-Editor), 1966-72; Glasgow Sonnets, 1972, Wi the Haill Voice, 1972, The Whittrick, 1973, From Glasgow to Saturn, 1973, Fifty Renascence Love-Poems, 1975, Rites of Passage, 1976, The New Divan, 1977,

Colour Poems, 1978, Platen: Selected Poems, 1978, Star Gate, 1979, Scottish Satirical Verse (Editor), 1980, Poems of Thirty Years, 1982, Grafts/Takes, 1983, Sonnets from Scotland, 1984, Selected Poems, 1985, From the Video Box, 1986, Themes on a Variation, 1988; Tales from Limerick Zoo, 1988; Collected Poems, 1990; Hold Hands Among the Atoms, 1991; prose: Essays, 1974, East European Poets, 1976, Hugh MacDiarmid, 1976, Twentieth Century Scottish Classics, 1987; Nothing Not Giving Messages, 1990; Crossing the Border, 1990; Evening Will Come They Will Sew The Blue Sail, 1991; plays: The Apple-Tree, 1982; Master Peter Pathelin, 1983; Cyrano de Bergerac, 1992; Sweeping Out the Dark, 1994. Address: (h.) 19 Whittingehame Court, Glasgow, G12 OBG; T.- 0141-339 6260.

Morgan, Leslie, DMS, DPE, FILAM, MIM. General Manager, Hoskyns Forres BPD (first Business Process Management Centre in Europe), since 1994; b. 7.8.53, Perth; m., Jill; 1 s.; 1 d. Educ. Perth Academy; Jordanhill College; Glasgow College of Technology. Sports Officer, Magnum Leisure Centre, Irvine; Deputy Manager, Bishopbriggs Sports Centre; Manager, Spectrum Leisure Centre, Co. Durham; Chief Leisure Officer, Wear Valley District Council; Director of Leisure and Economic Development, Wear Valley D.C.; Chief Executive, Moray District Council. British Leisure Personality of the Year, 1990. Recreations: basketball; skiing; squash. Address: (h.) The Orchard Dyke, near Forres, Moray, IV36 OTF; T.- 01309 641364.

Morgan, Tom, CBE, DL, OStJ, JP, NDD, CDD; b. 24.2.14, Aberdeenshire; m., Mary Montgomery McLauchlan (deceased); 2 s. Educ. Longside School; North and West of Scotland Colleges of Agriculture. Unigate PLC, 38 years (Regional Director, Scotland); Councillor, City of Edinburgh Corporation, 1954-71, City of Edinburgh District Council, 1977-84; City Treasurer, 1968-71; Lord Provost and Lord Lieutenant, 1980-84; Chairman, Edinburgh Military Tattoo and Edinburgh International Festival, 1980- 84. Recreations: golf; gardening. Address: (h.) 400 Lanark Road, Edinburgh, EH13 0LX; T.-0131-441 3245.

Morison, Hon. Lord (Alastair Malcolm Morison), QC, MA, LLB. Senator of the College of Justice, since 1985; b. 12.2.31, Edinburgh; m., Birgitte Hendil; 1 s., 1 d. by pr. m. Educ. Winchester College; Edinburgh University. Advocate, 1956; QC, 1965. Recreations: golf; fishing. Address: (b.) Court of Session, Edinburgh; T.-0131-225 2595.

Morison, Hugh, MA, DipEd. Director General, Scotch Whisky Association, since 1994; b. 22.11.43, Bognor Regis; m.; 2 d. Educ. Chichester High School for Boys; St. Catherine's College, Oxford. Assistant Principal, Scottish Home and Health Department, 1966-69; Private Secretary to Minister of State, Scottish Office, 1969-70; Principal: Scottish Education Department, 1971-73, Scottish Economic Planning Department, 1973-79 (seconded to Offshore Supplies Office, Department of Energy, 1974-75); Assistant Secretary, Scottish Economic Planning Department, 1979-82; Gwilym Gibbon Research Fellow, Nuffield College, Oxford, 1982-83; Assistant Secretary, Scottish Development Department, 1983-84; Under Secretary, Scottish Home and Health Department, 1984-88, Scottish Office Industry Department, 1988-93; Non- Executive Director, Weir Group PLC, 1988-93. Publication: The Regeneration of Local Economies, 1987. Publications: The Regeneration of Local Economics, 1987; Dauphine (Co-author), 1991. Recreations: hill-walking; archaeology; literature. Address: (b.) Scotch Whisky Association, 20 Atholl Crescent, Edinburgh, EH3; T.-0131-229 4383.

Morrice, Graeme. Leader, West Lothian Council, since 1995; Leader, Labour Group, West Lothian District Council, since 1992; b. 23.2.59, Edinburgh. Educ. Broxburn Academy; Napier University. Recreations: playing guitar; reading; listening to music. Address: (h.) 39 Burnside Road, Uphall, Broxburn, EH52 5DE; T.-01506 853266.

Morrice, Ken, MD, DPM, FRCPsych. Poet and Writer, since 1965; Psychiatrist, since 1956; b. 14.7.24, Aberdeen; m., Norah Thompson; 1 s.; 2 d. Educ. Robert Gordon's College; Aberdeen University. Hon. Fellow, Aberdeen University Mental Health Department; Psychotherapist in private practice. Publications: Crisis Intervention; Studies in Community Care; seven volumes of poetry; numerous papers; short stories. Recreations: golf; walking; TV. Address: (h.) 30 Carnegie Crescent, Aberdeen; T.-Aberdeen 310136.

Morris, Alexander Watt, BSc (Hons), MInstP. Principal, Edinburgh Tutorial College and American School of Edinburgh, since 1976; b. 24.11.46, Dunfermline; m., Moira Joan Watson; 1 s. Educ. Dunfermline High School; Edinburgh University. Began teaching career, Musselburgh Grammar School, 1972; Head of Physics, George Watson's Ladies College, 1973 (and to George Watson's College on merger of the schools); founded Edinburgh Tutorial College and American School of Edinburgh. Recreations: good food; hifi; cricket; skiing. Address: (b.) 29 Chester Street, Edinburgh, EH3 7EN; T.-0131-225 9888.

Morris, Alistair Lindsay, LLB, DipLP. Solicitor; Director, Sinclair Osborne Financial Services Ltd., since 1987; Director, Pagan Osborne & Grace Services Ltd., since 1986; b. 30.7.58, Dunfermline; m., Sandra Willins; 2 s. Educ. Queen Anne High School, Dunfermline; Aberdeen University. Council Member, Law Society of Scotland, since 1992. Recreations: motor sport; football; rugby. Address: (b.) 83 Market Street, St. Andrews, KY16 9PD; T.-01334 475001.

Morris, Professor Arthur Stephen, BA, MA, PhD. Professor, Department of Geography, Glasgow University; b. 26.12.36, Broadway, Worcestershire; m., Estela C.; 1 s.; 1 d. Educ. Chipping Campden; Exeter College, Oxford University; University of Maryland; University of Wisconsin. Instructor/Assistant Professor, Western Michigan University, 1964-67; Lecturer, Senior Lecturer, Reader, Glasgow University; Visiting Professor: Central University of Venezuela 1976-77, CEPEIGE, Quito, 1980, Colegie Mexiqueuse, Mexico, 1987. Publications: South America; Latin America. Recreations: gardening; music; sailing. Address: (h.) The Old Manse, Shandon, near Helensburgh; T.-0141-339 8855.

Morris, Professor Christopher David, BA, DipEd, MIFA, FSA, FSA Scot. Professor of Archaeology, Glasgow University, since 1990; b. 14.4.46, Preston; m., Dr. Colleen E. Batey. Educ. Queen Elizabeth's Grammar School, Blackburn; Durham University; Oxford University. Assistant Lecturer, Hockerill College of Education, Bishops Stortford, 1968-72; Lecturer, then Senior Lecturer in Archaeology, 1972-88, Reader in Viking Archaeology, 1989-90, Durham University; Member, Ancient Monuments Board for Scotland, since 1990. Council Member, Society of Antiquaries of Scotland, Glasgow Archaeological Society, Council for Scottish Archaeology Churches Committee, Whithorn Trust Research Committee. Recreations: classical music; opera; theatre; walking; skiing. Address: (b.) Department of Archaeology, 10 The Square, Glasgow University, Glasgow, G12 8QQ; T.-0141- 339 8855, Ext. 5690/4422.

Morris, James, CBE, BSc. Chief Executive, Scottish Society for the Prevention of Cruelty to Animals, since 1991; President, Scottish Area, Royal Air Forces Association, since 1991; Chairman, ATC Council for Scotland and NI, since 1995; President, Scottish Union Jack Association, since 1995; b. 8.7.36, Kirkcaldy; m., Anna W. Provan; 3 s. Educ. Kirkcaldy High School; Edinburgh

University. Entered RAF, 1957; commanded No. 201 Squadron, 1975-77; commanded RAF Kinloss, 1981-84; Director Operational Requirements (Air), 1986-89; Air Officer, Scotland and Northern Ireland, 1989-91 (Air Vice Marshal). Recreations: sailing; curling. Address: (b.) 19 Melville Street, Edinburgh, EH3 7PL; T.-0131-225 6418.

Morris, Jean Daveena Ogilvy, CBE, MA, MEd, LLD (Dundee and St. Andrews), OSStJ. Member, Court, University of St. Andrews, since 1994; Chairman, Parole Board for Scotland, 1980-92; b. 28.1.29, Kilmarnock; m., Rev. William J. Morris (qv); 1 s. Educ. Kilmarnock Academy; St. Andrews University. Clinical Psychologist: Royal Hospital for Sick Children, Edinburgh, St. David's Hospital, Cardiff, and Church Village, Pontypridd; Member, Bailie and Convener of Housing, Peterhead Town Council; Member, Aberdeen County Council; Columnist, Aberdeen Press and Journal; Chairman, Christian Action Housing Association; Member, Scottish Federation of Housing Associations; Chairman, Government Committee on Links Between Housing and Social Work (Morris Committee); Chairman, Local Review Committee, Barlinnie Prison; Chairman, Glasgow Abbeyfield Society; Vice Chairman, TSB Foundation; Director, Scottish Advisory Board, Abbey National; Chairman, Scotia House Development Company. Badminton Blue, St. Andrews University. Recreations: swimming; holidays in France. Address: (h.) 94 St. Andrews Drive, Glasgow, G41 4RX; T.-0141-427 2757.

Morris, Professor John Llewelyn, BSc, PhD, FIMA, CMath. Professor of Computer Science, Dundee University, since 1986; b. 19.9.43, Newtown, Wales; 2 s.; 1 d. Educ. Tywyn Grammar School; Leicester University; St. Andrews University. NCR Postdoctoral Fellow, Dundee University, 1967-69; Lecturer, Dundee University, 1969-75; Associate Professor, then Professor, University of Waterloo, Ontario, 1975-86. Publications: Computers and Computing (Co-author), 1973; Computational Methods in Elementary Numerical Analysis, 1983. Address: (b.) Dundee University, Dundee, DD1 4HN.

Morris, Professor Richard Graham Michael, MA, DPhil. Director, Centre for Neuroscience, Edinburgh University, (Professor, since 1993, Reader, 1989-93); b. 27.6.48, Worthing; m., Hilary Ann; 2 d. Educ. St. Albans, Washington DC; Marlborough College; Cambridge University; Sussex University. Addison Wheeler Fellow, Durham University, 1973-75; SSO, British Museum (Natural History), 1975-77; Researcher, BBC Television, 1977; Lecturer, St. Andrews University, 1977-86; MRC University Research Fellow, 1983-86. Member, MRC Neurosciences Grants Committee, 1981-85; MRC Neurosciences Board, since 1993; Hon. Secretary, Experimental Psychological Society, 1985-89; Chairman, Brain Research Association, 1990-94. Publications: academic papers and books; Learning and Memory (Co-Editor). Recreation: sailing. Address: (b.) Centre for Neuroscience, Edinburgh University, Crichton Street, Edinburgh, EH8 9LE; T.-0131-650 3518/4562.

Morris, Professor Robert John, BA, DPhil. Professor of Economic and Social History, Edinburgh University, since 1993; b. 12.10.43, Sheffield; m., Barbara; 1 s.; 1 d. Educ. Acklam Hall; Keble and Nuffield Colleges, Oxford. Lecturer and Senior Lecturer in Economic and Social History, Edinburgh University, since 1968. Editor, History and Computing. Recreation: watching vegetables grow. Address: (b.) 55 George Square, Edinburgh, EH8 9JU.

Morris, Professor Robert Lyle, BSc, PhD. Professor of Parapsychology, Edinburgh University, since 1985; b. 9.7.42, Canonsburg, Pennsylvania; m., Joanna Du Barry; 2 d. Educ. Crafton High School; University of Pittsburgh; Duke University. Research Fellow, Duke University, 1969-71; Research Co-ordinator, then Research Associate,

Psychical Research Foundation, 1971-74; Lecturer in Parapsychology, University of California, Santa Barbara, 1974-78; Lecturer, School of Social Sciences, University of California, Irvine, 1978-80; Reseach Coordinator, Communication Studies Laboratory, and Senior Research Scientist, School of Computer and Information Sciences, Syracuse University, 1980-85. Member, Council, Parapsychological Association; Member, Council, British Society for Psychical Research; President, Psychology Section, British Association for the Advancement of Science, 1995-96. Publication: Foundations of Parapsychology: Exploring the Boundaries of Human Capability (Co-author), 1986. Address: (h.) 2 Strathalmond Green, Edinburgh, EH4 8AQ; T.-0131-339 6461.

Morris, William, BA (Hons), FIOP, FSCOTVEC. Assistant General Secretary, Association of Principals of Colleges, since 1991; b. 15.5.24, Aberdare, Wales; m., Pauline; 1 s.; 2 d. Educ. Aberdare Boys' Secondary School; Cardiff School of Art; Garnet College, London; London School of Printing and Graphic Arts; Open University. Compositor/Typographer; Royal Artillery, 1942-45; Lecturer in Typography, LSP&GA, 1951-58; Head, Department of Typography and Related Subjects; Depute Principal, Glasgow College of Building and Printing; Principal, Anniesland College, 1981-89; Board Member, Printing and Publishing Industry Training Board, 1968-82; Member, City and Guilds of London Institute; Board Member and Director, Scottish Vocational Education Council, 1987-91; Past Chairman, Association of Principals of Colleges (Scottish Branch); Past Chairman, Association of College Management (Scottish Branch); Secretary, Employers' Association for Scottish Further Education Colleges, 1992-93; Secretary to the Vestry, St. Cyprian's Church, Lenzie, 1981-94. Recreations: golf; gardening; painting. Address: (h.) 26 Laurel Avenue, Lenzie, Kirkintilloch, Glasgow, G66 4RU; T.-0141-776 2716.

Morris, Rev. William James, JP, BA, BD, PhD, LLD, DD, Hon. FRCP&SGlas. Minister, Glasgow Cathedral, since 1967; Chaplain in Ordinary to The Queen in Scotland, since 1969; Chairman, Iona Cathedral Trust, since 1979; Dean, Chapel Royal in Scotland, since 1991; Chaplain to The Queen's Body Guard in Scotland (Royal Company of Archers), since 1994; b. 22.8.25, Cardiff; m., Jean Daveena Ogilvy Howie (see Jean Daveena Ogilvy Morris); 1 s. Educ. Cardiff High School; University of Wales (Cardiff and Aberystwyth); Edinburgh University. Ordained, 1951; Assistant, Canongate Kirk, Edinburgh, 1949-51; Minister, Barry Island and Cadoxton Presbyterian Church of Wales, 1951-53; Minister: St. David's, Buckhaven, 1953-57, Peterhead Old Parish Church, 1957-67; Chaplain, Peterhead Prison, 1963-67; Chaplain to Lord High Commissioner, 1975-76; Moderator, Deer Presbytery, 1965-66; Chaplain: Strathclyde Police, Glasgow Academy, High School of Glasgow, Glasgow District Council, Trades House of Glasgow, Glasgow YMCA, West of Scotland Engineers Association, Royal Scottish Automobile Club, Order of St. John; Member, Independent Broadcasting Authority, 1979-84 (Chairman, Scottish Advisory Committee); Member, Convocation, Strathclyde University; Honorary President, Glasgow Society of Social Service. Publication: A Walk Through Glasgow Cathedral, 1986. Recreation: being good, careful, and happy (not always simultaneously). Address: (h.) 94 St. Andrews Drive, Glasgow, G41 4RX; T.-0141-427 2757.

Morrison, Alexander Fraser, CBE, FRSA, BSc, CEng, FICE. Chairman, Highlands and Islands Enterprise; Chairman and Managing Director, Morrison Construction Group Ltd., since 1984; b. 20.3.48, Dingwall; m., Patricia Janice Murphy; 1 s.; 2 d. Educ. Tain Royal Academy; Edinburgh University. Morrison Construction Group, since 1970; Managing Director, 1976-84. National Federation of Civil Engineering Contractors: Chairman, 1993-94, Vice President, 1994-95; Director, Aberforth Split Level Trust plc; winner, 1991 Scottish Business Achievement Award. Recreations: rugby; golf; skiing; opera; theatre; art. Address: (b.) Morrison House, 12 Atholl Crescent, Edinburgh, EH3 8HA; T.-0131-228 4188.

Morrison, Andrew Neil, QFSM, DTech, FIFireE. Her Majesty's Chief Inspector of Fire Services (Scotland), since 1994; b. 8.9.37, Arbroath; m., Kathleen; 1 s. Educ. Arbroath High School; Dundee College of Technology. Grampian Fire Brigade: Deputy Firemaster, 1980, Firemaster, 1985. Chairman, Phoenix Club for Disabled Young Persons (Aberdeen). Recreations: curling; golf; reading. Address: (b.) Scottish Office Home and Health Department, St. Andrew's House, Edinburgh; T.-0131-244 2342.

Morrison, Rev. Angus, MA, BD. Minister, Associated Presbyterian Churches, Viewforth Congregation, Edinburgh, since 1989; b. 30.8.53, Oban; m., Marion Jane Matheson; 2 s.; 1 d. Educ. Oban High School; Glasgow University; London University. Minister, Free Presbyterian Church of Scotland Oban Congregation, 1979-86; Edinburgh Congregation, 1986-89; Moderator, Southern Presbytery, Free Presbyterian Church, 1987-88; Moderator, APC Scottish Presbytery, 1993-94. Secretary, Scottish Evangelical Theology Society; Member, Council, Rutherford House, Edinburgh; Contributor, Dictionary of Scottish Church History and Theology, 1993; Member, Gaelic Panel, National Bible Society of Scotland. Recreations: reading; swimming. Address: (h.) 6 Frogston Grove, Edinburgh, EH10 7AG; T.-0131-445 3673.

Morrison, Rev. Angus Wilson, MA, BD. Minister, Kildalton and Oa Parish, Islay, since 1989 (Minister, Braid Parish Church, Edinburgh, 1977-89); b. 14.2.34, Glasgow; m., Isobel M.S. Taylor; 1 s.; 2 d. Educ. Epsom College, Surrey; Trinity College, Oxford; New College, Edinburgh. Minister: Whithorn, 1961-67, Cults West, Aberdeen, 1967-77; various periods of service on General Assembly Committees, including Overseas Council, Inter-Church Relations, Board of Education and Selection Schools; Observer for World Alliance of Reformed Churches, Vatican Council II, 1963. Recreations: travel; family. Address: The Manse, Port Ellen, Isle of Islay, PA42 7DB; T.-01496 302447.

Morrison, Professor Arnold, BA, MEd, FBPsS, CPsychol. Emeritus Professor of Education, Stirling University, since 1984; Educational Consultant, since 1986; b. 29.3.28, Birmingham; m., Katharine Neil; 2 s.; 1 d. Educ. Birmingham College of Arts and Crafts; Birmingham University. Army, 1946-48; Schoolmaster, 1950-62; Lecturer, Moray House College of Education, 1962-66; Lecturer, Edinburgh University, 1966-70; Senior Lecturer, Dundee University, 1970-75; Professor of Education, Stirling University, 1975-84; Member, Consultative Committee on the Curriculum, 1980-86. Publications: Teachers and Teaching; Schools and Socialisation; various contributions on social psychology of education. Recreations:mountaineering; genealogy. Address: (h.) 4 Victoria Place, Stirling, FK8 2QX; T.-01786 74053.

Morrison, Colin Andrew, BA, MEd, DipM, MCIM, CertEd. Director of Education, Chartered Institute of Bankers in Scotland, since 1991; b. 14.10.61, Ellon; m., Stella Ross Ingram. Educ. Peterhead Academy; Robert Gordon's Institute of Technology; Aberdeen College of Education; Edinburgh University. Former Outdoor Pursuits Instructor and F.E. Lecturer/Senior Lecturer; Head of Business Studies, Stevenson College, 1990-91. Recreations: dinghy sailing; skiing. Address: (b.) 19 Rutland Square, Edinburgh, EH1 2DE; T.-0131-229 9869.

Morrison, David Ralston. Writer; b. 4.8.41, Glasgow; m., Edna May Wade; 1 s.; 1 d. Educ. Glasgow High School for Boys; Hamilton Academy; Strathclyde University. Librarian: Lanark County, Edinburgh College of Art,

Caithness. Founded and ran Scotia Review, Wick Folk Club, Wick Festival of Poetry, Folk and Jazz; author of numerous books of poetry; edited Essays on Neil M. Gunn, Essays on Fionn MacColla. Recreations: walking; drystanedyking; reading; music. Address: (h.) 18 MacArthur Street, Wick, KW1 5AX; T.-01955 3703.

Morrison, Hamish Robertson, OBE. Chief Executive, Scottish Council Development and Industry, since 1981; b. 24.5.44, Irvine; m., Denise Mary; 1 s.; 2 d. Educ. Kilmarnock Academy; Britannia Royal Naval College, Dartmouth. Royal Navy, 1961-69; Scottish Council: London Office, 1969-72, Highland Area Manager, 1972-75, Policy Director, Edinburgh, 1975-80; European Commission, Brussels, 1980-81. Recreations: hill-walking; industrial history of Scotland. Address: (h.) 43 Coates Gardens, Edinburgh, EH12 5LF; T.-0131-337 1476; (b.) 23 Chester Street, Edinburgh, EH3 7ET; T.-0131-225 7911.

Morrison, James, RSA, RSW, DA, DUniv (Stirling). Painter in oil and watercolour; b. 11.4.32, Glasgow; m., Dorothy McCormack; 1 s.; 1 d. Educ. Hillhead High School; Glasgow School of Art. Taught part-time, 1955-58; won Torrance Memorial Prize, RGI, 1958; Visiting Artist, Hospitalfield, 1962-63; Council Member, SSA, 1964-67; staff, Duncan of Jordanstone College of Art, 1965-87; won Arts Council Travelling Scholarship to Greece, 1968; painting in various regions of France, 1976-82; numerous one-man exhibitions since 1956, in Scotland, London, Italy, West Germany, Canada; four works in private collection of Duke of Edinburgh and numerous other works in public and private collections; several group exhibitions since 1980 in UK and Europe; regular series of expeditions to paint in Canadian and Greenland High Arctic, since 1990. Publication: Aff the Squerr. Recreation: playing in a chamber music group. Address: (h.) Craigview House, Usan, Montrose, Angus; T.-Montrose 672639.

Morrison, Jean Turner, DipHE. National President, The Girls' Brigade in Scotland, since 1993; b. 14.5.41, Hamilton. Educ. Eastbank Academy, Glasgow; Glasgow and West of Scotland College of Domestic Science. Assistant Principal Teacher, Garthamlock Secondary School, Glasgow. Elder, Shettleston Old Parish Church, Glasgow. Recreations: walking; gardening; reading; travelling. Address: (b.) B.B. House, 168 Bath Street, Glasgow, G2 4TQ; T.-0141-778 1148.

Morrison, Neil, MA (Hons), DipEd. Rector, Eyemouth High School, since 1990; b. 5.10.47, Aberdeen; m., Lorna; 2 d. Educ. Robert Gordon's College, Aberdeen; Aberdeen University. Teacher, Principal Teacher, 1971-81; Assistant Rector, Mintlaw Academy, 1981-87; Depute Rector, Culloden Academy, 1987-90. Recreation: gardening. Address: (b.) Eyemouth High School, Eyemouth, TD14 5BY.

Morrison, Nigel Murray Paton, QC. Queen's Counsel, since 1988; b. 18.3.48, Paisley. Educ. Rannoch School. Called to the Bar of England and Wales, Inner Temple, 1972; admitted to Scottish Bar, 1975; Assistant Editor, Session Cases, 1976-82; Assistant Clerk, Rules Council, 1978-84; Clerk of Faculty, Faculty of Advocates, 1979-86; Standing Junior Counsel to Scottish Development Department (Planning), 1982-86; Temporary Sheriff, since 1982; Chairman, Social Security Appeal Tribunals, 1982-91; Second (formerly Junior) Counsel to the Lord President of the Court of Session, 1984-89; First Counsel to the Lord President, since 1989; Counsel to Secretary of State under Private Legislation Procedure (Scotland) Act 1936, since 1986; Chairman, Medical Appeal Tribunals, since 1991; Trustee, National Library of Scotland, since 1989. Publications: Green's Annotated Rules of the Court of Session; Green's Civil Practice Bulletin; Stair Memorial Encyclopaedia of the Laws of Scotland (Contributor); Recreations: music; riding; Scottish country dancing; being taken by his black labrador for walks. Address: 11 India Street, Edinburgh EH3 6HA; T.-0131-225 8030.

Morrison, Peter, MA, LLB. Singer and Solicitor; b. 14.8.40, Greenock; m., Irene; 1 s.; 1 d. Educ. Greenock Academy; Glasgow University. Town Clerk's Department: Paisley, 1965, Clydebank, 1966-68; private legal practice thereafter; established own legal practice, 1977; began professional singing engagements at University; passed BBC audition, 1969, and began solo broadcasts; first television series, Castles in the Air, 1971; numerous radio, television and theatre appearances in UK and abroad. Recreations: golf; tennis; non-participating cricket and rugby supporter. Address: (b.) 65 Bath Street, Glasgow; T.-0141-331 1029.

Morrison, Peter Angus. Director, Lewis Land Services Ltd.; Director and Vice-Chairman, Western Isles Enterprise; Vice-Chairman, Board of Management, Lews Castle College; Member, Crofters Commission, 1984-93; b. 31.12.45, Isle of Lewis; m., Murdina; 2 d. Educ. Shawbost School; Lews Castle College. Mechanical engineering apprenticeship, then draughtsman, William Beardmore & Co., Glasgow; contracts draughtsman, John Brown Engineering, Clydebank; Lecturer in Mechanical Engineering, Springburn College of Engineering; Senior Lecturer, Engineering Department, Lews Castle College. Recreation: travel. Address: (h.) 52 Newmarket, Stornoway, Lewis; T.-01851 5338.

Morrison, Rev. Roderick, MA, BD. Minister, Partick Gardner Street Church, Glasgow, since 1994; b. 3.7.43, Lochmaddy; m., Christina Ann MacDonald; 1 s.; 1 d. Educ. Lochportan Public School; Glasgow University and Trinity College. Assistant Minister, Drumchapel Old Parish Church, Glasgow, 1973-74; Minister, Carinish Parish Church, North Uist, 1974-81; Minister, High Church, Stornoway, Lewis, 1981-94. Recreations: sailing; fishing; shooting. Address: 148 Beechwood Drive, Broomhill, Glasgow G11 7DX; T.-0141-339 2816.

Morrison, William Garth, CBE, BA, CEng, MIEE, DL. Farmer; Chief Scout, since 1988; Member, World Scout Committee, since 1992; Chief Commissioner of Scotland, The Scout Association, 1981-88; b. 8.4.43, Edinburgh; m., Gillian Cheetham; 2 s.; 1 d. Educ. Pangbourne College; Pembroke College, Cambridge. Service, Royal Navy, 1961-73, retiring with rank of Lt.; farming, since 1973; Member, Lothian Region Children's Panel, 1976-83 (Chairman, Midlothian/East Lothian Area Panel, 1978-81); Lamp of Lothian Trustee, 1978; Member, Lothian, Borders and Fife Committee, Prince's Trust, 1979, Lothian and Borders Committee, Prince's and Royal Jubilee Trusts, 1983-88; Member, Society of High Constables of Holyroodhouse, 1979; Deputy Lieutenant, East Lothian, 1984; Member, Scottish Community Education Council, 1988-95; Chairman, East and Midlothian NHS Trust, since 1993. Recreations: golf; sailing; Scouting. Address: West Fenton, North Berwick, East Lothian; T.-01620 842154.

Morrocco, Alberto, OBE, RSA, RSW, RP, RGI, LLD, DUniv. Painter, since 1938; b. 14.12.17, Aberdeen; 2 s.; 1 d. Educ. Sunnybank School, Aberdeen; Gray's School of Art, Aberdeen. Former Member, Grants Committee, Scottish Arts Council; former Member, Royal Fine Art Commission for Scotland. Carnegie Award, Royal Scottish Academy: Guthrie Award, San Vito Romano Prize. Address: Binrock, 456 Perth Road, Dundee; T.-01382 69319.

Morrow, Digby Wilson, LLB, CA. Chief Executive, Sidlaw Group plc, since 1988; b. 4.5.49, Barrhead; m., Margaret; 2 s.; 1 d. Educ. Paisley Grammar School; Glasgow University. European Controller, then Assistant VP Operations, Gray Tool Co., 1973-80; Finance Director, IMS Ltd., Singapore, 1980-83; Group Controller, Flopetrol

Schlumberger, Paris, 1983-85; Finance Director, Sidlaw Group plc, 1985-88; Director, Scottish Development Finance Ltd.; Member, Scottish Council, CBI. Recreations: sailing; golf. Address: (b.) Keith House, South Gyle, Edinburgh EH12 9DQ; T.-0131-317 2600.

Morton, Rev. Alasdair J., MA, BD, DipEd, DipRE, FEIS. Minister, Bowden linked with Newtown St. Boswells, since 1991; b. 8.6.34, Inverness; m., Gillian M. Richards; 2 s.; 2 d. Educ. Bell-Baxter School, Cupar; St. Andrews University; Hartford Theological Seminary. District Missionary/Minister, Zambia (Northern Rhodesia), 1960-65; Chaplain and Religious Education Lecturer, Malcolm Moffat Teachers' College, Serenje, Zambia, 1966-67; Principal, David Livingstone Teachers' College, Livingstone, Zambia, 1968-72; Minister, Greyfriars Parish Church, Dumfries, 1973-77; General Secretary, Department of Education, Church of Scotland, 1977-91. Recreations: choral singing; gardening. Address:The Manse, Newtown St. Boswells, TD6 0SG; T.-01835 822106.

Morton, Rev. Andrew Reyburn, MA, BD. Deputy General Secretary, Board of World Mission and Unity, Church of Scotland, 1988-93; b. 24.5.28, Kilmarnock; m., Marion Armstrong Chadwin; 2 s.; 2 d. Educ. Kilmarnock Academy; Glasgow University; Edinburgh University; Bonn University. Scottish Secretary, Student Christian Movement, 1953-56; Minister, Moncreiff Parish, East Kilbride, 1956-64; Chaplain, Edinburgh University, 1964-70; Warden, Wolfson Hall and Co-ordinating Warden, Halls of Residence, Glasgow University, 1970-74; Social Responsibility Secretary and, latterly, Secretary, Division of Community Affairs and Assistant General Secretary, British Council of Churches, 1974-81; Secretary, Inter-Church Relations Committee and Assistant Secretary, Overseas Council, subsequently Assistant Secretary, Board of World Mission and Unity, Church of Scotland, 1982-88; Associate Director, Centre for Theology and Public Issues, University of Edinburgh. Recreation: walking. Address: (h.) 11 Oxford Terrace, Edinburgh, EH4 1PX; T.-0131-332 6592.

Morton, 22nd Earl of (John Charles Sholto Douglas), DL; b. 19.3.27. Lord-Lieutenant, West Lothian, since 1985.

Morton, Tom, MA. Writer and Broadcaster; Presenter, daily show, BBC Radio Scotland, since 1994; Weekly Columnist, The Scotsman, since 1992; b. 31.12.55, Carlisle; m., Susan J. Bowie; 4 s.; 1 d. Educ. Marr College, Troon; Glasgow University. Reporter, Project Scotland, 1977-79; musician/evangelist, British Youth for Christ, 1979-83; hi-fi salesman, 1983; Reporter, Project Scotland, 1983-85; Reporter, BBC Scotland, 1983-86; Scottish Correspondent, Melody Maker, 1985-86; News Editor, Shetland Times, 1986-88; freelance, 1988-90; Highland Reporter, The Scotsman, 1990-94. Publications: Going Home: the Runrig Story, 1992; Spirit of Adventure, 1993; Red Guitars in Heaven, 1994; Hell's Golfer, 1995. Recreations: motorcycles; boats; books; music. Address: (b.) Radio Scotland, BBC, 7 Culduthel Road, Inverness, IV2 4AD; T.-01463 720720.

Morton, William John Keirs, DipTP, MRTPI. Chief Executive, Forth Valley Enterprise, since 1990; b. 14.6.49, Glasgow; m., Jan; 2 s.; 1 d. Educ. Bearsden Academy; Glasgow College of Art. Planning Assistant, Royal Burgh of Inverness, 1973-75; Project Officer, East Kilbride Development Corporation, 1975-76; SDA, 1976-87, latterly as Project Manager (Coatbridge Project); Chief Executive, Aberdeen Beyond 2000, 1987-89; Head of Urban Regeneration, SDA, 1989-90. Recreations: family; travel; cycling; reading. Address: (b.) Laurel House, Laurelhill Business Park, Stirling, FK7 9JQ; T.-01786 51919.

Moss, Michael Stanley, MA. Archivist, Glasgow University, since 1974; b. 11.4.47, Harrogate; m.; 2 d. Educ. King Edward's School, Bath; Worcester College,

Oxford. Registrar, Western Survey, National Register of Archives (Scotland). Publications include: The Workshop of the British Empire (Co-author); The Making of Scotch Whisky (Co-author); Shipbuilders to the World (Co-author); An Invaluable Treasurer (Co-author); The Royal (Co-author). Recreations: swimming; climbing; gardening; stable management. Address: (b.) The Archives, Glasgow University, Glasgow, G12 8QQ; T.-0141-330 5516.

Mounfield, J. Hilary, MA (Hons), MICFM. National Director, Epilepsy Association of Scotland, since 1995; Chair, Bighearted Scotland, since 1993; b. 19.7.41, Edinburgh; 2 s.; 1 d. Educ. Boroughmuir School; Edinburgh University. Research, Scottish Development Department and Ministry of Housing, 1963-66; teaching, London, 1973-84; fund-raising for charities, 1984-91; Appeals Director, Penumbra, 1991-95. Chair, ICFM, Scotland, 1993-95; Advisory Board Member, Edinburgh Common Purpose. Recreations: gardening; reading; walking. Address: (b.) 48 Govan Road, Glasgow, G51 1JL; T.-0141-427 4911.

Mowat, James Rennie, BSc, FEng, FIMinE. Chairman, Invercoe Engineering Ltd., since 1990; Chairman, Butters Engineering Services Ltd., since 1990; Board Member, East Kilbride Development Corporation, since 1990; b. 7.5.36, Glasgow; m., Gillian; 3 s. Educ. High School of Glasgow; Royal Technical College, Glasgow; Administrative Staff College, Henley. Various technical and managerial appointments, Anderson Strathclyde (Managing Director, 1980-89); Non-Executive Director: Invercoe Engineering Ltd., Butters Engineering Services Ltd.; Past President: Scottish Engineering, Mining Institute of Scotland. Recreations: sailing; occasional golf. Address: (h.) Cruive Cottage, Kinkell Bridge, Auchterarder, PH3 1LD.

Mowat, Sheriff Principal John Stuart, MA, LLB, QC. Sheriff Principal of South Strathclyde, Dumfries and Galloway, 1988-93; b. 30.1.23, Manchester; m., Anne Cameron Renfrew; 2 s.; 2 d. Educ. High School of Glasgow; Merchiston Castle School; Glasgow University. Served RAF Transport Command, 1942-46 (Flt.-Lt.); Journalist, 1947-52; Advocate, 1952-60; Sheriff of Fife and Kinross, at Dunfermline, 1960-72, at Cupar and Kinross, 1972-74, of Glasgow and Strathkelvin, 1974-88; Chairman, Sheriff Court Rules Council, 1989-92; Office-Bearer, Scottish Liberal Party, 1954-58; Parliamentary candidate, Caithness and Sutherland, 1955; Secretary, Sheriffs Association, 1968-75 (President, 1988); Trustee: Carnegie Dunfermline Trust, 1967-74, Carnegie United Kingdom Trust, 1970-74. Recreations: golf; curling; watching football. Address: (h.) Drummond View, 2 New Cottages, Fortingall, Perthshire.

Mowat, Norman Ashley George, MB, ChB, MRCP (UK), FRCP, FRCP (Edin). Consultant Physician and Gastroenterologist, Aberdeen Teaching Hospitals, since 1975; Clinical Senior Lecturer in Medicine, Aberdeen University, since 1975; b. 11.4.43, Cullen; m., Kathleen Mary Cowie; 1 s.; 2 d. Educ. Fordyce Academy; Aberdeen University. House Officer, then Senior House Officer, then Registrar, Aberdeen Teaching Hospitals, 1966-72; Lecturer in Medicine, Aberdeen University, 1972-73; Lecturer in Gastroenterology and Research Associate, Medical College of St. Bartholomew's, London, 1973-75. Visiting Physician to Shetland Islands; publications include Integrated Clinical Sciences: Gastroenterology (Co-Editor), 1985. Recreations: sailing; golf; soccer; reading; photography. Address: (h.) Bucholie, 13 Kings Cross Road, Aberdeen, AB2 4BF; T.-01224 319223.

Mowat, William George, JP. Honorary Sheriff, Caithness; Chairman, Caberfeidh Court, Royal British Legion Housing Association Ltd., 1978-93; Chairman, Caithness Voluntary Group, since 1991; Chairman, Caithness Justices, 1992-94; b. 12.5.28, Lybster; m., Aline Cameron Johnston; 3 d. Educ. Robert Gordon's College, Aberdeen. Provost of Wick,

1967-75; Chairman, Royal Burgh of Wick Community Council, 1977-91; Member, Caithness County Council, 1957-75. Vice Chairman, Civilian Committee, ATC Wick Squadron; Chairman, Friends of Hempriggs Residential Home, Wick; Elder, Church of Scotland. Recreations: golf; flying; used to fish a little. Address: (h.) Buchollie, Coronation Street, Wick, KW1 5LS; T.-01955 4794.

Mowat, William Stewart, FCCA. Director of Finance, Argyll and Clyde Health Board, since 1993; b. 28.12.46, Tobermory; m., Lynda; 1 s.; 1 d. Educ. Ellon Academy; Aberdeen College of Commerce. BP, London; C.F. Wilson, Aberdeen; John Wood Group; NHS, Aberdeen; Highland Health Board, Wick. Recreation: golf. Address: (h.) 7 Balmore Court, Kilmacolm, PA13 4LL; T.-01505 873182.

Moyes, William, BSc, PhD. Director of Strategic Planning and Performance Management, Management Executive, NHS in Scotland, 1990-94, now seconded from Scottish Office to British Linen Bank; b. 18.9.49, Dundee; m., Barbara Ann Rice; 1 s. Educ. Lawside Academy, Dundee; Edinburgh University. Entered Civil Service, 1974; Department of Environment and Transport, 1974-80; promoted to Principal, 1978; seconded to Economic Secretariat, Cabinet Office, 1980-83; joined Scottish Office Finance Division, 1983; Assistant Secretary, Scottish Education Department, 1985-87, Department of Agriculture and Fisheries for Scotland, 1987-90. Recreations: gardening; food and wine; talking. Address: (b.) 4 Melville Street, Edinburgh; T.-0131-243 8439.

Muir, Alastair James, BA (Hons). Chief Executive, Clydebank Economic Development Company, since 1989; b. 21.10.57, Paisley; m., Dr. Sarah Louise Davidson; 2 d. Educ. John Neilson, Paisley; Paisley College. Centre for Study of Public Policy, Strathclyde University, 1984-86; Depute Chief Executive, ASSET, 1986-89. Recreations: skiing; sailing; hill-walking. Address: (b.) Phoenix House, 7 South Avenue, Clydebank, G81 2LG; T.-0141-951 1131.

Muir, Richard. Chairman and Chief Executive, James Finlay PLC. Address: (b.) 10 West Nile Street, Glasgow, G1.

Muir, Trevor. Chief Executive, Midlothian District Council, since 1987; b. 10.7.49, Glasgow; m., Christine Ann; 1 s.; 1 d. Educ. High School of Glasgow; Langside College; Strathclyde University. Scottish Special Housing Association, 1973-77; City of Glasgow District Council, 1977-81; Director of Housing, City of Aberdeen District Council, 1981-87. Recreations: squash; family life. Address: (b.) Midlothian House, Buccleuch Street, Dalkeith, Midlothian, EH22 1DJ.

Muir Wood, Professor David, MA, PhD, CEng, FICE. Cormack Professor of Civil Engineering, Glasgow University, since 1987; Associate, Geotechnical Consulting Group, since 1983; b. 17.3.49, Folkestone; m., Helen Rosamond Piddington; 2 s. Educ. Royal Grammar School, High Wycombe; Peterhouse, Cambridge. William Stone Research Fellow, Peterhouse, Cambridge, 1973-75; Royal Society Research Fellow, Norwegian Geotechnical Institute, Oslo, 1975; Fellow, Emmanuel College, Cambridge, 1975-87; University Lecturer in Soil Mechanics, Cambridge University, 1975-87. British Geotechnical Society Prize, 1978. Publications: Offshore Soil Mechanics (Co-author); Pressuremeter Testing (Co-author); Soil Behaviour and Critical State Soil Mechanics. Recreations: music; travel; walking. Address: (b.) Department of Civil Engineering, Rankine Building, Glasgow University, Glasgow, G12 8LT; T.-0141-330 5202.

Mulholland, Henry, JP. Leader, Inverclyde District Council, since 1990; b. 10.5.30, Greenock; m., Mary Ann McNeil Scullion; 1 s.; 3 d. Educ. St. Columba's, Greenock.

Councillor, Greenock, since 1970; Director, Renfrewshire Enterprise Company; Director, Inverclyde Enterprise Company. Address: (h.) 119 Mallard Crescent, Greenock, PA16 7BE; T.-01475 723665.

Mullen, Frank, BSc, MPhil, MCP. Director, Scottish Convention Bureau, since 1994; b. 12.5.58, Kilmarnock. Educ. James Hamilton Academy, Kilmarnock; Glasgow University; University of Pennsylvania. Policy Researcher, Strathclyde Regional Council, 1980-85; Area Manager, Scottish Tourist Board, 1985-87; Marketing Director, Greater Glasgow Tourist Board and Convention Bureau, 1987-94. Recreations: keep-fit; theatre. Address: (b.) 23 Ravelston Terrace, Edinburgh, EH4 3EU; T.-0131-332 2433.

Mullen, Ian M., BSc, MRPharmS. Freelance consultant on healthcare and pharmaceutical issues; freelance writer and broadcaster; b. 11.5.46, Stirling; m., Veronica Drummond; 2 s.; 1 d. Educ. St. Modan's High School, Stirling; Heriot-Watt University. Registered MPS, 1970; self-employed community pharmacist, since 1971; elected to Pharmaceutical General Council, 1974; Vice-Chairman, 1983; Chairman, Pharmaceutical General Council (Scotland), 1986-88; Vice-Chairman, National Pharmaceutical Consultative Committee, 1987-89; Member, UK Advisory Committee on Borderline Substances, 1986-89; Vice-Chairman, Forth Valley Health Board, 1989-91; Director, Common Services Agency of the NHS in Scotland, 1991-94, Vice-Chairman, 1993; Director, Scottish Aids Research Foundation; contributor to All-Party Parliamentary Group on Aids; Director, Central Scotland Chamber of Commerce, 1990-93; Chairman, St. Andrew's School Board, 1990-94; Chairman, Falkirk and District Royal Infirmary NHS Trust. Recreations: walking; golf; swimming. Address: (h.) Ardenlea, 11 Arnothill, Falkirk, FK1 5RZ; T.-01324 621806.

Munn, Charles William, BA, PhD, FCIBS, FRSA. Chief Executive, Chartered Institute of Bankers in Scotland; b. 26.5.48, Glasgow; m., Andrea Cuthbertson; 1 s.; 1 d. Educ. Queen's Park Secondary School, Glasgow; Langside College; Strathclyde University; Glasgow University; Jordanhill College. British Linen Bank, 1964-67; Glasgow College of Technology, Department of Finance and Accounting, 1975-78; Lecturer in Economic History, Glasgow University, 1978-86, Senior Lecturer, 1986-88. Editor, The Scottish Banker; Member, Church of Scotland Church and Nation Committee, 1990-94. Publications: Clydesdale Bank: the First 150 Years, 1988; The Scottish Provincial Banking Companies 1747-1864, 1981. Recreation: golf. Address: (b.) 19 Rutland Square, Edinburgh, EH1 2DE; T.-0131-229 9869.

Munn, Sir James, OBE, MA, DEd, LLD, DUniv; b. 27.7.20, Bridge of Allan; m., Muriel Jean Millar Moles; 1 d. Educ. Stirling High School; Glasgow University. Indian Civil Service, 1941-48; various teaching appointments, Glasgow, 1949-57; Principal Teacher of Modern Languages, Falkirk High School, 1957-66 (Depute Rector, 1962-66); Principal Examiner in Modern Languages, Scottish Examination Board, 1965-66; Rector: Rutherglen Academy, 1966-70, Cathkin High School, 1970-83; Member, University Grants Committee, 1973-82; Member, Consultative Committee on the Curriculum, 1968-80, Chairman, 1980-87; Chairman, Committee to review the Structure of the Curriculum at S3 and S4, 1975-77; Member of Court, Strathclyde University, 1983-91; Manpower Services Commission/Training Commission Chairman for Scotland, 1984-88, Chairman, GB, 1987-88; University Commissioner, 1988-95. (h.) 4 Kincath Avenue, Rutherglen, Glasgow, G73 4RP; T.-0141-634 4654.

Munn, Professor Walter Douglas, MA, PhD, DSc, FRSE. Emeritus Professor of Mathematics, Glasgow University; b. 24.4.29, Kilbarchan; m., Margaret Clare Barlow. Educ.

Marr College, Troon; Glasgow University; St. John's College, Cambridge. Scientific Officer, Royal Naval Scientific Service; Assistant in Mathematics, then Lecturer in Mathematics, Glasgow University; Visiting Assistant Professor, Tulane University; Senior Lecturer in Computing Science, then Senior Lecturer in Mathematics, Glasgow University; Professor of Mathematics, Stirling University; Thomas Muir Professor of Mathematics, Glasgow University, 1973-95. Recreations: music; gardening; hill-walking. Address: (b.) Department of Mathematics, Glasgow University, Glasgow, G12 8QW.

Munro, Alexander, MB, ChB, ChM, FRCS. Consultant General Surgeon, Raigmore Hospital, Inverness, since 1978; Clinical Senior Lecturer in Surgery, Aberdeen University, since 1978; b. 5.6.43, Ross and Cromarty; m., Maureen E. McCreath; 2 s.; 1 d. Educ. Fortrose Academy; Aberdeen University. Training in General Surgery at Registrar and Senior Registrar level, Aberdeen Hospitals, 1971-78; specialist training, St. Mark's Hospital, 1977. Recreation: gardening. Address: (h.) 23 Eriskay Road, Inverness; T.-Inverness 223804.

Munro, Alison, MA. Secretary, Scots Ancestry Research Society, since 1990; b. 23.10.55, Edinburgh; m., Roger Richard. Educ. St. Denis, Edinburgh; St. Andrews University. Recreations: walking; gardening; sailing; music. Address: (b.) 29b Albany Street, Edinburgh; T.-0131-556 4220.

Munro, Angus Cunningham, BSc, PhD. Director, Scottish Antibody Production Unit, since 1984; b. 12.1.44, Dundee; m., Christine Renwick; 2 s.; 1 d. Educ. Harris Academy, Dundee; Edinburgh University. Senior Scientist and Project Manager, Beecham Pharmaceuticals, 1969-74; Principal Scientist, Glasgow and West of Scotland Blood Transfusion Service, 1974-84. Recreations: music; astronomy; collecting. Address: (b.) Scottish Antibody Production Unit, Law Hospital, Carluke, Lanarkshire, ML8 5ES; T.-01698 351161.

Munro, Professor Colin Roy, BA, LLB. Professor of Constitutional Law, Edinburgh University, since 1990; Dean, Faculty of Law, since 1992; Chief Examiner, London University LLB (External) Degree, since 1991; b. 17.5.49, Aberdeen; m., Ruth Elizabeth Pratt; 1 s.; 1 d. Educ. Aberdeen Grammar School; Aberdeen University. Lecturer in Law, Birmingham University, 1971-72, Durham University, 1972-80; Senior Lecturer in Law, then Reader in Law, Essex University, 1980-85; Professor of Law, Manchester University, 1985-90. Publications: Television, Censorship and the Law; Studies in Constitutional Law. Recreations: sport; cinema and theatre; real ale. Address: (b.) Faculty of Law, Old College, South Bridge, Edinburgh, EH8 9YL; T.-0131-650 2056.

Munro, Rev. David P, MA, BD, STM. Convener, Assembly Council, General Assembly, Church of Scotland; Minister, Bearsden North. Address: (b.) 121 George Street, Edinburgh, EH2 4YN.

Munro, Donnie, DA. Artist, Guitarist and Lead Singer, Runrig; b. Skye; m.; 3 children. Former Art Teacher, Inverness and Edinburgh; Rector, Edinburgh University, 1991-94. Dr. HC, Edinburgh, 1994.

Munro, Graeme Neil, MA. Director, Historic Scotland, since 1990; b. 28.8.44, Edinburgh; m., Nicola Susan Wells (qv); 1 s.; 1 d. Educ. Daniel Stewart's College, Edinburgh; St. Andrews University. Assistant Principal, Scottish Development Department, 1968-72; Principal, Scottish Development Department and Scottish Home and Health Department, 1972-79; Assistant Secretary, Department of Agriculture and Fisheries for Scotland, SHHD, and Central Services, 1979-90. Recreations: walking; reading; local history; gardening; swimming. Address: (b.) Longmore

House, Salisbury Place, Edinburgh EH9 1SH; T.-0131-668 8696.

Munro of Foulis, Hector William, ARICS. 31st Chief of Clan Munro; b. 20.2.50; m., Sarah Duckworth; 1 s.; 2 d. Educ. Oratory School; Agricultural College, Cirencester. Farmer and Landowner. Address: (h.) Foulis Castle, Evanton, Ross-shire.

Munro, Jack, DPE. Chief Executive, Greater Glasgow Tourist Board and Convention Bureau, since 1993; b. 18.9.49, Cromarty; m., Lynn Prentice Roberts. Educ. Fortrose Academy; Jordanhill College of Education. Assistant Director of Tourism and Recreation, North East Fife District Council, 1975-82; Conference Manager, Inverness District Council, 1984-86; Director, Greater Glasgow Convention Bureau, 1986-90; Director, Edinburgh Convention Bureau, 1990-93. Chairman, British Association of Conference Towns, 1992-93; Director, Mayfest International Arts Festival; Director, Glasgow International Jazz Festival. Recreations: rugby; golf; Scottish history; gardening. Address: (b.) 39 St. Vincent Place, Glasgow, G1 2ER; T.-0141-204 4480.

Munro, Jean Mary, BA (Hons), PhD. Chairman, Council, Scottish History Society, 1989-93; b. 2.12.23; m., Robert William Munro. Educ. London University; Edinburgh University. WRNS, 1944-47; freelance historical researcher; Member, Council, National Trust for Scotland, 1964-69 and 1987-92 (Executive, 1968-80); Chairman, Council, Scottish Genealogy Society, 1983-86 (Vice-President, since 1987); Chairman, Council, Scottish Local History Forum, 1984-88. Publications (as Jean Dunlop): the British Fisheries Society; the Clan Chisholm; the Clan Mackenzie; the Clan Gordon; the Scotts; the Clan Mackintosh; (with R.W. Munro): Tain through the Centuries; The Scrimgeours; The Acts of the Lords of the Isles. Recreations: reading; walking. Address: (h.) 15a Mansionhouse Road, Edinburgh, EH9 1TZ; T.-0131-667 4601.

Munro, Jennifer Margaret Cochrane, MA (Hons), DipRE. Headmistress, St. Denis and Cranley School, Edinburgh, since 1984; b. 13.8.37, Edinburgh. Educ. Edinburgh University; Moray House College of Education. History Teacher, Kelso High School, Ottawa (Ontario), James Gillespie's (Edinburgh); History and Deputy Head, St. Denis and Cranley; Elder, Church of Scotland; President, Scottish Women's Hockey Association, 1980-83; player, manager or delegate to IFWHA tournaments and conferences. Recreations: European travel; history; gardening. Address: (b.) St. Denis and Cranley, Ettrick Road, Edinburgh, EH10 5BJ; T.-0131-229 1500.

Munro, Professor J. Forbes, MA, PhD. Professor in Economic History, since 1990, and Clerk of Senate, since 1991, Glasgow University; b. 15.3.40, Grantown-on-Spey. Educ. Dingwall Academy; Edinburgh University; Wisconsin University. Lecturer in Economic History, then Senior Lecturer, then Reader, Glasgow University, 1965-90. Editor, Journal of African History, 1982-87; Dean of Social Sciences, Glasgow University, 1987-89. Publications: Colonial Rule and the Kamba, 1975; Africa and the International Economy, 1976; Britain in Tropical Africa, 1984. Recreation: curling. Address: (b.) 4 University Gardens, Glasgow University, Glasgow, G12 8QQ.

Munro, John Forbes, OBE, FRCPEdin. Registrar, Royal College of Physicians, Edinburgh, since 1993; Honorary Fellow, Edinburgh University, since 1992; b. 25.6.33, Edinburgh; m., Elizabeth Jean Durell Caird; 3 d. Educ. Edinburgh Academy; Chigwell School, Essex; Edinburgh University. Former Consultant Physician, Eastern General and Edenhall Hospitals and part-time Senior Lecturer, Edinburgh University. Recreations: art; gardening. Address:

(h.) Backhill, Carberry, near Musselburgh, East Lothian; T.-0131-663 4935.

Munro, Kenneth Alexander, MA, FRSA. Head of Representation in Scotland, European Commission, since 1988; b. 17.12.36, Glasgow; m., Elizabeth Coats Forrest McCreanor; 2 d. Educ. Hutchesons' Boys' Grammar School; Glasgow University. Economic research, Scottish American Investment Company, 1963-66; Senior Research Officer, ETU, 1966-67; Secretary, Economic Development Committee, NEDO, 1967-69; Industrial Relations Manager, Ford Motor Co., 1969-74; joined European Commission, 1974. Recreations: walking; swimming; cinema; theatre. Address: (b.) 9 Alva Street, Edinburgh, EH2 4PH; T.-0131-225 2058.

Munro, Nicola Susan, BA (Hons). Head, Curriculum and Assessment 5-14, Education/Industry Links and Careers Service Division, Scottish Office Education Department, since 1992; b. 11.1.48, Hitchin; m., Graeme Neil Munro (qv); 1 s.; 1 d. Educ. Harrogate Grammar School; Warwick University. Joined Scottish Office, 1970. Recreations: travel; reading; gardening. Address: (b.) New St. Andrews House, Edinburgh, EH1 3TA; T.-0131-244 4624.

Munro, Robert William. Author and Journalist; b. 3.2.14, Kiltearn, Ross-shire; m., Jean Mary Dunlop. Educ. Edinburgh Academy. War Service, Seaforth Highlanders and Inter-Services Public Relations Directorate (India), 1940-46; Editorial Staff, The Scotsman, 1933-59 and 1963-69; Editor-in-Chief, Highland News Group, 1959-63; Chairman, Edinburgh Press Club, 1955-57 (President, 1969-71); Honorary Editor, Clan Munro Association, 1939-71 (Vice-President, since 1963); former Council Member: Society of Antiquaries of Scotland, Scottish History Society, Scottish Genealogy Society; Trustee, National Museum of Antiquities of Scotland, 1982-85. Publications: Lachlan MacQuarrie of Ulva, 1944; Donald Monro's Western Isles of Scotland and Genealogies of the Clans 1549 (Editor), 1961; Tain Through the Centuries (Co-author, with wife), 1966; The Glorious Privilege: the History of The Scotsman (Co-author), 1967; Kinsmen and Clansmen, 1971; The Northern Lighthouses, 1976; Highland Clans and Tartans, 1977; Edinburgh and the Borders, 1977; The Munro Tree 1734, 1978; Scottish Lighthouses, 1979; Taming the Rough Bounds, Knoydart 1745-1784, 1984; Acts of the Lords of the Isles 1336-1493 (Co-author, with wife), 1986; More about MacQuarries, 1994. Recreations: historical research and writing; walking; visiting islands. Address: (h.) 15A Mansionhouse Road, Edinburgh, EH9 1TZ; T.-0131-667 4601.

Munro, Shona, BSc (Hons), DipEd, MAppSci. Director, Edinburgh Book Festival, since 1991; b. 7.9.57, Edinburgh. Educ. James Gillespie's High School, Edinburgh; Aberdeen University; Jordanhill College; Glasgow University. Depute, then Co-Director, Edinburgh Book Festival, 1987-91. Recreations: reading; cinema; walking; sport. Address: (b.) Scottish Book Centre, 137 Dundee Street, Edinburgh, EH11 1BG; T.-0131-228 5444.

Murchison, Lilian Elizabeth, MB, ChB, PhD, FRCPE, FRCP(Lond). Consultant Physician and Honorary Clinical Senior Lecturer in Medicine, Aberdeen University, since 1976; b. 29.4.36, Aultbea. Educ. Invergordon Academy; Edinburgh University; Glasgow University. Member, Scientific Staff, Atheroma Research Unit, Western Infirmary, Glasgow, 1963-68; Senior Tutor/Senior Registrar, Department of Medicine, Queen's University, Belfast, 1969-71; Lecturer, Department of Therapeutics and Clinical Pharmacology, Aberdeen University, 1971-76. Recreations: overseas travel; hill-walking. Address: (h.) 9 Highgate Gardens, Aberdeen, AB1 2TZ; T.-01224 588532.

Murchison, Maurine, OBE, MA (Hons); b. 25.11.35, London; m., Dr. Murdoch Murchison (qv); 3 s.; 2 d. Educ.

James Allen's Girls School, Dulwich; Edinburgh University. Secondary school teaching, 1958-59; homemaker and mother, since 1960; Member, Inverness County Children's Panel, 1971-75 (Chairman, 1972-75); Chairman, Highland Region Children's Panel, 1975-80; Member, Inverness Prison Visiting Committee, 1984-85; Member, Panel for Appeals Tribunal, set up under Social Work Scotland Act 1968, since 1983; Assessor under Race Relations Act, since 1982; Church Representative, Grampian Education Committee, 1990-94; Trustee, Aberdeen School of Christian Studies; Mediator, Family Mediation Grampian, since 1988; Chairman, Children's Panel Advisory Committee, Highland Region, 1980-85; Member, Consultative Committee on the Curriculum, 1980-87; Member, Highlands and Islands Development Consultative Council, 1978-86; Member, Police Advisory Board for Scotland, 1985-93; Lay Member, Schools Inspectorate, 1994. Recreations: embroidery; group Bible study; reading (ethics and theology). Address: (h.) Riverdale, 22 Hillview Road, Cults, Aberdeen, AB1 9HB; T.-01224 868327.

Murdoch, Alex, TD, FCIS. Chief Executive, C.J. Lang & Son Ltd., since 1985; b. 22.6.40, Perth; m., Ina; 2 s. Educ. Perth Academy. Chairman, Dundee Enterprise Trust; Chairman, Eastern Area, Highland TA & VR Association. Recreations: watching rugby; playing golf. Address: (b.) C.J. Lang & Son Ltd., 78 Longtown Road, Dundee, DD4 8DU; T.-01382 512000.

Murdoch, Professor Brian Oliver, BA, PhD, LittD, AMusTCL. Professor of German, Stirling University, since 1991; b. 26.6.44, London; m., Ursula Irene Riffer; 1 s.; 1 d. Educ. Sir George Monoux Grammar School, London; Exeter University; Jesus College, Cambridge. Lecturer in German, Glasgow University; Assistant/Associate Professor of German, University of Illinois; Lecturer/Senior Lecturer in German, Stirling University; Visiting Fellow, Trinity Hall, Cambridge, 1989; Visiting Fellow and Waynflete Lecturer, Magdalen College, Oxford, 1994; author of a number of books and articles on medieval German and Celtic literature, also on literature of the World Wars. Recreations: jazz; numismatics; books. Address: (b.) German Department, Stirling University, Stirling, FK9 4LA; T.-01786 467546.

Murdoch, Professor George, MBChB, FRCS (Edin), DSc. Professor Emeritus of Orthopaedic Surgery, since 1966; Visiting Professor, Strathclyde University; b. 30.11.20, Denny; m., Elizabeth Ann Rennie; 2 s.; 3 d. Educ. Falkirk High School; St. Andrews University. Squadron Leader, RAF; Consultant Orthopaedic Surgeon; Professor of Orthopaedic Surgery, Dundee University. Travelling Fellow, World Health Association; Honorary Fellow and Past President, International Society for Prosthetics and Orthotics. Publications: papers on surgery, prosthetics, orthotics; Editor of four books on prosthetics, orthotics. Recreations: reading; writing. Address: (h.) Pitfour Castle, Flat 3, St. Madoes, Perthshire, PH2 7NJ.

Murdoch, John, FCMA, JDipMA, CIPFA. Managing Director, Irvine Development Corporation, since 1994 (Director of Finance and Management Services 1972-94); b. 31.12.34, Glassford; m., Ann McTaggart Jack; 3 s.; 1 d. Educ. Hamilton Academy; School of Accountancy. Bank Clerk, Bank of Scotland, Hamilton, 1951-53 and 1955-58; National Service, Cameronians (Scottish Rifles), 1953-55; Trainee Cost Accountant, Colvilles Steel Industry, Motherwell, 1958-63; Budget Controller, East Kilbride Development Corporation, 1963-68; Financial Controller, Irvine Development Corporation, 1968-72. Recreations: writing; fungi-hunting; bird-watching. Address: (b.) Irvine Development Corporation, Perceton House, Girdle Toll, Irvine, Ayrshire; T.-Irvine 214100.

Mure, Kenneth Nisbet, QC. Advocate, Scotland, since 1975; Barrister, Grays Inn, since 1990; Fellow, Institute of Taxation, since 1981; b. 11.4.47, Glasgow. Educ. Glasgow High School; Glasgow University. Address: (b.) Advocates' Library, Edinburgh.

Murning, Ian Henry, TD, LLB (Hons), DPA, FRICS, MIMgt. Partner, Ian H. Murning Associates, Chartered Surveyors, since 1994; Lecturer, Napier University; b. 24.12.43, Chapelhall; m., Seona Jean Meiklejon; 1 s.; 2 d. Educ. Dalziel High School; Glasgow University; London University College of Estate Management. Valuer, Stirling Valuation Office, Highlands and Islands; Office of Chief Valuer (Scotland); District Valuer, Dumfries and Galloway, 1988-94. Chairman, Royal Institution of Chartered Surveyors, 1995-96; Commander, Royal Engineers (Home Defence), Army HQ Scotland, 1991-95, with rank of Lt. Col.; Member, Society of High Constables of Edinburgh, 1993. Address: (b.) 86 Craiglockhart Drive South, Otterburn Park, Edinburgh, EH14 1JY; T.-0131-443 8839.

Murphy, Sheriff Andrew John, MA, LLB. Sheriff of Tayside, Central and Fife at Falkirk, since 1991; b. 16.1.46. Called to Scottish Bar, 1970; called to Bar, Middle Temple, 1990. Address: (b.) Sheriff Court House, Main Street, Camelon, Falkirk, FK1 4AR.

Murphy, James Barrie, MB, ChB, DPM, FRCPsych. Medical Director, Greater Glasgow Community Mental Health Services NHS Trust; Honorary Clinical Senior Lecturer; b. 27.7.42, Glasgow; m., Jean Wynn Kirkwood; 1 s.; 1 d. Educ. High School of Glasgow; Glasgow University. Consultant Psychiatrist, Dykebar Hospital, Paisley, 1973-80; Medical Executive, Community and Mental Health Unit, Gartnavel Royal Hospital, Glasgow. Address: (b.) Gartnavel Royal Hospital, 1055 Great Western Road, Glasgow, G12 0XH; T.-0141-211 3824.

Murphy, Sheriff James Patrick, BL. Sheriff of Glasgow and Strathkelvin, since 1989; (Sheriff of North Strathclyde, 1976-89); b. 24.1.32.

Murphy, Peter Alexander, MA, MEd. Rector, Whitfield High School, Dundee, 1976-93; b. 5.10.32, Aberdeen; m., Margaret Christie; 3 s.; 1 d. Educ. Aberdeen Grammar School; Aberdeen University. Assistant Principal Teacher of English, Aberdeen Grammar School, 1963-65; Principal Teacher of English, Summerhill Academy, Aberdeen, 1965-71; Head Teacher, Logie Secondary School, Dundee, 1971-76. Chairman, Carnoustie Branch, Labour Party; Elder, Carnoustie Church. Publication: Life and Times of Logie School (Co-author). Recreations: hill-walking; hockey; bee-keeping; gardening. Address: (h.) Ashlea, 44 Burnside Street, Carnoustie, Angus; T.-Carnoustie 52106.

Murphy, Vernon Leslie, MA (Cantab), FCIT. Chairman and Managing Director, Scottish Airports Ltd., since 1988; Deputy Chairman, Renfrewshire Enterprise, since 1993; b. 28.7.44, Shrewsbury; m., Joan Bridget Mary; 2 d. Educ. Westminster; Gonville and Caius College, Cambridge. Joined B.A.A., 1966; former General Manager, Aberdeen Airport, and Deputy Managing Director, Gatwick Airport Ltd. Recreations: steam engines; photography; music; cricket. Address: (b.) St. Andrews Drive, Glasgow Airport, Paisley, PA3 2SW; T.-0141-848 4581.

Murray, Professor Alan Fraser, BSc, PhD, CEng, MIEE, SMIEEE. Professor of Neural Electronics, Edinburgh University, since 1994; b. 26.2.53, Edinburgh; m., Glynis Ruth; 1 s.; 1 d. Educ. Currie High School; Edinburgh University. NATO Fellow, Atomic Energy of Canada, 1978-80; Research Fellow, Edinburgh University, 1980-81; Wolfson Microelectronics Institute, 1981-84; Lecturer, then Reader, Department of Electrical Engineering, Edinburgh University, 1984-94. Publications: 133. Recreations: singer; guitarist, songwriter. Address: (b.) Department of Electrical Engineering, Edinburgh University, Mayfield Road, Edinburgh, EH9 3JL; T.-0131-650 5589.

Murray, Alexander George, KStG, KLJ, BSc, FBSC(Lond), FSA Scot. Former National Director, Crossroads (Scotland) Care Attendant Schemes; m., Margaret Elizabeth; 1 d. Educ. Whitehill School, Glasgow; Glasgow University. Former Scottish Manager, British subsidiary of Chase Manhatten Bank of America; formed several companies in investment/credit field. Led first Scottish delegation to UNESCO, 1955-56; established Scottish Worldfriends Society and became its first National Director; active in Highland societies; Scot of the Year, 1986; Founder and Convener, Caledonian Country Dancing Clubs; former Secretary, West of Scotland Refugee Committee; Past President, East Kilbride Sea Cadet Corps; Member, Organising Committee, East Kilbride National Mod, 1974-75; Provincial Grand Master Mason. Publications: A History of Scottish Contra Dancing; 40 Popular Scottish Dances. Recreations: bowling; swimming; walking. Address: (h.) Failte, 51 Eaglesham Road, Clarkston, Glasgow, G76 7TR.

Murray, Athol Laverick, PhD, MA, LLB, FRHistS, FSA Scot. Vice-President, Society of Antiquaries of Scotland, 1989-92; Keeper of the Records of Scotland, 1985-90; b. 8.11.30, Tynemouth; m., Irene Joyce Cairns; 1 s.; 1 d. Educ. Lancaster Royal Grammar School; Jesus College, Cambridge; Edinburgh University. Research Assistant, Foreign Office, 1953; Scottish Record Office: Assistant Keeper, 1953-83, Deputy Keeper, 1983-84. Recreations: historical research; bowling. Address: (h.) 33 Inverleith Gardens, Edinburgh, EH3 5PR; T.-0131-552 4465.

Murray, David Edward. Chairman, Murray International Holdings; Chairman, The Rangers Football Club plc; b. 14.10.51, Ayr; m., Louise (deceased); 2 s. Educ. Fettes College; Broughton High School. Young Scottish Business Man of the Year, 1984; Hon. Doctorate, Heriot-Watt University, 1986; Chairman, UK 2000 (Scotland), 1987; Governor, Clifton Hall School, 1987. Recreations: sports sponsorship; snooker; collecting wine. Address: (b.) South Gyle, Edinburgh; T.-0131-317 7000.

Murray, Donald, MA. Head Teacher, Sir Edward Scott School, Tarbert, Isle of Harris, since 1981; b. Port of Ness, Isle of Lewis; 2 d. Educ. Nicolson Institute, Stornoway; Glasgow University. Teacher, Calder Street Secondary School, Glasgow; Teacher, Achnamara Residential School, Argyll; Principal Teacher of Guidance, Victoria Drive Secondary School, Glasgow; Assistant Head Teacher (Curriculum), Kingsridge Secondary School, Glasgow. Recreations: angling; gardening; reading. Address: (h.) Balranald, West Tarbert, Isle of Harris; T.-01859 502339.

Murray, Rev. Douglas Millar, MA, BD, PhD. Lecturer in Church History, Glasgow University, since 1989; b. 1946, Edinburgh; m., Dr. Freya M. Smith. Educ. George Watson's College, Edinburgh; Edinburgh University; New College, Edinburgh; Fitzwilliam and Westminster Colleges, Cambridge. Minister: St. Bride's Church, Callander, 1976-80, John Ker Memorial Church in deferred union with Candlish Church, Edinburgh, 1980-81, and Polwarth Church, 1981-89. Editor, Liturgical Review, 1979-81; Associate Editor, Scottish Journal of Theology, 1981-87; Convener, Panel on Doctrine, General Assembly, Church of Scotland, 1986-90. Publication: Studies in the History of Worship in Scotland (Co-Editor); Freedom to Reform, 1993. Recreations: golf; Scottish country dancing; hillwalking. Address: 7 Newark Drive, Glasgow, G41 4QJ; T.-0141-423 7276.

Murray, Frank McDonald, EurEng, BSc (Hons), CEng, FIMinE. Secretary-General, Federation of European Explosives Manufacturers; Director, Ayrshire Chamber of Commerce; Chairman, Kilmarnock College; Director, Employers Association of F.E. Colleges; Director, Scottish Training and Targets Board; b. 7.9.36, Dunfermline; m., Nancy McDermott; 1 s.; 1 d. Educ. Kirkcaldy High School;

Edinburgh University. Coal mining/gold mining, 1957-62; joined ICI as explosives engineer, 1962; Managing Director, ICI Nobel's Explosives Co., 1988-93. Recreation: golf. Address: (b.) Ardeer Site, Stevenston, Ayrshire; T.-01294 487287.

Murray, George Malcolm, CBE, FFA. Chief General Manager, Scottish Life Assurance Company, since 1987; President, Faculty of Actuaries in Scotland, since 1994; Chairman, Baillie Gifford Japan Trust PLC, since 1981; b. 25.12.37, Hawick; m., Muriel; 2 s.; 1 d. Educ. Hawick High School. Joined Scottish Life, 1955; Assistant Actuary, 1962; held various appointments, including Investment Manager. Memb er, Scottish Sports Council; Trustee, Edinburgh University Trust Funds. Recreations: almost all sports and cultural activities, especially rugby, golf, jogging, and theatre. Address: (b.) 19 St. Andrew Square, Edinburgh, EH2 1YE; T.-0131-225 2211.

Murray, Gordon, BSc (Hons), PhD. Director, Scottish Courts Administration, since 1986; b. 25.8.35, Aberdeen; m., Janet Yerrington; 2 s.; 1 d. Educ. Kirkcaldy High School; Edinburgh University. Research Fellow, Atomic Energy Authority of Canada, 1960-62, UKAEA, 1962-65; Lecturer in Physics, Manchester University, 1965-69; Principal, Scottish Home and Health Department, 1970-77; Assistant Secretary, Scottish Education Department, 1977-79, Central Services, 1979-86. Recreations: reading; walking. Address: 26 Royal Terrace, Edinburgh, EH7 5AH; T.-0131-556 0755.

Murray, Gordon Lindsay Kevan. Partner, W.J. Burness WS, since 1982; Secretary, Scottish National Orchestra Society Ltd., 1985-90, Director, since 1990; b. 23.5.53, Glasgow; m., Susan Patricia; 1 s.; 3 d. Educ. Lenzie Academy; Edinburgh University. President, Scottish Young Lawyers Association, 1977-78. Address: (b.) 16 Hope Street, Charlotte Square, Edinburgh, EH2 4DD; T.-0131-226 2561.

Murray, Gregor Cumming, MA, MBA. Executive Director, Midlothian Enterprise Trust, since 1992; b. 16.4.57, Edinburgh; m., Kate; 2 d. Educ. George Watson's College, Edinburgh; Trinity College, Oxford; Edinburgh University Management School. Bank of Scotland; Investors in Industry; Leith Enterprise Trust. Board Member: Jewel and Esk Valley College, Lothian Investment Fund for Enterprise. Recreations: fly fishing; golf; music; chess. Address: (b.) 29A Eskbank Road, Dalkeith, EH22 1HJ; T.-0131-654 1234.

Murray, Isobel (Mary), MA, PhD. Writer and Critic; Senior Lecturer in English, Aberdeen University, since 1974; b. 14.2.39, Alloa; m., Bob Tait. Educ. Dollar Academy; Edinburgh University. Assistant Lecturer, then Lecturer and Senior Lecturer, Department of English, Aberdeen University; books include several editions of Oscar Wilde, introductions to new editions of J. MacDougall Hay's Gillespie, Ian MacPherson's Shepherd's Calendar and Robin Jenkins's Guests of War; edited, Beyond This Limit: Selected Shorter Fiction of Naomi Mitchison; A Girl Must Live: stories and poems by Naomi Mitchison; Ten Modern Scottish Novels (with Bob Tait), 1984. Address: (b.) Department of English, King's College, Old Aberdeen, Aberdeen, AB9 2UB; T.-Aberdeen 272644.

Murray, Professor James, BSc, ARCST, CEng, FIMechE, FIEE, FIM. Vice Principal, Napier University, since 1992; b. 25.7.30, Glasgow; m., Emily Lamb Beveridge; 1 s.; 1 d. Educ. Allan Glen's School, Glasgow; Glasgow University. Development Engineer, Ferranti, Edinburgh; Lecturer, Department of Mechanical Engineering, Heriot Watt University; Head, Department of Production Engineering, Napier Polytechnic. Former Member, Council, SCOTEC and EITB; Past Chairman, IProdE Scotland Region and CEI Scotland; Governor, Moray House College of Education;

Member of Convocation, Heriot-Watt University. Recreations: watching rugby; light rail transport. Address: (b.) Napier University, Colinton Road, Edinburgh, EH10 5DT; T.-0131-455 4602.

Murray, Professor James Lothian, BSc, MSc, FIMechE, CEng, FRSA. Professor Emeritus, Heriot-Watt University, since 1995; Senior Associate, Murray Technology Management Associates, since 1994; b. 11.6.38, Loanhead; m., Anne Walton; 1 d. Educ. Lasswade Senior Secondary School; Heriot-Watt University. Student apprentice, then Design Engineer, Ferranti Ltd., 1956-66; Heriot-Watt University: Lecturer in Engineering Design, 1966-78, Senior Lecturer in Design and Manufacture, 1978-85, Head, Department of Mechanical Engineering, 1984-89, Director, CAE Centre, 1991-94, Director, Institute of Technology Management, 1991-94. Member, Academic Board, Napier Polytechnic. Recreation: hill-walking. Address: 32 Westgarth Avenue, Edinburgh EH13 0BD; T.-0131-441 1288.

Murray, John, BA, DipEd, MEd. Headteacher, Harlaw Academy, Aberdeen, since 1993; b. 2.2.52, Irvine; m., Margaret McLaughlin; 2 s.; 1 d. Educ. St. Michael's Academy, Kilwinning; Strathclyde University; Glasgow University; Stirling University. Teacher of Modern Studies, then Principal Teacher of Modern Studies; Assistant Rector, Woodmill High School, Dunfermline, 1986-89; Depute Rector, Kirkcaldy High School, 1989-93. Recreations: family; football; theatre. Address: (b.) Harlaw Academy, Albyn Place, Aberdeen; T.-01224 589251.

Murray, John Kenneth, BCom, CA. Partner, Price Waterhouse, since 1985; Chairman, Aberdeen Enterprise Trust, since 1992; Chairman, Head Start Capital Fund, since 1993; b. 9.8.51, Bridge of Allan; m., Morag; 1 s.; 1 d. Educ. Dollar Academy; Edinburgh University. Trained as CA with Price Waterhouse.; Partner, Price Waterhouse, Aberdeen. Recreations: golf; shooting; cricket. Address: (h.) Bogarn House, Inchmarlo, Banchory; T.-01330 824476.

Murray, Professor Sir Kenneth, BSc, PhD, FRS, FRSE, FRCPath. Professor of Molecular Biology, Edinburgh University, since 1976; b. 30.12.30, East Ardsley; m., Noreen E. Parker (see Noreen Elizabeth Murray). Educ. Henry Mellish Grammar School; Birmingham University. Postdoctoral work, Stanford University, California, 1959-64; MRC Scientific Staff, Cambridge, 1964-67; joined Edinburgh University, 1967; leave of absence at European Molecular Biology Laboratory, Heidelberg, 1979-82. Recreations: musical appreciation; reading. Address: (b.) Institute of Cell and Molecular Biology, Edinburgh University, Mayfield Road, Edinburgh, EH9 3JR; T.-0131-650 5387.

Murray, Leonard G., JP, BL, SSC. Solicitor; former Senior Partner, now Consultant to, Levy & McRae, Solicitors; b. 16.8.33, Glasgow; m., Elizabeth Wilson; 3 s. Educ. St. Mungo's Academy, Glasgow; Glasgow University. Director, Murray Inns Ltd. After-dinner speaker; founder Director, Speakeasy (Scotland) Ltd., 1987; part-time Chairman, Industrial Tribunals, Medical Appeal Tribunals, Disability Appeal Tribunals. Recreation: golf. Address: (h.) 23 Courthill, Bearsden, Glasgow G61 3SN.

Murray, Professor Maxwell, BVMS, DVM, FRCPath, FRSE, PhD. Professor of Veterinary Medicine, Glasgow University, since 1985; b. 3.5.39, Glasgow; m., Christine Madelaine; 1 s.; 2 d. Educ. Shawlands Senior Secondary School; Glasgow University. Animal Health Trust Research Scholarship, 1962-63; Lecturer in Veterinary Pathology, University of Nairobi, 1963-65; Lecturer in Veterinary Pathology, then Senior Lecturer, Glasgow University, 1965-75; Senior Scientist, International Laboratory for Research on Animal Diseases, Nairobi, 1975-85. Address: (b.) Department of Veterinary Medicine, Glasgow University

Veterinary School, Bearsden Road, Bearsden, Glasgow, G61 1QH; T.-0141-339 8855, Ext. 5734.

Murray, Professor Noreen Elizabeth, FRS, PhD, FRSE. Professor, Institute of Cell and Molecular Biology, Edinburgh University; b. 26.2.35, Burnley; m., Kenneth Murray (qv). Educ. Lancaster Girls' Grammar School; King's College, London; Birmingham University. Research Associate, Department of Biological Sciences, Stanford University, 1960-64; Research Fellow, Botany School, Cambridge, 1964-67; Edinburgh University: Member, MRC Molecular Genetics Unit, Department of Molecular Biology, 1968-74, Lecturer, then Senior Lecturer, Department of Molecular Biology, 1974-80; Group Leader, European Molecular Biology Laboratory, Heidelberg, 1980-82; joined Edinburgh University as Reader, 1982. Recreation: gardening. Address: (b.) Institute of Cell and Molecular Biology, Edinburgh University, Mayfield Road, Edinburgh, EH9 3JR; T.-0131-650 5374.

Murray, Norman Loch, BA, CA, FRSA. Deputy Chief Executive, Morgan Grenfell Development Capital Limited, since 1989; Executive Director, Morgan Grenfell & Co. Ltd., since 1989; Non-Executive Director: Bristow Helicopter Group Ltd., Beni Food Group Ltd; former directorships (non-executive): Eurodollar (Holdings) Ltd., Taunton Cider plc, Burn Stewart Group Ltd., Dalmore Distillers Ltd.; b. 17.3.48, Kilmarnock; m., Pamela Ann Low; 2 s. Educ. George Watson's College; Heriot-Watt University; Harvard University Graduate School of Business Administration. Scottish & Newcastle Breweries PLC, 1971-73; Arthur Young, 1973-76; Peat Marwick Mitchell & Co., 1977-80; Royal Bank of Scotland PLC, 1980-85; Director, Charterhouse Development Capital Ltd., 1985-89. Institute of Chartered Accountants of Scotland: Member, Finance and General Purposes Committee, Chairman, Lothian, Borders and Central Area Committee, formerly Member, Research Committee; Chairman, British Venture Capital Association Legal and Technical Committee; Member, University of Glasgow External Review Group (Department of Accounting and Finance). Publication: Making Corporate Reports Valuable (Co-author), 1988. Recreations: squash; golf; hill-walking; travel. Address: (b.) 35 St. Andrew Square, Edinburgh, EH2 2AD; T.-0131-557 8600.

Murray, Patrick, VRD, WS. Landowner; b. 13.5.11, Edinburgh; m., Doris Herbert Green; 2 d. Educ. Ardvreck, Crieff; Marlborough College. Royal Naval Volunteer Reserve, 1935-55 (Commander); Partner, Murray, Beith & Murray, WS, Edinburgh, 1937-77. Recreations: gardening; forestry. Address: (h.) Townhead of Cavers, Hawick, Roxburghshire, TD9 8LJ; T.-01450 373604.

Murray, Robert John, MSc, MCIBS. Depute Leader, Angus Council, since 1995; Convenor, Personnel Committee, Tayside Regional Council, since 1994; b. 3.2.51, Montrose; m., Linda; 1 s.; 1 d. Educ. Montrose Academy; University of Abertay, Dundee. Recreations: cycling; golf. Address: (h.) 26 Adderley Terrace, Monifieth, DD5 4DR; T.-01382 534908.

Murray, Rt. Hon. Lord (Ronald King Murray), PC (1974), MA, LLB. Senator of the College of Justice in Scotland, since 1979; b. 15.6.22; m., Sheila Winifred Gamlin. Educ. George Watson's College; Edinburgh University; Jesus College, Oxford. Advocate, 1953; QC, 1967; MP (Leith), 1970-79; Lord Advocate, 1974-79. Assessor, Edinburgh University Court, 1981-93 (Vice-Chairman, 1990-93). Recreation: sailing. Address: (h.) 1 Inverleith Grove, Edinburgh, EH3 5PB; T.-0131-551 5330.

Murray, Professor Thomas Stuart, MD, PhD, FRCGP, FRCPGlas, FRCPEdin, DRCOG. West of Scotland Adviser in General Practice, since 1985; Titular Professor of General Practice, Glasgow University, since 1992; b.

22.7.43, Muirkirk; m., Anne Smith; 1 s.; 2 d. Educ. Cumnock Academy. Trained in medicine and cardiology, then general practice; principal in general practice, 1971; Senior Lecturer in General Practice, Glasgow University, 1977. Chairman, UK Conference of Regional Advisers; Member, Joint Committee for Postgraduate Training in General Practice. Recreations: sport; travel; reading. Address: (b.) Glasgow University, Glasgow, G12 8QQ; T.-0141-330 5276.

Murray, William Hutchison, OBE. Author and Mountaineer; b. 18.3.13, Liverpool; m., Anne Burnet Clark. Educ. Glasgow Academy. Union Bank of Scotland, until 1939; Captain, HLI, Western Desert (Prisoner of War, 1942-45); Leader, Scottish Himalayan Expedition, 1950; Deputy Leader, Everest Expedition, 1951; Leader, NW Nepal Expedition, 1953; Commissioner, Countryside Commission for Scotland, 1968-80; Mungo Park Medal, RSGS, 1950; Literary Award, USA Education Board, 1954; Honorary Doctorate, Stirling University, 1975; DLitt, Strathclyde University, 1991. Publications: Mountaineering in Scotland, 1947; Rock Climbs, Glencoe and Ardgour, 1949; Undiscovered Scotland, 1951; Scottish Himalayan Expedition, 1951; Story of Everest, 1953; Five Frontiers, 1959; The Spurs of Troodos, 1960; Maelstrom, 1962; Highland Landscape, 1962; Dark Rose the Phoenix, 1965; The Hebrides, 1966; Companion Guide to West Highlands, 1968; The Real MacKay, 1969; The Islands of Western Scotland, 1973; The Scottish Highlands, 1976; The Curling Companion, 1981; Rob Roy MacGregor, 1982; Scotland's Mountains, 1987. Recreations: mountaineering; sailing. Address: Lochwood, Loch Goil, Argyll.

Murray-Smith, Professor David James, MSc, PhD, CEng, FIEE, MInstMC. Titular Professor in Electronics and Electrical Engineering, Glasgow University; b. 20.10.41, Aberdeen; m., Effie Smith; 2 s. Educ. Aberdeen Grammar School; Aberdeen University; Glasgow University. Engineer, Inertial Systems Department, Ferranti Ltd., Edinburgh, 1964-65; Glasgow University: Assistant, Department of Electrical Engineering, 1965-67, Lecturer, 1967-77, Senior Lecturer, 1977-83, Reader, 1983-85. Past Chairman, United Kingdom Simulation Council. Recreations: hill-walking; photography; strong interest in railways. Address: (b.) Department of Electronics and Electrical Engineering, Glasgow University, Glasgow, G12 8QQ; T.-0141-339 8855.

Musgrave, Ralph Gilbert, BSc, PhD, IPM. Director of Management and Information Services, Lothian Regional Council, since 1986; b. 10.4.39, Edinburgh; m., Patricia E. Smith; 2 s. Educ. Broughton High School, Edinburgh; Edinburgh University. ICI Ltd., 1965; Lecturer, Falkirk College of Technology, 1966-71; Depute Director of Education, East Lothian County Council, 1971-75; Assistant Director of Education, Lothian Regional Council, 1975-86. Recreations: rugby; golf. Address: (b.) Lothian Regional Council, George IV Bridge, Edinburgh, EH1 1UQ; T.-0131-469 3003.

Musson, John Nicholas Whitaker, MA (Oxon).Governor, George Watson's College, Edinburgh, since 1989; Governor and Member of Council, Clifton College, Bristol, since 1989; Member, Scottish Council of Independent Schools' Governing Board, since 1993; b. 2.10.27; m., Ann Priest; 1 s.; 3 d. Educ. Clifton College; Brasenose College, Oxford. Served as Guardsman and Lt., Lancashire Fusiliers, 1945-48; HM Overseas Service, 1951-59 (District Officer, N. Nigeria and Lecturer, Institute of Administration, Nigeria); British Petroleum Co., London, 1959-61; Assistant Master and Housemaster, Canford School, Dorset, 1961-72; Warden, Glenalmond College, 1972-87; Scottish Division Chairman, Headmasters' Conference, 1981-83; Scottish Director, Independent Schools Careers Organisation, 1987-93. Recreations: hill-walking; fishing; painting. Address: (h.) 47 Spylaw Road, Edinburgh, EH10 5BP; T.-0131-337 0089.

Mutch, Alexander Fyvie, CBE, JP. Member, Grampian Regional Council, 1974-90 (first Convener, 1974-82); b. 23.3.24, Aberdeen; m., Freda Mutch; 1 d. Educ. Aberdeen Central School. Convener, Aberdeen Corporation Cleansing Committee, 1963; Vice-Chairman, North-East Water Board, 1968-70; Magistrate, Aberdeen, 1967; Senior Magistrate, 1968; Chairman, Aberdeen Licensing Court, 1968; Member, Aberdeen University Court, 1974-82; Chairman, South Aberdeen Conservative Association, 1964-68 (President, 1968-72); Senior Vice-President, Conservative Party in Scotland, 1972-73 (President, 1973-74); Leader, Conservative Group, Aberdeen Town Council, 1974-75; Governor, Robert Gordon's College, Aberdeen, 1968-70 and since 1974; Honorary President, Grampian-Houston Association; Honorary Citizen, Houston, Texas. Address: (h.) 28 Salisbury Terrace, Aberdeen; T.-Aberdeen 591520.

Mutch, William Edward Scott, OBE, BSc, PhD, FRSE, FICFor. Forestry and Land Use Consultant; b. 14.8.25, Salford; m., Margaret Isobel McKay; 1 d. Educ. Royal High School, Edinburgh; Edinburgh University. HM Colonial Service (Forest Department, Nigeria, as Assistant Conservator of Forests and Silviculturist), 1946; Research Assistant, Oxford University, 1952; Lecturer in Forestry, Edinburgh University, 1953. Head, Department of Forestry and Natural Resources, Edinburgh University, 1981-87; President, Institute of Chartered Foresters, 1982-84 (Institute Medal, 1986); Member: Countryside Commission for Scotland, 1988-92; National Forestry Research Advisory Committee; Nature Conservancy Council, 1988-91; NCC for Scotland, 1991-92; Scottish Natural Heritage, Chairman S.E. Scotland, 1992-94; Director, Central Scotland Woodlands Ltd., since 1989. Publication: Farm Woodland Management. Recreations: cabinet making; travel; painting. Address: (h.) 19 Barnton Grove, Edinburgh, EH4 6EQ; T.-0131-339 1400.

Myatt, Mary Elizabeth, BSc (Hons). Headmistress, The Park School, Glasgow, since 1986; b. 4.1.41, Belfast; m., Thomas Myatt. Educ. Omagh Academy; Queen's University, Belfast. Head, Mathematics Department: Dungannon High School for Girls, 1963-66, International School of Hamburg, 1966-68, Ashleigh House School, Belfast, 1968-70, Maida Vale High School, London, 1970-71; Wellington School, Ayr: Head, Mathematics Department, 1971-86, Director of Studies, 1984-86. Area Chairman, National Association of Ladies' Circles, 1978-79. Recreations: bridge; golf. Address: (b.) 25 Lynedoch Street, Glasgow, G3 6EX; T.-0141-332 0426.

Myles, Andrew Bruce, LLB, MA (Hons). Chief Executive, Scottish Liberal Democrats, since 1992; b. 25.10.57, Edinburgh. Educ. Holt School; Merchiston Castle School; Dundee University. Former General Services Manager (Mental Illness), Tayside Mental Health Unit. Designer/Director, E.I.F. Fringe Productions, 1976-79. Recreations: gardening; films; books; cats; holidays. Address: (b.) 4 Clifton Terrace, Edinburgh, EH13 5DR; T.-0131-337 2314.

Myles, David Fairlie, CBE. Hill Farmer; Member, Angus District Council, since 1984; Chairman, Dairy Produce Quota Tribunal for Scotland, since 1984; Member, Potato Marketing Board, since 1988; b. 30.5.25, Cortachy, Kirriemuir; m., Janet I. Gall; 2 s.; 2 d. Educ. Brechin High School. Auctioneer's clerk, 1941-43; Royal Marines, 1943-46; Tenant Hill Farmer, since 1946; Director of auction company, 1963-81; Member, Transport Users Consultative Committee for Scotland, 1973-79; Council Member, NFU of Scotland, 1970-79 (Convener, Organisation and Publicity Committee, 1976-79); Member, Meat Promotion Executive, MLC, 1975-79; Chairman, North Angus and Mearns Constituency Conservative Party, 1971-74; MP (Conservative), Banff, 1979-83; Joint Secretary, Backbench Conservative Agriculture Committee, 1979-83; Secretary, Backbench Conservative European Committee, 1980-83;

Member, Select Committee on Agriculture and Select Committee on European Legislation, 1979-83; Member, North of Scotland Hydro-Electric Board, 1985-89; Member, Angus Tourist Board, 1984-92; Dean, Guildry of Brechin, 1993-94. Elder, Edzell-Lethnot Parish Church. Recreations: curling; traditional Scottish fiddle music; works of Robert Burns. Address: (h.) The Gorse, Dunlappie Road, Edzell, Brechin, DD9 7UB; T.-0135 64 207.

Myles, William Mackay Stanley, TD (with bar). Senior Partner, Myles Brothers, Wholesale Ironmongers, Edinburgh, since 1954; Member, Executive Committee, National Trust for Scotland, since 1988; b. 6.3.27, Edinburgh; m., Margaret Shiela Grace Bruce; 3 s. Educ. Sciennes and James Clark's, Edinburgh; Bell-Baxter, Cupar. Royal Scots, 1945-66; India & Pakistan 1st Bn., 1946-47, 7/9 and 8/9 TA Bns., 1948-66, as Rifle Company Commander, 1951-66; Member, Regimental Council, since 1977; Mountaineering Council of Scotland: Training Officer, 1974-90, Hon. Secretary, 1977-83, Vice-President, 1984-88; Chairman, The Royal Scots Club, Edinburgh, since 1977; Chairman, Edinburgh West End Community Council; Director, Lord Roberts Workshops for Disabled Ex-Servicemen; Council Member, Earl Haig Fund; Elder, Church of Scotland, since 1950; Director, Drumsheugh Baths Club Ltd., Edinburgh, since 1972; President, Rotary Club of Edinburgh, 1983-84. Recreations: hill-walking; swimming; painting in oils; gardening. Address: (h.) 12 Douglas Crescent, Edinburgh, EH12 2BB; T.-0131-337 4781.

N

Nairn, Tom. Sociologist; b. 1932, Freuchie, Fife. Educ. Edinburgh University; Oxford University. Taught social philosophy, Birmingham University, and sociology, Hornsey College of Art; Editor, Bulletin of Scottish Politics, 1981-82; Columnist, The Scotsman. Publications: The Left Against Europe; The Break-Up of Britain?; The Enchanted Glass: Britain and its Monarchy.

Nairne, Andrew, MA (Hons). Visual Arts Director, Scottish Arts Council, since 1993; b. 10.2.60, Guildford; m., Nicola Dandridge. Educ. Radley College; St. Andrews University. Assistant Curator, Kettle's Yard, Cambridge University, 1984-85; Deputy Director, Ikon Gallery, Birmingham, 1985-86; Exhibitions Director, Centre for Contemporary Arts, Glasgow, 1986-93. Recreations: modern history; jazz. Address: (b.) 12 Manor Place, Edinburgh, EH3 7DD; T.-0131-226 6051.

Nandy, Kashinath, BSc, MSc (Calcutta), MSc (Edinburgh), PhD, FRAS, FRSE. Deputy Chief Scientific Officer, Royal Observatory, Edinburgh, 1977-86; Visiting Professor, Rome University, 1987; Honorary Professor, School of Mathematics, University of Wales, Cardiff, since 1994; b. 1.12.27, Santipur, West Bengal, India; m., Smritilekha; 1 d. Educ. Calcutta University; Edinburgh University. Observatory Assistant, Presidency College Observatory, Calcutta, 1952-59; received International Astronomical Union Grant for Studies Abroad, 1959-60; held Robert Cormack Bequest Fellowship (Royal Society of Edinburgh), 1960-63; Royal Observatory, Edinburgh: Research Fellow, 1963-68, Principal Scientific Officer, 1968-72, Senior Principal Scientific Officer, 1972-77. Fellow, Royal Astronomical Society; Member, International Astronomical Union; Founder Member, European Astronomical Society; Honorary Fellow, Edinburgh University, 1973-87; Honorary Research Fellow, University College, London, 1979-86, re-elected, 1989; elected Fellow, Royal Society of Edinburgh, 1973; Fellow, Royal Society of Liege, 1989. Recreations: reading; travel; photography; surfing. Address: (h.) 36 West Mains Road, Edinburgh, EH9 3BG; T.-0131-667 6131.

Nanjiani, Shereen, MA (Hons). Journalist, Scottish Television, since 1983; b. 4.10.61, Elderslie. Educ. John Neilson High School, Paisley; Glasgow University. Joined STV as a trainee journalist, 1983; moved to reporting two years later; became presenter of Scotland Today, 1985; also presented Eikon (religious magazine); chaired debate programmes on youth issues. Address: (b.) Scottish Television, Cowcaddens, Glasgow, G2 3PR; T.-0141-332 9999.

Napier, 14th Lord, and Ettrick, 5th Baron (Francis Nigel Napier), KCVO, DL. Private Secretary, Comptroller and Equerry to Princess Margaret, Countess of Snowdon, since 1973; b. 5.12.30; m.; 2 s.; 2 d. Address: Thirlestane, Ettrick, Selkirkshire.

Nash, Professor Andrew Samuel, BVMS, PhD, CBiol, FIBiol, MRCVS. Titular Professor, Department of Veterinary Medicine, Glasgow University Veterinary School, since 1992, and Director of the Veterinary Hospital, since 1993; Royal College of Veterinary Surgeons Recognised Specialist in Small Animal Medicine, since 1993; b. 1.8.44, Birmingham; m., Rosemary Truscott Hamilton; 1 s.; 1 d. Educ. Judd School, Tonbridge; Glasgow University. General veterinary practice, Ilfracombe, 1967-72; House Physician, Glasgow University Veterinary School, 1973-75, then Lecturer/Senior Lecturer, 1975-92. Silver Medal in Veterinary Clinical Medicine, 1967; RSPCA Humane Award, 1970; Member, Board of Directors, Glasgow Dog and Cat Home, 1981-95; Hon. President, Scottish Cat Club, since 1990; Member, Glasgow Presbytery, 1991-94; President, European Society of Veterinary Nephrology and Urology, 1992-94; Member, Board of Directors, Scottish Society for the Prevention of Cruelty to Animals, since 1995; author of more than 100 papers, articles, book chapters. Recreations: music; gardening; DIY; church work (church organist). Address: (b.) University of Glasgow Veterinary School, Bearsden Road, Glasgow, G61 1QH; T.-0141-330 5700.

Nash, Professor Anthony A., BSc, MSc, PhD. Professor and Head, Department of Veterinary Pathology, Edinburgh University, since 1994; b. 6.3.49, Coalville; m., Marion Eileen Bazeley; 4 d. Educ. London University; Birmingham University. Research Fellow, then Lecturer, Department of Pathology, Cambridge University; Eleanor Roosevelt Fellow, Scripps Research Institute, San Diego. Publications: two books; 80 scientific publications. Recreations: cricket; soccer. Address: (h.) Kinard, Links Road, North Berwick.

Nash, Victoria Jane, BSc, PhD. Assistant Chief Executive, Fife Regional Council, since 1988; b. 17.6.57, Northampton; m., Robin Campbell; 2 step d. Educ. Cheadle Hulme School; Oxford Polytechnic; Stirling University. Senior Research Officer, Scottish Office Education Department, 1982-83; Project Co-ordinator, Scottish Council for Educational Technology, 1983-85; Policy Analyst, then Assistant to the Chief Executive, Fife Regional Council, 1985-88. Recreations: cat worshipping; swimming; singing; antiques. Address: (b.) Fife House, North Street, Glenrothes, KY7 5LT; T.-01592 414141.

Naumann, Laurie M. Director, Scottish Council for Single Homeless, currently on secondment to the Scottish Office Social Work Services Inspectorate; b. 1943, Saffron Walden; m., Barbara; 2 s.; 3 d. Educ. Edinburgh, Gloucester and Nuremberg Rudolf Steiner; Leicester University. Furniture maker, Gloucestershire; Probation and After Care Officer, Leeds; Social Worker, Edinburgh. Council of Europe Social Fellowship to Finland to study services for the drunken offender, 1976; jointly won Rosemary Delbridge Memorial Trophy for influencing Parliament to legislate, 1983; Secretary, Hamish Allan Trust; Board Member, Kingdom and Old Town Housing Associations. Recreations: travel; reading; walking; woodwork. Address: (h.) St. Ann's, Alexander III Street, Kinghorn, Fife, KY3 9SD; T.-01592 890346.

Naylor, Brian, BSc, MPhil. Director (Properties in Care), Historic Scotland, since 1995; b. 10.2.49, Altrincham; m., 1, Mary Halley (deceased); 2 s.; 2, Moira Hillen; 2 step s. Educ. Lymm Grammar School; Leicester University; Edinburgh University. Scottish Office: graduate trainee, 1976-82; Principal, 1982-89; Assistant Secretary, 1989-95. Partner, Naylor's Delicatessen, Gullane. Recreations: fishing; theatre; swimming; walking. Address: (b.) Longmore House, Salisbury Place, Edinburgh, EH9 1SH; T.-0131-668 8735.

Neal, Andrew, BSc. Marketing Director, United Distillers UK, since 1993; b. 6.12.58, London; m., Janet; 1 s.; 2 d. Educ. Eastwood High School; Strathclyde University. Recreation: sport. Address: (b.) United Distillers UK, Cherrybank, Perth, PH2 0NG; T.-01738 21111.

Neil, Alex., MA (Hons). Policy Vice-Convener, Scottish National Party, since 1994; Prospective Parliamentary candidate, Kilmarnock; Economic Consultant; b. 22.8.51, Irvine; m., Isabella Kerr; 1 s. Educ. Dalmellington High School; Ayr Academy; Dundee University. Scottish Research Officer, Labour Party, 1975; General Secretary, Scottish Labour Party (SLP), 1976; Marketing Manager, 1979-83; Director, Cumnock and Doon Enterprise Trust, 1983-87; Director, Prince's Scottish Youth Business Trust,

1987-89; Chairman, Network Scotland Ltd., 1987-93. Recreations: family; golf; gardening; travel. Address: (h.) 26 Overmills Road, Ayr, KA7 3LQ; T.-01292 286675.

Neill, David Lindsay. Master Mariner; Ship's Captain, since 1973; Captain, P.S. Waverley, since 1975; b. 21.5.44, Glasgow; 1 s.; 2 d. Educ. various schools; Glasgow School of Nautical Studies. Deck Apprentice, 1960-64; Ship's Navigating Officer, 1964-70; Ferry Manager (Isle of Skye), 1970-71; Ship's Navigating Officer, 1971-73. Life Member, Paddle Steamer Preservation Society. Recreations: out of door. Address: (b.) Waverley Excursions Ltd., Anderston Quay, Glasgow, G3 8HA; T.-0141-221 8152.

Neill, Gordon Webster McCash, DSO, SSC, NP, FInstD. Solicitor and Notary Public; Honorary Sheriff; b. Arbroath; m., Margaret Mary Lamb; 1 s.; 1 d. Educ. Edinburgh Academy. Legal apprenticeship, 1937-39; Pilot, RAF, 1939-46 (DSO, French Croix de Guerres with silver gilt star and silver star); Partner, Neill & Gibb, SSC, 1947; Chairman, Dundee Area Board, British Law Insurance Co. Ltd., 1954; Principal, Neill & Mackintosh, SSC, 1967; Consultant, Thorntons WS, 1989; Past Chairman, Scottish Gliding Association and Angus Gliding Club Ltd.; Past President, Chamber of Commerce, Arbroath Rotary Club and Society of Solicitors and Procurators in Angus. Recreations: gliding; shooting; fishing. Address: (h.) 29 Duncan Avenue, Arbroath, Angus DD11 2DA; T.-01241 872221.

Neill, William Wilson, MA (Hons). Poet; b. 22.2.22, Prestwick; m., Doris Marie; 2 d. (by pr. m.). Educ. Ayr Academy; Edinburgh University. Served, RAF; won Sloane Verse Prize and Grierson Verse Prize while at Edinburgh University; Teacher; crowned Bard, Aviemore Mod, 1969; former Editor, Catalyst; former Editor, Lallans (Scots Language magazine); SAC Book Award, 1985; broadcasts, essays in Scotland's three tongues. Publications: Scotland's Castle, 1969; Poems, 1970; Four Points of a Saltire (Co-author), 1970; Despatches Home, 1972; Buile Shuibhne, 1974; Galloway Landscape: Poems, 1981; Cnu a Mogaill: Poems, 1983; Wild Places: Poems, 1985; Blossom, Berry, Fall: Poems 1986; Making Tracks: Poems, 1988; Straight Lines, 1992; Tales frae the Odyssey, 1992; Selected Poems, 1994. Address: (h.) Burnside, Crossmichael, Castle Douglas, DG7 3AP; T.-055-667 265.

Neilson, Rev. Peter, MA, BD. National Adviser in Mission and Evangelism, Church of Scotland, since 1986, and Director of Training, St. Ninian's Centre, Crieff, since 1992; b. 8.1.48, Lanark; m., Dorothy Jane; 3 d. Educ. Hamilton Academy; Glasgow University; Edinburgh University. Assistant Minister, Dunblane Cathedral, 1972-75; Minister, Mount Florida Parish Church, 1975-86. Recreation: singing. Address: (b.) St. Ninian's Centre, Crieff, PH7 4BG; T.-01764 653766.

Nelson, John, MBE, TD, DL. Convener, Stewartry District Council, since 1976; Chairman, Solway River Purification Board, since 1986; b. 26.12.18, Irongray, Dumfries; m., Margaret M.C. Shedden; 4 s. Educ. Castle Douglas High School. Farming, 1934-84, except for War years spent with Royal Artillery and Indian Mountain Artillery in Burma; NFU Committee Member, 40 years (Chairman, Stewartry Area, 1960-61); County Councillor, 1971-74; appointed Deputy Lieutenant, 1983. Recreation: horse riding. Address: (h.) Greentop, 4 Castle View, Castle Douglas; T.-Castle Douglas 503143.

Nelson, (Peter) Frederick, BSc, CEng, MIEE. Chairman, Scottish Sports Association, since 1990; Member, Scottish Sports Council, since 1990; b. 2.9.52, Glasgow; m., (Caroline) Ann; 3 s. Educ. John Neilson; Strathclyde University. President, Scottish Canoe Association, 1980-90; Member, Commonwealth Games Council for Scotland, since 1982. Recreations: canoeing; walking; DIY. Address:

(h.) 11 Barnton Park Place, Edinburgh, EH4 6ET; T.-0131-336 4779.

Neumann, Jan, CBE, BSc, FEng, FIMechE, FIMarE, FIES. Director, Scottish Nuclear Ltd.; b. 26.6.24, Prague; m., 1, Barbara Joyce Gove (deceased); 2 s.; 2, Irene McCusker. Educ. Friends' School, Great Ayton; London University. Flight Engineer, RAF; Design Engineer, English Electric Co., Rugby; various engineering design and management positions in Yarrow Admiralty Research Department; Director, YARD Ltd., 1969-88 (Managing Director, 1978-87); Director, Yarrow PLC, 1978-86; Board Member: SSEB, 1986-88, Scottish Nuclear, 1989-93; President, Institution of Engineers and Shipbuilders in Scotland, 1993-95; received Denny Gold Medal, IMarE, and Thomas Lowe Gray Prize, IMechE. Recreations: swimming; bowls. Address: (h.) 38 Norwood Park, Bearsden, Glasgow, G61 2RZ.

Newall, John, LLB, WS, NP. Solicitor, since 1966; Member, Council, Law Society of Scotland, since 1993; b. 6.8.42, Dumfries; m., Gaye Tuddenham; 1 s.; 2 d. Educ. Dumfries Academy; Edinburgh University. Solicitor, 1966; WS, 1970; Partner, Skene, Edwards and Garson, 1970-78; Partner, McGrigor, Donald, since 1978. Recreations: flying; golf; music. Address: (b.) McGrigor Donald, Erskine House, 68-73 Queen Street, Edinburgh; T.-0131-226 7777.

Newall, Stephen Park, DL, Hon. LLD (Strathclyde). Chairman, Lomond Healthcare NHS Trust, since 1995; Deputy Chairman, Court, University of Strathclyde, since 1993 (Chairman, Court, 1988-93); Deputy Lieutenant, Dunbartonshire, since 1985; b. 12.4.31, Bearsden, Dunbartonshire; m., Gay Sommerville Craig; 4 s.; 1 d. Educ. Loretto. Commissioned and served with Parachute Regiment, National Service, 1949-51; Sales Manager, A.P. Newall & Co., 1951-57; Managing Director, Bulten-Kanthal Stephen Newall Co. Ltd., 1957-80. Chairman, Epilepsy Association of Scotland, 1982-86; Chairman, Finance Committee, University of Strathclyde, 1985-88; Council Member, Quarrier's Homes, 1983-88; Council Member, Scottish Business School, 1983-85; Secretary of State for Scotland's Nominee on Court of Cranfield, 1985-92; Deacon Convener, Trades of Glasgow, 1983-84. Recreations: farming; hill-walking; sailing; music. Address: (h.) Rowaleyn, Rhu, Dunbartonshire; T.-01436 820 521.

Newell, Professor Alan F., BSc, PhD, FIEE, CEng, FBCS, FRSE, HonFCSLT. NCR Professor of Electronics and Microcomputer Systems, Dundee University, since 1980 (Director, Dundee University Microcomputer Centre, since 1980, Head of Applied Computer Studies Division, since 1994); Deputy Principal, since 1993; b. 1.3.41, Birmingham; m., Margaret; 1 s.; 2 d. Educ. St. Philip's Grammar School; Birmingham University. Research Engineer, Standard Telecommunication Laboratories; Lecturer, Department of Electronics, Southampton University. Recreations: family life; skiing; sailing. Address: (b.) Micro Centre, Department of Mathematics and Computer Science, The University, Dundee, DD1 4HN; T.-Dundee 223181.

Newis, Kenneth, CB, CVO, MA, FRSAMD. President, Queen's Hall (Edinburgh) Ltd.; Trustee, RSAMD Trust; Director, Scottish Churches Housing Agency; b. 9.11.16, Crewe; m., Kathleen Barrow; 2 d. Educ. Manchester Grammar School; St. John's College, Cambridge. HM Office of Works, London, 1938-70; Under Secretary, Scottish Development Department, 1970-73; Secretary, 1973-76. Recreation: music. Address: (h.) 11 Abbotsford Park, Edinburgh, EH10 5DZ; T.-0131-447 4138.

Newlands, Professor Rev. George McLeod, MA, BD, PhD. Professor of Divinity, Glasgow University, since 1986 (Dean, Faculty of Divinity, 1988-90); Principal, Trinity College, since 1991; 12.7.41, Perth; m., Mary Elizabeth

Wallace; 3 s. Educ. Perth Academy; Edinburgh University; Heidelberg University; Churchill College, Cambridge. Assistant Minister, Muirhouse, Edinburgh, 1969; Lecturer in Divinity, Glasgow University, 1969; University Lecturer in Divinity, Cambridge, 1973; Dean, Trinity Hall, Cambridge, 1982. Publications: Hilary of Poitiers; Theology of the Love of God; The Church of God; Making Christian Decisions; God in Christian Perspective. Recreations: walking; music; golf. Address: (b.) Faculty of Divinity, 4 The Square, Glasgow University, Glasgow G12 8QQ.

Newlands, William Jeffrey, MB, ChB, FRCSEdin. Consultant Ear, Nose and Throat Surgeon, Grampian Health Board and Orkney and Shetland Health Boards, since 1981; Clinical Senior Lecturer in Otolaryngology, Aberdeen University, since 1981; b. 9.9.29, Edinburgh; m., Patricia Kathleen St. Quintin Gee; 2 s.; 2 d. Educ. Daniel Stewart's College, Edinburgh; Edinburgh University. House Physician and House Surgeon, Western General Hospital, Edinburgh, 1952-53; Captain, RAMC, 1953-55; specialist training, 1958-65, Royal Infirmary, Edinburgh, Western Infirmary, Glasgow, Royal National Throat, Nose and Ear Hospital, London; Otolaryngologist, Brown Clinic, Calgary, 1966; Consultant ENT Surgeon: Grampian Health Board, 1967-77, County Hospital, Uddevalla, Sweden, 1977-78, Lothian Health Board, 1978-79; Professor of Otolaryngology, King Faisal University College of Medicine, Saudi Arabia, 1979-81. Examiner in Otolaryngology, Part 2 Examination, FRCSEdin, 1975-90. Recreations: travel; music. Address: (h.) 4 Camperdown Road, Aberdeen, AB2 4NU; T.-01224 633784.

Nicholls, Brian, BSc (Econ). Senior Business Consultant, Scottish Enterprise, since 1991; Vice President, Scottish Council Development and Industry, since 1991; Director, Scottish Opera, since 1993; b. 21.9.28, London; m., Mary Elizabeth Harley; 1 s.; 2 d. Educ. Haberdashers' Aske's School; London University; Harvard Business School. George Wimpey Ltd., 1951-55; Constructors John Brown Ltd., 1955-75; Director, CJB Projects Ltd., 1972-75; Director, CJB Pipelines Ltd., 1974-75; Deputy Chairman, CJB Mohandessi Iran Ltd., 1974-75; Industrial Adviser to Secretary of State for Scotland, 1975-78; Director, John Brown Engineering Ltd., 1978-91; Director, John Brown Engineering Gas Turbines Ltd., 1978-91; Director, Rugby Power Company Ltd., 1990-91; Vice President, John Brown Power Ltd., 1987-90; Vice President, John Brown Power Ltd., 1987-90; Member, Council, British Railway Export Group, 1976-78; Member, British Overseas Trade Board, 1978. Recreations: music; reading; walking. Address: (h.) Croy, Shandon, by Helensburgh, G84 8NN; T.-01436 820388.

Nicholson, Sheriff Principal (Charles) Gordon (Brown), QC, MA, LLB. Sheriff Principal of Lothian and Borders, since 1990; Commissioner, Scottish Law Commission, 1982-89; b. 11.9.35, Edinburgh; m., Hazel Mary Nixon; 2 s. Educ. George Watson's College, Edinburgh; Edinburgh University. Admitted to Faculty of Advocates, 1961; Advocate Depute, 1968-70; Sheriff of Dumfries and Galloway, at Dumfries, 1970-76; Sheriff of Lothian and Borders, at Edinburgh, 1976-82. Honorary President, Scottish Association for the Study of Delinquency; Hon. President, Scottish Association of Victim Support Schemes; Commissioner, Northern Lighthouse Board, since 1990 (Chairman, 1994-95). Publication: The Law and Practice of Sentencing in Scotland, 1981 (2nd edition, 1992). Recreation: music. Address: (h.) 1A Abbotsford Park, Edinburgh, EH10 5DX; T.-0131-447 4300.

Nicholson, Liz, MA. Depute Chief Executive, Citizens Advice Scotland, since 1992; b. 27.9.46, Birmingham; m., Colin Nicholson; 2 s.; 1 d. Educ. Our Lady of Mercy Grammar School, Wolverhampton; Edinburgh University. Research Associate, Edinburgh University, 1988-89;

Housing Campaign Worker, Shelter, 1989-92. Publications: Students and the Private Rented Sector; Odds against Health — Children and Temporary Accommodation. Address: (b.) Citizens Advice Scotland, 26 George Square, Edinburgh, EH8 9LD; T.-0131-667 0156.

Nicholson, Peter Alexander, LLB (Hons). Managing Editor, W. Green, The Scottish Law Publisher, since 1989; General Editor, Scots Law Times, since 1985; Scottish Editor, Current Law, since 1985; General Editor, Greens Weekly Digest, since 1986; b. 22.5.58, Stirling; m., Morag Ann Fraser; 1 s.; 2 d. Educ. St. David's RC High School, Dalkeith; Edinburgh University. Admitted as Solicitor, 1981. Lay Minister of the Eucharist. Recreations: choral singing; gardening; keeping fit. Address: (h.) 91 Greenbank Road, Edinburgh, EH10 5RT; T.-0131-447 1842.

Nickson, Baron cr. 1994 (Life Peer), of Renagour in the District of Stirling (David Wigley), KBE (1987), CBE (1981), DL, CBIM, FRSE. Life Peer; Chairman, Clydesdale Bank, since 1991 (Director, since 1981); Chairman, Senior Salaries Review Body, 1989-95; Director, Scottish & Newcastle Breweries plc, 1981-95 (Chairman, 1983-89); Deputy Chairman, General Accident Fire and Life Assurance Corporation plc; Director, National Australia Bank Ltd., since 1991; Director, National Australian Group (UK) Ltd., since 1993; Director, Edinburgh Investment Trust, 1983-94; b. 27.11.29, Eton; m., Helen Louise Cockcraft; 3 d. Educ. Eton College; Royal Military Academy, Sandhurst. Commissioned, Coldstream Guards, 1949-54; William Collins: joined, 1954, Director, 1961-85, Joint Managing Director, 1967, Vice-Chairman, 1976-83, Group Managing Director, 1979-82; Director: Scottish United Investors plc, 1970-83, Radio Clyde Ltd., 1982-85; Chairman, Pan Books, 1982-83; Chairman, Scottish Enterprise, 1990-93 (SDA, 1988-90); President, CBI, 1986-88; Chairman, CBI in Scotland, 1979-81; Chairman, Countryside Commission for Scotland, 1983-86; Member: Scottish Industrial Development Advisory Board, 1975-80, Scottish Economic Council, 1980-95, Scottish Committee, Design Council, 1978-81; Chairman, Atlantic Salmon Trust; Brigadier, Queen's Bodyguard for Scotland (Royal Company of Archers); Deputy Lieutenant, Stirling and Falkirk, since 1982. Recreations: fishing; bird-watching; the countryside. Address: (h.) Renagour House, Aberfoyle, Stirling, FK8 3TF; T.-Aberfoyle 275.

Nicol, Alexander David, CA. Director and Deputy Chief Executive, British Linen Bank Ltd.; Managing Director, Capital Leasing Ltd.; Managing Director, British Linen Assets plc; b. 11.7.38, Kirkcaldy; m., Sheila Giffen; 1 s.; 2 d. Educ. Buckhaven High School; Harvard AMP. Managing Director, NEI Peebles, 1976-83. Member, Edinburgh University Advisory Committee on Business Studies. Address: (b.) 4 Melville Street, Edinburgh, EH3 7NZ; T.-0131-243 8304.

Nicol, Rev. Douglas Alexander Oag, MA, BD (Hons). General Secretary, Church of Scotland Department of National Mission; b. 5.4.48, Dunfermline; m., Anne Wilson Gillespie; 2 s.; 1 d. Educ. Kirkcaldy High School; Edinburgh University; Glasgow University. Assistant Warden, St. Ninian's Centre, Crieff, 1972-76; Minister, Lochside, Dumfries, 1976-82; Minister, St. Columba, Kilmacolm, 1982-91. Chairman, Board of Directors, National Bible Society of Scotland, 1984-87; Convener, Board of National Mission, Church of Scotland, 1990-91. Recreations: family life; hill-walking. Address: (h.) 24 Corbiehill Avenue, Blackhall, Edinburgh, EH4 5DR; T.-0131-336 1965.

Nicol, Rev. James Gerard, PhB, STB, JCL. President, Roman Catholic Scottish National Tribunal, since 1992; Priest, Motherwell Diocese, since 1978; Judicial Vicar of all Scottish R.C. Dioceses, since 1992; b. 8.10.54, Coatbridge. Educ. St. Patrick's High School, Coatbridge; Blairs

College, Aberdeen; Pontifical Gregorian University, Rome; Scots College, Rome. Parochial appointments, since 1979; Tribunal: Judge Instructor, 1979-81, Co-ordinator, Motherwell Diocese, 1981-84; Defender of the Bond, 1984-86; Instructor/Defender, 1986-89; Vice-President, 1989-92; Assistant Youth Co-ordinator, Motherwell Diocese, 1979-85. Recreations: cooking; travel; reading; collecting ducks; listening to music. Address: R.C. Scottish National Tribunal, 22 Woodrow Road, Glasgow, G41 5PN; T.-0141-427 3036.

Nicol, Rev. Thomas James Trail, LVO, MBE, MC, MA, DD. Minister, Church of Scotland; Extra Chaplain to The Queen, since 1979; b. 24.1.17, Skelmorlie, Ayrshire; m., Mary Barnfather Taylor; 2 d. Educ. Edinburgh Academy; Dundee High School; Glasgow Academy; Aberdeen Grammar School; Aberdeen University. OCTU and Commission, Black Watch, 1939-42; ordained as Chaplain to the Forces, 1942; RAChD, 1942-46, attached 51 (H) Division; Minister, St. Luke's, Broughty Ferry, 1946-49; regular commission, RAChD, 1949-72; Assistant Chaplain-General, HQ Scotland, 1967-72; Minister, Crathie, 1972-77; Domestic Chaplain in Scotland to the Queen, 1972-79. Recreations: hill-walking; gardening; golf. Address: (h.) Beech Cottage, Dalginross, Comrie, Perthshire, PH6 2HB; T.-01764 670430.

Nicol, William, CBE, BSc, Hon.DEd, FCIOB, FInstR, FSCOTVEC. Chairman, Scottish Committee, and Member of Council, CNAA, 1985-93; former Chairman and Managing Director, Craig-Nicol Limited; b. 9.9.24, Glasgow; m., Margaret Jean McNeill; 2 s.; 1 d. Educ. High School of Glasgow; Gresham House; Glasgow University. President, Glasgow Master Wrights and Builders' Association, 1953-54; Chairman, Glasgow Local Joint Apprenticeship Committee, 1952-61; Chairman, Scottish Building Apprenticeship Council, 1959-67 and since 1992; Member, Board of Governors, Jordanhill College of Education, 1959-67; Deacon, Incorporation of Wrights in Glasgow, 1963-64; Director, Glasgow Chamber of Commerce, 1965-70 (Chairman, Education Committee); Founder Chairman, Scottish Branch, Chartered Institute of Building, 1963-65 (National President, 1970-71, Honorary Treasurer, 1972-76); Member, Construction Industry Training Board, 1964-85 (Chairman, Building Committee, 1967-72); President, Scottish National Federation of Building Trades' Employers, 1969-70 and 1972-73; Governor, Glasgow College of Building and Printing, 1966-75 (first Chairman, Board of Governors) and Vice-Chairman, then Chairman, new College Council, 1976-82; Vice-Chairman, Scottish Technical Education Council, 1973-78, Chairman, 1978-85; Chairman, British Refrigeration Association, 1975-77, President, 1986-88; Chairman, Commercial Section, CECOMAF, 1974-77 (President, CECOMAF, 1979-83); Committee Member, Scottish Branch, Institute of Refrigeration, 1977-81 (elected Vice-Chairman, 1979); Member, Heating, Ventilating, Air Conditioning and Refrigeration Equipment - Economic Development Committee, NEDO, 1984-87; Governor, Glasgow Polytechnic, 1985-93; Member, Court, Glasgow Caledonian University, since 1993; Chairman, Sector Board 4, SCOTVEC, since 1989, Member of Council, since 1993. Recreations: gardening; walking; reading; music; bridge. Address: (h.) 27 Burnhead Road, Glasgow, G43 2SU; T.-0141-637 4097.

Nicoll, Douglas Alexander Smith, JP. Honorary Sheriff, Forfar; b. 24.6.18, Forfar; m., Ella Mary Grant (deceased); 1 s.; 2 d. Educ. Forfar Academy. Partner, joinery manufacturing firm, from 1936; Managing Director and Chairman upon retirement, 1972; Member, Forfar Town Council, seven years; served on Magistrates' Bench, three years; served on Steering Committee for Community Councils in Angus; Elder, Church of Scotland. Recreations: music; bowling. Address: (h.) Dunvegan, 11 Turfbeg Avenue, Forfar, DD8 3LJ; T.-01307 463232.

Nicoll, Eric Hamilton, CBE, FSA Scot, BSc (Hons), FICE, FIWEM (Dip). Deputy Chief Engineer, Scottish Development Department, 1976-85; b. 15.5.25, Edinburgh; m., Helen Elizabeth Barnes; 1 s.; 1 d. Educ. George Heriot's School, Edinburgh; Edinburgh University. Engineering Assistant: Midlothian County Council Roads Department, 1945-46, Edinburgh Corporation Water Department, 1946-51; Chief Assistant County Engineer, Midlothian County Council, 1951-62; Scottish Development Department: Engineering Inspector, 1962-68, Senior Engineering Inspector, 1968-72, Assistant Chief Engineer, 1972-75. US Water Pollution Control Federation Arthur Sidney Bedell Award, 1985; Chairman, Edinburgh Recorded Music Society, 1993-95; Chairman, Pictish Arts Society and Archivist, 1992-95. Publication: Small Water Pollution Control Works: Design and Practice, 1988. Recreations: wood sculpture; music; antiquities. Address: (h.) 35 Wardie Road, Edinburgh, EH5 3LJ.

Nicolson, David M., CA. Office Managing Partner, KPMG Edinburgh, since 1988; b. 22.4.42, Edinburgh; m., Elizabeth Finlay Smith; 1 s.; 1 d. Educ. Royal High School, Edinburgh. Qualified as CA with Robertson & Maxtone Graham, Edinburgh, 1964; Peat Marwick Mitchell & Co., London, 1964-67; returned to Robertson & Maxtone Graham, 1967 (now KPMG). President, Edinburgh Junior Chamber of Commerce, 1975-76; President, Edinburgh Chamber of Commerce and Manufactures, since 1994; former Member of Council, Institute of Chartered Accountants of Scotland. Recreations: golf; tennis; skiing; gardening. Address: (b.) Saltire Court, 20 Castle Terrace, Edinburgh, EH1 2EG; T.-0131-222 2000.

Nicolson, Roy Macdonald, FFA, FPMI. Managing Director, Scottish Amicable, since 1990; b. 12.6.44, Glasgow; m., Jennifer; 1 s.; 1 d. Educ. Paisley Grammar School. Joined Scottish Amicable, 1960. Recreations: golf; bridge. Address: (b.) Scottish Amicable, Amicable House, 150 St. Vincent Street, Glasgow; T.-0141-248 2323.

Nimmo, Professor Myra A., BSc, PhD. Professor of Exercise Physiology, Faculty of Education, Strathclyde University; b. 5.1.54, Edinburgh; m., Dr. J.A. Macaskill; 2 s. Educ. Westbourne School for Girls; Glasgow University. Temporary Lecturer, Glasgow University, 1978-80; Wellcome Research Fellow, 1980-82; Lecturer in Physiology, Queen's College, Glasgow, 1982-84, Senior Lecturer in Physiotherapy and research, 1984-87, Acting Head, Department of Physiotherapy, 1987-88; Assistant Director, Scottish Vocational Education Department, 1988-91. Member, Scottish Sports Council, 1990-94; Olympic athlete. Recreation: general fitness. Address: (b.) Strathclyde University, Jordanhill Campus, Southbrae Drive, Glasgow, G13 1PP; T.-0141-950 3722.

Nimmo Smith, William Austin, QC, BA, LLB. Advocate, since 1969; Scottish Law Commissioner, since 1988; b. 6.11.42, Edinburgh; m., Dr. Jennifer Nimmo Smith; 1 s.; 1 d. Educ. Eton; Balliol College, Oxford; Edinburgh University. Standing Junior Counsel, Department of Employment, 1977-82; QC, 1982; Advocate Depute, 1983-86; Chairman, Medical Appeal Tribunals and Vaccine Damage Tribunals, 1986-91; Member (part-time), Scottish Law Commission, since 1988. Recreations: hill-walking; music. Address: (h.) 29 Ann Street, Edinburgh, EH4 1PL.

Nisbet, Brenda, BSc, PhD. Secretary, Scottish Countryside Activities Council, since 1991; b. 2.6.26, Leeds; m., John D. Nisbet; 1 s.; 1 d. Educ. West Leeds High School; Leeds University. Senior Scientific Officer, Rowett Research Institute, 1951-53; Lecturer in Zoology, Aberdeen University, 1955-89. Secretary, Scottish Orienteeering Association, 1985-94. Recreations: orienteering; hill-walking; gardening. Address: (h.) 7 Lawson Avenue, Banchory, AB31 3TW; T.-01330 823145.

Nisbet, Hugh Haddow, MA (Hons), DipEd. Headteacher, Paisley Grammar School, since 1989; b. 20.4.40, Barrhead; m., Lilian; 1 s.; 1 d. Educ. Paisley Grammar School; Glasgow University. Teacher, Crookston Castle Secondary School, Glasgow, 1963-69; Principal Teacher of History, Glenwood Secondary School, Glasgow, 1969-71; Assistant Head Teacher: Riverside Secondary School, Glasgow, 1971-75, Crookston Castle Secondary School, 1975-77; Headteacher, Stanely Green High School, Paisley, 1977-89. Recreations: reading; tropical fish-keeping; junior football; golf. Address: (b.) Paisley Grammar School, Glasgow Road, Paisley, PA1 3RP; T.-0141-889 3484.

Nisbet, James Barry Consitt, LLB, NP, JP. Stipendiary Magistrate, Glasgow, since 1984; b. 26.7.42, Forfar; m., Elizabeth McKenzie; 2 d. Educ. Forfar Academy; Edinburgh University. Legal Assistant, Warden Bruce & Co., WS, Edinburgh, 1967-68; Legal Assistant, then Junior Depute Town Clerk, then Depute Town Clerk, Perth City Council, 1968-75; Senior Depute Director of Administration, Perth and Kinross District Council, 1975-84. Secretary of Vestry, Lay Elector and Head Server, St. Ninian's Episcopal Cathedral, Perth; Secretary-General, Scottish Guild of Servers. Recreations: transport, especially railways and tramways; archaeology; music; foreign travel; genealogy. Address: (b.) District Court Chambers, 21 St. Andrews Street, Glasgow, G1 5PW; T.-0141-227 5424.

Nisbet, Professor John Donald, OBE, MA, BEd, PHD, FEIS. Professor of Education, Aberdeen University, 1963-88; b. 17.10.22, Rosyth; 1 s.; 1 d. Educ. Dunfermline High School; Edinburgh University; Aberdeen University. RAF, 1943-46; Teacher, 1946-48; Lecturer, 1949-63; Visiting Professor, San Jose, 1961, 1964, Monash, Australia, 1974, Waikato, New Zealand, 1978. Chairman: Educational Research Board, 1972-75, Scottish Committee on Primary Education, 1974-80, Scottish Council for Research in Education, 1975-78; President, British Educational Research Association, 1975; Editor, British Journal of Educational Psychology, 1967-74; Editor, Studies in Higher Education, 1979-84; Editor, World Yearbook of Education, 1985. Recreations: golf; orienteering. Address: (h.) 7 Lawson Avenue, Banchory, AB31 3TW; T.-01330 823145.

Niven, Catharine, BSc, AMA, FSA(Scot). Curator, Inverness Museum and Art Gallery, since 1984; b. 23.9.52, Denbigh; m., Roger Niven. Educ. Loughton High School; Leicester University. Freelance archaeologist, working in Britain and Scandinavia; Keeper of Antiquities, Rotherham Museum, 1979-81; Assistant Curator (Archaeology), Inverness Museum and Art Gallery, 1981-84. Recreation: music. Address: (b.) Castle Wynd, Inverness, IV2 3ED; T.-01463 237114.

Niven, Stuart Matthew, BSc, DipEd, FIMgt. Director, Scottish School of Further Education, Strathclyde University; b. 1.3.36, Clydebank; m., Jean K. McPhee; 1 s.; 1 d. Educ. Clydebank High School; Glasgow University. Teacher of Mathematics and Physics: Clydebank High School, 1959, Stow College of Engineering, 1961; Head, Department of Mathematics and Physics, Kilmarnock College, 1964; Jordanhill College of Education: Lecturer in Mathematics, 1967, Senior Lecturer in Further Education, 1968, Principal Lecturer, 1970. Member, CNAA Further Education Board, 1978-84; Chairman, Editorial Board, Journal for Further and Higher Education in Scotland, 1976-83; Chairman, National Liaison Committee on Training of Teachers of Nursing, Midwifery and Health Visiting, 1983-88; Member, National Board for Scotland for Nursing, Midwifery and Health Visiting, 1989-93; Member, UK Central Council for Nursing, Midwifery and Health Visiting, since 1989; President, International Vocational Education and Training Association, since 1994 (Vice President, Europe, 1990-92, President (Elect), 1992-94); President, International Section, American Vocational Association; Member, Royal Philosophical Society of

Glasgow. Publications: Vocational Further Education in Scotland, 1982; Professional Development of Further Education Lecturers in Scotland: Towards Comprehensive Provision, 1987. Recreation: golf. Address: University of Strathclyde, Jordanhill Campus, 76 Southbrae Drive, Glasgow, G13 1PP; T.-0141-950 3121.

Nixon, Christopher William, NDA, CertEd, ARAgs. Principal, Oatridge Agricultural College, since 1985; b. 7.11.45, Grappenhall; m., Susan Doreen Presley; 1 s.; 2 d. Educ. Normain College, Chester; Harper Adams Agricultural College. Lecturer in Agriculture/Extra Mural Lecturer, Newton Rigg, Penrith; Lecturer in Sheep Production/Senior Lecturer, Extra Mural, Bishop Burton; Depute Principal, Oatridge Agricultural College. Address: (h.) Bridgehill Farm, Harthill, Shotts, Lanarkshire, ML7 5TR; T.-01501 751257.

Nixon, Mary MacKenzie, OBE, MA (Hons), DipEd. Archivist, Scottish Girl Guides Association, 1979-90; b. Port Arthur, Canada. Educ. High School of Stirling; St. Andrews University. Assistant English Teacher, Riverside School, Stirling; Responsible Assistant, History, High School of Stirling, Falkirk High School; Responsible Assistant, English, Falkirk High School; Head, English Department, Grangemouth High School. Girl Guides Association: County Camp Adviser and Chairman, Training Committee, Stirlingshire; Scotland: Ranger Adviser, Training Adviser, Deputy Scottish Chief Commissioner; Co-ordinator, Silver Jubilee Scheme for Unemployed; Chairman, Netherurd Committee, Scottish Girl Guides Association Training Centre, 1981-85. Recreations: genealogy; archaeology; poetry. Address: (h.) Gartlea, 19 Station Road, Bannockburn, FK7 8LE.

Noakes, Robert Ogilvie. Executive Producer, BBC Radio Scotland, 1989-95, formed Neon Productions Limited, 1995; b. 13.5.47, St. Andrews. Educ. Bell Baxter School, Cupar. Various unskilled jobs, 1963-69; self-employed musician, songwriter, performer, recording artist, broadcaster, record producer, music publisher, 1969-87; Producer, BBC Radio, 1987-89. Recreations: travel (all modes, purposeful and otherwise); music; theatre; radio; cinema; reading; bargain hunting. Address: (b.) Festival Business Centre, 150 Brand Street, Glasgow G51 1DH; T.-0141-314 0051.

Noble, Sheriff Alistair William, LLB. Sheriff of North Strathclyde at Dunoon, since 1992; b. 10.1.54. Advocate, 1978. Address: (b.) Sheriff Court House, George Street, Dunoon, PA23 8BQ.

Noble, Sheriff David, MA, LLB, WS, JP. Sheriff at Oban and Fort William, since 1983; b. 11.2.23, Inverness; m., Marjorie Scott Smith; 2 s.; 1 d. Educ. Inverness Royal Academy; Edinburgh University. RAF Bomber Command, 1942-46; Miller Thomson & Robertson, WS, Edinburgh, 1950-83. Recreation: sailing. Address: (h.) Woodhouselee, North Connel, Argyll; T.-Connel 710678.

Noble, David Hillhouse, LLB, DipMan. Chief Executive, Skye and Lochalsh District Council, since 1974; b. 27.4.48, Paisley; m., Hilary; 1 s.; 2 d. Educ. Greenock Academy; Glasgow University. Legal and Administrative Assistant, Argyll County Council, 1972-73; Senior Legal and Administrative Assistant, Inverness County Council, 1973-74. Non-Executive Director, Skye and Lochalsh Enterprise, since 1991. Address: (b.) Tigh na Sgire, Park Lane, Portree, IV51 9EP; T.-01478 612341.

Noble (or Nobail), Sir Iain, Bt. of Ardkinglas and Eilean Iarmain, OBE, MA. Chairman, Noble and Company Ltd.; b. 8.9.35, Berlin. Educ. in China, Argentina and England; University College, Oxford. Scottish Council (Development and Industry), 1964-69; Co-founder and Joint Managing Director, Noble Grossart Ltd., Edinburgh, 1969-72.

Chairman, Seaforth Maritime Ltd., 1972-77; Director: Adam and Company plc, 1983-94, Independent Insurance Group PLC, since 1986, Premium Trust PLC, since 1993; and other companies; Chairman: Skye Bridge Ltd., since 1994, Pràban na Linne Ltd (Proprietor of The Gaelic Whiskies); Proprietor, Fearann Eilean Iarmain, since 1972; Member, Edinburgh University Court, 1970-73; Co-founder, Governor and Trustee, College of Sabhal Mor Ostaig, 1974-84; Trustee, National Museums of Scotland, 1986-90; Trustee of NMS Charitable Trust, since 1990; Chairman, Club Gniomhachas nan Gaidheal, 1989-90; Scotsman of the Year Award, 1982 (Knights Templar); President, Saltire Society, since 1992; Editor, Sources of Finance, 1967-69. Recreations: deasbad, comhradh, orain is ceol le deagh chompanaich. Address: An Oifig, Eilean Iarmain, An t-Eilean Sgitheanach, IV43 8QR; T.-01471 833 266; and 5 Darnaway Street, Edinburgh, EH3.

Noble, Lillias Mary, BEd. Director, LEAD-Scotland (Linking Education and Disability), since 1988; part-time Commissioner, Mental Welfare Commission, since 1992; b. 11.9.54, Vancouver. Educ. Larkhall Academy; Hamilton College of Education; Strathclyde University. Teacher of English and Assistant Principal Teacher, Thurso High School, 1975-80; Assistant Principal Teacher, Wester Hailes Education Centre, 1980-85; Save the Children Fund (Scotland), 1985-88. Recreations: climbing mountains; reading feminist literature. Address: (b.) LEAD-Scotland, Queen Margaret College, Clerwood Terrace, Edinburgh, EH12 8TS; T.-0131-317 3439.

Noble, Sir (Thomas Alexander) Fraser, Kt (1971), MBE (1947), MA, LLD, FRSE; b. 29.4.18, Cromdale; m., Barbara A.M. Sinclair; 1 s.; 1 d. Educ. Nairn Academy; Aberdeen University. Indian Civil Service, 1940-47; Lecturer in Political Economy, Aberdeen University, 1948-57; Secretary, Carnegie Trust for Scottish Universities, 1957-62; Vice-Chancellor, Leicester University, 1962-76; Principal, Aberdeen University, 1976-81; Past Chairman of numerous public service committees, including Scottish Standing Conference of Youth Service Organisations, Home Office Advisory Committee for Probation and After Care, Television Research Committee; Chairman, UK Committee of Vice Chancellors, 1970-72; former Member of Council, Association of Commonwealth Universities. Recreations: golf; listening to music. Address: (h.) Hedgerley, Victoria Street, Nairn; T.-Nairn 453151.

Noble, Timothy Peter, MA, MBA. Director: Noble Group Ltd., Waverley Mining Finance plc, Premium Underwriting plc, British Ski Federation Ltd.; Chairman: Business Archives Council of Scotland, Royal Scottish National Orchestra Endowment Trust; b. 21.12.43; m., Elizabeth Mary Aitken; 2 s.; 1 d. Educ. University College, Oxford; Gray's Inn, London; INSEAD, Fontainebleau. Recreations: skiing; tennis; bridge; wine; astronomy. Address: (h.) Ardnahane, Barnton Avenue, Edinburgh; T.-0131-336 3565.

Noel-Paton,(Frederick) Ranald, BA. Group Managing Director, John Menzies plc, since 1986; b. 7.11.38, Bombay; m., Patricia Anne Stirling; 4 d. Educ. Rugby School; McGill University. Investment Analyst, Greenshields Inc., 1962-63; Management Trainee, United Biscuits, 1964; various posts, British United Airways Ltd., 1965-70; various senior executive posts, British Caledonian Airways, 1970-86 (General Manager, West Africa, 1975-79, General Manager, Far East, 1980-86, Director, Caledonian Far East Airways, 1984-86); Director: Pacific Assets Trust plc, since 1986, General Accident plc, since 1987, Macallan Glenlivet plc, since 1990. Recreations: fishing; walking; bird-watching; the arts. Address: (b.) 108 Princes Street, Edinburgh, EH2 3AA; T.-0131-225 8555.

Normand, Andrew Christie, MA, LLB, LLM. Regional Procurator Fiscal, Glasgow and Strathkelvin, since 1990; b.

7.2.48, Edinburgh; m., Barbara Jean Smith; 2 d. Educ. George Watson's College, Edinburgh; Edinburgh University; Queen's University, Kingston, Ontario. Address: (b.) Procurator Fiscal's Office, 10 Ballater Street, Glasgow, G5 9PS; T.-0141-429 5566.

North, Michael James, MA, PhD. Reader in Biochemistry, Stirling University, since 1989; b. 20.1.48, London; m., Barbara Lockwood (deceased); 1 d. Educ. East Barnet Grammar School; Hertford College, Oxford; Newcastle upon Tyne University. SRC Postdoctoral Fellow, Leicester University and Essex University, 1973-75; Lecturer in Biochemistry, Stirling University, 1975-85; Senior Lecturer, 1985-89. Convener, Scottish Branch, Society for General Microbiology, 1988-93; Editor, Microbiology (formerly Journal of General Microbiology), 1988-94. Publication: Biochemical Protozoology (Joint Editor). Recreations: gardening; music; supporting Tottenham Hotspur FC. Address: (b.) Department of Biological and Molecular Sciences, Stirling University, Stirling, FK9 4LA; T.-01786 467764.

Norwell, Peter Smith, OBE, TD, JP. Honorary Sheriff, Perth; b. 14.4.12, Perth; m., Elisabeth May Edwards; 3 d. Educ. Dollar Academy. Lt.-Col., RASC, 1944; Secretary, Perthshire Territorial Army Association, 1960-62; Assistant Secretary, Angus, Perthshire and Fife Territorial Army Association, 1962-67; Managing Director, Norwells Perth Footwear Ltd., 1935-60; Town Councillor, Perth, 1946-52; Chairman, Perth Theatre Company, 1968-72. Address: (h.) Dura Den, Pitcullen Terrace, Perth, PH2 7EQ; T.-Perth 26789.

O

O'Brien, Sir Frederick William Fitzgerald, QC, MA, LLB. Sheriff Principal, Lothian and Borders, 1978-89; Convener of Sheriffs Principal, 1972-89; b. 19.7.17, Edinburgh; m., Audrey Muriel Owen; 2 s.; 1 d. Educ. Royal High School, Edinburgh; Edinburgh University. Called to Scottish Bar, 1947; QC, 1960; Commissioner, Mental Welfare Commission, 1962-65; Senior Advocate Depute, Crown Office, 1964-65; Sheriff Principal, Caithness, Sutherland, Orkney and Shetland, 1965-75; Interim Sheriff Principal, Aberdeen, Kincardine and Banff, 1969-71; Sheriff Principal, North Strathclyde, 1975-78; Interim Sheriff Principal, South Strathclyde, 1981; Member, Scottish Medical Practices Committee, 1973-76; Member, Scottish Records Advisory Council, 1974-83; Chairman, Sheriff Court Rules Council, 1975-81; Convener, General Council Business Committee, Edinburgh University, 1980-84; Past President, Royal High School FP Club (Honorary President, 1982-91); Chairman, Edinburgh Sir Walter Scott Club, 1989-92; Commissioner, Northern Lighthouse Board, 1965-89. Recreations: music; golf. Address: (h.) 22 Arboretum Road, Edinburgh, EH3 5PN; T.-0131-552 1923.

O'Brien, James Paul, MA (Hons), MEd, DipEdTech. Vice-Principal, Moray House Institute of Education, Heriot-Watt University, since 1993; b. 23.4.50, Stirling; m., Elaine Margaret Kathleen Smith; 1 d. Educ. St. Mirin's Academy, Paisley; Glasgow University. Teacher, 1973-85; Lecturer, St. Andrew's College of Education, 1985-88, Director, 1988-93, Assistant Principal, 1992-93. Recreations: golf; music; reading. Address: (b.) Holyrood Campus, Holyrood Road, Edinburgh, EH8 8AQ; T.-0131-558 6164.

O'Brien, Most Rev. Keith Michael Patrick, BSc, DipEd. Archbishop of St. Andrews and Edinburgh, since 1985; b. 17.3.38, Ballycastle, Northern Ireland. Educ. Saint Patrick's, Dumbarton; Holy Cross Academy, Edinburgh; Edinburgh University; St. Andrew's College, Drygrange; Moray House College of Education. Teacher, St. Columba's High School, Fife; Assistant Priest, Kilsyth, then Bathgate; Spiritual Director, St. Andrew's College, Drygrange; Rector, Blairs College, Aberdeen; ordained Archbishop by Cardinal Gray, 1985. Recreations: music; walking. Address: Saint Bennet's, 42 Greenhill Gardens, Edinburgh, EH10 4BJ.

O'Callaghan, Michael John, MBA, DipM (Hons), AInstM. Managing Director, Jetstream Aircraft Ltd., since 1992; b. 13.4.52, London; m., Susan; 2 d. Educ. St. Bonaventure's Grammar School; Cranfield Institute of Technology. Ford Motor Co., 1984-90; Director of Manufacturing, Jetstream Aircraft Ltd., 1991-92.

Odoni, Professor Robert W.K., BSc (Econ), PhD (Cantab). Professor of Pure Mathematics, Glasgow University, since 1989; b. 14.7.47, London; m., Josephine Ann; 2 s.; 1 d. Educ. Queen Elizabeth Grammar School, Barnet; Exeter University; Downing College, Cambridge. Temporary Lecturer in Pure Mathematics, Liverpool University, 1971-72; Research Fellow, Glasgow University, 1972-73;Exeter University: Lecturer in Pure Mathematics, 1973-79, Reader in Number Theory, 1979-85, Professor of Number Theory, 1985-89. Editorial Adviser, London Mathematical Society. Publications: 50 research papers. Recreations: country walks; swimming; cricket; music; literature; history; languages. Address: (b.) Department of Mathematics, University Gardens, Glasgow, G12 8QW; T.-0141-339 8855, Ext. 5179.

O'Farrell, Professor Patrick Neil, BA, PhD, MIPI. Professor of Economics, Heriot-Watt University, since 1986 (Assistant Principal, since 1995, Dean, Faculty of Economic and Social Studies, 1992-95); b. 18.4.41; m.; 3 d. Educ.

Trinity College, Dublin. Assistant in Geography, Trinity College, Dublin, 1963-65; Assistant Lecturer and Lecturer in Geography, Queen's University, Belfast, 1965-70; Lecturer in Geography, New University of Ulster, 1971-73; Lecturer, Senior Lecturer and Reader in Planning, UWIST, 1973-86. Recreations: golf; talking; music. Address: (b.) Heriot-Watt University, Riccarton, Edinburgh, EH14 4AS.

Ogden, Professor Raymond William, MA, PhD, FRSE. George Sinclair Professor of Mathematics, Glasgow University, since 1984 (Head of Department, 1986-94); b. 19.9.43, Lytham; m., Susanne; 2 s.; 2 d. Educ. Leamington College; Gonville and Caius College, Cambridge. Science Research Council Research Fellow, East Anglia University, 1970-72; Lecturer, then Reader in Mathematics, Bath University, 1972-80; Professor of Mathematics, Brunel University, 1981-84. Publication: Non-linear Elastic Deformations, 1984. Recreations: walking; music; gardening. Address: (b.) Department of Mathematics, Glasgow University, Glasgow, G12 8QW; T.-0141-339 8855.

Ogilvie, Lorna Margaret, BSc, MSc, FRMetS. Headmistress, St. Margaret's School for Girls, Aberdeen, since 1989; b. 22.3.47, Edinburgh. Educ. Mary Erskine School for Girls; Edinburgh University; University of Calgary; Moray House College of Education. Geography Teacher, Inverness High School, 1972-73; Head of Geology and Teacher of Geography, Royal Russell School, Croydon, 1973-82; Assistant Rector, Morrison's Academy, Crieff, 1982-88. Recreations: Scottish country dancing; skiing; golf; theatre; travel; reading. Address: (b.) 17 Albyn Place, Aberdeen, AB9 1RH; T.-01224 584466.

Ogilvie, Margaret Elizabeth. Owner/Gardener, Pitmuies Gardens, since 1966; b. 21.12.29, Co. Down; m., Douglas Farquhar Ogilvie (deceased); 1 s.; 2 d. Educ. Central School of Art and Crafts, London. Prior to marriage, advertising manager and book designer/typographer; National Trust for Scotland: Member, Council (twice), Member, Executive Committee (twice), Vice Convenor, Gardens Committee; Historic Houses Association: Member, Executive Council, Scottish Representative, Gardens Committee; Association for Protection of Rural Scotland: Member, Representative Committee, Member, judging panel for Annual Award; Member, Scottish Council for National Parks; Member, Committee, Scottish Museums of Year Award. Recreations: riding; skiing; music; travelling. Address: (h.) House of Pitmuies, by Forfar, Angus; T.-0124 12 245.

Ogilvie-Laing of Kinkell, Gerald, NDD, FRBS. Sculptor; b. 11.2.36; 4 s.; 1 d. Educ. Berkhamsted School; RMA, Sandhurst. Commissioned Fifth Fusiliers, 1955-60; resigned commission and attended St. Martin's School of Art, 1960-64; lived in New York, 1964-69; Artist in Residence, Aspen Institute for Humanistic Studies, Colorado, 1966; moved to north of Scotland, 1969, and restored ruins of Kinkell Castle; Civic Trust Award, 1971; established a tapestry workshop in north of Scotland; Visiting Professor, University of New Mexico, 1976-77; set up bronze foundry, Kinkell Castle, to produce own work; Member, Art Committee, Scottish Arts Council, 1978-80; Professor of Sculpture, Columbia University, New York, 1986-87; Commissioner, Royal Fine Art Commission for Scotland, 1987-95; divides time between north of Scotland and New York; public sculpture includes Callanish, 1971; Frieze of the Wise and Foolish Virgins, 1980; Fountain of Sabrina, 1982; Conan Doyle Memorial, 1991; Axis Mundi, 1991; Bank Underground Station Dragons, 1995. Address: (h.) Kinkell Castle, Ross and Cromarty, IV7 8AT; T.-01349 61485.

Ogilvy, Sir Francis (Gilbert Arthur), 14th Bt. Surveyor and Farmer; b. 22.4.69. Educ. Edinburgh Academy; Glenalmond College; Royal Agricultural College, Cirencester; BSc (Hons) (Reading). Address: (h.) Winton Cottage, Pencaitland, East Lothian, EH34 5AT.

O'Grady, Richard John Peard, MA (Hons). Director/Secretary, Zoological Society of Glasgow and West of Scotland, since 1972; b. 6.7.49, Cambridge; m., Maria Ann; 2 s. Educ. King's School, Bruton; Dundee University. Weekly pets feature, Daily Record, since 1976; D. of E. Inspector of Zoos, since 1982; Member, Clyde/Calders Conservation Committee. Recreations:reading and writing; visiting zoos, parks, reserves; natural history. Address: (b.) Glasgow Zoo, Calderpark, Uddingston, Glasgow, G71 7RZ; T.-0141-771 1185.

Ogston, Rev. David Dinnes, MA, BD. Minister, St. John's Kirk of Perth, since 1980; b. 25.3.45, Ellon, Aberdeenshire; m., Margaret Macleod; 2 d. Educ. Inverurie Academy; King's College and Christ's College, Aberdeen. Assistant Minister, St. Giles' Cathedral, Edinburgh, 1969-73; Minister, Balerno, 1973-80. Publication: White Stone Country; Dry Stone Days. Recreations: late-night films on TV; Greek and Russian Ikons. Address: 15 Comely Bank Perth; T.-Perth 621755.

Ogston, Professor Derek, MA, MD, PhD, DSc, FRCPEdin, FRCP, FIBiol, FRSE, FRSA. Professor of Medicine, Aberdeen University, since 1983 (Dean, Faculty of Medicine, 1984-87; Vice-Principal, since 1987); b. 31.5.32, Aberdeen; m., Cecilia Marie; 1 s.; 2 d. Educ. King's College School, Wimbledon; Aberdeen University. Aberdeen University: Lecturer in Medicine, 1962-69, Senior Lecturer in Medicine, 1969-75, MRC Travelling Fellow, 1967-68, Reader in Medicine, 1975-76, Regius Professor of Physiology, 1977-83. Member, Grampian Health Board, since 1991 (Vice-Chairman, since 1993); Member, General Medical Council, 1985-94. Publications: Haemostasis: Biochemistry, Physiology and Pathology (Joint Editor), 1977; The Physiology of Hemostasis, 1983; Antifibrinolytic Drugs: Chemistry, Pharmacology and Clinical Usage, 1984; Venous Thrombosis: Causation and Prediction, 1987. Recreation: gardening. Address: (h.) 64 Rubislaw Den South, Aberdeen, AB2 6AX; T.-Aberdeen 316587.

Ohara, Noriko. Principal Ballerina, Scottish Ballet; b. Japan. London Ballet, 1974; London Festival Ballet (as principal dancer), 1975; joined Scottish Ballet, 1976; has danced all the major roles in the company's repertoire; regular jury member, Prix de Lausanne; Associate Director, Asami Maki Ballet Company, Tokyo. Address: (b.) 261 West Princes Street, Glasgow, G4 9EE.

Oliver, Ian Thomas, QPM, LLB, MPhil, PhD, FRSA. Chief Constable, Grampian Police; b. 24.1.40, London; m., Elsie; 2 s.; 1 d. Educ. Grammar School, Hampton, Middlesex; Nottingham University; Strathclyde University. RAF, 1959-61; Constable to Superintendent, Metropolitan Police, 1961-77; Northumbria Police: Chief Superintendent, 1977, Assistant Chief Constable (Management Services), 1978; Chief Constable, Central Scotland, 1979. President, Association of Chief Police Officers in Scotland, 1983 and 1993; Churchill Fellow, 1986. Publication: Police, Government and Accountability, 1987. Address: (b.) Police Headquarters, Queen Street, Aberdeen; T.-Aberdeen 639111.

Oliver, James Kenneth Murray. Farmer; b. 1.2.14, Hawick; m., Rhona Mary Purdom Wilkinson; 1 s.; 1 d. Educ. Merchiston Castle, Edinburgh. Army, 1939-46; as racehorse trainer, trained 1,000 winners under National Hunt Rules; rode winner, Scottish Grand National, 1950; trained five winners, Scottish Grand National; four times runner-up, Grand National; trained winners for the Queen Mother; Honorary Vice President, Royal Highland and Agricultural Society of Scotland, since 1962; Director, Doncaster Bloodstock Sales Ltd.; Secretary, Teviotdale Farmers Club. Recreations: hunting; racing; golf; tennis; squash; gardening. Address: (h.) Hassendean Bank, Hawick; T.-01450 87 216.

Oliver, Professor Michael Francis, CBE, MD, MDhc (Bologna and Stockholm), FRCP, FRCPEdin, FFCM, FACC, FRSE. Honorary Professor, National Heart and Lung Institute, London, since 1989; Director, Wynn Institute for Metabolic Research, London 1989-93; Duke of Edinburgh Professor of Cardiology, Edinburgh University, 1979-89; Senior Cardiologist and Physician, Edinburgh Royal Infirmary, 1978-89; b. 3.7.25, Borth; m., 1, Margaret Y. Abbey; 2 s.; 1 s. (deceased); 1 d.; 2, Helen L. Daniel. Educ. Marlborough College, Wiltshire; Edinburgh University. Consultant Physician, Royal Infirmary, and Senior Lecturer in Medicine, Edinburgh University, 1961; Reader in Medicine, 1973; Personal Professor of Cardiology, 1977; Member, Scientific Board, International Society of Cardiology, 1968-78 (Chairman and Council on Atherosclerosis); Chairman, British Atherosclerosis Group, 1970-75; Member, Cardiovascular Panel, Government Committee on Medical Aspects of Food Policy, 1971-74 and 1982-84; UK Representative, Advisory Panel for Cardiovascular Diseases, World Health Organisation, since 1972; Chairman, BBC-Medical Advisory Group in Scotland, 1975-81; Council Member, British Heart Foundation, 1976-84; Convener, Cardiology Committee, Scottish Royal Colleges, 1978-81; President, British Cardiac Society, 1981-85; President, Royal College of Physicians of Edinburgh, 1985-88; Chairman, Honorary Advisory Panel, Cardiovascular Conditions for Fitness to Drive, 1983-90; Purkinje Medal, 1981; Polish Cardiac Society Medal, 1984; FRACP, 1988; FRCPI, 1988. Publications: 350 medical and scientific papers and five books. Recreations: questioning; all things Italian. Address: (h.) Barley Mill House, Pencaitland, East Lothian, EH34 5EP.

Olver, Professor Richard Edmund, BSc, MB, FRCP, FRCPE. James Mackenzie Professor of Child Health, Dundee; b. 26.10.41, Ayr; m.; 2 s.; 2 d. Educ. London University. House Officer and Senior House Officer posts, St. Thomas's, Addenbrookes and Brompton Hospitals, 1966-69; Lecturer, Senior Lecturer, Reader, Department of Paediatrics, University College, London, 1969-85; MRC Travelling Fellow, Cardiovascular Research Institute, San Francisco, 1973-74; Consultant Paediatrician, University College Hospital, London, 1975-85. Address: (b.) Dundee University, Dundee.

O'Neill, James, MSc, BEd, FSA (Scot). Regional Official (Scotland), National Association of Schoolmasters and Union of Women Teachers, since 1981; Secretary, Scottish Money Management Association, since 1991; b. 29.12.51, Glasgow; m., Angela Harris; 1 s.; 2 d. Educ. Our Lady's High School, Motherwell; Hamilton College of Education; Strathclyde University. Teacher, 1974-81; NASUWT: Branch Secretary, Glasgow, 1977-81; Chair, Education Committee (Scotland), 1979-81; Chair, NASUWT (UK) MSF Group, 1988-95; Member, Teachers' Superannuation Working Party (UK), since 1987; Kilmarnock and Loudoun District Council: Member, 1984-88, Chair, Manpower Committee, 1984-88, Secretary, Labour Group, 1984-86; Chair, Stewarton Branch, Labour Party. Recreations: rugby; reading (especially archaeology and science fiction/fantasy); politics. Address: (b.) 34 West George Street, Glasgow, G2 1DA; T.-0141-332 2688.

O'Neill, Rev. Professor John Cochrane, BA, BD, PhD. Professor of New Testament Language, Literature and Theology, Edinburgh University, since 1985; b. 8.12.30, Melbourne; m., Judith Beatrice Lyall (see Judith Beatrice O'Neill); 3 d. Educ. Melbourne Church of England Grammar School; Melbourne University; Ormond College Theological Hall; University of Göttingen; Clare College, Cambridge. Senior Tutor in History, Melbourne University, 1953-55; Lecturer in New Testament Studies, Ormond College Theological Hall, Melbourne, 1960-64; Dunn Professor of New Testament Language, Literature and Theology, Westminster College, Cambridge, 1964-85.

Publications: Paul's Letter to the Romans, 1975; The Bible's Authority: a portrait gallery of thinkers from Lessing to Bultmann, 1991. Recreations: swimming; walking. Address: (h.) 9 Lonsdale Terrace, Edinburgh, EH3 9HN; T.-0131-229 6070.

O'Neill, Judith Beatrice, MA, PGCE. Author of fiction for older children; b. 30.6.30, Melbourne; m., John Cochrane O'Neill (qv); 3 d. Educ. University of Melbourne; University of London. University Tutor, 1954-56, Melbourne, 1970-72, UK; School Teacher, Cambridge, 1974-82, and part-time author; full-time author, since 1982. Publications: Jess and the River Kids; Stringybark Summer; Deepwater; The Message; So Far from Skye. Recreations: reading; walking; music. Address: (h.) 9 Lonsdale Terrace, Edinburgh, EH3 9HN; T.-0131-229 6070.

O'Neill, Martin (John), BA (Econ). MP (Labour), Clackmannan, since 1983 (East Stirlingshire and Clackmannan, 1979-83); b. 6.1.45; m., Elaine Samuel; 2 s. Educ. Trinity Academy, Edinburgh; trades union and evening classes; Heriot-Watt University; Moray House College of Education. President, Scottish Union of Students, 1970-71; school teacher, 1974-79; Tutor, Open University, 1976-79. Member, Select Committee, Scottish Affairs, 1979-80; Opposition Spokesman, Scottish Affairs, 1980-84; Opposition Spokesman on Defence, 1984-88; Shadow Defence Secretary, 1988-92; Shadow Spokesman on Energy, since 1992. Recreations: watching football; reading; listening to jazz; cinema. Address: (b.) 19 Mar Street, Alloa, FK10 1HR; T.-01259 721536.

O'Neill, Maureen Patricia, BA (Hons), DMS. Director, Age Concern Scotland, since 1993; b. 11.5.48, Uganda; m., Jonathan Clogston-Willmott; 1 s.; 1 d. Educ. St. Margaret's School, Hastings; Charlton Park School, Cheltenham; Birkbeck College, London University. General Secretary, Edinburgh YWCA, 1982-87; Principal Officer, Policy, Research and Development, Scottish Association for Mental Health, 1987-93. Recreations: reading; theatre; sport. Address: (b.) 113 Rose Street, Edinburgh EH2 3DT; T.-0131-220 3345.

O'Neill, Patrick. Provost, Dumbarton District, since 1992; Magistrate and Justice of the Peace, since 1970; b. 3.5.28, Dumbarton; m., Mary Kane Connolly; 1 s.; 1 d. Educ. St. Patrick's High School, Dumbarton. AEU Branch Secretary, Dumbarton No. 2, 1967-92; AEU Award of Merit, 1992, for 39 years service; Chairman, West Dumbarton Constituency Labour Party, 12 years; Burgh and District Councillor intermittently since 1962; Director: Scottish Maritime Museum, Leven Valley Workspace Ltd., Dumbarton District Enterprise Trust; Chairman, Leven Valley Initiative. Recreations: chess; photography; opera; former amateur boxer (boxed for Queen's Own Cameron Highlanders). Address: (h.) 26 Bellsmyre Avenue, Dumbarton G82 3AR; T.-01389 63783.

O'Neill, Thomas (Tam), CA. Managing Director, Barr and Stroud Ltd., Glasgow, since 1990; Managing Director, Pilkington P.E. Ltd., since 1992; Deputy Chief Executive, Pilkington Optronics Ltd., since 1993; b. 30.8.43, Methlick; m., Maureen Jane McGinnis; 1 s.; 1 d. Educ. St. Mungo's Academy, Glasgow; Glasgow University. PA to Chairman, Reed International Ltd., London; Finance Director, Scott Lester Ltd., London; Finance Director, Southern Construction Ltd., Portsmouth; Divisional Finance Director, Norcros Ltd., Reading; Divisional Finance Director, N.E.I. Ltd., Newcastle; Finance Director, Barr & Stroud, Glasgow, 1988-90. Council Member, CBI Scotland; Council Member, Scottish Engineers. Recreations: golf (bandit); horse-racing (victim); reading. Address: (b.) Barr & Stroud Ltd., 1 Linthouse Road, Glasgow, G51 4BZ; T.-0141-440 4000.

Oppenheim, Professor Charles, BSc, PhD, DipInfSc, CertEd, FIInfSc, FLA. Head, Department of Information

Science, Strathclyde University, since 1991; b. 25.4.46, London. Educ. Orange Hill Boys' Grammar School; Manchester University. Information Officer, Glaxo Holdings; Lecturer, Plymouth Polytechnic; Lecturer, City University; Director of R&D, Derwent Publications Ltd.; Product Development Manager, Pergamon Infoline; Business Development Manager, Reuters Ltd. President, Institute of Information Scientists; Vice-President, ASLIB. Publications: 140 articles and many books. Recreations: chess; philately; socialising with students. Address: (b.) 26 Richmond Street, Glasgow, G1 1XH; T.-0141-552 4400.

O'Reilly, Denis St. John, MSc, MD, MRCPath. Consultant Clinical Biochemist, Royal Infirmary, Glasgow, since 1984; b. 30.3.51, Cork; m., Margaret M.P. Lucey; 2 s.; 1 d. Educ. Presentation Brothers College, Cork; University College, Cork; Birmingham University. Registrar, Queen Elizabeth Medical Centre, Birmingham, 1976-78; Senior Registrar, Bristol Royal Infirmary, 1978-84; Ainsworth Scholar-Research Fellow, Norsk Hydro Institute for Cancer Research, Oslo, 1982. Recreation: hill-walking. Address: (h.) 47 Strathblane Road, Milngavie, G62 8HA.

Ormiston, Linda, MA, DRSAMD. Singer — Mezzo Soprano; b. 15.1.48, Motherwell. Educ. Dalziel High School, Motherwell; Glasgow University; Royal Scottish Academy of Music and Drama; London Opera Centre. Has sung all over Britain, France, Belgium, Italy, Germany, Austria, Holland and Yugoslavia; has sung regularly at Scottish Opera, Opera North, and Glyndebourne; also well-known in lighter vein and as a member of The Music Box; recordings include Noyes Fludde, HMS Pinafore and Ruddigore with New Sadlers Wells Opera and Tell Me Pretty Maiden; has appeared at New York, Vancouver, Monte Carlo, Brussels and Tokyo; debut, Frankfurt Opera, 1993; debut, Salzburg Festival, 1994; Presenter, BBC Radio 3 and Radio Scotland. Recreations: playing the piano; skating; golf. Address: (h.) 39 Colinhill Road, Strathaven, ML10 6HF.

O'Rourke, Daniel (Donny), MA. Poet, journalist, film-maker, broadcaster, and teacher; Executive Producer, BBC Scotland, 1994-95; b. 5.7.59, Port Glasgow. Educ. St. Mirin's Academy, Paisley; Glasgow University. Chairman, British Youth Film Council, 1982-84; Producer, BBC TV and Radio Scotland, 1984-86; Reporter, Scottish Television, 1986-87, Producer, 1987-92, Head of Arts, 1992-93, Head of Arts and Documentaries, 1993-94. Member, Manpower Services Commission Youth Training Board, 1982-84; Member, Scottish Community Education Council, 1981-84. Publications: Second City, 1991; Rooming Houses of America, 1993; Dream State, the new Scottish poets, 1994; chapter in Burns Now, 1994. Recreations: playing guitar; Irish literature; Americana. Address: (h.) 63 Barrington Drive, Glasgow, G4 9ES.

Orr, David Campbell, MA. Director, Scottish Federation of Housing Associations, since 1990; b. 27.3.55, Kirkconnel; m., Carol; 1 s.; 2 d. Educ. Dundee University. Deputy Warden, Iona Community, Community House, 1976-77; Team Leader, then Co-ordinator, Centrepoint, Soho, 1977-86; Director, Newlon Housing Trust, 1986-90. Former Chair, Young Homelessness Group, Homeless Network, Threshold H.A. Recreations: watching sport — playing badly; cinema. Address: (b.) 38 York Place, Edinburgh, EH1 3HY; T.-0131-556 5777.

Orr, Ian, MRPS. Pharmacist; Honorary Sheriff, South Strathclyde, Dumfries and Galloway, since 1980; Lord Cornet (Standard Bearer), Lanark, since 1961; b. 14.3.26, Lanark; m., Dora Hickey; 1 s. Educ. Lanark Grammar School; Strathclyde University. National Service, RAMC, Egypt, 1947-49. Past President, Lanark Rotary Club; President, Dante Alighieri Society (Diploma Di Benemerenza and Silver Medal). Recreations: fox-hunting; gardening; golf; foreign travel. Address: (h.) Gezira, St. Patrick's Road, Lanark; T.-01555 662810.

Orr, John, OBE, BA, DipFM, FIMgt. Chief Constable, Strathclyde, from 1996; Deputy Chief Constable, Dumfries and Galloway, since 1990; b. 3.9.45, Kilmarnock; m., Joan; 2 s.; 1 d. Educ. James Hamilton Academy, Kilmarnock; Open University; Glasgow University. Entered police as cadet, Renfrew and Bute, 1961; progressed through ranks to rank of Detective Chief Superintendent and Joint Head of Strathclyde CID; seconded 1994 to HM Inspectorate of Constabulary as Assistant Inspector of Constabulary for Scotland. Recreations: Rotary; reading; gardening; angling. Address: (b.) Police Headquarters, Cornwall Mount, Dumfries, DG1 1PZ.

Orr Ewing, Major Edward Stuart, DL, JP. Lord Lieutenant, Wigtown District, since 1989; b. 28.9.31, London; m., 1, F.A.B. Farquhar (m. dissolved); 2, Diana Mary Waters; 1 s.; 2 d. Educ. Sherborne; RMCS, Shrivenham. Black Watch RHR, 1950-69 (Major); Farmer and Landowner, since 1964. Recreations: country sports; skiing; sailing; painting. Address: (h.) Dunskey, Portpatrick, Stranraer; T.-01776 810211.

Orr Ewing, Major Sir Ronald Archibald, 5th Bt; b. 14.5.12; m., Marion Hester Cameron of Lochiel; 2 s.; 2 d. Educ. Eton; Sandhurst. Scots Guards, 1932-53 (Major); DL, Perthshire, 1963; JP, Perthshire; Grand Master Mason of Scotland, 1965-69. Address: (h.) Cardross, Kippen, Stirling, FK8 3DY.

Osborne, Avril, MA, MSc, PhD. Director, Social Work, Orkney, since 1993; b. 9.4.47, Johnstone. Educ. Gourock High School; St. Andrews University; Nottingham University; Lancaster University; Aberdeen University. Child Care Officer, 1969-72; Senior Social Worker, 1972-76; Senior Lecturer, 1976-79; Consultant, 1979-82; Leverhulme Fellow, 1982-84; Assistant Director, Social Work, Highland, 1984-93; seconded to Scottish Office, 1991-93. Recreation: walking. Address: (b.) Orkney Islands Council, School Place, Kirkwall, Orkney; T.-01856 873535.

Osborne, Hon. Lord (Kenneth Hilton Osborne), QC (Scot). Senator of the College of Justice, since 1990; b. 9.7.37. Advocate, 1962; QC, 1976; Chairman, Local Government Boundary Commission, since 1990.

Osborne, Michael, BSc, MICFor. Director, Royal Scottish Forestry Society, since 1992; b. 11.8.52, Solihull. Educ. Prices Grammar School, Fareham; University College of North Wales, Bangor. Head Forester, Haddington Estates, Dunbar, 1981-93. Recreation: bird-watching. Address: (b.) 62 Queen Street, Edinburgh, EH2 4NA; T.-0131-225 8142.

Osler, Douglas Alexander, MA (Hons), FRSA. HM Depute Senior Chief Inspector of Schools, Scottish Office Education Department; b. 11.10.42, Edinburgh; m., Wendy I. Cochrane; 1 s.; 1 d. Educ. Royal High School, Edinburgh; Edinburgh University; Moray House College of Education. Assistant Teacher of History/Careers Master, Liberton Secondary School, Edinburgh, 1965-68; Principal Teacher of History, Dunfermline High School, 1968-74. English Speaking Union Fellowship to USA, 1966; International Visitor Program to USA, 1989. Publications: Queen Margaret of Scotland; Sources for Modern Studies, Volumes 1 and 2. Address: (b.) Room 4/115, New St. Andrew's House, Edinburgh.

Ovens, Iain Stanley, BA, MA, DMS, MIPD. Principal, Angus College, since 1993; b. 9.10.47, Glasgow; m., June Sangster. Educ. Duncanrig Senior Secondary School, East Kilbride; Strathclyde University. Lecturer, Barmulloch College of F.E.; Senior Lecturer, Head of Department, Head of Centre for Industrial Studies, Assistant Principal, Depute Principal, Glenrothes College of F.E. Address: (b.) Angus College, Keptie Road, Arbroath, DD11 3EA; T.-01241 72056.

Ovens, Nancy L.G. Chairman, Scottish National Committee, English-Speaking Union in Scotland, since 1989; m., A. Allan Ovens; 2 d. Educ. Bo'ness Academy; Kirkcudbright Academy; Morrison's Academy; College of Domestic Science. Teacher of Home Economics; Training Adviser, Scottish Association of Youth Clubs; Lecturer, Moray House College of Education; Senior Lecturer and Co-ordinator, National Centre for Play at Moray House Institute of Education. Vice-Chairman, Lothian Association of Youth Clubs; Trustee, John Watson Trust, Lamp of Lothian; Assessor to BBC Children in Need Appeal, Scotland. Recreations: gardening; theatre; rugby; Scottish music; good food and wine. Address: (b.) 23 Atholl Crescent, Edinburgh, EH3 8HQ; T.-0131-229 1528.

Owen, Professor David Gareth, MA, BD (Hons), PhD, FICE, CEng. Professor of Offshore Engineering, Heriot-Watt University, since 1986; b. 6.11.40, Brecon, Wales; m., Ann Valerie Wright; 2 d. Educ. Christ College, Brecon; Downing College, Cambridge. Graduate Engineer, John Laing & Son, London; Aerospace Engineer, Marconi Space and Defence Systems, Portsmouth; Lecturer in Civil Engineering, Heriot-Watt University; Visiting Professor, University of New Hampshire; Senior Lecturer, Department of Offshore Engineering, Heriot-Watt University. Recreations: music; travelling; skiing. Address: (h.) 7 Oak Lane, Edinburgh, EH12 6XH; T.-0131-339 1740.

Owen, Professor Douglas David Roy, MA, PhD. Professor of French, St. Andrews, 1972-88; b. 17.11.22, Norton, Suffolk; m., Berit Mariann; 2 s. Educ. Cambridge and County High School; Nottingham High Pavement School; Nottingham University; St. Catharine's College, Cambridge. St. Andrews University: Lecturer, 1951-64; Senior Lecturer, 1964-71; Reader, 1971-72; General Editor, Forum for Modern Language Studies. Publications: Fabliaux (Joint Editor), 1957; The Evolution of the Grail Legend, 1968; The Vision of Hell, 1970; Arthurian Romance: Seven Essays (Editor), 1970; Two Old French Gauvain Romances (Joint Editor), 1972; The Song of Roland (Translator), 1972 (new edition, 1990); The Legend of Roland, 1973; Noble Lovers, 1975; Chrétien de Troyes, Arthurian Romances (Translator), 1987; A Chat Round the Old Course, 1990; Guillaume le Clerc, Fergus of Galloway (Translator), 1991; Eleanor of Aquitaine: Queen and Legend, 1993; The Romance of Reynard the Fox (Translator), 1994. Recreation: golf. Address: (h.) 7 West Acres, St. Andrews, KY16 9UD; T.-01334 473329.

Owens, Agnes. Author; b. 24.5.26, Milngavie; m., Patrick Owens; 2 s.; 4 d. Educ. Bearsden Academy. Worked in shops, factories and offices; came to writing by accident; author of Gentlemen of the West (Autumn Book Award, 1984), Like Birds in the Wilderness, A Working Mother; short stories in Lean Tales, The Seven Deadly Sins and The Seven Cardinal Virtues; wrote a play with Liz Lochhead which toured Scotland for three months. Recreations: walking; reading. Address: (h.) 21 Roy Young Avenue, Balloch, Dunbartonshire; T.-Alexandria 50921.

Oxby, Dennis, BA, CA. Management Consultant; b. 18.8.55, Helensburgh. Educ. Dumbarton Academy; Strathclyde University. Director: SSA Investment Co. Ltd., Glasgow Arena Ltd., Dow Consolidated Holdings Ltd., Joles Systems Ltd., Mortiere Property and Investment Co. Ltd., The Dow Engineering Co. Ltd., Willflo Investments Ltd., Quinquennium Properties Ltd., Second City Associates Ltd; Principal Consultant, Zaraband Ltd; formerly Director: Scottish Exhibition Centre Ltd., Greater Glasgow Tourist Board and Convention Bureau Ltd., Associated Events and Exhibitions Ltd (Eventex). Recreation: reading Tom Shields' Diary. Address: (h.) 15 Riverview Drive, The Waterfront, Glasgow; T.-01836 737754.

P

Pacione, Professor Michael, MA, PhD. Professor of Geography, Strathclyde University, since 1990; b. 14.10.47, Dundee; m., Christine Hopper; 1 s.; 1 d. Educ. Lawside Academy, Dundee; Dundee University. Lecturer in Geography, Queens University, Belfast, 1973-75; Lecturer, Senior Lecturer, Reader, Strathclyde University, Glasgow, 1975-89. Publications: three books; editor of 13 books; 80 research papers. Recreations: sport; travel; photography. Address: (b.) Department of Geography, Strathclyde University, 50 Richmond Street, Glasgow, G1 1XH; T.-0141-552 4400.

Pack, Professor Donald Cecil, CBE, MA, DSc, FIMA, FEIS, FRSE. Emeritus Professor, Strathclyde University, since 1986; b. 14.4.20, Higham Ferrers; m., Constance Mary Gillam; 2 s.; 1 d. Educ. Wellingborough School; New College, Oxford. Ordnance Board, Cambridge, 1941-43; Armament Research Department, Ministry of Supply, Fort Halstead, 1943-46; Lecturer in Mathematics, St. Andrews University, 1947-52; Visiting Research Associate, Maryland University, 1951-52; Lecturer in Mathematics, Manchester University, 1952-53; Professor of Mathematics, Strathclyde University, 1953-82 (Vice-Principal, 1968-72); Honorary Professor, 1982-86; Member, various Government scientific boards and committees, 1952-84; First Hon. Member, European Consortium for Mathematics in Industry, 1988; Chairman, Scottish Certificate of Education Examination Board, 1969-77; Chairman, Committee of Inquiry into Truancy and Indiscipline in Scottish Schools, 1974-77 ("Pack Report" published by HMSO, 1977); Hon. President, National Youth Orchestra of Scotland (Chairman from foundation, 1978-88); Member, Scottish Arts Council, 1980-85; Member, UK Committee for European Music Year 1985 and Chairman, Scotland Advisory Committee, 1983-86; Member: General Teaching Council for Scotland, 1966-73, Dunbartonshire Education Committee, 1960-66; Governor, Hamilton College of Education, 1976-81; Council Member, Royal Society of Edinburgh, 1960-63; Honorary Treasurer and Council Member, Institute of Mathematics and its Applications, 1964-72; Member, International Advisory Committee on Rarefied Gas Dynamics Symposia, 1976-88; Member, British National Committee for Theoretical Mechanics, 1973-78; Council Member, Gesellschaft fuer angewandte Mathematik und Mechanik, 1977-83; Guest Professor: Technische Universitaet, Berlin, 1967, Bologna University and Politechnico Milan, 1980, Technische Hochschule, Darmstadt, 1981; other visiting appointments, Warsaw University, 1977, Kaiserslautern University, 1980-84. Past President: Edinburgh Mathematical Society, Glasgow Mathematical Association; Honorary President, Milngavie Music Club (President, 1983-93). Recreations: music; gardening; golf. Address: (h.) 18 Buchanan Drive, Bearsden, Glasgow, G61 2EW; T.-0141-942 5764.

Pagan, Graeme Henry, BL, WS. Solicitor, Hosack & Sutherland, Oban, since 1960; Chairman, Oban Housing Association, since 1971; Honorary Sheriff of North Strathclyde at Oban, since 1988; b. 20.3.36, Cupar; m., Heather; 1 s.; 2 d. Educ. New Park, St. Andrews; Bedford School; Edinburgh University. Part-time Procurator Fiscal, Oban, 1970-79; Regional Organiser, Shelter Campaign for the Homeless, 1968-75; Founder Member, Oban Abbeyfield Society; Organiser, Scottish Solicitors Will Aid; Chairman, Argyll and Bute Liberal Democrats. Recreations: family; jazz; sport; malt whisky; politics; wandering in the Highlands on foot and bike. Address: (h.) Neaveton, Oban, Argyll; T.-01631 63737.

Page, Professor Alan Chisholm, LLB, PhD. Professor of Public Law, Dundee University, since 1985 (Head, Department of Law, since 1986); b. 7.4.52, Broughty Ferry; m., Sheila Duffus; 1 s.; 1 d. Educ. Grove Academy; Edinburgh University. Lecturer in Law, University College, Cardiff, 1975-80; Senior Lecturer in Law, Dundee University, 1980-85. Publications: Legislation; Investor Protection. Recreation: mountaineering. Address: (h.) Westlands, Westfield Road, Cupar, Fife, KY15 5DR.

Page, Christopher Nigel, BSc, PhD, FLS. Principal Scientific Officer, Royal Botanic Garden, Edinburgh, since 1971; Honorary Lecturer, Department of Botany, Edinburgh University, since 1983; b. 11.11.42, Gloucester; m., 1, Pauline Ann (m. diss.); 1 s.; 2 d.; 2, Jane Clare; 1 d. Educ. Cheltenham Grammar School; Kings College, Durham; Newcastle-upon-Tyne University. NATO Overseas Research Fellow, Queensland University, 1968-70; Department of Rural Economy, Oxford University, 1970-71. Nuffield/Leverhulme Overseas Travel Fellow, 1976-77; Tutor, Scottish Field Studies Council, since 1973; Editor, British Fern Gazette, 1974-84; Specialist Adviser and Chairman, Conifer Conservation Committee, International Union for the Conservation of Nature, since 1986; Honorary Life Vice President, British Pteridological Society, since 1991. Publications: The Ferns of Britain and Ireland, 1982; Biology of Pteridophytes, 1984; Ferns (New Naturalist), 1988. Recreations: photography; walking; writing. Address: (h.) 17 Silverknowes Crescent, Edinburgh, EH4 5JE; T.-0131-336 1142.

Pain, Gillian (Jill) Margaret, MA, DipTP, MRTPI. Chief Inquiry Reporter, Scottish Office, since 1993; b. 29.5.36, Southborough. Educ. Felixstowe College; St. Andrews University; University College, London. Teacher, 1957-58; Hunting Aerosurveys, 1958-60; Assistant Map Research Officer, War Office, 1960-62; Planning Assistant — Chief Assistant Planning Adviser, Essex County Council, 1962-73; Senior Inspector — Assistant Chief Planning Inspector, The Planning Inspectorate, DOE, 1973-93. President, Town & Country Planning Summer School, 1992-94. Recreation: sailing; skiing; hill-walking; ice dance; classical music. Address: (b.) 2 Greenside Lane, Edinburgh, EH1 3AG; T.-0131-244 5643.

Paine, Nigel, Chief Executive, Scottish Council for Educational Technology, since 1990; b. 25.4.52. Educ. Haberdasher's Aske's Hatcham Boys' School; Reading University; East Anglia University. English Speaking Union Thyne Scholar, 1984; Trustee, National Extension College, since 1987; Vice-Chair, Anniesland College, since 1993. Board Member: Network Scotland, LEAD, LEAD Telematics; Fellow, Institute of Training and Development. Recreations: running; reading. Address: 74 Victoria Crescent Road, Glasgow G12 9JN; T.-0141-337 5000.

Palmer, Sheriff Charles William, LLB. Sheriff of Tayside, Central and Fife at Dunfermline, since 1992; b. 17.12.45. Sheriff of North Strathclyde at Dunoon and Dumbarton, 1986-92. Address: (b.) Dunfermline Sheriff Court, 1/6 Carnegie Drive, Dunfermline, KY12 7HJ.

Palmer, Professor Godfrey Henry Oliver, MIBiol, BSc, PhD, DSc, FIBrew. Professor, International Centre for Brewing and Distilling, Heriot-Watt University (previously Reader); Research Consultant; Visiting Professor and Research Scholar, University of Kyoto, Japan, 1991; b. 9.4.40, Elizabeth, Jamaica; m., Margaret Ann Wood. Educ. Shelbourne Secondary Modern School; Highbury County School; Leicester University; Edinburgh University; Heriot-Watt University. Technician, 1958-61; Brewing Research Foundation, 1968-77. Chairman, Scottish Section, Institute of Brewing, 1991-93; Chairman, Racial Incident Committee, East and Mid-Lothian, since 1993. Publication: Cereal Science and Technology, 1989. Recreations: reading; watching cereal fields; education of deprived children; friends; ball games; music. Address: (b.) Heriot-Watt University, Department of Biological Sciences,

International Centre for Brewing and Distilling, Edinburgh; T.-0131-449 5111.

Palmer, Robert Allen, BA (Hons). Director of Performing Arts, Glasgow City Council, since 1991; Director, Glasgow Cultural Capital of Europe 1990 and Festivals Director, Glasgow City Council, 1987-91; Theatre Director, since 1971; b. 3.6.47, Toronto; 1 s.; 1 d. Educ. Forrest Hill Collegiate; York University; Central London Polytechnic. Teacher of English and Drama, Inner London Education Authority and Surrey County Council, 1970-72; Director, Theatre Centre for Young People, 1971-73; Director, Theatremakers, MacRobert Arts Centre, Stirling, 1973-75; Director, Theatre Workshop, Edinburgh, 1975-80; Drama and Dance Director, Scottish Arts Council, 1980-87. Member, Advisory Panel for Drama and Dance, British Council, 1980-87; Board Member, London International Festival of Theatre, since 1992; Vice-Chairman, Arts Executive Committee, Institute of Leisure and Amenity Management, since 1992; Chairman, Network of Cultural Cities of Europe, since 1990; FRSA. Recreations: cooking; walking; music. Address: (h.) 28 Cathkin Road, Glasgow, G42.

Panton, John, MBE. Professional Golfer; b. 9.10.16, Pitlochry. Won PGA Match-Play Championship, 1956 (Runner-up, 1968); PGA British Seniors', 1967-69; World Seniors', 1967 (defeated Sam Snead for title); Silver King, 1950; Daks, 1951; North British-Harrogate, 1952; Goodwin Foursomes, 1952; Yorkshire Evening News, 1954; Gleneagles-Saxone Am.-Pro. Foursomes, 1956; Woodlawn Invitation Open (West Germany), 1958-59-60; leading British player, Open Championship, 1956; Leader, PGA Order of Merit (Vardon Trophy), 1951; won Scottish Professional Championship, seven times (and joint Champion, once); Ryder Cup player, 1951-53-61; awarded Golf Writers' Trophy, 1967; Hon. Professional, Royal and Ancient Golf Club, St. Andrews.

Paolozzi, Professor Sir Eduardo Luigi. Her Majesty's Sculptor in Ordinary for Scotland, since 1986; b. Leith, 7.3.24; 3 d. Full-time study, Edinburgh College of Art, Slade School of Fine Art, 1943-47; first exhibition, 1947; Instructor, Central School of Art and Design, 1949-55; Lecturer, St. Martin's School of Art, 1955-58; Tutor in Ceramics, Royal College of Art, London, 1968-89; Professor of Ceramics, Cologne, 1977-81; Professor of Sculpture, Munich, 1981-91; numerous awards, commissions, one-man and group exhibitions. Lives in London.

Park, Ian Michael Scott, CBE, MA, LLB. Partner, Paull & Williamsons, Advocates, Aberdeen, 1961-91, Consultant, since 1991; Member, Criminal Injuries Compensation Board, since 1983; Council Member, Law Society of Scotland, 1974-85; b. 7.4.38, Aberdeen; m., Elizabeth M.L. Struthers; 2 s. Educ. Aberdeen Grammar School; Aberdeen University. Assistant to, subsequently Partner, in, Paull & Williamsons; Member, Society of Advocates in Aberdeen, since 1962, Treasurer, 1991-92, President, 1992-93; sometime part-time Assistant, Department of Public Law, Aberdeen University; President, Law Society of Scotland, 1980-81; Chairman, Aberdeen Citizens Advice Bureau, until 1988; Secretary, Aberdeen Granite Association, 1962-84; Temporary Sheriff, 1976-84; part-time Chairman, Medical Appeals Tribunals; frequent broadcaster on legal topics. Recreations: golf; gardening. Address: (h.) 46 Rubislaw Den South, Aberdeen.

Park, Neil Ferguson, BSc. Administrator, Scottish Athletics Federation, since 1993; b. 26.9.62, Gosport; m., Judith Frances; 1 s. Educ. Daniel Stewart's and Melville College, Edinburgh; Aberdeen University. Former Assistant Secretary, Royal Highland and Agricultural Society. Recreations: rugby; golf; road-running. Address: (b.) Caledonia House, South Gyle, Edinburgh, EH12 9DQ.

Parker, Cameron Holdsworth, OBE, DL, BSc. Managing Director, Lithgows Limited, 1984-92, Vice-Chairman, since 1992; b. 14.4.32, Dundee; m., Marlyne Honeyman; 3 s. Educ. Morrison's Academy, Crieff; Glasgow University. Managing Director, latterly also Chairman, John G. Kincaid & Co. Ltd., Greenock, 1967-80; Chairman and Chief Executive, Scott Lithgow Ltd., Port Glasgow, 1980-83; Board Member, British Shipbuilders, 1977-80, 1981-83; Chief Executive, Prosper Enginering Ltd., Irvine, 1983-84. Liveryman, Worshipful Company of Shipwrights; Member, Council, CBI Scotland, 1986-92; Member, Argyll and Clyde Health Board, 1991-95; Board Member, Scottish Homes, since 1992; Director, Clyde Shaw Ltd., 1992-94. Recreation: golf. Address: (b.) Netherton, Langbank, Renfrewshire, PA14 6YG; T.-01475 540692.

Parker, Nicholas Sherren, MA (Cantab), FCA. Chartered Accountant; Partner, Coopers & Lybrand, since 1978 (Partner in charge, Corporate Finance Scotland); b. 11.6.46, Edinburgh; m., Julia Caroline Hamilton Dunlop; 1 s.; 2 d. Educ. Edinburgh Academy; St. Catharine's College, Cambridge. Recreations: shooting; golf; squash; fishing. Address: (b.) Erskine House, 68/73 Queen Street, Edinburgh, EH2 4NH; T.-0131-226 4488.

Parker, Richard Carmichael, Phd. Production Director, Shell UK Exploration and Production, since 1994; b. 18.12.39, Southampton; m. Irene Vehling; 2 s.; 1 d. Educ. Manchester University. Joined Shell as Petroleum Engineer, 1965; technical and managerial appointments, Europe, Middle East, Far East, South America,1965-94. Recreations: squash; rugby; golf. Address: (b.) 1 Altens Farm Road, Nigg, Aberdeen, AB9 2HY.

Parker, Timothy Robert Walter, LLB. Depute Secretary to Church of Scotland General Trustees, since 1982; b. 7.10.44, Aberdeen; m., Janet Helen Nicol; 3 d. Educ. Trinity College, Glenalmond; Aberdeen University. Private practice as Solicitor, 1969-82. Chairman, Lothian Primary Schools Chess League; Past Chairman, Trinity Academy P.T.A.; Secretary, Lothian Federation of P.T.A.s; Director, Parents Coalition; Committee Member, Viewpoint Housing Association. Recreations: bowling; walking; watching other sports; listening to music. Address: (h.) 35 Dudley Avenue, Edinburgh, EH6 4PL; T.-0131-554 2076.

Parkins, James J., BSc (Hons), PhD, CBiol, FIBiol. Head, Veterinary Animal Husbandry, Glasgow Veterinary School, since 1991; University Farm Director, since 1990; b. 27.7.45, Tynemouth; m., Elma; 1 s.; 1 d. Educ. Wolverhampton Grammar School; Glasgow University. Lecturer in Veterinary Animal Husbandry, 1970; Senior Lecturer, 1983, Reader, 1990, Glasgow University Veterinary School. Publications: over 100 papers. Recreations: the country; golf; music. Address: (b.) Glasgow University Veterinary School, Bearsden Road, Glasgow, G61 1QH; T.-0141-339 8855, Ext. 5720.

Parnell, Brian K., BSc, ACGI, DipTP, FRTPI. Planning Consultant; Vice-Chairman and Hon. Secretary, Scottish Council for National Parks, since 1991; Visiting Professor, Centre for Planning, Strathclyde University, since 1991; b. 18.12.22, Brighton; 2 s.; 1 d. Educ. Varndean School, Brighton; London University; Edinburgh College of Art. Captain, EME, 1943-47; Department of Planning, Midlothian County Council, 1949-57; Depute Planning Officer, Stirling County Council, 1957-64; joined Glasgow School of Art, 1964, Head, Department of Planning, 1976-87; Commissioner, Countryside Commission for Scotland, 1968-80; part-time Planning Inquiry Reporter, Scottish Office, 1982-93. Chairman, Association of Scientific Workers (Scottish Area), 1949-69; Member, Board of Governors, Heriot-Watt College, 1954-56; Chairman, Scottish Branch, Royal Town Planning Institute, 1972-73; Executive Committee Member, National Trust for Scotland, 1973-83; Trustee, Scottish Civic Trust, since 1985.

Recreations: sailing; swimming; hill-walking; travel. Address: (h.) 15 Park Terrace, Stirling, FK8 2JT; T.-01786 465714.

Parr, Professor John Brian, BSc (Econ), MA, PhD. Titular Professor in Applied Economics, Glasgow University, since 1989; Chairman, British Section, Regional Science Association, 1981-85; b. 18.3.41, Epsom; m., Pamela Jean Harkins; 2 d. Educ. Henry Thornton School; London University; University of Washington. Instructor, University of Washington, 1966; Assistant Professor/Associate Professor, University of Pennsylvania, 1967-75; joined Glasgow University as Lecturer, 1975. Editor, Papers of the Regional Science Association, 1968-75; Associate Editor, Journal of Regional Science, since 1979; Co-Editor, European Research in Regional Science, since 1990; Member, Board of Management, Urban Studies, since 1981; Associate Editor, Annals of Regional Science, since 1993. Publications: Christaller Central Place Structures (Co-author); Regional Policy: Past Experience and New Directions (Co-Editor); Analysis of Regional Structure: Essays in Honour of August Lösch (Co-Editor); Market Centers and Retail Location (Co-author). Address: (b.) Department of Social and Economic Research, Glasgow University, Glasgow, G12 8RT; T.-0141-339 8855, Ext. 4724.

Parratt, Professor James Roy, BPharm, MSc, PhD, DSc, MD (h.c.), FRCPath, DipRelStudies (Cantab), FRPharmS, FESC, FIBiol, FRSE. Professor of Cardiovascular Pharmacology, Strathclyde University, since 1983 (Head, Department of Physiology and Pharmacology, 1986-90); b. 19.8.33, London; m., Pamela Joan Lyndon Marels; 2 s.; 1 d. Educ. St. Clement Danes Holborn Estate Grammar School; London University. Spent nine years in Nigeria as Head of Pharmacology, Nigerian School of Pharmacy, then in Physiology, University Medical School, Ibadan; joined Strathclyde University, 1967; appointed Reader, 1970; Personal Professor, Department of Physiology and Pharmacology, 1975-83. Chairman, Cardiac Muscle Research Group, 1980-83; Gold Medal, Szeged University, 1975; Honorary Member, Hungarian Pharmacological Society, 1983; Honorary Doctorate, Albert Szent-Gyorgi Medical University, Hungary, 1989; Chairman, Universities and Colleges Christian Fellowship, 1984-90; former Vice-Chairman, Scripture Union; Past Chairman, SUM Fellowship; Lay Preacher, Baptist Unions of Scotland and Great Britain; Honorary President, Baptist Lay Preachers Association of Scotland, 1985-90. Recreation: music. Address: (h.) 16 Russell Drive, Bearsden, Glasgow, G61 3BD; T.-0141-942 7164.

Parry, David, BSc, MSc. Managing Director, AIAI (Artificial Intelligence Applications Institute), since 1992; b. 6.2.52, Oswestry; m., Joyce; 1 s.; 1 d. Educ. Oswestry High School for Boys; Queens University of Belfast. SDRC, Hitchin, Herts, 1979-88; Managing Director, Ferranti Infographics Ltd., Livingston, 1988-92. Recreations: golf; travel. Address: (b.) 80 South Bridge, Edinburgh, EH1 1HN; T.-0131-650 2732.

Parry-Jones, Professor William Llywelyn, MA, MD (Camb), BChir, FRCPsych, FRCP Glas, DPM Eng. Professor of Child and Adolescent Psychiatry, Glasgow University, since 1987; Honorary Consultant Psychiatrist, Greater Glasgow Health Board, since 1987; Supernumerary Fellow, Linacre College, Oxford, since 1987; b. 22.6.35, Ilford; m., Brenda Griffiths; 1 s.; 2 d. Educ. Llangefni Grammar School; Gonville and Caius College, Cambridge; London Hospital Medical College, London University. Lecturer in Psychiatry, Oxford University, 1969; Fellow, Linacre College, Oxford, 1969; Consultant in Adolescent Psychiatry, Highfield Adolescent Unit, Warneford Hospital, Oxford, 1972; Visiting Fellow, Gonville and Caius College, 1991. Publications include: The Trade in Lunacy, 1972. Recreations: collecting antiquarian medical books; travel;

gardening. Address: (b.) Royal Hospital for Sick Children, Yorkhill, Glasgow, G3 8SJ; T.-0141-201 0223.

Parsons, Professor Ian, BSc, PhD, FRSE. Professor of Mineralogy, Edinburgh University, since 1988, Head, Department of Geology and Geophysics, since 1993; b. 5.9.39, Manchester; m., Brenda Mary Reah; 3 s. Educ. Beckenham and Penge Grammar School; Durham University. DSIR Research Fellow, Manchester University, 1963-64; Aberdeen University: Assistant Lecturer, 1964-65, Lecturer, 1965-77, Senior Lecturer, 1977-83, Professor, 1983-88. Member, NERC Earth Sciences Research Grants and Training Awards Committee; President, Mineralogical Society; Member, NCC Committee for Scotland, 1985-90. Recreations: skiing; hill-walking; music. Address: (b.) Department of Geology and Geophysics, Edinburgh University, West Mains Road, Edinburgh, EH9 3JW; T.-0131-650 4839.

Paternoster, Rev. Canon Michael Cosgrove, MA. Rector, St. James' Episcopal Church, Aberdeen, since 1990; Honorary Canon, St. Paul's Cathedral, Dundee, since 1981; b. 13.5.35, East Molesey, Surrey; m., Careth Osborne. Educ. Kingston Grammar School; Pembroke College, Cambridge; Cuddesdon Theological College. Deacon, 1961; Priest, 1962; Curate, St. Andrew's, Surbiton, 1961-63; Chaplain to Anglican students in Dundee, 1964-68; Secretary, Fellowship of St. Alban and St. Sergius, 1968-71; Rector, St. James', Dollar, 1971-75; Rector, St. James's, Stonehaven, 1975-90; Secretary, Inter-Church Relations Committee, Scottish Episcopal Church, 1975-82; Member, Doctrine Committee, Scottish Episcopal Church, 1980-91; Aberdeen and N.E. Wing Chaplain, Air Training Corps, 1985-92; Director of Ordinands, Diocese of Aberdeen and Orkney, since 1995. Publications: Thou art There Also, 1967; Stronger Than Death, 1972. Recreations: reading; sketching; bird-watching; listening to music. Address: 31 Gladstone Place, Aberdeen, AB1 6UX; T.-01224 322631.

Paterson, Professor Alan Alexander, LLB (Hons), DPhil (Oxon). Professor of Law, Strathclyde University, since 1984; b. 5.6.47, Edinburgh; m., Alison Jane Ross Lowdon; 2 s.; 1 d. Educ. Edinburgh Academy; Edinburgh University; Pembroke College, Oxford. Research Associate, Oxford Centre for Socio-Legal Studies, 1972-73; Lecturer, Law Faculty, Edinburgh University, 1973-84; Visiting Professor, University of New Mexico Law School, 1982, 1986. Former Chairman, Scottish Legal Action Group; Chairman, British and Irish Legal Education and Technology Association; Chairman, Legal Services Group, Citizens Advice Scotland. Publications: The Law Lords, 1982; The Legal System of Scotland (Co-author), 1993. Address: (b.) Strathclyde University Law School, 173 Cathedral Street, Glasgow, G4 ORQ; T.-0141-552 4400, Ext. 3341.

Paterson, Colin Stuart, CBE, FCIT, MICS. Managing Director, Caledonian MacBrayne Ltd., since 1983; b. 29.7.32, London; m., Marcella; 2 s.; 2 d. Educ. Haberdashers' Aske's. Assistant General Manager, North Sea Ferries Ltd., 1967-83. Chairman, Marine Shipping Mutual Insurance Ltd.; Chairman, North of England Protection and Indemnity Association Ltd. Recreations: golf; rugby; church. Address: (h.) 11 MacLeod Drive, Helensburgh, G84 9QS; T.-01436 676245.

Paterson, Douglas McCallum, MA, MEd, DMS, DipM, MIM. Chief Executive, Aberdeen City Council, since 1995; b. 20.11.49, Macduff; m., Isobel Beaton; 2 d. Educ. Banff Academy; Aberdeen University. John Wood Group, 1971-75; Grampian Regional Council: Teacher, 1976-81, Head Teacher, 1981-86, Advisor, 1986-90, Depute Director of Education, 1990-92, Senior Depute Director, 1992-94, Director of Education, 1994-95. Recreations: local history; fishing industry; music; walking; theatre. Address: (b.) Town House, Aberdeen; T.-01224 522502.

Paterson, Lt. Col. Howard Cecil, TD, FSA Scot, FRSA. International Tourism Consultant and Artist; b. 16.3.20, Edinburgh; m., Isabelle Mary; 1 s. Educ. Daniel Stewart's College, Edinburgh; Edinburgh College of Art. Army, 1939-49; combat duties during War; personnel selection afterwards; Territorial Army, 1949-70; serves on East Scotland TAVR Committee; Founder, Gunner Heritage Appeal; Member, City of Edinburgh Artillery Officers' Association; Member, 52nd Lowland Division Officers' Club; Assistant Personnel Manager, Jute Industries Ltd., Dundee, 1949-51; Organising Secretary, Scottish Country Industries Development Trust, 1951-66; Senior Director, Scottish Tourist Board, 1966-81. Chairman, Taste of Scotland Ltd., 1984-86; Vice-Chairman, John Buchan Society; Member, Scottish Committee, British Horse Society; Chairman, Trekking and Riding Society of Scotland. Publications: Tourism in Scotland; Flavour of Edinburgh (with Catherine Brown). Recreations: fishing; shooting; riding; writing; drawing and painting; natural history; history. Address: (h.) Dovewood, West Linton, Peeblesshire, EH46 7DS; T.-01968 60346.

Paterson, (James Edmund) Neil, MA. Author; b. 31.12.15, Greenock; m., Rosabelle MacKenzie; 2 s.; 1 d. Educ. Banff Academy; Edinburgh University. Lt., RNVR minesweepers, 1940-45; variously Member, Chairman of Production, Director, Consultant, Films of Scotland, 1954-79; Governor, British Film Institute, 1958-60; Chairman, Literature Committee, Scottish Arts Council, 1967-76; Member, Planning Committee, National Film School, 1969; Governor, Pitlochry Festival Theatre, 1966-76; Governor, National Film School, 1970-80; Member, Arts Council of GB, 1974-76; Director, Grampian Television, 1960-86; Atlantic Award in Literature, 1946; American Film Academy Award, 1959; author of: The China Run, Behold Thy Daughter, And Delilah, Man on the Tight-Rope, The Kidnappers; various stories and screenplays. Recreations: golf; fishing; bridge. Address: (h.) St. Ronans, Crieff, Perthshire; T.-01764 652615.

Paterson, Sheriff James Veitch, MA (Oxon), LLB (Edin). Sheriff of Lothian and Borders at Jedburgh, Selkirk and Duns, since 1963; b. 16.4.28; m., Ailie Campbell Clark Hutchison; 1 s.; 1 d. Educ. Edinburgh Academy; Lincoln College, Oxford; Edinburgh University. Admitted Faculty of Advocates, 1953.

Paterson, Rev. John Love, MA, BD, STM, FSA Scot. Minister, St. Michael's Parish Church, Linlithgow, since 1977; b. 6.5.38, Ayr; m., Lorna Begg (see Lorna Marion Paterson). Educ. Ayr Academy; Glasgow University; Edinburgh University; Union Theological Seminary, New York. Minister: Presbyterian Church of East Africa, 1964-72, St. Andrew's, Nairobi, 1968-72; Chaplain, Stirling University, 1973-77. Moderator, West Lothian Presbytery, 1985. Recreation: gardening. Address: St. Michael's Manse, Linlithgow, West Lothian; T.-01506 842195.

Paterson, Very Rev. John Munn Kirk, ACII, MA, BD, DD. Minister Emeritus, St. Paul's Church, Milngavie; b. 8.10.22, Leeds; m., Geraldine Lilian Parker; 2 s.; 1 d. Educ. Hillhead High School; Edinburgh University. Pilot, RAF, 1940-46; Insurance official, 1946-58; ordained Minister, Church of Scotland, 1964; Minister, St. John's Church, Bathgate, 1964-70; Minister, St. Paul's Church, Milngavie, 1970-87. Moderator, General Assembly, Church of Scotland, 1984-85; Life Member, Chartered Insurance Institute; Hon. Doctorate, Aberdeen University, 1986. Recreations: fishing; gardening. Address: (h.) 58 Orchard Drive, Edinburgh, EH4 2DZ; T.-0131-332 5876.

Paterson, Lorna Marion, MA. General Secretary, Church of Scotland Woman's Guild, since 1985; b. 26.1.38, Unst; m., Rev. John L. Paterson (qv). Educ. Inverurie Academy; Aberden University; Aberdeen College of Education. Teacher of English, History, Geography and Religious Education, 1960-62; Teacher of English, 1962-66; Administrative Assistant, Strathclyde University, 1966-68; Deputy Academic Registrar, then Education Administrator, Stirling University, 1968-79. Guider (Division Commissioner, West Lothian, 1982-85); Secretary, Linlithgow Arts Guild, 1979-84. Recreations: singing; homemaking; church activities; the arts; people. Address: (h.) St. Michael's Manse, Kirkgate, Linlithgow, EH49 7AL; T.-0131-225 5722.

Paterson, Robert Archibald, MA, LLB. Solicitor of the Church of Scotland, 1968-95; b. Tarbolton; m., Jean Marshall Stewart; 2 d. Educ. Ayr Academy; Edinburgh University. Qualified Assistant, then Partner, James M. & A. Inglis & Wilkie, Solicitors, Kilmarnock, 1956-64; Principal Assistant, Law Department, Church of Scotland, 1964-67; Contributor, Stair Memorial Encyclopaedia. Recreations: the Scottish scene; hill-walking; travel; music.

Paterson, (Thomas) Michael, DA. Artist; Educational Television Consultant; Chairman, The Educational Television Association; b. 14.4.38, Kirkcaldy; m., Joan; 1 s.; 2 d. Educ. George Watson's Boys' College; Edinburgh College of Art; Moray House College of Education. Teacher of Art, Waid Academy, Anstruther, 1960-64; Special Assistant, George Heriot's, Edinburgh, 1964-67; Head of Art, Marr College, Troon, 1967-69; Lecturer and Programme Director, College Television Service, Craigie College of Education, 1969-80, Governor, 1979-80; Assistant Head of Educational Programmes, Scottish Television, 1981-89, Head of Education, 1989-91. ETA: Chairman (Scotland), 1979-80 and since 1993, National Executive, since 1978, Deputy Chairman, 1993-94; RTS Awards Convener, 1981-86, Chairman, Scottish Centre, and Member of Council, 1986-88; Member, Publicity Committee, General Assembly, Church of Scotland, 1983-86; Member, Board of Communication, 1986-90, 1994-95, Convener, A/V Production Unit, Church of Scotland, 1986-88. Publication: A Primary Art Course (Co-author). Recreations: golf; travel; gardening; reading. Address: (h.) 1 Laurelbank Road, Maybole, KA19 8BE.

Paterson, William, BSc (Eng), CEng, FIEE, MRAeS. Engineer in Chief, Northern Lighthouse Board, since 1987; b. 24.7.40, Neilston; m., Margaret Quirie Forrest Gerrard; 2 s.; 2 d. Educ. Paisley Grammar School; Strathclyde University. Radio Officer, Merchant Navy; Technician, then Engineer, Civil Aviation Authority; Head, Radio Department, Northern Lighthouse Board. Recreation: gardening; golf. Address: (b.) 84 George Street, Edinburgh, EH2 3DA; T.-0131-226 7051.

Paterson, (William) Guthrie (Wilson), BSc, MSc, CertEd. Deputy Principal and Dean of Centre, Scottish Agricultural College, since 1989; b. 5.6.40, Blantyre; m., Mary Isobel; 1 s.; 1 d. Educ. Hamilton Academy; Glasgow University; Jordanhill College of Education; Aberdeen University. Lecturer in Crop Husbandry, North of Scotland College of Agriculture, 1965-73; Senior Agronomy Specialist, West of Scotland Agricultural College, 1973-83; Head, Crop Production Department, North of Scotland College of Agriculture, 1983-93. Recreations: golf; gardening; music; reading. Address: (b.) Scottish Agricultural College, 581 King Street, Aberdeen, AB9 1UD; T.-01224 480291.

Paterson, Wilma, DRSAM. Freelance Composer/ Writer/Journalist; b. 23.4.44, Dundee; 1 s.; 1 d. Educ. Harris Academy; Royal Scottish Academy of Music. Composition study with Luigi Dallapiccola in Florence; writes all types of music (chamber, orchestral, incidental); music reviews for Glasgow Herald and The Independent; broadcasts and writes on food, plants, travel. Publications: A Country Cup; Was Byron Anorexic?; Shoestring Gourmet; Flowers and Herbs of the Bible; Lord Byron's Relish; Salmon & Women, The Feminine Angle. Address: 27 Hamilton Drive, Glasgow, G12 8DN; T.-0141-339 2711.

Paterson-Brown, June, CBE, MBChB. Commonwealth Chief Commissioner, Girl Guides Association, 1985-90; Vice-Chairman, Princes Trust, 1982-92; Non-Executive Director, Border Television plc, since 1980; b. 8.2.32, Edinburgh; m., Peter Neville Paterson-Brown (qv); 3 s.; 1 d. Educ. Esdaile School; Edinburgh University. Medical Officer, Family Planning and Well Woman's Clinics, 1959-85; Past Chairman: County of Roxburghshire Youth Committee, Roxburgh Duke of Edinburgh Award Committee; Scottish Chief Commissioner, Girl Guides Association, 1977-82; Chairman, Borders Region Children's Panel Advisory Committee, 1982-85; Chairman, Scottish Standing Conference of Voluntary Youth Organisations, 1983-85; Trustee, MacRobert Trusts, since 1987; Trustee, Prince's Trust, 1982-94; Paul Harris Fellow, 1990; Deputy Lieutenant, Roxburgh, Ettrick and Lauderdale, since 1990. Address: (h.) Norwood, Hawick, Roxburghshire TD9 7HP; T.-01450 372352.

Paterson-Brown, Peter Neville, MBChB, DObst RCOG. Medical Practitioner, since 1957; b. 23.3.51, Hawick; m., June Garden (see June Paterson-Brown); 3 s.; 1 d. Educ. Merchiston Castle School; Edinburgh University. Medical Adviser, Red Cross Scotland, 1981-94; Member, Scottish Committee, Medical Commission on Accident Prevention, since 1978; Director, Children's Hospice Association Scotland, since 1993; Vice President, React, since 1991. Red Cross Badge of Honour, 1995. Publication: A Matter of Life or Death. Recreations: skiing; shooting; golf; fishing. Address: (h.) Norwood, Hawick, Roxburghshire; T.-01450 72352.

Paton, Alasdair Chalmers, BSc, CEng, FICE, FIWEM. Chief Executive, Scottish Environment Protection Agency, from 1996; Director and Chief Engineer, Engineering, Water and Waste Directorate, Scottish Office Environment Department, since 1991; b. 28.11.44, Paisley; m., Zona G. Gill; 1 s.; 1 d. Educ. John Neilson Institution, Paisley; Glasgow University. Assistant Engineer, Clyde Port Authority, 1967-71; Assistant Engineer, DAFS, 1971-72; Senior Engineer, SDD, 1972-77; Engineer, Public Works Department, Hong Kong Government, 1977-80; Senior Engineer, then Principal Engineer, SDD, 1980-87; Deputy Chief Engineer, 1987-91. Recreations: Rotary; sailing; golf. Address: (b.) 27 Perth Street, Edinburgh; T.-0131-244 3035.

Paton, Ann, QC, MA, LLB. Admitted to Scottish Bar, 1977. Address: (b.) Advocates' Library, Parliament House, Edinburgh.

Paton, David Romer, FRICS, IRRV, FSA (Scot). Chartered Surveyor; b. 5.3.35, Aberdeen; m., Juliette Burney; 2 s. Educ. Gordonstoun School; Keble College, Oxford. Scottish Director, Leslie Lintott & Associates, 1979-86, Consultant, 1986-89; Past President, Aberdeen Chamber of Commerce; Past Chairman: Gordon Conservative and Unionist Association, Royal Northern & University Club, Association of Scottish Chambers of Commerce, Aberdeen Beyond 2000, Grampian-Houston Association; Chairman: North East Scotland Preservation Trust, Don District Salmon Fishery Board, Aberdeen Harbour Board; President, Friends of Grampian Stones, Aberdeen Civic Society; Chairman, NE Committee and Vice President, Scottish Council (Development and Industry); Secretary of State Appointee, North East River Purification Board; Minister of State Appointee, HMG Salmon Advisory Committee; Member, Grampian Initiative; Member, Committee, Architectural Heritage Society of Scotland; Member of Council, Association of Scottish District Salmon Fishery Boards; Member, St. John's Hospital Committee; Director, Aberdeen Maritime Museum Appeal Co. Ltd.; Director, Aberdeen Chamber of Commerce, Aberdeen Salmon Company Ltd. Recreations: fishing; conservation; music; bridge. Address: Grandhome, Aberdeen, AB22 8AR; T.-01224 722202.

Paton, George, MA, MEd, FEIS, FITD. Director, Scottish Council for Educational Technology, 1986-90; b. 5.12.31, Rutherglen; m., 1, Barbara Thomson (deceased); 2 s.; 2, J. Honor Smith. Educ. Rutherglen Academy; Glasgow University. National Service, RAEC, 1953-55; Schoolteacher, 1955-61; Lecturer in English, Jordanhill College of Education, 1961-63; Principal Lecturer in English, then Assistant Principal, Dundee College of Education, 1963-69; Principal, Hamilton College of Education, 1970-81; Assistant Principal, Jordanhill College of Education, 1981-82; Depute Director, Scottish Council for Educational Technology, 1982-86. President, International Council for Educational Media, 1989-91; Member, Library Information Service Committee (Scotland), 1984-91; Executive Committee Member, Commonwealth Institute in Scotland, since 1985; Governor, David Livingstone Memorial Trust, since 1971 (Chairman, since 1994); former Convener, Education Committee, General Teaching Council for Scotland; Member, Consultative Committee on the Curriculum, 1980-83; Member, SCE Examination Board, 1977-81; Past President, Association of Higher Academic Staff in Colleges of Education in Scotland; Chairman, Strathclyde Committee, Tenovus–Scotland (for medical research in Scotland), since 1991; Elder, Church of Scotland. Recreations: singing; drama; gardening. Address: (h.) 16 Old Bothwell Road, Bothwell, Glasgow, G71 8AW.

Paton, Rev. Iain Ferguson, BD, FCIS. Minister, Newlands South, Glasgow, since 1985; Convener, Church of Scotland Board of Stewardship and Finance, since 1984; b. 28.1.41, Edinburgh; m., Marjorie Vickers Macdonald; 1 s.; 1 d. Educ. George Watson's College, Edinburgh; Edinburgh University. Royal Bank of Scotland Ltd., 1957-66; Assistant Secretary, John Menzies (Holdings) Ltd., 1966-68; Senior Registrar, Charlotte Registrars Ltd., 1968-70; Secretary, Scottish Sports Council, 1970-75; Faculty of Divinity, Edinburgh University, 1975-79; Assistant Minister, St. Ninians Church, Corstorphine, 1979-80; Minister, Banchory-Ternan West Parish Church, 1980-85. Address: Newlands South Manse, 24 Monreith Road, Glasgow, G43 2NY; T.-0141-632 2588.

Paton, William, BSc (Hons). Director of Operations, National Engineering Laboratory; b. 29.11.41, Kilwinning; m., Elizabeth Anne; 2 s. Educ. Douglas Ewart School, Newton Stewart; Glasgow University. Consulting Geophysicist, Seismograph Services Ltd., 1963; Management Trainee, Colvilles Ltd., Ravenscraig, 1964; Research Scientist in Materials, NEL, 1965-76; Offshore Supplies Office, 1976-77; Divisional Manager, Materials Engineering Division, then Controller, Design, Materials and Systems Department, NEL, 1977-87. Recreation: golf. Address: (b.) National Engineering Laboratory, East Kilbride, Glasgow; T.-East Kilbride 20222.

Patrick, James McIntosh, RSA, LLD, ROI, ARE. Artist and Landscape Painter; b. 4.2.07, Dundee; m., Janet Watterston (deceased); 1 s.; 1 d. Educ. Morgan Academy, Dundee; Glasgow School of Art. Guthrie Award, RSA, 1935; paintings in numerous national and municipal collections; Hon. LLD, Dundee, 1973; Fellowship: Duncan of Jordanstone College of Art, Glasgow School of Art. Address: (h.) The Shrubbery, Magdalen Yard Road, Dundee.

Patrick, Sheriff (Lilian) Gail, MA, LLB. Sheriff of Tayside, Central and Fife at Kirkcaldy, since 1991; b. 24.12.41. Enrolled as Solicitor, 1966; former Lecturer and Tutor, Glasgow University and Edinburgh University; admitted to Faculty of Advocates, 1981; called to the Bar, Lincoln's Inn, 1990.

Patterson, Lindy Ann, LLB (Hons), ACIArb. Lawyer; Partner, Bird Semple, since 1988; b. 12.9.58, Berwick-upon-Tweed. Educ. Eyemouth High School; Edinburgh

University. UK National Vice-President, Association Internationale de Jeunes Avocats, since 1991; Member, Commercial Law Working Party; Scotland's first female Solicitor Advocate (May, 1993); Member, Judicial Procedure Committee and Rights of Audience Working Party, Law Society of Scotland. Recreations: skiing; hill-walking. Address: (b.) Napier House, 27 Thistle Street, Edinburgh; T.-0131-459 2345.

Patterson, Walter Moffat, MSc, BSc. HM Staff Inspector (Computing Studies); b. 14.6.45, Airdrie; m., Colleen McCrone (Toronto); 1 s.; 1 d. Educ. Coatbridge High School; Strathclyde University. Lecturer in Statistics, Paisley College; Development Officer, Glacier Metal Co., Kilmarnock, 1973-74; Lecturer in Statistics, Paisley College, 1974-83; Senior Lecturer in Information Technology, MEDC, Paisley College, 1983-86. Recreations: gardening; computing; golf. Address: (b.) Room 3/27, New St. Andrews House, Edinburgh, EH1 3SY; T.-0131-244 4528.

Pattison, David Arnold, BSc, PhD. Director of Leisure and Tourism Consulting, Cobham Resource Consultants; Hon. Vice-President, Scottish Youth Hostels Association; Hon. Professor, Queen Margaret College, Edinburgh; b. 9.2.41, Kilmarnock; m., Anne Ross Wilson; 2 s.; 1 d. Educ. Kilmarnock Academy; Glasgow University. Planning Assistant, Ayr County Council, 1963-64; PhD studies, Glasgow University, 1964-66; Planning Assistant, Dunbarton County Council, 1966-67; Lecturer, Strathclyde University, 1967-70; Head of Tourism, Highlands and Islands Development Board, 1970-81; Chief Executive, Scottish Tourist Board, 1981-85; Director Leisure & Tourism Consulting, Ernst & Young, 1985-89. External Examiner for postgraduate tourism courses, Strathclyde University, 1981-84. Recreations: reading; watching soccer and rugby; golf; gardening. Address: (h.) 7 Cramond Glebe Gardens, Cramond, Edinburgh, EH4 6NZ.

Pattison, Rev. Kenneth John, MA, BD, STM. Associate Minister, St. Andrew's and St. George's, Edinburgh, since 1990; Convener, Chaplaincies Committee, Church of Scotland, since 1993; b. 22.4.41, Glasgow; m., Susan Jennifer Brierley Jenkins; 1 s.; 2 d. Educ. Lenzie Academy; Glasgow University; Union Theological Seminary, New York. Minister, Church of Central Africa Presbyterian, Malawi, 1967-77; Minister, Park Parish Church, Ardrossan, 1977-84; Chaplain, Glasgow Royal Infirmary, 1984-90. Recreations: hill-walking; swimming; gardening; family history. Address: (h.) 11 Westhall Gardens, Edinburgh, EH10 4JJ; T.-0131-229 0008.

Pattullo, Sir (David) Bruce, Kt, CBE, BA, FRSE, FCIB (Scot). Governor and Group Chief Executive, Bank of Scotland, since 1991; Director (Non-Executive): British Linen Bank, since 1977, Standard Life, since 1985, Bank of Wales PLC, since 1986, NWS Bank, since 1986; Group Chief Executive and a Deputy Governor, Bank of Scotland, 1988-91; b. 2.1.38, Edinburgh; m., Fiona Jane Nicholson; 3 s.; 1 d. Educ. Belhaven Hill School; Rugby; Hertford College, Oxford. National Service commission, Royal Scots (seconded to West Africa); joined Bank of Scotland, 1961; winner, first prize, Institute of Bankers in Scotland, 1964; Manager, Investment Services Department, 1967-71; Deputy Manager, Bank of Scotland Finance Co. Ltd., 1971-73; Chief Executive, Group Merchant Banking Activities, 1973-78; Deputy Treasurer, 1978; Treasurer and General Manager, 1979-88; Group Chief Executive and a Deputy Governor, 1988-91. Chairman, Committee of Scottish Clearing Bankers, 1987-89. Recreations: tennis; hill-walking. Address: (b.) Bank of Scotland, Head Office, The Mound, Edinburgh, EH1 1YZ; T.-0131-243 5555.

Paul, Eur Ing Professor John P., BSc, PhD, ARCST, FEng, FIMechE, FISPO, cFBOA, FRSA, FRSE, FBES. Professor, Bioengineering Unit, Strathclyde University,

since 1972; Visiting Professor, Queen Margaret College, Edinburgh, since 1992; Chairman, British Standard, European Standard and International Standard Committees on Joint Replacements, 1992; b. 26.6.27, Sunderland; m., Elizabeth R. Graham; 1 s.; 2 d. Educ. Aberdeen Grammar School; Allan Glen's School, Glasgow; Royal College of Science and Technology, Glasgow; Glasgow University. Successively Research Assistant, Lecturer and Senior Lecturer in Mechanics of Materials, Royal College of Science and Technology, subsequently Strathclyde University, 1949-69; Visiting Professor, West Virginia University, 1969-70; Reader, then Professor, Bioengineering Unit, Strathclyde University, since 1970. President, International Society of Biomechanics, 1987-89. Publications: Computing in Medicine (Senior Editor), 1981; Biomaterials in Artificial Organs (Senior Editor), 1984; Disability (Co-Editor), 1979; Total Knee Joint Replacement (Co-Editor), 1988. Recreations: formerly rugby; gardening; home maintenance; light reading. Address: (h.) 25 James Watt Road, Milngavie, Glasgow, G62 7JX; T.-0141-956 3221.

Pawley, Professor G. Stuart, MA, PhD, FRSE, FRS. Professor of Computational Physics, Edinburgh University, since 1985; b. 22.6.37, Ilford; m., Anthea Jean Miller; 2 s.; 1 d. Educ. Bolton School; Corpus Christi College, Cambridge. Lecturer, Edinburgh University, 1964; Reader, 1970; Personal Chair, 1985; Guest Professor, Aarhus University, Denmark, 1969-70. Recreations: choral singing; mountain walking. Address: (b.) Physics Department, Kings Buildings, Edinburgh University, EH9 3JZ; T.-0131-650 5300.

Paxton, Professor Roland Arthur, MSc, CEng, FICE, FRSE, AMCST. Chairman, Institution of Civil Engineers Panel for Historical Engineering Works, since 1990; Commissioner, Royal Commission on the Ancient and Historic Monuments of Scotland, since 1993; Hon. Professor, Civil and Offshore Engineering, Heriot Watt University, since 1994; b. 29.6.32, Altrincham; m., Ann; 2 d. Educ. Altrincham Grammar School; Manchester College of Science and Technology; Heriot Watt University. Cartographical surveyor, Ordnance Survey, 1953-55; Civil Engineer, Corporations of Manchester, Leicester, Edinburgh, and Lothian Regional Council, retiring as Senior Principal Engineer, 1959-90; Hon. Senior Research Fellow, Heriot Watt University, 1990-94. Trustee, Forth Bridges Visitor Centre; Secretary and Director, Laigh Milton Viaduct Conservation Project; President, Edinburgh Bibliographical Society, 1992-95; author of books and papers on technical innovation and historical engineering. Address: (b.) Civil and Offshore Engineering, Heriot Watt University, Edinburgh, EH14 4AS; T.-0131-449 5111.

Payne, Professor Peter Lester, BA, PhD, FRHistS, FRSE. Professor of Economic History, Aberdeen University, since 1969; b. 31.12.29, London; m., Enid Christine Rowntree; 1 s.; 1 d. Educ. Brockley County School, London; Nottingham University. Visiting Lecturer in American Economic History, Johns Hopkins University, 1957-58; Lecturer in Economic and Social History, Nottingham University, 1958-59; Colquhoun Lecturer in Business History, Glasgow University, 1959-69; Senior Lecturer in Economic History, Glasgow University, 1964-69; Sherman Fairchild Distinguished Scholar, California Institute of Technology, Pasadena, 1977-78. Vice-President, Business Archives Council; Member, Business Archives Council of Scotland; Vice-President, Aberdeen and North of Scotland Philatelic Society. Publications include: Rubber and Railways in the Nineteenth Century; British Entrepreneurship in the Nineteenth Century; Colvilles and the Scottish Steel Industry; The Early Scottish Limited Companies; The Hydro; Growth and Contraction: Scottish Industry c. 1860-1990; Northern Scotland (Editor). Recreations: philately; woodwork. Address: (h.) 7 Kirkton Road, Westhill, Skene, Aberdeenshire, AB32 6LF; T.-01224 744703.

Peacock, Professor Sir Alan Turner, Kt (1987), DSC (1945), MA, Hon. DUniv (Stirling), Hon. DEcon (Zurich), Hon. DScEcon (Buckingham), HonDUniv (Brunel), HonLLD (St. Andrews), HonLLD (Dundee), HonDSc (Edinburgh), Hon. Fellow (LSE), Lib Doc (Catania), FBA, FRSE. Research Professor in Public Finance, Esmee Fairbairn Centre, Heriot-Watt University, since 1985; b. 26.6.22, Ryton-on-Tyne; m., Margaret Martha Astell-Burt; 2 s.; 1 d. Educ. Grove Academy; Dundee High School; St. Andrews University. Royal Navy, 1942-45; Lecturer in Economics, St. Andrews, 1947-48; Lecturer, then Reader in Economics, London School of Economics, 1948-56; Professor of Economic Science, Edinburgh University, 1956-62; Professor of Economics, York University, 1962-78 (Deputy Vice Chancellor, 1963-69); Professor of Economics, University College, Buckingham, 1978-80; Principal, then Vice Chancellor, Buckingham University, 1980-84; Chief Economic Adviser, Department of Trade and Industry (on secondment), 1973-76. Member, Royal Commission on the Constitution, 1970-73; Member, Inquiry into Retirement Provision, 1983-85; SSRC Council, 1972-73; President, International Institute of Public Finance, 1966-69; Chairman, Committee on Financing the BBC, 1985-86; Chairman, Rowntree Inquiry on Takeovers, 1989-91; Executive Director, David Hume Institute, Edinburgh, 1985-91; Chairman, Scottish Arts Council, 1986-92; Chairman, Academic Advisory Council, Institute of Economic Affairs, 1991-93; Head, UN Advisory Mission to Russia on Social Protection, 1992; Non-Executive Director, Caledonian Bank, since 1991; Chairman, Hebrides Ensemble, since 1994. Scottish Free Enterprise Award, 1987. Publications: 25 books, over 200 articles on economic questions. Recreations: attempting to write music; jogging; hill-walking. Address: (h.) Clinton Grange, 146/4 Whitehouse Loan, Edinburgh, EH9 2AN; T.-0131-447 5917.

Peacock, Peter James. Member, Highland Regional Council, since 1982 (Vice-Convener and Chairman, Policy and Resources Committee); Training, Organisation and Policy Consultant; Board Member, Centre for Highlands and Islands Policy Studies; Board Member, Scottish Natural Heritage (N.W. Region); b. 27.2.52, Edinburgh; 2 s. Educ. Hawick High School; Jordanhill College of Education, Glasgow. Community Worker, Orkney Islands, 1973-75. Co-author, Vice-Chairman, subsequently Chairman of successful applicant group for Independent Local Radio franchise, Moray Firth; Member,Highland Area Committee, SCDI; former Area Officer, Highlands, Islands, Grampian, Scottish Association of Citizens Advice Bureaux; former Chairman, Scottish Library and Information Council; Appointed Member, European Committee of the Regions, 1993. Recreations: ornithology; golf; watching rugby union. Address: (h.) 68 Braeside Park, Balloch, Inverness; T.-01463 790371.

Peaker, Professor Malcolm, DSc, PhD, FZS, FLS, FIBiol, FRSE. Director, Hannah Research Institute, Ayr, since 1981; Hannah Professor, Glasgow University, since 1981; b. 21.8.43, Stapleford, Nottingham; m., Stephanie Jane Large; 3 s. Educ. Henry Mellish Grammar School, Nottingham; Sheffield University, BSc Zoology; DSc; University of Hong Kong, SRC NATO Scholar; PhD. ARC Institute of Animal Physiology, 1968-78; Head, Department of Physiology, Hannah Research Institute, 1978-81. Member, Editorial Board: Journal of Dairy Science, 1975-78, International Zoo Yearbook, 1978-82, Journal of Endocrinology, 1981-91; Editor, British Journal of Herpetology, 1977-81. Publications: Salt Glands in Birds and Reptiles, 1975; Avian Physiology (Editor), 1975; Comparative Aspects of Lactation (Editor), 1977; Physiological Strategies in Lactation (Co-Editor), 1984; papers. Recreations: vertebrate zoology; natural history; golf; grumbling about bureaucrats. Address: (h.) Hannah Research Institute, Ayr, KA6 5HL.

Pearson, Donald William Macintyre, BSc (Hons), MB, ChB, FRCP(Glas), FRCP(Edin). Consultant Physician, Aberdeen Teaching Hospitals, since 1984; Clinical Senior Lecturer, Aberdeen University, since 1984; b. 5.9.50, Kilmarnock; m., Margaret J.K. Harris; 2 s.; 1 d. Educ. Cumnock Academy; Glasgow University. Registrar, University Department of Medicine, Glasgow Royal Infirmary; Lecturer in Medicine with Aberdeen University, Raigmore Hospital, Inverness; Senior Registrar in General Medicine, Diabetes and Endocrinology, Grampian Health Board. Past President, New Cumnock Burns Club. Recreations: music; Scottish poetry and literature. Address: (b.) Diabetic Clinic, Woolmanhill, Aberdeen Royal Infirmary, Aberdeen; T.-01224 681818, Ext. 55491.

Pearson, Francis Salmond Gillespie, MA (Oxon). Painter in oils, since 1984; b. 31.7.35, Edinburgh. Educ. Fettes College, Edinburgh; University College, Oxford; Edinburgh University. National Service, Cameron Highlanders; Assistant Master, Harrow School, 1960-61 and 1967-73; Member, Faculty of Advocates, since 1964; Headmaster, Truro Cathedral School, 1974-79; Head of Arts and Languages, Welbeck College, 1979-83. Trustee, Hopetoun House Preservation Trust. Address: (h.) 28 Douglas Crescent, Edinburgh, EH12 5BA; T.-0131-225 4736.

Pearson, Keith Philip, MA (Cantab), FRSE, CertEd, DipEstHisp. Headmaster, George Heriot's School, since 1983; b. 5.8.41, Preston; 2 d. Educ. Preston Grammar School; Madrid University; St. Catharine's College, Cambridge. Assistant Teacher, then Head of Modern Languages, Rossall School, 1964-72; Head of Modern Languages, then Deputy Principal, George Watson's College, 1972-83. Member, HMC; twice Member, SCCML; Member, Scottish Consultative Council on the Curriculum, 1987-91; Member, Council, Scottish Headteachers Association. Recreations: sport; hill-walking; music; DIY; foreign travel. Address: (h.) 11 Pentland Avenue, Edinburgh, EH13 0HZ; T.-0131-441 2630.

Pearson of Rannoch, Lord (Malcolm Everard MacLaren Pearson). Life Peer; b. 20.7.42; m.; 2 d.; 1 d. by pr. m. Chairman, PWS Holdings plc; founded Rannoch Trust, 1984. Address: Rannoch Barracks, Rannoch Station, PH17 2QE.

Peart, Geoff, BA, MA, MIED, MRTPI. Director of Development and Planning, Central Regional Council, since 1991; Director, Stirling Enterprise Park Ltd., since 1991; Director, Stirling University Innovation Park, since 1991; b. 25.10.46, Jarrow; m., Kathryn; 1 s.; 1 d. Educ. Dame Allan's Boys Grammar School, Newcastle upon Tyne; Southampton University; Nottingham University. Member, Scottish Office/COSLA Scottish Statistical Liaison Committee, 1975-91; Technical Adviser to Scottish Office/COSLA Local Government Finance Distribution Committee, 1985-91; Member, COSLA European Policy Advisory Group, 1989-91; Member, Royal Town Planning Institute Retail Working Party, 1986-87. Recreations: hill-walking; squash; cricket; reading. Address: (b.) Viewforth, Stirling; T.-Stirling 442989.

Peat, Jeremy Alastair, BA, MSc. Chief Economist, Royal Bank of Scotland, since 1993; Honorary Professor, Heriot-Watt University; b. 20.3.45, Haywards Heath; m., Philippa Ann; 2 d. Educ. St. Paul's School, London; Bristol University; University College London. Economic Assistant/Economic Adviser, Ministry of Overseas Development, 1969-77; Economic Adviser, Manpower Services Commission, 1978-80; Head, Employment Policy Unit, Ministry of Finance and Development Planning, Government of Botswana, 1980-84; Economic Adviser, HM Treasury, 1984-85; Senior Economic Adviser, Scottish Office, 1985-93. Recreations: walking; reading; tennis; listening to music. Address: (b.) 42 St. Andrew Square, Edinburgh, EH2 2YE; T.-0131-523 2277.

Peat, William Wood Watson, CBE, JP, FRAgS. Farmer; National Governor for Scotland, BBC, and Chairman, Broadcasting Council for Scotland, 1984-89; b. 14.12.22, Denny; m., Jean McHarrie; 2 s.; 1 d. Educ. Denny Public School. Lt., Royal Signals, NW Europe and India, 1940-46; Broadcaster; National Chairman, subsequently President, Scottish Association of Young Farmers Clubs; Member, Stirling County Council, 1959-75 (Vice Convener, 1967-70); Council Member, NFU of Scotland, 1959-78 (President, 1966-67); Member, Scotish River Purification Advisory Committee, 1960-79; Board of Management, RSNH, 1960-72; General Commissioner of Income Tax, since 1962; Chairman, Scottish Advisory Committee, Association of Agriculture, 1974-79 (Vice-President, since 1979); Council, Hannah Research Institute, 1963-82; Council Member, Scottish Agricultural Organisation Society Ltd., since 1963 (President, 1974-77); Member, British Agricultural Council, 1974-84; Member, Board of Management, Oatridge Agricultural College, 1967-75; Governor, West of Scotland Agricultural College (Chairman, 1983-88); Chairman, Scottish Agricultural Colleges Ltd., 1987-90; Director, FMC plc, 1974-83; Member, Central Council for Agricultural and Horticultural Co-operation, 1967-83; Member, Co-operative Development Board, 1983-89; Member, Board of Management, British Farm Produce Council, 1964-83, BFP Committee, Food from Britain, 1984-87; Chairman, BBC Scottish Agricultural Advisory Committee, 1971-76. Recreations: amateur radio; flying. Address: (h.) 61 Stirling Road, Larbert, FK5 4SG.

Peckham, Professor Gordon E., MA, PhD. Professor, Department of Physics, Heriot Watt University, since 1992; b. 29.10.36, Bristol; 1 s.; 1 d. Educ. Bristol Grammar School; Trinity College, Cambridge. Lecturer: Reading University, 1966, Heriot Watt University, 1971; Reader, Heriot Watt, 1972. Address: (b.) Physics Department, Heriot Watt University, Riccarton, Edinburgh, EH14 4AS; T.-0131-451 3028.

Peddie, Richard L., MA, MEd, AFBPsS. Hon. Lecturer, Strathclyde University, since 1988; formerly Vice Principal, Craigie College of Education; b. 11.6.28, Grangemouth; m., Nan K. Bell; 1 s.; 2 d. Educ. Grangemouth High School; Glasgow University. Royal Signals Officer, Allied Supreme HQ (SHAPE), 1951-53; Teacher, Stirlingshire, 1953-56; Educational Psychologist, Ayrshire, 1956-59; Lecturer, Jordanhill College, 1959-64; Head, Psychology Department, Assistant Principal, Vice-Principal, Craigie College of Education, 1964-88; Member, General Teaching Council for Scotland, 1970-78; External Examiner in Education, London University Institute, 1971-76; External Examiner, Hamilton College of Education, 1977-80; Member, Scottish Examination Board, 1980-84; Member, Education Committee, British Psychological Society, 1964-68; Chairman, Glasgow University Educational Colloquium, 1966-67; Chairman, Association of Lecturers in Colleges of Education in Scotland (ALCES), 1967-69; Captain, 51 (H) Infantry Division Signals Regiment (TA), 1953-60; Vice-Chairman, Ayr Children's Panel, 1970-74; Member, Scottish Council for Research in Education, 1962-78; Member, Executive Committee, Scottish Division of Educational and Child Psychology, 1979-84; Chairman, Association of Higher Academic Staff in Colleges of Education, 1984-87; Paul Harris Fellow, Rotary Award, 1986; Church of Scotland Elder; Dean of Guild, Burgh of Ayr, 1992-93. Recreations:reading; Rotary; driving; golf. Address: (h.) 14 Glenpark Place, Alloway, Ayr, KA7 4SQ; T.-01292 441996.

Peden, Professor George Cameron, MA, DPhil. Professor of History, Stirling University, since 1990; b. 16.2.43, Dundee; m., Alison Mary White; 3 s. Educ. Grove Academy, Broughty Ferry; Dundee University; Brasenose College, Oxford. Sub-Editor, Dundee Evening Telegraph, 1960-68; mature student, 1968-75; Tutorial Assistant, Department of Modern History, Dundee University, 1975-76; Temporary Lecturer, School of History, Leeds University, 1976-77; Lecturer in Economic and Social History, then Reader in Economic History, Bristol University, 1977-90; Visiting Fellow, All Souls College, Oxford, 1988-89. Publications: British Rearmament and the Treasury 1932-39, 1979; British Economic and Social Policy: Lloyd George to Margaret Thatcher, 1985; Keynes, The Treasury and British Economic Policy, 1988. Recreation: hill-walking. Address: (h.) Ardvurich, Leny Feus, Callander, FK17 8AS; T.-01877 30488.

Peebles, Gillian Margaret, LLB, WS. Board Member, Scottish Legal Aid Board, since 1992; Advocate, since 1995; b. 31.1.55, Glasgow; m., Sheriff Iain A.S. Peebles. Educ. Laurel Bank School; Glasgow University. Solicitor, 1977-94; WS, 1988. First woman president, Glasgow University Conservative Club, 1975. Recreations: travel; the arts. Address: (h.) 70 Dublin Street, Edinburgh, EH3 6NP; T.-0131-556 1150.

Peggie, Robert Galloway Emslie, CBE, FCCA, FBCS. Chairman, Local Government Staff Commission for Scotland, since 1994; b. 5.1.29, Bo'ness; 1 s.; 1 d. Educ. Lasswade High School. Trainee Accountant, 1946-52; Accountant in industry, 1952-57; Edinburgh Corporation, 1957-72: O. and M. Officer, Assistant City Chamberlain, Deputy City Chamberlain, Reorganisation Steering Committee; Chief Executive, Lothian Regional Council, 1974-86; Commissioner (Ombudsman) for Local Administration in Scotland, 1986-94. Member, Court, Heriot-Watt University (Convener, Finance Committee). Recreation: golf. Address: (b.) 23 Walker Street, Edinburgh, EH3 7HX; T.-0131-225 5300.

Pelham Burn, Angus Maitland, JP, DL. Director, Bank of Scotland, since 1977, Chairman, Aberdeen Local Board; Chairman, Scottish Provident, since 1995; Chairman, Aberdeen Trust PLC; Director, Abtrust Scotland Investment Company, since 1989; b. 13.12.31, London; m., Anne; 4 d. Educ. Harrow; North of Scotland College of Agriculture. Hudson's Bay Company, 1951-58; Farmer and Company Director, since 1958; Member, Kincardine County Council, 1967-75 (Vice Convener, 1973-75); Member, Grampian Regional Council, 1974-94; Member, Accounts Commission for Scotland, 1980-94 (Deputy Chairman, 1987-94); Chairman, Aberdeen Airport Consultative Committee, since 1986; Director, Aberdeen Association for Prevention of Cruelty to Animals, since 1975; Chairman, Order of St. John (Aberdeen) Ltd.; Council Member, Winston Churchill Memorial Trust, 1984-93; Member, Queen's Bodyguard for Scotland (Royal Company of Archers), since 1968; Vice Lord Lieutenant, Kincardineshire, since 1978. Recreations: gardening; photography; deer-stalking. Address: (b.) 68 Station Road, Banchory, AB31 3JS; T.-01330 823343.

Pelly, Frances, RSA. Sculptor; b. 21.7.47, Edinburgh. Educ. Morrison's Academy, Crieff; Duncan of Jordanstone College of Art, Dundee. Part-time lecturing, Dundee, 1974-78; full-time lecturing, Grays School of Art, Aberdeen, 1979-83. Recreations: riding; wildlife; gardening. Address: Costa Schoolhouse, Evie, Orkney; T.-0185 675 1326.

Peltenburg, Professor Edgar, BA, PhD, FSA (Scot). Professor of Archaeology, Edinburgh University, since 1993; b. 28.5.42, Montreal; m., Marie Wright; 3 s.; 1 d. Educ. Montreal; Birmingham University. Assistant Lecturer, Classics, McGill University, Montreal, 1963-66; Research Fellow in Archaeology, Birmingham University, 1966-69; Lecturer in Archaeology, Glasgow University, 1969-78; Lecturer in Near Eastern Archaeology, then Reader, Edinburgh University, 1978-93; director of excavations, Syria and Cyprus. Publications: six books; many scientific papers. Recreations: jazz; skiing. Address:

(b.) Department of Archaeology, Old High School, Infirmary Street, Edinburgh; T.-0131-650 4141.

Penman, David Roland, DA (Edin), DipTP (Edin), FRTPI, ARIAS, FSAScot. Reporter, Scottish Office Inquiry Reporters' Unit, 1994-95; b. 6.6.36, Manchester; m., Tamara Scott; 2 s.; 1 d. Educ. George Watson's Boys' College, Edinburgh; Edinburgh College of Art. Assistant Architect, private practices, 1960-67; Partner, Bamber Hall & Partners, Edinburgh, 1967-71; Depute County Planning Officer, Argyll County Council, 1971-73; County Planning Officer, Perth & Kinross Joint County Council, 1973-75; Director of Planning, Perth and Kinross District Council, 1975-94. Chairman, RTPI Scotland, 1984, Member of Council, 1978-85; President, Dundee Institute of Architects, 1988, Member of Council, 1980-90; Chairman, Scottish Urban Archaeological Trust, 1990-95; former Chairman, Duncan of Jordanstone College of Art; former Vice-Chairman, Scottish Conservation Projects Trust; former Council Member, National Trust for Scotland. Recreations: hill-walking; art galleries; theatre; DIY; Scots history; travel. Address: (h.) 17 Gannochy Road, Perth, PH2 7EF; T.-01738 627775.

Penn, Ian Devis, CBiol, FIBiol. Depute Principal, Dumfries and Galloway College, since 1983; b. 20.3.40, Bromley; m., Valerie Jane Rolston; 1 s.; 1 d. Educ. Colfe's Grammar School, London; North East Surrey College of Technology. Laboratory technician; Assistant Lecturer in Biology, Chelmsford, Essex; Lecturer B in Biology, Bristol Technical College; Senior Lecturer in Science, then Head, Department of Science, Stevenson College, Edinburgh. Institute of Biology: Chairman, Education Division, 1984-86, Chairman, Scottish Branch, 1985-8; Secretary, Dumfries Baptist Church, since 1989. Recreation: gardening. Address: (h.) Nithsdale, Edinburgh Road, Dumfries; T.-01387 262269.

Pennington, Christopher Royston, BSc (Hons), MB, ChB, MRCP, MD, FRCP, FRCPEdin. Consultant Physician (General Medicine and Gastroenterology), since 1979; Honorary Senior Lecturer in Medicine, Dundee University, since 1979; Examiner, MRCP (UK), since 1986; b. 22.2.46, Chard; m., Marcia Jane Barclay; 1 d. Educ. Shebbear College; Manchester University. House Officer, Manchester Royal Infirmary, 1970-71; Registrar in Medicine, Aberdeen Royal Infirmary, 1971-74; Lecturer in Medicine, Dundee University, 1974-79. External Examiner in Medicine, Aberdeen University, 1983-86; Examiner, Edinburgh College of Physicians; Specialty Adviser, Medical Defence Union of Scotland. Publications: Therapeutic Nutrition: A Practical Guide, 1988; book chapters and papers. Address: (h.) Balnagowan, Braehead, Invergowrie, Dundee.

Penrose, Hon. Lord (George William Penrose), QC (Scot). Senator of the College of Justice, since 1990; b. 2.6.38. Advocate, 1964; QC, 1978; Procurator to General Assembly of Church of Scotland, 1984-90.

Pentland, Brian, BSc, MB, ChB, FRCPE. Consultant Neurologist in Rehabilitation Medicine, since 1982; Senior Lecturer in Rehabilitation Studies, Edinburgh University, since 1983; b. 24.6.49, Glasgow; m., Gillian Mary Duggua; 4 s. Educ. Liberton High School, Edinburgh; Edinburgh University. Junior hospital appointments in Edinburgh, Cumbria and Dundee; formerly Lecturer in Neurology in Edinburgh. Recreation: hill-walking. Address: (b.) Astley Ainslie Hospital, Grange Loan, Edinburgh, EH9 2HL; T.-0131-537 9039.

Peoples, Robin (Robert John), MA (Hons). Artistic Director, Brunton Theatre, since 1992; b. 9.9.54, Londonderry; m., Lamorna Hutchison; 1 s.; 1 d. Educ. Foyle College, Derry; St. Andrews University. Youth and community work in Northern Ireland; taught at University of Erlangen-Nuremberg, Germany; awarded Scottish Arts Council Director's Bursary; directed and designed with various theatre companies throughout Scotland; Artistic Director, Scottish Youth Theatre, 1983-91; Member, Board, Federation of Scottish Theatre; Member, Board, Winged Horse Touring Productions; Patron, Voluntary Arts Network. Recreations: theatre; painting; reading. Address: (b.) Brunton Theatre, Musselburgh, EH21 6AA; T.-0131-665 3711.

Percy, Professor John Pitkeathly (Ian), CA, FRSA. Senior Partner, Grant Thornton, Scotland, since 1991; Chairman: W. & J.R. Watson (Holdings) Ltd., The Accounts Commission, MacDonald Orr Ltd.; Deputy Chairman, Caledonian Bank PLC; Non-Executive Director: Scottish Provident, Morgan Grenfell (Scotland) Ltd., William Wilson (Holdings) Ltd., The Edinburgh Academy; Vice Chairman, UK Auditing Practices Board; b. 16.1.42, Southport; m., Sheila; 2 d. Educ. Edinburgh Academy; Edinburgh University. Managing Partner, Grant Thornton, London, 1981-88; Honorary Professor of Accounting, Aberdeen University, 1988. Freeman, City of London; Member, British Academy of Experts; Elder, St. Cuthbert's Church of Scotland; President, Institute of Chartered Accountants of Scotland, 1990-91. Recreations: golf; fishing. Address: (h.) 30 Midmar Drive, Edinburgh; T.-0131-447 3645.

Perfect, Hugh Epton, BSc. Senior Assistant Principal, Moray House Institute of Education, Heriot-Watt University; b. 9.4.41, London; m., Susan; 2 d. Educ. Haberdasher's Askes' School, Hampstead; Imperial College, London. Teacher, Windsor Grammar School; Lecturer, Bulmershe College of Education, Reading; Lecturer/Senior Lecturer, Biology Department, Moray House College of Education. Recreations: badminton; gardening; micro-computers. Address: (b.) Moray House Institute of Education, Holyrood Road, Edinburgh, EH8 8AQ; T.-0131-558 6168.

Perman, Raymond John, BA, MBA. Development Director, Caledonian Publishing, since 1994; Chairman: Caledonian Magazines, Caledonian Information and Media Services, Insider Publications Ltd; b. 22.8.47, London; m., Fay Young; 3 s. Educ. Hemel Hempstead Grammar School; St. Andrews University; Open University; Edinburgh University. Oxford Mail, 1969-71; The Times, 1971-75; The Scotsman, 1975-76; Scottish Correspondent, Financial Times, 1976-81; Deputy Editor, Sunday Standard, 1981-83; Managing Director, Insider Publications Ltd, 1985-93. Address: Caledonian Publishing Ltd., 195 Albion Street, Glasgow G1 1QP; T.-0141-552 6255.

Perrie, Walter, MA, MPhil. Poet and Critic; b. 5.6.49, Quarter. Educ. Hamilton Academy; Edinburgh University; Stirling University. Full-time writer since 1975; six collections of poetry, one of which, A Lamentation for the Children, won a Scottish Arts Council book award; critical writings on aesthetics, philosophy of language, Hugh MacDiarmid, W.H. Auden, Muriel Spark and Lord Byron; held Scottish-Canadian writer's exchange fellowship, 1984-85; has lectured widely in Europe and North America; received a Gregory Award for poetry and bursaries from the Merrill-Ingram Foundation (New York) and Scottish Arts Council; Editor, Margin, a quarterly of arts and ideas, 1986-90; Writer-in-Residence, Strathkelvin District, 1992; author, Roads that Move: a journey through Eastern Europe, 1991; Writer in Residence, Stirling University, 1991. Address: (h.) 10 Croft Place, Dunning, PH2 0SB.

Perry, Professor Clive Graham, MA (Cantab), Hon. MA (Leicester). Festival Director, Pitlochry Festival Theatre, since 1986; Professor and Head, Department of Drama, Queen Margaret College, Edinburgh, since 1990; b. 17.3.36, Harrow. Educ. Wolverhampton Grammar School; Harrow County Grammar School; Cambridge University. Awarded Thames TV Scholarship to regional theatre, 1960-

360 WHO'S WHO IN SCOTLAND

61; Assistant Director, Derby Playhouse; Associate Director, Castle Theatre, Farnham; Director of Productions, Phoenix Theatre, Leicester; Director, Royal Lyceum Theatre, Edinburgh, 1966-76 (Director of Theatres in Edinburgh, 1971-76); Director, Birmingham Repertory Theatre, 1976-86. Recreation: theatre. Address: (b.) Pitlochry Festival Theatre, Port-Na-Craig, Pitlochry, PH16 5DR; T.-01796 473054.

Perth, 17th Earl of (John David Drummond), PC (1957); b. 13.5.07; m., Nancy Seymour Fincke; 2 s. Educ. Downside; Cambridge University. Lt., Intelligence Corps, 1940; War Cabinet Offices, 1942-43; Ministry of Production, 1944-45; Minister of State for Colonial Affairs, 1957-62; First Crown Estate Commissioner, 1962-77; Member, Court, St. Andrews University, 1967-86; Trustee, National Library of Scotland, since 1968. Hon. LLD; Hon. FRIBA; Hon. FRIAS. Address: (h.) Stobhall, by Perth, PH2 6DR; T.-01821 640 332.

Peterken, Laurence Edwin, CBE, MA. Director, Special Projects, NHS in Scotland, since 1993; General Manager, Greater Glasgow Health Board, 1986-93; b. 2.10.31, London; m., 1, Hanne Birgithe Von Der Recke (deceased); 1 s.; 1 d.; 2, Margaret Raynal Blair; 1 s.; 1 d. Educ. Harrow School (Scholar); Peterhouse, Cambridge (Scholar). Pilot Officer, RAF Regt., Adjt. No. 20 LAA Sqdn., 1950-52; Service Divisional Manager, Hotpoint Ltd., 1961-63; Commercial Director, then Managing Director, British Domestic Appliances Ltd., 1963-68; Director, British Printing Corporation Ltd., 1969-73; Managing Director, Fashion Multiple Division, Debenhams Ltd., 1974-76; Management Auditor, 1976-77; Controller, Operational Services, GLC, 1977-85; President, GLC Chief Officers' Guild, 1983-85; Acting Director, Royal Festival Hall, 1983-85. Chairman, Glasgow and West of Scotland Institute of Public Administration, since 1993. Recreations: opera; swimming. Address: (h.) 25 Kingsborough Gardens, Glasgow, G12 9NH.

Peters, David Alexander, OBE, MA, DSA, FHSM. General Manager, Borders Health Board, since 1985; b. 18.10.38, Glasgow; m., Moira Cullen Macpherson; 2 s.; 1 d. Educ. King's Park School, Glasgow; Glasgow University; Manchester University. Hospital Secretary, Greenock Royal Infirmary, Eye Infirmary, ENT Hospital, 1963-66; Eastern Regional Hospital Board, Dundee: Principal Administrative Assistant, 1966-68, Assistant Secretary, 1968-71, Principal Assistant Secretary, 1971-74; District Administrator, Renfrew District, Argyll and Clyde Health Board, 1974-81; Secretary, Borders Health Board, 1981-85. Recreations: curling; tennis; sailing; golf; gardening. Address: (h.) Wildcroft, Gattonside, Melrose, TD6 9NP.

Peters, Kenneth Jamieson, CBE, JP, DL, FRSA, FSA Scot, Assoc. MCIT. Vice-Chairman, Peterhead Bay Authority, since 1989; Deputy Lieutenant, City of Aberdeen, since 1978; b. 17.1.23, London; m., Arunda Merle Jane Jones. Educ. Aberdeen Grammar School; Aberdeen University. Served Second World War; commissioned Queen's Own Cameron Highlanders; also King's Own Scottish Borderers; editorial staff, Scottish Daily Record and Evening News Ltd., 1947-51; Assistant Editor, Aberdeen Evening Express, 1951-52; Assistant Editor, Manchester Evening Chronicle, 1952-53; Editor, Aberdeen Evening Express, 1953-56; Editor, Press and Journal, Aberdeen, 1956-60; Managing Director, Aberdeen Journals Ltd., 1960-80, Chairman, 1980-81; Director: Thomson North Sea, 1981-88, Thomson Scottish Petroleum, 1981-86, Thomson Forestry Holdings, 1982-88, Highland Printers Ltd., 1968-83; President, Scottish Daily Newspaper Society, 1964-66 and 1974-76; Member, Press Council, 1974-77; Director, Thomson Regional Newspapers, 1974-81; Director, Aberdeen Association of Social Service, 1973-78; Member, British Railways (Scottish) Board, 1982-92; Member, Girobank, Scotland

Board, 1984-90; Member, Executive, Scottish Council (Development and Industry), 1982-88 (Chairman, Aberdeen and North-East Committee, 1982-88); Fellow, SCDI, 1989; Member, Scottish Advisory Committee, British Council, 1967-84; National Committee Member, Films of Scotland, 1970-82; Burgess of Guild, City of Aberdeen, 1963. Publications: The Northern Lights, 1978; Burgess of Guild, 1982; Great North Memories, Vol. 1 and Vol. 2 (Editor). Recreations: walking; cricket; rugby football. Address: 47 Abergeldie Road, Aberdeen, AB1 6ED; T.-01224 587647.

Peterson, George Sholto, NP. Solicitor and Notary Public, since 1956; Honorary Sheriff, since 1982; b. 18.9.27, Lerwick; m., Dorothy Hilda Spence; 2 s.; 4 d. Educ. Lerwick Central Public School; Edinburgh University. Secretary, The Shetland Trust; Factor for the Marquess of Zetland; Senior Partner, Tait & Peterson, Solicitors and Estate Agents, Lerwick; Dean, Faculty of Solicitors in Shetland; Honorary Pastor, Ebenezer Church, Lerwick. Recreations: studying theology; reading; fishing. Address: (b.) Bank of Scotland Buildings, Lerwick, Shetland; T.-01595 693010.

Pethrick, Professor Richard Arthur, BSc, PhD, DSc, FRSC, FRSE. Professor in Chemistry, Strathclyde University, since 1983 (Head of Department, since 1992); b. 26.10.42; m., Joan Knowles Hume; 1 s. Educ. North Gloucestershire College, Cheltenham; London University; Salford University. Editor: British Polymer Journal, Polymer Yearbook, Polymer International, International Journal of Polymer Materials; Member, Polymer Committee, European Science Foundation; Member, Committee, MACRO Group, 1979-84; Member, SERC Polymer Materials Committee, since 1994. Address: (h.) 40 Langside Drive, Newlands, Glasgow, G43 2QQ; T.-0141-552 4400.

Petrie, Professor James Colquhoun, MB, ChB, FRCPEdin, FRCP, FFPM. Professor of Clinical Pharmacology, since 1985, Head, Department of Medicine and Therapeutics, Aberdeen University, since 1994; Honorary Consultant Physician, Aberdeen Teaching Hospitals, since 1971; b. 18.9.41, Aberdeen; m., Dr. M. Xanthe P.; 2 s.; 2 d. Educ. Anieres, Geneva; Robert Gordon's College, Aberdeen; Aberdeen University. Senior Lecturer, 1971-81, Reader, 1981-85, Aberdeen University. Chairman, Lecht Ski Company, since 1976. Recreations: ski; golf; fishing. Address: (b.) Department of Medicine and Therapeutics, Aberdeen Royal Infirmary, Foresterhill, Aberdeen, AB9 2ZB; T.-01224 681818.

Peyton Jones, Professor Simon Loftus, MA (Cantab), DipCompSci, MBCS, CEng. Professor of Computing Science, Glasgow University, since 1989; b. 18.1.58, Cape Town, South Africa; m., Dorothy Helen. Educ. Marlborough College; Trinity College, Cambridge. Systems Engineer, Beale Electronic Systems Ltd, 1980-82; University College London: Lecturer in Computer Science, 1982-86, Senior Lecturer in Computer Science, 1986-89. Publication: The Implementation of Functional Programming Languages, 1987. Recreations: cycling; reading; singing. Address: (b.) Department of Computing Science, University of Glasgow, Glasgow G12 8QQ; T.-0141-330 4500.

Philip, Hon. Lord (Alexander Morrison). Chairman, Scottish Land Court, since 1993; President, Lands Tribunal for Scotland, since 1993; b. 3.8.42, Aberdeen; m., Shona Mary MacRae; 3 s. Educ. Glasgow High School; St. Andrews University; Glasgow University. Solicitor, 1967-72; Advocate, 1973; Standing Junior Counsel, Scottish Education Department, 1982; Advocate Depute, 1982-85; QC, 1984; Chairman, Medical Appeal Tribunals, 1988-92. Recreations: piping; golf. Address: (b.) 1 Grosvenor Crescent, Edinburgh, EH12 5ER; T.-0131-225 3595.

Philips, Douglas John, MHSM, DipHSM. Director of Community Care Development, Argyll and Clyde Health Board, since 1992 (Unit General Manager, Argyll and Dumbarton Unit, 1989-92); b. 30.4.53, Edinburgh; m., Morag S. Hall. Educ. Dalkeith High School. Formerly General Manager, Northern Unit, Highland Health Board. Recreations: walking the Dalmatians; hill-walking; rambling; cycling; gardening; reading fiction; music; Coronation Street. Address: (h.) Windsong, Blairuskinmore, Kinlochard, Stirling FK8 3TP; T.-01877 387236.

Phillips, Professor John Clifford, BSc, CMath, FIMA, FRSA, MIMgt. Vice-Principal, Glasgow Caledonian University, since 1993; Chief Executive, Glasgow Caledonian University Company, since 1995; b. 29.1.43, Dyfed; m., Anne Margaret; 1 s.; 1 d. Educ. Llandeilo Grammar School; University of Wales, Aberystwyth. Lecturer, Lancashire Polytechnic, 1967-69; Leeds Polytechnic, 1969-71; Leeds Polytechnic: Senior Lecturer, 1971-77, Principal Lecturer, 1977-86, Head, School of Mathematics and Computing, 1986-87, Dean, Faculty of Engineering and Computing, 1988-90; Senior Executive, External Development, 1988-90; Principal, The Queen's College, Glasgow, 1991-93. Former Member, North Yorkshire County Council. Recreations: reading; walking; architectural conservation. Address: (b.) Glasgow Caledonian University, Cowcaddens Road, Glasgow, G4 0BA.

Phillips, Professor John H., MA, PhD. Professor of Biology Teaching and Head, Department of Biochemistry, Edinburgh University, since 1993; b. 19.2.41, York; m., Kerstin B. Halling; 2 d. Educ. Leighton Park School, Reading; Christ's College, Cambridge. Lecturer in Biochemistry, Makerere University, Uganda, 1967-69; scientific staff, MRC Laboratory of Molecular Biology, Cambridge, 1969-74; Department of Biochemistry, Edinburgh University, 1974-88, Director of Biology Teaching, 1988-93. Recreations: natural history; Scottish mountains; visits to Sweden. Address: (h.) 46 Granby Road, Edinburgh, EH16 5NW; T.-0131-667 5322.

Pickard, Willis Ritchie, MA (Hons), Hon. LLD (Aberdeen). Editor, Times Educational Supplement Scotland, since 1977; Rector, Aberdeen University, 1988-90; b. 21.5.41, Dunfermline; m., Ann; 2 d. Educ. Daniel Stewart's College; St. Andrews University. The Scotsman: Leader Writer, 1967-72, Features Editor, 1972-77. Former Member, Scottish Arts Council; Chairman, Children's Book Committee for Scotland; Chairman, Book Trust Scotland; Liberal candidate, East Fife, 1970 and February, 1974. Address: (b.) 37 George Street, Edinburgh, EH2 2HN; T.-0131-220 1100.

Pidgeon, Professor Carl R., BSc, PhD, FRSE. Professor of Semiconductor Physics and Deputy Head, Physics Department, Heriot Watt University; b. 27.11.37, London; 1 s.; 1 d. Educ. Reading University. Staff Member, National Magnet Laboratory, MIT, 1964-71; Reader in Physics, Heriot Watt University, 1971-83. Recreations: golf; skiing. Address: (b.) Physics Department, Heriot Watt University, Edinburgh.

Pignatelli, Frank, MA, MEd, DUniv, FBIM, FRSA. Director of Education, Strathclyde Regional Council, since 1988; Visiting Professor of Education, Glasgow University, since 1989; b. 22.12.46, Glasgow; m., Rosetta; 1 s.; 1 d. Educ. St. Mungo's Academy, Glasgow; Glasgow University. Chairman, Scottish Advisory Group on Technical and Vocational Initiative; Member, UK National Steering Group on TVEI; Member, CBI UK Policy Group on Understanding British Industry; Consultant to Egyptian Government on Vocational Education; Consultant to Queensland Catholic Education Commission; Member, Council, Association of Directors of Education in Scotland; Director and Member, Scottish Consultative Council on the Curriculum; Director, Scottish Vocational Education Council; President, British Institute of Management, Renfrewshire Branch; Chairman, Royal Institute of Public Administration, Glasgow and West of Scotland Branch. Recreations: genealogy; reading. Address: (b.) Strathclyde Regional Council, Department of Education, 20 India Street, Glasgow, G2 4PF; T.-0141-249 4170.

Pigott, David. Chief Executive, Edinburgh Healthcare NNS Trust. Address: (b.) Astley Ainslie Hospital, 133 Grange Loan, Edinburgh, EH9 2HL.

Pike, (Kathryn) Lorna, MA (Hons). Editor, Dictionary of the Older Scottish Tongue, since 1986; b. 8.8.56, Fort William. Educ. Lochaber High School, Fort William; Edinburgh University. Editor, Concise Scots Dictionary, 1979-83; Assistant Editor, Dictionary of the Older Scottish Tongue, 1984-86. Secretary, Scottish Text Society. Recreations: riding; photography; handicrafts. Address: (b.) 27 George Square, Edinburgh, EH8 9LD; T.-0131-650 4147.

Pilcher, Rosamunde. Author; b. 22.9.24, Lelant, Cornwall. Began publishing short stories in Woman and Home, 1945; since then has published hundreds of short stories and 25 novels, including Sleeping Tiger, Under Gemini, Wild Mountain Thyme, The Carousel, Voices in Summer, The Shell Seekers, September, The Blue Bedroom, Flowers in the Rain; play, The Dashing White Sergeant. Address: (h.) Over Pilmore, Invergowrie, by Dundee; T.-Longforgan 239.

Piper, Ronald Allen, BA, BD, PhD. Principal, St. Mary's College, St. Andrews University, since 1992, Head, School of Divinity, since 1992, Reader in New Testament, since 1992; b. 27.3.48, U.S.A.; m., Faith Elizabeth Woodhouse; 1 d. Educ. Pomona College, Claremont, California; London University. Lecturer in New Testament Studies, Aberdeen University, 1979-80; Lecturer in New Testament Language and Literature, St. Andrews University, 1980-92. Secretary, British New Testament Society. Publications: Wisdom in the Q-Tradition, 1989; The Gospel Behind the Gospels, 1995; numerous journal articles. Address: (b.) St. Mary's College, St. Andrews, KY16 9JU; T.-01334 462851.

Pippard, Professor Martin John, BSc, MB, ChB, FRCPath, FRCP. Professor of Haematology, Dundee University, since 1989; Honorary Consultant Haematologist, Dundee Teaching Hospitals Trust, since 1989; b. 16.1.48, London; m., Grace Elizabeth; 2 s.; 1 d. Educ. Buckhurst Hill County High School; Birmingham University. House Physician and House Surgeon, 1972-73; Senior Medical House Officer, 1973-75; Research Fellow, Nuffield Department of Clinical Medicine, Oxford, 1975-78; MRC Travelling Research Fellow, University of Washington, Seattle, 1978-80; Wellcome Trust Research Fellow and Clinical Lecturer, Nuffield Department of Clinical Medicine, 1980-83; Consultant Haematologist, MRC Clinical Research Centre and Northwick Park Hospital, 1983-88. Recreations: gardening; fell-walking. Address: (b.) Department of Haematology, Ninewells Hospital and Medical School, Dundee, DD1 9SY; T.-01382 660111.

Pirie, Henry Ward, OStJ, MA, LLB. Crossword Compiler, Glasgow Herald, and various publications; b. 13.2.22, Edinburgh; m., Jean Jardine; 4 s. Educ. George Watson's College; Edinburgh University. Royal Scots; Indian Army (Grenadiers), 1944; Advocate, 1947; Standing Junior Counsel to the Admiralty in Scotland, 1951; Sheriff-Substitute of Lanarkshire, at Airdrie, 1954-55; Sheriff-Substitute (later Sheriff) of Lanarkshire, at Glasgow, 1955-74. Past President: Glasgow and West of Scotland Watsonian Club, The Lenzie Club. Recreations: opera; bridge; dog-walking. Address: (h.) 16 Poplar Drive, Lenzie, Glasgow, G66 4DN.

Pirie, Professor Hugh Munro, BVMS, PhD, MRCVS, FRCPath. Professor, Department of Veterinary Pathology, Glasgow University, since 1982; b. 10.4.36, Glasgow; m., Myrtle Elizabeth Stewart Levack; 1 d. Educ. Coatbridge High School; Glasgow University. Scientific Editor, Research in Veterinary Science, 1981-88; British Council Specialist, Argentina, 1982, Ethiopia, 1986-88. President, Association of Veterinary Teachers and Research Workers, 1984; Secretary, European Association of Establishments for Veterinary Education, 1988-92; Chairman, Veterinary Panel, Royal College of Pathologists, 1988-93; Member, Council, Royal College of Veterinary Surgeons, 1993-97. Recreations: travel; gardening; hill-walking; swimming; gastronomy. Address: (h.) North East Corner, Buchanan Castle Estate, Drymen, G63 0HX; T.-01361 660781.

Pirie, Sheriff Iain Gordon, MA, LLB. Sheriff of Glasgow and Strathkelvin, since 1982; b. 15.1.33, Dundee; m., Dr. Sheila B. Pirie; 2 s.; 1 d. Educ. Harris Academy, Dundee; St. Andrews University. Procurator Fiscal, Dumfries, 1971-76, Ayr, 1976-79; Sheriff of South Strathclyde, Dumfries and Galloway, 1979-82. Address: (b.) Sheriff Court, 1 Carlton Place, Glasgow, G5 9DA; T.-0141-429 8888.

Pirrett, David, LLB, NP. Solicitor; Partner, Ross Harper at Hamilton, since 1973; b. 25.8.46, Glasgow; m., Catherine; 1 s.; 1 . Educ. Uddingston Grammar School; St. Andrews University. Secretary, Society of Solicitors of Hamilton, 1983-91, Vice-Dean, 1991-93, Dean, since 1993; Member, Council, Law Society of Scotland, since 1990, and Convener, Criminal Law Committee, since 1992. Deacon, Incorporation of Cordiners of Trades House of Glasgow, 1987-88. Recreations: golf; yachting. Address: (h.) 6 Lochaber Road, Strathaven, ML10 6HZ; T.-01357 22706.

Pitt, Professor Douglas Charles, BA, MA, PhD, FBIM. Professor of Organisational Analysis, Strathclyde University, since 1989; Dean, Strathclyde Business School; b. 13.7.43, Greenock; m., Jean Hamilton Spowart. Educ. Varndean Grammar School, Brighton; Exeter University; Manchester University. Executive Officer, Civil Service, 1961-64; Lecturer, then Senior Lecturer and Reader, Strathclyde University, 1973-89. Current research interest: telecommunications deregulation in Britain and the USA. Publications: The Post Office Telecommunications Function, 1980; Public Administration: An Introduction, 1980; Government Departments: An Organisational Analysis, 1981; The Computer Revolution in Public Administration, 1984. Recreations: German; riding; swimming; fishing; skiing; sailing; traditional jazz; bluegrass; opera. Address: (h.) 19 Waterfoot Road, Newton Mearns, Glasgow, G77 5RU; T.-0141-639 5359.

Pittock-Wesson, Joan Hornby, BA (Hons), MA, PhD. Director of Research, Thomas Reid Institute for Interdisciplinary Research in the Humanities, Sciences and Medicine, Aberdeen University, since 1990; b. 1.5.30, Featherstone; 1 s. Educ. Normanton High School for Girls; Victoria University of Manchester. Extra-Mural and Adult Education Lecturer, 1955-64; Lecturer in English, Senior Lecturer, Aberdeen University, 1966-95; founder Director, Cultural History Centre, Aberdeen University, 1985-94; founder Director, Institute for Cultural Studies (Thomas Reid Institute), 1990-94. Founder Editor, British Journal for Eighteenth Century Studies, 1978-80; President, British Society for Eighteenth Century Studies, 1980-82; British Representative, International Executive Committee, Eighteenth Century Studies, 1980-84. Publications: Ascendancy of Taste, 1973; Poetry and The Redemption of History, 1995. Recreation: walking. Address: (b.) Thomas Reid Institute, Humanity Manse, Aberdeen University, Aberdeen; T.-01224 272629.

Pitts, Professor Nigel Berry, BDS (Hons), PhD, FDS, RCSEng, FDS, RCSEdin. Director, Dental Health Services Research Unit, since 1985; Head, Department of Dental Health, Dundee University, since 1990, and Professor of Dental Health, since 1991; b. 1954, London; m., Elizabeth Ann; 3 s. Educ. Royal Liberty School; London Hospital Medical College Dental School, London University. House Officer/Senior House Officer, The London Hospital; Lecturer, Department of Conservative Dentistry, London Hospital Medical College Dental School; Lecturer, then Senior Lecturer, Department of Conservative Dentistry, University of Hong Kong; Director, Chief Scientist's Office Dental Health Services Research Unit. President, British Association for the Study of Community Dentistry; President, Diagnostic Systems Group, International Association for Dental Research. Recreations: family; photography. Address: (b.) Department of Dental Health, Dental School, Park Place, Dundee, DD1 4HR; T.-01382 635959.

Platt, Joseph, LLB. Founding Partner, Philpott Platt and Niblett, Solicitors, Dumbarton, and amalgamated firm of Crozier Philpott Platt and Niblet; part-time Tutor, Glasgow University; Member, Council, Law Society of Scotland; b. 22.5.51, Dumbarton; m., Christina Susan; 2 s. Educ. Dumbarton Academy; Glasgow University. Qualified as Solicitor, 1974; Partner, J.W. Dunn & Co., 1976. Recreations: hill-walking; photography; reading. Address: (b.) 21 Station Road, Dumbarton; T.-01389 730666.

Plotkin, Professor Gordon David, BSc, PhD, FRS, FRSE. Professor in Computer Science, Edinburgh University; Director, Laboratory for the Foundation of Computer Science; b. 9.9.46, Glasgow; m.; 1 s. Educ. Glasgow High School for Boys; Glasgow University; Edinburgh University. Lecturer, then Reader, Edinburgh University; Director, Laboratory for the Foundation of Computer Science; Member, Academia Europaea; Editor, Information and Control, Mathematical Structures in Computer Science, Theoretical Computer Science; Series Editor, Oxford University Press. Recreations: chess; hill-walking. Address: (b.) Department of Computer Science, King's Buildings, Edinburgh University, Edinburgh; T.-0131-650 5158.

Pollacchi, Derek Albert Paterson. Chief Executive, Central Scotland Healthcare NHS Trust, since 1994; b. 23.7.51, Dumbarton; m., Jean Lindsay Mullan; 2 d. Educ. St. Mungo's Academy, Glasgow. Various junior/middle management positions, 1972-79; Senior Administrator, Mearnskirk General Hospital, Glasgow, 1979-83, Leverndale Hospital, Glasgow, 1983-84; Director of Administrative Services, Lennox Castle Hospital/Stobill General Hospital and associated community health services, 1984-87; General Manager, Mental Handicap Services, Forth Valley Health Board, 1987-92; Chief Executive, Royal Scottish National Hospital and Community NHS Trust, 1993-94. Recreations: swimming; badminton; hill-walking; reading. Address: (b.) Old Denny Road, Larbert, FK5 4SD; T.-01324 570700.

Pollock, Sheriff Alexander, MA (Oxon), LLB. Sheriff of Grampian, Highland and Islands, at Aberdeen and Stonehaven, since 1993; b. 21.7.44, Glasgow; m., Verena Francesca Gertraud Alice Ursula Critchley; 1 s.; 1 d. Educ. Rutherglen Academy; Glasgow Academy; Brasenose College, Oxford; Edinburgh University; Perugia University. Partner, Bonar Mackenzie & Kermack, WS, 1971-73; called to Scottish Bar, 1973; Conservative candidate: West Lothian, General Election, February 1974, Moray and Nairn, General Election, October 1974; MP, Moray and Nairn, 1979-83, Moray, 1983-87; Parliamentary Private Secretary to Secretary of State for Scotland, 1982-86; PPS to Secretary of State for Defence, 1986-87; Advocate Depute, 1990-91; Sheriff (Floating) of Tayside, Central and Fife, at Stirling, 1991-93. Member, Queen's Bodyguard for Scotland (Royal Company of Archers), since 1984. Recreations: walking; music. Address: (h.) Drumdarrach, Forres, Moray.

Pollock, James A., FRICS. Chief Executive, Livingston Development Corporation. Address: (b.) Sidlaw House, Almondvale North, Livingston, EH54 6QA.

Polwarth, Lord (Henry Alexander Hepburne-Scott), TD, DL, FRSE. Vice-Lord-Lieutenant, Borders Region, 1975-91; Member, Queen's Bodyguard for Scotland (Royal Company of Archers); Chartered Accountant; b. 17.11.16; m., 1, Caroline Margaret Hay (m. diss.); 1 s.; 3 d.; 2, Jean Jauncey; 2 step s.; 1 step d. Educ. Eton College; King's College, Cambridge. Served Second World War as Captain, Lothians and Border Yeomanry; former Partner, Chiene and Tait, CA, Edinburgh; Governor, Bank of Scotland, 1966-72, Director, 1974-87; Chairman, General Accident, Fire & Life Assurance Company, 1968-72; Director, ICI Ltd., 1969-72, 1974-81; Director, Halliburton Co., 1974-87; Director, Canadian Pacific Ltd., 1975-86; Director, Sun Life Assurance Co. of Canada, 1975-84; Minister of State, Scottish Office, 1972-74; Chairman, later President, Scottish Council (Development and Industry), 1955-72; Chairman, Scottish Forestry Trust, 1987-89; Member, Franco-British Council, 1981-89; Chairman, Scottish National Orchestra Society, 1975-79; Chancellor, Aberdeen University, 1966-86; Hon. LLD: St. Andrews, Aberdeen; Hon. DLitt, Heriot-Watt; DUniv, Stirling. Address: Easter Harden, Hawick; T.-Hawick 372069.

Ponton, Professor John Wylie, BSc, PhD, FIChemE, FEng. ICI Professor of Chemical Engineering, Edinburgh University, since 1989; b. 2.5.43, Edinburgh; m., Katherine Jane Victoria Eachus. Educ. Melville College, Edinburgh; Edinburgh University. Recreations: engineering; amateur radio; music. Address: (b.) Department of Chemical Engineering, Edinburgh University, EH9 3JL; T.-0131-650 4860.

Poodle, Thomas, CEng, MICE, FIWEM. Depute Director (Chief Engineer), Clyde River Purification Board, since 1989; b. 25.7.43, Denny; m., Joan; 1 s.; 1 d. Educ. Denny High School; Graeme High School, Falkirk; Strathclyde University. Clyde River Purification Board: Assistant Hydrologist, 1968-75, Hydrologist, 1975-88. Member, British Standards Technical Committee. Recreations: sailing; skiing. Address: (b.) Rivers House, Murray Road, East Kilbride, Glasgow, G75 0LA; T.-013552 38181.

Poole, Sheriff Isobel Anne, LLB. Sheriff of Lothian and Borders; b. 9.12.41, Oxford. Educ. Oxford High School for Girls; Edinburgh University. Advocate. Recreations: country; arts; gardens; friends. Address: (b.) Sheriffs' Chambers, Sheriff Court, Edinburgh.

Pople, Andrew Howard, MBA. Chief Executive, Scottish Mutual, since 1994; Director, Life Division, Abbey National, since 1994; b. 15.11.57, Liverpool; m., Jane Hoskins; 1 s.; 2 d. Educ. Merchant Taylors' School, Crosby; Sussex University. Ministry of Defence, 1982-83; Bank of England, 1983-88. Recreations: swimming; cycling. Address: (b.) 301 St. Vincent Street, Glasgow, G2 5HN; T.-0141-275 9400.

Porteous, Brian William, BSc (Hons), MILAM, DipILAM. Depute Director, Parks and Recreation, Glasgow City Council, since 1994; b. 6.2.51, Falkirk; m., Shena; 3 s. Educ. Falkirk High School; St. Andrews University; Moray House College of Education; Loughborough University of Technology. Joined Scottish Sports Council as Development Officer, 1979, appointed Director of Operations, 1989. Honorary Secretary, British Orienteering Federation, 1974-76; former Member, Board, National Coaching Foundation. Publication: Orienteering, 1979. Recreations: golf; orienteering; amateur opera/musicals; caravanning. Address: (h.) Rannoch Lodge, 11a Marmion Road, North Berwick, East Lothian, EH39 4PG; T.-01620 893482.

Porter, Professor Richard William, MB, ChB, FRCSE. Director of Education and Training, Royal College of Surgeons of Edinburgh, since 1995; b. 16.2.35, Doncaster; m., Christine; 4 s. Educ. Oundle School; Edinburgh University. Consultant Orthopaedic Surgeon, Doncaster Royal Infirmary, 1978-91; Sir Harry Platt Chair of Orthopaedic Surgery, Aberdeen University, 1991-95. Chairman, Educational Committee, British Orthopaedic Association. Publication: Management of Back Pain, 1993. Address: (b.) Royal College of Surgeons of Edinburgh, Nicolson Street, Edinburgh EH8 9DW.

Potter, Brian Thomas, BSc, MB, ChB, MRCGP. Scottish Secretary, British Medical Association, since 1995; b. 25.8.52, Edinburgh; 1 s.; 2 d. Educ. Scotus Academy, Edinburgh; Edinburgh University Medical School. Registrar posts, Accident and Emergency Medicine, Renal Medicine, Royal Infirmary, Edinburgh, and Geriatric Medicine, City Hospital, Edinburgh; Principal in General Practice, Edinburgh; Medical Officer, Marks and Spencer, Edinburgh; Medical Practitioner, Glencorse Army Depot; Occupational Physician, City Hospital; Senior Medical Officer, Scottish Office Home and Health Department, 1992-95. Former Secretary, Lothian Division, BMA; Secretary, Lothian Area Medical Committee; former Member, Scottish Council, BMA. Recreations: swimming; keep-fit; singing. Address: (b.) BMA, Scottish Office, 3 Hill Place, Edinburgh EH8 9EQ; T.-0131-662 4820.

Pounder, Professor Derrick John, MB, ChB, FRCPA, FFPathRCPI, FCAP, MRCPath, FHKCPath. Professor of Forensic Medicine, Dundee University, since 1987; b. 25.2.49, Pontypridd; m., Georgina Kelly; 1 s.; 2 d. Educ. Pontypridd Boys' Grammar; Birmingham University. Senior Lecturer (Forensic Pathology), University of Adelaide; Deputy Chief Medical Examiner, Edmonton, Alberta, and Associate Professor, Universities of Alberta and Calgary, 1985-87. Freeman of Llantrisant. Recreations: photography; medieval architecture; almost lost causes. Address: (b.) Department of Forensic Medicine, Royal Infirmary, Dundee, DD1 9ND; T.-01382 200794.

Power, Graham, QPM, MA (Oxon). Deputy Chief Constable, Lothian and Borders Police, since 1994; b. 2.6.47, Middlesbrough; m.; 2 s.; 1 d. Educ. Stainsby Boys School, Middlesbrough; Queen's College, Oxford. Constable to Superintendent, Cleveland, 1966-88; Chief Superintendent, North Yorks, Harrogate, 1988-91; Assistant Chief Constable, Lothian and Borders, 1991-94. Recreation: trout fishing. Address: (b.) Police HQ, Fettes Avenue, Edinburgh, EH4 1RB; T.-0131-311 3100.

Prag, Thomas Gregory Andrew, MA, FIMgt. Managing Director, Moray Firth Radio; b. 2.1.47, London; m., Angela; 3 s. Educ. Westminster School; Brasenose College, Oxford. Joined BBC, 1968, as Studio Manager; Producer, BBC Radio Oxford; Programme Organiser, BBC Radio Highland; first Chief Executive, Moray Firth Radio, 1981. Director, Inverness, Loch Ness and Nairn Tourist Board; Trustee, Highland Community Foundation; Council Member, Radio Academy; Director, Association of Independent Radio Companies. Recreations: good intentions towards restoration of 1950 Daimler; keeping clock collection wound; family; growing vegetables; chasing deer off vegetables. Address: (b.) Moray Firth Radio, PO Box 271, Inverness, IV3 6SF.

Pratt, Roger Allan. Director, The Conservative Party in Scotland, since 1993; b. 28.12.50, Birmingham; m., Lynn. Educ. King Edwards Five Ways Grammar School. YC Organiser and Youth Officer, 1971-74; Conservative Party Agent, 1975-76; National YC Organiser, 1976-79; Agent, 1980-84; Deputy Central Office Agent, N.W. Area, 1984-89; Central Office Agent, then Regional Director, North West Area, 1989-93. Address: (b.) Suite 1/1, 14 Links Place, Leith, Edinburgh, EH6 7EZ; T.-0131-555 2900.

Prescott, Professor Laurie F., MA, MB, BChir, MD, FRCPEdin, FRSE, FRCP, FFPM. Honorary Consultant Physician, Edinburgh Royal Infirmary, since 1969; Professor of Clinical Pharmacology, Edinburgh University, since 1985; b. 13.5.34; London; m.; 1 s.; 3 d. Educ. Hitchin Boys Grammar School; Cambridge University; Middlesex Hospital Medical School, London. Research Fellow, Johns Hopkins Hospital, Baltimore, 1963-65; Lecturer in Therapeutics, Aberdeen University, 1965-69; Senior Lecturer in Clinical Pharmacology, Edinburgh University, 1969-74, Reader, 1974-85. British Pharmacological Society Lilly Prize, 1978. Recreations: music; gardening; sailing. Address: (h.) Redfern, 24 Colinton Road, Edinburgh, EH10 5EQ; T.-0131-447 2571.

Prescott, Paul G., PhD. Director, Railtrack Scotland Zone, since 1993; b. 12.1.51, Oldbury; m.; 1 s.; 1 d. Educ. King Edward's School, Birmingham; Gonville and Caius College, Cambridge; Imperial College, London. Water Resources Board, 1973-76; Marketing Manager, BR Provincial Sector, 1985-90; Planning and Marketing Manager, ScotRail, 1990-93. Recreations: hill-walking; genealogy; linguistics; travel. Address: (b.) Buchanan House, 58 Port Dundas Road, Glasgow, G4 0LQ; T.-0141-335 2424.

Presslie, Sheriff George. Sheriff of Lothian and Borders. Address: (b.) Edinburgh Sheriff Court, 27 Chambers Street, Edinburgh, EH1 1LB.

Preston, David Michael, LLB, NP. Solicitor, since 1976; b. 26.8.52, Glasgow; m., Sheila Elizabeth; 2 s. Educ. Hillhead High School; Dundee University. Part-time Depute Procurator Fiscal, 1976-79; Clerk to General Commissioners of Income Tax, since 1976; Registrar, Episcopal Diocese of Argyll and the Isles, since 1977; Partner, Hosack and Sutherland, since 1978; Member, Council, Law Society of Scotland, since 1990 (Convenor, Update Committee, since 1992). Past Chairman and first Hon. President, Oban Round Table; Chairman, Oban Youth and Community Association, since 1980; Commodore, Oban Sailing Club, 1992-93; Secretary, Atlantis Leisure, since 1991. Recreations: sailing; skiing; rugby spectating; logistical supporter (travel and finance) of two sons. Address: (h.) Westbank, Duncraggan Road, Oban; T.-01631 563228.

Preston, George Dawson Chrystal, MA. Secretary and Treasurer, Queen's Nursing Institute Scotland, since 1992; b. 20.4.31, Hampton; m., Elizabeth Anne Rennie; 1 d. Educ. Fettes College; Gonville and Caius College, Cambridge. Science Staff, Fettes College, 1955-91, Housemaster, 1959-64, and 1969-81, Senior Master, 1981-91. Keeper of Records, Fettes College. Recreations: gardening; computing; social court games. Address: (b.) 31 Castle Terrace, Edinburgh, EH1 2EL; T.-0131-229 2333.

Preston, Ian Mathieson Hamilton, CBE, BSc, PhD, FEng, MInstP, FIEE. Chief Executive, Scottish Power, 1990-95; Chairman, Scottish Council Development and Industry, since 1993; Chairman, Mining (Scotland), since 1995; Chairman Designate, East of Scotland Water Authority, since 1995; b. 18.7.32, Bournemouth; m., Sheila Hope Pringle; 2 s. Educ. Kilmarnock Academy; Glasgow University. University Assistant Lecturer, 1957-59; joined SSEB as Assistant Reactor Physicist, 1959; various appointments until Chief Engineer, Generation Design and Construction Division, 1972; Director General, Central Electricity Generating Board, Generation Development and Construction Division, 1977-83; Deputy Chairman, South of Scotland Electricity Board, 1985-90. Non Executive Director: Morgan Grenfell (Scotland), since 1994, Clydeport PLC, since 1994, Motherwell Bridge, since 1995. Chairman, British Hydromechanics Research Association, 1985-89. Recreations: angling; gardening. Address: (b.) Scottish Power PLC, 1 Atlantic Quay, Glasgow, G2 8SP; T.-0141-248 8200.

Preston, Robert John, ACIS. Finance Director/Company Secretary, Marshall Food Group Ltd., since 1989; b. 23.2.44, Watlington; m., Sandra Lena; 1 s. Educ. Grove Academy, Dundee; Dundee Institute of Art and Technology. Joined Marshall Food Group, 1989. Member, Council, CBI Scotland. Recreations: golf; reading; sports spectating. Address: (b.) Marshall Food Group Ltd., Newbridsge, Midlothian; T.-0131-333 3341.

Price, Rev. Peter Owen, CBE, QHC, BA, FPhS. Minister, Blantyre Old Parish Church, Glasgow, since 1985; b. 18.4.30, Swansea; m., 1, Margaret Winifred Trevan (deceased); 3 d. Educ. Wyggeston School, Leicester; Didsbury Theological College, Bristol; Open University. Chaplain, Royal Navy, 1960-84, latterly Principal Chaplain, Church of Scotland and Free Churches (Naval), Ministry of Defence, 1981-84; appointed Honorary Chaplain to the Queen, 1981. Recreations: clay pigeon shooting; rugby; warm water sailing. Address: The Manse of Blantyre, High Blantyre, Glasgow, G72 9UA; T.-01698 823130.

Prickett, Professor (Alexander Thomas) Stephen, MA, PhD, DipEd, FAHA. Regius Professor of English Language and Literature, Glasgow University, since 1990; b. 4.6.39, Freetown, Sierra Leone; m., Maria Angelica; 2 d. Educ. Kent College, Canterbury; Trinity Hall, Cambridge; University College, Oxford. English Teacher, Methodist College, Uzuakoli, E. Nigeria, 1962-64; Lecturer/Reader, Sussex University, 1967-82; Professor of English, Australian National University, Canberra, 1983-89. Publications: Do It Yourself Doom, 1962; Coleridge and Wordsworth: the Poetry of Growth, 1970; Romanticism and Religion, 1976; Victorian Fantasy, 1979; Words and the Word: language poetics and Biblical interpretation, 1986; England and the French Revolution, 1988; Reading the Text: Biblical criticism and literary theory, 1991. Recreations: walking; skiing; tennis; drama. Address: (b.) Department of English Literature, Glasgow University, Glasgow; T.-0141-339 8855.

Pride, Professor Stephen James, BSc, PhD, FRSE. Titular Professor in Mathematics, Glasgow University, since 1993 (Reader in Mathematics, 1987-93); b. 8.1.49, Melbourne. Educ. Hampton High School, Melbourne; Monash University, Melbourne; Australian National University, Canberra. Research Fellow, Open University, 1974-78; Temporary Lecturer in Mathematics, King's College, London University, 1978-79; Lecturer in Mathematics, Glasgow University, 1979-87. Member, Editorial Board, London Mathematical Society. Publications: more than 50 articles on group theory. Recreations: sport and outdoor activities; travelling; cinema; gardening. Address: (h.) 54 Airlie Street, Glasgow, G12 9SN; T.-0141-339 7395.

Priest, Professor Eric Ronald, BSc, MSc, PhD, FRSE. Professor of Theoretical Solar Physics, St. Andrews University, since 1983; b. 7.11.43, Birmingham; m., Clare Wilson; 3 s.; 1 d. Educ. King Edward VI School, Birmingham; Nottingham University; Leeds University. St. Andrews University: Lecturer in Applied Mathematics, 1968, Reader, 1977; SERC Senior Fellow, 1992-97. Elected Member, Norwegian Academy of Sciences and Letters, 1994. Recreations: bridge; walking; swimming; swingnastics; children. Address: (b.) Mathematical and Computational Sciences Department, St. Andrews University, St. Andrews, KY16 9SS; T.-01334 463709.

Pringle, Reginald Vincent, MA, MLitt. Librarian, Aberdeen University, since 1988; b. 23.12.42, Edinburgh; m., Pamela Margaret; 3 s. Educ. George Heriot's School; Edinburgh University. Associate Librarian, St. Andrews University, 1981-88. Project Director, Grampian Information, since 1990. Recreations: music; hill-walking; squash. Address: (h.) 47 Malcolm's Mount, Stonehaven, AB3 2SR; T.-01569 766405.

Pringle, Robert, MB, ChB, ChM, FRCS(Eng), FRCS(Edin), FRCS(Glas). Consultant Surgeon, Ninewells Hospital, Dundee, 1974-92; Honorary Senior Lecturer, Dundee University, 1967-92; Member, Council, Medical and Dental Defence Union of Scotland, since 1979; b. 23.8.27, Paisley; m., Margaret Anne Mitchell; 1 s.; 2 d. Educ. Camphill School, Paisley; Glasgow University. RAF, 1951-55 (Squadron Leader); Hall Fellow in Surgery, then Registrar in Surgery, Glasgow Royal Infirmary, 1956-59; Senior Registrar in Surgery, Royal Victoria Infirmary, Newcastle upon Tyne, 1960-63; First Assistant in Surgery, Newcastle upon Tyne University, 1963-64; Senior Lecturer in Surgery, St. Andrews University, 1964-67; Consultant Surgeon, Dundee Royal Infirmary, 1964-74. Chairman, Surgical Section, National Medical Consultative Committee, 1987-89; Member, Scottish Sub-Committee on Distinction and Meritorious Service Awards, 1991-93. Publications: papers and books on various gastroenterological, surgical and scientific topics. Recreations: flying; piano; golf; cycling. Address: (h.) Taynuilt, Kilspindie, Rait, Perthshire, PH2 7RX; T.-01821 670289.

Pritchard, Kenneth William, OBE, BL, WS. Secretary, The Law Society of Scotland, since 1976; b. 14.11.33, London; Honorary Sheriff, Dundee; m., Gretta Murray; 2 s.; 1 d. Educ. Dundee High School; Fettes College; St. Andrews University. National Service, Argyll and Sutherland Highlanders, 1955-57; 2nd Lt., 1956; TA, 1957-62 (Captain); joined J. & J. Scrimgeour, Solicitors, Dundee, 1957; Senior Partner, 1970-76; Member: Sheriff Court Rules Council, 1973-76, Lord Dunpark's Committee considering Reparation upon Criminal Conviction, 1973-77; Hon. Visiting Professor, Law School, Strathclyde University; Hon. Member, Law Institute of Victoria, 1985; Hon. Member, Law Society of New Zealand, 1987; Hon. Member, Faculty of Procurators and Solicitors in Dundee; Member, University Court of Dundee, 1983-93; President, Dundee High School Old Boys Club, 1975-76. Recreation: golf. Address: (h.) 36 Ravelston Dykes, Edinburgh, EH4 3EB; T.-0131-332 8584.

Procter, Rev. Robert Hendy, MA. Secretary, Scottish Council, The Scout Association, since 1982; b. 22.1.31, Alloa; m., Elizabeth Rosemary; 1 s.; 2 d. Educ. Fettes College; Trinity Hall, Cambridge. Commissioned, Royal Corps of Signals, 1950; Patons & Baldwins Ltd., 1954-79 (General Manager, from 1969); Director, John Gladstone & Co. Ltd., Galashiels, 1980-82. General Commissioner of Income Tax, Clackmannan Division, 1976-80; Honorary Sheriff, Tayside Central and Fife, at Alloa, 1975; Edinburgh Diocese training for ministry, 1988-91; Member, Christ Church Morningside Ministry Team, 1991; ordained priest, 1994; Member, Lothian Region Valuation Appeal Committee, 1994. Recreations: hill-walking; choral singing. Address: (h.) 2 Braid Avenue, Morningside, Edinburgh, EH10 6DR; T.-0131-447 1140.

Prosser, Professor James Anthony William (Tony), LLB. John Millar Professor of Law, Glasgow University, since 1992; b. 3.5.54, Ludlow. Educ. Ludlow Grammar School; Liverpool University. Research Assistant in Law, Southampton University, 1974-76; Lecturer in Law, Hull University, 1976-79; Lecturer, Senior Lecturer, Sheffield University, 1980-92; Jean Monnet Fellow, European University Institute, Florence, 1987-88. Publications: Test Cases for the Poor; Nationalised Industries and Public Control; Privatizing Public Enterprises (Co-author); Waiving the Roles (Co-editor). Recreations: walking; cinema; jazz. Address: (b.) School of Law, Glasgow University, Glasgow, G12 8QQ; T.-0141-339 8855, Ext. 4180.

Prosser, (Leslie) Charles, DFA, DAEd. Secretary, Royal Fine Art Commission for Scotland, since 1976; b. 27.10.39, Harrogate; m., Coral; 1 s.; 2 d. Educ. Bath Academy of Art at Corsham Court; Slade School of Fine Art, London University. Assistant Lecturer in Fine Art, Blackpool School of Art, 1962-64; Fine Art research, Royal Academy, Stockholm, 1964-65; Lecturer in Fine Art, Leeds/Jacob Kramer College of Art, 1965-76; research in Art Education, Leeds University, 1974-75. Leverhulme European Arts Research Award, 1964. Recreations: Scottish dancing and hill-walking. Address: (h.) 28 Mayfield Terrace, Edinburgh, EH9 1RZ; T.-0131-668 1141.

Prosser, Hon. Lord QC, MA (Oxon), LLB, HonFRIAS. Senator of the College of Justice in Scotland and Lord of Session, since 1986; b. 23.11.34, Edinburgh; m., Vanessa Lindsay; 2 s.; 2 d. Educ. Edinburgh Academy; Corpus Christi College, Oxford; Edinburgh University. Advocate, 1962; Queen's Counsel, 1974; Vice-Dean, Faculty of Advocates, 1979-83, Dean of Faculty, 1983-86. Chairman, Royal Lyceum Theatre Company, 1987-92; Chairman, Scottish Architectural Education Trust; Chairman, Scottish Historic Buildings Trust; Chairman, Chamber Group of Scotland; Chairman, Royal Fine Art Commission for Scotland, 1980-95. Address: 7 Randolph Crescent, Edinburgh, EH3 7TH; T.-0131-225 2709.

Proudfoot, Edwina Valmai Windram, MA, DipEd, FSA, FSA Scot, MIFA. Archaeologist; Director, St. Andrews Heritage Services, since 1988; Honorary Research Fellow, St. Andrews University, since 1985; b. 9.3.35, Dover; m., Professor V. Bruce Proudfoot (qv); 2 s. Educ. Invergordon Academy; Inverness Royal Academy; Edinburgh University. Lecturer (including Adult Education) in Archaeology, since 1959; director of excavations, numerous projects; Editor, Discovery and Excavation in Scotland, 1977-87; President, Council for Scottish Archaeology, 1983-89; Founder, first Chairman, Tayside and Fife Archaeological Committee, 1975-82; Member, Ancient Monuments Board for Scotland, since 1986; Chairman, St. Andrews Preservation Trust, 1988-93; Council Member, National Trust for Scotland, 1984-89 and since 1993; Member, Executive Committee, NTS, since 1994. Recreations: gardening; music; walking. Address: 12 Wardlaw Gardens, St. Andrews, KY16 9DW; T.-01334 473293.

Proudfoot, Professor V. Bruce, BA, PhD, FSA, FRSE, FRSGS, FSA Scot. General Secretary, Royal Society of Edinburgh; Emeritus Professor of Geography, St. Andrews University; b. 24.9.30, Belfast; m., Edwina Valmai Windram Field; 2 s. Educ. Royal Belfast Academical Institution; Queen's University, Belfast. Research Officer, Nuffield Quaternary Research Unit, Queen's University, Belfast, 1954-58; Lecturer in Geography: Queen's University, Belfast, 1958-59, Durham University, 1959-67; Hatfield College, Durham: Tutor, 1960-63, Librarian, 1963-65; Visiting Fellow, University of Auckland and Commonwealth Visiting Fellow, Australia, 1966; Alberta University, Edmonton: Associate Professor, 1967-70, Professor, 1970-74; Co-ordinator, Socio-Economic Opportunity Studies and Staff Consultant, Alberta Human Resources Research Council, 1971-72; Professor of Geography, St. Andrews University, 1974-93. Royal Society of Edinburgh: Convener, Earth Sciences Committee, 1983-85, Vice-President, 1985-88, Convener, Grants Committee, 1988-91; Chairman, Society for Landscape Studies, 1979-83; Vice-President, Society of Antiquaries of Scotland, 1982-85; President, Section H, BAAS, 1985; Chairman, Rural Geography Study Group, Institute of British Geographers, 1980-84; Vice-President and Chairman of Council, since 1993, Chairman of Dundee Centre, since 1993, Royal Scottish Geographical Society; Hon. President, Scottish Association of Geography Teachers, 1982-84; Trustee, National Museum of Antiquities of Scotland, 1982-85. Recreation: gardening. Address: (h.) Westgate, Wardlaw Gardens, St. Andrews, KY16 9DW; T.-01334 473293.

Provan, James Lyal Clark. Member, European Parliament, South Downs West, since 1994 (Chief Whip Conservative Group), Member: Fisheries Committee, Agricultural Committee, Transport and Tourism Committee; Chairman, EP Tourism Group; Member (Conservative), European Parliament, NE Scotland, 1979-89; Chairman, Rowett Research Institute, Aberdeen (Board Member, since 1990); Farmer; b. 19.12.36, Glenfarg, Perthshire; m., Roweena Adele Lewis; 2 s.; 1 d. Educ. Ardvreck School, Crieff; Oundle School, Northants; Royal Agricultural College, Cirencester. National Farmers Union of Scotland: Area President, Kinross, 1965, Fife and Kinross, 1971; Tayside Regional Councillor, 1978-81; Member, Tay River Purification Board, 1978-81; European Democratic (Conservative) Spokesman on Agriculture and Fisheries, 1981-87; Questor of European Parliament, 1987-89; former Executive Director, Scottish Financial Enterprise; Chairman, McIntosh of Dyce Ltd., McIntosh Donald Ltd., 1989-94; Member, Agriculture and Food Research Council, 1990-94. Recreations: country pursuits; sailing; flying; politics; agriculture. Address: Summerfield, Glenfarg, Perthshire PH2 9QD; Middle Lodge, Barns Green, Horsham, West Sussex RH13 7NL.

Pugh, Professor John Richard, BSc, PhD, CPhys, CEng, MInstP, MIEE. Head, Department of Physical Sciences and Professor of Physics, Glasgow Caledonian University, since 1992; Member, Board of Directors, Centre for Industrial Bulk Solids Handling, since 1993; b. 16.4.52, Shrewsbury; m., Christine Haldane; 3 s. Educ. Cumbernauld High School; Whitley Bay Grammar School; Glasgow University. Research Fellow, Glasgow University, 1976-80; Physicist, Barr and Stroud Ltd., Glasgow, 1980-91; Lecturer, then Senior Lecturer, Glasgow College, 1981-90; Professor of Physics and Depute Head, Glasgow Polytechnic, 1990-92. Tuba player, Bellshill Brass Band. Recreations: music; house restoration; gardening. Address: (b.) Department of Physical Sciences, Glasgow Caledonian University, Cowcaddens Road, Glasgow, G4 0BA; T.-0141-331 3670.

Punter, Professor David Godfrey, BA, MA, PhD. Professor of English Studies, Stirling University, since 1988; b. 19.11.49, London; m., Caroline Mary Case-Punter; 1 s.; 2 d. Educ. John Lyon School, Harrow; Fitzwilliam College, Cambridge. Lecturer, University of East Anglia, 1973-84; Professor, Fudan University, Shanghai, 1983; Senior Lecturer, University of East Anglia, 1984-86; Director, Development of University English Teaching Project, 1985-86; Professor, Chinese University of Hong Kong, 1986-88. Publications: eight books; 31 articles; 26 chapters contributed; two books edited. Recreations: child-minding; dog-minding; walking; squash. Address: (b.) Stirling University, Stirling; FK9 4LA; T.-01786 467495, Ext. 2362.

Punter, Professor John Vincent, BA, MA, PhD, MRTPI. Professor of Urban and Regional Planning, Centre for Planning, Strathclyde University, since 1993; b. 15.12.45, Bristol; m., Lesley B.V.; 2 d. Educ. Bristol and Thornbury Grammar Schools; universities of Newcastle upon Tyne and Toronto. Assistant Professor, York University, Toronto, 1972-75; Lecturer/Senior Lecturer, Reading University, 1975-93. British Planning Education Award, 1992. Publications: DOE, Planning Control in Western Europe, 1989; Design Control in Bristol, 1990. Recreations: mountain scrambling; football. Address: (b.) Centre for Planning, 50 Richmond Street, Glasgow, G1 1XN; T.-041-552 4400, Ext. 3906.

Purser, John Whitley, MA, PhD. Composer and Lecturer; Poet, Playwright, Musicologist, and Broadcaster; b. 10.2.42, Glasgow; 1 s.; 1 d. Educ. Fettes College; Glasgow University; Royal Scottish Academy of Music and Drama. Part-time Lecturer in English Literature, Glasgow University, 1981-85; Manager, Scottish Music Information Centre, 1985-87; compositions include two operas, numerous orchestral and chamber works; three books of poetry, The Counting Stick, A Share of the Wind and Amoretti; six radio plays and two radio series, A Change of Tune and Scotland's Music; music history: Is the Red Light On?, Scotland's Music; literary criticism: The Literary Works of Jack B. Yeats; awards: McVitie Scottish Writer of the Year, 1992; Glenfiddich Living Scotland Award, 1991; Giles Cooper Award, 1992; New York International Radio Festival Gold Medal, 1992; Sony Gold Medal, 1993; Oliver Brown Award, 1993; Scottish Heritage Award, 1993; Hon. Life Member, Saltire Society, 1993. Recreations: numerous. Address: (b.) 29 Banavie Road, Glasgow, G11 5AW; T.-0141-339 5292.

Purslow, Christopher George, BArch, RIBA, FRSA. Director of Architecture and Related Services, City of Glasgow, since 1988; b. 27.3.46, Shrewsbury. Educ. High School, Newcastle under Lyme; Bristol University. Courtaulds Ltd., Coventry, 1967; Tarmac Ltd., Wolverhampton, 1968; Philip Johnson, Architect, New York, 1969; Rice/Roberts, Architects, London, 1972; LB of Islington, 1974; Borough Architect, Islington, 1983-88. Recreations: theatre; music; mountains; architecture. Address: (b.) 20 Trongate, Glasgow, G1 5EY; T.-0141-227 5379.

Purton, Patricia. Director, Royal College of Midwives, Scottish Board. Address: (b.) 37 Frederick Street, Edinburgh, EH2 1EP.

Purves, David, BSc, PhD. Editor, Lallans Magazine, since 1987; Playwright; b. 9.4.24, Selkirk; m., Lilian Rosemary; 3 s. Educ. Galashiels Academy; Edinburgh University. Head, Trace Element Department, Edinburgh School of Agriculture, 1956-82; Supervisor, Central Analytical Department, 1982-87; author of Trace Element Contamination of the Environment, 1977; poetry collection: Thrawart Threipins, 1976; many poems in Scots published; Fringe First play, The Puddock an the Princess and rendering in Scots of Macbeth published, 1992; Past Preses, Scots Language Society. Address: (h.) 8 Strathalmond Road, Edinburgh, EH4 8AD; T.-0131-339 7929.

Purves-Hume, Ian Campbell, FIMgt. Director, Royal Scottish Agricultural Benevolent Institution, since 1990; b. 22.7.38, London; m., Jill Cairns Fairbairn; 2 d. Educ. Ottershaw; Royal Military Academy, Sandhurst. Army Officer, Argyll and Sutherland Highlanders, 1958-90, to rank of Brigadier. Recreations: walking; bird-watching. Address: (b.) RSABI, Ingliston, Edinburgh, EH28 8NB; T.-0131-333 1023.

Purvis, John Robert, CBE, MA (Hons). International Business Consultant (Managing Partner, Purvis & Co.), since 1973; Director, James River UK Holdings Ltd., since 1984; Director, Johnson Fry European Utilities Trust PLC, since 1994; Director, Jamont NV, since 1994; Director, AFV (UK) Ltd, since 1995; b. 6.7.38, St. Andrews; m., Louise Spears Durham; 1 s.; 2 d. Educ. Glenalmond; St. Andrews University. 2nd Lt., Scots Guards, 1956-58; First National City Bank (Citibank NA), London, New York City, Milan, 1962-69; Treasurer, Noble Grossart Ltd., Edinburgh, 1969-73; Director and Secretary, Brigton Farms Ltd., 1969-86; Managing Director, Founder, Owner, Gilmerton Management Services Ltd., 1973-92; Member, European Parliament, Mid Scotland and Fife, 1979-84 (Deputy Chief Whip, Group Spokesman on Monetary Affairs, Energy, Research and Technology) Vice Chairman, European Parliament Delegation to the Gulf States; Chairman, IBA Scottish Advisory Committee, 1985-89; Member for Scotland, IBA, 1985-89; Member of Council, St. Leonards School, St. Andrews, 1981-89; Chairman, Economic Affairs Committee, Scottish Conservative and Unionist Association, since 1986, Vice-President of Association, 1987-89; Member, Scottish Advisory

Committee on Telecommunications, since 1990. Recreations: Italy and Scotland. Address: Gilmerton House, Dunino, St. Andrews, KY16 8NB; T.-01334 75830.

Pyper, Mark Christopher Spring-Rice, BA. Headmaster, Gordonstoun School, since 1990; b. 13.8.47, Seaford; m., Jennifer L.; 1 s.; 2 d. Educ. Winchester College; Oxford University; London University. Assistant Master, Stoke Brunswick School, East Grinstead, 1966-68; Assistant Master, then Joint Headmaster, St. Wilfrid's School, Seaford, 1969-79; Registrar, Housemaster, then Deputy Headmaster, Sevenoaks School, 1979-90; Director, Sevenoaks Summer Festival, 1979-90. Address: (h.) Headmaster's House, Gordonstoun School, Elgin, IV30 2RF; T.-01343 830445.

Q

Quinault, Francis Charles, BSc, PhD. Hebdomadar, St. Andrews University, since 1994; former Assistant Principal for External Affairs and Senior Lecturer in Psychology, St. Andrews University; b. 8.5.43, London; m., Wendy Ann Horton; 1 s.; 2 d. Educ. Dulwich College; St. Catharine's College, Cambridge; Bristol University. Ford Foundation Scholar, Oslo University, 1969-70. Member, National Committee for the Training of University Teachers, 1981-87. Recreations: theatre; singing; Japanese; hill-walking. Address: (b.) University of St. Andrews, 71 North Street, St. Andrews, KY16 9AJ; T.-01334 462240.

Quinn, Terence James. Editor, Daily Record, since 1994; b. 17.11.51; m., Patricia Anna-Maria Gillespie; 1 s.; 1 d. Educ. St. Aloysius College, Glasgow. Editor: Telegraph & Argus, Bradford, 1984-89, Evening News, Edinburgh, 1989-92; Deputy Editorial Director, 1992-94, Editorial Director, 1994, Thomson Regional Newspapers. Recreations: tennis; reading; newspapers. Address: (b.) Daily Record, Anderston Quay, Glasgow, G3 8DA; T.-0141-248 7000.

R

Racey, Professor Paul Adrian, MA, PhD, DSc, FIBiol, FRSE. Regius Professor of Natural History, Aberdeen University, since 1993 (Professor of Zoology, 1985-93); b. 7.5.44, Wisbech, Cambridgeshire; m., Anna Priscilla Notcutt; 3 s. Educ. Ratcliffe College, Leicester; Downing College, Cambridge. Rothamsted Experimental Station, Harpenden, 1965-66; Zoological Society of London, 1966-70; Unit of Reproductive Biology, Liverpool University, 1970-73; joined Department of Zoology, Aberdeen University, 1973. Recreations: riding; sailing; skiing. Address: (b.) Department of Zoology, Aberdeen University, Aberdeen, AB9 2TN; T.-01224 272858.

Rae, Hugh Craufurd. Novelist; b. 22.11.35, Glasgow; m., Elizabeth Dunn; 1 d. Educ. Knightswood School. Prolific popular novelist; author of more than 50 tiles, under a variety of pseudonyms, including Stuart Stern, James Albany and Jessica Stirling; books include (as Hugh C. Rae) Skinner, The Marksman, The Shooting Gallery, Harkfast and Privileged Strangers and (as Jessica Stirling) The Spoiled Earth, The Hiring Fair, The Dark Pasture, Treasures on Earth, Creature Comforts, Hearts of Gold, The Good Provider, The Asking Price, The Wise Child, The Welcome Light. Recreation: golf. Address: (h.) Drumore Farm Cottage, Balfron Station, Stirlingshire.

Rae, Rita Emilia Anna, QC, LLB (Hons). Advocate. Educ. St. Patrick's High School, Coatbridge; Edinburgh University. Apprentice, Biggart, Lumsden & Co., Glasgow, 1972-74; Assistant Solicitor: Balfour & Manson, Edinburgh, 1974, Biggart, Baillie & Gifford, Glasgow, 1974-76; Solicitor and Partner, Ross Harper & Murphy, Glasgow, 1976-81; Advocate, 1982. Recreations: theatre; driving; walking; opera; music. Address: (h.) 73 Fotheringay Road, Glasgow; T.-0141-423 0781.

Rae, Scott Alexander, LLB (Hons), WS, NP, TEP. Partner, Morton Fraser Milligan WS, Edinburgh, since 1970; b. 17.12.44, Edinburgh; m., Annabel Riach; 3 s. Educ. Daniel Stewarts College, Edinburgh; Edinburgh University. Sometime Tutor and Course Leader, Edinburgh University; Law Society of Scotland Examiner in Taxation and Chairman, Board of Examiners. Member, VAT Tribunal (Scotland); Clerk, Incorporated Trades of Edinburgh; Secretary, International Academy of Estate and Trust Law; Collector, Society of Writers to the Signet. Recreations: fishing; farming; travel. Address: (b.) 15-19 York Place, Edinburgh; T.-0131-556 8444.

Raeburn, James B., FCIS. Director, Scottish Print Employers' Federation and Scottish Newspaper Publishers' Association, since 1984; b. 18.3.47, Jedburgh; m., Rosemary Bisset; 2 d. Educ. Hawick High School. Edinburgh Corporation, 1964-69; Roxburgh County Council, 1969-71; Electrical Contractors' Association of Scotland, 1972-83 (Secretary, 1975-83). Consultative Member, The Press Council, 1984-90; Director, Press Standards Board of Finance Ltd., since 1990; Director, Advertising Standards Board of Finance Ltd., since 1988; Director, National Council for the Training of Journalists, since 1993. Recreations: golf; squash. Address: (b.) 48 Palmerston Place, Edinburgh, EH12 5DE; T.-0131-220 4353.

Raeburn, Emeritus Professor John Ross, CBE, FRSE, FIBiol, BSc, MA, PhD. Consultant; b. 20.11.12, Kirkcaldy; m., Mary Roberts; 1 s.; 3 d. Educ. Manchester Grammar School; Edinburgh University; Cornell University. Professor, Agricultural Economics, Nanking University, 1936-37; Research Officer, Oxford University, 1938-39; Statistician, then Head of Agricultural Plans Branch, Ministry of Food, 1939-46; Senior Research Officer, Oxford University, 1946-49; Reader in Agricultural Economics, London University, 1949-59; Professor and Head, Department of Agriculture, Aberdeen University, 1959-78; Principal, North of Scotland College of Agriculture, 1963-78; Consultant to World Bank, 1979-88; Vice-President, International Association of Agricultural Economists, 1964-70; President, Agricultural Economics Society, 1964-65. Publications: Agriculture: Foundations, Principles and Development; The History of the International Association of Agricultural Economists (Co-author). Recreations: travel; gardening; photography. Address: (h.) 30 Morningfield Road, Aberdeen, AB2 4AQ; T.-01224 314010.

Raeburn, Sheriff Susan Adiel Ogilvie, LLB, QC. Sheriff of Glasgow and Strathkelvin, since 1993; b. 23.4.54, Ellon. Educ. St. Margaret's School for Girls, Aberdeen; Edinburgh University. Admitted, Faculty of Advocates, 1977; took silk, 1991; part-time Chairman, Social Security Appeal Tribunals, 1986-91; Temporary Sheriff, 1988-92; part-time Chairman, Medical Appeal Tribunals, 1992-93; Reporter to Scottish Legal Aid Board, 1990-93. Recreations: salmon fishing; the arts; travel. Address: (b.) Sheriff Court, P.O. Box 23, 1 Carlton Place, Glasgow, G5 9DA; T.-0141-429 8888.

Raffe, Professor David James, BA, BPhil. Professor of Sociology of Education, Edinburgh University, since 1992 (Co-Director, Centre for Educational Sociology, since 1987); b. 5.5.51, Felixstowe; m., Shirley Paine; 1 s.; 1 d. Educ. The Leys School; New College, Oxford; Nuffield College, Oxford. Edinburgh University: Research Fellow, Centre for Educational Sociology, 1975-79, Lecturer in Education, 1979-85; Reader in Education, 1985-92; Deputy Director, Centre for Educational Sociology, 1979-87. Publications: Reconstructions of Secondary Education, 1983; Fourteen to Eighteen, 1984; Education and the Youth Labour Market, 1988. Recreations: squash; hill-walking. Address: (b.) 7 Buccleuch Place, Edinburgh, EH8 9LW; T.-0131-650 4191.

Rafferty, George Campbell, BSc, MRCVS, DL. Veterinary Surgeon in general practice, since 1948; b. 1.3.26, Glasgow; m., Jane Lilian Sarsons; 2 s.; 2 d. Educ. Rutherglen Academy; Royal Dick Veterinary College. Qualified, 1948; in practice: Suffolk, 1948-49, Hampshire, 1949-50, Fife, 1951-52, Strathspey, since 1953; appointed Veterinary Zoo Inspector, 1984; Deputy Lieutenant, Inverness-shire, since 1985; Honorary Vice-President, Strathspey Farmers Club. Recreation: work. Address: Seaforth, Seafield Avenue, Grantown-on-Spey, Morayshire; T.-01479 2847.

Rafferty, Rt. Rev. Mgr. Lawrence. Bishop Auxiliary to Archbishop of St. Andrews and Edinburgh, since 1990; b. 24.6.33.

Rainey, John Bruce, BSc, MB, ChB, ChM, FRCSEdin. Consultant Surgeon, St. John's Hospital, Howden, Livingston, since 1988; Honorary Senior Lecturer in Surgery, Edinburgh University, since 1988; b. 18.5.52, Belfast; m., Dr. Linda Margaret King; 2 s.; 1 d. Educ. Royal Belfast Academical Institution; Edinburgh University. Trained in general surgery; Examiner in surgery and accident and emergency medicine for Royal College of Surgeons of Edinburgh. Aris and Gale Lecturer, Royal College of Surgeons of England, 1985. Recreations: family; sport; history and military history. Address: (h.) 9 Blackford Hill View, Edinburgh, EH9 3HD; T.-0131-667 6216.

Raistrick, Evlyn, MA. Chairman, Scottish Hockey Union, since 1992; Tournament Director, Atlanta Olympics, from 1996; Member, Rules Board, Competitions Committee, International Federation, since 1990; Member, Scottish Sports Council, since 1993; Member, Executive, Scottish

Sports Association, since 1993; b. 13.8.42, Edinburgh; m., David William; 3 s. Educ. Boroughmuir School; Edinburgh University. Maths Teacher, Liberton High, 1964-72. Recreations: hockey; squash; golf. Address; (h.) St. Michaels, Inveresk, Musselburgh, EH21 7UA; T.-0131-665 3055.

Ramage, Professor Robert, BSc, PhD, DSc, FRSE, FRS. Forbes Professor of Organic Chemistry, Edinburgh University, since 1984; b. 4.10.35, Glasgow; m., Joan Fraser Paterson; 3 d. Educ. Whitehill Senior Secondary School, Glasgow; Glasgow University. Fellow of Harvard College, 1961-63; Woodward Research Institute, Basel, 1963-64; Liverpool University, 1964-77; UMIST, 1977-84. Tilden Lectureship, Royal Society of Chemistry; award for synthesis, Royal Society of Chemistry. Recreations: sport; gardening. Address: (h.) 26 Craigleith View, Edinburgh, EH4 3JZ; T.-0131-337 1952.

Ramsay, Major General Charles Alexander, CB, OBE. Landowner and Farmer, since 1965; Chief Executive, Caledonian Eagle (GB) and Caledonian Eagle (Caribbean), since 1991; b. 12.10.36, North Berwick; m., Hon. Mary Margaret Hastings MacAndrew; 2 s.; 2 d. Educ. Eton; Sandhurst. Commissioned Royal Scots Greys, 1956; Staff College, Canada, 1967-68; Commanded Royal Scots Dragoon Guards, 1977-79; Commander 12th Armoured Brigade, 1980-82; Dep DMO MOD, 1983-84; GOC Eastern District, 1984-87; Director, General Army Organisation and Territorial Army, 1987-89; resigned from Army; Chairman, Eagle Enterprises Ltd. (Bermuda), The Wine Company (Scotland) Ltd., 1992-93, Cockburns of Leith PLC, 1993; Director, John Menzies Plc, Grey Horse Properties Ltd., Edinburgh Military Tattoo Ltd., Potomac Holdings Inc (USA), Morningside Holdings Inc (USA); Colonel, The Royal Scots Dragoon Guards, 1992; Member, Royal Company of Archers (Queen's Bodyguard for Scotland). Recreations: field sports; equitation; travel; motor-yachting; motoring. Address: (h.) Bughtrig, Coldstream, Berwickshire, TD12 4JP; T.-01890 840678.

Randall, Rev. David James, MA, BD, ThM. Minister, Church of Scotland, Macduff, since 1971; b. 5.6.45, Edinburgh; m., Nan Wardlaw; 3 s.; 1 d. Educ. George Heriot's School; Edinburgh University; Princeton Theological Seminary. Vice-Convener, General Assembly Mission and Evangelism Resources Committee. Recreations: jogging; reading. Address: The Manse, Macduff, AB45 3QL; T.-01261 832316.

Randall, John Norman, BA, MPhil. Assistant Secretary, Rural Affairs and Natural Heritage Division, Scottish Office Environment Department, since 1995; b. 1.8.45, Bromley, Kent; 1 s.; 1 d. Educ. Bromley Grammar School; Bristol University; Glasgow University. Department of Economic Affairs; Scottish Office. Recreation: hill-walking. Address: (b.) New St. Andrew's House, Edinburgh; T.-031-244 4066.

Rankeillour, Rt. Hon. Lord. Peer; Member, House of Lords, since 1968; Rear Commodore, House of Lords Yacht Club; Farmer and Landowner; b. 29.5.35. Educ. Ampleforth. Recreations: agricultural and horticultural equipment/ machinery inventor; hunting; landscaping on the grand scale. Address: (h.) The Achaderry Estate, Roy Bridge, Western Inverness-shire; T.-Spean Bridge 206.

Rankin, Sir Alick Michael, CBE (1986). Chairman, Scottish & Newcastle plc, since 1989; Director: Christian Salvesen PLC, since 1986 (Chairman, since 1992), Bank of Scotland, since 1987, Sears plc, since 1991, Scottish Financial Enterprise, since 1991, Securities Trust of Scotland plc, since 1991, James Finlay PLC, since 1994, General Accident PLC, since 1995 (Deputy Chairman); b. 23.1.35, London; m., Suzetta Nelson; 1 s.; 3 d. Educ. Eton College; Oxford University. Scots Guards, 1953-55; investment banking, Toronto, 1956-59; Scottish &

Newcastle Breweries plc, since 1960. Past President, The Brewers' Society. Recreations: fishing; shooting; golf; tennis. Address: (b.) Abbey Brewery, 111 Holyrood Road, Edinburgh, EH8 8YS; T.-0131-556 2591.

Rankin, Professor David W.H., MA, PhD, FRSE. Professor of Structural Chemistry, Edinburgh University, since 1989; b. 8.6.45, Birkenhead; m., Stella M. Thomas; 3 s.; 1 d. Educ. Birkenhead School; King's College, Cambridge. Edinburgh University: ICI Research Fellow, 1969, Demonstrator, 1971, Lecturer, 1973, Reader, 1980, Professor, 1989. Publication: Structural Methods in Inorganic Chemistry. Address: (b.) Department of Chemistry, Edinburgh University, West Mains Road, Edinburgh, EH9 3JJ; T.-0131-650 4728.

Rankin, Donald Watson, MB, ChB, MPhil, FRCPsych, DObstRCOG. Director, Scottish Health Advisory Service, since 1992; b. 19.10.39, Inverness; m., Sheila Frances Menzies; 2 s. Educ. Fort William Senior Secondary School; Edinburgh University. General Practitioner, 1967-76; Lecturer in Psychiatry, Edinburgh University, 1980-82; Consultant Psychiatrist, Fife Health Board, 1982-92. Appointed Doctor, Mental Welfare Commission for Scotland, 1986-90; Examiner, Royal College of Psychiatrists, 1988-93. Recreations: cooking; cycling; music; reading. Address: (h.) 58 Bennochy Road, Kirkcaldy, KY2 5RB; T.-01592 267847.

Rankin, Emeritus Professor Robert Alexander, MA, PhD, ScD, FRSAMD, FRSE. Emeritus Professor of Mathematics, Glasgow University, since 1982; b. 27.10.15, Garlieston, Wigtownshire; m., Mary Ferrier Llewelyn; 1 s.; 3 d. Educ. Whithorn School; Fettes College; Clare College, Cambridge. Fellow, Clare College, 1939-51; War work on rockets, 1940-45; Lecturer, Cambridge University, 1945-51; Assistant Tutor, Clare College, 1947-51; Mason Professor of Pure Mathematics, Birmingham University, 1951-54; Professor of Mathematics, Glasgow University, 1954-82 (Clerk of Senate, 1971-78, Dean of Faculties, 1985-88). Vice-President, Royal Society of Edinburgh, 1960-63; Keith Prize, RSE, 1961-63; Member, Secretary of State's Advisory Council on Education, 1959-61; Honorary President, Gaelic Society of Glasgow, since 1969; Vice-President, London Mathematical Society, 1966-68; LMS Senior Whitehead Prize, 1987; President, Edinburgh Mathematical Society, 1957-58 and 1978-79, Honorary member, since 1990. Recreations: music; hill-walking; Gaelic studies. Address: (h.) 98 Kelvin Court, Glasgow, G12 OAH; T.-0141-339 2641.

Rankin, Thomas John, MA, MAEdMan, AdvDipEd, FCollP. Head Teacher, Sgoil Dhalabroig, South Uist, since 1981; b. 29.3.47, Glasgow; m., Jean Helen Adams; 2 d. Educ. Strathbungo Secondary School, Glasgow; Glasgow University. Teacher, Bernard Street Junior Secondary School, Glasgow; Teacher, Chizongwe Secondary School, Chipata, Zambia; Deputy Head, Kabulonga School for Boys, Lusaka, Zambia; Examinations Officer, i/c Cambridge School Certificate and London University External Degree Examinations, Ministry of Education, Lusaka; Acting Headmaster, Libala Secondary School, Lusaka; Teacher: West Derby Comprehensive School, Liverpool, Chryston High School, near Glasgow. Address: (b.) Sgoil Dhalabroig, Daliburgh, Isle of South Uist, HS8 5SS; T.-01878 700276.

Ransford, Tessa, MA. Director, Scottish Poetry Library; Poet; Editor, Lines Review; b. 8.7.38, Bombay; 1 s.; 3 d. Educ. St. Leonard's School, St. Andrews; Edinburgh University; Craiglockhart College of Education. Publicity Department, Oxford University Press, 1958; in Pakistan as wife of missionary, 1960-68; Assistant to the Director, Scottish Institute of Adult Education, 1982-83; books of poetry: Poetry of Persons, 1975, While It Is Yet Day, 1976, Light of the Mind, 1980, Fools and Angels, 1984; Shadows from the Greater Hill, 1987; A Dancing Innocence, 1988; Seven Valleys, 1991; The Medusa Dozen and other poems, 1994; first prize, Jubilee poetry competition, Scottish Association for the Speaking of Verse, 1974; Scottish Arts Council Book Award, 1980; Howard Sergeant Award for services to poetry, 1989; Honorary Member, The Saltire Society, 1993; Founder and Organiser, School of Poets (open learning workshop for practising poets). Recreation: hill-walking. Address: (b.) Scottish Poetry Library, Tweeddale Court, 14 High Street, Edinburgh, EH1 1TE; T.-0131-557 2876.

Rea, John Malcolm, OBE, BA, MSc, CQSW. Director of Fundraising, Children's Hospice Association Scotland, since 1993; Scottish Member, Anglican Consultative Council, since 1993; Provincial Mission Board Convenor, Scottish Episcopal Church, since 1992; b. 28.2.44, Bradford; m., Della; 1 s.; 1 d. Educ. Bradford and Circencester Grammar Schools; Durham University; Newcastle University; Stirling University. Principal Adviser for Children, Newcastle Social Services, 1973-76; Scottish Director (Child Care), Barnardos, 1976-91; Director-General, Quarriers, 1991-93; founding Chairman, Edinburgh Stopover, 1981-85; founding Vice-Chair, Scottish Child and Family Alliance, 1982-87; Consultant to Lambeth Conference, 1988; Management Group, Anglican International Family Network, since 1988; Scottish Consultant, Charities Effectiveness Review Trust, since 1991; Member, Anglican International Refugees Network, since 1991. Recreations: voluntary work; tennis; sailing; skiing; walking; travel; church social and political action. Address: (h.) Beaconhill, Kirknewton, Midlothian, EH27 8AA; T.-01506 880637.

Read, Edward Reginald, MIMgt. Chairman, Royal Scottish Automobile Club, since 1994; Consultant, Ayrshire Marketing Executive, since 1989; General Secretary, Tenovus Scotland, since 1986; b. 6.12.29, Sydenham; 1 s.; 3 d. Educ. Ilkley Grammar School; Marr College, Troon. National Service, 1948-50; J. & P. Coats Ltd., 1950-85. Town Councillor, Troon, 1964-71. Recreations: travel; cars; golf. Address: (h.) 3 Windyhaugh, 119 South Beach, Troon, KA10 6EH; T.-01292 311276.

Read, Professor Paul, BSc, MSc, PhD, CBiol, FIBiol, MIWEM. Associate Head, Department of Biological Sciences, Napier University, since 1990; b. 1.1.48, Saffron Walden; m., Jane. Educ. Palmers Grammar School, Grays; Hull University; Aston University. Research Technician, Essex Water Authority, 1969-70; Research Assistant, University of Aston, 1971-72; Research Fellow, then Lecturer, Napier College, 1972-82; Senior Lecturer, Napier Polytechnic, 1982-90. Fifty publications. Recreations: offshore sailing/cruising; gardening; hill-walking. Address: (b.) Department of Biological Sciences, Napier University, Colinton Road, Edinburgh, EH10 5DT; T.-0131-455 2625.

Reavley, Edwin, BJur, DipCrim. Head, Air and General Environment Protection Division, Scottish Office Environment Division, since 1989; b. 9.10.43, Oxford; m., Coral Hilary; 4 d. Educ. Huddersfield New College; Magdalen College School, Oxford; Sheffield University; Cambridge University. Joined Scottish Office, 1970. Recreations: Oxford United; tai chi; theatre; walking. Address: (h.) 19 Nelson Street, Edinburgh, EH3 6LJ; T.-0131-556 7312.

Reed, Gavin Barras, BA. Vice Chairman, Scottish & Newcastle plc, 1991-94; b. 13.11.34, Newcastle upon Tyne; m. Muriel Joyce; 1 s.; 3 d. Educ. Eton; Trinity College, Cambridge. National Service, Fleet Air Arm; joined The Newcastle Breweries, 1958. Director: Wainholmes plc (Chairman), John Menzies plc, Ivory & Sime Enterprise Capital plc, Ivory & Sime Trustlink Ltd. (Chairman), Milburn Estates Ltd. (Chairman). Recreations: shooting; tennis. Address (h.) Whitehill, Aberdour, Burntisland, Fife

KY3 0RW; Broadgate, West Woodburn, Northumberland NE48 2RN.

Reed, Professor Peter, BA, RIBA, FRIAS, FRSA. Professor of Architecture, Strathclyde University; b. 31.1.33, Hayes, Middlesex; m., Keow Chim Lim; 2 d. Educ. Southall Grammar School; Manchester University; Open University. Commissioned Officer, RAF, 1960-61; Assistant Lecturer, University of Hong Kong, 1961-64; Architect in practice, Malaysia, 1964-70; joined Strathclyde University as Lecturer, 1970; Professor, 1986; Dean, Faculty of Engineering, 1988-90; Vice-Principal Elect, 1990-92; Vice-Principal, 1992-94. Secretary, Kilsyth Civic Trust, 1975-80; Chairman, Kilsyth Community Council, 1975-78; GIA Council, 1982-84; ARCUK Board of Education, 1985-95; Governor, Glasgow School of Art, 1982-94; Director, Glasgow West Conservation Trust, since 1990; Chairman, Council, Charles Rennie Mackintosh Society, 1991-94. Publications include Glasgow: The Forming of the City (Editor). Recreations: opera; Italian language and culture; wine; cricket. Address: (b.) Department of Architecture and Building Science, Strathclyde University, 131 Rottenrow, Glasgow, G4 0NG; T.-0141-552 4400.

Reekie, Iain Robert, BA. Artistic Director, 7:84 Theatre Company Scotland; b. 14.2.67, Edinburgh; 1 s. Educ. Firhill High School, Edinburgh; RSAMD. Freelance director, 1989-90; Publicity Officer, Mayfest, 1990; Assistant Director, 7:84 Theatre Company Scotland, 1990-91; Assistant Director, Nottingham Playhouse, 1991. Address: (b.) 2 Port Dundas Place, Glasgow, G2 3LB.

Rees, Alan Tait, MA (Cantab), CQSW; b. 4.8.31, Shanghai, China; m., Alison Margaret; 2 s.; 2 d. Educ. Kingswood School, Bath; Gonville and Caius College, Cambridge; London School of Economics; University College, Swansea. Community Development Officer, Tanzania; Lecturer in Youth and Community Studies, Moray House College; Organising Secretary, Board for Information in Youth and Community Service, Scotland; Senior Community Development Officer, Council of Social Service for Wales; Assistant Director, Edinburgh Voluntary Organisations Council. Chair, Scotland Yard Adventure Centre, Edinburgh; Member, Scottish Committee, British Association of Social Workers and Editor, Rostrum; Trustee, Seagull Trust; Director, Handicabs; Scottish National Representative, International Association for the Child's Right to Play. Recreations: gardening; painting; DIY. Address: (h.) 20 Seaforth Drive, Edinburgh, EH4 2BZ; T.-0131-332 7317.

Rees, Professor Elmer Gethin, BA (Cantab), PhD (Warwick), MA (Oxon), FRSE. Professor, Department of Mathematics, Edinburgh University, since 1979; Chairman, Executive Committee, International Centre for Mathematical Sciences, since 1993; b. 19.11.41, Llandybie, Wales; m., Mary Elene; 2 s. Educ. Llandeilo Grammar School; St. Catharine's College, Cambridge; Warwick University. Lecturer, Department of Pure Mathematics, Hull University, 1967-69; Member, Institute for Advanced Study, Princeton, 1969-70; Lecturer, Department of Pure Mathematics, University College of Swansea, 1970-71; Tutorial Fellow, St. Catherine's College, Oxford and Lecturer in Mathematics, Oxford University, 1971-79. Vice President, London Mathematical Society, 1994-96. Publications: Notes on Geometry; Homotopy Theory. Address: (h.) 23 Blacket Place, Edinburgh, EH9 1RJ; T.-0131-667 2747.

Rees, Jennifer Linda, BSc, MIMgt. Head, Department of Management Studies, Scottish College of Textiles, since 1989; b. 2.7.51, Edinburgh; m., Richard; 1 s.; 1 d. Educ. George Watson's Ladies College, Edinburgh; Edinburgh University. Operational Research Analyst, then Statistical Quality Control Manager, Scottish & Newcastle Breweries

Ltd.; Lecturer, Department of Business Studies, Edinburgh University. Recreations: swimming; skiing; playing piano badly. Address: (b.) Scottish College of Textiles, Galashiels, TD1 3HF.

Reeves, Philip Thomas Langford, RSA, RSW, RE, RGI, ARCA. Artist; b. 7.7.31, Cheltenham; m., Christine MacLaren (deceased); 1 d. Educ. Naunton Park School, Cheltenham; Cheltenham School of Art; Royal College of Art, London. Lecturer in Graphic Design, Glasgow School of Art, 1954-70, Head of Printmaking, 1970-91. Address: (h.) 13 Hamilton Drive, Glasgow, G12 8DN; T.-0141-339 0720.

Reid, Daniel, OBE, MD, FRCPEd, FRCPGlas, FFPHM, FRSH, DPH. Director, Scottish Centre for Infection and Environmental Health; former Director, Communicable Diseases (Scotland) Unit; Visiting Professor, Strathclyde University, since 1989; Honorary Clinical Senior Lecturer, Department of Infectious Diseases, Glasgow University, since 1969; Honorary Senior Lecturer, Edinburgh University, since 1991; Honorary Professor, Glasgow University, since 1993; m., Eileen Simpson (deceased); 2 d. Educ. Allan Glen's School, Glasgow; Glasgow University. House Surgeon, Victoria Infirmary, Glasgow; House Physician, Southern General Hospital, Glasgow; House Surgeon, Stobhill Hospital, Glasgow; Lt./Captain, Royal Army Medical Corps (attached Royal Northumberland Fusiliers, Hong Kong); Registrar, University Department of Infectious Diseases, Ruchill Hospital, Glasgow; Senior Registrar, Epidemiological Research Laboratory, London. Forbes Fellow, Fairfield Hospital, Melbourne, 1982; Chairman, Advisory Group on Infection, Scottish Health Services Planning Council. Address: (b.) Scottish Centre for Infection and Environmental Health, Ruchill Hospital, Glasgow, G20; T.- 0141-946 7120.

Reid, David C., MA, MEd. Rector, Kinross High School, since 1985; b. 4.9.43, Motherwell; m., Alison W. Ewing; 1 s.; 1 d. Educ. Wishaw High School; Glasgow University; Jordanhill College; Edinburgh University. Teacher of English, Kirkcaldy High School, 1966-71; Principal Teacher of English, Currie High School, 1971-80; Assistant Rector, Inverkeithing High School, 1980-85. Member/Chairman, English Panel, Scottish Examination Board, 1976-82; Member, IBA Educational Advisory Council (Schools Panels), 1975-86; Chairman, Joint Working Party (English "S" Grade), 1982-83; Member, Channel 4 Scottish Schools Committee. Recreations: hill-walking; angling; conversation; reading; Scottish traditional architecture. Address: (b.) Kinross High School, Kinross, Kinross-shire, KY13 7AW; T.-01577 862430.

Reid, Derek Donald, MA. Chief Executive, Scottish Tourist Board, since 1994; b. 30.11.44, Aberdeen; m., Janice; 1 s.; 1 d. Educ. Inverurie Academy; Aberdeen University. Joined Cadbury Schweppes, 1968, as management trainee; Director, Cadbury-Typhoo; Director in charge, foods and tea businesses; founding member, Premier Brands; returned to Scotland; Director, various small companies; Fellow, George Thomas Society; Hon. doctorate, Robert Gordon University, Aberdeen. Recreations: golf; fishing; art appreciation. Address: (h.) Bonhard House, Scone, Perth, PH2 7PQ; T.-01738 552471.

Reid, Professor Gavin Clydesdale, MA, MSc, PhD. Professor in Economics, St. Andrews University, since 1991; Director, Centre for Research into Industry, Enterprise, Finance and the Firm (CRIEFF), since 1992; b. 25.8.46, Glasgow; m., 1, Margaret Morrice or McGregor (m. diss.); 1 s.; 1 step-s.; 2, Maureen Johnson or Bagnall; 1 s.; 2 d.; 1 step.-s. Educ. Lyndhurst School; Frimley and Camberley Grammar School; Aberdeen University; Southampton University; Edinburgh University. Lecturer, Senior Lecturer, Reader in Economics, Edinburgh

University, 1971-91; Visiting Associate Professor: Queen's University, Ontario, 1981-82, Denver University, Colorado, 1984; Visiting Scholar, Darwin College, Cambridge, 1987-88; Leverhulme Trust Research Fellowship, 1989. Review Editor, 1981-87, Editorial Board, since 1986, Scottish Journal of Political Economy; Member, Council, Scottish Economic Society, since 1990. Publications: The Kinked Demand Curve Analysis of Oligopoly, 1981; Theories of Industrial Organization, 1987; The Small Entrepreneurial Firm (Co-author), 1988; Classical Economic Growth, 1989; Small Business Enterprise, 1993; Profiles in Small Business (Co-author), 1993. Recreations:music; reading; running; badminton. Address: (h.) 23 South Street, St. Andrews, KY16 9QS; T.-01334 72932.

Reid, Harry William, BA (Hons). Deputy Editor, The Herald, since 1983; b. 23.9.47, Glasgow; m., Julie Davidson (qv); 1 d. Educ. Aberdeen Grammar School; Fettes College; Oxford University. The Scotsman: Education Correspondent, 1973-77, Features Editor, 1977-81; Sports Editor, Sunday Standard, 1981-82; Executive Editor, Glasgow Herald, 1982-83. Publication: Dear Country: a quest for England, 1992. Recreations: reading; walking; supporting Aberdeen Football Club. Address: (h.) 15 Albion Buildings, Ingram Street, Glasgow; T.-0141-552 8403.

Reid, James Gordon, LLB (Hons), FCIArb. Queen's Counsel (Scotland), since 1993; Barrister, Gray's Inn, London, since 1995; b. 24.7.52, Edinburgh; m., Hannah Hogg Hopkins; 3 s.; 1 d. Educ. Melville College, Edinburgh; Edinburgh University. Solicitor, 1976-80; Advocate, 1980-93; Standing Junior Counsel, Scottish Office Environment Department, 1986-93; admitted as Barrister, Inner Temple, 1991. Recreations: general fitness; computers and music. Address: (h.) Lower Bunzion, by Pitlessie, Cupar, KY15 7TE; T.-01337 830844.

Reid, Jimmy. Journalist and Broadcaster; b. 1932. Former Engineer; prominent in campaign to save Upper Clyde Shipbuilders; former Convener of Shop Stewards, AUEW; former (Communist) Member, Clydebank Town Council; joined Labour Party and contested Dundee East, General Election, 1979; Rector, Glasgow University, 1971-74; Founder, Seven Days magazine; Columnist, The Herald, Glasgow.

Reid, John, PhD. MP (Labour), Motherwell North, since 1987; b. 8.5.47, Bellshill; m., Catherine McGowan; 2 s. Educ. St. Patrick's Senior Secondary School, Coatbridge; Stirling University. Scottish Research Officer, Labour Party, 1979-83; Political Adviser to Rt. Hon. Neil Kinnock, 1983-85; Scottish Organiser, Trade Unionists for Labour, 1986-87. Recreations: crosswords; football; reading. Address: (b.) Parliamentary Office, 114 Manse Road, Newmains, ML2 9BD; T.-01698 383866.

Reid, Rev. John Kelman Sutherland, CBE, TD, MA, DD. Member, Editorial Board, Scottish Journal of Theology, since 1948; b. 31.3.10, Leith; m., Margaret Winifrid Brookes (deceased). Educ. George Watson's College, Edinburgh; Edinburgh University; Heidelberg University; Basel University; Marburg University; Strasburg University. Professor of Philosophy, Calcutta University, 1935-37; Minister, Craigmillar Park Parish Church, Edinburgh, 1939-52; Chaplain to the Forces with Parachute Regiment, 1942-46; Professor of Theology, Leeds University, 1952-61; Chaplain, Territorial Army, 1948-62; Professor of Systematic Theology, Aberdeen University, 1961-76. Publications: Calvin's Theological Treatises (Editor and Translator), 1954; The Biblical Doctrine of the Ministry, 1955; The Authority of Scripture, 1957; Calvin's Concerning the Eternal Predestination of God (Editor and Translator), 1961; Our Life in Christ, 1963; Presbyterians and Unity, 1966; Christian Apologetics, 1969. Recreation:

golf. Address: (h.) 8 Abbotsford Court, 18 Colinton Road, Edinburgh, EH10 5EH; T.-0131-447 6855.

Reid, Professor John Low, MA, DM, FRCP. Regius Professor of Medicine and Therapeutics, Glasgow University, since 1989; Consultant Physician, Western Infirmary; b. 1.10.43, Glasgow; m., Randa Pharaon; 1 s.; 1 d. Educ. Fettes College; Oxford University. MRC Research Fellow, Royal Post Graduate Medical School, London, 1970-73; Travelling Fellow, US National Institutes of Health, Washington, USA, 1973-75; Senior Wellcome Fellow in Clinical Science and Reader in Clinical Pharmacology, Royal Post Graduate Medical School, London, 1975-78; Regius Professor of Materia Medica, Glasgow University, 1978-89; Editor, Journal of Hypertension. Publications: Lecture Notes in Clinical Pharmacology (Co-author); Clinical Science, 1982-84 (Editor); Handbook of Hypertension (Editor). Recreations: outdoors; gardening. Address: (b.) Gardiner Institute, Western Infirmary, Glasgow; T.-0141-211 2886.

Reid, Professor John William, MEd, FCII, FIRM, MIOSH. Professor and Head, Department of Risk and Financial Services, Glasgow Caledonian University, since 1993; b. 7.12.39, Liverpool; m., Mary McKenna; 3 s. Educ. De La Salle Grammar School, Liverpool; Edinburgh University. Joined Glasgow Polytechnic as Lecturer, 1977. Recreation: hill-walking. Address: (b.) Department of Risk and Financial Services, Caledonian University, Cowcaddens Road, Glasgow, G4 0BA; T.-0141-331 3152.

Reid, Professor Kenneth Gilbert Cameron, MA, LLB. Professor of Property Law, Edinburgh University, since 1994; b. 25.3.54, Glasgow; m., Elspeth Christie Reid; 2 s.; 1 d. Educ. Loretto; St. John's College, Cambridge; Edinburgh University. Admitted as a Solicitor, 1980; Lecturer in Law, Edinburgh University, 1980. Author of numerous books and papers on the law of property. Recreation: classical music. Address: (b.) Department of Private Law, Old College, South Bridge, Edinburgh, EH8 9YL; T.-0131-650 2015.

Reid, Patricia Maureen, BL. Member, Scottish Community Education Council; b. 29.8.39, Glasgow; m., Graham Douglas Melville Reid; 1 s.; 1 d. Educ. Laurel Bank School, Glasgow; Glasgow University. Qualified as Solicitor, 1961; employed as an Associate in private practice. County Commissioner, City of Glasgow Girl Guides, 1979-82; Scottish Chief Commissioner, 1982-87; Chairman, Programme and Training, The Girl Guides Association, 1990-93. Address: (h.) 64 Crown Road North, Glasgow, G12 9HW; T.-0141-357 1351.

Reid, Robert Russell, JP. Chairman, Argyll and Bute NHS Trust, formerly Chairman, Argyll and Clyde Health Board; Member, Argyll and Bute District Council, since 1975; Honorary Sheriff; Farmer; b. 26.12.32, Campbeltown; m., Rebecca Simpson Hunter; 3 s.; 1 d. Educ. Campbeltown Grammar School; Thorpe House; Rothesay Academy. Address: (h.) Ardmaleish Farm, Rothesay, Bute, PA20 0QL; T.-01700 503058.

Reid, Seona Elizabeth, BA, FRSA. Director, Scottish Arts Council, since 1990; b. 21.1.50, Paisley. Educ. Park School, Glasgow; Strathclyde University; Liverpool University. Business Manager, Theatre Royal, Lincoln, 1972-73; Press Officer, Northern Dance Theatre, Manchester, 1973-76; PRO, Ballet Rambert, London, 1976-79; freelance arts consultant, 1979-81; Director, Shape, London, 1981-87; Assistant Director, Greater London Arts, 1987-90. Recreations: walking; travel; the arts. Address: (b.) 12 Manor Place, Edinburgh, EH3 7DD; T.-0131-226 6051.

Reid, William James, ACII, FBIBA. Chairman, Reid Enterprise Ltd., Passport to Scotland Ltd., W.J. Reid (Underwriting Agents) Ltd., City Business Venue (Scotland) Ltd., Roadsense Ltd., Nickleby & Co. (Scotland)

Ltd.; b. 18.9.32, Edinburgh; m., Patricia; 2 s. Educ. George Heriot's School. Director, Collins Halden & Co. Ltd., 1960-68, Joint Managing Director, 1968-72, Chairman and Chief Executive, 1972-78; Director, Halden McQuaker & Co. Ltd., Glasgow, 1964-73; Director, Collins Halden & Burnett Ltd., Aberdeen, 1962-74; Director, Hogg Robinson Ltd., London, 1978-84; Chief Executive, Hogg Robinson (Scotland) Ltd., 1978-84; Chairman and Chief Executive: Collins Halden (Scotland) Ltd., 1984-90, Heath Collins Halden (Scotland) Ltd., 1990-92, C.E. Heath (Scotland) Ltd., 1990-92; President, Insurance Society of Edinburgh, 1978-79; Chairman, Corporation of Insurance Brokers Scotland, 1969-70; Member, National Council, Corporation of Insurance Brokers, 1968-71; Freeman of the City of London. Address: (h.) Ravensworth, 38 Pentland Avenue, Edinburgh, EH13 0HY; T.-0131-441 3942.

Reid, Sheriff William Macpherson, MA, LLB. Sheriff of Tayside, Central and Fife, since 1983; b. 6.4.38. Advocate, 1963; Sheriff of Lothian and Borders, 1978, Glasgow and Strathkelvin, 1978-83. Address: (b.) Sheriff Court House, County Buildings, Mar Street, Alloa, FK10 1HR.

Reid, (William) Russell. Editor, The Sunday Post, since 1989; b. 27.1.36, Dundee; m., Patricia Rutherford (deceased); 2 d. Educ. Harris Academy, Dundee; Arbroath High School. Joined D.C. Thomson & Co. Ltd. as Reporter on Courier and Evening Telegraph, 1953; joined Sunday Post as Reporter and Feature Writer, 1957; Deputy Editor, 1983. Member, Code Committee, Press Complaints Commission, since 1994. Recreations: music; walking; reading; talking. Address: (b.) Albert Square, Dundee, DD1 9QJ; T.-01382 223131.

Reith, David Stewart, LLB, NP, WS. Partner, Lindsays WS, Solicitors, Edinburgh, since 1976, Managing Partner, since 1994; b. 15.4.51, Edinburgh; m., Elizabeth Julia Hawkins; 1 s.; 1 d. Educ. Edinburgh Academy; Fettes College; Aberdeen University. Director, Scottish Historic Buildings Trust, since 1985; Cockburn Conservation Trust, since 1993; Scottish Lime Centre Trust, since 1994; Secretary: Lothian Building Preservation Trust, since 1984, Ponton House Trust, since 1982, Cockburn Conservation Trust, since 1993; Clerk, Incorporation of Cordiners; Honorary Solicitor, Architectural Heritage Society of Scotland and Fet-Lor Youth Centre. Recreations: curling; swimming; photography; wine. Address: (h.) Hawthorn Cottage, Oxton, Berwickshire, TD2 6PP; T.-01578 750233.

Remp, Stephen Edward, BA, MA. Chairman and Chief Executive, Ramco Energy plc, since 1977; b. 5.5.47, California, USA; m., Janine Beverley; 2 s. Educ. American International School; Claremont Men's College; John Hopkins University. Saltire Award, 1977, and Civic Trust Award, 1977 (Harthill Castle); Scottish Business Achievement Award, 1984; Burgess of Guild of City of Aberdeen. Recreations: skiing; tennis; shooting; swimming; music. Address: (b.) 4 Rubislaw Place, Aberdeen AB1 1XN; T.-01224 626224.

Rennie, Archibald Louden, CB, LLD; b. 4.6.24, Guardbridge, Fife; m., Kathleen Harkess; 4 s. Educ. Madras College, St. Andrews; St. Andrews University. Experimental Officer, Minesweeping Research Division, 1944-47; joined Department of Health for Scotland, 1947; Private Secretary to Secretary of State for Scotland, 1962-63; Assistant Secretary, Scottish Home and Health Department, 1963-69; Registrar General for Scotland, 1969-73; Under Secretary, Scottish Economic Planning Department, 1973-77; Secretary, Scottish Home and Health Department, 1977-84. Vice-Chairman, Advisory Committee on Distinction Awards, 1985-94; Chancellor's Assessor, St. Andrews University, 1985-89; Member, Scottish Records Advisory Council, 1985-93; Member, Council on Tribunals, and its Scottish Committee, 1987-88; Trustee, Lockerbie Air Disaster Appeal, 1988-91; Chairman, Disciplined

374 WHO'S WHO IN SCOTLAND

Services Pay Review Committee, Hong Kong, 1988; Chairman, Blacket Association, 1971-73. Recreations: sailing; sea-fishing; walking; reading. Address: (h.) Well Wynd House, South Street, Elie, Fife, KY9 1DN; T.-01333 330741.

Rennie, James Alexander Norris, MD, FRCP. Consultant Physician (Rheumatology), since 1979; b. 28.1.47, Dunfermline; m., Margaret; 2 s.; 1 d. Educ. Dunfermline High School; Aberdeen University. Lecturer, Department of Medicine, Aberdeen University, 1973-76; Senior Registrar, General Medicine/Rheumatology, Glasgow, 1976-79. Recreations: DIY; china painting; football. Address: (h.) 13 Belvidere Street, Aberdeen, AB2 4QS; T.-Aberdeen 632172.

Rennie, Professor Robert, LLB, PhD. Partner, Ballantyne & Copland, Solicitors, Motherwell, since 1972; Professor of Conveyancing, Glasgow University, since 1993; b. 30.6.47, Glasgow; m., Catherine Mary; 1 s.; 3 d. Educ. Lenzie Academy; Glasgow University. Apprentice then Legal Assistant, Bishop Milne Boyd & Co., Solicitors, Glasgow; joined Ballantyne & Copland as Legal Assistant, 1971; Convener, Law Society of Scotland Conveyancing Committee; Trustee, Lanarkshire Spastics Association; Board Member, Scottish Council for Spastics; Member, Local Interview Committee, Prince's Scottish Youth Business Trust; Director, Taggarts (Motor Holdings) Limited. Recreation: classical music. Address: (b.) Torrance House, Knowetop, Motherwell, ML1 2AF; T.-01698 66200.

Renshaw, Professor Eric, BSc, ARCS, DipStats, MPhil, PhD, CStat, FRSE. Professor of Statistics, Strathclyde University, since 1991; b. 25.7.45, Preston; m., Anne Renshaw. Educ. Arnold School, Blackpool; Imperial College, London; Manchester University; Sussex University; Edinburgh University. Lecturer, then Senior Lecturer in Statistics, Edinburgh University, 1969-91. Publication: Modelling Biological Populations in Space and Time. Recreations: skiing; golf; hill-walking; photography. Address: (b.) Department of Statistics and Modelling Science, Livingstone Tower, Strathclyde University, 26 Richmond Street, Glasgow, G1 1XH; T.-0141-552 4400.

Renton, Rev. Ian Paterson, OStJ, FSA Scot, JP. Minister, St. Colm's Parish Kirk, Dalry, Edinburgh, 1966-91; b. 22.3.26, Kirkcaldy; m., Ann Gordon Mutter Macpherson; 2 s.; 1 d. Educ. Sinclairtown and Viewforth Schools, Kirkcaldy; Newbattle Abbey College; Glasgow University; St. Mary's College, St. Andrews. Shipping Clerk, Robert Wemyss & Co., Kirkcaldy, 1941-44; Sergeant, 3rd Bn., Scots Guards, 1944-47; Ministry of Labour, Kirkcaldy, 1947-48; Newbattle Abbey College, 1948-50; Youth Clubs Organiser, Roxburghshire, 1950-53; divinity studies, 1953-58; Assistant Minister, North Kirk, Aberdeen, 1958-60; Minister, St. Mark's Church, Greenwich, London, 1960-66. Member, Edinburgh City Education Committee, 1970-76; Governor: Moray House College, 1971-79, Donaldson's School, Edinburgh, 1972-75, Newbattle Abbey College, 1973-76; Member, General Assembly Committee on Education, 1973-79; Joint Chairman, Scottish Joint Committee on Religious Education, 1974-79; Member, Lothian Region Education Committee, 1977-78; Member, Edinburgh Children's Panel, 1971-74; Executive Member, Broadcasting Council, Radio Forth, 1976-79; Member, DHSS Social Security Tribunal, 1978-84; Member, Church of Scotland Board of Education, 1983-85; Member, Committee on Medical Ethics, Lothian Health Board, since 1984; regular Contributor, BBC, STV, Radio Forth, since 1973; Moderator, Edinburgh Presbytery, 1989-90; Chaplain to Astley Ainslie Hospital, Edinburgh. Recreations: gardening; drystane diking; tai chi. Address: Roseneath, Newbattle Terrace, Edinburgh, EH10 4SF.

Renton, Janice Helen, LLB. Deputy Commissioner for Local Administration in Scotland, since 1991; Deputy Local Government Adjudicator for Scotland, since 1990; b. 20.4.47, Falkirk. Educ. Bo'ness Academy; Edinburgh University. Legal Assistant, Clackmannan County Council, 1969; Depute Reporter, Children's Panel, Glasgow Corporation, 1971; Senior Legal Assistant, Aberdeen County Council, 1972; Depute Director of Law and Administration, Grampian Regional Council, 1974; Senior Depute Director of Administration, City of Edinburgh, 1976-84; joined Commissioner's Office, 1989. Secretary, Edinburgh International Festival Society, 1982-84. Recreations: eating; talking. Address: 23 Walker Street, Edinburgh EH3 7HX.

Renton, Stuart, MBE, ARSA, DA, FRIBA, FRIAS. Architect; Chairman, Board of Governors, Edinburgh College of Art, since 1992; Visiting Professor, Department of Architecture, Strathclyde University, since 1992; b. 15.9.29, Edinburgh; m., Ethnie Sloan; 1 s.; 1 d. Educ. Royal High School, Edinburgh; Edinburgh College of Art. Military Service, RAF and RAFVR; Partner, Alan Reiach and Partners, Architects, Edinburgh, 1959; Partner, Reiach and Hall, 1965, Senior Partner, 1982-91; Consultant, 1991-94. External Examiner, several universities; Assessor for architectural awards schemes; Member, Visiting Board Panel, RIBA Education Board, 1984-92; Governor, Edinburgh College of Art, since 1985. Recreations: skiing; game fishing; Italian hill villages. Address: Grianan, Killichonan, Rannoch, Perthshire PH17 2QW; T.-01882 633247.

Renwick, Professor John Peter, MA, PhD, DLitt, Officier des Palmes Academiques. John Orr Professor of French, Edinburgh University, since 1980; b. 25.5.39, Gillingham; m., Claudette Gorse; 1 s.; 1 d. Educ. Gillingham Grammar School; St. Bartholomew's Grammar School, Newbury; St. Catherine's College, Oxford; Sorbonne; British Institute in Paris (Leverhulme Research Scholar). Assistant Lecturer, then Lecturer, Glasgow University, 1964-66; Fellow, Churchill College, Cambridge, 1966-72; Maitre de Conferences Associe, Departement de Francais, Universite de Clermont-Ferrand, 1970-71, 1972-74; Professor of French, New University of Ulster, 1974-80 (Pro-Vice-Chancellor, 1978-80). Publications: La destinee posthume de Jean-Francois Marmontel, 1972; Marmontel, Memoires, 1972; Marmontel, Voltaire and the Belisaire affair, 1974; Marmontel, Correspondence, 1974; Catalogue de la bibliotheque de Jean-Baptiste Massillon, 1977; Voltaire et Morangies, ou les Lumieres l'ont echappe belle, 1982; Chamfort devant La Posterite, 1986; Catalogue de la Bibliotheque du Comte D'Espinchal, 1988; Language and Rhetoric of the French Revolution, 1990. Address: (b.) 60 George Square, Edinburgh, EH8 9JU.

Rettie, James Philip, CBE, TD. Farmer; Partner, Rettie Farming Co.; Director, Rettie & Co.; Director, Edinburgh and Glasgow Investment Co.; Trustee, Scottish Civic Trust, since 1982; b. 7.12.26, Dundee; m., 1, Helen Grant; 2 Diana Harvey; 2 s.; 1 d. Educ. Trinity College, Glenalmond. Royal Engineers, 1945-48. Chairman, Sea Fish Industry Authority, 1981-87; Chairman, William Low & Co. PLC, 1980-85. Hon. Colonel, 117 and 277 FD8QNS RE (V), 1983-89. Recreations: shooting; gardening; walking. Address: (h.) Hill House, Ballindean, Inchture, Perthshire, PH14 9QS; T.-01828 686337.

Reynolds, Professor Siân, BA, MA. Professor of French, Stirling University, since 1990; Translator; b. 28.7.40, Cardiff; m., Peter France; 3 d. Educ. Howell's School, Llandaff; St. Anne's College, Oxford. Lecturer and Senior Lecturer, Sussex University, 1974-89; Lecturer, Edinburgh University, 1989-90. Publications: Women, State and Revolution (Editor); Britannica's Typesetters; translations. Address: (b.) Stirling University, Stirling, FK9 4LA; T.-01786 467530.

Rhind, William, MA (Hons), BSc. Honorary Sheriff, Grampian, Highlands and Islands; b. 11.9.07, Inverurie; m., Georgia L. Ollason; 1 d. Educ. Inverurie Academy; Aberdeen University; Aberdeen Teacher Training College. Anderson High School, Lerwick: Principal Teacher of Mathematics, 1931-47, Deputy Headmaster, 1947-52, Headmaster, 1952-70. Recreations: bridge; music; reading; angling. Address: (h.) Kelda, 6 Lovers Loan, Lerwick, Shetland; T.-01595 692238.

Richards, Professor Bryan Edward, BSc (Eng), DIC, PhD, CEng, FRAeSoc, AFAIAA. Mechan Professor of Aerospace, Glasgow University, since 1980; b. 30.6.38, Hornchurch; m., Margaret Owen; 2 s.; 2 d. Educ. Palmer's School, Grays; Queen Mary College, London University. Aerodynamicist, Bristol Aeroplane Company, Filton, 1960-62; Research Assistant, Imperial College, London University, 1962-66; Assistant Professor, Associate Professor, Professor, Von Karman Institute, Belgium, 1967-79; Head, Department of Aerospace Engineering, Glasgow University, 1980-90; Dean of Engineering, 1984-87. Publications: 110 articles. Recreations: sailing; hill-walking. Address: (h.) Ravenswood, 32 Suffolk Street, Helensburgh, G84 9PA; T.-01436 672112.

Richards, John Deacon, CBE, AADip, DUniv, RSA, RIBA, PPRIAS. Architect; Principal, John Richards Associates, Architects, since 1986; b. 7.5.31, Shanghai; m., Margaret Brown; 1 s.; 3 d. Educ. Cranleigh School, Surrey; Architectural Association School of Architecture, London. Partner, Robert Matthew, Johnson-Marshall & Partners, 1964-86 (Chairman, 1983-86); Member, Royal Fine Art Commission for Scotland, 1975-89; Agrement Board, 1980-83; Member, Williams Committee on National Museums and Galleries, 1981; Gold Medallist, RSA, 1972; Past President, Royal Incorporation of Architects in Scotland, 1983-85; Trustee, National Galleries of Scotland, 1986-90; Chairman, Scottish Committee, Housing Corporation, 1983-89; Board Member, Scottish Homes, 1988-93, Deputy Chairman, 1989-93; Housing Association Ombudsman for Scotland, since 1993. Recreation: country life. Address: (h.) Lady's Field, Whitekirk, East Lothian; T.-01620 870206.

Richardson, David, BA (Hons), DipEd, FIPD, MICFM. RNLI Organising Secretary Scotland, since 1991; b. 9.10.46, Gateshead; m., Sandra; 2 s.; 3 d. Educ. St. Cuthbert's Grammar School, Newcastle upon Tyne; Birmingham University; Newcastle upon Tyne University. Schoolmaster, 1968-81; Deputy National Secretary, National Federation of Young Farmers Clubs, 1981-89; Field Manager, N.E. Region, National Farmers Union, 1989-90. Fellow, Institute of Training and Development, since 1988; FA Coaching Certificate. Recreations: soccer; golf; folk dance, music and song. Address: (b.) RNLI, Bellevue House, Hopetoun Street, Edinburgh, EH7 4ND; T.-0131-557 9171.

Richardson, Professor John Stuart, MA, DPhil. Professor of Classics, Edinburgh University, since 1987, Dean, Faculty of Arts, and Provost, Faculty Group of Arts, Divinity and Music, since 1992; b. 4.2.46, Ilkley; m., Patricia Helen Robotham; 2 s. Educ. Berkhamsted School; Trinity College, Oxford. Lecturer in Ancient History, Exeter College, Oxford, 1969-72, St. Andrews University, 1972-87; Priest, Scottish Episcopal Church, since 1980; Anglican Chaplain, St. Andrews University, 1980-87; Team Priest, St. Columba's, Edinburgh, since 1987. Publications: Roman Provincial Administration, 1976; Hispaniae, 1986; papers on ancient history. Recreation: choral singing. Address: (h.) 29 Merchiston Avenue, Edinburgh EH10 4PH; T.-0131-228 3094.

Richardson, Penny (Penelope Jane), MA, DipGS, Certificate in Community Education. Director, Edinburgh and Lothian Council on Alcohol, since 1994; b. 31.7.46, Edinburgh. Educ. Edinburgh University; Edinburgh College

of Commerce; Moray House College of Education. Secretary/PA, then General Manager, Traverse Theatre, 1968-74; Articled Clerk, London, 1974-75; Community Animateur, Third Eye Centre, Glasgow, 1976; General Manager, Theatre Workshop, Edinburgh, 1977-82; various consultancies and short term posts, 1983-88; Secretary, West Lothian Health Council, 1988-90; Director, Scottish Association of Health Councils, 1990-94. Founder Member, Cervical Smear Campaign; Vice-Chair, Scottish Convention of Women, 1988-92; Convener, Executive Committee, Public Health Alliance in Scotland, since 1990. Address: (b.) Edinburgh and Lothian Council on Alcohol, 40 Shandwick Place, Edinburgh, EH2 4RT.

Riches, Professor John Kenneth, MA. Professor of Divinity and Biblical Criticism and Head, Department of Biblical Studies, Glasgow University; b. 30.4.39, London; m., Renate Emmy Therman; 2 s.; 1 d. Educ. Cranleigh School; Corpus Christi College, Cambridge. Assistant Curate, St. Edmund's, Norfolk, 1965-68; Chaplain, Fellow and Director of Studies in Theology, Sidney Sussex College, Cambridge, 1968-72; Lecturer, Department of New Testament Language and Literature, Glasgow University, 1973-86; Senior Lecturer, Department of Biblical Studies, Glasgow University, 1986-91; Chairman, Balmore Trust, since 1980; Convener, Doctrine Committee, Scottish Episcopal Church, since 1991. Publications: Jesus and the Transformation of Judaism; The World of Jesus; A Century of New Testament Study. Recreations: hill-walking; third world trading. Address: (h.) Viewfield, Balmore, Torrance, Glasgow, G64 4AE; T.-01360 620254.

Richmond, Professor John, CBE, MD, FRCPE, FRCP, FRCPSG, FRCPI, FACP(Hon), FFPM(Hon), FRCSE, FFPHM(Hon), FCP(SA)(Hon), FRACP(Hon), FRSE. President, Royal College of Physicians of Edinburgh, 1988-91; Emeritus Professor of Medicine, Sheffield University, since 1989; b. 30.5.26, Doncaster; m., Jenny Nicol; 2 s.; 1 d. Educ. Doncaster Grammar School; Edinburgh University. Junior hospital appointments, Edinburgh and Northants, 1948-49, 1952-53; RAMC, 1949-50; rural general practice, Galloway, 1950-52; Lecturer, Senior Lecturer, Reader in Medicine, Edinburgh University, 1954-73; Professor of Medicine, Sheffield University, 1973-89 (Dean of Medicine, 1985-88). Senior Censor and Senior Vice-President, Royal College of Physicians of London, 1984-85; Chairman, MRCP (UK) Examining Board, 1984-88; Member, Board of Advisors in Medicine, London University, since 1984; External Advisor, Chinese University of Hong Kong, since 1982; Member, Council of Management, Yorkshire Cancer Research Campaign, 1989-93; Member, Sheffield Health Authority, 1981-84; Member, Department of Health Clinical Standards Advisory Group, 1991-94; Member, Scottish Advisory Board, British Council, since 1991; Member, Scottish Committee, Marie Curie Memorial Foundation, since 1992. Address: (h.) 15 Church Hill, Edinburgh, EH10 4BG.

Richmond, John Kennedy, JP, DL. Chairman, Glasgow Airport Consultative Committee, since 1979; b. 23.4.37, Glasgow; m., Elizabeth Margaret; 1 s.; 1 d. Educ. King's Park Secondary School. Conservative Member, Glasgow Corporation, 1963-75; Member, Glasgow District Council, 1975-84; Deputy Lord Provost, 1977-80; Conservative Group Leader, 1975-77. Recreations: tennis; music; travel. Address: (h.) 84 Merrylee Road, Newlands, Glasgow, G43 2QZ; T.-0141-637 7705.

Rickets, Brigadier Reginald Anthony Scott. Managing Director, Irvine Development Corporation, 1981-95; Director, Ayrshire Chamber of Industries (President, 1986); Trustee, Scottish Maritime Museum (Irvine); Vice President, Ayrshire Chamber of Industry and Commerce, since 1991; Director, Enterprise Ayrshire, since 1990; Chairman, Scottish Committee, German Chamber of Industry and Commerce in UK; Director, ASSET Enterprise

Trust; b. 13.12.29; m., Elizabeth Ann Serjeant; 1 s.; 1 d. Educ. St. George's College, Weybridge; Royal Military Academy, Sandhurst. 2nd Lt., RE, 1949; served with Airborne, Armoured and field Engineers, UK, Cyrenaica, Egypt, Malaya, Borneo, Hong Kong and BAOR; special employment military forces, Malaya, 1955-59; Staff College, Camberley, 1962; Brigade Major, BAOR, 1963-66; Gurkha Independent Field Squadron, 1966-68; Directing Staff, Army Staff College, 1968-70; Commandant, Gurkha Engineers, and Commander, Royal Engineers Far East, 1970-73; Chief of Staff, Berlin, 1973-77; Brigadier Chief Engineer, UK Land Forces, 1978-81. Recreation: sailing (DTI Ocean Skipper, RYA Coach/Examiner, Commodore REYC, 1979). Address: 10 Waterside Street, Largs KA30 9LN; T.-01475 672838.

Rickman, Professor Geoffrey Edwin, MA, DPhil (Oxon), FBA, FSA. Professor of Roman History, St. Andrews University, since 1981; Master of the United College of St. Salvator and St. Leonard, since 1992; b. 9.10.32, Cherat, India; m., Ann Rosemary Wilson; 1 s.; 1 d. Educ. Peter Symonds' School, Winchester; Brasenose College, Oxford. Junior Research Fellow, Queen's College, Oxford; St. Andrews University: Lecturer in Ancient History, Senior Lecturer, Professor; Visiting Fellow, Brasenose College, Oxford. Council Member, Society for Promotion of Roman Studies; Member, Faculty of Archaeology, History and Letters, British School at Rome (Chairman, 1984-87). Publications: Roman Granaries and Storebuildings, 1971; The Corn Supply of Ancient Rome, 1980. Recreations: opera; swimming. Address: (h.) 56 Hepburn Gardens, St. Andrews, Fife; T.-St. Andrews 472063.

Riddle, Gordon Stewart, MA. Principal and Chief Ranger, Culzean Country Park, since 1976 (Deputy Administrator, Culzean Castle and Country Park, since 1982); b. 2.10.47, Kelso; m., Rosemary Robb; 1 s.; 1 d. Educ. Kelso High School; Edinburgh University; Moray House College of Education. Biology and History Teacher, Lasswade High School, 1970-71; National Ranger Training Course, 1971-72; Ranger and Depute Principal, Culzean Country Park, 1972-75; National Park Service (USA) Training Course, 1978; Winston Churchill Travelling Fellowship, USA, 1981. Member, Royal Society for the Protection of Birds, Scottish Committee, since 1995. Publications: The Kestrel; Seasons with the Kestrel. Recreations: sport; gardening; birds of prey; photography; hill-walking; music; writing. Address: (h.) Swinston, Culzean Country Park, by Maybole, Ayrshire; T.-01655 760 662.

Riddle, Robert William, OBE, DL. General Secretary, Royal British Legion Scotland/Earl Haig Fund (Scotland)/Officers' Association (Scottish Branch), 1983-94; b. 19.1.33, Galashiels; m., Ann Mary Munro Millar; 3 d. Educ. Stonyhurst. 2nd Lt., King's Own Scottish Borderers, 1953; Staff College, 1963; Brigade Major, 157 (L) Brigade TA, Glasgow, 1964; Commanding Officer, 1st Bn., King's Own Scottish Borderers, 1971; Military Secretary, CINC BAOR, 1974; Colonel AQ 3rd Armoured Division, 1977; Brigadier Scottish Division, 1980; retired, 1983; Colonel, King's Own Scottish Borderers, 1985-90; Colonel, The Lowland Volunteers (TA); Member, Queen's Bodyguard for Scotland (Royal Company of Archers). Recreations: field sports; golf; tennis. Address: (h.) Old Harestanes, Blyth Bridge, West Linton, Peeblesshire, EH46 7AH; T.-01721 752255.

Riddoch, Lesley, BA (Hons). Assistant Editor, The Scotsman, since 1994; Broadcaster; Speaker, The People's Parliament, Channel 4, since 1994; b. 21.2.60, Wolverhampton; m., George Gunn. Educ. High School of Glasgow; Wadham College, Oxford; University College, Cardiff. Sabbatical President, Oxford University Students Union, 1980-81; Co-Founder, Lilith (feminist magazine in Oxford), 1980; Reporter, BBC Radio Scotland, 1985-88; Co-Presenter, Head On, 1988-90; Presenter, Speaking Out,

1990-94. Member, Isle of Eigg Trust, since 1993. Norman McEwen Award, 1992; Cosmopolitan Woman of the Year (Communications), 1992; Plain English Award, 1993. Recreations: drinking; playing pool; walking. Address: (h.) Crannach Ha', Fowlis Wester, Crieff, PH7 3NL.

Ridley, Nicholas John, OBE. Managing Director, MA Associates, since 1995; b. 25.3.41, India; m., Isabel Susan Spencer-Nairn; 1 s.; 1 d. Educ. Edinburgh Academy; Shrewsbury School; R.M.A., Sandhurst. Enlisted Queen's Own Cameron Highlanders, 1959; commissioned, Queen's Own Highlanders, 1962; Lt. Col., 1980, and commanded 1st Bn., 1982; Col., 1984, and Military Director of Studies, Royal Military College of Science, Shrivenham, 1984-87; Brigadier and Commander, 54 Infantry Brigade, 1988-81; Deputy Commandant, RMCS, Shrivenham, 1991-93; Chief Executive, Faculty of Advocates, 1993-94. Recreations: field sports; music; golf; cabinet-making. Address: (h.) 5 Grant Avenue, Edinburgh, EH13 ODS; T.-0131-441 7674.

Ridley, Professor Tom, BSc (Eng), BArch, DIC, FRSE, Hon.FRIAS, FRSA, RIBA, FICE, FIStructE. Chartered Architect and Engineer, in private practice; Visiting Professor, Strathclyde University; Member, Royal Fine Art Commission for Scotland, since 1992; Consultant to Royal Scottish Academy; b. 15.8.27, Gateshead-on-Tyne; m., Carolyn Anne; 3 d. Educ. Imperial College, London University; Strathclyde University. Yorkshire Hennibique Contracting Co., 1948-54; Ove Arup & Partners, 1954-91; opened Scottish Office for Arups, 1960, and responsible for all work in Scotland; won Leverhulme Scholarship. Recreations: fishing; golf. Address: (h.) Marlyn, West Linton, EH46 7HW; T.-01968 660604.

Riemersma, Rudolph Arend, BSc, MSc, PhD. Assistant Director, Cardiovascular Research Unit, Edinburgh University, since 1975 (British Heart Foundation Senior Lecturer in Cardiac Biochemistry, since 1979); b. 9.5.43, Hengelo, Netherlands; m., Eva J. Nieuwenhuis; 1 s.; 1 d. Educ. Charlois Lyceum, Rotterdam; Leyden University; Edinburgh University. Biochemist, Department of Cardiology, Academic Hospital, Utrecht; postgraduate research, Royal Postgraduate Medical School, Hammersmith Hospital, London; Research Fellow, Edinburgh University, 1973. Former Vice-President, European Society of Clinical Investigation. Recreations: orienteering; skiing; hill-walking; botany. Address: (b.) Cardiovascular Research Unit, Hugh Robson Building, George Square, Edinburgh; T.-0131-650 3699.

Rifkind, Malcolm Leslie, QC, LLB, MSc. Secretary of State for Foreign and Commonwealth Affairs, since 1995; Secretary of State for Defence, 1992-95; Secretary of State for Transport, 1990-92; MP (Conservative), Edinburgh Pentlands, since 1974; b. 21.6.46, Edinburgh; m., Edith Amalia Steinberg; 1 s.; 1 d. Educ. George Watson's College, Edinburgh; Edinburgh University. Lecturer, University of Rhodesia, 1967-68; called to Scottish Bar, 1970; Opposition Front-Bench Spokesman on Scottish Affairs, 1975-76; Member, Select Committee on European Secondary Legislation, 1975-76; Chairman, Scottish Conservatives' Devolution Committee, 1976; Joint Secretary, Conservative Parliamentary Foreign and Commonwealth Affairs Committee, 1977-79; Member, Select Committee on Overseas Development, 1978-79; Parliamentary Under-Secretary of State, Scottish Office, 1979-82; Parliamentary Under-Secretary of State, Foreign and Commonwealth Office, 1982-83; Minister of State, Foreign and Commonwealth Office, 1983-86; Secretary of State for Scotland, 1986-90; Member, Queen's Bodyguard for Scotland (Royal Company of Archers). Address: (b.) House of Commons, London, SW1.

Rigg, David, MA (Hons). University Registrar and Depute Secretary, Paisley University, since 1987; b. 15.3.48, Insch; m., Margaret Taylor Mechie; 1 s.; 1 d. Educ. Daniel

Stewart's, Edinburgh; West Calder High School; Dundee University. British Gas, 1971-73; Administrative Assistant, Strathclyde University, 1973-79; Assistant Secretary, Paisley College, 1979-87. Recreations: gardening; reading; theatre. Address: (b.) Paisley University, High Street, Paisley, PA1 2BE; T.-0141-848 3677.

Rigg, John Alexander, BA, MA, PhD. Senior Economic Adviser, Scottish Office Industry Department, since 1995; b. 16.11.54, Leeds; m., Angela Mary English; 1 s.; 1 d. Educ. Roundhay School, Leeds; Trinity College, Cambridge. Research Assistant, Queen Mary College, London University, 1981-82; Senior Economic Analyst, Henley Centre for Forecasting, London, 1982-95; Director, Henley Centre, 1986-92; Economic Adviser, Scottish Office, 1992-95. Recreations: cinema; cricket; family history; rugby league. Address: (b.) Scottish Office Industry Department, Meridian Court, 5 Cadogan Street, Glasgow, G2 6AT; T.-0141-242 5565.

Rinning, Andrew, Secretary, Red Deer Commission, since 1990; b. 15.9.49, Balerno; m., Jeanette Legg; 1 s.; 1 d. Educ. Currie Senior Secondary School. Department of Agriculture and Fisheries for Scotland, 1969-75; Scottish Office Finance Division, 1975-78; Scottish Development Department, 1978-82; Scottish Office Finance Division, 1982-85; Assistant Private Secretary to Secretaries of State for Scotland, 1985-88; Scottish Office Finance Division, 1988-90. Recreations: curling; gardening; golf. Address: (b.) Knowsley, 82 Fairfield Road, Inverness, IV3 5LH; T.-01463 231751.

Risk, Sheriff Douglas James, QC, MA, LLB. Sheriff Principal of Grampian, Highland and Islands, since 1993; Honorary Professor, Faculty of Law, Aberdeen University, since 1993; b. 23.1.41; m., Jennifer Hood Davidson; 3 s.; 1 d. Educ. Glasgow Academy; Gonville and Caius College, Cambridge; Glasgow University. Admitted Advocate, 1966; Standing Junior Counsel to Scottish Education Department, 1975; Sheriff of Lothian and Borders at Edinburgh, 1977-79; Sheriff of Grampian, Highland and Islands, at Aberdeen and Stonehaven, 1979-93; Temporary Judge, Court of Session and High Court, 1992-93; QC, 1992; Honorary Lecturer, Faculty of Law, Aberdeen University, since 1981. Address: (b.) Sheriff Court House, The Castle, Inverness, IV2 3EG; T.-01463 230782.

Risk, Sir Thomas Neilson, BL, LLD (Glasgow), Dr. h.c. (Edin), FRSE; b. 13.9.22, Glasgow; m., Suzanne Eiloart; 4 s. (1 dec.) Educ. Kelvinside Academy, Glasgow; Glasgow University. Flt. Lt., RAF, 1941-46; RAFVR, 1946-53; Partner, Maclay, Murray & Spens, Solicitors, 1950-81; Governor, Bank of Scotland, 1981-91; Chairman, Standard Life Assurance Company, 1969-77; Director, Shell UK Ltd., 1983-92; Director, MSA (Britain) Ltd., since 1958; Director, The Merchants Trust plc, 1973-94; Director, British Linen Bank Limited, 1977-91 (Governor, 1977-86); Director, Bank of Wales, 1986-91; Director, Howden Group, 1971-87; Chairman, Scottish Financial Enterprise, 1986-89; Director, Barclays Bank, 1983-85; Member, Scottish Economic Planning Council, 1983-91; Member, National Economic Development Council, 1987-91; Member, Scottish Industrial Development Board, 1972-75; Trustee, Hamilton Bequest; Chairman, University of Glasgow Trust. Address: (h.) 10 Belford Place, Edinburgh, EH4 3DH.

Ritchie, Adam B., BSc, FMA. Curator, Dundee Art Galleries and Museums, since 1982; b. 24.10.43, Lewes; m., Ann M. Educ. Hemel Hempstead Grammar School; Gosforth Grammar School; Weston Super Mare Grammar School; Leicester University. Assistant Keeper of Biology, Leicester Museum; Keeper of Natural Museum, Dundee Museum; Depute Curator, Dundee Art Galleries and Museums. Recreations: travel; hill-walking; wildlife photography. Address: (h.) 43 Albany Terrace, Dundee; T.-01382 225733.

Ritchie, Alastair Newton Bethune; b. 30.4.21, London; m., Isobel Sinclair; 1 s.; 1 d. Educ. Harrow School; Corpus Christi College, Cambridge; Stirling University. Scots Guards, 1940-58; campaign North-West Europe, 1944-45; wounded; mentioned in Despatches; active service, Malaya and Far East, 1947-49; Canadian Army Staff College, 1951; Assistant Military Attache, Canada, 1952-53; active service, Canal Zone, Egypt, 1954; retired as Major, 1958; Argyll and Sutherland Highlanders TA, 1966-68; Partner, Drunkie Farms, Callander, 1967-81; Partner, Sheppards and Chase, Stock and Money Brokers and Member, Stock Exchange, 1960-85; Member, Stirling District Council, 1977-90; Member, Queen's Bodyguard for Scotland (Royal Company of Archers), since 1966; Deputy Lieutenant, Central Region (Stirling and Falkirk), since 1979. Recreations: gardening; fishing; music. Address: (h.) Avonbeith, Callander, Perthshire, FK17 8BN; T.-01877 330078.

Ritchie, Alexander John, BSc, DipEd. General Manager, Scottish Cricket Union, since 1991; b. 2.4.35, Alloa; m., Margaret; 1 s.; 1 d. Educ. Dollar Academy; St. Andrews University. Teacher, Larbert High School, 1958-63; Principal Teacher, Grangemouth High School, 1963-69; Assistant Director of Education, Dumfries-shire, 1969-75, Dumfries and Galloway, 1975-82; Senior Education Officer, Strathclyde (Argyll and Bute Division), 1982-91. Recreations: golf; gardening. Address: (h.) 22 South Street, Cambuskenneth, Stirling, FK9 5NL; T.-01786 448743.

Ritchie, Andrew, BD, DipMin. Minister, Craiglockhart Parish Church, Edinburgh, since 1991; Convener, Field Staff Committee, Church of Scotland, since 1993; b. 17.4.52, Dunfermline; m., Sheila; 3 s. Educ. Queen Anne School, Dunfermline; Edinburgh University and New College. Assistant Minister, Dundee Parish Church, 1983-84; Minister, Clarkston Parish Church, Airdrie, 1984-91; Convener, Parish Assistance Committee, 1988-90; Vice-Convener, Parish Reappraisal Committee, 1990-93. Recreations: music; reading; walking. Address: (h.) 202 Colinton Road, Edinburgh, EH14 1BP; T.-0131-443 2020.

Ritchie, Anna, BA, PhD, FSA, FSA Scot. Freelance archaeologist; Member, Ancient Monuments Board for Scotland, since 1990; Trustee, National Museums of Scotland, since 1993; b. 28.9.43, London; m., Graham Ritchie; 1 s.; 1 d. Educ. Woking Grammar School for Girls; University of Wales; Edinburgh University. Excavations on Neolithic, Pictish and Viking sites in Orkney; public and university lectures; archaeological research and writing; Editor, Proceedings of the Society of Antiquaries of Scotland, 1972-79; Secretary, Society of Antiquaries of Scotland, 1986-88; Vice-President, Society of Antiquaries of London, 1988-92; President, Society of Antiquaries of Scotland, 1990-93. Publications: The Kingdom of the Picts, 1977; Orkney and Shetland, 1985; Scotland BC, 1988; Picts, 1989; Viking Scotland, 1993; Prehistoric Orkney, 1995; co-author with Graham Ritchie of several works including Scotland: Archaeology and Early History, 1981. Recreations: walking; early music. Address: (h.) 50/1 Spylaw Road, Edinburgh, EH10 5BL; T.-0131-228 5962.

Ritchie, Anne Clarke, MA (Hons), DipEd. Scottish Director, Independent Schools' Careers Organisation, since 1993; b. 5.12.44, Glasgow. Educ. Hutchesons' Girls' Grammar School, Glasgow; Glasgow University. Assistant Teacher of Modern Languages, Allan Glen's School; Head of Modern Languages, St. Columba's School, Kilmacolm; Principal Teacher of Modern Languages, Jordanhill College School; Senior Mistress, Giggleswick School; Headmistress: Sutherland House School, Norfolk, Runton and Sutherland School, Norfolk. Director, Craigholme School, Glasgow. Recreations: music; painting; theatre; reading; travel; hill-walking. Address: 18 Castlemains Road, Milngavie, Glasgow, G62 7QQ; T.-0141-956 5027.

378 WHO'S WHO IN SCOTLAND

Ritchie, Anthony Elliot, CBE, MA, DSc, MD, FCSP, FRCPEd, FRSE, LLD. Secretary and Treasurer, Carnegie Trust for the Universities of Scotland, 1969-86; b. 30.3.15, Edinburgh; m., Elizabeth Lambie Knox; 1 s.; 3 d. Educ. Edinburgh Academy; Aberdeen University; Edinburgh University. Carnegie Scholar, Lecturer and Senior Lecturer in Physiology, Edinburgh University, 1941-48; Professor of Physiology, St. Andrews University, 1948-69; Honorary Consultant, Eastern Regional Hospital Board, 1950-69; Chairman, Scottish Committee on Science Education, 1970-78; Chairman, Scottish University Entrance Board, 1963-69; Member, British Library Board, 1973-80; Member, Houghton Committee on Teachers' Pay; Trustee, National Library of Scotland, Carnegie Trust; Royal Society of Edinburgh: Fellow, 1951, General Secretary, 1966-76, Bicentenary Gold Medal, 1983; Hon. DSc (St. Andrews); Hon. LLD (Strathclyde). Recreations: reading; hill-walking; mechanics; electronics. Address: (h.) 12 Ravelston Park, Edinburgh, EH4 3DX; T.-0131-332 6560.

Ritchie, Astrid Ilfra, JP, MA, FRSA, DipSocAdmin. Member, Scottish Community Education Council; Chairman, Scottish Adult Education Forum; Member, Scottish Examination Board; Chairman, Scottish Conservative Party Education Policy Committee; m., 1, Martin Huggins (m. dissolved); 2 d.; 2, Professor David Scarth Ritchie. Educ. Harrogate College; Edinburgh University. Former Lothian Regional Councillor; former Editor, Focus on Social Work and Service in Scotland; former Member, Broadcasting Council for Scotland; former Member, Mental Welfare Commission for Scotland; former Member, General Teaching Council. Address: (h.) 11 Ann Street, Edinburgh, EH4 1PL; T.-0131-332 1455.

Ritchie, Professor David Scarth, MA (Cantab), FRMetS. Governor, Paisley University; Trustee and Director, James Clerk Maxwell Founation; m., 1 Heather McLennan (deceased); 2 s.; 2 d.; 2, Astrid Ilfra Chalmers Watson. Educ. Edinburgh Academy; Cambridge University; Royal Naval College, Greenwich. Lt., Royal Navy, 1944-47; Technical Director, Barr & Stroud Ltd., 1969-85; Chairman, Scottish Education Department survey on industrial liasion in Central Institutions, 1985-88. Visiting Professor in Management of Technological Innovation, Strathclyde University, 1986-94. Address: (h.) Southwood, Newbyth, East Linton, EH40 3DU; T.-01620-860-211.

Ritchie, James S., BA. Secretary, Scottish CASEC, since 1995 (Secretary, Confederation of Associations of Specialist Engineering Contractors, Scottish Branch, 1991-94); Secretary, Scottish Joint Consultative Committee for Building, 1991-94; b. 20.12.36, Dunfermline; m., Patricia; 2 s.; 1 d. Joined Electrical Contractors' Association of Scotland (ECAS), 1990, following an eclectic career in contracting. Member, Scottish Building Contracts Committee; Member, Committee, Scottish Construction Industry Group. Recreations: reading; contemplating exercise; drafting letters to the editor. Address: (b.) Bush House, Bush Estate, Midlothian, EH26 0SB; T.-0131-445 5577.

Ritchie, John Douglas, CA. Partner, Pannell Kerr Forster, since 1985 (Chairman, Edinburgh office, since 1993); b. 9.10.52, Edinburgh; m., Joan Moira. Educ. George Watson's College. Barstow & Millar, CA, 1971-85 (Partner, 1978-85); Member, National Board for Nursing, Midwifery and Health Visiting for Scotland, 1988-93, Hon. Consultant, since 1993; Member, Management Committee, Viewpoint Housing Association, since 1991; Trustee, Viewpoint Trust, since 1991; President, Rotary Club of Braids, 1991-92; Member, Church of Scotland Board of Parish Education, since 1994; Member, Merchant Company of the City of Edinburgh, since 1985; Trustee, Bequest Fund for Ministers in Outlying Districts of the Church of Scotland, since 1994. Address: (b.) 17 Rothesay Place, Edinburgh, EH3 7SQ; T.-0131-225 3688.

Ritchie, Professor William, OBE, BSc, PhD, FRSGS, FRSE, FRICS. Vice Principal, since 1990, Professor of Physical Geography, since 1979, Aberdeen University (Head, Department of Geography, 1982-90); b. 22.3.40, Wishaw; m., Elizabeth Armstrong Bell; 2 s.; 1 d. Educ. Wishaw High School; Glasgow University. Research Assistant, Glasgow University, 1963; Assistant Lecturer, Lecturer, Senior Lecturer, Professor, Aberdeen University, since 1964; Dean, Faculty of Social Sciences, 1988; Visiting Professor/Research Scientist, Lousiana State University. Sometime Member: Nature Conservancy Advisory Committee for Scotland, Scottish Examination Board, Council of Royal Society of Edinburgh; Past Chairman, Royal Scottish Geographical Society (Aberdeen); Chairman, SCOVACT, since 1989; Vice-Chairman, SOTEAG; Member, Environmental Committee, American Association of Petroleum Geologists; Chairman, Ecological Steering Groups for the Oil Spill in Shetland; Member, Fulbright Commission; Vice-President, Royal Scottish Geographical Society. Address: (b.) Department of Geography, Aberdeen University, Old Aberdeen; T.-01224 272328.

Ritson, Bruce, MD, FRCPsych, FRCP(Ed), DipPsych. Clinical Director and Consultant Psychiatrist, Royal Edinburgh Hospital, since 1972; Senior Lecturer in Psychiatry, Edinburgh University, since 1972; Consultant, Royal Edinburgh Hospital, since 1972; b. 20.3.37, Elgin; m., Eileen Carey; 1 s.; 1 d. Educ. Edinburgh Academy; Edinburgh University; Harvard University. Trained in medicine, Edinburgh; postgraduate training in psychiatry, Edinburgh, Harvard and California; Director, Sheffield Region Addiction Unit, 1968-71; at present Consultant with special responsibility for alcohol-related problems; World Health Organisation consultant; Chairman, Howard League in Scotland; Chairman, Medical Council on Alcoholism; Secretary, Substance Misuse Section, Royal College of Psychiatrists; Member, Advisory Group on Alcohol Problems to Health and Safety Executive, EEC. Recreations: friends; squash; theatre. Address: (b.) Andrew Duncan Clinic, Royal Edinburgh Hospital, Morningside Park, Edinburgh; T.-0131-447 2011.

Roach, Professor Alan Colin, BSc, PhD, FRSC, CChem. Head, Department of Chemistry and Chemical Engineering, Paisley University, since 1990; Dean, Faculty of Science and Technology, since 1989; b. 16.6.42, Hull; m., Anne Bolton; 1 s.; 2 d. Educ. Greenock High School; Glasgow University; Oxford University. Lecturer in Theoretical Chemistry, Manchester University, 1968-70; Lecturer in Physical Chemistry, Paisley College, 1970-79, Senior Lecturer, 1979-90. Recreations: walking; running; rowing; politics. Address: (h.) 93 Octavia Terrace, Greenock; T.-01475 630213.

Roach, Professor Gary Francis, BSc, MSc, PhD, DSc, ScD. Professor of Mathematics, Strathclyde University, since 1979 (Dean, Faculty of Science, since 1982); b. 8.10.33, Penpedairheol, South Wales; m., Isabella Grace Willins Nicol. Educ. University College, South Wales and Monmouthshire; London University; Manchester University. RAF (Education Branch), Flying Officer, 1955-58; Research Mathematician, British Petroleum Co. Ltd., 1958-61; Lecturer, Manchester University Institute of Science and Technology, 1961-66; Visiting Professor, University of British Columbia, 1966-67; Strathclyde University: Lecturer, 1967-70, Senior Lecturer, 1970-71, Reader, 1971-79. Fellow, Royal Astronomical Society; Fellow, Institute of Mathematics and its Applications; Fellow, Royal Society of Arts; Fellow, Royal Society of Edinburgh; Past President, Edinburgh Mathematical Society. Recreations: mountaineering; photography; philately; gardening; music. Address: (b.) Department of Mathematics, Strathclyde University, Livingstone Tower, 26 Richmond Street, Glasgow, G1 1XH; T.-0141-552 4400, Ext. 3800.

Roads, Elizabeth Ann, MVO, FSA (Scot). Lyon Clerk and Keeper of the Records, since 1986; Carrick Pursuivant of Arms, since 1992; b. 5.7.51; m., Christopher George William Roads; 2 s.; 1 d. Educ. Lansdowne House School, Edinburgh; Cambridge College of Technology; Study Centre for Fine Art, London. Christie's, Art Auctioneers, 1971-74; Court of the Lord Lyon, 1975-86; temporarily Linlithgow Pursuivant Extraordinary, 1987. Recreations: history; reading; countryside activities. Address: (h.) 9 Denham Green Place, Edinburgh; T.-(b.) 0131-556 7255.

Robb, Professor Alan, DA, MA, RCA. Head, School of Fine Art, Duncan of Jordanstone College of Art, Dundee, since 1983; b. 24.2.46, Glasgow; m., Cynthia J. Neilson; 1 s.; 1 d. Educ. Robert Gordon's College, Aberdeen; Grays School of Art; Royal College of Art. Assistant Art Master, Oundle School, 1972-75; Crawford School of Art: Lecturer in Painting, 1975-78, Head of Painting, 1978-80, Head of Fine Art, 1980-83. Member, Fine Art Panel, CNAA, 1986-87; Specialist Advisor, CNAA, since 1987; Director, Art in Partnership, 1987-92; Director, British Health Care Arts Centre, 1988-93; Member, SHEFC Research Advisory Group, since 1993; first one-man exhibition, New 57 Gallery; exhibitions, 1973 and 1976; Arts Council touring two-man exhibition, 1978-79; regularly exhibits in Scotland. Publication: Irish Contemporary Art, 1980. Address: (b.) Duncan of Jordanstone College, University of Dundee, Perth Road, Dundee, DD1 4HT.

Robb, Kenneth Richard, LLB (Hons), NP. Solicitor; Partner, Marshall, Wilson, Falkirk; b. 3.9.54, Larbert; m., Susan Margaret Ringrose; 1 d. Educ. Falkirk High School; Edinburgh University. Private legal practice, since 1976; Member, Council, Law Society of Scotland, since 1987; Member, Board, Scottish Child Law Centre; part-time Chairman, Child Support Appeal Tribunals. Recreations: history; hill-walking; gardening. Address: (h.) 9 Bryanston Drive, Dollar, Clackmannanshire; T.-01259 743430.

Robbins, Oliver Charles Gordon, BA (Hons), MIMgt. Principal, Cambuslang College of Further Education, since 1992; b. 28.4.36, Edinburgh; m., Andrewena Henderson Briggs; 4 s.; 1 d. Educ. Bellevue Secondary School; Open University; Napier College. Apprentice engineer, 1952-57; draughtsman, 1957-60; design draughtsman, Rolls Royce/Ferranti Ltd., 1960-69; Lecturer, Senior Lecturer, Head of Department, Moray College of FE. Recreations: caravanning; martial arts. Address: (h.) 11 Strathaven Road, Lesmahagow, Lanarkshire; T.-Lesmahagow 894617.

Roberton, Esther A., BA. Coordinator, Scottish Constitutional Covention, since 1995; Member, Executive, Scottish Council Development and Industry, since 1991; Member, Tayside and Fife Committee, SCDI; since 1994; b. 24.6.56, Kirkcaldy; m., William J. Roberton; 1 s. Educ. Buckhaven High School; Edinburgh University. Education and Training Executive, Scottish Development Agency, 1985-88; Project Manager, Scottish Council Development and Industry, 1988-90; Executive Director, Scottish Community Education Council, 1990-93. Member, Executive, Campaign for a Scottish Parliament. Recreations: juggling; piano-playing; singing; yoga; walking; travel. Address: (h.) 23 High Street, Aberdour, KY3 0SH; T.-01383 860909.

Roberts, Professor Bernard, BSc, PhD, FRAS. Professor of Solar Magnetohydrodynamics, since 1994; Chairman, UK Solar Physics Community, since 1992; b. 19.2.46, Cork; m., Margaret Patricia Cartlidge; 4 s. Educ. Bletchley Grammar School; Hull University; Sheffield University. Lecturer in Applied Mathematics, St. Andrews University, 1971-87, Reader, 1987-94. Recreations: hill-walking; squash. Address: (b.) Mathematical Sciences, St. Andrews University, St. Andrews, KY16 9SS; T.-01334 463716.

Roberts, Professor Ronald John, BVMS, FRCVS, PhD, FRCPath, FIBiol, FRSE. Professor of Aquatic Pathobiology

and Director, Institute of Aquaculture, Stirling University, since 1971; b. 28.3.41; m., Helen Macgregor; 2 s. Educ. Campbeltown Grammar School; Glasgow University. Lecturer, Glasgow University, 1964-71; Consultant: Department of Agriculture and Fisheries for Scotland, 1967-70, Overseas Development Administration, since 1974, United Nations, since 1976; World Bank, since 1989; Council Member, Royal Society of Edinburgh, 1980-83; Member, Cabinet Office, Scientific Advisory Panel, 1994; Buckland Professor of Fisheries, Buckland Foundation, 1985; BVA Dalrymple-Champneys Medallist, 1990; Scientific Director, Machrihanish Marine Environmental Research Laboratory; Director, Kintyre Enterprise Trust; Chairman, Argyll and Bute Countryside Trust; Editor, Journal of Fish Diseases, Aquaculture Research. Publications: Fish Pathology; Handbook of Salmon and Trout Diseases; Bacterial Diseases of Fishes; Recent Advances in Aquaculture; Diseases of Asian Catfishes (Co-author). Recreations: golf at Machrihanish Golf Club; squash; forestry; rhododendron culture. Address: (b.) Institute of Aquaculture, Stirling University, Stirling; T.-Stirling 73171.

Roberts, Stewart Muir, OBE, DL, JP, FEIS, BA, MA. Honorary Sheriff, Ettrick and Lauderdale; Governor, Merchiston Castle School, 1962-90; b. 4.2.08, Selkirk; m., Marguerite Hugh Considine; 1 s.; 2 d. Educ. Merchiston Castle School; Clare College, Cambridge; Scottish Woollens' Technical College, Galashiels. Director, George Roberts & Co. Ltd., 1936-62 (Managing Director, 1956-62); Director, Roberts, Thorburn and Noble, 1962-73; Army Service, 1943-46; Standard Bearer, Royal Burgh of Selkirk, 1934; Member, Selkirk Town Council, 1935-75 (Provost, 1955-61); Member, Selkirk County Council, 1937-75 (Chairman, County Education Committee, 1948-75); Member and Chairman, Education Committee, Borders Regional Council, 1974-78; Vice-Convenor, Borders Regional Council, 1974-78. Recreations: golf; fishing; curling; bee-keeping. Address: (h.) The Know, Selkirk; T.-01750 20224.

Robertson, Alistair John, BMedBiol (Hons), MB, ChB, FRCPath, MIAC. Clinical Director in Pathology, Dundee Teaching Hospitals NHS Trust, since 1993; Consultant Histopathologist, Tayside Health Board, since 1982; Honorary Senior Lecturer in Pathology, Dundee University, since 1982; b. 29.6.50, Aberdeen; m., Frances Elizabeth Smith. Educ. Aberdeen Grammar School; Aberdeen University. House Physician, Ninewells Hospital, Dundee, 1975; House Surgeon, Aberdeen Royal Infirmary, 1976; Senior House Officer in Pathology, Ninewells Hospital, 1976; Lecturer in Pathology, Ninewells Hospital, 1977; Consultant in Administrative Charge, Perth and Kinross Unit Laboratories, 1982. Recreations: golf; curling; caravanning; philately; photography; theatre. Address: (b.) Pathology Department, Ninewells Hospital and Medical School, Dundee; T.-Dundee 660111.

Robertson, Alistair Raeburn, RD (and clasp), DPA, DSA, FHSM, FBIM. Director, Strathcarron Hospice, since 1991; Chairman, Scottish Partnership Agency for Palliative Cancer Care, since 1994; b. 29.5.33, Glasgow; m., Mary Gilchrist Smith; 2 s.; 1 d. Educ. Hyndland Senior Secondary School; Glasgow University; Manchester University. Corporation of Glasgow Education Department, 1949-56; Royal Navy, 1951-53; miscellaneous appointments, Scottish Health Service, 1956-71; Group Secretary and Treasurer, Board of Management for Angus Hospitals, 1971-74; District Administrator, South Eastern District, Greater Glasgow Health Board, 1974-85; Acting Secretary, Greater Glasgow Health Board, 1985-86; General Manager, Forth Valley Health Board, 1986-91. Royal Naval Reserve, 1951-79, Captain (Retd); Member, National Board for Nursing, Midwifery and Health Visiting for Scotland, 1988-91; Member, Management Committee, Common Services Agency, Scottish Health Service, 1987-91; Chairman,

Scottish Division, Institute of Health Services Management 1983-86, and former Member, National Council. Recreations: curling; gardening; Rotary. Address: (b.) Strathcarron Hospice, Randolph Hill, Denny, FK6 5HJ; T.-01324 826222.

Robertson, Andrew Ogilvie, LLB. Partner, T.C. Young & Son, Solicitors and Notaries, since 1968; Secretary, Erskine Hospital, since 1976; Chairman, Post Office Users Council for Scotland, since 1988; Secretary, Princess Royal Trust for Carers, since 1990; Chairman, Greater Glasgow Community and Mental Health Services NHS Trust, since 1993; b. 30.6.43, Glasgow; m., Sheila Sturton; 2 s. Educ Glasgow Academy; Sedbergh School; Edinburgh University. Director, Merchants House of Glasgow, 1978-85 and 1988; Secretary, Clydeside Federation of Community Based Housing Associations, 1978-93; Secretary, The Briggait Company Ltd., 1982-88; Director, Glasgow Chamber of Commerce, 1982-93. Recreations: climbing; skiing; sailing; running; fishing. Address: (b.) 30 George Square, Glasgow, G2 1LH; T.-0141-221 5562.

Robertson, Avril Margaret, FHCIMA. Director, Strathclyde Region Catering Services, since 1988; b. 17.7.35, Edinburgh; 2 s. Educ. Eastwood Secondary School; Queen's College, Glasgow. Began career as assistant housekeeper, 1956; former domestic science teacher and catering manager; Principal Officer (Catering), Strathclyde Regional Council, 1982-88. Member, College Council, Glasgow College of Food Technology; Member, Court, Glasgow Caledonian University. Industrial Caterer of the Year, 1992. Recreations: walking; reading; studying Portuguese; gardening. Address: (h.) 2 Rosehill Drive, Condorrat, Cumbernauld, Glasgow; T.-01236 738130.

Robertson, Brenda Margaret, JP. Member, Orkney Islands Council, 1974-94; b. 8.9.24, Scarborough; m., John MacDonald Robertson, BL, NP; 1 s.; 1 d. Educ. Scarborough Girls' High School; University College, St. Andrews. Wartime service, WRNS (Naval Intelligence); formerly: District Commissioner for Guides, Stromness and West Mainland; Member, Stromness Town Council, 1961-74; Orkney County Councillor; Member, Executive Council, NHS; Governor, Aberdeen College of Education. Recreations: reading; arts generally. Address: (h.) Berridale, Stromness, Orkney.

Robertson, Rev. Charles, JP, MA. Minister, Canongate Kirk, since 1978; Chaplain to The Queen, since 1991; b. 22.10.40, Glasgow; m., Alison Margaret Malloch; 1 s.; 2 d. Educ. Camphill School, Paisley; Edinburgh University. Assistant Minister, North Morningside Church, Edinburgh, 1964-65; Minister, Kiltearn, Ross and Cromarty, 1965-78. Secretary, Panel on Worship, General Assembly, since 1982; Church of Scotland Representative on Joint Liturgical Group, since 1984; Chaplain to Lord High Commissioner, 1990, 1991; Chaplain to: High Constables and Guard of Honour, since 1993, Clan Donnachaidh Society, since 1981, Elsie Inglis Memorial Maternity Hospital, 1982-89, New Club, since 1986, Moray House, since 1986, No. 2 (City of Edinburgh) Maritime HQ Unit RAAF, since 1987; President, Church Service Society, 1988-91 (Hon. President, since 1991); Chairman, Board, Queensberry House Hospital, since 1989; Governor, St. Columba's Hospice, Edinburgh, since 1986; Member, Executive Committee, Scottish Veteran's Residences, since 1978; Lecturer in Church Praise, St. Colm's College, 1980-93; Member, Broadcasting Standards Council, 1988-91 and 1992-93; Member, Historic Buildings Council for Scotland, 1990-93 and since 1993; Trustee, Church Hymnary Trust, since 1987; Trustee, Edinburgh Old Town Trust, 1987-91; Trustee, Edinburgh Old Town Charitable Trust, since 1991; edited Singing the Faith, 1990, Common Order, 1994; St. Margaret Queen of Scotland and Her Chapel, 1994. Recreations: Recreations: books; music; history; Canongate.

Address: Manse of Canongate, Edinburgh, EH8 8BR; T.-0131-556 3515.

Robertson, Sheriff Daphne Jean Black, MA, LLB, WS. Sheriff of Glasgow and Strathkelvin, since 1979; b. 31.3.37. Address: 1 Carlton Place, Glasgow, G5 9DA.

Robertson, David Alexander, CA, IRRV. Director of Finance, Orkney Islands Council, since 1994; Finance Director, Orkney Ferries Ltd., since 1992; b. 31.12.59, Glasgow; m., Ruth Elizabeth; 1 s. Educ. Inverness Royal Academy; Dundee College of Technology. Address: (b.) Council Offices, Kirkwall, Orkney; T.-01856 873535.

Robertson, David Greig, CBE, MA, MEd. Chairman of Court, Dundee University, since 1993; Chairman, LEAD — Scotland, since 1991; b. 29.12.24, Dundee; m., Margaret J.D. Keay; 3 s. Educ. Morgan Academy, Dundee; St. Andrews University. Education Officer, Royal Navy, 1945-47; Teacher, Dundee High School, 1952-54, Dollar Academy, 1954-58; Assistant Director of Education, Berwickshire, 1958-61, Dundee, 1961-64; Director of Education, Selkirkshire, 1964-72, Dundee, 1972-75, Tayside, 1975-89. President, Association of Directors of Education in Scotland, 1977-78; Trustee, Central Bureau for Educational Visits and Exchanges, 1975-84; Member, Scottish Consultative Council on the Curriculum, 1980-90; President, Scottish Amateur Music Association, since 1984; Vice-President, British Association for Early Childhood Education, since 1988; President, Scottish Institute of Adult Education, 1987-90; Vice Chairman, National Youth Orchestra of Scotland, 1988-94; Member, Scottish Commission on Education, since 1994. Recreations: reading; music. Address: (h.) 4 Glamis Terrace, Dundee, DD2 1NA; T.-01382 665586.

Robertson, George F., FRICS, FCIArb. Chartered Surveyor, Arbiter; Sole Principal, G.F. Robertson, Chartered Surveyors, Edinburgh; President, Rent Assessment Panel for Scotland, since 1987; b. 14.7.32, Edinburgh; m., Anne McGonigle; 3 d. Educ. George Heriot's School, Edinburgh; Heriot-Watt College, Edinburgh. Partner, Robertson and Dawson, Chartered Surveyors, Edinburgh, 1970-93; Lecturer (part-time), School of Architecture, Edinburgh College of Art/Heriot-Watt University, 1964-84; Chairman, Joint Standing Committee of Architects, Surveyors and Building Contractors in Scotland, 1976-78; Chairman, Board of Governors, Leith Nautical College, 1976-78; Chairman, Scottish Branch, Royal Institution of Chartered Surveyors, 1984-85; Director, Queensberry House Hospital, Edinburgh, 1983-86; Chairman, Scottish Building Contract Committee, 1983-88; Board Member, Scottish Development Agency, 1987-91; Hon. Secretary, Royal Institution of Chartered Surveyors in Scotland, 1988-90; Lay Member, Scottish Solicitors Discipline Tribunal, 1976-94. Recreations: working; gardening; Greece; researching Scottish market crosses. Address: (h.) Gladsheil, Campbell Court, Longniddry, East Lothian, EH32 0NR.

Robertson, George Islay MacNeill, MA. MP (Labour), Hamilton, since 1978; Member, Shadow Cabinet, since 1993; Shadow Scottish Secretary, since 1993; b. 12.4.46, Port Ellen, Islay; m., Sandra Wallace; 2 s.; 1 d. Educ. Dunoon Grammar School; Dundee University; St. Andrews University. Tayside Study Economics Group, 1968-69; Scottish Organiser, General, Municipal, Boilermakers Union, 1969-78; Chairman, Scottish Labour Party, 1977-78; Member, Scottish Executive, Labour Party, 1973-79; PPS to Secretary of State for Social Services, 1979; Opposition Spokesman on Scottish Affairs, 1979-80, on Defence, 1980-81, on Foreign and Commonwealth Affairs, 1981-93, on Scottish Affairs, 1993; Principal Spokesman on Europe, 1984-93; Member of Board, Scottish Development Agency, 1976-78, Scottish Tourist Board, 1974-76; Board of Governors, Scottish Police College, 1975-78; Vice

Chairman, British Council, 1985-93; Vice-Chairman, Westminster Foundation for Democracy, 1992-93. Recreations: family; photography. Address: (h.) 3 Argyle Park, Dunblane.

Robertson, George Slessor, MD, FFARCS, SBStJ. Consultant Anaesthetist, since 1969; Honorary Senior Lecturer in Anaesthesia, Aberdeen University; b. 30.12.33, Peterhead; m., Audrey E. McDonald; 1 s.; 2 d. Educ. Peterhead Academy; Aberdeen University. Early medical training, Aberdeen, London and Winnipeg. Publications: papers on the ethical dilemmas of non-treatment decisions in the demented elderly and advance directives. Recreations: golf; hill-walking; picture-framing. Address: (b.) Department of Anaesthesia, Royal Infirmary, Foresterhill, Aberdeen, AB9 2ZB; T.-01224 681818.

Robertson, Gillian Mary Ormond. Scottish Chief Commissioner, The Guide Association, since 1992; Member, National Council, The Guide Association, since 1989; Company Director; b. 7.5.41, Aberdeen; m., William Gordon Robertson; 1 s.; 3 d. Educ. St. George's School for Girls, Edinburgh; Froebel Educational Institute, London. County Commissioner, Kincardine and Deeside Guide Association, 1987-92; Past Chairman, Montrose Ladies Circle. Recreations: skiing; hill-walking; fishing; upholstery; gardening. Address: (h.) Pitgarvie Farm, Laurencekirk, Kincardineshire, AB30 1RB; T.-0167 4840281.

Robertson, Harry, IPFA. Chief Executive, Perth and Kinross District Council, since 1992; b. 7.9.49, Dunfermline; m., Rosemary Elizabeth; 2 s. Educ. Dunfermline High School; Glasgow College of Commerce. Trainee Accountant, Burgh of Burntisland; Accountancy Assistant, Assistant Town Chamberlain, Depute Town Chamberlain, Burgh of Barrhead; Depute Director of Finance, then Director of Finance/Depute Chief Executive, Perth and Kinross District Council. Secretary/Treasurer, Perth Repertory Theatre Ltd.; Chairman, Scottish Branch, CIPFA, 1987-88; Treasurer, Perthshire Tourist Board; Clerk to Lieutenancy, Perth and Kinross; Chief Executive and Secretary, Perth and Kinross Recreational Facilities Ltd.; Hon. Secretary, Bowerswell Memorial Homes (Perth) Ltd.; Member, Society of High Constables of the City of Perth. Recreations: golf; theatre; badminton; tropical fish. Address: (b.) 2 High Street, Perth, PH1 5PH; T.-01738 39911.

Robertson, Iain Alasdair, LLB. Chief Executive, Highlands and Islands Enterprise, since 1990; Board Member, Scottish Tourist Board, since 1993; b. 30.10.49, Perth; m., Judith Helen Stevenson; 2 s.; 1 d. Educ. Perth Academy; Aberdeen University. Qualified as a Solicitor, 1973; service at home and abroad with British Petroleum, 1975-90, latterly as BP America's Director of Acquisitions. Recreations: skiing; sailing; music. Address: (b.) Bridge House, Bridge Street, Inverness; T.-01463 244204.

Robertson, Maj.-Gen. Ian Argyll, CB (1968), MBE (1947), MA, DL. Deputy Lieutenant, Highland Region (Nairn), 1973-88; b. 17.7.13, Richmond, Surrey; m., Marjorie Violet Isobel Duncan; 2 d. Educ. Winchester College; Trinity College, Oxford. Commissioned Seaforth Highlanders, 1934; commanded 1st Bn., 1954-57; commanded School of Infantry, 1963-64; commanded 51 Highland Division, 1964-66; retired, 1968. Vice-Chairman and Chairman, Royal British Legion Scotland, 1971-74. Recreations: golf; gardening. Address: (h.) Brackla House, Nairn; T.-Cawdor 220.

Robertson, Ian Barr, MA, LLB. Solicitor (retired); Advocate in Aberdeen; Honorary Sheriff, Grampian, Highland and Islands, at Stonehaven; b. Aberdeen; m., Vi L. Johnston; 2 s.; 1 d. Educ. Mackie Academy; Fettes College; Aberdeen University. King's Regiment and KAR,

1939-46 (Captain); Partner, Cunningham & Robertson, Solicitors, Stonehaven, 1951-89; Joint Town Clerk, then Town Clerk, Stonehaven, 1957-75; President, Society of Town Clerks in Scotland, 1973-75; Member, Grampian Regional Council, 1974-86 (Chairman, Transportation and Roads, 1978-86); Member, Aberdeen Harbour Board, 1975-86; Member, Peterhead Bay Authority, 1978-88; Elder, Stonehaven South. Address: (h.) 15 Bath Street, Stonehaven; T.-Stonehaven 762879.

Robertson, Hon. Lord (Ian Macdonald Robertson), TD (1946), BA, LLB, QC. Senator of the College of Justice in Scotland, 1966-87; Chairman of Governors, Merchiston Castle School, since 1970; b. 30.10.12, Edinburgh; m., Anna Love Glen; 1 s.; 2 d. Educ. Merchiston Castle School, Edinburgh; Balliol College, Oxford; Edinburgh University. Admitted Faculty of Advocates, 1939; served War of 1939-45, 8th Bn., The Royal Scots (The Royal Regiment) — commissioned 1939; Captain/Staff Officer, 44th Lowland Infantry Brigade (15th Scottish Division); Normandy and North West Europe, 1944-45; mentioned in Despatches; Advocate Depute, 1949-51; QC, 1954; Sheriff Principal of Ayr and Bute, 1961-66; Sheriff Principal of Perth and Angus, 1966; Chairman, Medical Appeals Tribunal, 1957-63; Chairman, Scottish Joint Council for Teachers Salaries, 1965-81; Chairman, Scottish Valuation Advisory Council, 1977-86; UK Representative on Central Council, International Association of Judges, 1974-87; General Council Assessor, Edinburgh University Court, 1967-81; Chairman, Edinburgh Centre of Rural Economy and Edinburgh Centre for Tropical Veterinary Medicine, 1967-86; Governor, Merchiston Castle School, 1954-95; Captain, Honourable Company of Edinburgh Golfers at Muirfield, 1970-72. Recreation: golf. Address: (h.) 13 Moray Place, Edinburgh, EH3 6DT; T.-0131-225 6637.

Robertson, John. Regional Sheriff Clerk, Grampian, Highland and Islands. Address: (b.) Sheriff Court House, The Castle, Inverness, IV2 3EG.

Robertson, John Davie Manson, CBE, BL. Chairman, Robertson Group of Companies, since 1980; Director, Stanley Services Ltd., since 1987; Chairman, North of Scotland Water Authority, since 1995; Chairman, Highland Health Board, since 1991; b. 6.11.29, Golspie; m., Elizabeth Amelia Macpherson; 2 s.; 2 d. Educ. Kirkwall Grammar School; Edinburgh University. Member, National Health Service Tribunal, 1990; Trustee, TSB Scotland Foundation, 1989; Honorary Sheriff, Grampian, Highland and Islands, 1977; Honorary Vice Consul for Denmark, 1972; Honorary Consul, Federal Republic of Germany, 1976; Chairman, SCOTMEG, 1985-95; Chairman, Orkney Health Board, 1983-91 (Vice Chairman, 1979-83); Member, Board of Management, Orkney Hospitals, 1970-74; Board Member, Highlands and Islands Enterprise, 1990-95; Member, Highlands and Islands Development Consultative Council, 1989-91; Chairman, Highlands and Islands Savings Committee, 1975-78; Chairman, Children's Panel for Orkney, 1971-76; Chairman, Children's Panel, Orkney Advisory Committee, 1977-82. OBE, 1978; Royal Order of Knight of Dannebrog, 1982; Cavalier's Cross of the Order of Merit, 1986. Publications: Uppies and Doonies, 1967; An Orkney Anthology, 1991. Recreations: fishing; rough shooting. Address: (h.) Spinningdale House, Spinningdale, Sutherland, IV24 3AD; T.-01862 881223.

Robertson, John Shaw, MA. Rector, Dollar Academy, since 1994; b. 7.4.50, Glasgow; m., Mary; 1 s.; 1 d. Educ. Jordanhill College School; Glasgow University. English Master, Housemaster, Assistant Headmaster, Stewart's Melville, Edinburgh, 1973-87; Deputy Rector, Dollar Academy, 1987-94. Publication: Stewart's Melville: the first Ten Years (Co-author). Recreations: cricket (Scottish); music (English); literature (international). Address: 2 Academy Place, Dollar, FK14 7DZ; T.-01259 742511.

Robertson, John William, WS, MA. Secretary, British Linen Bank Ltd., since 1986; Solicitor, since 1971; b. 12.11.43, Dunfermline; m., Alice Rudland; 1 s.; 3 d. Educ. Dunfermline High School; Edinburgh University. Assistant Law Secretary, Bank of Scotland, 1975; Manager, Law Department, Bank of Scotland, London, 1978; Assistant Secretary, British Linen Bank Ltd., 1983. Address: (h.) 52 Findhorn Place, Edinburgh, EH9 2NS; T.-0131-667 4229.

Robertson, Sir Lewis, CBE, FRSE, FRSA. Chairman, Posteru Ltd., since 1991; b. 28.11.22, Dundee; m., Elspeth Badenoch; 2 s.; 1 s. (dec.); 1 d. Educ. Trinity College, Glenalmond. Apprentice Chartered Accountant, 1939-42; RAF Intelligence, 1942-46; entered family textile business, 1946; appointed Managing Director, Robertson Industrial Textiles, 1954; first Managing Director, Scott & Robertson, 1965 (Chairman, 1968); resigned, 1970; Chief Executive, Grampian Holdings, Glasgow, 1971-76 (also Deputy Chairman, 1972-76); Non-Executive Director, Scottish & Newcastle Breweries, 1975-87; Chairman: Triplex Lloyd plc, 1982-90, Borthwicks plc, 1985-89, Lilley plc, 1986-93, Havelock Europe plc, 1989-92, Stakis plc, 1991-95; Director, Whitman International, Geneva, 1987-90; Chairman, Scottish Board (and UK Council Member), British Institute of Management, 1981-83; Chairman, Eastern Regional Hospitals Board, 1960-70; Member, Committee of Enquiry into the Relationship of the Pharmaceutical Industry with the NHS, 1965-67; Member, Monopolies (later Monopolies and Mergers) Commission, 1969-76; Deputy Chairman and first Chief Executive, Scottish Development Agency, 1976-81; Member, Scottish Economic Council, 1977-83; Member, Restrictive Practices Court, since 1983; Member, Scottish Post Office Board, 1984-90; Trustee, since 1963, Member, Executive Committee, since 1964, Chairman, since 1990, Carnegie Trust for the Universities of Scotland; Member, Court, Dundee University, 1967-70 (first Finance Chairman); Council Member, Scottish Business School, 1978-83; Chairman, Scottish Arts Council, and Member, Arts Council of GB, 1970-71; Chairman, Scottish Advisory Committee, British Council, 1978-87; Council Member, Scottish History Society, 1984-89; first Chairman, Policy Committee, Scottish Episcopal Church, 1974-76; Trustee, Foundation for the Study of Christianity and Society, 1983-89; Member, Advisory Board, Edinburgh Edition of the Waverley Novels, since 1986; Director, Friends of Royal Scottish Academy since 1986; Royal Society of Edinburgh: Member, Council, since 1992, Treasurer, since 1994; Chairman, Scottish Division, Imperial Society of Knights Bachelor, since 1995; Hon. Doctorate of Laws, Dundee University, 1971; Hon. Doctorate of Business Administration, Napier University, 1992; Hon. DUniv, Stirling, 1993. Recreations: work; foreign travel; computer use; music; list-making. Address: 32 Saxe Coburg Place, Edinburgh, EH3 5BP; T.-0131-332 5221.

Robertson, Professor Noel Farnie, CBE, MA, BSc, PhD, FRSE, FIBiol; b. 24.12.23, Dundalk; m., Doreen Colina Gardner; 2 s.; 2 d. Educ. Trinity Academy; Edinburgh University; Trinity College, Cambridge. Plant Pathologist, West African Cacao Research Institute, Ghana, 1946-48; Lecturer, Plant Pathology, Cambridge University, 1948-59; Professor of Botany, Hull University, 1959-69; Professor of Agriculture, Edinburgh University, and Principal, East of Scotland College of Agriculture, 1969-83. Publications: Britain's First Chair in Agriculture (Co-author), 1990; From Dearth to Plenty (Co-author), 1995. Recreations: gardening; natural history. Address: (h.) Woodend, Juniper Bank, Walkerburn, Peebles-shire, EH43 6DE; T.-01896 810523.

Robertson, Raymond. MP (Conservative), Aberdeen South, since 1992; Minister for Education, Housing and Fisheries, Scottish Office. Former Vice-Chairman, Scottish Conservative Party. Address: (b.) House of Commons, London, SW1A 0AA.

Robertson, Richard Ross, RSA, FRBS, DA. Sculptor; b. 10.9.14, Aberdeen; m., Kathleen May Matts; 2 d. Educ. Paisley Grammar School; Glasgow School of Art; Aberdeen Art School. Work exhibited in Aberdeen public parks and several public buildings in city and county of Aberdeen; also exhibited in several private collections in Britain, America and Holland; retired Lecturer in Sculpture, Gray's School of Art, Aberdeen. Recreations: carving; gardening; walking. Address: (h.) Creaguir, Woodlands Road, Rosemount, Blairgowrie, Perthshire; T.-01250 4970.

Robertson, Robert, CBE, JP, FEIS. Member, Strathclyde Regional Council, 1974-86; b. 15.8.09, Shapensay, Orkney; m., Jean Murdoch Moffatt; 1 s.; 1 d. Educ. Forres Academy; Royal Technical College, Glasgow. Local government service since 1952; Convener, former Renfrewshire County Council; Chairman, former Renfrewshire Education Committee, 13 years; Chairman, Standing Committee for the Supply and Training of Teachers in Further Education (Robertson Report); Member, Board of Governors, Jordanhill College of Education; Member, various College Councils. Recreations: fishing; painting. Address: (h.) 24 Broadwood Park, Alloway, Ayrshire; T.-0292443820; Castlehill, near Maybole, Ayrshire; T.-01292 50337.

Robertson, Roderick. Managing Director, Robertsons of Tain Ltd.; Honorary Sheriff, Tain and Dingwall, 1976; b. 24.8.35, Tain; m., Elizabeth Martin Steele; 1 s. Educ. Tain Royal Academy. Agricultural engineering, 1951-56; Army, 1956-59; commenced business (agricultural engineering), 1959; elected, Tain Town Council, 1965 (Chairman of Development, Dean of Guild and Senior Bailie); JP, 1975; appointed Member, Valuation Appeal Committee, Ross and Cromarty, Skye and Lochalsh, 1980; Director, Royal Highland and Agricultural Society of Scotland; Director, Ross and Cromarty Enterprise, 1991; Chairman, Justice of the Peace Committee, Ross and Cromarty, 1980; Chairman, Local Royal British Legion Housing Association, 1984; Chairman, Tain Community Council. Recreations: flying; shooting; fishing; judo. Address: (h.) Viewfield Farm, Tain, Ross-shire, IV19 1PX; T.-01862 892151.

Robertson, Brigadier Sidney Park, MBE, TD, JP, DL, BCom. Director, S. & J.D. Robertson Group Ltd. (Chairman, 1965-79); Honorary Sheriff, Grampian, Highlands and Islands, since 1969; Vice Lord Lieutenant of Orkney, 1987-90; b. 12.3.14, Kirkwall; m., Elsa Miller Croy; 1 s.; 1 d. Educ. Kirkwall Grammar School; Milburn Edinburgh University. Commissioned, Royal Artillery, 1940 (Despatches, NW Europe, 1945); managerial posts, Anglo-Iranian Oil Co., Middle East, 1946-51; Manager Operations/Sales, Southern Division, Shell-Mex and BP, 1951-54; founder, Robertson firm, 1954; Major Commanding 861 (Independent) Light Anti-Aircraft Battery RA (Orkney and Zetland), TA, 1956-61; Lt. Col. Commanding Lovat Scouts, 1962-65; Brigadier, CRA 51st Highland Division, 1966-67; Chairman, Orkney Hospitals Board of Management/Orkney Health Board, 1965-79; DL, 1968; Honorary Area Vice-President (Orkney), Royal British Legion, since 1975; Honorary Colonel, 102 (Ulster and Scottish) Light Air Defence Regiment, Royal Artillery, 1975-80; Hon. Colonel Commandant, Royal Regiment of Artillery, 1977-80; Vice President, National Artillery Association, since 1977; Chairman, Royal Artillery Council of Scotland, 1980-84; Honorary President, Orkney Bn., Boys' Brigade; Vice-President, RNLI, since 1985; President, Villars Curling Club, 1978-80, 1986-88; Honorary President, Friends of St. Magnus Cathedral, since 1994; Freedom of Orkney, 1990. Recreations: travel; hill-walking; angling. Address: (h.) Daisybank, Kirkwall, Orkney; T.-01856 87 2085.

Robertson, Stephen Andrew Cormack, MBE, MUniv, MA, LLB, NP. Humorist and Actor; founder Member, Scotland The What?; b. 21.4.33, Aberdeen; m., Eva Mary

Stephen; 1 s.; 1 d. Educ. Aberdeen Grammar School; Aberdeen University. National service (2nd Lt.), 1957-59; supply teaching and legal and administrative assistant in various offices, 1960-63; Solicitor in Aberdeen, 1964-83; full-time participation in Scotland The What?, 1983-95. Recreations: watching sport; country pottering and hill-walking; golf; theatre; reading; drystane dyking. Address: (h.) 17 Rubislaw Den South, Aberdeen; T.-01224 317064.

Robertson, Sue, BA, MSocSci. Director, Scottish Council for Single Parents, since 1988; b. 12.7.50, Carlisle; m., David Hare; 1 s.; 2 d. Educ. Penrith Queen Elizabeth Grammar School; Oxford University; Birmingham University. Senior Economic Assistant, Scottish Economic Planning Department, 1973-78; Co-ordinator, Scottish Women's Aid, 1978-83; Training Officer, Scottish Council for Single Parents, 1983-88. Committee Member, Cairn Housing Association. Recreations: hill-walking; cycling; reading. Address: (b.) 13 Gayfield Square, Edinburgh, EH1 3NX; T.-0131-556 3899.

Robertson, William Nelson, MA, FCII. Group Chief Executive, General Accident, since 1990; Director, since 1984; Board Member, Association of British Insurers, since 1991; b. 14.12.33, Berwick upon Tweed; m., Sheila Catherine; 2 d. Educ. Berwick Grammar School; Edinburgh University. Joined General Accident, 1958; Deputy Chief General Manager, 1989-90. Recreations: hill-walking; gardening. Address: (b.) General Accident PLC, Pitheavlis, Perth, PH2 0NH; T.-01738 621202.

Robins, Professor David John, BSc, PhD, DSc, CChem, FRSC, FRSE. Professor of Chemistry, Glasgow University, since 1990; b. 12.8.45, Purley; m., Helen Dorothy Skinner; 1 s.; 1 d. Educ. Purley Grammar School; Exeter University. NIH Postdoctoral Fellowship, University of Pittsburgh, 1969-71; SRC Fellowship, Surrey University, 1971-72; Tutorial Fellow in Organic Chemistry, Reading University, 1973-74; Lecturer in Organic Chemistry, Glasgow University, 1974-87, Senior Lecturer, 1987-88, Reader, 1988-90. Recreations: badminton; gardening; music; hill-walking; cycling. Address: (b.) Department of Chemistry, Glasgow University, Glasgow, G12 8QQ; T.-0141-339 8855.

Robins, John F. Company Secretary, Animal Concern, since 1988 (Company Secretary, Scottish Anti-Vivisection Society, 1981-88); Co-ordinator, Scottish Animal Rights Network, since 1983; Managing Director, Ethical Promotions Ltd., since 1988; Co-ordinator, Save Scotland's Seals Funds, since 1988; b. 2.1.57, Glasgow; m., Mary E.; 1 s.; 1 d. Educ. St. Ninian's High School. Co-ordinator, Glasgow Energy Group, 1978-80; Green Party activist and candidate, 1978-81; Delegate, Anti-Nuclear Campaign, 1978-81; Vice-Chair, Friends of the Earth (Scotland) Ltd., 1981-82. Recreations: campaigning against hunting, shooting and fishing; catching up on lost sleep. Address: (b.) 62 Old Dumbarton Road, Glasgow, G3 8RE; T.-0141-334 6014.

Robinson, Douglas Robert. Convener, Dumfries and Galloway Regional Council, since 1990; b. 8.9.22, Lancashire; m., Isabel Nicol (deceased); 2, Milijana; 3 s.; 1 d.; 1 step d. Educ. Hutton Grammar School. Continuous local government service, since 1962; Chairman, Wigtown District Council, 1974; elected Member, Dumfries & Galloway Regional Council, 1974. Recreations: travelling; flying. Address: (h.) 34 Kirkland Road, Calside, Dumfries, DG1 4EZ; T.-01387 267984.

Robinson, Ernest Thomson, TD, MB, ChB, FRCGP, DRCOG. Chairman, Council, St. Andrew's Ambulance Association, since 1994; retired General Medical Practitioner; b. 18.3.34, Gartcosh; 4 s.; 3 d. Educ. Coatbridge Secondary School; Glasgow University. House Physician, Gartloch Hospital, 1958; House Surgeon, then

Senior House Officer, Accident and Emergency, Western Infirmary, Glasgow, 1959-61; Trainee G.P., Glasgow, 1961; House Officer, Obstetrics, Ayrshire Central Hospital, 1962; Principal General Medical Practitioner, Woodside Health Clinic, Glasgow (retired); former Regimental Medical Officer, 154 Lowland Regiment RCT (TA). Recreations: salmon and trout fishing. Address: (h.) 132 Prestonfield, Milngavie, Glasgow, G62 7QA; T.-0141-956 4926.

Robinson, Helen Mairi Johnstone, MA. Senior Dictionaries Editor, Larousse plc, formerly W. & R. Chambers, since 1990; Research Associate, Edinburgh Edition of the Waverley Novels, 1987-91; Kerr-Fry Award holder, Edinburgh University, 1985-90; b. 21.1.45, Glasgow; 1 s.; 1 d. Educ. George Watson's Ladies' College, Edinburgh; Edinburgh University. Scottish National Dictionary: Junior Assistant Editor, 1966, Assistant Editor, 1967, Senior Assistant Editor, 1972; Editor-in-Chief, Concise Scots Dictionary, 1973-85; Member, Advisory Committee, Private Papers of James Boswell, Yale University, since 1987. Publication: Concise Scots Dictionary, 1985. Recreations: music; theatre; reading; travel. Address: (b.) 43-45 Annandale Street, Edinburgh.

Robinson, Krystyna Irena, BA, MRTPI. Executive Director, Economic Development and Estates, City of Edinburgh District Council, since 1994; b. 30.6.46, Germany; 2 s. Educ. Newland High School, Hull; King's College, London University. Research Officer, Centre for Environmental Studies, London, 1968-70; Assistant Planning Officer, then Senior Planning Officer, East Sussex County Council, 1970-74; Assistant Borough Planning Officer, Hove Borough Council, 1974-82; Assistant to Chief Executive, then Principal Officer, Training and Employment, East Sussex County Council, 1982-89; County Economic Development Officer, Humberside County Council, 1989-94. Address: (b.) 375 High Street, Edinburgh, EH1 1QE; T.-0131-529 3402.

Robinson, Stanley Scott, MBE (Mil), TD, BL, SSC. Sheriff of Grampian, Highland and Islands (retired); Honorary Sheriff of Inverness; Honorary Sheriff of Angus; b. 27.3.13, Edinburgh; m., Helen Annan Hardie; 3 s. Educ. Boroughmuir School, Edinburgh; Edinburgh University. Admitted Solicitor, 1935; TA commission, 1936; War service, Royal Artillery, 1939-45; Major; mentioned in Despatches (2); France and Belgium, 1939-40, France and Germany, 1944-45; admitted SSC, 1962; Vice President, Law Society of Scotland, 1970-72; appointed Sheriff, Fort William/Skye/Inverness/Western Isles, 1972; retired, 1985. Publications: Law of Interdict, 1987; Law of Game and Salmon Fishing, 1990; Encyclopedia of Laws of Scotland (Contributor). bowling; caravanning. Address: (h.) Drumalin House, 16 Drummond Road, Inverness, IV2 4NB; T.-01463 233488.

Robson, Agnes, MA. Director, Directorate of Primary Care, NHS Management Executive, Scottish Office Home and Health Department, since 1992; b. 6.10.46, Edinburgh; 1 s. Educ. Holy Cross Academy; Edinburgh University. Civil Servant, since 1968; Head, Energy Division, 1988-89; Head, Nuclear Energy Division, 1989-90; Head, Urban Policy Division, 1990-92. Recreations: music; theatre. Address: (b.) New St. Andrews House, Edinburgh.

Robson, Euan Macfarlane, BA, MSc, MICA. Scottish Manager, Gas Consumers' Council, since 1986; b. 17.2.54, Northumberland; m., Valerie; 2 d. Educ. Trinity College, Glenalmond; Newcastle-upon-Tyne University; Strathclyde University. Teacher, 1976-79; Deputy Secretary, Gas Consumers' Northern Council, 1981-86. Member, Northumberland County Council, 1981-89; Honorary Alderman, Northumberland CC, since 1989; Liberal/SDP Alliance candidate, Hexham, 1983, 1987; Vice Chairman, Consumer Safety International; River Tweed Commissioner. Address: (h.) Elmbank, Tweedsyde Park, Kelso, TD5 7RF; T.-01573 225279.

Robson, Godfrey. Under Secretary, Industrial Expansion, Scottish Office, since 1993; b. 5.11.46. Scottish Fisheries Secretary, 1989-93.

Robson, Professor James Scott, MB, ChB (Hons), MD, FRCPEdin, FRCP. Emeritus Professor; Professor of Medicine, Edinburgh University, 1977-86; Physician in charge, Medical Renal Unit, Edinburgh Royal Infirmary, 1959-86; b. 19.5.21, Hawick; m., Mary Kynoch MacDonald; 2 s. Educ. Hawick High School; Edinburgh University; New York University. RAMC (Captain), India, Palestine and Egypt, 1945-48; Rockefeller Research Fellow, Harvard University, 1949-50; Edinburgh University:Senior Lecturer in Therapeutics, 1959, Reader in Therapeutics, 1961, in Medicine, 1968; Honorary Associate Professor of Medicine, Harvard, 1962; Merck Sharpe & Dome Visiting Professor to Australia, 1968. President, Renal Association, London, 1977-80; sometime Member, Editorial Board, and Deputy Chairman, Clinical Science and other medical journals; Member, Biomedical Research Committee, SH&HD; Chairman, Sub-Committee in Medicine, National Medical Consultative Committee. Publications: Companion to Medical Studies (Co-Editor); many scientific papers on renal physiology and disease. Recreations: gardening; theatre; reading; contemporary art; writing. Address: (h.) 1 Grant Avenue, Edinburgh, EH13 ODS; T.-0131-441 3508.

Rochester, Professor Colin Herbert, BSc, PhD, DSc, CChem, FRSC, FRSE. Baxter Professor of Chemistry, Dundee University, since 1980; b. 20.3.37, Coventry; m., Jennifer Mary Orrell; 2 s.; 2 d. Educ. Hymers College, Hull; Royal Liberty School, Romford; King's College, London University. Nottingham University: Assistant Lecturer in Physical Chemistry, 1962-64, Lecturer, 1964-72, Reader, 1972-80. Publication: Acidity Functions, 1970. Recreations: fossil collecting; swimming. Address: (b.) Chemistry Department, The University, Dundee, DD1 4HN; T.-01382 344327.

Rochford, Professor Gerard, BA, BSc. Psychotherapist; b. 17.12.32, Dorking; m., Anne Prime (dec.); 3 s.; 7 d. Educ. Worcester Royal Grammar School; Hull University; Oxford University. Medical Research Council, 1960-63; Lecturer in Psychology: Aberdeen University, 1963-67, Hong Kong University, 1967-70; Lecturer/Senior Lecturer, 1970-78, Professor of Social Work Studies, 1978-88, Aberdeen University. Member, Scottish Association of Psychoanalytical Psychotherapists. Recreations: family; friends; poetry. Address: (h.) 47 Waverley Place, Aberdeen; T.-Aberdeen 644873.

Rodger of Earlsferry, Rt. Hon. Lord (Alan Ferguson Rodger), QC, MA, LLB, DCL. Lord Advocate, since 1992; b. 18.9.44. Educ. Kelvinside Academy, Glasgow; Glasgow University; New College, Oxford. Fellow, New College, Oxford, 1970-72; Member, Faculty of Advocates, 1974; Clerk of Faculty, 1976-79; Advocate Depute, 1985-88; Home Advocate Depute, 1986-88; Member, Mental Welfare Commission for Scotland, 1981-84; UK Delegation to CCBE, 1984-89; Maccabaean Lecturer, British Academy, 1991; Solicitor General for Scotland, 1989-92. Address: (b.) Crown Office, 25 Chambers Street, Edinburgh, EH1 1LA.

Rodger, Willie, ARSA, RGI, DA (Glas). Printmaker; b. 3.3.30, Kirkintilloch; m., Anne Charmian Henry; 2 s.; 2 d. Educ. Lenzie Academy; Glasgow School of Art. Visualiser, London advertising agency, 1953-54; Art Teacher, Lenzie Acacady, 1955-68; Head, Art Department, Clydebank High School, 1968-87. Artist in Residence, Sussex University, 1971; Scottish Historical Playing Cards, 1975; Saltire Awards for Art in Architecture, 1984-89. Recreations: gardening; jazz. Address: Stenton, Bellevue Road, Kirkintilloch, Glasgow, G66 1AP; T.-0141-776 2116.

Rodgers, Professor Eamonn Joseph, BA (Hons), MA, PhD. Professor of Spanish and Latin-American Studies, Strathclyde University, since 1990; b. 4.6.41, Belfast; m., Valerie Ann Goodman; 2 s. Educ. St. Mary's Grammar School, Belfast; Queen's University, Belfast. Junior Lecturer in Spanish, Trinity College, Dublin, 1964-66; Lecturer, 1966-78; Senior Lecturer, 1978-89. Publication: From Enlightenment to Realism: The Novels of Galdos 1870-1887, 1987. Recreations: country walks; music. Address: (b.) Strathclyde University, Glasgow, G1 1XH; T.-0141-552 4400.

Roebuck, Michael Stuart, BSc, MEd, CertEd. Principal, Lews Castle College, since 1992; b. 5.12.49, Huddersfield; m., Margaret Jane; 1 s.; 1 d. Educ. Marlborough Grammar School; University of Ulster; Edinburgh University. Trainee Town Planner; Lecturer/Senior Lecturer/Deputy Head of Department, Stevenson College of F.E.; Assistant to the Director of Education, Lothian Region; TVEI Coordinator, Senior Adviser, Lothian Region. Recreation: cricket (retired). Address: (b.) Lews Castle College, Stornoway, Isle of Lewis; T.-01851 703311.

Roger, Alan Stuart, MBE (Mil), JP. Vice-President, National Trust for Scotland, 1984-95; Council Member, Contemporary Art Society, 1980-90; President, Bonsai Kai, since 1965; b. 27.4.09, London. Educ. Loretto School; Trinity College, Oxford. Partner, Norris Oakley Bros. and Director, various public companies, 1933; BRC and St. John Ambulance, France, 1940; Ministry of Supply mission to India, 1940-41; Indian Army, 1941-45 and War Office, 1945-52, serving India, Persia, Iraq, Hong Kong; Director of various public companies in UK and Portugal, 1953-79. Trustee, National Galleries of Scotland, 1967-82; former Trustee, Crarae Garden Trust; Member, Countess of Perth's Committee for Awards to Museums and Galleries, 1987-91. Recreations: gardening; reading. Address: (h.) Dundonnell, by Garve, Ross & Cromarty; T.-0185 483 206.

Roger, Peter Charles Marshall, CA. Director, Speirs & Jeffrey Ltd., since 1974; b. 11.4.42, Glasgow; m., Fiona Ann Murray; 2 s.; 1 d. Educ. Glasgow High School. Qualified CA, 1964; Thomson McLintock & Co., 1964-71; joined Speirs & Jeffrey Ltd., 1971. Recreation: golf. Address: (b.) 36 Renfield Street, Glasgow, G2 1NA; T.-0141-248 4311.

Rogerson, Robert William Kelly Cupples, OBE, BArch, FRIBA, FRIAS, FSA Scot, MRSH. Vice Chairman, Scottish Council on Disability, 1987-89; Chairman, Committee on Access for Scotland, 1980-89; Council Member, National Trust for Scotland, 1980-86; b. 14.5.17, Glasgow; m., Mary Clark MacNeill; 1 s.; 1 d. Educ. High School of Glasgow; Strathclyde University. Architect in private practice, 1955-56 and 1958-82 (Partner, Watson Salmond & Gray, 1956-58); Lecturer, School of Architecture, Glasgow School of Art; Past Chairman, Glasgow Building Guardian Committee; Past Chairman, RIAS Trustees of The Hill House, Helensburgh; Founder and Chairman, Glasgow Summer School; former Member, Committee on Artistic Matters, Church of Scotland. Publications: A Place at Work (Co-author); Jack Coia, His Life & Work. Recreations: gardening; travelling abroad. Address: (h.) Benn Bhuidhe House, Glen Shira, Inverary, Argyll PA32 8XH; T.-01499 302472.

Rolfe, Mervyn James, FRSA, JP, FSAScot. Deputy Leader of the Labour Group, Tayside Regional Council, since 1994; Member, Executive Committee, COSLA, since 1990; b. 31.7.47, Wisbech; m., Christine; 1 s. Educ. Buckhaven High School. Civil servant, until 1983; Co-ordinator, Dundee Resources Centre for the Unemployed, 1983-87; Vice-Chair, Dundee Trades Council, 1981-82; Convener, Education Committee, Tayside Region, 1986-94; Governor, Dundee (now Northern) College of Education, 1986-94; Member, Dundee University Court, since 1986; Member,

Scottish Community Education Council, 1986-88; Member, General Teaching Council, since 1986; Member, Scottish Committee for Staff Development in Education, 1987-91; Board Member, Scottish Enterprise, Tayside, since 1991; Member, Scottish Cooperative Development Committee, since 1984; Member, Dundee Heritage Trust, since 1986; Executive Member, Campaign for a Scottish Assembly, 1989-91. Recreations: reading; politics. Address: (h.) 17 Mains Terrace, Dundee; T.-01382 450073.

Rolfe, William David Ian, PhD, FRSE, FGS, FMA. Keeper of Geology, National Museums of Scotland, since 1986; b. 24.1.36; m., Julia Mary Margaret Rayer; 2 d. Educ. Royal Liberty Grammar School, Romford; Birmingham University. Geology Curator, University Lecturer, then Senior Lecturer in Geology, Hunterian Museum, Glasgow University, 1962-81; Deputy Director, 1981-86. President, Geological Society of Glasgow, 1973-76; Editor, Scottish Journal of Geology, 1967-72; President, Edinburgh Geological Society, 1989-91; President, Palaeontological Association, 1992-94. Recreations: visual arts; walking; swimming; music. Address: 4A Randolph Crescent, Edinburgh, EH3 7TH; T.-0131-226 2094.

Rollinson, Timothy John Denis, BSc, FICFor. Secretary, Forestry Commission, since 1994; b. 6.11.53, London; m., Dominique Christine; 1 s.; 2 d. Educ. Chigwell School, Essex; Edinburgh University. Joined Forestry Commission, 1976; Head of Growth and Yield Studies, 1981-88; Head of Land Use Planning, 1988-90; Head of Parliamentary and Policy Division, 1990-94. Recreations: golf; tennis; swimming; food; France. Address: (b.) Forestry Commission, 231 Corstorphine Road, Edinburgh; T.-0131-334 0303.

Rollo, 13th Lord (Eric John Stapylton Rollo); b. 3.12.15; m.; 2 s.; 1 d. Address: Pitcairns, Dunning, Perthshire, PH2 9BX.

Romanis, William Wright. Director, Administration and Services, National Farmers' Union of Scotland, since 1994; Organiser, ScotGrow, since 1987; Organiser, DairyScot, since 1994; b. 15.10.42, Musselburgh; m., Fiona MacGregor; 1 s.; 1 d. Educ. Musselburgh Grammar School. Administrative staff, Royal Highland & Agricultural Society of Scotland, 1957-65; Assistant Secretary, Scottish Association of Young Farmers' Clubs, 1965-67; Sales Officer/Promotion Officer, Scottish Milk Marketing Board, 1967-77; Organiser, then Director of Services, National Farmers' Union of Scotland, since 1977. Recreations: golf; hill-walking. Address: (b.) Rural Centre, West Mains, Ingliston, Newbridge, Midlothian, EH28 8LT; T.-0131-335 3111.

Rooke, Matthew Andre Paul, MA (Hons). Music Director, Scottish Arts Council, since 1991; b. 14.2.63, Oxford; m., Georgina Verity Dawson. Educ. St. Andrews University; Berklee College of Music. Music Officer, Arts Council of G.B., 1989-91. Recreation: cookery. Address: (b.) 12 Manor Place, Edinburgh, EH3 7PD; T.-0131-225 6051.

Rorke, Professor John, CBE, PhD, BSc, DEng, CEng, FIMechE, FRSE. Professor Emeritus, formerly Professor of Mechanical Engineering, Heriot-Watt University, 1980-88, and Vice-Principal, 1984-88; b. 2.9.23, Dumbarton; m., Jane Craig Buchanan; 2 d. Educ. Dumbarton Academy; Royal Technical College, Glasgow. Lecturer, Strathclyde University, 1946-51; Assistant to Engineering Director, Alexander Stephen & Sons Ltd., 1951-56; Technical Manager, then General Manager and Engineering Director, William Denny & Bros. Ltd., 1956-63; Technical Director, then Sales Director, Managing Director and Chairman, Brown Bros. & Co. Ltd. and Chairman, John Hastie of Greenock Ltd., 1963-78; Managing Director, Vickers Offshore Group, 1978 (Director of Planning, Vickers PLC,

1979-80). President, Institution of Engineers and Shipbuilders in Scotland, 1985-87; Chairman, Institute of Offshore Engineering Group, 1990-94. Recreations: bridge; golf. Address: (h.) 3 Barnton Park Grove, Edinburgh; T.-0131-336 3044.

Rose, Barry Michael, BSc, FIA. Chief Executive, Scottish Provident UK, since 1993; b. 10.3.45, Southend; m., Sandra Jane; 2 d. Educ. Manchester University. Assistant Investment Manager, Cooperative Insurance Society, 1971-76; Investment Secretary, then Investment Manager, Scottish Life Assurance, 1976-88; General Manager (Investment), Scottish Provident Institution, 1988-93. Address: (b.) 6 St. Andrew Square, Edinburgh, EH2 2YA; T.-0131-556 9181.

Rose, David, BA, NDA, CertEd, ARAgS. Principal, The Barony College, Dumfries, since 1980; b. 6.7.40, Denton, Manchester; m., Pauline Anne Rose; 1 s.; 1 d. Educ. Seale-Hayne College of Agriculture; Open University. Assistant Farm Manager, Wiltshire, 1962-66; Lecturer in Agriculture, Cumbria College of Agriculture and Forestry, 1967-70; Senior Lecturer in Agriculture, Bishop Burton College of Agriculture, 1970-74; Vice-Principal, Oatridge College of Agriculture, 1974-80. Recreation: hill-walking. Address: (b.) Parkgate, Dumfries; T.-01387 860251.

Rose, Professor Richard, BA, DPhil, FBA. Director and Professor of Public Policy, Centre for the Study of Public Policy, Strathclyde University, since 1976; b. 9.4.33; m., Rosemary J.; 2 s.; 1 d. Educ. Clayton High School, Missouri, USA; Johns Hopkins University; London School of Economics; Lincoln and Nuffield Colleges, Oxford University. Political public relations, Mississippi Valley, 1954-55; Reporter, St. Louis Post-Dispatch, 1955-57; Lecturer in Government, Manchester University, 1961-66; Professor of Politics, Strathclyde University, 1966-82; Consultant Psephologist, The Times, Independent Television, Daily Telegraph, STV, UTV, etc., since 1964; American SSRC Fellow, Stanford University, 1967; Visiting Lecturer in Political Sociology, Cambridge University, 1967; Director, ISSC European Summer School, 1973; Secretary, Committee on Political Sociology, International Sociological Association, 1970-85; Founding Member, European Consortium for Political Research, 1970; Member: US/UK Fulbright Commission, 1971-75, Eisenhower Fellowship Programme, 1971; Guggenheim Foundation Fellow, 1974; Visiting Scholar: Woodrow Wilson International Centre, Washington DC, 1974, Brookings Institute, Washington DC, 1976, American Enterprise Institute, Washington, 1980, Fiscal Affairs Department, IMF, Washington, 1984; Visiting Professor, European University Institute, Florence, 1977, 1978; Visitor, Japan Foundation, 1984; Hinkley Professor, Johns Hopkins University, 1987; Guest Professor, Wissenschaftzentrum, Berlin, 1988, 1990, Central European University, Prague, 1992-95; Ransome Lecturer, University of Alabama, 1990; Consultant Chairman, NI Constitutional Convention, 1976; Home Office Working Party on Electoral Register, 1975-77; Co-Founder, British Politics Group, 1974; Convenor, Work Group on UK Politics, Political Studies Association, 1976-88; Member, Council, International Political Science Association, 1976-82; Keynote Speaker, Australian Institute of Political Science, Canberra, 1978; Technical Consultant, OECD, World Bank, Scottish Opera; Director, ESRC (formerly SSRC) Research Programme, Growth of Government, 1982-86; Honorary Vice President, Political Studies Association, UK, 1986; Editor, Journal of Public Policy, since 1985 (Chairman, 1981-85); Foreign Member, Finnish Academy of Science and Letters, 1985; Member, American Academy of Arts and Sciences, 1994; Robert Marjolin AMEX Prize in International Economics, 1992. Publications: The British General Election of 1959 (Co-author), 1960; Must Labour Lose? (Co-author), 1960; Politics in England, 1964; Studies in British Politics (Editor), 1966; Influencing Voters, 1967;

Policy Making in Britain (Editor), 1969; People in Politics, 1970; European Politics (Joint Editor), 1971; Governing Without Consensus — An Irish Perspective, 1971; International Almanack of Electoral History (Co-author), 1974; Electoral Behaviour — A Comparative Handbook (Editor), 1974; Lessons From America (Editor), 1974; The Problem of Party Government, 1974; The Management of Urban Change in Britain and Germany (Editor), 1974; Northern Ireland — A Time of Choice, 1976; Managing Presidential Objectives, 1976; The Dynamics of Public Policy (Editor), 1976; New Trends in British Politics (Joint Editor), 1977; Comparing Public Policies (Joint Editor), 1977; What is Governing? — Purpose and Policy in Washington, 1978; Elections Without Choice (Joint Editor), 1978; Can Government Go Bankrupt? (Co-author), 1978; Britain — Progress and Decline (Joint Editor), 1980; Do Parties Make a Difference?, 1980; Challenge to Governance (Editor), 1980; Electoral Participation (Editor), 1980; Presidents and Prime Ministers (Joint Editor), 1980; Understanding the United Kingdom, 1982; United Kingdom Facts (Co-author), 1982; The Territorial Dimension in United Kingdom Politics (Joint Editor), 1982; Fiscal Stress in Cities (Joint Editor), 1982; Understanding Big Government, 1984; The Nationwide Competition for Votes (Co-author), 1984; Public Employment in Western Nations, 1985; Voters Begin to Choose (Co-author), 1986; Patterns of Parliamentary Legislation (Co-author), 1986; The Welfare State East and West (Joint Editor), 1986; Ministers and Ministries, 1987; Taxation By Political Inertia (Co-author), 1987; The Post-Modern President — The White House Meets the World, 1988; Ordinary People in Public Policy, 1989; Training Without Trainers? (Co-author), 1990; The Loyalty of Voters (Co-author), 1990; Lesson-Drawing in Public Policy, 1993; Inheritance before Choice, 1994; What Is Europe?, 1995. Recreations: architecture (historical, Britain; modern, America); music; writing. Address: (b.) CSPP, Strathclyde University, Livingstone Tower, Glasgow, G1 1XH; T.-0141-552 4400.

Rosebery, 7th Earl of (Neil Archibald Primrose), DL; b. 11.2.29; m., Alison Mary Deirdre Reid; 1 s.; 4 d. Educ. Stowe; New College, Oxford. Address: (h.) Dalmeny House, South Queensferry, West Lothian.

Rosie, Alexander. Director, Corporate Planning and Resources, Historic Scotland, since 1992; b. 13.8.50, Edinburgh; m., Ruth; 1 s. Educ. George Heriot's School, Edinburgh. Trainee Engineer, 1968-70; Civil Servant in the Scottish Office, since 1971. Recreations: sailing; tennis; playing piano. Address: (b.) Longmore House, Salisbury Place, Edinburgh EH9 1SH.

Rosie, George. Freelance Writer and Broadcaster; b. 27.2.41, Edinburgh; m., Elizabeth Ann Burness; 2 s.; 1 d. Educ. Trinity Academy, Edinburgh; Edinburgh School of Architecture. Editor, Interior Design magazine, 1966-68; freelance magazine writer, 1968-76; Scottish Affairs Correspondent, Sunday Times, 1976-86; Reporter, Channel 4 TV series Down the Line, 1986-87, Scottish Eye, 1988; Reporter/Writer, The Englishing of Scotland, 1988, Selling Scotland, 1989; Scotching the Myth, 1990; Losing the Heid, 1991; Editor, Observer Scotland, 1988-89; award winner, RSPB birds and countryside awards, 1988. Publications: British in Vietnam, 1970; Cromarty, 1975; The Ludwig Initiative, 1978; Hugh Miller, 1982; The Directory of International Terrorism, 1986; as contributor: Headlines, the Media in Scotland, 1978; Scottish Government Yearbook, 1982; Scotland, Multinationals and the Third World, 1982; World Offshore Oil and Gas Industry Report, 1987; stage plays: The Blasphemer, 1990; Carlucco and the Queen of Hearts, 1991 (winner, Fringe First, The Independent Theatre Award); It Had To Be You, 1994. Recreation: hill-walking. Address: (h.) 70 Comiston Drive, Edinburgh, EH10 5QS; T.-0131-447 9660.

Rosin, Leslie, BL, JP. Company Director; Member: Eastwood District Council, since 1984, Provost, since 1992;

Director, Scottish Chamber Orchestra; Director, Scottish Rights of Way Society; Vice-Chairman, Isobel Mair School; Chairman, Eastwood Branch, Scottish Mentally Handicapped Association; b. 31.8.31, London; m., Hilary Langman; 1 s.; 2 d. Educ. Hutchesons' Grammar School; Glasgow University. Member, Strathclyde Regional Council, 1986-90; former Vice-Chairman, Hillhead Conservative Association; former Chairman, Eastwood Conservative Association; former Member, Management Committee, Tron Theatre; former Chairman, Glasgow Chamber Music Society; Member, Music Committee, Scottish Arts Council; Delegate to COSLA; Chairman, Sports Advisory Group Eastwood; Board Member, Scottish Opera; Chairman, Eastwood Festival of the Arts. Recreation: harpsichord maker. Address: (h.) 26 Glenpark Avenue, Glasgow, G46 7JF; T.-0141-638 3333.

Ross, Alastair Robertson, OStJ, DA, ARSA, FRBS, FSA Scot, FRSA, MBIM, Hon. FRIAS. Artist; Lecturer in Fine Art, Duncan of Jordanstone College University of Dundee, since 1994; Lecturer in Fine Art, Duncan of Jordanstone College of Art, Dundee, 1966-94; Honorary Lecturer, Dundee University, 1969-94; Vice President, Royal Society of British Sculptors, 1988-90; Council Member, British School at Rome, since 1990; b. 8.8.41, Perth; m., Kathryn Margaret Greig Wilson; 1 d. Educ. St. Mary's Episcopal School, Dunblane; McLaren High School, Callander; Duncan of Jordanstone College of Art, Dundee. SED Postgraduate Scholarship, 1965-66; Dickson Prize for Sculpture, 1962; Holokrome (Dundee) Sculpture Prize and Commission, 1962; SED Travelling Scholarship, 1963; Royal Scottish Academy Chalmers Bursary, 1964; Royal Scottish Academy Carnegie Travelling Scholarship, 1965; Duncan of Drumfork Scholarship, 1965; award winner, Paris Salon, 1967; Medaille de Bronze, Societe des Artistes Francais, 1968; Professional Member, Society of Scottish Artists, 1969; Medaille D'Argent, 1970; Membre Associe, Societe des Artistes Francais, 1970; Scottish Representative and Member, Council, Royal Society of British Sculptors, since 1972; Sir Otto Beit Medal, Royal Society of British Sculptors, 1988; Freeman, City of London, 1989; Sir William Gillies Bequest Award, Royal Scottish Academy, 1989; Council Member, Society of Scottish Artists, 1972-75; Hon. Fellow, Royal Incorporation of Architects in Scotland, 1992; exhibited work widely in UK and abroad; work in: Scottish Arts Council Collection, Dundee Education Authority Collection, private collections in Austria, Switzerland, Egypt, USA, Norway, Bahamas, Canada, Portugal, India, UK. Recreations: genealogy; heraldry; travel. Address: (h.) Ravenscourt, 28 Albany Terrace, Dundee, DD3 6HS; T.-01382 24235.

Ross, Alexander (Sandy), LLB, CYCW. Deputy Chief Executive, Scottish Television Enterprises, since 1995; b. 17.4.48, Grangemouth; m., Alison Fraser; 2 s.; 1 d. Educ. Grangemouth High School; Edinburgh University; Moray House College. Apprentice lawyer, 1971-73; Lecturer, Paisley College, 1974-75; Producer, Granada TV, 1978-86; Controller, Arts and Entertainment, Scottish Television, 1986-95. Member, Edinburgh Town Council, 1971-74; Member, Edinburgh District Council, 1974-78; President, Moray House Students Union, 1976. Recreations: golf; music; reading; watching football. Address: (h.) 7 Murrayfield Avenue, Edinburgh, EH12 6AU; T.-0131-337 3679.

Ross, Rev. Andrew Christian, MA, BD, STM, PhD. Senior Lecturer in Ecclesiastical History, Edinburgh University, since 1966 (Principal of New College and Dean, Faculty of Divinity, 1978-84); b. 10.5.31, Millerhill, Lothian; m., I. Joyce Elder; 4 s.; 1 d. (deceased). Educ. Dalkeith High School; Edinburgh University; Union Theological Seminary, New York. RAF, 1952-54; Minister, Church of Central Africa Presbyterian (Malawi), 1958-65; Chairman, Lands Tribunal of Nyasaland, then Malawi Government, 1963-65; Vice Chairman, National Tenders

Board, Nyasaland, then Malawi Government, 1963-65. Member, University Court, 1971-73; Convener, Student Affairs Committee, 1977-83; Kerr Lecturer, Glasgow University, 1984; Lecturer, Assembly's College, Belfast, 1985; Visiting Professor, Yale University and Dartmouth College, 1992. Publications: John Philip: Missions, Race and Politics in South Africa; Vision Betrayed: the Jesuits in China and Japan. Recreation: coaching and watching football. Address: (h.) 27 Colinton Road, Edinburgh; T.-0131-447 5987.

Ross, Professor David Alexander, BSc (Hons), PhD, DipEdTech, CChem, FRSC. Head, Department of Molecular and Life Sciences, University of Abertay, Dundee, since 1991; b. 6.7.52, Stirling; m., Lyn; 3 d. Educ. Kilsyth Academy; Strathclyde University. Procter and Gamble Ltd., Newcastle, 1977-85; Senior Lecturer, University of Abertay, Dundee, 1985-91. Recreations: golf; fishing; gardening. Address: (h.) 32 Broadlands, Carnoustie, Angus; T.-01241 859905.

Ross, Donald Forrester, MA, CA. General Treasurer, Church of Scotland, since 1995; Secretary, Church of Scotland Trust, since 1975; b. 14.6.42, Aberdeen; m., Dorothy Reid Nelson; 2 s. Educ. Aberdeen Grammar School; Aberdeen University. CA Apprentice, G. & J. McBain, CA, Aberdeen, 1963-67; Audit Assistant, Thomson McLintock, CA, Glasgow, 1967-69; Assistant Treasurer, Church of Scotland, 1969-75; Deputy General Treasurer, Church of Scotland, 1975-95. Recreation: golf. Address: (b.) 121 George Street, Edinburgh, EH2 4YN; T.-0131-225 5722.

Ross, Rt. Hon. Lord (Donald MacArthur Ross), PC, MA, LLB. Lord Justice Clerk and President of the Second Division of the Court of Session, since 1985; a Senator of the College of Justice, since 1977; Lord High Commissioner to the General Assembly of the Church of Scotland, 1990 and 1991; b. 29.3.27, Dundee; m., Dorothy Margaret Annand; 2 d. Educ. High School of Dundee; Edinburgh University. Advocate, 1952; QC, 1964; Vice-Dean, Faculty of Advocates, 1967-73; Dean of Faculty, 1973-76; Sheriff Principal of Ayr and Bute, 1972-73; Member, Scottish Committee, Council of Tribunals, 1970-76; Member, Committee on Privacy, 1970; Deputy Chairman, Boundary Commission for Scotland, 1977-85. Member, Court, Heriot-Watt University, 1978-90; Chairman, 1984-90. Hon. LLD, Edinburgh, Dundee, Abertay Dundee; Hon. DUniv, Heriot-Watt; FRSE. Recreation: gardening; walking; travel. Address: Parliament House, Edinburgh, EH1 1RQ; T.-0131-225 2595.

Ross, Ernest. MP (Labour), Dundee West, since 1979; Chair, PLP Foreign Affairs Committee; Member, Employment Select Committee; b. 27.7.42, Dundee; m., June; 2 s.; 1 d. Educ. St. John's Junior Secondary School. Apprentice Marine Fitter, Caledon Shipyard; Quality Control Inspector/Engineer, Timex. Recreations: football; cricket. Address: (b.) Constituency Office, 13 Cowgate, Dundee; T.-01382 200329.

Ross, Graham Tullis, LVO, OBE. Chairman, Edinburgh Old Town Renewal Trust, since 1991; Chairman, Edinburgh Old Town Charitable Trust, since 1990; Chairman, Leith School of Art, since 1993; b. 5.7.28, Edinburgh; m., Margot; 1 s.; 2 d. Educ. George Watson's College, Edinburgh. Director, Macvitties Guest & Co. Ltd., Edinburgh, 1955-65; Managing Director, Macvitties Guest (Edinburgh), A.F. Reid (Glasgow), 1965-71; Managing Director, A.A. Laing Ltd. and Ross Restaurants Ltd., 1971-76; Managing Director, D.S. Crawford (Catering) Ltd., 1976-82; Director, Scottish Business in the Community, 1982-90. Chairman, Scottish Hotel and Catering Institute, 1968-72; Chairman, Napier College Advisory Committee, 1970-85. Recreation: hill-walking. Address: (h.) 20 Munro Drive, Edinburgh; T.-0131-225 8818.

Ross, Helen Elizabeth, BA, MA (Oxon), PhD (Cantab), FBPsS, CPsychol, FRSE. Honorary Senior Research Fellow, Stirling University, since 1994; b. 2.12.35, London. Educ. South Hampstead High School; Somerville College, Oxford; Newnham College, Cambridge. Assistant Mistress, schools in London and Oxfordshire, 1959-61; Research Assistant and student, Psychological Laboratory, Cambridge University, 1961-65; Lecturer in Psychology: Hull University, 1965-68, Stirling University, 1969-72; Senior Lecturer in Psychology, Stirling University, 1972-83; Research Fellow, DFVLR Institute for Aerospace Medicine, Bonn, 1980-81; Leverhulme Fellowship, 1983-84; Reader in Psychology, Stirling University, 1983-94. Member, S.E. Regional Board, Nature Conservancy Council for Scotland, 1991-92; Fellowship Secretary, Royal Society of Edinburgh, since 1994. Publications: Behaviour and Perception in Strange Environments, 1974; E.H. Weber: The Sense of Touch (Co-translator), 1978. Recreations: skiing; curling; hill-walking; traditional music. Address: (b.) Department of Psychology, Stirling University, Stirling, FK9 4LA; T.-01786 467647.

Ross, John Alexander, CBE, FRAgS. President, National Farmers' Union of Scotland, 1990; b. 19.2.45, Stranraer; m., Alison Jean Darling; 2 s.; 1 d. Educ. George Watson's College, Edinburgh. NFU of Scotland: Convener, Hill Farming Sub-Committee, 1984-90, Convener, Livestock Committee, 1987-90, Vice-President, 1986-90, Wigtown Area President, 1985-86. Chairman, Stranraer School Council, 1980-89; Session Clerk, Portpatrick Parish Church, 1975-80; Elder, Church of Scotland; Director, Animal Diseases Research Association. Recreations: golf; curling. Address: (b.) Rural Centre, West Mains, Ingliston, Newbridge, Midlothian EH28 8LT.

Ross, Michael David, FFA, CIMgt. Group Chief Executive, Scottish Widows, since 1991; b. 9.7.46, Edinburgh; m., Pamela Marquis Speakman. Educ. Daniel Stewart's College. Joined Scottish Widows, 1964; General Manager, 1968, Deputy Managing Director, 1990. FRSA. Recreations: curling; golf; skiing. Address: (b.) 15 Dalkeith Road, Edinburgh, EH16 5BU; T.-0131-655 6000.

Ross, Philip Wesley, TD, MB, ChB, MD, FRCPE, FRCPath, CBiol, FIBiol, FLS. Consultant, Edinburgh Royal Infirmary, and Reader in Medical Microbiology, Edinburgh University; b. 6.6.36, Aberdeen; m., Stella Joyce Shand; 2 s.; 1 d. Educ. Turriff Academy; Robert Gordon's College, Aberdeen; Aberdeen University. Senior Warden, Edinburgh University, 1972-83. Lt.-Col., RAMC (TA); Officer Commanding Medical Division and Edinburgh Detachment 205 Scottish General Hospital, 1975-80; Scottish Chairman, Institute of Biology; Examiner, Royal College of Surgeons, Edinburgh, Royal College of Pathologists; Chairman, Lothian Area Division of Laboratory Medicine, 1986-89; Elder, Duddingston Kirk, Edinburgh; Liberal Democrat candidate, Monklands East, 1992. Publications: textbooks and papers in scientific and medical journals on streptococci, diseases of mouth, throat and genital tract, antibiotics and cross infection. Recreations: music; playing church organs (formerly organist in three Aberdeen churches); walking; travel; art galleries; museums; politics. Address: (h.) 18 Old Church Lane, Duddingston Village, Edinburgh, EH15 3PX; T.-0131-661 5415.

Ross, Robert Fowler. Farming Editor, The Herald, since 1994; b. 9.3.40, Crossgates; m., Jeanette Miller; 1 s.; 1 d. Educ. Dunfermline High School. Trainee Reporter, Dunfermline Press; Reporter, Glasgow Herald, Scottish Daily Mail, Scotsman; Scottish Office Correspondent, The Herald, 1972-87; Edinburgh News Editor, The Herald, 1987-94. Recreations: gardening; walking. Address: (h.) 57 Oatlands Park, Linlithgow, EH49 6AS; T.-01506 842892.

Ross, Thomas Alexander, KStJ, BL, PhD. Former Senior Partner, Russel & Aitken, WS, Falkirk, Edinburgh and

Denny; Honorary Sheriff, Tayside, Central and Fife; b. 18.7.06, Selkirk; m., Eleanor Tyson; 1 s. Educ. Selkirk School; Edinburgh University. Director of Administration, Far Eastern Bureau of Political Intelligence, Department of the Foreign Office in Delhi and Chungking, 1944; Governor, Christ's Hospital. Recreations: travelling; shooting. Address: (b.) Russel & Aitken, WS, King's Court, Falkirk; T.-Falkirk 622888.

Ross, William, FRICS. Chief Executive, Edinburgh Development and Investment Limited; b. 2.2.41, Rutherglen; m., Margaret; 2 s.; 1 d. Educ. Rutherglen Academy; Glasgow University. Trainee, London County Council; Negotiator, Hillier Parker May and Rowden; Valuer, Glasgow Corporation; District Surveyor, British Rail Property Board; Group Development Surveyor, Maxwell Property Development Company; self-employed; Principal Surveyor (Development), Grampian Regional Council; Depute Director of Estates, then Director of Economic Development and Estates, City of Edinburgh District Council. Address: (b.) 1 Broughton Market, Edinburgh; T.-0131-556 5003.

Ross Stewart, David Andrew, OBE, BA (Cantab). Chairman, Scottish Provident Institution; b. 30.11.30, Edinburgh; m., Susan Olive Routh; 2 s. Educ. Rugby School; Cambridge University. Assistant General Manager, Alex. Cowan & Sons (NZ) Ltd., 1959-62; General Manager, Alex. Cowan & Sons (Stationery) Ltd., 1962-66; General Manager, Spicers (Stationery) Ltd., 1966-68; Managing Director, John Bartholomew & Son Ltd., 1968-89. Chairman, St. Andrew Trust plc; Chairman, EFM Income Trust plc; Chairman, Quayle Munro plc; Director, Lothian Investment Fund for Enterprise Ltd.; Fellow, Scottish Council (Development and Industry). Recreations: fishing; gardening; golf. Address: (b.) 13 Blacket Place, Edinburgh, EH9 1RN; T.-0131-667 3221.

Rotter, Professor John Michael, BA, MA, PhD. Professor of Civil Engineering, Edinburgh University, since 1989; Head, Department of Engineering Planning Unit, since 1992; b. 31.10.48, Chesterfield; 1 s.; 1 d. Educ. Monkton Combe School, Bath; Cambridge University. Temporary Lecturer in Civil Engineering, then Lecturer, then Senior Lecturer, University of Sydney, 1975-89. Visiting Professor, University of Washington, St. Louis, 1983-84; Visiting Research Fellow, Liverpool University, 1984. Publications: 133 papers; 35 major specialist reports; 51 presentations. Recreations: classical music; theatre; travelling; walking. Address: (b.) Edinburgh University, King's Buildings, Edinburgh, EH9 3JN; T.-0131-650 5719.

Rowallan, 4th Baron (John Polson Cameron Corbett); b. 8.3.47; 2 s.; 2 d. Address: Meiklemosside, Fenwick, Ayrshire, KA3 6AY.

Rowan, John O'Donnell, PhD, CPhys, FInstP, CEng, FIEE, FIPSM. Deputy Director, West of Scotland Health Boards Department of Clinical Physics and Bio-Engineering, since 1983; Honorary Clinical Senior Lecturer in Clinical Physics, Glasgow University, since 1991; Member, National Panel of Assessors for NHS Scientists in Scotland, since 1982; b. 5.4.36, Glasgow; m., Anne Kerr Wotherspoon; 2 d. by pr. m. Educ. Victoria Drive Senior Secondary School, Glasgow; Glasgow University. Research Physicist, Barr and Stroud, Glasgow, 1961-63; Electronics Engineer, Scottish Research Reactor Centre, East Kilbride, 1963-66; West of Scotland Health Boards Department of Clinical Physics and Bio-Engineering: Senior Physicist, 1966-71, Principal Physicist, 1971-81, Top Grade Physicist, 1981-83. Honorary Treasurer, Scottish Branch, Institute of Physics, 1972-77; Honorary Secretary, Hospital Physicists Association, 1976-78, and President, 1982-84; Deputy Editor, Physics in Medicine and Biology, 1980-82; President, Institute of Physical Sciences in Medicine, 1982-84; Member, Scottish Health Service National Scientific Services Advisory Committee, since 1989. Address: (b.) Glasgow Royal Infirmary, Glasgow, G4; T.-0141-304 4934.

Rowan-Robinson, Professor Richard Jeremy, MA, LLM, FRSA. Solicitor (England and Wales); Legal Associate, Royal Town Planning Institute; Professor of Planning and Environmental Law, Aberdeen University, since 1989; Director, Aberdeen University Centre for Environmental Law and Policy; Consultant in Planning and Environmental Law, Paull and Williamsons, Solicitors, Aberdeen, since 1992; b. 29.3.44, Edinburgh; m., Yvonne Joan Elizabeth; 2 s. Educ. University of Kent; Aberdeen University; Law Society College of Law. Assistant Solicitor, LB of Redbridge, 1966; Senior Assistant Solicitor, LB of Hillingdon, 1969; Deputy Clerk, Westmorland County Council, 1972; Solicitor, Lake District Special Planning Board, 1975; Lecturer, then Senior Lecturer, Department of Land Economy, Aberdeen University, 1978-89. Address: (b.) Department of Land Economy, Aberdeen University, St. Mary's, King's College, Old Aberdeen; T.-01228 272358.

Rowe, Michael, BA (Hons). Director (Scotland), Advisory Conciliation and Arbitration Service, since 1989; b. 30.5.37, Stoke-on-Trent; m., Kathleen Marie; 2 s. Educ. High School, Newcastle-under-Lyme; St. Catherine's College, Oxford University. Various posts, Department of Employment, 1961-70; First Secretary, UK Delegation to European Communities in Brussels, 1970-72; various posts, London, 1972-81; Benefit Manager, Scotland, Department of Employment, 1981-87; Deputy Director Scotland, Employment Service, 1987-89. Recreations: family; involvement in youth club activities; enjoying good food and wine. Address: (b.) Advisory, Conciliation and Arbitration Service, 123 Bothwell Street, Glasgow; T.-0141-248 1400.

Rowley, Alexander A.P., MA (Hons), MSc. Leader of Administration, Fife Council, since 1995; Chair, Finance, Fife Regional Council, since 1994; Scottish Co-ordinator, National Local Government Forum Against Poverty, since 1994; b. 30.11.63, Dunfermline; m., Susan Carden; 2 d. Educ. St. Columba's High School, Dunfermline; Newbattle Abbey College, Dalkeith; Edinburgh University. Recreations: reading; swimming. Address: (b.) Fife House, North Street, Glenrothes, Fife; T.-01592 414141.

Rowley, Professor David Ian, MB, ChB, BMedBiol, MD, FRCS. Professor of Orthopaedic and Trauma Surgery, Dundee University, since 1988; b. 4.7.51, Dewsbury; m., Ingrid Ginette; 1 s.; 1 d. Educ. Wheelwright Grammar School, Dewsbury; Aberdeen University; Sheffield University. Lecturer in Orthopaedic Surgery, Sheffield University, 1981; Senior Lecturer in Orthopaedic Surgery, Manchester University, and Senior Lecturer in Orthopaedic Mechanics, Salford University, 1985-88. Orthopaedic Editor, Journal of Royal College of Surgeons of Edinburgh; Regional Advisor in Surgery, NE Region, Royal College of Surgeons of Edinburgh; Examiner, Royal College of Surgeons, Edinburgh. Recreations: gardening; reading history. Address: (h.) Marclann Cottage, Kellie Castle, Arbroath; T.-01241 76466.

Rowson, John Tyldesley, BSc, CEng, FICE, FIHT. Director of Engineering, Fife Regional Council, since 1984; b. 4.4.38, Pendleton, Lancs; m., Diana Valerie Snelson; 2 s.; 1 d. Educ. Bolton School; Manchester University. Early appointments in Bolton, Macclesfield and Manchester; appointed Assistant City Engineer, Dundee, 1972; Depute Director of Roads, Tayside Region, 1975. Chairman, Association of Municipal Engineers, 1993-94; Vice-President, Institution of Civil Engineers, 1993-94; Past Chairman, County Surveyors' Society (Scottish Branch); Past Chairman, Dundee Branch, Institution of Civil Engineers and AME (Scotland). Recreations: golf; garden. Address: (b.) Fife Regional Council, Fife House, North Street, Glenrothes, Fife; T.-01592 414141.

Roxburgh, John Hampton, DPE. Technical Administrator, Scottish Rugby Union, since 1974; b. 20.6.38, Glasgow; m., Irene; 1 s.; 1 d. Educ. Jordanhill College School; Jordanhill College of Education. Taught in various Glasgow schools as Assistant Teacher of PE; transferred to further education; Head of Physical Education, Barmulloch College of Further Education. Captained Jordanhill, nine seasons; represented Glasgow in three positions; appointed SRU Advisory Coach, 1968. Recreation: golf. Address: (b.) Scottish Rugby Union, Murrayfield, Edinburgh, EH12 5PJ; T.-0131-346 5000.

Roxburghe, 10th Duke of (Guy David Innes-Ker), b. 18.11.54; m., 1, Lady Jane Meriel Grosvenor (m. diss.); 2 s.; 1 d.; 2, Virginia Mary Wynn-Williams; 1 d. Educ. Eton; Sandhurst; Magdalene College, Cambridge. Address: (h.) Floors Castle, Kelso.

Roy, Kenneth. Editor, The Scottish Review, since 1994; weekly Columnist, The Observer, since 1995; b. 26.3.45, Falkirk; m., Margaret H. Campbell; 2 s. Educ. Denny High School. Local journalism, 1962-1965; Glasgow Herald, 1965-67; public relations, 1967-69; Editor, Scottish Theatre magazine, 1969-72; BBC Scotland, 1972-80; Managing Director, West Sound, 1980-82; Proprietor, Carrick Media, since 1983; Editor, Journalist's Handbook, 1985-93; weekly Columnist, Scotland on Sunday, 1988-94. Critic of the Year, Scottish Press Awards, 1990, 1993; Columnist of the Year, British Regional Press Awards, 1994. Publications: Travels in a Small Country, 1987; Conversations in a Small Country, 1989; The Closing Headlines (autobiography), 1993; Scenes from a Small Country (collected journalism), 1994. Address: (b.) Carrick Media, 2/7 Galt House, 31 Bank Street, Irvine, KA12 0LL; T.-01294 311322.

Roy, Lindsay Allan, BSc. Rector, Inverkeithing High School, since 1989; b. 19.1.49, Perth; m., Irene Elizabeth Patterson; 2 s.; 1 d. Educ. Perth Academy; Edinburgh University. Assistant Rector, Kirkcaldy High School, 1983-86; Depute Rector, Glenwood High School, Glenrothes, 1986-89; Chairman, Modern Studies Association, 1976-79; Chairman, Modern Studies Panel, Scottish Examination Board, 1980-83; Member, Consultative Committee on the Curriculum Central Committee for Social Subjects, 1978-85. Recreation: angling. Address: (b.) Inverkeithing High School, Hillend Road, Inverkeithing, Fife; T.-01383 313400.

Royan, Bruce, BA (Hons), ALA, MBA, MIInfSc, FIMgt. Director of Information Services and University Librarian, Stirling University, since 1989; Principal Consultant, Infologistix Ltd., since 1988; b. 22.1.47, Luton; m., Ann Elizabeth Wilkins; 1 s.; 1 d. Educ. Dunstable Grammar School; North West Polytechnic; Glasgow University. Systems Development Manager, British Library, 1975-77; Head of Systems, National Library of Scotland, 1977-85; Director, Singapore Integrated Library Automation Service, 1985-88. Secretary, Working Party on Access to the National Database, 1980-83; Member, Council, Library Association of Singapore, 1987-88; Member, Universities and Colleges Information Systems Association, since 1989; Convenor, Higher Education IT Directors in Scotland, 1991-93; Executive Chairman, Bath Information and Data Services, since 1991; Councillor, The Library Association. Recreations: choral singing; antique maps; travel. Address: (b.) Stirling University, Stirling, FK9 4LA; T.-01786 467227.

Royle, Trevor Bridge, MA, FRSE. Author and Broadcaster; Associate Editor, Scotland on Sunday; b. 26.1.45, Mysore, India; m., Dr. Hannah Mary Rathbone; 3 s. Educ. Madras College, St. Andrews; Aberdeen University. Editor, William Blackwood & Sons Ltd.; Literature Director, Scottish Arts Council, 1971-79; Council Member, Scottish National Dictionary Association; Scottish Arts Council Book Award, 1983. Publications: We'll Support You Evermore: The Impertinent Saga of Scottish Fitba' (Co-Editor), 1976; Jock Tamson's Bairns (Editor), 1977; Precipitous City: The Story of Literary Edinburgh, 1980; A Diary of Edinburgh, 1981; Edinburgh, 1982; Death Before Dishonour: The True Story of Fighting Mac, 1982; The Macmillan Companion to Scottish Literature, 1983; James and Jim: The Biography of James Kennaway, 1983; The Kitchener Enigma, 1985; The Best Years of their Lives: The Post-War National Service Experience, 1986; War Report: The War Correspondents' View of Battle from the Crimea to the Falklands, 1987; The Last Days of the Raj, 1989; A Dictionary of Military Quotations, 1989; Anatomy of a Regiment, 1990; In Flanders Fields: poetry and prose of the First World War, 1990; Glubb Pasha, 1992; Mainstream Companion to Scottish Literature, 1993; Orde Wingate: Irregular Soldier, 1995; radio plays: Magnificat, 1984; Old Alliances, 1985; Foreigners, 1987; Huntingtower, 1988; A Man Flourishing, 1988; The Pavilion on the Links, 1991; The Suicide Club, 1992; stage play: Buchan of Tweedsmuir, 1991. Recreations: rugby football; hill-walking; restoring Craigiemeg. Address: (h.) 6 James Street, Edinburgh, EH15 2DS; T.-0131-669 2116.

Ruckley, Professor Charles Vaughan, MB, ChM, FRCSEdin, FRCPEdin. Consultant Surgeon, Royal Infirmary, Edinburgh, since 1971; Professor of Vascular Surgery, Edinburgh University, since 1992; President, Vascular Surgical Society, Great Britain and Ireland, 1993-94; b. 14.5.34, Wallasey; m., Valerie Anne Brooks; 1 s.; 1 d. Educ. Wallasey Grammar School; Edinburgh University. Research Fellow, University of Colorado, 1967-68. Secretary/Treasurer, Vascular Surgical Society of Great Britain and Ireland; Member, Council, Association of Surgeons of Great Britain and Ireland. Recreations: angling; music; skiing. Address: (b.) Vascular Surgery Unit, Royal Infirmary, Edinburgh; T.-0131-229 2477.

Rugg, Professor Michael Derek, BSc, PhD. Professor of Psychology and Wellcome Research Fellow, School of Psychology, St. Andrews University, since 1994; b. 23.9.54, Ely; m., Elizabeth Louise. Educ. Leicester University. Lecturer, Department of Psychology, St. Andrews University, 1979-88, Reader, 1988-92, Professor and Head of School, 1992-94. Committee Member, European Brain and Behaviour Society; Henri Hecaen Award for contributions to neuropsychology, 1989. Publications: 90 scientific articles. Recreations: rock climbing; mountaineering; skiing. Address: (b.) School of Psychology, St. Andrews University, St. Andrews, KY16 9JU; T.-01334 462069.

Runcie, Geoff. Chief Executive, Glasgow Chamber of Commerce. Address: (b.) 30 George Square, Glasgow, G2 1EQ.

Runciman, William Chisholm, LLB. Secretary, Carnegie Dunfermline and Hero Fund Trusts; b. 15.11.41, Greenock; m., Eileen; 2 s. Educ. Greenock Academy; Edinburgh University. Police Officer in Edinburgh and Lothian & Borders, retiring in 1987 as Chief Superintendent; former Director, National Playing Fields Association — Scotland. Recreations: mountaineering; fishing; photography. Address: (h.) 11 East Harbour Road, Charlestown, Fife, KY11 3EA.

Rundell, David Richard, BSc, MSc, CStat. Director of Computing Services, Heriot-Watt University, since 1990; b. 5.9.48, Plymouth; 3 d. Educ. Harwich County High, Harwich, Essex; St. Andrews University; Heriot-Watt University. Statistician, Medical School, Edinburgh University, 1970-76; Applications Team, Regional Computing Centre, University of Bath, 1976-79; User Services Manager, Computer Centre, Heriot-Watt University, 1979-90. Address: (b.) Computer Centre, Heriot-Watt University, Riccarton, Edinburgh EH14 4AS; T.-0131-449 5111.

Runnalls, Professor Graham Arthur, BA, MA, DipGenLing, DLitt. Professor of French, Edinburgh University; b. 21.11.37, Exmouth; m., Anne K.; 2 d. Educ. Exmouth Grammar School; Exeter University. Assistant Lecturer in French, Exeter University, 1962-63; Lecturer in French, North London Polytechnic, 1963-66; joined Edinburgh University as Lecturer, 1966. Honorary President, International Society for the Study of Medieval Theatre. Recreations: opera; sport, especially tennis and running. Address: (h.) 85A Colinton Road, Edinburgh, EH10 5DF; T.-0131-337 1737.

Rusby, Sir Cameron, KCB, LVO. Director, Freedom Food Ltd; Vice President, World Society for the Protection of Animals, since 1994; b. 20.2.26, Sliema, Malta; m., Marion Elizabeth Bell; 2 d. Educ. Wootton Court School, near Canterbury; Royal Naval College, Dartmouth. Thirty nine years in Royal Navy, reaching rank of Vice Admiral; retired, 1982; Chief Executive, Scottish Society for the Prevention of Cruelty to Animals, 1983-91, Legislative Adviser to the Society, 1991-94; . Recreations: sailing; skiing; equitation. Address: c/o Bank of Scotland, 70 High Street, Peebles, EH45 8AQ.

Rush, Christopher, MA (Hons). Writer; Teacher, George Watson's College, Edinburgh, since 1972; b. 23.11.44, St. Monans; m., Patricia Irene Boyd (deceased); 1 s.; 1 d. Educ. Waid Academy; Aberdeen University. Has won two Scottish Arts Council bursaries, two SAC book awards, twice been short-listed for Scottish Book of the Year Award; shortlisted for McVitie Scottish Writer of the Year, 1988; Screenwriter, Venus Peter (based on own book). Publications include: Peace Comes Dropping Slow; A Resurrection of a Kind; A Twelvemonth and A Day; Two Christmas Stories; Into the Ebb; With Sharp Compassion; Venus Peter Saves the Whale; Last Lesson of the Afternoon. Recreations: music; reading; cross-country running; sea-watching. Address: (h.) 2 Peel Terrace, Edinburgh, EH9 2AY; T.-0131-667 1248.

Russell, (Alastair) Muir, BSc. Secretary and Head of Department, Scottish Office Agriculture, Environment and Fisheries Department, since 1995; b. 9.1.49; m., Eileen Alison Mackay (qv). Educ. High School of Glasgow; Glasgow University. Joined Scottish Office, 1970; seconded as Secretary to Scottish Development Agency, 1975-76; Assistant Secretary, 1981; Principal Private Secretary to Secretary of State for Scotland, 1981-83; Under Secretary, 1990; seconded to Cabinet Office, 1990-92; Under Secretary (Housing), Scottish Office Environment Department, 1992-95; Deputy Secretary, Secretary, Scottish Office Agriculture and Fisheries Department, February-October, 1995. Non-Executive Director, Stagecoach Holdings, 1992-95. Recreations: music; food; wine. Address: (b.) Pentland House, 47 Robb's Loan, Edinburgh, EH14 1TY; T.-0131-244 6021.

Russell, Sheriff Albert Muir Galloway, CBE, QC, BA (Oxon), LLB. Sheriff, Grampian, Highland and Islands, at Aberdeen, 1971-91; b. 26.10.25, Edinburgh; m., Margaret Winifred Millar; 2 s.; 2 d. Educ. Edinburgh Academy; Wellington College; Brasenose College, Oxford; Edinburgh University. Lt., Scots Guards, 1944-47; Member, Faculty of Advocates, 1951; Standing Junior Counsel to Board of Trade, Department of Agriculture and Forestry Commission; QC (Scot), 1965; Vice Chairman, Board of Management, Southern Group of Hospitals, Edinburgh, 1966-70; Governor, Moray House College of Education, 1965-70. Recreations: golf; music. Address: (h.) Tulloch House, 1 Aultbea, Ross-shire, IV22 2JA.

Russell, Sheriff Dan Chapman, MA, LLB. Sheriff of South Strathclyde, Dumfries and Galloway at Hamilton, since 1992; b. 25.12.39. Qualified as Solicitor, 1963; in private practice, 1963-92.

Russell, Professor Elizabeth Mary, MD, DipSocMed, DObstRCOG, FFCM, FRCPGlas, FRCPEdin. Professor of Social Medicine, Aberdeen University, and Head, Department of Public Health, since 1990; Hon. Consultant in Public Health Medicine, since 1972; b. 27.1.36, Preston. Educ. Marr College, Troon; Glasgow University. General practice until 1964; medical management and social medicine, 1964-72; academic community medicine and public health, since 1972. Recreations: skiing; gardening; music. Address: (b.) Department of Public Health, Medical School, Foresterhill, Aberdeen, AB9 2ZD; T.-01224 681818, Ext. 53861.

Russell, George, MB, ChB, FRCP. Consultant Paediatrician, Grampian Health Board, since 1969; Honorary Senior Lecturer in Child Health, Aberdeen University, since 1970; b. 2.7.36, Insch; m., Gillian Douglas Simpson; 2 s.; 2 d. Educ. Robert Gordon's College; Aberdeen University. Junior hospital appointments, Aberdeen teaching hospitals; Research Fellow, University of Colorado; Lecturer in Child Health, Aberdeen University; Professor of Paediatrics, University of Riyad, Saudi Arabia. Regional Adviser in Paediatrics, British Paediatric Association, since 1988; Chairman, Scottish Cystic Fibrosis Group, since 1988; Member, British Paediatric Association Working Party on Cystic Fibrosis. Publications: numerous chapters and papers on paediatric respiratory and metabolic problems. Recreations: walking; photography; DIY. Address: (h.) 12 Pinewood Avenue, Aberdeen, AB1 8NB; T.-01224 315448.

Russell, George Stuart, OBE, BL, CA, WS. Former Senior Partner, Strathern and Blair WS, now Anderson Strathern, WS; b. 21.1.14, Edinburgh; m.; 1 s.; 3 d. Educ. Edinburgh Academy; Belhaven Hill; Harrow; Edinburgh University. CA, 1937; served Second World War, 1939-45 (Lt. Col.); then pursued a legal career; Fiscal, WS Society, 1973-79; closely involved in work of National Trust for Scotland, 1951-82, now Councillor Emeritus; Treasurer, Iona Community, 1947-65; President, Edinburgh Abbeyfield Society, 1978-92, now Vice-President; Vice President, UK, Abbeyfield Society, 1975-83; Trustee, New Club; Trustee, Scottish Churches Architectural Heritage Trust, 1982-95; Member, Queen's Bodyguard for Scotland (Royal Company of Archers). Recreations: fishing; walking; erecting plaques and indicators. Address: 59 Braid Road, Edinburgh, EH10; T.-0131-447 6009.

Russell, Rev. John, MA. Minister, Tillicoultry Parish Church, since 1978; b. 29.5.33, Glasgow; m., Sheila Spence; 2 s. Educ. Cathedral School, Bombay; High School of Glasgow; Glasgow University. Licensed by Glasgow Presbytery, 1957; ordained by United Church of Canada, 1959; Assistant Minister: Trinity United Church, Kitchener, Ontario, 1958-60, South Dalziel Church, Motherwell, 1960-62; Minister: Scots Church, Rotterdam, 1963-72, Southend Parish Church, Kintyre, 1972-78; Member of various General Assembly Committees, since 1972; Convener, General Assembly's Committee on Unions and Readjustments, 1987-90; Convener, Parish Reappraisal Committee, 1990-94; Vice Convener, Board of National Mission, 1994; Moderator, Presbytery of Stirling, 1993-94. Recreations: travel; reading. Address: The Manse, Dollar Road, Tillicoultry, Clackmannanshire, FK13 6PD; T.-01259 50340.

Russell, John Graham, FCIT. Chairman and Managing Director, John G. Russell (Transport) Ltd., since 1969; Chairman, Fife Warehousing Ltd., since 1988; Director, Combined Transport Ltd., since 1991; Director, Freight Transport Association, since 1994; b. Edinburgh; m., Isobel Margaret Hogg; 2 s.; 2 d. Educ. Merchiston Castle School, Edinburgh. Address: (b.) Gartcosh, Glasgow, G69 8ES; T.-01236 873511.

Russell, Michael William, MA. Chief Executive, Scottish National Party; b. 9.8.53; m., Cathleen Macaskill; 1 s. Educ.

Marr College, Troon; Edinburgh University. Creative Producer, Channel of Scotland, 1974-77; Director, Cinema Sgire, Western Isles, 1977-81; Founder and first Director, Celtic Film and Television Festival, 1980; Secretary General, Association for Film and Television in the Celtic Countries, 1981-83; Chief Executive, Network Scotland Ltd., 1983-91; Director, Eala Bhan Ltd., since 1991. Parliamentary candidate (SNP), Clydesdale, 1987; Executive Vice Convenor in charge of Publicity, SNP, 1987-91; Chairman, Save a Life in Scotland Campaign, 1986-88; Trustee, Celtic Film and TV Association, 1990-95; Board Director, Glasgow Film Theatre, since 1992. Recreations: gardening; cookery. Address: (h.) Feorlean, Glendaruel, Argyll, PA22 3AH; T.-01369 82 319.

Russell, Peter MacLeod, MA. Director, North East, Scottish Prison Service; b. 22.1.51, Edinburgh; m., Patricia Anne Kelly; 4 s.; 1 d. Educ. Royal High School, Edinburgh; Edinburgh University. Entered Scottish Office, 1973; Private Secretary to Parliamentary Under Secretary of State, 1976-78; Principal, 1978-86: Royal Commission on Legal Services in Scotland, 1978-80, SDD, 1980-84, Industry Department for Scotland, 1985-86; appointed Assistant Secretary, Scottish Office Home and Health Department, 1986. Address: (b.) Calton House, 5 Redheughs Rigg, Edinburgh EH12 9HW; T.-0131-244 8741.

Russell, Sir Robert Mark, MA (Oxon), KCMG. Chairman, Commonwealth Institute Scotland, since 1990; Chairman, Margaret Blackwood Housing Association, since 1990; Chairman, Martin Currie European Investment Trust PLC, since 1990; Chairman, C-Mist Ltd. (Centre for Maritime and Industrial Safety Technology), since 1993; b. 3.9.29, India; m., Virginia Mary Rogers; 2 s.; 2 d. Educ. Trinity College, Glenalmond; Exeter College, Oxford University. Royal Artillery, 1952-54; H.M. Diplomatic Service, 1954-89; Assistant Under Secretary of State, F.C.O., 1978-82; H.M. Ambassador to Turkey, 1983-86; Deputy Under Secretary of State, F.C.O., 1986-89. Recreations: music; travel. Address: (h.) 20 Meadow Place, Edinburgh, EH9 1JR; T.-0131-229 0732.

Russell, Robin Irvine, MD, PhD, FRCPEdin, FRCPGlas, FACN. Consultant in Charge, Department of Gastroenterology, Royal Infirmary, Glasgow, since 1970; Consultant Physician, Royal Infirmary, Glasgow, and Glasgow University, since 1970; b. 21.12.36, Wishaw; m., Ann Tindal Wallace; 1 s.; 1 d. Educ. Glasgow University. Member, medical and scientific staff, Medical Research Council Gastroenterology Unit, London. Chairman, British Digestive Diseases Foundation (Scotland); Member: Association of Physicians, British Society of Gastroenterology, American Gastroenterological Association. Publications: Elemental Diets; Investigative Tests and Techniques in Gastroenterology; Nutrition in Gastro-Intestinal Disease. Recreations: golf; travel; literature; music. Address: (h.) 28 Ralston Road, Bearsden, Glasgow, G61 3BA; T.-0141-942 6613.

Russell, Sheriff Terence Francis, BL. Sheriff, North Strathclyde, at Kilmarnock, since 1983; b. 12.4.31, Glasgow; m., Mary Ann Kennedy; 2 d. Educ. St. Mungo's Academy, Glasgow; Glasgow University. Solicitor: Glasgow, 1955-58, Bombay High Court, 1958-63, Glasgow, 1963-81; Sheriff, North Strathclyde, at Oban and Campbeltown and Grampian, Highland and Islands, at Fort William, 1981-83. Recreations: gardening; painting.

Russell, Thomas, BSc (Hons), MB, ChB, FRCS Edin, FRCS Glas. Consultant Neurosurgeon, since 1987; Senior Lecturer in Neurosurgery, Edinburgh University, since 1989; b. 8.3.50, Lanark; m., Donna; 1 d. Educ. Wishaw High School; Glasgow University. MRC Fellow in Neurosurgery, Institute of Neurological Sciences, Glasgow; Senior Registrar, Neurosurgery, Bristol; Exchange Neurosurgical Resident, Memphis; Consultant

Neurosurgeon, Western General Hospital, Edinburgh. Recreation: medical ethics/philosophy. Address: (h.) 15 White Dales, Edinburgh EH10 7JQ; T.-0131-445 5920.

Russell, Professor William C., BSc, PhD, FRSE. Professor of Biochemistry, St. Andrews University, since 1984; b. 9.8.30, Glasgow; m., 1, Dorothy Ada Brown (deceased); 1 s.; 1 d.; 2, Reta McDougall. Educ. Allan Glen's School, Glasgow; Glasgow University. Locke Research Fellow, Institute of Virology, Glasgow, 1959-63; Eleanor Roosevelt International Cancer Fellow, Toronto University, 1963-64; Member, MRC Scientific Staff, National Institute for Medical Research, London, 1964-84; Head, Division of Virology, 1977-84. Editor, Journal of General Virology, 1972-77; Convener, Virus Group, Society for General Microbiology, 1984-89; Member, Council, Society for General Microbiology, 1988-91; Chair, National Organising Committee, International Congress of Virology, Glasgow, 1993. Address: (b.) School of Biological and Medical Sciences, Irvine Building, St. Andrews University, North Street, St. Andrews, KY16 9AL; T.-01334 463405.

Rutherford, Alan Gray, BSc, PhD, CChem, CEng, FRSC, CEng, FInstE, FRSA. Scotch Whisky Production Director, United Distillers plc, since 1988; b. 9.10.42, Cramlington; m., Roslyn Anne Moore; 1 s.; 1 d. Educ. Gosforth Grammar School, Newcastle upon Tyne; Sheffield University; Newcastle upon Tyne University. Cookson Group of companies, three years; Scottish & Newcastle Breweries, 14 years, latterly as Group Personnel Director; joined Distillers Company Ltd. as Head of Research and Development, 1984. Executive Member, Scottish Council Development & Industry; Council Member, Scotch Whisky Association; President, Malt Distillers' Association of Scotland, 1991-94; Hon. Col., 4 Para (V); Member, Parachute Regimental Council; President, Ayrshire Branch, Parachute Regimental Association; Member, Board of Management, International Centre for Brewing and Distilling. Recreations: TA; hill-walking; rugby football. Address: (b.) United Distillers plc, 33 Ellersly Road, Edinburgh, EH12 6JW; T.-0131-337 7373.

Rutherford, Rev. Brian Craig, BSc, BD. Minister, Mastrick Parish, Aberdeen, since 1990; Councillor, Aberdeen District Council, since 1992; b. 8.6.47, Glasgow; m., Jean Walker; 2 s. Educ. King's Park Secondary School, Glasgow; Glasgow University; Edinburgh University. Assistant Minister, Carrick Knowe Parish, Edinburgh, 1976-77; Minister, Strathbrock Parish, West Lothian, 1977-83; Minister, Greyfriars/St. Ann's Church, Trinidad, 1983-87; General Treasurer, Blantyre Synod, Church of Central Africa Presbyterian, Blantyre, Malawi, 1988-89. Former Member, Edinburgh Corporation, Edinburgh District Council (JP, 1977-80), West Lothian District Council. Address: (h.) 13 Beechgrove Avenue, Aberdeen, AB2 4EZ; T.-01224 638011.

Rutherford, William Hay, MA, LLB. Advocate in Aberdeen, since 1949; Consultant, Raeburn Christie & Co. (Partner, 1978-87); Honorary Sheriff, Grampian, Highland and Islands, since 1974; b. 9.11.16, Forres; m., Dr. Jean Aitken Steel Wilson; 1 s.; 2 d. Educ. Forres Academy; Aberdeen University. Law Apprentice, James & George Collie, Advocates, Aberdeen, 1936-39; 51st Highland Division, Royal Signals, 1939-46 (taken prisoner, St. Valery, France, 1940; held prisoner, Stalag VIIIB, Upper Silesia, 1940-45); Legal Assistant, John Angus, Advocate, Aberdeen, 1946-61; Partner, Christie, Buthlay & Rutherford, Advocates, Aberdeen, 1962-78; President, Society of Advocates, Aberdeen, 1985-86; Session Clerk, Kirk of St. Nicholas (City Kirk of Aberdeen), since 1954; President, Royal Northern Agricultural Society, 1980; holder of British Horse Society 1994 Horse Trials Award for outstanding service to the sport. Recreations: country walking and wildlife study. Address: 38 Gladstone Place, Queen's Cross, Aberdeen.

Ruthven, Ian Scott, MB, ChB, FRCPEdin, FRCPGlas, DObstRCOG. Consultant Paediatrician, Ayrshire and Arran Health Board, since 1969; b. 9.3.37, Glasgow; m., Louisa Mary Jolly; 1 s.; 2 d. Educ. High School of Glasgow; Glasgow University. Junior hospital appointments, various Glasgow hospitals and in New Jersey, USA; Clinical Director, Hospital Paediatric Services in Ayrshire; Chairman, Ayrshire and Arran Division, BMA, 1987-88, currently Ayrshire Representative, Scottish Council, BMA; National Panellist for paediatric appointments in Scotland. Recreations: golf; angling; hill-walking. Address: (h.) Westholme, 10 Victoria Drive, Troon, KA10 6EN; T.-01292 313006.

Ryall, Michael Leslie (Mike), BSc, CEng, FIMechE, MInstPet, FRSA. Engineering Consultant (independent and retained by Weir Group), since 1991; Chairman, Scottish Design, since 1994; b. 25.3.31, Carshalton; m., Patricia; 2 s. Educ. George Watson's College; Watford Grammar School; Glasgow University. Research Director, Weir Pumps, 1971-75; Technical Director, Weir Pumps, 1975-91. National runner-up, Prince of Wales Award for Innovation and Production, 1984. Recreations: skiing; windsurfing; hill-walking; music; singing; gardening. Address: 18 Drumbeg Loan, Killearn, Glasgow, G63 9LG; T.-01360 550713.

Ryder, Jane. Director, Scottish Museums Council. Address: (b) County House, 20-22 Torphichen Street, Edinburgh, EH3 8JB.

S

Sagar, David Nigel, BSc (Econ), MBA, DipM, CertEd. Head, Aberdeen Business School, Robert Gordon University, since 1991; b. 12.6.43, Isleworth; m., Angela; 1 s.; 2 d. Educ. Latymer Upper School, Hammersmith; London School of Economics; London Business School. Former General Manager, Taylor Woodrow's St. Katharine's Dock development; entered education, 1981. Recreations: hill-walking; genealogy. Address: (h.) 83 Duthie Terrace, Aberdeen, AB1 6LS; T.-01224 318304.

Salmond, Alexander Elliot Anderson, MA (Hons). Economist; MP (SNP), Banff and Buchan, since 1987; National Convener, Scottish National Party, since 1990; b. 31.12.54, Linlithgow; m., Moira McGlashan. Educ. Linlithgow Academy; St. Andrews University. Vice-President: Federation of Student Nationalists, 1974-77, St. Andrews University SRC, 1977-78; Founder Member, SNP 79 Group, 1979; Assistant Agricultural and Fisheries Economist, DAFS, 1978-80; Economist, Royal Bank of Scotland, 1980-87. Hon. Vice-President, Scottish Centre for Economic and Social Research; former Member, Select Committee on Energy; Parliamentary Spokesman on Energy, Treasury, Fishing, Education and Nuclear Dumping. Recreations: golf; reading; football. Address: (b.) 17 Maiden Street, Peterhead, AB42 6EE; T.-01779 470444.

Salmond, Rev. James Sommerville, BA, BD, MTh, ThD. Minister, Holytown Parish Church, since 1979; b. 13.1.51, Broxburn; m., Catherine F. Wildy; 1 s.; 4 d. Educ. West Calder High School; Whitburn Academy; Leeds University; Edinburgh University; Central School of Religion. Serves on the Committees of Scottish Reformation Society, National Church Association, etc. Publications: Evangelicals within the Kirk 1690-1843; Moody Blues. Recreations: field sports; riding. Address: The Manse, Holytown, Motherwell; T.-Holytown 832622.

Salter, Professor Stephen Hugh, MA (Cantab), FRSE. Professor of Engineering Design, Edinburgh University, since 1986; b. 7.12.38, Johannesburg; m., Professor Margaret Donaldson. Educ. Framlingham College; Sidney Sussex College, Cambridge. Apprentice aircraft fitter and tool-maker; Research Assistant, Department of Psychology, Cambridge University; Research Fellow, then Lecturer, Department of Artificial Intelligence, then Reader in Mechanical Engineering, Edinburgh University. Recreations: photography; inventing and designing instruments and tools. Address: (b.) Department of Mechanical Engineering, Mayfield Road, Edinburgh University, Edinburgh, EH9 3JL; T.-0131-650 5703.

Saltoun, Lady (Flora Marjory Fraser). Chief of the name of Fraser; b. 18.10.30; m., Captain Alexander Ramsay of Mar; 3 d. Address: (h.) Cairnbulg Castle, Fraserburgh, Aberdeenshire, AB43 5TN.

Salzen, Professor Eric Arthur, BSc, PhD, FBPsS, FRSE. Professor of Psychology, Aberdeen University, since 1973 (Head, Department of Psychology, 1977-88); b. 28.4.30, London; m., Heather Ann Fairlie; 2 d. Educ. Wanstead County High School; Edinburgh University. Assistant in Zoology, Edinburgh University, 1954-55; Scientific Officer, HM Overseas Civil Service, 1955-56; Research Assistant and Lecturer in Psychology, Durham University, 1956-60; Lecturer in Zoology, Liverpool University, 1960-64; Associate Professor and Professor of Psychology, Waterloo University, Ontario, 1964-68; Senior Lecturer and Reader in Psychology, Aberdeen University, 1968-73. Recreation: travel. Address: (b.) Psychology Department, King's College, Aberdeen University, Aberdeen; T.-01224 272230.

Samson, Brian George. Director of Operations, Scottish Sports Council, since 1994; b. 9.9.47, Cupar; m., Penny Ann; 2 s.; 1 d. Educ. Bell Baxter High School, Cupar; Jordanhill College of Education; Napier College; diplomas in physical education, management studies, youth work. Teacher of Physical Education, 1970-74; Principal Teacher of P.E., 1974-84; Development Officer, then Senior Development Officer, Scottish Sports Council, 1984-94. Vice-President, Leith Academicals Rugby Club. Recreations: rugby; jogging/keep fit; skiing; walking; cycling; music; theatre; ornithology. Address: (h.) 15 Denham Green Terrace, Edinburgh; T.-0131-552 3694.

Samsova, Galina. Artistic Director, The Scottish Ballet, since 1991; b. Stalingrad. Began her career in Kiev; principal dancer, National Ballet of Canada; leading ballerina, London Festival Ballet; principal dancer, Sadler's Wells Royal Ballet; produced her first full-length work for Scottish Ballet, The Sleeping Beauty, 1994; Hon. Professor of Choreography in the Ukraine.

Sandeman, Mary. Singer; b. 10.7.47, Edinburgh; 2 s. Educ. St. Denis School, Edinburgh. Began to learn Gaelic and singing at aged 10; gained diploma in domestic science, secretarial training, National Institute of Broadcasting (Canada); worked in TV Department, Heriot-Watt University; in 1981, had a "No 1" hit record in nine countries with song called Japanese Boy under the stage name of Aneka.

Sandeman, Robert John, LLB, NP, WS, DL. Solicitor, since 1979; Deputy Lieutenant, Stirling and Falkirk Districts, since 1986; Chairman, Southern Area Committee, Highland TA&VRA, since 1991; b. 8.1.29, India; m., Enid; 1 s.; 1 d. Educ. Trinity College, Glenalmond; RMA, Sandhurst; Glasgow University. Infantry Officer, 1948-76; Second-in-Command, 1st Bn., The Royal Scots (The Royal Regiment), 1965-67; staff appointments, 1967-76; retired from Regular Army as Major, 1976; law student, 1976-79; commanded Number One Company, Home Service Force (Black Watch), Territorial Army, 1982-85. Member, Queen's Bodyguard for Scotland (Royal Company of Archers), since 1967; former Director, Glasgow, Stirlingshire and Sons of the Rock Society; Chairman, Stirling Members' Centre, National Trust for Scotland, 1990-94. Recreations: archery; walking; shooting. Address: (h.) Khyber House, Upper Glen Road, Bridge of Allan, FK9 4PX; T.-01786 832180.

Sanders, Samuel Chandrarajan, MBBS, FRCP, DMJ. Consultant Physician, Geriatric Medicine, Glasgow West, since 1976; Honorary Senior Clinical Lecturer, Geriatric Medicine, Glasgow University, since 1977; b. 1.7.32, Jaffna, Sri Lanka; m., Irene Saravanamuttu; 1 s.; 2 d. Educ. Jaffna College, Sri Lanka; Ceylon University. Resident HO, Ceylon, 1957-58; varied experience in medicine, surgery, neurosurgery, public health and forensic medicine, Sri Lanka, 1958-70; postgraduate training, forensic medicine and clinical therapeutics, Glasgow University, Guy's Hospital, London and Edinburgh Royal Infirmary, 1971-72; Registrar, then Senior Registrar, Glasgow Western District, 1973-76. Recreations: sport; reading; fishing. Address: (h.) 28 Hillfoot Drive, Bearsden, Glasgow, G61 3QF; T.-0141-942 9388.

Sanderson, David McLean, JP, LLD, FRSA. Chairman, General Purposes and Cultural Development, Strathclyde Regional Council (Convener, 1990-94); b. Glasgow; m., Ethel; 2 d. Chairman, Strathclyde Regional Finance Comittee, 1978-86; Vice-Convener of Council, 1986-90; Vice-Convener, Scottish Local Government Information Unit; Member, Board, East Kilbride Development Corporation, since 1975; Director: Scottish Chamber Orchestra, Scottish National Orchestra, Greater Glasgow Tourist Board; Chairman, Scottish TV Box 2000 Advisory Committee; former Member, Lanark County Council.

Recreation: playing the piano. Address: (b.) Strathclyde Regional Council, 20 India Street, Glasgow; T.-0141-227 3395.

Sanderson, Eric Fenton, LLB, CA, FCIBS. Director, The British Linen Bank Ltd., since 1984, Chief Executive, since 1989; Non-Executive Director, Airtours PLC, English and Overseas Properties plc, Dunedin Enterprise Investment Trust plc, United Artists Communications Scotland Ltd.; b. 14.10.51, Dundee; m., Patricia Ann Shaw; 3 d. Educ. Morgan Academy, Dundee; Dundee University. Qualified CA with Touche Ross & Co.; joined British Linen Bank Ltd., 1976. Recreations: gardening; photography. Address: (b.) 4 Melville Street, Edinburgh, EH3 7NZ; T.-0131-243 8301.

Sanderson, Professor Jeffrey John, BSc, PhD. Professor of Theoretical Plasma Physics, St. Andrews University, since 1985 (Reader in Applied Mathematics, 1975-85); b. 25.4.37, Birmingham; m., Mirjana Adamovic; 1 s.; 1 d. Educ. George Dixon Grammar School, Birmingham; Birmingham University; Manchester University. Research Associate, Maryland University, 1961-64; Theoretical Physicist, English Electric Co., Whetstone, 1964-66; Lecturer, then Senior Lecturer in Applied Mathematics, St. Andrews University, 1966-75; Visiting Professor, Department of Physics, College of William and Mary, USA, 1976-77. Publications: Plasma Dynamics (Co-author), 1969; Laser Plasma Interactions (Joint Editor), 1979. Recreations: chess; Scottish country dancing; five-a-side football; cricket. Address: (b.) North Haugh, St. Andrews, KY16 9SS; T.-01334 476161, Ext. 8135.

Sanderson, William. Farmer; Director, Royal Highland and Agricultural Society of Scotland; b. 9.3.38, Lanark; m., Netta; 4 d. Educ. Dalkeith High School. Past Chairman, South Midlothian and Lothians and Peeblesshire Young Farmers Clubs; Past Chairman, Dalkeith Agricultural Society; President, Royal Caledonian Curling Club, 1984-85; Past President, Oxenfoord and Edinburgh Curling Clubs; Scottish Curling Champion, 1971 and 1978 (2nd, World Championship, 1971). Recreations: curling; exhibiting livestock. Address: (h.) Blackshiels Farm, Blackshiels, Pathhead, Midlothian; T.-Humbie 833288.

Sanderson, Very Rev. William Roy, MA, DD. Minister, Church of Scotland; Extra Chaplain to The Queen in Scotland, since 1977 (Chaplain-in-Ordinary, 1965-77); b. 23.9.07, Leith; m., Muriel Easton; 3 s.; 2 d. Educ. Fettes College; Oriel College, Oxford; New College, Edinburgh. Ordained, 1933; Assistant Minister, St. Giles' Cathedral, 1932-34; Minister: St. Andrew's, Lochgelly, 1935-39, The Barony of Glasgow, 1939-63, Stenton with Whittingehame, 1963-73; Moderator, Glasgow Presbytery, 1958 and Haddington and Dunbar Presbytery, 1972-74; Moderator, General Assembly, 1967; Hon. DD (Glasgow), 1959; Chairman, Scottish Religious Advisory Committee, BBC, 1961-71; Member, Central Religious Advisory Committee, BBC and ITA, 1961-71; Governor, Fettes College, 1967-77; Honorary President, Church Service Society; President, New College Union, 1975. Recreations: reading; walking. Address: (h.) 1A York Road, North Berwick, EH39 4LS; T.-01620 892780.

Sanderson of Bowden, Lord (Charles Russell Sanderson), KB. Life Peer; Chairman, Scottish Mortgage and Trust, since 1993; Chairman, Hawick Cashmere Co., since 1990; Chairman, Scottish Pride Holdings, since 1994; Director: Illingworth Morris, United Auctions Ltd., Edinburgh Woollen Mills, Clydesdale Bank PLC, Watson and Philip PLC; Chairman, Scottish Conservative Party, 1990-93; b. 30.4.33, Melrose; m., Frances Elizabeth Macaulay; 1 s.; 1 s. deceased; 2 d. Educ. St. Mary's School, Melrose; Glenalmond College; Bradford University; Scottish College of Textiles. Commissioned, Royal Signals; Partner, Charles P. Sanderson, 1958-87; former Director,

Johnston of Elgin; former Chairman, Shires Investment PLC and Edinburgh Financial Trust; President, Scottish Conservative and Unionist Association, 1977-79; Chairman, National Union of Conservative and Unionist Associations Executive Committee, 1981-86; Minister of State, Scottish Office, 1987-90; Chairman, Eildon Housing Association, 1976-83; Member, Court, Napier University; Chairman, Glenalmond Council, since 1994; DL. Recreations: golf; amateur dramatics. Address: (h.) Becketts Field, Bowden, Melrose, Roxburgh.

Sandison, Bruce Macgregor. Writer and Journalist; b. 26.9.38, Edinburgh; m., Dorothy Ann Rhodes; 2 s.; 2 d. Educ. Royal High School, Edinburgh. Commissioned into Royal Army Service Corps, 1956-60; sometime poultry farmer and agricultural contractor; full-time writing, since 1981; Angling Correspondent, The Scotsman; Columnist, The Herald; writer on hill-walking and environmental matters; regular contributor to UK game fishing magazines and other journals; Tales of the Loch (series), Radio Scotland and Radio 4. Publications: The Trout Lochs of Scotland; The Sporting Gentleman's Gentleman; Game Fishing in Scotland; The Hillwalker's Guide to Scotland; The Heather Isles; Tales of the Loch; Long Walks with Little People. Recreations: hill-walking; game fishing; photography; swimming; music; reading; chess; bridge. Address: Hysbackie, Tongue, by Lairg, IV27 4XJ; T.-01847 55 274.

Sanford, Professor Anthony John, BSc, PhD, FBPsS, CPsychol. Professor of Psychology, Glasgow University, since 1982 (Head, Department of Psychology, 1983-86); b. 5.7.44, Birmingham; m., Linda Mae Moxey; 1 d. Educ. Waverley Grammar School; Leeds University; Cambridge University. MRC Research Scholar, Applied Psychology Unit, Cambridge; Postdoctoral Research Fellow, then Lecturer in Psychology, Dundee University; Senior Lecturer, then Reader in Psychology, Glasgow University. Gifford Lecturer in Natural Theology, Glasgow, 1983. Publications: Understanding Written Language (Co-author); Models, Mind and Man; Cognition and Cognitive Psychology; The Mind of Man; Communicating Quantities (Co-author). Recreations: hill-walking; industrial archaeology; music; cooking. Address: (b.) Department of Psychology, Glasgow University, Glasgow; T.-0141-330 4085.

Sang, Christopher T.M., MB, ChB, FRCSEdin, FRCPEdin. Consultant Cardiothoracic Surgeon, Lothian Health Board, since 1982; b. 14.6.43, Georgetown, Guyana; m., Jean Cowan (divorced); 1 s.; 2 d. Educ. George Watson's College, Edinburgh; Edinburgh University. General surgery training, Edinburgh, and general medicine and cardiology training, Edinburgh and Canada, 1966-73; cardiovascular and thoracic surgery training, Toronto, Edinburgh, London (Guy's) and Baltimore (Johns Hopkins), 1973-82. Address: (h.) 29 Blackford Hill Grove, Edinburgh, EH2 3HA; T.-0131-667 6046.

Sangster, Professor Alan John, BSc (Eng), MSc, PhD, CEng, FIEE. Professor, Electromagnetic Engineering, Heriot Watt University, since 1990; b. 21.11.40, Aberdeen; m., Barbara Macleod Wilkie; 1 s.; 1 d. Educ. Aberdeen Grammar School; Aberdeen University. Research Engineer, Ferranti Ltd., Edinburgh, 1964-69; Plessey Radar Ltd., 1969-72; Lecturer, Heriot Watt University, 1972-79, Senior Lecturer, 1979-86, Reader, 1986-90. Publications: 90 papers. Recreation: golf. Address: (b.) Computing and Electrical Engineering Department, Heriot Watt University, Edinburgh; T.-0131-451 3358.

Sarkar, Professor Susanta, BTech (Hons), DCT, PhD, CEng, MIStructE. Professor and Head, Department of Civil Engineering, Surveying and Building, University of Abertay Dundee, since 1978; b. 22.9.34, West Bengal; m., Delphine; 2 s. Educ. Indian Institute of Technology; Leeds

University. Postdoctoral Fellow, Leeds University; Senior Scientific Officer and Head of Concrete Structures, Structural Engineering Research Centre, 1965-68; Senior Lecturer/Acting Head, Department of Civil Engineering, National University of Singapore, 1968-71; Director of Studies, Civil Engineering, Hatfield Polytechnic, 1971-78. Past Chairman, Tayside Community Relations Council; Past Chairman, Dundee Voluntary Association. Recreations: travelling; photography; squash; badminton. Address: (h.) Carphin, 81 Camphill Road, Broughty Ferry, Dundee, DD5 2NA; T.-01382 730777.

Saunders, Professor Alison Marilyn, BA, PhD. Professor of French, Aberdeen University, since 1990; b. 23.12.44, Darlington. Educ. Wimbledon High School GPDST; Durham University. Lectrice, the Sorbonne, 1968-69; Lecturer in French, Aberdeen University, 1970-85; Senior Lecturer in French, 1985-90. Recreations: swimming; gardening; DIY; cooking; antiquarian book-collecting. Address: (h.) 75 Dunbar Street, Old Aberdeen, Aberdeen; T.-01224 494806.

Saunders, Professor David Stanley, BSc, PhD. Professor of Insect Physiology, Edinburgh University, since 1990; b. 12.3.35, Pinner; m., Jean Margaret Comrie Doughty; 3 s. Educ. Pinner County Grammar School; King's College, London; London School of Hygiene and Tropical Medicine. Joined academic staff, Zoology Department, Edinburgh, 1958; Visiting Professor: Stanford University, California, 1971-72, North Carolina University, 1983. Publications: Insect Clocks; Introduction to Biological Rhythms. Recreations: cycling; gardening; photography. Address: (b.) Institute of Cell, Animal and Population Biology, West Mains Road, Edinburgh, EH9 3JT.

Saunders, Professor William Philip, BDS, PhD, FDSRCS(Edin), FDSRCPS(Glas), MRD. Professor in Clinical Dental Practice, Glasgow University, since 1993; b. 12.10.48, Carlisle; m., Elizabeth; 1 s.; 2 step s.; 1 d.; 1 step d. Educ. Maidstone Grammar School; Royal Dental Hospital of London. Dental Officer, RAF, 1970-75; general dental practice, 1975-81; Lecturer, Department of Conservative Dentistry, Dundee University, 1981-88; Senior Lecturer in Clinical Practice, Glasgow Dental Hospital and School, 1988-93. Postgraduate Dental Hospital Tutor, Glasgow Dental Hospital, 1992-95; Editor, International Endodontic Journal. Publications: numerous papers. Recreations: ornithology; natural history; Scottish art; golf; endodontics. Address: (h.) The Old Smiddy, Knapp, Inchture, PH14 9SW; T.-01828 86478.

Savin, John Andrew, MA, MD (Cantab), FRCP, FRCPEdin, DIH. Consultant Dermatologist, Edinburgh Royal Infirmary, since 1971; Senior Lecturer, Dermatology Department, Edinburgh University, since 1971; b. 10.1.35, London; m., Patricia Margaret Steel; 2 s.; 2 d. Educ. Epsom College; Trinity Hall, Cambridge; St. Thomas's Hospital, London. Royal Naval Medical Service, 1960-64; Registrar to Skin Department, St. George's Hospital, London; Senior Registrar, St. John's Hospital for Diseases of the Skin, and St. Thomas's Hospital, London; Co-Editor, Recent Advances in Dermatology; Associate Editor, British Journal of Dermatology; former Secretary, Scottish Dermatological Society; President, British Association of Dermatologists, 1993-94; President, Section of Dermatology, Royal Society of Medicine, 1987-88. Recreations: golf; literature. Address: (h.) 86 Murrayfield Gardens, Edinburgh; T.-0131-337 7768.

Saxon, Professor David Harold, MA, DPhil, DSc, CPhys, FInstP, FRSE. Kelvin Professor of Physics, Glasgow University, since 1990; b. 27.10.45, Stockport; m., Margaret Flitcroft; 1 s.; 1 d. Educ. Manchester Grammar School; Balliol College, Oxford; Jesus College, Oxford. Research Officer, Nuclear Physics Department, Oxford University, 1969-70; Research Associate, Columbia University, New York, 1970-73; Rutherford Appleton Laboratory, Oxon: Research Associate, 1974-75, Senior Scientific Officer, 1975-76, Principal Scientific Officer, 1976-89; Chairman, PPARC Particle Physics Committee, since 1992; Member: Scientific Policy Committee, CERN, Geneva, since 1993, Physics Research Committee,DESY, Hamburg, since 1993. Address: (b.) Department of Physics and Astronomy, Glasgow University, Glasgow, G12 8QQ; T.-0141-330 4673.

Scaife, Geoffrey Richard. Chief Executive, NHS in Scotland, since 1993; Board Member, National Development Team for People with Learning Disabilities, since 1992; b. 12.1.49, Workington; m. Janet Elizabeth Woodward; 2 s.; 2 d. Educ. Workington Grammar School. Department of Health, London, 1968-71 and 1975-83; secondment to Prime Minister's Private Office, 1971-74; NHS Manager, Mersey Region, 1983-93 (including 1989-93 as Chief Executive, Mersey Regional Health Authority). Recreations: sport; countryside. Address: (b.) St. Andrew's House, Regent Road, Edinburgh, EH1 3DS; T.-0131-244 2410.

Schaw-Miller, Jean-Clare. Deputy Lieutenant, West Lothian, since 1980; Member, Scottish Youth Work Forum, SCEC, since 1991; Council Member (representing Scotland), Guide Dogs for the Blind Association, since 1992; Executive Committee Member, The Trefoil Holiday Centre for the Disabled, since 1993; Member, The Prince's Trust and Royal Jubilee Trusts Committee for Lothian and Borders, 1983-89 and 1995; b. 22.2.37, Gloucestershire; m., Robert Grant Schaw-Miller; 1 s.; 1 d. Educ. Clifton High School for Girls, Bristol; Edinburgh College of Domestic Science. Scottish Chief Commissioner, Girl Guides Association, 1987-92; Member, Scottish Youth Work Forum, SCEC, 1991-95; Chairman, South East Scotland Training Association, 1979-85; WRVS Family Welfare Organiser (Scotland), 1985-86. Address: (h.) Newgardens House, Dalmeny, South Queensferry, West Lothian, EH30 9TF; T.-0131-331 4612.

Schlesinger, Philip Ronald, BA, PhD, FRSA. Professor of Film and Media Studies, Stirling University, since 1989; b. 31.8.48, Manchester; m., Sharon Joy Rose; 2 d. Educ. North Manchester Grammar School; Queen's College, Oxford; London School of Economics. Thames Polytechnic: Lecturer, 1974, Senior Lecturer, 1977, Principal Lecturer, 1981; Head, Division of Sociology, 1981-88, Professor of Sociology, 1987-89; Social Science Research Fellow, Nuffield Foundation, 1982-83; Jean Monnet Fellow, European University Institute, Florence, 1985-86; Visiting Professor of Media and Communication, University of Oslo, since 1993; Co-Editor, Media, Culture and Society, since 1982. Publications: Putting "Reality" Together, 1978, 1987; Televising "Terrorism", 1983; Communicating Politics, 1986; Media, Culture and Society, 1986; Los Intelectuales en la Sociedad de la Informacion, 1987; Media, State and Nation, 1991; Women Viewing Violence, 1992; Culture and Power, 1992; Reporting Crime, 1994; European Transformations, 1994. Recreations: the arts; walking; travel. Address: Department of Film and Media Studies, Stirling University, Stirling FK9 4LA; T.-01786 46752.

Schofield, Rev. Melville Frederick, MA. Chaplain to Western General and Associated Hospitals, Edinburgh, since 1988; b. 3.10.35, Glasgow; m., Christina Skirving Crookston. Educ. Irvine Royal Academy; Dalkeith High School; Edinburgh University and New College. Ordained Assistant, Bathgate High, 1960-61; Minister, Canal Street, Paisley, 1961-67; Minister, Laigh Kirk, Kilmarnock, 1967-88. Former Moderator, Presbytery of Irvine and Kilmarnock; former Moderator, Synod of Ayr; radio and TV broadcaster; Past President, No. 0 Kilmarnock Burns Club. Recreations: international Burns engagements; golf; after-dinner speaking. Address: (h.) 25 Rowantree Grove, Currie, Midlothian, EH14 5AT; T.-0131-449 4745.

Scholes, Thomas Alexander, MSc, IPFA, IRRV, MIMgt. Chief Executive, Renfrewshire Council, since 1995; b. 30.4.49, Glasgow; m., Irene Elizabeth; 2 d. Educ. Hamilton Academy; Central College of Commerce; Strathclyde University. Strathclyde Regional Council: Principal Officer, 1975-80, Assistant Director of Finance, 1981-85, Senior Depute Director of Finance, 1986-95. Recreations: football supporting; watercolour painting; DIY. Address: (H.) 18 Glenfield Crescent, Paisley, PA2; T.-0141-884 5596.

Sclater, Robert Chalmers. Director of Harbours, Orkney Islands Council, since 1989; Oil Pollution Officer, Orkney, since 1989; Executive Director, Orkney Towage Company, since 1989; Executive Director, Orkney Islands Shipping Co.; Master Mariner; b. 7.8.41, Kirkwall; m., Anna Margaret; 1 s.; 2 d. Educ. Kirkwall Grammar School; Leith Nautical College; Robert Gordon's Institute of Technology. Merchant Navy, 1956-76; Marine Officer/1st Class Pilot, Orkney Islands Council, 1976-85; Depute Director of Harbours and Pilotage Superintendent, 1985-89. Member, Orkney Maritime Planning Committee; Kirkwall Sea Cadets Management Committee; DLA, RNLI, for Kirkwall Lifeboat; Elder, St. Magnus Cathedral. Recreations: swimming; gardening; walking. Address: (b.) Council Offices, Kirkwall, Orkney, KW15 1NY.

Scobie, Rev. Andrew John, MA, BD. Minister, Cardross Parish Church, since 1965; b. 9.7.35, Windygates; m., Elizabeth Jeannette; 1 s.; 1 d. Educ. Whitehill Senior Secondary School, Glasgow; Glasgow University (Medal in Systematic Theology); Gottingen University; Tubingen University; Marburg University. Assistantship, New Kilpatrick Church, Bearsden; Moderator, Dumbarton Presbytery, 1973-74; Convener, General Assembly's Parish Education Commitee, 1978-80; Convener, General Assembly's Panel on Worship, 1986-90; Member, Joint Liturgical Group, 1987-91; Chairman or Vice-Chairman, Cardross Community Council, since inception; former Co-Chairman, Presbytery of Dumbarton/Archdiocese of Glasgow Liaison Group; Vice-Convener, General Assembly's Artistic Matters Committee, since 1995. Publications: Studies in the Historical Jesus (Translator); contributions to New Ways to Worship, 1980, Prayers for Sunday Services, 1980, Three Orders for Holy Communion, 1986, Songs of God's People, 1988; Worshipping Together, 1991; Common Order, 1994. Recreations: golf; photography; wine making; visual arts. Address: The Manse, Cardross, Dumbarton G82 5LB; T.-01389 841289.

Scobie, William Galbraith, MB, ChB, FRCSEdin, FRCSGlas. Consultant Paediatric Surgeon, Lothian Health Board, since 1971; part-time Senior Lecturer, Department of Clinical Surgery, Edinburgh University, since 1971; Assistant Director, Edinburgh Postgraduate Board for Medicine, since 1986; b. 13.10.36, Maybole; m., Elizabeth Caldwell Steel; 1 s.; 1 d. Educ. Carrick Academy, Maybole; Glasgow University. Registrar, General Surgery, Kilmarnock Infirmary; Senior Registrar, Royal Hospital for Sick Children, Glasgow; Senior Registrar, Hospital for Sick Children, London; Senior Paediatric Surgeon, Abu Dhabi, 1980-81. Recreations: fishing; golf; gardening; music. Address: (h.) 598 Queensferry Road, Edinburgh, EH4 6AT; T.-0131-339 2306.

Scothorne, Professor Raymond John, BSc, MD, FRSE, FRCSG. Regius Professor of Anatomy, Glasgow University, 1973-90; b. 13.6.20, Nottingham; m., Audrey Gillott; 1 s.; 2 d. Educ. Royal Grammar School, Newcastle-upon-Tyne; Leeds University; Chicago University. Lecturer in Anatomy, Leeds University, 1944-50; Senior Lecturer, Glasgow University, 1950-60; Professor of Anatomy, Newcastle-upon-Tyne University, 1960-73. Anatomical Society of Gt. Britain and Ireland: Honorary Secretary, 1967-71, President, 1971-73; President, British Association of Clinical Anatomists, 1986-89; Foundation Editor, Clinical Anatomy, since 1988. Recreations: the countryside; labrador dogs. Address: (b.) Southern Knowe, Friars Brae, Linlithgow, West Lothian, EH49 6BQ.

Scothorne, Richard Mark, MA, MPhil. Managing Director, Partners in Economic Development Ltd., since 1992; b. 17.7.53, Glasgow; m., Dr. Sarah Gledhill; 1 s. Educ. Royal Grammar School, Newcastle upon Tyne; St. Catherine's College, Cambridge; Edinburgh University. Various posts in local government, 1977-86; Scottish Director, British Shipbuilders Enterprise Ltd., 1986-87; Economic Development Manager (Depute Director of Planning), Lothian Regional Council, 1987-92. Publication: The Vital Economy: integrating training and enterprise, 1990. Recreations: hill-walking; Scottish art; windsurfing. Address: (h.) 71 Murrayfield Gardens, Edinburgh, EH12 6DL; T.-0131-337 5476.

Scott, Alan W.A., AIB (Scot). Secretary, The Committee of Scottish Clearing Bankers. Address: (b.) 19 Rutland Square, Edinburgh, EH1 2DD; T.-0131-229 1326.

Scott, Alastair, BA. Travel writer, freelance photographer, and broadcaster; b. 19.3.54, Edinburgh; m., Sheena. Educ. Blairmore; Sedbergh; Stirling University. Travelled around the world, 1978-83; wrote three travel books, 1984-87 – Scot Free, A Scot Goes South, A Scot Returns; cycled 5,000 miles in E. Europe, 1987-88; wrote Tracks Across Alaska (800-mile sled dog journey), 1988-90; travelled Scotland, 1993-94, writing Native Stranger; presented BBC film version of Native Stranger, 1995. Recreations: reading; running; camping; carpentry; sailing; gardening. Address: Arroch, Kylerhea, Isle of Skye, IV40 8NH; T.-01599 522329.

Scott, Alexander, MA, MSc, PhD. Professorial Fellow, Heriot-Watt University, since 1989; b. 7.3.45, Lerwick; m., Anne Elliot; 3 d. Educ. Anderson Educational Institute; Boroughmuir Secondary; Edinburgh University. Research Assistant, Edinburgh University, 1967-70; Research Fellow, Heriot-Watt University, 1970-89; Tutor, Open University, 1971-75; Director, The Polecon Co., 1972-89; External Examiner, CNAA, 1981-85; Member, Joint Working Party on Economics, Scottish Examination Board, 1989-90; Chairman, Southfield Housing Society, 1977-80. Publications: Economics in Action (Co-author); Running the British Economy (Co-author); numerous papers. Recreations: squash; hill-walking; swimming; music. Address: (b.) The Esmee Fairbairn Research Centre, Heriot-Watt University, Riccarton, Edinburgh; T.-0131-451 3090.

Scott, Professor Bill, RSA. Sculptor; Head, School of Sculpture, Edinburgh College of Art (Lecturer, since 1962); b. 16.8.35, Moniaive; m., Phyllis Owen Scott; 1 s.; 2 d. Educ. Dumfries Academy; Edinburgh College of Art. One-man exhibitions: Compass Gallery, 1972, Stirling Gallery, 1974, New 57 Gallery, 1979, Lamp of Lothian, 1980, Artspace Gallery, 1980, Kirkcaldy Museum and Gallery, 1985, Talbot Rice Gallery, Edinburgh, 1995; numerous group exhibitions. Address: (h.) 45 St. Clair Crescent, Roslin, Midlothian, EH25 9NG.

Scott, Donald Bruce, MD, FRCPEdin, FFARCS. Consultant Anaesthetist, Edinburgh Royal Infirmary, 1959-86; President, European Society of Regional Anaesthesians, 1982-89; b. 16.12.25, Sydney; m., Joan Isobel White; 4 s.; 2 d. Educ. Hove Grammar School; Edinburgh University. Colonial Medical Service, Ghana, four years; training in anaesthesia, Edinburgh, six years; Consultant, NHS, Edinburgh Royal Infirmary, since 1959. Past President, Scottish Society of Anaesthetists; Past President, Obstetric Anaesthetists Association. Publication: Handbook of Epidural Anaesthesia (Co-author); Techniques of Regional Anaesthesia. Recreations: golf; food and wine. Address: (h.) 1 Zetland Place, Edinburgh, EH5 3HU; T.-0131-552 3317.

Scott, Esme (Lady Scott), CBE, WS, MA, LLB, NP. Chair, The Volunteer Centre UK; b. 7.1.32, Edinburgh; m.,

1, Ian Macfarlane Walker (deceased); 1 s.; 2, Kenneth Bertram Adam Scott, KCVO, CMG; 1 step-s.; 1 step-d. Educ. St. George's School for Girls, Edinburgh; Edinburgh University. Lawyer; Vice Chairman, National Consumer Council, 1984-87; Chairman, Scottish Consumer Council, 1980-85; Member, Equal Opportunities Commission, 1985-90; Past Chair, Scottish Association of Citizens Advice Bureaux; Chair, Volunteer Development Scotland, 1989-92; Member, Securities and Investments Board, 1991-93; Member, Court, Edinburgh University, 1989-92; Member, Scottish Committee, Council on Tribunals, 1986-92; Member, Social Security Advisory Committee; Member, National Council for Voluntary Organisations Board. Address: (h.) 13 Clinton Road, Edinburgh.

Scott, Gavin William Thomson, BCom, CA. Company Secretary and Treasurer, Scottish Agricultural College, since 1991; b. 19.7.55, Edinburgh; m., Elizabeth Moira Davidson; 2 s. Educ. George Watson's College; Edinburgh University. Deloitte Haskins & Sells, CAs, 1979-82; Keir International Ltd., 1982-87; United Nations Adviser, West Africa, 1987-91. Captain, Gambian Rugby Team, 1987; Scottish International Swimming and Water Polo, 1970s. Recreation: almost any sport. Address: (b.) S.A.C., West Mains Road, Edinburgh, EH9 3JG; T.-0131-535 4000.

Scott, Gordon Ramsay, OBE, BSc, MS, PhD, FRCVS. Honorary Fellow, Edinburgh University; Consultant Virologist, Food and Agricultural Organisation, since 1963; b. 6.7.23, Arbroath; m., Joan Henderson Walker; 1 s.; 2 d. Educ. Arbroath High School; Royal (Dick) Veterinary College, Edinburgh; Wisconsin University. Private practice, 1946-49; Virologist, Veterinary Laboratory, Kabete, Kenya, 1950-52 (Head, Virus Section, 1952-56); Head, Division of Virus Diseases, East African Veterinary Research Organisation, 1956-62; Acting Director, EAVRO, Kenya, 1959, 1962; Lecturer, Senior Lecturer, then Reader in Tropical Veterinary Medicine, Edinburgh University, 1963-90. Recreations: biometry; travel. Address: (h.) 2/12 Craufurdland, Braepark Road, Edinburgh, EH4 6DL.

Scott, Hugh Johnstone, DA, CertEd. Writer; b. Paisley; m., Mary (Margo) Smith Craig Hamilton; 1 s.; 1 d. Educ. Paisley Grammar School; Glasgow School of Art. Various jobs, then art school; art teacher, until 1984; full-time writing since 1984, including Writing Fellow, City of Aberdeen, 1991; Lecturer in Creative Writing, Glasgow University Adult and Continuing Education Department, since 1988; Tutor in Creative Writing; winner, Woman's Realm children's short story competition, 1982; winner, children's category, Whitbread Book of the Year, 1989, for Why Weeps the Brogan?; short-listed, Mcvitie's Prize, 1990; Tutor, Arvon Foundation Ltd., 1994. Recreations: weight training; exploring England; day-dreaming; reading, of course.

Scott, Iain William St. Clair, CA, FCIBS. General Manager, Personal Financial and Card Services, Bank of Scotland, since 1994; Chairman, Stevenson College, Edinburgh, since 1991; b. 14.5.46, Edinburgh; m., Noelle Margaret Gilmour; 1 s.; 1 d. Educ. George Watson's College. J.W. & R.N. Oswalds, CAs, 1963-70; joined Bank of Scotland, 1970. Recreations: golf; squash; curling. Address: (b.) 101 George Street, Edinburgh EH2 3JH; T.-0131-243 8021.

Scott, Ian Edward. Deputy Chief Executive, Scottish Court Service, since 1995; Regional Sheriff Clerk, Lothian and Borders, 1992-95; Sheriff Clerk, Edinburgh, since 1992; Sheriff Clerk of Chancery, since 1992; b. 18.10.42, Glasgow; m., Maureen Ferrie; 1 s.; 1 d. Educ. Bellahouston Academy. Recreations: amateur astronomy; rugby; making changes. Address: (h.) Meadowbank, Annandale Avenue, Lockerbie; T.-01576 203132.

Scott, Rev. Ian Gray, BSc, BD, STM. Minister, Greenbank Parish Church, Edinburgh, since 1983; b. 31.5.41,

Kirkcaldy; m., Alexandrina Angus; 1 d. Educ. Kirkcaldy High School; St. Andrews University; Union Theological Seminary, New York. Assistant Minister, St. Mungo's, Alloa, 1965-66; Minister: Holy Trinity Church, Bridge of Allan, 1966-76, Holburn Central, Aberdeen, 1976-83; Convener, Panel on Doctrine, General Assembly, 1978-82; part-time Lecturer, Faculty of Divinity, Aberdeen University, 1977-79; founder Member, Ministry and Psychotherapy Group; Convener, Board of Parish Education, Church of Scotland, since 1993; Member, Joint Commission on Doctrine, Church of Scotland/Roman Catholic Church. Recreations: reading; photography; caravanning; golf (so called). Address: 112 Greenbank Crescent, Edinburgh, EH10 5SZ; T.-0131-447 4032.

Scott, James David, BSc (Hons), DipEd. Rector, Graeme High School, Falkirk, since 1994; b. 30.9.52, Brechin; m., Rosalind; 1 s. Educ. Arbroath High School; Dundee University. Teacher of Mathematics, Lawside Academy, 1975-79; Assistant Principal Teacher of Mathematics, then Principal Teacher of Computing, St. Saviour's High School, Dundee, 1979-86; Assistant Project Co-ordinator, TVEI, Tayside, 1986-90; Depute Rector, Glenwood High School, Glenrothes, 1990-94. Recreations: computing; reading; hill-walking; aviation. Address: (b.) Graeme High School, Callendar Road, Falkirk; T.-01324 622576.

Scott, James Inglis. Director, Dunfermline Building Society, since 1961 (Chairman, 1981-95); b. 14.8.24, Dunfermline; m., Mabel Easson; 1 s.; 2 d. Educ. Merchiston Castle School. James Scott Engineering Group, 1947-78 (Director, 1955-78). Life Trustee: Carnegie Dunfermline Trust, since 1963 (Chairman, 1983-86); Carnegie United Kingdom Trust, since 1970; President, Electrical Contractors Association of Scotland, 1969-71. Address: (h.) 7/3 Rocheid Park, East Fettes Avenue, Edinburgh, EH9 1RP; T.-0131-332 8991.

Scott, James Orrock, FCCA. Partner, Henderson, Loggie, Pringle & Watt, Accountants, since 1967; Board Member, Angus, East of Scotland Housing Association, since 1988; Treasurer, SHARP (Scottish Heart and Arterial Disease Risk Prevention), since 1992; b. 13.12.40, Dundee; m., Alva; 1 s. Educ. Grove Academy. Member, Scottish Branch Executive, Society of Certified Accountants; first President, Scottish Athletics Federation; Council Member, British Athletic Federation. Recreations: athletics; bowling. Address: (h.) 3 Menzieshill Road, Dundee, DD2 1PS; T.-01382 665813.

Scott, John, DL, JP. Member, Orkney Islands Council, 1962-94; Director, Orkney Islands Shipping Company, 1962-93, latterly as Chairman; b. 3.9.21, Papa Stronsay; m., Margaret Ann Pottinger; 4 d. Educ. Stromness Academy. Home Guard; Auxiliary in Charge, HM Coastguard, Westray (retired); Army Cadet Force (Honorary Captain, retired); Past President, Local Committee, National Farmers Union; Secretary, Westray Baptist Church, 1943-86; Treasurer, local branch, Gideons International. Recreations: flying (PPL); sailing; golf; badminton. Address: (h.) Leckmelm, Annfield Crescent, Kirkwall, Orkney, KW15 1NS; T.-01856 873917.

Scott, John. Editor, Evening Times, since 1994. Address: (b.) 195 Albion Street, Glasgow G1 1QP.

Scott, John Andrew Ross, JP. Member, Borders Regional Council, since 1985 (Leader, Liberal Democrat Group, since 1992, Chairman, Planning and Development Committee, 1989-90, Chairman, Roads and Transportation Committee, since 1994); Chief Reporter, Southern Reporter, since 1986; elected to Scottish Borders Unitary Council, 1995; b. 6.5.51, Hawick; 2 s. Educ. Hawick High School. Worked on father's farm, 1966-74; Journalist, Hawick News, 1977-78, Tweeddale Press Group, since 1978; first SDP Member, Roxburgh District Council (1980-

85) and Borders Regional Council; Chairman, Roxburgh District Licensing Board, 1984-85; first Chairman, Borders Area Party, SDP, 1981-84; Secretary, Roxburgh and Berwickshire Liberal Democrats, 1988-89, Vice Chairman, 1993-94. Recreations: writing; music; travel; tennis. Address: (h.) 8 Union Street, Hawick, Roxburghshire; T.-01450 76324.

Scott, John Hamilton. Farmer; Lord-Lieutenant, Shetland; Chairman, Wool Growers of Shetland Ltd.; Chairman, Shetland Arts Trust; Member, N.E. Scotland Board, Scottish Natural Heritage; b. 30.11.36; m., Wendy Ronald; 1 s.; 1 d. Recreations: hill-climbing; Up-Helly-Aa; music. Address: (h.) Gardie House, Bressay, Shetland, ZE2 9EL.

Scott, Rev. John Miller, MA, BD, DD, FSA (Scot). Minister, St. Andrew's Scots Memorial Church, Jerusalem, 1985-88; b. 14.8.22, Glasgow; m., Dorothy Helen Loraine Bushnell; 2 s.; 1 d. Educ. Hillhead High School; Glasgow University and Trinity College. War Service, Egypt, Italy, India, 1942-46; Assistant Minister, Barony of Glasgow, 1948-49; Minister: Baxter Park Parish, Dundee, 1949-54; High Kirk of Stevenston, 1954-63; Kirk of the Crown of Scotland (Crown Court Church, Westminster), 1963-85; Moderator, Presbytery of England, 1971, 1979; Moderator, Presbytery of Jerusalem, 1986-88; Chairman, Israel Council, 1986-88; various periods of service on General Assembly Committees; Representative, World Alliance of Reformed Churches, Ecumenical Patriarchate, Istanbul, 1988. President, Caledonian Society of London, 1983-84; instituted Kirking Service for Scottish MPs and peers, 1966; Member, UNA Religious Advisory Committee, 1983-85. Recreations: travel; historical research; reading; gardening. Address: (h.) St. Martins, 6 Trinity Place, St. Andrews KY16 8SG; T.-01334 479518.

Scott, Malcolm Charles Norman, QC, BA, LLB; b. 8.9.51. Advocate, 1978. Address: (b.) Advocates' Library, Parliament House, Edinburgh, EH1 1RF.

Scott, Paul Henderson, CMG, MA, MLitt. Vice-President, Scottish National Party, since 1992; President, Scottish Centre, International PEN, since 1992; Vice-Chairman, Saltire Society, since 1990; Convener, Advisory Council for the Arts in Scotland, since 1981; Member of Councils: Association for Scottish Literary Studies, and Saltire Society; Convener, Scottish Centre for Economic and Social Research, since 1990; b. 7.11.20, Edinburgh; m., B.C. Sharpe; 1 s.;, 1 d. Educ. Royal High School, Edinburgh; Edinburgh University. HM Forces, 1941-47 (Major, RA); HM Diplomatic Service in Foreign Office, Warsaw, La Paz, Havana, Montreal, Vienna, Milan, 1947-80. Rector, Dundee University, 1989-92. Publications: 1707, The Union of Scotland and England, 1979; Walter Scott and Scotland, 1981; John Galt, 1985; The Age of MacDiarmid (Co-Editor), 1980; In Bed with an Elephant: The Scottish Experience, 1985; A Scottish Postbag (Co-Editor), 1986; The Thinking Nation, 1989; Towards Independence — essays on Scotland, 1991; Andrew Fletcher and the Treaty of Union, 1992; Scotland in Europe: a dialogue with a sceptical friend, 1992; Scotland: a concise cultural history (Editor), 1993; Defoe in Edinburgh and Other Papers, 1995. Recreation: skiing. Address: (h.) 33 Drumsheugh Gardens, Edinburgh, EH3 7RN; T.-0131-225 1038.

Scott, Richard H. Chief Executive, Scottish Legal Aid Board, since 1995. Address: (b.) 44 Drumsheugh Gardens, Edinburgh, EH3 7SW.

Scott, Sheriff Richard John Dinwoodie, MA, LLB. Sheriff of Lothian and Borders at Edinburgh, since 1986 (of Grampian, Highland and Islands, at Aberdeen and Stonehaven, 1977-86); Honorary Reader, Aberdeen University, 1980-86; b. 28.5.39, Manchester; m., Josephine Moretta Blake; 2 d. Educ. Edinburgh Academy; Edinburgh

University. Lektor, Folkuniversitet of Sweden, 1960-61; admitted to Faculty of Advocates, 1965; Standing Junior Counsel, Ministry of Defence (Air), 1969; Parliamentary candidate, 1974. Address: (b.) Sheriffs' Chambers, Sheriff Court House, Edinburgh, EH1 1LB; T.-031-226 7181.

Scott, Professor Roger Davidson, BSc, PhD, CPhys, FInstP. Director, Scottish Universities Research and Reactor Centre, since 1991; Titular Professor, University of Glasgow, 1994; b. 17.12.41, Lerwick; m., Marion McCluckie; 2 s.; 1 d. Educ. Anderson Institute, Lerwick; Edinburgh University. Demonstrator, Edinburgh University, 1965-68; Lecturer, then Depute Director, SURRC, 1968-91. Recreations: watching football; walking dogs; home maintenance. Address: (b.) Scottish Universities Research and Reactor Centre, East Kilbride, Glasgow, G75 0QU; T.-013552 23332, Ext. 102.

Scott, Sheriff Thomas. Sheriff of North Strathclyde. Address: (b.) Dumbarton Sheriff Court, Sheriff Court House, Church Street, Dumbarton, G82 1QR.

Scott, Thomas Hardy, OBE, BPhil, DPS. Adviser for Scotland, Cancer Relief Macmillan Fund, since 1984; b. 11.5.32, Dundee; m., Dorothy K. Shields; 2 s.; 2 d. Educ. Sedbergh School; Edinburgh University; St. Andrews University. Assistant Minister, St. Giles Cathedral, Edinburgh, 1959-61; Minister, Bonnybridge Parish Church, 1961-66; Chaplain, Heriot-Watt University, 1966-79; Hospice Director, Strathcarron Hospice, Denny, 1979-91. Chairman, Edinburgh Council of Social Service, 1974-77; Chairman, Joint Committee on Alcohol Related Problems, Lothian Health Board and Social Work Department, 1978-81; Chairman, Scottish Partnership Agency for Palliative and Cancer Care, 1991-94. Publication: Everybody's Death Should Matter to Somebody (Co-author and Editor). Recreation: golf. Address: (b.) Cancer Relief Macmillan Fund, Suite 7, Block 20, Western Court, 100 University Place, Glasgow G12 8SQ; T.-0141-339 6616.

Scott, William, BSc, MSc, MRPharmS. Chief Pharmaceutical Officer, Scottish Office, since 1992; b. 26.10.49, Bellshill; m., Catherine Muir Gilmour; 1 s.; 1 d. Educ. Wishaw High School; Heriot Watt University; Strathclyde University. Resident Pharmacist, Nottingham City Hospital, 1975-76; Staff Pharmacist, Eastern General Hospital, Edinburgh, 1976-79; Principal Pharmacist, Western General Hospital, Edinburgh, 1979-86; Chief Administrative Pharmaceutical Officer, Tayside Health Board, 1986-90; Deputy Chief Pharmacist, Scottish Office, 1990-92. Recreations: walking; reading; golf. Address: (b.) St. Andrews House, Edinburgh; T.-0131-244 2518.

Scott, Professor William Talbot, MA, PhD, DipEd, CertEd. Professor and Head, Department of Language and Media, Glasgow Caledonian University, since 1984; b. 28.2.42, Glasgow; m., Wendy Elizabeth Murray; 1 s.; 1 d. Educ. Woodside Secondary, Glasgow; Glasgow University; Sheffield University. Features Writer, D.C. Thomson & Co.; Lecturer/Senior Lecturer/Principal Lecturer in Communication Studies, Sheffield City Polytechnic. Chairman, Epilepsy Association of Scotland; Chairman, SCOTVEC Sector Group (Communication, Media and Performing Arts). Publication: The Possibility of Communication, 1990. Recreations: running; gardening. Address: (b.) Department of Language and Media, Glasgow Caledonian University, Cowcaddens Road, Glasgow, G4 0BA; T.-0141-331 3260.

Scott Brown, Ronald, MA, LLB. Director, Aberdeen Trust PLC, since 1983, Chairman, 1989-91; Director, Abtrust Fund Managers Ltd.; b. 14.2.37, Madras; m., Jean Leslie Booth; 3 s. Educ. Aberdeen Grammar School; Aberdeen University. Qualified Solicitor, 1961; Assistant, then Partner, Brander & Cruickshank, Advocates, 1961-83. Member, Board of Governors, Northern College of

Education, since 1983; Member, Court, Aberdeen University, since 1990. Address: (b.) 10 Queen's Terrace, Aberdeen, AB9 1QJ; T.-01224 631999.

Scott Elliot, Lt. Col. Alastair William. Regimental Secretary, Argyll & Sutherland Highlanders, since 1987; b. 25.11.34, Berwick upon Tweed; m., Andrena Christian Anderson; 2 s. Educ. Wellington College. Joined Army, 1953; served as a regular officer until 1987; commanded 1 A&H, 1974-77. Recreations: golf; shooting. Address: (h.) Shoreland, Fintry Road, Kippen, by Stirling; T.-01786 870261.

Scrimgeour, John Beocher, MB, ChB, DObst, RCOG, FRCOG, FRCS(Edin), FRCP (Edin). Consultant Obstetrician and Gynaecologist, since 1972; Honorary Senior Lecturer in Obstetrics and Gynaecology, Edinburgh University, since 1972; Medical Director, Western General Hospitals Unit, Edinburgh, since 1993; b. 22.1.39, Elgin; m., Joyce Morrin; 1 s.; 1 d. Educ. Hawick High School; Edinburgh University. General Practitioner, Edinburgh, 1963-65; Senior House Officer: Stirling Royal Infirmary, 1965, and Registrar, Eastern General Hospital, Edinburgh, 1966-69; Senior Registrar, Edinburgh Royal Infirmary, 1970-72; Senior Secretary, Edinburgh Obstetrical Society, 1980-85; Chairman, Area Division of Obstetrics and Gynaecology, 1984-88; Member, Council, Royal College of Obstetricians and Gynaecologists, 1976-81. Publication: Towards the Prevention of Fetal Malformation, 1978. Recreations: gardening; golf; tennis. Address: (h.) 4 Kinellan Road, Edinburgh, EH12 6ES; T.-0131-337 6027.

Seafield, 13th Earl of (Ian Derek Francis Ogilvie-Grant), b. 20.3.39; m., 1, Mary Dawn Mackenzie Illingworth (m. diss.); 2 s.; 2, Leila Refaat. Educ. Eton. Address: (h.) Old Cullen, Cullen, Banffshire.

Seager, Professor David Lewis, BSc, PhD. Chief Executive, Lewis C. Grant Ltd.; Visiting Professor in Mechanical Engineering, Edinburgh University, since 1991; b. 6.3.41, Bournemouth; m., Margaret Lythgoe; 3 s. Educ. Fettes College; Glasgow University; Cambridge University. Development Engineer, Sikorsky Aircraft, 1967-68; Research Engineer, Westinghouse Electric, 1968-72; Lecturer in Engineering, Aberdeen University, 1972-75; Technical Director, then Managing Director, Lewis C. Grant Ltd., Kirkcaldy, 1975-90; Honorary Fellow, Edinburgh University, 1984-91; Non-Executive Director, Forsbergs Inc., USA, 1987-90. Recreations: linguistics; theatre; cross-country skiing. Address: (h.) 20 Lady Helen Street, Kirkcaldy, KY1 1PR; T.-01592 51035.

Seagrave, David Robert, LLB (Hons), SSC, NP. Solicitor and Notary Public; Council Member, Law Society of Scotland, 1981-87; Partner, Seagrave & Co., Solicitors, Dumfries; b. 29.4.43, Berwick-on-Tweed; m., Fiona Lesley Thomson; 1 s.; 1 d. Educ. Newcastle-upon-Tyne; Glasgow University. Banking, insurance, police; Secretary, Enterprise Trust for Nithsdale, Annandale/Eskdale and the Stewartry, 1984-92. Recreations: choral singing; shooting; fishing; golf. Address: (h.) Amulree, Islesteps, Dumfries; T.-Dumfries 64523.

Sealey, Barry Edward, CBE, BA (Hons) (Cantab), CBIM. Director: Wilson Byard PLC (Chairman), Interace Graphics Ltd. (Chairman), Stagecoach Holdings PLC, Warburtons Ltd., The Caledonian Brewing Company Ltd., Scottish Equitable plc, Scottish American Investment Trust plc, Morago Ltd., and other companies; b. 3.2.36, Bristol; m., Helen Martyn; 1 s.; 1 d. Educ. Dursley Grammar School; St. John's College, Cambridge. RAF, 1953-55. Joined Christian Salvesen as trainee, 1958; joined Board, Christian Salvesen PLC (responsible for Food Services Division), 1969; appointed Managing Director, 1981, Deputy Chairman and Managing Director, 1987; retired from Christian Salvesen, 1990. Council Member, The Industrial

Society. Address: (h.) 4 Castlelaw Road, Edinburgh, EH13 0DN.

Searle, Rev. David Charles, MA, DipTh. Minister of the Church of Scotland, since 1965; Warden, Rutherford House, Edinburgh, since 1993; b. 14.11.37, Swansea; m., Lorna Christine Wilson; 2 s.; 1 d. Educ. Arbroath High School; St. Andrews University; London University; Aberdeen University. Teacher, 1961-64; Assistant Minister, St. Nicholas Church, Aberdeen, 1964-65; Minister: Newhills Parish Church, 1965-75, Larbert Old, 1975-85, Hamilton Road Presbyterian Church, Bangor, Co. Down, 1985-93; Contributor, Presbyterian Herald. Publication: Be Strong in the Lord, 1995. Recreations: sail-boarding; gardening; hill-walking. Address: (b.) Rutherford House, 17 Claremont Park, Edinburgh, EH6 7PJ; T.-0131-554 1206.

Seaton, Professor Anthony, BA, MD (Cantab), FRCPLond, FRCPEdin, FFOM. Professor of Environmental and Occupational Medicine, Aberdeen University, since 1988; b. 20.8.38, London; m., Jillian Margaret Duke; 2 s. Educ. Rossall School, Fleetwood; King's College, Cambridge; Liverpool University. Assistant Professor of Medicine, West Virginia University, 1969-71; Consultant Chest Physician, Cardiff, 1971-77; Director, Institute of Occupational Medicine, Edinburgh, 1978-90. Editor, Thorax, 1977-82; Chairman, Department of Environment Expert Panel on Air Quality Standards, since 1992; Member, Department of Health Committee on Medical Aspects of Air Pollution, MRC Committee on Toxic Hazards in the Environment. Publications: books and papers on occupational and respiratory medicine. Recreations: rowing; painting. Address: (h.) 8 Avon Grove, Cramond, Edinburgh, EH4 6RF; T.-031-336 5113; 71 Urquhart Terrace, Aberdeen AB2 1NJ.

Seaton, James. Editor, The Scotsman, since 1995. Address: (b.) 20 North Bridge, Edinburgh.

Seaton, Robert, MA, LLB. Secretary of the University, Dundee University, since 1973; b. 2.8.37, Clarkston, Renfrewshire; m., Jennifer Graham Jack; 2 s.; 2 d. Educ. Eastwood Secondary School; Glasgow University; Balliol College, Oxford; Edinburgh University. Administrative Assistant, then Senior Administrative Officer, then Assistant Secretary, Edinburgh University, 1962-73. Director, Dundee University Research Limited. Recreations: tennis; squash; golf; bridge; hill-walking. Address: (h.) Dunarn, 29 South Street, Newtyle, Angus, PH12 8UQ; T.-01828 650330.

Sedgley, Jeffrey P., BA (Hons), MSc, MA. Head Teacher, Lionel School, Isle of Lewis, since 1990; b. 15.3.44, Birmingham; 1 s.; 1 d. Educ. Sheldon Heath School, Birmingham; Keele University. Teacher in Lewis and Shetland, 1971-75; Depute Head Teacher, Lionel School, 1975-90. Chairman, Lewis and Harris Local Health Council, 1986-95; Member, Western Isles Health Board, since 1995; Secretary, Western Isles Executive, EIS, since 1988. Recreations: reading; cooking; visiting Italy. Address: (h.) 23 Adabrock, Port of Ness, Isle of Lewis; T.-01851-810-453.

Sefton, Rev. Henry Reay, MA, BD, STM, PhD. Clerk, Aberdeen Presbytery, since 1993; Master, Christ's College, Aberdeen, 1982-92; Senior Lecturer in Church History, Aberdeen University, 1991-92; Alexander Robertson Lecturer, University of Glasgow, 1995; b. 15.1.31, Rosehearty. Educ. Brechin High School; St. Andrews University; Glasgow University; Union Theological Seminary, New York. Assistant Minister, Glasgow Cathedral, 1957-58, St. Margaret's, Knightswood, Glasgow, 1958-61; Acting Chaplain, Hope Waddell Training Institution, Nigeria, 1959; Associate Minister, St. Mark's, Wishaw, 1962; Minister, Newbattle, 1962-66; Assistant Secretary, Church of Scotland Department of Education,

1966-72; Lecturer in Church History, Aberdeen University, 1972-90. Moderator, Aberdeen Presbytery, 1982-83, Synod of Grampian, 1991-92; Chairman, Association of University Teachers (Scotland), 1982-84. Recreations: hill-walking; church architecture; stamp and coin collecting. Address: (h.) 25 Albury Place, Aberdeen, AB1 2TQ; T.-01224 572305.

Selkirk, 10th Earl of (George Nigel Douglas-Hamilton); b. 4.1.06. Paymaster-General, 1953-55; Chancellor of the Duchy of Lancaster, 1955-57; First Lord of the Admiralty, 1957-59.

Semple, Lady (Ann Moira Sempill); 20th in line; b. 19.3.20; 2 s.; 1 d. Address: East Lodge, Druminnor, Rhynie, AB5 4LT.

Semple, Peter d'Almaine, MD, FRCPGlas, FRCPEdin. Consultant Physician and Chest Specialist, Inverclyde District, since 1979; b. 30.10.45, Glasgow; m., Judith Mairi Abercromby; 2 d. Educ. Belmont House; Loretto School; Glasgow University. Consultant Physician, Inverclyde Royal Hospital, 1979; former Postgraduate Medical Tutor, Inverclyde District; Honorary Clinical Senior Lecturer, Glasgow University. Past Chairman, Medical Audit Sub-Committee, Scottish Office; Past President, Greenock and District Faculty of Medicine; Past Chairman, West of Scotland Branch, British Deer Society; Director, Medical Audit, Royal College of Physicians and Surgeons of Glasgow. Recreations: field sports; gardening; golf. Address: (h.) High Lunderston, Inverkip, PA16 0DU; T.-01475 522342.

Semple, Walter George, BL, NP, ACI Arb. Solicitor; Partner, Bird Semple, Solicitors; b. 7.5.42, Glasgow; m., Dr. Lena Ohrstrom; 3 d. Educ. Belmont House, Glasgow; Loretto School; Glasgow University. President, Glasgow Juridical Society, 1968; Tutor and Lecturer (part-time), Glasgow University, 1970-79; Council Member, Law Society of Scotland, 1976-80; Chairman, Scottish Lawyers European Group, 1978-81; Member, Commission Consultative des Barreaux Europeens, 1978-80, 1984-87; President, Association Internationale des Jeunes Avocats, 1983-84; Chairman, Scottish Branch, Institute of Arbitrators, 1989-91; Director, Franco-British Lawyers Society Limited. Recreations: golf; fishing; skiing; music. Address: (h.) 79 Lancefield Quay, Glasgow G3 8HA.

Sewell, Professor John Isaac, BSc, PhD, CEng, FIEEE. Professor of Electronic Systems, Glasgow University, since 1985 (Dean, Faculty of Engineering, 1990-93); b. 13.5.42, Kirkby Stephen; m., Ruth Alexandra Baxter; 1 d. Educ. Kirkby Stephen Grammar School; Durham University; Newcastle-upon-Tyne University. Lecturer, Senior Lecturer, Reader, Department of Electronic Engineering, Hull University, 1968-85. Publications: 114 papers. Recreations: swimming; climbing. Address: (h.) 16 Paterson Place, Bearsden, Glasgow, G61 4RU; T.-0141-943 0729.

Sewell, Professor Morley Hodkin, MA, PhD, VetMB, MRCVS. Dean, Faculty of Veterinary Medicine, since 1994; Director, Centre for Tropical Veterinary Medicine, 1990-94; Professor of Tropical Veterinary Medicine, Edinburgh University, since 1993; b. 1.9.32, Sheffield; m., Cynthia Margaret-Rose Hanson; 1 s.; 3 d. Educ. King Edward VII School, Sheffield; Cambridge University. Colonial Office Research Scholar, Cambridge, 1957-59; Veterinary Research Officer, Government of Nigeria, 1959-63; Lecturer/Senior Lecturer/Reader/Professor, Edinburgh University, since 1963. Local Preacher, Methodist Church, since 1958; Circuit Steward, Edinburgh and Forth Circuit; Vice-Chairman, Action Partners. Recreations: Church; politics; travel. Address: (h.) 14 Craigiebield Crescent, Penicuik, Midlothian.

Seymour, Professor Philip Herschel Kean, BA, MEd, PhD. Professor of Cognitive Psychology, Dundee University, since 1988; b. 9.3.38, London; m., Margaret Jean Dyson Morris; 2 s.; 2 d. Educ. Kelly College, Tavistock; Exeter College, Oxford; St. Andrews University. Dundee University: Lecturer, 1966-75, Senior Lecturer, 1975-82, Reader, 1982-88. Chairman, Scottish Dyslexia Association, 1982-85. Publications: Human Visual Cognition, 1979; Cognitive Analysis of Dyslexia, 1986. Address: (b.) Department of Psychology, Dundee University, Dundee; T.-Dundee 223181.

Shaffer, Neville D., MA, LLB, QC. Address: (h.) 25 Norwood Drive, Whitecraigs, Giffnock, Glasgow, G46 7LS; T.-0141-638 1322.

Shand, Jimmy, MBE. Musician and Scottish Country Dance Band Leader; b. 28.1.08, East Wemyss; m., Anne Anderson; 2 s. Educ. East Wemyss School. Has played the accordion and led Scottish danceband at thousands of concert and theatre performances at home and overseas; numerous recordings; several thousand broadcasts. Recreations: motor bikes; sailing.

Shanks, Duncan Faichney, RSA, RGI, RSW. Artist; b. 30.8.37, Airdrie; m., Una Brown Gordon. Educ. Uddingston Grammar School; Glasgow School of Art. Part-time Lecturer, Glasgow School of Art, until 1979; now full-time painter; one-man shows: Stirling University, Scottish Gallery, Fine Art Society, Talbot Rice Art Gallery, Edinburgh University, Crawford Centre, Maclaurin Art Gallery, Glasgow Art Gallery, Fine Art Society, touring exhibition (Wales); taken part in shows of Scottish painting, London, 1986, Toulouse, Rio de Janeiro, 1985, Wales, 1988; Scottish Arts Council Award; Latimer and MacAulay Prizes, RSA; Torrance Award, Cargill Award, MacFarlane Charitable Trust Award, RGI; May Marshall Brown Award, RSW; tapestry commissioned by Coats Viyella, woven by Edinburgh Tapestry Company, presented to Glasgow Royal Concert Hall, 1991. Recreations: music; gardening.

Shanks, Rev. Norman James, MA, BD. Leader, Iona Community, since 1995; b. 15.7.42, Edinburgh; m., Ruth Osborne Douglas; 2 s.; 1 d. Educ. Stirling High School; St. Andrews University; Edinburgh University. Scottish Office, 1964-79; Chaplain, Edinburgh University, 1985-88; Lecturer in Practical Theology, Glasgow University, 1988-95; Convener, Acts Commission on Justice, Peace, Social and Moral Issues, 1991-95; Chairman, Edinburgh Council of Social Service, 1985-88; Chairman, Secretary of State's Advisory Committee on Travelling People, 1985-88; Convener, Church and Nation Committee, Church of Scotland, 1988-92; Member, Broadcasting Council for Scotland, 1988-93; Member, Scottish Constitutional Convention and Executive Committee, since 1989. Recreations: armchair cricket; occasional golf. Address: (h.) 1 Marchmont Terrace, Glasgow, G12 9LT; T.-0141-339 4421.

Shanks, Thomas Henry, MA, LLB. Solicitor and Notary Public, since 1956; Honorary Sheriff, Lanark, since 1982; b. 22.10.30, Lanark; m., Marjorie A. Rendall; 1 s.; 1 d. (by pr. m.); 3 step s.; 1 step d. Educ. Lanark Grammar School; Glasgow University. Intelligence Corps (National Service), 1954-56. Depute Clerk of Peace, County of Lanark, 1961-74; Chairman, Royal Burgh of Lanark Community Council, 1977-80 and 1983-86; Captain, Lanark Golf Club, 1962; Lord Cornet, 1968. Recreation: golf. Address: (h.) Clydesholm Braes, Lanark.

Sharp, Professor David William Arthur, MA, PhD, CChem, FRSC, FRSE. Professor of Chemistry, Glasgow University, since 1968; Director, Office for International Programmes, Glasgow University, since 1988; Convener, Scottish Council for the Validation of Courses for Teachers, 1983-89; b. 8.10.31, Folkestone; m., 1, Margaret Cooper; 1

s.; 2 d.; 2, Mary Mercer. Educ. Harvey Grammar School, Folkestone; Sidney Sussex College, Cambridge. Lecturer, Imperial College, London, 1957-61; Strathclyde University, latterly as Professor, 1965-68; Chairman, Scottish Council for Educational Technology, 1975-81; Council Member, Scottish Universities Council on Entrance, 1974-83; Chairman, Committee of Heads of University Chemistry Departments, 1979-81; Governor, Jordanhill College, 1971-79; Member, Scottish Examination Board, 1977-84; Council Member, Royal Society of Chemistry, 1974-77; Member, Council, Royal Society of Edinburgh, 1985-88. Publications: A New Dictionary of Chemistry (Editor); Penguin Dictionary of Chemistry (Editor); J. Fluorine Chemistry (Editor). Recreation: walking. Address: (b.) Department of Chemistry, Glasgow University, Glasgow, G12 8QQ; T.-0141-330 5290.

Sharp, Sir George, Kt (1976), OBE, JP, DL. Chairman, Glenrothes Development Corporation, 1978-86; Member, Economic and Social Committee, EEC, 1982-86; b. 8.4.19; m., Elsie May Rodger; 1 s. Educ. Buckhaven High School. Fife County Council: Member, 1945-75, Chairman, Water and Drainage Committee, 1955-61, Chairman, Finance Committee, 1961-72, Convener, 1972-75; Convener, Fife Regional Council, 1974-78; President: Association of County Councils, 1972-74; COSLA, 1975-78; Chairman: Kirkcaldy District Council, 1958-75, Fife and Kinross Water Board, 1967-75, Forth River Purification Board, 1955-67 and 1975-78, Scottish River Purification Advisory Committee, 1967-75, Scottish Tourist Consultative Council, 1979-82; Vice-Chairman, Forth Road Bridge Committee, 1972-78; Member, Scottish Water Advisory Committee, 1962-69, Committee of Enquiry into Salmon and Trout Fishing, 1963, Scottish Valuation Advisory Committee, 1972, Committee of Enquiry into Local Government Finance, 1974-76, Scottish Development Agency, 1975-80, Royal Commission on Legal Services in Scotland, 1978-80; Director, Grampian Television, 1975-89; Member, Scottish Board, National Girobank, 1982-90; Managing Trustee, Municipal Mutual Insurance Ltd., 1979-91. Recreations: golf; reading; gardening; football spectating. Address: (h.) Strathlea, 56 Station Road, Thornton, Fife; T.-Glenrothes 774347.

Sharp, Leslie, QPM, LLB, CIMgt. Chief Constable, Strathclyde Police, 1991-95; b. 14.5.36, London; m., Audrey Sidwell; 4 d. Educ. Finchley County Grammar School; University College, London. MRC, 1952-54; Middlesex Regiment, 1954-56; Metropolitan Police, 1956-80; Assistant and Deputy Chief Constable, West Midlands Police, 1980-88; Chief Constable, Cumbria Constabulary, 1988-91. Recreations: angling; cricket umpire; water colour painting; gardening. Address: (b.) 173 Pitt Street, Glasgow, G2 4JS; T.-0141-204 2626.

Sharratt, John, DPA, DCA, MITSA. Chief Trading Standards Officer, Borders Regional Council, since 1988; b. 16.8.47, Manchester; m., Yvonne; 4 s. Educ. Horwich Secondary School; Bell College of Technology. Trainee, Lancashire CC, 1964-69; Senior Trading Standards Officer, Glasgow Corporation/Strathclyde RC, 1969-79; Assistant Divisional Trading Standards Officer, 1979-84, Principal TSO (Research, Development and Training), 1984-88, Strathclyde RC. Education Secretary, Institute of Trading Standards Administration (Scottish Branch), 1985-91, Chairman, 1991-92. Recreations: squash; golf; fishing; watching rugby. Address: (b.) St. Dunstan's, High Street, Melrose, TD6 9RU; T.-0189 682 3922.

Shaw, Rev. Professor Douglas William David, MA, LLB, BD, DD, WS. Professor of Divinity, St. Andrews University, 1979-91 (Dean, Faculty of Divinity, 1983-86, Principal, St. Mary's College, 1986-92; Minister, Church of Scotland, since 1960; b. 25.6.28, Edinburgh; m., Edinburgh Academy; Loretto; Ashbury College, Ottawa; St. John's College, Cambridge; Edinburgh University. Practised law

as WS (Partner, Davidson and Syme, WS, Edinburgh), 1952-57; Assistant Minister, St. George's West Church, Edinburgh, 1960-63; Official Observer, Second Vatican Council, Rome, 1962; Lecturer in Divinity, Edinburgh University, 1963-79; Principal, New College, and Dean, Faculty of Divinity, Edinburgh, 1973-78; Visiting Fellow, Fitzwilliam College, Cambridge, 1978; Visiting Lecturer, Virginia University, 1979. Publications: Who is God?, 1968; The Dissuaders, 1978, In Divers Manners (Editor), 1990; Dimensions, 1992; Theology in Scotland. Recreations: squash; golf; hill-walking. Address: (h.) 40 North Street, St. Andrews, Fife, KY16 9AQ; T.-01334 477254.

Shaw, Rev. Duncan, BD (Hons), MTh. Minister, St. John's, Bathgate, since 1978; b. 10.4.47, Blantyre; m., Margaret S. Moore; 2 s.; 1 d. Educ. St. John's Grammar School, Hamilton; Hamilton Academy; Trinity College, Glasgow University. Assistant Minister, Netherlee Parish Church, Glasgow, 1974-77. Clerk, West Lothian Presbytery, since 1982 (Moderator, 1989-90). Recreations: gardening; travel (in Scotland). Address: St. John's Parish Church Manse, Mid Street, Bathgate, EH48 1QD; T.-Bathgate 653146.

Shaw, Professor Sir John Calman, KStJ, BL, FRSE, CA, FCMA, MBCS. Deputy Governor, Bank of Scotland, since 1991; b. 10.7.32, Perth; m., Shirley Botterill; 3 d. Educ. Strathallan; Edinburgh University. Qualified as Chartered Accountant, 1954; Partner, Graham, Smart & Annan, CA, Edinburgh, latterly Deloitte Haskins & Sells, 1960-1987; Executive Director, Scottish Financial Enterprise, 1986-90; President, Institute of Chartered Accountants of Scotland, 1983-84; Johnstone Smith Professor of Accountancy, Glasgow University, 1977-83. Director: Scottish Mortgage and Trust PLC, Scottish American Investment Company PLC (Chairman), Scottish Metropolitan Property PLC, Templeton Emerging Markets Investment Trust PLC, Templeton Latin America Investment Trust PLC, TR European Growth Trust PLC, US Smaller Companies Trust PLC (Chairman); Director, Scottish Enterprise; Member, Scottish Industrial Development Advisory Board; Member, Financial Reporting Council; Chairman, Scottish Higher Education Funding Council; Lay Director, Scottish Chamber Orchestra; Deputy Chairman, Edinburgh Festival Society; Chairman, David Hume Institute; author of various texts and publications on accountancy. Recreations: music; walking; travel. Address: (b.) The Mound, Edinburgh, EH1 1YZ.

Shaw, John Campbell, BSc, MSc, MRTPI. Managing Director, East Kilbride Development Corporation, 1990-95; b. 2.8.49, Belfast; m., Sheila Kerr Thomson; 2 d. Educ. Grosvenor High School, Belfast; Queens University, Belfast; Heriot-Watt University, Edinburgh. Lanarkshire County Council, 1973-75; Motherwell District Council, 1975-78; East Kilbride Development Corporation, since 1978: Head of Planning, 1982, Technical Director, 1986. Board Member, Lanarkshire Development Agency; Member, Town and Country Planning Association; contributor to various international symposia on matters relating to new or expanded community development. Recreations: squash; tennis; golf; watersports. Address: (b.) Atholl House, East Kilbride, G74 1LU; T.-013552 41111.

Shaw, Mark Robert, BA, MA, DPhil. Keeper of Natural History, National Museums of Scotland, since 1983; b. 11.5.45, Sutton Coldfield; m., Francesca Dennis Wilkinson; 2 d. Educ. Dartington Hall School; Oriel College, Oxford. Research Assistant (Entomology), Zoology Department, Manchester University, 1973-76; University Research Fellow, Reading University, 1977-80; Assistant Keeper, Department of Natural History, Royal Scottish Museum, 1980-83. Recreations: field entomology; family life. Address: (h.) 48 St. Albans Road, Edinburgh, EH9 2LU; T.-0131-667 0577.

Shaw, Richard Wright, MA. Principal, University of Paisley; b. 22.9.41, Preston; m., Susan Angela; 2 s. Educ. Lancaster Royal Grammar School; Sidney Sussex College, Cambridge. Assistant Lecturer in Management, then Lecturer in Economics, Leeds University, 1964-69; Lecturer in Economics, then Senior Lecturer, Stirling University, 1969-84; part-time Lecturer, Glasgow University, 1978-79; Visiting Lecturer, Newcastle University, NSW, 1982; Head, Department of Economics, Stirling University, 1982-84; Professor and Head, Department of Economics and Management, Paisley College, 1984-86; Vice Principal, 1986. Director, Renfrewshire Enterprise; Member: Board of Management, Reid Kerr College; Scottish Economic Council. Recreations:walking; listening to music. Address: (b.) University of Paisley, High Street, Paisley, PA1 2BE; T.-0141-848 3670.

Shaw, Professor Susan Angela, MA (Cantab), FCIM. Deputy Principal, Strathclyde University, since 1995; Professor of Marketing, since 1991; b. 1.6.43, Bristol; m., Richard Shaw; 2 s. Educ. Kingswood Grammar School, Bristol; Girton College, Cambridge. Marketing Executive, ICI Fibres; Lecturer, Senior Lecturer, Professor, Stirling University. Council Member, Food from Britain; Member, Food Policy Directorate, BBSRC; Director, Strathclyde University Food Project. Recreations: hill-walking; tennis; opera. Address: (b.) Department of Marketing, Strathclyde University, Stenhouse Buulding, 173 Cathedral Street, Glasgow, G4 0RQ; T.-0141-552 4400.

Shaw-Dunn, Gilbert, BSc, MBChB, FRCP Glas, MRCPsych. Consultant Psychiatrist, Greater Glasgow Health Board, since 1985; b. 20.1.49, Glasgow. Educ. Hillhead High School, Glasgow; Glasgow University. Trained, Glasgow Royal Infirmary and Royal Edinburgh Hospital; Consultant in psychiatry of old age, Leverndale Hospital, Glasgow. Recreation: domesticity. Address: (h.) 2 Buchlyvie Road, Ralston, Paisley, Renfrewshire.

Shaw-Stewart, Sir Houston (Mark), 11th Bt, MC (1950), TD. Vice Lord Lieutenant, Strathclyde Region (Eastwood, Renfrew and Inverclyde Districts), since 1980; b. 24.4.31; m., Lucinda Victoria Fletcher; 1 s. Educ. Eton. Coldstream Guards, 1949; 2nd Lt., Royal Ulster Rifles, Korea, 1950; Ayrshire Yeomanry, 1952; Member, Queen's Bodyguard for Scotland (Royal Company of Archers). Address: (h.) Ardgowan, Inverkip, Renfrewshire, PA16 0DW.

Shaw-Stewart, Lady (Lucinda Victoria), FRSA. National Trust for Scotland: Vice President, since 1994, Member, Executive Committee, since 1985, Convener, Curatorial Committee, since 1993; Trustee, Wallace Collection, since 1987; Trustee, Burrell Collection, since 1992; b. 29.9.49, Harrogate; m., Sir Houston Shaw-Stewart Bt; 1 s. Educ. Cranborne Chase School; diploma from Study Centre for the History of the Fine and Decorative Arts. Freelance Lecturer in Fine and Decorative Arts, 1969-82; National Trust for Scotland: London Representative, 1978-82, Member, Council, 1983-88. President, Inverclyde Branch, Save the Children Fund; Honorary Vice President, Ardgowan Hospice, Greenock. Address: (h.) Ardgowan, Inverkip, Renfrewshire PA16 0DW; T.-01475 521226.

Shea, Michael Sinclair MacAuslan, CVO, MA, PhD. Chairman, MacInnes Younger, Executive Search, since 1992; Chairman, Connoisseurs Scotland, since 1992; Chairman, China Gateway, since 1994; Political Consultant, Hanson PLC, since 1993; b. 10.5.38, Carluke; m., Mona Grec Stensen; 2 d. Educ. Lenzie Academy; Gordonstoun; Edinburgh University. Entered Foreign Office, 1963; seconded to Cabinet Office; Deputy Director General, British Information Services, New York; Press Secretary to the Queen; Head of Political and Government Affairs, Hanson PLC; remains Vice-Chairman of Melody Radio Ltd. (wholly-owned Hanson subsidiary). Visiting Professor,

Graduate School, Strathclyde University; Trustee, National Galleries of Scotland; Governor, Gordonstoun; Board Member, Murray Johnstone companies; Non-Executive Director, Caledonian Newspapers Ltd. and P&A Group; Vice-Chairman, Foundation for Skin Research; has published 14 books of fiction and non-fiction. Address: (b.) 1 St. Colme Street, Edinburgh, EH3 6AA; T.-0131-220 1456.

Shearer, Professor Magnus, RGN, QIDN, RNT, BA (Hons), MPhil. Head, Department of Health and Nursing, University of Abertay, Dundee, since 1994; b. 16.12.42, Kirkwall; m., Joyce Barningham; 2 s. Educ. Kirkwall Grammar School; Open University. Former Health Visitor, District Nurse, Nurse Tutor; Lecturer in Health Visiting, Robert Gordon's Institute of Technology, 1977-80, Queen Margaret College, Edinburgh, 1980-84; Assistant Director of Nurse Education, Southampton University Hospitals Combined School of Nursing and Midwifery, 1984-89; Head, Division of Health Studies, King Alfreds College, Winchester, and Director of Nurse Education, Basingstoke and Winchester College of Nursing and Midwifery, 1989-90; Executive Director (Standards), National Board for Nursing, Midwifery and Health Visiting for Scotland, 1991-94. Recreations: arts; walking. Address: (b.) University of Abertay, Bell Street, Dundee, DD1 1HG; T.-01382 308445.

Shearer, Magnus MacDonald, JP. Lord Lieutenant of Shetland, 1982-94; Honorary Consul for Sweden in Shetland and Orkney, 1958-94; Honorary Consul for Federal Republic of Germany in Shetland, 1972-87; b. 27.2.24; m., Martha Nicolson Henderson; 1 s. Educ. Anderson Educational Institute, Shetland; George Watson's College, Edinburgh. Royal Navy, Atlantic, Mediterranean and Far East, 1942-46; Royal Artillery TA, commissioned 2nd Lt., 1949; TARO, rank Captain, 1959; Honorary Secretary, Lerwick Station, RNLI, 1968-92; Member, Lerwick Town Council, 1963-69; Deputy Lieutenant of Shetland, 1973-82. Recreations: reading; bird watching; ships. Address: (h.) Birka, Cruester, Bressay, Shetland, ZE2 9EL; T.-01595 820363.

Shedden, Alfred Charles, MA, LLB. Senior Partner, McGrigor Donald, since 1993; b. 30.6.44, Edinburgh; m., Irene; 1 s.; 1 d. Educ. Arbroath High School; Aberdeen University. McGrigor Donald: Apprentice, 1967-69, Assistant, 1969-70, Partner, 1971, Managing Partner, 1985-92. Director, Scottish Financial Enterprise, since 1989; Chairman, Legal Resources Group, since 1991; Director, Standard Life Assurance Society, since 1992. Address: (b.) Pacific House, 70 Wellington Street, Glasgow; T.-0141-248 6677.

Sheehan, Sheriff Albert Vincent, MA, LLB. Sheriff of Tayside, Central and Fife, at Falkirk, since 1983; b. 23.8.36, Edinburgh; m., Edna Georgina Scott Hastings; 2 d. Educ. Bo'ness Academy; Edinburgh University. 2nd Lt., 1st Bn., Royal Scots (The Royal Regiment), 1960; Captain, Directorate of Army Legal Services, 1961; Depute Procurator Fiscal, Hamilton, 1961-71; Senior Depute Procurator Fiscal, Glasgow, 1971-74; Deputy Crown Agent for Scotland, 1974-79; Scottish Law Commission, 1979-81; Sheriff of Lothian and Borders, at Edinburgh, 1981-83. Leverhulme Fellow, 1971. Publications: Criminal Procedure in Scotland and France, 1975; Criminal Procedure, 1990. Recreations: naval history; travel; curling. Address: (b.) Sheriff Court House, Falkirk; T.-Falkirk 20822.

Shelmerdine, David John Charles, BSc, FITD, FIPD. Chief Executive, Scottish Council, The Scout Association, since 1987; Member, Scottish Youth Work Forum, since 1991; Member, Management Committee, Scottish Standing Conference of Voluntary Youth Organisations, since 1989; b. 18.3.48, Canterbury; m., Anne Marie Flint; 1 s.; 1 d. Educ. Hastings Grammar School; Brighton University.

Director, International Department, The Scout Association, London, 1978-82; Communications Executive, World Scout Bureau, Geneva, 1982-87. Chairman, Dollar Community Council, since 1993; Governor, Dollar Academy, since 1993. Recreations: hill-walking; civil engineering. Address: (b.) Fordell Firs, Hillend, Dunfermline, KY11 5HQ; T.-01383 419073.

Shelton, Richard Graham John, BSc, PhD. Officer-in-Charge, Scottish Office Freshwater Fisheries Laboratory, Pitlochry, since 1982; b. 3.7.42, Aylesbury; m., Freda Carstairs; 2 s. Educ. Royal Grammar School, High Wycombe; St. Andrews University. Research work, Burnham-on-Crouch Laboratory, MAFF, 1968-72; Assistant to Controller of Fisheries Research and Development, MAFF Fisheries Laboratory, Lowestoft, 1972-76 and (from 1974) Marine Laboratory, Aberdeen; worked on the population ecology of Crustacea, 1976-82. Address: (b.) Scottish Office Freshwater Fisheries Laboratory, Faskally, Pitlochry, PH16 5LB; T.-01796 2060.

Shepherd, David Arnot, JP, BSc, FRICS, IRRV. Senior Partner, J. & E. Shepherd, Chartered Surveyor, since 1963; b. 28.2.30, Dundee; m., Irene; 2 s.; 3 d. Educ. High School of Dundee; Mill Hill School, London; London University. Commissioned 2nd Lt., Royal Engineers, 1949. President, Property Owners and Factors of Scotland, 1963; President, Rating and Valuation Association, 1968; Member, Glenrothes Development Corporation, 1970-76; Member, Scottish Local Government Property Commission, 1973-76; Member, Lands Tribunal for Scotland, 1987-89. Recreations: skiing; golf; swimming; travel. Address: (b.) 13 Albert Square, Dundee DD1 1XA; T.-01382 200454; (h.) Annat, Rait, Perthshire PH2 7SB; T.-01821 670297.

Shepherd, Professor James, BSc, MB, ChB, PhD, FRCPath, FRCP (Glas). Professor in Pathological Biochemistry, Glasgow University, since 1987 (Reader, 1984-87); b. 8.4.44, Motherwell; m., Janet Bulloch Kelly; 1 s.; 1 d. Educ. Hamilton Academy; Glasgow University. Lecturer, Glasgow University: Biochemistry, 1968-72, Pathological Biochemistry, 1972-77; Assistant Professor of Medicine, Baylor College of Medicine, Houston, Texas, 1976-77; Senior Lecturer in Pathological Biochemistry, Glasgow University, 1977-84; Visiting Professor of Medicine, Geneva University, 1984; Director, West of Scotland Coronary Prevention Study; Chairman, European Atherosclerosis Society, 1993-96; author of textbooks and papers on lipoprotein metabolism and heart disease prevention. Address: (b.) Department of Biochemistry, Royal Infirmary, Glasgow, G4 OSF; T.-0141-304 4628.

Shepherd, Peter Charles, LLB, NP. Solicitor; b. 7.2.58, Aberdeen; m., Sheila Catherine; 2 s.; 1 d. Educ. Robert Gordon's College; Aberdeen University. Apprentice, 1978-80; Assistant, 1980-83; Partner, Aberdein Considine & Co., since 1984. President, Aberdeen Bar Association, 1994-95. Recreations: golf; fishing; gardening. Address: (b.) 8 Bon Accord Crescent, Aberdeen; T.-01224 589700.

Shepherd, Robert Horne (Robbie), AScA. Freelance Broadcaster, since 1976; b. 30.4.36, Dunecht, Aberdeen; m., Agnes Margaret (Esma); 1 s. Educ. Robert Gordon's College, Aberdeen. Left school at 15 to work in accountant's office; National Service, two years; joined fish firm as Assistant Accountant, then with fish group for 13 years as Management Accountant; left to become self-employed in that capacity; now full-time on radio and television. Recreations: golf; gardening; traditional music.

Shepherd, Col. W.K. Commandant, Princess Louise Scottish Hospital (Erskine Hospital). Address: (b.) Bishopton, PA7 5PU.

Sherrard, Mary Stephen, MBE, BA. National President, Woman's Guild, Church of Scotland, since 1993; b.

22.4.23, Renfrew; m., Rev. John A. Sherrard; 2 s.; 1 d. Educ. Girls' High School, Glasgow; Open University. Journalist; service in W.R.N.S.; playgroup work; Citizens Advice Bureau Manager; Chairman, Angus Citizens Advice Bureau; Vice-Chair, Scottish CAB. Elder, Buckhaven Parish Church. Recreations: crosswords; writing; walking on holiday. Address: (h.) Fair Havens, West Wynd, Buckhaven, KY8 1AS; T.-01592 716457.

Sherwood, Professor John Neil, DSc, PhD, CChem, FRSC, FRSE. Burmah Professor of Physical Chemistry, Strathclyde University, since 1983; Deputy Principal, since 1988; b. 8.11.33, Redruth, Cornwall; m., Margaret Enid Shaw; 2 d. Educ. Aireborough Grammar School; Bede College, Durham University. Research Fellow, Hull University, 1958-60; Lecturer and Reader, Strathclyde University, 1960-83. Recreations: hill-walking; photography; gardening. Address: (b.) Department of Pure and Applied Chemistry, Strathclyde University, Glasgow, G1 1XL; T.-041-552 4400.

Shiach, Allan G., BA. Chairman, Macallan-Glenlivet PLC, since 1979; Chairman, Scottish Film Council, since 1991; Chairman, Scottish Film Production Fund, since 1991; b. Elgin; m., Kathleen Breck; 2 s.; 1 d. Educ. Gordonstoun School; McGill University, Montreal. Writer/Producer, since 1970; Writer/Co-Writer: Don't Look Now, The Girl from Petrovia, Daryl, Joseph Andrews, Castaway, The Witches, Cold Heaven, and other films; Member, Broadcasting Council for Scotland, 1988-91; Member, Council, Scotch Whisky Association, since 1984; Chairman, Writers' Guild of G.B., 1989-91; Director, Rafford Films, since 1982; Director, Scottish Television PLC, since 1993; Director, Caledonian Publishing Ltd., since 1994; Freeman, City of London, 1988.

Shiach, Sheriff Gordon Iain Wilson, MA, LLB, BA (Hons). Sheriff of Lothian and Borders, at Edinburgh, since 1984; b. 15.10.35, Elgin; m., Margaret Grant Smith; 2 d. Educ. Lathallan; Gordonstoun; Edinburgh University; Open University. Admitted Advocate, 1960; practised as Advocate, 1960-72; Sheriff of Fife and Kinross, later Tayside, Central and Fife, at Dunfermline, 1972-79; Sheriff of Lothian and Borders, at Linlithgow, 1979-84; Hon. Sheriff, Elgin, since 1986; Member: Council of Sheriffs' Association, since 1989 (President, since 1994); Standing Committee on Criminal Procedure, 1989-93; Board, Lothian Family Conciliation Service, 1989-93; Parole Board for Scotland, since 1990 (Vice Chairman, since 1995); Council, Faculty of Advocates, since 1993; Shrieval Training Group, since 1994; Review Group on Social Work National Standards for Throughcare, 1994-95. Recreations:walking; swimming; music; art; film; theatre. Address: (b.) Sheriff Court House, 27 Chambers Street, Edinburgh EH1 1LB; T.-0131-225 2525.

Shields, Sir Robert, Kt, DL, DSc, PRCSEd, FRCSEng, HonFACS, FRCPS(Glas), HonFCS(SA). President, Royal College of Surgeons of Edinburgh, since 1994; Professor of Surgery, Liverpool University, and Hon. Consultant Surgeon, Royal Liverpool University Hospital, since 1969; b. 8.11.30, Paisley; m., Marianne Swinburn; 1 s.; 2 d. Educ. John Neilson School; Glasgow University. Lecturer in Surgery, Glasgow University, 1960-63; Senior Lecturer and Reader in Surgery, Welsh School of Medicine, 1963-69. Recreations: reading; sailing. Address: Royal College of Surgeons of Edinburgh, Nicolson Street, Edinburgh, EH8 9DW.

Shirreffs, Murdoch John, MB, ChB, DObstRCOG, FRCGP. General Medical Practitioner, Aberdeen, since 1974; Medical Hypnotherapist and Homoeopathic Physician; b. 25.5.47, Aberdeen; m., Jennifer McLeod. Educ. Aberdeen Grammar School; Aberdeen University. General Practice Trainer, since 1977; Secretary, Grampian Division, British Medical Association, since 1978; Member,

BMA Scottish Council. Past President, North of Scotland Veterans' Hockey Club. Recreations: hockey; opera and classical music; big band jazz; DIY; gardening; food and wine; travel. Address: (h.) 72 Gray Street, Aberdeen, AB1 6JE; T.-01224 321998.

Short, Agnes Jean, BA (Hons), MLitt. Writer; b. Bradford, Yorkshire; m., Anthony Short (qv); 3 s.; 2 d. Educ. Bradford Girls' Grammar School; Exeter University; Aberdeen University. Various secretarial, research and teaching jobs, both in UK and abroad; took up writing, 1966; 18 novels, most of which have a Scottish setting; also short stories and radio; Constable Award, 1976. Recreations: dog-walking; whisky-tasting; good food; small hills. Address: (h.) Khantore, Crathie, by Ballater, Aberdeenshire, AB35 5TJ.

Short, Emeritus Professor David Somerset, MD, PhD, FRCP, FRCPEdin. Honorary Consultant Physician, Grampian Health Board, since 1983; Emeritus Professor in Clinical Medicine, Aberdeen University, since 1983; b. 6.8.18, Weston-super-Mare, Avon; m., Joan Anne McLay; 1 s.; 4 d. Educ. Bristol Grammar School; Cambridge University; Bristol University. RAMC, 1944-47; Senior Registrar in Medicine/Cardiology, Bristol, National Heart Hospital, London Hospital and Middlesex Hospital, London, 1948-59; Consultant Physician, Aberdeen Hospitals and Senior Lecturer, Aberdeen University, 1960-83; former Physician to The Queen in Scotland. Recreation: travel. Address: (h.) 48 Victoria Street, Aberdeen, AB9 2PL; T.-01224 645853.

Sibbett, Professor Wilson, BSc, PhD. Professor of Physics, St. Andrews University (Director of Research, since 1994, Chairman, Department of Physics and Astronomy, 1985-94); b. 15.3.48, Portglenone, N. Ireland; m., Barbara Anne Brown; 3 d. Educ. Ballymena Technical College; Queen's University, Belfast. Postdoctoral Research Fellow, Blackett Laboratory, Imperial College, London, 1973-76; Lecturer in Physics, then Reader, Imperial College, 1976-85. Fellow, Institute of Physics; Fellow, Royal Society of Edinburgh. Recreation: golf (to low standard). Address: (b.) Department of Physics and Astronomy, St. Andrews University, North Haugh, St. Andrews, KY16 9SS; T.-01334 463100.

Sidgwick, Richard Twining, JP, DL, MSc, FRICS. Partner, West Highland Estates Office, since 1974; b. 17.7.44; m., Alison Janet Baggallay; 1 s.; 2 d. Educ. Fort Augustus Abbey School; Reading University. Deputy Lieutenant, Lochaber, Inverness, Badenoch and Strathspey, 1991; Director, Lochaber Limited, 1991, Vice-Chairman, 1992; Member, Red Deer Commission, 1993; Honorary Sheriff Fort William, 1994. Recreations: country sports; gardening; amenity woodlands. Address: (h.) Inverlair Lodge, Roy Bridge, Inverness-shire, PH31 4AR; T.-01397 732 246.

Sillars, James. Management Consultant; Assistant to Secretary General, Arab-British Chamber of Commerce, since 1993; MP (SNP), Glasgow Govan, 1988-92; b. 4.10.37, Ayr; m., Margo MacDonald (qv); 1 s.; 3 d. Educ. Ayr Academy. Member, Ayr Town Council and Ayr County Council Education Committee, 1960s; Member, Western Regional Hospital Board, 1965-70; Head, Organisation Department, Scottish TUC, 1968-70; MP, South Ayrshire, 1970-79; Co-Founder, Scottish Labour Party, 1976.

Silver, Alan William, CEng, DipTE, FICE, FIHT. Director of Roads, Grampian Region, since 1993; b. 22.6.41, Aberdeen; m., Margaret Eileen; 2 s. Educ. Aberdeen Grammar School; Aberdeen University; Robert Gordon's Institute of Technology. Worked for Sir Robert McAlpine & Sons on M1 Motorway; former Design Engineer, Sir William Halcrow, and Site Agent, C. Bryant & Sons; joined City Engineer's Department, Aberdeen, 1971; Chief Assistant, Traffic/Transporation/Road Safety, Roads Department, Grampian Regional Council, 1975. Recreations: amateur opera; bowls; curling; steam vehicles. Address: (b.) Roads Department, Grampian Regional Council, Woodhill House, Westburn Road, Aberdeen, AB9 2LU; T.-01224 664800.

Silver, Frederick Philip, MA. Editor, Stornoway Gazette, since 1991; b. 15.7.54, Manchester; m., Stephanie Blyth Sargent; 2 d. Educ. Bolton School; Jesus College, Oxford; Victoria University, Wellington. Journalist: Reading Evening Post, Western Mail (Cardiff), Western Daily Press (Bristol), China Daily (Beijing), Dominion/Dominion Sunday Times, Wellington, New Zealand.

Sime, Martin, MA. Director, Scottish Council for Voluntary Organisations, since 1991; b. 23.9.53, Edinburgh. Educ. George Heriot's; St. Andrews University; Edinburgh University. Social and Economic History Researcher, 1976-78; Sheep Farmer, 1978-81; Freelance Researcher, 1982; Project Manager, Sprout Market Garden, 1983-85; Development/Principal Officer (Day Services), Scottish Association for Mental Health, then Director, 1985-91; Member, Executive Committee, Edinburgh Association for Mental Health; Council Member, Scottish Business in the Community. Recreations: cinema; food; bridge. Address: (b.) 18/19 Claremont Crescent, Edinburgh, EH7 4QD; T.-0131-556 3882.

Simmers, Brian Maxwell, CA. Managing Director, Scottish Highland Hotels; b. 26.2.40, Glasgow; m., Constance Ann Turner; 3 s. Educ. Glasgow Academy; Larchfield; Loretto. Past President, Glasgow Academical Club; Governor, Glasgow Academy; former Honorary Secretary, Rugby Internationals' Golfing Society. Played rugby for Scotland (seven caps) and Barbarians. Recreations: rugby-watching; golf; shooting;fishing. Address: (b.) 98 West George Street, Glasgow, G2 1PW; T.-0141-332 3033.

Simmers, Graeme Maxwell, OBE, CA. Chairman, Scottish Sports Council, since 1992; Non-Executive Director, Stirling Royal Infirmary NHS Trust, since 1993; b. 2.5.35, Glasgow; m., Jennifer M.H. Roxburgh; 2 s.; 2 d. Educ. Glasgow Academy; Loretto School. Qualified CA, 1959; commissioned Royal Marines, 1959-61. Former Partner, Kidsons Simmers CA; Chairman, Scottish Highland Hotels Group Ltd., 1972-92; Member, Scottish Tourist Board, 1979-86; Chairman, HCBA (Scotland), 1984-86; Past Chairman, Board of Management, Member of National Executive, BHA; Elder and Treasurer, Killearn Kirk; Governor, Queen's College, Glasgow, 1989-93; Chairman of Governors, Loretto School; Past Chairman, Championship Committee, Royal and Ancient Golf Club of St. Andrews. Recreations: rugby; golf; skiing; literary society. Address: (h.) Kincaple, Boquhan, Balfron, near Glasgow, G63 ORW; T.-01360 440375.

Simmons, Professor John Edmund Leonard, BSc, PhD, CEng, FIMechE, MIEE. Professor of Mechanical Engineering, Heriot Watt University, since 1992, and Head, Department of Mechanical and Chemical Engineering, since.1994; Vice-Chairman, Engineering Manufacturing Industries Division, IMechE, since 1995; b. 24.9.47, Faversham; m., Anne; 1 s.; 1 d. Educ. Birmingham University; Cambridge University. Production Manager, Baker Perkins Chemical Machinery, Stoke on Trent, 1977-80; Design Manager, Vickers plc–Mitchell Bearings, Newcastle upon Tyne, 1981-84; Lecturer in Engineering, Durham University, 1984-91. Recreations: gardening; walking; travelling; cinema. Address: (b.) Heriot Watt University, Edinburgh, EH14 4AS; T.-0131-451 3132.

Simpson, Andrew Rutherford, MB, ChB, D(Obst)RCOG. Principal, general practice, 1965-94; Non Executive

Director, Borders Community Health Services NHS Trust; b. 13.7.32, Hawick; m., Helen Margaret Douglas; 3 d. Educ. Merchiston Castle School, Edinburgh; Edinburgh University. BMA: former Member, Scottish Council; Past Chairman, Scottish Borders Division, 1980, former Representative for Borders on Scottish Council; Past President and Life Member, Hawick Rugby Club (club doctor, over 30 years); Past President, Hawick Callants Club; Chairman, Douglas Haig Court. Recreations: rugby involvement; golf; philately; Rotary. Address: (h.) Netherfield, Buccleuch Road, Hawick, TD9 0EL; T.-01450 372459.

Simpson, Brian Middleton, MIBiol. Chief Executive, Scotch Quality Beef and Lamb Association, since 1991; b. 24.9.52, Perth; m., Helena; 1 s.; 2 d. Educ. Perth High School; West of Scotland Agricultural College. Agricultural Adviser, Scottish Agricultural College; Marketing Adviser, Kemira Fertilisers; Senior Project Executive, Scottish Enterprise. Recreation: hill-walking. Address: (b.) Rural Centre, — West Mains, Ingliston, Newbridge, EH28 8NZ; T.-0131-333 5335.

Simpson, David, CBE, DSc, CEng, FIEE. Chairman: Electronic Book Factory Ltd., Simpson Research Ltd., Albacom Ltd., Isocom Components Ltd., Bookham Technology Ltd.; Director: Healthscribe Inc., DMS Ltd.; b. 23.11.26, Ceres; m., Janice Ann; 1 s.; 2 d. Educ. Bell Baxter School, Cupar; Dundee Technical College; Stanford University. R. & D. Engineer, Marconi, 1952-56; Managing Director, Microcell Electronics, 1956-60; General Manager, Hughes Microelectronics, 1960-62; Managing Director, Hewlett Packard Ltd., 1962-70; Director, George Kent Ltd., 1970-76; President, Gould Corp., Chicago, 1976-88; Chairman, various UK companies, 1988-92. Recreations: hill-walking; wood-carving. Address: (h.) Elvingston House, Tranent, EH33 1EH; T.-01875 52878.

Simpson, Eric William McIntyre, DipEdTech, ALA. Chairman, Glasgow and West Hospital Broadcasting Service, since 1975; Co-ordinator, Learning Resources, Anniesland College, since 1988; freelance broadcaster; b. 18.2.45, Glasgow. Educ. Victoria Drive School, Glasgow; Strathclyde University. Former Administrative Director, Glasgow and West Hospital Broadcasting Service; SCOTVEC Subject Assessor for National Certificate; Member, National Working Party on Resource Based Learning; Radio Judge, Television and Radio Industries Club of Scotland Radio Awards, 1987, 1988; Member, National Working Party on Standards for Performance and Resourcing for Libraries in Scottish Further Education Colleges, 1991-92. Recreations: reading; spectator sports; listening to radio. Address: (h.) 11 Victoria Park Drive South, Glasgow, G14.

Simpson, George Alexander. Chairman, Thainstone House Hotel Ltd., Carden Place Investments Ltd.; b. 13.1.43; m., Lorraine; 1 s.; 1 d. Educ. Peterhead Academy. Founded Kildonnan Investments Ltd., late '60s; sold, 1989; founded Craigendarroch Group, 1983; Director, North of Scotland Radio Ltd. (Northsound). Recreations: golf; swimming; football. Address: (h.) 22 Rubislaw Den North, Aberdeen, AB2 4AN; T.-01224 208584.

Simpson, Professor Hugh Walter, MB, ChB, MD, PhD, FRCPath, FRCP(Glas). Head of Pathology, Glasgow Royal Infirmary, 1984-93, now Senior Research Fellow, University Department of Surgery, Glasgow University and Royal Infirmary; b. 4.4.31, Ceres Fife; m., Myrtle Emslie (see Myrtle Simpson); 3 s.; 1 d. Educ. Bryanston; Edinburgh University. Leader of numerous expeditions to polar and tropical regions; awarded Polar Medal and Mungo Park Medal. Recreation: skiing. Address: (h.) 7 Cleveden Crescent, Glasgow, G12 0PD; T.-0141-357 1091.

Simpson, Ian Christopher, LLB. Sheriff of South Strathclyde, Dumfries and Galloway, since 1988, at Airdrie, since 1991; b. 5.7.49, Edinburgh; m., Christine Margaret Anne Strang; 2 s. Educ. Glenalmond; Edinburgh University. Admitted to Faculty of Advocates, 1974. Captain, Scottish Universities Golfing Society, 1989-90; President, All Sphere Club, 1989-90. Recreation: golf. Address: (b.) Airdrie Sheriff Court, Graham Street, Airdrie, ML6 6EE; T.-01236 751121.

Simpson, Rev. James Alexander, BSc (Hons), BD, STM, DD. Minister, Dornoch Cathedral, since 1976; Chaplain to the Queen in Scotland; Moderator, General Assembly of the Church of Scotland, 1994; b. 9.3.34, Glasgow; m., Helen Gray McCorquodale; 3 s.; 2 d. Educ. Eastwood Secondary School; Glasgow University; Union Seminary, New York. Minister: Grahamston Church, Falkirk, 1960-66, St. John's Renfield, Glasgow, 1966-76. Publications: There is a time to ....; Marriage Questions Today; Doubts are not Enough; Holy Wit; Laughter Lines; The Master Mind; Dornoch Cathedral; More Holy Wit; Keywords of Faith; All About Christmas. Recreations: golf; photography; writing. Address: Cathedral Manse, Dornoch, IV25 3HN; T.-0186 2810296.

Simpson, James Walter Thorburn, BArch, RIBA, FRIAS. Partner, Simpson & Brown, Architects, since 1977; b. 27.7.44, Edinburgh; m., Ann Mary Bunney; 2 d. Educ. Trinity College, Glenalmond; Edinburgh College of Art. Lecturer, Heriot Watt University, 1975-80; co-founded Simpson & Brown, 1977, and Acanthus Associated Architectural Practices, 1985; Architect to St. Giles' Cathedral, 1983-90; Member, Ancient Monuments Board for Scotland, 1983-95; Architectural Advisor, Scottish Historic Buildings Trust, since 1985; Surveyor of the Fabric of York Minster, 1994-95; Chairman, RIAS Conservation Committee, 1992-94; UK Committee Member, International Council for Monuments and Sites, since 1992. Recreations: architectural history and geography; walking; piping; Scotland. Address: (b.) 179 Canongate, Edinburgh, EH8 8BN; T.-0131-557 3880.

Simpson, J.W., BSc, MCIT, MRIN, MNI. Divisional Manager, Marine Services, Forth Ports PLC, since 1986 (Port Manager, Grangemouth, 1982-86); Director, Forth Estuary Towage Ltd., since 1986; b. 30.8.44, St. Andrews; m., Barbara Hutton; 1 s.; 1 d. Educ. Grangemouth High School; Buckhaven High School; Leith Nautical College; Plymouth Polytechnic. Cadet, Furness Prince Lines, 1961-64; Navigating Officer: Shaw Savill Line, 1965-68, Overseas Containers Ltd., 1969-70; Assistant Harbour Master, then Assistant to Port Superintendent, Grangemouth, 1973-77; Port Superintendent, Leith and Granton, 1978-82. Recreation: sailing. Address: (b.) Forth Ports PLC, Tower Place, Leith, EH6 7DB; T.-0131-554 6473.

Simpson, Professor John Alexander, MD Hon. (Glasgow), DSc (Edin), DSc (Glas), FRCPLond, FRCPEdin, FRCPGlas, FRSE. Emeritus Professor of Neurology, Glasgow University, since 1987 (Professor of Neurology, 1965-87); Senior Neurologist, Institute of Neurological Sciences, Southern General Hospital, Glasgow, 1965-87; Consultant Neurologist, Civil Service Commission, 1974-87; b. 30.3.22, Greenock; m., Dr. Elizabeth M.H. Simpson; 2 s.; 1 d. Educ. Greenock Academy; Glasgow University. Surgeon-Lieutenant, RNVR; Registrar in Medicine, Southern General Hospital, Glasgow; Lecturer in Medicine, Glasgow University; MRC Research Fellow, National Hospital for Nervous Diseases, London; Senior Lecturer in Medicine, Glasgow University; Consultant Physician, Western Infirmary, Glasgow; Reader in Neurology, Edinburgh University. President, Association of British Neurologists, 1985-86; Past Chairman, Scottish Epilepsy Association; former Consultant Neurologist to British Army in Scotland; Editor, Journal of Neurology, Neurosurgery and Psychiatry. Recreations: violinist (Glasgow Chamber Orchestra and Scottish Fiddle

Orchestra); painting; sailing. Address: (h.) 87 Glencairn Drive, Glasgow, G41 4LL; T.-0141-423 2863.

Simpson, John Douglas, BSc(Hons). Headteacher, Fortrose Academy, since 1989; b. 2.3.51, Kilbirnie; m., Linda; 2 s.; 2 d. Educ. Spier's School, Beith; Glasgow University. Teacher of Biology, 1975; Principal Teacher, 1979; Assistant Headteacher, Merksworth High School, Paisley, 1983; Depute Headteacher, Cowdenknowes High School, Greenock, 1985. Recreations: golf; snooker. Address: (b.) Fortrose Academy, Fortrose, Ross-shire; T.-01381 620310.

Simpson, John William, IPFA. Secretary General, General Synod, Scottish Episcopal Church, since 1993; b. 19.11.44, Bournemouth; m., Joyce Carol Pollock; 2 s. Bournemouth CBC, 1961-68; Basingstoke BC, 1968-70; Poole BC, 1970-74, Bournemouth BC, 1974-81; Open University, 1981-87; Scottish Hydro-Electric PLC, 1988-90; KPMG Peat Marwick, 1990-93. Address: 21 Grosvenor Crescent, Edinburgh, EH12 5EE.

Simpson, Myrtle Lillias. Author and Lecturer; Member, Scottish Sports Council; Past Chairman, Scottish National Ski Council; b. 5.7.31, Aldershot; m., Professor Hugh Simpson (qv); 3 s.; 1 d. Educ. 19 schools (father in Army). Writer/Explorer; author of 12 books, including travel, biography, historical and children's; first woman to ski across Greenland; attempted to ski to North Pole (most northerly point reached by a woman unsupported); numerous journeys in polar regions on ski or canoe; exploration in China and Peru; Mungo Park Medal; Editor, Avenue (University of Glasgow magazine). Recreations: climbing; skiing; canoeing. Address: (h.) 7 Cleveden Crescent, Glasgow, G12 0PD; T.-0141-357 1091.

Simpson, Robert Keith, FCCA, IPFA. Governor, Royal Scottish Academy of Music and Drama; Board Member, Beild Housing Association Trustees; b. 26.7.43, Barrow-in-Furness; m., Brenda Mary Baines; 2 s. Educ. Barrow-in-Furness Grammar School. Accountant, Barrow-in-Furness County Borough Council, 1959-72; Principal Auditor, Bristol City Council, 1972-74; Chief Auditor, Avon County Council, 1974-77; Assistant Director of Finance, South Yorkshire County Council, 1977-82; Depute Controller of Audit, Commission for Local Authority Accounts in Scotland, 1982-85; Controller of Audit, Commission for Local Authority Accounts in Scotland, 1985-89. Former Editor, Audit Bulletin, CIPFA. Publications: Internal Audit in the Public Sector; Audit in the Public Sector (Co-author). Recreations: golf; hill-walking; drama. Address: (h.) Torr Beag, Killiecrankie; T.-01796 473602.

Sims, Graeme Lindsay, BA (Hons). Deputy Director General (Scotland), Office of Electricity Regulation, since 1994; b. 31.10.63, Glasgow; m., June Kennedy Russell; 1 d. Educ. Calday Grange Grammar School, Wirral; Magdalen College, Oxford. Associate Consultant, Boston Consulting Group, 1985-87; Development Officer, Scottish Cooperatives Development Committee, 1988-91; Economic Adviser, OFFER, 1991-93. Recreations: cooking; eating out; film; music. Address: (b.) OFFER, Regent Court, 70 West Regent Street, Glasgow G2 2QZ.

Sinclair, Alexander, OBE, DL, FCII. President, The Golf Foundation, since 1991; b. 6.7.20, West Kilbride; m., Elizabeth Tennant; 2 s.; 1 d. Educ. Ardrossan Academy. Clerk, Norwich Union, 1938-40; Royal Artillery, 1940-46; joined Alexander Stenhouse Insurance Brokers, 1957 (Director, 1962); Chairman, British Insurance Brokers Association in Scotland, 1985; retired, 1985. Deputy Lieutenant, Lanarkshire, 1988; Captain, Royal & Ancient Golf Club, 1988-89; Chairman, R. & A. Selection Committee, 1969-75; President, European Golf Association, 1981-83; President, Scottish Golf Union, 1976-77; former Scottish golf internationalist and Scottish golf captain;

awarded Frank Moran Award, 1979, for contribution to golf; West of Scotland Champion, 1950; semi-finalist, Scottish Amateur Championship, 1947-56; Lanarkshire Champion, three times; Scottish Senior Champion, 1979-84. Recreations: golf; curling; painting. Address: (h.) 17 Blairston Avenue, Bothwell, G71 8RZ; T.-01698 853359.

Sinclair, 17th Lord (Charles Murray Kennedy St. Clair), CVO. Lord Lieutenant, Dumfries and Galloway Region (District of Stewartry), 1982- 89; Extra Equerry to the Queen Mother, since 1953; Member, Queen's Bodyguard for Scotland (Royal Company of Archers); b. 21.6.14; m., Anne Lettice Cotterell; 1 s.; 2 d. Educ. Eton; Magdalene College, Cambridge. Served Second World War (mentioned in Despatches); retired Major, Coldstream Guards. Address: (h.) Knocknalling, St. John's Town of Dalry, Castle Douglas, Kirkcudbrightshire.

Sinclair, Rev. Colin Andrew MacAlister, BA (Hons), BD (Hons). General Director, Scripture Union Scotland, since 1988; b. 16.9.53, Glasgow; m., Ruth Mary Murray; 1 s.; 2 d. Educ. Glasgow Academy; Stirling University; Edinburgh University. Training Officer, Scripture Union, Zambia, 1974-77; Assistant Minister, Palmerston Place Church of Scotland, Edinburgh, 1980-82; Church of Scotland Minister, Newton on Ayr, 1982-88. Chairman, Evangelical Alliance Scotland; Director, NBSS; Hon. Vice President, UCCF; National Co-ordinator, Mission Scotland School of Evangelism. Recreations: family; reading; sport. Address: (b.) Scripture Union, 9 Canal Street, Glasgow, G4 0AB; T.-0141-332 1162.

Sinclair, Derek Urquhart, MA (Hons), MB, ChB, MRCGP, DPM. Medical Director, Central Scotland Healthcare NHS Trust, since 1994; b. 10.10.40, Falkirk; m., Dorothy Aalbregt; 1 s.; 2 d. Educ. Grangemouth High School; Falkirk High School; Glasgow University. Norwegian State Stipendiary, 1965-66; Principal in general practice, Falkirk, 1972-86; Regional Medical Officer, 1986-87, Medical Officer, 1987-88, Senior Medical Officer, 1988-92, Scottish Office Home and Health Department; Royal Scottish National Hospital and Community NHS Trust, Larbert: Unit Medical Manager, 1992-93, Medical Director, 1993-94. Recreations: gardening; walking; fishing. Address: (b.) Central Scotland Healthcare NHS Trust, Larbert FK5 4SD; T.-01324 570700.

Sinclair, Douglas. Secretary General, Convention of Scottish Local Authorities. Address: (b.) Rosebery House, 9 Haymarket Terrace, Edinburgh, EH12 5XZ.

Sinclair, Eric T.A., MA, DipEd. Rector, Kirkwall Grammar School, since 1991; b. 20.9.48, Edinburgh; m., Johanna Beckley; 3 c. Educ. Bell Baxter High School, Cupar; St. Andrews University; Edinburgh University; Moray House College. Taught, Teacher Training Colleges, Cameroon, Nigeria; Head of English, English High School, Istanbul; Assistant Rector, Forres Academy; Depute Rector, Bridge of Don Academy. Recreations: orienteering; squash; chess; gardening; reading. Address: (h.) Inganess Cottage, St. Ola, Kirkwall, Orkney.

Sinclair, Isabel Lillias, MA, BL, QC. Honorary Sheriff of Lothian and Borders, since 1979; b. Glasgow; m., J. Gordon MacDonald, BL. Educ. Shawlands Academy; Glasgow University. Newspaperwoman, 1933-46; Scottish Editor, BBC Woman's Hour, 1948; called to Scottish Bar, 1949; appointed Queen's Counsel, 1964; Sheriff Substitute, Lanarkshire at Airdrie, 1966-68; Sheriff of Lothian and Borders at Selkirk and Peebles, then Peebles and Edinburgh, 1968-79. Address: 30 Ravelston Garden, Edinburgh, EH4 3LE; T.-0131-337 9797.

Sinclair, Martin Fraser, MA, CA. Partner, Chiene & Tait, CA, since 1973; Director, Albyn Trust Ltd., since 1973; Director, NESSCO Ltd., since 1982; b. 18.7.45, Greenock;

m., Patricia Anne Ogilvy Smith; 1 s.; 2 d. Educ. Edinburgh Academy; Edinburgh University. Apprentice, Chiene & Tait, CA; qualified, 1970; Peat Marwick Mitchell & Co., Vancouver, 1970-73. President, Institute of Chartered Accountants Benevolent Association, 1983-84. Athletics Blue, Edinburgh University; Captain, Scottish Universities Athletics Team, 1969. Recreations: skiing; squash; orienteering. Address: (b.) 3 Albyn Place, Edinburgh, EH2 4NQ; T.-0131-225 7515.

Sinclair, Professor Roy Stuart, BSc, MSc, PhD, FSDC, FRSC, CCol, CChem. Personal Professor, Chemistry and Chemical Engineering, Paisley University, since 1991; Assistant Chief Commissioner (Scotland West), Scout Association, since 1990; b. 21.4.33, Glasgow; m., Ellen Catherine Murray; 2 s. Educ. Allan Glen's School, Glasgow; London University (External); Paisley University; Strathclyde University. Research Assistasnt, J. & P. Coats, Paisley, 1950-56; Lecturer in Chemistry, Paisley College, 1956-80, Senior Lecturer, 1980-91. Vice President, Paisley Philosophical Institution. Recreations: Scouting; hill-walking; occasional golf. Address: (b.) Paisley University, High Street, Paisley, PA1 2BE; T.-0141-848 3210.

Sinfield, Professor Robert Adrian, BA, DipSocAdmin. Professor of Social Policy, Edinburgh University, since 1979; b. 3.11.38, Wallington, Surrey; m., Dorothy Anne Palmer; 2 d. Educ. Mercers' School, London; Balliol College, Oxford; London School of Economics. Assistant Lecturer/Lecturer/Senior Lecturer/Reader in Sociology, Essex University, 1965-79; Visiting Lecturer in Social Work, Bryn Mawr College and Columbia University, 1969-70; consultancies, OECD, 1965-68, 1970, 1983 and UN, 1970-71; Scientific Adviser to DHSS Chief Scientist, since 1980; Convener and Co-Founder, Unemployment Unit, 1981-91; Chair, Social Policy Association, 1986-89; President, Section N, British Association for the Advancement of Science, 1993-94. Publications: The Long-Term Unemployed, 1968; Which Way for Social Work?, 1969; Industrial Welfare, 1971; The Workless State (Co-Editor), 1981; What Unemployment Means, 1981; Excluding Youth (Co-author), 1991; The Sociology of Social Security (Co-Editor), 1991. Address: (h.) 12 Eden Lane, Edinburgh, EH10 4SD; T.-0131-447 2182.

Singleton, Major John Francis Maxwell, MA, DL. Deputy Lieutenant, Kincardineshire; b. 26.8.16, Colwall; m., Jean Osborne (deceased); 1 s.; 2 d. Educ. Uppingham; Pembroke College, Cambridge. Commissioned Royal Artillery, 1938; served Second World War, BEF, MEF, CMF, BLA; Instructor, Mons Officer Cadet School, 1949-52; Malayan emergency, 1953-54. Vice Chairman, NE TAVRA; County Commissioner for Scouts, Kincardineshire. Recreations: physical training; outdoor games. Address: Hillhead, St. Cyrus, Montrose.

Sischy, Judith, BA, MA. Director, Scottish Council of Independent Schools, since 1990; b. 20.12.47, Halifax; m., Sheriff Mark Sischy (qv); 2 d. Educ. Newcastle upon Tyne Church High School; Bristol University; University of Toronto. Previously: Teacher of Modern Languages, Assistant and Deputy Secretary, Edinburgh Merchant Company. Director, Edinburgh Chamber of Commerce and Edinburgh Common Purpose; Non-Executive Director, Edinburgh Sick Children's Trust. Recreations: walking; swimming; cinema; music. Address: (b.) Floor 2/1, 11 Castle Street, Edinburgh, EH2 3AH; T.-0131-220 2106.

Sischy, Sheriff Mark, MA, LLB, SSC, NP. Sheriff at Glasgow and Strathkelvin, since 1990; Past President, Society of Solicitors in the Supreme Courts of Scotland; b. 14.7.45, Johannesburg; m., Judith Lewis (see Judith Sischy); 2 d. Educ. George Watson's College, Edinburgh; Edinburgh University. Recreation: armchair sportsman.

Skinner, Professor Andrew, MA, BLitt, FRSE, FBA. Adam Smith Professor of Political Economy, since 1994;

Vice-Principal, since 1991, Glasgow University; b. 11.1.35, Glasgow; m., Margaret Mary Robertson. Educ. Keil School, Dumbarton; Glasgow University; Cornell University, New York. Address: (h.) Glen House, Cardross, G82 5ES; T.-0138 9841 603.

Skinner, Angus, MBA, BSc, CQSW. Chief Inspector of Social Work Services, Scotland, since 1992; b. 9.1.50, Pakistan; m., Kate; 1 s. Educ. Daniel Stewart's, Edinburgh; Edinburgh University; London University; Strathclyde University. Cheshire County Council, 1971-72; Kent County Council, 1973-75; Lothian Region Social Work Department, 1976-88; Borders Region Social Work Department, 1988-91.

Skinner, Basil Chisholm, OBE, MA, FSA. Former Director of Extra-Mural Studies, Edinburgh University; b. 1923, Edinburgh; m., Lydia Mary Mackinnon; 2 s. Educ. Edinburgh Academy; Edinburgh University. Army Service, Yorkshire Yeomanry and Intelligence Corps; Librarian, Glasgow School of Art, 1951-54; Assistant Keeper, Scottish National Portrait Gallery, 1954-66; joined Edinburgh University as Lecturer, 1966; Council Member, National Trust for Scotland, 1970-75; Governor, Edinburgh Academy, 1973-75; Vice-President, Society of Antiquaries of Scotland, 1975-78; Member, Board of Trustees, National Museum of Antiquities, 1975-78; Trustee, Sir Patrick Geddes Memorial Trust, since 1981; Past Chairman, Hopetoun House Preservation Trust; Past Chairman, Conservation Committee, Scottish Development Agency; recipient, George Waterston Memorial Award, 1982. Publications: Scottish History in Perspective, 1966; Scots in Italy, 1966; Lime Industry in Lothian, 1970. Recreations: gardening; walking; travel. Address: (h.) Southfield Farm, Duddingston, Edinburgh, EH15 1SR; T.-0131-669 2041.

Skinner, Robert Gordon, LLB (Hons). Advocate, since 1987; part-time Chairman, Social Security Appeals Tribunal, since 1988; part-time Chairman, Disability Appeals Tribunal, since 1991; b. 14.6.57, Glasgow; m., Eileen Mary Judith Paterson; 2 s. Educ. Bishopbriggs High School; Glasgow University. Law Apprentice, Hughes, Dowdall & Co., Solicitors, Glasgow; Solicitor, Dorman Jeffrey & Co., Solicitors, Glasgow, 1980-86; called to the Bar, 1987. Recreations: football; swimming; golf; opera. Address: (h.) Whitehall, Springkell Avenue, Pollokshields, Glasgow.

Skorupski, Professor John Maria, MA, PhD. Professor of Moral Philosophy, St. Andrews University, since 1990; b. 19.9.46, Italy; m., Barbara Mary; 2 d. Educ. St. Benedict's, Ealing; Christ's College, Cambridge. Visiting Lectureships, Nigeria and Belgium, 1971-74; University of Wales Research Fellow, University College of Swansea, 1974-76; Lecturer in Philosophy, Glasgow University, 1976-84; Professor of Philosophy, Sheffield University, 1984-90. Fellow, Royal Society of Edinburgh. Publications: Symbol and Theory, 1976; John Stuart Mill, 1989; English Language Philosophy 1750-1945, 1993. Recreations: music; walking; skiing. Address: (h.) Cedar Lodge, Hepburn Gardens, St. Andrews, KY16 9LP; T.-01334 477590.

Slane, John Kerr, BSc. Factory Manager, Tarka Controls Ltd., Inverness, since 1984; former Chairman, Highland Area Group, CBI; b. 16.2.53, Dundee; m., Linda Jean. Educ. Morgan Academy; Dundee College of Technology. Recreation: hill-walking. Address: (b.) Tarka Controls Ltd., Lochiel Road, Inverness, IV2 3XR; T.-01463 237311.

Slater, Professor Peter James Bramwell, BSc, PhD, DSc, FIBiol, FRSE. Kennedy Professor of Natural History, St. Andrews University, since 1984; Head, School of Biological and Medical Sciences, since 1992; b. 26.12.42, Edinburgh; m., Elisabeth Vernon Smith; 2 s. Educ. Edinburgh Academy; Glenalmond; Edinburgh University.

Demonstrator in Zoology, Edinburgh University, 1966-68; Lecturer in Biology, Sussex University, 1968-84. Secretary, Association for the Study of Animal Behaviour, 1973-78, President, 1986-89; European Editor, Animal Behaviour, 1979-82; Editor, Advances in the Study of Behavior. Recreations: walking; ornithology; music. Address: (b.) School of Biological and Medical Sciences, St. Andrews, Fife; T.-01334 463500.

Slater, Trevor, OBE. Director (Non-Executive), Scottish Business in the Community; Scottish Community Education Council; Capital Enterprise Trust; Chest, Heart and Stroke Scotland; Scottish Urban Regeneration Forum; Wester Hailes Partnership; b. 31.10.42, Accrington; m., Eileen; 1 s.; 1 d. Educ. Westminster City. Military intelligence, 1961-70; Inland Revenue, 1971; Goodyear, 1972; Federated Land PLC, 1973-84 (Managing Director, 1982-84); Tilbury Douglas PLC, 1984-92 (Director, 1986-92). Fellow, Royal Society of Arts. Recreations: walking; travel. Address: (h.) 1 Succoth Gardens, Edinburgh, EH12 6BR; T.-0131-337 6554.

Slavin, Rev. William J., MA, STL, CPsychol. Parish Priest, St. Alphonsus, The Barras, Glasgow, since 1993; b. 17.1.40, Bristol. Educ. Blairs College, Aberdeen; Scots College, Rome; Glasgow University. Assistant Priest, Broomhill, Glasgow, 1965-70; Educational Psychologist, Glasgow Child Guidance Service, 1970-75; Deputy Director, Jessore Training Centre, Bangladesh, 1975-80; Secretary, RC Justice and Peace Commission, 1980-85; Co-ordinator, Scottish Drugs Forum, 1986-92. Recreation: An rud Gaidhealach. Address: (b.) 18 Stevenson Street, Glasgow, G40 2ST; T.-0141-552 0519.

Slawson, Keith Brian, BSc, MB, ChB, FRCA. Part-time Consultant Anaesthetist, Eastern General Hospital, Edinburgh; former Honorary Senior Lecturer, Edinburgh University; b. 7.9.33, Birmingham; m., Nan; 1 s.; 1 d. Educ. Bradford Grammar School; Edinburgh University. MRC Scientific Assistant, Department of Therapeutics, Edinburgh Royal Infirmary, 1962-63; Lecturer in Anaesthesia, Edinburgh University, 1963-66. Honorary Medical Officer, Scottish Rugby Union; Deputy President, Edinburgh Branch, British Red Cross. Recreation: caravanning. Address: (h.) 27 Craigmount View, Edinburgh; T.-0131-339 4786.

Sleeman, Professor Brian David, BSc, PhD, DSc, CMath, FIMA, FRSE. Professor of Mathematics, Dundee University, 1978-93, Ivory Professor of Mathematics, since 1993; b. 4.8.39, London; m., Juliet Mary Shea; 2 s.; 1 d. Educ. Tiffin Boys School; Battersea College of Technology; London University. Department of Mathematics and Computer Science, Dundee University: Assistant Lecturer, 1965-67, Lecturer, 1967-71, Reader, 1971-78. Chairman, Scottish Branch, Institute of Mathematics and its Applications, 1982-84; Member, General Synod, Scottish Episcopal Church, 1984-90; President, Edinburgh Mathematical Society, 1988-89. Publications: Multiparameter Spectral Theory in Hilbert Space, 1978; Differential Equations and Mathematical Biology, 1983. Recreations: choral music; hill-walking. Address: (b.) Department of Mathematics and Computer Science, Dundee University, Dundee, DD1 4HN; T.-01382 223181.

Sleeman, Professor Derek Henry, BSc, PhD, FRSE. Professor of Computing Science, Aberdeen University, since 1986; b. 11.1.41, Penzance; m., Margaret G. Rankine; 1 d. Educ. Penzance Grammar School; King's College, London. Leeds University: Computing Assistant, 1965-67, Lecturer in Computational Science, 1967-82, Associate Director, Computer Based Learning Project, 1969-82; Visiting Scientist: Rutgers University, 1979, Carnegie-Mellon University, 1980-81; Senior Consultant, Teknowledge, Palo Alto, CA, 1983-86; Senior Research Associate/Associate Professor, Stanford University, 1982-86. Secretary, SS AISB, 1979-82; Academic Co-ordinator, European Network of Excellence in Machine Learning, 1992-94. Publications: 80 technical papers, including Intelligent Tutoring Systems (Co-Editor). Recreations: hill and coastal path walking; medieval architecture; photography. Address: (b.) Computing Science Department, King's College, Aberdeen University, Aberdeen, AB9 2FX; T.-01224 272288.

Sloan, Professor David McPheator, BSc, MSc, PhD, DSc. Professor of Mathematics, Strathclyde University; b. 24.12.38, Cronberry; m., Margaret Templeton Kirk; 3 s.; 1 d. Educ. Cumnock Academy; Glasgow University; Keele University; Strathclyde University. Mathematician, English Electric Co., Stafford, 1962-64; Lecturer, Stafford Polytechnic, 1964-65; Lecturer, Senior Lecturer, Reader, Professor, Strathclyde University, from 1965. Recreations: hill-walking; folk music; reading. Address: (b.) Department of Mathematics, Strathclyde University, Glasgow; T.-0141-552 4400, Ext. 3819.

Sloane, Professor Peter James, BA (Econ), PhD. Professor of Political Economy, Aberdeen University, since 1984; b. 6.8.42, Cheadle Hulme; m., Avril Mary Urquhart; 1 s. Educ. Cheadle Hulme School; Sheffield University; Strathclyde University. Assistant Lecturer and Lecturer, Department of Political Economy, Aberdeen University, 1966-69; Lecturer in Industrial Economics, Nottingham University, 1969-75; Economic Adviser, Department of Employment Unit for Manpower Studies (on secondment), 1973-74; Professor of Economics and Management, Paisley College, 1975-84. Member, Economic and Social Research Council, 1979-85; Council Member, Scottish Economic Society, since 1983; Member, Mergers Committee, Scottish Higher Education Funding Council, since 1994. Publications: Sex Discrimination in the Labour Market, 1976; Women and Low Pay, 1980; Sport in the Market?, 1980; Equal Employment Issues, 1981; Tackling Discrimination in the Workplace, 1982; Labour Economics, 1985. Recreation: sport. Address: (b.) Department of Economics, Aberdeen University, Edward Wright Building, Dunbar Street, Old Aberdeen, Aberdeen, AB9 2TY.

Slowey, Professor Maria, BComm, DipSocSci, MLitt. Professor and Director, Department of Adult and Continuing Education, Glasgow University, since 1992; b. 14.10.52, Dublin. Educ. Dominican Convent, Cabra; University College, Dublin; Trinity College, Dublin. Research Fellow, 1976-80; Research Officer, 1980-82; Head, Adult Education Centre, LB of Waltham Forest, 1982-83; Lecturer in Adult Education, St. Patrick's College, Maynooth, 1983-84; Senior Lecturer in Recurrent Education, subsequently Head, Centre for Continuing Education and External Relations, University of Northumbria, 1985-92. Member of numerous national committees, including: Executive, Universities Association of Continuing Education; Women Returners' Network; Grampian Linked Work and Training Trust; Higher Education Policy Group, National Institute for Adult and Continuing Education; Advisory Committee, Division of Credit and Access, Higher Education Quality Council; Advisory Group on the Funding of Continuing Education, Scottish Higher Education Funding Council; Chair, Society for Research into Higher Education Continuing Education Research Group. Publications: three books and numerous official reports, papers and articles. Address: (b.) Department of Adult and Continuing Education, Glasgow University, 59 Oakfield Avenue, Glasgow, G12 8LW; T.-0141-330 4392.

Smail, Peter James, MA, BM, BCh, FRCP, DCH. Consultant Paediatrician and Clinical Director of Child Health, Aberdeen Royal Hospitals Trust, since 1992; Honorary Senior Lecturer in Child Health, Aberdeen University, since 1980; b. 10.10.43, Harrow; m., Janice

Lockhart; 3 s.; 1 d. Educ. Merchant Taylors', Northwood; St. John's College, Oxford; Oxford Clinical Medical School. Paediatric House Officer, Inverness Hospitals, 1970; Medical Registrar, Royal Cornwall Hospital (Treliske), 1972; Lecturer in Child Health, Dundee University, 1975; Fellow in Paediatric Endocrinology, University of Manitoba, Winnipeg, 1979. Member, Health Services Human Growth Hormone Committee, 1982-87; Secretary, Scottish Study Group for the Care of Young Diabetics, 1984-89. Recreations: Member, Aberdeen Bach Choir; Lay Clerk, St. Andrew's Cathedral, Aberdeen. Address: (b.) Royal Aberdeen Children's Hospital, Aberdeen, AB9 2ZG; T.-0224 681818, Ext. 53037.

Small, Christopher. Writer; b. 15.11.19, London; 3 d. Educ. Dartington Hall; Pembroke College, Oxford. Journalist and miscellaneous writer; Literary Editor and Dramatic Critic, Glasgow Herald, 1955-80. Publications:Ariel Like A Harpy: Shelley, Mary & Frankenstein; The Road to Miniluv: George Orwell, the State & God; The Printed Word. Recreation: gardening. Address: (h.) 26 Bell Place, Edinburgh, EH3 5HT; T.-0131-332 6591.

Small, J.B. Chief Executive, Victoria Infirmary NHS Trust. Address: (b.) Queen's Park House, Langside Road, Glasgow, G42 9TT.

Small, Professor John Rankin, CBE, BSc (Econ), FCCA, FCMA. Professor, Department of Accountancy and Finance, Heriot-Watt University, since 1967; Chairman, Commission for Local Authority Accounts in Scotland, 1983-92; b. 28.2.33, Dundee; m., Catherine Wood; 1 s.; 2 d. Educ. Harris Academy; Dundee School of Economics. Industry and commerce; Lecturer, Edinburgh University; Senior Lecturer, Glasgow University. Consultant to various organisations; Council Member, Chartered Association of Certified Accountants (President, 1982-83); Vice-Principal, Heriot-Watt University, 1974-78, 1987-90, Deputy Principal, 1990-94; Chairman, National Appeal Panel for Entry to Pharmaceutical Lists (Scotland), since 1987; Board Member, Scottish Homes, since 1993. Recreation: golf. Address: (b.) Heriot-Watt University, Riccarton, Edinburgh; T.-0131-451 3001.

Small, Ramsay George, MB, ChB, FFCM, FRCPE, DPH. Chief Administrative Medical Officer, Tayside Health Board, 1986-89 (retired); Honorary Senior Lecturer in Community Medicine, Dundee University, 1974-89; b. 5.2.30, Calcutta; m., Aileen Stiven Masterton; 4 s. Educ. Harris Academy, Dundee; St. Andrews University. Assistant Medical Officer of Health, Ayr County Council, 1958-61; Senior Assistant Medical Officer of Health, then Principal Medical Officer, City of Dundee, 1961-74; Community Medicine Specialist, Tayside Health Board, 1974-85. Faculty Adviser, Scotland, Faculty of Community Medicine, 1980-83, Convener Scottish Affairs Committee, 1983-86; Member, National Medical Consultative Committee and Member, Board, Faculty of Community Medicine, 1985-89; Member, Council, Royal College of Physicians of Edinburgh, 1987-90; President, Baptist Union of Scotland, 1972-73; Chairman, Eastern Regional Postgraduate Medical Education Committee, 1980-83; Secretary, Broughty Ferry Baptist Church, 1969-93. Recreations: bird-watching; music. Address: 46 Monifieth Road, Broughty Ferry, Dundee, DD5 2RX; T.-01382 778408.

Smillie, Anne. Chief Executive, Scottish Badminton Union, since 1989; b. 17.8.56, Glasgow. Educ. Victoria Drive Secondary School; Anniesland College. Joined Scottish Badminton Union, 1980; Director of major badminton events, including 1992 European Championships and 1994 World Team Championships. Recreations: music; reading. Address: (h.) 55 Westerton Avenue, Westerton, Glasgow; T.-0141-942 9804.

Smillie, Ian R.D., BL. Chief Executive, Kyle and Carrick District Council, since 1983; b. 13.9.39, Kilmarnock; m., Margaret; 2 d. Educ. Kilmarnock Academy; Glasgow University. Private practice, 1958-68; Royal Burgh of Ayr, 1968-74 (latterly as Assistant Town Clerk); Director of Administration, Kyle and Carrick District Council, 1974-83. Chairman, BACT, 1981; Dean, Ayr Faculty of Solicitors, 1989-90; Director, Freeport Scotland Limited; Director, Ayrshire Hospice; Director, Ayr Town Centre Management Initiative. Address: (b.) Burns House, Burns Statue Square, Ayr, KA7 1UT; T.-01292 281511.

Smith, Professor Adam Neil, MD, FRCSE, FRCPE, FIBiol, FRSE. Wade Professor of Surgical Studies, RCSEd, since 1986; formerly Consultant Surgeon, Gastro-Intestinal Unit, Edinburgh (retired); b. 27.6.26, Hamilton; m., Sibyl Mary Veitch Johnstone; 1 s.; 3 d. Educ. Lanark Grammar School; Glasgow University. Academic and Health Service appointments, since 1948; Lecturer in Surgery, Glasgow University; Medical Research Council Fellow; Reader, Edinburgh University and Western General Hospital. Vice-President and Council Member, Royal College of Surgeons of Edinburgh; Council Member, Association of Coloproctology; Past President, British Group for Research into Pelvic Function and Disease; former Surgical Traveller, James IV Surgical Association. Recreation: golf. Address: (h.) 2 Ravelston House Park, Edinburgh, EH4 3LU; T.-0131-332 4077.

Smith, Sir Alan, Kt (1982), CBE (1976), DFC (1941) and Bar (1942), DL, JP. President, Dawson International plc, Kinross, since 1982; Chairman, Quayle Munro PLC, Edinburgh, 1982-93; b. 14.3.17, South Shields; m., 1, Margaret Stewart Todd (deceased); 2, Alice Elizabeth Moncur; 3 s.; 2 d. Educ. Bede College, Sunderland. Self-employed, 1931-36; Unilever, 1936-39; RAF, 1939-45; Managing Director, Todd & Duncan Ltd., Kinross, 1946-60; Chairman and Chief Executive, Dawson International, Kinross, 1960-82. Board Member, Scottish Development Agency, 1982-87; Kinross Burgh Councillor, 1952-65; Provost of Kinross, 1959-65; Tayside Regional Councillor, 1979-90; Financial Convenor, Tayside Region, 1980-86. Recreations: work; sailing. Address: (h.) Ardgairney House, Cleish, by Kinross; T.-01577 850265.

Smith, Professor Alan Gordon Rae, MA, PhD, FRHistS. Professor in Modern History, Glasgow University, since 1992; b. 22.12.36, Glasgow; m., Isabel Robertson; 1 s.; 1 d. Educ. Glasgow High School; Glasgow University; University College, London. Research Fellow, Institute of Historical Research, London University, 1961-62; Assistant in History, 1962-64, then Lecturer, Glasgow University, 1964-75; Senior Lecturer in Modern History, 1975-85; Reader, 1985-92; Review Editor, History (Journal of the Historical Association), 1984-87; Member, Council, Royal Historical Society, 1990-94. Publications: The Government of Elizabethan England, 1967; The New Europe, 1969; Science and Society in the Sixteenth and Seventeenth Centuries, 1972; Servant of the Cecils: The Life of Sir Michael Hickes, 1977; The Emergence of a Nation State: The Commonwealth of England 1529-1660, 1984; The Anonymous Life of William Cecil, Lord Burghley, 1990; The Last Years of Mary Queen of Scots, 1990; Tudor Government, 1990; William Cecil, Lord Burghley, Minister of Queen Elizabeth I, 1991. Recreation: watching sport. Address: (h.) 5 Cargil Avenue, Kilmacolm, Renfrewshire; T.-Kilmacolm 2055.

Smith, Alexander. Member (Labour), Scotland South, European Parliament, since 1989; b. 2.12.43.

Smith, Allan Keppie. CBE, BSc, FEng, FIMechE, FWeldI. Managing Director, Facilities Management Division, Babcock International Group PLC, Rosyth Royal Dockyard; b. 18.5.32. Joined Army for National Service, 1953; commissioned, REME, 1954; Babcock & Wilcox:

joined as Graduate Trainee, 1955; appointed: Industrial Engineering Manager, Renfrew Works, 1965, Production Director, Renfrew Works, 1974, Managing Director, Renfrew and Dumbarton Works, 1976; Managing Director, Babcock Thorn Limited and Chairman, Rosyth Royal Dockyard plc, 1986; Director, Babcock International Group PLC, 1989; Chairman: Tickford Rail Limited, since 1990, Babcock Rail Limited, since 1993, Babcock Rosyth Defence Limited, since 1994, Babcock New Zealand Limited, since 1994; Past President, Scottish Engineering; Past Chairman, Council of the Welding Institute; Chairman, Pailsey University Integrated Graduate Development Scheme Management Committee; Member, Board of Governors, BMT Quality Assessors Limited; Member, Board, Fife Enterprise; Fellow, Paisley University; Awarded Institute of Marketing Scottish Marketer of the Year, 1992. Address: (h.) The Forts, Hawes Brae, South Queensferry EH30 9TE; T.-0131-319 1668.

Smith, Anne, QC, LLB (Hons). Admitted, Faculty of Advocates, 1980. Address: (b.) Advocates' Library, Parliament House, Edinburgh, EH1 1RF.

Smith, Professor Brian Clive, BA, MA, PhD. Professor of Political Science and Social Policy, Dundee University, since 1989; b. 23.1.38, London; m., Jean Baselow; 1 s.; 1 d. Educ. Colfe's Grammar School; Exeter University; McMaster University, Canada. Lecturer in Politics, Exeter University; Lecturer in Public Administration, Civil Service College, 1970-72; Senior Lecturer/Reader in Politics, Bath University, 1972-89. Publications include: Decentralisation; Bureaucracy and Political Power. Recreations: walking; opera. Address: (b.) Dundee University, Dundee, DD1 4HN; T.-01382 223181.

Smith, Sheriff Charles, MA, LLB, NP. Sheriff of Tayside, Central and Fife, at Cupar, since 1991, at Perth, 1986-91; b. 15.8.30, Methil; m., Janet Elizabeth Hurst; 1 s.; 1 d. Educ. Perth Academy; St. Andrews University. Solicitor, 1956; private practice as Principal, 1962-82; Member, Perth Town Council, 1966-68; Interim Depute Procurator Fiscal, 1974-82; Tutor, Dundee University, 1980-82; Member, Council, Law Society of Scotland (Convener, various Committees), 1977-82; Temporary Sheriff, 1977-82; Honorary Tutor, Dundee University, since 1982; Sheriff of Glasgow and Strathkelvin, 1982-86; Member, Council, Sheriffs' Association, 1987-90. Recreations: tennis; golf; bridge. Address: (b.) c/o Sheriff Clerk, Sheriff Court, Cupar, KY15 4LX; T.-01334 652121.

Smith, C. Christopher, MB, FRCP, FRCPE. Consultant Physician, General Medicine, and Head of Service, Infection Unit, Aberdeen Royal Infirmary NHS Trust, since 1973; Honorary Senior Lecturer in Medicine, University of Aberdeen, Elected Member, Senatus Academicus, 1988-92; Member, Council, Royal College of Physicians of Edinburgh, 1991-94; External Examiner, Final MB, University of Dundee; b. 16.5.39, West Indies; m., Sheila Anne Calder, MRCPsych; 2 s., 1 d. by pr. m. Educ. Lodge School, Barbados; Edinburgh University. Registrar, Department of Medicine, Edinburgh Royal Infirmary; Registrar, Thoracic Medicine, then Senior Registrar, Infectious Diseases, City Hospital, Edinburgh; Senior Registrar, Department of Therapeutics and Clinical Pharmacology, Edinburgh Royal Infirmary; former Member, Part I MRCP Examination Board, Member, Examination Committee United Examining Board, and Chairman, Written Paper Panel; Chairman, Specialty Advisory Committee, (JCHMT) on Infection and Tropical Medicine, and Member, JCHMT; Visitor for JCHMT Accreditation in Internal Medicine, Infection/Tropical Medicine, and Public Health Medicine; Regional Adviser, RCPs and Member, Aberdeen and NE Scotland Postgraduate Medical Education Committee; author of papers, chapters and leading articles on topics on medicine, infection, post-infective phenomena, and antimicrobial

chemotherapy; Visiting Lecturer, Hong Kong, Singapore, Malaya, Kenya, Zimbabwe, Saudi Arabia, Iceland, South Africa, since 1982. Recreations: watching cricket; golf; live theatre; jazz music; Winston Churchill's literary output and his biographies. Address: (b.) Wards 25/26, Aberdeen Royal Infirmary, Foresterhill, Aberdeen, AB9 2ZB; T.-Aberdeen 681818.

Smith, David Bruce Boyter, OBE, MA, LLB, FRSA, FInstD, NP. Director and Chief Executive, Dunfermline Building Society, since 1987; b. 11.3.42, St. Andrews; m., Christine Anne; 1 s.; 1 d. Educ. High School, Dunfermline; Edinburgh University. Legal training, Balfour & Manson, Edinburgh; admitted Solicitor, 1968; Solicitor, Standard Life Assurance Co., 1969-73; Dunfermline Building Society: Secretary, 1974-81, General Manager (Admin.), 1981-86, Deputy Chief Executive, 1986. Past Chairman, Scottish Committee, Building Societies Association; Member, Council, NHBC (Scotland); Deputy Chairman, Glenrothes Development Corporation; Director, Fife Enterprise Ltd.; Director, Scottish Fisheries Museum; Member, Building Societies Investor Protection Board; Member of Court and Finance Convener, Edinburgh University; Vice Chairman, Lauder College; Life Trustee, Carnegie Trust. Recreations: golf; sailing; the arts. Address: (b.) Caledonia House, Carnegie Avenue, Dunfermline, Fife; T.-01383 627727.

Smith, Sheriff David Buchanan, MA, LLB, FSAScot. Sheriff of North Strathclyde at Kilmarnock, since 1975; b. 31.10.36, Paisley; m., Hazel Mary Sinclair; 1 s.; 1 d. Educ. Paisley Grammar School; Glasgow University; Edinburgh University. Advocate, 1961; Standing Junior Counsel to Scottish Education Department, 1968-75; Tutor, Faculty of Law, Edinburgh University, 1964-72; Trustee, Scottish Curling Museum Trust, since 1980. President, Kilmarnock and District History Group; Trustee Scottish National Dictionary Association, since 1994. Publications: Curling: An Illustrated History, 1981; The Roaring Game: Memories of Scottish Curling, 1985; contributions to The Laws of Scotand: Stair Memorial Encyclopedia, Vol. 6; George Washington Wilson in Ayrshire, 1991. Recreations:Scotland — history and culture; curling; collecting curliana; music; architecture. Address: (b.) Sheriff Court House, Kilmarnock, KA1 1ED; T.-01563 520211.

Smith, Sir David Cecil, Kt, MA, DPhil, FRS, FRSE. Principal and Vice-Chancellor, Edinburgh University, 1987-94; President, Wolfson College, Oxford, since 1994; m., Lesley Margaret Mollison Mutch; 2 s.; 1 d. Educ. St. Paul's School, London; Queen's College, Oxford. Browne Research Fellow, Queen's College, Oxford, 1956-59; Harkness Fellow, University of California, Berkeley, 1959-60; University Lecturer, Department of Agriculture, Oxford University, 1960-74; Fellow and Tutor, Wadham College, Oxford, 1964-74; Melville Wills Professor of Botany, Bristol University, 1974-80; Sibthorpian Professor of Rural Economy, Oxford University, 1980-87. President, British Lichen Society, 1972-74; President, British Mycological Society, 1980; President, Society for Experimental Biology, 1983-85. Publication: The Biology of Symbiosis (Co-author), 1987. Address: Wolfson College, Oxford OX2 6UD; T.-01865 274101; The Steading, Balquhidder, Perthshire FK19 8NY; T.-01877 384316.

Smith, Professor David John, MA. Professor of Criminology, Edinburgh University, since 1994; b. 10.7.41, Egypt; m., Colette Marie Smith Obadia; 1 s. Educ. Bootham School, York; Christ Church, Oxford. Trainee Research Executive, 1963-64; Research Officer, 1964-66; Senior Research Officer, then Board Director, Interscan Ltd., 1966-71; Senior Research Associate, Political and Economic Manning, 1972-78; Senior Fellow, Policy Studies Institute, and Head, Social Justice and Social Order Group, 1979-94. Additional Commissioner, Commission for Racial

Equality, 1978-84; Specialist Adviser to Home Affairs and Employment Committees, House of Commons, 1981-82, 1986; Visiting Fellow, Lincoln College, Oxford, 1988-89. Recreations: large format photography; piano. Address: (b.) Faculty of Law, Edinburgh University, Old College, South Bridge, Edinburgh, EH8 9YL; T.-0131-650 2027.

Smith, Very Rev. David Macintyre Bell Armour, MA, BD, DUniv, JP. Minister, Logie, 1965-89; Moderator, General Assembly of the Church of Scotland, 1985; b. 5.4.23, Fort Augustus; m., Mary Kulvear Cumming; 3 s. Educ. Monckton Combe; Peebles High School; St. Andrews University. Minister, Warrender Church, Edinburgh, 1951-61; Exchange Preacher, USA, 1958 and 1961; Minister, Old Partick, Glasgow, 1961-65; Moderator, Stirling and Dunblane Presbytery, 1972-73; Moderator, Perth and Stirling Synod, 1975-76; Vice Convener, Joint Working Party, Church of Scotland, 1980-82; Convener, Church of Scotland Board of Education, 1979-83; Church of Scotland Representative, Stirlingshire Education Committee, 1969-79; Governor, Moray House College of Education, 1983; Member, Central Regional Education Committee, 1986-94; Member, Church of Scotland Assembly Council, 1989-93, Board of Practice and Procedure, 1982-90; Honorary Brother, Guildry of Stirling, 1986. Recreations: philately; gardening. Address: (h.) 28 Millar Place, Stirling, FK8 1XD; T.-Stirling 475085.

Smith, (Edward) Alistair, CBE, MA, PhD. Director, Aberdeen University International Office, since 1990 (Director, Aberdeen University University Development Trust, 1982-90); Deputy Chairman, Scottish Conservative Party, 1981-86; b. 16.1.39, Aberdeen. Educ. Aberdeen Grammar School; Aberdeen University. Lecturer in Geography, Aberdeen University, 1963-88; President, Scottish Conservative and Unionist Association, 1979-81; Member, Grampian Health Board, 1983-91; Board Member, SCOTVEC, 1989-93; Member, Committee for Scotland, Nature Conservancy Council, 1989-91; Member, N.E. Regional Committee, Nature Conservancy Council, 1991-92; Trustee, British School in Colombo, Sri Lanka, since 1994. Publications: Europe: A Geographical Survey of the Continent (Co-author), 1979; Scotland's Future Development (Contributor), 1983. Recreations: travel; photography; music. Address: (h.) 68A Beaconsfield Place, Aberdeen, AB2 4AJ; T.-01224 642932.

Smith, Elaine Constance. Actress; b. 2.8.58, Baillieston; m., Robert Morton; 2 d. Educ. Braidhurst High School, Motherwell; Royal Scottish Academy of Music and Drama; Moray House College of Education. Teacher of Speech and Drama, Firrhill High School, Edinburgh, 1979-82; joined 7:84 Theatre Company, 1982; moved to Wildcat Stage Productions, 1982; since 1986, worked with Borderline Theatre Co., Royal Lyceum, Dundee Rep., Tron Theatre; TV work includes City Lights and Naked Video; plays Mary Nesbitt in Rab C. Nesbitt (BBC2); original cast member, The Steamie. Board Member, Scottish Youth Theatre; Patron West Lothian Youth Theatre. Recreations: swimming; aerobics; reading. Address: (b.) c/o Crossan Communications, 10 Bernard Street, Edinburgh, EH6 6PP.

Smith of Gilmorehill, Baroness (Elizabeth Margaret), Life Peer; m., John Smith, QC, MP (deceased); 3 d.

Smith, Gordon Matthew, DCA, MITSA. Director of Trading Standards, Dumfries and Galloway Regional Council, since 1982; b. 10.11.44, Ayr; m., Moyra; 1 s.; 1 d. Educ. Ayr Academy. Trainee Trading Standards Officer, Ayr County Council, 1962-66; Trading Standards Officer: Lindsey (Lincolnshire) County Council, 1966-68, Lanark County Council, 1968-72; District Trading Standards Officer, 1972-75; Senior Trading Standards Officer, Strathclyde Regional Council, 1975-79; Assistant Chief Trading Standards Officer, Central Regional Council, 1979-82. Recreation: golf. Address: (b.) 1 Newall Terrace, Dumfries, DG1 1LN; T.-01387 60091.

Smith, Graham Douglas, LLB (Hons). Director Customer Service, ScotRail, since 1994; b. 22.6.48, Broughty Ferry. Educ. Prince Edward School, Salisbury; Dundee University. British Airways, 1971-91; Head of Customer Service and Retail, InterCity, 1991-94. Director, Glasgow Chamber of Commerce, 1987-90. Recreations: golf; tennis; travel; gardening. Address: (b.) Caledonian Chambers, Central Station, Glasgow.

Smith, Professor Grahame Francis, MA, PhD. Professor, Department of English Studies, Stirling University, and Deputy Principal, since 1993; b. 30.5.33, London; m., Angela Mary; 2 s.; 1 d. Educ. Woodside Senior Secondary School, Glasgow; Aberdeen University; Cambridge University. Taught at California University, Los Angeles, 1963-65, University College, Swansea, 1965-70; secondment to Malawi University, 1982-83. Publications: Dickens, Money and Society, 1968; The Novel and Society: From Defoe to George Elliot, 1984; The Achievement of Graham Greene, 1985; A Literary Life of Charles Dickens, 1995. Recreations: cinema; opera; jazz; walking. Address: (b.) Department of English Studies, Stirling University, Stirling, FK9 4LA; T.-01786 863171.

Smith, Rev. G. Richmond N.R.K., OBE, MA, BD. Minister, Church of Scotland, since 1952; b. 2.3.27, Rendall, Orkney; m., Agnes Margaret Elliott Longden. Educ. Anderson Educational Institute, Lerwick; Edinburgh University. Minister: East Parish, Peterhead, 1952-60, West High Parish, Kilmarnock, 1960-65; Theological Secretary, World Alliance of Reformed Churches, Geneva, 1965-83; retired to Scotland, 1983. Recreations: ornithology; archaeology. Address: (h.) Aignish, Kippford, by Dalbeattie, DG5 4LL; T.-Kippford 624.

Smith, Hamilton, BSc, PhD, CChem, FRSC, FRCPath, FRSE. Titular Professor of Forensic Medicine (Toxicology), Glasgow University, since 1987; b. 27.4.34, Stirling; m., Jacqueline Ann Spittal. Educ. Kilsyth Academy; Glasgow University. Glasgow University: MRC Fellow, 1960, Special Research Fellow, 1963, Lecturer in Forensic Medicine Department, 1964, Senior Lecturer, 1973, Reader, 1984. Publication: Glaister's Medical Jurisprudence and Toxicology, 13th edition. Recreations: golf (New Club, St. Andrews); gardening. Address: (b.) Department of Forensic Medicine and Science, Glasgow University, Glasgow, G12 8QQ; T.-0141-339 8855.

Smith, Hugh, DipWEM, FIWEM. Director, Clyde River Purification Board, since 1994; b. 23.2.47, Glasgow; m., Jessie; 1 s.; 1 d. Educ. Glenwood Secondary School; Stow College; Paisley College of Technology. Junior Chemist, BSC, Motherwell, 1963-65; Clyde River Purification Board:Junior Chemist, 1965-69, Assistant Inspector, 1969-76, Senior Assistant Inspector, 1976-79, Divisional Inspector, 1979-89, Depute Director (Chief Inspector), 1989-94. Member, Scottish Industrial Waste Panel. Recreations: golf; badminton. Address: (b.) Rivers House, Murray Road, East Kilbride, Glasgow, G75 0LA; T.-013552 38181.

Smith, Iain Crichton, OBE, LLD (Dundee), DLitt (Glasgow), DLitt (Aberdeen), MA (Hons). Writer; b. 1.1.28, Glasgow; m., Donalda Gillies Logan; 2 step s. Educ. Nicolson Institute, Stornoway; Aberdeen University. Teacher, Oban High School, 1955-77; full-time Writer, since 1977; former Member, STV Gaelic Advisory Committee; Fellow, Royal Literary Society; books in English: 10 novels, six volumes of short stories, 13 volumes of poetry; books in Gaelic: two novels, five volumes of short stories, four volumes of poetry; translations from Gaelic into English; numerous radio plays in both languages; Poetry Book Society Choice and three recommendations; eight Arts Council awards; awards for Gaelic plays and short stories; award for Gaelic television play; PEN Award, 1970; Scotsman Short Story Award,

1983; Commonwealth Poetry Prize (European Section), 1986; Travelling Scholarship, Society of Authors, 1987; Saltire Prize, 1992. Recreation: reading detective stories. Address:Tigh Na Fuaran, Taynuilt, Argyll; T.-Taynuilt 463.

Smith, Ian Fraser, LLB. Chief Executive, Dumfries and Galloway Council, since 1995; Chief Executive, Dumfries and Galloway Regional Council, since 1992; Member, Executive, SOLACE; b. 27.6.50, Dunfermline; m., Pat; 1 s.; 1 d. Educ. Kirkcaldy High School; Dundee University. Solicitor; held posts, Fife Region; Depute Chief Executive, Clackmannan District Council, 1977, Chief Executive, 1985. Area President, Dumfriesshire Scouts, since 1994. Recreations: gardening; modern painting; sculpture; watching rugby. Address: (b.) Dumfries and Galloway Council, Council Offices, English Street, Dumfries, DG1 2DD; T.-01387 260000.

Smith, James Aikman, TD, BA, LLB. Advocate; Honorary Sheriff, since 1976; b. 13.6.14, Kilmarnock; m., Katharine Ann Millar; 3 d. Educ. Glasgow Academy; Oxford University; Edinburgh University. Admitted Faculty of Advocates, 1939; served Royal Artillery, 1939-46 (Lt. Col., 1944), North Africa, Italy and Austria; Despatches, Bronze Star US; Sheriff Substitute, Renfrew and Argyll, 1948-52, Roxburgh, Berwick and Selkirk, 1952-57, Aberdeen, Kincardine and Banff, 1957-68; Sheriff of Lothians and Borders, 1968-76; President, Sheriffs' Association, 1969-72; Member, UK Departmental Committee on Probation Service, 1959-62; Member, After Care Council (Scotland), 1962-65; UK Delegate to UN Congress on Crime, Japan, 1970; Chairman, Edinburgh and East of Scotland Branch, English Speaking Union, 1970-74; Vice-President, Cairngorm Club, 1962-65; Chairman, Allelon Society, 1970-76; Elder, Church of Scotland, since 1948; has served on various General Assembly Committees. Recreations: hill-walking; gardening; travel. Address: (h.) 16 Murrayfield Avenue, Edinburgh, EH12 6AX; T.-0131-337 8205.

Smith, James Boyd, GM, MA, BSc, CEng, FIEE, FRSE. Councillor, Royal Society of Edinburgh, since 1992; b. 9.2.20, Edinburgh; m., May Campbell; 1 s.; 1 d. Educ. George Heriot's School, Edinburgh; Edinburgh University. Captain, Corps of Royal Engineers, 1939-45, served in N. Africa, Sicily, Normandy, Germany; George Medal, 1943, for bomb disposal work; mentioned in Despatches, 1945; joined Ferranti Ltd., 1947; Assistant General Manager, 1980-83; Director of numerous subsidiary companies; Director, Wolfson Microelectronics Ltd., 1984-93. Chairman, IEE Scottish Centre, 1973-74; Member, Edinburgh University Court, 1975-84; Hon. Fellow, Edinburgh University, 1989. Recreations: organ playing; gardening; genealogy. Address: (h.) 28 Murrayfield Road, Edinburgh, EH12 6ER; T.-0131-346 8604.

Smith, James David, OBE, MA, LLB. Retired Solicitor; Honorary Sheriff of North Strathclyde at Greenock, since 1976; b. 27.10.19, Dumbarton; m., Margaret McGregor Grant; 2 s. Educ. Dumbarton Academy; Glasgow University. Commissioned Highland Light Infantry, 1940; Town Clerk, Dumbarton, 1951-67; Chief Executive, Corporation of Greenock, 1967-75; Visiting Lecturer in Law, Paisley College of Technology, 1976-87. Address: (h.) 42 Octavia Terrace, Greenock, PA16 7SR; T.-01475 723788.

Smith, John Michael, BA (Hons), DipEd, MBIM. Rector, Berwickshire High School, since 1982; b. 7.2.40, Barnsley; m., Elspeth Sheena; 2 d. Educ. Queen Elizabeth Grammar School, Wakefield; Durham University; Westminster College, Oxford. Assistant Teacher of Classics and RE, 1962-67; Head of Classics, Wallsend Upon Tyne Grammar School, 1967-70; Senior Housemaster, Dalziel High School, 1970-73; Depute Rector, Berwickshire High School, 1973-82. Methodist Church Lay Preacher, since 1960; Circuit Steward, Berwick Upon Tweed Methodist Church Circuit. Recreations: walking; golf; reading spy thrillers; camping abroad. Address: (b.) Berwickshire High School, Duns; T.-01361 83710.

Smith, Sheriff J.R., LLB. Sheriff of South Strathclyde, Dumfries and Galloway at Stranraer. Address: (b.) Sheriff Court House, Lewis Street, Stranraer, DG9 7AA.

Smith, Professor Keith, BA, PhD, FRSE. Professor of Environmental Science, Stirling University, since 1986; Head of School of Natural Sciences, Stirling University, since 1994; b. 9.1.38, Marple; m., Muriel Doris Hyde; 1 s.; 1 d. Educ. Hyde County Grammar School; Hull University. Tutor in Geography, Liverpool University, 1963-65; Lecturer in Geography, Durham University, 1965-70; Strathclyde University: Senior Lecturer, 1971-75, Reader, 1975-82, Personal Professor, 1982-84, Professor and Head of Department, 1984-86. Drapers' Company Visiting Lecturer, Adelaide University, 1978; Visiting Principal Scientist, Illinois State Water Survey, 1988; Visiting Professor of Geography, University of Illinois, 1988. Publications: Water in Britain; Principles of Applied Climatology; Human Adjustment to Flood Hazard; Environmental Hazards. Recreations: hill-walking; badminton. Address: (b.) Department of Environmental Science, Stirling University, Stirling, FK9 4LA; T.-01786 467840.

Smith, Professor Lawrence D., BSc. Professor of Agricultural Economics, Glasgow University, since 1989; b. 1939, Bedfordshire; m., Evelyn Mavis Stead; 1 s.; 2 d. Educ. Bedford Modern School; Wye College, London University; Linacre College, Oxford. Departmental Lecturer, Agricultural Economics Research Institute, Oxford University, 1963-66; Lecturer, Senior Lecturer, Reader in Agricultural Economics, Department of Political Economy, Glasgow University. Director, Scottish Agricultural College, since 1990. Recreation: gardening. Address: (b.) Department of Political Economy, Glasgow University, Glasgow; T.-0141-339 8855.

Smith, Professor Lorraine Nancy, BScN, MEd, PhD. Professor of Nursing Studies, Glasgow University, since 1990 (Head of Department, since 1990); b. 29.6.49, Ottawa; m., Christopher Murray Smith; 1 s.; 1 d. Educ. Hillcrest High School, Ottawa; University of Ottawa; Manchester University. Co-opted to English National Board, 1988-90; Member, Scottish Alcohol Advisory Group, since 1991; Member, Clinical and Biomedical Research Committee (Scotland), 1992-94; Member, Clinical Standards Advisory Group (UK), since 1994. Recreations: reading; bridge; sailing. Address: (b.) 68 Oakfield Avenue, Glasgow University, Glasgow, G12 8LS; T.-0141-330 4051.

Smith, Matt, JP. Scottish Secretary, Unison, since 1993; Member, STUC General Council, since 1989; b. 4.2.52, Irvine; m., Eileen; 1 s.; 1 d. Educ. Stevenson High School; Ardrossan Academy. NALGO: District Officer, 1973-81, Senior Scottish District Officer, 1981-88, Scottish Organiser, 1988-93; Chair, Local Government Committee, STUC; Member, Executive, Scottish Council Development and Industry; former Councillor; Parliamentary candidate, Labour, 1979. Recreations: reading; gardening; travel; politics; music; family. Address: (b.) Unison House, 14 West Campbell Street, Glasgow, G2 6RX; T.-0141-332 0006.

Smith, Nigel R. Managing Director, David Auld Valves Ltd., since 1976; b. 9.6.41, Girvan; m., Jody; 2 s.; 2 d. Educ. Dollar Academy. Lt., 4/5 Bn., Royal Scots Fusiliers (TA), 1960-67; staff and management appointments, Bowater Paper, Richard Costain, Rank Hovis McDougall. Member, Executive, Scottish Engineering Employers Association, 1985-90; Member, Broadcasting Council for Scotland, 1986-90; Member, BBC General Advisory

Council, 1991-93; Member, Glasgow Development Agency, Strategy Review Panel, 1993-94; Member, Scottish Constitutional Commission, 1993-94; Chairman, Broadcasting for Scotland Campaign, since 1993; Member, Scottish Office Action for Engineering Group, since 1995. Recreations: hill-walking; offshore sailing; opera and choral; reading, particularly biography. Address: (b.) David Auld Valves, Cowlairs Industrial Estate, Finlas Street, Glasgow, G22 5DQ; T.-0141-557 0515.

Smith, Norma Henderson. Headmistress, Albyn School for Girls, Aberdeen, since 1982; b. 10.8.39, Edinburgh. Educ. George Watson's Ladies' College; Edinburgh University. Assistant Teacher of Chemistry, St. Leonard's School, St. Andrews; Head of Chemistry: St. Christopher School, Letchworth, Gordonstoun School; Assistant Headteacher, Berwickshire High School. Address: (b.) 17/23 Queens Road, Aberdeen, AB9 2PA; T.-01224 322408.

Smith, Philip Morgans, BSc, PhD, FLS. Convener, Honours School of Botany, Edinburgh University, since 1990; b. 5.2.41, Halesowen; m., Eira; 2 s. Educ. Halesowen Grammar School; Birmingham University. Harkness Fellow, Commonwealth Fund, New York; Senior Lecturer in Botany, Edinburgh University; various examining appointments/offices, Scottish Examination Board and related Scottish Office services, since 1970; agrostologist. Past President, Botanical Society of Scotland; Director, Botany of the Lothians Survey. Recreations: canal boating; watching trains; singing; painting. Address: (b.) 7 Clayhills Park, Balerno, Midlothian, EH14 7BH; T.-0131-449 4345.

Smith, Rev. Ralph Colley Philip, MA, STM. Part-time Chaplain, Western General Hospital, Edinburgh; Minister, Church of Scotland, since 1960; b. 11.3.31, Edinburgh; m., Florence; 2 s. Educ. Edinburgh Academy; St. Andrews University; Edinburgh University; Union Seminary, New York. Minister, Gallatown Church, Kirkcaldy; Religious Broadcasting Assistant, then Producer, Religion, Television, BBC Scotland; Associate Minister, New Kilpatrick Parish Church, Bearsden; Director of Audio-Visual Productions, Church of Scotland, 1985-91. Recreations: cello; bowls; golf. Address: (h.) 2 Blackford Hill View, Edinburgh, EH9 3HD.

Smith, Robert Haldane, CA, FCIBS. Chairman and Chief Executive, Morgan Grenfell Development Capital Limited and Director, Morgan Grenfell & Co. Limited and Morgan Grenfell (Scotland) Limited; b. 8.8.44, Glasgow; m., Alison Marjorie Bell; 2 d. Educ. Allan Glen's School, Glasgow. Articled to Robb Ferguson & Co., CA, Glasgow, 1963-68; qualified CA, 1968; ICFC, now 3i, 1968-82; General Manager (Corporate Finance Division), The Royal Bank of Scotland plc, 1983-85; Managing Director, National Commercial & Glyns, 1983-85; Managing Director, Charterhouse Development Capital Limited and Executive Director, Charterhouse Bank Limited, 1985-89; current Directorships include: Bristow Helicopter Group Limited, MFI Furniture Group PLC; Chairman, Board of Trustees, National Museums of Scotland; Commissioner, Museums and Galleries Commission; President, British Association of Friends of Museums; Senior Vice-President, Institute of Chartered Accountants of Scotland, since 1995. Publication: Managing Your Company's Finances (Co-author). Recreations: historic and listed buildings; music. Address: (b.) 35 St. Andrew Square, Edinburgh EH2 2AD; T.-0131-557 8600.

Smith, Robert Lupton, OBE, FRICS. Vice-President and Consultant, Association for the Protection of Rural Scotland, since 1993 (Director, 1981-93); Chartered Surveyor in private practice, since 1954; b. 26.4.24, Cheadle Hulme; m.; 3 d. Educ. George Watson's College; College of Estate Management; Heriot-Watt College. Chairman, Scottish Junior Branch, RICS, 1952; Member,

Scottish Executive Committee, RICS, 1952-60; elected, Edinburgh Town Council, 1962-74 and Edinburgh District Council, 1974-77; Governor, Edinburgh College of Art, 1963-89; fought European Election, 1979, as Liberal; Deputy Traffic Commissioner, 1974-78; Chairman, Good Neighbours Housing Association, 1984-87; Scottish Liberal Party: Chairman, Executive Committee, 1971-74, Chairman, 1974, President, 1976-82; Council Member, Royal Scottish Geographical Society, 1957-92; Chairman, Scottish Liberal Club, 1984-91; Director, Cockburn Conservation Trust Ltd., 1976-90; Chairman, Logierait Bridge Co. Ltd. Recreations: visiting Orkney; reading; looking at fine art. Address: (h.) Charleston, Dalguise, near Dunkeld, PH8 0JX; T.-01350 728968.

Smith, Robert S., MA (Hons), DipEd. Head Teacher, Cumnock Academy, since 1989; b. 18.10.40, St. Monans; m., Roslyn Hulme; 1 s.; 1 d. Educ. Waid Academy, Anstruther; St. Andrews University; Aberdeen University; Aberdeen College of Education. Classics Teacher, Airdrie Academy, 1963-67; Principal Teacher of Classics: Armadale Academy, 1967-70, Dumbarton Academy, 1970-74; Assistant/Depute Head Teacher, Clydebank High School, 1974-78; Head Teacher, Allan Glen's Secondary, 1978-89. Chairman, Scottish Executive, Professional Association of Teachers, 1989-90 (Council Member, 1989-92 and 1992-95); Member, University of Strathclyde Faculty of Education Advisory Board, since 1995. Publications: Discovering the Greeks; Discovering Greek Mythology. Recreation: country activities. Address: (b.) Cumnock Academy, Ayr Road, Cumnock, Ayrshire; T.-01290 421228.

Smith, Roger. Writer and Editor; b. 28.11.38, London; 2 d. Educ. Latymer Upper School, London. Editor, The Great Outdoors, 1977-86; Editor, Environment Now, 1987-89; Editor, Scottish World, 1989-90; Past Chairman, Scottish Wild Land Group; Member, Executive Committee, National Trust for Scotland. Publications: Penguin Book of Orienteering, 1981; The Winding Trail, 1981; Weekend Walking, 1982; Visitor's Guide to Scottish Borders, 1983; Jet Guide to Scotland's Countryside, 1985; The Great Outdoors Book of the Walking Year, 1988; Classic Walks in Scotland (Co-author), 1988; Chambers Guide to the Highlands and Islands, 1992; Catastrophies and Disasters, 1992; The Great Flood of Perth, 1993; 25 Walks: Highland Perthshire 1994; 25 Walks: Edinburgh and Lothian, 1995. Recreations: hill-walking; running; orienteering; Scottish history. Address: (h.) 43 Kilnknowe Place, Galashiels TD1 1RH; T.-01896 751003.

Smith, Roger Galbraith, MB, ChB, FRCPEdin, FRCPLond, FRCPGlas. Consultant Physician in Geriatric Medicine, Royal Victoria Hospital, Edinburgh, and Honorary Senior Lecturer in Geriatric Medicine, Edinburgh University, since 1989; b. 7.7.42, Edinburgh; m., Margaret Lawson; 1 s.; 1 d. Educ. George Watson's College, Edinburgh; Edinburgh University. Surgeon Lieutenant, Royal Navy, 1967-72; Senior Registrar in Geriatric Medicine, 1973-76; Senior Lecturer, Department of Geriatric Medicine, Edinburgh University, 1976-89. Member, Board of Directors, Queensberry House Hospital, Edinburgh. Recreations: golf; curling. Address: (h.) 56 Alnwickhill Road, Edinburgh; T.-0131-664 1745.

Smith, Ronald A., MA. General Secretary, Educational Institute of Scotland, since 1995; Member, General Council, STUC, since 1995; Member, Executive Board, European Trade Union Committee for Education, since 1995; b. 9.6.51, Lerwick; m., Mae; 1 s.; 1 d. Educ. Anderson Educational Institute; Aberdeen University; Aberdeen College of Education. Teacher of Latin, then A.P.T. of Latin, then Principal Teacher of Modern Studies, Broxburn Academy, 1973-88; Assistant Secretary, EIS, 1988-95. Address: (b.) 46 Moray Place, Edinburgh, EH3 6BH.

Smith, Sheriff Ronald Good, BL. Sheriff of North Strathclyde, since 1984; b. 24.7.33. Address: (b.) Sheriff Court House, 106 Renfrew Road, Paisley, PA3 4DD.

Smith, Professor Stanley Desmond, BSc, PhD, DSc, FRS, FRSE. Professor of Physics and Head of Department, Heriot-Watt University, since 1970; Chairman, Edinburgh Instruments Ltd., since 1971; b. 3.3.31, Bristol; m., Gillian Anne Parish; 1 s.; 1 d. Educ. Cotham Grammar School; Bristol University; Reading University. SSO, RAE, Farnborough, 1956-58; Research Assistant, Department of Meteorology, Imperial College, London, 1958-59; Lecturer, then Reader, Reading University, 1960-70; Head, Department of Physics, Heriot-Watt University, since 1970. Member: Advisory Council for Applied Research and Development, 1985-87, Advisory Council on Science and Technology, 1987-88, Defence Scientific Advisory Council, 1985-91, SERC Astronomy and Planetary Science and Engineering Boards, 1985-88, Council, Institute of Physics, 1984-87. Recreations: tennis; skiing; mountaineering; golf; raising the temperature. Address: (h.) 29D Gillespie Road, Colinton, Edinburgh, EH13 0NW; T.-0131-441 7225.

Smith, Professor Stanley William, MA, PhD (Cantab). Chair of English, Dundee University, since 1989 (Reader in English, 1988-89, Head of Department, 1989-94); b. 12.1.43, Warrington; 2 s.; 1 d. Educ. Boteler Grammar School, Warrington; Jesus College, Cambridge. Assistant Lecturer in English, Aberdeen University, 1967-68; Lecturer in English, Dundee University, 1968-85; Senior Lecturer, 1985-88; Visiting Professor, University of Florence, 1987; Chair, Council for University English, 1991-93; British Representative, Board, European Society for the Study of English, 1992-93; Member, Board, Standing Committee for Arts and Social Sciences, since 1989; Member, Board, Scotscass, since 1992; Vice-Chair, Scottish Committee of Professors of English. Publications: A Sadly Contracted Hero: The Comic Self in Post-War American Fiction, 1981; Inviolable Voice: History and Twentieth Century Poetry, 1982; 20th Century Poetry, 1983; W.H. Auden, 1985; Edward Thomas, 1986; W.B. Yeats, 1990; The Origins of Modernism, 1994; General Editor, Longman Critical Reader series and Longman Studies in 20th-century Literature series. Recreations: the arts; classical music; history and archaeology; travel. Address: (b.) English Department, The University, Dundee, DD1 4HN; T.-01382 344412.

Smith, W. Gordon. Writer and Critic; b. 13.12.28, Edinburgh. Journalist; Radio/TV Producer, BBC, 25 years; author of plays: Vincent; Jock; Knox; Sweeter Than All The Roses; A North British Working Man's Guide to the Arts; Wizard; On the Road to Avizandum; Marie of Scotland; Xanadu.

Smith, William Angus, BEM, FEIS, JP. Chairman, Education Committee, Shetland Islands Council, since 1975 (Vice Chairman, Housing Committee, 1982-85); Vice-Chairman, Lerwick Harbour Trust; b. 20.8.19, Burra Isle, Shetland; m., Daisy Manson; 3 s. Educ. Anderson Educational Institute. Engineer, British Telecomms, 1937-83; Royal Signals, UK, Middle East, Burma, India, Germany, 1940-46; Member, Lerwick Town Council and Zetland County Council, 1967-75; Member, Lerwick Harbour Trust, since 1967 (except for short break); Provost of Lerwick, 1971-74; Member, Shetland Islands Council, since 1975; Member, Shetland Area Health Board, 1974-89; Member, Electricity Consultative Council for North of Scotland District, 1974-90; Member, Shetland Recreational Trust. Recreations: crosswords; reading. Address: (h.) 14 Bruce Crescent, Lerwick, Shetland, ZE1 OPB; T.-01595 696428.

Smith, William Leggat, CBE, MC, TD, JP, DL, BA (Oxon), LLB, LLD; b. 30.1.18, Kilmarnock; m., Yvonne Menna Williams; 1 s.; 2 d. Educ. Glasgow Academy; Queen's College, Oxford; Glasgow University. Commissioned (TA), Cameronians (Scottish Rifles), 1939; served Second World War in UK, Europe, USA; Solicitor, 1947-86; Chairman, Governors, Glasgow Academy, 1972-80; Deacon Convener, Trades of Glasgow, 1964-65; Dean, Royal Faculty of Procurators in Glasgow, 1976-79; Member, Reviewing Committee on Export of Works of Art, 1980-82; Convener, Retirement Scheme of Church of Scotland, 1976-80; Chairman, Charles Rennie Mackintosh Society, 1985-88; Chairman, Indigent Gentlewomen of Scotland Fund, 1985-93; Chairman, Glasgow School of Art, 1975-88. Recreations: gardening; salmon fishing. Address: (h.) The Cottage, Clachan of Campsie, Glasgow; T.-01360 311434.

Smith, William Wilson Campbell, MA (Cantab), LLB (Glas). Partner, Biggart Baillie & Gifford, Solicitors, Glasgow and Edinburgh, since 1974; b. 17.5.46, Glasgow; m., Elizabeth Margaret Richards; 2 d. Educ. Glasgow Academy; St. Catharine's College, Cambridge; Glasgow University. Qualified as a Solicitor, 1972; Assistant Solicitor, Herbert Smith & Co., London, 1972-73. Member, various committees, Law Society of Scotland; Member, Joint Insolvency Examination Board; Deacon, Incorporation of Barbers, Glasgow, 1989-90; Trustee, Glassford Sheltered Housing Trust; Member of Convocation, Strathclyde University. Recreations: croquet; golf; barbershop singing. Address: (b.) Dalmore House, 310 St. Vincent Street, Glasgow, G2 5QR; T.-0141-228 8000.

Smith, Professor William Ewen, BSc, DIC, PhD, DSc, FRSC, FRSE. Professor of Inorganic Chemistry, since 1987, and Head of Department, Strathclyde University, since 1995; b. 21.2.41, Glasgow; m., Frances Helen Williamson; 1 s.; 1 d. Educ. Hutchesons' Boys Grammar School; Strathclyde University. Visiting Scientist, Oak Ridge National Laboratory, 1965-67; SERC and ICI Fellow, University College, London, 1967-69; Lecturer, Reader, Professor, Strathclyde University, since 1969. Publications: 170 papers and reviews. Recreations: golf; sailing. Address: (b.) Department of Pure and Applied Chemistry, Strathclyde University, Glasgow, G1 1XL; T.-0141-552 4400.

Smout, Professor Thomas Christopher, CBE, MA, PhD, FRSE, FSA (Scot), FRSA, FBA. Director, St. John's House Centre for Advanced Historical Studies, St. Andrews University, since 1991; Professor of Scottish History, 1980-91; HM Historiographer in Scotland; b. 19.12.33, Birmingham; m., Anne-Marie; 1 s.; 1 d. Educ. Leys School, Cambridge; Clare College, Cambridge. Department of Economic History, Edinburgh University 1975-79. Deputy Chairman, Scottish Natural Heritage; Member, Royal Commission on the Ancient and Historic Monuments of Scotland. Address: (b.) St. Andrews University, St. Andrews, Fife.

Smuga, George Muirhead Russell, MA (Hons), DipEd. Headteacher, North Berwick High School, since 1990; b. 6.11.47, Broughty Ferry; m., Isabel Ann; 1 s.; 1 d. Educ. Kirkcaldy High School; Edinburgh University. Principal Teacher, Modern Studies, then Assistant Headteacher, Portobello High School; Depute Headteacher, Beeslack High School. Member, Understanding British Industry Scotland and Northern Ireland Advisory Committee; co-author of four modern studies textbooks. Recreations: golf; supporting Hibernian F.C. Address: (h.) 47 Morton Street, Edinburgh, EH15 2DA; T.-0131-669 9690.

Smyth, Professor John Crocket, OBE, BSc, PhD, DUniv (Paisley), DipEd, CBiol, FIBiol, FLS, FRSA. Emeritus Professor of Biology, Paisley University, since 1988; Honorary Professor (Department of Environmental Science), Stirling University, since 1988; Chairman, Scottish Environmental Education Council, 1983-91; President, since 1991; Chairman, Secretary of State for

Scotland's Working Group on Environmental Education, 1990-93; b. 21.3.24, Edinburgh; m., Elizabeth Wallace Learmond; 1 s.; 1 d. Educ. George Watson's College; Edinburgh University. Assistant Lecturer in Zoology, Edinburgh University; Lecturer to Head, Department of Biology, Paisley College; Commissioner, Countryside Commission for Scotland, 1990-92; Vice-President, Royal Zoological Society of Scotland; Institute of Biology Charter Award for 1989; former Secretary and Chairman, Scottish Branch, Institute of Biology; Member, IUCN Commission on Education and Communication; IUCN Tree of Learning Award, 1990; Chairman, N.W. Europe Committee, 1980-85; Consultant for UNESCO-UNEP and UNCED on environmental education; Founder-Leader, Scottish Boys' Club. Address: (h.) Glenpark, Johnstone, Renfrewshire, PA5 0SP; T.-01505 320219.

Smyth, Professor John Fletcher, MA, MB, BChir, MD (Cantab), MSc (Lond), FRCPE, FRCP, FRCSE. Professor of Medical Oncology, Edinburgh University, since 1979 (Head, Department of Clinical Oncology, since 1980); Honorary Director, Imperial Cancer Research Fund Medical Oncology Unit, Edinburgh University, since 1980; b. 26.10.45, Dursley; m., Catherine Ellis; 2 d. Educ. Bryanston School; Trinity College, Cambridge. Trained, St. Bartholomews Hospital, Royal Postgraduate Medical School and Institute of Cancer Research, London; National Cancer Institute, Bethesda; University of Chicago; Honorary Consultant Physician, Royal Marsden Hospital and Senior Lecturer, Institute of Cancer Research, London, 1976-79. Governor, Bryanston School. Recreations: flying; music. Address: (h.) 18 Inverleith Avenue South, Edinburgh, EH3 5QA; T.-0131-552 3775.

Snaith, David William, MSc, PhD, CEng, MIM, CChem, FRSC, FBIM. Principal, Stow College, Glasgow, since 1983; b. 30.6.40, Birmingham; m., Susan Willoughby Tucker; 1 s.; 2 d. Educ. Kings Norton Grammar School, Birmingham; Aston University. Research Chemist, Birmingham Small Arms Co. Ltd.; Assistant Lecturer in Chemistry, Matthew Boulton Technical College, Birmingham, 1965; Lecturer in Chemistry, Ipswich Civic College, 1969; Deputy Head, Department of Science and Metallurgy, North Lindsey College of Technology, Scunthorpe, 1974; Head, Department of Science, North East Liverpool Technical College, 1980. Royal Society of Chemistry: Assistant Secretary, East Anglian Section Committee, 1972-74, Chairman, Southumbria Section, 1977-78. Recreations: hill-walking; photography; music; rifle shooting. Address: (b.) Stow College, 43 Shamrock Street, Glasgow, G4 9LD; T.-0141-332 1786.

Sneader, Walter, BSc, PhD, MRPharmS. Honorary Vice-President, Glasgow Jewish Representative Council, since 1989 (President, 1986-89); Chairman, West of Scotland Council of Christians and Jews, 1987-89; Senior Lecturer in Pharmaceutical Chemistry, Strathclyde University; b. 2.11.39, Glasgow; m., Myrna Joan Levine; 2 s.; 1 d. Educ. Glasgow High School; Glasgow University. After a period with National Research Council of Canada, joined Strathclyde University; Member, National Pharmaceutical Advisory Committee; former Executive Member, Glasgow Board of Jewish Education; former Hon. Secretary, Jewish Representative Council; Member, BBC Religious Advisory Committee, since 1989; elected Member, Jewish Board of Deputies, 1988. Publications: Drug Discovery: The Evolution of Modern Medicines, 1985; Drug Development: From Laboratory to Clinic, 1986; Drug Prototypes and Their Exploitation. Address: (b.) Department of Pharmaceutical Sciences, Strathclyde University, Glasgow, G1 1XW; T.-0141-552 4400.

Sneddon, Hutchison Burt, CBE, JP, DL. Lord Lieutenant of Lanarkshire; b. 17.4.29, Wishaw; m., Elizabeth Jardine; 1 s.; 2 d. Educ. Wishaw High School. Former Scottish Divisional Director, Nationwide Anglia Building Society;

Chairman, Cumbernauld Development Corporation, 1979-83; Vice-Chairman, Scottish National Housing and Town Planning Council, 1965-71; Chairman, Burns Heritage Trail, 1971-83; President, World Federation of Burns Clubs, 1989-90; Deputy President, COSLA, 1974-76; Chairman, Motherwell District Council, 1974-77; Provost, Burgh of Motherwell and Wishaw, 1971-75. Recreations: football (watching); philately. Adrerss: (h.) 36 Shand Street, Wishaw, ML2 8HN; T.-01698 373685.

Sneddon, Ian Naismith, OBE (1969), BSc, DSc, BA, MA, FRS, FRSE, FIMA, FRSA. Honorary Senior Research Fellow and Emeritus Professor of Mathematics, Glasgow University; Vice-Chairman, Board of Directors, Citizens' Theatre, Glasgow; b. 8.12.19, Glasgow; m., Mary Campbell Macgregor; 2 s.; 1 d. Educ. Hyndland School, Glasgow; Glasgow University; Trinity College, Cambridge. Junior Scientific Officer, Ministry of Supply, 1942-45; William Bryce Fellow, Glasgow University, 1945-46; Lecturer in Natural Philosophy, Glasgow University, 1946-50; Professor of Mathematics, University College of North Staffordshire, 1950-56; Simson Professor of Mathematics, Glasgow University, 1956-85. Hon DSc: Warsaw University, Heriot-Watt University, Hull University, Strathclyde University; Kelvin Medal, Glasgow University; Makdougall-Brisbane Prize, Royal Society of Edinburgh, 1959; Eringen Medal, Society of Engineering Science, 1979; Copernicus Medal, Polish Academy of Sciences, 1973; Gold Medal for Culture (Poland), 1983; Member, Order of the Long Leaf Pine (North Carolina), 1964; Commander, Order of Polonia Restituta, 1969; Commander, Order of Merit of Poland, 1979. Recreations: music; painting in oils; photography. Address: (h.) 19 Crown Terrace, Glasgow, G12 9ES; T.-0141-339 4114.

Sneller, David Bruce, BSc (Hons). Leader, East Ayrshire Council, since 1995; Leader, Cumnock and Doon Valley District Council, since 1988; b. 16.1.58, Sheffield; m., Jean. Educ. Firth Park School, Sheffield; Nottingham University. Geologist, British Coal (Opencast), 1981-92; Area Geologist, Scottish Coal, since 1995. Board Member, Enterprise Ayrshire, since 1991; Chair, Carrick, Cumnock and Doon Valley C.L.P. Recreations: golf; reading; swimming. Address: (h.) 3 Kings Drive, Cumnock, KA18 1AG; T.-01290 421568.

Sole, David Michael Barclay, OBE, BA (Hons). Rugby Player; b. 8.5.62, Aylesbury; m., Jane; 2 s.; 1 d. Educ. Trinity College, Glenalmond; Exeter University. Played rugby for Scotland, 1986-92 (44 caps); also British Lions and Barbarians; Captain of Scotland, 1989-92; tour to New Zealand; 1991 World Cup; tour to Australia, 1992. Address: (b.) 33 Ellersly Road, Edinburgh; T.-0131-337 7373.

Somerville, Alan John, BSc, MBA, MIL. Commercial Director, ScotRail, since 1994; b. 26.6.55; 1 s.; 1 d. Educ. Bishopbriggs High School; Glasgow University; Strathclyde Business School. Petrologist, 1977-82; Distribution Manager, Spring Grove Services, 1983-85; Depot Manager, then Trunking Manager, BOC Transhield, 1986-89; Commercial General Manager, BOC Baker, 1990-92; Business Controller, BOC Baker, 1993.

Somerville, Donald Robert, LLB, NP. Director of Legal Services, Inverness District Council, since 1984; b. 19.3.53, Edinburgh; m., Margaret; 3 d. Educ. Scotus Academy, Edinburgh; Edinburgh University. Law Apprentice/Legal Assistant, private practice, 1974-77; Principal Legal Assistant, West Lothian District Council, 1977-84. Recreations: hill-walking; jogging; following the Hearts. Address: (b.) Town House, Inverness; T.-01463 239111.

Sommerville, John Kenneth, CA. Partner, French Jarvie Macharg, CA, Glasgow, since 1970; Council Member, Institute of Chartered Accountants of Scotland, 1984-90; Council Member, Association of Accounting Technicians, since 1989 (President, 1995-96); b. 1.3.42, Glasgow; m., Iris Alexa Hutchison; 3 d. Educ. Kelvinside Academy. Member, Board of Governors, Kelvinside Academy, 1976-94 (Chairman of Board, 1985-94). Recreations: golf; running. Address: (b.) Pegasus House, 375 West George Street, Glasgow, G2 4LH; T.-0141-221 2984.

Somerville, Lynda Margaret, RGN, SCM. Director, Mental Health Foundation Scotland, since 1991; b. Paisley. Educ. Paisley Grammar School. Registered general nurse; midwife; medical sales; Marketing Director, Ross Hall Hospital; Director, Mackay Somerville Marketing; Marketing Manager, Britannia Life Ltd. Recreations: studying; music; dance. Address: (b.) 24 George Square, Glasgow, G2 1EG; T.-0141-221 2092.

Souter, Ian Patrick, MA, CA. Partner, Ernst & Young, since 1975; Insolvency Practitioner; b. 15.3.43, Aberdeen; m., May; 1 s.; 1 d. Educ. Aberdeen Grammar School; Aberdeen University. Qualified CA, 1967; joined Whinney Murray & Co., London, 1967; Partner, 1975; established Aberdeen Office, Whinney Murray, 1975; Member, Board of Governors, RGU, since 1987 (Chairman); Member, Council, ICAS, 1988-91; Chairman, Grampian Committee, ICAS, 1988-91. Recreations: sport; holidays in France. Address: (b.) Ernst & Young, 50 Huntly Street, Aberdeen, AB9 1XN; T.-01224 640033.

Southam, Professor John Chambers, MA, MD, FRCPath, FDS. Professor of Oral Medicine and Pathology, Edinburgh University, 1977-93; Faculty of Dental Surgery, Royal College of Surgeons of Edinburgh: Secretary, 1991-94, Vice-Dean, 1994-97; b. 3.2.34, Leeds; m., Susan; 1 s.; 1 d. Educ. Leeds Grammar School; Cambridge University; Leeds University. Lecturer, Oral Pathology, Sheffield University, 1963-70; Lecturer, Dental Surgery, Edinburgh University, 1970-71; Senior Lecturer, 1971-77. Member, General Dental Council, 1984-94. Publication: Oral Pathology (Co-author). Recreations: gardening; walking; travel; Scouting. Address: (h.) 13 Corstorphine House Avenue, Edinburgh, EH12 7AD; T.-0131-334 3013.

Southcott, Barry John, BSc (Econ), AIIMR, ASI. Director, British Investment Trust PLC, Edinburgh Fund Managers plc, BZW Convertible Investment Trust, CW Management Ltd. (Chief Executive, since 1993); b. 27.3.50, London; m., Lesley Anne Parkinson. Educ. Latymer Upper School; Bradford University. Recreations: tennis; football; music. Address: (b.) Donaldson House, 97 Haymarket Terrace, Edinburgh, EH12 5HD.

Soutter, Patrick Eliot, BL, NP. Retired Solicitor; Chairman, Department of Health and Social Security Appeal Tribunal, Hamilton, 1980-91; Honorary Sheriff, Hamilton, since 1984; b. 13.4.19, Hamilton; m., Muriel Gettings Johnston; 1 d. Educ. Hamilton Academy; Glasgow University. RAF (Pilot), 1939-45; joined family legal business, 1951; retired as Senior Partner, 1984; Secretary and Treasurer, Hamilton Golf Club, since 1951 (now Joint Secretary and Treasurer). Recreations: golf (played for Glasgow University and Lanarkshire County); fishing; curling. Address: (h.) The Linn, Woodhead Gardens, Bothwell, Lanarkshire; T.-01698 853123.

Spalding, Julian, BA, FMA. Director, Glasgow Museums and Art Galleries, since 1989; b. 15.6.47, London; 1 s. Educ. Chislehurst and Sidcup Grammar School for Boys; Nottingham University. Art Assistant: Leicester Museum & Art Gallery, 1970-71, Durham Light Infantry Museum & Arts Centre, 1971-72; Keeper, Mappin Art Gallery, 1972-76, Deputy Director, 1976-82; Director of Arts, Sheffield City Council, 1982-85; Director, Manchester City Art Galleries, 1985-89; Director, National Museum of Labour History, 1987-89. Member, Arts Council of GB, 1978-82; Founder, Art Galleries Association, 1976; Director, Guild of St. George, since 1983; Director, Mayfest, since 1989;

Member, Crafts Council, since 1986; Member, British Council, since 1987; Advisory Member, new British Library; Director, Scottish Football Museum, since 1994; Director, Niki de St. Phalle Foundation, since 1994. Publications: L.S. Lowry, 1979; Three Little Books on Painting, 1984; various exhibition catalogues. Recreations: cycling; gardening; painting. Address: (b.) Art Gallery and Museum, Kelvingrove, Glasgow, G3 8AG; T.-0141-305 2600.

Spawforth, David Meredith, MA (Oxon), FRSA. Headmaster, Merchiston Castle School, since 1981; b. 2.1.38, Wakefield; m., Yvonne Mary Gude; 1 s.; 1 d. Educ. Silcoates School; Hertford College, Oxford. Assistant Master, Winchester College, 1961-64; Housemaster, Wellington College, 1964-80; BP Education Fellow, Keble College, Oxford, 1977. Recreations: travel - especially France and Italy; theatre; walking. Address: (b.) Merchiston Castle School, Colinton, Edinburgh.

Speirs, Norman Thomas, BSc, MB, ChB, DMRD, FACI. Consultant Radiologist, Lothian Health Board, since 1958; b. 31.8.24, London; m., Dorothy Glen; 1 d. Educ. George Watson's Boys' College; Edinburgh University. House Surgeon, Royal Infirmary, Edinburgh; Captain, RAMC; specialist training in Radiology; various Registrar appointments, Edinburgh; retired Consultant Radiologist, Princess Margaret Rose Orthopaedic Hospital, Edinburgh, and Roodlands Hospital, Haddington; private practice, Murrayfield Hospital, Edinburgh. Past Chairman, Scottish Association of Amateur Cinematographers; elected to National Council, Institute of Amateur Cinematographers (IAC) and awarded its Fellowship, 1981; National Chairman, IAC, 1990-92. Address: (h.) 24 Liberton Place, Edinburgh EH16 6NA; T.-0131-672 2662.

Speirs, Robert, ACIS, FRSA. Finance Director, Royal Bank of Scotland plc, since 1993; b. 23.10.36, Liverpool; m., Patricia; 2 s. Educ. Alleynes Grammar School. Inland Revenue, 1953-64; Coopers & Lybrand, 1964-68; Texaco Ltd., 1968-77; Treasurer, British National Oil Corporation, 1977-83; Treasurer/Finance Director, Britoil plc, 1983-88; Finance Director, Olympia and York Canary Wharf Ltd., 1988-93. Recreations: DIY; walking; music. Address: (b.) 42 St. Andrew's Square, Edinburgh; T.-0131-523 2033.

Speirs, William MacLeod, BA (Hons), FRSA. Deputy General Secretary, Scottish TUC; Chairperson, 7:84 Theatre Company (Scotland), since 1988; b. 8.3.52, Dumbarton; 1 s.; 1 d. Educ. John Neilson High School, Paisley; Strathclyde University. Assistant Secretary, Scottish TUC, 1979-88. Chairperson, Labour Party in Scotland, 1987-88; Chairperson, Scottish Friends of Palestine, since 1982; Board Member, Glasgow Mayfest, since 1982. Recreations: reading; losing money on horses; watching St. Mirren F.C. Address: (b.) STUC, 16 Woodlands Terrace, Glasgow, G3 6DF; T.-0141-332 4946.

Spence, Alan, MA. Writer (poet, playwright, novelist, short-story writer); b. 5.12.47, Glasgow; m., Janani (Margaret). Educ. Allan Glen's School, Glasgow; Glasgow University. Writer in Residence, Glasgow University, 1975-77, Deans Community School, 1978, Traverse Theatre, Edinburgh, 1983, City of Edinburgh, 1986-87, Edinburgh University, 1989-92; winner, People's Prize, 1991; Macallan/Scotland on Sunday Short Story competition, 1993. Publications: poetry: ah!; Glasgow Zen; short stories: Its Colours They Are Fine, Stone Garden; novel: The Magic Flute; plays: Sailmaker; Space Invaders; Changed Days. Recreations: meditation; running; playing flute. Address: 21 Waverley Park, Edinburgh, EH8 8ER; T.-0131-661 8403.

Spence, Professor Alastair Andrew, CBE, MD, FRCA, FRCP (Glas & Edin), FRCS (Ed & Eng), Hon FDS, RCS Eng. Professor of Anaesthetics, Edinburgh University, since 1984; Honorary Consultant Anaesthetist, Royal Infirmary,

Edinburgh; President, College of Anaesthetists; b. 18.9.36, Glasgow; m., Maureen Isobel Aitchison; 2 s. Educ. Ayr Academy; Glasgow University. Professor and Head, University Department of Anaesthesia, Western Infirmary, Glasgow, 1969-84; Editor, British Journal of Anaesthesia, 1973-83; Hunterian Professor, Royal College of Surgeons of England, 1974; Joseph Clover Lecturer, 1990. Recreations: golf; gardening. Address: (h.) Harewood, Kilmacolm, PA13 4HX; T.-Kilmacolm 872962.

Spence, Ian W., BSc, BA. Headteacher, Anderson High School, Lerwick, since 1995; b. 27.8.46, Unst; m., Audrey; 2 d. Educ. Anderson Educational Institute; Aberdeen University. Teacher of Mathematics, Bo'ness Academy, 1968-70; Principal Teacher of Mathematics, Golspie High School, 1970-75; Anderson High School: Principal Teacher, 1975-79, Assistant Head, 1979-86, Depute Head, 1986-95. Recreations: golf; gardening. Address: (h.) 40 Murrayston, Lerwick, Shetland; T.-01595 694176.

Spence, James William, KFO (Norway), RON (Netherlands), BSc, MNI, MICS, MRIN, DL. Master Mariner, since 1971; Shipbroker, since 1975; Company Director, since 1977; b. 19.1.45, St. Ola, Orkney; m., Margaret Paplay Stevenson; 3 s. Educ. Leith Nautical College, Edinburgh; Robert Gordon's Institute of Technology, Aberdeen; University of Wales, Cardiff. Merchant Navy, 1961-74 (Member, Nautical Institute, 1972, Member, Royal Institute of Navigation, 1971); Micoperi SpA, 1974-75 (Temporary Assistant Site Co-ordinator on Scapa Flow Project); John Jolly (Shipbrokers, Stevedores, Shipping and Forwarding Agents) since 1975 (Manager, 1975, Junior Partner, 1976-77, Proprietor and Managing Director, since 1977). Vice-Consul for Norway, 1976, Consul, 1978; Vice-Consul for the Netherlands, 1978-94; Member, Kirkwall Community Council, 1978-82; Member, Orkney Pilotage Committee, 1979-88; Chairman, Kirkwall Port Employers' Association, 1979-87 (Member, since 1975); Station Honorary Secretary, RNLI, Kirkwall Lifeboat, 1987 (Deputy Launching Authority, 1976-87); Chairman, Pier Arts Centre Trust, 1989-91 (Trustee, 1980-91); Chairman, Association of Honorary Norwegian Consuls in the UK and Ireland, 1993-95. Recreations: oenology; equestrian matters; Orcadian history. Address: (h.) Alton House, Kirkwall, Orkney KW15 1NA; T.-01856 872268.

Spence, Professor John, ARCST, BSc, MEng, PhD, DSc, FRSE, CEng, FIMechE. Deputy Principal, Department of Mechanical Engineering, Strathclyde University (Trades House of Glasgow Professor of Mechanics of Materials, since 1982); b. 5.11.37, Chapelhall; m., Margaret Gray Hudson; 2 s. Educ. Airdrie Academy; Royal College of Science and Technology; Sheffield University. Engineering apprenticeship, Stewarts & Lloyds (now British Steel Corporation); Senior Engineer, then Head of Stress Analysis, Babcock & Wilcox Research Division; Strathclyde University: Lecturer, 1966, Senior Lecturer, Reader, Professor since 1979. Serves on several national committees: Senior Vice-President, Institution of Mechanical Engineers; EPSRC College; British Standards Institution; Engineering Professors Council (Chairman). Address: (b.) Department of Mechanical Engineering, Strathclyde University, 75 Montrose Street, Glasgow, G1 1XJ; T.-0141-552 4400, Ext. 2324.

Spence, Roger Norman Abbot, Co-producer, Boxcar Film Productions, since 1994; Managing Director, Royal Lyceum Theatre Company, 1983-94; b. 28.9.47, Lincoln; m., Judith Marie Mohekey. Educ. Lincoln Grammar School; Lincoln College of Art. Early career in production and as Lighting Designer in theatre, opera and ballet; General Manager, The Scottish Ballet, 1975-80; Administrative Director, Tynewear Theatre Company, 1980-83. President, Theatrical Management Association; Board Director: Edinburgh Capital Group, Scottish International Children's Festival,

Scottish Arts Lobby (SALVO), Theatres Investment Fund, Arts Research and Development Scotland; Trustee, Theatres Investment Trust. Address: (h.) 21 Glencairn Crescent, Edinburgh EH12 5BT; T.-0131-337 3373.

Spence, William Arthur, QPM, LLB, BA. Chief Constable, Tayside Police, since 1995; b. 20.11.43, Ellon; m., Hazel; 2 d. Educ. Ellon Academy; Strathclyde University; Open University. Served in Renfrew and Bute Constabulary and Strathclyde Police from 1962 (Assistant Chief Constable, 1986); Deputy Chief Constable, Tayside Police, 1988-95. Member, Home Office Group on Racial Attacks and Harassment; Member, Funding Panel, Scottish Victim Support; responsible for Scottish Police liaison arrangements, 1992 European Cup Final, Sweden; represents Scottish Police in organisational health, welfare and life saving matters. Recreations: gardening; genealogy; reading. Address: (b.) Tayside Police, PO Box 59, West Bell Street, Dundee, DD1 9JU; T.-01382 223200.

Spencely, John Despenser, MA, BArch, DipTP, RIBA, PPRIAS, MRTPI, FCIArb. Chairman, Reiach and Hall; Chairman, Buildings Investigation Centre; b. 5.10.39, Westerham, England; m., Marilyn Anne Read; 1 d. (by pr. m.). Educ. Bryanston School; Cambridge University; Edinburgh University. Architect, Town Planner; Member, Council: RIBA, RIAS; former Member, Scottish Building Contract Committee; President: Edinburgh Architectural Association, 1984-86, Royal Incorporation of Architects in Scotland, 1989-91; Lay Member, Scottish Solicitors Discipline Tribunal; Member, Advisory Committee on Arbitration to Scottish Law Commission; Honorary Fellow, Faculty of Social Sciences, Edinburgh University, since 1989; Board Member, Scottish Homes; Freeman of the City of London; Liveryman, Worshipful Company of Arbitrators. Recreations: sailing; reading; collecting some unfashionable 20th century authors; making jam. Address: (b.) 6 Darnaway Street, Edinburgh EH3 6BG; T.-0131-225 8444.

Spencer, Alec P., BA (Hons), MA, FBIM. Governor, Peterhead Prison, since 1992; b. 12.3.46, London; m., Joan; 2 s.; 1 d. Educ. Dame Alice Owen School; Keele University. Joined Scottish Prison Service, 1972, as Assistant Governor: Polmont Borstal, Perth Prison, Glenochil; Deputy Governor, Aberdeen Prison, 1978; Prison Department HQ, 1981; Warden, Glenochil D.C., 1983; Deputy Governor, Glenochil Complex, 1987; Governor, Dungavel Prison, 1989. Chairman, Scottish Forum on Prisons and Families; Butler Trust Award, 1987; Editor, ASPG Journal, 1982-90; Chairman, Governors' Committee, NUCPS, 1991-92. Recreations: music; walking; golf. Address: (b.) H.M. Prison, Peterhead, AB42 6YY; T.-01779 79101.

Spiers, Rev. John McLaren, LTh. Minister, Orchardhill Church, Giffnock, since 1977; b. 12.12.43, Edinburgh; m., Janet Diane Watson; 2 d. Educ. George Watson's College, Edinburgh; Glasgow University. Trainee, Scottish Union and National Insurance Company, 1961-65; University, 1966-71; Probationer Assistant, Drumchapel Old Parish Church, Glasgow, 1971-72; Minister, South Church, Barrhead, 1972-77. Recreations: music; art; family life; various sports. Address: 23 Huntly Avenue, Giffnock, Glasgow, G46 6LW.

Spilg, Walter Gerson Spence, MB, ChB (Hons), FRCPath, FRCPG. Consultant Pathologist, Victoria Infirmary, Glasgow, since 1972, in Administrative Charge, since 1986; Honorary Clinical Senior Lecturer, Glasgow University, since 1973; b. 27.10.37, Glasgow; m., Vivien Anne Burns; 1 s.; 2 d. Educ. Hutchesons' Boys' Grammar School, Glasgow; Glasgow University. Registrar in Pathology, Glasgow Royal Infirmary, 1965-68; Senior Registrar in Pathology, Victoria Infirmary, Glasgow, 1968-69; Lecturer in Pathology, Glasgow University (Western Infirmary),

1969-72. Member, Greater Glasgow Health Board Area Medical Sub-Committee in Laboratory Medicine; Examiner, Royal College of Physicians and Surgeons of Glasgow; Member, Forensic Pathology Liaison Committee. Recreations: bridge; golf. Address: (h.) 98 Ayr Road, Newton Mearns, Glasgow, G77 6EJ; T.-0141-639 3130.

Spratt, Col. Douglas Norman, CBE, TD, DL. Director, Cameo of Edinburgh, since 1984; b. 18.9.20, Ramsgate; m., Margaret; 1 d. Educ. Sir Roger Manwood's Grammar School, Sandwich, Kent. President, Edinburgh Branch, Institute of Marketing; Chairman, Friends of the Reserve Forces Association, Scotland; Regional Chairman, Action Research in Scotland; Member, High Constables of Edinburgh; Deputy Lieutenant, City of Edinburgh; Member of the Military Attaches London. Recreations: fishing; sailing. Address: (h.) 6 Fernielaw Avenue, Edinburgh, EH13 OEE; T.-0131-441 1962.

Sprent, Professor Janet I., BSc, ARCS, PhD, DSc, FRSE. Professor of Plant Biology, Dundee University, since 1989; b. 10.1.34, Slough; m., Emeritus Professor Peter Sprent. Educ. Slough High School; Imperial College, London; Tasmania University. Has spent 28 years at Dundee University; research focussed on nitrogen fixing legumes, both tree and crop species; currently involved in international collaboration, mainly in Africa and Brazil; Dean of Science and Engineering, 1987-89. Council Member, NERC, 1991-95; Member, Scottish Higher Education Funding Council, since 1992; Member, Joint Nature Conservation Committee, since 1994. Publications:three books and over 100 chapters/papers. Recreations: flying; hill walking. Address: Department of Biological Sciences, Dundee University, Dundee DD1 4HN; T.-01382 344279.

Sprent, Professor Peter, BSc, PhD, FRSE. Statistician and Author; Professor of Statistics, Dundee University, 1972-85, Professor Emeritus, since 1985; b. 28.1.23, Hobart, Australia; m., Janet Irene Findlater. Educ. Hutchins School, Hobart, Tasmania; Tasmania University; London University. Lecturer in Mathematics, Tasmania University, 1948-57; Statistician, East Malling Research Station, 1958-67; Senior Lecturer in Statistics, Dundee University, 1967-72. Sometime Member, Editorial Boards, Journal of Royal Statistical Society, Journal of American Statistical Association, Biometrics. Publications: ten books and many papers on statistics and related topics. Recreations: hill-walking; gardening. Address: (h.) 32 Birkhill Avenue, Wormit, Newport-on-Tay, DD6 8PW; T.-01382 541706.

Sprigge, Professor Timothy Lauro Squire, FRSE. Emeritus Professor of, and Endowment Fellow at, Edinburgh University, since 1989 (Professor of Logic and Metaphysics, 1979-89); b. 14.1.32, London; m., Giglia Gordon; 1 s.; 2 d. Educ. Gonville and Caius College, Cambridge. Lecturer in Philosophy, University College, London, 1961-63; Lecturer, then Reader in Philosophy, Sussex University, 1963-79. Publications: The Correspondence of Jeremy Bentham, Volumes 1 and 2; Facts, Words and Beliefs; Santayana: An Examination of his Philosophy; The Vindication of Absolute Idealism; Theories of Existence; The Rational Foundations of Ethics; James and Bradley: American Truth and British Reality. Recreation:backgammon. Address: (b.) Philosophy Department, David Hume Tower, Edinburgh University, George Square, Edinburgh; T.-0131-650 1000.

Sprot of Haystoun, Lt.-Col. Aidan Mark, MC, JP. Landowner (Haystoun Estate) and Farmer, since 1965; b. 17.6.19, Lilliesleaf. Educ. Belhaven Hill; Stowe. Commissioned, Royal Scots Greys, 1940; served Palestine, 1941-42, Western Desert, 1942-43, Italy, 1943-44, NW Europe, 1944-45; continued serving with Regiment in Germany until 1952, Libya, Egypt and Jordan, 1952-55, UK, 1955-58, Germany, 1958-62; Adjutant, 1944-45;

Commanding Officer, 1959-62; retired, 1962. County Councillor, Peeblesshire, 1963-75; DL (Peeblesshire), 1966-80; Lord Lieutenant, Tweeddale, 1980-94; Member, Queen's Bodyguard for Scotland (Royal Company of Archers), since 1950; County Director, Peeblesshire Branch, Red Cross, 1966-74, Patron, since 1983; County Commissioner, Peeblesshire Scout Association, 1968-73, Chairman, 1975-80, President, 1980-94; President, Borders Area Scout Association, since 1994; Scout Medal of Merit, 1994; Honorary Secretary, Royal Caledonian Hunt, 1964-74; President, Lowlands of Scotland TA&VRA, 1986-89; President, Lothian Federation of Boys' Clubs, since 1989; Honorary Freeman, Tweeddale District, 1994. Recreations: country sports; motor cycle touring. Address: (h.) Crookston, by Peebles, EH45 9JQ; T.-Kirkton Manor 740209.

Sprott, Gavin Chappell, MA. Head, Working Life Section, National Museums of Scotland and Curator, Scottish Agricultural Museum, Ingliston; b. 23.7.43, Dundee; m., Maureen Turnbull; 2 s.; 1 d. Educ. Edinburgh University. Research Assistant, Scottish Country Life Section, National Museum of Antiquities of Scotland, 1972-79. Recreations: cycling; walking. Address: (b.) National Museums of Scotland, Queen Street, Edinburgh, EH2; T.-0131-225 7534.

Spy, Sheriff James, LLB (Hons). Sheriff of North Strathclyde at Paisley, since 1988; b. 1.12.52. Admitted Solicitor, 1976; Advocate, 1979. Address: (b.) Sheriff Court House, 106 Renfrew Road, Paisley, PA3 4DD.

Squire, Rachel Anne, BA, CQSW. MP (Labour), Dunfermline West, since 1992; b. 13.7.54, Carshalton, Surrey; m., Allan Mason. Educ. Godolphin and Latymer Girls' School; Durham University. Social Worker, Birmingham Social Services, 1975-81; National Union of Public Employees, 1981-92. Address: (b.) House of Commons, London, SW1A 0AA.

Stachura, Peter Desmond, MA, PhD, DLitt, FRHistS. Reader in Modern History, Stirling University, since 1983; b. 2.8.44, Galashiels; m., Kay Higgins; 1 s.; 1 d. Educ. St. Mirin's RC Academy, Paisley; Glasgow University; East Anglia University. Research Fellow, Institut fur Europaische Geschichte, Mainz, Germany, 1970-71; Lecturer in History, Stirling University, 1971-83. Publications: Nazi Youth in the Weimar Republic; The Weimar Era and Hitler: a critical bibliography; The Shaping of the Nazi State (Editor); The German Youth Movement, 1900-1945; Gregor Strasser and the Rise of Nazism; The Nazi Machtergreifung (Editor); Unemployment and the Great Depression in Weimar Germany (Editor); The Weimar Republic and the Younger Proletariat: an economic and social analysis; Political Leaders in Weimar Germany: a biographical study; Themes of Modern Polish History (Editor). Recreations: supporting Celtic FC; discovering Poland; gardening. Address: (h.) Ashcroft House, Chalton Road, Bridge of Allan, FK9 4EF; T.-01786 832793.

Stair, 13th Earl of (John Aymer Dalrymple), KCVO (1978), MBE (1941). Captain General, Queen's Bodyguard for Scotland (Royal Company of Archers), 1973-88; b. 9.10.06; m., Davina Bowes-Lyon; 3 s. Educ. Eton; Sandhurst. Colonel (retired), Scots Guards. Address: (h.) Lochinch Castle, Stranraer, Wigtownshire.

Stanforth, Professor Anthony William, BA, MA, Drphil. Professor of Languages, Heriot-Watt University, since 1981 (Head, Department of Languages, 1981-89; Dean, Faculty of Economic and Social Studies, 1989-92); b. 27.7.38, Ipswich; m., Susan Margaret Vale; 2 s. Educ. Ipswich School; King's College, Newcastle (Durham University); Marburg University. Earl Grey Memorial Fellow, Newcastle-upon-Tyne University, 1962-64; Assistant Lecturer, Manchester University, 1964-65; Lecturer, Senior

Lecturer, Newcastle-upon-Tyne University, 1965-81; Visiting Assistant Professor, Wisconsin University, 1970-71. Fellow, Royal Society of Arts; Honorary Fellow, Institute of Linguists. Recreation: opera. Address: (b.) Department of Languages, Heriot-Watt University, Riccarton, Edinburgh, EH14 4AS; T.-0131-449 5111.

Stanners, Ian Cram, FRICS. Chartered Quantity Surveyor; b. 30.11.38, Glasgow; m., Louise Robertson; 2 d. Educ. Hutchesons' Boys' Grammar School. Chairman, Quantity Surveyors Divisional Committee, Scottish Branch, RICS, 1980-81; Chairman, RICS in Scotland, 1986-87; Chairman, Scottish Building Contract Committee. Honorary Vice-President, Clyde Amateur Rowing Club. Recreations: rowing; curling. Address: (b.) 21 Woodlands Terrace, Glasgow, G3 6DF; T.-0141-332 6032.

Stansfeld, John Raoul Wilmot, JP, DL, MA (Oxon), MIFM. Director, Joseph Johnston & Sons Ltd., since 1962; b. 15.1.35, London; m., Rosalinde Rachel Buxton; 3 s. Educ. Eton; Christ Church, Oxford. Lt., Gordon Highlanders, 1954-58; Chairman, North Esk District Salmon Fishery Board, 1967-80; Esk Fishery Board Committee, 1980-85; Vice Chairman, Association of Scottish District Salmon Fishery Boards, 1970-85; Director and Chairman, Montrose Chamber of Commerce, since 1984; Editor, Salmon Net Magazine, 1978-85; Chairman, Scottish Fish Farmers Association, 1970-73; Secretary, Diocese of Brechin, 1968-76. Member, Royal Company of Archers (Queen's Bodyguard for Scotland). Recreations: reading; jigsaw puzzles; trees. Address: (h.) Dunninald, Montrose, Angus, DD10 9TD; T.-01674 672666.

Stapleton, Anna Louise. Drama and Dance Director, Scottish Arts Council, since 1987; b. 20.10.49, Hitchin, Herts. Educ. Michael Hall School, Forest Row; New College of Speech and Drama, London. Company/Stage Manager for a range of theatres, 1972-77; Administrator, 1978-82, for Belt and Braces Theatre Company, Liverpool Everyman, Half Moon Theatre and others; Arts Development Officer (Drama), Greater London Arts Association, 1983-87. Recreations: travel; reading; walking; wine; friends. Address: (b.) 12 Manor Place, Edinburgh, EH3 7DD; T.-0131-226 6051.

Stark, Edi, MA (Hons), ALA. Presenter, The Slice, BBC Radio Scotland; Moment of Truth, BBC Scotland; Smalltalk, Grampian TV; Radio 4; b. Edinburgh; m., Gavin Stark; 1 s.; 1 d. Educ. Aberdeen University; RGIT. Community Librarian, Glasgow and Livingston; Northsound Radio: Community Co-ordinator, 1981, Senior Producer, 1982, Head of Speech Programming, 1983-89; freelance journalist, since 1990. Recreations: nothing too physical – conversation, food and drink, travel, reading, contemporary art – all with the children not too far away. Address: (b.) c/o BBC Scotland, Beechgrove Terrace, Aberdeen, AB9 2ZT; T.- 01224 625233.

Starszakowna, Professor Norma, DA. Textile Designer/Artist; Course Director, Textiles and Fashion, Duncan of Jordanstone College of Art, since 1984; b. 9.5.45, Crosshill; m., Andrew Taylor; 2 s. Educ. Kirkcaldy High School; Duncan of Jordanstone College of Art. Design and production of printed and dyed textiles for fashion and interior; commissioned work includes Crest Hotel, Antwerp, General Accident HQ, Perth, Issey Miyake, Winchester, and Scottish Arts Council; exhibited widely, UK and abroad. SAC Award, 1977; Saltire Art in Architecture Award, 1983; Member: Crafts Council Index, Board of Texprint, AHDFT, CNAA and various other national bodies. Recreation: travel. Address: (h.) 9 Fort Street, Magdalen Green, Dundee, DD2 1BS; T.-01382 644654.

Steedman, Robert Russell, RSA, RIBA, FRSA, FRIAS, ALI, DA, MLA. Partner, Morris and Steedman, Architects and Landscape Architects; b. 3.1.29, Batu Gajah, Malaysia; m., 1, Susan Scott (m. diss.); 1 s.; 2 d.; 2, Martha Hamilton. Educ. Loretto School; School of Architecture, Edinburgh College of Art; Pennsylvania University. Governor, Edinburgh College of Art, since 1974; Commissioner, Countryside Commission for Scotland, 1980-88; ARSA, 1973, Academician, 1979; Council Member, RSA, 1981 (Deputy President, 1982-83, Secretary, 1983-91); Commissioner, Royal Fine Art Commission for Scotland, since 1983; former Member, Council, RIAS; nine Civic Trust Awards, 1963-78; British Steel Award, 1971; RIBA Award for Scotland, 1974; European Heritage Medal, 1975; Association for the Protection of Rural Scotland, 1977; Borders Region Award, 1984. Address: (h.) 11B Belford Mews, Edinburgh; T.-0131-225 1697.

Steel, Professor Christopher Michael, BSc, MB, ChB, PhD, DSc, FRCPEdin, FRCPath, FRCSEdin, FRSE. Professor in Medical Science, St. Andrews University, since 1994; b. 25.1.40, Buckhaven; m., Dr. Judith Maygard Spratt; 2 s.; 1 d. Educ. Prince of Wales School, Nairobi; George Watson's College, Edinburgh; Edinburgh University. House Physician/House Surgeon/Resident/Senior House Officer, Edinburgh Teaching Hospitals; Graduate Research Fellow in Medicine, 1968; joined MRC staff, 1971; MRC Travelling Research Fellow, University of Nairobi, 1972-73; Assistant Director, MRC Human Genetics Unit, Edinburgh, 1979. Member, International Advisory Board, Lancet; Editor, Disease Markers; Member, Editorial Board, Clinical Science; published over 200 scientific papers and book chapters; Member, Government Gene Therapy Advisory Committee. Recreations: golf; skiing; music; theatre. Address: (b.) Bute Medical Building, St. Andrews, KY16 9TS; T.-01334 476161.

Steel, Very Rev. David, MA, BD, DD, LLD. Minister Emeritus, St. Michael's, Linlithgow, since 1977; b. 5.10.10, Hamilton; m., Sheila E.N. Martin (deceased); 3 s. (eldest son: Sir David Steel, PC, MP (qv)); 2 d. Educ. St. John's Grammar School, Hamilton; Peterhead Academy; Robert Gordon's College, Aberdeen; Aberdeen University. Minister: Denbeath, Fife, 1936-41, Bridgend, Dumbarton, 1941-46; Associate Secretary, Foreign Mission Committee, Edinburgh, 1946-49; Minister, St. Andrew's, Nairobi and East Africa, 1949-57; Locum, St. Cuthbert's, Edinburgh, 1957-58; Minister, St. Michael's, Linlithgow, 1959-76; Moderator, General Assembly of the Church of Scotland, 1974-75; Visiting Preacher and Lecturer: in America, 1953-87, St. Columba's, Pont Street, 1977, Lausanne, 1978, Tanzania, 1980; Chairman, Callendar Park College of Education, 1972-78; Vice-President: Boys' Brigade, National Bible Society of Scotland, West Lothian Historical and Amenity Society. Publications: History of St. Michael's; The Belief; Preaching through the Year. Recreations: trout fishing; travel. Address: (h.) 39 Newbattle Terrace, Edinburgh, EH10 4SF; T.-0131-447 2180.

Steel, Rt. Hon. Sir David (Martin Scott), PC (1977). MP, Tweeddale, Ettrick and Lauderdale, since 1983 (Roxburgh, Selkirk and Peebles, 1965-83); Leader, Liberal Party, 1976-88; b. 31.3.38, Kirkcaldy; m., Judith MacGregor; 3 s.; 1 d. Educ. Prince of Wales School, Nairobi; George Watson's College, Edinburgh; Edinburgh University (MA, LLB). Assistant Secretary, Scottish Liberal Party, 1962-64; Interviewer, BBC TV Scotland, 1964-65; Presenter, weekly religious programme, STV, 1966-67, for Granada, 1969, for BBC, 1971-76; Liberal Chief Whip, 1970-75; Sponsor, Private Member's Bill to reform law on abortion, 1966-67; President, Anti-Apartheid Movement of Great Britain, 1966-69; Chairman, Shelter, Scotland, 1969-73; Member, British Council of Churches, 1971-75; Vice-President, Liberal International, since 1978; Rector, Edinburgh University, 1982-85; Chubb Fellow, Yale, 1987; Hon. DUniv (Stirling), 1991; DLitt, University of Buckingham,

1994; awarded Freedom of Tweeddale, 1988, and Ettrick and Lauderdale, 1990; The Commander's Cross of the Order of Merit (Germany), 1992; DL, 1989; contested Central Italy seat, European elections, 1989; President, Liberal International, since 1994. Publications: Boost for the Borders, 1964; Out of Control, 1968; No Entry, 1969; The Liberal Way Forward, 1975; Militant for the Reasonable Man, 1977; High Ground of Politics, 1979; A House Divided, 1980; Border Country (with Judy Steel), 1985; The Time Has Come (with David Owen), 1987; Mary Stuart's Scotland (with Judy Steel), 1987; Against Goliath, 1989. Recreations: angling; vintage motoring. Address: (b.) House of Commons, London, SW1A 0AA; T.-0171-219 3373.

Steel, David Robert, MA, DPhil. Director of Corporate Affairs, NHS in Scotland, since 1990; b. 29.5.48, Oxford; m., Susan Elizabeth Easton; 1 s.; 1 d. Educ. Birkenhead School; Jesus and Nuffield Colleges, Oxford. Lecturer in Public Administration, Exeter University, 1972-84; Assistant Director, National Association of Health Authorities, 1984-86; Secretary, Health Board Chairmen's and General Managers' Groups and SCOTMEG, 1986-90. Address: (b.) St. Andrew's House, Edinburgh, EH1 3DE; T.-0131-244 2223.

Steele, Alexander Allison, OBE (1986). Honorary Sheriff, Perth, since 1985; b. 5.10.25, Oakley, Fife; m., Patricia Joyce Hipkins; 1 s.; 2 d. Educ. Boroughmuir Secondary School. Entered Scottish Home Department, 1942; Royal Navy, 1943-46; Scottish Court Service (Sheriff Clerk's Branch), 1950; Sheriff Clerk: Dingwall, 1969-71, Perth, 1971-81, Dundee, 1981-85; Member, Lord Stewart's Committee on Alternatives to Prosecution, 1977-83; Honorary Life Member, Society of Sheriff Court Auditors. Recreations: gardening; swimming; wine-making. Address: (h.) Lyndhurst, Hillend Road, Perth; T.-01738 626611.

Steele, George Thomas, MA (Hons). Rector, Johnstone High School, since 1975; b. 19.8.39, Newquay; m., Janet Mary Craig; 4 d. Educ. Hutchesons' (Boys) Grammar School; Glasgow University; Jordanhill College of Education. Teacher, Queen's Park Secondary School, 1962-65; Teacher, Hutchesons' (Boys') Grammar School, 1965-67; Principal Teacher of Classics, Whitburn Academy, 1967-71; Assistant Head Teacher, then Depute Head Teacher, Hillpark Secondary School, 1971-75. Member, Advisory Council on Misuse of Drugs to Home Office, 1977-83; Member, GGHB Liaison Committee on Alcohol and Drug Misuse, 1977-85. Recreations: DIY; reading; walking; holidays abroad; playing drums. Address: (b.) Johnstone High School, Beith Road, Johnstone; T.-Johnstone 322173.

Steele, Thomas Graham. Director: Radio Forth, Radio Tay, Cliar Sheanachain; b. 11.5.45, Lanark; m., Fiona MacAuslane; 1 s.; 1 d. Educ. Larkhall Academy, Larkhall; Skerry's College, Glasgow. Lobby Correspondent, Scottish Daily Mail; TV and Radio Presenter, BBC Glasgow; Producer, BBC Local Radio; Broadcaster, then Deputy Head of News and Current Affairs, Radio Forth; Director of Programmes (Group); Creator, Festival City Radio. Recreations: sailing; walking; reading; conversation. Address: (b.) Forth House, Forth Street, Edinburgh; T.-0131-556 9255.

Steer, Christopher Richard, BSc (Hons), MB, ChB, DCH, FRCPE. Consultant Paediatrician; Clinical Tutor, Department of Child Life and Health, Edinburgh University; Hon. Senior Lecturer, Department of Child Life and Health, Aberdeen University; Hon. Senior Lecturer, Department of Biochemistry, St. Andrews University; Clinical Director of Obstetrics, Gynaecology and Paediatrics; b. 30.5.47, Clearbrook, near Plymouth; m., Patricia Mary Lennox. Educ. St. Olaves and St. Saviours Grammar School, London; Edinburgh University.

Publications: Textbook of Paediatrics (Contributor); Treatment of Neurological Disorders (Contributor). Recreation: our garden. Address: (b.) Paediatric Unit, Kirkcaldy Acute Hospitals NHS Trust, Victoria Hospital, Kirkcaldy, Fife; T.-01592 643355.

Stein, Sheriff Colin Norman Ralph, BA (Hons), LLB. Floating Sheriff of Tayside, Central and Fife at Arbroath, since 1991; b. 14.6.48. Advocate, 1975. Address: (b.) Sheriff Court House, 88 High Street, Arbroath, DD11 1HL.

Stein, Rev. Jock, MA, BD. Joint Warden, Carberry Tower, since 1986 (Minister, Steeple Church, Dundee, 1976-86); b. 8.11.41, Edinburgh; m., Margaret E. Munro; 3 d. Educ. Sedbergh School; Cambridge University; Edinburgh University. Work Study Officer, United Steel Companies, Sheffield; Assistant Warden, St. Ninian's Lay Training Centre, Crieff; publishing and lay training, Presbyterian Church of East Africa. Publications: Ministers for the '80s (Editor); Our One Baptism; In Christ All Things Hold Together (Co-author); Ministry and Mission in the City; Mission and the Crisis of Western Culture (Editor); Scottish Self-Government: Some Christian Viewpoints (Editor). Recreations: music; skiing. Address: Carberry Tower, Musselburgh, EH21 8PY.

Steiner, Eleanor Margaret, MB, ChB, DPH, MFCM, MRCGP, MICGP. General Practitioner at Appin and Easdale, formerly Principal in general practice in Perthshire; Executive Member, Scottish Child Law Centre; Medical Member, Disability Appeals Tribunal; Aeromedical Doctor, St. John International Air Ambulance; Member, SACOT (Scottish Advisory Committee on Telecommunications); Member, DIEL (OFTEL Committee for Advice on Disabled and Elderly); b. 21.5.37, Glasgow; m., Mark Rudie Steiner (qv); 1 s. Educ. Albyn School, Aberdeen; Aberdeen University. Surgical Assistant, Freiburg; worked in hospitals, Switzerland, Canada, USA; Departmental Medical Officer/Senior Medical Officer, Aberdeen City; Organiser, Family Planning Services, Aberdeen; Member, Rubella Working Party; Adviser, Aberdeen Telephone Samaritans; Assistant, Psychiatry, Murray Royal Hospital, Perth; Contributor, Scientific Congress, Institute of Advanced Medical Sciences, Moscow. Recreations: sailing; hill-walking; international contacts. Address: (h.) Atlantic House, Ellenabeich, Isle of Seil, by Oban, Argyll, PA34 4RF; T.-Balvicar 300 594.

Steiner, Mark Rudie, LLB, NP. Legal Consultant and Defence Lawyer; part-time Chairman, Social Security Appeal Tribunal and Disability Appeal Tribunal; Scottish Representative, Consumers in the European Community Group; Member, Potato Marketing Board Consumer Liaison Committee; Member, National Pharmaceutical Consultative Committee Working Group on Quality Assurance; m., Dr. Eleanor Steiner, DPH, MFCM, MRCGP, MICGP; 1 s. Educ. Aberdeen University. Editor, Canadian Broadcasting Corporation, Toronto and Montreal; Editor, Swiss Broadcasting Corporation, Berne; Procurator Fiscal in Scotland; Partner and Director of various firms and companies; Past Chairman, Perth Community Relations Council; Delegate, Scottish Council for Racial Equality; Chairman, Central Scotland Society of Conservative Lawyers; neutral observer at various overseas political trials; contributor to various international journals; retired Principal, Goodman Steiner & Co., Defence Lawyers and Notaries in Central Scotland; former Member, Scottish Consumer Council. Recreations: sailing; developing international exchanges. Address: (h.) Atlantic House, Ellenabeich, Isle of Seil, by Oban, Argyll, PA34 4RF; T.-Balvicar 300 593.

Stell, Geoffrey Percival, BA, FSA, FSA Scot. Head of Architecture, Royal Commission on the Ancient and Historical Monuments of Scotland, since 1991; b. 21.11.44, Keighley; m., Evelyn Florence Burns; 1 s.; 1 d. Educ.

Keighley Boys' Grammar School; Leeds University; Glasgow University. Historic Buildings Investigator, RCAHMS, since 1969; one-time Chairman, Scottish Vernacular Buildings Working Group; sometime Chairman, Scottish Urban Archaeological Trust; sometime Vice-President, Council for Scottish Archaeology. Publications include: Dumfries and Galloway, 1986; Monuments of Industry (Co-author); Buildings of St. Kilda (Co-author); Loads and Roads in Scotland (Co-editor); The Scottish Medieval Town (Co-editor); Galloway, Land and Lordship (Co-Editor); Materials and Traditions in Scottish Building (Co-Editor). Recreations: gardening; music; travel, particularly in Scotland and France. Address: (h.) Beechmount, Borrowstoun, Bo'ness, West Lothian, EH51 9RS; T.-01506 822441.

Stenning, Professor Keith, MA, PhD. Director, Human Communication Research Centre, Edinburgh and Glasgow Universities, since 1989; Professorial Fellow, Edinburgh University, since 1989; b. 15.6.48, London; m., Dr. Lynn Michell; 2 s. Educ. High Wycombe Grammar School; Oxford University; Rockefeller University, NY. Lecturer in Psychology, Liverpool University; Lecturer in Psychology and Cognitive Science, Edinburgh University, 1983-88. Publications: papers on human information processing. Recreation: being blown hither and thither. Address: (b.) H.C.R.C., 2 Buccleuch Place, Edinburgh, EH8 9LW; T.-0131-650 4444.

Stephen, Alex, FCCA. Chief Executive, City of Dundee District Council, since 1991; b. 17.9.48, Dundee; m., Joyce; 1 s.; 1 d. Local government since 1970. Recreation: voluntary work. Address: (b.) 21 City Square, Dundee; T.-01382 434198.

Stephen, Rev. Donald Murray, TD, MA, BD, ThM. Minister, Marchmont St. Giles' Parish Church, Edinburgh, since 1974; b. 1.6.36, Dundee; m., Hilda Swan Henriksen; 2 s.; 1 d. Educ. Brechin High School; Richmond Grammar School, Yorkshire; Edinburgh University; Princeton Theological Seminary. Assistant Minister, Westover Hills Presbyterian Church, Arkansas, 1962-64; Minister, Kirkoswald, 1964-74; Chaplain, TA, 1965-85 (attached to 4/5 Bn., RSF, 205 Scottish General Hospital, 2nd Bn., 52nd Lowland Volunteers); Convener, Committee on Chaplains to Her Majesty's Forces, General Assembly, 1985-89. Recreations: golf; curling. Address: 19 Hope Terrace, Edinburgh, EH9 2AP; T.-0131-447 2834.

Stephen, Eric John. Farmer; Director, McIntosh Donald Ltd., since 1995; Director, Aberdeen and Northern Marts Ltd., 1986-95; Director, Aberdeen and Northern Estates Ltd., since 1987; b. 2.1.38, Turriff; 1 s.; 3 d. Educ. Inverurie Academy. Member, Scottish Agricultural Wages Board; former Convener, Employment and Technology Committee, National Farmers Union of Scotland; Elder, Auchterless Parish Church, 32 years; Past President, Aberdeen and Kincardine Executive, NFU of Scotland; Past President, Royal Northern Agricultural Society; Vice President, Aberdeen Fatstock Club; President, Turriff Show, 1992; elected Grampian Regional Councillor, 1993; Regional Member, British Wool Marketing Board, since 1993. Recreation: bowling. Address: Lower Thorneybank, Rothienorman, Inverurie, AB5 8XT; T.-018884 233.

Stephen, Professor Frank H., BA, PhD. Professor, Department of Economics, Strathclyde University, since 1990 (Senior Lecturer, 1979-86, Reader, 1986-90); Managing Editor, Journal of Economic Studies, since 1982; b. 20.11.46, Glasgow; m., Christine Leathard; 2 d. Educ. Queen's Park Secondary School, Glasgow; Strathclyde University. Research Officer, then Head, Economics Department, STUC, 1969-71; Lecturer, Department of Economics, Strathclyde University, 1971-79. Publications: The Performance of Labour-Managed Firms (Editor), 1982; Firms Organisation and Labour (Editor), 1984; The

Economic Analysis of Producers' Cooperatives, 1984; The Economics of the Law, 1988. Address: (b.) Department of Economics, Strathclyde University, Glasgow; T.-0141-552 4400.

Stephen, Professor Kenneth William, BDS, DDSc, HDDRCPS, FDSRCS. Professor of Community Dental Health, Glasgow University, since 1992 (Head, Department of Oral Medicine and Pathology, since 1980); Consultant-in-charge, Glasgow School of Dental Hygiene, since 1979; b. 1.10.37, Glasgow; m., Anne Seymour Gardiner; 1 s.; 1 d. Educ. Hillhead High School, Glasgow; Glasgow University. General Dental Practitioner, 1960-64; House Officer, Department of Oral Surgery, Glasgow Dental Hospital, 1964-65; Lecturer, Department of Conservative Dentistry, 1965-68, Lecturer, Department of Oral Medicine and Pathology, Glasgow University, 1968-71; Visiting Lecturer, Department of Oral Physiology, Newcastle-upon-Tyne University, 1969-70; Senior Lecturer, Department of Oral Medicine and Pathology, Glasgow University, 1971-80; Reader, 1980-84. Co-President, European Organisation for Caries Research, 1978-79. Recreations: swimming; hill-walking; skiing; gardening. Address: (b.) Dental School, 378 Sauchiehall Street, Glasgow, G2 3JZ; T.-0141-211 9854.

Stephens, Professor William Peter, MA, BD, DesSR. Professor of Church History, Aberdeen University, since 1986 (Dean, Faculty of Divinity, 1987-89, Provost, Faculty of Divinity, 1989-90); Methodist Minister, since 1958; b. 16.5.34, Penzance. Educ. Truro School; Clare College, Cambridge, and Wesley House, Cambridge; Universities of Lund, Strasbourg, Muenster. Assistant Tutor, Hartley Victoria College, Manchester, 1958-61; Minister and University Chaplain, Nottingham University, 1961-65; Minister, Shirley Methodist Church, Croydon, 1967-71; Chair of Church History, Hartley Victoria College, Manchester, 1971-73; Chair of Historical and Systematic Theology, Wesley College, Bristol, 1973-80; Research Fellow, then Lecturer in Church History, The Queen's College, Birmingham, 1980-86. Secretary, Society for the Study of Theology, 1963-77. Publications: The Holy Spirit in the Theology of Martin Bucer; Faith and Love; Methodism in Europe; The Theology of Huldrych Zwingli; Zwingli: an Introduction to His Thought; The Bible, the Reformation and the Church (Editor). Recreations: squash; tennis; hill-walking; skiing; swimming; theatre. Address: (b.) Faculty of Divinity, King's College, Aberdeen University, Aberdeen; T.-01224 272383.

Stevely, Professor William Stewart, BSc, DPhil, DipEd, FIBiol. Vice Principal, Paisley University, since 1992; b. 6.4.43, West Kilbride; m., Sheila Anne Stalker; 3 s.; 2 d. Educ. Ardrossan Academy; Glasgow University; Oxford University. Lecturer and Senior Lecturer in Biochemistry, Glasgow University, 1968-88; Professor and Head, Department of Biology, Paisley College, 1988-92. Member, Scottish Higher Education Funding Council, since 1994; Member, National Board for Nursing, Midwifery and Health Visiting for Scotland, since 1993. Address: (b.) Paisley University, High Street, Paisley; T.-0141-848 3000.

Steven, John Douglas, MB, ChB, FRCOG. Consultant Obstetrician and Gynaecologist, Stirling Royal Infirmary, since 1981; Member, Scottish Council, British Medical Association; b. 20.4.46, Perth. Educ. Douglas Ewart High School, Newton Stewart; Edinburgh University. Registrar in Obstetrics and Gynaecology, Western General Hospital, Edinburgh; Senior Registrar, Obstetrics and Gynaecology, Ninewells Hospital, Dundee. Address: (b.) Stirling Royal Infirmary, Stirling, FK8 2AU; T.-01786 434000.

Stevens, Claire, BA (Hons). Director, Scottish Council for Single Homeless, since 1992; b. 26.7.58, Sudbury. Educ. Sudbury Upper School; Warwick University. Welfare Rights Officer, Strathclyde Regional Council, 1981-84;

Welfare Rights Officer, Basildon Council, 1984-85; Housing Campaigns Worker, Shelter (Scotland), 1985-89; Housing Policy and Projects Officer, Age Concern Scotland, 1989-92. Member, Management Committee, Muirhouse Housing Association, since 1992. Address: (b.) 9 Forrest Road, Edinburgh; T.-0131-226 4382.

Stevens, Professor Paul John, BA (Cantab), MA, PhD. Professor of Petroleum Policy and Economics, Dundee University, since 1993; b. 30.4.47, Liverpool; m., Cassie Stevens; 1 s.; 1 d. Educ. Alsop High School, Liverpool; Clare College, Cambridge; London University. Assistant Professor, American University of Beirut, 1973-75; oil consultant, Beirut, 1975-77; Assistant Professor, American University of Beirut, 1977-79; Lecturer in Economics, then Senior Lecturer, University of Surrey, 1979-93. Publications: numerous books and papers on oil and gas. Recreations: travel; food and drink; golf; carpentry. Address: (b.) CPMLP, Dundee University, Dundee, DD1 4HN; T.-01382 344300.

Stevenson, Celia Margaret Stirton. Director, Scottish Screen Locations, since 1995; b. Ballantrae; m., Charles William Forbes Judge; 2 s.; 1 d. Educ. Wellington School, Ayr; Edinburgh College of Art. Interior design business, 1970-80; Reporter/Presenter, West Sound, Ayr, 1981-84; Scottish Television: Reporter/Presenter, 1984-86, Promotions trailer-maker, 1987-89, Head of Programme Planning and Film Acquisition, 1990-95. Director, South West Scotland Screen Commission. Recreations: cooking; reading; study of 20th-century art; interior design. Address: (b.) Film House, 88 Lothian Road, Edinburgh, EH3 9BZ; T.-0131-229 1213.

Stevenson, Professor David, BA, PhD, DLitt. Honorary Research Professor, Scottish History, St. Andrews University, since 1994; b. 30.4.42, Largs; m., Wendy B. McLeod; 2 s. Educ. Gordonstoun; Dublin University; Glasgow University. Aberdeen University: Lecturer in History, 1970-80, Senior Lecturer in History, 1980-84; Reader in Scottish History, 1984-90; St. Andrews University: Reader in Scottish History, 1990-91; Professor of Scottish History, 1991-94. Honorary Secretary, Scottish History Society, 1976-84; Fellow, Royal Historical Society. Publications: The Scottish Revolution 1637-44, 1973; Revolution and Counter-Revolution in Scotland 1644-51, 1977; Alasdair MacColla and the Highland Problem in the 17th Century, 1980; Scottish Covenanters and Irish Confederates, 1981; The Government of Scotland under the Covenanters 1637-51, 1982; Scottish Texts and Calendars (with Wendy B. Stevenson), 1987; The Origins of Freemasonry, 1988; The First Freemasons: The Early Scottish Lodges and their members, 1988; The Covenanters: the National Covenant and Scotland, 1988; King's College, Aberdeen, 1560-1641, 1990. Address: (b.) St. John's House, South Street, St. Andrews KY16 9QW.

Stevenson, David Deas, CBE, DSc, BCom, CA. Chairman Edinburgh Woollen Mill; b. 28.11.41, Hawick; m., Alix Jamieson; 2 d. Educ. Langholm Academy; Dumfries Academy; Edinburgh University. British Steel Corporation, 1966-67; Langholm Dyeing Co., 1967-70. Recreations: squash; horses; running. Address: (b.) Waverley Mills, Langholm, Dumfriesshire, DG13 0EB; T.-013873 80611.

Stevenson, Gerda. Actress, Singer, Writer, Book Illustrator, Director; b. 10.4.56, West Linton; m., Aonghas MacNeacail; 1 s. Educ. Peebles High School; Royal Academy of Dramatic Art, London (DDA, Vanbrugh Award). Has performed with 7:84 Theatre Co., Scottish Theatre Company, Royal Lyceum Theatre (Edinburgh), Traverse Theatre, Communicado, Monstrous Regiment, Victoria Theatre (Stoke on Trent), Contact Theatre (Manchester) and with Freefall at Lilian Baylis Theatre, London, and Birmingham Rep; directed Uncle Jesus for Edinburgh Festival Fringe; Assistant Director, Royal Lyceum, on Merchant of Venice and A Doll's House; Founder Member, Stellar Quines Theatre Co.; TV work includes Clay, Smeddum and Greenden, Square Mile of Murder, Grey Granite, Horizon: Battered Baby, The Old Master, Taggart, Dr. Finlay, The Bill; films: The Stamp of Greatness, Tickets to the Zoo, Blue Black Permanent (BAFTA Scotland Best Film Actress Award, 1993); extensive radio work includes title roles in Bride of Lammermoor and Catriona; freelance producer for Radio Scotland; wrote and illustrated children's book, The Candlemaker. Recreation: walking in the country. Address: (h.) 1 Roseneath Terrace, Edinburgh, EH9 1JS; T.-0131-229 5652.

Stevenson, James Edward Mackenzie, MA, LLB, NP. retired solicitor; Honorary Sheriff Substitute, South Strathclyde, Dumfries and Galloway, at Dumfries; b. 9.11.19, Lockerbie; m., Maureen Mary; 2 s.; 2 d. Educ. Lockerbie Academy; George Watson's Boys College; Edinburgh University. Captain, 131st Field Regiment, RA, Second World War; Town Clerk and Chamberlain: Burgh of Lochmaben, 1949-75, Burgh of Lockerbie, 1957-75. Clerk, Lockerbie Branch, Earl Haig Fund; Secretary, Abbeyfield Lockerbie & District Society Ltd. Recreations: golf; curling. Address: (h.) Kinnaird, 1 Ashgrove Terrace, Lockerbie, Dumfriesshire.

Stevenson, John Meikle, DL, BSc (Agric), FInstD. Farmer; b. 20.1.31, Aberlady; m., Eileen A.; 2 s.; 1 d. Educ. Trinity College, Glenalmond; Aberdeen University. Councillor, East Lothian County Council, 1961-66; President, East Lothian, National Farmers' Union, 1968-69; Council Member, NFU, 1966-70; Member, Governing Body, British Society for Research in Agricultural Engineering, since 1968; Chairman, Committee, Scottish Centre of Agricultural Engineering, 1987-95; Governor, East of Scotland College of Agriculture; Chairman, Royal Scottish Agricultural Benevolent Institution; Deputy Lieutenant, East Lothian. Recreations: shooting; fishing; gardening; golf. Address: (h.) Luffness Mains, Aberlady, East Lothian EH32 0PZ; T.-01875 870212.

Stevenson, Miranda Faye, BA (Hons), PhD. Curator of Animals, Royal Zoological Society of Scotland, since 1979; b. 26.3.47, Glasgow. Educ. Wesley College, Dublin; Trinity College, Dublin; University of Wales, Aberystwyth. Keeper, Chester Zoo; Biologist, Welsh Plant Breeding Centre; Research Assistant, University of Wales, Aberystwyth. International studbook keeper for the Diana monkey; EEP (European Endangered Species Programme) Co-ordinator; Chair, EEP Primate and Penguin TAGs; Winston Churchill Travelling Fellowship, 1976; Chair, Federation of Zoos Joint Management of Species Committee; Member, two IUCN specialist groups. Recreations: country walking; theatre; film. Address: (b.) Royal Zoological Society of Scotland, Murrayfield, Edinburgh EH12 6TS; T-0131-334 9171.

Stevenson, Peter David, MA (Cantab); b. 6.3.47, Edinburgh; m., The Hon. Susan Blades; 1 s.; 1 d. Educ. Edinburgh Academy; Trinity College, Cambridge. Chairman: Mackays Stores (Holdings) PLC, Clydeside Holdings plc; Director, Scottish Nuclear Ltd. Address: (b.) 22 Rutland Street, Edinburgh EH1 2AN; T.-0131-229 0550.

Stevenson, Robert Orr, BA, FCIS. Secretary, Scottish Homes (formerly Secretary, Scottish Special Housing Association); b. 27.4.33, Glasgow; m., Anne. Educ. Trinity College, Glenalmond; Christ's College, Cambridge. Beaverbrook Newspapers Ltd.: General Manager, Sunday Express; General Manager, Daily Express; Group General Manager, Scotland; Director and General Manager, Felixstowe Dock and Railway Company (Chief Executive, Port of Felixstowe); Managing Director, A.M. Tweedie & Co. Ltd. Recreations: golf; opera. Address: (h.) 12 East Parkside, Edinburgh EH16 5XJ; T.-0131-668 3716.

Stevenson, Ronald, FRMCM, HonFRIAS. Composer and Pianist; Broadcaster; Author; b. 6.3.28, Blackburn; m., Marjorie Spedding; 1 s.; 2 d. Educ. Royal Manchester College of Music; Conservatorio Di Santa Cecilia, Rome. Senior Lecturer, Cape Town University, 1963-65; BBC Prom debut in own 2nd Piano Concerto, 1972; Aldeburgh Festival recital with Sir Peter Pears, 1973; Busoni documentary, BBC TV, 1974; BBC Radio Scotland extended series on the bagpipe, clarsach and fiddle music of Scotland, 1980-84; Artist in Residence: Melbourne University, 1980, University of W. Australia, 1982, Conservatory of Shanghai, 1985; York University, 1987; published and recorded compositions: Passacaglia for Piano, two Piano Concertos, Violin Concerto (commissioned by Menuhin), Prelude, Fugue and Fantasy for Piano, Prelude and Fugue for Organ, In Memoriam Robert Carver, St. Mary's May Songs, A Child's Garden of Verse (BBC commission), Voces Vagabundae, Salute to Nelson Mandela (march for brass band), Cello Concerto (RSNO commission). Publication:Western Music. Recreations: hill-walking; reading poetry, biographies and politics. Address: (h.) Townfoot House, West Linton, Peeblesshire; T.-01968 60511.

Stevenson, Ronald Harley, MA, LLB. Chief Executive, Highland Regional Council, since 1981; b. 6.1.34, Dunfermline. Educ. Dunfermline High School; Edinburgh University. County Clerk, Caithness County Council, 1967-75; Joint Director of Law and Administration, Highland Regional Council, 1975-81. Address: (b.) Regional Buildings, Inverness; T.-Inverness 702001.

Stevenson, Sir Simpson, LLD. Provost, Inverclyde District Council, 1984-88; Chairman, Scottish Health Services Common Services Agency, 1983-87; b. 18.8.21, Greenock; m., Jean Holmes Henry. Educ. Greenock High School. Provost of Greenock, 1962-65; Chairman, Western Regional Hospital Board, 1967-73; Chairman, Greater Glasgow Health Board, 1973-83; knighted, 1976; Hon. LLD, Glasgow University, 1982; Member, Royal Commission on NHS, 1976-79. Address: (h.) The Gables, Reservoir Road, Gourock; T.-01475 631774.

Stevenson, Sheriff W.G., QC, MA, LLB. Sheriff of Glasgow and Strathkelvin at Glasgow. Address: (b.) Sheriff Court House, 1 Carlton Place, Glasgow, G5 9DA.

Stevenson, William Trevor, CBE, DL, FCIT; b. 21.3.21, Peebles; m., Alison Wilson Roy. Educ. Edinburgh Academy. Apprentice Engineer, 1937-41; Engineer, 1941-45; entered family food manufacturing business, Cottage Rusks, 1945; Managing Director, 1948-54; Chairman, 1954-59; Chief Executive, Cottage Rusks Associates, 1965-69; Regional Director, Ranks Hovis McDougall, 1969-74; Director, various companies in food, engineering, hotel and aviation industries, since 1974; Chairman, Alex. Wilkie Ltd., 1977-90; founder Chairman, Gleneagles Hotels, 1981-83; Chairman, Scottish Transport Group, 1981-86; Master, Company of Merchants of City of Edinburgh, 1978-80; Vice President, Edinburgh Chamber of Commerce, 1983-87; Chairman, Scottish Export Association, since 1993. Recreations: flying; sailing; curling.

Stewardson, Raymond Richard, BA (Hons), FRSA. Headteacher, Castlehead High School, Paisley, since 1989; b. 26.9.37, Huyton, Merseyside; m., Aileen Agnes Mackie; 1 s.; 1 d. Educ. Prescot Grammar School; Sheffield University; London University (External). Assistant Teacher; Principal Teacher of Geography; Assistant Head Teacher; Depute Rector; Rector, John Neilson High School, 1983-89, when merged with Castlehead High School. Recreations: swimming; gardening. Address: (b.) Castlehead High School, Camphill, Canal Street, Paisley PA1 2HL; T.-0141-887 4261.

Stewart, Alan George. Chief Executive, Alloa Clackmannan Enterprise Ltd., since 1991; b. 21.8.49,

Glasgow; m., Allison; 1 s.; 2 d. Educ. Hutchesons', Glasgow; Glasgow School of Art. Manager of Planning, Victoria, Australia; Policy Unit, SDA; Head of Policy and Planning, Clackmannan District Council; Executive Member, Royal Town Planning Institute, Scotland, 1973-87, Chairman, 1985-86. Recreations: family; work; walking; photography; playing the drums. Address: (b.) Alloa Business Centre, Alloa FK10 3SA.

Stewart, A.J. (Ada F. Kay). Playwright and Author; b. 5.3.29, Tottington, Lancashire. Educ. Grammar School, Fleetwood. ATS Scottish Command; first produced play, 1951; repertory actress, 1952-54; BBC TV Staff Writer/Editor/Adaptor, Central Script Section, 1956-59; returned to Scotland, 1959, as stage and TV writer; winner, BBC New Radio Play competition, 1956; The Man from Thermopylae, presented in Festival of Contemporary Drama, Rheydt, West Germany, 1959, as part of Edinburgh International Festival, 1965, and at Masquers' Theatre, Hollywood, 1972; first recipient, Wendy Wood Memorial Grant, 1982; Polish Gold Cross for achievements in literary field. Publications: Falcon - The Autobiography of His Grace, James the 4, King of Scots, 1970; Died 1513-Born 1929 - The Autobiography of A.J. Stewart, 1978; The Man from Thermopylae, 1981. Recreation: work. Address: 15 Oxford Street, Edinburgh EH8.

Stewart, Sheriff Alastair Lindsay, BA (Oxon), LLB(Edin). Sheriff of Tayside, Central and Fife at Dundee, since 1990; b. 28.11.38, Aberdeen; m., 1, Annabel Claire Stewart (m. diss.); 2 s.; 2, Sheila Anne Mackinnon. Educ. Edinburgh Academy; St. Edmund Hall, Oxford; Edinburgh University. Admitted to Faculty of Advocates, 1963; Tutor, Faculty of Law, Edinburgh University, 1963-73; Standing Junior Counsel to the Registrar of Restrictive Trading Agreements, 1968-70; Advocate Depute, 1970-73; Sheriff of Lanarkshire (later South Strathclyde, Dumfries and Galloway) at Airdrie, 1973-79; Sheriff of Grampian, Highland and Islands at Aberdeen and Stonehaven, 1979-90. Chairman, Scottish Association of Family Conciliation Services, 1986-89; Editor, Scottish Civil Law Reports, since 1992. Publications: Sheriff Court Practice (Contributor), 1988; The Scottish Criminal Courts in Action, 1990. Recreations: music; reading; walking. Address: (b.) Sheriffs' Chambers, Sheriff Court House, PO Box 2, 6 West Bell Street, Dundee DD1 9AD; T.-01382 229961.

Stewart, Alexander Donald, BA, LLB, WS, DL. Director, Murray Split Capital Trust PLC; Chairman, Scottish Amicable Life Assurance Society; b. 18.6.33, Edinburgh; m., Virginia Mary Washington; 1 s.; 5 d. Educ. Wellington College, Berkshire; Oxford University; Edinburgh University. Hon. Consul for Thailand in Scotland; DL, Perthshire. Recreations: music; field sports; winter sports. Address: (h.) Ardvorlich, Lochearnhead, Perthshire.

Stewart, Alexander Reavell Macdonald, FRICS. Chartered Surveyor; Chairman, Scottish Branch, Royal Institution of Chartered Surveyors, 1985-86; b. 14.2.29, Bearsden; m., Keris Duguid Keir; 2 s.; 2 d. Educ. Merchiston Castle School. President: Property Owners and Factors Association Glasgow, 1968-69, National Federation of Property Owners Scotland, 1978-80. Recreations: trout fishing; piping. Address: (b.) 21 Winton Lane, Glasgow; T.-0141-332 2752.

Stewart, Angus, QC, BA, LLB; b. 14.12.46. Called to Scottish Bar, 1975; Keeper of the Library, Faculty of Advocates. Address: (b.) Advocates' Library, Parliament House, Edinburgh, EH1 1RF.

Stewart, Archibald Ian Balfour, CBE, BL (Dist), FSA (Scot). Retired Solicitor; Honorary Sheriff; b. 19.5.15, Campbeltown; m., Ailsa Rosamund Mary Massey; 3 s. Educ. Cheltenham College; Glasgow University. Solicitor, 1938; Town Clerk, Lochgilphead, 1939-46, Campbeltown,

1947-54; Procurator Fiscal of Argyll at Campbeltown, 1941-74; Temporary Sheriff, 1975-88; Secretary, Clyde Fishermen's Association, 1941-70; Churchill Fellow, 1966; President, Scottish Fishermen's Federation, 1970-75; Hon. President, Clyde Fishermen's Association and Scottish Fishermen's Federation; former Director, Scottish Fishermen's Organisation and Scottish Board, Phoenix Insurance Co. Ltd.; Past President, Kintyre Antiquarian Society; Past Chairman, Argyll and Bute National Insurance Committee, Kintyre Employment Committee; Adviser, North East Atlantic Fisheries Conference, UN Law of Sea Conference; Editor, Kintyre Antiquarian and Natural History Society Magazine; Editor, List of Inhabitants upon the Duke of Argyle's Kintyre Estates 1792. Recreations: local history; genealogy; wine; gardening; idling. Address: (h.) Askomel End, Campbeltown, Argyll PA28 6EP; T.-01586 52353.

Stewart (nee Muir), Professor Averil M., BA, FCOT, TDip, SROT. Head, Department of Occupational Therapy, Queen Margaret College, Edinburgh, since 1986; b. 7.4.43, Edinburgh; m., J. Gavin Stewart. Educ. Dunfermline High School; Occupational Therapy Training Centre, Edinburgh. Lecturer, Glasgow School of Occupational Therapy, 1972-74; Senior Occupational Therapist, Head and District Occupational Therapist, Worthing District, 1975-83; Educational Development Officer, Council for Professions Supplementary to Medicine (secondment), 1978-80; Senior Lecturer, Department of Occupational Therapy, Queen Margaret College, 1983-86. Member, Vice-Chairman and Chairman, Occupational Therapists Board, CPSM, 1980-92. Publications: Occupational Therapy Teaching Resources in UK; Contributor: Occupational Therapy in Short-Term Psychiatry; Occupational Therapy in Mental Health. Recreations: wilderness travel; gardening. Address: (b.) Queen Margaret College, Edinburgh EH12 8TS.

Stewart, Brian John, MSc, CA. Group Chief Executive, Scottish & Newcastle plc, since 1991; Director (Non-Executive), Standard Life and Booker PLC, since 1993; b. 9.4.45, Stirling; m., Shona (Seonaid); 2 s.; 1 d. Educ. Perth Academy; Edinburgh University. J. & R. Morrison, CA, Perth, 1962-67; Chief Management Accountant, Ethicon Ltd., 1969-76; joined Scottish & Newcastle plc, 1976; Corporate Development Director, 1985; Group Finance Director, 1988. Recreations: skiing; golf. Address: (b.) 111 Holyrood Road, Edinburgh EH8 8YS; T.-0131-556 2591.

Stewart, Brian West, BSc, MRTPI. Chief Executive, Western Isles Islands Council, since 1993; b. 27.6.58, Edinburgh; m., Alicia Dolores Giles-Stewart; 1 d. Educ. George Heriot's, Edinburgh; Heriot-Watt University, Edinburgh. Graduate Trainee, UK Atomic Energy Authority, Risley; entered local government with posts in Newbury, Farnborough, Dingwall and Stornoway. Recreations: reading; current affairs; planning foreign holidays. Address: (b.) Council Offices, Sandwick Road, Stornoway, Isle of Lewis; T.-01851 703773.

Stewart, Clement A., MA, MEd. Rector, Portlethen Academy, since 1986; b. 9.1.41, Strichen. Educ. Aberdeen Grammar School; Aberdeen University. Teacher of Mathematics, Aberdeen Grammar School, 1963-70; Principal Teacher of Mathematics, Assistant Rector, Deputy Rector, Dunoon Grammar School, 1970-77; Head Teacher, Lochgilphead High School, 1977-86. Recreations: church work (Elder); Ramblers Association; Rotary. Address: (b.) Portlethen Academy, Bruntland Road, Portlethen, Aberdeen, AB1 4QL; T.-01224 782174.

Stewart, David Roger, TD, MA, BA (Hons), FEIS. Honorary Sheriff, Selkirk, since 1983; b. 3.2.20, Glasgow; m., Gwyneth Ruth Morris; 2 s.; 1 d. Educ. Hyndland Secondary School; Glasgow High School; Glasgow University; London University. Army, 1939-46; Schoolmaster, 1947-65 (Kelvinside Academy, Galashiels Academy); Rector, Selkirk High School, 1965-81; Member: Selkirk Town Council, 1967-75, Borders Education Committee, 1975-81, Borders Regional Council, 1982-86; TA, 1939-64; Chairman, Selkirk Committee, Cancer Research Campaign. Recreations: golf; gardening; reading. Address: (h.) Cairncoed, Hillside Terrace, Selkirk TD7 4ND; T.-01750 21755.

Stewart, Douglas Fleming, MA, LLB, WS, NP, FSA Scot. Solicitor (Scotland), Crown Estate Commissioners, 1970-91; Partner, J.F. Anderson, WS, now Anderson Strathern, WS, 1961-92; Secretary, Stewart Society, 1968-87; b. 22.5.27, Sydney, Australia; m., Catherine Coleman; 2 d. Educ. George Watson's College, Edinburgh; Edinburgh University. RAF, 1945-48; Member, Business Committee, General Council, Edinburgh University, 1961-69; Session Clerk, Braid Church, Edinburgh, 1979-91; Treasurer, Friends of the Royal Scottish Museum, 1972-90; Council Member, Royal Celtic Society, since 1981; President, Watsonian Club, 1989-90; Vice Chairman, Church of Scotland Trust, 1995. Recreation: swimming. Address: (b.) 48 Castle Street, Edinburgh EH2 3LX; T.-0131-220 2345.

Stewart, Ena Lamont. Playwright; b. 10.2.12, Glasgow; m., Jack Stewart (deceased); 1 s. Educ. Woodside School, Glasgow; Esdaile School, Edinburgh. Assistant, Public Library, Aberdeen, 1930-34; Medical Secretary, Radcliffe, Lancashire, 1934-37; Secretary/Receptionist, Royal Hospital for Sick Children, Glasgow, 1937-41; Baillie's Reference Library, Glasgow: Assistant Librarian, 1953-57, Librarian-in-charge, 1957-66; author of plays: Starched Aprons, Men Should Weep, The Heir to Ardmally, Business in Edinburgh, After Tomorrow (unperformed), Walkies Time, Knocking on the Wall, Towards Evening, High Places. Recreations: reading; listening to music. Address: (h.) 5a Monkton Road, Prestwick KA9 1AP; T.-01292 479827.

Stewart, Francis John, MA (Oxon), LLB, TD. Writer to the Signet (retired); Member, Queen's Bodyguard for Scotland (Royal Company of Archers); b. 11.5.17, Edinburgh; m., Olga Margaret Mounsey; 3 s.; 1 d. Educ. Cargilfield School, Edinburgh; Loretto School; Trinity College, Oxford; Edinburgh University. 1st Bn., Lothians and Borders Yeomanry; Senior Partner, Murray Beith & Murray, WS, Edinburgh (retired); Past Chairman of Governors, Loretto School; Honorary Consul for Principality of Monaco, 1964-85; Chevalier of the Order of St. Charles. Recreation: gardening. Address: (b.) 39 Castle Street, Edinburgh; T.-0131-225 1200.

Stewart, Sir Frederick Henry, KB, BSc, PhD, FRSA, DSc Hon. (Aberdeen, Leicester, Heriot-Watt, Durham, Glasgow), FRS, FRSE, FGS. Professor Emeritus, Edinburgh University, since 1982; Trustee, British Museum (Natural History), 1983-88; Council Member, Scottish Marine Biological Association, 1983-89; b. 16.1.16, Aberdeen; m., Mary Florence Elinor Rainbow. Educ. Fettes College, Edinburgh; Robert Gordon's College, Aberdeen; Aberdeen University; Emmanuel College, Cambridge. Mineralogist, Research Department, Imperial Chemical Industries, 1941-43; Lecturer in Geology, Durham University, 1943-56; Regius Professor of Geology and Mineralogy, Edinburgh University, 1956-82; Member, Council for Scientific Policy, 1967-71 (Assessor, 1971-73); Chairman, Natural Environment Research Council, 1971-73; Chairman, Advisory Board for the Research Councils, 1974-79; Member, Advisory Council for Research and Development, 1976-79; University Grants Committee Earth Sciences Review, 1986-87. Lyell Fund Award, 1951 and Lyell Medal, 1970, Geological Society of London; Mineralogical Society of America Award, 1952; Clough Medal, Edinburgh Geological Society; Sorby Medal, Yorkshire Geological Society. Publications: The British Caledonides, 1963; Marine Evaporites, 1963. Recreations: fishing; collecting fossil fish. Address: (h.) 79 Morningside

Park, Edinburgh, EH10 5EZ; T.-0131-447 2620; House of Letterawe, Lochawe, Argyll, PA33 1AH; T.-01838 200 329.

Stewart, George Girdwood, CB, MC, TD, BSc, FICFor, Hon. FLI. Cairngorm Estate Adviser to Highlands and Islands Enterprise, since 1988; b. 12.12.19, Glasgow; m., Shelagh Jean Morven Murray; 1 s.; 1 d. Educ. Kelvinside Academy, Glasgow; Glasgow University; Edinburgh University. Royal Artillery, 1940-46 (mentioned in Despatches); Forestry Commission: District Officer, 1949-60, Assistant Conservator, 1960-67, Conservator (Glasgow), 1967-69, Commissioner, Forest and Estate Management, 1969-79. Commanding Officer, 278 (Lowland) Field Regiment RA (TA), 1956-59; President, Scottish Ski Club, 1971-75; Vice President, National Ski Federation of Great Britain, 1975-78; Forestry Consultant to National Trust for Scotland, 1989-93 (Regional Representative for Central and Tayside, 1984-88); Chairman, Scottish Wildlife Trust, 1981-87; Member, Countryside Commission for Scotland, 1981-88; Member, Environment Panel, British Railways Board, 1980-90; Associate Director, Oakwood Environmental, since 1990; Member, Cairngorm Recreation Trust, since 1986; President, Scottish National Ski Council, 1988-94; Specialist Adviser to House of Lords Select Committee on EEC Forestry Policy, 1986. Fellow, Royal Society of Arts. Recreations: skiing; tennis; studying Scottish painting. Address: (h.) Stormont House, 11 Mansfield Road, Scone, Perth PH2 6SA; T.-01738 551815.

Stewart, Gillian Mary, BA (Hons). Under Secretary, Scottish Office Home and Health Department, since 1992; b. 2.6.45, Gosforth; 2 s. Educ. Blyth Grammar School; Durham University. Joined Scottish Office, 1970, as Assistant Principal; posts held in Education, Social Work Services Group, Environment. Recreations: swimming; walking; theatre; music. Address: (b.) St. Andrew's House, Edinburgh EH1 3DG; T.-0131-244 2131.

Stewart, Professor Graham George, BSc, PhD, DSc, FIBrew. Director, International Centre for Brewing and Distilling, since 1994; b. 22.3.42, Cardiff; m., Olga Leonara. Educ. Cathays High School, Cardiff; University College Cardiff; Bath University. Lecturer in Biochemistry, Portsmouth College of Technology, 1967-69; various technical positions, J. Labatt Ltd., Canada, 1969-94. Recreations: rugby; music; travel. Address: (b.) Heriot-Watt University, Riccarton, Edinburgh, EH14 4AS; T.-0131-451 3184.

Stewart, John Allan. MP (Conservative), Eastwood, since 1983 (East Renfrewshire, 1979-83); b. 1.6.42, St. Andrews; m., Susie Gourlay; 1 s.; 1 d. Educ. Bell Baxter High School, Cupar; St. Andrews University; Harvard University. Lecturer in Political Economy, St. Andrews University, 1965-70; Confederation of British Industry: Head, Regional Development Department, 1971, Deputy Director (Economics), 1973, Scottish Secretary, 1976, Scottish Director, 1978; Under Secretary of State, Scottish Office, 1981-86, 1990-95. Recreations: bridge; reading; gardening; hedgehogs. Address: (b.) House of Commons, London, SW1A 0AA; T.-0171-219 5110.

Stewart, John Barry Bingham, OBE, BA, CA. Past Chairman, Martin Currie Ltd.; b. 21.2.31, Edinburgh; m., Ailsa Margaret Crawford. Educ. The Leys School, Cambridge; Magdalene College, Cambridge. Accountancy training, Edinburgh; worked in London, United States and Canada; joined Martin Currie, 1960. Recreations: fishing; shooting; golf; skiing. Address: 18 Hope Terrace, Edinburgh EH9 2AR; T.-0131-447 1626.

Stewart, John Carwin, IPFA. Director of Finance and Depute Chief Executive, Dumfries and Galloway Regional Council, since 1981; b. 17.7.39, Perth; m., Helen Barbara; 1

s.; 1 d. Educ. Perth Academy; Scottish College of Commerce. Trainee, Perth Town Council, 1957-65; Accountant, Stirling County Council, 1965-70; Depute County Treasurer, Wigtown County Council, 1970-75; Depute Director of Finance, Dumfries and Galloway Regional Council, 1975-81. Chairman, Local Authority (Scotland) Accounts Advisory Committee. Recreations: golf; bridge. Address: (b.) Council Offices, English Street, Dumfries, DG1 2DD; T.-01387 260250.

Stewart, Sheriff John Hall, LLB. Sheriff of Strathclyde, Dumfries and Galloway, at Airdrie, since 1985; b. 15.3.44, Bellshill; m., Marion MacCalman; 1 s.; 2 d. Educ. Airdrie Academy; St. Andrews University. Admitted Solicitor, 1971; Advocate, 1978. President, Uddingston RFC. Address: (b.) Sheriff's Chambers, Sheriff Court House, Graham Street, Airdrie ML6 6EE; T.-Airdrie 751121.

Stewart, Kathleen Margaret, MA, LLB, WS, NP. Partner, McGrigor Donald, Solicitors, Edinburgh, Glasgow and London, since 1988 (Partner, Balfour & Manson, Solicitors, Edinburgh, 1983-87); b. St. Andrews. Educ. Bell Baxter High School, Cupar; St. Andrews University; Sweet Briar College, USA; Edinburgh University. Assistant Lawyer (Corporate Department) in London firm of commercial lawyers, 1975-79, and Scottish firms of commercial lawyers, 1980-83. Member, Company Law Panel, CBI; Member, EEC Sub-Committee, Company Law Committee, Law Society of Scotland. Recreations: horse riding; tennis; squash; bad bridge. Address: (b.) Erskine House, Queen Street, Edinburgh; T.-0131-226 7777.

Stewart, Rev. Norma Drummond, MA, MEd, DipTh, BD. Minister, Strathbungo Queen's Park Church, Glasgow, since 1979; b. 20.5.36, Glasgow. Educ. Hyndland Secondary School, Glasgow; Glasgow University; Bible Training Institute, Glasgow; Trinity College, Glasgow. Teacher, Garrioch Secondary School, Glasgow, 1958-62; Missionary, Overseas Missionary Fellowship, West Malaysia, 1965-74; ordained to ministry, Church of Scotland, 1977. Selection School Assessor; Convener, Education for the Ministry Committee, Glasgow Presbytery; Member, Church of Scotland Panel on Doctrine; occasional Lecturer in Old Testament, Glasgow University; Participant in Congress on World Evangelisation, Manila, 1989; Member, Council, Evangelical Alliance Scotland; Pastoral Adviser, Glasgow Presbytery; Member, Council of Christians and Jews. Recreation: research in Old Testament studies. Address: 5 Newark Drive, Glasgow G41 4QJ; T.-0141-423 4818.

Stewart, Norman MacLeod, BL, SSC. Senior Partner, Allan, Black & McCaskie, Solicitors, Elgin, since 1984; Chairman, Elgin and Lossiemouth Harbour Board, since 1993; President, Law Society of Scotland, 1985-86; b. 2.12.34, Lossiemouth; m., Mary Slater Campbell; 4 d. Educ. Elgin Academy; Edinburgh University. Training and Legal Assistant, Alex. Morison & Co., WS, Edinburgh, 1954-58; Legal Assistant: McLeod, Solicitor, Portsoy, 1958-59, Allan, Black & McCaskie, Solicitors, Elgin, 1959-61 (Partner, 1961); Council Member, Law Society of Scotland, 1976-87 (Convener, Public Relations Committee, 1979-81, and Professional Practice Committee, 1981-84). Past President, Elgin Rotary Club; Past Chairman, Moray Crime Prevention Panel; President, Edinburgh University Club of Moray, 1987-89. Recreations: walking; golf; music; Spanish culture. Address: (h.) Argyll Lodge, Lossiemouth, Moray; T.-0134381 3150.

Stewart, Patrick Loudon McIain, LLB, WS, DL. Senior Partner, Stewart Balfour & Sutherland, Solicitors, since 1982; Secretary, Clyde Fishermen's Association, since 1970; b. 25.7.45, Campbeltown; m., Mary Anne McLellan; 1 s.; 1 d. Educ. Edinburgh Academy; Edinburgh University. Partner, Stewart Balfour & Sutherland, Campbeltown, 1970; former Executive Member, Scottish Fishermen's

Federation (currently Chairman, Environmental Issues Committee); former Director, Scottish Fishermen's Organisation Ltd.; member of many Scottish fishing industry committees; Chairman, Argyll & Bute Trust; Secretary, Campbeltown and Kintyre Enterprise Trust Ltd.; Clerk, General Commissioners of Income Tax — Islay; HQ Staff Officer Legal Affairs, Sea Cadet Corps; Honorary Legal Adviser, Sea Cadet Association; Cadet Forces Medal. Recreations: sailing; shooting; youth work. Address: Craigadam, Campbeltown, Argyll PA28 6EP; T.-01586 552161.

Stewart, Peter Duns, MD, FRCPath, DL. Deputy Lieutenant, Dunbartonshire, since 1973; b. 11.7.15, Oban; m., Doreen M. King; 2 d. Educ. Oban High School; Edinburgh University. Service in RAMC (Regular) — general duties, then Pathologist, 1937-59; Consultant Pathologist, Vale of Leven District General Hospital, 1959-80; Member, Argyll and Clyde Health Board, 1975-83; Territorial Army, 1960-67; Army Cadet Force, 1968-77; Medical Officer, Dunbartonshire BRCS, 1967-80, County Director, 1980-83. Recreation: fishing. Address: (h.) Burnside House, 38 Campbell Street, Helensburgh G84 8YG; T.-Helensburgh 672612.

Stewart, Robert Armstrong, BA, DipTP, FRTPI, MIMgt. Director of Planning and Development, Moray District Council, since 1979; b. Stirling. Planning Assistant, Lanark County Council, 1968-69; Planner, Glasgow, 1969-70; Senior Assistant, then Group Leader: Development Control, West Lothian County, 1970-75; Depute Director: Planning, East Lothian District, 1975-79. Address: (b.) District Headquarters, High Street, Elgin; T.-Elgin 545121.

Stewart, Lt. Col. Robert Christie, CBE, TD; Lord Lieutenant, Clackmannanshire, since 1994; b. 3.8.26, Dollar; m., Ann Grizel Cochrane; 3 s.; 2 d. Educ. Eton; University College, Oxford. Lt., Scots Guards, 1944-49; 7th Bn., Argyll and Sutherland Highlanders TA, 1951-66; Lt.-Col., 1963-66; Hon. Col., 1/51 Highland Volunteers, 1972-75; Landowner; Lord Lieutenant, Kinross-shire, 1966-74; Member, Perth and Kinross County Council, 1953-75; Chairman, Kinross County Council, 1963-73; Chairman and President, Board of Governors, East of Scotland College of Agriculture, 1970-83. Recreations: shooting; golf; the countryside. Address: (h.) Arndean, by Dollar, FK14 7NH; T.-07259 742527.

Stewart, Roger Alfred, MA, MBA, ACIS, MCIM. Commercial Manager, Edinburgh Healthcare NHS Trust, since 1994; Chairman, Scottish Health Service Income Generation Group, 1989-94; b. 13.10.48, London; m., Frances Abercromby; 2 d. Educ. St. Marylebone Grammar School, London; St. Andrews University; Union College, NY; Edinburgh University. Administrator, Scottish Special Housing Association, Edinburgh, 1973-75; Assistant Secretary, Queen Margaret College, Edinburgh, 1976-88; Commercial Manager, Lothian Health Board, 1989-94. Elected Member of Council, National Trust for Scotland, 1986-91. Address: (h.) 66 South Trinity Road, Edinburgh EH5 3NX; T.-0131-552 7467.

Stewart, Roger Black, MA (Hons), DipEd. Headteacher, Inveralmond Community High School, Livingston, since 1992; b. 21.10.45, Lochgelly; m., Anne; 3 d. Educ. Auchterderran Junior Secondary School; Dundee University; Open University. Electrician, 1961-74; Teacher and Principal Teacher, 1976-86; Divisional Education Officer, Caithness, 1986-92. Recreations: supporting Dunfermline Athletic and regretting it. Address: (h.) 13 Hermand Gardens, West Calder.

Stewart, William F., MA, DipEd, BA (Hons). Rector, Belmont Academy, Ayr, since 1975; b. 25.1.33, Dreghorn; m., Marion McMillan; 3 d. Educ. Irvine Royal Academy; Glasgow University. Irvine Royal Academy: Teacher (Maths), Special Assistant Teacher (Maths), Principal Assistant (Maths), Principal Teacher (Maths), Depute Rector. President, Headteachers Association of Scotland, 1989-90; Member, Ayr College Board of Management; Executive Member, Kyle and Carrick Sports Council; Member, UCCA Executive. Recreations: golf; bowling; curling. Address: (b.) Belmont Academy, Belmont Road, Ayr; T.-01292 281733.

Still, Ronald McKinnon, MB, ChB, FRCOG. Consultant Obstetrician and Gynaecologist, since 1967; Honorary Senior Clinical Lecturer, Glasgow University, since 1967; b. 20.3.32, Helensburgh; 1 s.; 2 d. Educ. Hermitage School, Helensburgh; Glasgow University. House Surgeon/House Physician, Royal Infirmary, Glasgow, 1956-57; Captain, RAMC, seconded Malaya Military Forces, 1957-60; Registrar, Queen Mother's Hospital/Stobhill General Hospital, Glasgow; Senior Registrar, Glasgow Teaching Hospitals. Recreations: golf; music. Address: (h.) 9/5 Whistlefield Court, 2 Canniesburn Road, Bearsden, Glasgow G61; T.-0141-942 3097.

Still, Rev. William. Minister, Gilcomston South Church, Aberdeen, since 1945; Chairman of Trustees, Rutherford House Study Centre, since 1981; b. 8.5.11, Aberdeen. Educ. Aberdeen University and Christ's College. Fish worker in family business; Teacher of music, pianoforte, singing, choral work; Cadet, Salvation Army College, London; Assistant Minister, Springburnhill Parish Church, Glasgow. President, Inter-Varsity Fellowship, 1975-76; President, local University Christian Union, on several occasions. Recreations: walking; music; gardening; art; architecture. Address: 18 Beaconsfield Place, Aberdeen; T.-Aberdeen 644037.

Stimson, Professor William Howard, BSc, PhD, CBiol, FIBiol, FRSE. Professor of Immunology and Head, Department of Immunology, Strathclyde University, since 1981; Research Director/Executive Director, Rhone-Poulenc Diagnostics Ltd., Glasgow; Director, Aquaculture Diagnostics Ltd., Glasgow; b. 2.11.43, Liverpool; m., Jean Scott Baird; 1 s.; 1 d. Educ. Prince of Wales School, Nairobi; St. Andrews University. Research Fellow, Department of Obstetrics and Gynaecology, Dundee University, 1970-72; Lecturer, then Senior Lecturer, Biochemistry Department, Strathclyde University, 1973-80. Patron, Scottish Motor Neurone Disease Association; holder, Glasgow Loving Cup, 1982-83; Member, Editorial Boards, five scientific journals. Recreations: mechanical engineering; walking; golf. Address: (b.) Department of Immunology, Strathclyde University, 31 Taylor Street, Glasgow G4 ONR; T.-0141-552 4400, Ext. 3729.

Stirling, George Scott, MB, ChB, FRCPGlas, FRCPsych, DPM. Former Medical Administrator, Crichton Royal Hospital, Dumfries; b. 20.4.26, Aberdeen; m., Yvonne; 1 s.; 1 d. Educ. Robert Gordon's College, Aberdeen; Aberdeen University. House Physician, Royal Cornhill Hospital, Aberdeen; Medical Branch, RAF; House Physician, Woodend General Hospital, Aberdeen; Fellow in Psychiatry, Crichton Royal, Dumfries; Past Chairman, Forensic Section, Scottish Division, Royal College of Psychiatrists; Council of Europe Travelling Fellow; former Vice-Chairman, SASD (Dumfries). Recreations: fishing; gardening. Address: (h.) Phyllis Park, Murraythwaite, Dalton, Lockberie DG11 1DW.

Stirling, Sheriff Hamish, MA, LLB. Sheriff of South Strathclyde Dumfries and Galloway, at Hamilton, since 1992; b. 9.7.38, Liverpool; m., Margaret Davidson Bottomley; 2 s.; 1 d. Educ. Liverpool College; Robert Gordon's College, Aberdeen; Aberdeen University. Solicitor, 1961-62; Procurator Fiscal Depute: Dundee, 1963-70, Borders, 1970-74, Glasgow, 1974-75; Advocate, 1975-92; Temporary Sheriff, 1987-92. Recreations: foreign travel; golf. Address: (b.) Sheriff Court House, Beckford Street, Hamilton ML3 6AA; T.-01698 282957.

Stirling of Garden, Col. James, CBE, TD, KStJ, BA, FRICS. Lord Lieutenant of Stirling and Falkirk, since 1983; Chartered Surveyor; b. 8.9.30; m., Fiona; 2 s.; 2 d. Educ. Rugby; Trinity College, Cambridge. Partner, Ryden and Partners, 1962-89; Director, Scottish Widows Life Assurance Society, since 1974; Director, Scottish Board, Woolwich Building Society, since 1976; President, ,Highland TAVRA, since 1990. Address: (h.) Garden, Buchlyvie, Stirlingshire.

Stirling, Robin Colin Baillie, OBE, JP; b. 6.4.25, Bo'ness; m., Jean R. Hendrie, MA. Educ. Dalziel High School, Motherwell. Editor: Motherwell Times, 1957-85, Motherwell Times Series, 1959-85. Former Secretary, Lanarkshire Branch, NUJ; elected Life Member, NUJ, 1985; Guild of British Newspaper Editors: former Scottish Secretary, Chairman, 1967-70; NCTJ: Member, Scottish Training Committee, 1961-85, Chairman, Scottish Committee, 1978-81. Convener, Motherwell Guild of Help, since 1953; Chairman, Strathclyde Police P Division Crime Prevention Panel, 1976-84; Member: Management Committee, Motherwell and Wishaw CAB, since 1971 (Chairman, 1978-80), Motherwell and District Christian Aid Committee 1970-82; Honorary Vice President: Motherwell ASC, since 1986, Motherwell CC, since 1985, Lanarkshire Little Theatre; President, Motherwell Probus Club, 1987-88; Founder Chairman, Motherwell and District Music Society (Chairman, 1984-93). Recreations: gardening; music (including jazz); steam locomotives; Motherwell FC; Scottish Opera; cinema organs. Address: (h.) 37 The Loaning, Motherwell ML1 3HE; T.-63762.

Stirling of Fairburn, Roderick William Kenneth, TD, JP. Lord Lieutenant, Ross and Cromarty and Skye and Lochalsh, since 1988; Landowner and Estate Manager; Member, Red Deer Commission, 1964-89; Chairman, Highland Region Valuation Appeal Committee, 1983-91; Chairman, Scottish Salmon and White Fish Co. Ltd., 1980-91; b. 17.6.32; m., Penelope Jane Wright; 4 d. Educ. Wellesley House; Harrow; Aberdeen University. National Service, Scots Guards, 1950-52 (commissioned, 1951); TA service, Seaforth and Queen's Own Highlanders, 1953-69 (retired with rank of Captain); Member, Regional Advisory Committee to Forestry Commission, 1964-85; Local Director, Eagle Star Insurance Co., 1966-85; Director, Moray Firth Salmon Fishing Co. Ltd., 1973-91; Member, Highland River Purification Board, 1975-90; Ross and Cromarty County Councillor, 1970-74 (Chairman of Highways, 1973-74); Member, Ross and Cromarty District Council, since 1984 (Vice-Chairman, Water and Leisure Services Committee); Ross and Cromarty Representative, Scottish Accident Prevention Council. Recreations: wild life management; gardening; curling. Address: (h.) Arcan, Muir of Ord, Ross-shire IV6 7UL; T.-01997 433207.

Stirrups, Professor David Robert, MSc, BA, BDS, FDS, DOrth(RCSEng), FDS, MOrth(RCPS) Glasgow. Professor of Orthodontics, Dundee University, since 1993; b. 23.6.48, Gillingham; m., Anne; 1 s.; 1 d. Educ. Gillingham Grammar School; Sheffield University. Senior Registrar, Northern Health Authority, 1977-80; Consultant Orthodontist, Greater Glasgow Health Board, 1980-93. Recreations: orienteering; mountain marathons; philately. Address: (b.) Dundee University, Dundee DD1 4HN; T.-01382 635961.

Stiven, Frederic William Binning, ARSA, MCSD, DA. Constructivist, Designer and Teacher; Head of Design, Grays School of Art, Aberdeen, 1982-87; b. 25.4.29, Cowdenbeath; m., Jenny Paton; 2 s.; 2 d. Trained Edinburgh College of Art. Constructivist work in numerous public and private collections; exhibited in Edinburgh, Glasgow, Leeds, London, Bergen, Helsinki, Venice and New York; freelance Designer. Address: (h.) Sheallagan, Golf Course Road, Rosemount, Blairgowrie, Perthshire; T.-01250 874863.

Stobie, David Henry, BSc, MSc, CEng, MIMechE, DMS, FIMgt. Head, Department of Management Studies, Napier University, since 1984; Chairman, Edinburgh Branch, British Institute of Management, 1988-91, Vice-President, since 1991; b. 21.10.41, Edinburgh; m., June Moffat; 1 s.; 1 d. Educ. Tynecastle Senior Secondary School, Edinburgh; Heriot-Watt University, Edinburgh. Production Planning Engineer, Ferranti Ltd., 1965; various line management positions, Hewlett-Packard Ltd., 1966-73; Works Manager, Hall and Hall Ltd., 1973-74; Senior Systems Analyst, Hewlett-Packard Ltd., 1974-75; joined Napier as Lecturer, 1975. Recreations: hill-walking; classical music; wine-tasting. Address: (b.) Napier Management Centre, Napier University, 66 Spylaw Road, Edinburgh EH10 5BR; T.-0131-455 5000.

Stobo, James, OBE, DL, FRAgS. Farmer; President, Animal Diseases Research Association, 1980-95; Chairman, The Moredun Foundation for Animal Health and Welfare, since 1994; Chairman of Governors, Longridge Towers School, since 1982; Chairman, Scottish Seed Potato Development Council, since 1988; Chairman, Moredun Animal Health Ltd.; b. 9.12.34, Lanark; m., Pamela Elizabeth Mary Herriot; 1 s.; 2 d. Educ. Edinburgh Academy. Farming, since 1951; Past Chairman and President, Scottish Association of Young Farmers Clubs; Member, Home-Grown Cereals Authority, 1971-76; President, National Farmers' Union of Scotland, 1973-74; Director, John Hogarth Ltd., Kelso Mills; Member, Secretary of State for Scotland's Panel of Agricultural Arbiters. Vice-President: Scottish National Fat Stock Club, Royal Smithfield Club; Deputy Lieutenant, County of Berwick, 1987. Recreations: game shooting; photography. Address: Nabdean, Berwick-upon-Tweed TD15 1SZ; T.-01289 386224.

Stockdale, Elizabeth Joan Noel, MB, ChB, DMRD, FRCR. Consultant Radiologist, Royal Aberdeen Children's Hospital and Aberdeen Royal Infirmary, since 1980; Clinical Senior Lecturer, Aberdeen University, since 1980; b. Chippenham; m., Christopher Leo Stockdale; 2 s.; 1 d. Educ. Aberdeen University. House Surgeon, Aberdeen Royal Infirmary; Senior House Surgeon, Professorial Surgical Unit, Hospital for Sick Children, Great Ormond Street; Registrar, St. George's Hospital; Senior Registrar, Royal National Orthopaedic Hospital, Royal Marsden Hospital, Atkinson Morley's Hospital. Recreations: theatre; classical music; travel. Address: (h.) 1 Grant Road, Banchory, Kincardineshire AB31 3UW; T.-013302 823096.

Stodart of Leaston, Rt. Hon. Lord (James Anthony Stodart), PC (1974); b. 6.6.16, Exeter; m., Hazel Usher. Educ. Wellington. MP (Conservative), Edinburgh West, 1959-74; Joint Under Secretary of State, Scottish Office, 1963-64; Parliamentary Secretary, later Minister of State, Ministry of Agriculture, Fisheries and Food, 1970-74; Chairman: Agricultural Credit Corporation Ltd., 1975-87, Committee of Enquiry into Local Government in Scotland, 1980, Manpower Review of Veterinary Profession in UK, 1984-85. Publication: Land of Abundance: a study of Scottish agriculture in the 20th century. Recreations: music; golf; preserving a sense of humour. Addresses: Lorimers, North Berwick; Leaston, Humbie, East Lothian.

Stoddart, Charles Norman, LLB, LLM, PhD, SSC. Sheriff of North Strathclyde at Paisley, since 1988; b. 4.4.48, Dunfermline; m., Anne Lees; 1 d. Educ. Dunfermline High School; Edinburgh University; McGill University. Private practice as Solicitor, 1972-73; Lecturer in Scots Law, Edinburgh University, 1973-80; private practice as Solicitor, 1980-88. Publications: The Law and Practice of Legal Aid in Scotland (Co-author); A Casebook on Scottish Criminal Law (Co-author); Cases and Materials on Scottish Criminal Procedure (Co-author); Criminal Warrants, 1991. Recreation: foreign travel. Address: (b.) Paisley Sheriff Court, 106 Renfrew Road, Paisley; T.-0141-887 5291.

Stone, Professor Frederick Hope, OBE, MB, ChB, FRCP, FRCPsych. Professor of Child and Adolescent Psychiatry, Glasgow University, 1977-86; Consultant Psychiatrist, Royal Hospital for Sick Children, Glasgow, since 1954; b. 11.9.21, Glasgow; m., Zelda Elston, MA; 2 s.; 1 d. Educ. Hillhead High School, Glasgow; Glasgow University. Acting Director, Lasker Mental Hygiene Clinic, Hadassah, Jerusalem, 1952-54; World Health Organisation Visiting Consultant, 1960, 1964; Member, Kilbrandon Committee, 1963-65; Secretary-General, International Association of Child Psychiatry, 1962-66; Member, Houghton Committee on Adoption, 1968-72; Chairman, Scottish Division, Royal College of Psychiatrists, 1981-84; President, Young Minds; Chairman, Strathclyde Children's Panel Advisory Committee, 1988-94. Publication: Child Psychiatry for Students (Co-author). Address: (h.) 14A Hamilton Avenue, Pollokshields, Glasgow, G41 4JF; T.-0141-427 0115.

Stone, Gordon Victor, MBChB, FFCM, MFCMI, DCM. General Manager, Highland Health Board, since 1994; b. 4.10.45, London; m., Aileen S. Wilson; 1 s.; 1 d. Educ. Aberdeen Grammar School; Aberdeen University; Edinburgh University. Medical Officer, RAF, 1970-75; Scottish Health Service Fellow in Community Medicine, 1975-78; Specialist in Community Medicine, Grampian Health Board, 1978-89; Chief Administrative Medical Officer/Director of Public Health Medicine, Highland Health Board, 1989-94. Recreations: golf; skiing. Address: (b.) Reay House, 17 Old Edinburgh Road, Inverness IV2 3HG; T.-01463 239851.

Stone, Sheriff Marcus, MA, LLB. Sheriff of Lothian and Borders, at Linlithgow, 1984-93; Accredited Mediator since 1994; b. 22.3.21, Glasgow; m., Jacqueline Barnoin; 3 s.; 2 d. Educ. High School of Glasgow; Glasgow University. Served Second World War; admitted Solicitor, 1949; admitted Faculty of Advocates, 1965; Sheriff of North Strathclyde, at Dumbarton, 1971-76; Sheriff of Glasgow and Strathkelvin, at Glasgow, 1976-84. Publications: Proof of Fact in Criminal Trials, 1984; Cross-examination in Criminal Trials, 1988; Fact-Finding for Magistrates, 1990. Recreations: swimming; music. Address: (b.) Advocates Library, Parliament House, Edinburgh.

Stone, Professor Trevor W., BPharm, PhD, DSc. Professor and Head of Pharmacology, Glasgow University, since 1989; b. 7.10.47, Mexborough; m., Anne Corina. Educ. Mexborough Grammar School; London University; Aberdeen University. Lecturer in Physiology, Aberdeen University, 1970-77; Senior Lecturer/Reader in Neuroscience, then Professor of Neuroscience, London University, 1977-86. Editor, British Journal of Pharmacology, 1980-86. Publications: Microiontophoresis and Pressure Ejection, 1985; Purines: Basic and Clinical Aspects, 1991. Recreations: photography; snooker; working. Address: (b.) Department of Pharmacology, Glasgow University, Glasgow G12; T.-0141-330 4481.

Storie, Roy G., MA (Hons), DipEd. Headteacher, Prestwick Academy, since 1987; b. 16.9.34, Edinburgh; m.; 1 s.; 1 d. Educ. Royal High School; Edinburgh University; Moray House College of Education. Address: (b.) Prestwick Academy, Newdykes Road, Prestwick KA9 2LB.

Stormonth Darling, Sir Jamie Carlisle, Kt, CBE, MC, TD, WS, LLB, MA, Hon. FRIAS, DUniv (Stirling), Hon. LLD (Aberdeen). Vice-President, Scottish Conservation Projects Trust (President, 1983-88); b. 8.7.18, Battle, Sussex; m., Mary Finella Gammell, BEM, DL; 1 s.; 2 d. Educ. Winchester College; Christ Church, Oxford; Edinburgh University. 2nd Lt., KOSB (Territorial), 1937; Adjutant, 1941, to Lt.-Col. Commanding 52nd (L) Division; Reconnaissance Regiment, RAC, 1945-46; studied law, Edinburgh University, 1946-49; appointed Chief Executive as Secretary, then Director, National Trust for Scotland, 1949-83, then Vice-President (Emeritus). Concerned with various Scottish charities such as Scotland's Churches Scheme (Vice Chairman, 1994), Scottish Churches Architectural Heritage Trust, Scotland's Gardens Scheme, Pollok Trust (Glasgow), Edinburgh Old Town Charitable Trust; Patron, The Woodland Trust, Edinburgh Green Belt Trust. Recreations: gardening; countryside; golf. Address: (h.) Chapelhill House, Dirleton, North Berwick EH39 5HG; T.-0162 085 296.

Stormonth Darling, Lady (Mary Finella), BEM, DL (East Lothian); b. 15.4.24, Farnborough; m., Sir Jamie Carlisle Stormonth Darling, qv; 1 s.; 2 d. Educ. Southover Manor School, Lewes; Architectural Association, London. Special Operations Executive (SOE), 1942-45. Designed own house, 1974; Elder, Dirleton Kirk and Convener, Fabric Committee, since 1976; Member, Church and Nation Committee, Church of Scotland, 1978-86; Convener, Sub-Committee on International Interests, 1982-84; Member, British Council of Churches, 1980-83; voluntary and charitable work. Recreations: painting, sculpting and gardening. Address: Chapelhill House, Dirleton, North Berwick EH39 5HG; T.-0162 085 296.

Stott, Rt. Hon. Lord (George Gordon Stott), PC (1964), QC (Scot), MA, LLB, DipEd; b. 22.12.09; m., Nancy Braggins; 1 s.; 1 d. Educ. Edinburgh Academy; Edinburgh University. Advocate, 1936; QC (Scot), 1950; Advocate Depute, 1947-51; Sheriff of Roxburgh, Berwick and Selkirk, 1961-64; Lord Advocate, 1964-67; Senator of the College of Justice, 1967-85. Publications: Lord Advocate's Diary, 1992; Editor, Edinburgh Clarion. Address: (h.) 12 Midmar Gardens, Edinburgh; T.-0131-447 4251.

Stoward, Professor Peter John, MA, MSc, DPhil, FInstBiol, DipRMS, FRSE. Professor of Histochemistry, Dundee University; b. 27.1.35, Birmingham; m., Barbara Essex Lewis (deceased); 1 d. Educ. King Edward's School, Birmingham; Oriel College, Oxford. Assistant Lecturer, University of Aston in Birmingham, 1958-61; Research Assistant, Department of Human Anatomy, Oxford University, 1961-63 and 1965-67; International Research Fellow, National Institutes of Health, Bethesda, Maryland, 1964, 1965; Lecturer, Nuffield Department of Orthopaedic Surgery, Oxford University, 1967-68; Senior Lecturer in Anatomy, Dundee University, 1968-75; Reader in Histology, Dundee University, 1975-89; Acting Head, Department of Anatomy, Dundee University, 1987-88; Head, Department of Anatomy, 1988-91; Visiting Professor, Pavia University, Italy, since 1980; Editor, Histochemical Journal, since 1967. Diocesan Reader, Scottish Episcopal Church. Publications: Histochemistry: The Widening Horizons (Co-author), 1981; Histochemistry of Secretary Processes (Co-author), 1977; Histochemistry: theoretical and applied, 4th ed., Vol. 3; Enzyme Histochemistry (Co-Editor), 1991. Recreations: sailing; walking; the performing arts; reading. Address: (b.) Department of Anatomy and Physiology, The University, Dundee, DD1 4HN; T.-01382 344212/344970.

Strachan, Professor Hew Francis Anthony, MA, PhD, FRHistS. Professor of Modern History, Glasgow University, since 1992; Life Fellow, Corpus Christi College, Cambridge, since 1992; b. 1.9.49, Edinburgh; m., Pamela Dorothy Tennant (née Symes); 1 s.; 1 step s.; 2 d.; 1 step d. Educ. Rugby School; Corpus Christi College, Cambridge. Senior Lecturer, Department of War Studies and International Affairs, Royal Military Academy, Sandhurst, 1978-79; Fellow, Corpus Christi College, Cambridge, since 1979: Tutor for Admissions, 1981-88, Director of Studies in History, 1986-92, Senior Tutor, 1987 and 1989-92. Governor, Rugby School, since 1985, and Stowe School, since 1990; Member, Council, Society for Army Historical Research, 1980-95, Army Records Society, 1990-94, Council, National Army Museum, since 1994; Joint Editor, War in History. Publications: British Military Uniforms; History of the Cambridge University Officers

Training Corps; European Armies and the Conduct of War; Wellington's Legacy: the Reform of the British Army 1830-54; From Waterloo to Balaclava: Tactics, Technology, and the British Army 1815-1854 (Templer Medal, 1986); numerous articles and reviews. Recreations: shooting; rugby fives; rugby football. Address: (b.) Department of Modern History, Glasgow University, Glasgow G12 8QQ; T.-0141-339 8855.

Strang, Gavin Steel, BSc (Hons), DipAgriSci, PhD. MP (Labour), East Edinburgh, since 1970; b. 10.7.43, Dundee; m., Bettina Smith; 1 s. Educ. Morrison's Academy, Crieff; Edinburgh University. Parliamentary Under Secretary of State, Department of Energy, February to October, 1974; Parliamentary Secretary, Ministry of Agriculture, 1974-79; Principal Labour Agriculture Spokesman, since 1992. Recreations: golf; swimming; the countryside. Address: (b.) House of Commons, Westminster, London; T.-0171-219 5155.

Strang Steel, Sir (Fiennes) Michael, 3rd Bt; b. 22.2.43; m., Sally Russell; 2 s.; 1 d. Educ. Eton. Retired Major, 17th/21st Lancers, 1962-80. Forestry Commissioner, since 1988; DL. Address: (h.) Philiphaugh, Selkirk, TD7 5LX.

Strang Steel, Malcolm Graham, BA (Cantab), LLB, WS. Partner, W. & J. Burness, WS, since 1973; Member, Council, Law Society of Scotland, 1984-90; Chairman, Scottish Dyslexia Trust; b. 24.11.46, Selkirk; m., Margaret Philippa Scott; 1 s.; 1 d. Educ. Eton; Trinity College, Cambridge; Edinburgh University. Sometime Chairman, Albyn Housing Society Ltd. Recreations: shooting; fishing; skiing; tennis; reading. Address: (b.) 16 Hope Street, Edinburgh EH2 4DD; T.-0131-226 2561.

Strathmore and Kinghorne, 18th Earl of (Michael Fergus Bowes Lyon); b. 7.6.57; m.; 3 s. President, Boys' Brigade, since 1994; DL, Angus, since 1993. Address: Glamis Castle, Forfar, DD8 1QJ.

Strathmore and Kinghorne, Mary, Countess of, DL. Deputy Lieutenant for Angus; b. 31.5.32, London; m., 17th Earl of Strathmore and Kinghorne (deceased); 1 s.; 2 d. Deputy Lieutenant. Address: (h.) c/o Glamis Castle, Forfar, Angus.

Straton, Timothy Duncan, TD, CA, ATII. Partner, Scott-Moncrieff, CA; Treasurer, Scottish Society for the Prevention of Cruelty to Animals; b. 1.10.42, Edinburgh; m., Gladys Margaret George; 1 s.; 1 d. Educ. Edinburgh Academy. Honorary Treasurer, Bruntsfield Links Golfing Society; National Treasurer, Royal British Legion Scotland; Major, AGC (SPS), TA. Recreations: TA; driving; photography; golf. Address: (b.) 17 Melville Street, Edinburgh EH3 7PH; T.-0131-226 6281.

Street, Margaret Dobson; b. 18.10.20, Hawick; m., Richard Andrew Rutherford Street (deceased); 2 s. Educ. Hawick High School; Alva Academy. Civil Servant, 1938-48; Ministry of Labour and National Service, 1938-47; Ministry of National Insurance (Inspectorate), 1947-48; voluntary work since 1948, apart from freelance writing on household and conservation topics; Honorary Secretary (Past Chairman), Leith Civic Trust; Convener, Friends of North Carr Lightship; Member, North East Fife District Council, North Carr Management Committee; Saltire Society Representative, Council, National Trust for Scotland; Secretary, Mungo Park Commemoration Committee; Trustee, Robert Hurd Memorial Fund; Appeal Convener, Wallace Statue, Lanark; Member, Steering Committee, Brownsbank; Appeal Convener, Wallace Statue, Dryburgh; Vice-Chairman, Saltire Society, 1983-94; Saltire Society's Andrew Fletcher of Saltoun Award for services to Scotland, 1992. Recreations: promotion of Scottish cultural activity; conservation; good cooking. Address: (h.) 115 Trinity Road, Edinburgh; T.-0131-552 2409.

Stretton, James, BA, FFA. Chief Executive (UK Operations), Standard Life Assurance Company, since 1994; b. 16.12.43, Peterborough; m., Isobel Robertson; 2 d. Educ. Laxton Grammar School, Oundle; Worcester College, Oxford. Joined Standard Life, 1965. Recreations: music; gardening; reading; golf. Address: (b.) 3 George Street, Edinburgh EH2 2XZ; T.-0131-225 2552.

Strong, Hilary. Director, Edinburgh Festival Fringe, since 1994; b. 3.6.57, Chichester. Educ. Chichester High School for Girls; Lombard School of Dancing, :Chichester; Avery Hill College of Education, London. Stage manager and actress, 1979-83; administration and PR, 1984-85; Administrator: Merlin Theatre, Frome, 1986-88, Natural Theatre Company, Bath, 1989-94; freelance lecturer and director, 1987-94. Member, Board of Directors, National Campaign for the Arts, 1991-93; Drama Adviser, Arts Council of England, 1991-94. Recreations: travel; cooking; dancing. Address: (b.) Festival Fringe Society Ltd., 180 High Street, Edinburgh, EH1 1QS; T.-0131-226 5257.

Struthers, Professor Allan David, BSc, MD, FRCP, FRCPG, FRCPE, FESC. Professor of Clinical Pharmacology, Dundee University, and Hon. Consultant Physician, since 1992; b. 14.8.52, Glasgow; m., Julia Elizabeth Anne Diggens; 1 s.; 1 d. Educ. Hutchesons' Grammar School, Glasgow; Glasgow University. Medical Registrar, University Department of Materia Medica, Stobhill Hospital, Glasgow; Senior Registrar, Royal Postgraduate Medical School, London. Address: (b.) Department of Clinical Pharmacology, Ninewells Hospital, Dundee; T.-01382 660111, Ext. 3181.

Stuart, Charles Murray. Chairman, Scottish Power PLC, since 1992; Chairman, Intermediate Capital Group, since 1993; b. 28.7.33, Gourock; m., Netta Caroline; 1 s.; 1 d. Educ. Glasgow Academy; Glasgow University. MB Group PLC (formerly Metal Box), 1981-90, latterly as Executive Chairman; Chief Executive, Berisford International plc, 1990-91. Recreations: sailing; ballet; theatre. Address: (b.) 1 Atlantic Quay, Glasgow G2 8SP; T.-0141-248 8200.

Stuart of Findhorn, 2nd Viscount (David Randolph Moray Stuart); b. 20.6.24; m.; 2 s.; 3 d. Address: Findhorn, Forres, IV36 0YE.

Stuart, Michael John, BSc (Hons), FRSA. Headteacher, Kincorth Avenue, since 1990; b. 24.11.46, Fraserburgh; m., Daniele Madeleine; 2 s.; 1 d. Educ. Fraserburgh Academy; Aberdeen University. Assistant Teacher, Fraserburgh Academy, 1970-71; Kelvinside Academy, Glasgow, 1971-72; Principal Teacher, Greenwood Academy, Irvine, 1972-81; Assistant Head Teacher, Loudoun Academy, Galston, 1981-89; Depute Head Teacher, Carrick Academy, Maybole, 1989-90. Recreations: golf; angling; hill-walking. Address: (b.) Kincorth Academy, Kincorth Circle, Aberdeen, AB1 5NL; T.-01224 872881.

Stubbs, Ian Michael, LLB, CA, FTII. Partner, Maclay Murray & Spens, Solicitors, since 1973; b. 14.11.43, Birmingham; m., Joan Baird Crowther; 2 s.; 1 d. Educ. Marr College, Troon; Glasgow University. Thomson McLintock, Glasgow, 1965-68; Apprentice/Assistant, Maclay Murray & Spens, 1968-73. Council Member, Institute of Chartered Accountants of Scotland, 1986-92; Past Chairman, Board of Examiners, Law Society of Scotland; Senior Tutor, Wills Trusts and Executries, Glasgow University, 1980-86. Address: (h.) Suffolk Lodge, Methven Road, Whitecraigs, Glasgow, G46; T.-0141-639 6580.

Sturgeon, David, BL. Registrar and Deputy Secretary, Heriot-Watt University, since 1967; b. 10.12.35, Kilwinning; m., Nancy McDougall; 1 d.; 2 s. Educ. Dalry High School, Ayrshire (Blair Medallist, 1950); Glasgow University. National Service (RASC - War Office), 1957-

59; Trainee Actuary, Scottish Widows Fund, 1959-61; Administrative Assistant, Royal College of Science and Technology (later, Strathclyde University), 1961-67. Secretary and Treasurer, Edinburgh Society of Glasgow University Graduates, since 1971. Recreations: golf; music (particularly Scottish country dance music). Address: (h.) 10 Dalhousie Road, Eskbank, Midlothian EH22 3AS; T.-0131-663 1059.

Sturrock, Professor Robert Ralph, MB, ChB, DSc. Professor of Anatomy, Dundee University, since 1992; b. 1.7.43, Dundee; m., Norma Duncan; 1 d. Educ. Dundee High School; St. Andrews University. House Surgeon, Perth Royal Infirmary, 1967-68; House Physician, Stirling Royal Infirmary, 1968; Demonstrator, then Lecturer, Anatomy Department, Dundee University, 1968-77; Visiting Associate Professor of Neuroanatomy, Iowa University, 1976; Senior Lecturer, Dundee, 1977-81, Reader in Anatomy, 1981-92. Symington Memorial Prize in Anatomy, 1978. Recreations: reading; running; swimming; hill-walking. Address: (h.) 6 Albany Terrace, Dundee; T.-01382 223578.

Sturrock, Professor Roger Davidson, MB, BS, MRCS, MD, FRCPLond, FRCPGlas. McLeod/ARC Professor of Rheumatology, Glasgow University, since 1990; b. 20.10.46, Dundee; m., Helen; 3 d. Educ. Llanelli Boys' Grammar School; Queen Mary's School, Basingstoke; London University. Senior Lecturer and Hon. Consultant, Westminster Medical School, 1977-79; Senior Lecturer in Medicine and Hon. Consultant, Centre for Rheumatic Diseases, Glasgow Royal Infirmary, 1979-90. Recreations: hill-walking; music; choral singing. Address: (b.) University Department of Medicine, Royal Infirmary, Glasgow G31 2ER; T.-0141-304 4687.

Subak-Sharpe, Professor John Herbert, CBE, FInstBiol, BSc, PhD, FRSE. Professor Emeritus, Glasgow University and Honorary Senior Research Fellow in Virology, since 1994; Professor of Virology, Glasgow University, 1968-94; Honorary Director, MRC Virology Unit, Institute of Virology, Glasgow, 1968-94; b. 14.2.24, Vienna; m., Barbara Naomi Morris; 2 s.; 1 d. Educ. Humanistisches Gymnasium, Vienna; Birmingham University. Assistant Lecturer, Glasgow University, 1954-56; Member, ARC scientific staff, AVRI Pirbright, 1956-61; Visiting Fellow, California Institute of Technology, 1961; Member, MRC Experimental Virus Unit scientific staff, Glasgow, 1961-68; Visiting Professor, NIH, Bethesda, 1967-68. Visiting Fellow, Clare Hall, Cambridge, 1986; elected Member (Past Chairman, Course and Workshops Committee), EMBO, since 1969; Trustee (former Secretary and Vice-President), Genetical Society, since 1971; Chairman, MRC Training Awards Panel, 1986-89; Member, Governing Body, West of Scotland Oncological Organisation, since 1974, and Governing Body, Animal Virus Research Institute, Pirbright, 1986-88; Member, Scientific Advisory Group, Equine Virology Research Foundation, since 1987; Member, Medical Research Council Cell Biology and Disorders Board, 1988-92; Biochemical Society CIBA Medal and Prize, 1994. Recreations: travel; bridge. Address: (h.) 63 Kelvin Court, Glasgow G12 0AG; T.-0141-339 1863.

Suckling, Professor Colin James, BSc, PhD, DSc, CChem, FRSC, FRSA, FRSE. Professor of Chemistry, Strathclyde University, since 1984 (Dean, Faculty of Science, 1992-96); b. 24.3.47, Birkenhead; m., Catherine Mary Faulkner; 2 s.; 1 d. Educ. Quarry Bank High School, Liverpool; Liverpool University. Lecturer, Department of Pure and Applied Chemistry, Strathclyde University, 1972; Royal Society Smith and Nephew Senior Research Fellow, 1980. Convener, RSE Chemistry Committee, 1989-91; Member of Council, RSE, 1989-92; Member, General Teaching Council, 1993-95; Member, Board, City of Glasgow Philharmonic Orchestra. Publications: Chemistry

Through Models (Co-author), 1978; Biological Chemistry (Co-author), 1980; Enzyme Chemistry, Impact and Applications (Co-author), 1984, 1989. Recreations: music; horn playing. Address: (b.) Department of Pure and Applied Chemistry, Strathclyde Universtiy, 295 Cathedral Street Glasgow, G1 1XL; T.-0141-552 4400.

Suckling, David E., JP, CBiol, MIBiol. Member, Scottish Borders Council, 1995; Convener, Tweeddale District Council, 1992-95; Member of Staff, Macaulay Land Use Research Institue, 1967-95; b. 6.4.43, New Quay, Dyfed; m., Anne E. Robertson; 1 s.; 1 d. Educ. Dulwich College. District Council 1988; Board Member, Garvald Home Farm, since 1989; Board Member, Scottish Museums Council, since 1991, Vice-Chair, since 1992; Chairman, West Linton Community Council, 1986-91; West Linton Whipman, 1987; President, Whipman Play, since 1992. Recreations: gardening; walking; MGBs, reading. Address: (h.) The Dean, West Linton, Peeblesshire EH46 7AU.

Sugden, Chris, BA. Rector, Buckie High School; b. 25.5.46, Paignton; m., Lynne; 1 s.; 1 d. Educ. Newcastle upon Tyne University. Gordonstoun School, Moray; Castlebrae High School, Edinburgh; Knox Academy, Haddington; Harlaw Academy, Aberdeen. Recreations: exploration and outdoor activities. Address: (b.) Buckie High School, West Cathcart Street, Buckie AB56 1QB; T.-Buckie 832605.

Sugden, Professor David Edward, MA, DPhil. Professor, Department of Geography, Edinburgh University, since 1987; b. 5.3.41, Paignton; m., Britta Valborg Stridsberg; 2 s.; 1 d. Educ. Warwick School; Jesus College, Oxford. Scientific Officer, British Antarctic Survey, 1965-66; Lecturer/Reader, Department of Geography, Aberdeen University, 1966-86. Recreations: hill-walking; gardening; squash. Address: (b.) Department of Geography, Edinburgh University, Edinburgh EH8; T.-0131-650 2521.

Sullivan, John, BA, MA. Senior Lecturer in Russian, St. Andrews University, and Chairman of Department, since 1990; b. 2.11.37, Sheffield; m., Veronica Margaret Jones; 2 s.; 1 d. Educ. Firth Park Grammar School, Sheffield; Manchester University; Moscow University; Linacre College, Oxford. Lecturer in Russian, St. Andrews University, 1964-83. Publications include: An Unpublished Religious Songbook of Mid Eighteenth Century Russia; Russian Love Songs in the Early Eighteenth Century, three volumes. Recreations: golf; ornithology. Address: (h.) Thorncroft, 1 Hepburn Gardens, St. Andrews, Fife; T.-01334 472614.

Summerhayes, Peter Frank, CEng, FIEE, MCIT. Operations and Engineering Director, ScotRail, since 1994; b. 1.4.44, Walmer; m., Kathleen. Educ. Borough Polytechnic. Joined B.R. as student apprentice. Recreations: caravanning; rambling; DIY; reading. Address: (b.) Caledonian Chambers, Union Street, Glasgow; T.-041-335 4389.

Surber, Elizabeth, MA (Hons). Headmistress, Laurel Bank School, Glasgow, since 1995; b. 10.5.54, Kingston upon Thames. Educ. Tiffin Girls' School, Kingston upon Thames; Exeter University; Oxford University. Teacher of French, Hadleigh High School, 1976-77; Lectrice, Universite de Haute, Bretagne, 1977-78; Teacher of French, Tiffin Girls' School, Kingston upon Thames, 1979-82, Cheltenham Ladies' College, 1982-88; Second Deputy Headmistress, Bedford High School, 1988-94. Recreations: ballet; walking; travel. Address: (b.) Laurel Bank School, 4 Lilybank Terrace, Glasgow, G12 8RX.

Sutherland, C.J.M., QC, LLB (Hons); b. 20.5.54. Advocate, 1977; Treasurer, Faculty of Advocates, since 1994. Address: (b.) Advocates' Library, Parliament House, Edinburgh, EH1 1RF.

Sutherland, David George Carr, CBE, MC and bar, TD. Landowner and Farmer, since 1962; Consultant, Control Risks Group Ltd., since 1985; b. 2.10.20, London; m., 1, Jean Henderson; 2, Christine Hotchkiss; 1 s.; 2 d. Educ. Eton; Sandhurst. War Service, Black Watch and Special Air Service Regiment, Dunkirk, Western Desert, Aegean, Adriatic; wounded; mentioned in Despatches; Greek War Cross; command and staff appointments, 1945-55, including British Military Mission to Greece, instructor at Sandhurst, Gold Staff Officer at The Queen's Coronation; retired from the Army, 1955; Ministry of Defence, 1955-80; commanded 21 SAS Regiment, Artists Rifles, TA, 1956-60; Deputy Lieutenant for Tweeddale, since 1974; Non-Executive Director, Asset Protection International Ltd., 1981-85. Member, Queen's Bodyguard for Scotland, Royal Company of Archers, since 1949; Fellow, Royal Geographical Society. Recreations: fishing; shooting; walking. Address: Ferniehaugh, Dolphinton, West Linton; T.-Dolphinton 82257.

Sutherland, David I.M., MA, MEd, FIMgt, FRSA. Registrar, The General Teaching Council for Scotland, since 1985; b. 22.1.38, Wick; m., Janet H. Webster; 2 s. Educ. Aberdeen Grammar School; Aberdeen University; University of Zurich. Teacher of Modern Languages, Aberdeen Grammar School, 1962-66; Lecturer in Education, Stranmillis College of Education, Belfast, 1966-69; Lecturer in Educational Psychology, Craigie College of Education, Ayr, 1969-72; Assistant Director of Education, Sutherland County Council, 1972-75; Divisional Education Officer (Inverness), then Depute Director of Education, Highland Regional Council, 1975-85. Assessor, Committee of Scottish Higher Education Principals (Teacher Education Committee); Member: Scottish Education Department Planning Group on Teacher Supply, Scottish Association for Educational Management and Administration, Council, British Educational Management and Administration Society, Board, Commonwealth Council for Educational Administration, Standing Conference on Studies in Education, Scottish Educational Research Association, Professional Advisory Committee to Department of Education, Stirling University; Associate Member: Association of Directors of Education in Scotland; Consultant, National Board for Nursing, Midwifery and Health Visiting for Scotland. Recreations: golf; walking; theatre; reading. Address: (b.) 5 Royal Terrace, Edinburgh EH7 5AF; T.-0131-556 0072.

Sutherland, Donald Gilmour, CA. Regional Managing Partner — South, Ernst & Young, since 1990; b. 15.4.40, Edinburgh; m., Linda Malone; 2 s.; 1 d. Educ. George Watson's College. Joined Brown Fleming & Murray, London, 1963; Partner, Whinney Murray & Co., Glasgow, 1968, Edinburgh, 1974; Managing Partner, Ernst & Whinney, Edinburgh, 1985; Regional Managing Partner, 1987; Director, Murray Johnstone Ltd., Murray International Trust plc, Murray Income plc, Murray Smaller Markets Trust plc, 1987-89; Regional Managing Partner — North, Ernst & Young, 1989-90; Director, Standard Life Assurance Company, since 1990; Vice-Chairman, Governing Council, George Watson's College. Recreations: conservation; golf; antiques. Address: (b.) Ten George Street, Edinburgh EH2 2DZ; T.-0131-226 6400.

Sutherland, Elizabeth (Elizabeth Margaret Marshall), FSA Scot. Writer; b. 24.8.26, Kemback, Cupar; m., Rev. John D. Marshall; 2 s.; 1 d. Educ. St. Leonard's Girls' School, St. Andrews; Edinburgh University. Social Worker for Scottish Episcopal Church, 1974-80; Curator, Groam House Museum, Rosemarkie, 1982-93; author of: Lent Term (Constable Trophy), 1973, The Seer of Kintail, 1974, Hannah Hereafter (Scottish Arts Council Book Award), 1976, The Eye of God, 1977, The Weeping Tree, 1980, Ravens and Black Rain: The Story of Highland Second Sight, 1985, The Gold Key and The Green Life, 1986; In Search of the Picts, 1994. Recreations: Highland history;

Gaelic language; the Picts; walking. Address: (h.) 17 Mackenzie Terrace, Rosemarkie, Ross-shire IV10 8UH; T.-Fortrose 620924.

Sutherland, Countess of (Elizabeth Millicent Sutherland). Chief of Clan Sutherland; b. 30.3.21; m., Charles Noel Janson; 2 s.; 1 s. (deceased); 1 d. Educ. Queen's College, London; abroad. Land Army, 1939-41; Laboratory Technician, Inverness and London, 1941-45. Address: (h.) Dunrobin Castle, Sutherland; House of Tongue, Lairg, Sutherland.

Sutherland, George O., CA, FIMgt. Director of Finance, Edinburgh University, since 1994; b. 5.11.44, Dundee; m., Jane; 1 s.; 3 d. Educ. Morgan Academy; St.Andrews University. TA, 1962-72. Shell International Petroleum Co. Ltd., 1969-92; organised and led expeditions in Sahara desert and Borneo jungle, the latter identifying historically significant aircraft wrecks. Recreations: military and aviation history; battlefields; flying; water-sports; a young family; an old Morgan sports car. Address: (b.) Old College, South Bridge, Edinburgh, EH8 9YL; T.-0131-650 2182.

Sutherland, Ian Douglas, FRICS. Managing Partner, D.M. Hall & Son, Chartered Surveyors, since 1975 (joined as Trainee Surveyor, 1965); b. 23.10.45, Colombo, Ceylon; m., Kathryn Wallace; 1 s.; 1 d. Educ. St. Bees School, Cumberland. Member, Company of Merchants of the City of Edinburgh. Address: (b.) 36 Melville Street, Edinburgh EH3 7HA; T.-0131-225 3631.

Sutherland, James, CBE (1974), MA, LLB, LLD. McClure Naismith Anderson & Gardiner, Solicitors, Glasgow, Edinburgh and London (Partner, 1951-87, Consultant, 1987-90); b. 15.2.20; m., 1, Elizabeth Kelly Barr; 2 s.; 2, Grace Williamson Dawson. Educ. Queens Park Secondary School, Glasgow; Glasgow University. Royal Signals, 1940-46; Examiner in Scots Law, 1951-55, and Mercantile Law and Industrial Law, 1968-69, Glasgow University; Chairman, Glasgow South National Insurance Tribunal, 1964-66; Member, Board of Management, Glasgow Maternity and Women's Hospitals, 1964-74 (Chairman, 1966-74); Council Member, Law Society of Scotland, 1959-77 (Vice-President, 1969-70, President, 1972-74); Council Member, International Bar Association, since 1972 (Chairman, General Practice Section, 1978-80, Secretary General, 1980-84, President, 1984-86); Vice-Chairman, Glasgow Eastern Health Council, 1975-77; Council Member, General Dental Council, 1975-89; Deacon, Incorporation of Barbers, Glasgow, 1962-65; Dean, Royal Faculty of Procurators in Glasgow, 1977-80; Member, Court, Strathclyde University, 1977-92. Recreation: golf. Address: (h.) Greenacres, 20/1 Easter Belmont Road, Edinburgh EH12 6EX; T.-0131-337 1888.

Sutherland, Margaret Helen. Rector, Dornoch Academy, 1989-94; b. 15.11.28. Educ. Wishaw High School; West of Scotland Agricultural College; Jordanhill College of Education. Lecturer, Cumberland/Westmorland Farm School; Assistant Teacher of Science, West Lothian; Depute Head, Beauly Secondary School; Head Teacher, Farr Secondary School, Bettyhill. Founder President, Soroptimist International of Easter Ross; Past Chairman, Ross and Cromarty Conservative Association. Recreations: golf; gardening; Soroptimists; charity work. Address: (h.) Runachloie, Drummuie Terrace, Golspie, Sutherland.

Sutherland, Hon. Lord (Ranald Iain Sutherland), QC (Scot). Senator of the College of Justice, since 1985; b. 23.1.32. Advocate Depute, 1962-64, 1971-77; QC (Scot), 1969.

Sutherland, Sinclair Stewart, MB, ChB, DPM, FRCPsych. Consultant Psychiatrist, Lanarkshire Health Board, since 1985; Physician Superintendent, Hartwood

Hospital, Shotts, since 1985; b. 4.1.30, Carluke; m., 1, Margaret Helen Christina Strachan; 3 s.; 2, Dr. Alice Andries; 1 s. Educ. Wishaw High School; Aberdeen University. General Practitioner, Shetland Isles and Aberdeenshire, 1957-60; Psychiatry trainee posts, North Eastern Regional Hospital Board, 1960-65; Research Fellow in Psychiatry, Harvard University, 1964; Consultant Psychiatrist, Greater Glasgow Health Board, Deputy Physician Superintendent, Woodilee and Stoneyetts Hospitals, Glasgow, and Honorary Clinical Lecturer, Glasgow University, 1966-85. Worked with Scottish and Glasgow Marriage Guidance Councils, since 1972; Group Discussion Leader, Lanarkshire MGC, since 1986; Chairman, Lanarkshire MGC, 1990. Recreations: golf; motor cycling; clarinet. Address: (h.) Meadow Cottage, 32 Dunlop Street, Strathaven ML10 6LA.

Sutherland, Professor Sir Stewart Ross, KBE, FBA, FRSE, MA. Principal and Vice-Chancellor, Edinburgh University, since 1994; b. 25.2.41, Aberdeen; m., Sheena Robertson; 1 s.; 2 d. Educ. Robert Gordon's College; Aberdeen University; Cambridge University. Assistant Lecturer, Philosophy, UCNW, 1965-68; Lecturer, Senior Lecturer, Reader, Stirling University, 1968-77; Professor, Philosophy of Religion, King's College, London, 1977-90 (Vice-Principal, 1981-85, Principal, 1985-90); Vice-Chancellor, London University, 1990-94, and HM Chief Inspector of Schools (England), 1992-94; Visiting Fellow, Australian National University, 1974; Chairman, Brit. Acad. Postgraduate Studentships, 1987-94; Member, Council for Science and Technology, since 1993; Editor, Religious Studies, 1984-90; Chairman, Secretary of State's Committee on Appeal Procedures, since 1994; Chairman, Royal Institute of Philosophy, since 1988; President, Society for Study of Theology, 1985, 1986. Publications: several books and papers. Recreations: jazz; theatre; rough gardening. Address: (b.) Edinburgh University, Old College, South Bridge, EH8 9YL; T.-0131-650 2150.

Sutherland, Sir William George MacKenzie, Kt. (1988), QPM. Chief Constable, Lothian and Borders Police, since 1983; b. 12.11.33, Inverness; m., Jennie Abbott; 2 d. Educ. Inverness Technical High School. Cheshire Police, 1954-73; Surrey Police, 1973-75; Hertfordshire Police, 1975-79; Chief Constable, Bedfordshire Police, 1979-83. Recreations: squash; hill-walking. Address: (b.) Police Headquarters, Fettes Avenue, Edinburgh, EH4 1RB; T.-0131-311 3131.

Sutherland, William James, IPFA, FCMA. Group Financial Controller, Scottish Power plc, since 1990; b. 10.6.35, Glasgow; m., Fiona Mackay Begg; 3 s.; 1 d. Educ. Victoria Drive Senior Secondary School, Glasgow; Strathclyde University. Glasgow Corporation, 1952-61; Depute Town Chamberlain, Burgh of Bearsden, 1961-64; Town Chamberlain: Burgh of Bishopbriggs, 1964-68, Burgh of Cumbernauld, 1968-75; Depute Director of Finance, Strathclyde Regional Council, 1975-82; Chief Financial Officer, South of Scotland Electricity Board, 1982-90. Recreations: golf; table tennis. Address: (b.) Scottish Power plc, 75 Waterloo Street, Glasgow G2 7BD.

Sutor, Margaret H.D., MA. Director of Tourism, Ayrshire Tourist Board, since 1991; b. 21.5.56, Glasgow. Educ. Girvan Academy; Glasgow University. Tourism Department, Kyle and Carrick District Council, 1979-82; Assistant Tourist Officer, then Marketing and Administration Officer, Ayrshire and Burns Country Tourist Board, 1982-91. Recreations: tennis; badminton. Address: (b.) Burns House, Burns Statue Square, Ayr KA7 1UP; T.-01292 262555.

Sutter, Art. Broadcaster; b. 27.8.41, Airdrie; m., Janette; 2 d. Educ. Airdrie Academy. Studied piano/organ/voice; most of career spent in Scotch whisky industry (sales); Presenter, BBC Radio Scotland, 1985-93; chatshow, Grampian TV, since 1989. Recreations: golf; badminton; gardening.

Suttie, James Michael Peter, MRTPI. Director of Planning and Development, Banff and Buchan District Council, since 1980; b. 24.3.48, Arbroath; m., Sylvia; 1 s.; 2 d. Educ. Dundee High School; Duncan of Jordanstone College of Art, Dundee. Principal Planning Officer, Dundee Corporation, 1973-75; Principal Planning Assistant, Tayside Regional Council, 1975; Chief Assistant Planning Officer, Fife Regional Council, 1975-80. Recreations: golf; hill-walking; orienteering; driving. Address: (b.) Town House, Low Street, Banff; T.-01261 812521.

Sutton, Ann. Director, Scottish Adoption Association. Address: (b.) 2 Commercial Street, Edinburgh, EH6 6JA.

Swaffield, Professor John Arthur, BSc, MPhil, PhD, CEng, MRAeS, FIWEM, MCIBSE. Professor of Building Services Engineering, Heriot-Watt University, Edinburgh, since 1985; b. 4.3.43, Aberystwyth; m., Jean Winnan; 2 d. Educ. Ardwyn Grammar School, Aberystwyth; Bristol University. Research Fellow, Mechanical Engineering Department, City University, London, 1966-70; Deputy Head, Systems Laboratory, British Aircraft Corporation, Filton, Bristol, 1970-72; Senior Lecturer, South Bank Polytechnic, 1972-74; Lecturer and Senior Lecturer, Department of Building Technology, Brunel University, 1974-83; Reader in Mechanical Engineering, Brunel University, 1983-85; Dean of Engineering, Heriot-Watt University, 1990-93. Recreations: skiing; hill-walking; cinema; political/military history. Address: (b.) Department of Building, Heriot-Watt University, Riccarton, Edinburgh EH14 4AS; T.-0131-449 5111.

Swanson, Alexander James Grenville, MB, ChB, FRCS Edin. Consultant Orthopaedic Surgeon, since 1980; Acting Head, Department of Orthopaedic Surgery, Dundee University, 1986-88; b. 18.10.41, Ecclefechan; 2 s. Educ. Dingwall Academy; St. Andrews University. Postgraduate training: St. Andrews, 1967-68, Edinburgh, 1968-69, Glasgow, 1969-70, Edinburgh, 1970-74, Dunfermline, 1974-75; Lecturer, then Senior Lecturer and Honorary Consultant, Dundee University, 1975-83. Recreations: downhill skiing; cross-country skiing; travel. Address: (b.) Department of Orthopaedic and Traumatic Surgery, Royal Infirmary, Dundee DD1 9ND; T.-01382 660111.

Swanson, Kenneth M., BSc, PhD, JP, DL. Farmer; Assistant Director, Technology, Dounreay Nuclear Power Development Establishment, 1986-91; b. 14.2.30, Canisbay, Caithness; m., Elspeth J.W. Paton; 2 s.; 1 d. Educ. Wick High School; St. Andrews University. Flying Officer, Pilot, RAF, 1952; Lecturer in Physics, University of Wales, 1955; joined UKAEA, Dounreay, on Fast Reactors, 1958; appointed JP, 1970; DL, Caithness, 1977; Chairman, Caithness Jobs Commission, 1988; Director, Caithness and Sutherland Local Enterprise Company, 1990 (Vice-Chairman, 1994); Member, N.W. Board, Scottish Natural Heritage, 1992; author of papers and patents on the development of plutonium fuels for electricity production. Address: Knockglass, Westfield, Thurso; T.-0184 787 1201.

Swanston, Professor Michael Timothy, MA (Cantab), PhD. Professor, University of Abertay, Dundee, since 1995; Reader in Psychology, since 1984; b. 6.6.47, Bristol; m., Georgina Mary; 1 s.; 2 d. Educ. Rugby School; Cambridge University (Pembroke College). Psychologist, Army Personnel Research Establishment, 1969-72; Lecturer in Psychology, Dundee Institute of Technology, 1972-84; Honorary Rersearch Fellow, Dundee university, since 1989. Publications: one book; 40 papers. Recreations: golf; gardening. Address: (b.) University of Abertay, Bell Street, Dundee, DD1 1HG; T.-01382 308462.

Swapp, George David, OBE, DL, MA (Hons), DipEd. Deputy Lieutenant, Kincardineshire, since 1990; Member, Grampian Regional Council, since 1986; Member Aberdeenshire Council, since 1995; b. 25.5.31, Labuan (of

Aberdeen parents); m., Eva Jane MacNab; 2 s.; 2 d. Educ. Mackie Academy, Stonehaven; Aberdeen University. RAF Staff College, graduate and directing staff, 1965-68; Ministry of Defence (Training Policy), 1971-74 and 1978-80; promoted Wing Commander, 1971; Board Chairman, RAF Officer and Aircrew Selection Centre, 1974-78; Head, RAF Officer Training Establishment, Bracknell, 1980-83; retired from RAF, 1983. Member, North East River Purification Board; President, Stonehaven Branch, Royal British Legion; founder Member, Stonehaven Heritage Society; Chairman, Stonehaven Harbour Committee; Church Elder. Recreations: hill-walking; local history; geography; protection and enhancement of amenities and woodlands. Address: (h.) 9 Urie Crescent, Stonehaven AB3 2DY; T.-Stonehaven 764124.

Sweeney, Sister Dorothea, MA (Hons), BA(Soc) (Hons), PhD. Vice Principal, St. Andrew's College, since 1985; b. Glasgow. Educ. Notre Dame High School, Glasgow; Glasgow University; Notre Dame College of Education; Bedford College and LSE, London University; Strathclyde University. Assistant Teacher of English, Our Lady & St. Francis Secondary School, Glasgow, 1960-63; entered Congregation of Sisters of Notre Dame, Sussex, 1963; Assistant Teacher of English, Notre Dame High School, London, 1966-67; Notre Dame College of Education: Lecturer, Department of Psychology, 1970-76, Senior Lecturer, Department of Educational Science, 1976-80, Assistant Principal, 1980-85. Member, Board of Governors, St. Andrew's College, since 1980; Member, CNAA Inservice Education Board, 1982-87, Committee for Teacher Education, 1987-89, and Committee for Scotland, 1990-92; Member, National Inter-College Committee for Educational Research, 1982-89; Convener, School Boards, Headteacher Training, Steering Committee, 1988-89; School Boards Members Training, 1989-90; Training Consultant, National Staff Development & Appraisal Training, 1991-92; Myers-Briggs Qualified Trainer, since 1990; part-time Counsellor, since 1968. Recreations: creative writing; dance; music; art; sport; drama; technology. Address: (b.) St. Andrew's College of Education, 6 Duntocher Road, Bearsden, Glasgow G61 4QA; T.-0141-943 1424.

Sweeney, Patrick, MA (Hons). Head Teacher, Holy Rood High School, Edinburgh, since 1994; b. 13.4.49, Wanlockhead; m., May. Educ. Blairs College, Aberdeen; Glasgow University. Taught French and Latin in various schools, 1973-85; Assistant Head Teacher, St. Augustine's High School, Edinburgh, 1985-88; on staff of Quality Assurance Division, Lothian Regional Council, 1988-94, as Co-ordinator of Lothian TVEI Project and then Regional Adviser. Recreations: travel; squash; poor golf; The Herald newspaper; books of all descriptions. Address: (h.) 9 Wheatland Drive, Lanark, ML11 7QG.

Swinfen, Professor David Berridge, MA, DPhil, FRHistS. Professor of Commonwealth History, Dundee University, since 1990 (Head, Department of Modern History, 1988-92, Deputy Principal, 1992-94, Vice Principal, 1994); b. 8.11.36, Kirkcaldy; m., Ann Pettit; 2 s.; 3 d. Educ. Fettes College, Edinburgh; Hertford College, Oxford. Assistant Lecturer in Modern History, then Lecturer, Queen's College, Dundee, 1963-75; Director, School of American Studies, Dundee University, 1970-85; Senior Lecturer, Modern History, Dundee University, 1975-90. Recreation: music. Address: (h.) 14 Cedar Road, Broughty Ferry, Dundee, DD5 3BB; T.-01382 776496.

Swinton, Major General Sir John, KCVO, OBE, JP. Lord Lieutenant, Berwickshire, since 1989; President, Royal Highland and Agricultural Society of Scotland, 1993-94; Brigadier, Queen's Bodyguard for Scotland (Royal Company of Archers), since 1977; President, Borders Branch, SSAFA, since 1993; Council Member, Commonwealth Ex-Services League, since 1984; Vice

Chairman, Scottish National War Memorial, since 1988; Chairman, Berwickshire Civic Society, since 1982; Trustee, Cairn Housing Association, since 1989; President, Lowland TA & VRA, since 1992; Chairman, St. Abbs Head National Nature Reserve Joint Management Committee, since 1991; b. 21.4.25, London; m., Judith Balfour Killen; 3 s.; 1 d. Educ. Harrow School. Enlisted Scots Guards, 1943; commissioned, 1944; served NW Europe (twice wounded); Malaya, 1948-51 (Despatches); ADC to Field Marshal Sir William Slim, Governor General of Australia, 1953-54; Regimental Adjutant, Scots Guards, 1960-62; Adjutant, RMA, Sandhurst, 1962-64; comd. 2nd Bn., Scots Guards, 1966-68; Lt.-Col. commanding Scots Guards, 1970-71; Commander, 4th Guards Armoured Brigade, BAOR, 1972-73; Brigadier, Lowlands and Commander, Edinburgh and Glasgow Garrisons, 1975-76; GOC London District and Major General comd. Household Division, 1976-79. Honorary Colonel, 2nd Bn., 52nd Lowland Volunteers, 1983-90; National Chairman, Royal British Legion Scotland, 1986-89; Coordinator for Scotland, Duke of Edinburgh's Award 25th Anniversary Appeal, 1980 (Honorary Liaison Officer for the Borders, 1983-85); Chairman, Roxburgh and Berwickshire Conservative Association, 1983-85; Chairman, Thirlestane Castle Trust, 1984-90; Trustee, Army Museums Ogilby Trust, 1978-91; Member, Central Advisory Committee on War Pensions, 1986-89. Address: (h.) Kimmerghame, Duns, Berwickshire; T.-01361 883277.

Sword, Ian Pollock, BSc, PhD, CChem, FRSC, FBIM. Chairman, Inveresk Research International, since 1979; Director, Inveresk Clinical Research, since 1988; Director, SGS UK Holding Ltd., since 1989; Senior Executive Vice President, SGS Geneva, since 1994; Member, Medical Research Council, since 1994; b. 6.3.42, Kilmarnock; m., Flora Collins; 2 s.; 1 d. Educ. Coatbridge High School; Glasgow University. Princeton University, New Jersey, 1967-69; Oxford University, 1969-70; Huntingdon Research Centre, 1970-73; Inveresk Research International, since 1973. Publications: editor of two books; scientific papers. Recreations: music; golf. Address: (b.) Inveresk Research International Ltd., Tranent EH33 2NE; T.-01875 614545.

Symington, Rev. Alastair Henderson, MA, BD. Minister, New Kilpatrick Parish Church, Bearsden, since 1985; b. 15.4.47, Edinburgh; m., Eileen Margaret Jenkins; 2 d. Educ. Daniel Stewart's College, Edinburgh; Edinburgh University; Tubingen University, West Germany. Assistant Minister, Wellington Church, Glasgow, 1971-72; Chaplain, RAF, 1972-76; Minister, Craiglockhart Parish Church, Edinburgh, 1976-85. Contributor, Scottish Liturgical Review. Publications: Westminster Church Sermons, 1984; Reader's Digest Family Guide to the Bible (Co-author), 1985; For God's Sake, Ask!, 1993. Recreations: golf; rugby; music; computing. Address: 51 Manse Road, Bearsden, Glasgow G61 3PN; T.-0141-942 0035.

T

Tait, A. Margaret, BSc. Vice Convenor, General Council, University of Edinburgh Business Committee; Member, St. Margaret's Chapel Guild; Lay Member, Lothian Medical Ethics Committee; Member, Lothian Health Council; Executive Member, British Federation of University Women; b. 8.10.44, Edinburgh; m., J. Haldane Tait; 1 s.; 1 d. Educ. George Watson's Ladies' College, Edinburgh; Edinburgh University; Jordanhill College of Education. Teacher of Mathematics, Bellahouston Academy, Glasgow; former Member, Lothian Children's Panel; former Secretary, Scottish Association of Children's Panels; former Chairman, Dean House Children's Home, Edinburgh; Volunteer, Edinburgh Citizens' Advice Bureau; former Member, Edinburgh Youth Orchestra Committee; formerly Secretary of State's Nominee to General Teaching Council; former Member, Scottish Legal Aid Board. Recreations: golf; music; country walks; speaking in Spanish; entertaining. Address: (h.) 6 Ravelston House Park, Edinburgh EH4 3LU; T.-0131-332 6795.

Tait, Professor Elizabeth Joyce, BSc, PhD, FRSA, MIEEM. Deputy Director, Research and Advisory Services, Scottish Natural Heritage; Visiting Professor, Centre for Technology Strategy, Open University; b. 19.2.38, Edinburgh; m., Alex. D. Tait; 1 s.; 2 d. Educ. Glasgow High School for Girls; Glasgow University; Royal College of Science and Technology. Lecturer and Senior Lecturer, Open University, 1979-91 (Director, Centre for Technology Strategy, 1990-91); Professor, Environmental and Technology Management, Strathclyde University, 1991-92. Address: (b.) Scottish Natural Heritage, 2 Anderson Place, Edinburgh EH6 5NP; T.-0131-446 2403.

Tait, Eric, MBE, BSc (Eng), MPhil.International Executive Director, Pannell, Kerr, Forster, since 1989; b. 10.1.45, Edinburgh; m., Jane; 1 s.; 1 d. Educ. George Heriot's School; London University; Royal Military Academy, Sandhurst; Cambridge University. Commissioned, 2nd Lt., Royal Engineers, 1965; mentioned in Despatches; GSO3 HQ 39 Infantry Brigade, 1976; student, Advanced Staff Course, RAF Staff College, Bracknell, 1977; GSO2 SD HQ1 (BR) Corps, 1977-79; Officer Commanding 7 Field Squadron, RE, 1979-81; Lt. Col., 1982; Directing Staff, Staff College, Camberley, 1982; retired from active list, 1983. Member, Executive, Scottish Council (Development and Industry), 1984-89; Secretary, Institute of Chartered Accountants of Scotland, 1984-89. Chairman, European Advisory Forum, University of Nottingham and Trent. Recreations: swimming; hill-walking; reading. Address: (b.) 16 Rothesay Place, Edinburgh EH3 7SQ; T.-0131-225 3688.

Tait, Emeritus Professor Eric Alexander, BSc. Honorary Sheriff, Kincardine and Deeside, since 1983; Emeritus Professor, Aberdeen University; b. 26.2.22, Edinburgh; m., Margaret Anna Rowter (deceased); 2 s.; 2 d. Educ. King Alfred's Grammar School, Wantage; Aberdeen University. War Service, 1940-46 (Captain, Royal Artillery); student, 1946-50; Colonial Service, Geological Survey, Nigeria, 1950-61 (Principal Geologist); Department of Geology and Mineralogy, Aberdeen University, 1961-82 (Professor and Head of Department, 1972-82). Member, Stonehaven Town Council, 1965-71; Chairman, Stonehaven Community Council, 1975-78; Chairman, Mackie Academy School Council, 1975-82; Vice-Chairman, Kincardine and Deeside Conservative Association, 1975-91; Director, Kincardine and Deeside Branch, British Red Cross Society, 1981-91; Member, Grampian Health Board, 1983-91. Recreations: travel; reading. Address: (h.) Hingston, 83B Cameron Street, Stonehaven AB3 2HF; T.-01569 62872.

Tait, Rev. Thomas William, BD, RAFVR (Rtd). Parish Minister, Rattray, Blairgowrie, since 1972; Chairman, Tayside Health Council, since 1992; b. 11.11.31, Dunfermline; m., Irene Pope; 1 s.; 2 d. Educ. Dunfermline High School; St. Colm's College, Edinburgh; Edinburgh University; Christ's College, Aberdeen; Aberdeen University. HQ Staff, Boys' Brigade, 1954-61; Missionary, Church of Scotland, South Arabia, 1962-67; ordained and inducted, 1972; Member, Assembly Council, 1984-88; Chaplain, 2519 (Strathmore) Squadron, Air Training Corps, since 1974; Chairman, Blairgowrie Schools Council, 1975-89; Member, Perth and Kinross Health Council, 1980-91 (Chairman, 1984-91); Chairman, Blairgowrie and District Branch, Royal British Legion Scotland, and Chaplain, Angus and Perthshire Area; commissioned RAFVR, 1977 (retired Flt. Lt., 1988); Member, Secretary of State's Consultative Panel on Registration of Nursing Homes and Private Hospitals, since 1993; Member, Tayside Health Board Quality Monitoring Team, since 1993. Recreations: encouraging others to work in voluntary organisations; swimming; reading; overseas travel. Address: Manse of Rattray, Blairgowrie, Perthshire; T.-01250 872462.

Tankel, Henry I., OBE, MD, FRCSEdin, FRCSGlas. Surgeon, Southern General Hospital, Glasgow, 1962-91; Chairman, Glasgow Board of Jewish Education, 1985-90; b. 14.1.26, Glasgow; m., Judith Woolfson; 2 s.; 2 d. Educ. High School of Glasgow; Glasgow University. Fulbright Scholar, 1954-55; President, Glasgow Jewish Representative Council, 1974-77; Chairman, Glasgow Hospital Medical Services Committee, 1974-79; Board of Science and Education, 1978-81; President, United Synagogues of Scotland, 1978-85; Treasurer, Scottish Committee for Hospital Medical Services, 1978-91; Member, National Panel of Specialists, 1978-82 and 1987-91; invited to address General Assembly of Church of Scotland, 1984; Chairman, Scottish Joint Consultants Committee, 1989-92; Member, Scottish Health Service Advisory Council, 1989-93; Non-Executive Director, Southern General Hospital NHS Trust, since 1993. Recreations: walking; making model boats. Address: (h.) 26 Dalziel Drive, Glasgow G41 4PU; T.-0141-423 5830.

Tannahill, Andrew James, MB, ChB, MSc, FFPHM, MHSM. General Manager, Health Education Board for Scotland, since 1991; Honorary Senior Lecturer, Department of Epidemiology and Public Health, University of Dundee, since 1993; Honorary Fellow, Department of Public Health Sciences, University of Edinburgh, since 1994; b. 28.4.54, Inchinnan; m., Carol Elizabeth Fyfe. Educ. John Neilson Institution, Paisley; Glasgow University; Edinburgh University. Lecturer in Pathology, Glasgow University; Senior Registrar in Community Medicine, Lothian Health Board/Honorary Clinical Tutor, Edinburgh University; Regional Specialist in Community Medicine, East Anglian Regional Health Authority/Associate Lecturer, Cambridge University; Senior Lecturer in Public Health Medicine, Glasgow University/Honorary Consultant in Public Health Medicine, Greater Glasgow Health Board. Publications: Health Promotion: Models and Values (Co-author); contributor to Health Promotion: Disciplines and Diversity; papers on health education, prevention and health promotion. Recreations: countryside and bird-watching; music; theatre; photography; drawing and painting; reading (especially humour). Address: (b.) Health Education Board for Scotland, Woodburn House, Canaan Lane, Edinburgh EH10 4SG; T.-0131-447 8044.

Tasker, George Leith, CA. Senior Partner, Bird, Simpson & Co., CA, Dundee; b. 28.9.30, Dundee; m., Norma Croll; 3 d. Educ. Morgan Academy, Dundee; Cambridge University. CA training, 1947-53; National Service, RAF, 1953-55; commissioned into RAF Intelligence as interpreter (Russian); Qualified Assistant, Norman J. Bird & Co., CA, 1955-57 (became Partner, 1957, Senior Partner, 1979); Council Member, Institute of Chartered Accountants of Scotland, 1982-88. Treasurer, Dundee Chamber Music

Club; Elder, Church of Scotland; Governor, Duncan of Jordanstone College of Art, Dundee, 1988-92; President, Boys' Brigade, Dundee Bn. Recreations: music; theatre; travel abroad; art; fishing. Address: (h.) Hammersrang, Pitroddie, Perthshire PH2 7RJ; T.-01821 670 279.

Tate, Professor Austin, BA (Hons), PhD, CEng, MBCS, FBIS. Technical Director, AIAI (Artificial Intelligence Applications Institute), since 1985; Chair in Knowledge-Based Systems, Edinburgh University, since 1995; b. 12.5.51, Knottingley; m., Margaret. Educ. King's School, Pontefract; Lancaster University; Edinburgh University. Member, European Space Agency Expert Advisory Group on Informatics and Automation; elected Fellow, American Association of Artificial Intelligence, since 1993. Recreations: skiing; theme parks; graphic art. Address: (b.) AIAI, Edinburgh University, 80 South Bridge, Edinburgh EH1 1HN; T.-0131-650 2732.

Tavener, Alan, MA, ARCO, ARCM. Director of Music, Strathclyde University, since 1980; Artistic Director, Cappella Nova, since 1982; b. 22.4.57, Weston-Super-Mare; m., Rebecca Jane Gibson. Educ. City of Bath Boys' School; Brasenose College, Oxford. Conducted several world premieres of choral works and several CDs of early and contemporary music. Recreations: architecture; exhibitions; Scottish country dancing; food and drink. Address: (b.) Strathclyde University, Livingstone Tower, Richmond Street, Glasgow G1 1XH; T.-0141-552 4400, Ext. 3444.

Taylor, Anthony Edward, BA, IPFA. Director of Finance, Fife Regional Council, since 1987; b. 13.4.43; m., Joan Elizabeth; 3 s. (2 by pr. m.); 1 d. Educ. Cowbridge Grammar School, Glamorgan; University College of Wales, Aberystwyth. Research Officer, Lancashire and Merseyside Industrial Development Association, 1966-68; Economist, Cardiff City Council, 1968-70; Assistant Chief Accountant, then Head of Economics Unit, Brighton County Borough Council, 1970-74; Chief Budget Officer, Brighton Borough Council, 1974-79; Assistant Director of Finance, Sandwell Metropolitan Borough Council, 1979-82; Senior Depute Director of Finance, Tayside Regional Council, 1982-87. Council Member, CIPFA; Past Chairman, CIPFA Scottish Branch; Chairman, CIPFA Scottish Weekend School; Member, Local Government Finance Working Party; Adviser, Scottish Local Authority Management Centre. Recreations: history; castles; gardening; golf; philately. Address: (b.) North Street, Glenrothes, Fife; T.-01592 754411.

Taylor, Brian, MA (Hons). Political Editor, BBC Television, Scotland, since 1990; b. 9.1.55, Dundee; m., Pamela Moira Niven; 2 s. Educ. High School of Dundee; St. Andrews University. Reporter, Press and Journal, Aberdeen, 1977-80; Lobby Correspondent, Thomson Regional Newspapers, Westminster, 1980-85; Reporter, BBC Scotland, Glasgow, 1985-86; Co-Presenter, Left, Right and Centre, BBC Scotland, 1986-88; Political Correspondent, BBC Scotland, 1988-90. Recreations: golf; theatre. Address: (b.) BBC Scotland, Queen Margaret Drive, Glasgow G12 8DG.

Taylor, Charles Edwin, CBE, BSc, PhD, FRSE, FIBiol. Director, Scottish Crop Research Institute, 1972-86; President, Association of Applied Biologists, 1989; NATO Senior Research Fellow, Istituto di Nematologia Agraria CNR, Bari, Italy; b. 11.9.23, Oystermouth; 1 d. Educ. Cardiff High School; University College, Cardiff. Pilot, RAF, 1943-46; Lecturer in Applied Zoology, Nottingham University School of Agriculture, 1949-56; Senior Entomologist, Federation of Rhodesia and Nyasaland, 1956-59; Head, Zoology Section, Scottish Horticultural Research Institute, 1959-72. President, European Society of Nematologists, 1980-84; Editor, Nematologica, since 1990. Address: (b.) Westcroft, Longforgan, Dundee DD2 5EX; T.-0182 622 243.

Taylor, David Alexander, LLB (Hons), MSc, MBA. Director, Scottish Trade International, since 1994; Chairman, Scottish Development Overseas Ltd.; Director, Trade Development Centre Ltd.; b. 14.3.54, Forfar; m., Catherine Taylor; 2 s. Educ. Dundee High School; Edinburgh University; Strathclyde University. Senior Solicitor, City of Glasgow Council, 1979-84; SDA, 1985-91; Head of Consumer Products, Scottish Enterprise, 1991-94 (also part-time Tutor, Open University). Recreations: all sports. Address: (b.) 123 Bothwell Street, Glasgow, G2 7JP; T.-0141-228 2747.

Taylor, Elizabeth (Liz) Dewar, MA (Hons). Journalist and Author; b. 25.4.31, Newport, Fife; m., Adam McNeill Taylor (deceased); 1 s.; 3 d. Educ. Morgan Academy, Dundee; Galashiels Academy; King's College, Aberdeen. Reporter, Edinburgh Evening Dispatch, 1954-56; freelance stringer, Bombay, 1960-65; freelance journalist and broadcaster, since 1971. Publications include: Living with Loss; Bringing Up Children On Your Own; Living Alone; The Writing Business; 20th Century Antiques; also several books as Elisabeth McNeill. Recreations: gardening; crossword puzzles; bridge; Scrabble; cinema; horse-racing. Address: (h.) Cairnhill, Newstead, Melrose TD6 9DX; T.-0189682 2972.

Taylor, Rev. Howard, BSc (Hons), BD (Hons). Minister, St. David's Church, Knightswood, Glasgow, since 1986; Part-time Lecturer in Apologetics, Glasgow Bible College, since 1989; b. 6.6.44, Stockport; m., Eleanor Clark; 3 s. Educ. Gravesend Technical School, Kent; Nottingham University; Edinburgh University. Maths and Physics Teacher, Malawi University; Missionary in Malawi (minister of town and rural African churches, theological teacher, teacher of African languages to missionaries); Minister, Toward and Innellan Churches, Argyll. Publications: Faith Seeks Understanding, 1980; Pray Today 1982/83, 1982; In Christ All Things Hold Together; World Hope in the Middle East; The Delusion of Unbelief in a Scientific Age; Faith and Understanding; Israel — People of God; The Uniqueness of Christ in a Pluralist World, 1994; Is the New Testament the Source of Anti-Semitism, 1994. Recreations: hill walking; reading; classical music. Address: 60 Southbrae Drive, Glasgow G13 1QD; T.-0141-959 2904.

Taylor, Rev. Ian, BSc, MA, LTh, DipEd. Minister, Abdie & Dunbog and Newburgh, since 1983; b. 12.10.32, Dundee; m., Joy Coupar, LRAM; 2 s.; 1 d. Educ. Dundee High School; St. Andrews University; Durham University; Sheffield University; Edinburgh University. Teacher, Mathematics Department, Dundee High School; Lecturer in Mathematics, Bretton Hall College of Education; Senior Lecturer in Education, College of Ripon and York St. John; Assistant Minister, St. Giles' Cathedral, Edinburgh. Secretary, History of Education Society, 1968-73; extensive work in adult education (appreciation of music and the arts); Director, Summer Schools in Music, St. Andrews University; numerous courses for St. Andrews, Edinburgh and Hull Universities and WEA; has played principal roles in opera and operetta; Producer, Gilbert and Sullivan Society of Edinburgh, 1979-87; compiled Theatre Music Quiz series, Radio Tay; presented own operetta, My Dear Gilbert...My Dear Sullivan, BBC; Writer of revues and documentary plays with music, including Tragic Queen (Mary Queen of Scots), St. Giles' Cathedral, Edinburgh Festival Fringe, 1982, and John Knox (Church of Scotland Video). Publications: How to Produce Concert Versions of Gilbert Sullivan; The Gilbert and Sullivan Quiz Book; The Opera Lover's Quiz Book. Address: The Manse, Cupar Road, Newburgh, Fife KY14 6HA; T.-01337 840275.

Taylor, James Bradley. Chief Executive, Northern Lighthouse Board, since 1993; b. 12.8.45, Paisley; m., Elizabeth Sherwood. Educ. George Watson's College, Edinburgh; Britannia Royal Naval College; Defence School of Languages; Royal College of Defence Studies. Royal Navy, 1963-93; commanded HM submarines: Grampus, 1974-75, Orpheus, 1975-77, Spartan, 1980-82, HM ship London, 1989-90; Chief of Staff, Submarine Flotilla, 1990-91; Royal College of Defence Studies, 1992. Recreations: shooting; stalking; history; classic cars. Address: (b.) 84 George Street, Edinburgh, EH2 3DA; T.-0131-226 7051.

Taylor, Rev. John Henry Bindon, MA, BD, DipEd. Chairman, Forum on Scottish Education, since 1989; Vice-President, Christian Education Movewment (Scotland), since 1990; b. 4.11.26, Swansea; m., Jean Taylor, MBE; 3 s.; 1 d. Educ. Swansea Grammar School; Worcester College, Oxford; Glasgow University. Minister, Lincluden, Cumfries, 1952-56; St. Mary's, Woolston, Southampton, 1956-60; St. Andrew's, Irvine, 1960-69; Teacher, Ravenspark Academy, Irvine, 1969 (Assistant Rector, 1974); Depute Rector, Garnock Academy, 1978; Rector, Auchenharvie Academy, Stevenston, 1980, till retirement, 1989; Convener, Scottish Examination Board Panel on Religious Studies, 1982-88; Convener, Church of Scotland Education Committee, 1989-95. Recreations: walking; railway history. Address: (h.) 62 Woodlands Grove, Kilmarnock; T.-01563 526698.

Taylor, Rt. Rev. John Mitchell, MA. Bishop of Glasgow and Galloway; b. 23.5.32, Aberdeen; m., Edna Elizabeth Maitland; 1 s.; 1 d. Educ. Banff Academy; Aberdeen University; Theological College, Edinburgh. Curate, St. Margaret's, Aberdeen; Rector: Holy Cross, Knightswood, Glasgow, St. Ninian's, Pollokshields, Glasgow, St. John the Evangelist, Dumfries; Canon, St. Mary's Cathedral, Glasgow. Recreations: angling; hill-walking; sketching; music. Address: Bishop's House, 25 Quadrant Road, Glasgow G43 2QP.

Taylor, John Murray, MA, DipEd, MIM, FRSA. Principal, Clackmannan College, since 1987; b. 18.7.42; m., Katie Forsyth; 2 d. Educ. Banchory Academy; Aberdeen University. Teacher, Dunfermline High School, 1965-70; Principal Teacher of Classics, Kirkcudbright, Liberton, Callander, 1970-78; Assistant Director of Education, Central Region, 1978-87. Recreations: music; cycling; skiing; railways; DX radio. Address: (b.) Clackmannan College of Further Education, Branshill Road, Alloa FK10 3BT; T.-01259 215121.

Taylor, Joseph Healy, Convener, West Lothian Council, since 1995; b. 13.10.36, Fauldhouse; m., Mary Anna Welsh; 2 s.; 3 d. Educ. St. Mary's Senior Secondary School, Bathgate; Falkirk Technical College. Councillor, Midlothian, 1965-74; West Lothian District, 1992-95 (Depute Leader, Labour Group); JP, 1977-95. Recreations: walking; reading; football. Address: (b.) Sidlaw House, Livingston; T.-01506 445903.

Taylor, Rt. Rev. Maurice, STD. Bishop of Galloway, since 1981; b. 5.5.26, Hamilton. Educ. St. Aloysius College, Glasgow; Our Lady's High School, Motherwell; Pontifical Gregorian University, Rome. Royal Army Medical Corps, UK, India, Egypt, 1944-47; Assistant Priest: St. Bartholomew's, Coatbridge, 1951-52, St. Bernadette's, Motherwell, 1954-55; Lecturer, St. Peter's College, Cardross, 1955-65; Rector, Royal Scots College, Spain, 1965-74; Parish Priest, Our Lady of Lourdes, East Kilbride, 1974-81. Episcopal Secretary, Bishops' Conference of Scotland; Vice President, Catholic Institute for International Relations; Vice-Chairman, Episcopal Board, International Commission on English in the Liturgy. Publications: The Scots College in Spain, 1971; Guatemala, A Bishop's Journey, 1991; El Salvador: Portrait of a Parish, 1992; Opening Our Lives to the Saviour (Co-Author), 1995. Address: 8 Corsehill Road, Ayr KA7 2ST; T.-01292 266750.

Taylor, Michael Alan, BA, MSc, MEd, PhD. Principal and Chief Executive, Edinburgh's Telford College, since 1985;

b. 22.12.45, London; m., Maureen Brown. Educ. Sir George Monoux Grammar School, Walthamstow; Middlesex Polytechnic; Lancaster University; Liverpool University; Keele University. Teacher, London secondary schools, 1968-71; Lecturer, Chorley College of Education, 1971-73; Senior and Principal Lecturer, Ulster Polytechnic, 1973-76; Head, School of Social Sciences and Dean, North East Wales Institute of Higher Education, 1976-82 (Director, Institute of Health Education); Depute Principal, Telford College, 1982-84. Recreations: mountaineering; canoeing; skiing; cycling. Address: (b.) Telford College of Further Education, Crewe Toll, Edinburgh EH4 2NZ; T.-0131-332 2491.

Taylor, Michael George, MA (Hons). Headmaster, Austin Friars School, since 1994; b. 22.2.43, Coleraine; m., Eileen Forde; 1 s.; 2 d. Educ. St. Aloysius' College, Glasgow; Glasgow University. Head, History Department, St. Conval's High School, Cumnock, 1970-71; Head, History Department, then Assistant Rector, St. Andrew's Academy, Saltcoats, 1971-81; seconded to Chief Executive's Department, Strathclyde Regional Council, 1981-82; Rector, St. Joseph's College, Dumfries, 1982-94. President, Ayrshire History Teachers' Association, 1978-81; Member, Catholic Education Commission, 1984-87 and since 1989; Vice-Convener, Scottish Parent Teacher Council; Vice Chairman/Chairman, Dumfries Schools' Council, 1987-88; Hon. President: St. Joseph's College Past Pupils' Association, St. Joseph's College Parents' and Friends' Association. Recreations: reading; education; historical research. Address: (h.) 10 Rotchell Park, Dumfries DG2 7RH; T.-01387 253674.

Taylor, Michael Thomas, MA, MEd. Rector, Dyce Academy, Aberdeen, since 1980; b. 17.2.47, Newcastle upon Tyne; m., Sheena Robertson; 1 s.; 2 d. Educ. Rutherford Grammar School, Newcastle upon Tyne; Trinity College, Cambridge; Aberdeen University. Teacher of Chemistry, Cannock Grammar School, 1969-75; Ellon Academy: Principal Teacher of Guidance, 1975-76, Assistant Head Teacher, 1977-78, Depute Rector, 1978-80. Secretary, Newmachar Community Council; Chairman, Ellon Hillwalking Club. Recreations: hill-walking; music. Address: (h.) Loch-An-Eilan, Newmachar, Aberdeen; T.-01651 862234.

Taylor, Paul Doyle, MA, MEd. Rector, Linlathen High School, Dundee, since 1994; b. 27.9.43, Bognor Regis; m., Jean; 1 s.; 1 d. Educ. Chichester High School for Boys; Edinburgh University; University of Manitoba; Stirling University. Teaching English in Canada, 1968-69; Teacher of History, Edinburgh, 1969-74; Principal Teacher of History, Edinburgh and Livingston, 1974-83, Assistant Head Teacher, 1983-89; Deputy Head Teacher, Edinburgh, 1989-94. Recreations: hill-walking; gardening; bird-watching. Address: (b.) Linlathen High School, Forfar Road, Dundee, DD4 8AX; T.-01382 455824.

Taylor, Peter Bruce, MB, ChB, FRCA. Consultant Anaesthetist, since 1979; Honorary Senior Lecturer in Anaesthesia, Dundee University, since 1979; b. 30.6.44, Newcastle-upon-Tyne; m.; 1 s.; 1 d. Educ. Aberdeen Grammar School; Aberdeen University. Short Service commission, RAF, 1968-74; Anaesthetic Registrar, Aberdeen Royal Infirmary, 1974-75; Anaesthetic Senior Registrar, Nottingham AHA, 1976-79; Instructor in Anaesthesia, Michigan University Hospital, 1977-78. Linkman (Tayside), Association of Anaesthetists of GB and Ireland; President, North East of Scotland Society of Anaesthetists, 1995-96; Senior Life Master, Scottish Bridge Union. Recreations: duplicate bridge; reading; philately (specialist in Machin definitives). Address: (b.) Anaesthetic Department, Ninewells Hospital, Dundee, DD1 9SY; T.-Dundee 660111, Ext. 2475.

Taylor, Ronald Shaw, BA. Chief Executive, Aberdeen Enterprise Trust, since 1994; Managing Director, Parklands

Ltd., since 1993; b. 15.2.59, Dumfries; m., Moira Margaret; 2 s.; 1 d. Educ. Buckie High School; Robert Gordon's University. Graduate Trainee, Unigate PLC, 1981-84; Partner, C.B. Milne, newsagents, 1984-91; Chief Executive, Moray Enterprise Trust, 1991-94. Recreations: fly fishing; skiing. Address: (h.) Bernera, 85 West Church Street, Buckie, AB56 1AY; T.-01542 832650.

Taylor, Professor Samuel Sorby Brittain, BA, PhD. Professor of French, St. Andrews University, 1977-95; b. 20.9.30, Dore and Totley, Derbyshire; m., Agnes McCreadie Ewan; 2 d. Educ. High Storrs Grammar School, Sheffield; Birmingham University; Paris University. Royal Navy, 1956-68 (Sub Lt., RNVR); Personnel Research Officer, Dunlop Rubber Co., 1958-60; Institut et Musee Voltaire, Geneva, 1960-63; St. Andrews University: Lecturer, 1963, Reader, 1972, Personal Chair, 1977; Chairman, National Council for Modern Languages, 1981-85; Member, Executive Committee, Complete Works of Voltaire, 1970-85; Project Leader, Inter-University French Language Teaching Research and Development Project, 1980-88; Director, Nuffield Foundation project (French for science students), 1991-94; Chairman, Scottish Joint Working Party for Standard Grade in Modern Languages, 1982-84. Recreations: athletics timekeeping; photography. Address: (h.) 11 Irvine Crescent, St. Andrews KY16 8LG; T.-01334 472588.

Taylor of Gryfe, Lord (Thomas Johnston Taylor), Hon. LLD (Strathclyde); b. 27.4.12, Glasgow; m., Isobel. Educ. Bellahouston Academy. Member, Board, Scottish Television, 1968-83; Director: Whiteaway Laidlaw (Bankers), since 1971, Friends Provident, 1972-83, Scottish Metropolitan Property, 1972-88; Member, International Advisory Board, Morgan Grenfell, 1972-88; Chairman, Forestry Commission, 1967-72; Chairman, Economic Forestry, 1972-82; Chairman, Scottish Railways Board, 1969-80; Chairman, Wolfson Trust (Scotland), since 1975; Trustee, Dulverton Trust, since 1979; Chairman, Scottish Peers Association, 1988; Chairman, All-Party Parliamentary Group on Forestry; Commander Order of merit — Federal Republic of Germany. Recreation: golf. Address: (h.) 33 Seagate, Kingsbarns, Fife KY16 8SR; T.- 0133 488 430.

Taylor, William Gordon, MA, DipTP, MRTPI, FBIM, FIIM. Director, Economic Development and Planning, Fife Regional Council, since 1985; b. 13.2.43, Edinburgh; m., Margaret Frances Carrick McKinnon; 1 s.; 1 d. Educ. George Watson's College; Edinburgh University; Heriot-Watt University. Planning Assistant, Edinburgh Corporation; Area Planning Officer, Fife County Council; Assistant City Planning Officer, Dundee Corporation; Depute Planning Officer, then Director of Economic Development and Planning, Fife Regional Council. Board Member, Fife Enterprise Company; Past Chairman, Scottish Society of Directors of Planning; Advisor, EEC Environment Directorate; Advisor on industry and the environment, WHO; External Examiner, Dundee University. Recreations: golf; walking; music; current affairs. Address: (h.) Langdale, 55 Main Street, Dairsie, Fife KY15 4SR; T.-01334 870503.

Teasdale, Professor Graham Michael, MB, BS, MRCP, FRCSEdin, FRCSGlas. Professor and Head, Department of Neurosurgery, Glasgow University, since 1981; Consultant Neurosurgeon, Institute of Neurological Sciences, Glasgow, since 1975; b. 23.9.40, Spennymoor; m.; 3 s. Educ. Johnston Grammar School, Durham; Durham University. Postgraduate clinical training, Newcastle-upon-Tyne, London and Birmingham, 1963-69; Assistant Lecturer in Anatomy, Glasgow University, 1969-71; specialist training in surgery and neurosurgery, Southern General Hospital, Glasgow, 1971-75; Senior Lecturer, then Reader in Neurosurgery, Glasgow University, 1975-81. Editor, Society of British Neurosurgeons. Publication: The

Management of Head Injuries. Recreations: hill-walking; inshore fishing. Address: (b.) University Department of Neurosurgery, Institute of Neurological Sciences, Southern General Hospital, Glasgow; T.-0141-445 2466.

Tedford, Professor David John, BSc, PhD, ScD, ARCST, CEng, FIEE, SMIEEE, CPhys, FInstP, FRSE, FRSA, Order of Merit of Poland. Professor of Electrical Engineering (Foundation Chair), Strathclyde University, since 1972; Chief Scientific Adviser to Secretary of State for Scotland, since 1994; Secretary of State Scientific Adviser to Scottish Office Industry Department, since 1992; b. 12.7.31, Coatbridge; m., Mary White Gardner; 3 s.; 1 d. Educ. Coatbridge High School; Royal Technical College; Glasgow University. Research Engineer, Ferranti Ltd., Edinburgh, 1955-57; joined Strathclyde University as Lecturer, 1957; Deputy Principal, 1982-84, Vice-Principal, 1986-88, Deputy Principal (International Affairs), 1988-91; Special Adviser to Principal, 1991-92; Member: Council, IEE, since 1992; British National Committee and Executive Committee, CIGRE; Council and Vice President, Royal Society of Edinburgh; International Relations Committee, Royal Society; Management Board, Bell College of Technology, Hamilton; Management Board, SCOTVEC. Recreations: hill-walking; tennis; music; amateur astronomy. Address: (b.) Department of Electronic and Electrical Engineering, Strathclyde University, Royal College Building, 204 George Street, Glasgow G1 1XW; T.-0141-552 4400, Ext. 2071.

Templeton, Ian Godfrey, MA, BA. Warden, Glenalmond College, Perth, since 1992; b. 1.2.44, Edinburgh; m., Elisabeth Aline Robin; 1 s.; 1 d. Educ. Gordonstoun; Edinburgh University; Bedford College, London University. Assistant Master, then Housemaster, Melville College, Edinburgh, 1969-73; Housemaster, Daniel Stewart's and Melville College, Edinburgh, 1973-78; Assistant Headmaster, Robert Gordon's College, Aberdeen, 1978-85; Headmaster, Oswestry School, 1985-92. Governor, Belhaven Preparatory School; Director, Lathallan Preparatory School. Recreations: golf; skiing; choral singing. Address: Glenalmond College, Glenalmond, Perth PH1 3RY; T.-01738 88 227.

Tennant, George, BSc, PhD, CChem, FRSC, FRSE. Reader in Organic Chemistry, Edinburgh University, since 1977; b. 22.2.36, Glasgow; 1 s.; 1 d. Educ. Whitehill Senior Secondary School, Glasgow; Glasgow University. ICI Research Fellow, Aberdeen University, 1961-63; Lecturer: Queen's College, St. Andrews, 1963-65, Edinburgh University, 1965-76; Senior Lecturer, Edinburgh University, 1976-77; Head of Organic Chemistry, 1979-80, 1981-84. Secretary, Heterocyclic Group, Royal Society of Chemistry, 1976-79; Chairman, Edinburgh and SE Scotland Section, Royal Society of Chemistry, 1981-83. Recreations: sport; music; art. Address: (b.) Department of Chemistry, Edinburgh University, West Mains Road, Edinburgh, EH9 3JJ; T.-0131-650 4709.

Tennant, Sir Iain Mark, KT (1986). Chairman, Grampian Television PLC, 1968-89 (Vice-Chairman, 1960-68); Director, Caledonian Associated Cinemas PLC, 1950-90; Director, Clydesdale Bank PLC, 1969-89; Director, Abbey National Building Society (Chairman, Scottish Advisory Board, 1969-89); Director, Moray and Nairn Newspaper Company Ltd.; Crown Estate Commissioner, 1969-89; Honorary Director, Seagram Company Ltd., Montreal; Lord Lieutenant of Morayshire, 1963-94; Lord High Commissioner to the General Assembly of the Church of Scotland, 1988, 1989; b. 11.3.19, North Berwick; m., Lady Margaret Ogilvy; 2 s.; 1 d. Educ. Eton College; Magdalene College, Cambridge. Learned about film production, Welwyn Garden City Film Studios; served in Egypt with 2nd Bn., Scots Guards, 1940-42; became Intelligence Officer, 201 Guard's Brigade; captured at the surrender of Tobruk; prisoner of war, Italy and Germany, until 1945;

Founder Member, Moray Sea School, 1949; Council Member, Outward Bound Trust, 15 years; joined Board, Gordonstoun School, 1951 (Chairman, 1957-72); Member, Moray and Nairn County Council, 1956-64 (latterly Vice-Chairman, Education Committee); Member, The Times Publishing Co. Ltd., 1962-66; Member, Board, Cairngorm Sports Development Ltd., 1964-76; appointed Chairman, local Disablement Advisory Committee, 1964; Chairman, Glenlivet and Glen Grant Distilleries Ltd., 1964-70; Chairman, Glenlivet Distillers Ltd., 1970-77; Trustee, King George's Jubilee Trust, London, 1967-71; FRSA, 1971; Trustee, Churchill Trust, 1973-76; Member, Board, Courage Ltd., 1974-77; Chairman, Seagram Distillers Ltd. (in London), 1977-82; CBIM, 1983. Recreations: shooting; fishing. Address: (b.) Lochnabo, Lhanbryde, Moray; T.-01343 842228.

Terrell, Harry, MA, JP. Chief Executive, Dundee and Tayside Chamber of Commerce and Industry, since 1978; Member, Industrial Tribunals, since 1986; b. 2.8.38, Dundee; m., Patricia Mary Milgate; 1 s. Educ. Royal High School, Edinburgh; Dundee University. H.M. Diplomatic Service, 1955-66; Confederation of British Industry, 1970-76; Export Group for the Constructional Industries, 1976-77. Member, Advisory Board, Salvation Army, Dundee; Member, Management Committee, Dundee Citizens' Advice Bureau. Recreations: curling; reading. Address: (b.) Panmure Street, Dundee, DD1 1ED; T.-01382 201122.

Terry, Peter Brian, MB, ChB, MD, FRCS Edin, FRCOG. Consultant Obstetrician and Gynaecologist, since 1986; b. 3.6.52, Hillingdon; m., Gillian Margaret; 3 s. Educ. Merchant Taylors'; Edinburgh University Medical School. SHO, Simpson Memorial Maternity Pavilion, Edinburgh, 1977, Cumberland Infirmary, Carlisle, 1978; Registrar, Obstetrics and Gynaecology, Dudley Road Hospital, Birmingham, 1979; Research Registrar, 1982; Senior Registrar, Obstetrics and Gynaecology, Aberdeen, 1983; Consultant, 1986. Recreations: gardening; golf; walking. Address: (h.) 60 Forest Road, Aberdeen, AB2 4RP; T.-01224 317560.

Tervet, David John, BSc, MSc, PhD, CChem, MRSC, FCIWEM. Director, Solway River Purification Board, since 1994; b. 29.6.47, Woodford Green; m., Janie; 3 s. Educ. Chigwell; Edinburgh University; Strathclyde University; Dundee University. Assistant Chemist, Fife and Kinross Water Board, 1973-74; Chemist, Chief Chemist, Chief Scientist/Depute Director, Solway River Purification Board, 1974-94. Publications: papers on water quality. Recreations: cricket; music; gardening; railways (Life Member, Festiniog Railway Society). Address: (b.) Rivers House, Irongray Road, Dumfries, DG2 0JE; T.-01387 261767.

Thin, David Ainslie, BSc. Chairman and Managing Director, James Thin Ltd., since 1962; Chairman, Book Tokens Ltd., since 1987; Director, Edinburgh Book Festival; Council Member, National Trust for Scotland; b. 9.7.33, Edinburgh; m., Elspeth J.M. Scott; 1 s.; 2 d. Educ. Edinburgh Academy; Loretto School; Edinburgh University. President, Booksellers Association of GB and Ireland, 1976-78. Recreations: golf; travelling; reading. Address: (h.) 60 Fountainhall Road, Edinburgh EH9 2LP; T.-0131-667 2725.

Thomaneck, Professor Jurgen Karl Albert, JP, MEd, Drphil, FRSA. Professor in German, Aberdeen University, since 1992; Grampian Regional Councillor, since 1984; President, Aberdeen Trades Council, since 1982; b. 12.6.41, Germany; m., Guinevere Ronald; 2 d. Educ. Universities of Kiel, Tubingen, Aberdeen. Lecturer in German, Aberdeen University, since 1968. Board Member, Grampian Enterprise Ltd.; President, KIMO; author/editor of ten books, eight contributions to books, 28 articles in learned journals, all in German studies. Recreation: football. Address: (b.) Aberdeen University, Aberdeen AB9 1FX.

Thomas, Jeremy St. John, MA (Oxon), FRCPE, MRCPath. Consultant Pathologist, Western General Hospital, Edinburgh, since 1988; Secretary, Royal College of Physicians of Edinburgh, since 1993; b. 29.8.53, Cardiff; m., Dr. Valerie Doherty; 1 s.; 1 d. Educ. Lincoln College, Oxford; St. Thomas's Hospital, London. Trained in general medicine and pathology, Western Infirmary, Glasgow, 1979-88. Recreations: rugby football; antique rugs; photography. Address: (b.) Department of Pathology, Western General Hospital, Edinburgh; T.-0131-537 1961.

Thomas, Professor Lyn Carey, MA, DPhil (Oxon), FIMA. Professor of Management Science, Edinburgh University, since 1985 (Head, Department of Business Studies, 1987-90); b. 10.8.46, Dowlais; m., Margery Wynn Bright; 2 s.; 1 d. Educ. Lewis School, Pengam; Jesus College, Oxford. Research Fellow, University College, Swansea, 1971-74; Lecturer in Decision Theory, then Senior Lecturer, Manchester University, 1974-85; Senior NRC Fellow, Naval Postgraduate School, Monterey, California, 1982-83; President, Operational Research Society, 1994-95; Editor, IMA Journal of Mathematics applied in Business and Industry. Publications: Games, Theory and Applications, 1984; Operational Research Techniques, 1986; Credit Scoring and Credit Control, 1992. Recreations: reading; rugby; walking. Address: (b.) Department of Business Studies, William Robertson Building, 50 George Square, Edinburgh; T.-0131-650 3798.

Thomas, Professor Michael Frederic, MA, PhD, FGS, FRSE. Professor of Environmental Science, Stirling University, since 1980; b. 15.9.33, London; m., Elizabeth Anne Dadley (deceased); 1 s.; 1 d. Educ. Royal Grammar School, Guildford; Reading University. Assistant Lecturer in Geography, Magee University College, Londonderry, 1957-60; Lecturer, Ibadan University, Nigeria, 1960-64; Lecturer, then Senior Lecturer, St. Andrews University, 1964-79; visiting appointments, Universities of Canterbury (New Zealand), New South Wales, Natal, and Sierra Leone. Council Member, Royal Scottish Geographical Society; Past Chairman, British Geomorphological Research Group; Vice Chairman, Scottish Environmental Education Council. Publications: Tropical Geomorphology, 1974; Geomorphology in the Tropics, 1994. Recreations: listening to music; hill-walking; travel. Address: (b.) Department of Environmental Science, Stirling University, Stirling FK9 4LA; T.-01786 67840.

Thomas, Professor Michael James, OM (Poland), BSc, MBA, FRSA, FCIM. Professor of Marketing, Strathclyde University, since 1987; National Chairman, Chartered Institute of Marketing; b. 15.7.33; m.; 1 s.; 1 d. Educ. University College London; Indiana University. Metal Box Co. Ltd., London, 1957-60; Syracuse University Management School, 1960-71; Lancaster University, 1972-86. Recreation: ornithology. Address: (b.) Strathclyde University, Glasgow G4 ORQ.

Thomas, Professor Phillip Charles, BSc, PhD, FIBiol, CBiol, ARAgS, FRSE. Principal and Chief Executive, The Scottish Agricultural College, since 1990; Professor of Agriculture, Glasgow University, since 1987; Honorary Professor, Edinburgh University, since 1991; b. 17.6.42, Pontypool; m., Pamela Mary Hirst; 1 s.; 1 d. Educ. Abersychan Grammar School; University College of North Wales, Bangor. Lecturer, Department of Animal Nutrition and Physiology, Leeds University, 1966-71; Research Scientist, Hannah Research Institute, Ayr, 1971-87; Principal, West of Scotland College, Ayr, 1987-90. Publications: Nutritional Physiology of Farm Animals, 1983; Silage for Milk Production, 1983. Recreations: watching the garden grow; rugby coaching. Address: (b.) The Scottish Agricultural College, Central Office, West Mains Road, Edinburgh EH9 3JG.

Thomason, Edward, OBE, ACII. Convener, Shetland Islands Council, 1986-94; b. 12.8.22, Lerwick; m., Dinah.

Educ. Anderson Educational Institute, Lerwick. Councillor, since 1960; Convener, Zetland County Council, 1970-73. Recreations: fiddle and accordion music; writing magazine articles. Address: (h.) 14 Mounthooly Place, Lerwick, Shetland; T.-01595 692901.

Thompson, Professor Alan Eric, MA (Hons), PhD, FRSA, FSA(Scot). Emeritus Professor of the Economics of Government, Heriot-Watt University; b. 16.9.24; m., Mary Heather Long; 3 s.; 1 d. Educ. Edinburgh University. Edinburgh University: Assistant in Political Economy, 1952-53, Lecturer in Economics, 1953-59 and 1964-71; Professor of the Economics of Government, Heriot-Watt University, 1972-87; MP (Labour), Dunfermline, 1959-64; Member, Royal Fine Art Commission for Scotland, 1975-80; Chairman, Northern Offshore Maritime Resources Study, 1974-83; Governor, Newbattle Abbey College, 1975-85 (Chairman, 1980-83); Member, Local Government Boundaries Commission for Scotland, 1975-80; Member, Scottish Council for Adult Education in HM Forces, since 1973; BBC National Governor for Scotland, 1975-79; Governor, Leith Nautical College, 1981-85; Trustee, Bell's Nautical Trust, 1981-85; Parliamentary Adviser, Scottish Pharmaceutical General Council, since 1984. Publication: Development of Economic Doctrine (Co-author), 1980. Recreation: writing children's stories and plays. Address: (h.) 11 Upper Gray Street, Edinburgh EH9 1SN; T.-0131-667 2140.

Thompson, Colin, CBE, DUniv, FRSE, MA, FMA. Writer, Lecturer and Broadcaster on art and museums; b. 2.11.19, Berkhamstead; m., Jean A.J. O'Connell; 1 s.; 1 d. Educ. Sedbergh; King's College, Cambridge; Chelsea Polytechnic. Lecturer, Bath Academy of Art, Corsham, 1948-54; joined National Gallery of Scotland as Assistant Keeper, 1954; Director, National Galleries of Scotland, 1977-84. Member, Scottish Arts Council, 1976-83; Member, Edinburgh Festival Society, since 1979; Chairman, Scottish Museums Council, 1984-87; Chairman, Board of Governors, Edinburgh College of Art, 1989-91; Trustee, Buccleuch Heritage Trust; Chairman, Scottish Mining Museum Trust, since 1992. Publications: Pictures for Scotland, 1972; Hugo Van Der Goes and the Trinity Panels in Edinburgh (Co-author), 1974; Exploring Museums: Scotland, 1990. Address: (h.) Edenkerry, Lasswade, Midlothian EH18 1LW; T.-0131-663 7927.

Thompson, David George, MITSA, MAPEA, DCA, FIMgt. Director of Trading Standards, Highland Regional Council, since 1986; b. 20.9.49, Lossiemouth; m., Veronica; 1 s.; 3 d. Educ. Lossiemouth High School. Trainee, then Trading Standards Officer, Banff, Moray and Nairn Joint CC, 1967-73; Assistant Chief Trading Standards Officer, Ross & Cromarty County Council, 1973-75; Chief Trading Standards Officer, Western Isles Islands Council, 1975-83; Depute Director of Trading Standards, Highland Regional Council, 1983-86. Secretary/Treasurer, Scottish Branch, Institute of Trading Standards Administration, 1985-87, Chairman, 1988-89; Secretary/Treasurer, Society of Directors of Trading Standards in Scotland, 1987-89, Chairman, 1991-93. Recreations: golf; DIY; reading; Speakers' Club. Address: (h.) Balnafettack Guest House, Leachkin Road, Inverness; T.-01463 221555.

Thompson, Francis George, IEng, FIElecIE, MIExE, FSA (Scot). Author of books on Highland subjects; retired Senior Lecturer, Lews Castle College, Stornoway; Director, Western Isles Development Fund; b. 29.3.31, Stornoway; m., Margaret Elaine Pullar; 1 s.; 3 d. Educ. Nicolson Institute, Stornoway. From 1946: supply maintenance electrician, technical writer, assistant publicity manager, lecturer; has held various offices within An Comann Gaidhealach, including editorship of Sruth, bilingual newspaper, 1967-71; books include: Harris and Lewis, 1968; Harris Tweed, 1969; Highlands and Islands, 1974; Crofting Years, 1985; Shell Guide to Northern Scotland,

1987; The Western Isles, 1988; The First Hundred, 1992. Recreation: writing! Address: Am Fasgadh, 5 Rathad na Muilne, Stornoway, Lewis; T.-01851 703812.

Thompson, Graham L.,BSc. Managing Director, United Distillers UK plc, since 1990; b. 7.7.44, Birmingham; m., Gwendoline Ann. Educ. Solihull School; Leeds University. Brand Manager, Pedigree Petfoods, 1973-75, Senior Buyer, 1975-77; General Manager Purchasing, Arthur Bell & Sons, 1977-78, General Manager Administration, 1978-86, Administration Director, 1986-87; Operations Director, Arthur Bell Distillers, 1987-90; Director, Edward Dillon & Co. Ltd.; Director, Scotch Whisky Association. Recreation: sport. Address: (h.) Glengyle, Comrie Road, Crieff PH7 4BW; T.-01764 654821.

Thompson, John Robert, LLB, NP. Director of Administration, Inverclyde District Council, since 1991; Clerk, Inverclyde Licensing Board and District Court; Clerk of the Peace; Solicitor; b. 23.5.38, Glasgow; 1 s.; 1 d. Educ. Hutchesons' Grammar School; Glasgow University. Address: (b.) Municipal Buildings, Clyde Square, Greenock, PA15 1LY; T.-01475 724400.

Thomson, Alan James Reid, FCIBS, MIPD. General Manager, Bank of Scotland, since 28.10.35, Airdrie; m., Eileen Isobel Millar; 1 s.; 1 d. Educ. Robert Gordon's College, Aberdeen. Bank of Scotland, since 1952; Staff Manager, 1974; Assistant General Manager (Staff), 1978. A Vice President and Convenor, Education Committee, Chartered Institute of Bankers in Scotland; Director, Edinburgh Chamber of Commerce (Chairman, Human Resource Development Group). Recreations: golf; swimming. Address: (b.) Bank of Scotland Head Office, The Mound, Edinburgh EH1 1YZ; T.-0131-243 5480.

Thomson, Alexander McEwan, SSC, NP. Solicitor; b. 13.11.17, Dublin; m., Marjorie May Wood; 2 s.; 1 d. Educ. Daniel Stewart's College; George Heriot's School; Edinburgh University. Partner, Drummond & Reid, 1960-69 and Drummond & Co., WS, 1969-83 (Senior Partner, 1970-83); retired, 1983; Solicitor to General Teaching Council for Scotland, 1966-83; Solicitor to Edinburgh (subsequently Lothian Regional) Assessor; President, Society of Solicitors in the Supreme Courts of Scotland, 1979-82. Recreation: gardening. Address: (h.) The Steading, Leithhead, by Kirknewton, West Lothian; T.-01506 883393.

Thomson, Colin, BSc (Hons), PhD, FRSC. Reader in Theoretical Chemistry, St. Andrews University, since 1978 (Senior Lecturer, 1970-88); Regional Director for Research, National Foundation for Cancer Research, since 1977; Director, Association for International Cancer Research, since 1984; b. 6.7.37, Whitby, Yorkshire; m., Maureen Margaret Green; 2 s.; 2 d. Educ. Whitby Grammar School; Leeds University. Postdoctoral Research Fellow, California University, 1961-63; Postdoctoral (NATO) Research Fellow, Cambridge University, 1963-64; Lecturer in Theoretical Chemistry, St. Andrews University, 1964-70; Committee Member, SERC Computational Chemistry Committee, since 1983; Editor, RSC specialist reports; Chairman, Board of Directors, Association for International Cancer Research, 1992; President, International Society of Quantum Biology, 1995-97. Recreations: jazz and dance band musician; walking; sailing. Address: (h.) 12 Drumcarrow Road, St. Andrews, KY16 8SE; T.-01334 474820.

Thomson, Professor Derick S., MA (Aberdeen), BA (Cantab), DLitt (Univ. of Wales), DLitt (Univ. of Aberdeen), FRSE, FBA. Professor of Celtic, Glasgow University, 1963-91; b. 5.8.21, Stornoway; m., Carol Galbraith; 5 s.; 1 d. Educ. Nicolson Institute, Stornoway; Aberdeen University; Cambridge University; University College of North Wales, Bangor. Taught at Edinburgh,

Glasgow and Aberdeen Universities before returning to Glasgow as Professor, 1963; Chairman, Gaelic Books Council, 1968-91; President, Scottish Gaelic Texts Society; former Member, Scottish Arts Council; first recipient, Ossian Prize, 1974; author of numerous books and articles, including An Introduction to Gaelic Poetry, The Companion to Gaelic Scotland, European Poetry in Gaelic and collections of Gaelic poetry, including collected poems Creachadh na Clarsaich and Meall Garbh/Rugged Mountain; Editor, Gairm, since 1952. Address: (h.) 263 Fenwick Road, Giffnock, Glasgow, G46 6JX; T.-0141-638 0957.

Thomson, Duncan, MA, PhD. Keeper, Scottish National Portrait Gallery, since 1982; b. 2.10.34, Killearn; m., Julia Jane Macphail; 1 d. Educ. Airdrie Academy; Edinburgh University; Edinburgh College of Art; Moray House College of Education. Teacher of Art; Assistant Keeper, Scottish National Portrait Gallery. Publications: The Life and Art of George Jamesone, 1974; Avigdor Arikha, 1994. Address: (b.) Scottish National Portrait Gallery, 1 Queen Street, Edinburgh EH2 1JD; T.-0131-556 8921.

Thomson, Sir (Frederick Douglas) David, Bt, BA. Chairman, Britannia Steamship Insurance Association Limited, since 1986 (Director, since 1965); Director, Cairn Energy PLC, since 1971; Chairman, Through Transport Marine Mutual Assurance Association (Bermuda) Ltd., since 1983 (Director, since 1973); Director, Danae Investment Trust Ltd., since 1979; Chairman, Jove Investment Trust PLC, since 1983; Director, Martin Currie Pacific Trust PLC, since 1985; Chairman, Abtrust European Index Investment Trust PLC, since 1990; Chairman, Ptarmigan International Capital Trust PLC, since 1990; Director, Kynoch Group PLC, since 1991; Director, James Fisher and Sons PLC, since 1993; Chairman, Laurence J. Smith Ltd., since 1993; Director, Asset Management Investment Company PLC, since 1994; Member, Royal Company of Archers (Queen's Bodyguard for Scotland); b. 14.2.40, Edinburgh; 2 s.; 1 d. Educ. Eton; University College, Oxford. Recreations: shooting; skiing; tennis. Address: (h.) Holylee, Walkerburn, Peeblesshire; T.-01896 870673.

Thomson, Geddes, MA (Hons). Writer, former teacher; b. 20.9.39, Dalry; m., Lucy Faulkner; 2 s. Educ. Dalry High School; Glasgow University. Principal Teacher of English, Allan Glen's School, Glasgow, 1972-89, Shawlands Academy, Glasgow, 1989-93; Extra-Mural Lecturer, Department of Adult and Continuing Education, Glasgow University, 1985-93. Publications include: A Spurious Grace, 1981; Identities (Editor), 1981; The Poetry of Edwin Morgan, 1986. Recreations: supporting Partick Thistle; fishing; browsing in bookshops. Address: (h.) 48 Windyedge Crescent, Glasgow G13 1YF; T.-0141-959 5277.

Thomson, George Buchanan, FCIBS. Honorary Treasurer, Scottish Civic Trust, since 1976; Director, Clydesdale Development Company, since 1988; Director and Chairman, Association for the Relief of Incurables; b. 10.1.24, Glasgow; m., Margaret Irene Williams. Educ. Eastwood Secondary School. Joined Union Bank of Scotland, 1940; War Service, 1942-46 with RAF (Navigator, Bomber Command); held various banking appointments, 1947-86; retired as Assistant General Manager (Branch Administration, West), Bank of Scotland; Past President, Institute of Bankers in Scotland; Director, Ian Skelly Holdings Ltd., 1986-89. Former Convener, Board of Stewardship and Finance, Church of Scotland. Recreations: curling; bowling. Address: (h.) Kingswood, 26 Waverley Avenue, Helensburgh G84 7JU; T.-01436 672915.

Thomson, Iain Marshall, FIA (Scot). Managing Director, Lawrie and Symington, since 1990; formerly Director,

United Auctions Ltd.; b. 28.9.38, Stirling; 2 d. Educ. Lanark Grammar School; George Watson's College, Edinburgh. Joined Macdonald, Fraser and Co. Ltd., 1955, appointed Director, 1970, Joint Managing Director, 1976; Council Member, Institute of Auctioneers and Appraisers in Scotland, since 1972, Vice President, 1986-88, President, 1988-90; Vice President, Royal Highland and Agricultural Society of Scotland, 1990; appointed by Secretary of State for Scotland to Panel of Arbiters, 1983; Past Chairman, Perth and District Junior Agricultural Club. Recreations: golf; fishing. Address: (b.) Muirglen, Lanark ML11 9AX.

Thomson, Professor John Aidan Francis, MA, DPhil, FRHistS. Titular Professor in Mediaeval History, Glasgow University, since 1994; b. 26.7.34, Edinburgh; m., Katherine J.V. Bell; 1 s.; 1 d. Educ. George Watson's Boys' College, Edinburgh; Edinburgh University; Balliol College, Oxford. Glasgow University: Assistant in Mediaeval History, 1960, Lecturer, 1961, Senior Lecturer, 1974, Reader, 1983. President, Glasgow Archaeological Society, 1978-81. Publications: The Later Lollards 1414-1520, 1965; Popes and Princes 1417-1517, 1980; The Transformation of Mediaeval England 1370-1529, 1983; Towns and Townspeople in the Fifteenth Century (Editor), 1988; The Early Tudor Church and Society, 1485-1529, 1993. Recreations: hill-walking; gardening. Address: (b.) Department of Medieval History, Glasgow University, Glasgow G12 8QQ; T.-0141-339 8855.

Thomson, John Alexander, MD, PhD, FRCPGlas, FRCPLond. Reader in Medicine, University Department of Medicine, Glasgow University, since 1981; Honorary Consultant Physician, Glasgow Royal Infirmary, since 1968; b. 19.4.33, Airdrie; m., Fiona Jane Reid; 2 s.; 2 d. Educ. Hamilton Academy; Glasgow University. House Physician, then House Surgeon, Glasgow Royal Infirmary, 1956-57; Royal Army Medical Corps, 1957-59 (Regimental Medical Officer, 13/18 Royal Hussars); House Surgeon, Glasgow Royal Maternity and Women's Hospital, 1959-60; McIntyre Clinical Research Scholar in Medicine, University Department of Medicine, 1960-61; Registrar in Medicine, then Senior Registrar, University Medical Unit, Glasgow Royal Infirmary, 1961-68; Senior Lecturer in Medicine and Consultant Endocrinologist, Glasgow Royal Infirmary, 1968-81. Address: (b.) University Department of Medicine, Royal Infirmary, 10 Alexandra Parade, Glasgow G31 2ER; T.-0141-552 3535.

Thomson, Professor Joseph McGeachy, LLB. Regius Professor of Law, Glasgow University, since 1991; Deputy General Editor, Stair Memorial Encyclopaedia of the Laws of Scotland, since 1985; b. 6.5.48, Campbeltown. Educ. Keil School, Dumbarton; Edinburgh University. Lecturer in Law, Birmingham University, 1970-74; Lecturer in Laws, King's College, London, 1974-84; Professor of Law, Strathclyde University, 1984-90. Recreations: opera; ballet; food and wine. Address: (h.) 140 Hyndland Road, Glasgow; T.-0141-334 6682.

Thomson, Professor Kenneth James, MA, MSc, MS. Professor of Agricultural Economics, Aberdeen University, since 1986; b. 30.9.45, Aberdeen; m., Lydia. Educ. Aberdeen Grammar School; Aberdeen University; London University; Iowa State University. Lecturer and Senior Lecturer, Department of Agricultural Economics, Newcastle upon Tyne University, 1972-86. Editor, Journal of Agricultural Economics, 1987-93. Publication: The Cost of the Common Agricultural Policy, 1982. Recreations: viola-playing; mountaineering. Address: (b.) School of Agriculture, 581 King Street, Aberdeen, AB9 1UD; T.-01224 480291.

Thomson, Malcolm George, QC, LLB; b. 6.4.50. Advocate, 1974; called to the Bar, Lincoln's Inn, 1991. Address: (b.) Advocates' Library, Parliament House, Edinburgh, EH1 1RF.

Thomson, Michael Scott, FRICS, IRRV. Commercial Director, Irvine Development Corporation, since 1972; b. 21.5.39, Newcastle; m., Elizabeth; 1 s.; 2 d. Educ. Allan Glen's School, Glasgow. Valuation Surveyor, Glasgow City Assessor's Department and Estates Department; Deputy Commercial Director, Redditch Development Corporation. Founder President, Irvine Junior Chamber; Past President, Irvine Burns Club; Director, Ayr United F.C., 1986-92. Recreations: golf (participant); most other sports (spectator). Address: (h.) 7 Finlas Avenue, Ayr.

Thomson, Michael Stuart MacGregor, MA, CA. Director of Finance and Administration, Royal Scottish Society for Prevention of Cruelty to Children, since 1991; b. 4.5.38, Perth; m., Rosemary; 2 s.; 1 d. Educ. Gordonstoun; St. Andrews University. CA apprenticeship, 1960-63; Director, then Managing Director, Peter Thomson (Perth) Ltd., 1963-85; Michael Thomson & Co., 1985-91; Balbirnie House Hotel Ltd., 1987-91. Lord Dean of the Guildry Incorporation of Perth, 1973-76; Governor, Balnacraig School. Publication: Background to Collecting Doulton Art Pottery. Recreations: grandparenting; footering; adventures; travel; sport. Address: (b.) 41 Polwarth Terrace, Edinburgh EH11 1NU; T.-0131-337 8539.

Thomson, Sheriff Nigel Ernest Drummond, CBE, MA, LLB. Sheriff of Lothian and Borders, at Edinburgh, since 1976, and at Peebles, since 1983; b. 19.6.26, Aberdeen; m., Snjolaug Magnusson; 1 s.; 1 d. Educ. George Watson's Boys' College; St. Andrews University; Edinburgh University. Called to Scottish Bar, 1953; appointed Sheriff at Hamilton, 1966; Member, Scottish Arts Council, 1978 (Chairman, Music Committee, 1979-84). Hon. President, Strathaven Arts Guild; Hon. Vice-President, Tenovus-Scotland; Hon. President, Scottish Association for Counselling, 1986-89; Vice President, British Association for Counselling, since 1992; Chairman, Edinburgh Youth Orchestra Society, 1986-92; Convenor, Council for Music in Hospitals in Scotland, since 1992. Recreations: music; woodwork; golf. Address: (h.) 50 Grange Road, Edinburgh; T.-0131-667 2166.

Thomson, Rev. Peter David, MA, BD. Minister, Comrie and Strowan with Dundurn, since 1978; b. 4.11.41, St. Andrews; m., Margaret Celia Murray; 1 s.; 1 d. Educ. Dundee High School; Edinburgh University; Glasgow University; Tubingen University. Minister, Balmaclellan with Kells, 1968-78; Moderator, Kirkcudbright Presbytery, 1974-75; Convener, Nomination Committee, General Assembly, 1982-85. Chairman, New Galloway and Kells Community Council, 1976-78; Moderator, Perth Presbytery, 1988-89. Recreations: haphazardly pursued interests in photography, wildlife, music, theology, current affairs. Address: The Manse, Comrie, Perthshire, PH6 2HE; T.-01764 670269.

Thomson, Robert Scott, OBE, BSc, CChem, MRCS, FRSA. Rector, Larkhall Academy, 1974-94; b. 9.6.33, Newtongrange; m., Helen Mary McIntosh; 1 d. Educ. Newbattle Secondary School; Dalkeith High School; Heriot-Watt University. Scientific Technical Officer, NCB, 1950-59; Chemistry Teacher, George Watson's College, 1963-67; Principal Teacher of Chemistry: Dalkeith High School, 1967-70, George Watson's College, 1970-74. Former Member, Scottish Consultative Council on the Curriculum; Chairman, Committee on Technology; Convener, Scottish Education Industry Committee; Member, Court, Heriot-Watt University; President, The Watt Club, 1994-95; Non-Executive Director, Lanarkshire Healthcare NHS Trust, since 1995. Recreations: reading; gardening; bowling; Larkhall Rotary Club; Larkhall Professional and Businessmen's Club.

Thomson, Roy Hendry, CStJ, MA (Hons). President, Scottish Liberal Democrats; President, Aberdeen and North East Association for Mental Health; Chairman, Friends of Aberdeen University Library; Director, Kaleidoscope, Aberdeen International Children's Festival; Marketing Director, Aberdeen International Youth Festival; b. 27.8.32, Aberdeen; m., Nancy; 3 d. Educ. Aberdeen Grammar School; Aberdeen University. National Service, Gordon Highlanders, 1955-57; personnel and market research, Rowntree & Co. Ltd., 1957-60; Chairman/Director, family motor business, until 1986; former Director, The Scottish Ballet (Chairman, 1983-87); former Member, City of Aberdeen District Council; Past President: Rotary Club of Aberdeen, Mountain Rescue Association, Aberdeen; former Chairman, Scottish Liberal Democrats. Recreations: skiing; hill-walking; bee-keeping. Address: (h.) 5 Baillieswells Grove, Bieldside, Aberdeen AB1 9BH; T.-Aberdeen 861628.

Thomson, Professor Samuel J., BSc, PhD, DSc, CChem, FRSC, FRSE. Professor Emeritus, Glasgow University, since 1987; Honorary Senior Research Fellow, since 1987; Member, British Railways Board, Scottish Committee, 1989-94; Adviser to BR Railfreight Distribution, since 1994; b. 27.9.22, Hamilton; m., Christina M. MacTaggart; 1 s.; 1 d. Educ. Hamilton Academy; Glasgow University. Lt., Royal Signals, 1944; Lecturer in Radiochemistry, Durham University, 1951; Lecturer, Senior Lecturer, Reader, Titular Professor, Glasgow University, 1957-87. Publications: books and papers on surface chemistry and catalysis, etc. Recreations: visual perception; reading. Address: (h.) 10 Balfleurs Street, Milngavie, Glasgow G62 8HW; T.-0141-956 2622.

Thomson, S. Kenneth, MHSM, DipHSM. Chief Executive, Law Hospital NHS Trust, since 1994; Conductor, Glasgow Gaelic Musical Association, since 1983; b. 20.8.49, Campbeltown; m., Valerie Ferguson; 1 s.; 1 d. Educ. Keil School, Dumbarton. Administrative trainee, Scottish Health Service; hospital administrator; Unit Administrator, Argyll and Clyde Health Board, Renfrew Unit; Unit General Manager, Argyll and Dumbarton Unit; Unit General Manager, Lanarkshire Health Board, Law Hospital Unit. National Mod Gold Medallist, 1979; Governor, Keil School, since 1995. Recreations: music; Gaelic language and culture; theatre; skiing; swimming. Address: (b.) Law Hospital, Carluke, Lanarkshire, ML8 5ER; T.-01698 364120.

Thomson, Stuart James, HND (Agric). General Secretary, Ayrshire Cattle Society of GB and Ireland, since 1984; Director, Cattle Services (Ayr) Ltd.; Director, World Federation Ayrshire Breed Societies; b. 29.8.54, Kirkwall; m., Carolynne Henderson; 1 s. Educ. Kirkwall Grammar School; School of Agriculture, Aberdeen. Regional Officer, North of Scotland Milk Marketing Board, 1976-84. Member, Executive Committee, National Cattle Breeders Association. Recreations: gardening; golf; fishing. Address: (b.) 1 Racecourse Road, Ayr KA7 2DE; T.-01292 267123.

Thomson, Sir Thomas James, Kt (1991), CBE (1983), OBE (1978), MB, ChB, FRCPGlas, FRCPLond, FRCPEdin, FRCPIre. Chairman, Greater Glasgow Health Board, 1987-93; Member, Court, University of Strathclyde, since 1992; b. 8.4.23, Airdrie; m., Jessie Smith Shotbolt; 2 s.; 1 d. Educ. Airdrie Academy; Glasgow University. Lecturer, Department of Materia Medica, Glasgow University, 1953-61; Postgraduate Adviser to Glasgow Northern Hospitals, 1961-80; Honorary Secretary, RCPSGlas, 1965-73; Secretary, Specialist Advisory Committee for General Internal Medicine for UK, 1970-74; Chairman: Medico-Pharmaceutical Forum, 1978-80 (Chairman, Education Advisory Board, 1979-83); Conference of Royal Colleges and Faculties in Scotland, 1982-85; National Medical Consultative Committee for Scotland, 1982-87; President, RCPSGlas, 1982-84; Hon.FACP, 1983; Hon. LLD, Glasgow University, 1988. Publications: Dilling's Pharmacology (Co-Editor); Gastroenterology - an integrated course. Recreations:

swimming; golfing. Address: (h.) 1 Varna Road, Glasgow G14 9NE; T.-0141-959 5930.

Thomson, Walter, MBE. Editor, Selkirk Advertiser, 1932-86; Rugby Writer, Sunday Post, since 1931; b. 20.3.13, Selkirk; m., Gerda; 2 d. Educ. Selkirk High School; Heriot-Watt. Army (Captain), 1940-46. Publication: Rummle Them Up!, 1989. Recreation: photography. Address: (h.) Cruachan, Murrayfield, Selkirk; T.-Selkirk 20261.

Thorley, George William Faulds, BA (Hons), DipTP, MSc, FRSA, MRTPI. Chief Executive, South Ayrshire Council, since 1995; Assistant Chief Executive, Strathclyde Regional Council, 1990-95; b. 19.1.48, Dundee; m., Anne; 2 d. Educ. St. Michael's Secondary School, Dundee; Lawside Academy, Dundee; Strathclyde University. Joined Strathclyde Regional Council, 1975, as Senior Planner/Economist; joined Chief Executive's Department, 1980, as Senior Executive (Economic Strategy). Recreations: gardening; badminton; music; visual arts. Address: (b.) P.O. Box 1996, Wellington Square, Ayr, KA7 1DS; T.-01292 612170.

Thornber, Iain, JP, DL, FRSA, FSA Scot, FSA. District Councillor, Morvern, Sunart and Ardgour, Lochaber, since 1988 (Chairman, Lochaber District Licensing Board); Deputy Lieutenant, Lochaber, Inverness, Badenoch and Strathspey, since 1988; b. 3.2.48, Falkirk. Educ. Glenhurich Public School. Company Factor, Glensanda Estate, Morvern, Argyll. Trustee, West Highland Museum, Fort William; Member, Local Advisory Panel, Forestry Commission; Member, Morvern Red Deer Management Group; Member, Inverness Prison Visiting Committee. Publications: The Castles of Morvern; The Gaelic Bards of Morvern; Rats; The Sculptures Stones of Cill Choluimchille, Morvern; Moidart or Among the Clanranalds (Editor); Bronze Age Cairns in the Aline Valley, Morvern (Co-author). Recreations: deer stalking; salmon fishing; photography; local history research. Address: (b.) Knock House, Morvern, by Oban, PA34 5UU.

Thorne, Roderick Hugh Frank, MA, CertEd, AdvCertEd. Head Teacher, Sanday School, Orkney, since 1984; b. 7.5.47, Maidenhead; m., Sylvia Mary Driscoll; 3 s. Educ. Leighton Park; Trinity, Cambridge; Christ Church, Oxford. Head Teacher, Fetlar, 1971-74, Fair Isle, 1976-81, Kent, 1981-84. Recreations: natural history; golf; photography. Address: (b.) Schoolhouse, Sanday, Orkney; T.-01857 600 404.

Thornton-Kemsley, Nigel Scott, CBE (1987), DL. Managing Director, Thornton Enterprises Ltd.; Managing Director, Thornton Farms Ltd., 1956-88; Chairman, North of Scotland College of Agriculture, 1982-88; Director, Royal Highland and Agricultural Society of Scotland, 1971-88; Director, Scottish Agricultural Colleges, 1987-88; Governor, Rowett Research Institute, 1981-88; b. 14.8.33, Chigwell, Essex; m., Judith Gay Sanders; 1 s.; 2 d. Educ. Fettes College; East of Scotland College of Agriculture. National Service: Royal Signals, 1954-56, TA 51st Highland Signal Regiment, 1957-63, 3rd Bn., Gordon Highlanders, 1963-71, OC TAVR Company; Major on retiral; Deputy Lieutenant, Kincardineshire, 1978; Member, Grampian Health Board, 1989-93; President, Aberdeen-Angus Cattle Society, 1981-82; Member, Scottish American Community Relations Council, 1971-80; Chairman, Council, Scottish Agricultural Colleges, 1982-84; Life Governor, Imperial Cancer Research Council, since 1978; Past President, Royal Northern Agricultural Society; Past President, Fettercairn Farmers' Club. Recreation: fishing. Address: Thornton Castle, Laurencekirk, Kincardineshire; T.-01561 377301.

Thorpe, John Elton, BA, PhD. Senior Principal Scientific Officer, Freshwater Fisheries Laboratory, Pitlochry, 1981-95; b. 24.1.35, Wolverhampton; m., Judith Anne Johnson; 2 s. Educ. Kingswood School, Bath; Jesus College, Cambridge. Cambridge Expedition to British Honduras, 1959-60 (Leader); Shell International Chemical Co. Ltd., London, 1960-62; joined DAFS Freshwater Fisheries Laboratory, Pitlochry, 1963. Vice-President, Fisheries Society of British Isles, 1988-93; Editor, Journal of Fish Biology, since 1991; Member, Editorial Board: Journal of Animal Ecology, since 1988, Reviews in Fish and Fisheries, since 1989, Fisheries Management, 1978-84, and Aquaculture and Fisheries Management, since 1985; Chairman, Killiecrankie and Fincastle Community Council, 1976-78. Special Medal, University of Lodz, Poland, 1992. Publications: eight books; 200 scientific papers. Recreations: travelling; Baroque music. Address: (h.) Piper's Croft, Killiecrankie, Perthshire PH16 5LW; T.-01796 47 3886.

Thrower, Rev. Charles George, BSc. Minister, Carnbee linked with Pittenweem, since 1970; Moderator, St. Andrews Presbytery, 1991-92; b. 22.11.37, Barton Turf, Norfolk; m., Dr. Stephanie A.M. Thrower; 1 s.; 3 d. Educ. King Edward VI School, Norwich; Britannia Royal Naval College, Dartmouth. Electrical branch training H.M.S. Girdle-Ness (Malta), 1960-61; divinity student, St. Mary's, 1961-64; probationer, St. Andrews Church, Dundee, 1964-65; missionary appointment, Hampden with Falmouth, Trelawny, Jamaica, 1966-70. Synod of Fife Youth Adviser, 1971-74; Chairman, East Neuk of Fife Committee, Children 1st, since 1974, and Member, Children 1st Policy and Staff Committee. Recreations: water colour painting; photography; sailing; gardening; local church history. Address: The Manse, 2 Milton Place, Pittenweem, Fife, KY10 2LR; T.-01333 311255.

Thrower, James Arthur, BLitt, MA, PhD, FRAS. Professor of the History of Religions and Director, Centre for the Study of Religions, Aberdeen University, since 1994; b. 5.10.36, Guisborough; m., Judith Elizabeth Gauss; 3 d. Educ. Guisborough Grammar School; St. Chad's College, Durham; St. Edmund Hall, Oxford. Staff-Tutor, Eastern District, WEA, 1962-64; Lecturer in Philosophy of Religion, Ghana University, 1964-68; Lecturer in Religious Studies, Bede College, Durham, 1968-70; Lecturer in Religious Studies, Aberdeen University, 1970 (Senior Lecturer, 1981, Reader, 1993, Head of Department, 1984-87); Riddoch Lecturer, since 1984; Visiting Professor: Helsinki University, 1974, Polish Academy of Sciences, 1976, Aligarh Muslim University, India, 1988; British Council Exchange Scholar, Leningrad University, 1976 and 1978; Visiting Scholar, Gdansk University, 1981 and 1982; British Academy exchange scholar Chinese Academy of Social Sciences, 1989; Warden, Balgownie Lodge, Aberdeen University, 1971-82. Author of a number of books and articles about the history of religions. Recreations: travel and exploration; classical music; opera; ballet. (h.) 2 Riverside Mill Cottages, Bridge of Don AB23 8LZ; T.-Aberdeen 822127.

Thyne, Malcolm Tod, MA, FRSE. Headmaster, Fettes College, since 1988; b. 6.11.42, Edinburgh; m., Eleanor Christine Scott; 2 s. Educ. The Leys School, Cambridge; Clare College, Cambridge. Assistant Master, Edinburgh Academy, 1965-69; Assistant Master, Oundle School, 1969-80 (Housemaster, 1972-80); Headmaster, St. Bees School, Cumbria, 1980-88. Publications: Periodicity, Atomic Structure and Bonding (Revised Nuffield Chemistry), 1976; contributions to Revised Nuffield Chemistry Handbook for Pupils and Teachers Guides, 1978. Recreations: mountaineering; ski-ing. Address: (b.) Fettes College, Edinburgh EH4 1QX; T.-0131-332 2281.

Tiefenbrun, Ivor Sigmund, MBE. Managing Director, Linn Products Ltd., Glasgow; Member, Design Council; b. 18.3.46, Glasgow; m., Evelyn Stella Balarksy; 2 s.; 1 d. Educ. Strathbungo Senior Secondary School; Strathclyde University (Sixties dropout). Worked overseas, 1971-73;

founded Linn Products, 1973. Chairman, Federation of British Audio, 1983-87. Recreations: thinking; music; reading; sailing. Address: (b.) Linn Products Ltd., Floors Road, Waterfoot, Eaglesham, Glasgow G76 0EP; T.-0141-644 5111.

Tierney, David A., BA (Hons). Rector, Speyside High School, Aberlour, since 1987; b. 15.1.50, Glasgow; m., Valerie Lauder; 2 s. Educ. Queen's Park School, Glasgow; Strathclyde University; Jordanhill College of Education; Glasgow University. Teacher, Govan High School, Glasgow, 1973-76; Principal Teacher of Modern Studies, Mackie Academy, 1976-83; Depute Rector, Speyside High School, 1983-87. Recreations: hill-walking; cycling; reading; gardening. Address: (h.) Sunningdale, Elgin; T.-01343 547945.

Tilbrook, Peter John, BSc, PhD, MIEEM. Director, North West Region, Scottish Natural Heritage, since 1992; b. 12.12.38, Romford; m., Frances Carol Brander; 2 d. Educ. Royal Liberty Grammar School; Durham University; Queen Mary College, London University. Research Scientist and Base Commander, Signy Island Base, South Orkney Islands, Falkland Islands Dependencies Survey; Head, Terrestrial Ecology Section, British Antarctic Survey; Deputy Regional Officer and Regional Officer, North West Scotland, Nature Conservancy Council; Director, North West Region, Nature Conservancy Council for Scotland. Polar Medal, 1967. Recreations: hill-walking; scuba diving; squash; photography; music; gardening. Address: (h.) Rosenberg, Cromarty, Ross-shire IV11 8YT; T.-01381 600239.

Tildesley, James Michael. Director, Scottish Maritime Museum, since 1989; b. 10.3.47, Southminster; m., Janet Birks; 2 s.; 1 d. Educ. Chelmsford Technical High School; Goldsmiths' College, London University. Assistant Master, Mayfield School, Redbridge; Assistant Curator, then Deputy Curator, Passmore Edwards Museum; Assistant Director of Leisure, L.B. of Newham. Vice-Chairman, Ayrshire Tourist Board; Chairman, TOCCATA; Chairman, Irvine and District Tourist Association. Address: (b.) Scottish Maritime Museum, Laird Forge, Gottries Road, Irvine, KA12 8QE; T.-01294 278283.

Timms, Professor Duncan William Graham, BA, PhD. Professor of Applied Social Science, Stirling University, since 1972; Director, SocINFO, since 1988; Director, Project Varsetile, since 1993; b. 11.10.38, Cheltenham; m., Elizabeth Anne Barnes; 1 s.; 1 d. Educ. Pate's Grammar School, Cheltenham; St. Catharine's College, Cambridge. Lecturer, Senior Lecturer, University of Queensland, 1963-68; Professor of Sociology, University of Auckland, 1968-72; Deputy Principal, Stirling University, 1978-84 (Acting Principal, 1980-81); Visiting Professor, University of Stockholm, since 1985. Publications: The Urban Mosaic, 1972; Family Structure in Childhood and Mental Health in Adolescence, 1991. Recreations: music; Swedish countryside. Address: (h.) 7 East Claremont Street, Edinburgh EH7 4HT; T.-0131-556 7481.

Timms, Professor Peter Kenneth, MBE. Chairman, Board of Management, Glasgow University Business School, since 1991; Managing Director, Flexible Technology Ltd., Bute, since 1981; Member, Highlands and Islands Enterprise, since 1990; Member, Scottish Industrial Development Advisory Board, since 1989; b. 2.12.43, Witney, Oxon; m., Patricia; 3 s. Educ. St. Edmund's School, Canterbury, Kent. Production Engineer, Texas Instruments Ltd., 1964; Manufacturing Engineer, then Process Engineering Manager, IBM UK Ltd., 1967; Director and General Manager, AFA Minerva, 1978. Non-Executive Director: Ferranti Technologies Ltd (Chairman, since 1995), Murray Enterprise plc, Scottish Electronics Technology Group Ltd. Recreations: boating; travel. Address: Millbrae, Ascog, Rothesay, Bute PA20 9ET; T.-01700 504515.

Titterington, Professor (Donald) Michael, BSc, PhD, DipMathStat, FRSE. Professor of Statistics, Glasgow University, since 1988; b. 20.11.45, Marple, Cheshire; m., Mary Hourie Philp; 1 s. Educ. High School of Stirling; Edinburgh University; Cambridge University. Lecturer, then Senior Lecturer, then Titular Professor, Department of Statistics, Glasgow University, 1972-88; visiting appointments: Princeton University, 1978, State University of New York, 1980, Wisconsin University, 1982, Australian National University, 1982; Associate Editor, Biometrika, 1979-85, Annals of Statistics, 1983-85 and since 1995, Journal, American Statistical Association, 1986-88 and since 1991, and IEEE Transactions on Pattern Analysis and Machine Intelligence, since 1994; Joint Editor, Journal of the Royal Statistical Society, Series B, 1986-89, and Statistical Science, 1992-94; Council Member, Royal Statistical Society, 1987-92; elected Fellow, Institute of Mathematical Statistics, 1986; elected Member, International Statistical Institute, 1991. Publications: Statistical Analysis of Finite Mixture Distributions (Co-author); many journal articles. Recreation: being a father. Address: (b.) Department of Statistics, Glasgow University, Glasgow, G12 8QQ; T.-0141-330 5022.

Tiusanen, Professor Tauno Juhani, PhD. Professor, Institute of Russian and East European Studies, Glasgow University, since 1992; Visiting Professor, Helsinki School of Economics, since 1992, and Northeastern University, Boston, since 1989; b. 30.4.41, Helsinki; m., Ritva Haukka; 1 s. Educ. Pori Lyceum, Finland; Glasgow University. Lecturer, University of Tampere, Finland, 1965-66; Journalist, Germany, 1966-69; Research Fellow, University of Technology, Zurich, 1969-73; Deputy Director, Business International, Vienna, 1974-76; Managing Director, Tietokarki, Helsinki, 1977-91. Publications: Western Direct Investments in European CMEA Countries, 1990; From Marx to Market Economy, 1991; The Baltic States, 1993. Recreations: liteature; swimming. Address: (b.) Institute of Russian and East European Studies, Glasgow University, 29 Bute Gardens, Glasgow G12 8QQ; T.-0141-330 4579.

Tobin, Patrick Francis John, MA, PGCE, FRSA. Principal, Mary Erskine School and Daniel Stewart's & Melville College, since 1989; Member, Scottish Consultative Council on the Curriculum; b. 4.10.41, London; m., Margery Ann Sluce; 1 s.; 3 d. Educ. St. Benedict's, Ealing; Christ Church, Oxford; London University. Head of Economics, St. Benedict's, Ealing, 1963-71; Head of History, Christ College, Brecon, 1971-75; Head of History, Tonbridge School, 1975-81; The King's School, Parramatta, NSW, 1980; Headmaster, Prior Park College, Bath, 1981-89. Recreations: reading; writing; canal boating; hill-walking; travel. Address: (h.) 11 Queensferry Terrace, Edinburgh EH4 3EQ.

Tod, Stewart, DA (Edin), RIBA, FRIAS, FSA Scot. Senior Partner, Stewart Tod & Partners, Architects, Edinburgh, since 1977; b. 30.4.27, West Wemyss; m., A. Vivienne J. Nixon; 2 s.; 2 d. Educ. Buckhaven High School; Edinburgh College of Art. RAF, 1945-48; Stratton Davis & Yates, 1952-55; Falkirk District Council, 1955-57; Carr and Matthew, 1957-60; David Carr Architects, 1960-77. Executive Committee Member, Association for the Protection of Rural Scotland; General Trustee, Church of Scotland. Recreations: bee-keeping; gardening; sketching. Address: (b.) 43 Manor Place, Edinburgh; T.-0131-225 7988.

Todd, Professor Adrian Christopher, BTech, PhD, CEng, FIChemE, FInstPet. Professor of Petroleum Engineering, Heriot Watt University, since 1990 (Head of Department, since 1991); b. 1.4.44, Leicester; m., Valerie H. Todd; 1 d. Educ. Lutterworth Grammar School; Loughborough University of Technology. Research Scientist, Shell, 1969-72; joined Heriot Watt University as Lecturer in Chemical Engineering, 1972. Recreation: Christian activities.

Address: (b.) Department of Petroleum Engineering, Heriot Watt University, Riccarton, Edinburgh; T.-0131-451 3124.

Todd, Rev. Andrew Stewart, MA, BD, DD. Minister, St. Machar's Cathedral, Old Aberdeen, 1967-93; Chaplain to The Queen in Scotland, since 1991; b. 26.5.26, Alloa; m., Janet Agnes Brown Smith; 2 s.; 2 d. Educ. High School of Stirling; Edinburgh University; Basel University. Assistant Minister, St. Cuthbert's, Edinburgh, 1951-52; Minister: Symington, Lanarkshire, 1952; North Leith, 1960; Member, Church Hymnary Revision Comittee, 1963-73; Convener, General Assembly's Committee on Public Worship and Aids to Devotion, 1974-78; Moderator, Aberdeen Presbytery, 1980-81; Convener, Panel on Doctrine; Member, Church Hymnary Trust; awarded Honorary Doctorate, Aberdeen University, 1982; translator of three theological books from German into English; Honorary President, Church Service Society; Honorary President, Scottish Church Society. Recreations: music; gardening. Address: (h.) Culearn, Balquhidder, Lochearnhead, Perthshire FK19 8FB; T.-01877 384662.

Todd, Jessie. Chief Executive, Youth Clubs Scotland, since 1990; b. 4.9.48, Dunfermline; 1 s.; 1 d. Educ. Dunfermline High School; Aberdeen College. Former Lecturer/Senior Lecturer, Aberdeen College; joined Scottish and Newcastle Breweries, developing its youth training scheme. Recreations: more work!; music; arts; social interaction; walking; family. Address: (b.) Youth Clubs Scotland, Balfour House, 19 Bonnington Grove, Edinburgh; T.-0131-554 2561.

Toft, Anthony Douglas, CBE, BSc, MD, FRCPE, FRCPGlas, FRCPLond, FRCPI, FACP(Hon), FRACP(Hon), FRCSE, FRCPC(Hon), FRCGP(Hon). Consultant Physician, Royal Infirmary, Edinburgh, since 1978; Chief Medical Officer, Scottish Equitable Life Assurance, since 1987; President, Royal College of Physicians of Edinburgh, 1991-94; b. 29.10.44, Perth; m., Maureen Darling; 1 s.; 1 d. Educ. Perth Academy; Edinburgh University. Chairman, Collegiate Members' Committee, Royal College of Physicians of Edinburgh, 1978; Vice-President, Royal College of Physicians, 1989-91; Chairman, Scottish Royal Colleges, 1992-94; Chairman, Joint Committee of Higher Medical Training, since 1993. Recreations: golf; gardening. Address: (h.) 41 Hermitage Gardens, Edinburgh EH10 6AZ; T.-0131-447 2221.

Togneri, Martin, MA (Hons), MBA. Director, Locate in Scotland, since 1995; b. 27.4.56, Stirling; m., Kathleen; 2 s. Educ. St. Modan's High School, Stirling; Glasgow University; Strathclyde University. Burroughs Machines Ltd., 1978-80; postgraduate study, 1980-83; Accounts Commission, 1983-94; joined Locate in Scotland, 1984. Recreations: reading; relaxing. Address: (b.) 120 Bothwell Street, Glasgow, G2 7JP; T.-0141-228 2247.

Tolley, David Anthony, MB, BS (Lond), FRCS, FRCSEdin. Consultant Urological Surgeon, Western General Hospital, Edinburgh, since 1980; Honorary Senior Lecturer, Department of Surgery/Urology, Edinburgh University, since 1980; Director, Scottish Lithotriptor Centre; b. 29.11.47, Warrington; m., Judith Anne Finn; 3 s.; 1 d. Educ. Manchester Grammar School; Kings College Hospital Medical School, London University. House Surgeon and Physician, Kings College Hospital; Lecturer in Human Morphology, Southampton University; Lecturer in Anatomy and Fulbright Fellow, University of Texas at Houston; Surgical Registrar, Hammersmith and Ealing Hospitals, London; Senior Surgical Registrar (Urology), Kings College Hospital, London; Senior Urological Registrar, Yorkshire Regional Training Scheme. Member: MRC Working Party on Urological Cancer; MRC Working Party on Superficial Bladder Cancer; Editorial Board, British Journal of Urology; Standing Commitee on Postgraduate Education, British Association of Urological Surgeons; Board, Minimal Access Therapy Training Unit

Scotland; Education Committee, Royal College of Surgeons of Edinburgh; Past Chairman, Scottish Urological Oncology Group. Recreations: golf; motor racing; sailing. Address: (b.) Murrayfield Hospital, Corstorphine Road, Edinburgh; T.-0131-334 0363.

Tombs, Sebastian Martineau, BArch, DipArch (Cantab), FRIAS, ACIArb. Secretary, Royal Incorporation of Architects in Scotland, since 1995; b. 11.10.49, Sussex; m., Eva Hierman; 4 s.; 2 d. Educ. Bryanston; Cambridge University. RMJM, Edinburgh, 1975-76; Roland Wedgwood, Edinburgh, 1976-77; Fountainbridge Housing Association, Edinburgh, 1977-78; Housing Corporation, 1978-81; Edinburgh District Council Housing Department, 1982-86; Depute Secretary, RIASI, 1986-94; Founder and first Secretary, Scottish Ecological Design Association, 1991-94, Chairman, 1994-95. Chair, Parents' Council, Edinburgh Rudolf Steiner School. Recreation: choral music. Address: (b.) 15 Rutland Square, Edinburgh, EH1 2BE; T.-0131-229 7545.

Topping, Professor Barry H.V., BSc, PhD, CEng, CMath, MBCS, MICE, MIStructE, FIMA. Professor, Department of Civil and Offshore Engineering, Heriot-Watt University, Edinburgh, since 1990; b. 14.2.52, Manchester. Educ. Bedford Modern School; City University, London. Lecturer in Civil Engineering, Edinburgh University, 1978-88; Von-Humboldt Research Fellow, Stuttgart University, 1986-87; Senior Lecturer, Heriot-Watt University, 1988-89, Reader, 1989-90. Co-Editor, Structural Engineering Review; Co-Editor, Computing Systems in Engineering. Address: (b.) Department of Civil and Offshore Engineering, Heriot-Watt University, Riccarton, Edinburgh EH14 4AS; T.-0131-449 5111.

Torrance, Rev. Dr. Iain Richard, TD, MA, BD, DPhil. Lecturer in Divinity, Aberdeen University, since 1993; Co-Editor, Scottish Journal of Theology, since 1982; b. 13.1.49, Aberdeen; m., Morag Ann McHugh; 1 s.; 1 d. Educ. Edinburgh Academy; Monkton Combe School, Bath; Edinburgh University; St. Andrews University; Oriel College, Oxford University. Minister, Northmavine, Shetland, 1982-85; Tutor in New Testament and Ethics, Queen's College, Birmingham, 1985-89; Lecturer in New Testament and Patristics, Birmingham University, 1989-93. Hon. Secretary, Aberdeen A.U.T., since 1995; Secretary, Society for the Study of Christian Ethics, since 1995; Judge, Templeton (UK) Awards, since 1994; TA Chaplain, since 1982. Publications: Christology after Chalcedon, 1988; Human Genetics: a Christian perspective (Co-author), 1995. Recreations: walking; Scottish history; reading. Address: (h.) Concraig Smiddy, Clinterty, Aberdeen, AB1 8RN; T.-01224 790902.

Torrance, Rev. Professor James Bruce, MA (Hons), BD. Professor of Systematic Theology, Aberdeen University, 1977-89 (Dean, Faculty of Divinity, 1978-81); Minister, Church of Scotland, since 1950; b. 3.2.23, Chengtu, Szechwan, West China; m., Mary Heather Aitken; 1 s.; 2 d. Educ. Royal High School, Edinburgh; Edinburgh University and New College; Marburg University; Basle University; Oxford University. RAF, 1943-45; ordained, Invergowrie, Dundee, 1954; Lecturer in Divinity and Dogmatics in History of Christian Thought, 1961, and Senior Lecturer in Christian Dogmatics, 1972, New College, Edinburgh; Visiting Professor of New Testament, Union Theological Seminary, Richmond, Virginia, 1960, of Theology, Columbia Theological Seminary, 1965, and Vancouver School of Theology, 1974-75; Visiting Professor in South Africa, USA, New Zealand, Australia, Fiji, W. Samoa, Canada. Convenor, Panel on Doctrine, General Assembly, 1982-86; Joint Convener, British Council of Churches Commission on Doctrine of the Trinity, 1983-89; Joint Convenor, World Alliance of Reformed Churches, Lutheran World Federation Conversations, 1985-88. Publications: John Duns Scotus in a Nutshell (Co-author), 1992; Worship, Community and the Triune God of Grace, 1994;

Nature of Atonement (Editor), 1995. Recreations: bee-keeping; fishing; swimming; gardening. Address: (h.) 3 Greenbank Crescent, Edinburgh EH10 5TE; T.-0131-447 3230.

Torrance, Very Rev. Thomas Forsyth, MBE, MA, BD, DrTheol, DLitt, DD, DrTeol, DTheol, DSc, FBA, FRSE. Emeritus Professor, Edinburgh University, since 1979; b. 30.8.13, Chengdu, Sichuan, China; m., Margaret Edith Spear; 2 s.; 1 d. Educ. Canadian School, Chengdu, China; Bellshill Academy, Lanarkshire; Edinburgh University; Basel University; Oriel College, Oxford. Minister: Alyth Barony Parish Church, 1940-47; served as Church of Scotland Chaplain, 1943-45; Minister, Beechgrove Parish Church, Aberdeen, 1947-50; Edinburgh University: Professor of Church History, 1950-52, Professor of Christian Dogmatics, 1952-79; Moderator, General Assembly of the Church of Scotland, 1976-77. Cross of St. Mark, First Class, 1970; Protoprebyter of Greek Orthodox Church (Hon.), 1973; President, Academie Internationale des Sciences Religieuses, 1972-81. Recreations: formerly golf, squash, fishing; now walking. Address: (h.) 37 Braid Farm Road, Edinburgh EH10 6LE; T.-0131-447 3224.

Toth, Professor Akos George, Dr. Jur., PhD. Professor of Law, Strathclyde University, since 1984; Jean Monnet Chair of European Law, since 1991; b. 9.2.36, Mezotur, Hungary; m., Sarah Kurucz. Educ. Budapest University; Szeged University; Exeter University. Strathclyde University: Lecturer in Law, 1971-76, Senior Lecturer, 1976-82, Reader, 1982-84; British Academy Research Readership, 1993-95. Publications: Legal Protection of Individuals in the European Communities, 1978; The Oxford Encyclopaedia of European Community Law, 1990. Recreations: travel; music; opera; theatre; swimming; walking. Address: (b.) Strathclyde University, Law School, 173 Cathedral Street, Glasgow, G4 ORQ; T.-0141-552 4400, Ext. 3338.

Toulmin, David. Hon. MLitt (Aberdeen). Writer; b. 1.7.13, Rathen, Aberdeenshire; m., Margaret Jane Willox; 3 s. Educ. five public/parish schools. From the age of 14 to 65, earned living by manual labour (farm worker); his first article was published by Farmer and Stock Breeder, 1947; wrote short stories in dialect for local newspapers and the Scots Magazine; five stories broadcast on radio by the BBC; a collection was published as Hard Shining Corn, 1972; has published a further eight books; awarded grant by the Scottish Arts Council, 1983; Spring Book Award, 1993, for Collected Short Stories; real name, John Reid. Recreations: writing; reading; popular music; cinema; video; television; antiquarian research. Address: (h.) 7 Pittodrie Place, Aberdeen; T.-Aberdeen 634058.

Townell, Nicholas Howard, MB, BS (Lond), FRCS (Eng), FRCS (Edin). Consultant General Surgeon and Urologist, Dundee and Angus Hospitals, since 1985; Honorary Senior Lecturer in Surgery, Dundee University Medical School, since 1985; b. 19.4.49, Redhill; m., Hoang Anh Vuong; 1 s.; 2 d. Educ. Davenant Foundation Grammar School; London University; Royal Free Hospital School of Medicine. Various House Surgeon, House Physician and Registrar posts; Senior Registrar in General Surgery and Urology, Royal Free Hospital. Fellow, Royal Society of Medicine. Specialist interest: minimally invasive urology. Recreations: classical music; golf; squash; hill-walking. Address: (h.) Rosebank, Hillside, Angus, DD10 9HZ; T.-0167 4830296.

Trabichoff, Geoffrey Colin, AGSM, LGSM. Violinist; Leader, BBC Scottish Symphony Orchestra, since 1982; Leader, The Paragon Ensemble of Scotland and the Salon Orchestra; Director/Soloist and Recitalist; b. 15.4.46, London; m., Judith Orbach; 1 step s.; 1 d. Leader, Gulbenkian Orchestra, Lisbon, 1974-76; Leader, Mannheim Chamber Orchestra, 1976-78; Leader, Hannover State Orchestra, 1978-81. Address: (h.) 40 Woodend Drive, Jordanhill, Glasgow G13; T.-0141-959 3496.

Trainer, Professor James, MA, PhD. Professor of German, Stirling University, since 1969 (Deputy Principal, 1973-78, 1981-87, 1989-92); b. 2.3.32; m., Barbara Herta Reinhard (deceased); 2 s.; 1 d. Educ. St. Andrews University; Free University of Berlin. Lecturer in German, St. Andrews University, 1958-67; Visiting Professor, Yale University, 1964-65; Visiting Scholar, University of California at Santa Barbara, 1989; Vice-Convener, SUCE, 1987-94; Convener, SUCE Modern Languages Panel, 1979-86; Member, Inter University and Polytechnic Council, since 1983; Member, Scottish Examination Board, 1975-82; Chairman, SED Postgraduate Awards Committee, since 1989; Member, UK Fulbright Committee, 1985-93; Trustee, National Library of Scotland, 1986-91; Chairman, Scottish Conference of University Teachers of German, 1978-80; Member, National Academic Audit Unit; Member, SHEFCO Quality Assessment Committee; Member Overseas Research Students Awards Committee, CVCP; Governor, Morrison's Academy, Creiff. Recreations: music; cricket; translating. Address: (b.) Stirling University, Stirling; T.-01786 473171.

Tranter, Nigel, OBE, KCLJ, DLitt, MA (Hon.). Author and Novelist, since 1935; b. 23.11.09, Glasgow; m., May Jean Campbell Grieve (deceased); 1 s. (deceased); 1 d. Educ. St. James' Episcopal School; George Heriot's, Edinburgh. Professional Writer, since 1946; published more than 120 books, including over 80 novels; Vice-Convener, Scottish Covenant Association, 1951-55; President, East Lothian Liberal Association, 1960-70; Chairman, National Forth Road Bridge Committee, 1953-57; Chairman, St. Andrew Society of East Lothian, since 1966; President, Scottish PEN, 1962-66 (now Honorary President); Chairman, Society of Authors, Scotland, 1966-70; Chairman, National Book League, Scotland, 1971-73. Vice-Chancellor, Order of St. Lazarus of Jerusalem, 1982-88; Hon. Vice-President, Scottish Association of Teachers of History; Honorary Freeman of Blackstone, Virginia, USA, 1980; BBC Radio Scot of the Year, 1989; Hon. President, Saltire Society; Trustee, Scottish Flag Fund; Chairman, St. Andrew Society of East Lothian. Recreations: walking; climbing; genealogy; castle architecture. Address: (h.) Quarry House, Aberlady, East Lothian; T.-Aberlady 258.

Travis, Christopher Douglas, BSc (Soc Sci). Chief Executive, Kincardine and Deeside Enterprise Trust Ltd.; b. 12.5.59, Kaduna, Nigeria. Educ. Dollar Academy; Edinburgh University. Previously: Lecturer in Economics/research student, Dundee College of Technology, Business Counsellor, SDA, Economic Development Manager, Gordon District Council, Executive Director, Clydesdale Development Co. Ltd., Chairman, Lanarkshire Enterprise Training Ltd. Recreations: cooking; reading; hill-walking; golf. Address: (b.) Unit 1, Aboyne Business Centre, Huntly Road, Aboyne AB34 5HE; T.-013398 87222.

Trayhurn, Professor Paul, BSc, DPhil, DSc, FIBiol. Head, Division of Biochemical Sciences, Rowett Research Institute, since 1988; Department of Biomedical Sciences and Department of Molecular and Cell Biology, Aberdeen University, since 1992 (Honorary); b. 6.5.48, Exeter; m., Deborah Hartland Gigg; 3 s.; 1 d. Educ. Colyton Grammar School, Devon; Reading University; Oxford University. Graduate student, Linacre College, Oxford, 1969-72; NATO European Research Fellow, Strasbourg, 1972-73; Postdoctoral Fellow, Oxford, 1973-75; MRC Scientific/Senior Scientific Staff, Dunn Nutrition Laboratory, Cambridge, 1975-86; Professor and Heritage Scholar, University of Alberta, 1986-88; Evelyn Williams Visiting Professor, University of Sydney, 1992. Member, Council, Nutrition Society, 1982-84, 1991-93; Chairman, Scottish Section, Nutrition Society, 1993-95; Chairman, BBSRC Human Nutrition Advisory Panel; Chairman, Scientific Committee, 8th European Congress on Obesity. Publications: over 250 scientific publications. Address: (b.) Division of Biochemical Sciences, Rowett Research

Institute, Bucksburn, Aberdeen, AB2 9SB; T.-01224 716610.

Tremmel, Ronald Ian, DA, MPhil, RIBA, ARIAS. Director of Property, Fife Regional Council, since 1991; President, LAMP (Local Authority Managers of Property), since 1994; External Examiner, Duncan of Jordanstone College of Art, since 1989; b. 25.6.50, Edinburgh; m., Susan Ruth Duckman; 1 d. Educ. North Berwick High School; Edinburgh University; Heriot Watt University. Worked briefly with private architectural firms in Edinburgh; moved into local government as a senior architect with Inverclyde District Council, 1979; Principal Architect, Fife Regional Council. Member, Scottish Vernacular Buildings Working Group. Recreations: curling; badminton; theatre. Address: (h.) Cargill House, Letham, Fife; T.-01592 414141.

Trewavas, Professor Anthony James, BSc, PhD, FRSE. Professor, Institute of Cell and Molecular Biology, Edinburgh University, since 1990; b. 17.6.39, London; m., Valerie; 1 s.; 2 d. Educ. Roan Grammar School; University College, London. Lecturer/Reader, Edinburgh University; Visiting Professor, Universities of Michigan State, Calgary, California (Davis), Bonn, Illinois, North Carolina, National University of Mexico; University of Milan. Publications: 140 scientific papers; two books. Recreations: music (particularly choral); reading. Address: (h.) 1 Rullion Road, Penicuik, Midlothian; T.-01948 673372.

Trotter, Alexander Richard. DL, FRSA. Vice President, Scottish Landowners Federation, since 1986 (Convenor, 1982-85); Member, Nature Conservancy Council and Chairman, its Committee for Scotland, 1985-90; b. 20.2.39, London; m., Julia Henrietta Greenwell; 3 s. Educ. Eton College. Royal Scots Greys, 1958-68; Member, Berwickshire County Council, 1968-74 (Chairman, Roads Committee, 1972-74); Member, UK Committee, European Year of the Environment, 1986-88; Chairman, Mortonhall Park Ltd., since 1973; Vice-Chairman, Border Grain Ltd., since 1984. Member, Queen's Bodyguard for Scotland (Royal Company of Archers). Recreations: skiing; tennis; hunting; shooting. Address: Charterhall, Duns, BerwickshireTD11 3RE; T.-01890 840301.

Trudgill, David L., BSc, PhD, CBiol, FBIBiol. Head, Zoology Department, Scottish Crop Research Institute, since 1972; b. 2.5.42, Leeds; m., Margaret Jean Luckraft; 3 s. Educ. Leeds Grammar School; Ulverston Grammar School; Leeds University; London University. Nematologist, Rothamsted Experimental Station, 1966-72. Chairman, European Plant Protection Organisation ad hoc committee on potato cyst nematodes. Recreations:hill-walking; fishing. Address: (b.) Zoology Department, Scottish Crop Research Institute, Invergowrie, Dundee DD2 5DA; T.-01382 562731.

Truman, Donald Ernest Samuel, BA, PhD, FIBiol, CBiol, FRSA. Vice-Dean and Vice-Provost, Faculty of Science and Engineering, University of Edinburgh, since 1989; b. 23.10.36, Leicester; m., Kathleen Ramsay; 1 s.; 1 d. Educ. Wyggeston School, Leicester; Clare College, Cambridge. NATO Research Fellow, Wenner-Grenn Institute, Stockholm, 1962-63; MRC Epigenetics Research Group, Edinburgh, 1963-72; Lecturer, Department of Genetics, Edinburgh University, 1972-78; Senior Lecturer, 1978-89; Head of Department, 1984-89, Director of Biology Teaching Unit, 1985-89; Aneurin Bevan Memorial Fellow, Government of India, 1978; Chairman, Edinburgh Centre for Rural Research, since 1993; Member, Council, Scottish Agricultural College, since 1995. Publications: The Biochemistry of Cytodifferentiation, 1974; Differentiation in Vitro (Joint Editor), 1982; Stability and Switching in Cellular Differentiation, 1982; Coordinated Regulation of Gene Expression, 1986. Recreation: gardening. Address: (b.) Faculty of Science and Engineering Office, West Mains Road, Edinburgh, EH9 3JY; T.-0131-650 5758.

Tuck, Ronald Moore Sinclair, MA, DMS. H.M. Chief Inspector of Schools, since 1992; b. 20.3.49, Edinburgh; m., Anne; 1 s.; 1 d. Educ. George Heriot's; Edinburgh University; Dundee Institute of Technology. Lecturer/Senior Lecturer, Angus College, 1974-85; H.M. Inspector of Schools, 1985-92. Recreations: watching football; bridge; keeping fit. Address: (b.) Room 4/108, New St. Andrews House, St. James Centre, Edinburgh; T.-0131-244 4513.

Tucker, Derek Alan. Editor, Press and Journal, Aberdeen, since 1992; b. 31.10.53, Liverpool; 1 s.; 1 d. Educ. Quarry Bank High School, Liverpool; Municipal Grammar School, Wolverhampton. Reporter/Chief Reporter/News Editor/Deputy Editor, Express and Star, Wolverhampton, 1972-92. Member, Press Complaints Commission, since 1995; Officer, RAFVR; avoids societies like the plague. Recreations: golf; travel; watching any sport not involving horses. Address: (b.) Lang Stracht, Mastrick, Aberdeen; T.-01224 690222.

Tucker, Professor John Barry, BA, MA, PhD. Professor of Cell Biology, St. Andrews University, since 1990; b. 17.3.41, Arundel; m., Janet Stephen Murray; 1 s. Educ. Queen Elizabeth Grammar School, Atherstone; Peterhouse, Cambridge. Fulbright Travel Scholar and Research Associate, Department of Zoology, Indiana University, 1966-68; SERC Research Fellow, Department of Zoology, Cambridge, 1968-69; Lecturer in Zoology, St. Andrews University, 1969-79 (Chairman, Zoology Department, 1982-84); Reader II in Zoology, 1979-90. Member: SERC Advisory Group II, 1977-80, SERC Molecular Biology and Genetics Sub-committee, 1986-89, Editorial Board of Development, 1979-88. Recreations: cycling; hill-walking; tennis; reluctant gardener. Address: (b.) School of Biological and Medical Sciences, Bute Building, St. Andrews University, St. Andrews, Fife KY16 9TS; T.-01334 463560.

Tumelty, Michael, MA (Hons). Music Critic, The Herald, since 1983; b. 31.5.46, Hexham; m., Frances McGinniss; 2 s.; 1 d. Educ. St. Aloysius College, Glasgow; Aberdeen University. Postgraduate research into the music of Debussy, 1974-75; entered teaching, St. Columba's High School, Clydebank (Principal Teacher, 1980-83); served on a variety of working groups on curriculum development; freelance Music Critic, Jewish Echo, 1979-82, and Daily Telegraph, 1982-83; Member, Scottish Central Committee on Music, 1982-83. Recreations: family; avid collector of records. Address: (b.) The Herald, Albion Street, Glasgow.

Tunstall-Pedoe, Professor Hugh David, MA, MD, FRCP, FRCPE, FFCM. Professor and Director, Cardiovascular Epidemiology Unit, and Senior Lecturer in Medicine, Ninewells Hospital and Medical School, Dundee, since 1981; Honorary Consultant Cardiologist, since 1981; Honorary Specialist in Public Health Medicine, since 1981; b. 30.12.39, Southampton; m., Jacqueline Helen; 2 s.; 1 d. Educ. Haberdashers' Aske's School; Dulwich College; King's College, Cambridge; Guy's Hospital Medical School. Junior hospital posts, Guy's, Brompton, National Queen Square and London Hospitals; MRC Social Medicine Unit, 1969-71; Lecturer in Medicine, The London Hospital, 1971-74; Senior Lecturer in Epidemiology and Honorary Physician, and Honorary Community Physician, St. Mary's Hospital and Medical School, London, 1974-81. Chairman, European Society of Cardiology Working Group on Epidemiology and Prevention, 1983-85. Recreations: hill-walking; bee-keeping; golf. Address: (b.) Cardiovascular Epidemiology Unit, Ninewells Hospital and Medical School, Dundee, DD1 9SY; T.-01382 644255.

Turley, Mark John, BSc (Hons), MBA, MCIOH. Director of Housing, City of Edinburgh Council, since 1996; Executive Director of Housing, City of Edinburgh District Council, since 1993; b. 25.6.60, Dudley. Educ. High Arcal

Grammar School, Sedgley; Leicester University. Sheffield City Council, 1981-91; Head of Tenant Services, York City Council, 1991-93. Recreations: playing violin; reading. Address: (b.) Housing Department, 23 Waterloo Place, Edinburgh, EH1 3BH; T.-0131-529 7325.

Turmeau, Professor William Arthur, CBE, FRSE, Dr. h.c., BSc, PhD, CEng, FIMechE. Principal and Vice-Chancellor, Napier University, 1982-94; b. 19.9.29, London; m., Margaret Moar Burnett; 1 d. Educ. Stromness Academy, Orkney; Edinburgh University; Moray House College of Education; Heriot-Watt University. Royal Signals, 1947-49; Research Engineer, Northern Electric Co. Ltd., Montreal, 1952-54; Mechanical Engineer, USAF, Goose Bay, Labrador, 1954-56; Contracts Manager, Godfrey Engineering Co. Ltd., Montreal, 1956-61; Lecturer, Bristo Technical Institute, Edinburgh, 1962-64; Napier College: Lecturer and Senior Lecturer, 1964-68, Head, Department of Mechanical Engineering, 1968-75, Assistant Principal and Dean, Faculty of Technology, 1975-82. Member, Scottish Economic Council, since 1988; Member, Council for Industry and Higher Education, since 1991; Member, Steering Committee, University of the Highlands and Islands Project; Member, IMechE Accreditation Committee; Member, Scottish Division Committee, Institute of Directors, since 1992; Member, British Council CICHE, since 1982; Patron, Lothian Children, since 1992. Recreations: modern jazz; Leonardo da Vinci. Address: (h.) 71 Morningside Park, Edinburgh, EH10 5EZ; T.-0131-447 4639.

Turnbull, Wilson Mark, DipArch, MLA, MBCS, RIBA, FRIAS, FLI. Turnbull Jeffrey Partnership, Landscape Architects, since 1982; b. 1.4.43, Edinburgh. Educ. George Watson's; Edinburgh College of Art; University of Pennsylvania. Assistant Professor of Architecture, University of Southern California, 1970-74; Partner, W.J. Cairns and Partners, Environmental Consultants, 1974-82; Partner, Design Innovations Research, 1976-81; Council Member, Cockburn Association (Edinburgh Civic Trust), 1986; Commissioner, Countryside Commission for Scotland, 1988-92; Chairman, Edinburgh Greenbelt Initiative, 1988-91; Director, Edinburgh Greenbelt Trust, since 1991, Vice-Chairman, since 1993. Recreation: sailing. Address: (b.) Sandeman House, 55 High Street, Edinburgh EH1 1SR; T.-0131-557 5050.

Turner, John R., MA, MusB, FRCO. Organist and Director of Music, Glasgow Cathedral, since 1965; Lecturer, Royal Scottish Academy of Music, since 1965; Organist, Strathclyde University, since 1965; b. Halifax. Educ. Rugby; Jesus College, Cambridge. Recreations: gardening; travel. Address: (h.) Binchester, 1 Cathkin Road, Rutherglen, Glasgow G73 4SE; T.-0141-634 7775.

Turner, Professor Kenneth John, BSc, PhD. Professor of Computing Science, Stirling University, since 1987; b. 21.2.49, Glasgow; m., Elizabeth Mary Christina; 2 s. Educ. Hutchesons' Boys Grammar School; Glasgow University; Edinburgh University. Data Communications Designer, International Computers Ltd., 1974-76; Senior Systems Analyst, Central Regional Council, 1976-77; Data Communications Consultant, International Computers Ltd., 1977-87. Recreations: choral singing; craft work; sailing. Address: (b.) Department of Computing Science, Stirling University, Stirling, FK9 4LA; T.-01786 467420.

Turner, Malcolm, OBE, JP, DL. Member, Strathclyde Regional Council, since 1974; Deputy Lieutenant, Dunbartonshire, since 1989; Vice Chairman, Scottish National Housing and Town Planning Council; Vice-President, Clydebank Rugby Club; b. 13.12.21, Clydebank; m., Margaret Balfour; 1 s. Educ. Clydebank High School. Member: Clydebank Town Council, 1957-75 (Provost, 1966-69), Dunbarton County Council, 1957-75; Member, Cumbernauld Development Corporation, 1975-83; former

Chairman, Central Water Development Board; Vice-Chairman, Convention of Royal Burghs, 1967-73; Hon. Freeman, Clydebank District. Recreations: angling; caravanning; bowling; golf. Address: (h.) 14 Mossgiel Drive, Clydebank, Dunbartonshire G81 2BY; T.-0141-952 3992.

Turner, Norman William, MILAM, ALA, FIMgt, FSA(Scot). Director of Leisure, Motherwell District Council, since 1985; Past Chairman, Association of Directors of Leisure, Recreation and Tourism; b. 12.4.48, Portsmouth. Educ. Portsmouth Technical High School; Brighton Polytechnic. District Librarian, Motherwell District Council; Depute Director of Libraries and Museums, Falkirk District Council; Deputy District Librarian, City of Southampton District; Deputy Borough Librarian, Andover Borough Council. Former Vice-Chairman, Public Libraries Group; former Hon. Treasurer, Scottish Library Association. Recreations: season ticket holder, Motherwell FC; sport; theatre; cinema; music; natural history. Address: (b.) Motherwell District Council, PO Box 14, Civic Centre, Motherwell ML1 1TW; T.-01698 266166.

Turner, Susan Morag, MA, DipEd, DIDCE, CTD, FISW, FCollP, FRSA. Director, Scottish Association for the Deaf, since 1991; b. 5.4.35, Glasgow. Educ. Rutherglen Academy; Glasgow University; Manchester University. Teacher of hearing-impaired children, Glasgow School for the Deaf; Head Teacher: Paisley School for the Deaf, Dundee School for the Deaf; Lecturer, Professional Curriculum Support Services Department, Moray House College; Director, Scottish Centre for the Education of the Deaf, 1971-91. Scottish Vice-President, National Association of Special Educational Needs; Council Member, International Centre for Special Education; Member, Board of Trustees, Royal National Institute for Deaf People; Member, Church Advisorate on Special Educational Needs; Chairman, J.S. Lochrie Memorial Trust. Address: (h.) 15 Bonaly Brae, Colinton, Edinburgh EH13 0QF; T.-0131-441 7520.

Turner Thomson, Ann Denise. Interior Designer; b. 23.5.29, Molesey; m., Gordon Turner Thomson; 1 s.; 3 d. Educ. Sherborne School for Girls, Dorset; St. James's Secretarial College, London. Council Member, National Trust for Scotland, 1990-95; Member, Council, Edinburgh International Festival; Member, Board of Directors, Art in Partnership; Member, Saltire Society Housing Awards Panel. Recreations: theatre; opera; visual arts. Address: 8 Middleby Street, Edinburgh EH9 1TD; T.-0131-667 3997.

Tyre, Alistair McKenzie, FHCIMA, DipSHS, MIMgt. Principal and Chief Executive, Langside College, Glasgow, since 1991; b. 6.12.40, Glasgow; m., Jenice Elizabeth Cleat; 1 d. Educ. Dunoon Grammar School; Strathclyde University. Hotel management, 1960-67; Lecturer and Head of Department, Ayr College, 1967-87; Depute Principal, James Watt College, Greenock, 1987-91. Director, Borderline Theatre Company; Director, Scottish Further Education Unit; Member, General Convocation, Strathclyde University. Recreations: golf; squash; hill-walking; gardening; theatre. Address: (b.) 50 Prospecthill Road, Glasgow, G42 9LB; T.-0141-649 4991.

Tyre, Colin Jack, LLB, DESU. Advocate, since 1987; b. 17.4.56, Dunoon; m., Elaine Patricia Carlin; 1 s.; 2 d. Educ. Dunoon Grammar School; Edinburgh University; Universite d'Aix Marseille. Admitted as Solicitor, 1980; Lecturer in Scots Law, Edinburgh University, 1980-83; Tax Editor, CCH Editions Ltd., Bicester, 1983-86. Publications: CCH Inheritance Tax Reporter; contributor to Stair Memorial Encyclopaedia. Recreations: orienteering; golf; mountain walking; contemporary music. Address: (b.) Advocates' Library, 1 Parliament Square, Edinburgh; T.-0131-226 5071.

U

Upton, Professor Anthony Frederick, MA (Oxon), AM, FRHistS. Professor of Nordic History, St. Andrews University, since 1984; b. 13.10.29, Stockton Heath, Cheshire; m., Sirkka R.; 3 s. Educ. County Boys' School, Windsor; Queen's College, Oxford. Assistant Lecturer in Modern History, Leeds University, 1952-56; St. Andrews University: Lecturer in Modern History, 1956, Senior Lecturer, 1966, Reader, 1974. Sundry offices, Labour Party in Fife and in educational bodies, e.g. St. Andrews School Council. Recreations: music; literature; politics. Address: (h.) 5 West Acres, St. Andrews, Fife.

U'ren, William Graham, BSc (Hons), DipTP, FRTPI. Director of Planning and Technical Services, Clydesdale District Council, since 1982; b. 28.12.46, Glasgow; m., Wendy; 2 d. Educ. Aberdeen Grammar School; Aberdeen University; Strathclyde University. Planning Assistant: Clackmannan County Council, 1970-72, Lanark County Council, 1972-75; Principal and Chief Planning Officer, Clydesdale District Council, 1975-82. Past Chairman, Scottish Society of Directors of Planning. Recreations: sport; bird watching; philately. Address: (b.) District Offices, South Vennel, Lanark ML11 7JT; T.-Lanark 661331.

Urquhart, Celia Margaret Lloyd. Proprietor, C U Developments; Chairman, Court, Glasgow Caledonian University; Board Member, Nursing Board for Scotland; a Director, Glasgow Chamber of Commerce; Chairman, Arran Haulage Services; Member, Advisory Committee, Imperial Cancer Rersearch; Patron, Arran Cancer Support; b. 7.4.47, Glasgow; 1 s.; 2 d. Trained as registered general Nurse; moved to business administration; joined BNOC as a corporate planner; founded C U Data, 1986. Won Scottish Free Enterprise Award, 1990. Recreations: hill-walking; sailing; gardening; golf. Address: (b.) C U Developments, Munro Business Centre, Munro Place, Anniesland, Glasgow, G13 2UP.

Urquhart, John Munro, CBE, MA, MEd, FEIS; b. 16.9.10, Gairloch; m., Adela Margaret Sutherland; 1 s.; 1 d. Educ. Lochgilphead Secondary School; Oban High School; Glasgow University. Schoolmaster, Hutchesons' Boys' Grammar School; Assistant Director of Education, Banffshire; Depute Director of Education, Glasgow; Director of Education, Selkirkshire; Director, Scottish Certificate of Education Examination Board, 1965-75; Consultant Registrar, Caribbean Examinations Council, 1977-78; President, Association of Directors of Education, 1963-64. Boy Scouts County Commissioner, Selkirkshire; edited Statistical Account of Selkirkshire, 1964; District Governor, Rotary District 102, 1980. Recreations: angling; walking; reading; gardening. Address: (h.) 29 Craiglockhart Drive South, Edinburgh EH14 1JA; T.-0131-443 3085.

Urwin, Professor Derek William, BA, MA (Econ), PhD. Professor of Politics and International Relations, Aberdeen University, since 1990; b. 27.10.39, Consett; m., Patricia Anne Ross; 2 s. Educ. Consett Grammar School; Wolsingham Grammar School; Keele University; Manchester University. Lecturer, Strathclyde University, 1963-72; Associate Professor, University of Bergen, 1972-80; Professor, Warwick University, 1981-90. Publications: Western Europe since 1945; The Community of Europe; From Ploughshare to Ballot Box; Politics in Western Europe Today; Centre-Periphery Structures in Europe; Scottish Political Behaviour. Recreations: walking; reading; marquetry. Address: (b.) Department of Politics and International Relations, Aberdeen University, Old Aberdeen, AB9 2TY; T.-01224 272716/272713.

V

Valentine, Ian Balfour, CA. Scottish Managing Partner, BDO Stoy Hayward, Chartered Accountants, since 1985; Non-Executive Board Member, Ayrshire and Arran Health Board, 1981-93; b. 17.10.40, Glasgow; m., Elaine; 1 s.; 1 d. Educ. Hutchesons' Boys' Grammar School. Partner, J. Wyllie Guild & Ballantine, 1965 (subsequently BDO Stoy Hayward). Member, Council, Institute of Chartered Accountants of Scotland and of South West Committee; Chairman, Ayrshire Association of Chartered Accountants of Scotland, 1976-78; President, Junior Chamber Ayr, 1972-73; Member, Ayr Schools Council, 1976-78; Director, Federation of Scottish Junior Chambers of Commerce, 1973-74; Honorary Secretary and Treasurer, Ayr Rugby Football Club, 1979-84. Recreations: golf; rugby (as spectator); bridge. Address: (b.) 64 Dalblair Road, Ayr; T.- 01292 263277.

Valentine, Keith, MA, LLB. Procurator Fiscal, Stirling, since 1976; b. 10.12.32, Perth; m., Anne Florence Ritchie; 1 s.; 2 d. Educ. Perth Academy; Edinburgh University. RAF Education Branch, 1956-59 (Flt.-Lt.); Procurator Fiscal Service, since 1961, Ayr, Glasgow, Edinburgh and Crown Office; other legal experience in private practice and with General Accident Fire and Life Assurance Corporation Ltd. Founder Chairman and former Scottish Branch Representative, Executive Committee, British Association for the Study and Prevention of Child Abuse and Neglect. Recreations: golf; gardening; swimming; holidays in the sun. Address: (h.) Muircroft, Chalton Road, Bridge of Allan FK9 4EF.

Vanderheijden, Professor Cornelius A.J.M. Professor of Strategic Management, Strathclyde University, since 1991; b. 31.10.32, Rotterdam; m., Haverkamp Henderika. Educ. Technological University, Delft. General and business planning, Shell Group; Head, Internal Consultancy, then Head, Scenario Planning, Shell International; Member, Shell's Planning Management Team. Address: (h.) Flat 7, 166 Ingram Street, Glasgow; T.-0141-552 7899.

Vandore, Peter Kerr, QC, MA (Hons), LLB; b. 7.6.43. Called to the Scottish Bar, 1968. Address: Advocates' Library, Parliament House, Edinburgh, EH1 1RF.

van Heyningen, Veronica, MA, MS, DPhil. Staff Scientist, MRC Human Genetics Unit, Edinburgh University, since 1977; Hon. Treasurer, The Genetical Society, since 1994; Co-Chair, Human Genome Organisation's Human Genome Mapping Committee; Trustee, National Museums of Scotland, since 1994; b. 12.11.46, Hungary; m., Dr. Simon van Heyningen; 1 s.; 1 d. Educ. Humphrey Perkins School, Leicestershire; Girton College, Cambridge; North Western University, Illinois; Lady Margaret Hall, Oxford. BEIT Memorial Fellow, 1973-76; Howard Hughes International Research Scholar, since 1993; Honorary Professor, Edinburgh University, 1995. Recreations: visiting museums; travel; talking to people. Address: (b.) MRC Human Genetics Unit, Edinburgh, EH4 2XU; T.-0131-467 8405.

Vannet, Alfred Douglas, LLB, FRSA. Regional Procurator Fiscal, Grampian, Highland and Islands, at Aberdeen, since 1994; b. 31.7.49, Dundee; m., Pauline Margaret Renfrew; 1 s.; 1 d. Educ. High School of Dundee; Dundee University. Procurator Fiscal Depute, Dundee, 1976-77; Procurator Fiscal Depute, then Senior Procurator Fiscal Depute, Glasgow, 1977-84; Assistant Solicitor, Crown Office, 1984-90; Deputy Crown Agent, 1990-94. Recreations: music; golf; walking.

van Raay, Stefan Bastiaan. Senior Curator of Art, Glasgow Museums and Art Galleries, since 1993; b.

3.12.54, Rotterdam. Educ. St. Franciscus College, Rotterdam; Leyden University; University of Amsterdam. PR Officer, Hollandse Beton Group, Netherlands, 1978-80; studied art history and archaeology, 1980-86; Co-Founder, D'Arts, Amsterdam, 1986-90; Deputy Director, Van Gogh Museum, Amsterdam, 1990-93. Member, Board of Advisers, Tableau (magazine of fine arts). Recreations: skiing; reading; classical music; angling. Address: (b.) The Burrell Collection, Pollok Country Park, Glasgow G43 1AT; T.-0141-649 7151.

Vardy, Professor Alan Edward, BSc, PhD, EurIng, CEng, FICE, MASCE, MIAHR, FRSA. Professor of Civil Engineering, Dundee University, since 1979 (Deputy Principal, 1985-89, Vice-Principal, 1988-89); Director, Wolfson Bridge Research Unit, 1980-90; b. 6.11.45, Sheffield; m., Susan Janet; 2 s.; 1 d. Educ. High Storrs Grammar School, Sheffield; Leeds University. Lecturer in Civil Engineering, Leeds University, 1972-75; Royal Society Warren Research Fellow, Cambridge University, 1975-79. Recreations: flying; wind-surfing; music. Address: (h.) Dunholm, 512 Perth Road, Dundee, DD2 1LW; T.- Dundee 566123.

Vas, Professor Peter, MSc, PhD, CSc, DSc, MIEEE, FIEE. Professor in Engineering, Department of Engineering, Aberdeen University, since 1990; b. 1.6.48, Budapest; m., S. Vasne; 2 s. Educ. Technical University of Budapest. United Electrical Machine Works, 1973-77; Newcastle University, 1977-87; Chalmers University of Technology, Lund University of Technology, 1987-90. Laureate of George Montefiore International Award, Belgium, 1990. Publications: over 100 papers; three books; several patents. Address: (b.) Department of Engineering, University of Aberdeen, Aberdeen; T.-01224 272818.

Vaughan, Barbara, BSc, MA. Chairman, Scottish Community Education Council, since 1988; b. 12.2.40, Thornton Heath; m., Dr. Robin A. Vaughan; 2 s.; 2 d. Educ. St. Anne's College, Sanderstead; Nottingham University; Dundee University. Teacher, Derbyshire, 1962-64; Lecturer in Economics, Dundee Institute of Technology, 1979-83; Councillor, Tayside Region, 1980; Chairman, Further Education Sub-Committee, 1981-82; Chairman, Education Committee, 1982-86; Member, MSC Committee for Scotland, 1983-86; Commissioner, MSC, 1986.

Veal, Sheriff Kevin Anthony, KSG, KHS, LLB. Sheriff of Tayside Central and Fife at Forfar, since 1993; b. 16.9.46, Chesterfield; m., Monica Flynn; 2 s.; 2 d. Educ. Lawside Academy, Dundee; St. Andrews University. Partner, Burns Veal and Gilland, Dundee, 1971-93; Legal Aid Reporter, 1978-93; Temporary Sheriff, 1984-93; Tutor, Department of Law, Dundee University, 1978-85; Dean, Faculty of Procurators and Solicitors in Dundee, 1991-93. Musical Director, Cecilian Choir, Dundee, since 1975. Recreations: organ and classical music; hill-walking. Address: (h.) Viewfield, 70 Blackness Avenue, Dundee, DD2 1JL; T.- 01382 668633.

Vernon, Kenneth Robert, CBE, BSc, FEng, FIEE, FIMechE. Deputy Chairman and Chief Executive, North of Scotland Hydro-Electric Board, 1973-88; b. 15.3.23, Dumfries; m., Pamela Hands; 1 s.; 3 d.; 1 d. deceased. Educ. Dumfries Academy; Glasgow University. BTH Co., Edinburgh Corporation, British Electricity Authority, 1948-55; South of Scotland Electricity Board, 1955-56; North of Scotland Hydro Electric Board: Chief Electrical and Mechanical Engineer, 1964, General Manager, 1966, Board Member, 1970; Director, British Electricity International Ltd., 1976-88; Board Member, Northern Ireland Electricity Service, 1979-85. Recreation: fishing. Address: (h.) 10 Keith Crescent, Edinburgh EH4 3NH; T.-0131-332 4610.

Vernon, Richard Geoffrey, BSc, PhD, FIBiol. Head, Department of Biochemistry and Molecular Biology,

Hannah Research Institute; Honorary Lecturer, Glasgow University; b. 19.2.43, Maidstone; m., Mary Christine Cunliffe; 1 s.; 1 d. Educ. Newcastle High School; Birmingham University. Consultant Editor, Journal of Dairy Research; Member, Editorial Board, Domestic Animal Endocrinology; Past President, Birmingham University Mountaineering Club; first ascent of Mount Mazinaw, first British ascent, Mount Nautilus. Publication: Physiological Strategies in Lactation (Joint Editor). Recreations: walking; ornithology; mountaineering; bridge; photography. Address: (h.) 29 Knoll Park, Ayr, KA7 4RH; T.-01292 42195.

Vettese, Raymond John, DipEd, BA (Hons). Teacher and Writer; b. 1.11.50, Arbroath; m., Maureen Elizabeth. Educ. Montrose Academy; Dundee College of Education; Open Univesity. Journalist, Montrose Review, 1968-72; student, 1972-75; barman, 1975-77; factory worker, 1977-78; clerical officer, 1978-85; teacher, since 1985; Preses, Scots Language Society; William Soutar Fellowship, 1990-93. Publications: Four Scottish Poets, 1985; The Richt Noise, 1988 (Saltire Society Best First Book); A Keen New Air, 1995. Recreations: reading; music; cooking; chess. Address: (h.) 9 Tayock Avenue, Montrose, DD10 9AP; T.-01674 678943.

Vickerman, Professor Keith, BSc, PhD, DSc, FLS, FRSE, FRS. Regius Professor of Zoology, Glasgow University, since 1984; Consultant Expert on Parasitic Diseases, World Health Organisation, since 1973; b. 21.3.33, Huddersfield; m., Moira Dutton; 1 d. Educ. King James Grammar School, Almondbury; University College, London (Fellow, 1985). Wellcome Lecturer in Protozoology, University College, London, 1958-63; Tropical Research Fellow, Royal Society, 1963-68; Glasgow University: Reader in Zoology, 1968-74; Professor of Zoology, 1974-84, Head, Department of Zoology, 1979-85. Leeuwenhoek Lecturer, Royal Society, 1994. Publications: The Protozoa (Co-author), 1967; many papers in scientific and medical journals. Recreations: drawing and painting; gardening. Address: (h.) 16 Mirrlees Drive, Glasgow G12 OSH; T.-0141-334 2794.

Vincent, Catherine Lindsey, BA (Hons). Joint Director of Marketing and Communications, Scottish Sports Council, since 1989; b. 30.7.56, Oxford; m., Jonathan Nicholas Crook; 2 d. Educ. Rosebery Grammar School, Epsom; Newnham College, Cambridge. Research Assistant, Sheffield University, 1978; Assistant Editor, Athlone Press, 1979; Freelance Writer, 1980; Development Officer, Scottish Community Education Council, 1981; Senior Policy Analyst, Fife Regional Council, 1986. Former Chairman, Spiritual Assembly of the Baha'is of Edinburgh; former Director, Baha'i Information Scotland. Publication: Discovering Edinburgh, 1981. Recreations: reading; walking; tennis; badminton; enjoying family. Address: (b.) Scottish Sports Council, Caledonia House, South Gyle, Edinburgh EH12 9DQ; T.-0131-317 7200.

W

Waddell, William A.H., BA (Hons). Head Teacher, Bishopbriggs High School, since 1994; b. 22.6.51, Paisley; m., Alison; 2 d. Educ. John Neilson, Paisley; Strathclyde University. Teacher of Mathematics, then Assistant Principal Teacher of Mathematics, Park Mains High School, 1974-80; Principal Teacher of Mathematics, Dumbarton Academy, 1980-85; Assistant Head Teacher, Boclair Academy, 1985-90; Depute Head Teacher, Hermitage Academy, 1990-94. Recreations: sport; gardening; family pursuits. Address: (h.) 66 Stuart Road, Bishopton, Renfrewshire.

Wade, Professor Nicholas James, BSc, PhD. Professor of Visual Psychology, Dundee University, since 1991; b. 27.3.42, Retford, Nottinghamshire; m., Christine Whetton; 2 d. Educ. Queen Elizabeth's Grammar School, Mansfield; Edinburgh University; Monash University. Postdoctoral Research Fellow, Max-Planck Institute for Behavioural Physiology, Germany, 1969-70; Lecturer in Psychology, Dundee University, 1970-78, Reader, 1978-91. Publications: The Art and Science of Visual Illusions, 1982; Brewster and Wheatstone on Vision, 1983; Visual Allusions: Pictures of Perception, 1990; Visual Perception: an introduction, 1991; Psychologists in Word and Image, 1995. Recreations: golf; cycling. Address: (h.) 36 Norwood, Newport-on-Tay, Fife DD6 8DW; T.-01382 543136.

Wade, Professor Terence Leslie Brian, BA, PhD, FIL. Professor in Russian Studies, Strathclyde University; b. 19.5.30, Southend-on-Sea; m., Mary Isobel McEwan; 2 d. Educ. Southend-on-Sea High School for Boys; Durham University. National Service, Intelligence Corps, 1953-55; War Office Language Instructor, 1955-63; Lecturer, Scottish College of Commerce, Glasgow, 1963-64; Lecturer, Senior Lecturer, Reader, Professor, Strathclyde University, from 1964; Chairman, Department of Modern Languages, 1986-94. Convener, West of Scotland Association of Teachers of Russian; Editor, Journal of Russian Studies, 1980-86: Chairman, Association of Teachers of Russian, 1986-89; President, Association of Teachers of Russian, 1989-90; Member, Presidium, International Association of Teachers of Russian Language and Literature, since 1991. Publications: Russian Exercises for Language Laboratories (Co-author); The Russian Preposition "do" and the Concept of Extent; Prepositions in Modern Russian; Russia Today (Co-Editor); The Gender of Soft-Sign Nouns in Russian; A Comprehensive Russian Grammar. Address: 1 Cleveden Crescent, Glasgow, G12 OPD; T.-0141-339 3947.

Waigh, Professor Roger David, BPharm, PhD, MRPharmS, CChem, FRSC. Professor of Medicinal Chemistry, Strathclyde University, since 1991; b. 8.8.44, Loughborough; m., Sally Joy Bembridge; 1 s.; 1 d. Educ. Sir George Monoux Grammar School, Walthamstow; Bath University. Lecturer, Strathclyde University, 1970-76; Lecturer, then Senior Lecturer, Manchester University, 1976-91. Recreations: bird-watching; golf; photography. Address: (b.) Department of Pharmaceutical Sciences, Strathclyde University, Glasgow G1 1XW; T.-0141-552 4400.

Waite, James A., MA. Rector, Perth Academy, since 1986; b. 9.10.42, Edinburgh; m., Sandra R. MacKenzie; 1 s.; 2 d. Educ. Royal High School, Edinburgh; Edinburgh University. Teacher of English, George Heriot's School, 1965-70; Principal Teacher of English, Campbeltown Grammar School, 1970-71; Principal Teacher of English, then Assistant Head Teacher, Boroughmuir High School, 1971-83; Depute Head Teacher, James Gillespie's High School, 1983-86. Recreations: theatre; literature; music;

hill-walking. Address: (b.) Perth Academy, Murray Place, Perth, PH1 1NJ; T.-01738 623491.

Wake, Joseph Robert, MA, CPA. Secretary, Scotland, Central Bureau for Educational Visits and Exchanges, since 1972; b. 16.5.42, Corbridge; 1 s.; 2 d. Educ. Royal Grammar School, Newcastle upon Tyne; Edinburgh University; Moray House College of Education. Teacher, Kirkcaldy High School, 1966-69, St. Modan's High School, Stirling, 1969-71; Principal Teacher of Modern Languages, Grangemouth High School, 1971-72. Recreations: cricket; philately; Scottish dancing. Address: (b.) 3 Bruntsfield Crescent, Edinburgh EH10 4HD; T.-0131-447 8024.

Wakeford, Air Marshal Sir Richard (Gordon), KCB (1976), LVO (1961), OBE (1958), AFC (1952). Chairman, MacRobert Trustees, 1982-94; b. 20.4.22, Torquay; m., Anne Butler; 2 s.; 1 d.; 1 d. (deceased). Educ. Montpelier School, Paignton; Kelly College, Tavistock. Entered RAF, 1941; Coastal Command, 1941-45; Transport Command, 1945-47; Training Command, 1947-52; staff duties, including Director of Ops Staff, Malaya, 1952-58; CO, The Queens' Flight, 1958-61; IDC, 1969; Director, Service Intelligence, 1970-73; Commander, Anzuk Force Singapore, 1974-75; Deputy Chief of Defence Staff (Intelligence), 1975-78; retired Air Marshal, 1978. Director, RAF Benevolent Fund, Scotland, 1978-89; Commissioner, Queen Victoria School, Dunblane, 1980-90; Director, Thistle Foundation; Director, Cromar Nominess; Commander, Order of St. John, 1986. Recreation: fishing. Address: (h.) Sweethome Cottage, Inchberry Road, Fochabers, IV32 7AQ; T.-0343 820 436.

Walde, Professor Thomas W., PhD, LLM, Driur. Professor of Petroleum, Mineral and International Investment Law, Dundee University, since 1991; Executive Director, Centre for Petroleum and Mineral Law and Policy; b. 1949, Germany; 1 s. Educ. Universities of Heildelberg, Frankfurt and Harvard. Institute for International Economic Law, Frankfurt, 1975-80; U.N. Natural Resources and Energy Division, 1980-85; Adviser to Governments on mineral development policies, legislation, and contract negotiations; Interregional Advisor on Petroleum and Mineral Legislation, U.N. (D.T.C.D.), 1985-90. Address: (b.) Park Place, Dundee DD1 4HN; T.-01382 344300.

Walkden, Gordon Mark, BSc, PhD. Member, Kincardine and Deeside District Council, since 1984 (Vice Convener and Chairman, Policy and Resources, since 1988); Head, Department of Geology and Petroleum Geology, Aberdeen University; Geological Consultant to industry; b. 8.6.44, Edinburgh; m., K. Mary M. Begg; 3 c. Educ. Quintin School, London; Manchester University. Past Chairman, Banchory Community Council; scientific author and local historian. Recreations: building restoration; palaeontology. Address: (h.) Banchory, Kincardineshire.

Walker, (Alexander) Percy, DL, MB, ChB, DObstRCOG, MRCGP. Deputy Lieutenant, Ayr and Arran; b. 2.7.16, Irvine; m., Aileen G. Digby; 1 s.; 3 d. Educ. Shrewsbury School; Glasgow University. Temporary Surgeon Lt., RNVR, 1940-46; General Medical Practitioner, Ayr, 1948-81; Adjudicating Medical Officer, DHSS, 1952-87; Senior Medical Officer, Western Meeting Club, Ayr Racecourse, 1955-87. Recreations: golf; gardening; curling; sailing. Address: (h.) Bentfield, Maryborough Road, Prestwick, Ayrshire KA9 1SW; T.-01292 477876.

Walker, Alexander William, MBE, JP. Honorary Sheriff, since 1970; Chairman, Finance and General Purposes Committee, Tweeddale District Council, 1977-92 (Member of Council, 1974-92; Chairman, Tweeddale Licensing Board, since 1975; Chairman, Tweeddale Local Sports Council; b. 10.5.24, Peebles; m., Dorothy Margaret. Educ. Kingsland School; Scottish Woollen and Worsted Technical

College. D.B. Ballantyne Bros., 1939-70; Air Training Corps, 1941-43, RAF, 1943-46 (Sergeant); former Director, Sonido International Ltd. (formerly Fidelitone International Ltd.); elected, Peebles Town Council, 1960-75; Provost, 1967-70; Burgh Treasurer, 1971-75; held every office, Peebles Town Council; Member, Peeblesshire County Council, 1960-70 (Vice Chairman, Finance Committee); Vice Chairman, Tweeddale District Council, 1974-77; Warden, Neidpath Castle, 1971; former Dean, Guildry Corporation of Peebles; Honorary President, Peebles Callants Club; Dean, Guildry Corporation of Peebles, since 1990-93. Recreations: football in younger days; now enjoys reading political biographies; and, of course, local government, which unfortunately is no longer local or indeed democratic. Address: (h.) Gadeni, 59 High Street, Peebles; T.-Peebles 21011.

Walker, Professor Andrew Charles, BA, MSc, PhD, FInstP, FRSE, CPhys. Professor of Modern Optics, Heriot-Watt University, since 1988; b. 24.6.48, Wembley; m., Margaret Elizabeth; 1 s.; 1 d. Educ. Kingsbury County Grammar School; Essex University. Postdoctoral Fellowship, National Research Council of Canada, 1972-74; SRC Research Fellowship, Essex University, 1974-75; Higher/Senior Scientific Officer, UKAEA Culham Laboratory, 1975-83; Lecturer/Reader, Heriot-Watt University, 1983-88. Honorary Secretary, Quantum Electronics Group, Institute of Physics, 1982-85; Chairman, Scottish Branch, Institute of Physics, 1993-95. Recreations: music; skiing; sailing. Address: (b.) Department of Physics, Heriot-Watt University, Riccarton, Edinburgh EH14 4AS; T.-0131-451 3036.

Walker, Professor David Maxwell, CBE, QC, MA, PhD, LLD, Hon. LLD, FBA, FRSE, FRSA. Regius Professor of Law, Glasgow University, 1958-90; Honorary Senior Research Fellow, since 1990; b. 9.4.20, Glasgow; m., Margaret Knox, OBE. Educ. High School of Glasgow; Glasgow University; Edinburgh University; London University. HLI and Indian Army, 1939-46; Advocate, 1948; in practice, Scottish Bar, 1948-54; Professor of Jurisprudence, Glasgow University, 1954-58; Barrister (Middle Temple), 1957; QC (Scot), 1958; Dean, Faculty of Law, Glasgow University, 1956-59; Convener, School of Law, 1984-88. Chairman, High School of Glasgow Trust. Publications: Law of Damages in Scotland; The Scottish Legal System; Law of Delict in Scotland; Law of Civil Remedies in Scotland; Law of Prescription in Scotland; Law of Contracts in Scotland; Oxford Companion to Law; Principles of Scottish Private Law (four volumes); The Scottish Jurists; Stair's Institutions (Editor); Stair Tercentenary Studies (Editor); A Legal History of Scotland, (3 Vols). Recreations: book collecting; Scottish history; motoring. Address: (b.) Department of Private Law, Glasgow University, Glasgow G12 8QQ; T.-0141-339 8855, Ext. 4556.

Walker, Professor David Morrison, OBE, DA, FSA, FSA Scot, FRSE, HFRIAS, Hon. LLD (Dundee). Associate Professor of Art History, University of St. Andrews, since 1994; Chief Inspector of Historic Buildings, Scottish Office Environment Department, 1988-93; b. 31.1.33, Dundee; m., Averil Mary Stewart McIlwraith; 1 s. Educ. Morgan Academy, Dundee; Dundee College of Art. Voluntary work for National Buildings Record, Edinburgh, 1952-56; National Service, Royal Engineers, 1956-58; Glasgow Education Authority, 1958-59; Dundee Education Authority, 1959-61; Historic Buildings Branch, Scottish Office: Senior Investigator of Historic Buildings, 1961-76, Principal Investigator of Historic Buildings, 1976-78; Principal Inspector of Historic Buildings, 1978-88. Alice Davis Hitchcock Medallion, 1970. Publications: Dundee Nineteenth Century Mansions, 1958; Architecture of Glasgow (Co-author), 1968 (revised and enlarged edition, 1987); Buildings of Scotland: Edinburgh (Co-author), 1984; Dundee: An Illustrated Introduction (Co-author), 1984; St.

Andrew's House: an Edinburgh Controversy 1912-1939, 1989; Central Glasgow: an illustrated architectural guide (Co-author), 1989. Address: (h.) 1 St. Vincent Street, Edinburgh EH3 6SW.

Walker, Drew, BSc, MB, ChB, MSc, MFCM. Director of Health Planning and Public Health, Chief Administrative Medical Officer, Executive Board Member, Ayrshire and Arran Health Board, since 1991; b. 30.8.54, Bridge of Allan. Educ. Perth Academy; Edinburgh University. House Officer/SHO, 1978-80; District Medical Officer, Zimbabwe, 1980-82; Registrar/Senior Registrar in public health, 1983-87; Consultant in public health, 1987-91. National Vice President, Medical Practitioners Union, 1988-90. Recreations: football; climbing; skiing; reading Viz. Address: (h.) Schaw House, by Stair, Ayrshire.

Walker, Ernest John Munro, CBE. Chairman, UEFA Stadia Committee; b. 20.7.28, Glasgow; m., Anne; 1 s.; 2 d. Educ. Queen's Park Secondary School. Army (Royal Horse Artillery), 1946-48; Assistant Secretary, industrial textile company, 1948-58; Assistant Secretary, Scottish Football Association, 1958-77, Secretary, 1977-90. Director, Euro-Sporting; Director, Scotball Travel and Leisure Ltd.; Director, Eastern European Assistance Bureau; Member: FIFA Board of Appeal; Chairman, Scottish Stadia Committee; Vice-President, Newspaper Press Fund. Recreations: golf (past Captain, Haggs Castle GC); fishing; music; travel.

Walker, Ian. Member, Gordon District Council, since 1984 (Convener, Leisure and Recreation Committee); Member, COSLA Arts and Recreation Commitee; Director, Scottish Sculpture Workshop; Trustee, North-East of Scotland Heritage Trust; Trustee, Action North East; Member, Gordon Sports Council; Vice-Chairman, Gordon Forum for the Arts; Member, Gordon Crime Prevention Panel; Member, Gordon Fishings Management Committee; Head Teacher, Westhill Primary School, since 1973; b. 1.6.40, Inverurie; m., Mildred Agnes Rose; 1 s.; 1 d. Educ. Daviot School; Inverurie Academy; Aberdeen College of Education. Assistant Teacher, Insch School, 1963-67; Head Teacher: Finzean School, 1967-69, Kinellar School, 1969-73; Member, Working Party on Mathematics in the Primary School, Grampian Regional Council; Elder, Church of Scotland; Chairman: Westhill and District Swimming Pool Association, Westhill Swimming Pool Trust, Lawsondale Playing Field Trust. Recreations: listening to all kinds of music, especially jazz and blues; indoor bowling; walking; watching cricket (Blue, Aberdeen College of Education), reading; theatre; films; golf. Address: (h.) 11A Arnhall Drive, Westhill, Skene, Aberdeenshire AB32 6TZ; T.-01224 741783.

Walker, Irene, MBA, BSc (Hons). Chief Executive, Dumfries and Galloway Enterprise Ltd., since 1994; b. 28.1.52, Larbert; m., Neil Walker. Educ. Larbert High School; Edinburgh University; St. Andrews University. Local government, 1975-86; Glasgow Garden Festival, 1986-88; Scottish Development Agency, 1989-91; Grampian Enterprise Ltd., 1991-93. Recreations: windsurfing; skiing. Address: (b.) Solway House, Dumfries Enterprise Park, Tinwald Downs Road, Heathhall, Dumfries DG1 3SJ. Tel.: 01387 245000.

Walker, Rev. James Bernard, MA, BD, DPhil. Chaplain, St. Andrews University, since 1993; b. 7.5.46, Malawi; m., Sheila Mary Easton; 3 s. Educ. Hamilton Academy; Edinburgh University; Merton College, Oxford. Church of Scotland Minister: Mid Craigie linked with Wallacetown, Dundee, 1975-78, Old and St. Paul's, Galashiels, 1978-87; Principal, The Queen's College, Birmingham, 1987-93. Publication: Israel — Covenant and Land, 1988. Recreations: hill-walking; tennis; squash; golf. Address: (b.) 3A St. Mary's Place, St. Andrews KY16 9UY; T.-01334 462865.

Walker, Leslie Gresson, MA, PhD, DipClinPsychol, CPsychol, AFBPsS. Senior Lecturer, Department of Mental Health, Aberdeen University, since 1989; Director, Behavioural Oncology Unit, Departments of Mental Health and Surgery, Aberdeen University; Honorary Consultant Clinical Psychologist, Aberdeen Royal Hospitals NHS Trust; b. 17.5.49, Glasgow; m., Mary Birnie; 2 s. Educ. Banff Academy; Aberdeen University. Clinical Psychologist, Grampian Health Board, 1974-76; Lecturer, Aberdeen University, 1976-89; elected Member, National Committee of Scientists in Professions Allied to Medicine (Clinical Psychology Sub-Committee), Scottish Home and Health Department, 1979-85; External Assessor, Children's Panel Advisory Committee, Grampian Regional Council, 1982-90; Council Member, British Society of Experimental and Clinical Hypnosis, since 1991; Consultant Editor, Contemporary Hypnosis, since 1991; Chairman Elect, British Psychosocial Oncology Group; Elder, Church of Scotland. Publications: numerous scientific papers and three books, including Police Stress at Work (Co-author), 1993. Address: (b.)Behavioural Oncology Unit, Departments of Mental Health and Surgery, Medical School, Foresterhill, Aberdeen AB9 2ZD; T.-01224 681818, Ext. 53881.

Walker, Margaret, OBE, MA. Vice-President, Scottish Conservative & Unionist Association, 1987-89; Chairman, Scottish Committee, National Social Affairs Forum, 1985-93; b. 4.5.26, Paisley; m., David Maxwell Walker (qv). Educ. Paisley Grammar School; Glasgow University. Manuscript Department, National Library of Scotland, 1948-54; Chairman, Hillhead Conservative & Unionist Association, 1982-86; West of Scotland Conservative Women's Area Committee: Vice-Chairman, 1980-81, Chairman, 1981-83; West of Scotland Conservative Area Council: Vice-Chairman, 1983-85, Chairman, 1985-87. Recreations: music; ballet; conservation; cookery. Address: (h.) 1 Beaumont Gate, Glasgow, G12 9EE; T.-0141-339 2802.

Walker, Michael Giles Neish, CBE, MA (Cantab). Chairman, Sidlaw Group, since 1988 (Chief Executive, 1976-88); b. 28.8.33, Fife; m., Margaret R. Hills; 2 s.; 1 d. Educ. Shrewsbury School; St. John's College, Cambridge. National Service, Royal Dragoons, 1952-54 (2nd Lt.); TA, Fife and Forfar Yeomanry, 1954-72 (Major); joined Jute Industries Ltd., 1958 (subsequently name changed to Sidlaw Group); Director, Dunedin Smaller Companies Trust, since 1982; Director, Scottish Hydro-Electric plc, since 1982; Chairman, I & S Smaller Companies Trust PLC, since 1992. Address: (b.) Sidlaw Group plc, Keith House, South Gyle, Edinburgh EH12 9DQ; T.-0131-317 2600.

Walker, William Connell, FIPM, FBIM, FRSA. MP (Conservative), Tayside North, since 1979; Company Director; b. 20.2.29, Dundee; m., Mavis Evelyn Lambert; 3 d. Educ. Logie School. Message boy; RAF (commissioned); Training and Education Officer; Director of Personnel; Managing Director. Vice-President, World Scout Parliamentary Union; President, Air Cadet Gliding; Vice President, British Gliding Association; RAF Volunteer Reserve, Squadron Leader. Recreations: gliding; flying; Scouting; walking; caravanning. Address: (h.) Longacres, Burrelton, Perthshire, PH13 9NY; T.-01250 874782.

Walker, Professor William Farquhar, DSc, ChM, FRCS (Edin and Eng), FRSE. Consultant General Surgeon, since 1965; Emeritus Professor of Vascular Surgery, Surgery, Dundee University; b. 26.5.25, Aberdeen; m., Bettie Stanley; 2 s.; 1 d. Educ. Forfar Academy; St. Andrews University. RAF, 1949-51; Senior Lecturer in Surgery (Consultant), Dundee Royal Infirmary, 1956-75. President, Association of Surgeons of Great Britain and Ireland, 1984; President, Vascular Society of Great Britain and Ireland, 1989. Recreations: golf; fishing; gardening. Address: (h.) 438 Blackness Road, Dundee; T.-01382 68179.

Walker, William M., QC, MA, LLB; b. 19.5.33. Advocate, 1957; Social Security Commissioner, since 1988; a Child Support Commissioner, since 1993.

Walkingshaw, Francis, NP. Solicitor; Procurator Fiscal, District of Wigtown, since 1983, and Kirkcudbright, since 1993; b. 9.12.42, Edinburgh; m., Penelope Marion Theodosia Brooks McKissock; 2 s. Educ. George Watson's College, Edinburgh. Private practice; joined Procurator Fiscal service, 1975. Dean, Faculty of Wigtown District Solicitors, 1985-87. Recreations: shooting; fishing; food and wine. Address: (b.) Sheriff Court House, Lewis Street, Stranraer; T.-01776 704321.

Wallace, Alan John, FRICS. Commercial Director, East Kilbride Development Corporation, since 1990; b. 9.7.51, Motherwell; m., Mary; 1 s.; 1 d. Educ. Wishaw High School. Valuation Surveyor, Lanark County Council, 1969-75; Estates Surveyor, Motherwell District Council, 1975-78; Depute Commercial Director, Livingston Development Corporation, 1978-90. Recreation: golf. Address: (b.) East Kilbride Development Corporation, Atholl House, East Kilbride G74 1LU; T.-013552 41111.

Wallace, Archibald Duncan, MB, ChB. Medical Practitioner, Campbeltown, since 1950; Hon. Sheriff of North Strathclyde at Campbeltown, since 1980; b. 4.1.26, Glasgow; m., Rona B. MacLennan; 1 s.; 2 d. Educ. High School of Glasgow; Glasgow University. Sector Medical Officer, Argyll and Clyde Health Board, until 1988; Civilian MO to RAF Machrihanish, until 1988. Chairman, Campbeltown Branch, RNLI; Past President, Campbeltown Rotary Club; Past Captain, Machrihanish Golf Club. Recreations: golf; gardening. Address: (h.) Lilybank House, Low Askomil, Campbeltown; T.-01586 52658.

Wallace, Professor David Alexander Ross, BSc, PhD, FRSA, FRSE. Professor of Mathematics, Strathclyde University, since 1986 (Professor, Stirling University, 1973-86); b. 24.11.33, Cupar. Educ. Stranraer High School; St. Andrews University; Manchester University. Instructor: Princeton University, 1958-59, Harvard University, 1959-60; Research Fellow, then Lecturer, Glasgow University, 1960-65; Senior Lecturer, Aberdeen University, 1965-73. Recreations: culture; tennis; swimming; skiing; badminton. Address: (b.) Department of Mathematics, Strathclyde University, Livingstone Tower, 26 Richmond Street, Glasgow G1 1XH; T.-0141-552 4400.

Wallace of Campsie, Baron (George Wallace), JP, DL. Life President, Wallace, Cameron (Holdings) Ltd., since 1981; b. 13.2.15; m. Educ. Queen's Park School, Glasgow; Glasgow University. Solicitor, since 1950; Honorary Sheriff, Hamilton, since 1971; Chairman, East Kilbride and Stonehouse Development Corporation, 1969-75; Member, South of Scotland Electricity Board, 1966-68; Member, Board, Scottish Development Agency, 1975-78; President, Glasgow Chamber of Commerce, 1974-76; Chairman, Scottish Executive Committee, British Heart Foundation, 1973-76; Patron, Scottish Retirement Council, since 1975. Address: (h.) 14 Fernleigh Road, Newlands, Glasgow G43 2UE.

Wallace, James Fleming, QC, MA, LL.B. Counsel (Draftsman), Scottish Law Commission, 1979-93; Part-time Chairman, Industrial Tribunals, since 1993; b. 19.3.31, Edinburgh; m., Valerie Mary Lawrence (deceased); 2 d.; 2, Linda Ann Lilleker. Educ. Edinburgh Academy; Edinburgh University. National Service, 1954-56 (2nd Lt., Royal Artillery); TA (Lt., Royal Artillery), 1956-60; practised at Scottish Bar, 1957-60; Parliamentary Draftsman and Legal Secretary to Lord Advocate, 1960-79. Publications: The Businessman's Lawyer (Scottish Supplement); Stair Memorial Encyclopaedia (Contributor). Recreations: hill-walking; choral singing; golf; badminton. Address: (h.) 24 Corrennie Gardens, Edinburgh EH10 6DB; T.-0131-447 1224.

Wallace, James Robert, MA (Cantab), LLB (Edinburgh). MP (Liberal Democrat, formerly Liberal), Orkney and Shetland, since 1983; Leader, Scottish Liberal Democrats, since 1992; Advocate, since 1979; b. 25.8.54, Annan; m., Rosemary Janet Fraser; 2 d. Educ. Annan Academy; Downing College, Cambridge; Edinburgh University. Called to Scottish Bar, 1979; contested Dumfries, 1979, and South of Scotland Euro Constituency, 1979; Member, Scottish Liberal Party Executive, 1976-85 (Vice-Chairman, Policy, 1982-85); Honorary President, Scottish Young Liberals, 1984-85; Liberal Democrat Spokesman on Fisheries, since 1988, and on Scotland, since 1992. Publication: New Deal for Rural Scotland (Co-Editor), 1983. Recreations: golf; reading; travelling (especially between London and the Northern Isles). Address: (h.) Northwood House, Tankerness, Orkney KW17 2QS; T.-01856 861383.

Wallace, John Anderson. Chief Executive, Tayside Regional Council, 1982-90; b. 10.7.29, Perth; m., Mary; 1 s.; 1 d. Educ. Perth Academy; Edinburgh University. Solicitor, private practice, 1951-54; Solicitor: Dundee Corporation, 1954-60, Cumbernauld Development Corporation, 1960-66; Depute Town Clerk, Dundee Corporation, 1966-75; Depute Chief Executive, Tayside, 1975-82. Recreations: bowls; golf; music. Address: (h.) Corrymeela, 17 Fintry Place, Broughty Ferry, Dundee DD5 3BG; T.-01382 778833.

Wallace, John David, MA, DipEd, FSA Scot. International Arbiter and Chairman, Arbiters Council, Federation Internationale des Echecs; President, Scottish Junior Chess Association, 1986-89; Council Member, Scottish Chess Association; b. 21.11.21, Bulford; m., Jenefer M.H. Bell (deceased); 1 s.; 1 d. Educ. Tonbridge School; St. Andrews University. Army Service, 1940-46 (Captain, Royal Artillery); teaching appointments in Orkney and Fife, 1954-73; Assistant Rector, Madras College, St. Andrews, 1971-73; founding Headmaster, Abbotsgrange Middle School, Grangemouth, 1974-84. Recreations: bridge; chess; curling; hill-walking. Address: (h.) Kirkheugh Cottage, The Shorehead, St. Andrews, Fife KY16 9RG.

Wallace, Rev. William Fitch, BDS, BD. Minister, Pultneytown and Thrumster Church, since 1990; Convener, Church of Scotland Board of Social Responsibility, since 1993; b. 6.10.39, Falkirk; m., Jean Wyness Hill; 1 s.; 3 d. Educ. Allan Glen's School; Glasgow University; Edinburgh University. Minister, Wick St. Andrew's and Thrumster Church, 1974-90; former missionary dentist. Vice-Convener, Board of Social Responsibility, 1989-92. Recreations: family; golf; gardening. Address: The Manse, Coronation Street, Wick KW1 5LS; T.-01955 603166.

Wallace, Professor William Villiers, MA, FRHistS. Director, Institute of Russian and East European Studies, Glasgow University, 1979-92, now Senior Research Fellow; Dean, Faculty of Social Sciences, Glasgow University, 1989-92; b. 15.12.26, Glasgow; m., Gulli Fyfe; 2 s.; 1 d. Educ. Hutchesons' Boys' Grammar School; Glasgow University; London University. RNVR, 1944-47; appointments in History, Pittsburgh University, London University, Aberdeen University, Durham University, 1953-67; Professor of History, New University of Ulster, 1967-79. Foreign Member, Russian Academy of Technological Sciences. Address: (b.) Institute of Russian and East European Studies, Glasgow University, 29 Bute Gardens, Glasgow G12 8RS; T.-0141-330 4579.

Walls, Professor Andrew Finlay, OBE, MA, BLitt, DD, FSA Scot. Director, Centre for the Study of Christianity in the Non-Western World, since 1982; b. 21.4.28; m., Doreen Mary Harden; 1 s.; 1 d. Librarian, Tyndale House, Cambridge, 1952-57; Lecturer in Theology, Fourah Bay College, Sierra Leone, 1957-62; Head, Department of Religion, Nigeria University, 1962-65; Aberdeen University: Lecturer in Church History, 1966-69, Senior Lecturer, 1969, first Head, Department of Religious Studies, and Riddoch Lecturer in Comparative Religion, 1970, Reader, 1975, Professor of Religious Studies, 1979-85, Emeritus Professor, 1985; Honorary Professor, Edinburgh University, since 1987; Visiting Professor of World Christianity, Yale University, 1988; Co-opted Member, Aberdeen Education Committee, 1971-74; Aberdeen City Councillor, 1974-80; Convener, Arts and Recreation, COSLA, 1978-80; Chairman, Council for Museums and Galleries in Scotland, 1978-81; Vice-Chairman, Committee of Area Museums Councils, 1980-81; Member, Williams Committee on the future of the national museums, 1979-82; Trustee, National Museum of Antiquities of Scotland, 1982-85; Member, Museums Advisory Board for Scotland, 1984-85; Trustee, National Museums of Scotland, 1985-87; Methodist Preacher; Past Chairman, Disablement Income Group, Scotland; President, British Association for the History of Religions, 1977-80; Secretary, Scottish Institute of Missionary Studies; Editor, Journal of Religion in Africa, 1967-86; Committee Member, European Ethnological Research Centre; Henry Martyn Lectures, Cambridge University, 1988; Margaret Harris Lectures, Dundee University, 1989. Address: (b.) Centre for the Study of Christianity in the Non-Western World, Edinburgh University, New College, Mound Place, Edinburgh EH1 2LX; T.-0131-650 8952.

Walsh, James Richard Thomas. Leader, Argyll and Bute Council, since 1995 (Chairman, Finance and Personnel, Chairman, Policy); Chairman, Finance and Manpower, Argyll and Bute District Council, since 1992; b. 19.12.46, Dunoon; m., Allison; 2 s. Educ. Dunoon Grammar School. Member, Strathclyde Regional Council, since 1982. Recreations: painting; golf; walking dogs. Address: (h.) Castleton Villa, Innellan, Dunoon, Argyll; T.-01369 830383.

Walters, Professor David Gareth, BA, PhD. Stevenson Professor of Hispanic Studies, Glasgow University, since 1995; b. 1.1.48, Neath; m., Christine Ellen Knott; 1 s.; 1 d. Educ. Rhondda County Grammar School for Boys; University College, Cardiff. Temporary Lecturer in Spanish, Leeds University, 1972-73; Glasgow University, 1973-95: Lecturer in Hispanic Studies, Senior Lecturer, Titular Professor. Publications: books on Francisco de Quevedo and Francisco de Aldana; editor, Poems to Lisi and collection of essays on Antonio Machado; numerous articles on Spanish, Portuguese and Catalan literature. Recreations:music; playing the piano; poetry; travel; most sports; antiques. Address: (h.) 32 Golf View, Bearsden, Glasgow G61 4HJ; T.-0141-942 4948.

Walton, Professor Henry John, MD, PhD, FRCPE, FRCPsych, DPM, Hon.MD. Physician; Professor of International Medical Education, Edinburgh, since 1986; b. 15.2.24, South Africa; m., Sula Wolff. Educ. University of Cape Town; London University; Columbia University, NY; Edinburgh University. Registrar in Neurology and Psychiatry, University of Cape Town, 1946-54; Head, Department of Psychiatry, 1957-60; Senior Registrar, Maudsley Hospital, London, 1955-57; Senior Lecturer in Psychiatry, then Professor of Psychiatry, Edinburgh University, 1962-85; Editor, Medical Education, since 1976; President, Association for Medical Education in Europe, 1972-86, Hon. Life President, since 1986; President, World Federation for Medical Education, since 1983; frequent Consultant to WHO; Member, Academies of Medicine of Argentina, Belgium and Poland. Publications: as Editor: Small Group Psychotherapy, 1974; Dictionary of Psychiatry, 1985; as Co-Editor: Newer Developments in Assessing Clinical Competence, 1986; as Co-Author: Alcoholism, 1988; Report of the World Conference on Medical Education; Report on World Summit of Medical Education, 1993. Recreations: literature; visual arts, particularly Western painting and Chinese and Japanese art.

Address: (b.) World Federation for Medical Education, Edinburgh University, 11 Hill Square, Edinburgh EH8 9DR; T.-0131-650 6209.

Walton, John Christopher, BSc, PhD, DSc. Reader in Chemistry, St. Andrews University, since 1986; b. 4.12.41, St. Albans; m., Jane Lehman; 1 s.; 1 d. Educ. Watford Grammar School for Boys; Sheffield University. Assistant Lecturer: Queen's College, St. Andrews, 1966-67; Dundee University, 1967-69; Lecturer in Chemistry, United College, St. Andrews, 1969-80; Senior Lecturer, 1980-86. Director, Good Health Association (Scotland) Ltd.; Elder, Seventh-day Adventist Church. Recreations: music; philosophy. Address: (b.) School of Chemistry, St. Andrews University, St. Andrews, Fife, KY16 9ST; T.-01334 463864.

Walton, Kenneth D., BMus, GMusRNCM, ARCO, AMIPR. Director – Corporate Affairs, Greater Glasgow Tourist Board and Convention Bureau, since 1989; b. 20.2.58, Paisley; m., Janis H. Goodfellow; 2 d. Educ. Paisley Grammar School; Glasgow University; Royal Northern College of Music, Manchester. Tutor in Music, Glasgow University, 1982-83; Lecturer in Academic Studies, RSAMD, 1985-86, 1988-89; on music staff, Hutchesons' Grammar School, 1987-88; Manager, Scottish Music Information Centre, 1988-89; Member, BBC Music Advisory Committee, Scotland, 1985-89; President, Glasgow Society of Organists, 1985-86; Secretary and Treasurer, Scottish Musicians Benevolent Fund, 1988-89; Member, Board of Directors, Chorus International Festival, since 1989, Glasgow Building Preservation Trust, since 1992, Scottish Early Music Consort, since 1992; Music Critic, Daily Telegraph, 1983-91. Recreations: gardening; golf. Address: (h.) Wraysbury, Watt Road, Bridge of Weir PA11 3DN; T.-01505 612981.

Wannop, Professor Urlan Alistair, MA, MCD, MRTPI. Professor of Urban and Regional Planning, Strathclyde University, since 1981; b. 16.4.31, Newtown St. Boswells; 1 s.; 1 d. Educ. Aberdeen Grammar School; Edinburgh University; Liverpool University. Appointments in public and private practice, 1956-68; Team Leader, Coventry-Solihull-Warwickshire Sub-Regional Planning Study, 1968-71; Director, West Central Scotland Plan, 1972-74; Senior Deputy Director of Planning, Strathclyde Regional Council, 1975-81; Member, Parliamentary Boundary Commission for Scotland, since 1983. Address: (h.) 43 Lomond Street, Helensburgh G84 7ES; T.-01436 74622.

Ward, David Romen, MA, CertEd. Rector, Hutchesons' Grammar School, since 1987; b. 21.12.35, Newcastle upon Tyne; m., Stella Barbara Anderson; 1 s.; 2 d. Educ. St. Mary's, Melrose; Sedbergh School; Emmanuel College, Cambridge. Assistant Master: Winchester College, Wellington College; Senior History Master, City of London School; Deputy Headmaster, Portsmouth Grammar School; Head Master, Hulme Grammar School. Member, Admiralty Interview Board; Member, Convocation, Strathclyde University; Member, Quality Assessment Committee, Scottish Higher Education Funding Council; Freeman, City of London. Publications: Fall of Metternich and the Revolution of 1848; British Foreign Policy 1815-1865; Explorations. Address: (h.) 192 Nithsdale Road, Glasgow, G41 5EU; (b.) Hutchesons' Grammar School, Beaton Road, Glasgow G41 4NW; T.-0141-423 2933.

Ward, Dorothy May Blair, MBChB, MRCGP, FRSM. Principal in general practice, Glasgow, since 1966; Hospital Practitioner, Geriatric Medicine, Cowglen Hospital, Glasgow, since 1974; b. 27.8.28, York; m., Thomas B. Begg; 1 s.; 2 d. Educ. Paisley Grammar School; Glasgow University. Past Chairman and Member, Joint Committee, Postgraduate Training for General Practice, 1977-92; Past Chairman and Member, Glasgow Local Medical Committee, 1966-92; BMA: Member, Board, Science and

Education; former Member, General Medical Services Committee; Fellow of BMA; Member, General Medical Council; President, Medical Women's International Association. Address: (h.) 3 Montgomery Drive, Giffnock, Glasgow G46 6PY.

Ward, Professor John Macqueen, CBE, CA, Companion, IEE. Resident Director, Scotland and North of England, IBM United Kingdom Ltd., since 1990; Professor, Heriot Watt University; b. 1.8.40, Edinburgh; m., Barbara Macintosh; 1 s.; 3 d. Educ. Edinburgh Academy; Fettes College. Joined IBM UK Ltd. at Greenock plant, 1966; worked in France and UK; appointed European Director of Information Systems, 1975, and Havant Site Director, 1981. Chairman, Scottish CBI; Chairman, Quality Scotland Foundation; Chairman, Advisory Scottish Council for Education and Training Targets; Chairman, Scottish Electronics Forum; Chairman, Institute of Technology Management; Director, Scottish Business in the Community; Member, Council, Institute of Chartered Accountants; Director, IIP Scotland; Director, Greater Easterhouse Development Company, 1991-93; Non Executive Director, European Assets Trust NV; Member, Scottish Committee, Association of Business Sponsorship of the Arts; Honorary Doctorate, Napier University. Address: (b.) 21 St. Andrew Square, Edinburgh EH2 1AY; T.-0131-556 9292.

Ward, Leslie Graeme. Director, Advocates for Animals, since 1979; Secretary, St.Andrew Animal Fund, since 1989; b. 12.1.51, Dunbar; m., Erika Gillian; 1 d. Educ. Dunbar Grammar School. RAF, 1969-79. Member, Executive Committee, League Against Cruel Sports; Member, Home Secretary's Animal Procedures Committee; Treasurer, Committee for the Reform of Animal Experiments; Fellow, Winston Churchill Travelling Fellowship Trust. Recreations: sports; walking the dogs. Address: (b.) 10 Queensferry Street, Edinburgh. EH2 4PG; T.-0131-225 6039.

Ward, Maxwell Colin Bernard, MA. Partner, Baillie Gifford & Co., since 1975; Director, Scottish Equitable Policyholders' Trust, since 1994; Director, Scottish Equitable plc, since 1995; Director, Scottish Equitable Life Assurance Society, 1988-94; b. 22.8.49, Sherborne; m., Sarah Marsham; 2 s.; 2 d. Educ. Harrow; St. Catharine's, Cambridge. Trainee, Baillie Gifford & Co., 1971-75. Board Member, Scottish Council for Spastics. Recreations: tennis; squash; bridge; country pursuits. Address: (h.) Stobshiel House, Humbie, East Lothian EH36 5PD; T.-01875 833646.

Wardlaw, Professor Alastair Connell, MSc, PhD, DSc, FRSE. Professor of Microbiology, Glasgow University, since 1970; b. 20.1.30, Port of Spain; m., Jacqueline Shirley Jones; 1 s.; 2 d. Educ. Manchester Grammar School; Manchester University. Research Fellow, Western Reserve University, Cleveland, Ohio, 1953-55; Sir Alexander Fleming Research Fellow, St. Mary's Hospital, London, 1955-58; Research Fellow and Research Member, Connaught Laboratories, Toronto, 1958-66; Professor of Microbiology, Toronto University, 1966-70. Member, Marshall Aid Commemoration Commission. Publications: Sourcebook of Experiments for the Teaching of Microbiology; Practical Statistics for Experimental Biologists; Pathogenesis and Immunity in Pertussis. Recreations: ceramics; gardening; cycle-camping. Address: (h.) 92 Drymen Road, Bearsden, Glasgow G61 2SY; T.-0141-942 2461.

Wardrop, James Arneil, DL, FCIBS, FSA (Scot). Vice Chairman, Japan Society of Scotland, since 1990; Vice Chairman, Accord, The Renfrewshire Hospice, since 1993; Deputy Lieutenant, Renfrewshire, since 1995; b. 19.4.40, Paisley. Educ. John Neilson Institution, Paisley. Joined National Bank of Scotland, by a process of mergers absorbed into Royal Bank of Scotland; Deputy Agent, San Francisco, 1978-81; Manager, Business Development International Division, 1981-94. Elder, Paisley Abbey; Trustee, Kibble Education Centre; Director, Past Chairman, Incorporated Glasgow Renfrewshire Society; Member, Master Court, Paisley Hammermen Society (Collector, 1995-96); Lay Member of Council, Paisley Art Institute; Director, Western Club, Glasgow. Recreations: country pursuits; gardening; music. Address: (h.) Saint Kevins, Meikleriggs, Paisley, PA2 9PT; T.-0141-887 3627.

Ward Thompson, Catharine J., BSc, DipLA, ALI. Head, School of Landscape Architecture, Edinburgh College of Art/Heriot Watt University, since 1989; b. 5.12.52; m., Henry Swift Thompson; 3 c. Educ. Holy Cross Convent, Chalfont St. Peter; Southampton University; Edinburgh University. Landscape Assistant/Landscape Architect/Senior Landscape Architect, 1973-81; Lecturer and Studio Instructor, School of Landscape Architecture, Edinburgh College of Art, 1981-88. Consultant, Landscape Design and Research Unit, Heriot-Watt University, since 1989. Recreations: dance; choreography. Address: (h.) 11 Douglas Crescent, Edinburgh EH12 5BB; T.-0131-337 6818.

Warhurst, A. Michael, BSc, MSc, PhD, CBiol, MIBiol. Chair, Friends of the Earth, Scotland, since 1995; Research Scientist; b. 17.1.68, London. Educ. Alleyn's School; York University; Glasgow University; Edinburgh University. Recreations: music; cinema; theatre; practical conservation; hill-walking. Address: (b.) Department of Civil and Environmental Engineering, Edinburgh University, Edinburgh; T.-0131-650 5812.

Wark, Kirsty. Presenter, Newsnight, BBC2, and other television programmes. Began her career with BBC Scotland; presented The Late Show, BBC2; partner, Wark Clements (production company).

Warlow, Professor Charles Picton, BA, MB, BChir, MD, FRCP (Lond), FRCP (Edin), FRCP (Glas). Professor of Medical Neurology, Edinburgh, since 1987; Honorary Consultant Neurologist, Lothian Health Board; b. 29.9.43; m.; 2 s.; 1 d. Educ. Cambridge University. Lecturer in Medicine, Aberdeen University, 1971-74; Registrar and Senior Registrar in Neurology, National Hospitals for Nervous Diseases, London, and University College Hospital, London, 1974-76; Clinical Lecturer in Neurology, then Clinical Reader, Oxford University, 1976-86. Recreations: sailing; photography; mountains. Address: 3 Mortonhall Hall Road, Edinburgh EH9 2HS.

Warner, Sheriff Graeme Christopher, LLB, WS, NP. Sheriff of Grampian, Highland and Islands, at Aberdeen and Stonehaven, since 1992; in private practice as a Solicitor, 1969-91; b. 20.10.48, Glasgow; divorced; 1 s.; 1 d. Educ. Strathallan; Edinburgh University. Recreations: staying alive. Address: (b.) Sheriff Court House, Aberdeen; T.-01224 648316.

Warren, Alastair Kennedy, TD, MA. President, Nithsdale Council of Voluntary Service; Director, Solway Community Business, 1987-91; Chairman, Loch Arthur Village for Mentally Handicapped Adults, 1985-91; Trustee, Dumfries and Galloway Care Trust, 1989-92; Freelance Journalist; b. 17.7.22, Glasgow; m., Ann Lindsay Maclean; 2 s. Educ. Laurel Bank School; Glasgow Academy; Loretto School; Glasgow University. Served at home and overseas, HLI, 1940-46 (from private to Major); Management Trainee, Stewarts and Lloyds, 1950-53; Glasgow Herald: joined, 1954, Business Editor, 1961-63, City Editor, 1964-65, Editor, 1965-74; Regional Editor, Scottish and Universal Newspapers Ltd., Southern Region, 1974-76; Editor, Dumfries and Galloway Standard, 1976-86. Served with 5/6th Bn., HLI (TA), 1947-63; first Chairman, Stewartry Mountaineering Club, 1976-78;

Provost, Royal Burgh of New Galloway and Kells Parish, 1978-81. Recreations: walking his dog; swimming; travel. Address: (h.) Rathan, High Street, New Galloway, Castle Douglas DG7 3RN; T.-New Galloway 257.

Waterman, Professor Peter George, BPharm (Hons), PhD, FLS, DSc, FRSE. Professor in Phytochemistry, Department of Pharmaceutical Sciences, Strathclyde University, since 1987; b. 28.4.46, Langley, Kent; m., Margaret Humble. Educ. Judd School, Tonbridge; London University. Postgraduate Research Assistant, London University, 1968-69; Lecturer, Senior Lecturer, Reader, Department of Pharmacy, Strathclyde University, 1969-87. Pharmaceutical Society Young Scientist of the Year Award, 1979; Phytochemical Society of Europe Tate & Lyle Award for contribution to Phytochemistry, 1984; Executive Editor, Journal of Biochemical Systematics and Ecology. Recreations: travel; ornithology; walking. Address: (b.) Phytochemistry Research Laboratories, Department of Pharmaceutical Sciences, Strathclyde University, Glasgow G1 1XW; T.-0141-552 4400.

Waters, Donald Henry. Deputy Chairman and Chief Executive, Grampian Television PLC, since 1993 (Chief Executive and Director, 1987-93); b. 17.12.37, Edinburgh; m., June Leslie Hutchison; 1 s.; 2 d. Educ. George Watson's, Edinburgh; Inverness Royal Academy. Director, John M. Henderson and Co. Ltd., 1972-75; Grampian Television PLC: Company Secretary, 1975, Director of Finance, 1979; Director: Moray Firth Radio Ltd., since 1982, Cablevision Scotland PLC, 1987-91; Chairman, Celtic Film and Television Association; Vice-Chairman, BAFTA Scotland; Visiting Professor of Film and Media Studies, Stirling University; Chairman, Police Dependant Trust for Grampian, since 1992; Past Chairman, Royal Northern and University Club, Aberdeen; Chairman, Glenburnie Properties Ltd., since 1993; Director: Central Scotland Radio Ltd., since 1994, GRT Bus Group PLC, since 1994, British Linen Bank Group Ltd., since 1995, British Linen Bank Ltd., since 1995; Member, ITV Council and ITV Broadcast Board; Fellow, Royal Society of Arts. Address: (h.) Balquhidder, 141 North Deeside Road, Milltimber, Aberdeen AB1 0JS; T.-Aberdeen 867131.

Waters, Rev. Robert, MA. General Secretary, Congregational Union of Scotland, since 1971; b. 8.7.30, Edinburgh; m., Magdalene Forrest; 1 s.; 1 d. Educ. Boroughmuir School, Edinburgh; Edinburgh University; Scottish Congregational College; Chicago University. Recreation: trout fishing. Address: (b.) 340 Cathedral Street, Glasgow G1 2BQ; T.-0141-332 7667.

Watkins, Trevor Francis, BA, PhD, FSA, FSA Scot. Senior Lecturer and Head of Department of Archaeology, Edinburgh University, since 1979; b. 20.2.38, Epsom, Surrey; m., Antoinette Marie; 1 s.; 2 d. Educ. Kingston Grammar School; Birmingham University. Research Fellow, Birmingham University; Lecturer, Edinburgh University. Council Member, British School of Archaeology in Iraq. Recreations: walking; bird-watching; music. Address: (b.) Department of Archaeology, Edinburgh University, 19 George Square, Edinburgh EH8 9JZ; T.-0131-650 4139.

Watson, Adam, BSc, PhD, DSc, FRSE. Senior Principal Scientific Officer and Leader of grouse research team, Institute of Terrestrial Ecology, 1971-90; b. 14.4.30, Turriff; m., Jenny; 1 s.; 1 d. Educ. Aberdeen University. Demonstrator in Zoology, McGill University, Montreal, 1952-53; Zoologist on Baird expedition to Baffin Island, 1953; Assistant Lecturer in Zoology, Aberdeen University, 1953-55; Teacher of Science, Aberdeen Academy, 1957; Senior Research Fellow, Aberdeen University, 1957-60; Senior Scientific Officer, then Principal Scientific Officer, Nature Conservancy, 1961-66; Officer in charge, Nature Conservancy Council Mountain and Moorland Ecology

Station, Banchory, 1968-71; Neill Prize, Royal Society of Edinburgh, for "outstanding contribution to natural history". Recreations: mountaineering; skiing. Address: (h.) Clachnaben, Crathes, Banchory AB31 3JE.

Watson, Professor Alan Albert, JP, MA, BD, MB, BS, FRCP, FRCPath, DMJ, DTM&H. Emeritus Regius Professor of Forensic Medicine, Glasgow University; Honorary Consultant in Forensic Medicine, Greater Glasgow Health Board, since 1978; Committee Member, Forensic Medicine (Scotland) Committee, since 1982; b. 20.2.29, Reading; m., Jeannette Anne Pitts; 3 s. Educ. Reading School; St. Mary's Hospital, London; Queens' College, Cambridge. Lecturer in Pathology, Glasgow University, 1964-69; University Senior Assistant Pathologist, Cambridge University, 1969-71; elected Fellow of Queen's College and Assistant Director of Studies, 1970; Consultant in Forensic Medicine, SE Asia Region, Delhi, WHO, 1977. Hon. President, Scottish Band of Hope Union. Recreations: Church activities (Baptist lay preacher). Address: (h.) Cessnock Castle, Galston, Ayrshire KA4 8LJ; T.-01563 820980.

Watson, Alexander Bell, MA, MEd, FIMgt, FSA Scot, FRSA. Chief Executive, Tayside Regional Council, since 1995; b. 20.5.45, Airdrie; m., Jean; 3 s. Educ. Airdrie Academy; Glasgow University; Jordanhill College of Education. Teacher of Classics, Morrison's Academy, Crieff, 1968; Principal Teacher of Classics: Portree High School, 1971, McLaren High School, Callander, 1973; Assistant Director of Education: Central, 1975, Strathclyde, 1983; Senior Depute Director of Education, Central Regional Council, 1986; Director of Education, Tayside Regional Council, 1990-95. General Secretary, Association of Directors of Education in Scotland, 1993-95. Recreations: music; reading; fishing; Scottish heritage; DIY. Address: (h.) Belmont, Lour Road, Forfar DD8 2BB; T.-01307 62718.

Watson, Antony Charles Harington, MB, ChB, FRCSEdin. Consultant Plastic Surgeon, Lothian Health Board, since 1972; Honorary Senior Lecturer, Department of Clinical Surgery, Edinburgh University, since 1972; Chairman, Specialist Advisory Committee in Plastic Surgery; b. 14.10.36, London; m., Anne Henderson Spence; 1 s.; 3 d. Educ. Barnard Castle School; Edinburgh University. Surgical training, Edinburgh and Florida. Council Member, British Association of Plastic Surgeons, since 1984; Examiner for Fellowship, Royal College of Surgeons of Edinburgh; Fellowship in Accident and Emergency Medicine and in Specialist Assessment in Plastic Surgery; President, British Association of Plastic Surgeons, 1991; Hon. Treasurer, Royal College of Surgeons of Edinburgh, 1991-93; Secretary, Scottish Melanoma Group, 1980-84. Recreations: playing and listening to music; boating; painting and sculpture. Address: (h.) 34 Mayfield Terrace, Edinburgh EH9 1RZ; T.-0131-668 3322.

Watson, David Robert, BA (Eng). Chief Executive, Oil and Gas Projects and Supplies Office, Department of Trade and Industry, since 1994; b. 9.4.52; m., Elizabeth Anne; 1 s.; 1 d. Educ. St. Anselm's, Bakewell, Oundle; Worcester College, Oxford. Peat Marwick Mitchell, 1973-76; various posts, British Petroleum, 1977-94. Recreations: cricket; music; gardening. Address: (b.) Tay House, 300 Bath Street, Glasgow, G2 4DX; T.-0141-228 3601.

Watson, Deirdre. Director, Scottish Child Law Centre. Address: (b.) Lion Chambers, 170 Hope Street, Glasgow, G2 2TU.

Watson, Garry S. Scottish Legal Services Ombudsman. Address: (b.) 2 Greenside Lane, Edinburgh, EH1 3AH.

Watson, Professor George Alistair, BSc, MSc, PhD, FIMA. Professor, Department of Mathematics and

Computer Science, Dundee University, since 1988; b. 30.9.42, Aberfeldy; m., Hilary Mackay; 1 d. Educ. Breadalbane Academy; Edinburgh University; Australian National University. Demonstrator, Computer Unit, Edinburgh University, 1964-66; Dundee University: Research Fellow, then Lecturer, Mathematics Department, 1969-82; Senior Lecturer, Mathematical Sciences Department, 1982-84; Reader, Department of Mathematics and Computer Science, 1984-88. Recreation: gardening. Address: (h.) 7 Albany Road, West Ferry, Dundee DD5 1NS; T.-Dundee 79473.

Watson, Harry Duff, MA, BA, DipEd. Senior Editor, Dictionary of the Older Scottish Tongue, Edinburgh University, since 1985; b. 17.6.46, Crail; m., Susan Margaret Saul; 2 s. Educ. Waid Academy, Anstruther; Edinburgh University; University College, London. Teacher of English/English as a Foreign Language, Scotland, England, Sweden, West Germany, 1970-79; appointed Editor, Dictionary of the Older Scottish Tongue, 1979. Past Senior Vice-President, Scottish Swedish Society; Member, Council, Scottish Text Society; Member, Board, Scottish Studies, Edinburgh University. Publication: Kilrenny and Cellardyke. Recreations: reading; writing; music; genealogy; languages. Address: (h.) 14 Braehead Grove, Edinburgh EH4 6BG; T.-0131-339 6911.

Watson, Hugh, QPM. Commandant, Scottish Police College, Tulliallan Castle, since 1991; b. 24.2.38, Edinburgh; m., Evelyn Scrimger; 1 s.; 2 d. Educ. Dunfermline High School. RAF, 1955-58; Lothian and Peebles Constabulary, 1958-75; Lothian and Borders Police, 1975-91; Assistant Chief Constable, 1984-91. Recreations: gardening; reading; DIY. Address: (b.) Tulliallan Castle, Kincardine-on-Forth FK10 4BE; T.-01259 730333.

Watson, Professor John, BSc, ARCST, PhD, DSc. Professor in Biochemistry, Strathclyde University, since 1988 (Reader, 1985-88); b. 17.6.42, Glasgow; m., Anne Brown; 2 d. Educ. Whitehill Secondary, Glasgow; Glasgow University; Strathclyde University. MRC Research Fellow, Glasgow University; Lecturer, Senior Lecturer, Reader, Professor, Strathclyde University. Recreations: golf; swimming; skiing; reading. Address: (b.) Bioscience and Biotechnology, Strathclyde University, Todd Centre, Glasgow G4 0NR; T.-0141-552 4400, Ext. 3825.

Watson, Captain John J., OBE, MInstD. Deputy Chairman, Dundee Port Authority (Chief Executive, since 1986); Immediate Past Chairman, British Ports Association; Chairman, Marine Operations Committee, International Association of Ports and Harbours; President, Dundee and Tayside Chamber of Commerce and Industry; Member, Tay River Purification Board; Member, Tayside Branch, Scottish Council (Development & Industry); Master Mariner; b. 19.1.39, Barr, Ayrshire; m., Maureen; 1 s. Educ. Girvan High School; Strathclyde University, Glasgow. Merchant Navy, 1954-66; British Transport Docks Board, 1966-80; Harbourmaster, Dundee Port Authority, 1980-86. Former District Commissioner for Scouting, Boothferry; Past President, Goole & District Junior Chamber. Recreations: shooting; golf; fishing. Address: (h.) 39 Elie Avenue, Broughty Ferry, Dundee DD5 3SF; T.-01382 738151.

Watson, Michael (Mike) Goodall, BA (Hons). MP (Labour), Glasgow Central, since 1989; b. 1.5.49, Cambuslang; m., Lorraine Therese McManus. Educ. Dundee High School; Heriot-Watt University. Development Officer, WEA East Midlands District, 1974-77; Industrial Officer, ASTMS, 1977-79; Regional Officer, ASTMS (latterly MSF), 1979-89. Member, Scottish Executive Committee, Labour Party, 1987-90. Publication: Rags to Riches: the official history of Dundee United FC. Recreations: watching Dundee United FC; jogging; reading, especially political biographies. Address: (b.) 58 Fox Street, Glasgow G1 4AU; T.-0141-204 4738.

Watson, Roderick, MA, PhD, FRSE. Poet; Literary Critic and Writer; Reader in English, Stirling University; Director, Stirling Institute for International Scottish Studies; b. 12.5.43, Aberdeen; m., Celia Hall Mackie; 1 s.; 1 d. Educ. Aberdeen Grammar School; Aberdeen University; Peterhouse, Cambridge. Lecturer in English, Victoria University, British Columbia, 1965-66; collections of poetry include Trio and True History on the Walls; other books include The Penguin Book of the Bicycle, The Literature of Scotland, MacDiarmid, The Poetry of Norman MacCaig and The Poetry of Scotland (Editor). Recreation: cycling. Address: (h.) 19 Millar Place, Stirling; T.-Stirling 475971.

Watt, Alison, BA (Hons). Painter; b. 11.12.65, Greenock. Educ. Glasgow School of Art. Prizes: British Institution Fund, 1st prize for painting, 1986; winner, John Player Portrait Award, 1987; Armour Prize for still life painting, Glasgow School of Art, 1987; Elizabeth Greenshields Foundation Award, 1989; commissioned to paint HM Queen Elizabeth the Queen Mother for National Portrait Gallery; recent exhibitions: one-woman show, Scottish Gallery, London; one-woman show, Glasgow Art Gallery and Museum, Kelvingrove.

Watt, Archibald, MBE, JP, MA, MEd, FEIS, FSA Scot. Honorary Sheriff, Grampian, Highlands and Islands, since 1979; b. 20.5.14, Aberdeen; m., 1, Anne D.M. Ashton (deceased); 2, Elizabeth P. White. Educ. Robert Gordon's College, Aberdeen; Aberdeen University; Aberdeen College of Education. Teacher of English, Elgin Academy, 1938; Flt.-Lt., RAF Administrative and Special Duties Branch and RAF Regiment, 1941-46; Mackie Academy: Principal Teacher of English, 1949, Deputy Rector, 1962, retired, 1977; Organist, HM Prison, Aberdeen, 1930-38; WEA Organiser for Adult Education, Elgin, 1946-49; WEA Tutor in Psychology, 1946-51; Founder and Organising Secretary, Stonehaven Music Club, since 1949; Member, National Council, and Chairman, Regional and District Committees, Scottish Community Drama Association, 1949-67; Member, National Executive and District Chairman, School Library Association in Scotland, 1952-73; Elder, Church of Scotland, since 1954; Chairman and/or Member, Kincardine District Committee, EIS, 1956-77; Member, Joint Consultative Committee, Kincardine County Council, 1965-77; Queen's Jubilee Medal, 1977; Organist, South Church, Stonehaven, 1976-94; Director, Kinneff Old Church Preservation Trust Ltd., since 1979; Founder Member and President, Stonehaven Probus Club, 1981-82; Committee Member, National Trust for Scotland (Kincardine and Deeside Centre), 1984-88; Member, Aberdeen Choral Society, 1978-91, Aberdeen Proms Chorus, since 1985, BB Centenary Band, since 1991; Chairman, Stonehaven Heritage Society, since 1988; author of Reading Lists for the Secondary School, 1966; Highways and Byways Round Stonehaven, 1976; Highways and Byways Round Kincardine, 1985; A Goodly Heritage, 1991; The Roman Camp of Raedykes, 1992; Early Stonehaven Settlers, 1994. Recreations: concert and theatre-going; travel; antiquities and archaeology; brass bands; research; golf; choral singing. Address: (h.) Rutlands, Arduthie Road, Stonehaven; T.-Stonehaven 762712.

Watt, Archibald Scott, LCH, MInstCH, SRCH. Member, Borders Regional Council, since 1974; Member, Lothian and Borders Police Board, since 1974; Member, Borders Health Board, 1978-91; Member, Borders Council, since 1995; Director, Borders Careers Co.; b. 21.8.29, Loanhead, Midlothian; m., Mary Corbett McNairn Brown; 1 d. RAF, 1947-49; Chiropodist, in private practice, since 1957; elected, Peebles Town Council and Peeblesshire County Council, 1973; TA, 1960-62; Past President, Peebles Rotary Club. Recreations: photography; archery. Address: East Rectory, Tweed Brae, Peebles; T.-Peebles 720803.

Watt, Brian, MD, FRCPath, FRCP Edin, CBiol, FIBiol. Consultant Bacteriologist, City Hospital, Edinburgh, since 1982; Honorary Senior Lecturer, Department of Bacteriology, Edinburgh University, since 1974; Clinical Director, Medical Microbiology Services, RIE Unit; b. 6.12.41, Edinburgh; m., Hilary Watt; 2 d. Educ. Rudolf Steiner School; Edinburgh University. Lecturer, Department of Bacteriology, Edinburgh University, 1968-73; Consultant Microbiologist, Western General Hospital, 1973-82. Recreations: fishing; gardening; golf; tennis; singing. Address: (h.) Silverburn House, by Penicuik, Midlothian; T.-01968 672085.

Watt, Jessie Lovie, BSc (Hons), PhD, DipRCPath, MRCPath. Crofters Commissioner for Orkney and Shetland, since 1993; Director, Shetland Marts Co-operative Ltd., since 1994; b. 20.1.51, Lerwick; m., Alan James Milne; 2 s. Educ. Anderson Educational Institute, Lerwick; Aberdeen University. Principal Cytogeneticist, Grampian Health Board, and Hon. Lecturer in Genetics, Aberdeen University, 1978; Top-Grade Cytogeneticist, West Midlands Regional Health Board, 1986; Principal, North Atlantic Fisheries College, Scalloway, Shetland, 1989. Recreation: floral art. Address: (h.) Hallibrig, Whiteness, Shetland, ZE2 9LL; T.-01595 840518.

Watt, Jim, MBE (1980). Boxer; b. 18.7.48, Glasgow. Turned professional, 1968; British Lightweight Champion, 1972-73, 1975-77; European Lightweight Champion, 1977-79; World Lightweight Champion, 1979-81; four successful defences of World title; Freedom of Glasgow, 1981.

Watt, John Gillies McArthur, QC, LLB. Advocate and Barrister; b. 14.10.49, Dumbarton; m., Susan Sparks; 2 d. Educ. Clydebank High School; Edinburgh University; Glasgow University. Solicitor, 1974; Advocate, 1979; Member of Middle Temple, 1992; QC, 1992; Advocate Depute ad hoc, since 1990; Temporary Sheriff, since 1991. Recreations: shooting; skiing; sailing; opera. Address: (b.) Advocates Library, Parliament House, Parliament Square, Edinburgh EH1 1RF; T.-0131-226 5071.

Watt, Robert Strachan, CBE, MA, FRSA, FBCS. Chairman, Livingston Development Corporation, since 1982; Chairman, West Lothian NHS Trust; b. 13.10.32, Aberdeen; m., Lorna Beattie; 1 s.; 2 d. Educ. Robert Gordon's College; Aberdeen University. Member, Glenrothes Development Corporation, 1971-78 (Deputy Chairman, 1978-81); Chairman, Management Committee, Scottish New Towns Computer Service, 1977-81; Member, Whitley Council, 1975-81; Council Member, British Computer Society, 1968-69.

Watt, Roger, BA, PhD, FRSE. Professor of Psychology and Head of Department, Stirling University, since 1990; b. 26.11.54, London; m., Helen; 2 s.; 1 d. Educ. St. Olaves Grammar School; Downing College, Cambridge. Research Fellow: Durham University, University College London, Cambridge University; Scientist, MRC Applied Psychology Unit, Cambridge; Royal Society of Edinburgh BP Research Fellow, Stirling University. Editor, Ben Ledi View (Callander local paper). Recreations: music; hill-walking; family life. Address: (b.) Department of Psychology, Stirling University, Stirling, FK9 4LA; T.-01786 467640.

Watts, John, PhD, FRSA, FSA Scot.. Rector, St. Kentigern's RC Academy, Blackburn, since 1988; b. 23.6.39; m., Moira McCallum; 3 s.; 3 d. Educ. Oxford University; Glasgow University. Teacher, 1960-74; Head Teacher, Daliburgh Primary/Secondary School, South Uist, 1974-81; Head Teacher, Bishop Challoner RC Secondary School, Birmingham, 1981-88. Research Fellow, Edinburgh University; Member, Scottish Catholic Heritage

Commission; former National Convener for Justice and Peace, C.T.F. Recreations: reading; Gaelic language and culture; family caravanning; watching football. Address: (b.) St. Kentigern's Academy, West Main Street, Blackburn, West Lothian EH47 7LX; T.-01506 56404.

Waugh, Alan, BSc (Hons), DipEd, FRSA. Head Teacher, Penicuik High School, since 1992; b. 9.2.49, Loanhead; m., Margo Watt; 1 s.; 1 d. Educ. Lasswade Senior Secondary School; Edinburgh University. Head of Chemistry, then Assistant Head Teacher, Lasswade High School Centre, 1976-86; Depute Head Teacher, James Gillespie's High School, 1986-92. Address: (b.) Penicuik High School, Carlops Road, Penicuik EH26 9EP; T.-Penicuik 674165.

Weatherhead, Alexander Stewart, OBE, TD, MA, LLB. Solicitor; Partner, Tindal Oatts, Solicitors, Glasgow, since 1960; b. 3.8.31, Edinburgh; m., Harriett Foye; 2 d. Educ. Glasgow Academy; Glasgow University. Royal Artillery, 1950-52; TA, 1952; Lt. Col. Commanding 277 (A&SH) Field Regiment, RA (TA), 1965-67, The Lowland Regiment, RA (T), 1967 and Glasgow and Strathclyde Universities OTC, 1970-73; Colonel, 1974; TAVR Colonel, Lowlands (West), 1974-76; ADC (TAVR) to The Queen, 1977-81; Honorary Colonel, Glasgow and Strathclyde Universities OTC, since 1982; Chairman, Lowlands TAVRA, 1990-93; Council Member, Law Society of Scotland, 1971-84 (Honorary Vice-President, 1983-84); Member, Royal Commission on Legal Services in Scotland, 1976-80; Council Member, Society for Computers and Law, 1973-86 (Chairman, 1981-84); Temporary Sheriff, 1985-92; Dean, Royal Faculty of Procurators in Glasgow, 1991-95; Commodore, Royal Western Yacht Club, since 1995. Recreations: tennis; sailing; reading; music. Address: (h.) 52 Partickhill Road, Glasgow, G11 5AB; T.-041-334 6277; (b.) 48 St. Vincent Street, Glasgow G2 5HS.

Weatherhead, Anne E., MB, ChB, MRCPsych. Medical Officer, Mental Welfare Commission for Scotland, since 1984; b. 3.5.37, Kirriemuir; m., Very Rev. James L. Weatherhead (qv); 2 s. Educ. Cheltenham Ladies' College; Edinburgh University. Former National Vice-President, Church of Scotland Woman's Guild; Elder, St. Giles Cathedral, Edinburgh. Recreations: music; art; relishing Edinburgh. Address: (h.) 28 Castle Terrace, Edinburgh.

Weatherhead, Very Rev. Dr. James Leslie, MA, LLB. Principal Clerk, General Assembly of the Church of Scotland, since 1985; Moderator, General Assembly, 1993; b. 29.3.31, Dundee; m., Dr. Anne Elizabeth Shepherd (see Anne E. Weatherhead); 2 s. Educ. High School of Dundee; Edinburgh University and New College, Edinburgh. Temporary Sub-Lt., RNVR (National Service), 1955-56. Licensed by Presbytery of Dundee, 1960, Presbytery of Ayr, 1960; Assistant Minister, Auld Kirk of Ayr, 1960-62; Minister: Trinity Church, Rothesay, 1962-69, Old Church, Montrose, 1969-85. Member, Broadcasting Council for Scotland, 1978-82. Recreations: music; sailing. Address: (b.) Church of Scotland Offices, 121 George Street, Edinburgh EH2 4YN; T.-0131-225 5722.

Weatherston, William Alastair Paterson, CB, MA. Under Secretary, Scottish Office Education Department, 1989-95; b. 20.11.35, Peebles; m., Margaret Jardine; 2 s.; 1 d. Educ. Peebles High School; Edinburgh University. Assistant Principal, Department of Health for Scotland and Scottish Education Department, 1959-63; Private Secretary to Permanent Under Secretary of State, Scottish Office, 1963-64; Principal, Scottish Education Department, 1964-72; Cabinet Office, 1972-74; Assistant Secretary, Scottish Home and Health Department, 1974-77; Scottish Education Department, 1977-79; Central Services, Scottish Office, 1979-82; Director, Scottish Courts Administration, 1982-86; Fisheries Secretary, Department of Agriculture and Fisheries for Scotland, 1986-89. Recreations: reading;

music. Address: (b.) Scottish Office Education Department, 43 Jeffrey Street, Edinburgh EH1 1DN; T.-0131-244 5322.

Webb, David John, MD, FRCP, FRCPE, FFPM. Senior Lecturer in Medicine, Edinburgh University, since 1990; Director, Clinical Research Centre and Honorary Consultant Physician, Western General Hospital, Edinburgh, since 1990; b. 1.9.53, Greenwich; m., Dr. Margaret Jane Cullen. Educ. Dulwich College, London; London University: Royal London Hospital. Junior hospital appointments, 1977-79; Medical Registrar, Royal London rotation, 1979-82; MRC Research Fellow, MRC Blood Pressure Unit, Glasgow, and Honorary Lecturer, Glasgow University, 1982-85; Lecturer in Pharmacology and Clinical Pharmacology, St. George's Hospital Medical School, London, and Honorary Medical Senior Registrar, St. George's Hospital, London, 1985-89. Executive Member, British Hypertension Society, since 1991; Honorary Trustee and Joint Research Director, High Blood Pressure Foundation and Endocrine Research Trust, since 1991; Member, Association of Physicians of Great Britain and Ireland. Recreations: opera; bridge; summer and winter mountaineering. Address: (h.) 26 Inverleith Gardens, Edinburgh EH3 5PS; T.-0131-332 1205.

Webb, Professor Jeffrey R.L., BSc, DPhil, FRSE. Titular Professor in Mathematics, Glasgow University, since 1987 (Reader, 1982-87); b. 19.12.45, Stourport-on-Severn; m., Angela Millard; 1 s.; 1 d. Educ. King Charles I School, Kidderminster; Sussex University. Royal Society European Programme Fellowship, 1970-71; Science Research Council Fellowship, Sussex University, 1971-73; Lecturer in Mathematics, Glasgow University, 1973-78 and 1979-82; Visiting Associate Professor, Indiana University, 1978-79; Visiting Professor, Tulane University, New Orleans, 1982. Member, Editorial Board, Glasgow Mathematical Journal. Recreations:chess; books; listening to music. Address: (b.) Mathematics Department, Glasgow University, Glasgow G12 8QW; T.-0141-339 8855, Ext. 5181.

Webster, David Pirie, OBE, DPE, LCSP (Phys). Author; Chairman, Commonwealth Games Council for Scotland, since 1991; Director of Leisure, Recreation and Tourism, Cunninghame District Council, 1975-87; b. 18.9.28, Aberdeen; 4 s.; 2 d. Educ. Crowlees Boys School; Aberdeen Training College; Woolmanhill College. Senior Technical Representative, Scottish Council of Physical Recreation, 1954-72; Head of Facilities Planning Division, Scottish Sports Council, 1972-74; Director/Administrator, Magnum Leisure Centre, 1974-75. Director of Weightlifting, Commonwealth Games; Secretary General, World Federation of Heavy Events Athletes. Recreations: writing (more than 30 books); Highland Games; fitness and weight training. Address: (h.) 43 West Road, Irvine KA12 8RE; T.- 01294 272257.

Webster, G.E. (Ted), FRICS. Managing Partner Scotland, Richard Ellis, Chartered Surveyors; b. 28.2.48, Glasgow; m.; 3 children. Joined Richard Ellis Glasgow, 1975, admitted to partnership, 1985. Executive Member, Scottish Council Development and Industry; Governor, Glasgow School of Art; Member, Court, Glasgow University. Recreations: Glasgow Art Club; Pollok and Western Gailes Golf Clubs. Address: (b.) Pacific House, 70 Wellington Street, Glasgow; T.-0141-204 1931.

Webster, Jack (John Barron). Author and Journalist; Columnist, The Herald; b. 8.7.31, Maud, Aberdeenshire; m., Eden Keith; 3 s. Educ. Maud School; Peterhead Academy; Robert Gordon's College, Aberdeen. Reporter, Turriff Advertiser; Reporter/Sub Editor, Aberdeen Press & Journal/Evening Express; Chief Sub-Editor, Scottish Sunday Express; Feature Writer, Scottish Daily Express; Feature Writer, Sunday Standard. Publications: The Dons, 1978; A Grain of Truth, 1981; Gordon Strachan, 1984; Another Grain of Truth, 1988; 'Tis Better to Travel, 1989;

Alistair MacLean (biography), 1991; Famous Ships of the Clyde, 1993; The Flying Scots, 1994; The Express Years, 1994; television films: The Roup, 1985; As Time Goes By, 1987; Northern Lights, 1989; Webster Goes West, 1991; John Brown: The Man Who Drew a Legend, 1994; video film: The Glory of Gothenburg, 1993. Address: (b.) The Herald, 195 Albion Street, Glasgow G1; T.-0141-552 6255.

Webster, Michael Alan, BA, DMS, MIMgt, FRSA. Principal, Perth College, since 1991; b. 7.12.45, Manchester. Educ. Chetham's School, Manchester; Moseley Hall Grammar School; Exeter University. Lecturer, Business Studies Department, Bridgnorth College, 1972-80, Head of Department, 1980-84; Education Adviser, Shropshire County Council, 1984-88, Principal Adviser, 1988-91. Recreations: hill-walking; skiing; theatre; fishing. Address: (b.) Perth College, Crieff Road, Perth, PH1 2NX; T.-01738 621171.

Webster, Professor Robin Gordon Maclennan, MA (Cantab), MA (Arch), RIBA, ARIAS, ARSA. Professor of Architecture and Head of School, Scott Sutherland School of Architecture, The Robert Gordon University, Aberdeen, since 1984; Senior Partner, Robin Webster & Associates, Aberdeen, since 1984; Commissioner, Royal Fine Art Commission for Scotland, since 1990; b. 24.12.39, Glasgow; m., Katherine S. Crichton; 1 s.; 2 d. Educ. Glasgow Academy; Rugby School; St. John's College, Cambridge. Assistant, Gillespie Kidd & Coia, Architects, Glasgow, 1963-64; National Building Agency, London, 1965-67; Senior Partner, Spence and Webster, Architects, 1972-84; Lecturer, Bartlett School of Architecture, 1969-74; Visiting Lecturer, Washington University, St. Louis, 1975, Cambridge University, 1976-77, and Mackintosh School, Glasgow School of Art, 1978-84. Winner, New Parliamentary Building Competition, Westminster, 1972; 1st prize, New York Waterfront Competition, 1988; Chairman, Association of Scottish Schools of Architecture, 1986-90; President, Aberdeen Society of Architects, 1989-91. Recreations: drawing and painting; sailing. Address: (b.) Scott Sutherland School of Architecture, The Robert Gordon University, Garthdee Road, Aberdeen; T.-01224 313247.

Weeple, Edward John, MA. Under Secretary, Scottish Office Industry Department, since 1990; b. 15.5.45, Glasgow; 3 s.; 1 d. Educ. St. Aloysius' College, Glasgow; Glasgow University. Entered DHSS, London, 1968; Assistant Principal, 1968-73 (Private Secretary to Minister of Health, 1971-73); Principal, 1973-78; transferred to Scottish Office, 1978; Principal (Industrial Development Division, SEPD), 1978-80; Assistant Secretary, Scottish Home and Health Department, 1980-85; Assistant Secretary, Department of Agriculture and Fisheries for Scotland, 1985-90. Address: (h.) 19 Lauder Road, Edinburgh; T.-0131-668 1150.

Weir, Alan David, MBA, CA. Finance Officer, Glasgow University, since 1982; b. 25.11.37, Edinburgh; m., Alys Taylor Macdonald; 2 s. Educ. Mill Hill; Edinburgh University; Strathclyde University. National Service (commissioned), Black Watch (RHR) and 4th QONR; served Articles with Touche Ross, London; commercial and industrial experience at Board level. Recreations: golf; hill-walking. Address: (h.) 3 Dumgoyne Drive, Bearsden, Glasgow G61 3AP; T.-0141-942 7936.

Weir, Professor Alexander Douglas, MA, MEd. Professor of Education, Strathclyde University, since 1993; Vice Dean (Research), Faculty of Education, since 1993; b. 2.9.42, Falkirk; m., Alison Marion Cook; 1 s.; 1 d. Educ. Falkirk High School; Edinburgh University. Lecturer, Falkirk College of Technology, 1965-67; Senior Research Officer, Scottish Council for Research in Education, 1967-74; Lecturer, Glasgow University, 1974-79; Director, Scottish Vocational Preparation Unit, 1979-85; Director,

Vocational Initiatives Unit, Glasgow University, 1985-88; Director of Research, Jordanhill College of Education, 1988-91. Member, National Executive, Boys' Brigade, 1976-84; Chair, Strathclyde Regional Conference of Voluntary Youth Organisations, 1991-94; author of five books and 70 articles. Recreation: youth work. Address: (b.) Faculty of Education, Strathclyde University, Southbrae Drive, Glasgow G13 1PP; T.-0141-950 3261.

Weir, Hon. Lord (David Bruce Weir), QC (Scot), MA, LLB. Senator of the College of Justice in Scotland, since 1985; b. 19.12.31. Advocate Depute, 1979-82; Chairman, Medical Appeal Tribunal, 1972-77; Chairman, Pensions Appeals Tribunal for Scotland, 1978-84; Chairman, NHS Tribunal Scotland, 1983-85; Member, Parole Board, Scotland, 1989-92; Governor, Fettes College.

Weir, Professor Donald Mackay, MB, ChB, FRCPEdin, MD (Hons). Emeritus Professor, Honorary Fellow, Department of Medical Microbiology, Edinburgh University; Professor of Microbial Immunology, Edinburgh University, 1983-93; Honorary Consultant, Lothian Health Board, 1967-93; b. 16.9.28, Edinburgh; m., Dr. Cecelia Caroline Blackwell, DSc; 3 s. Educ. Edinburgh Academy; Edinburgh University. Research Fellow, Medical Research Council, Rheumatism Research Unit, 1957-61; Edinburgh University: Lecturer, Department of Bacteriology, 1961-67, Senior Lecturer, 1967-78, Reader, 1978-83. Publications: Immunology (Co-author); Handbook of Experimental Immunology (Editor); Principles of Infection and Immunity in Patient Care (Co-author, with wife); research papers (with wife) on cot death, meningitis and peptic ulcers. Recreation: sailing. Address: (h.) 36 Drummond Place, Edinburgh; T.-0131-556 7656.

Weir, Robin Loudon. Honorary Sheriff; retired hotelier; b. 17.7.19, Muar, Malaya; m., Dorothy Isabella Urquhart; 2 s.; 1 d. Educ. Bellahouston Academy, Glasgow; Glasgow University. Address: (h.) Rose Cottage, Scorrybreck, Coolin Hills Estate, Portree, Isle of Skye; T.-01478 2135.

Weir, Sharman Elizabeth, BMus (Hons). General Manager, Citizens' Theatre, Glasgow, since 1994; b. 31.3.59, Barrhead. Educ. John Neilson High School, Paisley; Glasgow University. Professional musician, 1981-85; Project Manager and Consultant, BP Exploration, 1985-92; Business Manager, Citizens' Theatre, Glasgow, 1992-94. Director, Scottish Early Music Consort. Recreations: music (flute, singing, piano); travel. Address: (b.) Citizens' Theatre, 119 Gorbals Street, Glasgow, G5; T.-0141-429 5561.

Weir, Tom, MBE, FRSGS. Journalist and Photographer. Former Ordnance Surveyor; climbed in the Himalayas and began professional photography; author of several books on climbing and Scotland; Presenter, Weir's Way, Scottish Television.

Weir, Viscount (William Kenneth James Weir), BA, Hon. DEng (Glasgow), Hon. FEng. Chairman, The Weir Group PLC, since 1966; Vice-Chairman, St. James' Place Capital plc, since 1985; Deputy Chairman, BICC plc (Director, since 1977; Director, Canadian Pacific Limited; b. 9.11.33, Glasgow; m., 1, Diana MacDougall (m. diss.); 2 s.; 3, Marina Sevastopoulo; 2 s.; 1 d. Educ. Eton; Trinity College, Cambridge. Member, London Advisory Committee, Hongkong and Shanghai Banking Corporation, 1980-92; Deputy Chairman, Charterhouse J. Rothschild PLC, 1983-85; Member, Court, Bank of England, 1972-84; Co-Chairman, RIT and Northern PLC, 1982-83; Director, 1970, Chairman, 1975-82, Great Northern Investment Trust Ltd.; Member, Scottish Economic Council, 1972-85; Director, British Steel Corporation, 1972-76; Chairman, Patrons of National Galleries of Scotland; Member, Queen's Bodyguard for Scotland (Royal Company of Archers). Recreations:

WHO'S WHO IN SCOTLAND 461

shooting; golf; fishing. Address: (h.) Rodinghead, Mauchline, Ayrshire; T.-Fiveways 233.

Wells, W.J. Chief Executive, Dundee Healthcare NHS Trust. Address: (b.) Royal Dundee Liff Hospital, Dundee, DD2 5NF.

Welsh, Andrew Paton, MA (Hons), DipEd. MP (SNP), Angus East, since 1987; National Vice-President, SNP, since 1987; b. 19.4.44, Glasgow; m., Sheena Margaret Cannon (see Sheena Margaret Welsh); 1 d. Educ. Govan High School; Glasgow University. Member, Stirling District Council, 1974; MP (SNP), South Angus, 1974-79; SNP Parliamentary Spokesman on Housing, 1974-78 and since 1987, Self-Employed and Small Businesses, 1975-79 and since 1987, Agriculture, 1975-79 and since 1987, Parliamentary Chief Whip, 1977-79 and since 1987; SNP Executive Vice Chairman for Administration, 1979-83; Member, National Executive Committee, SNP, since 1983; Parliamentary candidate, East Angus, 1983; Member, Church and Nation Committee, Church of Scotland, 1984-85; Member, Dundee University Court, 1984-87; Provost, Angus District Council, 1984-87; Member, Angus District Health Council; Member, SCOTVEC Public Administration and Moderating Committees. Recreations: music; horse riding. Address: (h.) Montquhir, Carmyllie, Arbroath; T.-01241 860317.

Welsh, Frederick Wright, JP. Chairman, Community Services Committee, Dundee District Council, since 1990; Convenor of Housing, Dundee District Council, since 1992; elected to Dundee City Council, 1995; National Chair, Association of Direct Labour Organisations, 1991-92; Director, Local Government Information Unit, 1991-92; Director/Chairman, Taywide Services, Dundee, since 1991; Member, Central Advisory Committee on Justices of the Peace, since 1991; Member, Justices Committee, Dundee District; Member, Scottish Housing Forum; Vice-Chair, Post Office and Telecommunications Advisory Committee for Tayside; b. Dundee; m., Margaret; 3 s. Educ. Rockwell Secondary School, Dundee. Member, Dundee Corporation, 1973-75 (Convener, Public Libraries, Museums and Art Galleries, 1973-75); Member, Tayside Regional Council, 1974-77 (Labour Group Chief Whip and Further Education Opposition Spokesman, 1974-77); Chair, Dundee East Constituency Labour Party; Member, Dundee District Council, since 1977; Member, Central Committee, Gas Consumers Council for Scotland; Member, Perth Prison Visiting Committee; Member, Management Committee, Dundee Resources Centre for Unemployed; Chairman, ADLO Scottish Region and Member, National Council, ADLO; Vice Convener, COSLA Miscellaneous Services Committee; Depute Chair, Heat Development (Dundee) Ltd., since 1986; Member, Fire Services Scotland Examination Board, 1973-75; Member, British Standards Institute OC/4 Committee. Recreations: gardening; DIY; watching all sports; walking. Address: (h.) 2 McKinnon Street, Dundee DD3 6JN; T.-01382 27669.

Welsh, Gerard F.G., LLB. Regional Solicitor, Lothian Regional Council, since 1982; b. 20.2.41, Uddingston; m., Elizabeth Anne Wilde; 1 s.; 1 d. Educ. Our Lady's High School, Motherwell; Glasgow University. Apprenticeship, Scottish Gas Board; Legal Assistant and Principal Legal Assistant, Midlothian County Council; Assistant Director of Administration, Lothian Regional Council. Chairman, Society of Directors of Administration in Scotland, 1989-90. Recreations: rugby; golf; cricket. Address: (b.) 1 Parliament Square, Edinburgh EH1 1RF; T.-0131-469 3444.

Welsh, Ian, MA (Hons), DPSE. Leader, South Ayrshire Council; Assistant Head Teacher, Auchinleck Academy; b. 23.11.53, Ayr; m., Elizabeth; 2 s. Educ. Prestwick Academy; Ayr Academy; Glasgow University; Jordanhill College; Open University. Councillor, Kyle and Carrick,

1989-95, Leader, 1990-92. Former Governor, Craigie College of Education; former professional footballer; Director, Prestwick International Airport, since 1992; Director, Borderline Theatre Company, since 1990. Recreations: reading non-fiction, crime fiction. Address: (h.) 36 Ayr Road, Prestwick, Ayrshire; T.-01292 476502.

Welsh, Peter Brian, CertEd, BSc (Econ), DASE, MA. Director of Education, Fife Regional Council, since 1992; b. 1.6.43, Newry, Co. Down; m., Angela; 3 d. Educ. St. Colman's College, Newry; St. Joseph's College of Education, Belfast; Queen's University, Belfast; New University of Ulster, Coleraine. Teacher, Belfast, 1965-77; Vocational Guidance Adviser, Western Education and Library Board, Omagh, 1977-82; Senior Assistant Education Officer, Suffolk County Council, 1982-85; Fife Regional Council: Depute Director of Education, 1985-90; Senior Depute Director of Education, 1990-92. Recreations: reading; rugby (armchair). Address: (b.) Fife House, North Street, Glenrothes KY7 5LT; T.-01592 754411.

Wemyss and March, Earl of (Francis David Charteris), KT (1966), Hon. LLD (St. Andrews), Hon. DUniv (Edinburgh), JP, BA. Lord Lieutenant, East Lothian, 1967-87; b. 19.1.12, London; m., Mavis Lynette Gordon Murray (deceased); 1 s.; 1 d.; 1 s. (deceased); 1 d. (deceased); 2, Shelagh Kennedy. Educ. Eton; Balliol College, Oxford. Commissioned, Lovat Scouts (TA), 1932-44; Basutoland Administrative Service, 1937-44; War Service, African Auxiliary Pioneer Corps, Middle East, 1941-44; Chairman, Council, National Trust for Scotland, 1947-67 (President, 1967-91; Chairman, Scottish Churches Council, 1964-71; Chairman, Royal Commission on Ancient and Historical Monuments of Scotland, 1949-84; Vice-President, Marie Curie Memorial Foundation; President, Royal Scottish Geographical Society, 1958-62; President, National Bible Society of Scotland, 1960-83; Lieutenant, Queen's Bodyguard for Scotland (Royal Company of Archers). Recreations: countryside and conservation. Address: (h.) Gosford House, Longniddry, East Lothian; T.-0187 57 200.

West, Peter William Alan, MA. Secretary to the University, Strathclyde University, since 1990; b. 16.3.49, Edinburgh; m., Margaret Clark; 1 s.; 1 d. Educ. Edinburgh Academy; St. Andrews University. Administrator, Edinburgh University, 1972-77; Assistant Secretary, Leeds University, 1977-83; Deputy Registrar, Strathclyde University, 1983-89. Recreations: supporting Scotland's leading football team (Hibernian) through thick and thin. Address: (b.) Strathclyde University, McCance Building, 16 Richmond Street, Glasgow G1 1XQ; T.-0141-552 4400, Ext. 2001.

West, Professor Thomas Summers, CBE, BSc, PhD, DSc, FRSC, FRSE, FRS. Former Director, Macaulay Institute for Soil Research, Aberdeen; b. 18.11.27, Peterhead; m., Margaret O. Lawson; 1 s.; 2 d. Educ. Tarbat School, Portmahomack; Tain Royal Academy; Aberdeen University; Birmingham University. Lecturer in Chemistry, Birmingham University, 1955-63; Imperial College of Science and Technology, London: Reader in Chemistry, 1963-65, Professor of Chemistry, 1965-75. Meldola Medal, Royal Institute of Chemistry; Gold Medal, Society of Analytical Chemistry; President, Society for Analytical Chemistry, 1969-71; Honorary Secretary, Royal Society of Chemistry, 1972-75; President, Analytical Division, International Union of Pure and Applied Chemistry, 1979-81; Secretary General, IUPAC, 1983-91; Honorary Research Professor, Aberdeen University, since 1983. Recreations: gardening; motoring; reading; music; fishing. Address:(h.) 31 Baillieswells Drive, Bieldside, Aberdeen AB1 9AT; T.-01224 868294.

Westcott, Michael John Herbert, BSc (Hons) (Glasgow), Hon. MA (Edinburgh). University Administrative Fellow, Edinburgh University; b. 16.4.19, Plymouth. Educ. Hillhead

High School; Glasgow University. Ministry of Home Grown Timber Production, 1940-43; Army (Royal Signals), 1943-48 (retired as Major); Colonial Service, Sierra Leone (Administrative Officer), 1948-61; Administrative Officer, Edinburgh University, 1962-86. Vice-Chairman, Royal Lyceum Theatre Club; Honorary President, Edinburgh and SE Scotland VSO Group; Trustee, UK Foundation for the Peoples of the South Pacific. Recreations: walking; theatre; music. Address: (h.) 2 Kilgraston Court, Kilgraston Road, Edinburgh EH9 2ES; T.-0131-447 8282.

Westwood, Alan, BSc, MSc, PhD, CChem, MRSC, FRCPath. Director of Clinical and Diagnostic Services, since 1994, and Head, Department of Paediatric Biochemistry, since 1979, Royal Hospital for Sick Children, Edinburgh; Honorary Senior Lecturer, Edinburgh University, since 1981; b. 2.3.48, Luton; m., Jennifer Anne; 1 s.; 1 d. Educ. Luton Technical School; Liverpool University; Birmingham University. Clinical Biochemist: Broadgreen Hospital, Liverpool, 1969, Birmingham Children's Hospital, 1970, Liverpool Royal Infirmary, 1976, Edinburgh Royal Hospital for Sick Children, 1979. Chairman, Scottish Region, Association of Clinical Biochemists, 1984-87 (Member of Association Council, 1982-85). Recreations: cycling; curling; microcomputing. Address: (h.) Fawnspark, Loanstone, by Penicuik, Midlothian EH26 8PH; T.-Penicuik 78407.

Whatley, Christopher Allan, BA, PhD, FRHistS. Reader in Scottish History and Head, Department of Modern History, Dundee University, since 1995; b. 29.5.48, Birmingham; 1 s.; 1 d. Educ. Bearsden Academy; Strathclyde University. Lecturer, Ayr College, 1975-79, Dundee University, 1979-88, St. Andrews University, 1988-92, Dundee University, 1992-94; Senior Lecturer, 1994. Editor, Scottish Economic and Social History. Publications: The Scottish Salt Industry, 1570-1850; Onwards from Osnaburgs: the rise and progress of a Scottish textile company; Bought and Sold for English Gold?: explaining the union of 1707; The Manufacture of Scottish History (Co-author); The Life and Times of Dundee (Co-author); The Remaking of Juteopolis: Dundee 1891-1991 (Editor); John Galt. Recreations: walking; watching Dundee United FC; theatre. Address: (h.) Viewlands, 2 Moor Road, Ceres, KY15 5LR; T.-01382 223181.

Wheater, Professor Roger John, OBE, CBiol, FIBiol, FRSA, FRSE. Director, Royal Zoological Society of Scotland, since 1972; Honorary Professor, Edinburgh University, since 1993; b. 24.11.33, Brighton; m., Jean Ord Troup; 1 s.; 1 d. Educ. Brighton, Hove and Sussex Grammar School; Brighton Technical College. Commissioned, Royal Sussex Regiment, 1953; served Gold Coast Regiment, 1953-54; 4/5th Bn., Royal Sussex Regiment (TA), 1954-56; Colonial Police, Uganda, 1956-61; Chief Warden, Murchison Falls National Park, 1961-70; Director, Uganda National Parks, 1970-72; Member, Co-ordinating Committee, Nuffield Unit of Tropical Animal Ecology; Member, Board of Governors, Mweka College of Wildlife Management, Tanzania; Director, National Park Lodges Ltd.; Member, Uganda National Research Council; Vice Chairman, Uganda Tourist Association; Council Member, 1980, and President, 1988-91, International Union of Directors of Zoological Gardens; Chairman, Federation of Zoological Gardens of Great Britain and Ireland, 1993; Chairman, Anthropoid Ape Advisory Panel, 1977-91; Member, International Zoo Year Book Editorial Board, 1987; President, Association of British Wild Animal Keepers, 1984; Chairman, Membership and Licensing Committee, 1984-91; Chairman, Working Party on Zoo Licensing Act, 1981-84; Council Member, Zoological Society of London, 1991-92, 1995; Chairman, European Association of Zoos and Aquaria, 1994; Member of Council, National Trust for Scotland, 1973-78, Executive Committee, 1982-87; Chairman, Cammo Estate Advisory Committee, 1980; Member, Proceedings B Editorial Board,

Royal Society of Edinburgh, 1988-91; ESU William Thyne Scholar, 1975; Assessor, Council, Scottish Wildlife Trust, 1973-92; Consultant, World Tourist Organisation (United Nations), 1980; Member, Secretary of State for Scotland's Working Group on Environmental Education, since 1990; Board Member, Scottish Natural Heritage, since 1995; Vice-Chairman, Edinburgh Branch, English Speaking Union, 1977-81; President, Edinburgh Special Mobile Angling Club, 1982-86. Recreations: country pursuits; painting; gardening. Address: (b.) Scottish National Zoological Park, Edinburgh EH12 6TS; T.-0131-334 9171.

Wheatley, Sheriff John Francis, QC, BL. Sheriff, Perthshire and Kinross-shire, at Perth, since 1980; b. 9.5.41, Edinburgh; m., Bronwen Catherine Fraser; 2 s. Educ. Mount St. Mary's College, Derbyshire; Edinburgh University. Called to Scottish Bar, 1966; Standing Counsel to Scottish Development Department, 1968-74; Advocate Depute, 1974-78. Recreations: music; gardening. Address: Braefoot Farmhouse, Fossoway, Kinross-shire; T.-Fossoway 212.

Wheeler, Sir (Harry) Anthony, Kt (1988), OBE, PPRSA, Hon. RA, Hon. RHA, Hon. RGI, Hon. DDes, Hon. RBS, PPRIAS, FRIBA, FRSA, BArch, MRTPI, DipTP. Consultant, Wheeler & Sproson, Architects and Town Planners, Edinburgh and Kirkcaldy, since 1986; b. 7.11.19, Stranraer; m., Dorothy Jean Campbell; 1 d. Educ. Stranraer High School; Glasgow School of Architecture; Strathclyde University. War Service, Royal Artillery, 1939-46; John Keppie Scholar and Sir Rowand Anderson Studentship, RIBA Grissell Medallist, Neale Bursar; Assistant to City Architect, Oxford, to Sir Herbert Baker & Scott, London; Senior Architect, Glenrothes Development Corporation; began private practice in Fife; Senior Lecturer, Dundee School of Architecture, 1952-58; Saltire Awards and Commendations (22), Civic Trust Awards and Commendations (12); Trustee, Scottish Civic Trust, 1970-83; Member, Royal Fine Art Commission for Scotland, 1967-85; President, Royal Scottish Academy, 1983-90. Recreations: sketching and water colours; fishing; music; drama; gardens. Address: (h.) Hawthornbank House, Dean Village, Edinburgh EH4 3BH.

Wherrett, Professor Brian Spencer, BSc, PhD, FInstP, FRSE. Chair of Theoretical Physics, Heriot-Watt University, since 1986; b. 8.5.46, Bromley; m., Shirley Ruth; 1 s.; 1 d. Educ. Westcliff High School; Reading University. Lecturer, Department of Physics, Heriot-Watt University, 1971; promoted to Senior Lecturer and Reader; Visiting Professor, North Texas State University, 1981-82; Past Chairman, SERC Committee on Atomic, Molecular and Plasma Physics and Optical Sciences. Recreation: golf. Address: (b.) Department of Physics, Heriot-Watt University, Riccarton, Edinburgh EH14 4AS; T.-0131-451 3039.

Whitby, Professor Lionel Gordon, MA, PhD, MD, BChir, FRCP, FRCPEdin, FRCPath, FRSE, FIBiol. Emeritus Professor; Professor of Clinical Chemistry, Edinburgh University, 1963-91; Honorary Consultant in Clinical Chemistry, South Eastern Regional Hospital Board, 1963-74, and Lothian Health Board, 1974-91; Chairman, Advisory Committee on Distinction Awards, Scottish Sub-Committee, since 1993; b. 18.7.26, London; m., Joan Hunter Sanderson; 1 s.; 2 d. Educ. Eton College; King's College, Cambridge. MRC Scholar for Training in Research, Biochemistry Department, Cambridge University, 1948-51; Fellow, King's College, Cambridge, 1951-55; junior hospital appointments, Middlesex Hospital, London, etc., 1956-58; Registrar in Chemical Pathology, then Assistant Lecturer, Royal Postgraduate Medical School, London, 1958-60; Rockefeller Travelling Fellowship in Medicine, National Institutes of Health, Bethesda, 1959-60; University Biochemist, Addenbrooke's Hospital, Cambridge, 1960-63; Fellow, Peterhouse,

Cambridge, 1961-62; Dean, Faculty of Medicine, Edinburgh University, 1969-72 and 1983-86. Visiting Professor of Chemical Pathology, Royal Postgraduate Medical School, 1974; Vice-Principal, Edinburgh University, 1979-83; Member, General Medical Council, 1986-91; Medical Laboratory Technicians Board, Council for Professions Supplementary to Medicine, 1978-92. Publications: Lecture Notes on Clinical Chemistry (Co-author); Principles & Practice of Medical Computing (Co-editor); scientific papers. Recreations: gardening; photography. Address: (h.) 51 Dick Place, Edinburgh EH9 2JA; T.-0131-667 4358.

White, Glenda Ann, BA (Hons), MEd (Hons), MA, DCE. Chief Inspector of Schools, Department of Education, Strathclyde Regional Council (HM Inspector of Schools, 1985-90); b. 5.4.45, Wallasey. Educ. Queen Elizabeth's Girls' Grammar School, Barnet; Open University; Glasgow University; Manchester University. Teaching appointments, four primary schools in Liverpool and Glasgow, including Assistant Headteacher, Commonhead Primary School, Easterhouse, 1966-72; Lecturer, Callander Park College of Education, Falkirk, 1972-74; Lecturer/Senior Lecturer, Jordanhill College of Education, Glasgow, 1974-85. Member, Schools Advisory Committee, Independent Television Commission. Recreations:hill-walking; theatre; music. Address: (h.) 72 Great George Street, Glasgow G12 8RU; T.-0141-339 0893.

White, John, QFSM, BA, FIFireE. Firemaster, Fife Regional Council, since 1988; b. 23.3.36, Rosewell; 1 s.; 1 d. Educ. Lasswade Secondary; West Calder High School; Open University. South Eastern Fire Brigade, 1959; North Eastern (now Grampian) Fire Brigade, 1969; Fife Fire Brigade, 1979. Recreations: golf; hill-walking; sailing. Address: (b.) Fife Fire & Rescue Service Headquarters, Strathore Road, Thornton, Kirkcaldy; T.-01592 774451.

White, Paul Charles, BA, IPFA, MBA. Director of Finance/Deputy General Manager, Lothian Health Board, since 1993; b. 9.8.49, Londonderry; m., Alison Perry; 4 d. Educ. St. Columb's College, Londonderry; Queen's University, Belfast; Henley Business School. Director of Finance and Information, Western Health Board, N.I., 1985-90; General Manager, Altnagelvin Group of Hospitals, Londonderry, 1990-93. Board Member, Telford College, Edinburgh. Recreations: family; North Berwick; golf; theatre. Address: (h.) 13 Macnair Avenue, North Berwick, East Lothian.

White, Robert I.K., BSc, FRICS. Chief Estates Officer, Scottish Office, since 1985; b. 22.2.36, Comrie; m., Constance M. Jackson; 2 s. Educ. Larbert High School; Edinburgh University. Ministry of Public Buildings and Works/PSA, 1962-85, serving in Glasgow, Newcastle, London, Germany and Edinburgh. Recreations: golf; curling; gardening. Address: (b.) Room 39a, James Craig Walk, Edinburgh EH1 3SZ; T.-0131-244 3629.

White, Professor Stephen Leonard, MA, PhD, DPhil. Professor of Politics, Glasgow University, since 1991; b. 1.7.45, Dublin; m., Ishbel MacPhie; 1 s. Educ. St. Andrew's College, Dublin; Trinity College, Dublin; Glasgow University; Wolfson College, Oxford. Lecturer in Politics, Glasgow University, 1971-85, Reader, 1985-91; Head of Department, since 1992. President, British Association for Slavonic and East European Studies, since 1994; Joint Editor, Coexistence; Chief Editor, Journal of Communist Studies and Transition Politics. Publications include: Britain and the Bolshevik Revolution, 1980; Origins of Detente, 1986; The Bolshevik Poster, 1989; After Gorbachev, 1993; Russia Goes Dry, 1995. Address: (h.) 11 Hamilton Drive, Glasgow G12 8DN; T.-0141-334 9541.

Whitelaw, Brian Murray, LLB, DipLP, MIMgt, NP. Depute Chief Executive, Caithness District Council, since 1990; Solicitor and Notary Public; b. 25.12.53, Glasgow; m., Joan Harte; 1 s.; 2 d. Educ. St. Columba's, Clydebank; Strathclyde University. Trainee Solicitor, Joseph Mellick, Solicitors, Glasgow, 1981-83; Assistant Solicitor, Borders Regional Council, 1983-85; Senior Solicitor, Dumbarton District Council, 1985-86; Principal Solicitor, Dumbarton District Council, 1986-90. Recreations: flying light aircraft; rifle and pistol shooting; photography; cycling; drinking whisky. Address: (b.) Caithness District Council, Market Square, Wick KW1 4AB; T.-01955 603761.

Whitelaw, Ian Macleod. Assistant Secretary, The Scottish Office Agriculture and Fisheries Department, since 1984; b. 20.9.42, Edinburgh; m., Rhoda Margaret Thomson; 1 s.; 1 d. Educ. Royal High School, Edinburgh. Scottish Education Department, 1961-71; Secretary, Scottish Agricultural Development Council, 1971-74; SOAFD, since 1974. Recreations: sport; history (Scottish/military); hill-walking. Address: (b.) Department of Agriculture and Fisheries for Scotland, Pentland House, 47 Robbs Loan, Edinburgh EH14 1TW; T.-0131-244 6335.

Whitelaw, Robert George, MA, MD, FRCOG, DL. Deputy Lieutenant, Fife, since 1969; Honorary Sheriff, since 1978; b. 29.4.13, Motherwell; m., Cicely Mary Ballard; 1 s. Educ. Wishaw High School; Glasgow University. Consultant Obstetrician and Gynaecologist, West Fife Group of Hospitals, 1956-78; External Examiner, Edinburgh University, 1967-71; Examiner: Central Midwives Board for Scotland, General Nursing Council for Scotland, Royal College of Surgeons of Edinburgh, PLAB. Past President, Fife Branch, BMA; Past President, Dunfermline Rotary Club. Publications: various papers, mainly on obstetrical and gynaecological subjects. Recreations: golf; photography; travel. Address: (h.) 64 Garvock Hill, Dunfermline, Fife KY12 7UU; T.-01383 721209.

Whiteman, Professor Arthur John, BSc, PhD. Professor Emeritus, Aberdeen University, since 1993; Professor of Petroleum Geology, 1974-93; b. 1.1.28, Ormskirk; m., Sally Janet Peltet; 2 s.; 2 d. Educ. University College, London; Stanford University; Columbia University. Geologist, Humble Oil and Refining Co. Research Fellowship, Columbia University, 1949-51; Geologist, HM Geologist Survey, Great Britain, 1951-56; Exploration Geologist, Compagnie Des Petroles D'Algerie, Royal Dutch Shell, 1956-60; Consultant Petroleum Geologist, since 1960; Professor of Geology, Khartoum, 1960-68; Professor of Petroleum Geology, Ibadan University, 1968-72; Professor of Petroleum Geology, Bergen University, 1972-74. Publications: Geology of Sudan Republic, 1971; Nigeria: Its Petroleum Geology, Resources and Potential, 1982; Rift Systems — Hydrocarbon Habitat and Potential, 1989. Recreation: gardening. Address: (h.) Garden Cottage, Inchmarlo, Banchory AB31 4BT; T.-01330 825214.

Whiten, David Andrew, BSc, PhD, FBPS. Reader in Psychology, St. Andrews University, since 1990; b. 20.4.48, Grimsby; m., Dr. Susie Challoner; 2 d. Educ. Wintringham School, Grimsby; Sheffield University; Bristol University; Oxford University. Research Fellow, Oxford University, 1972-75; Lecturer, St. Andrews University, 1975-90; Visiting Professor, Zurich University, 1992. Publications: Machiavellian Intelligence (Co-author), 1988; Natural Theories of Mind, 1991; Foraging Strategies of Monkeys, Apes and Humans (Co-author), 1992. Recreations: painting; walking; wildlife; good-lifing. Address: (b.) School of Psychology, St. Andrews University, St. Andrews KY16 9JU.

Whitfield, Professor Charles Richard, MD, FRCOG, FRCPGlas. Regius Professor of Midwifery, Glasgow University, and Consultant Obstetrician, Queen Mother's Hospital, Glasgow, and Consultant Gynaecologist, Western Infirmary, Glasgow, 1976-92; b. 21.10.27, India; m.,

464 WHO'S WHO IN SCOTLAND

Marion Douglas McKinney; 1 s.; 2 d. Educ. Campbell College, Belfast; Queen's University, Belfast. Resident appointments, Belfast Teaching Hospitals, 1951-53; RAMC, 1953-64 (Senior Specialist in Obstetrics and Gynaecology, 1959-64); Consultant Obstetrician and Gynaecologist, Belfast Teaching Hospitals, 1968-74; Professor of Obstetrics and Gynaecology, Manchester University, 1974-76. Publication: Dewhurst's Postgraduate Textbook of Obstetrics and Gynaecology (Editor). Recreations: trying to remember what they were. Address: (h.) 23 Thorn Road, Bearsden, Glasgow G61.

Whiting, Professor Brian, MD, FRCPGlas, FFPM. Titular Professor (Clinical Pharmacology), Glasgow University, since 1986, Dean, Faculty of Medicine, since 1992; Consultant Physician (Clinical Pharmacology), since 1972, now at Western Infirmary, Glasgow; Member, General Medical Council, since 1991; b. 6.1.39, Manchester; 2 d. Educ. Stockport Grammar School; Glasgow University. Research and hospital posts, Stobhill General Hospital, Department of Materia Medica, 1965-77; Visiting Professor of Clinical Pharmacology, University of California, San Francisco, 1978-79; returned to Glasgow, 1979; Director, Clinical Pharmacokinetics Laboratory, Department of Materia Medica, Stobhill General Hospital, Glasgow, 1980-91; Treasurer, Clinical Section, British Pharmacological Society, 1987-91. Publication: Lecture Notes on Clinical Pharmacology (Co-author). Recreations: painting; music; mountaineering. Address: (h.) 2 Milner Road, Glasgow G13 1QL; T.-0141-959 2324.

Whitley, Rev. Laurence Arthur Brown, MA, BD, PhD. Minister, Montrose Old Parish, since 1985 (Busby East and West, 1975-85); b. 19.9.49, Port Glasgow; m., Catherine MacLean MacFadyen; 1 s.; 1 d. Educ. Edinburgh Academy; Edinburgh University; St. Andrews University. Assistant Minister, St. Andrews, Dundee, 1974-75. Parliamentary candidate (SNP), Dumfriesshire, February and October, 1974. Recreation: Heautontimorumenosis. Address: (h.) 2 Rosehill Road, Montrose, Angus DD10 8ST; T.-Montrose 672447.

Whittemore, Professor Colin Trengove, BSc, PhD, DSc, NDA, CBiol, FIBiol, FRSE. Head, Institute of Ecology and Resource Management, Edinburgh University, since 1990, and Professor of Agriculture and Rural Economy, since 1990; b. 16.7.42, Chester; m., Chris; 1 s.; 3 d. Educ. Rydal School; Newcastle-upon-Tyne University. Lecturer in Agriculture, Edinburgh University and Head, Animal Production, Advisory and Development, Edinburgh School of Agriculture; Professor of Animal Production, Head, Animal Division, Edinburgh School of Agriculture; Head, Department of Agriculture, Edinburgh University. Sir John Hammond Memorial Prize for scientific contribution to an understanding of nutrition and growth; Oxford University Blackman Lecture; Royal Agricultural Society of England Gold Medal for research; Mignini Oscar; David Black Award. Publications: author of five text books of animal sciences. Recreations: skiing; riding. Address: (b.) Edinburgh University, School of Agriculture, West Mains Road, Edinburgh EH9 3JG; T.-0131-667 1041.

Whittington, Professor Graeme Walter, BA, PhD. Professor in Geography, St. Andrews University, since 1995 (Chairman, Department of Geography, School of Geography and Geology, since 1993); b. 25.7.31, Cranleigh. Educ. King Edward VI Royal Grammar School, Guildford; Reading University. St. Andrews University: Assistant, 1959, Lecturer, 1962, Senior Lecturer, 1972, Reader, 1980; Visiting Lecturer, Natal University, 1971; Member, British Association Committee on Ancient Fields, 1958-73; Member, Council, Royal Scottish Geographical Society, since 1992. Publications: Environment and Land Use in Africa (Co-Editor); An Historical Geography of Scotland (Co-Editor). Recreations: gardening; classical

music. Address: (h.) 3 Leonard Gardens, St. Andrews, Fife KY16 8RD; T.-0334 476807.

Whyte, Christopher, MA (Hons), PhD. Writer and Critic; Lecturer in Scottish Literature, Glasgow University, since 1990; b. 29.10.52, Glasgow; m., Gay. Educ. St. Aloysius College, Glasgow; Pembroke College, Cambridge. Lector, Rome University, 1977-85; Lecturer in English Literature, Edinburgh University, 1986-89. Publications: In The Face of Eternity: Eight Gaelic Poets, 1991; Uirsgeul/Myth, 1991. Recreations: classical music; walking; cooking. Address: (h.) 15 Hart Street, Edinburgh EH1 3RN; T.-0131-558 3907.

Whyte, Donald, JP, FHG, FSG. Consultant Genealogist, Author and Lecturer; b. 13.3.26, Newtongrange; m., Mary Burton; 3 d. Educ. Crookston School, Musselburgh; Institute of Heraldic and Genealogical Studies, Canterbury. Agricultural and horticultural work, 1940-68; professional genealogist, 1968-76; Member, Kirkliston and Winchburgh District Council, 1964-75 (Chairman, 1970-73); Member, West Lothian County Council, 1970-75; founder Member and Vice-President, Scottish Genealogy Society; President, Association of Scottish Genealogists and Record Agents, since 1981. Publications: Kirkliston: A Short Parish History; Dictionary of Scottish Emigrants to USA; Introducing Scottish Genealogical Research; Dictionary of Scottish Emigrants to Canada before Confederation; Walter MacFarlane: Clan Chief and Antiquary; Scottish Clock and Watchmakers, 1453-1900. Address: (h.) 4 Carmel Road, Kirkliston EH29 9DD; T.-0131-333 3245.

Whyte, Duncan, CA, ATII. Chief Operating Officer — Energy Supply (formerly Finance Director), Scottish Power plc, since 1988; b. 27.7.46, Falkirk; m., Marion; 1 s. Educ. Kilsyth Academy. Qualified as CA, 1968; Arthur Andersen & Co., 1969-83 (Managing Partner, Edinburgh Office, 1980-83); Financial Director, Kwik-Fit Holdings PLC, 1983-88. Recreations: squash; golf; general sport; reading (history). Address: (b.) Corporate Office, 1 Atlantic Quay, Glasgow G2 8SP.

Whyte, Rev. Iain Alexander, BA, BD, STM. Chaplain, University of Edinburgh, since 1994; b. 3.9.40, Stirling; m., Isabel Helen Martin; 2 s.; 1 d. Educ. Sherborne School, Dorset; St. Peter's College, Oxford; Glasgow University; Union Theological Seminary, NY. Assistant Minister, Kildrum, Cumbernauld, 1967-69; Minister and Youth Worker in Ghana, 1969-71; Chaplain to Overseas Students in Glasgow, 1971-74; Lecturer, Falkirk Technical College, 1974-75; Minister, Merksworth Parish Church, Paisley, 1976-81; Chaplain, St. Andrews University, 1981-87; Minister, Blairhill Dundyvan Parish Church, Coatbridge, 1987-90; National Secretary for Scotland, Christian Aid, 1990-94. Scottish Churches Representative, Board, Christian Aid, 1980-86 (Chairman, Christian Aid Middle East Committee, 1982-86); Chairman, Scottish Churches Council Race and Community Relations Group, 1981-83; Scottish Representative, Britain/Zimbabwe Society; former Chair, Glasgow Anti-Apartheid Group. Recreations: travel; squash; watching St. Mirren; numismatics; candle-making. Address: (h.) 34 Shandon Crescent, Edinburgh EH11 1QF; T.-0131-337 3559.

Whyte, Iain Wilson, BA, DCE. Director and General Secretary, Church of Scotland Board of Parish Education, since 1993; b. 2.12.56, Johnstone; m., Elaine; 2 d. Educ. Paisley Grammar School; Jordanhill College; Open University. Adult Education Tutor, Glasgow, 1978-82; Development Officer, Priesthill, Glasgow, 1982-84; Adult Education Officer, European Social Fund Project, Strathclyde, 1984-86; Lecturer, Cardonald College, Glasgow, 1986-90, Senior Lecturer, 1990-93. Elder, Colinton Parish Church, Edinburgh. Recreations: playing guitar, piano, organ; singing; songwriting; golf. Address:

(b.) St. Colm's, 20 Inverleith Terrace, Edinburgh, EH3 5NS; T.-0131-332 0343.

Whyte, Rev. James, BD, DipCE. Parish Minister, Broom, Newton Mearns, since 1987; b. 26.4.46, Glasgow; m., Norma Isabella West; 1 s.; 2 d. Educ. Glasgow; Jordanhill College; Glasgow University. Trained as planning engineer; studied community education (Glasgow and Boston, Mass., USA); Community Organiser with Lamp of Lothian Collegiate Trust, Haddington; Organiser of Community Education, Dumbarton, 1971-73; Assistant Principal Community Education Officer, Renfrew Division, Strathclyde Region, 1973-77; entered ministry, Church of Scotland, 1977; Assistant Minister: Barrhead Arthurlie, 1977-78, St. Marks, Oldhall, Paisley, 1978-80; Minister, Coupar Angus Abbey, 1981-87. Recreations: gardening; reading. Address: Manse of Broom, 3 Laigh Road, Newton Mearns, Glasgow G77; T.-0141-639 2916.

Whyte, Very Rev. Professor James Aitken, MA, LLD, DD, DUniv. Moderator, General Assembly of the Church of Scotland, 1988-89; Professor of Practical Theology and Christian Ethics, St. Andrews University, 1958-87; b. 28.1.20, Leith; m., 1, Elisabeth Wilson Mill (deceased); 2 s.; 1 d.; 2, Ishbel Christina Macaulay or Rathie. Educ. Daniel Stewart's College, Edinburgh; Edinburgh University. Ordained and commissioned as Chaplain to the Forces, 1945; Minister: Dunollie Road Church, Oban, 1948-54, Mayfield North Church, Edinburgh, 1954-58; Dean of Divinity, St. Andrews University, 1968-72; Principal, St. Mary's College, 1978-82; Kerr Lecturer, Glasgow University, 1969-72; Croall Lecturer, Edinburgh University, 1972-73; Hon. LLD, Dundee University, 1981; Hon.DD, St. Andrews University, 1989; Hon. DUniv., Stirling University, 1994; President, Society for the Study of Theology, 1983-84; Margaret Harris Lecturer, Dundee University, 1990. Publication: Laughter and Tears, 1993. Address: (h.) 13 Hope Street, St. Andrews, Fife; T.-St. Andrews 472323.

Whyte, Robert, MB, ChB, FRCPsych, DPM. Consultant Psychotherapist, Carswell House, Glasgow, since 1979; b. 1.6.41, Edinburgh; m., Susan Frances Milburn; 1 s.; 1 d. Educ. George Heriot's, Edinburgh; St. Andrews University. House Officer in Surgery, Arbroath Infirmary, 1966; House Officer in Medicine, Falkirk and District Royal Infirmary, 1967; Trainee in Psychiatry, Dundee Psychiatric Services, 1967-73; Consultant Psychiatrist, Duke Street Hospital, Glasgow, 1973. Past Chairman, Scottish Association of Psychoanalytical Psychotherapists; Member, Scottish Institute of Human Relations. Address: (h.) Waverley, 70 East Kilbride Road, Busby, Glasgow G76 8HU; T.-0141-644 1659.

Wickham-Jones, Caroline R., MA, MIFA, FSA, FSA Scot. Archaeologist; b. 25.4.55, Middlesborough. Educ. Teesside High School; Edinburgh University. Freelance archaeologist and author with research interests in early (postglacial) settlement of Scotland, stone tools, and the preservation of the cultural heritage; former Council Member, National Trust for Scotland; Council Member, Institute of Field Archaeologists, 1986-90; former Secretary, Society of Antiquaries of Scotland; former Trustee, John Muir Trust; Livery Woman of the City of London (Skinners Company). Recreations: travel; wilderness walking; socialising. Address: (h.) 21 Dudley Gardens, Edinburgh EH6 4PU.

Wigglesworth, Rev. Chris, MBE, BSc, PhD, BD. General Secretary, Church of Scotland Board of World Mission; b. 8.4.37, Leeds; m., Ann Livesey; 1 s.; 3 d. Educ. Grangefield Grammar School, Stockton-on-Tees; University College, Durham; New College, Edinburgh. Church of North India, 1967-72; St. Andrew's and St. Columba's Church, Bombay, 1972-79; University Lecturer in Practical Theology, Aberdeen, 1979-86. Recreations: painting; hill-walking.

Address: (h.) 12 Leven Terrace, Edinburgh; T.-0131-228 6335.

Wight, Robin A.F., MA, FCA. Regional Executive Chairman — Scotland, Coopers & Lybrand, since 1989; b. 5.6.38, Edinburgh; m., Sheila; 3 s.; 1 d. Educ. Dollar Academy; Magdalene College, Cambridge. Partner, Coopers & Lybrand, since 1971; Regional Partner, Scotland, 1977-95; Member, Executive Committee, 1978-87; Member, Governing Board, 1987-89; Member, Council, 1989-93. Recreations: skiing; golf; reading; theatre. Address: (h.) 22 Regent Terrace, Edinburgh; T.-0131-556 2100.

Wightman, Very Rev. William David, BA (Hons). Provost, St. Andrews Cathedral, Aberdeen, since 1991, also Priest-in-Charge, St. Ninian's, Aberdeen; Hon. Canon, Christchurch Cathedral, Hartford, Conn., since 1991; b. 29.1.39, Leicester; m., Karen Elizabeth Harker; 2 s.; 2 d. Educ. Alderman Newton's Grammar School, Leicester; George Dixon Grammar School, Birmingham; Birmingham University; Wells Theological College. Ordained Deacon, 1963; ordained Priest, 1964. Director, Training for Ministry (Diocese of Aberdeen and Orkney), 1989-91. Recreations: fishing; swimming; choral music. Address: (h.) 15 Morningfield Road, Aberdeen AB2 4AP; T.-01224 314765.

Wild, John Robin, JP, BDS, DPD. Chief Dental Officer, Scottish Office Home and Health Department, and Director of Dental Services for the NHS in Scotland, since 1993 (Deputy Chief Dental Officer, 1987-93); b. 12.9.41, Scarborough; m., Eleanor Daphne Kerr; 1 s.; 2 d. Educ. Sedbergh School; Edinburgh University; Dundee University. General Dental Practitioner, Scarborough, 1965-71; Dental Officer, East Lothian, 1971-74; Chief Administrative Dental Officer, Borders Health Board, 1974-87; Regional Dental Postgraduate Adviser, S.E. Regional Committee for Postgraduate Medical Education, 1982-87; Hon. Member, clinical teaching staff, Edinburgh Dental School, 1975-94; Fellow, Edinburgh University; Past Chairman, Scottish Council, British Dental Association. Recreations: vintage cars (restoration and driving); music; gardening. Address: (h.) Braehead House, St. Boswells, Roxburghshire; T.-01835 823203.

Wildgoose, James Richmond, BSc, DPhil. Chief Agricultural Economist (Senior Economic Adviser), Scottish Office, since 1990; b. 17.4.49, Edinburgh; m., Charlotte Dorothy; 1 s.; 1 d. Educ. Melville College; Edinburgh University; Oxford University. Economic Assistant/Economic Adviser, Ministry of Agriculture, Fisheries and Food, 1976-86; Administrative Principal, MAFF Tropical Foods Division, 1986-90; Admnistrative Principal, Scottish Office (SDD), 1990. Recreations: local Baptist church; playing piano; music; walking. Address: (b.) Room 162, Pentland House, Robb's Loan, Edinburgh; T.-0131-244 6128.

Wilkie, Rev. James Lindsay, MA, BD. Secretary for relations with churches in Africa, Board of World Mission, Church of Scotland, since 1984; b. 30.1.34, Dunfermline; m., Dr. Irene A. Wilkie; 1 s.; 3 d. Educ. Aberdeen Grammar School; Aberdeen University and Christ's College. Assistant Minister, St. Machar's Cathedral, Aberdeen, 1959-60; District Missionary and Minister, United Church of Zambia, 1961-70; Chaplain, University of Zambia, 1970-76; Africa Secretary, then Divisional Secretary and Deputy General Secretary, British Council of Churches, 1976-84; member of team which translated Bible into Chinamwanga language of Zambia. Recreation: DIY. Address: (h.) 7 Comely Bank Avenue, Edinburgh EH4 1EW; T.-0131-343 1552.

Wilkie, Neil Keith, OBE, MA (Hons), FRSA. Headmaster, Gairloch High School, since 1978; b. 5.4.39, Perth; m., Margaret Rawlinson; 1 s. Educ. Perth Academy; Dundee

University; Dundee College of Education; East of Scotland College of Agriculture. Sugar planter, Trinidad, six years; resumed academic studies, 1966; Teacher of History and Modern Studies, then Principal Teacher of History, Golspie High School, 1972-78. Elder, Gairloch and Dundonnell Parish Church; Member, Gairloch Community Council. Recreations: sport; travel; gardening. Address: (h.) Rohallion, Achtercairn, Gairloch, Ross-shire; T.-01445 712221.

Wilkie, Professor (William) Roy, MA. Emeritus Professor, Department of Human Resource Management, Strathclyde University, since 1974; b. 10.6.30, Rutherglen; m., Jill Henzell; 1 s.; 3 d. Educ. Rutherglen Academy; Aberdeen University. Lecturer and Senior Lecturer, Department of Administration, Strathclyde University, 1963-66; Director, J. & J. Denholm (Management) Ltd., 1966-70; Reader and Head, Department of Administration, Strathclyde University, 1966-73. Publications: The Concept of Organization, 1974; Managing the Police, 1986. Recreations: swimming; movies; jazz; reading. Address: (b.) Graham Hill Building, 50 Richmond Street, Glasgow; T.-0141-552 4400.

Wilkins, Professor Malcolm Barrett, BSc, PhD, DSc, AKC, FRSE. Regius Professor of Botany, Glasgow University, since 1970 (Dean, Faculty of Science, 1985-87; Member, University Court, since 1993); b.27.2.33, Cardiff; m., Mary Patricia Maltby; 1 s.; 1 d. (deceased). Educ. Monkton House School, Cardiff; King's College, London University. Lecturer in Botany, King's College, London, 1958-64; Lecturer in Biology, then Professor of Biology, East Anglia University, 1964-67; Professor of Plant Physiology, Nottingham University, 1967-70. Rockefeller Foundation Fellow, Yale University, 1961-62; Corporation Research Fellow, Harvard University, 1962-63; Darwin Lecturer, British Association for the Advancement of Science, 1967; elected Corresponding (Honorary) Member, American Society of Plant Physiologists, 1984; Chairman, Life Science Working Group, European Space Agency, 1987-89; Trustee, Royal Botanic Garden, Edinburgh, since 1990, Chairman, since 1994; Vice President, Royal Society of Edinburgh, since 1994. Recreations: sailing; fishing; model engineering. Address: (b.) Botany Department, Glasgow University, Glasgow G12 8QQ; T.-0141-339 8855.

Wilkinson, Sheriff Alexander Birrell, QC, MA, LLB. Sheriff of Glasgow and Strathkelvin at Glasgow, since 1991; Temporary Judge, Court of Session, since 1993; b. 2.2.32, Perth; m., Wendy Imogen Barrett; 1 s.; 1 d. Educ. Perth Academy; St. Andrews University; Edinburgh University. Advocate, 1959; practised at Scottish Bar, 1959-69; Lecturer in Scots Law, Edinburgh University, 1965-69; Sheriff of Stirling, Dunbarton and Clackmannan, at Stirling and Alloa, 1969-72; Professor of Private Law, Dundee University, 1972-86 (Dean, Faculty of Law, 1974-76 and 1986); Sheriff of Tayside, Central and Fife at Falkirk, 1986-91; a Chairman, Industrial Tribunals (Scotland), 1972-86; Chancellor, Dioceses of Brechin and of Argyll and the Isles, Scottish Episcopal Church; Chairman, Scottish Marriage Guidance Council, 1974-77; Chairman, Legal Services Group, Scottish Association of CAB, 1979-83; Vice-President, Sheriffs' Association, since 1995. Publications: Gloag and Henderson's Introduction to the Law of Scotland, 8th and 9th editions (Co-editor); The Scottish Law of Evidence; The Law of Parent and Child in Scotland (Co-author). Recreations: collecting books and pictures; reading; travel. Address: (h.) 25 Glencairn Crescent, Edinburgh, EH12 5BT; T.-0131-346 1797.

Wilkinson, Andrew Peter Descarrieres, BSc, MB, ChB, DipObstRCOG. Senior Partner, general practice, Castle Douglas, since 1982; Governor, Strathallan School, since 1986; b. 19.2.44, Edinburgh; m., Patricia Jane Elliot; 2 s.; 1 d. Educ. Strathallan School; Edinburgh University. Former

HO and SHO, Edinburgh; general practice, since 1972. Member: Dumfries and Galloway Health Board, 1987-94 (Vice Chairman, 1989-94); Scottish Council, BMA, 1980-90; Scottish General Medical Services Committee, 1981-91; Chairman, Castle Douglas Branch, Royal Scottish Society for the Prevention of Cruelty to Children, 1982-92. Recreations: gardening; shooting; sailing. Address: Lochbank, Castle Douglas, Kirkcudbright; T.-01556 503413.

Wilkinson, Professor Paul, MA. Professor of International Relations and Head of School of History and International Relations, St. Andrews University; Writer on conflict and terrorism; b. 9.5.37, Harrow, Middlesex; m., Susan; 2 s.; 1 d. Educ. John Lyon School; University College, Swansea; University of Wales. RAF, 1959-65; Assistant Lecturer in Politics, University College, Cardiff, 1966-68; University of Wales: Lecturer, 1968-75, Senior Lecturer, 1975-77, Reader in Politics, 1978-79; Professor of International Relations, Aberdeen University, 1979-89; Editor, Terrorism and Political Violence; Member, Editorial Board, Security Handbook, Social Intelligence, and Violence and Aggression; Editor, Key Concepts in International Relations; Scottish Free Enterprise Award, 1982; Honorary Fellow, University College, Swansea, 1986; Special Consultant, CBS America, 1989-90, BBC, since 1989; Aviation Security Adviser to IFAPA, 1988; Safety Adviser, World Tourism and Travel Council. Publications: Social Movement, 1971; Political Terrorism, 1974; Terrorism and the Liberal State, 1986 (revised edition); The New Fascists, 1983; Terrorism: Theory and Practice (Co-author), 1979; British Perspectives on Terrorism (Editor), 1981; Contemporary Research on Terrorism (Joint Editor), 1987; Technology and Terrorism (Editor), 1994; Terrorism: British Perspectives (Editor), 1993. Recreations: modern art; poetry; walking. Address: (b.) Department of International Relations, St. Andrews University, St. Andrews KY16 9TR; T.-01334 462900.

Wilkinson, Professor Peter Charles, MD, FRSE, FIBiol. Professor in Immunology, Glasgow University, since 1982; Honorary Consultant in Immunology, Western Infirmary, Glasgow, since 1970; b. 10.7.32, London; m., Eileen Mary Baron; 2 s.; 1 d. Educ. London Hospital Medical College; London University. House appointments, London Hospital, 1956-58; Flt.-Lt., RAF (Medical Officer), 1958-60; Lecturer in Bacteriology, London Hospital Medical College, 1960-63; Lecturer and Senior Lecturer in Bacteriology and Immunology, Glasgow University, 1964-77; MRC Travelling Fellow, Swiss Research Institute, 1967-69; Reader, Glasgow University, 1977-82; Visiting Professor, Rockefeller University, New York, 1979. Publications: Chemotaxis and Inflammation; A Dictionary of Immunology (Co-author). Recreations: various interests in the arts. Address: (h.) 26 Randolph Road, Glasgow G11 7LG.

Wilkinson, (William) Roderick, DAA, FIPM. Novelist and Scriptwriter; b. 31.3.17, Glasgow; 1 s.; 2 d. Educ. North Kelvinside Secondary, Glasgow. Director of advertising agency, 1946-59; Director of Personnel, 1959-80. Publications: 10 books, fiction and non-fiction; plays, articles and stories. Recreation: fishing. Address: (h.) 61 Norwood Park, Bearsden, Glasgow G61 2RZ; T.-0141-942 2185.

Wilks, Antony Hugh Francis, MBE, FNI. Chief Harbourmaster, Firth of Forth; Chairman, Forth Estuary Forum; Member, Board, Forth River Purification; Member, Board, Scottish Natural Heritage (S.E.); b. 29.12.36, Watford; m., Susan; 1 s.; 1 d. Educ. Oundle. Royal Navy, 1958-90, latterly Naval Base Commander, Rosyth, 1985-90. Contributor, The Naval Review; knighthood, State of Brunei. Recreations: lawn tennis and rackets. Address: (b.) Easter Fossoway, Kinross-shire; T.-0131-554 3661.

Will, David Houston, BL, NP. Vice-President, FIFA, since 1990; Chairman, FIFA Referees Committee, and Legal Matters Committee; Member, FIFA Executive Committee, World Cup Organising Committee and Security Committee; b. 20.11.36, Glasgow; m., Margaret; 2 d. Educ. Brechin High School; Edinburgh University. Chairman, Brechin City FC, 1966-91; appointed to SFA Council, 1970; President, SFA, 1984-89; Vice-President, UEFA, 1986-90. Recreations: golf; curling. Address: (h.) Norandale, 32 Airlie Street, Brechin, Angus; T.-01356 622273.

Will, Ronald Kerr, WS. Retired Solicitor; b. 22.3.18, Edinburgh; m., Margaret Joyce Stevenson; 2 s. Educ. Merchiston Castle School; Edinburgh University. Served King's Own Scottish Borderers, 1940-46 (Major); mentioned in Despatches; WS, 1950; former Senior Partner, Dundas & Wilson, CS, Edinburgh; Deputy Keeper of Her Majesty's Signet, 1975-83; Director, Scottish Equitable Life Assurance Society, 1965-88 (Chairman, 1980-83); Director, Scottish Investment Trust PLC, 1963-88; Member, Council on Tribunals, 1971-76 and Chairman, Scottish Committee; Governor, Merchiston Castle School, 1953-76. Recreations: gardening; shooting; fishing. Address: (h.) Chapelhill Cottage, Dirleton, North Berwick, East Lothian; T.-0162085 0338.

Willett, Emeritus Professor Frank, CBE, MA, FRSE. Hon. Senior Research Fellow, since 1990, Director, Hunterian Museum & Art Gallery, Glasgow, 1976-90; b. 18.8.25, Bolton; m., Mary Constance Hewitt; 1 s.; 3 d. Educ. Bolton Municipal Secondary School; University College, Oxford. Keeper of Ethnology and General Archaeology, Manchester Museum, 1950-58; Government Archaeologist, Nigeria, 1958-63; Leverhulme Research Fellow, 1964; Research Fellow, Nuffield College, Oxford, 1964-66; Professor of Art History, African Studies and Interdisciplinary Studies, Northwestern University, Evanston, Illinois, 1966-76; Visiting Fellow, Clare Hall, Cambridge, 1970-71; Hon. Corresponding Member, Manchester Literary and Philosophical Society, since 1958; Vice Chairman, Scottish Museums Council, 1986-89; Fellow, Royal Anthropological Institute; Fellow, Royal Society of Edinburgh, Curator, RSE, since 1990. Publications: Ife in the History of West African Sculpture, 1967; African Art: An Introduction, 1971; Treasures of Ancient Nigeria, Co-author, 1980. Recreation: walking. Address: (h.) 583 Anniesland Road, Glasgow G13 1UX; T.-0141-959 3424.

Willetts, Professor Brian Benjamin, MA, PhD, CEng, FICE. Professor of Civil Engineering, Aberdeen University, since 1985 (Head, Engineering Department, 1991-94); b. 12.6.36, Old Hill; m., Patricia Margaret Jones; 1 s.; 1 d. Educ. King Edward VI School, Stourbridge; Emmanuel College, Cambridge. Assistant Engineer, City of Birmingham, 1959-61; Executive Engineer, Government of Northern Nigeria, 1961-63; Lecturer/Senior Lecturer, Lanchester Polytechnic, 1963-66; Lecturer/Senior Lecturer, Aberdeen University, 1967-85. Address: (h.) Mosscroft, Upper Lochton, Banchory, Kincardineshire; T.-0133 082 2674.

Willey, Professor Roger James, BSc, PhD, CPhys, MIOSH, MBIM. Chief Executive, Centre for Environmental and Waste Management, Paisley University, since 1992; b. 11.6.46, Rhondda; m., Jennifer; 2 d. Educ. Porth County Grammar School; University College, Swansea. Specialist in the treatment of hazardous materials, especially asbestos; consultancy work in Europe, USA, Canada, Middle East and Japan; presented at conferences in Europe, America and Japan; Chairman, Institute of Occupational Safety and Health (West of Scotland); Member, IOSH Professional Standards Committee; Member, Secretary of State for Scotland Advisory Committee on Sustainable Development; Board Member, South West Region, Scottish Natural Heritage. Publications:

50 papers/technical articles. Recreations: sport; travel. Address: (b.) Westerfield House, 25 High Calside, Paisley PA2 6BY; T.-0141-848 3146.

Williams, Sir Alwyn, Kt, PhD, FRS, FRSE, MRIA, FGS, Hon. FRCPS, Hon. DSc, Hon. LLD. Honorary Research Fellow, Department of Geology, Glasgow University (Principal and Vice-Chancellor, Glasgow University, 1976-88); Non-Executive Director, Scottish Daily Record and Sunday Mail Ltd., 1984-90; b. 8.6.21, Aberdare, Wales; m., Edith Joan Bevan; 1 s.; 1 d. Educ. Aberdare Boys' Grammar School; University College of Wales, Aberystwyth. Commonwealth Fund Fellow, US National Museum, 1948-50; Lecturer in Geology, Glasgow University, 1950-54; Professor of Geology, Queen's University, Belfast, 1954-74; Lapworth Professor of Geology, Birmingham University, 1974-76; Chairman, Scottish Hospital Endowments Research Trust, since 1989; Member, Scottish Tertiary Education Advisory Council, 1984-86; President, Palaeontological Association, 1968-70; President, Royal Society of Edinburgh, 1985-88; Trustee and Chairman, Board of British Museum (Natural History), 1971-79; Chairman, Committee on National Museums and Galleries of Scotland, 1979-81; Honorary Fellow, Geological Society of America, since 1970; Foreign Member, Polish Academies of Science, since 1981; Hon. DSc, Universities of Wales, Queen's (Belfast) and Edinburgh; Hon. DCL, Oxford; Hon. LLD, Glasgow, Strathclyde; Hon. DUniv, Paisley. Address: (h.) 25 Sutherland Avenue, Pollokshields, Glasgow G41 4HG; T.-0141-427 0589.

Williams, Arthur, OBE, FRPharmS. Chief Administrative Pharmaceutical Officer, Grampian, Orkney and Shetland Health Boards, since 1981; b. 5.11.32, Tarleton, near Preston; m., Barbara; 1 s.; 1 d. Educ. Hutton Grammar School, near Preston; School of Pharmacy, Leicester. Senior Pharmacist, United Manchester Hospitals, 1957-59; Chief Pharmacist: Jewish Hospital, 1959-62, Macclesfield Hospital, 1962-66; Group Chief Pharmacist to Area Pharmaceutical Officer, 1966-81. Merck, Sharp and Dohme Award, 1979; Evans Gold Medal, 1991; Evans Award for Innovation (Scotland), 1991. Recreations: gardening; fell-walking; natural history. Address: (b.) Grampian Health Board, 2 Eday Road, Aberdeen AB9 1RE; T.-01224 663456, Ext. 75135.

Williams, Professor Bryan Peter, BA (Hons), MA, CQSW. Professor of Social Work and Head, Department of Social Work, Dundee University; b. 18.11.45, Northampton; m., Anne Rosemary Dysart; 1 d. Educ. Northampton and Weston-Super-Mare Grammar Schools; Hull University; Bristol University. UK Atomic Energy Authority, 1963-66; residential social worker, Chile voluntary service, 1966-67; schoolteacher, 1967-68; probation officer, 1973-76; Lecturer in Social Work, Dundee University, 1976-89. Review Committee on Parole and Related Issues, 1988-89; Member, Council, Central Council for Education and Training in Social Work and Chair, UK Standards Panel, 1990-93; Member, Scottish Committee, Central Council for Education and Training in Social Work; Member, Council, Scottish Association for the Care and Resettlement of Offenders, 1982-91 (Chair, 1990-93); Chairman, Board of Governors, Aberlow House School; Member, Board of Governors, Gordonstoun School; Chair, Association of University Professors in Social Work. Publications: books and papers on research into social work and criminal justice. Recreations: mountaineering; skiing; rock climbing; sea canoeing; all types of music. Address: (b.) Department of Social Work, Dundee University, Dundee DD1 4HN; T.-0382 344651.

Williams, Professor Howard Peter, MSc. Professor, Management Science Department, Strathclyde University, since 1990; Director, Network and Resource Management Centre; b. 27.2.54, St. Albans. Educ. Exeter University;

Newcastle upon Tyne University. Economist, ICI Plant Protection Division, International Wool Secretariat, British Ship Research Association; Senior Research Fellow, Newcastle-upon-Tyne University. Member, Scottish Advisory Committee on Telecommunications, Glasgow Advisory Committee on Posts and Telecommunications. Recreations: windsurfing; opera; breadmaking. Address: (b.) Department of Management Science, Sir Graham Hills Building, Strathclyde University, Glasgow G1 1XH; T.-0141-552 4400, Ext. 3153.

Williams, Professor Morgan Howard, BSc Hons, PhD, DSc, CEng, FBCS, FRSA. Professor of Computer Science, Heriot-Watt University, since 1980 (Head of Department, 1980-88); b. 15.12.44, Durban; 2 s. Educ. Grey High School, Port Elizabeth; Rhodes University, Grahamstown. Physicist in Antarctic Expedition, 1968-69; Rhodes University: Lecturer in Computer Science, 1970-72, Senior Lecturer, 1972-77, Professor and Head of Department, 1977-80. Address: Department of Computing and Electrical Engineering, Heriot-Watt University, Riccarton, Edinburgh EH14 4AS; T.-0131-451 3430.

Williamson, David, CBE, BL. Honorary President, SSC (a club for the youth of Scotland), Chairman, 1964-89; Chairman, North Merchiston Club, Edinburgh, since 1982; Trustee, Stanley Nairne Memorial Trust, since 1969; b. 13.1.20, Edinburgh; m., Agnes Margaret. Educ. George Heriot's School, Edinburgh; Edinburgh University. Army Service, 1940-46 (Gunner, Lance Bombadier, Bombadier, Sergeant, Officer Cadet, Second Lieutenant, Lieutenant, Captain); Keeper of the Registers of Scotland, 1973-82 (supervised introduction of Registration of Title to Scotland, 1981); Honorary Member, Law Society of Scotland, since 1982; received Keystone Gold Award for services to Boys' Clubs, 1985. Publications: Registration of Title Practice Book (Co-author); The Story of the Scottish Schoolboys' Club (Editor and Co-author); Stanley Nairne, The Boys' Club Pioneer. Recreations: walking; enjoying countryside; reading; appreciating music (including opera); watching rugby. Address: (h.) 10 Homeross House, Mount Grange, Edinburgh EH9 2QX; T.-0131-447 3050.

Williamson, Professor Edwin Henry, MA, PhD. Professor of Hispanic Studies, Edinburgh University, since 1990; b. 2.10.49; m., Susan Jane Fitchie; 2 d. Educ. Edinburgh University. Lecturer in Spanish, Trinity College, Dublin, 1974-77; Lecturer in Spanish, Birkbeck College, London, 1977-90. Publications: The Half-Way House of Fiction: Don Quixote and Arthurian Romance, 1984; El Quijote Y Los Libros de Caballerias, 1991; The Penguin History of Latin America, 1992; Cervantes and the Modernists, 1994. Recreations: theatre; art; film; hill-walking. Address: (b.) Department of Hispanic Studies, Edinburgh University, David Hume Tower, George Square, Edinburgh EH8 9JX; T.-0131-650 3673.

Williamson, Professor James, CBE, MB, ChB, FRCPEdin, DSc (Hon.). Chairman, Chest, Heart and Stroke, Scotland, since 1993; Past President, British Geriatrics Society; Past Chairman, Age Concern Scotland; Professor Emeritus, Geriatric Medicine, Edinburgh University; b. 22.11.20, Wishaw; m., Sheila Mary Blair; 3 s.; 2 d. Educ. Wishaw High School; Glasgow University. General medical training in Glasgow hospitals; general practice; training in respiratory medicine, becoming Consultant in Edinburgh, 1954; converted to geriatric medicine, 1959; Consultant, Edinburgh, until 1973; first occupant, Chair of Geriatric Medicine, Liverpool University; first occupant, Chair of Geriatric Medicine, Edinburgh University, 1976-86; Visiting Professor to several North American medical schools. Recreations: reading; walking. Address: (h.) 8 Chester Street, Edinburgh EH3 7RA; T.-0131-477 0282.

Williamson, Raymond MacLeod, MA, LLB, FRSA. Solicitor, since 1968 (Partner, MacRoberts, Solicitors,

Glasgow and Edinburgh, since 1972); Governor, High School of Glasgow; Governor, Royal Scottish Academy of Music and Drama; Chairman, John Currie Singers Ltd.; b. 24.12.42, Glasgow; m., Brenda; 1 s.; 1 d. Educ. High School of Glasgow; Glasgow University. Chairman, Royal Scottish National Orchestra, 1985-91. Recreation: music. Address: (h.) 11 Islay Drive, Newton Mearns, Glasgow G77 6UD; T.-0141-639 4133.

Williamson, Richard John. Editor, Evening Express, Aberdeen, since 1986; b. 14.12.35, Dunphail, Moray; m., Lesley Paterson Mutch; 1 s.; 1 d. Educ. Forres Academy. Elder, Cathedral Church of St. Machar, Old Aberdeen; Trustee, Chris Anderson Trust, Aberdeen. Recreations: reading; walking. Address: (b.) Lang Stracht, Mastrick, Aberdeen; T.-01224 690222.

Williamson, W. David, MA. Rector, Whitburn Academy, since 1990; b. 4.6.47, Glasgow; m., Margaret McLaren; 1 s.; 2 d. Educ. Allan Glens School, Glasgow; Glasgow University; Jordanhill College. Teacher, then Principal Teacher of Modern Studies, John Neilson High School, Paisley, 1969-78; Assistant Headteacher, Castlebrae High School, Edinburgh, 1978-83; Depute Headteacher, Portobello High School, Edinburgh, 1983-90. Council Member, Headteachers Association of Scotland. Recreations: hill-walking; running. Address: (h.) 33/4 Orchard Brae Avenue, Edinburgh EH4 2UP.

Willock, Professor Ian Douglas, MA, LLB, PhD. Professor of Jurisprudence, Dundee University. Educ. Aberdeen University. Address: (b.) Department of Law, Dundee University, Dundee; T.-01382 223181.

Wills, Jonathan W.G., MA (Hons), PhD. Partner, Shetland News Agency; Writer, Illustrator and Painter; b. 17.6.47, Oxford; m., Lesley M. Roberts; 3 s.; 1 d. Educ. Warwick School; Anderson Educational Institute, Lerwick; Edinburgh University. Reporter, Shetland Times, 1969; Warden and boatman, Noss National Nature Reserve, 1970; Rector, Edinburgh University (first student Rector), 1971; Scottish and NI Organiser, Third World First (Oxfam), 1972; Boatman, Muckle Flugga Lighthouse, Unst, 1974; Reporter, Shetland Times, 1976; Senior Producer/Presenter, BBC Radio Shetland, 1977; News Editor, Shetland Times, 1981; Scottish Correspondent, The Times, 1982; Producer, BBC Radio Scotland, 1983; Freelance and Research Assistant to Alex. Falconer, MEP, 1984; Tutor, Media Studies, STUC and individual trade unions, 1984; Senior Reporter, Shetland Times, 1985, Editor, 1987-90; Fraser Press Award, 1981-82 and 1990, for work on Shetland Times; Labour candidate, Orkney and Shetland, 1974 (twice). Publications: Magnus Pole, 1975; Linda and the Lighthouse, 1976; A Place in the Sun — Shetland and oil, 1991; Innocent Passage — the wreck of the tanker Braer (Co-author), 1993. Recreations: sailing other people's boats; ornithology; painting; gardening. Address: (h.) Sundside, Bressay, Shetland ZE2 9ER.

Wilson, Alan Oliver Arneil, MB, ChB, DPM, FRCPsych. Consultant in private practice, Murrayfield Hospital, Edinburgh; Consultant Psychiatrist, Bangour Hospitals, 1977-89; former Member, Clinical Teaching Staff, Faculty of Medicine, Edinburgh University; Member, Executive Group, and Past President, Board of Directors, World Association for Psychosocial Rehabilitation; Consultant (in Scotland), Ex-Services Mental Welfare Society; b. 4.1.30, Douglas; m., Dr. Fiona Margaret Davidson; 3 s. Educ. Biggar High School; Edinburgh University. RAMC, 1953-55; psychiatric post, Stobhill General Hospital, Glasgow, and Garlands Hospital, Carlisle, 1955-63; Consultant Psychiatrist and Deputy Physician Superintendent, St. George's Hospital, Morpeth, 1963-77. Joint Honorary Secretary, Northern Counties Psychiatric Association; Chairman, Group for Study of Rehabilitation and Community Care, Scottish Division, RCPsych; Member,

Ethics Committee, World Association for Social Psychiatry; Chairman, Psychosocial Rehabilitation Scotland. V.M. Bekhterev Medal awarded by Bekhterev Psychoneurological Research Institute, St. Petersburg. Recreations: golf; folk singing; guitar; "blethering"; former Hibernian FC footballer. Address: (h.) 14 Cammo Hill, Edinburgh EH4 8EY; T.-0131-339 2244.

Wilson, Brian, MA (Hons), FSA (Scot). MP (Labour), Cunninghame North, since 1987; b. 13.12.48, Dunoon; m., Joni Buchanan; 1 s.; 1 d. Educ. Dunoon Grammar School; Dundee University; University College, Cardiff. Journalist; Publisher and Founding Editor, West Highland Free Press; Contributor to The Guardian, Glasgow Herald, etc.; first winner, Nicholas Tomalin Memorial Award for Journalism; contested Ross and Cromarty, Oct., 1974, Inverness, 1979, Western Isles, 1983; front-bench spokesman on Scottish Home Affairs etc., 1988-92, Transport, 1992-94, Trade and Industry, since 1994; Parliamentary Adviser to Scottish Professional Footballers Association. Address: (h.) Miavaig House, Uig, Isle of Lewis; T.-01851 672 357; (b.) 37 Main Street, Kilbirnie, Ayrshire; T.-0505 682847.

Wilson, Brian, LLB. Chief Executive, Inverness District Council, since 1978; Clerk, Highland River Purification Board, since 1989; b. 20.2.46, Perth; m., Isobel Esson; 3 d. Educ. Buckie High School; Aberdeen University. Management trainee, Marks and Spencer, 1966-68; Apprentice, then Legal Assistant, Banff County Council, 1969-72; Senior Legal Assistant, Inverness County Council, 1972-73; Depute County Clerk, Banff County Council, 1973-75; Director of Administration and Legal Services, Banff and Buchan District Council, 1975-78. Hon. Secretary SOLACE (Scottish Branch) since 1986; Clerk, JP Advisory Committee (Inverness). Recreations: garden; fishing. Address: (b.) Town House, Inverness IV1 1JJ; T.-01463 724202.

Wilson, Conrad. Music Critic, The Scotsman, 1963-91 (also restaurant reviewer, 1981-91); freelance music reviewer and feature writer, The Herald, since 1991; b. 7.11.32, Edinburgh; 1 s.; 1 d. Educ. Daniel Stewart's College, Edinburgh. Music Critic, Evening Dispatch, Edinburgh, 1954-58; Music Editor, Philips Records, Holland, 1958-61; Cultural Correspondent, The Scotsman, London Office, 1961-63. Programme Editor, Edinburgh Festival, 1966-82; freelance Music Lecturer, since 1964; Chairman, Critics' Committee, European Music Year, Arts Council of GB, 1985; Co-Director, Ramsay Head Press, since 1987; elected Member, International Association of Music Critics, since 1993. Publications: A Critic's Choice, 1966; Scottish Opera, the First Ten Years, 1972; Collins Encyclopedia of Music (revised), 1976; Good Food Facts (Co-author), 1986; Where to Eat Well in Scotland, 1988; Collins Dictionary of Music (revised), 1988; music section, Guinness Encyclopaedia of Music, 1990; Playing for Scotland, 1993; Alex, the authorised biography of Sir Alexander Gibson, 1993; Puccini, to be published 1996. Address: (h.) 7 Bangholm Terrace, Edinburgh; T.-0131-552 2550.

Wilson of Tillyorn, Baron (David Clive Wilson), GCMG, MA (Oxon), PhD. Life Peer (1992); Chairman, Scottish Hydro Electric PLC, since 1993; Chairman, Scottish Committee, British Council, since 1993; Chancellor's Assessor, Aberdeen University, since 1993; Member, Council, Glenalmond College, since 1994; President, Bhutan Society of the UK, since 1993; Member, Board, Martin Currie Pacific Trust; Member, Governing Body, School of Oriental and African Studies, since 1992; b. 14.2.34, Alloa; m., Natasha Helen Mary Alexander; 2 s. Educ. Trinity College, Glenalmond; Keble College, Oxford. Entered Foreign Service, 1958; Third Secretary, Vientiane, 1959-60; language student, Hong Kong, 1960-62; Second, later First Secretary, Peking, 1963-65; FCO, 1965-68; resigned, 1968; Editor, China Quarterly, 1968-74; Visiting Scholar, Columbia University, New York, 1972; rejoined Diplomatic Service, 1974; Cabinet Office, 1974-77; Political Adviser, Hong Kong, 1977-81; Head, S. European Department, FCO, 1981-84; Assistant Under Secretary of State, FCO, 1984-87. Hon.LLD (Aberdeen); Hon.DLitt (Sydney); Hon.DLitt (Abertay, Dundee); KStJ. Recreations: mountaineering; skiing; reading. Address: (b.) Scottish Hydro Electric plc, Dunkeld Road, Perth PH1 5WA; T.-01738 455200.

Wilson, David Rowan, OBE. Honorary Sheriff, Wigtown; retired Solicitor; b. 1.11.13, Hamilton; m., Helen Kirkland Benson; 1 s. Educ. Hamilton Academy; Glasgow University. Qualified as Solicitor, 1936; Depute County Clerk, then County Clerk, Wigtownshire, 1948-75; Chief Executive, Wigtown District Council, 1975-78. Justice of the Peace, Wigtown District. Recreations: golf; curling. Address: (h.) Benachie, Cairnryan Road, Stranraer; T.-0177670 2307.

Wilson, David Steel, DipM. Chef/Proprietor, The Peat Inn, since 1972; b. 21.1.36, Bishopbriggs; m., Patricia Ann; 1 s.; 1 d. Educ. Bishopbriggs High School; Glasgow College of Commerce. Sales/Marketing Manager in industry, 1967-71; trainee chef, 1971-72. Master Chef of G.B.; Chef Laureate; Fellow, RSA, 1992. Recreations: travel; art; sport; music; theatre. Address: (b.) The Peat Inn, by Cupar, Fife KY15 5LH; T.-0133840 206.

Wilson, Gerald R., CB, MA. Secretary, The Scottish Office Education Department, since 1988, and Deputy Secretary, The Scottish Office; b. 7.9.39, Edinburgh; m., Margaret; 1 s.; 1 d. Educ. Holy Cross Academy; Edinburgh University. Assistant Principal, Scottish Home and Health Department, 1961-65; Private Secretary, Minister of State for Scotland, 1965-66; Principal, Scottish Home and Health Department, 1966-72; Private Secretary to Lord Privy Seal, 1972-74, to Minister of State, Civil Service Department, 1974; Assistant Secretary, Scottish Economic Planning Department, 1974-77; Counsellor, Office of the UK Permanent Representative to the Economic Communities, Brussels, 1977-82; Assistant Secretary, Scottish Office, 1982-84; Under Secretary, Industry Department for Scotland, 1984-88. Recreation: music. Address: (b.) New St. Andrew's House, Edinburgh EH1 3TG; T.-0131-244 4409.

Wilson, Professor Gordon McAndrew, MA, PhD, FRSA. Assistant Principal, Dean of Education and Director of Craigie Campus in Ayr, Paisley University, since 1993; b. 4.12.39, Glasgow; m., Alison Rosemary Cook; 2 s.; 1 d. Educ. Eastwood Secondary School; Glasgow University; Jordanhill College of Education. Teacher of History and Modern Studies: Eastwood Secondary School, 1963-65, Eastwood High School, 1965-67; Lecturer in Social Studies, Hamilton College of Education, 1967-73 (Head of Department, 1973-81); Principal Lecturer in Inservice Education, then Assistant Principal, Jordanhill College of Education, 1981-88; Principal, Craigie College of Education, 1988-93; Member, General Teaching Council for Scotland, 1991-94; Chairman, Review and Development Group on English Language 5-14; Member, Committee on Curriculum and Examinations S5-S6 (Howie Committee), 1990-92; Chairman, Teacher Education Committee, Committee of Scottish Higher Education Principals, 1992-94; Specialist Adviser on Student Affairs, COSHEP, since 1993; Member: Board of Directors, Ayrshire Chamber of Commerce and Industry, since 1992, Board of Directors, Enterprise Ayrshire, since 1994. Publications: Teaching Local History in Lanarkshire, 1972; Alexander McDonald, Leader of the Miners, 1982; Dictionary of Scottish Business Biography (Contributor), 1986. Recreations: reading; gardening; walking; music. Address: (b.) Paisley University, Craigie Campus in Ayr, Beech Grove, Ayr KA8 0SR; T.-01292 260321/4.

Wilson, Hamish Robert McHattie, MA (Aberdeen), MA, PhD (Cantab), AHSM. Director of Service Planning and Contracts, Grampian Health Board, since 1991 (Unit General Manager, 1987-90); b. 19.1.46, Aberdeen. Educ. Robert Gordon's College, Aberdeen; Aberdeen University; Emmanuel College, Cambridge. Entered Health Service administration, 1972; held posts with Grampian Health Board in planning, primary care and as Secretary. Member, Scottish Society of the History of Medicine; Member, Scottish and National Divisional Councils, Institute of Health Services Management. Recreations: music; reading; theatre; cinema; good food and wine. Address: (b.) Summerfield House, 2 Eday Road, Aberdeen AB9 1RE; T.-01224 663456.

Wilson of Langside, Baron (Henry Stephen Wilson), PC, QC, LLB. Advocate, since 1946; b. 21.3.16, Glasgow; m., Jessie Forrester Waters. Educ. High School of Glasgow; Glasgow University. Army, 1939-46 (Regimental Officer, HLI and RAC); called to Scottish Bar, 1946; Labour candidate, Dumfries, 1950, 1955, West Edinburgh, 1951; Sheriff, Greenock, 1955-56, Glasgow, 1956-65; Solicitor-General for Scotland, 1965-67; Lord Advocate, 1967-70; Sheriff, Glasgow, 1971-75, Sheriff Principal, Glasgow and Strathkelvin, 1975-77.

Wilson, Ian Dunn. Farmer; Vice-President, Scottish Agricultural Organisation Society; Panel Member, Scottish Agricultural Arbiters Association; Director, Scottish Pride Holdings plc, since 1994; b. 25.4.46, Edinburgh; m., Agnes Jane; 1 s.; 1 d. Educ. Trinity College, Glenalmond; Royal Agricultural College, Cirencester. Director, Scottish Milk Marketing Board, 1988-94; Chairman, Scottish Dairy Council, 1990-91. Recreations: golf; shooting. Address: Drum, Beeswing, Dumfries DG2 8PB; T.-01387 76240.

Wilson, Ian Matthew, CB, MA. Secretary of Commissions for Scotland, 1987-92 (Under Secretary, Scottish Education Department, 1977-86); Member, RSAMD Governing Body, since 1992; President, University of Edinburgh Graduates' Association, since 1995; b. 12.12.26, Edinburgh; m., Anne Chalmers (deceased); 3 s. Educ. George Watson's College; Edinburgh University. Assistant Principal, Scottish Home Department, 1950; Private Secretary to Permanent Under Secretary of State, Scottish Office, 1953-55; Principal, Scottish Home Department, 1955; Assistant Secretary: Scottish Education Department, 1963, Scottish Home and Health Department, 1971; Assistant Under Secretary of State, Scottish Office, 1974-77. Address: (h.) 1 Bonaly Drive, Edinburgh EH13 OEJ; T.-0131-441 2541.

Wilson, Brigadier James, CBE. Executive Director, Edinburgh Old Town Trust, 1987-90; Chief Executive, Livingston Development Corporation, 1977-87; b. 12.3.22, Irvine; m., Audrie Veronica Haines; 3 d. Educ. Irvine Royal Academy; Edinburgh Academy. Served Royal Artillery, 1941-77. Chairman, Soldiers, Sailors and Airmen's Families Association, West Lothian, 1983-93; President, Royal Artillery Association Scotland, 1987-94; Vice Chairman, Royal Artillery Council for Scotland, 1988-94. Recreations: golf; bridge. Address: (h.) 2 The Gardens, Aberlady, East Lothian.

Wilson, James Wiseman, OBE, SBStJ. Director, Wilforge Foundation, since 1970; Director, Wilson Management Ltd., since 1970; b. 31.5.33, Glasgow; m., Valerie Grant; 1 s.; 3 d. Educ. Trinity College, Glenalmond; Harvard Business School. Marketing Director, Scottish Animal Products, 1959-63; Sales Director, then Managing Director, then Chairman, Robert Wilson & Sons (1849) Ltd., 1964-85. National Trust for Scotland: Member of Council, 1977-82 and 1984-89, President, Ayrshire Members' Centre; Chairman, Management Committee, Scottish Civic Trust; Honorary President, Skelmorlie Golf Club and Irvine Pipe Band; won Aims of Industry Free Enterprise Award (Scotland), 1980. Recreations: golf; backgammon; skiing;

bridge; travelling. Address: (h.) Skelmorlie Castle, Skelmorlie, Ayrshire PA17 5EY; T.-01475 521127.

Wilson, Janette Sylvia, LLB, NP. Solicitor of the Church of Scotland and Law Agent to the General Assembly, since 1995; b. 15.1.51, Inverness; m., Stuart Ronald Wilson. Educ. Inverness Royal Academy; Edinburgh University. Law Apprentice, then Assistant, Dundas & Wilson, CS, Edinburgh, 1973-77; Assistant, then Partner, Ross Harper & Murphy, Edinburgh, 1977-81; Depute Solicitor, Church of Scotland, 1981-95. Member, Law Society Public Service and Commerce Group. Recreations: keeping fit; reading; gardening. Address: (b.) 121 George Street, Edinburgh; T.-0131-225 5722.

Wilson, Peter Liddell, BSc, MA, FIMgt, FIPD. Secretary, Heriot-Watt University, since 1991; b. 8.12.42, Douglas; m., Joy Janet Gibson; 2 d. Educ. Lanark Grammar School; Glasgow University; Birkbeck College, London University. Mathematics Teacher, Lanark Grammar School, 1964-67; Royal Navy (Instructor Lieutenant), 1967-70; Army (Royal Army Educational Corps), 1970-90: Commander Education, 1st Armoured Division (Lt. Col.), 1983-85, SOI Education HQ BAOR (Lt. Col.), 1986-88, MOD (Resettlement) (Colonel), 1988-90. Chairman, Edinburgh Confrence Centre, since 1991; Member, Board of Management, Petroleum Science and Technology Institute, since 1992. Recreations: golf; jogging; hill-walking; theatre. Address: (b.) Heriot-Watt University, Riccarton, Edinburgh EH14 4AS; T.-0131-449 5111.

Wilson, Professor Peter Northcote, CBE, BSc, MSc, Dip. Animal Genetics, PhD, CBiol, FBiol, FRSE, FRSA. Emeritus Professor of Agriculture and Rural Economy, Edinburgh University; Scientific Director, Edinburgh Centre for Rural Research, since 1990; b. 4.4.28, Beckenham, Kent; m., Maud Ethel Bunn; 2 s.; 1 d. Educ. Whitgift School, Croydon; Wye College, London University; Edinburgh University. Lecturer in Agriculture, Makerere College, East Africa; Senior Lecturer in Agriculture, Imperial College of Tropical Agriculture, Trinidad; Professor of Tropical Agriculture, University of West Indies, Trinidad; Head of Biometrics, Unilever Research Laboratory, Bedford; Agricultural Development Director, SLF Ltd., Liverpool; Chief Agricultural Adviser, BOCM Silcock Ltd., Basingstoke. Past President, British Society of Animal Production; Past Vice President, Institute of Biology; Chairman, Frank Parkinson Agricultural Trust, since 1978; Hon. Secretary, Institute of Biology, since 1992; Past President, Edinburgh Agricultural Society; Member, Council, SAC, since 1995. Publications: Agriculture in the Tropics (Co-author); Improved Feeding of Cattle and Sheep (Co-author). Recreations: walking; photography; natural history. Address: (b.) Crew Building, Kings Buildings, West Mains Road, Edinburgh EH9 3JG.

Wilson, Robert Gordon, BL, LLD. Vice-President, Scottish National Party, since 1992; Solicitor; b. 16.4.38, Glasgow; m., Edith M. Hassall; 2 d. Educ. Douglas High School for Boys; Edinburgh University. National Secretary, SNP, 1963-71; MP, Dundee East, 1974-87; Chairman and National Convener, SNP, 1979-90; Rector, Dundee University, 1983-86; Member, Court, University of Abertay, Dundee. Recreation: reading; sailing; walking. Address: (h.) 48 Monifieth Road, Dundee DD5 2RX.

Wilson, Roy. General Manager, Pitlochry Festival Theatre, 1961-95; b. St. Andrews. Educ. Burgh School and Madras College, St. Andrews. Proprietor, grocer's business, St. Andrews, 1953-59; Assistant Manager, Pitlochry Festival Theatre, 1959-61. Recreations: plays and theatre in general; most forms of classical music, with particular interest in choral singing; listening to records; reading. Address: (h.) Kilrymont, Bruach Lane, Pitlochry, Perthshire PH16 5DG; T.-Pitlochry 472897.

Wilson, R. Ross, BSc, PhD, MInstP, CPhys. Managing Director, James Howden & Co. Ltd., since 1992; b. 13.3.47, Glasgow; m., Margaret; 2 s. Educ. Hamilton Academy; Glasgow University. Research Officer, then Vibration Group Leader, Central Electricity Research Laboratories, CEGB; Section Head, Design Analysis, Corporate Engineering Laboratory, British Steel; Design Manager, then Technical Director, James Howden Ltd. Recreations: golf; reading; gardening. Address: (b.) Old Govan Road, Renfrew PA4 8XJ; T.-0141-886 6711.

Wilson, Thomas Black, BSc (Hons), MBCS. Principal, Glasgow College of Building and Printing, since 1989; b. 23.12.43, Airdrie; m., Barbara Smith; 1 s.; 1 d. Educ. Cumnock Academy; Glasgow University; Jordanhill College. Principal Teacher, Prestwick Academy, 1969-74; Head, Computing Department, Ayr College, 1974-84; Depute Principal: Barmulloch College, Glasgow, 1984-86, Cardonald College, Glasgow, 1986-89. Member, Scottish Central Committee (Mathematics), 1975-82. Recreations: reading; writing; music. Address: (b.) 60 North Hanover Street, Glasgow G1 2BP; T.-0141-332 9969.

Wilson, Emeritus Professor Thomas Brendan, CBE, MA, BMus, ARCM, FRSE. Composer; b. 10.10.27, Trinidad, Colorado; m., Margaret Rayner; 3 s. Educ. St. Mary's College, Aberdeen; Glasgow University; Royal College of Music. RAF, 1945-48; Glasgow University: Lecturer in Music, Extra-Mural Studies, 1957, Reader in Music, Extra-Mural Studies, 1972, Professor, 1977; Member, Scottish Arts Council, 1966-72; Past Chairman, Composers Guild; President, Scottish Society of Composers; Member, Advisory Commitee, Scottish Music Information Centre; elected Member, Royal Society of Musicians; compositions include orchestral, choral-orchestral, chamber-orchestral, opera (including The Confessions of a Justified Sinner), ballet, brass band, vocal music of different kinds, and works for a wide variety of chamber ensembles and solo instruments; numerous commissions; Hon. Doctorate of Music, Glasgow University, 1991; Fellow, Royal Scottish Academy of Music and Drama, since 1991. Recreations: golf; talking shop. Address: (h.) 120 Downhill Street, Glasgow G12 9DN; T.-0141-339 1699.

Wilson, Professor Thomas Michael Aubrey, BSc (Hons), PhD, CBiol, MIBiol. Deputy Director, Scottish Crop Research Institute, since 1995; b. 10.10.51, Hawick; m., Judith Lindsey Dring; 2 s.; 1 d. Educ. Hawick High School; Edinburgh University; Cambridge University. Lecturer in Biochemistry, Liverpool University; Senior Scientific Officer, then Principal Scientific Officer, John Innes Institute, Norwich; Professor, AgBiotech Center, Rutgers University, NJ; Head, Virology Department, SCRI, Dundee, 1992-95; Senior Editor, Journal of General Virology; published 85 papers, reviews, and book chapters; edited or co-authored two books; first recipient, SGM Herpes Vaccine Research Trust Prize, 1985. Recreations: hill-walking; adventure films/books. Address: (b.) Invergowrie, Dundee, DD2 5DA; T.-01382 562731.

Wilson, William John McKinley, QPM. Chief Constable, Central Scotland Police, since 1990; b. 27.6.43, Kinghorn; m., Catherine; 3 s. Educ. Kirkcaldy High School. Joined Fife Constabulary, 1962: Chief Superintendent, 1981, Deputy Chief Constable, 1984. Recreations: football; golf. Address: (b.) Central Scotland Police, Randolphfield, Stirling; T.-01786 456300.

Wilson, William Murray, MB, ChB, MRCGP. General Medical Practitioner, Dalry, Ayrshire, 1949-89; Medical Advisor, Roche Products, Dalry, Ayrshire, since 1965; Medical Referee, Cunninghame District Council, since 1972; Member, Ayrshire and Arran Health Board; b. 19.1.25, Glasgow; m., Elizabeth Carbine; 3 s. Educ. Eastwood Secondary School; Glasgow University. Past Chairman, Local Medical Committee/GP Committee, Area Medical Committee, BMA Ayrshire Division; former Member, General Medical Services Committee, London and Edinburgh; Elder, St. Margaret's Church, Dalry; former Member, Education for the Ministry Committee, Church of Scotland; Honorary Lecturer, British Red Cross Society, St. Andrew's Ambulance Association. Recreations: travel; photography. Address: (h.) 22 Courthill Street, Dalry, Ayrshire KA24 5AN; T.-Dalry 832165.

Wilson, W. Stewart, BSc. Rector, Banchory Academy, since 1978; b. 15.5.37, Aberdeen; m., Elizabeth Gorrod; 1 s.; 1 d. Educ. Aberdeen Grammar School; Aberdeen University. Teacher, Aberdeen Grammar School, 1961-66; Principal Teacher of Mathematics, then Deputy Rector, Banchory Academy, 1966-78. Elder and Clerk, Congregational Board, Banchory Ternan West Parish Church; Past President: Banchory and District Round Table, Rotary Club of Banchory Ternan; Past Chairman, Kincardine and Deeside National Trust Members' Centre; former Scottish Headquarters Scout Commissioner for Adult Leader Training, now Assistant Chief Commissioner for Scotland. Recreations: philately; Robert Burns - his life and works; antique maps of Kincardineshire. Address: (h.) Ibiscus, Rosehill Crescent, Banchory; T.-01330 823194.

Windsor, Malcolm L., PhD, FRSC. Secretary, North Atlantic Salmon Conservation Organization, since 1984; b. 12.4.38, Bristol; m., Sally; 2 d. Educ. Cotham Grammar School, Bristol; Bristol University. Researcher, University of California, 1965-67; fisheries research, Humber Laboratory, Hull, 1967-75; Fisheries Adviser to Chief Scientist, Ministry of Agriculture and Fisheries, London, 1975-84. Secretary, Society for the Preservation of Duddingston Village. Publication: book on fishery products. Recreations: local conservation work; jazz; walking. Address: (b.) 11 Rutland Square, Edinburgh EH1 2AS; T.-0131-228 2551.

Windsor, Col. Rodney Francis Maurice, CBE, DL. Farmer; b. 22.2.25, Redhill; m., Deirdre Chichester (deceased); m. Angela Stainton; 2 s.; 1 d. Educ. Tonbridge School. Enlisted Royal Armoured Corps, 1943; commissioned The Queen's Bays, 1944-52; Captain, 1949; ADC to CINC and High Commissioner Austria, 1949-50; served in North Irish Horse (TA), 1959-67; Lt. Col. Commanding, 1964-67; Colonel TA N. Ireland, 1967-71; ADC (TA) to HM The Queen, 1970-75; Member, Highland TA Association, 1971-77; Member, Banff and Buchan District Valuation Appeal Committee, since 1982 (Chairman); Deputy Lieutenant, Aberdeenshire, since 1989. Recreations: field sports; golf. Address: (h.) Byth House, New Byth, Turriff, Aberdeenshire AB53 7XN; T.-01888 544230.

Winney, Robin John, MB, ChB, FRCPEdin. Consultant Renal Physician, Edinburgh Royal Infirmary, since 1978; b. 8.5.44, Dunfermline. Educ. Dunfermline High School; Edinburgh University. Recreations: badminton; curling. Address: (h.) 74 Lanark Road West, Currie, Midlothian EH14 5JZ.

Winning, His Eminence Thomas Joseph Cardinal, STL, DCL, DD, DUniv, GCHS, FEIS. Archbishop of Glasgow and Metropolitan, since 1974; President, Bishops' Conference of Scotland, since 1985; b. 3.6.25, Wishaw. Educ. Our Lady's High School, Motherwell; St. Mary's College, Blairs; St. Peter's College; Scots College; Gregorian University, Rome. Ordained Priest, Rome, 1948; Assistant Priest, Chapelhall, 1949-50; Rome (DCL, "Cum Laude"), 1953; Assistant Priest, St. Mary's Hamilton, 1953-57; Cathedral, Motherwell, 1957-58; Chaplain, Franciscans of the Immaculate Conception, Bothwell, 1958-61; Diocesan Secretary, Motherwell, 1956-61; Spiritual Director, Scots College, Rome, 1961-66; Advocate of the Sacred Roman Rota, 1965; Parish Priest, St. Luke's

Motherwell, 1966-70; Officialis and Vicar Episcopal, Motherwell Diocese, 1966-70; first President, Scottish Catholic Marriage Tribunal, 1970; nominated Titular Bishop of Louth and Bishop Auxiliary, 1971, and ordained by James Donald Scanlan, Archbishop of Glasgow, November, 1971; Parish Priest, Our Holy Redeemer's Clydebank, 1972-74; translated to Glasgow as Archbishop, 1974; created Cardinal Priest of the title of S. Andrea delle Frate, 1994; Honorary DD (Glasgow), 1983; awarded Glasgow Loving Cup, 1983; Grand Prior of Scotland, Equestrian Order of the Holy Sepulchre of Jerusalem, 1989; Hon. D.Univ. (Strathclyde), 1992. Recreations: watching football; listening to music. Address: (h.) 40 Newlands Road, Glasgow G43 2JD; T.-0141-226 5898.

Winter, Charles M., CBE, FCIBS. Director-General, The Scottish Chambers of Commerce; Director, Scottish Financial Enterprise; b. 21.7.33, Dundee; m., Audrey Hynd; 1 s.; 1 d. Educ. Harris Academy, Dundee. Joined Royal Bank of Scotland, 1949; Director, 1981; Director, Royal Bank of Scotland Group, 1981; Group Chief Executive, 1985-93; President, Institute of Bankers in Scotland, 1981-83; Director, Lloyds & Scottish PLC, 1983-84; Chairman, Committee of Scottish Clearing Bankers, 1983-85 and 1989-91; Member, Board of Governors, Leith Nautical College, 1979-82; Treasurer, Commonwealth Games, Scotland, 1986; Chairman, Steering Committee, Inter-Alpha Group of Banks, 1986; Senior Vice-President, Edinburgh Chamber of Commerce and Manufactures. Recreations: golf; choral music. Address: (h.) 4 Charteris Park, Longniddry EH32 0NX.

Winton, Alexander, CBE, QFSM, MIFireE. HM Chief Inspector of Fire Services for Scotland, 1990-93; b. 13.7.32, Perth; m., Jean; 2 s. Perth and Kinross Fire Brigade, 1958; Instructor, Scottish Fire Service Training School, 1962; Lancashire County Fire Brigade, 1967; East Riding of Yorkshire Fire Brigade, 1970; Angus Area Fire Brigade, 1973; Tayside Fire Brigade, 1975; Deputy Firemaster, Tayside Fire Brigade, 1981; Firemaster, 1985-89. Recreations:golf; curling. Address: (h.) 5 Ferndale Drive, Broughty Ferry, Dundee DD5 3DB; T.-Dundee 78156.

Wiseman, Alan William. Director and Chairman, Robert Wiseman Dairies, since 1979; President, Scottish Dairy Trade Federation, 1988-95; b. 20.8.50, Giffnock; m., Margaret. Educ. Duncanrig Senior Secondary School, East Kilbride. Left school to be one of his father's milkmen, 1967; has been a milkman ever since. Scottish Businessman of the Year, 1992; former Chairman, Scottish Dairy Council; Member, Council, Scottish CBI, since 1990; Scottish Business Achievement Award, 1994. Recreations: golf; shooting. Address: (b.) Cadzow House, High Parks Farm, Hamilton; T.-01698 425481.

Wishart, David, BSc, PhD, CEng, CStat. Director, Microcentre Ltd.; Director, Clustan Ltd.; b. 5.7.43, London; m., Doreen Pamela Craig Wishart; 3 s. Educ. Kilburn Grammar School; Truro School; St. Andrews University. Statistician, Civil Service Department, London, 1970-75; Principal, Scottish Office, 1975-77; Chief Statistician, Scottish Office, 1977-81; Director of Statistics, Scottish Office, 1981-84; Assistant Secretary, Scottish Office, 1984-95. Fellow: British Computer Society, Royal Statistical Society (Vice President, 1986-88), Royal Society of Arts; Member, Institute of Directors; Director, Wishart Society. Recreations: cricket; skiing; opera. Address: (h.) 16 Kingsburgh Road, Edinburgh EH12; T.-0131-337 1448.

Wishart, Ruth. Columnist, The Herald; Broadcaster, BBC Radio, since 1989 (Presenter, Speaking Out); b. Glasgow; m., Rod McLeod. Educ. Eastwood Senior Secondary School. TV Editor, Daily Record, 1970-73; Woman's Editor, Daily Record, 1973-78; Assistant Editor, Sunday Mail, 1978-82; Assistant Editor, Sunday Standard, 1982-83; Freelance Writer, 1983-86; Senior Assistant Editor, The

Scotsman, 1986-88. Member, Scottish Advisory Committee, British Council; Director, Assembly Theatre; Member, Scottish Committee, ABSA; Hon. Vice-President, Scottish Action on Dementia; Member, Council, Royal Glasgow Institute. Recreations: theatre; travel; curling. Address: (h.) Wilson Court, Wilson Street, Glasgow.

Withers, Professor Charles William John, BSc, PhD, FRGS. Professor of Geography, Edinburgh University, since 1992; b. 6.12.54, Edinburgh; m., Anne; 2 s.; 1 d. Educ. Daniel Stewart's College, Edinburgh; St. Andrews University; Cambridge University. Lecturer, Senior Lecturer, Principal Lecturer, Professor of Geography, College of St. Paul and St. Mary/Cheltenham and Gloucester College of Higher Education. Hon. Editor, Historical Geography Research series; Editor, History and Philosophy of Geography; author of five books, 80 academic articles. Recreations: reading; hill-walking. Address: (b.) Department of Geography, Edinburgh University, Drummond Street, Edinburgh; T.-0131-650 2559.

Withers, John Alexander (Jack), FCIL. Librarian and Writer-in-Residence, Scottish-German Centre/Goethe Institut, since 1974; Writer; b. Glasgow; m., Beate (Bea) Haertel. Educ. North Kelvinside School; Jordanhill College of Education (Youth and Community Diploma). Left school at 14; worked in garage, electrical industry, labouring, National Service, unemployment, razor-blade salesman; long periods abroad, wandering, wondering, working: France, FRG, Italy, Scandinavia, Spain, North Africa; youth worker; freelance writer; ski instructor; librarian; Scottish republican and radical; plays for radio, TV, theatre; James Kennoway Screenplay Award (shared); Scottish Arts Council Awards; short stories published in numerous journals in UK, Denmark and West Germany; Editor, Two Tongues — Two Cities; books: Glasgow Limbo, A Real Glasgow Archipelago. Address: (h.) 16 Belmont Crescent, Glasgow; T.-0141-339 9492.

Witney, Eur. Ing. Professor Brian David, BSc, MSc, PhD, CEng, FIMechE, FIAgrE, MemASAE. Director, Scottish Centre of Agricultural Engineering, since 1987, and Vice-Dean, Scottish Agricultural College, since 1990; b. 8.6.38, Edinburgh; m., Maureen M.I. Donnelly; 1 s.; 2 d. Educ. Daniel Stewart's College, Edinburgh; Edinburgh University; Durham University; Newcastle University. Senior Research Associate, Newcastle upon Tyne University, 1962-66; Research Fellow, US Army Research Office, Duke Univ., 1966-67; Senior Scientific Officer, Military Engineering Experimental Establishment, Christchurch, 1967-70; Head, Agricultural Engineering Department, East of Scotland College of Agriculture, Edinburgh, 1970-86. President, Institution of Agricultural Engineers, 1988-90; President, European Society of Agricultural Engineers, 1993-94. Publication: Choosing and Using Farm Machines. Address: (b.) Scottish Centre of Agricultural Engineering, SAC, Bush Estate, Penicuik, Midlothian EH26 0PH; T.-0131-535 3002.

Wolfe, William Cuthbertson, CA, JP. Member, National Council, Scottish National Party, since 1991; b. 22.2.24; 2 s.; 2 d. Educ. Bathgate Academy; George Watson's College, Edinburgh. Army Service, 1942-47, NW Europe and Far East; Air OP Pilot. Hon. Publications Treasurer, Saltire Society, 1953-60; Scout County Commissioner, West Lothian, 1960-64; Hon. President (Rector), Students' Association, Heriot-Watt University, 1966-69; contested (SNP) West Lothian, 1962, 1964, 1966, 1970, Feb. and Oct. 1974, 1979, North Edinburgh, Nov. 1973; Chairman, SNP, 1969-79, President, 1980-82; Treasurer, Scottish CND, 1982-85; Secretary, Scottish Poetry Library, 1985-91. Publication: Scotland Lives.

Wolfe Murray, Angus Malcolm. Film Critic, The Scotsman, since 1988; b. 20.5.37, Edinburgh; m.,

Stephanie; 4 s. Educ. Eton. Greensman, bank clerk, oil worker, insurance broker, journalist, novelist, publisher's editor, roadie for rock band, publisher, construction worker, long-distance lorry driver, fine art transporter, film critic. Recreations: skiing; cricket. Address: (h.) Stobo Hopehead, Peebles, EH45 8NY.

Wolfram, Professor Julian, BSc, CEng, PhD, FRINA, MSaRS. Total Oil Marine Chair of Offshore Research and Development, Heriot-Watt University, since 1990; b. 2.8.46, London; m., Margaret Mary Lockhart; 1 s., 1 d., by pr. m. Educ. Gordonstoun; Reading University; Newcastle University. Research and Development Officer, Vickers Shipbuilders Ltd.; Lecturer (latterly Senior Lecturer) in Naval Architecture, Sunderland Polytechnic; Lecturer (latterly Senior Lecturer) in Marine Technology, Strathclyde University; Tutor, Open University; Chief Examiner, Ship Structures and Dynamics, Engineering Council; Consultant to several companies in the marine field. Publications: over 30 technical papers. Recreations: sailing; squash; hill walking. Address: (b.) Heriot-Watt University, Edinburgh EH14 4AS; T.-0131-449 5111.

Wong, Professor Henry H.Y., BSc, PhD, DIC, CEng, FRAeS. Emeritus Professor, Department of Aeronautics and Fluid Mechanics, Glasgow University; Senior Research Fellow, since 1987; Adviser to the Guangdong Higher Education Bureau, China, since 1985; Adviser to Glasgow University on Chinese Affairs, since 1986; Chair Professor, Nanjing University of Aeronautics and Astronautics, since 1987; "Concurrent" Professor, National University of Defense Technology, Changsha, since 1989; b. 23.5.22, Hong Kong; m., Joan Anstey; 2 s.; 1 d. Educ. St. Stephen College, Hong Kong; Jiao-Tong University, Shanghai; Imperial College, London; Glasgow University. Assistant Lecturer, Jiao-Tong University, 1947-48; Engineer, Armstrong Siddeley, 1949; Structural Engineer, Hunting Percival Aircraft, 1949-51; Senior Structural Engineer, de Havilland Aircraft, 1952-57; Senior Lecturer, Hatfield Polytechnic, 1957-59; Lecturer, Senior Lecturer, then Reader in Aeronautics and Fluid Mechanics, Glasgow University, from 1960; Economic and Technological Consultant to Shantou Special Economic Zone, China, since 1988. Former Treasurer and Vice-Chairman, Kilmardinny Music Circle; Chairman, Glasgow Summer School, since 1979; City of Glasgow Lord Provost's Award, 1988. Recreations: reading; music; painting; swimming. Address: (h.) 77 Antonine Road, Bearsden, Glasgow; T.-0141-942 8346.

Wood, Arthur Murdoch Mactaggart, OBE, MA, LLB. Chief Executive, Children 1st, since 1968; b. 15.12.37, Kilbarchan; 2 s.; 2 d. Educ. George Watson's College, Edinburgh; Edinburgh University. Standard Life Assurance Company, 1960-61; Assistant Secretary, RSSPCC, 1961-68. Address: (b.) Children 1st, Melville House, 41 Polwarth Terrace, Edinburgh EH11 1NU; T.-0131-337 8539.

Wood, Brian Charles Thallon, BL (Dist.), NP. Solicitor, since 1955; Consultant, Charles Wood & Son, Solicitors, Kirkcaldy, since 1956; Honorary Sheriff; b. 8.8.34, Kirkcaldy; m., Tessa; 1 s.; 1 d. Educ. Fettes; Edinburgh University. Part-time Chairman, Industrial Tribunals, 1972-77; part-time Chairman, Rent Assessment Committee, 1987; Member, Council, Law Society of Scotland, since 1992-94; Accredited ADR Mediator. Recreations: gardens; skiing; curling; mending anything. Address: (h.) 4 Kilenuik Road, Kinghorn, Fife; T.-01592 891218.

Wood, Brian James, JP, BSc (Hons), FRSA. Rector, Hazlehead Academy, Aberdeen, since 1993 (Rector, Mearns Academy, 1989-93); b. 6.12.49, Banff; m., Doreen A. Petrie; 1 s.; 1 d. Educ. Banff Academy; Aberdeen Academy; Aberdeen University; Aberdeen College of Education. Teacher of Physics, George Heriot's School, Edinburgh, 1972-75; Mackie Academy, 1975-89, latterly as

Depute Rector. Chairman, Justices of the Peace for Kincardine and Deeside; Member, Chairmen of Justices Committee for Scotland; Elder, Church of Scotland. Recreations: sport; reading; music; travel; theatre; DIY. Address: (h.) 13 Edinview Gardens, Stonehaven; T.-01569 763888.

Wood, Emeritus Professor Hamish Christopher Swan, CBE, BSc, PhD, CChem, FRSC, FRSE, DUniv, LLD, FScotvec; b. 8.5.26, Hawick; m., Jean Dumbreck Mitchell; 1 s.; 1 d. Educ. Hawick High School; St. Andrews University. Lecturer in Chemistry, St. Andrews University, 1950-51; Research Fellow, Australian National University, 1951-53; Lecturer, Senior Lecturer and Reader, Strathclyde University, 1953-69, Professor of Organic Chemistry, 1969-91, Vice-Principal, 1984-86; Member, Universities Funding Council, 1989-92; Chairman, Court, Glasgow Caledonian University, 1993-94; Member, Council, Royal Society of Edinburgh, 1992-95. Address: (b.) Thomas Graham Building, Strathclyde University, 295 Cathedral Street, Glasgow G1 1XL; T.-0141-552 4400.

Wood, Sir Ian Clark, CBE (1982), LLD, BSc, CBIM. Chairman and Managing Director, John Wood Group PLC, since 1967; Chairman, J.W. Holdings, since 1982; b. 21.7.42, Aberdeen; m., Helen Macrae; 3 s. Educ. Robert Gordon's College, Aberdeen; Aberdeen University. Joined family business, John Wood & Sons, 1964; Member, Scottish Economic Council; Member, Scottish Enterprise Board; Member, Oil and Gas Projects and Supplies Office Board; Fellow, Royal Society of Arts; Member, Scottish Higher Education Funding Council; Board Director, Royal Bank of Scotland; Grampian Industrialist of the Year, 1978; Young Scottish Businessman of the Year, 1979; Scottish Free Enterprise Award, 1985; Scottish Business Achievement Award Trust — joint winner, 1992, corporate elite leadership award services category; Hon. LLD, 1984. Recreations: squash; family; art. Address: (b.) John Wood Group PLC, John Wood House, Greenwell Road, East Tullos, Aberdeen; T.-01224 851000.

Wood, Professor Robert Anderson, BSc, MB, ChB, FRCPEdin, FRCSEdin. Professor of Postgraduate Medicine, Aberdeen University, since 1992; Dean, Royal College of Physicians of Edinburgh, since 1992; b. 26.5.39, Edinburgh. Educ. Edinburgh Academy; Edinburgh University. Address: (h.) Ballomill House, Abernethy, Perthshire; T.-Abernethy 0201.

Wood, Stephen Charles, BA (Hons), MA, FSA Scot, FRSA, Chevalier de l'Ordre des Palmes Académiques, France. Keeper, Scottish United Services Museum, Edinburgh Castle, since 1983; b. 29.1.52, Wells, Somerset; 1 s. Educ. The Blue School, Wells; Bishop Wordsworth's School, Salisbury; Birkbeck College, London University. Curator, Department of Uniform, National Army Museum, London, 1971-83. Publications: The Scottish Soldier, 1987; In the Finest Tradition, 1988; The Auld Alliance, 1989; The Legendary 51st, 1990. Recreations: travel; gastronomy; historical research. Address: (b.) Edinburgh Castle, Edinburgh.

Woodruff, Professor Sir Michael (Francis Addison), Kt (1969), DSc, MD, MS, FRCS, FRCSE, FRACS, Hon. FACS, FRSE, FRS. Professor Emeritus, Surgery, Edinburgh University; b. 3.4.11, London; m., Hazel Gwenyth Ashby; 2 s.; 1 d. Educ. Wesley College, Melbourne; Queens College, Melbourne University. House Physician and House Surgeon, Royal Melbourne Hospital; Captain, Australian Army Medical Corps (PoW, Singapore); Tutor in Surgery, Sheffield University, 1946; Lecturer in Surgery, Aberdeen University, 1948; Professor of Surgery, Otago University, 1953, Edinburgh University, 1957-76; research worker, MRC Clinical and Population Cytogenetics Unit, Edinburgh, 1976-86. President, The Transplantation Society, 1972-74. Publications: Deficiency

Diseases in Japanese Prison Camps; Surgery for Dental Students; The Transplantation of Tissues and Organs; On Science and Surgery; The Interaction of Cancer and Host; Cellular Variation and Adaptation in Cancer, 1990. Recreations: sailing; music; tennis. Address: (h.) The Bield, 506 Lanark Road, Juniper Green, Edinburgh EH14 5DH; T.-0131-453 3653.

Woods, David. Managing Director, Scottish Provident. Address: (b.) 6 St. Andrew Square, Edinburgh, EH2 2YA.

Woodward, Michael Trevor, PhD, MA (Hons), MBA. Director, Ivory and Sime Investment Management plc; Investment Director, Ivory and Sime plc, 1990-94; b. 25.11.57, Birmingham; m., Anne McWalter Russell; 2 d. Educ. Dartmouth Comprehensive School; Aberdeen University; Edinburgh University. Ivory and Sime plc, since 1983. Recreations: family; golf; squash; racketball. Address: (b.) 1 Charlotte Square, Edinburgh EH2 4DZ; T.-0131-225 1357.

Worrall, Ernest Paterson, MB, ChB, FRCPsych, DPM. Consultant Psychiatrist, Southern General Hospital, Glasgow, since 1980; Medical Director, Langside Priory Hospital; b. 28.10.42, Hamilton; m., Jean Price; 1 s.; 1 d. Educ. Hamilton Academy; Glasgow University. Lecturer in Psychiatry, Dundee University, 1973-75; Senior Lecturer in Psychological Medicine, Glasgow University, 1975-80. Recreations: cycling; bowling. Address: (b.) Department of Psychiatry, Southern General Hospital, Glasgow G51 1TF; T.-0141-201 1900.

Worthington, Tony, BA, MEd. MP (Labour), Clydebank and Milngavie, since 1987; Front-bench Spokesman: Overseas Development, 1992-93, Foreign Office, 1993-94, Northern Ireland, since 1995; b. 11.10.41, Hertfordshire; m., Angela; 1 s.; 1 d. Educ. City School, Lincoln; London School of Economics; York University; Glasgow University. Recreations: running; fishing; gardening. Address: (h.) 24 Cleddans Crescent, Hardgate, Clydebank; T.-01389 73195.

Wotherspoon (John Munro) Iain, TD, DL. Senior Partner, MacAndrew & Jenkins, WS, since 1954; Deputy Lieutenant, Districts of Lochaber, Inverness, Badenoch and Strathspey, since 1982, and Clerk, since 1985; b. 19.7.24, Inverness; m., Victoria Avril Jean Edwards; 2 s.; 2 d. Educ. Inverness Royal Academy; Loretto School; Trinity College, Oxford; Edinburgh University. Lt., Royal Signals, Europe and Burma, 1944-46; TA, 1948-78; Lt.-Col. commanding 51 (Highland) Division Signals, 1963-70; Col. Dep. Cdr. 13 Signals Gp., 1970-72; Hon. Col. 32 (Scottish) Signal Regiment, 1972-78; ADC to The Queen, 1971-76; WS, 1950; Solicitor and Land Owner. Recreations: shooting; fishing; stalking. Address: (h.) Maryfield, 62 Midmills Road, Inverness IV2 3QL; T.-01463 233642.

Wray, Professor David, MD (Hons), BDS, MB, ChB, FDSRCPS, FDSRCS (Edin). Professor of Oral Medicine, Glasgow University, since 1993; Hon. Consultant, Greater Glasgow Health Board, since 1993; b. 3.1.51, Carshalton; m., Alison M.P. Wray; 2 s. Educ. Uddingston Grammar School; Glasgow University. Fogarty Fellow, N.I.H. Bethesda, USA, 1979-81; Wellcome Research Fellow, Royal Dental, London, 1982; Senior Lecturer, Edinburgh University, 1983-92. Chairman, Joint Advisory Committee for the Additional Dental Specialties. Recreations: golf; curling; skiing. Address: (h.) Flat 20, 18 Cleveland Street, Glasgow G3 7AE; T.-0141-248 8915.

Wray, James. MP (Labour), Glasgow Provan, since 1987; b. 28.4.38. Address: (b.) House of Commons, London, SW1A 0AA.

Wright, Andrew Paul Kilding, BArch, RIBA, PRIAS. Partner, Law & Dunbar-Nasmith, since 1981; President,

Royal Incorporation of Architects in Scotland, since 1995; Diocesan Architect, Diocese of Moray, Ross and Caithness, since 1989; b. 11.2.47, Walsall; m., Jean Patricia; 1 s.; 2 d. Educ. Queen Mary's Grammar School, Walsall; Liverpool University School of Architecture. Practising architect, since 1972; President, Inverness Architectural Association, 1986-88; Council, RIAS, 1985-94 and since 1995; External Examiner, Robert Gordon University, since 1990; Council, Royal Institute of British Architects, 1988-94 and since 1995. Recreations: music; railway history; fishing. Address: (b.) St. Leonards Road, Forres, IV36 0DN; T.-01309 673221.

Wright, David Frederick, MA (Cantab). Senior Lecturer in Ecclesiastical History, Edinburgh University, since 1973; b. 2.10.37, Hayes, Kent; m., Anne-Marie; 1 s.; 1 d. Educ. Christ's College, Cambridge; Lincoln College, Oxford. Edinburgh University: Lecturer, 1964-73, Associate Dean, Faculty of Divinity, 1972-76, Dean, 1988-92, Member, University Court, 1984-87; External Examiner, Universities of Sussex, Liverpool, Durham, Cambridge, etc.; Member, Council of Management, Keston College; Chairman, Tyndale Fellowship for Biblical and Theological Research; Associate Editor, Tyndale Bulletin; Editor, Scottish Bulletin of Evangelical Theology; Member of Praesidium, International Congress on Calvin Research. Publications: Common Places of Martin Bucer, 1972; Essays in Evangelical Social Ethics (Editor), 1979; Lion Handbook History of Christianity (Consultant Editor), 1977; New Dictionary of Theology (Joint Editor), 1988; The Bible in Scottish Life and Literature (Contributor and Editor), 1988; Chosen by God: Mary in Evangelical Perspective (Contributor and Editor), 1989; Dictionary of Scottish Church History and Theology (Chief General Editor), 1993; Calvin's Old Testament Commentaries (General Editor), 1993; Martin Bucer: Reforming Church and Community (Contributor and Editor), 1994. Recreations: walking; gardening; DIY. Address: (h.) 3 East Camus Road, Edinburgh EH10 6RE; T.-0131-445 1960.

Wright, David John, MB, BS, FRCA. Consultant Anaesthetist, Western General Hospital, Edinburgh, since 1979; b. 13.4.44, Oswestry; m., Bronwen; 2 s.; 1 d. Educ. Bristol Grammar School; St. Bartholomew's Hospital Medical College, London. Honorary Editor, Scottish Society of the History of Medicine. Address: (h.) 20 Lennox Row, Edinburgh EH5 3JW; T.-0131-552 3439.

Wright, Douglas Stewart. MBE, Director, Keep Scotland Beautiful, since 1973; Chairman, Beautiful Scotland in Bloom, since 1983; b. 22.7.32, Glasgow; m., May Carswell; 1 s.; 2 d. Educ. Albert Road Academy, Pollokshields. Representative, Scottish Field, 1947-58; National Service, 1st Bn., Cameronians Scottish Rifles (Malaya), 1950-52; General Manager, The Scottish Farmer, 1959-66; Appeals Director, Scottish Council for the Care of Spastics, 1966-73. Committee Member, Stars Organisation for Spastics (Scotland); Past President, Glasgow Haggis Club (No. 33); Member, Gideons International. Recreations: dog walking; specialist in China Tea Clippers; collecting ships in bottles. Address: (b.) Cathedral Square, Dunblane, Perthshire FK15 OAQ; T.-01786 823202.

Wright, Professor George, BSc, MPhil, PhD. Deputy Director and Professor of Business Administration, Strathclyde Graduate Business School, since 1991; b. 24.11.52, Louth; m., Josephine Elizabeth; 2 s. Educ. Queen Elizabeth II Grammar School; NE London Polytechnic; Brunel University. Research Assistant, Brunel University, 1974-79; Research Fellow, Huddersfield Polytechnic, 1979-81; Senior Lecturer, City of London Polytechnic, 1981-86; Reader, then Professor, Bristol Business School, 1986-91. Publications: seven books; 60 journal articles. Recreation: visiting public houses. Address: (b.) Strathclyde Graduate Business School, 130 Rottenrow, Glasgow G4 0GE; T.-0141-553 6000.

Wright, George Gordon. Publisher; b. 25.6.42, Edinburgh. Educ. Darroch Secondary School; Heriot Watt College. Started publishing as a hobby, 1969; left printing trade, 1973, to develop own publishing company; founder Member, Scottish General Publishers Association; Past Chairman, Scottish Young Publishers Society; Oliver Brown Award, 1994; Secretary/Treasurer, 200 Burns Club, since 1991. Publications: MacDiarmid: An Illustrated Biography, 1977; A Guide to the Royal Mile, 1979; Orkney From Old Photographs, 1981; A Guide to Holyrood Park and Arthur's Seat, 1987. Recreations: history of Edinburgh; photography; jazz. Address: (h.) 25 Mayfield Road, Edinburgh EH9 2NQ; T.-0131-667 1300.

Wright, Grahame Alan, BA (Econ), MPhil (Cantab). Assistant Principal External Relations, University of Abertay Dundee, since 1993; b. 5.8.47, Sunderland; m., Joan Margaret; 2 s.; 1 d. Educ. Mortimer County Secondary, South Shields; Open University; Newcastle Polytechnic; Clare College, Cambridge. Musical instrument retailer, 1963-77; Research Assistant, Lecturer, Senior Lecturer, Principal Lecturer, Newcastle Polytechnic, 1980-91; Head, Department of Accountancy, Economics and Law, Dundee Institute of Technology, 1991-93. Recreation: music. Address: (h.) 12 Woodlands Park, Blairgowrie, PH10 6UW; T.-01250 875243.

Wright, Professor Howard David, BEng, PhD, CEng, FIStructE, FICE. Professor of Structures (in association with Thorburn Colquhoun), Strathclyde University, since 1991; b. 5.10.52, Holmes Chapel; m., Elizabeth Mary Warren Baynham; 2 s.; 1 d. Educ. Sandbach School; Sheffield University. Assistant Engineer, CEGB, 1974-78; Structural Engineer, Boots the Chemists, 1978-82; Lecturer in Structural Design, University of Wales, Cardiff, 1982-91. Council Member, Institution of Structural Engineers, 1988-91; Committee Member, Building Standards Advisory Board, since 1991. Publications: papers on composite construction and engineering education. Recreations: hill-walking; music; mechanics. Address: (b.) Department of Civil Engineering, 107 Rottenrow, Glasgow G4 0NG; T.-0141-552 4400, Ext. 3251.

Wright, Ian William Weir, BSc, DRCST, CEng, MIChemE, CChem, MRIC. Chief Inspector, HM Industrial Pollution Inspectorate, since 1985; b. 22.4.35, Glasgow; m., Mary Stirling; 1 s.; 1 d. Educ. Allan Glen's School, Glasgow; Strathclyde University.Production Chemist, UKAEA, Windscale Works, 1959-63; Chemical Engineer, Scottish Pulp & Paper Mills, 1963-71 (Deputy Technical Manager); HM Industrial Pollution Inspectorate, since 1971. Recreations: DIY; gardening; reading; motoring. Address: (b.) 27 Perth Street, Edinburgh EH3 5RB; T.-0131-244 3056.

Wright, Rev. Kenyon Edward, MA, BA, BSc, MTh. Director, Kairos (Centre for a Sustainable Society), since 1990; Consultant on Justice and Peace to ACTS (Action of Churches Together in Scotland); Chair, Executive, Scottish Constitutional Convention; Vice-Chair, Scottish Environmental Forum; Co-ordinating Secretary, The Christian Peace Conference (International); Patron, Scottish Refugee Council; Canon Emeritus and Companion of the Order of the Cross of Nails, Coventry Cathedral; b. 31.8.32, Paisley; m., Betty Robinson; 3 d. Educ. Paisley Grammar School; Glasgow University; Cambridge University. Missionary in India, 1955-70; Director, Ecumenical Social and Industrial Institute, Durgapur, India, 1963-70; Director, Urban Ministry, Coventry Cathedral, 1970-74; Canon Residentiary and Director of International Ministry, Coventry Cathedral, 1974-81; General Secretary, Scottish Churches Council and Director, Scottish Churches House, 1981-90. Recreations: reading; walking; travel; living life to the full. Address: (b.) Kairos Centre, c/o The Rectory, Glencarse, Perth, PH2 7LX; T.-01738 860386.

Wright, Malcolm. Chief Executive, Edinburgh Sick Children's NHS Trust. Address: (b.) Royal Hospital for Sick Children, 9 Sciennes Road, Edinburgh, EH9 1LF.

Wright, Professor Michael, LLB, LLM, CIPD, FRSA, FIMgt. Vice Principal, Napier University, since 1992; b. 24.5.49, Newcastle-upon-Tyne; m., Pamela Stothart; 2 s.; 1 d. Educ. Durham Johnston Grammar School; Bearsden Academy; Birmingham University. Lecturer, University of West of England, 1970-79; Head of Department, Glasgow Caledonian University, 1980-83; Assistant Principal, Napier University, 1983-92; Vice-President, Institute of Personnel Management, 1991-93; Elder, Balerno Parish Church. Recreation: sport. Address: (b.) Napier University, 219 Colinton Road, Edinburgh, EH14 1DJ; T.-0131-455 4607.

Wright, Rt. Rev. Roderick. Roman Catholic Bishop of Argyll and the Isles, since 1991; b. 28.6.40. Ordained, 1964. Address: Bishop's House, Esplanade, Oban, PA34 5AB.

Wright, Very Rev. Ronald (William Vernon) Selby, CVO, ChStJ, TD, MA, DD, FRSE, JP. Chaplain, Edinburgh Castle and to the Governor, 1959-90; Chaplain, Queen's Bodyguard for Scotland (Royal Company of Archers), 1973-93 (Honorary Member, since 1994); Extra Chaplain to the Queen, since 1978 (Chaplain, 1961-78); b., 12.6.08, Glasgow. Educ. Edinburgh Academy; Melville College, Edinburgh; Edinburgh University and New College. Minister of the Canongate, 1937-77; Chaplain, 7/9 Royal Scots, 1938-42, 1946-48; Senior Chaplain, 52 Lowland Division, 1942-43; 1O Indian Division, 1944-45; Honorary Senior Chaplain to the Forces, since 1945; Founder Warden, St. Giles (later Canongate) Boys' Club, 1927-78; Moderator: Edinburgh Presbytery, 1963, General Assembly, 1972-73; Radio Padre, BBC, 1942-47; Extra-ordinary Director, Edinburgh Academy, since 1973; Hon. Member, New Club. Publications: Asking them Questions; Take Up God's Armour; Another Home. Address: (h.) The Queen's House, 36 Moray Place, Edinburgh EH3 6BX; T.-0131-226 5566.

Wright, Tom, BA (Hons). Writer; b. 8.3.23, Glasgow. Educ. Coatbridge High School; Strathclyde University. Served apprenticeship in embossing and stained glass; Army, 1943-47; served in Europe and Far East, including Japan; began to publish poems and short stories after demobilisation; had first play performed, Edinburgh Festival, 1960; author of There Was A Man; began to write radio and television drama, 1963; former Creative Writing Fellow; former Script Editor, BBC Scotland Drama Department; has also been Script Editor and Story Line Editor, Take The High Road, STV; won Festival Fringe Award, 1984, for Talk of the Devil; recent work includes The Hunter and the Hill, 1994, and Forgotten Army, 1995; Past Chairman, Scottish Committee, Writers' Guild, and Scottish Society of Playwrights. Recreation: listening to music. Address: 318 Churchill Drive, Glasgow G11.

Wyke, John Anthony, MA, PhD, VetMB, MRCVS, FRSE. Director, Beatson Institute for Cancer Research, since 1987; Honorary Professor, Glasgow University; b. 5.4.42, Cleethorpes. Educ. Dulwich College; Cambridge University; Glasgow University; London University. Leukemia Society of America Fellow, Universities of Washington and Southern California, 1970-72; Staff Scientist, Imperial Cancer Research Fund, 1972-85; Assistant Director of Research, 1985-87. Address: (b.) Beatson Institute for Cancer Research, CRC Beatson Laboratories, Garscube Estate, Switchback Road, Bearsden, Glasgow G61 1BD; T.-0141-942 9361.

Wylie, Alexander F., QC, LLB (Hons), FCIArb; b. 2.6.51. Called to the Scottish Bar, 1978. Address: (b.) Advocates' Library, Parliament House, Edinburgh, EH1 1RF.

Wylie, Rt. Hon. Lord (Norman Russell Wylie), PC (1970), VRD (1961), BA (Oxon), LLB (Glas). Senator of the College of Justice in Scotland, 1974- 90; b. 26.10.23, Elderslie; m., Gillian Mary Verney; 3 s. Educ. Paisley Grammar School; St. Edmund Hall, Oxford (Hon. Fellow, since 1975); Glasgow University; Edinburgh University. Fleet Air Arm, 1942-46 (subsequently RNR, Lt.-Cdr, 1954). Admitted Faculty of Advocates, 1952; Standing Junior Counsel to Air Ministry, 1956; Advocate Depute, 1958; QC, 1964; Solicitor General for Scotland, April to October, 1964; MP (Conservative), Edinburgh Pentlands, 1964-74; Lord Advocate, 1970-74. Chairman, Scottish National Committee, English Speaking Union of Commonwealth, 1978-84; Trustee, Carnegie Trust for Universities of Scotland, since 1975; Justice of Appeal, Republic of Botswana, since 1994. Recreations: shooting; sailing. Address: (h.) 30 Lauder Road, Edinburgh; T.-0131-667 8377.

Wylie, Rev. William Andrew, MA. Crisis Management Consultant; b. 17.5.27, London; m., Jennifer Barclay Mack; 4 d. by pr. m. Educ. Glasgow Academy; Glasgow University and Trinity College. Royal Navy, 1944-47; Chaplain, Clyde Division, RNVR, 1954-59; Minister: Stepps, 1953-59, Scots Kirk, Lausanne, 1959-67; General Secretary, Scottish Churches Council, 1967-71; Minister, St. Andrew's and St. George's, Edinburgh, 1972-85; Chaplain, Inverclyde Industrial Mission, 1985-86; Chaplain to the offshore oil industry, 1986-91; elected Hon. Fellow, Institute of Petroleum, 1990; elected Burgess of Aberdeen, 1990; Chairman of Governors, Aiglon College, Switzerland, 1984-91; Governor, Fettes College, 1978-85. Recreations: gardening; labradors; golf; music. Address: (h.) Chesterhill, Boarhills, by St. Andrews, KY16 8PP; T.- 01334 880440.

Wyllie, George. Artist; b. 1921, Glasgow. Installations; performances; events; best known for "paper boat" installation and exhibition, Glasgow, Liverpool, London and New York, 1989-90; Visiting Lecturer, Glasgow School of Art; Associate, Royal Scottish Academy; Hon. DLitt, Strathclyde University, Glasgow.

Wyllie, Gordon Malcolm, LLB, FSA Scot, NP, WS. Partner, Biggart Baillie & Gifford; Clerk to the Trades House of Glasgow and to Grand Antiquity Society of Glasgow; Clerk to General Commissioners of Inland Revenue, Glasgow North and South Divisions; b. Newton Mearns. Educ. Dunoon Grammar School; Glasgow University. Honorary Treasurer, Edinburgh Summer School in Ancient Greek; Director, Bailford Trustees Ltd.; Chairman, Edinburgh Subscription Ball Committee; Box Master, Incorporation of Hammermen of Edinburgh; wrote Scottish contribution to International Bar Association's International Dictionary of Succession Terms. Recreations: music; history and the arts generally; country walks; foreign travel. Address: (b.) 310 St. Vincent Street, Glasgow; T.- 0141-228 8000.

Wyllie, Very Rev. Hugh Rutherford, MCIBS, MA, Hon.DD (Aberdeen). Minister, Old Parish Church of Hamilton, since 1981; Moderator, General Assembly of the Church of Scotland, 1992-93; admitted as Hon. Freeman, District of Hamilton, 1992; b. 11.10.34, Glasgow; m., Eileen E. Cameron, MA; 2 d. Educ. Shawlands Academy; Hutchesons' Grammar School, Glasgow. Union Bank of Scotland, 1951-53; RAF, 1953-55; Glasgow University, 1956-62; Assistant Minister, Glasgow Cathedral, 1962-65; Minister, Dunbeth Church, Coatbridge, 1965-72; Minister, Cathcart South Church, Glasgow, 1972-81; Moderator, Presbytery of Hamilton, 1989-90, Convener, Business Committee, 1991-95; President, Hamilton Burns Club, 1990; founder Member, Hamilton Centre for Information for the Unemployed, 1983; introduced Dial-a-Fact on drugs and alcohol, 1986; established Hamilton Church History Project; Convener, General Assembly's Stewardship and Budget Committee, 1978-83; Convener, Stewardship and Finance Board, 1983-86; Convener, Assembly Council, 1987-91; Member, Board of Nomination to Church Chairs, since 1993; Member, General Assembly's Board of Practice and Procedure, since 1991; Non-Executive Director, Lanarkshire Health Care NHS Trust, since 1995; Dr William Barclay Memorial Lecturer, 1994. Recreations: gardening; DIY; two yellow labradors. Address: Mansewood, Union Street, Hamilton ML3 6NA; T.-01698 420002.

Wyllie, James Hogarth, BA, MA. Senior Lecturer in International Relations and Director, Postgraduate Strategic Studies Programme, Aberdeen University, since 1979; International Affairs Analyst, Grampian Television, since 1989; Specialist Correspondent, Jane's Intelligence Review, since 1992; Member, JDM Marketing Associates, Aberdeen, since 1992; b. 7.3.51, Dumfries; m., Claire Helen Beaton; 2 s. Educ. Sanquhar Academy; Dumfries Academy; Stirling University; Lancaster University. Research Officer, Ministry of Defence, 1974-75; Tutor in Politics, Durham University, 1975-77; Lecturer in Politics, University of East Anglia, 1977-79; freelance journalism; frequent current affairs comment and analysis, BBC Radio; Commonwealth Fellow, University of Calgary, 1988. Publications: Influence of British Arms; European Security in the Nuclear Age; Economist Pocket Guide to Defence (Co-author); International Politics since 1945 (Contributor). Recreations: travelling; cinema; badminton; walking; cycling. Address: (b.) Department of Politics and International Relations, Aberdeen University, Aberdeen AB9 2TY; T.-01224 272725.

Wynd, Andrew H.D., DipSW (CQSW). General Secretary, Scottish Spina Bifida Association, since 1989; b. 7.10.53, Hamilton. Educ. Bellshill Academy; Stirling University. Local government officer; Senior Officer, National Voluntary Childcare Organisation. Past Chair, Scottish Association of Voluntary Service Co-ordinators; former Chair, Strathclyde Regional Council Pre-five Voluntary Sector Forum. Address: (b.) Scottish Spina Bifida Association, 190 Queensferry Road, Edinburgh EH4 2BW; T.-0131-332 0743.

Y

Yang, Professor Eric Shih-Jung, BSc, MSc, PhD, CEng, FIEE, FIOA. Professor, Department of Computing and Electrical Engineering, Heriot-Watt University, since 1985; m., Fei Jeannette; 1 d. Educ. Hong Kong University; Queen Mary College, London University. Senior Scientific Officer, British Rail, 1970-72; Lecturer, then Senior Lecturer, Heriot-Watt University, 1972-85. Publications: Low-Noise Electrical Motors, 1981; Machinery Noise Measurement (Co-author), 1985; Handbook of Electric Machines (Co-author), 1987. Address: (h.) 14 Cherry Tree Park, Balerno, Edinburgh EH14 5AJ; T.-0131-449 2069.

Yarrow, Sir Eric Grant, MBE, DL, CEng, MRINA, FRSE. Chairman, Clydesdale Bank PLC, 1985-91 (Director, since 1962); Director, National Australia Bank Ltd., 1987-91; b. 23.4.20, Glasgow; m., 1, Rosemary Ann Young (deceased); 1 s. (deceased); 2, Annette Elizabeth Francoise Steven (m. diss.); 3 s.; 3, Joan Botting; 3 step d. Educ. Marlborough College; Glasgow University. Served engineering apprenticeship, G. & J. Weir, 1938-39; Royal Engineers, 1939-45; served Burma, 1942-45 (Major, RE, 1945); Yarrow & Co. Ltd. (later Yarrow PLC): Assistant Manager, 1946, Director, 1948, Managing Director, 1958-67, Chairman, 1962-85, President, 1985-87; Director, Standard Life Assurance Company, 1958-91; Chairman, Princess Louise Scottish Hospital, Erskine, 1980-86, Hon. President, since 1986; President, Scottish Convalescent Home for Children, 1957-70; Council Member, Royal Institution of Naval Architects, since 1957 (Vice President, 1965, Honorary Vice President, 1972); Member, General Committee, Lloyd's Register of Shipping, 1960-89; Deacon, Incorporation of Hammermen in Glasgow, 1961-62; Chairman, Yarrow (Shipbuilders) Ltd., 1962-79; Officer (Brother), Order of St. John, since 1965; Deputy Lieutenant, County of Renfrewshire, since 1970; Prime Warden, Worshipful Company of Shipwrights, 1970-71; Council Member, Institute of Directors, 1983-90; President, Smeatonian Society of Civil Engineers, 1983-84; President, The Marlburian Club, 1984; President, Scottish Area, Burma Star Association, since 1990; Vice President, Royal Highland and Agricultural Society for Scotland, 1990. Recreation: golf. Address: (h.) Cloak, Kilmacolm, Renfrewshire PA13 4SD; T.-Kilmacolm 2067.

Yates, Keith. Chief Executive, Stirling Council, since 1995. Address: (b.) c/o Viewforth, Stirling, FK8 2ET.

Yemm, Professor Robert, BDS, BSc, PhD, FDS RCS(Edin). Professor and Head, Department of Dental Prosthetics and Gerontology, Dundee University, since 1984; b. 31.1.39, Bristol; m., Glenys Margaret; 1 s.; 1 d. Educ. Bristol Grammar School; Bristol University. Lecturer in Dental Prosthetics, Bristol University; Associate Professor, Department of Oral Biology, Alberta University; Lecturer in Dental Medicine (Oral Biology), then Dental Prosthetics, Bristol University; Senior Lecturer (Honorary Consultant), Dental Prosthetics, Dundee University. Recreation: sailing. Address: (h.) 10 Birkhill Avenue, Wormit, Newport-on-Tay, Fife DD6 8PX; T.-01382 541819.

Yewe-Dyer, Mervyn Richard, BDS, BSc, FDS, MSc, MGDS. Deputy Chief Dental Officer, Scottish Office, since 1994; Director, Regional Dental Officer Service, since 1994; b. 4.8.43, London; m., Melanie Dorcas Gould; 1 s.; 2 d. Educ. Christ's Hospital; London University. Nuffield Research Fellow, 1966-68; Lecturer, Manchester University, 1969-73; general dental practice, 1974-93; Lecturer (part-time), Guy's Hospital Dental School, 1979-87; Board Member, Dental Practice Board England, 1985-91. Publication: Notes on Prosthetic Dentistry. Recreations:

photography; golf; bee-keeping. Address: (b.) Room 7, St. Andrew's House, Edinburgh, EH1 3DG; T.-0131-244 2305.

Young, Charles Whiteford, LLB, CA. Director, British Linen Bank Ltd., since 1991; Director, United Auctions (Scotland) Ltd., since 1993; b. 18.5.53, Glasgow; m., Sharon M.M. Stevenson; 3 d. Educ. Glasgow Academy; Trinity College, Glenalmond; Aberdeen University; Glasgow University. Arthur Young McClelland Moores & Co., Glasgow, 1975-78; Corporate Finance Department, British Linen Bank, since 1979. Recreations: golf; tennis; swimming. Address: (b.) 4 Melville Street, Edinburgh EH3 7NZ; T.-0131-243 8326.

Young, Professor Daniel Greer, MB, ChB, FRCSEdin, FRCSGlas, DTM&H. Professor of Paediatric Surgery, Glasgow University; Honorary Consultant Paediatric Surgeon; former President, British Association of Paediatric Surgeons; b. Skipness, Argyll; m., Agnes Gilchrist Donald; 1 s.; 1 d. Educ. Wishaw High School; Glasgow University. Resident Assistant Surgeon, Hospital for Sick Children, London; Senior Lecturer, Institute of Child Health, London University; Honorary Consultant Surgeon, Hospital for Sick Children, London, and Queen Elizabeth Hospital, Hackney, London; Senior Lecturer and Head, Department of Paediatric Surgery, Glasgow University, Honorary Consultant Surgeon, Royal Hospital for Sick Children and Stobhill General Hospital, Glasgow. Honorary Secretary, Lanarkshire Division, British Medical Association; Past President, Royal Medico-Chirurgical Society of Glasgow; Honorary President, Scottish Spina Bifida Association; Member of Council, Royal College of Physicians and Surgeons; Past Chairman, Intercollegiate Board in Paediatric Surgery; Honorary Member: Hungarian Paediatric Surgical Association, South African Paediatric Surgical Association, American Surgical Paediatric Association. Recreations: curling; fishing; gardening. Address: (b.) Department of Paediatric Surgery, Royal Hospital for Sick Children, Yorkhill, Glasgow G3 8SJ; T.-0141-201 0170.

Young, Lt.-Gen. Sir David (Tod), KBE (1980), CB (1977), DFC (1952). Chairman, Cairntech Ltd., Edinburgh, 1983-93, Director, since 1993; b. 17.5.26, Edinburgh; m., 1, Joyce Marian Melville (deceased); 2 s.; 2, Joanna Myrtle Oyler (nee Torin). Educ. George Watson's College, Edinburgh. Commissioned The Royal Scots, 1945; Brevet Lt.-Col., 1964; Mil. Assistant, MoD, 1964-67; commanded 1st Bn., The Royal Scots, 1967-69; Col. GS, Staff College, 1969-70; Commander, 12 Mechanized Brigade, 1970-72; Deputy Military Secretary, MoD, 1972-74; Commander Land Forces, Northern Ireland, 1975-77; Director of Infantry, MoD, 1977-80; GOC Scotland and Governor, Edinburgh Castle, 1980-82; Colonel, The Royal Scots, 1975-80; Colonel Commandant: Scottish Division, 1980-82, Ulster Defence Regiment, 1986-91; Honorary Colonel, Northern Ireland Regiment Army Air Corps, 1988-93; Vice President, Scottish Partnership Agency for Palliative and Cancer Care, since 1993; Member, Scottish Committee, Marie Curie Foundation, since 1983 (Chairman, 1986); President, Army Cadet Force Association Scotland, since 1984; HM Commissioner, Queen Victoria School, 1984-93; Chairman, St. Mary's Cathedral Workshop, 1986-92; Member, Board of Governors, St. Columba's Hospice, since 1986; Honorary President, St. Mary's Cathedral Workshop, since 1993. Recreations: golf; sports; music. Address: c/o Adam & Company plc, 22 Charlotte Square, Edinburgh EH2 4DF.

Young, Hugh Kenneth, TD, CA, FCIBS. General Manager and Secretary and Member, Management Board, Bank of Scotland; b. 6.5.36, Galashiels; m., Marjory Bruce Wilson; 2 s.; 1 d. Educ. Edinburgh Academy. National Service, 1959-61; commissioned as 2nd Lt., Royal Scots; TA service, 1957-59, 1961-69 and 1986-92, latterly as Major; with ICFC Ltd., 1962-67; with Schroders Ltd. group, 1967-

73, latterly as Manager, J. Henry Schroder Wagg & Co. Ltd.; Local Director in Edinburgh, Edward Bates & Sons Ltd., 1973-75; joined Bank of Scotland, 1975; Head of Corporate Finance, Bank of Scotland Finance Company Ltd., 1976; Director, The British Linen Bank Ltd., 1978-84 (Deputy Chief Executive, 1982-84). Director:Bank of Scotland (Jersey) Ltd., 1986 (Chairman), Bank of Wales (Jersey) Ltd., 1986, Scottish Agricultural Securities Corporation PLC, 1988, First Mortgage Securities Ltd., 1992, Bank of Scotland (Isle of Man) Ltd., 1993 (Chairman). Recreations: squash; tennis; hill-walking. Address: (b.) The Mound, Edinburgh EH1 1YZ; T.-0131-243 5562.

Young, John Henderson, OBE (1980), JP, MIMgt, DL. Deputy Lieutenant of Glasgow, since 1981; Chairman, Association of Scottish Conservative Councillors, 1991-94, Hon. President, since 1994; Bailie/Magistrate of Glasgow on four occasions; b. 21.12.30, Glasgow; m., Doris Paterson; 1 s. Educ. Hillhead High School, Glasgow; Scottish College of Commerce. RAF, 1949-51. Councillor, Glasgow Corporation, 1964-73, Glasgow District Council, 1974-96, City of Glasgow Council, from 1996; Leader, Glasgow City Council, 1977-79, Leader of the Opposition, 1979-80, 1988-92, from 1996 (new City of Glasgow Council); Parliamentary candidate (Conservative), Rutherglen, 1966, Cathcart, 1992; Chairman, Cathcart Conservatives, 1964-65, 1968-71, 1987-88; Chairman, Glasgow Euro Constituency, 1987-91; Vice-Chairman, Scottish Tory Reform Group, since 1993; Vice Chairman, Glasgow Conservatives, 1969-72; Public Relations Consultant; former Vice-Chairman, Scottish Pakistani Association; Secretary, Scottish/South African Society, 1986-88; Governor, Hutcheson's Educational Trust, since 1991; Member, Glasgow Sports Promotion Council; Member, Merchants House of Glasgow; Kentucky Colonel, 1984; Hon. Don Cossack (Russia), 1989; Lord Provost's Award, 1989. Publication: A History of Cathcart Conservative Association, 1918-93. Recreations: meeting people; history; reading; animal welfare. Address: (h.) 4 Deanwood Avenue, Muirend, Glasgow G44 3RJ; T.-0141-637 9535.

Young, John Maclennan, OBE (1987), JP. Convener, Caithness District Council, since 1974; Member, Highland Regional Council, 1974-90; Honorary Sheriff at Wick, since 1994; elected to Highland Council, 1995; b. 6.6.33, Thurso. Educ. Thurso Miller Academy. Farmer; Member, Caithness County Council, 1961-75; Member, Caithness Western District Council, 1961-75; Chairman, Housing Committee, 1968-73, and Planning Commitee, 1973-75, Caithness County Council; Conservative candidate, Caithness and Sutherland, 1970. Address: (h.) Sordale, Halkirk, Caithness; T.-Halkirk 228.

Young, Margaret Rose, JP, MPAH (Scot), CMH, CHyp. Hypnotherapist and Counsellor; Honorary Sheriff; b. 5.1.51, Canada; m., Simon George Young; 3 d. Educ. St. Mary's School, Calne; St. Andrews University. Member, Justices of the Peace Committee, Ross and Cromarty, since 1985. Recreations: reading; music; theatre; walking. Address: (h.) Tarrel, by Tain, Ross-shire, IV20 1SL; T.-01862 871248.

Young, Mark Richard, BSc, PhD, FRES, FIBiol, CBiol. Senior Lecturer, Aberdeen University, since 1989; Member, North East River Purification Board, since 1984; Chairman, National Reserves Committee, Scottish Wildlife Trust, since 1990; b. 27.10.48, Worcester; m., Jennifer Elizabeth Tully; 1 s.; 1 d. Educ. Kings School, Worcester; Birmingham University. Lecturer, Aberdeen University, 1973-89. Recreations: natural history; walking; ball sports; visiting Hebridean islands. Address: (b.) Culterty Field Station, Department of Zoology, University of Aberdeen, Newburgh, Ellon, Aberdeenshire AB41 0AA; T.-01358 789631.

Young, Raymond Kennedy, OBE, RIAS, BArch (Hons). Director, Research and Innovation Services, Scottish Homes, since 1992; b. 23.1.46, Newcastle upon Tyne; m., Jean; 3 s. Educ. High School of Glasgow; Strathclyde University. Architectural Research Unit, Strathclyde University, 1971-74; Housing Corporation in Scotland, 1974-89 (Director, 1982-89); Scottish Homes, since 1989. Recreations: theatre; opera; railways; a little swimming. Address: (b.) Rosebery House, 9 Haymarket Terrace, Edinburgh; T.-0131-479 5700.

Young, Robert W.J., BSc (Hons), PhD, CEng, MICE. HM Inspector of Schools (Staff Inspector), since 1970; b. 14.3.36, Falkirk; m., Cynthia; 2 d. Educ. Melville College, Edinburgh; Edinburgh University. Civil Engineer, British Rail, 1958-61; Edinburgh University, 1961-70, with period of secondment to Khartoum University, Sudan. Recreations: wind-surfing; sailing; skiing; bridge.

Young, Roger, BSc, MBA. Chief Executive, Scottish Hydro-Electric plc, since 1988; b. 14.1.44, Edinburgh; m., Susan; 1 s.; 2 d. Educ. Gordonstoun School; Edinburgh University; Cranfield Business School. Address: (b.) 10 Dunkeld Road, Perth PH1 5WA; Tel.: 01738 455040.

Young, Professor Stephen, BCom, MSc. Professor of International Business, Strathclyde University, since 1987, Head, Department of Marketing, 1992-96; b. 20.8.44, Berwick upon Tweed; 1 s.; 1 d. Educ. Berwick Grammar School; Liverpool University; Newcastle University. Economist, Government of Tanzania; Head, International Economics Department, Milk Marketing Board, 1969-73; Lecturer/Senior Lecturer, Paisley College of Technology, 1973-79; Senior Lecturer, Department of Marketing, Strathclyde Business School, 1980-87 (Director, Strathclyde International Business Unit, from 1983); Directorships: Scotmex Ltd., The Licensing Centre Ltd. Recreations: mountaineering; cycling; running. Address: (h.) 65 Russell Place, Linwood, Paisley PA3 3SS; T.-01505 327621.

Young, Sheriff Sir Stephen Stewart Templeton, 3rd Bt. Sheriff of North Strathclyde at Greenock, since 1984; b. 24.5.47; m.; 2 s. Educ. Rugby; Trinity College, Oxford; Edinburgh University. Sheriff, Glasgow and Strathkelvin, 1984. Address: (b.) Sheriff Court House, Nelson Street, Greenock, PA15 1TR.

Young, Rev. William Galbraith, MA (Hons), BD, PhD. Retired Bishop, Church of Pakistan; retired Minister, Church of Scotland; b. 10.10.17, Greenock; m., Elizabeth Crawford Wiseman; 1 s.; 2 d. Educ. Greenock Academy; Oban High School; Glasgow University. Private, RAMC, 1940-45 (War service overseas, India, Iraq, Persia, Cyprus); Missionary, Church of Scotland, Punjab, Pakistan, 1947-77; Principal, Murree Language School, 1954-55; Vice-President, West Pakistan Christian Council, 1963-64; Editor, Urdu Textbook Project, Theological Education Fund, 1963-77; Professor of Church History, Gujranwala Theological Seminary, 1966-70; Church of Pakistan: Bishop, 1970-77, Chairman, Liturgical Commission, 1970-77, Deputy Moderator, 1974-77; Minister, Resolis and Urquhart Parish Church, 1977-85; Moderator, Chanonry and Dingwall Presbytery, 1979-80; Moderator, Synod of Ross, Sutherland and Caithness, 1981-82; Chairman, Sialkot Inter-Aid Committee (Flood and Refugee Relief), 1973-77; Vice-Chairman, East Ross and Black Isle Council of Social Service, 1980-82. Publications: Handbook of Source Materials for Students of Church History up to 650 AD, 1969; Patriarch, Shah and Caliph, 1974; Church of Pakistan - Experimental Services, 1974; The Parish of Urquhart and Logie Wester, 1984; Life and Witness Through Sixty Years of Change, 1991; Days of Small Things?, 1992; various publications in Urdu. Recreations: (when young) tennis; (now) choral singing; walking; reading; listening to music. Address: (h.) 29 Ferry Brae, North Kessock, Inverness IV1 1YH; T.-0146 373 581.

Younger of Leckie, 3rd Viscount (Sir Edward George Younger), OBE (1940); b. 21.11.06; m., Evelyn Margaret McClure, MBE (deceased); 3 s.; 1 d. Educ. Winchester; New College, Oxford. Served Second World War; Colonel, Argyll and Sutherland Highlanders (TA); Lord Lieutenant, Stirling and Falkirk, 1964-79. Address: (h.) Leckie, Gargunnock, Stirling.

Younger of Prestwick, Rt. Hon. Lord (George Kenneth Hotson Younger), KCVO, TD, DL. Chairman, The Royal Bank of Scotland Group plc, since 1991; b. 22.9.31; m., Diana Rhona Tuck; 3 s.; 1 d. Educ. Cargilfield School, Edinburgh; Winchester College; New College, Oxford. Argyll and Sutherland Highlanders, 1950-51; 7th Bn., Argyll and Sutherland Highlanders (TA), 1951-65; Honorary Colonel, 154 (Lowland) Transport Regiment, RCT T&AVR, 1977-85; Director: George Younger & Son Ltd., 1958-68; J.G. Thomson & Co. Ltd., Leith, 1962-66; Maclachlans Ltd., 1968-70; Tennant Caledonian Breweries, 1977-79; Non Executive Director: The Royal Bank of Scotland Group plc, 1989; Murray International Trust PLC, 1989 (Chairman); Murray Smaller Markets Trust PLC, 1989 (Chairman); Murray Income Trust PLC, 1989 (Chairman); Murray Ventures PLC, 1989 (Chairman); Siemens Plessey Electronic Systems Ltd., 1990 (Chairman); Banco Santander S.A., 1991; SPEED, 1992 (Chairman); PIK Holdings Ltd., 1991 (Chairman); Scottish Equitable plc, 1993; Royal Armouries Board of Trustees, 1994 (Chairman); The Fleming Mercantile Investment Trust PLC, 1994; contested North Lanarkshire, 1959; Unionist Candidate, Kinross and West Perthshire, 1963 (stood down in favour of Sir Alec Douglas-Home); MP (Conservative), Ayr, 1964-92; Scottish Conservative Whip, 1965-67; Parliamentary Under-Secretary of State for Development, Scottish Office, 1970-74; Minister of State for Defence, 1974; Secretary of State for Scotland, 1979-86; Chairman, Conservative Party in Scotland, 1974-75 (Deputy Chairman, 1967-70); Secretary of State for Defence, 1986-89; President, National Union of Conservative and Unionist Associations, 1987-88. Brigadier, Queen's Bodyguard for Scotland (Royal Company of Archers); DL, Stirlingshire, 1968. Recreations: music; tennis; sailing; golf. Address: (b.) 42 St. Andrew Square, Edinburgh EH2 2YE; T.-0131-556 8555.

Younger, John David Bingham. Lord Lieutenant of Tweeddale, since 1994; Managing Director, Broughton Brewery Ltd., since 1979; b. 20.5.39, Doune; m., Anne Rosaleen Logan; 1 s.; 2 d. Educ. Eton College; Royal Military Academy, Sandhurst. Argyll and Sutherland Highlanders, 1957-69; Scottish and Newcastle Breweries, 1969-79; Broughton Brewery Ltd., since 1979; Deputy Lieutenant, Tweeddale, 1987. Chairman, Board of Governors, Belhaven Hill School Trust, 1988; Chairman, Scottish Borders Tourist Board, 1989; Member, A&SH Regimental Trust and Committee, 1985; Director, Queen's Hall (Edinburgh) Ltd; Member, Queen's Bodyguard for Scotland (Royal Company of Archers) 1969-73; Vice President, RHAAS, 1994. Recreation: the countryside. Address: (h.) Kirkurd House, Blyth Bridge, Peeblesshire EH46 7AH; T.-01721 752223.

Younger, Sheriff Robert Edward Gilmour, MA, LLB. Sheriff of Tayside, Central and Fife, at Stirling, since 1992 (Stirling and Alloa, 1987-92); b. 25.9.40, Stirling; m., Helen Jane Hayes; 1 s.; 1 d. Educ. Winchester; New College, Oxford; Edinburgh University; Glasgow University. Advocate, 1968-79; Sheriff of Glasgow and Strathkelvin, at Glasgow, 1979-82, and of Tayside, Central and Fife, at Stirling and Falkirk, 1982-87. Recreations: out of doors. Address: (h.) Old Leckie, Gargunnock, Stirling; T.-01786 860213.

Youngson, George Gray, MB, ChB, PhD, FRCSEdin. Consultant Surgeon, Royal Aberdeen Children's Hospital and Aberdeen Royal Infirmary, since 1985; Honorary Senior Lecturer in Clinical Surgery, Aberdeen University, since 1985; b. 13.5.49, Glasgow; m., Sandra Jean Lister; 1 s.; 2 d. Educ. Buckhaven High School; Aberdeen University. House Officer to Professor George Smith, 1973; Research Fellow, 1975; Registrar in General Surgery, 1975-77; Senior Resident in Cardiac and Thoracic Surgery, University Hospital, London, Ontario, 1979; Lecturer in Clinical Surgery, Aberdeen University, 1981; Clinical Fellow, Paediatric Surgery, Hospital for Sick Children, Toronto, 1983; Lecturer in Surgical Paediatrics and Transplantation, Aberdeen University, 1984; Regional Advisor and Examiner, Royal College of Surgeons of Edinburgh. Recreations: sport (tennis and squash); music (piobaireachd, guitar). Address: (h.) 10 Kennerty Park, Peterculter, Aberdeen.

Z

Zealley, Andrew King, MB, ChB, FRCP, FRCPsych, DPM. Medical Director, Edinburgh Healthcare NHS Trust, since 1994; Consultant Psychiatrist, Lothian Health Board, since 1971; b. 28.10.35, Stockton-on-Tees; m., Dr. Helen Elizabeth Zealley (qv); 1 s.; 1 d. Educ. Sherborne School; Edinburgh University. Chairman, Lothian Area Medical Committee, 1978-88; Chairman, Lothian Research Ethics Committee, since 1988. Publications include: Companion to Psychiatric Studies, 5th edition (Co-editor). Recreations: running; sailing; skiing. Address: (h.) Viewfield House, Tipperlinn Road, Edinburgh EH10 5ET; T.-0131-447 5545.

Zealley, Helen Elizabeth, MD, FRCPE, FFPHM. Chief Administrative Medical Officer and Director of Public Health, Lothian Health Board, since 1988; Honorary Senior Lecturer, Edinburgh University, since 1988; b. 10.6.40; m., Dr. Andrew Zealley (qv); 1 s.; 1 d. Educ. St. Albans High School; Edinburgh University. Member, Council, Royal College of Physicians, Edinburgh; Member, Board, Faculty of Public Health Medicine; Hon. President, Lothian Branch, British Association of Early Childhood; Member, Court, Edinburgh University. Recreations: family and home; sailing; skiing; travel. Address: (b.) Lothian Health Board, 148 Pleasance, Edinburgh EH8 9RS; T.-0131-668 3940.

von Zugbach de Sugg, Professor Reginald (Reggie) Gordon Leslie, CLJ, MA, PhD, MBIM, FMS, ACP. Professor in Management, Paisley University, since 1990; b. 20.2.44, Derbyshire; m., 1, Moira Doreen Murphy (m. dissolved); 2, Claudia Bettina Hein (m. dissolved). Educ. City of London School; Brighton Polytechnic; London University Institute of Education; UMIST. Regular Army Officer (Major), 1968-86; Director of Undergraduate Studies, Glasgow Business School, Glasgow University, 1986-90; author of numerous papers; books: Power and Prestige in the British Army, 1988; The Winning Manager, 1995. Commander, Military and Hospitaler Order of St. Lazarus of Jerusalem. Recreations: horses; dogs; real tennis; literature. Address: (h.) 7 Downside Road, Dowanhill, Glasgow; T.-0141-337 2228.